Funk & Wagnalls Standard Desk Dictionary

VOLUME 2

N–Z

Funk & Wagnalls, Inc.

Publishers since 1876

N

N (en) *n. pl.* **n's** or **ns**, **N's** or **Ns**, **ens** (enz) **1.** The fourteenth letter of the English alphabet. **2.** The sound represented by the letter *n*, a voiced, alveolar nasal. — *symbol* **. Printing** An en. **2.** *Chem.* Nitrogen (symbol N). **3.** *Math.* An indefinite number.

nab (nab) *v.t.* **nabbed, nab·bing** *Informal* **1.** To catch or arrest, as a fugitive or criminal. **2.** To take or seize suddenly; snatch. [Prob. of Scand. origin]

na·bob (nā'bob) *n.* **1.** A European who has become rich in India. **2.** Any very rich or powerful man. [< Hind. *nawwāb* < Arabic *nuwwab*, pl. of *nā'ib* viceroy]

na·celle (nə·sel') *n. Aeron.* A separate enclosure on an aircraft, esp. one for an engine. [< F, small boat]

na·cre (nā'kər) *n.* Mother-of-pearl. [< F < Ital. *naccara* < Arabic *naqqāra* drum]

na·cre·ous (nā'krē·əs) *adj.* **1.** Containing, resembling, or producing nacre. **2.** Iridescent; pearly.

Na-Dene (nä·dĕn') *n.* A group of related North American Indian languages. Also **Na-Dé·né** (-dä·nā').

na·dir (nā'dər, -dir) *n.* **1.** The point of the celestial sphere directly beneath the position of an observer, and opposite to the zenith. **2.** The lowest possible point: opposed to *zenith.* [< MF < Arabic *nazīr* (*as-samt*) opposite (the zenith)]

nae (nā) *adj. & adv. Scot.* No; not.

nag¹ (nag) *v.* **nagged, nag·ging** *v.t.* **1.** To bother or annoy by repeatedly urging, scolding, carping, etc. — *v.i.* **2.** To urge, scold, carp, etc., continually. — *n.* One who nags. [< Scand.] — **nag'ger** *n.* — **nag'ging·ly** *adv.*

nag² (nag) *n.* **1.** A pony or small horse used for riding. **2.** An old, broken-down, or worthless horse. [ME *nagge*]

Na·hua·tl (nä'wät'l) *n.* **1.** The Uto-Aztecan language of the Aztecs and certain other Indian peoples. **2.** The peoples whose native language is Nahuatl. — *adj.* Of or pertaining to Nahuatl or the people who speak it.

Na·hua·tlan (nä'wät·lən) *n.* **1.** A branch of the Uto-Aztecan linguistic family of North and Central American Indians, including the Aztec dialects. **2.** Nahuatl. — *adj.* Of or pertaining to Nahuatl or Nahuatlan.

Na·hum (nā'əm, -hum) Seventh-century B.C. Hebrew prophet. — *n.* A book of the Old Testament containing his prophecies. [< Hebrew, comfort]

na·iad (nā'ad, nī'-) *n. pl.* **·ads** or **·a·des** (-ə·dēz) **1.** In classical mythology, one of the water nymphs believed to dwell in and preside over fountains, springs, rivers, lakes, and wells. **2.** *Entomol.* The aquatic nymphal stage in the life cycle of certain insects. [< L < Gk. *Naias*, *-ados*.]

na·if (nä·ēf') *adj. French* Masculine form of NAIVE. Also **na·if'.**

nail (nāl) *n.* **1.** A slender piece of metal, usu. pointed at one end and broadened at the other, used for driving into or through wood, etc., so as to hold or fasten one piece to another or to project as a peg. **2.** Something resembling a nail in shape or function. **3.** A thin, horny plate growing on one side of the ends of the fingers and toes of men and other primates. **4.** An animal part corresponding to the nail of a primate, as a claw, talon, or hoof. — **hard as nails 1.** In good physical condition; rugged. **2.** Not to be moved by sentiment, pity, etc. — **to hit the nail on the head** To do or say something exactly to the point. — *v.t.* **1.** To fasten or fix in place with a nail or nails. **2.** To close up or shut in by means of nails: often with *up.* **3.** To secure or make certain through quick or decisive action: often with *down.* **4.** To fix firmly or immovably: Terror *nailed* him to the spot. **5.** *Slang* To catch or arrest; intercept. **6.** *Slang* To expose, as a lie or liar. [OE *nægl*, orig., fingernail.]

nail file A small, fine file for shaping the fingernails.

nail·fold (nāl'fōld') *n. Anat.* The cuticle (def. 3).

nail polish A clear or colored lacquer or other substance applied to the nails to give a glossy finish. Also **nail enamel.**

nail·set (nāl'set') *n.* A punch for driving the head of a nail below or even with a surface. Also **nail set.**

nain·sook (nān'sook, nan'-) *n.* A soft, lightweight cotton fabric. [< Hind. *nainsukh*, lit., pleasure of the eye]

na·ive (nä·ēv') *adj.* **1.** Having an unaffected or simple nature that lacks worldly experience; artless. **2.** Lacking or revealing the lack of deliberate or careful analysis; uncritical: a *naive* idea. **3.** Uninstructed: a *naive* observer. Also **na·ïve'.** [< F, fem. of *naïf* < L *nativus* natural, inborn] — **na·ive'ly** *adv.* — **na·ive'ness** *n.*

na·ive·té (nä·ēv'tā', nä·ēv'tā) *n.* **1.** The state or quality of being naive. **2.** An incident, remark, etc., of a naive character. Also **na·ïve·té'**, **na·ive·ty** (nä·ēv'tē). [< F]

na·ked (nā'kid) *adj.* **1.** Having no clothes on; nude. **2.** Having no covering, or lacking the usual covering; exposed. **3.** Bare or stripped, as of vegetation, furnishings, ornaments, etc. **4.** Without addition, adornment, or qualification; stark: the *naked* truth. **5.** Unaided by an optical instrument: the *naked* eye. **6.** Open or exposed to view: a *naked* sword. **7.** Without defense or protection; vulnerable. **8.** Being without means of sustenance; destitute. **9.** *Bot.* **a** Not enclosed in an ovary or case: said of seeds. **b** Without protective scales: said of buds. **c** Without a perianth: said of flowers. **d** Without leaves: said of stalks. **e** Having no hairs; smooth: said of leaves. **10.** *Zool.* Lacking fur, hair, feathers, etc. [OE *nacod*] — **na'ked·ly** *adv.* — **na'ked·ness** *n.*

nam·by-pam·by (nam'bē·pam'bē) *adj.* **1.** Full of or exhibiting weak sentimentality; insipid. **2.** Timid and irresolute. — *n. pl.* **·bies** One who is namby-pamby. [< The title of a satiric poem by Henry Carey, died 1743.]

name (nām) *n.* **1.** A word or group of words by which a person, thing, animal, class, or concept is distinctively known or referred to: esp., the proper appellation of a person or family. **2.** A usu. derogatory word or phrase evaluating character or quality: to call someone *names.* **3.** Popular or general reputation. **4.** A famous or important person, organization, or thing: a big *name* in industry. **5.** Mere semblance or outward form: a wife in *name* only. **6.** Fame or distinction. — **by the name of** Named. — **in the name of 1.** For the sake of. **2.** By the authority of. — **to make a name for oneself** To achieve distinction or fame. — **to one's name** Of one's own: He hasn't a friend *to his name.* — *v.t.* **named, nam·ing** *v.t.* **1.** To give a name to; call. **2.** To mention or refer to by name; cite. **3.** To identify. **4.** To fix or determine: to *name* the day. **5.** To nominate; appoint. — *adj.* **1.** Having or known by a name. **2.** *U.S. Informal* Famous. [OE *nama*] — **nam'er** *n.*

name day The feast day of the saint for whom one is named.

name·less (nām'lis) *adj.* **1.** Undistinguished or obscure: a *nameless* multitude. **2.** That cannot be named; indescribable: *nameless* terror. **3.** Not fit to be spoken of; unmentionable: *nameless* atrocities. **4.** Unmentioned by name. **5.** Having no name; esp., having no legal name; illegitimate. — **name'less·ly** *adv.* — **name'less·ness** *n.*

name·ly (nām'lē) *adv.* That is to say; to wit.

name·sake (nām'sāk') *n.* One who is named after or has the same name as another.

nan·keen (nan·kēn') *n.* **1.** A buff-colored Chinese cotton fabric. **2.** *pl.* Clothes made of nankeen. Also **nan·kin** (-kēn'). [after *Nanking*, where originally made]

nan·ny (nan'ē) *n. pl.* **·nies 1.** *Informal* A female goat: also **nanny goat.** **2.** *Brit.* A child's nurse. [after *Nanny*, a personal name, dim. of *Ann*]

nano- *combining form* **1.** Exceedingly small. **2.** In the metric system and in technical usage, one billionth of (a specified unit). Also, before vowels, **nan-.** [< Gk. *nānos* dwarf]

Nantes, Edict of (nants, *Fr.* nänt) An order granting political equality to the Huguenots, issued by Henry IV of France in 1598 and revoked by Louis XIV in 1685.

Na·o·mi (nā·ō'mē, nā'ə·mē, -mī) In the Bible, the mother-in-law of Ruth. *Ruth* i 2. [< Hebrew, my delight]

nap¹ (nap) *n.* A short sleep; doze. — *v.i.* **napped, nap·ping 1.** To take a nap; doze. **2.** To be unprepared or off one's guard. [OE *hnappian* to doze]

nap² (nap) *n.* **1.** The short fibers forming a downy or fuzzy surface on flannel and certain other fabrics. **2.** A covering resembling this, as upon some plants. — *v.t.* **napped, nap·ping** To raise a nap on. [< MDu. *noppe*]

na·palm (nā'päm) *n.* A jellylike mixture that is combined with gasoline to form an incendiary fuel, as in bombs, flame throwers, etc. [< *na(phthenic)* and *palm(itic)* acids, chemical compounds used in its manufacture]

nape (nāp) n. The back of the neck. [Origin uncertain]

na·per·y (nā′pər·ē) n. pl. **·per·ies** Household linen, esp. napkins, tablecloths, etc. [See NAPKIN.]

Naph·ta·li (naf′tə·lī, -lē) In the Old Testament, a son of Jacob and Bilhah, Rachel's maid. Gen. xxx 7–8. — n. **1.** A tribe of Israel. **2.** The land occupied by the tribe of Naphtali. [< Hebrew, my wrestling]

naph·tha (naf′thə, nap′-) n. **1.** A volatile, colorless petroleum distillate intermediate between gasoline and benzene, used as a solvent, cleaning fluid, fuel, etc. **2.** Any similar substance obtained from another source, as from coal tar. **3.** Petroleum. [< L < Gk., prob. < Persian naft petroleum]

naph·tha·lene (naf′thə·lēn, nap′-) n. Chem. A colorless, odorous coal-tar compound, $C_{10}H_8$, used in the making of dyes, moth balls, etc. Also **naph′tha·line** (-lin, -lēn).

naph·thol (naf′thol, -thol, nap′-) n. Chem. Either of two compounds, $C_{10}H_7OH$, derived from naphthalene and used in making dyes. Also **naph·tol** (naf′tol, -tōl, nap′-).

nap·kin (nap′kin) n. **1.** A small, usu. square cloth or paper, used at meals for wiping the hands and mouth or protecting the clothes. **2.** A small piece of toweling. **3.** Chiefly Brit. A diaper. [ME napekyn, < L mappa a cloth]

na·po·le·on (nə·pō′lē·ən, Fr. nȧ·pô·lā·ôṅ′) n. **1.** A rich pastry composed of layers of puff paste filled with cream, custard, etc. **2.** A former French gold coin. **3.** A card game. [after Napoleon Bonaparte]

Na·po·le·on·ic (nə·pō′lē·on′ik) adj. Characteristic of, pertaining to, or suggesting Napoleon Bonaparte.

Napoleonic Wars See table for WAR.

nappe (nap) n. **1.** The sheet of water overlying the top of a weir. **2.** Geom. In a cone, one of the two conical surfaces divided by the vertex. [< F, sheet]

nap·per¹ (nap′ər) n. One who takes naps.

nap·per² (nap′ər) n. One who or that which raises a nap.

nap·py¹ (nap′ē) adj. **·pi·er, ·pi·est 1.** Having or coated with nap. **2.** Having a coarse or kinky quality, as hair.

nap·py² (nap′ē) n. pl. **·pies** Brit. Informal A baby's diaper. Also **nap′pie.** [< NAPKIN]

nar·cis·sism (när′sis·iz·əm, när·sis′iz·əm) n. **1.** Excessive admiration for or fascination with oneself. **2.** Psychoanal. The infantile stage of development in which the self is the object of one's erotic interest. Also **nar·cism** (när′siz·əm). [< NARCISSUS] — **nar′cis·sist** n. — **nar′cis·sis′tic** adj.

nar·cis·sus (när·sis′əs) n. pl. **·cis·sus·es** or **·cis·si** (-sis′ī) Any of various bulbous flowering plants of the amaryllis family, including the daffodil and jonquil.

Nar·cis·sus (när·sis′əs) In Greek mythology, a youth who fell in love with his own image in water and pined away for it until he died and changed into the narcissus.

narco- combining form Torpor; insensibility. Also, before vowels, **narc-.** [< Gk. narkē numbness]

nar·co·sis (när·kō′sis) n. Deep stupor produced by a drug.

nar·co·syn·the·sis (när′kō·sin′thə·sis) n. Psychiatry Therapy using narcotics to enable the patient to recall and relive painful experiences and minimize their hidden effects.

nar·cot·ic (när·kot′ik) n. **1.** A drug, as opium or morphine, that relieves pain and induces sleep, but may be habit-forming. **2.** One who is addicted to the use of narcotics. **3.** Anything that deadens or soothes. — adj. **1.** Capable of producing narcosis or stupor. **2.** Pertaining to, like, or induced by a narcotic or narcotics. **3.** Of, relating to, or for narcotic addicts or their treatment. [< L < Gk. < narkē torpor] — **nar·cot′i·cal·ly** adv.

nar·co·tism (när′kə·tiz′əm) n. **1.** Addiction to narcotics. **2.** Narcosis.

nar·co·tize (när′kə·tīz) v.t. **·tized, ·tiz·ing** To bring under the influence of a narcotic; stupefy. — **nar′co·ti·za′tion** n.

nard (närd) n. **1.** Spikenard. **2.** Any of several aromatic plants or roots formerly used in medicine. [< OF < L < Gk. nardos, prob. < Semitic]

nar·es (nâr′ēz) n. pl. of **nar·is** (nâr′is) Anat. Openings into the nasal cavities; esp., the nostrils. [< L, nostrils] — **nar·i·al** (nâr′ē·əl), **nar·ine** (nâr′in, -īn) adj.

nar·ghi·le (när′gə·lā) n. A hookah. Also **nar′gi·le, nar′gi·leh.** [< F < Persian < nārgīl coconut]

Nar·ra·gan·set (nar′ə·gan′sit) n. pl. **·set** or **·sets 1.** One of a tribe of North American Indians of Algonquian stock, formerly inhabiting Rhode Island. **2.** The language of this tribe. Also **Nar′ra·gan·sett.**

nar·rate (na·rāt′, nar′āt) v. **·rat·ed, ·rat·ing** v.t. **1.** To tell or relate, as a story. **2.** To speak in accompaniment and explanation of (a motion picture, television program, etc.). — v.i. **3.** To tell a story, etc. [< L narratus, pp. of narrare to relate] — **nar·ra·tor** or **nar·rat·er** (na·rāt′ər, nar′ā·tər) n.

nar·ra·tion (na·rā′shən) n. **1.** The act of narrating. **2.** A narrative. **3.** An account that narrates, as in fiction, etc.

nar·ra·tive (nar′ə·tiv) n. **1.** Something narrated, as an account, story, or tale. **2.** The act, art, or process of narrating. — adj. Of the nature of, pertaining to, or dealing with narration: a narrative poem. — **nar′ra·tive·ly** adv.

nar·row (nar′ō) adj. **1.** Having little width, esp. in comparison with length: not broad. **2.** Limited or small, as extent or scope: narrow ambition. **3.** Narrow-minded. Nearly unsuccessful or disastrous: a narrow escape. **5.** Prohibiting or characterized by small means or resources. Minute or detailed; painstaking: narrow search. — v.t. & To make or become narrow or narrower, as in width scope. — n. **1.** Usu. pl. A narrow passage; esp., the n rowest part of a strait, isthmus, etc. **2.** A narrow or c tracted part, as of a street or valley. [OE nearu] — row·ness n.

nar·row-gauge (nar′ō·gāj′) adj. Designed for or having width of railroad track less than 56½ inches. Also **nar′ro gage′, nar′row-gaged′, nar′row-gauged′.**

narrow gauge A narrow-gauge railway, locomotive, or c

nar·row·ly (nar′ō·lē) adv. **1.** Barely; hardly. **2.** So as be narrow. **3.** In a narrow manner.

nar·row-mind·ed (nar′ō-mīn′did) adj. Having or chara terized by narrow views or sentiments; illiberal; bigoted. **nar′row-mind′ed·ly** adv. — **nar′row-mind′ed·ness** n.

nar·whal (när′wəl -hwəl) n. A large, arctic cetacean ha ing in the male a long, straight, spiral tusk, and valued its oil and ivory. Also **nar′wal, nar·whale** (när′wā -hwäl′). [< Dan. or Sw. narhval]

na·sal (nā′zəl) adj. **1.** Of or pertaining to the nose. Phonet. Produced with the voice passing partially or whol through the nose, as (m), (n), and (ng), and the Fren nasal vowels. **3.** Characterized by or suggestive of a sou so produced. — n. **1.** Phonet. A nasal sound. **2.** Anat. part of the nose, as a bone. [< NL < L nasus nose] — **sal·i·ty** (nā·zal′ə·tē) n. — **na′sal·ly** adv.

na·sal·ize (nā′zəl·īz) v. **·ized, ·iz·ing** v.t. **1.** To give a nas sound to. — v.i. **2.** To produce nasal sounds instead of or ones. — **na′sal·i·za′tion** n.

nas·cent (nā′sənt, nas′ənt) adj. **1.** Beginning to exist develop; newly conceived. **2.** Chem. Of, pertaining to, being in the nascent state. [< L nascens, -centis, ppr. nasci to be born] — **nas′cence, nas′cen·cy** n.

nascent state Chem. The uncombined condition of atom in its most active state at the moment of its liberatio from a compound. Also **nascent condition.**

naso- combining form **1.** Nose. **2.** Nasal and. [< L nas nose]

na·stur·tium (nə·stûr′shəm) n. **1.** Any of various garde plants with funnel-shaped flowers, commonly yellow, orang or red. **2.** A rich yellow or reddish orange color. [< cress < nasus nose + tortus, pp. of torquere to twist]

nas·ty (nas′tē) adj. **·ti·er, ·ti·est 1.** Offensive to the sense taste or smell; disgusting. **2.** Indecent; obscene: nasty la guage. **3.** Disagreeable; unpleasant: nasty weather. Mean, spiteful, or ill-natured: a nasty remark. **5.** Grievo or painful: a nasty cut. [< Du. nestig or Sw. naskug filth — **nas′ti·ly** adv. — **nas′ti·ness** n.

-nasty combining form Biol. An automatic response to (specified) stimulus, or in a (specified) direction or characte [< Gk. nastos close-pressed]

na·tal (nāt′l) adj. **1.** Of or pertaining to one's birth. Poetic Native: said of a place. [< L nasci to be born]

na·ta·to·ry (nā′tə·tôr′ē, -tō′rē) adj. Of, pertaining to, adapted for swimming. Also **na′ta·to′ri·al.**

Natch·ez (nach′iz) n. pl. **Natch·ez** One of a tribe of Nor American Indians of Muskhogean stock, formerly inhabitin the lower Mississippi valley.

Na·than (nā′thən) In the Bible, a prophet who denounce David for the death of Uriah. II Sam. xii 1. [< Hebre nāthān he gave]

Na·than·a·el (nə·than′ē·əl, -than′yəl) A disciple of Jesu John xxi 1. [< Hebrew, gift of God]

na·tion (nā′shən) n. **1.** A body of persons associated wit a particular territory, usu. organized under a governmen and possessing a distinctive cultural and social way of lif **2.** A body of persons having a common origin and languag **3.** A tribe or federation, esp. of American Indians. [< L nasci to be born]

— **Syn. 1.** A nation is primarily the people under one gover ment; a state is an independent nation. The words are often inte changed, but nation stresses ethnic unity, while state stresses p litical autonomy. We may speak of the many nations that ma up the ancient Roman state. Country is primarily geographical, region of the earth distinct from others by its topographical fe tures or political character; Montenegro is a country, but no long a state.

na·tion·al (nash′ən·əl, nash′nəl) adj. **1.** Of, belonging t or representative of a nation as a whole. **2.** Characterist of or peculiar to a particular nation. — n. A subject citizen of a nation. [< F] — **na′tion·al·ly** adv.

national bank 1. U.S. A commercial bank organized b federal statute and chartered by the national governmen **2.** A bank associated with the national finances.

National Guard An organized militia force of a State, Territory, or the District of Columbia, maintained in pa by the U.S. government and subject to federal service national emergencies.

na·tion·al·ism (nash′ən·əl·is′əm, nash′nəl-) *n.* **1.** Devotion, often chauvinistic, to one's own nation. **2.** The belief or doctrine that among nations the common welfare is best served by independent rather than collective or cooperative action. **3.** A desire or movement for national independence. **— na′tion·al·ist** *adj. & n.* **— na′tion·al·is′tic** *adj.* **— na′·tion·al·is′ti·cal·ly** *adv.*

na·tion·al·i·ty (nash′ən·al′ə·tē) *n. pl.* **·ties 1.** A body of people having the same traditions, language, or ethnic origin, and potentially or actually constituting a nation. **2.** The state or fact of being related to a particular nation, as by birth or citizenship. **3.** National character or quality. **4.** The fact or quality of existing as a nation.

na·tion·al·ize (nash′ən·əl·īz′, nash′nəl-) *v.t.* **·ized, ·iz·ing 1.** To place (the industries, resources, etc., of a nation) under the control or ownership of the state. **2.** To make national, in character or scope. **3.** To accept as a national; naturalize. Also *Brit.* **na′tion·al·ise′. — na′tion·al·i·za′tion** *n.* **— na′tion·al·iz′er** *n.*

National League See under MAJOR LEAGUE.

National Socialism See under NAZI.

Nation of Islam See under BLACK MUSLIM.

na·tion-wide (nā′shən·wīd′) *adj.* Extending throughout the nation.

na·tive (nā′tiv) *adj.* **1.** Born in a particular place or region: *a native* New Yorker. **2.** Linked to one by birth or by conditions existing at the time and place of one's birth: *native* language. **3.** Produced, originated, or grown in a particular region or country; indigenous. **4.** Of, pertaining to, or characteristic of any particular area or its inhabitants. **5.** Natural rather than acquired; inborn: *native* shrewdness. **6.** Of, pertaining to, or characteristic of the original inhabitants, chiefly nonwhites, of areas recently discovered or settled by foreigners: *native* ritual. **7.** Occurring in nature in a pure state: *native* copper. **— n. 1.** A permanent or lifelong resident of a country or region. **2.** One who was born in a specified country or place. **3.** An original inhabitant of a country or region; aborigine. **4.** An animal, plant, or mineral found only in a specified country or place. [< F < L < *nasci* to be born.] **— na′tive·ly** *adv.* **— na′tive·ness** *n.* **— Syn.** (adj.) **1, 3.** indigenous, endemic.

na·tive-born (nā′tiv·bôrn′) *adj.* Born in the region or country specified.

na·tiv·i·ty (nā·tiv′ə·tē, nə-) *n. pl.* **·ties 1.** Birth, esp. with regard to the time, place, or circumstances surrounding it. **2.** In astrology, a horoscope taken at the time of one's birth. [< OF < L *nativitas*]

Na·tiv·i·ty (nā·tiv′ə·tē, nə-) *n. pl.* **·ties 1.** The birth of Christ: with *the*. **2.** A representation in a painting, drama, etc., of the birth of Christ. **3.** Christmas Day.

NATO (nā′tō) North Atlantic Treaty Organization.

na·tri·um (nā′trē·əm) *n.* Sodium. [< NL < F, ult. < Gk. *nitron* niter]

nat·ty (nat′ē) *adj.* **·ti·er, ·ti·est** Neat and smart, as in dress or appearance: *a natty* vest. [? Akin to NEAT¹] **— nat′ti·ly** *adv.* **— nat′ti·ness** *n.*

nat·u·ral (nach′ər·əl, nach′rəl) *adj.* **1.** Produced by or existing in nature; not artificial. **2.** Of, pertaining to, or involving nature or the study of nature. **3.** Derived from or defined by nature: *natural* day. **4.** Belonging to or existing in one's nature; innate: *natural* talent. **5.** Being so because of one's inherent ability, disposition, etc.: *a natural* athlete. **6.** Conforming to nature or to its usual or expected course: death from *natural* causes. **7.** Closely resembling nature; lifelike: *a natural* pose. **8.** Untouched by man or by the influences of civilization; wild. **9.** Free from affectation or awkwardness: *natural* manner. **10.** Derived from or consistent with the nature or essence of a thing; expected: *natural* conclusion. **11.** *Music* A not sharped or flatted. **b** Denoting a scale or mode that is unaltered by accidentals. **12.** Physical or actual, as distinguished from spiritual, etc.: *natural* man. **13.** Determined by innate moral conviction: *natural* rights. **14.** Related by blood rather than through adoption: *natural* mother. **15.** Founded upon reason rather than faith: *natural* religion. **16.** Born out of wedlock. **— n. 1.** *Music* **a** A note that is affected by neither a sharp nor a flat. **b** A character (♮) that cancels a sharp or flat at a specific line or space on the staff. **2.** In keyboard musical instruments, a white key. **3.** *U.S. Informal* One who or that which is naturally gifted, esp., well suited to some purpose, or obviously destined for success. [< F < L < *natura* nature, character] **— nat′u·ral·ness** *n.*

natural gas A gas consisting chiefly of methane, generated naturally in underground oil deposits and used as a fuel.

natural history The observation and study of the phenomena of the material universe, esp. the biological and earth sciences.

nat·u·ral·ism (nach′ər·əl·iz′əm, nach′rəl-) *n.* **1.** Close adherence to nature or human life in literature, painting, etc. **2.** *Philos.* The doctrine that all phenomena are derived from natural causes and can be explained by scientific laws. **3.** Action or thought derived exclusively from natural desires and instincts.

nat·u·ral·ist (nach′ər·əl·ist, nach′rəl-) *n.* **1.** One who is versed in natural history, as a zoologist or botanist. **2.** An adherent of the doctrine of naturalism.

nat·u·ral·is·tic (nach′ər·əl·is′tik, nach′rəl-) *adj.* **1.** Of, according to, or characteristic of naturalism. **2.** In accordance with or closely resembling nature. **3.** Of or pertaining to naturalists or natural history.

nat·u·ral·ize (nach′ər·əl·īz′, nach′rəl-) *v.* **·ized, ·iz·ing** *v.t.* **1.** To confer the rights and privileges of citizenship upon, as an alien. **2.** To adopt (a foreign word, custom, etc.) into the common use of a country or area. **3.** To adapt (a foreign plant, animal, etc.) to the environment of a country or area. **4.** To explain by natural laws: to *naturalize* a miracle. **5.** To make natural or lifelike. **— v.i. 6.** To become as if native; adapt. **7.** To observe or study nature. Also *Brit.* **nat′u·ral·ise′. — nat′u·ral·i·za′tion** *n.*

nat·u·ral·ly (nach′ər·əl·ē, nach′rəl·ē) *adv.* **1.** In a natural, normal, or expected manner. **2.** By inherent nature. **3.** Of course; certainly.

natural number *Math.* A positive integer, as 1, 2, 3, etc.

natural philosophy 1. The study of nature in general. **2.** The physical sciences collectively.

natural resource *Usu. pl.* **1.** A source of wealth provided by nature, as forests, minerals, and water supply. **2.** Any natural ability or talent.

natural science 1. The sciences collectively that deal with the physical universe. **2.** Any one of these sciences, as biology, chemistry, or physics.

natural selection *Biol.* The process whereby individual variations advantageous to an organism in a certain environment tend to become perpetuated in later generations; survival of the fittest forms.

na·ture (nā′chər) *n.* **1.** The essential character of something: the *nature* of democracy. **2.** *Sometimes cap.* The overall pattern or system of natural objects, existences, forces, events, etc.; also, the principle or power that appears to guide it: laws of *nature*. **3.** The entire material universe and its phenomena. **4.** The basic character or disposition of a person or animal. **5.** *Sometimes cap.* A force, drive, or tendency that influences or determines the behavior or condition of a person or thing; instinct. **6.** Sort; kind; variety: nothing of that *nature*. **7.** A wild, naked, or uncivilized condition. **8.** That which is within the accepted or legal limits of morality: an act against *nature*. **9.** Natural aspect or appearance, as of a person or scene. **— by nature** By birth or disposition. [< OF < L < *nasci* to be born]

-natured *combining form* Possessing a (specified) nature, disposition, or temperament: *good-natured*.

naught (nôt) *n.* **1.** Nothing. **2.** A cipher; zero; the character 0. Also spelled *nought*. [OE < *nā* not + *wiht* thing]

naugh·ty (nô′tē) *adj.* **·ti·er, ·ti·est 1.** Mischievous; disobedient; bad. **2.** Indecent or improper: a *naughty* word. **— naugh′ti·ly** *adv.* **— naugh′ti·ness** *n.*

nau·se·a (nô′zē·ə, -zhə, -sē·ə, -shə) *n.* **1.** A sick feeling in the stomach accompanied by an impulse to vomit; queasiness. **2.** Strong disgust or loathing. [< L < Gk. *nausia, nautia* seasickness]

nau·se·ate (nô′zē·āt, -sē-, -zhē-, -shē-) *v.t. & v.i.* **·at·ed, ·at·ing** To affect with or feel nausea or disgust.

nau·seous (nô′shəs, -zhē·əs, -zē·əs, -sē·əs) *adj.* **1.** Affected with nausea; queasy; sick. **2.** Nauseating; disgusting. **— nau′seous·ly** *adv.* **— nau′seous·ness** *n.*

nau·ti·cal (nô′ti·kəl) *adj.* Pertaining to or involving ships, seamen, or navigation. **— Syn.** See MARINE. [< L < Gk. < *naus* ship] **— nau′ti·cal·ly** *adv.*

nau·ti·lus (nô′tə·ləs) *n. pl.* **·lus·es** or **·li** (-lī) **1.** Any of a group of mollusks with a spiral shell whose chambers are lined with mother-of-pearl; esp., the **chambered** or **pearly nautilus. 2.** The paper nautilus. [< L < Gk. *nautilos sailor*]

Nav·a·ho (nav′ə·hō) *n. pl.* **·hos, ·hoes** or **·ho** One of a tribe of North American Indians now living on reservations in Arizona, New Mexico, and Utah. Also **Nav′a·jo.**

na·val (nā′vəl) *adj.* **1.** Of, involving, or having a navy: a *naval* power. **2.** Of or pertaining to ships: a *naval* convoy. **— Syn.** See MARINE. [< L < *navis* ship]

nave¹ (nāv) *n. Archit.* The main body of a church, situated

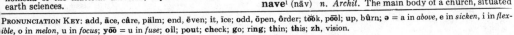

CHAMBERED NAUTILUS
(Cross-section; diameter to 10 inches)

between the side aisles [< L *navis* ship]

nave[2] (nāv) *n.* The hub of a wheel. [OE *nafu*]

na·vel (nā′vəl) *n.* **1.** The depression on the abdomen where the umbilical cord was attached; umbilicus. **2.** A central part or point. [OE < *nafu* nave[2]]

navel orange An orange, usu. seedless, having a navellike depression that contains a small, secondary fruit.

nav·i·cert (nav′ə·sûrt) *n. Brit.* A safe-conduct authorizing a vessel of a friendly or neutral nation to pass through a naval blockade.

nav·i·ga·ble (nav′ə·gə·bəl) *adj.* Capable of being navigated; as: **a** Broad or deep enough to admit of passage: said of a body of water. **b** Capable of being steered. **— nav′·i·ga·bil′i·ty**, **— nav′i·ga·ble·ness** *n.* **— nav′i·ga·bly** *adv.*

nav·i·gate (nav′ə·gāt) *v.* **·gat·ed**, **·gat·ing** *v.t.* **1.** To travel or move across, over, on, or through, as by ship or aircraft. **2.** To plot the course of (a ship, aircraft, etc.). **3.** To manage or direct the course of; guide: to *navigate* a missile. — *v.i.* **4.** To guide or steer a ship, aircraft, etc. **5.** To compute and plot the course, position, etc., as of a ship or aircraft. **6.** To travel by ship. [< L < *navis* boat + *agere* to direct]

nav·i·ga·tion (nav′ə·gā′shən) *n.* **1.** The act or practice of navigating. **2.** The art or science of charting the course of ships, aircraft, etc. **— nav′i·ga′tion·al** *adj.*

navigation light *Aeron.* One of the colored lights on an aircraft, indicating its size, position, and course at night: also called *running light.*

nav·i·ga·tor (nav′ə·gā′tər) *n.* **1.** One who navigates. **2.** One who is trained in or practices navigation. [< L]

nav·vy (nav′ē) *n. pl.* **·vies** *Brit.* A laborer, esp. in construction work on railways, roads, etc. [< NAVIGATOR]

na·vy (nā′vē) *n. pl.* **·vies** **1.** *Often cap.* The entire military sea force of a country, including vessels, servicemen, yards, etc.; also, the agency of government charged with its supervision. **2.** The warships of a nation, taken collectively. **3.** Navy blue. [< OF < L *navis* ship]

navy bean A small, dried, white bean related to the common kidney bean. [from its use in the U.S. Navy]

navy blue A very dark blue: also *navy.*

Navy Cross A decoration in the form of a bronze cross, awarded by the U.S. Navy for extraordinary heroism in action against the enemy. See DECORATION.

navy yard A government-owned dockyard for the building, repairing, docking, and equipping of warships.

nay (nā) *adv.* **1.** *Archaic* No. **2.** Not exactly that, but rather: She is a pretty, *nay,* a beautiful woman. — *n.* **1.** A negative vote or voter: opposed to *yea.* **2.** A denial or refusal. [ME < ON < *ne* not + *ei* ever]

Naz·a·rene (naz′ə·rēn) *n.* **1.** A native or inhabitant of Nazareth. **2.** A Christian. **3.** One of a sect of early Christians of Jewish origin who continued to observe much of the Jewish ritual. **— the Nazarene** Jesus Christ. — *adj.* Of Nazareth or the Nazarenes. Also **Naz′a·re′an** (-rē′ən).

Naz·a·rite (naz′ə·rīt) *n.* An ancient Hebrew who took vows of abstinence. *Num.* vi. Also **Naz′i·rite**. [< Hebrew < *nāzar* to abstain]

na·zi (nä′tsē, nat′sē, na′zē) *Often cap. n. pl.* **·zis** One who advocates or practices Nazism. — *adj.* Of the nature of, pertaining to, or involving Nazism. [< NAZI]

Na·zi (nä′tsē, nat′sē, na′zē) *n. pl.* **·zis** A member of the National Socialist German Workers' Party, founded in 1919, whose fascistic program (called **National Socialism**) was dominant in Germany from 1933 to 1945 under the dictatorship of Hitler. — *adj.* **1.** Of or pertaining to the Nazis or their party. **2.** Caused or committed by Nazis: *Nazi* atrocities. [< G, short for *nationalsozialist* National Socialist] **— Na′zism** or **Na′zi·ism** *n.*

Ne·an·der·thal (nē·an′dər·täl, -thôl, -thol; *Ger.* nā·än′dər·täl) *adj.* Of or characteristic of Neanderthal man.

Neanderthal man *Anthropol.* An extinct species of man that typifies the paleolithic cavedwellers preceding modern man. [< G *Neanderthal*, Neander valley, Germany, where the first bones of this species were found]

neap (nēp) *adj.* Designating or pertaining to a neap tide. — *n.* A neap tide. [OE *nēp-* in *nēpflod* low tide]

Ne·a·pol·i·tan (nē′ə·pol′ə·tən) *adj.* Of, relating to, or characteristic of Naples. — *n.* A native or resident of Naples.

neap tide The tide occurring shortly after the first and third quarters of the moon, when the rise and fall are minimal: also called *neap.*

near (nir) *adv.* **1.** At, to, or within a little distance; not remote in place, time, or degree. **2.** Nearly; almost: a team of *near* championship caliber. **3.** In a close relation; intimately. **4.** Stingily or frugally. — *adj.* **1.** Not distant in place, time, or degree. **2.** Closely approximating; almost achieved: a *near* success. **3.** Narrow; close: a *near* escape. **4.** Closely related, as by blood: someone *near* and dear. **5.** Closely touching one's interests or affections; intimate. **6.** That saves distance or time; short; direct. **7.** Stingy; miserly. **8.** On the left: used in riding or driving: the *near* ox: opposed to *off.* — *prep.* Close by or to. — *v.t. & v.i.* To come or

draw near (to); approach. [OE *nēar*, compar. of *nēah* nigh] **— near′ness** *n.*

near·by (nir′bī′) *adj. & adv.* Close by; near; adjacent.

Near East The countries lying east of the Mediterranea[n] mostly in SW Asia, including Turkey, Syria, Lebano[n] Israel, Jordan, Saudi Arabia, etc., and sometimes the Ba[l]kans and Egypt.

near·ly (nir′lē) *adv.* **1.** Almost; practically. **2.** Closely, in distance, time, degree, similarity, etc.

near·sight·ed (nir′sī′tid) *adj.* Able to see distinctly [at] short distances only; myopic. **— near′sight′ed·ly** *adv.* **— near′sight′ed·ness** *n.*

neat (nēt) *adj.* **1.** Characterized by or in a state of order[li]ness, tidiness, and cleanliness. **2.** Free from sloppines[s] vagueness, or embellishment; precise. **3.** Ingeniously do[ne] or said; clever: a *neat* trick. **4.** Free from admixture; u[n]diluted, as liquor. **5.** Remaining after all deductions; ne[t] [< OF < L *nitidus* shining] **— neat′ly** *adv.* **— neat′ness** *n.*

'neath (nēth) *prep. Dial.* or *Poetic* Beneath. Also **neat[h]**

neat's-foot oil (nēts′foot′) A pale yellow oil obtained b[y] boiling the shinbones and feet of cattle, used as a lubrica[nt] and softening agent for leather.

Neb·u·chad·nez·zar (neb′yōō·kəd·nez′ər), died 562 B.C[.] king of Babylonia 605–562 B.C.; conquered Jerusalem. *Kings* xxiv and xxv. Also **Neb′u·chad·rez′zar** (-rez′ər).

neb·u·la (neb′yə·lə) *n. pl.* **·lae** (-lē) or **·las** *Astron.* An interstellar mass of cloudlike appearance and vast exten[t] often luminous, and composed of gaseous matter. [< [mist,] vapor, mist] **— neb′u·lar** *adj.*

nebular hypothesis *Astron.* The hypothesis that th[e] solar system was formed from the consolidation of great ma[s]ses of matter thrown off by a rotating nebula.

neb·u·lose (neb′yə·lōs) *adj.* Nebulous.

neb·u·los·i·ty (neb′yə·los′ə·tē) *n. pl.* **·ties** **1.** The state [or] quality of being nebulous. **2.** A nebula.

neb·u·lous (neb′yə·ləs) *adj.* **1.** Vague or confused; haz[y] **2.** Cloudlike; misty. **3.** Of, pertaining to, or like a nebul[a.] **— neb′u·lous·ly** *adv.* **— neb′u·lous·ness** *n.*

nec·es·sar·i·ly (nes′ə·ser′ə·lē) *adv.* **1.** As a necessary co[n]sequence. **2.** Of necessity; unavoidably.

nec·es·sar·y (nes′ə·ser′ē) *adj.* **1.** Absolutely needed to a[c]complish a certain result; essential. **2.** Being of such a na[ture] that it must exist or occur; inevitable: a *necessary* b[e]lief. **3.** Caused by or acting under obligation or compulsio[n] required. **4.** That cannot be logically denied. — *n.* p[l.] **·sar·ies** *Often pl.* That which is indispensable; an essenti[al] requisite: the *necessaries* of life.

ne·ces·si·tate (nə·ses′ə·tāt) *v.t.* **·tat·ed**, **·tat·ing** **1.** To mak[e] necessary. **2.** To compel or oblige: No man is *necessitated* t[o] lie. **— ne·ces′si·ta′tion** *n.* **— ne·ces′si·ta′tive** *adj.*

ne·ces·si·tous (nə·ses′ə·təs) *adj.* **1.** Extremely needy; de[s]titute; poverty-stricken. **2.** Urgent; compelling. **— n[e·]ces′si·tous·ly** *adv.* **— ne·ces′si·tous·ness** *n.*

ne·ces·si·ty (nə·ses′ə·tē) *n. pl.* **·ties** **1.** *Often pl.* Tha[t] which is indispensable or requisite, esp. toward the attai[n]ment of some end. **2.** The quality, conditon, or fact [of] being necessary. **3.** The conditions that make compulso[ry] a particular course of action: to resign out of *necessity.* **4.** Urgent or desperate need, as because of poverty or acciden[t] also, a time of such need. **5.** That which is unavoidable b[e]cause it is part of an invariable process, as in nature, logi[c] etc.; also, the process itself. **— of necessity** By necessity inevitably. [< OF < L *necessitas*]

neck (nek) *n.* **1.** *Anat.* **a** The part of an animal that co[n]nects the head with the trunk. **b** Any similarly constricte[d] part of an organ, bone, etc.: the *neck* of the uterus. ◆ Co[m]lateral adjective: *cervical.* **2.** The narrowed part of an ob[ject,] esp. if near one end: the *neck* of a bottle. **3.** Somethin[g] likened to a neck; as: **a** A narrow passage of water betwee[n] two larger bodies of water. **b** A narrow strip of land, as [a] peninsula, isthmus, or cape. **4.** The part of a garment clos[e] to or covering the neck. **5.** The part of a violin, guitar, etc[.] that carries the fingerboard and tuning pegs. **6.** *Archit.* The upper part of the shaft of a column, just below the capita[l] **— neck and neck** Abreast of one another, as horses in [a] race. **— neck of the woods** *U.S. Informal* A neighborho[od] or region. **— to save one's (own) neck** To extricate onese[lf] from difficult or dangerous circumstances, often without co[n]cern for others. — *v.i.* **1.** *U.S. Slang* To kiss and cares[s] in lovemaking. — *v.t.* **2.** *U.S. Slang* To make love t[o] (someone) in such a manner. [OE *hnecca*]

neck·band (nek′band′) *n.* **1.** The part of a garment tha[t] fits around the neck. **2.** A band around the neck.

necked (nekt) *adj.* **1.** Having a neck or necks. **2.** Havin[g] or characterized by (a specified kind of) neck or (a specifie[d] number of) necks: used in combination: *long-necked.*

neck·er·chief (nek′ər·chif) *n.* A kerchief for the neck.

neck·ing (nek′ing) *n. U.S. Slang* Kissing and caressing [in] lovemaking.

neck·lace (nek′lis) *n.* An ornament worn around the nec[k] and usu. consisting of a string of beads, shells gems, etc.

ck·line (nek′līn′) *n.* The line or contour formed by the t of a garment around the neck.

ck·piece (nek′pēs′) *n.* An article of clothing, usu. of fur, orn around the neck like a scarf.

ck·tie (nek′tī′) *n.* **1.** A strip of material worn knotted round the neck or collar and hanging down the front of a' hirt. **2.** Any bow or tie worn under the chin.

ck·wear (nek′wâr′) *n.* Articles worn around the neck, as ies, collars, mufflers, etc.

cro- *combining form* Corpse; the dead; death. Also, be- ore vowels, **necr-**. [< Gk. *nekros* corpse]

·crol·o·gy (ne·krol′ə·jē) *n.* *pl.* ·**gies 1.** A list of persons ho have died in a certain place or time. **2.** An obituary otice. — **nec·ro·log·ic** (nek′rə·loj′ik) or ·**i·cal** *adj.* — **nec′·** **o·log′i·cal·ly** *adv.* — **ne·crol′o·gist** *n.*

·cro·man·cy (nek′rə·man′sē) *n.* **1.** The art of divining ne future through alleged communication with the dead. . Black magic; sorcery. [ME < OF < L < Gk. <*nekros* orpse + *manteia* divination] — **nec′ro·man′cer** *n.* — **ec′ro·man′tic** *adj.*

·ec·ro·phil·i·a (nek′rō·fil′ē·ə) *n.* An abnormal attraction, sp. of an erotic nature, to corpses. — **nec·ro·phile** (nek′rə- l, -fil) *n.* — **nec′ro·phil′ic** *adj.*

·crop·o·lis (ne·krop′ə·lis) *n.* A cemetery. [< Gk. < *ekros* corpse + *polis* city]

·cro·sis (ne·krō′sis) *n.* **1.** *Pathol.* The death of tissue in a ving animal, resulting from infection or burns; gangrene. . *Bot.* A decay and death of plant tissue. [< Gk. *nekrōsis* .eath] — **ne·crot′ic** (-krot′ik) *adj.*

·ec·tar (nek′tər) *n.* **1.** In Greek mythology, the drink of he gods. **2.** Any delicious drink. **3.** *Bot.* The saccharine ecretion of plants, collected by bees to make honey. [< L < Gk. *nektar*] — **nec·tar·e·an** (nek·târ′ē·ən), **nec·tar·e·ous** nek·târ′ē·əs), **nec·tar·ous** (nek′tər·əs) *adj.*

·ec·tar·ine (nek′tə·rēn′, nek′tə·rēn) *n.* A variety of peach aving a smooth, waxy skin and a firm pulp.

·ec·ta·ry (nek′tər·ē) *n.* *pl.* ·**ries** *Bot.* A gland that secretes ectar.

·e (nā) *adj.* Born with the name of: used chiefly to note he maiden name of a married woman: Mrs. Mary Lincoln, *ée* Todd. Also **nee**. [< F, pp. fem. of *naître* to be born]

·ed (nēd) *v.t.* **1.** To have an urgent or essential use for something lacking; want; require. — *v.i.* **2.** To be in vant. **3.** To be obliged or compelled; have to: He *need* not o. — *n.* **1.** The fact, quality, or condition of lacking or eeling the lack of something necessary or desirable. **2.** A esire or longing: the *need* for revenge. **3.** Obligation; ne- essity: no *need* to be afraid. **4.** A condition of want, dan- er, or helplessness. **5.** Something wanted or required: nodest *needs*. **6.** Poverty; hardship. — **Syn.** See POVER- Y. [OE *nīed*, *nēd*] — **need′er** *n.*

·ed·ful (nēd′fəl) *adj.* **1.** Needed; requisite; necessary. . *Archaic* Needy. — **need′ful·ly** *adv.* — **need′ful·ness** *n.* **·ed·i·ness** (nē′dē·nis, -di·nis) *n.* The state of being needy; overty; want.

·ee·dle (nēd′l) *n.* **1.** A small, slender, pointed instrument, usu. of steel, with an eye at one end to carry thread through abric in sewing. **2.** A hypodermic needle. **3.** A pointer or ndex, as in a gauge or compass. **4.** A small, pointed instru- nent of steel, diamond, etc., that traverses the grooves of a ·honograph record and transmits sound vibrations: some- imes called *stylus*. **5.** A slender, pointed rod of steel, bone, tc., used in knitting; also, a similar, hooked rod used in rocheting. **6.** A needleshaped leaf, as that of a pine tree. 7. Any object suggesting a needle in shape. **8.** A fine- ·ointed instrument used in etching. **9.** *Mech.* A needle valve (which see). — **on the needle** *U.S. Slang* Addicted to arcotics. — *v.* **dled, ·dling** *v.t.* **1.** To sew or pierce with needle. **2.** *Informal* To tease or heckle repeatedly. **3.** J.S. *Informal* To increase the alcoholic content of: to *needle* he beer. — *v.i.* **4.** To sew or work with a needle. **5.** To rystallize in the form of needles. [OE *nǣdle*]

·ee·dle·point (nēd′l·point′) *n.* **1.** Embroidery on canvas, as in a tapestry; also, a single stitch. **2.** Lace made with a ewing needle on a paper pattern: also called *point lace*.

·eed·less (nēd′lis) *adj.* Not needed or necessary; useless. — **need′less·ly** *adv.* — **need′less·ness** *n.*

·eedle valve *Mech.* A valve having a needlelike plug ·apable of closely regulating the flow of a liquid or gas.

·ee·dle·wom·an (nēd′l·wŏŏm′ən) *n.* *pl.* ·**wom·en** (-wim′- n) A seamstress.

·ee·dle·work (nēd′l·wûrk′) *n.* Work done with a needle.

·eed·n't (nēd′nt) Need not.

·eeds (nēdz) *adv.* *Archaic* Of necessity: often with *must*: He *needs* must go. [OE *niedes*]

·eed·y (nē′dē) *adj.* **need·i·er, need·i·est** Being in need, vant, or poverty; necessitous.

·e′er (nâr) *adv.* *Poetic* Never.

ne′er-do-well (nâr′dōō·wel′) *n.* A worthless, unreliable person. — *adj.* Shiftless; good-for-nothing.

ne·far·i·ous (ni·fâr′ē·əs) *adj.* Extremely wicked; vile. [< L < *ne-* not + *fas* divine law] — **ne·far′i·ous·ly** *adv.* — **ne·far′i·ous·ness** *n.*

ne·gate (ni·gāt′, nĕ′gāt) *v.t.* ·**gat·ed, ·gat·ing 1.** To render ineffective or void; nullify. **2.** To deny; contradict; rule out. [< L *negatus*, pp. of *negare* to deny]

ne·ga·tion (ni·gā′shən) *n.* **1.** The absence or opposite of something: Sleep is the *negation* of consciousness. **2.** The act of denying or contradicting. **3.** That which is negative.

neg·a·tive (neg′ə·tiv) *adj.* **1.** Expressing, containing, or characterized by negation, denial, or refusal. **2.** Marked by the absence of positive or affirmative qualities: a *negative* attitude. **3.** *Math.* Less than zero; to be subtracted; minus. **4.** *Electr.* Having the kind of electricity exhibited by a resinous object when rubbed with wool. **5.** *Med.* Not indi- cating the presence of a particular disease, organism, etc.: a *negative* blood test. **6.** *Photog.* Having the lights and darks reversed. — *n.* **1.** *Photog.* An image showing the lights and darks reversed; also, the film or plate on which it appears. **2.** An expression of denial or refusal. **3.** The side of a ques- tion that denies or contradicts what the other side affirms, as in a debate. **4.** *Math.* A negative symbol or quantity. **5.** *Electr.* A negative pole, plate, terminal, etc. **6.** *Gram.* A negative particle, as *not*. — *adv.* No; not so: a military usage. — **double negative** *Gram.* The use of two negatives in the same statement, as in "I didn't see nobody." ◆ This usage is now considered nonstandard. Such statements as "I am not unhappy," however, are standard English and have the effect of weak affirmatives. — **in the negative 1.** By or with an expression of refusal; no. **2.** On the negative or opposing side. — *v.t.* ·**tived, ·tiv·ing 1.** reject; veto. **2.** To deny; contradict. **3.** To prove to be false. **4.** To make ineffective. [< F < L *negare* to deny] — **neg′a·tive·ly** *adv.* — **neg′a·tive·ness, neg′a·tiv′i·ty** *n.*

neg·a·tiv·ism (neg′ə·tiv·iz′əm) *n.* **1.** An attitude charac- terized by the questioning of traditional beliefs; skepticism. **2.** A tendency to deny, contradict, etc. **3.** *Psychol.* An atti- tude characterized by resistance to suggestion. — **neg′a·** **tiv·ist** *n. & adj.* — **neg′a·tiv·is′tic** *adj.*

neg·lect (ni·glekt′) *v.t.* **1.** To fail to heed or take note of; disregard. **2.** To fail to give proper attention to: to *neglect* one's business. **3.** To fail to do or perform; leave undone. — *n.* **1.** Habitual want of attention or care; negligence. **2.** The act of neglecting, or the state of being neglected. **3.** An instance of neglect. [< L < *nec-* not + *legere* to gather] — **neg·lect′er** or **neg·lec′tor** *n.*

neg·lect·ful (ni·glekt′fəl) *adj.* Exhibiting or indicating neg- lect. — **neg·lect′ful·ly** *adv.* — **neg·lect′ful·ness** *n.*

neg·li·gee (neg′li·zhā′, neg′li·zhā) *n.* **1.** A loose, flowing, usu. decorative dressing gown worn by women. **2.** Any informal attire. Also **neg·li·gée′,** *French* **né·gli·gé** (nā·glē- zhā′). [< F *négligé*, pp. of *négliger* to neglect]

neg·li·gence (neg′lə·jəns) *n.* **1.** The state, quality, or fact of being negligent. **2.** A negligent act or omission. [< OF]

neg·li·gent (neg′lə·jənt) *adj.* **1.** Habitually neglecting to do what ought to be done; neglectful. **2.** Free-and-easy; in- formal; nonchalant. — **neg′li·gent·ly** *adv.*

neg·li·gi·ble (neg′lə·jə·bəl) *adj.* Not worth considering, as because of trifling size, amount, or extent. — **neg′li·gi·bil′·** **i·ty, neg′li·gi·ble·ness** *n.* — **neg′li·gi·bly** *adv.*

ne·go·ti·a·ble (ni·gō′shē·ə·bəl, -shə·bəl) *adj.* **1.** Capable of being negotiated. **2.** Open to negotiation. **3.** That can be legally transferred to another party. — **ne·go′ti·a·bil′i·ty** *n.*

ne·go·ti·ate (ni·gō′shē·āt) *v.* ·**at·ed, ·at·ing** *v.i.* **1.** To con- fer with another party with the aim of reaching an agree- ment. — *v.t.* **2.** To arrange or conclude by negotiation. **3.** To transfer (a note, bond, etc.) to another for a value re- ceived; sell. **4.** To manage to execute, traverse, or cope with (something difficult): to *negotiate* a steep hill. [< L *negotiari* to do business] — **ne·go′ti·a′tor** *n.*

ne·go·ti·a·tion (ni·gō′shē·ā′shən) *n.* **1.** The act or process of negotiating. **2.** A conference or discussion designed to produce an agreement.

Ne·gri·to (ni·grē′tō) *n.* *pl.* ·**tos** or ·**toes** *Anthropol.* One of the Pygmy peoples of the Malay Peninsula, the Philippine Islands, central Africa, and southeast Asia. [< Sp., dim. of *negro* black]

ne·gri·tude (nē′grə·tōōd′, -tyōōd′) *n.* Often cap. **1.** Aware- ness of and pride in one's black African heritage. **2.** The fact of being a Negro; Negroness. Also *French* **né·gri·tude** (nā′grə·tüd′). [< F < L *niger* black]

Ne·gro (nē′grō) *n.* *pl.* ·**groes 1.** A member of the Negroid ethnic division of mankind. **2.** One who is of Negroid stock or has Negro ancestors. — *adj.* **1.** Of, pertaining to, or having the characteristics of a Negro or Negroes. **2.** Of Ne- groid ethnic stock. Also **ne′gro.** [< Sp. < L *niger* black]

RONUNCIATION KEY: add, āce, câre, pälm; end, ēven; it, īce; odd, ōpen, ôrder; tŏŏk, pōōl; up, bûrn; ə = a in *above*, e in *sicken*, i in *flex- le*, o in *melon*, u in *focus*; yōō = u in *fuse*; oil; pout; check; go; ring; thin; this; zh, vision.

Ne·groid (nē′groid) *adj.* **1.** *Anthropol.* Of, pertaining to, or belonging to a major ethnic division of the human species characterized by skin color ranging from dark brown to almost black. **2.** Resembling, related to, or characteristic of Negroes. — *n.* A Negroid person.

Ne·gro·ness (nē′grō·nis) *n.* The fact of being a Negro.

Ne·he·mi·ah (nē′hə·mī′ə) Fifth-century B.C. Hebrew statesman and historian. — *n.* A book of the Old Testament: also, in the Douai Bible, II *Esdras.* [< Hebrew *Nehemyāh* Jehovah comforts]

neigh (nā) *v.i.* To utter the cry of a horse; whinny. — *n.* The cry of a horse. [OE *hnǣgan;* imit.]

neigh·bor (nā′bər) *n.* **1.** One who lives near another. **2.** One who or that which is near another. **3.** *Chiefly Dial.* Friend; mister: a term of address. — *adj.* Living nearby. — *v.t. & v.i.* To live or be near to or next to; adjoin: Also *Brit.* **neigh′bour.** [OE < *nēah* near + *gebur* dweller]

neigh·bor·hood (nā′bər·hŏŏd) *n.* **1.** A comparatively small region possessing some specific quality or character. **2.** The people who live in such a region. **3.** Any region or area; vicinity. Also *Brit.* **neigh′bour·hood.** — **in the neighborhood of 1.** Near. **2.** *Informal* Approximately.

neigh·bor·ing (nā′bər·ing) *adj.* Situated or living nearby.

neigh·bor·ly (nā′bər·lē) *adj.* Like a good neighbor; kind, sociable, etc. — **neigh′bor·li·ness** *n.*

nei·ther (nē′thər, nī′-) *adj.* Not the one nor the other; not either. — *pron.* Not the one nor the other: *Neither* of the hats is becoming. — *conj.* **1.** Not either; not: used with the correlative *nor* to list alternatives and to signify their negation: He *neither* reads nor writes. **2.** Nor yet: He cannot write: *neither* can he read. ◆ See usage note under EITHER. [ME *naither, neyther* < OE *nāhwaether*]

nemato- *combining form* Thread; filament: also, before vowels, **nemat-.** Also **nema-.** [< Gk. *nēma, -matos* thread]

nem·a·tode (nem′ə·tōd) *Zool. adj.* Of or belonging to a phylum or class of roundworms, as the hookworm. — *n.* A nematode worm. [< NL *Nematoda*]

nem·e·sis (nem′ə·sis) *n.* *pl.* **·ses** (-sēz) **1.** An unusually tenacious opponent or antagonist. **2.** An instrument of vengeance. [< Gk., retributive justice]

Nem·e·sis (nem′ə·sis) In Greek mythology, the goddess of retributive justice or vengeance. [< NEMESIS]

neo- *combining form* New; recent; a modern or modified form of. Also, before vowels, usu. **ne-.** [< Gk. < *neos* new]

ne·o·clas·sic (nē′ō·klas′ik) *adj.* Of, pertaining to, or denoting a revival of classical style in literature, art, music, etc. Also **ne′o·clas′si·cal.** — **ne′o·clas′si·cism** *n.* — **ne′o·clas′si·cist** *n.*

ne·o·dym·i·um (nē′ō·dim′ē·əm) *n.* A metallic element (symbol Nd) forming rose-colored salts, found in combination with cerium, etc. See ELEMENT. [< NEO- + (DI)DYMIUM]

Ne·o·lith·ic (nē′ə·lith′ik) *adj.* *Anthropol.* Of or pertaining to the period of human culture following the Mesolithic, characterized by polished stone implements and a settled agriculture. [< Gk. *neos* new + *lithos* stone]

ne·ol·o·gism (nē·ol′ə·jiz′əm) *n.* **1.** A new word or phrase. **2.** The use of new words or of new meanings for old words. Also **ne·ol′o·gy.** [< F *néologisme*] — **ne·ol′o·gist** *n.* — **ne·ol′o·gis′tic** or **·ti·cal** *adj.*

ne·o·my·cin (nē′ə·mī′sin) *n.* An antibiotic related to streptomycin, used in the treatment of certain infections.

ne·on (nē′on) *n.* A gaseous element (symbol Ne) occurring in the atmosphere in very small amounts. See ELEMENT. — *adj.* **1.** Of or pertaining to neon. **2.** Composed of or employing neon. [< NL < Gk., neut. of *neos* new]

ne·o·phyte (nē′ə·fīt) *n.* **1.** A recent convert, esp. in the early Christian Church. **2.** Any beginner. [< LL < Gk. *neophytos* newly planted] — **ne′o·phyt′ic** (-fit′ik) *adj.*

ne·o·plasm (nē′ə·plaz′əm) *n.* *Pathol.* Any abnormal growth of tissue in the body; a tumor. — **ne′o·plas′tic** *adj.*

ne·o·prene (nē′ə·prēn) *n.* *Chem.* Any of various types of synthetic rubber. [< NEO- + (CHLORO)PRENE]

Nep·a·lese (nep′ə·lēz′, -lēs′) *adj.* Of Nepal, its people, or their culture. — *n.* A native or inhabitant of Nepal.

ne·pen·the (ni·pen′thē) *n.* **1.** A drug or potion supposed by the ancient Greeks to banish pain and sorrow. **2.** Anything causing oblivion. [< L < Gk. < *nē-* not + *penthos* sorrow]

neph·ew (nef′yŏŏ, *esp. Brit.* nev′yŏŏ) *n.* The son of a brother or brother-in-law or of a sister or sister-in-law. [< OF < L *nepos* grandson, nephew.]

nepho- *combining form* Cloud. Also, before vowels, **neph-.** [< Gk. *nephos* cloud]

neph·rite (nef′rīt) *n.* A very hard, compact, white to dark-green mineral formerly worn as a remedy for diseases of the kidney. [< G *nephrit* < Gk. *nephros* kidney]

ne·phrit·ic (ni·frit′ik) *adj.* **1.** Of or pertaining to the kidney or kidneys; renal: also **neph′ric. 2.** Of, pertaining to, or suffering from nephritis. Also **ne·phrit′i·cal.** — *n.* Any medicine applicable to disease of the kidney.

ne·phri·tis (ni·frī′tis) *n.* *Pathol.* Inflammation of the kid-

neys. [< LL < Gk. *nephros* kidney]

nephro- *combining form* A kidney. Also, before vowel **nephr-.** [< Gk. *nephros* kidney]

ne·phro·sis (ni·frō′sis) *n.* *Pathol.* Disease of the kidney

ne plus ul·tra (nē plus ul′trə) *Latin* The extreme or u most point; perfection; literally, nothing more beyond.

nep·o·tism (nep′ə·tiz′əm) *n.* Favoritism; esp. governme tal patronage to relatives. [< F < L *nepos, -potis* grandso nephew] — **ne·pot·ic** (ni·pot′ik) *adj.* — **nep′o·tist** *n.*

Nep·tune (nep′tŏŏn, -tyŏŏn) In Roman mythology, the g of the sea: identified with the Greek *Poseidon.* — *n.* T fourth largest planet and eighth in order from the sun. S PLANET. [< L *Neptunus*] — **Nep·tu′ni·an** *adj.*

nep·tu·ni·um (nep·tŏŏ′nē·əm, -tyŏŏ′-) *n.* A radioacti element (symbol Np), artificially produced from a uraniu isotope by neutron bombardment and decaying to plutor um by emission of a beta particle. See ELEMENT.

Ne·re·id (nir′ē·id) *pl.* **Ne·re·i·des** (ni·rē′ə·dēz) or **Ne·re·i** In Greek mythology, one of the fifty daughters of Nereus

Ne·reus (nir′ŏŏs, -ē·əs) In Greek mythology, a sea go father of the Nereides.

nerve (nûrv) *n.* **1.** *Physiol.* Any of the cordlike bundles fibers that convey impulses of sensation, etc., between t brain or spinal cord and other parts or organs. **2.** Coura or boldness; daring. **3.** *Informal* Arrogant assurance; bras ness. **4.** *Usu. pl.* Unsteadiness of mind and muscle; nervo ness: a case of *nerves.* **5.** Muscle; sinew: now only in t phrase **to strain every nerve.** — **to get on one's nerves** *I formal* To irritate; exasperate; upset. — *v.t.* **nerved, ner ing** To provide with nerve or nerves. — **to nerve onese** To summon up one's courage. [< L *nervus* sinew]

nerve cell *Physiol.* A neuron.

nerve center 1. *Physiol.* An aggregation of neurons havir a specific function, as hearing, sight, etc. **2.** The focus command and communication; headquarters.

nerve impulse *Physiol.* A wave of electrical disturbanc along a nerve fiber and continuing until it has been di charged into the appropriate sensory or motor channels.

nerve·less (nûrv′lis) *adj.* **1.** Lacking force; feeble. **2** Completely controlled and calm in crises; cool. **3.** *Ana* Having no nerves. — **nerve′less·ly** *adv.* — **nerve′less·ness** *n*

nerve-rack·ing (nûrv′rak′ing) *adj.* Extremely irritating harrowing. Also **nerve′-wrack′ing.**

ner·vous (nûr′vəs) *adj.* **1.** Characterized by or exhibitin restlessness, anxiety, tension, etc.; high-strung; excitable. **2** Neural. **3.** Caused by or acting on the nerves or nervo system. — **ner′vous·ly** *adv.* — **ner·vos′i·ty** (-vos′ə·tē ner′vous·ness** *n.* — **Syn.** 1. uneasy, fidgety, jittery, skittish.

nervous breakdown Popularly, any severe mental o emotional disturbance, usu. requiring hospitalization.

nervous system *Physiol.* A system in animals that coo dinates, controls, and regulates various organic activities b means of the reception and transmission of stimuli.

ner·vure (nûr′vyŏŏr) *n.* *Biol.* A vein, as on a leaf or an i sect's wing. Also **ner′vule** (-vyŏŏl). [< F < L *nervus* sinew — **ner·vu·ra·tion** (nûr′vyə·rā′shən) *n.*

nerv·y (nûr′vē) *adj.* **nerv·i·er, nerv·i·est 1.** *U.S. Inform* Brazen; impudent; brash. **2.** *Brit. Informal* Nervou jumpy. **3.** Having or requiring courage.

nes·cience (nesh′əns, -ē·əns) *n.* Lack or absence of know edge; ignorance. [< L < *ne-* not + *scire* to know] — **nes′cient** *adj. & n.* — **nes′cient·ist** *n.*

-ness *suffix of nouns* **1.** State or quality of being: *darkne* **2.** An example of this state or quality: to do someone a *kin ness.* [OE *-nes(s), -nis(s)*]

nest (nest) *n.* **1.** The habitation prepared or the place se lected by a bird for the hatching of its eggs and the rearin of its young. **2.** A place used by fishes, insects, turtles, etc for laying eggs. **3.** The group of animals, birds, etc., oc cupying such a place. **4.** A cozy or snug place. **5.** A haun or den; also, those occupying such a place: a *nest* of thieve **6.** A series or set of similar things designed to fit into one ar other, as bowls, boxes, etc. — *v.t.* **1.** To place in or as in nest. **2.** To pack or place one inside another. — *v.i.* **3.** T build or occupy a nest. **4.** To hunt for nests. [OE]

n'est-ce pas (nes pä′) *French* Isn't that so?

nest egg 1. A sum of money set aside for emergencies, et **2.** An artificial egg kept in a nest to induce a hen to lay egg

nes·tle (nes′əl) *v.* **·tled, ·tling** *v.i.* **1.** To lie or press close and snugly; cuddle; snuggle. **2.** To lie or be embedded, half-hidden. — *v.t.* **3.** To press snugly or lovingly **4.** To place, or shelter in or as in a nest. [OE *nestlian* t nest] — **nes′tler** *n.*

nest·ling (nest′ling, nes′-) *n.* **1.** A bird too young to leav the nest. **2.** A young child. — *adj.* Recently hatched.

Nes·tor (nes′tər) In Greek legend, the oldest and wises Greek chief in the Trojan War. — *n.* Any wise old ma

net¹ (net) *n.* **1.** A fabric of thread, cord, rope, etc., woven o knotted to form an open pattern or meshwork and used t catch fish, birds, etc. ◆ Collateral adjective: *reticular.*

anything that traps or entangles; a snare.   **3.** A piece of
fine lace.   **4.** Any of various devices constructed with meshes: cargo *net*; tennis *net*.   **5.** Something resembling a net.
— *v.t.* **net·ted, net·ting 1.** To catch in or as in a net; ensnare.
2. To make into a net.   **3.** To cover, enclose, or shelter with
a net.   **4.** In tennis, etc., to hit (the ball) into the net.   [OE]

net² (net) *adj.* **1.** Obtained after deducting all expenses,
losses, taxes, etc.: distinguished from *gross*: *net* proceeds.   **2.**
Free from anything extraneous; fundamental; basic: *net* results.   — *n.* A net profit, amount, weight, etc.   — *v.t.* **net·
ed, net·ting** To earn or yield as clear profit.   [< F]

neth·er (neth′ər) *adj.* Situated beneath or below.   [OE
nither < Gmc.]

neth·er·most (neth′ər·mōst′) *adj.* Lowest.

nether world 1. The world of the dead.   **2.** The world of
punishment after death; hell.

net·ting (net′ing) *n.* **1.** A net; network.   **2.** The act or operation of making net.   **3.** The right of using fishing nets.

net·tle (net′l) *n.* **1.** An herb having minute stinging hairs.
2. Any of various plants having some real or fancied resemblance to this herb.   — *v.t.* **·tled, ·tling 1.** To annoy or irritate; provoke.   **2.** To sting like nettle.   [OE *netle* < Gmc.]

nettle rash Urticaria.   Also **nettle fever.**

net ton A short ton.   See under TON¹.

net·work (net′wûrk′) *n.* **1.** A system of interlacing lines,
tracks, or channels.   **2.** An openwork fabric; netting.   **3.**
Telecom. A chain of broadcasting stations.   **4.** Any interconnected system: an espionage *network*.

Neuf·châ·tel (nœ′shə·tel′, *Fr.* nœ·shä·tel′) *n.* A soft, white
cheese produced in Neufchâtel, a town in northern France.

neu·ral (nŏor′əl, nyŏor′-) *adj.* Of or pertaining to the nerves
or nervous system.   [< Gk. *neuron* cord, sinew]

neu·ral·gi·a (nŏor·ral′jē·ə, -jə, nyŏor-) *n. Pathol.* Acute
pain along the course of a nerve.   — **neu·ral′gic** *adj.*

neu·ras·the·ni·a (nŏor′əs·thē′nē·ə, -then′yə, nyŏor′-)   *n.*
A condition marked by general debility, depression, and bodily disturbances, formerly believed to be due to weakness or
exhaustion of the nervous system.   [< NL < Gk. *neuron*
cord, sinew + *astheneia* weakness]   — **neu′ras·then′ic**
(-then′ik) *adj. & n.*

neu·ri·tis (nŏor·rī′tis, nyŏor-)   *n. Pathol.* Inflammation of a
nerve.   — **neu·rit′ic** (-rit′ik) *adj.*

neuro- *combining form* Nerve.   Also **neur-** (before vowels),
neuri-.   [< Gk. *neuron* sinew]

neu·rol·o·gy (nŏo·rol′ə·jē, nyŏo-)   *n.* The branch of medicine that deals with the nervous system and its disorders.
[< NL *neurologia*]   — **neu·ro·log′i·cal** (nŏor′ə·loj′i·kəl,
nyŏor′-) *adj.*   — **neu·rol′o·gist** *n.*

neu·ron (nŏor′on, nyŏor′-)   *n. Physiol.* The fundamental
cellular unit of the nervous system, consisting of a nucleus
with all its processes and extensions: also called *nerve cell.*
Also **neu′rone** (-ōn).   [< NL < Gk. *neuron* sinew]   — **neu·
ron′ic** (nŏo·ron′ik, nyŏo-) *adj.*

neu·rop·ter·an (nŏo·rop′tər·ən, nyŏo-)   *n.* A neuropterous
insect.   Also **neu·rop′ter, neu·rop′ter·on** (-on).   — *adj.* Neuropterous.   Also **neu·rop′ter·oid.**

neu·rop·ter·ous (nŏo·rop′tər·əs, nyŏo-) *adj.* Of or pertaining to an order of insects having two pairs of membranous
net-veined wings and chewing mouth parts.   Also **neu·rop′·
er·al.**   [< NL *Neuroptera*]

neu·ro·sis (nŏo·rō′sis, nyŏo-)   *n. pl.* **·ses** (-sēz) *Psychiatry*
Any of various emotional disturbances, less severe than the
psychoses, and usu. involving anxiety, depression, and unre-
solved psychic conflicts: also called *psychoneurosis.*   [< NL]

neu·rot·ic (nŏo·rot′ik, nyŏo-)   *adj.* **1.** Pertaining to or suffering from neurosis.   **2.** Neural.   — *n.* A neurotic person.

neu·ter (nŏo′tər, nyŏo′-) *adj.* **1.** *Gram.* Neither masculine
nor feminine in gender.   **2.** *Biol.* Having nonfunctioning or
imperfectly developed sex organs, as a worker bee.   — *n.* **1.**
Biol. A neuter plant or animal.   **2.** A castrated animal.   **3.**
Gram. **a** The neuter gender.   **b** A word in this gender.   [ult.
< L < *ne*- not + *uter* either]

neu·tral (nŏo′trəl, nyŏo′-) *adj.* **1.** Not taking the part of
either side in a dispute or war.   **2.** Of or belonging to neither
side in a dispute, war, etc.: *neutral* territory.   **3.** Neither one
thing nor the other; indefinite; middling.   **4.** Having no decided hue or color; grayish.   **5.** *Biol.* Neuter; esp., without
stamens or pistils.   **6.** *Chem.* Neither acid nor alkaline: a
neutral solution.   **7.** *Electr.* Neither positive nor negative.
8. *Phonet.* Produced with the tongue in a relaxed, midcen-
tral position, as the *a* in *about*.   — *n.* **1.** One who or that
which is neutral.   **2.** *Mech.* The state in which transmission
gears are disengaged: a car in *neutral*.   [< L < *neuter*
either]   — **neu′tral·ly** *adv.*

neu·tral·ism (nŏo′trəl·iz′əm, nyŏo′-)   *n.* In foreign affairs,
the policy of not associating or aligning a nation with any
side of a power conflict.   — **neu′tral·ist** *adj. & n.*

neu·tral·i·ty (nŏo·tral′ə·tē, nyŏo′-)   *n. pl.* **·ties** Neutral con-

dition, status, attitude, policy, etc., as of a nation during a
war.   [< F < Med.L *neutralitas*]

neu·tral·ize (nŏo′tral·īz, nyŏo′-)   *v.t.* **·ized, ·iz·ing 1.** To
counteract or destroy the force, influence, effect, etc., of.   **2.**
To declare (a nation, area, etc.) neutral during a war.   **3.**
Chem. To make neutral or inert.   **4.** *Electr.* To render electrically neutral by combining equal negative and positive
units.   [< F *neutraliser*]   — **neu′tral·i·za′tion** (-ə·zā′shən,
-ī·zā′-) *n.*   — **neu′tral·iz′er** *n.*

neu·tri·no (nŏo·trē′nō, nyŏo-)   *n. pl.* **·nos** *Physics* An
atomic particle associated with the radioactive emission of
beta rays, carrying no electric charge and having a mass approaching zero.   [< Ital., little neutron]

neu·tron (nŏo′tron, nyŏo′-)   *n. Physics* An electrically neutral particle of the atomic nucleus having a mass approximately equal to that of the proton.

neutron star *Astron.* A hypothetical star of great density
that is a source of strong X-rays and believed to be a
collapsed large star.

nev·er (nev′ər) *adv.* **1.** Not at any time; not ever: also used
in combination to form adjectives: *never-ending*.   **2.** Not at
all; positively not: *Never* fear.   [OE *nǣfre*]

nev·er·more (nev′ər·môr′, -mōr′) *adv.* Never again.

nev·er·the·less (nev′ər·thə·les′) *adv.* Nonetheless; however; yet.   — **Syn.** See BUT¹.

ne·vus (nē′vəs)   *n. pl.* **·vi** (-vī) A birthmark or congenital
mole.   [< L *naevus* blemish]   — **ne′void** *adj.*

new (nŏo, nyŏo) *adj.* **new·er, new·est 1.** Having recently
been made, used, developed, etc.   **2.** Having never existed,
occurred, etc., before.   **3.** Recently discovered, observed,
etc.: a *new* river.   **4.** Different from that which is older or
previous: a *new* dispensation.   **5.** Unfamiliar; strange.   **6.**
Not accustomed or experienced: *new* at the job.   **7.** Having
recently come into a certain place, condition, relationship,
etc.: a *new* member.   **8.** Built, made, etc., in place of something older: a *new* post office.   **9.** Fresh; unspoiled.   **10.** Repeated; renewed: a *new* plea.   **11.** Additional; increased: a
new supply.   **12.** Rejuvenated; refreshed: a *new* man.   **13.**
Modern; current; fashionable.   **14.** *Usu. cap.* Designating
the most recent form or period: said of languages.   — *adv.*
Newly; freshly; recently.   — *n.* That which is new.   [OE
nīwe < Gmc.]   — **new′ish** *adj.*   — **new′ness** *n.*

new·born (nŏo′bôrn′, nyŏo′-) *adj.* **1.** Just lately born.   **2.**
Reborn.   — *n.* A newborn infant or animal.

New·burg (nŏo′bûrg, nyŏo′-)   See À LA NEWBURG.

new·com·er (nŏo′kum′ər, nyŏo′-)   *n.* One who has recently
arrived.

New Deal The political, economic, and social policies of the
administration under Franklin D. Roosevelt.

new·el (nŏo′əl, nyŏo′-)   *n. Archit.* **1.** The post that terminates the handrail of a staircase.   **2.** The central pillar or
upright of a spiral staircase.   Also **newel post.**   [< OF <
LL < L *nux* nut]

New England The NE section of the United States, including Maine, New Hampshire, Vermont, Massachusetts,
Rhode Island, and Connecticut.   — **New Englander**

new-fan·gled (nŏo′fang′gəld, nyŏo′-)   *adj.* Lately come
into fashion; novel: a derogatory term.   [ME < *newe* new +
fangel contrivance, prob. < *fōn* to seize, grasp]

New·found·land (nŏo′fənd·lənd, nyŏo′-)   *n.* A large dog of
a breed originating in Newfoundland, having a broad head,
square muzzle, and thick, abundant, usu. black coat.

New·gate (nŏo′git, -gāt, nyŏo′-)   Formerly, a London prison.

New Jerusalem The city of God; heaven.   *Rev.* xxi 2.

New Latin See under LATIN.

new·ly (nŏo′lē, nyŏo′-)   *adv.* **1.** Very recently; lately.   **2.**
Once more; anew; afresh.   **3.** In a new or different way.

new·ly·wed (nŏo′lē·wed′, nyŏo′-)   *n.* A person recently
married.

new moon 1. The phase of the moon when it is directly
between the earth and the sun, its disk then being invisible;
also, the first visible crescent of the disk.   **2.** The period
when the moon is new.

new-mown (nŏo′mōn′, nyŏo′-) *adj.* Recently mown, as hay.

New Neth·er·land (neth′ər·lənd)   The Dutch colony in
North America, 1613–1664, near the mouth of the Hudson
River; capital, New Amsterdam.

new penny A penny (def. 3).

news (nŏoz, nyŏoz)   *n.pl.* (*construed as sing.*) **1.** Information of a recent event, development, etc., esp. as reported in
a newspaper, on the radio, etc.   **2.** Any new or unfamiliar
information.   [< NEW]

news·boy (nŏoz′boi′, nyŏoz′-)   *n.* A boy who sells or delivers newspapers.

news·cast (nŏoz′kast′, -käst′, nyŏoz′-)   *n.* A radio or television broadcast of news.   — **news′cast′er** *n.*

news·let·ter (nŏoz′let′ər, nyŏoz′-)   *n.* A brief, specialized,
periodical news report or set of reports sent by mail.

---

news·mag·a·zine (nōōz′mag′ə·zēn, -mag′ə·zēn′, nyōōz′-) n. A periodical, especially a weekly, that summarizes the news.

news·man (nōōz′man′, -mən, nyōōz′-) n. pl. ·men (-men′, -mən) 1. A news reporter. 2. A newsdealer.

news·pa·per (nōōz′pā′pər, nyōōz′-) n. 1. A printed publication usu. issued daily or weekly, containing news, editorials, advertisements, etc. 2. Newsprint.

news·print (nōōz′print′, -nyōōz′-) n. The thin, unsized paper on which the ordinary newspaper is printed.

news·reel (nōōz′rēl′, nyōōz′-) n. A short motion picture showing current events.

news·stand (nōōz′stand′, nyōōz′-) n. U.S. A stand or stall at which newspapers and periodicals are offered for sale.

New Style See (Gregorian) CALENDAR.

news·worth·y (nōōz′wûr′thē, nyōōz′-) adj. Having sufficient importance to be reported in a newspaper or newscast.

news·y (nōō′zē, nyōō′-) Informal adj. news·i·er, news·i·est Full of news. — n. pl. news·ies U.S. A newsboy.

newt (nōōt, nyōōt) n. Any of various semiaquatic salamanders. [Earlier ewt; in ME an ewt was taken as a newt]

New Testament That portion of the Bible containing the life and teachings of Christ and his followers.

New World The Western Hemisphere.

New Year The first day of the year; in the Gregorian calendar, January 1. Also **New Year's Day** (yirz).

New Year's Eve The night of December 31.

New York·er (yôr′kər) An inhabitant of New York; esp., a native or resident of New York City.

New Zea·land·er (zē′lən·dər) 1. A resident of New Zealand. 2. Formerly, a Maori.

next (nekst) adj. 1. Coming directly after in time, order, position, etc. 2. Nearest or closest in space. 3. Adjacent or adjoining: in the next room. — adv. 1. Immediately afterward. 2. On the first succeeding occasion: when next we meet. — prep. Nearest to: next his heart. — **next door** 1. The adjacent house, building, apartment, etc. 2. In, at, or to the adjacent house, etc. — **next to** Almost; nearly: next to impossible. [OE niehst, superl. of neah near]

next of kin The person most closely related to one.

nex·us (nek′səs) n. pl. ·us·es or ·us 1. A bond or tie between the several members of a group or series; link. 2. A connected series. [< L, pp. of nectere to tie]

ni·a·cin (nī′ə·sin) n. Nicotinic acid.

nib (nib) n. 1. The point of a pen. 2. The projecting, pointed part of anything; tip. — v.t. **nibbed**, **nib·bing** To furnish with a nib. [Var. of NEB < OE nebb beak]

nib·ble (nib′əl) v. ·bled, ·bling v.t. 1. To eat with small, quick, gentle bites: to nibble grass. 2. To take little, soft bites of: to nibble an ear. — v.i. 3. To eat or bite, esp. with small, gentle bites: often with at. — n. 1. A little bit or morsel. 2. The act of one who or that which nibbles. [< Gmc] — **nib′bler** n.

Ni·be·lung (nē′bə·lŏŏng) n. pl. ·lungs or ·lung·en (-lŏŏng′-en) In Teutonic mythology, one of a dwarf people who held a magic ring and a hoard of gold, taken from them by Siegfried.

Ni·be·lung·en·lied (nē′bə·lŏŏng′ən·lēt′) The lay of the Nibelungs, a Middle High German epic poem written by an unknown author during the early 13th century.

nib·lick (nib′lik) n. In golf, a nine iron. [? < Du. < knep-pel club]

Nic·a·ra·guan (nik′ə·rä′gwən) adj. Of or pertaining to Nicaragua. — n. A native of Nicaragua.

nice (nīs) adj. nic·er, nic·est 1. Agreeable; pleasing; respectable; suitable. 2. Friendly; kind. 3. Characterized by, revealing, or demanding discrimination, delicacy, or subtlety: a nice distinction. 4. Precise, accurate, or minute, as an instrument. — **nice and** Gratifyingly; properly: nice and dry. [< OF, innocent, foolish < L nescius ignorant] — **nice′ly** adv. — **nice′ness** n.

Ni·cene Creed (nī′sēn, nī·sēn′) Eccl. 1. A Christian confession of faith, adopted by the first Council of Nicaea, A.D. 325. 2. Any of several other creeds later adopted by Christian churches. [after Nicaea, an ancient town in Asia Minor]

ni·ce·ty (nī′sə·tē) n. pl. ·ties 1. Usu. pl. A minute or subtle point, detail, or distinction. 2. Usu. pl. A delicacy or refinement: niceties of living. 3. The quality of requiring careful and delicate treatment. 4. Precision or accuracy; exactness. 5. The quality of being nice. — **to a nicety** Exactly.

niche (nich) n. 1. A recessed space or hollow, usu. in a wall, for a statue or the like. 2. Any position specially adapted to its occupant: to find one's niche. — v.t. **niched, nich·ing** To put in a niche. [Prob. < F, ult. < L nidus nest]

Nich·o·las (nik′ə·ləs, -lus) Saint See SANTA CLAUS.

nick (nik) n. A slight cut, chip, or indentation on a surface or edge. — **in the nick of time** At the exact or crucial moment. — v.t. To make a nick in or on.

NICHE

nick·el (nik′əl) n. 1. A hard, ductile, malleable, silver-white metallic element (symbol Ni) having a wide variety of uses. See ELEMENT. 2. A five cent coin of the U.S., made of an alloy of nickel and copper its ore looks like copper — v.t. ·eled or ·elled, ·el·ing or ·el·ling To plate with nick [< Sw. < G < (kupfer)nickel, lit., copper demon; becau its ore looks like copper]

nick·el·o·de·on (nik′əl·ō′dē·ən) n. U.S. 1. Formerly, motion-picture theater charging an admission fee of five cen 2. Formerly, a jukebox or other automatic music machi [< NICKEL (def. 2) + odeon < F odéon theater]

nick·el-plate (nik′əl-plāt′) v.t. ·plat·ed, ·plat·ing To cov with nickel by electroplating.

nickel plate A thin layer of nickel deposited on the surfa of objects by electroplating.

nickel silver German silver.

nick·er (nik′ər) n. 1. A neigh. 2. A neighing laugh. — v 1. To neigh. 2. To snicker. [Imit.]

nick·nack (nik′nak′) See KNICKKNACK.

nick·name (nik′nām′) n. 1. A familiar form of a prop name, as Tom for Thomas. 2. A descriptive name given i stead of or in addition to the actual name of a person, plac or thing, as Honest Abe. — v.t. ·named, ·nam·ing 1. To giv a nickname to or call by a nickname. 2. To misname. [M ekename surname, an ekename becoming a nickname]

nic·o·tine (nik′ə·tēn, -tin) n. An acrid, poisonous, oily alk loid, $C_{11}H_{14}N_2$, contained in the leaves of tobacco. Al **nic′o·tin.** [< F, after Jean Nicot, 1530–1600, French coun ier, who introduced tobacco into France from Portugal] — **nic·o·tin·ic** (nik′ə·tin′ik) adj.

nicotinic acid Biochem. A colorless, water-soluble con pound, $C_6H_5NO_2$, prepared by the oxidation of nicotine an forming part of the vitamin B complex, used to prevent pe lagra: also called niacin.

nic·ti·tate (nik′tə·tāt) v.i. ·tat·ed, ·tat·ing To wink. Al **nic′tate.** [< Med.L, freq. of L nictare to wink] — **nic**′ **ta′tion** n.

nictitating membrane A transparent third eyelid at th inner corner of the eye in various birds, reptiles, etc.

niece (nēs) n. The daughter of a brother or sister. [< O ult. < L neptis niece, granddaughter]

Nie·tzsche·an (nē′chi·ən) adj. Of or relating to Friedri Nietzsche, or to his philosophy. — n. A follower of Ni tzsche, or of his philosophy. — **Nie′tzsche·an·ism, Nie tzsche·ism** n.

nif·ty (nif′tē) adj. ·ti·er, ·ti·est Slang Stylish; pleasing.

nig·gard (nig′ərd) n. A stingy person. — adj. Niggardl [? < AF, ? ult. < ON hnøggr]

nig·gard·ly (nig′ərd·lē) adj. 1. Stingy; parsimonious. Meanly insufficient; scanty. — adv. In the manner of niggard. — **nig′gard·li·ness** n.

nig·ger (nig′ər) n. A Negro or member of any dark-skinne people: a vulgar and offensive term. [See NEGRO.]

nig·gle (nig′əl) v.i. ·gled, ·gling To occupy oneself wit trifles; behave trivially. [Cf. dial. Norw. nigla]

nig·gling (nig′ling) adj. 1. Fussy; overprecise. 2. Mean petty. 3. Annoying; nagging. — n. Overelaborate or ove precise work or behavior. — **nig′gling·ly** adv.

nigh (nī) Chiefly Archaic & Dial. adj. **nigh·er, nigh·est** next 1. Close; near. 2. Convenient; direct. — adv. Near in time or place. 2. Almost: often with on or ont nigh on a year. — prep. Near. — v.t. & v.i. To draw nea approach. [OE nēah, nēh] — **nigh′ness** n.

night (nīt) n. 1. The period from sunset to sunrise, esp. th part that is dark. ◆ Collateral adjective: nocturnal. 2. Th period of evening and darkness before midnight of a give day. 3. Darkness; the dark. 4. A condition of ignoranc gloom, painful confusion, etc. [OE niht, neaht]

night blindness Vision that is abnormally poor in di light but normal in daylight.

night-bloom·ing ce·re·us (nīt′blōō′ming sir′ē·əs) A tro tropical cactus having large white flowers that open at nigh

night·cap (nīt′kap′) n. 1. A cap to be worn in bed. 2. I formal A drink of liquor taken just before going to bed.

night·clothes (nīt′klōz′, -klōthz′) n.pl. Clothes to be wor in bed.

night club A restaurant open until late at night, providin entertainment, food, and drink.

night crawler Any large earthworm that emerges at nigh

night·fall (nīt′fôl′) n. The close of day.

night·gown (nīt′goun′) n. A loose gown worn in bed b women and children. Also **night′dress′** (-dres′).

night·hawk (nīt′hôk′) n. 1. Any of various birds relate to the whippoorwill. 2. The nightjar.

night·in·gale (nīt′ən·gāl, nī′ting-) n. A small, Old Worl migratory bird allied to the thrushes and noted for the melo dious song of the male. [OE < niht night + galan to sing]

night·jar (nīt′jär′) n. Any of various goatsuckers of Eu rope: also called nighthawk.

night letter A telegram sent at night, at reduced rates.

night-light (nīt'līt') *n.* A usu. dim light kept on at night.

night-long (nīt'lông', -long') *adj.* Lasting through the night. — *adv.* Through the whole night.

night-ly (nīt'lē) *adj.* 1. Of, pertaining to, or occurring each night. 2. Pertaining to or occurring at night. — *adv.* 1. By night. 2. Each night: to take place *nightly*.

night-mare (nīt'mâr) *n.* 1. A horrible and frightening dream. 2. Any experience or condition resembling a nightmare. [< NIGHT + MARE²] — **night'mar-ish** *adj.*

night owl One who stays up late.

nights (nīts) *adv. Informal* At night. [OE *nihtes*]

night school A school that holds classes during the evening, esp. for those who cannot attend day school.

night-shade (nīt'shād') *n.* 1. Any of various flowering plants typical of a family that includes tobacco, pepper, jimsonweed, the potato, and the tomato. 2. Belladonna.

night-shirt (nīt'shûrt') *n.* A long, loose garment worn in bed, usu. by men or boys.

night-spot (nīt'spot') *U.S. Informal* A night club.

night-stick (nīt'stik') *n. U.S.* A long, heavy club carried by policemen.

night table A bedside table or stand.

night-time (nīt'tīm') *n.* The time from sunset to sunrise, or from dark to dawn.

night-walk-er (nīt'wô'kər) *n.* A night crawler.

night watch 1. A watch or guard kept at night. 2. A night watchman. 3. A period of watch or guard.

night-wear (nīt'wâr') *n.* Nightclothes.

night-y (nī'tē) *n. pl.* **night-ies** *U.S. Informal* A nightgown.

nigri- *combining form* Black. Also, before vowels, **nigr-**. [< L *niger, nigris* black]

ni-hil-ism (nī'əl-iz'əm, nī'hil-) *n.* 1. *Philos.* **a** A doctrine that denies existence. **b** A doctrine that denies any basis for knowledge or truth. **c** Total denial of all traditional principles, values, and institutions. 2. In politics: **a** A doctrine advocating the destruction of all political, economic, and social institutions. **b** *Usu. cap.* A revolutionary movement in Russia in the 19th century advocating violence and terror. 3. Any revolutionary movement advocating terror and violence. — **ni'hil-ist** *n.* — **ni-hil-is'tic** *adj.*

Ni-ke (nī'kē) In Greek mythology, the winged goddess of victory: identified with the Roman *Victoria*. — *n.* An antiaircraft guided missile. [< Gk. *Nikē* victory]

nil (nil) *n.* Nothing. [< L, contr. of *nihil* nothing]

Nile green Any of several light green tints.

nil-gai (nil'gī) *n.* A large, short-maned antelope of India. Also **nil'gau** (-gô), **nil'ghai, nil'ghau** (-gô). [< Hind. < *nīl* blue + *gāi* cow]

nim-ble (nim'bəl) *adj.* **-bler, -blest** 1. Light and quick in movement; lively. 2. Characterized by a quick and ready intellect. [OE *numel* quick at grasping] — **nim'ble-ness** *n.* — **nim'bly** *adv.*

nim-bo-stra-tus (nim'bō-strā'təs, -strat'əs) *n. Meteorol.* A low, formless, dark gray cloud layer, precipitating continuous rain or snow.

nim-bus (nim'bəs) *n. pl.* **-bus-es** or **-bi** (-bī) 1. A luminous emanation believed to envelop a deity or holy person. 2. Any atmosphere or aura, as of fame, glamor, etc. 3. Formerly, a nimbostratus. [< L, cloud]

Nim-rod (nim'rod) Grandson of Ham, described as a mighty hunter. *Gen.* x 8. — *n.* A hunter. Also **nim'rod.**

Ni-ña (nē'nə, *Sp.* nē'nyä) *n.* One of the three ships of Columbus on his first voyage to America.

nin-com-poop (nin'kəm-pōōp) *n.* An idiot; fool. [Origin unknown]

nine (nīn) *n.* 1. The sum of eight and one: a cardinal number. 2. Any symbol of this number, as 9, ix, IX. 3. Anything consisting of or representing nine units, as a baseball team, etc. — **the Nine** The Muses. — *adj.* Being one more than eight. [OE *nigon*] — **ninth** *adj. & n.*

nine iron In golf, an iron with an extremely slanted face, used for lofting the ball: also called *niblick.*

nine-pence (nīn'pəns) *n. Brit.* 1. The sum of nine pennies. 2. A coin of this value, no longer minted.

nine-pins (nīn'pinz') *n.pl.* (*construed as sing.*) A bowling game similar to tenpins, using nine large wooden pins.

nine-teen (nīn'tēn') *n.* 1. The sum of eighteen and one: a cardinal number. 2. Any symbol of this number, as 19, xix, XIX. 3. Anything consisting of or representing nineteen units. — *adj.* Being one more than eighteen. [OE *nigon-tiene*] — **nine'teenth'** *adj. & n.*

nine-ty (nīn'tē) *n. pl.* **-ties** 1. The sum of eighty and ten: a cardinal number. 2. Any symbol of this number, as 90, xc, XC. 3. Anything consisting of or representing ninety units, as an organization, game token, etc. — *adj.* Being ten more than eighty. [OE *nigontig*] — **nine'ti-eth** *adj. & n.*

Nin-e-veh (nin'ə-və) An ancient city on the Tigris, capital of Assyria. — **Nin'e-vite** (-vīt) *n.*

Ni-o-be (nī'ə-bē) In Greek mythology, the mother whose children were killed by Apollo and Artemis after she had vaunted their superiority. She was turned by Zeus into a stone from which tears continued to flow.

ni-o-bi-um (nī-ō'bē-əm) *n.* A rare, steel gray, metallic element (symbol Nb), valuable as an alloy metal: formerly called *columbium.* See ELEMENT. [< NIOBE]

nip¹ (nip) *v.* **nipped, nip-ping** *v.t.* 1. To pinch or compress between two surfaces; bite. 2. To sever or remove by pinching, biting, or clipping: usually with *off.* 3. To check, arrest, or destroy the growth or development of. 4. To affect painfully or injuriously, as by cold. 5. *Slang* To steal; pilfer. 6. *Slang* To catch; take. — *v.i.* 7. *Brit. Informal* To move nimbly or rapidly: with *off, away,* etc. — *n.* 1. The act of one who or that which nips. 2. That which is nipped off. 3. Any small portion: a *nip* of tea. 4. A sharp, stinging quality. 5. Severe cold or frost. 6. A cutting remark. 7. A sharp, pungent flavor. — **nip and tuck** *U.S.* Very close or even; precariously uncertain. [Cf. Du. *nijpen* to pinch]

nip² (nip) *n.* A small quantity of liquor. — *v.t. & v.i.* To sip (liquor). [? < earlier *nipperkin* a small liquid measure]

nip-per (nip'ər) *n.* 1. One who or that which nips. 2. *pl.* Any of various implements used for nipping, as pliers, pincers, etc. 3. The large claw of a crab or lobster. 4. *pl. Slang* Handcuffs. 5. *Brit. Informal* A small boy; lad.

nip-ple (nip'əl) *n.* 1. The protuberance on the breasts of higher mammals, esp. that of the female; teat. 2. The rubber teatlike mouthpiece of a nursing bottle. 3. Something resembling a nipple, as a short pipe coupling with threaded ends. [Earlier *nible,* ? dim. of NIB]

nip-py (nip'ē) *adj.* **-pi-er, -pi-est** 1. Biting or sharp, as cold weather. 2. *Brit. Informal* Active; alert. — **nip'pi-ly** *adv.* — **nip'pi-ness** *n.*

nir-va-na (nir-vä'nə, nər-van'ə) *n.* 1. In Buddhism, the state of absolute felicity attained through the annihilation of the self. 2. Freedom from care and pain; bliss. [< Skt. *nirvāna* extinction]

Ni-san (nē-sän', nis'ən) *n.* The seventh month of the Hebrew year. Also **Nis'san.** See (Hebrew) CALENDAR.

Ni-sei (nē-sā') *n. pl.* **-sei** or **-seis** A native American of immigrant Japanese parentage.

ni-si (nī'sī) *conj. Law* Unless: used after the word *order, rule, decree,* etc., signifying that it shall become effective at a certain time, unless modified or avoided. [< L]

Nis-sen hut (nis'ən, nēs'-) A prefabricated sheet steel building resembling a long half-cylinder lying flat on the ground. [after P. N. *Nissen,* 1871–1930, who invented it]

nit (nit) *n.* 1 The egg of a louse or other parasitic insect. 2. An immature louse. [OE *hnitu*] — **nit'ty** *adj.*

ni-ter (nī'tər) *n.* 1. Potassium or sodium nitrate; saltpeter. 2. *Obs.* Natron. Also **ni'tre.** [< OF < L < Gk. *nitron*]

ni-ton (nī'ton) *n.* Radon. [< L (*nit*)*ere* to shine) + -ON]

nit-pick (nit'pik') *Informal v.t.* 1. To fuss over or find fault with. — *v.i.* 2. To engage in nit-picking. Also **nit'-pick.** [Back formation < NIT-PICKING] — **nit'-pick'er** *n.*

nit-pick-ing (nit'pik'ing) *n. Informal* A fussing over trivial details, often with the aim of finding fault.

ni-trate (nī'trāt) *Chem. n.* 1. A salt or ester of nitric acid. 2. Niter. — *v.t.* **-trat-ed, -trat-ing** To treat or combine with nitric acid or a compound. See NITER.]

ni-tric (nī'trik) *adj. Chem.* 1. Of, pertaining to, or obtained from nitrogen. 2. Containing nitrogen in the higher valence.

nitric acid *Chem.* A colorless, highly corrosive liquid, HNO_3, having strong oxidizing properties.

ni-tride (nī'trīd, -trid) *n. Chem.* A compound of nitrogen with some more electropositive element. Also **ni'trid** (-trid)

ni-tri-fy (nī'trə-fī) *v.t.* **-fied, -fy-ing** *Chem.* 1. To treat or combine with nitrogen. 2. To convert, as ammonium salts in the soil, into nitrates or nitrites by oxidation. 3. To treat or impregnate (soil, etc.) with nitrates. [< F *nitrifier*] — **ni'tri-fi'a-ble** *adj.* — **ni'tri-fi-ca'tion** *n.*

ni-trite (nī'trīt) *n. Chem.* A salt of nitrous acid.

nitro- *combining form Chem.* Containing the univalent radical NO_2. Also, before vowels, **nitr-.** Also **nitri-.** [< L *nitrum* < Gk. *nitron*]

ni-tro-ben-zene (nī'trō-ben'zēn, -ben-zēn') *n. Chem.* A yellow, oily compound, $C_6H_5NO_2$, formed by the nitration of benzene and used in the making of aniline.

ni-tro-gen (nī'trə-jən) *n.* An odorless, colorless, gaseous element (symbol N) forming about four-fifths of the atmosphere by volume and playing a decisive role in the formation of compounds essential to life. See ELEMENT. [< F *nitrogène* < *nitro*- NITRO- + -*gène* -GEN]

nitrogen fixation 1. The conversion of atmospheric nitrogen into nitrates by soil bacteria. 2. The production of nitrogen compounds, as for fertilizers and explosives, by processes utilizing free nitrogen. — **ni'tro-gen-fix'ing** *adj.*

ni-trog-en-ize (nī-troj'ən-īz, nī'trə-jən-īz') *v.t.* **ized, -iz-ing**

To treat or combine with nitrogen.

ni·trog·e·nous (nī-troj′ə-nəs) *adj.* Pertaining to or containing nitrogen. Also **ni·tro·ge·ne·ous** (nī′trō-jē′nē-əs).

ni·tro·glyc·er·in (nī′trō-glis′ər-in) *n. Chem.* A colorless to pale yellow, oily liquid, $C_3H_5(ONO_2)_3$, made by nitrating glycerol, used as an explosive and propellant, etc. Also **ni′. tro, ni′tro·glyc′er·ine.** [< NITRO- + GLYCERIN]

nitro group *Chem.* The univalent NO_2 radical.

ni·trous (nī′trəs) *adj. Chem.* Of, pertaining to, or derived from nitrogen: esp. applied to those compounds containing less oxygen than the nitric compounds.

nitrous oxide A gas, N_2O, used as an anesthetic in dental surgery, etc., and sometimes having an exhilarating effect when inhaled: also called *laughing gas.*

nit·ty-grit·ty (nit′ē-grit′ē) *U.S. Slang n.* The basic questions or details; essence. — *adj.* Down-to-earth; basic.

nit·wit (nit′wit′) *n.* A silly or stupid person.

ni·val (nī′vəl) *adj.* Of or pertaining to the snow; also, growing under the snow. [< L *nivalis* < *nix, nivis* snow]

nix¹ (niks) *n.* In Germanic mythology, a water sprite.

nix² (niks) *Slang n.* **1.** Nothing. **2.** No. — *adv.* No. — *interj.* Stop! Watch out! — *v.t.* To forbid or disagree with: He *nixed* our suggestions. [< G *nichts* nothing]

Ni·zam (ni-zäm′, -zam′, nī-) *n.* The title of the former hereditary rulers of Hyderabad, India.

no¹ (nō) *adv.* **1.** Nay; not so. **2.** Not at all; not in any wise: *no* better than the other. **3.** Not: used to express an alternative after *or:* whether or *no.* — *n. pl.* **noes 1.** A negative reply; a denial. **2.** A negative vote or voter: The *noes* have it. [OE *nā* < *ne* not + *ā* ever]

no² (nō) *adj.* Not any; not one. [OE < *ne* not + *ān* one]

no³ (nō) *n. pl.* **no** *Sometimes cap.* The classical drama of Japan, traditionally tragic or noble in theme, having music and dancing: also spelled *noh.* Also **nō.** Compare KABUKI.

No·ah (nō′ə) In the Old Testament, a patriarch who built an ark that saved him, his family, and every kind of animal from the Flood. *Gen.* v-ix. [< Hebrew]

nob¹ (nob) *n.* **1.** *Slang* The head. **2.** In cribbage, the jack of trumps. [Var. of KNOB]

nob² (nob) *n. Slang* One who is rich, influential, etc.

No·bel Prizes (nō-bel′) Any of five prizes founded by the will of Alfred Nobel and awarded annually in the fields of physics, chemistry, medicine, literature, and the furtherance of world peace.

no·be·li·um (nō-bē′lē-əm) *n.* An unstable radioactive element (symbol No) originally produced by the bombardment of curium by an isotope of carbon. See ELEMENT. [after A. B. *Nobel*]

no·bil·i·ty (nō-bil′ə-tē) *n. pl.* **·ties 1.** A class in society composed of persons having hereditary title, rank, and privileges. **2.** In Great Britain, the peerage. **3.** The state or quality of being noble.

no·ble (nō′bəl) *adj.* **·bler, ·blest 1.** Having excellence or dignity; eminent; illustrious; worthy. **2.** Characterized by or displaying superior moral qualities. **3.** Magnificent and imposing in appearance; grand; stately. **4.** Of or pertaining to the nobility; aristocratic. **5.** Chemically inert. — *n.* **1.** A nobleman. **2.** In Great Britain, a peer. [< MF < L *nobilis* noble, well-known] — **no′ble·ness** *n.* — **no′bly** *adv.*

no·ble·man (nō′bəl-mən) *n. pl.* **·men** (-mən) A man of noble rank; in England, a peer.

no·blesse o·blige (nō-bles′ ō-blēzh′) *French* Those of high birth, wealth, or social position must behave generously or nobly toward others; literally, nobility obligates.

no·ble·wom·an (nō′bəl-wŏŏm′ən) *n. pl.* **·wom·en** (-wim′-in) A woman of noble rank. **2.** In England, a peeress.

no·bod·y (nō′bod′ē, -bəd-ē) *pron.* Not anybody. — *n. pl.* **·bod·ies** A person of no importance or influence.

nock (nok) *n.* **1.** The notch for the bowstring on the butt end of an arrow. **2.** The notch on the horn of a bow for securing the bowstring. [ME *nocke*]

nocti- *combining form* By or at night. Also, before vowels, **noct-.** [< L *nox, noctis* night]

noc·tu·id (nok′chŏŏ-id) *n.* Any of a large family of medium-sized moths, esp. those whose larvae are destructive. — *adj.* Of this family of moths. [< NL < L *noctua* night owl]

noc·tur·nal (nok-tûr′nəl) *adj.* **1.** Of, pertaining to, or occurring at night. **2.** *Biol.* Active, blooming, etc., by night. [< LL < L *nocturnus* nightly] — **noc·tur′nal·ly** *adv.*

noc·turne (nok′tûrn) *n.* **1.** In painting, a night scene. **2.** *Music* A composition of a pensive or romantic nature.

nod (nod) *v.* **nod·ded, nod·ding** *v.i.* **1.** To lower the head forward briefly, as in agreement, assent, invitation, etc. **2.** To let the head fall forward slightly and involuntarily, as when drowsy. **3.** To be inattentive or careless. **4.** To sway or bend the top or upper part, as trees. — *v.t.* **5.** To lower (the head) by nodding. **6.** To express or signify (assent, agreement, etc.) by nodding the head. — *n.* The act of one who or that which nods. — **to give** (or **get**) **the nod** *U.S. Slang* To give (or receive) the sign to go ahead, assent, approval, etc. [ME *nodden*] — **nod′der** *n.*

nod·dle (nod′l) *Informal n.* The head; noodle. — *v.t. & v.i.* **·dled, ·dling** To nod frequently. [Freq. of NOD]

nod·dy (nod′ē) *n. pl.* **·dies 1.** A dunce; a fool. **2.** One of several terns of the Atlantic coast. [? < NOD]

node (nōd) *n.* **1.** A knot, knob, or swelling; protuberance. **2.** *Bot.* A joint or knob of a stem. **3.** *Math.* A point at which a curve crosses itself. **4.** *Astron.* Either of two points at which the orbit of a heavenly body intersects the ecliptic. **5.** *Physics* A point, line, or surface in a standing wave system at which some component wave has virtually zero amplitude. **6.** *Anat.* A swelling. [< L *nodus* knot] — **nod·a** (nōd′l) *adj.* — **nod′al·ly** *adv.*

nod·ule (noj′ōōl, nod′yōōl) *n.* **1.** A little knot or node. **2.** *Bot.* A little knot. [< L < *nodus* knot] — **nod·u·lar** (noj′ŏŏ-lər), **nod′u·lose** (-lōs), **nod′u·lous** (-ləs) *adj.*

no·ël (nō-el′) *n.* A Christmas carol. Also **no·el′.**

No·ël (nō-el′) *n.* Christmas. Also **No·el′.** [< F < LL (*dies*) *natalis* birthday]

nog (nog) *n.* **1.** Eggnog (which see). **2.** *Brit. Dial.* A strong ale. Also **nogg.** [Origin unknown]

nog·gin (nog′in) *n.* **1.** *Informal* A person's head. **2.** A small mug or cup. **3.** A measure of liquor equal to about one fourth of a pint or a gill. [Origin unknown]

noh (nō) See NO³.

no·how (nō′hou′) *adv. Dial.* In no way; not by any means.

noise (noiz) *n.* **1.** Loud, confused, or disturbing sound of any kind. **2.** In communication theory, any random disturbance that causes a received signal to differ from what was transmitted. — *v.* **noised, nois·ing** *Rare v.t.* **1.** To spread, report, or rumor: often with *about* or *abroad.* — *v.i.* **2.** To be noisy; make a noise. [< OF, ? < L *nausea*] — **Syn.** (noun) **1.** din, clamor, uproar, hubbub, racket, clatter, blare. See SOUND¹.

noise·less (noiz′lis) *adj.* Causing or making little or no noise; quiet; silent. — **noise′less·ly** *adv.* — **noise′less·ness** *n.*

noise·mak·er (noiz′mā′kər) *n.* A horn, bell, etc., for making noise at celebrations. — **noise′mak′ing** *n. & adj.*

noi·some (noi′səm) *adj.* **1.** Offensive or disgusting, esp. in smell; stinking. **2.** Injurious; noxious. [ME < *noy* annoyance + OE *-sum* like, resembling] — **noi′some·ly** *adv.* — **noi′some·ness** *n.*

nois·y (noi′zē) *adj.* **nois·i·er, nois·i·est 1.** Making a loud noise. **2.** Characterized by or full of noise. — **nois′i·ly** *adv.* — **nois′i·ness** *n.*

no·li-me-tan·ge·re (nō′li-mē-tan′jə-rē) *n.* A warning against touching or meddling. [< L, touch me not]

nol·le pros·e·qui (noi′ē pros′ə-kwī) *Law* An entry of record in a civil or criminal case, to signify that the plaintiff or prosecutor will not press it. [< L, to be unwilling to prosecute]

no·lo con·ten·de·re (nō′lō kən-ten′də-rē) *Law* A plea by a defendant in a criminal action that has the same legal effect as an admission of guilt but does not debar him from denying the truth of the charges in any other proceedings. [< L, I am unwilling to contend]

nol-pros (nol′pros′) *v.t.* **-prossed, -pros·sing** *Law* To subject to a nolle prosequi. [Short for NOLLE PROSEQUI]

no·mad (nō′mad, nom′ad) *n.* **1.** One of a group of people that habitually shifts its abode to find food, avoid drought, etc. **2.** One who constantly moves about, usu. without purpose; a wanderer. — *adj.* Nomadic. [< L < Gk. *nomas* < *nemein* to graze] — **no′mad·ism** *n.*

no·mad·ic (nō-mad′ik) *adj.* Of, pertaining to, or like nomads. Also **no·mad′i·cal.** — **no·mad′i·cal·ly** *adv.*

no man's land 1. A tract of waste or unowned land. **2.** In war, the land between opposing armies. **3.** An area of human activity characterized by ambiguity or peril.

nom de guerre (nôn də gâr′) *French* A pseudonym; literally, a war name.

nom de plume (nom′ də plŏŏm′, Fr. nôn də plüm′) A pen name; a writer's assumed name. — **Syn.** See PSEUDONYM. [< F *nom* name + *de* of + *plume* pen]

no·men·cla·ture (nō′mən-klā′chər, nō-men′klə-) *n.* **1.** The system of names used to describe the various elements of a science, art, etc.; terminology. **2.** The specific names for the parts or stages of a device, process, etc.

nom·i·nal (nom′ə-nəl) *adj.* **1.** Existing in name only; not actual. **2.** Slight or inconsiderable; trifling. **3.** Of or like a name. **4.** *Gram.* Of, pertaining to, or like a noun. [< L *nomen* name]

nom·i·nal·ism (nom′ə-nəl-iz′əm) *n. Philos.* The doctrine that universals (abstract concepts) exist only as names and without a basis in reality: opposed to *realism.* [< F *nominalisme*] — **nom′i·nal·ist** *adj. & n.*

nom·i·nal·ly (nom′ə-nəl-ē) *adv.* In name only; not actually.

nom·i·nate (nom′ə-nāt) *v.t.* **-nat·ed, -nat·ing 1.** To name or propose as a candidate for elective office. **2.** To appoint to some office or duty. — *adj.* Having a particular or special name. [< L *nominare* to name] — **nom′i·na′tion** *n.* — **nom′i·na′tor** *n.*

nom·i·na·tive (nom′ə-nə-tiv, nom′ə-nā′-) *adj.* **1.** *Gram.*

Designating the case of the subject of a finite verb, or of a word agreeing with or in apposition to the subject. **2.** Appointed by nomination; nominated. — *n. Gram.* **1.** The nominative case. **2.** A word in this case.

nom·i·nee (nom/ə·nē′) *n.* One who receives a nomination.

nomy *combining form* The science or systematic study of: *astronomy, economy.* [< Gk. *nomos* law]

non- *prefix* Not. [< F < L *non* not]
◆ *Non-* is the Latin negative adverb adopted as an English prefix. It denotes in general simple negation or absence of, as in *nonheroic,* not heroic, *nonattendance,* lack of attendance.

non·age (non/ij, nō/nij) *n.* **1.** The period of legal minority. **2.** A period of immaturity. [< OF < *non* not + *age* age]

non·a·ge·nar·i·an (non/ə·jə·nâr/ē·ən, nō/nə-) *n.* A person between 90 and 100 years of age. — *adj.* **1.** Being ninety years old, or between 90 and 100. **2.** Of or pertaining to a nonagenarian. [< L *nonagenarius* of ninety]

non·a·gon (non/ə·gon) *n. Geom.* A polygon having nine sides and nine angles. [< L *nonus* ninth + Gk. *gōnia* angle]

nonce (nons) *n.* Present time or occasion: now chiefly in the phrase **for the nonce.** [ME *for then ones* for the one (occasion), misread as *for the nones*]

nonce word A word coined for a single occasion.

non·cha·lant (non/shə·lənt, non/shə·länt′) *adj.* Marked by or exhibiting a lack of interest or excitement; casually indifferent. [< OF < *non* not + *calere* to be warm, to be desirous] — **non/cha·lance** *n.* — **non/cha·lant·ly** *adv.*

non·com (non/kom′) *U.S. Informal n.* A noncommissioned officer. — *adj.* Noncommissioned.

non·com·bat·ant (non/kəm·bat/ənt, non/kom/bə·tənt, -kum/-) *n.* **1.** One whose duties as a member of a military force do not entail fighting, as a chaplain or medical officer. **2.** A civilian in wartime.

non·com·mis·sioned (non/kə·mish/ənd) *adj.* Not holding a commission: said of certain grades of the armed forces.

noncommissioned officer *Mil.* An enlisted man appointed to a noncommissioned grade, as from corporal to sergeant major in the U.S. Army. See table for GRADE.

non·com·mit·tal (non/kə·mit/l) *adj.* Not involving or revealing a commitment to any particular attitude, opinion, etc. — **non/com·mit/tal·ly** *adv.*

non·com·pli·ance (non/kəm·plī/əns) *n.* Failure or neglect to comply. — **non/com·pli/ant** *adj. & n.*

non com·pos men·tis (non kom/pəs men/tis) *Law* Not of sound mind; mentally unbalanced: often **non compos.** [< L]

non·con·duc·tor (non/kən·duk/tər) *n.* A substance that offers resistance to the passage of some form of energ , as of heat or electricity. — **non/con·duct/ing** *adj.*

non·con·form·ist (non/kən·fôr/mist) *n.* **1.** One who does not conform to an approved manner of behaving or thinking. **2.** *Often cap.* An English Protestant who refuses to conform to the Church of England. — **non/con·form/ing** *adj.* — **non/con·for/mi·ty** *n.*

non·co·op·er·a·tion (non/kō·op/ə·rā/shən) *n.* Failure to cooperate; esp., resistance to a government through civil disobedience, including the refusal to pay taxes. — **non/co·op/er·a/tion·ist** *n.* — **non/co·op/er·a·tive** (-kō·op/rə·tiv, -kō·op/ə·rā/tiv) *adj.* — **non/co·op/er·a/tor** *n.*

non·de·script (non/di·skript) *adj.* Not distinctive enough to be described; lacking individual character. — *n.* A nondescript person or thing: often used disparagingly. [< NON- + L *descriptus,* pp. of *describere* to describe]

none (nun) *pron.* (construed as *sing.* or *pl.*) **1.** Not one; no one. **2.** No or not one (specified person or thing); not any (of a class of things). **3.** No part or portion; not any: It is *none* of my business. — *adv.* By no means; not at all: He is *none* too bright. [OE < *ne* not + *an* one]

non·ef·fec·tive (non/i·fek/tiv) *adj.* **1.** Not effective. **2.** Unfit or unavailable for active service or duty, as in the army or navy. — *n.* A noneffective soldier, sailor, etc.

non·en·ti·ty (non·en/tə·tē) *n. pl.* **·ties 1.** One who or that which is of little or no account; a nothing. **2.** That which does not exist, or exists solely in the imagination. **3.** The negation of being; nonexistence.

nones (nōnz) *n.pl.* **1.** In the ancient Roman calendar, the ninth day before the ides. **2.** *Often cap. Eccl.* Prescribed prayers constituting the fifth of the seven canonical hours. [< OF < L *nonae,* fem. pl. of *nonus* ninth]

none·such (nun/such′) *n.* **1.** One who or that which has no equal; nonpareil. **2.** A variety of apple. Also *nonsuch.*

none·the·less (nun/thə·les′) *adv.* In spite of everything; nevertheless. Also **none the less.**

non·fea·sance (non·fē/zəns) *n. Law* The nonperformance of some act that one is legally bound to perform. — **non·fea/sor** *n.*

non·fer·rous (non·fer/əs) *adj.* Not containing iron; esp., pertaining to metals other than iron, as copper, tin, platinum, etc.

non·fic·tion (non/fik/shən) *n.* Prose literature other than fiction, as historical works, biographies, etc. — **non/fic/tion·al** *adj.* — **non/fic/tion·al·ly** *adv.*

non·flam·ma·ble (non/flam/ə·bəl) *adj.* Not flammable.

no·nil·lion (nō·nil/yən) *n.* **1.** *U.S.* A thousand octillions, written as 1 followed by thirty zeros: a cardinal number. **2.** *Brit.* A million octillions (def. 2), written as 1 followed by fifty-four zeros: a cardinal number. — *adj.* Being a nonillion in number. [< MF < L *nonus* ninth + F (*m*)*illion* million] — **no·nil/lionth** (-yənth) *adj. & n.*

non·in·ter·ven·tion (non/in·tər·ven/shən) *n.* **1.** The refusal or failure to intervene; esp., the policy or practice of a nation of not intervening in the affairs of other nations. **2.** An instance of this. — **non/in·ter·ven/tion·ist** *adj. & n.*

non·join·der (non·join/dər) *n. Law* An omission to join an action or suit, as by a person who should be a party to it.

non·ju·ror (non·jŏŏr/ər) *n.* One who refuses to take an oath, as of allegiance, supremacy, or abjuration. [< NON- + JUROR, in obs. sense "one who takes an oath"]

non·met·al (non·met/l) *n. Chem.* Any element, as nitrogen, carbon, or sulfur, that has acid rather than basic properties.

non·mor·al (non·môr/əl, -mor/-) *adj.* Having no relation to morals; neither moral nor immoral. — **non/mo·ral/i·ty** *n.*

non·ob·jec·tive (non/əb·jek/tiv) *adj.* Not objective; esp., denoting a style of nonrepresentational art.

non·pa·reil (non/pə·rel′) *adj.* Having no equal; unrivaled. — *n.* **1.** One who or that which has no equal; a paragon. **2.** Any of various brilliantly colored finches of the southern U.S. **3.** *Printing* A size of type, 6 points, between agate and minion. [< MF < *non* not + OF *pareil equal*]

non·par·ti·san (non·pär/tə·zən) *adj.* Not partisan; esp., not controlled by, associated with, or in support of the interests of any one political party. Also **non·par/ti·zan.**

non·plus (non·plus′, non/plus) *v.t.* **·plused** or **·plussed, ·plusing** or **·plussing** To cause to be at a loss; baffle; perplex. — *n.* A mental standstill; bewilderment, esp. as causing speechlessness or indecision. [< L *non plus* no further]

non·pro·duc·tive (non/prə·duk/tiv) *adj.* **1.** Not productive; esp., pertaining to that part of the labor force that does not directly contribute to the production of goods, as office workers, salesmen, etc. **2.** Unproductive. — **non/pro·duc/tive·ly** *adv.* — **non/pro·duc/tive·ness** *n.*

non·prof·it (non·prof/it) *adj.* Not organized or maintained for the making of a profit: *nonprofit* charities.

non·pros (non·pros′) *v.t.* **·prossed, ·pros·sing** *Law* To enter judgment against (a plaintiff who fails to prosecute). [Short for NON PROSEQUITUR]

non pro·se·qui·tur (non prō·sek/wi·tər) *Law* A judgment entered against a plaintiff who fails to prosecute an action. [< L, lit., he does not prosecute]

non·rep·re·sen·ta·tion·al (non/rep/ri·zen·tā/shən·əl) *adj.* Not representational; esp., denoting a style of art that does not seek to represent objects as they appear in nature.

non·res·i·dent (non·rez/ə·dənt) *adj.* Not resident; esp., not residing permanently in the locality where one works, owns property, attends school, etc. — *n.* One who is nonresident. — **non/res/i·dence, non/res/i·den·cy** *n.*

non·re·sis·tant (non/ri·zis/tənt) *adj.* **1.** Not resistant; esp., incapable of resistance, as to infection. **2.** Of, pertaining to, or characteristic of a nonresistant. — *n.* One who is passive in the face of violence. — **non/re·sis/tance** *n.*

non·re·stric·tive (non/ri·strik/tiv) *adj.* **1.** Not restrictive. **2.** *Gram.* Denoting a word or word group, esp. an adjective clause, that describes its antecedent, but may be omitted without loss of essential meaning, as *which is for sale* in *Our house, which is for sale, needs repairs.*

non·sec·tar·i·an (non/sek·târ/ē·ən) *adj.* Not restricted to or associated with any one religion, sect, or faction.

non·sense (non/sens, -səns) *n.* **1.** That which is without sense, or without good sense; esp., words or actions that are meaningless or absurd. **2.** Things of no importance or use; trifles. **3.** Foolish or frivolous conduct. — **non·sen/si·cal** *adj.* — **non·sen/si·cal·ly** *adv.* — **non·sen/si·cal·ness** *n.*

non se·qui·tur (non sek/wə·tər) **1.** *Logic* An inference that does not follow from the premises. **2.** Any comment not relevant to what has preceded it. [< L, it does not follow]

non·skid (non/skid′) *adj.* Having a surface that resists skidding.

non·stan·dard (non/stan/dərd) *adj.* **1.** Varying or deviating from the standard. **2.** *Ling.* Designating those usages or varieties of a language that differ from the standard.

nonstandard English *Ling.* Those usages in English that differ from standard English: also *substandard English.*

non·stop (non/stop′) *adj.* Making, having made, or scheduled to make no stops: a *nonstop* flight; *nonstop* train.

non·such (non/such′) See NONESUCH.

non·suit (non/sōōt′) *Law v.t.* To order the dismissal of the suit of. — *n.* **1.** The abandonment of a suit. **2.** A judgment dismissing a suit, when the plaintiff either abandons it or fails to establish a cause of action.

non·sup·port (non/sə·pôrt/, -pôrt/) *n.* Failure to provide for the support of a legal dependent.

non trop·po (non trop/ō) *Music* Not too much. [< Ital.]

non·un·ion (non·yōōn/yən) *adj.* **1.** Not belonging to or associated with a trade union. **2.** Not recognizing or contracting with any trade union; also, not employing the members of any union: *nonunion* shop. **3.** Not produced or maintained by union labor.

non·un·ion·ism (non·yōōn/yən·iz/əm) *n.* Opposition to trade unions. — **non·un/ion·ist** *n.*

non·white (non/hwīt/) *n.* One who is not a member of the Caucasoid ethnic division of mankind. — *adj.* **1.** Of or pertaining to nonwhites. **2.** Not white.

noo·dle[1] (nōōd/l) *n.* **1.** A simpleton. Also **noo/dle·head/** (-hed/). **2.** *Informal* The head. [? < NOD]

noo·dle[2] (nōōd/l) *n.* A thin strip of dried dough, usu. containing egg, used in soup, etc. [< G *nudel*]

nook (nōōk) *n.* **1.** An interior corner or angle, as in a room. **2.** Any narrow or retired place, as a recess. [ME *nok* corner]

noon (nōōn) *n.* **1.** The middle of the day; twelve o'clock in the daytime. **2.** The highest or culminating point; zenith: the *noon* of life. — *adj.* Of, pertaining to, or ocurring at or about noon. [OE < L *nona* (*hora*) ninth (hour)]

noon·day (nōōn/dā/) *n.* Noon. — *adj.* Of or at noon.

no one Not any person; nobody.

noon·time (nōōn/tīm/) *n.* **1.** Midday. **2.** The culminating point or period. Also *Archaic* **noon/tide/**. [OE *nōntīd*]

noose (nōōs) *n.* **1.** A loop furnished with a running knot, as in a hangman's halter or a snare. **2.** Anything that entraps, restrains, or binds. — *v.t.* **noosed, noos·ing 1.** To capture or secure with a noose. **2.** To make a noose in or with. [< Provençal < L *nodus* knot]

Noot·ka fir (nōōt/kə) The Douglas fir.

no-par (nō/pär/) *adj.* Having no par or face value, as certain stock.

nope (nōp) *adv. Chiefly U.S. Slang* No.

nor (nôr) *conj.* And not; likewise not. ♦ *Nor* is used chiefly as a correlative of a preceding negative, as *neither, not,* or *never*: He is neither tall *nor* short; He has not come, *nor* will he. *Nor* is also used to introduce a clause following an affirmative clause: He hates me, *nor* does he hide it. [Contr. of ME *nother* neither]

Nor·dic (nôr/dik) *adj. Anthropol.* Pertaining or belonging to the tall, long-headed, blond-haired subdivision of the Caucasian ethnic stock, distributed mainly in NW Europe. — *n.* A Nordic person. [< NL *nordicus*]

nor'·east·er (nôr·ēs/tər), etc. See NORTHEASTER, etc.

Nor·folk jacket (nôr/fək) A loose-fitting men's jacket with a belt and two box pleats at the back and front.

no·ri·a (nō/rē·ə) *n.* An undershot water wheel having buckets on its rim to raise water, used in Spain and the Orient: also called *Persian wheel*. [< Sp. < Arabic *nā'ūrah*]

norm (nôrm) *n.* **1.** A pattern, model, or standard regarded as typical of a specified group. **2.** *Psychol.* The standard of performance in a given function or test, usu. the average achievement for the group concerned. **3.** *Stat.* The mode. [< L *norma* rule]

NORIA

nor·mal (nôr/məl) *adj.* **1.** Conforming to or consisting of a pattern, process, or standard regarded as usual or typical; natural. **2.** *Psychol.* **a** Well adjusted; without marked or persistent mental aberrations. **b** Of average skill, intelligence, etc. **3.** *Chem.* **a** Denoting a solution containing one gram equivalent weight of solute per liter: used as a unit, as *two normal, three normal*, etc. **b** Denoting a hydrocarbon having a straight, unbranched chain of carbon atoms: *normal* butane. **4.** *Math.* Perpendicular. — *n.* **1.** *Math.* A perpendicular; esp., a perpendicular to a tangent line or plane at the point of tangency. **2.** The common or natural condition, form, degree, etc. **3.** The usual or accepted rule or process. [< L < *norma* rule] — **nor/mal·cy, nor·mal·i·ty** (nôr·mal/ə·tē), **nor/mal·ness** *n.*

normal curve *Stat.* A bell-shaped curve representing the distribution of a series of values of a variable.

normal distribution *Stat.* A frequency distribution represented by a normal curve.

nor·mal·ize (nôr/məl·īz) *v.t.* **·ized, ·iz·ing** To bring into accord with a norm or standard form; make normal. — **nor/·mal·i·za/tion** *n.* — **nor/mal·iz/er** *n.*

nor·mal·ly (nôr/mə·lē) *adv.* **1.** As a rule; usually: The mail *normally* comes before noon. **2.** In a normal manner.

normal school A school that prepares secondary-school graduates to become teachers.

Nor·man (nôr/mən) *n.* **1.** One of the Scandinavian people who conquered Normandy in the tenth century. **2.** One of the people of mixed Scandinavian and French descent who

conquered England in 1066. **3.** A resident of Normandy **4.** Norman French. — *adj.* Of or pertaining to Normandy or the Normans. [< OF *Normans* Northmen]

Norman Conquest The subjugation of England by William the Conqueror in 1066. See table for WAR.

Norman French 1. The dialect of French spoken by the Normans in the Middle Ages. **2.** The legal parlance of England from the Norman Conquest to the 17th century. **3.** The dialect of French spoken in Normandy. Also *Norman.*

nor·ma·tive (nôr/mə·tiv) *adj.* **1.** Of, pertaining to, or based upon a norm, esp. one regarded as a standard or rule of usage. **2.** Implying, supporting, or establishing a norm.

Norse (nôrs) *adj.* **1.** Scandinavian. **2.** Of or pertaining to Norway, Iceland, and the Faroe Islands; West Scandinavian. — *n.* **1.** The Scandinavians or West Scandinavians collectively: used with *the.* **2.** The Scandinavian or North Germanic group of the Germanic languages; esp., Norwegian. **3.** The West Scandinavian languages. — **Old Norse 1.** The ancestor of the North Germanic languages, best represented by Old Icelandic: also called *Old Scandinavian.* **2.** Old Icelandic: see under ICELANDIC. [< Du. < MDu. *nordsch, nortsch* northern]

Norse·man (nôrs/mən) *n. pl.* **·men** (-mən) A Scandinavian of Viking times.

north (nôrth) *n.* **1.** The direction along a meridian that falls to the left of an observer on earth facing the sun at sunrise. **2.** One of the four cardinal points of the compass, directly opposite *south* and 90° counterclockwise from *east.* See COMPASS CARD. **3.** Any direction near this point. **4.** *Sometimes cap.* Any region north of a specified point. — **the North** In the U.S.: **a** The population or territory of the northern or northeastern States; esp., the region north of Maryland, the Ohio River, and Missouri. **b** The Free States opposed to the Confederacy (*the South*) in the Civil War. — *adj.* **1.** To, toward, facing, or in the north. **2.** Coming from the north. — *adv.* In or toward the north. [OE]

North American Indian An Indian of any of the tribes formerly inhabiting North America north of Mexico, now the United States and Canada. Abbr. *N.Am.Ind.*

North Atlantic Drift The terminal current of the Gulf Stream system, flowing from near Newfoundland northeast to Western Europe. Also **North Atlantic Current.**

North Atlantic Treaty Organization A military and naval alliance of Belgium, Canada, Denmark, France, Greece, Iceland, Italy, Luxemburg, the Netherlands, Norway, Portugal, Turkey, the United Kingdom, the U.S., and West Germany, organized under the **North Atlantic Treaty** of Washington, Apr. 4, 1919. Abbr. *NATO*

north·bound (nôrth/bound/) *adj.* Going northward. Also **north/-bound/.**

north·east (nôrth/ēst/, *Naut.* nôr·ēst/) *n.* **1.** The direction midway between north and east. **2.** A point on the mariner's compass, four points or 45° clockwise from due north. See COMPASS CARD. **3.** Any region lying in or toward this point. — *adj.* **1.** To, toward, facing, or in the northeast. **2.** Coming from the northeast. — *adv.* In or toward the northeast. — **north/east/ern** *adj.*

north·east·er (nôrth/ēs/tər, *Naut.* nôr·ēs/tər) *n.* **1.** A gale or storm from the northeast. **2.** A sailor's hat with a sloping brim worn in stormy weather. Also spelled *nor'easter.*

north·east·er·ly (nôrth/ēs/tər·lē, *Naut.* nôr·ēs/tər·lē) *adj.* **1.** In, of, or toward the northeast. **2.** From the northeast, as wind. — *adv.* Toward or from the northeast. — *n.* A wind or storm from the northeast. Also spelled *nor'easterly.*

north·east·ward (nôrth/ēst/wərd, *Naut.* nôr·ēst/wərd) *adv.* Toward the northeast. Also **north/east/wards** (-wərdz). — *adj.* To, toward, facing, or in the northeast. — *n.* Northeast.

north·east·ward·ly (nôrth/ēst/wərd·lē, *Naut.* nôr·ēst/wərd·lē) *adj. & adv.* Toward or from the northeast.

north·er (nôr/thər) *n.* **1.** A gale or storm from the north. **2.** *U.S.* A violent, cold north wind blowing over the plains of the SW States.

north·er·ly (nôr/thər·lē) *adj.* **1.** In, of, toward, or pertaining to the north. **2.** From the north, as a wind. — *adv.* Toward or from the north. — *n.* A wind or storm from the north. — **north/er·li·ness** *n.*

north·ern (nôr/thərn) *adj.* **1.** To, toward, or in the north. **2.** Native to or inhabiting the north: a *northern* species. **3.** *Sometimes cap.* Of, pertaining to, or characteristic of the north or the North. **4.** From the north, as a wind.

north·ern·er (nôr/thər·nər) *n.* **1.** One who is native to or lives in the north. **2.** *Usu. cap.* One who lives in or comes from the North.

northern lights The aurora borealis.

north·ern·most (nôr/thərn·mōst/) *adj.* Farthest north.

Northern Spy A large, yellowish red variety of apple.

north·land (nôrth/lənd) *n.* A land or region in the north [OE] — **north/land·er** *n.*

North·man (nôrth/mən) *n. pl.* **·men** (-mən) A Scandinavian; esp., a Scandinavian of the Viking period. [OE]

North Star Polaris.

Nor·thum·bri·a (nôr·thum′brē·ə) An ancient Anglo-Saxon kingdom, extending from the Humber to the Firth of Forth. **Nor·thum·bri·an** (nôr·thum′brē·ən) *adj.* **1.** Of or pertaining to Northumbria or to its inhabitants. **2.** Of or pertaining to the Old English dialect used in Northumbria. — *n.* **1.** A native or inhabitant of Northumbria. **2.** The Old English Northumbrian dialect.

north·ward (nôrth′wərd, *Naut.* nôr′thərd) *adv.* Toward the north. Also **north′wards** (-wərdz). — *adj.* To, toward, facing, or in the north. — *n.* A northward direction or point; also, a northern part or region.

north·ward·ly (nôrth′wərd·lē, *Naut.* nôr′thərd·lē) *adj. & adv.* **1.** Toward the north. **2.** Coming from the north.

north·west (nôrth·west′, *Naut.* nôr·west′) *n.* **1.** The direction midway between north and west. **2.** A point on the mariner's compass, four points or 45° counterclockwise from due north. See COMPASS CARD. **3.** Any region, lying in or toward this point. — *adj.* **1.** To, facing, or in the northwest. **2.** Coming from the northwest. — *adv.* In or toward the northwest. — **north′west′ern** *adj.*

north·west·er (nôrth′wes′tər, *Naut.* nôr·wes′tər) *n.* A gale or storm from the northwest: also spelled *nor′wester*.

north·west·er·ly (nôrth′wes′tər·lē, *Naut.* nôr·wes′tər·lē) *adj.* **1.** In, of, or toward the northwest. **2.** From the northwest, as a wind. — *adv.* Toward or from the northwest.

north·west·ward (nôrth′west′wərd, *Naut.* nôr·west′wərd) *adv.* Toward the northwest. Also **north′west′wards.** — *adj.* To, toward, or in the northwest. — *n.* Northwest.

north·west·ward·ly (nôrth′west′wərd·lē, *Naut.* nôr·west′wərd·lē) *adj. & adv.* Toward or from the northwest.

Nor·way maple (nôr′wā) A tall European maple.

Nor·we·gian (nôr·wē′jən) *adj.* Of or pertaining to Norway, its people, or their language. — *n.* **1.** A native or inhabitant of Norway. **2.** The North Germanic language of Norway. [< Med.L < ON < *nor(thr)* north + *vegr* way]

nor′west·er (nôr·wes′tər), etc. See NORTHWESTER, etc.

nose (nōz) *n.* **1.** The part of the face or forward end of an animal that contains the nostrils and the organ of smell, and that in man encloses cavities used in the respiratory process. ◆ Collateral adjectives: *nasal, rhinal.* **2.** The sense of smell or the power of smelling; scent. **3.** The ability to perceive or discover by or as if by the sense of smell: a *nose* for scandal. **4.** Something resembling a nose, as a spout or nozzle. **5.** *Aeron.* The forward part of an aircraft. **6.** The prow of a ship. **7.** *Informal* The nose (def. 1), considered as its owner's agent for prying or interfering: Keep your *nose* out of this. — **by a nose** *Slang* By a narrow margin. — **on the nose** *Slang* **1.** Designating a racing bet on a horse, etc., to win. **2.** Exactly; precisely. — **to pay through the nose** *Slang* To pay an excessively high price. — *v.* **nosed, nos·ing** *v.t.* **1.** To nuzzle. **2.** To make (one's way) carefully with the front end foremost. **3.** To perceive or discover by or as if by smell; scent. — *v.i.* **4.** To pry or interfere; snoop: with *around* or *about.* **5.** To move forward, esp. carefully. **6.** To smell; sniff. — **to nose out** To defeat by a narrow margin. [OE *nosu*]

nose·band (nōz′band′) *n.* The part of a bridle that passes over the nose of a horse: also called *nosepiece.*

nose·bleed (nōz′blēd′) *n.* Bleeding from the nose.

nose cone *Aerospace* The cone-shaped forward section of a rocket or missile, separable from the main body and carrying the payload, and able to withstand great heat.

nose·dive (nōz′dīv′) *v.i.* **-dived, -div·ing** To take a nose dive; plunge downward.

nose dive 1. A steep, downward plunge of an aircraft, nose end foremost. **2.** Any steep, sudden drop.

nose·gay (nōz′gā′) *n.* A small bunch of flowers; bouquet. [< NOSE + GAY, in obs. sense "a pretty thing"]

nose·piece (nōz′pēs′) *n.* **1.** Any piece or part, as of a helmet, that covers or protects the nose. **2.** A noseband.

nos·ey (nō′zē) See NOSY.

nos·tal·gi·a (nos·tal′jə, -jē·ə) *n.* **1.** A longing for familiar or beloved circumstances that are now remote or irrecoverable. **2.** Any longing for something far away or long ago. **3.** Severe homesickness. [< NL < Gk. *nostos* return home + *algos* pain] — **nos·tal′gic** *adj.*

nos·tril (nos′trəl) *n.* One of the external openings of the nose. [OE *nos(u)* nose + *thyrel* hole]

nos·trum (nos′trəm) *n.* **1.** A medicine of one's own preparation; also, a quack medicine. **2.** A favorite remedy or plan. **3.** A cure-all. [< L *noster* our own]

nos·y (nō′zē) *adj.* **nos·i·er, nos·i·est** *Informal* Prying; snooping; inquisitive: also spelled *nosey.*

not (not) *adv.* In no way, or to no extent or degree: used to note the absence, reverse, or opposite of something or to express negation, prohibition, or refusal. [OE < *ne* not + *ā* ever + *wiht* thing however small]

not- Var. of NOTO-.

no·ta·ble (nō′tə·bəl) *adj.* Worthy of note; remarkable; distinguished. — *n.* One who is distinguished, famous, etc. [< OF < L *nota* mark] — **no′ta·bil′i·ty** *n.* — **no′ta·ble·ness** *n.* — **no′ta·bly** *adv.*

no·ta·rize (nō′tə·rīz) *v.t.* **·rized, ·riz·ing** To attest to or authenticate as a notary public. — **no′ta·ri·za′tion** *n.*

no·ta·ry public (nō′tə·rē) *pl.* **no·ta·ries public** One who is legally authorized to administer oaths, certify contracts, etc. Also **notary.** — **no·tar′i·al** (-târ′ē·əl) *adj.*

no·ta·tion (nō·tā′shən) *n.* **1.** A system of signs, figures, or abbreviations used for convenience in recording a quantity, relation, process, etc.: musical *notation*; algebraic *notation.* **2.** The act or process of using notation. **3.** A note or comment. [< L < *notare* to note] — **no·ta′tion·al** *adj.*

notch (noch) *n.* **1.** A V-shaped cut in a surface. **2.** A nick cut into a stick, etc., as for keeping count. **3.** A narrow passage between mountains; a defile. **4.** *Informal* A degree; level: He is a *notch* above the others. — *v.t.* **1.** To make a notch or notches in. **2.** To record by or as if by notches; score. [Prob. ME < OF *oschier* to notch]

note (nōt) *n.* **1.** *Often pl.* A brief record or summary of facts set down for future study or reference: to take *notes.* **2.** A brief account or jotting to aid the memory. **3.** *Music* **a** A symbol representing a tone or sound of a given duration and pitch. **b** A tone or sound of a definite pitch. **c** A key of the keyboard. **4.** Any more or less musical sound, as the call of a bird. **5.** Any distinctive vocal sound, as the cry of an animal. **6.** A distinctive mark: a *note* of sadness; a *note* of spring in the air. **7.** A piece of paper currency issued by a government or authorized bank and negotiable as money: a bank *note.* **8.** A promissory note (which see). **9.** A formal, written communication of an official or diplomatic nature. **10.** A brief letter, esp. of an informal character. **11.** *pl.* A record of impressions, observations, reflections, etc. **12.** A marginal comment amending, criticizing, or explaining a passage in a book, etc.; annotation. **13.** Distinction; importance; reputation: a gentleman of *note.* **14.** Notice; attention: worthy of *note.* **15.** *Archaic* or *Poetic* A melody or song. — *v.t.* **not·ed, not·ing** **1.** To become aware of; observe. **2.** To pay attention to; heed carefully: to *note* well. **3.** To make special mention of. **4.** To set down for remembering; make a note of. **5.** To point out or indicate. [< OF < L *nota* mark] — **not′er** *n.*

note·book (nōt′book′) *n.* **1.** A book with blank pages on which notes may be entered. **2.** A book in which notes of hand are registered; bill book.

not·ed (nō′tid) *adj.* **1.** Well known by reputation; famous. **2.** Taken note of. — **not′ed·ly** *adv.* — **not′ed·ness** *n.*

note paper Paper for writing notes or letters.

note·wor·thy (nōt′wûr′thē) *adj.* Remarkable; significant. — **note′wor′thi·ly** *adv.* — **note′wor′thi·ness** *n.*

noth·ing (nuth′ing) *n.* **1.** Not anything; naught. **2.** No part or element: He knew *nothing* of it. **3.** One who or that which is of little or no importance. **4.** Insignificance or unimportance: to rise from *nothing.* **5.** Zero. **6.** A state of nonexistence; also, that which is nonexistent. — **for nothing 1.** Without charge; free. **2.** To no avail. **3.** Without cause. — *adv.* In no degree; not at all: now only in the expression **nothing like.** [ME < OE *nān thing*]

noth·ing·ness (nuth′ing·nis) *n.* **1.** The condition, quality, or fact of being nothing; nonexistence. **2.** Utter worthlessness or insignificance. **3.** That which is petty, trivial, or nonexistent. **4.** Unconsciousness.

no·tice (nō′tis) *v.t.* **·ticed, ·tic·ing 1.** To pay attention to or become aware of. **2.** To refer to or comment on. **3.** To treat courteously or with favor. — *n.* **1.** The act of noticing or observing. **2.** Announcement; information; warning. **3.** A formal announcement: to give *notice.* **4.** A written or printed communication publicly displayed. **5.** A short advertisement or review. **6.** Respectful treatment; civility. [< OF < L *notitia* fame, renown]

no·tice·a·ble (nō′tis·ə·bəl) *adj.* **1.** That can be noticed; perceptible. **2.** Worthy of notice. — **no′tice·a·bly** *adv.*

no·ti·fi·ca·tion (nō′tə·fə·kā′shən) *n.* **1.** The act of notifying. **2.** Notice given. **3.** A sign, advertisement, etc., by which notice is conveyed.

no·ti·fy (nō′tə·fī) *v.t.* **·fied, ·fy·ing 1.** To give notice to; inform. **2.** *Chiefly Brit.* To make known. [< OF < L *notus* known + *facere* to make] — **no′ti·fi′er** *n.*

no·tion (nō′shən) *n.* **1.** A general idea or impression; a vague conception. **2.** An opinion, belief, or idea. **3.** Intention; inclination. **4.** *pl. U.S.* Small miscellaneous articles for sale. — **Syn.** See IDEA. [See NOTIFY.]

no·tion·al (nō′shən·əl) *adj.* **1.** Pertaining to, expressing, or consisting of notions or concepts. **2.** Existing in imagination only. — **no′tion·al·ly** *adv.*

noto- *combining form* Back. Also, before vowels, **not-.** [< Gk. *nōton* back]

no·to·chord (nō′tə·kôrd) *n. Biol.* In invertebrate embryos, a flexible rod of cells along the median line on the dorsal side, a precursor of the spinal column.

no·to·ri·e·ty (nō′tə·rī′ə·tē) *n. pl.* **·ties 1.** The state or character of being notorious. **2.** One who or that which is notorious.

no·to·ri·ous (nō·tôr′ē·əs, -tō′rē-) *adj.* **1.** Widely known and generally disapproved of or deplored. **2.** Generally known; acknowledged. [< Med.L < *noscere* to know] — **no·to′ri·ous·ly** *adv.*

no-trump (nō′trump′) *n.* **1.** In bridge, a bid calling for play without a trump suit. **2.** Play without a trump suit. — *adj.* Of or denoting a bid or play of no-trump.

not·with·stand·ing (not′with·stan′ding, -with-) *prep.* In spite of: He left *notwithstanding* your orders. — *adv.* All the same; nevertheless: Though closely guarded, he escaped *notwithstanding.* — *conj.* In spite of the fact that; although. — **notwithstanding that** Although.

nou·gat (nōō′gət, *Fr.* nōō·gä′) *n.* A confection made with chopped almonds, pistachios, etc., mixed in a honey or sugar paste. [< F < Provençal]

nought (nôt) See NAUGHT.

noun (noun) *n. Gram.* **1.** A word used as the name of a thing, quality, or action. **2.** Anything that can be used either as subject, object, or appositive, as a noun clause. — *adj.* Of or pertaining to a noun or nouns: also **noun′al.** [< AF, OF < L *nomen* name] — **noun′al·ly** *adv.*

noun clause *Gram.* A dependent clause that functions as a noun in a sentence, as *Whoever finds my wallet* in *Whoever finds my wallet will be rewarded.*

nour·ish (nûr′ish) *v.t.* **1.** To furnish food or other material to sustain the life and promote the growth of (a living plant or animal). **2.** To support; maintain; foster. [< OF < L *nutrire* to nourish] — **nour′ish·a·ble** *adj.* — **nour′ish·er** *n.* — **nour′ish·ing·ly** *adv.*

nour·ish·ment (nûr′ish·mənt) *n.* **1.** That which nourishes; nutriment. **2.** The act of nourishing, or the state of being nourished.

nou·veau riche (nōō′vō′ rēsh′) *French pl.* **nou·veaux riches** (nōō′vō′ rēsh′) One who has recently become rich.

no·va (nō′və) *n. pl.* **·vae** (-vē) or **·vas** *Astron.* A star that suddenly flares up and fades away after a period of a few months or years. [< L, fem. of *novus* new]

nov·el (nov′əl) *adj.* New, strange, or unusual. — *n.* A fictional prose narrative of considerable length, usu. having an overall pattern or plot. [< F < Ital. < L *novus* new]

nov·el·ette (nov′əl·et′) *n.* A short novel: also *novella.*

nov·el·ist (nov′əl·ist) *n.* A writer of novels.

nov·el·is·tic (nov′əl·is′tik) *adj.* Of, pertaining to, characteristic of, or found in novels. — **nov′el·is′ti·cal·ly** *adv.*

nov·el·ize (nov′əl·īz) *v.t.* **·ized, ·iz·ing** To put into the form of a novel. — **nov′el·i·za′tion** *n.*

no·vel·la (nō·vel′ə, *Ital.* nō·vel′lä) *n. pl.* **·vel·las,** *Ital.* **·vel·le** (-vel′lā) **1.** A short tale or narrative, usu. with a moral. **2.** A novelette. [< Ital. See NOVEL.]

nov·el·ty (nov′əl·tē) *n. pl.* **·ties 1.** Something novel or unusual. **2.** The quality of being novel or new. **3.** *Usu. pl.* A small manufactured article.

No·vem·ber (nō·vem′bər) The eleventh month of the year, containing 30 days. [< L, ninth month (of the old Roman calendar) < *novem* nine]

no·ve·na (nō·vē′nə) *n.* In the Roman Catholic Church, devotions made on nine successive days, for some special religious purpose. [< Med.L < L *novem* nine]

nov·ice (nov′is) *n.* **1.** A beginner in any occupation; an inexperienced person. **2.** *Eccl.* One who enters a religious order or community on probation. [< F < L *novicius* new] — **Syn. 1.** *Novice* is a general term, often used as the official designation for those who have yet to demonstrate proficiency in a game or sport. *Beginner* is a homelier synonym for *novice,* sometimes implying depreciation; even more depreciatory is *tyro.*

no·vi·ti·ate (nō·vish′ē·it, -āt) *n.* **1.** The state or period of being a novice. **2.** *Eccl.* **a** The period of probation of a novice in a religious order or community. **b** The quarters occupied by such novices. **3.** A novice (defs. 1 and 2). Also **no·vi′ci·ate.** [< F *novicat* or Med.L *novitiatus*]

No·vo·cain (nō′və·kān) *n.* Proprietary name for a brand of procaine used as a local anesthetic, less toxic than cocaine. Also **no′vo·cain, no′vo·caine, No′vo·caine.**

now (nou) *adv.* **1.** At once. **2.** At or during the present time. **3.** Nowadays. **4.** In the immediate past: He said so just *now.* **5.** In the immediate future: He is going just *now.* **6.** In such circumstances: *Now* we can be sure of getting home. **7.** At this point in the proceedings, narrative, etc.: The war was *now* virtually over. — *conj.* Seeing that; since: *Now* that you've come, stay a while. — *n.* The present time, moment, or occasion. — **now and then** From time to time; occasionally: also **now and again.** [OE *nū*]

now·a·days (nou′ə·dāz′) *adv.* In the present time or age.

no·way (nō′wā′) *adv.* **1.** In no way, manner, or degree. **2.** *U.S. Dial.* By any means. Also **no′ways′** (-wāz′).

no·where (nō′hwâr′) *adv.* In no place; not anywhere. — *n.* No place. Also *U.S. Dial.* **no′wheres′** (-hwârz′).

no·wise (nō′wīz′) *adv.* In no manner or degree.

nox·ious (nok′shəs) *adj.* Causing or tending to cause injur[y] to health or morals; hurtful. — **Syn.** See PERNICIOUS. [< L< *noxa* harm] — **nox′ious·ly** *adv.* — **nox′ious·ness** *n.*

noz·zle (noz′əl) *n.* A projecting spout or pipe serving as an outlet, as of a teapot, hose, or rifle. [Dim. of NOSE]

nth (enth) *adj.* **1.** *Math.* Representing an ordinal equiva[lent] to *n.* **2.** Infinitely or indefinitely large (or small); mos[t] extreme: to the *nth* degree.

nu (nōō, noo) *n.* The thirteenth letter in the Greek alpha[bet] (N, ν), corresponding to English *n.* See ALPHABET.

nu·ance (nōō·äns′, nōō′äns, nyōō′-; *Fr.* nü·äns′) *n.* A fin[e] or subtle variation, as in color, tone, or meaning; grada[tion]. [< F < OF *nuer* to shade < *nue* cloud]

nub (nub) *n.* **1.** A knob or protuberance. **2.** A small piec[e] as of coal. **3.** *U.S. Informal* Core; gist; point: the *nub* of th[e] story. [Var. of KNOB] — **nub′by** *adj.*

nub·bin (nub′in) *n. U.S.* **1.** An imperfectly developed fru[it] or ear of corn. **2.** Anything small or stunted. [< NUB]

nub·ble (nub′əl) *n.* A small protuberance or lump; nub [Dim. of NUB] — **nub′bly** *adj.*

Nu·bi·an (nōō′bē·ən, nyōō′-) *adj.* Of Nubia, its people, o[r] their language. — *n.* **1.** A native of Nubia; esp., a membe[r] of any of the tribes formerly ruling the territory betwee[n] Egypt and Abyssinia. **2.** The language of the Nubians.

nu·bile (nōō′bil, nyōō′-) *adj.* Ready or suitable for ma[r]riage: said of young women. [< L < *nubere* to wed] — **nu·bil′i·ty** *n.*

nu·cle·ar (nōō′klē·ər, nyōō′-) *adj.* **1.** Of, pertaining to, o[r] resembling a nucleus or nuclei. Also **nu′cle·al** (-klē·əl). **2.** O[f] or using atomic energy: *nuclear* reactor. [< F *nucléaire*]

nuclear fission *Physics* Fission.

nuclear fusion *Physics* Fusion.

nuclear physics The branch of physics that investigate[s] the structure and properties of the atomic nucleus.

nuclear reaction *Physics* A change in the properties o[f] one or more atomic nuclei, esp. as a result of a collision be[-] tween two nuclei.

nu·cle·ase (nōō′klē·ās, nyōō′-) *n. Biochem.* An enzym[e] that hydrolyzes nucleic acids.

nu·cle·ate (nōō′klē·āt, nyōō′-) *adj.* Having a nucleus. — *v.t. & v.i.* **·at·ed, ·at·ing** To form or gather into a nucleu[s] [< L *nucleare* to form a kernel] — **nu′cle·a′tion** *n.* — **nu[′]cle·a′tor** *n.*

nu·cle·ic acid (nōō·klē′ik, nyōō-) *Biochem.* Any of a grou[p] of complex noncrystalline acids derived from nucleoprotein and containing carbohydrates combined with phosphor[ic] acids and bases derived from purine or pyrimidine.

nu·cle·in (nōō′klē·in, nyōō′-) *n. Biochem.* A colorles[s] amorphous protein containing nucleic acid, found as a no[r]mal constituent of cell nuclei.

nucleo- *combining form* Nucleus. [< L *nucleus* kernel[]

nu·cle·o·late (nōō′klē·ə·lāt, nyōō′-) *adj.* Having a nucleo[-] lus or nucleoli. Also **nu′cle·o·lat′ed.**

nu·cle·o·lus (nōō·klē′ə·ləs, nyōō′-) *n. pl.* **·li** (-lī) *Biol.* [A] rounded body sometimes found within the nucleus of a ce[ll] Also **nu′cle·ole** (-ōl). For illus. see CELL. [< L, dim. o[f] NUCLEUS] — **nu·cle′o·lar** *adj.*

nu·cle·on (nōō′klē·on, nyōō′-) *n. Physics* Any of the par[-] ticles composing the nucleus of an atom, as the proton, ne[u]tron, neutrino, etc.

nu·cle·on·ics (nōō′klē·on′iks, nyōō′-) *n.pl. (usually co[n]strued as sing.)* The practical applications of nuclear physi[cs] in any field of science, engineering, or technology. — **nu′cle[·]on′ic** *adj.*

nu·cle·o·plasm (nōō′klē·ə·plaz′əm, nyōō′-) *n. Biol.* Th[e] protoplasm of a cell nucleus. — **nu′cle·o·plas′mic** *adj.*

nu·cle·o·pro·te·in (nōō′klē·ə·prō′tē·in, -tēn, nyōō′-) [n.] *Biochem.* Any of a class of substances found in the nuclei o[f] plant and animal cells, containing one or more protein mol[e]cules combined with nucleic acid.

nu·cle·us (nōō′klē·əs, nyōō′-) *n. pl.* **·cle·i** (-klē·ī) **1.** A cen[-] tral point or part around which other things are gathere[d] core. **2.** A center of growth or development. **3.** *Biol.* [A] complex spherical body surrounded by a thin membrane an[d] embedded in the protoplasm of most plant and animal cells containing chromatin and essential to the processes of hered[-] ity and to other vital activities of the cell. For illus. see CEL[L] **4.** *Astron.* The brightest portion in the head of a comet or i[n] the center of a nebula. **5.** *Physics* The central core of a[n] atom, containing nucleons that provide its effective mas[s] and carrying a positive electric charge balanced by the nega[-] tive charge of the surrounding electrons. **6.** *Chem.* A grou[p] or ring of atoms so related structurally that their funda[-] mental arrangement remains intact through a series of chem[-] ical changes. [Contr. of L *nuculeus,* dim. of *nux, nucis* nut[]

nu·clide (nōō′klīd, nyōō′-) *n. Physics* A specific, relativel[y] stable atom as defined by the composition and properties o[f] its nucleus.

nude (nōōd, nyōōd) *adj.* Without clothing or covering; naked. — *n.* **1.** A nude figure, esp. in painting, sculpture, etc. **2.** The state of being nude. [< L *nudus* naked, bare] — **nude/ly** *adv.* — **nude/ness** *n.*

nudge (nuj) *v.t.* **nudged, nudg·ing** To touch or push gently, as with the elbow, in order to attract attention, etc. — *n.* A gentle push, as with the elbow. [? < Scand.]

nudi- *combining form* Without covering; naked; bare. [< L *nudus* naked]

nud·ism (nōō/diz·əm, nyōō/-) *n.* The doctrine or practice of living in the state of nudity.

nud·ist (nōō/dist, nyōō/-) *n.* One who believes in or practices nudism. — *adj.* Of or pertaining to nudism.

nu·di·ty (nōō/də·tē, nyōō/-) *n.* *pl.* **·ties** **1.** The state or fact of being nude. **2.** A naked part; anything uncovered.

nud·nik (nōōd/nik) *n.* *U.S. Slang* A pestiferous or annoying person. Also **nud/nick.** [< Yiddish]

nug·get (nug/it) *n.* A lump; esp., a lump of gold found in its native state. [? Dim. of dial. E *nug* lump]

nui·sance (nōō/səns, nyōō/-) *n.* Anything that annoys, bothers, or irritates. [< F *nuire* to harm]

nuisance tax A tax on various consumer goods and services, etc., regarded as more of a bother than a burden.

null (nul) *adj.* **1.** Of no legal force or effect; void; invalid. **2.** Nonexistent; negative. **3.** Of no avail; useless. — **null and void** Without legal force or effect. [< L < *ne* not + *ullus* any]

nul·li·fi·ca·tion (nul/ə·fə·kā/shən) *n.* **1.** The act of nullifying, or the state of being nullified. **2.** In U.S. history, the refusal of a State to obey an act of Congress, or the doctrine that such refusal is legal.

nul·li·fy (nul/ə·fī) *v.t.* **·fied, ·fy·ing** **1.** To make useless or ineffective; undo. **2.** To deprive of legal force or effect. — **Syn.** See ANNUL. [< LL < *nullus* none + *facere* to make] — **nul/li·fi/er** *n.*

nul·li·ty (nul/ə·tē) *n.* *pl.* **·ties** **1.** The state of being null. **2.** That which is null.

numb (num) *adj.* **1.** Having no sensation; without feeling. **2.** Unable to move. — *v.t.* To make numb. [ME < OE < *niman* to take] — **numb/ly** *adv.* — **numb/ness** *n.*

num·ber (num/bər) *n.* **1.** A specific quantity or place in a sequence, usu. designated by one of a series of symbols or words called *numerals*. **2.** A symbol or word used to designate number; a numeral. **3.** *Often pl.* A sizable collection or grouping: *numbers* of people. **4.** An indefinite quantity or collection: a *number* of facts. **5.** A specific sum or total count. **6.** *pl.* A large group; multitude. **7.** One of a series of things to which numbers are assigned: the March *number* of a magazine. **8.** A part of a program of music or entertainment. **9.** Quantity, as composed of units. **10.** A particular group, esp. of a privileged character. **11.** *Gram.* The representation in a language, by inflection or otherwise, of singleness or plurality. English has the singular and the plural number. **12.** *pl.* In poetry, metrical feet or rhythm; also, verse or verses. **13.** *Informal* An item or article, as of merchandise. Symbol #. — **any number of** A good many; rather a lot. — **beyond** (or **without**) **number** Too numerous to be counted. — **to get** (or **have**) **one's number** *Informal* To have insight into a person's motives, character, etc. — *v.t.* **1.** To determine the total number of; reckon. **2.** To assign a number to. **3.** To include as one of a collection or group. **4.** To amount to; total. **5.** To set or limit the number of. **6.** To be (a number of years, etc.) old or older. — *v.i.* **7.** To make a count; total. **8.** To be included, as in a particular group. **9.** To count off or call out numbers. [< OF < L *numerus*] — **num/ber·er** *n.*

num·ber·less (num/bər·lis) *adj.* **1.** Very numerous; countless. **2.** Having no number.

Num·bers (num/bərz) *n.pl.* (*construed as sing.*) The fourth book of the Old Testament.

num·bles (num/bəlz) *n.pl.* *Archaic* The entrails of an animal, as a deer. [< OF, ult. < LL *lumbellus*, dim. of L *lumbus* loin]

numb·skull (num/skul/) See NUMSKULL.

nu·mer·a·ble (nōō/mər·ə·bəl, nyōō/-) *adj.* That can be numbered. [< L *numerare* to count]

nu·mer·al (nōō/mər·əl, nyōō/-) *n.* A symbol, letter, or word that is used alone or in combination with others to express a number. — *adj.* **1.** Used in expressing or representing a number. **2.** Of or pertaining to number. [< LL < *numerus* number] — **nu/mer·al·ly** *adv.*

nu·mer·ate (nōō/mə·rāt, nyōō/-) *v.t.* **·at·ed, ·at·ing** **1.** To numerate; count. **2.** To read, as a numerical expression. [< L *numerare* to number]

nu·mer·a·tion (nōō/mə·rā/shən, nyōō/-) *n.* **1.** The act, process, or system of reading or naming numbers. **2.** An instance or example of this.

nu·mer·a·tor (nōō/mə·rā/tər, nyōō/-) *n.* **1.** *Math.* The term

of a fraction indicating how many of the parts of a unit are to be taken. In a common fraction it appears above or to the left of the line. **2.** One who or that which numbers.

nu·mer·i·cal (nōō·mer/i·kəl, nyōō-) *adj.* **1.** Of or denoting number. **2.** Numerable. **3.** Represented by or consisting of numbers or figures rather than letters. [< NL < L *numerus* number] — **nu·mer/i·cal·ly** *adv.*

nu·mer·ous (nōō/mər·əs, nyōō/-) *adj.* Consisting of a great number of units; being many. — **nu/mer·ous·ly** *adv.* — **nu/mer·os/i·ty** (nōō/mə·ros/ə·tē, nyōō/-), **nu/mer·ous·ness** *n.*

Nu·mid·i·a (nōō·mid/ē·ə, nyōō-) An ancient kingdom and Roman province in northern Africa. — **Nu·mid/i·an** *adj. & n.*

nu·mis·mat·ics (nōō/miz·mat/iks, -mis-, nyōō/-) *n.pl.* (*construed as sing.*) The study of coins, medals, and related objects, as paper money. [< F < L *numisma* coin < Gk. < *nomos* law] — **nu/mis·mat/ic** *adj.* — **nu·mis/ma·tist** *n.*

num·skull (num/skul/) *n.* A blockhead; dunce: also spelled **numbskull.**

nun (nun) *n.* A woman belonging to a religious order and living in a convent under vows of poverty, chastity, and obedience. [OE < LL *nonna* child's nurse, fem. of *nonnus*, orig., old man] — **nun/nish** *adj.*

nun·ci·o (nun/shē·ō, -sē·ō, nōōn/-) *n.* *pl.* **·ci·os** A permanent diplomatic envoy of the Pope to a foreign government. — **Syn.** See AMBASSADOR. [< Ital. < L *nuntius* messenger]

nun·ner·y (nun/ər·ē) *n.* *pl.* **·ner·ies** A convent for nuns.

nun's veiling (nunz) A soft, thin fabric, usu. of worsted, used for veiling and as a dress material.

nup·tial (nup/shəl) *adj.* Of or pertaining to marriage or the marriage ceremony. — *n.* *Usu. pl.* A marriage or wedding. [< L *nubere* to marry] — **nup/tial·ly** *adv.*

nurse (nûrs) *n.* **1.** A person who cares for the sick, injured, or infirm; esp., one who is trained to do such work. **2.** One who is a graduate of a school of nursing. **3.** A nursemaid. **4.** One who or that which fosters, nourishes, protects, or promotes. — *v.* **nursed, nurs·ing** *v.t.* **1.** To take care of (the sick, injured, or infirm). **2.** To feed (an infant) at the breast; suckle. **3.** To promote the growth and development of; foster; cherish. **4.** To feed and care for, as a child. **5.** To take steps to cure. **6.** To use or operate carefully: to *nurse* a weak wrist. **7.** To preserve or prolong deliberately. **8.** To fondle. **9.** To suckle at the breast of. — *v.i.* **10.** To act or serve as a nurse. **11.** To take nourishment from the breast. **12.** To suckle an infant. [Earlier *nurice* < OF < LL < L *nutrix* nursing mother] — **nurs/er** *n.*

nurse·maid (nûrs/mād/) *n.* A woman employed to care for children. Also **nurs·er·y·maid** (nûr/sər·ē·mād/, nûrs/rē-).

nurs·er·y (nûr/sər·ē, nûrs/rē) *n.* *pl.* **·er·ies** **1.** A place where trees, shrubs, etc., are raised, as for sale. **2.** A room or area set apart for the use of children. **3.** A nursery school. **4.** Anything that fosters, breeds, or develops.

nurs·er·y·man (nûr/sər·ē·mən, nûrs/rē-) *n.* *pl.* **·men** (-mən) One who raises or cultivates plants in a nursery.

nursery rhyme A simple story, riddle, proverb, etc., presented in rhymed·verse or jingle for children.

nursery school A place where children of preschool age regularly meet for training and supervised play.

nursing home A residence for persons who are unable to care for themselves, as the aged or the infirm.

nurs·ling (nûrs/ling) *n.* **1.** An infant or animal in the stage of being nursed. **2.** Anything that is carefully/tended or supervised. Also **nurse/ling.**

nur·ture (nûr/chər) *n.* **1.** That which nourishes; food; sustenance. **2.** Training; breeding; education. — *v.t.* **·tured, ·tur·ing** **1.** To feed or support; nourish; rear. **2.** To bring up or train; educate. [< OF < LL < L *nutrire* to nourish]

nut (nut) *n.* **1.** A dry fruit consisting of a kernel or seed enclosed in a woody shell, as a walnut, pecan, acorn, etc. **2.** The kernel of such fruit, esp. when edible. **3.** A small block of metal having an internal screw thread so that it may be fitted upon a bolt, screw, or the like. **4.** A person or matter difficult to deal with; a problem. **5.** *U.S. Slang* A crazy, irresponsible, or eccentric person. **6.** *Slang* The head. **7.** *Usu. pl. Slang* A testicle. — *v.i.* **nut·ted, nut·ting** To gather nuts. [OE *hnutu*] — **nut/ter** *n.*

nut-brown (nut/broun/) *adj.* Of a dark shade of brown suggesting the color of certain nuts, as the walnut.

nut·crack·er (nut/krak/ər) *n.* **1.** *Sometimes pl.* A device for cracking the hard shells of nuts. **2.** Any of certain crowlike birds, as the common nutcracker of Europe.

nut·gall (nut/gôl/) *n.* A nut-shaped gall, as on an oak tree.

nut·hatch (nut/hach/) *n.* A small, short-tailed bird related to the titmouse and feeding on nuts.

nut·meg (nut/meg) *n.* **1.** The aromatic kernel of the fruit of various tropical trees, esp. of the nutmeg tree of the Molucca Islands. **2.** The tree itself. [ME < OF < *nois* nut + *mugue* musk]

Nutmeg State Nickname of Connecticut.

nut·pick (nut'pik') *n.* A small, sharp-pointed instrument for picking out the kernels of nuts.

nu·tri·a (nōō'trē·ə, nyōō'-) *n.* The soft brown fur of the coypu, often dyed to resemble beaver. [< Sp., otter]

nu·tri·ent (nōō'trē·ənt, nyōō'-) *adj.* **1.** Giving nourishment; nutritious. **2.** Conveying nutriment. —*n.* Something that nourishes; food. [< L < *nutrire* to nourish]

nu·tri·ment (nōō'trə·mənt, nyōō'-) *n.* **1.** That which nourishes; food. **2.** Anything that promotes development. [< L < *nutrire* to nourish] —**nu'tri·men'tal** *adj.*

nu·tri·tion (nōō·trish'ən, nyōō-) *n.* **1.** The act or process of nourishing; esp., the processes by which food is converted into tissue in living organisms. **2.** That which nourishes. [< L < *nutrire* to nourish] —**nu·tri'tion·al** *adj.* —**nu·tri'tion·al·ly** *adv.* —**nu·tri'tion·ist** *n.*

nu·tri·tious (nōō·trish'əs, nyōō-) *adj.* Promoting growth and repairing the waste of living organisms; nourishing. —**nu·tri'tious·ly** *adv.* —**nu·tri'tious·ness** *n.*

nu·tri·tive (nōō'trə·tiv, nyōō'-) *adj.* **1.** Having nutritious properties. **2.** Of or relating to nutrition. —**nu'tri·tive·ly** *adv.* —**nu'tri·tive·ness** *n.*

nuts (nuts) *Chiefly U.S. Slang adj.* **1.** Crazy; demented; eccentric. **2.** Extremely enthusiastic or in love: with *about*. —*interj.* An exclamation of contempt, disappointment, etc. [< pl. of NUT]

nut·shell (nut'shel') *n.* The shell of a nut. —**in a nutshell** In brief and concise statement or form.

nut·ty (nut'ē) *adj.* **·ti·er**, **·ti·est 1.** Abounding in or producing nuts. **2.** Having the flavor of nuts. **3.** *Chiefly U.S. Slang* Crazy; nuts. —**nut'ti·ly** *adv.* —**nut'ti·ness** *n.*

nux vom·i·ca (nuks' vom'i·kə) **1.** The silky disklike seed of an Indian tree containing strychnine and other poisons. **2.** The tree itself. [< L *nux* nut + *vomere* to vomit]

nuz·zle (nuz'əl) *v.* **·zled**, **·zling** *v.i.* **1.** To rub, press, or dig with or as with the nose. **2.** To nestle or snuggle; lie close. —*v.t.* **3.** To push or rub the nose, etc., into or against. **4.** To root up with the nose or snout. [Freq. of NOSE, v.]

nyc·to- *combining form* Night; nocturnal. Also, before vowels, **nyct-**. Also **nycti-**. [< Gk. *nyx, nyktos* night]

ny·lon (nī'lon) *n.* **1.** A synthetic material yielding fibers and bristles of great toughness, strength, and elasticity; esp., cloth made from these fibers. **2.** *pl. Informal* Stockings made of nylon, a trade name]

nymph (nimf) *n.* **1.** In Greek and Roman mythology, any of a class of minor female divinities dwelling in groves, forests, fountains, etc. **2.** *Chiefly Poetic.* A young woman or girl. **3.** *Entomol.* The young of an insect undergoing incomplete metamorphosis, at which stage the wing pads are first evident: also **nym·pha** (nim'fə). [< OF < L < Gk. *nymphē* nymph, bride] —**nymph'al, nym·phe·an** (nim·fē'·ən) *adj.*

nympho- *combining form* Nymph; bride. Also, before vowels, **nymph-**. [< Gk. *nymphē* bride, nymph]

nym·pho·ma·ni·a (nim'fə·mā'nē·ə, -mān'yə) *n. Psychiatry* An extreme and ungovernable sexual desire in women. —**nym'pho·ma'ni·ac** *adj. & n.*

Nyx (niks) In Greek mythology, the goddess of night.

O

o, O (ō) *n. pl.* **o's** or **os, O's** or **Os, oes** (ōz) **1.** The fifteenth letter of the English alphabet. **2.** Any sound represented by the letter *o*. **3.** Anything shaped like an *O*. —*symbol* **1.** *Math.* Zero or nought. **2.** *Chem.* Oxygen.

o' (ō, ə) *prep.* Of: one o'clock, man-o'-war, jack-o'-lantern.

o- Var. of OB-.

O (ō) *interj.* **1.** An exclamation used in direct address, as in prayer or invocation: *O* Lord! **2.** An exclamation of surprise, disappointment, fear, longing, etc.: *O* dear! —*n. pl.* **O's** An exclamation or lamentation.

O' (ō) A descendant of: *O'Conor*: a patronymic prefix commonly used in Irish surnames, equivalent to the English and Scandinavian suffixes *-son, -sen.* Compare FITZ-, MAC-.

oaf (ōf) *n. pl.* **oafs** or *Rare* **oaves** (ōvz) A stupid, bungling person. [Earlier *auf* < ON *álfr* elf] —**oaf'ish** *adj.* —**oaf'ish·ly** *adv.* —**oaf'ish·ness** *n.*

oak (ōk) *n.* **1.** An acorn-bearing tree or shrub of the beech family, valued for the hardness, strength, and durability of its timber. ◆ Collateral adjective: *quercine.* **2.** The wood of the oak. **3.** Any of various plants resembling the oak. [OE *āc*] —**oak'en** *adj.*

oak apple A rounded gall produced on an oak by an insect. Also **oak gall.**

oak leaf cluster A bronze decoration given to holders of certain U.S. military medals in recognition of further merit.

oak·um (ō'kəm) *n.* Hemp fiber obtained by untwisting and picking out the fibers of old rope, used for caulking seams, etc. [OE *ācumba* < *ā-* out + *cemban* to comb]

oar (ôr, ōr) *n.* **1.** A wooden implement for propelling or steering a boat, consisting of a long shaft with a blade at one end. **2.** A person using an oar. **3.** An oarlike part or appendage, as in certain worms. —*v.t.* **1.** To propel with or as with oars; row. **2.** To make (one's way) or traverse (water) with or as with oars. —*v.i.* **3.** To proceed by or as by rowing; row. [OE *ār*]

oared (ôrd, ōrd) *adj.* Having or equipped with oars.

oar·lock (ôr'lok', ōr'-) *n.* A device on the side of a boat for keeping an oar in place. Also, *Brit.*, **rowlock.**

oars·man (ôrz'mən, ōrz'-) *n. pl.* **·men** (-mən) One who rows.

o·a·sis (ō·ā'sis, ō'ə·sis) *n. pl.* **·ses** (-sēz) An area in a desert made fertile by groundwater or by irrigation. [< L < Gk.]

oat (ōt) *n.* **1.** *Usu. pl.* A cereal grass widely cultivated for its edible grain. **2.** *Usu. pl.* The grain itself. **3.** Any similar grass, as the wild oat. **4.** A musical pipe made from the stem of an oat. —**to feel one's oats** *Informal* **1.** To be exuberant or high-spirited. **2.** To feel bold or self-assured. —**to sow one's wild oats** *Informal* To experience the adventures and follies characteristic of youth. [OE *āte*] —**oat'en** *adj.*

oat·cake (ōt'kāk') *n.* A thin, hard cake of oatmeal.

oath (ōth) *n. pl.* **oaths** (ōths, ōthz) **1.** A formal declaration in support of a pledge or promise, usu. based on an appeal to God or some other higher institution or figure; also, the form of the declaration. **2.** The careless or profane use of the name of God or other sacred person or thing. **3.** A profane or vulgar utterance. [OE *āth*]

oat·meal (ōt'mēl') *n.* A cereal food made from the cooked meal of oats; also, the meal itself. Also **oat meal.**

ob- *prefix* **1.** Toward; to; facing: *obvert.* **2.** Against; in opposition to: *object, obstruct.* **3.** Over; upon: *obliterate.* **4.** Completely: *obdurate.* **5.** Inversely: prefixed to adjectives in scientific terms. Also: *o-* before *m*, as in *omit; oc-* before *c*, as in *occur; of-* before *f*, as in *offend; op-* before *p*, as in *oppress.* [< L *ob* toward, for, against]

O·ba·di·ah (ō'bə·dī'ə) Sixth-century B.C. minor Hebrew prophet. —*n.* A book of the Old Testament containing his prophecies.

ob·bli·ga·to (ob'lə·gä'tō, *Ital.* ôb'blē·gä'tō) *Music adj.* Denoting a part or accompaniment essential to the performance of a composition. —*n.* An obbligato part. Also spelled **obligato.** [< Ital. < L *obligare.* See OBLIGE.]

ob·du·rate (ob'dyə·rit, -rāt) *adj.* **1.** Unmoved by or hardened against human feelings or moral influence; hardhearted. **2.** Difficult to handle or manage; intractable. [< L < *ob-* against + *durare* to harden] —**ob'du·rate·ly** *adv.* —**ob'du·ra·cy** (-rə·sē), **ob'du·rate·ness** *n.*

o·be·di·ence (ō·bē'dē·əns, ə·bē'-) *n.* The act of obeying, the condition of being obedient; submission; compliance.

o·be·di·ent (ō·bē'dē·ənt, ə·bē'-) *adj.* Complying with or conforming to a command, restraint, etc.; dutiful. **2.** Deferring habitually to laws, superiors, etc.; docile; compliant. [See OBEY.] —**o·be'di·ent·ly** *adv.*

o·bei·sance (ō·bā'səns, ō·bē'-) *n.* **1.** Courtesy, reverence, homage; also, an act or gesture expressing this: chiefly in phrases **to do** (**make,** or **pay**) **obeisance.** [< OF < *obeissant*, ppr. of *obeir* to obey] —**o·bei'sant** *adj.*

ob·e·lisk (ob'ə·lisk) *n.* **1.** A square shaft of stone with pyramidal top, usu. tapering, and often used as a monument in ancient Egypt. **2.** *Printing* The dagger sign (†), used as a mark of reference: also **ob·e·lus** (ob'ə·ləs). [< L < Gk. *obelos* a spit, hence pointed pillar] —**ob'e·lis'cal, ob'e·lis·koid** (-koid) *adj.*

O·ber·on (ō'bə·ron) In medieval legend and folklore, the king of the fairies, husband of Titania.

o·bese (ō·bēs') *adj.* Very fat or corpulent. [< L *obesus* fat] —**o·bese'ly** *adv.*

o·bes·i·ty (ō·bēs'sə·tē, ō·bēs'ə-) *n.* The condition of being obese; corpulence. Also **o·bese'ness** *n.*

bey (ō-bā′, ə-bā′) *v.t.* **1.** To comply with or carry out the ommand, request, etc., of. **2.** To comply with or execute a command, request, etc.). **3.** To be guided, controlled, or ctuated by. — *v.i.* **4.** To be obedient; comply. [< OF < L *oboedire* to give ear, obey] — **o·bey′er** *n.*

·fus·cate (ob-fus′kāt, ob′fəs-) *v.t.* **·cat·ed, ·cat·ing 1.** To onfuse or perplex; bewilder. **2.** To darken or obscure. [< *obfuscare* to darken, obscure] — **ob′fus·ca′tion** *n.*

bi (ō′bē) *n.* A broad sash tied with a stylized bow or loop n the back, worn by Japanese women. [< Japanese *ōbi*]

bit (ō′bit, ob′it) *n. Informal* An obituary.

·i·ter dic·tum (ob′ə·tər dik′təm) *Latin pl.* **ob·i·ter dic·ta** dik′tə) **1.** *Law* A judicial opinion that is not binding. **2.** Any incidental remark.

bit·u·ar·y (ō-bich′ōō·er′ē) *n. pl.* **·ar·ies** A published no- ice of a person's death, usu. including a biographical sketch. — *adj.* Of or recording a death. [< Med.L < L *obitus* a oing down, death]

·ject[1] (əb-jekt′) *v.i.* **1.** To offer an argument in opposition r disagreement. **2.** To feel or state disapproval. — *v.t.* **.** To offer in opposition or criticism. [< L < *ob-* towards, gainst + *jacere* to throw] — **ob·jec′tor** *n.*

·ject[2] (ob′jikt, -jekt) *n.* **1.** Anything that is or may be pprehended by the senses. **2.** The purpose or end of an ction. **3.** One who or that which is the focus or center of hought, action, etc. **4.** *Gram.* **a** A substantive that receives r is affected by the action of the verb, called the **direct bject** when it receives the direct action, as *pie* in *She gave im the pie*, and the **indirect object** when it receives the econdary action, as *him* in the same sentence. **b** A substan- ive following a preposition, as *mountain* in the phrase *on he mountain*. — **Syn.** See PURPOSE. [< Med.L *objectum* omething thrown in the way]

ject glass *Optics* An objective (*n.* def. 3).

·jec·ti·fy (əb-jek′tə-fī) *v.t.* **·fied, ·fy·ing** To make objec- ive. — **ob·jec′ti·fi·ca′tion** *n.*

·jec·tion (əb-jek′shən) *n.* **1.** A statement or feeling of isagreement, opposition, etc. **2.** The cause or reason for isagreement, etc. **3.** The act of objecting.

·jec·tion·a·ble (əb-jek′shən·ə·bəl) *adj.* Deserving of dis- pproval; offensive. — **ob·jec′tion·a·bil′i·ty** *n.* — **ob·jec′- ion·a·bly** *adv.*

·jec·tive (əb-jek′tiv) *adj.* **1.** Free from personal feelings, pinions, prejudice, etc.; unbiased. **2.** Pertaining to what s external to or independent of the mind; real: opposed to *ubjective*. **3.** Treating of or stressing external or actual henomena, as distinct from inner or imaginary feelings or houghts. **4.** *Gram.* Denoting the case of the object of a ransitive verb or preposition; accusative. **5.** Pertaining to goal or end. — *n.* **1.** That which is striven for or aimed t; a goal; end. **2.** *Gram.* **a** The objective or accusative ase. **b** A word in this case. **3.** *Optics* A lens or lenses, as n a telescope, that is nearest to the object being viewed: lso called *object glass*. — **ob·jec′tive·ly** *adv.*

·jec·tiv·i·ty (ob′jek·tiv′ə·tē) *n.* **1.** The state or quality of eing objective. **2.** Material reality. Also **ob·jec′tive·ness.**

ject lesson An example of a principle or moral in a con- rete form or striking instance.

·jet d'art (ōb-zhe′ dàr′) *French pl.* **ob·jets d'art** (ōb- he′) Any work of artistic value.

·jur·gate (ob′jər-gāt, əb-jûr′-) *v.t.* **·gat·ed, ·gat·ing** To ebuke severely; scold sharply. [< L < *ob-* against + *urgare* to scold] — **ob′jur·ga′tion** *n.* — **ob′jur·ga′tor** *n.* — **ob·jur·ga·to·ri·ly** (ob-jûr′gə-tôr′ə-lē, -tō′rə-lē) *adv.* — b·jur′ga·to·ry (-tôr′ē, -tō′rē) *adj.*

·late[1] (ob′lāt, ob-lāt′) *adj.* Flattened at the poles. [< NL < L *ob-* towards + (*pro*)*latus* lengthened out] — **ob· ate·ly** (ob′lāt·lē, ob-lāt′-) *adv.*

·late[2] (ob′lāt, ob-lāt′) *adj.* Consecrated or devoted to a eligious life. — *n.* A person so devoted, as in a monastery. < Med.L *oblatus* < L, pp. of *offerre* to present]

·la·tion (ob-lā′shən) *n.* **1.** The act of offering religious vorship, sacrifice, etc., esp. in the Eucharist. **2.** That which is offered, esp. the elements of the Eucharist. **3.** Any olemn offering. [See OBLATE[2].] — **ob·la′tion·al** *adj.*

b·la·to·ry (ob′lə-tôr′ē; for *adj.*, also -git) *v.t.* **·gat·ed, ·gat·ing** *f* o bind or compel, as by contract, conscience, promise, etc. — *adj.* Bound or restricted. — **ob′li·ga′tor** *n.*

·li·ga·tion (ob′lə-gā′shən) *n.* **1.** The act of obligating, or he state of being obligated. **2.** The duty, promise, contract, tc., by which one is bound. **3.** Any duty or requirement. **.** The constraining or binding power of a law, promise, onscience, etc. **5.** What one owes in return for a service, avor, etc.; also, the service or favor itself. [< OF < LL < *lig·are*. See OBLIGE.]

b·li·ga·tive (ob′lə-gā′tiv) *adj.* Implying or expressing ob- igation.

ob·li·ga·to (ob′lə-gä′tō, *Ital.* ōb′blē-gä′tō) See OBBLIGATO.

ob·lig·a·to·ry (ə-blig′ə·tôr′ē, -tō′rē, ob′lĭ·gə-) *adj.* Of the nature of or constituting a duty or obligation; imperative.

o·blige (ə-blīj′) *v.t.* **o·bliged, o·blig·ing 1.** To place (one) under obligation, as for a service, favor, etc.: with *to.* **2.** To compel, bind, or constrain, as by command, request, etc. **3.** To do a favor or service for. [< OF < L *obligare*, orig., to tie around] — **o·blig′er** *n.*

o·blig·ing (ə-blī′jing) *adj.* Disposed to do favors; accommo- dating; kind. — **o·blig′ing·ly** *adv.* — **o·blig′ing·ness** *n.*

ob·lique (ə-blēk′, *in military usage* ·ə-blīk′) *adj.* **1.** Deviat- ing from the perpendicular or horizontal; slanting. **2.** Not direct or straightforward in meaning, expression, etc.: *oblique praise.* **3.** Indirectly aimed at or attained. **4.** *Geom.* Having an acute or obtuse angle. **5.** Not in the direct line of descent; collateral. — *n.* **1.** An oblique thing, as a line. **2.** *Naut.* The act of veering less than ninety degrees. — *v.i.* **·liqued, ·li·quing** To deviate from the perpendicular or horizontal; slant. [< L *obliquus*] — **ob·lique′ly** *adv.* — **ob·liq·ui·ty** (ə-blik′wə-tē), **ob·lique′ness** *n.*

oblique angle *Geom.* An angle not a right angle; an acute or obtuse angle.

ob·lit·er·ate (ə-blit′ə-rāt) *v.t.* **·at·ed, ·at·ing 1.** To destroy utterly. **2.** To blot or wipe out, as writing. [< L < *obli- terare* to efface] — **ob·lit′er·a′tion** *n.* — **ob·lit′er·a′tive** *adj.* — **ob·lit′er·a′tor** *n.*

ob·liv·i·on (ə-bliv′ē-ən) *n.* **1.** The state or fact of being com- pletely forgotten. **2.** The state or fact of forgetting com- pletely. [< OF < L *oblivisci* to forget]

ob·liv·i·ous (ə-bliv′ē-əs) *adj.* **1.** Not conscious or aware; un- mindful: with *of* or *to.* **2.** Forgetful or given to forgetfulness. [< L *obliviosus*] — **ob·liv′i·ous·ly** *adv.* — **ob·liv′i·ous- ness** *n.*

ob·long (ob′lông, -long) *adj.* Longer in one dimension than in another: said usually of rectangles. — *n.* An oblong figure, object, etc. [< L *oblongus* somewhat long]

ob·lo·quy (ob′lə-kwē) *n. pl.* **·quies 1.** Abusive and defam- atory language, esp. by a large group of people; vilification. **2.** Disgrace resulting from such abuse. [< LL < *ob- against + *loqui* to speak]

ob·nox·ious (əb-nok′shəs) *adj.* Highly disagreeable; ob- jectionable; offensive. [< L < *ob-* towards + *noxius* harm- ful] — **ob·nox′ious·ly** *adv.* — **ob·nox′ious·ness** *n.*

o·boe (ō′bō, ō′boi) *n.* A double-reed woodwind instrument with a conical bore, having a high, penetrating tone. [< Ital. < F *hautbois.* See HAUTBOY.] — **o′bo·ist** *n.*

ob·scene (əb-sēn′, ob-) *adj.* **1.** Offensive or abhorrent to prevailing concepts of morality or decency; indecent; lewd. **2.** Disgusting; loathsome; foul. [< MF < L *obscenus* ill- omened, filthy] — **ob·scene′ly** *adv.* — **ob·scene′ness** *n.*

ob·scen·i·ty (əb-sen′ə-tē, -sē′nə-, ob-) *n. pl.* **·ties 1.** The quality or state of being obscene. **2.** Something obscene.

ob·scur·ant (əb-skyoor′ənt) *n.* One who or that which ob- scures, esp. by opposing or hindering educational progress, free thought, etc. — *adj.* **1.** Causing obscurity. **2.** Of an obscurant. [< L < *obscurare* to darken]

ob·scur·ant·ism (əb-skyoor′ən·tiz′əm) *n.* **1.** The act or principles of an obscurant. **2.** Opposition to learning and inquiry. — **ob·scur′ant·ist** *n. & adj.*

ob·scure (əb-skyoor′) *adj.* **·scur·er, ·scur·est 1.** Not clear or plain to the mind; hard to understand. **2.** Not clear or distinct to the senses; difficult to discern. **3.** Not readily discovered; hidden; remote. **4.** Without distinction or fame; inconspicuous. **5.** Having little or no light; dark. — *v.t.* **·scured, scur·ing 1.** To render obscure, vague, indefinite, etc. **2.** To cover or darken so as to make dim, indistinct, etc. [< OF < L *obscurus* covered over] — **ob·scure′ly** *adv.* — **ob·scure′ness** *n.*

ob·scu·ri·ty (əb-skyoor′ə-tē) *n. pl.* **·ties 1.** The state or quality of being obscure. **2.** An obscure person or thing.

ob·se·quies (ob′sə-kwēz′) *n.pl.* Funeral rites. [< OF *obse- ques* < Med.L *obsequiae*, pl. funeral rites]

ob·se·qui·ous (əb-sē′kwē-əs) *adj.* Excessively obedient or submissive; sycophantic; servile. [< L < *obsequi* to comply with] — **ob·se′qui·ous·ly** *adv.* — **ob·se′qui·ous·ness** *n.*

ob·serv·a·ble (əb-zûr′və-bəl) *adj.* **1.** Capable of being ob- served; noticeable. **2.** Worthy of notice or mention; note- worthy. **3.** That may or must be observed, as a holiday. — **ob·serv′a·bly** *adv.* — **ob·serv′a·ble·ness** *n.*

ob·serv·ance (əb-zûr′vəns) *n.* **1.** The act of observing a command, law, etc. **2.** The act of celebrating a holiday, ceremony, rite, etc. **3.** A customary rite, ceremony, etc. **4.** Observation; notice; attention. **5.** *Eccl.* The rule or constitu- tion of a religious order.

ob·ser·vant (əb-zûr′vənt) *adj.* **1.** Attentive or quick in observing; heedful; alert. **2.** Strict or careful in obeying or keeping a custom, law, ceremony, etc.: often with *of: obser- vant* of ritual. — **ob·ser′vant·ly** *adv.*

---

ob·ser·va·tion (ob'zər·vā'shən) *n.* **1.** The act of observing, or the fact of being observed; also, that which is observed. **2.** Close examination for the purpose of scientific study. **3.** An opinion or judgment. **— to take** (or **work out**) **an observation** *Naut.* To calculate the latitude and longitude from the altitude and position of the sun or other celestial body. **— ob'ser·va'tion·al** *adj.* **— ob'ser·va'tion·al·ly** *adv.*

ob·ser·va·to·ry (ab·zûr'va·tôr'ē, -tō'rē) *n. pl.* **·ries 1.** A building or station for the systematic observation of natural phenomena; esp., one for astronomical observation. **2.** A place affording a panoramic view.

ob·serve (ab·zûrv') *v.* **·served, ·serv·ing** *v.t.* **1.** To see or notice; perceive. **2.** To watch attentively. **3.** To make careful observation of, esp., for scientific purposes. **4.** To say or comment; remark. **5.** To follow or comply with (a law, custom, etc.); abide by. **6.** To celebrate as a holiday. **—** *v.i.* **7.** To make a remark; comment: often with *on* or *upon*. **8.** To take notice. **9.** To look on or attend without taking part, as at a meeting. [< OF < L *observare* to watch] **— ob·serv'er** *n.* **— ob·serv'ing·ly** *adv.*

ob·sess (ab·ses') *v.t.* To occupy or trouble the mind of to an excessive degree; preoccupy; harass; haunt. [< L *obsidere* to occupy, besiege] **— ob·ses'sive** *adj.* **— ob·ses'sor** *n.*

ob·ses·sion (ab·sesh'ən) *n.* **1.** That which obsesses, as a persistent idea or feeling. **2.** *Psychiatry* An unwanted or compulsive idea or emotion persistently coming to awareness. **3.** The act of obsessing, or the state of being obsessed.

ob·sid·i·an (ab·sid'ē·ən, ob-) *n.* A glassy volcanic rock, usu. black. [< L *obsidianus*]

ob·so·les·cent (ob'sə·les'ənt) *adj.* Growing obsolete. **— ob'so·les'cence** *n.* **— ob'so·les'cent·ly** *adv.*

ob·so·lete (ob'sə·lēt, ob'sə·lēt') *adj.* **1.** Gone out of fashion; out-of-date. **2.** No longer used or practiced. **3.** *Biol.* Imperfectly developed; atrophied or vestigial. [< L *obsolescere* to wear out] **— ob'so·lete'ly** *adv.* **— ob'so·lete'ness** *n.* **— ob'so·let'ism** *n.*
— Syn. 1. An *obsolete* word is no longer used either in speech or writing, usually because it has been supplanted by a different word. *Archaic* words were current at some time in the past, and appear in the works of Shakespeare, the Bible, etc., but unlike obsolete words they are still used for effect because they have an unmistakable flavor of their period or milieu. *Rare* words may be *archaic* or current, but are little used.

ob·sta·cle (ob'sta·kəl) *n.* That which stands in the way; a hindrance or obstruction. [< OF < L *ob-* before, against + *stare* to stand]

ob·stet·ric (ab·stet'rik) *adj.* Of or pertaining to obstetrics or childbirth. Also **ob·stet'ri·cal.** [< L *obstetrix, -icis* midwife, lit., one who stands by] **— ob·stet'ri·cal·ly** *adv.*

ob·ste·tri·cian (ob'stə·trish'ən) *n.* A medical and surgical specialist in obstetrics.

ob·stet·rics (ab·stet'riks) *n.pl.* (*construed as sing.*) The branch of medicine dealing with pregnancy and childbirth.

ob·sti·na·cy (ob'stə·nə·sē) *n. pl.* **·cies 1.** The state or quality of being obstinate. **2.** An obstinate act, feeling, etc.

ob·sti·nate (ob'stə·nit) *adj.* **1.** Unreasonably fixed in one's purpose or opinion; unyielding; stubborn. **2.** Difficult to overcome or cure: an *obstinate* habit. [< L *obstinare* to persist] **— ob'sti·nate·ly** *adv.* **— ob'sti·nate·ness** *n.*

ob·strep·er·ous (ab·strep'ər·əs) *adj.* Unruly, noisy, or boisterous, esp. in resistance to control, advice, etc. [< L < *ob-* towards + *strepere* to make noise] **— ob·strep'er·ous·ly** *adv.* **— ob·strep'er·ous·ness** *n.*

ob·struct (ab·strukt') *v.t.* **1.** To stop or impede movement through (a way or passage) by obstacles or impediments; barricade. **2.** To block or retard the progress or way of; impede. **3.** To come or be in front of so as to prevent a clear view. [< L < *ob-* before + *struere* to pile, build] **— ob·struct'er** or **ob·struc'tor** *n.* **— ob·struc'tive** *adj.* **— ob·struc'tive·ly** *adv.* **— ob·struc'tive·ness** *n.*

ob·struc·tion (ab·struk'shən) *n.* **1.** That which obstructs. **2.** The act of obstructing, or the state of being obstructed.

ob·struc·tion·ist (ab·struk'shən·ist) *n.* One who makes a practice of obstructing, esp. in politics, one who obstructs debate, legislation, etc. **— ob·struc'tion·ism** *n.*

ob·tain (ab·tān') *v.t.* **1.** To gain possession of, esp. by effort; acquire; get. **—** *v.i.* **2.** To be prevalent or in effect. **— Syn.** See GET. [< OF < L < *ob-* towards + *tenere* to hold] **— ob·tain'a·ble** *adj.* **— ob·tain'er** *n.* **— ob·tain'ment** *n.*

ob·trude (ab·trood') *v.* **·trud·ed, ·trud·ing** *v.t.* **1.** To thrust or force (oneself, an opinion, etc.) upon another without request or warrant. **2.** To push forward or out; eject. **—** *v.i.* **3.** To intrude oneself. [< L < *ob-* towards + *trudere* to thrust] **— ob·trud'er** *n.* **— ob·tru'sion** *n.*

ob·tru·sive (ab·troo'siv) *adj.* Tending to obtrude. **— ob·tru'sive·ly** *adv.* **— ob·tru'sive·ness** *n.*

ob·tuse (ab·toos', -tyoos') *adj.* **1.** Lacking acuteness of intellect or feeling; insensible. **2.** Not clear or distinct to the senses; dull, as a sound or pain. **3.** *Bot.* Blunt or rounded at the extremity, as a leaf or petal. [< L *obtusus* blunt, ¹ulled] **— ob·tuse'ly** *adv.* **— ob·tuse'ness** *n.*

obtuse angle *Geom.* An angle greater than a right angle and less than a straight angle.

ob·verse (ob'vûrs; *for adj., also* ob·vûrs') *adj.* **1.** Turned toward or facing one. **2.** Narrower at the base than at the apex: an *obverse* leaf. **3.** Constituting a counterpart. **—** *n.* **1.** The front or principal side of anything; esp., the side of a coin bearing the main design or device: distinguished from *reverse.* **2.** A counterpart. [< L < *ob-* towards + *vertere* to turn] **— ob·verse'ly** *adv.*

ob·vi·ate (ob'vē·āt) *v.t.* **·at·ed, ·at·ing** To prevent or counter (an objection, difficulty, etc.) by effective measures; provide for. [< L *obviatus,* pp. of *obviare* to meet, withstand] **— Syn.** preclude, forestall, avert.

ob·vi·ous (ob'vē·əs) *adj.* **1.** Immediately evident; palpably true; manifest. **2.** Behaving without equivocation or subtlety. [< L < *ob-* before + *via* way] **— ob'vi·ous·ly** *adv.* **— ob'vi·ous·ness** *n.*

oc- Assimilated var. of OB-.

oc·a·ri·na (ok'ə·rē'nə) *n.* A small musical instrument in the shape of a sweet potato, with a mouthpiece and finger holes and yielding soft, sonorous notes. [< Ital., dim. of *oca* goose < L *auca;* so called with ref. to its shape]

oc·ca·sion (ə·kā'zhən) *n.* **1.** The particular time of an event or occurrence; also, the event or occurrence itself. **2.** An important or extraordinary event. **3.** A favorable time or condition; opportunity. **4.** The immediate cause or ground for some action or state: to give one *occasion* to complain. **5.** A need or requirement. **— on occasion** On suitable opportunity; now and then. **— to take the** (this, etc.) *occasion* To avail oneself of the (this, etc.) opportunity. **—** *v.t.* To cause or bring about, esp. in an accidental or incidental manner. [< L < *ob-* towards + *cadere* to fall]

oc·ca·sion·al (ə·kā'zhən·əl) *adj.* **1.** Occurring, appearing, etc., irregularly or now and then. **2.** Made, intended, or suitable for a particular occasion: *occasional* verse. **3.** Pertaining to or designating a small chair, table, etc., that is not part of a set. **— oc·ca'sion·al·ly** *adv.*

oc·ci·dent (ok'sə·dənt) *n.* The west: opposed to *orient.* [< OF < L *occidens, -entis* region where the sun sets.]

Oc·ci·dent (ok'sə·dənt) **1.** The countries west of Asia; esp. Europe. **2.** The western hemisphere.

oc·ci·den·tal (ok'sə·den'təl) *adj.* Of or belonging to the west, or to the countries constituting the Occident: distinguished from *oriental.* **—** *n.* One born or living in a western country. Also **Oc'ci·den'tal.**

oc·cip·i·tal (ok·sip'ə·təl) *adj.* Pertaining to the occiput. **—** *n.* The occipital bone.

occipital bone *Anat.* The hindmost bone of the skull, between the parietal and temporal bones.

oc·ci·put (ok'sə·put, -pət) *n. pl.* **oc·cip·i·ta** (ok·sip'ə·tə) *Anat.* The lower back part of the skull. [< L, back of the head < *ob-* against + *caput* head]

oc·clude (ə·klood') *v.* **·clud·ed, ·clud·ing** *v.t.* **1.** To shut up or close, as pores or openings. **2.** To shut in, out, or off. **3.** *Chem.* To take up, either on the surface or internally, but without change of properties. **4.** *Meteorol.* To displace, as a mass of warm air by an advancing front of cold air. **—** *v.i.* **5.** *Dent.* To meet so that the corresponding cusps fit close together: said of the teeth of the upper and lower jaw. [< L < *ob-* against + *claudere* to close] **— oc·clu'dent** *adj.* **— oc·clu·sion** (ə·kloo'zhən) *n.*

oc·clu·sive (ə·kloo'siv) *adj.* **1.** Characterized by or bringing about occlusion or closure. **2.** *Phonet.* Pertaining to stop. **—** *n. Phonet.* A stop.

oc·cult (ə·kult', ok'ult) *adj.* **1.** Of or pertaining to various magical arts and practices, as astrology, alchemy, etc. **2.** Beyond human understanding; mysterious. **3.** Not divulged or disclosed; secret. **— Syn.** See MYSTERIOUS. **—** Occult arts or practices: usu. with *the.* **—** *v.t.* To hide; conceal from view. **—** *v.i.* To become hidden or concealed from view. [< L *occultus,* pp. of *occulere* to cover over, hide] **— oc·cult'ism** *n.* **— oc·cult'ist** *n.* **— oc·cult'ly** *adv.*

oc·cul·ta·tion (ok'ul·tā'shən) *n. Astron.* Concealment of one celestial body by another interposed in the line of vision.

oc·cu·pan·cy (ok'yə·pən·sē) *n. pl.* **·cies 1.** The act of occupying, or the state of being occupied. **2.** *Law* The act of taking possession of something previously unowned. **3.** The condition of being an occupant or tenant. **4.** The time during which something is occupied.

oc·cu·pant (ok'yə·pənt) *n.* **1.** One who occupies a place, position, etc. **2.** A tenant. [See OCCUPY.]

oc·cu·pa·tion (ok'yə·pā'shən) *n.* **1.** One's regular, principal, or immediate business or job. **2.** The act of occupying or the state of being occupied. **3.** The taking and holding of land by a military force: the *occupation* of Germany. **— Syn. 1.** *Occupation* and *vocation* are general terms, meaning little more than line of work. A *profession* requires special knowledge and training: Law and medicine are *professions.* A *business* is usually industrial, commercial, or mercantile, but may also be general: the clothing *business,* the *business* of government. A *trade* requires manual skill, as does a *craft,* but the latter suggests greater degree of skill and even artistic creation: the bricklayer's *trade*, the jeweler's *craft*.

oc·cu·pa·tion·al (ok/yə-pā/shən-əl) *adj.* Of, pertaining to, or caused by an occupation. — **oc/cu·pa/tion·al·ly** *adv.*

occupational therapy *Med.* The treatment of nervous, mental, or physical disabilities by means of work designed to promote recovery or readjustment.

oc·cu·py (ok/yə-pī) *v.t.* **·pied, ·py·ing** **1.** To take and hold possession of, as by conquest. **2.** To fill or take up (space or time). **3.** To inhabit; dwell in. **4.** To hold; fill, as an office or position. **5.** To busy or engage; employ. [< OF < L *ob-* against + *capere* to take] — **oc/cu·pi/er** *n.*

oc·cur (ə-kûr/) *v.i.* **·curred, ·cur·ring** **1.** To happen or take place. **2.** To be found or met with; appear. **3.** To suggest itself; come to mind. [< L < *ob-* towards, against + *currere* to run]

oc·cur·rence (ə-kûr/əns) *n.* **1.** The act or fact of occurring. **2.** That which occurs; an event. — **oc·cur/rent** *adj.*

o·cean (ō/shən) *n.* **1.** The great body of salt water that covers about 70 percent of the earth's surface. **2.** *Often cap.* Any one of the divisions of this body of water, usu. reckoned as five, the Atlantic, Pacific, Indian, Arctic, and Antarctic. **3.** A very large expanse or quantity. [< OF < L *ōkeanos*]

ocean current Any of a large number of riverlike masses of water flowing in all oceans, each having a characteristic direction, length, depth, speed, and temperature.

o·ce·an·ic (ō/shē-an/ik) *adj.* **1.** Of, relating to, or living in the ocean; pelagic. **2.** Resembling an ocean; vast.

O·ce·an·ic (ō/shē-an/ik) *n.* A subfamily of the Austronesian family of languages, including the Melanesian languages of the Solomon Islands, Fiji, New Caledonia, the New Hebrides, etc., and the Micronesian group of languages.

o·ce·an·og·ra·phy (ō/shē-ən-og/rə-fē, ō/shən-og/-) *n.* The branch of physical geography that treats of oceanic life and phenomena. — **o/ce·an·og/ra·pher** *n.* — **o/ce·an·o·graph/ic** (-ə-graf/ik) *or* **·i·cal** *adj.* — **o/ce·an·o·graph/i·cal·ly** *adv.*

o·cel·lat·ed (os/ə-lā/tid, ō-sel/ā-tid) *adj.* **1.** Having an ocellus or ocelli. **2.** Resembling an ocellus. **3.** Spotted. Also **o·cel·late** (os/ə-lāt, ō-sel/āt). [< L *ocellatus* small-eyed]

o·cel·lus (ō-sel/əs) *n.* *pl.* **·li** (-lī) **1.** *Biol.* A minute simple eye, as of many invertebrates. **2.** An eyelike spot, as in the tail of a peacock. [< L, dim. of *oculus* eye] — **o·cel/lar** *adj.*

oc·e·lot (ō/sə-lət, -lot, os/ə-) *n.* A large cat of Central and South America, having a spotted yellowish or reddish gray coat. [< F, short for Nahuatl *tlaocelotl* < *tlalli* field + *ocelotl* jaguar]

o·cher (ō/kər) *n.* **1.** A naturally occurring iron oxide mixed with various earthy materials and varying from light yellow to deep orange or red, largely used as a pigment. **2.** A dark yellow color derived from or resembling ocher. Also *Brit.* **o·chre.** [< OF < L < Gk. *ōchra* yellow ocher < *ōchros* pale yellow] — **o/cher·ous, o·chre·ous** (ō/krē-əs), **o/cher·y, ·chry** (ō/krē) *adj.*

-ock *suffix of nouns* Small: *hillock*. [OE *-oc, -uc*]

o·clock (ə-klok/) Of or according to the clock: six *o'clock*.

oct- See OCTO-.

oc·ta·gon (ok/tə-gon) *n.* *Geom.* A polygon having eight sides and eight angles. [< L < Gk. < *oktō* eight + *gōnia* angle] — **oc·tag·o·nal** (ok-tag/ə-nəl) *adj.* — **oc·tag/o·nal·ly** *adv.*

oc·ta·he·dron (ok/tə-hē/drən) *n.* *pl.* **·dra** (-drə) *Geom.* A polyhedron bounded by eight plane faces. [< Gk. < *oktō* eight + *hedra* seat] — **oc/ta·he/dral** *adj.*

oc·tane (ok/tān) *n.* *Chem.* One of a group of saturated hydrocarbons that have the formula C_8H_{18}.

octane number A measure of the antiknock properties of gasoline, expressed as the percentage, by volume, of isooctane that must be blended with normal heptane until the mixture has the same knock rating as the gasoline under test.

oc·tant (ok/tənt) *n.* An eighth part of a circle; an arc subtending an angle of 45 degrees. [< LL *octans, -antis* an eighth part < L *octo* eight] — **oc·tant/al** (-tan/təl) *adj.*

oc·tave (ok/tiv, -tāv) *n.* **1.** *Music* **a** The interval between a tone and another having twice as many or half as many vibrations per second. **b** A tone at this interval above or below any other, considered in relation to that other. **c** Two tones at this interval, sounded together; also, the resulting consonance. **d** An organ stop giving tones an octave above those normally corresponding to the keys played. **2.** *Eccl.* The eighth day from a feast day, beginning with the feast day as one; also, the lengthening of a festival so as to include a period of eight days. **3.** Any group or series of eight. **4.** In prosody, an octet. — *adj.* **1.** Composed of eight. **2.** *Music* Producing tones an octave higher. [< L *octavus* eighth < *octo* eight] — **oc·ta·val** (ok-tā/vəl, ok/tə-) *adj.*

oc·ta·vo (ok-tā/vō, -tä/-) *n.* *pl.* **·vos 1.** The page size (6 x 9½ inches except where otherwise specified) of a book made

up of printer's sheets folded into eight leaves. **2.** A book consisting of pages of this size. — *adj.* In octavo. Also *eightvo*. Also written **8vo** or **8°**. [< L *in octavo* in an eighth]

oc·tet (ok-tet/) *n.* **1.** A musical composition for eight singers or instrumentalists. **2.** A group of eight singers or instrumentalists. **3.** Any group of eight. Also **oc·tette/.** [< Ital. < L *octo* eight]

oc·til·lion (ok-til/yən) *n.* **1.** *U.S.* A thousand septillions, written as 1 followed by 27 zeros: a cardinal number. **2.** *Brit.* A million septillions (def. 2), written as 1 followed by 48 zeros: a cardinal number — *adj.* Being an octillion in number. [< MF < *octo* eight + F (*m*)*illion*]

octo- *combining form* Eight: also, before vowels, *oct-*. Also *octa-*. [< L *octo* and Gk. *oktō* eight]

Oc·to·ber (ok-tō/bər) The tenth month of the year, containing 31 days. [< L, eighth month of early Roman calendar < *octo* eight]

October Revolution See RUSSIAN REVOLUTION under REVOLUTION.

oc·to·dec·i·mo (ok/tə-des/ə-mō) *n.* *pl.* **·mos 1.** The page size (approximately 4 x 6½ inches) of a book made up of printer's sheets folded into 18 leaves. **2.** A book consisting of pages of this size. — *adj.* In octodecimo; consisting of pages of this size. Also *eighteenmo*. Also written **18mo** or **18°**. [< L *in octodecimo* in an eighteenth]

oc·to·ge·nar·i·an (ok/tə-jə-nâr/ē-ən) *adj.* Being eighty or from eighty to ninety years of age. — *n.* One between eighty and ninety years of age. Also **oc·tog·e·nar·y** (ok-toj/ə-ner/ē) *adj. & n.* [< L < *octoginta* eighty]

oc·to·pod (ok/tə-pod) *n. Zool.* Any of a group of eight-armed cephalopods, as the octopus.

oc·to·pus (ok/tə-pəs) *n.* *pl.* **·pus·es** *or* **·pi** (-pī) *or* **oc·top·o·des** (ok-top/ə-dēz) **1.** An eight-armed marine mollusk having a large oval head and rows of suckers along the arms; a devilfish. **2.** Any organized power regarded as far-reaching and potentially destructive; esp., a powerful business organization. [< NL < Gk. < *oktō* eight + *pous* foot]

oc·to·roon (ok/tə-rōōn/) *n.* A person who is one-eighth Negro. [< L *octo* eight + (QUAD)ROON]

oc·u·lar (ok/yə-lər) *adj.* Of, like, or related to the eye or sight. — *n.* The lenses forming the eyepiece of an optical instrument. [< L < *oculus* eye] — **oc/u·lar·ly** *adv.*

oc·u·list (ok/yə-list) *n.* A physician skilled in treating diseases of the eye; ophthalmologist. [< MF < L *oculus* eye]

o·da·lisque (ō/də-lisk) *n.* A female slave or concubine in an Oriental harem. Also **o/da·lisk.** [< F < Turkish *ōdaliq* chambermaid]

odd (od) *adj.* **1.** Strange or unusual in appearance, behavior, etc.; peculiar; queer. **2.** Not part of what is regular, usual, required, etc.: an odd job. **3.** Constituting a member of an incomplete pair, set, etc.: an odd slipper. **4.** Leaving a remainder when divided by two; not even: Five is an odd number; also, characterized by such a number. **5.** Additional to a specified round number: seventy odd dollars. [< ON *oddi* point, hence, third point of a triangle, hence, odd number] — **odd/ly** *adv.* — **odd/ness** *n.*

odd·i·ty (od/ə-tē) *n.* *pl.* **·ties 1.** One who or that which is odd. **2.** An odd or peculiar quality or trait; an eccentricity. **3.** The state of being odd; singularity; strangeness.

odd·ment (od/mənt) *n.* *Usu. pl.* A fragment, scrap, or leftover; odds and ends.

odds (odz) *n.pl.* (*sometimes construed as sing.*) **1.** An equalizing allowance or advantage given to a weaker opponent. **2.** The proportion by which one bet differs from that of another. **3.** The ratio between the probability for and the probability against something being true or happening. **4.** A difference to the advantage of one side. — **at odds** At variance; disagreeing. [< plural of ODD]

odds and ends Miscellaneous things; fragments; scraps.

ode (ōd) *n.* A lyric poem often in the form of an elaborate address and usually characterized by loftiness of tone, feeling, and style. [< MF < LL < Gk. *ōidē* song]

-ode¹ *combining form* Way; path: *anode, cathode*. [< Gk. *hodos* way]

-ode² *suffix* Like; resembling; having the nature of. [< Gk. *-ōdēs < eidos* form]

O·din (ō/din) In Norse mythology, the supreme deity, god of war, art, culture, and the dead.

o·di·ous (ō/dē-əs) *adj.* Exciting hate, repugnance, or disgust; offensive; abhorrent. [< OF < L < *odium* hatred] — **o/di·ous·ly** *adv.* — **o/di·ous·ness** *n.*

o·di·um (ō/dē-əm) *n.* **1.** The state of being odious. **2.** Extreme dislike or aversion; hatred. **3.** The reproach, disgrace, or stigma associated with something hateful; opprobrium. [< L, hatred]

o·dom·e·ter (ō-dom/ə-tər) *n.* A device for measuring distance traveled by a vehicle. [< Gk. < *hodos* way, road + *metron* a measure] — **o·dom/e·try** *n.*

-odont *combining form* Toothed. [< Gk. *odous, odontos* tooth]

odonto- *combining form* Tooth; of the teeth. Also, before vowels, **odont-**. [< Gk. *odous, odontos* tooth]

o·don·tol·o·gy (ō′don·tol′ə·jē) *n.* The body of scientific knowledge that relates to the structure, health, and growth of the teeth. — **o·don·to·log·i·cal** (ō·don′tə·loj′i·kəl) *adj.* — **o·don′to·log′i·cal·ly** *adv.* — **o′don·tol′o·gist** *n.*

o·dor (ō′dər) *n.* **1.** That quality of a substance that renders it perceptible to the sense of smell; smell; scent. **2.** Regard or estimation. **3.** A perfume; incense. — **Syn.** See SMELL. Also *Brit.* **o′dour.** [< OF < L] — **o′dored** *adj.*

o·dor·if·er·ous (ō′də·rif′ər·əs) *adj.* Having or giving off an odor, especially a pleasant odor. [< L < *odor* odor + *ferre* to bear] — **o′dor·if′er·ous·ly** *adv.* — **o′dor·if′er·ous·ness** *n.*

o·dor·less (ō′dər·lis) *adj.* Having no odor. — **o′dor·less·ly** *adv.* — **o′dor·less·ness** *n.*

o·dor·ous (ō′dər·əs) *adj.* Having an odor, esp. a fragrant odor. — **o′dor·ous·ly** *adv.* — **o′dor·ous·ness** *n.*

-odynia *combining form Med.* Pain; chronic pain in a (specified) part of the body. [< Gk. *odynē* pain]

O·dys·seus (ō·dis′yōōs, -ē·əs) In Greek legend, king of Ithaca, one of the Greek leaders in the Trojan War and hero of the *Odyssey:* Latin *Ulysses.*

Od·ys·sey (od′ə·sē) An ancient Greek epic poem attributed to Homer, describing the wanderings of Odysseus during the ten years after the fall of Troy. — *n.* A long, wandering journey: often **od′ys·sey.** — **Od′ys·sey′an** *adj.*

oe- See also words beginning E-.

oe·de·ma (i·dē′mə) See EDEMA.

Oed·i·pus (ed′ə·pəs, ē′də-) In Greek legend, the son of Laius and Jocasta, rulers of Thebes, who unwittingly killed his father and married his mother.

Oedipus complex *Psychoanal.* A strong, typically unconscious attachment of a child to the parent of the opposite sex, esp. of a son to his mother, with antagonism toward the other parent. — **Oed·i·pal** (ed′ə·pəl, ē′də-) *adj.*

o′er (ôr, ōr) *prep. & adv. Poetic* Over.

oe·soph·a·gus (i·sof′ə·gəs) See ESOPHAGUS.

oes·tro·gen (es′trə·jən, ēs′-) See ESTROGEN.

oes·trous (es′trəs, ēs′-) See ESTROUS.

of (uv, ov; *unstressed* əv) *prep.* **1.** Coming from: Anne of Cleves; an actor *of* noble birth. **2.** Included among: Is he *of* your party? **3.** Located at: the Leaning Tower *of* Pisa. **4.** Away or at a distance from: within six miles *of* home. **5.** Named; specified as: the city *of* Newark; a fall *of* ten feet. **6.** Characterized by: a man *of* strength. **7.** With reference to; as to: quick *of* wit. **8.** About; concerning: Good is said *of* him. **9.** Because of: dying *of* pneumonia. **10.** Possessing: a man *of* means. **11.** Belonging to: the lid *of* a box. **12.** Pertaining to: the majesty *of* the law. **13.** Composed of: a ship *of* steel. **14.** Containing: a glass *of* water. **15.** From the number or class of: six *of* the seven conspirators. **16.** So as to be without: relieved *of* anxiety. **17.** Produced by: the plays *of* Shakespeare. **18.** Directed toward; exerted upon: a love *of* opera. **19.** During, on, or at a specified time or occasion: *of* recent years. **20.** Set aside for or devoted to: a program *of* music. **21.** *U.S.* Before; until: used in telling time: ten minutes *of* ten. **22.** *Archaic* By: loved *of* all men. [OE, away from, off]

of- Assimilated var. of OB-.

of course 1. In the usual order of procedure; naturally; as expected. **2.** Doubtless; certainly.

off (ôf, of) *adj.* **1.** Farther or more distant; remote: an *off* chance. **2.** In a (specified) circumstance or situation: to be well *off.* **3.** Not in accordance with the facts; wrong: Your reckoning is *off.* **4.** Not up to standard: an *off* season for roses. **5.** No longer considered active or effective: The deal is *off.* **6.** Away from work; not on duty: *off* hours. **7.** In riding or driving, on the right: opposed to *near:* Pass on the *off* side. **8.** *Naut.* Seaward. — *adv.* **1.** To a distance; so as to be away: My horse ran *off.* **2.** To or at a (specified) future time: to put it *off* for a week. **3.** To or at a (specified) distance: to stand five feet *off.* **4.** So as to be no longer in place, connection, etc.: Take *off* your hat. **5.** So as to be no longer functioning, continuing, or in operation: to break *off* talks. **6.** So as to be away from one's work, duties, etc.: to take the day *off.* **7.** So as to be completed, exhausted, etc.: to kill *off* one's enemies. **8.** So as to deviate from or be below what is regarded as standard: His game dropped *off.* **9.** *Naut.* Away from land, a ship, the wind, etc. — **off and on** Now and then; intermittently. — **to be off 1.** To leave; depart. **2.** *Informal* To be insane. — *prep.* **1.** So as to be separated, detached, distant, or removed from (a position, source, etc.): twenty miles *off* course. **2.** Not engaged in or occupied with; relieved from: *off* duty. **3.** Extending away or out from; no longer on: *off* Broadway. **4.** So as to deviate from or be below (what is regarded as standard): to be *off* one's game. **5.** On or from (the material or substance of): living *off* nuts and berries. **6.** *Informal* No longer using, engaging in, or advocating: to be *off* drinking. **7.** *Naut.*

Opposite to and seaward of: the battle *off* the eastern cap — **off of** *Informal* Off; from: He fell *off of* the horse. — The state or condition of being off. [ME]

of·fal (ôf′fəl) *n.* **1.** The waste parts of a butchered anima **2.** Rubbish or refuse of any kind. [ME *ofall* < OFF + FALL

off·beat (ôf′bēt′, of′-) *n. Music* Any secondary or wea beat in a measure. — *adj. U.S. Slang* Out of the ordinar strange; unconventional; unusual.

off-Broad·way (ôf′brôd′wā) *adj.* **1.** Not situated in th Broadway entertainment district: an *off-Broadway* theate **2.** Designating a play that is regarded as experimental, no commercial, etc. — *n.* Any area in New York City in whi off-Broadway plays are produced.

off·cast (ôf′kast′, -käst′, of′-) *adj.* Rejected; castoff. — Anything thrown away or rejected.

off chance A bare possibility.

off-col·or (ôf′kul′ər, of′-) *adj.* **1.** Unsatisfactory in colo as a gem. **2.** Indelicate or indecent; risqué.

of·fence (ə·fens′) See OFFENSE.

of·fend (ə·fend′) *v.t.* **1.** To give displeasure or offense t **2.** To be disagreeable to (the sense of smell, sight, etc — *v.i.* **3.** To give displeasure or offense; be offensive. [L < *ob-* against + *fendere* to hit] — **of·fend′er** *n.* — **Syn. 1.** Insult, affront, exasperate, outrage.

of·fense (ə·fens′; *for defs. 4 & 5, also* ō′fens, of′ens) *n.* Any violation of a rule, duty, propriety, etc.; esp., a brea of law. **2.** The act of offending or causing displeasur **3.** That which offends: an *offense* to the ear. **4.** The act attacking or assaulting; attack. **5.** In football, hockey, et the team possessing the ball or puck. — **to give offense** To offend or cause anger, resentment, etc. — **to take offen** To be offended; feel angry, hurt, etc. Also *esp. Brit.,* **offen**

of·fen·sive (ə·fen′siv) *adj.* **1.** Unpleasant or disagreeab obnoxious; disgusting. **2.** Causing anger, resentment, et insulting. **3.** Of, pertaining to, or characterized by attac distinguished from *defensive.* — *n.* The movement, attitu or position of offense or attack. — **of·fen′sive·ly** *adv.* — **of·fen′sive·ness** *n.*

of·fer (ôf′fər, of′ər) *v.t.* **1.** To present for acceptance or jection. **2.** To suggest for consideration or action; propo **3.** To make an offering of: often with *up.* **4.** To show rea ness to do or attempt; propose or threaten: to *offer* batt **5.** To attempt to do or inflict; also, to do or inflict. **6.** suggest as payment; bid. **7.** To present for sale. — **8.** To present itself; appear. **9.** To make an offering worship or sacrifice. — *n.* **1.** The act of offering. **2.** Th which is offered, as a bid, suggestion, etc. [OE *offrian* < *ob-* before + *ferre* to bring] — **of′fer·er** or **of′fer·or** *n*

of·fer·ing (ôf′fər·ing, of′ər-) *n.* **1.** The act of making offer. **2.** That which is offered, as a sacrifice or contributi

of·fer·to·ry (ôf′fər·tôr′ē, -tō′rē, of′ər-) *n. pl. -ries* E **1.** *Usu. cap.* A section of the eucharistic liturgy during wh the bread and wine to be consecrated are offered, and t alms of the congregation are collected. **2.** Any collecti taken during a religious service. **3.** An antiphon, hymn, anthem sung during this service. **4.** A prayer of oblati said by the celebrant over the bread and wine to be con crated. [< Med.L *offertorium* < LL, place of offerings]

off·hand (ôf′hand′, of′-) *adv.* Without preparation; unce moniously; extempore. Also **off′hand′ed·ly.** — *adj.* Done, said, or made offhand. **2.** Casual; informal; cu Also **off′hand′ed.**

of·fice (ôf′fis, of′is) *n.* **1.** A place in which the business o individual, corporation, government bureau, etc., is carri out; also, the staff and administrative officials working such a place. **2.** *Usu. cap. U.S.* An executive branch the federal government ranking below the departmen **3.** Any post or position held by a person; especially, a po tion of authority or trust in the government, a corporati etc. **4.** The duty, charge, or trust of a person. **5.** Any done or intended to be done for another; a service; fav through his kind *offices.* **6.** *Eccl.* A prescribed religiou devotional service, as: **a** The canonical hours. **b** The Mo ing or Evening Prayer. **7.** Any ceremony or rite, esp. rite for the dead. [< OF < L *officium* service]

of·fice·hold·er (ôf′fis·hōl′dər, of′-) *n.* One who holds office under a government.

of·fi·cer (ôf′fə·sər, of′ə-) *n.* **1.** In the armed forces, one pointed to a certain rank and authority; esp., one holdin commission. **2.** One elected or appointed to a position authority or trust in a corporation, government, institut etc. **3.** On a merchant or passenger ship, the captain any of the mates. **4.** One who enforces the law, as a poli man. — *v.t.* **1.** To furnish with officers. **2.** To comma direct; manage.

officer of the day At a military installation, the officer w on a given day is responsible for the performance of t guard, maintenance of order or security, etc.

of·fi·cial (ə·fish′əl, ō-) *adj.* **1.** Of or relating to an office position of authority. **2.** Supported by or derived fr authority. **3.** Authorized to carry out some special du

. Formal: *official* banquets. — *n.* One who holds an office r position; esp., one who is authorized to act for a corpora-on, government agency, etc., in a subordinate capacity. — of·fi′cial·ly *adv.*

fi·cial·dom (ə-fish′əl-dəm, ō-) *n.* **1.** Officials collectively r as a class. **2.** Rigid adherence to official forms, routines, t.c.: also **of·fi′cial·ism**.

fi·ci·ate (ə-fish′ē-āt, ō-) *v.i.* **·at·ed, ·at·ing 1.** To act or rve as a priest or minister. **2.** To perform the duties or inctions of any office or position. — **of·fi′ci·a′tion** *n.* — of·fi′ci·a′tor *n.*

fic·i·nal (ə-fis′ə-nəl) *adj.* Prepared and kept in stock by pharmacy. — *n.* Any drug or medicine kept ready for ale. [< Med.L < officina workshop]

fi·cious (ə-fish′əs, ō-) *adj.* Unduly forward in offering ne's services or advice; obtrusive; meddling. [< L offi-osus obliging < officium service] — **of·fi′cious·ly** *adv.* — of·fi′cious·ness *n.*

·ing (ô′fing, of′ing) *n.* **1.** That part of the visible sea fshore but beyond anchorage. **2.** A position some distance fshore. — **in the offing 1.** In sight and not very distant. . Ready or soon to happen, arrive, etc.

·ish (ô′fish, of′ish) *adj.* Inclined to be distant in manner; loof. — **off′ish·ly** *adv.* — **off′ish·ness** *n.*

·scour·ing (ôf′skour′ing, of′-) *n.* **1.** *Usu. pl.* Trash; arbage. **2.** A social outcast; wretch.

·set (*n.* ôf′set′, of′-; *v.* ôf′set′, of′-) *n.* **1.** That which alances or compensates for something else. **2.** That which erives, develops, or springs from something else; offshoot. . *Archit.* A ledge formed along a wall by a reduction in nickness above; setoff. **4.** *Printing* **a** Offset printing. An impression made by offset printing. **5.** A bend or urve made in a pipe, rod, etc., to allow it to pass an ob-acle. — *v.* **·set, ·set·ting** *v.t.* **1.** To balance or compensate r. **2.** *Printing* **a** To reproduce by offset printing. **b** To ansfer (an impression) by offset printing. **3.** *Archit.* To ake an offset in. — *v.i.* **4.** To branch off or project as an fset.

·set printing A method of printing in which the inked npression from a lithographic plate is transferred to a abber-coated cylinder, and then onto the paper.

·shoot (ôf′shōōt′, of′-) *n.* **1.** *Bot.* A lateral shoot or branch om the main stem of a plant. **2.** Anything that derives branches off from a principal source, stock, etc.

·shore (ôf′shôr′, -shōr′, of′-) *adj.* **1.** Moving or directed way from the shore. **2.** Situated or occurring at some dis-nce from the shore. — *adv.* From or away from the shore.

·side (ôf′sīd′, of′-) *adj.* In football, in front of the ball efore it is put into play: said of a player, team, or play. lso **off side.**

·spring (ôf′spring′, of′-) *n. pl.* **·spring** or **·springs 1.** e progeny or issue of a person, animal, or plant; descend-nt. **2.** Any result or product: the *offspring* of his mind.

·stage (ôf′stāj, of′-) *n.* The area behind or to the side a stage, out of the view of the audience. — *adj.* In or om this area: *off-stage* dialogue. — *adv.* To this area.

·white (ôf′hwīt′, of′-) *n.* Oyster white.

t (ôft, oft) *adv.* Often: archaic or poetic except in certain ombinations, as **oft-repeated, oft-recurring,** etc. [OE]

t·en (ôf′ən, of′-) *adv.* Frequently or repeatedly. [Var. ME *ofte*, OE *oft*]

t·en·times (ôf′ən-tīmz′, of′-) *adv. Archaic* Frequently; ften. Also **oft·times** (ôf′tīmz′, of′-).

gee (ō′jē, ō-jē′) *n. Archit.* **1.** Any S-shaped curve used a construction. **2.** An arch having two S-shaped curves eeting at the apex: also **ogee arch.** [OF *ogive*]

give (ō′jīv, ō-jīv′) *n. Archit.* **1.** A diagonal rib of a aulted arch or bay. **2.** A pointed arch. [< OF *ogive*]

gle (ō′gəl, og′əl) *v.* **o·gled, o·gling** *v.t.* **1.** To look at with dmiring or impertinent glances. **2.** To stare at; eye. — i. **3.** To look or stare in an admiring or impertinent man-er. — *n.* An amorous or coquettish look. [< LG *oegeln*, eq. of *oegen* to look at < *oege* eye] — **o′gler** *n.*

gre (ō′gər) *n.* **1.** In fairy tales, a man-eating giant or nonster. **2.** One who is brutal, hideous, or feared. [< F] — **o·gre·ish** (ō′gər-ish), **o·grish** (ō′grish) *adj.* — **o′gress** (-grəs) *n.fem.*

(ō) *interj.* An exclamation expressing surprise, sudden motion, etc. — *n.* The interjection *oh.*

m (ōm) *n.* The unit of electrical resistance, equal to the esistance of a conductor carrying a current of one ampere t a potential difference of one volt between the terminals.

m·age (ō′mij) *n.* Electrical resistance of a conductor, xpressed in ohms.

m·me·ter (ōm′mē′tər) *n.* A galvanometer for measuring he resistance of a conductor in ohms.

ho (ō-hō′) *interj.* An exclamation expressing astonishment, xultation, etc.

-oid *suffix* Like; resembling; having the form of: *ovoid, hydroid.* [< NL *-oides* < Gk. *-oeidēs* < *eidos* form]

oil (oil) *n.* **1.** A greasy or unctuous, sometimes combus-tible liquid of vegetable, animal, or mineral origin, soluble in alcohol and ether, but not in water, variously used as food, for lubricating, illuminating, and fuel, and in the manu-facture of soap, candles, cosmetics, perfumery, etc. **2.** Petroleum. **3.** An oil color; also, an oil painting. **4.** Any-thing of an oily consistency. — *v.t.* **1.** To smear, lubricate, or supply with oil. **2.** To bribe; flatter. — *adj.* **1.** Of or resembling oil. **2.** Using, obtained from, or yielding oil. [< OF < L prob. < Gk. *elaion* olive oil]

oil burner A heating unit that operates on oil fuel.

oil cake The mass of compressed seeds of cotton, flax, etc., or coconut pulp from which oil has been expressed, used as food (**oil meal**) for livestock, etc.

oil·cloth (oil′klôth′, -kloth′) *n.* A fabric waterproofed with oils and pigments, used as a covering for tables, etc.

oil color A color or paint made of pigment ground in linseed or other oil, used chiefly by artists.

oil of vitriol Sulfuric acid.

oil painting 1. A painting done in pigments mixed in oil. **2.** The art of painting in oils.

oil·paper (oil′pā′pər) *n.* Paper treated with oil for trans-parency and resistance against moisture and dryness.

oil·skin (oil′skin′) *n.* Cloth made waterproof with oil, or a garment of such material.

oil slick A smooth area on water caused by a film of oil.

oil·stone (oil′stōn) *n.* A whetstone moistened with oil.

oil well A well that is dug or drilled to obtain petroleum.

oil·y (oi′lē) *adj.* **oil·i·er, oil·i·est 1.** Of, pertaining to, or containing oil. **2.** Coated, smeared, or soaked with oil; greasy. **3.** Smooth or suave in behavior, speech, etc.; unctuous. — **oil′i·ly** *adv.* — **oil′i·ness** *n.*

oint·ment (oint′mənt) *n.* A fatty or unctuous preparation applied to the skin as a medicine or cosmetic; unguent. [< OF *oignement*, ult. < L *unguentum* < *ungere* to anoint]

O·jib·wa (ō-jib′wä, -wä) *n. pl.* **·wa** or **·was 1.** One of a tribe of North American Indians formerly inhabiting the regions around Lake Superior. **2.** Their Algonquian language. Also called *Chippewa*: also **O·jib′way.**

OK (*interj., adj., adv. & n.* ō′kā′; *v.* ō-kā′) *interj., adj., & adv.* All correct; all right: used to express approval, agreement, etc. — *v.t.* To approve, endorse, or agree to; especially, to sign with an *OK.* — *n.* Approval; agreement; endorsement. Also **O.K., o′kay′, o′keh′.** [? < *o(ll) k(orrect)*, humorous misspelling of "all correct," reinforced by *O(ld) K(inderhook)* in the name of a political club (1840) supporting Martin Van Buren of Kinderhook, N.Y.]

o·ka·pi (ō-kä′pē) *n.* An African ruminant related to the giraffe, but with a smaller body and a shorter neck. [< native African name]

O·kie (ō′kē) *n. U.S. Slang* A migrant farmworker, origi-nally one from Oklahoma.

o·kra (ō′krə) *n.* **1.** A tall annual herb of the mallow family. **2.** Its green mucilaginous pods, used in soups and stews, or as a vegetable. **3.** Gumbo. [< West African]

-ol¹ *suffix Chem.* Denoting an alcohol or phenol: *methanol, glycerol.* [< (ALCOH)OL]

-ol² *suffix Chem.* Var. of -OLE¹, as in *benzol.*

old (ōld) *adj.* **old·er** or **eld·er, old·est** or **eld·est 1.** Living, existing, made, known, etc., for a relatively long time. **2.** Exhibiting the characteristics of advanced life. **3.** Having a specified age or duration: a child two months *old.* **4.** Worn with age or repeated use; shabby. **5.** Familiar through long acquaintance or use: an *old* friend. **6.** Skilled through long experience: an *old* hand at politics. **7.** Belonging to or associated with a relatively remote period in history; ancient. **8.** *Usu. cap.* Denoting the earlier or earliest of two or more things, periods, developments, etc.; *Old* English; the *Old* Testament. **9.** *Informal* Good; cherished; dear: a general term of affection or endearment: *old* buddy of mine. **10.** *Informal* Plentiful; great; wonderful: used to ex-press intense pleasure, excess, etc.: a grand *old* time. **11.** *Geog.* In a late stage of a cycle of development: said of topo-graphic features, streams, etc. — *n.* Past time: days of *old.* [OE *ald*] — **old′ness** *n.*

— **Syn.** (adj.) **1.** *Old* and *aged* mean having lived a long time, but *old* more often suggests feebleness or senility than *aged.* An *elderly* man has passed middle age, but is generally regarded as younger than an *old* man, both in years and in vigor.

Old Bailey The central criminal court of London.

old country The native country of an immigrant, esp. a European country.

old·en (ōl′dən) *adj. Archaic & Poetic* Old; ancient.

Old English *Printing* Black letter.

old·fan·gled (ōld′fang′gəld) *adj.* Having a fondness for what is old-fashioned. [On analogy with NEWFANGLED]

---

old-fash·ioned (ōld'fash'ənd) *adj.* Of, pertaining to, characteristic of, or favoring former times, old customs, etc.

old fashioned A cocktail of whisky, sugar, fruit, etc.

old fo·gy (fō'gē) One who is extremely conservative or old-fashioned. Also **old fo'gey**. — **old'-fo'gy·ish** *adj.*

Old French See under FRENCH.

Old Glory The flag of the United States.

old guard The conservative element in a community, political party, etc.

old hat *U.S. Slang* Out of style; old-fashioned; obsolete.

Old Hickory Nickname of Andrew Jackson.

Old High German See under GERMAN.

Old Icelandic See under ICELANDIC.

old·ish (ōl'dish) *adj.* Somewhat old.

old lady *Slang* 1. One's mother. 2. One's wife.

old-line (ōld'līn') *adj.* 1. Traditional or conservative in action or thought. 2. Long-established; traditional.

Old Line State Nickname of Maryland.

old maid 1. A spinster. 2. *Informal* One who is prim, prudish, fastidious, etc.

old man *Slang* 1. One's father. 2. One's husband. 3. Any man in a position of authority, as an employer.

old master Any of the famous painters who lived between the 13th and 16th centuries, esp. in Italy and the Low Countries; also, any of their paintings.

Old Nick The devil.

Old Prussian See under PRUSSIAN.

old rose Any of various shades of grayish or purplish red.

old·ster (ōld'stər) *n. Informal* An old or elderly person.

Old Stone Age The Paleolithic period of human culture.

old-style (ōld'stīl') *adj.* Of a former or old-fashioned style.

old style *Printing* A style of type having the stems and the serifs of nearly the same thickness.

Old Style See (Gregorian) CALENDAR.

Old Testament The first of the two main divisions of the Bible, divided into the Pentateuch, the Prophets, and the Hagiographa.

old-time (ōld'tīm') *adj.* 1. Of or characteristic of a former time. 2. Of long standing; long-established.

old-tim·er (ōld'tī'mər) *n. Informal* 1. One who has been a member, resident, etc., for a long time. 2. An old-fashioned person.

Ol·du·vai Gorge (ōl'doō-vī', ōl'dŏŏ-vī') A gorge about 100 mi. SE of Lake Victoria in Tanzania; site of fossils of extinct mammals believed to be forerunners of early man.

old-wom·an·ish (ōld'wŏŏm'ən·ish) *adj.* Characteristic of or suitable for an old woman; fussy.

old-world (ōld'wûrld') *adj.* 1. Of or pertaining to the Old World or Eastern Hemisphere. 2. Ancient; antique.

Old World The Eastern Hemisphere, including Europe, Asia and Africa; esp., Europe.

-ole[1] *suffix Chem.* Denoting a closed-chain compound having a five-membered ring. Also spelled **-ol.** [< L *oleum* oil]

-ole[2] *suffix* Small; little: *nucleole.* [< L *-olus*, dim. suffix]

o·le·a·ceous (ō'lē·ā'shəs) *adj. Bot.* Pertaining or belonging to the olive family of plants and including the lilac, jasmine, and ash. [< NL *oleaceae* < L *olea* olive tree]

o·le·ag·i·nous (ō'lē·aj'ə·nəs) *adj.* Of or pertaining to oil; oily. [< F < L < *olea* olive tree] — **o'le·ag'i·nous·ly** *adv.*

o·le·an·der (ō'lē·an'dər) *n.* An Old World, evergreen shrub, having leaves that yield a poisonous glycoside and clusters of fragrant rose or white flowers. [< Med.L]

o·le·ate (ō'lē·āt) *n. Chem.* A salt or ester of oleic acid.

o·le·ic (ō·lē'ik, ō'lē-) *adj.* Of, pertaining to, or derived from oil. [< L *oleum* oil + -IC]

oleic acid *Chem.* An oily compound, $C_{17}H_{33}COOH$, contained as an ester in most mixed oils and fats.

o·le·o (ō'lē·ō) Short for OLEOMARGARINE.

oleo- *combining form* Oil; of oil. [< L *oleum* oil]

o·le·o·mar·ga·rine (ō'lē·ō·mär'jə·rin, -rēn) *n.* A substitute for butter made usu. from vegetable oils: also called *margarine.* Also **o'le·o·mar'ga·rin.**

o·le·o·res·in (ō'lē·ō·rez'in) *n.* 1. A naturally occurring compound of an essential oil and a resin. 2. A pharmaceutical preparation consisting of a resin and sometimes other active matter in solution with a fixed or volatile oil.

ol·fac·tion (ol·fak'shən) *n.* The act, sense, or process of smelling odors. [< L *olfactus.* See OLFACTORY.]

ol·fac·to·ry (ol·fak'tər·ē, -trē) *adj.* Of or pertaining to the sense of smell. — *n. pl.* **·ries** *Usu. pl.* The organ of smell. [< L *olere* to have a smell + *facere* to make]

ol·i·garch (ol'ə·gärk) *n.* A ruler in an oligarchy.

ol·i·gar·chy (ol'ə·gär'kē) *n. pl.* **·chies** 1. A form of government in which power is restricted to a few; also, a state so governed. 2. The ruling oligarchs. [< Gk. < *oligos* few + *archein* to rule] — **ol'i·gar'chic, ol'i·gar'chal, ol'i·gar'chi·cal** *adj.*

Ol·i·go·cene (ol'ə·gō·sēn') *Geol. adj.* Pertaining to the third oldest of the epochs or series comprised in the Tertiary system. — *n.* This epoch, with its included rock series. [< OLIGO- + Gk. *kainos* new, recent]

o·li·o (ō'lē·ō) *n. pl.* **o·li·os** A miscellaneous collection, as o musical pieces or numbers. [< Sp. *olla* pot, stew]

ol·ive (ol'iv) *n.* 1. A small, oily fruit native to Southern Europe and the Middle East. 2. The evergreen tree yielding this fruit, having leathery leaves and hard yellow wood. 3. The dull, yellowish green color of the unripe olive: also **olive green.** — *adj.* 1. Pertaining to or characteristic o the olive. 2. Having a dull, yellowish green color. 3. Tinged with this color: an *olive* complexion. [< L *oliva*]

olive branch 1. A branch of the olive tree as an emblem o peace. 2. Any peace offering.

olive drab 1. Any of several shades of greenish brown. 2. A woolen material of this color, formerly used by the arme services of the U.S. for uniforms. 3. *Often pl.* A uniform or a pair of trousers made of this cloth.

olive oil Oil pressed from olives, used in cooking, etc.

Olives, Mount of A hill just east of Jerusalem: *Matt.* xvi 1. Also **Ol·i·vet** (ol'ə·vet, -vit).

ol·i·vine (ol'ə·vēn, -vin) *n.* A vitreous, often transparent magnesium-iron silicate, often used as a gemstone.

ol·la (ol'ə, *Sp.* ō'lyä, ō'yä) *n.* 1. A wide-mouthed pot or jar usu. of earthenware. 2. A highly seasoned stew. [< Sp < L *olla* pot]

ol·o·gy (ol'ə·jē) *n. pl.* **·gies** *Informal* A science or branch o learning: a humorous term. [< -LOGY] — **ol'o·gist** *n.*

O·lym·pi·a (ō·lim'pē·ə) An ancient city in the wester Peloponnesus, Greece; scene of the Olympic games.

O·lym·pi·ad (ō·lim'pē·ad) *n.* 1. The interval of four year between two successive celebrations of the Olympic games 2. The modern Olympic games.

O·lym·pi·an (ō·lim'pē·ən) *adj.* 1. Of or pertaining to th great gods of Olympus, or to Mount Olympus. 2. Godlike 3. Of or pertaining to Olympia or the Olympic games. Als **O·lym·pic** (ō·lim'pik, ə-). — *n.* 1. One of the twelve highe gods who dwelt on Mount Olympus. 2. A contestant in th Olympic games. 3. A native of Olympia.

Olympic games 1. In ancient Greece, athletic games races, and contests in poetry held every four years at th plain of Olympia in Elis in honor of Zeus. 2. A modern in ternational revival of the ancient athletic games, held ever four years at some city chosen for the event. Also **Olympia games, O·lym'pics.**

-oma *suffix Med.* Tumor: *carcinoma.* [< Gk. *-ōma*]

o·ma·sum (ō·mā'səm) *n. pl.* **·sa** (-sə) The third stomac of a ruminant. [< L]

om·buds·man (om·budz'mən) *n. pl.* **·men** (-mən) government official appointed to receive and report griev ances against the government. [< Sw.]

-ome *combining form Bot.* Group; mass. [< Gk. *-ōma*]

o·me·ga (ō·mē'gə, ō·meg'ə, ō'meg·ə) *n.* 1. The twenty fourth and last letter in the Greek alphabet (Ω, ω), corre sponding to English long *o.* See ALPHABET. ◆ In the ety mologies in this dictionary, omega is transliterated as ō. 2 The end; the last. [< Gk. ō *mega* great o]

om·e·let (om'lit, om'ə·lit) *n.* A dish of eggs beaten togethe with milk and cooked in a frying pan, often with other in gredients. Also *Brit.* **om'e·lette.** [< F *omelette*]

o·men (ō'mən) *n.* A phenomenon or incident regarded as prophetic sign. — *v.t.* To foretell as or by an omen. [< L — **Syn.** (noun) portent, foretoken, augury, presage.

om·i·cron (om'ə·kron, ō'mə-) *n.* The fifteenth letter of th Greek alphabet (O, o), corresponding to English short Also **om'i·kron.** See ALPHABET. [< Gk. *o mikron* little o

om·i·nous (om'ə·nəs) *adj.* 1. Of the nature of or fore-shad owed by an omen or by a presentiment of evil; threatening 2. Serving as an omen; prognostic. [< L < *omen* omen] — **om'i·nous·ly** *adv.* — **om'i·nous·ness** *n.*

o·mis·si·ble (ō·mis'ə·bəl) *adj.* Capable of being omitted.

o·mis·sion (ō·mish'ən) *n.* 1. The act of omitting, or th state of being omitted. 2. Anything omitted or neglecte

o·mis·sive (ō·mis'iv) *adj.* Failing to do or include. — **o·mis'sive·ly** *adv.*

o·mit (ō·mit') *v.t.* **o·mit·ted, o·mit·ting** 1. To leave out; fa to include. 2. To fail to do, make, etc.; neglect. [< L *omi tere* to let go < *ob-* to, towards + *mittere* to send]

omni- *combining form* All; totally: *omnipotent.* [< *omnis* all]

om·ni·a vin·cit a·mor (om'nē·ə vin'sit ā'môr) *Latin* Lo conquers all things.

om·ni·bus (om'nə·bəs, -bus) *n.* 1. A bus. 2. A printed an thology: a Conrad *omnibus.* — *adj.* Covering a full colle tion of objects or cases. [< F < L, for all]

om·nif·er·ous (om·nif'ər·əs) *adj.* Producing all kinds. [L *omnifer* < *omnis* all + *ferre* to bear]

om·nip·o·tence (om·nip'ə·təns) *n.* 1. Unlimited and un versal power, esp. as a divine attribute. 2. *Usu. cap.* Go 3. Unlimited power. Also **om·nip'o·ten·cy.**

om·nip·o·tent (om·nip'ə·tənt) *adj.* 1. Almighty; havin in authority or power. — **the Omnipotent** God. [< O < L < *omnis* all + *potens, -entis* able, powerful] — **om·nip** **o·tent·ly** *adv.*

om·ni·pres·ence (om′nə-prez′əns) *n.* The quality of being everywhere present at the same time. [< Med.L < L *omnis* all + *praesens, -entis* present] **—om′ni·pres′ent** *adj.*

om·ni·range (om′nə-rānj′) *n. Aeron.* A network of very-high-frequency radio signals emitted simultaneously in all directions from a transmitting station, enabling aircraft pilots to plot their bearings from the station.

om·nis·cience (om-nish′əns) *n.* **1.** Infinite knowledge. **2.** *Usu. cap.* God. **3.** Extensive knowledge. Also **om·nis′·ien·cy.**

om·nis·cient (om-nish′ənt) *adj.* Knowing all things; all-knowing. **—the Omniscient** God. [< NL < L *omnis* all + *sciens, -entis,* ppr. of *scire* to know] **—om·nis′cient·ly** *adv.*

om·ni·um-gath·er·um (om′nē-əm-gath′ər-əm) *n.* A miscellaneous collection: a humorous pseudo-Latin term.

om·niv·o·rous (om-niv′ər-əs) *adj.* **1.** Eating both animal and vegetable food. **2.** Eating food of all kinds indiscriminately. **3.** That assimilates everything: an *omnivorous* taste or literature. [< L *omnis* all + *vorare* to devour] **—om·niv′o·rous·ly** *adv.* **—om·niv′o·rous·ness** *n.*

on (on, ôn) *prep.* **1.** Above and supported by. **2.** In contact with any surface or outer part of: a blow *on* the head. **3.** Attached to or suspended from: *on* a string. **4.** Directed or moving along the course of. **5.** Near; adjacent to. **6.** Within the duration of. **7.** At the occasion of; because of: *On* seeing her, I left. **8.** At the moment or point of: *on* the hour. **9.** In a state or condition of: *on* fire; *on* record. **10.** By means of: *on* wheels. **11.** Using as a means of sustenance, activity, etc.: living *on* fruit. **12.** In addition to: thousands *on* thousands. **13.** Sustained or confirmed by: *on* good authority. **14.** With reference to: to bet *on* a horse. **15.** Concerning; about: a work *on* economics. **16.** Engaged in; occupied with: *on* a journey; *on* duty. **17.** As a consequence or result of: making a profit *on* tips. **18.** In accordance with or relation to; in terms of. **19.** Directed, tending, or moving toward or against: making war *on* the enemy. **20.** Following after: disease on the heels of famine. **21.** *Informal* With, as about one's person: Do you have five dollars *on* you? **22.** *Informal* At the expense of: The joke is *on* them; drinks *on* the house. **23.** *Informal* So as to annoy or make difficulty for: The car stalled *on* me. **—Syn.** See AT. ◆ See note under UPON. **—to have something on** *U.S. Informal* To have knowledge, possess evidence, etc., against. **—adv. 1.** In or into a position or condition of contact, adherence, covering, etc.: He put his hat *on.* **2.** In the direction of an activity, performance, etc.: He looked *on* while they played. **3.** In advance; ahead, in space or time: later *on.* **4.** In continuous course or succession: The music went *on.* **5.** In or into operation, performance, or existence. **—and so on** And so like what has gone before; et cetera. **—on and on** Without interruption; continuously. **—to be on to** *Informal* To be aware of, informed about, or alert to. **—adj. 1.** Being in operation, progress, or application. **2.** Near; located nearer. [OE *on, an*]

-on *suffix* **1.** *Physics* Atomic or charged particle: *meson.* **2.** *Chem.* Inert gas; neon. [< Gk., neuter *-on*]

on·an·ism (ō′nən-iz′əm) *n.* **1.** Withdrawal before orgasm; incomplete coitus. **2.** Masturbation. [after *Onan.* Cf. *Gen.* xxxviii 9.] **—o′nan·ist** *n.* **—o′nan·is′tic** *adj.*

once (wuns) *adv.* **1.** One time; without repetition. **2.** At or during some past time. **3.** At any time; ever. **—once (and) for all** Finally. **—once in a while** Occasionally. **—adj.** Former; formerly existing; quondam. **—conj.** As soon as; whenever. **—n.** One time. **—all at once 1.** All at the same time. **2.** All of a sudden. **—at once 1.** Simultaneously. **2.** Immediately. [ME < OE *ānes,* genitive of *ān* one]

once-o·ver (wuns′ō′vər) *n. Slang* **1.** A quick glance or survey. **2.** A quick putting of things in order.

on·com·ing (on′kum′ing, ôn′-) *adj.* Approaching. **—n.** An approach.

one (wun) *adj.* **1.** Being a single individual, object, or unit. **2.** Being or designating an unspecified or not precisely identified individual, thing, or time. **3.** Designating a person, thing, or group as contrasted with another or others. **4.** Single in kind; the same; closely united or alike. **—n. 1.** A single unit, the first and lowest integer in the numerical series, preceding two: a cardinal number. **2.** Any symbol of this number, as 1, i, I. **3.** A single person or thing. **—pron. 1.** Someone or something; anyone or anything. **2.** An individual or thing among persons or things already mentioned. **—all one 1.** Of equal consequence. **2.** Unimportant; of no significance. **—at one** In harmony or accord. **—one another** Each other. **—one by one** Singly and in succession. [OE *ān*]

◆ Expressions like *one of those who* may be followed by a plural or a singular verb, either *one* or *those* being regarded as the antecedent of *who* according to the sense or emphasis of the idea expressed. One may say *He is one of those who never*

break rules* or *He is one of those who is always sure of what he is doing.*

One must work at one's own pace* and *One must work at his own pace* are both correct, but the latter form is more common in the U.S.

-one *suffix Chem.* Denoting an organic compound of the ketone group: *acetone.* [< Gk. *-ōnē,* fem. patronymic]

one-horse (wun′hôrs′) *adj.* **1.** Drawn or adapted to be worked by one horse. **2.** *Informal* Of inferior resources or capacity; small; unimportant: a *one-horse* town.

O·nei·da (ō-nī′də) *n.* A member of a tribe of North American Indians of Iroquoian stock.

one·ness (wun′nis) *n.* **1.** Singleness; unity; sameness. **2.** Agreement; concord. **3.** Quality of being unique.

on·er·ous (on′ər-əs) *adj.* **1.** Burdensome or oppressive. **2.** *Law* Legally subject to an obligation. [< OF < L *onus* burden] **—on′er·ous·ly** *adv.* **—on′er·ous·ness** *n.*

one·self (wun-self′, wunz′-) *pron.* A form of the indefinite pronoun *one,* used as a reflexive or as object of a preposition. Also **one′s self.**

one-sid·ed (wun′sī′did) *adj.* **1.** Having, involving, or on one side. **2.** Biased; unfair. **3.** Having unequal or unbalanced sides. **—one′-sid′ed·ly** *adv.* **—one′-sid′ed·ness** *n.*

on-the-job (on·thə-job′, ôn′-) *adj.* Pertaining to skills acquired while actually doing the job: *on-the-job* training.

one-time (wun′tīm′) *adj.* Former: a *one-time* winner.

one-track (wun′trak′) *adj.* **1.** Having or consisting of a single track. **2.** *Informal* Limited to a single idea or pursuit: a *one-track* mind.

one-way (wun′wā′) *adj.* Moving, or permitting movement, in one direction only: *one-way* traffic.

on·ion (un′yən) *n.* **1.** The edible, succulent bulb of an herb of the lily family, having a pungent odor and taste. **2.** Any of various allied plants. [< OF < L *unio* pearl, onion]

on·ion-skin (un′yən-skin′) *n.* A thin, translucent paper.

on·look·er (on′look′ər, ôn′-) *n.* One who looks on; a spectator. **—on′look′ing** *adj.*

on·ly (ōn′lē) *adv.* **1.** In one manner or for one purpose alone. **2.** Solely; exclusively. **3.** Merely; just. **—adj. 1.** Alone in its class; sole; single. **2.** Standing alone by reason of superior excellence. **—conj.** Except that; but. [OE *ānlīc*]

on·o·mat·o·poe·ia (on′ə-mat′ə-pē′ə, ō-nom′ə-tə-) *n.* **1.** The formation of words in imitation of natural sounds, as *crack, splash,* or *bow-wow.* **2.** An imitative word. **3.** The use of such words. Also **on′o·mat′o·po·e′sis** (-pō-ē′sis), **on′·o·mat·o·py** (-mat′ə-pē). [< L < Gk. < *onoma* name + *poieein* to make] **—on′o·mat′o·po·e′ic** or **-i·cal, on′o·mat′o·po·et′ic** (-pō-et′ik) *adj.* **—on′o·mat′o·po·et′i·cal·ly** *adv.*

On·on·da·ga (on′ən-dô′gə, -dä′-) *n. pl.* **-ga** or **-gas 1.** A tribe of North American Indians of Iroquoian stock formerly living in New York and Ontario. **2.** A member of this tribe.

on·rush (on′rush′, ôn′-) *n.* An onward rush or flow.

on·set (on′set′, ôn′-) *n.* **1.** An attack; assault. **2.** An initial stage, as of illness. **3.** A setting about; outset; start.

on·shore (on′shôr′, -shōr′, ôn′-) *adv. & adj.* To, toward, or on the shore.

on·slaught (on′slôt′, ôn′-) *n.* A violent, often hostile assault. [< Du. *annslag,* or < ON + ME *slaught* slaughter]

on·to (on′tōō, ôn′-) *prep.* **1.** Upon the top of; to and upon. **2.** *Informal* Aware of: I'm *onto* your tricks. Also **on to.**

onto- *combining form* Being; existence: *ontogeny.* Also, before vowels, **ont-.** [< Gk. *ōn, ontos,* ppr. of *einai* to be]

on·tog·e·ny (on-toj′ə-nē) *n. pl.* **-nies** *Biol.* The history of the development of the individual organism. Also **on·to·gen·e·sis** (on′tō-jen′ə-sis). **—on·to·ge·net·ic** (on′tō-jə-net′ik), **on′to·gen′ic** *adj.* **—on·tog′e·nist** *n.*

on·tol·o·gy (on-tol′ə-jē) *n. pl.* **-gies** The branch of metaphysics dealing with the philosophical theory of reality. **—on′to·log′i·cal** *adj.* **—on·tol′o·gist** *n.*

o·nus (ō′nəs) *n.* A burden or responsibility. [< L]

on·ward (on′wərd, ôn′-) *adv.* In the direction of progress; forward in space or time; ahead. Also **on′wards. —adj.** Moving or tending to be forward or ahead. [ME]

on·yx (on′iks) *n.* A variety of chalcedony having layers of different colors, used as a semiprecious gemstone. [< L < Gk., nail, onyx]

oo- *combining form* **1.** Egg; pertaining to eggs: *oology.* **2.** *Biol.* An ovum: *oogenesis.* [< Gk. *ōon* egg]

oo·dles (ōōd′lz) *n.pl. Informal* A great deal; many. [< dial. E *oodle,* var. of HUDDLE, n.]

o·o·lite (ō′ə-līt) *n.* A granular variety of limestone made up of round grains resembling the roe of a fish. [< F < Gk. *ōon* egg + *lithos* stone] **—o′o·lit′ic** (-lit′ik) *adj.*

o·ol·o·gy (ō-ol′ə-jē) *n.* The branch of ornithology that deals with the study of eggs. **—o·o·log′ic** (ō′ə-loj′ik) or **-i·cal** *adj.* **—o·ol′o·gist** *n.*

oo·long (ōō′lông) *n.* A dark tea that is partly fermented before being dried. [< Chinese *wu-lung* black dragon]

oo·mi·ak (ōō/mē·ak) See UMIAK.

oophoro- *combining form* Ovary; ovarian. Also, before vowels, **oophor-**. [< Gk. *ōophoros* egg-bearing]

ooze[1] (ōōz) *v.* **oozed, ooz·ing** *v.i.* **1.** To flow or leak out slowly or gradually. **2.** To exude moisture. **3.** To escape or disappear little by little. —*v.t.* **4.** To give off or exude in or as in droplets or a trickle. —*n.* **1.** A slow, gradual leak. **2.** That which oozes. [ME < OE *wāse* slimy mud]

ooze[2] (ōōz) *n.* **1.** Slimy mud or moist, spongy soil. **2.** A deposit of calcareous matter found on the ocean bottom and largely made up of the remains of foraminifers. **3.** Muddy or marshy ground; bog; fen. [OE *wāse* slimy mud]

oo·zy[1] (ōō/zē) *adj.* **·zi·er, ·zi·est** Slowly leaking.

oo·zy[2] (ōō/zē) *adj.* **·zi·er, ·zi·est** Of or resembling mud or ooze; slimy. —**oo/zi·ly** *adv.* —**oo/zi·ness** *n.*

op- Assimilated var. of OB-.

o·pac·i·ty (ō·pas/ə·tē) *n.* *pl.* **·ties 1.** The state or quality of being opaque. **2.** That which is opaque.

o·pal (ō/pəl) *n.* An amorphous, variously colored hydrous silica, including some iridescent varieties esteemed as gemstones. [< L < Gk. < Skt. *upala* precious stone]

o·pal·esce (ō/pəl·es/) *v.i.* **·esced, ·esc·ing** To exhibit opalescence.

o·pal·es·cence (ō/pəl·es/əns) *n.* An iridescent play of brilliant or milky colors, as in an opal. —**o/pal·es/cent** *adj.*

o·pal·ine (ō/pəl·ēn, -in) *adj.* Resembling or characteristic of an opal; opalescent. —*n.* A milky variety of glass.

o·paque (ō·pāk/) *adj.* **1.** Impervious to light; not translucent or transparent. **2.** Impervious to reason; unintelligent. **3.** Impervious to radiant heat, electric radiation, etc. **4.** Having no luster; dull. **5.** Unintelligible; obscure. —*n.* **1.** That which is opaque. **2.** A pigment used to darken or eliminate portions of a print, photographic negative, etc. [ME *opake* < L *opacus* dark] —**o·paque/ly** *adv.* —**o·paque/ness** *n.*

op art (op) A style of art of the 1960's characterized by complex geometric patterns. [< *op(tical) art*]

o·pen (ō/pən) *adj.* **1.** Affording approach, view, passage, or access. **2.** Public; accessible to all. **3.** Not secret or hidden: *open* hostility. **4.** Expanded; unfolded: an *open* flower. **5.** Not enclosed or covered: an *open* car. **6.** Ready for business, appointment, etc. **7.** Not settled or decided; pending: an *open* question. **8.** Available: The job is still *open*. **9.** Unbiased; receptive: often with *to*: an *open* mind; *open* to conviction. **10.** Generous; liberal: an *open* hand. **11.** *Phonet.* **a** Produced with a wide opening above the tongue; low: said of vowels, as the *a* in *father* and *calm*: opposed to *close*. **b** Ending in a vowel or diphthong: said of a syllable. **12.** Not deceptive: an *open* face. **13.** Eager or willing to receive: with *open* arms. **14.** In hunting or fishing, without prohibition: *open* season. **15.** Liable to attack, robbery, temptation, etc. **16.** Having openings, holes, or perforations, as needlework. **17.** *Music* **a** Not stopped by the finger, as a string. **b** Not produced by the stopping of a string or hole, or the use of a valve or slide; not fingered, as the tone of an instrument. **c** Not stopped by the hand or by a mute, as a brass instrument or its tone. **18.** Unrestricted by union regulations in employment: an *open* shop. **19.** *U.S. Informal* Permitting illicit activities, as gambling and prostitution: an *open* town. **20.** Out of doors. **21.** Not to be defended in war: *open* city. **22.** Not restricted by rigid classes, control, etc.: an *open* society. —*v.t.* **1.** To set open or ajar, as a door; unclose; unfasten. **2.** To make passable; free from obstacles. **3.** To make or force (a hole, passage, etc.). **4.** To remove the covering, lid, etc., of. **5.** To expand, as for viewing; unroll; unfold, as a map. **6.** To make an opening or openings into: to *open* an abscess. **7.** To make or declare ready for commerce, use, etc.: to *open* a store. **8.** To make or declare public or free of access, as a park. **9.** To make less compact; expand: to *open* ranks. **10.** To make more receptive to ideas or sentiments; enlighten: to *open* the mind. **11.** To bare the secrets of; divulge; reveal: to *open* one's heart. **12.** To begin, as negotiations. **13.** *Law* To undo or recall (a judgment or order) so as to permit its validity to be questioned. —*v.i.* **14.** To become open. **15.** To come apart or break open; rupture. **16.** To come into view; spread out; unroll. **17.** To afford access or view: The door *opened* on a courtyard. **18.** To become receptive or enlightened. **19.** To begin: The season *opened* with a ball. **20.** In the theater, to begin a season or tour. —*n.* Any wide space not enclosed, obstructed, or covered, as by woods, rocks, etc.: usu. with the definite article: in the open. [OE] —**o/pen·er** *n.* —**o/pen·ly** *adv.* —**o/pen·ness** *n.*

o·pen-air (ō/pən·âr/) *adj.* Occurring, done, etc., out of doors: an *open-air* concert.

o·pen-and-shut (ō/pən·ən·shut/) *adj. Informal* Obvious; easily determined.

open door 1. The policy or practice of giving to all nations the same commercial privileges in a region or area open for trade or exploitation. **2.** Admission to all without charge.

o·pen-door (ō/pən·dôr/, -dōr/) *adj.* Of or characterized b the commercial policies or practices of the open door.

o·pen-eyed (ō/pən·īd/) *adj.* **1.** Having the eyes ope aware; watchful. **2.** Amazed: in *open-eyed* wonder.

o·pen-faced (ō/pən·fāst/) *adj.* **1.** Having an honest fac **2.** Having a face or side uncovered.

o·pen-hand·ed (ō/pən·han/did) *adj.* Giving freely; libera —**o/pen·hand/ed·ly** *adv.* —**o/pen·hand/ed·ness** *n.*

o·pen-heart·ed (ō/pən·här/tid) *adj.* Disclosing th thoughts and intentions plainly; frank; candid. —**o/pe heart/ed·ly** *adv.* —**o/pen·heart/ed·ness** *n.*

o·pen-hearth (ō/pən·härth/) *adj. Metall.* Designating steel-making process in which the material is melted in shallow furnace open at each end to admit fuel and air.

open house 1. A house or a social event in which hospita ity is extended to all who wish to come. **2.** An occasio when a school, factory, institution, etc., is open to visitor

o·pen·ing (ō/pən·ing) *n.* **1.** The act of becoming open or causing to be open. **2.** A vacant or unobstructed space, a hole, passage, or gap. **3.** An aperture in a wall, esp. on for the admission of light or air. **4.** The first part or stag as of a period, act, or process. **5.** A first time for or t beginning of something: the play's *opening*. **6.** In ches checkers, etc., a specific series of opening moves. **7.** An o portunity for action, esp. in business.

open market A market accessible to all buyers and selle

o·pen-mind·ed (ō/pən·mīn/did) *adj.* Free from prejudic conclusions; amenable to reason; receptive. —**o/pe mind/ed·ly** *adv.* —**o/pen·mind/ed·ness** *n.*

o·pen-mouthed (ō/pən·mouthd/, -moutht/) *adj.* **1.** Havi the mouth open; gaping, as in wonder or surprise. **2.** Nois clamorous. **3.** Greedy; voracious.

open sesame An unfailing means or formula for openi secret doors and gaining entrance: an allusion to the tale *Ali Baba and the Forty Thieves* in the *Arabian Nights.*

open shop 1. An establishment employing both union a nonunion labor. **2.** An establishment whose policy is to hi only nonunion labor.

open stock In merchandising, extra or additional parts o set, as of dishes, that are always kept in stock.

o·pen·work (ō/pən·wûrk/) *n.* Any product of art or han craft containing numerous small openings.

op·er·a (op/ər·ə, op/rə) Plural of OPUS. —*n.* **1.** A form drama in which music is a dominant factor, made up of ari recitatives, choruses, etc., with orchestral accompanimen scenery, acting, and sometimes dance. **2.** A particul musical drama or its music or libretto. **3.** An opera hou [< Ital. < L, service, work < *opus* work] —**op·er·at** (op/ə·rat/ik) *adj.* —**op/er·at/i·cal·ly** *adv.*

op·er·a·ble (op/ər·ə·bəl) *adj.* **1.** Capable of treatment surgical operation. **2.** Practicable. —**op/er·a·bil/i·ty** *n*

o·pé·ra bouffe (ô·pā·rä bōōf/) *French* A farcical com opera. Also *Ital.* **o·pe·ra buf·fa** (ō/pä·rä bōōf/fä).

opera glass Small binoculars suitable for use at the theat Also **opera glasses.**

opera hat A man's top hat, having a collapsible crown.

opera house A theater adapted for performance of opera

op·er·ate (op/ə·rāt) *v.* **·at·ed, ·at·ing** *v.i.* **1.** To act function; work. **2.** To bring about the proper or intend effect. **3.** *Surg.* To perform an operation. **4.** To carry or military or naval operation: usu. with *against*. —*v.t.* **5.** To control the working of, as a machine. **6.** To manage conduct the affairs of. **7.** To bring about or cause; effe [< L *operari* to work] —**op/er·at/a·ble** *adj.*

op·er·a·tion (op/ə·rā/shən) *n.* **1.** The act or process operating. **2.** A method of operating; mode of action. An act or transaction, esp. in the stock market. **4.** A cou or series of acts to effect a certain purpose; process. **5.** T state of being in action: to be in *operation*. **6.** *Surg.* A manipulation upon or within the body, performed with without instruments, to restore disunited or deficient par to remove diseased or injured parts, etc. **7.** *Math.* **a** T act of making a change in the value or form of a quanti **b** The change itself as indicated by symbols or rules. **8.** military or naval campaign.

op·er·a·tion·al (op/ə·rā/shən·əl) *adj.* **1.** Pertaining to operation. **2.** Checked and serviced for ready operatio

operations research The application of scientific metho and skills to insure maximum efficiency in industry and go ernment. Also called **operational research.**

op·er·a·tive (op/ər·ə·tiv, -ə·rā/tiv) *adj.* **1.** Exerting fo or influence. **2.** Moving or working efficiently; effecti **3.** Being in operation or in force. **4.** Connected with sur cal operations. **5.** Concerned with practical work, mecha cal or manual. —*n.* **1.** A skilled worker, as in a mill factory. **2.** *Informal* A detective. —**op/er·a·tive·ly** *adv*

op·er·a·tor (op/ə·rā/tər) *n.* **1.** One who operates a machi or mechanism. **2.** One who runs a commercial or industr establishment. **3.** A broker. **4.** *Math.* A symbol th briefly indicates a mathematical process. **5.** *Slang* One w craftily obtains things with little or no cost to himself.

er·cu·late (ō-pûr′kyŏŏ-lit, -lāt) *adj.* Having an opercu-
m. Also **o·per′cu·lat′ed.**

er·cu·lum (ō-pûr′kyŏŏ-ləm) *n.* *pl.* **·la** (-lə) *Biol.* A
like part or organ in certain plants, esp. one serving to
ose an aperture or provide protection. Also **o·per·cele**
·pûr′sēl), **o·per′cule** (-kyŏŏl). [< L, a covering, lid <
erire to cover] — **o·per′cu·lar** *adj.*

e·re ci·ta·to (op′ə·rē si·tā′tō) *Latin* In the work cited,
quoted. Abbr. *o.c., op. cit.*

e·ret·ta (op′ə·ret′ə) *n.* A type of short, humorous opera
th dialogue: also called *light opera.* [< Ital., dim. of *opera*]

hid·i·an (ō·fid′ē·ən) *n.* One of a group of limbless rep-
les with jaws connected by elastic ligaments; a serpent or
ake. — *adj.* Snakelike. [< NL < Gk. *ophis* serpent]

h·thal·mi·a (of·thal′mē·ə) *n.* *Pathol.* Inflammation of
e eye, its membranes, or its lids. Also **oph·thal′my** (-mē).
< LL < Gk. < *ophthalmos* eye] — **oph·thal′mic** *adj.*

h·thal·mic (of·thal′mik) *adj.* Of or pertaining to the eye.

h·thal·mi·tis (of′thal·mī′tis) *n.* *Pathol.* Inflammation
the eye, including the outer and internal structures.

hthalmo- *combining form* Eye; pertaining to the eyes.
< Gk. *ophthalmos* eye]

h·thal·mol·o·gy (of′thal·mol′ə·jē) *n.* The science deal-
g with the structure, functions, and diseases of the eye. —
h·thal′mo·log′ic (-mə·loj′ik) or **·i·cal** *adj.* — **oph′thal·**
ol′o·gist *n.*

n·thal·mo·scope (of·thal′mə·skōp) *n.* An optical instru-
ent for illuminating and viewing the center of the eye. —
h·thal′mo·scop′ic (-skop′ik) or **·i·cal** *adj.* — **oph·thal·**
os·co·py (of′thal·mos′kə·pē) *n.*

ia *combining form* *Med.* A (specified) defect of the eye,
condition of sight: *myopia.* Also spelled *-opy.* [< Gk.
pia < *ōps, ōpos* the eye]

l·ate (*n.* & *adj.* ō′pē·it, -āt; *v.* ō′pē·āt) *n.* 1. Medicine
ntaining opium or one of its derivatives. 2. Something
ducing relaxation or sleep. — *adj.* 1. Consisting of opi-
m. 2. Tending to induce sleep. — *v.t.* **·at·ed, ·at·ing** 1.
o treat with opium or an opiate. 2. To deaden; dull.

ine (ō·pīn′) *v.t.* & *v.i.* **o·pined, o·pin·ing** To hold or ex-
ress as an opinion; think; conjecture: now usu. humorous.
< MF < L *opinari* to think, suppose]

in·ion (ə·pin′yən, ō-) *n.* 1. A conclusion or judgment
eld with confidence, but falling short of positive knowledge.
. An expert judgment given more or less formally. 3. An
valuation. 4. A prevailing sentiment: public *opinion.* 5.
aw The formal announcement of the conclusions of a court.
< OF < L *opinari* to think]

in·ion·at·ed (ə·pin′yən·ā′tid, ō-) *adj.* Obstinately at-
ched to one's own opinion. — **o·pin′ion·at′ed·ness** *n.*

in·ion·a·tive (ə·pin′yən·ā′tiv, ō-) *adj.* 1. Opinionated.
. Of the nature of opinion. — **o·pin′ion·a·tive·ly** *adv.* —
pin′ion·a′tive·ness *n.*

l·um (ō′pē·əm) *n.* A narcotic drug obtained from the
nripe capsules of the **opium poppy,** containing a mixture of
kaloids, including morphine. [< L < Gk. *opion* opium,
m. of *opos* vegetable juice]

os·sum (ə·pos′əm, pos′əm) *n.* An American marsupial
largely arboreal and nocturnal habits, having a prehensile
il and feet adapted for grasping. [< Algonquian]

·po·nent (ə·pō′nənt) *n.* One who opposes another, as in
ttle; antagonist. — **Syn.** See ENEMY. — *adj.* 1. Acting
gainst something or someone; opposing. 2. *Anat.* Bringing
e part, as of a muscle, into opposition to another. 3.
tanding in front; opposite. [< L < *ob-* against + *ponere*
place] — **op·po′nen·cy** *n.*

·por·tune (op′ər·tōōn′, -tyōōn′) *adj.* 1. Meeting some
eed; esp. right or fit. 2. Occurring at the right moment;
mely. [< MF < L *opportunus* favorable, lit., (a wind)
lowing towards port] — **op′por·tune′ly** *adv.* — **op′por·**
ine′ness *n.*

·por·tu·nist (op′ər·tōō′nist, -tyŏŏ′-) *n.* One who uses
very opportunity to contribute to the achievement of some
nd, and who is relatively uninfluenced by moral principles
r sentiment. — **op′por·tu·nis′tic** *adj.* — **op′por·tu′nism** *n.*

·por·tu·ni·ty (op′ər·tōō′nə·tē, -tyŏŏ′-) *n.* *pl.* **·ties** A fit
r convenient time; favorable occasion or circumstance.

·pos·a·ble (ə·pō′zə·bəl) *adj.* 1. Capable of being placed
pposite something else: said esp. of the thumb. 2. That
an be opposed. — **op·pos′a·bil′i·ty** *n.*

·pose (ə·pōz′) *v.* **·posed, ·pos·ing** *v.t.* 1. To act or be in
pposition to; resist; combat. 2. To set in opposition to
ontrast: to *oppose* love to hatred. 3. To place before or in
ont. — *v.i.* 4. To act or be in opposition. [< OF < L
ob- against + *ponere* to place] — **op·pos′er** *n.*
— **Syn.** 1. Combat, fight, resist, withstand, dispute, contradict,
ontravene.

·po·site (op′ə·zit) *adj.* 1. Situated or placed on the other
de, or on each side, of an intervening space or thing. 2.

Facing or moving the other way: *opposite* directions. 3.
Contrary in tendency or character: *opposite* opinions. 4.
Bot. **a** Arranged in pairs, as leaves on a stem. **b** Having one
part or organ immediately before or vertically over another,
as a stamen before a petal. — *n.* Something or someone
that is opposite, opposed, or contrary. — *adv.* In an opposite or complementary direction or position. — *prep.* 1.
Across from; facing. 2. Complementary to, as in theatrical
roles: He played *opposite* her. [< OF < L *oppositus.* See
OPPOSE.] — **op′po·site·ly** *adv.* — **op′po·site·ness** *n.*

op·po·si·tion (op′ə·zish′ən) *n.* 1. The act of opposing or resisting. 2. The state of being opposite or opposed; antithe-
sis. 3. A position confronting another or a placing in contrast. 4. That which is or furnishes an obstacle to some result: The stream flows without *opposition.* 5. *Often cap.*
The political party opposed to the party or administration in
power. — **op′po·si′tion·al** *adj.* — **op·po·si′tion·ist** *n.* —
op′po·si′tion·less *adj.*

op·pos·i·tive (ə·poz′ə·tiv) *adj.* Placed or capable of being
placed in contrast. — **op·pos′i·tive·ly** *adv.*

op·press (ə·pres′) *v.t.* 1. To burden or keep down by harsh
and unjust use of force or authority. 2. To lie heavy upon
physically or mentally. [< OF < Med.L *oppressare,* ult.
< L *ob-* against + *premere* to press] — **op·pres′sor** *n.*

op·pres·sion (ə·presh′ən) *n.* 1. The act of oppressing, or the
state of being oppressed. 2. A sense of weight or constriction; mental depression. 3. That which oppresses.

op·pres·sive (ə·pres′iv) *adj.* 1. Burdensome; tyrannical;
harsh; cruel. 2. Producing a state of oppression. — **op·**
pres′sive·ly *adv.* — **op·pres′sive·ness** *n.*

op·pro·bri·ous (ə·prō′brē·əs) *adj.* 1. Contemptuously abusive; imputing disgrace. 2. Shameful; disgraceful. — **op·**
pro′bri·ous·ly *adv.* — **op·pro′bri·ous·ness** *n.*

op·pro·bri·um (ə·prō′brē·əm) *n.* 1. The state of being
scornfully reproached; ignominy. 2. Reproach mingled
with disdain. 3. A cause of disgrace or reproach. [< L <
ob- against + *probum* disgrace]
— **Syn.** 1. odium, obloquy, infamy, disgrace.

op·pugn (ə·pyōōn′) *v.t.* To assail or oppose with argument;
call in question; controvert. [< L < *ob-* against + *pugnare*
to fight] — **op·pugn′er** *n.*

-opsia *combining form* *Med.* A (specified) type or condition
of sight. Also **-opsy.** [< NL < Gk. *opsis* aspect, sight]

opt (opt) *v.i.* To choose; decide. [< F < L *optare*]

op·ta·tive (op′tə·tiv) *adj.* 1. Expressing desire or choice.
2. *Gram.* Denoting the mood that expresses wish or desire.
— *n.* *Gram.* 1. The optative mood. 2. A word or construction in this mood. [< F < LL < L *optare* to wish] — **op′·**
ta·tive·ly *adv.*

op·tic (op′tik) *adj.* Pertaining to the eye or vision. — *n.*
Informal The eye. [< MF < Med.L < Gk. *optikos* < stem
op- as in *opsomai* I shall see]

op·ti·cal (op′ti·kəl) *adj.* 1. Pertaining to optics. 2. Of or
pertaining to eyesight. 3. Designed to assist or improve vision. — **op′ti·cal·ly** *adv.*

optical fiber Any of various fibers of glass or other clear
plastic through which light may be conducted along any desired path and in compact bundles will transmit images of
high fidelity and resolution.

optical maser *Physics* A laser.

op·ti·cian (op·tish′ən) *n.* One who makes or deals in optical goods.

optic nerve *Anat.* The special nerve of vision, connecting
the retina with the cerebral centers. For illus. see EYE.

op·tics (op′tiks) *n.pl.* (construed as *sing.*) The science that
treats of the phenomena of light, vision, and sight.

op·ti·mal (op′tə·məl) *adj.* Most favorable; best.

op·ti·mism (op′tə·miz′əm) *n.* 1. A disposition to look on
the bright side of things. 2. The doctrine that everything
is ordered for the best. 3. The doctrine that the universe is
constantly tending toward a better state. [< F < L *opti-
mus* best] — **op′ti·mist** *n.* — **op′ti·mis′tic** or **·ti·cal** *adj.* —
op′ti·mis′ti·cal·ly *adv.*

op·ti·mum (op′tə·məm) *n.* *pl.* **·ma** (-mə) or **·mums** The
condition or degree producing the best result. — *adj.* Producing or conducive to the best results. [< L, neut. of *opti-
mus* best]

op·tion (op′shən) *n.* 1. The right, power, or liberty of
choosing; discretion. 2. The act of opting or choosing. 3.
The purchased privilege of either buying or selling something
at a specified price within a specified time. 4. A thing that is
or can be chosen. [< MF < L < *optare* to choose]

op·tion·al (op′shən·əl) *adj.* Left to one's preference; not required; elective. — **op′tion·al·ly** *adv.*

op·tom·e·try (op·tom′ə·trē) *n.* The profession or occupation of measuring vision and prescribing corrective lenses to
compensate for visual defects. — **op·tom′e·trist** *n.*

op·u·lence (op′yə·ləns) *n.* 1. Wealth; affluence. 2. Luxuriance; abundance. Also **op'u·len·cy** (-lən·sē). — **Syn. 1.** riches, fortune, means, prosperity.

op·u·lent (op'yə·lənt) *adj.* **1.** Possessing great wealth; rich; affluent. **2.** Plentiful; abundant; profuse. [< L *opulentus* < *ops, opis* power, wealth] — **op'u·lent·ly** *adv.*

o·pus (ō'pəs) *n. pl.* **op·er·a** (op'ər·ə, op'rə) A literary or musical work or composition. Abbr. *op.* [< L, work]

-opy See -OPIA.

or (ôr, *unstressed* ər) *conj.* **1.** Introducing an alternative: stop or go. **2.** Offering a choice of a series: Will you take milk *or* coffee *or* chocolate? **3.** Introducing an equivalent: the culinary art *or* art of cookery. **4.** Indicating uncertainty: He lives in Chicago *or* thereabouts. **5.** Introducing the second alternative of a choice limited to two: with *either* or *whether*: It must be either black *or* white; I don't care whether he goes *or* not. **6.** *Poetic* Either; whether: *or* in the heart *or* in the head. [ME contraction, of *other, auther* either, OE *āther*; infl. in meaning by OE *olhthe* or]

-or[1] *suffix of nouns* The person or thing performing the action expressed in the root verb: *competitor.* ◆ See note under -ER[1]. [< AF *-our*, OF *-or* < L *-or, -ator*]

-or[2] *suffix of nouns* Quality, state, or condition: *favor.* [< OF < L]

or·a·cle (ôr'ə·kəl, or'-) *n.* **1.** The seat of worship of some ancient divinity, as of Apollo at Delphi, where prophecies were given out by the priests in answer to inquiries. **2.** A prophecy thus given. **3.** The deity whose prophecies were given. **4.** A person of unquestioned wisdom or knowledge, or something regarded as of infallible authority. **5.** A wise saying. [< OF < L *oraculum* < *orare* to speak, pray]

o·rac·u·lar (ō·rak'yə·lər, ō-) *adj.* **1.** Of or pertaining to an oracle. **2.** Obscure; enigmatical. **3.** Prophetic; farseeing. — **o·rac'u·lar'i·ty** *n.* — **o·rac'u·lar·ly** *adv.*

o·ral (ôr'əl, ō'rəl) *adj.* **1.** Uttered through the mouth; spoken. **2.** Of or pertaining to the mouth; also, situated at or near the mouth. **3.** Of, pertaining to, or using speech. **4.** Taken or administered by mouth. — **Syn.** See VERBAL. — *n. Usu. pl.* An academic examination in which the student speaks his answers aloud. [< L *os, oris* mouth] — **o'ral·ly** *adv.*

o·rang (ō·rang') *n.* An orang-utan.

or·ange (ôr'inj, or'-) *n.* **1.** A round, juicy fruit of a low, much-branched, evergreen tree with a reddish yellow rind enclosing membranous divisions and a refreshing, sweetish or subacid pulp. **2.** Any of the trees yielding this fruit. **3.** Any of many related species. **4.** A reddish yellow color; also, a pigment of this color. — *adj.* **1.** Reddish yellow. **2.** Of an orange. [< OF < Provençal < Sp. < Arabic < Persian *nārang*]

or·ange·ade (ôr'inj·ād', or'-) *n.* A beverage made of orange juice, sugar, and water. [< F]

orange blossom The white, fragrant blossom of the orange tree, often worn by brides: State flower of Florida.

Or·ange·man (ôr'inj·mən, or'-) *n. pl.* **·men** (-mən) A member of a secret society founded in northern Ireland in 1795 for upholding Protestant ascendancy and succession in England. [named in honor of William III, king of England and Prince of Orange]

orange pekoe A black tea from India, Ceylon, and Java.

or·ange·wood (ôr'inj·wŏŏd', or'-) *n.* The fine-grained, yellowish wood of the orange tree, used in lathe work.

o·rang-u·tan (ō·rang'ə·tan, -ŏŏ·tan) *n. pl.* **·tans** or **·tan** A large, anthropoid ape of Borneo and Sumatra, having brownish red hair and extremely long arms: also called *orang, ourang.* Also **o·rang'-ou·tang** (-ə·tang, -ŏŏ·tang). [< Malay < *oran* man + *utan* forest]

o·rate (ôr'āt, ō·rāt', ō'rāt, ō·rāt') *v.i.* **o·rat·ed, o·rat·ing** To talk oratorically or pompously; speechify. [See ORATION.]

o·ra·tion (ō·rā'shən, ō·rā'-) *n.* An elaborate public speech, esp. one given at a formal occasion. [< L < *orare* to speak]

or·a·tor (ôr'ə·tər, or'-) *n.* **1.** One who delivers an oration; an eloquent public speaker. **2.** *Law* The complainant in a chancery proceeding. — **or'a·tor·ship'** *n.*[1]

or·a·to·ri·o (ôr'ə·tôr'ē·ō, -tō'rē·ō, or'-) *n. pl.* **·os** A large musical composition for solo voices, chorus, and orchestra, usu. dramatizing a sacred story, but without scenery or acting. [< Ital. < LL. See ORATORY[2].]

or·a·to·ry[1] (ôr'ə·tôr'ē, -tō'rē, or'-) *n.* **1.** The art of public speaking; eloquence. **2.** Eloquent language. [< L *oratoria* (*ars*) the oratorical (art)] — **or'a·tor'i·cal** (-tôr'i·kəl, -tor'-) *adj.* — **or'a·tor'i·cal·ly** *adv.*

or·a·to·ry[2] (ôr'ə·tôr'ē, -tō'rē, or'-) *n. pl.* **·ries** A place for prayer; private chapel. [< LL *oratorium* (*templum*) (temple) for prayer < *orare* to pray]

orb (ôrb) *n.* **1.** A rounded mass; a sphere or globe. **2.** A circle or orbit; anything circular. **3.** A sphere topped by a cross, used as a symbol of royal power. **4.** *Poetic* The eye. — *v.t.* **1.** To shape into a sphere or circle. **2.** *Poetic* To enclose; encircle. [< L *orbis* circle]

or·bic·u·lar (ôr·bik'yə·lər) *adj.* **1.** Having the form of an orb or orbit. **2.** Well-rounded. **3.** *Bot.* Circular, as a leaf.

[< F, or < L < *orbiculus*, dim. of *orbis* circle] — **or·bi·lar'i·ty** (-lar'ə·tē) *n.* — **or·bic'u·lar·ly** *adv.*

or·bic·u·late (ôr·bik'yə·lit, -lāt) *adj.* Having a round form; orbicular. Also **or·bic'u·lat'ed.** — **or·bic'u·late·ly** *adv.*

or·bit (ôr'bit) *n.* **1.** The path in space along which a heavenly body or artificial satellite moves about its center of traction. **2.** A range of influence or action: the *orbit* of imperialism. — *v.t.* **1.** To cause to move in an orbit, as artificial satellite. **2.** To revolve around (the earth, etc. as a satellite. — *v.i.* **3.** To move in or as in an orbit. [< L *orbita* track of a wheel < *orbis* wheel, circle] — **or'bi·tal** *adj.*

or·chard (ôr'chərd) *n.* A plantation of trees grown for their products, as fruit, nuts, oils, etc.; also, the enclosure of ground containing them. [OE < *ort-geard* garden]

or·ches·tra (ôr'kis·trə) *n.* **1.** A comparatively large group of musicians playing together; esp., a symphony orchestra; also, the instruments they play. **2.** *U.S.* In theaters, the place immediately before the stage, occupied by the musicians: also **orchestra pit. 3.** The main floor of a theater. [< L < Gk. *orchēstra* dancing space] — **or·ches·tral** (ôr·kes'trəl) *adj.* — **or·ches'tral·ly** *adv.*

or·ches·trate (ôr'kis·trāt) *v.t. & v.i.* **·trat·ed, ·trat·ing** To compose or arrange (music) for an orchestra. — **or·ches·tra'tion** *n.*

or·chid (ôr'kid) *n.* **1.** Any of a family of herbs of temperate regions, having bulbous roots and often very showy flowers. **2.** Any of various delicate, rosy purple colors. [< NL < *orchis* orchid < Gk., orig., a testicle; so called because of shape of its rootstocks]

orchio- *combining form* Testicle; pertaining to the testicle. Also, before vowels, **orchi-.** [< Gk. *orchis* testicle]

or·chis (ôr'kis) *n.* Any of various plants having dense spikes of small flowers. [< L, orchid]

or·dain (ôr·dān') *v.t.* **1.** To order or decree; enact. **2.** To predestine; destine: said of God, fate, etc. **3.** To invest with ministerial or priestly functions. [< OF < L *ordinare* to set in order] — **or·dain'er** *n.*

or·deal (ôr·dēl', -dē'əl, ôr'dēl) *n.* **1.** A severe test of character or endurance. **2.** A former method of judicial trial in which the accused was subjected to painful physical tests that were supposed to do him no harm if he were innocent. [OE *ordāl, ordēl* judgment < *or-* out + *dǣl* a deal]

or·der (ôr'dər) *n.* **1.** A condition in which there is a methodical, proper, or harmonious arrangement of things. **2.** The disposition or arrangement of things. **3.** Established method, procedure, or condition. **4.** A proper or working condition. **5.** A command, direction, or regulation. **6.** *Law* Any direction of a court, entered in the record but not included in the final judgment. **7.** A commission or instruction to supply, purchase, or sell something; also, that which is supplied or purchased. **8.** A body of persons united by some common bond: the *Order* of Odd Fellows. **9.** A monastic or religious body. **10.** A group of persons upon whom an honor has been conferred, entitling them to wear special insignia; also, the insignia so worn. **11.** *Eccl.* **a** *Usu. pl.* Any of the various grades or degrees of the Christian ministry. **b** The rite or sacrament of ordination. **c** A liturgical form for a service or the performance of a rite. **12.** *Archit.* **a** A system of classical architecture, as Doric, Ionic, or Corinthian, usu. represented by the general character of its columns. **b** A column with its entablature. **13.** *Biol.* A taxonomic category ranking next below the class, and above the family. — **in order 1.** In accordance with rule or proper procedure. **2.** Neat; tidy. — **in order that** So that; to the end that. — **in order to** For the purpose of. — **in short order** Quickly; without delay. — **on order** Ordered but not yet delivered. — **on the order of** Similar to. — **out of order 1.** Not in working condition. **2.** Not in proper arrangement or sequence. **3.** Not according to rule. **4.** Not suitable or appropriate. — **to order** According to the buyer's specifications. — *v.t.* **1.** To give a command or direction to. **2.** To command to go, come, etc. **3.** To give an order that (something) be done. **4.** To give an order for. **5.** To put in orderly or systematic arrangement. **6.** To ordain. — *v.i.* **7.** To give an order or orders. — **to order arms** *Mil.* To bring a rifle against the right side, with the butt on the ground. [OF < L *ordo, -inis* row, series, order] — **or'der·er** *n.*

or·der·ly (ôr'dər·lē) *adj.* **1.** Having regard for arrangement, method, or system. **2.** Peaceful. **3.** Characterized by neatness and order. **4.** Pertaining to orders. — *n. pl.* **·lies** **a** A hospital attendant. **2.** A soldier detailed to carry orders. — *adv.* Methodically; regularly. — **or'der·li·ness** *n.*

or·di·nal[1] (ôr'də·nəl) *adj.* **1.** Denoting position in an order or succession. **2.** Pertaining to an order, as of plants, animals, etc. [< LL < L *ordo, -inis* order]

or·di·nal[2] (ôr'də·nəl) *n. Eccl.* A book of rites for certain church services. [< Med.L < LL < L *ordo, -inis* order]

ordinal number *Math.* A number that shows the order of a unit in a given series, as first, second, third, etc.: distinguished from *cardinal number.*

or·di·nance (ôr'də·nəns) *n.* **1.** An order, decree, or law.

municipal body. **2.** A religious rite or ceremony. [< OF Med.L < L < *ordinare* to set in order]

di·nar·i·ly (ôr′də·ner′ə·lē, ôr′də·nâr′ə·lē) *adv.* **1.** In ordinary cases; usually. **2.** In the usual manner. **3.** To the usual extent; normally.

di·nar·y (ôr′də·ner′ē) *adj.* **1.** Of common or everyday occurrence; customary; usual. **2.** According to an established order; normal. **3.** Common in rank or degree; average; commonplace. — *n. pl.* **·nar·ies 1.** That which is usual or common. **2.** *Brit.* **a** A meal provided regularly at a fixed price. **b** An eating house where such meals are served. **3.** *Law* One who exercises jurisdiction in his own right, and not by delegation. **4.** *Eccl.* **a** A rule or book prescribing the form for saying Mass. **b** The practically unchangeable part of the Mass: with *the*: distinguished from the *proper*. — **in ordinary 1.** In actual and constant service. **2.** *Naut.* Out of commission; laid up: said of a ship. — **out of the ordinary** not common or usual; extraordinary. [< OF < L *ordinarius* regular, usual] — **or′di·nar′i·ness** *n.*

di·nate (ôr′də·nit) *adj.* Characterized by order; regular. — *n. Math.* **1.** The distance of any point from the X-axis, measured on a line parallel to the Y-axis in a coordinate system. **2.** The line or number indicating such distance.

di·na·tion (ôr′də·nā′shən) *n.* **1.** *Eccl.* The rite of consecration to the ministry. **2.** The state of being ordained, regulated, or settled.

·nance (ôrd′nəns) *n.* **1.** Military weapons, ammunition, and associated equipment and materiel. **2.** Cannon or artillery. [Contr. of ORDINANCE]

do·vi·cian (ôr′də·vish′ən) *adj. Geol.* Of or designating a period of the Paleozoic era, following the Cambrian and preceding the Silurian. — *n.* An epoch of the Paleozoic era. • chart for GEOLOGY. [< L *Ordovices* the Ordovices, an ancient Celtic tribe]

dure (ôr′jər, -dyŏor) *n.* Excrement; feces. [< OF < ord dull, nasty < L *horridus* bristling]

(ôr, ōr) *n.* **1.** A natural substance, as a mineral or rock, containing a valuable metal. **2.** A natural substance containing a nonmetallic mineral: sulfur *ore.* [OE *ār, ǣr* brass, copper; infl. in meaning by OE *ōra* unwrought metal]

(œ′rə) *n. pl.* **ö·re** A coin or monetary unit equivalent to one hundredth of a krone in Denmark and Norway, and of a krona in Sweden. [< Norw., Dan., and Sw.]

g·a·no (ō·reg′ə·nō) *n.* A perennial herb of the mint family, having aromatic leaves used as a seasoning. [< Sp. < L *origanum* wild marjoram]

gon grape An evergreen shrub having dark blue berry clusters resembling grapes: the State flower of Oregon.

es·tes (ô·res′tēz, ō-) In Greek legend, the son of Agamemnon and Clytemnestra who, together with his sister Electra, avenged his father's murder by killing his mother and her lover. [< L < Gk.]

ray (ôr′frā) See ORPHREY.

an (ôr′gən) *n.* **1.** A musical instrument consisting of a collection of pipes and reeds made to sound by means of compressed air controlled by one or more keyboards and by various knobs used to vary registration: often called *pipe organ.* **2.** Any musical instrument resembling this, either in sound or in some aspect of its mechanism. **3.** Any part of a plant or animal, as a stamen, the heart, etc., performing some definite function. **4.** An instrument or agency of communication; esp., a newspaper or periodical published in the interest of a political party, religious denomination, etc. [< L *organa*, or < OF < L < Gk. *organon* instrument]

an·dy (ôr′gən·dē) *n. pl.* **·dies** A thin, crisp, transparent, cotton muslin, used for dresses, collars, cuffs, etc. Also **or·gan·die.** [< F *organdi*; ult. origin uncertain]

o organ grinder A street musician playing a hand organ.

an·ic (ôr·gan′ik) *adj.* **1.** Of, pertaining to, or of the nature of animals and plants. **2.** Affecting or altering the structure of an organ or part: *organic* disease: distinguished from *functional.* **3.** Serving the purpose of an organ. **4.** *Chem.* Of or pertaining to compounds containing carbon. **5.** Inherent in or pertaining to the fundamental structure of anything; constitutional. **6.** Of or characterized by systematic coordination of parts; organized; systematized. **7.** *Law* Designating the system of laws or principles forming the foundation of a government. Also **or·gan′i·cal.** [< L < organon instrument] — **or·gan′i·cal·ly** *adv.*

anic chemistry The branch of chemistry that relates to the structure, formation, and properties of compounds containing carbon.

anic disease *Pathol.* A disease that affects or alters the structure of some particular organ or part.

an·ism (ôr′gən·iz′əm) *n.* **1.** An animal or plant considered as a totality of interdependent parts functioning to maintain vital activities. **2.** Anything that is analogous in structure and function to a living thing: the social *organism.*

---

or·gan·ist (ôr′gən·ist) *n.* One who plays the organ.

or·gan·i·za·tion (ôr′gən·ə·zā′shən, -ī·zā′-) *n.* **1.** The act of organizing, or the state of being organized; also, that which is organized. **2.** A number of individuals systematically united for some end or work. **3.** The officials, committeemen, etc., who control a political party. Also *Brit.* **or′gan·i·sa′tion.**

or·gan·ize (ôr′gən·īz) *v.* **·ized, ·iz·ing** *v.t.* **1.** To bring together or form as a whole or combination, as for a common objective. **2.** To arrange systematically; order. **3.** To furnish with organic structure. **4.** To enlist (workers) in a trade union. **5.** To unionize the workers of (a factory, etc.). — *v.i.* **6.** To form or join an organization. Also *Brit.* **or′gan·ise.** — **or·gan·iz′a·ble** *adj.* — **or′gan·iz′er** *n.*

organo- *combining form* **1.** *Biol.* Related to an organ or to the organs of the body. **2.** *Chem.* Organic. [< Gk. *organon* instrument, organ]

or·ga·no·me·tal·lic (ôr′gə·nō·mə·tal′ik) *adj. Chem.* Designating or pertaining to a compound of metal and carbon.

organ pipe One of the tubes of a pipe organ in which a column of air is made to vibrate so as to produce a tone.

or·gasm (ôr′gaz·əm) *n. Physiol.* The acme of excitement at the culmination of a sexual act. [< NL < Gk. *orgaein* to swell] — **or·gas·tic** (ôr·gas′tik) *adj.*

or·gi·as·tic (ôr′jē·as′tik) *adj.* **1.** Pertaining to or resembling an orgy. **2.** Marked by orgies.

or·gy (ôr′jē) *n. pl.* **·gies 1.** Wild or wanton revelry. **2.** Any immoderate or excessive indulgence. **3.** *pl.* The secret rites in honor of certain Greek and Roman deities, marked by frenzied songs and dances. [Earlier *orgies*, pl. < MF < L *orgia* < Gk., secret rites]

o·ri·el (ôr′ē·əl, ō′rē-) *n. Archit.* A bay window, esp. one built out from a wall and resting on a bracket or similar support. [< OF *oriol* porch, gallery, ? < Med.L *oriolum*]

o·ri·ent (*n. & adj.* ôr′ē·ənt, ō′rē-, -ent; *v.* ôr′ē·ent, ō′rē-) *n.* **1.** The east: opposed to *occident.* **2.** The eastern sky; also, sunrise. — *v.t.* **1.** To cause to face or turn to the east. **2.** To place or adjust, as a map, in exact relation to the points of the compass. **3.** To adjust in relation to something else. Also **orientate.** — *adj.* **1.** Resembling sunrise; bright. **2.** Ascending; rising. [< OF < L (*sol*) *oriens, -entis* rising (sun), east, ppr. of *oriri* to rise]

O·ri·ent (ôr′ē·ənt, ō′rē-, -ent) **1.** The countries east of Europe; esp., eastern Asia. **2.** The eastern hemisphere.

o·ri·en·tal (ôr′ē·en′tal, ō′rē-) *adj.* **1.** Of or pertaining to the East, or to the countries constituting the Orient: distinguished from *occidental.* **2.** Very bright, clear, and pure: said of gems. **3.** Denoting a variety of precious corundum, esp. sapphire: an *oriental* topaz. — **o′ri·en·tal·ly** *adv.*

O·ri·en·tal (ôr′ē·en′tal, ō′rē-) *adj.* Of or pertaining to the Orient; Eastern. — *n.* An inhabitant of Asia; an Asian.

O·ri·en·tal·ism (ôr′ē·en′tal·iz′əm, ō′rē-) *n.* **1.** An Oriental quality, mannerism, characteristic, etc. **2.** Knowledge of or proficiency in Oriental languages, literature, etc. Also **o′ri·en′tal·ism.** — **O′ri·en′tal·ist** *n.*

Oriental rug 1. A rug or carpet hand-woven in one piece in the Orient. **2.** Any rug having a design or texture resembling those made in the Orient.

o·ri·en·tate (ôr′ē·en·tāt′, ō′rē-) *v.* **·tat·ed, ·tat·ing** *v.t.* **1.** To orient. — *v.i.* **2.** To face or turn eastward or in some specified direction. **3.** To become adjusted or oriented.

o·ri·en·ta·tion (ôr′ē·en·tā′shən, ō′rē-) *n.* **1.** The act of orienting, or the state of being oriented. **2.** The determination or adjustment of one's position with reference to circumstances, ideals, etc.

or·i·fice (ôr′ə·fis, or′-) *n.* An opening into a cavity; aperture. [< MF < LL < L *os, oris* mouth + *facere* to make]

or·i·flamme (ôr′ə·flam, or′-) *n.* **1.** The red banner of the abbey of St. Denis, used as a battle standard by the kings of France until the 15th century. **2.** Any flag or standard. [< F < OF < *orie* golden (< L *aureus*) + *flambe* banner]

or·i·ga·mi (ôr′i·gä′mē) *n.* The ancient Japanese art of folding single sheets of paper into realistic animal forms, usu. without the aid of scissors or paste. [< Japanese]

or·i·gan (ôr′ə·gən, or′-) *n.* The wild marjoram. [< OF < L < Gk. *origanon*, an herb like marjoram]

or·i·gin (ôr′ə·jin, or′-) *n.* **1.** The beginning of the existence of anything. **2.** A primary source; cause. **3.** Parentage; ancestry. **4.** *Math.* **a** The point at which the axes of a Cartesian coordinate system intersect. **b** The point in a polar coordinate system where the radius vector equals zero. [< OF < L *origo, -inis* source, beginning]

o·rig·i·nal (ə·rij′ə·nəl) *adj.* **1.** Of or belonging to the beginning, origin, or first stage of existence of a thing. **2.** Produced by one's own mind and thought; not copied or imitative. **3.** Able to produce works requiring thought without copying or imitating others; creative; inventive. — *n.* **1.** The first form of anything. **2.** An original work, as a paint-

---

ing, sculpture, etc., as distinct from a reproduction or copy. **3.** A person or thing represented in a painting, biography, etc. **4.** A person of unique character or genius. **5.** An eccentric. — **Syn.** See NEW.

o·rig·i·nal·i·ty (ə·rij′ə·nal′ə·tē) *n. pl.* **·ties** **1.** The power of originating; inventiveness. **2.** The quality of being original or novel. **3.** Something original.

o·rig·i·nal·ly (ə·rij′ə·nəl·ē) *adv.* **1.** At the beginning. **2.** In a new and striking manner.

original sin *Theol.* The corruption and depravity held to be inherent in all mankind as a consequence of Adam's first sinful disobedience.

o·rig·i·nate (ə·rij′ə·nāt) *v.* **·nat·ed, ·nat·ing** *v.t.* **1.** To bring into existence; create; initiate. — *v.i.* **2.** To come into existence; have origin; arise. — **o·rig′i·na′tion** *n.* — **o·rig′i·na′tive** *adj.* — **o·rig′i·na′tive·ly** *adv.* — **o·rig′i·na′tor** *n.* — **Syn.** 1. institute, propagate, produce.

o·ri·ole (ôr′ē·ōl, ō′rē-) *n.* **1.** Any of a family of black and yellow birds of the Old World, related to the crows. **2.** Any of various black and yellow American songbirds that build hanging nests; esp., the Baltimore oriole and the orchard oriole. [< OF < Med.L < L *aureolus*, dim. of *aureus* golden]

O·ri·on (ō·rī′ən) In Greek and Roman mythology, a giant hunter who pursued the Pleiades and was killed by Diana. — *n.* A constellation. [< L < Gk.]

or·i·son (ôr′i·zən, or′-) *n. Usu. pl.* A devotional prayer. [< OF < LL *oratio, -onis* prayer]

Or·lon (ôr′lon) *n.* A synthetic fiber woven from an acrylic resin, having high resistance to heat, light, and chemicals, widely used as a textile material: a trade name. Also **or′lon.**

or·mo·lu (ôr′mə·lōō) *n.* Any of various alloys of copper, tin, and zinc that resemble gold in appearance, used in furniture decorations, jewelry, etc. [< F < *or* gold + *moulu*, pp. of *moudre* to grind]

or·na·ment (*n.* ôr′nə·mənt; *v.* ôr′nə·ment) *n.* **1.** Something that adorns or beautifies; a.decoration. **2.** Ornaments, collectively. **3.** A person regarded as a source of honor or credit. **4.** The act of adorning, or the state of being adorned; ornamentation. **5.** *Music* A tone or group of tones used to embellish a melody without materially affecting its harmonic content. — *v.t.* **1.** To furnish with ornaments; decorate. **2.** To be an ornament to. [< OF < L < *ornare* to adorn] — **or′na·ment′er** (-ment′ər) *n.*

or·na·men·tal (ôr′nə·men′təl) *adj.* Of the nature of or serving as an ornament. — *n.* An ornamental object; esp., a plant used as decoration. — **or′na·men′tal·ly** *adv.*

or·na·men·ta·tion (ôr′nə·men·tā′shən) *n.* **1.** The act or result of ornamenting. **2.** The state of being ornamented. **3.** That which ornaments; also, ornaments, collectively.

or·nate (ôr·nāt′) *adj.* **1.** Elaborately or excessively ornamented; overdecorative. **2.** Florid or showy, as a style of writing. [< L *ornatus*, pp. of *ornare* to adorn] — **or·nate′ly** *adv.* — **or·nate′ness** *n.*

or·ner·y (ôr′nər·ē, ôrn′rē) *adj. Dial.* **1.** *U.S.* Disposed to be contrary or stubborn. **2.** *U.S.* Mean; ugly; low; snide: an *ornery* trick. **3.** Ordinary; common. [Alter. of ORDINARY] — **or′ner·i·ness** *n.*

ornitho- *combining form* Bird; of or relating to birds. Also, before vowels, **ornith-.** [< Gk. *ornis, onithos* bird]

or·ni·thol·o·gy (ôr′nə·thol′ə·jē) *n.* The branch of zoology that treats of birds. [< NL < Gk. *ornithologos* treating of birds] — **or′ni·tho·log′ic** (-thə·loj′ik) or **·i·cal** *adj.* — **or′· ni·tho·log′i·cal·ly** *adv.* — **or′ni·thol′o·gist** *n.*

oro-[1] *combining form* Mouth; oral: *oropharynx.* [< L *os, oris* mouth]

oro-[2] *combining form Geol.* Mountain; of mountains. [< Gk. *oros* mountain]

o·ro·tund (ôr′ə·tund, ō′rə-) *adj.* **1.** Full, clear, rounded, and resonant: said of the voice. **2.** Pompous; inflated, as a manner of speech. [< L < *os, oris* mouth + *rotundus* round] — **o·ro·tun·di·ty** (ôr′ə·tun′də·tē) *n.*

or·phan (ôr′fən) *n.* **1.** A child whose parents are dead; also, less commonly, a child with one surviving parent. **2.** A cast-off or waif. — *adj.* **1.** That is an orphan. **2.** Of or for orphans. — *v.t.* To make an orphan of. [< L < Gk. *orphanos* orphaned] — **or′phan·hood** (-hŏŏd) *n.*

or·phan·age (ôr′fən·ij) *n.* **1.** An institution for the care of orphans or other abandoned children. **2.** The condition of being an orphan; also, orphans collectively.

Or·phe·us (ôr′fē·əs) In Greek mythology, the son of a Muse, whose singing to the lyre could charm beasts and even rocks and trees. When his wife Eurydice died he was permitted to lead her back from Hades provided he did not turn to look at her until they had arrived in the upper world, but he did look back and she was lost. — **Or′phe·an** *adj.*

or·phic (ôr′fik) *adj. Sometimes cap.* Of a mystical nature; oracular. Also **or′phi·cal.** — **or′phi·cal·ly** *adv.*

Or·phic (ôr′fik) *adj.* **1.** Of, pertaining to, or associated with Orpheus. **2.** Having the quality of the music of Orpheus; enchanting. Also **Or′phi·cal.** [< L < Gk. < *Orpheus*]

or·pine (ôr′pin) *n.* Any of a large, widely distributed family

of plants including the sedums and houseleeks as the c mon or **garden orpine,** having succulent stems and lea and clusters of whitish flowers. Also **or′pin.**

Or·ping·ton (ôr′ping·tən) *n.* Any of a variety of large mestic fowls having single combs and unfeathered l [after *Orpington,* a village in Kent, England]

or·ris (ôr′is, or′-) *n.* Any of the several species of iris hav a scented root; esp. one whose dried rootstock is used medicine, as a perfume, etc. Also **or′rice.** [Prob. alter Ital. *ireos* < L *iris* iris]

ort (ôrt) *n. Usu. pl. Archaic* or *Dial.* A worthless scra leaving, as of food. [ME; ult. origin uncertain]

or·thi·con (ôr′thə·kon) *n.* A sensitive television cam tube using low-velocity electrons in scanning: also ca *image orthicon.* Also **or·thi·con·o·scope** (or′thi·kon′ə·sk

ortho- *combining form* **1.** Straight; upright; in line: or *dontics.* **2.** At right angles; perpendicular: *orthorhombic.* Correct; proper; right: *orthography.* **4.** *Med.* The correc of irregularities or deformities of: *orthopedics.* **5.** *Chen* Designating that one of a series of acids that is most f hydrated: *orthophosphoric* acid: distinguished from *meta* Noting a benzene derivative in which the substituted ar or radicals occupy adjoining positions. Also, before vow **orth-.** [< Gk. *orthos* straight]

or·tho·clase (ôr′thō·klās, -klāz) *n.* A brittle, vitreous, tassium-aluminum silicate of the feldspar group, a const ent of many igneous rocks: also called *potash feldspar.* ORTHO- + Gk. *klasis* fracture]

or·tho·don·tics (ôr′thə·don′tiks) *n.* The branch of dent ry concerned with the prevention and correction of irre larities of the teeth. Also **or′tho·don′tia** (-don′sha, -shē [< NL < Gk. *orthos* right, straight + *odous, odontos* too — **or′tho·don′tic** *adj.* — **or′tho·don′tist** *n.*

or·tho·dox (ôr′thə·doks) *adj.* **1.** Holding the commonly cepted or established faith, esp. in religion; correct or so in doctrine. **2.** Conforming to the Christian faith as re sented in the early ecumenical creeds. **3.** Adhering to ditional practice or belief. [< LL < Gk. < *orthos* right *doxa* opinion] — **or′tho·dox′ly** *adv.*

Or·tho·dox (ôr′thə·doks) *adj.* **1.** Of, belonging to, or ch acteristic of the Eastern Orthodox Church. **2.** Designat any of the bodies in this Church.

Orthodox Church The Eastern Orthodox Church.

Orthodox Judaism The branch of Judaism that accepts Mosaic Laws and their authoritative rabbinical interpr tions in the Talmud and elsewhere as binding for today

or·tho·dox·y (ôr′thə·dok′sē) *n. pl.* **·dox·ies** **1.** Ortho belief or practice; also, an instance of it. **2.** The quality condition of being orthodox. — **or′tho·dox′i·cal** *adj.*

or·thog·ra·phy (ôr·thog′rə·fē) *n. pl.* **·phies** **1.** A mod system of spelling, esp. of spelling correctly. **2.** The st dealing with letters and spelling. [< OF < L < Gk. < or *graphos*] — **or·thog′ra·pher, or·thog′ra·phist** *n.* — or **graph·ic** (ôr′thə·graf′ik), **or′tho·graph′i·cal** *adj.* — **or′ graph′i·cal·ly** *adv.*

or·tho·pe·dics (ôr′thə·pē′diks) *n.pl. (construed as si* The branch of surgery concerned with the correction of formities of the skeletal system. Also **or′tho·pae′dics, tho·pe·dy** (ôr′thə·pē′dē). [< F < Gk. *orthos* right + *deia* rearing of children] — **or′tho·pe′dic** *adj.* — **or′ pe′dist** *n.*

or·thop·ter·on (ôr·thop′tə·ron) *n.* An orthopterous ins

or·thop·ter·ous (ôr·thop′tər·əs) *adj.* Designating any o order of insects with membranous hind wings and leathe usually straight, fore wings, including locusts, crick grasshoppers, etc. [< NL < Gk. *orthos* straight + *pte* wing] — **or·thop′ter·an** *adj. & n.*

or·to·lan (ôr′tə·lən) *n.* A bunting of Europe, having olive-green head and a yellow throat. [< F < Provença Ital. < L *hortulus,* dim. of *hortus* garden]

-ory[1] *suffix of nouns* A place or instrument for (perform the action of the main element): *dormitory, lavatory.* [< *-oir, -oire.* See -ORY[2].]

-ory[2] *suffix of adjectives* Related to; like; resembling: *a tory, laudatory.* [< F *-oir, -oire,* or < L *-orius, -oria, -oriu*

o·ryx (ôr′iks, or′-, ō′riks) *n. pl.* **o·ryx·es** or **o·ryx** An several long-horned antelopes, such as the **Arabian oryx** a gemsbok. [< NL < L < Gk.]

os[1] (os) *n. pl.* **o·ra** (ôr′ə, ō′rə) *Anat.* A mouth or openi [< L]

os[2] (os) *n. pl.* **os·sa** (os′ə) *Anat.* A bone. [< L]

O·sage (ō′sāj) *n.* **1.** One of a tribe of North American dians of Siouan stock now living in Oklahoma. **2.** The l guage of this tribe. [< Siouan *Wazhazhe* war people]

Osage orange **1.** A showy tree of the mulberry family, tive to Arkansas and adjacent regions, widely used a hedge. **2.** Its orangelike fruit.

Os·car (os′kər) *n.* One of the gold statuettes awarded nually in the U.S. for outstanding achevements in mot pictures. [Origin uncertain]

os·cil·late (os′ə·lāt) *v.i.* **·lat·ed, ·lat·ing** **1.** To swing b d forth, as a pendulum. **2.** To fluctuate between various urses of action or thought; waver. [< L *oscillare* to ing] **— os'cil·la'tor** *n.*

cil·la·tion (os'ə-lā'shən) *n.* **1.** The act or state of oscil-ting. **2.** A single swing of an oscillating body. **3.** *Physics* periodic fluctuation between extreme values of a quantity force. **— os'cil·la·to'ry** (-lə-tôr'ē, -tō'rē) *adj.*

cil·lo·graph (ə-sil'ə-graf, -gräf) *n.* A device for record-g and measuring any oscillating system convertible into ave forms, as sound, light, heartbeats, etc.

cil·lo·scope (ə-sil'ə-skōp) *n.* Any of various electronic struments for projecting the forms of electromagnetic aves on the fluorescent screen of a cathode-ray tube.

cine (os'in, -īn) *adj.* Of or belonging to a suborder of rds, including those having the most highly developed vo-l ability, as thrushes, sparrows, etc. Also **os'ci·nine. —** *n.* n oscine bird. [< NL < L *oscen, oscinis* singing bird]

·co·Um·bri·an (os'kō-um'brē-ən) *n.* A branch of the alic subfamily of Indo-European languages.

cu·late (os'kyə-lāt) *v.t. & v.i.* **·lat·ed, ·lat·ing 1.** To kiss: ed humorously. **2.** To come into close contact or union. *Biol.* To have (characteristics) in common. [< L *osculari* kiss]

cu·la·tion (os'kyə-lā'shən) *n.* The act of kissing; also, kiss. **— os'cu·la·to'ry** (-lə-tôr'ē, -tō'rē) *adj.*

e[1] *suffix of adjectives* **1.** Full of or abounding in (the main ement): *verbose.* **2.** Like; resembling (the main element): *andiose.* Compare **-OUS.** [< L *-osus*]

e[2] *suffix Chem.* Indicating a sugar or other carbohydrate: *:lose, fructose.* [< (GLUC)OSE]

see (ō'zē, ō'sē) The Douai Bible name for HOSEA.

ier (ō'zhər) *n.* Any of various willows producing long, xible shoots used in wickerwork. [< OF]

si·ris (o·sī'ris) In Egyptian mythology, the god of the un-rworld and lord of the dead, husband of his sister Isis.

is *suffix of nouns* **1.** The condition, process, or state of: *:lamorphosis.* **2.** *Med.* **a** A diseased or abnormal condi-on of: *neurosis.* **b** A formation of: *sclerosis.* [< L < Gk. *sis*; or directly < Gk.]

ity *suffix of nouns* Forming nouns corresponding to ad-ctives in *-ose*: *verbosity.* [< F *-osité* < L *-ositas*; or directly L]

·man·li (oz·man'lē, os-) *n.* *pl.* **·lis 1.** An Ottoman Turk. The language of the Ottoman Turks; Turkish. *— adj.* **ttoman.** [< Turkish *Osman* Osman < Arabic *'Othmān*]

mi·rid·i·um (os'mə-rid'ē-əm, oz'-) *n.* A mixture of iridi-m and osmium that occurs naturally, used in pen points: al-called *iridosmine, iridosmium.* [< OSM(IUM) + IRIDIUM]

mi·um (oz'mē-əm, os'-) *n.* A hard, brittle, extremely :avy, metallic element (symbol Os) of the platinum oup. See ELEMENT. [< Gk. *osmē* odor]

mose (oz'mōs, os'-) *v.t. & v.i.* **·mosed, mos·ing** To sub-ct to or undergo osmosis.

mo·sis (oz·mō'sis, os-) *n.* *Chem.* **1.** The diffusion of a uid through a semipermeable membrane, resulting in equal-ation of the pressures on each side. **2.** The tendency of a uid to act in such a manner. Also **os'mose.** [< Gk. *ōsmos ōthein* to impel] **— os·mot·ic** (oz·mot'ik, os-) *adj.* **— os-ot'i·cal·ly** *adv.*

prey (os'prē) *n.* An American hawk, brown above and hite below, that preys upon fish: also called *fish hawk.* ME < L < *os, ossis* bone + *frangere* to break]

si- *combining form* Bone: *ossify.* [< L *os, ossis* bone]

·sian (osh'ən, os'ē·ən) *n.* A legendary Irish hero and bard the third century. **— Os·si·an·ic** (os'ē·an'ik) *adj.*

sif·er·ous (o·sif'ər·əs) *adj.* Yielding or containing bones. < L *os, ossi*(s) + -FEROUS]

si·fy (os'ə·fī) *v.t. & v.i.* **·fied, ·fy·ing 1.** To convert or be onverted into bone. **2.** To make or become rigid or inflexi-le in habits, beliefs, etc.; harden. [< L *os, ossis* + *facere* to ake] **— os·sif'ic** (o·sif'ik) *adj.* **— os'si·fi·ca'tion** *n.*

·te·al (os'tē·əl) *adj.* Of, pertaining to, or like bone; ony. [< Gk. *osteon* bone]

ten·si·ble (os·ten'sə·bəl) *adj.* Offered as real or genuine; pparent. [< F < L *ostendere* to show] **— os·ten'si·bly** *dv.*

·ten·sive (os·ten'siv) *adj.* Manifest; apparent; ostensible. **- os·ten'sive·ly** *adv.*

·ten·ta·tion (os'tən·tā'shən) *n.* **1.** The act of displaying ainly or pretentiously in order to excite admiration, awe, tc. **2.** Excessive or uncalled-for exhibition; showiness. [< F < L *ostendere* to show]

·ten·ta·tious (os'tən·tā'shəs) *adj.* **1.** Intended to at-act notice; showy. **2.** Marked by ostentation. **— os'ten-a'tious·ly** *adv.* **— os'ten·ta'tious·ness** *n.*

teo- *combining form* Bone; pertaining to bone or bones. lso, before vowels, **oste-.** [< Gk. *osteon* bone]

·te·ol·o·gy (os'tē·ol'ə·jē) *n.* The study of the skeleton and

of the structure of bones. **— os'te·o·log'i·cal** (-ə·loj'i·kəl) *adj.* **— os'te·ol'o·gist** *n.*

os·te·o·ma (os'tē·ō'mə) *n.* *pl.* **·o·mas** or **·o·ma·ta** (-ō'mə-tə) *Pathol.* A tumor of bony tissue. [< OSTE(O)- + -OMA]

os·te·o·my·e·li·tis (os'tē·ō·mī'ə·lī'tis) *n. Pathol.* Suppura-tive inflammation of the bone, sometimes involving the mar-row. [< OSTEO- + MYEL(O)- + -ITIS]

os·te·op·a·thy (os'tē·op'ə·thē) *n.* A system of healing based on the theory that most diseases are the result of structural abnormalities of the body and may be cured by manipulation of the affected parts. **— os'te·o·path'**, **os·te·op·a·thist** (os'-te·op'ə·thist) *n.* **— os'te·o·path·ic** (os'tē·ə·path'ik) *adj.*

Os·ti·a (os'tē·ə, *Ital.* ō'styä) An ancient port city of Rome.

ost·ler (os'lər) See HOSTLER.

os·tra·cism (os'trə·siz'əm) *n.* **1.** In ancient Greece, tem-porary banishment by popular vote. **2.** The act of ostraciz-ing or the state of being ostracized.

os·tra·cize (os'trə·sīz) *v.t.* **·cized, ·ciz·ing 1.** To shut out or exclude, as from society or from a particular group; banish. **2.** To exile by ostracism. Also *Brit.* **os'tra·cise.** [< Gk. *os-trakizein* < *ostrakon* potsherd, shell, voting tablet]

os·trich (ôs'trich, os'-) *n.* *pl.* **·trich·es** or **·trich 1.** A large, two-toed, flightless bird of Africa and Arabia, the largest of existing birds, having long, power-ful legs and a plumage highly valued for orna-mental purposes. **2.** A rhea. [< OF < LL < L *avis* bird + LL *struthio* ostrich]

Os·tro·goth (os'trə·goth) *n.* A member of the eastern branch of the Goths, who established a kingdom in Italy from 493 to 555. [< LL *Os-trogothi*] **— Os'tro·goth'ic** *adj.*

Os·ty·ak (os'tē·ak) *n.* **1.** One of a Finno-Ugric people inhabiting western Siberia and the Ural Mountains. **2.** The Ugric language of these people. Also **Os'ti·ak.**

Os·we·go tea (os·wē'gō) A species of mint with bright red flowers, found in the eastern U.S. [after *Oswego*, city in New York State]

ot- Var. of OTO-.

O·thel·lo (ō·thel'ō, ə-) In Shakespeare's play of this name, the hero, a Moor of Venice, whose jealousy, inspired by Iago, provokes him to kill his innocent wife Desdemona.

ostrich drawing label:
OSTRICH
(To about 8 feet high)

oth·er (uth'ər) *adj.* **1.** Different from the one or ones speci-fied or implied. **2.** Noting the remaining one of two persons or things: the *other* eye. **3.** Additional; more: Have you no *other* children? **4.** Alternate; second: every *other* day. **5.** Different: The truth is *other* than what you suppose. **6.** Former: in *other* times. *— pron.* **1.** Another or different person or thing. **2.** The other person or thing: this hand, not the *other.* *— adv.* Differently; otherwise: with *than.* [OE *ōther*] **— oth'er·ness** *n.*

oth·er·wise (uth'ər·wīz') *adv.* **1.** In a different manner; by other means. **2.** In other circumstances or conditions. **3.** In all other respects: an *otherwise* sensible person. *— adj.* **1.** Other than supposed; different: The facts are *otherwise.* **2.** Other: He could not be *otherwise* than proud.

other world A world peopled by the dead.

oth·er·world·ly (uth'ər·wûrld'lē) *adj.* Concerned with matters of the spirit or intellect, esp. to the neglect of ma-terial things. **— oth'er·world'li·ness** *n.*

Oth·man (oth'mən, *Arabic* ŏŏth·män') Ottoman.

-otic *suffix of adjectives* **1.** *Med.* Of, related to, or affected by: corresponding to nouns in *-osis*: *sclerotic.* **2.** Causing or producing: *narcotic.* [< Gk. *-ōtikos*, suffix of adjectives]

o·ti·ose (ō'shē·ōs, -tē-) *adj.* **1.** Being at rest; indolent; lazy. **2.** Having no use or effect; futile. [< L *otiosus* idle] **— o'ti·ose'ly** *adv.* **— o'ti·os'i·ty** (-os'ə·tē) *n.*

o·ti·tis (ō·tī'tis) *n. Pathol.* Inflammation of the ear. [< OT(O)- + -ITIS]

oto- *combining form* Ear; pertaining to the ear: *otology.* Also, before vowels, **ot-.** [< Gk. *ous, ōtos* ear]

o·tol·o·gy (ō·tol'ə·jē) *n.* The science of the ear and its dis-eases. **— o·to·log'i·cal** (ō'tə·loj'i·kəl) *adj.* **— o·tol'o·gist** *n.*

ot·ta·va (ŏt·tä'vä) *n. Ital.* An octave.

ottava ri·ma (rē'mä) In prosody, a stanza form of Italian origin consisting of eight lines in iambic pentameter and rhyming in the pattern *ababbcc.* [< Ital., octave rhyme]

Ot·ta·wa (ot'ə·wə) *n.* One of a tribe of North American In-dians of Algonquian stock, originally inhabiting the region around Georgian Bay, Lake Huron and Ontario. [< dial. F *otauan*; ult. < Algonquian. Akin to Cree *atāweu* a trader.]

ot·ter (ot'ər) *n.* **1.** Any of various web-footed mammals of aquatic habits, related to the weasel and having a long, flat-tened tail. **2.** Its valuable, dark brown fur. [OE *otor*]

ot·to·man (ot'ə·mən) *n.* **1.** An upholstered, armless seat or sofa, usu. without a back. **2.** A cushioned footrest. [< F *ottomane*, orig. fem. of *ottoman* Ottoman]

Ot·to·man (ot/ə·mən) *n. pl.* **·mans** A Turk: also *Othman.*
— *adj.* Of or pertaining to the Turks. [< F < Ital. *Otto-mano* < Med.L *Ottomanus* < Arabic *'Othmāni* of Osman]

Ottoman Empire A former empire (1300–1919) of the Turks in Asia Minor, NE Africa, and SE Europe; capital, Constantinople: also *Turkish Empire.*

ouch (ouch) *interj.* An exclamation of sudden pain.

ought[1] (ôt) *v. Present 3rd person sing.* **ought** An auxiliary followed by the infinitive with *to* expressed or understood, meaning: **1.** To have a moral duty: A person *ought* to keep his promises. **2.** To be advisable: You *ought* to be careful. **3.** To be expected as something probable, natural, or logical: The engine *ought* to run. ◆ A past is formed by placing the following verb in the perfect infinitive, as in *He ought to have been there.* [OE past tense of *āgan* to owe]

ought[2] (ôt) See AUGHT[1].

ought[3] (ôt) See AUGHT[2].

oui (wē) *adv. French* Yes.

oui·ja (wē/jə) *n.* A device consisting of a large board inscribed with the alphabet and other characters and over which moves a small rectangular board resting on three legs, the pointer of which is thought to spell out mediumistic communications. [< F *oui* yes + G *ja* yes]

ounce (ouns) *n.* **1.** A unit of weight; one sixteenth of a pound avoirdupois, or 28.349 grams; one twelfth of a pound troy, or 31.1 grams. See table front of book. **2.** A fluid ounce. **3.** A small quantity. [< OF < L *uncia* twelfth part (of a pound or foot)]

our (our) *pronominal adj.* The possessive case of the pronoun *we,* used attributively: *our* child. [OE *ūre,* gen. of *wē*]

ours (ourz) *pron.* **1.** The possessive case of the pronoun *we,* used predicatively: That dog is *ours.* **2.** The one or ones belonging or relating to us: their country and *ours.* — **of ours** Belonging or relating to us: a double possessive.

our·self (our·self/) *pron.* Myself or ourselves, considered collectively: used in formal or regal contexts.

our·selves (our·selvz/) *pron.pl.* A form of the first person plural pronoun, used: **1.** As a reflexive: We helped *ourselves.* **2.** As an emphatic or intensive form of *we:* We *ourselves* want to know. **3.** As a designation of a normal, proper, or usual state: We weren't *ourselves* then.

-ous *suffix of adjectives* **1.** Full of, having, given to, like: *joyous, glorious.* **2.** *Chem.* Having a lower valence than that indicated by *-ic:* said of elements in compounds: *nitrous* oxide. [< OF < L *-osus*]

ou·sel (ōō/zəl) See OUZEL.

oust (oust) *v.t.* To force out or remove, as from a place or position. [< AF < LL < ob- against + *stare* to stand]

oust·er (ous/tər) *n.* **1.** The act or condition of ousting. **2.** One who ousts. **3.** *Law* The act of putting one out of possession or occupancy of real property to which he is legally entitled; wrongful dispossession.

out (out) *adv.* **1.** Away from the inside or center: to branch *out.* **2.** In or into the open air: to go *out.* **3.** Away from a specified or usual place, as from one's home or place of business: *out* to lunch. **4.** From a receptacle or source: to pour *out* wine. **5.** From among others: to pick *out.* **6.** So as to remove, deplete, or exhaust: to sweep *out;* to dry *out.* **7.** Thoroughly: tired *out.* **8.** Into extinction or inactivity: The flame went *out;* The excitement died *out.* **9.** To a conclusion; to the end: Hear me *out.* **10.** Into being or activity, or into a state manifest to the senses: An epidemic broke *out.*

out- *combining form* **1.** Living or situated outside; away from the center; detached: *outlying, outpatient.* **2.** Going forth; outward: *outbound, outstretch.* **3.** Denoting the time, place, or result of the action expressed by the root verb: *outcome, outcry.* **4.** To a greater extent; more; better. *Out* is widely used to form compounds.

out-and-out (out/ənd-out/) *adj.* Unqualified; outright.

out·bid (out·bid/) *v.t.* **·bid, ·bid·den** or **·bid, ·bid·ding** To bid more than; offer a higher bid than: also *overbid.*

out·board (out/bôrd/, -bōrd/) *adj. & adv. Naut.* **1.** Outside the hull. **2.** Away from the center line of a vessel.

outboard motor A portable gasoline or electric motor for temporary attachment to the stern of a small boat.

out·bound (out/bound/) *adj.* Outward bound.

out·break (out/brāk/) *n.* A sudden bursting forth, as of an emotion or a disease; an eruption.

out·build·ing (out/bil/ding) *n.* A building separate from and subordinate to a main building, as a woodshed or barn: also called *outhouse.*

out·burst (out/bûrst/) *n.* A bursting out; esp., a sudden and violent display, as of anger.

out·cast (out/kast/, -käst/) *n.* **1.** One who is cast out or excluded. **2.** A homeless person or vagabond. **3.** Anything cast out, as refuse. — *adj.* Rejected; discarded; forlorn.

out·class (out·klas/, -kläs/) *v.t.* To surpass decisively.

out·come (out/kum/) *n.* Consequence or result.

out crop (*n.* out/krop/; *v.* out·krop/) *Geol. n.* **1.** The exposure at or above the surface of the ground of any rock stra-

tum, vein, etc. **2.** The rock so exposed. — *v.i.* **·crop ·crop·ping** To crop out above the ground, as rocks.

out·cry (*n.* out/krī/; *v.* out·krī/) *n. pl.* **·cries 1.** A loud or clamor. **2.** A vehement outburst of alarm, indigna etc. — *v.t.* **·cried, ·cry·ing** To surpass in noise or cryi

out·date (out·dāt/) *v.t.* **·dat·ed, ·dat·ing** To make obsc or out-of-date.

out·dat·ed (out·dā/tid) *adj.* Out-of-date; old-fashione

out·dis·tance (out·dis/təns) *v.t.* **·tanced, ·tanc·ing 1.** outrun, as in a race; outstrip. **2.** To surpass complete

out·do (out·dōō/) *v.t.* **·did, ·done, ·do·ing** To exceed in formance; surpass. — **out·do/er** *n.*

out·done (out·dun/) *adj. U.S. Dial.* Provoked; exaspera

out·door (out/dôr/, -dōr/) *adj.* **1.** Being or done in the c air. **2.** Intended for the outdoors. Also *out-of-door.*

out·doors (out·dôrz/, -dōrz/) *adv.* Outside of the house the open air. — *n.* The world beyond the house; the c air. Also *out-of-doors.*

out·er (ou/tər) *adj.* **1.** Being on the exterior side. **2.** ther from a center or from something regarded as the ins

out·er·most (ou/tər·mōst) *adj.* Most remote from the side or inner part; farthest out.

outer space The space beyond the extreme limits of earth's atmosphere; interplanetary and interstellar spac

out·face (out·fās/) *v.t.* **·faced, ·fac·ing 1.** To face or s down. **2.** To defy or confront fearlessly or impudently

out·field (out/fēld/) *n.* In baseball: **a** The space beyond infield. **b** The outfielders collectively.

out·field·er (out/fēl/dər) *n.* In baseball, any of three pla whose positions are in the outfield.

out·fit (out/fit/) *n.* **1.** The tools or equipment needed any particular purpose, as a trade, etc. **2.** *U.S. Inform* group of persons regarded as a unit; esp., a military unit. *U.S. Informal* A set of clothing. — *v.t. & v.i.* **·fit·ted, ·fit·** To provide with or acquire an outfit. — **out/fit/ter** *n.*

out·flank (out·flangk/) *v.t.* To get around and in back of flank of (an opposing force or army); flank.

out·flow (out/flō/) *n.* **1.** That which flows out. **2.** The or process of flowing out.

out·fox (out·foks/) *v.t. U.S. Informal* To outwit.

out·go (*v.* out·gō/; *n.* out/gō/) *v.t.* **·went, ·gone, ·go·ing** go farther than; exceed. — *n. pl.* **·goes 1.** That wh goes out; outlay. **2.** The act of going out. — **out/go/e**

out·go·ing (out/gō/ing) *adj.* **1.** Going out; leaving. **2.** Friendly; expansive. — *n.* The act of going out.

out·group (out/grōōp/) *n. Sociol.* Those not in an ,n-gr

out·grow (out·grō/) *v.t.* **·grew, ·grown, ·grow·ing 1.** grow too large for. **2.** To lose or get rid of in the cours time or growth: to *outgrow* a habit. **3.** To surpass in grow

out·growth (out/grōth/) *n.* **1.** That which grows ou something else; an excrescence. **2.** A natural result or de opment. **3.** The process of growing out.

out·house (out/hous/) *n.* **1.** An outdoor privy or toilet. An outbuilding.

out·ing (ou/ting) *n.* **1.** A short pleasure trip; an excurs **2.** The act of going out; an airing.

out·land·er (out/lan/dər) *n.* **1.** A foreigner. **2.** A stran

out·land·ish (out·lan/dish) *adj.* **1.** Strange or unfamil as in appearance or manners. **2.** *Informal* Freakish; cr **3.** Far-off; remote. [OE *ūtland*] — **out·land/ish·ly** *adv.* **out·land/ish·ness** *n.*

out·last (out·last/, -läst/) *v.t.* To last longer than.

out·law (out/lô/) *n.* **1.** One who habitually breaks or de the law; a criminal. **2.** A person deprived of the protec or benefit of the law. — *v.t.* **1.** To prohibit; ban. **2.** deprive of legal force or protection, as a contract. **3.** To clare an outlaw. [OE < ON *ūtlagi*] — **out/law/ry** *n.*

out·lay (*n.* out/lā/; *v.* out·lā/) *n.* **1.** The act of disbursin spending. **2.** The amount spent; expenditure. — *v.t.* **·lay·ing** To expend (money, etc.).

out·let (out/let) *n.* **1.** A passage or vent for escape or charge. **2.** A channel of expression or escape: an *outlet* creative energy. **3.** In commerce, a market for any co modity; also, a store handling the goods of a particular m ufacturer. **4.** *Electr.* The point in a wiring system at wh the current is taken to supply electrical apparatus.

out·line (out/līn/) *n. Sometimes pl.* A preliminary ske showing the principal features of a thing; general plan. A systematic statement of the structure or content of an say, etc. **3.** The bordering line that serves to define a figu **4.** A sketch made only of such lines. — *v.t.* **·lined, ·lin 1.** To make or give an outline of. **2.** To draw the outline

out·live (out·liv/) *v.t.* **·lived, ·liv·ing 1.** To live longer th (another). **2.** To live through; survive.

out·look (out/lŏŏk/) *n.* **1.** A point of view. **2.** The prosp of a thing. **3.** A place where something is viewed. **4.** expanse in view. **5.** The act of looking out.

out·man (out·man/) *v.t.* **·manned, ·man·ning 1.** To surp in number of men. **2.** To excel in manliness.

out·mo·ded (out·mō/did) *adj.* Out of fashion.

most (out'mōst') *adj.* Farthest out; outermost.

-of-date (out'əv-dāt') *adj.* Old-fashioned; archaic.

-of-door (out'əv-dôr', -dōr') *adj.* Outdoor.

-of-doors (out'əv-thə-mä') *adv. & n.* Outdoors.

-of-the-way (out'əv-thə-wä') *adj.* **1.** Remote; difficult reach; secluded. **2.** Out of the common range; odd.

-pa·tient (out'pā'shənt) *n.* A patient treated at but not mally admitted to a hospital, dispensary, etc.

-play (out-plā') *v.t.* To play better than; defeat.

-point (out-point') *v.t.* **1.** To score more points than. **2.** *ut.* To sail closer to the wind than.

-post (out'pōst') *n.* **1.** A detachment of troops stationed a distance from the main body as a guard against surprise ack. **2.** The station occupied by such troops. **3.** Any *:*lying settlement, as at a frontier.

-pour (*v.* out-pôr', -pōr'; *n.* out'pôr', -pōr') *v.t. & v.i.* To *ur* out. — *n.* A free outflow. — **out'pour'er** *n.*

-put (out'pŏot') *n.* **1.** The amount of anything produced *a* given time, as by a mine, factory, mill, etc. **2.** The effective work done by a machine. **3.** *Electr.* The electrical rgy delivered by a generator, circuit, amplifier, etc.

-rage (*n.* out'rāj'; *v.* out-rāj') *n.* **1.** An act of shocking *:*lence or cruelty. **2.** A gross violation of morality or decy. **3.** A profound insult or injury. — *v.t.* **·raged, ·rag·** **1.** To commit an outrage upon. **2.** To subject to an *:*rage. **3.** To rape. [ME < OF ult. < L *ultra* beyond] — **Syn.** (noun) **1.** crime, atrocity. — (verb) See OFFEND.

·ra·geous (out-rā'jəs) *adj.* **1.** Of the nature of an outrage; awful; atrocious. **2.** Heedless of authority or decency. — **out·ra'geous·ly** *adv.* — **out·ra'geous·ness** *n.*

tré (ōō-trā') *adj. French* Strikingly odd; exaggerated.

·reach (*v.* out-rēch'; *n.* out'rēch') *v.t.* **1.** To reach or go *:*ond; surpass. **2.** To extend (something). — *v.i.* **3.** To *:*ch out. — *n.* The act or extent of reaching out.

·ride (out-rīd') *v.t.* **·rode, ·rid·den, ·rid·ing** To ride fastfarther, or better than.

·rid·er (out'rī'dər) *n.* A mounted attendant who rides in *:*vance or to one side of a carriage.

·rig·ger (out'rig'ər) *n.* **1.** A part built or arranged to *:*ject beyond a natural outline, as of a vessel or machine. A projecting contrivance terminating in a boatlike float, *:*ced to the side of a canoe to prevent capsizing. **3.** A *:*cket projecting from the side of a narrow rowboat, and *:*vided with a rowlock for an oar; also, a boat so equipped.

·right (*adj.* out'rīt'; *adv.* out'rīt') *adj.* **1.** Free from re*:*ve or restraint; downright. **2.** Complete; entire. **3.** Going straight on. — *adv.* **1.** Without reservation or limita*:*n; openly. **2.** Entirely; utterly. **3.** Without delay.

·sell (out-sel') *v.t.* **·sold, ·sell·ing** **1.** To sell more readily for a higher price than. **2.** To sell more goods than.

·set (out'set') *n.* A setting out; beginning.

·shine (out-shīn') *v.* **·shone, ·shin·ing** *v.t.* **1.** To shine *:*ghter than. **2.** To surpass. — *v.i.* **3.** To shine forth.

·side (*n., adj., & adv.* out'sīd'; *prep.* out'sīd') *n.* **1.** The *:*ter or exterior surface or side. **2.** The space beyond a *:*unding line or surface. **3.** The part that is seen; outward *:*pearance. **4.** Something empty of significance or sub*:*nce; mere outward display. — **at the outside** *Informal* *:* the farthest, longest, or most. — *adj.* **1.** Pertaining to, *:*ated on, or restricted to the outside. **2.** Originating, *:*used by, or situated beyond designated limits.

·sid·er (out'sī'dər) *n.* One who is outside or excluded. — **Syn.** stranger, alien, foreigner.

·size (out'sīz') *n.* An irregular size, as of clothing; esp., uncommonly large size. — *adj.* Being of an outsize: also *t'sized'.*

·skirts (out'skûrts') *n.pl.* A place remote from the main central area; an outlying district.

t·smart (out-smärt') *v.t. Informal* To outwit; fool.

·spo·ken (out'spō'kən) *adj.* **1.** Bold or free in speech; *:*ank. **2.** Spoken boldly or frankly. · **out'spo'ken·ly** *adv.* · **out'spo'ken·ness** *n.*

·spread (*v.* out-spred'; *n.* out'spred') *v.t. & v.i.* **·spread,** **·read·ing** To spread out; extend. — *n.* The act of spread*:* out.

t·stand·ing (out-stan'ding) *adj.* **1.** Prominent; excel*:*nt. **2.** Still standing or unsettled, as a debt. **3.** Project*:*; abutting.

·stretch (out-strech') *v.t.* **1.** To stretch out; expand. *:*tend. **2.** To extend beyond.

·strip (out-strip') *v.t.* **·stripped, ·strip·ping** **1.** To leave *:*hind; outrun. **2.** To excel; surpass.

·ward (out'wərd) *adj.* **1.** Of or pertaining to the out*:*de; external. **2.** Relating to the physical as distinguished *:*m the mental or spiritual aspect. **3.** Readily apparent, *:*p. to sight: no *outward* sign of trouble. **4.** Superficially evi*:*nt: *outward* display of wealth. **5.** Not inherent; extrinsic:

outward grace. — *adv.* **1.** In an outward direction. **2.** In an outward manner. **3.** Away from a place regarded as central, as home. [OE *ūtweard*] — **out'ward·ness** *n.*

out·ward·ly (out'wərd-lē) *adv.* **1.** On or toward the outside. **2.** In outward form or aspect; seemingly.

out·wards (out'wərdz) *adv.* Outward.

out·wear (out-wâr') *v.t.* **·wore, ·worn, ·wear·ing** **1.** To wear or stand use longer than; outlast. **2.** To wear out.

out·weigh (out-wā') *v.t.* **1.** To weigh more than. **2.** To exceed in importance, value, etc.

out·wit (out-wit') *v.t.* **·wit·ted, ·wit·ting** To trick or baffle by superior ingenuity or cunning.

out·work¹ (out-wûrk') *v.t.* **·worked** or **·wrought, ·work·ing** To work faster or better than.

out·work² (out'wûrk') *n. Mil.* Any outer defense, as beyond the ditch of a fort.

out·worn (out-wôrn') Past participle of OUTWEAR.

ou·zel (ōō'zəl) *n.* **1.** One of various European thrushes, as the blackbird. **2.** The water ouzel. Also spelled *ousel.* [OE *ōsle*]

o·va (ō'və) Plural of OVUM.

o·val (ō'vəl) *adj.* **1.** Having the shape of an egg. **2.** Resembling an ellipse. — *n.* An oval shape or figure. [< MF < L *ovum* egg] — **o'val·ly** *adv.* — **o'val·ness** *n.*

o·va·ry (ō'və-rē) *n. pl.* **·ries** **1.** *Zool.* The genital gland of female animals in which the ova are produced. **2.** *Bot.* In plants, that organ in which the ovules are contained. For illus. see FLOWER. [< NL < L *ovum* egg] — **o·var'i·an,** **o·var'i·al** *adj.*

o·vate (ō'vāt) *adj. Bot.* Egg-shaped: said of leaves. [< L *ovum*] — **o'vate·ly** *adv.*

o·va·tion (ō-vā'shən) *n.* A spontaneous acclamation of popularity; enthusiastic applause. [< L *ovare* to rejoice, exult] — **o·va'tion·al** *adj.*

ov·en (uv'ən) *n.* An enclosed chamber in which substances are heated in order to cook or dry them. [OE *ofen*]

ov·en·bird (uv'ən-bûrd') *n.* A North American warbler with an olive-colored back and a golden crown, having a grassy nest suggesting an oven.

o·ver (ō'vər) *prep.* **1.** In or to a place or position above; higher than. **2.** So as to pass or extend across: walking *over* the bridge. **3.** On the other side of: lying *over* the ocean. **4.** Upon the surface or exterior of. **5.** Here and there upon or within; throughout all parts of: traveling *over* land and sea. **6.** At or up to a level higher than: The mud is *over* my boots. **7.** So as to close or cover: Put the lid *over* the jar.

over- *combining form* **1.** Above; superior: *overlord.* **2.** Passing above; going beyond the top or limit of: *overflow.* **3.** Moving or causing to move downward, as from above: *overturn.* **4.** Excessively; excessive; too much: *overcharge.* *Over-* is widely used to form compounds.

o·ver·act (ō'vər-akt') *v.t. & v.i.* To act with exaggeration.

o·ver·age¹ (ō'vər-ij) *n.* In commerce, an amount of money or goods in excess of that which is listed as being on hand.

o·ver·age² (ō'vər-āj') *adj.* **1.** Over the usual or specified age. **2.** Too old to be of use: *overage* guns.

o·ver·all (ō'vər-ôl') *adj.* **1.** From one end to the other. **2.** Including or covering everything.

o·ver·alls (ō'vər-ôlz') *n.pl.* Loose, coarse trousers, often with suspenders and a piece extending over the breast, worn over the clothing as protection against soiling and wear.

o·ver·arm (ō'vər-ärm') *adj.* Done with the arm above the level of the shoulder, as a swimming stroke.

o·ver·awe (ō'vər-ô') *v.t.* **·awed, ·aw·ing** To subdue or restrain by awe.

o·ver·bal·ance (ō'vər-bal'əns) *v.* **·anced, ·anc·ing** *v.t.* **1.** To exceed in weight, importance, etc. **2.** To cause to lose balance. — *v.i.* **3.** To lose one's balance. — *n.* Excess of weight or value.

o·ver·bear (ō'vər-bâr') *v.* **·bore, borne, ·bear·ing** *v.t.* **1.** To crush or bear down by physical weight or force. **2.** To prevail over; domineer. — *v.i.* **3.** To be too fruitful.

o·ver·bear·ing (ō'vər-bâr'ing) *adj.* **1.** Arrogant; domineering. **2.** Overwhelming. — **o·ver·bear'ing·ly** *adv.*

o·ver·bid (ō'vər-bid') *v.t. & v.i.* **·bid, ·bid·den** or **·bid, ·bid·ding** **1.** To bid more than the value of (something). **2.** To outbid (someone).

o·ver·blown (ō'vər-blōn') *adj.* **1.** Blown up or swollen, as with conceit or pretentiousness; inflated; bombastic. **2.** Past full bloom, as a flower.

o·ver·board (ō'vər-bôrd', -bōrd') *adv.* Over the side of or out of a boat or ship. — **to go overboard** *U.S. Informal* To be extremely enthusiastic about someone or something.

o·ver·bur·den (ō'vər-bûr'dən) *v.t.* To load with too much weight, care, etc. — *n.* That which overburdens.

o·ver·cap·i·tal·ize (ō'vər-kap'i·təl·īz') *v.t.* **·ized, ·iz·ing** **1.** To invest capital in to an extent not warranted by actual prospects. **2.** To affix an unjustifiable or unlawful value to the nominal capital of (a corporation). **3.** To estimate the value of (a property, company, etc.) too highly. — o′ver·cap′i·tal·i·za′tion *n.*

o·ver·cast (ō′vər·kast′, -käst′; *for v. defs. 1, 2, & 4, also* ō′vər·kast′, -käst′) *adj.* **1.** Covered or obscured, as with clouds. **2.** Gloomy; melancholy. **3.** Sewn with long wrapping stitches to prevent raveling. — *n.* **1.** A covering or mantle, as of clouds. **2.** *Meteorol.* A cloud or clouds covering more than nine-tenths of the sky. — *v.* ·cast, ·cast·ing *v.t.* **1.** To make overcast. **2.** To cast beyond. **3.** To sew with an overcast stitch. — *v.i.* **4.** To become overcast.

o·ver·charge (*v.* ō′vər·chärj′; *n.* ō′vər·chärj′) *v.t.* ·charged, ·charg·ing **1.** To charge (someone) too high a price. **2.** To overburden. **3.** To overdo. — *n.* An excessive charge.

o·ver·cloud (ō′vər·kloud′) *v.t.* **1.** To cover with clouds; darken. **2.** To make gloomy. — *v.i.* **3.** To become cloudy.

o·ver·coat (ō′vər·kōt′) *n.* An outdoor coat worn over a suit, etc., esp. in cold weather.

o·ver·come (ō′vər·kum′) *v.t.* ·came, ·come, ·com·ing **1.** To get the better of in any conflict or struggle; defeat; conquer. **2.** To prevail over or surmount, as difficulties, obstacles, etc. **3.** To render (someone) helpless, as by emotion, sickness etc. — *v.i.* **4.** To gain mastery; win. [OE *ofercuman*]

o·ver·com·pen·sa·tion (ō′vər·kom′pən·sā′shən) *n.* *Psychol.* Excessive or abnormal reaction, esp. to compensate for the fact or feeling of inferiority.

o·ver·de·vel·op (ō′vər·di·vel′əp) *v.t.* **1.** To develop excessively. **2.** *Photog.* To develop (a plate or film) to too great a degree. — o′ver·de·vel′op·ment *n.*

o·ver·do (ō′vər·dōō′) *v.* ·did, ·done, ·do·ing *v.t.* **1.** To do excessively; exaggerate. **2.** To overtax the strength of; exhaust. **3.** To cook too much, as meat. [OE *oferdōn*]

o·ver·dose (*v.* ō′vər·dōs′; *n.* ō′vər·dōs′) *v.t.* ·dosed, ·dos·ing To dose to excess. — *n.* An excessive dose.

o·ver·draft (ō′vər·draft′, -dräft′) *n.* **1.** The act of overdrawing an account, as at a bank. **2.** The amount by which an account is overdrawn. Also o′ver·draught′.

o·ver·draw (ō′vər·drô′) *v.t.* ·drew, ·drawn, ·draw·ing **1.** To draw against (an account) beyond one's credit. **2.** To draw or strain excessively, as a bow. **3.** To exaggerate.

o·ver·drive (*v.* ō′vər·drīv′; *n.* ō′vər·drīv′) *v.t.* ·drove, ·driv·en, ·driv·ing To drive too hard or too far. — *n.* *Mech.* A gearing device that turns a drive shaft at a speed greater than that of the engine, thus decreasing power output.

o·ver·due (ō′vər·dōō′, -dyōō′) *adj.* **1.** Remaining unpaid after becoming due. **2.** Past due: an *overdue* plane or train.

o·ver·eat (ō′vər·ēt′) *v.i.* ·ate (-āt′, *Brit.* -et′) or *Archaic* ·eat (-et′, -ēt′), ·eat·en, ·eat·ing To eat to excess.

o·ver·es·ti·mate (*v.* ō′vər·es′tə·māt; *n.* ō′vər·es′tə·mit) *v.t.* ·mat·ed, ·mat·ing To value or estimate too highly. — *n.* An estimate that is too high. — o′ver·es′ti·ma′tion *n.*

o·ver·ex·pose (ō′vər·ik·spōz′) *v.t.* ·posed, ·pos·ing **1.** To expose excessively. **2.** *Photog.* To expose (a film or plate) too long. — o′ver·ex·po′sure (-spō′zhər) *n.*

o·ver·flow (*v.* ō′vər·flō′; *n.* ō′vər·flō′) *v.* ·flowed, ·flown, ·flow·ing *v.i.* **1.** To flow or run over the brim or bank, as water, rivers, etc. **2.** To be filled beyond capacity; superabound. — *v.t.* **3.** To flow over the brim or bank of. **4.** To flow or spread over; cover; flood. **5.** To cause to overflow. — *n.* **1.** The act or process of overflowing. **2.** That which flows over. **3.** The amount by which a capacity is exceeded; surplus. **4.** An outlet for liquid. [OE *oferflōwan*]

o·ver·grow (ō′vər·grō′) *v.* ·grew, ·grown, ·grow·ing *v.t.* **1.** To grow over; cover with growth. **2.** To grow too big for; outgrow. — *v.i.* **3.** To increase excessively; grow too large.

o·ver·hand (ō′vər·hand′) *adj.* **1.** In baseball, etc., executed with the hand above the level of the elbow or the shoulder. Also o′ver·hand′ed (-han′did). **2.** In sewing, made by carrying the thread over both edges, as a seam. — *adv.* In an overhand manner. — *n.* **1.** An overhand stroke or delivery, as in tennis. **2.** A kind of knot. For illus. see KNOT[1].

o·ver·hang (ō′vər·hang′) *v.* ·hung (-hung′), ·hang·ing *v.t.* **1.** To hang or project over (something); jut over. **2.** To threaten; menace. **3.** To adorn with hangings. — *v.i.* **4.** To hang or jut over something. — *n.* An overhanging portion of a structure; also, the amount of such projection.

o·ver·haul (*v.* ō′vər·hôl′; *n.* ō′vər·hôl′) *v.t.* **1.** To examine carefully for needed repairs. **2.** To make all needed repairs in; renovate. **3.** To catch up with; gain on. — *n.* A thorough inspection and repair. Also o′ver·haul′ing.

o·ver·head (*adj. & n.* ō′vər·hed′; *adv.* ō′vər·hed′) *adj.* **1.** Situated or working above the level of one's head: an *overhead* light. **2.** Of or relating to the overhead of a business. — *n.* The operating expenses of a business, as rent, light, heat, taxes, etc. — *adv.* Over or above the head.

o·ver·hear (ō′vər·hir′) *v.t.* ·heard (-hûrd′), ·hear·ing To hear (something said or someone speaking) without the knowledge or intention of the speaker. — o′ver·hear′er *n.*

o·ver·joy (ō′vər·joi′) *v.t.* To delight or please greatly.

o·ver·kill (ō′vər·kil′) *n.* The military capacity for dest tion far beyond the resources and population of an ene

o·ver·land (ō′vər·land′) *adj.* Proceeding over or acc plished by land. — *adv.* Across, over, or via land.

o·ver·lap (*v.* ō′vər·lap′; *n.* ō′vər·lap′) *v.t. & v.i.* ·lap ·lap·ping **1.** To lie or extend partly over or upon (anothe each other); lap over. **2.** To cover and project bey (something). — *n.* **1.** The state or extent of overlapp **2.** The part that overlaps.

o·ver·lay (*v.* ō′vər·lā′; *n.* ō′vər·lā′) *v.t.* ·laid, ·lay·ing **1.** spread something over, as with a decorative pattern or la **2.** To lay or place over or upon something else. **3.** To o burden. — *n.* **1.** *Printing* A piece of paper placed on tympan of a press to make the impression heavier or to c pensate for a depression. **2.** Anything that covers or pa covers something. **3.** An ornamental layer, as veneer, plied to wood, etc. **4.** A transparent sheet laid over a r to add or emphasize certain features.

o·ver·leaf (ō′vər·lēf′) *adv.* On the other side of a page.

o·ver·leap (ō′vər·lēp′) *v.t.* ·leaped or ·leapt, ·leap·ing **1.** leap over or across. **2.** To omit; overlook. **3.** To leap ther than; outleap. — **to overleap oneself** To miss o purpose by going too far. [OE *oferhlēapan*]

o·ver·lie (ō′vər·lī′) *v.t.* ·lay (-lā′), ·lain (-lān′), ·ly·ing **1.** lie over or upon. **2.** To suffocate by lying upon.

o·ver·load (*v.* ō′vər·lōd′; *n.* ō′vər·lōd′) *v.t.* To load ex sively; overburden. — *n.* **1.** An excessive burden. **2.** *El* An amperage in excess of that which can be safely carrie

o·ver·look (*v.* ō′vər·lŏŏk′; *n.* ō′vər·lŏŏk′) *v.t.* **1.** To fai see or notice; miss. **2.** To disregard purposely or indulge ly; ignore. **3.** To look over or see from a higher place. To afford a view of: The castle *overlooks* the harbor. **5.** supervise; oversee. **6.** To examine or inspect. — *n.* The act of looking over, as from a height; an inspection; s vey. **2.** An elevated place affording a view.

o·ver·lord (ō′vər·lôrd′) *n.* **1.** A superior lord or chief. One who holds supremacy over others. — o′ver·lord′shi

o·ver·ly (ō′vər·lē) *adv.* *Chiefly U.S.* To an excessive degr too much; too.

o·ver·man (ō′vər·man′) *v.t.* ·manned, ·man·ning To p vide with more men than necessary.

o·ver·mas·ter (ō′vər·mas′tər, -mäs′-) *v.t.* To overcor overpower. — o′ver·mas′ter·ing *n. & adj.*

o·ver·match (*v.* ō′vər·mach′; *n.* ō′vər·mach′) *v.t.* To be m than a match for; surpass. — *n.* One who or that whic superior in strength, skill, etc.

o·ver·much (ō′vər·much′) *adj.* Excessive; too much. *adv.* In too great a degree. — *n.* An excess; too much.

o·ver·night (*adj. & adv.* ō′vər·nīt′) *adj.* **1.** Done dur the previous evening; lasting all night. **2.** Away from ho for one night: *overnight* trip. **3.** Used for nighttime use or for short visits: an *overnight* bag. — *adv.* **1.** During through the night. **2.** On the previous evening.

o·ver·pass (*n.* ō′vər·pas′, -päs′; *v.* ō′vər·pas′, -päs′) *n.* elevated section of highway crossing other lines of travel. *v.t.* **1.** To pass over, across, or through; cross. **2.** To s pass. **3.** To overlook. **4.** To transgress.

o·ver·play (ō′vər·plā′) *v.t.* **1.** To play or act (a part or r to excess. **2.** To rely too much on the strength or value **3.** In golf, to send (the ball) beyond the putting green.

o·ver·pow·er (ō′vər·pou′ər) *v.t.* **1.** To gain suprema over; subdue. **2.** To render wholly helpless or ineffecti overcome. **3.** To supply with more power than necessa

o·ver·pow·er·ing (ō′vər·pou′ər·ing) *adj.* **1.** That ov powers. **2.** Intense. — o′ver·pow′er·ing·ly *adv.*

o·ver·print (*v.* ō′vər·print′; *n.* ō′vər·print′) *v.t.* To print ditional material of another color on (sheets already printe — *n.* Any word, symbol, etc., printed on a postage star changing its value or use.

o·ver·pro·duce (ō′vər·prə·dōōs′, -dyōōs′) *v.t.* ·duced, · ing To produce too much of or so as to exceed demand.

o·ver·pro·duc·tion (ō′vər·prə·duk′shən) *n.* Production excess of demand, or of the possibility of profitable sale.

o·ver·rate (ō′vər·rāt′) *v.t.* ·rat·ed, ·rat·ing To rate or va too highly; credit with undue merit; overestimate.

o·ver·reach (ō′vər·rēch′) *v.t.* **1.** To reach over or beyo **2.** To spread over; cover. **3.** To defeat (oneself), as by tempting something beyond one's capability. **4.** To miss stretching or reaching too far. **5.** To outwit; cheat. — **6.** To reach too far. **7.** To cheat. — o′ver·reach′er *n.*

o·ver·ride (ō′vər·rīd′) *v.t.* ·rode (-rōd′), ·rid·den (-rid′ı ·rid·ing **1.** To disregard summarily, as if trampling dov supersede. **2.** To ride (a horse, etc.) to exhaustion. **3.** ride over. **4.** To trample down; suppress.

o·ver·rule (ō′vər·rōōl′) *v.t.* ·ruled, ·rul·ing **1.** To dec against or nullify; set aside; invalidate. **2.** To disallow arguments of (someone). **3.** To have control over; rule. To prevail over.

o·ver·run (*v.* ō′vər·run′; *n.* ō′vər·run′) *v.* ·ran (-ran′), ·r ·run·ning *v.t.* **1.** To spread or swarm over, as vermin in

...ders. **2.** To overflow. **3.** To spread rapidly across or ...roughout, as a fashion or fad. **4.** To run beyond; pass ...e limit of. **5.** *Printing* To shift or rearrange (words, lines ...type, etc.) from one line, page, or column to another. — **6.** To run over; overflow. **7.** To pass the usual or de-...ed limit. — *n.* An instance of overrunning; also, the ...ount of overrunning.

er·score (ō′vər-skôr′, -skōr′) *v.t.* ·**scored**, ·**scor·ing** To ...aw a line or lines over a word, letter, etc.

er·seas (ō′vər-sēz′) *adv.* Beyond the sea; abroad. — ...j. Situated, coming from, or for use beyond the sea; for-...gn: also **o′ver·sea′**.

er·see (ō′vər-sē′) *v.t.* ·**saw**, ·**seen**, ·**see·ing** **1.** To direct; ...perintend. **2.** To survey; watch. [OE *ofersēon*]

er·se·er (ō′vər-sē′ər, -sir′) *n.* A person who oversees; ...p., one who superintends laborers at their work.

er·sell (ō′vər-sel′) *v.t.* ·**sold** (-sōld′), ·**sell·ing** **1.** To sell ...excess. **2.** To sell more of (a stock, etc.) than one can pro-...de.

er·set (*v.* ō′vər-set′; *n.* ō′vər-set′) *v.* ·**set**, ·**set·ting** *v.t.* **1.** ...) disconcert. **2.** *Printing* To set too much (type or copy). — *v.i.* **3.** To overturn; fall over. — *n.* **1.** A turning over; ...set. **2.** *Printing* Excess of composed type.

er·shad·ow (ō′vər-shad′ō) *v.t.* **1.** To render unimpor-...nt or insignificant by comparison; loom above; dominate. ... To throw a shadow over; obscure.

er·shoe (ō′vər-shōō′) *n.* A shoe worn over another for ...otection against water, mud, cold, etc.; a galosh.

er·shoot (ō′vər-shōōt′) *v.* ·**shot**, ·**shoot·ing** *v.t.* **1.** To ...oot or go over or beyond (the mark, target, etc.). **2.** To ... beyond; exceed, as a limit. **3.** To drive or force (some-...ing) beyond the proper limit. — *v.i.* **4.** To shoot or go ...er or beyond the mark. **5.** To go too far.

er·shot (ō′vər-shot′) *adj.* **1.** Surpassed in any way. **2.** ...rojecting, as the upper jaw beyond the lower jaw. **3.** ...riven by water flowing over from above: an *overshot* wheel.

er·sight (ō′vər-sit′) *n.* **1.** An inadvertent mistake or ...nission. **2.** Watchful supervision; superintendence.

er·size (ō′vər-sīz′) *adj.* Of a larger size than necessary ... normal: also **o′ver·sized′**. — *n.* A large size.

er·skirt (ō′vər-skûrt′) *n.* A skirt or drapery worn over ...e skirt of a dress.

er·sleep (ō′vər-slēp′) *v.* ·**slept**, ·**sleep·ing** *v.i.* To sleep ...o long.

er·spread (ō′vər-spred′) *v.t.* ·**spread**, ·**spread·ing** To ...read or extend over; cover completely.

er·state (ō′vər-stāt′) *v.t.* ·**stat·ed**, ·**stat·ing** To state in ...o strong terms; exaggerate. — **o′ver·state′ment** *n.*

er·stay (ō′vər-stā′) *v.t.* To stay beyond the limits or ...uration of.

er·step (ō′vər-step′) *v.t.* ·**stepped**, ·**step·ping** To step ...ver or go beyond; exceed, as a limit or restriction.

er·stock (*v.* ō′vər-stok′; *n.* ō′vər-stok′) *v.t.* To stock to ...xcess. — *n.* An excessive supply.

er·strung (ō′vər-strung′) *adj.* Too tense or sensitive.

er·stuff (ō′vər-stuf′) *v.t.* **1.** To stuff to excess. **2.** To ...ver completely with deep upholstery: said of furniture.

er·sup·ply (*n.* ō′vər-sə-plī′; *v.* ō′vər-sə-plī′) *n.* *pl.* ·**plies** ...n excessive supply. — *v.t.* ·**plied**, ·**ply·ing** To supply in ...xcess.

ert (ō′vûrt, ō·vûrt′) *adj.* **1.** Open to view; observable. ... *Law* Done with criminal intent. [< OF, pp. of *ovrir* to ...pen] — **o·vert·ly** (ō′vûrt·lē, ō·vûrt′lē) *adv.* — **Syn. 1.** evident, plain, open. See MANIFEST. — **Ant.** covert, ...dden, secret.

er·take (ō′vər-tāk′) *v.t.* ·**took** (-tōōk′), ·**tak·en**, ·**tak·ing** ... To catch up with. **2.** To come upon suddenly.

ver-the-count·er (ō′vər-thə-koun′tər) *adj.* Not sold on ...he floor of a stock exchange: said of stocks, bonds, etc.

er·throw (*v.* ō′vər-thrō′; *n.* ō′vər-thrō′) *v.t.* ·**threw** ...(-thrōō′), ·**thrown**, ·**throw·ing** **1.** To bring down or remove ...om power by force; defeat; ruin. **2.** To throw over or down; ...pset. — *n.* **1.** The act of overthrowing; destruction; demo-...tion. **2.** In baseball, etc., a throwing of the ball over and ...eyond the player or base aimed at.

ver·time (*n., adj., & adv.* ō′vər-tīm′; *v.* ō′vər-tīm′) *n.* ...ime used in working beyond the specified hours. — *adj.* ...During or for extra working time: *overtime* pay. — *adv.* Be-...ond the stipulated time. — *v.t.* ·**timed**, ·**tim·ing** *Photog.* ...'o expose too long, as a plate or film.

ver·tone (ō′vər-tōn′) *n.* **1.** *Music* An upper partial tone: ...o called because it is heard with and above the fundamental ...one produced by a musical instrument. **2.** Connotations, ...mplications, etc., of language, thoughts, etc.

ver·top (ō′vər-top′) *v.t.* ·**topped**, ·**top·ping** **1.** To rise ...bove the top of; tower over. **2.** To surpass; excel.

ver·ture (ō′vər-chər) *n.* **1.** *Music* An instrumental prel-...de to an opera or other large work. **b** Any of various orches-

---

tral pieces, often having programmatic content. **2.** An act or proposal intended to initiate a relationship, negotiations, etc. — *v.t.* ·**tured**, ·**tur·ing** **1.** To offer as an overture or pro-posal. **2.** To introduce with or as an overture. [See OVERT.]

o·ver·turn (*v.* ō′vər-tûrn′; *n.* ō′vər-tûrn′) *v.t.* **1.** To turn or throw over; capsize; upset. **2.** To overthrow; defeat; ruin. — *v.i.* **3.** To turn over; capsize; upset. — *n.* **1.** The act of overturning, or the state of being overturned. **2.** A subver-sion or destruction. **3.** Turnover (def. 6).

o·ver·ween·ing (ō′vər-wē′ning) *adj.* **1.** Presumptiously proud or conceited. **2.** Excessive; exaggerated. [OE *ofer-wēnan* to become insolent] — **o′ver·ween′ing·ly** *adv.*

o·ver·weigh (ō′vər-wā′) *v.t.* **1.** To outweigh; overbalance. **2.** To overburden; oppress.

o·ver·weight (*n.* ō′vər-wāt′; *adj. & v.* ō′vər-wāt′) *n.* **1.** Ex-cess weight, as beyond the legal or customary amount. **2.** Greater importance; preponderance. — *adj.* Being more than the usual or permitted weight. — *v.t.* To overburden.

o·ver·whelm (ō′vər-hwelm′) *v.t.* **1.** To bury or submerge completely, as with a wave or flood. **2.** To overcome or de-feat; crush. [ME *oferwhelmen* to turn upside down] — **Syn. 1.** inundate, bury. **2.** rout, vanquish.

o·ver·whelm·ing (ō′vər-hwel′ming) *adj.* Crushing by rea-son of force, weight, or numbers; irresistible. — **o′ver·whelm′ing·ly** *adv.*

o·ver·work (*v.* ō′vər-wûrk′; *n.* ō′vər-wûrk′) *v.* ·**worked** (*Ar-chaic* ·**wrought**), ·**work·ing** *v.t.* **1.** To cause to work too hard. **2.** To work on or elaborate excessively: to *overwork* an argument. — *v.i.* **3.** To work too hard; do too much work. — *n.* Excessive work. [OE *oferwiercan*]

o·ver·write (ō′vər-rīt′) *v.t. & v.i.* ·**wrote** (-rōt′), ·**writ·ten** (-rit′ən), ·**writ·ing** **1.** To write in too elaborate or labored a style. **2.** To write too much about (a subject) or at too great length. **3.** To write over other writing.

o·ver·wrought (ō′vər-rôt′) *adj.* **1.** Worked up or excited excessively; overstrained. **2.** Worked all over, as with em-broidery. **3.** Worked too hard. **4.** Too elaborate.

ovi- *combining form* Egg; of or pertaining to eggs: *oviparous.* Also **ovo-**. [< L *ovum* egg]

o·vi·duct (ō′vi-dukt′) *n.* *Anat.* A Fallopian tube.

o·vi·form (ō′vi-fôrm) *adj.* Shaped like an egg or ovum.

o·vi·pa·ra (ō-vip′ər-ə) *n.pl.* Animals that lay eggs. [< NL < L < *ovum* egg + -*parus* < *parere* to bring forth]

o·vip·a·rous (ō-vip′ər-əs) *adj.* *Zool.* Producing eggs or ova that mature and are hatched outside the body, as birds, most fishes, and reptiles. — **o·vip′a·rous·ly** *adv.* — **o·vip′·a·rous·ness** *n.*

o·vi·pos·i·tor (ō′vi-poz′ə-tər) *n.* *Entomol.* The tubular or-gan at the extremity of the abdomen in many insects by which the eggs are deposited. [< OVI- + L *ponere* to place]

o·void (ō′void) *adj.* Egg-shaped: also **o·voi′dal.** — *n.* An egg-shaped body.

o·vo·vi·vip·a·rous (ō′vō-vī-vip′ər-əs) *adj.* *Zool.* Producing eggs that are hatched within the parent's body, but without formation of a placenta, as some reptiles and fishes. — **o′vo·vi·vip′a·rous·ly** *adv.* — **o′vo·vi·vip′a·rous·ness** *n.*

o·vu·late (ō′vyə-lāt) *v.i.* ·**lat·ed**, ·**lat·ing** To produce ova; discharge ova from an ovary. [See OVULE.]

o·vu·la·tion (ō′vyə-lā′shən) *n.* *Biol.* **1.** The formation and discharge of ova. **2.** The period when this occurs.

o·vule (ō′vyōōl) *n.* **1.** *Bot.* The body within the ovary that upon fertilization becomes the seed. For illus. see FLOWER. **2.** *Zool.* An immature ovum. [< F < NL *ovulum*, dim. of L *ovum* egg] — **o′vu·lar, o·vu·lar·y** (ō′vyə-ler′ē) *adj.*

o·vum (ō′vəm) *n.* *pl.* **o·va** (ō′və) *Biol.* The female repro-ductive cell of animals, produced in the ovary. [< L]

owe (ō) *v.* **owed** (*Obs.* **ought**), **ow·ing** *v.t.* **1.** To be indebted to the amount of. **2.** To be obligated to render or offer: to *owe* an apology. **3.** To have or possess by virtue of some condition or cause: with *to*: He *owes* his success to his own efforts. **4.** To cherish (a certain feeling) toward another. — *v.i.* **5.** To be in debt. [OE *āgan* to own]

ow·ing (ō′ing) *adj.* Due; yet to be paid. — **owing to** At-tributable to; on account of; in consequence of.

owl (oul) *n.* **1.** A predatory nocturnal bird, having large eyes and head, short, sharply hooked bill, long powerful claws, and a circular facial disk of radiating feathers. **2.** A person with nocturnal habits. [OE *ūle*]

owl·et (ou′lit) *n.* A small or young owl.

owl·ish (ou′lish) *adj.* **1.** Like an owl. **2.** *Brit. Dial.* Stu-pid. — **owl′ish·ly** *adv.* — **owl′ish·ness** *n.*

own (ōn) *adj.* **1.** Belonging or relating to oneself: following the possessive (usu. a possessive pronoun) as an intensive or to indicate the exclusion of others: my *own* horse; his *own* idea. **2.** Being of the nearest degree: *own* cousin. — **to come into one's own 1.** To obtain possession of one's property. **2.** To receive one's reward. — **to hold one's own 1.** To maintain one's place or position. **2.** To keep up with one's

---

work, or remain undefeated. — **on one's own** Entirely dependent on one's self for support or success. — *v.t.* **1.** To have or hold as one's own; possess. **2.** To admit or acknowledge. — *v.i.* **3.** To confess: with *to*. — **to own up** *Informal* To confess forthrightly and fully. — **Syn.** See CONFESS. [OE *āgan* to possess, have] — **own'a·ble** *adj.*

own·er (ō′nər) *n.* One who has the legal title or right to or has possession of a thing. — **own'er·less** *adj.*

own·er·ship (ō′nər·ship) *n.* The state of being an owner.

ox (oks) *n.* *pl.* **ox·en** (ok′sən) **1.** An adult castrated male of the genus *Bos*, used for draft and food. **2.** Any bovine quadruped, as a buffalo, bison, or yak. [OE *oxa*]

ox·al·ic acid (ok·sal′ik) *Chem.* A white, crystalline, poisonous compound, $C_2H_2O_4 \cdot 2H_2O$, found in plant tissues and made artificially, used in bleaching, dyeing, etc.

ox·blood (oks′blud′) *n.* A deep red color.

ox·bow (oks′bō′) *n.* **1.** A bent piece of wood in an ox yoke, that forms a collar for the ox. **2.** A bend in a river shaped like this.

ox·eye (oks′ī′) *n.* **1.** Any of several plants of the composite family having large yellow heads. **2.** The oxeye daisy. **3.** Any of various shore birds, as the sandpiper. **4.** An oval dormer window.

ox·eyed (oks′īd) *adj.* Having large, calm eyes, as an ox.

ox·ford (oks′fərd) *n.* *U.S.* **1.** A low shoe laced at the instep. Also **oxford shoe**. **2.** A cotton cloth of basket weave, used for men's shirts. Also **Oxford**. [after *Oxford*]

oxford gray **1.** A very dark gray. **2.** A woolen fabric of this color.

ox·heart (oks′härt′) *n.* A variety of sweet cherry.

ox·i·da·tion (ok′sə·dā′shən) *n.* *Chem.* **1.** The process or state of undergoing combination with oxygen. **2.** The process by which atoms lose or are deprived of valence electrons, or begin sharing them with a more electronegative element.

ox·ide (ok′sīd, -sid) *n.* *Chem.* Any binary compound of oxygen with another element: iron *oxide*. Also **ox'id** (-sid). [< F < *ox(ygène)* oxygen + *(ac)ide* acid]

ox·i·dize (ok′sə·dīz) *v.* **·dized**, **·diz·ing** *Chem.* *v.t.* **1.** To convert (an element) into its oxide; combine with oxygen. **2.** To increase the valence of an atom or group of atoms by the loss of electrons. — *v.i.* **3.** To become oxidized. Also **ox·i·date** (ok′sə·dāt). Also *Brit.* **ox'i·dise**. — **ox'i·diz'a·ble** *adj.*

ox·lip (oks′lip′) *n.* A species of primrose, closely resembling the cowslip: also called *five-fingers*. [OE < *oxa, oxan* ox + *slyppe* slime]

Ox·o·ni·an (ok·sō′nē·ən) *adj.* Of or pertaining to Oxford, England, or to its university. — *n.* A student or graduate of Oxford University. [< LL *Oxonia* Oxford]

ox·tail (oks′tāl′) *n.* The tail of an ox, esp. when skinned for use in soup.

oxy-¹ *combining form* **1.** Sharp; pointed; keen. **2.** Acid: *oxygen*. [< Gk. *oxys* sharp, acid]

oxy-² *combining form* *Chem.* **1.** Oxygen; of or containing oxygen, or one of its compounds. **2.** An oxidation product. **3.** Containing the hydroxyl group. [< OXYGEN]

ox·y·a·cet·y·lene (ok′sē·ə·set′ə·lēn) *adj.* Designating or pertaining to a mixture of acetylene and oxygen, used to tain high temperatures, as in welding.

ox·y·gen (ok′sə·jin) *n.* A colorless, tasteless, odorless g eous element (symbol O), occurring free in the atmosphe of which it forms about one-fifth by volume. It is an ab dant and active element, combining with hydrogen to fo water, supporting combustion, and essential in the respir tion of plants and animals. See ELEMENT. [< F < *oxy-¹* + -*gène* -gen]

ox·y·gen·ate (ok′sə·jən·āt′) *v.t.* **·at·ed**, **·at·ing** To tre combine, or impregnate with oxygen. — **ox'y·gen·a'tion**

ox·y·gen·ize (ok′sə·jən·īz′) *v.t.* **·ized**, **·iz·ing** To oxidize.

oxygen mask A device worn over the nose and mouth means of which the user can inhale oxygen as an aid breathing.

oxygen tent A tentlike canopy placed over a patient's he and shoulders, within which pure oxygen may be circula for the purpose of facilitating respiration.

ox·y·hy·dro·gen (ok′si·hī′drə·jən) *n.* A mixture of oxy and hydrogen.

ox·y·mo·ron (ok′si·môr′on, -mō′ron) *n.* *pl.* **·mo·ra** (-mô -mō′rə) A figure of speech in which contradictory terms brought together, as in the phrase, *"O heavy lightness, s ous vanity!"* [< Gk. < *oxys* sharp + *moros* foolish]

o·yez (ō′yes, ō′yez) *interj.* Hear! hear ye! an introduct word to call attention to a proclamation, as by a court cr usu. repeated three times. Also **o'yes**. [< OF *oyez*, perative of *oir*, ult. < L *audire* to hear]

oys·ter (ois′tər) *n.* **1.** A bivalve mollusk, found in salt a brackish water and moored by the shell to stones, of shells, etc.; esp., a common edible species of Europe a America. **2.** An analogous bivalve, as the **pearl oyster**. Some delicacy; tidbit; prize. — *v.i.* To gather or farm o ters. [< OF < L < Gk. *ostreon*]

oyster bed A place where oysters breed or are grown.

oyster crab A smooth-bodied crab living nonparasitica in the mantle of the oyster.

oyster cracker A small biscuit or hard, salted cracker.

oyster plant Salsify.

oyster white Any of several very light gray tints.

O·zark State (ō′zärk) Nickname of Missouri.

o·zo·ce·rite (ō·zō′kə·rīt, -sə-, ō′zō·sir′īt) *n.* A waxy, tra lucent mixture of natural hydrocarbons, used in candles, e Also **o·zo'ke·rite**. [< G < Gk. *ozein* to smell + *keros* w

o·zone (ō′zōn) *n.* **1.** An unstable allotropic form of oxyg O_3, with a pungent odor like that of chlorine, formed va ously, as by the passage of electricity through the air. It i powerful oxidizing agent, and is used for bleaching oils, w es, ivory, flour, and starch, and for sterilizing drinking wat **2.** *Informal* Fresh air. [< F < Gk. *ozein* to smell]

o·zon·ic (ō·zon′ik, ō·zō′nik), **o·zo·nous** (ō′zə·nəs) *adj.*

o·zo·nize (ō′zō·nīz) *v.t.* **·nized**, **·niz·ing** **1.** To treat or cha with ozone. **2.** To convert (oxygen) into ozone. — **o'zo za'tion** *n.* — **o'zo·niz'er** *n.*

o·zon·o·sphere (ō·zon′ə·sfir) *n.* *Meteorol.* A narrow la in the stratosphere, containing a high concentration of ozo Also **ozone layer**. — **o·zon'o·spher'ic** or **·i·cal** *adj.*

P

p, P (pē) *n.* *pl.* **p's** or **ps**, **P's** or **Ps**, **pees** (pēz) **1.** The sixteenth letter of the English alphabet. **2.** The sound represented by the letter *p*, the voiceless bilabial stop. — *symbol* **1.** *Chem.* Phosphorus (symbol P). **2.** *Genetics* The parental generation: followed by a subscript numeral, as P_1, P_2, to indicate the first, second, etc., parental generation. — **to mind one's P's and Q's** To be careful of one's behavior.

pa (pä) *n.* *Informal* Papa.

pa·ba or **PABA** *Biochem.* Para-aminobenzoic acid.

pab·u·lum (pab′yə·ləm) *n.* Any substance giving nourishment; aliment. [< L *pabulum* fodder] — **pab'u·lar** *adj.*

pace (pās) *n.* **1.** A step in walking; also, the distance covered in one such movement. **2.** A conventional measure of length approximating the average length of stride in walking: usu. 3 feet, but sometimes making 5 paces to the rod. The U.S. Army **regulation pace** is 30 inches, quick time; 36 inches, double time. **3.** The manner or speed of movement in going on the legs; carriage and action, esp. of a horse. **4.** Rate of speed, as in movement, work, etc. **5.** A gait of a horse, etc., in which both feet on the same side are lifted and moved forward at once. — **to put (one) through his paces** To test the abilities, speed, etc., of. — *v.* **paced, pac**

v.t. **1.** To walk back and forth across. **2.** To measure paces. **3.** To set or make the pace for. **4.** To train to a c tain gait or pace. — *v.i.* **5.** To walk with slow or regu steps. **6.** To move at a pace (def. 5). [< F < L *passus*, of *pandere* to stretch.] — **pac'er** *n.*

paced (pāst) *adj.* **1.** Having a particular pace: used in co pounds: slow-*paced*. **2.** Measured in paces or by pacing. Done after or with the help of a pacemaker.

pace·mak·er (pās′mā′kər) *n.* **1.** One who makes or se the pace for another in a race. **2.** *Anat.* A mass of tissue the right atrium of the heart that normally regulates t heartbeat. — **pace'mak'ing** *n.* & *adj.*

pa·cha (pə·shä′, pash′ə), **pa·cha·lic** (pə·shä′lik) See PASH PASHALIK.

pach·ou·li (pach′ŏŏ·lē, pə·chōō′lē) See PATCHOULI.

pachy- *combining form* Thick; massive. [< Gk. *pach* thick]

pach·y·derm (pak′ə·dûrm) *n.* **1.** Any of certain thic skinned, nonruminant hoofed animals, esp. an elephant, h popotamus, or rhinoceros. **2.** A thick-skinned, insensiti

erson. [< F < Gk. < *pachys* thick + *derma* skin] —
ach′y·der′ma·tous (-dûr′mə-təs), **pach′y·der′mous** *adj.*
·cif·ic (pə-sif′ik) *adj.* 1. Tending or leading to peace or
nciliation. 2. Peaceful. Also **pa·cif′i·cal.** [< MF < L
pax, pacis peace + *facere* to make] — **pa·cif′i·cal·ly** *adv.*
·cif·ic (pə-sif′ik) *adj.* Pertaining to the Pacific Ocean.
cif·i·cate (pə-sif′ə-kāt) *v.t.* ·**cat·ed,** ·**cat·ing** To pacify;
lm. — **pac·i·fi·ca·tion** (pas′ə-fə-kā′shən) *n.* — **pa·cif′i·**
·**tor** *n.* — **pa·cif′i·ca·to′ry** (-kə-tôr′ē, -tō′rē) *adj.*
c·i·fi·er (pas′ə-fī′ər) *n.* 1. One who or that which pacifies.
. A rubber nipple or ring, for babies to suck or bite on.
c·i·fist (pas′ə-fist) *n.* One who opposes war or military
eparedness, and proposes that all disputes be settled by
bitration. — **pac′i·fism** *n.* — **pac′i·fis′tic** *adj.*
c·i·fy (pas′ə-fī) *v.t.* ·**fied,** ·**fy·ing** 1. To bring peace to (an
ea). 2. To allay the anger or agitation of; quiet; soothe.
< F < L < *pax, pacis* peace + *facere* to make]
ck[1] (pak) *n.* 1. A bundle or large package, esp. one to be
rried on the back of a man or animal. 2. A collection of
ything; heap. 3. A full set of like or associated things
su. handled collectively, as cards. 4. A group of dogs or
olves that hunt together. 5. Any gang or band, esp. a
iminal gang. 6. An ice pack. 7. A cosmetic paste for the
ce. 8. A wrapping of sheets or blankets used in certain
ater-cure treatments; also, the sheets or blankets used. 9.
parachute, fully assembled and folded for use. 10. The
uantity of something, as foods, put in containers for preser-
ation at one time or in one season. — **Syn.** See FLOCK. —
. 1. To make a pack or bundle of. 2. To place compactly
a trunk, box, etc., for storing or carrying. 3. To fill com-
actly, as for storing or carrying. 4. To put up for preserva-
on or sale. 5. To compress tightly; crowd together. 6.
o fill completely or to overflowing; cram. 7. To cover, fill,
surround so as to prevent leakage, damage, etc.: to *pack*
piston rod. 8. To load with a pack; burden. 9. To carry
transport on the back or on pack animals. 10. To carry
wear habitually: to *pack* a gun. 11. To send or dispatch
ummarily: with *off* or *away.* 12. To treat with a pack (def.
. 13. *Slang* To be able to inflict: He *packs* a wallop. —
. 14. To place one's clothes and belongings in trunks,
oxes, etc., for storing or carrying. 15. To be capable of
eing stowed or packed. 16. To crowd together. 17. To
ttle in a hard, firm mass. 18. To leave in haste: often with
* or *away.* — **to send packing** To send away or dismiss
ummarily. [ME *pakke,* appar. < LG *pak*] — **pack′er** *n.*
ck[2] (pak) *v.t.* To arrange, select, or manipulate to one's
wn advantage: to *pack* a jury. [? < PACK[1]]
ck·age (pak′ij) *n.* 1. Something packed, wrapped up, or
ound together, as for transportation. 2. A box, case, or
ther receptacle used for packing. 3. The act of packing.
. A combination of items considered as a unit. — *v.t.*
ged, ·**ag·ing** To arrange or tie into a package..
ckage store *U.S.* A store that sells liquor by the bottle.
ck animal An animal used to carry packs or burdens.
ck·et (pak′it) *n.* 1. A small package; parcel. 2. A steam-
ip for conveying mails, passengers, and freight at stated
mes: also **packet boat.** — *v.t.* To make into a packet or
arcel. [< AF *pacquet,* dim. of ME *pakke*]
ck·ing (pak′ing) *n.* 1. The act or operation of one who
r that which packs. 2. The canning or putting up of meat,
sh, fruit, etc. 3. Any material used in packing, closing a
int, stopping a wound, etc.
cking box 1. A stout box in which goods are packed.
lso **packing case.** 2. *Mech.* A stuffing box.
cking plant *U.S.* A factory where meats and meat prod-
cts are processed and packed. Also *U.S.* **packing house.**
ck rat A North American rat that carries off and hides
mall articles in its nest.
ck·sad·dle (pak′sad′l) *n.* A saddle for a pack animal, to
hich the packs are fastened so as to balance evenly.
ck·thread (pak′thred′) *n.* Strong thread used for wrapping.
ct (pakt) *n.* An agreement; compact. [< OF < L *pac-
um* agreement]
d[1] (pad) *n.* 1. A cushion; also, any stuffed, cushionlike
ing serving to protect from jarring, friction, etc. 2. A
umber of sheets of paper gummed together at one edge; a
ablet. 3. A large floating leaf of an aquatic plant: a lily
ad. 4. A soft cushionlike enlargement of skin on the under-
urface of the toes of many animals. 5. The foot of a fox,
tter, etc. 6. The footprint of an animal. 7. A launching
ad. — *v.t.* **pad·ded, pad·ding** 1. To stuff, line, or protect
ith pads or padding. 2. To lengthen (speech or writing)
y inserting unnecessary matter. 3. To add to (an expense
ccount, voting register, etc.) for fraudulent purposes. [Ori-
in unknown]
d[2] (pad) *v.i.* **pad·ded, pad·ding** 1. To travel by walking.
. To move with soft, almost noiseless footsteps. — *n.* A
ull, padded sound, as of a footstep. [Akin to PAD[3]]

pad[3] (pad) *n.* 1. An easy-paced road horse. 2. A highway-
man. [< LG *pad* path]
pad·ding (pad′ing) *n.* 1. The act of one who or that which
pads. 2. Material with which to pad. 3. Extraneous matter used in writing, etc., merely to fill space.
pad·dle (pad′l) *n.* 1. A broad-bladed implement resembling
a short oar, used without a rowlock in propelling a canoe or
small boat. 2. The distance covered during one trip in a
canoe over a given time. 3. A flat board for inflicting bodily
punishment. 4. A small, rounded, flat piece of wood with a
handle, used in table tennis. 5. The act of paddling. — *v.*
·**dled,** ·**dling** *v.i.* 1. To move a canoe, etc., on or through
water by means of a paddle. 2. To row gently or lightly.
3. To swim with short, downward strokes, as ducks do. 4.
To play in water with the hands or feet; wade. — *v.t.* 5.
To propel by means of a paddle or paddles. 6. To convey
by paddling. 7. To beat with a paddle; spank. 8. To stir.
— **to paddle one's own canoe** To be independent. [ME, ?
var. of *patel* < L *patella* shallow pan] — **pad′dler** *n.*
paddle board One of the broad, paddlelike boards set on
the circumference of a paddle wheel or water wheel.
pad·dle·fish (pad′l-fish′) *n.* *pl.* ·**fish** or ·**fish·es** A large fish
having a scaleless body and paddle-shaped snout, found in
the Mississippi Valley streams.
paddle wheel A wheel having projecting floats or boards
for propelling a vessel.
pad·dling (pad′ling) *n.* 1. The act of propelling with a paddle. 2. A beating or spanking.
pad·dock (pad′ək) *n.* 1. A pasture, lot, or enclosure for exercising horses, adjoining a stable. 2. A grassed enclosure
at a racecourse where horses are walked and saddled. — *v.t.*
To confine in a paddock, as horses. [Alter. of dial. E *parrock,*
OE *pearruc* enclosure]
pad·dy[1] (pad′ē) *n.* *pl.* ·**dies** The ruddy duck. [after *Paddy,*
a proper name]
pad·dy[2] (pad′ē) *n.* *pl.* ·**dies** Rice in the husk, whether gathered or growing. [< Malay *pādĭ*]
paddy wagon *U.S. Slang* A patrol wagon.
pa·di·shah (pä′di·shä) *n.* Lord protector; chief ruler: a title
of the shah of Iran. Also **pad·shah** (päd′shä). [< Persian
< *pati* master + *shāh* king]
pad·lock (pad′lok′) *n.* A detachable lock, having a pivoted
hasp to be passed through a staple or ring and then locked.
— *v.t.* To fasten with or as with a padlock. [ME]
pa·dre (pä′drā) *n.* 1. Father: a title used in Italy, Spain,
and Spanish America in addressing or speaking of priests.
2. An army or navy chaplain. [< L *pater, patris* father]
pae·an (pē′ən) *n.* A song of joy or exultation. Also spelled
pean. [< L < Gk. *paian* hymn addressed to Apollo]
paed-, paedo- See PEDO-.
paed·e·rast (ped′ər·ast), etc. See PEDERAST, etc.
pa·gan (pā′gən) *n.* 1. One who is neither a Christian, a Jew,
nor a Moslem; a heathen. 2. In early Christian use, an idol
worshiper. 3. An irreligious person. —*adj.* Of, pertaining
to, or like pagans; heathenish. [< L < L, orig., villager <
pagus the country] — **pa′gan·dom** *n.* — **pa′gan·ish** *adj.*
— **pa′gan·ism** *n.*
pa·gan·ize (pā′gən·īz) *v.t. & v.i.* ·**ized,** ·**iz·ing** To make or
become pagan.
page[1] (pāj) *n.* 1. A male attendant; esp., in chivalry, a lad
or young man in training for knighthood, or a youth attending a royal or princely personage. 2. In Congress or other
legislatures, a boy who attends upon legislators while in session. 3. A boy employed in a hotel, club, etc., to perform
light duties. — *v.t.* **paged, pag·ing** 1. To seek or summon
(a person) by calling his name. 2. To wait on as a page. [<
OF < Ital. < Gk., < *pais, paidos* boy]
page[2] (pāj) *n.* 1. One side of a leaf of a book, letter, etc. 2.
The printing or the type used on one side. 3. Any event or
events worthy of being noted or recorded: a sad *page* in history. 4. *Usu. pl.* Any source or record of knowledge. — *v.*
paged, pag·ing *v.t.* 1. To mark the pages of with numbers.
—*v.i.* 2. To turn pages: usu. with *through.* [< F < L *pagina* written page < *pangere* to fasten]
pag·eant (paj′ənt) *n.* 1. A community outdoor celebration
presenting scenes from local history and tradition. 2. An
exhibition or spectacular parade devised for a public celebration. 3. A theatrical spectacle. 4. Unsubstantial display.
[< Med.L *pagina* scaffold of a stage]
pag·eant·ry (paj′ən·trē) *n.* *pl.* ·**ries** 1. Pageants collectively. 2. Ceremonial splendor or display. 3. Empty or
showy display.
pag·i·nate (paj′ə·nāt) *v.t.* ·**nat·ed,** ·**nat·ing** To number the
pages of (a book) consecutively. [< L *pagina* page + -ATE[1]]
pag·i·na·tion (paj′ə·nā′shən) *n.* 1. The numbering of the
pages, as of a book. 2. The system of figures and marks
used in paging.
pa·go·da (pə·gō′də) *n.* In the Far East, a sacred tower or

temple, usu. pyramidal. Also **pag·od** (pag′əd, pə·god′).
[< Pg. < Tamil < Skt. *bhagavati* belonging to a deity]

paid (pād) Past tense and past participle of PAY.

pail (pāl) *n.* **1.** A cylindrical vessel for carrying liquids, etc., properly having a handle; bucket. **2.** The amount carried in this vessel. [OE *paegel* wine measure] — **pail′ful′** *n.*

pail·lasse (pal·yas′, pal′yas) *n.* A mattress of straw, excelsior, etc.: also spelled *palliasse*. [< MF < L *palea* chaff]

pain (pān) *n.* **1.** The unpleasant sensation or feeling resulting from or accompanying some injury, overstrain, or obstruction of the physical powers. **2.** Any distressing or afflicting emotion. **3.** *pl.* Care, effort, etc. expended on anything: with much *pains*. **4.** *pl.* The pangs of childbirth. — **on** (or **upon** or **under**) **pain of** With the penalty of (some specified punishment). — **to take pains** To be careful; to make an effort. — *v.t.* **1.** To cause pain to; hurt. — *v.i.* **2.** To cause pain. [< OF < L *poine* fine, penalty]

pained (pānd) *adj.* **1.** Hurt physically or mentally; distressed. **2.** Showing pain: a *pained* expression.

pain·ful (pān′fəl) *adj.* **1.** Giving pain; distressing. **2.** Requiring labor or care; arduous. **3.** Affected with pain: said of the body. — **pain′ful·ly** *adv.* — **pain′ful·ness** *n.*

pain·less (pān′lis) *adj.* Free from pain; causing no pain. — **pain′less·ly** *adv.* — **pain′less·ness** *n.*

pains·tak·ing (pānz′tā′king, pān′stā′-) *adj.* Careful; assiduous. — *n.* Careful effort. — **pains′tak′ing·ly** *adv.*

paint (pānt) *n.* **1.** A color or pigment, either dry or mixed with oil, water, etc. **2.** A cosmetic, as rouge. **3.** Grease paint. **4.** A film, layer, or coat of pigment applied to the surface of an object; also, the dry coating of such a pigment: cracked *paint*. — *v.t.* **1.** In art: **a** To make a representation of in paints or colors. **b** To make, as a picture, by applying paints or colors. **2.** To describe vividly, as in words. **3.** To cover, coat, or decorate with paint. **4.** To apply cosmetics to. **5.** To apply (medicine, etc.) with or as with a swab. — *v.i.* **6.** To practice the art of painting; paint pictures. **7.** To apply cosmetics to the face, etc. [< OF < L *pingere* to paint] — **paint·y** (pān′tē) *adj.*

paint·brush (pānt′brush′) *n.* A brush for applying paint.

paint·ed (pān′tid) *adj.* **1.** Coated with paint. **2.** Depicted in colors. **3.** Having no reality, truth, or value; artificial.

painted bunting A brilliantly colored finch widely distributed in the southern U.S. Also **painted finch.**

paint·er¹ (pān′tər) *n.* **1.** One who covers surfaces with a coat of paint. **2.** An artist who paints in oils, etc.

paint·er² (pān′tər) *n.* *Naut.* A rope with which to fasten a boat by its bow. [Prob. < OF < L *pendere* to suspend]

paint·er³ (pān′tər) *n.* *U.S. Dial.* The puma, or cougar. [Var. of PANTHER]

paint·ing (pān′ting) *n.* **1.** The act of laying on paints with a brush. **2.** The art of creating meaningful effects on a surface by the use of pigments. **3.** A picture.

pair (pâr) *v.t.* **1.** To bring together or arrange in a pair or pairs; match; couple; mate. — *v.i.* **2.** To come together as a couple or pair. **3.** To marry or mate. — **to pair off 1.** To separate into couples. **2.** To arrange by pairs. — *n.* **1.** Two persons or things of a kind, that are joined, related, or associated; a couple; brace. **2.** A single thing having two correspondent parts dependent on each other: a *pair* of scissors. **3.** A married couple; also, two animals mated. **4.** In legislative bodies, two opposed members who agree to abstain from voting, and so offset each other. **5.** A set of similar things making a whole: a *pair* of pajamas. **6.** In some games of cards, two cards of the same denomination: a *pair* of queens. ◆ Current usage calls for *pair* in the plural after a numeral of two or more, as, four *pairs* of shoes, though informally the singular is often used, as, four *pair* of shoes. [< F < L neut. plural of *par* equal]

Pais·ley (pāz′lē) *adj.* Made of or resembling a patterned woolen fabric originally made in Paisley, Scotland. — *n.* **1.** Paisley fabric. **2.** A Paisley shawl.

pa·ja·mas (pə·jä′məz, -jam′əz) *n.* *pl. cf* **pa·ja·ma** (-mə) **1.** A garment consisting of loose trousers of silk, cotton, etc., and an accompanying jacket or blouse, used for sleeping. **2.** In the Orient, similar trousers worn by both men and women Also, *Brit.*, *pyjamas*. [< Hind. < Persian *pāi* leg + *jāmah* garment]

PAISLEY DESIGN

pal (pal) *Informal n.* A friend or chum. — *v.i.* **palled, pal·ling** To associate as pals. [< Romany ult. < Skt. *bharatr* brother]

pal·ace (pal′is) *n.* **1.** A royal residence, or the official residence of some high dignitary, as of a bishop. **2.** Any splendid residence or stately building. [< OF < L *Palatium* Palatine Hill at Rome, on which stood the palace of Caesar Augustus]

pal·a·din (pal′ə·din) *n.* **1.** Any of the twelve peers of Charlemagne. **2.** A paragon of knighthood. [< F < Ital. < L < *palatium*. See PALACE.]

palae- Var. of PALEO-.

palaeo- See PALEO-.

pal·an·quin (pal′ən·kēn′) *n.* A type of covered litter us[...] as a means of conveyance in the Orient, borne by poles [...] the shoulders of two or more men. Also **pal′an·keen′.** [...] Pg. < Javanese < Skt. *palyanka*]

pal·at·a·ble (pal′it·ə·bəl) *adj.* **1.** Agreeable to the taste [...] palate; savory. **2.** Acceptable. — **pal′at·a·bil′i·ty, pal′[...] a·ble·ness** *n.* — **pal′at·a·bly** *adv.*

pal·a·tal (pal′ə·təl) *adj.* **1.** Pertaining to the palate. [...] *Phonet.* **a** Produced by placing the front (not the tip) of t[...] tongue near or against the hard palate, as *y* in English *yo*[...] **b** Produced with the blade of the tongue near the hard p[...] ate, as *ch* in *child*, *j* in *joy*. — *n.* *Anat.* **1.** A bone of t[...] palate. **2.** *Phonet.* **a** A palatal consonant. **b** A front vow[...] [< F < L *palatum* palate]

pal·a·tal·ize (pal′ə·təl·īz) *v.t. & v.i.* ·ized, ·iz·ing *Phon*[...] To change a nonpalatal sound to a palatal by assimilatio[...] as (-yōŏr) to (-shər) in *censure*. — **pal′a·tal·i·za′tion** *n.*

pal·ate (pal′it) *n.* **1.** *Anat.* The roof of the mouth, consi[...] ing of the anterior **hard palate**, having a bony skeleton, a[...] the posterior **soft palate**, that is composed of muscular t[...] sue. For illus. see MOUTH, THROAT. **2.** The sense of tas[...] [< L *palatum.*]

pa·la·tial (pə·lā′shəl) *adj.* Of, like, or befitting a palac[...] magnificent. — **pa·la′tial·ly** *adv.*

pa·lat·i·nate (pə·lat′ə·nāt, -nit) *n.* A political division rul[...] over by a prince possessing certain prerogatives of royal[...] within his own domain.

pal·a·tine¹ (pal′ə·tīn, -tin) *adj.* Of or pertaining to the p[...] ate. — *n.* *Anat.* Either of the two bones forming the ha[...] palate. [< F < L *palatum* palate]

pal·a·tine² (pal′ə·tīn, -tin) *adj.* **1.** Of or pertaining to [...] royal palace or its officials. **2.** Possessing royal prerogativ[...] a count *palatine*. — *n.* **1.** A lord exercising sovereign pow[...] over a province. **2.** A vassal exercising royal privileges ov[...] his territory. **3.** The ruler of a palatinate or county pa[...] tine. [< F < L < *palatium* palace]

pa·lav·er (pə·lav′ər) *n.* **1.** Empty talk, esp. that intend[...] to flatter or deceive. **2.** A public discussion or conferen[...] **3.** Originally, a parley with native or aboriginal inhabitan[...] as by explorers. — *v.t.* **1.** To flatter; cajole. — *v.i.* **2.** [...] talk idly and at length. [< Pg. < LL *parabola* story, wor[...] — **pa·lav′er·er** *n.*

pale¹ (pāl) *n.* **1.** A pointed stick or stake. **2.** A fence [...] closing a piece of ground. **3.** Any boundary or limit. [...] That which is enclosed within bounds. — *v.t.* **paled, pal·i[...]** To enclose with pales; fence in. [< OF < L *palus* stak[...]

pale² (pāl) *adj.* **1.** Of a whitish or ashen appearance. [...] Of a very light shade of any color; lacking in brightness [...] intensity of color. **3.** Feeble or weak. — *v.t. & v.i.* **pale[...]** **pal·ing** To make or turn pale; blanch. [< OF < L < *[...]* *lere* to be pale] — **pale′ly** *adv.* — **pale′ness** *n.*

pale·face (pāl′fās′) *n.* A white person: a term alleged[...] originated by North American Indians.

paleo- *combining form* **1.** Ancient; old. **2.** Primitive. Al[...] before vowels, **pale-.** Also **palae-, palaeo-.** [< Gk. *pala*[...] old, ancient]

Pa·le·o·cene (pā′lē·ə·sēn′) *Geol. adj.* Of or pertaining [...] the oldest epoch of the Tertiary period, preceding the E[...] cene. — *n.* This epoch. See chart for GEOLOGY.

pa·le·og·ra·phy (pā′lē·og′rə·fē) *n.* **1.** An ancient mode [...] writing; ancient writings collectively. **2.** The science [...] describing or deciphering ancient writings. — **pa′le·og′[...]** **pher** *n.* — **pa′le·o·graph′ic** (-ə·graf′ik) or **·i·cal** *adj.*

Pa·le·o·lith·ic (pā′lē·ō·lith′ik) *adj.* *Anthropol.* Pertain[...] ing, pertaining to, or associated with a period of human c[...] ture preceding the Mesolithic and characterized by chipp[...] or flaked stone implements, cave paintings, etc.

pa·le·ol·o·gy (pā′lē·ol′ə·jē) *n.* The study of antiquity [...] antiquities; archeology. — **pa′le·o·log′i·cal** (-ə·loj′i·kəl) *a*[...] — **pa′le·ol′o·gist** *n.*

pa·le·on·tol·o·gy (pā′lē·on·tol′ə·jē) *n.* *pl.* **·gies 1.** The s[...] ence that treats of ancient forms of life or of fossil organi[...] **2.** A work dealing with this subject. [< PALEO- + Gk. [...] *ontos* being, ppr. of *einai* to be + -LOGY] — **pa′le·on·to·lo[...]** **ic** (-on′tə·loj′ik) or **·i·cal** *adj.* — **pa′le·on·tol′o·gist** *n.*

Pa·le·o·zo·ic (pā′lē·ō·zō′ik) *adj.* *Geol.* Of or pertaining [...] the era following the Pre-Cambrian and preceding the Mes[...] zoic. — *n.* The Paleozoic era, with its life forms and ro[...] systems. See chart for GEOLOGY. [< PALEO- + Gk. *zōē* li[...]

Pal·es·tine (pal′is·tīn) In Biblical times, a territory on t[...] eastern coast of the Mediterranean, the country of the Jew[...] Old Testament *Canaan*: also *Holy Land*. — **Pal′es·tin′i·[...]** (-tin′ē·ən) *adj. & n.*

pa·les·tra (pə·les′trə) *n.* *pl.* **·trae** (-trē) In ancient Gree[...] a school or practice place for athletics. [< L < Gk. < *[...]* *laiein* to wrestle] — **pa·les′tral, pa·les′tri·an** *adj.*

pal·ette (pal′it) *n.* **1.** A thin board or tablet with a hole [...] the thumb, upon which artists lay and mix their colors [...] The range of colors characteristic of a particular arti[...] painting, etc. Also spelled *pallet*. [< F < L *pala* spade]

·li (pä′lē) *n.* The sacred language of the early Buddhist ·ritings, still surviving in the religious literature of Burma ·d Thailand. [< Skt. *pāli* (*bhasa*) canonical (language)]

·imp·sest (pal′imp·sest) *n.* A parchment, manuscript, ·., written upon two or three times, the earlier writing hav-·g been wholly or partially erased to make room for the ·xt. [< L < Gk. < *palin* again + *psaein* to rub]

·in·drome (pal′in·drōm) *n.* A word, sentence, verse, ·., that is the same read forward or backward, as "Madam, ·m Adam." [< Gk. < *palin* again + *dromos* run]

·ing (pā′ling) *n.* **1.** One of a series of upright pales form-·g a fence. **2.** Pales or pickets collectively. **3.** A fence or ·closure made of pales or pickets. **4.** The act of erecting a ·nce with pales.

·i·sade (pal′ə·sād′) *n.* **1.** A barrier or fortification made ·strong timbers set in the ground. **2.** One of the stakes ·rming such a barrier. **3.** *pl.* An extended cliff or rocky ·ecipice. — *v.t.* **·sad·ed, ·sad·ing** To enclose or fortify with ·palisade. [< MF < Provençal < L *palus* stake]

·ish (pāl′ish) *adj.* Somewhat pale.

·l¹ (pôl) *n.* **1.** A covering, usu. of black cloth, thrown over ·coffin or over a tomb. **2.** A dark, heavy covering, cloud, ·c. **3.** A gloomy or oppressive atmosphere, effect, etc. **4.** ·ccl. **a** A chalice cover, consisting of a square piece of card-·ard faced on both sides with lawn or linen. **b** An altar ·oth. — *v.t.* To cover with or as with a pall. [OE < L *pal-·um* cloak]

·l² (pôl) *v.i.* **1.** To become insipid or uninteresting. **2.** ·o have a dulling or displeasing effect: followed by *on*. — **3.** To satiate; cloy. [Appar. aphetic var. of APPALL]

·la·di·an (pə·lā′dē·ən) *adj.* **1.** Pertaining to or charac-·ristic of the goddess Pallas. **2.** Characterized by wisdom ·learning. [< L < Gk. *Palladios* of Pallas]

·la·di·um¹ (pə·lā′dē·əm) *n.* *pl.* **·di·a** (-dē·ə) Any object ·nsidered essential to the safety of a community or organ-·ation; a safeguard. [< PALLADIUM]

·la·di·um² (pə·lā′dē·əm) *n.* A rare, silver-white, malle-·le and ductile metallic element (symbol Pd) occurring in ·mbination with platinum, iridium, and rhodium. See ELE-·ENT. [< NL, after the asteroid *Pallas*]

·la·di·um (pə·lā′dē·əm) In Greek and Roman legend, a ·atue of Pallas Athena, esp. one in Troy, on the preserva-·on of which the safety of the city depended.

·las (pal′əs) In Greek mythology, a name of Athena, the ·ddess of wisdom: often **Pallas Athena.** — *n.* The second ·rgest asteroid. [< Gk., prob. orig. maiden]

·l·bear·er (pôl′bâr′ər) *n.* One who forms part of an es-·rt for a coffin at a funeral.

·let¹ (pal′it) *n.* **1.** *Mech.* **a** A click or pawl used to regu-·te the motion of a ratchet wheel, etc., as by converting re-·procating into rotary motion, or the reverse. **b.** The lip or ·int of a pawl. **2.** A paddle for mixing and shaping clay ·r crucibles, etc. **3.** A tool used in gilding the backs of ·oks or for taking up gold leaf. **4.** A painter's palette. ·< F < L *pala* spade]

·let² (pal′it) *n.* **1.** A small, mean bed or mattress, usu. ·straw. **2.** A blanket laid on the floor for a bed. [< OF ·L *palea* chaff, straw]

·liasse (pal·yas′, pal′yas) See PAILLASSE.

·li·ate (pal′ē·āt) *v.t.* **·at·ed, ·at·ing 1.** To cause (a crime, ·ult, etc.) to appear less serious or offensive. **2.** To relieve ·e symptoms or effects of (a disease, etc.) without curing. ·< L *palliatus*, pp. of *palliare* to cloak] — **pal′li·a′tion** *n.* ·**pal′li·a·tive** *adj. & n.* — **pal′li·a·tor** *n.*

·lid (pal′id) *adj.* Of a pale or wan appearance; weak or ·cking in color. [< L *pallere* to be pale] — **pal′lid·ly** ·*v.* — **pal′lid·ness** *n.*

·lor (pal′ər) *n.* The state of being pale or pallid; pale-·ss. [< L < *pallere* to be pale]

·lm¹ (päm) *n.* **1.** The inner surface of the hand between ·e wrist and the base of the fingers. **2.** A linear measure ·ual to the approximate breadth (3 or 4 inches) or length ·bout 8½ inches) of the hand. **3.** That which covers the ·lm, as part of a glove. **4.** The flattened terminal portion ·the antler of a moose, etc. **5.** The flat, expanding end of ·y armlike projection, as the blade of an oar. — *v.t.* **1.** To ·de (cards, dice, etc.) in or about the hand, as in sleight of ·and. **2.** To handle or touch with the palm. — **to palm off** ·o pass off or impose fraudulently. [< F < OF < L *palma*]

·lm² (päm) *n.* **1.** Any of a large and varied group of tropi-·l evergreen trees or shrubs usu. having an unbranched ·unk topped by a crown of large palmate or pinnate leaves. ·a leaf or branch of the palm, used as a symbol of victory ·joy. **3.** Triumph; victory. [OE < L *palma* palm tree]

·l·ma·ceous (pal·mā′shəs, pä·mā′-) *adj.* Belonging to or ·aracteristic of the group of plants comprising the palms.

·l·mar (pal′mər, pä′mər) *adj.* Of, pertaining to, or similar ·the palm of the hand.

pal·mate (pal′māt, pä′māt) *adj.* **1.** Resembling an open hand. **2.** Broad and flat, with fingerlike projections, as the antlers of the moose, or some corals. **3.** *Bot.* Having lobes that diverge from the apex of the petiole: a *palmate* leaf. **4.** *Zool.* Webbed, as a bird's foot. Also **pal′mat·ed.** [< L *palmatus*, pp. of *palmare* to mark with the palm of the hand] — **pal′mate·ly** *adv.* — **pal·ma′tion** *n.*

palm·er (pä′mər) *n.* In the Middle Ages, one who had visit-ed Palestine and brought back a palm branch as a token of the pilgrimage.

pal·met·to (pal·met′ō) *n.* *pl.* **·tos** or **·toes** Any of various palms having fanlike foliage. [< Sp. *palmito*, dim. of *palma* palm tree < L]

Palmetto State Nickname of South Carolina.

palmi- *combining form* Palm. [< L *palma* palm]

palm·ist (pä′mist) *n.* One who practices palmistry.

palm·is·try (pä′mis·trē) *n.* The art or practice of supposed-ly discovering a person's past or future from the lines and marks in the palm of the hand. [ME < *palme* palm + *-estrie*, prob. < OF *maistrie* mastery]

palm oil A yellowish, butterlike oil obtained from the fruit of several varieties of palm, and used in the manufacture of soap, candles, etc.

palm sugar Sugar made from palm sap.

Palm Sunday The Sunday before Easter, being the last Sunday in Lent and the first day in Holy Week. [Named for Christ's triumphal entry into Jerusalem, when palm branches were strewn before him]

palm·y (pä′mē) *adj.* **palm·i·er, palm·i·est 1.** Marked by prosperity; flourishing. **2.** Abounding in palms.

pal·my·ra (pal·mī′rə) *n.* An East Indian palm having large fan-shaped leaves. [< Pg. *palmeira* palm tree]

pal·o·mi·no (pal′ə·mē′nō) *n.* *pl.* **·nos** A light tan or golden brown horse with a cream-colored mane and tail. [< Am. Sp., orig., dove-colored horse < Sp. < L *palumbus* ringdove]

pa·loo·ka (pə·lōō′kə) *n.* *U.S. Slang* **1.** An inferior or bun-gling pugilist. **2.** A lout; lummox. [Coined by Jack Con-way, U.S. journalist, d. 1928; ult. origin uncertain]

palp (palp) *n.* A palpus. [< F < L *palpus* feeler]

pal·pa·ble (pal′pə·bəl) *adj.* **1.** Capable of being touched or felt. **2.** Readily perceived; obvious. **3.** Perceptible by touching. [< L < L *palpare* to touch] — **pal′pa·bil′i·ty, pal′pa·ble·ness** *n.* — **pal′pa·bly** *adv.*

pal·pate (pal′pāt) *v.t.* **·pat·ed, ·pat·ing** To feel or examine by touch, esp. for medical diagnosis. — *adj.* Having a pal-pus or palpi. [< L *palpare* to touch] — **pal·pa′tion** *n.*

pal·pi·tate (pal′pə·tāt) *v.i.* **·tat·ed, ·tat·ing 1.** To quiver; tremble. **2.** To beat more rapidly than normal; flutter: said esp. of the heart. [< L *palpitatus*, pp. of *palpitare* to trem-ble, freq. of *palpare* to touch] — **pal′pi·ta′tion** *n.*

pal·pus (pal′pəs) *n.* *pl.* **·pi** (-pī) *Zool.* A feeler; esp., one of the jointed sense organs attached to the mouth parts of arthropods: also called *palp.* [< NL < L *palpus* feeler]

pal·sied (pôl′zēd) *adj.* Affected with palsy; trembling.

pal·sy (pôl′zē) *n.* *pl.* **·sies 1.** Paralysis. **2.** Any impair-ment or loss of ability to control movement. — *v.t.* **·sied, ·sy·ing 1.** To paralyze. **2.** To cause to tremble or become helpless, as from fear or rage. [< OF < L *paralysis*]

pal·ter (pôl′tər) *v.i.* **1.** To speak or act insincerely; equivo-cate; lie. **2.** To be fickle or capricious; trifle. **3.** To haggle or quibble. [Origin unknown] — **pal′ter·er** *n.*

pal·try (pôl′trē) *adj.* **·tri·er, ·tri·est 1.** Having little or no worth or value; trifling; trivial. **2.** Contemptible; petty. [< LG < *palte* rag.] — **pal′tri·ly** *adv.* — **pal′tri·ness** *n.*

pa·lu·dal (pə·lōōd′l) *adj.* Pertaining to a marsh; swampy. [< L *palus, paludis* marsh]

pam·pas (pam′pəz, *Sp.* däs′) *n.pl.* The great treeless plains south of the Amazon river, extending from the At-lantic to the Andes. [< Sp. < Quechua *pampa* plain]

pam·pe·an (pam′pē·ən, pam·pē′ən) *adj.* Of or pertaining to the pampas or to their native inhabitants. — *n.* An Indian of the pampas.

pam·per (pam′pər) *v.t.* To treat very indulgently; gratify the whims or wishes of; coddle. [Appar. < LG < *pampen* to live luxuriously] — **pam′per·er** *n.*

pam·phlet (pam′flit) *n.* **1.** A printed work stitched or past-ed, but not permanently bound. **2.** A brief treatise or essay, often on a subject of current interest, printed and published without a binding. [< OF *pamphlet*, dim. of *Pamphilus*, title of a 12th c. Latin love poem]

pam·phlet·eer (pam′flə·tir′) *n.* One who writes pamphlets: sometimes a term of contempt. — *v.i.* To write and issue pamphlets.

pan¹ (pan) *n.* **1.** A wide, shallow vessel, usu. of metal, used for holding liquids or in cooking. **2.** Any similar receptacle or vessel, as one used for boiling and evaporating. **3.** A cir-cular iron dish with sloping sides, in which gold is separated. **4.** The powder cavity of a flintlock. **5.** The skull; brainpan.

6. Hardpan. **7.** Either of the two receptacles on a pair of scales or a balance. — *v.* **panned, pan·ning** *v.t.* **1.** To separate (gold) by washing gold-bearing earth in a pan. **2.** To wash (earth, gravel, etc.) for this purpose. **3.** To cook and serve in a pan. **4.** *Informal* To criticize severely. — *v.i.* **5.** To search for gold by washing earth, gravel, etc., in a pan. **6.** To yield gold, as earth. — **to pan out** *U.S. Informal* To succeed. [OE < Gmc. < LL < L < Gk. *patanē*]

pan² (pan) *v.t.* **panned, pan·ning** To move (a motion-picture or television camera) so as to photograph an entire scene, follow a particular character, etc. [< PANORAMA]

pan- *combining form* **1.** All; every; the whole: *panchromatic*. **2.** Comprising, including, or applying to all: usually capitalized when preceding proper nouns or adjectives, as in: **Pan-African, Pan-Asia, Pan-Arab.** [< Gk., neut. of *pas* all]

Pan (pan) In Greek mythology, a god identified with the Roman *Faunus*.

pan·a·ce·a (pan'ə-sē'ə) *n.* A remedy for all diseases or ills; a cure-all. [< L < Gk. < *pan*, neut. of *pas* all + *akos* cure] — **pan'a·ce'an** *adj.*

Panama hat A hat woven from the leaves of a palmlike tree of Central and South America.

Pan·a·ma·ni·an (pan'ə-mā'nē-ən, -mä'-) *adj.* Of or pertaining to the Isthmus of Panama or its inhabitants. — *n.* A native or naturalized inhabitant of Panama. Also **Pan·a·man** (pan'ə-män').

Pan-A·mer·i·can (pan'ə-mer'ə-kən) *adj.* Including or pertaining to the whole of America, both North and South, or to all Americans. Also **Pan American.**

Pan-A·mer·i·can·ism (pan'ə-mer'ə-kən·iz'əm) *n.* The advocacy of a closer political and economic cooperation among the republics of the western hemisphere.

Pan American Union A bureau established in Washington, D.C., in 1890, by the 21 American republics to promote mutual peace.

pan·a·tel·a (pan'ə-tel'ə) See PANETELA.

pan-broil (pan'broil') *v.t. & v.i.* To cook in a heavy frying pan placed over direct heat, using little or no fat.

pan·cake (pan'kāk') *n.* **1.** A thin, flat cake made from batter fried in a pan or baked on a griddle. **2.** A cosmetic resembling face powder: also **pancake make-up. 3.** *Aeron.* An abrupt landing in which an airplane is leveled off and stalled well above the surface so that it drops flat. — *v.i.* **·caked, ·cak·ing** *Aeron.* To make a pancake landing.

pan·chro·mat·ic (pan'krō·mat'ik) *adj. Photog.* Sensitive to light of all colors of the spectrum, as film or a plate. — **pan·chro'ma·tism** (-krō'mə·tiz'əm) *n.*

pan·cre·as (pan'krē·əs, pang'-) *n. Anat.* A large gland situated behind the lower part of the stomach, secreting digestive enzymes into the duodenum and producing insulin in the islands of Langerhans. [< NL < Gk. < *pan-* all + *kreas* flesh] — **pan'cre·at'ic** (-at'ik) *adj.*

pan·da (pan'də) *n. pl.* **·das** or **·da 1.** A small, raccoonlike carnivore of the southeastern Himalayas, with long reddish brown fur and ringed tail: also called *bearcat.* **2.** A large, bearlike mammal of Tibet and China, with black-and-white coat and rings around the eyes: also called *giant panda.* [Prob. < Nepalese]

GIANT PANDA
(5 feet long; 2 feet high at shoulder)

Pan·de·an (pan·dē'ən) *adj.* Of or pertaining to the god Pan.

pan·dem·ic (pan·dem'ik) *adj.* **1.** *Med.* Widely epidemic. **2.** Universal; general. — *n.* A pandemic disease. [< Gk. < *pan-* all + *dēmos* people]

pan·de·mo·ni·um (pan'də·mō'nē·əm) *n.* **1.** The abode of all demons. **2.** Loosely, hell. **3.** A place marked by disorder and uproar. **4.** Riotous uproar. Also **pan'dae·mo'ni·um.** [< NL < Gk. *pan-* all + *daimōn* demon]

pan·der (pan'dər) *n.* **1.** A go-between in sexual intrigues; pimp. **2.** One who ministers to the passions or base desires of others. Also **pan'der·er.** — *v.i.* **1.** To act as a pander. — *v.t.* **2.** To act as a pander for. [< L < Gk. *Pandaros*; or < *Pandare*, character in Chaucer's Troilus and Criseyde]

Pan·do·ra (pan·dôr'ə, -dō'rə) In Greek mythology, the first mortal woman, who brought with her a box (**Pandora's box**) containing all human ills which, when she opened the lid, escaped into the world. [< Gk., all-gifted]

pan·dow·dy (pan·dou'dē) *n. pl.* **·dies** *U.S.* A deep-dish pie or pudding make of baked sliced apples and having only a top crust. Also **apple pandowdy.** [Origin unknown]

pane (pān) *n.* **1.** One of the sections of a window, door, etc., filled with a sheet of glass. **2.** A sheet of glass for such a section. **3.** One of the flat surfaces on an object having several sides, as a nut, bolthead, or cut diamond. **4.** A panel in a door, ceiling, etc. [< OF < L *pannus* piece of cloth]

pan·e·gyr·ic (pan'ə·jir'ik) *n.* **1.** A formal public eulogy, either written or spoken. **2.** Elaborate praise; laudation. [< MF < L < Gk. < *pan-* all + *agyris* assembly] — **pan'·e·gyr'i·cal** *adj.* **pan'e·gyr'i·cal·ly** *adv.*

pan·e·gyr·ist (pan'ə·jir'ist) *n.* One who panegyrizes.

pan·e·gy·rize (pan'ə·jə·rīz') *v.* **·rized, ·riz·ing** *v.t.* **1.** deliver or write a panegyric upon; eulogize. — *v.i.* **2.** make panegyrics.

pan·el (pan'əl) *n.* **1.** A rectangular or square piece form part of a wainscot, ceiling, door, etc., usu. raised above sunk below the general level, surrounded by a molding, **2.** A window pane. **3.** One or more pieces of the same different fabric inserted lengthwise in a woman's sk **4.** A tablet of wood used as the surface for an oil painti also, the picture painted on such a tablet. **5.** A picture v long for its width. **6.** *Law* **a** The official list of pers summoned for jury duty. **b** The body of persons compos a jury **7.** A small group of persons selected to hold a cussion, judge a contest, etc. **8.** An instrument panel. *v.t.* **pan·eled** or **·elled, pan·el·ing** or **·el·ling 1.** To fit, nish, or adorn with panels. **2.** To divide into panels. [< OF < Med.L < L *pannus* piece of cloth]

panel discussion A discussion before an audience of a cific topic by a group of selected speakers.

pan·el·ing (pan'əl·ing) *n.* **1.** Wood or other materials u in making panels. **2.** Panels collectively. Also **pan'el·li**

pan·el·ist (pan'əl·ist) *n.* A person serving on a panel.

pan·e·te·la (pan'ə·tel'ə) *n.* A long, slender cigar: a spelled *panatela.* Also **pan'e·tel'la.** [< Sp.]

pan fish Any little fish that can be fried whole.

pang (pang) *n.* **1.** A sudden sharp pain. **2.** A spasm mental anguish. [Origin unknown]

pan·go·lin (pang·gō'lin) *n.* A heavily armored, typica long-tailed toothless mammal of Asia and Africa: also ca *scaly anteater.* [< Malay *peng-gōling* roller, in ref. to power of rolling itself up]

pan·han·dle¹ (pan'han'dəl) *v.i.* **·dled, ·dling** *U.S. Infor* To beg, esp. on the street. [PAN-HAN-DLER]

pan·han·dle² (pan'han'dəl) *n.* **1.** The handle of a pan. *Usu. cap. U.S.* A narrow strip of land shaped like the han of a pan, as in Texas or West Virginia.

pan·han·dler (pan'han'dlər) *n. U.S. Informal* A begg [< PAN¹ (receive to receive alms) + HANDLE, v.]

Pan-Hel·len·ic (pan'he·len'ik) *adj.* **1.** Of or pertain to all Greeks. **2.** Of college fraternities or sororities.

pan·ic (pan'ik) *n.* **1.** A sudden, unreasonable, overpower fear, esp. when affecting a large number simultaneous **2.** An instance of such fear. — *adj.* **1.** Of the nature or resulting from panic. **2.** *Usu. cap.* Of or pertaining the Greek god Pan. — *v.t. & v.i.* **·icked, ·ick·ing** To aff or become affected with panic. [< MF < Gk. *panikos* or for the god Pan, who was believed to cause sudden groundless fear] — **pan'ick·y** *adj.*

pan·i·cle (pan'i·kəl) *n. Bot.* A loose compound flower cl ter, produced by irregular branching. [< L *panicula*, d of *panus* swelling]

pan·ic-strick·en (pan'ik·strik'ən) *adj.* Overcome by pa Also **pan'ic-struck'** (-struk').

pa·nic·u·late (pə·nik'yə·lāt, -lit) *adj. Bot.* Arrang in panicles. Also **pa·nic'u·lat'ed.** — **pa·nic'u·late·ly** *a*

pan·jan·drum (pan·jan'drəm) *n.* A mock title for an c cial of exaggerated importance or great pretensions. [Coir by Samuel Foote, 1720–1777, English dramatist and act

pan·nier (pan'yər) *n.* **1.** One of a pair of baskets adap to be slung on both sides of a beast of burden. **2.** A bas for carrying a load on the back. **3.** A light framework extending a woman's dress at the hips; also, a skirt or ov skirt so extended. [< MF < L *panarium* bread basket

pa·no·cha (pə·nō'chə) *n.* A coarse Mexican sugar. Also **pa·no'che.** [< Am. Sp., dim. of Sp. *pan*]

pan·o·ply (pan'ə·plē) *n. pl.* **·plies 1.** The complete equ ment of a warrior. **2.** Any complete covering that prote or arrays. [< Gk. *panoplia* full armor] — **pan'o·plied** *a*

pan·o·ram·a (pan'ə·ram'ə, -rä'mə) *n.* **1.** A series of p tures representing a continuous scene, arranged to unroll a pass before the spectator. **2.** A complete view in every rection; also, a complete or comprehensive view of a subj or of passing events. [< PAN- + Gk. *horama* sight] — **pan'o·ram'ic** *adj.* — **pan'o·ram'i·cal·ly** *adv.*

pan·pipe (pan'pīp') *n. Sometimes cap. Often pl.* An inst ment consisting of a graduated series of short flutes, origin ly reeds, joined together in proper order to produce a sca

Pan-Slav·ism (pan'slō'viz·əm) *n.* The idea of uniting Slavic peoples, esp. under the hegemony of Russia. — **Pa Slav'ic** *adj.* — **Pan'-slav'ist** *n.*

pan·sy (pan'zē) *n. pl.* **·sies 1.** A garden violet havi blossoms of a variety of colors. **2.** *U.S. Slang* An effemin or homosexual man. [< MF *pensée* thought]

pant (pant) *v.i.* **1.** To breathe rapidly or spasmodical gasp for breath. **2.** To emit smoke, steam, etc., in lo puffs. **3.** To gasp with desire; yearn: with *for* or *after.* To beat or pulsate rapidly. — *v.t.* **5.** To breathe out utter gaspingly. — *n.* **1.** The act of panting. **2.** A gas **3.** A throb, as of the heart. **4.** A puff, as from an engir [Appar. < OF, ult. < L *phantasiare* to have a nightmare

nt- Var. of PANTO-.

n·ta·lets (pan'tə·lets') *n.pl.* 1. Formerly, long ruffled or nbroidered drawers extending below the hem of the skirt Separate frilled leg coverings to be attached to drawers. lso **pan'ta·lettes'.** [Dim. of PANTALOON]

n·ta·loon (pan'tə·lōōn') *n. pl.* Formerly, a tight-fitting rment for the hips and legs; trousers. [< MF < Ital. *intalone* clown < *Pantaleone*, popular Venetian saint]

n·ta·loon (pan'tə·lōōn') In early Italian comedy, a skin-, foolish old man wearing pantaloons.

1·the·ism (pan'thē·iz'əm) *n.* 1. The doctrine that the hole universe is God, or that every part of the universe is a anifestation of God. 2. Worship of all the gods. [<PAN- Gk. *theos* god] — **pan'the·ist** *n.* — **pan'the·is'tic,** an'the·is'ti·cal *adj.* — **pan'the·is·ti·cal·ly** *adv.*

n·the·on (pan'thē·on) *n.* 1. All the gods of a people col-ctively. 2. A mausoleum or temple commemorating the eat of a nation. [< L < Gk. < *pan-* all + *theios* of or cred to a god]

n·the·on (pan'thē·on) A circular domed temple at Rome, dicated to all the gods, built in 27 B.C., rebuilt A.D. 120– 4, and since A.D. 609 used as a church.

n·ther (pan'thər) *n.* 1. A leopard, esp. the black variety Asia. 2. The puma or cougar. 3. The jaguar. [< OF L < Gk. *panthēr*] — **pan'ther·ess** *n.fem.*

nt·ies (pan'tēz) *n.pl.* A woman's or child's underpants. **nto-** *combining form* All; every. Also, before vowels, *nt-*. [< Gk. *pantos,* genitive of *pas* all]

n·to·graph (pan'tə·graf, -gräf) *n.* An instrument used r copying drawings, maps, etc., to any scale. — **pant'o-aph'ic** or **·i·cal** *adj.* — **pan·tog·ra·phy** (pan·tog'rə·fē) *n.*

n·to·mime (pan'tə·mīm) *n.* 1. Any play in which the tors express their meaning by action without dialogue. 2. estures without speech. 3. In ancient Roman drama, a rt of a play in which the actor used only gestures to the companiment of the chorus. — *v.t. & v.i.* **·mimed, ·mim·** To act or express in pantomime. [< F < L < Gk. *nto(s)* of all + *mimos* imitator] — **pan'to·mim'ic** (-mim'-) or **·i·cal** *adj.* — **pan'to·mi'mist** (-mī'mist) *n.*

n·try (pan'trē) *n. pl.* **·tries** A room or closet for provi-ns, dishes, table linen, etc. [ME < OF < L *panis* bread] **nts** (pants) *n.pl. Chiefly U.S.* 1. Trousers. 2. Drawers. nderpants. [Short for PANTALOONS]

n·ty·waist (pan'tē·wāst') *n.* 1. A child's waist on which fasten short pants. 2. *Slang* An effeminate young man.

n·zer (pan'zər, *Ger.* pän'tsər) *adj.* Armored; also, using mored tanks or mechanized troops. [< G, armor plating MHG < OF < Ital. *panzia* belly]

p¹ (pap) *n. Archaic* A teat; nipple. [ME *pappe*]

p² (pap) *n.* 1. Any soft food for babies. 2. *Slang* The es and privileges of public office. [Prob. akin to L *pūppa*]

·pa (pä'pə, pə·pä') *n.* Father: used familiarly. [< F < Gk. *papas,* child's word for father]

·pa·cy (pā'pə·sē) *n. pl.* **·cies** 1. The dignity, office, or risdiction of the pope. 2. The succession of popes. 3. he period during which a pope is in office. [< Med.L Gk. *papas* father]

·pa·cy (pā'pə·sē) *n.* The Roman Catholic system of urch government.

·pal (pā'pəl) *adj.* 1. Of, pertaining to, or ordered by the pe. 2. Of or pertaining to the papacy. 3. Of or pertain-g to the Roman Catholic Church.

pal cross A cross having three crossbars or transoms, e top one the shortest and the bottom one the longest.

·paw (pə·pô', pô'pô) *n.* 1. The fleshy, edible fruit of a orth American shrub or small tree. 2. The tree bearing is fruit. Also spelled *pawpaw.* [< PAPAYA]

·pa·ya (pä·pä'yä, pə·pä'yə) *n.* 1. The yellow, melonlike uit of a tropical American evergreen tree, valued for its avor and nutritious qualities. 2. The tree bearing this uit. [< Sp. and Pg.; ult of Carib origin]

·per (pā'pər) *n.* 1. A substance made from pulp obtained om rags, wood, bark, etc., usu. formed into thin sheets for riting, printing, wrapping, etc. 2. A sheet of this material. Something similar in appearance to paper, as papier-âché. 4. Wallpaper. 5. A small paper wrapper or card lding a limited number or amount: a *paper* of pins. A printed or written document. 7. A newspaper. 8. A ritten discourse or treatise. 9. In schools and colleges, a ece of written work, as an assignment, a report, etc. 0. *pl.* A collection of letters, diaries, and other writings, pecially by one person. 11. *pl.* Personal documents or entification; credentials. 12. *pl.* A ship's papers. 13. business, written or printed pledges to pay, that are nego-able. 14. *Slang* Free passes to a theater, etc.; also, an idience so admitted. 15. *pl. U.S.* Documents leading naturalization: see FIRST PAPERS, SECOND PAPERS. — **paper** 1. In written or printed form. 2. In theory, as

distinguished from fact. — *v.t.* 1. To cover with wallpaper. 2. To fold or enclose in paper. 3. To supply with paper. 4. *Slang* To issue free tickets of admission to (a place of amusement). — *adj.* 1. Made of paper. 2. Existing only in writing. [< OF < L *papyrus*] — **pa'per·y** *adj.*

pa·per·back (pā'pər·bak') *adj.* Of books, having a flexible paper cover or binding. — *n.* A book so bound.

pa·per·hang·er (pā'pər·hang'ər) *n.* One whose business is to cover walls, etc., with paper. — **pa'per·hang'ing** *n.*

pa·per·knife (pā'pər·nīf') *n. pl.* **·knives** (-nīvz') A dull blade for opening letters, leaves of books, etc.

paper money Currency consisting of paper imprinted with certain fixed values issued by a government or by authorized banks for circulation as a substitute for metallic money.

paper nautilus One of various eight-armed marine mol-lusks having delicate shells.

pa·per·weight (pā'pər·wāt') *n.* A small, heavy object, of-ten ornamental, placed on loose papers to secure them.

pap·er·work (pā'pər·wûrk') *n.* Work involving the prep-aration or handling of reports, letters, forms, etc.

pa·pier-mâ·ché (pā'pər·mə·shā', *Fr.* pá·pyä'·mä·shā') *n.* A material consisting of paper pulp mixed with size, paste, oil, resin, etc., that can be molded into various shapes when wet and that becomes hard when dry. [< F *papier* paper + *mâché,* pp. of *mâcher* to chew]

pa·pil·la (pə·pil'ə) *n. pl.* **·pil·lae** (-pil·ē) 1. *Anat.* **a** The nipple. **b** Any small nipplelike process of connective tissue, as on the tongue or at the root of a hair. 2. *Bot.* A small nipple-shaped projection. [< L] — **pap·il·la·ry** (pap'ə-ler'ē) *adj.*

pap·il·lo·ma (pap'ə·lō'mə) *n. pl.* **·ma·ta** (-mə·tə) *Pathol.* An abnormality of the skin or mucous membrane consisting of tumorous outgrowths, as corns, warts, etc. [< PAPILLA] — **pap·il·lose** (pap'ə·lōs) *adj.* Having many papillae. — **pap·il'los'i·ty** (-los'ə·tē) *n.*

pa·pist (pā'pist) *n.* An adherent of the papacy; a Roman Catholic: usu. a disparaging term. [See PAPACY.] — **pa·pis·ti·cal** (pə·pis'ti·kəl), **pa·pis'tic** *adj.* — **pa·pis·try** *n.*

pa·poose (pa·pōōs') *n.* A North American Indian infant or small child. Also **pap·poose'.** [< Algonquian *papoos*]

pap·pus (pap'əs) *n. pl.* **pap·pi** (pap'ī) *Bot.* A downy tuft of hairs, as in thistles, or on certain fruits. [< NL < Gk. *pappos* grandfather] — **pap'pose** (-ōs), **pap'pous** (-əs) *adj.*

pap·py (pap'ē) *n. pl.* **·pies** Papa; father. [Dim. of PAPA¹]

pa·pri·ka (pa·prē'kə, pap'rə·kə) *n.* A condiment made from the ripe fruit of a mild variety of red pepper. Also **pa·pri'ca.** [< Magyar, red pepper]

Pap·u·an (pä'pōō·ən, pap'ōō·ən) *adj.* Of or pertaining to the Island of Papua or to the Papuan peoples. — *n.* A member of any of the dark peoples inhabiting Melanesia.

pap·u·la (pap'yə·lə) *n. pl.* **·lae** (-lē) *Pathol.* A pimple. Also **pap'ule** (-yōōl). [< L, pimple] — **pap'u·lan** *adj.*

pa·py·rus (pə·pī'rəs) *n. pl.* **·ri** (-rī) 1. A tall rushlike aqua-tic plant of the sedge family, formerly common in Egypt. 2. A type of writing paper made by the ancient Egyptians from this plant. 3. A manuscript written on this material. [< L < Gk. *papyros*]

par (pär) *n.* 1. An accepted standard or level used for com-parison: usu. preceded by *on* or *upon*: His work is on a *par* with that of the other students. 2. The normal average in amount, quality, or degree: His health is up to *par*. 3. In commerce, the state of equality between the nominal, or face, value and the market value of shares of stock, bonds, bills of exchange, etc: also *parity*. 4. In golf, the number of strokes allotted to a hole or round when played perfectly. — *adj.* 1. Normal; average. 2. In commerce, having the face value normal. [< L, equal]

para-¹ *prefix* 1. Beside; nearby; along with: *paradigm*. 2. Beyond; aside from; amiss: *paradox*. 3. *Chem.* A modifi-cation of or a compound similar to (not necessarily isomeric or polymeric): *paramorphine*. 4. *Med.* **a** A functionally disordered or diseased condition: *paraplegia*. **b** Similar to but not identical with a true condition or form: *paratyphoid*. Also, before vowels and *h*, usu. **par-**. [< Gk. *para* beside]

para-² *combining form* Shelter or protection against: *parasol*. [< Ital *para,* imperative of *parare* to defend]

par·a·mi·no·ben·zo·ic acid (par'ə·ə·mē'nō·ben·zō'ik, -am'ə·nō-) *Biochem.* A colorless crystalline compound, $C_7H_7NO_2$, forming part of the vitamin B complex, present in yeast and also made synthetically.

par·a·ble (par'ə·bəl) *n.* A short narrative making a moral or religious point by comparison with natural or homely things. [< OF < LL < Gk. *parabolē* a placing side by side]

pa·rab·o·la (pə·rab'ə·lə) *n. Math.* The curve formed by the edges of a plane when cutting through a right circular cone at an angle parallel to one of its sides. [< L < Gk. *parabolē* a placing side by side]

par·a·bol·ic (par'ə·bol'ik) *adj.* 1. Pertaining to or having the nature of a parable. **2.** Pertaining to or like a parabola. Also **par·a·bol/i·cal.** — **par·a·bol/i·cal·ly** adv.

pa·rab·o·lize (pə·rab/ə·līz) v.t. **·lized,** **·liz·ing** **1.** To relate in parable form. **2.** Math. To give the form of a parabola to.

par·a·chute (par/ə·shoot) n. A large, umbrella-shaped apparatus for retarding the speed of a body descending through the air, esp. from an airplane. — v, **·chut·ed, ·chut·ing** v.t. **1.** To land (troops, materiel, etc.) by means of parachutes. — v.i. **2.** To descend by parachute. [< F < PARA²- + chute fall] — **par/a·chut/ist** n.

par·a·clete (par/ə·klēt) n. One called to the aid of another. — **the Paraclete** The Holy Spirit as a helper or comforter. [< OF < LL < LGk. paraklētos comforter, advocate]

pa·rade (pə·rād/) n. **1.** A procession or march for ceremony or display. **2.** A marshaling and maneuvering of troops for display or inspection. **3.** A ground where military reviews are held. **4.** A promenade or public walk; also, the persons promenading. **5.** Pompous show, ostentation. — **on parade** On display. — v. **·rad·ed, ·rad·ing** v.t. **1.** To walk or march through or about. **2.** To display ostentatiously; flaunt. **3.** To cause to assemble for military parade. — v.i. **4.** To march formally. **5.** To walk in public for the purpose of showing oneself. **6.** To assemble in military order for inspection or review. [< MF < Sp. parada stopping place, exercise ground] — **pa·rad/er** n.

par·a·digm (par/ə·dim, -dīm) n. Gram. **1.** A list or table of all the inflected forms of a word or class of words, as a particular declension, conjugation, etc. **2.** Any pattern or example. [< LL < Gk. paradeigma pattern] — **par/a·dig·mat/ic** (-dig·mat/ik) adj.

par·a·dise (par/ə·dīs) n. **1.** Heaven. **2.** A place or state of great beauty or delight. [< F < LL < Gk. paradeisos park] — **par/a·di·sa/ic** (-di·sā/ik) or **·i·cal, par/a·dis/i·ac** (-dis/ē·ak) or **par·a·di·si·a·cal** (par/ə·di·sī/ə·kəl) adj.

Par·a·dise (par/ə·dīs) Eden or heaven.

par·a·dox (par/ə·doks) n. **1.** A statement seemingly absurd or contradictory, yet in fact true. **2.** A statement essentially self-contradictory, false, or absurd. **3.** One whose character or behavior is inconsistent or contradictory. [< F < L < Gk. paradoxos incredible] — **par/a·dox/i·cal** adj. — **par/a·dox/i·cal·i·ty** (-kal/ə·tē), **par/a·dox/i·cal·ness** n. — **par/a·dox/i·cal·ly** adv.

par·a·drop (par/ə·drop) n. Mil. The dropping of supplies equipment, etc., by parachute.

par·af·fin (par/ə·fin) n. Chem. **1.** A waxy mixture of hydrocarbons, distilled from petroleum and widely used for candles, as a preservative, etc. **2.** Any hydrocarbon of the methane series — v.t. To treat or impregnate with paraffin. Also **par/af·fine** (-fin, -fēn). [< G < L par(um) too little + affin(is) related to; so named because it has little affinity for other substances]

paraffin series Chem. The methane series.

paraffin wax Paraffin in its solid state.

par·a·gon (par/ə·gon) n. A model or pattern of excellence, esp. of a specific excellence: a paragon of manhood. [< OF < Ital. paragone touchstone, prob. < Gk. parakonan to sharpen one thing against another]

par·a·graph (par/ə·graf, -gräf) n. **1.** A distinct part or section of a written discourse, begun on a new and usu. indented line and generally containing a unified statement of a particular point. **2.** A short article, item, or comment, as in a newspaper. **3.** A mark (¶) used to indicate where a para graph is to be begun. — v.t. **1.** To arrange in or into paragraphs. **2.** To comment on or express in a paragraph. [< OF < LL < Gk. < para beside + graphein to write] — **par/a·graph/er** n. — **par/a·graph/ic, par/a·graph/i·cal** adj.

par·a·keet (par/ə·kēt) n. Any of certain small parrots, with long, wedge-shaped tails: also spelled paraquet, paroquet, parrakeet, parroket, parroquet. [< OF < Ital. parrochetto]

Par·a·li·pom·e·non (par/ə·li·pom/ə·non) n. The Douai Bible name for CHRONICLES.

par·al·lax (par/ə·laks) n. The apparent displacement of an object, esp. of a star or other heavenly body, when it is viewed successively from two points not in the same line of sight. [< F < Gk. parallassein to deviate]

par·al·lel (par/ə·lel) adj. **1.** Being a uniform distance away or apart throughout a certain area or extent. **2.** Geom. Not meeting, however far extended: said of straight lines and of planes. **3.** Having a close resemblance. **4.** Music **a** Denoting consecutive identical or similar intervals in the same two voices. **b** Denoting consecutive identical chords. **5.** Electr. Connected between like terminals, as a group of cells, condensers, etc. — n. **1.** An object or surface equidistant from another. **2.** Geom. A parallel line or plane. **3.** Essential likeness. **4.** A counterpart; match. **5.** Comparison: to draw a parallel between two things. **6.** Geog. Any of the circles imagined as drawn upon the earth's surface at right angles to its axis, every point on which marks a given latitude north or south of the equator. **7.** Electr. Connection between like terminals: usu. in the phrase **in parallel:** also called multiple. — v.t. **·leled** or **·lelled, ·lel·ing**

or **·lel·ling 1.** To place in parallel; make parallel. **2.** be, go, or extend parallel to. **3.** To furnish with a para or equal; find a parallel to. **4.** To be a parallel to; cor spond to. **5.** To compare; liken. [< MF < L < Gk. para beside + allēlos one another]

parallel bars Two horizontal crossbars, parallel to ea other and supported by upright posts, used for gymnast

par·al·lel·e·pi·ped (par/ə·lel/ə·pī/pid, -pip/id) n. A pri with six faces, each of which is a parallelogram. Also **par·lel/o·pi/ped, par/al·lel/e·pip/e·don, par/al·lel/o·pip/e·d** (-pip/ə·don, -pī/pə-). [< Gk. < parallēlos parallel + epi don a plane surface]

par·al·lel·ism (par/ə·lel·iz/əm) n. **1.** The state or qual of being parallel. **2.** Likeness; similarity. **3.** A comparis

par·al·lel·o·gram (par/ə·lel/ə·gram) n. **1.** Geom. A fo sided plane figure whose opposite sides are parallel a equal. **2.** Any area or object having such form. [< M < L < Gk. < parallēlos parallel + grammē line]

pa·ral·y·sis (pə·ral/ə·sis) n. pl. **·ses** (-sēz) **1.** Pathol. P tial or complete loss of motor function, esp., voluntary n tion, resulting from injury to the nervous system or t muscular mechanism. **2.** Cessation or crippling of norn activities. [< L < Gk. < paralyein to disable] — **a·lyt·ic** (par/ə·lit/ik) adj. & n.

par·a·lyze (par/ə·līz) v.t. **·lyzed, ·lyz·ing 1.** To bring ab paralysis in; make paralytic. **2.** To render powerless, in fective, or inactive. [< F paralyser, back formation paralysie palsy] — **par/a·lyz/er** n. — **par/a·ly·za/tion** n.

par·a·me·ci·um (par/ə·mē/shē·əm, -sē·əm) n. pl. **·c** (shē·ə, -sē·ə) Any of various species of ciliate protoz having a flattened, elongate body, and feeding by a pri tive oral groove. [< NL < Gk. paramēkēs oblong, oval

pa·ram·e·ter (pə·ram/ə·tər) n. **1.** Math. A constant wh values determine the operation or characteristics of a s tem. **2.** A fixed limit or guideline. [< NL < Gk. para side + metron measure]

par·a·mil·i·tar·y (par/ə·mil/ə·ter/ē) adj. Having a milit structure although not officially military; capable of beco ing, replacing, or supplementing a military force: said of c tain political movements, etc. [< PARA-¹ + MILITARY]

par·a·mount (par/ə·mount) adj. **1.** Superior to all othe chief in importance. **2.** Having the highest authority rank. — n. A supreme lord; highest ruler. [< AF < par by + à mont up, above] — **par/a·mount·ly** adv.

par·a·mour (par/ə·moor) n. A lover, esp. one who onl fully takes the place of a husband or wife. [< OF par am with love]

par·a·noi·a (par/ə·noi/ə) n. Psychiatry A form of men disorder characterized by delusions of persecution or grandeur. [< NL < Gk. < para beside + noos, nous mi — **par·a·noi·ac** (par/ə·noi/ak) adj. Relating to or affected paranoia. — n. One affected by paranoia.

par·a·noid (par/ə·noid) adj. Resembling or suggestive paranoia. — n. One affected by paranoia.

par·a·pet (par/ə·pit, -pet) n. A low wall about the edge a roof, terrace, bridge, etc. [< MF, or < Ital. parapet — **par/a·pet·ed** adj.

par·a·pher·na·li·a (par/ə·fər·nā/lē·ə, -nāl/yə, -fə-) n.pl. Personal effects. **2.** A group of articles, esp. as used in so activity; equipment; gear. [< Med.L paraphernalia (bo a wife's own (goods)]

par·a·phrase (par/ə·frāz) n. A restatement of the mean of a passage, work, etc., as for clarity. — v.t. & v.i. **·phras ·phras·ing** To express in or make a paraphrase. [< MF L < Gk. < para beside + phrazein to tell] — **par/a·phra er, par/a·phrast** (-frast) n. — **par/a·phras/tic** or **·ti adj.** — **par/a·phras/ti·cal·ly** adv.

par·a·ple·gi·a (par/ə·plē/jē·ə) n. Pathol. Paralysis of t lower half of the body, due to disease or injury of the spi cord. Also **par/a·ple/gy** (-plē/jē). [< NL < Gk. < p beside + plēssein to strike] — **par·a·ple/gic** adj. & n.

par·a·psy·chol·o·gy (par/ə·sī·kol/ə·jē) n. The study extrasensory perception and related psychic phenomena.

pa·ra·quet (par/ə·kēt) See PARAKEET.

par·a·site (par/ə·sīt) n. **1.** Biol. An animal or plant th lives in or on another organism, the host, and from whom obtains nourishment. **2.** One who lives at another's pense without making proper return. [< L < Gk. pa sitos, lit., one who eats at another's table] — **par/a·sit par/a·sit/i·cal** adj. — **par/a·sit/i·cal·ly** adv.

par·a·sit·ism (par/ə·sī/tiz·əm) n. The condition of be a parasite; parasitic mode of existence.

par·a·sol (par/ə·sôl, -sol) n. A small, light umbrella carr by women, used as protection against the sun. [< MF Ital. < para- para-² + sole sun]

par·a·sym·pa·thet·ic (par/ə·sim/pə·thet/ik) adj. A Denoting a part of the nervous system originating in cranial and sacral regions and having among its functi the constriction of the pupil, the slowing of the heart, dilation of the blood vessels, and the stimulation of digestive and genitourinary systems.

r·a·thy·roid (par′ə·thī′roid) *adj. Anat.* **1.** Lying near
he thyroid gland. **2.** Of or pertaining to any of the several,
su. four, small glands found near the thyroid gland and
erving to control the amount of calcium in the blood. — *n.*
ne of the parathyroid glands.

r·a·troops (par′ə·trōōps) *n.pl.* Troops trained and equip-
ed to drop behind enemy lines by parachute. — **par′a·**
·oop·er *n.*

r a·ty·phoid (par′ə·tī′foid) *Pathol. adj.* Of or pertaining
ɔ paratyphoid fever. — *n.* Paratyphoid fever.

ratyphoid fever *Pathol.* An infectious disease having
ymptoms resembling those of typhoid fever, but caused by
different bacterium.

r a·vi·on (pär′ ə·vyöñ′) *French* By airmail.

r·boil (pär′boil′) *v.t.* **1.** To boil partially. **2.** To make
ncomfortable with heat. [< OF < LL *perbullire* to boil
ɔoroughly]

r·buck·le (pär′buk′əl) *n.* A sling for vertically raising a
eavy object by passing a doubled rope around it, the free
ɔds being pulled through the loop. — *v.t.* ·led, ·ling To
ɔist or lower by means of a parbuckle. [Earlier *parbunkle*;
rigin uncertain]

r·cel (pär′səl) *n.* **1.** Something that is wrapped up; pack-
ge. **2.** A quantity of some commodity put up for sale; lot.
. An indefinite number of persons or things. **4.** A distinct
ortion of land. — *v.t.* par·celed or ·celled, par·cel·ing or
el·ling **1.** To divide or distribute in parts or shares: usu.
rith *out.* **2.** To make up a parcel or parcels. — *adj. & adv.*
art; partly. [< F < L *pars, partis* part]

rcel post A postal service for the conveying and deliver-
ɔg of parcels not exceeding a specified weight and size.

rch (pärch) *v.t.* **1.** To make extremely dry. **2.** To make
ery thirsty. **3.** To dry (corn, peas, etc.) by exposing to
reat heat. **4.** To dry up or shrivel by exposing to cold. —
i. **5.** To become dry. **6.** To become dry with thirst. [ME
archen; ult. origin uncertain]

r·chee·si (pär·chē′zē) *n.* A board game derived from pa-
ɔisi. Also par·che′si, par·chi′si.

rch·ment (pärch′mənt) *n.* **1.** The skin of sheep, goats,
ɔd other animals prepared and polished with pumice stone,
sed as a material for writing or painting upon. **2.** A writ-
ɔg on this material. **3.** Any of several types of paper made
ɔ imitation of parchment. [< OF < L *pergamenus* of
ergamum, the city where it was first used]

rd¹ (pärd) *n. Archaic* A leopard or panther. [< OF
< L < Gk. *pardos*]

rd² (pärd) *n. Slang* A partner. [Short for PARDNER]

rd·ner (pärd′nər) *n. U.S. Dial* Chum; friend. [Alter.
f PARTNER]

r·don (pär′dən) *v.t.* **1.** To remit the penalty of (an of-
ɔnse, insult, etc.). **2.** To forgive (a person) for an offense.
. To grant courteous allowance for or to. — *n.* **1.** The act
f pardoning; forgiveness. **2.** An official warrant declaring
uch a remission. **3.** In the Roman Catholic Church, an
ɔdulgence. [< OF < LL < *per-* through + *donare* to give]
— **par′don·a·ble** *adj.* — **par′don·a·bly** *adv.*

r·don·er (pär′dən·ər) *n.* **1.** One who pardons. **2.** In the
Iiddle Ages, a layman who sold ecclesiastical indulgences.

re (pâr) *v.t.* pared, par·ing **1.** To cut off the covering
ɔyer or part of. **2.** To cut off or trim away (a covering
ɔyer or part): often with *off* or *away* **3.** To diminish gradu-
lly. [< OF *parer* to prepare, trim] — **par′er** *n.*

r·e·gor·ic (par′ə·gôr′ik, -gor′ik) *n. Med.* A camphorated
ɔncture of opium, used primarily to treat diarrhea. [< LL
< Gk. < *parēgoros* soothing]

·ren·chy·ma (pə·reng′ki·mə) *n.* **1.** *Biol.* The essential
ɔnctioning cellular substance of an animal organ, as distin-
uished from connective tissue. **2.** *Bot.* The soft cell tissue
f higher plants, as found in stem pith or fruit pulp. Also
·ren′chyme (-kīm). [< NL < Gk. < *para* beside +
nchyma infusion] — **par·en·chym·a·tous** (par′eng·kim′ə-
ɔs) *adj.*

r·ent (pâr′ənt) *n.* **1.** A father or mother **2.** One exer-
ɔsing the functions of a father or mother. **3.** A progenitor;
ɔrefather. **4.** Any organism that generates another. **5.**
ource; cause. [< OF < L *parere* to beget] — **pa·ren·tal**
pa.ren′tal) *adj.* — **pa·ren′tal·ly** *adv.* — **par′ent·hood** *n.*

r·ent·age (pâr′ən·tij) *n.* **1.** Descent or derivation from
ɔrents; lineage; origin. **2.** Derivation from a source or
rigin. **3.** Parenthood. [< OF]

·ren·the·sis (pə·ren′thə·sis) *n. pl.* ·ses (-sēz) **1.** Either
ɔr both of the upright curved lines ( ) used to enclose an in-
erjected, explanatory, or qualifying remark, mathematical
uantities, etc. **2.** *Gram.* A word, phrase, or clause inserted
ɔ a sentence that is grammatically complete without it, set
ɔff usu. by commas, dashes, or upright curved lines. **3.** An
ɔtervening episode or incident. [< Med. L < Gk. < *para*
eside + *en* in + *tithenai* to place]

pa·ren·the·size (pə·ren′thə·sīz) *v.t.* ·sized, ·siz·ing **1.** To
insert as a parenthetical statement. **2.** To insert parentheses in. **3.** To place within parentheses (def. 1).

par·en·thet·i·cal (par′ən·thet′i·kəl) *adj.* **1.** Thrown in;
episodic. **2.** Abounding in or like parentheses; also, given
to using parentheses. — **par′en·thet′i·cal·ly** *adv.*

pa·re·sis (pə·rē′sis, par′ə·sis) *n. Pathol.* **1.** Partial paralysis affecting muscular motion but not sensation. **2.** General
paresis. [< NL < Gk., a letting go] — **pa·ret·ic** (pə·
ret′ik, -rē′tik) *adj.* — **pa·ret′i·cal·ly** *adv.*

par ex·cel·lence (pär ek′sə·läns, *Fr.* pár ek·se·läns′) Beyond comparison; preeminently. [< F, lit., by excellence]

par·fait (pär·fā′) *n.* A frozen dessert or confection made
with eggs, sugar, whipped cream, and fruit or other flavoring. [< F, perfect]

par·he·li·on (pär·hē′lē·ən) *n. pl.* ·li·a (-lē·ə) *Meteorol.* One
of two bright images sometimes appearing on a solar halo.
Also **par·he′li·um** (-əm). [< L < Gk. < *para* beside +
hēlios sun] — **par·he′lic, par·he·li·a·cal** (pär′hi·lī′ə·kəl) *adj.*

pari- *combining form* Equal. [< L *par, paris* equal]

pa·ri·ah (pə·rī′ə, par′ē·ə) *n.* **1.** A member of an extensive
low caste of southern India and Burma. **2.** A social outcast.
[< Tamil *paraiyon*, lit., (hereditary) drummer]

pa·ri·e·tal (pə·rī′ə·təl) *adj.* **1.** *Anat.* **a** Of, pertaining to, or
forming the walls of a cavity or hollow organ. **b** Of or pertaining to the parietal bones. **2.** *Bot.* Attached to the wall
of the ovary. **3.** *U.S.* Pertaining to residence or authority
within the walls of a college. — *n.* A parietal bone. [<
MF < L *paries* wall]

parietal bone *Anat.* Either of two bones that form a part
of the top and sides of the cranium.

par·i·mu·tu·el (par′i·myōō′chōō·əl) *n.* **1.** A system of betting at races in which those who have bet on the winners
share in the total amount wagered. Also **par′i·mu′tu·el.** **2.**
A pari-mutuel machine. [< F, stake or mutual wager]

pari-mutuel machine A machine for recording pari-mutuel
bets: also called *totalizator, totalizer.*

par·ing (pâr′ing) *n.* **1.** The act of one who pares. **2.** *Often
pl.* The part pared off.

Par·is (par′is) In Greek mythology, a son of Priam whose
abduction of Helen caused the Trojan War.

Paris green A poisonous compound prepared from copper
acetate and arsenic trioxide, used chiefly as an insecticide.

par·ish (par′ish) *n.* **1.** *Eccl.* In the Anglican, Roman Catholic, and some other churches, a district with its own church.
2. *U.S.* All those who worship at the same church. **3.** *Brit.*
A political subdivision of a county. **4.** In Louisiana, a civil
district corresponding to a county. **5.** The people of a
parish. ◆ Collateral adjective: *parochial.* [< OF < LL
< Gk. *paroikia*, orig., residence away from one's people <
Gk. *paroikos*, orig., neighboring, later diocese]

pa·rish·ion·er (pə·rish′ən·ər) *n.* A member of a parish.

Pa·ri·sian (pə·rizh′ən, -riz′ē·ən) *adj.* Of or pertaining to the
city of Paris. — *n.* A native or resident of Paris.

par·i·ty (par′ə·tē) *n. pl.* ·ties **1.** Equality, as of condition,
rank, value, etc.; also, a like state or degree. **2.** The equiva-
lence in legal weight and quality of the legal tender of one
class of money to another. **3.** Par (def. 3). **4.** Equality
between the currency or prices of commodities of two countries or cities. **5.** Perfect analogy; close resemblance. **6.**
U.S. A level for farm prices that gives to the farmer the
same purchasing power that he averaged during each year of
a chosen base period. [< MF < *paritas* equality]

park (pärk) *n.* **1.** A tract of land for public use in or near a
city. **2.** An open square in a city. **3.** A national park
(which see). **4.** An amusement park (which see). **5.** A
large tract of land surrounding a country estate. **6.** *Mil.*
An open area where guns, trucks, etc., are assembled for
servicing and storage. **7.** In English law, a tract of land
held through royal grant or by prescription. — *v.t.* **1.** To
place or leave (an automobile, etc.) standing for a time, as
on a street. **2.** *U.S. Slang* To place; set. **3.** To assemble
or mass together: to *park* artillery. **4.** To enclose in or as
in a park. — *v.i.* **5.** To park an automobile, etc. [< OF
parc game preserve]

par·ka (pär′kə) *n. U.S. & Canadian* **1.** A hooded outer
garment of undressed skins worn by Eskimos. **2.** A similar
garment worn for skiing and other winter sports. [< Aleut]

Par·kin·son's disease (pär′kən·sənz) *Pathol.* A form of
paralysis characterized by muscular rigidity, tremor, and
weakness. Also **Park′in·son·ism.** [after James *Parkinson*,
1755–1824, English physician]

park·land (pärk′land′) *n. Often pl.* **1.** Land used or designated as a park. **2.** Grassland with trees.

park·way (pärk′wā) *n.* A wide thoroughfare adorned with
spaces planted with turf and trees.

par·lance (pär′ləns) *n.* Manner of speech; language: legal
parlance. [< OF < *parler* to speak]

par·lay (pär·lā′, pär′lē) *v.t. & v.i.* To place (an original bet and its winnings) on a later race, contest, etc. — *n.* Such a bet. [< F < Ital *paroli* grand cast at dice]

par·ley (pär′lē) *n.* A conference, as with an enemy; a discussion of terms. — *v.i.* To hold a conference, esp. with an enemy. [< F *parlée*, fem. pp. of *parler* to speak]

par·lia·ment (pär′lə·mənt) *n.* 1. An assembly for consultation and deliberation. 2. A national legislature, esp. when composed of various estates. [< OF *parlement* speaking < *parler* to speak]

Par·lia·ment (pär′lə·mənt) *n.* 1. The supreme legislature of Great Britain and Northern Ireland, composed of the House of Lords and the House of Commons. 2. The legislature in any of Great Britain's colonies or dominions.

par·lia·men·tar·i·an (pär′lə·men·târ′ē·ən) *n.* One versed in parliamentary procedure or debate.

par·lia·men·ta·ry (pär′lə·men′tər·ē) *adj.* 1. Of, pertaining to, or enacted by a parliament. 2. According to the rules of a parliament: *parliamentary* procedure. 3. Of a government, having a parliament.

parliamentary procedure The rules by which meetings of deliberative assemblies, societies, boards, clubs, etc., are formally conducted. Also **parliamentary law.**

par·lor (pär′lər) *n.* 1. A room for reception of callers or entertainment of guests. 2. A room in an inn, hotel, etc., for private conversation, appointments, etc. Also *Brit.* **par′lour.** [< AF < Med.L < ML *parabolare* to speak]

parlor car A railway car fitted with luxurious chairs, and run as a day coach: also called *chair car.*

par·lous (pär′ləs) *Archaic adj.* 1. Dangerous or exciting. 2. Shrewd. — *adv.* Exceedingly. [Var. of PERILOUS]

Par·me·san cheese (pär′mə·zan′) A hard, dry Italian cheese made from skim milk, grated and used to flavor spaghetti, soups, etc. [after *Parma*, a city in Italy]

Par·nas·sus (pär·nas′əs), **Mount** 1. A mountain in central Greece, anciently regarded as sacred to Apollo and the Muses. 2. The domain of poetry or of literature. 3. A collection of poems or other literary works. — **Par·nas·si·an** (pär·nas′ē·ən) *adj.*

pa·ro·chi·al (pə·rō′kē·əl) *adj.* 1. Pertaining to, supported by, or confined to a parish. 2. Narrow; provincial; restricted in scope. [See PARISH.] — **pa·ro′chi·al·ism** *n.* — **pa·ro′chi·al·ly** *adv.*

parochial school A school, usu. elementary, supported and directed by the parish of a church.

par·o·dy (par′ə·dē) *n. pl.* **·dies** 1. A humorous or burlesque imitation of a literary or musical work or style. 2. An incompetent attempt to imitate another's work or style. — *v.t.* **·died, ·dy·ing** To make a parody of. [Ult. < Gk. *parōidia* burlesque poem or song] — **pa·rod·ic** (pə·rod′ik) or **·i·cal** *adj.* — **par′o·dist** *n.*

pa·rol (pə·rōl′) *n.* A word: now only in phrase **by parol,** by word of mouth. [< OF *parole* word]

pa·role (pə·rōl′) *n.* 1. The conditional release of a prisoner before his sentence has expired. 2. The duration of such conditional freedom. 3. *Mil.* A pledge of honor by a prisoner of war that he will not seek to escape or will not serve against his captors until exchanged. — **on parole** Freed from prison under conditions of parole. — *v.t.* **·roled, ·rol·ing** To release (a prisoner) on parole. [< F *parole* (d'honneur) word (of honor)]

pa·rol·ee (pə·rō′lē) *n.* One released from prison on parole.

pa·ro·quet (par′ə·ket) See PARAKEET.

pa·rot·id (pə·rot′id) *Anat. adj.* 1. Situated near the ear. 2. Designating one of the paired salivary glands in front of and below the ear. — *n.* A parotid gland. [< F < L < Gk. *parōtis,* < *para-* beside + *ous, ōtos* ear]

par·ox·ysm (par′ək·siz′əm) *n.* 1. A sudden and violent outburst, as of emotion or action: a *paroxysm* of tears. 2. *Pathol.* A sudden intensification of the symptoms of a disease, usu. occurring at intervals. [< MF < Med.L < Gk. < *para-* beside + *oxynein* to goad < *oxys* sharp] — **par·ox·ys′mal** (-siz′məl) *adj.* — **par·ox·ys′mal·ly** *adv.*

par·quet (pär·kā′, -ket′) *n.* 1. Flooring of parquetry. 2. The main floor of a theater, esp. the section from the orchestra pit to the parquet circle: also called *orchestra.* — *v.t.* **·quet·ed** (-kād′, -ket′id), **·quet·ing** (-kā′ing, -ket′ing) To make (a floor, etc.) of parquetry. [< F < OF *parchet* small compartment, dim. of *parc*]

parquet circle The section of theater seats at the rear of the parquet and under the balcony.

par·quet·ry (pär′kit·rē) *n. pl.* **·ries** Inlaid mosaic of wood, used esp. for floors.

parr (pär) *n.* 1. A young salmon before its first migration seaward. 2. The young of some other fishes, as the cod or pollack. [? < dial. E (Scottish)]

par·ra·keet (par′ə·kēt) See PARAKEET.

PARQUETRY

par·ri·cide (par′ə·sīd) *n.* 1. The killing of a parent. 2. One who has killed a parent. [< F < L *paricida* killer of relative] — **par′ri·ci′dal** *adj.* — **par′ri·ci′dal·ly** *adv.*

par·ro·ket (par′ə·ket) See PARAKEET.

par·ro·quet (par′ə·ket) See PARAKEET.

par·rot (par′ət) *n.* 1. Any of certain birds native in warm regions, having a hooked bill, and often brilliant plumage, including the macaws, parakeets, etc., some of which imitate human speech and laughter. 2. One who repeats without understanding. — *v.t.* To repeat or imitate by rote. [MF var. of *Perrot* < F < LL *Petrus*] — **par′rot·er** *n.*

parrot fish Any of many small fishes inhabiting warm seas and having vivid coloring and beaklike jaws.

par·ry (par′ē) *v.* **·ried, ·ry·ing** *v.t.* 1. To ward off (a thrust, blow, etc.) in fencing. 2. To avoid or evade. — *v.i.* 3. To ward off a thrust or blow. — *n. pl.* **·ries** 1. A defensive movement, as in fencing. 2. An evasion or diversion in a contest of wits. [< Ital. *parare* to ward off]

parse (pärs) *v.t.* **parsed, pars·ing** 1. To analyze (a sentence) grammatically by giving the form, function, and syntactical relation of each of its words. 2. To describe and analyze (a word) grammatically. [< L *pars, partis* part]

par·sec (pär′sek) *n. Astron.* A unit of length used in expressing stellar distances, corresponding to an annual parallax of one second of arc, or 3.26 light-years.

Par·see (pär′sē, pär·sē′) *n.* A member of a religious sect practicing a form of Zoroastrianism, descendants of Persians who fled to India in the eighth century to escape Moslem persecution. Also **Par′si.** [< Persian *Pārsī* a Persian] — **Par′see·ism, Par′si·ism, Par′sism** *n.*

Par·si·fal (pär′si·fäl, -fəl) A knight in Wagner's opera (1882) of this name.

par·si·mo·ni·ous (pär′sə·mō′nē·əs) *adj.* Characterized by or showing parsimony; penurious; niggardly. — **par′si·mo′ni·ous·ly** *adv.* — **par′si·mo′ni·ous·ness** *n.*

par·si·mo·ny (pär′sə·mō′nē) *n. pl.* **·nies** Undue sparingness in the expenditure of money; stinginess. [< L *parsus,* pp. of *parcere* to spare]

pars·ley (pärs′lē) *n.* A cultivated herb, having aromatic leaves, widely used to garnish and flavor foods. [< OF < LL < L < Gk. < *petra* rock + *selinon* parsley]

pars·nip (pärs′nip) *n.* A European herb of the parsley family, with a large, sweetish, edible root. [ME < OF *pasnaie* + OE *nǣp* turnip]

par·son (pär′sən) *n.* 1. A clergyman; minister. 2. In the Anglican Church, a clergyman having full charge of a parish; a rector. [< OF < Med.L *persona* rector] — **par·son·ic** (pär·son′i·kəl), **par·son′ic** *adj.*

par·son·age (pär′sən·ij) *n.* 1. A clergyman's dwelling; esp., a free official residence provided by the church. 2. In English ecclesiastical law, the benefice of a parson.

part (pärt) *n.* 1. A portion of a whole; segment. 2. Math. One of a specified number of equal divisions; an aliquot division. 3. A distinct piece or portion of a machine that fulfills a specific function in the working of the whole. Something less than the whole. 5. An organ, member, or other portion of an animal or plant body. 6. *Usu. pl.* region; territory: in foreign *parts.* 7. One's proper share, as of obligation or performance: to do one's *part.* 8. Individual concern or participation in something. 9. The role or lines assigned to an actor in a play. 10. *Usu. pl.* An endowment of mind or character: a man of *parts.* 11. *Music* a The melody intended for a single voice or instrument in a concerted piece: sometimes called *voice.* b The written or printed copy for the performer's use. 12. Division, section, or installment of a literary work. 13. The dividing line on the scalp made by combing sections of the hair in opposite directions. — **for one's part** As far as one is concerned. — **for the most part** To the greatest extent; in general. — **in good part** With good grace; good-naturedly. — **part** Partly. — **part and parcel** An essential part: an emphatic phrase. — **to take part** To participate; share; cooperate: usu. with *in.* — **to take someone's part** To support someone in a contest or disagreement. — *v.t.* 1. To divide or break (something) into parts. 2. To sever or discontinue (a relationship or connection). 3. To separate by being or coming between; keep or move apart. 4. To comb (the hair) so as to leave a dividing line on the scalp or elsewhere on the scalp. 5. To separate (mingled substances) chemically or mechanically. — *v.i.* 6. To become divided or broken into parts. 7. To go away from one another; cease associating. 8. To depart. — **to part from** To separate from; leave. — **to part with** 1. To give up; relinquish. 2. To part from. — *adv.* To some extent; partly. [< OF and OE < L *pars, partis*]

par·take (pär·tāk′) *v.* **·took, ·tak·en, ·tak·ing** *v.i.* 1. To take part or have a share: with *in.* 2. To receive or take a portion or share: with *of.* 3. To have something of the quality or character: with *of.* — *v.t.* 4. To take or have a part in; share. [Back formation < *partaker* < L < *pars, part* part + *capere* to take] — **par·tak′er** *n.*

art·ed (pär′tid) *adj.* **1.** Situated or placed apart; separated. **2.** *Bot.* Cut almost but not quite to the base, as certain leaves. **3.** Divided into parts.

ar·terre (pär-târ′) *n.* **1.** A flower garden having beds arranged in a pattern. **2.** The part of a theater on the main floor under the balcony and behind the parquet. [< MF < L *per* through, all over + *terra* land]

ar·the·no·gen·e·sis (pär′thə-nŏ-jĕn′ə-sis) *n. Biol.* Reproduction by means of unfertilized eggs, seeds, or spores, as in many rotifers, insects, and algae. Also **par′the·nog′e·ny** -noj′ə-nē). [< Gk. *parthenos* virgin + GENESIS] — **par′·he·no·ge·net′ic** (-jə·nĕt′ik), **par′the·no·gen′ic** *adj.* — **par′·he·no·ge·net′i·cal·ly** *adv.*

ar·the·non (pär′thə-non) The temple of Athena on the Acropolis at Athens, dedicated in 438 B.C., regarded as one of the finest examples of Doric architecture.

ar·thi·a (pär′thē·ə) An ancient kingdom occupying what s now NE Iran.

ar·thi·an (pär′thē·ən) *n.* An inhabitant of Parthia. — *adj.* Of or pertaining to Parthia or the Parthians. — **Parthian shot** Any aggressive remark or action made in eaving or fleeing, after the manner of Parthian cavalry who hot at their enemies while retreating.

ar·tial (pär′shəl) *adj.* **1.** Pertaining to, constituting, or nvolving a part only. **2.** Favoring one side; biased. **3.** Having a special liking: usu. with *to.* — *n.* In acoustics, a partial tone. [< OF < LL < L *pars, partis* part] — **par′·ial·ly** *adv.*

artial eclipse *Astron.* An eclipse in which only part of he disk of a celestial body is obscured from view.

ar·ti·al·i·ty (pär′shē·al′ə·tē) *n. pl.* **·ties** **1.** The state of being partial. **2.** Unfairness; bias. **3.** A particular fondness; predilection. Also **par′tial·ness** (-shəl·nis).

artial tone Any of the simple or pure tones that, taken collectively, constitute a complex tone

ar·tic·i·pant (pär·tis′ə·pənt) *adj.* Sharing; taking part n. — *n.* One who participates; a sharer.

ar·tic·i·pate (pär·tis′ə·pāt) *v.* **·pat·ed,** **·pat·ing** *v.i.* To ake part or have a share in common with others: with *in.* < L < *pars, partis* part + *capere* to take] — **par·tic′i·a′tion, par·tic′i·pance** *n.* — **par·tic′i·pa′tor** *n.*

ar·ti·cip·i·al (pär′tə·sip′ē·əl) *Gram. adj.* **1.** Having the ature, form, or use of a participle. **2.** Characterized by, consisting of, or based on a participle. — *n.* A participle. — **par′ti·cip′i·al·ly** *adv.*

ar·ti·ci·ple (pär′tə·sip′əl) *n. Gram.* A verbal adjective, often retaining some of the attributes of a verb, such as ense and the power of taking an object, but often also aving the adjectival function of qualifying nouns. The **resent participle** ends in *-ing* and the **past participle** ommonly in *-d, -ed, -en, -n,* or *-t.* — **dangling participle** A articiple that modifies the wrong substantive, as in "*Open*-ng the door, the *room* looked large." [< OF, var. of *par-icipe* < L *participium* a sharing, partaking]

ar·ti·cle (pär′ti·kəl) *n.* **1.** A minute part, piece, or portion, as of matter. **2.** A very small amount or slight degree. **.** *Physics* One of the elementary components of an atom, s an electron, proton, neutron, meson, etc. **4.** *Gram.* **a** A hort, uninflected part of speech, as an article, preposition, nterjection, or conjunction. **b** A prefix or suffix. **5.** A mall section or clause, as of a document. [< L *particula,* lim. of *pars, partis* part]

ar·ti·col·ored (pär′tē·kul′ərd) *adj.* **1.** Differently col-red in different parts. **2.** Diversified. Also spelled *party-olored.* [< F *parti,* to divide + COLORED]

ar·tic·u·lar (pər·tik′yə·lər) *adj.* **1.** Peculiar or pertaining o a specified person, thing, time, or place; specific. **2.** Re-erring to one as distinguished from others. **3.** Especially oteworthy: of *particular* importance. **4.** Comprising all etails or circumstances: a *particular* description. **5.** Re-uiring or giving minute attention to details; fastidious: *articular* in dress. **6.** *Logic* Including some, not all, of a lass: opposed to *universal.* — *n.* **1.** *Usu. pl.* An item; etail. **2.** An individual instance; a single or separate case. **.** *Logic* A particular proposition. — **in particular** Particu-arly. [< OF < LL *particularis* concerning a part]

ar·tic·u·lar·i·ty (pər·tik′yə·lar′ə·tē) *n. pl.* **·ties** **1.** The tate or quality of being particular, as: **a** Exactitude in escription. **b** Strict or careful attention to details; fastidi-usness. **2.** That which is particular, as: **a** A circumstance r detail. **b** A special characteristic; peculiarity.

ar·tic·u·lar·ize (pər·tik′yə·lə·rīz′) *v.* **·ized, ·iz·ing** *v.t.* **1.** To make out or treat individually or in detail. — *v.i.* **2.** To ive particular details; be specific. — **par·tic′u·lar·i·za′-ion** *n.* — **par·tic′u·lar·iz′er** *n.*

ar·tic·u·lar·ly (pər·tik′yə·lər·lē) *adv.* **1.** With specific eference; distinctly. **2.** In an unusually great degree. **.** Part by part; in detail. **4.** Severally; personally.

par·tic·u·late (pər-tik′yə-lāt) *adj.* Consisting of minute, separate particles.

part·ing (pär′ting) *adj.* **1.** Given or done at parting: a *parting* glance. **2.** Of or pertaining to a parting or a going away. **3.** Departing; declining. **4.** Separating; dividing. — *n.* **1.** The act of separating, or the state of being separated. **2.** A leave-taking; esp., a final separation. **3.** A place, line, or surface of separation. **4.** That which serves to part or separate objects.

parting shot Any retort or aggressive action made as one is leaving or fleeing. [< PARTHIAN SHOT by folk etymology]

par·ti·san (pär′tə-zən) *n.* **1.** One who supports or upholds a party, cause, etc.; esp., an overly zealous adherent or devotee. **2.** *Mil.* A member of a body of detached or ir-regular troops; a guerrilla. — *adj.* **1.** Of, relating to, or characteristic of a partisan. **2.** Advocated by or composed of members of one party. **3.** *Mil.* Of or carried on by par-tisans. Also **par′ti·zan.** — **Syn.** See ADHERENT. [< F < Ital. < L *pars, partis* part] — **par′ti·san·ship** *n.*

par·tite (pär′tīt) *adj.* Divided into or composed of parts: used in combination: *bipartite, tripartite.* [< L *partitus,* pp. of *partire* to divide]

par·ti·tion (pär-tish′ən) *n.* **1.** The act of dividing, separat-ing, distributing; also, the state of being divided, etc. **2.** Something that divides or separates, as a light interior wall dividing a room, an enclosure, a septum in a plant or animal structure, etc. **3.** One of the parts, sections, com-partments, etc., into which a thing is divided. — *v.t.* **1.** To divide into parts, sections, segments, etc. **2.** To separate by a partition: often with *off.* [< OF < L *partire* to divide] — **par·ti′tion·er** *n.* — **par·ti′tion·ment** *n.*

par·ti·tive (pär′tə-tiv) *adj.* **1.** Separating into integral parts or distinct divisions. **2.** *Gram.* Denoting a part as distinct from the whole. Example: *Of them* is the *partitive* genitive in the sentence "Many of them were there." — *n. Gram.* A partitive word or case. [< F *partitif* or L < *par-titus,* pp. of *partire* to divide] — **par′ti·tive·ly** *adv.*

part·ly (pärt′lē) *adv.* In some part; partially.

part·ner (pärt′nər) *n.* One who is united or associated with another or others in some action, enterprise, etc.; as: **a** *Law* A member of a partnership. **b** A husband or wife; spouse. **c** One of a couple who dance together. **d** One of two or more players on the same side in a game. **e** A colleague or associate in some undertaking; a sharer. — *v.t. Rare* **1.** To make a partner. **2.** To be the partner of. [ME < fusion of *parcener* and *part*]

part·ner·ship (pärt′nər·ship) *n.* **1.** The state or relation-ship of being a partner; association. **2.** *Law* **a** A contractual relationship in which two or more persons combine capital, labor, etc., to carry on a business. **b** The contract that creates such a relationship. **c** The persons associated.

part of speech *Gram.* One of the eight traditional classes of words in English, noun, pronoun, verb, adverb, adjective, conjunction, preposition, and interjection.

par·took (pär-tŏŏk′) Past tense of PARTAKE.

par·tridge (pär′trij) *n.* **1.** Any of certain small, plump game birds of the Old World. **2.** Any of various similar birds, as the ruffed grouse or the bobwhite. [< OF < L < Gk. *perdix, -ikos* partridge]

part song A song of three or more parts; esp., a secular choral piece without accompaniment.

part-time (pärt′tīm′) *adj.* For, during, or by part of the time: a *part-time* student.

par·tu·ri·ent (pär-tyŏŏr′ē-ənt, -tŏŏr′-) *adj.* **1.** Bringing forth or about to bring forth young. **2.** Of or pertaining to parturition. **3.** Producing or about to produce an idea, discovery, etc. [< L *parturiens, -entis,* ppr. of *parturire* to be in labor] — **par·tu′ri·en·cy** *n.*

par·tu·ri·tion (pär′tyŏŏ-rish′ən, -chŏŏ-) *n.* The act of bringing forth young; delivery; childbirth.

par·ty (pär′tē) *n. pl.* **·ties** **1.** A social gathering for pleas-ure or entertainment. **2.** A group of persons associated or gathered together for some common purpose; as: **a** A group united in promoting or maintaining a cause, policy, system, etc.; esp., a political group organized to gain control of a government through the election of its candidates to public office. **b** A small body of persons selected for some special mission or assignment: a demolition *party.* **c** A group formed for a sport or other diversion. **3.** *Law* Either of the persons or groups involved in legal proceedings. **4.** One who takes part or participates in an action, plan, etc.: a *party* to his crime. **5.** *Informal* A person. — *adj.* Of or pertaining to a party or parties. [< OF *partir* to divide]

par·ty-col·ored (pär′tē·kul′ərd) See PARTI-COLORED.

party line **1.** A telephone line or circuit serving two or more subscribers. Also **party wire.** **2.** A boundary line between the properties of two or more owners. **3.** The essential beliefs or policies of a political party.

party politics Policies and acts aimed at furthering the interests of one political party.

party whip A whip (def. 4).

par value The nominal or stated value of stock; face value: distinguished from *market value*.

par·ve·nu (pär/və-nōō, -nyōō) *n.* One who has risen above his class through the sudden attainment of wealth or position; an upstart. — *adj.* 1. Being a parvenu. 2. Characteristic of or resembling a parvenu. [< F, orig., pp. of *parvenir* to arrive < L *pervenire*]

pas (pä) *n.* A dance step. [< F < L *passus* step]

pas·chal (pas/kəl) *adj.* Pertaining to the Jewish Passover or to Easter: *paschal* sacrifice. [< OF < LL < Gk. < Hebrew *pesakh* a passing over]

paschal flower The pasqueflower.

Paschal Lamb 1. Jesus Christ. 2. Any symbolic representation of Christ.

pas de deux (pä də dœ/) *French* A dance or ballet figure for two persons.

pa·sha (pə·shä/, pash/ə, pä/shə) *n.* Formerly, a Turkish honorary title placed after the name of generals, governors of provinces, etc.: also *pacha*. [< Turkish *bāsh* head]

pa·sha·lik (pə·shä/lik) *n.* The province or jurisdiction of a pasha: also spelled *pachalic*. Also **pa·sha/lic.** [< Turkish]

Pash·to (push/tō) *n.* The Iranian language dominant in Afghanistan: also called *Afghan*: also *Pushtu*.

pasque·flow·er (pask/flou/ər) *n.* Any of several plants of the crowfoot family, having white, red, or purple flowers blooming about Easter, the State flower of South Dakota: also called *paschal flower*. Also **pasch/flow/er.**

pas·quin·ade (pas/kwin·ād/) *n.* An abusive or coarse personal satire posted in a public place. — *v.t.* **·ad·ed, ·ad·ing** To attack or ridicule in pasquinades; lampoon. [< Ital. < *Pasquino*, orig., a disinterred statue at Rome on which satirical verses were pasted] — **pas/quin·ad/er** *n.*

pass (pas, päs) *v.* **passed** (*Rare*, **past**), **passed** or **past**, **pass·ing** *v.t.* 1. To go by or move past. 2. To succeed in meeting the requirements of (a test, trial, etc.). 3. To go beyond or surpass. 4. To spend (a specified period of time). 5. To cause or allow to move, go past, proceed, advance, etc.: to *pass* him through the ranks. 6. To approve or sanction; enact: to *pass* a bill. 7. To be approved or sanctioned by: The bill *passed* the senate. 8. To cause or allow to get through (a test, trial, etc.). 9. To convey or transfer from one to another; transmit: to *pass* a bad check. 10. In football, hockey, etc., to transfer (the ball, etc.) to another player on the same team. 11. In baseball, to walk (a batter). 12. To utter or pronounce, esp. judicially: to *pass* sentence. 13. To discharge or excrete (waste); void. 14. To omit paying (a dividend). 15. *Law* To transfer ownership or title of to another; make over. 16. *Rare* To permit to go unnoticed or unmentioned. 17. *Rare* To pledge or promise. — *v.i.* 18. To go or move; proceed; advance. 19. To go by or move past. 20. To obtain or force a way: to *pass* through a crowd. 21. To lead or extend; run: The river *passes* under a bridge. 22. To go by or elapse: The years *passed* slowly. 23. To come to an end; terminate. 24. To die. 25. To go about or circulate; be current. 26. To change or move from one condition, place, form, etc., to another: to *pass* from hot to cold. 27. To be mutually exchanged or transacted: Whispers *passed* between them. 28. To take place; occur: It came to *pass*. 29. To be allowed or permitted without challenge, censure, etc. 30. To undergo a test, etc., successfully. 31. To be approved, sanctioned, ratified, etc. 32. To be excreted or voided. 33. *Law* To give or pronounce sentence, judgment, etc.: with *on* or *upon*. 34. In football, hockey, etc., to transfer the ball, etc., to another player on the same team. 35. In fencing, to make a pass or thrust; lunge. 36. In card games, to decline to make a play, bid, etc. — **to pass away** 1. To come to an end. 2. To die. 3. To allow (time) to elapse. — **to pass for** To be accepted or regarded as, usu. erroneously. — **to pass off** 1. To come to an end; disappear. 2. To give out or circulate as genuine; palm off. 3. To be emitted, as vapor. — **to pass out** 1. To distribute or circulate. 2. *Informal* To faint. — **to pass over** To fail to notice or consider, as an applicant. — **to pass up** *U.S. Informal* 1. To reject or fail to take advantage of, as an offer or opportunity. 2. To pass over. — *n.* 1. A way or opening through which one can pass; esp., a narrow passage between the peaks of a mountain range. 2. A permit, order, or license giving the bearer authority to enter, move about, depart, etc., without the usual restrictions; as: **a** *Mil.* A written form granting permission to the holder to be absent from duty; also, the permission itself or the period of absence covered by it. **b** A ticket allowing one to enter a theater, movie, train, etc., free of charge. 3. The passing of an examination or course. 4. In magic, hypnotism, etc.: **a** A movement of the hand, a wand, etc., over a person or thing. **b** The manipulation of objects by sleight of hand. 5. A state of affairs; situation: to bring events to a critical *pass*. 6. In fencing, a thrust or

lunge. 7. In cards, a refusal to bid or raise a bid. 8. I baseball, a walk. — **to bring to pass** To cause to be fu filled or accomplished. — **to come to pass** To happe — **to make a pass** 1. To attempt to hit. 2. *Slang* To in vite intimacies; proposition. [< OF < L *passus* step]

pass·a·ble (pas/ə·bəl, päs/-) *adj.* 1. Capable of bein passed, penetrated, crossed, etc.: *passable* rivers. 2. Fairl good or acceptable; tolerable. 3. Fit for general circulatio as money. — **pass/a·ble·ness** *n.* — **pass/a·bly** *adv.*

pas·sage (pas/ij) *n.* 1. A portion of a writing, speech, o musical composition, usu. of small or moderate length. 2 *Music* A short section of a composition designed primaril to display the performer's skill, as a run or flourish. 3. way, channel, duct, etc., by which a person or thing ma pass. 4. A hall, corridor, etc., between apartments in building. 5. The act of passing, changing, etc.; esp., th transition from one state or period to another: the *passag* from winter to summer. 6. A journey, esp. by sea: a storm *passage*; also, the right or privilege of making a journey: t secure *passage*. 7. The right, power, or freedom to pass. The passing or enactment of a legislative measure. 9. A evacuation of the bowels. — *v.i.* **·saged, ·sag·ing** *Rare* 1. To make a journey. 2. To fight or quarrel. [< OF]

pas·sage·way (pas/ij·wā/) *n.* A way affording passag esp. a hall or corridor.

pass·book (pas/bŏŏk/, päs/-) *n.* A bankbook.

pas·sé (pa·sā/, pas/ā; *Fr.* pà·sā/) *adj.* 1. Past the prim faded. 2. Out-of-date; old-fashioned. [< F, orig., pp. o *passer* to pass] — **pas·sée/** *adj. fem.*

passed ball (past, päst) In baseball, a misplay charged t the catcher for allowing a runner to advance by failing t catch a pitch that passes reasonably close to him.

pas·sen·ger (pas/ən·jər) *n.* One who travels in a convey ance. [< MF *passager* < *passage* passage]

passe par·tout (pas pär·tōō/, *Fr.* pàs pàr·tōō/) In pictur framing: **a** A light frame consisting of a glass, the pictur and a pasteboard back put together with strips of tap pasted around the edges. **b** The tape. [< MF < *passer* t pass + *partout* everywhere]

pas·ser·by (pas/ər·bī/, päs/-) *n.* *pl.* **pas·sers·by** One wh passes by, usu. casually.

pas·ser·ine (pas/ər·ēn, -in) *adj.* 1. Of or pertaining to a order of birds including all singing birds, and more than ha of the living birds of various sizes. 2. Resembling or chara teristic of a sparrow. — *n.* A passerine bird. [< L *pass* sparrow + -INE[1]]

pas·sim (pas/im) *adv.* *Latin* Here and there; in variou passages: a reference note in books.

pass·ing (pas/ing, päs/-) *adj.* 1. Going by or away. 2 Transitory; fleeting. 3. Happening or occurring; curren 4. Done, said, etc., in a cursory or casual manner. 5. filling all requirements: a *passing* grade. — **Syn.** See TRAI SIENT. — *n.* 1. The act of one who or that which passes. A means or place of passing, as a ford. — **in passing** Inc dentally. — *adv.* *Archaic* In a surpassing degree or manne

pas·sion (pash/ən) *n.* 1. Any intense, extreme, or ove powering emotion or feeling. 2. Ardent affection or lov 3. Intense sexual desire or lust. 4. Overwhelming anger rage. 5. An outburst of strong feeling, esp. of violence anger. 6. A strong desire or affection for some objec cause, etc. 7. The object of such a desire or affection. [OF < L < *passus* pp. of *pati* to suffer] — **pas/sion·less** *ad*

Pas·sion (pash/ən) *n.* 1. The sufferings of Christ, esp. aft the Last Supper and on the Cross. 2. The part of the Go pels that relates the sufferings and death of Christ. 3. representation of Christ's sufferings in art, music, etc.

pas·sion·ate (pash/ən·it) *adj.* 1. Capable of or incline to strong passion; excitable. 2. Easily moved to ange quick-tempered. 3. Expressing, displaying, or characte ized by passion or strong emotion; ardent. 4. Strong vehement, as a feeling or emotion. — **Syn.** See ARDEN — **pas/sion·ate·ly** *adv.* — **pas/sion·ate·ness** *n.*

pas·sion·flow·er (pash/ən·flou/ər) *n.* Any of various vine or shrubs having showy flowers and sometimes edible berrie so called from the fancied resemblance of certain parts t the wounds, crown of thorns, etc., of Christ. [Trans. of Med. *flos passionis*]

passion fruit The berries of the passion flower.

Passion play A religious drama representing the Passio of Christ.

pas·sive (pas/iv) *adj.* 1. Not acting, working, or operatin inactive; inert. 2. Acted upon, affected, or influenced b something external. 3. Receiving or receptive to an e ternal force, etc. 4. Submitting or yielding without resis ance or opposition; submissive. 5. *Gram.* Designatin voice of the verb that indicates that the subject is receiver the action, as *was killed* in the passive voice in *Caesar wa killed by Brutus*: distinguished from *active*. — *n.* *Gram.* The passive voice. 2. A verb or construction in this voic [< L *passus* pp. of *pati* to suffer] — **pas/sive·ly** *adv.* — **pas/sive·ness** *n.*

assive resistance A method of opposing some authority or law by nonviolent acts, as voluntary fasting, etc.

pas·siv·i·ty (pa·siv′ə·tē) *n.* The state of being passive.

pass·key (pas′kē′, pās′-) *n.* A master key.

pass·o·ver (pas′ō′vər, pās′-) *n.* A Jewish feast commemorating the night when God, smiting the first-born of the Egyptians, "passed over" the houses of the children of Israel.

pass·port (pas′pôrt′, -pōrt′, pās′-) *n.* 1. An official warrant certifying the citizenship of the bearer and affording protection to him when traveling abroad. 2. A permit to travel or convey goods through a foreign country. 3. Anything that enables one to gain entrance, acceptance, etc. [< MF < *passer* to pass + *port* harbor]

pass·word (pas′wûrd′, pās′-) *n.* 1. A secret word or phrase enabling the speaker to pass a guard or sentry. 2. Anything that gains entrance or access for one.

ast (past, pāst) *adj.* 1. Ended or finished; done with. 2. Having existed in or belonging to a former time: *past* civilizations. 3. Just passed or gone by: the *past* few days. 4. Having formerly served in a public office, committee, etc.: a *past* governor. — *n.* 1. Past or antecedent time, conditions, or events: usu. with *the*. 2. Something, as a former life or career, that is kept secret. 3. *Gram.* **a** A verb tense denoting any action or condition that occurred at a former time. **b** A verb or construction in this tense. — *adv.* In such a manner as to go by: to run *past.* — *prep.* 1. Beyond in time; after. 2. Beyond in place or position; farther than. 3. Beyond the reach, power, or influence of: *past* hope. 4. Beyond in amount or degree. [Orig. pp. of PASS]

as·ta (päs′tə) *n.* A noodlelike paste or dough, as spaghetti, macaroni, etc. [< Ital. < LL, dough, paste]

aste (pāst) *n.* 1. A mixture, usu. of flour and water, used as an adhesive for paper, etc. 2. Any of various soft, moist, smooth preparations used as foods, in cooking, etc.; as: **a** Dough used in making pastry. **b** A soft, creamy mass made from fish, fruit, etc. 3. A vitreous composition used in making imitation gems; also, a gem made of this composition. — *v.t.* **past·ed, past·ing** 1. To stick or fasten with or as with paste. 2. To cover by applying pasted material. [< OF < LL < Gk. *pastē* barley porridge] — **past′er** *n.*

aste·board (pāst′bôrd′, -bōrd′) *n.* 1. Paper pulp pressed, or paper pasted together and rolled into a stiff sheet. 2. A board on which dough for pastry is rolled. 3. *Informal* A visiting card; also, a playing card. — *adj.* Flimsy.

as·tel (pas·tel′, pas′tel) *n.* 1. A picture drawn with colored crayons. 2. The art of drawing such pictures. 3. A dried paste made of pipe clay, pigment, and gum water, used for crayons; also, a hard crayon made of this paste: also called *pastille.* 4. A delicate, soft, or slightly grayish tint. — *adj.* 1. Of or pertaining to a pastel. 2. Having a delicate, soft, or slightly grayish tint. [See PASTE.] — **pas′·tel·ist** or **pas′tel·list** *n.*

as·tern (pas′tərn) *n.* 1. The part of a horse's foot that is between the fetlock and the hoof. 2. A hobble for a horse's foot. [< OF < *pasture* tether for a grazing animal]

as·teur·i·za·tion (pas′tər·ə·zā′shən, -chər-) *n.* A process of arresting or preventing fermentation in liquids, as beer, milk, wine, etc., by heating so as to destroy the vitality of the ferment. Also *Brit.* **pas′teur·i·sa′tion.**

as·teur·ize (pas′tə·rīz, -chə·rīz) *v.t.* **·ized, ·iz·ing** To treat by pasteurization. Also *Brit.* **pas′teur·ise.**

as·tic·cio (päs·tē′chō) *n.* *pl.* **·ci** (-chē) A work of art, music, or literature made up of fragments from various sources. [< Ital., paste]

as·tiche (pas·tēsh′, päs-) *n.* A pasticcio, esp. one imitating or satirizing the style of other artists. [< F]

as·tille (pas·tēl′, -til′) *n.* 1. A compound of aromatic substances with niter for fumigating. 2. A troche; lozenge. 3. A flavored confection. 4. Pastel (def. 3). Also **pas·til** (pas′til). [< MF < L *pastillus* little loaf, lozenge]

as·time (pas′tīm′, päs′-) *n.* Something that serves to make time pass agreeably. [Trans. of F *passe-temps*]

ast master 1. One who has held the office of master in certain social or benevolent organizations. 2. One who has thorough experience in something; an expert; adept.

as·tor (pas′tər, päs′-) *n.* A Christian clergyman who has church or congregation under his charge. [< AF, OF < *pastor, -oris* shepherd, lit., feeder] — **pas′tor·ship** *n.*

as·tor·al (pas′tər·əl, päs′-) *adj.* 1. Of or pertaining to shepherds, rustics, or rural life. 2. Having the characteristics usu. associated with rural life, as innocence, simplicity, etc. 3. Dealing with or portraying rural life. 4. Pertaining to a clergyman or his duties. — *n.* 1. A literary work, esp. a poem, dealing with rural life, scenes, etc. 2. A picture illustrating rural scenes. 3. *Eccl.* A letter from a pastor or bishop to his flock. [< L *pastor* shepherd] — **pas′tor·al·ism** *n.* — **pas′tor·al·ist** *n.* — **pas′tor·al·ly** *adv.*

as·tor·ate (pas′tər·it, päs′-) *n.* 1. The office or jurisdiction of a pastor. 2. The duration of a pastoral charge. 3. Pastors collectively.

past participle See under PARTICIPLE.

past perfect *Gram.* The verb tense indicating an action completed prior to the occurrence of some other past action or specified past time, as *had finished* is the past perfect in *He had finished before the bell rang.* Also called *pluperfect.*

pas·tra·mi (pə·strä′mē) *n.* Heavily seasoned, smoked beef, usu. cut from the shoulder. [< Yiddish < Rumanian]

pas·try (pās′trē) *n.* *pl.* **·tries** Articles of food that are sweet, baked, and are usu. made with a crust of shortened dough, as pies, tarts, etc.; also, any sweet baked foods.

pas·tur·age (pas′chər·ij, päs′-) *n.* 1. Grass and herbage for cattle. 2. Ground used or suitable for grazing.

pas·ture (pas′chər, päs′-) *n.* 1. Ground for the grazing of domestic animals. 2. Grass or herbage that grazing domestic animals eat. — *v.t.* **·tured, ·tur·ing** 1. To put in a pasture to graze. 2. To graze on (grass, etc.). 3. To provide pasturage for (cattle, etc): said of land. [< OF < LL < L < *pascere* to feed] — **pas′tur·a·ble** *adj.*

past·y[1] (pās′tē) *adj.* **past·i·er, past·i·est** Like paste. — **past′i·ness** *n.*

past·y[2] (pās′tē, *Brit.* pas′tē, päs′tē) *n.* *pl.* **pas·ties** A pie; esp., a meat pie. [< OF < LL *pasta* paste]

pat (pat) *v.* **pat·ted, pat·ting** *v.t.* 1. To touch or tap lightly with something flat, esp. with the hand in caressing, etc. 2. To shape or mold by a pat or pats. — *v.i.* 3. To run or walk with light steps. — *n.* 1. A light, caressing stroke; a gentle tap. 2. The sound of patting or pattering. 3. A small, molded mass, as of butter. — *adj.* 1. Exactly suitable; apt. 2. Needing no change: a *pat* hand in a card game. 3. Glib; facile. — *adv. Informal* 1. Firm; steadfast: to stand *pat.* 2. Aptly. [ME *patte*] — **pat′ness** *n.* — **pat′ter** *n.*

patch (pach) *n.* 1. A small piece of material used to repair a garment, etc. 2. A piece of courtplaster or the like, applied to the skin to hide a blemish or to set off the complexion. 3. A small piece of ground; also, the plants growing on it: a *patch* of corn. 4. A piece of material worn over an injured eye. 5. Any small part of a surface not sharing the general character of the whole. 6. A shred or scrap. — *v.t.* 1. To put a patch or patches on. 2. To repair or put together, esp. hurriedly or crudely: often with *up* or *together.* 3. To make of patches, as a quilt. [ME *pacche*] — **patch′·a·ble** *adj.* — **patch′er** *n.*

patch·ou·li (pach′ŏŏ-le, pə·chŏŏ′le) *n.* 1. An East Indian herb of the mint family. 2. A perfume obtained from it. Also spelled *pachouli.* Also **patch′ou·ly.** [< F < Tamil < *paccu* green + *ilai* leaf]

patch pocket A pocket sewn to the outside of a garment.

patch·work (pach′wûrk′) *n.* 1. A fabric made of patches of cloth, as for quilts, etc. 2. Work made up of heterogeneous materials; work done hastily or carelessly; a jumble.

patch·y (pach′ē) *adj.* **patch·i·er, patch·i·est** 1. Made up of or abounding in patches. 2. Careless; jumbled. 3. Peevish; irritable. — **patch′i·ly** *adv.* — **patch·i·ness** *n.*

pate (pāt) *n.* The head or top of the head; also, the brains or intellect: usu. humorous or derogatory. [ME]

pâté de foie gras (pä·tā′ də fwä grä′) *French* A paste of fat goose liver.

pa·tel·la (pə·tel′ə) *n.* *pl.* **·tel·lae** (-tel′ē) *Anat.* The flat, movable, oval bone in front of the knee joint; kneecap. For illus. see SKELETON. [< L, dim. of *patina* pan, bowl] — **pa·tel′lar** *adj.* — **pa·tel·late** (pə·tel′ăt, -it) *adj.*

pat·en (pat′n) *n.* 1. A plate; esp., a plate for the eucharistic bread: also called *patina:* also spelled *patin, patine.* 2. A thin, metallic plate or disk. [< OF < L *patina* pan]

pa·ten·cy (pāt′n·sē) *n.* 1. The condition of being patent or evident. 2. *Chiefly Med.* The state of being open, spread, enlarged, or without obstruction.

pat·ent (pat′nt, *Brit.* pāt′nt; *for adj. defs. 1, 4, & 5, usu.* pāt′nt) *n.* 1. A government protection to an inventor, securing to him for a specific time the exclusive right of manufacturing, exploiting, using, and selling an invention; also, the right granted. 2. Any official document securing a right. 3. That which is protected by a patent or its distinctive marks or features. — *v.t.* To obtain a patent on (an invention). — *adj.* 1. Manifest or apparent to everybody. 2. Protected or conferred by letters patent. 3. Open for general inspection or use: letters *patent.* 4. Expanded; spreading widely, as leaves from the stem of a plant. 5. *Chiefly Med.* Open; unobstructed, as an intestine. [< F < L < *patere* to lie open] — **pat′ent·a·bil·i·ty** *n.* — **pat′ent·a·ble** *adj.*

pat·en·tee (pat′n·tē′) *n.* One who holds a patent.

patent leather Leather with a glossy, varnishlike finish.

pa·tent·ly (pāt′nt·lē, pat′nt-) *adv.* Manifestly; clearly.

patent medicine A medicine manufactured and sold under patent and usu. of secret composition.

pat·en·tor (pat′n·tər) *n.* One who grants a patent.

pa·ter (pā'tər) *n. Brit. Informal* Father. [< L]

pa·ter·fa·mil·i·as (pā'tər·fə·mil'ē·əs) *n.* The father of a family. [< L < *pater* father + *familia* family]

pa·ter·nal (pə·tûr'nəl) *adj.* 1. Of, pertaining to, or characteristic of a father; fatherly. 2. Derived from, related through, or connected with one's father. [< LL < L < *pater* father] — **pa·ter'nal·ly** *adv.*

pa·ter·nal·ism (pə·tûr'nəl·iz'əm) *n.* The care or control of a country, community, group of employees, etc., in a manner suggestive of a father looking after his children. — **pa·ter'·nal·is'tic** *adj.* — **pa·ter'nal·is'ti·cal·ly** *adv.*

pa·ter·ni·ty (pə·tûr'nə·tē) *n.* 1. The condition of being a father. 2. Parentage on the male side. 3. Origin in general.

pa·ter·nos·ter (pā'tər·nos'tər) *n.* 1. The Lord's Prayer. *Matt.* vi 9–13. Also **Pa'ter Nos'ter.** 2. A large bead of the rosary, indicating that a paternoster is to be recited. [< L *pater noster* our father]

path (path, päth) *n. pl.* **paths** (pathz, päthz, paths, päths) 1. A walk or way used by man or animals on foot. 2. A track or course. 3. A course of life or action. [OE *pæth*]

Pa·than (pə·tän', pət·hän') *n.* An Afghan; esp., one of a people of Afghanistan of Indo-Iranian stock and Moslem religion. [< Hind. < Afghan *Pēstūn* an Afghan]

pa·thet·ic (pə·thet'ik) *adj.* Of the nature of, expressing, or arousing sadness, pity, tenderness, etc. Also **pa·thet'i·cal.** [< LL < Gk. < *pathos* suffering] — **pa·thet'i·cal·ly** *adv.* — **pa·thet'i·cal·ness** *n.*

pathetic fallacy The ascribing of human emotions and characteristics to nature or things of nature, as a *sad day.*

path·find·er (path'fīn'dər, päth'-) *n.* One skilled in leading or finding a way, esp. in unknown regions.

-pathia See **-PATHY.**

path·less (path'lis, päth'-) *adj.* Trackless; untrodden.

patho- *combining form* Suffering; disease. Also, before vowels, **path-.** [< Gk. *pathos* suffering]

path·o·gen (path'ə·jən) *n.* Any disease-producing bacterium or microorganism. Also **path'o·gene** (-jēn).

path·o·gen·e·sis (path'ə·jen'ə·sis) *n. Med.* The production or development of any diseased condition. Also **pa·thog·e·ny** (pə·thoj'ə·nē).

path·o·gen·ic (path'ə·jen'ik) *adj. Med.* Productive of or pertaining to the production of disease. Also **path'o·ge·net'·ic** (-jə·net'ik).

path·o·log·i·cal (path'ə·loj'i·kəl) *adj.* 1. Of pathology. 2. Related to, involving, concerned with, or caused by disease. Also **path'o·log'ic.** — **path'o·log'i·cal·ly** *adv.*

pa·thol·o·gist (pə·thol'ə·jist) *n.* One skilled in pathology.

pa·thol·o·gy (pə·thol'ə·jē) *n. pl.* **·gies** 1. The branch of medical science that treats of the origin, nature, causes, and development of disease. 2. The sum of the conditions, processes, and effects in the course of a disease.

pa·thos (pā'thos) *n.* The quality, esp. in literature or art, that arouses feelings of pity, sorrow, compassion, etc. — **Syn.** See FEELING. [< Gk. < *pathein* to suffer]

path·way (path'wā', päth'-) *n.* A path; footway.

-pathy *combining form* 1. Suffering; affection. 2. *Med.* Disease, or the treatment of disease: *psychopathy.* Also spelled *-pathia.* [< Gk. *pathos* suffering]

pa·tience (pā'shəns) *n.* 1. The state, quality, or fact of being patient; also, the ability to be patient. 2. *Chiefly Brit.* Solitaire (def. 2). [< OF < L *pati* to suffer]

pa·tient (pā'shənt) *adj.* 1. Possessing or demonstrating quiet, uncomplaining endurance under distress or annoyance. 2. Tolerant, tender, and forbearing. 3. Capable of tranquilly awaiting results. 4. Persevering; diligent. — *n.* A person undergoing treatment for disease or injury. [< OF < L *pati* to suffer] — **pa'tient·ly** *adv.*

pat·in (pat'n) See PATEN (def. 1).

pat·i·na[1] (pat'ə·nə, pə·tē'nə) *n. pl.* **·nae** (-nē) 1. An earthen ware or metal bowl or basin used as a domestic utensil by the Romans. 2. A paten (def. 1). [< L < Gk. *patanē*]

pat·i·na[2] (pat'ə·nə, pə·tē'nə) *n.* 1. A green rust that covers ancient bronzes, copper coins, medals, etc. 2. Any surface of antique appearance. Also called *patine.* [< F, prob. < L *patina* plate]

pat·ine (pa·tēn' *for def. 1,* pat'n *for def. 2*) *n.* 1. Patina[2]. 2. See PATEN (def. 1).

pa·ti·o (pä'tē·ō, pat'ē·ō; *Sp.* pä'tyō) *n. pl.* **·ti·os** 1. The open inner court of a Spanish or Spanish-American dwelling. 2. *U.S.* A paved area adjoining a house, used for parties, barbecues, etc. [< *Sp.,* ? < L *patere* to lie open]

pat·ois (pat'wä, *Fr.* pȧ·twä') *n. pl.* **pat·ois** (pat'wäz, *Fr.* pȧ·twä') A type of local dialect, esp. one that is rustic or illiterate. [< F; origin uncertain]

patri- *combining form* Father: *patricide.* [< L *pater, -tris* father]

pa·tri·arch (pā'trē·ärk) *n.* 1. The leader of a family or tribe who rules by paternal right. 2. One of the fathers of the Hebrew race, Abraham, Isaac, or Jacob. 3. One of the twelve sons of Jacob considered as the progenitors of the tribes of Israel. 4. A venerable man; esp., the founder of a religion, order, etc. 5. *Eccl.* **a** In the primitive Christian church, any of the bishops of Antioch, Alexandria, Rome, Constantinople, or Jerusalem. **b** In the Greek Orthodox Church, any of the bishops of Constantinople, Alexandria, Antioch, or Jerusalem. [< OF < L < Gk. < *patria* family, clan + *archein* to rule]

pa·tri·ar·chal (pā'trē·är'kəl) *adj.* 1. Of, pertaining to, or governed by a patriarch. 2. Of the nature of a patriarchy. 3. Having the nature or character of a patriarch. — **pa'tri·ar'chal·ly** *adv.*

pa·tri·ar·chate (pā'trē·är'kit) *n.* 1. The office, dominion, or residence of a patriarch. 2. A patriarchal system of government.

pa·tri·ar·chy (pā'trē·är'kē) *n. pl.* **·chies** 1. A system of government in which the father or the male heir of his choice rules. 2. Government by men.

pa·tri·cian (pə·trish'ən) *adj.* 1. Of or pertaining to the aristocracy. 2. Noble or aristocratic. — *n.* 1. An aristocrat; esp., in ancient Rome, a member of the hereditary aristocracy. 2. Any one of the upper classes. 3. An honorary title bestowed by the later Roman emperors. [< OF < L *pater, -tris* senator, lit., father] — **pa·tri'cian·ly** *adv.*

pat·ri·cide (pat'rə·sīd) *n.* 1. The killing of one's father. 2. One who has killed his father. [< LL *patricidium*] — **pat·ri·ci'dal** *adj.*

pat·ri·lin·e·al (pat'rə·lin'ē·əl) *adj.* Derived from or descending through the male line.

pat·ri·mo·ny (pat'rə·mō'nē) *n. pl.* **·nies** 1. An inheritance from a father or an ancestor; also, anything inherited. 2. An endowment, as of a church. [< OF < L < *pater, -tris* father] — **pat'ri·mo'ni·al** *adj.* — **pat'ri·mo'ni·al·ly** *adv.*

pa·tri·ot (pā'trē·ət, -ot) *n.* One who loves his country and zealously guards its welfare; esp., a defender of popular liberty. [< F < LL < Gk. *patris* fatherland] — **pa'tri·ot'ic** *adj.* — **pa'tri·ot'i·cal·ly** *adv.*

pa·tri·ot·ism (pā'trē·ə·tiz'əm) *n.* Devotion to one's country.

pa·tris·tic (pə·tris'tik) *adj.* Of or pertaining to the fathers of the Christian church or to their writings. Also **pa·tris'ti·cal.** — **pa·tris'ti·cal·ly** *adv.*

pa·trol (pə·trōl') *v.t. & v.i.* **·trolled, ·trol·ling** To walk or go through or around (an area, town, etc.) for the purpose of guarding or inspecting. — *n.* 1. One or more soldiers, policemen, etc., patrolling a district. 2. A reconnaissance of combat group sent out from the main body in air, ground, or naval warfare. 3. The act of patrolling. 4. A division or troop of Boy Scouts. [< MF < *patrouiller,* var. of *patouiller* orig., to paddle in mud] — **pa·trol'ler** *n.*

patrol car A squad car.

pa·trol·man (pə·trōl'mən) *n. pl.* **·men** (-mən) 1. One who patrols. 2. *U.S.* A policeman assigned to a beat.

patrol torpedo boat A small, highly maneuverable vessel armed with torpedoes for action against enemy shipping: also called *PT boat.*

patrol wagon *U.S.* A police wagon for conveying prisoners.

pa·tron (pā'trən) *n.* 1. One who protects, fosters, or supports some person, thing, or enterprise. 2. A regular customer. 3. A patron saint. [< OF < L *patronus* protector] — **pa'tron·al** *adj.* — **pa'tron·ess** *n.fem.*

pa·tron·age (pā'trən·ij, pat'rən-) *n.* 1. The protection, support, or position of a patron. 2. In the public service, the power or right to distribute offices, esp. political offices; also, the offices so distributed. 3. The financial support given by customers to a commercial establishment. 4. An overly condescending manner.

pa·tron·ize (pā'trən·īz, pat'rən-) *v.t.* **·ized, ·iz·ing** 1. To act as a patron toward; give support to. 2. To treat in a condescending manner. 3. To trade with as a regular customer frequent. — **pa'tron·iz'er** *n.* — **pa'tron·iz'ing·ly** *adv.*

patron saint A saint regarded as the special protector of a country, city, person, cause, etc.

pat·ro·nym·ic (pat'rə·nim'ik) *adj.* Pertaining to or derived from the name of one's father or paternal ancestor. — *n.* 1. A family name. 2. A name formed by adding a prefix or suffix to a proper name, as *Johnson,* son of John. [< L < Gk. < *pater* father + *onoma* name] — **pat'ro·nym'i·cal·ly** *adv.*

pa·troon (pə·trōōn') *n.* Formerly, under the old Dutch law, a holder of entailed estates, having some manorial rights. [< Du. < F < L *patronus* protector]

pat·ter[1] (pat'ər) *v.i.* 1. To make a succession of light, sharp sounds. 2. To move with light, quick steps. — *v.t.* 3. To cause to patter. — *n.* The act or sound of pattering. [Freq. of PAT[1]]

pat·ter[2] (pat'ər) *v.t. & v.i.* To speak or say glibly or rapidly; mumble mechanically or indistinctly. — *n.* 1. Glib and rapid talk, as used by comedians, etc. 2. Patois or dialect. 3. Any professional jargon. 4. Rapid speech set to music. [Short for PATERNOSTER] — **pat'ter·er** *n.*

pat·tern (pat'ərn) *n.* 1. An original or model proposed for or worthy of imitation. 2. Anything shaped or designed to serve as a model or guide in making something else. 3. A ecorative design or figure; also, such design worked on something. **4.** Arrangement of natural or accidental markings: he *pattern* of a butterfly's wings. **5.** The stylistic composition or design of a work of art. **6.** A complex of integrated arts functioning as a whole: the behavior *pattern* of a five-ear-old. **7.** A representative example, sample, or instance. — *v.t.* **1.** To make after a model or pattern: with *on, upon,* r *after.* **2.** To decorate or furnish with a pattern. [< F *atron* patron]

at·ty (pat′ē) *n.* *pl.* **·ties 1.** A small, flat piece of chopped neat, fish, etc. **2.** A small pie. [Alter. of F *pâté*]

tty shell A small puff-paste shell in which creamed meat, ish, vegetables, or fruit are served.

u·ci·ty (pô′sə-tē) *n.* **1.** Smallness of number or quantity. . Scarcity; insufficiency. [< OF or < L *paucus* few]

aul (pôl), died 67? A.D., one of the apostles; the chief early 'hristian missionary to the Gentiles; author of several New 'estament epistles: original name *Saul.* Also **Saint Paul, 'aul the Apostle, Saul of Tarsus.**

aul Bunyan The famous hero lumberjack of American olklore, of superhuman size and strength.

aul·ine (pô′lēn, -līn) *adj.* Of the apostle Paul, his teachngs, or writings. — **Paul′in·ism** *n.* — **Paul′in·ist** *n.*

unch (pônch) *n.* **1.** The abdomen or the belly, esp. if proruding. **2.** A rumen (def. 1). [< OF < L *pantex, -ticis* elly] — **paunch′y** *adj.* — **paunch′i·ness** *n.*

u·per (pô′pər) *n.* **1.** One who receives, or is entitled to reeive, public charity. **2.** Any very poor person. [< Med.L pauper* poor] — **pau′per·ism** *n.*

u·per·ize (pô′pər-īz) *v.t.* **·ized, ·iz·ing** To make a pauper f.

use (pôz) *v.i.* **paused, paus·ing 1.** To cease action or utterance temporarily; hesitate. **2.** To dwell or linger: with *n* or *upon.* — *n.* **1.** A temporary ceasing of action; rest. . A holding back because of doubt or irresolution; hesitaon. **3.** A momentary cessation in speaking or music for he sake of meaning or expression; also, a sign indicating uch cessation. **4.** *Music* A hold. **5.** In prosody, a calulated interval of silence in a meter, or the place at which he voice naturally pauses in reading a verse: see CAESURA. < OF < L < Gk. < *pauein* to stop] — **paus′er** *n.*

v·an (pə·van′, -vän′) *n.* **1.** A slow, stately dance of the 6th and 17th centuries. **2.** Music for or in the manner of his dance. Also **pav·ane** (pə·van′, -vän′; *Fr.* pȧ·vȧn′). < MF < Sp. ? < L *pavo, -onis* peacock]

ve (pāv) *v.t.* **paved, pav·ing 1.** To cover or surface with as-halt, gravel, concrete, etc., as a road. — **to pave the way or)** To make preparation (for); lead up to. [< OF < L *avire* to ram down] — **pav′er** *n.*

ve·ment (pāv′mənt) *n.* **1.** A hard, solid, surface covering r a road or footway. **2.** A paved road or footway. **3.** The aterial with which a surface is paved.

vil·ion (pə·vil′yən) *n.* **1.** A movable or open structure, s a large tent or summerhouse. **2.** A related or connected art of a principal building, as for hospital patients. **3.** A anopy. — *v.t.* **1.** To provide with a pavilion. **2.** To shelr by a pavilion. [< OF < L *papilio, -onis* butterfly, tent]

v·ing (pā′ving) *n.* **1.** The laying of a pavement. **2.** A avement; also, the material used for pavement.

·vo (pā′vō) A constellation, the Peacock. [< L]

v·o·nine (pav′ə·nīn, -nin) *adj.* **1.** Resembling or characristic of the peacock. **2.** Iridescent like the tail of a pea-ock. [< L *pavo, -onis* peacock]

w (pô) *n.* **1.** The foot of an animal having nails or claws. . *Informal* A human hand. — *v.t. & v.i.* **1.** To strike or rape with the feet or paws: to *paw* the air. **2.** *Informal* To andle or caress rudely or clumsily; maul. [< OF *powe,* rob. of Gmc. origin] — **paw′er** *n.*

wl (pôl) *n.* *Mech.* A hinged or pivoted member shaped to ngage with ratchet teeth, either to drive a ratchet wheel or stop its reverse motion. [Origin uncertain]

wn¹ (pôn) *n.* **1.** A chessman of lowest rank, that moves file but captures diagonally. **2.** Any insignificant person sed at another's will. [< AF, OF *peon* foot soldier]

wn² (pôn) *n.* **1.** Something pledged as security for a loan. . The condition of being held as a pledge for money loaned. . The act of pawning. — *v.t.* **1.** To give as security for a an. **2.** To risk or stake. [< OF *pan,* var. of early Frisian *ind* pledge] — **pawn′a·ble** *adj.* — **pawn′age** *n.* — **pawn′-**, **pawn′or** *n.*

wn·brok·er (pôn′brō′kər) *n.* One engaged in the business lending money at interest on pledged personal property.

w·nee (pô·nē′) *n.* *pl.* **·nees** or **·nee** A member of one of ur tribes of North American Indians formerly inhabiting e region between the Arkansas River and the Platte River, ebraska, now living in Oklahoma.

wn·shop (pôn′shop′) *n.* The shop of a pawnbroker.

wn ticket A receipt for goods pawned.

paw·paw (pô′pô) See PAPAW.

pay¹ (pā) *v.* **paid** or (*Obs.* except for def. 2 of *to pay out*) **payed, pay·ing** *v.t.* **1.** To give (someone) what is due for a debt, purchase, etc.; remunerate. **2.** To give (money, etc.) for a purchase, service rendered, etc. **3.** To provide or hand over the amount of, as a debt, bill, etc. **4.** To yield as return or recompense. **5.** To afford profit or benefit to. **6.** To defray, as expenses. **7.** To requite, as for an insult. **8.** To render or give, as a compliment, attention, etc. **9.** To make, as a call or visit. — *v.i.* **10.** To make recompense or payment. **11.** To be worthwhile: It *pays* to be honest — **to pay back** To repay. — **to pay off 1.** To pay the entire amount of (a debt, mortgage, etc.). **2.** To pay the wages of and discharge. **3.** To gain revenge upon or for. **4.** *U.S. Informal* To afford full return. **5.** *Naut.* To turn or cause to turn to leeward. **6.** *U.S. Slang* To bribe. — **to pay out 1.** To disburse or expend. **2.** *Naut.* To let out by slackening, as a rope or cable. — **to pay up** To make full payment (of). — *n.* **1.** That which is given as a recompense; wages. **2.** The act of paying, or the state of being paid. **3.** Paid employment. **4.** Requital; reward; also, retribution. — *adj.* **1.** Of or pertaining to payments, persons who pay, or services paid for: *pay* day. **2.** Constructed so as to require payment on use. **3.** Yielding enough metal to be worth mining: *pay* dirt. [< OF < L *pacare* to appease] — **pay′er** *n.* — **Syn.** (verb) **1.** compensate, indemnify. **2.** spend, expend. **3.** settle, liquidate.

pay² (pā) *v.t.* **paid** or **payed, pay·ing** To coat with a waterproof substance, as pitch. [< AF < L < *pix, picis* pitch]

pay·a·ble (pā′ə·bəl) *adj.* **1.** Due and unpaid. **2.** That can or will be paid. **3.** Likely to be profitable. — **pay′a·bly** *adv.*

pay·day (pā′dā′) *n.* The day on which wages are distributed.

pay dirt 1. Soil containing enough metal, esp. gold, to be profitable to mine. **2.** Anything profitable.

pay·ee (pā·ē′) *n.* A person to whom money has been or is to be paid.

pay·load (pā′lōd′) *n.* **1.** That part of a cargo producing revenue. **2.** The warhead of a guided missile.

pay·mas·ter (pā′mas′tər, -mäs′-) *n.* One who has charge of paying employees. — **pay′mis′tress** (-mis′tris) *n.fem.*

pay·ment (pā′mənt) *n.* **1.** The act of paying, or that which is paid. **2.** Recompense. **3.** Punishment.

pay·off (pā′ôf′, -of′) *n.* **1.** *Informal* Any settlement, reward, or punishment. **2.** *Informal* The climax or outcome of an incident or narrative. **3.** *U.S. Slang* A bribe.

pay·roll (pā′rōl′) *n.* A list of those entitled to receive pay, with the amounts due them; also, the total sum of money needed to make the payments. Also **pay roll.**

pays (pās) See PAIS.

pea (pē) *n.* *pl.* **peas** or **pease 1.** A climbing annual leguminous herb having pinnate leaves and round, green, usu. edible seeds. **2.** The seed of any one of various related plants. [< PEASE, incorrectly taken as a plural]

peace (pēs) *n.* **1.** A state of mental or physical quiet or tranquillity; calm. **2.** The absence or cessation of war. **3.** Public order and tranquillity. **4.** A state of reconciliation after strife or enmity. **5.** Freedom from mental agitation or anxiety. — **at peace 1.** In a quiet state; tranquil. **2.** In a state or condition of order and harmony. — **to hold** (or **keep**) **one's peace** To be silent. — *v.i.* *Obs. except as an imperative* To be or become quiet. [< OF < L *pax, pacis*]

Peace Corps A U.S. government organization, established in 1961, that trains and sends volunteers to live in and aid underdeveloped countries by teaching, farming, building, etc.

peace·a·ble (pē′sə·bəl) *adj.* **1.** Inclined to peace. **2.** Peaceful; tranquil. — **peace′a·ble·ness** *n.* — **peace′a·bly** *adv.*

peace·ful (pēs′fəl) *adj.* **1.** Not in a state of war, riot, or commotion; undisturbed. **2.** Averse to strife. **3.** Inclined to or characteristic of peace. — **peace′ful·ly** *adv.* — **peace′ful·ness** *n.*

peace·mak·er (pēs′mā′kər) *n.* One who effects a reconciliation between unfriendly parties. — **peace′mak′ing** *n. & adj.*

peace pipe The calumet.

peace·time (pēs′tīm′) *n.* A time of peace. — *adj.* Of, characterized by, or used in such a time.

peach¹ (pēch) *n.* **1.** The edible fruit of a tree of the rose family, wildly cultivated in many varieties. **2.** The tree itself. **3.** The yellowish pink color characteristic of the fruit. **4.** *Slang* Any particularly beautiful, pleasing, or excellent person or thing. [< OF < LL < L < Gk. *Persikon (mēlon)* Persian (fruit)]

peach² (pēch) *v.i.* *Slang* To inform against an accomplice; turn informer. [Aphetic var. of obs. *appeach* to accuse]

peach·y (pē′chē) *adj.* **peach·i·er, peach·i·est 1.** Resembling a peach, esp. in color or downiness. **2.** *Slang* Delightfully pleasant, beautiful, etc. — **peach′i·ness** *n.*

pea·coat (pē′kōt′) *n.* A pea jacket. Also **pea coat.**

pea·cock (pē′kok′)   *n.* The male of a gallinaceous crested bird having erectile, brilliantly iridescent tail coverts enormously elongated and marked with eyelike spots, and the neck and breast of a greenish blue.   ♦ Collateral adjective: *pavonine.*   — *v.i.*   To strut vainly; make a display.   [OE *pēa, pāwa* peacock (< L *pavo*) + COCK¹]

peacock blue   A vivid greenish blue.

pea·fowl (pē′foul′)   *n.* A peacock or peahen.

pea green   A light yellowish green.

pea·hen (pē′hen′)   *n.* A female peafowl.

pea jacket   A short coat of thick woolen cloth, worn by seamen. Also called *peacoat.*   [< Du. *pij* coat of coarse wool + JACKET]

MALE PEACOCK
(Body to 36 inches long; tail coverts to 6 feet)

peak (pēk)   *n.* **1.** A projecting point or edge; an end terminating in a point. **2.** A conspicuous or precipitous mountain; also, the summit of such a mountain. **3.** A point formed by the growth or cut of hair. **4.** The maximum development, strength, value, etc., of something.   [OE **5.** *Naut.* **a** The after upper corner of a fore-and-aft sail. **b** The upper end of a gaff. **c** The sharply narrowed part of a vessel at the bow or stern.   — *v.t.* **1.** *Naut.* To raise to or almost to a vertical position, as a gaff or yard. **2.** To make into a peak or point.   — *v.i.* **3.** To assume the form of a peak.   [Var. of PIKE⁴]

peak·ed (pē′kid, pēkt)   *adj.* Having a thin or sickly appearance.   [Origin uncertain]

peal (pēl)   *n.* **1.** A prolonged, sonorous sound, as of a bell or thunder. **2.** A set of large bells. **3.** A change rung on a set of bells.   — *v.t. & v.i.* To sound with a peal or peals.   [ME *pele,* aphetic var. of *apele* < OF *apeler* to appeal]

pe·an (pē′ən)   See PAEAN.

pea·nut (pē′nut′)   *n.* **1.** The nutlike seed or seed pod of an annual herbaceous vine ripening underground from the flowers that bury themselves after fertilization. **2.** The plant bearing this nut.

peanut brittle   A hard candy containing roasted peanuts.

peanut butter   A spread resembling butter in consistency, made from ground, roasted peanuts.

pear (pâr)   *n.* **1.** The juicy, edible, fleshy fruit of a tree of the rose family. **2.** The tree bearing this fruit.   [OE < W Gmc. < LL < L *pira,* pl. of *pirum* pear]

pearl¹ (pûrl)   *n.* **1.** A smooth, rounded, variously tinted nacreous concretion formed as a deposit around a foreign body in the shells of various mollusks, and largely used as a gem. **2.** Something like or likened to such a jewel in form, luster, value, etc. **3.** Nacre or mother-of-pearl. **4.** A very pale bluish gray: also **pearl blue, pearl gray. 5.** *Printing* A size of type smaller than agate, 5 points.   — *adj.* **1.** Pertaining to, consisting of, set with, or made of pearl or mother-of-pearl. **2.** Shaped like a pearl.   — *v.i.* **1.** To seek or fish for pearls. **2.** To form beads like pearls.   — *v.t.* **3.** To adorn or set with or as with pearls. **4.** To color or shape like pearls. **5.** To make into small round grains, as barley.   [< OF < Med.L *perna* pearl < L, mussel]   — **pearl′ly** *adj.*

pearl² (pûrl)   See PURL².

pearl·ash (purl′ash)   *n.* Commercial potassium carbonate.

peas·ant (pez′ənt)   *n.* **1.** In Europe, a farmer, farm laborer, or rustic workman. **2.** *Informal* A boorish, uncouth, or simple-minded person.   [< AF < OF *pais* country < LL < *pagus* district]

peas·ant·ry (pez′ən·trē)   *n.* **1.** The peasant class; a body of peasants. **2.** Rusticity.

pease (pēz)   Alternate plural of PEA: now used only in the collective sense.   [OE < LL < L, pl. of *pisum* < Gk. < *pisos,* pulse, pease]

pease·cod (pēz′kod)   *n.* A pea pod. Also **peas′cod.**

pea·soup·er (pē′soop′ər)   *n.* **1.** *Canadian* A French Canadian. **2.** *Brit.* A thick fog.

peat (pēt)   *n.* **1.** A substance consisting of partially carbonized vegetable material, found usu. in bogs. **2.** A block of this substance, pressed and dried for fuel: also called *turf.*   [ME < Med.L *peta* piece of peat]   — **peat′y** *adj.*

peat bog   A marsh with an accumulation of peat.

peat moss   **1.** A moss of which peat is largely composed. **2.** *Brit.* A peat bog.

pea·vey (pē′vē)   *n. pl.* **·vies** An iron-pointed lever fitted with a movable hook and used for handling logs. Also **pea′vy.**   [after Joseph Peavey, its inventor]

peb·ble (peb′əl)   *n.* **1.** A small, rounded fragment of rock, shaped by the action of water, ice, etc. **2.** Quartz crystal; also, a lens made of it. **3.** Leather that has been pebbled.   — *v.t.* **·bled, ·bling 1.** To impart a rough grain to (leather). **2.** To cover or pelt with pebbles.   [Back formation of OE *papol(stān)* pebble(stone)]

peb·bly (peb′lē, peb′əl·ē)   *adj.* **·bli·er, ·bli·est 1.** Covered with or full of pebbles. **2.** Having a texture resembling pebbles.

pe·can (pi·kan′, -kän′, pē′kan)   *n.* **1.** A large hickory of the central and southern U.S., with edible, oval, thin-shelled nuts. **2.** The nut of this tree.   [Earlier *paccan* < Algonquian (Cree) *pacan*]

pec·ca·dil·lo (pek′ə·dil′ō)   *n. pl.* **·los** or **·loes** A slight, trifling sin.   [< Sp., dim. of *pecado* sin < L < *peccare* to sin]

pec·cant (pek′ənt)   *adj.* **1.** Guilty of sin; sinful. **2.** Corrupt and offensive.   — **pec′can·cy** *n.*   — **pec′cant·ly** *adv.*

pec·ca·ry (pek′ər·ē)   *n. pl.* **·ries** A hoglike animal of Central and South America.   [< Sp. < Carib *pakira*]

pec·ca·vi (pe·kä′vī, -kä′vē)   *n. pl.* **·vis** *Latin* A confession of guilt; literally, I have sinned.

peck¹ (pek)   *v.t.* **1.** To strike with the beak, as a bird does or with something pointed. **2.** To make by striking thus: *peck* a hole in a wall. **3.** To pick up, as food, with the beak.   — *v.i.* **4.** To make strokes with the beak or with something pointed. **5.** To eat in small amounts or without appetite: with *at.*   — *n.* **1.** A quick, sharp blow, as with a beak. **2.** A mark or hole made by such a blow. **3.** *Informal* A quick kiss.   [ME. Var. of PICK.]   — **peck′er** *n.*

peck² (pek)   *n.* **1.** A measure of capacity: the fourth of a bushel. See table front of book. **2.** A vessel for measuring a peck. **3.** *Slang* A great quantity.   [< OF *pek*]

pec·tin (pek′tin)   *n. Biochem.* Any of a class of carbohydrates contained in the cell walls of various fruits as apples, lemons, etc., used as the basis of fruit jellies.

pec·to·ral (pek′tər·əl)   *adj.* **1.** Of or pertaining to the breast or chest. **2.** Of or for diseases of the lungs or chest.   — *n.* **1.** A pectoral organ, fin, or muscle. **2.** Any medicine for ailments of the chest.   [< L < *pectus, -oris* breast]

pectoral fin   *Zool.* One of the anterior paired fins of fish, homologous with the anterior limb of higher vertebrates.

pec·u·late (pek′yə·lāt)   *v.t. & v.i.* **·lat·ed, ·lat·ing** To steal or appropriate wrongfully (funds, esp. public funds entrusted to one's care); embezzle.   [< L *peculatus,* pp. of *peculari* embezzle]   — **pec′u·la′tion** *n.*   — **pec′u·la′tor** *n.*

pe·cu·liar (pi·kyool′yər)   *adj.* **1.** Having a character exclusively its own; specific. **2.** Singular; strange. **3.** Select; special; separate. **4.** Belonging particularly or exclusively to one.   — *n.* A person or thing that is peculiar; former any private possession.   [< MF *peculier* or < L < *peculium* private property]   — **pe·cul′iar·ly** *adv.*

pe·cu·li·ar·i·ty (pi·kyoo′lē·ar′ə·tē, -kyool′yar′-)   *n.* **·ties 1.** A characteristic. **2.** The quality of being peculiar.   — **syn.** See CHARACTERISTIC.

pe·cu·ni·ar·y (pi·kyoo′nē·er′ē)   *adj.* **1.** Consisting of or relating to money. **2.** Having a monetary penalty; entailing a fine.   [< L < *pecunia* money < *pecus* cattle]

ped-¹   Var. of PEDI-¹.

ped-²   Var. of PEDO-.

-ped   Var. of -PEDE.

ped·a·gog·ic (ped′ə·goj′ik, -gō′jik)   *adj.* **1.** Of or pertaining to the science or art of teaching. **2.** Of or belonging to a pedagogue; affected with a conceit of learning. Also **ped′a·gog′i·cal.**   — **ped′a·gog′i·cal·ly** *adv.*

ped·a·gog·ism (ped′ə·gog/iz·əm, -gŏg′-)   *n.* The nature, character, or business of a teacher. Also **ped′a·gogu′ism.**

ped·a·gogue (ped′ə·gog, -gôg)   *n.* **1.** A schoolmaster; educator. **2.** A pedantic, narrow-minded teacher. Also **ped′a·gog.**   [< OF < L < Gk. < *pais, paidos* child + *agō* leader]

ped·a·go·gy (ped′ə·gō′jē, -goj′ē)   *n.* **1.** The science or profession of teaching. **2.** The theory of how to teach.

ped·al (ped′l)   *adj.* **1.** Of or pertaining to a foot, feet, or a footlike part. **2.** Of or pertaining to a pedal.   — *n. Mech.* A lever operated by the foot and having various functions: a bicycle *pedal;* a piano *pedal.*   — *v.t. & v.i.* **ped·aled, ·ped·al·ing** or **·al·ling** To move or operate by working pedals.   [< L < *pes, pedis* foot]

ped·al-push·ers (ped′l·poosh′ərz)   *n.pl.* Slacks that come to just below the knees, worn by women and girls.

ped·ant (ped′ənt)   *n.* One who makes needless display of his learning, or who insists upon the importance of trifling points of scholarship.   [< MF < Ital. *pedante,* prob. < Med.L *paedagogans, -antis,* ppr. of *paedagogare* to teach]   — **pe·dan·tic** (pi·dan′tik)   *adj.*   — **pe·dan′ti·cal·ly** *adv.*

ped·ant·ry (ped′ən·trē)   *n. pl.* **·ries 1.** Ostentatious display of knowledge. **2.** Slavish adherence to forms or rules.

ped·ate (ped′āt)   *adj.* **1.** Resembling or having the functions of a foot; also, having feet. **2.** *Bot.* Divided or parted as a fan, the lateral divisions being subdivided: said of leaves.   [< L *pedatus* having feet]   — **ped′ate·ly** *adv.*

ped·dle (ped′l)   *v.* **·dled, ·dling** *v.i.* **1.** To travel about selling small wares. **2.** To piddle.   — *v.t.* **3.** To carry about and sell in small quantities. **4.** To sell or dispense in small quantities.   [Appar. back formation < ME *pedlere* peddler]

ped·dler (ped′lər)   *n.* One who peddles; a hawker.   [ME *ped* basket]   — **ped′dler·y** *n.*

-pede   *combining form* Footed: *centipede.* Also spelled *-pede* as in *quadruped.*   [< L *pes, pedis* foot]

ped·er·ast (ped′ə·rast, pē′də-)   *n.* One addicted to pederasty: also spelled *paederast.*

ed·er·as·ty (ped′ə·ras′tē, pē′də-) *n.* Sex relations between men, esp. between men and boys. [< NL < Gk. < *pais, aidos* boy + *erastēs* lover] — **ped′er·as′tic** *adj.*

·d·es·tal (ped′is·təl) *n.* **1.** A base or support for a column, tatue, or vase. **2.** Any foundation or support. — **to put n a pedestal** To hold in high estimation; to put in the position of an idol or hero. — *v.t.* **·taled** or **·tailed, ·tal·ing** or **·al·ling** To place on a pedestal. [< MF < Ital. < *piè, iede* foot + *di* of + *stallo* stall, standing place]

·des·tri·an (pə·des′trē·ən) *adj.* **1.** Moving on foot; walk-ng. **2.** Pertaining to common people; plebeian. **3.** Com-nonplace, prosaic, or dull, as prose. — *n.* One who journeys r moves from place to place on foot; a walker. [< L *pedes-r, -tris* on foot] — **pe·des′tri·an·ism** *n.*

·di-[1] *combining form* Foot; related to the foot or feet. Also, before vowels, ped-. [< L *pes, pedis* foot]

di-[2] Var. of PEDO-.

·di·a·tri·cian (pē′dē·ə·trish′ən, ped′ē-) *n.* A physician pecializing in pediatrics. Also **pe·di·at·rist** (pē′dē·at′rist).

·di·at·rics (pē′dē·at′riks, ped′ē-) *n.pl.* (construed as *sing.*) hat branch of medicine dealing with the diseases and hy-ienic care of children: also spelled *paediatrics*. [< Gk. *pais, aidos* child + -IATRICS] — **pe′di·at′ric** *adj.*

·d·i·cab (ped′i·kab) *n.* A three-wheeled vehicle operated y pedaling and used for public hire, esp. in Asia.

·di·cel (ped′ə·səl) *n.* **1.** A stalk or supporting part. **2.** *lot.* The stalk supporting a single flower in an inflorescence omposed of flowers arranged upon a common peduncle. **3.** *ool.* A footlike sucker or part. [< NL *pedicellus*, dim. of *pediculus*, dim. of *pes, pedis* foot]

·di·cel·late (ped′ə·sə·lit, -lāt′) *adj.* On or having a pedicel.

·di·cle (ped′i·kəl) *n.* A pedicel.

·dic·u·lo·sis (pə·dik′yə·lō′sis) *n. Pathol.* The condition f being infested with lice; lousiness. [< L *pediculus* little use + -OSIS] — **pe·dic′u·lous** *adj.*

·di·cure (ped′i·kyŏor) *n.* **1.** Chiropody. **2.** A chiropo-ist; podiatrist. **3.** The cosmetic treatment of the feet and enails. [< F < L *pes, pedis* foot + *curare* to care for]

·di·gree (ped′ə·grē) *n.* **1.** A line of ancestors; lineage. **2.** list or table of descent and relationship, esp. of an animal f pure breed. [< MF *pié de grue* a crane's foot; from a aree line mark denoting succession in pedigrees] — **ped′i·reed** *adj.*

·di·ment (ped′ə·mənt) *n. Archit.* **1.** A broad triangular art above a portico or door. **2.** Any similar piece sur-nounting a door, screen, bookcase, etc. [Earlier *periment*, rob. alter. of PYRAMID; infl. in form by L *pes, pedis* foot] — **ped′i·men′tal** (-men′təl) *adj.*

PEDIMENT
(Supreme Court Building, Washington, D.C.)

do- *combining form* Child; children; offspring: also, be-re vowels, ped-, as in *pedagogy*. Also spelled *paedo-*. [< k. *pais, paidos* child]

·dom·e·ter (pi·dom′ə·tər) *n.* An instrument that records e number of steps taken by the person who carries it. [< < L *pes, pedis* foot + Gk. *metron* measure]

·dun·cle (pi·dung′kəl) *n. Bot.* The general stalk or pport of an inflorescence. **2.** *Zool.* A stalk or stalklike art. [< NL *pedunculus* footstalk, dim. of *pes, pedis* foot] — **pe·dun′cu·lar** (-kyə·lər) *adj.* — **pe·dun′cu·late** (-kyə·lit, āt), **pe·dun′cu·lat′ed** *adj.*

ek (pēk) *v.i.* To look furtively, slyly, or quickly; peep. — A peep, glance. [ME *piken*; origin uncertain]

ek·a·boo (pē′kə·bōō′) *n.* A children's game in which one des one's face and calls out "peekaboo!"

el[1] (pēl) *n.* The natural coating of certain kinds of fruit, s oranges and lemons; skin; rind. — *v.t.* **1.** To strip off the ark, skin, etc., of. **2.** To strip off; remove. — *v.i.* **3.** To se bark, skin, etc. **4.** To come off: said of bark, skin, etc. *Slang* To undress. — **to keep one's eye peeled** *Informal* o keep watch; be alert. — **to peel off** *Aeron.* To veer off om a flight formation so as to dive or prepare for a landing. ME < L *pilare* to deprive of hair] — **peel′er** *n.*

el[2] (pēl) *n.* A long-handled implement used in moving read, etc., about an oven. [< OF < L *pala* shovel]

el·ing (pē′ling) *n.* Something peeled off, as rind, skin, etc.

en (pēn) *n.* The end of a hammer head opposite the flat, riking face, usu. shaped like a wedge. — *v.t.* To beat, end, or shape with the peen. [< ON]

peep[1] (pēp) *v.i.* **1.** To utter the small, sharp cry of a young bird or chick; chirp; cheep. **2.** To speak in a weak, small voice. — *n.* **1.** The cry of a chick or small bird, or of a young frog; chirp. **2.** A small sandpiper. [ME *pepen*; imit.]

peep[2] (pēp) *v.i.* **1.** To look through a small hole, from concealment, etc.; peek. **2.** To look furtively or quickly; peek. **3.** To begin to appear; be just visible. — *n.* **1.** A furtive look; a glimpse or glance. **2.** A peephole. **3.** The earliest appearance: the *peep* of day. [Prob. alter. of PEEK]

peep·er[1] (pē′pər) *n.* An animal that peeps, as a chick or any of several tree frogs.

peep·er[2] (pē′pər) *n.* **1.** One who peeps or peeks; a spying person. **2.** *Slang* An eye.

peep·hole (pēp′hōl′) *n.* An aperture, as a hole or crack, through which one may peep; also, a small window in a door.

peep·ing Tom (pē′ping tom′) An overly inquisitive or prying person; esp., one who peeps in at windows.

Peeping Tom of Coventry In British legend, a curious tailor who peeped at Lady Godiva and was struck blind.

peep·show (pēp′shō′) *n.* An exhibition of pictures, etc., viewed through a small orifice fitted with a magnifying lens.

peer[1] (pir) *v.i.* **1.** To look narrowly or searchingly, as in an effort to see clearly. **2.** To come partially into view. **3.** *Poetic* To appear. [Origin uncertain]

peer[2] (pir) *n.* **1.** An equal, as in natural gifts or in social rank. **2.** An equal before the law. **3.** A noble, esp. a British duke, marquis, earl, viscount, or baron; also, a prelate in the House of Lords. [< OF < L *par* equal]

peer·age (pir′ij) *n.* **1.** The office or rank of a peer or noble-man. **2.** Peers collectively. **3.** A book containing a genea-logical list of the nobility.

peer·ess (pir′is) *n.* A woman who holds a title of nobility, either in her own right or by marriage with a peer.

peer·less (pir′lis) *adj.* Of unequaled excellence. — **peer′-less·ly** *adv.* — **peer′less·ness** *n.*

peer of the realm One of the lords of Parliament.

peeve (pēv) *v.t.* **peeved, peev·ing** *Informal* To make pee-vish. — *n. Informal* A complaint, annoyance, or grievance. [Back formation < PEEVISH]

pee·vish (pē′vish) *adj.* **1.** Irritable or querulous; cross. **2.** Showing discontent and vexation. [ME *pevische*; origin un-certain] — **pee′vish·ly** *adv.* — **pee′vish·ness** *n.*

pee·wee (pē′wē) *n.* **1.** See PEWEE. **2.** *Informal* Anything or anyone small or diminutive. — *adj.* Tiny. [Imit.]

peg (peg) *n.* **1.** A pin, usu. of wood or metal, used to fasten articles together, to stop a hole, etc. **2.** A projecting pin upon which something may be hung, or which may serve to keep a score, etc. **3.** In a stringed musical instrument, a pin for holding fast the end of a string and adjusting its tension. **4.** A reason or excuse. **5.** A degree or step, as in rank or estimation. **6.** *Brit.* A drink of brandy or whisky and soda. **7.** *Informal* A leg, often of wood. **8.** *Informal* A throw, as in baseball. — **to take (one) down a peg** To lower the self-esteem of (a person). — *v.* **pegged, peg·ging** *v.t.* **1.** To drive or force a peg into; fasten with pegs. **2.** To mark with pegs. **3.** To strike or pierce with a peg or sharp instrument. **4.** *Informal* To throw. — *v.i.* **5.** To work or strive hard and perseveringly: usu. with *away*. **6.** In croquet, to hit a peg. **7.** To mark the score with pegs. — *adj.* Peg-top. [ME < MDu. *pegge*]

Peg·a·sus (peg′ə·səs) In Greek mythology, a winged horse, symbol of poetic inspiration. — *n.* A constellation, the Winged Horse. [< L < Gk. *Pēgasos*]

peg·board (peg′bôrd) *n.* **1.** Any perforated board into which pegs may be inserted for holding things, keeping score, etc. **2.** *Brit.* A game in which a player arranges pegs in cer-tain patterns on a perforated board: also called *solitaire*.

peg leg *Informal* **1.** An artificial leg of rodlike or tapering shape. **2.** A person with such a leg.

peg·top (peg′top′) *adj.* Wide at the hip and narrow at the ankle: said of trousers: also *peg*. Also **pegged**.

peg top A child's wooden spinning top, pear-shaped and having a sharp metal peg.

pei·gnoir (pān·wär′, pān′wär) *n.* A loose dressing gown or negligee worn by women. [< F < *peigner* to comb]

pe·jo·ra·tion (pē′jə·rā′shən, pej′ə-) *n.* The condition of be-coming worse; deterioration.

pe·jo·ra·tive (pē′jə·rā′tiv, pej′ə-, pi·jôr′ə·tiv, -jor′-) *adj.* Having or giving a derogatory or disparaging meaning or sense: a *pejorative* statement. — *n.* A pejorative word. [< LL *pejorare* to make worse] — **pe′jo·ra′tive·ly** *adv.*

Pe·king·ese (pē′kə·nēz′ for def. 1; pē′king·ēz′ for defs. 2, 3) *n. pl.* **·ese** **1.** A variety of a pug dog, having long, silky hair, snub nose, and short legs. **2.** A native or inhabitant of Peking. **3.** The dialect spoken in Peking. — *adj.* Of or pertaining to Peking. Also **Pe·kin·ese** (pē′kə·nēz′).

Pe·king man (pē′king′) *Paleontol.* An extinct manlike pri-mate whose fossil remains were found near Peking, China.

pe·koe (pē′kō, *Brit.* pek′ō) *n.* A superior black tea of India, Ceylon, and Java, made from the downy tips of the young buds of the tea plant. [< dial. Chinese *pek* white + *ho* hair]

pe·lag·ic (pə·laj′ik) *adj.* Of, pertaining to, or inhabiting the sea or ocean far from land. [< L < Gk. < *pelagos* the sea]

pel·ar·go·ni·um (pel′är·gō′nē·əm) *n.* Any of a number of strong-scented, ornamental herbs or shrubs generally known as *geraniums*, having handsome, variously colored flowers. [< NL < Gk. *pelargos* stork]

pelf (pelf) *n.* Money; wealth, esp. if dishonestly acquired. [< OF *pelfre* booty; ult. origin uncertain]

pel·i·can (pel′i·kən) *n.* A large, gregarious, web-footed bird of warm regions, having a pouch on the lower jaw for the temporary storage of fish. [OE < LL < Gk. *pelekan*]

Pelican State Nickname of Louisiana.

pe·lisse (pə·lēs′) *n.* A long outer garment or cloak, originally made of fur or lined with fur. [< F < Med.L < L (*vestis*) *pellicia* (a garment) of skins or fur]

pel·la·gra (pə·lā′grə, -lag′rə) *n. Pathol.* A disease characterized by gastric disturbance, skin eruptions, etc., caused by a deficiency of nicotinic acid. [< NL, prob. < Ital. *pelle agra* rough skin] —**pel·la′grous** *adj.*

pel·let (pel′it) *n.* 1. A small round ball, as of wax, paper, etc. 2. A small bullet. 3. A very small pill. 4. A stone. 5. A cannonball. —*v.t.* 1. To make into pellets. 2. To strike or hit with pellets. [< OF < Med.L < L *pila* ball]

pell-mell (pel′mel′) *adv.* 1. In a confused or disordered way or manner. 2. With a headlong rush; in wild haste. —*adj.* Devoid of order or method; confused. —*n.* A jumble; disorder. Also spelled **pell′mell′.** [< F *pêlemêle* < OF *pesle-mesle*]

pe·lu·cid (pə·lōō′sid) *adj.* 1. Permitting to a certain extent the passage of light. 2. Transparently clear and simple: a *pellucid* style. [< L < *per-* through + *lucere* to shine] —**pel·lu′cid·ly** *adv.* —**pel·lu′cid·ness, pel·lu·cid·i·ty** (pel′-ōō·sid′ə·tē) *n.*

Pel·o·pon·ne·sian (pel′ə·pə·nē′zhən, -shən) *adj.* Of or pertaining to the Peloponnesus. —*n.* A native or inhabitant of the Peloponnesus.

Peloponnesian War See table for WAR.

pe·lo·ta (pe·lō′tə) *n.* A game popular among Basques, Spaniards, and Spanish Americans. It is played in a walled court with a hard rubber ball and a curved, wicker racquet. [< Sp., lit., a ball, aug. of *pella* < L *pila*]

pelt[1] (pelt) *n.* 1. The skin of an animal, usu. with the fur left on. 2. A garment made of skin. 3. The human skin: a humorous term. [< OF < L *pellis* skin]

pelt[2] (pelt) *v.t.* 1. To strike repeatedly with or as with blows. 2. To throw or hurl (missiles). 3. To assail with words. —*v.i.* 4. To beat or descend with violence. 5. To move rapidly; hurry. —*n.* 1. A blow. 2. A swift pace. [ME *pelten,* ? var. of *pulten* to thrust] —**pelt′er** *n.*

pel·tate (pel′tāt) *adj. Bot.* Attached at or near the center of the lower surface, as a leaf. Also **pel′tat·ed.** [< L *peltatus* armed with a shield] —**pel′tate·ly** *adv.*

pel·try (pel′trē) *n. pl.* **·ries** 1. Pelts collectively. 2. A pelt. 3. A place for keeping or storing pelts.

pelvi- *combining form* Pelvis. [< L *pelvis* basin]

pel·vic (pel′vik) *adj.* Of, pertaining to, or near the pelvis.

pelvic arch *Anat.* In vertebrates, that part of the skeleton to which the hind limbs (in man, the lower limbs) are attached. Also **pelvic girdle.**

pel·vis (pel′vis) *n. pl.* **·ves** (-vēz) 1. *Anat.* **a** The part of the skeleton that forms a bony girdle joining the lower or hind limbs to the body, composed, in man, of the two innominate bones and the sacrum. **b** The hollow interior portion of the kidney, into which the urine is discharged. For illus. see KIDNEY. 2. A basinlike structure. [< L, basin]

pem·mi·can (pem′ə·kən) *n. U.S. & Canadian* 1. Lean meat, usu. venison, cut into strips, dried, pounded into paste with fat and a few berries, and pressed into cakes. 2. A similar concentrated and nutritious food made from beef and dried fruits, used by Arctic explorers, etc. Also **pem′i·can.** [< Algonquian (Cree) *pimekan* < *pime* fat]

pen[1] (pen) *n.* 1. An instrument for writing with fluid ink, usu. a metal point split in the middle and fitted to a holder. 2. A ball-point pen. 3. The quality of one's penmanship. 4. The profession of writing. 5. The style of writing. 6. A writer. —*v.t.* **penned, pen·ning** To write with a pen. [< OF < LL < L, wing, feather] —**pen′ner** *n.*

pen[2] (pen) *n.* 1. A small enclosure, as for pigs; also, the animals contained in a pen. 2. Any small place of confinement. 3. *Slang* A penitentiary. —*v.t.* **penned** or **pent, pen·ning** To enclose in or as in a pen; confine. [OE *penn*]

HUMAN PELVIS
a Crest of ilium. *b* Ilium. *c* Coccyx. *d* Acetabulum. *e* Ischium. *f* Pubic symphysis. *g* Head of femur. *h* Sacrum. *i* Lumbar vertebrae.

pe·nal (pē′nəl) *adj.* 1. Of or pertaining to punishment. 2. Liable, or rendering liable, to punishment. 3. Enacting or prescribing punishment: a *penal* code. 4. Relating to the means, or place of punishment. [< OF < L *poena* penalty]

pe·nal·ize (pē′nəl·īz, pen′əl-) *v.t.* **·ized, ·iz·ing** 1. To subject to a penalty, as for a violation. 2. To declare, as an action, subject to a penalty. Also *Brit.* **pe′nal·ise.** —**pe′nal·i·za′tion** *n.*

pen·al·ty (pen′əl·tē) *n. pl.* **·ties** 1. The legal punishment for having violated a law. 2. A sum of money to be forfeited as punishment for illegal acts; fine. 3. The disadvantage, loss, or suffering incurred by some act, error, state of being, etc.: the *penalty* of sin. 4. In sports and games, a handicap imposed for a violation of rules.

pen·ance (pen′əns) *n.* 1. *Eccl.* A sacramental rite involving contrition, confession of sins to a priest, the acceptance of penalties, and absolution; also, the penalty imposed. Any penalty, mortification, or act of piety voluntarily undertaken as an atonement for sin. —**to do penance** To perform an act or acts of penance. —*v.t.* **·anced, ·anc·ing** To impose a penance upon. [< OF < L *paenitere* to repent]

pence (pens) *Brit.* The plural of PENNY: used mostly in combination: *twopence.*

pen·chant (pen′chənt, *Fr.* pän·shän′) *n.* A strong liking or inclination for something. [< F *pencher* to incline]

pen·cil (pen′səl) *n.* 1. A writing, drawing, or marking implement consisting of a stick or thin strip of graphite, colored chalk, slate, etc., encased in wood or inserted in a mechanically operated holder. 2. A pencillike instrument for applying cosmetics. 3. A small stick of some substance: a styptic *pencil.* 4. A set of rays, as of light, diverging from or converging upon a given point. 5. In drawing or painting, the artist's skill or style. —*v.t.* **pen·ciled** or **·cilled, pen·cil·ing** or **·cil·ling** 1. To mark, write, draw, or color with or as with a pencil. 2. To use a pencil on. [< OF < L *penicillum* paintbrush] —**pen′cil·er** or **pen′cil·ler** *n.*

pend (pend) *v.i.* 1. To await adjustment or settlement. *Dial.* To hang; depend. [< MF < L *pendere* to hang]

pen·dant (pen′dənt) *n.* 1. Anything that hangs from something else, either for ornament or for use. 2. Something hanging from a chandelier, ceiling, lamp, etc., by which a light is turned on and off. 3. *Archit.* An ornament hanging from a ceiling, roof, etc. Also spelled *pendent.* —*adj.* See PENDENT. [See PEND.]

pen·dent (pen′dənt) *adj.* 1. Hanging downward; suspended. 2. Projecting; overhanging. 3. Undetermined; pending. Also spelled *pendant.* —*n.* See PENDANT. [Var. PENDANT] —**pen′dent·ly** *adv.*

pend·ing (pen′ding) *adj.* 1. Remaining unfinished or undecided. 2. Imminent; impending. —*prep.* 1. During the process or continuance of. 2. While awaiting; until.

pen·drag·on (pen·drag′ən) *n.* In ancient Britain, a supreme ruler or chief. [< Welsh, a chief leader in war]

pen·du·lous (pen′jōō·ləs) *adj.* 1. Hanging, esp. so as to swing. 2. Undecided; wavering. [< L *pendere* to hang] —**pen′du·lous·ly** *adv.* —**pen′du·lous·ness** *n.*

pen·du·lum (pen′jōō·ləm, -də-) *n.* 1. A suspended body free to oscillate between two extremes. 2. Such a device serving to regulate the movement of a clock. 3. Something that changes often. [See PENDULOUS.]

Pe·nel·o·pe (pə·nel′ə·pē) In the *Odyssey,* the faithful wife of Odysseus, who, during his absence kept her many suitors in check under pretext of having to weave a shroud.

pen·e·tra·ble (pen′ə·trə·bəl) *adj.* That can be penetrated. —**pen′e·tra·bil′i·ty** *n.* —**pen′e·tra·bly** *adv.*

pen·e·trate (pen′ə·trāt) *v.* **·trat·ed, ·trat·ing** *v.t.* 1. To force a way into or through; pierce; enter. 2. To spread or diffuse itself throughout. 3. To perceive the meaning of; understand. 4. To affect or move profoundly. —*v.i.* 5. To enter or pass through something. 6. To have an effect on the mind or emotions. [< L *penetrare* to put within] —**pen′e·tra·ble** (-trə·bəl) *adj.* —**pen′e·tra·bil′i·ty** *n.*

pen·e·trat·ing (pen′ə·trā′ting) *adj.* 1. Tending or having power to penetrate. 2. Acute; discerning: a *penetrating* mind. Also **pen′e·tra·tive.** —**pen′e·trat′ing·ly** *adv.* **pen′e·trat′ing·ness** *n.*

pen·e·tra·tion (pen′ə·trā′shən) *n.* 1. The act or power of penetrating physically. 2. Ability to penetrate mentally; acuteness; discernment. 3. The depth to which a bullet sinks in a target.

pen·guin (pen′gwin, peng′-) *n.* A web-footed, flightless aquatic bird of the southern hemisphere, with flipperlike wings and short legs. [< Welsh *pen* head + *gwyn* white]

pen·hold·er (pen′hōl′dər) *n.* 1. A handle with a device for inserting a metallic pen. 2. A rack for pens.

pen·i·cil·lin (pen′ə·sil′in) *n.* A powerful antibiotic found in a mold fungus, used to treat bacterial infections.

pen·i·cil·li·um (pen′ə·sil′ē·əm) *n. pl.* **·cil·li·a** (-sil′ē·ə) Any of various fungi growing on decaying fruits, ripening cheeses, etc.; one of which is the principal source of penicillin. [< L *penicillus* paintbrush]

·nin·su·la (pə·nin'sə·lə, -syə-) *n.* A piece of land almost ·rrounded by water, and connected with the mainland by ɪ isthmus. [< L < *paene* almost + *insula* island] — **pe·n'su·lar** *adj.*

·ninsula State A nickname for FLORIDA.

·nis (pē'nis) *n. pl.* **·nis·es** or **·nes** (-nēz) The copulatory ·gan of male animals. [< L, orig., tail] — **pe'ni·al** (-nē-), **pe'nile** (-nil, -nīl) *adj.*

n·i·tence (pen'ə·təns) *n.* The state of being penitent; ·ntrition. [< OF < L < *paenitere* to repent]

n·i·tent (pen'ə·tənt) *adj.* Affected by a sense of one's ·vn guilt, and resolved on amendment. — *n.* **1.** One who is ·nitent. **2.** One who confesses his sins to a priest and subits to the penance prescribed. — **pen'i·tent·ly** *adv.* See PENITENCE.

n·i·ten·tial (pen'ə·ten'shəl) *adj.* Of or expressing peni·nce or penance. — *n.* A penitent. — **pen'i·ten'tial·ly** *adv.*

n·i·ten·tia·ry (pen'ə·ten'shər·ē) *n. pl.* **·ries** A prison, p. one operated by a state or federal government for those ·nvicted of serious crimes. — *adj.* **1.** Of or pertaining to ·nance. **2.** Relating to or used for the punishment of crim·als. **3.** Rendering the offender liable to imprisonment. ˌee PENITENCE.

n·knife (pen'nīf') *n. pl.* **·knives** (-nīvz') A small pocket ·ife.

n·man (pen'mən) *n. pl.* **·men** (-mən) **1.** A person con·dered with regard to his handwriting. **2.** An author.

n·man·ship (pen'mən·ship) *n.* **1.** The art of writing. The style or quality of handwriting.

n name An author's assumed name; pseudonym; nom de ·ume. — **Syn.** See PSEUDONYM.

ɪ·nant (pen'ənt) *n.* **1.** A long, narrow flag, usu. triangu·r, used as a school emblem, etc. **2.** A similar flag awarded sports winners. [< PENNON]

n·nate (pen'āt) *adj.* Having wings or feathers. Also **·n'nat·ed.** [< L *pennatus* winged < *penna* feather]

ɪnnate *combining form* Having wings or feathers.

n·ni (pen'ē) *n. pl.* **pen·nis** or **pen·ni·a** (pen'ē-ə) A Finn·ɪ coin and monetary unit, the hundredth part of a markka. ˌ Finnish < G *pfennig* penny]

ɪ·ni·less (pen'i·lis) *adj.* Poverty-stricken.

ɪ·non (pen'ən) *n.* **1.** A small, pointed flag, borne by ·dieval knights on their lances. **2.** Any banner or flag. **3.** wing. [< OF *penon* streamer < L *penna* feather]

ɪnnsylvania Dutch 1. Descendants of immigrants from ·V Germany and from Switzerland, who settled in Penn·lvania in the 17th and 18th centuries. **2.** The language ·oken by these people, a High German dialect with an ad·ixture of English. [< early and dial. E *Dutch* (< G ·eutsch) German] — **Penn'syl·va'ni·a-Dutch** *adj.*

nn·syl·va·ni·an (pen'səl·vā'nē·ən, -vān'yən) *adj.* **1.** Of relating to the State of Pennsylvania. **2.** *Geol.* Belonging or denoting a Paleozoic period following the Mississippian ·d preceding the Permian periods. See table for GEOLOGY. · *n.* **1.** A native or inhabitant of Pennsylvania. **2.** *Geol.* ·e Pennsylvanian period or rock system.

ɪ·ny (pen'ē) *n. pl.* **pen·nies** or *Brit.* **pence** (pens) **1.** In ·e U.S. and Canada, a cent. **2.** A coin of Great Britain, ·eland, and various Commonwealth Nations, equivalent to shilling. **3.** In the United Kingdom, a coin equal in value ¹⁄₁₀₀ pound: also *new penny.* **4.** Money in general. — **a ·etty penny** *Informal* A large or relatively large amount of ·oney. [OE *penning, penig, pending*]

nny *combining form* Costing (a specified number of) ·nnies: formerly designating the cost of nails per hundred, ·t now denoting their length, beginning at 1 inch for two·nny nails. [< PENNY]

ɪny ante 1. A poker game in which the ante is limited to ·e cent. **2.** *Informal* Any piddling transaction.

ɪny pincher A parsimonious person. — **pen·ny-pinch· ɪ** (pen'ē-pinch'ing) *adj. & n.*

ɪ·ny·roy·al (pen'ē-roi'əl) *n.* A low, erect, strong-scented ·rb of North America yielding **oil of pennyroyal**, used in ·dicine. [Alter. of earlier *pulyole ryale*]

ɪ·ny·weight (pen'ē·wāt') *n.* In troy weight, the twenti·ɪ part of an ounce, 24 grains, or 1.56 grams. See table ·nt of book.

ɪ·ny-wise (pen'ē-wīz') *adj.* Unduly economical in small ·tters. — **penny-wise and pound-foolish** Economical in ·all matters, but wasteful in large ones.

ɪ·ny·worth (pen'ē-wûrth') *n.* **1.** As much as can be ·ught for a penny. **2.** A bargain. **3.** A small amount.

ɪnob·scot (pə-nob'skot) *n.* One of a tribe of North Amer·ɪn Indians of the Algonquian confederacy of 1749.

nol·o·gy (pē-nol'ə·jē) *n. pl.* **·gies** The science that treats crime and of the management of prisons and reforma·ies. [< L *poena* penalty + -LOGY] — **pe·no·log·i·cal** ·/nə·loj'i·kəl) *adj.* — **pe·nol'o·gist** *n.*

ɪ·sile (pen'sil) *adj.* **1.** Hanging loosely. **2.** Constructing

---

pensile nests: said of birds. [< L < *pendere* to hang] — **pen'sile·ness, pen·sil'i·ty** *n.*

pen·sion[1] (pen'shən) *n.* **1.** A periodic allowance to an individual or to his family, given when certain conditions, as age, length of service, etc., have been fulfilled. **2.** A grant or allowance paid to someone of recognized ability in the arts or sciences. — *v.t.* **1.** To grant a pension to. **2.** To dismiss with a pension: with *off.* [< OF < L *pensio, -onis* payment] — **pen'sion·a·ble** *adj.*

pen·sion[2] (pen'shən, *Fr.* pän·syôn') *n. French* A boarding house; also, a boarding school. [< OF, payment, rent]

pen·sion·ar·y (pen'shən·er'ē) *adj.* **1.** Living by means of a pension. **2.** Consisting of or like a pension. — *n. pl.* **·ar·ies 1.** A pensioner. **2.** A hireling.

pen·sion·er (pen'shən·ər) *n.* **1.** One who receives a pension or is dependent on the bounty of another. **2.** At Cambridge University, a student who pays his own expenses. **3.** A boarder, as in a convent or school.

pen·sive (pen'siv) *adj.* **1.** Engaged in or addicted to serious, quiet reflection. **2.** Expressive of, suggesting, or causing a melancholy thoughtfulness. [< OF < L *pensare* to think] — **pen'sive·ly** *adv.* — **pen'sive·ness** *n.*

pen·stock (pen'stok') *n.* **1.** A trough or conduit for carrying water to a water wheel. **2.** A sluice or floodgate controlling the discharge of water, as from a pond.

pent (pent) Past participle of PEN[2]. — *adj.* Penned up or in; closely confined.

penta- *combining form* Five: *pentagon.* Also, before vowels, **pent-.** [< Gk. *pente* five]

pen·ta·gon (pen'tə·gon) *n. Geom.* A polygon having five sides and five angles. [< L < Gk. < *pente* five + *gōnia* angle] — **pen·tag·o·nal** (pen·tag'ə·nəl) *adj.* — **pen·tag'o·nal·ly** *adv.*

Pentagon, the 1. A five-sided building in Arlington, Virginia, housing the U.S. Department of Defense and other offices. **2.** The military leadership of the U.S.

pen·ta·he·dron (pen'tə·hē'drən) *n. pl.* **·dra** (-drə) *Geom.* A polyhedron bounded by five plane faces. — **pen'ta·he'·dral** *adj.*

pen·tam·e·ter (pen·tam'ə·tər) *n.* **1.** A line of verse consisting of five metrical feet. **2.** Verse comprised of pentameters. — *adj.* Having five metrical feet. [< L < Gk. < *pente* five + *metron* a measure]

pen·tane (pen'tān) *n. Chem.* Any one of three isomeric, volatile, liquid hydrocarbons of the methane series, C_5H_{12}, two of which are contained in petroleum.

Pen·ta·teuch (pen'tə·tōok, -tyōok) *n.* The first five books of the Old Testament collectively, consisting of Genesis, Exodus, Leviticus, Numbers, and Deuteronomy. [< LL < Gk. < *pente* five + *teuchos* book] — **Pen'ta·teuch'al** *adj.*

pen·tath·lon (pen·tath'lən) *n.* An athletic contest consisting of five separate events, in all of which each contestant must participate. [< Gk. < *pente* five + *athlos* contest]

pen·ta·va·lent (pen'tə·vā'lənt, pen·tav'ə-) *adj. Chem.* Having a valence of five. [< PENTA- + L *valere* to have power or value]

Pen·te·cost (pen'tə·kôst, -kost) *n.* **1.** A Christian festival, the seventh Sunday after Easter, commemorating the descent of the Holy Ghost upon the apostles (*Acts* ii): also called *Whitsunday.* **2.** A Jewish festival, fifty days after the first day of Passover: also called *Shabuoth.* [< LL < Gk. *pentēkostē* (*hēmera*) the fiftieth (day)]

pen·te·cos·tal (pen'tə·kôs'tal, -kos'-) *adj. Often cap.* Of, pertaining to, or occurring at Pentecost.

pent·house (pent'hous') *n.* An apartment or other structure on the roof of a building. [< OF, ? < LL *appendicium* appendage]

Pen·to·thal Sodium (pen'tə·thôl) A proprietary name for a brand of thiopental sodium.

pent-up (pent'up') *adj.* Repressed: *pent-up emotions.*

pe·nuch·le (pē'nuk·əl), **pe·nuck·le** See PINOCHLE.

pe·nult (pē'nult, pi·nult') *n.* The syllable next to the last in a word. Also **pe·nul·ti·ma** (pi·nul'tə·mə). [Short for *penultima* < L < *paene* almost + *ultimus* last]

pe·nul·ti·mate (pi·nul'tə·mit) *adj.* **1.** Next to the last. **2.** Of or belonging to the next to the last syllable. — *n.* A penultimate part. [< L *paene* almost + ULTIMATE]

pe·num·bra (pi·num'brə) *n. pl.* **·brae** (-brē) or **·bras 1.** A partial shadow, as in an eclipse, within which the rays of light from an illuminating body are partly but not wholly intercepted. **2.** The dark fringe around the central part of a sunspot. [< NL < L *paene* almost + *umbra* shadow] — **pe·num'bral, pe·num'brous** (-brəs) *adj.*

pe·nu·ri·ous (pə·nŏor'ē·əs, -nyŏor'-) *adj.* **1.** Excessively sparing in the use of money; stingy. **2.** Extremely poor; needy. **3.** Affording or yielding little; scanty. [< MF < Med.L < L *penuria* want, poverty] — **pe·nu'ri·ous·ly** *adv.* — **pe·nu'ri·ous·ness** *n.*

pen·u·ry (pen′yə·rē) *n.* Extreme poverty or want. [< OF < L *penuria* want]

pe·on (pē′ən) *n.* **1.** In Latin America, a laborer; servant. **2.** Formerly, a debtor kept in servitude until he had worked out of his debt. [< Sp. < LL *pedo, -onis* foot soldier < L *pes, pedis* foot]

pe·on·age (pē′ən·ij) *n.* **1.** The condition of being a peon. **2.** The system by which debtors are held in servitude until they have worked out their debt. Also **pe′on·ism** (-iz′əm).

pe·o·ny (pē′ə·nē) *n.* *pl.* **·nies** **1.** A plant of the crowfoot family, having large crimson, rose, or white flowers. **2.** The flower. [OE < L < Gk. *Paion* Paeon, the Healer]

peo·ple (pē′pəl) *n.* *pl.* **peo·ple;** *for defs. 1 & 2, also* **peo·ples** **1.** The entire body of human beings living in the same country, under the same government, and speaking the same language: the *people* of England. **2.** A body of human beings having the same history, culture, and traditions, and usu. speaking the same language: the Polish *people*. **3.** In a state or nation, the body of persons invested with political rights. **4.** A group of persons having the same interests, profession, condition of life, etc.: poor *people*. **5.** Persons considered collectively: *people* say. **6.** Ordinary persons; the populace: usu. with *the*. **7.** One's family or relatives. **8.** Human beings as distinguished from animals. **9.** Animals collectively: the ant *people*. — *v.t.* **·pled, ·pling** To fill with inhabitants; populate. [< OF < L *populus* populace] — **peo′pler** *n.*

— **Syn.** A group having a common descent, language, culture, habitat, or government may be called a *people*. *Folk* is a homelier word for *people*, nearly as broad, and usu. stressing common traditions, customs, or behavior. A *nation* is a political entity, comprising the *people* (or *peoples*) under one government.

People's Party A political organization formed in the U.S. in 1891, advocating public control of railways, an income tax, and limitation of ownership of land.

pep (pep) *n.* *Informal* Energy and high spirits; vigorous activity. — *v.t.* **pepped, pep·ping** To fill or inspire with energy or pep: usu. with *up*. [Short for PEPPER]

pep·lum (pep′ləm) *n.* *pl.* **·lums** or **·la** (-lə) A short overskirt, ruffle, or flounce attached to a blouse or coat at the waist. [< L < Gk. *peplos* a woman's shawl]

pep·per (pep′ər) *n.* **1.** A pungent, aromatic condiment consisting of the dried immature berries of a plant. When ground entire it is **black pepper**, but when the outer coating of the seeds is removed, the product is **white pepper**. **2.** Any plant of the pepper family. **3.** Red pepper. **4.** Green pepper. — *v.t.* **1.** To sprinkle or season with pepper. **2.** To sprinkle freely. **3.** To shower, as with missiles; spatter; pelt. **4.** To make (speech or writing) vivid or pungent, as with humor, sarcasm, etc. — *v.i.* **5.** To discharge missiles at something. [OE, ult. < L < Gk. *peperi*]

pep·per-and-salt (pep′ər·ən·sôlt′) *adj.* Having or consisting of a mixture of white and black, so as to present a grayish appearance. — *n.* A pepper-and-salt cloth.

pep·per·box (pep′ər·boks′) . **1.** A container for sprinkling pepper. **2.** A quick-tempered person.

pep·per·corn (pep′ər·kôrn′) *n.* **1.** A berry of the pepper plant. **2.** Anything trifling or insignificant.

pep·per·grass (pep′ər·gras′, -gräs′) *n.* A plant of the mustard family, having a pungent flavor, and used as a salad vegetable. Also **pep′per·wort** (-wûrt).

pepper mill A hand mill, often designed for table use, in which peppercorns are ground.

pep·per·mint (pep′ər·mint′) *n.* **1.** A pungent, aromatic herb used in medicine and confectionery. **2.** An oil made from this herb. **3.** A confection flavored with peppermint.

pepper pot **1.** A pepperbox. **2.** A stew of meat or fish with vegetables, flavored with peppers.

pepper tree A tree of Central and South America whose seeds are used as a spice.

pep·per·y (pep′ər·ē) *adj.* **1.** Pertaining to or like pepper; pungent. **2.** Quick-tempered; hasty. **3.** Spicy and vivid, as speech or writing. — **pep′per·i·ness** *n.*

pep·py (pep′ē) *adj.* **·pi·er, ·pi·est** *Informal* Full of energy; lively. — **pep′pi·ness** *n.*

pep·sin (pep′sin) *n.* **1.** *Biochem.* An enzyme secreted by the gastric juices that promotes the digestion of proteins. **2.** A medicinal preparation obtained from the stomachs of various animals, as the pig and the calf, used to aid digestion. Also **pep′sine** (-sin). [< G < Gk. *pepsis* digestion]

pep talk *Informal* A brief, vigorous talk meant to inspire.

pep·tic (pep′tik) *adj.* **1.** Of, pertaining to, or promotive of digestion. **2.** Of, pertaining to, or caused by pepsin. **3.** Able to digest. — *n.* An agent that promotes digestion. [< Gk. *pepsis* digestion]

pep·tone (pep′tōn) *n.* *Biochem.* Any of the soluble compounds into which proteins are converted when acted upon by pepsin, by acids and alkalis, by putrefaction, etc. [< G < Gk. *peptos* digested] — **pep·ton·ic** (pep·ton′ik) *adj.*

Pe·quot (pē′kwot) *n.* One of a tribe of Algonquian Indians, formerly inhabiting southern New England.

per (pûr) *prep.* **1.** By; by means of; through: used in commercial and business English: *per* bearer. **2.** To or for each: ten cents *per* yard. **3.** By the; every: esp. in Latin phrase *per diem.* [< L, through, by]

per- *prefix* **1.** Through; throughout: *per*vade, *per*ennial. **2.** Thoroughly: *per*turb. **3.** Away: *per*vert. **4.** Very: *per*fe *vid.* **5.** *Chem.* Indicating an excess amount of a specified el ment in a compound: hydrogen *per*oxide. [< L *per* throug

per·ad·ven·ture (pûr′əd·ven′chər) *adv.* *Archaic* Perchance perhaps. [< OF *par aventure* by chance]

per·am·bu·late (pə·ram′byə·lāt) *v.* **·lat·ed, ·lat·ing** *v.t.* To walk through or over. **2.** To walk through or around as to inspect, etc. — *v.i.* **3.** To stroll. [< L < *per* throu + *ambulare* to walk] — **per·am·bu·la·tion** (pə·ram′byə·lā shən) *n.* — **per·am′bu·la·to′ry** (-tôr′ē, -tō′rē) *adj.*

per·am·bu·la·tor (pə·ram′byə·lā′tər) *n.* **1.** One who pe ambulates. **2.** *Chiefly Brit.* A baby carriage.

per an·num (pûr an′əm) *Latin* By the year.

per·cale (pər·kāl′, -kal′) *n.* A closely woven cotton fabr without gloss. [< F, prob. < Persian *pergālah*]

per cap·i·ta (pûr kap′ə·tə) *Latin* For each person; literall by heads.

per·ceive (pər·sēv′) *v.t. & v.i.* **·ceived, ·ceiv·ing** **1.** To b come aware of (something) through the senses; see, hear feel, taste, or smell. **2.** To come to understand; apprehen with the mind. [< OF < L < *per-* thoroughly + *capere* take] — **per·ceiv′a·ble** *adj.* — **per·ceiv′a·bly** *adv.*

— **Syn. 1.** sense. Compare SEE, DISCERN. **2.** comprehend.

per·cent (pər·sent′) *n.* **1.** Number of parts in or to ev hundred, often specified: fifty *percent* of the people. Amount or quantity commensurate with the number of un in proportion to one hundred: ten *percent* of fifty is fiv symbol, %. **3.** *pl.* Securities bearing a certain percentage interest. Also **per cent., per cent** [Short for L *per centum* the hundred]

per·cent·age (pər·sen′tij) *n.* **1.** Rate per hundred, or p portion in a hundred parts. **2.** A proportion or part consi ered in its quantitative relation to the whole. **3.** In co merce, the allowance, commission, duty, or interest on hundred. **4.** *Informal* Advantage; profit.

per·cen·tile (pər·sen′til, -til) *n.* *Stat.* Any of 100 poin spaced at equal intervals within the range of a plotted var ble, each point denoting that percentage of the total cas lying below it in the series. — *adj.* Of a percentile.

per·cept (pûr′sept) *n.* *Psychol.* **1.** Something perceiv **2.** Immediate knowledge derived from perceiving. [< *percipere* to perceive]

per·cep·ti·ble (pər·sep′tə·bəl) *adj.* That can be perceive appreciable. — **per·cep′ti·bil′i·ty** *n.* — **per·cep′ti·bly** *a*

per·cep·tion (pər·sep′shən) *n.* **1.** The act or process of p ceiving. **2.** The result or effect of perceiving. **3.** Any sight, knowledge, etc., arrived at by or as by perceiving. The capacity for perceiving. — **per·cep′tion·al** *adj.* **per·cep′tu·al** (-chōō·əl) *adj.*

per·cep·tive (pər·sep′tiv) *adj.* **1.** Having the power of p ception. **2.** Having a quick capacity for perceiving. **3.** or pertaining to perception. — **per·cep′tive·ly** *adv.* — **p cep·tiv′i·ty** (pûr′sep·tiv′ə·tē), **per·cep′tive·ness** *n.*

perch¹ (pûrch) *n.* **1.** A horizontal staff or pole used a roost for poultry. **2.** Any place on which birds alight or re **3.** Any place for sitting or standing, esp. if elevated. **4.** rod (def. 9). — *v.i.* **1.** To alight or sit on or as on a per roost. — *v.t.* **2.** To set on or as on a perch. [< OF < *pertica* pole] — **perch·er** (pûr′chər) *n.*

perch² (pûrch) *n.* *pl.* **perch** or **perches** **1.** A small, spi finned fresh-water food fish. **2.** Any of various other related fishes. [< OF < L < Gk. *perkē*]

per·chance (pər·chans′, -chäns′) *adv.* Possibly; perha [< OF *par chance* by chance]

Per·che·ron (pûr′chə·ron, -shə-) *n.* A breed of large dr horses. [after *Perche*, a region of nothern France]

per·cip·i·ent (pər·sip′ē·ənt) *adj.* **1.** Having the power perception. **2.** Perceiving rapidly or keenly. — *n.* C who or that which perceives. [< L < *per-* thoroughly capere to take] — **per·cip′i·ence** or **·en·cy** *n.*

per·coid (pûr′koid) *adj.* Of or pertaining to an order spiny-finned fishes, including the fresh-water perches; per like. — *n.* A percoid fish. Also **per·coi·de·an** (pər·koi′dē-ə [< L *perca* perch² + -OID]

per·co·late (pûr′kə·lāt; *for n.*, also pur′kə·lət) *v.t. & .lat·ed, ·lat·ing** Of a liquid, to pass or cause to pass throu fine interstices; filter. — *n.* That which has percolated. L < *per-* through + *colare* to strain] — **per′co·la′tion** *n*

per·co·la·tor (pûr′kə·lā′tər) *n.* A type of coffeepot in wh boiling water rises to the top in a tube and then filters dow through finely ground coffee in a container below.

per·cus·sion (pər·kush′ən) *n.* **1.** The sharp striking of body against another. **2.** The shock, vibration, or sou produced by a striking of one body against another. **3.** *M* A light, quick tapping of the finger tips upon the back, che or abdomen, for determining by resonance the condition the organ beneath. **4.** The act of striking the percussion cap in a firearm. **5.** *Music* Percussion instruments. — *adj.* Of, pertaining to, or operating by percussion. [< L < *per-through* + *quatere* to shake]

ercussion cap A small cap of thin metal, containing mercury fulminate or some other detonator, formerly used in ammunition to explode the propelling charge.

ercussion instruments Musical instruments whose tone is produced by striking, as the timpani, cymbals, drums, etc. **er·di·em** (per dē′əm, dī′əm) **1.** By the day. **2.** An allowance for expenses each day. [< L]

er·di·tion (pər·dish′ən) *n.* **1.** Eternal damnation; the utter loss of a soul. **2.** The place of eternal damnation; hell. [< OF < L *per-* through, away + *dare* to give]

ère (pâr) *n. French* Father: often used after a surname to distinguish father from son: Dumas *père.*

er·e·gri·nate (per′ə·gri·nāt′) *v.* ·**nat·ed**, ·**nat·ing** *v.i.* **1.** To travel from place to place. — *v.t.* **2.** To travel through or along. [< L *peregrinari* to travel abroad] — **per′e·gri·na′· ion** *n.* — **per·e·gri·na′tor** *n.*

er·e·grine (per′ə·grin) *adj.* **1.** Coming from foreign regions. **2.** Wandering. — *n.* The peregrine falcon. [< L < *eregre* abroad < *per-* through + *ager* land]

eregrine falcon **1.** A falcon generally blackish blue above and white or gray below, formerly much used in falconry. **2.** An American subspecies of this falcon.

er·emp·to·ry (pə·remp′tər·ē, per′əmp·tôr′ē, -tō′rē) *adj.* **1.** Not admitting of appeal; decisive; absolute. **2.** Positive in opinion, etc.; imperious. **3.** Intolerant of opposition; dictatorial. **4.** *Law* Precluding or putting an end to debate or discussion; final. [< L < *per-* entirely + *emere* to take] — **er·emp′to·ri·ly** *adv.* — **per·emp′to·ri·ness** *n.*

er·en·ni·al (pə·ren′ē·əl) *adj.* **1.** Continuing or enduring through the year or through many years. **2.** Perpetual; everlasting; unceasing. **3.** *Bot.* Lasting more than two years. — *n.* A plant that grows for three or more years, isu. blossoming and fructifying annually. [< L < *per-* through + *annus* year] — **per·en′ni·al·ly** *adv.*

er·fect (*adj. & n.* pûr′fikt; *v.* pər·fekt′) *adj.* **1.** Having all the elements or qualities requisite to its nature or kind; complete. **2.** Without defect; flawless: *perfect* weather. **3.** Thoroughly and completely skilled or informed: a *perfect* violinist. **4.** Accurately corresponding to a type or original; exact: a *perfect* replica. **5.** Thorough; utter: He made a *perfect* nuisance of himself. **6.** Completely effective: a *perfect* answer. **7.** *Informal* Very great: a *perfect* horror of spiders. **8.** *Gram.* Denoting the tense of a verb expressing action completed in the past. Grammarians note in English a present perfect, past perfect (or pluperfect), and a future perfect ense. **9.** *Music* **a** Denoting the three intervals whose accuracy of intonation the human ear can recognize within precise limits, the **perfect octave**, the **perfect fifth**, and the **perfect fourth**. **b** Complete: a *perfect* cadence. — *n. Gram.* The perfect tense; also, a verb in this tense. — *v.t.* **1.** To bring to perfection; complete. **2.** To make thoroughly skilled or accomplished: to *perfect* oneself in an art. [< OF < L < *per-* thoroughly + *facere* to do, make] — **per·fect′er** *n.* — **per′fect·ly** *adv.* — **per′fect·ness** *n.*

er·fect·i·ble (pər·fek′tə·bəl) *adj.* Capable of being made perfect or of arriving at perfection. — **per·fect′i·bil′i·ty** *n.*

er·fec·tion (pər·fek′shən) *n.* **1.** The state or quality of being perfect. **2.** The embodiment of something that is perfect: As a hostess, she is *perfection.* **3.** Any quality, characteristic, or trait considered to be perfect. **4.** The highest degree of something. **5.** The act or process of perfecting.

er·fec·tion·ist (pər·fek′shən·ist) *n.* One who demands of himself or of others an exceedingly high degree of excellence.

er·fec·tive (pər·fek′tiv) *adj.* Tending to make perfect. — **er·fec′tive·ly** *adv.* — **per·fec′tive·ness** *n.*

er·fec·to (pər·fek′tō) *n. pl.* ·**tos** A cigar of medium size, shaped to taper at either end. [< Sp., perfect]

erfect participle Past participle.

erfect pitch Absolute pitch.

er·fer·vid (pər·fûr′vid) *adj.* Excessively fervid; ardent; zealous. [< NL < L *per-* thoroughly + *fervidus* burning]

er·fid·i·ous (pər·fid′ē·əs) *adj.* Marked by or guilty of perfidy; treacherous. [< L *perfidia*] — **per·fid′i·ous·ly** *adv.* — **per·fid′i·ous·ness** *n.*

er·fi·dy (pûr′fə·dē) *n. pl.* ·**dies** The act of violating faith, trust, or allegiance; treachery. [< MF < L < *per* through, under pretext of + *fides* faith]

er·fo·li·ate (pər·fō′lē·it, āt) *adj. Bot.* Growing so that the stem seems to pass through it, as a leaf. [< NL < L *per-* through + *folium* leaf] — **per·fo′li·a′tion** *n.*

er·fo·rate (*v.* pûr′fə·rāt; *adj.* pûr′fə·rit) *v.t.* ·**rat·ed**, ·**rat·ing** **1.** To make a hole or holes through, by or as by stamping or drilling. **2.** To pierce with holes in rows or patterns. — *adj.* Perforated. [< L < *per-* through + *forare* to bore]

— **per′fo·ra·ble** *adj.* — **per′fo·ra′tive, per′fo·ra·to′ry** (-rə·tôr′ē, -tō′rē) *adj.* — **per′fo·ra′tor** *n.*

per·fo·rat·ed (pûr′fə·rā′tid) *adj.* Pierced with a hole or holes; esp., pierced with lines of holes, as sheets of stamps.

per·fo·ra·tion (pûr′fə·rā′shən) *n.* **1.** The act of perforating, or the state of being perforated. **2.** A hole or series of holes drilled in or stamped through something.

per·force (pər·fôrs′, -fōrs′) *adv.* By or of necessity; necessarily. [< OF < *par* by (< L *per-*) + *force* force]

per·form (pər·fôrm′) *v.t.* **1.** To carry out in action; execute; do. **2.** To fulfill; discharge, as a duty or command. **3.** To act (a part) or give a performance of (a play, piece of music, etc.). — *v.i.* **4.** To carry through to completion an action, undertaking, etc. **5.** To give an exhibition or performance. [< OF < *par-* thoroughly (< L *per-*) + *fournir* to accomplish] — **per·form′a·ble** *adj.*

per·form·ance (pər·fôr′məns) *n.* **1.** An entertainment of some kind before an audience or spectators. **2.** A public presentation: The music had its first *performance* here. **3.** The act or manner of performing a play, part, piece of music, etc. **4.** Manner of operating or functioning: The car's *performance* improved. **5.** Any act, deed, or accomplishment.

per·form·er (pər·fôr′mər) *n.* One who performs; esp., an actor, musician, etc.

per·fume (pər·fyōōm′; *for n., usu.* pûr′fyōōm) *n.* **1.** A fragrant substance, usu. a volatile liquid, prepared to emit a pleasant odor; scent. **2.** A pleasant odor, as from flowers; fragrance. — **Syn.** See SMELL. — *v.t.* **fumed, fum·ing** To fill or scent with a fragrant odor. [< MF < Ital. < *per-* through (< L) + *fumare* to smoke < LL *fumus* smoke]

per·fum·er (pər·fyōō′mər) *n.* **1.** One who makes or deals in perfumes. **2.** One who or that which perfumes.

per·fum·er·y (pər·fyōō′mər·ē) *n. pl.* ·**er·ies** **1.** The art or business of preparing perfumes. **2.** Perfumes in general, or a specific perfume. **3.** A place where perfumes are made.

per·func·to·ry (pər·fungk′tər·ē) *adj.* **1.** Done mechanically; careless; cursory. **2.** Having no zest or enthusiasm; dull. [< LL < L < *per-* through + *fungi* to perform] — **per·func′to·ri·ly** *adv.* — **per·func′to·ri·ness** *n.*

per·fuse (pər·fyōōz′) *v.t.* **fused, fus·ing** **1.** To permeate, suffuse, or sprinkle with a liquid, color, etc. **2.** To spread (a liquid, etc.) over or through something; diffuse. [< L < *per-* throughout + *fundere* to pour] — **per·fu′sion** (-fyōō′· zhən) *n.* — **per·fu′sive** (-fyōō′siv) *adj.*

per·go·la (pûr′gə·lə) *n.* An arbor or covered walk made of trelliswork covered with vegetation or flowers. [< Ital., arbor < L *pergula* projecting roof, arbor]

per·haps (pər·haps′) *adv.* Maybe; possibly. [< PER + *happes,* pl. of *hap* chance]

peri- *prefix* **1.** Around; encircling: *periphery.* **2.** Situated near; adjoining: *perihelion.* [< Gk. *peri* around]

per·i·anth (per′ē·anth) *n. Bot.* The envelope of a flower, esp. one in which the calyx and corolla are so alike as to be indistinguishable. [< F < NL < Gk. *peri-* around + *anthos* flower]

per·i·car·di·al (per′ə·kär′dē·əl) *adj.* Of or pertaining to the pericardium. Also **per′i·car′di·ac** (-ak), **per′i·car′di·an.**

per·i·car·di·tis (per′ə·kär·dī′tis) *n. Pathol.* Inflammation of the pericardium.

per·i·car·di·um (per′ə·kär′dē·əm) *n. pl.* ·**di·a** (-dē·ə) *Anat.* A membranous bag that surrounds and protects the heart. [< NL < Gk. < *peri-* around + *kardia* heart]

per·i·carp (per′ə·kärp) *n. Bot.* The wall of a ripened ovary or fruit, usu. in three layers, the epicarp, mesocarp, and endocarp: also called *seedcase, seed vessel.* [< NL < Gk. < *peri-* around + *karpos* fruit] — **per′i·car′pi·al** *adj.*

Per·i·cle·an (per′ə·klē′ən) *adj.* Pertaining to, characteristic of, or named after Pericles, or the period of his supremacy, when Greek art, drama, and statesmanship are considered to have been at their height.

per·i·cra·ni·um (per′ə·krā′nē·əm) *n. pl.* ·**ni·a** (-nē·ə) *Anat.* The periosteum of the external surface of the cranium. [< NL < Gk. < *peri-* around + *kranion* skull] — **per′i·cra′· ni·al** *adj.*

per·i·gee (per′ə·jē) *n. Astron.* The point in the orbit of the moon or of an artificial satellite at which it is nearest the earth: opposed to *apogee.* [< MF < Med.L < Gk. < *peri-,* near + *gē* earth] — **per′i·ge′al, per′i·ge′an** *adj.*

per·i·gon (per′ə·gon) *n. Geom.* An angle equal to two straight angles or 360 degrees.

per·i·he·li·on (per′ə·hē′lē·ən) *n. pl.* ·**li·a** (-lē·ə) *Astron.* The point in the orbit of a planet or comet where it is nearest the sun: opposed to *aphelion.* [< NL < Gk. *peri-* around, near + *hēlios* sun]

per·il (per′əl) *n.* Exposure to the chance of injury; danger; risk. — *v.t.* ·**iled** or ·**illed, ·il·ing** or ·**il·ling** To expose to danger; imperil. [< OF < L *periculum* trial, danger]

per·i·lous (per′əl·əs) *adj.* Involving, or attended with peril;

hazardous; risky. — **per'il·ous·ly** *adv.* — **per'il·ous·ness** *n.*

pe·rim·e·ter (pə·rim'ə·tər) *n.* **1.** The boundary line of any figure of two dimensions. **2.** The sum of the sides of a plane figure. [< L < Gk. < *peri-* around + *metron* measure] — **per·i·met·ric** (per'ə·met'rik) or **·ri·cal** *adj.*

per·i·ne·um (per'ə·nē'əm) *n.*, *pl.* **·ne·a** (-nē'ə) *Anat.* **1.** The region of the body between the genital organs and the rectum. **2.** The entire region comprising the anus and the internal genitals. Also **per'i·nae'um.** [< LL < Gk. < *peri-* around + *inein* to empty out] — **per'i·ne'al** *adj.*

pe·ri·od (pir'ē·əd) *n.* **1.** A portion of time marked or defined by certain conditions, events, etc.: a *period* of rest. **2.** A portion or lapse of time, as in a process or development, a stage. **3.** A portion of time into which something is divided: Our new school day has seven *periods.* **4.** *Astron.* The time it takes a planet or satellite to revolve once about its primary. **5.** *Geol.* One of the divisions of geologic time. **6.** *Physics* The time that elapses between any two successive similar phases of an oscillation or other regularly repeated cyclical motion. **7.** A dot (.) placed on the line, used as a mark of punctuation after every complete declarative sentence, after most abbreviations, etc. **8.** The pause at the end of a sentence. **9.** *Pathol.* A stage distinguishable in the course of a disease. **10.** Menstruation. **11.** The completion of something. [< OF < L < Gk. < *peri-* around + *hodos* way]

pe·ri·od·ic (pir'ē·od'ik) *adj.* **1.** Of, pertaining to, or like a period. **2.** Recurring at regular intervals. **3.** Intermittent. **4.** Of or expressed in periodic sentences. **5.** *Physics* Recurring after a definite interval. — **pe'ri·od'i·cal·ly** *adv.*

pe·ri·od·i·cal (pir'ē·od'i·kəl) *adj.* **1.** Of or pertaining to publications that appear at fixed intervals of more than one day; also, published at regular intervals. **2.** Periodic. — *n.* A periodical publication.

pe·ri·o·dic·i·ty (pir'ē·ə·dis'ə·tē) *n.* The quality of being periodic or of recurring at definite intervals of time.

periodic law *Chem.* The statement that the physical and chemical properties of the elements are related to their atomic numbers, and that they recur periodically when the elements are arranged in the order of these numbers.

periodic sentence A sentence so constructed as to suspend completion of both sense and structure until the close.

periodic table *Chem.* A table in which the elements are arranged in groups as determined by the periodic law.

per·i·os·te·um (per'ē·os'tē·əm) *n.* *Anat.* A tough, fibrous vascular membrane that surrounds and nourishes the bones. [< NL < LL < Gk. < *peri-* around + *osteon* bone] — **per'i·os'te·al, per'i·os'te·ous** *adj.*

per·i·pa·tet·ic (per'i·pə·tet'ik) *adj.* Walking about from place to place. — *n.* One given to walking about. [< MF < L < Gk. < *peri-* around + *patein* to walk]

Per·i·pa·tet·ic (per'i·pə·tet'ik) *adj.* Of or pertaining to the philosophy of Aristotle, who lectured to his disciples while walking. — *n.* A disciple of Aristotle.

pe·riph·er·al (pə·rif'ər·əl) *adj.* **1.** Of or consisting of a periphery. **2.** Capable of perceiving images laterally that are not directly in one's line of sight: *peripheral* vision. **3.** Not central; marginal: of *peripheral* importance. **4.** *Anat.* Outer; external. — **pe·riph'er·al·ly** *adv.*

pe·riph·er·y (pə·rif'ər·ē) *n.*, *pl.* **·er·ies** **1.** The outer part surface, or boundary of something. **2.** A surrounding region, area, or country. [< OF < LL < Gk. < *peri-* around + *pherein* to carry]

pe·riph·ra·sis (pə·rif'rə·sis) *n.*, *pl.* **·ses** (-sēz) A roundabout about or instance of expressing something; circumlocution. Also **per·i·phrase** (per'i·frāz'). [< L < Gk. < *peri-* around + *phrazein* to declare]

per·i·phras·tic (per'ə·fras'tik) *adj.* **1.** Of the nature of or involving periphrasis; circumlocutory. **2.** *Gram.* Denoting a construction in which a phrase is substituted for an inflected form, as, *the hat of John* for *John's hat.* Also **per'i·phras'ti·cal.** — **per'i·phras'ti·cal·ly** *adv.*

pe·rique (pə·rēk') *n.* A dark, strongly flavored tobacco grown in Louisiana. [after nickname of Pierre Chenet, American tobacco grower who introduced this variety]

per·i·scope (per'ə·skōp) *n.* An instrument consisting of prisms or mirrors so arranged as to reflect light rays down a vertical tube, used to guide submarines, etc. [< Gk. *peri-* around + *skopeein* to look] — **per·i·scop·ic** (per'ə·skop'ik) or **·i·cal** *adj.*

per·ish (per'ish) *v.i.* **1.** To suffer a violent or untimely death. **2.** To pass from existence. [< OF < L < *per-* away + *ire* to go]

per·ish·a·ble (per'ish·ə·bəl) *adj.* **1.** Liable to perish. **2.** Liable to speedy decay, as fruit in transportation. — *n.* *Usu. pl.* Something liable to decay, as food. — **per'ish·a·ble·ness, per'ish·a·bil'i·ty** *n.* — **per'ish·a·bly** *adv.*

per·i·stal·sis (per'ə·stôl'sis, -stal'-) *n.*, *pl.* **·ses** (-sēz) *Physiol.* A contractile muscular movement of any hollow organ, as of the alimentary canal, whereby the contents are gradually propelled toward the point of expulsion.

PERISCOPE

[< NL < Gk. < *peri-* around + *stellein* to place] — **per·stal'tic** *adj.*

per·i·style (per'ə·stīl) *n.* *Archit.* **1.** A system of colum about a building or an internal court. **2.** An area or space enclosed. [< MF < L < Gk. < *peri-* around + *stylos* pilla — **per'i·sty'lar** *adj.*

per·i·to·ne·um (per'ə·tə·nē'əm) *n.*, *pl.* **·ne·a** (-nē'ə) *An* A serous membrane that lines the abdominal cavity and is more or less complete covering for the viscera. Also **per'i· nae'um.** [< LL < Gk. < *peri-* around + *teinein* to stretc — **per'i·to·ne'al** or **·nae'al** *adj.*

per·i·to·ni·tis (per'ə·tə·nī'tis) *n.* *Pathol.* Inflammation the peritoneum.

per·i·wig (per'ə·wig) *n.* A peruke or wig. [Earlier *perywy* alt. of *perruck* < MF *perruque*]

per·i·win·kle[1] (per'ə·wing'kəl) *n.* Any of several sm. marine snails, some of which are edible. [OE *pinewincle* < L *pina* mussel + OE *wincle* a shellfish]

per·i·win·kle[2] (per'ə·wing'kəl) *n.* A plant having shinir evergreen leaves and blue or sometimes white flowers: al called *myrtle.* [OE < L *pervinca*]

per·jure (pûr'jər) *v.t.* **·jured, ·jur·ing** **1.** To make (onese guilty of perjury. **2.** To find guilty of or involved in pe jury. [< OF < L < *per-* thoroughly + *jurare* to swear] — **per'jur·er** *n.*

per·jured (pûr'jərd) *adj.* Guilty of or constituting perjur

per·ju·ry (pûr'jə·rē) *n.*, *pl.* **·ries** *Law* The wilful giving false testimony or the withholding of material facts or e dence while under oath in a judicial proceeding.

perk[1] (pûrk) *v.i.* **1.** To recover one's spirits or vigor: wi *up.* **2.** To carry oneself or lift one's head jauntily. — *t* **3.** To raise quickly or smartly, as the ears: often with *up*. To make (oneself) trim and smart in appearance: often wi *up* or *out.* — *adj.* Perky. [ME *perken;* ? var. of PERCH

perk[2] (pûrk) *v.i.* *Informal* To percolate.

perk·y (pûr'kē) *adj.* **perk·i·er, perk·i·est** **1.** Jaunty; sprigh ly; pert. **2.** Spirited and self-assured. Also **perk.** — **per i·ly** *adv.* — **perk'i·ness** *n.*

per·ma·frost (pûr'mə·frôst, -frost) *n.* The part of t earth's surface in arctic regions that is permanently froze

per·ma·nence (pûr'mə·nəns) *n.* The state or quality of b ing permanent.

per·ma·nen·cy (pûr'mə·nən·sē) *n.*, *pl.* **·cies** **1.** Permanenc **2.** Something permanent.

per·ma·nent (pûr'mə·nənt) *adj.* Continuing in the sar state or without essential change; enduring; durable; fixe — *n.* A permanent wave. [< OF < L < *per-* through *manere* to remain] — **per'ma·nent·ly** *adv.*

Permanent Court of International Justice An inte national tribunal established under the Covenant of t League of Nations (1921) and superseded in 1945 by the I ternational Court of Justice: also called *World Court.*

permanent wave An artificial wave mechanically or che ically set in the hair and lasting several months.

per·man·ga·nate (pər·mang'gə·nāt) *n.* *Chem.* A dark pu ple salt of permanganic acid.

per·man·gan·ic acid (pûr'man·gan'ik) *Chem.* An aci $HMnO_4$, that is a powerful oxidizer in aqueous solutions.

per·me·a·bil·i·ty (pûr'mē·ə·bil'ə·tē) *n.* The quality or co dition of being permeable, as by liquids, gases, etc.

per·me·a·ble (pûr'mē·ə·bəl) *adj.* Allowing passage, esp. fluids. — **per'me·a·bly** *adv.*

per·me·ance (pûr'mē·əns) *n.* **1.** The act of permeatir **2.** *Electr.* The ability to be traversed by magnetic lines force.

per·me·ate (pûr'mē·āt) *v.* **·at·ed, ·at·ing** *v.t.* **1.** To spre thoroughly through; pervade. **2.** To pass through the po or interstices of. — *v.i.* **3.** To spread itself. [< L < *p* through + *meare* to pass] — **per'me·ant** *adj.* — **per'm a'tion** *n.* — **per'me·a'tive** *adj.*

Per·mi·an (pûr'mē·ən) *Geol.* *adj.* Of or pertaining to t latest period of the Paleozoic era. — *n.* The Permian ro system or period. See table for GEOLOGY. [after *Perm, fc* mer E. Russian province]

per·mis·si·ble (pər·mis'ə·bəl) *adj.* That can be permitte allowable. — **per·mis'si·bil'i·ty** *n.* — **per·mis'si·bly** *adv.*

per·mis·sion (pər·mish'ən) *n.* **1.** The act of permitting allowing. **2.** Formal authorization or consent.

per·mis·sive (pər·mis'iv) *adj.* **1.** Permitting; granting p mission. **2.** Permitted; optional. **3.** Not strict in dis pline. — **per·mis'sive·ly** *adv.* — **per·mis'sive·ness** *n.*

per·mit (*v.* pər·mit'; *n.* pûr'mit) *v.* **·mit·ted, ·mit·ting** *v.t.* To allow the doing of; consent to. **2.** To give (someor leave or consent; authorize. **3.** To afford opportunity f — *v.i.* **4.** To afford possibility or opportunity. **5.** To low. — *n.* **1.** Permission to do something. **2.** An offic document or certificate authorizing performance of a spe fied activity; license. [< L < *per-* through + *mittere* send, let go] — **per·mit'ter** *n.*

per·mut·a·ble (pər·myōō'tə·bəl) *adj.* Capable of bei changed or of undergoing change or interchange.

r·mu·ta·tion (pûr′myōō·tā′shən) n. 1. The act of re-ranging; transformation. 2. *Math.* Change in the order of equence of elements or objects in a series; esp., the making f all possible changes of sequence of sequence, as *abc, acb, bac*, etc.

r·mute (pər·myōōt′) v.t. ·mut·ed, ·mut·ing To subject to ermutation, esp., to change the order of. [< OF < L < er- thoroughly + *mutare* to change]

r·ni·cious (pər·nish′əs) adj. 1. Having the power of de-troying or injuring; very injurious; deadly. 2. Malicious; icked. [< MF < L < *per-* thoroughly + *nex, necis* death] - per·ni′cious·ly adv. — per·ni′cious·ness n.
— Syn. 1. Noxious, baneful, deleterious, detrimental.

rnicious anemia *Pathol.* Severe anemia characterized y inadequate development of red blood corpuscles and pro-ressive disturbances in the muscular, nervous, and gastro-ntestinal systems.

r·nick·e·ty (pər·nik′ə·tē) adj. Persnickety.

r·o·rate (per′ə·rāt) v.i. ·rat·ed, ·rat·ing 1. To speak at ngth; harangue. 2. To sum up or conclude a speech.

r·o·ra·tion (per′ə·rā′shən) n. The concluding portion of n oration or the summing up of an argument. [< L < *per-* rough + *orare* to speak]

r·ox·ide (pə·rok′sid) n. *Chem.* 1. An oxide having the ighest proportion of oxygen for a given series. 2. Hydro-en peroxide. Also **per·ox′id** (-sid). — v.t. ·id·ed, ·id·ing o bleach, as hair, with peroxide.

r·pen·dic·u·lar (pûr′pən·dik′yə·lər) adj. 1. Being at ght angles to the plane of the horizon; upright or vertical. *Math.* Meeting a given line or plane at right angles — n. . A perpendicular line or plane. 2. A plumb rule. 3. A ne at right angles to another line or to a plane. [< OF < L *rpendiculum* plumb line] — per′pen·dic′u·lar′i·ty (-lar′ə-) n. — per′pen·dic′u·lar·ly adv.

r·pe·trate (pûr′pə·trāt) v.t. ·trat·ed, ·trat·ing To do, per-rm, or commit (a crime, etc.). [< L < *per-* thoroughly + *itrare* to accomplish] — per′pe·tra′tion n. — per′pe-a′tor n.

r·pet·u·al (pər·pech′ōō·əl) adj. 1. Continuing or lasting rever or for an unlimited time. 2. Incessant. [< OF < L *per-* through + *petere* to seek] — per·pet′u·al·ly adv.
— Syn. (adj.) 1. eternal, endless, interminable.

rpetual motion Continuous motion of a mechanism, nceived of as a capacity of doing work indefinitely by the ergy supplied through its own operation.

r·pet·u·ate (pər·pech′ōō·āt) v.t. ·at·ed, ·at·ing 1. To ake perpetual or enduring. 2. To cause to remain known, irrent, etc.: to perpetuate a myth. [< L < *perpetuare* to per-tuate] — per·pet′u·a′tion n. — per·pet′u·a′tor n.

r·pe·tu·i·ty (pûr′pə·tōō′ə·tē, -tyōō′-) n. pl. ·ties 1. The uality or state of being perpetual. 2. Something perpetual, a perpetual annuity. 3. Unending or unlimited time. ee PERPETUAL.]

r·plex (pər·pleks′) v.t. 1. To cause to hesitate or become nfused, as from doubt, difficulties encountered, etc.; puz-e. 2. To make complicated, intricate, or confusing.
— Syn. 1. bewilder, mystify, confound. Compare BAFFLE.

r·plexed (pər·plekst′) adj. 1. Confused; puzzled; bewil-red. 2. Of a complicated character; involved. [Appar. ter. of obs. *perplex,* adj., intricate < L *perplexus* involved] - per·plex′ed·ly (-plek′sid·lē) adv.

r·plex·ing (pər·plek′sing) adj. Confusing; puzzling. — r·plex′ing·ly adv.

r·plex·i·ty (pər·plek′sə·tē) n. pl. ·ties 1. The state, iality, or condition of being perplexed; doubt; confusion; wilderment. 2. That which perplexes. 3. The quality or ndition of being intricate or complicated.

r·qui·site (pûr′kwə·zit) n. 1. Any incidental profit, pay-ent, etc., beyond what is earned as salary or wages. 2. ny privilege or benefit owed or claimed as one's due. [< L *requisitum* a thing diligently sought]

rse (pûrs) adj. Dark grayish blue. — n. A dark grayish ue. [< OF *pers* < LL *persus* < *Persicus* Persian]

r se (pûr sē′, sā′) *Latin* By itself; intrinsically.

r·se·cute (pûr′sə·kyōōt) v.t. ·cut·ed, ·cut·ing 1. To annoy harass persistently. 2. To maltreat or oppress because of ce, religion, or beliefs. [< F < L *persecutus,* pp. of *perse-i* to pursue] — per′se·cu′tion n. — per′se·cu′tive adj. - per′se·cu′tor n.

r·seph·o·ne (pər·sef′ə·nē) In Greek mythology, the ughter of Zeus and Demeter, abducted to the underworld y Pluto, but allowed to return to the earth for part of each ar: identified with the Roman *Proserpine.*

r·seus (pûr′syōōs, -sē·əs) In Greek mythology, the son of us and Danae, slayer of Medusa and rescuer of Androm-a. A northern constellation. See CONSTELLATION.

r·se·ver·ance (pûr′sə·vir′əns) n. 1. The act or habit of rsevering. 2. *Theol.* In Calvinism, the continuance in ace and certain salvation of those chosen by God.

---

per·se·vere (pûr′sə·vir′) v.i. ·vered, ·ver·ing To persist in any purpose or enterprise; strive in spite of difficulties, etc. [< OF < L < *per-* thoroughly + *severus* strict] — per′se·ver′ing adj. — per′se·ver′ing·ly adv.

Per·sian (pûr′zhən, -shən) adj. Of or pertaining to Persia (now Iran), or its people, language, or culture. — n. 1. A native or inhabitant of Persia or Iran. 2. The Iranian lan-guage of the Persians. [< OF < L *Persia* Persia]

Persian Empire An empire of SW Asia, extending from the Indus to the Mediterranean, destroyed by Alexander the Great (331 B.C.).

Persian lamb 1. The lamb of the karakul sheep. 2. Its black, gray, or brown curled fur.

Persian wheel A noria.

per·si·flage (pûr′sə·fläzh) n. A light, flippant style of con-versation or writing. [< F < *persifler* to banter]

per·sim·mon (pər·sim′ən) n. 1. Any of several trees hav-ing reddish orange fruit with an astringent taste when not ripe. 2. The fruit of these trees. [< Algonquian]

per·sist (pər·sist′, -zist′) v.i. 1. To continue firmly in some course, state, etc., esp. despite opposition or difficulties. 2. To be insistent, as in repeating or continuing an action. 3. To continue to exist; endure. [< L < *per-* thoroughly + *sistere* causative of *stare* to stand]

per·sis·tence (pər·sis′təns, -zis′-) n. 1. The act, condition, or quality of persisting. 2. Perseverance. 3. The continu-ance of an effect longer than the cause that first produced it. Also **per·sis′ten·cy.**

per·sis·tent (pər·sis′tənt, -zis′-) adj. 1. Persevering or stubborn in a course or resolve. 2. Enduring; permanent. 3. Constantly repeated. — per·sis′tent·ly adv.

per·snick·e·ty (pər·snik′ə·tē) adj. *Informal* 1. Unduly fas-tidious; fussy. 2. Demanding minute care or pains. Also *pernickety.* [< dial. E] — per·snick′e·ti·ness n.

per·son (pûr′sən) n. 1. Any human being considered as a distinct entity or personality; an individual. 2. The body of a human being. 3. One's characteristic appearance or phys-ical condition. 4. *Law* Any human being, corporation, or body politic having legal rights and duties. 5. *Theol.* One of the three individualities in the Trinity 6. *Gram.* a A modification of the pronoun and verb that distinguishes the speaker (**first person**), the person or thing spoken to (**second person**), and the person or thing spoken of (**third person**). b Any of the forms or inflections indicating this, as *I* or *we, you, he, she, it.* — in person 1. Physically present. 2. Acting for oneself. [< F < L *persona* actor's mask, character]

per·so·na (pər·sō′nə) n. pl. ·nae (-nē) *Usu. pl.* A charac-ter in a drama, novel, etc. [L, person]

per·son·a·ble (pûr′sən·ə·bəl) adj. Attractive or pleasing in personal appearance. — per′son·a·bly adv.

per·son·age (pûr′sən·ij) n. 1. A man or woman of impor-tance or rank. 2. A person; individual. 3. A character in fiction, drama, history, etc.

per·so·na gra·ta (pər·sō′nə grä′tə, grā′tə) *Latin* An ac-ceptable or welcome person.

per·son·al (pûr′sən·əl) adj. 1. Pertaining to or concerning a particular person; not general or public. 2. Relating to, having the qualities of, or constituting a person or persons. 3. Done in person: a *personal* service. 4. Of or pertaining to the body or appearance: *personal* beauty. 5. Directly refer-ring to an individual, esp. in a critical or disparaging man-ner: *personal* remarks. 6. *Law* Pertaining to property re-garded as movable or temporary: distinguished from *real.* 7. *Gram.* Denoting or indicating person: *personal* pronouns. — n. 1. *Law* A movable or temporary article or property; chattel. 2. A paragraph or advertisement of personal refer-ence or application. [< OF < LL < L *persona* a person]

per·son·al·i·ty (pûr′sən·al′ə·tē) n. pl. ·ties 1. Distinctive qualities or characteristics of a person. 2. A person of out-standing or distinctive qualities. 3. That which constitutes a person; personal existence. 4. *Often pl.* A remark or ref-erence, often disparaging, of a personal nature.

per·son·al·ize (pûr′sən·əl·īz′) v.t. ·ized, ·iz·ing 1. To make personal. 2. To personify. 3. To mark with one's name, initials, etc., as stationery or handkerchiefs.

per·son·al·ly (pûr′sən·əl·ē) adv. 1. In person; not through an agent. 2. As regards one's own opinions, tastes, etc. 3. With regard to a person as an individual. 4. As though in-tended for or directed toward oneself.

personal pronoun *Gram.* A pronoun that varies in form according to person, gender, case, and number, as *we, their, him.*

per·son·al·ty (pûr′sən·əl·tē) n. pl. ·ties *Law* Personal property.

per·so·na non gra·ta (pər·sō′nə non grä′tə, grā′tə) *Latin* A person who is not welcome or acceptable.

per·son·ate (pûr′sən·āt) v.t. ·at·ed, ·at·ing 1. To act the part of, as a character in a play. 2. *Law* To impersonate

with intent to deceive. [See PERSON.] — **per′son·a′tion** n.
— **per′son·a′tive** adj. — **per′son·a′tor** n.
per·son·i·fi·ca·tion (pər·son′ə·fə·kā′shən) n. 1. The figurative endowment of inanimate objects or qualities with personality or human attributes. 2. Exemplification of a quality or attribute in one's person; embodiment: She was the *personification* of joy. 3. Impersonation.
per·son·i·fy (pər·son′ə·fī) v.t. **·fied**, **·fy·ing** 1. To think of or represent as having life or human qualities. 2. To represent (an abstraction or inanimate object) as a person. 3. To be the embodiment of; typify. [< F < L *persona* mask, person + *facere* to make] — **per·son′i·fi′er** n.
per·son·nel (pûr′sə·nel′) n. The persons employed in a business, in military service, etc. [See PERSONAL.]
per·spec·tive (pər·spek′tiv) n. 1. The art or theory of representing solid objects on a flat surface in such a way as to convey the impression of depth and distance. 2. The effect of distance upon the appearance of objects. 3. The relative importance of facts or matters from any special point of view. 4. Judgment of facts, circumstances, etc., with regard to their importance. 5. A distant view, vista, or prospect. — adj. Pertaining to, characterized by, or represented in perspective. [< Med.L < LL < L < *per-* through + *specere* to look] — **per·spec′tive·ly** adv.
per·spi·ca·cious (pûr′spə·kā′shəs) adj. 1. Keenly discerning or understanding. 2. *Archaic* Sharp-sighted. [< L *perspicax, -acis* sharp-sighted] — **per′spi·ca′cious·ly** adv. — **per′spi·ca′cious·ness** n.
per·spi·cac·i·ty (pûr′spə·kas′ə·tē) n. Keenness in mental penetration or discernment.
per·spi·cu·i·ty (pûr′spə·kyoo′ə·tē) n. 1. Clearness of expression or style; lucidity. 2. Perspicacity.
per·spic·u·ous (pər·spik′yoo·əs) adj. Having the quality of perspicuity; clear; lucid. — **per·spic′u·ous·ly** adv. — **per·spic′u·ous·ness** n.
per·spi·ra·tion (pûr′spə·rā′shən) n. 1. The act or process of perspiring. 2. The fluid excreted; sweat. 3. Arduous physical effort. — **per·spir·a·to·ry** (pər·spī′rə·tôr′ē) adj.
per·spire (pər·spīr′) v. **·spired**, **·spir·ing** v.i. 1. To give off a saline fluid through the pores of the skin; sweat. — v.t. 2. To give off through pores; exude. [< MF < L < *per-* through + *spirare* to breathe]
per·suade (pər·swād′) v.t. **·suad·ed**, **·suad·ing** 1. To induce (someone) to do something. 2. To induce to a belief; convince. [< MF < L < *per-* thoroughly + *suadere* to advise] — **per·suad′a·ble** adj. — **per·suad′er** n.
per·sua·sion (pər·swā′zhən) n. 1. The act of persuading or of using persuasive methods. 2. Ability to persuade. 3. The state of being persuaded; settled opinion; conviction. 4. An accepted creed or belief. 5. A religious sect. 6. Party; group; faction.
per·sua·sive (pər·swā′siv) adj. Having power or tendency to persuade. — n. That which persuades or tends to persuade. — **per·sua′sive·ly** adv. — **per·sua′sive·ness** n.
pert (pûrt) adj. 1. Impertinent; saucy. 2. *Dial.* Handsome and lively. [Apheptic var. of ME *apert* < OF, open, impudent] — **pert′ly** adv. — **pert′ness** n.
per·tain (pər·tān′) v.i. 1. To have reference; relate. 2. To belong as an adjunct, function, quality, etc. 3. To be fitting or appropriate. — **pertaining to** Having to do with; belonging or relating to. [< OF < L < *per-* through + *tenere* to hold]
per·ti·na·cious (pûr′tə·nā′shəs) adj. 1. Tenacious of purpose; adhering fixedly to a pursuit or opinion. 2. Stubbornly or doggedly persistent. [< L < *per-* thoroughly, very + *tenax, -acis* tenacious] — **per′ti·na′cious·ly** adv.
per·ti·nac·i·ty (pûr′tə·nas′ə·tē) n. pl. **·ties** 1. Tenacity of purpose; unyielding adherence. 2. Obstinacy.
per·ti·nent (pûr′tə·nənt) adj. Related to or properly bearing upon the matter in hand; relevant. [See PERTAIN.] — **per′ti·nence, per′ti·nen·cy** n. — **per′ti·nent·ly** adv.
per·turb (pər·tûrb′) v.t. 1. To disquiet or disturb greatly; alarm; agitate. 2. To throw into disorder; cause confusion in. [< OF < L < *per-* thoroughly + *turbare* to disturb] — **per·turb′a·ble** adj. — **per′tur·ba′tion** n.
pe·ruke (pə·rook′) n. A wig; esp. one worn by men in the 17th and 18th centuries: also *periwig*. [< MF *perruque* < Ital. *perrucca*]
pe·rus·al (pə·roo′zəl) n. The act or procedure of reading or examining carefully; a thorough reading or scrutiny.
pe·ruse (pə·rooz′) v.t. **·rused**, **·rus·ing** 1. To read carefully or attentively. 2. To read. 3. To examine; scrutinize. [< PER- + USE, v.] — **pe·rus′a·ble** adj. — **pe·rus′er** n.
Pe·ru·vi·an (pə·roo′vē·ən) adj. Of or pertaining to Peru or its inhabitants, etc. — n. A native or inhabitant of Peru.
Peruvian bark Cinchona.
per·vade (pər·vād′) v.t. **·vad·ed**, **·vad·ing** To spread through every part of; be diffused throughout; permeate. [< L < *per-* through + *vadere* to go] — **per·va′sion** (-zhən) n.
per·va·sive (pər·vā′siv) adj. Thoroughly penetrating or permeating. — **per·va′sive·ly** adv. — **per·va′sive·ness** n.

per·verse (pər·vûrs′) adj. 1. Willfully deviating from acceptable or conventional behavior, opinion, etc. 2. Refractory; capricious. 3. Petulant; cranky. 4. Morally wrong or erring; wicked; perverted. [See PERVERT.] — **per·verse′ly** adv. — **per·verse′ness** n.
per·ver·sion (pər·vûr′zhən, -shən) n. 1. The act of perverting, or the state of being perverted. 2. A perverted form of act, use, etc. 3. Deviation from the normal in sexual desire or activities.
per·ver·si·ty (pər·vûr′sə·tē) n. pl. **·ties** 1. The state or quality of being perverse. 2. An instance of perverseness.
per·vert (v. pər·vûrt′; n. pûr′vərt) v.t. 1. To turn to an improper use or purpose; misapply. 2. To distort the meaning or intent of; misconstrue. 3. To turn from approved opinions or conduct; lead astray. 4. To deprave; debase; corrupt. — n. One characterized by or practicing sexual perversion. [< F < L < *per-* away + *vertere* to turn] — **per·vert′er** n. — **per·vert′i·ble** adj.
per·vert·ed (pər·vûr′tid) adj. 1. Deviating widely from what is right or acceptable; distorted. 2. Characterized by viciousness, sexual perversion, etc. — **per·vert′ed·ly** adv.
per·vi·ous (pûr′vē·əs) adj. 1. Capable of being penetrated. 2. Open to reason, suggestions, etc. [< L *pervius* having way through] — **per′vi·ous·ly** adv. — **per′vi·ous·ness** n.
pe·se·ta (pə·sā′tə, *Sp.* pā·sā′tä) n. The standard monetary unit of Spain, equivalent to 100 centimos: in 1960 worth about 2 U.S. cents; also, a silver coin of this value. [< S. dim. of *pesa* weight]
pes·ky (pes′kē) adj. **·ki·er, ·ki·est** U.S. Informal Annoying; troublesome. [Prob. < PEST + -Y²] — **pes′ki·ly** adv.
pe·so (pā′sō) n. pl. **·sos** 1. The standard monetary unit of various Spanish-speaking countries, as Argentina, Mexico, or the Philippines, equivalent to 100 centavos. 2. A coin or note of this denomination. [< Sp., orig., a weight < L *pensum*, orig. pp. neut. of *pendere* to weigh]
pes·sa·ry (pes′ə·rē) n. pl. **·ries** Med. 1. A device worn internally to remedy a uterine displacement. 2. A contraceptive device worn over or in the uterine cervix. [< Med.L < Gk. *pessos* oval stone]
pes·si·mism (pes′ə·miz′əm) n. 1. A disposition to take a gloomy or cynical view of affairs: opposed to *optimism*. 2. The doctrine that the world and life are essentially evil. [< L *pessimus* worst + -ISM] — **pes′si·mist** n. — **pes′si·mis′tic** or **·ti·cal** adj. — **pes′si·mis′ti·cal·ly** adv.
pest (pest) n. 1. An annoying person or thing. 2. A destructive or injurious insect, plant, etc. 3. A virulent epidemic, esp. of plague. [< MF < L *pestis* plague]
pes·ter (pes′tər) v.t. To harass with petty and persistent annoyances; bother; plague. [< OF < em- in + LL *pastorium* foot shackles] — **pes′ter·er** n.
pest·hole (pest′hōl′) n. A squalid or insanitary place which disease is likely to occur and spread.
pes·ti·cide (pes′tə·sīd) n. A chemical or other substance used to destroy plant and animal pests. — **pes′ti·ci′dal** adj.
pes·tif·er·ous (pes·tif′ər·əs) adj. 1. *Informal* Annoying; bothersome. 2. Carrying or spreading infectious disease. 3. Having an evil or harmful influence. [< L < *pe* plague + *ferre* to bear] — **pes·tif′er·ous·ly** adv. — **pes·tif′er·ous·ness** n.
pes·ti·lence (pes′tə·ləns) n. 1. Any widespread, often fatal, infectious or contagious disease, as cholera or the bubonic plague. 2. A noxious or malign doctrine, influence, etc.
pes′ti·len′tial (-len′shəl) adj.
pes·ti·lent (pes′tə·lənt) adj. 1. Tending to produce infectious or epidemic disease. 2. Having a malign influence or effect. 3. Making trouble; vexatious. [< OF < L < *pe* plague] — **pes′ti·lent·ly** adv.
pes·tle (pes′əl) n. 1. An implement used for crushing, pulverizing, or mixing substances in or as in a mortar. 2. A vertical moving bar employed in pounding, as in a stamp mill, etc. — v.t. & v.i. **·tled, ·tling** To pound, grind, or mix with or as with a pestle. [< OF < L < *pistus*, pp. of *pinsere* to pound]
pet¹ (pet) n. 1. A tame animal treated lovingly or kept as a companion or playmate. 2. Any loved and cherished creature or thing. 3. A favorite: teacher's *pet*. — adj. 1. Tamed or kept as a pet. 2. Regarded as a favorite; cherished. — v. **pet·ted, pet·ting** — v.t. To stroke or caress. 2. To treat indulgently; coddle. — v.i. 3. U.S. *Slang* To make love by kissing and caressing. [< dial. E (Scottish), ? < F *petit* little one]
pet² (pet) n. A fit of pique or ill temper. [Origin unknown]
pet·al (pet′l) n. *Bot.* One of the divisions or leaflike parts of a corolla. For illus. see FLOWER. [< NL < Gk. *petalon* leaf] — **pet′aled** or **pet′alled** adj.
-petal combining form Seeking: *centripetal*. [< L *petere* seek]
pet·a·lif·er·ous (pet′ə·lif′ər·əs) adj. Bearing petals.
pe·tard (pi·tärd′) n. 1. An explosive device formerly used to break through walls, gates, etc. 2. A small firecracker

PESTLE IN MORTAR

ploding with a loud report. [< MF < OF < L _peditum_, g. pp. neut. of _pedere_ to break wind]

·cock (pet'cock') _n. Mech._ A small valve or faucet, used · draining, releasing pressure, etc. Also **pet cock.** [? < s. _pet_ a fart + COCK¹]

ter (pē'tər) _v.i. Informal_ To diminish gradually and en cease or disappear: followed by _out._ [Orig. U.S. mining ng, ? < F _péter (dans la main)_ to come to nothing]

ter (pē'tər) One of the twelve apostles, reputed author two New Testament epistles: called **Saint Peter.** Also _mon Peter._ **— n.** Either of the two books of the New stament that bear his name. [< LL < Gk. _petros_ stone]

er Pan The hero of J. M. Barrie's play (1904) of the me name, a little boy who remained perpetually a child.

er Pan collar A flat collar with rounded ends, used on ·ls' and women's blouses, dresses, etc.

·i·o·late (pet'ē-ə-lāt) _adj._ Having a petiole. Also **pet/i·o·** /ed.

·i·ole (pet'ē-ōl) _n._ **1.** _Bot._ The stem or slender stalk of a f; a leafstalk. **2.** _Anat._ A peduncle. [< L _petiolus,_ orig. n. of _pes, pedis_ foot] **— pet/i·o·lar** _adj._

·it (pet'ē) _adj. Law_ Small; lesser; minor: also _petit_ jury: also elled _petty._ [< OF, small]

tite (pə·tēt') _adj. fem._ Diminutive; little. [< F]

·it four (pet'ē fōr', fôr'; _Fr._ pə·tē'fōōr') _pl._ **pet·its fours pet·it fours** (pet'ē fōrz', fôrz'; _Fr._ pə·tē'fōōr') A little, coratively iced cake. [< F, lit., little oven]

·ti·tion (pə·tish'ən) _n._ **1.** A formal request or prayer. **2.** formal request addressed to a person or group in authority d asking for some benefit, the redress of a grievance, etc. _Law_ A formal application in writing made to a court, re-esting judicial action concerning some matter therein set rth. **4.** Something formally requested or entreated. **—** . **1.** To make a petition to. **2.** To ask for. **—** _v.i._ **3.** To ake a petition. [< OF < L < _petere_ to seek] **— pe·ti'· n·ar'y** _adj._ **— pe·ti/tion·er** _n._

it jury The jury that sits at a trial in civil and criminal ses: also called _trial jury:_ also spelled _petty jury._

it larceny See under LARCENY.

tit mal (pə·tē' mäl') _Pathol._ A mild form of epilepsy aracterized by a momentary loss of consciousness: distin-ished from _grand mal._ [< F, lit., little sickness]

·it point (pet'ē) **1.** A fine tapestry stitch used in deco-tive needlework: also called _tent stitch._ **2.** Needlework ne in this stitch.

trar·chan sonnet (pə·trär'kən) A sonnet having the yme scheme _abbaabba_ in the octave, and having in the stet a set of two or three different, variously combined ymes, as _cdcdcd,_ or _cdecde,_ etc.

·rel (pet'rəl) _n._ Any of various small sea birds as the ·rm petrel. [? < LL _Petrellus,_ dim. of _Peter,_ after St. Pe-·, in an allusion to his walking on the water. _Matt._ xiv 29]

·ri·fac·tion (pet'rə·fak'shən) _n._ **1.** The act or process petrifying, or the state of being petrified. **2.** Anything trified. Also **pet/ri·fi·ca/tion** (-fə·kā/shən). [< PETRIFY.] **pet/ri·fac/tive** _adj._

·ri·fy (pet'rə·fī) _v._ **·fied, ·fy·ing** _v.t._ **1.** To convert (organ-material) into a substance of stony character. **2.** To ake fixed and unyielding. **3.** To daze or paralyze with r, surprise, etc. **—** _v.i._ **4.** To become stone or like stone. : MF < L _petra_ a rock + _facere_ to make]

ro- _combining form_ Rock; stone. Also, before vowels, **tr-.** [< F < L < Gk. _petra_ rock and _petros_ stone]

·ro·chem·is·try (pet'rō·kem'is·trē) _n._ The chemistry of troleum and its derivatives, esp. the natural and synthetic drocarbons. **— pet/ro·chem/i·cal** _adj. & n._

trog·ra·phy (pə·trog'rə·fē) _n._ The systematic descrip-n and classification of rocks. **— pe·trog/ra·pher** _n._ **—** t·ro·graph·ic (pet'rə·graf'ik) or **·i·cal** _adj._ **— pet/ro· aph/i·cal·ly** _adv._

·rol (pet'rəl) _n. Brit._ Gasoline.

·ro·la·tum (pet'rə·lā'təm) _n._ A greasy, semisolid sub-ance obtained from petroleum, used as a stabilizer for cer-n explosives and in ointments. Also **petroleum jelly.**

tro·le·um (pə·trō'lē·əm) _n._ An oily, liquid mixture of merous hydrocarbons, found in subterranean deposits, ed in its natural state for heat and light, and as the source gasoline, benzine, kerosene, paraffin, etc.: also called _naph-_ _l, rock oil._ [< Med.L < L _petra_ rock (< Gk.) + _oleum_ oil] **roleum ether** _Chem._ A distillate of petroleum used as a lvent of fats, waxes, etc.

trol·ic (pə·trol'ik) _adj._ Of or pertaining to petroleum.

trol·o·gy (pə·trol'ə·jē) _n._ The science of the origin, struc-re, constitution, and characteristics of rocks. **— pet·ro· g·ic** (pet'rə·loj'ik) or **·i·cal** _adj._ **— pet/ro·log/i·cal·ly** _adv._ **· pe·trol/o·gist** _n._

·ti·coat (pet'ē·kōt) _n._ **1.** A skirt or skirtlike garment nging from the waist; esp., a woman's underskirt. **2.**

Something resembling a petticoat. **3.** A woman: a humor-ous or disparaging term. **4.** An electric insulator shaped like an inverted cup, for use on high-tension wires. **—** _adj._ Of or influenced by women: _petticoat_ politics.

pet·ti·fog (pet'i·fog, -fôg) _v.i._ **·fogged, ·fog·ging** **1.** To be unduly concerned over trivial matters; fuss. **2.** To be a pet-tifogger. [Appar. back formation < PETTIFOGGER]

pet·ti·fog·ger (pet'i·fog'ər, -fôg'ər) _n._ **1.** An inferior law-yer, esp. one dealing with insignificant cases, or resorting to tricks. **2.** One who quibbles or fusses over trivialities. [Ear-lier _petty fogger_ < PETTY + obs. _fogger_ a trickster for gain] **— pet'ti·fog'ger·y** _n._

pet·tish (pet'ish) _adj._ Capriciously ill-tempered; petulant; peevish. [Prob. < PET² + -ISH] **— pet/tish·ly** _adv._

pet·ty (pet'ē) _adj._ **·ti·er, ·ti·est** **1.** Having little worth or importance; trifling; insignificant. **2.** Having little scope or generosity; narrow-minded. **3.** Mean; spiteful. **4.** Having a comparatively low rank or position; minor. **5.** _Law_ Petit. [< F _petit_ small] **— pet/ti·ly** _adv._ **— pet/ti·ness** _n._

petty cash A supply of money kept for minor expenses, as in a business office.

petty jury See PETIT JURY.

petty larceny See under LARCENY.

petty officer _Naval_ Any of a class of noncommissioned of-ficers. See table at GRADE.

pet·u·lant (pech'ōō·lənt) _adj._ Displaying or characterized by capricious fretfulness; peevish. [< OF < L _petulans,_ -antis_ forward, ult. < _petere_ to rush at] **— pet/u·lant·ly** _adv._ **— pet/u·lance, pet/u·lan·cy** _n._

pe·tu·ni·a (pə·tōō'nē·ə, -tyōō'-) _n._ Any of various tropical American plants cultivated widely for their funnel-shaped, variously colored flowers. [< NL < F _petun_ tobacco]

pew¹ (pyōō) _n._ **1.** A bench for seating people in church, fre-quently with a kneeling rack attached. **2.** Formerly, a box-like enclosure with seats on three sides, occupied by a family attending church. [ME < OF < LL _podia,_ pl. of _podium_ height, balcony < Gk. _podion_ base]

pew² (pyōō) _interj._ An expression of disgust or displeasure, as at a bad odor. [Origin unknown]

pe·wee (pē'wē) _n._ Any of various small, greenish gray fly-catchers: also spelled _peewee._ [Imit.]

pe·wit (pē'wit, pyōō'it) _n._ Any of various birds having a high or shrill cry. [Imit.]

pew·ter (pyōō'tər) _n._ **1.** An alloy, usu. of tin and lead, for-merly much used for tableware. **2.** Pewter articles collec-tively. **3.** The characteristic dull gray of pewter. **—** _adj._ **1.** Made of pewter. **2.** Dull gray. [< OF _peutre,_ plural]

pe·yo·te (pā·ō'tē, _Sp._ pā·yō'tā) _n._ Mescal. Also **pe·yo'tl** (-yot'l). [< Am. Sp. < Nahuatl _peyotl,_ lit., caterpillar]

pfen·nig (pfen'ikh) _n._ _pl._ **·nigs** or **pfen·ni·ge** (pfen'i·gə) A small bronze coin of Germany, equivalent to one hundredth of a deutschemark. [< G, penny]

Phae·dra (fē'drə) In Greek mythology, the wife of Theseus, who fell in love with her stepson and killed herself because he spurned her. Also **Phæ/dra.**

Pha·e·thon (fā'ə·thon) In Greek mythology, the son of Helios, who borrowed his father's chariot of the sun, and would have set heaven and earth on fire by his careless driv-ing if Zeus had not slain him with a thunderbolt.

pha·e·ton (fā'ə·tən, _esp. Brit._ fā'tən) _n._ **1.** A light, four-wheeled carriage, open at the sides, and sometimes having a top. **2.** An open automobile having front and back seats. [< F, ult. < Gk. _Phaethōn_ Phaethon]

-phage _combining form_ One who or that which eats or con-sumes: _bacteriophage._ [< Gk. _phagein_ to eat]

phago- _combining form_ Eating. Also, before vowels, **phag-.** [< Gk. _phagein_ to eat]

phag·o·cyte (fag'ə·sīt) _n._ _Physiol._ A leucocyte that ingests and destroys harmful bacteria, etc., in the blood and tissues of the body. **— phag/o·cyt/ic** (-sit/ik) or **·i·cal** _adj._

-phagous _combining form_ Consuming; tending to eat. [< Gk. _phagein_ to eat]

-phagy _combining form_ The consumption or eating of. Also **-phagia.** [< Gk. _phagein_ to eat]

phal·ange (fā·lanj', fə·lanj') _n._ _Anat._ A phalanx.

pha·lan·ge·al (fə·lan'jē·əl) _adj._ Of, pertaining to, or re-sembling the phalanges of the fingers and toes. Also **pha-lan/gal** (-gəl), **pha·lan/ge·an.**

pha·lan·ger (fə·lan'jər) _n._ Any one of a family of small marsupials of Australia and New Guinea, having long, often prehensile tails. [< NL < _phalanges,_ pl. of _phalanx_ phalanx]

pha·lanx (fā'langks, _esp. Brit._ fal'angks) _n._ _pl._ **pha·lan·ges** (fə·lan'jēz) or **pha·lanx·es** **1.** In ancient Greece, a marching order of heavy infantry, with close ranks and files, joined shields, and spears overlapping. **2.** Any massed or compact body or corps. **3.** _Anat._ One of the bones articulating with the joints of the fingers or toes: also called _phalange._ [< L < Gk. _phalanx, phalangos_ line of battle]

---

phal·a·rope (fal′ə·rōp) *n.* Any of several swimming birds resembling the sandpiper, but having lobate toes. [< F < NL < Gk. *phalaris* coot + *pous* foot]

phal·lism (fal′iz·əm) *n.* Worship of the generative power in nature as symbolized by the phallus. Also **phal′li·cism.** — **phal′li·cist, phal′list** *n.*

phal·lus (fal′əs) *n. pl.* **·li** (-ī) **1.** A representation of the male generative organ, often used as a symbol of the generative power of nature. **2.** *Anat.* The penis or the clitoris. [< L < Gk. *phallos* penis] — **phal′lic** *adj.*

-phane *combining form* Something resembling or similar to (a specified substance or material): *cellophane.* [< Gk. *-phanēs* < *phainein* to show]

phan·tasm (fan′taz·əm) *n.* **1.** An imaginary appearance; phantom. **2.** A mental image; fancy. [< Gk. *phantasma*]

phan·tas·ma·go·ri·a (fan·taz′mə·gôr′ē·ə, -gō′rē·ə) *n.* **1.** A changing, incoherent series of apparitions or phantasms, as in a dream. **2.** An exhibition of pictures projected on a screen and made to increase or diminish in size rapidly while continuously in focus; also, any exhibition of optical effects. **3.** An apparition. Also **phan·tas′ma·go·ry.** [< NL < Gk. *phantasma* appearance + (prob.) *agora* crowd] — **phan·tas′ma·go′ri·al, phan·tas′ma·gor′ic** (-gôr′ik, -gor′ik) or **·i·cal** *adj.*

phan·tas·mal (fan·taz′məl) *adj.* Of or like a phantasm; unreal or illusive; spectral. Also **phan·tas′mic.**

phan·ta·sy (fan′tə·sē, -zē) See FANTASY.

phan·tom (fan′təm) *n.* **1.** Something that exists only in appearance. **2.** An apparition; specter. **3.** The visible representative of an abstract state or incorporeal person. — *adj.* Illusive; ghostlike. Also spelled *fantom.* [< OF < L < Gk. *phantasma* apparition < *phainein* to show]

-phany *combining form* Appearance; manifestation: *epiphany.* [< Gk. < *phainein* to appear]

Phar·aoh (fâr′ō, fā′rō, fär′ē·ō) *n.* Any one of the monarchs of ancient Egypt. [< LL < Gk. < Hebrew < Egyptian *pr-ʿōh* the great house] — **Phar′a·on′ic** (-ē·on′ik) or **·i·cal** *adj.*

phar·i·sa·ic (far′ə·sā′ik) *adj.* **1.** Of or pertaining to the Pharisees. **2.** Observing the form, but neglecting the spirit, of religion; self-righteous. Also **phar′i·sa′i·cal** — **phar′i·sa′i·cal·ly** *adv.* — **phar′i·sa′i·cal·ness** *n.*

phar·i·sa·ism (far′ə·sā·iz′əm) *n.* **1.** *Often cap.* The principles of the Pharisees. **2.** Formality, self-righteousness, or hypocrisy. Also **Phar′i·see·ism** (-sē·iz′əm).

Phar·i·see (far′ə·sē) *n.* **1.** A member of an ancient Jewish sect that accepted the Mosaic law and the oral traditions associated with it, and emphasized strict observance of ritual. **2.** A formal, sanctimonious, hypocritical person: also **phar′i·see.** [OE *fariseus,* infl. by OF *pharise,* both < L < Gk. < Aramaic *perīshayā,* pl. of *perīsh*]

phar·ma·ceu·ti·cal (fär′mə·sōō′ti·kəl) *adj.* Pertaining to, using, or relating to pharmacy or the pharmacopoeia: also **phar·ma·cal** (fär′mə·kəl). Also **phar′ma·ceu′tic.** — *n.* A pharmaceutical product. [< L < Gk. < *pharmakon* drug] — **phar′ma·ceu′ti·cal·ly** *adv.* — **phar′ma·ceu′tist** *n.*

phar·ma·ceu·tics (fär′mə·sōō′tiks) *n.pl. (construed as sing.)* Pharmacy (def. 1).

phar·ma·cist (fär′mə·sist) *n.* A qualified druggist.

pharmaco- *combining form* A drug; of or pertaining to drugs. Also, before vowels, **pharmac-.** [< Gk. *pharmakon* drug]

phar·ma·col·o·gy (fär′mə·kol′ə·jē) *n.* The science of the nature, preparation, administration, and effects of drugs. — **phar′ma·co·log′ic** (-kə·loj′ik) or **·i·cal** *adj.* — **phar′ma·co·log′i·cal·ly** *adv.* — **phar′ma·col′o·gist** *n.*

phar·ma·co·poe·ia (fär′mə·kə·pē′ə) *n.* **1.** A book, usu. published by an authority, containing standard formulas and methods for the preparation of medicines, drugs, and other remedial substances. **2.** A collection of drugs. [< NL < Gk. < *pharmakon* drug + *poieein* to make] — **phar′ma·co·poe′ial** *adj.* — **phar′ma·co·poe′ist** *n.*

phar·ma·cy (fär′mə·sē) *n. pl.* **·cies** **1.** The art or business of compounding and identifying drugs, and of compounding and dispensing medicines: also called *pharmaceutics.* **2.** A drugstore. [< OF < LL < Gk. < *pharmakon* drug]

pha·ryn·ge·al (fə·rin′jē·əl, far′in·jē′əl) *adj.* Of or pertaining to the pharynx. Also **pha·ryn′gal** (-gəl).

phar·yn·gi·tis (far′in·jī′tis) *n.* *Pathol.* Inflammation of the pharynx, as in diphtheria and sore throat.

pharyngo- *combining form* The throat; related to the throat. Also, before vowels, **pharyng-.** [< Gk. *pharynx* throat]

phar·ynx (far′ingks) *n. pl.* **pha·ryn·ges** (fə·rin′jēz) or **phar·ynx·es** *Anat.* The part of the alimentary canal between the palate and the esophagus, serving as a passage for air and food. For illus. see MOUTH, THROAT. [< NL < Gk. *pharynx, -yngos* throat]

phase (fāz) *n.* **1.** The view that anything presents to the eye; any one of varying distinctive manifestations of an object. **2.** *Astron.* One of the appearances or forms presented periodically by the moon and planets. **3.** *Physics* **a** Any particular stage in the complete cycle of a periodic system. **b**

The fraction of a cycle through which a wave has passed any instant. **4.** *Chem.* Any homogeneous part of a mater system separated from other parts by physical boundar: as ice in water. **5.** *Biol.* Any characteristic or decisive sta in the growth, development, or life pattern of an organis Also **pha·sis** (fā′sis). — **in phase** Reaching correspond phases simultaneously, as two waves. — **to phase out** in) *U.S.* To plan and execute the orderly and gradual co pletion or initiation of an enterprise. [< NL < Gk. *phainein* to show] — **pha·sic** (fā′zik) *adj.* — **Syn.** (noun) **1.** Aspect, side, fact.

-phasia *combining form Med.* Defect or malfunction speech: *dysphasia.* Also **-phasy.** [< Gk. < *phanai* to spea

pheas·ant (fez′ənt) *n.* **1.** A long-tailed, gallinaceous bi originally of Asia, noted for the gorgeous plumage of male; esp. the **ring-necked pheasant,** widely bred in U.S. **2.** One of various other birds, as the ruffed grouse. AF < L < Gk. *Phasianos (ornis)* the Phasian (bird) < *P sis* the Phasis, a river in the Georgian S.S.R.]

Phe·be (fē′bē) See PHOEBE.

phen- Var. of PHENO-.

phe·nac·e·tin (fə·nas′ə·tin) *n. Chem.* A white, crystalli coal-tar compound, $C_{10}H_{13}NO_2$, used in medicine as an tipyretic. Also **phe·nac′e·tine.**

phe·nix (fē′niks) See PHOENIX.

pheno- *combining form Chem.* Related to benzene; a der ative of benzene. Also, before vowels, **phen-.** [< Gk. *phai shining* < *phainein* to show]

phe·no·bar·bi·tal (fē′nō·bär′bə·tal, -tôl) *n. Chem.* A wh odorless, slightly bitter, crystalline powder, $C_{12}H_{12}O_3$ used as a sedative. Also **phe′no·bar′bi·tone** (-tōn).

phe·nol (fē′nōl, -nol) *n. Chem.* A white, crystalline, cau compound, C_6H_5OH, derived from coal tar and used as a infectant: also called *carbolic acid.* [< Gk. *phaino-* shin < *phainein* to show + -OL[1]]

phe·nol·phthal·ein (fē′nōl·thal′ēn, fē′nolf·thal′ē·in) *Chem.* A yellowish white derivative of phenol, $C_{20}H_{14}$ used as a laxative, an indicator in acid-base titrations, e

phe·nom·e·na (fi·nom′ə·nə) Plural of PHENOMENON.

phe·nom·e·nal (fi·nom′ə·nəl) *adj.* **1.** Pertaining to p nomena. **2.** Extraordinary or marvelous. **3.** *Philos.* I ceptible through the senses. — **phe·nom′e·nal·ly** *adv.*

phe·nom·e·nal·ism (fi·nom′ə·nəl·iz′əm) *n. Philos.* doctrine that denies either our knowledge or the existenc a reality beyond phenomena. — **phe·nom′e·nal·ist** *n.* **phe·nom′e·nal·is′tic** *adj.* — **phe·nom′e·nal·is′ti·cal·ly** ad

phe·nom·e·non (fi·nom′ə·non) *n. pl.* **phe·nom·e·na** (- for defs. 2 & 3, often **phe·nom·e·nons 1.** Something visible directly observable, as an appearance, action, change, etc Any unusual occurrence; marvel. **3.** *Informal* A person h ing some remarkable talent, power, or ability; prodigy. *Med.* Any notable characteristic or disease. [< LL < < *phainein* to show]

phe·no·type (fē′nə·tīp) *n. Biol.* The aggregate of gen characteristics visibly manifested by an organism. [< Gk. *phainein* to show + -TYPE] — **phe′no·typ′ic** (-tīp or **·i·cal** *adj.* — **phe′no·typ′i·cal·ly** *adv.*

phen·yl (fen′əl, fē′nəl) *n. Chem.* The univalent rad C_6H_5, the basis of numerous aromatic compounds.

phew (fyōō, fōō) *interj.* An exclamation of disgust or : prise.

phi (fī, fē) *n.* The twenty-first letter in the Greek alpha (Φ, ϕ): corresponding to English *ph* and *f.* See ALPHABE

phi·al (fī′əl) See VIAL.

Phi Be·ta Kap·pa (fī bā′tə kap′ə, bē′tə) An American h orary society founded in 1776, having its membership ba on conditions of high academic standing.

phil- Var. of PHILO-.

phi·lan·der (fi·lan′dər) *v.i.* To make love without seri intentions: said of a man. — *n.* A male flirt: also **phi·l der·er.** [< Gk. *philandros,* orig., loving men < *phileei love* + *anēr, andros* man]

phi·lan·thro·py (fi·lan′thrə·pē) *n. pl.* **·pies 1.** The eff to promote the happiness or social elevation of mankind by making donations, etc. **2.** Love or benevolence tow mankind in general. [< LL < Gk. < *phileein* to love + *thropos* man] — **phil·an·throp·ic** (fil′ən·throp′ik) or **·i** *adj.* — **phil·an·throp′i·cal·ly** *adv.* — **phi·lan′thro·pist** *n.*

phi·lat·e·ly (fi·lat′ə·lē) *n.* The study and collection of p age stamps, stamped envelopes, etc.; stamp collecting. F < Gk. *philos* loving + *ateleia* exemption from tax as ir cated by a stamp] — **phil·a·tel·ic** (fil′ə·tel′ik) or **·i·cal** — **phil·a·tel′i·cal·ly** *adv.* — **phi·lat′e·list** (-lat′ə·list) *n.*

-phile *combining form* One who supports or is fond of; devoted to: *bibliophile.* Also **-phil.** [< Gk. *-philos* lovin

Phi·le·mon (fi·lē′mon) A Greek of Colossae, converted Christianity by Saint Paul. — *n.* A book of the New Te ment consisting of an epistle addressed by Saint Paul to **phil·har·mon·ic** (fil′här·mon′ik, -ər·mon′-) *adj.* Someti *cap.* Fond of music: often used in the names of musical s eties. [< F < Ital. < Gk. *philos* loving + *harmonia* mu

ilia *combining form* **1.** A tendency toward: *hemophilia*. An excessive affection or fondness for: *necrophilia*. Also -lled -*phily*. [< Gk. -*philia* < *phileein* to love]

l·ip (fil′ip) One of the twelve apostles: called **Saint** ilip.

·lip·pi (fi·lip′ī) An ancient town in northern Macedonia, eece; scene of the defeat of Brutus and Cassius by Octavi- and Antony, 42 B.C., and of Saint Paul's first preaching in rope. *Acts* xvi 12. **— Phi·lip′pi·an** *adj. & n.*

·lip·pi·ans (fi·lip′ē·ənz) *n.pl. (construed as sing.)* A book the New Testament consisting of an epistle of Saint Paul lressed to Christians at Philippi.

lip·pic (fi·lip′ik) *n.* An impassioned speech character- d by invective. **— the Philippics** A series of twelve eches in which Demosthenes denounced Philip of Mace- 1. [< L < Gk. *Philippikos* pertaining to Philip]

·lis·ti·a (fi·lis′tē·ə) An ancient region on the Mediter- ean, SW Palestine. *Ps.* lx 8.

·lis·tine (fi·lis′tin, -tēn, -tīn, fil′əs-) *n.* One of a warlike e of ancient Philistia. I *Sam.* xvii 23. [< F < LL < Gk. Hebrew *p'lishtim*]

·lis·tine (fi·lis′tin, -tēn, -tīn, fil′əs-) *n.* An ignorant, nar- v-minded person, devoid of culture and indifferent to art. G student slang *Philister* one of the ancient Philistines] **Phi·lis′tin·ism** *n.*

lo- *combining form* Loving; fond of. Also, before vowels, *l-*. [< Gk. *philos* < *phileein* to love]

·o·den·dron (fil′ə·den′drən) *n.* Any of various climbing nts of the arum family, having glossy, evergreen leaves l cultivated as an ornamental house plant. [< NL < , neut. of *philodendros* fond of trees.]

·log·y·ny (fi·loj′ə·nē) *n.* Fondness for or devotion to men. [< Gk. < *philos* loving + *gynē* woman] **— phi· ′y·nist** *n.* **— phi·log′y·nous** *adj.*

lol·o·gy (fi·lol′ə·jē) *n.* **1.** The study of written records, efly literary works, to set up accurate texts and deter- ne their meaning. **2.** Linguistics, esp. comparative and torical. [< F < L < Gk. < *philologos* fond of argument words.] **— phil·o·log·ic** (fil′ə·loj′ik) or -**i·cal** *adj.* **— phil′· g·i·cal·ly** *adv.* **— phi·lol′o·gist, phi·lol′o·ger** *n.*

·o·mel (fil′ə·mel) *n. Poetic* The nightingale. Also **phil′· ıe′la** (-mē′lə). [< F < L < Gk. ? < *philos* loving + *los* song]

·los·o·pher (fi·los′ə·fər) *n.* **1.** A student of or specialist philosophy. **2.** One who lives, makes judgments, etc., ac- ding to a philosophy. **3.** One who is calm and patient ler all circumstances. [< OF < L < Gk. *philosophos* er of wisdom]

osopher's stone An imaginary stone or substance ca- ble of transmuting the baser metals into gold.

·o·soph·i·cal (fil′ə·sof′i·kəl) *adj.* **1.** Of or founded on e principles of philosophy. **2.** Proper to or characteristic a philosopher. **3.** Self-restrained; rational; thoughtful. o **phil′o·soph′ic.** **— phil′o·soph′i·cal·ly** *adv.* **— phil′o· h′i·cal·ness** *n.*

·los·o·phize (fi·los′ə·fīz) *v.i.* -**phized, ·phiz·ing** To spec- te like a philosopher; moralize. **— phi·los′o·phiz′er** *n.*

·los·o·phy (fi·los′ə·fē) *n. pl.* -**phies. 1.** The inquiry into most comprehensive principles of reality in general, or of ne sector of it, as human knowledge or human values. **2.** e love of wisdom, and the search for it. **3.** A philosophi- system; also, a treatise on such a system. **4.** The general vs that furnish the rational explanation of anything: the *losophy* of banking. **5.** Practical wisdom; fortitude. [< ′ < L < Gk. *philosophos* lover of wisdom]

lous *combining form* Loving; fond of. [< Gk. -*philos*] **·ter** (fil′tər) *n.* **1.** A charmed draft supposed to have wer to excite sexual love. **2.** Any magic potion. **—** *v.t.* charm with a philter. Also **phil′tre.** [< MF < L < Gk. *phileein* to love]

ly Var. of -PHILIA.

e·bi·tis (fli·bī′tis) *n. Pathol.* Inflammation of the inner mbrane of a vein. [< Gk. *phleps, phlebos* blood ssel + -ITIS] **— phle·bit′ic** (-bit′ik) *adj.*

ebo- *combining form* Venous. Also, before vowels, leb-. [< Gk. *phleps, phlebos* blood vessel]

e·bot·o·mize (fli·bot′ə·mīz) *v.t.* -**mized, ·miz·ing** To at by phlebotomy.

e·bot·o·my (fli·bot′ə·mē) *n. Surg.* The practice of open- g a vein for letting blood as a remedial measure; bloodlet- ıg. [< OF < L < Gk. < *phleps, phlebos* blood vessel + *mein* to cut] **— phleb·o·tom·ic** (fleb′ə·tom′ik) or -**i·cal** j. **— phle·bot′o·mist** *n.*

egm (flem) *n.* **1.** *Physiol.* A viscid, stringy mucus secret- in the air passages, esp. when produced as a discharge ough the mouth. **2.** Cold, undemonstrative temper. **3.** e of the four natural humors in ancient physiology. [< F < LL < Gk., flame, phlegm < *phlegein* to burn]

phleg·mat·ic (fleg·mat′ik) *adj.* Not easily moved or ex- cited. Also **phleg·mat′i·cal.** **— phleg·mat′i·cal·ly** *adv.*

phlo·em (flō′əm) *n. Bot.* The complex tissue serving for the conduction of the sap in plants. [< G < Gk. *phloos* bark]

phlo·gis·ton (flō·jis′tən) *n.* The hypothetical substance formerly assumed to be a necessary constituent of all com- bustible bodies, and to be given up by them in burning. [< NL < Gk., < *phlogizein* to set on fire]

phlox (floks) *n.* Any of various herbs with opposite leaves and clusters of variously colored flowers. [< NL < L < Gk., wallflower, lit., flame]

-phobe *combining form* One who fears or has an aversion to. [< LL < Gk. *phobeesthai* to fear]

pho·bi·a (fō′bē·ə) *n.* **1.** A compulsive and persistent fear of any specified type of object, stimulus, or situation. **2.** Any strong aversion or dislike. [< L < Gk. < *phobos* fear] **— pho′bic** (-bik) *adj.*

-phobia *combining form* An exaggerated and persistent dread of or aversion to. [< Gk. *phobos* fear]

In the following list each entry denotes a phobia for what is indicated:

acrophobia high places	**hemophobia** blood
agoraphobia open spaces	**musophobia** mice
ailurophobia cats	**necrophobia** dead bodies
androphobia men	**nyctophobia** night, darkness
astraphobia thunderstorms	**ophidiophobia** reptiles
autophobia self, being alone	**phonophobia** noise
bathophobia depths	**pyrophobia** fire
cynophobia dogs	**taphephobia** being buried alive
demophobia crowds	**thanatophobia** death
gynophobia women	**zoophobia** animals

phoe·be (fē′bē) *n.* An American bird, a flycatcher, having grayish brown plumage and a slightly crested head. [Imit. of its cry; infl. in form by PHOEBE]

Phoe·be (fē′bē) In Greek mythology, Artemis as goddess of the moon. **—** *n. Poetic* The moon. Also spelled *Phebe*. [< L < Gk., bright]

Phoe·bus (fē′bəs) In Greek mythology, Apollo as god of the sun. Also **Phoebus Apollo.** **—** *n. Poetic* The sun.

Phoe·ni·cian (fə·nē′shən. -nish′ən) *adj.* Of ancient Phoe- nicia, its people, or its language. **—** *n.* **1.** One of the people of ancient Phoenicia or any of its colonies. **2.** The North- west Semitic language of these people.

phoe·nix (fē′niks) *n.* In Egyptian mythology, a bird of great beauty, said to live for 500 or 600 years and then con- sume itself by fire, rising from its ashes to live through another cycle, often used as a symbol of immortality. Also spelled *phenix*. [OE < Med.L < L < Gk. *phoinix* phoenix, Phoenician, purple red, crimson]

phon- Var. of PHONO-.

pho·nate (fō′nāt) *v.i.* -**nat·ed, ·nat·ing** To make speech sounds. [< Gk. *phōnē* voice] **— pho·na′tion** *n.*

phone[1] (fōn) *Informal n.* A telephone. **—** *v.t. & v.i.* **phoned, phon·ing** To telephone. [Short for TELEPHONE]

phone[2] (fōn) *n. Phonet.* A sound used in human speech. [< Gk. *phōnē* a sound, voice]

-phone *combining form* Voice; sound: *microphone*. [< Gk. *phōnē* voice]

pho·neme (fō′nēm) *n. Ling.* A class of phonetically similar phones that alternate with each other according to phonetic environment and that function to distinguish utterances from one another, as /t/ and /p/ in the words *tin* and *pin*. See ALLOPHONE. [< Gk. *phōnēma* utterance]

pho·ne·mic (fə·nē′mik, fō-) *adj.* **1.** Of or referring to pho- nemes. **2.** Involving distinctive speech sounds: a *phonemic* difference. **— pho·ne′mi·cal·ly** *adv.*

pho·ne·mics (fə·nē′miks, fō-) *n.pl. (construed as sing.)* **1.** A phonemic system. **2.** The study of phonemic systems.

pho·net·ic (fə·net′ik, fō-) *adj.* **1.** Of or pertaining to pho- netics, or to speech sounds and their production. **2.** Rep- resenting the sounds of speech. Also **pho·net′i·cal.** [< NL < Gk. *phōnē* sound] **— pho′net/i·cal·ly** *adv.*

pho·ne·ti·cian (fō′nə·tish′ən) *n.* A specialist in phonetics. Also **pho·net·i·cist** (fə·net′ə·sist), **pho′ne·tist.**

pho·net·ics (fə·net′iks, fō-) *n.pl. (construed as sing.)* **1.** The branch of linguistics dealing with the analysis, description, and classification of the sounds of speech. **2.** The system of sounds of a language: the *phonetics* of American English. **3.** Loosely, phonetic transcription.

pho·ney (fō′nē) See PHONY.

-phonia See -PHONY.

phon·ic (fon′ik, fō′nik) *adj.* Pertaining to or of the nature of sound, esp. speech sounds.

phon·ics (fon′iks, fō′niks) *n.pl. (construed as sing.)* **1.** The phonetic rudiments used in teaching reading and pronuncia- tion. **2.** The science of sound; acoustics.

phono- *combining form* Sound; speech; voice. Also, before vowels, *phon-*. [< Gk. *phōnē* voice]

pho·no·gram (fō′nə·gram) *n.* A character symbolizing a speech sound, word, etc. — **pho′no·gram′ic** or **·gram′mic** *adj.* — **pho′no·gram′i·cal·ly** or **·gram′mi·cal·ly** *adv.*

pho·no·graph (fō′nə·graf, -gräf) *n.* A record player.

pho·no·graph·ic (fō′nə·graf′ik) *adj.* 1. Pertaining to or produced by a phonograph. 2. Pertaining to or written in phonography. — **pho′no·graph′i·cal·ly** *adv.*

phonograph record A grooved disk that reproduces sounds on a record player.

pho·nog·ra·phy (fō·nog′rə·fē, fə-) *n.* 1. The art or science of representing words according to a system of sound elements; esp. a style of shorthand. 2. The art of representing speech sounds by marks or letters.

pho·nol·o·gy (fō·nol′ə·jē) *n.* 1. Phonemics. 2. Phonemics and phonetics taken together. 3. The history of the sound changes that have taken place in a language, or the study thereof. — **pho·no·log·ic** (fō′nə·loj′ik) or **·i·cal** *adj.* — **pho′·no·log′i·cal·ly** *adv.* — **pho·nol′o·gist** *n.*

pho·ny (fō′nē) *U.S. Slang adj.* **·ni·er, ·ni·est** Fake; false; spurious; counterfeit. — *n. pl.* **·nies** 1. Something fake or not genuine. 2. One who tries to be something he is not. Also spelled *phoney.* [? < British slang *fawney man* peddler of imitation jewelry, ult. < Irish *fainne* ring]

-phony *combining form* A (specified) type of sound or sounds: *cacophony.* Also *-phonia.* [< Gk. *phōnē* sound, voice]

-phore *combining form* A bearer or producer of: *semaphore.* [< NL < Gk. < *pherein* to bear]

-phorous *combining form* Bearing or producing: found in adjectives corresponding to nouns in *-phore.*

phos·gene (fos′jēn) *n. Chem.* A colorless, highly toxic gas, $COCl_2$, having a suffocating odor, used in organic chemistry and in warfare. [< Gk. *phōs* light + *-gene* -GEN]

phosph- Var. of PHOSPHO-.

phos·phate (fos′fāt) *n.* 1. *Chem.* A salt or ester of phosphoric acid. 2. *Agric.* Any fertilizer valued for its phosphoric acid. 3. A beverage of carbonated water, containing small amounts of phosphoric acid. [< F]

phos·phat·ic (fos·fat′ik) *adj.* 1. Relating to the phosphates. 2. Containing some phosphate.

phos·phide (fos′fīd, -fid) *n. Chem.* A compound of phosphorus with a metal, as **calcium phosphide**, Ca_3P_2. Also **phos′phid** (-fid).

phos·phite (fos′fīt) *n.* A salt of phosphorous acid.

phospho- *combining form* Phosphorus; of or containing phosphorus, or any of its compounds. Also, before vowels, *phosph-.*

phos·phor (fos′fər) *n.* Any of a class of substances that will emit light under the action of certain chemicals or radiations. [< L < Gk. *phōs* light + *pherein* to bear]

Phos·phor (fos′fər) *n. Poetic* The morning star, esp. Venus. [< L *Phosphorus* morning star < Gk. *phōsphoros*]

phos·pho·rate (fos′fə·rāt′) *v.t.* **·rat·ed, ·rat·ing** To combine with phosphorus.

phos·phor·esce (fos′fə·res′) *v.i.* **·esced, esc·ing** To glow with a faint light unaccompanied by perceptible heat.

phos·phor·es·cence (fos′fə·res′əns) *n.* 1. The emission of light without sensible heat; also, the light so emitted. 2. The property of continuing to shine in the dark after exposure to light, shown by many mineral substances.

phos·phor·es·cent (fos′fə·res′ənt) *adj.* Exhibiting phosphorescence.

phos·phor·et·ed (fos′fə·ret′id) *adj. Chem.* Combined with phosphorus. Also **phos′phor·et′ted, phos′phu·ret′ed** (-fyə·ret′id) or **·ret′ted.**

phos·phor·ic (fos·fôr′ik, -for′-) *adj. Chem.* Pertaining to or derived from phosphorus, esp. in its highest valence.

phosphoric acid *Chem.* One of three acids of phosphorus, esp. *orthophosphoric acid* (H_3PO_4), used as a reagent.

phos·pho·rous (fos′fər·əs, fos·fôr′əs, -fō′rəs) *adj. Chem.* Of, pertaining to, resembling, containing, or derived from phosphorus, esp. in its lower valence.

phosphorous acid *Chem.* A crystalline acid, H_3PO_3, with a garlic taste, obtained by the oxidation of phosphorus.

phos·pho·rus (fos′fər·əs) *n.* A soft, nonmetallic element (symbol P), found only in combination; white or yellow phosphorus is luminous in the dark, highly flammable, and poisonous; red phosphorus does not glow, is less flammable, and nonpoisonous. See ELEMENT. [< NL < L *Phosphorus* morning star < Gk. *phōs* light + *pherein* to bear]

pho·tic (fō′tik) *adj.* 1. Of or relating to light or to the production of light. 2. Designating those underwater regions penetrated by sunlight: the *photic* zone.

pho·to (fō′tō) *n. pl.* **·tos** *Informal* A photograph.

photo- *combining form* 1. Light; of, pertaining to, or produced by light. 2. Photograph; photographic: *photoengrave.* [< Gk. *phōs* light]

pho·to·cell (fō′tō·sel′) *n.* A photoelectric cell.

pho·to·chem·is·try (fō′tō·kem′is·trē) *n.* The branch of chemistry dealing with chemical reactions produced or influenced by light. — **pho′to·chem′i·cal** *adj.*

pho·to·e·lec·tric (fō′tō·i·lek′trik) *adj.* Of or pertainin the electrical or electronic effects due to the action of li Also **pho′to·e·lec′tri·cal.**

photoelectric cell An electron tube, one of whose e trodes is sensitive to variations in the intensity of light, corporated in electrical circuits as a controlling, testing, counting device: also *electric eye, photocell, phototube.*

pho·to·e·lec·tron (fō′tō·i·lek′tron) *n.* An electron emi from a metal surface when exposed to suitable radiatio

pho·to·en·grave (fō′tō·in·grāv′) *v.t.* **·graved, ·grav·in** reproduce by photoengraving. — **pho′to·en·grav′er** *n.*

pho·to·en·grav·ing (fō′tō·in·grā′ving) *n.* 1. The ac process of producing by the aid of photography a relief b or plate for printing. 2. A plate or picture so produce

photo finish 1. A race so closely contested that only a tograph of the finish can determine the winner. 2. *Infor* Any race or competition decided by a slim margin.

pho·to·flash bulb (fō′tō·flash′) *Photog.* A flash bulb.

pho·to·flood lamp (fō′tō·flud′) *Photog.* An electric la operating at excess voltage to give high illumination.

pho·to·gen·ic (fō′tō·jen′ik) *adj.* 1. Being a good sub for a photograph, esp. for esthetic reasons. 2. *Biol.* Pro ing phosphorescence. — **pho′to·gen′i·cal·ly** *adv.*

pho·to·gram·me·try (fō′tō·gram′ə·trē) *n.* The art technique of making surveys or maps by photographs.

pho·to·graph (fō′tə·graf, -gräf) *n.* A picture taken by tography. — *v.t.* 1. To take a photograph of. — *v.i.* To practice photography. 3. To be depicted in ph graphs: He *photographs* beautifully. — **pho·tog·ra·pher** tog′rə·fər) *n.*

pho·to·graph·ic (fō′tə·graf′ik) *adj.* 1. Pertaining to, u in, or produced by photography. 2. Of or like a photogra Also **pho′to·graph′i·cal.** — **pho′to·graph′i·cal·ly** *adv.*

pho·tog·ra·phy (fə·tog′rə·fē) *n.* 1. The process of form and fixing an image of an object or objects by the chem action of light and other forms of radiant energy on ph sensitive surfaces. 2. The art or business of producing printing photographs.

pho·to·gra·vure (fō′tō·grə·vyŏŏr′, -grāv′yər) *n.* 1. process of making an intaglio plate from a photograph use in printing. 2. A picture so produced. [< F]

pho·to·lith·o·graph (fō′tō·lith′ə·graf, -gräf) *v.t.* To re duce by photolithography. — *n.* A picture produced photolithography.

pho·to·li·thog·ra·phy (fō′tō·li·thog′rə·fē) *n.* The ar operation of producing on stone, largely by photogra means, a printing surface from which impressions may taken by a lithographic process. — **pho′to·lith′o·grap** (-lith′ə·graf′ik) *adj.*

pho·tol·y·sis (fō·tol′ə·sis) *n.* Chemical or biological dec position due to the action of light. [< NL < Gk. *phōs* li + *lyein* to loosen] — **pho·to·lyt·ic** (fō′tə·lit′ik) *adj.*

pho·to·map (fō′tō·map′) *n.* A map composed of one more aerial photographs.

pho·tom·e·ter (fō·tom′ə·tər) *n.* Any instrument for me uring or comparing the intensity of light.

pho·tom·e·try (fō·tom′ə·trē) *n.* 1. The measurement of intensity of light, esp. with a photometer. 2. The branc optics that treats of such measurement. — **pho·to·met** (fō′tə·met′rik) or **·ri·cal** *adj.* — **pho·to′me′trist** *n.*

pho·to·mi·cro·graph (fō′tō·mī′krə·graf, -gräf) *n.* A p tograph taken through a microscope; a microphotogra — **pho·to·mi·crog·ra·phy** (fō′tō·mī·krog′rə·fē) *n.*

pho·to·mon·tage (fō′tō·mon·täzh′, -môn-) *n.* Mont produced by photography.

pho·to·mu·ral (fō′tō·myŏŏr′əl) *n.* A photograph enlar to a considerable size, used for wall decoration.

pho·ton (fō′ton) *n. Physics* A quantum of radiant ene moving with the velocity of light and an energy proportic to its frequency: also called *light quantum.* — **pho·ton′ic** e

pho·to·nu·cle·ar (fō′tō·nōō′klē·ər, -nyōō′-) *adj. Phy* Of, pertaining to, or designating a reaction initiated in atomic nucleus by a photon.

pho·to·off·set (fō′tō·ôf′set, -of′-) *n.* Offset printing fro metal surface on which the text or design has been imprin by photography.

pho·to·play (fō′tō·plā′) *n.* A play arranged for or presen in a motion-picture performance.

pho·to·sen·si·tive (fō′tō·sen′sə·tiv) *adj.* Sensitive to lig — **pho′to·sen′si·tiv′i·ty** *n.*

pho·to·sphere (fō′tō·sfir′) *n. Astron.* The visible shin surface of the sun. — **pho′to·spher′ic** (-sfir′ik, -sfer′-) *a*

pho·to·stat (fō′tə·stat) *v.t. & v.i.* **·stat·ed** or **·stat·ted, ·st ing** or **·stat·ting** To make a reproduction (of) with a Pho stat. — *n.* The reproduction so produced. — **pho′to·st** **ic** *adj.* — **pho′to·stat′i·cal·ly** *adv.*

Pho·to·stat (fō′tə·stat) *n.* A camera designed to reprod facsimiles of documents, drawings, etc., directly as positiv a trade name. Also **photostat.**

pho·to·syn·the·sis (fō′tō·sin′thə·sis) *n. Biochem.* T process by which plants form carbohydrates from carbon de, inorganic salts, and water through the agency of sunlight acting upon chlorophyll. — **pho′to·syn·thet′ic** (-sin′·t′ik) adj.

·to·tel·e·graph (fō′tō·tel′ə·graf, -gräf) v.t. & v.i. To nsmit by phototelegraphy. — n. Something so transtted.

·to·te·leg·ra·phy (fō′tō·tə·leg′rə·fē) n. The electrical telegraphic transmission of messages, photographs, etc., facsimile; telephotography. — **pho′to·tel′e·graph′ic** əl′ə·graf′ik) adj.

·to·trop·ic (fō′tə·trop′ik) adj. Biol. Turning in a parular direction under the influence of light. — **pho′to·p′i·cal·ly** adv.

·tot·ro·pism (fō·tot′rə·piz′əm) n. Biol. Phototropic wth or response.

·to·tube (fō′tō·tōōb′, -tyōōb′) n. A photoelectric cell.

·to·type (fō′tə·tīp′) n. **1.** A relief plate made for printby photography. **2.** The process by which it is produced: o **pho·to·typ·y** (fō′tō·tī′pē). **3.** A picture printed from ′h a plate. — **pho′to·typ′ic** (-tip′ik) adj.

·ase (frāz) n. **1.** Gram. A group of two or more associ·d words, not containing a subject and predicate: distinshed from clause. **2.** A word or group of words spoken in ∍ breath. **3.** A concise, catchy expression. **4.** Music A ′rt division of time comprising several statements of one more motifs. — v.t. & v.i. **·phrased, ·phras·ing 1.** To ′ress in words or phrases. **2.** To divide (a sentence, etc.) ɔ phrases when speaking. **3.** Music To divide (a melody) ɔ phrases. [< LL < Gk. phrazein to point out] — **·as·al** (frā′zəl) adj. — **phras′ing** n.

a·se·ol·o·gy (frā′zē·ol′ə·jē) n. pl. **·gies 1.** The choice ι arrangement of words and phrases in expressing ideas. A compilation or handbook of phrases. [< NL < Gk. asis speech + logos word] — **phra′se·o·log′i·cal** (-ə·loj′·•l) adj. — **phra′se·o·log·ist** (-jist) n.

·en·ic (fren′ik) adj. **1.** Of or pertaining to the mind. **2.** at. Of or pertaining to the diaphragm: the phrenic nerve. NL < Gk. phrēn, phrenos diaphragm, mind]

·eno- combining form **1.** Mind; brain. **2.** Diaphragm; ɔr related to the diaphragm. Also, before vowels, **phren-**. Gk. phrēn, phrenos the diaphragm (thought to be the ′t of intellect)]

·e·nol·o·gy (fri·nol′ə·jē) n. The doctrine that the contmation of the human skull allegedly indicates the degree ′evelopment of various mental faculties and characteris-s. [< Gk. phrēn, phrenos mind + -LOGY] — **phren·o··ic** (fren′ə·loj′ik) or **·i·cal** adj. — **phre·nol′o·gist** n.

yg·i·a (frij′ē·ə) An ancient country in west central Asia nor. — **Phryg′i·an** n. & adj.

hal·e·in (thal′ē·in, -ēn, fthal′-) n. Chem. Any of a series compounds formed by combining a phenol with phthalic ′d or its anhydride, and yielding dyes in some derivatives. o **phthal′e·ine.** [< PHTHAL(IC) + -ein, var. of -IN]

hal·ic acid (thal′ik, fthal′-) Chem. One of three arotic crystalline compounds, $C_8H_6O_4$, derived variously.

hi·sis (thī′sis, fthī′-) n. Pathol. Tuberculosis of the gs. Also **phthis′ic.** [< L < Gk., a wasting away < phthi-ι to decay] — **phthis′i·cal, phthis·ick·y** (fiz′ik-ē) adj.

yceae combining form Bot. Seaweed: used in the names various classes of algae. [< Gk. phykos seaweed]

′co- combining form Seaweed; of or related to seaweed. Gk. phykos seaweed]

·la (fī′lə) Plural of PHYLUM.

·lac·ter·y (fi·lak′tər·ē) n. pl. **·ter·ies 1.** In traditional laism, one of two small leather cases containing a strip or ıps of parchment inscribed with Scriptural passages, and ınd on the forehead or around the left arm during mornprayer. [< LL < Gk. phylaktērion safeguard]

·llo- combining form Leaf; pertaining to a leaf. Also, be-∍ vowels, **phyll-**. [< Gk. phyllon leaf]

·l·o·tax·is (fil′ə·tak′sis) n. Bot. **1.** The arrangement of ʋes upon a stem. **2.** The laws of this arrangement. Also **y′lo·tax′y.** [< NL < Gk. phyllon leaf + taxis arrange-nt] — **phyl′lo·tac′tic** (-tak′tik) adj.

yllous combining form Having (a specified kind or num-′ of) leaves. [< Gk. phyllon leaf]

·lo- combining form Tribe; race; species. Also, before wels, **phyl-**. [< Gk. phylē, phylon tribe]

·log·e·ny (fi·loj′ə·nē) n. pl. **·nies 1.** Biol. The history ′the evolution of a species or group: distinguished from on-∍ny. **2.** Tribal or racial history. Also **phy·lo·gen·e·sis** ′lə·jen′ə·sis). [< Gk. phylon race + -geneia birth, origin] **phy′lo·ge·net′ic** (-jə·net′ik) adj. — **phy′lo·ge·net′i·cal·ly** ʋ. — **phy′lo·gen′ic** adj.

·lum (fī′ləm) n. pl. **·la** (-lə) Biol. A great division of imals or plants of which the members are believed to have ′ɔmmon evolutionary ancestor. [< NL < Gk. phylon ′ɛe]

-**phyre** combining form Geol. A porphyritic rock. [See PORPHYRY.]

physi- Var. of PHYSIO-.

phys·ic (fiz′ik) n. A cathartic; a purge. — v.t. **·icked, ·ick·ing 1.** To treat with medicine, esp. with a cathartic. **2.** To cure or relieve. [< L < Gk. physikē (epistēmē) (the knowledge) of nature]

phys·i·cal (fiz′i·kəl) adj. **1.** Of or relating to the human body, as distinguished from the mind or spirit. **2.** Of the nature of or pertaining to matter or material things. **3.** Of or relating to the material universe or to the sciences that treat of it. **4.** Of or pertaining to physics: a physical law. **5.** Apparent to the senses; external: physical changes. [See PHYSIC.] — **phys′i·cal·ly** adv.

physical chemistry The branch of chemistry that deals with the physical properties of substances, esp. with reference to the laws governing their quantitative energy transformations and chemical interactions.

physical education Athletic training and development of the human body; also, education in hygiene.

physical geography Geography dealing with the natural features of the earth, as vegetation, land forms, drainage, ocean currents, climate, etc.: also called physiography.

physical science Any of the sciences that treat of inanimate matter or energy, as physics, astronomy, chemistry, geology, etc.

physical therapy The treatment of disability, injury, and disease by external physical means, as by electricity, heat, light, massage, exercise, etc.: also called physiotherapy.

phy·si·cian (fi·zish′ən) n. **1.** One who is legally authorized to practice medicine; a doctor. **2.** A doctor engaged in general practice. **3.** Any healer. [See PHYSIC.]

phys·i·cist (fiz′ə·sist) n. A specialist in physics.

physico- combining form Physics. [< Gk. physikos < physis nature. See PHYSIC.]

phys·i·co·chem·i·cal (fiz′i·kō·kem′i·kəl) adj. **1.** Of or pertaining to the physical and chemical properties of matter. **2.** Pertaining to physical chemistry.

phys·ics (fiz′iks) n.pl. (construed as sing.) The science that treats of motion, matter, and energy, and of their interactions.

physio- combining form Nature; related to natural functions or phenomena. Also, before vowels, physi-. [< Gk. physis nature. See PHYSIC.]

phys·i·og·no·my (fiz′ē·og′nə·mē, esp. Brit. fiz′ē·on′ə·mē) n. pl. **·mies 1.** The face or features considered as revealing character or disposition. **2.** The outward look of a thing. **3.** The practice of discerning character in the features of the face or form of the body. [< OF < Med.L phisnomia < Gk. physiognōmonia the judging of a man's nature (by his features)] — **phys′i·og·nom′ic** (-og·nom′ik, esp. Brit. -ə·nom′ik) or **·i·cal** adj. — **phys′i·og·nom′i·cal·ly** adv. — **phys′i·og·nom′ist** n.

phys·i·og·ra·phy (fiz′ē·og′rə·fē) n. **1.** A description of nature. **2.** Physical geography. — **phys′i·og·raph′ic** (-ə·graf′ik) or **·i·cal** adj. — **phys′i·o·graph′i·cal·ly** adv.

phys·i·ol·o·gy (fiz′ē·ol′ə·jē) n. pl. **·gies 1.** The science that treats of the processes and mechanisms by which living animals and plants function under varied conditions. **2.** The aggregate of vital processes: the physiology of the frog. [< F < L < Gk. < physiologos speaker on nature] — **phys′i·o·log′i·cal, phys′i·o·log′ic** adj. — **phys′i·o·log′i·cal·ly** adv. — **phys′i·ol′o·gist** n.

phys·i·o·ther·a·py (fiz′ē·ō·ther′ə·pē) n. Physical therapy.

phy·sique (fi·zēk′) n. The structure, strength, or appearance of the body. [< F, orig. adj., physical]

-**phyte** combining form A (specified) kind of plant; a plant having a (specified) habitat. [< Gk. phyton plant]

phyto- combining form Plant; of or related to vegetation. Also, before vowels, **phyt-**. [< Gk. phyton plant]

pi¹ (pī) n. **1.** The sixteenth letter in the Greek alphabet (Π, π): corresponding to English p. See ALPHABET. **2.** Math. a This letter used to designate the ratio of the circumference of a circle to its diameter. **b** The ratio itself (3.14159 . . .). [def. 2 < Gk. p(eripheria) periphery]

pi² (pī) n. **1.** Printing Type that has been thrown into disorder. **2.** Any jumble or disorder. — v.t. **pied, pie·ing** To jumble or disorder, as type. Also spelled pie. [Var. of PIE¹]

pi·a ma·ter (pī′ə mā′tər) Anat. The delicate inner membrane that envelops the brain and spinal cord. [< Med.L, tender mother]

pi·a·nis·si·mo (pē′ə·nis′i·mō, Ital. pyä·nēs′sē·mo) Music adj. & adv. Very soft or very softly: a direction to the performer. — n. pl. **·mos** A passage so played. [< Ital. < L planissimus, superl. of planus soft]

pi·an·ist (pē·an′ist, pē′ə·nist) n. One who plays the piano; esp., an expert or professional performer on the piano. [< F pianiste and < Ital. pianista]

---

pi·an·o¹ (pē·an′ō) *n. pl.* **·os** A musical instrument having felt-covered hammers operated from a manual keyboard that strike upon steel wires to produce musical tones; a pianoforte. [< Ital. < L *planus* flat, soft]

pi·a·no² (pē·ä′nō, *Ital.* pyä′nō) *Music adj. & adv.* Soft or softly: a direction to the performer. — *n. pl.* **·os** A passage so played. [< Ital. < L *planus* flat, soft]

pi·an·o·for·te (pē·an′ə·fôr′tā, -fôr′-, -fôrt′, -fôrt′) *n.* A piano. [< Ital. < *piano e forte* soft and loud]

pi·as·ter (pē·as′tər) *n.* 1. A monetary unit of various countries, as Egypt, Libya, Sudan, and Syria: the hundredth part of a pound. 2. A Turkish coin and monetary unit: also called *kurus.* 3. The Spanish peso or dollar. Also **pi·as′tre.** [< F < Ital. *piastra,* lit., plate of metal]

pi·az·za (pē·az′ə, *Ital.* pyät′tsä) *n.* 1. An open area or public square in a city or town, esp. in Italy. 2. A covered outer walk or gallery. 3. *Chiefly U.S.* A veranda or porch. [< Ital., square, market place]

pi·broch (pē′brokh) *n.* A martial air played on the bagpipe. [< Gaelic *piobaireachd* art of playing the bagpipe]

pi·ca (pī′kə) *n.* 1. A size of type; 12-point; about ⅙ inch; also, a standard unit of measurement for thickness and length of leads, borders, etc. 2. A size of typewriter type equivalent to 12-point, with 10 characters to the inch. [< Med.L, a book of church rules]

pic·a·dor (pik′ə·dôr, *Sp.* pē′kä·thôr′) *n.* In bullfighting, a horseman who seeks to weaken the bull by pricking him with a lance. [< Sp., lit., pricker < *picar* to prick]

pic·a·resque (pik′ə·resk′) *adj.* 1. Of or involving rogues or vagabonds. 2. Denoting a form of fiction involving rogues and vagabonds. [< Sp. *picaresco* roguish]

pic·a·roon (pik′ə·rōōn′) *n.* 1. One who lives by cheating or robbery; a pirate, rogue, or adventurer. 2. A pirate vessel. [< Sp. *picarón,* aug. of *picaro* rogue]

pic·a·yune (pik′i·yōōn′) *adj. U.S.* 1. Of small value; paltry; contemptible. 2. Petty; niggling; mean. Also **pic′a·yun′ish.** — *n.* 1. *U.S.* A coin of little value. 2. *U.S.* Anything of trifling value. [< F *picaillon* farthing]

pic·ca·lil·li (pik′ə·lil′ē) *n.* A relish of chopped vegetables.

pic·co·lo (pik′ə·lō) *n. pl.* **·los** A small flute pitched an octave higher than the ordinary flute. [< Ital., small]

pick¹ (pik) *v.t.* 1. To choose; select, as from a group or number. 2. To detach or pluck, as with the fingers. 3. To clear (a field, tree, etc.) in such a manner. 4. To clear of or harvest; gather. 5. To prepare for removing the feathers, hulls, leaves, etc. 6. To remove extraneous matter from (the teeth, etc.), as with the fingers or with a pointed instrument. 7. To touch, irritate, or remove (something) with a fingernail, etc. 8. To nibble at or peck. 9. To eat in a dainty or overfastidious manner. 10. To break up, penetrate, or indent with or as with a pointed instrument. 11. To form in this manner: to *pick* a hole. 12. To pull apart, as rags. 13. To seek or point out critically: to *pick* flaws. 14. To remove the contents of by stealth: to *pick* a pocket. 15. To open (a lock) by means other than the key. 16. To provoke: to *pick* a fight. — *v.i.* 17. To work with a pick. 18. To pluck or remove fruit, flowers, etc.; harvest. 19. To eat daintily or without appetite; nibble. 20. To select carefully. 21. To steal. — **to pick apart** (or **to pieces**) 1. To pull apart. 2. To destroy by shrewd or critical analysis. — **to pick at** 1. To touch or toy with. 2. To eat without appetite. 3. *U.S. Informal* To nag at. — **to pick off** 1. To remove by picking. 2. To hit, as with a bullet. 3. In baseball, to catch (a base runner) off base. — **to pick on** 1. To determine on; choose. 2. *Informal* To tease or annoy. — **to pick one's way** (or **steps**) To advance by careful selection of one's course. — **to pick out** 1. To choose or select. 2. To distinguish (something) from its surroundings. 3. To produce the notes of (a tune, etc.) singly or slowly, as by ear. — **to pick over** To examine carefully or one by one. — **to pick up** 1. To take up, as with the hand. 2. To take up or receive into a group, vehicle, etc. 3. To acquire casually or by chance. 4. To gain speed; accelerate. 5. To be able to perceive or receive, as a radio station. 6. To break (ground, etc.) with a pick. 7. *U.S.* To make (a room, etc.) tidy. 8. *Informal* To recover spirits, health, etc.; improve. 9. *Informal* To make the acquaintance of (a stranger, esp. of the opposite sex) under casual circumstances. — *n.* 1. Right of selection; choice. 2. That which is selected, esp. the choicest part. 3. The quantity of certain crops that are picked by hand. 4. The act of picking. [ME *piken, pikken* < OE *pican, pīcian*] — **pick′er** *n.*

pick² (pik) *n.* 1. A double-headed, pointed metal tool mounted on a wooden handle, used for breaking ground, etc. 2. Any of various implements for picking. 3. A plectrum. [Appar. var. of PIKE¹]

pick·a·back (pik′ə·bak′) *adv.* Piggyback. [Earlier *pickback, pickpack*]

pick·a·nin·ny (pik′ə·nin′ē) *n. pl.* **·nies** A Negro child: a condescending or offensive term. Also **pic′ca·nin′ny.** [Dim. of Sp. *pequeño* little, small]

pick·ax (pik′aks′) *n.* A pick or mattock with one end of head edged like a chisel and the other pointed; also, a with both ends pointed. Also **pick′axe′.**

picked (pikt) *adj.* 1. Carefully selected. 2. Cleaned picking out refuse, stalks, etc.

picked-o·ver (pikt′ō′vər) *adj.* Handled; left after best have been removed.

pick·er·el (pik′ər·əl, -rel) *n.* Any of various North Am can fresh-water fishes of the pike family, esp. the small cies having a narrow snout and sharp teeth. [Dim. of PIK

pick·er·el·weed (pik′ər·əl·wēd′) *n.* Any of various pe nial plants found in the shallows of North American la

pick·et (pik′it) *n.* 1. A pointed stick or post, used as a fe paling, tent peg, etc.; a stake. 2. A person stationed at outside of a place affected by a strike, for the purpose of p licizing alleged grievances, etc. 3. A person engaged in p licly protesting a proposed law, policy, etc. 4. *Mil.* A dier or detachment of soldiers posted to guard a ca army, etc. — *v.t.* 1. To be a picket or station pickets side of. 2. To fence or fortify with pickets. 3. To tie picket, as a horse. 4. *Mil.* **a** To guard by means of a pic **b** To post as a picket. — *v.i.* 5. To act as a picket (def & 3). [< F *piquet* pointed stake]

pick·et·er (pik′it·ər) *n.* A picket (defs. 2 & 3).

picket fence A fence made of upright pickets.

picket line A line of people picketing a business, etc.

pick·ing (pik′ing) *n* 1. The act of picking; also, that wh is or may be picked. 2. *pl.* That which is left: scanty p ings. 3. *Usu. pl.* That which is taken by question means; spoils.

pick·le (pik′əl) *n.* 1. A cucumber that has been preser and flavored in a liquid solution, usu. of brine or vinegar. Any article of food so preserved or flavored. 3. A liquid servative, as brine or vinegar, sometimes spiced, for me fish, etc. 4. Diluted acid used in cleaning metal casti etc. 5. *Informal* An embarrassing condition or position. *v.t.* **·led, ·ling** 1. To preserve or flavor in pickle. 2. *Me* To treat with a pickle. [Appar. < MDu. *pekel, peeckel*]

pick·led (pik′əld) *adj.* 1. Preserved in pickle. 2. Of w work, etc., having a bleached finish. 3. *Slang* Drunk.

pick·lock (pik′lok′) *n.* 1. A special implement for open a lock. 2. One who picks locks, esp. illegally.

pick-me-up (pik′mē′up′) *n. Informal* A drink, esp. an coholic drink, taken to renew one's energy or spirits.

pick·pock·et (pik′pok′it) *n.* One who steals from pock

pick·up (pik′up′) *n.* 1. Acceleration, as in the speed of automobile, engine, etc. 2. *Electronics* A crystal, ceran or magnetic device that converts the oscillations of a nee in a record groove into electrical impulses. 3. The tone a of a record player. 4. A small, usu. open truck for li loads. 5. *Telecom.* **a** In radio, the location of microphc in relation to program elements. **b** The place where a bro cast originates. **c** In television, the scanning of an image the electron beam. **d** The scanning apparatus. 6. In ba ball, the act of fielding a ball that has touched the grou 7. *Informal* A period of renewed or increased activity *pickup* in business. 8. *Informal* Something that stimula or renews in spirit. 9. *Slang* A stranger with whom a cas acquaintance is made.

pic·nic (pik′nik) *n.* 1. An outdoor social outing for wh food is usu. provided by the people participating. 2. *Sl* An easy or pleasant time or experience. — *v.i.* **·nick ·nick·ing** To have or attend a picnic. [< F *pique-nic* prob. reduplication of *piquer* to pick, peck] — **pic′nick·er**

pico- *combining form* One trillionth (10⁻¹²) of a speci quantity or dimension. [< NL < Sp., small quantity]

pi·cot (pē′kō) *n.* A small thread loop on ornamental edg ribbon, etc. — *v.t. &v.i.* **·coted** (-kōd). **·cot·ing** (-kō·ing) sew with this edging. [< F, dim. of OF *pic* point]

pic·ric acid (pik′rik) *Chem.* A yellow, crystalline, bit compound, C₆H₂(NO₂)₃OH, used in dyeing and in cert explosives.

picro- *combining form* Bitter. Also, before vowels, **pic** [< Gk. *pikros* bitter]

Pict (pikt) *n.* One of an ancient people of uncertain ori who inhabited Britain and the Scottish Highlands.

Pict·ish (pik′tish) *n.* The language of the Picts, of undef mined relationship. — *adj.* Of or pertaining to the Pie

pic·to·graph (pik′tə·graf, -gräf) *n.* 1. A picture represe ing an idea, as a hieroglyph. 2. A record of such pictu [< L *pictus* painted + -GRAPH] — **pic′to·graph′ic** *adj.* **pic′to·graph′i·cal·ly** *adv.* — **pic·tog·ra·phy** (pik·tog′rə·fē)

pic·to·ri·al (pik·tôr′ē·əl, -tō′rē-) *adj.* 1. Pertaining to, c posed of, or concerned with pictures. 2. Graphic; vi 3. Containing or illustrated by pictures. — *n.* A periodi that devotes considerable space to pictures. [< LL < *pictus,* pp. of *pingere* to paint] — **pic·to′ri·al·ly** *adv.*

pic·ture (pik′chər) *n.* 1. A visual representation of an ob ject or scene upon a flat surface, as a painting, drawing, graving, or photograph. 2. A vivid or graphic verbal scription. 3. A mental image or impression of the nature

situation, event, etc. **4.** An overall situation, esp. as
rceived from a particular vantage point. **5.** One who or
at which resembles or embodies another person or thing:
e is the *picture* of despair. **6.** A motion picture. **7.** Some-
ing attractive or pleasant: pretty as a *picture.* — *v.t.*
red, ·tur·ing **1.** To form a mental image of. **2.** To
scribe graphically; depict verbally. **3.** To make a picture
  [< L *pictus,* pp. of *ping*ere to paint]
ture gallery A room or hall for exhibiting pictures.
ture hat A woman's hat having a very wide brim and
en trimmed with plumes.
·tur·esque (pik′chə·resk′) *adj.* **1.** Having a striking,
egular beauty, quaintness, or charm. **2.** Abounding in
riking or original expression or imagery; richly graphic. **3.**
ke or suitable for a picture; having pictorial quality. —
′tur·esque′ly *adv.* — pic′tur·esque′ness *n.*
ture tube Kinescope.
ture window A large window consisting of a single pane
glass, designed to frame a view of the outside.
ture writing **1.** The use of pictures or pictorial symbols
writing. **2.** A writing so made.
·**dle** (pid′l) *v.* ·**dled, ·dling** *v.t.* **1.** To trifle; dawdle: usu-
y with *away.* — *v.i.* **2.** To trifle; dawdle. **3.** To urinate.
rigin uncertain]
·**dling** (pid′ling) *adj.* Unimportant; trivial; trifling.
g·in (pij′in) *n.* A mixed language combining the vo-
bulary and grammar of dissimilar languages. [< Chinese
onun. of *business*]
gin English A jargon composed of English and ele-
ents of local non-English dialects, used as the language of
mmerce in areas of China, Melanesia, Northern Australia,
d West Africa. Also called **Pidgin.**
¹ (pī) *n.* **1.** A baked food consisting of one or two layers
crusts of pastry with a filling of fruit, custard, meat, etc.
A layer cake filled with cream, jam, etc. **3.** See PI². **4.**
ang Anything very good or very easy. **5.** *Slang* Political
aft. [? < PIE²; with ref. to the variety of objects collected
 magpies]
² (pī) *n.* A magpie. [< OF < L *pica* magpie]
·**bald** (pī′bôld′) *adj.* Having spots, esp. of white and
ack. — *n.* A spotted or mottled animal, esp. a horse.
< PIE² + BALD; because like a magpie's plumage]
·**ce** (pēs) *n.* **1.** A portion or quantity existing as an indi-
dual entity or mass: a *piece* of paper. **2.** A small portion
sidered as forming or having formed a distinct part of a
ole. **3.** A coin: a fifty-cent *piece.* **4.** An instance; ex-
ple: a *piece* of luck. **5.** One of a class or group: a *piece*
furniture. **6.** A work of esthetic interest, as a literary or
sical composition, a play, etc. **7.** Point of view; opinion:
 speak one's *piece.* **8.** One of the disks or counters used
checkers, backgammon, etc. **9.** A quantity or length,
of wallpaper, in which an article is manufactured or sold.
. *Dial.* A short time, space, or distance: to walk a *piece.*
. *Dial.* A snack between regular meals. **12.** *Archaic or
al.* A person; individual. — **a piece of one's mind** *In-
mal* Criticism or censure frankly expressed. — **of a** (or
e) **piece 1.** Of the same kind, sort, or class. **2.** Of the
me piece; undivided. — **to go to pieces 1.** To fall apart.
Informal To lose moral or emotional self-control. —
have a piece of *U.S. Slang* To have a financial interest in.
 v.t. **pieced, piec·ing 1.** To add or attach a piece or pieces
, as for enlargement. **2.** To unite or reunite the pieces of,
in mending. **3.** To unite (parts) into a whole. [< OF
Med.L *pecia;* ult. origin uncertain] — piec′er *n.*
ce de ré·sis·tance (pyes də rä·zē·stäns′) *French* **1.** A
incipal or most important item. **2.** The chief dish of a
nner.
ce goods Fabrics made in standard lengths.
·**ce·meal** (pēs′mēl′) *adv.* **1.** Piece by piece; gradually.
In pieces. — *adj.* Made up of pieces. [ME < *pece*
ece + ·*mele* a part]
·**ce·work** (pēs′wûrk′) *n.* Work done or paid for by the
ece or quantity. — piece′work′er *n.*
 chart *Stat.* A graph in the form of a circle divided into
ctors.
·**d** (pīd) *adj.* Spotted; piebald; mottled. [< PIE²]
·**d-à·terre** (pyä·dà·târ′) *n. French* A temporary or sec-
dary lodging; literally, foot on the ground.
·**d·mont** (pēd′mont) *adj. Geog.* At the foot of a mountain.
< L < *pes, pedis* foot + *mons, montis* mountain]
 plant *U.S. Dial.* The common variety of rhubarb.
r (pir) *n.* **1.** A structure extending over the water, secured
 y piles and serving as a landing place for vessels; wharf. **2.**
 plain, detached mass of masonry, usu. serving as a sup-
rt: the *pier* of a bridge. **3.** An upright projecting portion
 a wall; a buttress. **4.** A solid portion of a wall between
indow openings, etc. [< OF *per* < Med.L *pera*]
·**rce** (pirs) *v.* **pierced, pierc·ing** *v.t.* **1.** To pass into or

through, with or as if with a pointed instrument; puncture;
stab. **2.** To force a way into or through: to *pierce* the wilderness. **3.** To make an opening or hole in, into, or through.
4. To make or cut (an opening or hole) in or through something. **5.** To cut through as if stabbing; cleave. **6.** To
affect sharply or deeply, as with emotion, pain, etc. **7.** To
solve; understand: to *pierce* a mystery. — *v.i.* **8.** To enter;
penetrate. [< OF *percer*] — pierc′er *n.* — pierc′ing·ly
adv. — pierc′ing·ness *n.*
pier glass A large, high mirror intended to fill the space,
or pier, between two windows.
Pi·e·ri·a (pī·ir′ē·ə) A coastal region of ancient Macedon, at
the base of Mount Olympus, legendary birthplace of the nine
Muses. — Pi·e′ri·an *adj.*
Pier·rot (pye·rō′) Formerly, a stock character in French
pantomimes, wearing white pantaloons and a loose white
jacket with big buttons. [< F, dim. of *Pierre* Peter]
Pie·tà (pyä·tä′) *n.* In painting, sculpture, etc., a representation of Mary mourning over the body of Christ in her arms.
[< Ital., lit., pity]
pi·e·tism (pī′ə·tiz′əm) *n.* **1.** Piety or godliness; devotion.
2. Affected or exaggerated piety. [< G *pietismus*] — pi′e·
tist *n.* — pi′e·tis′tic or ·ti·cal *adj.* — pi·e·tis/ti·cal·ly *adv.*
pi·e·ty (pī′ə·tē) *n. pl.* ·ties **1.** Reverence toward God or
the gods. **2.** Honor and obedience due to parents, etc.
3. A pious act, wish, etc. **4.** The state or quality of being
pious. [< OF < L < *pius* dutiful]
piezo- *combining form* Pressure; related to or produced by
pressure. [< Gk. *piezien* to press]
pi·e·zo·e·lec·tric·i·ty (pī·ē′zō·i·lek′tris′ə·tē, -ē′lik-) *n.* Electricity or electric phenomena resulting from pressure upon
certain bodies, esp. crystals. — pi·e′zo·e·lec′tric or ·tri·cal
adj. — pi·e′zo·e·lec′tri·cal·ly *adv.*
pif·fle (pif′əl) *Informal v.i.* ·**fled, ·fling** To talk nonsensi-
cally; babble. — *n.* Nonsense; babble. [? Blend of PID-
DLE and TRIFLE]
pig (pig) *n.* **1.** A cloven-hoofed mammal having a long,
mobile snout; esp., a small, young one: also called *hog,
swine.* ♦ Collateral adjective: *porcine.* **2.** The flesh of a
pig; pork. **3.** An oblong mass of metal, esp. iron or lead,
just run from the smelter and cast in a rough mold; also,
the mold. **4.** Pig iron or iron pigs in general. **5.** *Informal*
A person who is filthy, gluttonous, or coarse. **6.** *Informal*
A railroad locomotive. — *v.i.* **pigged, pig·ging 1.** To bring
forth pigs. **2.** To act or live like pigs: with *it.* [ME *pigge;*
ult. origin uncertain]
pig·eon (pij′ən) *n.* **1.** A bird having short legs, a small head
and a sturdy body; esp., the domestic pigeon or rock dove.
2. *Slang* One who is easily swindled. [< OF < LL *pipio,
-onis* young chirping bird]
pigeon breast *Pathol.* A deformity in which the chest is
narrow and pointed. — pi′geon-breast′ed *adj.*
pigeon hawk A small American falcon.
pig·eon·heart·ed (pij′ən·här′tid) *adj.* Timid; fearful.
pig·eon·hole (pij′ən·hōl′) *n.* **1.** A hole for pigeons to nest
in. **2.** A small compartment, as in a desk, for filing papers.
— *v.t.* ·holed, ·hol·ing **1.** To place in a pigeonhole; file. **2.**
To file away and ignore. **3.** To place in categories.
pig·eon-toed (pij′ən·tōd′) *adj.* Having the toes or feet
turned inward.
pig·ger·y (pig′ər·ē) *n. pl.* ·ger·ies A place for keeping or
raising pigs.
pig·gish (pig′ish) *adj.* Like a pig; greedy; dirty; selfish. —
pig′gish·ly *adv.* — pig′gish·ness *n.*
pig·gy (pig′ē) *n. pl.* ·gies A little pig. Also pig′gie.
pig·gy·back (pig′ē·bak′) *adv.* **1.** On the back or shoulders:
to ride *piggyback:* also *pickaback.* **2.** On a railway flat car; to
ship trailers *piggyback.* — pig′gy·back′ing *n.*
piggy bank A coin bank in the shape of a pig.
pig·head·ed (pig′hed′id) *adj.* Stupidly obstinate. — pig′-
head′ed·ly *adv.* — pig′head′ed·ness *n.*
pig iron Crude iron poured from a blast furnace into variously shaped molds or pigs of sand or the like.
pig latin A jargon in which the initial sound of a word is
usu. transposed to the end and to which -*ay* (ā) is added,
as in *Illkay the umbay* for *Kill the bum.* Also pig Latin.
pig·ment (pig′mənt) *n.* **1.** Any of a class of finely powdered,
insoluble coloring matters suitable for making paints, enam-
els, etc. **2.** Any substance that imparts color to animal or
vegetable tissues, as melanin and chlorophyll. [< L *pingere*
to paint] — pig′men·tar·y (-ter′ē) *adj.*
pig·men·ta·tion (pig′mən·tā′shən) *n.* **1.** Coloration resulting from pigment. **2.** *Biol.* Deposition of pigment by cells.
pig·ment·ed (pig′mən·tid) *adj.* Having pigmentation.
pig·my (pig′mē) See PYGMY.
Pig·my (pig′mē) See PYGMY.
pig·nut (pig′nut′) *n.* **1.** The fruit of a species of hickory
common in the U.S. **2.** The tree.

pig·pen (pig′pen′) *n.* A pen or sty where pigs are kept.
pig·skin (pig′skin′) *n.* **1.** The skin of a pig. **2.** Something made of this skin, as a saddle. **3.** *U.S. Informal* A football.
pig·sty (pig′stī′) *n. pl.* **·sties** A sty or pen for pigs.
pig·tail (pig′tāl′) *n.* **1.** A braid or plait of hair extending down from the back of the head. **2.** A twist of tobacco.
pike[1] (pīk) *n.* A long pole having a metal spearhead. — *v.t.* **piked, pik·ing** To run through or kill with a pike. [< MF *pique*]
pike[2] (pīk) *n.* **1.** A widely-distributed, voracious fresh-water food fish having a slender body and a long snout. **2.** Any of several other fishes resembling the pike. [< PIKE[5] with ref. to its pointed snout]
pike[3] (pīk) *n.* **1.** A turnpike. **2.** The fee for using a turn-pike road. — *v.i.* **piked, pik·ing** *Slang* To go in haste: usu. with *along.* [Short for TURNPIKE]
pike[4] (pīk) *n. Brit. Dial.* A mountain peak or pointed hill.
pike[5] (pīk) *n.* A spike or sharp point, as the end of a spear.
piked (pīkt, pī′kid) *adj.* Having a pike; pointed. [< PIKE[5]]
pik·er (pī′kər) *n. U. S. Slang* **1.** One who bets or speculates in a small, niggardly way. **2.** One who acts in a petty or nig-gling way. [Origin uncertain]
pike·staff (pīk′staf′, -stäf′) *n. pl.* **·staves** (-stāvz′) The wooden handle of a pike. [< PIKE[5] + STAFF[1]]
pi·laf (pi·läf′) *n.* An Oriental dish of rice, raisins, spice, and a meat or fowl sauce. Also **pi·laff′, pi·lau** (pi·lou′, -lô′), **pi·law′** (-lô′). [< Persian and Turkish *pilāw*]
pi·lar (pī′lər) *adj.* Of, pertaining to, or covered with hair. [< NL < L *pilus* hair]
pi·las·ter (pi·las′tər) *n. Archit.* A rectangular column, with capital and base, engaged in a wall. [< MF < Ital. < L *pila* column]
pil·chard (pil′chərd) *n.* A small, herringlike food fish, the sardine of Mediterranean and Euro-pean Atlantic waters. [Earlier *pilcher*; origin uncertain]
pile[1] (pīl) *n.* **1.** A quantity of anything gath-ered or thrown together in one place; a heap. **2.** A funeral pyre. **3.** A massive building or group of buildings. **4.** *Informal* A large ac-cumulation, quantity, or number of something. **5.** *Physics* A reactor. **6.** *Slang* A large amount of money. — *v.* **piled, pil·ing** *v.t.* **1.** To make a heap or pile of: often with *up.* **2.** To cover or burden with a pile or piles: to *pile* a plate with food. — *v.i.* **3.** To form a heap or pile. **4.** To proceed or go in a confused mass: with *in, on, off, out,* etc. — **to pile up** To accumulate. [< OF < L *pila* pillar, pier]

PILASTER

pile[2] (pīl) *n.* **1.** A heavy timber forced into the earth to form a foundation for a building, pier, etc.: also called *spile.* **2.** Any similar supporting structure, as of steel or concrete. — *v.t.* **piled, pil·ing 1.** To drive piles into. **2.** To furnish or strengthen with piles. [OE *pil* dart, pointed stake]
pile[3] (pīl) *n.* **1.** The cut or uncut loops that form the surface of certain fabrics, as velvets, plushes, and corduroys. **2.** The surface so formed. **3.** Hair collectively; fur; wool. **4.** Soft, fine hair; down. [< L *pilus* hair] — **piled** *adj.*
pi·le·at·ed (pī′lē·ā′tid, pil′ē-) *adj.* **1.** *Bot.* Provided with a pileus or cap. **2.** *Ornithol.* Having the feathers of the pileum elongated or conspicuous; crested. Also **pi′le·ate.** [< L *pileatus* capped]
pile driver A machine for driving piles.
pi·le·ous (pī′lē·əs) *adj.* Pilose.
piles (pīlz) *n.pl.* Hemorrhoids. [< LL *pila* ball]
pi·le·um (pī′lē·əm, pil′ē-) *n. pl.* **·le·a** (-lē·ə) *Ornithol.* The top of the head of a bird, from the base of the bill to the nape and above the eyes. [< L, var. of *pileus* felt cap]
pi·le·us (pī′lē·əs, pil′ē-) *n. pl.* **·le·i** (-lē·ī) *Bot.* The um-brella-shaped portion of a mushroom. [< L felt cap]
pil·fer (pil′fər) *v.t. & v.i.* To steal in small quantities [< OF *pelfrer* to rob] — **pil′fer·age** (-fər·ij) *n.* — **pil′fer·er** *n.*
pil·grim (pil′grim) *n.* **1.** One who journeys to some sacred place from religious motives. **2.** Any wanderer or wayfarer. [ME < OF < L < *per-* through + *ager, agri* land]
Pil·grim (pil′grim) *n.* One of the English Puritans who founded Plymouth Colony in 1620.
pil·grim·age (pil′grə·mij) *n.* **1.** A journey made to a shrine or sacred place. **2.** Any long or arduous journey.
Pilgrim Fathers The founders of Plymouth Colony, Mas-sachusetts, in 1620.
Pilgrim's Progress A religious allegory by John Bunyan.
pil·ing (pī′ling) *n.* **1.** Piles collectively. **2.** A structure formed of piles. **3.** The act or process of driving piles.
pill (pil) *n.* **1.** A pellet or globule containing medicine, con-venient for swallowing whole. **2.** A disagreeable necessity. **3.** *Slang* A person difficult to bear with; a bore. **4.** *Slang* A ball or disk, as a baseball or golfball. — **the pill** or **the Pill** Any of various oral contraceptive drugs in tablet form, taken by women. — *v.t.* **1.** To form into pills. **2.** To dose with pills. [< L *pila* ball]

pil·lage (pil′ij) *n.* **1.** The act of taking money or prope by open violence; looting. **2.** Spoil; booty. — *v.* **lag ·lag·ing** *v.t.* **1.** To plunder. **2.** To take as loot. — *v.i.* To take plunder. [< OF < *piller* to plunder] — **pil′l** er *n.*
pil·lar (pil′ər) *n.* **1.** A vertical, freestanding support, u slender in relation to its height; column; shaft. **2.** A str ture of similar form used as a decoration or monument. Anything resembling a pillar in form or function. **4.** who strongly supports a work or cause. — **from pillar post** From one predicament to another. — *v.t.* To supp or adorn with pillars. [< OF < LL < L *pila* pillar]
pill·box (pil′boks′) *n.* **1.** A small box for pills. **2.** A sm round, concrete emplacement for a machine gun, antita gun, etc. **3.** A small, round hat with a flat top.
pil·lion (pil′yən) *n.* A pad or seat behind the saddle o horse or motorcycle for a second rider. [Appar. < Scott Gaelic *pillean,* dim. of *pell* cushion]
pil·lo·ry (pil′ə·rē) *n. pl.* **·ries** A framework in which offender was fastened by the neck and wrists and exposed public scorn. — *v.t.* **·ried, ·ry·ing 1.** To set in the pillo **2.** To hold up to public scorn or ridicule. [< OF *pellor*
pil·low (pil′ō) *n.* **1.** A case, usu. of cloth, filled with a s or yielding material, as feathers or foam rubber, used cushion the head, as during sleep. **2.** A small, usu. deco tive cushion. **3.** Any body rest. **4.** Anything resemblin pillow. — *v.t.* **1.** To rest on or as on a pillow. **2.** To ac a pillow for. — *v.i.* **3.** To recline on or as on a pillow. [< OE < L *pulvinus* cushion] — **pil′low·y** *adj.*
pil·low·case (pil′ō·kās′) *n.* A covering drawn over a pill Also **pillow slip.**
pi·lose (pī′lōs) *adj.* Hairy; also *pileous, pilous.* [< L *p* hair] — **pi·los·i·ty** (pī·los′ə·tē) *n.*
pi·lot (pī′lət) *n.* **1.** One who operates or guides an airc or spacecraft during flight. **2.** One who is trained and censed to conduct ships in and out of port or through cert waters difficult to navigate. **3.** The helmsman of a sh **4.** Any guide. **5.** *Mech.* A part that steadies or guides action of a tool or other part. **6.** A pilot light (which se — *v.t.* **1.** To act as the pilot of; steer. **2.** To guide or c duct, as through difficult circumstances. **3.** To serve a pilot on, over, or in. — *adj.* **1.** Serving as a guide or cont **2.** Serving as a trial situation. **3.** Of or pertaining to pilot or pilots. [< MF *pillotte, pilot* < Ital. *pilota*]
pi·lot·age (pī′lət·ij) *n.* **1.** The act of piloting a vesse aircraft. **2.** The fee for such service.
pilot balloon A small balloon sent aloft to show the direct and velocity of the wind.
pilot fish An oceanic fish often seen in warm latitudes company with sharks.
pi·lot·house (pī′lət·hous′) *n.* An enclosed structure, u in the forward part of a ship, containing the steering wh and compass: also called *wheelhouse.*
pilot lamp A small electric light that shows whether a gi circuit, motor, etc., is functioning: also called *pilot light.*
pilot light 1. A minute jet of gas kept burning for ignit an ordinary burner as soon as the gas is turned on: a **pilot burner. 2.** A pilot lamp (which see).
pilot officer In the Royal, Royal Canadian, and other Co monwealth air forces, a commissioned officer ranking n below a flight officer. See table at GRADE.
pi·lous (pī′ləs) *adj.* Pilose.
pil·sner (pil′znər) *n. Often cap.* Beer of a kind origina brewed in Pilsen, Czechoslovakia. Also **pil′sen·er** (-zə·nə
Pilt·down man (pilt′doun) A spurious type of early m postulated from skull fragments planted by a hoaxer n Piltdown, England.
Pi·ma (pē′mə) *n. pl.* **Pi·mas** or **Pi·ma 1.** One of a tribe North American Indians of southern Arizona and North Mexico. **2.** The Uto-Aztecan language of this tribe.
Pi·man (pē′mən) *n.* A branch of the Uto-Aztecan st of North American Indians. — *adj.* Of or pertaining to t linguistic branch.
pi·men·to (pi·men′tō) *n. pl.* **·tos 1.** The dried, unripe, a matic berries of a West Indian tree of the myrtle family. Pimien to, [< Sp. < Med.L *pigmentum* spiced drink, spi
pimento cheese A cheese with pimentos added.
pi·mien·to (pi·myen′tō) *n. pl.* **·tos** A sweet pepper or ripe fruit, used as a relish and as a stuffing in olives: a called *pimento.* [< Sp. < *pimienta* pepper]
pimp (pimp) *n.* A pander; esp., one who solicits for a pro tute in exchange for part of her earnings. — *v.i.* To act pimp. [? < F < MF < L *pipire* to murmur seductively
pim·per·nel (pim′pər·nel) *n.* A plant of the primrose fa ily, usu. with red flowers, as the common **scarlet pimpern** [< OF < Med.L < LL, ? < L *piper* pepper]
pim·ple (pim′pəl) *n.* A small swelling or elevation of skin, with an inflamed base. [ME < OE *piplian* from out in pimples] — **pim′pled, pim′ply** *adj.*
pin (pin) *n.* **1.** A short, stiff piece of wire with a sharp po and a round, usu. flattened head, used for fastening toget

s of clothing, sheets of paper, etc. **2.** An ornament inted on a pin or having a pin with a clasp. **3.** Anything mbling a pin in form or use, as a hairpin or clothespin. A peg or bar, as of metal or wood, used in fastening or porting, as the bolt of a door, a linchpin, etc. **5.** A roll-pin. **6.** Something of no importance; a trifle. **7.** In ling and other ball-throwing games, one of the rounded den clubs, that are set up as the target. **8.** In golf, a with a small flag attached to mark the position of a **9.** *pl. Informal* The legs. **10.** *Music* A peg. **11.** *Naut.* belaying pin. **b** A thole. **— on pins and needles** Uneasy nxious; nervous. **—** *v.t.* **pinned, pin·ning 1.** To fasten or as with a pin or pins. **2.** To seize and hold firmly; e unable to move. **3.** To transfix with a pin, spear, etc. 'o force (someone) to make up his mind, follow a definite rse of action, etc.: usu. with *down.* **5.** *U.S. Slang* In col-s and universities, to give one's fraternity pin to (a girl) n expression of the intention to become engaged. **6.** *Slang* To hold responsible for (a wrongdoing, etc.); ase of: with *on.* [OE *pinn* peg] **— pin′ner** *n.*

·ceous (pī-nā′shəs) *adj. Bot.* Pertaining or belonging he pine family of widely distributed coniferous trees and bs having needlelike leaves and bearing hard, woody es. [< NL < L *pinus* pine]

·fore (pin′ə-fôr, -fōr) *n.* A sleeveless apronlike gar-t, esp. one for protecting a child's dress.

·all (pin′bôl′) *n.* A game in which a ball is propelled spring to the top of an inclined board, and in its descent hes any of various numbered pins, holes, etc., the con-s so made determining the player's score.

e-nez (pans′nā′, pins′-, *Fr.* pans·nā′) *n. pl.* **pince-nez** glasses held upon the nose by a spring. [< F, lit., pinch-e < *pincer* to pinch + *nez* nose]

er·like (pin′sər-līk′) *adj.* Resembling the action or 1 of one or both jaws of pincers: a *pincerlike* movement.

ers (pin′sərz) *n.pl.* (*sometimes construed as sing.*) **1.** nstrument having two handles and a pair of jaws work-on a pivot, used for holding objects. **2.** *Zool.* A nipper-organ, as the claw of a lobster. Also **pinch·ers** (pin′-z). [ME *pinsours*, appar. < AF *pincer* to pinch]

h (pinch) *v.t.* **1.** To squeeze between two hard edges rfaces, as a finger and thumb, etc. **2.** To bend or com-s painfully. **3.** To affect with pain or distress: The cold hed his fingers. **4.** To contract or make thin, as from or hunger. **5.** To reduce in means; distress, as for lack oney. **6.** *Slang* To capture or arrest. **7.** *Slang* To steal. .i. **8.** To squeeze; hurt. **9.** To be careful with money; tingy. **— to pinch pennies** To be economical or stingy . **1.** The act of pinching, or the state of being pinched. o much of a substance as can be taken between the finger thumb; a small amount. **3.** An emergency. **4.** *Slang* A t. **5.** *Slang* An arrest or raid. [< AF *pincher*, OF *pin-* **— pinch′er** *n.*

h·beck (pinch′bek) *n.* **1.** An alloy of copper, zinc, and forming a cheap imitation of gold. **2.** Anything spurious retentious. **—** *adj.* **1.** Made of pinchbeck. **2.** Cheap; rious. [after Christopher *Pinchbeck,* 1670?–1732, Eng-inventor]

h-hit (pinch′hit′) *v.i.* **-hit, -hit·ting 1.** In baseball, to o bat in place of a regular player. **2.** *U.S. Informal* To stitute for another in an emergency. **— pinch hitter**

cush·ion (pin′kŏŏsh′ən) *n.* A small cushion into which s are stuck when they are not in use.

¹ (pīn) *n.* **1.** Any of various cone-bearing trees having lle-shaped evergreen leaves growing in clusters, and in-ling many important timber trees. **2.** Loosely, any tree he pine family. **3.** The wood of any pine tree. [Fusion E *pin* and OF *pin,* both < L *pinus* pine tree]

² (pīn) *v.* **pined, pin·ing** *v.i.* **1.** To grow thin or weak h longing, grief, etc. **2.** To have great longing; usu. with *r.* [OE *pin* torment, ult. < L *poena* punishment]

e-al (pin′ē-əl) *adj.* **1.** Shaped like a pine cone. **2.** Per-ing to the pineal body. [< F < L *pinea* pine cone]

al body *Anat.* A small, reddish gray, vascular, conical y of rudimentary glandular structure found in the brain having no known function. Also **pineal gland.**

·ap·ple (pīn′ap′əl) *n.* **1.** A tropical erican plant having spiny, recurved ves and a cone-shaped fruit tipped with psette of spiked leaves. **2.** Its edible it. **3.** *Slang* A hand grenade.

e cone The cone-shaped fruit of the e tree.

e needle The needle-shaped leaf of a e tree.

tar A dark, viscous tar obtained by destructive distillation of the wood of e trees, used to treat skin ailments.

PINEAPPLE

Pine-Tree (pīn′trē′) **State** Nickname of Maine.

pine·y (pī′nē) See PINY.

pin·feath·er (pin′feth′ər) *n. Ornithol.* A rudimentary feather, esp. one just beginning to grow through the skin.

pin·fold (pin′fōld′) *n.* A pound for stray animals, esp. for cattle. **—** *v.t.* To shut in a pinfold. [OE *pundfald*]

ping (ping) *n.* A brief, sharp, high-pitched sound. **—** *v.i.* To make this sound. [Imit.]

ping-pong (ping′pong′, -pông′) *n.* The game of table ten-nis. [< *Ping Pong,* a trade name]

pin·head (pin′hed′) *n.* **1.** The head of a pin. **2.** Any small or insignificant object. **3.** A small minnow. **4.** A micro-cephalic. **5.** *Slang* A brainless or stupid person.

pin·hole (pin′hōl′) *n.* A minute puncture made by or as by a pin.

pin·ion¹ (pin′yən) *n.* **1.** The wing of a bird. **2.** A feather; quill. **3.** The outer segment of a bird's wing, bearing the flight feathers. **4.** The anterior border of the wing of an insect. **—** *v.t.* **1.** To cut off one pinion or bind the wings of (a bird) so as to prevent flight. **2.** To cut or bind (the wings) of a bird. **3.** To bind or hold the arms of (someone). **4.** To shackle; confine. [< OF < L *penna, pinna* feather]

pin·ion² (pin′yən) *n. Mech.* A toothed wheel driving or driven by a larger cogwheel. For illus. see DIFFERENTIAL GEAR. [< F < OF < L *pinna,* orig., pinnacle]

pink¹ (pingk) *n.* **1.** A pale hue of crimson. **2.** Any of several garden plants with narrow, grasslike leaves and fra-grant flowers. **3.** The flower of any of these plants, as the carnation. **4.** The highest or best condition, degree, or ex-ample. **5.** *Informal* A person who holds somewhat radical economic or political views: a contemptuous term. **— in the pink (of condition)** *Informal* In excellent health. **—** *adj.* **1.** Being pink in color. **2.** *Informal* Moderately radical. [Origin uncertain] **— pink′ish** *adj.*

pink² (pingk) *v.t.* **1.** To prick or stab with a pointed weap-on. **2.** To decorate, as cloth or leather, with a pattern of holes. **3.** To cut or finish the edges of (cloth) with a notched pattern, as to prevent raveling or for decoration. **4.** *Brit.* To adorn; deck. [ME *pynken*]

pink·eye (pingk′ī′) *n.* **1.** *Pathol.* An acute, contagious con-junctivitis marked by redness of the eyeball. **2.** *Vet.* A febrile, contagious keratitis of sheep.

pink·ie (pingk′ē) *n. U.S. Informal* The little or fifth finger. Also **pink′y.** [Prob. < obs. *pink* small]

pink·ing shears (pingk′ing) Shears with serrated blades for scalloping the edges of fabrics.

pink rhododendron A tall rhododendron having rosy purple flowers: State flower of Washington.

pin money 1. An allowance of money for minor incidental expenses. **2.** An allowance made by a husband to his wife for her personal expenses.

pin·na (pin′ə) *n. pl.* **pin·nae** (pin′ē) **1.** *Bot.* A single leaflet of a pinnate leaf. **2.** *Anat.* The auricle of the ear. **3.** *Zool.* A feather, wing, fin, or the like. [< NL < L *pinna, penna* feather] **— pin′nal** *adj.*

pin·nace (pin′is) *n. Naut.* **1.** Any ship's boat. **2.** For-merly, a small vessel used as a tender, scout, etc. [< OF < Ital. *pinaccia,* prob. < L *pinus* pine]

pin·na·cle (pin′ə-kəl) *n.* **1.** A small turret or tall ornament, as on a parapet. **2.** Anything resembling a pinnacle, as a mountain peak. **3.** The highest point or place; apex; sum-mit. **—** *v.t.* **-cled, -cling 1.** To place on or as on a pinnacle. **2.** To furnish with a pinnacle; crown. [< OF < LL *pin-naculum,* dim. of L *pinna* wing, pinnacle]

pin·nate (pin′āt, -it) *adj.* **1.** Like a feather. **2.** *Bot.* Hav-ing the shape or arrangement of a feather: said of compound leaves or leaflets arranged on each side of a common axis. Also **pin′nat·ed.** [< L < *pinna* feather, wing] **— pin′nate·ly** *adv.* **— pin·na′tion** *n.*

pinnati- *combining form* **1.** *Bot.* Feathered; resembling a feather. **2.** *Zool.* Pinni-. [< L *pinna* feather]

pinni- *combining form Zool.* Web; fin: *pinniped.* Also *pinnati.* [< L *pinna* feather]

pi·noch·le (pē′nuk·əl, -nok-) *n.* A card game for two, three, or four persons, played with a double deck of 48 cards with no card below a nine: also spelled *penuchle, penuckle.* Also **pi′noc·le.** [Origin uncertain]

pi·ñon (pin′yən, pēn′yōn; *Sp.* pē-nyōn′) *n.* **1.** Any of various pine trees of the southwestern U.S., having edible seeds: also spelled *pinyon.* **2.** A seed from such a tree. [< Sp] < L *pinea* pine cone]

pin·point (pin′point′) *n.* **1.** The point of a pin. **2.** Some-thing extremely small. **—** *v.t.* To locate or define precisely.

pin·scher (pin′shər) *n.* A Doberman pinscher. [< G, terrier]

pint (pīnt) *n.* **1.** A dry and liquid measure of capacity equal to half a quart. See table front of book. **2.** A con-tainer having such a capacity. [< OF *pinte*]

Pin·ta (pin'tə, *Sp.* pēn'tä) *n.* One of the three ships of Columbus on his initial voyage to America.

pin·tail (pin'tāl') *n.* **1.** A duck of the northern hemisphere, the male of which has a long, sharp tail. **2.** A sharp-tailed grouse of North America.

pin·tle (pin'təl) *n.* A pin upon which anything pivots, as a rudder, hinge, etc. [OE *pintel* penis]

pin·to (pin'tō) *adj. SW U.S.* Piebald; pied, as an animal. — *n. pl.* **·tos** **1.** *SW U.S.* A pied animal: said esp. of a horse or pony. **2.** A kind of spotted bean of the southwestern U.S.: also **pinto bean.** [< Am. Sp. < Sp., lit., painted, ult. < L *pingere* to paint]

pin·up (pin'up') *n. Slang* **1.** A picture of a sexually attractive young woman hung on a wall. **2.** A young woman who is the subject of such a picture. — *adj.* **1.** Capable of being affixed to a wall, etc.: a *pinup* lamp. **2.** *U.S. Slang* Having the qualities of or suitable for a pinup: a *pinup* girl.

pin·wheel (pin'hwēl') *n.* **1.** A firework that revolves when ignited, forming a wheel of fire. **2.** A child's toy resembling a windmill, revolving on a pin attached to a stick.

pin·worm (pin'wûrm') *n.* A nematode worm parasitic in the lower intestines and rectum of man, esp. of children.

pin·y (pī'nē) *adj.* **pin·i·er, pin·i·est** Pertaining to, suggestive of, or covered with pines: also *piney.*

pin·yon (pin'yən) See PIÑON (def. 1).

pi·o·neer (pī'ə·nir') *n.* **1.** One of the first explorers, settlers, or colonists of a new country or region. **2.** One of the first investigators or developers in a new field of research, enterprise, etc. **3.** *Mil.* An engineer who goes before the main body, building roads, bridges, etc. — *v.t.* **1.** To prepare (a way, etc.). **2.** To prepare the way for. **3.** To be a pioneer of. — *v.i.* **4.** To act as a pioneer. [< OF *peonier* foot soldier < ML < L *pes, pedis* foot]

pi·ous (pī'əs) *adj.* **1.** Actuated by reverence for a Supreme Being; religious; godly. **2.** Marked by a reverential spirit. **3.** Practiced in the name of religion. [< L *pius* dutiful, respectful] — **pi'ous·ly** *adv.* — **pi'ous·ness** *n.*

pip¹ (pip) *n.* The seed of an apple, orange, etc. [Short for PIPPIN]

pip² (pip) *n.* **1.** A spot, as on a playing card, domino, or die. **2.** A sharp audible or visible signal produced mechanically or electronically, as in radar. [< earlier *peep;* origin unknown]

pip³ (pip) *v.* **pipped, pip·ping** *v.t.* **1.** To break through (the shell), as a chick in the egg. — *v.i.* **2.** To peep; chirp. [Prob. var. of PEEP¹]

pip⁴ (pip) *n.* **1.** *Vet.* A contagious disease of fowls marked by mucus in the throat or by a scale on the tongue. **2.** *Slang* A mild human ailment: used humorously. [< MDu. < LL < L *pituita* mucus, the pip]

pipe (pīp) *n.* **1.** An apparatus, usu. a small bowl with a hollow stem, for smoking tobacco, opium, etc. **2.** Enough tobacco to fill the bowl of a pipe. **3.** A long conducting passage of wood, metal, tiling, etc., for conveying a fluid. **4.** A single tube or long, hollow case. **5.** Any hollow or tubular part in an animal or plant body. **6.** *Music* **a** A tubular flute or woodwind instrument. **b** An organ pipe. **c** *pl.* The bagpipe. **7.** The voice; also, a bird's note or call. **8.** A large cask for wine; also, a liquid measure of half a tun. **9.** A boatswain's whistle. — *v.* **piped, pip·ing** *v.i.* **1.** To play on a pipe. **2.** To make a shrill sound. **3.** *Naut.* To signal the crew by means of a boatswain's pipe. — *v.t.* **4.** To convey by or as by means of pipes. **5.** To provide with pipes. **6.** To play, as a tune, on a pipe. **7.** To utter shrilly or in a high key. **8.** *Naut.* To call to order by means of a boatswain's pipe. **9.** To lead, entice, or bring by piping. **10.** To trim, as a dress, with piping. — **to pipe down** *Slang* To become silent; stop talking or making noise. — **to pipe up** **1.** To start playing or singing. **2.** To speak out, esp. in a shrill voice. [OE, ult. < L *pipare* to cheep]

pipe-clay (pīp'klā') *v.t.* To whiten with pipe clay.

pipe clay A white clay used for pottery, for making tobacco pipes, and for whitening military accouterments.

pipe dream A groundless hope or wish; a daydream.

pipe·fit·ting (pīp'fit'ing) *n.* **1.** A piece of pipe used to connect two or more pipes together. **2.** The work of joining pipes together. — **pipe'fit'ter** *n.*

pipe·line (pīp'līn') *n.* **1.** A line of pipe, as for the transmission of water, oil, etc. **2.** A channel for the transmission of information, usu. private or secret. — *v.t.* **·lined, ·lin·ing** **1.** To convey by pipeline. **2.** To furnish with a pipeline.

pipe organ An organ having pipes, as distinguished from an electric organ, etc.

pip·er (pī'pər) *n.* **1.** One who plays upon a pipe, esp. a bagpipe. **2.** One who installs pipes.

pipe stem **1.** The stem of a tobacco pipe. **2.** Anything resembling this. Also **pipe-stem** (pīp'stem').

pi·pette (pī·pet', pi-) *n.* A small tube, often graduated, for removing or transferring measured quantities of a liquid. Also **pi·pet'.** [< F, dim. of *pipe* pipe]

pip·ing (pī'ping) *adj.* **1.** Playing on the pipe. **2.** Hissing or sizzling: *piping* hot. **3.** Having a shrill sound. **4.** Char-

acterized by peaceful rather than martial music. — The act of one who pipes. **2.** Music of or suggesting th pipes; a wailing or whistling sound. **3.** A system of p as for drainage. **4.** A narrow strip of cloth folded on bias, used for trimming dresses, etc.

pip·it (pip'it) *n.* One of various larklike singing birds w distributed in North America. [Prob. imit. of its call]

pip·kin (pip'kin) *n.* A small earthenware jar. [? Dir PIPE]

pip·pin (pip'in) *n.* **1.** An apple of many varieties. seed; pip. [< OF *pepin* seed of a fruit]

pip·sis·se·wa (pip-sis'ə·wə) *n.* An evergreen of the h family, with white or pink flowers and thick leaves, use medicine as an astringent and diuretic. [< Algonquia

pip-squeak (pip'skwēk') *n.* **1.** A petty and contemp person or thing. **2.** A small, insignificant person.

pip·y (pī'pē) *adj.* **pip·i·er, pip·i·est** **1.** Pipelike; tub containing pipes. **2.** Piping; thin and shrill.

pi·quant (pē'kənt, -känt, -kwänt, pē·känt') *adj.* **1.** Ha an agreeably pungent or tart taste. **2.** Tart; racy. **3.** ly and interesting. — **Syn.** See RACY. [< F, orig. pp *piquer* to sting]

pique (pēk) *n.* A feeling of irritation or resentment. *v.t.* **piqued, pi·quing** **1.** To excite resentment in. **2** stimulate or arouse; provoke. **3.** To pride (oneself): *on* or *upon.* [< MF < *piquer* to sting, prick] — **Syn.** (noun) displeasure, offense, umbrage, huff.

pi·qué (pē·kā') *n.* A fabric of cotton, rayon, or silk, raised cord or welts running lengthwise in the fabric. [lit., quilted, orig. pp. of *piquer* to prick, backstitch]

pi·ra·cy (pī'rə·sē) *n. pl.* **·cies** **1.** Robbery on the high **2.** The unauthorized publication, reproduction, or us another's invention, idea, or literary creation.

pi·ra·nha (pi·rä'nyə) *n.* A small fish of tropical S America with massive jaws and sharp teeth, known t tack man and larger animals. [< Pg. (Brazilian) < ̃ toothed fish]

pi·rate (pī'rit) *n.* **1.** A rover and robber on the high **2.** A vessel engaged in piracy. **3.** A person who a priates without right the work of another. — *v.t.* **·rat·ed, ·rat·ing** **1.** To practice or commit piracy (uɲ **2.** To plagiarize. [< L < Gk. *peiran* to attempt] — **rat·ic** (pī·rat'ik) or **·i·cal** *adj.* — **pi·rat'i·cal·ly** *adv.*

pir·ou·ette (pir'ōō·et') *n.* A rapid whirling upon the in dancing. — *v.i.* **·et·ted, ·et·ting** To make a pirou [< F spinning top, origin uncertain]

pis·ca·to·ri·al (pis'kə·tôr'ē·əl, -tō'rē-) *adj.* **1.** Perta to fishes or fishing. **2.** Engaged in fishing. Also **pis·ca·t** [< L < *piscator* fisherman] — **pis·ca·to'ri·al·ly** *adv.*

Pis·ces (pis'ēz, pī'sēz) *n.pl.* A constellation, the Fis Fishes; also, the twelfth sign of the zodiac. See ZODIAC. L, pl. of *piscis* a fish]

Pis·cis Aus·tri·nus (pis'is ô·strī'nəs) A constellation taining the star Fomalhaut. [< L]

pisci- *combining form* Fish; of or related to fish. Also fore vowels, **pisc-.** [< L *piscis* fish]

pis·ci·cul·ture (pis'i·kul'chər) *n.* The hatching and rea of fish. — **pis'ci·cul'tur·al** *adj.* — **pis'ci·cul'tur·ist** *n.*

pis·cine (pis'īn, -ēn, -in) *adj.* Of, pertaining to, or re bling a fish or fishes [< L *piscis* a fish + -INE¹]

pis·civ·o·rous (pi·siv'ər·əs) *adj.* Feeding on fish.

pis·mire (pis'mīr) *n. Archaic & Dial.* An ant. Also **pis** (pis'ant). [ME < *pisse* urine + *mire* an ant]

pis·ta·chi·o (pis·tä'shē·ō, -tash'ē·ō) *n. pl.* **·chi·os** small tree of western Asia and the Levant. **2.** Its edible **3.** The flavor produced by the pistachio nut. **4.** A del shade of green, the color of the pistachio nut. Also **pis·ta** (-täsh'). [< Ital. < L < Gk. < *pistakē* a pistachio prob. < OPersian *pistah* a pistachio nut]

pis·til (pis'til) *n. Bot.* The seed-bearing organ of flowe plants, composed of the ovary, with its contained ovules the stigma, usu. with a style. For illus. see FLOWER. [< L *pistillum* pestle]

pis·til·late (pis'tə·lit, -lāt) *adj. Bot.* **1.** Having a pistil Having pistils and no stamens. Also **pis'til·lar'y** (-lər'ē

pis·tol (pis'təl) *n.* A small firearm having a stock to fi hand, and a short barrel, and fired from one hand. — **pis·toled** or **·tolled, pis·tol·ing** or **·tol·ling** To shoot w pistol. [< MF < MHG < Czechoslovakian *pišt'al*]

pis·tole (pis·tōl') *n.* A former European gold coin of v ing value. [< F, short for MF *pistolet* pistol]

pis·ton (pis'tən) *n.* **1.** *Mech.* A rigid disk fitted to slide cylinder, and connected with a rod for receiving the pres of or exerting pressure upon a fluid in the cylinder. valve in a wind instrument for altering the pitch of t [< F < Ital. < LL *pistare*, freq. of L *pinsere* to pound

piston ring *Mech.* An adjustable metal ring fitted in groove around the piston and designed to prevent lea between the piston and the cylinder wall.

pit¹ (pit) *n.* **1.** A natural or artificial cavity in the gro esp. when relatively wide and deep. **2.** A pitfall for sn nals; snare. **3.** An abyss so deep that one cannot return ɪ it, as the grave. **4.** Great distress or trouble. **5.** The ɪ floor of the auditorium of a theater, esp. the rear part; , the audience occupying this area. **6.** An enclosed space ɪhich fighting cocks, etc., are pitted against each other. ɪny natural cavity or depression in the body: the *pit* of stomach. **8.** Any slight depression or excavation, as a ɪmark. **9.** That part of the floor of an exchange where ecial line of trading is done: the wheat *pit*. **10.** A min-ɪxcavation, or the shaft of a mine. — *v*. **pit·ted, pit·ting** ɪ. To mark with dents, pits, or hollows. **2.** To put, bury, ɪore in a pit. **3.** To match as antagonists; set in opposi-— *v.i.* **4.** To become marked with pits. [OE < L *us* a well]

ɪoit) *n*. The kernel of certain fruits, as the plum. — *v.t.* ɪed, **pit·ting** To remove pits from, as fruits. [< Du. < ɪ. *pitte* kernel, pith]

ɪ**pat** (pit′ə-pat′) *v.i.* **·pat·ted, ·pat·ting** To move or ɪd with light, quick steps or pulsations. — *n*. A tapping ɪccession of taps, steps, or similar sounds. — *adv*. With ɪapat; flutteringly. Also *pitty-pat*. [Imit.]

ɪ¹ (pich) *n*. **1.** A thick, viscous, dark substance ob-ɪed by boiling down tar from the residues of distilled tur-ɪine, etc., used in coating seams. **2.** Any of a class of ɪues obtained from the refining of fats, oils, and greases. ɪhe resinous sap of pines. **4.** Bitumen or asphalt, esp. ɪ unrefined. — *v.t.* To smear, cover, or treat with or as ɪ pitch. [OE < L *pix, picis* pitch]

ɪ² (pich) *v.t.* **1.** To throw or hurl; fling. **2.** To erect ɪet up (a tent, camp, etc.). **3.** To set the level, angle, ɪee, etc., of. **4.** To put in a definite place or position. **5.** ɪet in order; arrange: now chiefly in the phrase **pitched** ɪe. **6.** In baseball, to deliver (the ball) to the batter. **7.** ɪet or be set in a pitch or key. — *v.i.* **8.** To fall or ɪge forward or headlong. **9.** To lurch; stagger. **10.** To ɪ and fall alternately at the bow and stern, as a ship. **11.** ɪncline downward; slope. **12.** To encamp; settle. **13.** ɪaseball, to deliver the ball to the batter; act as pitcher. ɪ **pitch in** *Informal* **1.** To work together; cooperate. **2.** ɪtart vigorously. — **to pitch into** To attack; assail. — ɪ. Point or degree of elevation or depression. **2.** The ɪme top or bottom point. **3.** The degree of descent of a ɪvity; also, a descent, slope, or inclination to the horizon. ɪn building, the inclination of a roof. **5.** *Aeron.* The ɪement of an aircraft about its lateral axis. **6.** *Mech.* **a** ɪ amount of advance of a screw thread in a single turn. **b** ɪ distance between two corresponding points on the teeth ɪ gearwheel. **7.** *Physics* The dominant frequency of a ɪd wave perceived by the ear, ranging from a low tone ɪout 20 cycles per second to a maximum high approach-ɪ0,000 cycles. **8.** *Music* **a** The sensory impression of the ɪeness or gravity of a tone or sound. **b** The exact vibra-ɪ frequency of a tone expressed in cycles per second. ɪhe act of pitching; a throw. **10.** In baseball: **a** The ɪvery of the ball by the pitcher. **b** The place of pitching. **c** ɪ distance pitched. **11.** The act of dipping or plunging ɪnward, as a ship. **12.** *U.S. Slang* A practiced talk or ɪal intended to influence or persuade. [ME *picchen*] ɪ**-black** (pich′blak′) *adj.* Intensely black, as pitch. ɪ**·blende** (pich′blend′) *n*. A black or brown variety of ɪineral occurring in the massive form and resembling ɪh in luster, the chief source of uranium and radium. [< ɪ. *pech* pitch¹ + *blende* blende]

ɪ**·dark** (pich′därk′) *adj.* Very dark; as black as pitch. ɪ**·er¹** (pich′ər) *n*. One who pitches: esp., in baseball, the ɪer who delivers the ball to the batter. [< PITCH²]

ɪ**·er²** (pich′ər) *n*. **1.** *Chiefly U.S.* A container with a ɪt and a handle, used for holding liquids to be poured ɪ. **2.** A form of leaf suggestive of a pitcher. [< OF < LL ɪk. *bikos* wine jar]

ɪ**er plant** Any of several carnivorous plants having ɪular leaves arranged in the form of ɪhers that function as insect traps.

ɪ**·fork** (pich′fôrk′) *n*. A large fork ɪ which to handle hay, straw, etc. — ɪ To lift and throw with or as with a ɪhfork.

ɪ**·man** (pich′mən) *n. pl.* **·men** (-mən) ɪg One who sells small articles from a ɪporary stand, as at a fair, etc.; a side-ɪk vender.

ɪ **pine** Any of several American pines ɪt yield pitch or turpentine.

ɪ **pipe** *Music* A small pipe that ɪnds a particular tone when blown, used ɪadjust the pitch of a voice or instru-ɪt; also, a group of such pipes com-ɪed in a unit.

PITCHER PLANT
(About 2 feet tall)

pitch·y (pich′ē) *adj.* **pitch·i·er, pitch·i·est** **1.** Resembling pitch; intensely dark; pitchlike. **2.** Full of or daubed with pitch. — **pitch′i·ly** *adv.* — **pitch′i·ness** *n*.

pit·e·ous (pit′ē-əs) *adj.* Exciting pity, sorrow, or sympathy. [See PITY] — **pit′e·ous·ly** *adv.* — **pit′e·ous·ness** *n*.

pit·fall (pit′fôl′) *n*. **1.** A hidden danger or unexpected difficulty. **2.** A pit for entrapping wild beasts or men. [ME < PIT¹ + *falle, fal* < OE *fealle* a trap]

pith (pith) *n*. **1.** *Bot.* The cylinder of soft, spongy tissue in the center of the stems and branches of certain plants. **2.** *Ornithol.* The spongy substance of the interior of the shaft of a feather. **3.** The marrow of bones or of the spinal cord. **4.** Concentrated force; vigor. **5.** The essential part; gist. — *v.t.* **1.** To destroy the central nervous system or spinal cord of (a frog, etc.) by passing a wire through the vertebral column. **2.** To remove the pith from. **3.** To kill (cattle) by severing the spinal cord. [OE *pitha*]

Pith·e·can·thro·pus (pith′ə-kan′thrə-pəs, -kan-thrō′pəs) *n. pl.* **·pi** (-pī) *n. Paleontol.* An extinct manlike primate represented by skeletal remains discovered in central Java: also called *Java man*. [< NL < Gk. *pithēkos* ape + *anthropos* man] — **Pith′e·can′thro·pine** (-pēn, -pin) *adj.*

pith helmet A topi.

pith·less (pith′lis) *adj.* Having no pith; lacking force.

pith·y (pith′ē) *adj.* **pith·i·er, pith·i·est** **1.** Consisting of pith; like pith. **2.** Forceful; effective: a *pithy* remark. — **Syn.** See TERSE. — **pith′i·ly** *adv.* — **pith′i·ness** *n*.

pit·i·a·ble (pit′ē-ə-bəl) *adj.* **1.** Arousing or meriting pity or compassion. **2.** Insignificant; contemptible. — **pit′i·a·ble·ness** *n*. — **pit′i·a·bly** *adv.*

pit·i·ful (pit′i-fəl) *adj.* **1.** Calling forth pity or compassion; wretched. **2.** Evoking a feeling of contempt. — **pit′i·ful·ly** *adv.* — **pit′i·ful·ness** *n*.

pit·i·less (pit′i-lis) *adj.* Having no pity; ruthless. — **pit′i·less·ly** *adv.* — **pit′i·less·ness** *n*.

pit·man (pit′mən) *n. pl.* **·men** (-mən) *for def 1,* **·mans** (-mənz) *for def. 2* **1.** One who works in a pit, as in a mine. **2.** *Mech.* A connecting rod.

pit·tance (pit′əns) *n*. A small allowance of money. [< OF *pitance*, monk's food allotment, pity]

pit·ter-pat·ter (pit′ər-pat′ər) *n*. A rapid series of light sounds or taps. [Varied reduplication of PATTER¹]

pit·ty-pat (pit′ē-pat′) See PITAPAT.

pi·tu·i·tar·y (pi-too′ə-ter′ē, -tyoo′-) *adj. Physiol.* **1.** Secreting mucus. **2.** *Anat.* Of the pituitary gland. — *n. pl.* **·tar·ies** **1.** *Anat.* The pituitary gland. **2.** *Med.* Any of various preparations made from extracts of the pituitary gland. [< L < *pituita* mucus]

pituitary gland *Anat.* A small, rounded body at the base of the brain that secretes hormones affecting growth, metabolism, and other functions of the body. Also **pituitary body**.

pit viper Any of various venomous snakes, as the rattlesnake, bushmaster, copperhead, etc., characterized by a small depression between the nostril and the eye.

pit·y (pit′ē) *n. pl.* **pit·ies** **1.** Grief or pain awakened by the misfortunes of others; compassion. **2.** That which arouses compassion; misfortune. — *v.t. & v.i.* **pit·ied, pit·y·ing** To feel pity (for). [< OF < L *pietas, -tatis* dutiful conduct] — **pit′i·er** *n*. — **pit′y·ing·ly** *adv.*

— **Syn.** (noun) **1.** Both *pity* and *compassion* are keen regret or sorrow, but *compassion* more strongly suggests the inclination to give aid or support, or to show mercy. *Sympathy* is a sharing of the feelings of another; it becomes akin to *pity* when those feelings are sorrow, chagrin, disappointment, etc.

più (pyoo) *adv. Music* More: a direction. [< Ital. < L *plus*]

piv·ot (piv′ət) *n*. **1.** *Mech.* Something upon which a related part turns, oscillates, or rotates, as a pin or short cylindrical bearing fixed on only one end, for carrying or rotating a swinging part. **2.** A person or thing upon which an important matter hinges or turns. — *v.t.* **1.** To place on, attach by, or provide with a pivot or pivots. — *v.i.* **2.** To turn on a pivot; swing. [< F, origin unknown] — **piv′ot·al** *adj.* — **piv′ot·al·ly** *adv.*

pix·i·la·ted (pik′sə-lā′tid) *adj.* **1.** Affected by the pixies; mentally unbalanced; fey. **2.** *Slang* Drunk. [Prob. alter. of dial. E (Cornish) *pixy-led* bewitched]

pix·y (pik′sē) *n. pl.* **pix·ies** A fairy or elf. Also **pix′ie**. [< dial. E *pixey, pisky*; origin uncertain]

piz·za (pēt′sə, *Ital.* pēt′sä) *n*. An Italian food comprising a doughy crust overlaid with a mixture of cheese, tomatoes, spices, etc., and baked. [< Ital.]

piz·ze·ri·a (pēt′sə-rē′ə) *n*. A place where pizzas are prepared, sold, and eaten. [< Ital. < *pizza* pizza]

piz·zi·ca·to (pit′sə-kä′tō, *Ital.* pēt′tsē-kä′tō) *Music adj.* Plucked with the fingers. — *adv.* In a pizzicato manner. — *n. pl.* **·ti** (-tē) A tone or passage played in a pizzicato manner. [< Ital., pp. of *pizzicare* to pluck, pinch]

pla·ca·ble (plā′kə·bəl, plak′ə-) *adj.* Appeasable; yielding; forgiving. [< OF < L < *placare* to appease] — **pla′ca·bil′i·ty, pla′ca·ble·ness** *n.* — **pla′ca·bly** *adv.*

plac·ard (plak′ärd; *for v.*, *also* plə·kärd′) *n.* **1.** A paper publicly displayed, as a poster. **2.** A tag or plate bearing the owner's name. — *v.t.* **1.** To announce by means of placards. **2.** To post placards on or in. [< F *plaquer* to veneer, plate]

pla·cate (plā′kāt, plak′āt, plak′ət) *v.t.* **·cat·ed, ·cat·ing** To appease the anger of; pacify. [< L < *placare* to appease] — **pla′cat·er** *n.* — **pla·ca′tion** *n.*

pla·ca·to·ry (plā′kə·tôr′ē, -tō′rē, plak′ə-) *adj.* Tending or intended to placate. Also **pla′ca·tive.**

place (plās) *n.* **1.** A particular point or portion of space, esp. that part occupied by or belonging to a thing under consideration; a definite locality or location. **2.** An occupied situation or building; space regarded as abode or quarters. **3.** An open space or square in a city; also, a court or street. **4.** Position in a sequence or series. **5.** Station in life; rank. **6.** An office, appointment, or employment; position. **7.** Room for occupation. **8.** Room; way: One thing gives *place* to another. **9.** A particular passage or page in a book, etc. **10.** The second position among the first three finishers in a race, as in a horse race. **11.** *Math.* The position of a figure in relation to the other figures of a given arithmetical series or group. — **in place 1.** In a natural or suitable position. **2.** In its original site. — **in place of** Instead of. — **out of place** Removed from or not situated in the natural or appropriate place, order, or relation. — **to take place** To happen; occur. — *v.* **placed, plac·ing** *v.t.* **1.** To put in a particular place or position. **2.** To put or arrange in a particular relation or sequence. **3.** To find a place, situation, home, etc., for. **4.** To appoint to a post or office. **5.** To identify; classify. **6.** To arrange for the satisfaction, handling, or disposition of. **7.** To bestow or entrust. — *v.i.* **8.** In racing: **a** To finish second: distinguished from *show, win.* **b** To finish among the first three finishers. [< OF, ult. < L < Gk. < *platys* wide]

pla·ce·bo (plə·sē′bō) *n. pl.* **·bos** *or* **·boes 1.** *Med.* Any harmless substance given to humor a patient or as a test in controlled experiments. **2.** Anything said in order to flatter. [< L < *placere* to please]

place kick In football, a kick for a goal in which the ball is placed on the ground for kicking.

place mat A mat on which a table setting is placed.

place·ment (plās′mənt) *n.* **1.** The act of placing, or the state of being placed. **2.** Relative position; arrangement. **3.** The business of placing persons in jobs. **4.** In football, the setting of the ball for a place kick; also, the kick itself.

pla·cen·ta (plə·sen′tə) *n. pl.* **·tas** *or* **·tae** (-tē) **1.** *Anat.* In higher mammals, the vascular, spongy organ of interlocking fetal and uterine structures by which the fetus is nourished in the uterus. **2.** *Bot.* The part of the ovary that supports the ovules. [< L, cake < Gk. < *plax, plakos* flat object] — **pla·cen′tal, plac·en·tar·y** (plas′ən·ter′ē, plə·sen′tər·ē) *adj.*

pla·cen·tate (plə·sen′tāt) *adj.* Having a placenta.

plac·er¹ (plā′sər) *n.* One who or that which places.

plac·er² (plas′ər) *n. Mining* **1.** An alluvial or glacial deposit of sand, gravel, etc., containing gold in particles large enough to be obtained by washing. **2.** Any place where deposits are washed for valuable minerals. [Var. of Sp. *placel* sandbank < *plaza* place]

plac·id (plas′id) *adj.* Having a smooth face or nature; unruffled; calm. [< L < *placere* to please] — **pla·cid·i·ty** (plə·sid′ə·tē), **plac′id·ness** *n.* — **plac′id·ly** *adv.*

plack·et (plak′it) *n.* The opening in the upper part of a dress, blouse, or skirt to make it easy to put on and take off. Also **placket hole.** [Origin unknown]

pla·gia·rism (plā′jə·riz′əm, -jē·ə-) *n.* **1.** The act of plagiarizing. **2.** Something plagiarized. — **pla′gia·rist** *n.* — **pla′gia·ris′tic** *adj.*

pla·gia·rize (plā′jə·rīz, -jē·ə-) *v.* **·rized, ·riz·ing** *v.t.* **1.** To appropriate and pass off as one's own (the writings, ideas, etc., of another). **2.** To appropriate and use passages, ideas, etc., from. — *v.i.* **3.** To commit plagiarism. — **pla′gia·riz′er** *n.*

pla·gia·ry (plā′jər·ē, -jē·ər·ē) *n. pl.* **·ries 1.** The act or result of plagiarism. **2.** One who plagiarizes; a plagiarist. [< L *plagium* kidnapping < Gk. *plagios* treacherous]

plagio- *combining form* Oblique; slanting. Also, before vowels, **plagi-.** [< Gk. *plagios* oblique]

pla·gi·o·clase (plā′jē·ə·klās′) *n.* Feldspar consisting chiefly of the silicates of sodium, calcium, and aluminum, and crystallizing in the triclinic system. [< PLAGIO- + Gk. *klasis* cleavage] — **pla′gi·o·clas′tic** (-klas′tik) *adj.*

plague (plāg) *n.* **1.** Anything troublesome or harassing; affliction; calamity. **2.** *Pathol.* Any of various forms of a virulent, febrile, highly contagious, and often pandemic disease, esp. the bubonic plague. **3.** The Black Death. **4.** *Informal* Nuisance; bother. — *v.t.* **plagued, plagu·ing 1.** To vex; annoy. **2.** To afflict with plague or disaster. [< OF < LL < L *plaga*, prob. < Gk. *plēssein* to strike]

pla·guy (plā′gē) *Informal adj.* Troublesome. — *adv.* tiously; intolerably: also **pla′gui·ly.** Also **pla′guey.**

plaice (plās) *n.* **1.** A flounder of European waters. **2.** of various American flatfishes. [< OF < LL *platessa* fish, ult. < Gk. *platys* broad]

plaid (plad) *adj.* Having a tartan pattern; checkered. An oblong woolen scarf of tartan or checkered pattern, in the Scottish Highlands as a cloak over one shoulder; any fabric of this pattern. [< Scottish Gaelic *plaide* ket] — **plaid′ed** *adj.*

plain (plān) *adj.* **1.** Flat; smooth. **2.** Presenting few culties; easy. **3.** Clear; understandable. **4.** Straig ward; guileless. **5.** Lowly in condition or station. **6.** adorned; without ornamentation. **7.** Not figured, tw or variegated: *plain* cloth. **8.** Homely. **9.** Not rich; ple: *plain* food. — *n.* An expanse of level land; a pr [< OF < L *planus* flat] — **plain′ly** *adv.* — **plain′ne**

plain·clothes man (plān′klōz′, -klōthz′) A member police force not in uniform; esp., a detective.

plains·man (plānz′mən) *n. pl.* **·men** (-mən) A dwell the plains.

plain·song (plān′sông, -song) *n.* The old ecclesia chant, having simple melody, not governed by strict ru meter but by accentuation of the words. Also **plain·** (plān′chant, -chänt). [Trans. of Med.L *cantus planus*

plain-spo·ken (plān′spō′kən) *adj.* Candid; frank.

plaint (plānt) *n.* **1.** A lamentation. **2.** A complaint. OF < L *planger* to lament]

plain·tiff (plān′tif) *n. Law* The party that begins an a at law; the complaining party in an action: opposed to *dant.* [< OF < L *plangere* to lament]

plain·tive (plān′tiv) *adj.* Expressing a subdued sad mournful. [< OF, fem. of *plaintif*] — **plain′tive·ly** *ad* **plain′tive·ness** *n.*

plait (plāt, plat) *v.t.* **1.** To braid (hair, etc.). **2.** To — *n.* **1.** A braid, esp. of hair. **2.** A pleat. [< OF < *plicare* to fold]

plan (plan) *n.* **1.** A scheme, method, or design for th tainment of some object. **2.** A drawing showing the pr tion and relation of parts, as of a building. **3.** Any sk draft. **4.** A mode of action. — *v.* **planned, plan·nin 1.** To form a scheme or method for doing, achieving, etc To make a plan of, as a building; design. **3.** To have intention or purpose. — *v.i.* **4.** To make plans. [< M OF < L < *planus* flat] — **plan′ner** *n.*

pla·nar·i·an (plə·nâr′ē·ən) *n. Zool.* Any of an ord chiefly aquatic flatworms having elongate flattened b and the power of regenerating themselves when cut a [< NL < L *planus* flat]

plane¹ (plān) *n.* **1.** *Geom.* A surface such that a straigh joining any two of its points lies wholly within the su **2.** Any flat surface. **3.** A grade of development; lev *plane* of thought. **4.** *Aeron.* A supporting surface of a plane. **5.** An airplane. — *adj.* **1.** Lying in a plane. Level; flat. **3.** Dealing only with flat surfaces: *plan* ometry. [< L *planus* flat] — **pla·nar** (plā′nər) *adj.*

plane² (plān) *n.* A tool used for smoothing boards or surfaces of wood. — *v.* **planed, plan·ing** *v.t.* **1.** To smooth or even with a plane. **2.** To remove with a p — *v.i.* **3.** To use a plane. **4.** To do the work of a plane F < L < OF < L *planare* to level] — **plan·er** (plā′nər

plane³ (plān) *v.i.* **planed, plan·ing 1.** To rise partly o the water, as a power boat when driven at high speed. **2** glide; soar. [< F < OF < L < *planus* flat]

plan·et (plan′it) *n.* **1.** *Astron.* One of the celestial b revolving around the sun and shining only by reflected Those within the Earth's orbit, Mercury and Venus called **inferior planets.** Those beyond it, the **superior** ets, are Mars, Jupiter, Saturn, Uranus, Neptune, and P Between Mars and Jupiter are the asteroids or **minor** ets. **2.** In ancient astronomy, one of the seven hea bodies (the Sun, Moon, Mercury, Venus, Mars, Jupiter Saturn) having a motion relative to the fixed stars. astrology, a planet considered as an influence on huma ings. [< OF < LL < Gk. < *planaesthai* to wander]

plan·e·tar·i·um (plan′ə·târ′ē·əm) *n. pl.* **·i·ums** *or* **·i·a 1.** An apparatus for exhibiting the features of the h ens as they exist at any time and for any place on earth, sisting of an array of suitably mounted stereopticon stalled in a room having a circular dome. **2.** A roo building having such an apparatus. **3.** An apparatu model representing the planetary system.

plan·e·tar·y (plan′ə·ter′ē) *adj.* **1.** Of or pertaining planet or the planets. **2.** Mundane; terrestrial. **3.** V dering; erratic. **4.** *Mech.* Pertaining to or denoting a ty gearing in which one or more small wheels mesh with toothed circumference of a larger wheel, around which revolve, at the same time rotating axially.

plan·e·tes·i·mal (plan′ə·tes′ə·məl) *Astron. adj.* Of or taining to very small, solid, planetary bodies. — *n.* such bodies.

TABLE OF PLANETS

Name	MERCURY	VENUS	EARTH	MARS	JUPITER	SATURN	URANUS	NEPTUNE	PLUTO
Symbol	☿	♀	⊕	♂	♃	♄	♅	♆	♇
Distance from sun, millions of miles	36	67	93	142	483	886	1780	2790	3670
Mean diameter, miles	3000	7600	7918	4200	87,000	72,000	33,200	31,000	4000
Period of sidereal revolution	88 days	225 days	365.25 days	687 days	12 years	29.5 years	84 years	165 years	248 years
Period of rotation	88 days	20–30 days?	23 hr., 56 min.	24 hr., 37 min.	9 hr., 50 min.	10 hr., 14 min.	10 hr., 45 min.	15 hr., 48 min.	?
No. of satellites	0	0	1	2	12	9	5	2	0
Mass, Earth considered as 1.	0.0543	0.8148	1.0000	0.1069	318.35	95.3	14.58	17.26	0.1?
Escape velocity, miles per second	2	6.3	6.95	3.1	37	22	13	15	?
Mean density, water = 1	5.3	4.95	5.52	3.95	1.33	0.69	1.56	2.27	5?
Surface gravity, Earth = 1	0.38	0.87	1.00	0.39	2.65	1.17	1.05	1.23	0.5?
Mean orbital velocity, miles per second	29.76	21.78	18.52	15.00	8.12	6.00	4.23	3.37	2.95

anetesimal hypothesis *Astron.* The hypothesis that he solar system developed from large masses of planetesimals that coalesced to form planets and satellites.

an·et·fall (plan′it·fôl′) *n.* The descent of a rocket or artificial satellite to the surface of a planet.

an·e·toid (plan′ə·toid) *n. Astron.* An asteroid. **— plan′·toi′dal** *adj.*

ane tree Any of various large deciduous trees characterized by broad, lobed leaves and spreading growth. [< OF < Gk. *platys* broad]

an·et-struck (plan′it·struk′) *adj.* Affected by the influence of planets. Also **plan′et-strick′en** (-strik′ən).·

anet wheel One of the smaller wheels in an epicyclic ·rain.

an·gent (plan′jənt) *adj.* Dashing noisily; resounding, as he sound of bells. [< L *plangens, -entis,* ppr. of *plangere* ιment, strike] **— plan′gen·cy** *n.* **— plan′gent·ly** *adv.*

an·gor·ous (plang′gər-əs) *adj.* Wailing; lamenting. [< *plangor* lamentation < *plangere.* See PLANGENT.]

a·ni·form (plā′nə·fôrm, plan′ə-) *adj.* Having the surfaces early flat.

a·nim·e·ter (plə·nim′ə·tər) *n.* An instrument for measuring the area of any plane surface, however irregular, by ιoving a pointer around its boundary and reading the indications of a scale. [< F *planimètre*] **— pla·ni·met·ric** (plā′· ə·met′rik, plan′ə-) or **·ri·cal** *adj.* **— pla·nim′e·try** *n.*

an·i·sphere (plan′ə·sfir) *n.* A plane projection of the ohere; especially, a polar projection of the heavens on a ιart, showing the stars visible at a given time. [< OF < Med.L *planisphaerium* < L *planus* flat + *sphaera* sphere]

an·ish (plan′ish) *v.t.* To condense, smooth, toughen, or oolish, as metal, by hammering, rolling, etc. [< MF < L *lanus* flat]

ank (plangk) *n.* 1. A broad piece of sawed timber, thicker ιan a board. 2. A support. 3. One of the principles of a olitical platform. **— to walk the plank** To walk off a ·ank projecting from the side of a ship, a method once used y pirates for executing prisoners. **— v.t.** 1. To cover, irnish, or lay with planks. 2. To broil or bake and serve ιn a plank, as fish. 3. *Informal* To put down forcibly. 4. *nformal* To pay: with *out, down,* etc. [< OF < LL *planca*]

ank·ing (plangk′ing) *n.* 1. The act of laying planks. 2. .nything made of planks. 3. Planks collectively.

ank·ton (plangk′tən) *n. Biol.* The marine animal and ιant organisms that drift or float with currents, waves, etc., ιnable to influence their own course and ranging in size from ιicroorganisms to jellyfish. [< G < Gk. *plazesthai* to ·ander] **— plank·ton′ic** *adj.*

ano-[1] *combining form* Roaming; wandering. Also, before owels, **plan-**. [< Gk. *planos* wandering]

plano-[2] *combining form* Flat; level; plane: *plano-concave, planometer.* Also, before vowels, **plan-**. Also **plani-**. [< L *planus* flat]

pla·no-con·cave (plā′nō·kon′kāv) *adj.* Plane on one side and concave on the other.

pla·no-con·vex (plā′nō·kon′veks) *adj.* Plane on one side and convex on the other.

pla·nom·e·ter (plə·nom′ə·tər) *n.* A device for gauging a plane surface, especially as used in metalworking. [< PLANO-[2] + -METER] **— pla·nom′e·try** *n.*

plant (plant, plänt) *n.* 1. A living organism belonging to the vegetable kingdom, as distinguished from the animal kingdom, having typically rigid cell walls and characterized by growth chiefly from the synthesis of simple, usually inorganic food materials from soil, water, and air. 2. One of the smaller forms of vegetable life, as distinct from shrubs and trees. 3. A set of machines, tools, apparatus, etc., necessary to conduct a manufacturing enterprise or other business: a chemical *plant.* 4. The buildings, grounds, and permanent appliances needed for any institution, as a post office, college, etc. 5. A slip or cutting from a tree or bush; sapling. 6. A person placed in a theater audience to encourage applause, speak lines, or contribute to the action of a play. 7. An apparently trivial passage early in a story or play that later becomes important in shaping the outcome of the action. 8. *Slang* A trick; dodge; swindle. **— v.t.** 1. To set in the ground for growing. 2. To furnish with plants or seed: to *plant* a field. 3. To set or place firmly; put in position. 4. To found; establish. 5. To introduce into the mind; implant, as an idea or principle. 6. To introduce into a country, as a breed of animal. 7. To deposit (fish or spawn), in a body of water. 8. To stock, as a river. 9. To bed (oysters). 10. *Slang* To deliver, as a blow. 11. *Slang* To place or station for purposes of deception, observation, etc.: to *plant* evidence. 12. *Slang* To hide; bury: Where did you *plant* the loot? [OE *plante* < L *planta* a sprout, cutting; ult. origin uncertain]

Plan·tag·e·net (plan·taj′i·net) A patronymic of the Angevin dynasty of English sovereigns from Henry II (1154) to the accession of the House of Tudor (1485). [< Med.L *planta genista* sprig of broom; with ref. to the habit of Geoffrey of Anjou, founder of the line, of wearing one]

plan·tain[1] (plan′tin) *n.* An annual or perennial herb (genus *Plantago*) widely distributed in temperate regions; especially, the **common** or **greater plantain** (*P. major*) with large, ovate, ribbed leaves. [< OF < L *plantago, -ginis* < *planta* sole of the foot; with ref. to the shape of the leaves]

plan·tain[2] (plan′tin) *n.* 1. A tropical, perennial herb (*Musa paradisiaca*), sometimes growing to 30 feet. 2. The long, bananalike fruit of this plant, edible when cooked. [< Sp. *plátano*; infl. in form by PLANTAIN[1]]

plan·tar (plan'tər) *adj.* Pertaining to the sole of the foot. [< L *planta* sole of the foot]

plan·ta·tion (plan·tā'shən) *n.* **1.** Any place that is planted. **2.** A farm or estate of many acres, planted in cotton, tobacco, etc., worked by resident laborers. **3.** A colony. **4.** A grove cultivated for its wood. [< L < *plantare* to plant]

plant·er (plan'tər) *n.* **1.** One who plants. **2.** An early settler or colonizer. **3.** An owner of a plantation. **4.** An agricultural implement for dropping seed in soil. **5.** A decorative container in which shrubs and flowers are planted, especially outdoors. **6.** *Canadian* In Newfoundland, a trader who hires and provisions fishermen in return for a share of the catch.

plan·ti·grade (plan'tə·grād) *Zool. adj.* Walking on the whole sole of the foot: distinguished from *digitigrade*. [< F < L *planta* sole of the foot + *gradi* to walk]

plant louse **1.** An aphid. **2.** Any of a family of leaping insects that infest plants and suck their juices.

plaque (plak) *n.* **1.** A plate, disk, or slab of metal, porcelain, ivory, etc., artistically ornamented, as for wall decoration. **2.** A small disk or brooch worn as a badge of membership, etc. [< F < MDu. *placke* flat disk, tablet]

plash[1] (plash) *n.* A slight splash. — *v.t. & v.i.* To splash lightly, as water. [Prob. imit.] — **plash'y** *adj.*

plash[2] (plash) *n.* A small pool. [OE *plæsc* pool]

-plasia *combining form* Growth; development; formative action. Also **-plasis.** [< Gk. *plassein* to mold, form]

-plasm *combining form* *Biol.* The viscous material of an animal or vegetable cell: *protoplasm.* [< LL < Gk. *plassein* to mold, form]

plas·ma (plaz'mə) *n.* **1.** The liquid portion of nutritive animal fluids, as blood, lymph, or intercellular fluid. **2.** The clear, fluid portion of blood, freed from blood cells and used for transfusions. **3.** The viscous material of a cell; protoplasm. **4.** *Physics* **a** The region in a gas-discharge tube in which there are approximately equal numbers of positive ions and electrons. **b** Any gas composed of such particles. Also **plasm** (plaz'əm). [< LL < Gk. *plassein* to mold, form] — **plas·mat·ic** (plaz·mat'ik), **plas'mic** *adj.*

plasma engine A reaction engine producing a small but sustained thrust by emission of a plasma jet.

plasma jet *Physics* A beam of plasma ejected from a specially constructed generator that forms a brilliantly luminous jet of extremely high energy and temperature.

plasmo- *combining form* Plasma; of or pertaining to plasma. Also, before vowels, **plasm-.** [See -PLASM]

plas·mo·di·um (plaz·mō'dē·əm) *n.* *pl.* **·di·a** (-dē·ə) **1.** A mass of protoplasm resulting from the fusion of ameboid organisms, typical of the slime molds. **2.** Any of a genus of parasitic protozoans that include the causative agents of malaria. [< NL < PLASM(O)- + Gk. *eidos* form]

-plast *combining form* An organized living particle or cell. [< Gk. < *plassein* to form]

plas·ter (plas'tər, pläs'-) *n.* **1.** A composition of lime, sand, and water, sometimes mixed with hair, for coating walls and partitions. **2.** Plaster of Paris. **3.** A viscid substance spread on linen, silk, etc., and applied to some part of the body, used for healing. — *v.t.* **1.** To cover or overlay with or as with plaster. **2.** To apply a plaster to, as a part of the body. **3.** To apply like plaster or a plaster: to *plaster* posters on a fence. **4.** To cause to adhere or lay flat like plaster. [OE reinforced by OF *plastre* < LL < L < Gk. *emplessain* < *en* upon, into + *plassein* to mold] — **plas'ter·er** *n.* — **plas'ter·ing** *n.* — **plas'ter·y** *adj.*

plas·ter·board (plas'tər·bôrd', pläs'-, -bōrd') *n.* A wallboard made of gypsum or plaster and fibrous paper.

plaster cast **1.** A cast or model of a person or object made by molding plaster of Paris. **2.** *Surg.* A cast.

plaster of Paris Calcined gypsum, setting readily when mixed with water, useful in making molds, casts, bandages, etc. [With ref. to use of gypsum from Paris]

plas·tic (plas'tik) *adj.* **1.** Giving form or fashion to matter. **2.** Capable of being molded; pliable. **3.** Pertaining to modeling or molding. **4.** *Surg.* Efficacious in recreating or remodeling injured or destroyed parts: *plastic* surgery. — *n.* **1.** Any substance or material that may be molded. **2.** *Chem.* One of a large class of synthetic organic compounds capable of being molded, extruded, cast, or otherwise fabricated into various shapes, or of being drawn into filaments for textiles. [< L < Gk. *plastikos* moldable] — **plas'ti·cal·ly** *adv.*

-plastic *combining form* Growing; developing; forming. [< Gk. *plastikos* plastic, moldable]

plas·tic·i·ty (plas·tis'ə·tē) *n.* **1.** The quality or state of being plastic. **2.** Capacity for being shaped or molded.

plas·ti·ciz·er (plas'tə·sī'zər) *n.* That which functions to make a substance plastic, preserve softness, etc.

plastic surgery Surgery that deals with the restoration or healing of lost, wounded, or deformed parts of the body.

plas·tid (plas'tid) *n.* *Biol.* **1.** A small, specialized mass in the cytoplasm of a cell. For illus. see CELL. **2.** An elementary organism, as a cell. [< G < Gk. < *plassein* to mold]

plas·tron (plas'trən) *n.* **1.** A leather shield worn on th[e] breast by fencers. **2.** *Zool.* The ventral part of the shell a turtle or tortoise: also **plas'trum.** [< F, < Ital. < *piast* sheet of metal] — **plas'tral** (-trəl) *adj.*

-plasty *combining form* *Surg.* An operation involving: **a** (specified) part of the body: *osteoplasty.* **b** Tissue from a (spe[c] ified) source: *zooplasty.* **c** A (specified) process or formatio[n] *neoplasty.* [< Gk. *-plastia* formation]

-plasy See -PLASIA.

plat (plat) *v.t.* **plat·ted, plat·ting** To plait or braid. — [n.] A plait; braid. [Var. of PLAIT]

plat- Var. of PLATY-.

plate (plāt) *n.* **1.** A flat, extended, rigid body of metal any material of slight but even thickness. **2.** A shallow ve[s] sel made of crockery, wood, glass, etc., in which food served or from which it is eaten at table. **3.** Household a[r] ticles, as trays, carving sets, etc., that are plated with a pr[e] cious metal. **4.** A portion of food served at table; platef[ul] **5.** A piece of flat metal bearing a design or inscription or i[n] tended for reproduction, as in a bookplate. **6.** Metal sheets. **7.** An impression from an engraving, woodcut, et[c] as reproduced in a book. **8.** An electrotype or stereoty[pe] **9.** A horizontal timber laid on a wall to receive a framewor[k] **10.** *Dent.* A piece of metal, vulcanite, or plastic fitted to th[e] mouth and holding one or more artificial teeth. **11.** A th[in] part of the brisket or beef. **12.** *Photog.* A sensitized sheet glass, metal, or the like, for taking photographs. **13.** [In] baseball, the home base. **14.** *Biol.* A platelike part or stru[c] ture; a lamina. **15.** A dish used in taking up collections, i[n] churches; also, a collection. **16.** *Electronics* The princi[pal] anode in an electron tube. — *v.t.* **plat·ed, plat·ing 1.** [To] coat with a thin layer of gold, silver, etc. **2.** To cover sheathe with metal plates for protection. **3.** In papermak[ing,] ing, to give a high gloss to (paper) by pressure betwe[en] metal plates. **4.** *Printing* To make an electrotype or stere[o] type from. [< OF < LL *plattus* flat] — **plat'er** *n.*

pla·teau (pla·tō', *esp. Brit.* plat'ō) *n.* *pl.* **·teaus** or **·tea[ux]** (-tōz') **1.** An extensive stretch of elevated and comparativ[e] ly level land; mesa. **2.** A stage or period of leveling off the development of something or in the process of learnin[g] [< F < OF *plat* flat]

plat·ed (plā'tid) *adj.* **1.** Coated with a layer of gold, silve[r] etc.: often used in combination: *gold-plated.* **2.** Provid[ed] with plates, as of metal.

plate·ful (plāt'fool') *n.* *pl.* **·fuls** The quantity that fills plate.

plate glass Glass in clear, thick sheets, suitable for mirro[rs] display windows, etc.

plate·let (plāt'lit) *n.* **1.** A small, platelike object. **2.** *Ph[ys] iol.* A blood platelet. [Dim. of PLATE]

plat·en (plat'n) *n.* *Mech.* **1.** The part of a printing pre[ss] typewriter, or the like, on which the paper is supported receive the impression. **2.** In a machine tool, the adjustab[le] table that carries the work. [See PLATE]

plat·form (plat'fôrm) *n.* **1.** Any floor or flat surface raise[d] above the adjacent level, as a stage for public speaking or raised walk upon which railroad passengers alight. **2.** [A] projecting stage at the end of a car or similar vehicle. **3.** [A] formal scheme of principles put forth by a religious, poli[ti] cal, or other body; also, the document stating the princip[les] of a political party. [< MF < *plate* flat + *forme* form]

plat·ing (plā'ting) *n.* **1.** A layer or coating of metal. **2.** [The] sheathing of metal plates, as armor. **3.** The act or process sheathing or coating something with plates of metal.

pla·tin·ic (plə·tin'ik) *adj.* *Chem.* Of, pertaining to, or co[n] taining platinum, esp. in its higher valence.

plat·i·nize (plat'ə·nīz) *v.t.* **·nized, ·niz·ing** To coat or co[m] bine with platinum, esp. by electroplating.

platino- *combining form* Platinum; of or containing pla[ti] num. Also, before vowels, **platin-.** [< PLATINUM]

plat·i·nous (plat'ə·nəs) *adj.* *Chem.* Of, pertaining to, containing platinum, esp. in its lower valence.

plat·i·num (plat'ə·nəm) *n.* **1.** A heavy, steel-gray, malle[able] able and ductile metallic element (symbol Pt) that is ve[ry] infusible, resistant to most acids, and that has a high elect[ri] cal resistance. It is widely used as a catalyst, in industry a[nd] the arts, and in jewelry. See ELEMENT. **2.** A color resem[ling] bling that of platinum. [< NL < Sp. *plata* silver]

platinum blond **1.** A very light, almost white blond. One having platinum blond hair.

plat·i·tude (plat'ə·tōōd, -tyōōd) *n.* **1.** A flat, dull, or co[m] monplace statement; an obvious truism. **2.** Dullness; trit[e] ness. [< F *plat* flat] — **plat'i·tu'di·nous** *adj.*

plat·i·tu·di·nize (plat'ə·tōō'də·nīz, -tyōō'-) *v.i.* **·nized, ·n[iz]** ing To utter platitudes.

pla·ton·ic (plə·ton'ik) *adj. Often cap.* Purely spiritual, devoid of sensual feeling. — **pla·ton'i·cal·ly** *adv.*

Pla·ton·ic (plə·ton'ik) *adj.* Of, pertaining to, or characte[r] istic of Plato or of Platonism; academic; theoretical. — **Pla·ton'i·cal.** — **Pla·ton'i·cal·ly** *adv.*

Pla·to·nism (plā'tə·niz'əm) *n.* The philosophy of Plat[o]

.., the doctrine that objects are merely copies or images of rnal ideas and that these ideas are the ultimate realities. **Pla′to·nist** *n.*

·toon (plə·tōon′) *n.* **1.** A subdivision of a company, op, or other military unit, commanded by a lieutenant. A company of people; esp., in football, a defensive or ensive unit. — *v.t.* In football, to use as or in a platoon. [F *peloton* ball, group of men]

toon sergeant In the U.S. Army, the senior noncomssioned officer in a platoon. See table for GRADE.

tt·deutsch (plät′doich′) *n.* The low German vernacuof the north of Germany. [< G]

·ter (plat′ər) *n.* **1.** *Chiefly U.S.* An oblong shallow dish which meat or fish is served. **2.** *Informal* A phonograph ord. [< AF *plat* dish]

ty- *combining form* Flat. Also, before vowels, *plat-*. Gk. *platys* flat]

·y·pus (plat′ə·pəs) *n.* A burrowing, egg-laying, aquatic notreme of Australia, having a ducklike : also called *duckbill*. [< NL < Gk. < tus* flat + *pous* foot]

u·dit (plô′dit) *n.* An expression of apuse; praise bestowed. [< L *plaudite*, imperative of *plaudere* to applaud]

u·si·ble (plô′zə·bəl) *adj.* **1.** Seeming be likely or probable, but open to doubt. Apparently trustworthy or believable. L *plausibilis* deserving applause] —

PLATYPUS
(To 2 feet long; tail about 5½ inches)

u/si·bil′i·ty, plau/si·ble·ness *n.* — **plau′si·bly** *adv.*
y (plā) *v.i.* **1.** To engage in sport or diversion; amuse eself. **2.** To take part in a game of skill or chance. **3.** To in a way that is not to be taken seriously. **4.** To act or ave in a specified manner: to *play* false. **5.** To behave ntly or insincerely: with *with*. **6.** To make love sportively. To move quickly or irregularly as if frolicking: lights *play* along a wall. **8.** To discharge or be discharged freely or tinuously: a fountain *playing* in the square. **9.** To perm on a musical instrument. **10.** To give forth musical nds. **11.** To be performed or exhibited. **12.** To act on as on a stage; perform. **13.** To move freely or loosely, , within limits, as part of a mechanism. — *v.t.* **14.** To gage in (a game etc.). **15.** To imitate in play: to *play* vboys and Indians. **16.** To perform sportively or wantonto *play* a trick. **17.** To oppose in a game or contest. **18.** move or employ (a piece, card, etc.) in a game. **19.** To ploy (someone) in a game as a player. **20.** To cause: to y havoc. **21.** To perform upon (a musical instrument). **.** To perform or produce, as a piece of music, a play, etc. **.** To act the part of on or as on the stage: to *play* the fool. **.** To perform or act in: to *play* Chicago. **25.** To cause to ve quickly or irregularly. **26.** To put into or maintain in ion. **27.** In angling, to let (a hooked fish) tire itself by intaining pressure on the line. **28.** To bet or bet on. — **play at 1.** To take part in. **2.** To pretend to be doing; do f-heartedly. — **to play down** To minimize. — **to play** o the hands of To act to the advantage of (a rival or opnent). — **to play off 1.** To oppose against one another. To decide (a tie) by playing one more game. — **to play** **1.** To take unscrupulous advantage of (another's hopes, otions, etc.) for one's own advantage. **2.** To continue. **to play out 1.** To come to an end; be exhausted. **2.** To tinue to the end. — **to play the game** To behave in a r manner. — **to play up** *Informal* To emphasize. — **to** y up to *Informal* To try to win the favor of by flattery, **.** — *n.* **1.** A dramatic composition; drama. **2.** The permance of such a composition. **3.** Exercise or action for reation or diversion. **4.** A maneuver or turn in a game. Manner of playing: rough *play*. **6.** In sports, a state of ng actively and legitimately in use or motion: in *play*. **7.** e act of playing a game, esp. gambling. **8.** Fun; joking: say something in *play*. **9.** The active operation of someng: the *play* of one's mind. **10.** Action or operation that ight, free, and unencumbered. **11.** Light, quick, fitful vement. **12.** Manner of acting toward or dealing with ers: fair *play*. — **to make a play for** *Informal* **1.** To empt to gain something, as a favor, votes, etc. **2.** To atnpt to seduce. [OE *plegan*] — **play′a·ble** *adj.*

y·back (plā′bak′) *n.* **1.** The act of reproducing a sound ording, as from a record or tape. **2.** A method or mane for reproducing sound recordings.

y·bill (plā′bil′) *n.* **1.** A bill or poster advertising a play. A program of a play.

y·boy (plā′boi′) *n.* *Informal* One who constantly seeks asure at nightclubs, social gatherings, etc.

y-by-play (plā′bī·plā′) *adj.* Dealing with each play or ent as it happens: a *play-by-play* report.

y·er (plā′ər) *n.* **1.** One who takes part or specializes in a me: a tennis *player*. **2.** An actor. **3.** A performer on a

musical instrument. **4.** A gambler. **5.** An automatic device for playing a musical instrument.

player piano A piano having a mechanical device by which it may be played automatically.

play·fel·low (plā′fel′ō) *n.* An associate in play; playmate.

play·ful (plā′fəl) *adj.* **1.** Lightly humorous; joking: a *playful* remark. **2.** Full of high spirits and play; frolicsome: a *playful* puppy. — **play′ful·ly** *adv.* — **play′ful·ness** *n.*

play·go·er (plā′gō′ər) *n.* One who goes often to the theater.

play·ground (plā′ground′) *n.* An area, usu. adjoining a school, used for playing games and for recreation.

play·house (plā′hous′) *n.* **1.** A theater. **2.** A small house for children to play in. **3.** A toy house.

playing card One of a pack of cards used in playing various games, the pack usu. consisting of four suits (spades, hearts, diamonds, clubs) of 13 cards each.

play·let (plā′lit′) *n.* A short play.

play·mate (plā′māt′) *n.* A companion in sports or in play.

play·off (plā′ôf′, -of′) *n.* In sports: **a** A decisive game or contest to break a tie. **b** A series of games to decide a championship, award, etc.

play·pen (plā′pen′) *n.* A small, usu. collapsible enclosure in which a baby or small child is left to amuse himself.

play·thing (plā′thing′) *n.* A thing to play with; a toy.

play upon words Words used with double meaning; a pun.

play·wright (plā′rīt′) *n.* A writer of plays.

pla·za (plä′zə, plaz′ə) *n.* An open square or market place in a town or city. [< Sp. < L *platea* wide street]

plea (plē) *n.* **1.** An appeal or entreaty. **2.** An excuse, pretext, or justification: the tyrant's *plea*. **3.** *Law* **a** An allegation made by either party in a cause: a pleading. **b** A statement made by or for the defendant concerning the charge or indictment against him. [< OF < L *placitum* opinion, orig. pp. of *placere* to please]

plead (plēd) *v.* **plead·ed** or **pled** (pled), **plead·ing** *v.i.* **1.** To make earnest entreaty; beg. **2.** *Law* **a** To advocate a case in court. **b** To file a pleading. — *v.t.* **3.** To allege as an excuse or defense. **4.** *Law* To discuss or maintain (a case) by argument. [See PLEA.] — **plead′a·ble** *adj.* — **plead′er** *n.*

plead·ing (plē′ding) *n.* **1.** The act of making a plea. **2.** *Law* **a** The art, science, or system of preparing the formal written statements of the parties to an action. **b** *Usu. pl.* Any one of such statements. — **plead′ing·ly** *adv.*

pleas·ant (plez′ənt) *adj.* **1.** Giving or promoting pleasure; pleasing. **2.** Agreeable in manner, act, appearance, etc. **3.** Merry; gay. [< OF < L *placere* to please] — **pleas′ant·ly** *adv.* — **pleas′ant·ness** *n.*

pleas·ant·ry (plez′ən·trē) *n.* *pl.* **·tries 1.** A playful, amusing, or good-natured remark, jest, or trick. **2.** The quality or spirit of pleasant conversation or companionship.

please (plēz) *v.* **pleased, pleas·ing** *v.t.* **1.** To give pleasure to; be agreeable to. **2.** To be the wish or will of. **3.** To be so kind as to; be willing to: usu. in the imperative: *Please* pass the bread. — *v.i.* **4.** To give satisfaction or pleasure. **5.** To have the will or preference; wish: Go when you *please*. [< OF < L *placere* to please] — **Syn. 1.** cheer, gladden, delight, rejoice, exhilarate.

pleas·ing (plē′zing) *adj.* Affording pleasure or satisfaction; gratifying. — **pleas′ing·ly** *adv.* — **pleas′ing·ness** *n.*

pleas·ur·a·ble (plezh′ər·ə·bəl) *adj.* Gratifying; pleasant; satisfying. — **pleas′ur·a·ble·ness** *n.* — **pleas′ur·a·bly** *adv.*

pleas·ure (plezh′ər) *n.* **1.** An agreeable sensation or emotion; enjoyment. **2.** Something that gives a feeling of enjoyment, delight, or satisfaction. **3.** Amusement or diversion: a search for *pleasure*. **4.** Sensual gratification. **5.** One's preference; choice. [See PLEASE.]

pleat (plēt) *n.* A fold of cloth doubled on itself and pressed or sewn in place. — *v.t.* To make a pleat or pleats in. Also *plait*. [Var. of PLAIT] — **pleat′er** *n.*

plebe (plēb) *n.* *U.S.* A member of the freshman class in the U.S. Military Academy at West Point or the U.S. Naval Academy at Annapolis. [Short for PLEBEIAN]

ple·be·ian (pli·bē′ən) *adj.* **1.** Of or pertaining to the common people, esp. those of ancient Rome. **2.** Common or vulgar. — *n.* **1.** One of the common people, esp. of ancient Rome. **2.** Anyone who is coarse or vulgar. [< L < *plebs* the common people] — **ple·be′ian·ism** *n.*

pleb·i·scite (pleb′ə·sīt, -sit) *n.* An expression of the popular will by means of a vote by the whole people, as to change a constitution. [< F < L < *plebs* common people + *scitum* decree] — **ple·bis·ci·tar·y** (plə·bis′ə·ter′ē) *adj.*

plec·trum (plek′trəm) *n.* *pl.* **·trums** or **·tra** (-trə) A small implement with which the player on a lyre, guitar, etc., picks or strikes the strings: also called *pick*. Also **plec′tron** (-tron). [< L < Gk. < *plessein* to strike]

pled (pled) Alternate past tense and past participle of PLEAD.

pledge (plej) *n.* **pledged, pledg·ing 1.** To give or deposit as security for a loan, etc. **2.** To bind by or as by a pledge.

3. To promise solemnly, as assistance. **4.** To offer (one's word, life, etc.) as a guaranty or forfeit. **5.** To drink a toast to. **6.** To promise to join (a fraternity). **7.** To accept (someone) as a pledge (def. 6). — *n.* **1.** A promise or agreement to perform or fulfill some act, contract, or duty. **2.** A formal promise to do or not to do something. **3.** The drinking of a toast to one's health, etc. **4.** Something given as security for a debt or obligation. **5.** The state of being given or held as security: to put property in *pledge.* **6.** One who has promised to join a fraternity but who has not yet been formally inducted. [< OF < Med.L *plebium,* prob. < Gmc.] — **pledg′er** *n.*

pledg·ee (plej·ē′) *n.* **1.** One to whom something is pledged. **2.** One with whom a pledge is deposited.

pledg·or (plej′ər) *n. Law* A pledger. Also **pledge′or.**

-plegia *combining form Pathol.* A (specified) kind of paralysis, or paralytic condition: *hemiplegia.* Also **-plegy.** [< Gk. < *plēgē* stroke]

Plei·a·des (plē′ə-dēz, plī′-) *n.pl.* **1.** In Greek mythology, the seven daughters of Atlas, who were set by Zeus among the stars. **2.** *Astron.* A loose cluster of many hundred stars in the constellation Taurus, six of which are visible to ordinary sight.

Plei·o·cene (plī′ə-sēn) See PLIOCENE.

Pleis·to·cene (plīs′tə-sēn) *Geol. adj.* Of or pertaining to the earlier of the two epochs of the Quaternary, characterized by the glacial epoch of northern Asia, Europe, and North America. — *n.* The rock series of this epoch. See chart for GEOLOGY. [< Gk. *pleistos* most + *kainos* recent]

ple·na·ry (plē′nə-rē, plen′ə-) *adj.* **1.** Full in all respects or requisites; complete. **2.** Fully or completely attended, as an assembly. [< LL < L *plenus* full] — **ple′na·ri·ly** *adv.* — **ple′na·ri·ness** *n.*

plenary indulgence In the Roman Catholic Church, the remission of all temporal penalties incurred by sin.

plen·i·po·ten·ti·ar·y (plen′i·pə·ten′shē·er′ē, -shə·rē) *adj.* Possessing or conferring full powers. — *n. pl.* **·ar·ies** A person fully empowered to represent a government, as an ambassador, minister, or envoy. [< Med.L < LL < L *plenus* full + *potens* powerful < *potere* to be able]

plen·i·tude (plen′ə-tood, -tyood) *n.* The state of being full, complete, or abounding.

plen·te·ous (plen′tē-əs) *adj.* **1.** Characterized by plenty; amply sufficient. **2.** Yielding an abundance. — **plen′te·ous·ly** *adv.* — **plen′te·ous·ness** *n.*

plen·ti·ful (plen′ti·fəl) *adj.* **1.** Existing in great quantity; abundant. **2.** Yielding or containing plenty; affording ample supply. — **plen′ti·ful·ly** *adv.* — **plen′ti·ful·ness** *n.*
— **Syn. 1.** *Plentiful* suggests comparison with a need or demand, and can be applied to almost anything concrete: wheat is *plentiful* this year, aspirants for movie jobs are always *plentiful.* *Abundant* suggests, in the concrete, the works of nature rather than of man: *abundant* foliage. *Ample* means both just enough and more than enough, and so tends to imply an amount between enough and *plenty.* — **Ant.** scanty, scarce.

plen·ty (plen′tē) *n.* **1.** The state of being sufficient and in abundance. **2.** As much as can be required; an abundance or sufficiency: I have *plenty.* — *adj.* Existing in abundance; plentiful. — *adv. Informal* In a sufficient degree: The house is *plenty* large enough. [< OF < L *plenus* full]

ple·o·nasm (plē′ə-naz′əm) *n.* **1.** The use of needless words; redundancy; also, an instance of it. **2.** A redundant word or phrase. **3.** Superabundance. [< L < Gk. < *pleōn* more] — **ple′o·nas′tic** (-nas′tik) *adj.* — **ple′o·nas′ti·cal·ly** *adv.*

pleth·o·ra (pleth′ər·ə) *n.* **1.** A state of excessive fullness; superfluity. **2.** *Med.* Superabundance of blood in the whole system or in an organ or part. [< LL < Gk. < *plēthein* to be full] — **ple·thor′ic** (plē-thôr′ik) *adj.* — **ple·thor′i·cal·ly** *adv.*

pleu·ra (ploor′ə) *n. pl.* **pleu·rae** (ploor′ē) *Anat.* The serous membrane that envelops the lungs and is folded back upon the walls of the thorax and upon the diaphragm. [< Gk. *pleura* side] — **pleu′ral** *adj.*

pleu·ri·sy (ploor′ə·sē) *n. Pathol.* Inflammation of the pleura, commonly attended with fever, pain in the chest, difficult breathing, exudation, etc. [< OF < LL < L < Gk. *pleura* side] — **pleu·rit·ic** (ploo-rit′ik) *adj.*

pleuro- *combining form* **1.** Of or pertaining to the side. **2.** *Med.* Of, related to, or affecting the pleura. Also, before vowels, **pleur-.** [< Gk. *pleura* side]

Plex·i·glas (plek′si·glas′, -gläs′) *n.* A lightweight thermoplastic acrylic resin, very weather-resistant and highly transparent: a trade name. Also **plex′i·glas, plex′i·glass.**

plex·us (plek′səs) *n. pl.* **plex·us·es** or **plex·us** **1.** A network or complicated interlacing of parts. **2.** *Anat.* A network of cordlike structures, as blood vessels or nerves. [< L, pp. of *plectere* to intertwine]

pli·a·ble (plī′ə-bəl) *adj.* **1.** Easily bent or twisted; flexible. **2.** Easily persuaded or controlled; tractable. — **pli′a·bil′i·ty, pli′a·ble·ness** *n.* — **pli′a·bly** *adv.*

pli·an·cy (plī′ən-sē) *n.* The state or quality of being pliant.

pli·ant (plī′ənt) *adj.* **1.** Capable of being bent or twisted with ease. **2.** Easily yielding to influence; compliant. OF, ppr. of *plier* < L *plicare* to fold] — **pli′ant·ly** *adv.*

pli·cate (plī′kāt) *adj.* Folded or pleated, as a fan. Also **cat·ed.** — **pli′cate·ness** *n.* — **pli′cate·ly** *adv.* — **pli·ca′tion, plic·a·ture** (plik′ə-choŏr) *n.*

pli·er (plī′ər) *n.* **1.** *pl.* Small pincers for bending, holding, cutting: also **pair of pliers. 2.** One who or that which pl

plight¹ (plīt) *n.* A condition, state, or circumstance, usu a dangerous or complicated nature. [< AF *plit* fold, co tion < OF *pleit*]

plight² (plīt) *v.t.* **1.** To pledge (one's word, faith, etc.). To promise, as in marriage; betroth. — **to plight one's t 1.** To pledge one's solemn word. **2.** To promise onese marriage. [OE *plihtan* to expose to danger] — **plight′**

Plim·soll mark (plim′sol, -səl) A mark painted on the side of the hull of a British vessel to show how deeply may be loaded. Also **Plimsoll line.** [after Samuel *Plim* 1824–98, English statesman]

plinth (plinth) *n. Archit.* **1.** The slab, block, or stone, square, on which a column, pedestal, or statue rests. thin course, as of slabs, usu. projecting beneath a wall: **plinth course.** [< L < Gk. *plinthos* brick]

Pli·o·cene (plī′ə-sēn) *Geol. adj.* Of or pertaining to the est epoch of the Tertiary, and succeeded by the Pleistoc — *n.* The Pliocene epoch or rock series. Also spelled P *cene.* See chart for GEOLOGY. [< Gk. *pleiōn* more + *ka* new] — **Pli′o·cen′ic** (-sen′ik) *adj.*

plod (plod) *v.* **plod·ded, plod·ding** *v.i.* **1.** To walk hea or laboriously. **2.** To work in a steady, laborious man — *v.t.* **3.** To walk along heavily or laboriously. — *n.* **1.** act or duration of plodding. **2.** The sound of a heavy s as of a horse. [Imit.] — **plod′der** *n.* — **plod′ding·ly**

-ploid *combining form Biol.* In cytology and genetics, ing a (specified) number of chromosomes: *polyploid.* C sponding nouns end in **-ploidy.** [< Gk. *-ploos* fold + -

plop (plop) *v.t. & v.i.* **plopped, plop·ping** To drop wi sound like that of something striking the water without m ing a splash. — *n.* The act or sound of plopping. — Suddenly with a plopping sound. [Imit.]

plo·sion (plō′zhən) *n. Phonet.* The sudden release of br after closure of the oral passage in the articulation of a consonant, as after the *p* in *pat.* [< EXPLOSION]

plo·sive (plō′siv) *Phonet. adj.* Designating a sound duced by plosion. — *n.* A consonant so produced; a

plot (plot) *n.* **1.** A piece or patch of ground, usu. use some special purpose. **2.** A chart or diagram, as of a b ing, for showing certain data; also, a surveyor's map. secret plan to accomplish some questionable purpose; spiracy. **4.** The scheme or pattern of the events, incid or situations of a story, play, etc. — *v.* **plot·ted,** plot *v.t.* **1.** To make a map, chart, or plan of, as of a ship's co a building, etc. **2.** To plan for secretly. **3.** To arrange plot of (a novel, etc.). **4.** *Math.* **a** To represent graphi the position of (a measured value) by a point located reference to its coordinates on graph paper. **b** To dra curve) through a series of such points. — *v.i.* **5.** To fo plot; scheme. [OE] — **plot′ter** *n.*

plov·er (pluv′ər, plō′vər) *n.* **1.** Any of various shore b having long, pointed wings and a short tail. **2.** Any of tain related shore birds, as the **upland plover.** [< *plovier,* ult. < L *pluvia* rain]

plow (plou) *n.* **1.** An implement for cutting, turning stirring, or breaking up the soil, usu. drawn by hors oxen, or by mechanical power. **2.** Any implement tha erates like a plow: often in combination: a *snowplow.* — **1.** To turn up the surface of (land) with a plow. **2** make or form (a furrow, one's way, etc.) by or as by m of a plow. **3.** To furrow or score the surface of: Shot pl the field. **4.** To dig out or remove with a plow: with *out.* **5.** To move or cut through (water). — *v.i.* **6.** To up soil with a plow. **7.** To undergo plowing in a spec way, as land. **8.** To move or proceed as a plow does: with *through* or *into.* **9.** To advance laboriously; plod. **to plow into** *Informal* **1.** To hit hard. **2.** To under vigorously to accomplish, finish, or solve (a meal, prob etc.). Also, *esp. Brit.,* **plough.** [OE *plōh,* prob. < ON p — **plow′a·ble** *adj.* — **plow′er** *n.*

plow·boy (plou′boi′) *n.* **1.** A boy who drives or guid team in plowing. **2.** A country boy. Also **plough′boy**

plow·man (plou′mən) *n. pl.* **·men** (-mən) **1.** One plows. **2.** A farmer; rustic. Also **plough′man.**

plow·share (plou′shâr′) *n.* The blade of a plow. **plough′share.**

ploy (ploi) *n.* A maneuver or stratagem, as in a game or versation. [< EMPLOY]

pluck (pluk) *v.t.* **1.** To pull out or off; pick. **2.** To with force; snatch or drag: with *off, away,* etc. **3.** To out the feathers, hair, etc., of. **4.** To give a twitch or to, as a sleeve. **5.** To cause the strings (of a musical in ment) to sound by quickly pulling or picking them. *Slang* To rob; swindle. — *v.i.* **7.** To give a sudden

ug: with *at*. — **to pluck up** To rouse or summon (one's
ourage). — *n*. **1**. Confidence and spirit in the face of dif-
culty or danger. **2**. A sudden pull; twitch. — **pluck'er** *n*.
OE *pluccian* to pick out, ? ult. < LL *pilus* hair]
uck·y (pluk'ē) *adj*. **pluck·i·er, pluck·i·est** Brave and
pirited; courageous. — **pluck'i·** y *adv*. — **pluck'i·ness** *n*.
ug (plug) *n*. **1**. Anything, as a piece of wood or a cork,
sed to stop a hole. **2**. *Electr.* A usu. two-pronged device at-
ached to the end of a wire or cable and inserted in a socket
r jack to make a connection. **3**. A spark plug. **4**. A fire-
lug. **5**. A flat cake of pressed or twisted tobacco. **6**. A
iece of tobacco for chewing. **7**. *Informal* Anything useless
r defective. **8**. *Informal* An old, worn-out horse. **9**. *Slang*
. favorable word, recommendation, or piece of publicity for
omeone or something. **10**. *Geol.* A core of hard, igneous
ock that has filled the neck of a volcano. — *v*. **plugged,
lug·ging** *v.t.* **1**. To stop or close, as a hole, by inserting a
lug; often with *up*. **2**. To insert as a plug. **3**. *Slang* To
hoot a bullet into. **4**. *Slang* To hit or punch. **5**. *Slang* To
dvertise frequently or insistently. — *v.i.* **6**. *Informal* To
vork doggedly. **7**. *Slang* To hit or shoot. **8**. *Slang* To
avor or work for a cause, person, etc.: usu. with *for*. — **to
lug in** To insert the plug of (a lamp, etc.) in an electrical
utlet. [< MDu. *plugge*] — **plug'ger** *n*.
ug·ly (plug'ug'lē) *n*. *pl.* **·lies** *U.S. Slang* A gangster,
uffian, or rowdy.
um[1] (plum) *n*. **1**. The edible fruit of any of various trees
f the rose family. **2**. The tree itself. **3**. The plumlike
ruit of any of various other trees; also, a tree bearing such
ruit. **4**. A raisin, esp. as used in cooking. **5**. Any of varius shades of dark, reddish purple. **6**. The best or most
hoice part of anything. **7**. Something desirable, as a post
r appointment. **8**. A sugarplum. [OE *plūme* < LL < L
runum < Gk. *prounon*]
um[2] (plum) See PLUMB (*adj*. def. 2 and *adv*. def. 2).
um·age (plōō'mij) *n*. **1**. The feathers of a bird; esp., a
ird's entire covering of feathers. **2**. Gaudy costume or
dornment. [< F < *plume* plume]
umb (plum) *n*. A lead weight (*plumb bob*) on the end of a
ne (*plumb line*) used to find the exact perpendicular, to
ound the depth of water, etc. — **off** (or **out of**) **plumb** Not
xactly vertical; not in alignment. — *adj*. **1**. Conforming
o a true vertical or perpendicular. **2**. *Informal Sheer*; ab-
olute; complete: also spelled *plum*. — *adv*. **1**. In a line
erpendicular to the plane of the horizon; vertically. **2**. *In-
ormal* Utterly; completely; entirely: also spelled *plum*. —
.t. **1**. To test the perpendicularity of with a plumb. **2**. To
nake vertical; straighten: usu. with *up*. **3**. To test the
epth of; sound. **4**. To reach the lowest level or extent of:
o *plumb* the depths of despair. [< F < L *plumbum* lead]
umb- Var. of PLUMBO-.
umb bob The weight used at the end of a plumb line.
umb·er (plum'ər) *n*. One whose occupation is
he installing or repairing of plumbing.

umb·er's friend (plum'ərz) A plunger
def. 3).
umb·ing (plum'ing) *n*. **1**. The art or trade
f putting into buildings the tanks, pipes, etc.,
or water, gas, sewage, etc. **2**. The pipe system
f a building. **3**. The act of sounding for depth,
tc., with a plumb line.
umb line 1. A cord by which a weight is sus-
ended to test the perpendicularity or depth of
omething. **2**. Such a cord.
umbo- *combining form* Lead; of or contain-
ng lead. Also, before vowels, *plumb-*. [< L
lumbum lead]
ume (plōōm) *n*. **1**. A feather, esp. when long
nd ornamental. **2**. A large feather or tuft of
eathers used as an ornament. **3**. *Biol.* A feath-
·r-like form or part. **4**. Plumage. **5**. Anything
esembling a plume. **6**. A decoration of honor
r achievement. — *v.t.* **plumed, plum·ing 1**.
o adorn, dress, or furnish with or as with plumes. **2**. To
mooth (itself or its feathers); preen. **3**. To congratulate
r pride (oneself): with *on* or *upon*. [< F < L *pluma*]
um·met (plum'it) *n*. **1**. A plumb bob. **2**. Something
nat oppresses or weighs down. — *v.i.* To drop straight
own; plunge. [< OF *plom* < L *plumbum* lead]
u·mose (plōō'mōs) *adj*. **1**. Bearing feathers or plumes.
2. Plumelike; feathery. [< L *pluma* feather] — **plu'mose·**
y *adv*. — **plu·mos·i·ty** (plōō·mos'ə·tē) *n*.
ump[1] (plump) *adj*. **1**. Somewhat fat; chubby. **2**. Well
lled or rounded out. — *v.t. & v.i.* To make or become
lump: often with *up* or *out*. [< MDu., var. of *plomp* blunt]
— **plump'ly** *adv*. — **plump'ness** *n*.
ump[2] (plump) *v.i.* **1**. To fall suddenly or heavily; drop
vith full impact. **2**. To give one's complete support: with

for. **3**. To come or go abruptly or in a hurry: with *in* or *out*.
— *v.t.* **4**. To drop or throw down heavily or all at once. **5**.
To utter bluntly or abruptly: often with *out*. — *n*. **1**. The
act of plumbing or falling. **2**. The sound made by this. —
adj. Containing no reservation or qualification; blunt; downright. — *adv*. **1**. With a sudden impact or fall. **2**. Straightforwardly; bluntly. **3**. Straight down. [< MDu. *plompen*;
ult. imit.] — **plump'er** *n*. — **plump'ly** *adv*.
plum·y (plōō'mē) *adj*. **plum·i·er, plum·i·est 1**. Made of, covered, or adorned with feathers. **2**. Like a plume or feather.
plun·der (plun'dər) *v.t.* **1**. To rob of goods or property by
open violence, as in war; pillage. **2**. To despoil by robbery
or fraud. **3**. To take as plunder. — *v.i.* **4**. To take plunder.
— *n*. **1**. That which is taken by plundering; booty. **2**.
The act of plundering or robbing. [< G < MHG *plundern*,
orig., to remove household goods] — **plun'der·er** *n*.
plunge (plunj) *v*. **plunged, plung·ing** *v.t.* **1**. To thrust or
force suddenly into a fluid, penetrable substance, hole, etc.
2. To force into some condition or state: to *plunge* a nation
into debt. — *v.i.* **3**. To dive, jump, or fall into a fluid,
chasm, etc. **4**. To move suddenly or with a rush. **5**. To
move violently forward and downward, as a horse or ship.
6. To descend abruptly or steeply, as a road or cliff. **7**. *Informal* To gamble or speculate heavily. — *n*. **1**. The act of
plunging; a leap; dive. **2**. A sudden and violent motion, as
of a breaking wave. **3**. A place for diving or swimming. **4**.
A swim. **5**. A heavy or extravagant bet, expenditure, or
speculation. [< OF *plonger*, ult. < L *plumbum* lead]
plung·er (plun'jər) *n*. **1**. One who or that which plunges.
2. *Informal* One who gambles recklessly. **3**. A cuplike device made of rubber and attached to a stick, used to clean
out clogged drains, etc.: also called *plumber's friend*. **4**.
Mech. Any appliance having a plunging motion, as a piston.
plunk (plungk) *Informal v.t.* **1**. To pluck, as a banjo or its
strings; strum. **2**. To place or throw heavily and suddenly:
with *down*. — *v.i.* **3**. To emit a twanging sound. **4**. To
fall heavily. — *n*. A heavy blow, or its sound. — *adv*.
Directly; exactly: *plunk* in the middle. [Imit.]
plu·per·fect (plōō·pûr'fikt) *n. Gram.* The past perfect. [<
L *plus quam perfectus*, lit., more than completed]
plu·ral (plōōr'əl) *adj*. **1**. Containing, consisting of, or designating more than one. **2**. *Gram.* Of or designating a linguistic term that denotes more than one (in languages that
have dual number, as Sanskrit and Greek, more than two):
distinguished from *dual, singular*. — *n. Gram.* The plural
number or a word in this number. [< OF < L *plus, pluris*
more] — **plu'ral·ly** *adv*.
◆ English nouns regularly form their plurals by adding *s*
to the singular. However, nouns that end in *y* preceded either
by a consonant or by *qu* form their plurals by changing the
y to *i* and adding *es*, as, body, *bodies*, city, *cities*, colloquy,
colloquies; if the *y* is preceded by a vowel (other than *u*), the
plural is formed by adding *s*, as, day, *days*, monkey, *monkeys*. Nouns ending in *ss*, *sh*, *ch*, *s*, *x*, and *zz* usually form
their plurals by adding *es*, as, brass, *brasses*, crash, *crashes*,
crutch, *crutches*, gas, *gases*, box, *boxes*, buzz, *buzzes*. Many
nouns ending in *f* change the *f* to *v* and add *es*, as, wolf,
wolves, half, *halves*. Nouns ending in *o* form their plurals by
adding either *s* or *es*, and the preferable form will be found
at the word entry. Some nouns of Old English origin have an
irregular plural in *en*, as, child, *children*, and some form the
plural by a vowel change, as mouse, *mice*; goose, *geese*; man,
men. A few nouns retain the singular form unchanged in the
plural, as, deer, hose, moose, series. Some such nouns, especially the names of animals, have also an alternative plural
regularly formed, as fish, fish or fishes. Fish is the usual collective plural; *fishes* is used to indicate more than one genus,
variety, species, etc. Many words of foreign derivation retain the plural forms peculiar to the languages from which
they are derived, as, addendum, *addenda*; crisis, *crises*; datum, *data*. Many nouns of this class have also a plural in the
regular English form, as, appendix, *appendixes* or *appendices*;
beau, *beaus* or *beaux*; cherub, *cherubs* or *cherubim*; focus,
focuses or *foci*. Compounds commonly form the plural regularly by adding *s* or *es* to the complete word, as, armful, *arm-
fuls*; football, *footballs*. If the last element of the compound
forms its plural irregularly, the same form usually appears in
the plural of the compound, as, footman, *footmen*. Some
nouns that end in *-man*, but are not compounds, form the
plural regularly by adding *s*, as, Mussulman, *Mussulmans*.
Hyphenated compounds in which the principal word forms
the first element change that element to form the plural, as,
father-in-law, *fathers-in-law*.
plu·ral·ism (plōōr'əl·iz'əm) *n*. **1**. The condition of being
plural. **2**. A social condition in which disparate religious,
ethnic, and racial groups are part of a common community.
3. *Eccl.* The holding at the same time of more than one
office. **4**. *Philos.* The doctrine that there are several ulti-

Captions for plumb bob illustration:
PLUMB BOB
a Plumb line.
b Plumb bob.
c Wall.

mate substances. Compare DUALISM, MONISM. — **plu′ral·ist** n. — **plu′ral·is′tic** adj.

plu·ral·i·ty (ploō·ral′ə·tē) n. pl. **·ties** 1. In U.S. politics: **a** The number of votes cast for a candidate over and above the number cast for his nearest opponent. **b** In a contest having more than two candidates, the greatest number of votes cast for any one candidate but not more than half the total number of votes cast. Distinguished from *majority*. 2. The larger or greater portion of anything. 3. The state or condition of being plural or numerous.

plu·ral·ize (ploōr′əl·īz) v.t. **·ized, ·iz·ing** 1. To make plural. 2. To express in the plural. — **plu′ral·i·za′tion** n.

pluri- combining form More; many; several. [< L plus, pluris more]

plus (plus) prep. 1. Added to: Three plus two equals five. 2. Increased by: salary plus commission. — adj. 1. Of, pertaining to, or involving addition. 2. Extra; supplemental. 3. Denoting a value higher than ordinary in a specified grade: B plus. 4. Positive: a plus quantity. 5. Informal More of something than can be stated or described: He has personality plus. 6. Electr. Positive. — n. pl. **plus·es** 1. The plus sign. 2. An addition or an extra quantity. 3. A positive quantity. — adv. Electr. Positively. [< L, more]

plus fours Knickerbockers cut very full and bagging below the knees. [Orig. tailor's cant; because they were four inches longer than ordinary knickerbockers]

plush (plush) n. A pile fabric of silk, rayon, mohair, etc., having a deeper pile than velvet. — adj. 1. Of plush. 2. Slang Luxurious. [< MF < OF < Ital. < L pilus hair]

plush·y (plush′ē) adj. plush·i·er, plush·i·est Of or resembling plush. — **plush′i·ly** adv.

plus sign A sign (+) denoting addition or a positive quantity.

Plu·to (ploō′tō) In Greek and Roman mythology, the god of the dead. — n. A planet of the solar system, ninth in order from the sun. See PLANET. [< L < Gk. Ploutōn]

plu·toc·ra·cy (ploō·tok′rə·sē) n. pl. **·cies** 1. Government by the wealthy. 2. A wealthy class that controls the government. [< Gk. ploutos wealth + kratein to rule]

plu·to·crat (ploō′tə·krat) n. 1. A member of a plutocracy. 2. Informal Any wealthy person. — **plu′to·crat′ic, plu′to·crat′i·cal** adj. — **plu′to·crat′i·cal·ly** adv.

plu·ton·ic (ploō·ton′ik) adj. Geol. Deeply subterranean in original position: said of igneous rocks. [< L Pluto, -onis]

plu·to·ni·um (ploō·tō′nē·əm) n. A radioactive element (symbol Pu), formed in the bombardment of neptunium by deuterons. See ELEMENT. [< NL < Pluto (the planet)]

Plu·tus (ploō′təs) In Greek mythology, the god of riches, blinded by Zeus. [< L < Gk. Ploutos < ploutos wealth]

plu·vi·al (ploō′vē·əl) adj. 1. Of or pertaining to rain. 2. Caused by the action of rain. [< L pluvia rain]

pluvio- combining form Rain; pertaining to rain. Also before vowels, **pluvi-**. [< L pluvia rain]

ply[1] (plī) v.t. **plied, ply·ing** To bend; mold; shape. — n. pl. **plies** 1. A layer, fold, or thickness, as of cloth, etc. 2. A strand of rope, yarn, thread, etc.; used in combination to mean a (certain) number of folds, twists, or strands: three-ply yarn. 3. A bent; inclination. [< F < L plicare to fold]

ply[2] (plī) v. **plied, ply·ing** v.t. 1. To use in working, fighting, etc.; wield; employ. 2. To work at; be engaged in. 3. To supply with or offer repeatedly: to ply a person with drink. 4. To address (a person) repeatedly with questions, requests, etc. 5. To strike or assail persistently: He plied the donkey with a whip. 6. To traverse regularly: ferryboats that ply the river. — v.i. 7. To make regular trips; sail: usu. with between. 8. To work steadily. 9. To proceed; steer. 10. Naut. To beat; tack. [< APPLY]

Plymouth Rock One of a breed of domestic fowls. [after Plymouth Rock]

ply·wood (plī′wood′) n. A structural material consisting of sheets or layers of wood glued together, the grains of adjoining layers usu. being at right angles to each other.

pneu·mat·ic (noō·mat′ik, nyoō-) adj. 1. Pertaining to pneumatics. 2. Operated by compressed air. 3. Pertaining to or containing air or gas. 4. Spiritual. 5. Containing air, as cavities in the bones of certain birds. Also **pneu·mat′i·cal**. — n. A tire inflated with compressed air. [< L < Gk. < pneuma breath, wind] — **pneu·mat′i·cal·ly** adv.

pneu·mat·ics (noō·mat′iks, nyoō-) n.pl. (construed as sing.) The branch of physics that treats of the mechanical properties of air and other gases.

pneumato- combining form 1. Air. 2. Breath; breathing. 3. Spirit; spirits. Also, before vowels, **pneumat-**. [< Gk. pneuma, pneumatos air, spirit, breath < pnein to blow]

pneu·ma·tol·o·gy (noō′mə·tol′ə·jē, nyoō-) n. pl. **·gies** The doctrine or study of the nature and operation of spirit and spiritual beings. — **pneu′ma·to·log′ic** (-tə·loj′ik) or **·i·cal** adj. — **pneu′ma·tol′o·gist** n.

pneumono- combining form Lung; related to the lungs; respiratory. Also **pneum-** (before vowels), **pneumono-**. [< Gk. pneumōn, pneumonos a lung]

pneu·mo·coc·cus (noō′mə·kok′əs, nyoō′-) n. pl. **·coc·ci** (-kok′sī) Any of a group of bacteria that inhabit the respiratory tract, some of which cause lobar pneumonia. — **pneu·mo·coc′cal, pneu′mo·coc′cic** (-kok′sik) adj.

pneu·mo·nia (noō·mōn′yə, nyoō-) n. Pathol. Inflammation of the lungs, a disease of bacterial or viral origin occurring in many forms, as **bronchial pneumonia** or **lobar pneumonia**. [< NL < Gk. < pneumōn lung]

pneu·mon·ic (noō·mon′ik, nyoō-) adj. 1. Of, pertaining to, or affected with pneumonia. 2. Pulmonary. [< NL pneumonicus < Gk. pneumonikos < pneumōn lung]

poach[1] (pōch) v.t. To cook (eggs, fish, etc.) in boiling water, milk, or other liquid. [< OF poche pocket, pouch; because the egg white forms a pouch around the yolk]

poach[2] (pōch) v.i. 1. To trespass on another's property, etc. esp. for the purpose of taking game or fish. 2. To take game or fish unlawfully. — v.t. 3. To trespass on, as for taking game or fish. 4. To take (game or fish) unlawfully. [< OF pocher to thrust, encroach upon] — **poach′er** n.

pock (pok) n. 1. A pustule in an eruptive disease, as in smallpox. 2. A pockmark. [OE pocc]

pock·et (pok′it) n. 1. A small pouch inserted in a garment for carrying money, etc. 2. A small bag or pouch. 3. An opening, receptacle, or container. 4. Money, means, or financial interests. 5. Mining a A cavity containing ore. An accumulation of ore. 6. One of the pouches in a billiard or pool table. 7. An air pocket (which see). 8. A region or area, usu. small and differentiated in some way from the surrounding area. — **in one's pocket** 1. On terms of close intimacy. 2. Under one's influence or control. — adj. 1. Diminutive, as if pocketable. 2. Pertaining to, for, or carried in a pocket: pocket lining. — v.t. 1. To put into or confine in a pocket. 2. To appropriate as one's own, esp. dishonestly. 3. To enclose as if in a pocket. 4. To conceal; suppress: Pocket your pride. 5. To retain without signing. 6. In billiards, etc., to drive (a ball) into a pocket. [< A pokete, dim. of OF poque, poche pouch] — **pock′et·a·ble** adj.

pocket billiards Pool[2] (def. 5).

pock·et·book (pok′it·book′) n. 1. A wallet. 2. A woman's purse or handbag. 3. A book, usu. paperbound and smaller than standard size: also **pocket book**. 4. Money or financial resources.

pock·et·ful (pok′it·fool′) n. pl. **·fuls** As much as a pocket will hold.

pock·et·knife (pok′it·nīf′) n. pl. **·knives** (-nīvz′) A knife having one or more blades that fold into the handle.

pocket money Money for small expenses.

pocket veto U.S. An act whereby the President, on being presented a bill by Congress for his signature of approval, retains ("pockets") it unsigned until the session has adjourned, thus causing it to fail without a direct veto.

pock·mark (pok′märk′) n. A pit or scar left on the skin by smallpox or a similar disease. — **pock′-marked′** adj.

pock·y (pok′ē) adj. pock·i·er, pock·i·est 1. Pertaining to, resembling, or affected with smallpox. 2. Marked by pocks.

po·co (pō′kō) adv. Music Slightly; a little. [< Ital.]

pod[1] (pod) n. 1. A seed vessel or capsule, esp. of a leguminous plant. 2. Aeron. A separate enclosure on an aircraft, esp. one beneath the wing for a jet engine. — v.i. **pod·ded, pod·ding** To produce pods. [Origin unknown]

pod[2] (pod) n. A flock or collection of animals, esp. of seals, whales, or walruses. [Origin unknown]

-pod combining form 1. One who or that which has (a specified number or kind of) feet: arthropod. 2. A (specified kind of) foot. Also **-pode**. [< Gk. pous, podos foot]

-poda combining form Zool. Plural of -POD: used in names of phyla, orders, classes, etc.: Arthropoda.

podg·y (poj′ē) adj. podg·i·er, podg·i·est Pudgy. [< dial. podge to walk slowly and heavily] — **podg′i·ness** n.

po·di·a·try (pə·dī′ə·trē, pō-) n. Chiropody. [< Gk. pous, podos foot + -IATRY] — **po·di′a·trist** n.

po·di·um (pō′dē·əm) n. pl. **·di·ums** or **·di·a** (-dē·ə) 1. A small platform or dais for the conductor of an orchestra, speaker, etc. 2. Zool. A foot, or any footlike structure. [< L < Gk. podion, dim. of pous, podos foot]

-podium combining form A footlike part. [< NL < Gk. podion, dim. of pous, podos a foot]

-podous combining form -footed: used in adjectives corresponding to nouns in -pod and -poda: arthropodous.

Po·dunk (pō′dungk) n. Any small town regarded as dull and nonprogressive. [? after Podunk, Massachusetts]

po·em (pō′əm) n. 1. A composition in verse, characterized by the imaginative treatment of experience and a condensed use of language. 2. Any composition in verse. 3. Any composition or work of art characterized by intensity and beauty. [< F < L < Gk. poiein to make]

po·e·sy (pō′ə·sē, -zē) n. pl. **·sies** 1. Poetic Poetry taken collectively. 2. Poetic The art of writing poetry.

po·et (pō′it) n. 1. One who writes poems. 2. One esp. endowed with imagination and the creative faculty or power of artistic expression. — **po′et·ess** n.fem.

·et·as·ter (pō′it·as′tər) *n.* An inferior poet. [< NL]
·et·ic (pō·et′ik) *adj.* **1.** Of or pertaining to a poet or po-
·ry. **2.** Having the nature or quality of or expressed in
)etry: a *poetic* theme. **3.** Having or showing the sensibil-
y, feelings, faculty, etc., of a poet. Also **po·et′i·cal.**
etic justice The ideal distribution of rewards to the good
·d punishment to the evil as often represented in literature.
etic license The departure from fact or rigid rule for the
·ke of an artistic effect.
·et·ics (pō·et′iks) *n.pl.* (*usu.* construed as *sing.*) **1.** The
·ture, principles, and forms of poetry or, by extension, of
·y art. **2.** A treatise on poetry.
·et·ize (pō′it·īz) *v.t. & v.i.* **·ized, ·iz·ing** To write or ex-
·ess in poetry. — **po′et·iz′er** *n.*
·et laureate *pl.* **poets laureate 1.** In Great Britain, the
·icial poet of the realm, a member of the royal household
·arged with writing verses for particular occasions. **2.** A
)et acclaimed as the most eminent in a locality.
·et·ry (pō′it·rē) *n.* **1.** The art or craft of writing poems.
. Poems collectively. **3.** The quality, effect, or spirit of a
·em or of anything poetic. **4.** Something that is poetic.
·go stick (pō′gō) A stiltlike toy, with a spring at the base
·d fitted with two projections for the feet, on which a per-
·n may stand and propel himself in a series of hops.
·grom (pō′grəm, pō·grom′) *n.* An organized and often
·icially instigated local massacre, esp. one directed against
·e Jews. [< Russian, destruction]
·gy (pō′gē, pog′ē) *n.* *pl.* **·gies** or **·gy** The menhaden, a
·h. [< Algonquian *pauhagen*]
(poi, pō′ē) *n.* A native Hawaiian food made from the
·ot of the taro that is first cooked, ground to a paste, then
·rmented. [< Hawaiian]
·ietic *combining form* Making; producing; creating. [<
·k. *poiētikos* forming < *poieein* to make]
·gn·ant (poin′yənt, poin′nənt) *adj.* **1.** Painful and afflict-
·g to the feelings: *poignant* grief. **2.** Piercing, sharp, and
·tting: *poignant* sarcasm. **3.** Penetrating and apt: *poign-
·t* observations. [< OF, ppr. of *poindre* to prick] —
·ign′an·cy *n.* — **poign′ant·ly** *adv.*
·lu (pwȧ·lü′) *French adj.* Hairy. — *n.* A French sol-
·er, esp. of World War I.
·in·ci·a·na (poin/sē·a′nə, -än/ə) *n.* **1.** A tropical tree or
·rub of the bean family. **2.** A similar tree, the **royal
·inciana**, having bright orange and scarlet flowers. [< N
·after M. de *Poinci,* a 17th c. governor of the West Indies]
·in·set·ti·a (poin·set′ē·ə) *n.* Any of various American
·ants of the spurge family, having large, showy red bracts.
·fter J. R. *Poinsett,* 1779–1851, U.S. statesman]
·nt (point) *n.* **1.** The sharp, tapering end of a thing. **2.**
)mething sharp or tapering, as a needle or dagger. **3.** In
·inting or writing, a dot, mark, etc. **4.** Any mark of punc-
·ation, esp. a period. **5.** That which is conceived to have
·sition, but not parts, dimension, or extent, as the extrem-
·y of a line. **6.** A spot, place, or locality. **7.** A tapering
·act of land extending into water. **8.** A fixed place from
·hich position and distance are reckoned. **9.** A particular
·gree, state, or limit reached or determined: the boiling
·*int.* **10.** One of the 32 equal divisions that indicate direc-
·on on a mariner's compass card, each division equal to an
·gular distance of 11° 15′, reckoning from north at 0°. For
·ustration see COMPASS CARD. **11.** A particular moment of
·me: on the *point* of starting; at the *point* of death. **12.** The
·nportant or main purpose or aim: the whole *point* of the in-
·iiry. **13.** Advantage: What's the *point* of telling her? **14.**
·e main idea; gist: the *point* of the joke. **15.** An impor-
·nt, striking, or effective fact, idea, etc.: She has some good
·)ints in her argument. **16.** A tip, idea, or suggestion. **17.**
·ny single item or particular; detail. **18.** A prominent or
·stinguishing feature, attribute, or peculiarity. **19.** *pl.* The
·xtremities of an animal, as a horse. **20.** A spike or prong
·1 the antler of a deer. **21.** A unit, as in measuring, evalu-
·ing, rating, scoring, etc.: A touchdown equals six *points.*
2. In schools and colleges, a unit of credit equal to a certain
·imber of hours of academic work. **23.** *Printing* A unit of
·pe size, about ½2 of an inch. **24.** In commerce, one dollar,
·ed in quoting prices of stocks, etc.: Wheat fell four
·)ints. **25.** The attitude of a pointer or setter when it finds
·ame: The dog came to a *point.* **26.** *Electr.* **a** A contact or
·)nducting part for making or breaking a circuit, as in a dis-
··ibutor, relay, etc. **b** *Brit.* An outlet or socket. **27.** *Brit.*
·ilroads, a movable rail that tapers to a point, as in a switch.
8. *Mil.* The individual or group that goes ahead of an
·lvance guard. **29.** The act of pointing. **30.** *Electr.* An
·f a set of contacts determining the direction of current flow
· a circuit. — **at** (or **on, upon) the point of** On the verge
·t. — **beside the point** Irrelevant. — **in point** Pertinent.
·- **in point of** In the matter of; as regards. — **to make a
·oint of** To treat as vital or essential. — **to see the point**

To understand the purpose of a course of action; get the important meaning of a story, joke, etc. — **to stretch a point**
To make an exception. — **to the point** Relevant; apt. —
v.t. **1.** To direct or aim, as a finger or weapon. **2.** To indicate; direct attention to: often with *out:* to *point* the way; to
point out errors. **3.** *Chiefly U.S.* To give force or point to, as
a meaning or remark: often with *up.* **4.** To shape or sharpen
to a point. **5.** To punctuate, as writing. **6.** To mark or separate with points, as decimal fractions: with *off.* **7.** In hunting, to indicate the presence or location of (game) by standing rigid and directing the muzzle toward it: said of dogs **8.**
In masonry, to fill and finish the joints of (brickwork) with
mortar. — *v.i.* **9.** To call attention or indicate direction by
or as by extending the finger: usually with *at* or *to.* **10.** To
direct the mind: Everything *points* to your being wrong. **11.**
To be directed; have a specified direction; tend; face: with *to*
or *toward.* **12.** To point game: said of hunting dogs. **13.**
Med. To come to a head, as an abscess. **14.** *Naut.* To sail
close to the wind. [< OF *point* dot and *pointe* sharp tip]
point·blank (point′blangk′) *adj.* **1.** Aimed directly at the
mark; in gunnery, fired horizontally. **2.** Close enough to
aim directly at the mark: *pointblank* range. **3.** Direct; plain:
a *pointblank* question. — *n.* A shot with direct aim. —
adv. **1.** In a straight line; from close range. **2.** Directly;
without circumlocution. [? < F *de pointe en blanc* from a
point into the white (of a target)]
point·ed (poin′tid) *adj.* **1.** Having a point. **2.** Sharply
precise and cutting, as an epigram. **3.** Made clearly evident; emphasized. **4.** Directed or aimed, as at a particular
person. — **point′ed·ly** *adv.* — **point′ed·ness** *n.*
point·er (poin′tər) *n.* **1.** One who or that which points.
2. A hand, index finger, or other indicator, as on a clock or
scale. **3.** A long tapering rod used in classrooms to point out
things. **4.** One of a breed of smooth-haired dogs trained to
scent and point out game. **5.** *Informal* A hint; tip.
pointes (points) *n.pl.* In ballet, dancing on tiptoe. [< F]
poin·til·lism (pwan′tə·liz′əm) *n.* In painting, a method of
producing effects of light by placing small spots of varying
hues close together on a surface. [< F < *pointiller* to mark
with dots] — **point′til·list** *n.*
point lace Needlepoint (def. 2).
point·less (point′lis) *adj.* **1.** Having no point; blunt. **2.**
Having no relevance or meaning. **3.** Having no force; ineffective. **4.** Having no points scored. — **point′less·ly** *adv.*
— **point′less·ness** *n.*
point of honor Something that vitally affects one's honor.
point of no return That stage or position in any enterprise,
course, action, etc., beyond which there can be no return to
the starting point; a state of total commitment.
point of order A question as to whether or not the correct
parliamentary procedure is being observed.
point of view 1. The place or position from which one views
an object, situation etc. **2.** An attitude or viewpoint.
poise (poiz) *v.* **poised, pois·ing** *v.t.* **1.** To bring into or hold
in balance; maintain in equilibrium. **2.** To hold; support,
as in readiness. — *v.i.* **3.** To be balanced or suspended;
hover. — *n.* **1.** The state or quality of being balanced;
equilibrium. **2.** Repose and dignity of manner; self-possession. **3.** Physical ease or balance. **4.** Any condition of hov-
ering or suspended motion. **5.** Indecision; suspense. [<
OF < L *pendere* to weigh, suspend]
poi·son (poi′zən) *n.* **1.** Any substance that, either taken internally by or coming into contact with an organism, acts
chemically upon the tissues in such a way as to harm or destroy. **2.** Anything that tends to harm, destroy, or corrupt.
— *v.t.* **1.** To administer poison to; kill or injure with poison.
2. To put poison into or on. **3.** To corrupt; pervert: to *poison* one's mind. — *adj.* Poisonous. [< OF < L *potio, -onis*
drink, esp. a poisonous one] — **poi′son·er** *n.*
poison dogwood Poison sumac. Also **poison elder.**
poison ivy A climbing shrub related to sumac, having
glossy, variously notched, trifoliate leaves, greenish flowers,
whitish berries, and blistering poison.
poison oak 1. Any of various shrubs related to poison ivy
or poison sumac. **2.**
A species of poison
ivy common in the
western U.S.
poi·son·ous (poi′zən-
əs) *adj.* **1.** Containing or being a poison.
2. Having the effect
of a poison; toxic. —
poi′son·ous·ly *adv.* —
poi′son·ous·ness *n.*
poison sumac A
shrub or small tree
growing in swamps in

POISON IVY (*a*) AND
POISON SUMAC (*b*)

the U.S. and Canada, having smooth, entire leaflets, panicles of greenish yellow berries, and a strong poison.

poke[1] (pōk) v. **poked, pok·ing** v.t. 1. To push or prod, as with the elbow; jab. 2. To make by or as by thrusting. 3. To thrust or push in, out, through, from, etc.: to *poke* one's head from a window. 4. To stir (a fire, etc.) by prodding: often with *up*. — v.i. 5. To make thrusts, as with a stick: often with *at*. 6. To intrude or meddle. 7. To go or look curiously; pry. 8. To appear or show. 9. To proceed slowly; dawdle; putter: often with *along*. — **to poke one's nose into** To meddle in. — **to poke fun at** To ridicule, esp. slyly. — n. 1. A push; prod. 2. One who moves sluggishly; a dawdler. 3. *Informal* A punch. [< MLG *poken*]

poke[2] (pōk) n. A pocket or small bag. [< OF < Gmc.]

poke[3] (pōk) n. A large bonnet with projecting front or brim. Also **poke bonnet**. [Prob. < POKE[1]]

poke·ber·ry (pōk'ber'ē) n. pl. ·ries 1. A berry of the pokeweed. 2. The pokeweed plant.

pok·er[1] (pō'kər) n. 1. One who or that which pokes. 2. A metal rod for poking a fire.

po·ker[2] (pō'kər) n. Any of several games of cards in which the players bet on the value of the cards dealt to them, the winner being he whose hand contains the cards of highest value. [Cf. G *pochspiel*, lit., boast game < *pochen* to boast]

poker face *Informal* A face that reveals nothing: so called from the inscrutable faces of skillful poker players.

poke·weed (pōk'wēd') n. A stout perennial North American herb, having purple berries, edible shoots, and a medicinal root: also called *pokeberry*. Also **poke·root'** (-rōōt', -rōŏt'). [< Algonquian (Virginian) *pakon* weed used for staining < *pak* blood]

pok·y (pō'kē) adj. **pok·i·er, pok·i·est** *Informal* 1. Lacking briskness; dull; slow. 2. Shabby or dowdy, as dress. 3. Cramped; stuffy. Also **poke'y**.

Poland China An American mixed breed of large pigs.

po·lar (pō'lər) adj. 1. Of the poles of a sphere, magnet, etc. 2. Of, from, or near the North or South Pole. 3. Directly opposite in character, etc. 4. *Chem.* Exhibiting ionization. [< Med.L < Gk. *polos* pivot, pole]

polar bear A large, white bear of arctic regions.

Po·lar·is (pō·lar'is, -lâr'-) n. One of the 20 brightest stars, 2.12 magnitude; Alpha in the constellation Ursa Minor: also called *Cynosure, polestar, North Star*. [< L]

po·lar·i·scope (pō·lar'ə·skōp) n. An optical instrument for exhibiting or measuring the polarization of light, or for examining substances in polarized light.

po·lar·i·ty (pō·lar'ə·tē, -lâr'-) n. pl. ·ties 1. The quality or condition of having poles. 2. *Physics* The possession by a body of two poles, the properties at one pole being at opposite or contrasting nature to the properties at the other pole, as in a magnet. 3. The quality or condition of being attracted to one pole and repelled from the other. 4. The possession of two contrary qualities, tendencies, etc.

po·lar·i·za·tion (pō'lər·ə·zā'shən, -ī·zā'-) n. 1. The possession or bestowal of polarity. 2. *Physics* A condition of electromagnetic waves, most noticeable in light, in which one component of its oscillation is limited to a certain plane, as by transmission through variously oriented crystals or other suitable media. 3. *Electr.* A change in the potential of a cell due to the accumulation of liberated gases.

po·lar·ize (pō'lə·rīz) v. **·ized, ·iz·ing** v.t. 1. To develop polarization in; give polarity to. — v.i. 2. To acquire polarity. — **po'lar·iz'a·ble** adj. — **po'lar·iz'er** n.

Po·lar·oid (pō'lə·roid) n. A plastic capable of polarizing the light passing through: a trade name. Also **po'la·roid**.

Polar Regions The areas within the Arctic and Antarctic circles.

pole[1] (pōl) n. 1. Either of the two extremities of the axis of a sphere or any spheroidal body. 2. One of the two points where the earth's axis of rotation meets the surface, called the North *Pole* and the South *Pole*. 3. *Physics* One of the two points at which opposite qualities or forces are concentrated, as in a magnet. 4. Either of two diametrically opposite forces, tendencies, etc. — **to be poles apart** (or **asunder**) To differ greatly. [< OF < L < Gk. *polos* pivot, pole]

pole[2] (pōl) n. 1. A long, comparatively slender piece of wood or metal. 2. A unit of linear measure, usu. equal to 16.5 feet. 3. A unit of square measure equal to a square rod or 30.25 square yards. — v.t. & v.i. **poled, pol·ing** To propel or push (a boat, raft, etc.) with a pole. [OE < L *palus* stake]

Pole (pōl) n. A native or inhabitant of Poland.

pole·ax (pōl'aks') n. An ax, or a combined ax and pick, set on a long pole; a battle-ax. — v.t. To strike or fell with a poleax. Also **pole'axe'**. [ME *pol* poll + AX]

pole·cat (pōl'kat') n. 1. A European carnivore allied to the weasel, noted for its offensive odor. 2. *U.S.* A skunk. [< F *poule* pullet + CAT; from its predacity]

po·lem·ic (pō·lem'ik) n. 1. An argument or controversy; disputation. Also **po·lem'i·cal**. — n. 1. An argument or controversy. 2. One who engages in argument or controversy. [< Gk. < *polemos* war]

po·lem·ics (pō·lem'iks) n.pl. (*construed as sing.*) The art practice of disputation, esp., theological disputation. — p **lem'i·cist** (-ə·sist) n.

pole·star (pōl'stär') n. Polaris.

pole-vault (pōl'vōlt') v.i. To perform a pole vault. **pole'-vault'er** n.

pole vault An athletic event in which a vault or jump ov a high, horizontal bar is made with the help of a long po

po·lice (pə·lēs') n. 1. An official civil force or departme organized to maintain order, prevent and detect crime. a enforce law. 2. (*construed as pl.*) The members of such force. 3. In a community, the maintenance of order, la health, safety, etc. 4. In the U.S. Army: **a** The cleaning keeping clean of a camp or garrison. **b** A group of soldiers signed to some specific duty or duties: kitchen *police*. — ·**liced, ·lic·ing** 1. To protect, regulate, or maintain order (a city, etc.) with or as with police. 2. *U.S.* To make cle or orderly, as a military camp. [< MF < LL < Gk. < *lites* citizen < *polis* city]

police dog A German shepherd dog.

po·lice·man (pə·lēs'mən) n. pl. ·**men** (-mən) A mem of a police force.

police state A country whose citizens are rigidly supervis by a national police, often working secretly.

po·lice·wom·an (pə·lēs'wŏŏm'ən) n. pl. ·**wom·en** (-wir in) A woman member of a police force.

pol·i·clin·ic (pol'i·klin'ik) n. The department of a hospi in which outpatients are treated. Compare POLYCLINIC. G < Gk. *polis* city + *klinik* clinic]

pol·i·cy[1] (pol'ə·sē) n. pl. ·**cies** 1. Any plan of action, e in governmental or business administration: a nation's f eign *policy*. 2. Prudence, wisdom, or shrewdness, as in co duct or the management of one's affairs; also, any act or p based on such principles: It was his *policy* always to be sile [< OF < LL < Gk. *politeia* polity]

pol·i·cy[2] (pol'ə·sē) n. pl. ·**cies** A written contract of ins ance. [< MF < Ital. < Med.L < Gk. *apodeiknynai* to sh forth] — **pol'i·cy·hol'der** n.

po·li·o (pō'lē·ō) n. *Informal* Poliomyelitis.

polio- *combining form Med.* Of or pertaining to the g matter of the brain or the spinal cord. [< Gk. *polios* gr

pol·i·o·my·e·li·tis (pol'ē·ō·mī'ə·lī'tis, pō'lē-) n. *Pathol.* acute, infectious virus disease, occurring esp. in children, a characterized by inflammation of the gray matter of spinal cord, followed by paralysis and atrophy of vari muscle groups: also called *infantile paralysis*. [< NL Gk. *polios* gray + *myelos* marrow + -ITIS]

pol·ish (pol'ish) n. 1. Smoothness or glossiness of surfa 2. A substance used to produce a smooth or glossy surfa 3. Refinement or elegance. 4. The process of polishing. v.t. 1. To make smooth or lustrous, as by rubbing. 2. complete; perfect. 3. To free from crudity, etc. — v.i. To take a gloss. 5. To become elegant or refined. — **polish off** 1. To do or finish completely. 2. To dispose **to polish up** To improve. [< OF < L *polire* to smoo — **pol'ished** adj. — **pol'ish·er** n.

Po·lish (pō'lish) adj. Of or pertaining to Poland, its habitants, or their language. — n. The West Slavic l guage of the Poles.

Po·lit·bu·ro (pol'it·byŏŏr'ō) n. The leading committee the Communist party in the Soviet Union, replaced in 1 by the Presidium. [< Russian *polit(icheskoe) buro*]

po·lite (pə·līt') adj. ·**lit·er, ·lit·est** 1. Courteous; manne 2. Refined; cultured; polished: *polite* society. [< L *po* to polish] — **po·lite'ly** adv. — **po·lite'ness** n.

— **Syn.** 1. *Polite* implies punctilious observance of the fo of speech and action customary among well-bred persons. *Civ* weaker, implying little more than the avoidance of rudeness. *T courteous* is to be *polite* while having also a warmer regard for feelings and dignity of others. — **Ant.** impolite, rude, boorish

po·li·tesse (pō·lē·tes') n. *French* Politeness; civility.

pol·i·tic (pol'ə·tik) adj. 1. Skillful, ingenious, or shre 2. Crafty; sly; cunning. 3. Wise, prudent, or expedient *politic* move. 4. Political: see BODY POLITIC. [< OF < I Gk. *polites* citizen < *polis* city] — **pol'i·tic·ly** adv. — **Syn.** 1. diplomatic, discreet. 2. wily. 3. See EXPEDIENT

po·lit·i·cal (pə·lit'i·kəl) adj. 1. Of or concerned with g ernment. 2. Of, relating to, or involved in politics. Characteristic of or similar to politics or politicians. Having an organized system of government. [< L < *polites* citizen] — **po·lit'i·cal·ly** adv.

political economist A person skilled in political econom

political economy Economics.

political science The science of the form, principles, a conduct of civil government.

pol·i·ti·cian (pol'ə·tish'ən) n. 1. One who is engaged politics, esp. professionally. 2. One who engages in poli for personal or partisan aims. 3. One who is skilled in science of government or politics; a statesman.

po·lit·i·co (pə·lit'i·kō) n. pl. ·**cos** A politician. [< Sp. < *politicus*]

·tics (pol′ə·tiks) *n.pl.* (*Usu. construed as sing.*) **1.** The nce or art of government. **2.** The affairs or activities of e engaged in controlling or seeking to control a govern- t; also, the profession or area of activity of such persons. 'he principles, aims, or policies of a government. **4.** The or practices of those who seek any position of power or antage. **5.** Political opinions. [< OF < L < Gk. *politēs* en]

·ty (pol′ə·tē) *n.* *pl.* **·ties 1.** The form or method of ernment of a nation, state, church, etc. **2.** Any commu- living under some definite form of government. [< L < Gk. *politeia* polity]

κa (pōl′kə, pō′-) *n.* **1.** A lively round dance consisting ree quick steps and a hop. **2.** Music for this dance, in le meter. — *v.i.* **·kaed, ·ka·ing** To dance the polka. [< Czech *pulka* half step < *Polak* a Pole]

a dot 1. One of a series of round dots decorating a tex- fabric. **2.** A pattern or fabric made up of such dots.

(pōl) *n.* **1.** The voting at an election. **2.** The total iber of votes cast or registered. **3.** *pl.* The place where es are cast and counted. **4.** A survey of public opinion given subject, usu. obtained from a sample group. **5.** t of persons. **6.** The head, esp. the top or back of the d where hair grows. — *v.t.* **1.** To receive (a specified iber of votes). **2.** To enroll, as for taxation or voting; ster. **3.** To cast (a vote) at the polls. **4.** To canvass in ll (def. 4). **5.** To cut off or trim, as hair, horns, etc. **6.** ·ut off or trim the hair, horns, top, etc., of: to *poll* cattle. ·*i.* **7.** To vote at the polls; cast one's vote. [< MDu. · top of the head] — **poll′er** *n.*

·ack (pol′ək) *n.* A food fish of the North Atlantic: also led *pollock*. [< Scot. *podlok*]

·en (pol′ən) *n.* The male or fertilizing element in a seed t, consisting of fine yellowish powder formed within the ier of the stamen. [< L, fine flour]

·n count A measure of the relative concentration of en grains in the atmosphere at a given locality and date, ally expressed as the number of grains per cubic yard.

·nate (pol′ə·nāt) *v.t.* **·nat·ed, ·nat·ing** *Bot.* To supply onvey pollen to. Also **pol′len·ate.** — **pol′li·na′tion** *n.*

·wog (pol′ē·wog) *n.* A tadpole. Also **pol′ly·wog.** [ME *ygle*]

·ster (pōl′stər) *n.* One who takes polls. Also **poll′ist.**

·tax A tax on a person, as distinguished from that on erty, esp. as a prerequisite for voting.

·ute (pə·loōt′) *v.t.* **·lut·ed, ·lut·ing** To make unclean or ure; dirty; corrupt; profane. [< L < *polluere* to defile] **·ol·lut′er** *n.* — **pol·lu′tion** *n.*

·lux (pol′əks) In Greek mythology, the twin brother of tor. See CASTOR AND POLLUX. — *n.* One of the 20 htest stars, 1.21 magnitude; Beta in the constellation iini.

·ly·an·na (pol′ē·an′ə) *n.* One who persistently finds i in everything. [after stories by Eleanor H. Porter, 8–1920]

· (pō′lō) *n.* **1.** A hockeylike game played on horseback, with a light wooden ball and long-handled mallets. **2.** milar game played on ice, roller skates, in the water, etc. ob. < Tibetan *pulu* ball] — **po′lo·ist** *n.*

·naise (pol′ə·nāz′, pō′lə-) *n.* **1.** A stately, marchlike sh dance. **2.** Music for this dance, in triple meter. [< F *ise*) *polonaise* Polish (dance)]

·ni·um (pə·lō′nē·əm) *n.* A radioactive element (sym- Po) produced by the disintegration of various uranium erals, discovered in 1898 by Pierre and Marie Sklodow- Curie. See ELEMENT. [< NL < Med.L *Polonia* Poland]

·er·geist (pōl′tər·gīst) *n.* A ghost or spirit reputed to ke much noise. [< G, lit., noisy ghost]

·roon (pol·troōn′) *n.* A mean-spirited coward; craven; d. — *adj.* Cowardly; contemptible. [< F < Ital. *rone* coward < *poltro* colt] — **pol·troon′er·y** *n.*

· *combining form* **1.** Many; several; much: *polygamy.* Excessive; abnormal. [< Gk. *polys* much, many]

·an·dry (pol′ē·an′drē) *n.* The condition of having more n one husband at the same time. [< L < *poly-* many *ēr, andros* man, husband] — **pol′y·an′· drous** *adj.*

·y·cen·trism (pol′ē·sen′triz·əm) *n.* The existence of eral centers of power in the Communist world, as Peking Belgrade, where Moscow had formerly been the single disputed center. — **pol′y·cen′trist** *n. & adj.*

·yg·a·mous (pə·lig′ə·məs) *adj.* **1.** Of, pertaining to, cticing, or characterized by polygamy. **2.** *Bot.* Bearing sexual and bisexual or hermaphrodite flowers on the same nt. — **po·lyg′a·mous·ly** *adv.*

·yg·a·my (pə·lig′ə·mē) *n.* **1.** The condition or practice iaving more than one wife or husband at the same time.

2. *Zool.* The state of having more than one mate at the same time. [< F < LL < Gk. < *poly-* many + *gamos* marriage] — **po·lyg′a·mist** *n.*

pol·y·glot (pol′i·glot) *adj.* Expressed in several tongues or speaking several languages; multilingual. — *n.* **1.** A poly- glot book or person. **2.** A mixture of several languages. [< Gk. < *poly-* many + *glōtta* tongue] — **pol′y·glot′ism** *n.*

pol·y·gon (pol′i·gon) *n.* *Geom.* A closed, usu. plane, figure bounded by straight lines or arcs, esp. by more than four. [< L < Gk. < *poly-* many + *gōnia* angle] — **po·lyg·o·nal** (pə·lig′ə·nəl), **po·lyg′o·nous** *adj.* — **po·lyg′o·nal·ly** *adv.*

pol·y·graph (pol′i·graf, -gräf) *n.* **1.** A device for multiply- ing or reproducing a drawing or writing. **2.** A versatile or prolific author. **3.** An electrical device for simultaneously recording variations in the heartbeat, blood pressure, muscle reflexes, and respiratory movements, sometimes used as a lie detector. [< Gk. *polygraphos* writing much] — **pol′y· graph′ic** or **·i·cal** *adj.* — **po·lyg·ra·phy** (pə·lig′rə·fē) *n.*

po·lyg·y·ny (pə·lij′ə·nē) *n.* The condition of having more than one wife at the same time. [< POLY- + Gk. *gynē* woman] — **po·lyg′y·nous** (pə·lij′ə·nəs) *adj.*

pol·y·he·dron (pol′i·hē′drən) *n.* *pl.* **·dra** (-drə) or **·drons** *Geom.* A solid bounded by plane faces, esp. by more than four. [< NL < Gk. < *poly-* many + *hedra* base, side] — **pol′y·he′dral** *adj.*

Pol·y·hym·ni·a (pol′i·him′nē·ə) The Muse of sacred song. Also **Po·lym·ni·a** (pə·lim′nē·ə).

pol·y·mer (pol′i·mər) *n.* *Chem.* Any of two or more com- pounds formed by polymerization. [< Gk. *polymerēs* mani- fold < *poly-* many + *meros* part]

pol·y·mer·ic (pol′i·mer′ik) *adj.* *Chem.* Having the same chemical composition but different molecular weights and different properties, as acetylene and benzene.

po·lym·er·ism (pə·lim′ə·riz′əm, pol′i·mə-) *n.* *Chem.* The condition of being polymeric.

po·lym·er·i·za·tion (pə·lim′ər·ə·zā′shən, pol′i·mər·ə-) *n.* *Chem.* The process of changing the molecular arrangement of a compound so as to form new compounds having the same percentage composition as the original, but of greater molecular weight and different properties.

po·lym·er·ize (pə·lim′ə·rīz, pol′i·mə·rīz′) *v.t. & v.i.* **·ized, ·iz·ing** To subject to or undergo polymerization. Also *Brit.* **po·lym′er·ise.**

pol·y·morph (pol′i·môrf) *n.* A substance or organism that exhibits polymorphism. [< Gk. < *poly-* many + *morphē* form]

pol·y·morph·ism (pol′i·môr′fiz·əm) *n.* The property of having, assuming, or passing through several forms or char- acters. — **pol′y·mor′phic, pol′y·mor′phous** *adj.*

Pol·y·ne·sian (pol′i·nē′zhən, -shən) *n.* **1.** One of the native brown-skinned people of Polynesia. **2.** A subfamily of the Austronesian family of languages spoken by these people. — *adj.* Of or pertaining to Polynesia, its people, or their languages.

pol·y·nom·i·al (pol′i·nō′mē·əl) *adj.* Of, pertaining to, or consisting of many names or terms. — *n.* **1.** *Math.* An ex- pression, as in algebra, containing two or more terms. **2.** *Biol.* A scientific name consisting of more than two terms. [< POLY- + *-nomial*, as in BINOMIAL]

pol·yp (pol′ip) *n.* **1.** *Pathol.* **a** A smooth growth of hyper- trophied mucus found in mucous membrane, as in the nasal passages. **b** A tumor. **2.** *Zool.* **a** A single individual forming part of a colonial marine animal, esp. a hydrozoan. **b** A hy- dra. [< MF < L < Gk. < *poly-* many + *pou-* foot] — **pol′y·pous** *adj.*

pol·y·pet·al·ous (pol′i·pet′əl·əs) *adj.* *Bot.* Having the pet- als free and distinct. [< NL *polypetalus* < Gk. *poly-* many + *petalon* leaf]

pol·y·phase (pol′i·fāz) *adj.* *Electr.* Having or producing several phases, as an alternating current.

pol·y·phon·ic (pol′i·fon′ik) *adj.* **1.** Consisting of many sounds or voices. **2.** *Music* Designating or involving the simultaneous combination of two or more independent melodic parts. Also **po·lyph·o·nous** (pə·lif′ə·nəs). [< Gk. < *poly-* many + *phōnē* voice]

po·lyph·o·ny (pə·lif′ə·nē, pol′i·fō′nē) *n.* *pl.* **·nies 1.** Mul- tiplicity of sounds, as in an echo. **2.** The representation by one written character or sign of more than one sound. **3.** Polyphonic music.

pol·y·ploid (pol′i·ploid′) *adj.* *Genetics* Having more than twice the normal number of chromosomes. — *n.* An organ- ism with more than two chromosome sets.

pol·y·pod (pol′i·pod) *adj.* **1.** Having many feet. **2.** *Zool.* Pertaining to many-footed organisms. — *n.* A myriapod. [< POLY- + -POD]

pol·y·pus (pol′i·pəs) *n.* *pl.* **·pi** (-pī) *Pathol.* A polyp.

pol·y·syl·lab·ic (pol′i·si·lab′ik) *adj.* **1.** Having or pertain- ing to several syllables, esp. to more than three. **2.** Characterized by words of more than three syllables. Also **pol′y·syl·lab′i·cal.** [< MF < Med.L < Gk. < *poly-* many + *syllabē* syllable]

pol·y·syl·la·ble (pol′i·sil′ə·bəl) *n.* A polysyllabic word. — **pol′y·syl′la·bism** or **·syl·lab′i·cism** (pol′i·si·lab′ə·siz′əm) *n.*

pol·y·tech·nic (pol′i·tek′nik) *adj.* Embracing many arts: also **pol′y·tech′ni·cal.** — *n.* A school of applied science and the industrial arts. [< F < Gk. < *poly-* many + *technē* craft, art]

pol·y·the·ism (pol′i·thē·iz′əm) *n.* The belief in and worship of more gods than one. [< F < Gk. < *poly-* many + *theos* god] — **pol′y·the′ist** *n.* — **pol′y·the·is′tic** or **·is′ti·cal** *adj.*

pol·y·va·lent (pol′i·vā′lənt) *adj.* 1. *Bacteriol.* Designating a type of vaccine containing antibodies derived from two or more different strains of microorganisms. 2. *Chem.* Multivalent. — **pol′y·va′lence** *n.*

pom·ace (pum′is) *n.* 1. The pulpy substance of apples or similar fruit after grinding. 2. The pulpy substance of anything ground. [< Med.L *pomacium* cider < L *pomum* apple]

po·ma·ceous (pō·mā′shəs) *adj.* 1. Relating to or made of apples. 2. Of or pertaining to a pome.

po·made (pō·mād′, -mäd′) *n.* A perfumed dressing for the hair or scalp. — *v.t.* **·mad·ed, ·mad·ing** To anoint with pomade. [< MF < Ital. < L *pomum* apple]

pome (pōm) *n.* *Bot.* A fleshy fruit with a core, as an apple, quince, pear, or the like. [< OF, apple < L *pomum*]

pome·gran·ate (pom′gran·it, pum′-, pəm·gran′it) *n.* 1. The fruit of a tropical Asian and African tree about the size of an orange and having many seeds. 2. The tree itself. [< OF *pome* apple + *grenate* < L *granatum* seeded]

Pom·e·ra·ni·an (pom′ə·rā′nē·ən) *adj.* Relating to Pomerania or its inhabitants. — *n.* 1. A native or inhabitant of Pomerania. 2. One of a breed of small dog with pointed ears, a bushy tail, and long, straight, silky coat.

pom·mel (pum′əl, pom′-) *n.* 1. A knob, as on the hilt of a sword, bayonet, etc. 2. A knob at the front and on the top of a saddle. — *v.t.* **pom·meled** or **·melled, pom·mel·ing** or **·mel·ling** To beat with or as with the fists or a pommel. Also spelled *pummel.* [< OF *pomel* rounded knob]

po·mol·o·gy (pō·mol′ə·jē) *n.* The science that deals with fruits and fruit culture. [< NL < L *pomum* an apple, fruit + -LOGY] — **po·mo·log·i·cal** (pō′mə·loj′i·kəl) *adj.* — **po′·mo·log′i·cal·ly** *adv.* — **po·mol′o·gist** *n.*

pomp (pomp) *n.* 1. Magnificent or stately display; splendor. 2. Ostentatious display; vain show. [< OF < L < Gk. *pompē* a sending, procession]

pom·pa·dour (pom′pə·dôr, -dôr, -dōr) *n.* A style of arranging hair by puffing it over the forehead. [after the Marquise de *Pompadour,* 1721–64]

pom·pa·no (pom′pə·nō) *n.* *pl.* **·nos** Any of various spiny-finned food fishes of warm seas. [< Sp. *pámpano*]

pom·pon (pom′pon, *Fr.* pôṅ·pôṅ′) *n.* 1. A tuft or ball, as of wool, ribbon, etc., worn on hats, on costumes, etc. 2. A small, compact variety of chrysanthemum or dahlia. [< F]

pom·pos·i·ty (pom·pos′ə·tē) *n.* *pl.* **·ties** The state or quality of being pompous in manner or speech.

pom·pous (pom′pəs) *adj.* 1. Marked by exaggerated dignity or self-importance. 2. Bombastic and florid, as speech. 3. Full of pomp. [See POMP.] — **pom′pous·ness** *n.* — **pom′· pous·ly** *adv.*

pon·cho (pon′chō) *n.* *pl.* **·chos** 1. A South American cloak like a blanket with a hole in the middle for the head. 2. A similar waterproofed garment, used as a raincoat. [< Sp.]

pond (pond) *n.* A body of still water, smaller than a lake. [ME *ponde,* var. of POUND²]

pon·der (pon′dər) *v.t.* 1. To weigh in the mind; consider carefully. — *v.i.* 1. To meditate; reflect. [< OF < L *ponderare* to weigh] — **pon′der·er** *n.*

pon·der·a·ble (pon′dər·ə·bəl) *adj.* Capable of being weighed; having appreciable weight. — **pon′der·a·bil′i·ty** *n.*

pon·der·ous (pon′dər·əs) *adj.* 1. Having great weight; also, huge; bulky. 2. Heavy to the extent of dullness; lumbering. [< F < L < *pondus, ponderis* weight] — **pon′der·os′i·ty** (-də·ros′ə·tē), **pon′der·ous·ness** *n.* — **pon′der·ous·ly** *adv.*

pond lily Any of various plants of the water-lily family.

pond scum Any of a group of free-floating, fresh-water green algae that form a scum on ponds.

pond·weed (pond′wēd′) *n.* Any of various perennial aquatic plants that grow in ponds and streams.

pone (pōn) *n.* *Southern U.S.* Corn pone.

pon·gee (pon·jē′) *n.* A thin, natural, unbleached silk with a rough weave, originally made in China from wild silk-worms. [? < Chinese *pen chi* home loom]

pon·iard (pon′yərd) *n.* A dagger. — *v.t.* To stab with a poniard. [< MF < OF *poing* fist < L *pugnus*]

pons (ponz) *n.* *pl.* **pon·tes** (pon′tēz) 1. A bridge: used in Latin phrases. 2. The pons Varolii. [< L]

pons Va·ro·li·i (ponz və·rō′lē·ī) *Anat.* A broad band of nerve fibers that connect the cerebrum, cerebellum, and medulla oblongata. [< NL, bridge of Varoli; after Costanzo *Varoli,* 1543?–75, Italian anatomist]

pon·ti·fex (pon′tə·feks) *n.* *pl.* **pon·tif·i·ces** (pon·tif′ə- In ancient Rome, a priest belonging to the Pontifical Co [< L *pons, pontis* bridge + *facere* to make]

pon·tiff (pon′tif) *n.* 1. In the Roman Catholic Churc The Pope. b Any bishop. 2. In ancient Rome, a pon [< MF *pontife* < L *pontifex* pontifex] — **pon·tif′ic a**

pon·tif·i·cal (pon·tif′i·kəl) *adj.* 1. Of, pertaining t suitable for a pope or bishop. 2. Haughty; pompous; matic. — **pon·tif′i·cal·ly** *adv.*

Pontifical College In ancient Rome, the highest pri group that had supreme jurisdiction in religious matte

pon·tif·i·cate (*n.* pon·tif′ə·kit, -kāt′; *v.* -kāt′) *v.i.* **·ca ·cat·ing** 1. To act or speak pompously or dogmatically To perform the office of a pontiff. — *n.* The office or of a pontiff.

pon·ton (pon′tən) *n.* *U.S. Mil.* A pontoon.

pon·toon (pon·tōōn′) *n.* 1. *Mil.* A flat-bottomed boat tight metal cylinder, or the like, used in the constructi temporary floating bridges over rivers. 2. A pontoon br 3. Either of the floats on the landing gear of a seaplane. MF < L *pons, pontis* bridge]

pontoon bridge A bridge supported on pontoons. **ponton bridge.**

po·ny (pō′nē) *n.* *pl.* **·nies** 1. A breed of very small h esp. one not over 14 hands high. 2. Any small horse. *U.S. Slang* A translation used to prepare foreign lang lessons: also called *trot.* 4. Anything that is small fo kind. 5. *Informal* A very small glass for liquor o contents. — *v.t.* & *v.i.* **·nied, ·ny·ing** *U.S. Slang* 1 translate lessons with the aid of a pony. 2. To pay (mo that is due: with *up.* [< dial. E (Scottish) *powney*]

pony express A former postal system by which mai relayed by riders mounted on swift ponies.

pooch (pōōch) *n.* *Slang* A dog; esp., a small mongrel. dial. E and obs. *pooch,* var. of POUCH]

poo·dle (pōōd′l) *n.* One of a breed of dogs of high in gence, with long, curly, usu. white or black hair. [*pudel* < *pudeln* to splash in water]

pooh (pōō) *interj.* An exclamation of contempt, disdain

Pooh-Bah (pōō′bä′) *n.* *Informal* A pretentious, pom official. [after a character in Gilbert and Sullivan's *Mikado*]

pooh-pooh (pōō′pōō′) *v.t.* To reject or speak of dis fully. [Reduplication of POOH]

pool¹ (pōōl) *n.* 1. A small body of fresh water, as a sp 2. A deep place in a stream. 3. Any small, isolated bo liquid: a pool of blood. 4. A swimming pool. [OE p

pool² (pōōl) *n.* 1. In certain gambling games, a colle stake. 2. In business, a combination whereby comp agree to fix prices in order to overcome competition. finance, any combination formed for a speculative opera as in stocks. 4. Any combining of efforts or resourc typists' *pool.* 5. Any of various games played on a pocket billiard table: also *pocket billiards.* See BILLIA — *v.t.* 1. To combine in a mutual fund or pool. — *v.* To form a pool. [< F < L *pulla* stake]

pool·room (pōōl′rōōm′, -rōōm′) *n.* A commercial estab ment or room equipped for the playing of pool, billiards

pool table A six-pocket billiard table for playing pool.

poop¹ (pōōp) *Naut.* *n.* 1. The after part or stern of a 2. A short deck built over the main deck at the stern ship: also *poop deck.* — *v.t.* 1. To break over the ste poop of: said of a wave. 2. To take (a wave) over the s [< OF < OProvençal < L *puppis*]

poop² (pōōp) *U.S. Slang* *v.t.* To tire: usu. in the passive was *pooped* by the long climb. [Origin unknown]

poor (pōōr) *adj.* 1. Lacking means of comfortable sub ence; needy. 2. Characterized by poverty: a *poor* neigh hood. 3. Lacking in abundance; scanty; meager: a crop. 4. Lacking in fertility; sterile: *poor* soil. 5. Inf in workmanship or quality. 6. Feeble; frail: *poor* he 7. Thin from bad feeding; lean, as cattle. 8. Contempt mean. 9. Lacking proper ability; unsatisfactory. 10. serving of pity. — *n.* Indigent or needy people collecti preceded by *the.* [< OF < L *pauper* poor] — **poor′ly** & *adj.* — **poor′ness** *n.*

poor·house (pōōr′hous′) *n.* A public establishment m tained as a dwelling for paupers.

poor-spir·it·ed (pōōr′spir′it·ed) *adj.* Having little spir courage. — **Syn.** See COWARDLY. — **poor′-spir′it·ed·ne**

poor white In the southern U.S., a member of a cla poverty-stricken white farmers or laborers: an offe term. Also **poor white trash.**

pop¹ (pop) *v.* **popped, pop·ping** *v.i.* 1. To make a sharp plosive sound. 2. To burst open or explode with su sound. 3. To move or go suddenly or quickly: with *in* etc. 4. To bulge: His eyes *popped.* — *v.t.* 5. To caus burst or explode, as kernels of corn. 6. To thrust or suddenly: with *in, out,* etc. 7. To fire (a gun, etc.). shoot. — **to pop the question** *Informal* To make a pro of marriage. — *n.* 1. A sharp, explosive noise. 2.

th a firearm. **3.** Soda (def. 2). —*adv.* **1.** Like, or with e sound of a pop. **2.** Suddenly. [Imit.]

²(pop) *n. Slang* **1.** Papa. **2.** A familiar term of address for an old man. [Short for *poppa*, var. of PAPA]

³(pop) *n.* A concert of popular or light classical music. —*adj.* Featuring popular or light classical music: a *pop* ncert; a *pop* orchestra. Also **pops.** [Short for POPULAR]

art *Sometimes cap.* A style of art of the 1960's influced by popular commercial art.

•corn (pop'kôrn') *n.* A variety of maize, the kernels of nich explode when heated, forming large white balls; also, e corn after popping, eaten as a confection.

e (pōp) *n. Often cap.* In the Roman Catholic Church, the shop of Rome and the head of the Church. [OE < LL < Jk. < Gk. *pappas* father] —**pope'dom** *n.*

•er·y (pō'par·ē) *n.* The practices, doctrines, etc., of the oman Catholic Church: an offensive term.

•eyed (pop'īd') *adj.* **1.** Having bulging or protruding es. **2.** Filled with astonishment; amazed.

•gun (pop'gun') *n.* A child's toy gun that expels a pellet th a popping sound by compressed air.

•in·jay (pop'in·jā) *n.* A pretentious, conceited person. [< OF *papegai* < Sp. < Arabic *babaghā*]

•ish (pō'pish) *adj.* Pertaining to popes or popery: an fensive term. —**pop'ish·ly** *adv.* —**pop'ish·ness** *n.*

•lar (pop'lar) *n.* **1.** Any of a genus of dioecious trees and ashes of the willow family. **2.** The wood of any of these es. [< OF < L *populus*]

•lin (pop'lin) *n.* A durable silk, cotton, or rayon fabric th a ribbed surface, used for dresses, etc. [< F < Ital. *palina* papal; because made in Avignon, a papal residence]

•o·ver (pop'ō'vər) *n.* A very light egg muffin.

•per (pop'ər) *n.* **1.** One who or that which pops. **2.** A ntainer or device for popping corn.

•pet valve (pop'it) *Mech.* A valve that rises and falls rpendicularly, used in gasoline engines.

•py (pop'ē) *n. pl.* **·pies 1.** Any of various plants having bed or toothed leaves and showy red, violet, orange, or nite flowers, as the **opium poppy. 2.** A medicinal extract, opium, from such a plant. **3.** The bright scarlet color of rtain poppy blossoms: also **poppy red.** [OE < L *papaver*]

•py·cock (pop'ē·kok) *n. Informal* Pretentious talk; mbug; nonsense. [< Dial. Du. *pappekak*, lit., soft dung]

•py seed The small, black seed of the poppy plant used flavor and top rolls, bread, etc.

•u·lace (pop'yə·lis) *n.* The common people; the masses. [< MF < Ital. < L *populus* people]

•u·lar (pop'yə·lər) *adj.* **1.** Approved of, admired, or ked by most people: *popular* music. **2.** Having many ends. **3.** Of, pertaining to, or engaged in by the people at rge: *popular* government. **4.** Suited to the intelligence of dinary people. **5.** Prevalent among the people in general. Suited to the means of the people: *popular* prices [< L *pularis* of the people] —**pop'u·lar·ly** *adv.*

pular front A coalition of leftist, labor, and liberal parties formed to combat fascism and promote reform.

•u·lar·i·ty (pop'yə·lar'ə·tē) *n.* The condition of being pular. [See POPULAR.]

•u·lar·ize (pop'yə·lə·rīz') *v.t.* **·ized, ·iz·ing** To make pular. Also *Brit.* **pop'u·lar·ise'.** —**pop'u·lar·i·za'tion** *n.* —**pop'u·lar·iz·er** *n.*

•u·late (pop'yə·lāt) *v.t.* **·lat·ed, ·lat·ing 1.** To furnish th inhabitants, as by colonization; people. **2.** To inhabit. [< Med.L < L *populus* the people]

•u·la·tion (pop'yə·lā'shən) *n.* **1.** The total number of rsons living in a country, city, or other specified area. **2.** he total number of persons of a particular group, class, ce, etc., residing in a place. **3.** The act or process of populating or furnishing with inhabitants. **4.** *Stat.* A group of ems or individuals. [< LL < L *populus* the people]

•u·list (pop'yə·list) *adj.* Of or pertaining to the Populist or People's Party. —*n.* A member of the People's arty. —**Pop'u·lism** *n.* —**Pop'u·lis'tic** *adj.*

pulist Party People's Party.

•u·lous (pop'yə·ləs) *adj.* Containing many inhabitants; ickly settled. —**pop'u·lous·ly** *adv.* —**pop'u·lous·ness** *n.*

rce·lain (pôrs'lin, pōrs'-, pôr'sə-, pōr'-) *n.* **1.** A white, rd, translucent ceramic ware, usu. glazed; chinaware. **2.** n object made of this material. [< MF < Ital. *porcellana* ell < L *porcella*, dim. fem. of *porcus* pig] —**por·ce·la·ne· us** (pôr'sə·lā'nē·əs, por'-) or **por'cel·la'ne·ous** *adj.*

rch (pôrch, pōrch) *n.* **1.** A covered structure or recessed ace at the entrance to a building; a stoop. **2.** *U.S.* A randa. **3.** A covered walk or portico. [< OF < L *porti- s* colonnade < *porta* gate]

r·cine (pôr'sīn, -sin) *adj.* **1.** Of, pertaining to, or characteristic of swine. **2.** Swinish; hoggish; piggish. [< F, fem. *porcin* < L < *porcus* pig]

por·cu·pine (pôr'kyə·pīn) *n.* Any of various large, clumsy rodents covered with erectile spines or quills used for defense: also, *U.S.* **hedgehog.** [< OF < OProvençal < It. < L *porcus* pig + *spina* thorn]

pore¹ (pôr, pōr) *v.i.* **pored, por·ing 1.** To gaze steadily or intently. **2.** To study or read with care and application: with *over: to pore over* one's accounts. **3.** To meditate; ponder: with *on, over,* or *upon.* [ME *pouren*]

pore² (pôr, pōr) *n.* **1.** A minute orifice or opening, as in the skin or a leaf, serving as an outlet for perspiration or as a means of absorption. **2.** Any similar opening, as in rock. [< OF < L < Gk. *poros* pore, passage]

por·gy (pôr'gē) *n. pl.* **·gies** or **·gy 1.** Any of various saltwater food fishes, esp. the **red porgy** of Mediterranean and European waters. **2.** Any of various related fishes, as the scup. [Origin uncertain]

pork (pôrk, pōrk) *n.* **1.** The flesh of swine used as food. **2.** *U.S. Slang* Government money, favors, etc., obtained through political patronage. [< OF < L *porcus* pig]

pork barrel *U.S. Slang* A Federal appropriation for some local enterprise that will favorably impress a representative's constituents.

pork·er (pôr'kər, pōr'-) *n.* A pig or hog, esp. one fattened for slaughter.

pork·pie (pôrk'pī, pōrk'-) *n.* **1.** A pie filled with chopped pork and having a thick crust. **2.** A man's hat with a low, flat crown. Also **pork pie.**

pork·y (pôr'kē, pōr'-) *adj.* **pork·i·er, pork·i·est 1.** Of or like pork. **2.** Obese; fat, as from overeating.

por·nog·ra·phy (pôr·nog'rə·fē) *n. pl.* **·phies** Obscene literature or art. [< Gk. < *pornē* prostitute + *graphein* to write] —**por·no·graph·ic** (pôr'nə·graf'ik) *adj.*

po·ros·i·ty (pô·ros'ə·tē, pō-) *n. pl.* **·ties 1.** The property of being porous; porousness. **2.** A porous part or structure.

po·rous (pôr'əs, pōr'əs) *adj.* **1.** Having pores. **2.** Permeable by fluids or light. —**po'rous·ly** *adv.* —**po'rous·ness** *n.*

por·phy·ry (pôr'fə·rē) *n. pl.* **·ries** An igneous rock that has a groundmass enclosing crystals of feldspar or quartz. [< OF < Med.L < Gk. *porphyros* purple]

por·poise (pôr'pəs) *n. pl.* **·pois·es** or **·poise 1.** A dolphinlike animal with a blunt, rounded snout; esp., the **harbor porpoise** of the North Atlantic and Pacific, blackish above and white below. **2.** Loosely, any small cetacean, as the common dolphin. [< OF < L *porcus pisces,* lit., hog fish]

PORPOISE (def. 1)
(To 6 feet long)

por·ridge (pôr'ij, por-) *n.* **Chiefly Brit.** A soft food made by boiling oatmeal or other meal in water or milk until thickened. **2.** Originally, pottage. [Alter. of POTTAGE]

por·rin·ger (pôr'in·jər, por'-) *n.* A small, relatively shallow bowl for porridge or soup; esp., such a bowl used by small children. [Earlier *pottanger* < MF *potager* soup bowl]

port¹ (pôrt, pōrt) *n.* **1.** A city or place of customary entry and exit of ships, esp. for commerce. **2.** A harbor or haven. **3.** *Law* A port of entry. [OE < L *portus* harbor]

port² (pôrt, pōrt) *Naut. n.* The left side of a vessel as one faces the front or bow: formerly called *larboard:* opposed to *starboard.* —*v.t. & v.i.* To put or turn to the port or larboard side. —*adj.* Left: *port* side. [Prob. < PORT¹]

port³ (pôrt, pōrt) *n.* **1.** *Naut.* **a** A porthole. **b** A covering for a porthole. **2.** *Mech.* An orifice for the passage of air, gas, etc.: a steam *port.* [Prob. < OF < L *porta* gate, door]

port⁴ (pôrt, pōrt) *n.* A variety of sweet wine, usu. dark red. [Short for *Oporto* wine, after *Oporto,* Portugal]

port⁵ (pôrt, pōrt) *v.t. Mil.* To carry (a rifle, saber, etc.) diagonally across the body and sloping to the left shoulder. —*n.* **1.** *Mil.* The position of a rifle or other weapon when ported. **2.** The way in which one bears or carries himself. [< MF < L *portare* to carry]

port·a·ble (pôr'tə·bəl, pōr'-) *adj.* That can be readily carried or moved. —*n.* Something portable, as a typewriter or radio. [< MF < LL < L *portare* to carry] —**port'a·bil'i·ty, port'a·ble·ness** *n.* —**port'a·bly** *adv.*

port·age (pôr'tij, pōr'-) *n.* *U.S. & Canadian* **1.** The act of transporting (canoes, boats, and goods) from one navigable water to another; also, that which is transported. **2.** The route over which and the place where such transportation is made. **3.** The charge for transportation.

por·tal (pôr'təl, pōr'-) *n.* **1.** *Often pl.* An entrance, door, or gate, esp. one that is grand and imposing. **2.** The portal vein. —*adj.* Pertaining to the portal vein. [< MF < Med.L, ult. < L *porta* gate]

por·ta·tive (pôr'tə·tiv, pōr'-) *adj.* **1.** Of or pertaining to carrying; capable of carrying. **2.** Portable. [< OF < L *portatus,* pp. of *portare* to carry]

port authority Any official body having charge of the ordination of all rail and water traffic of a port.

port·cul·lis (pôrt·kul′is, pōrt-) *n.* A grating made of strong bars of wood or iron that can be let down suddenly to close the gateway of a fortified place. [< OF < *porte* gate + fem. of *coleis,* pp. of *couler* to slide]

Porte (pôrt, pōrt) *n.* The former Ottoman Turkish government: with *the.* [< F (*la Sublime*) *Porte* (the High) Gate, trans. of Turkish *Babi Ali*]

porte-co·chère (pôrt′kō·shâr′, pōrt′-; *Fr.* pôrt·kô·shâr′) *n.* **1.** A large covered gateway for vehicles, leading into a courtyard. **2.** A porch over a driveway at the entrance of a building for sheltering persons entering or leaving vehicles. [< F < *porte* gate + *cochère,* fem. adj. < *coche* coach]

por·tend (pôr·tend′, pōr-) *v.t.* To warn of as an omen; forebode. [< L < *pro-* forth + *tendere* to stretch]

por·tent (pôr′tent, pōr′-) *n.* **1.** An indication or sign of what is to happen, esp. of something momentous or calamitous. **2.** Ominous significance. **3.** A prodigy; marvel.

por·ten·tous (pôr·ten′təs, pōr-) *adj.* **1.** Having the nature of a portent; foreboding. **2.** Causing astonishment or awe; extraordinary. **— por·ten′tous·ly** *adv.* **— por·ten′tous·ness** *n.*

por·ter¹ (pôr′tər, pōr′-) *n.* **1.** One who carries travelers' luggage, etc., for hire, as at a railroad station. **2.** *U.S.* An attendant in a Pullman car. [< OF < LL *portator* to carry]

por·ter² (pôr′tər, pōr′-) *n.* A keeper of a door or gate; janitor. [< OF < LL < L *porta* gate, door]

por·ter³ (pôr′tər, pōr′-) *n.* A dark brown, heavy, English liquor resembling ale, formerly drunk chiefly by porters.

por·ter·house (pôr′tər·hous′, pōr′-) *n.* **1.** A place where porter, ale, etc., are retailed. **2.** A restaurant; chophouse. **3.** A choice cut of beefsteak including a part of the tenderloin, usu. next to the sirloin: also **porterhouse steak.**

port·fo·li·o (pôrt·fō′lē·ō, pōrt-) *n. pl.* **·li·os 1.** A portable case for holding drawings, papers, etc. **2.** Such a case for carrying documents of a department of state. **3.** The office of a minister of state or a cabinet member. **4.** An itemized list of investments, securities, etc., of a bank or investor. [< Ital. < L *portare* to carry + *folium* leaf, sheet of paper]

port·hole (pôrt′hōl′, pōrt′-) *n.* **1.** A small opening in a ship's side for admitting light and air, for shooting a weapon through, or for loading cargo. **2.** A loophole in the wall of a fort for shooting through; embrasure. **3.** An opening into a furnace, engine, or the like, shaped like a porthole.

por·ti·co (pôr′ti·kō, pōr′-) *n. pl.* **·coes** or **·cos** An open space or ambulatory with roof upheld by columns; a porch. [< Ital. < L *porticus* < *porta* door] **— por′ti·coed** *adj.*

por·tière (pôr·tyâr′, pōr-; *Fr.* pôr·tyâr′) *n.* A curtain for a doorway, used instead of a door. Also **por·tiere′.** [< F]

por·tion (pôr′shən, pōr′-) *n.* **1.** A part of a whole, whether separated from it or not. **2.** An allotment or share. **3.** The quantity of food usu. served to one person. **4.** The part of an estate coming to an heir or next of kin. **5.** A dowry (def. 1). **— v.t. 1.** To divide into shares for distribution; parcel: usu. with *out.* **2.** To give a dowry or inheritance to. **3.** To assign; allot. [< OF < L *portio, -onis*] **— por′tion·a·ble** *adj.* **— por′tion·less** *adj.*

— Syn. (noun) **1.** *Portion, fraction,* and *section* denote a part of a whole. A *portion* was originally an alloted share, and so suggests a measured quantity: to devote a *portion* of one's time to study. A *fraction,* originally a very small part, now denotes a part taken away: the first *fraction* in the distillation of petroleum. Unlike the other synonyms, *fraction* has little or no suggestion of measurement. A *section* is the part lying between two cuts; hence, any clearly demarcated part: a *section* of a book.

por·tion·er (pôr′shən·ər, pōr′-) *n.* One who divides in shares or holds a share or shares.

port·ly (pôrt′lē, pōrt′-) *adj.* **·li·er, ·li·est 1.** Somewhat corpulent; stout. **2.** Having a stately appearance and carriage; impressive. [< PORT⁵ + -LY] **— port′li·ness** *n.*

port·man·teau (pôrt·man′tō, pōrt-) *n. pl.* **·teaus** or **·teaux** (-tōz) *Chiefly Brit.* A large, leather suitcase hinged at the back to form two distinct compartments. [< MF < *porter* to carry + *manteau* coat < L *mantellum*]

port of call A port where vessels put in for supplies, repairs, discharge or taking on of cargo, etc.

port of entry *Law* A place, whether on the coast or inland, designated as a point at which persons or merchandise may enter or pass out of a country: also called *port.*

por·trait (pôr′trit, pōr′-, -trāt) *n.* **1.** A likeness of a person, esp. of the face, produced, usu. from life, by an artist or photographer. **2.** A vivid word description, esp. of a person. [See PORTRAY.] **— por′trait·ist** *n.*

por·trai·ture (pôr′tri·chər, pōr′-) *n.* **1.** The art or practice of making portraits. **2.** A portrait. **3.** Portraits collectively.

por·tray (pôr·trā′, pōr-) *v.t.* **1.** To represent by drawing, painting, etc. **2.** To describe or depict in words. **3.** To represent, as in a play; act. [< OF < Med.L < L *pro-* forward + *trahere* to draw] **— por·tray′a·ble** *adj.* **— por·tray′al** *n.* **— por·tray′er** *n.*

por·tress (pôr′tris, pōr′-) *n.* A woman porter or doorkeeper. Also **por·ter·ess** (pôr′tris, -tər·is, pōr′-).

Por·tu·guese (pôr′chə·gēz′, -gēs′, pōr′-) *adj.* Pertaining to Portugal, its inhabitants, or their language. **— n. 1.** A tive or inhabitant of Portugal. **2.** The people of Portu **3.** The Romance language of Portugal and Brazil.

Portuguese man-of-war Any of several large ma organisms, having long, stinging tentacles hanging d from a bladderlike float.

pose¹ (pōz) *n.* **1.** The position of the whole or part of body, esp. such a position assumed for or represented by artist or photographer. **2.** A mental attitude adopted effect. **— v. posed, pos·ing** *v.i.* **1.** To assume or hold attitude or position, as for a portrait. **2.** To affect me attitudes. **3.** To represent oneself: to *pose* as an exp **— v.t. 4.** To cause to assume an attitude or position, as artist's model. **5.** To state or propound; put forward a question, etc. [< OF, fusion of LL *pausare* to place < L pause and *pos-,* stem of L *ponere* to put]

pose² (pōz) *v.t.* **posed, pos·ing** To puzzle or confuse asking a difficult question. [< obs. *appose,* var. of OPPO

Po·sei·don (pō·sī′dən) In Greek mythology, brother of Z god of the sea and of horses: identified with the Ro *Neptune.* **— Po′sei·do′ni·an** (-dō′nē·ən) *adj.*

pos·er¹ (pō′zər) *n.* One who poses. [< POSE¹, v.]

pos·er² (pō′zər) *n.* A question that baffles. [< POSE²]

po·seur (pō·zœr′) *n.* One who affects a particular attit to make an impression on others. [< F < *poser* to pose]

pos·it (poz′it) *v.t.* **1.** To put in position; place. **2.** To down or assume as a fact or basis of argument; postul [< L *positus,* pp. of *ponere* to place]

po·si·tion (pə·zish′ən) *n.* **1.** The manner in which a th is placed. **2.** Disposition of the body or parts of the bo **3.** The locality or place occupied by a person or thing. *Med.* The placement or arrangement of the body of a pati in order to facilitate therapeutic, surgical, or obstetr procedures. **5.** The proper or appropriate place: in *positi* **6.** State or situation in relation to other conditions: to in a false *position.* **7.** An attitude or point of view; sta **8.** Relative social standing; status; also, high social sta ing. **9.** Employment; job. **10.** In sports, the assignm of an area covered by a particular player. **— to be i position** To have the means or opportunity to. **— v.t.** place in a particular or appropriate position. [< OF < *ponere* to place] **— po·si′tion·al** *adj.*

— Syn. (noun) **1.** See PLACE. **9.** office, post, situation.

pos·i·tive (poz′ə·tiv) *adj.* **1.** That is or may be directly firmed; actual. **2.** Expressing, containing, or characteri by affirmation: a *positive* attitude. **3.** Inherent in a th by and of itself, regardless of its relations to other thir **4.** Openly and plainly expressed: a *positive* denial. **5.** perative. **6.** Not admitting of doubt or denial. **7.** Not one of two opposite directions, qualities, properties, e which is taken as primary, or as indicating increase or p gression. **8.** *Math.* Greater than zero; plus: said of qu tities and usu. denoted by the sign (+). **9.** *Med.* Denot the presence of a specific condition or organism: a *posi* Wasserman reaction. **10.** *Photog.* Having the lights a darks in their original relation, as in a print made from negative. **11.** *Biol.* Noting the response of an organ toward a stimulus: a *positive* tropism. **12.** *Electr.* Hav the kind of electricity exhibited by a glass object wl rubbed with silk; characterized by a deficiency of electr on a charged body. **13.** *Chem.* Basic. **14.** *Gram.* Denot the simple, uncompared degree of the adjective or adve **15.** *Stat.* Designating a correlation in which the values two variables tend to increase or decrease together: a *direct.* **— n. 1.** That which is positive or capable of be directly or certainly affirmed. **2.** *Math.* A positive sym or quantity. **3.** *Electr.* A positive pole, terminal, etc. *Photog.* A positive picture or print. **5.** *Gram.* The posit degree of an adjective or adverb; also, a word in this degr [< OF, fem. of *positif* < L < *ponere* to place] **— pos′i·ti ly** *adv.* **— pos′i·tive·ness** *n.*

pos·i·tiv·ism (poz′ə·tiv·iz′əm) *n.* **1.** A way of thinking t regards nothing as ascertained or ascertainable beyond facts of physical science or of sense. **2.** *Philos.* A system philosophy elaborated by Auguste Comte, holding that m can have no knowledge of anything but actual phenome and facts and their interrelations. **3.** Certitude, or claim of certitude, in knowledge. **— pos′i·tiv·ist** *n.* **— po i·tiv·is′tic** *adj.*

pos·i·tron (poz′ə·tron) *n. Physics* The positive counterp of an electron.

pos·se (pos′ē) *n.* **1.** A posse comitatus. **2.** A force men; squad. [< Med.L, armed force < L, to be able]

pos·se com·i·ta·tus (pos′ē kom′ə·tā′təs) The body of m that a sheriff or other peace officer calls or may call to his sistance in the discharge of his official duty, as to quell a ri [< Med.L < *posse* power + *comitatus* county]

pos·sess (pə·zes′) *v.t.* **1.** To have as property; own. **2.** have as a quality, attribute, etc. **3.** To enter and take control over; dominate: often used passively: The id *possessed* him. **4.** To maintain control over (oneself, on d, etc.). **5.** To put in possession, as of property, news, with *of*. **6.** To have knowledge of; gain mastery of, language. **7.** To imbue or impress, as with wonder or dea: with *with*. **8.** To have sexual intercourse with. F < L < *potis* master + *sedere* to sit (as)]

·essed (pə·zest′) *adj*. **1.** Having; owning: *possessed* of ady tongue. **2.** Calm; cool: to be *possessed* in time of ger. **3.** Controlled by or as if by evil spirits; beyond self-rol; frenzied.

·es·sion (pə·zesh′ən) *n*. **1.** The act or fact of possess- **2.** The state of being possessed. **3.** That which is pos-ed or owned. **4.** *pl*. Property; wealth. **5.** The state of g possessed by, or as by, evil spirits. **6.** Self-possession.

·es·sive (pə·zes′iv) *adj*. **1.** Of or pertaining to posses-or ownership. **2.** Having a strong desire for complete tional domination of another person. **3.** *Gram*. Desig-ng a case of the noun or pronoun that denotes possession, n, or the like. In English, this is formed in nouns by add-'s to the singular and to irregular plurals: *John's* book; 's souls; and a simple apostrophe to the regular plural sometimes to singulars and proper names ending in a ant: *boys'* shoes; *James'* (or *James's*) brother. Pronouns he possessive case have special forms, as *my, mine, his, hers, its, our, ours, your, yours, their, theirs, whose.* — *ram*. **1.** The possessive case. **2.** A possessive form or struction. **— pos·ses′sive·ness** *n*.

·et (pos′it) *n*. A drink of hot milk curdled with wine or sweetened and spiced. [< ME *poshote, possot*]

·si·bil·i·ty (pos′ə·bil′ə·tē) *n*. *pl*. **·ties 1.** The fact or e of being possible. **2.** That which is possible.

·si·ble (pos′ə·bəl) *adj*. **1.** Capable of happening or prov-true: not contrary to fact, natural laws, or experience. Capable of being done or of coming about; feasible. That may or may not happen. [< OF < L < *posse* to able + *esse* to be] **— pos′si·bly** *adv*.

·sum (pos′əm) *n*. *Informal* An oppossum. **— to play ·sum** To feign death, illness, etc. [< OPOSSUM.]

·¹ (pōst) *n*. An upright piece of timber or other material; a A support for a sign. **b** A bearing or framing member building. **c** An indicator of the starting or finishing point racecourse, etc. **—** *v.t.* **1.** To put up (a poster, etc.) in ne public place. **2.** To fasten posters upon. **3.** To ounce by or as by a poster: to *post* a reward. **4.** To ·lish the name of on a list. [OE < L *postis* door post]

·² (pōst) *n*. **1.** A position or employment, esp. a public ce. **2.** *Mil*. **a** A place occupied by a detachment of ps. **b** The buildings and grounds of such a place. **3.** An gned beat, position, or station, as of a sentry, policeman, **4.** A trading post or settlement. **5.** *U.S.* A local unit veterans' organization. **—** *v.t.* To assign to a particular t; station, as a sentry. [< MF < Ital. < LL *postum*, tr. of L *positum*. pp. neut. of *ponere* to place]

·³ (pōst) *n*. **1.** *Chiefly Brit*. A single delivery of mail to a ne office, etc.; also, the mail itself. **2.** *Chiefly Brit*. An blished, usu. government, system, for transporting the ils; also, a local post office. **3.** *Brit*. A mailbox. **4.** A er or courier who carries mail over a fixed route. **5.** Any he stations furnishing relays of men and horses on such a te. **—** *v.t.* **1.** *Chiefly Brit*. To place in a mailbox or post ce; mail. **2.** To inform. **3.** In bookkeeping: **a** To trans-(items or accounts) to the ledger. **b** To make the proper ries in (a ledger). **—** *v.i.* **4.** To travel with post horses. To travel with speed; hasten. **—** *adv*. **1.** By post horses. Speedily; rapidly. [< MF < Ital. *posta*, orig., a station LL, contr. of L *posita*, pp. fem. of *ponere* to place]

·t- *prefix* **1.** After in time or order; following: *postdate, twar*. **2.** Chiefly in scientific terms, after in position; be-d. [< L *post* behind, after]

·t·age (pōs′tij) *n*. **1.** The charge levied on mail matter. The act of going by post.

·tage stamp A small, printed label issued and sold by a ernment to be affixed to letters, parcels, etc., in payment postage.

·tal (pōs′təl) *adj*. Pertaining to the mails or to mail vice. **—** *n*. A postal card.

·tal card A card, issued officially, for carrying a written printed message through the mails.

·t-bel·lum (pōst′bel′əm) *adj*. Occurring after a war, ., after the Civil War. [< L < *post* after + *bellum* war]

·t·box (pōst′boks′) *n*. A mailbox (def. 1).

·t card 1. A postal card. **2.** An unofficial one card of any ulation size, usu. having a picture on one side, trans-ssible through the mails on prepayment of postage.

·t chaise A closed carriage used for traveling and drawn post horses.

·t·date (pōst′dāt′) *v.t.* **·dat·ed, ·dat·ing 1.** To assign or a date later than the actual date to (a check, document, .). **2.** To follow in time.

post·er (pōs′tər) *n*. **1.** A placard or bill used for advertis-ing, public information, etc., to be posted on a wall or other surface. **2.** A billposter. [< POST¹]

pos·te·ri·or (pos·tir′ē·ər) *adj*. **1.** Situated behind or toward the hinder part. **2.** Coming after another in a series. **3.** Subsequent in time; later. **4.** *Anat*. **a** In animals, pertain-ing to the tail end of the body. **b** In man, pertaining to the back side of the body. **—** *n*. Sometimes *pl*. The buttocks. [< L, compar. of *posterus* coming after < *post* after, behind] **— pos·te′ri·or′i·ty** (-ôr′ə·tē, -or′ə-) *n*. **— pos·te′ri·or·ly** *adv*.

pos·ter·i·ty (pos·ter′ə·tē) *n*. **1.** Future generations taken collectively. **2.** All of one's descendants. [< OF < L < *posterus* coming after]

pos·tern (pōs′tərn, pos′-) *n*. A small back gate or door, esp. in a fortification or castle. **—** *adj*. Situated at the back or side. [< OF < LL < *postera* back door, gate]

post exchange *Mil*. An establishment for the sale of mer-chandise and services to military personnel. Abbr. *PX*

post·grad·u·ate (pōst′graj′ōō·it, -āt) *adj*. Of or pertaining to studies pursued after the taking of an advanced degree. **—** *n*. One who pursues such studies.

post·haste (pōst′hāst′) *Archaic* **—** *n*. Great haste or speed, like that of the post. **—** *adv*. With utmost speed.

post horse A horse kept at a post house.

post house A house where post horses were kept for relay; also, formerly, a post office.

post·hu·mous (pos′chōō·məs) *adj*. **1.** Denoting a child born after the father's death. **2.** Published after the au-thor's death, as a book. **3.** Arising or continuing after one's death. [< LL < L *postumus* latest, last] **— post′hu·mous·ly** *adj*.

pos·til·lion (pōs·til′yən, pos-) *n*. One who guides a team drawing a carriage or other heavy vehicle by riding the near horse when one pair is used or the near horse of the leaders when two or more pairs are used. Also **pos·til′lion**. [< MF < Ital. < *posta* post, station]

post·im·pres·sion·ism (pōst′im·presh′ən·iz′əm) *n*. The theories and practice of a group of expressionist painters of the late 19th century, who rejected the objective naturalism of the Impressionists and emphasized the subjective point of view of the artist. **— post′im·pres′sion·ist** *n. & adj*. **— post′im·pres′sion·is′tic** *adj*.

post·lude (pōst′lōōd) *n*. *Music* **1.** An organ voluntary con-cluding a church service. **2.** Loosely, a coda.

post·man (pōst′mən) *n*. *pl*. **·men** (-mən) A mailman.

post·mark (pōst′märk′) *n*. Any official mark stamped on mail to cancel stamps and to give the date and place of send-ing or receiving. **—** *v.t.* To stamp with a postmark.

post·mas·ter (pōst′mas′tər, -mäs′-) *n*. **1.** An official hav-ing charge of a post office. **2.** One who provides horses for posting. **— post′mis′tress** (-mis′tris) *n.fem*.

postmaster general *pl*. **postmasters general** The execu-tive head of the postal service of a government.

post·me·rid·i·an (pōst′mə·rid′ē·ən) *adj*. Pertaining to or occurring in the afternoon. Also **post′me·rid′i·o·nal**. [< L < *post* after + *meridies* noon]

post me·rid·i·em (pōst mə·rid′ē·əm) After midday. Abbr. *p.m., P.M.* [< L]

post-mortem (pōst′môr′təm) *adj*. **1.** Happening or per-formed after death. **2.** Of or pertaining to a post-mortem examination. **—** *n*. **1.** A post-mortem examination. **2.** *Informal* An analysis or discussion of an accomplished fact. [< L *post mortem* after death]

post-mortem examination *Med*. A thorough examina-tion of a human body after death: also called *autopsy*.

post·na·tal (pōst·nāt′l) *adj*. Occurring after birth.

post office 1. The branch of the civil service of a govern-ment charged with carrying and delivering the mails. **2.** Any local office that receives, sorts, and delivers mail, sells stamps, etc. **3.** Any town or place having a post office.

post·op·er·a·tive (pōst·op′ər·ə·tiv, -ə·rā′-) *adj*. *Surg*. Oc-curring or done after a surgical operation: *postoperative* care.

post·paid (pōst′pād′) *adj*. Having postage prepaid.

post·par·tum (pōst′pär′təm) *adj*. *Med*. After childbirth. [< POST- + L *partus* childbirth < *parere* to bear]

post·pone (pōst·pōn′) *v.t.* **·poned, ·pon·ing 1.** To put off to a future time; defer; delay. **2.** To subordinate. [< L < *post-* after + *ponere* to put] **— post·pon′a·ble** *adj*. **post·pone′ment** *n*. **— post·pon′er** *n*.
   —Syn. 1. Delay, defer, procrastinate, adjourn, stay.

post·pran·di·al (pōst·pran′dē·əl) *adj*. After-dinner. [< POST- + L *prandium* lunch + -AL¹]

post road A road built for the transportation of mail, formerly having post houses at specified distances.

post·script (pōst′skript′) *n*. **1.** A sentence or paragraph added to a letter after the writer's signature. **2.** A supple-mental addition to a written or printed document. Abbr. *p.s., P.S.* [< L *postscriptum*, pp. of *postscribere* to write after]

pos·tu·lant (pos′chə·lənt) *n.* **1.** One who presents a request. **2.** *Eccl.* An applicant for admission into a religious order. [< L < *postulare*, freq. of *poscere* to ask] — **pos′·tu·lant·ship** *n.*

pos·tu·late (*v.* pos′chə·lāt; *n.* pos′chə·lit) *v.t.* **·lat·ed, ·lat·ing** **1.** To claim, demand, or require. **2.** To set forth as self-evident. **3.** To assume the truth or reality of. — *n.* **1.** A self-evident truth. **2.** A prerequisite. **3.** A fundamental principle. — **pos′tu·la′tion** *n.* — **pos′tu·la′tor** *n.*

pos·ture (pos′chər) *n.* **1.** The position or carriage of the body or parts of the body. **2.** Such a position assumed during posing for an artist, etc. **3.** The visible disposition of the various parts of a material thing. **4.** A mental attitude; frame of mind. **5.** A situation or condition, esp. if a consequence of policy: national defense posture. — *v.t.* **1.** To place (a person) in a specific position or pose. — *v.i.* **2.** To assume or adopt a bodily pose or a character not natural to one. [< F < L *positura* position] — **pos′tur·al** *adj.* — **pos′tur·er, pos′tur·ist** *n.*

pos·tur·ize (pos′chə·rīz) *v.t. & v.i.* **·ized, ·iz·ing** To posture; pose.

post·war (pōst′wôr′) *adj.* After a war.

po·sy (pō′zē) *n.* *pl.* **·sies** A single flower or a bouquet. [Contr. of POESY]

pot (pot) *n.* **1.** A round, fairly deep vessel of metal, earthenware, or glass, generally having a handle, used for cooking and other domestic purposes. **2.** Such a vessel and its contents. **3.** The amount a pot will hold. **4.** A large drinking cup, as a tankard; also, drink or liquor. **5.** In cardplaying, the amount of stakes wagered or played for, esp. in poker. **6.** *Informal* A large sum of money. **7.** In fishing, a basketlike trap for catching lobsters, eels, etc. — **to go to pot** To deteriorate. — *v.* **pot·ted, pot·ting** *v.t.* **1.** To put into a pot or pots: to *pot* plants. **2.** To preserve (meat, etc.) in pots or jars. **3.** To cook in a pot. **4.** To shoot (game) for food rather than for sport. **5.** To shoot or kill with a pot shot. **6.** *Informal* To secure, capture, or win; bag. — *v.i.* **7.** To take a pot shot; shoot. [OE *pott*]

po·ta·ble (pō′tə·bəl) *adj.* Suitable for drinking: said of water. — *n.* Often *pl.* Something drinkable; a drink. [< MF < LL < *potare* to drink]

po·tage (pō·täzh′) *n.* French Any thick soup.

pot·ash (pot′ash′) *n.* **1.** Potassium hydroxide. **2.** Crude potassium carbonate. **3.** The oxide of potassium, K_2O. [< Du. *potasch*]

po·tas·si·um (pə·tas′ē·əm) *n.* A bluish white, highly reactive, metallic element (symbol K), never found free in nature, but yielding many compounds of great practical value in industry, medicine, etc.: also called *kalium*. See ELEMENT. [< NL < *potass* potash] — **po·tas′sic** *adj.*

potassium bitartrate *Chem.* A white crystalline compound, $HKC_4H_4O_6$, having an acid taste; an ingredient of baking powder: also called *cream of tartar*.

potassium bromide *Chem.* A crystalline compound, KBr, used in photography, and in medicine as a sedative.

potassium carbonate *Chem.* A white, strongly alkaline compound, K_2CO_3, used in making soap and glass.

potassium cyanide *Chem.* An intensely poisonous compound, KCN, used in photography, and as a reagent.

potassium hydroxide *Chem.* A whitish deliquescent solid, KOH, yielding a strong caustic solution: used in saltmaking, electroplating, as a chemical reagent, etc. Also called *caustic potash, potash.*

potassium nitrate *Chem.* A crystalline white salt, KNO_3, used in gunpowder, fertilizers, and in medicine. Also called *niter, saltpeter.*

potassium permanganate *Chem.* A purple red crystalline salt, $KMnO_4$, used as an oxidizing agent in antiseptics and deodorizing substances.

potassium sulfate *Chem.* A salt, K_2SO_4, used in the manufacture of glass and alum, and in the crude state as a component of fertilizer.

po·ta·tion (pō·tā′shən) *n.* **1.** The act of drinking; also, a drink, esp. of an alcoholic beverage. **2.** A drinking bout. [< OF < L < *potare* to drink]

po·ta·to (pə·tā′tō) *n.* *pl.* **·toes** **1.** One of the edible tubers of a plant of the nightshade family: also called *Irish potato, white potato.* **2.** The plant. **3.** The sweet potato. [< Sp. *patata* < Arawakan (Taino) *batata*]

potato beetle A beetle having long black stripes on the wing covers, that feeds on the leaves of the potato, tomato, and similar plants. Also **potato bug.**

potato chip *U.S.* A very thin slice of potato fried crisp and salted.

pot·bel·ly (pot′bel′ē) *n.* *pl.* **·lies** **1.** A protuberant belly. **2.** An upright wood- or coal-burning stove with bulging sides: also **potbellied stove.** — **pot′bel′lied** *adj.*

pot·boil·er (pot′boi′lər) *n.* *Informal* A literary or artistic work produced simply to obtain the means of subsistence.

po·tent (pōt′nt) *adj.* **1.** Physically powerful. **2.** Having great authority. **3.** Exerting great influence on mind or morals; very convincing: a *potent* argument. **4.** Of a liquor, etc., strong in its physical and chemical eff **5.** Sexually competent: said of the male. [< L < able + *esse* to be] — **po′ten·cy, po′tence** *n.* — **po′te** *adv.* — **po′tent·ness** *n.*

po·ten·tate (pōt′n·tāt) *n.* One having great power or s a sovereign. [< LL *potentatus*]

po·ten·tial (pə·ten′chəl) *adj.* **1.** Possible but not ac **2.** Having capacity for existence, but not yet exis latent. **3.** *Gram.* Indicating possibility, power, or lib as a verb phrase including *may, can, must*, etc. — *n* A possible development; potentiality. **2.** *Electr.* The ch on a body as referred to another body or to a given stan as the earth, considered as having zero potential. [< *potentialis*] — **po·ten′tial·ly** *adv.*

po·ten·ti·al·i·ty (pə·ten′chē·al′ə·tē) *n.* *pl.* **·ties** **1.** herent capacity for development or accomplishment. That which is potential ro capable of being realized.

poth·er (poth′ər) *n.* Excitement mingled with confu bustle; fuss. — *v. & v.i.* To worry; bother.

pot·herb (pot′ûrb, -hûrb) *n.* Any plant or herb, greens, when cooked or used to flavor boiled foods.

pot·hole (pot′hōl′) *n.* A deep hole, as in a road.

pot·hook (pot′hŏŏk′) *n.* **1.** A curved or hooked pie iron for lifting or hanging pots. **2.** A curved mark or mentary stroke used in teaching penmanship.

pot·house (pot′hous′) *Brit.* *n.* An alehouse; saloon.

po·tion (pō′shən) *n.* A draft, as a large dose of liquid r cine: often used of a magic or poisonous draft. [< OF < *potare* to drink]

pot·luck (pot′luk′) *n.* Whatever food may have been pared for the family: usu. in the phrase **to take potluck.**

pot·pie (pot′pī′) *n.* **1.** A meat pie baked in a deep **2.** Meat stewed with dumplings.

pot·pour·ri (pot·pŏŏr′ē, *Fr.* pō·pōō·rē′) *n.* **1.** A mi: of dried flower petals kept in a jar and used to perfu room. **2.** A musical medley or literary miscellany. Any incongruous mixture. [< F, lit., rotten pot]

pot roast Meat braised and cooked in a covered pot.

pot·sherd (pot′shûrd) *n.* A bit of broken earthenwa

pot shot **1.** A shot fired to kill, without regard to the of sports. **2.** A shot fired, as from ambush, at a perso animal within easy range. **3.** A random shot.

pot·stone (pot′stōn′) *n.* A variety of steatite or soaps

pot·tage (pot′ij) *n.* A thick broth or stew of veget with or without meat. [< OF *pot* pot]

pot·ted (pot′id) *adj.* **1.** Placed or kept in a pot. **2.** Co or preserved in a pot. **3.** *Slang* Drunk.

pot·ter[1] (pot′ər) *v.t. & v.i.* Chiefly *Brit.* To putter. [F of dial, *pote*] — **pot′ter·er** *n.*

pot·ter[2] (pot′ər) *n.* One who makes earthenware or celain vessels.

potter's field A piece of ground appropriated as a b ground for the destitute and the unknown. *Matt.* xxvi

potter's wheel A horizontal rotating disk used by po for holding and manipulating prepared clay.

pot·ter·y (pot′ər·ē) *n.* *pl.* **·ter·ies** **1.** Ware molded from clay and hardened by intense heat. **2.** The art of making earthenware or porcelain. **3.** A place where pottery is made. [< OF < Med.L *pot* pot]

pot·tle (pot′l) *n.* **1.** A drinking vessel, pot, or tankard holding about half a gallon. **2.** An old liquid measure of half a gallon. **3.** Liquor. [< OF *pot* pot)

pot·ty[1] (pot′ē) *adj.* *Brit. Informal* **1.** Insignificant. **2.** Slightly drunk; also, a little silly.

pot·ty[2] (pot′ē) *n.* *pl.* **·ties** A receptacle that fits under a child's toilet seat; also, the toilet seat.

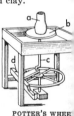

POTTER'S WHEE
a Molding clay. *b* -
tating wheel. *c* Dia
d Treadle.

pouch (pouch) *n.* **1.** A small bag, sack, or other conta used for carrying money, pipe tobacco, ammunition, **2.** *Zool.* **a** A saclike part for temporairly containing foo in gophers and pelicans. **b** A marsupium. **3.** *Bot.* Any like cavity, as the pod of the mustard plant. **4.** A mai — *v.t.* **1.** To put in a pouch. **2.** To fashion in pouc form. — *v.i.* **3.** To form a pouchlike cavity. [< OF *p* — **pouch′y.** *adj.*

poul·tice (pōl′tis) *n.* A moist, mealy mass of flour, must etc., applied hot to a sore part of the body. — *v.t.* **·ti ·tic·ing** To cover with a poultice. [< L *puls* porridge]

poul·try (pōl′trē) *n.* Domestic fowls, generally or co tively, as hens, ducks, etc. [< OF *poule* hen]

pounce[1] (pouns) *v.i.* **pounced, pounc·ing** To swoo spring in or as in seizing prey: with *on, upon,* or *at.* — **1.** A talon or claw of a bird of prey. **2.** The act of poun

pounce[2] (pouns) *n.* **1.** A powder, as of cuttlebone, merly used to absorb excess of ink, as on a manusc

, A finely pulverized substance used in transferring designs. — *v.t.* To sprinkle, smooth, or rub with pounce. [< F < L *pumex* pumice]

und[1] (pound) *n.* **1.** A unit of weight varying in different :untries and at different periods. **2.** In Great Britain and e U.S., either of two legally fixed units, the avoirdupois >und and the troy pound. See table front of book. . The standard monetary unit of the United Kingdom, |uivalent to 20 shillings: in 1960 worth about $2.81: also >und sterling. Symbol £. **4.** A similar monetary unit of eland and several members of the Commonwealth of ations. **5.** A standard monetary unit of various other :untries; esp. Egypt, Israel, and Turkey. [OE < L *pondus* eight]

und[2] (pound) *n.* **1.** A place, enclosed by authority, in hich stray animals or distrained possessions are left until laimed or redeemed. **2.** A place of confinement for law-·eakers. **3.** A trap for wild animals. **4.** An area or place , which to catch or stow fish. — *v.t.* To confine in a pound; ipound. [OE *pund*-]

und[3] (pound) *v.t.* **1.** To strike heavily and repeatedly; :at. **2.** To reduce to a pulp or powder by beating. — *v.i.* . To strike heavy, repeated blows: with *on*, *at*, etc. **4.** To .ove or proceed heavily. **5.** To throb heavily or resound-gly. — *n.* **1.** A heavy blow. **2.** The act of pounding.)E *pūnian* to bruise] — **pound'er** *n.*

und·age (poun'dij) *n.* A rate on the pound sterling.

und·al (poun'dəl) *n.* *Physics* A unit of force that, acting 1 a mass of one pound, imparts to it a velocity of one foot :r second.

und·cake (pound'kāk') *n.* A rich cake having ingre-.ents equal in weight, as a pound each of flour, butter, and igar, with eggs added.

und·er (poun'dər) *n.* **1.** Anything weighing a pound. . One who or that which weighs, has, etc., a given number : pounds: used in combination: an eight-*pounder*.

und-fool·ish (pound'foo'lish) *adj.* Extravagant with rge sums, but watching small sums closely.

ur (pôr, pōr) *v.t.* **1.** To cause to flow in a continuous ·ream, as water, sand, etc. **2.** To send forth, emit, or utter ·ofusely or continuously. — *v.i.* **3.** To flow in a continu-.us stream; gush. **4.** To rain heavily. **5.** To move in great .umbers; swarm. — *n.* A pouring, flow, or downfall. [ME *>uren*] — **pour'er** *n.* — **pour'ing·ly** *adv.*

·ur·boire (poor·bwär') *n.* *French* A gratuitous gift of .oney, as a tip. [< F, lit., in order to drink]

ut[1] (pout) *v.i.* **1.** To thrust out the lips, esp. in ill humor. . To be sullen; sulk. **3.** To swell out; protrude. — *v.t.* . To thrust out (the lips, etc.). **5.** To utter with a pout. – *n.* **1.** A pushing out of the lips as in pouting. **2.** A fit : ill humor. [ME *pouten*]

ut[2] (pout) *n.* Any of various fresh-water catfishes. [OE *ēle) pūte* eelpout]

ut·er (pou'tər) *n.* **1.** One who pouts. **2.** A breed of igeon having the habit of puffing out the crop.

·v·er·ty (pov'ər·tē) *n.* **1.** The condition or quality of :ing poor. **2.** Scantiness of supply: a *poverty* of imagina-.on. **3.** Absence or scarcity of necessary qualities, elements, :c.: *poverty* of soil. [< OF < L < *pauper* poor] — **Syn.** **1.** Privation, indigence, penury.

·v·er·ty-strick·en (pov'ər·tē·strik'ən) *adj.* Suffering from overty; destitute.

·w·der (pou'dər) *n.* **1.** A finely ground or pulverized .ass of loose particles formed from a solid substance in the ·ry state. **2.** Any of various substances prepared in this .rm, as a cosmetic, medicine, or explosive. — *v.t.* **1.** To educe to powder; pulverize. **2.** To sprinkle or cover with or .s with powder. — *v.i.* **3.** To be reduced to powder. **4.** o use powder as a cosmetic. [< OF < L *pulvis* dust] — ·ow'der·er *n.*

·wder blue A soft medium blue.

·wder horn The hollow horn of an ox or cow, formerly .tted with a cover and used for holding gunpowder.

·wder puff A soft pad used to apply powder to the skin.

·w·der·y (pou'dər·ē) *adj.* **1.** Consisting of or like fine ·owder or dust. **2.** Covered with or as with powder; mealy; .usty. **3.** Capable of being easily powdered; friable.

·w·er (pou'ər) *n.* **1.** Ability to act; capability. **2.** Po-.ential capacity. **3.** Strength or force actually put forth. :. The right, ability, or capacity to exercise control; legal .uthority. **5.** Any agent that exercises power, as in con-·rol or dominion; an important and influential sovereign ·ation. **6.** Great or telling force or effect. **7.** *Often pl.* :. A mental or physical faculty. **8.** Any form of energy avail-.ble for doing work; esp., electrical energy. **9.** *Physics* The ime rate at which energy is transferred, or converted into vork. **10.** *Math.* **a** The product of a number multiplied .y itself a given number of times: The third *power* of 2 is 8.

b An exponent. **11.** *Optics* Magnifying capacity, as of a lens. — *v.t.* To provide with means of propulsion. [< OF < LL < L *posse* to be able]

power boat A motorboat.

pow·er·ful (pou'ər·fəl) *adj.* **1.** Possessing great force or energy; strong. **2.** Exercising great authority, or manifest-ing high qualities. **3.** Having great effect on the mind. — *adv.* *Dial. & Informal* Very. — **pow'er·ful·ly** *adv.*

pow·er·house (pou'ər·hous') *n.* *Electr.* A station where electricity is generated.

pow·er·less (pou'ər·lis) *adj.* **1.** Destitute of power; un-able to accomplish an effect; impotent. **2.** Without au-thority. — **pow'er·less·ly** *adv.* — **pow'er·less·ness** *n.*

power of attorney *Law* **1.** The authority or power to act conferred upon an agent. **2.** The instrument or docu-ment by which that power or authority is conferred.

power politics The use or threatened use of superior force to exact international concessions.

pow·wow (pou'wou') *n.* *U.S. n.* **1.** *Informal* Any meeting or conference. **2.** A North American Indian. ceremony to cure the sick or effect success in war, etc. **3.** A conference with or of American Indians. — *v.i.* To hold a powwow. [< Algonquian (Massachusetts) *pauwaw*, lit., he dreams]

pox (poks) *n.* **1.** Any disease characterized by purulent eruptions: *chickenpox*. **2.** Syphilis. [Var. of *pocks*, pl. of POCK]

prac·ti·ca·ble (prak'ti·kə·bəl) *adj.* **1.** That can be put into practice; feasible. **2.** That can be used; usable. [< F < Med.L < LL < Gk. *prassein* to do] — **prac'ti·ca·bil'i·ty**, **prac'ti·ca·ble·ness** *n.* — **prac'ti·ca·bly** *adv.*

prac·ti·cal (prak'ti·kəl) *adj.* **1.** Pertaining to or governed by actual use and experience or action, as contrasted with speculation. **2.** Trained by or derived from practice or experience. **3.** Applicable to use. **4.** Manifested in prac-tice. **5.** Being such to all intents and purposes; virtual. — **Syn.** See PRACTICABLE. [< MF < LL < Gk. *prassein* to do] — **prac'ti·cal·i·ty** (-kal'ə·tē), **prac'ti·cal·ness** *n.*

practical joke A trick having a victim or victims.

prac·ti·cal·ly (prak'tik·lē) *adv.* **1.** In a practical manner. **2.** To all intents and purposes; in fact or effect; virtually.

practical nurse One who has some training and practice in nursing but who is not a registered nurse.

prac·tice (prak'tis) *v.* **·ticed**, **·tic·ing** *v.t.* **1.** To make use of habitually or often: to *practice* economy. **2.** To apply in action; make a practice of. **3.** To work at a profession. **4.** To do or perform repeatedly in order to acquire skill or training; rehearse. **5.** To instruct, as pupils, by repeated exercise or lessons. — *v.i.* **6.** To repeat or rehearse some-thing in order to acquire skill or proficiency. **7.** To work at a profession. — *n.* **1.** Any customary action or proceeding; habit. **2.** An established custom or usage. **3.** The act of doing or performing: distinguished from *theory*. **4.** The regular prosecution of a profession. **5.** Frequent and con-peated exercise in any matter. **6.** *pl.* Stratagems or schemes for bad purposes; tricks. **7.** The rules by which legal pro-ceedings are governed. Also **prac'tise**. [< MF < Med.L < LL < Gk. *praktikos* < *prassein* to do] — **prac'tic·er** *n.* — **Syn.** (noun) **5.** *Practice* is the putting into action of what one has learned in theory, to gain skill and facility. *Exercise* is primarily physical action to acquire and maintain strength. *Drill* is systematic and rigorous *practice* under an instructor.

prac·ticed (prak'tist) *adj.* **1.** Expert by practice; experi-enced. **2.** Acquired by practice. Also **prac'tised**.

prac·ti·tion·er (prak·tish'ən·ər) *n.* One who practices an art or profession.

prae- See PRE-.

prae·fect (prē'fekt) See PREFECT.

prae·no·men (prē·nō'mən) *n.* *pl.* **·nom·i·na** (-nom'ə·nə) The first name of an ancient Roman; also, any given name: also spelled *prenomen*. [< L]

praeter- See PRETER-.

prae·tor (prē'tər) *n.* A city magistrate of ancient Rome; also spelled *pretor*. [< L < *praeire* to go before] — **prae-to·ri·al** (pri·tôr'ē·əl, -tō'rē-) *adj.* — **prae'tor·ship** *n.*

prae·to·ri·an (pri·tôr'ē·ən, -tō'rē-) *adj.* Of a praetor; praetorial. — *n.* A praetor or ex-praetor. Also spelled *pretorian*.

Prae·to·ri·an (pri·tôr'ē·ən, -tō'rē-) *adj.* Denoting the Praetorian Guard. — *n.* A soldier of the Praetorian Guard. Also spelled *Pretorian*.

Praetorian Guard **1.** The bodyguard of the Roman emperors. **2.** A member of this bodyguard.

prag·mat·ic (prag·mat'ik) *adj.* **1.** Pertaining to the study of events with emphasis on cause and effect. **2.** *Philos.* Pertaining to pragmatism. **3.** Pragmatical. [< L < Gk. < *pragma, pragmatos* thing done < *prassein* to do]

prag·mat·i·cal (prag·mat'i·kəl) *adj.* Relating to everyday business; practical; commonplace.

prag·mat·i·cal·ly (prag-mat′i-kəl-ē) *adv.* In a pragmatic or pragmatical manner. **— prag·mat′i·cal·ness** *n.*

prag·ma·tism (prag′mə-tiz′əm) *n.* 1. *Philos.* The doctrine that ideas have value only in terms of their practical consequences, and that results are the sole test of the validity or truth of one's beliefs. 2. The quality or condition of being pragmatic. **— prag′ma·tist** *n.*

prai·rie (prâr′ē) *n.* *U.S. & Canadian* A tract of grassland; esp., the broad, grassy plain of central North America. [< F < L *pratum* meadow]

prairie chicken Either of two gallinaceous game birds inhabiting the plains of western North America. Also **prairie hen.**

prairie dog A burrowing rodent of the plains of North America. Also **prairie squirrel.**

prairie schooner *U.S.* A covered wagon used for travel by pioneers.

Prairie State Nickname of ILLINOIS.

prairie wolf A coyote.

praise (prāz) *n.* 1. An expression of approval or commendation. 2. The glorifying and honoring of a god, ruler, hero, etc. **—** *v.t.* **praised, prais·ing** 1. To express approval and commendation of; applaud. 2. To express adoration of; glorify, esp. in song. [< OF < LL *pretiare* to prize] **— prais′er** *n.*

  — Syn. (verb) 1. *Praise* is a weak word, and may refer to the mere speaking of compliments. To *laud* is to *praise* highly. *Extol* stresses the intention to elevate or magnify a person or thing by praise. *Applaud* and *acclaim* point to a public show of approval, as by clapping the hands or shouting. **— Ant.** blame, decry.

praise·wor·thy (prāz′wûr′thē) *adj.* Worthy of praise. **— praise′wor·thi·ly** *adv.* **— praise′wor·thi·ness** *n.*

Pra·krit (prä′krit) *n.* Any of several vernacular languages of ancient India. [< Skt. *prakrtā* natural]

pra·line (prä′lēn, prā′-) *n.* A confection made of pecans or other nuts browned in boiling sugar. [< F, after Marshal Duplessis-*Praslin*, 1598–1675, whose cook invented it]

pram (pram) *n.* *Chiefly Brit. Informal* A baby carriage. [Short for PERAMBULATOR]

prance (prans, präns) *v.* **pranced, pranc·ing** *v.i.* 1. To move proudly with high steps, as a spirited horse; spring from the hind legs; also, to ride a horse moving thus. 2. To move in an arrogant or elated manner; swagger. 3. To gambol; caper. **—** *v.t.* 4. To cause to prance. **—** *n.* The act of prancing; a high step; caper. [ME *prauncen*] **— pranc′er** *n.*

pran·di·al (pran′dē-əl) *adj.* Of or pertaining to a meal, esp. dinner. [< L *prandium* breakfast or lunch]

prank[1] (prangk) *v.t.* 1. To decorate gaudily. **—** *v.i.* 2. To make an ostentatious show. [Prob. < MLG *prank* pomp]

prank[2] (prangk) *n.* A mischievous or frolicsome act; a trick. **—** *v.i.* To play pranks or tricks. [Origin uncertain; ? < PRANK[1]] **— prank′ish** *adj.*

pra·se·o·dym·i·um (prā′zē-ō-dim′ē-əm, prā′sē-) *n.* A yellowish white metallic element (symbol Pr) of the lanthanide series, having olive-green salts. See ELEMENT. [< NL < Gk. *prasios* light green + (DI)DYMIUM]

prate (prāt) *v.* **prat·ed, prat·ing** *v.i.* 1. To talk idly and at length; chatter. **—** *v.t.* 2. To utter idly or emptily. **—** *n.* Idle talk; prattle. [< MDu.-MLG *praten*] **— prat′er** *n.* **— prat′ing·ly** *adv.*

prat·fall (prat′fôl′) *n.* *U.S. Slang* A fall on the buttocks.

prat·tle (prat′l) *v.* **·tled, ·tling** *v.i.* 1. To talk foolishly or like a child. **—** *v.t.* 2. To utter in a foolish or childish way. **—** *n.* 1. Childish speech. 2. Idle or foolish talk. [See PRATE.] **— prat′tler** *n.*

prawn (prôn) *n.* Any of various shrimplike crustaceans of tropical and temperate waters, used as food. **—** *v.i.* To fish for prawns. [ME *prane, prayne*]

pray (prā) *v.i.* 1. To address prayers to a deity, idol, etc. 2. To make earnest request or entreaty; beg. **—** *v.t.* 3. To say prayers to. 4. To ask (someone) earnestly; entreat. 5. To ask for by prayers or entreaty. [< OF < LL < L *prex, precis* request, prayer] **— pray′er** *n.*

prayer[1] (prâr) *n.* 1. A devout request or petition to a deity. 2. The act of praying, esp. to God. 3. A set form of words used for a devout request, petition, etc. 4. Spiritual and wordless communion with God. 5. *Often pl.* A religious service. 6. Something prayed for. 7. Any earnest request.

prayer book 1. A book of prayers for divine service. 2. *Usu. cap.* The Book of Common Prayer.

prayer·ful (prâr′fəl) *adj.* Inclined or given to prayer; devotional. **— prayer′ful·ly** *adv.* **— prayer′ful·ness** *n.*

prayer wheel A wheel, cylinder, or vertical drum containing written prayers, used by the Buddhists of Tibet.

praying mantis The mantis (which see).

pre- *prefix* 1. Before in time or order; prior to; preceding; as in: *prearrange, pre-Roman.* 2. Before in position; anterior: chiefly in scientific terms; as in: *preabdomen, preanal.* 3. Preliminary to; preparing for; as in: *precollege.* Also **prae-.** [< L *prae* before]

preach (prēch) *v.t.* 1. To advocate or recommend urgent 2. To proclaim or expound upon: to *preach* the gospel. To deliver (a sermon, etc.). **—** *v.i.* 4. To deliver a serm 5. To give advice, esp. in an officious or moralizing manr [< OF < L *praedicare* to proclaim]

preach·er (prē′chər) *n.* 1. *Informal* A clergyman, esp Protestant minister. 2. One who preaches.

preach·i·fy (prē′chə-fī) *v.i.* **·fied, ·fy·ing** *Informal* preach or discourse tediously. **— preach′i·fi·ca′tion** *n.*

preach·ment (prēch′mənt) *n.* A sermon or moral lectu esp. a tedious one.

preach·y (prē′chē) *adj.* **preach·i·er, preach·i·est** Given preaching; sanctimonious.

pre·am·ble (prē′am-bəl) *n.* 1. An introductory stateme or preface, esp. to a formal document. 2. An introducto act, event, fact, etc. [< OF < Med.L < L *prae-* before *ambulare* to walk] **— pre·am′bu·lar·y** (-byə-ler′ē) *adj.*

pre·am·pli·fi·er (prē-am′plə-fī′ər) *n.* In a sound reprod tion system, an auxiliary amplifier used to reinforce v weak signals before sending them into the main amplifi Also **pre·amp** (prē′amp).

preb·end (preb′ənd) *n.* 1. A stipend allotted from revenues of a cathedral or conventual church to a clergym 2. The land or tithe yielding the stipend. 3. A prebenda [< MF < Med.L < L *praebere* to supply] **— preb′ dal** *adj.*

preb·en·dar·y (preb′ən-der′ē) *n. pl.* **·dar·ies** A canon clergyman who holds a prebend. Also called *prebend.*

Pre-Cam·bri·an (prē-kam′brē-ən) *adj. Geol.* Of or p taining to all geological time and rock formations preced the Cambrian. See table for GEOLOGY. **—** *n.* Pre-Cambr era or rocks.

pre·can·cel (prē-kan′səl) *v.t.* **·celed** or **·celled, ·cel·ing ·cel·ling** To cancel (stamps) before use on mail. **—** *n.* precanceled stamp.

pre·car·i·ous (pri-kâr′ē-əs) *adj.* 1. Subject to continu risk; uncertain. 2. Subject or exposed to danger; hazardo **— Syn.** See RISKY. 3. Without foundation or basis. [< *precarius* obtained by prayer]

pre·cau·tion (pri-kô′shən) *n.* 1. A step or preparati taken to avoid a possible danger, evil, etc. 2. Cauti observed in preparation for a possible emergency. [< < LL < L < *prae-* before + *cavere* to take care] **—** p **cau′tion·ar·y** *adj.*

pre·cau·tious (pri-kô′shəs) *adj.* Exercising precauti **— pre·cau′tious·ly** *adv.* **— pre·cau′tious·ness** *n.*

pre·cede (pri-sēd′) *v.* **·ced·ed, ·ced·ing** *v.t.* 1. To go or before in order, place, rank, time, etc. 2. To preface; int duce. **—** *v.i.* 3. To go or be before; take precedence. [< < L < *prae-* before + *cedere* to go]

prec·e·dence (pri-sēd′əns, pres′ə-dəns) *n* 1. The act, rig or state of preceding in place, time, or rank. 2. The ce monial order observed by persons of different ranks formal occasions. Also **prec·e·den·cy** (pri-sēd′ən-sē, pres dən-sē).

prec·e·dent (*n.* pres′ə-dənt; *adj.* pri-sēd′nt) *n.* An act instance capable of being used as a guide or standard evaluating future actions. **—** *adj.* Former; preceding. **prec′e·den′tial** *adj.*

pre·ced·ing (pri-sē′ding) *adj.* Going before, as in tim place, or rank; earlier; foregoing. **— the preceding** Th which precedes or has been mentioned before.

pre·cen·tor (pri-sen′tər) *n.* One who leads the singi of a church choir or congregation. [< LL < L < *pre* before + *canere* to sing] **— pre·cen·to·ri·al** (prē′sen-tôr′ē əl, -tō′rē-) *adj* **— pre·cen′tor·ship** *n.*

pre·cept (prē′sept) *n.* 1. A rule prescribing a particula kind of conduct or action. 2. A proverbial standard guide to morals; a maxim. [< L *praecipere* to prescribe

pre·cep·tive (pri-sep′tiv) *adj.* 1. Consisting of or expres ing a precept or precepts. 2. Pertaining to or of the natu of a precept.

pre·cep·tor (pri-sep′tər) *n.* A teacher; instructor. [< *praeceptor*] **— pre·cep·to·ri·al** (prē′sep-tôr′ē-əl, -tō′rē *adj.* **— pre·cep′tress** (-tris) *n.fem.*

pre·ces·sion (pri-sesh′ən) *n.* The act of preceding. **pre·ces′sion·al** *adj.*

pre·cinct (prē′singkt) *n.* 1. *U.S.* An election district of town, township, county, etc. 2. *U.S.* **a** A subdivision of city or town under the jurisdiction of a police unit. **b** T police station for such an area. 3. A place marked off l fixed limits; also, the boundary of such a place. 4. *pl* Neighborhood; environs. 5. A limited area of though action, etc. [< Med.L < L *praecingere* < *prae-* before *cingere* to encircle]

pre·ci·os·i·ty (presh′ē-os′ə-tē) *n. pl.* **·ties** Extreme fa tidiousness or affected refinement, as in speech, style, etc.

pre·cious (presh′əs) *adj.* 1. Highly priced or prize valuable. 2. Greatly esteemed: truth is *precious.* 3. B loved; cherished. 4. Affectedly delicate or sensitive, as style of writing. 5. *Informal* Flagrant; surpassing: a *p*

ıs scoundrel. — *n.* Precious one; sweetheart. — *adv.*
remely; very. [< OF < L < *pretium* price] — **pre′·**
ıs·ly *adv.* — **pre′cious·ness** *n.*
ıous stone A valuable, rare gem, as the diamond,
y, sapphire, or emerald.
·i·pice (pres′i·pis) *n.* **1.** A high vertical or overhang-
face of rock; the brink of a cliff. **2.** A perilous situation.
F < L < *prae-* before + *caput* head]
cip·i·ta·ble (pri·sip′ə·tə·bəl) *adj. Chem.* Capable of
ng precipitated: a *precipitable* salt.
cip·i·tant (pri·sip′ə·tənt) *adj.* **1.** Rushing or falling
ckly or heedlessly. **2.** Rash; overhasty; impulsive. **3·** Very
den; abrupt. — *n. Chem.* Any substance that, when added
 solution, results in the formation of a precipitate. — **pre·**
′i·tance, pre·cip′i·tan·cy *n.* — **pre·cip′i·tant·ly** *adv.*
cip·i·tate (pri·sip′ə·tāt; *for adj. & n.,* also pri·sip′ə·tit) *v.*
·ed, ·tat·ing *v.t.* **1.** To hasten the occurrence of. **2.** To
l from or as from a height; throw headless. **3.** *Meteorol.*
 cause (vapor, etc.) to condense and fall as dew, rain, etc.
Chem. To separate (a substance) in solid form, as from a
 ıtion. — *v.i.* **5.** *Meteorol.* To fall as condensed vapor,
  6. *Chem.* To separate and settle, as a substance held
 ıolution. **7.** To fall headlong. — *adj.* **1.** Moving speed-
 or hurriedly; rushing headlong. **2.** Lacking due de-
 ıration; hasty; rash. **3.** Sudden and brief, as a disease.
n. Chem. A deposit of solid matter formed by precipita-
ı. [< L < *praeceps.* See PRECIPICE.] — **pre·cip′i·tate·**
ı. *adv.* — **pre·cip′i·tate·ness** *n.* — **pre·cip′i·ta′tive** *adj.*
pre·cip′i·ta′tor *n.*
cip·i·ta·tion (pri·sip′ə·tā′shən) *n.* **1.** *Meteorol.* **a** The
 ıositing of moisture from the atmosphere upon the sur-
 e of the earth. **b** The amount of rain, snow, etc., depos-
 ı. **2.** *Chem.* The process of separating any of the con-
 ıuents of a solution. **3.** The act of precipitating, or the
 te of being precipitated. **4.** Rash haste or hurry.
cip·i·tous (pri·sip′ə·təs) *adj.* **1.** Consisting of or like a
 ıcipice; very steep. **2.** Having many precipices. **3.** Hasty.
pre·cip′i·tous·ly *adv.* — **pre·cip′i·tous·ness** *n.*
cis (prā′sē, prā·sē′) *n. pl.* **pré·cis** (prā′sēz, prā·sēz′) A
 ıcise summary of a book, article, or document; abstract.
Syn. See ABRIDGMENT. [< F]
cise (pri·sīs′) *adj.* **1.** Sharply and clearly determined
 defined. **2.** No more and no less than; exact in amount.
 Noting or confined to a certain thing; particular. **4.**
 ıact or distinct in sound, statement, etc. **5.** Scrupulously
 ıervant of rule. [< F < L < *prae-* before + *caedere* to
 ı.] — **pre·cise′ly** *adv.* — **pre·cise′ness** *n.*
·ci·sion (pri·sizh′ən) *n.* The state or quality of being
 ıcise; accuracy; definition. — *adj.* **1.** Designed for ex-
 ımely accurate measurement: *precision* instruments. **2.**
 ıaracterized by precision. — **pre·ci′sion·ist** *n.*
·clude (pri·klood′) *v.t.* **·clud·ed, ·clud·ing 1.** To make
 ıpossible or ineffectual by prior action. **2.** To shut out;
 ılude. — **Syn.** See PREVENT. [< L < *prae-* before +
 udere to shut] — **pre·clu′sion** (-kloo′zhən) *n.* — **pre·**
sive (-kloo′siv) *adj.* — **pre·clu′sive·ly** *adv.*
·co·cious (pri·kō′shəs) *adj.* **1.** Unusually developed or
 ıvanced for one's age. **2.** Pertaining to or showing pre-
 ıture development. [< L < *prae-* beforehand, early +
 ıuere to cook] — **pre·co′cious·ly** *adv.* — **pre·co′cious·**
 ıss, pre·coc′i·ty (-kos′ə·tē) *n.*
·con·ceive (prē′kən·sēv′) *v.t.* **·ceived, ·ceiv·ing** To conve in advance; form an idea or opinion of beforehand.
·con·cep·tion (prē′kən·sep′shən) *n.* **1.** An idea or opin-
 ı formed or conceived in advance. **2.** A prejudice or mis-
 ınception; bias. — **pre′con·cep′tion·al** *adj.*
·con·di·tion (prē′kən·dish′ən) *n.* A condition that must
 met before a certain result is attained; prerequisite.
·cur·sor (pri·kûr′sər) *n.* One who or that which precedes
 ı suggests the course of future events. [< L < *prae-*
 fore + *currere* to run]
·cur·so·ry (pri·kûr′sər·ē) *adj.* Going before as a precur-
 ı or harbinger; preliminary. Also **pre·cur′sive** (-kûr′siv).
·da·cious (pri·dā′shəs) *adj.* Living by preying upon
 hers, as a beast or bird; raptorial: also *predatory.* Also
 e·da′ceous. [< L *praeda* prey] — **pre·da′cious·ness,**
 e·dac′i·ty (-das′ə·tē) *n.*
·date (prē′dāt′) *v.t.* **·dat·ed, ·dat·ing 1.** To date before
 e actual time. **2.** To precede in time.
d·a·tor (pred′i·tər) *n.* A predatory person or animal.
d·a·to·ry (pred′ə·tôr′ē, -tō′rē) *adj.* **1.** Of, relating to, or
 ıaracterized by plundering. **2.** Accustomed to or living by
 laging. **3.** Predacious. [< L *praeda* prey] — **pred′a·**
 r·ly *adv.* — **pred′a·to′ri·ness** *n.*
·de·cease (prē′di·sēs′) *v.t.* **·ceased, ·ceas·ing** To die be-
 e: She *predeceased* her husband by five years.
d·e·ces·sor (pred′ə·ses′ər) *n.* **1.** One who goes or has
 ne before another in point of time. **2.** A thing succeeded

by something else. **3.** An ancestor. [< OF < LL < *prae-*
before + *decessor* withdrawer]
pre·des·ti·nate (prē·des′tə·nāt) *v.t.* **·nat·ed, ·nat·ing 1.**
Theol. To foreordain by divine decree or purpose. **2.** To
predestine. [< L < *prae-* before + *destinare* to determine]
pre·des·ti·na·tion (prē·des′tə·nā′shən) *n.* **1.** The act of
predestinating, or the state of being predestined; destiny; fate.
2. *Theol.* The foreordination of all things by God, including
the salvation or damnation of men.
pre·des·tine (prē·des′tin) *v.t.* **·tined, ·tin·ing** To destine or
decree beforehand; foreordain; predestinate.
pre·de·ter·mine (prē′di·tûr′min) *v.t.* **·mined, ·min·ing 1.**
To determine beforehand; foreordain. **2.** To urge to accept
(a point of view, etc.) beforehand; influence. — **pre′de·**
ter′mi·nate (-mə·nit, -nāt) *adj.* — **pre′de·ter′mi·na′tion** *n.*
pred·i·ca·ble (pred′i·kə·bəl) *adj.* Capable of being predicated or affirmed. — *n.* **1.** Anything predicable. — **pred′·**
i·ca·bil′i·ty, pred′i·ca·ble·ness *n.*
pre·dic·a·ment (pri·dik′ə·mənt) *n.* **1.** A trying or embarrassing situation; plight. **2.** A specific state, position, or
situation. [< LL < *praedicare* to proclaim. See PREACH.]
pred·i·cate (*v.* pred′i·kāt; *n. & adj.* pred′i·kit) *v.* **·cat·ed,**
·cat·ing *v.t.* **1.** *U.S.* To found or base (an argument, proposition, etc.): with *on* or *upon.* **2.** To affirm as a quality or
attribute of something. **3.** To imply or connote. **4.** To declare; proclaim. **5.** *Logic* To state or affirm concerning the
subject of a proposition. — *v.i.* **6.** To make a statement or
affirmation. — *n.* **1.** *Gram.* The verb in a sentence or clause
together with its complements and modifiers. **2.** *Logic*
In a proposition, that which is stated about a subject. —
adj. **1.** That predicates. **2.** *Gram.* Belonging to, relating to,
or of the nature of a predicate. [< L < *praedicare* to pro-
claim] — **pred′i·ca′tive** *adj.* — **pred′i·ca′tive·ly** *adv.*
predicate adjective *Gram.* An adjective that describes the
subject of a linking verb, as *sad* in *He is sad.*
predicate noun *Gram.* A noun that designates or identifies
the subject of a linking verb, as *king* in *He was king.*
pred·i·ca·tion (pred′i·kā′shən) *n.* **1.** The act of predicating.
2. Something predicated. — **pred′i·ca′tion·al** *adj.*
pre·dict (pri·dikt′) *v.t.* **1.** To make known beforehand;
prophesy. **2.** To assert on the basis of data, theory, or experience but in advance of proof. — *v.i.* **3.** To make a prediction. [< L < *prae-* before + *dicere* to say] — **pre·dict′a·**
ble *adj.* — **pre·dict′a·bly** *adv.* — **pre·dic′tor** *n.*
pre·dic·tion (pri·dik′shən) *n.* **1.** The act of predicting. **2.**
Something predicted. — **pre·dic′tive** *adj.* — **pre·dic′·**
tive·ly *adv.*
pre·di·gest (prē′di·jest′, -dī-) *v.t.* To treat (food) by a process of partial digestion before introduction into the stomach.
pre·di·lec·tion (prē′də·lek′shən, pred′ə-) *n.* A preference
or bias in favor of something; a partiality: with *for.* [< F <
Med.L < L *prae-* before + *diligere* to love, choose]
pre·dis·pose (prē′dis·pōz′) *v.t.* **·posed, ·pos′ing 1.** To give
a tendency or inclination to; make susceptible: Exhaustion
predisposes one to sickness. **2.** To dispose of beforehand.
pre·dom·i·nant (pri·dom′ə·nənt) *adj.* Superior in power,
influence, effectiveness, number, or degree; prevailing over
others. — **pre·dom′i·nance, pre·dom′i·nan·cy** *n.* — **pre·**
dom′i·nant·ly *adv.*
pre·dom·i·nate (pri·dom′ə·nāt) *v.i.* **·nat·ed, ·nat·ing 1.** To
have governing influence or control; be in control: often with
over. **2.** To be superior to all others. **3.** To prevail. —
pre·dom′i·nat′ing·ly *adv.* — **pre·dom′i·na′tion** *n.*
pre·em·i·nent (prē·em′ə·nənt) *adj.* Supremely eminent;
distinguished above all others; outstanding; conspicuous.
[< L < *prae-* before + *eminere* to stand out] — **pre·em′i·**
nent·ly *adv.* — **pre·em′i·nence** *n.*
pre·empt (prē·empt′) *v.t.* **1.** To acquire or appropriate beforehand. **2.** To occupy (public land) so as to acquire by
preemption. — *v.i.* **3.** In bridge, to make a preemptive
bid. — **pre·emp′tor** *n.* — **pre·emp′to·ry** (-tə·rē) *adj.*
pre·emp·tion (prē·emp′shən) *n.* **1.** The right to purchase
something before others; also, the act of so purchasing. **2.**
Public land obtained by exercising this right. [< Med.L
< L *prae-* before + *emptus,* pp. of *emere* to buy]
pre·emp·tive (prē·emp′tiv) *adj.* **1.** Pertaining to or capable of preemption. **2.** In bridge, designating a bid that is unnecessarily high, intended to discourage subsequent bidding.
preen (prēn) *v.t.* **1.** To trim and dress (feathers, etc.) with
the beak, as a bird. **2.** To dress or adorn (oneself) carefully.
3. To pride or congratulate (oneself): with *on.* — *v.i.*
4. To primp; prink. [ME *proyne, preyn, prene*]
pre·ex·ist (prē′ig·zist′) *v.i. & v.t.* To exist before. — **pre′·**
ex·is′tence *n.* — **pre′ex·is′tent** *adj.*
pre·fab (prē′fab′) *n.* A prefabricated structure or part.
pre·fab·ri·cate (prē·fab′rə·kāt) *v.t.* **·cat·ed, ·cat·ing 1.** To
build beforehand. **2.** To manufacture in standard sections
that can be rapidly assembled. — **pre·fab′ri·ca′tion** *n.*

pref·ace (pref′is) *n.* **1.** A statement or brief essay, included in the front matter of a book, etc., and dealing primarily with the purpose and scope of the work. **2.** Any introductory speech, writing, etc. — *v.t.* ·aced, ·ac·ing **1.** To introduce or furnish with a preface. **2.** To serve as a preface for. [< OF < L < *prae*- before + *fari* to speak]

pref·a·to·ry (pref′ə·tôr′ē, -tō′rē) *adj.* Of the nature of a preface; introductory. Also **pref′a·to′ri·al.** — **pref′a·to′ri·ly** *adv.*

pre·fect (prē′fekt) *n.* **1.** In ancient Rome, any of various civil and military officials. **2.** Any magistrate, chief official, etc.; esp., in France: **a** The chief administrator of a department. **b** The head of the Paris police. **3.** The dean of certain private or religious schools. Also spelled *praefect*. [< OF < L *praeficere* to set over]

pre·fec·ture (prē′fek·chər) *n.* The office, jurisdiction, or province of a prefect. — **pre·fec′tur·al** *adj.*

pre·fer (pri·fûr′) *v.t.* ·ferred, ·fer·ring **1.** To hold in higher regard or esteem; value more. **2.** To choose (something or someone) over another or others; like better. **3.** To give priority to, as certain securities over others. — **Syn.** See CHOOSE. [< F < L < *prae*- before + *ferre* to carry] — **pre·fer′rer** *n.*

pref·er·a·ble (pref′ər·ə·bəl) *adj.* That is preferred; more desirable; worthy of choice. — **pref′er·a·ble·ness, pref′er·a·bil′i·ty** *n.* — **pref′er·a·bly** *adv.*

pref·er·ence (pref′ər·əns) *n.* **1.** The choosing of one person or thing over another or others; also, the privilege of so choosing. **2.** One who or that which is preferred. **3.** The granting of special advantage to one over others, as to one country or group of countries. **4.** The act of preferring, or the state of being preferred.

pref·er·en·tial (pref′ə·ren′shəl) *adj.* **1.** Showing or arising from preference or partiality. **2.** Giving preference, as in tariffs. — **pref′er·en′tial·ism** *n.* — **pref′er·en′tial·ly** *adv.*

preferential shop A shop that gives preferential treatment to union members when hiring, laying off, promoting, etc.

pre·fer·ment (pri·fûr′mənt) *n.* **1.** The act of promoting to higher office; advancement. **2.** A position, rank, or office of social prestige or profit. **3.** The act of preferring.

preferred stock Stock on which dividends must be paid before dividends can be paid on common stocks, usu. also receiving preference in the distribution of assets on liquidation. Also *Brit.* **preference shares.**

pre·fig·u·ra·tion (prē·fig′yə·rā′shən) *n.* **1.** The act of prefiguring. **2.** That which prefigures; a prototype. — **pre·fig·ur·a·tive** (prē·fig′yər·ə·tiv) *adj.* — **pre·fig′ur·a·tive·ly** *adv.* — **pre·fig′ur·a·tive·ness** *n.*

pre·fig·ure (prē·fig′yər) *v.t.* ·ured, ·ur·ing **1.** To serve as an indication or suggestion of; foreshadow. **2.** To imagine or picture to oneself beforehand. [< LL < L *prae*- before + *figurare* to form]

pre·fix (*n.* prē′fiks; *v.* prē·fiks′) *n.* **1.** *Gram.* A bound form affixed to the beginning of a base, stem, or root, altering or modifying its meaning, as *re*- in *renew.* Compare COMBINING FORM, SUFFIX. **2.** Something placed before, as a title before a name. — *v.t.* To put or attach before or at the beginning; add as a prefix. [< OF < L < *prae*- before + *figere* to fasten, fix] — **pre′fix·al** *adj.* — **pre′fix·al·ly** *adv.* — **pre·fix·ion** (prē·fik′shən) *n.*

preg·na·ble (preg′nə·bəl) *adj.* **1.** Capable of being captured, as a fort. **2.** Open to attack; vulnerable; assailable. [< OF < L *prehendere* to seize] — **preg′na·bil′i·ty** *n.*

preg·nan·cy (preg′nən·sē) *n. pl.* ·cies The state or quality of being pregnant.

preg·nant (preg′nənt) *adj.* **1.** Carrying a growing fetus in the uterus. **2.** Having considerable weight or significance; full of meaning. **3.** Teeming with ideas. **4.** Bearing issue or results; fruitful; prolific. [< L < *prae*- before + *gnasci* to be born] — **preg′nant·ly** *adv.*

pre·hen·si·ble (pri·hen′sə·bəl) *adj.* Capable of being grasped.

pre·hen·sile (pri·hen′sil) *adj.* Adapted for grasping or holding, as the tail of a monkey. [See PREHENSION.] — **pre·hen·sil·i·ty** (prē′hen·sil′ə·tē) *n.*

pre·hen·sion (pri·hen′shən) *n.* The act of grasping, physically or mentally. [< L < *prehendere* to seize]

pre·his·tor·ic (prē′his·tôr′ik, -tor′-) *adj.* Of or belonging to the period before written history. Also **pre′his·tor′i·cal.** — **pre′his·tor′i·cal·ly** *adv.*

pre·his·to·ry (prē·his′tə·rē) *n. pl.* ·ries The history of mankind in the period preceding written records.

pre·judge (prē·juj′) *v.t.* ·judged, ·judg·ing To judge beforehand or without proper inquiry. [< F < Med.L < *prae*- before + *judicare* to judge] — **pre·judg′er** *n.* — **pre·judg′ment** or **pre·judge′ment** *n.*

prej·u·dice (prej′oo·dis) *n.* **1.** A judgment or opinion formed before the facts are known; esp., an unfavorable, irrational opinion. **2.** The act or state of holding preconceived, irrational opinions. **3.** Hatred of or dislike for a particular group, race, religion, etc. **4.** Injury or damage to a person

arising from a hasty and unfair judgment by others. (or **to**) **the prejudice of** To the injury or detriment of. *v.t.* ·diced, ·dic·ing **1.** To cause to have a prejudice; influence. **2.** To damage or impair by some act, judgment, etc. [< OF < L < *prae*- before + *judicium* judgment] — **Syn.** (noun) *Prejudice, bias,* and *partiality* are compared they denote an attitude of mind that interferes with fair judgment. Only *prejudice* is necessarily a term of opprobrium; literally it signifies prejudgment without adequate hearing or consideration, but it is chiefly used to refer to a strong emotional *bias*. *bias* is an imbalance of mind, an inclination in some direction that prevents a fair weighing of issues. *Partiality* is an inclination to favor one person or view unfairly. A *bias* may be for or against someone or something, but *partiality* always implies favor.

prej·u·di·cial (prej′oo·dish′əl) *adj.* Tending to prejudice; injure; detrimental. — **prej′u·di·cial·ly** *adv.*

prel·a·cy (prel′ə·sē) *n. pl.* ·cies **1.** The system of church government by prelates: sometimes used disparagingly. The dignity or function of a prelate; also, prelates collectively: also **prel·a·ture** (prel′ə·chər).

prel·ate (prel′it) *n.* An ecclesiastic of high rank, as a bishop, archbishop, etc. [< OF *prelat* < L *praelatus* set over] — **prel′ate·ship** *n.* — **pre·lat·ic** (pri·lat′ik) or **·i·cal** *adj.*

pre·lim·i·nar·y (pri·lim′ə·ner′ē) *adj.* Before or introductory to the main event, proceeding, or business; prefatory; preparatory. — *n. pl.* ·nar·ies **1.** A preparatory step or act. **2.** A preliminary examination. **3.** In sports, a minor introductory event, as a boxing match. [< F *pré-* pre- + *liminaire* prefactory] — **pre·lim′i·nar′i·ly** *adv.*

pre·lit·er·ate (prē·lit′ər·it) *adj.* Of a culture, lacking or predating the existence of written language or records.

prel·ude (prel′yood, prē′lood) *n.* **1.** *Music* **a** An instrumental composition of moderate length, in a free style. **b** An opening section or movement of a musical composition. **2.** Any introductory or opening performance or event. — **·ud·ed, ·ud·ing** *v.t.* **1.** To introduce with a prelude. **2.** To serve as a prelude to. — *v.i.* **3.** To serve as a prelude. **4.** To provide or play a prelude. [< Med.L < L < *prae*- before + *ludere* to play] — **pre·lud·er** (pri·lōō′dər, prel′yoo·dər) *n.* — **pre·lu·di·al** (pri·lōō′dē·əl) *adj.*

pre·ma·ture (prē′mə·chōōr′, -tōōr′, -tyōōr′; *Brit.* prem′ə·tyōōr′) *adj.* Existing, happening, or developed before its natural or proper period; untimely. [< L < *prae*- before + *maturus* ripe] — **pre′ma·ture′ly** *adv.* — **pre′ma·ture′ness, pre′ma·tu′ri·ty** *n.*

pre·med·i·cal (prē·med′i·kəl) *adj.* Preparatory to or preparing for the study of medicine. Also *Informal* **pre·med.**

pre·med·i·tate (prē·med′ə·tāt) *v.t. & v.i.* ·tat·ed, ·tat·ing To plan or consider beforehand. [< L < *prae*- before + *meditari* to muse, ponder] — **pre·med′i·tat′ed·ly** *adv.* — **pre·med′i·ta′tive** *adj.* — **pre·med′i·ta′tor** *n.*

pre·med·i·ta·tion (prē·med′ə·tā′shən) *n.* **1.** The act of meditating. **2.** *Law* The deliberation and planning of a crime before its commission, showing intent to commit it.

pre·mi·er (prē′mē·ər, *esp. Brit.* prem′yər; *for n.,* also pri·mir′) *adj.* **1.** First in rank or position; principal. **2.** First in order of occurrence; senior. — *n.* **1.** Prime minister. **2.** In Canada, the head of a Provincial cabinet. [< L *primus* first] — **pre′mi·er·ship′** *n.*

pre·mière (pri·mir′, *Fr.* prə·myâr′) *n.* The first performance of a play, movie, etc. [< F, fem. of *premier* first]

pre·mil·len·ni·al (prē′mi·len′ē·əl) *adj.* Pertaining to or occurring before the millennium.

prem·ise (prem′is; *for v.,* also pri·mīz′) *n.* **1.** A proposition that serves as a ground for argument or for a conclusion. *pl.* A definite portion of real estate; land with its appurtenances; also, a building or part of a building. **3.** In a logism, either of the two propositions that combine to form a conclusion. **4.** *pl. Law* That part in a deed that sets forth the date, names of parties, the land or thing conveyed or granted, etc. Also **prem′iss.** — *v.* ·mised, ·mis·ing *v.t.* **1.** To state beforehand, as by way of introduction or explanation. **2.** To state or assume as a premise or basis of argument. — *v.i.* **3.** To make a premise. [< MF < Med.L < *prae*- before + *mittere* to send]

pre·mi·um (prē′mē·əm) *n.* **1.** An object or service offered free as an inducement to buy, rent, or contract for another object or service. **2.** The amount paid or payable for insurance, usu. in periodical installments. **3.** An extra amount or bonus paid in addition to a fixed price, wage, etc. **4.** A price paid for a loan, usu. in addition to interest. **5.** The or price at which stocks, shares, or money are valued in excess of their nominal or par value: bank shares at a premium of five percent. **6.** High regard or value. **7.** A reward or prize awarded in a competition. — **at a premium 1.** Valuable and in demand. **2.** Above par. [< L ult. < *prae*- before + *emere* to take]

pre·mo·lar (prē·mō′lər) *Anat. n.* One of the teeth situated in front of the molars and behind the canines: also called *bicuspid*. — *adj.* Situated in front of the molar teeth.

pre·mo·ni·tion (prē′mə·nish′ən, prem′ə-) *n.* **1.** A presenti-

nt of the future not based on information received; an in-
ictive foreboding. **2.** An actual warning of something
, to occur. [< LL < *prae-* before + *monere* to advise] —
•mon·i·to·ry (pri·mon′ə·tôr′ē, -tō′rē) *adj.* — **pre·mon′·**
/**ri·ly** *adv.*
·na·tal (prē-nāt′l) *adj.* Prior to birth: *prenatal* care.
·na′tal·ly *adv.*
·no·men (prē·nō′mən) See PRAENOMEN.
oc·cu·pied (prē·ok′yə/prēd) *adj.* **1.** Engrossed in thought
in some action. **2.** Previously occupied.
oc·cu·py (prē·ok′yə·pī) *v.t.* ·**pied,** ·**py·ing 1.** To engage
y; engross the mind. **2.** To occupy or take possession of
t. [< L *praeoccupare* to seize beforehand] — **pre·oc′u·**
·**cy** (-pən·sē), **pre·oc′cu·pa′tion** *n.*
or·dain (prē·ôr′dān) *v.t.* To ordain beforehand; fore-
·ain. — **pre·or·di·na′tion** (prē·ôr′də·nā′shən) *n.*
) (prep) *adj. Informal* Preparatory: a *prep* school.
pack·age (prē·pak′ij) *v.t.* ·**aged,** ·**ag·ing** To package
·eats, etc.) before offering them for sale.
)·a·ra·tion (prep′ə·rā′shən) *n.* **1.** The act or process of
·paring. **2.** An act or proceeding undertaken in advance
·ome event; provision. **3.** The fact or state of being pre-
·ed. **4.** Something made or prepared, as a medicine.
par·a·to·ry (pri·par′ə·tôr′ē, -tō′rē) *adj.* **1.** Serving as
·paration. **2.** Occupied in preparation: a *preparatory*
·olar. — *adv.* As a preparation: *Preparatory* to writing, I
consider this: also **pre·par′a·to′ri·ly.**
·aratory school A private school that prepares stu-
·ts for college admission.
pare (pri·pâr′) *v.* ·**pared,** ·**par·ing** *v.t.* **1.** To make
·ly, fit, or qualified; put in readiness. **2.** To provide with
·at is needed; equip: to *prepare* an expedition. **3.** To
·g to a state of completeness: to *prepare* a meal. — *v.i.*
·'o make preparations; get ready. [< OF < L < *prae-* be-
·+ *parare* to produce] — **pre·par′ed·ly** (pri·pâr′id·lē)
·, **pre·par′er** *n.*
par·ed·ness (pri·pâr′id·nis, -pârd′-) *n.* Readiness; esp.,
·ndition of military readiness for war.
pay (prē·pā′) *v.t.* ·**paid,** ·**pay·ing** To pay or pay for in
·ance. — **pre·pay′ment** *n.*
pense (pri·pens′) *adj.* Considered beforehand; pre-
·litated: chiefly in the phrase **malice prepense.** [< OF <
·ro- ahead + *pensare* to think] — **pre·pense′ly** *adv.*
pon·der·ant (pri·pon′dər·ənt) *adj.* Having superior
·e, weight, importance, quantity, etc.. — **pre·pon′der·**
·e, **pre·pon′der·an·cy** *n.* — **pre·pon′der·ant·ly** *adv.*
pon·der·ate (pri·pon′də·rāt) *v.i.* ·**at·ed,** ·**at·ing 1.** To
·f greater weight. **2.** To incline downward or descend, as
·scale of a balance. **3.** To be of greater power, impor-
·ce, quantity, etc.; predominate; prevail. [< L < *prae-*
·ore + *ponderare* to weigh] — **pre·pon′der·a′tion** *n.*
·o·si·tion (prep′ə·zish′ən) *n. Gram.* **1.** In some lan-
·ges, a word as *by, for, from,* functioning to indicate the re-
·on of a substantive (the object of the preposition) to
·ther substantive, verb, or adjective and usu. placed be-
·· its object. Together they constitute a prepositional
·ase that serves as an adjectival or an adverbial modifier
·sitting *beside the fire*; a man *of honor*. **2.** Any word or
·struction that functions in a similar manner, as *in refer-*
·· *to* in He telephoned *in reference* to your letter.
·· It was once maintained that a sentence should never
· with a preposition, but natural English sentences often
·· *What did you laugh at?* is good English. *At what did you
·h?* is awkward and unnatural. [< F < L < *prae-* before
·*onere* to place] — **prep′o·si′tion·al** *adj.* — **prep′o·si′·**
·**al·ly** *adv.*
pos·sess (prē′pə·zes′) *v.t.* **1.** To preoccupy to the ex-
·ion of other ideas, beliefs, etc.; prejudice; bias. **2.** To
·ress or influence beforehand or at once, esp. favorably.
·**re′pos·ses′sion** *n.*
pos·sess·ing (prē′pə·zes′ing) *adj.* Inspiring a favora-
·opinion; pleasing. — **pre′pos·sess′ing·ly** *adv.*
pos·ter·ous (pri·pos′tər·əs) *adj.* Contrary to nature,
·on, or common sense; utterly absurd or impracticable.
·L < *prae* before + *posterus* last] — **pre·pos′ter·ous·ly**
· — **pre·pos′ter·ous·ness** *n.*
·puce (prē′pyoōs) *n. Anat.* The fold of skin covering
·glans of the penis or clitoris: also called *foreskin.* [< F
·· *praeputium*] — **pre·pu′tial** (pri·pyoō′shəl) *adj.*
·Raph·a·el·ite (prē·raf′ē·ə·līt, -rā′fē-) *n.* **1.** A follower
·he **Pre-Raphaelite Brotherhood,** a society of artists
·ned in England, 1847–49, stressing characteristics sup-
·edly typical of Italian art before the time of Raphael. **2.**
·· modern artist with similar aims. — *adj.* Of or pertain-
·to the Pre-Raphaelites. — **Pre-Raph′a·el·it′ism** *n.*
req·ui·site (prē·rek′wə·zit) *adj.* Required as an ante-
·ent condition; necessary to something that follows. — *n.*
·ething prerequisite.

pre·rog·a·tive (pri·rog′ə·tiv) *n.* **1.** An exclusive and unquestionable right belonging to a person or body of persons;
esp., a hereditary or official right. **2.** Any characteristic
privilege peculiar to a person or class. **3.** Precedence; pre-
eminence. — *adj.* Of, pertaining to, or possessing a prerogative. [< OF < L < *prae-* before + *rogare* to ask]
pres·age (n. pres′ij; v. pri·sāj′) *n.* **1.** An indication of something to come; omen. **2.** A presentiment; foreboding. **3.**
Prophetic meaning or import. — *v.* ·**saged,** ·**sag·ing** *v.t.* **1.**
To give a presage or portent of; foreshadow. **2.** To have a
presentiment of. **3.** To predict; foretell. — *v.i.* **4.** To
make a prediction. [< MF < L < *prae-* before + *sagire*
to perceive keenly] — **pre·sag′er** *n.*
pres·by·ter (prez′bə·tər, pres′-) *n. Eccl.* **1.** In the early
Christian church, one of the elders of a church. **2.** In various hierarchical churches, a priest. **3.** In the Presbyterian
Church: **a** An ordained clergyman: also called *teaching elder.*
b A layman who is a member of the governing body of a congregation. [< LL < Gk. *presbyteros* elder, compar. of *pres-
bys* old, important]
pres·by·te·ri·al (prez′bə·tir′ē-əl, pres′-) *adj.* Pertaining to
a presbytery or a presbyter. Also **pres·byt′er·al.** — **pres′·**
by·te′ri·al·ly *adv.*
pres·by·te·ri·an (prez′bə·tir′ē-ən, pres′-) *adj.* Pertaining
to or characterized by church government by presbyters. —
pres′by·te′ri·an·ism *n.*
Pres·by·te·ri·an (prez′bə·tir′ē-ən, pres′-) *adj.* Pertaining
to any of various Protestant churches that have church government by presbyters. — *n.* A member of a Presbyterian
church. — **Pres′by·te′ri·an·ism** *n.*
pres·by·ter·y (prez′bə·ter′ē, pres′-) *n. pl.* ·**ter·ies 1.** In
the Presbyterian Church, a court composed of the ministers
and one or two presbyters of each church in a district. **2.**
Presbyters collectively. **3.** Government of a church by
presbyters. **4.** That part of a church set apart for the clergy.
[< OF < LL *presbyterium* assembly of elders]
pre·school (prē′skoōl′) *adj.* Of, intended for, or designating
a child past infancy but under school age.
pre·sci·ence (prē′shē-əns, presh′ē-) *n.* Knowledge of events
before they take place; foreknowledge. [< OF < L < *prae-*
before + *scire* to know]
pre·sci·ent (prē′shē-ənt, presh′ē-) *adj.* Having prescience;
farseeing. — **pre′sci·ent·ly** *adv.*
pre·scribe (pri·skrīb′) *v.* ·**scribed,** ·**scrib·ing** *v.t.* **1.** To set
down as a direction or rule to be followed; enjoin. **2.** *Med.*
To order the use of (a medicine, treatment, etc.). — *v.i.* **3.**
To lay down laws or rules; give directions. **4.** *Med.* To order a remedy; give prescriptions. [< L < *prae-* before +
scribere to write] — **pre·scrib′er** *n.*
pre·script (prē′skript; *for adj.,* also pri·skript′) *n.* Something prescribed; a rule or regulation, esp. a rule of conduct.
— *adj.* Laid down, prescribed.
pre·scrip·tion (pri·skrip′shən) *n.* **1.** *Med.* **a** A physician's
order for a medicine including directions for its use. **b** The
remedy so prescribed. **2.** The act of prescribing. **3.** That
which is prescribed; a prescript.
pre·scrip·tive (pri·skrip′tiv) *adj.* **1.** Making strict requirements or rules: *prescriptive* grammar. **2.** Sanctioned by
custom or long use. — **pre·scrip′tive·ly** *adv.*
pres·ence (prez′əns) *n.* **1.** The state or fact of being present. **2.** The area immediately surrounding a person or
thing; close proximity. **3.** The immediate vicinity of a person of superior rank, esp., a sovereign; also, the person or
personality of a sovereign, ruler, etc. **4.** Personal appearance; bearing; esp., a pleasing or dignified bearing. **5.** An
invisible spirit or influence felt to be near.
presence of mind Full command of one's faculties, esp. in
an emergency; coolness, alertness, and readiness.
pres·ent[1] (prez′ənt) *adj.* **1.** Now going on; not past or future. **2.** Of or pertaining to time now occurring; current.
3. Being in the place or company referred to or considered;
being at hand. **4.** Being actually considered, written, discussed, etc.: the *present* issue. **5.** *Gram.* Denoting a tense or
verb form that expresses a current or habitual action or
state. — *n.* **1.** Present time; the time being; now. **2.**
Gram. The present tense; also, a verb form denoting it. **3.**
pl. Law Present writings: a term for the document in which
the word occurs: Know all men by these *presents.* — **at
present** Now. [< OF < L < *prae-* before + *esse* to be]
pre·sent[2] (v. pri·zent′; *n.* prez′ənt) *v.t.* **1.** To bring into the
presence or acquaintance of another; introduce, esp. to one
of higher rank. **2.** To exhibit to view or notice. **3.** To suggest to the mind: This *presents* a problem. **4.** To put forward for consideration or action; submit, as a petition. **5.**
To make a gift or presentation of or to, esp. formally. **6.** To
aim or level (a weapon, etc). — **to present arms** *Mil.* To
salute by holding a gun vertically in front of one's body with
the muzzle up and the trigger facing forward. — *n.* Some-

thing presented or given; a gift. [< OF < L *praeesse* to be before] — **pre·sent′er** *n.*

pre·sent·a·ble (pri·zen′tə·bəl) *adj.* **1.** Fit to be presented; in suitable condition or attire for company. **2.** Capable of being offered, exhibited, or bestowed. — **pre·sent′a·bil′i·ty, pre·sent′a·ble·ness** *n.* — **pre·sent′a·bly** *adv.*

pres·en·ta·tion (prez′ən·tā′shən, prē′zen-) *n.* **1.** The act of presenting or proffering for acceptance, approval, etc., or the state of being presented. **2.** The formal offering of a complimentary gift. **3.** The act of introducing or bringing to notice, esp. to one of higher rank: *presentation* at court. **4.** An exhibition or representation, as of a play.

pres·ent-day (prez′ənt·dā′) *adj.* Modern; current.

pre·sen·ti·ment (pri·zen′tə·mənt) *n.* A prophetic sense of something to come; a foreboding. [< F < L < *prae-* before + *sentire* to perceive]

pres·ent·ly (prez′ənt·lē) *adv.* **1.** After a little time; shortly. **2.** At the present time; now.

pre·sent·ment (pri·zent′mənt) *n.* **1.** The act of presenting. **2.** Something represented or exhibited.

present participle See under **PARTICIPLE**.

present perfect *Gram.* The verb tense expressing an action completed by the present time, usu. constructed with a form of the verb *to have*, as *has finished* in *By now he has finished the task.*

present tense *Gram.* The verb tense marking present time, as *am* in *I am here*, or *are going* in *You are going home.*

pre·ser·va·tive (pri·zûr′və·tiv) *adj.* Serving or tending to preserve. — *n.* A preservative agent; esp., a chemical substance added to food to retard spoilage.

pre·serve (pri·zûrv′) *v.* **·served, ·serv·ing** *v.t.* **1.** To keep in safety; guard: May the gods *preserve* you. **2.** To keep intact or unimpaired; maintain. **3.** To prepare (food) for future consumption, as by boiling with sugar or by salting. **4.** To keep from decomposition or change, as by chemical treatment. **5.** To keep for one's private hunting or fishing: to *preserve* foxes. — *v.i.* **6.** To make preserves, as of fruit. **7.** To maintain a game preserve. — *n.* **1.** *Usu. pl.* Fruit that has been cooked, usu. with sugar, to prevent its fermenting. **2.** Something that preserves or is preserved. **3.** An area set apart for the protection of wildlife, forests, etc.; also, such an area reserved for restricted or private hunting or fishing. [< OF < LL < L *prae-* before + *servare* to keep] — **pre·serv′·a·bil′i·ty** *n.* — **pre·serv′a·ble** *adj.* — **pres·er·va′tion** (prez′ər·vā′shən) *n.* — **pre·serv′er** *n.*

pre·shrunk (prē′shrungk′) *adj.* Shrunk during manufacture to minimize later shrinkage during cleaning.

pre·side (pri·zīd′) *v.i.* **·sid·ed, ·sid·ing** **1.** To sit in authority, as over a meeting; act as chairman or president. **2.** To exercise direction or control. **3.** To occupy a featured place, as an instrumentalist on a program. [< F < L < *prae-* before + *sedere* to sit] — **pre·sid′er** *n.*

pres·i·den·cy (prez′ə·dən·sē) *n.* *pl.* **·cies** **1.** The office, function, or term of office of a president. **2.** *Often cap.* The office of president of the U.S.

pres·i·dent (prez′ə·dənt) *n.* **1.** One who is chosen to preside over an organized body. **2.** *Often cap.* The chief executive of a republic. **3.** The chief executive officer of a government department, corporation, society, or similar body. **4.** The chief officer of a college or university. **5.** The chairman of a meeting conducted under parliamentary rules. [< OF < L *praesidens, -entis,* ppr. of *praesidere* to preside] — **pres·i·den·tial** (prez′ə·den′shəl) *adj.* — **pres′i·dent·ship′** *n.*

pre·sid·i·o (pri·sid′ē·ō) *n.* *pl.* **·sid·i·os** A garrisoned post; fortified settlement; fort. [< Am. Sp. < L *praesidium*]

pre·sid·i·um (pri·sid′ē·əm) *n.* An executive committee in the Soviet Union serving as the permanent organ of a larger governmental body.

Pre·sid·i·um (pri·sid′ē·əm) *n.* **1.** A governmental body of the Soviet Union that exercises the powers of the Supreme Soviet between plenary sessions. **2.** The supreme policy-making committee of the Communist party of the Soviet Union, headed by the party secretary. See **POLITBURO**.

pre·sig·ni·fy (prē·sig′nə·fī) *v.t.* **·fied, ·fy·ing** To signify or give token of in advance; presage; foreshadow.

press¹ (pres) *v.t.* **1.** To act upon by weight or pressure: to *press* a button. **2.** To compress so as to extract the juice: to *press* grapes. **3.** To extract by pressure, as juice. **4.** To exert pressure upon so as to smooth, shape, make compact, etc. **5.** To smooth or shape by heat and pressure, as clothes; iron. **6.** To embrace closely; hug. **7.** To force or impel. **8.** To distress or harass; place in difficulty. **9.** To urge persistently; entreat: They *pressed* me for an answer. **10.** To advocate persistently; emphasize. **11.** To put forward insistently: to *press* a claim. **12.** To urge onward; hasten. **13.** To proceed further in, as a lawsuit. **14.** To produce (a phonograph record) from a matrix. — *v.i.* **15.** To exert pressure; bear heavily. **16.** To advance forcibly or with speed. **17.** To press clothes, etc. **18.** To crowd; cram. **19.** To be urgent or importunate. — *n.* **1.** Newspapers or periodical literature collectively, or the persons concerned

with such publications, as editors, reporters, etc. **2.** Criticism, news, etc., in newspapers and periodicals. **3.** A place of business where printing is carried on. **4.** The process, or business of printing. **5.** A printing press. **6.** An apparatus by which pressure is applied, as for crushing grapes to make wine. **7.** The act of crowding together. **8.** Hurry; pressures of affairs: the *press* of business. **9.** The proper crease and folds in a pressed garment. **10.** A movable upright closet [< OF < L *pressare,* freq. of *premere* to press] — **press′er**

ess² (pres) *v.t.* **1.** To force into military or naval service. **.** To put to use in a manner not intended or desired. — *n.* commission to impress men into the public service; also, he impressment of men. [< obs. *prest* enlistment for advance pay < OF < L < *prae-* before + *stare* to stand]

ess agent A person employed to advance the interests of a actor, singer, etc., by means of publicity.

ess conference An interview granted by a celebrity, official, etc., to a number of journalists at the same time.

ess gang A detachment of men detailed to press men into aval or military service. Also **press-gang** (pres/gang′).

ess·ing (pres/ing) *adj.* **1.** Demanding immediate attention; urgent. **2.** Importunate. — **press/ing·ly** *adv.*

ess·man (pres/mən) *n.* *pl.* **·men** (-mən) **1.** A man in charge of a press, as a printing press. **2.** *Brit.* A journalist.

ess of canvas *Naut.* The maximum spread of sail that an be carried with safety. Also **press of sail**.

ess·or (pres/ər) *adj.* *Physiol.* Increasing the functional ctivities of an organ, as a nerve. [< PRESS¹]

ess release A bulletin prepared by a public relations department, etc., announcing an event, decision, etc.

ess·ure (presh/ər) *n.* **1.** The act of pressing, or the state being pressed. **2.** Any force that acts against an opposing rce. **3.** An impelling or constraining moral force. **4.** Urgent demands on one's time or strength. **5.** The oppressive fluence or depressing effect of something hard to bear; eight. **6.** *Physics* The force acting upon a surface per unit area. — *v.t.* **·sured**, **·sur·ing** *Informal* To compel, as by rceful persuasion. [< OF < L < *premere* to press]

essure cabin *Aeron.* An enclosed compartment in an rcraft in which air is pressurized.

essure cooker A strong, airtight pot for cooking food at gh temperature under pressure: also called *autoclave*.

essure group A group that seeks to influence legislators d public opinion in behalf of its own special interests.

es·sur·ize (presh/ər·īz) *v.t.* **·ized**, **·iz·ing** **1.** To subject to gh pressure. **2.** To establish (in an aircraft compartment, ecial suit, etc.) an air pressure higher than the low atmosheric pressure at high altitudes. — **pres/sur·i·za/tion** *n.*

ess·work (pres/wûrk′) *n.* **1.** The operating or management of a printing press. **2.** The work done by it.

es·ti·dig·i·ta·tion (pres/tə·dij/ə·tā/shən) *n.* The practice sleight of hand; legerdemain. [< F < Ital. < LL *praestus* mble + L *digitus* finger] — **pres/ti·dig/i·ta/tor** *n.*

es·tige (pres·tēzh′, pres/tij, pres·tēj′) *n.* **1.** Authority or aportance based on past achievements, reputation, power, c. **2.** Importance, respect, etc., due to the appearance of ealth or power. [< F < L *praestigium* illusion < *prae-* bere + *stringere* to bind]

es·tig·ious (pres·tij/əs, -tē/jəs) *adj.* Having a famous putation or name; honored or well-known; illustrious. — **es·tig/ious·ly** *adv.* — **pres·tig/ious·ness** *n.*

es·to (pres/tō) *adj.* *Music* Quick; faster than allegro. — *v.* **1.** *Music* In a presto manner: a direction to the perrmer. **2.** At once; speedily. — *n.* *Music* A presto movement or passage. [< Ital. < L *praesto* at hand]

e·sum·a·ble (pri·zōō/mə·bəl) *adj.* That may be assumed presumed; reasonable. — **pre·sum/a·bly** *adv.*

e·sume (pri·zōōm′) *v.* **·sumed**, **·sum·ing** *v.t.* **1.** To take r granted; assume to be true until disproved. **2.** To take on oneself without warrant or permission; venture: usu. ith the infinitive. **3.** To indicate the probability of; seem to ove: A concealed weapon *presumes* the intent to commit a ime. — *v.i.* **4.** To act or proceed presumptuously or overnfidently. **5.** To make excessive demands: with *on* or oon. [< OF < L < *prae-* before + *sumere* to take] — re·sum·ed·ly (pri·zōō/mid·lē) *adv.* — **pre·sum/er** *n.*

e·sump·tion (pri·zump/shən) *n.* **1.** Offensively forward arrogant conduct or speech; insolence. **2.** The act of preming; also, something presumed. **3.** A ground or reason r presuming. **4.** That which may be logically assumed ue until disproved. **5.** *Law* The inference of a fact from rcumstances that usually or necessarily attend such a fact. — **Syn. 1.** arrogance, boldness, impudence, impertinence.

e·sump·tive (pri·zump/tiv) *adj.* **1.** Creating or affording asonable grounds for belief. **2.** Based upon presumption: heir *presumptive*. — **pre·sump/tive·ly** *adv.*

e·sump·tu·ous (pri·zump/chōō·əs) *adj.* Unduly confint or bold; audacious; arrogant. — **pre·sump/tu·ous·ly** *v.* — **pre·sump/tu·ous·ness** *n.*

e·sup·pose (prē/sə·pōz′) *v.t.* **·posed**, **·pos·ing** **1.** To asme to start with. **2.** To imply as a necessary antecedent ndition. — **pre·sup·po·si·tion** (prē/sup·ə·zish/ən) *n.*

e·tend (pri·tend′) *v.t.* **1.** To assume or display a false aparance of; feign. **2.** To claim or assert falsely. **3.** To ign in play; make believe. — *v.i.* **4.** To make believe, as play or deception. **5.** To put forward a claim: with *to*. < L < *prae-* before + *tendere* to spread out]

pre·tend·ed (pri·ten/did) *adj.* **1.** Alleged or asserted; professed. **2.** Deceptive; false. — **pre·tend/ed·ly** *adv.*

pre·tend·er (pri·ten/dər) *n.* **1.** One who advances a claim or title; a claimant to a throne. **2.** One who pretends.

pre·tense (pri·tens′, prē/tens) *n.* **1.** A pretended claim; pretext. **2.** A false assumption of a character or condition. **3.** The act or state of pretending. **4.** A right or title asserted. **5.** The condition of being a claimant. Also *Brit.* **pretence/**. [< AF < Med.L < L *praetendere* to pretend]

pre·ten·sion (pri·ten/shən) *n.* **1.** A claim put forward, as to an office, privilege, rank, etc. **2.** Affectation; display. **3.** A bold or presumptuous pretention.

pre·ten·tious (pri·ten/shəs) *adj.* **1.** Making an ambitious outward show; ostentatious. **2.** Making claims, esp. when exaggerated or false. [< F *prétentieux*] — **pre·ten/tious·ly** *adv.* — **pre·ten/tious·ness** *n.*

preter- *prefix* Beyond; past; more than: also spelled *praeter-*. [< L *praeter* beyond < *prae* before]

pret·er·it (pret/ər·it) *Gram. adj.* Signifying past time or completed past action. — *n.* The tense that expresses absolute past time; also, a verb in this tense. Also **pret/er·ite.** [< OF < L < *praeter-* beyond + *ire* to go]

pret·er·i·tive (pri·ter/ə·tiv) *adj.* *Gram.* Used only in a past tense or past tenses: said of certain verbs.

pre·ter·mit (prē/tər·mit′) *v.t.* **·mit·ted**, **·mit·ting** To fail or cease to do; neglect; omit. [< L < *praeter-* beyond + *mittere* to send] — **pre/ter·mis/sion** (-mish/ən) *n.*

pre·ter·nat·u·ral (prē/tər·nach/ər·əl) *adj.* **1.** Diverging from or exceeding the common order of nature, but not outside the natural order: distinguished from *supernatural*. **2.** Outside the natural order. — **Syn.** See SUPERNATURAL. — **pre/ter·nat/u·ral·ism** *n.* — **pre/ter·nat/u·ral·ly** *adv.*

pre·text (prē/tekst) *n.* **1.** A fictitious reason or motive advanced to conceal a real one. **2.** A specious excuse or explanation. [< L < *prae-* before + *texere* to weave]

pre·tor (prē/tər), **pre·to·ri·an** (pri·tôr/ē·ən, -tō/rē-), etc. See PRAETOR, etc.

pret·ti·fy (prit/i·fī) *v.t.* **·fied**, **·fy·ing** To make pretty; embellish overmuch.

pret·ty (prit/ē) *adj.* **·ti·er**, **·ti·est** **1.** Characterized by delicacy, gracefulness, or proportion rather than by striking beauty. **2.** Pleasant; attractive: a *pretty* melody. **3.** Decent; good; sufficient: often used ironically: A *pretty* mess you've made of it! **4.** *Informal* Rather large in size or degree; considerable. **5.** Foppish. — *adv.* To a fair extent; rather: He looked *pretty* well. — **sitting pretty** *Informal* In good circumstances. — *n.* *pl.* **·ties** (-tēz) A pretty person or thing. [OE *prættig* sly, cunning] — **pret/ti·ly** *adv.* — **pret/ti·ness** *n.*

pret·zel (pret/səl) *n.* A glazed, salted biscuit, usu. baked in the form of a loose knot. [< G *brezel*]

pre·vail (pri·vāl′) *v.i.* **1.** To gain mastery; triumph: with *over* or *against*. **2.** To be effective or efficacious. **3.** To use persuasion or influence successfully: with *on*, *upon*, or *with*. **4.** To be or become a predominant feature or quality; be prevalent. **5.** To have general or widespread use or acceptance. [< OF or L < *prae-* before + *valere* to be strong]

pre·vail·ing (pri·vā/ling) *adj.* **1.** Current; prevalent. **2.** Having effective power or influence; efficacious. — **pre·vail/ing·ly** *adv.* — **pre·vail/ing·ness** *n.*

prev·a·lent (prev/ə·lənt) *adj.* **1.** Of wide extent or frequent occurrence; common. **2.** Predominant; superior. **3.** Efficacious; effective. — **prev/a·lence** *n.* — **prev/a·lent·ly** *adv.*

pre·var·i·cate (pri·var/ə·kāt) *v.i.* **·cat·ed**, **·cat·ing** To speak or act in a deceptive, ambiguous, or evasive manner; lie. [< L < *prae-* before + *varicare* to straddle] — **pre·var/i·ca/tion** *n.* — **pre·var/i·ca/tor** *n.*

pre·vent (pri·vent′) *v.t.* **1.** To keep from happening, as by previous measures or preparations; preclude; thwart. **2.** To keep from doing something; forestall; hinder. [< L < *prae-* before + *venire* to come] — **pre·vent/a·ble** or **pre·vent/i·ble** *adj.* — **pre·vent/a·bil/i·ty** or **pre·vent/i·bil/i·ty** *n.* — **pre·vent/er** *n.*

— **Syn. 1.** *Prevent* suggests forcible restraint and complete stoppage. The sense of anticipation, originally understood in *prevent*, is now to be found in *preclude* and *forestall*. An event is *precluded* by circumstances which make its occurrence impossible; to *forestall* is to make advance preparation to deal with, esp. to restrain. *Avert* suggests a warding off of something. — **Ant.** permit, facilitate.

pre·ven·tion (pri·ven/shən) *n.* **1.** The act of preventing. **2.** A hindrance; obstruction.

pre·ven·tive (pri·ven/tiv) *adj.* Intended or serving to ward off harm, disease, etc.: *preventive* medicine. — *n.* That which prevents or hinders. Also **pre·vent·a·tive** (pri·ven/tə·tiv). — **pre·ven/tive·ly** *adv.* — **pre·ven/tive·ness** *n.*

pre·view (prē/vyōō′) *n.* **1.** An advance showing of a motion picture, a fashion show, etc., to invited guests. **2.** Any advance display or viewing. — *v.t.* To view in advance. Also spelled *prevue*.

pre·vi·ous (prē′vē-əs) *adj.* **1.** Existing or taking place before something else in time or order; antecedent; prior to. **2.** *Informal* Acting or occurring too soon; premature. — **previous to** Antecedent to; before. [< L < *prae*- before + *via* way] — **pre′vi·ous·ly** *adv.* — **pre′vi·ous·ness** *n.*

pre·vise (prē-vīz′) *v.t.* ·**vised**, ·**vis·ing** **1.** To foresee. **2.** To notify beforehand. [< L < *prae*- before + *videre* to see]

pre·vi·sion (prē-vizh′ən) *n.* **1.** The act or power of foreseeing; prescience; foresight. **2.** An anticipatory vision.

pre·vue (prē′vyōo′) See PREVIEW.

pre·war (prē′wôr′) *adj.* Of or pertaining to a condition, arrangement, time, etc., before a war.

prex·y (prek′sē) *pl.* ·**ies** *n.* *Slang* A president; esp., a college president. Also **prex.**

prey (prā) *n.* **1.** Any animal seized by another for food. **2.** A victim of a harmful or hostile person or influence. — *v.i.* **1.** To seek or take prey for food. **2.** To make someone a victim, as by cheating. **3.** To exert a wearing or harmful influence. Usu. with *on* or *upon.* [< OF < L *praeda* booty] — **prey′er** *n.*

Pri·am (prī′əm) In Greek legend, the father of Hector and Paris, the last king of Troy who was killed at the end of the Trojan War.

price (prīs) *n.* **1.** The amount of money, goods, etc., for which something is bought or sold. **2.** The cost at which something is obtained. **3.** Value; worth. **4.** A bribe, or anything used for a bribe. **5.** A reward for the capture or death of someone. — **beyond price 1.** Invaluable; priceless. **2.** Not bribable. — **to price out of the market** To lose one's share of a market by overpricing. — **to set a price on one's head** To offer a reward for the capture of a person, dead or alive. — *v.t.* **priced**, **pric·ing 1.** To set a price on; establish a price for. **2.** *Informal* To ask the price of. [< OF < L *pretium*]

price cutting The act of reducing the price of an article below the price at which it is usually advertised or sold.

price fixing 1. The establishment and maintenance of a scale of prices by specified groups of producers or distributors. **2.** The establishing by law of maximum or minimum or fixed prices for certain goods and services. **3.** The fixing of the retail price of a product by a manufacturer or producer. — *adj.* Pertaining to price fixing.

price·less (prīs′lis) *adj.* **1.** Beyond price or valuation; invaluable. **2.** *Informal* Wonderfully amusing or absurd.

price list A catalogue of goods listing their prices.

price rigging The concealed illegal fixing of prices.

prick (prik) *v.t.* **1.** To pierce slightly, as with a sharp point; puncture. **2.** To affect with sharp mental pain; sting; spur. **3.** To outline or indicate by punctures. **4.** To transplant (young plants) preparatory to later planting. **5.** To trace (a ship's course, etc.) on a chart: with *off.* **6.** To urge on with or as with a spur; goad. — *v.i.* **7.** To have or cause a stinging or piercing sensation. — **to prick up one's** (or **its**) **ears 1.** To raise the ears erect. **2.** To listen attentively. — *n.* **1.** The act of pricking; also, the sensation of being pricked. **2.** A mental sting or spur. **3.** A slender, sharp-pointed thing, as a thorn or weapon. **4.** A puncture; dot. [OE *prica* point, dot] — **prick′er** *n.*

prick·le (prik′əl) *n.* **1.** A small, sharp point, as on the bark of a plant. **2.** A tingling or stinging sensation. — *v.* ·**led**, ·**ling** *v.t.* **1.** To prick; pierce. **2.** To cause a tingling or stinging sensation in. — *v.i.* **3.** To have a stinging sensation; tingle. [OE *pricel*]

prick·ly (prik′lē) *adj.* **1.** Furnished with prickles. **2.** Stinging, as if from a prick or sting: a *prickly* sensation.

prickly heat A rash characterized by redness, itching, and small eruptions: also called *heat rash.*

prickly pear 1. A flat-stemmed cactus bearing a pear-shaped and often prickly fruit. **2.** The fruit itself.

pride (prīd) *n.* **1.** An undue sense of one's own superiority; arrogance; conceit. **2.** A proper sense of personal dignity and worth. **3.** That of which one is justly proud. **4.** The most excellent part of anything: the nation's *pride.* **5.** The best time or the flowering of something: the *pride* of summer. **6.** A group or company: said of lions. — *v.t.* **prid·ed**, **prid·ing** To take pride in (oneself) for something: with *on* or *upon.* [OE *prūt* proud]
— **Syn.** (noun) **1.** *Pride* manifests itself in disdain or haughtiness toward others; *self-esteem*, in more deference to one's opinions than others grant. *Conceit* is an exaggerated opinion of one's ability or worth. *Vanity* is seen in an excessive desire for admiration, while *vainglory* points to undue boasting about one's accomplishments. **6.** See FLOCK. — **Ant.** humility, modesty.

pride·ful (prīd′fəl) *adj.* Full of pride; haughty; disdainful.

prie-dieu (prē-dyœ′) *n.* A small desk with a shelf for a book, at which to kneel at prayers. [< F, pray God]

pri·er (prī′ər) *n.* One who pries: also spelled *pryer.*

priest (prēst) *n.* **1.** One esp. consecrated to the service of a divinity, and serving as mediator between the divinity and

his worshipers. **2.** In the Anglican, Greek, and Roman Catholic churches, a clergyman in the second order of the ministry, ranking next below a bishop, and having authority to administer the sacraments. [OE < L *presbyter*]

priest·craft (prēst′kraft′, -kräft′) *n.* **1.** Priestly arts and wiles: a disparaging term. **2.** The knowledge of priests.

priest·ess (prēs′tis) *n.* A woman or girl who exercises priestly functions.

priest·hood (prēst′hŏŏd) *n.* **1.** The priestly office or character. **2.** Priests collectively. [OE *prēosthad*]

priest·ly (prēst′lē) *adj.* Of, pertaining to, or befitting priest or the priesthood. — **priest′li·ness** *n.*

priest-rid·den (prēst′rid′n) *adj.* Completely under the influence or domination of priests.

prig (prig) *n.* A formal and narrow-minded person who assumes superior virtue and wisdom. [Origin uncertain]

prig·gish (prig′ish) *adj.* Like a prig; smug. — **prig′gish·ly** *adv.* — **prig′gish·ness** *n.*

prim (prim) *adj.* Minutely or affectedly precise and formal; stiffly proper and neat. — *v.t.* **primmed**, **prim·ming** To fix (the face, mouth, etc.) in a precise or prim expression. [Origin uncertain] — **prim′ly** *adv.* — **prim′ness** *n.*

pri·ma·cy (prī′mə-sē) *n.* *pl.* ·**cies 1.** The state of being first, as in rank or excellence. **2.** The office or province of a primate; archbishopric: also **pri′mate·ship** (-mit-ship). **3.** In the Roman Catholic Church, the office of the Pope. [< OF < Med.L < LL *primas, primatis* one of the first]

pri·ma don·na (prē′mə don′ə) **1.** A leading female singer as in an opera company. **2.** *Informal* A temperamental, vain person. [< Ital., lit., first lady]

pri·ma fa·ci·e (prī′mə fā′shi·ē, fā′shē) *Latin* At first view so far as at first appears. — **pri′ma-fa′ci·e** *adj.*

prima-facie evidence Evidence that, if unexplained or uncontradicted, would establish the fact alleged.

pri·mal (prī′məl) *adj.* **1.** Being at the beginning or foundation; first; original. **2.** Most important; chief. [< Med.L < L *primus*]

pri·ma·ri·ly (prī-mâr′ə·lē, prī′mə·rə·lē) *adv.* In the first place; originally; essentially.

pri·ma·ry (prī′mer·ē, -mər·ē) *adj.* **1.** First in time or origin; primitive. **2.** First in a series or sequence. **3.** First in rank or importance; chief. **4.** Constituting the fundamental original elements of which a whole is composed; basic; elemental. **5.** Of the first stage of development; elementary; lowest: *primary* school. **6.** *Electr.* Of, pertaining to, or not having an inducing current or its circuit: a *primary* coil. *Chem.* **a** Having some characteristic in the first degree, as in initial replacement of one atom or radical. **b** Having a carbon atom directly joined to only one other carbon atom in a molecule. — *n.* *pl.* ·**ries 1.** That which is first in rank, dignity, or importance. **2.** *Usu. pl.* A direct primary election. **3.** One of the primary colors. **4.** A primary cell. **5.** *Ornithol.* One of the large flight feathers of the pinion of a bird's wings. **6.** *Astron.* A body, as a planet, as distinguished from another body that revolves around it, as a satellite. [< L *primus* first]

primary cell *Electr.* Any of several devices consisting of two electrodes immersed in an electrolyte and capable of generating a current by chemical action when the electrodes are in contact through a conducting wire. Also called *voltaic cell.*

primary colors Any of several sets of colors considered basic to all other colors, as red, green, and blue (**physiological, fundamental,** or **additive primaries**); red, yellow, green blue, black, and white (**psychological** or **subtractive primaries**); and red, yellow, and blue (**painting primaries**).

primary election A direct primary election.

primary school A school for very young pupils, usu. the first four grades of elementary school.

pri·mate (prī′mit, -māt) *n.* **1.** The prelate highest in rank in a nation or province. **2.** Any of an order of mammals, including the tarsiers, lemurs, marmosets, monkeys, apes, and man. [< OF < LL < L *primus*] — **pri·ma·tial** (prī-mā′shəl) *adj.*

pri·ma·tol·o·gy (prī′mə·tol′ə·jē) *n.* The study of the origin, structure, evolution, and classification of primates. — **pri·ma·tol′o·gist** *n.*

prime¹ (prīm) *adj.* **1.** First in rank, dignity, or importance. **2.** First in value or quality; first-rate. **3.** First in time order; original; primitive. **4.** *Math.* Divisible by no whole number except itself and unity. Two or more numbers are said to be *prime* to each other when they have no common factor except unity. **5.** Not derived; first. — *n.* **1.** The period of full vigor, beauty, and power succeeding youth and preceding age. **2.** The period of full perfection in anything. **3.** The beginning of anything; dawn; spring. **4.** The best anything: a *prime* grade. **5.** *Math.* A prime number. **6.** A mark or accent (′) written above and to the right of a letter or figure; also, an inch, a minute, etc., as indicated by this sign. **7.** *Music* Unison. — *v.* **primed**, **prim·ing** *v.t.* **1.** prepare; make ready. **2.** To put a primer into (a gun, as preparatory to firing. **3.** To pour water into (a pump) to displace air and promote suction. **4.** To cover (a surface) with sizing, a first coat of paint, etc. **5.** To supply beforehand with facts, information, etc.; brief. — *v.i.* **6.** To make something ready, as for firing, pumping, etc. [< OF L *primus*] — **prime′ly** *adv.* — **prime′ness** *n.*

prime[2] (prīm) *n. Often cap. Eccl.* The second of the seven canonical hours. [OE < LL *prima* (*hora*) first (hour)]

prime meridian A meridian from which longitude is reckoned, now, generally, the one that passes through Greenwich, England.

prime minister The chief minister and head of a cabinet, and often the chief executive of a government.

prim·er[1] (prim′ər) *n.* **1.** An elementary textbook; esp., a beginning reading book. **2.** *Printing* Either of two sizes of type, **great primer** (18-point) and **long primer** (10-point). Med.[L < L *primus*]

prim·er[2] (prī′mər) *n.* **1.** Any device, as a cap, tube, etc., used to detonate the main charge of a gun, mine, etc. **2.** One who or that which primes.

pri·me·val (prī·mē′vəl) *adj.* Belonging to the first ages; primitive. [< L *primus* first + *aevum* age] — **pri·me′val·ly** *adv.*

primi· *combining form* First. [< L *primus* first]

pri·mi·ge·ni·al (prī′mə·jē′nē·əl) *adj.* Being the first or first-born; primal; original. [< L *primus* + *genus* kind]

prim·ing (prī′ming) *n.* **1.** That with which anything is primed. **2.** A combustible composition used to ignite an explosive charge. **3.** The first layer of paint laid on a surface.

prim·i·tive (prim′ə·tiv) *adj.* **1.** Pertaining to the beginning or origin; earliest; primary; not derived. **2.** Resembling the manners or style of early times; simple; crude. **3.** *Anthropol.* of or pertaining to the earliest anthropological forms or civilizations. **4.** *Biol.* **a** Being or occurring at an early stage of development or growth; first-formed; rudimentary. **b** Not much changed by evolution: a *primitive* species. — *n.* **1.** An artist, or a work of art, belonging to an early period; also, a work resembling such art, or an artist producing it. **2.** One who or that which is primitive. [< F < L < *primus* first] **prim′i·tive·ly** *adv.* — **prim′i·tive·ness, prim′i·tiv′i·ty** *n.*

prim·i·tiv·ism (prim′ə·tiv·iz′əm) *n.* Belief in or adherence to primitive forms and customs.

pri·mo·gen·i·tor (prī′mə·jen′ə·tər) *n.* An earliest ancestor; forefather. [< Med.L < L *primo* first + *genitor* father]

pri·mo·gen·i·ture (prī′mə·jen′ə·chər) *n.* **1.** The state of being the first-born child. **2.** The exclusive right of the eldest son to inherit the property, title, etc., of a parent. [< d.L < L *primo* first + *gignere* to beget]

pri·mor·di·al (prī·môr′dē·əl) *adj.* **1.** First in time; original; elemental. **2.** *Biol.* First in order or appearance in the growth or development of an organism. [< LL < L *primus* + *ordiri* to begin a web] — **pri·mor′di·al·ly** *adv.*

primp (primp) *v.t. & v.i.* To prink; dress up, esp. with superfluous attention to detail.

prim·rose (prim′rōz) *n.* **1.** An early-blossoming perennial herb with tufted basal leaves and variously colored flowers. The evening primrose. **3.** A pale yellow color, named for the common primrose of England. — *adj.* **1.** Pertaining to the primrose. **2.** Of primrose color. **3.** Flowery; gay. [ME *primrose* < Med.L < L *primus* first]

prince (prins) *n.* **1.** A nonreigning male member of a royal family. **2.** A male monarch or sovereign. **3.** *Brit.* The son of a sovereign or of a son of the sovereign. **4.** One of a high order of nobility. **5.** The ruler of a small state. **6.** One of highest rank of any class: a merchant *prince*. [< OF < *primus* first + stem of *capere* to take]

Prince Al·bert (al′bûrt) A long, double-breasted frock coat.

prince consort The husband of a reigning female sovereign.

prince·ling (prins′ling) *n.* **1.** A young prince. **2.** A subordinate prince. Also **prince′let** (-lit).

prince·ly (prins′lē) *adj.* **-li·er, -li·est** **1.** Liberal; generous. Like or suitable for a prince. **3.** Having the rank of a prince. — *adv.* In a princely manner. — **prince′li·ness** *n.*

Prince of Darkness Satan.

Prince of Peace Jesus Christ.

Prince of Wales The title conferred on the eldest son of the British sovereign, to make that son heir apparent.

prin·cess (prin′sis) *n.* **1.** A nonreigning female member of a royal family. **2.** The consort of a prince. **3.** Formerly, a female sovereign. **4.** *Brit.* A daughter of the sovereign or of a son of the sovereign. [< F *princesse*]

prin·cesse (prin·ses′, prin′sis) *adj.* Designating a woman's close-fitting garment hanging in an unbroken line from shoulder to flared hem. Also **prin′cess.** [< F, princess]

princess royal The eldest daughter of a sovereign.

prin·ci·pal (prin′sə·pəl) *adj.* First in rank, character, or importance. — *n.* **1.** One who takes a leading part in some action. **2.** *Law* **a** The actor in a crime, or one present aiding and abetting. **b** The employer of one who acts as an agent. **c** One primarily liable for whom another has become surety. **d** The capital or body of an estate. **3.** One who is at the head of some body or society. **4.** The head teacher, master, or officer of a school. **5.** Property or capital, as opposed to interest or income. **6.** The chief truss or rafter of a roof. [< F < L *princeps* first, principal] — **prin′ci·pal·ly** *adv.* — **prin′ci·pal·ship′** *n.*

principal axis *Optics* The imaginary line passing through the center of a lens or mirror at right angles to each surface.

principal clause *Gram.* An independent clause. See under CLAUSE.

prin·ci·pal·i·ty (prin′sə·pal′ə·tē) *n. pl.* **·ties** **1.** The territory of a reigning prince, or one that gives to a prince a title of courtesy. **2.** The state, office, or jurisdiction of a prince.

principal parts The inflected forms of a verb from which all other inflected forms may be derived. In English, the principal parts of a verb are the infinitive (*go, walk*), the past tense (*went, walked*), and the past participle (*gone, walked*). In this dictionary, when appropriate, the past, past participle, and present participle are shown (*gave, given, giving*). When, however, the principal parts are entirely regular in formation, adding *-ed* and *-ing* directly to the infinitive without spelling modification, they are not shown. In cases where the past tense and past participle are identical, only the one is shown (*behaved, behaving*).

prin·ci·ple (prin′sə·pəl) *n.* **1.** A general truth or law, basic to other truths. **2.** A rule of personal conduct. **3.** Moral standards collectively: a man of *principle*. **4.** That which is inherent in anything, determining its nature. **5.** A primary source or fundamental cause. **6.** An established mode of action or operation in natural phenomena: the *principle* of relativity. **7.** *Chem.* An essential constituent of a compound or substance. [< L *principium* a beginning]

prin·ci·pled (prin′sə·pəld) *adj.* Having or characterized by ethical principles: often in combination: *high-principled*.

prink (pringk) *v.t.* **1.** To dress (oneself) for show. — *v.i.* **2.** To dress oneself showily or fussily. — **prink′er** *n.*

print (print) *n.* **1.** An impression with ink from type, plates, etc.; printed characters collectively; also, any printed matter. **2.** Anything printed from an engraved plate or lithographic stone; a proof; also, a printed picture or design. **3.** An impression or mark made upon a substance by pressure; imprint: the *print* of a shoe in the snow. **4.** Any fabric stamped with a design. **5.** Any tool or device bearing a pattern or design, or that upon which it is impressed. **6.** *Photog.* A positive picture made from a negative. — **in print** Printed; also, for sale in printed form. — **out of print** No longer on sale, the edition being exhausted: said of books, etc. — *v.t.* **1.** To mark, as with inked type, a stamp, die, etc. **2.** To stamp or impress (a mark, seal, etc.) on or into a surface. **3.** To fix as if by impressing: The scene is *printed* on my memory. **4.** To produce (a book, newspaper, etc.) by the application of inked type, plates, etc., to paper or similar material. **5.** To cause to be put in print; publish. **6.** To write in letters similar to those used in print. **7.** *Photog.* To produce (a positive picture) by transmitting light through a negative onto a sensitized surface. — *v.i.* **8.** To be a printer. **9.** To take or give an impression in printing. **10.** To form letters similar to printed ones. [< OF < L *premere* to press] — **print′a·ble** *adj.* — **prin′ter** *n.*

printer's devil Devil (def. 7).

print·ing (prin′ting) *n.* **1.** The making and issuing of printed matter. **2.** The act of reproducing a design upon a surface. **3.** That which is printed. **4.** The number of copies of anything printed at one time. **5.** Writing that resembles printed matter. **6.** The act of one who or that which prints.

printing press A mechanism for printing from an inked surface, operating by pressure.

pri·or[1] (prī′ər) *adj.* Preceding in time, order, or importance. — **prior to** Before. [< L, earlier, superior]

pri·or[2] (prī′ər) *n.* A monastic officer next in rank below an abbot. [OE < L] — **pri′or·ate** (-it) *n.*

pri·or·ess (prī′ər·is) *n.* A woman holding a position corresponding to that of a prior; a nun next below an abbess.

pri·or·i·ty (prī·ôr′ə·tē, -or′-) *n. pl.* **·ties** **1.** Antecedence; precedence. **2.** A first right established on emergency or need. **3.** A certificate giving a first right to a manufacturer or contractor.

pri·or·y (prī′ər·ē) *n. pl.* **·or·ies** A monastic house presided over by a prior or prioress. [< OF *priorie* < Med.L *prioria*]

prism (priz′əm) *n.* **1.** *Geom.* A solid whose bases or ends are any similar equal and parallel plane figures, and whose lateral faces are parallelograms. **2.** *Optics* A prism made of glass or other transparent substance and usually having triangular ends, used to produce a spectrum or to refract light beams. [< LL < Gk., < *prixein* to saw]

pris·mat·ic (priz·mat′ik) *adj.* **1.** Refracted or formed by a prism. **2.** Resembling the spectrum; exhibiting rainbow tints. **3.** Pertaining to or shaped like a prism. Also **pris·mat/i·cal. — pris·mat/i·cal·ly** *adv.*

pris·on (priz/ən) *n.* **1.** A public building for the safekeeping of persons in legal custody; a penitentiary. **2.** Any place of confinement. **3.** Imprisonment. — *v.t.* To imprison. [< OF < F < *prehendere* to seize]

pris·on·er (priz/ən·ər, priz/nər) *n.* **1.** One who is confined in a prison or whose liberty is forcibly restrained. **2.** A person confined for any reason. [< OF *prisonier*]

pris·sy (pris/ē) *Informal adj.* **·si·er, ·si·est** Effeminate; overprecise; prim. [Blend of PRIM or PRECISE + SISSY]

pris·tine (pris/tēn, -tin; *Brit.* pris/tīn) *adj.* **1.** Of or pertaining to the earliest state or time; primitive. **2.** Extremely pure; untouched; unspoiled. [< L *pristinus* primitive]

prith·ee (prith/ē) *interj. Archaic* I pray thee.

pri·va·cy (prī/və·sē) *n.* *pl.* **·cies 1.** The condition of being private; seclusion. **2.** The state of being secret; secrecy.

pri·vate (prī/vit) *adj.* **1.** Removed from public view; secluded. **2.** Not for public or common use. **3.** Having no official rank, character, office, etc.: a *private* citizen. **4.** Not generally known; secret. **5.** Not common or usual; special: a *private* interpretation. **6.** Individual; personal: one's *private* opinion. — *n.* **1.** *Mil.* An enlisted man ranking below a corporal. *Abbr. Pvt.* See table at GRADE. **2.** *pl.* The genitals. — **in private** In secret. [< L *privatus* apart from the state] — **pri/vate·ly** *adv.* — **pri/vate·ness** *n.*

private detective A detective employed by a private citizen, business enterprise, etc., rather than by a city or state.

private enterprise Free enterprise.

pri·va·teer (prī/və·tir/) *n.* **1.** A vessel owned and commanded by private persons, but carrying on maritime war under letters of marque. **2.** The commander or one of the crew of a privateer: also **pri/va·teers/man** (-tirz/mən). — *v.i.* To cruise in or as a privateer. — **pri/va·teer/ing** *n.*

private eye *Informal* A private detective.

private first class A soldier ranking next above a private and below a corporal. *Abbr. Pfc, Pfc.* See table at GRADE.

private school *U.S.* A school maintained under private or corporate management, usu. for profit.

private secretary A secretary who works for one individual only and is usu. entrusted with confidential matters.

pri·va·tion (prī·vā/shən) *n.* The state of lacking something necessary or desirable; esp., want of the common comforts of life. [< L *privare* to set apart]

priv·a·tive (priv/ə·tiv) *adj.* **1.** Causing privation, want, or destitution; depriving. **2.** *Gram.* Altering a word so as to express a negative instead of a positive meaning: *privative* particles (such prefixes and suffixes as *a-, an-, in-, -less*). — *n. Gram.* A privative prefix or suffix. [< L *privativus*] — **priv/a·tive·ly** *adv.* — **priv/a·tive·ness** *n.*

priv·et (priv/it) *n.* An ornamental, bushy shrub of the olive family, with white flowers and black berries, used for hedges. [Earlier *primet*; origin unknown]

priv·i·lege (priv/ə·lij) *n.* **1.** A special or peculiar benefit, favor, or advantage. **2.** An exemption or immunity by virtue of one's office or station. **3.** A fundamental or basic civil, legal, or political right; the *privilege* of voting. — *v.t.* **·leged, ·leg·ing 1.** To grant a privilege to. **2.** To exempt or free: with *from*. [< OF < L < *privus* one's own + *lex* law]

priv·i·leged (priv/ə·lijd) *adj.* Having or enjoying a privilege.

priv·y (priv/ē) *adj.* **1.** Participating with another or others in the knowledge of a secret transaction: with *to: privy* to the plot. **2.** *Archaic* Secret. — *n. pl.* **priv·ies 1.** *Law* One who is concerned with another in a matter affecting the interests of both. **2.** A small toilet or outhouse. [< F < L *privatus.* See PRIVATE.] — **priv/i·ly** *adv.*

privy council Any body of advisers or counselors, as appointed by a sovereign for his personal use.

Privy Council 1. In Great Britain, the sovereign's personal council whose duties have been largely assumed by the cabinet. **2.** In Canada, a body that advises the Governor General.

privy seal In Great Britain, the seal used by the sovereign on papers that later pass under the great seal or do not demand the great seal.

prix fixe (prē fēks/) A meal served at a fixed price; table d'hôte. Compare À LA CARTE. [< F, fixed price]

prize¹ (prīz) *n.* **1.** That which is offered or won as a reward for superiority or success, as in a contest. **2.** Anything to be striven for. **3.** Anything offered or won, as in a lottery, etc. — *adj.* **1.** Offered or awarded as a prize: a *prize* medal. **2.** Having drawn a prize; entitled to a prize. **3.** Highly valued or esteemed. — *v.t.* **prized, priz·ing 1.** To value highly. **2.** To estimate the value of; appraise. [Var. of PRICE.]

prize² (prīz) *n.* In international law, property, as a vessel and cargo, captured by a belligerent at sea in conformity with the laws of war. — *v.t.* **prized, priz·ing 1.** To seize as a prize, as a ship. **2.** To raise or force with a lever; pry: also spelled *prise.* [< F *prise* something taken, booty]

prize court A court sitting for the adjudication of prizes taken at sea in wartime.

prize fight A fight between professional boxers for a pr a certain sum of money, etc., generally limited to a speci number of rounds. — **prize fighter** — **prize fighting**

prize ring A roped enclosure within which boxers fight.

pro¹ (prō) *n. pl.* **pros 1.** An argument or vote in favo something: in the phrase *pros and cons.* **2.** *Usu. pl.* One v votes for or favors a proposal. — *adv.* In behalf of; in fa of; for: to argue pro and con. [< L, for]

pro² (prō) *n. pl.* **pros** *Informal* **1.** A professional athl **2.** Any expert in any field.

pro-¹ *prefix* **1.** Forward; to or toward the front from a p tion behind; forth: *produce*, to lead forth; *project*, to th forth. **2.** Forth from its place; away: *profugate*, to flee aw **3.** To the front of; forward and down: *prolapse*, to slip ward and down. **4.** Forward in time or direction: *proc* to go forward. **5.** In behalf of: *prolocutor.* **6.** In place substituted for: *proconsul.* **7.** In favor of: *pro-Russ* [< L *pro- < pro* before, forward, for]

pro-² *prefix* **1.** Prior; occurring earlier in time: *progno* **2.** Situated in front; forward; before: *prognathous.* [*pro- < pro* before, in front]

pro·a (prō/ə) *n.* A swift Malaysian vessel, propelled by s or oars. Also called *prahu.* [< Malay *prāū*]

prob·a·bil·i·ty (prob/ə·bil/ə·tē) *n. pl.* **·ties 1.** The stat quality of being probable; likelihood. **2.** A probable ev statement, condition, etc.

prob·a·ble (prob/ə·bəl) *adj.* **1.** Likely to be true or to h pen, but leaving room for doubt. **2.** That renders so thing worthy of belief, but falls short of demonstrat *probable* evidence. — *Syn.* See APPARENT. [< OF < *probare* to prove, test]

prob·a·bly (prob/ə·blē) *adv.* In all probability.

pro·bate (prō/bāt) *adj.* **1.** Of or pertaining to a prol court. **2.** Pertaining to making proof. — *n.* **1.** Fori legal proof, as of a will. **2.** The right or jurisdiction of p ing wills. — *v.t.* **·bat·ed, ·bat·ing** To obtain probate of, will. [< L < *probare* to prove]

probate court A court having jurisdiction of the proc wills, of guardianships, and of the settlement of estates.

pro·ba·tion (prō·bā/shən) *n.* **1.** *Law* A method of allow a person convicted of a minor offense to go at large but under the supervision of a probation officer. **2.** A proc ing or period designed to test character, qualifications, as of a new employee. **3.** The status or condition of one ing tried out, or free under suspension of sentence: to b *probation.* **4.** The act of proving; also, proof. — **pro tion·al, pro·ba/tion·ar/y** *adj.*

pro·ba·tion·er (prō·bā/shən·ər) *n.* One on probation.

probation officer A person delegated to supervise ar fender on suspended sentence.

pro·ba·tive (prō/bə·tiv) *adj.* **1.** Serving to prove or **2.** Pertaining to probation; proving. Also **pro·ba·t** (prō/bə·tôr/ē, -tō/rē).

probe (prōb) *v.* **probed, prob·ing** *v.t.* **1.** To explore wi probe. **2.** To investigate or examine thoroughly. — *v.t* To penetrate; search. — *n.* **1.** *Surg.* An instrument fo ploring cavities, wounds, etc. **2.** That which proves or t **3.** *U.S.* A searching investigation or inquiry, esp. into cr [< LL *proba* proof] — **prob/er** *n.*

pro·bi·ty (prō/bə·tē, prob/ə-) *n.* Virtue or integrity te and confirmed. [< F < L < *probus* good, honest]

prob·lem (prob/ləm) *n.* **1.** A perplexing question or so tion, esp. when difficult or uncertain of solution. **2.** puzzling or difficult circumstance or person. **3.** *Mat* proposition in which some operation or construction is quired, as to bisect an angle. — *adj.* **1.** Presenting dealing with a problem. **2.** Being a problem. [< OF < Gk. < *pro-* forward + *ballein* to throw]

prob·lem·at·ic (prob/ləm·at/ik) *adj.* Constituting volving a problem; questionable; contingent. Also p **lem·at/i·cal.** — **prob/lem·at/i·cal·ly** *adv.*

pro·bos·cis (prō·bos/is) *n. pl.* **·bos·cis·es** or **·bos·ci** (-bos/ə·dēz) **1.** *Zool.* **a** A long flexible snout, as of the t **b** The trunk of an elephant. **2.** *Entomol.* Any of var tubular feeding structures of certain insects, as those mosquitoes. **3.** A human nose: a humorous term. [< Gk. < *pro-* before + *boskein* to feed]

pro·caine (prō·kān/, prō/kān) *n.* A white crystalline c pound, $C_{13}H_{20}O_2N_2$, used chiefly in its hydrochloride as a local anesthetic. [< PRO-¹ + (CO)CAINE]

pro·ce·dure (prə·sē/jər) *n.* **1.** A manner of proceedin acting in any course of action. **2.** The methods or forn conducting a business, parliamentary affairs, etc. course of action; a proceeding. — **pro·ce/du·ral** *adj.*

pro·ceed (prə·sēd/) *v.i.* **1.** To go on or forward, esp. af stop. **2.** To begin and carry on an action or process. issue or come, as from some cause, source, or origin: with *f* **4.** *Law* To institute and carry on legal proceedings. [< L < *pro-* forward + *cedere* to go] — **pro·ceed/er** *n.*

pro·ceed·ing (prə·sē/ding) *n.* **1.** An act or course of act also, a particular act or course of action. **2.** The act of who or that which proceeds. **3.** *pl.* The records or minutes of the meetings of a society, etc. **4.** *Law* Any action instituted in a court.

ro·ceeds (prō'sēdz) *n.pl.* The amount derived from the disposal of goods, work, or the use of capital; return; yield.

roc·ess (pros'es, *esp. Brit.* prō'ses) *n.* **1.** A course or method of operations in the production of something. **2.** A series of continuous actions that bring about a particular result, end, or condition: the *process* of growth. **3.** A forward movement; advance; course. **4.** *Law* **a** Any judicial writ or order. **b** A writ issued to bring a defendant into court. **c** The whole course of proceedings in a cause. **5.** *Biol.* An accessory outgrowth or prominence of an organism or any of its parts: vertebral *process.* — *adj.* **1.** Produced by a special method: *process* butter; *process* cheese. **2.** Pertaining to, for, or made by a mechanical or chemical photographic process: a *process* illustration. — *v.t.* **1.** To subject to a routine procedure: to *process* an application. **2.** To treat or prepare by a special method. **3.** *Law* **a** To issue or serve a process on. **b** To proceed against. [See PROCEED.] — **proc'**·**es·sor** or **proc'ess·er** *n.*

ro·ces·sion (prə·sesh'ən, prō-) *n.* **1.** An array, as of persons or vehicles, arranged in succession and moving in a formal manner; a parade; also, any continuous course: the *procession* of the stars. **2.** The act of proceeding or issuing forth: the *procession* of the Holy Ghost from the Father. — *v.i.* To march in procession. [See PROCEED.]

ro·ces·sion·al (prə·sesh'ən·əl) *adj.* Of, pertaining to, or moving in a procession. — *n.* **1.** A hymn sung at the opening of a church service, during the entrance of the choir, etc. **2.** The music played or sung during a procession. — **pro·****ces'sion·al·ly** *adv.*

ro·claim (prō·klām') *v.t.* **1.** To announce or make known publicly or officially; declare. **2.** To make plain; manifest. **3.** To outlaw, prohibit, or restrict by proclamation. [< L < *pro-* before + *clamare* to call] — **pro·claim'er** *n.*

roc·la·ma·tion (prok'lə·mā'shən) *n.* **1.** The act of proclaiming. **2.** That which is proclaimed.

ro·cliv·i·ty (prō·kliv'ə·tē) *n.* *pl.* **·ties** Natural tendency: usu. with *to.* [< L < *pro-* before + *clivus* slope]

ro·con·sul (prō·kon'səl, prō'kon'-) *n.* **1.** In ancient Rome, an official who exercised authority over a province or an army. **2.** A governor of a dependency; a viceroy. [< L] — **pro·con'su·lar** (-sə·lər,-syə-) *adj.* — **pro·con'su·late** (-sə·, -syə-), **pro·con'sul·ship** *n.*

ro·cras·ti·nate (prō·kras'tə·nāt) *v.* **·nat·ed, ·nat·ing** *v.i.* **1.** To put off taking action until a future time; be dilatory. — *v.t.* **2.** To defer or postpone. [< L *procrastinare*] — **pro·cras'ti·na'tion** *n.* — **pro·cras'ti·na'tor** *n.*

ro·cre·ate (prō'krē·āt) *v.t.* **·at·ed, ·at·ing** **1.** To engender or beget (offspring). **2.** To originate; produce. [< L < *pro-* before + *creare* to create] — **pro'cre·ant** *adj.* — **pro'cre·****a'tion** *n.* — **pro'cre·a'tor** *n.*

ro·cre·a·tive (prō'krē·ā'tiv) *adj.* **1.** Possessed of generative power; reproductive. **2.** Pertaining to procreation.

ro·crus·te·an (prō·krus'tē·ən) *adj.* **1.** Pertaining to or characteristic of Procrustes. **2.** Ruthlessly or violently bringing about conformity.

ro·crus·tes (prō·krus'tēz) In Greek mythology, a giant of Attica, who tied travelers to an iron bed and amputated or stretched their limbs until they fitted it.

rocto- *combining form Med.* Related to or affecting the rectum. Also, before vowels, **proct-**. [< Gk. *proktos* anus]

roc·tol·o·gy (prok·tol'ə·jē) *n.* The branch of medicine that treats of the diseases of the rectum. — **proc·to·log·i·cal** (prok'tə·loj'i·kəl) *adj.* — **proc·tol'o·gist** *n.*

roc·tor (prok'tər) *n.* **1.** An agent acting for another; attorney; proxy. **2.** A university or college official charged with maintaining order, supervising examinations, etc. — *v.t. & v.i.* To supervise (an examination). [ME *proketour, procutour*] — **proc·to·ri·al** (prok·tôr'ē·əl, -tō'rē-) *adj.*

ro·cum·bent (prō·kum'bənt) *adj.* **1.** *Bot.* Lying on the ground; trailing, as certain vines and plants. **2.** Lying down on or on the face; prone; prostrate. [< L < *pro-* forward + *cumbere* to lie down]

ro·cur·a·ble (prō·kyŏor'ə·bəl) *adj.* That can be procured.

ro·cur·ance (prō·kyŏor'əns) *n.* The process of procuring.

roc·u·ra·tor (prok'yə·rā'tər) *n.* **1.** A person authorized to act for and manage the affairs of another. **2.** In ancient Rome, one who had charge of the imperial revenues or, in a province, was an administrator. [See PROCURE.] — **proc'u·****ra·to'ri·al** (-rə·tôr'ē·əl, -tō'rē-) *adj.* — **proc'u·ra'tor·ship** *n.*

ro·cure (prō·kyŏor') *v.* **·cured, ·cur·ing** *v.t.* **1.** To obtain by some effort or means; acquire. **2.** To bring about; cause. **3.** To obtain (women) for the gratification of the lust of others. — *v.i.* **4.** To be a procurer or procuress. — **Syn.** See GET. [< OF < L < *pro-* on behalf of + *curare* to attend to] — **pro·cure'ment** *n.*

pro·cur·er (prō·kyŏor'ər) *n.* One who procures for another, as to gratify lust; a pimp. — **pro·cur'ess** *n.fem.*

Pro·cy·on (prō'sē·on) *n.* One of the 20 brightest stars, 2.12 magnitude; Alpha in the constellation Canis Minor: also called *Dog Star.* [< L < Gk. *Prokyōn*]

prod (prod) *v.t.* **prod·ded, prod·ding** **1.** To punch or poke with or as with a pointed instrument. **2.** To arouse mentally; urge; goad. — *n.* **1.** Any pointed instrument used for prodding; a goad. **2.** A thrust or punch; a poke. **3.** A reminder. [Origin unknown] — **prod'der** *n.*

prod·i·gal (prod'ə·gəl) *adj.* **1.** Addicted to wasteful expenditure, as of money, time, or strength; extravagant. **2.** Yielding in profusion; bountiful. **3.** Lavish; profuse. — *n.* One who is wasteful or profligate; a spendthrift. [< L *prodigus* wasteful] — **prod'i·gal·ly** *adv.*

prod·i·gal·i·ty (prod'ə·gal'ə·tē) *n.* *pl.* **·ties 1.** Extravagance; wastefulness. **2.** Great abundance; lavishness. **3.** Extreme generosity; bounteousness.

pro·di·gious (prə·dij'əs) *adj.* **1.** Enormous or extraordinary in size, quantity, or degree; vast. **2.** Marvelous; amazing. [< L *prodigium* omen] — **pro·dig'ious·ly** *adv.* — **pro·dig'ious·ness** *n.*

prod·i·gy (prod'ə·jē) *n.* *pl.* **·gies 1.** A person having remarkable qualities or powers: a violin *prodigy.* **2.** Something extraordinary. **3.** Something out of the ordinary course of nature; a monstrosity. [< L *prodigium*]

pro·duce (*v.* prə·dōōs', -dyōōs'; *n.* prod'ōōs, -yōōs, prō'dōōs, -dyōōs) *v.* **·duced, ·duc·ing** *v.t.* **1.** To bring forth or bear; yield, as young or a natural product. **2.** To bring forth by mental effort; compose, write, etc. **3.** To bring about: His words *produced* a violent reaction. **4.** To bring to view; exhibit: to *produce* evidence. **5.** To manufacture; make. **6.** To bring to performance before the public, as a play. **7.** To extend or lengthen, as a line. **8.** *Econ.* To create (anything with exchangeable value). — *v.i.* **9.** To yield or generate an appropriate product or result. — *n.* That which is produced; a product; esp. farm products collectively. [< L < *pro-* forward + *ducere* to lead] — **pro·duc'i·ble** *adj.*

pro·duc·er (prə·dōō'sər, -dyōō'-) *n.* **1.** One who or that which produces, esp. one who makes things for sale and use. **2.** One who finances and generally controls the production of a play, concert, motion picture, etc.

prod·uct (prod'əkt, -ukt) *n.* **1.** Anything produced or obtained as a result of some operation or work, as by generation, growth, labor, study, or skill. **2.** A result. **3.** *Math.* The result obtained by multiplication.

pro·duc·tion (prə·duk'shən) *n.* **1.** The act or process of producing. **2.** That which is produced. **3.** Any tangible result of industrial, artistic, or literary effort.

pro·duc·tive (prə·duk'tiv) *adj.* **1.** Producing or tending to produce; fertile; creative, as of artistic things. **2.** Producing or tending to produce profits or increase in quantity, quality, or value. **3.** Causing; resulting in: with *of.* — **pro·****duc'tive·ly** *adv.* — **pro·duc·tiv·i·ty** (prō'duk·tiv'ə·tē), **pro·****duc'tive·ness** *n.*

pro·em (prō'əm) *n.* An introductory statement; preface. [< OF < L < Gk. *prooimion* overture] — **pro·e·mi·al** (prō·ē'mē·əl) *adj.*

prof·a·na·tion (prof'ə·nā'shən) *n.* **1.** The act of profaning; also, an instance of it. **2.** Abusive or improper treatment of anything.

pro·fane (prə·fān', prō-) *v.t.* **·faned, ·fan·ing 1.** To treat (something sacred) with irreverence or abuse; desecrate; pollute. **2.** To put to an unworthy or degrading use; debase. — *adj.* **1.** Manifesting irreverence or disrespect toward the Deity or sacred things. **2.** Not religious or concerned with religious things; secular. **3.** Vulgar; common; coarse. [< F < L < *profanus* before or outside the temple, hence, unsacred] — **pro·fan·a·to·ry** (prə·fan'ə·tôr'ē, -tō'rē) *adj.* — **pro·fane'ly** *adv.* — **pro·fan'er** *n.* — **pro·fane'ness** *n.*

pro·fan·i·ty (prə·fan'ə·tē) *n.* *pl.* **·ties 1.** The state of being profane. **2.** Profane speech or action.

—Syn. 2. *Profanity* may refer to irreverent use of a sacred name, as well as to the use of words considered lewd or coarse. *Blasphemy* is a much stronger word; *profanity* may be thoughtless or careless speech, but *blasphemy* denotes a degree of malicious insult to sacred things. *Cursing* and *swearing* are types of *profanity; cursing* involves the uttering of imprecations in the name of God, generally as an expression of rage or frustration, while *swearing* is the uttering of rash or empty oaths.

pro·fess (prə·fes') *v.t.* **1.** To declare openly; avow; affirm. **2.** To assert, usu. insincerely: to *profess* remorse. **3.** To declare or affirm faith in. **4.** To have as one's profession: to *profess* the law. **5.** To receive into a religious order. — *v.i.* **6.** To make open declaration; avow. **7.** To take the vows of a religious order. [< L < *pro-* before < *fateri* to confess]

pro·fess·ed·ly (prə·fes'id·lē) *adv.* **1.** By open profession; avowedly. **2.** Pretendedly.

pro·fes·sion (prə-fesh′ən) *n.* **1.** An occupation that properly involves a liberal, scientific, or artistic education. **2.** The collective body of those following such occupations. **3.** The act of professing or declaring; declaration: *professions* of good will. **4.** That which is avowed or professed; a declaration. **5.** The act of binding oneself to a religious order; also, the condition of being so bound. — **Syn.** See OCCUPATION.

pro·fes·sion·al (prə-fesh′ən-əl) *adj.* **1.** Connected with, preparing for, engaged in, appropriate to, or conforming to a profession: *professional* courtesy. **2.** Of or pertaining to an occupation pursued for gain: a *professional* ball player. — *n.* **1.** One who pursues as a business some vocation or occupation. **2.** One who engages for money to compete in sports. **3.** One skilled in a profession, craft, or art. — **pro·fes′sion·al·ism** *n.* — **pro·fes′sion·al·ly** *adv.*

pro·fes·sor (prə-fes′ər) *n.* **1.** A teacher of the highest rank in a university or college, or in an institution where professional or technical studies are pursued. ◆ *Professor* may be abbreviated *Prof.* before the full name but is usu. written out before the surname, as *Professor Smith.* **2.** One who professes skill and offers instruction in some sport or art. — **pro·fes′sor·ship** *n.*

pro·fes·so·ri·al (prō′fə-sôr′ē-əl, -sō′rē-, prof′ə-) *adj.* Of, pertaining to, or characteristic of a professor; pedagogic; academic. — **pro′fes·so′ri·al·ly** *adv.*

prof·fer (prof′ər) *v.t.* To offer for acceptance. — *n.* The act of proffering, or that which is proffered. [< AF, OF < L *pro-* in behalf of + *offere* to offer] — **prof′fer·er** *n.*

pro·fi·cien·cy (prə-fish′ən-sē) *n. pl.* **·cies** A high state of attainment in some knowledge, art, or skill; expertness.

pro·fi·cient (prə-fish′ənt) *adj.* Thoroughly versed, as in an art or science. — *n.* An expert. [< L < *pro-* forward + *facere* to do] — **pro·fi′cient·ly** *adv.*

pro·file (prō′fil, *esp. Brit.* prō′fēl) *n.* **1.** The outline of a human face or figure as seen from the side; also, a drawing of this outline. **2.** Any outline or contour. **3.** A short biographical sketch vividly presenting the most striking characteristics of a personality. **4.** *Archit.* The outline of a perpendicular section of a building, etc., or the contour of an architectural member. **5.** *Geol.* A vertical section of the earth's crust. — *v.t.* **·filed, ·fil·ing 1.** To draw a profile of. **2.** To write or make a profile of. [< Ital. *proffilare* to draw in outline < L *pro-* forward + *filum* thread, line]

prof·it (prof′it) *n.* **1.** Any advantage or gain; benefit. **2.** *Often pl.* Excess of returns over outlay or expenditure. **3.** The return from the employment of capital after deducting the amount paid for raw material and for wages, rent, interest, etc. **4.** That part of the amount received for goods which exceeds the sum originally paid for them with or without all secondary expenses involved. — **gross profit** The excess of receipts from sales over expenditures for production or purchase. — **net profit** The surplus remaining after all necessary deductions, as for interest, bad debts, etc. — *v.i.* **1.** To be of advantage or benefit. **2.** To derive gain or benefit. — *v.t.* **3.** To be of profit or advantage to. [< L *profectus,* pp. of *proficere* to go forward] — **prof′it·less** *adj.*

prof·it·a·ble (prof′it-ə-bəl) *adj.* Bringing profit or gain; advantageous. — **prof′it·a·ble·ness** *n.* — **prof′it·a·bly** *adv.*

prof·i·teer (prof′ə-tir′) *v.i.* To seek or obtain excessive profits. — *n.* One who is given to making excessive profits, esp. to the detriment of others. — **prof′i·teer′ing** *n.*

profit sharing A system of remuneration by which workmen are given a share of the net profits of a business. — **prof·it-shar·ing** ((prof′it-shâr′ing) *adj.*

prof·li·ga·cy (prof′lə-gə-sē) *n. pl.* **·cies** The state or quality of being profligate.

prof·li·gate (prof′lə-git, -gāt) *adj.* **1.** Lost or insensible to principle, virtue, or decency. **2.** Recklessly extravagant; in great profusion. — *n.* **1.** A depraved or dissolute person. **2.** A reckless spendthrift. [< L, pp. of *profligare* to destroy < *pro-* forward + *fligere* to dash] — **prof′li·gate·ly** *adv.* — **prof′li·gate·ness** (-git·nis, -gāt′nis) *n.*

prof·lu·ent (prof′lōō-ənt) *adj.* Flowing smoothly or plentifully. [< L < *pro-* before + *fluere* to flow] — **prof′lu·ence** *n.*

pro·found (prə-found′, prō-) *adj.* **1.** Intellectually deep or penetrating. **2.** Reaching to, arising from, or affecting the depth of one's nature: *profound* respect. **3.** Situated far below the surface; unfathomable. **4.** Deep. **5.** Thorough; exhaustive: *profound* changes. — *n.* **1.** A fathomless depth. **2.** The ocean; the deep. [< OF < L *pro-* very + *fundus* deep] — **pro·found′ly** *adv.* — **pro·found′ness** *n.*

pro·fun·di·ty (prə-fun′də-tē, prō-) *n. pl.* **·ties 1.** The state or quality of being profound, in any sense. **2.** A deep place or thing. **3.** A profound or abstruse statement, theory, etc.

pro·fuse (prə-fyōōs′, prō-) *adj.* **1.** Giving or given forth lavishly; liberal; extravagant. **2.** Copious; overflowing; abundant: *profuse* vegetation. [< L < *pro-* forward + *fundere* to pour] — **pro·fuse′ly** *adv.* — **pro·fuse′ness** *n.*

pro·fu·sion (prə-fyōō′zhən, prō-) *n.* **1.** A lavish supply or condition: a *profusion* of ornaments. **2.** The act of pouring forth or supplying in great abundance; prodigality.

pro·gen·i·tor (prō-jen′ə-tər) *n.* A forefather or parent. [< F < L < *pro-* forth + *gignere* to beget]

prog·e·ny (proj′ə-nē) *n. pl.* **·nies** Offspring.

pro·ges·ter·one (prō-jes′tə-rōn) *n. Biochem.* A female hormone, isolated as a white, crystalline compound, $C_{21}H_{30}$ O_2, and also made synthetically. It is active in preparing the uterus for the fertilized ovum. Also **pro·ges·tin** (prō-jes′tin).

prog·na·thous (prog′nə-thəs, prog-nā′thəs) *adj.* Having abnormally projecting jaws. Also **prog·nath·ic** (prog-nath′-ik). — **prog·na·thism** (prog′nə-thiz′əm) *n.*

prog·no·sis (prog-nō′sis) *n. pl.* **·ses** (-sēz) **1.** *Med.* a A prediction or conclusion regarding the course of a disease and the probability of recovery. b Likelihood of recovery: The *prognosis* is excellent. **2.** Any prediction or forecast. [< NL < Gk. < *pro-* before + *gignōskein* to know]

prog·nos·tic (prog-nos′tik) *adj.* **1.** Of, pertaining to, or serving as a prognosis. **2.** Predicting or foretelling. — *n.* **1.** A sign of some future occurrence; an omen. **2.** *Med.* A symptom indicative of the course of a disease.

prog·nos·ti·cate (prog-nos′tə-kāt) *v.t.* **·cat·ed, ·cat·ing 1.** To foretell (future events, etc.) by present indications. **2.** To indicate beforehand. — **prog·nos′ti·ca′tion** *n.* — **prog·nos′ti·ca′tor** *n.*

pro·gram (prō′gram, -grəm) *n.* **1.** A performance or show, esp. one given at a scheduled time on television or radio. **2.** A printed announcement or schedule of events, esp. one for a theatrical performance. **3.** Any prearranged, proposed, or desired plan or course of proceedings. **4.** *Electronics* A sequence of instructions set up on the control panels of an electronic computer as guides in the performance of a desired operation or group of operations. Also *Brit.* **pro·gramme.** — *v.t.* **·gramed** or **·grammed, ·gram·ing** or **·gram·ming 1.** To arrange or include in a program. **2.** To make up a program for (a radio station, a computer, etc.). [< LL < Gk. < *pro-* before + *graphein* to write] — **pro·gram·mat·ic** (prō′grə-mat′ik) or **pro′gram·at′ic** *adj.*

pro·gram·mer (prō′gram·ər) *n.* One who makes up a computer program. Also **pro′gram·er.**

program music See under MUSIC.

prog·ress (*n.* prog′res, *esp. Brit.* prō′gres; *v.* prə-gres′) **1.** A moving forward in space; movement forward nearer a goal. **2.** Advancement toward maturity or completion; improvement. — *v.i.* **1.** To move forward or onward. **2.** To advance toward completion or fuller development. [< L *pro-* forward + *gradi* to walk]

pro·gres·sion (prə-gresh′ən) *n.* **1.** The act of progressing; advancement. **2.** *Math.* A sequence of numbers or quantities, each of which is derived from the preceding by a constant relationship. **3.** *Music* a A movement from one tone or chord to another. b A succession of tones, chords, etc. **4.** Course or lapse of time; passage. — **pro·gres′sion·al** *adj.* — **pro·gres′sion·ism** *n.*

pro·gres·sive (prə-gres′iv) *adj.* **1.** Moving forward; advancing. **2.** Proceeding gradually or step by step. **3.** Aiming at or characterized by progress. **4.** Spreading from one part to others; increasing: said of a disease: *progressive* paralysis. **5.** Striving for or favoring progress or reform, esp. social, political, educational, or religious. **6.** Denoting or pertaining to a tax or taxes in which the tax rate increases as the amount taxed increases. **7.** *Gram.* Designating an aspect of the verb that expresses the action as being in progress at some time in the past, present, or future: formed with any tense of the auxiliary *be* and the present participle; as, He *is* speaking; he *had been* speaking; he *will be* speaking. — *n.* **1.** One who believes in progress or in progressive methods; esp., one who favors or promotes reforms or changes as in politics or religion. **2.** *Gram.* A progressive verb form. [< OF *progressif*] — **pro·gres′sive·ly** *adv.* — **pro·gres′sive·ness** *n.* — **pro·gres′siv·ism** *n.* — **pro·gres′siv·ist** *n.*

Pro·gres·sive-Con·ser·va·tive Party (prə-gres′iv-kən-sûr′və-tiv) In Canada, one of the principal political parties, formerly called the Conservative Party.

Progressive Party 1. A political party formed under the leadership of Theodore Roosevelt in 1912. **2.** A political party formed in 1924 under the leadership of Robert M. LaFollette. **3.** A political party formed in 1948, which nominated Henry A. Wallace for president.

pro·hib·it (prō-hib′it) *v.t.* **1.** To forbid, esp. by authority or law; interdict. **2.** To prevent or hinder. [< L < *pro-* before + *habere* to have] — **pro·hib′it·er** *n.*

pro·hi·bi·tion (prō′ə-bish′ən) *n.* **1.** The act of prohibiting, preventing, or stopping; also, a decree or order forbidding anything. **2.** The forbidding of the manufacture, transportation, and sale of alcoholic liquors as beverages.

pro·hi·bi·tion·ist (prō′ə-bish′ən·ist) *n.* One who favors legal prohibition of the manufacture and sale of alcoholic liquors.

pro·hib·i·tive (prō-hib′ə-tiv) *adj.* **1.** Prohibiting or serving to prohibit. **2.** Preventing the sale, purchase, etc., of something: *prohibitive* costs. Also **pro·hib′i·to·ry** (-tôr′ē, -tō′rē). — **pro·hib′i·tive·ly** *adv.*

·ect (*n.* proj′ekt; *v.* prə-jekt′)   *n.*   **1.** Something projected or mapped out in the mind, as a course of action; a 'n.   **2.** In schools, a problem, task, or piece of work given a student or group of students.   **3.** A housing project. — *v.t.*   **1.** To cause to extend forward or out.   **2.** To throw th or forward, as missiles.   **3.** To visualize as an external lity.   **4.** To cause (an image, shadow, etc.) to fall on a face.   **5.** To propose or plan.   **6.** *Math.* **a** To make a jection (of a solid, etc.) on a plane. **b** To reproduce (a re) by drawing lines from a vertex through every point the figure) to the corresponding point of the reproduc-1.   **7.** To use or produce (one's voice, words, etc.) so as to heard clearly and at a distance. — *v.i.*   **8.** To protrude. *Psychol.* To attribute one's own ideas, impulses, etc., to ers.   **10.** To speak or sing so as to be heard clearly and at istance.   [< L < *pro*- before + *jacere* to throw]

jec·tile (prə-jek′təl, *esp. Brit.* -tīl)   *adj.*   **1.** Projecting, mpelling forward.   **2.** Capable of being or intended to be jected or shot forth.   **3.** Protrusile. — *n.*   **1.** A body jected or thrown forth by force.   **2.** *Mil.* A missile for charge from a gun or cannon.   [< NL < L *projectus* own out]

jec·tion (prə-jek′shən)   *n.*   **1.** The act of projecting; tting, throwing, or shooting out or forth.   **2.** That which jects; a projecting part.   **3.** A scheme; project.   **4.** A tem of lines drawn on a given fixed plane, as in a map, resenting point for point a given terrestrial or celestial face.   **5.** *Psychol.* **a** The unconscious process of attribut-one's own feelings, attitudes, etc., to others. **b** An in-nce of this process.   **6.** *Photog.* **a** The process of exhibit-motion pictures or slides on a screen. **b** The picture so duced.   — **pro·jec′tive** *adj.*   — **pro·jec′tive·ly** *adv.*

jec·tor (prə-jek′tər)   *n.*   **1.** An apparatus for throwing minated images or motion pictures upon a screen.   **2.** A rror or combination of lenses for projecting a beam of t.   **3.** One who devises projects; schemer; promoter.

lapse (prō-laps′)   *Pathol.*   *v.i.* **lapsed, ·laps·ing** To fall of place, as an organ or part. — *n.* The falling down of organ or part, as the uterus, from its normal position. o **pro·lap·sus** (prō-lap′səs).   [< L < *pro*- forward + *labi* glide, fall]

late (prō′lāt)   *adj.*   **1.** Extended lengthwise.   **2.** Length-d toward the poles, as a spheroid.   [< L < *pro*- forward *ferre* to carry]

·le·gom·e·non (prō′lə-gom′ə-non)   *n.*   *pl.* **·na** (-nə) *Often* An introductory remark or remarks; a preface.   [< Gk. *pro*- before + *legein* to say]   — **pro′le·gom′e·nous** *adj.*

le·tar·i·an (prō′lə-târ′ē-ən)   *adj.*   Of or pertaining to the letariat.   — *n.* A member of the proletariat.   [< L < *les* offspring: so called because they served the Roman te only by having children]   — **pro′le·tar′i·an·ism** *n.*

le·tar·i·at (prō′lə-târ′ē-ət)   *n.*   **1.** Wageworkers collec-ely; the working class: a term used esp. in Marxism.   **2.** ancient Rome, the lowest class of the state.

lif·er·ate (prō-lif′ə-rāt)   *v.t. & v.i.* **·at·ed, ·at·ing** To pro-e, reproduce, or grow, esp. with rapidity, as cells in tissue mation.   — **pro·lif′er·a′tion** *n.*   — **pro·lif′er·a′tive** *adj.*

lif·er·ous (prō-lif′ər-əs)   *adj.*   **1.** Producing offspring ely.   **2.** *Bot.* **a** Developing buds, branches, and flowers m unusual places. **b** Bearing progeny in the way of off-ots, buds, etc.   [< Med.L < L *proles, prolis* offspring + *re* to bear]

lif·ic (prō-lif′ik)   *adj.*   **1.** Producing abundantly, as off-ing or fruit; fertile.   **2.** Producing results abundantly: a *lific* writer.   [< F < Med.L < L *proles, prolis* offspring stem of *facere* to make]   — **pro·lif′i·ca·cy** (-i-kə-sē), pro· **ic·ness** *n.*   — **pro·lif′i·cal·ly** *adv.*

— **Syn.** 1. fruitful, fecund. 2. productive.

lix (prō′liks, prō-liks′)   *adj.*   **1.** Unduly long and verbose, an address.   **2.** Indulging in long and wordy discourse. F < L < *pro*- before + stem of *liquere* to flow]   — **pro·** i·ty (prō-lik′sə-tē), **pro′lix·ness** *n.*   — **pro′lix·ly** *adv.*

logue (prō′lôg, -log)   *n.*   **1.** A prefatory statement to a m, discourse, or performance; esp., an introduction, often verse, spoken or sung before a play or opera.   **2.** Any icipatory act or event.   — *v.t.* To introduce with a pro-ue or preface. Also **pro′log.**   [< OF < L < Gk. < *pro*-ore + *logos* discourse]

·logu·ize (prō′lôg-īz, -log-)   *v.i.* **·ized, ·iz·ing** To make or er a prologue. Also **pro′lo·gize.**   — **pro′logu·iz′er** *n.*

·long (prə-lông′, -long′)   *v.t.* To extend in time or space; tinue; lengthen.   Also **pro·lon′gate** (-lông′gāt, -long′-). OF < LL < L *pro*- forth + *longus* long]   — **pro·lon·ga′·** n *n.*   — **pro·long′er** *n.*   — **pro·long′ment** *n.*

m (prom)   *n.*   *U.S. Informal* A formal college or school nce or ball.   [Short for *promenade*]

m·e·nade (prom′ə-nād′, -näd′)   *n.*   **1.** A walk for amuse-nt or exercise, or as part of a formal or social entertain-ment.   **2.** A place for promenading.   **3.** A concert or ball opened with a formal march; also, the march.   — *v.* **·nad·ed, ·nad·ing** *v.i.*   **1.** To take a promenade. — *v.t.*   **2.** To take a promenade through or along.   **3.** To take or exhibit on or as on a promenade.   [< MF < LL < *pro*- before + *minare* to drive (cattle)]   — **prom′e·nad′er** *n.*

Pro·me·theus (prə-mē′thyōōs, -thē-əs)   In Greek mytholo-gy, a Titan who stole fire from heaven for mankind and as a punishment was chained to a rock, where an eagle daily de-voured his liver, which was made whole again at night.   [< L < Gk. *Promētheus*]   — **Pro·me′the·an** *adj. & n.*

pro·me·thi·um (prə-mē′thē-əm)   *n.*   A radioactive element (symbol Pm), separated from uranium fission products and belonging to the lanthanide series: formerly called *illinium.* See ELEMENT.   [< NL < PROMETHEUS]

prom·i·nence (prom′ə-nəns)   *n.*   **1.** The state of being prom-inent.   **2.** That which is prominent.   **3.** *Astron.* One of the great tongues of flame shooting out from the sun's surface, seen during total eclipses. Also **prom′i·nen·cy.**

prom·i·nent (prom′ə-nənt)   *adj.*   **1.** Jutting out; projecting; protuberant.   **2.** Conspicuous in position, character, or im-portance.   **3.** Well-known; eminent.   [< L < *prominere* to project]   — **prom′i·nent·ly** *adv.*

pro·mis·cu·ous (prə-mis′kyōō-əs)   *adj.*   **1.** Composed of in-dividuals or things confusedly or indiscriminately mingled.   **2.** Indiscriminate, esp. in sexual relations.   **3.** *Informal* Lacking plan or purpose; casual; irregular.   [< L < *pro*-thoroughly + stem of *miscere* to mix]   — **pro·mis·cu·i·ty** (prō′mis·kyōō′ə-tē, prom′is-) *n.*   — **pro·mis′cu·ous·ly** *adv.*   — **pro·mis′cu·ous·ness** *n.*

prom·ise (prom′is)   *n.*   **1.** An assurance given by one person to another that the former will or will not perform a specified act.   **2.** Reasonable ground for hope or expectation, esp. of future excellence or satisfaction.   **3.** Something promised.   — *v.* **·ised, ·is·ing** *v.t.*   **1.** To engage or pledge by a promise: used with the infinitive or a clause.   **2.** To make a promise of (something) to someone.   **3.** To give reason for expecting.   **4.** *Informal* To assure (someone).   — *v.i.*   **5.** To make a promise.   **6.** To give reason for expectation.   [< L < *pro*-forth + *mittere* to send]   — **prom′is·ee** *n.*   — **prom′is·er** *n.*

Promised Land   **1.** Canaan, promised to Abraham by God. *Gen.* xv 18.   **2.** Any longed-for place of happiness or im-provement.   **3.** Heaven; paradise. Also *Land of Promise.*

prom·is·ing (prom′is-ing)   *adj.*   Giving promise of good re-sults: a *promising* sign.   — **prom′is·ing·ly** *adv.*

prom·is·so·ry (prom′ə-sôr′ē, -sō′rē)   *adj.*   **1.** Containing or of the nature of a promise.   **2.** Indicating what is to be re-quired after the signing of an insurance contract.

promissory note   A written promise by one party to pay another party a certain sum of money at a specified time, or upon demand.

prom·on·to·ry (prom′ən-tôr′ē, -tō′rē)   *n.*   *pl.* **·ries**   **1.** A high point of land extending into the sea; headland.   **2.** *Anat.* A rounded projection or part.   [< Med.L < L, ? < *promi-nere* to project]

pro·mote (prə-mōt′)   *v.t.* **·mot·ed, ·mot·ing**   **1.** To contribute to the progress, development, or growth of; further; encour-age.   **2.** To advance to a higher position, grade, or honor.   **3.** To work in behalf of; advocate actively.   **4.** In educa-tion, to advance (a pupil) to the next higher school grade.   **5.** To seek to make (a commercial product, business ven-ture, etc.) popular or successful, as by securing capital or by advertising.   [< L < *pro*- forward + *movere* to move]   — **pro·mot′er** *n.*   — **pro·mo′tion** *n.*   — **pro·mo′tion·al** *adj.*   — **pro·mo′tive** *adj.*

prompt (prompt)   *v.t.*   **1.** To incite to action; instigate.   **2.** To suggest or inspire (an act, thought, etc.).   **3.** To remind of something forgotten or next in order; give a cue to.   — *v.i.*   **4.** To give help or suggestions.   — *adj.*   **1.** Acting or ready to act at the moment; punctual.   **2.** Done or rendered with readiness or alacrity; taking place at the appointed time.   — *n.*   **1.** An act of prompting.   **2.** The information imparted by prompting.   [< OF < L < *pro*- forth + *emere* to take]   — **prompt′ness** *n.*

prompt·er (promp′tər)   **1.** In a theater, one who follows the lines and prompts the actors.   **2.** One who or that which prompts.

prompt·i·tude (promp′tə-tōōd, -tyōōd)   *n.*   The quality, habit, or fact of being prompt; promptness.

prompt·ly (prompt′lē)   *adv.*   In a prompt manner; at once.

pro·mul·gate (prō-mul′gāt, prom′əl-gāt)   *v.t.* **·gat·ed, ·gat·ing** To make known or announce officially and formally; put into effect by public proclamation, as a law or dogma.   [< L < *pro*- forth + *vulgus* people]   — **pro′mul·ga′tion** *n.*   — **pro·mul·ga·tor** (prō-mul′gā-tər, prom′əl-) *n.*

prone (prōn)   *adj.*   **1.** Lying flat, esp. with the face, front, or palm downward; prostrate.   **2.** Leaning forward or down-ward; also, moving or sloping sharply downward.   **3.** Mentally inclined or predisposed: with *to*. [< L *pronus* prostrate] — **prone′ly** *adv.* — **prone′ness** *n.*

prong (prông, prong) *n.* **1.** A pointed end of an instrument, as the tine of a fork. **2.** Any pointed, projecting part, as the end of an antler. — *v.t.* To prick or stab with or as with a prong. [Cf. LG *prange* pointed stick, Du. *prangen* to pinch]

prong·horn (prông′hôrn′, prong′-) *n.* *pl.* **·horns** or **·horn** A ruminant of western North America, resembling an antelope, with deciduous branched horns.

pro·nom·i·nal (prō-nom′ə-nəl) *adj.* Of, pertaining to, or of the nature of a pronoun. — **pro·nom′i·nal·ly** *adv.*

pronominal adjective The possessive case of a personal pronoun used attributively, as *my, your, his, her*, etc.

pro·noun (prō′noun) *n.* *Gram.* A word that may be used instead of a noun or noun phrase, as an adjective, or to introduce a question. [< OF < L < *pro-* in place of + *nomen* name, noun]

pro·nounce (prə-nouns′) *v.* **·nounced, ·nounc·ing** *v.t.* **1.** To utter or deliver officially or solemnly; proclaim: to *pronounce* judgment. **2.** To assert; declare, esp. as one's judgment. **3.** To enunciate or articulate (sounds). **4.** To utter the constituent sounds of (a word or phrase) in a particular sequence or with a particular accentual pattern. **5.** To utter (the sound of a letter). — *v.i.* **6.** To make a judgment or pronouncement. **7.** To articulate words; speak. [< OF < LL < L < *pro-* forth + *nuntiare* to announce] — **pro·nounce′a·ble** *adj.* — **pro·nounc′er** *n.*

pro·nounced (prə-nounst′) *adj.* Of marked or clearly indicated character. — **pro·nounc·ed·ly** (prə-noun′sid·lē) *adv.*

pro·nounce·ment (prə-nouns′mənt) *n.* **1.** The act of pronouncing. **2.** A formal declaration or announcement.

pron·to (pron′tō) *adv. U.S. Informal* Quickly; promptly; instantly. [< Sp. < L *promptus* brought forth]

pro·nun·ci·a·men·to (prə-nun′sē-ə-men′tō, -shē-ə-) *n.* *pl.* **·tos** A public announcement; proclamation; manifesto. [< Sp. < L *pronuntiare* to pronounce]

pro·nun·ci·a·tion (prə-nun′sē·ā′shən) *n.* **1.** The act or manner of uttering words. **2.** Articulation.

proof (proof) *n.* **1.** The act or process of proving; esp., the establishment of a fact by evidence or a truth by other truths. **2.** A trial of strength, truth, excellence, etc. **3.** Evidence and argument sufficient to induce belief. **4.** *Law* Anything that serves to determine a verdict. **5.** The state or quality of having successfully undergone a test. **6.** Impenetrability; also, impenetrable armor. **7.** The standard of strength of alcoholic liquors. **8.** *Printing* A printed trial sheet showing the contents or condition of matter in type or of a plate, or the like. **9.** In engraving and etching, a trial impression taken from an engraved plate, stone, or block; also, a perfect impression from such a plate, etc., when finished. **10.** *Photog.* A trial print from a negative. **11.** *Math.* A process to check a computation by using its result; also, a demonstration. **12.** In philately, an experimental printing of a stamp. — *adj.* **1.** Employed in or connected with proving or correcting. **2.** Capable of resisting successfully: with *against*. **3.** Of standard alcoholic strength, as liquors. [< OF < LL < *probare* to test]

-proof *combining form* **1.** Impervious to; able to withstand; not damaged by: *bombproof*. **2.** Protected against: *mothproof*. **3.** As strong as: *armorproof*. **4.** Resisting; showing no effects of: *panicproof*. Adjectives formed with *-proof* may also be used as verbs. [< PROOF, adj.]

proof·read (proof′rēd′) *v.t. & v.i.* **·read** (-red′), **·read·ing** (-rē′ding) To read and correct (printers' proofs). — **proof′·read′er** *n.* — **proof′read′ing** *n.*

proof spirit An alcoholic liquor that contains a standard amount of alcohol. In the U.S. 100 proof indicates a liquor half of whose volume is ethyl alcohol having a specific gravity of 0.7939 at 60° F.

prop[1] (prop) *n.* **1.** A rigid object, as a beam or pole, that bolsters or sustains an incumbent weight. **2.** One who gives support to an institution, organization, etc. — *v.t.* **propped, prop·ping 1.** To support or keep from falling with or as with a prop. **2.** To lean or place: usu. with *against*. **3.** To support; sustain. [< MDu. *proppe* a support]

prop[2] (prop) *n.* A property (def. 7.).

prop·a·ga·ble (prop′ə-gə-bəl) *adj.* That can be propagated.

prop·a·gan·da (prop′ə-gan′də) *n.* **1.** A systematic effort to persuade a body of people to support or adopt a particular opinion, attitude, or course of action. **2.** Any selection of facts, ideas, or allegations forming the basis of such an effort. **3.** An institution or scheme for propagating a doctrine or system. ◆ *Propaganda* is now often used in a disparaging sense, as of a body of distortions and half-truths calculated to bias one's judgment or opinions. [< PROPAGANDA] — **prop′a·gan′dism** *n.* — **prop′a·gan′dist** *n. & adj.*

Prop·a·gan·da (prop′ə-gan′də) *n.* In the Roman Catholic Church, a society of cardinals charged with overseeing the foreign missions. [< NL (*congregatio de*) *propaganda* (*fide*) (the council for) propagating (the faith)]

prop·a·gan·dize (prop′ə-gan′dīz) *v.* **·dized, ·diz·ing** *v.t.* **1.**

To spread by means of propaganda. **2.** To subject to propaganda. — *v.i.* **3.** To carry on or spread propaganda.

prop·a·gate (prop′ə-gāt) *v.* **·gat·ed, ·gat·ing** *v.t.* **1.** To cause (animals, plants, etc.) to multiply by natural reproduction. **2.** To spread from person to person, as a doctrine or belief; disseminate. **3.** To transmit through a medium: to *propagate* heat. **4.** To reproduce (itself), as a species, plant or animal. **5.** To pass on (traits, qualities, etc.), as one's offspring. — *v.i.* **6.** To have offspring; breed. [< pro- forth + *pag-* root of *pangere* to fasten] — **prop′a·ga′tion** *n.* — **prop′a·ga′tive** *adj.* — **prop′a·ga′tor** *n.*

pro·pane (prō′pān) *n. Chem.* A gaseous hydrocarbon of the methane series, C_3H_8, obtained from petroleum and sometimes used as a fuel gas.

pro pa·tri·a (prō pā′trē·ə) *Latin* For one's country.

pro·pel (prə-pel′) *v.t.* **·pelled, ·pel·ling** To cause to move forward or ahead; drive or urge forward. [< L < *pro-* forward + *pellere* to drive]

pro·pel·lant (prə-pel′ənt) *n.* **1.** One who or that which propels. **2.** *Mil.* An explosive that upon ignition propels a projectile from a gun. **3.** A solid or liquid fuel that serves to propel a rocket, guided missile, etc.: also spelled *propellent*.

pro·pel·lent (prə-pel′ənt) *adj.* Able to propel; propelling. — *n.* See PROPELLANT.

pro·pel·ler (prə-pel′ər) *n.* **1.** One who or that which propels. **2.** Any device for propelling a craft through water or air; esp., one having blades mounted at an angle on a power-driven shaft and producing a thrust by their rotary action on the medium.

pro·pe·no·ic acid (prō′pə-nō′ik) *Chem.* Acrylic acid.

pro·pen·si·ty (prə-pen′sə-tē) *n.* *pl.* **·ties** A natural position or tendency; bent. [< L < *pro-* forward + *pen-* to hang]

prop·er (prop′ər) *adj.* **1.** Specially suited or adapted to some end; appropriate. **2.** Conforming to a prevailing standard of conduct or manners; fitting. **3.** Understood in a strict or literal sense: usu. following the noun modified: part of the book *proper*. **4.** Naturally belonging to a particular person, thing, or class: Crying is *proper* to babies. **5.** Modest; decent. **6.** *Gram.* Designating a particular person, place, or the like: a *proper* name. **7.** *Brit. Informal* Thorough; unmitigated: a *proper* bore. — *n.* *Sometimes cap. Eccl.* The portion of the breviary, missal, or Mass containing the prayers and collects suitable to special occasions or feasts: with *the*: distinguished from *ordinary*. [< OF < L *propius* one's own] — **prop′er·ly** *adv.* — **prop′er·ness** *n.*

proper fraction *Math.* A fraction in which the numerator is less than the denominator.

proper noun *Gram.* A noun that names a particular person, place, or thing, and is always capitalized, as *Paul, Venus, U.S.S. Nautilus*: distinguished from *common noun*.

prop·er·tied (prop′ər-tēd) *adj.* Owning property.

prop·er·ty (prop′ər-tē) *n.* *pl.* **·ties 1.** Any object of value that a person may lawfully acquire and hold; that which may be owned, as stocks, land, etc. **2.** The legal right to possession, use, enjoyment, and disposal of a thing. **3.** Holdings, land, etc., owned; wealth. **4.** A parcel of land. **5.** Any of the qualities or characteristics that together make up the nature or basic structure of a thing. **6.** A quality or feature that belongs distinctively to a particular object or class; a peculiarity. **7.** In the theater, any portable article used in a performance other than scenery and the costumes, as books, dishes, etc.: also called *prop*. [< OF < L *proprius* one's own.] — **prop′er·ty·less** *adj.* — **Syn. 3.** chattels, goods, estate. **6.** See CHARACTERISTIC.

proph·e·cy (prof′ə-sē) *n.* *pl.* **·cies 1.** A prediction made under divine influence and direction. **2.** Any prediction. **3.** Discourse delivered by a prophet under divine inspiration. **4.** A book of prophecies. [< OF < LL < Gk. < *pro* before + *phanai* to speak]

proph·e·sy (prof′ə-sī) *v.* **·sied, ·sy·ing** *v.t.* **1.** To utter or foretell with or as with divine inspiration. **2.** To predict (a future event). **3.** To point out beforehand. — *v.i.* **4.** To speak by divine influence, or as a medium between God and man. **5.** To foretell the future. **6.** To explain or teach religious subjects; preach. [See PROPHECY] — **proph′e·si·er** *n.*

— **Syn. 1.** *Prophesy* and *foretell* are often interchangeable. In Scriptural sense *prophesy* refers to the uttering of religious truth under divine inspiration, and does not necessarily include prediction of future events. *Foretell* always bears the latter sense.

proph·et (prof′it) *n.* **1.** One who delivers divine messages or interprets the divine will. **2.** One who foretells the future, esp., an inspired predictor. **3.** A religious leader. **4.** An interpreter or spokesman for any cause. **5.** A mantis.

the Prophet According to Islam, Mohammed.

Prophets The second of the three ancient divisions of the Old Testament, containing all those books not found in the Pentateuch or the Hagiographa. [< OF < LL < Gk. < *pro-* before + *phanai* to speak] — **proph′et·ess** *n.fem.*

pro·phet·ic (prə-fet′ik) *adj.* **1.** Of or pertaining to a prophet r prophecy. **2.** Pertaining to or involving prediction or resentment; predictive. Also **pro·phet′i·cal.** — **pro·phet′i·al·ly** adv. — **pro·phet′i·cal·ness** n.

o·phy·lac·tic (prō′fə-lak′tik, prof′ə-) adj. Tending to rotect against or ward off something, esp. disease; preentive. — n. A prophylactic medicine or appliance. [< ik. < pro- before + phylassein to guard]

o·phy·lax·is (prō′fə-lak′sis, prof′ə-) n. Preventive treatnent for disease. [< NL < Gk. pro- before + phylaxis uarding]

o·pin·qui·ty (prō-ping′kwə-tē) n. **1.** Nearness in place or ime. **2.** Kinship. — **Syn.** See APPROXIMATION. [< L < rope near]

o·pi·ti·ate (prō-pish′ē-āt) v.t. **·at·ed, ·at·ing** To cause to e favorably disposed; conciliate. [See PROPITIOUS.] — **pro·i·ti·a·ble** (prō-pish′ē-ə-bəl) adj. — **pro·pi′ti·at′ing·ly** adv. — **pro·pi′ti·a′tion** n. — **pro·pi′ti·a′tive** adj. — **pro·pi′ti·a′** or n.

o·pi·ti·a·to·ry (prō-pish′ē-ə-tôr′ē, -tō′rē) adj. Pertaining o or causing propitiation.

o·pi·tious (prō-pish′əs) adj. **1.** Attended by favorable ircumstances; auspicious. **2.** Kindly disposed; gracious. [< OF < L propitious favorable, ? < pro- before + petere o seek] — **pro·pi′tious·ly** adv. — **pro·pi′tious·ness** n. — **Syn. 1.** Propitious may be applied to persons, while auspiious is not so used.

op·jet (prop′jet′) n. Aeron. A turboprop.

o·po·nent (prə-pō′nənt) n. **1.** One who makes a proposal r proposition. **2.** One who advocates or supports a cause r doctrine. [< L < pro- forth + ponere to put]

o·por·tion (prə-pôr′shən, -pōr′-) n. **1.** Relative magniude, number, or degree, as existing between parts, a part nd a whole, etc. **2.** Fitness and harmony; symmetry. **3.** proportionate or proper share. **4.** An equality or identity etween ratios. **5.** Math. The relationship among four erms such that the product of the second and third terms is qual to the product of the first and fourth. **6.** pl. Size; imensions. — v.t. **1.** To adjust properly as to relative nagnitude, amount, or degree. **2.** To form with a harmonius relation of parts. [< OF < L < pro- for + portio, -onis hare] — **pro·por′tion·a·ble** adj. — **pro·por′tion·a·bly** adv. — **pro·por′tion·er** n. — **pro·por′tion·ment** n.

o·por·tion·al (prə-pôr′shən-əl, -pōr′-) adj. **1.** Of or being proportion. **2.** Math. **a** Constituting the terms of a proortion. **b** Varying so that corresponding values form a proortion. — n. Any quantity or number in proportion to nother or others. — **pro·por′tion·al·ly** adv. — **pro·por′·on·al′i·ty** (-al′ə-tē) n.

o·por·tion·ate (adj. prə-pôr′shən-it, -pōr′-; v. prə-pôr′·hən·āt, -pōr′-) adj. Being in due proportion; proportional. — v.t. **·at·ed, ·at·ing** To make proportionate. — **pro·por′·on·ate·ly** adv. — **pro·por′tion·ate·ness** n.

o·po·sal (prə-pō′zəl) n. **1.** An offer proposing something o be accepted or adopted. **2.** An offer of marriage. **3.** omething proposed, as a scheme or plan.

o·pose (prə-pōz′) v. **·posed, ·pos·ing** v.t. **1.** To put forard for acceptance or consideration. **2.** To nominate, as or appointment. **3.** To intend; aim. **4.** To suggest the rinking of (a toast or health). — v.i. **5.** To form or anounce a plan or design. **6.** To make an offer, as of marage. [< OF < pro- forth (< L) + poser to put down, rest] — **pro·pos′er** n. — **Syn. 3.** What we propose to do is subject to further considration. What we purpose to do is settled; the word suggests that he mind has been made up.

op·o·si·tion (prop′ə-zish′ən) n. **1.** A scheme or proposal ffered for consideration or acceptance. **2.** U.S. Informal ny matter or person to be dealt with. **3.** A subject or tatement presented for discussion. **4.** Logic A statement n which something (the subject) is affirmed or denied in erms of something else (the predicate). **5.** Math. A statenent of a truth to be demonstrated (a theorem) or of an operation to be performed (a problem). [< OF < L < pro- orth + ponere to put] — **prop′o·si′tion·al** adj. — **prop′·si′tion·al·ly** adv.

o·pound (prə-pound′) v.t. To put forward for considera-ion, solution, etc.; submit. [Earlier propone < L proponere o set forth] — **pro·pound′er** n.

o·pri·e·tar·y (prə-prī′ə·ter′ē) adj. **1.** Of or belonging to proprietor. **2.** Subject to exclusive ownership. **3.** Desig-ating an article, as a medicine, protected by copyright, atent, secrecy, etc. — n. pl. **·tar·ies 1.** A proprietor or roprietors collectively. **2.** Proprietorship; ownership. [< L < L proprius one's own]

o·pri·e·tor (prə-prī′ə·tər) n. A person having the exclu-ve title to anything. — **pro·pri′e·tor·ship′** n. — **pro·pri′·tress** n.fem.

o·pri·e·ty (prə-prī′ə·tē) n. pl. **·ties** The character or

quality of being proper; esp., accordance with recognized usage or principles. — **the proprieties** The standards of good society. [< OF propriete < L proprius one's own]

pro·pul·sion (prə-pul′shən) n. **1.** The act or operation of propelling. **2.** A propelling force. — **pro·pul′sive** (-siv) adj.

pro·pyl (prō′pil) n. Chem. The univalent radical, C_3H_7, de-rived from propane.

pro ra·ta (prō rā′tə, rat′ə, rä′tə) In proportion. [< L pro rata (parte) according to the calculated (share)]

pro·rate (prō-rāt′, prō′rāt′) v.t. & v.i. **·rat·ed, ·rat·ing** To distribute or divide proportionately. [< PRO RATA] — **pro·rat′a·ble** adj. — **pro·ra′tion** n.

pro·ro·ga·tion (prō′rə-gā′shən) n. **1.** The act of proro-guing. **2.** The act of prolonging; also, continuance.

pro·rogue (prō-rōg′) v.t. **·rogued, ·ro·guing** To discontinue a session of (an assembly). [< MF < L < pro- forward + rogare to ask]

pro·sa·ic (prō-zā′ik) adj. **1.** Unimaginative; commonplace; dull. **2.** Of or like prose. Also **pro·sa′i·cal.** [< LL < L prosa prose] — **pro·sa′ic·ness** n.

pro·sce·ni·um (prō-sē′nē-əm) n. pl. **·ni·a** (-nē-ə) The part of a theater stage in front of the curtain, sometimes including the curtain and its arch. [< L < Gk. < pro- before + skēnē stage, tent]

pro·scribe (prō-skrīb′) v.t. **·scribed, ·scrib·ing 1.** To de-nounce or condemn; prohibit. **2.** To outlaw or banish. **3.** In ancient Rome, to publish the name of (one condemned or exiled). [< L proscribere to write publicly] — **pro·scrib′er** n. — **pro·scrip′tion** (-skrip′shən) n. — **pro·scrip′tive** adj.

prose (prōz) n. **1.** Speech or writing without metrical struc-ture: distinguished from verse. **2.** Commonplace or tedious discourse. — adj. **1.** Of or pertaining to prose. **2.** Tedious; tiresome. — v.t. & v.i. **prosed, pros·ing** To write or speak in prose. [< OF < L prosa (oratio) straightforward (discourse)]

pros·e·cute (pros′ə-kyōōt) v. **·cut·ed, ·cut·ing** v.t. **1.** To go on with as to complete. **2.** To carry on or engage in, as a trade. **3.** Law **a** To bring suit against. **b** To seek to enforce, as a claim, by legal process. — v.i. **4.** To begin and carry on a legal proceeding. — **Syn.** See PUSH. [< L < pro- for-ward + sequi to follow]

prosecuting attorney The attorney empowered to act in behalf of the state, county, or national government in prose-cuting for penal offenses.

pros·e·cu·tion (pros′ə-kyōō′shən) n. **1.** The act or process of prosecuting. **2.** Law The instituting and carrying for-ward of a judicial or criminal proceeding. **3.** The party in-stituting and conducting it.

pros·e·cu·tor (pros′ə-kyōō′tər) n. **1.** One who prosecutes. **2.** Law **a** One who institutes and carries on a suit, esp. a criminal suit. **b** A prosecuting attorney.

pros·e·lyte (pros′ə-līt) n. One who has been brought over to any opinion, belief, sect, or party, esp. from one religious belief to another. — v.t. & v.i. **·lyt·ed, ·lyt·ing** To proselyt-ize. [< LL < Gk. proselytos, orig., a newcomer] — **pros′e·lyt′ism** (-lə-tiz′əm, -līt′iz-) n.

pros·e·lyt·ize (pros′ə-lit·īz′) v. **·ized, ·iz·ing** v.i. **1.** To make proselytes. — v.t. **2.** To make a convert of. Also proselyte: also Brit. **pros′e·lyt·ise′.**

pros·en·ceph·a·lon (pros′en-sef′ə-lon) n. Anat. The an-terior segment of the three divisions of the brain in embryos, developing into the cerebrum and the optic thalamus, with related structures: also called forebrain. [< NL < Gk. pros toward + encephalon brain] — **pros′en·ce·phal′ic** (-sə-fal′ik) adj.

Pros·er·pine (pros′ər-pīn, prō-sûr′pə-nē) In Roman mythol-ogy, the daughter of Ceres and wife of Pluto: identified with the Greek Persephone. Also **Pro·ser·pi·na** (prō-sûr′pə-nə).

pro·sit (prō′sit, Ger. prō′zit) interj. To your good health: used as a drinking toast, esp. by the Germans. Also **prost** (prōst). [< L, lit., may it benefit]

pro·slav·er·y (prō-slā′vər-ē, -slāv′rē) adj. In U.S. history, advocating Negro slavery.

pro·sod·ic (prō-sod′ik) adj. Of or pertaining to prosody. Also **pro·sod′i·cal.**

prosodic symbols In the scansion of verse, those signs used to indicate the various kinds of syllables, stresses, feet, etc.: these include the breve (˘), macron (¯), acute (′), caesura (‖), and vertical bar (|).

pros·o·dy (pros′ə-dē) n. The science of poetical forms, in-cluding quantity and accent of syllables, meter, versifica-tion, and metrical composition. [< L < Gk. prosōidia a song sung to music] — **pro·so·di·ac** (prō-sō′dē-ak), **pro·so·di·al** (prō-sō′dē-əl) adj. — **pros′o·dist** n.

pros·pect (pros′pekt) n. **1.** A future probability; esp., often in the plural, the chance for future success. **2.** An extended view. **3.** An exposure; outlook. **4.** A prospective buyer. — v.t. & v.i. To explore (a region) for gold, oil, etc. [< L < pro- forward + specere to look]

pro·spec·tive (prə·spek′tiv) adj. 1. Anticipated. 2. Looking toward the future. — **pro·spec′tive·ly** adv.

pros·pec·tor (pros′pek·tər) n. One who searches or examines a region for mineral deposits or precious stones.

pro·spec·tus (prə·spek′təs) n. pl. **·tus·es** 1. A paper containing information of a proposed undertaking. 2. A summary; outline. [< L < pro- forward + specere to look]

pros·per (pros′pər) v.i. To be prosperous; thrive; flourish. [< OF < L prosperus favorable, prosperous]

pros·per·i·ty (pros·per′ə·tē) n. pl. **·ties** The state of being prosperous; material well-being.

pros·per·ous (pros′pər·əs) adj. 1. Successful; flourishing. 2. Auspicious. 3. Favorable. [< MF < L prosperus favorable] — **pros′per·ous·ly** adv. — **pros′per·ous·ness** n.

pros·tate (pros′tāt) Anat. adj. Of or designating the prostate gland. — n. The prostate gland. [< NL < Gk. prostatēs stander before < pro- before + histanai to set]

prostate gland Anat. A partly muscular gland at the base of the bladder and surrounding the urethra in male mammals, providing some of the chemicals necessary to maintain the sperm for reproduction. — **pro·stat·ic** (prō·stat′ik) adj.

pros·the·sis (pros′thə·sis) n. pl. **·ses** (-sēz) 1. Surg. The fitting of artificial parts to the body. 2. A part so fitted, as an artificial limb, false tooth, etc. [< L < Gk. < pros- to + tithenai to put] — **pros·thet·ic** (pros·thet′ik) adj.

pros·thet·ics (pros·thet′iks) n.pl. (construed as sing.) The branch of surgery that specializes in artificial parts. — **pros·the·tist** (pros′thə·tist) n.

pros·tho·don·tics (pros′thə·don′tiks) n. The branch of dentistry concerned with the making of crowns, bridges, dentures, and artificial teeth; dental prosthetics. Also **pros′·tho·don′ti·a.** (-thə·don′shē·ə). [< NL < Gk. prosthesis addition + odous tooth] — **pros·tho·don·tist** (pros′thə·don′tist) n.

pros·ti·tute (pros′tə·tōōt, -tyōōt) n. 1. A woman who offers her body for hire for purposes of sexual intercourse. 2. One who sells his services for unworthy purposes. — v.t. **·tut·ed, ·tut·ing** 1. To apply (talent, etc.) to unworthy purposes. 2. To offer (oneself or another) for lewd purposes, esp. for hire. [< L < pro- forward + statuere to place] — **pros′ti·tu′tion** n. — **pros′ti·tu′tor** n.

pros·trate (pros′trāt) adj. 1. Lying prone, or with the face to the ground. 2. Brought low in mind or spirit. 3. Lying at the mercy of another. 4. Bot. Trailing along the ground. — v.t. **·trat·ed, ·trat·ing** 1. To bow or cast (oneself) down, as in adoration or pleading. 2. To throw flat; lay on the ground. 3. To overcome; make helpless. [< L < pro- before + sternere to stretch out] — **pros·tra′tion** n.

pros·y (prō′zē) adj. **pros·i·er, pros·i·est** 1. Like prose; prosaic. 2. Dull; tedious. — **pros′i·ly** adv. — **pros′i·ness** n.

prot- Var. of PROTO-.

pro·tac·tin·i·um (prō′tak·tin′ē·əm) n. A radioactive metallic element (symbol Pa) of the actinide series, intermediate between thorium and uranium: also called protoactinium. See ELEMENT.

pro·tag·o·nist (prō·tag′ə·nist) n. 1. The actor who played the chief part in a Greek drama. 2. Any leading character, contender, etc. [< Gk. < prōtos first + agōnistēs actor]

pro·te·an (prō′tē·ən, prō·tē′ən) adj. Readily assuming different forms or various aspects; changeable. [< PROTEUS]

pro·te·ase (prō′tē·ās) n. Biochem. An enzyme that digests proteins.

pro·tect (prə·tekt′) v.t. 1. To shield or defend from attack, harm, or injury. 2. Econ. To assist (domestic industry) by means of protective tariffs. 3. In commerce, to provide funds to guarantee payment of (a draft, etc.). [< L < pro- before + tegere to cover] — **pro·tect′ing·ly** adv.

pro·tec·tion (prə·tek′shən) n. 1. The act of protecting, or the state of being protected. 2. One who or that which protects. 3. Econ. A system aiming to protect the industries of a country by imposing duties. See PROTECTIVE TARIFF. — **pro·tec′tive** adj. — **pro·tec′tive·ly** adv.

pro·tec·tion·ism (prə·tek′shən·iz′əm) n. The economic doctrine or system of protection. — **pro·tec′tion·ist** n.

protective tariff A tariff that is intended to insure protection of domestic industries against foreign competition.

pro·tec·tor (prə·tek′tər) n. 1. One who protects; a defender. 2. In English history, one appointed as a regent of the kingdom during minority or incapacity of the sovereign. Also **pro·tect′er.** — **pro·tec′tress** n.fem.

Pro·tec·tor (prə·tek′tər) n. The title borne by Oliver Cromwell, 1653–58, and by Richard Cromwell, his son, 1658–59 during the Protectorate: in full, **Lord Protector.**

pro·tec·tor·ate (prə·tek′tər·it) n. 1. A relation of protection and partial control by a strong nation over a weaker power. 2. A country or region under the protection of another. 3. The office, or period of office, of a protector of a kingdom. Also **pro·tec′tor·ship.**

Pro·tec·tor·ate (prə·tek′tər·it) n. The English government during the rule of the Cromwells, 1653–59.

pro·té·gé (prō′tə·zhā, Fr. prō·tā·zhā′) n. One specially cared

for by another who is older or more powerful. [< F < protegere to protect] — **pro′té·gée** n.fem.

pro·te·in (prō′tē·in, -tēn) n. Biochem. Any of a class highly complex nitrogenous compounds originally synth sized by plants, and forming an essential constituent in t processes of animal metabolism. Also **pro′te·id** (-id). [< < Gk. prōtos first]

pro tem·po·re (prō tem′pə·rē) Latin For the time bein

Prot·er·o·zo·ic (prot′ər·ə·zō′ik) Geol. adj. Of or designing the geological era following the Archeozoic and succeed by the Paleozoic. See chart for GEOLOGY. — n. The Prot ozoic era. [< Gk. proteros former + ZOIC]

pro·test (n. prō′test; v. prə·test′) n. 1. A solemn or form objection or declaration. 2. A public expression of disser 3. A formal notarial certificate attesting the fact that a nc or bill of exchange has been presented for acceptance or pa ment and that it has been refused. 4. The act of protestir — adj. Of or relating to public protest: protest demonstr tions. — v.t. 1. To assert earnestly or positively. 2. U To make a protest against; object to. 3. To declare formal that payment of (a promissory note, etc.) has been du submitted and refused. — v.i. 4. To make solemn affirm tion. 5. To make a protest; object. [< OF < L < p forth + testari to testify] — **pro·test′er** n. — **pro·test′in ly** adv.

prot·es·tant (prot′is·tənt, prə·tes′-) n. One who makes protest. [< MF < L < protestari]

Prot·es·tant (prot′is·tənt) n. A member of one of tho bodies of Christians that adhere to Protestantism, as disti guished from Roman Catholicism. — adj. Pertaining Protestants or Protestantism.

Protestant Episcopal Church A religious body in t United States that is descended from the Church of Englan also called Episcopal Church.

Prot·es·tant·ism (prot′is·tənt·iz′əm) n. 1. The princip and common system of doctrines of the Protestants. 2. T ecclesiastical system founded upon this faith; also, Prot tants, collectively. 3. The state of being a Protestant.

prot·es·ta·tion (prot′is·tā′shən) n. 1. The act of protes ing; also, that which is protested. 2. A formal declarati of dissent. 3. Any solemn or urgent avowal.

Pro·te·us (prō′tē·əs, -tyōōs) In Greek mythology, a sea g who had the power of assuming different forms.

pro·tist (prō′tist) n. Biol. Any member of a large divisi or kingdom of one-celled or noncellular plants and anima including bacteria, flagellates, rhizopods, and ciliates. [NL < Gk. prōtos first] — **pro·tis′tan** adj. & n. — **p tis′tic** adj.

pro·ti·um (prō′tē·əm) n. Chem. The hydrogen isotope atomic mass 1 (symbol, H^1): sometimes so called in distin tion from deuterium and tritium. [< NL < Gk. prōtos firs

proto- combining form 1. First in rank or time; chief; ty cal. 2. Primitive; original: prototype. Also, before vowe prot-. [< Gk. prōtos first]

pro·to·ac·tin·i·um (prō′tō·ak·tin′ē·əm) n. Protactinium

pro·to·col (prō′tə·kōl, -kol) n. 1. The rules of diplomac and state etiquette and ceremony. 2. The prelimina draft of diplomatic negotiation or of an official docume as a treaty. — v.i. **·coled** or **·colled, ·col·ing** or **·col·ling** write or form protocols. [< OF < Med.L < LGk. prō kollon the first sheet glued to a papyrus roll enumerati the contents < prōtos first + kolla glue]

pro·ton (prō′ton) n. Physics One of the elementary par cles in the nucleus of an atom, having a unitary positi charge and a mass of approximately 1.672×10^{-24} gram [< NL < Gk. < prōtos first]

pro·to·plasm (prō′tə·plaz′əm) n. Biol. The physic chemical basis of living matter, a viscid, grayish, transluce substance of complex composition that forms the essenti part of plant and animal cells. [< G < Gk. prōtos first plasma form] — **pro′to·plas′mic** adj.

pro·to·type (prō′tə·tīp) n. 1. Biol. A primitive or ancest organism; an archetype. 2. An original model on whi subsequent forms are to be based. [< F < NL < Gk. prōtos first + typos form] — **pro′to·typ′al** (-tī′pəl), **pro′· typ′ic** (-tip′ik), **pro′to·typ′i·cal** adj.

pro·to·zo·an (prō′tə·zō′ən) n. Any of a phylum of micr scopic, single-celled organisms, largely aquatic and includi many parasites. Also **pro·to·zo′on.** [< NL < Gk. prōtos first + zōion animal] — **pro′to·zo′an** adj. — **pro′to·zo′ic a**

pro·tract (prō·trakt′) v.t. 1. To extend in time; prolon 2. In surveying, to draw or map by means of a scale and pr tractor; plot. 3. Anat. To protrude or extend. [< L pro- forward + trahere to draw] — **pro·trac′tion** n. — **pro·trac′tive** adj.

pro·trac·tile (prō·trak′til) adj. Capable of being protract or protruded.

pro·trac·tor (prō·trak′tər) n. 1. One who protracts. An instrument for measuring and laying off angles. Anat. A muscle that extends a limb or moves it forward.

pro·trude (prō·trōōd′) v.t. & v.i. **·trud·ed, ·trud·ing** To pu

thrust out; project outward. [< L < *pro-* forward + *dere* to thrust] — **pro·tru′sion** (-trōō′zhən) *n.*
tru·sile (prō·trōō′sil) *adj.* Adapted to being thrust out, the tongue of an anteater. Also **pro·tru′si·ble.**
tru·sive (prō·trōō′siv) *adj.* **1.** Tending to protrude; **truding. 2.** Pushing or driving forward. — **pro·tru′· e·ly** *adv.* — **pro·tru′sive·ness** *n.*
tu·ber·ance (prō·tōō′bər·əns, -tyōō′-) *n.* **1.** Something **t** protrudes; a knob; prominence. **2.** The state of being **tuberant.** Also **pro·tu′ber·an·cy, pro·tu′ber·a′tion.**
tu·ber·ant (prō·tōō′bər·ənt, -tyōō-) *adj.* Swelling out **ond** the surrounding surface; bulging. [< LL < L *pro- th + tuber* a swelling] — **pro·tu′ber·ant·ly** *adv.*
ud (proud) *adj.* **1.** Actuated by, possessing, or manifest-pride; arrogant; also, self-respecting. **2.** Sensible of **ıor** and personal elation: generally followed by *of* or by a **b** in the infinitive. **3.** High-mettled, as a horse. **4.** Pro-ding from or inspired by pride. **5.** Being a cause of **ıorable** pride, as a distinction. — **to do oneself proud** To extremely well. [OE < OF, prob. ult. < L < *pro-* for *esse* to be] — **proud′ly** *adv.*
ud flesh *Pathol.* A granulated growth resembling flesh a wound or sore. [So called from its swelling up]
ve (prōōv) *v.* **proved, proved** or **prov·en, prov·ing** *v.t.* **1.** show to be true or genuine, as by evidence or argument. To determine the quality or genuineness of; test: to *prove* un. **3.** To establish the authenticity or validity of, as a **l. 4.** *Math.* To verify the accuracy of (a calculation, etc.). *v.i.* **5.** To be shown to be by the result or outcome; turn to be. [< OF < L < *probus* upright] — **prov′a·ble** **. — prov′er** *n.*
-ven·cal (prō′vən·säl′, *Fr.* prō·vän·sàl′) *n.* **1.** A native resident of Provence, France. **2.** The Roman language Provence, used esp. in the 12th and 13th centuries in the **ıc** literature of the troubadours. — *adj.* Of or pertaining Provence, its inhabitants, or their language.
v·en·der (prov′ən·dər) *n.* **1.** Food for cattle; esp., dry **d**, as hay. **2.** *Rare* Provisions generally. — *v.t.* To pro-**e** with food, as cattle. [< OF < L *praebere* to supply]
v·erb (prov′ərb) *n.* **1.** A pithy saying, esp. one con-**ısing** the wisdom of experience; adage; saw; maxim. An enigmatic saying. **3.** A typical example; byword. OF < L < *pro-* before + *verbum* word]
– Syn. 1. A *proverb* is usually a homely illustration of a gen-truth, as: A rolling stone gathers no moss. An *adage* is a time-**ored** and generally accepted *proverb*, as: A man is known by company he keeps. Any ancient and hackneyed *adage* is a *saw*, All that glitters is not gold.
ver·bi·al (prə·vûr′bē·əl) *adj.* **1.** Pertaining to, or like a verb. **2.** Well-known; notorious. — **pro·ver′bi·al·ly** *adv.*
v·erbs (prov′ərbz) *n.pl.* (*construed as sing.*) An Old **tament** book of moral sayings.
vide (prə·vīd′) *v.* **vid·ed, vid·ing** *v.t.* **1.** To supply or **ınish. 2.** To afford; yield. **3.** To prepare, make ready, or **ıcure** beforehand. **4.** To set down as a condition; stipu-**. — *v.i.* 5.** To take measures in advance: with *for* or *inst.* **6.** To furnish means of subsistence: usu. with *for.* To make a stipulation. [< L < *pro-* before + *videre* to **] — pro·vid′er** *n.*
vid·ed (prə·vī′did) *conj.* On condition; if: He will get loan *provided* he offers good security.
v·i·dence (prov′ə·dəns) *n.* **1.** The care exercised by God **r** the universe. **2.** An event or circumstances ascribable divine interposition. **3.** The exercise of foresight and **e** for the future. [< OF < L *providere* to foresee]
v·i·dence (prov′ə·dəns) God; the Deity.
v·i·dent (prov′ə·dənt) *adj.* Anticipating and making **dy** for future wants. — **prov′i·dent·ly** *adv.*
v·i·den·tial (prov′ə·den′shəl) *adj.* Resulting from or **olving** God's providence. — **prov′i·den′tial·ly** *adv.*
vid·ing (prə·vī′ding) *conj.* On condition; provided.
v·ince (prov′ins) *n.* **1.** A country incorporated with a **gdom** or empire and subject to central administration. Any large administrative division of a country with a **ınanent** local government. **3.** *pl.* Regions lying at a **ıance** from the capital or most populous part of a country. A sphere of knowledge, activity, or endeavor. [< OF *L provincia* province]
vin·cial (prə·vin′shəl) *adj.* **1.** Of or pertaining to a **ıvince. 2.** Confined to a province; rustic; local. **3.** Nar-**v;** uncultured; illiberal. — *n.* **1.** A native or inhabitant a province. **2.** One who is provincial. — **pro·vin′ci·al′·** (-shē·al′ə·tē) *n.* — **pro·vin′cial·ly** *adv.*
vin·cial·ism (prə·vin′shəl·iz′əm) *n.* **1.** The quality of **ng** provincial. **2.** A provincial custom, esp. of speech.
vi·sion (prə·vizh′ən) *n.* **1.** The act of providing, or the **te** of being provided. **2.** Measures or means made **dy** in advance. **3.** *pl.* Food or a supply of food. **4.**

Something provided or prepared, as against future need. **5.** The part of an agreement, instrument, etc., referring to one specific thing; a stipulation. — *v.t.* To provide with food or provisions. [< OF < L < *pro-* before + *videre* to see] — **pro·vi′sion·er** *n.*
pro·vi·sion·al (prə·vizh′ən·əl) *adj.* Provided for a present service or temporary necessity; adopted tentatively. Also **pro·vi′sion·ar′y.** — **pro·vi′sion·al·ly** *adv.*
pro·vi·so (prə·vī′zō) *n.* *pl.* **·sos** or **·soes** A stipulation or clause, as in a contract or statute, limiting, modifying, or rendering conditional its operation. [< Med.L *proviso* it being provided < L *providere* to foresee]
pro·vi·so·ry (prə·vī′zər·ē) *adj.* **1.** Conditional. **2.** Provisional. — **pro·vi′so·ri·ly** *adv.*
prov·o·ca·tion (prov′ə·kā′shən) *n.* **1.** The act of provok-ing. **2.** An incitement to action; stimulus.
pro·voc·a·tive (prə·vok′ə·tiv) *adj.* Serving to provoke; stim-ulating. — *n.* That which provokes or tends to provoke. — **pro·voc′a·tive·ly** *adv.* — **pro·voc′a·tive·ness** *n.*
pro·voke (prə·vōk′) *v.t.* **·voked, ·vok·ing 1.** To stir to anger or resentment; irritate; vex. **2.** To arouse or stimulate to some action. **3.** To stir up or bring about: to *provoke* a quar-rel. **4.** To induce or cause; elicit: to *provoke* a smile. [< OF < L < *pro-* forth + *vocare* to call] — **pro·vok′ing·ly** *adv.* — **pro·vok′ing·ness** *n.*
prov·ost (prov′əst) *n.* **1.** A person having charge or au-thority over others. **2.** The chief magistrate of a Scottish city. **3.** In some English and American colleges, the head of the faculty. **4.** The head of a collegiate chapter or a cathedral; a dean. [< OE and OF, both < LL *propositus*, var. of L *praepositus* chief] — **prov′ost·ship** *n.*
pro·vost marshal (prō′vō) A military or naval officer exer-cising police functions: also called *provost.*
prow (prou) *n.* **1.** The fore part of the hull of a vessel; the bow. **2.** Any projection. [< MF < L < Gk. *prōira*]
prow·ess (prou′is) *n.* **1.** Strength, skill, and courage, esp. in battle. **2.** A daring and valiant deed. [< OF *prouesse, proece < prou* brave]
prowl (proul) *v.t. & v.i.* To roam about stealthily, as in search of prey or plunder. — *n.* The act of prowling. [ME *prollen* to search] — **prowl′er** *n.*
prowl car *U.S.* A police patrol car.
prox·i·mal (prok′sə·məl) *adj.* **1.** *Anat.* Relatively nearer the central portion of the body or point of origin. **2.** Proxi-mate. — **prox′i·mal·ly** *adv.*
prox·i·mate (prok′sə·mit) *adj.* Being in immediate relation with something else; next: also *proximal.* [< LL < L *proximus*, superl. of *prope* near] — **prox′i·mate·ly** *adv.*
prox·im·i·ty (prok·sim′ə·tē) *n.* The state or fact of being near or next; nearness. [See PROXIMATE.]
proximity fuse A fuse in a projectile, usu. activated by an electronic device, that detonates by simple proximity to the target: also called *VT fuse.*
prox·i·mo (prok′sə·mō) *adv.* In or of the next or coming month. [See PROXIMATE.]
prox·y (prok′sē) *n.* *pl.* **prox·ies 1.** A person empowered by another to act for him. **2.** The office or right to so act, or the instrument conferring it. [ME *prokecie*]
prude (prōōd) *n.* A person who makes an affected display of modesty and propriety, esp. in matters relating to sex. [< F *preude* (*femme*) strong, hence, modest (woman)] — **prud′ish** *adj.* — **prud′ish·ly** *adv.* — **prud′ish·ness** *n.*
pru·dence (prōōd′ns) *n.* The quality or state of being pru-dent; sagacity; discretion.
pru·dent (prōōd′nt) *adj.* **1.** Cautious; worldly-wise. **2.** Exercising sound judgment. **3.** Not extravagant. **4.** Decorously discreet. [< OF < L *prudens, -entis* knowing, foreseeing] — **pru′dent·ly** *adv.*
– Syn. 1. discreet, circumspect, wary. **3.** thrifty, economical, frugal. — **Ant.** imprudent, indiscreet, rash, reckless.
pru·den·tial (prōō·den′shəl) *adj.* **1.** Proceeding from or marked by prudence. **2.** Exercising prudence and wisdom. — **pru·den′tial·ly** *adv.*
prud·er·y (prōō′dər·ē) *n.* *pl.* **·er·ies 1.** Extreme priggish-ness; primness. **2.** Prudish action or language.
prune¹ (prōōn) *n.* The dried fruit of the plum. [< OF < LL < L *prunum*]
prune² (prōōn) *v.t. & v.i.* **pruned, prun·ing 1.** To trim or cut branches or parts (from) so as to improve growth, ap-pearance, etc. **2.** To cut off (branches or parts). [< OF *proöignier, proignier, ? < provaignier* to cut] — **prun′er** *n.*
pru·ri·ent (prōōr′ē·ənt) *adj.* **1.** Having lustful cravings or desires. **2.** Lewd. [< L *pruriens, -entis,* ppr. of *prurire* to itch] — **pru′ri·ence, pru′ri·en·cy** *n.* — **pru′ri·ent·ly** *adv.*
pru·ri·tus (prōō·rī′təs) *n. Pathol.* Intense itching. [< L < *prurire* to itch] — **pru·rit·ic** (-rit′ik) *adj.*
Prus·sian (prush′ən) *adj.* **1.** Of or pertaining to Prussia, its inhabitants, or their language. **2.** Characteristic of the

Junkers of Prussia; militaristic; overbearing. — *n.* A native or inhabitant of Prussia.

Prussian blue 1. *Chem.* Any one of a group of cyanogen compounds containing chiefly ferric ferrocyanide, formerly much used in dyeing. 2. A deep blue pigment.

prus·sic acid (prus/ĭk) Hydrocyanic acid.

pry[1] (prī) *v.i.* **pried, pry·ing** To look or peer carefully, curiously, or slyly; snoop. — *n.* *pl.* **pries** 1. A sly and searching inspection. 2. One who pries; an inquisitive, prying person. [ME *prien*] — **pry/ing·ly** *adv.*

pry[2] (prī) *v.t.* **pried, pry·ing** *Chiefly U.S.* 1. To raise, move, or open by means of a lever; prize. 2. To obtain by effort. — *n.* A lever, as a bar, stick, or beam; also, leverage. [Back formation < *prize* lever]

pry·er (prī/ər) See PRIER.

psalm (säm) *n.* 1. *Often cap.* A sacred song or lyric contained in the Old Testament Book of Psalms. 2. Any sacred song. — *v.t.* To celebrate or praise in psalms. [OE < LL < Gk. *psalmos* song accompanied by a harp]

psalm·ist (sä/mist) *n.* A maker or composer of psalms. — **the Psalmist** King David, as the traditional author of many of the Scriptural psalms.

psalm·o·dy (sä/mə·dē, sal/-) *n.* *pl.* **·dies** 1. The use of psalms in divine worship. 2. A collection of psalms. [< OF < LL < Gk. < *psalmos* psalm + *aeidein* to sing]

Psalms (sämz) A lyrical book of the Old Testament, containing 150 hymns. Also **Book of Psalms.**

psal·ter (sôl/tər) *n.* The psalms appointed to be read or sung at any given service. [See PSALTERY.] — **psal·te·ri·an** (sôl·tir/ē·ən, sal-) *adj.*

Psal·ter (sôl/tər) *n.* The Book of Psalms, esp. for use in religious services. Also **Psal/ter·y.**

psal·ter·y (sôl/tər·ē) *n.* *pl.* **·ter·ies** An ancient stringed musical instrument played by plucking with a plectrum. [< OF < L < Gk. < *psallein* to pluck]

pseu·do (sōō/dō) *adj.* Pretended; sham.

pseudo- *combining form* 1. False; pretended: *pseudonym*. 2. Counterfeit; not genuine. 3. Closely resembling: *pseudopodium*. 4. Illusory; apparent. 5. Abnormal; erratic. Also, before vowels, **pseud-.** [< Gk. < *pseudēs* false]

pseu·do·nym (sōō/də·nim) *n.* A fictitious name; pen name. [< F < Gk. < *pseudēs* false + *onoma* name] — **pseu·don·y·mous** (sōō·don/ə·məs) *adj.* — **pseu·don/y·mous·ly** *adv.* — **pseu·don/y·mous·ness, pseu/do·nym/i·ty** *n.*

— **Syn.** *Pseudonym, alias, pen name,* and *nom de plume* denote an assumed name. Pseudonym is the general term, including all the others. An *alias* is a name taken to conceal one's true identity, most often for some wrongful purpose. *Pen name* and *nom de plume* refer to a fictitious name signed to a literary work by its author.

pseu·do·po·di·um (sōō/də·pō/dē·əm) *n.* *pl.* **·di·a** (-dē·ə) *Zool.* A temporary extension of the protoplasm of a cell or of a protozoan, used for taking in food, locomotion, etc. Also **pseu/do·pod** (-pod), **pseu/do·pode** (-pōd). [< NL]

pshaw (shô) *interj.* An exclamation of annoyance, disapproval, disgust, or impatience. — *v.t. & v.i.* To exclaim *pshaw* at (a person or thing).

psi (sī, psī, psē) *n.* The twenty-third letter in the Greek alphabet (Ψ, ψ): equivalent to English *ps.* See ALPHABET.

psit·ta·co·sis (sit/ə·kō/sis) *n.* An acute, infectious virus disease of parrots and related birds, transmissible to man and resembling influenza: also called *parrot fever.* [< NL < Gk. *psittakos* parrot + -OSIS]

pso·ri·a·sis (sə·rī/ə·sis) *n.* *Pathol.* A noncontagious, inflammatory skin disease, chronic or acute, characterized by reddish patches and white scales. [< NL < Gk. *psōra* an itch] — **pso·ri·at·ic** (sôr/ē·at/ik, sō/rē-) *adj.*

psych- Var. of PSYCHO-.

psy·che (sī/kē) *n.* 1. The human soul. 2. *Psychoanal.* The mind, often regarded as an entity functioning apart from or independently of the body. [< Gk. *psychē* soul]

Psy·che (sī/kē) In Greek and Roman mythology, a maiden who is united with Eros and is a personification of the soul.

psy·che·del·ic (sī/kə·del/ik) *adj.* Causing or having to do with an abnormal stimulation of consciousness or perception. [< Gk. *psychē* soul + *del(os)* manifest + -IC]

psy·chi·a·trist (sī·kī/ə·trist, si-) *n.* A physician specializing in the practice of psychiatry.

psy·chi·a·try (sī·kī/ə·trē, si-) *n.* The branch of medicine that deals with the diagnosis and treatment of mental disorders. — **psy·chi·at·ric** (sī/kē·at/rik) or **·ri·cal** *adj.*

psy·chic (sī/kik) *adj.* 1. Pertaining to the mind. 2. Pertaining to mental phenomena that appear to be independent of normal sensory stimuli, as clairvoyance, telepathy, and extrasensory perception. 3. Caused by, proceeding from, or attributed to a nonmaterial or occult agency. 4. Sensitive to mental or occult phenomena. Also **psy/chi·cal.** — *n.* One sensitive to extrasensory phenomena. [See PSYCHE.] — **psy/chi·cal·ly** *adv.*

psycho- *combining form* Mind; soul; spirit: *psychosomatic.* Also, before vowels, **psych-.** [< Gk. *psychē.* See PSYCHE.]

psy·cho·a·nal·y·sis (sī/kō·ə·nal/ə·sis) *n.* A system of psy-

chotherapy that seeks to alleviate neuroses and other me[ntal] disorders by the analysis of unconscious factors as reve[aled] in dreams, free association, lapses of memory, etc. — **p[sy·]cho·an/a·lyt/ic** (-an/ə·lit/ik) or **·i·cal** *adj.* — **psy/cho· a·lyt/i·cal·ly** *adv.*

psy·cho·an·a·lyst (sī/kō·an/ə·list) *n.* One who pract[ices] psychoanalysis.

psy·cho·an·a·lyze (sī/kō·an/ə·līz) *v.t.* **·lyzed, ·lyz·ing** To treat by psychoanalysis. Also *Brit.* **psy/cho·an/a·lyse.**

psy·cho·chem·i·cal (sī/kō·kem/i·kəl) *n.* *Chem.* A d[rug] or compound that affects consciousness and behavior. — *adj.* Consisting or of the nature of a psychochemical.

psy·cho·gen·ic (sī/kō·jen/ik) *adj.* Having mental origin[or] being affected by mental conflicts and states.

psy·cho·log·i·cal (sī/kə·loj/i·kəl) *adj.* 1. Of or pertain[ing] to psychology. 2. Of or in the mind. Also **psy/cho·lo[g·ic]** — **psy/cho·log/i·cal·ly** *adv.*

psy·chol·o·gist (sī·kol/ə·jist) *n.* A student of or a speci[alist] in psychology.

psy·chol·o·gize (sī·kol/ə·jīz) *v.i.* **·gized, ·giz·ing** 1. [To] study psychology. 2. To theorize on psychology.

psy·chol·o·gy (sī·kol/ə·jē) *n.* *pl.* **·gies** 1. The scienc[e of] the human mind in any of its aspects, operations, powers[or] functions. 2. The systematic investigation of mental p[he]nomena, especially those associated with consciousness, [be]havior, and the problems of adjustment to the environm[ent.] 3. The behavior patterns regarded as characteristic of[an] individual, type, group, etc. 4. A work on psychology[.]

psy·cho·mo·tor (sī/kō·mō/tər) *adj.* *Physiol.* Of or pert[ain]ing to muscular movements resulting from mental proce[sses.]

psy·cho·neu·ro·sis (sī/kō·nŏŏ·rō/sis, -nyŏŏ-) *n.* *pl.* **·ses** (-sēz) *Psychiatry* Neurosis. — **psy/cho·neu·rot/ic** (-rot[/ik]) *adj. & n.*

psy·cho·path (sī/kō·path) *n.* One who is mentally unsta[ble,] esp. in a criminal or antisocial manner.

psy·cho·path·ic (sī/kō·path/ik) *adj.* Of or characterize[d by] psychopathy.

psy·cho·pa·thol·o·gy (sī/kō·pə·thol/ə·jē) *n.* The patho[logy] of the mind. — **psy/cho·path/o·log/i·cal** (-path/ə·loj/[i·kəl)] *adj.* — **psy/cho·pa·thol/o·gist** *n.*

psy·chop·a·thy (sī·kop/ə·thē) *n.* Mental disorder.

psy·cho·phar·ma·col·o·gy (sī/kō·fär/mə·kol/ə·jē) *n.* [A] branch of pharmacology dealing with drugs that affect [the] mind. — **psy/cho·phar/ma·co·log/ic** (-kə·loj/ik) *adj.*

psy·cho·sis (sī·kō/sis) *n.* *pl.* **·ses** (-sēz) *Psychiatry* A se[vere] mental disorder, often involving disorganization of the t[otal] personality, with or without organic disease. [< NL < *psychōsis* giving of life < *psychoein* to animate]

psy·cho·so·mat·ic (sī/kō·sō·mat/ik) *adj.* 1. Of or pert[ain]ing to the effect of emotional states upon the body, [with] special reference to certain disorders. 2. Designati[ng a] branch of medicine that treats such disorders with a psy[cho]logical approach.

psy·cho·ther·a·py (sī/kō·ther/ə·pē) *n.* *pl.* **·pies** The tr[eat]ment of nervous and mental disorders, by psycholog[ical] methods, as hypnosis, re-education, psychoanalysis, [etc.] Also **psy/cho·ther/a·peu/tics** (-ther/ə·pyōō/tiks). — **psy[·]cho·ther/a·peu/tic** *adj.* — **psy/cho·ther/a·pist** *n.*

psy·chot·ic (sī·kot/ik) *n.* One suffering from a psych[osis.] — *adj.* Of or characterized by a psychosis.

psy·chot·o·mi·met·ic (sī·kot/ō·mi·met/ik, -mī·met/ik) *adj.* Designating a group of drugs capable of inducing alt[ered] states of consciousness and having possible therapeutic va[lue.]

psychro- *combining form* Cold. [< Gk. *psychros* cold]

ptar·mi·gan (tär/mə·gən) *n.* *pl.* **·gans** or **·gan** A gr[ouse] of the northern hemisphere, having a white winter plum[age] and feathered toes. [< Scottish Gaelic *tarmachan*]

PT boat A patrol torpedo boat.

ptero- *combining form* Wing; feather; winglike. Also, [be]fore vowels, **pter-.** [< Gk. *pteron* wing]

pter·o·dac·tyl (ter/ə·dak/til) *n. Paleontol.* Any of a ge[nus] of extinct flying reptiles of the Jurassic period. [< NL < Gk. *pteron* wing + *daktylos* finger]

-pterous *combining form* Having (a specified numbe[r or] kind of) wings: *dipterous.* [< Gk. *pteron* wing]

Ptol·e·ma·ic (tol/ə·mā/ik) *adj.* Of or pertaining to P[tol]emy, the astronomer, or to the dynasty of Egyptian k[ings] that began with Ptolemy I. [< Gk. *Ptolemaïkos*]

Ptolemaic system The ancient astronomical syste[m of] Ptolemy. It assumed that the earth was the central b[ody] around which the sun, planets, and celestial bodies revol[ved.]

Ptol·e·ma·ist (tol/ə·mā/ist) *n.* A believer in or adhe[rent] of the Ptolemaic system.

pto·maine (tō/mān, tō·mān/) *n. Biochem.* Any of a c[lass] of basic nitrogenous compounds, some of which are poi[son]ous, derived from decomposing animal or vegetable pro[tein.] Also **pto/main.** [< Ital. < Gk. *ptōma* corpse]

ptomaine poisoning An erroneous term for food poison[ing.]

pty·a·lin (tī/ə·lin) *n. Biochem.* An enzyme, containe[d in] saliva, that converts starch into dextrin and maltose. [< Gk. *ptyalon* saliva < *ptuein* to spit + -IN]

pub (pub) *n. Brit. Informal* A public house; inn; tavern.

pu·ber·ty (pyōō'bər·tē) *n. pl.* **·ties** The period during which an individual becomes physiologically capable of reproduction. [< L < *pubes, puberis* an adult]

pu·bes (pyōō'bēz) *n.* **1.** *Anat.* The part of the lower abdomen covered with hair in the adult; the pubic region. **2.** The hair that appears on the body at puberty; esp., the hair in the pubic region. [< L, pubic hair]

pu·bes·cent (pyōō·bes'ənt) *adj.* **1.** Arriving or having arrived at puberty. **2.** Having a growth of soft, fine hairs, as certain plants. [< MF < L *pubescens, -entis,* ppr. of *pubescere* to grow hair, attain puberty] — **pu·bes'cence** *n.*

pu·bic (pyōō'bik) *adj.* Of or pertaining to the region in the lower part of the abdomen: the *pubic* bones.

pu·bis (pyōō'bis) *n. pl.* **·bes** (-bēz) *Anat.* Either of the two bones that join with a third to form an arch on either central side of the pelvis. [See PUBES.]

pub·lic (pub'lik) *adj.* **1.** Of, pertaining to, or affecting the people at large or the community. **2.** Maintained by or for the public: *public* parks. **3.** Participated in by the people: *public* demonstration. **4.** For the use of the public; especially, for hire: a *public* cab, hall, etc. **5.** Well-known; open; notorious: a *public* scandal. **6.** Acting before or for the community: a *public* official. — *n.* **1.** Those who may be grouped together for any given purpose. **2.** An audience; esp., the admirers of an actor or other celebrity. — **the public** The people of a locality or nation. [< MF < L *publicus*] — **pub'lic·ly** *adv.* — **pub'lic·ness** *n.*

pub·lic-ad·dress system (pub'lik-ə-dres') An apparatus for the amplification of speech, music, etc., in public places.

pub·li·can (pub'lə·kən) *n.* **1.** In England, the keeper of a public house. **2.** In ancient Rome, a tax collector. [< OF < L < *publicanus* public revenue, orig. neut. of *publicus*]

pub·li·ca·tion (pub'lə·kā'shən) *n.* **1.** The act of publishing or offering to public notice. **2.** Any printed work placed on sale or otherwise distributed or offered for distribution. **3.** Notification to people at large orally or by writing or print; promulgation; proclamation. [See PUBLISH.]

public domain Lands owned by a state or national government; public lands. — **in the public domain** Available for unrestricted use: said of material on which copyright or patent right has expired.

public enemy **1.** A person, esp. a criminal, regarded as a menace to the public. **2.** An enemy state.

public house **1.** An inn, tavern, or hotel. **2.** In England, a place licensed to sell intoxicating liquors; a saloon.

pub·li·cist (pub'lə·sist) *n.* **1.** A writer on international law or on topics of public interest. **2.** A public-relations man or publicity agent.

pub·lic·i·ty (pub·lis'ə·tē) *n.* **1.** Information or personal news intended to promote the interests of individuals, institutions, etc. **2.** The state of being public, or the act of making or becoming public; exposure; notoriety. **3.** The attention or interest of the public gained by any method.

pub·li·cize (pub'lə·sīz) *v.t.* **·cized, ·ciz·ing** To advertise.

public library **1.** A library maintained for the use of the public. **2.** The building in which it is contained.

public opinion The prevailing ideas, beliefs, and aims of the people, collectively.

public relations The activities and techniques used by organizations and individuals to establish favorable attitudes and responses in their behalf on the part of the general public or of special groups; also, the occupation of establishing such attitude and responses.

public school **1.** *U.S.* A school maintained by public funds for the free education of the children of the community, usu. covering elementary and secondary grades. **2.** *Brit.* A private or endowed school not run for profit, esp. one preparing students for the universities, as Eton, Harrow, etc.

public servant A government official.

public utility A business organization or industry that supplies water, electricity, gas, etc., to the public, and is subject to particular governmental regulations.

public works Architectural or engineering works or improvements built with public money, as parks, roads, etc.

pub·lish (pub'lish) *v.t.* **1.** To print and issue (a book, magazine, map, etc.) to the public. **2.** To make known or announce; promulgate; proclaim. [See PUBLIC.] — **pub'lish·a·ble** *adj.*

pub·lish·er (pub'lish·ər) *n.* One who publishes; esp., one whose business is publishing books, etc.

puce (pyōōs) *adj.* Of a dark brown or purplish brown. [< flea color, flea < L *pulex, -icis* flea]

puck[1] (puk) *n.* An evil sprite or hobgoblin. [OE *pūca*]

puck[2] (puk) *n.* The black, hard, rubber disk used in playing ice hockey. [? < dial. E, to strike]

Puck (puk) A mischievous elf or goblin in Shakespeare's *Midsummer Night's Dream.* [< PUCK[1]]

puck·a (puk'ə) See PUKKA.

puck·er (puk'ər) *v.t. & v.i.* To gather or draw up into small folds or wrinkles. — *n.* A wrinkle or group of wrinkles. [Appar. freq. of POKE[2]] — **puck'er·y** *adj.*

puck·ish (puk'ish) *adj.* Mischievous; impish.

pud·ding (pŏŏd'ing) *n.* **1.** A sweetened and flavored dessert of soft food, usu. made of milk, flavoring, a thickening agent, etc. **2.** A sausage of seasoned minced meat, blood, or the like, usu. boiled or broiled. [ME *poding,* orig., sausage, black pudding]

pud·dle (pud'l) *n.* **1.** A small pool of water, esp. dirty water. **2.** A small pool of any liquid. — *v.t.* **·dled, ·dling** **1.** *Metall.* To convert (molten pig iron) into wrought iron by melting and stirring in the presence of oxidizing substances. **2.** To mix (clay, etc.) with water so as to obtain a watertight paste. **3.** To make muddy; stir up. [ME *podel,* dim. of OE *pudd* ditch] — **pud'dly** *adj.*

pud·dle-ball (pud'l-bôl') *n. Metall.* A ball of iron reduced to a pasty condition in the puddling furnace and ready for hammering or rolling.

pud·dler (pud'lər) *n.* **1.** One who puddles. **2.** A device for stirring fused metal.

pud·dling (pud'ling) *n. Metall.* The operation or business of making wrought iron from pig iron in a puddling furnace.

puddling furnace A reverberatory furnace for puddling pig iron: also called *hearth.*

pudg·y (puj'ē) *adj.* **pudg·i·er, pudg·i·est** Short and fat; dumpy; chubby: also *podgy.* [< Scot.]

pueb·lo (pweb'lō *for def. 1;* pwä'blō *for def. 2*) *n. pl.* **·los** **1.** A communal adobe or stone building or group of buildings of the Indians of the SW U.S. **2.** A town or village of Indians or Spanish Americans, as in Mexico. [< Sp., village]

Pueb·lo (pweb'lō) *n.* A member of one of the Indian tribes of Mexico and the SW U.S., as a Zuni, Hopi, etc.

pu·er·ile (pyōō'ər·il, pyōō'rəl, -rīl, pwer'əl, -īl) *adj.* **1.** Pertaining to or characteristic of childhood; juvenile. **2.** Immature; weak; silly: a *puerile* suggestion. [< L < *puer* boy, child] — **pu'er·ile·ly** *adv.* — **pu'er·ile·ness** *n.*

pu·er·il·i·ty (pyōō'ə·ril'ə·tē, pyōō·ril'-, pwer·il'-) *n. pl.* **·ties** **1.** Puerile state. **2.** A childish act or expression.

pu·er·per·al (pyōō·ûr'pər·əl) *adj. Med.* Of or connected with childbirth. [< L < *puer* child + *parere* to bear]

puff (puf) *n.* **1.** A breath emitted suddenly and with force; also, a sudden emission, as of air, smoke, or steam. **2.** A light, air-filled piece of pastry. **3.** A light ball, tuft, wad, or pad for dusting powder on the hair or skin. **4.** A loose roll of hair in a coiffure, or a light cushion over which it is rolled. **5.** A quilted bed coverlet; a comforter. **6.** In dressmaking, a part of a fabric so gathered as to produce a loose, fluffy distention. **7.** Excessive praise, as in a newspaper or advertisement. **8.** A puffball. — *v.i.* **1.** To blow in puffs, as the wind. **2.** To breathe hard, as after violent exertion. **3.** To emit smoke, steam, etc., in puffs. **4.** To smoke a cigar, etc., with puffs. **5.** To move, act, or exert oneself while emitting puffs: with *away, up,* etc. **6.** To swell, as with air or pride; dilate: often with *up* or *out.* — *v.t.* **7.** To send forth or emit with short puffs or breaths. **8.** To move, impel, or stir up with or in puffs. **9.** To smoke, as a pipe or cigar, with puffs. **10.** To swell or distend. **11.** To praise excessively. **12.** To arrange (hair, etc.) in a puff. [ME *puf*]

puff adder A large, sluggish, venomous African viper with a habit of violently puffing out its breath.

puff·ball (puf'bôl') *n.* Any of various globular fungi that puff out dustlike spores when broken open.

puff·er (puf'ər) *n.* One who or that which puffs.

puf·fin (puf'in) *n.* A sea bird allied to the auk and having a deep, compressed, highly colored bill. [ME *poffin*]

puff·y (puf'ē) *adj.* **puff·i·er, puff·i·est** **1.** Swollen with or as with air, etc. **2.** Inflated in manner; bombastic. **3.** Blowing in puffs. — **puff'i·ly** *adv.* — **puff'i·ness** *n.*

pug[1] (pug) *n.* Clay worked with water, for molding pottery or bricks. — *v.t.* **pugged, pug·ging** **1.** To knead or work (clay) with water, as in brickmaking. **2.** To fill in with clay, etc. [Origin unknown]

pug[2] (pug) *n.* **1.** A breed of dog characterized by a short square body, upturned nose, curled tail, and short smooth coat. **2.** A pug nose. [Prob. alter. of PUCK]

pug[3] (pug) *n. Anglo-Indian* An animal's footprint; trail. [< Hind. *pag* foot]

pug[4] (pug) *n. Slang* A professional pugilist. [Short for PUGILIST]

pugh (pyōō, pōō) *interj.* An exclamation of disgust.

pu·gi·lism (pyōō'jə·liz'əm) *n.* The art or practice of boxing or fighting with the fists. [< L *pugil* boxer] — **pu'gi·list** *n.* — **pu'gi·lis'tic** *adj.*

pug·na·cious (pug·nā'shəs) *adj.* Disposed or inclined to fight; quarrelsome. [< L *pugnare* to fight] — **pug·na'cious·ly** *adv.*

pug·nac·i·ty (pug·nas′ə·tē) *n. pl.* **·ties** The quality of being pugnacious; quarrelsome disposition; combativeness. Also **pug·na′cious·ness** (-nā′shəs·nis).

pug nose A short nose tilted upward at the end. [< PUG²] — **pug-nosed** (pug′nōzd′) *adj.*

puis·ne (pyōō′nē) *adj. Law* Junior as to rank; younger. [< OF < *puis* afterwards + *né* born]

pu·is·sant (pyōō′ə·sənt, pyōō·is′ənt, pwis′ənt) *adj.* Powerful; mighty. [< OF < L *posse* to be able] — **pu′is·sance** *n.* — **pu′is·sant·ly** *adv.*

puke (pyōōk) *v.t. & v.i.* **puked, puk·ing** To vomit or cause to vomit. — *n.* Vomit. [Origin unknown]

puk·ka (puk′ə) *adj. Anglo-Indian* **1.** Made of good materials; substantial. **2.** Genuine; superior. Also spelled *pucka.* [< Hind. *pakkā* substantial, cooked, ripe]

pul·chri·tude (pul′krə·tōōd, -tyōōd) *n.* Beauty; grace; physical charm. [< L *pulchritudo, -inis* < *pulcher* beautiful]

pul·chri·tu·di·nous (pul′krə·tōō′də·nəs, -tyōō′-) *adj.* Beautiful; lovely; esp., having physical beauty.

pule (pyōōl) *v.i.* **puled, pul·ing** To cry plaintively, as a child; whimper; whine. [Prob. imit.] — **pul′er** *n.*

Pul·itz·er Prize (pyōō′lit·sər, pool′it-) One of several annual awards for outstanding work in American journalism, letters, music, and art, established by Joseph Pulitzer, 1847–1911, U.S. journalist.

pull (pool) *v.t.* **1.** To apply force so as to cause motion toward or in the direction of the source of force; drag; tug. **2.** To draw or remove from a natural or fixed place. **3.** To give a pull or tug to. **4.** To pluck, as a fowl. **5.** To rip; tear; rend. **6.** To strain so as to cause injury. **7.** In golf, etc., to strike (the ball) so that it curves obliquely from the direction in which the striker faces. **8.** In baseball, to hit (the ball) to the field that the batter faces on completing his swing. **9.** *Slang* To put into effect; carry out: often with *off.* **10.** *Slang* To make a raid on; arrest. **11.** *Slang* To draw out so as to make. **12.** *Printing* To make or obtain by impression from type: to *pull* a proof. **13.** In boxing, to deliver (a punch, etc.) with less than one's full strength. **14.** In rowing: **a** To operate (an oar) by drawing toward one. **b** To propel or transport by rowing. **c** To be propelled by: The gig *pulls* four oars. — *v.i.* **15.** To use force in hauling, dragging, moving, etc. **16.** To move: with *out, in, away, ahead,* etc. **17.** To drink or inhale deeply. **18.** To propel a boat with oars; row. — **to pull for 1.** To strive in behalf of. **2.** *Informal* To declare one's allegiance to. — **to pull oneself together** To regain one's composure. — **to pull out** To withdraw, as from established position. — **to pull through** To manage to succeed, recover, etc. — **to pull up** To come to a halt. — **to pull up with** To advance to a position even with. — *n.* **1.** The act of pulling. **2.** Something that is pulled, as the handle of a drawer. **3.** An impression made by pulling the lever of a hand press. **4.** A long swallow, or a deep puff. **5.** Any steady, continuous effort. **6.** *Slang* A means of influencing those in power; influence. **7.** Attraction; appeal. **8.** The amount of resistance met in drawing a bowstring, pulling a trigger or the like, usu. measured in pounds. [OE *pullian* to pluck] — **pull′er** *n.*

pull·back (pool′bak′) *n.* **1.** A restraint or drawback. **2.** A device for drawing or holding something back, as part of a dress, or a window.

pul·let (pool′it) *n.* A young hen, or one not fully grown. [< OF *polete, poulet,* dim. of *poule* hen]

pul·ley (pool′ē) *n. pl.* **·leys 1.** A wheel grooved to receive a rope, and usu. mounted in a block, used to increase the mechanical advantage of an applied force. **2.** A block with its pulleys or tackle. **3.** A wheel driving, carrying, or being driven by a belt. [< OF < Med.L *poleia,* prob. ult. < Gk. *polos* pivot, axis]

Pull·man (pool′mən) *n.* A sleeping car or chair car on a passenger train: a trade name. Also **Pullman car.** [after George M. Pullman, 1831–97, U.S. inventor]

pull·out (pool′out′) *n.* **1.** A withdrawal, as of troops. **2.** *Aeron.* The maneuver of an airplane in passing from a dive to horizontal flight.

pull·o·ver (pool′ō′vər) *adj.* Put on by being drawn over the head. — *n.* A garment so put on, as a sweater or shirt.

pulmo- *combining form* Lung. [< *pulmo, -onis* lung]

pul·mo·nar·y (pul′mə·ner′ē) *adj.* **1.** Of, pertaining to, or affecting the lungs: also *pneumonic.* **2.** Having lunglike organs. [< L *pulmo, -onis* lung]

pulmonary artery *Anat.* An artery that conveys venous blood from the right ventricle of the heart to the lungs.

pulmonary tuberculosis Tuberculosis.

pul·mon·ic (pul·mon′ik) *adj.* Pulmonary.

Pul·mo·tor (pool′mō′tər, pool′-) *n.* An apparatus for producing artificial respiration by forcing oxygen into the lungs: a trade name. Also **pul′mo′tor.** [< PUL(MO)- + MOTOR]

pulp (pulp) *n.* **1.** A moist, soft, slightly cohering mass of matter, as the succulent part of fruit. **2.** A mixture of wood fibers or rags reduced to a pulpy consistency and forming the substance of paper. **3.** *Often pl.* A magazine printed on rough, unglazed paper, and usu. having contents of a cheap sensational nature: distinguished from *slick.* **4.** *Dent.* The soft tissue of vessels and nerves that fills the central cavity of a tooth. — *v.t.* **1.** To reduce to pulp. **2.** To remove the pulp or envelope from. — *v.i.* **3.** To be or become of a pulp consistency. [< MF < L *pulpa* flesh, pulp of fruit, pith] — **pulp′i·ness** *n.* — **pulp′y** *adj.*

pul·pit (pool′pit) *n.* **1.** An elevated stand or desk for a preacher in a church. **2.** The office or work of preaching. **3.** The clergy as a class. [< L *pulpitum* scaffold, stage]

pulp·wood (pulp′wood′) *n.* The soft wood of certain trees, as the spruce, used in the manufacture of paper.

pul·que (pul′kē, pool′-; *Sp.* pool′kä) *n.* A fermented drink made from various species of agave, esp. from the juice of the maguey. [< Am. Sp.]

pul·sar (pul′sär) *n.* A rotating neutron star, a source of regularly pulsing radio waves. [< PULSE + QUASAR]

pul·sate (pul′sāt) *v.i.* **·sat·ed, ·sat·ing 1.** To move or throb with rhythmical impulses, as the pulse or heart. **2.** To vibrate; quiver. [< L *pellere* (pp. *pulsus*) to beat] — **pul·sa′tion** *n.* — **pul′sa·tive** (-sə·tiv) *adj.* — **pul′sa·tor** *n.* — **pul·sa·to·ry** (pul′sə·tôr′ē) *adj.*

pulse¹ (puls) *n.* **1.** *Physiol.* The rhythmical beating of the arteries resulting from the successive contractions of the heart. **2.** Any throbbing or pulsation. **3.** *Telecom.* A brief surge of electrical or electromagnetic energy, usu. transmitted as a signal in communication. **4.** An indication of general opinion or sentiment. — *v.i.* **pulsed, puls·ing** To pulsate; throb. [< OF < L *pulsus (venarum)* the beating (of the veins)] — **pulse′less** *adj.*

pulse² (puls) *n.* Leguminous plants collectively, as peas, beans, etc.; also, their edible seeds. [< OF < L *puls* pottage of meal or pulse]

pulse·jet (puls′jet′) *n. Aeron.* A jet engine having movable vanes that intermittently take in air to develop power in rapid bursts. Also **pul′so·jet′** (-sō-jet′).

pul·som·e·ter (pul·som′ə·tər) *n.* A device for pumping liquids by steam pressure, consisting of two pear-shaped chambers connected by valves: also called *vacuum pump.*

pul·ver·ize (pul′və·rīz) *v.* **·ized, ·iz·ing** *v.t.* **1.** To reduce to powder or dust, as by crushing. **2.** To demolish; annihilate. — *v.i.* **3.** To become reduced to powder or dust. Also Brit. **pul′ver·ise.** [< MF < LL < L *pulvis, pulveris* powder, dust] — **pul′ver·iz′a·ble** *adj.* — **pul′ver·i·za′tion** *n.* — **pul′ver·iz′er** *n.*

pu·ma (pyōō′mə) *n.* A reddish carnivore of the cat family ranging from Canada to Patagonia: also called *cougar, mountain cat, mountain lion.* [< Sp. < Peruvian]

pum·ice (pum′is) *n.* Spongy volcanic lava, used as an abrasive and polishing material, esp. when powdered. Also **pumice stone.** — *v.t.* **·iced, ·ic·ing** To smooth, polish, clean with pumice. [< OF < L *pumex, pumicis*] — **pumi·ceous** (pyōō·mish′əs) *adj.*

pum·mel (pum′əl) *v.t.* **·meled** or **·melled, ·mel·ing** or **·mel·ling** To pommel. — *n.* A pommel.

pump¹ (pump) *n.* A mechanical device for raising, circulating, exhausting, or compressing a liquid or gas by drawing or pressing it through openings and pipes. — *v.t.* **1.** To raise with a pump, as water or other liquid. **2.** To remove the water, etc., from. **3.** To inflate with air by means of a pump. **4.** To propel, discharge, force, etc., from or as from a pump. **5.** To obtain information from persistently or subtly: to *pump* a witness. **6.** To obtain (information) in such a manner. — *v.i.* **7.** To work a pump; raise water or other liquid with a pump. **8.** To move up and down like a pump handle. [Prob. < MDu. *pompe*] — **pump′er** *n.*

pump² (pump) *n.* A low-cut shoe without a fastening, having either a high or a low heel. [Origin uncertain]

pum·per·nick·el (pum′pər·nik′əl) *n.* A coarse, dark, sour bread made from unsifted rye. [< G]

pump·kin (pump′kin, pung′-) *n.* **1.** A large, round, edible, yellow-orange fruit borne by a coarse trailing vine with heart-shaped leaves. **2.** The vine. **3.** Any of several related European plants. [< MF < L < Gk. *pepon* melon]

pun (pun) *n.* The humorous use of two words having the same or similar sounds but different meanings, or of two different, more or less incongruous meanings of the same word. — *v.i.* **punned, pun·ning** To make a pun. [Origin uncertain] — **pun′ning·ly** *adv.*

punch¹ (punch) *n.* **1.** A tool for perforating or indenting, or for driving out or in an object inserted in a hole, as a bolt or pin. **2.** A machine for impressing a design or stamping a die. — *v.t.* To perforate, shape, indent, etc., with a punch. [Prob. short for PUNCHEON¹]

punch² (punch) *v.t.* **1.** To strike sharply, esp. with the fist. **2.** To poke with a stick; prod. **3.** To operate; work; use: *punch* a time clock. **4.** *U.S.* In the West, to drive (cattle). — *n.* **1.** A swift blow with the fist; also, a thrust or nudge. **2.** *Slang* Vitality; force: an editorial with *punch.* [Prob. var. of POUNCE²] — **punch′er** *n.*

punch³ (punch) *n.* A beverage having wine or spirits, mixed

-a, or fruit juices as a basic ingredient, sweetened, some-
mes spiced, and diluted with water. [? < Hind. < Skt.
iñchan five; from the five original ingredients]
inch (punch) The quarrelsome, grotesque hero of a comic
uppet show, **Punch and Judy,** who habitually fights with
s wife, Judy. **— pleased as Punch** Extremely pleased;
ghly gratified. [Short for PUNCHINELLO]
nch card In data processing, a card marked by an ar-
ngement of positions to record information indicated by
e presence or absence of punched holes. Also **punched card.**
nch-drunk (punch′drungk′) *adj.* **1.** Groggy, slow in
ovement, speech, etc., from repeated blows to the head: said
prize fighters. **2.** Confused; dazed.
n·cheon¹ (pun′chən) *n.* **1.** An upright supporting timber.
A punch or perforating tool. **3.** A broad, heavy piece of
ughly dressed timber. [< OF *poncon, poinchon* a punch]
n·cheon² (pun′chən) *n.* **1.** A liquor cask of variable ca-
acity, from 72 to 120 gallons. **2.** A liquor measure of vary-
g amount. [< OF *ponçon, poinchon*]
n·chi·nel·lo (pun′chə·nel′ō) *n.* *pl.* **·los** or **·loes** A comic
aracter; buffoon, esp. in an Italian puppet show. Also
n′chi·nel′lo. [< dial. Ital. (Neapolitan) *Polcenella*]
nch·ing bag (pun′ching) An inflated or stuffed ball, usu.
spended, that is punched with the fists for exercise.
nch press A machine equipped to cut or form metal.
nc·til·i·o (pungk·til′ē·ō) *n.* *pl.* **·til·i·os 1.** A fine point of
iquette. **2.** Preciseness in the observance of etiquette or
remony. [< Sp. < Ital. < L *punctum* point]
nc·til·i·ous (pungk·til′ē·əs) *adj.* **1.** Very careful in the
servance of forms of etiquette, etc. **2.** Very precise. —
· **punc·til′i·ous·ly** *adv.* **— punc·til′i·ous·ness** *n.*
nc·tu·al (pungk′chōō·əl) *adj.* **1.** Acting or arriving
omptly. **2.** Done or made precisely at an appointed time.
Punctilious; exact. [< Med.L < L *punctus* pricking,
int] **— punc′tu·al·ly** *adv.*
nc·tu·al·i·ty (pungk′chōō·al′ə·tē) *n.* *pl.* **·ties** The qual-
, characteristic, act, or habit of being punctual.
nc·tu·ate (pungk′chōō·āt) *v.* **·at·ed, ·at·ing** *v.t.* **1.** To di-
de or mark with punctuation. **2.** To interrupt at inter-
ls. **3.** To emphasize; stress. **—** *v.i.* **4.** To use punctua-
n. [< Med.L < L *punctus* point] **— punc′tu·a′tor** *n.*
nc·tu·a·tion (pungk′chōō·ā′shən) *n.* The use of points or
arks in written or printed matter to indicate the separation
the words into sentences, clauses, and phrases, and to aid
the better comprehension of the meaning; also, the marks
used (**punctuation marks**). **— punc′tu·a′tive** *adj.* The
ief punctuation marks are:

period	.	parentheses	( )
colon	:	brackets	[ ]
semicolon	;	dash (em-dash)	—
comma	,	(en-dash)	–
question mark	?	hyphen	-
(interrogation point)		quotation marks	" "
exclamation mark	!	virgule (virgil)	/

nc·ture (pungk′chər) *v.* **·tured, ·tur·ing** *v.t.* **1.** To pierce
th a sharp point. **2.** To make by pricking, as a hole. **3.**
cause to collapse: to *puncture* a tire. **—** *v.i.* **4.** To be
erced or punctured. **—** *n.* **1.** A small hole made by pierc-
g with a sharp point. **2.** A minute depression; pit. **3.**
e act of puncturing. [< L *pungere* to prick]
n·dit (pun′dit) *n.* **1.** In India, one versed in Sanskrit
re and in the science, laws, and religion of the Hindus. **2.**
y learned man. [< Hind. < Skt. *pandita*]
n·gent (pun′jənt) *adj.* **1.** Sharp or acrid to taste or
ell; keen; penetrating: a *pungent* odor. **2.** Affecting the
nd or feelings so as to cause pain; poignant. **3.** Caustic;
ting: *pungent* sarcasm. [< L *pungere* to prick] **— pun′.**
nce (-jəns), **pun′gen·cy** *n.* **— pun′gent·ly** *adv.*
nic (pyōō′nik) *adj.* **1.** Of or pertaining to ancient Car-
age or the Carthaginians. **2.** Untrustworthy, as the Car-
aginians. **—** *n.* The language of the Carthaginians. [<
< *Poenus* Carthaginian, Phoenician]
nic Wars See table for WAR.
n·ish (pun′ish) *v.t.* **1.** To subject (a person) to pain, con-
ement, or other penalty for a crime or fault. **2.** To im-
se a penalty on. **3.** To use roughly; injure. **4.** To de-
ete, as a stock of food. [< OF < L *punire* to punish] **—**
n′ish·a·ble *adj.* **— pun′ish·a·bil′i·ty** *n.* **— pun′ish·er** *n.*
n·ish·ment (pun′ish·mənt) *n.* **1.** A penalty imposed, as
r transgression of law. ◆ Collateral adjective: *penal.* **2.**
y ill suffered in consequence of wrongdoing. **3.** The act of
nishing. **4.** *Informal* Rough handling, as in a prize fight.
·ni·tive (pyōō′nə·tiv) *adj.* **1.** Pertaining to or inflicting
nishment: *punitive* measures. **2.** *Law* Of a character to
nish or vindicate. Also **pu′ni·to·ry** (-tôr′ē, -tō′rē). **— pu′.**
tive·ly *adv.* **— pu′ni·tive·ness** *n.*
n·ja·bi (pun·jä′bē) *n.* **1.** A native of the Punjab. **2.** The
nskritic language of the Punjab: also spelled *Panjabi.*

punk¹ (pungk) *n.* **1.** Wood decayed through the action of a
fungus, useful as tinder. **2.** An artificial preparation that
will smolder without flame. [< Algonquian]
punk² (pungk) *U.S. Slang n.* **1.** Nonsense. **2.** A petty hoodlum.
3. A young, inexperienced boy or man: a contemptuous term.
— *adj.* **1.** Worthless. **2.** Unwell. [Origin uncertain]
pun·ka (pung′kə) *n.* A fan; esp., a rectangular strip of
cloth, etc., swung from the ceiling and moved by a servant or
by machinery. Also **pun′kah.** [< Hind. *pankhā* fan]
pun·ster (pun′stər) *n.* One who puns. Also **pun′ner.**
punt¹ (punt) *n.* A flat-bottomed,
square-ended boat, often propelled by
a pole, used in shallow waters. **—**
v.t. **1.** To propel (a boat) by pushing
with a pole against the bottom of a
shallow stream, lake, etc. **2.** To convey in a punt. **—** *v.i.* **3.** To go or
hunt in a punt. [OE < L *ponto, -onis*
punt, pontoon] **— punt′er** *n.*

PUNT

punt² (punt) *v.i.* In certain card games, to gamble or bet,
esp. against a bank. [< F < Sp. < L *punctum* point] **—**
punt′er *n.*
punt³ (punt) *n.* In football, a kick made by dropping the
ball from the hands and kicking it before it strikes the
ground. **—** *v.t. & v.i.* In football, to propel (the ball) with a
punt. [? Var. of BUNT] **— punt′er** *n.*
pun·ty (pun′tē) *n.* *pl.* **·ties** An iron rod used in glassmak-
ing to handle the hot glass. [< F *pontil*]
pu·ny (pyōō′nē) *adj.* **·ni·er, ·ni·est** Of small and feeble development or importance; weak and insignificant. [See
PUISNE.] **— pu′ni·ly** *adv.* **— pu′ni·ness** *n.*
pup (pup) *n.* **1.** A puppy (def. 1). **2.** The young of the seal,
the shark, and certain other animals. **—** *v.i.* **pupped, pup·**
ping To bring forth pups. [Short for PUPPY]
pu·pa (pyōō′pə) *n.* *pl.* **·pae** (-pē) *Entomol.* **1.** The quies-
cent stage in the development of an insect, following the lar-
val and preceding the adult stage. **2.** An insect in such a
stage. [< NL < L, girl, doll, puppet] **— pu′pal** *adj.*
pu·pil¹ (pyōō′pəl) *n.* A person of any age under the care of
a teacher; learner. **— Syn.** see STUDENT. [< OF < L *pu·*
pillus, dim. of *pupus* boy and *pupilla,* dim. of *pupa* girl]
pu·pil² (pyōō′pəl) *n. Anat.* The contractile opening in the
iris of the eye, through which light reaches the retina. [<
OF < L *pupilla* pupil of the eye]
pup·pet (pup′it) *n.* **1.** A small figure of a person, animal,
etc., and animated by the hand. **2.** A marionette. **3.** One
slavishly subject to the will of another; a tool. **—** *adj.* **1.**
Of or pertaining to puppets. **2.** Not autonomous: a *puppet*
state. [< OF < L *pupa* girl, doll, puppet]
pup·pet·eer (pup′i·tir′) *n.* One who manipulates puppets.
puppet show A drama with puppets for the actors.
pup·py (pup′ē) *n.* *pl.* **·pies 1.** A young dog: also called
pup. **2.** A pup (def. 2). [< OF < L *pupa* girl, doll] **—**
pup′py·ish *adj.*
puppy love Sentimental, adolescent love or infatuation.
pup tent A shelter tent.
pur·blind (pûr′blīnd′) *adj.* **1.** Partly blind. **2.** Having
little or no insight or understanding. [ME] **— pur′blind′ly**
adv. **— pur′blind′ness** *n.*
pur·chase (pûr′chəs) *v.t.* **·chased, ·chas·ing 1.** To acquire
by paying money or its equivalent; buy. **2.** To obtain by
exertion, sacrifice, flattery, etc. **3.** To move, hoist, or hold
by a mechanical purchase. **—** *n.* **1.** Something purchased.
2. The act of purchasing. **3.** A device that holds or grips
something so as to prevent slipping, etc. **4.** A device that
gives a mechanical advantage, as a tackle or lever; also,
leverage. **5.** Any means of increasing influence or advantage. **6.** Value; worth. [< OF *porchacier* to seek for] **—**
pur′chas·a·ble *adj.* **— pur′chas·er** *n.*
pur·dah (pûr′də) *n. Anglo-Indian* **1.** A curtain or screen
used to seclude women. **2.** The state or system of such seclusion. [< Urdu and Persian *pardah*]
pure (pyōōr) *adj.* **pur·er, pur·est 1.** Free from anything
that weakens, impairs, or pollutes. **2.** Free from adulteration; clear; clean. **3.** Genuine; stainless: *pure* food; pure
motives. **4.** Free from moral defilement; innocent; chaste.
5. Free from foreign or imported elements, as a language.
6. Free of harsh qualities, as music; also, correct in form or
style; finished. **7.** Abstract; nonobjective: *pure* form. **8.**
Phonet. Having a single, unvarying tone or sound: said of
vowels. **9.** Concerned with fundamental research, as distinguished from practical application; theoretical: said of
sciences. **10.** *Genetics* Breeding true with respect to one or
more characters; purebred. **11.** Nothing but; sheer: *pure*
luck. [< OF < L *purus* clean, pure] **— pure′ness** *n.*
pure·bred (*adj.* pyōōr′bred′; *n.* pyōōr′bred′) *adj. Biol.*
Bred from stock having had no admixture for many generations: said especially of livestock. **—** *n.* A purebred animal.

pu·rée (pyŏŏ·rā′, pyŏŏr′ā; *Fr.* pü·rā′) *n.* A thick pulp, usu. of vegetables, boiled and strained. [< F < OF < L *purare* to purify]

pure·ly (pyŏŏr′lē) *adv.* 1. So as to be free from admixture, taint, or any harmful substance. 2. Chastely; innocently. 3. Completely; totally. 4. Merely; simply.

pur·ga·tion (pûr·gā′shən) *n.* The act of purging; catharsis.

pur·ga·tive (pûr′gə·tiv) *adj.* Tending to purge; esp., precipitating a bowel movement. — *n.* A purgative agent.

pur·ga·to·ry (pûr′gə·tôr′ē, -tō′rē) *n. pl.* **·ries** 1. In Roman Catholic theology, a state or place where the souls of those who have died penitent are made fit for paradise by expiating venial sins and undergoing any punishment remaining for previously forgiven sins. 2. Any place or state of temporary banishment, suffering, or punishment. [See PURGE.] — **pur′ga·to′ri·al** *adj.*

purge (pûrj) *v.* **purged, purg·ing** *v.t.* 1. To cleanse of what is impure or extraneous; purify. 2. To remove (impurities, etc.) in cleansing: with *away, off,* or *out.* 3. To rid (a group, nation, etc.) of elements regarded as undesirable or inimical, esp. by killing. 4. To cleanse or rid of sin, fault, or defilement. 5. *Med.* **a** To cause evacuation of (the bowels, etc.). **b** To induce evacuation of the bowels of. — *v.i.* 6. To become clean or pure. 7. *Med.* To have or induce evacuation of the bowels, etc. — *n.* 1. The act or process of purging. 2. That which purges, esp. a cathartic. [< OF < L *purgare* to cleanse < *purus* pure] — **purg′er** *n.* — **purg′ing** *n.*

pu·ri·fy (pyŏŏr′ə·fī) *v.* **·fied, ·fy·ing** *v.t.* 1. To make pure or clean. 2. To free from sin. 3. To free of foreign or debasing elements, as a language. — *v.i.* 4. To become pure or clean. [< OF < L < *purus* pure + *facere* to make] — **pu′ri·fi·ca′tion** *n.* — **pu·rif′i·ca·to·ry** (pyŏŏ·rif′ə·kə·tôr′ē, -tō′rē) *adj.* — **pu′ri·fi′er** *n.*

Pu·rim (pŏŏr′im, pyŏŏr′im; *Hebrew* pŏŏ·rēm′) *n.* A Jewish festival commemorating the defeat of Haman's plot to massacre the Jews (*Esth.* ix 26), observed about the first of March. [< Hebrew *pūrīm*, pl. of *pūr* lot]

pur·ist (pyŏŏr′ist) *n.* 1. One who believes in or practices exact or meticulous usage, as of a language, style, etc. 2. One who practices or advocates an art form in which primary stress is placed on structural simplicity, as in works of a geometric nature. — **pur′ism** *n.* — **pu·ris′tic** *adj.*

pu·ri·tan (pyŏŏr′ə·tən) *n. Sometimes cap.* One who is scrupulously strict or exacting in his religious or moral life: often used disparagingly. — *adj.* Puritanical. — **pu′ri·tan·ism** *n.*

Pu·ri·tan (pyŏŏr′ə·tən) *n.* One of a group of English Protestants who in the 16th and 17th centuries advocated simpler forms of creed and ritual in the Church of England. — *adj.* Of or pertaining to the Puritans or to their beliefs or customs. [< LL < L *purus* pure] — **Pu′ri·tan·ism** *n.*

pu·ri·tan·i·cal (pyŏŏr′ə·tan′i·kəl) *adj.* 1. Rigidly scrupulous or exacting in religious observance or morals; strict. 2. *Often cap.* Of or characteristic of the Puritans. Also **pu′ri·tan′ic.** — **pu′ri·tan′i·cal·ly** *adv.* — **pu′ri·tan′i·cal·ness** *n.*

pu·ri·ty (pyŏŏr′ə·tē) *n.* 1. The quality or state of being pure. 2. Saturation: said of a color.

purl[1] (pûrl) *v.i.* 1. To whirl; turn. 2. To flow with a bubbling sound. 3. To move in eddies. — *n.* 1. A circling movement of water; an eddy. 2. A gentle, continued murmur, as of a rippling stream. [Cf. Norw. *purla* to gush out]

purl[2] (pûrl) *v.t.* 1. In knitting, to make (a stitch) backward. 2. To edge with lace, embroidery, etc. Also spelled *pearl.* — *v.i.* 3. To do edging with lace, etc.: also spelled *pearl.* — *n.* 1. An edge of lace, embroidery, etc. 2. In knitting, the inversion of the knit stitch, giving a horizontal rib effect. Also spelled *pearl.* 3. A spiral of gold or silver wire used in lacework. [Earlier *pyrle* < *pyrl* twist]

pur·lieu (pûr′lōō) *n.* 1. *pl.* The outlying districts or outskirts of any place. 2. A place in which one is free to come and go. 3. Formerly, ground unlawfully taken for a royal forest, but afterward disafforested and restored to its rightful owners. [< AF < OF < *puraler* to go through]

pur·lin (pûr′lin) *n.* A horizontal timber supporting rafters. Also **pur′line** (-lin). For illus. see ROOF. [ME *purlyn*]

pur·loin (pûr·loin′) *v.t. & v.i.* To steal; filch. [< OF *porloignier* to remove, put far off] — **pur·loin′er** *n.*

pur·ple (pûr′pəl) *n.* 1. A color of mingled red and blue, between crimson and violet. 2. Cloth or a garment of this color, worn formerly by sovereigns. 3. Royal power or dignity: usu. in the phrase **born to the purple.** 4. The office of a cardinal, from the official red hat and robes. 5. The office of a bishop. — *v.t. & v.i.* **·pled, ·pling** To make or become purple. — *adj.* 1. Of the color of purple. 2. Imperial; regal. 3. Ornate; flowery: a *purple* passage of prose. [OE < OF < L *purpura*, orig., shellfish yielding Tyrian purple dye, or cloth dyed with it]

Purple Heart A decoration, the **Order of the Purple Heart,** awarded to members of the armed forces or to citizens of the U.S. honorably wounded in action. See DECORATION.

pur·plish (pûr′plish) *adj.* Somewhat purple.

pur·port (pûr′pôrt, -pōrt; *for v.,* also pər·pôrt′, -pōrt′) *v.t.*

1. To have or bear as its meaning; signify; imply. 2. To claim or profess (to be), esp. falsely. — *n.* 1. That which conveyed or suggested to the mind as the meaning or intention; import. 2. The substance of a statement, etc., given in other than the exact words. [< AF or OF < L *pro-* for + *portare* to carry] — **pur·port′ed·ly** *adv.*

pur·pose (pûr′pəs) *n.* 1. An idea or ideal kept before the mind as an end of effort or action; design; aim. 2. A particular thing to be effected or attained. 3. Practical advantage or result; use: words to little *purpose.* 4. Settled resolution; determination. 5. Purport; intent, as of spoken or written language. 6. A proposition; question at issue — **on purpose** Intentionally. — *v.t. & v.i.* **·posed, ·pos-** To have the intention of doing or accomplishing (something); intend; aim. [< OF *pro-* forth + *poser* to put] **pur′pose·ful** *adj.* — **pur′pose·ful·ly** *adv.* — **pur′pose·f ness** *n.* — **pur′pose·less** *adj.* — **pur′pose·less·ly** *adv.* — **Syn.** (noun) 1. Intent, intention, aim, goal, design, end.

pur·pose·ly (pûr′pəs·lē) *adv.* For a purpose; intentional

pur·po·sive (pûr′pəs·siv) *adj.* 1. Pertaining to, having, indicating purpose. 2. Functional; useful. — **pur′po·si ly** *adv.* — **pur′po·sive·ness** *n.*

purr (pûr) *n.* A murmuring sound, such as a cat ma when pleased. — *v.i.* 1. To make such a sound. — *v.t.* To express by or as by purring. [Imit.]

purse (pûrs) *n.* 1. A small bag or pouch, one for car ing money. 2. Available resources or means; treasury: public *purse.* 3. A sum of money offered as a prize. — **pursed, purs·ing** To contract into wrinkles or folds: to p the lips. [OE < LL < Gk. *byrsa* skin, hide]

purs·er (pûr′sər) *n.* 1. An officer having charge of the counts, etc., of a vessel. 2. Formerly, a naval paymas

purs·lane (pûrs′lin, -lān) *n.* A common garden herb w reddish green stem and leaves and small yellow flowers, u as a salad: also called *pussley.* [< OF < L *porcilaca*]

pur·su·ance (pər·sōō′əns) *n.* The act of pursuing; a follc ing up; prosecution: usu. in the phrase **in pursuance of**

pur·su·ant (pər·sōō′ənt) *adj.* Done in accordance with by reason of something; conformable. — *adv.* In acco ance; conformably: usu. with *to*: also **pur·su′ant·ly.**

pur·sue (pər·sōō′) *v.* **·sued, ·su·ing** *v.t.* 1. To follow in attempt to overtake or capture; chase. 2. To seek or atta 3. To advance along the course of; keep to the direction provisions of, as a path, plan, or system. 4. To apply on energies to or have as one's profession or chief interest: *pursue* one's studies. 5. To follow persistently; harass. *v.i.* 6. To follow; chase. 7. To continue; persist. — [< A OF < LL < L < *pro-* forth + *sequi* to follow] — **pur·su ble** *adj.* — **pur·su′er** *n.*

pur·suit (pər·sōōt′) *n.* 1. The act of pursuing; a chase. That which is followed as a continued employment, pasti etc. — **Syn.** See OCCUPATION.

pursuit plane *Mil.* A fighter plane.

purs·y (pûr′sē) *adj.* **purs·i·er, purs·i·est** 1. Short-breath asthmatic. 2. Fat; hefty. [Earlier *pursive* < AF *pur* OF *polsif* < *polser* to pant, gasp] — **purs′i·ness** *n.*

pu·ru·lent (pyŏŏr′ə·lənt, -yə·lənt) *adj.* Consisting of or creting pus; suppurating. [< L < *pus, puris* pus] — **ru·lence** or **·len·cy** *n.* — **pu′ru·lent·ly** *adv.*

pur·vey (pər·vā′) *v.t. & v.i.* To furnish (provisions, et [< AF < L *providere*] — **pur·vey′or** *n.*

pur·vey·ance (pər·vā′əns) *n.* 1. The act of purveying. That which is purveyed or supplied; provisions.

pur·view (pûr′vyōō) *n.* 1. Extent, sphere, or scope of a thing, as of official authority. 2. Range of view, experien or understanding; outlook. 3. *Low* The body or the sc or limit of a statute. [< AF *purveu* provided]

pus (pus) *n.* A yellowish secretion from inflamed tissu [< L] — **pus·sy** (pus′ē) *adj.*

push (pŏŏsh) *v.t.* 1. To exert force upon or against (an ject) for the purpose of moving. 2. To force (one's way) through a crowd, jungle, etc. 3. To press forward, pro cute, or develop with vigor and persistence. 4. To u advocate, or promote vigorously and persistently: to p a new product. 5. To bear hard upon; harass: I am *pus* for time. — *v.i.* 6. To exert steady pressure against sor thing so as to move it. 7. To move or advance vigorou or persistently. 8. To exert great effort. — *n.* 1. The of pushing; a shove. 2. *Informal* An extremity; exigen at a *push* for money. 3. Determined activity; energy. Anything pushed to cause action. 5. An influential cliq [< OF < L *pusare* to beat]

push button A button or knob that on being pushed op or closes a circuit in an electric system. — **push·but** (pŏŏsh′but′n) *adj.*

push·cart (pŏŏsh′kärt′) *n.* A two- or four-wheeled c pushed by hand, used by fruit venders, peddlers, etc.

push·er (pŏŏsh′ər) *n.* 1. One who or that which pushes esp., an active, energetic person. 2. *Aeron.* An airpl with the propeller in the rear of the wings. 3. *U.S. Sl* One who illegally sells narcotics to addicts.

ing (pŏŏsh′ing) *adj.* **1.** Possessing enterprise and gy. **2.** Aggressive; impertinent. **— push′ing·ly** *adv.*

·o·ver (pŏŏsh′ō′vər) *n. Slang* **1.** One who is easily de-ed, overcome, taken advantage of, etc.; an easy mark. nything that can be done with little or no effort.

·pin (pŏŏsh′pin′) *n.* A pin with a large head, inserted humb pressure and used for mounting papers, etc.

·pull (pŏŏsh′pŏŏl′) *adj. Electronics* Designating a cir-or system that uses two similar components operating in osite phase.

·tu (push′tŏŏ) *n.* Pashto.

·y (pŏŏsh′ē) *adj.* **·i·er, ·i·est** *Informal* Offensively ag-sive; bossy. **— push′i·ly** *adv.* **— push′i·ness** *n.*

il·lan·i·mous (pyŏŏsə·lan′ə·məs) *adj.* **1.** Lacking age, or spirit; cowardly. **2.** Characterized by weakness urpose or lack of courage. [< LL < L *pusillus* very little *mimus* soul] **— pu′sil·la·nim′i·ty** (-lə-nim′ə-tē) *n.* — **il·lan′i·mous·ly** *adv.* **— pu′sil·lan′i·mous·ness** *n.*

· (pŏŏs) *n. Informal* **1.** A cat. **2.** A child or young an: a term of affection. [< LG *puus*, name for a cat]

² (pŏŏs) *n. Slang* The mouth; face. [< Irish *pus* mouth]

·ley (pŭs′lē) *n.* Purslane. [Alter. of PURSLANE]

sy (pŏŏs′ē) *n. pl.* **·sies** *Informal* **1.** A cat. **2.** A fuzzy in, as of a willow, birch, etc. [Dim. of PUSS¹]

sy·foot (pŏŏs′ē·fŏŏt′) *v.i.* **1.** To move softly and stealth-as a cat does. **2.** To act or proceed without committing elf or revealing one's intentions.

sy willow (pŏŏs′ē) A small American wil-with silky catkins in early spring.

tu·late (pŭs′chŏŏ·lāt; *for adj., also* pŭs′-ə·lit) *v.t. & v.i.* **·lat·ed, ·lat·ing** To form into ecome pustules. **—** *adj.* Covered with pus-s. [< L *pustulatus*, pp. of *pustulare* to blis-**— pus′tu·la′tion** *n.*

tule (pŭs′chŏŏl) *n.* **1.** *Pathol.* A small ele-on of the skin with an inflamed base contain-ous. **2.** Any elevation resembling a pimple blister. [< L *pustula*] **— pus′tu·lar, pus′/ us** *adj.*

· (pŏŏt) *v.* **put, put·ting** *v.t.* **1.** To bring into et in a specified or implied place or position; lay. **2.** To g into a specified state or relation: to *put* a prisoner to ch. **3.** To bring to bear; apply: *Put* your back into it! 'o impose. **5.** To ascribe or attribute, as the wrong in-retation on a remark. **6.** To place according to one's es-ation: I *put* the time at five o'clock. **7.** To throw with a hing motion of the arm: to *put* the shot. **8.** To incite; mpt. **9.** To bring forward for debate, answer, considera-, etc. **10.** To subject. **11.** To express in words: That's *ing* it mildly. **12.** To bet: I'll *put* six dollars on that se. **—** *v.i.* **13.** To go; proceed: to *put* to sea. **— to put** ut *Naut.* To change to the opposite tack; change direc-. **— to put aside** (or **away** or **by**) **1.** To place in re e; save. **2.** To thrust aside; discard. **— to put down 1.** repress; crush. **2.** To degrade; demote. **3.** To write n; record. **4.** *Slang* To disparage. **— to put forth 1** extend, as the arm or hand. **2.** To grow, as shoots or s. **3.** To exert. **4.** To set out; leave port. **— to put for-** d To advance; urge, as a claim. **— to put in 1.** *Naut.* enter a harbor or place of shelter. **2.** To interpolate; in-ose. **3.** *Informal* To devote; expend, as time. **4.** To ance (a claim, etc.). **5.** To submit, as an application. **— ut off 1.** To delay; postpone. **2.** To discard. **— to on 1.** To don. **2.** To bring into action; turn on. **3.** To ulate; pretend. **4.** To give a representation of; stage. *Slang* To deceive; mock. **— to put out 1.** To extinguish. 'o expel; eject. **3.** To disconcert; embarrass. **4.** To in venience. **5.** In baseball, to retire (a batter or base run-. **— to put over 1.** To place in command or charge. **2.** *rmal* To accomplish successfully. **— to put one** (or *ething*) **over on** *Informal* To deceive or dupe. **— to put ugh 1.** To bring to successful completion. **2.** To cause ndergo. **— to put up 1.** To erect; build. **2.** To pre-e or can. **3.** To wager; bet. **4.** To provide (money, tal, etc.). **5.** To sheathe, as a weapon. **— to put upon** take advantage of. **— to put up with** To endure. **—** The act of putting, as a throw. **—** *adj. Informal* Fixed; led: My hat won't stay *put*. [Fusion of OE *pūtian* to igate, *potian* to push, and *pȳtan* to put out]

a·tive (pyŏŏ′tə·tiv) *adj.* Supposed; reputed. [< MF *LL*, L, pp. of *putare* to think] **— pu′ta·tive·ly** *adv.*

off (pŏŏt′ŏf′, -ôf′) *n.* An evasion; excuse.

on (pŏŏt′on′) *n. Slang* A hoax or deception.

out (pŏŏt′out′) *n.* In baseball, the act of causing an , as of a batter or base runner.

re·fac·tion (pyŏŏ′trə·fak′shən) *n.* **1.** The decomposi-of organic matter. **2.** The state of being putrefied. **3.** rescent or putrefied matter.

pu·tre·fac·tive (pyŏŏ′trə·fak′tiv) *adj.* **1.** Of or pertaining to putrefaction. **2.** Producing putrefaction.

pu·tre·fy (pyŏŏ′trə·fī) *v.t. & v.i.* **·fied, ·fy·ing 1.** To decay or cause to decay with a fetid odor; rot. **2.** To make or become gangrenous. **— Syn.** See DECAY. [< F < L < *putrere* to decay + *facere* to make] **— pu′tre·fi′er** *n.*

pu·tres·cent (pyŏŏ·tres′ənt) *adj.* **1.** Becoming putrid; **2.** Pertaining to putrefaction. **— pu·tres′cence** *n.*

pu·trid (pyŏŏ′trid) *adj.* **1.** Being in a state of putrefaction; rotten. **2.** Indicating or produced by putrefaction: a *putrid* smell. **3.** Rotten; corrupt. [< L *putrere* to decay] **— pu·trid′i·ty** *n.* **— pu′trid·ly** *adv.* **— pu′trid·ness** *n.*

Putsch (pŏŏch) *n.* An outbreak or rebellion; an attempted *coup d'état.* [< G < dial. G (Swiss), lit., push, blow]

putt (put) *n.* In golf, a light stroke made on a putting green to place the ball in or near the hole. **—** *v.t. & v.i.* To strike (the ball) with such a stroke. [Var. of PUT]

put·tee (pŭt′ē, pŭ·tē′) *n.* A strip of cloth wound spirally about the leg from knee to ankle, used by soldiers, sportsmen, etc.; also, a leather gaiter strapped around the leg. Also **put′ty.** [< Hind. < Skt. *patta* strip of cloth]

put·ter¹ (pŭt′ər) *n.* **1.** In golf, one who putts. **2.** An up-right, stiff-shafted golf club used on the putting green.

put·ter² (pŭt′ər) *v.i.* **1.** To act or work in a dawdling man-ner. **—** *v.t.* **2.** To waste (time, etc.) in dawdling or putter-ing. [Var. of POTTER¹]

put·ting green (put′ing) In golf: **a** Green (*n.* def. 5). **b** A place set aside for putting practice.

put·ty (pŭt′ē) *n.* **1.** Whiting mixed with linseed oil to the consistency of dough, used for filling holes or cracks in wood surfaces, securing panes of glass in the sash, etc. **2.** Any of various similar substances. **—** *v.t.* **·tied, ·ty·ing** To fill, stop, fasten, etc., with putty. [< OF *potée* calcined tin, lit., pot-ful] **— put′ti·er** *n.*

putty knife A knife with a spatulalike blade, used in apply-ing putty.

put-up (pŏŏt′up′) *adj. Informal* Prearranged or contrived in an artful manner: a *put-up* job.

puz·zle (puz′əl) *v.* **·zled, ·zling** *v.t.* **1.** To confuse or per-plex. **2.** To solve by investigation and study, as something perplexing: with *out.* **—** *v.i.* **3.** To be perplexed or confused. **— to puzzle over** To attempt to understand or solve. **—** *n.* **1.** Something that puzzles; enigma. **2.** A toy, word game, etc., designed to test one's ingenuity or patience. **3.** The state of being puzzled; perplexity. [Origin unknown] **— puz′zler** *n.* **— puz′zle·ment** *n.*

— Syn. (verb) **1.** confound, bewilder, baffle, daze. **—** (noun) **1.** A *puzzle* is usually intricate but can be solved by ingenuity and patience; many *puzzles* are made for amusement. An *enigma* is something said or written whose meaning is hidden and can only be inferred from clues. A *conundrum* is a baffling question, the answer to which depends upon some trick of words. *Conundrums* are also *riddles*, but a *riddle* is usually less playful in character.

py- Var. of PYO-.

pyelo- *combining form* Pelvis. Also, before vowels, **pyel-.** [< Gk. *pyelos* pelvis, trough]

py·e·mi·a (pī·ē′mē·ə) *n. Pathol.* A type of blood poisoning characterized by many abscesses. [< NL < Gk. *pyon* pus + *haima* blood] **— py·e′mic** *adj.*

Pyg·ma·li·on (pig·mā′lē·ən, -māl′yən) In Greek mythology, a sculptor of Cyprus who fell in love with his statue, Galatea, which Aphrodite later brought to life.

pyg·my (pig′mē) *adj.* **1.** Diminutive; dwarfish. **2.** Trivial; unimportant. **—** *n. pl.* **·mies** A small person or thing re-garded as insignificant. Also spelled *pigmy.* [< L < Gk. *pygmē* the length from elbow to knuckles]

Pyg·my (pig′mē) *n. pl.* **·mies 1.** A member of a Negroid people of equatorial Africa, ranging in height from four to five feet. **2.** Any of the Negrito peoples of the Philippines, Andaman Islands, and Malaya.

py·ja·mas (pə·jä′məz, -jam′əz) See PAJAMAS.

py·lon (pī′lon) *n.* **1.** *Archit.* A monumental structure con-stituting an entrance to an Egyptian temple, consisting of a central gateway, flanked on each side by a truncated pyra-midal tower. **2.** A stake marking the course in an airport or turning point in an air race. **3.** One of the steel towers sup-porting a high-tension electric power line. **4.** *Surg.* An arti-ficial leg, usu. temporary.

py·lo·rus (pī·lôr′əs, -lō′rəs, pi-) *n. pl.* **·ri** (-rī) *Anat.* The opening between the stomach and the duodenum, surround-ed by a sphincter. [< LL < Gk. < *pylē* gate + *ouros* watcher] **— py·lor′ic** (-lôr′ik, -lor′ik) *adj.*

pyo- *combining form* Pus; of or related to pus. Also, before vowels, **py-.** [< Gk. *pyon* pus]

py·or·rhe·a (pī′ə·rē′ə) *n. Pathol.* A continuous discharge of pus; esp., from the gums, with loosening of the teeth. [< NL < Gk. *pyon* pus + *rheein* to flow] **— py′or·rhe′al** *adj.*

pyr- Var. of PYRO-.

---

pyr·a·mid (pir′ə·mid) *n.* **1.** *Archit.* A structure of masonry typically having a square base and tri-angular sides meeting in an apex, sometimes vast in size, as those used as tombs or tem-ples in ancient Egypt. **2.** Something pyra-midal in form. **3.** *Geom.* A solid con-sisting of a polygonal base and triangular sides, having a common vertex. **4.** *Mineral.* A crystal form consisting of three or more similar planes having a common point of intersection. — *v.t. & v.i.* **1.** To arrange or form in the shape of a pyramid. **2.** To buy or sell (stock) with paper profits, and to continue so buying or selling. [ME *piramis* (pl. *pyramids*) and later borrowing of F *pyramide*, both < L < Gk. *pyramis, -idos*] — **py·ram·i·dal** (pi·ram′ə-dəl), **pyr′a·mid′ic** or **·i·cal** *adj.* — **py·ram′i·dal·ly** *adv.*

pyre (pīr) *n.* **1.** A heap of combustibles arranged for burn-ing a dead body. **2.** Any pile or heap of combustible materi-al. [< L *pyra* hearth, funeral pile < Gk. *pyr* fire]

py·reth·rum (pī·reth′rəm, -rē′thrəm) *n.* The powdered flowers of a chrysanthemum, used medically as an ointment, and as an insecticide. [< L, feverfew < Gk. *pyrethron*]

py·ret·ic (pī·ret′ik) *adj.* **1.** Affected with or relating to fever. **2.** Remedial in fevers. [< NL < Gk. *pyretos* fever]

Py·rex (pī′reks) *n.* A type of heat-resisting glass having a high silica content, with additions of soda, aluminum, and boron: a trade name. Also **py′rex.**

pyr·i·dox·ine (pir′ə·dok′sēn, -sin) *n. Biochem.* Vitamin B₆, a water-soluble compound, $C_8H_{10}NO_3$, occurring in cereal grains, vegetable oils, legumes, yeast, meats, and fish, and also made synthetically. [PYRID(INE) + OX(Y)⁻² + -INE²]

py·rite (pī′rīt) *n. pl.* **py·ri·tes** (pī·rī′tēz) A metallic, pale yellow iron disulfide, FeS₂, a source of sulfuric acid: also called *fool's gold, iron pyrites.* [< L < Gk. < *pyritēs* (*lithos*) fire (stone)] — **py·rit′ic** (-rit′ik) or **·i·cal** *adj.*

py·ri·tes (pī·rī′tēz) *n.pl.* Any of various metallic sulfides.

pyro- *combining form* Fire; heat. Also, before vowels, *pyr-.* [< Gk. *pyr, pyros* fire]

py·ro·e·lec·tric (pī′rō·i·lek′trik, pir′ō-) *adj.* Of, pertaining to, or manifesting pyroelectricity; developing poles when heated. — *n.* A pyroelectric substance.

py·ro·e·lec·tric·i·ty (pī′rō·i·lek′tris′ə·tē, -ē′lek-, pir′ō-) *n.* Electrification or electric polarity developed in certain min-erals by a change in temperature.

py·ro·gen·ic (pī′rə·jen′ik, pir′ō-) *adj.* **1.** Causing or pro-duced by heat. **2.** Caused by or inducing fever. Also **py·rog·e·nous** (pī·roj′ə·nəs, pi-).

py·rog·ra·phy (pī·rog′rə·fē, pi-) *n.* The art or process of producing a design, as on wood or leather, by a red-hot point or fine flame. — **py·ro·graph** (pī′rə·graf, -gräf, pir′ə-) *n.* — **py·rog′ra·pher** *n.* — **py′ro·graph′ic** *adj.*

py·rol·y·sis (pī·rol′ə·sis) *n. Chem.* Decomposition of or-ganic compounds or other substances by the action of heat. [< NL < Gk. *pyr, pyros* fire + *lysis* loosing] — **py·ro·lit·ic** (pī′rə·lit′ik, pir′ə-) *adj.*

py·ro·mag·net·ic (pī′rō·mag·net′ik, pir′ō-) *adj.* Of, per-taining to, or produced by changes in magnetic prop-caused by change of temperature.

py·ro·ma·ni·a (pī′rə·mā′nē·ə, -mān′yə, pir′ə-) *n.* A com-pulsion to set things on fire. — **py′ro·ma′ni·ac** (-ak) *adj.* — **py·ro·ma·ni·a·cal** (pī′rō·mə·nī′ə·kəl, pir′ō-) *adj.*

py·rom·e·ter (pī·rom′ə·tər) *n.* An instrument for measur-high degrees of heat. — **py·ro·met·ric** (pī′rə·met′rik, p or **·ri·cal** *adj.* — **py·rom′e·try** *n.*

py·ro·tech·nic (pī′rə·tek′nik, pir′ə-) *adj.* Pertaining to works or their manufacture. Also **py′ro·tech′ni·cal.**

py·ro·tech·nics (pī′rə·tek′niks, pir′ə-) *n.pl.* (*constru sing. in defs.* 1, 4) **1.** The art of making or using firew Also **py·ro·tech·ny** (pī′rə·tek′nē, pir′ə-) **2.** A display o works. **3.** An ostentatious display, as of oratory. **4.** Rockets, flares, or the like, that produce flame or smok signaling, lighting, screening, etc. [< MF < Gk. *pyr, fire + technē* art] — **py′ro·tech′nist** *n.*

py·ro·tox·in (pī′rə·tok′sin, pir′ə-) *n. Biochem.* Any of ous toxins found in the body and inducing a rise of b temperature or symptoms of fever.

py·rox·y·lin (pī·rok′sə·lin) *n. Chem.* A cellulose ni mixture, less explosive than guncotton, and widely us making Celluloid, collodion, lacquers, adhesives, etc. **py·rox′y·line** (-lēn, -lin). [< F < Gk. *pyr, pyros* fire + wood + F *-in -in*]

Pyr·rhic victory (pir′ik) A victory gained at a ruinous such as that of Pyrrhus over the Romans in 279 B.C. [*Pyrrhus* king of Epirus]

Py·thag·o·re·an·ism (pi·thag′ə·rē′ən·iz/əm) *n.* The mystical philoso-phy taught by Pythagoras, including the idea that number is the essence of all things. — **Py·thag·o·re·an** (pi·thag′ə·rē′ən) *n. & adj.*

Pythagorean theorem *Geom.* The theorem that the sum of the squares of the legs of a right triangle is equal to the square of the hypotenuse.

Pyth·i·an (pith′ē·ən) *adj.* **1.** Relat-ing to Delphi, to Apollo's temple there, its oracle, or its priestess. **2.** Relating to the Pythian games. — *n.* **1.** A native or inhabitant of Delphi. **2.** The priestess of A lo. **3.** An epithet of the Delphic Apollo. [< L *Py < Gk. Pythios*]

PYTHAGOREAN THEOREM
Sum of squares AB and BCGF equa square ACHK
$(a^2 + b^2 = c^2)$

Pythian games In ancient Greece, games held every years at Delphi in honor of Apollo.

Pyth·i·as (pith′ē·əs) See DAMON AND PYTHIAS.

py·thon (pī′thon, -thən) *n.* **1.** A large, nonvenomou pent that crushes its prey. **2.** Any nonvenomous con-tor. [< L < Gk. *Python,* a serpent slain by Apollo]

py·tho·ness (pī′thə·nis, pith′ə-) *n.* **1.** The priestess o Delphic oracle. **2.** Any woman supposed to be possess the spirit of prophecy.

pyx (piks) *n. Eccl.* A vessel or casket, usu. of precious m in which the Host is preserved. [< L < Gk. *pyxos* box]

pyx·i·di·um (pik·sid′ē·əm) *n. pl.* **·i·a** (-ē·ə) *Bot.* A vessel with two parts, the upper separating as a lid.

pyx·is (pik′sis) *n. pl.* **pyx·i·des** (pik′sə·dēz) **1.** A b pyx; esp., an ancient form of ornamental jewel case or box. **2.** An emollient ointment. **3.** *Bot.* A pyxidium. [

Q

q, Q (kyōō) *n. pl.* **q's** or **qs, Q's** or **Qs, cues** (kyōōz) **1.** The 17th letter of the English alphabet. **2.** The sound repre-sented by the letter *q.* In English *q* is always followed by *u* and represents (kw), as in *quack, quest, quote, equal,* etc. In some words borrowed from French, however, English follows the French pronunciation with (k) alone, as in *appliqué, con-quer, coquette, pique.* Final *-que* always represents (k), as in *antique, oblique, physique, unique,* etc.

qua (kwā, kwä) *adv.* In the capacity of; by virtue of being; insofar as. [< L, ablative sing. fem. of *qui* who]

quack¹ (kwak) *v.i.* To utter a harsh, croaking cry, as a duck. — *n.* The sound made by a duck, or a similar croak-ing noise. [Imit.]

quack² (kwak) *n.* **1.** A pretender to medical knowledge or skill. **2.** One who falsely poses as an expert; a charlatan. — *adj.* Of or pertaining to quacks or quackery. — *v.i.* To play the quack. [Short for QUACKSALVER] — **quack′ish** *ad quack′ish·ly adv.*

quack·er·y (kwak′ər·ē) *n. pl.* **·er·ies** Ignorant or fraud practice. Also **quack′hood** (-hŏŏd), **quack′ism.**

quack·sal·ver (kwak′sal′vər) *n.* A medical quack. MDu. < *quacken* quack¹ + *salf* salve]

quad¹ (kwod) *n. Informal* A quadrangle, as of a colleg

quad² (kwod) *n. Printing* A piece of type metal of height than the letters, used for spacing: also called *quad*

quad·ran·gle (kwod′rang·gəl) *n.* **1.** *Geom.* A plane f having four sides and four angles. **2.** A court, esp. a square or oblong; also, the building or buildings that surround a court. [< OF < LL < L < *quattuor* four + *angulus*] — **quad·ran′gu·lar** (-gyə·lər) *adj.*

quad·rant (kwod′rənt) *n.* **1.** A quarter section of a c subtending an arc of 90°; also, the arc subtended. **2.** A

rument having a graduated arc of 90°, with a movable radi-
s for measuring angles on it, used in navigation, surveying,
nd astronomy for measuring altitudes. [< L *quattuor* four]
· quad·ran·tal (kwod·ran′təl) *adj.*

·ad·ra·phon·ic (kwod′rə·fon′ik) *adj.* Designating a
stem of stereophonic sound that uses four loudspeakers.

·ad·rat (kwod′rat) *n.* *Printing* A quad².

·ad·rate (kwod′rāt; *for n., also* kwod′rit) *n.* 1. In astrolo-
y, an aspect of two heavenly bodies in which they are dis-
int from each other 90°. 2. A cubical or square object. —
j. Square; four-sided. [< L *quadrare* to square]

·ad·rat·ic (kwod·rat′ik) *adj.* 1. Pertaining to or resem-
ing a square. 2. *Math.* Pertaining to or designating an
juation, curve, surface, etc., of the second degree. — *n.*
ath. A quadratic equation, curve, etc.

·ad·rat·ics (kwod·rat′iks) *n.pl.* (construed as sing.) *Rare*
he branch of algebra dealing with quadratic equations.

·ad·ren·ni·al (kwod·ren′ē·əl) *adj.* 1. Occurring once in
ur years. 2. Lasting four years. — **quad·ren′ni·al·ly** *adv.*

·adri- *combining form* Four: *quadrilateral.* Also *quadru-:*
so **quadr-** (before vowels). [< L *quattuor* four]

·ad·ri·lat·er·al (kwod′rə·lat′ər·əl) *adj.* Formed or bound-
1 by four lines; four-sided. — *n.* *Geom.* A figure bounded
y four straight lines terminated at four angles. [< L *quat-
ior* four + *latus* side]

·a·drille (kwə·dril′) *n.* 1. A square dance for four cou-
es, having five figures. 2. Music for or in the manner of
is dance. [< F < Sp. < L *quattuor* four]

·ad·ril·lion (kwod·ril′yən) *n.* 1. *U.S.* A thousand tril-
ons, written as 1 followed by fifteen zeros: a cardinal num-
er. 2. *Brit.* A million trillions (def. 2), written as 1 fol-
wed by twenty-four zeros: a cardinal number. — *adj.* Be-
g a quadrillion in number. [< MF < *quadri-* four +
ni)llion million] — **quad·ril′lionth** *adj. & n.*

·ad·ri·no·mi·al (kwod′rə·nō′mē·əl) *n.* *Math.* An alge-
raic expression having four terms.

·ad·ri·va·lent (kwod′rə·vā′lənt) *adj.* *Chem.* Having a
alence of four, as carbon: also *tetratomic, tetravalent.* [<
UADRI- + L *valere* to be worth] — **quad′ri·va′lence,**
uad′ri·va′len·cy *n.*

·ad·roon (kwod·ro͞on′) *n.* A person having one Negro
randparent. [< Sp. *cuarto* fourth]

·adru- Var. of QUADRI-.

·ad·ru·ped (kwod′ro͞o·ped) *n.* An animal having four
et; esp., a four-footed mammal. — *adj.* Having four feet.
< L *quattuor* four + *pes* foot] — **quad·ru·pe·dal** (kwod·
o͞o′pə·dəl, kwod′ro͞o·ped′l) *adj.*

·ad·ru·ple (kwod′ro͞o·pəl, kwod·ro͞o′pəl) *v.t. & v.i.* **·pled,**
ling To multiply by four; make or become four times
rger. — *adj.* 1. Consisting of four. 2. Multiplied by four.
— *n.* A sum four times as great as another. — *adv.* So as
make four times larger. [< OF < L *quadruplus*]

·ad·ru·plet (kwod′ro͞o·plit, kwod·ro͞o′-) *n.* 1. A com-
ound or combination of four things or objects. 2. One of
ur offspring born of the same mother at one birth.

·ad·ru·pli·cate (kwod·ro͞o′plə·kāt; *for adj. & n., also* kwod·
o͞o′plə·kit) *adj.* Quadruple; fourfold. — *n.* One of four
ke things. [< L *quattuor* four + stem of *plicare* to fold] —
uad·ru′pli·cate·ly *adv.* — **quad·ru′pli·ca′tion** *n.*

·aff (kwaf, kwof, kwôf) *v.t. & v.i.* To drink, esp. copiously
r with relish. — *n.* A drink; swallow. — **quaff′er** *n.*

·ag·gy (kwag′ē, kwog′ē) *adj.* **·gi·er, ·gi·est** Yielding to or
aaking under the foot, as soft, wet earth; boggy.

·ag·mire (kwag′mīr′, kwog′-) *n.* 1. Marshy ground that
ves way under the foot. 2. A difficult situation. [< obs.
uag to shake + MIRE] — **quag′mired′, quag′mir′y** *adj.*

·a·hog (kwô′hôg, -hog, kwə·hôg′, -hog′) *n.* An edible
merican clam called *hard-shelled clam.* Also **qua′haug.** [<
lgonquian (Narraganset) *poquauhock*]

·ail¹ (kwāl) *n.* Any of various small American game birds
:lated to the partridge, esp. the bobwhite. [< OF *quaille,*
rob. of Gmc. origin]

·ail² (kwāl) *v.i.* To shrink with fear; lose heart or courage.
ME *quailen*]

·aint (kwānt) *adj.* 1. Combining an antique appearance
ith a pleasing oddity, fancifulness, or whimsicalness. 2.
leasingly odd or old-fashioned; fanciful. [< OF < L <
>gnoscere to ascertain] — **quaint′ly** *adv.* — **quaint′ness** *n.*

·ake (kwāk) *v.i.* **quaked, quak·ing** 1. To shake, as with
iolent emotion or cold. 2. To shake or tremble, as earth
uring an earthquake. — **Syn.** See SHAKE. — *n.* 1. The
ct of quaking. 2. An earthquake. [OE *cwacian* to shake]

·uak·er (kwā′kər) *n.* A member of the Society of Friends:
riginally a term of derision. [< QUAKE, v.; with ref. to the
ounder's admonition to tremble at the word of the Lord] —
uak′er·ish *adj.* — **Quak′er·ish·ly** *adv.* — **Quak·er·ism**
wā′kə·riz′əm) *n.* — **Quak′er·ly** *adj. & adv.*

·al·i·fi·ca·tion (kwol′ə·fə·kā′shən) *n.* 1. The act of quali-

fying, or the state of being qualified. 2. Any ability, training, etc., that fits a person for a specific office, role, position,
etc. 3. A restriction: to accept without *qualification.*

qual·i·fied (kwol′ə·fīd) *adj.* 1. Competent or fit, as for public office. 2. Restricted or modified. — **qual′i·fied′ly** *adv.*

qual·i·fy (kwol′ə·fī) *v.* **·fied, ·fy·ing** *v.t.* 1. To make fit or capable, as for an office, occupation, or privilege. 2. To make
legally capable. 3. To limit or restrict. 4. To attribute a
quality to; describe; characterize. 5. To make less strong or
extreme. 6. To change the strength or flavor of. 7. *Gram.*
To modify. — *v.i.* 1. To be or become qualified or fit; meet
the requirements, as for entering a race. [< MF < Med.L
< L *qualis* of such a kind + *facere* to make] — **qual′i·fi′a·
ble** *adj.* — **qual′i·fi′er** *n.*

qual·i·ta·tive (kwol′ə·tā′tiv) *adj.* Of or pertaining to quality: distinguished from *quantitative.* [< LL < L *qualis* of
such a kind] — **qual′i·ta·tive·ly** *adv.*

qualitative analysis *Chem.* The process of determining
the kind and number of ingredients present in a substance.

qual·i·ty (kwol′ə·tē) *n.* *pl.* **·ties** 1. That which makes
something such as it is; a distinguishing element or characteristic. 2. The basic or essential character, nature, etc., of
something. 3. Excellence: *quality* rather than quantity.
4. The degree of excellence. 5. A moral or personality trait
or characteristic. 6. *Music* The timbre of a voice or musical
instrument. 7. ~~Archaic~~ High ~~or superior social rank or birth;~~
~~also, persons of superior rank collectively.~~ — *adj.* Of superior quality. [< F < L *qualis* of such a kind]

qualm (kwäm, kwôm) *n.* 1. A feeling of sickness. 2. A
twinge of conscience; moral scruple. 3. A sensation of fear
or misgiving. [? OE *cwealm* death] — **qualm′ish** *adj.* —
qualm′ish·ly *adv.* — **qualm′ish·ness** *n.* — **qualm′y** *adj.*

quan·da·ry (kwon′dər·ē, -drē) *n.* *pl.* **·da·ries** A state of
hesitation or perplexity; predicament.

quan·ta (kwon′tə) Plural of QUANTUM.

quan·ti·ta·tive (kwon′tə·tā′tiv) *adj.* 1. Of or pertaining to
quantity. 2. Having to do with quantities only: distinguished from *qualitative.* — **quan′ti·ta′tive·ly** *adv.* — **quan′·
ti·ta′tive·ness** *n.*

quantitative analysis *Chem.* The process of finding the
amount or percentage of each element or ingredient present
in a material or compound.

quan·ti·ty (kwon′tə·tē) *n.* *pl.* **·ties** 1. A specified or indefinite number, amount, weight, etc. 2. The property of a
thing that admits of exact measurement. 3. *Often pl.* A
large amount: abundance: *quantities* of food. 4. Measure;
amount: *quantity* rather than quality. 5. *Math.* An entity
regarded as possessing a certain determinable magnitude, as
length, size, volume, or number. 6. The relative length of a
speech sound, prosodic syllable, or musical tone. 7. *Electr.*
The amount of current. [< OF < L *quantus* how much]

quan·tize (kwon′tīz) *v.t.* **·tized, ·tiz·ing** *Physics* 1. To restrict the possible values of (an observable quantity or magnitude). 2. To express as multiples of a given quantity or
quantum. — **quan′ti·za′tion** *n.*

quan·tum (kwon′təm) *n.* *pl.* **·ta** (-tə) *Physics* A fundamental unit of energy as provided for in the quantum theory.
[< L, neuter of *quantus* how much]

quantum theory *Physics* The theory that energy is not a
smoothly flowing continuum but is manifested by the emission from radiating bodies of discrete particles or *quanta,* the
values of which are expressed as the product of Planck's constant multiplied by the frequency of the given radiation.

quar·an·tine (kwôr′ən·tēn, kwor′-) *n.* 1. The enforced isolation for a fixed period of time of persons, ships, or goods arriving from places infected with or exposed to contagious
disease. 2. A place designated for the enforcement of such
interdiction. 3. The enforced isolation of any person or
place infected with contagious disease. 4. Any enforced isolation. 5. A period of forty days. — *v.t.* **·tined, ·tin·ing** To
subject to or retain in quarantine; isolate by or as by quarantine. [< Ital. < ult. < L *quadraginta* forty]

quark (kwärk, kwôrk) *n. Physics* A hypothetical elementary
particle. [after "Three quarks for Muster Mark" in James
Joyce's *Finnegans Wake*]

quar·rel¹ (kwôr′əl, kwor′-) *n.* 1. An unfriendly, angry, or
violent dispute. 2. A falling out; breach of amity. 3. The
cause for dispute. — *v.i.* **quar·reled** or **·relled, quar·rel·ing**
or **·rel·ling** 1. To engage in a quarrel. 2. To break off a mutual friendship. 3. To find fault. [< F < L *queri* to com-
plain] — **quar′rel·er** or **quar′rel·ler** *n.*
— **Syn.** (noun) 1. Wrangle, bicker, squabble, altercation, scrap.

quar·rel·some (kwôr′əl·səm, kwor′-) *adj.* Inclined to quarrel. — **quar′rel·some·ly** *adv.* — **quar′rel·some·ness** *n.*

quar·ry¹ (kwôr′ē, kwor′ē) *n.* *pl.* **·ries** 1. A beast or bird
hunted or killed, as in the chase. 2. Anything hunted,
slaughtered, or pursued. [< OF < L *corium* hide]

quar·ry² (kwôr′ē, kwor′ē) *n.* *pl.* **·ries** An excavation from which stone is taken by cutting, blasting, or the like. — *v.t.* ·ried, ·ry·ing **1.** To cut, dig, or take from or as from a quarry. **2.** To establish a quarry in. [< OF < L *quadrus* square] — **quar′ri·er** *n.*

quart (kwôrt) *n.* **1.** A measure of capacity, the fourth part of a gallon, or two pints. In the U.S., the dry quart is equal to 1.10 liters and the liquid quart is equal to 0.946 liter. See table inside back cover. **2.** A container having such a capacity. [< OF < L *quartus* fourth]

quar·ter (kwôr′tər) *n.* **1.** One of four equal parts into which anything is or may be divided. **2.** In the U.S. and Canada, a coin having the value of 25 cents. **3.** Fifteen minutes or the fourth of an hour; also, the moment such a period begins or ends. **4.** Three months or a fourth of a year. **5.** A term of school, usu. one fourth of a year. **6.** *Astron.* A fourth part of the moon's revolution about the earth. **7.** One of the four periods into which a game, as football, is divided. **8.** One of the four principal points of the compass. **9.** A particular district or locality, as of a city: the native *quarter*. **10.** A place or source from which something comes: on authority of the highest *quarter*. **11.** *Usu. pl.* Proper or assigned station, as of officers and crew on a warship. **12.** *pl.* A place of lodging or residence. **13.** Mercy shown to a vanquished enemy. **14.** Either of the four limbs of a quadruped, together with the adjacent parts. **15.** *Naut.* The upper part of a vessel's side, near the stern. **16.** *Heraldry* **a** Any of four equal divisions into which a shield is divided. **b** An ordinary occupying such a division. — **at close quarters** Close by; at close range. — *adj.* **1.** Being one of four equal parts. **2.** Having one fourth of a standard value. — *v.t.* **1.** To divide into four equal parts. **2.** To divide into a number of parts or pieces. **3.** To cut the body of (an executed person) into four parts. **4.** To range from one side to the other of (a field, etc.) while advancing. **5.** To furnish with quarters or shelter; lodge. **6.** *Heraldry* **a** To divide (a shield) into quarters. **b** To bear or arrange (different coats of arms) quarterly upon a shield. — *v.i.* **7.** To be stationed or lodged. **8.** To range from side to side of an area, as dogs in hunting. **9.** *Naut.* To blow on a ship's quarter: said of the wind. [< OF < L < *quartus* fourth]

quar·ter·back (kwôr′tər·bak′) *n.* In American football, one of the backfield, who often calls the signals.

quarter day Any of the four days of the year when quarterly payments are due.

quar·ter·deck (kwôr′tər·dek′) *n.* *Naut.* The rear part of a ship's upper deck, reserved for officers.

quar·tered (kwôr′tərd) *adj.* **1.** Divided into four quarters. **2.** Lodged; stationed; also, having quarters. **3.** Quarter-sawed. **4.** *Heraldry* Divided into quarters.

quar·ter·ly (kwôr′tər·lē) *adj.* **1.** Containing or being a fourth part. **2.** Occurring at intervals of three months. — *n. pl.* ·lies A publication issued once every three months. — *adv.* **1.** Once in a quarter of a year. **2.** In or by quarters.

quar·ter·mas·ter (kwôr′tər·mas′tər, -mäs′-) *n.* **1.** *Usu. cap. Mil.* An officer responsible for the supply of food, fuel, clothing, etc. **2.** On shipboard, a petty officer responsible for steering and related functions.

quar·tern (kwôr′tərn) *n.* A fourth part of certain measures or weights, as of a peck or pound. [< OF < L < *quartus* fourth]

quarter note *Music* A note having one fourth the time value of a whole note: also called *crotchet*.

quar·ter·saw (kwôr′tər·sô′) *v.t.* ·sawed, ·sawed or ·sawn, ·saw·ing To saw (a log) lengthwise into quarters so that each face corresponds with one of the log's radii.

quarter section A tract of land half a mile square, containing one fourth of a square mile, or 160 acres.

quarter sessions A court held quarterly.

quar·ter·staff (kwôr′tər·staf′, -stäf′) *n. pl.* ·staves (-stāvz′) A stout, iron-tipped staff about 6½ feet long, formerly used in England as a weapon; also, the use of the quarterstaff.

quarter tone *Music* Half of a semitone. Also **quar·ter·tone** (kwôr′tər·tōn′).

quar·tet (kwôr·tet′) *n.* **1.** A composition for four voices or instruments. **2.** The four persons who perform such compositions. **3.** Any group or set of four things of a kind. Also **quar·tette′**. [< F *quartette* < Ital.]

quar·to (kwôr′tō) *adj.* Having four leaves or eight pages to the sheet: a *quarto* book. — *n. pl.* ·tos A book or pamphlet having pages the size of a fourth of a sheet: often written **4to** or **4°**. [< L (*in*) *quarto* (in) fourth]

quartz (kwôrts) *n.* Silicon dioxide, SiO_2, a hard, vitreous mineral occurring in many varieties, sometimes massive, as jasper and chalcedony, or sometimes in colorless and transparent or diversely colored forms crystallizing in the hexagonal system. [< G *quarz*; ult. origin uncertain]

quartz crystal A thin section of pure quartz, accurately ground and polished for use in certain optical instruments and as a high-frequency oscillator in some electron tubes.

quartz lamp A mercury-vapor lamp that is enclosed in a quartz tube and transmits ultraviolet wavelengths.

qua·sar (kwā′zär) *n.* A galaxylike formation in rem space that emits radio waves and vast energy. [QUA STELL]AR(RADIO SOURCE)]

quash¹ (kwosh) *v.t. Law* To make void or set aside, as indictment; annul. — **Syn.** See ANNUL. [< OF < *quassare* to shatter; meaning infl. by SQUASH¹]

quash² (kwosh) *v.t.* To put down or suppress forcibly summarily: to *quash* a rebellion. [< OF < L *quassare* shatter]

quasi- *prefix* **1.** (With nouns) Resembling; not genuine in *quasi-adult*, *quasi-insight*. **2.** (With adjectives) Nea almost, as in *quasi-complex*, *quasi-official*. [< L, as if]

qua·si·ju·di·cial (kwā′si·jōō·dish′əl, -zī-, kwä′sē-) *adj.* ercising functions of a judicial nature as a guide for off action, as a committee investigating facts and drawing clusions from them.

quas·si·a (kwosh′ē·ə, kwosh′ə) *n.* **1.** The wood of eithe two tropical American trees yielding a variety of econo products. **2.** A bitter drug prepared from this wood, use medicine as a tonic, etc. **3.** The tree itself. [< NL, a Graman *Quassi* who discovered its use in 1730]

qua·ter·na·ry (kwə·tûr′nə·rē) *adj.* **1.** Consisting of f **2.** Fourth in order. — *n. pl.* ·ries **1.** The number fou group of four things. **2.** *Math.* A quantic function ha four variables. [< L *quaternarius* < *quaterni* by fours

Qua·ter·na·ry (kwə·tûr′nə·rē) *adj. Geol.* Of, pertaining or designating a geological period and system of the Ce zoic era, following the Tertiary and still continuing. chart for GEOLOGY. — *n.* The Quaternary system or per

qua·ter·ni·on (kwə·tûr′nē·ən) *n.* A set, system, or fil four. [< LL < *quattuor* four < L *quattor*]

quat·rain (kwot′rān) *n.* A stanza or poem of four lines. F < *quatre* four]

quat·re·foil (kat′ər·foil′, kat′rə-) *n.* **1.** A leaf, etc., ha four leaflets. **2.** *Archit.* An ornament with four foils or lobes. [< OF *quatre* four + *foil* leaf]

quat·tro·cen·to (kwat′rō·chen′tō) *n.* The 15th century as connected with the revival of art and literature, esp. in Italy. — *adj.* Of or pertaining to the quattrocento. [< Ital.]

QUATREFOILS

qua·ver (kwā′vər) *v.i.* **1.** To tremble or shake: said usu. of the voice. **2.** To produce trill quavers in singing or in playing a musical instrument. *v.t.* **3.** To utter or sing in a tremulous voice. — *n.* quivering or tremulous motion. **2.** A shake or trill, a singing. **3.** *Music Chiefly Brit.* An eighth note. [Freq obs. *quave*, ME *cwafian* to tremble] — **qua′ver·y** *adj.*

quay (kē) *n.* A wharf or artificial landing place where sels may load or unload. [< OF *cai* hedge, wall]

quean (kwēn) *n.* A brazen or ill-behaved woman; har prostitute. [OE *cwene* prostitute]

quea·sy (kwē′zē) *adj.* **quea·si·er**, **quea·si·est 1.** Sick at stomach. **2.** Nauseating; also, caused by nausea. **3.** Ea nauseated. **4.** Fastidious; squeamish. **5.** Requiring to carefully treated; delicate. **6.** Hazardous. [ME *coisy*; gin unknown] — **quea′si·ly** *adv.* — **quea′si·ness** *n.*

Quech·ua (kech′wä) *n.* **1.** One of a tribe of South Am can Indians. **2.** The language of the Quechuas: also ca *Incan*. Also spelled *Kechua*. — **Quech′uan** (kech′wən) & *n.*

queen (kwēn) *n.* **1.** The wife of a king. **2.** A female eign or monarch. **3.** A woman preeminent in a given sph **4.** In chess, the most powerful piece, capable of moving number of squares in a straight or diagonal line. **5.** A p ing card bearing a conventional picture of a queen. **6.** *tomol.* The single fully developed female in a colony of so insects, as bees, ants, etc. — *v.t.* **1.** To make a queen **2.** In chess, to make a queen of (a pawn) by moving it to eighth row. — *v.i.* **3.** To reign as or play the part queen. — **to queen it** To act in a domineering, que manner. [OE *cwēn* woman, queen]

Queen Anne's lace The wild carrot.

Queen Anne's War See WAR OF THE SPANISH SUCCESS in table for WAR.

queen consort The wife of a reigning king, who does share his sovereignty.

queen dowager The widow of a king.

queen·ly (kwēn′lē) *adj.* **queen·li·er**, **queen·li·est 1.** O like a queen. **2.** Fit for a queen. — *adv.* In the manne a queen. — **queen′li·ness** *n.*

queen mother A queen dowager who is mother of a re ing sovereign.

queen's English King's English.

queer (kwir) *adj.* **1.** Unusual; singular; odd. **2.** Of q tionable character. **3.** *Slang* Counterfeit. **4.** *Slang* Ho sexual. — *n. Slang* **1.** Counterfeit money. **2.** *Slang* A mosexual person. — *v.t. U.S. Slang* To jeopardize or sp [Origin unknown] — **queer′ly** *adv.* — **queer′ness** *n.*

quell (kwel) *v.t.* **1.** To put down or suppress by force;

uish. **2.** To quiet; allay, as pain. [OE *cwellan* to kill]
— **Syn. 1.** subdue, crush. **2.** soothe, still.

·que chose (kel′kə shōz′) *French* A trifle; something.

ıch (kwench) *v.t.* **1.** To put out or extinguish, as a fire.
'o put an end to. **3.** To slake or satisfy (thirst). **4.** To
ɔress or repress, as emotions. **5.** To cool, as heated iron
teel, by thrusting into water or other liquid. [OE
ıcan to grow less, disappear] — **quench′a·ble** *adj.* —
ıch′er *n.* — **quench′less** *adj.*

·u·lous (kwer′ə·ləs, -yə·ləs) *adj.* **1.** Disposed to com-
ı or be fretful; captious. **2.** Indicating or expressing a
plaining or whining disposition. [< LL < *queri* to com-
ı] — **quer′u·lous·ly** *adv.* — **quer′u·lous·ness** *n.*

ry (kwir′ē) *v.* ·ried, ·ry·ing *v.t.* **1.** To inquire into; ask
ıt. **2.** To ask questions of; interrogate. **3.** To express
ɔt concerning the correctness or truth of. — *v.i.* **4.** To
e or express doubt; question. — **Syn.** See ASK. — *n.*
ries 1. An inquiry or question. **2.** A doubt; interroga-
. [< L < *quaerere* to ask]

t (kwest) *n.* **1.** The act of seeking or looking for some-
g; a search. **2.** An adventure or expedition, as in medi-
romance. **3.** The person or persons engaged in a quest.
·t. & *v.i.* To go on a quest or to search for (something).
OF < L < *quaerere* to ask, seek] — **quest′er** *n.*

·tion (kwes′chən) *n.* **1.** An interrogative sentence
ng for an answer; an inquiry. **2.** A subject of inquiry or
ate; a matter to be decided; problem. **3.** A subject of
ute; a controversy. **4.** A proposition under discussion in
·liberative assembly. **5.** Possibility of disagreement or
ive; doubt: no *question* about it. **6.** The act of asking or
uiring. — **beside the question** Irrelevant; not pertinent.
·eyond (all) question** Not open to dispute; settled. —
of the question Not to be thought of; impossible. — *v.t.*
1. To put a question or questions to; interrogate. **2.** To
ıncertain of; doubt. **3.** To make objection to; challenge;
ute. — *v.i.* **4.** To ask a question or questions. — **Syn.**
ASK. [< L < *quaerere* to ask] — **ques′tion·er** *n.*

·tion·a·ble (kwes′chən·ə·bəl) *adj.* **1.** Characterized by
btful integrity, honesty, respectability, etc. **2.** Liable to
alled in question; debatable. **3.** Uncertain; difficult to
de. — **ques′tion·a·bil′i·ty, ques′tion·a·ble·ness** *n.* —
·/tion·a·bly** *adv.*

·tion mark A mark of punctuation (?) indicating that
sentence it closes is a direct question: also called *interro-
on point.*

·tion·naire (kwes′chə·nâr′) *n.* A written or printed
ı comprising a series of questions submitted to a number
ersons to obtain data for a survey or report. [< F]

·zal (ket·säl′) *n.* *pl.* ·**zal·es** (-sä′lās) **1.** A bird of long,
ıiant plumage, the national symbol of Guatemala, re-
ded as a deity by the Mayas. **2.** The standard monetary
t of Guatemala: in 1962 worth about one U.S. dollar.
ɔ **que·zal** (kā·säl′). [< Sp.]

ıe (kyōō) *n.* **1.** A pigtail. **2.** A line of persons or vees. — *v.i.* queued, queu·ing *Brit.* To form a line: usu.
h *up.* Also **cue.** [< MF < L *cauda* a tail]

·ble (kwib′əl) *n.* **1.** An evasion of a point or question.
a trivial distinction or objection; cavil. — *v.i.* **·bled,**
ng To evade the truth or the point in question, as by
ing trivial objections. [< obs. *quib* < L *quibus,* ablative
of *qui* who, which] — **quib′bler** *n.*

·k (kwik) *adj.* **1.** Done or occurring in a short time;
id; swift. **2.** Responding readily or eagerly to impres-
ıs or instruction: a *quick* mind. **3.** Alert; sensitive; per-
tive: a *quick* ear. **4.** Easily aroused or excited; hasty: a
ck temper. **5.** Nimble: *quick* fingers. **6.** Pregnant; with
ld. **7.** Refreshing; bracing. **8.** Burning briskly. — *n.*
Those who are alive: chiefly in the phrase **the quick and
dead. 2.** The living flesh, esp. the tender flesh under a
ɡernail. **3.** The feelings: cut to the *quick.* **4.** A plant
able for hedges. — *adv.* Quickly; rapidly. [OE *cwic*
ʾe] — **quick′ness** *n.*

ck bread Any bread, biscuits, etc., whose leavening
nt makes immediate baking possible.

ck·en (kwik′ən) *v.t.* **1.** To cause to move more rapidly;
ten or accelerate. **2.** To give or restore life to. **3.** To ex-
e or arouse; stimulate: to *quicken* the appetite. — *v.i.* **4.**
move or act more quickly; become more rapid. **5.** To
ıe or return to life; revive. **6.** To begin to manifest signs
life: said of the fetus. — **quick′en·er** *n.*

ck-freeze (kwik′frēz′) *v.t.* ·**froze, ·fro·zen, ·freez·ing** To
ɔject (food) to rapid refrigeration for storing at or below
ɛzing temperatures.

ck·ie (kwik′ē) *n.* *U.S. Slang* Anything done hastily, as
short cuts or makeshift methods.

ck·lime (kwik′līm′) *n.* See under LIME[1].

ck·ly (kwik′lē) *adv.* In a quick manner; rapidly; soon.

ck march A march in quick time; quickstep.

quick·sand (kwik′sand′) *n.* A bed of sand, often of considerable depth, so water-soaked as to engulf any object, person, or animal resting or moving upon it.

quick·set (kwik′set′) *n.* **1.** A plant suitable for hedges, esp.
hawthorn. **2.** A hedge made of it.

quick·sil·ver (kwik′sil′vər) *n.* **1.** Mercury in its liquid
form. **2.** An amalgam of tin, used for the backs of mirrors.
[OE *cwicseolfor.* Trans. of L *argentum vivum.*]

quick·step (kwik′step′) *n.* A march or dance written in a
rapid tempo; also, a quick march.

quick-tem·pered (kwik′tem′pərd) *adj.* Easily angered.

quick time A marching step of 120 paces a minute, each
pace of 30 inches, used in military drills and ceremonies.

quick-wit·ted (kwik′wit′id) *adj.* Having a ready wit or
quick discernment; keen; alert. — **quick′-wit′ted·ly** *adv.* —
quick′-wit′ted·ness *n.*

quid[1] (kwid) *n.* **1.** A small portion of chewing tobacco. **2.**
A cud, as of a cow. [OE *cwudu.* Var. of CUD.]

quid[2] (kwid) *n.* *pl.* **quid** *Brit. Slang* A pound sterling, or a
sovereign. [? Suggested by L QUID PRO QUO]

quid·di·ty (kwid′ə·tē) *n.* *pl.* **·ties 1.** The essence of a thing.
2. A quibble; cavil. [< LL < L *quid* which, what]

quid·nunc (kwid′nungk′) *n.* One who seeks to know all
that is going on; a busybody. [< L *quid nunc* what now]

quid pro quo (kwid′ prō kwō′) *Latin* **1.** Something for
something; an equivalent in return. **2.** A substitution.

qui·es·cent (kwī·es′ənt) *adj.* **1.** Being in a state of repose or
inaction; quiet; still. **2.** Resting free from anxiety, emotion,
or agitation. [< L *quiescere* to be quiet] — **qui·es′cence** *n.*
— **qui·es′cent·ly** *adv.*

qui·et (kwī′ət) *adj.* **1.** Making little or no noise. **2.** Having little or no motion; still; calm. **3.** Characterized by silence; also, retired or secluded: a *quiet* nook. **4.** Free from
excessive activity, turmoil, or vexation: a *quiet* day at the office. **5.** Gentle; mild: a *quiet* temperament. **6.** Restful to
the eye; reposeful: a *quiet* scene. **7.** Not showy or pretentious; modest: *quiet* decorations. **8.** Not loud or brash; reserved: a *quiet* sense of humor. **9.** In commerce, not busy or
active. — **Syn.** See CALM. — *n.* **1.** The quality or condition of being quiet. **2.** Peace; tranquillity; calmness. — *v.t.*
& *v.i.* To make or become quiet: often with *down.* — *adv.*
In a quiet or peaceful manner. [< OF < L *quies, quietis*
rest, repose] — **qui′et·ly** *adv.* — **qui′et·ness** *n.*

qui·et·ism (kwī′ə·tiz′əm) *n.* **1.** A form of religious mysti-
cism in which the will and the intellect fix themselves in a
passive contemplation of God. **2.** A state of quiet.

qui·et·ist (kwī′ə·tist) *n.* **1.** An advocate or practicer of qui-
etism. **2.** One who seeks or enjoys quiet.

qui·e·tude (kwī′ə·tōōd, -tyōōd) *n.* A state or condition of
calm or tranquillity; repose; rest.

qui·e·tus (kwī·ē′təs) *n.* **1.** A silencing or suppressing, as of
a rumor. **2.** Anything that kills, as a blow. **3.** A final discharge, as of a debt. [< L *quietus est* is quit]

quill (kwil) *n.* **1.** *Ornithol.* One of the large, strong flight
feathers or tail feathers of a bird. **2.** Something made from a
quill, as a pen or plectrum. **3.** *Zool.* One of the large, sharp
spines of a porcupine or hedgehog. [ME *quil*]

quilt (kwilt) *n.* **1.** A bedcover made by stitching together
firmly two layers of cloth or patchwork with some soft and
warm substance (as wool or cotton) between them. **2.** Any
bedcover, esp. if thick. **3.** A quilted skirt or other quilted
article. — *v.t.* **1.** To stitch together (two pieces of material)
with a soft substance between. **2.** To stitch in ornamental
patterns or crossing lines. **3.** To pad or line with something
soft. — *v.i.* **4.** To make a quilt or quilted work. [< OF <
L *culcita* bed, cushion]

quilt·ing (kwil′ting) *n.* **1.** The act or process of making a
quilt, or of stitching as in making a quilt. **2.** Material for
quiltwork. **3.** A quilting bee or party.

quilting bee A social gathering of women for working on a
quilt or quilts. Also **quilting frolic, quilting party.**

quince (kwins) *n.* **1.** The hard, acid, applelike fruit of a
small tree of the rose family, used for preserves. **2.** The
tree. [< MF < OF *cooin* < L < Gk. *kydōnion*]

qui·nine (kwī′nīn, *esp. Brit.* kwi·nēn′) *n. Chem.* A white,
amorphous or slightly crystalline, very bitter alkaloid,
$C_{20}H_{24}N_2O_2$, contained in cinchona barks, the salts of which
are used in medicine for their tonic and antipyretic qualities
and in the treatment of malaria. Also **quin·in** (kwin′in). [<
Sp. *quina* cinchona bark and its extract]

quinine water A carbonated beverage flavored with quinine: also called *tonic.*

quin·qua·ge·nar·i·an (kwin′kwə·jə·nâr′ē·ən) *adj.* Of or
pertaining to the age of 50 years, or to the decade between 50
and 60 years of age. — *n.* One who is of this age.

Quin·qua·ges·i·ma Sunday (kwin′kwə·jes′ə·mə) The
Sunday before Ash Wednesday: also called *Shrove Sunday.*
[< L *quinquagesima* (*dies*) fiftieth (day)]

quinque- *combining form* Five: *quinquennial.* Also, before vowels, **quinqu-.** [< L *quinque* five]

quin·quen·ni·al (kwin-kwen′ē-əl) *adj.* Occurring every five years, or once in five years; also, lasting five years. — *n.* A quinquennial anniversary. [< L *quinque* five + *annus* year]

quin·sy (kwin′zē) *n. Pathol.* A suppurative inflammation of the tonsils. [< Med.L < Gk. *kynanchē* dog's collar]

quint (kwint) *n.* **1.** A fifth. **2.** A set of five. **3.** *Informal* A quintuplet. [< L *quintus* fifth]

quin·tal (kwin′təl) *n.* **1.** A measure of weight, a hundred-weight. **2.** In the metric system, 100 kilograms. [< MF < Med.L *quintale* < Arabic *quintar* < LL *centarium* one hundred pieces of gold]

quin·tes·sence (kwin-tes′əns) *n.* **1.** An extract from anything, containing in concentrated form its most essential principle. **2.** The purest and most essential part of anything. [< F < Med.L *quinta essentia* fifth essence] — **quin·tes·sen·tial** (kwin′tə-sen′shəl) *adj.*

quin·tet (kwin-tet′) *n.* **1.** A musical composition for five voices or instruments; also, the five persons performing it. **2.** Any group of five persons or things. Also **quin·tette′.** [< F < Ital. *quintetto,* dim. of *quinto* fifth]

quin·til·lion (kwin-til′yən) *n.* **1.** *U.S.* A thousand quadrillions, written as 1 followed by 18 zeros: a cardinal number. **2.** *Brit.* A million quadrillions (def. 2), written as 1 followed by 30 zeros: a cardinal number. — *adj.* Being a quintillion in number. [< *quinti-* five + (*mi*)*llion*] — **quin·til′lionth** *adj. & n.*

quin·tu·ple (kwin′tŏŏ-pəl, -tyŏŏ-, kwin-tŏŏ′pəl, -tyŏŏ′-) *v.t. & v.i.* **·pled, ·pling** To multiply by five; make or become five times as much or as large. — *adj.* **1.** Consisting of five things united or of five parts. **2.** Multiplied by five. — *n.* A number or a sum five times as great as another. [< F < LL *quintuplex* fivefold]

quin·tu·plet ((kwin′tŏŏ-plit, -tyŏŏ-, kwin-tŏŏ′plit, -tyŏŏ′-, -tup′lit) *n.* **1.** Five things of a kind used or occurring together. **2.** One of five born of the same mother at one birth.

quin·tu·pli·cate (*adj.* kwin-tŏŏ′plə-kit, -tyŏŏ′-; *v.* kwin-tŏŏ′plə-kāt, -tyŏŏ′-) *adj.* **1.** Fivefold. **2.** Raised to the fifth power. — *v.t. & v.i.* **·cat·ed, ·cat·ing** To multiply by five; quintuple. — *n.* One of five identical things. — **in quintuplicate** So as to have five identical copies. — **quin·tu′pli·cate·ly** *adv.* — **quin·tu′pli·ca′tion** *n.*

quip (kwip) *n.* **1.** A sarcastic or witty jest or retort. **2.** A quibble. **3.** An odd, fantastic action or object. — *v.i.* **quipped, quip·ping** To make a witty remark; jest. [Prob. < L *quippe* indeed] — **quip′pish** *adj.*

quip·ster (kwip′stər) *n.* One who makes quips.

quire (kwīr) *n.* **1.** The twentieth part of a ream of paper; 24 (or 25) sheets. **2.** A set of all the sheets necessary to make a book. — *v.t.* **quired, quir·ing** To fold or separate into quires. [< OF *quaer,* ult. < L *quaterni* a set of four]

Quir·i·nal (kwir′ə-nəl) *n.* **1.** One of the Seven Hills of Rome, containing the **Quirinal palace,** after 1870 the official residence of the kings of Italy. **2.** The monarchical or civil government of Italy: distinguished from the *Vatican.* — *adj.* Pertaining to or situated on the Quirinal.

quirk (kwûrk) *n.* **1.** A personal peculiarity, mannerism, or caprice. **2.** A quibble. **3.** A sharp turn or twist. **4.** A sudden curve or flourish, as in writing. **5.** A bright retort; quip. [Origin uncertain] — **quirk′y** *adj.*

quirt (kwûrt) *n.* A short-handled riding whip with a braided lash. — *v.t.* To strike with a quirt. [< Am. Sp. *cuarta*]

quis·ling (kwiz′ling) *n.* One who betrays his country to the enemy and is then given political power by the conquerors. [after Vidkun *Quisling,* 1887–1945, Norwegian Nazi party leader and traitor] — **quis′ling·ism** *n.*

quit (kwit) *v.* **quit** or **quit·ted, quit·ting** *v.t.* **1.** To cease or desist from; discontinue. **2.** To give up; renounce. **3.** To go away from; leave. **4.** To let go of (something held). — *v.i.* **5.** To stop; cease; discontinue. **6.** To leave; depart. **7.** *Informal* To resign from a position, etc. — *adj.* Released, relieved, or absolved from something; clear; free; rid. — *n.* The act of quitting. — **to be quits** To be even (with another). — **to cry quits** To declare (oneself) willing to stop competing. [< OF < Med.L < L *quietus* at rest]

quit·claim (kwit′klām′) *n. Law* A full release and acquittance given by one to another in regard to a certain demand, suit, or right of action. Also **quit′claim′ance** (-əns). — *v.t.* To relinquish or give up claim or title to; release from a claim. [< MF *quite clamer* to declare quit or free]

quite (kwīt) *adv.* **1.** To the fullest extent; totally: *quite dead.* **2.** Really; truly. **3.** *Informal* To a great or considerable extent; noticeably; very; *quite ill.* ◆ The phrase *quite a* is used in many idioms to indicate considerable but indefinite number, size, quantity, etc., as in *quite a lot* (a good deal), *quite a few* (many), *quite a while* (a long while). It is also used in informal expressions with the sense of "wonderful, great, etc.," as in *quite a guy.* [ME; var. of QUIT, adj.]

quit·rent (kwit′rent′) *n.* A fixed rent formerly paid by a freeholder, whereby he was released from feudal services.

quit·tance (kwit′ns) *n.* **1.** Discharge or release, as from debt or obligation. **2.** A document or receipt certifying t **3.** A recompense or repayment. [< OF < *quitter* to qu

quit·ter (kwit′ər) *n.* One who quits needlessly; a shir

quiv·er[1] (kwiv′ər) *v.i.* To shake with a slight, tremul motion; vibrate; tremble. — *n.* The act or fact of qui ing; a trembling or shaking. [Var. of QUAVER]

quiv·er[2] (kwiv′ər) *n.* A portable case for arrows; also, contents. [< AF *quivier,* OF *cuivre* < OHG *kochar*]

quix·ot·ic (kwik-sot′ik) *adj.* **1.** Of, pertaining to, or Don Quixote. **2.** Ridiculously chivalrous or romantic; h ing high but impractical sentiments, aims, etc. — **quix i·cal·ly** *adv.* — **quix·ot·ism** (kwik′sə-tiz′əm) *n.*

quiz (kwiz) *n.* **1.** The act of questioning; esp., an infor oral or written examination of a class or individual. **2.** eccentric person or thing. **3.** A hoax; practical joke. — **quizzed, quiz·zing 1.** To examine by asking question question. **2.** *Brit.* To make fun of; ridicule. — **Syn.** ASK. [Origin unknown] — **quiz′zer** *n.*

quiz·zi·cal (kwiz′i-kəl) *adj.* **1.** Given to chaffing or ban ing. **2.** Queer; odd. **3.** Questioning; puzzled: a *quizz* smile. — **quiz′zi·cal·ly** *adv.*

quoin (koin, kwoin) *n.* **1.** An external angle or corner of a building. **2.** A stone or stones forming such an angle. **3.** A wedge or wedgelike piece, as one of the stones in an arch. **4.** *Printing* A wedge or pair of wedges for locking type in a chase or galley. — *v.t.* To provide, secure, or support with a quoin or quoins. [Var. of COIN]

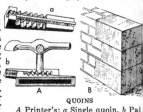

QUOINS

A Printer's: *a* Single quoin, *b* Pai ready for locking with key. *B* Quoins of dressed stone.

quoit (kwoit, *esp. Brit.* koit) *n.* **1.** A ring of metal, r etc., thrown in a game at a short stake, either encirclir or coming as close to it as possible. **2.** *pl. (construed as si* The game so played. — *v.t.* To pitch as a quoit. [< *coite,* ? flat stone < OF *cuilte.* See QUILT.]

quon·dam (kwon′dəm) *adj.* Having been forme former. [< L]

Quon·set hut (kwon′sit) A prefabricated, metal struc the roof of which is half of a cylinder cut lengthwise resting on the ground: a trade name. [after *Quonset,* Rh Island, where first made]

quo·rum (kwôr′əm, kwō′rəm) *n.* The number of mem of any deliberative or corporate body as is necessary for legal transaction of business, commonly, a majority. [< genitive plural of *qui* who]

quo·ta (kwō′tə) *n.* A proportional part or share requ from each person, group, state, etc., for making up a cer number or quantity. [< Med.L < L *quotus* how man

quot·a·ble (kwō′tə-bəl) *adj.* Suitable for quotation. — **quot′a·bil′i·ty** *n.*

quo·ta·tion (kwō-tā′shən) *n.* **1.** The act of quoting. The words quoted or cited. **3.** A price quoted or curr as of securities, etc.: the *quotations* for wheat. — **quo tion·al** *adj.* — **quo·ta′tion·al·ly** *adv.* — **quo·ta′tion·ist**

quotation mark Either of the marks placed at the be ning and end of a word or passage that is an exact quota of the original. In English usage, one or two inverted c mas (" ") mark the beginning of a quotation, and cc spondingly, one or two apostrophes (' ") the close, the si marks being used to set off a quotation within a quotat

quote (kwōt) *v.* **quot·ed, quot·ing** *v.t.* **1.** To reproduce words of. **2.** To repeat or cite (a rule, author, etc.), as authority or illustration. **3.** In commerce: **a** To stat price). **b** To give the current or market price of. **4.** *Printi* To enclose within quotation marks. — *v.i.* **5.** To ma quotation, as from a book. — *n.* **1.** Loosely, a quotat **2.** A quotation mark. [< Med.L *quotare* to distinguis number < L *quot* how many] — **quot′a·ble** *adj.* — **qu** *n.* — **quote′wor′thy** (-wûr′thē) *adj.* — **quot′ing·ly** *ad*

quoth (kwōth) *v.t.* Said or spoke; uttered: the imper tense of the obsolete verb *queth,* used only in the first third persons, the subject always following the verb: *qu* he. [OE *cwæth,* pt. of *cwethan* to say]

quo·tid·i·an (kwō-tid′ē-ən) *adj.* Recurring or occur every day. — *n.* A fever that returns every day. [< or < L *quotidianus* daily]

quo·tient (kwō′shənt) *n. Math.* The result obtaine division; a number indicating how many times one quar is contained in another. [< L *quotiens* how often]

quo war·ran·to (kwō wô·ran′tō, wō-) *Law* A proceed usu. criminal in form but in substance civil, by which a ernment or sovereign seeks to recover an office or franchi [< L, by what warrant]

R

(är) *n.* *pl.* **r's** or **rs, R's** or **Rs, ars** (ärz) **1.** The 18th
er of the English alphabet. **2.** The sound represented
the letter *r.* — *symbol* **1.** *Chem.* An alkyl group. **2.**
h. Ratio. **3.** *Electr.* Resistance. — **the three R's** Read-
writing, and arithmetic regarded as the essential ele-
nts of a primary education.

(rä) The supreme Egyptian deity, the sun god, usu.
resented as a hawk-headed man crowned with the solar
and the sacred serpent: also *Re.*

bet (rab'it) *n.* **1.** A recess or groove
r near the edge of one piece of wood,
, cut so as to receive the edge of another
e. **2.** A joint so made. — *v.* **·bet·ed,**
·ing *v.t.* **1.** To cut a rabbet in. **2.** To

RABBET JOINTS

te in a rabbet. — *v.i.* **3.** To be jointed by a rabbet. [<
< *rabattre* to beat down]

bi (rab'ī) *n.* *pl.* **·bis** or **·bies** In Judaism: **a** The spiritual
d of a Jewish community, authorized to perform religious
ies. **b** Master; teacher: a title for one learned in the Law.
o **rab'bin** (-in). [< Hebrew *rabbī* my master]

bin·ate (rab'in·āt) *n.* **1.** The office or term of office of a
bi. **2.** Rabbis collectively.

·bin·ic (rə·bin'ik) *n.* The Hebrew language as used in
ancient and early medieval periods.

bin·i·cal (rə·bin'i·kəl) *adj.* Pertaining to the rabbis or
heir opinions, languages, or writings. Also **rab·bin'ic.** —
·bin'i·cal·ly *adv.*

bit (rab'it) *n.* **1.** Any of a family of various small,
g-eared mammals allied to but smaller than the hare, as
common American cottontail. **2.** The pelt of a rabbit
nare. **3.** Welsh rabbit. — *v.i.* To hunt rabbits. [Akin
o Walloon *robett,* Flemish *robbe*] — **rab'bit·er** *n.*

bit fever Tularemia.

bit foot The left hind foot of a rabbit, carried as a good-
k charm. Also **rab·bit's foot.**

bit hutch A coop in which domestic rabbits are bred.

bit punch A short chopping blow at the base of the
ull or back of the neck.

ble (rab'əl) *n.* A disorderly crowd or mob. — **the rab-
** The populace or lower classes: a contemptuous term.
dj. Of, suited to, or characteristic of a rabble; disorderly.
v.t. **·bled, ·bling** To mob. [? < RABBLE³]

ble-rous·er (rab'əl·rou'zər) *n.* One who tries to incite
bs by arousing prejudices and passions.

·e-lai·si·an (rab'ə·lā'zē·ən, -zhən) *adj.* **1.** Of, pertain-
to, or resembling Rabelais or his works. **2.** Bawdy and
sterous. — *n.* A student or imitator of Rabelais. —
b'e·lai'si·an·ism, Rab'e·la'ism *n.*

·id (rab'id) *adj.* **1.** Affected with, arising from, or per-
ning to rabies; mad. **2.** Unreasonably zealous; fanatical;
d] — **rab'id·ly** *adv.* — **rab'id·ness** *n.*

ies (rā'bēz, -bi·ēz) *n.* An acute, infectious, usu. fatal
ease of certain animals, esp. of dogs, readily transmissible
man by the bite of an affected animal: also called *hydro-
bia.* [< L, madness] — **ra/bi·et'ic** (-et'ik) *adj.*

·coon (ra·kōon') *n.* **1.** A North American nocturnal
nivore, grayish brown with a black cheek patch and a
ck-and-white-ringed bushy tail. **2.** The fur of this ani-
l. Also spelled *racoon.* [Alter. of Algonquian *arakunem*
nd-scratcher]

e¹ (rās) *n.* **1.** One of the major zoological subdivisions of
nkind, regarded as having a common origin and exhibit-
a relatively constant set of physical traits, such as pig-
ntation, hair form, and facial and bodily proportions. **2.**
y group of people or any grouping of peoples having, or
umed to have, common characteristics, habits, appear-
ce, etc. **3.** A nation: the German *race.* **4.** A genealogical
family stock; clan: the *race* of MacGregor. **5.** Pedigree;
eage: a noble *race.* **6.** Any class of beings having charac-
istics uniting them, or differentiating them from others:
e *race* of lawyers. **7.** *Biol.* A group of plants or animals,
ving distinct characteristics that are passed on to off-
ring. [< MF < Ital. *razza*; origin uncertain]

race² (rās) *n.* **1.** A contest to determine the relative speed
of the contestants. **2.** Any contest. **3.** Movement or progression, esp. when regular or swift. **4.** Duration of life;
course; career. **5.** A swift current of water or its channel.
6. A sluice or channel by which to conduct water to or from
a water wheel or around a dam. **7.** Any groove along which
some part of a machine slides or is guided. — *v.* **raced, rac·
ing** *v.i.* **1.** To take part in a contest of speed. **2.** To move
at great or top speed. **3.** To move at an accelerated or too
great speed: said of machinery. — *v.t.* **4.** To contend
against in a race. **5.** To cause to race. [< ON *rās*]

race-course (rās'kôrs', -kōrs') *n.* A racetrack.

race-horse (rās'hôrs') *n.* A horse bred and trained for contests of speed.

ra·ceme (rā·sēm', rə-) *n.* **1.** *Bot.* An inflorescence in which
the flowers are arranged singly at intervals on a common
axis. **2.** *Chem.* A racemic compound. [< L *racemus* cluster]

ra·ce·mic (rā·sē'mik, -sem'ik, rə-) *adj.* **1.** *Bot.* Of, pertaining to, or contained in racemes. **2.** *Chem.* Indicating any
compound that is optically inactive, but separable into two
isomers, one dextrorotatory, the other levorotatory. Also
rac·e·moid (ras'ə·moid).

rac·e·mose (ras'ə·mōs) *adj.* Like a raceme in form or nature. Also **rac'e·mous** (-məs). — **rac'e·mose·ly** *adv.*

rac·er (rā'sər) *n.* **1.** One who races. **2.** Anything designed
or used for racing, as a car, yacht, etc. **3.** One of various
colubrine snakes, as the blacksnake.

race riot A violent conflict between groups in the same community, based on differences of color or creed.

race suicide The slow reduction in numbers of a people
through voluntary failure on the part of individuals to maintain the birth rate at or above the level of the death rate.

race-track (rās'trak') *n.* A track or course over which a
horse race, dog race, etc., is run: also called *racecourse.*

race-way (rās'wā') *n.* **1.** A channel for conducting water.
2. A tube for protecting wires, as in a subway. **3.** *U.S.* A
racetrack for trotting horses.

Ra·chel (rā'chəl) The wife of Jacob; mother of Joseph and
Benjamin. *Gen.* xxix 6. [< Hebrew, lit., ewe]

ra·chi·tis (rə·kī'tis) *n.* *Pathol.* Rickets. [< NL < Gk. <
rachis spine] — **ra·chit'ic** (-kit'ik) *adj.*

ra·cial (rā'shəl) *adj.* Of, pertaining to, or characteristic of a
race, races, or descent. — **ra'cial·ly** *adv.*

ra·cial·ism (rā'shəl·iz'əm) *n.* Racism. — **ra'cial·ist** *n.*

ra·cism (rā'siz·əm) *n.* **1.** An irrational belief in or advocacy
of the superiority of a given group, people, or nation, usu.
one's own, on the basis of racial differences having no scientific validity. **2.** Social action or government policy based
upon such assumed differences. — **ra'cist** *n.*

rack¹ (rak) *n.* **1.** An open grating, framework, or the like, in
or on which articles may be placed. **2.** A triangular frame
for arranging the balls on a billiard table. **3.** A container or
framework in an airplane for carrying bombs. **4.** *Mech.* A
bar or the like having teeth that engage with those of a gearwheel, pinion, or worm gear. **5.** A machine for stretching or
making tense; esp., an instrument of torture that stretches
the limbs of victims. **6.** Torture or punishment as by the
rack; also, intense mental or physical suffering. **7.** A
wrenching or straining, as from a storm. — *v.t.* **1.** To place
or arrange in or on a rack. **2.** To torture on the rack. **3.** To
torment. **4.** To strain, as with the effort of thinking: to rack
one's brains. **5.** To raise (rents) excessively. — **to rack up**
U.S. Informal To achieve: to *rack up* a perfect score. [<
MDu. < *recken* to stretch] — **rack'er** *n.*

rack² (rak) *n.* **1.** Thin, flying, or broken clouds. **2.** Any
floating vapor. — *v.i.* To move rapidly; send, as clouds before the wind. Also spelled *wrack.* [< Scand.]

rack³ (rak) *n.* Destruction; wreck; demolition: now usu. in
the phrase **rack and ruin.** — **to rack up** *U.S. Slang* To
wreck. [Var. of WRACK²]

rack·et¹ (rak'it) *n.* **1.** A nearly elliptical hoop of bent wood,
usu. strung with catgut or nylon, and having a handle, used
in striking a tennis ball, etc. **2.** A large wooden sole or shoe
to support the weight of a man or horse on swampy ground.

3. A snowshoe. **4.** An organ stop. **5.** *Often pl.* A game resembling court tennis, played in a court with four walls. Often *racquet.* [< MF < Arabic *rāha* palm of the hand]
rack·et² (rak′it) *n.* **1.** A clattering, vociferous, or confused noise. **2.** *Informal* A scheme for getting money or other benefits by fraud, intimidation, or other illegitimate means. **3.** *Slang* Any business or occupation. **4.** Social activity or excitement. — *v.i.* **1.** To make a loud, clattering noise. **2.** To indulge in noisy sport or diversion. [Prob. imit.]
rack·et·eer (rak′ə·tir′) *n.* **1.** One engaged in a racket. **2.** Formerly, a bootlegger or rumrunner. — **rack′et·eer′ing** *n.*
rack·et·y (rak′it·ē) *adj.* Making a racket; noisy.
rac·on·teur (rak′on·tûr′, *Fr.* rá·kôn̄·tœr′) *n.* A skilled storyteller.
ra·coon (ra·kōōn′) See RACCOON.
rac·quet (rak′it) See RACKET¹.
rac·y (rā′sē) *adj.* **rac·i·er, rac·i·est** **1.** Having a spirited or pungent interest; spicy; piquant. **2.** Having a characteristic flavor assumed to be indicative of origin, as wine; rich, fresh, or fragrant. **3.** Suggestive; slightly immodest: a *racy* story. [< RACE] — **rac′i·ly** *adv.* — **rac′i·ness** *n.*
ra·dar (rā′där) *n.* *Telecom.* An electronic device that locates objects by beaming radio-frequency impulses that are reflected back from the object, and determines its distance by a measurement of the time elapsed between transmission and reception of the impulses. [< *ra(dio) d(etection) a(nd) r(anging)*]
radar beacon *Telecom.* The part of a radar that transmits radio-frequency waves. Also **ra·con** (rā′kon).
ra·dar·scope (rā′där·skōp) *n.* *Telecom.* The oscilloscope of a radar set.
rad·dle (rad′l) *v.t.* **·dled, ·dling** To intertwine or weave together. [< OF < MHG *reidel* stout stick]
ra·di·al (rā′dē·əl) *adj.* **1.** Pertaining to, consisting of, or resembling a ray or radius. **2.** Extending from a center like rays. **3.** Of or pertaining to the radius or a radiating part. **4.** *Anat.* Denoting the radius. **5.** Developing uniformly on all sides. — *n.* A radiating part. — **ra′di·al·ly** *adv.*
radial engine A multicylinder internal-combustion engine having its cylinders arranged like the spokes in a wheel.
ra·di·an (rā′dē·ən) *n.* *Math.* **1.** An arc equal in length to the radius of the circle of which it is a part. **2.** The angle subtended by such an arc, equal to 57° 17′ 44.80625″ +.
ra·di·ance (rā′dē·əns) *n.* The quality or state of being radiant; brightness; effulgence. Also **ra′di·an·cy, ra′di·ant·ness.**
ra·di·ant (rā′dē·ənt) *adj.* **1.** Emitting rays of light or heat. **2.** Beaming with light or brightness, kindness, or love: a *radiant* smile. **3.** Resembling rays. **4.** Consisting of or transmitted by radiation: *radiant* heat. — *n.* **1.** A straight line proceeding from and conceived as revolving around a given point. **2.** *Astron.* That point in the heavens from which, during a meteoric shower, the meteors seem to shoot. **3.** The luminous point from which light proceeds or is made to radiate. **4.** That which radiates. [< L *radians, -antis,* ppr. of *radiare* to emit rays] — **ra′di·ant·ly** *adv.*
radiant energy *Physics* The energy associated with and transmitted in the form of waves, esp. those of electromagnetic frequencies, as heat, light, radio waves, X-rays, etc.
ra·di·ate (*v.* rā′dē·āt; *adj. & n.* rā′dē·it) *v.* **·at·ed, ·at·ing** *v.i.* **1.** To emit rays or radiation; be radiant. **2.** To issue forth in rays, as light from the sun. **3.** To spread out from a center, as the spokes of a wheel. — *v.t.* **4.** To send out or emit in rays. **5.** To cause to spread as if from a center; diffuse. **6.** To show as if shining with. — *adj.* Divided or separated into rays; having rays; radiating. — **ra′di·a′tive** *adj.*
ra·di·a·tion (rā′dē·ā′shən) *n.* **1.** The act of radiating, or the state of being radiated. **2.** *Physics* **a** The emission and propagation of radiant energy, esp. by radioactive substances capable of affecting living tissue. **b** The stages of emission, absorption, and transmission involved in this.
radiation sickness *Pathol.* A condition due to absorption of excess radiation and marked by fatigue, vomiting, internal hemorrhage, and progressive tissue breakdown.
ra·di·a·tor (rā′dē·ā′tər) *n.* **1.** That which radiates. **2.** A chamber, coil, or flat hollow vessel, through which is passed steam or hot water for warming a building or apartment. **3.** In engines, a nest of tubes for cooling water flowing through them. **4.** *Physics* Any source of radiant energy, whether in the form of particles or of electromagnetic waves. — **ra′di·a·to′ry** (-ə·tôr′ē, -tō′rē) *adj.*
rad·i·cal (rad′i·kəl) *adj.* **1.** Of, proceeding from, or pertaining to the root or foundation; fundamental. **2.** Thoroughgoing; extreme: *radical* measures. **3.** *Math.* Pertaining to the root or roots of a number. **4.** In etymology, belonging or referring to a root or a root syllable. **5.** *Chem.* Pertaining to a radical. **6.** Of or pertaining to political radicals. — *n.* **1.** One who carries his theories or convictions to their furthest application. **2.** In politics, one who advocates widespread governmental changes and reforms at the earliest opportunity. **3.** The primitive or underived part of a word; a root. **4.** *Math.* **a** A quantity that is the root of another

quantity. **b** The radical sign. **5.** *Chem.* A group of at that acts as a unit in a compound and may pass uncha through a series of reactions. [< LL *radicalis* having r — **rad′i·cal·ly** *adv.* — **rad′i·cal·ness** *n.*
rad·i·cal·ism (rad′i·kəl·iz′əm) *n.* **1.** The state of being ical. **2.** Advocacy of radical measures.
radical sign *Math.* The symbol √ placed before a qua to indicate that a designated root is to be taken.
rad·i·cle (rad′i·kəl) *n.* **1.** *Bot.* **a** The embryonic root b the cotyledon of a plant. **b** A small root or rootlet. **2.** A rootlike part, as the initial fiber of a nerve. [< L *radi* dim. of *radix, -icis* root]
ra·di·i (rā′dē·ī) Plural of RADIUS.
ra·di·o (rā′dē·ō) *n.* *pl.* **·os** **1.** The science and technic communicating by means of radio waves that have modulated to carry information either in the form of s or of a code. **2.** A radio program or broadcast. **3.** A re er, transmitter, or other radio apparatus. **4.** A radio sage or radiogram. **5.** The radio business and industry *adj.* Of, pertaining to, designating, employing, or prod by radiant energy, esp. in the form of electromagnetic w — *v.t. & v.i.* **ra·di·oed, ra·di·o·ing** To transmit (a mes etc.) or communicate with (someone) by radio. Also, *wireless.* [< RADIO(TELEGRAPHY)]
radio- *combining form* **1.** Radial. **2.** Radio; produc obtained by or related to radio. **3.** Radioactive. **4.** R tion. [< L *radius* ray]
ra·di·o·ac·tive (rā′dē·ō·ak′tiv) *adj.* Pertaining to, ex ing, caused by, or characteristic of radioactivity.
radioactive series *Physics* The sequence of disintegr products through which a radioactive element passes b reaching a stable form as an isotope of lead. The three cipal series are those of uranium, thorium, and actiniu
ra·di·o·ac·tiv·i·ty (rā′dē·ō·ak·tiv′ə·tē) *n. Physics* The s taneous nuclear disintegration of certain elements anc topes, with the emission of nucleons or of electromagnet diation; also, a particular form of such disintegration.
radio astronomy The branch of astronomy and astro ics that studies celestial objects by the analysis of waves intercepted by radio telescopes.
radio beacon A stationary radio transmitter that send characteristic signals for the guidance of ships and air
radio beam *Aeron.* A continuous radio signal along a way to guide aircraft.
ra·di·o·bi·ol·o·gy (rā′dē·ō·bī·ol′ə·jē) *n.* The study o effects of radiation upon living organisms.
ra·di·o·broad·cast (rā′dē·ō·brôd′kast′, -käst′) *v.t.* **·cast** or **·cast·ed, ·cast·ing** To broadcast by radio. — broadcast. — **ra′di·o·broad′cast′er** *n.*
ra·di·o·car·bon (rā′dē·ō·kär′bən) *n. Physics* The rad tive isotope of carbon of mass 14 with a half life of a 5570 years, much used in the dating of fossils, artifacts certain kinds of geological formations: also called *carbo*
radio compass *Aeron.* A directional radio receiver th dicates the bearing of a radio transmitting station.
ra·di·o·dat·ing (rā′dē·ō·dā′ting) *n.* The technique of ing objects by measuring their radioactivity.
ra·di·o·el·e·ment (rā′dē·ō·el′ə·mənt) *n. Physics* An tope or element exhibiting radioactivity.
radio fix The position of an aircraft, ship, or radio tran ter, as determined by use of radio signals.
radio frequency Any wave frequency lying between a 10 kilocycles and 30,000 megacycles.
ra·di·o·gram (rā′dē·ō·gram′) *n.* **1.** A message sent b dio. **2.** A radiograph.
ra·di·o·graph (rā′dē·ō·graf′, -gräf′) *n.* A picture mad means of radioactivity; an X-ray photograph. — *v.t.* make a radiograph of. — **ra′di·og′ra·pher** (-og′rə·fər) **ra′di·o·graph′ic** or **·i·cal** *adj.* — **ra′di·og′ra·phy** *n.*
ra·di·o·i·so·tope (rā′dē·ō·ī′sə·tōp) *n. Physics* A radioa isotope, usu. one produced artificially from a normally s element, used in biological and physical research ar medicine for diagnostic and therapeutic purposes.
ra·di·ol·o·gy (rā′dē·ol′ə·jē) *n.* The branch of science relates to radiant energy and its applications, especia the diagnosis and treatment of disease. — **ra·di·o·log** (rā′dē·ə·loj′i·kəl) or **ra′di·o·log′ic** *adj.* — **ra′di·ol′o·gi**
ra·di·om·e·ter (rā′dē·om′ə·tər) *n.* An instrument fo tecting and measuring radiant energy by converting it mechanical energy, as by the rotation of blackened v suspended in a vacuum and exposed to sunlight. — r o·met′ric (-ō·met′rik) *adj.* — **ra′di·om′e·try** *n.*
ra·di·o·phone (rā′dē·ō·fōn′) *n.* **1.** Any device for the duction or transmission of sound by radiant energy. radiotelephone. — **ra′di·o·phon′ic** (-fon′ik) *adj.* — oph′o·ny (-of′ə·nē) *n.*
ra·di·o·pho·tog·ra·phy (rā′dē·ō·fə·tog′rə·fē) *n.* The t mission of a photograph by radio waves. — **ra′di·o·p graph** (-fō′tə·graf, -gräf) *n.*
radio pill *Med.* A tiny radio transmitter that can be i duced into the body to transmit physiological data.

...o·scope (rādē-ō-skōp′) *n.* An apparatus detecting radioactivity or X-rays.

...os·co·py (rā′dē-os′kə-pē) *n.* Examination of opaque bodies with the aid of X-rays or other form of radiant energy. — **ra′di·o·** **/ic** (-skop′ik) or **·i·cal** *adj.*

...o·sonde (rā′dē-ō-sond′) *n. Meteorol.* An orne device, usu. attached to a balloon, radios meteorological data to the ground. F < *radio* radio + *sonde* sounding]

o spectrum The full range of frequencies aining to and associated with radiant energy; esp., the radio frequencies.

o star Any of a large number of stars that be identified and studied by means of the o waves they emit.

o station An installation of all the equipment needed for effective radio broadcasting, when used for commercial or educational poses and licensed to employ an assigned uency and power.

...o·stron·tium (rā′dē-ō-stron′shəm, -tē-əm) *Physics* Strontium 90.

...o·tel·e·gram (rā′dē-ō-tel′ə-gram) *n.* A sage sent by radiotelegraphy.

...o·te·leg·ra·phy (rā′dē-ō-tə-leg′rə-fē) *n.* egraphic communication using radio waves. — **ra′di·o·** **·graph′ic** (-tel′ə-graf′ik) *adj.* — **ra′di·o·tel′e·graph** al, -gräf) *n.*

...o·tel·e·phone (rā′dē-ō-tel′ə-fōn) *n.* A telephone that rates by means of radio waves. — **ra′di·o·tel′e·phon′ic** l/ə-fon′ik) *adj.* — **ra′di·o·te·leph′o·ny** (-tə-lef′ə-nē) *n.*

o telescope *Astron.* A highly sensitive radio receiver, gned to receive radio waves from outer space.

...o·ther·a·py (rā′dē-ō-ther′ə-pē) *n. Med.* The treatent of disease by X-rays and other forms of radioactivity.

...o·ther·my (rā′dē-ō-thûr′mē) *n. Med.* Diathermy.

...o·tho·ri·um (rā′dē-ō-thôr′ē-əm, -thō′rē-əm) *n.* A ractive isotope of thorium, with a half life of 1.9 years.

o tube An electron tube.

o wave Any electromagnetic wave having a radio frency; a Hertzian wave.

...ish (rad′ish) *n.* **1.** The pungent, edible root of a tall, nching herb of the mustard family. **2.** The herb yielding root. [OE *rædic* < L *radix, radicis* root]

...um (rā′dē-əm) *n.* A powerfully radioactive metallic nent (symbol Ra), obtained principally as a disintegraproduct of uranium. It has a half life of about 1,600 rs, emitting alpha and beta particles and gamma rays in a cession of stages beginning with radon and continuing to num G, a stable isotope of lead. See ELEMENT. [< NL < *idius* ray + -IUM]

um therapy The treatment of diseases, esp. cancer, means of radium.

...i·us (rā′dē-əs) *n. pl.* **·di·i** (-dē-ī) **1.** A straight line n the center of a circle or sphere to the circumference or face. **2.** *Anat.* The thicker and shorter bone of the fore-, on the same side as the thumb. **3.** *Zool.* A similar bone he forelimb of other vertebrates. **4.** *Bot.* A ray floret composite flower. **5.** A ray or radiating part. **6.** A cir-ar area or boundary measured by the length of its radius. Sphere, scope, or limit, as of activity. **8.** A fixed limit of vel or operation under specified conditions: the cruising *ius* of a ship. [< L, orig. rod, hence spoke of a wheel]

...ius vector *pl.* **radius vectors** or **ra·di·i vec·to·res** (rā′dē-ī -tôr′ēz, -tō′rēz) *Math.* The straight-line distance from a d origin to any point of a curve.

...ix (rā′diks) *n. pl.* **rad·i·ces** (rad′ə-sēz, rā′də-) or **ra·dix·** **1.** *Math.* A number or symbol used as the basis of a scale numeration. **2.** *Bot.* The root of a plant. [< L, root]

...ome (rā′dōm) *n.* A protective housing for the antenna a radar assembly. [< RA(DAR) + DOME]

...on (rā′don) *n.* A heavy, gaseous, radioactive element mbol Rn), an emanation of radium with a half life of out 14 days: formerly called *niton.* See ELEMENT.

... (raf) *n.* The rabble; riffraff. [< dial. *raff* to rake < OF *ler* < *rafle*]

...fi·a (raf′ē-ə) *n.* A cultivated palm of Madagascar, leafstalks of which furnish fiber for making hats, mats, skets, etc. **2.** Its fiber. [< Malagasy]

...·ish (raf′ish) *adj.* **1.** Tawdry; gaudy; flashy. **2.** Dis-utable.

...fle (raf′əl) *n.* A form of lottery in which one buys a ance on an object. — *v.* **·fled, ·fling** *v.t.* **1.** To dispose of a raffle: often with *off.* — *v.i.* **2.** To take part in a raffle. [< OF *rafle* a game of dice < Du. *rafelen*] — **raf′fler** *n.*

... (raft, räft) *n.* **1.** A float of logs, planks, etc., fastened gether for transportation by water. **2.** A life raft. — *v.t.*

1. To transport on a raft. **2.** To form into a raft. — *v.i.* **3.** To travel by, be employed on, or manage a raft. [< ON *raptr* rafter]

raft² (raft, räft) *n. Informal* A large number or indiscriminate collection of any kind. [< RAFF]

raft·er (raf′tər, räf′-) *n.* A beam giving form, slope, and support to a roof. For illus. see ROOF. [OE *ræfter*]

rafts·man (rafts′mən, räfts′-) *n. pl.* **·men** (-mən) One who manages or works on a raft.

rag¹ (rag) *v.t.* **ragged, rag·ging** *Slang* **1.** To tease or annoy. **2.** To scold. — *n. Brit.* A ragging. [Origin uncertain]

rag² (rag) *n.* **1.** A torn or discarded piece of cloth. **2.** A small cloth used for washing, cleaning, etc. **3.** A fragment of anything. **4.** *pl.* Cotton or linen textile remnants used in the making of rag paper. **5.** *pl.* Tattered or shabby clothing. **6.** Any clothing: a jocular usage. **7.** Anything resembling a rag in appearance or worth: used humorously or in disparagement. — **.ad rags** *Slang* One's best clothes. — **to chew the rag** *Slang* To talk or argue at great length. [OE < ON *rögg* tuft]

rag³ (rag) *v.t.* **ragged, rag·ging** To compose or play in rag-time. — *n.* Ragtime.

rag·a·muf·fin (rag′ə-muf′in) *n.* Anyone, esp. a child, wearing very ragged clothes. [after *Ragamoffyn,* demon in William Langland's *Piers Plowman,* 1393]

rage (rāj) *n.* **1.** Violent anger; wrath; fury. **2.** Any great violence or intensity, as of a fever or a storm. **3.** Extreme eagerness or emotion; great enthusiasm. **4.** Something popular or in demand; a fad. — *v.i.* **raged, rag·ing 1.** To speak, act, or move with unrestrained anger. **2.** To act or proceed with great violence. **3.** To spread or prevail un-controlled, as an epidemic. [< OF < LL < L *rabere* to rage] — **rag′ing·ly** *adv.*

rag·ged (rag′id) *adj.* **1.** Rent or worn into rags; frayed. **2.** Wearing worn, frayed, or shabby garments. **3.** Of rough or uneven character or aspect. **4.** Naturally of a rough or shaggy appearance. — **rag′ged·ly** *adv.* — **rag′ged·ness** *n.*

ragged edge *Informal* The extreme or precarious edge; the verge; the *ragged edge* of starvation. — **on the ragged edge** Dangerously near to losing one's self-control, sanity, etc.

rag·lan (rag′lən) *n.* An overcoat or topcoat, the sleeves of which extend in one piece up to the collar. — *adj.* Denoting a garment with such sleeves. [after Lord *Raglan,* 1788–1855, English field marshal]

rag·man (rag′man′, -mən) *n. pl.* **·men** (-men′, -mən) One who buys and sells old rags and other waste; a ragpicker.

ra·gout (ra·gōō′) *n.* A highly seasoned dish of stewed meat and vegetables. — *v.t.* **ra·gouted** (-gōōd′), **ra·gout·ing** (-gōō′ing) To make into a ragout. [< F]

rag·pick·er (rag′pik′ər) *n.* One who picks up rags and other junk for a livelihood.

rag·time (rag′tīm′) *n.* **1.** A kind of American dance music, developed from about 1890 to 1920, characterized by highly syncopated rhythm in fast time. **2.** The rhythm of this music. Also called *rag.* [< *ragged time*]

rag·weed (rag′wēd′) *n.* A coarse, very common annual or perennial herb, the pollen of which induces hay fever.

rag·wort (rag′wûrt′) *n.* Any of several herbs of the composite family, with bright yellow flowers.

rah (rä) *interj.* Hurrah: a cheer used chiefly in college yells.

raid (rād) *n.* **1.** A hostile or predatory incursion by a rapid-ly moving body of troops or an armed vessel; a foray. **2.** An air raid. **3.** Any sudden invasion, capture, or seizure. **4.** An attempt by speculators to lower stock prices. — *v.t.* **1.** To make a raid on. — *v.i.* **2.** To participate in a raid. [< Scottish form of OE *rād* a riding] — **raid′er** *n.*

rail¹ (rāl) *n.* **1.** A bar of wood, metal, etc., resting on supports, as in a fence, at the side of a stair-way, or capping the bulwarks of a ship; a railing. **2.** One of a series of parallel bars of iron or steel, resting upon crossties and forming a support and guide for wheels, as of a railroad. **3.** A railroad considered as a means of transportation: to ship by rail. — *v.t.* To furnish or shut in with rails; fence. [< OF < L *regula* wooden ruler]

RAIL FENCE

rail² (rāl) *n.* Any of numerous marsh birds having very short wings, moderately long legs and toes, and a short turned-up tail. [< OF *raale*]

rail³ (rāl) *v.i.* **1.** To use scornful, insolent, or abusive lan-guage; scold: with *at* or *against.* — *v.t.* **2.** To drive or force by railing. [< MF < Provençal *ralhar* to jest at] — **rail′** **er** *n.*

rail·ing (rā′ling) *n.* **1.** A series of rails; a balustrade. **2.** Rails, or material from which rails are made.

rail·ler·y (rā′lər-ē) *n. pl.* **·ler·ies** Merry jesting or teasing; banter. [< F *raillerie* jesting]

rail·road (rāl′rōd′) *n.* **1.** A graded road having metal rails supported by ties or sleepers, for the passage of trains or rolling stock drawn by locomotives. **2.** The system of tracks, stations, etc., used in transportation by rail. **3.** The corporation or persons owning or operating such a system. — *v.t.* **1.** To transport by railroad. **2.** *U.S. Informal* To rush or force with great speed or without deliberation: to *railroad* a bill through Congress. **3.** *U.S. Slang* To cause to be imprisoned on false charges or without fair trial. — *v.i.* **4.** To work on a railroad. — **rail/road/er** *n.* — **rail/road/ing** *n.*

rail·split·ter (rāl/split/ər) *n.* One who splits logs into fence rails.

rail·way (rāl/wā/) *n.* **1.** *Chiefly Brit.* A railroad. **2.** Rails similar to those of a railroad, as for streetcars. **3.** A track or set of rails, as in a factory, for handling heavy articles, etc.

rai·ment (rā/mənt) *n.* *Archaic* Wearing apparel; clothing; garb. [Aphetic var. of *arrayment* < ARRAY + -MENT]

rain (rān) *n.* **1.** The condensed water vapor of the atmosphere falling in drops. ◆ Collateral adjective: *pluvial.* **2.** The fall of such drops. **3.** A fall or shower of anything in the manner of rain. **4.** A rainstorm; shower. **5.** *pl.* The rainy season, as in a tropical country. — *v.i.* **1.** To fall from the clouds in drops of water: usu. with *it* as the subject. **2.** To fall like rain, as tears. **3.** To send or pour down rain, as clouds. — *v.t.* **4.** To send down like rain; shower. — **to rain out** To cause (a game, outdoor event, etc.) to be canceled or postponed because of rain. [OE *regn*]

rain·bow (rān/bō/) *n.* **1.** An arch of prismatic colors formed in the sky opposite the sun and caused by refraction, reflection, and dispersion of light in raindrops falling through the air. **2.** Any similar display of color. [OE *regnboga*]

rain check *U.S.* **1.** The stub of a ticket to an outdoor event, as a baseball game, entitling the holder to admission at a future date if for any reason the event is called off. **2.** A postponed invitation.

rain·coat (rān/kōt/) *n.* A coat, often waterproof, intended to be worn in rainy weather. Also, *Brit., waterproof.*

rain·fall (rān/fôl/) *n.* **1.** A fall of rain. **2.** *Meteorol.* The amount of water, measured in inches, precipitated in a given region over a stated time, as rain, hail, snow, or the like.

rain gauge An instrument for measuring the amount of rainfall at a given place or time. Also **rain gage.**

rain·mak·er (rān/mā/kər) *n.* One reputedly able to cause rain; esp., among certain American Indians, one who uses incantations to produce rain. — **rain/mak/ing** *n.*

rain·out (rān/out/) *n.* *Physics* Precipitation of radioactive water droplets following an underwater nuclear explosion.

rain·proof (rān/proof/) *adj.* Shedding rain, as garments.

rain·storm (rān/stôrm/) *n.* A storm accompanied by rain.

rain·wa·ter (rān/wô/tər, -wot/-) *n.* Water that falls or has fallen in the form of rain. Also **rain water.**

rain·y (rā/nē) *adj.* **rain·i·er, rain·i·est** Characterized by, abounding in, or bringing rain. — **rain/i·ness** *n.*

rainy day A time of need; hard times.

raise (rāz) *v.* **raised, rais·ing** *v.t.* **1.** To cause to move upward or to a higher level; elevate. **2.** To place erect; set up. **3.** To construct or build. **4.** To make greater in amount, size, or value: to *raise* prices. **5.** To advance or elevate in rank, estimation, etc. **6.** To increase the strength, intensity, or degree of. **7.** To breed; grow: to *raise* tomatoes. **8.** *U.S.* To rear (children, a family, etc.). **9.** To cause to be heard: to *raise* a hue and cry. **10.** To cause; occasion, as a smile or laugh. **11.** To stir to action or emotion. **12.** To waken; animate or reanimate. **13.** To gather together; obtain or collect, as an army, capital, etc. **14.** To bring up for consideration, as a question. **15.** To cause to swell or become lighter; leaven. **16.** To put an end to, as a siege. **17.** In poker, to bet more than. **18.** *Naut.* To cause to appear above the horizon, as land or a ship, by approaching nearer. — *v.i.* **19.** *Informal* To cough up phlegm. **20.** In poker, to make a raise. — **to raise the devil** (or **the dickens, hell, the roof, a rumpus,** etc.) *Informal* To make a great disturbance; stir up confusion. — *n.* **1.** The act of raising. **2.** An increase, as of wages or a bet. ◆ In British usage, a *rise* is an increase in wages. [< ON *risa* to rise] — **rais/er** *n.*

raised (rāzd) *adj.* **1.** Elevated in low relief. **2.** Made with yeast or leaven.

rai·sin (rā/zən) *n.* A grape of a special sort dried in the sun or in an oven. [< OF < L *racemus* bunch of grapes]

rai·son d'ê·tre (re·zôn/ de/tr/) *French* Reason or excuse for existing; literally, reason for being.

raj (räj) *n.* In India, sovereignty; rule. [< Hind. *rāj*]

ra·jah (rä/jə) *n.* A Hindu prince or chief of a tribal state in India; also, a Malay or Javanese ruler: often used as a courtesy title. Also **ra/ja.** [< Hind. < Skt. *rājan* king]

Raj·put (räj/pōōt) *n.* One of a powerful and warlike Hindu caste. Also **Raj/poot.** [< Hind. < Skt. < *rājan* king + *putra* son]

rake¹ (rāk) *n.* A toothed implement for drawing together loose material, loosening the surface of the soil, etc. — *v.* **raked, rak·ing** *v.t.* **1.** To scrape or gather together with or as with a rake. **2.** To smooth, clean, or prepare with a rake.

3. To gather by diligent effort; scrape together. **4.** search or examine carefully. **5.** To direct heavy gu[...] along the length of, as a ship or column of troops; enf[...] — *v.i.* **6.** To use a rake. **7.** To scrape or pass rough[...] violently: with *across, over,* etc. **8.** To make a search.

rake in *Informal* To earn or acquire (money, etc.) in [...] quantities. [OE *raca*] — **rak/er** *n.*

rake² (rāk) *v.* **raked, rak·ing** *v.i.* **1.** To lean from the pendicular, as a ship's masts. — *v.t.* **2.** To cause to incline. — *n.* Inclination from the perpendicular or [...] zontal, as of the edge of a cutting tool. [Origin uncer[...]

rake³ (rāk) *n.* A dissolute, lewd man; a roué. [Earlier [...] *hell* < ME *rakel* rash, wild]

rake-off (rāk/ôf/, -of/) *n.* *U.S. Slang* **1.** A share, as of its; commission. **2.** A rebate, usu. illegitimate.

rak·ish¹ (rā/kish) *adj.* **1.** Dashing; jaunty; smart. **2.** [...] Having the masts unusually inclined, so as to suggest s[...] [< RAKE²] — **rak/ish·ly** *adv.* — **rak/ish·ness** *n.*

rak·ish² (rā/kish) *adj.* Characteristic of a rake; disso[...] profligate. — **rak/ish·ly** *adv.* — **rak/ish·ness** *n.*

râle (räl) *n.* *Pathol.* A sound additional to that of no[...] respiration, heard on auscultation of the chest and indic[...] of the presence, nature, or stage of a disease. [< F, ra[...]

ral·len·tan·do (räl/ən·tän/dō, *Ital.* räl/len·tän/dō) [...] *adj. & adv.* Gradually slower. [< Ital.]

ral·ly¹ (ral/ē) *n. pl.* **·lies 1.** A meeting or assembly of sons for a common purpose. **2.** A rapid recovery of a no[...] condition as after exhaustion, depression, etc. **3.** A re[...] as of scattered troops, to order or action. **4.** In tennis interchange of several strokes before one side wins the p[...] **5.** A driving competition or procession over a fixed, ofte[...] tensive course, as for sports cars, antique automobiles[...] — *v.* **·lied, ·ly·ing** *v.t.* **1.** To bring together and resto[...] effective discipline: to *rally* fleeing troops. **2.** To sum[...] up or revive: to *rally* one's spirits. **3.** To bring togethe[...] common action. — *v.i.* **4.** To return to effective disci[...] or action: The enemy *rallied.* **5.** To unite for commo[...] tion. **6.** To make a partial or complete return to a no[...] condition; improve. **7.** In tennis, to engage in a rally. F < *re-* again + *allier* to join] — **ral/li·er** *n.*

ral·ly² (ral/ē) *v.t. & v.i.* **·lied, ·ly·ing** To mock or tease raillery; banter. [< F *railler* to banter] — **ral/li·er** *n.*

ram (ram) *n.* **1.** A male sheep. **2.** A device for dri[...] forcing, or crushing by heavy blows or thrusts. **3.** A[...] draulic ram. — *v.t.* **rammed, ram·ming 1.** To strike or as with a ram; dash against. **2.** To drive or force do[...] into something. **3.** To cram; stuff. [OE *ramm*] — [...] mer *n.* — **ram/mish** *adj.*

ram·ble (ram/bəl) *v.i.* **·bled, ·bling 1.** To walk about f[...] and aimlessly; roam. **2.** To write or talk aimlessly or [...] out sequence of ideas. **3.** To proceed with turns and tw[...] meander. — **Syn.** See WANDER. — *n.* **1.** The act of bling; an aimless or leisurely stroll. **2.** A meandering [...] maze. [? ME *romblen,* freq. of *romen* to roam]

ram·bler (ram/blər) *n.* **1.** One who or that which ram[...] **2.** Any of several varieties of climbing roses, with cluste[...] deep red flowers.

ram·bunc·tious (ram·bungk/shəs) *adj.* *U.S. Informal* [...] terous; rough. [Prob. var. of *robustious* < ROBUST]

ram·e·kin (ram/ə·kin) *n.* **1.** A seasoned dish of b[...] crumbs with eggs and cheese, baked and served in a sha[...] dish. **2.** A dish, usu. with a handle, in which ramekin[...] baked. **3.** Any dish used both for baking and serving. **ram/e·quin.** [< F *ramequin* < Du.]

ram·ie (ram/ē) *n.* The fiber yielded by a shrubby Chi[...] and East Indian perennial of the nettle family, used for [...] age and certain textiles. Also **ram/ee.** [< Malay *ram[...]*

ram·i·fi·ca·tion (ram/ə·fə·kā/shən) *n.* **1.** The act or pr[...] of ramifying. **2.** An offshoot or subdivision. **3.** A re[...] consequence, etc., stemming from a main source.

ram·i·form (ram/ə·fôrm) *adj.* **1.** Branch-shaped. [...] Branched. [< L *ramus* branch + -FORM]

ram·i·fy (ram/ə·fī) *v.t. & v.i.* **·fied, ·fy·ing** To div[...] spread out into or as into branches; branch out. [< [...] Med.L < L *ramus* branch + *facere* to make]

ram jet (ram/jet/) *n.* A type of jet engine that provides tinuous jet propulsion.

ra·mose (rā/mōs, rə·mōs/) *adj.* **1.** Branching. **2.** Con[...] ing of or having branches. [< L < *ramus* branch]

ra·mous (rā/məs) *adj.* **1.** Of or like branches. **2.** Ram[...] [See RAMOSE]

ramp¹ (ramp) *n.* **1.** An inclined passageway or roadwa[...] between floors of a building. **2.** A movable stairwa[...] which passengers enter or leave an airplane. [< F [...] *ramper* to climb]

ramp² (ramp) *v.i.* **1.** To rear up on the hind legs and thr[...] out the forelegs, as a horse. **2.** To act in a violent or th[...] ening manner; rampage. — *n.* The act of ramping. [< *ramper* to climb]

ram·page (*n.* ram/pāj; *v.* ram·pāj/) *n.* Boisterous agita[...] or excitement. — *v.i.* **·paged, ·pag·ing 1.** To rush or[...]

ently. 2. To storm; rage. [Orig. Scot., ? < RAMP²] —
m·pag'er n. — **ram·pa'geous** adj.
n·pant (ram/pənt) adj. 1. Exceeding all bounds; wild.
Widespread or unchecked, as an erroneous belief. 3.
anding on the hind legs; rearing: said of a quadruped. 4.
eraldry Standing on the hind legs, with both forelegs ele-
ted. [< OF, ppr. of *ramper*. See RAMP².] — **ram/pan·cy**
— **ram/pant·ly** adv.
n·part (ram/pärt, -pərt) n. 1. The embankment sur-
unding a fort, on which the parapet is raised. 2. A bul-
ark or defense. — v.t. To supply with or as with ramparts;
rtify. [< F *remparer* to fortify]
n·rod (ram/rod/) n. 1. A rod used to drive home the
arge of a muzzleloading gun or pistol. 2. A similar rod
ed for cleaning the barrel of a rifle, etc.
n·shack·le (ram/shak/əl) adj. Likely to go to pieces, as
om age or neglect. [< *ransackle*, freq. of RANSACK]
1 (ran) Past tense of RUN.
ich (ranch) n. 1. An establishment for raising or grazing
ttle, sheep, horses, etc., in large herds. 2. The buildings,
rsonnel, and lands connected with it. 3. A large farm. —
i. To manage or work on a ranch. [< Sp. *rancho* soldiers'
ess] — **ranch/er, ranch/man** n.
ich house 1. The main building of a ranch .2. *U.S.* A
ie-story house usu. having a low roof with a wide overhang.
1·cid (ran/sid) adj. Having the unpleasant taste or smell
oily substances that have begun to spoil; rank; sour. [<
< *rancere* to be rank] — **ran·cid/i·ty, ran/cid·ness** n.
1·cor (rang/kər) n. Bitter enmity; spitefulness. Also *Brit.*
in/cour. [< OF < LL < L *rancere* to be rank] — **ran/·**
r·ous adj. — **ran/cor·ous·ly** adv. — **ran/cor·ous·ness** n.
id (rand, ränd) n. The monetary unit of South Africa.
1·dom (ran/dəm) n. Lack of definite aim or intention:
ow chiefly in the phrase **at random**, without definite pur-
ose or aim; haphazardly. — adj. Done at random. [<
F *random* rapidity, impetuosity] — **ran/dom·ly** adv.
nge (rang) Past tense of RING².
nge (ränj) n. 1. The area over which anything moves,
erates, or is distributed. 2. *U.S.* An extensive tract of
nd over which cattle, sheep, etc., roam and graze. 3. Ex-
nt or scope: the whole *range* of politics. 4. The extent to
hich any power can be made effective: *range* of influence.
The extent of variation of anything: the temperature
nge. 6. A line, row, or series, as of mountains. 7. The
aximum distance that an aircraft, ship, vehicle, etc., can
avel before its fuel is exhausted; also, the maximum dis-
nce at which a weapon, transmitter, etc., is effective. 8. A
ace for shooting at a mark: a rifle *range.* 9. A large cook-
g stove. — adj. Of or pertaining to a range. — v. **ranged**,
ng·ing v.t. 1. To arrange in definite order, as in rows. 2.
o assign to a class, division, or category. 3. To move about
over (a region, etc.). 4. To put (cattle) to graze on a
nge. 5. To adjust or train, as a telescope or gun. — v.i.
. To move over an area in a thorough, systematic manner.
To rove; roam. 8. To extend or proceed: The shot *ranged*
the right. 9. To exhibit variation within specified limits.
0. To lie in the same direction, line, etc. [< OF < *ranc* row]
nge finder An instrument for determining the distance
an object from a given point.
ng·er (rän/jər) n. 1. One who or that which ranges; a
ver. 2. One of an armed band designed to protect large
acts of country. 3. One of a herd of cattle that feeds on a
nge. 4. *U.S.* A warden employed in patrolling forest
acts. — **ranger·ship** n.
ng·er (rän/jər) n. One of a select group of U.S. soldiers
ained for raiding action on enemy territory.
ng·y (rän/jē) adj. **rang·i·er, rang·i·est** 1. Disposed to
am, or adapted for roving, as cattle. 2. Having long,
ender limbs, as a person. 3. Affording wide range; roomy.
Resembling a mountain range.
ni (rä/nē) n. 1. The wife of a raja or prince. 2. A reign-
g Hindu queen or princess. Also spelled **ra'nee.** [< Hind. <
kt. *rājni*, fem. of *rajan* king]
nk¹ (rangk) n. 1. A series of objects ranged in a line
row; a range. 2. Degree of official standing, esp. in the
med forces. See table for GRADE. 3. A line of soldiers
awn up side by side in close order. 4. *pl.* An army; also,
e mass of soldiery. 5. Relative position or status; degree;
ade. 6. High degree or position: a lady of *rank.* — **Syn.**
ee CLASS. — v.t. 1. To arrange in a rank or ranks. 2. To
ace in a class, order, etc. 3. To outrank: Sergeants *rank*
rporals. — v.i. 4. To hold a specified place or rank. 5.
o have the highest rank or grade. [< OF *ranc*]
nk² (rangk) adj. 1. Very vigorous and flourishing in
owth, as vegetation. 2. Strong and disagreeable to the
ste or smell. 3. Utter; complete: *rank* injustice. 4. Pro-
ucing a luxuriant growth; fertile. [OE *ranc* strong] —
ank/ly adv. — **rank/ness** n.

rank and file 1. The common soldiers of an army, including
all from the corporals downward. 2. Those who form the
bulk of any organization, as distinct from officers or leaders.
rank·ing (rangk/ing) adj. Superior in rank; taking precedence over others in the same category: a *ranking* senator.
ran·kle (rang/kəl) v. **·kled, ·kling** v.i. 1. To cause continued resentment: The defeat *rankles* in his breast. 2. To become irritated or inflamed; fester. — v.t. 3. To irritate;
embitter. [< OF *rancler* to fester]
ran·sack (ran/sak) v.t. 1. To search through every part of.
2. To search throughout for plunder; pillage. [< ON *rann-
saka* to search a house] — **ran/sack·er** n.
ran·som (ran/səm) v.t. 1. To secure the release of (a person, property, etc.) for a required price, as from captivity or
detention. 2. To set free on payment of ransom. — n. 1.
The payment for the release of a person or property detained. 2. Release purchased. [< OF < L *re-* back +
emere to buy] — **ran/som·er** n.
rant (rant) v.i. 1. To speak in loud, violent, or extravagant
language; rave. — v.t. 2. To utter in a ranting manner. —
n. Bombastic talk. [< MDu. *ranten* rave] — **rant/er** n.
rap¹ (rap) v. **rapped, rap·ping** v.t. 1. To strike sharply and
quickly; hit. 2. To utter in a sharp manner: with *out.*
3. *Slang* To criticize severely. — v.i. 4. To strike sharp,
quick blows. 5. *Slang* To have a frank discussion; talk.
— n. 1. A sharp blow. 2. A sound caused by or as by
knocking. 3. *Slang* A charge of wrongdoing; blame.
4. *Slang* A talk; discussion. [ME, prob. imit.] — **rap/per** n.
rap² (rap) n. The least bit: I don't care a *rap.* [< RAPT]
ra·pa·cious (rə·pā/shəs) adj. 1. Given to plunder or rapine.
2. Grasping; greedy. 3. Subsisting on prey seized alive, as
hawks, etc. [< L *rapere* to seize] — **ra·pa/cious·ly** adv. —
ra·pa/cious·ness n. — **ra·pac/i·ty** (-pas/ə·tē) n.
rape¹ (rāp) v. **raped, rap·ing** v.t. 1. To commit rape upon;
ravish. 2. *Archaic* To carry off by force. — n. 1. The forcible and unlawful carnal knowledge of a woman against her
will. 2. *Archaic* A capturing or snatching away by force.
[< AF < L *rapere* to seize] — **rap/ist** n.
rape² (rāp) n. A plant related to the cabbage, grown as a
forage crop for sheep and hogs, and having seeds that yield
rape oil. [< L *rapum* turnip]
rape oil An oil obtained from rapeseed, and used as a lubri-
cant, etc.: also called *colza oil.*
rape·seed (rāp/sēd/) n. The seed of the rape.
Raph·a·el (raf/ē·əl, rā/fē-) One of the archangels.
rap·id (rap/id) adj. 1. Having or moving with great speed;
swift. 2. Characterized by rapidity: a *rapid* style. 3. Done
or completed in a short time: *rapid* growth. — **Syn.** See
SWIFT¹. — n. *Usu. pl.* A swift-running descent in a river.
[< L *rapere* to seize, rush] — **ra·pid·i·ty** (rə·pid/ə·tē) n. —
rap/id·ly adv. — **rap/id·ness** n.
rapid eye movement Rapid movement of the closed eyes
during sleep, associated with dreaming and a characteristic
pattern of electrical activity of the brain. Also REM.
rap·id-fire (rap/id·fīr/) adj. 1. Firing or designed for firing
shots in rapid succession. 2. Characterized by speed.
ra·pi·er (rā/pē·ər, rāp/yər) n. 1. A long, straight, two-edged
sword with a large cup hilt, used for dueling, chiefly for
thrusting. 2. A shorter straight sword without cutting edge
and therefore used for thrusting only. [< MF *rapière*]
rap·ine (rap/in) n. The taking of property by force, as in
war; spoliation; pillage. [< OF < L *rapere* to seize]
rap·port (ra·pôr/, -pōr/) n. Harmony or sympathy of relation; agreement; accord. — **en rapport** (äṅ rȧ·pôr/)
French In close accord. [< F *rapporter* to bring back]
rap·proche·ment (rȧ·prôsh·mäṅ/) n. *French* A state of
harmony or reconciliation; restoration of cordial relations.
rap·scal·lion (rap·skal/yən) n. A rogue; scamp; rascal. [<
earlier *rascallion*, extension of RASCAL]
rapt (rapt) adj. 1. Carried away with lofty emotion; enrap-
tured; transported. 2. Engrossed; intent; deeply engaged.
[< L < *rapere* to seize]
rap·to·ri·al (rap·tôr/ē·əl, -tō/rē-) adj. 1. Seizing and devouring living prey; predatory. 2. Having talons adapted for
seizing prey: said esp. of hawks, vultures, eagles, and other
carnivorous birds. [< L < *rapere* to seize]
rap·ture (rap/chər) n. 1. The state of being rapt or transported; ecstatic joy; ecstasy. 2. *Often pl.* An act or expression of excessive delight. — v.t. **·tured, ·tur·ing** *Poetic* To
enrapture. [< RAPT] — **rap/tur·ous** adj. — **rap/tur·ous·**
ly adv. — **rap/tur·ous·ness** n.
rare¹ (râr) adj. **rar·er, rar·est** 1. Infrequent in occurrence,
distribution, etc. 2. Highly esteemed because of infrequency or uncommonness. 3. Rarefied: now said chiefly of the
atmosphere, etc. [< L *rarus* rare] — **rare/ness** n.
— **Syn.** 1. scarce, unusual, exceptional. See OBSOLETE.
rare² (râr) adj. Not thoroughly cooked, as roasted or broiled
meat retaining its redness and juices. [OE *hrēre*]

rare·bit (râr′bit) *n.* Welsh rabbit.

rare earth *Chem.* Any of the metallic oxides of the lanthanide series of elements.

rare-earth element (râr′ûrth′) *Chem.* Any of a group of metallic elements constituting the lanthanide series. Also **rare-earth metals.**

rar·e·fy (râr′ə·fī) *v.* **-fied, -fy·ing** *v.t.* **1.** To make rare, thin, less solid, or less dense. **2.** To refine or purify. — *v.i.* **3.** To become rare, thin, or less solid. **4.** To become pure. [< F < L < *rarus* rare + *facere* to make] — **rar′e·fac′tion** (-fak′shən) *n.* — **rar′e·fac′tive** *adj.* — **rar′e·fi′a·ble** *adj.*

rare·ly (râr′lē) *adv.* **1.** Not often; infrequently. **2.** With unusual excellence or effect; finely **3.** Exceptionally.

rar·ing (râr′ing) *adj.* *U.S. Informal* Extremely eager or enthusiastic. [< Pres. part. of *rare,* dial. of REAR²]

rar·i·ty (râr′ə·tē) *n.* *pl.* **-ties 1.** That which is exceptionally valued because of scarceness. **2.** The state of being rare.

ras·cal (ras′kəl) *n.* An unprincipled fellow; rogue; knave: sometimes used playfully. — *adj. Obs.* Base; mean. [< OF, ult. < L *radere* to scratch] — **ras·cal′i·ty** (-kal′ə·tē) *n.* — **ras′cal·ly** *adj. & adv.*

rase (rāz) *v.t.* **rased, ras·ing** To raze.

rash¹ (rash) *adj.* **1.** Acting without due caution or regard of consequences; reckless. **2.** Exhibiting recklessness or precipitancy. [Prob. < MLG < OHG *rasc* lively] — **rash′ly** *adv.* — **rash′ness** *n.*

rash² (rash) *n.* A superficial eruption of the skin, often localized. [< OF, ult. < L *radere* to scratch]

rash·er (rash′ər) *n.* A thin slice of meat, esp. bacon.

rasp (rasp, räsp) *n.* **1.** A file having coarse pyramidal projections for abrasion. **2.** The act or sound of rasping. — *v.t.* **1.** To scrape or rub with or as with a rasp. **2.** To affect unpleasantly; irritate. **3.** To utter in a rough voice. — *v.i.* **4.** To grate; scrape. **5.** To make a rough, harsh sound. [< OF *rasper* to scrape] — **rasp′er** *n.* — **ras′py** *adj.*

rasp·ber·ry (raz′ber′ē, -bər·ē, räz′-) *n. pl.* **-ries 1.** The round fruit of certain brambles of the rose family, composed of drupes clustered around a fleshy receptable. **2.** Any plant yielding this fruit. **3.** *Slang* A Bronx cheer: also spelled *razzberry.* [< earlier *raspis* (berry)]

rat (rat) *n.* **1.** A destructive and injurious rodent of worldwide distribution, larger and more aggressive than the mouse. **2.** *Slang* A cowardly or selfish person who deserts or betrays his associates. **3.** A pad over which a woman's hair is combed to give a coiffure body. — **to smell a rat** To suspect that something is wrong. — *v.i.* **rat·ted, rat·ting 1.** To hunt rats. **2.** *Slang* To desert one's party, etc. **3.** *Slang* To inform; betray: with *on.* [OE *ræt*]

rat·a·ble (rā′tə·bəl) *adj.* **1.** *Brit.* Legally liable to taxation. **2.** Estimated proportionally; pro rata: a *ratable* distribution. **3.** That may be rated or valued. Also **rate′a·ble.** — **rat′a·bil′i·ty, rat′a·ble·ness** *n.* — **rat′a·bly** *adv.*

ra·tan (ra·tan′) See RATTAN.

ratch·et (rach′it) *n.* **1.** A mechanism consisting of a notched wheel, the teeth of which engage with a pawl, permitting motion of the wheel in one direction only. **2.** The pawl or the wheel thus used. Also **ratchet wheel.** [< F *rochet* bobbin]

rate¹ (rāt) *n.* **1.** The measure of a variable in relation to some fixed unit: a *rate* of 5 miles per hour. **2.** Degree of value; price; also, the unit cost of a commodity or service. **3.** Comparative rank or class. **4.** *Brit.* A local tax on property. **5.** Proportion, as of an incidence, to some fixed number of cases: the death *rate* per 100,000 adults. **6.** A fixed allowance, amount, or ratio. — **at any rate** In any case; anyhow. — *v.* **rat·ed, rat·ing** *v.t.* **1.** To estimate the value or worth of; appraise. **2.** To place in a certain rank or grade. **3.** To consider; regard. **4.** To fix the rate for the transportation of (goods), as by rail. **5.** *Informal* To deserve. — *v.i.* **6.** To have rank, rating, or value. **7.** *Informal* To stand in comparison with others. [< OF < L < *reri* to calculate] — **rat′er** *n.*

rate² (rāt) *v.t. & v.i.* **rat·ed, rat·ing** To reprove with vehemence; rail at.

rath·er (rath′ər, rä′thər) *adv.* **1.** More willingly. **2.** With more reason, justice, wisdom, etc. **3.** More precisely, strictly, or accurately. **4.** Somewhat; in a greater or less degree: *rather* cold. **5.** On the contrary. **6.** *Brit.* Yes indeed! ◆ Both *had rather* and *would rather* are acceptable forms. [OE *hrathor,* compar. of *hrathe* soon, quickly]

raths·kel·ler (rath′skel·ər, räts′kel·ər) *n.* A beer hall or similar restaurant, usu. located in a cellar. [< G *rat* council, town hall + *keller* cellar]

rat·i·fy (rat′ə·fī) *v.t.* **-fied, -fy·ing** To give sanction to, esp. official sanction; confirm. [< OF < Med.L < L *ratus* fixed, calculated + *facere* to make] — **rat′i·fi·ca′tion** (-fə·kā′shən) *n.* — **rat′i·fi′er** *n.*

— **Syn.** The U.S. Senate *ratifies* a proposed treaty; Congress *confirms* Presidential appointments; notarization *validates* a bill of sale. These words are chiefly used of governmental process.

rat·i·ne (rat·ə·nā′) *n.* A heavy, loosely woven fabric with a nubby surface. [< F < *ratiner* to make nubby]

rat·ing (rā′ting) *n.* **1.** Classification according to a standard; grade; rank; status. **2.** An evaluation of the financial standing of a business firm or an individual. **3.** Any specialist grade held by an enlisted man or officer: the *rating* of in the Air Force.

ra·tio (rā′shō, -shē·ō) *n. pl.* **-tios 1.** Relation of degree, number, etc.; proportion; rate. **2.** The relation of two quantities, esp. the quotient of the first divided by the second: ratio of 3 to 5 is expressed as 3 : 5 or ⅗. [< L *reri* to think]

ra·ti·oc·i·nate (rash′ē·os′ə·nāt) *v.i.* **-nat·ed, -nat·ing** make a deduction from premises; reason. [< L *reri* to think] — **ra′ti·oc′i·na′tion** *n.* — **ra′ti·oc′i·na′tive** *adj.* — **ra′ti·oc′i·na′tor** *n.*

ra·tion (rash′ən, rā′shən) *n.* **1.** A portion; share. **2.** A fixed allowance or portion of food, etc., allotted in time of scarcity. **3.** *Mil.* Food for one person for one day. — *v.t.* **1.** To issue rations to, as an army. **2.** To give out or allot rations. **3.** To restrict to limited rations. [< F < L *ratio, -onis*] — **ra′tion·ing** *n.*

ra·tion·al (rash′ən·əl) *adj.* **1.** Possessing the faculty of reasoning. **2.** Having full possession of one's mental faculties; sane. **3.** Conformable to reason; judicious; sensible. **4.** Attained by reasoning. **5.** *Math.* Denoting an algebraic expression containing no variables within irreducible radicals. [See RATIO.] — **ra′tion·al′i·ty** (rash′ən·al′ə·tē) *n.* — **ra′tion·al·ly** *adv.* — **ra′tion·al·ness** *n.*

ra·tion·ale (rash′ən·al′, -ä′lē, -ä′lē) *n.* **1.** The rational or logical basis of something. **2.** A rational explanation of principles.

ra·tion·al·ism (rash′ən·əl·iz′əm) *n.* **1.** The formation of opinions by reason alone, independently of authority or revelation. **2.** *Philos.* The theory that truth and knowledge are attainable through reason rather than by empirical means. — **ra′tion·al·ist** *n.* — **ra′tion·al·is′tic** or **-ti·cal** *adj.* — **ra′tion·al·is′ti·cal·ly** *adv.*

ra·tion·al·ize (rash′ən·əl·īz′) *v.* **-ized, -iz·ing** *v.t.* **1.** *Psychol.* To explain or base (one's behavior) on grounds ostensibly rational but not in accord with the actual or unconscious motives. **2.** To explain or treat from a rationalistic point of view. **3.** To make rational or reasonable. — *v.i.* **4.** To think in a rational or rationalistic manner. Also *Brit.* **ra′tion·al·ise′.** — **ra′tion·al·i·za·tion** (rash′ən·əl·ə·zā′shən or -ī·zā′shən) *n.* — **ra′tion·al·iz′er** *n.*

rat·ite (rat′īt) *adj.* Designating a group of flightless birds including ostriches, cassowaries, kiwis, emus, etc. — *n.* A ratite bird. [< L *ratis* raft + -ITE¹]

rat·line (rat′lin) *n.* *Naut.* **1.** One of the small ropes fastened across the shrouds of a ship, used as a ladder for going aloft or descending. **2.** The rope so used. Also **rat′lin** (-lin). [Origin unknown]

RA·TO (rā′tō) *n.* An airplane takeoff assisted by an auxiliary rocket motor or unit; also, the rocket motor or unit used. Also **ra′to.** [< r(ocket) + a(ssisted) + t(ake)o(ff)]

rat race *Slang* A frantic, usu. fruitless, struggle.

rats·bane (rats′bān′) *n.* Rat poison.

rat's nest *Informal* A cluttered and messy place.

rat·tan (ra·tan′) *n.* **1.** The long, tough, flexible stem of various tropical palms, used in making wickerwork, light furniture, etc. **2.** The palm itself. Also spelled **ratan.** [< Malay *rotan*]

rat·ter (rat′ər) *n.* **1.** A dog or cat that catches rats. **2.** *Slang* A deserter; traitor.

rat·tle (rat′l) *v.* **-tled, -tling** *v.i.* **1.** To make a series of noises in rapid succession, as of hard objects striking one another. **2.** To move or act with such noises; also, to make a gurgling sound in the throat. **3.** To talk rapidly and foolishly; chatter. — *v.t.* **4.** To cause to rattle: to *rattle* pennies in a tin cup. **5.** To utter or perform rapidly or noisily. **6.** *Informal* To confuse; disconcert; agitate. — *n.* **1.** A series of short, sharp sounds in rapid succession. **2.** A plaything, implement, etc., made to produce a rattling noise. **3.** Any of the jointed horny rings in the tail of a rattlesnake. **4.** Rapid and noisy talk; chatter. [Imit.]

rat·tle·brain (rat′l·brān′) *n.* A talkative, flighty person; foolish chatterer. Also **rat′tle·head′** (-hed′), **rat′tle·pate′** (-pāt′). — **rat′tle·brained′** *adj.*

rat·tler (rat′lər) *n.* **1.** One who or that which rattles. **2.** A rattlesnake.

rat·tle·snake (rat′l·snāk′) *n.* Any of several venomous American snakes with a tail ending in a series of horny, loosely connected, modified joints, that make a rattling noise when the tail is vibrated.

RATTLESNAKE
(To 8 feet long)

rat·tle·trap (rat′l·trap′) *n.* Any rickety, clattering, or worn-out vehicle or article.

rat·trap (rat′trap′) *n.* **1.** A trap for catching rats. **2.** A hopeless or involved predicament.

rat·ty (rat′ē) *adj.* **-ti·er, -ti·est 1.** Ratlike. **2.** Abounding in rats. **3.** *Slang* Disreputable; shabby.

cous (rô'kəs) *adj.* **1.** Rough in sound; hoarse; harsh. Boisterous; unruly; disorderly. [< L *raucus*] — **rau'·** (-sə·tē), rau'cous·ness *n.* — rau'cous·ly *adv.*

wol·fi·a (rou·wŏŏl'fē·ə) *n.* Any of a genus of tropical s or shrubs, several of which contain alkaloids having able medicinal properties. [after Leonard *Rauwolf*, a c. German botanist]

age (rav'ij) *v.* **·aged, ·ag·ing** *v.t.* **1.** To lay waste, as by aging or burning; despoil. — *v.i.* **2.** To wreak havoc; be ructive. — *n.* Violent and destructive action, or its re-; ruin. [See RAVISH.] — rav'ag·er *n.*

e (rāv) *v.* **raved, rav·ing** *v.i.* **1.** To speak wildly or inco-ently. **2.** To speak with extravagant enthusiasm. **3.** To ke a wild, roaring sound; rage. — *v.t.* **4.** To utter wildly ncoherently. — *n.* The act or state of raving; a frenzy. *dj. Informal* Extravagantly enthusiastic: *rave* reviews. *f raver* to wander, to be delirious]

el (rav'əl) *v.* **rav·eled** or **·elled, rav·el·ing** or **·el·ling** *v.t.* To separate the threads or fibers of; unravel. **2.** To make r or plain; explain: often with *out.* — *v.i.* **3.** To become arated, as threads or fibers; unravel; fray. — *n.* **1.** A ken or rejected thread. **2.** A raveling. [< MDu. *ravelen* angle] — rav'el·er or rav'el·ler *n.*

el·ing (rav'əl·ing) *n.* A thread or threads raveled from bric. Also **rav'el·ling.**

en¹ (rā'vən) *n.* A large, omnivorous, widely distributed ine bird, having lustrous black plumage. — *adj.* Black shining, like a raven. [OE *hræfn*]

en² (rav'ən) *v.t.* **1.** To devour hungrily or greedily. **2.** take by force; ravage. — *v.i.* **3.** To search for prey or der. **4.** To eat voraciously. — *n.* The act of plunder-spoliation; pillage. [< OF *raviner* < L *rapina* < *rapere* eize] — rav'en·er *n.*

en (rā'vən) *n.* The constellation Corvus.

en·ing (rav'ən·ing) *adj.* **1.** Seeking eagerly for prey; cious. **2.** Devouring; voracious. **3.** Mad.

en·ous (rav'ən·əs) *adj.* **1.** Violently voracious or hun-**2.** Extremely eager for gratification. [See RAVEN².]

av'en·ous·ly *adv.* — rav'en·ous·ness *n.*

ine (rə·vēn') *n.* A deep gorge or gully, esp. one worn by ow of water. [< F]

ing (rā'ving) *adj.* **1.** Furious; delirious; frenzied. **2.** *rmal* Outstandingly attractive: a *raving* beauty. — *n.* rious, incoherent, or irrational utterance.

lo·li (rä·vyō'lē, rä'vē·ō'lē, rav'ē-) *n.pl.* Little envelopes ough for encasing meat or cheese, boiled, and often served tomato sauce. [< Ital. pl. of *raviolo* little turnip]

ish (rav'ish) *v.t.* **1.** To fill with strong emotion, esp. de-t; enrapture. **2.** To commit a rape upon. **3.** *Archaic* seize and carry off by force. [< OF < L *rapere* to seize] av'ish·er *n.* — rav'ish·ment *n.*

ish·ing (rav'ish·ing) *adj.* Filling with delight; enchant-— rav'ish·ing·ly *adv.*

(rô) *adj.* **1.** Not changed or prepared by cooking; un-ked. **2.** Having the skin irritated or abraded. **3.** Bleak; ling: a *raw* wind. **4.** In a natural state; crude. **5.** Newly e; fresh: *raw* paint, *raw* work. **6.** Inexperienced; un-iplined. **7.** Obscene; coarse; off-color. **8.** Harshly un-; ruthless. — *n.* A sore or abraded spot: with *the.* — **in raw 1.** In a raw, unrefined, or untempered state. **2.**

U.S. Informal Naked; nude. [OE *hrēaw.*] — raw'ly *adv.* — raw'ness *n.*

raw·boned (rô'bônd') *adj.* Bony; gaunt.

raw·hide (rô'hīd') *n.* **1.** A hide dressed without tanning. **2.** A whip made of such hide.

ray¹ (rā) *n.* **1.** A narrow beam of light. **2.** Anything repre-senting or suggesting this. **3.** A slight manifestation; glim-mer; hint. **4.** *Geom.* One of several straight lines emerging from a point and unlimited in one direction. **5.** *Zool.* **a** One of the rods supporting the membrane of a fish's fin. **b** One of the radiating parts of a radiate animal, as a starfish. **6.** *Bot.* A ray flower. **7.** *Physics* **a** A line of propagation of any form of radiant energy. **b** A stream of particles spontaneous-ly emitted by a radioactive substance. — *v.i.* **1.** To emit rays; shine. **2.** To issue forth as rays; radiate. — *v.t.* **3.** To send forth as rays. **4.** To mark with rays or radiating lines. **5.** To treat with X-rays, etc. [< OF < L *radius* rod]

ray² (rā) *n.* Any of various fishes having a flattened body with expanded pectoral fins and gill openings on the lower surface. [< OF < L *raia*]

ray flower *Bot.* Any of the flat marginal flowers surround-ing the disk, as the daisy or sunflower. Also **ray floret.**

ray·on (rā'on) *n.* **1.** A synthetic fiber produced from cellu-lose, the material being forced through fine jets to produce threadlike filaments. **2.** A fabric made from such fibers. [Coined from RAY¹; prob. infl. by F *rayon* ray]

raze (rāz) *v.t.* **razed, raz·ing 1.** To demolish, as a building. **2.** *Rare* To scrape or shave off. Also spelled *rase.* — **Syn.** See DEMOLISH. [< OF < L *radere* to scrape]

ra·zor (rā'zər) *n.* A sharp cutting implement used for shav-ing off the beard or hair, etc. [< OF < LL *rasorium* scraper]

ra·zor·back (rā'zər·bak') *n.* **1.** The rorqual, a whale. **2.** A lean, long-legged, half-wild hog, common in the southeastern U.S. **3.** A hill with a sharp, narrow ridge.

razor blade A thin, metal blade, having either one or two sharpened edges, inserted in a safety razor.

razz (saz) *Slang n.* A Bronx cheer. — *v.t.* To heckle; de-ride. [< RAZZBERRY]

razz·ber·ry (raz'ber'ē, -bər·ē, räz'-) *n. pl.* **·ries** *U.S. Slang* A Bronx cheer. [< RASPBERRY]

raz·zle-daz·zle (raz'əl·daz'əl) *n. U.S. Slang* Bewildering, exciting, or dazzling activity or performance. Also **razz·ma·tazz** (raz'mə·taz'). [Varied reduplication of DAZZLE]

re¹ (rā) *n. Music* The second of the syllables used in solmi-zation; the second degree of a major scale; also, the tone D. [< L *re(sonare)*. See GAMUT.]

re² (rē) *prep.* Concerning; about; in the matter of: used in business letters, law, etc. [< L, ablative of *res* thing]

re- *prefix* **1.** Back: *rebound, remit.* **2.** Again; anew; again and again. [< L *re-, red-* back, again]

◆ Sense 2 of *re-* is freely used in forming words, particu-larly verbs or words derived from verbs. Some words thus formed are hyphenated to prevent confusion with similarly spelled words, as *recoil,* to spring back, and *re-coil,* to coil again, but in current usage most other words using *re-* as a prefix are written solid. However, many writers still prefer to hyphenate some combinations of *re-* and a word beginning with a vowel, especially *e.*

A list of self-explanatory words containing the prefix *re-* (def. 2) appears below.

andon	reappointment	reblossom	recondense	rediscover	reengage
sorb	reapportion	reboil	reconduct	rediscovery	reengagement
sorption	reapportionment	reborn	reconfirm	redissolve	reengrave
cept	reargue	rebuild	reconquer	redistill	reenjoy
commodate	reargument	rebuilt	reconquest	redistribute	reenjoyment
company	reascend	rebury	reconsecrate	redivide	reenkindle
cuse	reascension	recapitalize	reconsolidate	redivision	reenlist
quire	reascent	recarry	reconvene	redo	reenlistment
apt	reassemble	recelebrate	recopy	redraw	reenslave
dress	reassembly	rechallenge	recoronation	redrive	reenter
journ	reassert	rechange	recross	redry	reentrance
journment	reassertion	recharge	recrown	redye	reerect
just	reassign	recharter	recrystallization	reecho	reestablish
justment	reassimilate	recheck	recrystallize	reedit	reestablishment
mission	reassimilation	rechoose	recultivate	reelect	reexamination
mit	reassociate	rechristen	recultivation	reelection	reexamine
opt	reassume	recircle	rededicate	reelevate	reexchange
orn	reassumption	recirculate	rededication	reembark	reexhibit
vance	reattach	reclasp	redefeat	reembody	reexpel
irm	reattack	reclean	redefine	reembrace	reexperience
irmation	reattain	reclothe	redemand	reemerge	reexport
ign	reattempt	recoin	redemonstrate	reemergence	reexpulsion
ignment	reavow	recoinage	redeny	reemigrate	reface
nex	reawake	recolonize	redeposit	reenact	refashion
noint	reawaken	recolor	redescend	reenaction	refasten
pear	rebaptism	recombine	redescent	reenactment	refertilize
pearance	rebaptize	recombination	redescribe	reencourage	refire
ply	rebind	recommence	redetermine	reencouragement	reflow
point	rebloom	recommission	redigest	reendow	reflower

reach (rēch) *v.t.* **1.** To stretch out or forth, as the hand; extend. **2.** To present or hand over. **3.** To be able to touch or grasp: *Can you reach the top shelf?* **4.** To arrive at or come to by motion or progress. **5.** To achieve communication with; gain access to. **6.** To amount to; total. **7.** To strike or hit, as with a blow or missile. — *v.i.* **8.** To stretch the hand, foot, etc., out or forth. **9.** To attempt to touch or grasp something: *He reached for his wallet.* **10.** To have extent in space, time, etc.: *The ladder reached to the ceiling.* **11.** *Naut.* To sail on a tack with the wind on or forward of the beam. — *n.* **1.** The act or power of reaching. **2.** The distance one is able to reach, as with the hand, an instrument, or missile. **3.** Extent of thought, influence, etc.; scope; range. **4.** An unbroken stretch, as of a stream; a vista or expanse. **5.** *Naut.* The sailing, or the distance sailed, by a vessel on one tack. [OE *rǣcan*] — **reach′er** *n.*

re·act (rē·akt′) *v.i.* **1.** To act in response, as to a stimulus. **2.** To act in a manner contrary to some preceding act. **3.** *Physics* To exert an opposite and equal force on an acting or impinging body. **4.** *Chem.* To undergo a reaction.

re·act (rē·akt′) *v.t.* To act again.

re·act·ance (rē·ak′təns) *n. Electr.* In a circuit, the opposition to an alternating current caused by inductance and capacitance.

re·ac·tion (rē·ak′shən) *n.* **1.** Responsive action, attitude, etc. **2.** Tendency toward a former state of things; esp., a trend toward an earlier social, political, or economic policy or condition. **3.** The action of a muscle, nerve, organ, etc., in response to a stimulus; reflex action. **4.** *Psychol.* A response to an experience, situation, influence, etc. **5.** *Physics* **a** The equal and opposite force exerted on an agent by the body acted upon. **b** A nuclear reaction. **6.** *Chem.* The reciprocal action of substances subjected to chemical change. **7.** *Med.* The effect upon an organism of any foreign substance introduced for therapeutic purposes, or for testing, immunizing, etc.

re·ac·tion·ar·y (rē·ak′shən·er′ē) *adj.* Pertaining to, favoring, or characterized by reaction (def. 2). — *n. pl.* **·ar·ies** One who favors political or social reaction; one hostile toward change or progress. Also **re·ac′tion·ist.**

re·ac·ti·vate (rē·ak′tə·vāt) *v.t.* **·vat·ed, ·vat·ing** To make active or effective again. — **re·ac′ti·va′tion** *n.*

re·ac·tive (rē·ak′tiv) *adj.* **1.** Reacting or tending to react. **2.** Resulting from reaction. **3.** Responsive to a stimulus.

re·ac·tiv·i·ty (rē′ak·tiv′ə·tē) *n.* **1.** The state or quality of being reactive. **2.** *Chem.* The relative tendency of an element to enter into chemical reactions.

re·ac·tor (rē·ak′tər) *n.* **1.** One who or that which reacts. **2.** *Electr.* A device for introducing reactance into a circuit, as for starting motors, controlling current, etc. **3.** *Physics* Any of various assemblies for the generation and control of atomic energy: formerly called *pile.*

read (*v. & n.* rēd; *adj.* red) *v.* **read** (red), **read·ing** (rē′ding) *v.t.* **1.** To apprehend the meaning of (a book, writing, etc.) by perceiving the form and relation of the printed or written characters. **2.** To utter aloud (something printed or written). **3.** To understand the significance, intent, etc., as if by reading: *to read the sky.* **4.** To apprehend the mea of something written in (a foreign language). **5.** To ma study of: *to read law.* **6.** To discover the true nature person, character, etc.) by observation or scrutiny. **7.** interpret (something read) in a specified manner. **8.** take as the meaning of something read. **9.** To have wording: *The passage reads "principal,"* not *"princi* **10.** To indicate or register, as an instrument or device. To bring into a specified condition by reading: *I read h sleep.* — *v.i.* **12.** To apprehend written or printed ch ters, as of words, music, etc. **13.** To utter aloud the w or contents of a book, etc. **14.** To gain information by a ing: with *of* or *about.* **15.** To learn by means of books; st **16.** To have a specified wording: *How does the con read?* **17.** To admit of being read in a specified manner first verse *reads* well. **18.** To have the quality of a spe style or manner of writing: *His work reads* like poetry. To give a public reading or recital. — **to read betwee lines** To perceive or infer what is not expressed or obv — **to read out** **1.** To read aloud. **2.** To expel from a gious body, political party, etc., by proclamation or certed action. — **to read up** (or **up on**) To learn by rea — *adj.* Informed by books: well *read.* [OE *rǣdan* to rea

read·a·ble (rē′də·bəl) *adj.* **1.** Legible. **2.** Interesti enjoyable to read. — **read′a·bil′i·ty, read′a·ble·ness** *n* **read′a·bly** *adv.*

read·er (rē′dər) *n.* **1.** One who reads. **2.** A profession citer. **3.** One who reads and criticizes manuscripts of to publishers. **4.** A textbook containing exercises in rea **5.** *Eccl.* A church functionary authorized to read in ch services.

read·ing (rē′ding) *n.* **1.** The act or practice of one reads. **2.** A public or formal recital of something wr **3.** Literary research; study; scholarship. **4.** Matter th read or is designed to be read. **5.** The indication of a m dial, graduated instrument, etc. **6.** The form in which passage or word appears in any copy of a work. **7.** A cific interpretation. — *adj.* **1.** Pertaining to or suitab reading. **2.** Of or pertaining to a reader or readers.

read·y (red′ē) *adj.* **read·i·er, read·i·est** **1.** Prepared fo or action. **2.** Prepared in mind; willing. **3.** Likely or li with *to: ready to sink.* **4.** Quick to act, follow, occur, o pear; prompt. **5.** Immediately available or at hand; venient; handy. **6.** Designating the standard positi which a rifle is held just before aiming. **7.** Quick to per or understand; alert; facile: *a ready wit.* — *n.* The pos in which a rifle is held before aiming. — *v.t.* **read·ied,** *i* **y·ing** To make ready; prepare. [ME < OE *rǣde, gerǣ ig,* suffix of adverbs] — **read′i·ly** *adv.* — **read′i·ness** *i*

read·y-made (red′ē·mād′) *adj.* **1.** Not made to order: pared or kept on hand for general demand: said especia clothing. **2.** Prepared beforehand; not impromptu.

read·y-mix (red′ē·miks) *adj. U.S.* Ready to use after ing liquid, etc.: *ready-mix* pancake flour.

ready money Money on hand; cash.

read·y-to-wear (red′ē·tə·wâr′) *adj.* Ready-made: sa clothing.

refold	reinaugurate	reinvite	renavigate	repurify	restrive
reforge	reincite	reinvolve	renominate	repursue	restudy
reformulate	reincorporate	rejudge	renomination	requicken	resubject
refortification	reincur	rekindle	renotify	reradiate	resubjecti
refortify	reinduce	relabel	renumber	reread	resummon
reframe	reinfect	relace	reobtain	rerecord	resummon
refreeze	reinfection	relaunch	reobtainable	rerise	resupply
refuel	reinflame	relaunder	reoccupation	reroll	resurvey
refurnish	reinform	relearn	reoccupy	reroute	reteach
regather	reinfuse	relight	reoccur	resaddle	retell
regear	reinhabit	reline	reoccurrence	resail	retest
regerminate	reinoculate	reliquidate	reopen	resalute	retie
regermination	reinoculation	reliquidation	reoppose	reseal	retranslat
regild	reinscribe	relive	reordain	reseed	retraverse
reglaze	reinsert	reload	reordination	reseek	retrim
reglorify	reinsertion	reloan	repacify	resegregate	retype
reglue	reinspect	relocate	repack	reseize	reuse
regrade	reinspection	relocation	repaint	reseizure	reutilize
regraft	reinspire	remade	repaper	resell	reutter
regrant	reinstall	remake	repass	resend	revaluate
regroup	reinstruct	remanufacture	repave	resettle	revalue
rehandle	reintegrate	remarriage	repenalize	resettlement	revarnish
rehear	reintegration	remarry	replant	reshape	reverificat
rehearing	reinter	rematch	replantation	resharpen	reverify
reheat	reinterment	remeasure	replay	reshuffle	revictual
reheel	reinterrogate	remelt	repledge	resift	revictualm
rehire	reintrench	remerge	replunge	resolder	revindicat
reignite	reintroduce	remigrate	repolish	resolidify	revindicat
reimplant	reintroduction	remigration	repopulate	resow	revisit
reimpose	reinundate	remilitarization	repopulation	respread	revitalize
reimposition	reinvent	remilitarize	repour	restack	rewarm
reimpregnate	reinvest	remix	reprocess	restipulate	rewash
reimpress	reinvestigate	remodification	reproclaim	restipulation	reweigh
reimprint	reinvestigation	remodify	republication	restrengthen	rewin
reimprison	reinvigorate	remold	republish	restrike	rewind
reimprisonment	reinvigoration	rename	repurchase	restring	rework

·gent (rē·ā′jənt) *n. Chem.* Any substance used to ascertain the nature or composition of another by means of their procal chemical action. [< RE- + AGENT]

¹ (rēl, rē′əl) *adj.* **1.** Having existence or actuality as a ng or state; not imaginary: a *real* event. **2.** Not artificial ounterfeit; genuine. **3.** Representing the true or actual, pposed to the apparent or ostensible: the *real* reason. **4.** affected; unpretentious: a *real* person. **5.** *Philos.* Having ual existence. **6.** *Law* Pertaining to property regarded as novable or pérmanent, as land or tenements: distinshed from *personal.* — *adv. Informal* Very; extremely: e *real* glad. [< OF < LL *realis* < L *res* thing] — **real**′. **s** *n.*

¹² (rē′əl, *Sp.* rā·äl′) *n. pl.* **re·als** or **re·a·les** (rā·ä′lās) *for 1*, **reis** (rās) *for def.* 2 **1.** A former small silver coin of in and various Latin-American countries. **2.** A former tuguese and Brazilian coin. [< Sp., lit., royal]

estate Land, including whatever is made part of or atned to it by man or nature, as trees, houses, etc. — **real**-**ate** (rēl′ə·stāt′, rē′əl-) *adj.*

·ism (rē′əl·iz′əm) *n.* **1.** The tendency to be concerned n and act in accordance with actual facts rather than ls, feelings, etc. **2.** In literature and art, the treatment abject matter in conformance with nature or real life and nout idealization: opposed to *idealism.* **3.** *Philos.* **a** The trine that abstract concepts have objective existence and more real than concrete objects: opposed to *nominalism.* he doctrine that things have reality apart from the conus perception of them. — **re′al·ist** *n.* — **re′al·is′tic** *adj.* **e·al·is′ti·cal·ly** *adv.*

·i·ty (rē·al′ə·tē) *n. pl.* **·ties 1.** The fact, state, or quali-f being real or genuine. **2.** That which is real; an actual ng, situation, or event. **3.** The sum or totality of real gs. **4.** *Philos.* The absolute or ultimate, as contrasted n the apparent. [< Med.L < L *realis* real]

·ize (rē′əl·īz, rē′liz) *v.* **·ized, ·iz·ing** *v.t.* **1.** To under-d or appreciate fully. **2.** To make real or concrete. **3.** :ause to appear real. **4.** To obtain as a profit or return. 'o obtain money in return for: He *realized* his holdings a profit. — *v.i.* **6.** To sell property for cash. Also *Brit.* **l·ise.** — **re′al·iz′a·ble** *adj.* — **re′al·i·za′tion** *n.*

·life (rē′əl·līf′, rēl′-) *adj. U.S. Informal* Actual; true. **·ly** (rē′ə·lē, rē′lē) *adv.* **1.** In reality; as a matter of fact; ally; indeed. **2.** Honestly; truly: used for emphasis: *lly,* the situation is impossible.

l·ly (rē·ə·lī′) *v.t. & v.i.* **-al·lied, -al·ly·ing** To ally again. **m** (relm) *n.* **1.** A kingdom or domain. **2.** The scope or ge of any power or influence: the *realm* of imagination. **ʌ** primary zoogeographical division of the globe: also ed *region.* [< OF *realme*]

l·tor (rē′əl·tər, -tôr) *n. U.S.* A realty broker who is a nber of the National Association of Real Estate Boards: ade name. Also **re′al·tor.** [< REALTY + -OR¹] **·ty** (rē′əl·tē) *n. pl.* **·ties** *Law* Real estate or real perty in any form. [< REAL¹ (def. 6) + -TY¹]

wages Wages evaluated in terms of purchasing power. **n¹** (rēm) *n.* **1.** A unit of quantity for sheets of paper sisting of twenty quires or 480 sheets (**short ream**), 500 ts (**long ream**), or 516 sheets (**printer's** or **perfect ream**). *l. Informal* A prodigious amount of printed, written, or ken material: *reams* of footnotes. [< OF < Sp. < Ara-*rizmah* bundle]

n² (rēm) *v.t.* **1.** To increase the size of (a hole). **2.** To rge or taper (a hole) with a rotating cutter or reamer. **3.** get rid of (a defect) by reaming. [? OE *ryman* to enlarge] **n·er** (rē′mər) *n.* **1.** One who or that which reams. **2.** nishing tool with a rotating cutting edge for reaming: etimes called *rimmer.* **3.** A device with a ridged cone extracting juice from citrus fruits.

n·i·mate (rē·an′ə·māt) *v.t.* **·mat·ed, ·mat·ing 1.** To ng back to life; resuscitate. **2.** To give renewed strength /igor to; revive. — **re′an·i·ma′tion** *n.*

ɔ (rēp) *v.t.* **1.** To harvest or gather (a crop) with a the, reaper, etc. **2.** To cut the growth from or gather the t of, as a field. **3.** To obtain as the result of action or ef-; receive as a return or result. — *v.i.* **4.** To harvest n, etc. **5.** To receive a return or result. [OE *rēopan,* ɪn] — **reap′a·ble** *adj.*

·er (rē′pər) *n.* **1.** One who reaps. **2.** A reaping machine. **·ing machine** A machine for harvesting nding grain, often equipped with appliances for pressing, dling, and binding the cut grain: also called *harvester.*

¹ (rir) *n.* **1.** The back or hind part. **2.** A place or posi-t behind any person or thing. **3.** The portion of a mili-y force that is last or farthest from the front: opposed to . — *adj.* Being in the rear. [Var. of ARREAR]

² (rir) *v.t.* **1.** To place upright; raise. **2.** To build; :t. **3.** To care for and bring to maturity. **4.** To breed or

grow. — *v.i.* **5.** To rise upon the hind legs, as a horse. **6.** To rise high; tower, as a mountain. [OE *rǣran,* causative of *rīsan* to rise] — **rear′er** *n.*

rear admiral *Naval* A commissioned officer ranking next below a vice admiral. Also *Brit. & Canadian* **rear-ad·mi·ral** (rir′ad′mər·əl). See tables at GRADE.

rear guard A body of troops to protect the rear of an army. **re·arm** (rē·ärm′) *v.t. & v.i.* **1.** To arm again. **2.** To arm with more modern weapons. — **re·ar′ma·ment** *n.*

rear·most (rir′mōst′) *adj.* Coming or stationed last. **re·ar·range** (rē′ə·rānj′) *v.t. & v.i.* **·ranged, ·rang·ing** To arrange again or in some new way. — **re′ar·range′ment** *n.* **rear·ward** (rir′wərd) *adj.* Coming last or toward the rear; hindward. — *adv.* Toward or at the rear; backward: also **rear′wards.** — *n.* Hindward position; the rear; end.

rea·son (rē′zən) *n.* **1.** A motive or cause for an action, belief, thought, etc. **2.** An explanation for or defense of an action, belief, etc.; justification. **3.** The faculty of thinking logically. **4.** Good judgment; common sense. **5.** A normal state of mind; sanity. — **by reason of** Because of. — **in reason** In accordance with reason or good sense. — **it stands to reason** It is logical or reasonable. — **with reason** Justifiably; properly. — *v.i.* **1.** To think logically; obtain inferences or conclusions from known or presumed facts. **2.** To talk or argue logically. — *v.t.* **3.** To think out carefully and logically; analyze: with *out.* **4.** To influence by means of reason; persuade or dissuade. **5.** To argue; debate. [< OF *raison* < L < *reri* to think, reckon] — **rea′son·er** *n.* — **rea′son·less** *adj.*

— **Syn.** (noun) A *reason* seeks to explain or justify an action by citing facts, circumstances, inducement, and the like, together with the workings of the mind upon them. The *purpose* of an action is the effect that it is intended to produce; its *motive* is the inner impulse that sets it in motion and guides it. *Grounds* are the facts, data, etc., that the mind weighs in reaching a decision; and *argument* is the logical demonstration of how these facts and data determine the decision. **3.** See INTELLECT.

rea·son·a·ble (rē′zən·ə·bəl) *adj.* **1.** Conformable to reason; sensible. **2.** Having the faculty of reason; rational. **3.** Governed by reason. **4.** Moderate, as in price; fair. — **rea**′-**son·a·bil′i·ty, rea′son·a·ble·ness** *n.* — **rea′son·a·bly** *adv.*

rea·son·ing (rē′zən·ing) *n.* **1.** The mental process of drawing conclusions from known or presumed facts. **2.** The proofs, data, etc., employed in or resulting from this process. **re·as·sure** (rē′ə·shōōr′) *v.t.* **·sured, ·sur·ing 1.** To restore to courage or confidence. **2.** To assure again. **3.** To reinsure. — **re′as·sur′ance** *n.* — **re′as·sur′ing·ly** *adv.*

re·bate (rē′bāt, ri·bāt′) *v.t.* **·bat·ed, ·bat·ing 1.** To allow as a deduction. **2.** To make a deduction from. **3.** *Obs.* To blunt, as an edge. — *n.* A deduction from a gross amount; discount: also **re·bate′ment.** [< OF *rabattre* to beat down < *re-* again + *abattre.* See ABATE.] — **re′bat·er** *n.*

re·bec (rē′bek) *n.* An early violinlike instrument. Also **re**′. **beck.** [< F, alter. of OF *rebebe* < Arabic *rabāb*] **Re·bec·ca** (ri·bek′ə) In the Bible, the wife of Isaac, and mother of Esau and Jacob. *Gen.* xxiv 15.

re·bel (*v.* ri·bel′; *n. & adj.* reb′əl) *v.i.* **·belled, ·bel·ling 1.** To rise in armed resistance against the established government or ruler of one's land. **2.** To resist any authority or established usage. **3.** To react with violent aversion: usu. with *at.* — *n.* One who rebels. — *adj.* Rebellious; refractory. [< OF < L < *re-* again + *bellare* to make war]

re·bel·lion (ri·bel′yən) *n.* **1.** The act of rebelling. **2.** Organized resistance to a lawful government or authority.

re·bel·lious (ri·bel′yəs) *adj.* **1.** Being in a state of rebellion; insubordinate. **2.** Of or pertaining to a rebel or rebellion. **3.** Resisting control; refractory: *rebellious* curls. — **re·bel′lious·ly** *adv.* — **re·bel′lious·ness** *n.*

re·birth (rē·bûrth′, rē′bûrth′) *n.* **1.** A new birth. **2.** A revival or renaissance.

re·bound (ri·bound′; *for n.,* also rē′bound′) *v.i.* **1.** To bound back; recoil. — *v.t.* **2.** To cause to rebound. — *n.* **1.** Recoil. **2.** Something that rebounds or resounds. **3.** *Informal* Reaction of feeling after a disappointment: to fall in love on the *rebound.* [< F < *re-* back + *bondir* to bound]

re·broad·cast (rē·brôd′kast′, -käst′) *v.t.* **·cast** or **·cast·ed, ·cast·ing 1.** To broadcast (the same program) more than once. **2.** To broadcast (a program received from another station). — *n.* A program so transmitted.

re·buff (ri·buf′) *v.t.* **1.** To reject or refuse abruptly or rudely. **2.** To drive or beat back; repel. — *n.* **1.** A sudden repulse; curt denial. **2.** A sudden check; defeat. **3.** A beating back. [< MF < Ital. *ribuffare* to reprimand]

re·buke (ri·byōōk′) *v.t.* **·buked, ·buk·ing** To reprove sharply; reprimand. — *n.* A strong expression of disapproval. [< AF < OF < *re-* back + *buchier* to beat] — **re·buk′a·ble** *adj.* — **re·buk′er** *n.*

re·bus (rē′bəs) *n. pl.* **·bus·es** A puzzle representing a word, phrase, sentence, etc., by letters, numerals, pictures, etc., whose names have the same sounds as the words represented. [< L, ablative pl. of *res* thing]

re·but (ri·but′) *v.t.* **·but·ted, ·but·ting** To refute by contrary evidence or proof, as in formal argument; disprove. — **Syn.** see REFUTE. [< OF < *re-* back + *bouter* to strike, push] — **re·but′ter** *n.*

re·but·tal (ri·but′l) *n.* The act of rebutting; refutation.

re·cal·ci·trant (ri·kal′sə·trənt) *adj.* Not complying; obstinate; rebellious; refractory. — *n.* One who is recalcitrant. [< L < *re-* back + *calcitrare* to kick < *calx* heel] — **re·cal′ci·trance, re·cal′ci·tran·cy** *n.*

re·call (ri·kôl′; *for n., also* rē′kôl) *v.t.* **1.** To call back; order or summon to return. **2.** To summon back in awareness or attention. **3.** To recollect; remember. **4.** To take back; revoke. — *n.* **1.** A calling back or to mind. **2.** Revocation. **3.** A system whereby officials may be removed from office by popular vote.

re·cant (ri·kant′) *v.t.* **1.** To withdraw formally one's belief in (something previously believed or maintained). — *v.i.* **2.** To disavow an opinion or belief previously held. [< L < *re-* back + *cantare* to sing] — **re·can·ta·tion** (rē′kan·tā′shən) *n.* — **re·cant′er** *n.*

re·cap (*v.* rē′kap′, rē·kap′; *n.* rē′kap′) *v.t.* **·capped, ·cap·ping** To recondition (an automobile tire) by vulcanizing new rubber onto the surface that comes in contact with the road. — *n.* A tire that has been recapped.

re·ca·pit·u·late (rē′kə·pich′ŏō·lāt) *v.t. & v.i.* **·lat·ed, ·lat·ing 1.** To review briefly; sum up. **2.** *Zool.* To reproduce (typical ancestral forms) in the course of embryonic development. [< LL < *re-* again + *capitulare* to draw up in chapters] — **re′ca·pit′u·la′tion** *n.* — **re′ca·pit′u·la′tive** (-lā′-tiv), **re′ca·pit′u·la·to′ry** (-lə·tôr′ē, -tō′rē) *adj.*

re·cap·ture (rē·kap′chər) *v.t.* **·tured, ·tur·ing 1.** To capture again; obtain by recapture. **2.** To recall; remember. — *n.* **1.** The act of retaking. **2.** Anything recaptured.

re·cast (*v.* rē·kast′, -käst′; *n.* rē′kast′, -käst′) *v.t.* **·cast, ·cast·ing 1.** To form anew; cast again. **2.** To fashion anew by changing style, arrangement, etc., as a discourse. **3.** To calculate anew. — *n.* Something that has been recast.

re·cede (ri·sēd′) *v.i.* **·ced·ed, ·ced·ing 1.** To move back, as flood waters. **2.** To withdraw, as from an agreement, etc. **3.** To slope backward: a *receding* forehead. **4.** To become more distant. [< L < *re-* back + *cedere* to go]

re·cede (rē·sēd′) *v.t.* **·ced·ed, ·ced·ing** To cede back.

re·ceipt (ri·sēt′) *n.* **1.** The act or state of receiving anything. **2.** *Usu. pl.* That which is received: cash *receipts*. **3.** A written acknowledgment of the payment of money, of the delivery of goods, etc. **4.** A recipe. — *v.t.* **1.** To give a receipt for the payment of. **2.** To write acknowledgment of payment on, as a bill. [< OF < L < *re-* back + *capere* to take]

re·ceiv·a·ble (ri·sē′və·bəl) *adj.* **1.** Capable of being received; fit to be received, as legal tender. **2.** Maturing for payment: said of a bill. — *n. pl.* Outstanding accounts listed among the assets of a business.

re·ceive (ri·sēv′) *v.* **·ceived, ·ceiv·ing** *v.t.* **1.** To take into one's hand or possession (something given, delivered, etc.); acquire. **2.** To gain knowledge of: He *received* the news at breakfast. **3.** To take from another by hearing or listening: The king *received* his oath of fealty. **4.** To bear; support: These columns *receive* the weight of the building. **5.** To experience; meet with: to *receive* abuse. **6.** To undergo; suffer: He *received* a wound. **7.** To contain; hold. **8.** To allow entrance to; admit; greet. **9.** To accept as true, proven, etc. — *v.i.* **10.** To be a recipient. **11.** To welcome visitors or callers. **12.** *Telecom.* To convert radio waves into some useful form by means of a receiver. [< OF < L < *re-* back + *capere* to take]

— **Syn.** *Receive* has no close synonym; he who *receives* takes what is given and what comes entirely passively. *Acquire* implies an active role, or some effort to obtain; the same is true of *get*, for the most part, but this word is broad enough to include some of the sense of *receive*.

re·ceiv·er (ri·sē′vər) *n.* **1.** One who receives; a recipient. **2.** An official assigned to receive money due. **3.** *Law* A person appointed by a court to take into his custody, control, and management the property or funds of another pending judicial action concerning them. **4.** Something that receives; a receptacle. **5.** *Telecom.* **a** An instrument serving to receive and reproduce signals transmitted from another part of a circuit: a telephone *receiver*. **b** Any of various electronic devices that convert radio waves into audio signals, video signals, etc., or into forms useful as a basis for observation, as in radio telescopes or radar: also **receiving set.**

re·ceiv·er·ship (ri·sē′vər·ship) *n.* **1.** The office and functions pertaining to a receiver under appointment of a court. **2.** The state of being in the hands of a receiver.

re·cent (rē′sənt) *adj.* Pertaining to, or formed, developed, or created in time not long past; modern. [< MF < L *recens*] — **re′cent·ly** *adv.* — **re′cen·cy, re′cent·ness** *n.*

Re·cent (rē′sənt) *adj. Geol.* Pertaining to or designa[...] the present geological epoch, succeeding the Pleistoc[...] See chart for GEOLOGY.

re·cep·ta·cle (ri·sep′tə·kəl) *n.* **1.** Anything that serve[...] contain or hold something else. **2.** *Bot.* The base to w[...] the parts of the flower, fruit, or seeds are fixed. For illus FLOWER. [< L < *re-* back + *capere* to take] — **re·cep[...] u·lar** (rē′sep·tak′yə·lər) *adj.*
— **Syn. 1.** container, repository.

re·cep·tion (ri·sep′shən) *n.* **1.** The act of receiving, or state of being received. **2.** A formal social entertainme[...] guests: a wedding *reception*. **3.** The manner of receivi[...] person or persons: a warm *reception*. **4.** *Telecom.* The a[...] process of receiving, or the quality of reproduction achie[...] [< OF < L < *re-* back + *capere* to take]

re·cep·tion·ist (ri·sep′shən·ist) *n.* One employed to me[...] callers at the entrance to an office.

re·cep·tive (ri·sep′tiv) *adj.* **1.** Able or inclined to rec[...] as truths or impressions. **2.** Able to take in or hold. — **cep′tive·ly** *adv.* — **re·cep·tiv·i·ty** (rē′sep·tiv′ə·tē), **re·** **tive·ness** *n.*

re·cep·tor (ri·sep′tər) *n. Anat.* The terminal structure neuron, specialized to receive stimuli and transmit the[...] the spinal cord and brain. [< OF or L, receiver]

re·cess (*n.* ri·ses′, rē′ses; *for def. 2. usu.* rē′ses; *v.* ri·ses′[...] **1.** A depression or indentation in any otherwise contin[...] line or surface, esp. in a wall; niche. **2.** A time of cess[...] from employment or occupation: The school took a re[...] **3.** *Usu. pl.* A secluded spot; withdrawn or inner place[...] *recesses* of the mind. — *v.t.* **1.** To place in or as in a re[...] **2.** To make a recess in. — *v.i.* **3.** To take a recess. [...] [< *re-* back + *cedere* to go]

re·ces·sion (ri·sesh′ən) *n.* **1.** The act of receding; a w[...] drawal. **2.** The procession of the clergy, choir, etc., a[...] leave the chancel after a church service. **3.** An econ[...] setback in commercial and industrial activity, esp. on[...] curring as a downward turn during a period of generall[...] ing prosperity.

re·ces·sion (rē·sesh′ən) *n.* The act of ceding again; a g[...] back.

re·ces·sion·al (ri·sesh′ən·əl) *adj.* Of or pertaining to r[...] sion. — *n.* A hymn sung as the choir or clergy leav[...] chancel after service.

re·ces·sive (ri·ses′iv) *adj.* **1.** Having a tendency to re[...] or go back; receding. **2.** *Genetics* Designating one of a[...] of hereditary characters that, appearing in a hybri[...] spring, is masked by a contrasting character. — *n. Ge[...]* A recessive character. — **re·ces′sive·ly** *adv.*

re·cher·ché (rə·sher·shā′) *adj. French* **1.** Rare and e[...] site; choice. **2.** Elegant and refined; also, overrefined.

rec·i·pe (res′ə·pē) *n.* **1.** A formula or list of ingredient[...] mixture, giving proper directions for compounding, coo[...] etc. **2.** A medical prescription: usu. abbreviated to ℞. method prescribed for attaining a desired result. [< L[...] back + *capere* to take]

re·cip·i·ent (ri·sip′ē·ənt) *adj.* Receiving or ready to rec[...] receptive. — *n.* One who or that which receives. [<[...] *re-* back + *capere* to take] — **re·cip′i·ence, re·cip′i·en[...]**

re·cip·ro·cal (ri·sip′rə·kəl) *adj.* **1.** Done or given by ea[...] two to the other; mutual. **2.** Mutually interchangeabl[...] Alternating; moving to and fro. **4.** Expressive of mutu[...] lationship or action: used in connection with certain[...] nouns and verbs or their meaning. **5.** *Math.* Of or pe[...] ing to various types of mutual relations between two qu[...] ties. — *n.* **1.** That which is reciprocal. **2.** *Math.* The tient obtained by dividing unity by a number or expres[...] as ½ is the *reciprocal* of *x*. In a fraction, this reverses th[...] merator and denominator, as ⅗ is the *reciprocal* of ⅗. [...] *reciprocus*] — **re·cip·ro·cal·i·ty** (-kal′ə·tē), **re·cip′r[...] ness** *n.* — **re·cip′ro·cal·ly** *adv.*

reciprocal pronouns *Gram.* Pronouns or phrases den[...] reciprocal action or relation, as *each other, one another.*

re·cip·ro·cate (ri·sip′rə·kāt) *v.* **·cat·ed, ·cat·ing** *v.t.* [...] cause to move backward and forward alternately. **2** give and receive mutually; interchange. **3.** To give, fee[...] etc., in return; requite, as an emotion. — *v.i.* **4.** To[...] backward and forward. **5.** To make a return in kind. [...] give and receive favors, gifts, etc., mutually. [< L < r[...] *rocus* reciprocal] — **re·cip′ro·ca′tion** *n.* — **re·cip′ro·c[...] tive** *adj.* — **re·cip′ro·ca′tor** *n.* — **re·cip′ro·ca·to′ry** (tôr′ē, -tō′rē) *adj.*

rec·i·proc·i·ty (res′ə·pros′ə·tē) *n.* **1.** Reciprocal obliga[...] action, or relation. **2.** A trade relation between two c[...] tries by which each makes concessions favoring the imp[...] tion of the other's products. [< F *réciprocité*]

re·cit·al (ri·sīt′l) *n.* **1.** A telling over in detail, or that v[...] is thus told. **2.** A public delivery of something previo[...] memorized. **3.** A musical program performed usu. by[...] person or several appearing as soloists.

rec·i·ta·tion (res′ə·tā′shən) *n.* **1.** The act of repeating memory. **2.** The reciting of a lesson, or the meeting

ass for that purpose. **3.** That which is allotted for recital
· actually recited. [< L < *re-* again + CITE]

·i·ta·tive (res/ə·tə·tēv′, rə·sit/ə·tiv) *n. Music* **1.** Lan-
·age uttered in the phrasing of ordinary speech, but set to
·usic. **2.** This style of singing, or a passage so rendered. Also
·*alian re·ci·ta·ti·vo* (rä′chē·tä·tē′võ). [< Ital. *recitativo*]

·cite (ri·sīt′) *v.* **·cit·ed, ·cit·ing** *v.t.* **1.** To declaim or say
·ɔm memory, esp. formally, as a lesson in class. **2.** To tell
· particular detail; relate. **3.** To enumerate. — *v.i.* **4.** To
·claim or speak something from memory. **5.** To repeat or
· examined in a lesson or part of a lesson in class. [< OF <
< *re-* again + CITE] — **re·cit′er** *n.*

— **Syn. 1.** repeat. **2.** recount, narrate, recapitulate.

·k (rek) *v.t. & v.i. Archaic* **1.** To have a care (for); heed;
·nd. **2.** To be of concern (to). [OE *reccan*]

·k·less (rek/lis) *adj.* **1.** Foolishly heedless of danger;
·sh. **2.** Proceeding from carelessness or rashness. [OE
·*cceléas*] — **reck′less·ly** *adv.* — **reck′less·ness** *n.*

·k·on (rek/ən) *v.t.* **1.** To count; compute; calculate. **2.**
·ɔ look upon as being; regard: They *reckon* him a fool. —
·i. **3.** To make computation; count up. **4.** To rely or de-
·nd: with *on* or *upon*: to *reckon* on help. — **to reckon with**
·, To settle accounts with. **2.** To take into consideration.
·ɔE *recenian* to explain] — **reck′on·er** *n.*

·k·on·ing (rek/ən·ing) *n.* **1.** The act of counting; com-
·utation; a settlement of accounts. **2.** Account; score; bill,
·, at a hotel. **3.** *Naut.* Dead reckoning (which see).

·claim (ri·klām′) *v.t.* **1.** To bring (swamp, desert, etc.)
·to a condition to support cultivation or life, as by draining
· irrigating. **2.** To obtain (a substance) from used or waste
·oducts. **3.** To cause to return from wrong or sinful ways
· life. — *n.* The act of reclaiming, or state of being re-
·aimed. [< OF < L < *re-* back + *clamare* to cry out] —
·claim′a·ble *adj.* — **re·claim′ant, re·claim′er** *n.*

·claim (rē·klām′) *v.t.* To claim again.

·la·ma·tion (rek/lə·mā′shən) *n.* **1.** The act of reclaim-
·g. **2.** Restoration, as to usefulness or a moral life.

·cline (ri·klīn′) *v.* **·clined, ·clin·ing** *v.i. & v.t.* To assume or
·use to assume a recumbent position; lie or lay down or
·ack. [< L < *re-* back + *clinare* to lean] — **rec·li·na·tion**
·ek/lə·nā′shən) *n.* — **re·clin′er** *n.*

·luse (ri·kloos′; *for n.*, *also* rek/loos) *n.* **1.** One who lives
· retirement or seclusion. **2.** A religious devotee who lives
·ɔluntarily shut up in a cell. — *adj.* Secluded or retired
·om the world. [< OF < L < *re-* back + *claudere* to shut]
· **re·clu′sion** *n.* — **re·clu′sive** *adj.*

·og·ni·tion (rek/əg·nish′ən) *n.* **1.** The act of recogniz-
·g, or the state of being recognized. **2.** Acknowledgment of
· fact or claim. **3.** Friendly notice; salutation; attention.
·. Acknowledgment and acceptance on the part of one gov-
·nment of the independence of another. [< L < *re-* again
· *cognoscere* to know] — **re·cog′ni·to·ry** (ri·kog/nə·tôr′ē,
·′rē) **re·cog′ni·tive** *adj.*

·cog·ni·zance (ri·kog/nə·zəns, -kon/ə-) *n. Law* **1.** An
·ɔligation of record, with condition to do some particular
·t, as to appear and answer. **2.** A sum of money deposited
· surety for fulfillment of such act or obligation, and for-
·ited by its nonperformance. [< OF < L. See RECOGNI-
·ON] — **re·cog′ni·zant** *adj.*

·og·nize (rek/əg·nīz) *v.t.* **·nized, ·niz·ing** **1.** To perceive
· identical with someone or something previously known.
·. To identify, as by previous experience: I *recognize* poor
·ɔetry when I see it. **3.** To perceive as true; realize: to *rec-*
·*nize* the facts in a case. **4.** To acknowledge the indepen-
·nce and validity of, as a newly constituted government.
·. To indicate appreciation or approval of. **6.** To regard as
·lid or genuine: to *recognize* a claim. **7.** To give (someone)
·rmission to speak, as in a legislative body. **8.** To admit
·e acquaintance of; greet. [Back formation < RECOGNI-
·ANCE] — **rec·og·niz·a·ble** (rek/əg·nī′zə·bəl) *adj.* — **rec′·**
·**g·niz′a·bly** *adv.* — **rec′og·niz′er** *n.*

·coil (v. ri·koil′; *n.* rē′koil′) *v.i.* **1.** To start back, as in fear
· loathing; shrink. **2.** To spring back, as from force of dis-
·arge or impact. **3.** To return to the source; react: with *on*
· *upon*: Crime *recoils* upon its perpetrator. — *n.* A back-
·ard movement, as of a gun at the moment of firing; also, a
·rinking. [< OF < *re-* backwards + *cul* backside < L
·*lus*] — **re·coil′er** *n.*

·coil (rē′koil′) *v.t. & v.i.* To coil again.

·c·ol·lect (rek/ə·lekt′) *v.t.* **1.** To call back to the mind. —
·i. **2.** To have a recollection of something. [< L < *re-*
·gain + COLLECT]

·col·lect (rē/kə·lekt′) *v.t.* **1.** To collect again, as things
·attered. **2.** To collect or compose (one's thoughts or
·erves); compose or recover (oneself). — **re′·col·lec′tion** *n.*

·c·ol·lec·tion (rek/ə·lek′shən) *n.* **1.** The act or power of
·membering. **2.** Something remembered. — **rec′ol·lec′·**
·ve *adj.* — **rec′ol·lec′tive·ly** *adv.*

rec·om·mend (rek/ə·mend′) *v.t.* **1.** To commend with favorable representations. **2.** To make attractive or acceptable. **3.** To advise; urge. **4.** To give in charge; commend.
[< Med.L < L *re-* again + COMMEND] — **rec′om·mend′er** *n.*

rec·om·men·da·tion (rek/ə·men·dā′shən) *n.* **1.** The act of
recommending, or of being recommended. **2.** A letter recommending a person.

re·com·mit (rē/kə·mit′) *v.t.* **·mit·ted, ·mit·ting** **1.** To commit again. **2.** To refer back to a committee, as a bill. —
re′com·mit′tal *n.*

rec·om·pense (rek/əm·pens) *v.t.* **·pensed, ·pens·ing** **1.** To
give compensation to; pay or repay; reward. **2.** To compensate for, as a loss. — *n.* **1.** An equivalent for anything
given or done; payment. **2.** Compensation or reward. [<
OF < LL < L *re-* again + *compensare*. See COMPENSATE.]
— **Syn.** (verb) **1.** reimburse. **2.** indemnify.

rec·on·cil·a·ble (rek/ən·sī′lə·bəl) *adj.* Capable of being
reconciled, adjusted, or harmonized. — **rec′on·cil′a·bil′i·ty,
rec′on·cil′a·ble·ness** *n.* — **rec′on·cil′a·bly** *adv.*

rec·on·cile (rek/ən·sīl) *v.t.* **·ciled, ·cil·ing** **1.** To bring back
to friendship after estrangement. **2.** To settle or adjust, as a
quarrel. **3.** To bring to acquiescence, content, or submission. **4.** To make or show to be consistent or congruous;
harmonize: often with *to* or *with*: Can he *reconcile* his statement with his conduct? [< OF < L < *re-* again + *conciliare*
to unite] — **rec′on·cile′ment** *n.* — **rec′on·cil′er** *n.* — **rec·
on·cil·i·a·tion** (rek/ən·sil′ē·ā′shən) *n.*

rec·on·dite (rek/ən·dīt, ri·kon/dīt) *adj.* **1.** Remote from ordinary or easy perception; abstruse; secret. **2.** Dealing in
abstruse matters. **3.** Hidden. [< L < *recondere* to hide]
— **rec′on·dite′ly** *adv.* — **rec′on·dite′ness** *n.*

re·con·di·tion (rē/kən·dish′ən) *v.t.* To put into good or
working condition, as by making repairs; overhaul.

re·con·nais·sance (ri·kon/ə·səns, -säns) *n.* **1.** A reconnoi-
tering; a preliminary examination or survey, as of the territory and resources of a country. **2.** *Mil.* The act of obtaining information of military value, especially regarding the
position, strength, and movement of enemy forces. Also **re·
con′nois·sance.** [< F]

re·con·noi·ter (rē/kə·noi′tər, rek/ə-) *v.t.* To examine or survey, as for military, engineering, or geological purposes. —
v.i. To make a reconnaissance. [< OF < L < *re-* again +
cognoscere to know] — **re′con·noi′ter·er** *n.*

re·con·sid·er (rē/kən·sid′ər) *v.t. & v.i.* To consider again,
esp. with a view to a reversal of previous action. — **re′con·
sid′er·a′tion** *n.*

re·con·sti·tute (rē·kon/stə·tōōt, -tyōōt) *v.t.* **·tut·ed, ·tut·ing**
To constitute again; make over. — **re·con′sti·tu′tion** *n.*

re·con·struct (rē/kən·strukt′) *v.t.* To build again; rebuild.

re·con·struc·tion (rē/kən·struk′shən) *n.* **1.** The act of re-
constructing, or the state of being reconstructed. **2.** *Often
cap.* The restoration of the seceded States as members of the
Union under the **Reconstruction Acts** of March 2 and 23,
1867. — **re′con·struc′tive** *adj.*

Reconstruction period *U.S.* The period following the
Civil War during which the seceded Southern States were reorganized in accordance with the Congressional program.

re·con·vert (rē/kən·vûrt′) *v.t.* **1.** To change back to a state
or form previously possessed. **2.** To convert back to a previously held religious belief. — **re′con·ver′sion** *n.*

rec·ord (*n. & adj.* rek/ərd; *v.* ri·kôrd′) *n.* **1.** An account in
written or other permanent form serving as a memorial or
authentic evidence of a fact or event. **2.** Something on
which such an account is made, as a document or monument.
3. Information preserved and handed down: the heaviest
rainfall on *record.* **4.** The known career or performance of a
person, animal, organization, etc. **5.** The best listed achievement, as in a competitive sport. **6.** *Law* **a** A written account
of an act, statement, or transaction made by an officer acting
under authority of law, and intended as permanent evidence
thereon. **b** An official written account of a judicial or legislative proceeding. **7.** A phonograph record. — **off the record** **1.** Unofficial or unofficially. **2.** Not for quotation or
publication, or not from a source to be identified. — *adj.*
Surpassing any previously recorded achievement or performance of its kind. — *v.t.* **1.** To write down or otherwise
inscribe, as for preserving a record. **2.** To indicate; register,
esp. in permanent form, as a cardiograph does. **3.** To make
a tape or phonograph record of. — *v.i.* **4.** To record something. [< OF < L *recordari* to remember]

— **Syn.** (noun) **1.** note, memorandum, register, roll, catalogue.

record changer A device on some record players that automatically feeds successive records onto the turntable.

re·cord·er (ri·kôr′dər) *n.* **1.** One who records. **2.** A magistrate having criminal jurisdiction in a city or borough. **3.** A
registering apparatus. **4.** Any of a group of fipple flutes
having eight finger holes, and various ranges. **5.** A tape or
wire recorder. — **re·cord′er·ship** *n.*

re·cord·ing (ri-kôr′ding) *n.* **1.** *Telecom.* The process of registering a relatively permanent physical record of sounds or other communicable signals. **2.** A phonograph record.

record player A motor-driven turntable with a pickup attachment and auxiliary equipment for the playing of phonograph records: also called *gramophone, phonograph.*

re·count (ri-kount′) *v.t.* **1.** To relate the particulars of; narrate in detail. **2.** To enumerate; recite. [< OF *reconter* to relate]

re-count (rē-kount′; *for n., also* rē′kount′) *v.t.* To count again. — *n.* A repetition of a count; esp., a second count of votes cast. — **re·count′al** *n.*

re·coup (ri-kōōp′) *v.t.* **1.** To recover or obtain an equivalent for; make up, as a loss. **2.** To reimburse for a loss; indemnify. — *n.* The act or process of recouping. [< OF < *re-* back + *couper* to cut] — **re·coup′a·ble** *adj.* — **re·coup′ment** *n.*

re·course (rē′kôrs, -kōrs, ri·kôrs′, -kōrs′) *n.* **1.** Resort to or application for help or security. **2.** One who or that which is resorted to for help or supply. [< OF < L < *re-* back + *currere* to run]

re·cov·er (ri·kuv′ər) *v.t.* **1.** To regain after losing. **2.** To make up for; retrieve, as a loss. **3.** To restore (oneself) to natural balance, health, etc. **4.** To reclaim, as land. **5.** *Law* To gain or regain in legal proceedings. — *v.i.* **6.** To gain health, composure, etc. [< OF < L < *re-* back + *capere* to take] — **re·cov′er·a·ble** *adj.* — **re·cov′er·er** *n.*

re-cov·er (rē·kuv′ər) *v.t.* To cover again.

re·cov·er·y (ri·kuv′ər·ē) *n., pl.* ·er·ies **1.** The act of recovering. **2.** The state of being or having recovered. **3.** Restoration from sickness or from a condition of evil. **4.** The extraction of valuable substances from original sources, byproducts, waste, etc.

rec·re·ant (rek′rē·ənt) *adj.* **1.** Unfaithful to a cause or pledge; false. **2.** Craven; cowardly. — *n.* A cowardly or faithless person; also, a deserter. [< OF < Med.L < L *re-* back + *credere* to believe] — **rec′re·ance, rec′re·an·cy** *n.* — **rec′re·ant·ly** *adv.*

rec·re·ate (rek′rē·āt) *v.* ·at·ed, ·at·ing *v.t.* **1.** To impart fresh vigor to; refresh. — *v.i.* **2.** To take recreation. [< L < *re-* again + *creare* to create] — **rec′re·a′tive** *adj.*

re-cre·ate (rē′krē·āt′) *v.t.* ·at·ed, ·at·ing To create anew. — **re′-cre·a′tion** *n.*

rec·re·a·tion (rek′rē·ā′shən) *n.* **1.** Refreshment of body or mind; diversion; amusement. **2.** Any pleasurable exercise or occupation. — **rec′re·a′tion·al** *adj.*

re·crim·i·nate (ri·krim′ə·nāt) *v.* ·nat·ed, ·nat·ing *v.t.* **1.** To accuse in return. — *v.i.* **2.** To repel one accusation by making another in return. [< Med.L < L *re-* again + *criminare* to accuse of crime] — **re·crim′i·na′tive, re·crim′i·na·to·ry** (ri·krim′ə·nə·tôr′ē, -tō′rē) *adj.* — **re·crim′i·na′tor** *n.*

re·crim·i·na·tion (ri·krim′ə·nā′shən) *n.* **1.** The act of recriminating. **2.** A countercharge.

re·cru·desce (rē′krōō·des′) *v.i.* ·desced, ·desc·ing To break out afresh. [< L < *re-* again + *crudescere* to become raw] — **re′cru·des′cence** *n.* — **re′cru·des′cent** *adj.*

re·cruit (ri·krōōt′) *v.t.* **1.** To enlist (men) for military or naval service. **2.** To muster; raise, as an army, by enlistment. **3.** To supply with recruits. **4.** To regain or revive (lost health, strength, etc.). — *v.i.* **5.** To enlist new men for military or naval service. **6.** To regain lost health or strength. **7.** To gain or raise new supplies of anything lost or needed. — *n.* A newly enlisted member of an organization, esp. of the armed forces. See tables at GRADE. [< F < OF < L < *re-* again + *crescere* to grow] — **re·cruit′er** *n.* — **re·cruit′ment** *n.*

rec·tal (rek′təl) *adj. Anat.* Of, for, or in the rectum.

rec·tan·gle (rek′tang′gəl) *n.* A parallelogram with all its angles right angles. [< F < LL < L *rectus* straight + *angulus* angle]

rec·tan·gu·lar (rek·tang′gyə·lər) *adj.* **1.** Having one or more right angles. **2.** Resembling a rectangle in shape. — **rec·tan′gu·lar·i·ty** (-lar′ə·tē) *n.* — **rec·tan′gu·lar·ly** *adv.*

recti- *combining form* Straight: *rectilinear.* Also, before vowels, **rect-.** [< L *rectus* straight < *regere* to guide]

rec·ti·fi·er (rek′tə·fī′ər) *n.* **1.** One who or that which rectifies. **2.** *Electr.* A device used to convert an alternating current into a direct current.

rec·ti·fy (rek′tə·fī) *v.t.* ·fied, ·fy·ing **1.** To make right: correct; amend. **2.** *Chem.* To refine and purify, as a liquid, by repeated distillations. **3.** *Electr.* To change (an alternating current) into a direct current. **4.** To allow for errors or inaccuracies in, as a compass reading. [< MF < LL < L *rectus* straight] — **rec′ti·fi′a·ble** *adj.* — **rec′ti·fi·ca′tion** (rek′tə·kā′shən) *n.*

rec·ti·lin·e·ar (rek′tə·lin′ē·ər) *adj.* Pertaining to, consisting of, moving in, or bounded by a straight line or lines; straight. Also **rec′ti·lin′e·al** (-ē·əl). — **rec′ti·lin′e·ar·ly** *adv.*

rec·ti·tude (rek′tə·tōōd, -tyōōd) *n.* **1.** Uprightness in principles and conduct. **2.** Correctness, as of judgment. [< F < LL < L *rectus* straight]

rec·to (rek′tō) *n., pl.* ·toes A right-hand page, as of a boo opposed to *verso.* [< L *recto* (*folio*) on the right (page)]

recto- *combining form Anat.* Rectal; pertaining to or loca ed in the rectum. Also, before vowels **rect-.** [See RECTU

rec·tor (rek′tər) *n.* **1.** In the Church of England, a prie who has full charge of a parish, and receives the paroch tithes. **2.** In the Protestant Episcopal Church, a priest charge of a parish. **3.** In the Roman Catholic Church: **a** priest in charge of a congregation or church, esp. one having parochial status. **b** The head of a seminary or re gious house. **4.** In certain universities, colleges, and schoo the head or chief officer. [< L < *regere* to guide, rule] — **rec′tor·ate** (-it) *n.* — **rec·to·ri·al** (rek·tôr′ē·əl, -tō′rē-) *a*

rec·to·ry (rek′tər·ē) *n., pl.* ·ries **1.** A rector's dwelling. In England, a parish domain with its buildings, revenue, e

rec·tum (rek′təm) *n., pl.* ·ta (-tə) *Anat.* The terminal p tion of the large intestine, connecting the colon with t anus. [< NL *rectum* (*intestinum*) straight (intestine)]

re·cum·bent (ri·kum′bənt) *adj.* **1.** Lying down, wholly partly. **2.** *Biol.* Tending to rest upon or extend from a su face, as certain plant or animal organs. [< L < *re-* back *-cumbere* < *cubare* to lie down] — **re·cum′bence, re·cu ben·cy** *n.* — **re·cum′bent·ly** *adv.*

re·cu·per·ate (ri·kōō′pə·rāt, -kyōō′-) *v.* ·at·ed, ·at·ing **1.** To regain health or strength. **2.** To recover from loss, of money. — *v.t.* **3.** To obtain again after loss; recover. To restore to vigor and health. — **Syn.** See RECOVER. [< L < *re-* back + *capere* to take] — **re·cu′per·a′tion** *n.* **re·cu′per·a′tive, re·cu′per·a·to·ry** (-pər·ə·tôr′ē, -tō′rē) *a* — **re·cu′per·a′tor** *n.*

re·cur (ri·kûr′) *v.i.* ·curred, ·cur·ring **1.** To happen ag or repeatedly, esp. at regular intervals. **2.** To come back return; esp., to return to the mind or in recollection. [< < *re-* back + *currere* to run]

re·cur·rent (ri·kûr′ənt) *adj.* **1.** Happening or appeari again or repeatedly; recurring. **2.** *Anat.* Running back: s of arteries and nerves. — **re·cur′rence, re·cur′ren·cy** *n.* **re·cur′rent·ly** *adv.*

re·cur·vate (ri·kûr′vit, -vāt) *adj.* Bent back. — **re·cur** ture (-və·char) *n.*

re·curve (ri·kûrv′) *v.t. & v.i.* ·curved, ·curv·ing To curve bend back or down. [< L < *re-* back + *curvus* curved] **re·cur·va·tion** (rē′kûr·vā′shən) *n.*

red (red) *adj.* **red·der, red·dest 1.** Being of or havin bright color resembling that of blood. **2.** Communistic. *n.* **1.** One of the primary colors, occurring at the oppos end of the spectrum from violet; the color of blood. **2.** A pigment or dye having or giving this color. **3.** An ultrara cal in political views, esp. a communist. **4.** A red object c sidered with reference to its color. — **in the red** *Infor* Operating at a loss; owing money. — **to see red** *Infor* To be very angry. [OE *rēad*] — **red′dish** *adj.* — **red** *adv.* — **red′ness** *n.*

Red (red) *n.* **1.** A member of the Communist party of R sia. **2.** A member of the Communist party of any count **3.** Any person who supports or approves of the aims of t Communist party. **4.** An ultraradical; anarchist.

re·dact (ri·dakt′) *v.t.* **1.** To prepare, as for publication; ed revise. **2.** To draw up or frame, as a message or edict. L < *re-* back + *agere* to drive] — **re·dac′tion** *n.* — **dac′tor** *n.*

red algae Any of a class of algae of a red, brownish red, purplish color.

Red Army The army of the Soviet Union.

red-bait·ing (red′bā′ting) *n.* The practice of denounci groups or individuals as communist or sympathetic to co munism, often with little evidence. — **red′bait′er** *n.*

red·bird (red′bûrd′) *n.* **1.** The cardinal (def. 2). **2.** T scarlet tanager.

red-blood·ed (red′blud′id) *adj.* Having vitality and vig

red·breast (red′brest′) *n.* A bird having a red breast, as American or European robin.

red·cap (red′kap′) *n. U.S.* A railroad porter.

red cedar 1. An American juniper tree of the cypress fa ily, having a fine-grained, durable wood of a bright or de red color resembling cedar. **2.** The wood of this tree.

Red Chamber The chamber of the Canadian Senate Ottawa.

Red China *Informal* The People's Republic of China.

red·coat (red′kōt′) *n.* A British soldier of the period whe red coat was part of the uniform, esp. during the Americ Revolution and the War of 1812.

Red Cross An international organization for the care of t sick and wounded in war, formed in accordance with the ternational convention signed at Geneva in 1864, the me bers wearing a red Geneva cross as a badge of neutrali These societies are now national organizations, as the Am ican Red Cross, and continue their activities in times peace, as in fighting disease, etc.

red deer 1. The common European and Asian stag. **2.** T white-tailed deer in its rufous summer coat.

·den (red'n) *v.t.* **1.** To make red. —*v.i.* **2.** To grow d; flush; blush.

·dec·o·rate (ri-dek'ə-rāt) *v.t. & v.i.* **·rat·ed, ·rat·ing** To novate or remodel, as an apartment. — **re'dec'o·ra'tion** *n.*

·deem (ri-dēm') *v.t.* **1.** To regain possession of by paying price; esp., to recover, as mortgaged property. **2.** To pay ; receive back and satisfy, as a promissory note. **3.** To free; ransom. **4.** *Theol.* To rescue from sin and its penal- s. **5.** To fulfill, as an oath or promise. **6.** To compensate : The play was *redeemed* by its acting. [< MF < L < re- ck + *emere* to buy] — **re·deem'a·ble, re·demp'ti·ble** (emp'tə·bəl) *adj.*

·deem·er (ri-dē'mər) *n.* One who redeems. — **The Re- emer** Jesus Christ.

·deem·ing (ri-dē'ming) *adj.* Compensating for faults, ks, poor qualities, etc.: the *redeeming* feature.

·le·liv·er (rē'di-liv'ər) *v.t.* **1.** To deliver again, as a mes- ge or a speech. **2.** To give back; return; restore. — **re'- ·liv'er·ance, re·de·liv'er·y** *n.*

·demp·tion (ri-demp'shən) *n.* **1.** The act of redeeming, the state of being redeemed. **2.** The recovery of what is rtgaged or pledged. **3.** The payment of a debt or obliga- n; esp., the paying of the value of its notes, warrants, etc., a government. [< OF < L < *redimere* to redeem.]

·demp·tive (ri-demp'tiv) *adj.* Serving to redeem, or con- cted with redemption. Also **re·demp'to·ry** (-tər·ē).

·l Ensign The Canadian flag, bearing both the Union ck and the arms of Canada.

·e·vel·op (rē'di·vel'əp) *v.t.* **1.** To develop again. **2.** *Pho- .* To intensify with chemicals and put through a second veloping process. — *v.i.* **3.** To develop again. Also **re'de- l'ope.** — **re'de·vel'op·er** *n.* — **re'de·vel'op·ment** *n.*

·eye (red'ī') *n.* **1.** *U.S. Informal* The danger signal in a lroad semaphore system. **2.** *U.S. Slang* Inferior whisky.

·fin (red'fin') *n. pl.* **·fins** or **·fin** One of various cyprinoid es; esp., the common shiner of eastern North America.

·hand·ed (red'han'did) *adj.* **1.** Having just committed y crime. **2.** Caught in the act of doing some particular ng. — **red'hand'ed·ly** *adv.* — **red'-hand'ed·ness** *n.*

·head (red'hed') *n.* **1.** A person with red hair. **2.** An erican duck, sometimes mistaken for the canvasback.

·herring 1. Herring dried and smoked to a reddish color. A diverting of attention from the main subject by intro- cing some irrelevant topic.

·hot (red'hot') *adj.* **1.** Heated to redness. **2.** New, as if t from the fire: *red-hot* news. **3.** Heated; excited.

·in·gote (red'ing·gōt) *n.* An outer coat with long full rts. [< F *rédingote*, alter. of E *riding coat*]

·lin·te·grate (ri·din'tə·grāt) *v.t.* **·grat·ed, ·grat·ing** To tore to a perfect state. — *adj.* Restored. [< L < red- in + *integrare* to make whole] — **re·din'te·gra'tion** *n.*

·li·rect¹ (rē'di·rekt') *v.t.* To direct again or anew: to *re- ect* a letter. — **re'di·rec'tion** *n.*

·li·rect² (rē'di·rekt') *adj. Law* Designating the examina- n of a witness, after cross-examination, by the party who t examined him.

·lis·trict (rē·dis'trikt) *v.t.* To district again; esp., to re- w the boundaries of the election districts of.

·lead (led) Minium.

·let·ter day (red'let'ər) A memorable occasion: from the on calendars of red letters to indicate holidays.

·light A red traffic or signal light meaning "stop."

·light district (red'līt') A part of a city or town in ich brothels, often marked by a red light, are numerous.

·man An American Indian.

·neck (red'nek') *n.* In the rural South, a poor, unedu- ed white person: a disparaging term.

·oak 1. Any of several oaks having a dense, cross-grained od. **2.** The wood of any of these oaks.

·o·lent (red'ə·lənt) *adj.* Full of or diffusing a pleasant grance. [< OF < L < red- thoroughly + *olere* to smell] — **red'o·lence, red'o·len·cy** *n.* — **red'o·lent·ly** *adv.*

·loub·le (rē·dub'əl) *v.t. & v.i.* **·led, ·ling 1.** To make or ome double. **2.** To increase greatly. **3.** To echo or re- o. **4.** To fold or turn back. **5.** In bridge, to double (an onent's double). — *n.* In bridge, the doubling of an op- ent's double.

·loubt (ri·dout') *n.* **1.** An enclosed fortification, esp. a nporary one of any form. **2.** An earthwork or simple tification placed within the main rampart line of a per- nent fortification. [< F < Ital. < Med.L < L *reductus* ret place, pp. of *reducere* to reduce]

·loubt·a·ble (ri·dou'tə·bəl) *adj.* **1.** Inspiring fear; for- lable. **2.** Deserving respect or deference. Also **re·doubt'- (-dou'tid).** [< F, ult. < L re- thoroughly + *dubitare* to bt] — **re·doubt'a·ble·ness** *n.* — **re·doubt'a·bly** *adv.*

·lound (ri·dound') *v.i.* To have an effect, as by reaction, ch credit, discredit, advantage, etc., of the original agent;

accrue. — *n.* A return by way of consequence; requital. [< F < L < red- back + *undare* to surge]

red pepper A species of capsicum cultivated in many varie- ties and used as a condiment: also called *cayenne pepper.*

red·poll (red'pōl') *n.* Any of various small finches of north- ern regions, having a reddish crown.

re·draft (*n.* rē'draft', -dräft'; *v.* rē·draft', -dräft') *n.* **1.** A second draft or copy. **2.** A bill of exchange drawn by the holder of a protested bill on the drawer or endorsers for the reimbursement of the amount of the original bill with costs and charges. — *v.t. & v.i.* To make a redraft (of).

re·dress (ri·dres'; for *n.*, also rē'dres) *v.t.* **1.** To set right, as a wrong, by compensation or by punishment of the wrong- doer; make reparation for. **2.** To make reparation to; com- pensate. **3.** To remedy; correct. **4.** To adjust, as balances. — *n.* **1.** Satisfaction for wrong done; reparation; amends. **2.** A restoration; correction. [< F < re- again + *dresser* to arrange] — **re·dress'er** or **re·dres'sor** *n.*

re·dress (rē·dres') *v.t. & v.i.* To dress again.

red salmon The sockeye.

red·skin (red'skin') *n.* A North American Indian.

red snapper A reddish fish found in Atlantic waters and esteemed as a food fish.

red·start (red'stärt') *n.* **1.** A small European singing bird allied to the warblers; having a black throat, white forehead, and rust-red breast, sides, and tail. **2.** A small fly-catching warbler of eastern North America, with bright orange-red patches against black and white.

red tape Rigid official procedure involving delay or inac- tion: from the tying of public documents with red tape.

re·duce (ri·dōōs', -dyōōs') *v.* **·duced, ·duc·ing** *v.t.* **1.** To make less in size, amount, number, intensity, etc.; diminish. **2.** To bring to a lower condition; degrade. **3.** To bring to submission; conquer. **4.** To bring to a specified condition or state: with *to*: to *reduce* a person to desperation. **5.** To thin (paint, etc.) with oil or turpentine. **6.** *Math.* To change (an expression) to a more elementary form. **7.** *Surg.* To restore (displaced parts) to normal position. **8.** *Chem.* **a** To de- crease the valence of (an atom or group of atoms) by adding electrons. **b** To remove oxygen from (a compound). **9.** *Metall.* To extract (a metal) from a combined state, as in an ore. — *v.i.* **10.** To become less in any way. **11.** To decrease one's weight, as by dieting. — **Syn.** See DECREASE. [< L < re- back + *ducere* to lead] — **re·duc'er** *n.* — **re·duc'i- bil'i·ty** *n.* — **re·duc'i·ble** *adj.* — **re·duc'i·bly** *adv.*

reducing agent *Chem.* A substance that effects reduction, while increasing its valence and becoming oxidized.

re·duc·ti·o ad ab·sur·dum (ri·duk'shē·ō ad ab·sûr'dəm) *Latin* Reduction to an absurdity; disposal of a proposition by showing that its logical conclusion is absurd.

re·duc·tion (ri·duk'shən) *n.* **1.** The act or process of reduc- ing, or its results. **2.** *Chem.* **a** The process of depriving a compound of oxygen. **b** The process by which atoms gain valence electrons or cease to share them with a more electro- negative element. — **re·duc'tion·al** *adj.* — **re·duc'tive** (-tiv) *adj.*

re·dun·dance (ri·dun'dəns) *n.* **1.** The condition or quality of being redundant. **2.** That which is redundant.

re·dun·dan·cy (ri·dun'dən·sē) *n. pl.* **·cies 1.** Redundance. **2.** In information theory, the extent to which a signal re- peats the same message, reducing the probability of error and reducing the effective capacity of the channel.

re·dun·dant (ri·dun'dənt) *adj.* **1.** Being more than is re- quired; constituting an excess. **2.** Unnecessarily verbose; tautological. [< L *redundans, -antis*, ppr. of *redundare* to overflow] — **re·dun'dant·ly** *adv.*

re·du·pli·cate (*v.* ri·dōō'plə·kāt, -dyōō'-; *adj.* ri·dōō'plə·kit, -dyōō'-) *v.* **·cat·ed, ·cat·ing** *v.t.* **1.** To repeat again and again; redouble; iterate. **2.** *Ling.* To affix a reduplication to. — *v.i.* **3.** To undergo reduplication. — *adj.* **1.** Repeated again and again; duplicated. **2.** *Bot.* Valvate with the mar- gins reflexed. [< L < re- again + *duplicare* to double] — **re·du'pli·ca'tive** *adj.*

re·du·pli·ca·tion (ri·dōō'plə·kā'shən, -dyōō'-) *n.* **1.** The act of reduplicating, or the state of being reduplicated; a re- doubling. **2.** *Ling.* **a** The repetition of an initial element or elements in a word. **b** The doubling of all or part of a word, often with vowel or consonant change, as in *razzle-dazzle.*

red·wing (red'wing') *n.* **1.** An American blackbird with bright scarlet patches on the wings of the male. Also **red'- winged' blackbird. 2.** An Old World red-winged thrush, with bright reddish orange on the sides and underwings.

red·wood (red'wŏŏd') *n.* **1.** A sequoia. **2.** Its durable red- dish wood. **3.** Any of various similar trees.

re·ech·o (ri·ek'ō) *v.t.* **1.** To echo back, as a sound. **2.** To echo again; repeat, as an opinion. — *v.i.* **3.** To echo again; reverberate. — *n.* That which is reechoed.

reed (rēd) *n.* **1.** The slender, frequently jointed stem of certain tall grasses growing in wet places, or the grasses themselves. **2.** A thin, elastic plate of reed, wood, or metal nearly closing an opening, as in a pipe, used in reed organs, oboes, clarinets, etc., to produce a musical tone. **3.** A musical pipe made of the hollow stem of a plant. **4.** *Archit.* A semicylindrical ornamental molding or bead. **5.** An arrow. **6.** The abomasum. — *v.t.* **1.** To fashion into or decorate with reeds. **2.** To thatch with reeds. [OE *hrēod*]

reed·ing (rē'ding) *n.* **1.** Beading or semicylindrical moldings collectively. **2.** Ornamentation by such moldings. **3.** A molding of this kind. **4.** The knurling on the edge of a coin, as distinguished from milling.

reed organ A keyboard musical instrument sounding by means of free reeds vibrated by air currents.

reed pipe An organ pipe that acts as a resonator for a tuned reed. Compare FLUE PIPE.

re·ed·u·cate (rē·ej'oo̅·kāt) *v.t.* ·cat·ed, ·cat·ing **1.** To educate again. **2.** To rehabilitate, as a criminal, by education.

reed·y (rē'dē) *adj.* reed·i·er, reed·i·est **1.** Full of reeds. **2.** Like a reed. **3.** Having a thin, sharp tone, like a reed instrument. — **reed'i·ness** *n.*

reef¹ (rēf) *n.* **1.** A ridge of sand or rocks, or esp. of coral, at or near the surface of the water. **2.** A lode, vein, or ledge. Compare SHOAL¹. [< ON *rif*] — **reef'y** *adj.*

reef² (rēf) *Naut. n.* **1.** The part of a sail that is folded and secured or untied and let out in regulating its size on the mast. **2.** The tuck taken in a sail when reefed. — *v.t.* **1.** To reduce (a sail) by folding a part and fastening it to a yard or boom. **2.** To shorten or lower, as a topmast by taking part of it in. [< ON *rif* rib]

reef·er¹ (rē'fər) *n.* **1.** One who reefs. **2.** A close-fitting, often double-breasted coat or jacket of heavy material.

reef·er² (rē'fər) *n. U.S. Slang* A marihuana cigarette. [? from its resemblance to the reef of a sail]

reef knot A square knot.

reek (rēk) *v.i.* **1.** To give off smoke, vapor, etc. **2.** To give off a strong, offensive smell. **3.** To be pervaded with anything offensive. — *v.t.* **4.** To expose to smoke or its action. **5.** To give off or emit (fumes, an odor, etc.) [OE *rēocan* to smoke] — **reek'er** *n.* — **reek'y** *adv.*

reel¹ (rēl) *n.* **1.** A rotary device or frame for winding rope, film, or other flexible substance. **2.** Motion picture film wound on one reel, used as a unit of length. **3.** A wooden spool for wire, thread, etc. **4.** Material, as thread, paper, etc., wound on a reel. — *v.t.* **1.** To wind on a reel or bobbin, as a line. **2.** To pull by reeling a line: with *in*: to *reel* a fish in. **3.** To say, do, etc., easily and fluently: with *off*. [OE *hrēol*] — **reel'a·ble** *adj.* — **reel'er** *n.*

reel² (rēl) *v.i.* **1.** To stagger, sway, or lurch, as when giddy or drunk. **2.** To whirl round and round. **3.** To have a sensation of giddiness or whirling. **4.** To waver or fall back, as attacking troops. — *v.t.* **5.** To cause to reel. — *n.* A staggering motion; giddiness. [< REEL¹] — **reel'er** *n.*

reel³ (rēl) *n.* A lively dance, chiefly Scottish or Irish; also, the music for this dance. [? < REEL¹]

re·en·force (rē'en·fôrs', -fōrs'), **re·en·force·ment** (rē'en·fôrs'mənt, -fōrs'-), etc. See REINFORCE, etc.

re·en·try (rē·en'trē) *n. pl.* ·tries **1.** The act of entering again. **2.** In whist and bridge, an entry. **3.** *Aerospace* The return of a rocket or other object to the atmosphere of the earth after travel to very high altitudes.

re·e·val·u·ate (rē'i·val'yoo̅·āt) *v.t.* ·at·ed, ·at·ing To evaluate or consider anew. — **re/e·val/u·a'tion** *n.*

reeve¹ (rēv) *v.t.* reeved or rove, reev·ing *Naut.* **1.** To pass, as a rope or rod, through a hole, block, or aperture. **2.** To fasten in such manner. **3.** To pass a rope, etc., through (a block or pulley). [Origin uncertain]

reeve² (rēv) *n.* **1.** In Canada, the elected head of a rural municipal council. **2.** In medieval England: **a** A high administrative official. **b** A bailiff; steward. [OE *gerēfa*]

reeve³ (rēv) *n.* The female of the ruff, a sandpiper.

re·fec·tion (ri·fek'shən) *n.* **1.** Refreshment with food and drink. **2.** A light meal. [< OF < L < *re-* again + *facere* to make]

re·fec·to·ry (ri·fek'tə·rē) *n. pl.* ·ries A room or hall for eating, esp. in a religious house or college.

re·fer (ri·fûr') *v.* ·ferred, ·fer·ring *v.t.* **1.** To direct or send for information, assistance, etc. **2.** To hand over or submit for consideration, settlement, etc. **3.** To assign or attribute to a source, cause, class, period, etc. — *v.i.* **4.** To make reference; allude. **5.** To turn, as for information, help, or authority. — **Syn.** See ATTRIBUTE. [< OF < L < *re-* back *ferre* to carry] — **ref·er·a·ble** (ref'ər·ə·bəl), **re·fer'ra·ble** or **re·fer'ri·ble** *adj.* — **re·fer'ral** *n.* — **re·fer'rer** *n.*

ref·e·ree (ref'ə·rē') *n.* **1.** A person to whom something is referred, esp. for settlement or arbitration. **2.** In certain sports, as football, a supervisory official. — **Syn.** See JUDGE. — *v.t. & v.i.* ·reed, ·ree·ing To judge as a referee.

ref·er·ence (ref'ər·əns, ref'rəns) *n.* **1.** The act of referring. **2.** An incidental allusion or direction of the attention: *reference* to a recent event. **3.** A note or other indication in a

book, referring to some other book or passage. Comp CROSS-REFERENCE. **4.** One who or that which is or may referred to. **5.** The state of being referred or related: used the phrases **with** (or **in**) **reference to**. **6.** The person or p sons to whom one seeking employment may refer for reco mendation. — **ref'er·enc·er** *n.*

ref·er·en·dum (ref'ə·ren'dəm) *n. pl.* ·dums or ·da (-də) **1.** The submission of a proposed public measure or law that been passed upon by a legislature or convention to a vot the people for ratification or rejection. **2.** The vote in s a procedure. [< L, gerund of *referre* to refer]

ref·er·ent (ref'ər·ənt) *n.* The object, concept, etc., to wh reference is made in a statement or its symbolic equivale

re·fill (*v.* rē·fil'; *n.* rē'fil') *v.t.* To fill again. — *n.* Any co modity packaged to fit and fill a container originally cont ing that commodity: a *refill* for a lipstick case.

re·fine (ri·fīn') *v.* ·fined, ·fin·ing *v.t.* **1.** To make fine or p free from impurities or extraneous matter. **2.** To make ished or cultured. **3.** To improve or change by subtle or cise alterations. — *v.i.* **4.** To become fine or pure. **5.** become more polished or cultured. **6.** To make fine dist tions. [< RE- + FINE¹, v.] — **re·fin'er** *n.*

re·fined (ri·fīnd') *adj.* **1.** Characterized by refinement; tivated; polished. **2.** Free from impurity; purified. **3.** ceedingly precise or exact; subtle.

re·fine·ment (ri·fīn'mənt) *n.* **1.** Fineness of thought, ta language, etc.; freedom from coarseness or vulgarity; cacy; culture. **2.** The act, effect, or process of refining. nice distinction; subtlety. **4.** Fastidiousness.
— **Syn. 1.** *Refinement* implies not only the elimination of garity and grossness but also the development of delicate per tion and understanding. *Cultivation* is the self-discipline, st and exercise that bring urbanity, learning, esthetic taste, *Culture* primarily contrasts the enlightenment of the civilized with that of a savage or a child; *breeding* suggests the training manifests itself in good manners, tact, and consideration for oth — **Ant.** coarseness, grossness, vulgarity.

re·fin·er·y (ri·fī'nər·ē) *n. pl.* ·er·ies A place where s crude material, as sugar or petroleum, is purified.

re·fit (rē·fit') *v.t. & v.i.* ·fit·ted, ·fit·ting To make or be m fit or ready again, as by repairs, replacing equipment, etc. *n.* The repair of damages or wear, esp. of a ship.

re·flect (ri·flekt') *v.t.* **1.** To turn or throw back, as wave light, heat, or sound. **2.** To give back an image of; mir **3.** To cause as a result of one's actions, character, etc.; He *reflects* credit on his teacher. **4.** To manifest as a re of influence, imitation, etc. — *v.i.* **5.** To send back ray of light or heat. **6.** To shine back. **7.** To give back an age; be mirrored. **8.** To think carefully; ponder. **9.** bring blame, discredit, etc.: with *on* or *upon*. **10.** *Anat.* fold back upon itself, as a membrane or tissue. [< O L < *re-* back + *flectere* to bend]

re·flec·tion (ri·flek'shən) *n.* **1.** The act of reflecting, or state of being reflected. **2.** *Physics* The throwing off or from a surface of impinging light, heat, sound, or any for radiant energy. **3.** The result of reflecting; reflected ray an image thrown by reflection. **4.** Meditation; careful sideration. **5.** An imputation of blame or censure. **6.** The folding of a part upon itself. Also **re·flex'ion**. — **flec'tion·al** or **re·flex'ion·al** *adj.*
— **Syn. 4.** rumination, reverie, thought. **5.** aspersion, madversion

re·flec·tive (ri·flek'tiv) *adj.* **1.** Given to reflectio thought; meditative. **2.** Of, pertaining to, or caused b flection. **3.** Having the quality of throwing back light, etc. — **re·flec'tive·ly** *adv.* — **re·flec'tive·ness** *n.* — **re tiv'i·ty** *n.*

re·flec·tor (ri·flek'tər) *n.* **1.** That which reflects. **2.** A ished surface for reflecting light, heat, sound, etc. **3.** A scope that transmits an image from a reflecting surface t eyepiece. **4.** *Physics* A substance placed around the co a nuclear reactor for the purpose of maintaining the lev the chain reaction.

re·flex (*adj. & n.* rē'fleks; *v.* ri·fleks') *adj.* **1.** *Physiol* pertaining to, or produced by involuntary response to a s ulus. **2.** Turned, thrown, or directed backward or in the posite direction. **3.** Bent back; reflexed. — *n.* **1.** *Ph* An involuntary movement or response to a stimulus, winking, sneezing, shivering, etc.: also **reflex action**. **2.** flection, or an image produced by reflection, as from a m or like surface. **3.** Light reflected from an illuminated face to a shady one. — *v.t.* To bend back; turn back o flect. [See REFLECT.]

reflex angle *Geom.* An angle greater than 180 degre

reflex arc *Physiol.* The entire path of a nerve impulse f the receptors to the nerve center, and thence to the effec

re·flex·ive (ri·flek'siv) *adj.* **1.** *Gram.* **a** Of verbs, havin object that is identical with the subject, as "dresses" in dresses himself." **b** Of pronouns in the objective case, h identical with the subject, as "herself" in "She hurt hers **2.** Of or pertaining to a reflex or reflection. — *n.* *Gra*

lexive verb or pronoun. — **re·flex'ive·ly** adv. — **re·flex'·ness, re·flex·iv·i·ty** (rē'flek·siv'ə·tē) n.

lu·ent (ref'lōō·ənt) adj. Flowing back; ebbing, as the e. [< L < re- back + fluere to flow] — **ref'lu·ence** n.

lux (rē'fluks') n. A flowing back; ebb: the flux and reflux fortune. [< L refluxus, pp. of refluere. See REFLUENT.]

or·est (rē·fôr'ist, -for'-) v.t. & v.i. To replant (an area) h trees. — **re'for·es·ta'tion** n.

orm (ri·fôrm') v.t. **1.** To make better by removing uses, altering, etc. **2.** To improve morally; persuade or ucate to a better life. **3.** To put an end to (an abuse, malctice, etc.). — v.i. **4.** To give up sin or error; become ter. — n. **1.** An act or result of reformation; change for better, esp. in administration. **2.** Improvement in one's sonal life, esp. by abandonment of bad habits. [< OF < re- again + formare to form] — **re·form'a·tive** adj. — **form'er, re·form'ist** n.

orm (rē'fôrm') v.t. & v.i. To form again. — **re'·for'tion** n.

or·ma·tion (ref'ər·mā'shən) n. The act of reforming, or state of being reformed; esp., moral improvement.

or·ma·tion (ref'ər·mā'shən) n. The 16th-century reous revolution that aimed at reforming Catholicism and led with the establishment of Protestantism.

or·ma·to·ry (ri·fôr'mə·tôr'ē, -tō'rē) n. pl. **·ries** An inution for the reformation and instruction of juvenile ofders. Also **reform school.** — adj. Tending to reform.

ormed (ri·fôrmd') adj. **1.** Restored to a better state; rected or amended. **2.** Improved in conduct, habits, etc.

orm Judaism The branch of Judaism that does not act in entirety the Mosaic Laws, the Talmud, and rabbini-interpretations as binding in modern times.

ract (ri·frakt') v.t. **1.** To deflect (a ray) by refraction. Optics To determine the degree of refraction of (an eye or s). [< L < refringere to turn aside]

rac·tion (ri·frak'shən) n. **1.** Physics The change of direc-a of a ray, of light or heat, in passage m one medium to another of different sity. **2.** Optics The refracting of light s by the eye so as to form an image upon retina. — **re·frac'tive** adj. — **re·c'tive·ly** adv. — **re·frac'tive·ness, re·c·tiv·i·ty** (rē'frak·tiv'ə·tē) n.

active index Optics The ratio of the city of a specific radiation in a vacuum ts velocity in a given medium.

rac·tor (ri·frak'tər) n. **1.** That which acts. **2.** A refracting telescope. See ler TELESCOPE.

LIGHT REFRACTION

rac·to·ry (ri·frak'tər·ē) adj. **1.** Not amenable to con-; unmanageable; obstinate. **2.** Resisting heat or ordi-y methods of reduction, as an ore. **3.** Resisting treat-nt, as a disease. — n. pl. **·ries 1.** One who or that which efractory. **2.** Any of various materials highly resistant to action of great heat, as fire clay. [See REFRACT.] — **re·c'to·ri·ly** adv. — **re·frac'to·ri·ness** n.

rain¹ (ri·frān') v.i. To keep oneself back; abstain ion. [< OF < L refrenare to curb] — **re·frain'er** n.

rain² (ri·frān') n. **1.** A phrase or strain in a poem or g repeated at the end of each stanza. **2.** Any saying re-ted over and over. [< OF < L refringere to turn aside]

ran·gi·ble (ri·fran'jə·bəl) adj. Capable of being re-ted, as light. [< RE- + L frangere to break + -IBLE] — **ran'gi·bil'i·ty, re·fran'gi·ble·ness** n.

resh (ri·fresh') v.t. **1.** To make fresh or vigorous again, by food or rest; reinvigorate; revive. **2.** To make fresh, n, cool, etc. **3.** To stimulate, as the memory. **4.** To re-y or replenish with or as with new supplies. — v.i. **5.** To ome fresh again; revive. **6.** To take refreshment. [< < re- again + fres fresh]

resh·er (ri·fresh'ər) adj. Reviewing material previously died. — n. One who or that which refreshes.

resh·ing (ri·fresh'ing) adj. **1.** Serving to refresh. **2.** joyably novel or unusual. — **re·fresh'ing·ly** adv.

resh·ment (ri·fresh'mənt) n. **1.** The act of refreshing, he state of being refreshed. **2.** That which refreshes, as d or drink. **3.** pl. Food, or food and drink.

rig·er·ant (ri·frij'ər·ənt) adj. Cooling or freezing. Allaying bodily heat or fever. — n. **1.** Any medicine or terial, as ice, that reduces abnormal heat of the body. **2.** ubstance used for obtaining and maintaining a low tem-ature, as frozen carbon dioxide or ammonia.

rig·er·ate (ri·frij'ə·rāt) v.t. **·at·ed, ·at·ing 1.** To keep or ke cold. **2.** To freeze or chill (foodstuffs, etc.) for pre-vative purposes. [< L < re- thoroughly + frigerare to l] — **re·frig'er·a'tion** n. — **re·frig'er·a'tive** adj. & n. **re·frig'er·a·to·ry** (-tôr'ē, -tō'rē) adj.

rig·er·a·tor (ri·frij'ə·rā'tər) n. A box, cabinet, room,

railroad car, etc., equipped with a cooling apparatus for pre-serving perishable foods, etc.

reft (reft) Past tense and past participle of REAVE.

ref·uge (ref'yōōj) n. **1.** Shelter or protection, as from dan-ger or distress. **2.** One who or that which shelters or pro-tects. **3.** A safe place; asylum. [< OF < L < re- back + fugere to flee]
— **Syn.** (noun) **3.** sanctuary, retreat, haven.

ref·u·gee (ref'yōō·jē', ref'yōō·jē') n. One who flees from in-vasion, persecution, or political danger.

re·ful·gent (ri·ful'jənt) adj. Shining brilliantly; radiant. [< L < re- back + fulgere to shine] — **re·ful'gence, re·ful'·gen·cy** n. — **re·ful'gent·ly** adv.

re·fund¹ (v. ri·fund'; n. rē'fund) v.t. **1.** To give or pay back (money, etc.). **2.** To repay; reimburse. — v.i. **3.** To make repayment. — n. A repayment; also, the amount repaid. [< OF < L < re- back + fundere to pour] — **re·fund'er** n.

re·fund² (rē·fund') v.t. To fund anew; replace (an old loan) by issuing new securities.

re·fur·bish (re·fûr'bish) v.t. To furbish again; renovate or freshen; polish up; brighten.

re·fus·al (ri·fyōō'zəl) n. **1.** The act of refusing; declination. **2.** The privilege of accepting or rejecting; option.

re·fuse¹ (ri·fyōōz') v.t. **·fused, ·fus·ing 1.** To decline to do, permit, take, or yield. **2.** Mil. To turn back (the wing of a line of troops), so that it stands at an angle with the main body. **3.** To decline to jump over: said of a horse at a ditch, hedge, etc. — v.i. **4.** To decline to do, permit, take, or yield something. [< OF < L refusus, pp. of refundere to re-fund]

ref·use² (ref'yōōs) n. Anything worthless; rubbish. — adj. Rejected as worthless. [See REFUSE¹.]

re·fute (ri·fyōōt') v.t. **·fut·ed, ·fut·ing 1.** To prove the incor-rectness or falsity of (a statement). **2.** To prove (a person) to be in error; confute. [< L refutare to repulse] — **re·fut'·a·bil·i·ty** n. — **re·fut'a·ble** adj. — **re·fut'a·bly** adv. — **ref·u·ta·tion** (ref'yōō·tā'shən), **re·fu'tal** n. — **re·fut'er** n.
— **Syn. 1.** Refute, disprove, rebut, and confute mean to show to be incorrect or fallacious. Refute emphasizes the fact of opposing a statement or argument; disprove emphasizes the result of such opposition. To rebut is to refute in formal debate, while to confute is to disprove, overthrow, or put to confusion; confute may include the use of ridicule, as well as of logical argument.

re·gain (ri·gān') v.t. **1.** To get possession of again, as some-thing lost; recover. **2.** To reach again; get back to: He re-gained the street. [< MF regaigner] — **re·gain'er** n.

re·gal (rē'gəl) adj. **1.** Of a king; royal. **2.** Stately. [< OF < L regalis < rex, regis king] — **re'gal·ly** adv.

re·gale (ri·gāl') v. **·galed, ·gal·ing** v.t. **1.** To give unusual pleasure to; delight. **2.** To entertain sumptuously; feast. — v.i. **3.** To feast. [< F < ré- again + OF gale pleasure] — **re·gale'ment** n.

re·ga·li·a (ri·gā'lē·ə, -gāl'yə) n.pl. **1.** The insignia and em-blems of royalty, as the crown, scepter, etc. **2.** The distinc-tive symbols, insignia, etc., of any society, order, or rank. **3.** Fine clothes; fancy trappings. [See REGAL]

re·gard (ri·gärd') v.t. **1.** To look at or observe closely or at-tentively. **2.** To look on or think of in a certain or specified manner; consider: I regard him as a friend. **3.** To take into account; consider. **4.** To have relation or pertinence to; concern. — v.i. **5.** To pay attention. **6.** To gaze or look. — n. **1.** Careful attention or notice; heed; consideration. **2.** Esteem; respect. **3.** Reference; relation: in regard to this matter. **4.** A look or aspect. **5.** Usu. pl. Good wishes; af-fection. [< OF < re- again + garder to guard, heed]

re·gard·ful (ri·gärd'fəl) adj. **1.** Having or showing regard; heedful. **2.** Respectful; deferential. — **re·gard'ful·ly** adv.

re·gard·ing (ri·gär'ding) prep. In reference to; concerning.

re·gard·less (ri·gärd'lis) adj. Having no regard or consid-eration; heedless; negligent: often with of. — adv. Informal In spite of everything. — **re·gard'less·ly** adv.

re·gat·ta (ri·gat'ə, -gä'tə) n. **1.** A boat race, or a series of such races. **2.** Originally, a gondola race. [< Ital.]

re·gen·cy (rē'jən·sē) n. pl. **·cies 1.** The government or of-fice of a regent or body of regents. **2.** The period during which a regent governs. **3.** A body of regents. **4.** The dis-trict under the rule of a regent. Also **re'gent·ship.**

re·gen·er·ate (v. ri·jen'ə·rāt; adj. ri·jen'ər·it) v. **·at·ed, ·at·ing** v.t. **1.** To cause complete moral and spiritual reforma-tion or regeneration in. **2.** To produce or form anew; re-create; reproduce. **3.** To make use of (heat or other energy that might otherwise be wasted) by means of various de-vices. **4.** Biol. To grow or form by regeneration. **5.** Tele-com. To return (part of the output of an amplifier) to the in-put in reinforcing phase to control gain, selectivity, etc. — v.i. **6.** To form anew; be reproduced. **7.** To become spiritu-ally regenerate. **8.** To effect regeneration. — adj. **1.** Hav-ing new life; restored. **2.** Spiritually renewed; regenerated.

[< L < re- again + generare to generate] — re·gen′er·a·cy, re·gen·er·a′tion n. — re·gen·er·a·tive (ri-jen′ə-rā′tiv, -ər-ə-tiv) adj. — re·gen′er·a′tive·ly adv. — regen′er·a′tor n.

re·gent (rē′jənt) n. 1. One who rules in the name and place of a sovereign. 2. A resident master who takes part in the government of a university or college. 3. One of various educational officers, as of a state. — adj. 1. Exercising authority in another's place. 2. Governing; ruling. [< OF < L < regere to rule]

reg·i·cide (rej′ə-sīd) n. 1. The killing of a king or sovereign. 2. One who has killed a king or sovereign. [< L rex, regis king + -CIDE] — reg′i·ci′dal adj.

re·gime (ri-zhēm′) n. 1. System of government or administration. 2. A social system. 3. Regimen. Also ré·gime (rā-zhēm′). [< F < L < regere to rule, guide]

reg·i·men (rej′ə-mən) n. A systematized course of living, as to food, clothing, etc.: also regime. [< L regere to rule]

reg·i·ment (rej′ə-mənt) n. 1. Mil. An administrative and tactical unit of infantry, artillery, etc., larger than a battalion and smaller than a division, usu. commanded by a colonel. 2. Any large body of persons. — v.t. 1. To form into a regiment or regiments; organize. 2. To assign to a regiment. 3. To form into well-defined units or groups; systematize. 4. To make uniform. [< OF < LL < L regere to rule] — reg′i·men′tal adj. — reg′i·men·ta′tion n.

reg·i·men·tals (rej′ə-men′təlz) n.pl. 1. A military uniform. 2. The uniform worn by a regiment.

re·gion (rē′jən) n. 1. An indefinite portion of territory or space, usu. of considerable extent. 2. A particular area or place: the delta region of the Nile. 3. General area; scope; province: in the region of literature. 4. A portion of the body. 5. A realm (def. 3). [< AF < L < regere to rule]

re·gion·al (rē′jən-əl) adj. 1. Of or pertaining to a particular region; sectional; local: regional planning. 2. Of or pertaining to an entire region or section. — re′gion·al·ly adv.

reg·is·ter (rej′is-tər) n. 1. A formal or official record or account, as of names or transactions; also, a book containing such a record. 2. An individual entry in a register. 3. Any of various devices for counting or recording: a cash register. 4. An official keeper of records; registrar. 5. Music A A portion of the compass of a voice or instrument having tones of a relatively homogeneous timbre. b A full set of organ pipes or harpsichord strings controlled by a single stop. 6. A device by which heated or cooled air is admitted to a room. 7. Printing a Exact correspondence of the lines and margins on the opposite sides of a printed sheet. b Correct relation of the colors in color printing. 8. The act of recording or registering; registry. — v.t. 1. To enter in or as in a register; record officially or exactly. 2. To indicate, as on a scale. 3. To express; show: His face registered shock. 4. To cause (mail) to be recorded, on payment of a fee, when deposited with the postal system, so as to insure delivery. 5. Printing To effect the exact correspondence of; put in register. — v.i. 6. To enter one's name in a register. 7. To cause one's name to be included on a list of eligible voters by fulfilling certain requirements. 8. Informal To have effect; make an impression. 9. Printing To be in register. [< OF < Med.L < LL < L < re- back + gerere to carry] — reg·is·tra·ble (rej′is-trə-bəl) adj. — reg′is·trant n.

reg·is·tered (rej′is-tərd) adj. 1. Recorded, as a birth, a voter, an animal's pedigree, etc. 2. Having a required or official certificate, as a nurse.

registered nurse A graduate nurse licensed to practice by the appropriate State authority and entitled to add R.N. after her name.

reg·is·trar (rej′is-trär, rej′is·trär′) n. An authorized keeper of a register or of records; esp., a college or university officer who records the enrollment of students, their grades, etc.

reg·is·tra·tion (rej′is·trā′shən) n. 1. The act of entering in a registry; also, such an entry. 2. The registering of voters; also, the number of voters registered. 3. Enrollment in a school, college, or university. 4. Music The combination of stops used in playing a composition on the organ.

reg·is·try (rej′is-trē) n. pl. ·tries 1. The act of registering; registration. 2. A register, or the place where it is kept.

reg·nant (reg′nənt) adj. 1. Reigning in one's own right. 2. Dominant. [< L regnum reign] — reg′nan·cy n.

re·gorge (ri-gôrj′) v.t. ·gorged, ·gorg·ing To vomit up; disgorge. [< F < re- again + gorger to gorge]

re·gress (n. rē′gres; v. ri-gres′) n. 1. Passage back; return. 2. The power or right of passing back. 3. Withdrawal; retrogression. — v.i. To go back; move backward; return. [< L < re- back + gradi to walk] — re·gres′sor n.

re·gres·sion (ri-gresh′ən) n. 1. The act of regressing. 2. Psychoanal. A retreat of the libido to earlier and less mature forms of behavior. 3. Stat. The return to a mean or average value. 4. Med. The subsidence of a disease.

re·gres·sive (ri-gres′iv) adj. 1. Tending to regress. 2. Of or marked by regression. 3. Denoting or pertaining to a tax or taxes in which the tax rate decreases as the amount taxed increases. — re·gres′sive·ly adv.

re·gret (ri-gret′) v.t. ·gret·ted, ·gret·ting 1. To look ba upon with a feeling of distress or loss. 2. To feel sorrow grief concerning. — n. 1. Distress of mind over loss or cumstances beyond one's control. 2. Remorseful sorro compunction. 3. pl. A polite refusal in response to an in tation. [< OF regreter < Gmc.] — re·gret′ta·ble adj. re·gret′ta·bly adv. — re·gret′ter n.

re·gret·ful (ri-gret′fəl) adj. Feeling, expressive of, or ful regret. — re·gret′ful·ly adv. — re·gret′ful·ness n.

reg·u·lar (reg′yə-lər) adj. 1. Made according to rule; sy metrical; normal. 2. Acting according to rule; methodi orderly: regular habits. 3. Constituted, appointed, or c ducted in the proper manner; duly authorized: a regu meeting. 4. Gram. Undergoing the inflection that is norm or most common to the class of words to which it belon said esp. of weak verbs. 5. Bot. Having all the parts or gans of the same kind uniform in structure or shape and si said mainly of flowers. 6. Eccl. Bound by a religious r 7. Mil. Pertaining or belonging to the permanent milit services. 8. In politics, adhering loyally to a party org zation or platform. 9. Geom. Having equal sides and ang 10. Math. Controlled or governed by one law or operat throughout: a regular equation. 11. Informal Thorou unmitigated; absolute. 12. U.S. Designating the com nent of the armed services that consists of persons in con uous service on active duty in both peace and war: the regu Army. — n. 1. A regular soldier. 2. Informal One re larly employed or engaged; also, a habitual customer. Eccl. A member of a religious or monastic order. 4. A p son loyal to a certain political party. [< OF < L < reg rule] — reg′u·lar·ly adv. — reg′u·lar·ness n.

reg·u·lar·i·ty (reg′yə-lar′ə-tē) n. pl. ·ties The state, q ity, or character of being regular; also, an instance of th

reg·u·lar·ize (reg′yə-lə-rīz′) v.t. ·ized, ·iz·ing To make ular. Also Brit. reg′u·lar·ise′. — reg′u·lar·i·za′tion n.

reg·u·late (reg′yə-lāt) v.t. ·lat·ed, ·lat·ing 1. To direc control according to certain rules, principles, etc. 2. adjust according to a standard, degree, etc.: to regulate rency. 3. To adjust to accurate operation. 4. To put in der. [< LL < regulare to rule] — reg′u·la′tive, reg′u to′ry adj.

reg·u·la·tion (reg′yə-lā′shən) n. 1. The act of regulat or the state of being regulated. 2. A rule of conduct.

reg·u·la·tor (reg′yə-lā′tər) n. 1. One who or that wh regulates. 2. A device for regulating the rate of a wa 3. Mech. A contrivance for regulating or equalizing mot or flow. — reg′u·la′tor·ship n.

Reg·u·lus (reg′yə-ləs) A white star, one of the 20 bright 1.34 magnitude; Alpha in the constellation Leo. [< L]

re·gur·gi·tate (ri-gûr′jə-tāt) v. ·tat·ed, ·tat·ing v.i. rush, pour, or surge back. — v.t. 2. To cause to surge ba as partially digested food; vomit. [< Med.L < re- back LL gurgitare to swallow, engulf] — re·gur′gi·tant adj. re·gur′gi·ta′tion n.

re·ha·bil·i·tate (rē′hə-bil′ə-tāt) v.t. ·tat·ed, ·tat·ing 1. restore to a former state, capacity, privilege, rank, etc.; r state. 2. To restore to a state of health, useful activity, e through training, therapy, guidance. [< Med.L < re- b + HABILITATE] — re′ha·bil′i·ta′tion n.

re·hash (v. rē-hash′; n. rē′hash′) v.t. To work into a form; go over again. — n. Something hashed over, or m or served up from something used before.

re·hear·ing (rē-hir′ing) n. A new hearing, as in court.

re·hears·al (ri-hûr′səl) n. 1. A practice session or perfo ance of a play, etc. 2. The act of practicing or drilling public performance. 3. The act of telling over again.

re·hearse (ri-hûrs′) v. ·hearsed, ·hears·ing v.t. 1. To form privately in preparation for public performance, play or song. 2. To instruct by rehearsal. 3. To say c again; repeat aloud; recite. 4. To give an account of; late. — v.i. 5. To rehearse a play, song, dance, etc. OF < re- again + hercier to harrow] — re·hears′er n.

Reich (rīkh) n. Germany or its government. — First R The Holy Roman Empire from its establishment in the n century to its collapse in 1806. — Second Reich Eithe two German governments in the period 1871–1933. Third Reich The Nazi state under Adolf Hitler, 1933– [< G, realm]

reichs·mark (rīkhs′märk′) n. A former standard monet unit of Germany, worth about 24 U.S. cents.

Reichs·tag (rīkhs′täkh) n. The former legislative assem of Germany. [< G]

reign (rān) n. 1. The possession or exercise of supr power, esp. royal power; sovereignty. 2. The time or d tion of a sovereign's rule. — v.i. 1. To hold and exer sovereign power. 2. To hold sway; prevail: Winter rei [< F < L regnum rule]

Reign of Terror The period of the French Revolution f May, 1793, to August, 1794, during which thousands w guillotined, including Louis XVI and Marie Antoinette.

re·im·burse (rē′im-bûrs′) v.t. ·bursed, ·burs·ing 1. To

ack (a person) an equivalent for what has been spent or lost; compense; indemnify. **2.** To pay back; refund. [< RE- obs. *imburse*] **— re/im·burs/a·ble** *adj.* **— re/im·burse/·ent** *n.* **— re/im·burs/er** *n.*

·im·port (*v.* rē/im·pôrt/, -pōrt/, rē·im/·pôrt, -pōrt; *n.* rē·im/·ōrt, -pōrt) *v.t.* To import (goods, etc., previously export-) again. **— n. 1.** The act of importing again. **2.** That hich is reimported. **— re/im·por·ta/tion** *n.*

n (rān) *n.* **1.** *Usu. pl.* A strap attached to the bit to con-ol a horse or other draft animal. **2.** Any means of restraint control; a check. **— v.t. 1.** To guide, check, or halt with as with reins. **2.** To furnish with reins. **— v.i. 3.** To eck or halt a horse by means of reins: with *in* or *up.* [< **F** < L *retinere* to retain]

in·car·nate (rē/in·kär/nāt) *v.t.* **·nat·ed, ·nat·ing** To cause undergo reincarnation.

in·car·na·tion (rē/in·kär·nā/shən) *n.* **1.** A rebirth of the ul in successive bodies; also, the belief in such rebirth. **2.** Vedic religions, the becoming of an avatar again.

n·deer (rān/dir/) *n.* *pl.* **·deer** A deer of northern re-ons, having branched antlers in both sexes, long domesti-ted for its milk, hide, and flesh, and used as a pack animal. < ON < *hreinn* reindeer + *dȳr* deer]

in·force (rē/in·fôrs/, -fōrs/) *v.t.* **·forced, ·forc·ing 1.** To ve new force or strength to. **2.** *Mil.* To strengthen with ad-tional personnel or equipment. **3.** To add some strength-ing part or material to. **4.** *Psychol.* To strengthen (a sponse) by the addition of another stimulus, as a reward. so spelled **reenforce.** [< RE- + *inforce*, var. of ENFORCE]

nforced concrete Concrete containing metal bars, rods, netting disposed through the mass to increase its tensile ength and durability: also called *ferro-concrete.*

in·force·ment (rē/in·fôrs/mənt, -fōrs/-) *n.* **1.** The act of inforcing. **2.** *Often pl. Mil.* A fresh body of troops or addi-nal vessels. Also spelled *reenforcement.*

in·state (rē/in·stāt/) *v.t.* **·stat·ed, ·stat·ing** To restore to ormer state, position, etc. **— re/in·state/ment** *n.*

in·sure (rē/in·shŏŏr/) *v.t.* **·sured, ·sur·ing 1.** To protect e risk on a policy already issued) by obtaining insurance m a second insurer: said of a first insurer. **2.** To insure ew. **— re/in·sur/ance** *n.* **— re/in·sur/er** *n.*

·s·sue (rē·ish/ōō) *n.* **1.** A second or subsequent issue, as a publication changed in form or price. **2.** A second print-g of postage stamps from the same plates. **— v.t. ·sued,** ·ing To issue again.

·t·er·ate (rē·it/ə·rāt) *v.t.* **·at·ed, ·at·ing** To say or do ain and again. [< L *re-* again + ITERATE] **— re·it/er-ion** *n.* **— re·it/er·a/tive** *adj.* **— re·it/er·a/tive·ly** *adv.*

·ect (*v.* ri·jekt/; *n.* rē/jekt) *v.t.* **1.** To refuse to accept, rec-nize, believe, etc. **2.** To refuse to grant; deny, as a peti-n. **3.** To refuse (a person) recognition, acceptance, etc. To expel, as from the mouth; vomit. **5.** To cast away as rthless; discard. **— n.** One who or that which has been ected. [< L < *re-* back + *jacere* to throw] **— re·ject/er** re·jec/tor *n.* **— re·jec/tion** *n.*

oice (ri·jois/) *v.* **·joiced, ·joic·ing** *v.i.* **1.** To feel joyful; glad. **— v.t. 2.** To fill with joy; gladden. [< OF < *re-* ain + *esjoir* to be joyous] **— re·joic/er** *n.*

oic·ing (ri·joi/sing) *adj.* Pertaining to or characterized joyfulness. **— n.** The feeling or expression of joy.

oin[1] (ri·join/) *v.t.* **1.** To say in reply; answer. **— v.i. 2.** answer; respond. [< F < *re-* again + *joindre* to join]

oin[2] (rē/join/) *v.t.* **1.** To come again into company with. To join together again; reunite. **— v.i. 3.** To come to-ther again. [< RE- + JOIN]

oin·der (ri·join/dər) *n.* **1.** An answer to a reply; also, y reply or retort. **2.** *Law* The answer filed by a defendant a plaintiff's replication.

u·ve·nate (ri·jōō/və·nāt) *v.t.* **·nat·ed, ·nat·ing** To give w vigor or youthfulness to. Also **re·ju/ve·nize.** [< RE- + *juvenis* young + -ATE¹] **— re·ju/ve·na/tion** *n.*

lapse (ri·laps/; *for n., also* rē/laps) *v.i.* **lapsed, ·laps·ing** To lapse back, as into a disease. **2.** To return to bad bits or ways; backslide. **— n.** The act or condition of re-sing. [< L < *re-* back + *labi* to slide] **— re·laps/er** *n.*

ate (ri·lāt/) *v.* **·lat·ed, ·lat·ing** *v.t.* **1.** To tell the events the particulars of; narrate. **2.** To bring into connection relation. **— v.i. 3.** To have relation: with *to.* **4.** To have erence: with *to.* [< F *relater*] **— re·lat/er, re·la/tor** *n.* **— Syn. 1.** report, recount, recite, rehearse, state. **2.** connect, k, join, associate. **3.** pertain, apply.

at·ed (ri·lā/tid) *adj.* **1.** Standing in relation; connected. Connected by blood or marriage; of common ancestry; n. **3.** Narrated; told. **— re·lat/ed·ness** *n.*

a·tion (ri·lā/shən) *n.* **1.** The fact or condition of being ated or connected in some way. **2.** Connection by blood marriage; kinship. **3.** A person connected by blood or rriage; kinsman. **4.** Reference; regard; allusion: in *rela-*

tion to that matter. **5.** The position of one person with respect to another: the *relation* of ruler to subject. **6.** *pl.* Conditions or connections that bring an individual in touch with his fellows; also, any conditions or connections by which one country may come into contact with another politically and commercially. **7.** The act of narrating; also, that which is narrated. [< F < L. See REFER.] **— re·la/tion·al** *adj.*

re·la·tion·ship (ri·lā/shən·ship) *n.* The state of being re-lated; connection.
  — Syn. *Relationship, kinship, consanguinity,* and *affinity* are compared as they apply to persons of the same descent or family. *Relationship* is the most general term, embracing all the others and also the connection between things. *Kinship* is *relationship* by blood or marriage, and suggests mutual regard and affection. *Consanguinity* is *relationship* by blood only, and *affinity, relation-ship* by marriage only.

rel·a·tive (rel/ə·tiv) *adj.* **1.** Having connection; pertinent: an inquiry *relative* to one's health. **2.** Resulting from or de-pending upon relation; comparative: a *relative* truth. **3.** In-telligible only in relation to each other: the *relative* terms "father" and "son." **4.** Referring to, relating to, or qualify-ing an antecedent term: a *relative* pronoun. **— n. 1.** One who is related; a kinsman. **2.** A relative word or term, esp. a relative pronoun. [< OF < Med.L < L *relatus*] **— rel/a-tive·ly** *adv.* **— rel/a·tive·ness** *n.*

relative clause *Gram.* An adjective clause.

relative pronoun *Gram.* A pronoun that relates to an an-tecedent and introduces a qualifying clause, as *who* in *We found a boatman who ferried us.*

rel·a·tiv·i·ty (rel/ə·tiv/ə·tē) *n.* **1.** The quality or condition of being relative. **2.** *Philos.* Existence only as an object of, or in relation to, a thinking mind. **3.** A condition of depend-ence or of close relation, as of the solar system on the sun. **4.** *Physics* The principle of the interdependence of matter, energy, space, and time, as mathematically formulated by Albert Einstein. The **special theory of relativity** states that the velocity of light is the maximum velocity possible in the universe, that it is constant and independent of the motion of its source, and that energy and mass are interconvertible in accordance with the equation *energy = mass* $\times$ *the square of the speed of light* or $E = mc^2$. The **general theory of rela-tivity** extends these principles to the law of gravitation and the motions of the heavenly bodies.

re·lax (ri·laks/) *v.t.* **1.** To make lax or loose; make less tight or firm. **2.** To make less stringent or severe, as discipline. **3.** To abate; slacken, as efforts. **4.** To relieve from strain or effort. **— v.i. 5.** To become lax or loose; loosen. **6.** To be-come less stringent or severe. **7.** To rest; repose. **8.** To be-come less formal; unbend. [< L < *re-* again + *laxare* to loosen] **— re·lax/a·ble** *adj.* **— re/lax·a/tion** *n.* **— re·lax/-er** *n.*

re·lay (rē/lā, ri·lā/) *n.* **1.** A fresh set, as of men, horses, or dogs, to replace or relieve a tired set. **2.** A supply of any-thing kept in store for anticipated use or need. **3.** A relay race, or one of its laps or legs. **4.** *Electr.* A device that uti-lizes variations in the condition of a current in a circuit to effect the operation of similar devices in the same or another circuit. **— v.t. 1.** To send onward by or as by relays. **2.** To provide with relays. **3.** *Electr.* To operate or retransmit by means of a relay. [< MF < L *relaxare* to loosen again]

re·lay (rē·lā/) *v.t.* **-laid, -lay·ing** To lay again.

relay race A race between teams each member of which races a set part of the course and is relieved by a teammate.

re·lease (ri·lēs/) *v.t.* **·leased, ·leas·ing 1.** To set free; lib-erate. **2.** To deliver from worry, pain, obligation, etc. **3.** To free from something that holds, binds, etc. **4.** To permit the circulation, sale, performance, etc., of, as a motion pic-ture, phonograph record, or news item. **— n. 1.** The act of releasing or the state of being released. **2.** A discharge from responsibility or penalty, as from a debt. **3.** *Law* An instru-ment of conveyance by which one surrenders and relinquish-es all claim to something; quitclaim. **4.** Anything formally released to the public, as news, a motion picture, etc. **5.** *Mech.* Any catch or device to hold and release a mechanism, weights, etc. [< OF < L *relaxare* to relax] **— re·leas/er** *n.*

re·lease (rē/lēs/) *v.t.* **·leased, ·leas·ing** To lease again.

released time *U.S.* A period during which school children are released from classes to receive religious instruction.

rel·e·gate (rel/ə·gāt) *v.t.* **·gat·ed, ·gat·ing 1.** To send off or consign, as to an obscure position or place. **2.** To assign, as to a particular class or sphere. **3.** To refer (a matter) to someone for decision **4.** To banish; exile. [< L < *re-* back + *legare* to send] **— rel/e·ga/tion** *n.*

re·lent (ri·lent/) *v.i.* To soften in temper; become more gen-tle or compassionate. [< L < *re-* again + *lentus* soft]

re·lent·less (ri·lent/lis) *adj.* **1.** Unremitting; continuous. **2.** Indifferent to the pain of others; pitiless. **— re·lent/less-ly** *adv.* **— re·lent/less·ness** *n.*

rel·e·vant (rel′ə·vənt) *adj.* Fitting or suiting given requirements; pertinent; applicable: usu. with *to*. [< Med.L ppr. of *relevare* to bear upon] — **rel′e·vance, rel′e·van·cy** *n.* — **rel′e·vant·ly** *adv.*

re·li·a·ble (ri·lī′ə·bəl) *adj.* That may be relied upon; worthy of confidence; trustworthy. — **re·li′a·bil′i·ty, re·li′a·ble·ness** *n.* — **re·li′a·bly** *adv.*

re·li·ance (ri·lī′əns) *n.* **1.** The act of relying, or the condition of being reliant. **2.** Something relied upon.

re·li·ant (ri·lī′ənt) *adj.* Manifesting reliance, esp. upon oneself. — **re·li′ant·ly** *adv.*

rel·ic (rel′ik) *n.* **1.** Some remaining portion or fragment of that which has vanished or been destroyed. **2.** A keepsake or memento. **3.** The body or part of the body of a saint, or any sacred memento. **4.** Any outworn custom, institution, etc. [< OF < L *reliquiae* remains, leavings.]

re·lief (ri·lēf′) *n.* **1.** The act of relieving, or the state of being relieved. **2.** That which relieves. **3.** Charitable aid, as food or money. **4.** The release, as of a sentinel or guard, from his post or duty, and the substitution of some other person or persons; also, the person or persons so substituted. **5.** In architecture and sculpture, the projection of a figure, ornament, etc., from a surface: also, any such figure. **6.** In painting, the apparent projection of forms and masses. **7.** *Geog.* **a** The elevations and unevenness of land surface. **b** The parts of a map that portray the configuration of the district represented; contour lines. [See RELIEVE.]

re·lieve (ri·lēv′) *v.t.* **·lieved, ·liev·ing 1.** To free wholly or partly from pain, embarrassment, etc. **2.** To lessen or alleviate, as pain or anxiety. **3.** To give aid or assistance to. **4.** To free from obligation, injustice, etc. **5.** To release from duty, as a sentinel, by providing or serving as a substitute. **6.** To make less monotonous, harsh, or unpleasant; vary. **7.** To bring into relief or prominence. **8.** To rid (oneself) of urine or excrement. [< OF < L < *re-* again + *levare* to lift, raise] — **re·liev′a·ble** *adj.* — **re·liev′er** *n.*

re·li·gion (ri·lij′ən) *n.* **1.** The beliefs, attitudes, emotions, behavior, etc., constituting man's relationship with the powers and principles of the universe, esp. with a deity or deities. **2.** An object of conscientious devotion or scrupulous care: *His work is a religion to him.* [< OF < L < *re-* back + *ligare* to bind]

re·li·gious (ri·lij′əs) *adj.* **1.** Feeling and manifesting religion; devout; pious **2.** Of or pertaining to religion: a *religious* teacher. **3.** Strict in performance; conscientious: a *religious* loyalty. **4.** Belonging to the monastic life. — *n. pl.* **·ious** A person devoted to a life of piety; a monk or nun. [< OF < Med.L *religiosus*] — **re·li′gious·ly** *adv.* — **re·li′gious·ness** *n.*

re·lin·quish (ri·ling′kwish) *v.t.* **1.** To give up; abandon. **2.** To renounce: to *relinquish* a claim. **3.** To let go (a hold, etc.). [< OF < L < *re-* back, from + *linquere* to leave] — **re·lin′quish·er** *n.* — **re·lin′quish·ment** *n.*

rel·i·quar·y (rel′ə·kwer′ē) *n. pl.* **·quar·ies** A repository for relics, as a casket, coffer, or shrine. [< F < L < *re-* back, from + *linquere* to leave]

rel·ish (rel′ish) *n.* **1.** Appetite; appreciation; liking. **2.** The flavor, esp. when agreeable, in food and drink. **3.** The quality in anything that lends spice or zest: Danger gives *relish* to adventure. **4.** Something taken with food to lend it flavor, as chopped pickles and spices. **5.** A small but important characteristic; flavoring. — *v.t.* **1.** To like the savor of; enjoy. **2.** To give pleasant flavor to. — *v.i.* **3.** To have an agreeable flavor; afford gratification. [ME < OF *relaissier* to leave behind] — **rel′ish·a·ble** *adj.* — **Syn.** (noun) **1.** gusto, zest.

re·luc·tance (ri·luk′təns) *n.* **1.** The state of being reluctant. **2.** *Electr.* Capacity for opposing magnetic induction. Also **re·luc′tan·cy.** — **Syn. 1.** disinclination, unwillingness.

re·luc·tant (ri·luk′tənt) *adj.* **1.** Marked by unwillingness or rendered unwillingly. **2.** Disinclined to yield to some requirement. [< L < *re-* back + *luctari* to fight] — **re·luc′tant·ly** *adv.* — **Syn. 1.** averse, hesitant, indisposed, loath.

rel·uc·tiv·i·ty (rel′ək·tiv′ə·tē) *n. pl.* **·ties** *Electr.* The specific electrical resistance to magnetization, of a given substance per unit of length or cross section.

re·ly (ri·lī′) *v.i.* **·lied, ·ly·ing** To place trust or confidence: with *on* or *upon*. [< OF < L < *re-* again + *ligare* to bind]

rem (rem) *n.* *Physics* The quantity of absorbed ionizing radiation that has the same biological effect as one roentgen of X-ray or gamma ray radiation. [< R(OENTGEN) + E(QUIVALENT) + M(AN)]

REM *n.* Rapid eye movement.

re·main (ri·mān′) *v.i.* **1.** To stay or be left behind after the removal, departure, or destruction of other persons or things. **2.** To continue in one place, condition, or character: *He remained* in office. **3.** To be left as something to be done, dealt with, etc.: *It remains* to be proved. **4.** To endure or last; abide. [< OF < L < *re-* back + *manere* to stay]

re·main·der (ri·mān′dər) *n.* **1.** That which remain **2.** *Math.* The quantity left after subtraction or divisi **3.** A book disposed of by a publisher at a reduced pri — *adj.* Left over. — *v.t.* To sell (books) as remainders.

re·mains (ri·mānz′) *n.pl.* **1.** That which is left after a p has been removed or destroyed. **2.** The body of a deceas person. **3.** Writings of an author published after his dea **4.** Survivals of the past, as fossils, etc.

re·mand (ri·mand′, -mänd′) *v.t.* **1.** To order or send ba **2.** *Law* To recommit to custody, as an accused person afte preliminary examination. — *n.* **1.** A remanding, or be remanded. **2.** A remanded person. [< OF < LL < L back + *mandare* to order] — **re·mand′ment** *n.*

re·mark (ri·märk′) *n.* **1.** An oral or written comment saying; a casual observation. **2.** The act of observing or ticing; observation; notice. — *v.t.* **1.** To say or write way of comment. **2.** To take particular notice of. — **3.** To make remarks: with *on* or *upon*. [< F < *re-* again *marquer* to mark] — **re·mark′er** *n.*

re·mark·a·ble (ri·mär′kə·bəl) *adj.* **1.** Worthy of not **2.** Extraordinary; unusual; conspicuous; distinguished. — **re·mark′a·ble·ness** *n.* — **re·mark′a·bly** *adv.*

re·me·di·a·ble (ri·mē′dē·ə·bəl) *adj.* Capable of being cu or remedied. [< MF < L *remediabilis*] — **re·me′di·a·ble ness** *n.* — **re·me′di·a·bly** *adv.*

re·me·di·al (ri·mē′dē·əl) *adj.* Of the nature of or adap to be used as a remedy: *remedial* measures. [< L < *re diare* to remedy] — **re·me′di·al·ly** *adv.*

rem·e·dy (rem′ə·dē) *n. pl.* **·dies 1.** That which cures affords relief to bodily disease or ailment; a medicine; a remedial treatment. **2.** A means of counteracting or rem ing an error, evil, etc. **3.** *Law* A legal mode for enforcin right or redressing or preventing a wrong. — *v.t.* **·died ing 1.** To cure or heal, as by medicinal treatment. **2.** make right; correct. **3.** To overcome or remove (an e defect, etc.). [< AF < OF < L < *re-* again + *meder heal*]

re·mem·ber (ri·mem′bər) *v.t.* **1.** To bring back or re again to the mind or memory. **2.** To keep in mind carefu as for a purpose. **3.** To bear in mind as worthy of a rewa gift, etc.: *She remembered* me in her will. **4.** To reward; — *v.i.* **5.** To have or use one's memory. — **to remem (one) to** To inform a person of the regard of: *Remember to your wife.* [< OF < LL < L < *re-* again + *memorar bring to mind*] — **re·mem′ber·er** *n.*

re·mem·brance (ri·mem′brəns) *n.* **1.** The act or powe remembering, or the state of being remembered. **2.** period within which one can remember. **3.** That whic remembered. **4.** *Often pl.* A memento; keepsake. **5.** ful regard. [< OF]

re·mind (ri·mīnd′) *v.t.* To bring to (someone's) mind; ca to remember. — **re·mind′er** *n.* — **re·mind′ful** *adj.*

rem·i·nisce (rem′ə·nis′) *v.i.* **·nisced, ·nisc·ing** *Chiefly* To recall incidents or events of the past; indulge in rem cences. [Back formation < REMINISCENCE]

rem·i·nis·cence (rem′ə·nis′əns) *n.* **1.** The recalling to n of past incidents and events. **2.** The narration of past periences. **3.** A feature, etc., serving as a reminder of s thing else. [< MF or LL < L < *re-* again + *memini* to member] — **rem′i·nis′cent** *adj.* — **rem′i·nis′cent·ly** a

re·miss (ri·mis′) *adj.* Slack or careless in matters requi attention; dilatory; negligent. [< L < *re-* back + *m to send*] — **re·miss′ness** *n.*

re·mis·si·ble (ri·mis′ə·bəl) *adj.* Capable of being remi or pardoned, as sins. [< F *rémissible*] — **re·mis′si·bil′i** *n.*

re·mis·sion (ri·mish′ən) *n.* **1.** The act of remitting, or state of being remitted. **2.** Discharge from penalty; par deliverance, as from a debt or obligation. **3.** *Med.* T porary abatement of a disease or pain. Also **re·mit·ta** mit′l). [See REMIT.]

re·mit (ri·mit′) *v.* **·mit·ted, ·mit·ting** *v.t.* **1.** To sen money in payment for goods; transmit. **2.** To refrain fi exacting or inflicting, as a penalty. **3.** To pardon; for as a sin or crime. **4.** To abate; relax, as vigilance. **5** refer or submit for judgment, settlement, etc., as to or authority. **6.** *Law* To refer (a legal proceeding) to a l court for further consideration. **7.** *Rare* To send back, prison. — *v.i.* **8.** To send money, as in payment. **9** diminish; abate. [< L < *re-* back + *mittere* to send] **re·mit′ta·ble** *adj.* — **re·mit′ter** or **re·mit′tor** *n.*

re·mit·tance (ri·mit′əns) *n.* The act of sending mone credit; also, the money or credit so sent.

re·mit·tent (ri·mit′ənt) *adj.* Having temporary dim tions of energy or action, as a fever. — *n.* A remittent f — **re·mit′tence, re·mit′ten·cy** *n.* — **re·mit′tent·ly** *adv.*

rem·nant (rem′nənt) *n.* **1.** That which remains of a thing. **2.** The piece of cloth, etc., left over after the last ting. **3.** Any small piece or quantity. — *adj.* Remai [< OF < L < *re-* back + *manere* to stay, remain]

re·mod·el (rē·mod′l) *v.t.* **·eled** or **·elled, ·el·ing** or **·el·lin** To model again. **2.** To make over or anew.

mon·e·tize (ri·mon'ə·tīz) *v.t.* **·tized, ·tiz·ing** To reinstate (p. silver) as lawful money. — **re·mon'e·ti·za'tion** *n.*

mon·strance (ri·mon'strəns) *n.* **1.** The act of remonstrating; protest; expostulation. **2.** Expostulatory counsel.

mon·strant (ri·mon'strənt) *adj.* Having the character of a remonstrance; expostulatory. — *n.* One who presents signs a remonstrance.

mon·strate (ri·mon'strāt) *v.* **·strat·ed, ·strat·ing** *v.t.* **1.** to say or plead in protest. — *v.i.* **2.** To urge strong reasons against any course or action; protest; object. [< Med.L < *re-* again + *monstrare* to show] — **re·mon·stra·tion** (ē'mon·strā'shən, rem'ən-) *n.* — **re·mon'stra·tive** (-strə-) **·) *adj.* — **re·mon'stra·tor** (-strā·tər) *n.*

norse (ri·môrs') *n.* The keen or hopeless anguish caused by a sense of guilt; distressing self-reproach. [< OF < LL L < *re-* again + *mordere* to bite] — **re·morse'ful** *adj.* — **morse'ful·ly** *adv.* — **re·morse'ful·ness** *n.* — **re·morse'- is** *adj.* — **re·morse'less·ly** *adv.* — **re·morse'less·ness** *n.*

note (ri·mōt') *adj.* **·mot·er, ·mot·est** **1.** Located far from specified place. **2.** Distant in time. **3.** Having slight relation or connection: a *remote* cousin. **4.** Not obvious; slight. Distant in manner; aloof. [< L < *re-* again + *movere* move] — **re·mote'ly** *adv.* — **re·mote'ness** *n.*

note control Control from a distance by electrical or lio circuits, as in the operation of a machine, aircraft, ided missile, etc.

mount (*v.* ri·mount'; *n.* rē'mount') *v.t. & v.i.* To mount ain. — *n.* **1.** A new setting or framing. **2.** A fresh riding rse. [< OF < *re-* again (< L) + *monter* to climb]

nov·a·ble (ri·mōo'və·bəl) *adj.* Capable of being re·ved. — **re·mov'a·bil'i·ty, re·mov'a·ble·ness** *n.* — **re· v'a·bly** *adv.*

nov·al (ri·mōo'vəl) *n.* **1.** The act of removing, or the .te of being removed. **2.** Dismissal, as from office. **3.** anging of place, as of residence or business.

nove (ri·mōov') *v.* **·moved, ·mov·ing** *v.t.* **1.** To take or ve away, as from one place to another. **2.** To take off; ff, as a hat. **3.** To get rid of; do away with: to *remove* uses. **4.** To kill. **5.** To displace or dismiss, as from office. To take out; extract: with *from.* — *v.i.* **7.** To change 's place of residence or business. **8.** *Poetic* To go away. *n.* **1.** The act of removing, as one's business or belongings. The space moved over in changing an object from one sition to another. **3.** A degree of difference; step: He is a fool *remove* from a fool. [< OF < L < *re-* again + *vere* to move] — **re·mov'er** *n.* — **Syn.** (verb) **1.** transfer, transplant, transpose. **3.** eliminate, iterate, eradicate. **5.** depose, disestablish.

noved (ri·mōovd') *adj.* Separated, as by intervening ace, time, or relationship, or by difference in kind: a cousin ice *removed.* — **re·mov·ed·ness** (ri·mōo'vid·nis) *n.*

nu·ner·ate (ri·myōo'nə·rāt) *v.t.* **·at·ed, ·at·ing** To make t or adequate return to or for; pay or pay for. [< L < *re-* ain + *munus* gift] — **re·mu'ner·a·bil'i·ty** *n.* — **re·mu'· r·a·ble** *adj.* — **re·mu'ner·a'tion** *n.* — **re·mu'ner·a'tive** ə·rā'tiv, -nər·ə·tiv) *adj.* — **re·mu'ner·a'tive·ly** *adv.*

mus (rē'məs) In Roman mythology, the twin brother of mulus. See ROMULUS.

· Var. of RENI-.

·ais·sance (ren'ə·säns', -zäns', ri·nā'səns; *Fr.* rə·ne·säns') A new birth; resurrection; renas· ice. [< F < L < *re-* again + *sci* to be born]

1·ais·sance (ren'ə·säns', -zäns', nā'səns; *Fr.* rə·ne·säns') *n.* **1.** ue revival of letters and art in Eu· oe, marking the transition from dieval to modern history. **2.** The riod of this revival, roughly from e 14th through the 16th century. The style of art, literature, etc., at was developed in and charac· istic of this period. Also *Renas· ice.* — *adj.* **1.** Of the Renais· ice. **2.** Pertaining to a style of ihitecture developed in Italy in e 15th century, and based on the ssic Roman style.

al (rē'nəl) *adj.* Of, pertaining affecting, or near the kidneys. [F < LL < L *renes* kidneys]

n·ard (ren'ərd) See REYNARD.

nas·cence (ri·nas'əns) *n.* A re· ·th; revival. [< L < *re-* again + *nasci* to be born] — **re· s/cent** *adj.*

nas·cence (ri·nas'əns) *n.* The Renaissance.

id (rend) *v.* **rent or rend·ed, rend·ing** *v.t.* **1.** To tear art forcibly. **2.** To pull or remove forcibly: with *away,*

from, off, etc. **3.** To pass through (the air) violently and noisily. **4.** To distress (the heart, etc.). — *v.i.* **5.** To split; part. [OE *rendan* to tear] — **rend'er** *n.*

ren·der (ren'dər) *v.t.* **1.** To give, present, or submit for action, approval, payment, etc. **2.** To provide; give: to *render* aid to the poor. **3.** To give as due: to *render* obedience. **4.** To perform; do: to *render* great service. **5.** To give or state formally. **6.** To give by way of requital: to *render* double for one's sins. **7.** To represent or depict, as in music or painting. **8.** To cause to be: to *render* a ship seaworthy. **9.** To translate. **10.** To melt and clarify, as lard. **11.** To give back; return: often with *back.* **12.** To surrender; give up. [< F < LL < L < *re-* back + *dare* to give] — **rend'er·a· ble** *adj.* — **ren'der·er** *n.*

ren·dez·vous (rän'dā·vōo, -də-; *Fr.* rän·dā·vōo') *n. pl.* **·vous** (-vōoz, *Fr.* -vōo') **1.** An appointed place of meeting. **2.** A meeting or an appointment to meet. — *v.t. & v.i.* **·voused** (-vōod), **·vous·ing** (-vōo'ing) To assemble or cause to assemble at a certain place or time. [< F < *se rendre* to betake oneself]

ren·di·tion (ren·dish'ən) *n.* **1.** The interpretation of a text; a translation. **2.** Artistic, dramatic, or musical interpretation; also, the performance or execution of a dramatic or musical composition. **3.** The act of rendering; also, that which is rendered. [< obs. F < *rendre* to render]

ren·e·gade (ren'ə·gād) *n.* **1.** One who forsakes his faith, etc. **2.** A traitor; deserter. Also **ren·e·ga'do** (-gā'dō). — *adj.* Of or characteristic of a renegade; traitorous. [< Sp. < Med.L < L *re-* again + *negare* to deny]

re·nege (ri·nig', -neg', -nēg') *v.i.* **·neged, ·neg·ing** **1.** In card games, to fail to follow suit when able and required by the rules to do so; revoke. **2.** *Informal* To fail to fulfill a promise. [See RENEGADE.] — **re·neg'er** *n.*

re·new (ri·nōo', -nyōo') *v.t.* **1.** To make new or as if new again; restore to a former or sound condition. **2.** To begin again; resume. **3.** To repeat: to *renew* an oath. **4.** To regain (vigor, strength, etc.). **5.** To cause to continue in effect; extend. **6.** To revive; reestablish. **7.** To replenish or replace, as provisions. — *v.i.* **8.** To become new again. **9.** To begin or commence again. [< RE- + NEW] — **re·new'· a·ble** *adj.* — **re·new'al** *n.* — **re·new'ed·ly** *adv.*

reni- *combining form* Kidney; of or related to the kidneys. Also **ren-** (before vowels): also **reno-.** [< L *ren, renis* kidney]

ren·i·form (ren'ə·fôrm, rē'nə-) *adj.* Kidney-shaped.

ren·net (ren'it) *n.* **1.** The mucous membrane lining the fourth stomach of a suckling calf or sheep. **2.** *Biochem.* A substance that yields rennin, obtained from the stomach of such an animal. [ME *rennen* to cause to run]

ren·nin (ren'in) *n. Biochem.* A milk-curdling enzyme present in rennet. [< RENN(ET) + -IN]

re·nounce (ri·nouns') *v.* **·nounced, ·nounc·ing** *v.t.* **1.** To give up, esp., by formal statement. **2.** To disown; repudiate. [< F < L < *re-* back, against + *nuntiare* to report] — **re·nounce'ment** *n.* — **re·nounc'er** *n.* — **Syn.** **1.** *Renounce* and *abjure* are often used in the general sense of put aside or abandon: to *renounce* one's citizenship, to *abjure* vice. *Forswear* has acquired an implication of perjury, esp. in the reflexive form: he *forswore* himself, that is, he swore falsely.

ren·o·vate (ren'ə·vāt) *v.t.* **·vat·ed, ·vat·ing** **1.** To make as good as new; repair. **2.** To renew; refresh. [< L < *re-* again + *novare* to make new] — **ren'o·va'tion** *n.* — **ren'o· va'tor** *n.*

re·nown (ri·noun') *n.* Exalted reputation; celebrity; fame. [< AF < OF < L *re-* again + *nominare* to name]

re·nowned (ri·nound') *adj.* Having renown; famous.

rent¹ (rent) *n.* **1.** Compensation made in any form by a tenant to a landlord or owner for the use of land, buildings, etc., esp., when paid in money at regular or specified intervals. **2.** Similar payment for the use of any property, movable or fixed. **3.** *Econ.* Income derived by the owner from the use or cultivation of his land or property. — **for rent** Available for use or occupancy by the paying of rent. — *v.t.* **1.** To obtain temporary possession and use of for a rent. **2.** To grant such temporary possession and use. — *v.i.* **3.** To be let for rent. [< OF < L < *re-* back + *dare* to give] — **rent'a·ble** *adj.* — **rent'er** *n.*

rent² (rent) Alternative past tense and past participle of REND. — *n.* **1.** A hole or slit made by rending or tearing; rip; fissure. **2.** A violent separation; schism.

rent·al (ren'təl) *n.* **1.** The revenue from rented property **2.** A schedule of rents. — *adj.* Of or for rent. [< AF]

ren·tier (rän·tyā') *n. French* One who owns or derives a fixed income from invested capital or lands.

re·nun·ci·a·tion (ri·nun'sē·ā'shən, -shē-) *n.* **1.** The act of renouncing or disclaiming; repudiation. **2.** A declaration or statement in which something is renounced. [< L *renunciatio, -onis* proclamation] — **re·nun'ci·a'tive** *adj.* — **re· nun·ci·a·to·ry** (ri·nun'sē·ə·tôr'ē, -tō'rē, -shē-) *adj.*

re·or·der (rē-ôr′dər) *v.t.* **1.** To order (goods) again. **2.** To put back into order. **3.** To give a different order to; rearrange. — *n.* Goods ordered again.

re·or·gan·i·za·tion (rē′ôr·gən·ə·zā′shən, -ī·zā′-) *n.* **1.** The act of reorganizing, or the condition of being reorganized. **2.** The legal reconstruction of a corporation.

re·or·gan·ize (rē·ôr′gən·īz) *v.t.* & *v.i.* **·ized, ·iz·ing** To organize anew. — **re·or′gan·iz′er** *n.*

rep[1] (rep) *n.* A silk, cotton, rayon, or wool fabric having a crosswise rib: also spelled *repp*. [< F *reps*, prob. < E *ribs*]

rep[2] (rep) *n. Slang* Reputation.

re·pair[1] (ri·pâr′) *v.t.* **1.** To restore to sound or good condition after damage, decay, etc.; mend. **2.** To make amends for (an injury); remedy. **3.** To make up, as a loss; compensate for. — *n.* **1.** The act or process of repairing. **2.** Condition after use or after repairing: in good *repair*. [< OF < L *re-* again + *parare* to prepare, make ready] — **re·pair′er** *n.*

re·pair[2] (ri·pâr′) *v.i.* To betake oneself; go: to *repair* to the garden. [< OF < LL < L *re-* again + *patria* native land]

re·pair·man (ri·pâr′mən, -mən) *n. pl.* **·men** (-men′, -mən) A man whose work is to make repairs.

rep·a·ra·ble (rep′ər·ə·bəl) *adj.* Capable of being repaired. Also **re·pair·a·ble** (ri·pâr′ə·bəl). — **rep′a·ra·bil′i·ty** *n.* — **rep′a·ra·bly** *adv.*

rep·a·ra·tion (rep′ə·rā′shən) *n.* **1.** The act of making amends; atonement. **2.** That which is done by way of amends or satisfaction. **3.** The act of repairing or the state of being repaired. **4.** *pl.* Indemnities paid by defeated countries for acts of war. [< OF < LL < L. See REPAIR.[1]] — **re·par·a·tive** (ri·par′ə·tiv) *adj.*

rep·ar·tee (rep′ər·tē′, -är-, -tā′) *n.* **1.** Conversation marked by quick and witty replies. **2.** Skill or quickness in such conversation. **3.** A witty or quick reply; a sharp rejoinder. [< OF < *repartir* to depart again, reply]

re·past (ri·past′, -päst′) *n.* **1.** Food taken at a meal. **2.** A meal. [< OF < Med.L < LL < L *re-* again + *pascere* to feed]

re·pa·tri·ate (*v.* rē·pā′trē·āt; *n.* rē·pā′trē·it) *v.t.* **·at·ed, ·at·ing** To send back to one's own country or to the place of citizenship. — *n.* One who has been repatriated. [< LL < L *re-* again + *patria* native land] — **re·pa′tri·a′tion** *n.*

re·pay (ri·pā′) *v.* **·paid, ·pay·ing** *v.t.* **1.** To pay back; refund. **2.** To pay back or refund something to. **3.** To give a reward or inflict a penalty for; recompense or retaliate for. — *v.i.* **4.** To make repayment or requital. [< OF *repaier*] — **re·pay′a·ble** *adj.* — **re·pay′ment** *n.*

re·peal (ri·pēl′) *v.t.* To rescind, as a law; revoke. — **Syn.** See ANNUL. — *n.* The act of repealing; revocation. [< OF < *re-* back, again + *apeler* to call, summon] — **re·peal′a·ble** *adj.* — **re·peal′er** *n.*

re·peat (ri·pēt′) *v.t.* **1.** To say again; iterate. **2.** To recite from memory. **3.** To say (what another has just said) **4.** To tell, as a secret, to another. **5.** To do, make, or experience again. — *v.i.* **6.** To say or do something again; esp., to vote more than once in an election. — *n.* **1.** The act of repeating; a repetition. **2.** *Music* A passage that is repeated; also, any notations indicating this. **3.** Anything repeated. [< OF < L *re-* again + *petere* to seek, demand]

re·peat·ed (ri·pē′tid) *adj.* Occurring or spoken again and again; reiterated. — **re·peat′ed·ly** *adv.*

re·peat·er (ri·pē′tər) *n.* **1.** One who or that which repeats. **2.** A repeating firearm. **3.** *U.S.* One who votes, or attempts to vote, more than once at the same election. **4.** One who has been repeatedly imprisoned.

re·peat·ing decimal (ri·pē′ting) A decimal in which a series of digits is repeated indefinitely, as 0.16353535. . . .

repeating firearm A gun, rifle, or pistol capable of shooting several bullets without reloading.

re·pel (ri·pel′) *v.* **·pelled, ·pel·ling** *v.t.* **1.** To force or drive back; repulse. **2.** To reject; refuse, as a suggestion. **3.** To cause to feel distaste or aversion. **4.** To refuse to mix with or adhere to. **5.** To push or keep away, esp. with invisible force. — *v.i.* **6.** To act so as to drive something back or away. **7.** To cause distaste or aversion. [< L *re-* back + *pellere* to drive] — **re·pel′ler** *n.*

re·pel·lent (ri·pel′ənt) *adj.* **1.** Serving, tending, or having power to repel. **2.** Waterproof. **3.** Repugnant; repulsive. — *n.* Something that repels, as a compound to repel insects. — **re·pel′lence, re·pel′len·cy** *n.*

re·pent (ri·pent′) *v.i.* **1.** To feel remorse or regret, as for something one has done or failed to do; be contrite. **2.** To change one's mind concerning past action: with *of*: He *repented* of his generosity. — *v.t.* **3.** To feel remorse or regret for (an action, sin, etc.). **4.** To change one's mind concerning (a past action). [< OF < L *re-* again + *poenitere* to cause to repent] — **re·pent′er** *n.*

re·pen·tance (ri·pen′təns) *n.* The act of repenting or the condition of being repentant.

re·pen·tant (ri·pen′tənt) *adj.* Showing, feeling, or characterized by repentance. [< OF] — **re·pen′tant·ly** *adv.*

re·peo·ple (rē·pē′pəl) *v.t.* **·pled, ·pling 1.** To people and **2.** To provide again with animals; restock.

re·per·cus·sion (rē′pər·kush′ən) *n.* **1.** The act of driving back, or the state of being driven back; repulse. **2.** Echo; reverberation. **3.** A stroke or blow given in return; also, the recoil after impact. **4.** The indirect result of something; aftereffect. [< L *re-* again + *percutere* to strike] — *n.* **per·cus′sive** *adj.*

rep·er·toire (rep′ər·twär, -twôr) *n.* A list of songs, plays, operas, or the like, that a person or company is prepared to perform; also, such pieces collectively: also called *reperto-* [See REPERTORY.]

rep·er·to·ry (rep′ər·tôr′ē, -tō′rē) *n. pl.* **·ries 1.** Repertoire. **2.** A place where things are gathered together. **3.** The things as gathered. [< LL *repertorium* inventory < L *re-rire* to discover]

repertory company A theatrical group having a repertoire of productions, each typically running for a few weeks. A repertory theater.

rep·e·ti·tion (rep′ə·tish′ən) *n.* **1.** The act of repeating; the doing, making, or saying of something again. **2.** Recital from memory. **3.** That which is repeated; a copy. — **rep·e·ti·tive** (ri·pet′ə·tiv) *adj.* — **re·pet′i·tive·ly** *adv.*

rep·e·ti·tious (rep′ə·tish′əs) *adj.* Characterized by or containing repetition, esp. useless or tedious repetition. — **rep′e·ti′tious·ly** *adv.* — **rep′e·ti′tious·ness** *n.*

re·phrase (rē·frāz′) *v.t.* **·phrased, ·phras·ing** To phrase again; esp., to express in a new way.

re·pine (ri·pīn′) *v.i.* **·pined, ·pin·ing** To be discontented or fretful; complain; murmur. [< RE- + PINE[2]] — **re·pin′er** *n.*

re·place (ri·plās′) *v.t.* **·placed, ·plac·ing 1.** To put back in place. **2.** To take or fill the place of; supersede. **3.** To fund; repay. — **re·place′a·ble** *adj.* — **re·plac′er** *n.*

re·place·ment (ri·plās′mənt) *n.* **1.** One who or that which takes the place of another person or thing. **2.** The act of placing or the state of being replaced.

re·plen·ish (ri·plen′ish) *v.t.* **1.** To fill again, as something wholly or partially emptied. **2.** To bring back to fullness or completeness, as supplies. [< OF < L *re-* again + *ple- full*] — **re·plen′ish·er** *n.* — **re·plen′ish·ment** *n.*

re·plete (ri·plēt′) *adj.* **1.** Full or supplied to the uttermost. **2.** Gorged with food or drink; sated. [< L < L *re-* again + *plere* to fill] — **re·ple′tion** *n.*

re·plev·in (ri·plev′in) *Law n.* **1.** An action to regain possession of personal property unlawfully retained, on giving security to try the title and respond to the judgment; also recovery of property by such action **2.** The writ or process by which such proceedings are instituted. — *v.t.* To recover (goods) by a writ of replevin. Also **re·plev·y** (ri·plev′ē). [AF < OF < *re-* back + *plevir* to pledge]

rep·li·ca (rep′lə·kə) *n.* Any close copy or reproduction, esp. of a work of art, etc. [< Ital. < L *replicare* to reply]

rep·li·ca·tion (rep′lə·kā′shən) *n.* **1.** A reply. **2.** *Law* A plaintiff's reply to a defendant's plea or answer. [< OF L < *replicare* to answer to] — **rep′li·ca·tive** *adj.*

re·ply (ri·plī′) *v.* **·plied, ·ply·ing** *v.i.* **1.** To give an answer orally or in writing. **2.** To respond by some act, gesture, etc. **3.** To bounce back, as a sound; echo. **4.** *Law* To make a pleading in answer to the statement of the defense. — *v.t.* **5.** To say in answer: often with a clause as object. — *n. pl.* **·plies** Something said, written, or done by way of answer. [< OF < L *replicare* to fold back, answer to] — **re·pli′er** *n.*

re·port (ri·pôrt′, -pōrt′) *n.* **1.** To make or give an account of, often formally. **2.** To relate, as information obtained by investigation. **3.** To repeat to another, as an answer. **4.** To complain about, esp. to a superior. **5.** To state the result of consideration concerning: The committee *reported* the bill. — *v.i.* **6.** To make a report. **7.** To act as a reporter. **8.** To present oneself, as for duty. — *n.* **1.** That which is reported. **2.** A statement or record of an investigation, transaction, etc. **3.** Common talk; rumor. **4.** Fame; reputation or character. **5.** An explosive sound. [< OF < L *re-* back + *portare* to carry] — **re·port′a·ble** *adj.*

report card *U.S.* A periodic statement of a pupil's scholastic record, which is presented to the parents or guardian.

re·port·ed·ly (ri·pôr′tid·lē, -pōr′-) *adv.* According to report.

re·port·er (ri·pôr′tər, -pōr′-) *n.* **1.** One who reports; esp. one who reports news for a newspaper, magazine, etc. One who reports cases in court for official publication. — **rep·or·to·ri·al** (rep′ər·tôr′ē·əl, -tō′rē-) *adj.*

re·pose[1] (ri·pōz′) *n.* **1.** The act of taking rest or the state of being at rest. **2.** Calm; peace. **3.** Ease of manner; grace and dignified calmness. **4.** That which conduces to rest or calm. — *v.* **·posed, ·pos·ing** *v.t.* **1.** To lay or place in a position of rest. — *v.i.* **2.** To lie at rest. **3.** To rely; depend: with *on, upon*, or *in*. [< F < LL < L *re-* again *pausare* to pause] — **re·pos′al** *n.* — **re·pose′ful** *adj.* — **re·pos′er** *n.*

re·pose[2] (ri·pōz′) *v.t.* **·posed, ·pos·ing** To place, as confidence or hope: with *in*. [ME < L *reponere* to put back] — **re·pos′al** *n.*

pos·i·to·ry (ri·poz/ə·tôr/ē, -tō/rē) *n. pl.* **-ries 1.** A place which goods are or may be stored. **2.** A person to whom secret is entrusted **3.** A burial vault. **4.** A receptacle for dics. [< L < *re-* back, again + *ponere* to place]
pos·sess (rē/pə·zes/) *v.t.* **1.** To have possession of again; gain possession of. **2.** To give back possession or owner-up to. — **re/pos·ses/sion** (-zesh/ən) *n.*
pous·sé (rə·pōō·sā/) *adj.* **1.** Formed in relief, as a design metal. **2.** Adorned with such designs. [< F]
·p (rep) *n.* Rep, the fabric.
·re·hend (rep/ri·hend/) *v.t.* To criticize sharply; find ult with; blame. [< L < *re-* back + *prehendere* to hold]
·re·hen·si·ble (rep/ri·hen/sə·bəl) *adj.* Deserving blame censure. — **rep/re·hen/si·bil/i·ty, rep/re·hen/si·ble·ness** — **rep/re·hen/si·bly** *adv.*
·re·hen·sion (rep/ri·hen/shən) *n.* The act of reprehend-; also, an expression of blame; a rebuke. — **rep/re·hen/·e** *adj.* — **rep/re·hen/sive·ly** *adv.*
·re·sent (rep/ri·zent/) *v.t.* **1.** To serve as the symbol, pression, or designation of; symbolize. **2.** To express or mbolize in this manner. **3.** To depict; portray, as in nting or sculpture. **4.** To produce on the stage, as an era. **5.** To act the part of; impersonate. **6.** To serve as be the delegate, agent, etc., of. **7.** To describe: They *resented* him as a genius. **8.** To set forth in words; state; olain. **9.** To bring before the mind; present clearly. **10.** set up as an example, specimen, type, etc., of. [< OF < < *re-* again + PRESENT²] — **rep/re·sent/a·ble** *adj.* — **·/re·sent/a·bil/i·ty** *n.*
·resent (rē/pri·zent/) *v.t.* To present again. — **re/-pre/·** **·ta/tion** *n.*
·re·sen·ta·tion (rep/ri·zen·tā/shən) *n.* **1.** The act of resenting or the state of being represented. **2.** Anything t represents, as a picture, a statue, etc. **3.** A dramatic formance. **4.** The right of acting authoritatively for ers, esp. in a legislative body. **5.** Representatives collec-ely. **6.** A setting forth by statement or account, esp. to ect or propose. [< OF]
·re·sen·ta·tion·al (rep/ri·zen·tā/shən·əl) *adj.* **1.** Serv-to represent; esp., denoting a style of art that seeks to resent objects realistically. **2.** Of, pertaining to, or of the ure of representation.
·re·sen·ta·tive (rep/ri·zen/tə·tiv) *adj.* **1.** Typifying or ical of a group or class. **2.** Acting as a qualified agent. Made up of representatives. **4.** Based on or pertaining he political principle of representation. **5.** Presenting, traying, or representing, or capable of so doing — *n.* **1.** e who or that which is fit to stand as a type; a typical in-nce. **2.** One who is a qualified agent of any kind. **3.** A mber of a legislative body, esp. a member of the lower se of Congress or of a State legislature. — **rep/re·sen/ta·** **·ly** *adv.* — **rep/re·sen/ta·tive·ness** *n.*
·ress (ri·pres/) *v.t.* **1.** To keep under restraint or control. To put down; quell, as a rebellion. **3.** *Psychoanal.* To ct the repression of, as fears, impulses, etc. [< L < *re-* **k** + PRESS] — **re·press/er** or **re·pres/sor** *n.* — **re·** **ss/i·ble** *adj.*
— **Syn. 1.** check, curb, rein, restrain, subdue, suppress.
·ress (rē/pres/) *v.t. & v.i.* To press again.
·res·sion (ri·presh/ən) *n.* **1.** The act of repressing or the dition of being repressed. **2.** That which holds in check; straint. **3.** *Psychoanal.* The exclusion from conscious-s of painful or unacceptable memories, etc.
·res·sive (ri·pres/iv) *adj.* **1.** Tending to repress. **2.** able of repressing. — **re·pres/sive·ly** *adv.* — **re·pres/·** **·ness** *n.*
·rieve (ri·prēv/) *v.t.* **·prieved, ·priev·ing 1.** To suspend porarily the execution of a sentence upon. **2.** To relieve a time from suffering, danger, or trouble. — *n.* **1.** The porary suspension of a sentence, or the instrument order-such a suspension. **2.** Temporary relief or cessation of 1 or ill. **3.** The act of reprieving or the state of being re-ved. [< earlier *repry* < F *repris*, pp. of *reprendre* to back] — **re·priev/a·ble** *adj.*
·ri·mand (rep/rə·mand, -mänd) *v.t.* To reprove sharply ormally. — *n.* Severe reproof or censure. [< F *répri-de* reprod]
·rint (*n.* rē/print/; *v.* rē·print/) *n.* An edition of a printed k that is a verbatim copy of the original. — *v.t.* To t a new edition or copy of. — **re·print/er** *n.*
·ri·sal (ri·prī/zəl) *n.* **1.** The application of force short of by one nation against another in retaliation for acts mitted; also, an instance of such use of force. **2.** Any of retaliation. [< OF *reprendre* < L < *re-* back + *pre-lere* to hold]
·rise (rə·prēz/, -prīz/) *n. Music* A repeated phrase; esp., repetition of or return to the subject after an intermediate vement. [See REPRISAL.]

re·proach (ri·prōch/) *v.t.* **1.** To charge with or blame for something wrong; rebuke; censure. **2.** To bring discredit and disgrace upon; to disgrace. — *n.* **1.** The act of re-proaching, or the words of one who reproaches; censure; re-proof; rebuke. **2.** A cause of blame or disgrace. **3.** Disgrace; discredit. [< F *reprocher*; ult. origin uncertain.] — **re·proach/a·bly** *adj.* — **re·proach/a·ble·ness** *n.* — **re·proach/·** **a·bly** *adv.* — **re·proach/er** *n.*
re·proach·ful (ri·prōch/fəl) *adj.* Containing or full of re-proach; expressing reproach. — **re·proach/ful·ly** *adv.* — **re·proach/ful·ness** *n.*
rep·ro·bate (rep/rə·bāt) *adj.* **1.** Having lost all sense of duty; depraved. **2.** Abandoned to punishment; condemned. — *n.* A depraved or profligate person. — *v.t.* **·bat·ed, ·bat·ing** To disapprove of heartily; condemn. [See REPROVE.] — **rep/ro·ba/tion** *n.* — **rep/ro·ba/tive** *adj.*
re·pro·duce (rē/prə·dōōs/, -dyōōs/) *v.* **·duced, ·duc·ing** *v.t.* **1.** To make a copy, image, or reproduction of. **2.** *Biol.* **a** To give rise to (offspring) by sexual or asexual generation. **b** To replace (a lost part or organ) by regeneration. **3.** To produce again. **4.** To recall to the mind; visualize again. — *v.i.* **5.** To produce offspring. **6.** To undergo copying, re-production, etc. — **re/pro·duc/er** *n.* — **re/pro·duc/i·ble** *adj.*
re·pro·duc·tion (rē/prə·duk/shən) *n.* **1.** The act or power of reproducing. **2.** *Biol.* The process by which an animal or plant gives rise to another of its kind **3.** That which is re-produced, as a revival of a play or a copy of a picture.
re·pro·duc·tive (rē/prə·duk/tiv) *adj.* Pertaining to, em-ployed in, or tending to reproduction. — **re/pro·duc/tive·ly** *adv.* — **re/pro·duc/tive·ness** *n.*
re·proof (ri·prōōf/) *n.* **1.** The act of reproving. **2.** A re-buke; blame; censure. Also **re·prov·al** (ri·prōō/vəl).
re·prove (ri/prōōv/) *v.t.* **proved, ·prov·ing 1.** To censure, as for a fault; rebuke. **2.** To express disapproval of (an act). [< OF < LL < *re-* again + *probare* to test] — **re·prov/a·ble** *adj.* — **re·prov/er** *n.* — **re·prov/ing·ly** *adv.*
— **Syn. 1.** chide, upbraid, reprimand.
re·prove (rē·prōōv/) *v.t.* **·proved, -prov·ing** To prove (a theory, assertion, etc.) anew.
rep·tile (rep/til, -tīl) *n.* **1.** Any of a class of cold-blooded, air-breathing vertebrates, including the snakes, crocodiles, lizards, and turtles. **2.** A groveling, abject person. — *adj.* **1.** Crawling on the belly. **2.** Groveling morally; sly and base; treacherous. **3.** Of or resembling a reptile [< LL < *reptus*, pp. of *repere* to creep]
rep·til·i·an (rep·til/ē·ən) *adj.* Of, pertaining to, or charac-teristic of a reptile or reptiles. — *n.* Any reptile.
re·pub·lic (ri·pub/lik) *n.* **1.** A state in which the sovereignty resides in the people and the legislative and administrative powers are lodged in officers elected by them; also, such a government. [< F < L *respublica* commonwealth]
re·pub·li·can (ri·pub/li·kən) *adj.* **1.** Of, like, or suitable for a republic. **2.** Supporting republican government. — *n.* One who advocates a republican form of government.
Re·pub·li·can (ri·pub/li·kən) *adj.* Pertaining to or belong-ing to the Republican Party of the U.S. — *n.* A member of the Republican Party.
Republican calendar See under CALENDAR.
re·pub·li·can·ism (ri·pub/li·kən·iz/əm) *n.* **1.** The theory or principles of republican government. **2.** Advocacy of or adherence to republican principles.
Re·pub·li·can·ism (ri·pub/li·kən·iz/əm) *n.* The policy and principles of the Republican Party of the U.S.
Republican Party One of the two major political parties of the United States, founded in 1854 in opposition to the ex-tension of slavery.
re·pu·di·ate (ri·pyōō/dē·āt) *v.t.* **·at·ed, ·at·ing 1.** To refuse to accept as valid or binding; reject. **2.** To refuse to ac-knowledge or pay. **3.** To cast off; disown, as a son. [< L < *repudiare* to divorce] — **re·pu/di·a/tion** *n.* — **re·pu/di·a/tive** *adj.* — **re·pu/di·a/tor** *n.*
re·pug·nance (ri·pug/nəns) *n.* The state of feeling aversion and resistance; antipathy. Also **re·pug/nan·cy.**
re·pug·nant (ri·pug/nənt) *adj.* **1.** Offensive to taste or feel-ing; exciting aversion or repulsion **2.** Being inconsistent or opposed; antagonistic. **3.** Hostile; resisting. [< OF < L < *re-* back + *pugnare* to fight]
re·pulse (ri·puls/) *v.t.* **·pulsed, ·puls·ing 1.** To drive back; repel, as an attacking force. **2.** To repel by coldness, dis-courtesy, etc.; reject; rebuff. — *n.* **1.** The act of repulsing or the state of being repulsed. **2.** Rejection; refusal [< L *repulsus*, pp. of *repellere*. See REPEL.] — **re·puls/er** *n.*
re·pul·sion (ri·pul/shən) *n.* **1.** The act of repelling, or the state of being repelled. **2.** Aversion; repugnance **3.** *Phys-ics* The mutual action of two bodies that tends to drive them apart.
re·pul·sive (ri·pul/siv) *adj.* **1.** Exciting feelings of dislike, disgust, or horror; grossly offensive. **2.** Such as to forbid ap-

proach or familiarity; forbidding. **3.** Acting by repulsion: *repulsive* forces. **— re·pul′sive·ly** *adv.* **— re·pul′sive·ness** *n.*

rep·u·ta·ble (rep′yə·tə·bəl) *adj.* **1.** Having a good reputation; estimable; honorable. **2.** Consistent with proper usage, as words **— rep′u·ta·bil′i·ty** *n.* **— rep′u·ta·bly** *adv.*

rep·u·ta·tion (rep′yə·tā′shən) *n.* **1.** The general estimation in which a person or thing is held by others. **2.** The state of being in high regard or esteem **3.** A particular credit or character ascribed to a person or thing: a *reputation* for honesty. [See REPUTE.]

re·pute (ri·pyoot′) *v.t.* **·put·ed, ·put·ing** To regard or consider to be as specified; esteem: usu. in the passive: They are *reputed* to be an intelligent people. **— n. 1.** Reputation (defs. 1 and 2). **2.** Public opinion; general report. [< OF < L *reputare* to reckon, be reputed]

re·put·ed (ri·pyoo′tid) *adj.* Generally thought or supposed: a *reputed* criminal **— re·put′ed·ly** *adv.*

re·quest (ri·kwest′) *v.t.* **1.** To express a desire for. **2.** To ask (a person) to do a favor, answer an inquiry, etc. **— Syn.** See ASK. **— n. 1.** The act of requesting; petition. **2.** That which is requested. **3.** The state of being in demand: in *request.* **— adj.** Having been asked for: a *request* program. [See REQUIRE.]

re·qui·em (rē′kwē·əm, rek′wē-) *n.* **1.** Any musical composition, or service for the dead. **2.** *Often cap. Eccl.* In the Roman Catholic Church, a solemn mass sung for the dead: also **Requiem mass. 3.** *Often cap.* A musical setting for such a mass. [< L *Requiem* (aeternam dona eis, Domine) rest (eternal give unto them, O Lord)]

req·ui·es·cat in pa·ce (rek′wē·es′kat in pä′sē) May he rest in peace Abbr. *R.I.P.* [< L]

re·quire (ri·kwīr′) *v.* **·quired, ·quir·ing** *v.t.* **1.** To have need of; find necessary. **2.** To demand authoritatively; insist upon. **— v.i. 3.** To make demand or request. [< OF < L < *re-* again + *quaerere* to ask, seek] **— re·quir′a·ble** *adj.* **— re·quir′er** *n.* **— re·quire′ment** *n.*

req·ui·site (rek′wə·zit) *adj.* Required by the nature of things or by circumstances; indispensable. **— n.** That which cannot be dispensed with; a necessity. [See REQUEST.] **— req′ui·site·ly** *adv.* **— req′ui·site·ness** *n.*

req·ui·si·tion (rek′wə·zish′ən) *n.* **1.** A formal request, summons, or demand, as for supplies. **2.** A necessity or requirement. **3.** The state of being required. **— v.t.** To make a requisition for or upon; demand or take upon requisition. [See REQUIRE.]

re·quite (ri·kwīt′) *v.t.* **·quit·ed, ·quit·ing 1.** To make equivalent return for, as kindness, service, or injury; make up for. **2.** To make return to; compensate or repay in kind. **3.** To give or do in return. [< RE- + *quite*, obs. var. of QUIT] **— re·quit·al** (ri·kwīt′l) *adj.* **— re·quit′er** *n.*

rere·dos (rir′dos) *Chiefly Brit. n.* **1.** An ornamental screen behind an altar. **2.** The back of an open fire hearth. [< AF < *rere* rear + *dos* back]

re·run (*n.* rē′run; *v.* rē·run′) *n.* The presenting of a motion picture, play, etc., after its original run is over; also, the motion picture, play, etc., so presented. **— v.t. ·ran, ·run·ning** To run again or a second time.

re·sale (rē′sāl, rē·sāl′) *n.* The act of selling again.

re·scind (ri·sind′) *v.t.* To make void, as an act; abrogate; repeal. **— Syn.** See ANNUL. [< L < *re-* back + *scindere* to cut] **— re·scind′a·ble** *adj.* **— re·scind′er** *n.*

re·scis·sion (ri·sizh′ən) *n.* The act of rescinding or abrogating. **— re·scis′si·ble** (-sis′-) *adj.* **— re·scis′so·ry** *adj.*

re·script (rē′skript) *n.* **1.** A formal answer to questions of state, law, morality, etc., as given by a Roman emperor or a Pope. **2.** Any decree, edict or formal announcement. [< L < *re-* back + *scribere* to write]

res·cue (res′kyoo) *v.t.* **·cued, ·cu·ing 1.** To save or free from danger, captivity, evil, etc.; deliver. **2.** *Law* To remove forcibly from the custody of the law. **— n.** The act of rescuing; deliverance. [< OF *rescourre* < *re-* back + *escorre* to move, shake] **— res′cu·a·ble** *adj.* **— res′cu·er** *n.*

re·search (ri·sûrch′, rē′sûrch) *n.* **1.** Diligent, protracted investigation; studious inquiry. **2.** A systematic investigation of some phenomenon **— v.i.** To undertake research. [< F < *re-* back + *chercher* to seek] **— re·search′·er** *n.*

re·seat (rē·sēt′) *v.t.* **1.** To seat again. **2.** To put a new seat or seats in or on.

re·sect (ri·sekt′) *v.t. Surg.* To cut or pare off. [< L < *re-* back + *secare* to cut] **— re·sec′tion** *n.*

re·sem·blance (ri·zem′bləns) *n.* **1.** The quality of similarity in nature, form, etc.; likeness. **2.** A semblance or likeness of a person or thing. **— Syn.** See ANALOGY.

re·sem·ble (ri·zem′bəl) *v.t.* **·bled, ·bling** To be similar to in appearance, quality, or character. [< OF < *re-* again + *sembler* to seem] **— re·sem′bler** *n.*

re·sent (ri·zent′) *v.t.* To feel or show resentment at; be indignant at. [< F < *re-* again + *sentir* to feel] **— re·sent′·ful** *adj.* **— re·sent′ful·ly** *adv.* **— re·sent′ful·ness** *n.*

re·sent·ment (ri·zent′mənt) *n.* Anger and ill will in view of real or fancied wrong or injury.

re·ser·pine (ri·sûr′pēn, -pin, res′ər-) *n.* A drug origina prepared from alkaloids found in rauwolfia, used as a tr quilizer. [< NL *Rauwolfia serpentina*, genus name + -I]

res·er·va·tion (rez′ər·vā′shən) *n.* **1.** The act of reserv **2.** That which is reserved, kept back, or withheld. **3** qualification or condition, as to an opinion or commitme **4.** An agreement by which a seat on a train, hotel room, e is reserved in advance. **5.** A tract of government land served for a special purpose, as for the use and occupanc an Indian tribe, or for the preservation of forests, wild etc. [< OF < LL *reservatio, -onis*]

re·serve (ri·zûrv′) *v.t.* **·served, ·serv·ing 1.** To hold bac set aside for special or future use. **2.** To keep as one's o retain. **3.** To arrange for ahead of time; have set aside one's use. **— n. 1.** Something stored up for future us set apart for a particular purpose. **2.** A reservation of la **3.** In banking, the amount of funds reserved in order to m regular or emergent demands. **4.** The act of reserving. Silence or reticence as to one's feelings, opinions, or aff **6.** A fighting force held back from action to meet poss emergencies. **7.** A branch of the armed forces compose persons trained for military service and subject to ca emergencies. **— adj.** Held in reserve; constituting a serve. [< OF < L < *re-* back + *servare* to keep] **— serv′a·ble** *adj.* **— re·serv′er** *n.*

re·serve (rē·sûrv′) *v.t. & v.i.* **·served, -serv·ing** To s again.

re·served (ri·zûrvd′) *adj.* **1.** Characterized by reserv manner; distant; undemonstrative. **2.** Retained; kept b **— re·serv·ed·ly** (ri·zûr′vid·lē) *adv.* **— re·serv′ed·ness**

Reserve Officers' Training Corps In the U.S., a mili corps to train students at colleges and universities to qu as officers in a reserve. Abbr. *ROTC, R.O.T.C.*

re·serv·ist (ri·zûr′vist) *n.* A member of a military rese

res·er·voir (rez′ər·vwôr, -vwär, -vôr) *n.* **1.** A lake, ei natural or artificial, for collecting and containing a supp water, as for use in a city or for water power. **2.** An att ment to a stove, machine, or instrument, for containi fluid to be used in its operation. **3.** An extra supply; a s of anything. [< F *réservoir*]

re·set (*v.* rē·set′; *n.* rē′set′) *v.t.* **·set, ·set·ting** To set ag **— n.** The act of resetting, or that which is reset.

re·ship (rē·ship′) *v.* **·shipped, ·ship·ping** *v.t.* **1.** To again. **2.** To transfer (oneself) to another vessel. **— v** To go on a vessel again. **4.** To sign for another voyage crew member or a passenger. **— re·ship′ment** *n.*

re·side (ri·zīd′) *v.i.* **·sid·ed, ·sid·ing 1.** To dwell for a co erable time; make one's home; live. **2.** To exist as ar tribute or quality: with *in.* **3.** To be vested: with *in.* **Syn.** See LIVE. [< F < L *residere* to abide]

res·i·dence (rez′ə·dəns) *n.* **1.** The place or the house w one resides. **2.** The act of residing. **3.** The fact of bein ficially present, esp. in the phrase **in residence. 4.** The of power of government. **5.** The length of time one re in a place. Also *residency.* [< OF < LL *residentia*]

res·i·den·cy (rez′ə·dən·sē) *n. pl.* **·cies 1.** Residence. An official abode of the representative of a government. *Med.* The period of clinical training served by a physici his chosen specialty.

res·i·dent (rez′ə·dənt) *n.* **1.** One who resides or dwells place. **2.** A diplomatic representative residing at a for seat of government. **3.** *Med.* One serving a residency *adj.* **1.** Having a residence. **2.** Abiding in a place in nection with one's official work: a *resident* physician. **3** herent: Pungency is *resident* in pepper. **4.** Not migra said of certain birds.

res·i·den·tial (rez′ə·den′shəl) *adj.* **1.** Of, pertaining t resulting from residence; having residence. **2.** Of, consi of, or suitable for residences or living quarters.

re·sid·u·al (ri·zij′oo·əl) *adj.* **1.** Pertaining to or havin nature of a residue or remainder. **2.** Left over as a res **— n.** Something left over.

re·sid·u·ar·y (ri·zij′oo·er′ē) *adj.* Of or pertaining to a r uum or remainder; residual.

res·i·due (rez′ə·doo, -dyoo) *n.* **1.** A remainder or su after a part has been separated or otherwise treated. *Chem.* Insoluble matter left after filtration or separ from a liquid. **3.** *Law* The portion of an estate that rem after all charges, debts, and particular bequests have satisfied. Also **re·sid·u·um** (ri·zij′oo·əm). [< OF < L back + *sedere* to sit]

re·sign (ri·zīn′) *v.t.* **1.** To give up, as a position, offic trust. **2.** To relinquish (a privilege, claim, etc.). **3.** T over (oneself, one's mind, etc.), as to fate or dominatio *v.i.* **4.** To resign a position, etc. [< OF < L < *re-* ba *signare* to seal] **— re·sign′er** *n.*

re·sign (rē·sīn′) *v.t.* To sign again.

res·ig·na·tion (rez′ig·nā′shən) *n.* **1.** The act of resig as a position or office. **2.** A written statement decl one's intention to resign. **3.** The quality of being su sive or acquiescent.

signed (ri·zīnd′) *adj.* Characterized by resignation; sub-
ssive. — **re·sign·ed·ly** (ri·zī′nid·lē) *adv.*

sil·ience (ri·zil′yəns) *n.* The quality or power of being
silient; elasticity; rebound. Also **re·sil′ien·cy.**

sil·ient (ri·zil′yənt) *adj.* **1.** Springing back to a former
ape or position. **2.** Capable of recoiling from pressure or
ock unchanged or undamaged; buoyant. [< MF < L <
back + *salire* to leap] — **re·sil′ient·ly** *adv.*

in (rez′in) *n.* **1.** An amorphous organic substance exud-
from certain plants and trees, yellowish or dark in color.
Any of a class of similar substances made by chemical
nthesis, esp. those used in the making of plastics. **3.**
sin (def. 1). — *v.t.* To apply resin to. [< OF < L < Gk.
tinē] — **res·i·na·ceous** (rez′ə·nā′shəs) *adj.*

i·nous (rez′ə·nəs) *adj.* **1.** Like or containing resin. **2.**
tained from resin. Also **res·in·y** (rez′ən·ē).

ist (ri·zist′) *v.t.* **1.** To strive against; act counter to. **2.**
be proof against; withstand. — *v.i.* **3.** To offer opposi-
n. [< OF < L *resistere* to withstand] — **re·sist′er** *n.*

sis·tance (ri·zis′təns) *n.* **1.** The act of resisting. **2.** Any
ce tending to hinder motion. **3.** *Electr.* The opposition
at a conductor offers to the passage of a current, resulting
m the conversion of energy into heat, light, etc. **4.** *Psy-
anal.* The action of the ego in preventing the return to
sciousness of unpleasant incidents and experiences. **5.**
e underground and guerrilla movement opposing an occu-
ng power. — **re·sis′tant** *n.*

ist·i·ble (ri·zis′tə·bəl) *adj.* Capable of being resisted. —
sist′i·bil′i·ty *n.* — **re·sist′i·bly** *adv.*

is·tive (ri·zis′tiv) *adj.* Having or exercising the power
resistance. — **re·sis′tive·ly** *adv.*

is·tiv·i·ty (rē′zis·tiv′ə·tē) *n.* **1.** The capacity to resist,
the degree of that capacity. **2.** *Electr.* Specific resistance
electric or magnetic force of a substance as tested in a cube
asuring one centimeter.

ist·less (ri·zist′lis) *adj.* **1.** Incapable of resisting; irre-
ible. **2.** Offering no resistance; powerless. — **re·sist′-
s·ly** *adv.* — **re·sist′less·ness** *n.*

is·tor (ri·zis′tər) *n.* *Electr.* A device, as a coil of wire,
introducing resistance into an electrical circuit.

na·tron (rez′nə·tron) *n.* *Electronics* A tetrode electron
e operating on the resonance principle and capable of gen-
ting large power at high frequency and maximum efficien-
[< RES(O)NA(TOR) + -TRON]

ole (rē·sōl′) *v.t.* **·soled, ·sol·ing** To sole (a shoe, etc.)
in.

o·lute (rez′ə·lōot) *adj.* **1.** Having a fixed purpose; de-
mined. **2.** Bold; unflinching. [See RESOLVE.] — **res′o·
e·ly** *adv.* — **re·o·lute·ness** *n.*

o·lu·tion (rez′ə·lōo′shən) *n.* **1.** The act of resolving or
reducing to a simpler form. **2.** The state of being reso-
e; active fortitude. **3.** The making of a resolve; also, the
pose or course resolved upon. **4.** The separation of any-
ng into component parts. **5.** A proposition offered to or
pted by an assembly. **6.** *Med.* The termination of an ab-
mal condition. — **res′o·lu′tion·er, res′o·lu′tion·ist** *n.*

olve (ri·zolv′) *v.* **·solved, ·solv·ing** *v.t.* **1.** To decide or
settle. **2.** *v.* **·solved, ·solv·ing** *v.t.* **1.** To cause to decide or de-
mine. **3.** To separate or break down into constituent
ts. **4.** To make clear; explain or solve, as a problem. **5.**
explain away; remove (doubts, etc.). **6.** To state or de-
e by vote, as in a legislative assembly. **7.** To transform;
vert: He *resolves* his anger into pride. **8.** *Optics* To make
tinguishable the structure or parts of, as in a microscope
telescope. — *v.i.* **9.** To make up one's mind; arrive at a
ision: with *on* or *upon.* **10.** To become separated into
stituent parts. — *n.* **1.** Fixity of purpose; resolution.
A fixed determination; a resolution. **3.** The action of a
iberative body expressing formally its intention or pur-
e. [< L < *re-* again + *solvere* to loosen] — **re·solv′a·
adj.** — **re·solv·a·bil′i·ty** *n.* — **re·solv′er** *n.*

olve (rē·solv′) *v.t.* **·solved, ·solv·ing** To solve anew.

olved (ri·zolvd′) *adj.* Fixed or set in purpose; deter-
ned. — **re·solv·ed·ly** (ri·zol′vid·lē) *adv.*

o·nance (rez′ə·nəns) *n.* **1.** The state or quality of being
onant. **2.** *Physics* The property whereby any vibratory
tem responds with maximum amplitude to an applied
ce having a frequency equal or nearly equal to its own. **3.**
ctr. The condition of an electric circuit in which maximum
w of current is obtained by impressing an electromotive
ce of given frequency.

o·nant (rez′ə·nənt) *adj.* **1.** Sending back or having the
ality of sending back or prolonging sound. **2.** Resound-
. **3.** Having resonance. [< L < *re-* again + *sonare* to
nd] — **res′o·nant·ly** *adv.*

o·nate (rez′ə·nāt) *v.i.* **·nat·ed, ·nat·ing** **1.** To exhibit
onance. **2.** To manifest sympathetic vibration, as a res-
ator. [< L *resonatus*, pp. of *resonare.* See RESONANT.]

res·o·na·tor (rez′ə·nā′tər) *n.* **1.** That which resounds. **2.**
Any device utilizing the effects of resonance, esp. in connection with sound or electromagnetic waves. [< NL]

re·sorb (ri·sôrb′) *v.t.* To absorb again. [< L < re- back +
sorbere to suck up] — **re·sorp·tion** (ri·sôrp′shən) *n.*

re·sor·cin·ol (ri·zôr′sin·ōl, -ol) *n.* *Chem.* A colorless crystalline compound, $C_6H_6O_2$, used as an antiseptic and in the
making of dyes. Also **re·sor′cin.** — **re·sor′cin·al** *adj.*

re·sort (ri·zôrt′) *v.i.* **1.** To go frequently or habitually; repair. **2.** To have recourse; apply or betake oneself for relief
or aid: with *to.* — *n.* **1.** A place frequented for recreation
or rest: health *resort.* **2.** The use of something as a means; a
recourse. **3.** The act of frequenting a place. [< OF < *re-
again + sortir* to go out] — **re·sort′er** *n.*

re·sort (rē·sôrt′) *v.t. & v.i.* To sort anew or again.

re·sound (ri·zound′) *v.i.* **1.** To be filled with sound; echo;
reverberate. **2.** To make a loud, prolonged, or echoing
sound. **3.** To ring; echo: said of sounds. — *v.t.* **4.** To give
back (a sound, etc.); re-echo. **5.** *Poetic* To extol. [ME <
OF < L *resonare* to echo]

re·sound (rē·sound′) *v.t. & v.i.* To sound again.

re·source (ri·sôrs′, -zôrs′, -sōrs′, rē′sôrs, -sōrs) *n.* **1.** That
which is resorted to for aid or support; resort. **2.** *pl.* Available means or property; any natural advantages or products.
3. Capacity for finding or adapting means; power of achievement. **4.** Fertility in expedients; skill or ingenuity in meeting any situation; resourcefulness. [< OF < *re-* again +
sourdre < L *surgere* to rise]

re·source·ful (ri·sôrs′fəl, -sōrs′-, -zôrs′-, -zors′-) *adj.* **1.** Fertile in
resources or expedients. **2.** Full of resources. — **re·source′-
ful·ly** *adv.* — **re·source′ful·ness** *n.*

re·spect (ri·spekt′) *v.t.* **1.** To have deferential regard for;
esteem. **2.** To treat with propriety or consideration. **3.** To
regard as inviolable; avoid intruding upon. **4.** To have relation or reference to; concern. — *n.* **1.** Regard for and appreciation of worth; honor and esteem. **2.** Demeanor or de-
portment indicating deference; courteous regard. **3.** *pl.* Expressions of consideration or esteem; compliments: to pay
one's *respects.* **4.** Conformity to duty or obligation: *respect*
for the law. **5.** The condition of being honored or respected.
6. A specific aspect: In what *respect* is he wanting? **7.** Reference or relation: usu. with *to:* with *respect* to profits. [<
L < *re-* again + *specere* to look] — **re·spect′er** *n.*

re·spect·a·ble (ri·spek′tə·bəl) *adj.* **1.** Deserving of respect;
being of good name or repute; also, respected. **2.** Being of
moderate excellence; average. **3.** Considerable in number,
size, quality, etc. **4.** Having a good appearance; presentable. **5.** Conventionally correct or socially acceptable in conduct. — **re·spect′a·bil′i·ty** *n.* — **re·spect′a·bly** *adv.*

re·spect·ful (ri·spekt′fəl) *adj.* Marked by or manifesting
respect. — **re·spect′ful·ly** *adv.* — **re·spect′ful·ness** *n.*

re·spect·ing (ri·spek′ting) *prep.* In relation to; regarding.

re·spec·tive (ri·spek′tiv) *adj.* Pertaining or relating severally to each of those under consideration; particular.

re·spec·tive·ly (ri·spek′tiv·lē) *adv.* As singly or severally
considered; singly in the order designated: The first three go
to John, James, and William *respectively.*

re·spell (rē·spel′) *v.t.* To spell again, esp. in a system whereby pronunciation is indicated.

res·pi·ra·tion (res′pə·rā′shən) *n.* **1.** The act of inhaling
and exhaling; breathing. **2.** The process by which a plant or
animal takes in oxygen from the air and gives off carbon dioxide and other products of oxidation. [< MF < L < *re-* again
+ *spirare* to breathe]

res·pi·ra·tor (res′pə·rā′tər) *n.* **1.** A screen, as of fine gauze,
worn over the mouth or nose, as a protection against dust,
etc. **2.** A device worn over the nose and mouth for the inhalation of medicated vapors, or oxygen for lung patients.
3. An apparatus for artificial respiration.

re·spir·a·to·ry (ri·spir′ə·tôr·ē, -tō′rē, res′pər·ə-) *adj.* Of,
pertaining to, used in, or caused by respiration.

re·spite (res′pit) *n.* **1.** Postponement; delay. **2.** Temporary intermission of labor or effort; an interval of rest. **3.**
Law Temporary suspension of the execution of a sentence for
a capital offense; reprieve. — *v.t.* **·pit·ed, ·pit·ing** **1.** To relieve by a pause or rest. **2.** To grant delay in the execution
of (a penalty, sentence, etc.). **3.** To postpone. [< OF < L
respectus regard, refuge]

re·splen·dent (ri·splen′dənt) *adj.* Shining with brilliant
luster; vividly bright; splendid; gorgeous. [< L < *re-* back
+ *splendere* to shine] — **re·splen′dence, re·splen′den·cy** *n.*
— **re·splen′dent·ly** *adv.*

re·spond (ri·spond′) *v.i.* **1.** To give an answer; reply. **2.**
To act in reply or return; react. **3.** *Law* To be liable or answerable. — *v.t.* **4.** To say in answer; reply. — *n.* **1.** *Archit.* A pilaster or similar feature placed against a wall, to receive an arch. **2.** *Eccl.* A response (def. 2). [< OF < *re-* back
+ *spondere* to pledge] — **re·spon′der** *n.*

re·spon·dence (ri·spon′dəns) n. 1. The character or condition of being respondent. 2. The act of responding. Also **re·spon′den·cy.**

re·spon·dent (ri·spon′dənt) adj. 1. Giving response, or given as a response; answering; responsive. 2. Law Occupying the position of defendant. — n. 1. One who responds or answers. 2. Law A defendant.

re·sponse (ri·spons′) n. 1. The act of responding, or that which is responded; reply; reaction. 2. Eccl. a A portion of a liturgy or church service said or sung by the congregation or choir in reply to the officiating priest. b An anthem sung or said during or after a reading. Also called **respond.** 3. Biol. The behavior of an organism resulting from a stimulus or influence; a reaction. 4. In bridge, the play of a high or low card in following suit, as a signal to one's partner.

re·spon·si·bil·i·ty (ri·spon′sə·bil′ə·tē) n. pl. ·ties 1. The state of being responsible or accountable. 2. That for which one is answerable; a duty or trust. 3. Ability to meet obligations or to act without superior authority or guidance. Also **re·spon′si·ble·ness.**

re·spon·si·ble (ri·spon′sə·bəl) adj. 1. Answerable legally or morally for the discharge of a duty, trust, or debt. 2. Having capacity to perceive the distinctions of right and wrong. 3. Able to meet legitimate claims; having sufficient property or means for the payment of debts. 4. Involving accountability or obligation. [See RESPOND.] — **re·spon′si·bly** adv.

re·spon·sive (ri·spon′siv) adj. 1. Inclined or ready to respond; being or reacting in accord, sympathy, or harmony; responding. 2. Constituting, or of the nature of, response or reply. 3. Characterized by or containing responses. — **re·spon′sive·ly** adv. — **re·spon′sive·ness** n.

rest[1] (rest) v.i. 1. To cease working, exerting oneself, etc., so as to refresh oneself. 2. To cease from effort or activity for a time. 3. To seek or obtain ease or refreshment by lying down, sleeping, etc. 4. To sleep. 5. To be at peace; be tranquil. 6. To lie in death; be dead. 7. To remain unchanged. 8. To be supported; stand, lean, lie, or sit: with against, on, or upon. 9. To be founded or based: with on or upon. 10. To rely; depend: with on or upon. 11. To be placed as a burden or responsibility: with on or upon. 12. To be or lie in a specified place. 13. To be directed; remain, as the gaze or eyes, on something. 14. Law To cease presenting evidence in a case. 15. Agric. To lie fallow. — v.t. 16. To give rest to; refresh by rest. 17. To put, lay, lean, etc., as for support or rest. 18. To found; base. 19. To direct (the gaze, eyes, etc.). 20. Law To cease presenting evidence in (a case). — n. 1. The act or state of resting; repose; quiet. 2. Freedom from disturbance or disquiet; tranquillity. 3. Sleep; also, death. 4. That on which anything rests; a support. 5. In billiards and pool, a support for a cue; a bridge. 6. A place of repose or quiet; a stopping place; abode. 7. Music A pause or interval of silence that corresponds to the time value of a note; also, the character indicating such a pause. 8. In prosody, a pause in a verse; caesura. 9. Mil. A command given troops, allowing them to relax. — **at rest** 1. In a state of repose, as in sleep or death. 2. Not in motion; still. 3. Free from anxiety or worry: to set one's mind at rest. [OE restan] — **rest′er** n.

rest[2] (rest) n. 1. That which remains or is left over; a remainder. 2. (construed as pl.) Those remaining or not enumerated; the others. — v.i. To be and remain; stay: Rest content. [< OF < L < re- back + stare to stand]

re·state (rē·stāt′) v.t. ·stat·ed, ·stat·ing To state again or anew. — **re·state′ment** n.

res·tau·rant (res′tər·ənt, -tə·ränt) n. A place where refreshments or meals are provided; a public dining room. [< F, lit., restoring]

res·tau·ra·teur (res′tər·ə·tûr′, Fr. res·tō·rä·tœr′) n. The proprietor or keeper of a restaurant. [< F]

rest·ful (rest′fəl) adj. 1. Full of or giving rest; affording freedom from disturbance, work, or trouble. 2. Being at rest or in repose; quiet. — **rest′ful·ly** adv. — **rest′ful·ness** n.

rest·ing (res′ting) adj. 1. In a state of rest; reposing; also, dead. 2. Bot. Dormant: a resting spore.

res·ti·tu·tion (res′tə·too′shən, -tyoo′-) n. 1. The act of restoring something that has been taken away or lost. 2. The act of making good or rendering an equivalent for injury or loss. 3. Restoration to, return to, or recovery of a former position or condition. 4. Physics The tendency of elastic bodies to recover their shape after compression. [< OF < L < re- again + statuere to set up]

res·tive (res′tiv) adj. 1. Impatient of control; unruly. 2. Restless; fidgety. [< F < L restare to stand] — **res′tive·ly** adv. — **res′tive·ness** n.

rest·less (rest′lis) adj. 1. Having no rest; never quiet. 2. Unable or disinclined to rest. 3. Constantly seeking change; discontented. 4. Obtaining no rest or sleep; sleepless. — **rest′less·ly** adv. — **rest′less·ness** n.

re·stock (rē·stok′) v.t. To stock again or anew.

res·to·ra·tion (res′tə·rā′shən) n. 1. The act of restoring a person or thing to a former place or condition. 2. The state

of being restored; renewal. 3. The reconstruction or repa of something so as to restore it to its original or former stat also, an object that has been so restored. — **the Restorati** The return of Charles II to the English throne in 1660, aft the overthrow of the Protectorate; also, the following peri until 1685.

re·sto·ra·tive (ri·stôr′ə·tiv, -stō′rə-) adj. 1. Tending able to restore. 2. Pertaining to restoration. — n. Th which restores; esp. something to restore consciousness.

re·store (ri·stôr′, -stōr′) v.t. ·stored, ·stor·ing 1. To bri into existence or effect again. 2. To bring back to a form or original condition, appearance, etc., as a painting. 3. put back in a former place or position; reinstate, as a depos monarch. 4. To bring back to health and vigor. 5. To gi back (something lost or taken away). [< OF < L < re again + -staurare to make firm] — **re·stor′er** n.

re-store (rē·stôr′, -stōr′) v.t. -stored, -stor·ing To sto again or anew.

re·strain (ri·strān′) v.t. 1. To hold back from acting, pr ceeding, or advancing; repress. 2. To deprive of freedom liberty, as by placing in a prison. 3. To restrict or limit. OF < L < re- back + stringere to draw tight] — **re·strai a·ble** adj. — **re·strain′ed·ly** adv. — **re·strain′er** n.

re·straint (ri·strānt′) n. 1. The act of restraining. 2. T state of being restrained; confinement. 3. That which strains; a restriction. 4. Self-repression; constraint.

restraint of trade Interference with the free flow of goo or with fair competition, as by price fixing.

re·strict (ri·strikt′) v.t. To hold or keep within limits bounds. [< L restrictus, pp. or restringere to restrain]

re·strict·ed (ri·strik′tid) adj. 1. Limited; confined. 2. N available to the general public; limited to a specific gro restricted information. 3. Excluding people of certain rac religions, or nationalities. — **re·strict′ed·ly** adv.

re·stric·tion (ri·strik′shən) n. 1. The act of restricting, the state of being restricted. 2. That which restricts.

re·stric·tive (ri·strik′tiv) adj. 1. Serving, tending, or op ating to restrict. 2. Gram. Denoting a word or word gro esp. an adjective clause, that limits the identity of its an cedent and is therefore essential to the meaning of the s tence, as who votes for Jones in Any man who votes for Jone a fool. — **re·stric′tive·ly** adv.

rest room A toilet and washroom in a public building.

re·sult (ri·zult′) n. 1. The outcome of an action, cou process, or agency; consequence; effect; conclusion. Math. A quantity or value ascertained by calculation. — v.i. 1. To be a result or outcome; be a physical or logical c sequent; follow: with from. 2. To have an issue; termina end: with in. [< L < re- back + salire to leap]

re·sul·tant (ri·zul′tənt) adj. Arising or following as a sult. — n. 1. That which results; a consequence. 2. Ph ics A force, velocity, or other quantity, resulting from a equivalent in effect to the action of two or more quantitie the same kind.

re·sume (ri·zoom′) v. ·sumed, ·sum·ing v.t. 1. To take again after cessation or interruption; begin again. 2. take or occupy again. 3. To take for oneself again: to sume a title. — v.i. 4. To continue after cessation or in ruption. [< MF < L < re- again + sumere to take] — **sum′a·ble** adj. — **re·sum′er** n.

ré·su·mé (rez′oo̅·mā′, rez′oo̅·mā) n. A summary, a one's employment record. [< F]

re·sump·tion (ri·zump′shən) n. The act of resuming.

re·sur·face (rē·sûr′fis) v.t. ·faced, ·fac·ing To provide a new surface.

re·surge (ri·sûrj′) v.i. ·surged, ·surg·ing 1. To rise ag be resurrected. 2. To surge or sweep back again, as the t [< L < re- again + surgere to rise]

re·sur·gent (ri·sûr′jənt) adj. 1. Rising again. 2. Surg back or again. — **re·sur′gence** n.

res·ur·rect (rez′ə·rekt′) v.t. 1. To bring back to life; r from the dead. 2. To bring back into use or to notice. v.i. 3. To rise again from the dead. [Back formatio RESURRECTION]

res·ur·rec·tion (rez′ə·rek′shən) n. 1. A rising again f the dead. 2. The state of those who have risen from dead. 3. Any revival or renewal, as of a practice or cust after disuse, decay, etc.; restoration. — **the Resurrec** Theol. 1. The rising of Christ from the dead. 2. The ri again of all the dead at the day of judgment. [See RESUR — **res′ur·rec′tion·al** adj. — **res′ur·rec′tion·ar·y** adj.

re·sus·ci·tate (ri·sus′ə·tāt) v.t. & v.i. ·tat·ed, ·tat·ing bring or come back to life; revive from unconscious [< L < re- again + suscitare to revive] — **re·sus′ci·ta** n. — **re·sus′ci·ta′tive** adj. — **re·sus′ci·ta′tor** n.

ret (ret) v.t. ret·ted, ret·ting To steep or soak, as fla separate the fibers: also rot. [ME < MDu. reten]

re·tail (n. & adj. rē′tāl; v. ri·tāl′) n. The selling of goo small quantities, esp. to the ultimate consumer: dis guished from wholesale. — adj. Pertaining to, involvin engaged in the sale of goods at retail. — v.t.

l. 2. To repeat, as gossip. — *v.i.* **3.** To be sold at retail. [OF < *re-* back + *tailler* to cut] — **re·tail·er** *n.*

ain (ri·tān′) *v.t.* **1.** To keep or continue to keep in one's possession; hold. **2.** To maintain in use, practice, etc. **3.** keep in a fixed condition or place. **4.** To keep in mind; member. **5.** To hire; also, to engage (an attorney or other representative) by paying a retainer. [< OF < L < *re-* ck + *tenere* to hold] — **re·tain′a·ble** *adj.*

ain·er¹ (ri·tā′nər) *n.* **1.** A servant. **2.** One who retains keeps. **3.** *Mech.* A device for holding the parts of ball or er bearings in place.

ain·er² (ri·tā′nər) *n.* **1.** The fee paid, or the agreement de, to employ an attorney to serve in a suit; a retaining . **2.** A similar fee paid to anyone to retain his services. OF *retenir* to hold back, used as noun]

ain·ing wall (ri·tā′ning) A wall to prevent the material an embankment or cut from sliding, as a revetment.

ake (*v.* rē·tāk′; *n.* rē′tāk′) *v.t.* **·took, ·tak·en, ·tak·ing 1.** take back; receive again. **2.** To recapture. **3.** To photograph again. — *n.* A motion-picture or television scene, 't of a musical or other recording, etc., done again.

al·i·ate (ri·tal′ē·āt) *v.* **·at·ed, ·at·ing** *v.i.* **1.** To return for like; esp., to repay evil with evil. — *v.t.* **2.** To repay injury, wrong, etc.) in kind; revenge. [< L < *re-* back punishment in kind] — **re·tal′i·a·tive** *adj.* — **re·'i·a·to′ry** *adj.*

al·i·a·tion (ri·tal′ē·ā′shən) *n.* The act of retaliating; re-sal; requital. — **Syn.** See REVENGE.

ard (ri·tärd′) *v.t.* **1.** To cause to move or proceed slow-hinder the advance or course of; delay. — *v.i.* **2.** To be ayed. — *n.* The act of retarding; delay. [< MF < L *re-* back + *tardare* to make slow] — **re·tard′ant** *n.* & *adj.*

re·tar·da·tion *n.* — **re·tard′a·tive** (-ə·tiv) *adj.* & *n.*

ard·ed (ri·tär′did) *adj. Psychol.* Slowed down or back-rd in mental development or school achievement.

ard·er (ri·tärd′ər) *n.* **1.** One who or that which retards. *Chem.* A substance that slows a chemical reaction, usu. en added in small quantity: compare CATALYST.

·h (rech) *v.i.* To make an effort to vomit; strain; heave. *E hræcan* to clear one's throat]

en·tion (ri·ten′shən) *n.* **1.** The act of retaining, or the te of being retained. **2.** The ability to remember. **3.** e capacity or ability to retain. **4.** *Med.* A retaining with-the body of materials normally excreted, as urine.

en·tive (ri·ten′tiv) *adj.* Having the power or tendency retain. — **re·ten′tiv′i·ty** *n.* — **re·ten′tive·ness** *n.*

i·cent (ret′ə·sənt) *adj.* Habitually silent or reserved in erance. [< L < *re-* again + *tacere* to be silent] — **ret′i·ce, ret′i·cen·cy** *n.* — **ret′i·cent·ly** *adv.*

ic·u·lar (ri·tik′yə·lər) *adj.* Like a network; reticulate; ricate. Also **re·tic′u·lar·ly.**

ic·u·late (ri·tik′yə·lāt; *for adj., also* ri·tik′yə·lit) *v.* **·lat-·lat·ing** *v.t.* **1.** To make a network of. **2.** To cover with as with lines of network. — *v.i.* **3.** To form a network. *adj.* **1.** Having the form or appearance of a network. **2.** . Having lines or veins crossing: also **re·tic′u·lat′ed.** — **tic′u·la′tion** *n.*

i·cule (ret′ə·kyool) *n.* A small bag formerly used by men for carrying personal articles, etc. [See RETICULUM.]

ic·u·lum (ri·tik′yə·ləm) *n. pl.* **·la** (-lə) **1.** A netlike ucture; network. **2.** *Zool.* The second stomach of a rumi-t. [< L, dim. of *rete* net]

·i·na (ret′ə·nə, ret′nə) *n. pl.* **·nas** *or* **·nae** (-nē) *Anat.* The er membrane at the back of the eyeball, containing light-sitive rods and cones that transmit the image to the optic ve. For illus. see EYE. [< Med.L < L *rete* net] — **ret′i·nal** *adj.*

·i·ni·tis (ret′ə·nī′tis) *n. Pathol.* Inflammation of the 'na.

·i·nue (ret′ə·noo, -nyoo) *n.* The body of retainers at-ding a person of rank; cortège. [< F < *retenir* to retain]

·ire (ri·tīr′) *v.* **·tired, ·tir·ing** *v.i.* **1.** To go away or with-w, as for privacy, solitude, or rest. **2.** To go to bed. **3.** withdraw oneself from business, public life, or active vice. **4.** To fall back; retreat, as troops under attack. To move back; recede or appear to recede. — *v.t.* **6.** To ove from active service. **7.** To pay off and withdraw m circulation: to *retire* bonds. **8.** To withdraw (troops,) from action. **9.** In baseball, etc., to put out (a batter side). [< MF < *re-* back + *tirer* to draw]

·ired (ri·tīrd′) *adj.* **1.** Withdrawn from public view; tary; secluded: a *retired* life. **2.** Withdrawn from active vice, business, office, etc. **3.** Due to or received by a son withdrawn from active service: *retired* pay.

·ire·ment (ri·tīr′mənt) *n.* **1.** The act of retiring, or the te of being retired. **2.** A secluded place; a retreat.

·ir·ing (ri·tīr′ing) *adj.* **1.** Shy; modest; reserved; unob-sive. **2.** Pertaining to retirement: a *retiring* pension.

re·tort¹ (ri·tôrt′) *v.t.* **1.** To direct (a word or deed) back upon the originator. **2.** To reply to, as an accusation or ar-gument, by a similar accusation, etc. — *v.i.* **3.** To make answer, esp. sharply. — *n.* **1.** A keen rejoinder or retalia-tory speech; caustic repartee. **2.** The act of retorting. [< L < *re-* back + *torquere* to twist] — **re·tort′er** *n.*

re·tort² (ri·tôrt′) *n.* **1.** *Chem.* A vessel with a bent tube for the heating of substances, or for dis-tillation. **2.** *Metall.* A vessel in which ore may be heated for the removal of its metal content. [< L *retortus* bent back.]

RETORTS

a Retort with re-ceiver. *b* Common retort.

re·touch (rē·tuch′; *for n., also* rē′-tuch) *v.t.* **1.** To add new touches to; modify; revise. **2.** *Photog.* To change or improve, as a print. — *n.* An ad-ditional touch, as to a picture, model, or other work of art. — **re·touch′er** *n.*

re·trace (ri·trās′) *v.t.* **·traced, ·trac-ing 1.** To go back over; follow back-ward, as a path. **2.** To trace the whole story of, from the beginning. **3.** To go back over with the eyes or mind. [< F *retracer*] — **re·trace′a·ble** *adj.*

re·trace (rē·trās′) *v.t.* **·traced, ·trac·ing** To trace again, as an engraving, drawing, or map.

re·tract (ri·trakt′) *v.t.* & *v.i.* **1.** To take back (an assertion, admission, etc.); make a disavowal (of); recant. **2.** To draw back or in, as the claws of a cat. [< F < L < *re-* again + *tractare* to handle, freq. of *trahere* to draw] — **re·tract′a·ble** *or* **·i·ble** *adj.* — **re·trac·ta·tion** (rē′trak·tā′shən), **re·trac′-tion** *n.*

re·trac·tile (ri·trak′til) *adj. Zool.* Capable of being drawn back or in, as a cat's claws or the head of a tortoise. — **re-trac·til·i·ty** (rē′trak·til′ə·tē) *n.*

re·trac·tive (ri·trak′tiv) *adj.* Having the power or tenden-cy to retract; retracting.

re·trac·tor (ri·trak′tər) *n.* **1.** One who or that which re-tracts. **2.** *Surg.* An instrument used to hold apart the edges of a wound, incision, etc.

re·tread (*n.* rē′tred′; *v.* rē·tred′) *n.* A pneumatic tire fur-nished with a new tread. — *v.t.* **·tread·ed, ·tread·ing** To fit or furnish (an automobile tire) with a new tread.

re·tread (rē·tred′) *v.t.* **·trod, -trod·den, -tread·ing** To tread again.

re·treat (ri·trēt′) *v.i.* **1.** To go back or backward; with-draw; retire. **2.** To curve or slope backward. — *v.t.* **3.** In chess, to move (a piece) back. — *n.* **1.** The act of retreat-ing. **2.** The retirement of a military force from a position of danger or from an enemy; also, a signal for retreating, made by a trumpet or drum **3.** *Mil.* A signal, as by bugle, for the lowering of the flag at sunset. **4.** Retirement; seclusion; soli-tude. **5.** A place of retirement, quiet, or security; a refuge; haunt. **6.** Religious retirement; also, the time spent in reli-gious retirement. — **to beat a retreat 1.** To give a signal for retreat, as by the beat of drums. **2.** To turn back; flee. [< OF < L < *re-* back + *trahere* to draw]

re·trench (ri·trench′) *v.t.* **1.** To cut down or reduce; curtail (expenditures). **2.** To cut off or away; remove; omit. — *v.i.* **3.** To make retrenchments; economize. [< MF < *re-* back + *trencher* to cut]

re·trench·ment (ri·trench′mənt) *n.* **1.** The act of retrench-ing. **2.** Reduction, as of expenses, for the sake of economy. **3.** *Mil.* An interior fortification from which the enemy can be resisted should the outer line be taken.

re·tri·al (rē·trī′əl) *n.* A second or succeeding trial, as of a judicial case.

ret·ri·bu·tion (ret′rə·byoo′shən) *n.* **1.** The act of requiting; esp., impartial infliction of punishment. **2.** That which is done or given in requital, as a reward or punishment. [< OF < L < *re-* back + *tribuere* to divide, grant]

re·trib·u·tive (ri·trib′yə·tiv) *adj.* Tending to reward or punish. Also **re·trib′u·to′ry** (-tôr′ē, -tō′rē).

re·triev·al (ri·trē′vəl) *n.* **1.** The act or process of retriev-ing. **2.** Possibility of restoration or recovery.

re·trieve (ri·trēv′) *v.* **·trieved, ·triev·ing** *v.t.* **1.** To get back; regain. **2.** To restore; revive, as flagging spirits. **3.** To make up for. **4.** To call to mind. **5.** To find and bring in (wounded or dead game): said of dogs. **6.** *Electronics* To obtain or extract (specific information) from the storage unit of an electronic computer. — *v.i.* **7.** To retrieve game. — *n.* The act of retrieving; recovery. [ME < OF < *re-* again + *trouver* to find] — **re·triev′a·bil′i·ty** *n.* — **re·triev′a·ble** *adj.* — **re·triev′a·bly** *adv.*

re·triev·er (ri·trē′vər) *n.* **1.** A sporting dog specifically trained to retrieve game. **2.** One who retrieves.

retro- *prefix* **1.** Back; backward. **2.** Behind. [< L *retro* back, backward]

ret·ro·ac·tive (ret'rō·ak'tiv, rē'trō-) *adj.* Taking effect at a (usu. specified) time prior to its enactment, ratification, etc., as a provision in a law or contract; applying retrospectively. — **ret'ro·ac'tive·ly** *adv.* — **ret'ro·ac·tiv'i·ty** *n.*

ret·ro·cede (ret'rō·sēd') *v.* **·ced·ed, ·ced·ing** *v.t.* **1.** To cede or give back — *v.i.* **2.** To recede. [< L < *retro-* back + *cedere* to go] — **ret'ro·ces'sion** (-sesh'ən) *n.*

ret·ro·fire (ret'rə·fīr') *n. Aerospace* The operation or moment of firing a retrorocket.

ret·ro·flex (ret'rə·fleks) *adj.* Bent backward; reflexed: said esp. of the tongue. Also **ret·ro·flexed** (ret'rə·flexst). [< LL < L *retro-* back + *flectere* to bend]

ret·ro·grade (ret'rə·grād) *adj.* **1.** Going or tending backward; reversed. **2.** Declining to or toward a worse state or character. **3.** *Astron.* Apparently moving from east to west relative to the fixed stars. **4.** Reversed; inverted. — *v.* **·grad·ed, ·grad·ing** *v.i.* **1.** To move or appear to move backward. **2.** To degenerate. **3.** *Astron.* To have a retrograde motion. — *v.t.* **4.** To cause to move backward; reverse. [< L < *retro-* backward + *gradi* to walk] — **ret'ro·gra·da'tion** (-grā·dā'shən) *n.*

ret·ro·gress (ret'rə·gres) *v.i.* To go back to an earlier or worse state. [< L < *retro-* backward + *gradi* to walk] — **Syn.** In strict usage, *retrogress* suggests a return to a former place or condition, while *degenerate* implies a passing into a worse condition.

ret·ro·gres·sion (ret'rə·gresh'ən) *n.* **1.** The act or process of retrogressing. **2.** *Biol.* Return to or toward an earlier form or structure. — **ret'ro·gres'sive** *adj.*

ret·ro·rock·et (ret'rō·rok'it) *n. Aerospace* An auxiliary rocket whose reverse thrust decelerates a rocket or spaceship.

re·trorse (ri·trôrs') *adj.* Turned or directed backward. [< L *retrorsus,* contr. of *retroversus* < *retro-* backward + *versus,* pp. of *vertere* to turn] — **re·trorse'ly** *adv.*

ret·ro·spect (ret'rə·spekt) *n.* A view or contemplation of something past. [< L < *retro-* back + *specere* to look] — **ret'ro·spec'tion** *n.*

ret·ro·spec·tive (ret'rə·spek'tiv) *adj.* **1.** Looking back on the past. **2.** Looking or facing backward. **3.** Applying retroactively, as legislation. **4.** Characterized by retrospection. — **ret'ro·spec'tive·ly** *adv.*

ret·rous·sé (ret'rōō·sā', *Fr.* rə·trōō·sā') *adj.* Turned up at the end: said of a nose. [< F, pp. of *retrousser* to turn up]

re·try (rē·trī') *v.t.* **·tried, ·try·ing** To try again, as a judicial case.

re·turn (ri·tûrn') *v.i.* **1.** To come or go back, as to or toward a former place or condition. **2.** To come back or revert in thought or speech. **3.** To revert to a former owner. **4.** To answer; respond. — *v.t.* **5.** To bring, carry, send, or put back; replace. **6.** To give in return for something. **7.** To repay or requite, esp. with an equivalent: to *return* a compliment. **8.** To yield or produce, as a profit or interest. **9.** To send back; reflect, as light or sound. **10.** To render (a verdict, etc.). **11.** To submit, as a report or writ, to one in authority. **12.** To report or announce officially. **13.** In card games, to lead (a suit previously led by one's partner). — *n.* **1.** The act, process, state, or result of coming back or returning. **2.** That which is returned. **3.** That which accrues, as from investments, labor, or use; profit. **4.** A coming back, reappearance, or recurrence, as of a periodical event. **5.** A report, list, etc.; esp., a formal or official report. **6.** *pl.* A set of tabulated statistics: election *returns.* **7.** In card games, a lead in a suit formerly led, esp. by one's partner **8.** In tennis, etc., the act of returning a ball to one's opponent; also, the ball, etc., so returned. — *adj.* **1.** Of, pertaining to, or for a return: a *return* ticket. **2.** Given, taken, or done in return: a *return* visit. **3.** Occurring or presented a second time or again. **4.** Reversing direction; doubling back, as a U-shaped bend. [< OF < *re-* back + *torner* to turn] — **re·turn'a·ble** *adj.* — **re·turn'er** *n.*

re·turn (rē'tûrn') *v.t. & v.i.* To turn or fold back again.

return ticket A round-trip ticket.

Reu·ben (rōō'bin) In the Old Testament, the eldest son of Jacob and Leah. *Gen.* xxix 32. — *n.* The tribe of Israel descended from Reuben.

re·un·ion (rē·yōon'yən) *n.* **1.** The act of reuniting. **2.** A gathering of persons who have been separated.

re·u·nite (rē'yōo·nīt') *v.t. & v.i.* **·nit·ed, ·nit·ing** To unite, cohere, or combine again after separation. — **re'u·nit'er** *n.*

Reu·ters (roi'tarz) *n.* A British organization for collecting news and distributing it to member newspapers. Also **Reuter's News Agency.** [after Baron P. J. von *Reuter,* 1816–99, born in Germany]

rev (rev) *n.* A revolution, as of a motor. — *v.t. & v.i.* **revved, rev·ving** To alter the speed of (a motor): with *up.*

re·vamp (rē·vamp') *v.t.* **1.** To patch up; make over; renovate. **2.** To vamp (a boot or shoe) anew.

re·veal (ri·vēl') *v.t.* **1.** To make known; disclose; divulge. **2.** To make visible; expose to view; show. [< OF < L to unveil < *re-* back + *velum* veil] — **re·veal'a·ble** *adj.* — **re·veal'er** *n.* — **re·veal'ment** *n.*

re·veil·le (rev'i·lē) *n.* **1.** A morning signal by drum or gle, notifying soldiers or sailors to rise. **2.** The hour at wh this signal is sounded. [< F, ult. < L < *re-* again + *vigil* to keep watch]

rev·el (rev'əl) *v.i.* **rev·eled** or **·elled, rev·el·ing** or **·el·ling 1.** To take delight: with *in:* He *revels* in his freedom. **2.** To gage in boisterous festivities; make merry. — *n.* **1.** Mer making; carousing. **2.** *Often pl.* An occasion of boisterous tivity; a celebration. [< OF *reveler* to make an uproar < *rebellare*] — **rev'el·er** or **rev'el·ler** *n.*

rev·e·la·tion (rev'ə·lā'shən) *n.* **1.** The act or process of vealing. **2.** That which is or has been revealed. **3.** *Th* **a** The act of revealing or communicating divine truth, e by divine agency. **b** That which has been so revealed, as c cerning God in his relations to man.

Rev·e·la·tion (rev'ə·lā'shən) *n. Often pl.* The Apocaly or book of Revelation, the last book of the New Testame in full, **The Revelation of Saint John the Divine.**

rev·el·ry (rev'əl·rē) *n. pl.* **·ries** Noisy or boisterous me ment.

re·venge (ri·venj') *v.* **·venged, ·veng·ing** *v.t.* **1.** To inf punishment, injury, or loss in return for. **2.** To take or s vengeance in behalf of. — *n.* **1.** The act of revenging. A means of avenging oneself or others. **3.** A desire for v geance. [< OF < *re-* again + *vengier* to take vengeance] **re·veng'er** *n.* — **Syn.** (noun) **1.** *Revenge* stresses personal bitterness seeks relief in harming or humiliating an enemy. *Vengea* originally the indignant vindication of justice, is now applie any furious and thoroughgoing *revenge. Retaliation* suggests repayment of an act by a like act.

re·venge·ful (ri·venj'fəl) *adj.* Disposed to or full of rever vindictive. — **re·venge'ful·ly** *adv.* + **re·venge'ful·ness**

rev·e·nue (rev'ə·nyōo, -nōo) *n.* **1.** Total current inc of a government, except duties on imports: also called *in nal revenue.* **2.** Income from any form of property. **3** source of income. [< F < L < *re-* back + *venire* to com

re·ver·ber·ant (ri·vûr'bər·ənt) *adj.* Reverberating.

re·ver·ber·ate (ri·vûr'bə·rāt) *v.* **·at·ed, ·at·ing** *v.i.* **1.** To sound or re-echo. **2.** To be reflected. **3.** To rebound or coil. — *v.t.* **4.** To echo back (a sound); re-echo. **5.** To flect. [< L < *re-* back + *verberare* to beat]

re·ver·ber·a·tion (ri·vûr'bə·rā'shən) *n.* **1.** The act process of reverberating. **2.** That which is reverbera **3.** The rebound or reflection of light, heat, or sound wav — **re·ver'ber·a'tive** *adj.* — **re·ver'ber·a·to·ry** (-bər·ə·tô -tō'rē) *adj.*

re·vere (ri·vir') *v.t.* **·vered, ·ver·ing** To regard with re ence; venerate. — **Syn.** See VENERATE. [< L < *re-* ag + *vereri* to fear] — **re·ver'er** *n.*

rev·er·ence (rev'ər·əns) *n.* **1** A feeling of profound res often mingled with awe and affection; veneration. **2.** act of respect; an obeisance. — *v.t.* **·enced, ·enc·ing** To gard with reverence. — **Syn.** See VENERATE.

Rev·er·ence (rev'ər·əns) *n.* A title or form of address clergymen: often preceded by *His, Your,* etc.

rev·er·end (rev'ər·ənd) *adj.* **1.** Worthy of reverence. *Often cap.* A title of respect often used with the name clergyman. — *n. Informal* A clergyman; minister. REVERE.]

rev·er·ent (rev'ər·ənt) *adj.* **1.** Feeling reverence. **2.** pressing reverence. [See REVERE.] — **rev'er·ent·ly** ad

rev·er·en·tial (rev'ə·ren'shəl) *adj.* Proceeding from or pressing reverence. — **rev'er·en'tial·ly** *adv.*

rev·er·ie (rev'ə·rē) *n. pl.* **·er·ies 1.** Abstracted mus dreaming. **2.** A product of such musing. Also **rev'er·y.** F < MF *resver* to be delirious, dream]

re·vers (rə·vir', -vâr') *n. pl.* **·vers** (-virz', -vârz') A pa a garment folded over to show the inside, as the lapel coat. Also **re·vere'.** [< OF. See REVERSE.]

re·ver·sal (ri·vûr'səl) *n.* The act of reversing, or the s of being reversed.

re·verse (ri·vûrs') *adj.* **1.** Having a contrary or oppo direction, character, order, etc.; turned backward. **2.** C ing backward motion: the *reverse* gear of an automobile. *n.* **1.** That which is directly opposite or contrary. **2.** back or secondary side of anything: distinguished from *verse.* **3.** A change to an opposite position, directio state. **4.** A change for the worse; a check or partial de **5.** *Mech.* A reversing gear or movement. — *v.* **·ver ·vers·ing** *v.t.* **1.** To turn upside down or inside out. To turn in an opposite direction. **3.** To change into so thing different or opposite. **4.** To set aside; annul: to *verse* a decree. **5.** *Mech.* To cause to have an opposite tion or effect. — *v.i.* **6.** To move or turn in the opp direction. **7.** To reverse its action, as an engine. [< O L < *re-* back + *vertere* to turn] — **re·verse'ly** *adv.* — vers'er *n.*

re·vers·i·ble (ri·vûr'sə·bəl) *adj.* **1.** Capable of being versed in direction or position. **2.** Capable of going e forward or backward, as a chemical reaction or physiolog

...ess. **3.** Capable of being used or worn inside out or ...kward, as a coat. **4.** Having the finish on both sides, as ...bric. — *n.* A reversible coat. — **re·vers′i·bil′i·ty, re·** **s′i·ble·ness** *n.* — **re·vers′i·bly** *adv.*

er·sion (ri·vûr′zhən, -shən) *n.* **1.** A return to or toward ...e former state, condition, practice, or belief. **2.** The act ...eversing, or the state of being reversed. **3.** *Biol.* **a** The ...ppearance in an individual of characteristics that had not ...n evident for two or more generations: also called *atavism.* ...n example of such reappearance. **4.** *Law* **a** The return of ...state to the grantor or his heirs after the expiration of the ...nt. **b** The right of succession to an estate. [See REVERT.] **·e·ver′sion·al,** — **re·ver′sion·ar·y** (-er′ē) *adj.*

·ert (ri·vûrt′) *v.i.* **1.** To go or turn back to a former place, ...dition, attitude, etc. **2.** *Biol.* To return to or show char-...ristics of an earlier type. **3.** *Law* To return to the for-...owner or his heirs. [< OF < L < *re-* back + *vertere* to ...] — **re·vert′i·ble** *adj.* — **re·vert′ive** *adj.*

·et·ment (ri·vet′mənt) *n.* A facing or sheathing, as of ...onry, for protecting earthworks, river banks, etc. [< F ...)F < LL < L < *re-* again + *vestire* to clothe]

·iew[1] (ri·vyoo′) *v.t.* **1.** To go over or examine again; look ...r study again. **2.** To look back upon; think of retro-...tively. **3.** To make an inspection of, esp. formally. **4.** ...write or make a critical review of, as a new book. **5.** *Law* ...eexamine (something done or adjudged by a lower court). ...*i.* **6.** To write a review or reviews, as for a magazine. ...RE- + VIEW]

·iew[2] (ri·vyoo′) *n.* **1.** A repeated or new view or study of ...ething; a retrospective survey. **2.** A lesson studied or ...ed again. **3.** Critical study or examination. **4.** An ar-...e containing a critical discussion of some work. **5.** A peri-...al devoted to essays in criticism and on general subjects. ...t formal inspection, as of troops. **7.** *Law* A judicial revi-... by a superior court of the order or decree of a subordi-... court. See REVUE. [< MF < L < *re-* again + *videre* ...e]

·iew·al (ri·vyoo′əl) *n.* The act of reviewing; a review. **·iew·er** (ri·vyoo′ər) *n.* One who reviews; esp., one who ...ically reviews new books, plays, movies, etc.

·le (ri·vīl′) *v.* **·viled, ·vil·ing** *v.t.* **1.** To assail with abu-... or contemptuous language; vilify; abuse. — *v.i.* **2.** To ... abusive or contemptuous language. — **Syn.** See SCOLD. ...OF *reviler* to despise] — **re·vile′ment** *n.* — **re·vil′er** *n.* **·vil′ing·ly** *adv.*

·s·al (ri·vī′zəl) *n.* The act of revising; revision. **·se** (ri·vīz′) *v.t.* **·vised, ·vis·ing** **1.** To read or read over ... to correct errors, suggest or make changes, etc. **2.** To ...nge; alter. — *n.* **1.** The act or result of revising; a revi-... **2.** A corrected proof after revision. [< MF < L < ...gain + *visere* to scrutinize] — **re·vis′er** or **re·vi′sor** *n.* **·sion** (ri·vizh′ən) *n.* **1.** The act or process of revising. ...omething revised, as a new version of a book. — **re·vi′-** ...al, **re·vi′sion·ar·y** *adj.* **·so·ry** (ri·vī′zər·ē) *adj.* Effecting, or capable of effect-...revision; revising: *revisory* powers.

·val (ri·vī′vəl) *n.* **1.** The act of reviving or, the state of ...g revived. **2.** A recovery, as from depression. **3.** A res-...tion, as after neglect or obscurity. **4.** A renewal of in-...st in religion. **5.** A series of evangelical meetings to re-...ken faith. **·val·ist** (ri·vī′vəl·ist) *n.* A preacher or leader in a reli-...s revival movement.

·ive (ri·vīv′) *v.* **·vived, ·viv·ing** *v.t.* **1.** To bring back to ...or to consciousness. **2.** To give new health, etc., to. **3.** ...bring back into use. **4.** To make effective or operative ...n. **5.** To renew in the mind or memory. **6.** To produce ...n, as an old play. — *v.i.* **7.** To come back to life again. ...'o assume new vigor, health, etc. **9.** To come back into ... **10.** To become effective or operative again. [< MF ...< *re-* again + *vivere* to live] — **re·viv′er** *n.* **·vi·fy** (ri·vīv′ə·fī) *v.t.* **·fied, ·fy·ing** To give new life to; ...ve. [< L < *re-* again + *vivus* alive + *facere* to make] ...e·viv′i·fi·ca′tion *n.*

·ca·ble (ri·vōk′ə·bəl) *adj.* Capable of being revoked. ...**re·vok·a·ble** (ri·vō′kə·bəl). — **rev/o·ca·bil′i·ty** *n.* — **′o·ca·bly** *adv.* **·ca·tion** (rev′ə·kā′shən) *n.* The act of revoking, or the ...e of being revoked; repeal; reversal; annulment. **·oke** (ri·vōk′) *v.* **·voked, ·vok·ing** *v.t.* **1.** To annul or ...e void by recalling; cancel; rescind. — *v.i.* **2.** In card ...es, to fail to follow suit when possible and when required ...the rules. — **Syn.** See ANNUL. — *n.* In card games, ...ect to follow suit; a renege. [< OF < L < *re-* back + ...re to call] — **re·vok′er** *n.* **·olt** (ri·vōlt′) *v.i.* **1.** An uprising against authority; re-...ion. **2.** An act of protest, refusal, or disgust. **3.** The ...e of a person or persons who revolt: to be in *revolt.* —

v.i. **1.** To rise in rebellion against constituted authority; mu-tiny. **2.** To turn away in disgust: with *against, at,* or *from.* — *v.t.* **3.** To cause to feel disgust; repel. [< MF < Ital. < L < *re-* back + *volvere* to roll] — **re·volt′er** *n.* **re·volt·ing** (ri·vōl′ting) *adj.* Abhorrent; loathsome; nause-ating. — **re·volt′ing·ly** *adv.*

rev·o·lu·tion (rev′ə·loo′shən) *n.* **1.** The act or state of re-volving. **2.** A motion in a closed curve around a center, or a complete circuit made by a body in such a course. **3.** *Mech.* Rotation about an axis, as in a spiral, so as to come to a point corresponding to the starting point. **4.** *Astron.* The movement of a planet around the sun or of any celestial body around a center of attraction. **5.** A cycle of successive events or changes. **6.** The overthrow and replacement of a government or political system by those governed. **7.** A drastic change in a condition, method, idea, etc.: a *revolution* in industry. [< OF < LL < L < *re-* back + *volvere* to roll] — **American Revolution** The war for independence carried on by the thirteen American colonies against Great Britain, 1775–83. Also *Revolutionary War.* See table for WAR. — **Chinese Revolution** The events in China during the years 1911–12, inspired by Sun Yat-sen, that overthrew the Man-chu Empire and established a republic. — **English Revolution** The course of events in England in 1642–89 that brought about the execution of Charles I, the rise of the Commonwealth, the dethronement of James II, and the establishment of a constitutional government. — **French Revolution** The revolution that began in France in 1789, overthrew the French monarchy, and culminated in the start of the Napoleonic era in 1799. — **Russian Revolution** The conflict (1917–22), beginning in a Petrograd uprising on March 12, 1917, that resulted in a provisional moderate government and the abdication of Nicholas II. On November 6, the Bolsheviks under Lenin overthrew this government (the **October Revolution**), and in December, 1922, united the soviet states in the Union of Soviet Socialist Republics under Communist (Bolshevik) control.

rev·o·lu·tion·ar·y (rev′ə·loo′shən·er′ē) *adj.* **1.** Pertaining to or of the nature of revolution, esp. political; causing or tending to produce revolution. **2.** Rotating; revolving. **Revolutionary calendar** See (Republican) CALENDAR. **Revolutionary War** The American Revolution. See un-der REVOLUTION. **rev·o·lu·tion·ize** (rev′ə·loo′shən·īz) *v.t.* **·ized, ·iz·ing** To effect a radical change in the character, operation, etc., of. **re·volve** (ri·volv′) *v.* **·volved, ·volv·ing** *v.i.* **1.** To move in an orbit about a center. **2.** To spin around on an axis; rotate. **3.** To recur periodically. — *v.t.* **4.** To cause to move in a circle or orbit. **5.** To cause to rotate. **6.** To turn over men-tally; consider. [< L < *re-* back + *volvere* to roll] — **re·volv′a·ble** *adj.* **re·volv·er** (ri·vol′vər) *n.* **1.** A type of pistol having a re-volving cylinder in the breech chambered to hold several cartridges that may be fired in succession without reloading. **2.** One who or that which revolves. **revolving door** A door rotating like a turnstile about a cen-tral post and consisting of three or four adjustable leaves so encased in a doorway as to exclude drafts of air. **re·vue** (ri·vyoo′) *n.* A musical show consisting of songs, dances, and skits that lampoon or burlesque contemporary people and events: also spelled *review.* [< F] **re·vul·sion** (ri·vul′shən) *n.* **1.** A sudden change of or strong reaction in feeling. **2.** The drawing back from something; violent withdrawal or recoil. [< OF < L < *re-* back + *vel-lere* to pull] — **re·vul′sive** (-siv) *adj.* **re·ward** (ri·wôrd′) *n.* **1.** Something given or done in return; esp., a gift, prize, etc., for merit, service, or achievement. **2.** Money offered for information, for the return of lost goods, etc. **3.** Profit; return. — *v.t.* **1.** To give a reward to or for. **2.** To be a reward for. [< OF < *re-* back (< L) + *warder* to guard] — **re·ward′er** *n.* **re·wire** (rē·wīr′) *v.t.* **·wired, ·wir·ing** To wire again, as a house or a machine. **re·word** (rē·wûrd′) *v.t.* **1.** To say again in other words; ex-press differently. **2.** To utter or say again in the same words. **re·write** (*v.* rē·rīt′; *n.* rē′rīt′) *v.t.* **·wrote, ·writ·ten, ·writ·ing** **1.** To write over again. **2.** In American journalism, to put into publishable form (a story submitted by a reporter). — *n.* A news item written in this manner. **rex** (reks) *n. pl.* **re·ges** (rē′jēs) *Usu. cap. Latin* King. **Rey·nard** (ren′ərd, rā′närd) *n.* The fox, esp. as the personi-fication of cunning: also spelled *Renard.* [< MDu. < OHG, name of fox in medieval legend] **-rhage, -rhagia, -rhagy** See -RRHAGIA. **-rhaphy** See -RRHAPHY. **rhap·so·dize** (rap′sə·dīz) *v.t. & v.i.* **·dized, ·diz·ing** To ex-press or recite rhapsodically. — **rhap′so·dist** *n.*

rhap·so·dy (rap′sə·dē) n. pl. ·dies 1. A series of disconnected and often extravagant sentences, extracts, or utterances, gathered or composed under excitement. 2. Music An instrumental composition of irregular form, often suggestive of improvisation. 3. A miscellaneous collection. [< L < Gk. < rhaptein to stitch together + ōidē song] — rhap·sod·ic (rap·sod′ik) or ·i·cal adj. — rhap·sod′i·cal·ly adv.

rhe·a (rē′ə) n. A flightless bird of the plains of South America, smaller than true ostriches, and having three toes: also called ostrich. [< NL < L < Gk.]

Rhe·a (rē′ə) In Greek mythology, the daughter of Uranus and Gaea and mother of Zeus.

-rhea See -RRHEA.

Rhen·ish (ren′ish) adj. Pertaining to the river Rhine, or to the adjacent lands. — n. Rhine wine. [< L Rhenus Rhine]

rhe·ni·um (rē′nē·əm) n. A heavy, lustrous, rare metallic element (symbol Re) of the manganese group. See ELEMENT. [< NL < L Rhenus Rhine]

rheo- combining form Current or flow, as of water or electricity. [< Gk. rheos a current]

rhe·o·stat (rē′ə·stat) n. Electr. A variable resistor used to control current and voltage strength in a circuit. [< RHEO- + Gk. statos standing] — rhe′o·stat′ic adj.

rhe·sus (rē′səs) n. A monkey with a short tail, common throughout India and widely used in biological and medical research. [< NL < Gk. Rhēsos Rhesus]

Rhe·sus factor (rē′səs) Rh factor.

rhet·o·ric (ret′ə·rik) n. 1. The art of discourse, both written and spoken. 2. The power of pleasing or persuading. 3. Affected and exaggerated display in the use of language. 4. The art of prose as distinct from verse. [< MF < Gk. < rhētōr public speaker]

rhe·tor·i·cal (ri·tôr′i·kəl, -tor′-) adj. 1. Pertaining to rhetoric; oratorical. 2. Designed for showy oratorical effect. — rhe·tor′i·cal·ly adv. — rhe·tor′i·cal·ness n.

rhetorical question A question put only for oratorical or literary effect, the answer being implied in the question.

rhet·o·ri·cian (ret′ə·rish′ən) n. 1. A master of rhetoric. 2. One who writes or speaks eloquently. [< F rhétoricien]

rheum (room) n. Pathol. 1. A thin, watery discharge from the nose and eyes. 2. A cold. [< OF < L < Gk. rheuma stream < rheein to flow] — rheum′y adj.

rheu·mat·ic (roo·mat′ik) adj. 1. Of or relating to rheumatism. 2. Affected with rheumatism. — n. One affected with rheumatism. [< OF < L < Gk. rheuma a stream]

rheumatic fever Pathol. An infectious disease chiefly affecting children, characterized by painful inflammation around the joints, typically intermittent fever, and inflammation of the pericardium and valves of the heart.

rheu·ma·tism (roo′mə·tiz′əm) n. Pathol. 1. A painful inflammation and stiffness of the muscles, joints, etc. 2. Rheumatoid arthritis. [< L < Gk. rheumatismos < rheuma a stream]

rheu·ma·toid (roo′mə·toid) adj. Pathol. 1. Resembling rheumatism. 2. Rheumatic. Also rheu′ma·toi′dal (-toid′l). — rheu′ma·toi′dal·ly adv.

rheumatoid arthritis Pathol. A persisting inflammatory disease of the joints, marked by atrophy, rarefaction of the bones, and deformities.

Rh factor Biochem. An agglutinogen present in the blood of most persons (who are said to be **Rh positive**) and that may cause hemolytic reactions under certain conditions, as during pregnancy or following transfusions with persons lacking this factor (who are said to be **Rh negative**): also called Rhesus factor.

rhin- Var. of RHINO-.

rhi·nal (rī′nəl) adj. Of or pertaining to the nose; nasal.

rhine·stone (rīn′stōn′) n. A refractive, colorless glass or paste, used as an imitation gemstone. [Trans. of F caillou du Rhin; so called because orig. made at Strasbourg]

Rhine wine 1. Wine made from grapes grown in the neighborhood of the Rhine: also called Rhenish. 2. Any of various white, dry, still wines.

rhi·ni·tis (rī·nī′tis) n. Pathol. Inflammation of the mucous membranes of the nose.

rhi·no¹ (rī′nō) n. pl. ·nos A rhinoceros.

rhi·no² (rī′nō) n. Slang Money; cash. [Origin unknown]

rhino- combining form Nose; nasal. Also, before vowels, rhin-. [< Gk. rhis, rhinos nose]

rhi·noc·e·ros (rī·nos′ər·əs) n. pl. ·ros·es or ·ros A large, herbivorous mammal of Africa and Asia, having one or two horns on the snout and a very thick hide. [< LL < Gk. < rhis, rhinos nose + keras horn]

rhizo- combining form Root; pertaining to a root or roots. Also, before vowels, rhiz-. [< Gk. rhiza root]

rhi·zoid (rī′zoid) adj. Rootlike. — n. Bot. A hairlike, branching organ by which mosses and liverworts obtain nourishment and support. — rhi·zoi·dal (rī·zoid′l) adj.

rhi·zome (rī′zōm) n. Bot. A subterranean rootlike stem, producing roots from its lower surface and leaves or shoots from its upper surface: also called rootstalk, rootstock. Also

rhi·zo·ma (rī·zō′mə). [< NL rhizoma < Gk. rhizōma, < rhiza root] — rhi·zom·a·tous (rī·zom′ə·təs, -zō′mə-)

rhi·zo·pod (rī′zə·pod) n. Any of a class or subclass of tozoans with rootlike pseudopodia. — rhi·zop·o·dan zop′ə·dən) adj. & n. — rhi·zop′o·dous adj.

rho (rō) n. The seventeenth letter in the Greek alph (P, ρ), corresponding to the English r aspirated. See AL BET. [< Gk. rhō]

Rhode Island Red An American breed of domestic fo reddish and black in color, with yellow smooth legs.

Rhodes scholarship One of a number of scholarshi Oxford University, provided for in the will of Cecil Rh for selected scholars (**Rhodes scholars**) from the U.S. the British dominions and colonies.

Rho·di·an (rō′dē·ən) adj. Of or pertaining to the islar Rhodes. — n. A native of Rhodes.

rho·di·um (rō′dē·əm) n. A whitish gray, metallic eler (symbol Rh) of the platinum group, whose salts are fo most part rose-colored, used in electroplating to prevent rosion. See ELEMENT. [< NL < Gk. rhodon rose]

rho·do·den·dron (rō′də·den′drən) n. Any of a gen evergreen shrubs or small trees of the heath family, clusters of white, pink, or purple flowers: the State flow West Virginia. [< L < Gk. < rhodon rose + dendron t

-rhoea See -RRHEA.

rhomb (rom, romb) n. A rhombus. [< F rhombe]

rhom·ben·ceph·a·lon (rom′ben·sef′ə·lon) n. Anat. A ment of the embryonic brain that divides into the me cephalon and myelencephalon: also called hindbrain. NL]

rhom·bic (rom′bik) adj. Pertaining to or having the s of a rhombus. Also **rhom′bi·cal**.

rhom·boid (rom′boid) n. Geom. 1. A parallelogram ha opposite sides and opposite angles equal but having no angle. 2. A solid bounded by such parallelograms. 1. Having the character or shape of a rhomboid. 2. Ha a shape approaching that of a rhombus. [< F rhomb — **rhom·boi·dal** (rom·boid′l) adj.

rhom·bus (rom′bəs) n. pl. ·bus·es or ·bi (-bī) Geom equilateral parallelogram having the angles usu., but necessarily, oblique. [< L < Gk. rhombos spinning to

rhu·barb (roo′bärb) n. 1. A stout, coarse, perennial having large leaves and small clusters of flowers on tall st esp. one whose acid leafstalks are used in cooking. 2. Slang A heated argument or quarrel. [< MF < LL < rha rhubarb, ? < Rha the Volga River + L barbarus fore

rhumb (rum, rumb) n. Naut. 1. One of the 32 points o mariners' compass, separated by arcs of 11° 15′. 2. these arcs or divisions. [< OF rumb]

rhum·ba (rum′bə) See RUMBA.

rhumb line A line or course along the surface of a spr crossing successive meridians at the same angle.

rhyme (rīm) n. 1. A correspondence of sounds in tw more words, esp. at the ends of lines of poetry. 2. A whose lines have a correspondence of sounds in the words. 3. Poetry; verse. — v. rhymed, rhym·ing v To make rhymes or verses. 2. To correspond in sound terminal sounds. — v.t. 3. To put or write in rhym verse. 4. To use as a rhyme. Also spelled rime. [< rime < L < Gk. rhythmus rhythm] — rhym′er n.

rhyme·ster (rīm′stər) n. A writer of jingles: also sp rimester.

rhythm (rith′əm) n. 1. The recurrence or repetiti stress, beat, sound, accent, motion, etc., usu. occurring regular or harmonious pattern or manner. 2. Music a relative duration and accent of musical sounds. b Any cific arrangement of the accents or durations of mu sounds. 3. In poetry, the cadenced flow of sound as d mined by the succession of long and short syllables (clas rhythm), or accented and unaccented syllables (mo rhythm). 4. In painting, sculpture, etc., a regular or monious recurrence of lines, forms, colors, etc. [< MF < Gk. rhythmos < rheein to flow]

rhyth·mi·cal (rith′mə·kəl) adj. Of or possessing rhy Also **rhyth·mic** (rith′mik). — **rhyth′mi·cal·ly** adv.

rhythm method Birth control by sexual abstinence d the woman's estimated monthly period of fertility.

ri·al (rī′al) n. A standard monetary unit and coin of in 1961 worth about 13 U.S. cents. [< OF rial, real r

ri·al·to (rē·al′tō) n. pl. ·tos A market or place of exch [< RIALTO]

Ri·al·to (rē·al′tō, Ital. rē·äl′tō) In New York City theater district. [after Rialto, the ancient business qu of Venice]

rib (rib) n. 1. Anat. One of the series of bony rods atta to the spine of most vertebrates, and nearly encirclin thoracic cavity. In man there are twelve ribs on each forming the walls of the thorax. For illus. see SKELETON Collateral adjective: costal. 2. Something likened to a the rib of an umbrella. 3. A curved side timber ber away from the keel in a boat or ship. 4. A raised on

ipe in cloth or knit goods. **5.** *Bot.* A vein of a leaf, esp.
entral one. **6.** A cut of meat including one or more ribs.
v.t. **ribbed, rib·bing 1.** To make with ridges: to *rib* a piece
knitting. **2.** To strengthen or protect by or enclose within
s. **3.** *Slang* To make fun of; tease. [OE]

ald (rib′əld) *adj.* Pertaining to or indulging in coarse
guage or vulgar jokes. — *n.* One who uses coarse or abu-
e language. [< OF *ribauld* < Gmc.]

ald·ry (rib′əl·drē) *n. pl.* **·ries** Ribald language.

and (rib′ənd) *n. Archaic* A decorative ribbon.

bing (rib′ing) *n.* An arrangement or collection of ribs,
in ribbed cloth, etc.

bon (rib′ən) *n.* **1.** A narrow strip of fine fabric, usu. silk
satin, having finished edges and made in a variety of
aves, used as trimming. **2.** Something shaped like or sug-
sting a ribbon, as a watch spring. **3.** *Often pl.* A narrow
ip; a shred: torn to *ribbons.* **4.** An ink-bearing strip of
th for giving the impression in a typewriter or similar
vice. **5.** A colored strip of cloth worn to signify member-
p in an order, the award of a prize, or as a military badge.
v.t. To ornament with ribbons; also, to form or tear into
bons. [< MF *riban* < Gmc.]

o·fla·vin (rī′bō·flā′vin) *n. Biochem.* A member of the
amin B complex, vitamin B₂, an orange-yellow, crystal-
e compound, $C_{17}H_{22}N_4O_6$, found in milk, leafy vegetables,
gs, and meats: also *vitamin G.* [< RIBO(SE) + FLAVIN]

o·nu·cle·ase (rī′bō·nōō′klē·ās, -nyōō′-, -āz) *n. Biochem.*
pancreatic enzyme, effective in splitting ribonucleic acid.

o·nu·cle·ic acid (rī′bō·nōō·klē′ik, -nyōō-) *Biochem.* A
cleic acid of high molecular weight found in the cytoplasm
d nuclei of cells and associated with DNA in the synthesis
cell proteins. Abbr. *RNA*

ose (rī′bōs) *n. Chem.* A sugar, $C_5H_{10}O_5$, derived from
ntose and occurring in certain nucleic acids. [< G *ribon-*
ᵣe, arbitrary alteration of ARABINOSE + -*söure* acid]

o·some (rī′bə·sōm) *n. Biol.* One of a class of minute
tein particles found in the cytoplasm of plant and animal
ls, associated with ribonucleic acid in the transmission of
netic characteristics. — **ri·bo·so·mal** (rī′bə·sō′məl) *adj.*

combining form Realm: *bishopric.* [OE *rīce*]

e (rīs) *n.* **1.** The edible seeds of an annual cereal grass,
h in carbohydrates and forming a staple food throughout
world. **2.** The grass itself, cultivated in warm climates.
OF < Ital. < L < Gk. *oryza*]

paper 1. Paper made from rice straw. **2.** A delicate
getable paper made from the pith of a Chinese shrub,
ed into thin rolls and flattened into sheets.

er (rī′sər) *n.* A kitchen utensil consisting of a container
forated with small holes through which potatoes and
er vegetables are pressed.

**** (rich) *adj.* **1.** Having large possessions, as of money,
ds, or lands; wealthy; opulent. **2.** Composed of rare or
cious materials; valuable; costly: *rich* fabrics. **3.** Lus-
us to the taste, often implying an excess of fats, flavoring,
. **4.** Full, satisfying, and pleasing, as a tone, voice, color,
. **5.** Luxuriant; abundant: *rich* hair; *rich* crops. **6.**
lding abundant returns; fruitful. **7.** Abundantly sup-
ed: often with *in* or *with*. **8.** Abounding in desirable qual-
s; of full strength, as blood. **9.** *Informal* Exceedingly
morous; amusing or ridiculous: a *rich* joke. **10.** Of a fuel-
mixture, containing a relatively high ratio of fuel to air.
[< OE *rīce* powerful, rich and OF *riche* < Gmc.] —
h′ly *adv.* — **rich′ness** *n.*

es (rich′iz) *n.pl.* **1.** Abundant possessions; wealth. **2.**
undance of whatever is precious.

h·ter scale (rikh′tər) A scale for measuring the magni-
de of earthquakes. [after C. F. *Richter*, born 1900, U.S.
smologist]

**** (rik) *n.* A stack, as of hay, having the top covered to
tect the interior from rain. — *v.t.* To pile in ricks. [OE
ac]

ets (rik′its) *n. Pathol.* A disease of early childhood,
efly due to a deficiency of calcium salts or vitamin D,
aracterized by softening of the bones and consequent de-
mity: also called *rachitis.* [? Alter. of Gk. *rachitis* inflam-
tion of the spine]

ett·si·a (rik·et′sē·ə) *n. pl.* **·si·ae** (-si·ē) Any of a genus
microorganisms typically parasitic in the bodies of certain
ks and lice, but transmissible to other animals and to man
d the causative agent of typhus, Rocky Mountain spotted
er, etc. [after Howard T. *Ricketts*, 1871–1910, U.S. pa-
ologist] — **rick·ett′si·al** *adj.*

et·y (rik′it·ē) *adj.* **·et·i·er, ·et·i·est 1.** Ready to fall;
ttering. **2.** Affected with or like rickets. **3.** Irregular, as
otion. **4.** Feeble; infirm; unsteady. — **rick′et·i·ly** *adv.*
rick′et·i·ness *n.*

k·ey (rik′ē) *n. pl.* **·eys** A cooling drink of which a liquor,
gin, lime juice, and carbonated water are the chief ingre-

dients. [Said to be after a Colonel *Rickey*]

rick·rack (rik′rak′) *n.* Flat braid in zigzag form, made of
cotton, rayon, silk, or wool; also, the openwork trimming
made with this braid. [Reduplication of RACK¹]

rick·shaw (rik′shô) *n.* A jinriksha. Also **rick′sha.**

ric·o·chet (rik′ə·shā′, -shet′) *v.i.* **·cheted** (-shād′) or **·chet·**
ted (-shet′id), **·chet·ing** (-shā′ing) or **·chet·ting** (-shet′ing)
To glance from a surface, as a stone thrown over the water;
make a series of skips or bounds. — *n.* **1.** A bounding, as of
a projectile over or off a surface. **2.** A projectile so bounding. [< F; origin uncertain]

rid (rid) *v.t.* **rid** or **rid·ded, rid·ding** To free, as from a burden or annoyance: usu. with *of.* — *adj.* Free; clear; quit:
with *of*: We are well *rid* of him. [< ON *rythja* to clear land]

rid·dance (rid′ns) *n.* A ridding of something undesirable,
or the state of being rid. — **good riddance** A welcome deliverance from something undesirable.

rid·den (rid′n) Past participle of RIDE.

rid·dle¹ (rid′l) *v.t.* **·dled, ·dling 1.** To perforate in numerous
places, as with shot. **2.** To sift through a coarse sieve. **3.**
To damage, injure; criticize, etc., as if by perforating. — *n.*
A coarse sieve. [OE *hriddel* sieve] — **rid′dler** *n.*

rid·dle² (rid′l) *n.* **1.** A puzzling question stated as a problem to be solved by clever ingenuity; a conundrum. **2.** Any
puzzling object or person. — **Syn.** See PUZZLE. — *v.* **·dled,**
·dling *v.t.* **1.** To solve; explain. — *v.i.* **2.** To utter or
solve riddles. [OE *rædels* advice, interpretation]

ride (rīd) *v.* **rode** (*Archaic* **rid**), **rid·den** (*Archaic* **rid**), **rid·ing**
v.i. **1.** To sit on and be borne along by a horse or other ani-
mal. **2.** To be borne along as if on horseback. **3.** To travel
or be carried on or in a vehicle or other conveyance. **4.** To
be supported in moving: The wheel *rides* on the shaft. **5.**
To support and carry a rider in a specified manner: This car
rides easily. **6.** To seem to float in space, as a star. **7.** *Naut.*
To lie at anchor, as a ship. **8.** To work or move upward out
of place: with *up.* **9.** *Slang* To continue unchanged: Let it
ride. — *v.t.* **10.** To sit on and control the motion of (a
horse, bicycle, etc.). **11.** To move or be borne or supported
upon. **12.** To overlap or overlie. **13.** To travel or traverse
(an area, etc.) on horseback, in an automobile, etc. **14.** To
control imperiously or oppressively: usually in the past participle: a king-*ridden* people. **15.** To accomplish by riding: to
ride a race. **16.** To cause to ride. **17.** *Naut.* To keep at
anchor. **18.** *Informal* To tease or harass by ridicule or petty
criticisms; tyrannize. — **to ride out** To survive; endure successfully. — *n.* **1.** An excursion by any means of conveyance, as on horseback, by car, etc. **2.** A road intended for
riding. [OE *rīdan*] — **rid′a·ble** *adj.*

rid·er (rī′dər) *n.* **1.** One who or that which rides. **2.** One
who breaks in horses. **3.** Any device that rides upon or
weighs down something else. **4.** A separate piece of writing
or print added to a document, record, or the like. **5.** An addition or proposed addition to a legislative bill.

ridge (rij) *n.* **1.** An elevation long in proportion to its width
and height and generally having sloping sides. **2.** A long,
relatively narrow elevation of land. **3.** That part of a roof
where the rafters meet the ridgepole. **4.** Any raised strip,
as on fabric, etc. **5.** The back or backbone of an animal, especially of a whale. — *v.* **ridged, ridg·ing** *v.t.* **1.** To mark
with ridges. **2.** To form into ridges. — *v.i.* **3.** To form
ridges. [OE *hrycg*] — **ridg′y** *adj.*

ridge·pole (rij′pōl′) *n.* A horizontal timber at the ridge of a
roof. Also **ridge beam, ridge piece, ridge plate.** For illus.
see ROOF.

rid·i·cule (rid′ə·kyōōl) *n.* **1.** Language or actions calculated
to make a person or thing the object of contemptuous or humorous derision or mockery. **2.** An object of mocking mer-
riment; butt. — *v.t.* **·culed, ·cul·ing** To make fun of; deride.
[< OF < L *ridiculum* a joke] — **rid′i·cul′er** *n.*

ri·dic·u·lous (ri·dik′yə·ləs) *adj.* Exciting ridicule; absurd
and unworthy of consideration. — **ri·dic′u·lous·ly** *adv.* —
ri·dic′u·lous·ness *n.*

rid·ing¹ (rī′ding) *n.* The act of one who rides; a ride. — *adj.*
1. Suitable for riding. **2.** For use while at anchor.

rid·ing² (rī′ding) *n.* **1.** One of the three administrative divisions into which Yorkshire, England, was formerly divided. **2.** In Canada, an administrative or electoral district.
[OE *thrithing* < ON *thrithjungr* third part]

rife (rīf) *adj.* **1.** Great in number or quantity; plentiful;
abundant. **2.** Prevalent; current. **3.** Containing in abundance: followed by *with.* [OE *rȳfe*]

riff (rif) *n.* In jazz music, a melodic phrase or motif, played
repeatedly as background or used as the main theme. [?
Back formation < RIFFLE, or ? < REFRAIN]

Riff (rif) *n.* One of a Berber tribe inhabiting the mountainous region of northern Morocco. — **Rif′fi·an** *adj. & n.*

rif·fle (rif′əl) *n.* **1.** *U.S.* A shoal or rocky obstruction lying
beneath the surface of a river or other stream. **2.** A stretch

of shallow, choppy water caused by such a shoal. **3.** The act or a way of shuffling cards. — *v.t. & v.i.* **·fled, ·fling 1.** To cause or form a rapid. **2.** To shuffle (cards) by bending up adjacent corners of two halves of the pack, and permitting the cards to slip together as they are released. **3.** To thumb through (the pages of a book). [? Alter. of RUFFLE]

riff·raff (rif'raf') *n.* **1.** The populace; rabble. **2.** Miscellaneous rubbish. [ME *riff and raff* one and all < OF *rif et raf*]

ri·fle[1] rī'fəl) *n.* **1.** A firearm having a rifled or spirally grooved bore, fired from the shoulder. **2.** An artillery piece having a rifled bore. *pl.* A body of soldiers equipped with rifles. — *v.t.* **·fled, ·fling.** To cut a spirally grooved bore in (a firearm, etc.). [< *rifled gun* < OF *rifler* to file]

U.S. RIFLES

A Springfield, 1903. *B* Garand semi-automatic, World War II. *C* M-14 automatic, 1958.

ri·fle[2] (rī'fəl) *v.t.* **·fled ·fling 1.** To search through and rob, as a safe. **2.** To search and rob (a person). **3.** To seize and take away by force. [< OF *rifler* to plunder] — **ri'fler** *n.*

ri·fle·man (rī'fəl·mən) *n.* *pl.* **·men** (-mən) One armed or skilled with the rifle.

rifle range An area used for shooting rifles at a target.

ri·fling (rī'fling) *n.* **1.** The operation of forming the grooves in a rifle. **2.** The grooves of a rifle collectively.

rift[1] (rift) *n.* **1.** An opening made by riving or splitting; a cleft; fissure. **2.** Any disagreement or lack of harmony, as between friends, nations, etc. — *v.t.* To rive; burst open; split. [< Scand. Cf. Dan. *rift*, ON *rifa*.]

rift[2] (rift) *n.* A shallow place in a stream.

rig[1] (rig) *v.t.* **rigged, rig·ging 1.** To fit out; equip. **2.** *Naut.* **a** To fit, as a ship, with rigging. **b** To fit (sails, stays, etc.) to masts, yards, etc. **3.** *Informal* To dress; clothe, esp. in finery. **4.** To make or construct hurriedly: often with *up.* — *n.* **1.** *Naut.* The arrangement of sails, rigging, spars, etc., on a vessel. **2.** *Informal* A style of dress; costume. **3.** *U.S. Informal* A horse or horses and vehicle. **4.** Any apparatus, gear, or tackle: an oil-well *rig.* **5.** Fishing tackle. [< Scand. Cf. Norwegian and Sw. *rigga.*]

rig[2] (rig) *v.t.* **rigged, rig·ging** To control fraudulently; manipulate: to *rig* an election. [Origin uncertain]

rig·a·doon (rig'ə·dōon') *n.* **1.** A gay, quick dance for two, originating in Provence. **2.** Music for this dance. [< F]

Ri·gel (rī'jəl, -gəl) One of the 20 brightest stars, 0.34 magnitude; Beta in the constellation Orion. [< Arabic *rijl* foot]

rig·ger (rig'ər) *n.* **1.** One who rigs. **2.** One who fits the rigging of ships. **3.** A ship having a specified rig: used in combination: a *square-rigger.*

rig·ging (rig'ing) *n.* **1.** *Naut.* The entire cordage system of a vessel. **2.** Tackle used in logging. **3.** The act of one who or that which rigs.

right (rīt) *adj.* **1.** Done in accordance with or conformable to moral law or to some standard of rightness; equitable; just; righteous. **2.** Conformable to truth or fact. **3.** Conformable to a standard of propriety or to the conditions of the case; proper; fit; suitable. **4.** Most desirable or preferable; also, fortunate. **5.** Pertaining to, designating, or situated on the side of the body that is toward the south when one faces east. **6.** Holding one direction, as a line; straight; direct. **7.** Properly placed, disposed, or adjusted; well-regulated; orderly. **8.** Sound in mind or body; healthy; well. **9.** *Geom.* Formed with reference to a line or plane perpendicular to another line or plane: a *right* angle. **10.** Designed to be worn outward or when in use placed toward an observer: the *right* side of cloth. **11.** *Sometimes cap.* Designating a person, party, faction, etc., having absolutely or relatively conservative or reactionary views and policies. — **to rights** In a proper or orderly condition: to put a room to *rights.* — *adv.* **1.** In accordance with justice or moral principle. **2.** According to the fact or truth; correctly. **3.** In a straight line; directly. **4.** Very: used dialectally or in some titles: a *right* good time, *Right* Reverend. **5.** Suitably; properly. **6.** Precisely; just; also, immediately. **7.** Without delay or evasion. **8.** Toward the right. **9.** Completely or quite: The house burned *right* to the ground. — *n.* **1.** That which is right; moral rightness; also, justice. **2.** *Often pl.* A just and proper claim or title to anything. **3.** The right hand, side, or direction. **4.** Anything adapted for right-hand use or position. **5.** *Often cap.* A group, party, etc., whose views and policies are right (adj. def. 11) or, in Europe, whose members sit to the presiding officer's right in a deliberative assembly. **6.** In boxing, a blow delivered with the right hand. — *v.t.* **1.** To restore to an upright or normal position. **2.** To put in order; set right. **3.** To make

correct or in accord with facts. **4.** To make reparation f **5.** To make reparation to (a person). — *v.i.* **1.** To reg an upright or normal position. [OE *riht*] — **right'er** *n*

right·a·bout (rīt'ə·bout') *n.* **1.** The opposite direction. A turning in or to the opposite direction.

right angle *Geom.* An angle whose sides are perpendic to each other; an angle of 90°.

right-an·gled (rīt'ang'gəld) *adj.* Forming or containin right angle or angles: a *right-angled* triangle.

right·eous (rī'chəs) *adj.* **1.** Conforming to a standar right and justice; virtuous. **2.** Morally right; equitabl *righteous* act. [OE < *riht* right + *wîs* wise] — **right'ec ly** *adv.* — **right'eous·ness** *n.*

right face In military drill, a 90-degree pivot to the rig using the ball of the left foot and the heel of the right.

right·ful (rīt'fəl) *adj.* **1.** Characterized by or conformin a right or just claim: *rightful* heritage. **2.** Consonant v moral right or with justice and truth. **3.** Proper. **4.** right; just. [OE *rihtful*] — **right'ful·ly** *adv.* — **right** ness *n.*

right-hand (rīt'hand') *adj.* **1.** Of, for, pertaining to situated on the right side or right hand. **2.** Chiefly depe ed on: *right-hand* man. **3.** Toward the right.

right-hand·ed (rīt'han'did) *adj.* **1.** Using the right h more easily than the left. **2.** Done with the right hand. Moving from left to right, as the hands of a clock. **4.** Ad ed for use by the right hand. — **right'-hand'ed·ness** *n.*

right·ist (rī'tist) *n.* One whose views and policies are r (adj. def. 11). — *adj.* Right (adj. def. 11). — **right'is**

right·ly (rīt'lē) *adv.* **1.** Correctly. **2.** Honestly; uprigh **3.** Properly; aptly.

right-mind·ed (rīt'mīn'did) *adj.* Having right feeling opinions. — **right'mind'ed·ly** *adv.* — **right'mind'ed·ne**

right·ness (rīt'nis) *n.* **1.** The quality or condition of b right. **2.** Rectitude. **3.** Correctness. **4.** Straightness.

right·o (rī'tō) *interj.* *Brit. Informal* Right: All right!

right of asylum In international law, the right to pro tion from arrest in a place recognized by law or custom

right of search In international law, the right of a be erent vessel in time of war to verify the nationality of a sel and to ascertain, if neutral, whether it carries contrab goods. Also **right of visit and search.**

right of way 1. *Law* The right of a person to pass over land of another; also, the path or piece of land. **2.** The s of land over which a railroad lays its tracks, on which a p lic highway is built, or above which a high-tension po line is built. **3.** The legal or customary precedence whic lows one vehicle or vessel to cross in front of another.

right-of-way (rīt'əv·wā')

right triangle A triangle containing one right angle.

right whale Any of several whales of polar seas, havi large head and elastic whalebone plates in its mouth.

right wing 1. *Sometimes cap.* A party, group, faction, having rightist policies. **2.** The wing, division, part, etc the right side. — **right-wing** (rīt'wing') *adj.* — **rig wing'er** *n.*

rig·id (rij'id) *adj.* **1.** Resisting change of form; stiff. Rigorous; inflexible; severe. **3.** Not moving; fixed. **4.** St exact, as reasoning. **5.** *Aeron.* Designating a dirigible w cells are enclosed within a rigid framework. [< L *rigio* be stiff] — **rig'id·ly** *adv.* — **ri·gid'i·ty, rig'id·ness** *n.*

Rig·il Cen·tau·rus (rig'il ken·tôr'əs) *n.* One of th brightest stars, 0.6 magnitude; Beta in the constella Centaurus.

rig·ma·role (rig'mə·rōl) *n.* Incoherent talk or writing; sense. Also **rig'a·ma·role'** (-ə·mə-). [Alter. of *ragman* deed on parchment]

rig·or (rig'ər) *n.* **1.** The condition of being stiff or rigid. Stiffness of opinion or temper; harshness. **3.** Exactness out allowance or indulgence; inflexibility; strictness; se ty. **4.** Inclemency, as of the weather; hardship. Also *I* **rig'our.** [< OF < L < *rigere* to be stiff] — **rig'or·ist** *adj.* **rig'or·is'tic** *adj.*

rig·or mor·tis (rig'ər·môr'tis, rī'gər) The muscular rig that ensues shortly after death. [< L, stiffness of deat

rig·or·ous (rig'ər·əs) *adj.* **1.** Marked by or acting with or; uncompromising; severe. **2.** Logically accurate; ex strict. **3.** Inclement; severe: a *rigorous* climate. — **rig ous·ly** *adv.* — **rig'or·ous·ness** *n.*

rile (rīl) *v.t.* **riled, ril·ing** *Informal* To vex; to tate. **2.** To make (a liquid) muddy. Also *roil.* [Va ROIL]

rill (ril) *n.* **1.** A small stream. **2.** A long, narrow valle the face of the moon: also **rille.** [Prob. < LG *rille*]

rim (rim) *n.* **1.** The edge of an object, usu. of a circula ject. **2.** The peripheral part of a wheel, connected to hub by spokes. **3.** The frame of a pair of spectacles, rounding the lenses. — *v.t.* **rimmed, rim·ming 1.** To vide with a rim; border. **2.** In sports, to roll around the of (the basket, cup, etc.) without falling in. [OE *rima*

rime[1] (rīm) See RHYME.

ne² (rīm) *n.* **1.** A milky white, granular deposit of ice ▪rmed on objects by fog or water vapor that has frozen. **2.** ▪rost. — *v.i. & v.t.* **rimed, rim·ing** To cover with or congeal ▪to rime. [OE *hrīm* frost] — **rim′y** *adj.*

n·er (rī′mər) See RHYMER.

ne·ster (rīm′stər) See RHYMESTER.

n·mer (rīm′ər) *n.* A reamer (def. 2).

▪d (rīnd) *n.* The skin or outer coat that may be peeled or ▪ken off, as of bacon, fruit, cheese, etc. [OE *rind* bark]

▪·der·pest (rin′dər·pest) *n. Vet.* An acute intestinal ▪rus disease of cattle and sometimes of sheep. [< G]

▪g¹ (ring) *n.* **1.** Any circular object, line, mark, etc. **2.** A ▪rcular band, usu. of precious metal, worn on a finger. **3.** ny metal or wooden band used for holding or carrying ▪mething. **4.** A group of persons or things in a circle; also, circular movement. **5.** A group of persons, as in business ▪ politics; a clique. **6.** One of a series of concentric layers ▪ wood in the trunk of a tree, formed by annual growth. **7.** ▪n area or arena, usu. square, as that in which boxers fight; ▪e fighting in general. **8.** Political competition or rivalry: ▪e tossed his hat into the *ring.* **9.** *Chem.* An arrangement ▪ atoms in a closed chain: the benzene *ring.* **10.** The space ▪tween two concentric circles. — **to run rings around** ▪formal To be superior to in some way. — *v.* **ringed, ring·** **g** *v.t.* **1.** To surround with a ring; encircle. **2.** To form ▪o a ring or rings. **3.** To provide or decorate with a ring or ▪gs. **4.** To cut a ring of bark from (a branch or tree). **5.** ▪o hem in (cattle, etc.) by riding in a circle around them. **6.** ▪ certain games, to cast a ring over (a peg or pin). — *v.i.* **7.** To form a ring or rings. **8.** To move or fly in rings or ▪irals; circle. [OE *hring*]

▪g² (ring) *v.* **rang** (*Archaic* or *Dial.* **rung**), **rung, ring·ing** ▪. **1.** To give forth a resonant, sonorous sound, as a bell ▪nen struck. **2.** To sound loudly or be filled with sound or ▪sonance; reverberate; resound. **3.** To cause a bell or bells ▪ sound. **4.** To have or suggest a sound expressive of a spe- ▪fied quality: His story *rings* true. **5.** To have a continued ▪nsation of ringing or buzzing: My ears *ring.* — *v.t.* **6.** To use (a bell, etc.) to ring. **7.** To produce, as a sound, by or ▪ by ringing. **8.** To announce or proclaim by ringing: to ▪g the hour. **9.** To summon, escort, usher, etc., in this ▪anner: with *in* or *out*: to *ring* out the old year. **10.** To ▪ll on the telephone: often with *up.* — *n.* **1.** The sound ▪oduced by a bell or other vibrating, sonorous body. **2.** ▪e act of sounding a bell. **3.** A telephone call. **4.** Any re-▪rberating sound, as of acclamation. **5.** Characteristic ▪und or impression: the *ring* of truth. **6.** A set, chime, or ▪al of bells. [OE *hringan*; imit.]

g·bolt (ring′bōlt′) *n.* A bolt having a ring through an ▪e in its head.

g·dove (ring′duv′) *n.* One of several other pigeons hav-▪g a black ring partially surrounding the neck.

ged (ringd) *adj.* **1.** Having a wedding ring; lawfully ▪arried. **2.** Encircled by raised or depressed lines or bands. Marked by a ring or rings. **4.** Composed of rings.

·gent (rin′jənt) *adj. Biol.* Gaping, as a corolla in which ▪e lips are widely separated. [< L < *ringi* to gape]

g·er¹ (ring′ər) *n.* **1.** One who or that which rings (a bell ▪ chime). **2.** *Slang* An athlete, horse, etc., illegally entered ▪ a contest by concealing disqualifying facts, as age, pro-▪ssional status, etc. **3.** *Slang* A person who bears a marked ▪emblance to another: You are a *ringer* for Jones.

g·er² (ring′ər) *n.* **1.** One who or that which rings. **2.** A ▪oit or horseshoe that falls around one of the posts.

g·lead·er (ring′lē′dər) *n.* A leader or organizer of any ▪dertaking, esp. of an unlawful one, as a riot.

g·let (ring′lit) *n.* **1.** A long, spiral lock of hair; a curl. ▪ A small ring.

g·mas·ter (ring′mas′tər, -mäs′-) *n.* One who has charge ▪ a circus ring and of the performances in it.

g·side (ring′sīd′) *n.* The space or seats immediately sur-▪nding a ring, as at a prize fight.

g·worm (ring′wûrm′) *n. Pathol.* Any of several con-▪gious skin diseases, caused by certain fungi, and marked ▪ the appearance of discolored, scaly patches on the skin.

▪k (ringk) *n.* **1.** A smooth, artificial surface of ice, used ▪ ice-skating or hockey. **2.** A smooth floor, used for roller-▪ating. **3.** A building containing a surface for ice-skating ▪ roller-skating. [< Scot., course, race]

▪se (rins) *v.t.* **rinsed, rins·ing** **1.** To remove soap from ▪ putting through clear water. **2.** To wash lightly, as by ▪ping in water or by running water over or into. **3.** To ▪move (dirt, etc.) by this process. — *n.* **1.** The act of rins-▪:, or the solution in which something is rinsed. **2.** A hair ▪loring agent. [< OF < L *recens* fresh] — **rins′er** *n.*

▪·ing (rin′sing) *n.* **1.** A rinse. **2.** The liquid in which ▪ything is rinsed. **3.** That which is removed by rinsing.

▪t (rī′ət) *n.* **1.** A disturbance consisting of wild and tur-

bulent conduct of a large number of persons, as a mob. **2.** A brilliant or sometimes confusing display: a *riot* of color. **3.** Boisterous festivity; revelry. **4.** Loose or profligate liv-ing or activity. **5.** *U.S. Slang* An uproariously amusing per-son, thing, or performance. — **to run riot 1.** To act or move wildly and without restraint. **2.** To grow profusely or luxuriantly, as vines. — *v.i.* **1.** To take part in a riot or public disorder. **2.** To live a life of feasting, drinking, etc.; revel. — *v.t.* **3.** To spend (time, money, etc.) in riot or rev-elry. [< F < *rioter* to quarrel] — **ri′ot·er** *n.*

riot act Any forceful or vigorous warning or reprimand. — **to read the riot act to** To reprimand bluntly and severely.

ri·ot·ous (rī′ət·əs) *adj.* **1.** Of, pertaining to, or like a riot. **2.** Engaged in a riot. **3.** Loud; uproarious. **4.** Profligate: *riotous* spending. — **ri′ot·ous·ly** *adv.* — **ri′ot·ous·ness** *n.*

riot squad A group of policemen specially trained, armed, and equipped to deal with riots.

rip¹ (rip) *v.* **ripped, rip·ping** *v.t.* **1.** To tear or cut apart roughly or violently; slash. **2.** To tear or cut from some-thing else in a rough or violent manner: with *off, away, out,* etc. **3.** To saw or split (wood) in the direction of the grain. — *v.i.* **4.** To be torn or cut apart; split. **5.** *Informal* To utter with vehemence: with *out.* **6.** *Informal* To rush head-long. — *n.* **1.** A place torn or ripped open; a tear. **2.** A ripsaw. [Cf. MLG *reppen*, MDu. *rippen*] — **rip′per** *n.*

rip² (rip) *n.* **1.** A ripple; a rapid in a river. **2.** A riptide. [? < RIP¹]

ri·par·i·an (ri·pâr′ē·ən, rī-) *adj.* Of or growing on a bank of a river or stream. [< L < *ripa* river bank]

rip·cord (rip′kôrd′) *n. Aeron.* The cord, together with the handle and fastening pins, that when pulled releases a para-chute from its pack.

ripe (rīp) *adj.* **1.** Grown to maturity and fit for food, as fruit or grain. **2.** Brought by keeping and care to a condi-tion for use, as wine or cheese. **3.** Fully developed; matured. **4.** Advanced in years. **5.** In full readiness to do or try; pre-pared; ready. **6.** Fit; opportune. **7.** Resembling ripe fruit; rosy; luscious. [OE *rīpe*] — **ripe′ly** *adv.* — **ripe′ness** *n.*

rip·en (rī′pən) *v.t. & v.i.* To make or become ripe; mature.

ri·poste (ri·pōst′) *n.* **1.** A return thrust, as in fencing. **2.** A quick, clever reply; repartee. — *v.i.* **·post·ed, ·post·ing** **1.** To make a riposte. **2.** To reply quickly. Also **ri·post′.** [< F < Ital. *risposta* reply]

rip·ping (rip′ing) *Brit. Slang adj.* Splendid; excellent. — *adv.* Very; extraordinarily: a *ripping* good time.

rip·ple (rip′əl) *v.* **·pled, ·pling** *v.i.* **1.** To become slightly agitated on the surface, as water blown on by a light breeze. **2.** To flow with small waves or undulations on the surface. **3.** To make a sound like water flowing in small waves. — *v.t.* **4.** To cause to form ripples. — *n.* **1.** One of the wave-lets on the surface of water. **2.** Any sound like that made by rippling. **3.** Any appearance like a wavelet. [? Fusion of RIFFLE + RIP²] — **rip′pler** *n.* — **rip′ply** *adj.*

rip·plet (rip′lit) *n.* A small ripple.

rip·roar·ing (rip′rôr′ing, -rōr′-) *adj. U.S. Slang* Good and lively; boisterous.

rip·roar·i·ous (rip·rôr′ē·əs, -rōr′-) *adj. U.S. Slang* Uproar-ious; boisterous; violent. — **rip·roar′i·ous·ly** *adv.*

rip·saw (rip′sô′) *n.* A coarse-toothed saw used for cutting wood in the direction of the grain: also called *rip.*

rip·snort·er (rip′snôr′tər) *n. Archaic Slang* Any person or thing excessively noisy, violent, or striking.

rip·tide (rip′tīd′) *n.* Water agitated and made dangerous for swimmers by conflicting tides or currents: also called *rip, tiderip.*

rise (rīz) *v.* **rose, ris·en, ris·ing** *v.i.* **1.** To move upward; go from a lower to a higher position. **2.** To slope gradually up-ward. **3.** To have height or elevation: The city *rises* above the plain. **4.** To gain elevation in rank, status, fortune, or reputation. **5.** To swell up: Dough *rises.* **6.** To become greater in force, intensity, height, etc.; also, to become high-er in pitch, as the voice. **7.** To become greater in amount, value, etc. **8.** To become erect after lying down, sitting, etc.; stand up. **9.** To get out of bed. **10.** To return to life. **11.** To revolt; rebel. **12.** To adjourn. **13.** To appear above the horizon: said of heavenly bodies. **14.** To come to the surface, as a fish after a lure. **15.** To have origin; begin. **16.** To become perceptible to the mind or senses. **17.** To occur; happen. **18.** To be able to cope with an emergency, danger, etc. — *v.t.* **19.** To cause to rise. — **to rise above** To prove superior to; show oneself indifferent to. — *n.* **1.** The act of rising; ascent. **2.** Degree of ascent; elevation; also, an ascending course. **3.** The act of beginning to be: the *rise* of a stream. **4.** An elevated place; a small hill. **5.** The act of appearing above the horizon. **6.** Increase or advance, as in price or value. **7.** Advance or elevation, as in rank, prosperity, or importance. **8.** The spring or height of an arch above the impost level. **9.** The height of a stair step.

10. Ascent in a musical scale; also, increase in volume of tone. **11.** The ascent of a fish to food or bait; also, the flying up of a game bird. **12.** *Informal* An emotional reaction; a response or retort. **13.** *Brit.* An increase in salary. [OE *rīsan*]

ris·en (riz′ən) Past participle of RISE.

ris·er (rī′zər) *n.* **1.** One who rises or gets up, as from bed: He is an early *riser.* **2.** The vertical part of a step or stair.

ris·i·bil·i·ty (riz′ə·bil′ə·tē) *n.* *pl.* **·ties** **1.** A tendency to laughter. **2.** *pl.* Impulses to laughter: also **ris′i·bles** (-bəlz).

ris·i·ble (riz′ə·bəl) *adj.* **1.** Having the power of laughing. **2.** Of a nature to excite laughter. **3.** Pertaining to laughter. [< F < LL < L *rīdere* to laugh] — **ris′i·bly** *adv.*

ris·ing (rī′zing) *adj.* **1.** Increasing in wealth, power, or distinction. **2.** Ascending; also, sloping upward: a *rising* hill. **3.** Advancing to adult years or to a state of vigor and activity; growing: the *rising* generation. — *n.* **1.** The act of one who or that which rises. **2.** That which rises above the surrounding surface. **3.** An insurrection or revolt. **4.** Yeast or leaven used to make dough rise.

risk (risk) *n.* **1.** A chance of encountering harm or loss; hazard; danger. **2.** In insurance: **a** The hazard or chance of loss. **b** The degree of exposure to loss. **c** An insurance applicant who is considered a hazard to the insurer. — *v.t.* **1.** To expose to a chance of injury or loss. **2.** To incur the risk of. [< F < Ital. *risco*] — **risk′er** *n.*

risk·y (ris′kē) *adj.* **risk·i·er, risk·i·est** Attended with risk; hazardous; dangerous.

ri·sot·to (rē·sôt′tō) *n.* Rice cooked in broth and served with meat, cheese, etc. [< Ital. < *riso* rice]

ris·qué (ris·kā′, *Fr.* rēs·kā′) *adj.* Bordering on or suggestive of impropriety; bold; daring; off-color: a *risqué* story or play. [< F, pp. of *risquer* to risk] — **Syn.** racy, ribald, suggestive.

ris·sole (ris′ōl, *Fr.* rē·sôl′) *n.* In cookery, a sausagelike roll consisting of minced meat or fish, enclosed in a thin puff paste and fried. [< F, ult. < LL *russeolus* reddish]

ri·tar·dan·do (rē′tär·dän′dō) *Music adj.* Slackening in tempo gradually; retarding. — *n.* *pl.* **·dos** A gradual slackening of tempo. [< Ital.]

rite (rīt) *n.* **1.** A solemn or religious ceremony performed in an established or prescribed manner, or the words or acts constituting or accompanying it. **2.** Any formal practice or custom. [< L *rītus*]

rit·u·al (rich′ŏō·əl) *n.* **1.** A prescribed form or method for the performance of a religious or solemn ceremony; any body of rites or ceremonies. **2.** A book setting forth such a system of rites. — *adj.* Of, pertaining to, or practiced as a rite or rites. [< L *rītus* rite] — **rit′u·al·ly** *adv.*

rit·u·al·ism (rich′ŏō·əl·iz′əm) *n.* **1.** Insistence upon ritual; adherence to ritual. **2.** The study of religious ritual. **3.** A love of ritual. — **rit′u·al·ist** *n.* — **rit′u·al·is′tic** *adj.* — **rit′· u·al·is′ti·cal·ly** *adv.*

ritz·y (rit′sē) *adj.* **ritz·i·er, ritz·i·est** *U.S. Slang* Smart; elegant; classy. [< the *Ritz*-Carlton Hotel, New York; after César *Ritz*, 1850–1918, who founded it]

ri·val (rī′vəl) *n.* **1.** One who strives to equal or excel another, or is in pursuit of the same object as another; a competitor. **2.** One equaling or nearly equaling another, in any respect. — *v.* **ri·valed** or **·valled, ri·val·ing** or **·val·ling** *v.t.* **1.** To strive to equal or excel; compete with. **2.** To be the equal of or a match for. — *v.i.* **3.** Being a rival; competing. [< L *rīvalis,* pl. *rīvales* those living near the same stream]

ri·val·ry (rī′vəl·rē) *n.* *pl.* **·ries** **1.** The act of rivaling. **2.** The state of being a rival or rivals; competition.

rive (rīv) *v.* **rived, rived** or **riv·en, riv·ing** *v.t.* **1.** To split asunder by force; cleave. **2.** To break (the heart, etc.). — *v.i.* **3.** To become split. [< ON *rīfa*] — **riv·er** (rī′vər) *n.*

riv·er (riv′ər) *n.* **1.** A large, natural stream of water, usu. fed by converging tributaries along its course and discharging into a larger body of water, as the ocean, a lake, or another stream. ◆ Collateral adjective: *fluvial.* **2.** A large stream of any kind; copious flow — **to sell down the river** To betray the trust of; deceive. — **to send up the river** To send to the penitentiary. [< OF *rivière*]

river basin *Geog.* An extensive area of land drained by a river and its branches.

riv·er·ine (riv′ə·rīn, -ər·in) *adj.* Pertaining to or like a river; riparian.

riv·er·side (riv′ər·sīd′) *n.* The space alongside of or adjacent to a river.

riv·et (riv′it) *n.* A short, soft metal bolt, having a head on one end, used to join objects, as metal plates, by passing the shank through holes and forming a new head by flattening out the other end. — *v.t.* **1.** To fasten with or as with a rivet. **2.** To batter the headless end of (a bolt, etc.) so as to make fast. **3.** To fasten firmly. **4.** To engross or attract (the eyes, attention, etc.). [< OF, prob. < MDu. *wriven* to cause to turn] — **riv′et·er** *n.*

riv·u·let (riv′yə·lit) *n.* A small stream or brook; streamlet. [< Ital. < L *rivulus,* dim. of *rivus* stream]

roach[1] (rōch) *n.* **1.** A European fresh-water fish of the carp

family, with a greenish back. **2.** Any of various relat[ed] fishes. [< OF *roche.*]

roach[2] (rōch) *n.* A cockroach.

road (rōd) *n.* **1.** An open way for public passage, esp. fr[om] one city, town, or village to another; a highway. **2.** A way of advancing or progressing: the *road* to fame. **3.** U[sed] *pl.* A roadstead: Hampton *Roads.* **4.** *U.S.* A railroad. — **on the road** **1.** On tour: said of circuses, theatrical co[m]panies, etc. **2.** Traveling, as a canvasser or salesman. Living the life of a tramp or hobo. [OE *rād* journey < rī[dan] to ride]

road·bed (rōd′bed′) *n.* **1.** The graded foundation of grav[el,] etc., on which the ties, rails, etc., of a railroad are laid. **2.** The graded foundation or surface of a road.

road·block (rōd′blok′) *n.* **1.** An obstruction in a road. **2.** Any arrangement of men and materials for blocking passa[ge,] as of enemy troops.

road·house (rōd′hous′) *n.* A restaurant, dance hall, e[tc.,] located at the side of the road in a rural area.

road metal Broken stone or the like, used for making [or] repairing roads.

road runner A long-tailed ground cuckoo inhabiting open regions of southwestern North America, and running with great swiftness.

road·side (rōd′sīd′) *n.* The area along the side of a road. — *adj.* Situated on the side of a road.

road·stead (rōd′sted) *n. Naut.* A place of anchorage offshore, but less sheltered than a harbor. [< ROAD + *stead,* a place]

ROAD RUNNE[R] (Body to 2[4] inches; tail 12 inches)

road·ster (rōd′stər) *n.* A light, open automobile, usu. with a single seat for two people and a luggage compartment or rumble seat in the re[ar.]

road·way (rōd′wā′) *n.* A road, esp. that part over wh[ich] vehicles pass.

roam (rōm) *v.i.* **1.** To move about purposelessly from p[lace] to place; rove. — *v.t.* **2.** To wander over; range. — *n.* [The] act of roaming. [ME *romen*] — **roam′er** *n.*

roan (rōn) *adj.* Of a horse, having a color consisting of [bay,] sorrel, or chestnut, thickly interspersed with gray or wh[ite.] — *n.* **1.** A roan color. **2.** An animal of a roan color. MF < Sp. *roano.*]

roar (rôr, rōr) *v.i.* **1.** To utter a deep, prolonged cry, a[s of] rage or distress. **2.** To make a loud noise or din, as the [sea] or a cannon. **3.** To laugh loudly. **4.** To move, proceed[, or] function with a roar, as an automobile. — *v.t.* **5.** To u[tter] or express by roaring. — *n.* **1.** A full, deep, resonant [cry,] as of a beast, or of a human being in pain, grief, anger, [etc.] **2.** Any loud, prolonged sound, as of wind or waves. [< L *rārian*] — **roar′er** *n.*

roast (rōst) *v.t.* **1.** To cook (meat, etc.) by subjecting to [the] action of heat, as in an oven. **2.** To cook before an open [fire,] or by placing in hot ashes, embers, etc. **3.** To heat to an ex[-]treme degree. **4.** To dry and parch under the action of h[eat.] **5.** *Metall.* To heat (ores) with access of air for the purpos[e of] dehydration, purification, or oxidation. **6.** *Informal* [To] criticize or ridicule severely. — *v.i.* **7.** To roast food i[n an] oven, etc. **8.** To be cooked or prepared by this method. [—] To be uncomfortably hot. — *n.* **1.** Something roasted; [esp.,] a piece of roasted meat. **2.** A piece of meat adapted or [pre]pared for roasting. **3.** The act of roasting. — *adj.* Ro[ast]ed. [< OF *rostir* < Gmc.]

roast·er (rōs′tər) *n.* **1.** One who or that which roasts. [2.] A pan or contrivance for roasting something. **3.** Someth[ing] suitable for roasting, esp. a pig.

rob (rob) *v.* **robbed, rob·bing** *v.t.* **1.** To seize and carr[y off] the property of by unlawful violence or threat of viole[nce.] **2.** To deprive of something belonging or due. **3.** To p[lun]der; rifle, as a house. **4.** To steal. ◆ — *v.i.* **5.** To co[mmit] robbery. [< OF *robe* booty] — **rob′ber** (-ər) *n.*

robber baron *U.S.* One of the powerful and unscrupu[lous] financial adventurers of the late 19th century.

rob·ber·y (rob′ər·ē) *n.* *pl.* **·ber·ies** The act of one [who] robs; the taking away of the property of another un[law]fully, by force or fear. — **Syn.** see THEFT.

robe (rōb) *n.* **1.** A long, loose, flowing garment, worn [over] other dress; a gown. **2.** A bathrobe. **3.** *pl.* Such a garm[ent] worn as a badge of office or rank. **4.** Anything that co[vers] in the manner of a robe. **5.** *U.S.* A blanket or covering [used] for use in an automobile: lap *robe.* — *v.* **robed, rob·ing** *v.t.* **1.** To put a robe upon; dress. — *v.i.* **2.** To put on ro[be.] [< OF, orig. booty < Gmc.]

rob·in (rob′in) *n.* **1.** A large North American thrush [with] black head and tail, grayish wings and sides, and red[dish] brown breast and underparts. **2.** A small European bir[d of] the thrush family, with the cheeks, and breast yellowish [red.] Also **robin redbreast.** [< OF *Robin,* dim. of *Robert*]

Robin Hood A legendary medieval outlaw of Engl[and,] famed for his chivalry and daring, who lived in Sherw[ood] Forest and robbed from the rich to help the poor.

n's-egg blue (rob'inz·eg') A light greenish blue.
in·son Cru·soe (rob'in·sən krōō'sō) The hero of De-
Robinson Crusoe (1719), a sailor shipwrecked on a tropi-
sland.
t (rō'bət, rob'ət) n. 1. A mechanical man constructed
erform work in the place of human beings. 2. One who
ks mechanically; automaton. 3. Any mechanism or de-
that operates automatically or is remotely controlled.
Czechoslovakian robota forced labor]
t bomb A high-explosive bomb provided with a jet
ne or rocket permitting it to travel under its own power
being launched on the target, as the German V-1 of
ld War II: also called buzz bomb.
ist (rō·bust', rō'bust) adj. 1. Possessing or charac-
:ed by great strength or endurance; rugged. 2. Re-
ing strength. 3. Violent; rude. [< L < robur oak,
:e strength] — ro·bust'ly adv. — ro·bust'ness n.
rok) n. In Arabian and Persian legend, an enormous
powerful bird of prey. [< Arabic < Persian rukh]
helle salt (rō·shel') A white crystalline tartrate of po-
um and sodium, KNaC₄H₄O₆·4H₂O, used as a cathartic.
er La Rochelle]
(rok) n. 1. A large mass of stone or stony material.
fragment of rock small enough to be thrown; stone. 3.
The material forming the essential part of the earth's
t, classified principally according to mode of formation,
neous or sedimentary. 4. Something resembling or sug-
ing a rock, as a firm support, source of strength, etc. 5.
Slang A gemstone, esp. a large diamond. — on the
:s U.S. Informal 1. Ruined; also, destitute or bankrupt.
erved with ice cubes but without soda or water: said of
sky or other liquors. — adj. Made or composed of rock.
OF roque, roche]
² (rok) v.i. 1. To move backward and forward or from
to side; sway 2. To sway, reel, or stagger, as from a
r; shake. — v.t. 3. To move backward and forward or
1 side to side, esp. so as to soothe or put to sleep. 4. To
ie to sway or reel. — n. The act of rocking; a rocking
ion. [OE roccian]
·a·by (rok'ə·bī) interj. Go to sleep: from a nursery song
nded to lull a child to slumber. — n. A lullaby. Also
:'a·bye, rock'·a·bye.
·and-roll (rok'ən·rōl') adj. Denoting a form of popu-
music derived from hillbilly styles, characterized by rep-
ous melody and rhythm and exaggerated vocal manner-
3. — n. Rock-and-roll music. Also rock 'n' roll.
bottom The very bottom; the lowest possible level:
:es hit rock bottom. — rock-bot·tom (rok'bot'əm) adj.
·bound (rok'bound') adj. Encircled by or bordered
l rocks.
candy Large crystals of sugar.
crystal Colorless transparent quartz.
dove The wild pigeon of Europe, the parent of domes-
varieties.
·er (rok'ər) n. 1. One who rocks, as a cradle or rocking
ir. 2. One of the curved pieces on which a rocking chair
cradle rocks. 3. A rocking chair. 4. A rocking horse.
ff one's rocker Slang Mentally unbalanced; nuts.
·et (rok'it) n. 1. A firework, projectile, missile, or other
ice, usu. cylindrical in form, that is propelled by the reac-
of escaping gases produced during flight. 2. A type of
icle operated by rocket propulsion and designed for space
·el. — v.i. 1. To move like a rocket. 2. To fly straight
nto the air, as a bird. — v.t. 3. To propel by means of a
:et. [< Ital. rocchetta, dim. of rocca distaff < Gmc.]
et bomb A bomb delivered to its target by means of a
:et.
·et·eer (rok'ə·tir') n. One who designs or launches
:ets; a student of rocket flight.
et engine A reaction engine fueled by a liquid or solid
pellant containing its own oxidizing agent.
et gun Any gunlike device used for the discharge of
:et projectiles, as a bazooka.
·et·ry (rok'it·rē) n. The science, art, and technology of
:et flight, design, construction, etc.
·et·sonde (rok'it·sond') n. Meteorol. A radiosonde
pted for use on high-altitude rockets.
·fish (rok'fish') n. pl. ·fish or ·fish·es Any of several
iy finned fishes of the Pacific coast of North America.
garden A garden with flowers and plants growing in
:y ground or among rocks.
ing chair A chair having the legs set on rockers.
ing horse A toy horse mounted on rockers, large
ugh to be ridden by a child: also called hobbyhorse.
lobster The spiny lobster.
maple The sugar maple.
oil Petroleum.
:oon (rok·ōōn') n. A small rocket equipped with vari-

ous meteorological recording devices and attached to a balloon, from which it is released at predetermined altitudes.
[< ROCK(ET) + (BALL)OON]
rock·ribbed (rok'ribd') adj. 1. Having rocky ridges. 2.
Unyielding; inflexible.
rock salt Halite.
rock·shaft (rok'shaft', -shäft') A shaft made to rock on its
bearings; esp., such a shaft for operating a slide valve in
an engine.
rock wool Mineral wool.
rock·y¹ (rok'ē) adj. rock·i·er, rock·i·est 1. Consisting of,
abounding in, or resembling rocks. 2. Tough; unfeeling;
hard. — rock'i·ness n.
rock·y² (rok'ē) adj. rock·i·er, rock·i·est 1. Inclined to rock
or shake; unsteady. 2. Informal Dizzy or weak, as from dissipation. — rock'i·ness n.
Rocky Mountain goat A goatlike, shaggy white ruminant
with short black horns, found in the mountains of NW North
America: also called mountain goat.
Rocky Mountain sheep The bighorn.
Rocky Mountain spotted fever Pathol. An acute infectious disease caused by a microorganism transmitted by the
bite of certain ticks, and marked by skin eruptions.
ro·co·co (ra·kō'kō, rō'kə·kō') n. 1. A style of art that developed in France in the 18th century and spread throughout
Europe; esp., architecture and ornament characterized by
curvilinear designs, often imitating shells, foliage, and scrolls
in asymmetrical arrangements. 2. Music The elegant, formal style of European music from about 1726 to 1775, immediately following the baroque. 3. Florid, fantastic, or odd
style, as in literature. — adj. 1. In the rococo style. 2.
Overelaborate; florid. [< F, alter. of rocaille shellwork]
rod (rod) n. 1. A straight, slim piece of wood, metal, or
other material. 2. A shoot or cane of any woody plant. 3. A
switch or several switches together, used as an instrument of
punishment. 4. Discipline; correction: with the. 5. A scepter or badge of office; a wand. 6. Dominion; power. 7. A
bar, typically of metal, forming part of a machine: a connecting rod. 8. A light pole used to suspend and manipulate a
fishing line. 9. A measure of length, equal to 5.5 yards; also,
a square rod: sometimes called perch, pole. See table front
of book. 10. A measuring rule. 11. One of the rodlike
bodies of the retina sensitive to faint light. 12. A rod-
shaped bacterium. 13. In Biblical usage, a line of family
descent. 14. A lightning rod. 15. The drawbar of a freight
train. 16. U.S. Slang A pistol. [OE rodd]
rode (rōd) Past tense of RIDE.
ro·dent (rōd'nt) n. Any of a large cosmopolitan order of
gnawing mammals, having in each jaw two (rarely four) incisors growing continually from persistent pulps, and no ca-
nine teeth, as a squirrel, beaver, or rat. — adj. 1. Gnawing; corroding. 2. Of or pertaining to a rodent or rodents.
[< L rodens, -entis, ppr. of rodere to gnaw]
rodent ulcer Pathol. A malignant ulcer that progressively
destroys soft tissues and bones, especially of the face.
ro·de·o (rō'dē·ō, rō·dā'ō) n. pl. ·os 1. The driving of cattle
together to be branded, counted, inspected, etc.; a roundup.
2. A public spectacle in which the more exciting features of
a roundup are presented, as the riding of broncos, branding,
lariat throwing, etc. 3. An enclosure for cattle. [< Sp. ro-
dear to go around < L rota wheel]
roe¹ (rō) n. 1. The spawn or eggs of female fish. 2. The milt
of male fish. 3. The eggs of crustaceans. [Var. of dial. roan,
appar. < ON hrogn or MDu. roch]
roe² (rō) n. A small, graceful deer of Europe and western
Asia. Also roe deer. [OE rā]
roe·buck (rō'buk') n. The male of the roe deer.
roent·gen (rent'gən, runt'-; Ger. rœnt'gən) n. A measure
of the intensity of gamma or X-rays, being the quantity of
radiation that will produce 1 electrostatic unit of electricity
in 1 cubic centimeter of air at normal temperature and pressure: also spelled röntgen. [after Wilhelm Konrad Roentgen]
roent·gen·ize (rent'gən·īz, runt'-) v.t. ·ized, ·iz·ing To subject to the action of X-rays. — roent·gen·i·za'tion n.
roentgeno- combining form X-rays; using, produced by, or
producing X-rays. Also, before vowels, roentgen-. [<
ROENTGEN]
roent·gen·o·gram (rent'gən·ə·gram', runt'-) n. An X-ray
photograph. Also roent'gen·o·graph' (-graf', -gräf').
roent·gen·og·ra·phy (rent'gən·og'rə·fē, runt'-) n. Med.
Photography means of X-rays; radiography. — roent'·
gen·o·graph'ic (-ə·graf'ik) adj. — roent'gen·o·graph'i·cal-
ly adv.
Roentgen rays X-rays.
Ro·gal·lo wing (rō·gal'ō) Aeron. A kitelike triangular flexible wing that can be used on simple aircraft, as a kite, or type
of parachute. [after F. M. Rogallo, U.S. engineer, the in-
ventor]

ro·ga·tion (rō·gā′shən) *n. Often pl.* Litany; supplication, esp. as part of the rites of the Rogation Days. [< L < *rogatus*, pp. of *rogare* to ask]

Rogation Days *Eccl.* The three days immediately preceding Ascension Day, observed as days of special supplication.

rog·er (roj′ər) *interj.* 1. *Often cap.* Message received: used in radio communication. 2. *Informal* All right; O.K. [after *Roger*, personal name representing *r* in telecommunication]

rogue (rōg) *n.* 1. A dishonest and unprincipled person; rascal. 2. One who is innocently mischievous or playful. 3. *Biol.* A variation from a standard. 4. A fierce and dangerous animal, as an elephant, separated from the herd. 5. *Archaic* A vagrant. — *v.* **rogued, ro·guing** *v.t.* 1. To practice roguery upon; defraud. 2. *Bot.* To eliminate (inferior individuals) from a plot of plants undergoing selection. [Origin uncertain]

ro·guer·y (rō′gər·ē) *n. pl.* **·guer·ies** 1. Conduct characteristic of a rogue; trickery. 2. A roguish act.

rogues′ gallery A collection of photographs of criminals taken to aid the police in identification.

ro·guish (rō′gish) *adj.* 1. Playfully mischievous. 2. Knavish; dishonest. — **ro′guish·ly** *adv.* — **ro′guish·ness** *n.*

roil (roil) *v.t.* 1. To make muddy or turbid, as by stirring up sediment. 2. To vex; irritate; rile. [< F *rouiller*, *ruiler*]

roil·y (roi′lē) *adj.* **roil·i·er, roil·i·est** Turbid; muddy.

roist·er (rois′tər) *v.i.* 1. To act in a blustery manner; swagger. 2. To engage in tumultuous merrymaking; revel. [< OF < L *rusticus* rustic] — **roist′er·er** *n.*

Ro·land (rō′lənd, *Fr.* rô·län′) Legendary nephew of Charlemagne and hero of the medieval French epic *Chanson de Roland*, in which he dies fighting the Saracens.

role (rōl) *n.* 1. A part or character taken by an actor. 2. Any assumed character or function. Also **role**. [< F *rôle*]

roll (rōl) *v.i.* 1. To move forward on a surface by turning round and round, as a ball or wheel. 2. To move or be moved on wheels or rollers. 3. To move or appear to move in undulations or swells, as waves. 4. To assume the shape of a ball or cylinder by turning over and over upon itself, as a ball of yarn. 5. To pass; elapse: with *on* or *by*. 6. Of sounds: **a** To make a deep, prolonged sound, as thunder. **b** To trill, as a bird. **c** To produce a roll, as on a drum. 7. To rotate wholly or partially: his eyes *rolled.* 8. To sway or move from side to side, as a ship. 9. To wander or travel about. 10. To walk with a swaying motion; also, to stagger. 11. To become spread or flat because of pressure applied by a roller, etc.: The metal *rolls* easily. 12. To perform a periodic revolution or cycle, as the seasons. 13. To move ahead; progress. — *v.t.* 14. To cause to move along a surface by turning round and round, as a ball, log, etc. 15. To move, push forward, etc. on wheels or rollers. 16. To wrap round and round upon itself or on an axis: often with *up.* 17. To cause to assume the shape of a ball or cylinder by means of rotation and pressure: to *roll* a cigarette. 18. To impel or cause to move onward with a steady, surging motion. 19. To spread or make flat by pressing with a roller or rollers, as dough. 20. To impart a swaying motion to. 21. To wrap or envelop in or as in a covering. 22. To rotate, as the eyes. 23. Of sounds: **a** To utter with a trilling sound: to *roll* one's r's. **b** To emit in a full and swelling manner. **c** To beat a roll upon (a drum, etc.). 24. To cast (dice) in the game of craps. 25. *Printing* To apply ink to (a form) by means of a roller or rollers. 26. *U.S. Slang* To rob (a drunk or a person who is asleep). — **to roll back** In commerce, to cause (prices, wages, etc.) to return to a previous, lower level, as by government direction. — **to roll in** *Informal* 1. To arrive, in numbers; congregate. 2. To wallow; luxuriate: to *roll in* money. — **to roll up** *Informal* 1. To accumulate; amass, as profits. 2. To arrive, as an automobile. — *n.* 1. Anything rolled up in cylindrical form. 2. A register or list of names. 3. A roller; esp., a cylinder in fixed bearings used as a roller. 4. A strip of material, as of ribbon or carpeting, that is rolled upon itself or upon a core, often of an agreed length for use as a measure. 5. Any food rolled up in preparation for use; also, a small, individually shaped portion of bread. 6. A rolling gait or movement, as of a ship. 7. Of sounds: **a** A reverberation, as of thunder. **b** A rapid sustained series of short sounds: a drum *roll.* **c** A trill, as of a bird. 8. A swell or undulation of a surface, as of land or water. 9. *U.S. Slang* **a** A wad of paper money. **b** Money in general. 10. The act of rolling, or the state of being rolled. 11. *Aeron.* A complete rotation of an airplane about its longitudinal axis without change in the direction of flight. [< OF < L *rotula* < *rota* wheel]

roll·a·way (rōl′ə·wā′) *adj.* Mounted on rollers for easy movement into storage: a *rollaway* bed.

roll call 1. The act of calling a roll or list of the names of a number of persons, as soldiers, to determine which are present. 2. The time or signal for calling the roll.

roll·er (rō′lər) *n.* 1. One who or that which rolls. 2. Any of various cylindrical devices that roll or rotate. 3. The wheel of a caster or roller skate. 4. A rod on which a win-

dow shade, towel, map, etc., is rolled. 5. A heavy cyl for rolling, smoothing, or crushing something: a steam *r* 6. *Surg.* A long rolled bandage. 7. One of a series of swelling waves that break on a coast, esp. after a storm *Ornithol.* **a** Any of various European birds having gaudy ors and remarkable for their rolling and tumbling flight canary having a trilling song.

roller bearing A bearing employing steel rollers to l friction between the parts of a mechanism.

roller coaster *U.S.* A railway with small, open car over a route of steep inclines and sharp turns, comm amusement parks.

roller skate A skate having wheels instead of a runr

rol·lick (rol′ik) *v.i.* To romp or behave in a careless, f some manner. [? Blend of ROLL and FROLIC]

rol·lick·ing (rol′ik·ing) *adj.* 1. Acting in a carefree, s gering manner. 2. Jovial; light-hearted; merry. Also **lick·some** (-səm), **rol′lick·y.**

roll·ing (rō′ling) *adj.* 1. Turning round and round, es as to move forward on a surface. 2. Having a success sloping elevations and depressions: *rolling* hills. 3. Tu on or as if on wheels; rotating. 4. Turned back or dowr over a roll: a *rolling* collar. 5. Surging in puffs, billov waves, as smoke, water, etc. 6. Of sounds: a Trilled. sounding; reverberating. 7. Swaying from side to side Recurring; elapsing. — *n.* The act of one who or that v rolls or is rolled.

rolling hitch A knot having one or more intermediate between the first and last hitch. For illus. see HITCH.

rolling mill 1. An establishment in which metal is r into sheets, bars, etc. 2. A machine used to roll meta

rolling pin A cylindrical device, usu. of wood and w handle at each end, for rolling out dough, etc.

rolling stock The wheeled transportation equipment railroad, as locomotives and passenger cars.

roll-top (rōl′top′) *adj.* Designating a type of desk ha\ flexible, slatted cover that rolls back out of the way.

ro·ly-po·ly (rō′lē·pō′lē) *adj.* Short and fat; pudgy; du — *n. pl.* **-pol·ies** 1. A roly-poly person or thing. 2. C *Brit.* A pudding made of pastry dough spread with fruit serves, etc., rolled up and cooked. [Reduplication of F

Ro·ma·ic (rō·mā′ik) *adj.* Pertaining to or characteris the language or people of modern Greece. — *n.* M\ Greek, esp. the popular spoken form. [< LL < Gk. *maikos* Roman]

ro·maine (rō·mān′) *n.* A variety of lettuce characte by long, crisp leaves. [< F, fem. of *romain* Roman]

ro·man (rō′mən) *Sometimes cap. n.* A common style of or lettering characterized by serifs, perpendicularity, thicker vertical strokes than horizontal strokes: This I set in roman. — *adj.* Pertaining to, designating, or pr in roman. Distinguished from *italic.* [< ROMAN]

Ro·man (rō′mən) *adj.* 1. Of, pertaining to, or chara istic of modern or ancient Rome or its people. 2. Of c longing to the Roman Catholic Church. 3. Of, perta to, or characteristic of the language of ancient Rome; L 4. Of or pertaining to the Holy Roman Empire. — *n.* native, resident, or citizen of ancient or modern Rome The language of ancient Rome; Latin. 3. *Informal A* man Catholic. [< OF < L *Roma* Rome]

Roman calendar See under CALENDAR.

Roman candle A firework consisting of a tube filled v composition that discharges colored balls and sparks

Roman Catholic A member of the Roman Cat Church. — **Roman Catholicism**

Roman Catholic Church The Christian church tha ognizes the Pope as its supreme head: also called *Ca Church, Church of Rome.*

ro·mance (rō·mans′; *for n., also* rō′mans) *n.* 1. A lo\ fair. 2. A kind of love between the sexes, usu. youthfu nonmarital, characterized by high ideals of purity and tion, strong ardor, etc. 3. Adventurous, heroic, or pi esque character or nature: the *romance* of faraway p 4. A tendency toward the mysterious or adventurous. long narrative, sometimes in verse, presenting chiva ideals and usu. involving heroes in strange adventure affairs of love. 6. Any long fictitious narrative embo scenes and events filled with extravagant adventures. An extravagant or fanciful falsehood. — *v.* **·manced, ·n** *ing v.i.* 1. To tell or write romances. 2. To think or ac romantic manner. 3. *Informal* To make love. — *v.* *Informal* To make love to; woo. [< OF *romans* story ten in French < L < *Romanicus* Roman] — **ro·manc**

Ro·mance (rō·mans′, rō′mans) *adj.* Pertaining or be ing to one or more, or all, of the languages that have c oped from Vulgar Latin and that exist now as French, ian, Spanish, Portuguese, Catalan, Provençal, and manian. — *n.* One or all collectively, of the Romance guages.

Roman Empire The empire of ancient Rome, establ in 27 B.C. and continuing until A.D. 395.

an·esque (rō'mən·esk') *adj.* Of, pertaining to, or des-
.ing a style of Western architec-
that developed from Roman
iples, prevailed from the 5th to
2th century, and was character-
by round arches and general
iveness. — *n.* The Roman-
e style of architecture.

an holiday 1. Enjoyment or
t derived from the suffering of
rs. 2. A day of gladiatorial and
· contests in ancient Rome.

an·ic (rō·man'ik) *adj.* 1. Ro-
2. Romance.

an·ism (rō'mən·iz'əm) *n.* The
las, forms, etc., of the Roman
olic Church: often used dispar-
.ly. — **Ro'man·ist** *n.*

an·ize (rō'mən·īz) *v.t. & v.i.*
, ·iz·ing 1. To make or become
an or Roman Catholic. 2. To
· in the Roman style, language,
— **Ro'man·i·za'tion** *n.*

an nose A nose that is somewhat aquiline.

an numerals The letters used by the ancient Ro-
s as symbols in arithmetical notation. The basic letters
(1), V(5), X(10), L(50), C(100), D(500), and M(1000),
ntermediate and higher numbers are formed as follows:
symbol following another of equal or greater value adds
s value, as II = 2, XI = 11; any symbol preceding one
eater value subtracts from its value, as IV = 4, IX = 9,
= 90. When a symbol stands between two of greater
e, it is subtracted from the second and the remainder
d to the first, as XIV = 14, LIX = 59.

a·nov (rō'mə·nôf, *Russian* rô·mä'nôf) A Russian dy-
y founded in 1613, and ended in 1918 with the execution
icholas II. Also **Ro'ma·noff.**

ans (rō'mənz) *n.pl.* (*construed as sing.*) One of the
s of the New Testament, a letter from the apostle Paul
ie Christians at Rome: in full **Epistle to the Romans.**

an·tic (rō·man'tik) *adj.* 1. Of, characterized by, or of
nature of romance. 2. Characterized by or given to
ngs or thoughts of love or romance. 3. Suitable for or
ucive to love or amorousness. 4. Visionary; impracti-
5. Not based on fact; imaginary; fictitious. 6. Of or
aining to romanticism in art, literature, and music. —
ine who is romantic. [< F *romant* romance, novel] —
.an'ti·cal·ly *adv.*

an·ti·cism (rō·man'tə·siz'əm) *n.* 1. *Usu. cap.* A
ement in art, music, and literature originating in Europe
ie late 18th century, characterized by a revolt against
neoclassic adherence to rules, forms, and traditions, an
ting of the feelings, and a marked preference for indi-
alism, etc.: distinguished from *classicism.* Also **Roman-**
ovement. 2. Romantic quality. — **ro·man'ti·cist** *n.*

an·ti·cize (rō·man'tə·sīz) *v.* ·cized, ·ciz·ing *v.t.* To re-
or interpret in a romantic manner.

·a·ny (rom'ə·nē, rō'mə-) *n. pl.* ·**nies** 1. A Gypsy (def.
2. The Indic language of the Gypsies: also called *Gypsy.*
lj. Of or pertaining to the Gypsies or their language. —
· **Rom'ma·ny** (rom'ə·nē). [< *Romany* < *rom* man]

e (rōm) 1. Capital of the former Roman republic, the
ian Empire, and the States of the Church: Italian and
n *Roma.* 2. The Roman Catholic Church.

ie·o (rō'mē·ō) The hero of Shakespeare's *Romeo and*
et.

) (rōmp) *v.i.* 1. To play boisterously. 2. To win easily.
. 1. One who romps, esp. a girl. 2. Noisy, exciting
c or play. 3. *Informal* An easy win. — **romp'ish** *adj.*
omp'ish·ly *adv.* — **romp'ish·ness** *n.*

o·er (rom'pər) *n.* 1. One who romps. 2. *pl.* A garment
bining a waist and bloomers, worn by young children.

·u·lus (rom'yə·ləs) In Roman mythology, a son of
·s and founder of Rome, who with his twin brother Re-
was reared by a she-wolf. Later Romulus slew his
her to become the first ruler of Rome.

deau (ron'dō, ron·dō') *n. pl.* ·**deaux** (-dōz, -dōz') A
m of thirteen (or sometimes ten) lines with only two
nes, and in which the opening words are repeated in two
es as an unrhymed refrain. [< F *rond* round]

del (ron'dəl, -del) *n.* A verse form consisting of 13 or
ines, the first two lines being repeated, as a refrain, in the
enth and eighth lines, and again in the thirteenth and
-teenth. [< F *rond* round]

do (ron'dō, ron·dō') *n. Music* A composition or move-
t having a main theme and several contrasting episodes,
main theme being repeated after each subordinate
ie. [< Ital. < F *rond* round]

rönt·gen (rent'gən, runt'-; *Ger.* rœnt'gən) See ROENTGEN.

rood (rōōd) *n.* 1. A cross or crucifix; esp., a large crucifix or
representation of the Crucifixion over the altar screen of a
church. 2. A land measure equivalent to one-fourth of an
acre, or 40 square rods: also **square rood.** [OE *rōd* rod,
measure of land, cross]

roof (rōōf, rŏŏf) *n.* 1. The exterior upper covering of a
building. For other il-
lustrations see GABLE
ROOF, GAMBREL ROOF.
2. Any top covering,
as of a car or oven. 3.
The most elevated
part of anything. —
v.t. To cover with or
as with a roof. [OE
hrōf] — **roof'less** *adj.*
roof·er (rōō'fər, rŏŏf'-
ər) *n.* One who makes
or repairs roofs.

roof garden 1. A
garden on the roof of
a building. 2. A space
on a roof including a
garden and used as a
restaurant, etc.

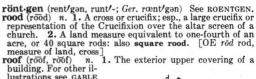

ROOF, KINGPOST TYPE
a Common rafter. *b* Purlin. *c* Kingpost. *d* Ridge pole. *e* Principal
rafter. *f* Strut. *g* Pole plate.
h Tie beam.

roof·ing (rōō'fing, rŏŏf'ing) *n.* 1. The act of covering with
a roof. 2. Material for roofs. 3. A roof; covering.

roof·tree (rōōf'trē', rŏŏf'-) *n.* 1. The ridgepole of a roof;
also, the roof itself. 2. A home or dwelling.

rook¹ (rŏŏk) *n.* 1. An Old World crow noted for its gregari-
ousness. 2. A trickster or cheat; a sharper. — *v.t. & v.i.* To
cheat; defraud. [OE *hrōc*]

rook² (rŏŏk) *n.* A castle-shaped chessman that can move
any number of unoccupied squares parallel to the sides of the
board: also called *castle.* [< OF *roc* ult. < Persian *rukh*]

rook·er·y (rŏŏk'ər·ē) *n. pl.* ·**er·ies** 1. A colony or breeding
place of rooks. 2. A breeding place of sea birds, seals, etc.

rook·ie (rŏŏk'ē) *n. Slang* 1. A raw recruit in the army, etc.
2. Any novice, as in baseball. [Prob. alter. of RECRUIT]

room (rōōm, rŏŏm) *n.* 1. An extent of space used for some
implied or specified purpose. 2. A space for occupancy or
use enclosed on all sides, as in a building. 3. *pl.* Lodgings.
4. Warrantable occasion; opportunity: *room* for doubt. —
v.i. To occupy a room; lodge. [OE *rūm* space]

room·er (rōō'mər, rŏŏm'ər) *n.* A lodger; esp., one who
rents a room and eats elsewhere.

room·ette (rōōm·et', rŏŏm·et') *n.* A small compartment in
a railroad sleeping car furnished with a folding bed.

room·ful (rōōm'fŏŏl', rŏŏm'-) *n. pl.* ·**fuls** 1. As many or as
much as a room will hold. 2. A number of persons present
in a room.

room·ing house (rōō'ming, rŏŏm'ing) *U.S.* A house for
roomers.

room·mate (rōōm'māt', rŏŏm'-) *n. U.S.* One who shares
lodgings with another or others.

room·y (rōō'mē, rŏŏm'ē) *adj.* **room·i·er, room·i·est** Having
abundant room; spacious. — **room'i·ness** *n.*

roor·back (rŏŏr'bak) *n. U.S.* A slanderous report circu-
lated for political purposes. [after *Roorback,* purported author of a (nonexistent) book of travel that was cited as authority for certain defamatory charges made against President Polk in the 1844 campaign]

roost (rōōst) *n.* 1. A perch upon which fowls rest at night;
also, any place where birds resort to spend the night. 2.
Any temporary resting place. — *v.i.* 1. To sit or perch upon
a roost. 2. To come to rest; settle. [OE *hrōst*]

roost·er (rōōs'tər) *n.* The male of the chicken; cock.

root¹ (rōōt, rŏŏt) *n.* 1. The underground portion of a plant,
that absorbs moisture, obtains or stores nourishment, and
provides support. 2. Any underground growth, as a tuber
or bulb. 3. That from which anything derives origin,
growth, or support, or life and vigor: Money is the *root* of
evil. 4. An ancestor. 5. A rootlike part of an organ or
structure: the *root* of a tooth or nerve. 6. *Ling.* A base to
which affixes and thematic vowels may be added to form
words, as *know* in *unknown, knowable,* and *unknowingly.* See
STEM. 7. *Math.* A quantity that, multiplied by itself a specified number of times, will give a given quantity: 3 is the
square *root* of 9 and the cube *root* of 27. 8. *Music* The fundamental tone of a chord. — *v.i.* 1. To put forth roots and
begin to grow. 2. To be or become firmly fixed. — *v.t.* 3.
To fix by or as by roots. 4. To pull, dig, or tear up by or as
by the roots; with *up* or *out.* [OE *rōt* < ON] — **root'less**
adj. — **root'y** *adj.*

root² (rōōt, rŏŏt) *v.t.* 1. To dig with the snout, as swine. —
v.i. 2. To turn up the earth with the snout. 3. To search;
rummage. 4. To toil. [OE *wrōtan* to root up] — **root'er** *n.*

root[3] (root, root) *v.i. U.S. Informal* To cheer for or encourage a contestant, team, etc., with *for.* [Prob. var. of ROUT[2]] — **root′er** *n.*

root beer A beverage made with yeast and root extracts.

root hair *Bot.* Hairlike outgrowths of plant roots, having an absorbent and protective function.

root·let (root′lit, root′-) *n.* A small root.

root·stalk (root′stok′, root′-) *n. Bot.* A rhizome.

root·stock (root′stok′, root′-) *n.* **1.** Original source; origin. **2.** *Bot.* A rhizome.

rope (rōp) *n.* **1.** A construction of twisted fibers, as of hemp, cotton, flax, etc., so intertwined in several strands as to form a thick cord. **2.** A collection of things plaited or united in a line. **3.** A slimy or glutinous filament or thread. **4.** A cord or halter used in hanging. **5.** Execution or death by hanging: to die by the *rope.* **6.** *U.S.* A lasso. — **to give (one) plenty of rope** To allow (a person) to pursue unchecked a course that will end in disaster. — **to know the ropes** *Informal* To be familiar with all the conditions in any sphere of activity. — *v.* **roped, rop·ing** *v.t.* **1.** To tie or fasten with or as with rope. **2.** To enclose or divide with a rope: usu. with *off.* **3.** *U.S.* To catch with a lasso. — *v.i.* **4.** To become drawn out or extended into a filament or thread. [OE *rāp*]

rope·danc·er (rōp′dan′sər, -dän′-) *n.* A tightrope walker.

rope·walk (rōp′wôk′) *n.* A long alley or building used for the spinning of rope yarn.

rope·walk·er (rōp′wô′kər) *n.* A tightrope walker.

rop·y (rō′pē) *adj.* **rop·i·er, rop·i·est 1.** That may be drawn into threads, as a glutinous substance; stringy. **2.** Resembling ropes or cordage. — **rop′i·ly** *adv.* — **rop′i·ness** *n.*

Roque·fort cheese (rōk′fərt, *Fr.* rôk·fôr′) A strong cheese with a blue mold, made from ewe's and goat's milk in the town of Roquefort, France.

ror·qual (rôr′kwol) *n.* A whalebone whale of the Atlantic and Pacific oceans: also called *finback, razorback.* [< F < Norw. *röyrkval*]

Ror·schach test (rôr′shäk, -shäkh, rōr′-) *Psychol.* A test in which personality characteristics are made capable of analysis by the subject's interpretation of a series of standard inkblot patterns. [after Hermann *Rorschach,* 1884–1922, Swiss psychiatrist]

ro·sa·ceous (rō·zā′shəs) *adj.* **1.** *Bot.* Of, pertaining to, or designating the rose family of trees, shrubs, and herbs. **2.** Resembling a rose. [< L < *rosa* rose]

ro·sa·ry (rō′zə·rē) *n. pl.* **·ries 1.** *Eccl.* **a** A series of prayers. **b** A string of beads for keeping count of these prayers. **2.** A garden or bed of roses. [< L *rosa* rose]

rose[1] (rōz) *n.* **1.** Any of a large genus of hardy, erect or climbing shrubs, with rodlike, prickly stems: the national flower of England and the State flower of New York, North Dakota, and Iowa. **2.** The flower of such a shrub, usu. having five sepals and exhibiting a wide range of colors, principally white, yellow, pink, or red. **3.** Any of various other plants or flowers likened to the true rose. **4.** A light pinkish red. **5.** An ornamental knot; a rosette. **6.** A form in which gems, esp. diamonds, are often cut; also, a diamond so cut. — **bed of roses** A peaceful or carefree time, place, or condition. — *v.t.* **rosed, ros·ing** To cause to blush; redden; flush. [OE < L *rosa,* prob. < Gk. *rhodea*]

rose[2] (rōz) Past tense of RISE.

ro·se·ate (rō′zē·it, -āt) *adj.* **1.** Rosy; rose-colored. **2.** Cheerful; optimistic. [< L *roseus*] — **ro′se·ate·ly** *adv.*

rose·bud (rōz′bud′) *n.* The bud of a rose.

rose·bush (rōz′bŏŏsh′) *n.* A rose-bearing shrub or vine.

rose campion An herbaceous plant, cultivated for its pink or crimson flowers.

rose chafer A hairy, fawn-colored beetle injurious to roses: also called *rose beetle.* Also **rose bug.**

rose-col·ored (rōz′kul′ərd) *adj.* Pink or crimson, as a rose. — **to see through rose-colored glasses** To see things in an unduly favorable light.

rose fever *Pathol.* A variety of hay fever, assumed to be caused by rose pollen. Also **rose cold.**

rose·mar·y (rōz′mâr′ē) *n. pl.* **·mar·ies** An evergreen, fragrant Old World shrub of the mint family, commonly with blue flowers, cultivated for use in making perfume and in cookery. [ME < L < *ros* dew + *marinus* of the sea]

rose of Sharon 1. A hardy shrub of the mallow family: also called *shrub althea.* **2.** A species of St. Johnswort having large, yellow flowers.

rose quartz A semitransparent variety of quartz, pink or rose in color and often used for ornament and as a gemstone.

Ro·set·ta stone (rō·zet′ə) A tablet of basalt inscribed with two forms of Egyptian hieroglyphics and in Greek, found near Rosetta, Egypt, in 1799. It supplied the key to the ancient inscriptions of Egypt.

ro·sette (rō·zet′) *n.* **1.** An ornament or badge having some resemblance to a rose; esp., an architectural ornament with parts circularly arranged. **2.** A flowerlike cluster of leaves, organs, or markings, arranged in circles, as in certain plants. [< F, dim. of *rose*]

rose water A fragrant preparation made variously by distillation of rose petals or rose oil with water, used as toilet water and in cooking.

rose window A circular window filled with tracery, radiating from the center like spokes.

rose·wood (rōz′wŏŏd′) *n.* **1.** A hard, close-grained, colored, fragrant wood yielded by certain tropical American trees. **2.** Any of various other woods resembling true wood. **3.** Any tree yielding such a wood.

Rosh Ha·sha·na (rosh hə·shä′nə, rösh) The Jewish Year, celebrated in September or early October. Also **Ha·sho′nah** (-shō′-). [< Hebrew *rōsh* head + *hash-sh* of the year]

ros·in (roz′in) *n.* **1.** The hard, amber-colored resin for the residue after the distillation of oil from crude turpen also called *resin.* **2.** Resin (defs. 1 & 2). — *v.t.* To a rosin to. [Alter. of RESIN] — **ros′in·y** *adj.*

ros·ter (ros′tər) *n.* **1.** A list of officers and men enrolle duty; also, a list of active military organizations. **2.** list of names. [< Du. *rooster* list, lit. gridiron]

ros·trum (ros′trəm) *n. pl.* **·trums** or **·tra** (-trə) *for defs 3,* **·tra** *for def. 2* **1.** A pulpit or platform. **2.** In an Rome: **a** A beaklike part on the prow of a ship. **b** The tors′ platform in the Roman forum, embellished with parts. **3.** *Biol.* A beaklike process or part. [< L *ros* beak] — **ros′tral, ros′trate** (-trāt) *adj.*

ros·y (rō′zē) *adj.* **ros·i·er, ros·i·est 1.** Like a rose; rose blushing. **2.** Bright, pleasing, or flattering. **3.** Made ornamented with roses. **4.** Auguring success; optim — **ros′i·ly** *adv.* — **ros′i·ness** *n.*

rot (rot) *v.* **rot·ted, rot·ting** *v.i.* **1.** To undergo decom tion; decay. **2.** To become morally rotten. — *v.t.* **3** cause to decompose; decay. **4.** To ret. — **Syn.** See DF — *n.* **1.** The process of rotting or the state of being ro **2.** That which is rotten. **3.** Any of various diseases in ing decay in humans, plants, and animals, esp., sheep. *Informal* Trashy and nonsensical opinions or expression *interj.* Nonsense. [< L *rotian*]

Ro·tar·i·an (rō·târ′ē·ən) *n.* A member of a Rotary — *adj.* Of or pertaining to Rotary Clubs or their mem — **Ro·tar′i·an·ism** *n.*

ro·ta·ry (rō′tər·ē) *adj.* **1.** Turning or designed to around its axis, like a wheel. **2.** Having some part turns on its axis. **3.** Characterized by movement aroun axis; rotatory. — *n. pl.* **·ries** A rotary device or part. LL < L *rota* wheel]

Rotary Club A club belonging to an international ass tion of clubs, **Rotary International,** whose aim is to imp civic service.

rotary engine *Mech.* **1.** An engine in which rotary m is directly produced, as in a turbine. **2.** In internal-con tion engines, a radial engine revolving about a fixed cr shaft.

rotary press A printing press using curved type plates revolve against the paper.

ro·tate (rō′tāt) *v.t. & v.i.* **·tat·ed, ·tat·ing 1.** To tu cause to turn on or as on its axis. **2.** To alternate in a nite order or succession. [< L *rotare* to turn < *rota* wh — **ro′tat·a·ble, ro·ta·tive** (rō′tə·tiv) *adj.* — **ro′ta·tor** *n* — **Syn.** (verb) **1.** spin, whirl, twirl, turn, gyrate. See REVO

ro·ta·tion (rō·tā′shən) *n.* **1.** The act or state of rotati rotary motion. **2.** Change or alternation in a particula quence; regular variation. [< L *rotatio, -onis*] — **r tion·al** *adj.*

ro·ta·to·ry (rō′tə·tôr′ē, -tō′rē) *adj.* **1.** Having, perta to, or producing rotation. **2.** Following in succession. Alternating or recurring.

rote (rōt) *n.* **1.** Mechanical routine. **2.** Repetition of w as a means of learning them, with slight attention to sense. — **by rote** Mechanically, without intelligent a tion: to learn *by rote.* [ME; origin uncertain]

ro·te·none (rō′tə·nōn) *n. Chem.* A crystalline compo $C_{23}H_{22}O_6$, the effective principle in insecticides and fish sons, obtained from the roots of various plants. [Origi known]

rot·gut (rot′gut′) *U.S.* An inferior raw whisky.

ro·ti·fer (rō′tə·fər) *n.* One of a division of microscopi ganisms usu. found in stagnant fresh water, having rin cilia that in motion resemble revolving wheels. [< NL *rota* wheel + *ferre* to bear] — **ro·tif′er·al** (rō·tif′ər·əl) tif′er·ous *adj.*

ro·tis·se·rie (rō·tis′ər·ē) *n.* **1.** A restaurant where pat select uncooked food and have it roasted and served. shop where food is roasted and sold. **3.** A rotating devic roasting meat, etc. [< F < *rôtir* to roast]

ro·to·gra·vure (rō′tə·grə·vyŏŏr′, -grāv′yər) *n.* **1.** The p ess of printing photographs, letters, etc., from cylin etched from photographic plates and run through a ro press. **2.** A picture printed by this process. **3.** The se of a newspaper containing such pictures. [< L *rota* wh + GRAVURE]

tor (rō'tər) n. 1. The rotating section of a motor, dyna-o, turbine, or other power generator: distinguished from *tor.* 2. *Aeron.* The horizontally rotating unit of a helicop-r or autogiro, consisting of the airfoils and hub. [Contrac-n of ROTATOR]

·ten (rot'n) adj. 1. Decomposed by natural process; pu-id. 2. Untrustworthy; treacherous. 3. Corrupt; venal. Liable to break; unsound. 5. *Informal* Worthless. [< N *rotinn*] **— rot/ten·ly** adv. **— rot/ten·ness** n. **— Syn. 1.** decayed, putrefied, putrescent, carious, fetid. Com-re DECAY. **— Ant.** fresh, sweet, sound, wholesome, healthy.

·ter (rot'ər) n. *Chiefly Brit. Slang* A worthless or objec-nable person; scoundrel.

tund (rō·tund') adj. 1. Rounded out; spherical; plump. Full-toned, as a voice or utterance; sonorous. [< L *ro-ndus* round] **— ro·tun/di·ty** n. **— ro·tund/ly** adv. **— ro-nd/ness** n.

tun·da (rō·tun'də) n. A circular building or an interior ll, surmounted with a dome. [< Ital. < L *rotundus*. See TUND.]

·ble (rōō'bəl) See RUBLE.

·é (rōō·ā') n. A sensualist; debauchee. [< F < *rouer* to eak on the wheel]

ge (rōōzh) n. 1. Any cosmetic used for coloring the eeks or lips pink or red. 2. A ferric oxide used in polishing etals and glass. **— v. rouged, roug·ing** *v.t.* 1. To color th rouge. **— v.i.** 2. To apply rouge. [< F < L *rubeus* by]

gh (ruf) adj. 1. Having an uneven surface; not smooth polished. 2. Coarse in texture; shabby. 3. Disordered ragged; shaggy. 4. Having the surface broken; uneven. Characterized by rude or violent action. 6. Boisterous tempestuous; stormy. 7. Characterized by harshness of irit; brutal. 8. Lacking the finish and polish bestowed by t or culture; crude. 9. Done or made hastily and without tention to details, as a drawing. 10. Harsh to the ear; ating; inharmonious. **— n.** 1. A low, rude, and violent llow; a rowdy. 2. A crude, incomplete, or unpolished ob-t, material, or condition. 3. Any part of a golf course on nich tall grass, bushes, etc., grow. **— in the rough** In a ude or unpolished state. **— v.t.** 1. To make rough; ughen. 2. To treat roughly. 3. To make, cut, or sketch ughly: with *in* or *out.* **— v.i.** 4. To become rough. 5. To have roughly. **— to rough it** To live, camp, or travel der rough, hard, or impoverished conditions. **— adv.** In a de manner; roughly. [OE *rūh*] **— rough/ly** adv. **— ugh/ness** n.

gh·age (ruf'ij) n. 1. Any coarse or tough substance. Food material containing a high percentage of indigesti-e constituents, as cellulose.

ugh-and-read·y (ruf'ən·red'ē) adj. 1. Characterized by acting with rude but effective promptness. 2. Unpol-ned but good enough.

ugh-and-tum·ble (ruf'ən·tum'bəl) adj. 1. Marked by e disregard of all rules, as a fight. 2. Scrambling; disorder-. **— n.** A rough-and-tumble fight or scuffle.

igh·cast (ruf'kast', -käst') *v.t.* **·cast, ·cast·ing** 1. To ape or prepare in a preliminary or incomplete form. 2. o coat, as a wall, with coarse plaster, and cover with thin ortar by dashing it on. **— n.** 1. Very coarse plaster for e outside of buildings. 2. A form or model of something in s first rough stage. **— rough/cast'er** n.

igh·draw (ruf'drô') *v.t.* **·drew, ·drawn, ·draw·ing** To etch hastily or crudely.

igh·dry (ruf'drī') *v.t.* **·dried, ·dry·ing** To dry without oning, as washed clothes.

igh·en (ruf'ən) *v.t. & v.i.* To make or become rough.

igh·hew (ruf'hyōō') *v.t.* **·hewed, ·hewed** or **·hewn, ·hew-g** 1. To hew or shape roughly or irregularly. 2. To make udely; roughcast.

igh·house (ruf'hous') *Slang* n. A noisy, boisterous, or olent game; rough play. **— v. ·housed, ·hous·ing** **— v.i.** 1. o make a disturbance; engage in horseplay or violence. **— '.** 2. To handle or treat roughly but without hostile intent. **igh·neck** (ruf'nek') n. *U.S. Slang* A rowdy.

igh·rid·er (ruf'rī'dər) n. *U.S.* One skilled in breaking roncos or performing dangerous feats in horsemanship.

ugh Riders The 1st U.S. Volunteer Cavalry in the panish-American War of 1898, mainly organized and sub-quently commanded by Theodore Roosevelt.

igh·shod (ruf'shod') adj. Shod with rough shoes to pre-ent slipping, as a horse. **— to ride roughshod (over)** To t overbearingly; domineer without consideration.

u·lette (rōō·let') n. 1. A game played at a table divided to spaces numbered and colored red and black, and having rotating disk (**roulette wheel**) on which a ball is rolled un-l it drops into one of 37 or 38 correspondingly marked baces. 2. An engraver's disk of tempered steel, as for trac-

ing points on a copperplate; also, a draftsman's wheel for making dotted lines. **— v.t. ·let·ted, ·let·ting** To perforate or mark with a roulette. [< F < *roue* wheel]

round (round) adj. 1. Having a contour that is circular or approximately so; spherical, ring-shaped, or cylindrical. 2. Having a curved contour or surface; not angular or flat; con-vex or concave. 3. Liberal; ample; large. 4. Easy and free, as in motion; brisk. 5. Of full cadence; well-balanced; full-toned. 6. Made without reserve; outspoken. 7. Open; just. 8. Formed or moving in rotation or a circle. 9. Re-turning to the point of departure: a *round* trip. 10. Of a number, increased or decreased by a relatively small amount for the sake of simplicity: 3,992 is 4,000 in *round* numbers. 11. Semicircular: a *round* arch. 12. *Phonet.* Labialized; rounded. **— n.** 1. Something round, as a globe, ring, or cylinder, a rung of a ladder, a portion of the thigh of a beef, etc. 2. *Often pl.* A circular course or range; circuit; beat. 3. A single revolution; also revolving motion. 4. A series of recurrent movements; routine; order: the daily *round* of life. 5. One of a series of concerted actions performed in succes-sion: a *round* of applause. 6. One of the divisions of a box-ing match; a bout. 7. In golf, a number of holes or an inter-val of play in a match. 8. *Music* A short canon in the oc-tave or unison, in which each voice enters in turn and re-turns to the beginning upon reaching the end. 9. A firing by a company or squad in which each soldier fires once; volley. 10. A single shot or complete unit of ammunition. 11. The state of being carved out on all sides: sculpture in the *round.* 12. The state or condition of being circular; roundness. 13. A thick slice from a haunch. **— to go** (or **make**) **the rounds** 1. To take a usual walk or tour, as of inspection. 2. To pass from person to person of a certain group. **— v.t.** 1. To make round. 2. To bring to completion; perfect: usually with *off* or *out.* 3. To free of angularity; fill out to fullness of form. 4. *Phonet.* To utter (a vowel) with the lips in a rounded position; labialize. 5. To travel or go around; make a circuit of. **— v.i.** 6. To become round. 7. To come to completeness or perfection. 8. To fill out; become plump. 9. To make a circuit; travel a circular course. 10. To turn around. **— to round off** 1. To make round or rounded. 2. To make into a round number. **— to round up** 1. To col-lect (cattle, etc.) in a herd, as for driving to market. 2. *In-formal* To assemble. **— adv.** 1. On all sides; in such a man-ner as to encircle. 2. With a circular or rotating motion. 3. Through a circle or circuit, as from person to person or point to point: provisions enough to go *round.* 4. In circum-ference: a log 3 feet *round.* 5. From one view or position to another; to and fro. 6. In the vicinity: to hang *round.* **— prep.** 1. Enclosing; encircling. 2. On every side of, or from every side toward; surrounding. 3. Toward every side from; about. [< OF < L *rotundus* round] **— round/ish** adj. **— round/ish·ness** n. **— round/ness** n.

round·a·bout (round'ə·bout') adj. 1. Circuitous; indirect. 2. Encircling. **— n.** 1. An outer garment reaching to the waist; a jacket. 2. *Brit.* A merry-go-round.

round·ed (roun'did) adj. 1. Round or spherical. 2. *Pho-net.* Formed or uttered with the lips rounded; labialized.

roun·de·lay (roun'də·lā) n. 1. A simple melody. 2. A musical setting of a poem with a recurrent refrain. [< OF < *rond* round]

round·er (roun'dər) n. 1. A tool for rounding. 2. *U.S. Slang* A drunkard, drifter, or petty criminal. 3. *pl.* (con-strued *as sing.*) An English game somewhat resembling base-ball.

Round·head (round'hed') n. A member of the parliamen-tary party in England in the civil war of 1642–49.

round·house (round'hous') n. 1. A cabin on the after part of the quarter-deck of a vessel. 2. A round building with a turntable in the center for housing and switching locomo-tives. 3. In pinochle, a meld of four kings and four queens.

round·ly (round'lē) adv. 1. In a round manner or form; cir-cularly; spherically. 2. Severely; vigorously: to be *roundly* denounced. 3. Frankly; bluntly. 4. Thoroughly.

round number A number expressed to the nearest ten, hundred, thousand, etc. Also **round figure.**

round robin 1. A tournament, as in tennis or chess, in which each player meets every other player. 2. A letter cir-culated among the members of a group. 3. A number of sig-natures, as to a petition, written in a circle so as to avoid giving prominence to any one name.

round-shoul·dered (round'shōl'dərd) adj. Having the back rounded or the shoulders stooping.

round table 1. A meeting place for conference. 2. Any discussion group. **— round-ta·ble** (round'tā'bəl) adj.

Round Table 1. The table around which King Arthur and his knights sat. 2. King Arthur and his knights.

round-the-clock (round'thə-klok') adj. Through all twenty-four hours of the day.

round trip A trip to a place and back again; a two-way trip. — **round′-trip′** adj.

round·up (round′up′) n. U.S. 1. The bringing together of cattle scattered over a range, as for inspection or branding. 2. The cowboys, horses, etc., employed in this work. 3. Informal A bringing together of persons or things.

round·worm (round′wûrm′) n. A nematode worm, esp. one parasitic in the human intestines.

rouse (rouz) v. **roused, rous·ing** v.t. 1. To cause to awaken from slumber, repose, unconsciousness, etc. 2. To excite to vigorous thought or action; stir up. 3. To startle or drive (game) from cover. — v.i. 4. To awaken. 5. To become active. 6. To start from cover: said of game. — n. The act of rousing. [Orig. technical term in hawking and hunting] — **rous′er** n.

rous·ing (rou′zing) adj. 1. Able to rouse or excite: a rousing speech. 2. Lively; active; vigorous: a rousing trade. 3. Informal Outrageous; astonishing: a rousing lie.

roust (roust) v.t. & v.i. Informal To arouse and drive (a person or thing); stir up: usu. with out. [< ROUSE]

roust·a·bout (roust′a·bout′) n. 1. A laborer on river craft or on the waterfront. 2. One who is employed for casual work; esp., a transient laborer on a cattle ranch, etc. 3. A laborer in a circus.

rout¹ (rout) n. 1. A disorderly and overwhelming defeat or flight. 2. A boisterous crowd. — v.t. To defeat disastrously; put to flight. [< OF < L rumpere to break]

rout² (rout) v.i. 1. To root, as swine. 2. To search; rummage. — v.t. 3. To dig or turn up with the snout. 4. To turn up as if with the snout; disclose to view: with out. 5. To hollow, gouge, or scrape, as with a scoop. 6. To drive or force out. [Var. of ROOT²]

route (root, rout) n. 1. A course, road, or way taken in traveling from one point to another. 2. The specific course over which mail is sent. 3. The territory covered by a newsboy. — v.t. **rout·ed, rout·ing** To dispatch or send by a certain way, as passengers, goods, etc. [< OF < L rupta (via) broken (road), fem. of ruptus. See ROUT¹.]

rout·er (rou′tər) n. 1. One who scoops or routs. 2. A tool for routing. 3. A plane devised for working a molding around a circular sash. [< ROUT²]

rou·tine (roo·tēn′) n. 1. A detailed method of procedure, regularly followed: an official routine. 2. Habitual methods of action induced by circumstances. — adj. Customary; habitual. [< F < route way, road] — **rou·tine′ly** adv.

rou·tin·ism (roo·tē′niz·əm) n. Adherence to routine or routine methods in general. — **rou·tin′ist** n.

rou·tin·ize (roo·tē′nīz) v.t. **ized, ·iz·ing** To reduce or fit to a routine.

roux (roo) n. French Butter and an equal portion of flour mixed and browned together, used for sauces, etc.

rove¹ (rōv) v. **roved, rov·ing** v.i. 1. To wander from place to place; go or move without any definite destination. — v.t. 2. To roam over, through, or about. — n. The act of roving; a ramble. [ME roven] — **rov′er** n.

rove² (rōv) Alternate past tense and past participle of REEVE¹.

row¹ (rō) n. 1. An arrangement or series of persons or things in a continued line; a rank; file. 2. A street lined with houses on both sides. 3. A line of seats, as in a theater. — **a long row to hoe** A hard task or undertaking. — v.t. To arrange in a row: with up. [OE rāw, var. of ræw line]

row² (rō) v.i. 1. To use oars, etc., in propelling a boat. — v.t. 2. To propel across the surface of the water with oars, as a boat. 3. To transport by rowing. 4. To be propelled by (a specific number of oars): said of boats. 5. To make use of (oars or rowers), esp. in a race. 6. To row against in a race. — n. 1. The act of rowing. 2. A turn at the oars. 3. A trip in a rowboat. [OE rōwan]

row³ (rou) n. 1. A noisy disturbance or quarrel; a brawl. 2. Any dispute or disturbance. — v.t. & v.i. To engage in a row or brawl. [Origin uncertain]

row·an (rō′ən, rou′-) A small tree native to Europe, having clusters of bright orange berries: also called mountain ash.

row·boat (rō′bōt′) n. U.S. A boat propelled by oars.

row·dy (rou′dē) n. pl. **·dies** One inclined to create disturbances; a rough, disorderly person. — adj. **·di·er, ·di·est** Rough and loud; disorderly. [Origin unknown] — **row′dy·ish** adj. — **row′dy·ism, row′di·ness** n.

row·el (rou′əl) n. A spiked or toothed wheel, as on a spur. — v.t. **row·eled** or **·elled, row·el·ing** or **·el·ling** To prick with a rowel; spur. [< OF roele < L rota wheel]

row·lock (rō′lok′) n. Brit. An oarlock.

roy·al (roi′əl) adj. 1. Pertaining to a monarch; kingly. 2. Under the patronage or authority of a king, or connected with a monarchical form of government: a royal governor. 3. Like or befitting a king; regal. 4. Of superior quality or size. 5. Informal Extraordinarily good, large, impressive, etc. — n. 1. A size of paper, 19 x 24 inches for writing, 20 x 25 inches for printing. 2. Naut. A sail next above the topgallant. [< OF < L < rex king] — **roy′al·ly** adv.

royal blue A brilliant blue, often with reddish overtor[...]

Royal Canadian Mounted Police The federal pol[...] force of Canada.

roy·al·ist (roi′əl·ist) n. A supporter of a royal dynasty. adj. Of or pertaining to royalists: also **roy′al·is′tic.**

Roy·al·ist (roi′əl·ist) n. 1. In English history, a Cavalier adherent of King Charles I. 2. In French history, a supporter of the Bourbon or Orléans claims to the throne si[...] 1793. 3. In the American Revolution, a supporter of [...] king; Loyalist; Tory.

roy·al·mast (roi′əl·mast′, -mäst′) n. Naut. The section a mast next above the topgallant mast.

royal palm Any of various palms native to tropical Am[...] ica, noted for their height and striking appearance.

royal purple 1. A very deep violet color verging tow[...] blue. 2. Originally, a rich crimson.

roy·al·ty (roi′əl·tē) n. pl. **·ties** 1. The rank, birth, lineage of a king or queen. 2. A royal personage; also, ro[...] persons collectively. 3. A share of proceeds paid to a p[...] prietor, author, or inventor. 4. A tax paid to the crown the produce of royal mines, or on gold and silver coina[...] 5. A royal possession or domain. 6. Any domain or pr[...] ince. [< OF roialte]

-rrhagia combining form Pathol. An abnormal or viol[...] discharge or flow; an eruption: also -rhage, -rhagia, -rho[...] Also **-rrhage, -rrhagy.** Corresponding adjectives [...] formed with **-rrhagic.** [< Gk. < rrhag-, root of rrhēgnyn[...] to burst]

-rrhaphy combining form A sewing together; a suture. [< -rrhaphie < Gk. rhaptein to sew together]

-rrhea combining form Pathol. An abnormal or excess[...] flow or discharge: also spelled -rhea, -rhoea. Also **-rrho[...]** [< Gk. -rrhoia < rheein to flow]

rub (rub) v. **rubbed, rub·bing** v.t. 1. To move or pass o[...] the surface of with pressure and friction. 2. To cause (sor[...] thing) to move or pass with friction; scrape; grate. 3. [...] cause to become frayed, worn, or sore from friction. 4. [...] clean, shine, burnish, etc., by means of pressure and fricti[...] 5. To apply or spread with pressure and friction. 6. [...] remove or erase by friction: with off or out. — v.i. 7. [...] move along a surface with friction; scrape. 8. To ex[...] pressure and friction. 9. To become frayed, worn, or s[...] from friction; chafe. 10. To undergo rubbing or removal rubbing: with off, out, etc. — **to rub it in** Slang To harp someone's errors, faults, etc. — **to rub out** Slang To k[...] — **to rub the wrong way** Slang To irritate; annoy. — [...] 1. A rubbing: Give it a rub. 2. A hindrance, doubt, e[...] There's the rub. 3. Something that rubs or is rough to [...] feelings; a sarcasm. 4. A roughness or unevenness of s[...] face, quality, or character. [ME rubben, prob. < LG]

ru·ba·to (roo·bä′tō) Music adj. Denoting the lengthen[...] of one note at the expense of another. — n. pl. **·tos** A [...] bato modification. — adv. In a rubato manner. [< It[...] robbed]

rub·ber¹ (rub′ər) n. 1. A resinous elastic material obtain[...] by coagulating the milky latex of certain tropical plants, a[...] also made synthetically: sometimes called India rubber. [...] Anything used for rubbing, erasing, polishing, etc. 3. [...] article made of rubber, as an elastic band or an oversh[...] 4. In baseball, the pitcher's plate. 5. Slang A condom. One who or that which rubs. — adj. Made of rubber. [RUB] — **rub′ber·y** adj.

rub·ber² (rub′ər) n. In bridge, whist, and other card gam[...] a series of two or three games terminated when one side [...] won two games; also, the odd game that breaks a tie betw[...] the players. [Origin unknown]

rubber check U.S. Slang A worthless check.

rub·ber·ize (rub′ər·īz) v.t. **ized, ·iz·ing** To coat, impr[...] nate, or cover with a preparation of rubber.

rub·ber·neck (rub′ər·nek′) U.S. Slang n. One who cra[...] his neck in order to see something; a sightseer; tourist. v.i. To stretch or crane one's neck; gape.

rubber plant 1. Any of several plants yielding rubber. [...] A house plant of the mulberry family, having large, glo[...] leathery leaves.

rub·ber-stamp (rub′ər·stamp′) v.t. 1. To endorse, init[...] or approve with the mark made by a rubber stamping devi[...] 2. Informal To pass or approve as a matter of routine.

rub·bish (rub′ish) n. 1. Waste refuse, or broken matt[...] trash. 2. Nonsense; rot. [ME rubbous] — **rub′bish·y** a[...]

rub·ble (rub′əl; for def. 3, also roo′bəl) n. 1. Rough, irr[...] ular pieces of broken stone. 2. The debris to which bu[...] ings of brick, stone, etc., are reduced by violent actions, by earthquakes or bombings. 3. Rough pieces of stone use in construction; also, masonry composed of such piec[...] [Origin uncertain] — **rub′bly** adj.

rub·down (rub′doun′) n. A type of massage.

rube (roob) n. Slang A farmer; rustic. [Abbreviation Reuben, a proper name]

ru·bel·la (roo·bel′ə) n. Pathol. German measles. [< [...] neut. pl. of L rubellus reddish, dim. of ruber red]

e·o·la (rōo-bē'ə-lə) *n. Pathol.* **1.** Measles (def. 1). **2.** **·man** measles. [< NL, neut. pl. dim. of L *rubeus* red] — **be'o·lar** *adj.*

bi·con (rōo'bi·kon) A river in north central Italy, form- the boundary separating Caesar's province of Gaul from **ly**, and by crossing it he committed himself to war with **mpey**. — **to cross the Rubicon** To be committed def- **ely** to some course of action.

i·cund (rōo'bə·kənd) *adj.* Red, or inclined to redness; **y**. [< L *rubicundus* red] — **ru'bi·cun'di·ty** *n.*

id·i·um (rōo-bid'ē·əm) *n.* A soft, rare, silvery white, **callic** element (symbol Rb) resembling potassium. See **:MENT**. [< NL < L *rubidus* red]

le (rōo'bəl) *n.* **1.** A standard monetary unit of the **S.R**.: in 1960 worth about 25 U.S. cents: also spelled **ble**. **2.** Formerly, a Russian silver coin.

ric (rōo'brik) *n.* **1.** A part of an early manuscript or a **k** that appears in red, used to indicate initial letters, **dings**, etc. **2.** *Eccl.* A direction or rule printed in a devo- **al** or liturgical office. **3.** A heading or title, as of a chap- **statute**, etc. **4.** Any direction or rule of conduct. — **1.** Red or reddish. [< F < L *ru- a* red earth] — **ru'bri·cal** *adj.* — **ru'bri·cal·ly** *adv.*

ri·cate (rōo'brə·kāt) *v.t.* **·cat·ed**, **·cat·ing** To mark or **with** red; illuminate with red, as a book. [< L *rubricare* **·edden**] — **ru'bri·ca'tion** *n.* — **ru'bri·ca'tor** *n.*

y (rōo'bē) *n.* *pl.* **·bies** **1.** A translucent, deep purplish **variety** of corundum, highly valued as a gemstone: also **ed** *Oriental ruby.* **2.** A rich red color like that of a ruby. **dj.** Pertaining to or like a ruby; being of a rich crimson. **v.t. ·bied**, **·by·ing** To tint with the color of a ruby; redden. **OF** *rubi*, ult. < L *rubeus* red]

ne (rōosh) *n.* A quilted or ruffled strip of fine fabric, **n** about the neck or wrists of a woman's costume. [< F, **hive**, frill]

h·ing (rōo'shing) *n.* Material for ruches; also, ruches **ectively**.

·sack (ruk'sak', rŏok'-) *n.* A canvas knapsack. [< **< rucken**, var. of *rücken* back + *sack* sack]

·us (ruk'əs) *n.* *U.S. Slang* An uproar; commotion; **npus**. [Prob. blend of RUMPUS and RUCTION]

der (rud'ər) *n.* **1.** *Naut.* A broad, flat, movable device **ged** vertically at the stern of a vessel to direct its course. **Anything** that guides or directs a course. **3.** *Aeron.* A **ged** or pivoted surface, used to control the position of an **raft** about its vertical axis. [OE *rōthor*, scull]

dy (rud'ē) *adj.* **·di·er**, **·di·est** **1.** Tinged with red. **2.** **ving** a healthy glow; rosy: a *ruddy* complexion. **3.** *Brit.* **ng** Bloody: a euphemism. [OE *rudig*] — **rud'di·ly** *adv.* **rud'di·ness** *n.*

dy duck A small North American duck having stiffened **feathers** and, in the adult male, a bright chestnut-colored **ly**.

e (rōod) *adj.* **rud·er**, **rud·est** **1.** Offensively blunt or un- **l**; rough or abrupt; impudent. **2.** Characterized by lack **polish** or refinement; uncultivated; uncouth. **3.** Unskill- **ly** made or done; crude; rough. **4.** Robust; strong. **5.** **rbarous**; savage. [< OF, or < L *rudis* rough] — **rude'ly** — **rude'ness** *n.*

i·ment (rōo'də·mənt) *n.* **1.** A first principle, step, **ge**, or condition. **2.** That which is as yet undeveloped or **y** partially developed. **3.** *Biol.* An undeveloped or func- **nless** organ or part. [< F < L *rudimentum* first attempt]

i·men·ta·ry (rōo'də·men'tər·ē) *adj.* **1.** Pertaining to **of** the nature of a rudiment or first principle; elementary. **Being** or remaining in an imperfectly developed state; **stigial**; abortive. Also **ru'di·men'tal**. — **ru'di·men'ta·ri- ·ness** *n.* — **ru'di·men'ta·ri·ness** *n.*

· (rōo) *v.* **rued**, **ru·ing** *v.t.* **1.** To feel sorrow or remorse **over**; govern. — **v.i.** **2.** To feel sorrow or be regretful. — **n**. See MOURN. — *n.* Sorrowful remembrance; regret. **E** *hrēowan* to be sorry] — **ru'er** *n.*

·² (rōo) *n.* **1.** A small, bushy herb with bitter, acrid leaves, **merly** much used in medicine. **2.** Any bitter draft. [< **< L** *ruta* < Gk. *rhytē*]

·ful (rōo'fəl) *adj.* **1.** Feeling or causing sorrow, regret, **pity**; deplorable; sorrowful. **2.** Expressing sorrow or pity. **rue'ful·ly** *adv.* — **rue'ful·ness** *n.*

¹ (ruf) *n.* **1.** A pleated, round, heavily starched collar **pular** in the 16th century. **2.** Ruffle¹ (defs. 1 and 2). **3.** **natural** collar of projecting feathers or hair around the **ck** of a bird or mammal. **4.** An Old World sandpiper of **ich** the male in the breeding season has an erectile frill of **thers** about the neck. [Short for RUFFLE¹]

·² (ruf) *n.* The playing of a trump upon another suit when **e** has no cards of that suit. — *v.t. & v.i.* To trump when **able** to follow suit. [< OF *roffle*, *rouffle*, *ronfle*]

ed (ruft) *adj.* Having a ruff, ruffle, or frill; ruffled.

ruffed grouse A North American grouse: called *partridge* in the northern and *pheasant* in the southern U.S.

ruf·fi·an (ruf'ē·ən, ruf'yən) *n.* A lawless, brutal fellow; a tough. — *adj.* Lawlessly or recklessly brutal or cruel. [< OF *ruffian*] — **ruf'fi·an·ism** *n.* — **ruf'fi·an·ly** *adj.*

ruf·fle¹ (ruf'əl) *n.* **1.** A pleated strip or frill of fabric, lace, etc., used as trim or ornament. **2.** Anything resembling such a strip. Also called *ruff*. **3.** A temporary discompo- sure. **4.** A slight disturbance, as a ripple. — *v.* **·fled**, **·fling** *v.t.* **1.** To disturb or destroy the smoothness or regularity of. **2.** To draw into folds or ruffles; gather. **3.** To furnish with ruffles. **4.** To erect (the feathers) in a ruff. **5.** To disturb or irritate; upset. **6.** To riffle (the pages of a book). **7.** To shuffle (cards). — *v.i.* **8.** To be or become rumpled or dis- ordered. **9.** To become disturbed or irritated. [< RUFFLE²]

ruf·fle² (ruf'əl) *n.* A low continuous beat of a drum, not as loud as a roll. — *v.t.* **·fled**, **·fling** To beat a ruffle upon, as a drum. [< earlier *ruff*; prob. imit.]

ru·fous (rōo'fəs) *adj.* Dull red. [< L *rufus* red]

rug (rug) *n.* **1.** A heavy textile fabric, made in one piece, to cover a portion of a floor. **2.** A covering made from the skins of animals. **3.** *Chiefly Brit.* A heavy coverlet or lap robe. [< Scand. Cf. Norw. *rugga* coarse coverlet.]

rug·by football (rug'bē) **1.** *Usu. cap. Brit.* A form of foot- ball in which the ball is propelled toward the opponents' goal by kicking or carrying. **2.** *Canadian* Football (def. 3).

rug·ged (rug'id) *adj.* **1.** Having a surface full of abrupt ine- qualities; broken into irregular points or crags; rough; un- even. **2.** Shaggy; unkempt; ragged. **3.** Rough in temper, character, or action. **4.** Having strongly marked features; wrinkled. **5.** Lacking culture or refinement; rude. **6.** Rough to the ear; grating. **7.** Robust; sturdy; hale. **8.** Tempestuous; stormy. [< Scand.] — **rug'ged·ly** *adv.* — **rug'ged·ness** *n.*

ru·gose (rōo'gōs) *adj.* Full of wrinkles, as some leaves. Also **ru'gous** (-gəs). [< L < *ruga* wrinkle]

ru·in (rōo'in) *n.* **1.** Total destruction of value or usefulness. **2.** Loss of honor, position, wealth, etc.; degradation. **3.** *Often pl.* That which remains of something demolished or de- cayed. **4.** A condition of desolation or destruction. **5.** That which causes destruction, downfall or injury. — *v.t.* **1.** To bring to ruin; destroy. **2.** To bring to bankruptcy or poverty. **3.** To deprive of chastity; seduce. — *v.i.* **4.** To fall into ruin. — **Syn.** See DEMOLISH. [< OF < L < *ruere* to fall] — **ru'in·a·ble** *adj.* — **ru'in·er** *n.*

ru·in·a·tion (rōo'in·ā'shən) *n.* **1.** The act of ruining, or the state of being ruined. **2.** Something that ruins.

ru·in·ous (rōo'in·əs) *adj.* **1.** Causing or tending to ruin. **2.** Falling to ruin; decayed. — **ru'in·ous·ly** *adv.* — **ru'in·ous· ness** *n.*

rule (rōol) *n.* **1.** Controlling power, or its possession and exercise; government; dominion; authority. **2.** A method or principle of action: I make early rising my *rule*. **3.** An authoritative direction or enactment respecting the doing or method of doing something: the *rules* of a game. **4.** A regu- lation or body of directions laid down by or for a religious order. **5.** A prescribed form, method, or set of instructions for solving a given class of mathematical problems. **6.** An established usage or law, fixing the form or use of words or the construction of sentences. **7.** Something belonging to the ordinary course of events or condition of things. **8.** Reg- ular or proper method; propriety, as of conduct; regularity. **9.** *Law* A judicial decision on some motion or special appli- cation: a *rule* to show cause. **10.** A straightedged instru- ment for use in measuring, or as a guide in drawing lines. **11.** *Printing* A strip of type-high metal for handling type or for printing a rule or line. — **as a rule** Ordinarily; usually. — *v.* **ruled**, **rul·ing** *v.t.* **1.** To have authority or control over; govern. **2.** To influence greatly; dominate. **3.** To decide or determine judicially or authoritatively. **4.** To re- strain; keep in check. **5.** To mark with straight, parallel lines. **6.** To make (a straight line) with or as with a ruler. — *v.i.* **7.** To have authority or control; be in command. **8.** To maintain a standard of rates. **9.** To form and express a decision. [< OF < L *regula* ruler, rule] — **rul'a·ble** *adj.*

rule of thumb **1.** Measurement by the thumb. **2.** Rough- ly practical rather than scientifically accurate measure.

rul·er (rōo'lər) *n.* **1.** One who rules or governs, as a sover- eign. **2.** A straight-edged instrument for use in measuring, or as a guide in drawing lines, usu. marked in inches.

rul·ing (rōo'ling) *adj.* Exercising dominion; controlling; predominant. — *n.* **1.** The act of one who rules or governs. **2.** A decision, as of a judge or presiding officer.

rum¹ (rum) *n.* **1.** An alcoholic liquor distilled from ferment- ed molasses or cane juice. **2.** Any alcoholic liquor. [Origin uncertain; ? short for obs. *rumbullion* rum]

rum² (rum) *adj.* *Brit. Slang* Queer; strange; peculiar. [? < Romany *rom* man]

Ru·ma·ni·an (rōō·mā′nē·ən, -mān′yən) *adj.* Of Rumania, its people, or their language. — *n.* **1.** A native or inhabitant of Rumania. **2.** The Romance language of the Rumanians.

rum·ba (rum′bə, *Sp.* rōōm′bä) *n.* **1.** A dance having its origin among Cuban Negroes. **2.** A modern ballroom dance based on this; also, music for or in the manner of such a dance. Also spelled *rhumba.* [< Am.Sp.]

rum·ble (rum′bəl) *v.* **·bled, ·bling** *v.i.* **1.** To make a low, heavy, rolling sound, as thunder. **2.** To move or proceed with such a sound. — *v.t.* **3.** To cause to make a low, heavy, rolling sound. **4.** To utter with such a sound. — *n.* **1.** A continuous low, heavy, rolling sound. **2.** A seat or baggage compartment in the rear of a carriage. **3.** A folding seat in the back of a coupé or roadster: in full **rumble seat. 4.** *U.S. Slang* A gang fight, usu. involving teenagers. [ME romblen] — **rum′bler** *n.* — **rum′bling·ly** *adv.* — **rum′bly** *adj.*

ru·men (rōō′men) *n. pl.* **ru·mi·na** (rōō′mə·nə) The first stomach or the cud of a ruminant. [< L gullet]

ru·mi·nant (rōō′mə·nənt) *n.* One of a division or suborder of even-toed, cud-chewing mammals, as the deer, sheep, cow, camel, etc., having a stomach with four cavities, the rumen, reticulum, omasum, and abomasum. — *adj.* **1.** Chewing the cud. **2.** Of or pertaining to a ruminant. **3.** Meditative or contemplative. [< L < *ruminare* to chew over]

ru·mi·nate (rōō′mə·nāt) *v.t. & v.i.* **·nat·ed, ·nat·ing 1.** To chew (food previously swallowed and regurgitated) over again; chew (the cud). **2.** To meditate or reflect (upon); ponder. [See RUMINANT.] — **ru′mi·nat′ing·ly** *adv.* — **ru′mi·na′tion** *n.* — **ru′mi·na′tive** *adj.* — **ru′mi·na′tive·ly** *adv.* — **ru′mi·na′tor** *n.*

rum·mage (rum′ij) *v.* **·maged, ·mag·ing** *v.t.* **1.** To search through (a place, box, etc.) by turning over and disarranging the contents; ransack. **2.** To find or bring out by searching: with *out* or *up.* — *v.i.* **3.** To make a thorough search. — *n.* **1.** Any act of rummaging. **2.** An upheaval or stirring up; bustle. [< MF < *arrumer* to stow cargo] — **rum′mag·er** *n.*

rummage sale 1. A sale of second-hand objects to obtain money for some charitable purpose. **2.** A sale of unclaimed articles, or a sale for clearing out articles prior to restocking.

rum·my¹ (rum′ē) *n.* A card game in which each player draws a card and discards another card, the object being to combine or get rid of one's hand in sequences of three cards or more of the same suit. [? < Brit. slang *rummy*, queer]

rum·my² (rum′ē) *n. pl.* **·mies** *Slang* A drunkard. — *adj.* **·mi·er, ·mi·est** Of or resembling rum: a *rummy* flavor.

ru·mor (rōō′mər) *n.* **1.** An unverified or unfounded report, story, etc., circulating from person to person. **2.** Common gossip; hearsay. — *v.t.* To tell or spread as a rumor; noise about. Also *Brit.* **ru′mour.** [< OF < L]

rump (rump) *n.* **1.** The rounded or fleshy upper part of the hind quarters of an animal. **2.** The analogous region in man; the buttocks. **3.** A cut of beef between the loin and the round. **4.** A legislative group, representative body, etc., having only a remnant of its original membership, and therefore regarded as unauthoritative. **5.** A last, often undesirable remnant. [ME *rumpe* < Scand.]

rum·ple (rum′pəl) *v.t. & v.i.* **·pled, ·pling** To form into creases or folds; wrinkle; ruffle. — *n.* **1.** An irregular fold; untidy wrinkling. **2.** The condition of being rumpled. [< MDu. *rumpelen*]

rum·pus (rum′pəs) *n. Informal* A row; wrangle; to-do. [Origin uncertain]

rumpus room A room for games, informal gatherings, etc.

rum·run·ner (rum′run′ər) *n.* A ship or person illicitly transporting alcoholic liquors across a border.

run (run) *v.* **ran** (*Archaic* or *Dial.* **run**), **run, run·ning** *v.i.* **1.** To move by rapid steps, faster than walking, in such a manner that both feet are off the ground for a portion of each step. **2.** To move rapidly; go swiftly. **3.** To flee; take flight. **4.** To make a brief or rapid journey. **5.** To make regular trips; ply. **6.** To be a candidate or contestant. **7.** To finish a race in a specified position. **8.** To move or pass easily: The rope *runs* through the block. **9.** To elapse: The hours *run* by. **10.** To proceed in direction or extent: This road *runs* north. **11.** To move in or as in a stream; flow. **12.** To become liquid and flow, as wax; also, to spread or mingle confusedly, as colors when wet. **13.** To move or pass into a specified condition: to *run* into trouble. **14.** To climb or grow in long shoots, as vines. **15.** To become torn by unraveling, as a knitted fabric. **16.** To suppurate. **17.** To leak. **18.** To continue or proceed: The conversation *ran* on and on. **19.** To be in operation; be operative; work: Will the engine *run*? **20.** To continue in existence or effect; extend in time: Genius *runs* in her family. **21.** To be reported or expressed: The story *runs* as follows. **22.** To migrate, as salmon from the sea. **23.** To occur or return, as to the mind. **24.** To incline; tend: Her taste *runs* to luxuries. **25.** To be performed or repeated in continuous succession, as a play. **26.** To make a rapid succession of demands for payment, as on a bank. **27.** To continue unexpired or unpaid, as a debt;

become payable. — *v.t.* **28.** To go along by running, a route, course, or path. **29.** To make one's way through, or past: to *run* rapids. **30.** To perform or accomplish by or as by running: to *run* an errand. **31.** To compete against in or as in a race. **32.** To enter (a horse, e for a race. **33.** To present and support as a candidate. To hunt or chase, as game. **35.** To bring to a specified dition by or as by running: to *run* oneself out of breath. To drive or force: with *out of, off, into, through,* etc. **37.** cause (a vessel) to move rapidly or freely. **38.** To move eye, hand, etc.) quickly or lightly. **39.** To cause to m slide, etc., as into a specified position. **40.** To cause to g ply: to *run* a train. **41.** To transport or convey in a ve or vehicle. **42.** To smuggle. **43.** To cause to flow. **44.** give forth a flow of, emit: Her eyes *ran* tears. **45.** To m as from melted metal. **46.** To sew or stitch in a continu line. **47.** To maintain or control the motion or opera of, as a machine. **48.** To direct or control; manage; o see. **49.** To allow to continue or mount up, as a bill: o with *up.* **50.** To become liable to; incur: to *run* a risk. In games, to make (a number of points, strokes, etc.) cessively. **52.** To publish in a magazine or newspaper *run* an ad. **53.** To mark, set down, or trace, as a boun line. **54.** To suffer from (a fever, etc.). — **to run ac** To meet by chance. — **to run down 1.** To pursue and o take, as a fugitive. **2.** To strike down while moving. **3.** speak of disparagingly; decry. — **to run in 1.** To ins include. **2.** *Printing* To print without a paragraph or bre **3.** *Slang* To arrest and place in confinement. — **to run** **1.** To meet by chance. **2.** To collide with. — **to run off** To produce on a typewriter, printing press, etc. **2.** To cide (a tied race, game, etc.) by the outcome of another, s sequent race, game, etc. **3.** To flee or escape; elope. — **run out** To come to an end; be exhausted, as supplies. — **run out of** To exhaust one's supply of. — **to run over** To ride or drive over; run down. **2.** To overflow. **3.** T over or examine hastily or quickly; rehearse. — **to** **through 1.** To spend wastefully; squander. **2.** To stab pierce. **3.** To run over (def. 3). — **to run up** To prod make hurriedly, as on a sewing machine. — *n.* **1.** An ac instance of running or going rapidly. **2.** The movemen gait of running: to break into a *run.* **3.** A distance cove by running. **4.** A distance traveled between two points by a train or vessel. **5.** A rapid, brief journey. **6.** A cou or route followed, as in reaching a destination. **7.** The p ilege of free use or access: to have the *run* of the place. **8** series, succession, or sequence, as of playing cards in cons tive order. **9.** A continuous spell of a specified conditio *run* of luck. **10.** A continuous period of consecutive formances, as of a theatrical production. **11.** A trend tendency: the *run* of the market. **12.** A broadly inclus category, type, or class: the general *run* of readers. **13** period of continuous operation, as of a machine or fact **14.** The output during such a period. **15.** A continu length or extent of something: a *run* of pipe. **16.** A leng wise rip in knitted fabric. **17.** Characteristic direction, tra ency, or linear form: the *run* of the grain in wood. **1** Flowing movement, as of a stream. **19.** The period of s flow. **20.** A swift stream or current. **21.** Mass migra or movement of animals, esp. of fish to spawn. **22.** A t burrow, or terrain frequented by a specific kind of anir **23.** An enclosure for animals or poultry. **24.** A steep co or runway, as for skiing or sledding. **25.** An unusua large number of demands for payment, as on a bank. Any great sustained demand, as for a commodity. **27.** sic A rapid succession of tones. **28.** In baseball, the sco of a point by a player's making a complete circuit of bases; also, a point so scored. **29.** In football, the ball rier's attempt to run through or around the line of the opp ing team. **30.** In cricket, the scoring of a point by b batsmen successfully reaching opposite popping creases a a hit. **31.** *Naut.* The after part of a ship's bottom. *Mining* A vein of ore or rock. **33.** An approach to a ta made by a bombing plane: also *bomb run.* — **a run for o** **money** A successful or satisfactory instance of activity, in competition. — **in the long run** As the ultimate outc of any train of circumstances. — *adj.* **1.** Made liqu melted. **2.** Made by a process of melting and casting molding: *run* metal; *run* butter. [OE *rinnan*]

run·a·bout (run′ə·bout′) *n.* **1.** A small, open automo **2.** A light, open wagon. **3.** A small motorboat.

run·a·round (run′ə·round′) *n.* **1.** *Slang* Artful decepti evasion. **2.** *Printing* Type set narrower than the body of text, as around illustrations.

run·a·way (run′ə·wā′) *adj.* **1.** Escaping or escaped fr restraint or control; fugitive. **2.** Brought about by runn away: a *runaway* marriage. **3.** Easily won as a horse r **4.** Of, pertaining to, or characterized by a rapid price r — *n.* **1.** One who or that which runs away; also, a he whose driver has lost control. **2.** An act of running aw **3.** *Informal* An easily won victory, as in a race.

·down (run′doun′) *n.* A summary; resumé.
·down (run′doun′) *adj.* **1.** Debilitated; physically ·ak; tired out. **2.** Dilapidated; shabby. **3.** Stopped be- ·se not wound: said of a timepiece.
e (rōōn) *n.* **1.** Any of the characters in the runic alpha- ·:. **2.** A Finnish ·em or one of its can- ·. **3.** *pl.* Old Norse ·e expressed in or as ·runes. **4.** Any ob- ·re or mystic song, ·em, verse, or say- ·. [< OE and ON ·a mystery, secret ·versation] — ru′· ·adj.

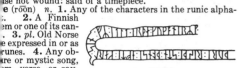

RUNES
(Tomb inscription, Sweden, 11th century)

g[1] (rung) *n.* **1.** A round crosspiece forming one of the ·ps of a ladder. **2.** A crosspiece used in chairs to strength- ·or support the legs or back. **3.** The spoke of a wheel. ·E *hrung* staff, pole]
g[2] (rung) Past participle of RING[2].
ic alphabet An old Germanic alphabet, probably origi- ·ing in both the Latin and Greek, consisting originally of ·characters, or runes.
-in (*n.* run′in′; *adj.* run′in′) *n.* **1.** A quarrel; bicker. **2.** ·nting Inserted or added matter. — *adj. Printing* In- ·ted or added.
nel (run′əl) *n.* A rivulet. [OE *rynel* < *rinnan* to run]
ner (run′ər) *n.* **1.** One who or that which runs, as one ·p runs a race. **2.** One who operates or manages anything. ·One who runs errands or goes about on any kind of busi- ·s. **4.** That part on which an object runs or slides: the ·ner of a skate. **5.** *Mech.* A device to assist sliding mo- ·n. **6.** Any of various fishes of warm and temperate seas. ·*Bot.* **a** A slender, procumbent stem rooting at the end and ·es, as in the strawberry. **b** Any of various twining plants. ·A smuggler. **9.** A long, narrow rug or carpeting, used in ·ways, etc. **10.** A narrow strip of cloth, used on tables, ·ssers, etc.
ner-up (run′ər-up′) *n.* A contestant or team finishing ·second place.
ning (run′ing) *adj.* **1.** Moving or going rapidly. **2.** In- ·ed or trained to run rather than to pace or trot: said of ·ses. **3.** Creeping or clinging, as a plant. **4.** Flowing: ·*ning* water. **5.** Slipping or untying easily: a *running* ·t. **6.** Moving or pulling easily and freely: a *running* ·e. **7.** Being or able to be in operation: a *running* engine. ·Cursive: a *running* handwriting. **9.** Liquid or fluid. **10.** ·charging, as pus from a sore. **11.** In a straight line: ·ee feet *running*. **12.** Current, as an account. **13.** Con- ·uous; repeated: a *running* design. **14.** Kept up continu- ·ly. **15.** Passing; cursory: a *running* glance. **16.** Fol- ·ing one another without intermission; successive: He ·ked three hours *running*. **17.** Accomplished or performed ·h a run. **18.** Of or pertaining to a trip or run: the train's ·*ning* time. — *n.* **1.** The act of one who or that which ·s. **2.** That which runs or flows. **3.** The amount or quan- ·y that runs. **4.** Ability or power to run. **5.** Competition ·race: He is out of the *running*.
ning board A footboard on the side of a locomotive, ·eet car, automobile, etc.
ning gear *Mech.* The wheels and axles of any vehicle ·l their immediate attachments, as distinguished from the ·ly that they support.
ning knot A knot made so as to slip along a noose and ·nten when pulled upon: also called *slipknot*.
ning light *Aeron.* A navigation light.
ning mate The candidate for the lesser of two offices ·sely linked by constitutional provisions, as the vice-pres- ·ncy with the presidency.
ning title *Printing* A title or headline repeated at the ·d of every page or every other page throughout a book or ·apter. Also **running head.**
i·ny·mede (run′i-mēd) A meadow in Surrey, England, ·ere King John is said to have signed the Magna Carta.
·off (run′ôf′, -of′) *n.* **1.** The part of the rainfall that is ·t absorbed directly by the soil but is drained off in rills or ·eams. **2.** A special contest held to break a tie.
·of-the-mill (run′əv-thə-mil′) *adj.* Not special in any ·y; average; ordinary. Also **run-of-the-mine.**
·on (run′on′, -ôn′) *n. Printing* Appended matter.
t (runt) *n.* **1.** An unusually small, weak, or stunted ani- ·l or plant. **2.** A small person: often a contemptuous ·m. [< Scot. *runt* old cow]
t·y (runt′ē) *adj.* **runt·i·er, runt·i·est** Dwarfish; stunted. **runt′i·ness** *n.*
·way (run′wā′) *n.* **1.** A way or path over or through ·ich something runs. **2.** A pathway extending from a

stage into the audience, used for certain types of theatrical entertainment. **3.** The channel or bed of a stream. **4.** In lumbering, a chute. **5.** Any track specially laid for wheeled vehicles. **6.** *Aeron.* An improved or unimproved roadlike surface, used for the takeoff and landing of aircraft.
ru·pee (rōō·pē′) *n.* **1.** The standard monetary unit of vari- ous countries; esp., the rupee of India and Pakistan, in 1960 worth about 21 U.S. cents. **2.** A coin of this denomination. [< Hind. < Skt. *rūpya* coined silver]
rup·ture (rup′chər) *n.* **1.** The act of breaking apart, or the state of being broken apart. **2.** *Pathol.* Hernia. **3.** Breach of friendship or concord between individuals or nations. — *v.t. & v.i.* **·tured, ·tur·ing 1.** To break apart; separate into parts. **2.** To affect with or suffer a rupture. [< Med.L *ruptura* < *rumpere* to break] — **rup′tur·a·ble** *adj.*
ru·ral (rōōr′əl) *adj.* **1.** Of or pertaining to the country as distinguished from the city or the town; rustic. **2.** Of or pertaining to farming or agriculture. [< MF < L < *rus, ruris* country] — **ru′ral·ism** *n.* — **ru′ral·ist** *n.* — **ru′ral· ly** *adv.*
— **Syn. 1.** Rustic, pastoral, bucolic. — **Ant.** urban.
rural free delivery A government service of house-to-house free mail delivery in rural districts.
ru·ral·i·ty (rōō-ral′ə-tē) *n. pl.* **·ties 1.** The condition or quality of being rural. **2.** A rural characteristic.
ru·ral·ize (rōōr′əl-īz) *v.* **·ized, ·iz·ing** *v.t.* **1.** To make rural. — *v.i.* **2.** To go into or live in the country; rusticate. — **ru′ral·i·za′tion** *n.*
ruse (rōōz) *n.* An action intended to mislead or deceive; a stratagem; trick. [< MF *ruser* to turn aside.]
rush[1] (rush) *v.i.* **1.** To move or go swiftly or with violence. **2.** To make an attack; charge: with *on* or *upon*. **3.** To pro- ceed recklessly or rashly; plunge: with *in* or *into*. **4.** To come, surge, flow, etc., suddenly. — *v.t.* **5.** To drive or push with haste or violence; hurry. **6.** To do or perform hastily or hurriedly. **7.** To make a sudden assault upon; also, to capture by such an assault. **8.** *Slang* To seek the favor of with assiduous attentions. **9.** In football, to move (the ball) toward the goal of the other team by a rush or rushes. **10.** *U.S.* To consider for membership in a fraternity or sorority. — *n.* **1.** The act of rushing; a sudden turbulent movement, drive, or onset. **2.** A state of pressed or impatient activity; hurry. **3.** A sudden surge, flow, or outpouring. **4.** A sud- den pressing demand. **5.** A sudden or urgent press of traffic, business, etc. **6.** A sudden flocking of people to a new re- gion, esp. to an area rumored to be rich in a precious min- eral: a gold *rush*. **7.** *U.S.* A general contest or scrimmage between students, as between sophomores and freshmen. **8.** In football, an attempt to take the ball through the opposing linemen and toward the goal. **9.** *pl.* In motion pictures, the first film prints of a scene or series of scenes, before editing or selection. — *adj.* **1.** Requiring urgency or haste: a *rush* order. **2.** Characterized by much traffic, business, etc. **3.** *U.S.* Denoting a time or function set aside for fraternity or sorority members to meet new students to consider them for membership: *rush* week. [< AF < OF *ruser, reuser* to push back < L *recusare* to refuse] — **rush′er** *n.*
rush[2] (rush) *n.* **1.** Any one of various grasslike, usu. aquatic herbs, growing in marshy ground and having pliant, cylin- drical, leafless stems, often used for making mats, etc. **2.** A thing of little or no value. **3.** A rushlight. [OE *risc*]
rush hour A time when traffic or business is at its height. — **rush-hour** (rush′our′) *adj.*
rush·light (rush′līt′) *n.* A candle made by dipping a rush in tallow. Also **rush candle.**
rush·y (rush′ē) *adj.* **rush·i·er, rush·i·est 1.** Abounding in, covered with, or made of rushes. **2.** Like a rush.
rusk (rusk) *n.* **1.** A light, sweetened bread or biscuit. **2.** Bread or cake that has been crisped and browned in an oven. [< Sp. *rosca*, twisted loaf of bread]
rus·set (rus′it) *n.* **1.** A reddish or yellowish brown. **2.** Coarse homespun cloth or clothing of this color. **3.** Russet leather. **4.** A winter apple of greenish color, mottled with brown. — *adj.* **1.** Of a reddish or yellowish brown color. **2.** Made of russet cloth; also, coarse; homespun. **3.** Finished, but not blacked: said of leather. [< OF < L *russus* red]
Rus·sian (rush′ən) *adj.* Of or pertaining to Russia, its peo- ple, or their language. — *n.* **1.** A native or citizen of the Soviet Union or the former Russian Empire; esp., a Great Russian, Ukrainian, or Byelorussian. **2.** The East Slavic language of Russia, including Great Russian, Ukrainian, and Byelorussian.
Russian dressing Mayonnaise dressing to which chili sauce, pimentos, chopped pickles, etc., have been added.
Rus·sian·ize (rush′ən-īz) *v.t.* **·ized, ·iz·ing** To make Rus- sian in manner, character, etc.
Russian leather A smooth, well-tanned, high-grade leath- er of calfskin or light cattle hide, dressed with birch oil.

Russian Orthodox Church An autonomous branch of the Eastern Orthodox Church in the Soviet Union, under the patriarch of Moscow.

Russian Revolution See under REVOLUTION.

Russian roulette A suicidal stunt in which one aims a revolver containing one cartridge at one's head and pulls the trigger, with one chance in six of being shot.

Russian wolfhound The borzoi.

Russo- *combining form* Russia; pertaining to the Russians.

Russo-Japanese War (rus'ō·jap'ə·nēz', -nēs') See table for WAR.

Rus·so·pho·bi·a (rus'ə·fō'bē·ə) *n.* Fear of the policy or influence of Russia. **— Rus'so·phobe** *n.*

rust (rust) *n.* **1.** The reddish or yellow coating formed on iron and steel by exposure to air and moisture, consisting of ferric hydroxide, Fe(OH)$_3$, and ferric oxide, Fe$_2$O$_3$. **2.** Any film formed on the surface of a metal by oxidation. **3.** A disease caused by a parasitic fungi living on the tissues of higher plants and characterized by the appearance of orange or reddish brown spots on the host plant. **4.** Any coating or accretion formed by a corrosive or degenerative process. **5.** A condition or tendency that destroys or weakens energy or active qualities: the *rust* of idleness. **6.** Any of several shades of reddish brown, somewhat like the color of rust, but containing more orange. **— v.t. & v.i. 1.** To become or cause to become rusty. **2.** To contract or cause to contract rust. **3.** To become or cause to become weakened or impaired because of inaction or disuse. **4.** To make or become rust-colored. [OE *rūst*]

rus·tic (rus'tik) *adj.* **1.** Typical of or appropriate to simple country life. **2.** Plain; simple; homely: *rustic* garments. **3.** Uncultured; rude; awkward. **4.** Unaffected; artless: *rustic* simplicity. **5.** Of or pertaining to any irregular style of work or decoration appropriate to the country; also, of or pertaining to work in natural, unpolished wood. **— Syn.** See RURAL. **— n. 1.** One who lives in the country. **2.** A country person of simple manners or character; also, a coarse or clownish person. **3.** Rusticwork. **4.** Country dialect. [< L < *rus* country] **— rus'ti·cal·ly** *adv.*

rus·ti·cate (rus'tə·kāt) *v.* **·cat·ed, ·cat·ing** *v.i.* **1.** To go to the country. **2.** To stay or live in the country. **— v.t. 3.** To send or banish to the country. **4.** To make rustic. **5.** To construct (masonry) with rusticwork. **— rus'ti·ca'tion** *n.* **— rus'ti·ca'tor** *n.*

rus·tic·i·ty (rus·tis'ə·tē) *n. pl.* **·ties 1.** Rustic condition, character, or manners; simplicity; homeliness; awkwardness. **2.** A rustic trait or peculiarity.

rus·tic·work (rus'tik·wûrk') *n.* **1.** Ashlar masonry having rough surfaces, and often deeply sunk grooves at the joints. **2.** Furniture, etc., made of the natural limbs and roots of trees. Also **rustic work.**

rus·tle[1] (rus'əl) *v.t. & v.i.* **·tled, ·tling** To fall, move, or ca to move with a quick succession of small, light, rubb sounds, as dry leaves or sheets of paper. **— n.** A rustl sound. [ME *rustel*, alter. of OE *hrūxlian* to make a noi **— rus'tler** *n.* **— rus'tling·ly** *adv.*

rus·tle[2] (rus'əl) *v.t. & v.i.* **·tled, ·tling 1.** *Informal* To with or obtain by energetic or vigorous action. **2.** *U.S. formal* To steal (cattle, etc.). [Blend of RUSH and HUST

rus·tler (rus'lər) *n.* *U.S. Informal* **1.** A cattle or ho thief. **2.** A pushing, energetic person.

rust·y (rus'tē) *adj.* **rust·i·er, rust·i·est 1.** Covered or fected with rust. **2.** Consisting of or produced by rust. Having the reddish or yellowish appearance of rust: s often of salted fish or meat that has become rancid. **4.** paired by inaction or want of exercise; also, stiff. **5.** Inef tive or weakened through neglect; also, having lost skill want of practice. **6.** *Biol.* Appearing as if covered with r brownish red. **— rust'i·ly** *adv.* **— rust'i·ness** *n.*

rut[1] (rut) *n.* **1.** A sunken track worn by a wheel, as i road; also, a groove forming a path for anything. **2.** A tled habit or course of procedure; routine. **— v.t.** rut **rut·ting** To wear or make a rut or ruts in. [Var. of ROU

rut[2] (rut) *n.* **1.** The sexual excitement of various anim esp. of deer and other ruminants; estrus. **2.** The period ing which this excitement lasts. **— v.** **rut·ted, rut·ting** To be in rut. [< MF < L < *rugire* to roar]

ru·ta·ba·ga (rōō'tə·bā'gə) *n.* **1.** A cultivated plant al to the turnip. **2.** Its edible root. [< dial. Sw. *rotabagg*

ruth (rōōth) *n.* *Archaic* **1.** Compassion; pity. **2.** Gr repentance; regret. [ME < OE *hrēow* sad]

Ruth (rōōth) A widow of Moab who left her own people went with her mother-in-law Naomi to Bethlehem. **—** The book of the Old Testament in which this story is t

Ru·the·ni·an (rōō·thē'nē·ən) *n.* **1.** One of a group Ukrainians living in eastern Czechoslovakia and the Tr carpathian Oblast, formerly Ruthenia. **2.** The Ukrair language. **— adj.** Of or pertaining to the Ruthenian their language.

ru·the·ni·um (rōō·thē'nē·əm) *n.* A gray, brittle, rare me lic element (symbol Ru) of the platinum group. See P MENT. [< NL, after *Ruthenia*]

ruth·less (rōōth'lis) *adj.* Having no compassion; merci [< RUTH] **— ruth'less·ly** *adv.* **— ruth'less·ness** *n.*

rut·tish (rut'ish) *adj.* Disposed to rut; lustful; libidin

rut·ty (rut'ē) *adj.* **·ti·er, ·ti·est** Full of ruts. **— rut'ti·nes -ry** Var. of -ERY.

rye (rī) *n.* **1.** The grain or seeds of a hardy cereal grass cl ly allied to wheat, used in the making of flour and whis and as a feed for livestock. **2.** The plant. **3.** Whisky tilled from rye or partly from rye. [OE *ryge*]

rye grass Darnel.

S

s, S (es) *n. pl.* **s's** or **ss, S's** or **Ss, ess·es** (es'iz) **1.** The 19th letter of the English alphabet. **2.** The sound represented by the letter *s*, usu. a voiceless sibilant, but often voiced between vowels, as in *easy*. **— symbol 1.** Anything shaped like an S. **2.** *Chem.* Sulfur (symbol S).

s- *Chem.* Symmetrical.

-s[1] A variant of *-es*[1], inflectional ending of the plurals of nouns, attached to nouns not ending in a sibilant or an affricate: *books, words, cars.* It represents (s) after a voiceless consonant, and (z) after a voiced consonant or a vowel. Compare -ES[1].

-s[2] An inflectional ending used to form the third person singular present indicative of verbs not ending in a sibilant, affricate, or vowel: *reads, walks, sings.* Compare -ES[2].

-s *suffix* On; of a; at: often used in adverbs without appreciable force: *nights, Mondays, always, towards.* [OE *-es*, forming adverbial genitives]

-'s[1] An inflectional ending used to form the possessive of singular nouns and of plural nouns not ending in *-s*: a *man's* world, *women's* fashions. In plurals ending in *-s* (or *-es*) a simple apostrophe is used as a sign of the possessive: a *girls'* school, the *churches'* steeples.

-'s[2] Contraction of: **a** Is: *He's* here. **b** Has: *She's* left. **c** Us: *Let's* go.

Sa *Chem.* Samarium.

Sab·ba·tar·i·an (sab'ə·târ'ē·ən) *adj.* Pertaining to the Sab-

bath or its strict observance. **— n. 1.** A Christian who serves Sunday strictly. **2.** A Christian who observes seventh day as the Sabbath. **— Sab'ba·tar'i·an·ism** *n.*

Sab·bath (sab'əth) *n.* **1.** The seventh day of the week, pointed in the Decalogue as a day of rest to be observed the Jews; now, Saturday. **2.** The first day of the wee observed by Christians; Sunday. **3.** The institution or servance of a day of rest; a time of rest, peace, or quiet. The sabbatical year of the Jews. *Lev.* xxv 4. [Fusio OE *sabat* and OF *sabbat, sabat,* both < L *sabbatum* < Gk Hebrew *shābath* to rest] **— Sab·bat'ic** or **·i·cal** *adj.* **— S bat'i·cal·ly** *adv.*

sab·bat·i·cal (sə·bat'i·kəl) *adj.* Of the nature of the S bath as a day of rest; offering rest at regular intervals. **sab·bat'ic. — n.** A sabbatical year. [See SABBATH]

sabbatical year 1. In the ancient Jewish economy, e seventh year, in which the people were required to ref from tillage. **2.** A year's vacation awarded to teacher some American educational institutions every seven ye

sa·ber (sā'bər) *n.* **1.** A heavy one-edged cavalry sw with a thick-backed blade, often curved. **2.** In fencin light swordlike instrument, used for both thrusting slashing, hits being scored with the point or either edge. *v.t.* To strike, wound, or kill with a saber. Also, *Brit.,* sa [< F < G, prob. < Hung. *szabni* to cut]

Sa·bine (sā'bīn) *n.* One of an ancient central Italian peo

nquered and absorbed by Rome in 290 B.C. — *adj.* Of or
rtaining to the Sabines.

ble (sā′bəl) *n.* **1.** A carnivore of northern Asia and Eu-
pe, related to the marten and prized for its valuable fur.
The dressed fur of a sable, esp. of the Asian sable. **3.** *pl.*
arments made wholly or partly of this fur. **4.** The color
ack; also, mourning or a mourning garment. — *adj.* **1.**
ack, esp. as the color of mourning. **2.** Made of or having
e color of sable fur; dark brown. [< OF < Med.L *sabelum*]

bot (sab′ō, *Fr.* så·bō′) *n.* **1.** A wooden shoe. **2.** A shoe
ving a wooden sole but flexible shank. [< F < OF *savate*,
t. < Arabic *sabbat* sandal]

o·tage (sab′ə·täzh, *Fr.* så·bô·tàzh′) *n.* An act of mali-
ous damage or destruction, as one intended to obstruct the
oduction of war materiel by the enemy. — *v.* **·taged, ·tag·**
g *v.i.* **1.** To engage in sabotage. — *v.t.* **2.** To damage or
stroy by sabotage. [< F < *sabot* sabot; with ref. to dam-
e done to machinery with sabots]

o·teur (sab′ə·tûr′, *Fr.* så·bô·tœr′) *n.* One who engages
sabotage. [< F]

bra (sä′brə) *n.* A native Israeli. [< Hebrew, cactus]

bre (sä′bər) See SABER.

(sak) *n.* Biol. A membranous pouch or receptacle in an
imal or plant, as for containing a liquid: the ink *sac* of a
uid. [< F < L *saccus* sack¹]

·cha·ride (sak′ə·rīd, -rid) *n.* *Chem.* Any of a large group
carbohydrates containing sugar, usu. classified as *mono-*
ccharide, disaccharide, etc.

·cha·rin (sak′ər·in) *n.* *Chem.* A white crystalline coal-
r compound, C₇H₅O₃NS, from 300 to 500 times sweeter
an cane sugar, used as a noncaloric sweetening agent. [<
< Gk. ult. < Skt. *sharkarā* grit, sugar]

·cha·rine (sak′ər·in, -ə·rīn) *adj.* **1.** Of, pertaining to, or
the nature of sugar; sweet. **2.** Cloyingly sweet: a *saccha-*
ne manner. — *n.* Saccharin. — **sac′cha·rine·ly** *adv.* —
.c′cha·rin′i·ty *n.*

·charo- *combining form* Sugar; of or pertaining to sugar.
so, before vowels, **sacchar-**. [See SACCHARIN]

·cha·rose (sak′ə·rōs) *n.* Sucrose.

·er·do·tal (sas′ər·dōt′l) *adj.* **1.** Pertaining to a priest or
iesthood; priestly. **2.** Believing in the divine authority of
e priesthood. [< MF < L *sacerdos, -dotis* priest] — **sac′·**
·do′tal·ly *adv.*

·er·do·tal·ism (sas′ər·dōt′l·iz′əm) *n.* **1.** The character
d methods of the priesthood; priestcraft. **2.** Zeal for
iestly things.

chem (sā′chəm) *n.* A North American Indian hereditary
ief. [< Algonquian (Narraganset)]

chet (sa·shā′, *esp. Brit.* sash′ā) *n.* A small ornamental
g for perfumed powder. [< MF, dim. of *sac* sack]

ck¹ (sak) *n.* **1.** A bag for holding bulky articles. **2.** A
easure or weight of varying amount. **3.** A loose jacket-
e garment, worn by women and babies: also **sacque**. **4.**
lang Dismissal: esp. in the phrases **to get the sack, to give**
omeone) **the sack. 5.** In baseball slang, a base. **6.** *U.S.*
lang A bed; mattress. — **to hit the sack** *U.S. Slang* To
 to bed. — **to sack out** *U.S. Slang* To go to bed. — *v.t.*
)E < L < Gk. < Hebrew *saq* sack, sackcloth]

ck² (sak) *v.t.* To plunder or pillage (a town or city) after
pturing. — *n.* **1.** The pillaging of a captured town or
ty. **2.** Loot or booty obtained by pillage. [< MF *sac* <
al. *sacco,* orig., plunder < Med.L < L *saccus* sack¹] —
ck′er *n.*

ck³ (sak) *n.* Light-colored Spanish dry wine; also, any
rong white wine from southern Europe. [Earlier (*wyne*)
ck < F (*vin*) *sec* dry (wine) < L *siccus* dry]

ck·but (sak′but) *n.* **1.** An early instrument resembling
e trombone. **2.** In the Bible, a stringed instrument. [<
F < OF *saquer* to draw + *bouter* to push]

ck·cloth (sak′klôth′, -kloth′) *n.* **1.** A coarse cloth used
r making sacks. **2.** Coarse cloth or haircloth worn in pen-
nce. — **in sackcloth and ashes 1.** In the Bible, wearing
arments of sackcloth and sprinkling ashes on one's head
 marks of penance or sorrow. **2.** In any state of sorrow,
enance, or self-abasement.

ck coat A short, loose-fitting coat with no waist seam.

ck·ful (sak′fŏol′) *n. pl.* **·fuls** Enough to fill a sack.

ck·ing (sak′ing) *n.* A coarse cloth made of hemp or flax
nd used for sacks.

ck race A race run with the feet in a sack.

·cral¹ (sā′krəl) *adj.* Of, pertaining to, or situated near the
icrum. — *n.* A sacral vertebra or nerve.

·cral² (sā′krəl) *adj.* Pertaining to sacred rites. [< L
icrum rite < *sacer* sacred]

c·ra·ment (sak′rə·mənt) *n.* **1.** *Eccl.* Any of certain rites
rdained by Christ or by the church, as baptism, the Eu-

charist, confirmation, etc. **2.** *Often cap. Eccl.* **a** The Eucharist; the Lord's Supper. **b** The consecrated bread and
wine of the Eucharist: often with *the*. **3.** Any sign or token
of a solemn covenant or pledge. **4.** Anything considered to
have a secret or mysterious meaning. [< OF < L *sacrare* to
consecrate]

sac·ra·men·tal (sak′rə·men′təl) *n.* **1.** One of certain rites,
such as the use of holy water, oil, or salt, employed as ad-
juncts to sacraments, or regarded as analogous to a sacrament. **2.** *pl.* The objects, words, or ceremonies used in administering a sacrament. — *adj.* **1.** Of or pertaining to a
sacrament. **2.** Constituting or composing a sacrament. **3.**
Having the influence or efficacy of a sacrament. **4.** Consecrated, as by sacred vows. — **sac′ra·men′tal·ism** *n.* —
sac′ra·men′tal·ist *n.* — **sac′ra·men′tal·ly** *adv.*

sa·cred (sā′krid) *adj.* **1.** Set apart or dedicated to religious
use; hallowed. **2.** Pertaining or related to deity, religion, or
hallowed places or things. **3.** Consecrated or dedicated to a
person or purpose. **4.** Entitled to reverence or respect; not
to be profaned; inviolable. [< OF < L *sacrare* to treat as
sacred] — **sa′cred·ly** *adv.* — **sa′cred·ness** *n.*

Sacred College The College of Cardinals.

sacred cow 1. *U.S. Informal* Something or someone regarded as above criticism or reproach. **2.** A cow when considered sacred, as by the Hindus.

sac·ri·fice (sak′rə·fīs) *n.* **1.** The act of making an offering
to a deity, in worship or atonement; also, that which is so
offered. **2.** A giving up of some cherished or desired object,
person, idea, etc., usu. for the sake of something else; also,
that which is so given up. **3.** Loss incurred or suffered without return. **4.** A reduction of price that leaves little or no
profit or involves loss. **5.** In baseball, a sacrifice hit. — *v.*
·ficed, ·fic·ing *v.t.* **1.** To make an offering or sacrifice of, as
to a god or deity. **2.** To give up, yield, permit injury to, or
relinquish (something valued) for the sake of something else,
as a person, thing, or idea. **3.** To sell at a reduced price;
part with at a loss. **4.** In baseball, to advance (one or more
runners) by means of a sacrifice hit. — *v.i.* **5.** To make a
sacrifice. **6.** To make a sacrifice hit. [< OF < L < *sacer*
sacred + *facere* to perform, do] — **sac′ri·fic′er** *n.* — **sac′·**
ri·fic′ing·ly *adv.*

sacrifice fly In baseball, a fly ball hit with less than two out
that enables a runner on third base to score after the catch.

sacrifice hit In baseball, a bunt made with less than two
out that enables a runner or runners to advance a base while
the batter is being retired. Also **sacrifice bunt.**

sac·ri·fi·cial (sak′rə·fish′əl) *adj.* Of, pertaining to, performing, or like a sacrifice. — **sac′ri·fi′cial·ly** *adv.*

sac·ri·lege (sak′rə·lij) *n.* The act of violating or profaning
anything sacred, including sacramental vows. [< OF < L
< *sacer, sacris* sacred + *legere* to gather, steal] — **sac′ri·**
le′gist (-lē′jist) *n.*

sac·ri·le·gious (sak′rə·lij′əs, -lē′jəs) *adj.* **1.** Having committed sacrilege; impious. **2.** Of, pertaining to, or like sacrilege. — **sac′ri·le′gious·ly** *adv.* — **sac′ri·le′gious·ness** *n.*

sac·ris·tan (sak′ris·tən) *n.* An officer having charge of the
sacristy of a church. [< Med.L < L *sacer, sacris* sacred]

sac·ris·ty (sak′ris·tē) *n. pl.* **·ties** A room in a religious
house for the sacred vessels and vestments; vestry.

sacro- *combining form Med.* Near, or related to the sacrum.
[< L (*os*) *sacrum* the sacral (bone)]

sac·ro·il·i·ac (sak′rō·il′ē·ak) *adj. Anat.* Pertaining to the
sacrum and the ilium and to the joints or ligaments connecting them. [< SACRO- + ILIAC]

sac·ro·sanct (sak′rō·sangkt) *adj.* Peculiarly and exceedingly sacred; inviolable: sometimes used ironically. [< L
< *sacro,* ablative of *sacrum* rite + *sanctus,* pp. of *sancire* to
make holy, inviolable] — **sac′ro·sanc′ti·ty** *n.*

sa·crum (sā′krəm) *n. pl.* **·cra** (-krə) *Anat.* A composite
bone formed by the union of the five vertebrae between the
lumbar and caudal regions, constituting the dorsal part of
the pelvis. For illus. see PELVIS. [< NL < L (*os*) *sacrum*
sacred (bone); from its use in sacrifices]

sad (sad) *adj.* **sad·der, sad·dest 1.** Sorrowful or depressed
in spirits. **2.** Causing sorrow or pity; unfortunate. **3.** *Informal* Pitifully inadequate; bad; contemptible. **4.** Dark-
hued; somber. [OE *sæd,* orig., sated] — **sad′ly** *adv.* —
sad′ness *n.*

sad·den (sad′n) *v.t. & v.i.* To make or become sad.

sad·dle (sad′l) *n.* **1.** A seat or pad for a rider, as on the back
of a horse or on a bicycle. **2.** A padded cushion for a horse's
back, used as part of a harness or to support a pack, etc. **3.**
A part of an animal that is similar to a saddle in shape, position, etc.; esp., the lower part of the back of a fowl. **4.** The
two hindquarters of a carcass, as of mutton, veal, or venison;
also, the undivided loins of such a carcass. **5.** Something
resembling a saddle in form or position, as a bearing for a car
axle. — **in the saddle** In control. — *v.* **·dled, ·dling** *v.t.*

ONUNCIATION KEY: add, āce, câre, pälm; end, ēven; it, īce; odd, ōpen, ôrder; tŏŏk, pōōl; up, bûrn; ə = a in *above,* e in *sicken,* i in *flex-*
e, o in *melon,* u in *focus;* yōō = u in *fuse;* oil; pout; check; go; ring; thin; this; zh, vision.

1. To put a saddle on. **2.** To load, as with a burden. **3.** To place as a burden or responsibility: with *upon.* — *v.i.* **4.** To get into a saddle. [OE *sadol*]

sad·dle-backed (sad′l-bakt) *adj.* **1.** Concave, as a saddle, in the back or upper part. **2.** Having a saddlelike mark, as some birds.

sad·dle-bag (sad′l-bag) *n.* One of a pair of pouches connected by a strap or band and slung over an animal's back or attached to a saddle.

sad·dle-cloth (sad′l-klôth′, -kloth′) *n.* A cloth placed under and attached to a saddle.

saddle horse A horse used with or trained for the saddle.

sad·dler (sad′lər) *n.* **1.** A maker of saddles, harness, etc. **2.** A saddle horse.

saddle roof A ridge roof having two gables.

sad·dler·y (sad′lər-ē) *n. pl.* **·dler·ies 1.** Saddles, harnesses, etc., collectively. **2.** A shop where such articles are sold. **3.** The craft or business of a saddler.

saddle shoe A white sport shoe having a dark band of leather across the instep.

saddle soap A softening and preserving soap for leather, containing pure white soap, as Castile, and neat's-foot oil.

Sad·du·cee (saj′ōō-sē, sad′yōō-sē) *n.* A member of an ancient Jewish sect that adhered to the written Mosaic law but repudiated oral tradition, rejecting the resurrection of the body, etc. Compare PHARISEE. [Appar. ult. after *Zadok,* a high priest (*Ezek.* xl 46)] — **Sad′du·ce′an, Sad·du·cae′an** *adj.* — **Sad′du·cee′ism** *n.*

sad·i·ron (sad′ī′ərn) *n.* An iron for pressing clothes.

sad·ism (sā′diz·əm, sad′iz·əm) *n.* **1.** *Psychol.* A condition in which sexual gratification depends largely on the infliction of pain upon others. **2.** A tendency to take delight in being cruel. Compare MASOCHISM. [after Comte Donatien de *Sade,* 1740–1814, who described such sexual aberrations in his writings] — **sad·ist** (sā′dist, sad′ist) *n. & adj.* — **sa·dis·tic** (sə-dis′tik, sā-) *adj.* — **sa·dis′ti·cal·ly** *adv.*

sad sack *U.S. Slang* A blundering, pitiable person.

sa·fa·ri (sə-fä′rē) *n. pl.* **·ris** An expedition or journey, often on foot, as for hunting. [< Swahili < Arabic *safara* to travel.]

safe (sāf) *adj.* **saf·er, saf·est 1.** Free or freed from danger or evil. **2.** Having escaped injury or damage; unharmed. **3.** Not involving risk or loss. **4.** Conferring safety. **5.** Prudent or trustworthy. **6.** Not likely to cause or do harm or injury. **7.** In baseball, having reached base without being retired. — *n.* **1.** A strong metal receptacle for protecting valuables. **2.** Any place of safe storage. [< OF < L *salvus* whole, healthy] — **safe′ly** *adv.* — **safe′ness** *n.*

safe·break·er (sāf′brā′kər) *n.* A safecracker.

safe-con·duct (sāf′kon′dukt) *n.* **1.** An official document assuring protection on a journey or voyage, as in time of war; a passport. **2.** The act of conducting in safety.

safe-crack·er (sāf′krak′ər) *n.* One who breaks into safes to rob them. — **safe′crack′ing** *n.*

safe-de·pos·it box (sāf′di-poz′it) A box or other fireproof receptacle for valuables, generally in a bank.

safe·guard (sāf′gärd′) *n.* One who or that which guards or protects against accident or injury. — *v.t.* To defend; protect; guard.

safe·keep·ing (sāf′kē′ping) *n.* The act or state of keeping or being kept in safety; protection.

safe·ty (sāf′tē) *n. pl.* **·ties 1.** Freedom from danger or injury. **2.** A device or catch designed as a safeguard, as in a firearm. **3.** In football, the act or play of touching the ball to the ground behind the player's own goal line when the impetus that sent the ball over the goal line was given to it by one of his own side. Also **safe′ty-touch′down′** (-tuch′doun′). [< OF < Med.L < L *salvus* sound]

safety belt 1. A strap or strip of strong belting encircling the user and fastened to a fixed object, worn by linemen, window cleaners, etc., as a safeguard against falling. **2.** A strap fixed to the seat of an aircraft or vehicle, by which the occupant is secured against sudden shocks or turning movements: also called *seat belt.*

safety glass Two sheets of glass having a film of transparent, adhesive plastic tightly pressed between them: also called *shatterproof glass.*

safety lamp A miner's lamp having the flame surrounded by fine wire gauze that prevents the ignition of explosive gases: also called *davy.*

safety match A match that will ignite only when struck upon a chemically prepared surface.

safety pin A pin whose point springs into place within a protecting sheath.

safety razor A razor provided with a guard or guards for the blade to prevent accidental gashing of the skin.

safety valve 1. *Mech.* A valve in a steam boiler, etc., for automatically relieving excessive pressure. **2.** Any outlet for pent-up energy or emotion.

saf·fron (saf′rən) *n.* **1.** An autumn-flowering species of crocus. **2.** The dried orange-colored stigmas of this plant,

used for coloring confectionery, etc., and as a flavoring ı cookery. **3.** A deep yellow-orange: also **saffron yellow.** *adj.* Yellow-orange. [< OF < Med.L < Arabic *za'farān*

sag (sag) *v.* **sagged, sag·ging** *v.i.* **1.** To bend or sink down ward from weight or pressure, esp. in the middle. **2.** T hang unevenly. **3.** To lose firmness or determination weaken, as from exhaustion, age, etc. **4.** To decline, as i price or value. — *v.t.* **5.** To cause to sag. — *n.* **1.** A sa ging. **2.** A sagging or sunken place or part. [ME *sagge*

sa·ga (sä′gə) *n.* **1.** A medieval Scandinavian prose narr tive dealing with legendary or historical exploits, usu. of single hero or family. **2.** A long story, sometimes poeti often chronicling the history of a family. [< ON]

sa·ga·cious (sə-gā′shəs) *adj.* **1.** Characterized by discern ment, shrewdness, and wisdom. **2.** Ready and apt to appr hend. [< L *sagax*] — **sa·ga′cious·ly** *adv.* — **sa·ga′ciou ness** *n.*

sa·gac·i·ty (sə-gas′ə-tē) *n.* The quality of being sagaciou discernment and judgment; shrewdness.

sag·a·more (sag′ə-môr, -mōr) *n.* A chief among the Algo quian Indians of North America, usu. inferior to sache [< Algonquian (Penobscot) *sagamo* he prevails]

sage[1] (sāj) *n.* A venerable man of recognized wisdom, e perience, prudence, and foresight. — *adj.* **sag·er, sag·** **1.** Characterized by or proceeding from calm, far-seei wisdom and prudence. **2.** Profound; learned. — **Syn.** S WISE[1]. [< OF, ult. < LL *sapius* prudent, wise] — **sage′** *adv.* — **sage′ness** *n.*

sage[2] (sāj) *n.* **1.** A plant of the mint family, having a green leaves used for flavoring meats. **2.** The leaves of th plant. **3.** The sagebrush. [< F < L *salvus* safe]

sage·brush (sāj′brush′) *n.* An aromatic, bitter, typical perennial herb or small shrub, widely distributed on t alkali plains of the western U.S.

Sagebrush State Nickname of Nevada.

sage hen A large grouse of the western U.S.

sag·it·tal (saj′ə-təl) *adj.* **1.** Of, pertaining to, or resen bling an arrow or arrowhead. **2.** *Anat.* Of or pertaining the longitudinal plane dividing an animal into right and le halves. [< L *sagitta* arrow] — **sag′it·tal·ly** *adv.*

Sag·it·ta·ri·us (saj′ə-târ′ē·əs) *n.* A constellation, t Archer; also, the ninth sign of the zodiac. See ZODIAC. [< *sagitta* arrow]

sag·it·tate (saj′ə-tāt) *adj. Bot.* Shaped like an arrowhea as certain leaves. [< L *sagitta* arrow]

sa·go (sā′gō) *n. pl.* **·gos 1.** Any of several varieties of Ea Indian palm. **2.** The pith of this palm, used as a thickenin agent in puddings, etc. [< Malay *sāgū*]

sa·gua·ro (sə-gwä′rō, -wä′-) *n. pl.* **·ros** A large desert ca tus with an erect, columnar trunk, strong spines, and flowe ing tops. Also **sa·hua′ro** (-wä′-). [< Sp. < Piman]

Sa·hib (sä′ib) *n.* Master; sir: used in India and Pakistan f people of rank and, esp. formerly, for Europeans. Also **S heb.** [< Urdu < Arabic *sāhib* lord, companion]

said (sed) Past tense and past participle of SAY. — a *Law* Previously mentioned; aforesaid.

sail (sāl) *n. pl.* **sails;** *for def. 3, often* **sail 1.** *Naut.* A pie of canvas, or other strong material, attached to a vessel that it may be spread to the wind and aid in the vesse propulsion. **2.** Sails collectively. **3.** A sailing vessel craft. **4.** A trip or passage in any watercraft. **5.** Anythi resembling a sail in form or use, as the broad part of the a of a windmill. — **to make sail 1.** To unfurl a sail or sa **2.** To set out on a voyage. — **to set sail** To begin a voyag get under way. — **under sail** Sailing; with sails spread. *v.i.* **1.** To move across the surface of water by the action wind or mechanical power. **2.** To travel over water in a sh or boat. **3.** To begin a voyage. **4.** To manage a saili craft. **5.** To glide or float in the air. **6.** To move along i stately or dignified manner. **7.** *Informal* To pass rapidly. *Informal* To proceed boldly into action: with *in.* — *v.t.* To move or travel across the surface of (a body of water) in ship or boat. **10.** To navigate (a ship, etc.). — **to sail in 1.** To begin with energy. **2.** To attack violently. [C *segl*] — **sail′a·ble** *adj.*

sail·boat (sāl′bōt′) *n. U.S.* A small boat propelled by sail or sails.

sail·cloth (sāl′klôth′, -kloth′) *n.* A very strong, firm woven cotton canvas suitable for sails.

sail·er (sā′lər) *n.* A vessel that sails; a ship having a spe fied sailing power: a fast *sailer.*

sail·fish (sāl′fish′) *n. pl.* **·fish** or **·fish·es** A marine fi allied to the spearfish, having a large or conspicuous dors fin likened to a sail.

sail·or (sā′lər) *n.* **1.** A seaman; mariner. **2.** A sailor ha

sailor hat A low-crowned, flat-topped straw hat with brim, worn by both sexes: also called *sailor.*

saint (sānt) *n.* **1.** A holy or godly person. **2.** In certa churches, such a person who has died and been canonize **3.** Any one of the blessed in heaven. **4.** A very patient, u selfish person. — *v.t.* To canonize; venerate as a saint.

Holy; canonized. [< OF < L *sancire* to make sacred]
aint'hood, saint'ship n.
.t For entries not found under *Saint*, see under ST.
.t (sānt) n. A member of one of the religious bodies
wn as **Saints**: Latter-day *Saint*.

.t **Bernard** A working dog of great
and strength, characterized by a
sive head, and a thick, white, red, or
dled coat, used to rescue travelers by
hospice at Great St. Bernard Pass in
Swiss Alps.

SAINT BERNARD
(About 27 inches
high at shoulder)

.t·ed (sān'tid) adj. 1. Canonized. 2.
oly character; saintly.
.t·ly (sānt'lē) adj. ·li·er, ·li·est Like,
erned with, or suitable for a saint. —
·t'li·ness n.
.t **Patrick's Day** March 17, a day
itionally celebrated by the Irish in honor of their patron
t.
.t **Valentine's Day** February 14, the anniversary of
beheading of St. Valentine by the Romans, and also a
when valentines are exchanged.
(seth) *Archaic* Present indicative third person singu-
of SAY.
l (sāk) n. 1. Purpose of obtaining or accomplishing:
peak slowly for the *sake* of clarity. 2. Interest; account;
antage: for your own *sake*. [OE *sacu* lawsuit]
Syn. 2. Something done for the *sake* of a person, or on his
lf, is intended to promote his welfare. But *sake* suggests the
evolence of a parent or friend, while *behalf* suggests a some-
t less personal relationship, as that of an attorney or patron.
e² (sä'kē) n. A fermented liquor made in Japan from
Also **sa'ki**. [< Japanese]
sal) n. Salt. [< L]
am (sə·läm') n. An oriental salutation or obeisance
le with a low bow, the palm of the right hand being held
he forehead; also, a respectful or ceremonious verbal
ting. — v.t. & v.i. To greet with or make a salaam.
Arabic *salām* peace, a salutation]
·ble (sā'lə·bəl) adj. Such as can be sold; marketable:
spelled *saleable*. — **sal·a·bil'i·ty, sal'a·ble·ness** n.
·cious (sə·lā'shəs) adj. 1. Lustful; lewd. 2. Obscene: a
cious joke. [< L < *salire* to leap] — **sa·la'cious·ly** adv.
a·la'cious·ness, sa·lac'i·ty (-las'ə·tē) n.
d (sal'əd) n. Green herbs or vegetables, usu. uncooked
served with a dressing, sometimes mixed with chopped
meat, fish, etc.; also, a similar dish made with fruit.
OF < Provençal < L *sal* salt]
·man·der (sal'ə·man'dər) n. 1. Any of a variety of
ed, lizardlike amphibians having a smooth, moist skin
two pairs of limbs. 2. A mythical lizard or other crea-
e fabled to live in fire. 3. Any person or thing that can
d great heat. 4. A large poker or other implement used
und or in fire, or when red-hot. [< OF < L *salamandra*
ēk.] — **sal'a·man'drine** (-drin) adj.
·mi (sə·lä'mē) n. A salted, spiced sausage, originally
ian. [< Ital., < L *sal* salt]
ammoniac *Chem.* A white, crystalline, soluble comnd, NH₄Cl, used in medicine and industry. [< L *sal*
moniacum, lit. salt of Ammon]
·ried (sal'ər·ēd, sal'rēd) adj. 1. In receipt of a salary.
Yielding a salary.
·ry (sal'ər·ē, sal'rē) n. pl. ·ries A periodic, fixed pay-
nt for services, esp. for official or professional services as
inguished from manual or menial labor. — v.t. ·ried,
ing To pay or allot a salary to. [< AF < L *salarium*
ney paid Roman soldiers for their salt]
(sāl) n. 1. The act of selling; the exchange or transfer
roperty of any kind for money or its equivalent. 2. An
tion. 3. The selling of something at bargain prices. 4.
portunity of selling; market. — **for sale** (or **on sale**)
ered or ready for sale. [OE *sala* < ON]
·a·ble (sā'lə·bəl) See SALABLE.
e·ra·tus (sal'ə·rā'təs) n. Sodium bicarbonate, for use in
kery; baking soda. [< NL *sal aëratus* aerated salt]
·s·girl (sālz'gûrl') n. U.S. A woman or girl hired to sell
rchandise, especially in a store.
·s·la·dy (sālz'lā'dē) n. pl. ·dies *Informal* A woman or
hired to sell merchandise, esp. in a store.
·s·man (sālz'mən) n. pl. ·men (-mən) A man hired to
goods, stock, etc., in a store or by canvassing.
·s·man·ship (sālz'mən·ship) n. 1. The work or profes-
n of a salesman. 2. Ability or skill in selling.
·s·peo·ple (sālz'pē'pəl) n.pl. Salespersons.
·s·per·son (sālz'pûr'sən) n. A person hired to sell mer-
andise, esp. in a store.
·s resistance The ability to resist any attempts to in-
e one to buy certain goods or services.

sales·room (sālz'rōōm', -rŏŏm') n. A room where merchandise is displayed for sale.
sales tax A tax on money received from sales of goods.
sales·wom·an (sālz'wŏŏm'ən) n. pl. ·wom·en (-wim'in) A
woman or girl hired to sell merchandise, esp. in a store.
sal·ic (sal'ik) adj. *Geol.* Belonging to a group of igneous
rocks composed chiefly of silica and alumina, as the feld-
spars, quartz, etc. [< S(ILICA) + AL(UMINUM) + -IC]
sal·i·cyl·ate (sal'ə·sil'āt, sə·lis'ə·lāt) n. *Chem.* A salt or
ester of salicylic acid.
sal·i·cyl·ic acid (sal'ə·sil'ik) *Chem.* A white crystalline
compound, C₇H₆O₃, occurring in many plants and also made
synthetically, one acetyl form of which is widely known as
aspirin. [< SALIC(IN) + -YL + -IC]
sa·li·ent (sā'lē·ənt) adj. 1. Standing out prominently;
striking; conspicuous. 2. Protruding; projecting. 3. Leaping; springing. — n. The part of a fortification, etc., that
most protrudes towards the enemy. [< L < *salire* to leap]
— **sa'li·ence** n. — **sa'li·ent·ly** adv. — **sa'li·ent·ness** n.
sa·line (sā'līn) adj. 1. Of, constituting, or characteristic of
salt. 2. Containing salt; salty. — n. 1. A metallic salt.
2. A salt solution used in the investigation of biological and
physiological processes, and also in medicine. [< F < LL
< L *sal, salis* salt] — **sa·lin'i·ty** (sə·lin'ə·tē) n.
Salisbury steak Hamburger (def. 2).
sa·li·va (sə·lī'və) n. *Physiol.* The slightly alkaline fluid secreted by the glands of the mouth, considered a promoter of
digestion. [< L] — **sal·i·var·y** (sal'ə·ver'ē) adj.
sal·i·vate (sal'ə·vāt) v. ·vat·ed, ·vat·ing v.i. To secrete saliva. — v.t. To produce salivation in. [< L < *saliva* saliva]
— **sal'i·va'tion** n.
sal·low (sal'ō) adj. Of an unhealthy yellowish color: said
chiefly of the human skin. [OE *salu*] — **sal'low·ish** adj.
— **sal'low·** y adv. — **sal'low·ness** n.
sal·ly (sal'ē) v.i. ·lied, ·ly·ing 1. To rush out suddenly. 2.
To set out energetically. 3. To go out, as from a room or
building. — n. pl. ·lies 1. A rushing forth, as of troops
against besiegers; sortie. 2. Any sudden rushing forth. 3.
A going forth, as on a walk. 4. A bantering remark or witti-
cism. [< OF < L *salire* to leap]
sal·ma·gun·di (sal'mə·gun'dē) n. 1. A saladlike dish of
chopped meat, anchovies, eggs, onions, oil, etc. 2. Any
medley or mixture. Also **sal'ma·gun'dy**. [< F *salmigondis*]
salm·on (sam'ən) n. 1. Any of various food fishes inhabiting the North Atlantic coastal waters and ascending to adjacent rivers to spawn, having a brownish color above, silvery
sides, black spots, and a delicate pink flesh. 2. Any of various other salmonoid fishes. 3. A reddish or pinkish orange
color: also **salmon pink**. — adj. Having a salmon color.
[< OF < L *salmo, -onis*, prob. akin to *salire* to leap] — **sal-
mo·noid** (sal'mə·noid) adj. & n.
salmon trout 1. The European brown trout. 2. The lake
trout. 3. The steelhead.
Sa·lo·me (sə·lō'mē) The daughter of Herodias, who asked
Herod for the head of John the Baptist in return for her
dancing. *Matt.* xiv 8.
sa·lon (sə·lon', *Fr.* sȧ·lôn') n. 1. A room in which guests are
received; a drawing room. 2. The periodic gathering of
noted persons, under the auspices of some distinguished figure. 3. A hall or gallery used for exhibiting works of art.
4. An establishment devoted to some specific purpose: a
beauty *salon*. [< F < Ital. < *sala* hall < Gmc.]
sa·loon (sə·lōōn') n. 1. A place where alcoholic drinks are
sold; a bar. 2. A large apartment or room for assemblies,
public entertainment, exhibitions, etc. 3. The main cabin
of a passenger ship. [< F *salon* salon]
sa·loon·keep·er (sə·lōōn'kē'pər) n. One who owns or manages a saloon (def. 1).
sal·si·fy (sal'sə·fē, -fī) n. pl. ·fies An Old World plant with
a white, edible root and an oysterlike flavor: also called *oyster plant*. [< F < Ital. *sassefrica*]
sal soda Sodium carbonate.
salt (sôlt) n. 1. Sodium chloride, NaCl, a compound found
in sea water and as a mineral, used as a seasoning and as a
preservative. ◆ Collateral adjective: *saline*. 2. *Chem.* Any
compound consisting of the cation of a base and the anion of
an acid, combined in proportions that give a balance of electropositive and electronegative charges. 3. pl. A salt used as
a laxative or cathartic; also, smelling salts. 4. Piquant humor; dry wit; repartee. 5. That which preserves or purifies.
6. *Informal* A sailor: an old *salt*. 7. A saltcellar. — **to take
with a grain of salt** To have doubts about. — adj. 1. Flavored with salt; briny. 2. Cured or preserved with salt. 3.
Containing, or growing or living in or near, salt water. —
v.t. 1. To season with salt. 2. To preserve or cure with salt.
3. To furnish with salt: to *salt* cattle. 4. To add zest or
piquancy to. 5. To add something to so as to increase the
value fraudulently: to *salt* a mine with gold. — **to salt away**

1. To pack in salt for preserving. **2.** *Informal* To store up; save. [OE *sealt*] — **salt′ness** *n.*

salt·cel·lar (sôlt′sel′ər) *n.* A small receptacle for salt; a saltshaker. [ME < *salt* + F *salière* saltcellar]

salt·ed (sôl′tĭd) *adj.* **1.** Treated with salt; preserved. **2.** *Informal* Experienced or expert in some occupation.

sal·tine (sôl·tēn′) *n.* A crisp, salty cracker.

salt lick A place to which animals go to lick salt from superficial deposits; a salt spring or dried salt pond.

salt·pe·ter (sôlt′pē′tər) *n.* Potassium nitrate. — **Chile saltpeter** Mineral sodium nitrate, found chiefly in Chile. [< OF < Med.L < L *sal* salt + *petra* a rock < Gk.]

salt·shak·er (sôlt′shā′kər) *n.* A container with small holes for sprinkling table salt.

salt·wa·ter (sôlt′wô′tər, -wot′ər) *adj.* Of, composed of, or living in salty water.

salt·works (sôlt′wûrks′) *n.* *pl.* **·works** An establishment where salt is made on a commercial scale.

salt·wort (sôlt′wûrt′) *n.* **1.** Any of various maritime plants of the goosefoot family. **2.** Any of various glassworts.

salt·y (sôl′tē) *adj.* **salt·i·er, salt·i·est** **1.** Of, containing, or tasting like salt. **2.** Reminiscent of the sea; smelling of the sea. **3.** Piquant; sharp; pungent, as literature or speech. — **salt′i·ly** *adv.* — **salt′i·ness** *n.*

sa·lu·bri·ous (sə·lōō′brē·əs) *adj.* Conducive to health; healthful; wholesome. [< L < *salus* health] — **sa·lu′bri·ous·ly** *adv.* — **sa·lu′bri·ous·ness, sal·u′bri·ty** *n.*

sal·u·tar·y (sal′yə·ter′ē) *adj.* **1.** Calculated to bring about a sound condition by correcting evil or promoting good; beneficial. **2.** Salubrious. [< F < L < *salus, salutis* health] — **sal′u·tar′i·ly** *adv.* — **sal′u·tar′i·ness** *n.*

sal·u·ta·tion (sal′yə·tā′shən, -yōō-) *n.* **1.** The act of saluting. **2.** Any form of greeting. **3.** The opening words of a letter, as *Dear Sir.* [< MF < L < *salus, salutis* health]

sa·lu·ta·to·ri·an (sə·lōō′tə·tôr′ē·ən, -tō′rē-) *n.* *U.S.* In schools, the graduating student, usu. receiving second highest honors, who delivers the salutatory. [< SALUTATORY]

sa·lu·ta·to·ry (sə·lōō′tə·tôr′ē, -tō′rē) *adj.* *pl.* **·ries** An opening oration, as at a school commencement. — *adj.* Of or consisting in greeting; esp., relating to a salutatory address. [< L < *salutare.* See SALUTE.]

sa·lute (sə·lōōt′) *n.* **1.** A greeting by display of military or other official honors, as by presenting arms, firing cannon, etc. **2.** The act of or attitude assumed in giving a military salute. **3.** A gesture of greeting, compliment, etc. — *v.* **·lut·ed, ·lut·ing** *v.t.* **1.** To greet with a sign of welcome, respect, etc. **2.** To honor in some prescribed way, as by raising the hand to the cap. — *v.i.* **3.** To make a salute. [< F < L *salus, salutis* health] — **sa·lut′er** *n.*

sal·va·ble (sal′və·bəl) *adj.* Capable of being saved or salvaged. [< LL < L *salvus* safe] — **sal′va·bil′i·ty** *n.*

sal·vage (sal′vij) *v.t.* **·vaged, ·vag·ing** To save, as a ship or its cargo, from wreck, capture, etc. — *n.* **1.** The saving of a ship, cargo, etc., from loss. **2.** Any act of saving property. **3.** Compensation to persons who save a vessel, her cargo, or the lives of those belonging to her. **4.** That which is saved from a wrecked or abandoned vessel or from a fire. **5.** Anything saved from destruction. [< MF < Med.L < L *salvus* safe] — **sal′vage·a·ble** *adj.* — **sal′vag·er** *n.*

sal·va·tion (sal·vā′shən) *n.* **1.** The process or state of being saved. **2.** *Theol.* Deliverance from sin and penalty, realized in a future state. **3.** Any means of deliverance from danger, evil, or ruin. [< OF < LL < L *salvus* safe]

Salvation Army A religious and charitable organization on semimilitary lines, founded by William Booth in 1865.

salve¹ (sav, säv) *n.* **1.** A thick, adhesive ointment for local ailments. **2.** Anything that heals, soothes, or mollifies. **3.** Praise or flattery. — *v.t.* **salved, salv·ing** **1.** To dress with ointment. **2.** To soothe; appease. [OE *sealf*]

salve² (salv) *v.t.* **salved, salv·ing** To save from loss; salvage. [< Med.L *salvare*]

sal·ve³ (sal′vē) *interj.* Hail. [< L < *salvere* to be well]

sal·ver (sal′vər) *n.* A tray, as of silver. [< OF < Sp. < *salvar* to taste]

sal·vi·a (sal′vē·ə) *n.* Any of a genus of ornamental plants of the mint family, as the sage. [< L. See SAGE².]

sal·vo (sal′vō) *n.* *pl.* **·vos** or **·voes** **1.** A simultaneous discharge of artillery, or of two or more bombs. **2.** A salute given by firing all the guns. **3.** Any salute or simultaneous outburst: a *salvo* of applause. [< Ital. *salva* salute]

sal vo·lat·i·le (sal vō·lat′ə·lē) Ammonium carbonate; also, an aromatic solution of ammonium carbonate, used as smelling salts. [< NL, volatile salt < L]

sam·a·ra (sam′ər·ə, sə·mâr′ə) *n.* *Bot.* A one-seeded fruit, as of the elm, ash, or maple, provided with a membrane or wing. [< L, elm seed]

Sa·mar·i·a (sə·mâr′ē·ə) In the Bible, a city of Palestine, capital of the northern kingdom of Israel, or, later, a restricted portion of central Palestine west of the Jordan occupied by the Samaritans.

Sa·mar·i·tan (sə·mar′ə·tən) *n.* **1.** One of the people of Sa-

maria. II *Kings* xvii. **2.** Good Samaritan (which see). *adj.* Of or pertaining to Samaria.

sa·mar·i·um (sə·mâr′ē·əm) *n.* A hard, brittle, yellow gray, metallic element (symbol Sm) of the lanthanide se See ELEMENT. [< NL < *samarskite*, an orthorhom vitreous, black mineral]

sam·ba (sam′bə, säm′bä) *n.* **1.** A popular dance of Br ian origin. **2.** Music for this dance, in duple meter. — To dance the samba. [< Pg. < native African name]

Sam Browne belt (sam′ broun′) A military belt wi shoulder strap running diagonally across the chest. [a Sir *Samuel J. Browne*, 1824–1901, British general]

same (sām) *adj.* **1.** Having individual or specific iden or quality; identical; equal: with *the.* **2.** Similar in kin quality. **3.** Similar in quantity or measure; equivalent. Aforesaid; identical: said of a person or thing just mentio — **all the same** **1.** Nevertheless; yet. **2.** Equally acc able or unacceptable. — **just the same** **1.** Nevertheless; **2.** Unchanged. — *pron.* The identical person, thing, — *adv.* In like manner; equally: with *the.* [< ON sar

same·ness (sām′nis) *n.* **1.** Lack of change or variety; notony. **2.** Close similarity; likeness. **3.** Identity; uni

Sam Hill (sam′ hil′) *U.S. Slang* Hell: a euphemism.

sam·i·sen (sam′i·sen) *n.* A Japanese guitarlike instrum with three strings, played with a plectrum. [< Japanese < Chinese *san hsien* three strings]

SAMISEN

sa·mite (sā′mīt, sam′ it) *n.* A rich medieval fabric of silk, often interwoven gold or silver. [< OF < Med.L < Gk. *hex* six + r thread]

Sa·mo·an (sə·mō′ən) *adj.* Of or pertaining to Samoa, t aboriginal Polynesian inhabitants, or to their language. *n.* **1.** A native of the Samoan islands. **2.** The Polyne language of the Samoans.

sam·o·var (sam′ə·vär, sam′ə·vär′) *n.* A metal urn for b ing water, as for making tea. [< Russian, lit., self-bo

Sam·o·yed (sam′ə·yed′) *n.* **1.** One of a Mongoloid pe inhabiting the Arctic coasts of Siberia. **2.** A large dog ing a thick white coat of long hair. — *adj.* Of the Samoy or their language; Samoyedic. Also **Sam′o·yede′** (-yed′). Russian, lit., self-eater]

Sam·o·yed·ic (sam′ə·yed′ik) *adj.* Of or pertaining to Samoyeds or their language. — *n.* A subfamily of the U ic languages, including the language of the Samoyeds.

samp (samp) *n.* Coarse Indian corn; also, a porridge m of it. [< Algonquian *nasaump* softened with water]

sam·pan (sam′pan) *n.* A small flat-bottomed boat or used along rivers and coasts of China and Japan. Chinese *san* three + *pan* board, plank]

sam·ple (sam′pəl) *n.* A portion, part, or piece take shown as a representative of the whole. — *v.t.* **·pled, ·** To test or examine by means of a sample. [See EXAMP

sam·pler¹ (sam′plər) *n.* One who tests by sampling.

sam·pler² (sam′plər) *n.* A piece of needlework, origi designed to show a beginner's skill. [See EXAMPLE.]

sam·pling (sam′pling) *n.* **1.** A small part of something number of items from a group selected for examinatio analysis in order to estimate the quality or nature of whole. **2.** The act or process of making such a selecti

Sam·son (sam′sən) A Hebrew judge of great strength trayed to the Philistines by Delilah. *Judges* xii–xvi.

Sam·u·el (sam′yōō·əl) A Hebrew judge and prophet. — Either of two historical books, I and II Samuel, of the Testament.

sam·u·rai (sam′ŏŏ·rī) *n.* *pl.* **·rai** Under the Japanese dal system, a member of the soldier class of the lower bility; also, the class itself. [< Japanese]

san·a·tive (san′ə·tiv) *adj.* Healing; sanatory; health-gi [< OF < Med.L < L *sanare* to heal]

san·a·to·ri·um (san′ə·tôr′ē·əm, -tō′rē-) *n.* *pl.* **·ri·um ·ri·a** (-tôr′ē·ə, -tō′rē·ə) **1.** An institution for the treat and care of invalids and convalescents. **2.** A health re Also called *sanitarium.* [< NL < LL < L *sanare* to h

sanc·ti·fied (sangk′tə·fīd) *adj.* **1.** Made holy; freed f sin; consecrated. **2.** Sanctimonious; self-righteous.

sanc·ti·fy (sangk′tə·fī) *v.t.* **·fied, ·fy·ing** **1.** To set apa holy or for holy purposes; consecrate. **2.** To purify or r holy. **3.** To render sacred or inviolable, as a vow. [< LL < L *sanctus* holy + *facere* to make] — **sanc′ti tion** *n.* — **sanc′ti·fi′er** *n.*

sanc·ti·mo·ni·ous (sangk′tə·mō′nē·əs) *adj.* Makin ostentatious display or pretense of sanctity. — **sanc′ti ni·ous·ly** *adv.* — **sanc′ti·mo′ni·ous·ness** *n.*

sanc·ti·mo·ny (sangk′tə·mō′nē) *n.* Assumed or out sanctity; a show of holiness or devoutness. [< OF *sanctimonia* holiness]

sanc·tion (sangk′shən) *v.t.* **1.** To approve authoritati confirm; ratify. **2.** To countenance; allow. — *n.* **1.**

d authoritative confirmation or ratification. **2.** A formal cree. **3.** A provision for securing conformity to law, as by e enactment of rewards or penalties or both. **4.** *Usu. pl.* international law, coercive measures adopted to force a tion that is violating international law to desist. **5.** In hics, that which makes virtue morally obligatory. [< L *sancire* to render sacred, inviolable]

ac·ti·ty (sangk'tə·tē) *n. pl.* **·ties 1.** The state of being nctified; holiness. **2.** Sacredness; solemnity.

ac·tu·ar·y (sangk'chōō·er'ē) *n. pl.* **·ar·ies 1.** A holy or cred place. **2.** The most sacred part of a place in a sacred ucture. **3.** A place of refuge; asylum; also, immunity. < OF < LL < L *sanctus* holy]

ac·tum (sangk'təm) *n. pl.* **·tums** or **·ta** (-tə) **1.** A sacred ace. **2.** A private room where one is not to be disturbed. : L, neut. of *sanctus* holy]

ac·tum sanc·to·rum (sangk'təm sangk·tôr'əm, -tō'rəm) The holy of holies. **2.** A place of great privacy: often ed humorously.

ac·tus (sangk'təs) *n. Eccl.* **1.** An ascription of praise to od, occurring at the end of the Preface in many eucharistic urgies. **2.** A musical setting for this. [< L *sanctus* holy]

d (sand) *n.* **1.** A hard, granular rock material finer than avel and coarser than dust. **2.** *pl.* Stretches of sandy ach, desert, etc. **3.** *pl.* Sandy grains in an hourglass. **4.** Moments of time or life. **5.** A reddish yellow color. — **1.** To sprinkle or cover with sand. **2.** To smooth or rade with sand or sandpaper. **3.** To mix sand with. **4.** fill with sand. [OE] — **sand'er** *n.*

·dal (san'dəl) *n.* **1.** A foot covering, consisting usu. of a e only, held to the foot by thongs. **2.** A light slipper. **3.** overshoe of rubber, cut very low. [< OF < Gk. *sanda-*] — **san'daled, san'dalled** *adj.*

·dal·wood (san'dəl·wŏŏd') *n.* **1.** The fine-grained, nse, fragrant wood of any of several East Indian trees. **2.** e similar wood of other trees, whose dark red wood is used a dyestuff. [< Med.L < Skt. *candana*]

d·bag (sand'bag') *n.* **1.** A bag filled with sand, used for lding fortifications, for ballast, etc. **2.** A long, narrow g filled with sand and used as a club or weapon. — *v.t.* **gged, ·bag·ging 1.** To fill or surround with sandbags. To strike with a sandbag. — **sand'bag'ger** *n.*

d·bar (sand'bär') *n.* A ridge of silt or sand in rivers, ng beaches, etc., formed by the action of currents or tides.

d·blast (sand'blast', -bläst') *n.* **1.** A fine jet of sand, pelled under pressure and used to clean, grind, or deco- e hard surfaces. **2.** The apparatus used in applying this st. — *v.t.* To clean or engrave by means of a sandblast.

d·box (sand'boks') *n.* **1.** A box on a locomotive or eetcar filled with sand to be poured on the rail treads to event slipping. **2.** A box of sand for children to play in.

d·cast (sand'kast', -käst') *v.t.* **·cast, ·cast·ing** To make casting) by pouring metal into a mold of sand.

d crack *Vet.* A crack running down from the coronet of orse's hoof and apt to cause lameness if neglected.

d flea Any of various fleas that live in sand, as the goe.

d·hog (sand'hôg', -hog') *n.* One who works under air essure, as in caisson sinking, tunnel building, etc.

d·lot (sand'lot') *adj.* Of or in a vacant lot in or near an an area: *sand-lot* baseball.

d·man (sand'man') *n.* In nursery lore, a person sup- ed to make children sleepy by casting sand in their eyes.

d painting A form of painting by the American Indians which fine colored sand is trickled on a ground base.

d·pa·per (sand'pā'pər) *n.* Heavy paper coated with d for smoothing or polishing. — *v.t.* To rub or polish h sandpaper.

d·pi·per (sand'pī'pər) *n.* Any of certain small wading ds related to the snipes and frequenting seashores. Also d'peep' (-pēp').

d·stone (sand'stōn') *n.* A rock consisting chiefly of artz sand cemented with silica, feldspar, lime, or clay.

d·storm (sand'stôrm') *n.* A high wind by which sand or st is carried along.

d·wich (sand'wich, san'-) *n.* **1.** Two thin slices of ad, having between them meat, cheese, etc. **2.** Any mbination of alternating dissimilar things pressed to- her. — *v.t.* **1.** To place between two layers or objects. To insert between dissimilar things. [after John ontagu, fourth Earl of *Sandwich*, 1718–92, who originated n order to eat without leaving the gaming table]

dwich man *n. pl.* **men** *Informal* A man carrying ad- rtising boards (**sandwich boards**) slung in front and be- d.

d·y (san'dē) *adj.* **sand·i·er, sand·i·est 1.** Consisting of characterized by sand; containing, covered with, or full of d. **2.** Yellowish red: a *sandy* beard. — **sand'i·ness** *n.*

sane (sān) *adj.* **1.** Mentally sound; not deranged. **2.** Pro- ceeding from a sound mind. [< L *sanus* whole, healthy] — **sane'ly** *adv.* — **sane'ness** *n.*

San·for·ize (san'fə·rīz) *v.t.* **·ized, ·iz·ing** To treat (cloth) so as to prevent shrinkage: a trade name. Also **san'for·ize.** [after Sanford L. Cluett, 1874–1968, U.S. inventor]

sang (sang) Past tense of SING.

sang-froid (säɴ·frwä') *n.* Calmness amid trying circum- stances; coolness; composure. [< F, lit., cold blood]

san·gri·a (säng·grē'ə) *n.* Red wine mixed with fruit and/or fruit juices. [< Sp. *sangría*, lit., bleeding]

sangui- combining form Blood. [< L *sanguis* blood]

san·gui·nar·y (sang'gwə·ner'ē) *adj.* **1.** Attended with bloodshed. **2.** Bloodthirsty. **3.** Consisting of blood. — **san'gui·nar'i·ly** *adv.* — **san'gui·nar'i·ness** *n.*

san·guine (sang'gwin) *adj.* **1.** Of cheerful, hopeful disposi- tion. **2.** Ruddy; robust. **3.** Of, like, or full of blood. **4.** *Obs.* Bloodthirsty; sanguinary. [< OF < L *sanguis, -inis* blood] — **san'guine·ly** *adv.* — **san'guine·ness** *n.*

san·i·tar·i·um (san'ə·târ'ē·əm) *n. pl.* **·tar·i·ums** or **·tar·i·a** (-târ'ē·ə) A sanatorium. [< NL < L *sanitas* health]

san·i·tar·y (san'ə·ter'ē) *adj.* **1.** Relating to the preserva- tion of health. **2.** Favorable to health; hygienic. [< F < L *sanitas* health] — **san'i·tar'i·ly** *adv.*

sanitary napkin An absorbent pad worn by women during menstruation.

san·i·ta·tion (san'ə·tā'shən) *n.* The use and practical ap- plication of sanitary measures; the removal or neutralization of elements injurious to health.

san·i·ta·tion·man (san'i·tā'shən·man') *n. pl.* **·men** (-män) A person, esp. a municipal employee, whose work is the collection of refuse and trash.

san·i·tize (san'ə·tīz) *v.t.* **·tized, ·tiz·ing 1.** To make san- itary. **2.** To make acceptable or unobjectionable.

san·i·ty (san'ə·tē) *n. pl.* **·ties 1.** The state of being sane; soundness of mind. **2.** Sane moderation or reasonableness.

San Jo·sé scale (san' hō·zā') A scale insect destructive to various fruit trees.

sank (sangk) Past tense of SINK.

sans (sanz, *Fr.* säɴ) *prep.* Without. [< OF *sanz*]

sans-cu·lotte (sanz'kyōō·lot', *Fr.* säɴ·kü·lôt') *n.* **1.** A rev- olutionary: originally a term of contempt applied by the aris- tocrats to the French revolutionaries in 1789. **2.** Any rev- olutionary or radical. [< F, lit., without knee breeches] — **sans-cu·lot'tic** *adj.* — **sans'-cu·lot'tism** *n.*

San·sei (sän·sā) *n. pl.* **·sei** or **·seis** An American citizen of Japanese descent whose grandparents settled in the U.S. [< Japanese, third generation]

san·se·vi·e·ri·a (san'sə·vi·ir'ē·ə) *n.* Any of several peren- nial herbs of the lily family, cultivated as an ornamental plant. [after the Prince of *Sanseviero*, 1710–71]

San·skrit (san'skrit) *n.* The ancient and classical language of the Hindus of India, belonging to the Indic branch of the Indo-Iranian subfamily of Indo-European languages. Also **San'scrit.** [< Skt. *samskrita* artificial, highly cultivated]

San·skrit·ic (san·skrit'ik) *adj.* **1.** Of, pertaining to, or writ- ten in Sanskrit. **2.** Designating a group of some 30 to 40 an- cient and modern languages and dialects of India.

sans ser·if (sanz ser'if) *Printing* A type face without serifs: also called *gothic.*

San·ta Claus (san'tə klôz') In nursery lore, a fat, jolly old man who brings presents at Christmas time. [< Du. *Sant Nikolaas* Saint Nicholas]

San·ta Ma·ri·a (san'tə mə·rē'ə) One of the three ships of Columbus on his maiden voyage to America.

sap[1] (sap) *n.* **1.** The juices of plants, that contain and trans- port the materials necessary to growth. **2.** Any vital fluid; vitality. **3.** *Slang* A foolish or gullible person. [OE *sæp*]

sap[2] (sap) *v.* **sapped, sap·ping** *v.t.* **1.** To weaken or destroy gradually and insidiously; enervate; exhaust. **2.** To ap- proach or undermine (an enemy fortification) by digging a sap. — *v.i.* **3.** To dig a sap or saps. — *n.* A deep, narrow trench or tunnel dug so as to approach or undermine a forti- fication. [< MF < Ital. *zappa* spade, goat]

sap·head (sap'hed') *n. Slang* A simpleton; sap. — **sap'- head'ed** *adj.*

sa·pi·ent (sā'pē·ənt) *adj.* Wise; sagacious: often used iron- ically. [< OF < L < *sapere* to have good taste] — **sa'pi- ence, sa'pi·en·cy** *n.* — **sa'pi·ent·ly** *adv.*

sap·less (sap'lis) *adj.* **1.** Destitute of sap; withered. **2.** Wanting vitality, spirit, or vivacity; insipid; dull.

sap·ling (sap'ling) *n.* **1.** A young tree. **2.** A youth. [Dim. of SAP[1]]

sap·o·dil·la (sap'ə·dil'ə) *n.* **1.** A large evergreen tree of the West Indies and tropical America. **2.** Its edible, apple- shaped fruit, a source of chicle: also **sapodilla plum.** Also **sa·po·ta** (sə·pō'tə), **sap'a·dil'lo, sap'o·dil'lo.** [< Sp. < Na- huatl *tzapotl*]

sap·o·na·ceous (sap/ə·nā/shəs) *adj.* Soapy.

sa·pon·i·fy (sə·pon/ə·fī) *v.t.* **·fied, ·fy·ing** *Chem.* To convert (a fat or oil) into soap by the action of an alkali. [< F < L *sapo, saponis* soap + *facere* to make] — **sa·pon/i·fi/a·ble** *adj.* — **sa·pon·i·fi·ca·tion** (sə·pon/ə·fə·kā/shən) *n.* — **sa·pon/i·fi/er** *n.*

sap·per (sap/ər) *n.* **1.** One who or that which saps. **2.** A soldier employed in making a sap². [< SAP² + -ER]

Sap·phic (saf/ik) *adj.* **1.** Pertaining to or in the manner of Sappho. **2.** In prosody, denoting a line of trochaic pentameter with a dactyl in the third foot, much used by Sappho. [after *Sappho*]

sap·phire (saf/īr) *n.* **1.** Any of the hard, translucent, colored varieties of corundum other than the red variety, that when cut are used as gems; esp., a deep blue corundum. **2.** Deep pure blue. [< OF < L < Gk. *sappheiros*]

sap·py (sap/ē) *adj.* **·pi·er, ·pi·est 1.** Full of sap; juicy. **2.** *Slang* Immature; silly. — **sap/pi·ly** *adv.* — **sap/pi·ness** *n.*

sapro- *combining form* **1.** Decomposition or putrefaction. **2.** Saprophytic. [< Gk. *sapros* rotten]

sap·ro·phyte (sap/rə·fīt) *n.* A vegetable organism that lives on dead or decaying organic matter, as certain funguses, various bacteria, etc. — **sap/ro·phyt/ic** (-fit/ik) *adj.*

sap·suck·er (sap/suk/ər) *n.* Any of various small black and white woodpeckers that damage orchard trees by exposing and drinking the sap.

sap·wood (sap/wŏŏd/) *n. Bot.* The new wood next to the bark of an exogenous tree.

sar·a·band (sar/ə·band) *n.* **1.** A slow, stately dance of the 17th and 18th centuries. **2.** Music for this dance, in triple meter. Also **sar/a·bande.** [< F < Sp. < Persian *sarband* a kind of dance and song]

Sar·a·cen (sar/ə·sən) *n.* **1.** Originally, a nomad Arab of the Syrian-Arabian desert. **2.** A Moslem, esp. during the Crusades. **3.** Any Arab. [< LL < LGk. *Sarakēnos*] — **Sar/a·cen/ic** (-sen/ik) or **·i·cal** *adj.*

Sar·ah (sâr/ə) The wife of Abraham. *Gen.* xvii 15.

sa·ran (sə·ran/) *n.* Any of a class of synthetic fibers and textile materials obtained by the polymerization of vinyl chloride. [Coined by Dow Chemical Co.]

sa·ra·pe (sə·räp/ē) See SERAPE.

Saratoga trunk A very large traveling trunk used formerly by ladies. [after *Saratoga* Springs]

sar·casm (sär/kaz·əm) *n.* **1.** An ironical or scornful utterance; contemptuous and taunting language. **2.** The use of biting gibes or cutting rebukes. [< LL < Gk. *sarkazein* to tear flesh, sneer < *sarx, sarkos* flesh]
— **Syn. 1.** *Sarcasm* may describe a man's weakness in subtly pejorative terms, or may show the vanity of his pretensions, or his absurdity. *Irony* is more limited, and is sometimes regarded as one of the methods of *sarcasm*; it consists of the assertion of the opposite of what is really meant.

sar·cas·tic (sär·kas/tik) *adj.* **1.** Characterized by or of the nature of sarcasm; taunting. **2.** Given to the use of sarcasm. Also **sar·cas/ti·cal.** — **sar·cas/ti·cal·ly** *adv.*

sarce·net (särs/nit) See SARSENET.

sarco- *combining form* Flesh; of or related to flesh. Also, before vowels, **sarc-.** [< Gk. *sarx, sarkos* flesh]

sar·co·carp (sär/kō·kärp) *n. Bot.* The succulent part of a stone fruit, as the fleshy edible part of a plum or peach.

sar·co·ma (sär·kō/mə) *n. pl.* **·ma·ta** (-mə·tə) *Pathol.* A tumor, often malignant, made up of cells resembling those of embryonic connective tissue. [< Gk. < *sarx, sarkos* flesh] — **sar·co/ma·toid, sar·co/ma·tous** (-kō/mə·təs, -kom/ə-) *adj.*

sar·coph·a·gus (sär·kof/ə·gəs) *n. pl.* **·gi** (-jī) **1.** A stone coffin or tomb. **2.** A large ornamental coffin of marble or stone placed in a crypt or exposed to view. **3.** A kind of limestone, used by the Greeks for coffins. [< L < Gk. < *sarx, sarkos* flesh + *phagein* to eat]

sar·cous (sär/kəs) *adj.* Of, pertaining to, or composed of flesh or muscle. [< Gk. *sarx, sarkos* flesh]

sard (särd) *n.* The deep brownish red variety of chalcedony, used as a gem. [< OF < L < Gk. *Sardeis* Sardis]

sar·dine (sär·dēn/) *n.* **1.** A small, herringlike fish commonly preserved in oil as a food delicacy, esp. the pilchard. **2.** Any of various related fishes similarly preserved. [< OF < L < Gk. *sardēnē, ?* < *Sardo* Sardinia]

Sar·dis (sär/dis) An ancient city of Asia Minor, capital of Lydia; destroyed by Tamerlane. Also **Sar/des.**

sar·don·ic (sär·don/ik) *adj.* Scornful or derisive; mocking; cynical. [< F < L < Gk. *sardanios* bitter, scornful] — **sar·don/i·cal·ly** *adv.* — **sar·don/i·cism** *n.*

sar·do·nyx (sär/də·niks) *n.* A variety of chalcedony in bands varying from light to reddish brown, with other colors. [< L < Gk., appar. < *sardios* sard + *onyx* onyx]

sar·gas·so (sär·gas/ō) *n.* An olive-brown seaweed having small air bladders on its stalks, native in tropical American waters: also called *gulfweed.* Also **sar·gas/sum.** [< Pg. < *sarga, ?* < L *salicastrum*]

sa·ri (sä/rē) *n. pl.* **·ris** A long piece of cotton or silk cloth, constituting the principal garment of Hindu women, worn round the waist, one end falling to the feet, and the oth[er] crossed over the bosom and shoulder, and sometimes ov[er] the head. Also **sa/ree.** [< Hind. *sarī* < Skt. *śāti*]

sa·rong (sə·rong/) *n.* **1.** A skirtlike garment of colored [s] or cotton cloth worn by both sexes in the Malay Archipela[go], etc. **2.** The material used for this garment. [< Ma[l.] *sārung,* prob. < Skt. *sāraṅga* variegated]

sar·sa·pa·ril·la (sas/pə·ril/ə, sär/sə·pə·ril/ə) *n.* **1.** The dr[ied] roots of certain tropical American climbing plants of the l[ily] family. **2.** A medicinal preparation or a beverage ma[de] from such roots. [< Sp. < *zarza* bramble + *parilla,* dim. [of] *parra* vine]

sarse·net (särs/net) *n.* A fine, thin silk, used for linin[g] also spelled *sarcenet.* [< AF, dim. of ME *sarzin* Sarace[n]]

sar·to·ri·al (sär·tôr/ē·əl, -tō/rē-) *adj.* **1.** Pertaining t[o a] tailor or his work. **2.** Pertaining to men's clothes. [< [L] *sartor* patcher, mender] — **sar·to/ri·al·ly** *adv.*

sash¹ (sash) *n.* An ornamental band or scarf, worn as a g[ir]dle, or around the waist or over the shoulder. [Orig. sh[awl] < Arabic *shāsh* muslin, turban]

sash² (sash) *n.* A frame, as of a window, in which glas[s is] set. — *v.t.* To furnish with a sash. [Alter. of CHASS[IS] taken as a pl.]

sa·shay (sa·shā/) *v.i. U.S. Informal* To move with a swi[sh]ing or gliding motion. [Alter. of *chassé,* a dance motion]

sass (sas) *Informal n.* Impudence; back talk. — *v.t.* [To] talk to impudently or disrespectfully. [Dial. alter. of SAU[CE]]

sas·sa·fras (sas/ə·fras) *n.* **1.** An aromatic, deciduous t[ree] of the laurel family. **2.** The root bark of this tree, used [as] flavoring, and yielding a volatile oil. [< Sp. *sasafrás,* pr[ob.] < N. Am. Ind. name]

sas·sy¹ (sas/ē) *adj.* **·si·er, ·si·est** *U.S. Dial.* Saucy; imp[er]tinent; cheeky.

sas·sy² (sas/ē) *n.* A West African tree having a bark t[hat] yields a poisonous alkaloid. Also **sas/sy·bark/** (-bär[k]) **sas/sy·wood/** (-wŏŏd/). [< native W. African name]

sat (sat) Past tense of SIT.

Sa·tan (sā/tən) In the Bible, the great adversary of God [and] tempter of mankind; the Devil: identified with Luci[fer] *Luke* iv 5–8; *Rev.* xii 7–9. Also **Sa/than** (sā/tən), **Sath·a·[nas]** (sath/ə·nəs). [< Hebrew *sātān* enemy]

sa·tan·ic (sā·tan/ik) *adj.* Devilish; infernal; wicked. A[lso] **sa·tan/i·cal.** — **sa·tan/i·cal·ly** *adv.*

satch·el (sach/əl) *n.* A small handbag or suitcase. [< [L] < L *sacellus,* dim. of *saccus* sack]

sate (sāt) *v.t.* **sat·ed, sat·ing** To satisfy the appetite [or] satiate. [Appar. alter. of obs. *sade* to sate, OE *sadian:* fashioned after L *sat, satis* enough]

sa·teen (sa·tēn/) *n.* A cotton fabric woven so as to giv[e] a satin surface. [Alter. of SATIN]

sat·el·lite (sat/ə·līt) *n.* **1.** *Astron.* A smaller body attend[ing] upon and revolving round a larger one; a moon. **2.** One [that] attends upon a person in power. **3.** Any obsequious atte[nd]ant. **4.** A small nation that is politically, economically [or] militarily dependent on a great power. **5.** A town or c[om]munity whose activities are largely determined by those [of a] neighboring metropolis. **6.** Any manmade object launc[hed] from and revolving around the earth. [< F < L *satel[les,]* *satellitis* attendant, guard]

sa·ti·a·ble (sā/shē·ə·bəl, -shə·bəl) *adj.* Capable of be[ing] satiated. — **sa/ti·a·bil/i·ty, sa/ti·a·ble·ness** *n.* — **sa/[ti·a·]** **bly** *adv.*

sa·ti·ate (sā/shē·āt) *v.t.* **·at·ed, ·at·ing 1.** To satisfy the [ap]petite or desire of; gratify. **2.** To fill or gratify beyond [nat]ural desire; glut. — **Syn.** See SATISFY. — *adj.* Filled [to] satiety; satiated. [< L < *satis* enough] — **sa/ti·a/tion** *n.*

sa·ti·e·ty (sə·tī/ə·tē) *n. pl.* **·ties** The state of being satia[ted.]

sat·in (sat/ən) *n.* A silk, cotton, rayon, or acetate fabri[c of] thick texture, with glossy face and dull back. — *adj.* O[f or] resembling satin; glossy; smooth. [< OF < Med.L *sati[nus,]* *setinus,* ult. < L *seta* silk] — **sat/in·y** *adj.*

sat·i·net (sat/ə·net/) *n.* **1.** A strong fabric with cotton w[arp] and woolen filling. **2.** A thin satin. Also **sat/i·nette/.** [< dim. of *satin* satin]

sat·in·wood (sat/ən·wŏŏd/) *n.* **1.** The satinlike wood of [an] East Indian tree of the mahogany family. **2.** The tree.

sat·ire (sat/īr) *n.* **1.** The use of sarcasm, irony, or wit in [ex]posing abuses or follies; ridicule. **2.** A written composi[tion] in which vice, folly, etc., is held up to ridicule. [< MF [< L] *satira, satura* satire, orig. medley < *(lanx) satura* fruit sa[lad,] lit., full (dish), fem. of *satur* full]
— **Syn. 1.** chaff, raillery, mockery, derision.

sa·tir·ic (sə·tir/ik) *adj.* Of, pertaining to, or resemb[ling] satire, esp. literary satire: *satiric* verse. Also **satiric[al.]**

sa·tir·i·cal (sə·tir/i·kəl) *adj.* **1.** Given to or character[ized] by satire. **2.** Severely sarcastic; caustic: a *satirical* la[sh.] **3.** Satiric. — **sa·tir/i·cal·ly** *adv.* — **sa·tir/i·cal·ness** *n.*

sat·i·rist (sat/ə·rist) *n.* **1.** A writer of satire. **2.** A satiric[al] person.

sat·i·rize (sat/ə·rīz) *v.t.* **·rized, ·riz·ing** To criticize by m[eans] of satire; subject to satire. — **sat/i·riz/er** *n.*

t·is·fac·tion (sat′is·fak′shən) _n._ **1.** The act of satisfying · the state of being satisfied; gratification. **2.** The making amends, reparation, or payment, as of a claim or obliga- on. **3.** That which satisfies; atonement; compensation.

t·is·fac·to·ry (sat′is·fak′tər·ē) _adj._ **1.** Giving satisfac- on; answering fully all desires, expectations, or require- ents. **2.** Atoning; expiatory. — _Syn._ See ADEQUATE. — ιt′is·fac′to·ri·ly _adv._ — **sat′is·fac′to·ri·ness** _n._

t·is·fy (sat′is·fī) _v._ **·fied, ·fy·ing** _v.t._ **1.** To supply fully ith what is desired, expected, or needed; gratify. **2.** To ee from doubt or anxiety; convince. **3.** To give what is ιe to. **4.** To pay or discharge (a debt, obligation, etc.). **5.** o answer sufficiently or convincingly, as a question or ob- ction. **6.** To fulfill the conditions or requirements of, as ι equation. **7.** To make reparation for; expiate. — _v.i._ **8.** o give satisfaction. [< OF < L < _satis_ enough + _facere_ · do] — **sat′is·fi′er** _n._ — **sat′is·fy′ing·ly** _adv._ — _Syn._ **1.** _Satisfy_ suggests the giving of just enough, and no ore, and a state of mind that is merely content. To _gratify_ is to ase, hence to give liberally, while _satiate_ is now chiefly used to dicate an excess or oversupply.

to·ri (sä·tôr′ē) _n._ The illumination of spirit sought by ιn Buddhists. [< Japanese]

trap (sä′trap, sat′rap) _n._ **1.** A governor of a province ancient Persia. **2.** A subordinate, often despotic, ruler or ιvernor. [< L < Gk. < OPersian _shathraparan_, lit., pro- ctor of a province]

trap·y (sä′tra·pē, sat′rə·pē) _n._ _pl._ **·trap·ies** The terri- ry or the jurisdiction of a satrap. Also **sa·trap·ate** (sä′trə- t, sat′rə-).

t·u·rate (sach′ə·rāt; _for adj., also_ sach′ə·rit) _v.t._ **·rat·ed, ·at·ing 1.** To soak or imbue thoroughly. **2.** To fill, im- egnate, or charge (a substance or material) to its full ca- city. — _adj._ **1.** Filled to repletion; saturated. **2.** Very tense; deep: said of colors. [< L _saturatus_, pp. of _saturare_ · fill up] — **sat·u·ra·ble** (sach′ər·ə·bəl) _adj._ — **sat′u·ra′ter** · **tor** _n._ — **sat′u·ra′tion** _n._

t·u·rat·ed (sach′ə·rā′tid) _adj._ **1.** Incapable of holding ore of a substance or material; completely satisfied; re- ete: _saturated_ vapor. **2.** _Chem._ Designating an organic ιmpound, as paraffin or methane, having no free valences ιd without double or triple bonds. **3.** Designating a color hue exhibiting high saturation.

t·ur·day (sat′ər·dē, -dā) _n._ The seventh or last day of the eek. [OE _Sæterdæg, Sæternesdæg_]

t·urn (sat′ərn) _n._ In Roman mythology, the god of agricul- ιre: identified with the Greek _Cronus._ — _n._ The second rgest planet of the solar system and sixth in order from the n. See PLANET. [< L _Saturnus_] — **Sa·tur·ni·an** (sə- ιr′nē·ən) _adj._

t·ur·na·li·a (sat′ər·nā′lē·ə) _n.pl._ (_Usu._ construed as _sing._) ny season or period of general license or revelry.

t·ur·na·li·a (sat′ər·nā′lē·ə) _n.pl._ The feast of Saturn, ιld at Rome in mid-December, and marked by wild revel- g and licentious abandon. — **Sat′ur·na′li·an** _adj._

t·ur·nine (sat′ər·nīn) _adj._ Having a grave, gloomy, or orose disposition or character. [< OF < Med.L _Saturnus_ ιd, Saturn]

t·yr (sat′ər, sā′tər) _n._ **1.** In Greek mythology, a lecher- ιs woodland diety in human form, having pointed ears, ιat's legs, and budding horns. **2.** A very lascivious man. < L < Gk. _satyros_] — **sa·tyr·ic** (sə·tir′ik) or **·i·cal** _adj._

t·yr·i·a·sis (sat′ə·rī′ə·sis) _n._ _Psychiatry_ An excessive and ιcontrollable sexual desire in men. [< NL < Gk. < _saty- s_ satyr]

uce (sôs) _n._ **1.** An appetizing dressing or liquid relish for od. **2.** Any appetizing garnish of a meal. **3.** Formerly, ιy condiment, as salt or pepper. **4.** A dish of fruit pulp ewed and sweetened. **5.** _Informal_ Pert or impudent lan- ιage. — _v.t._ **sauced, sauc·ing 1.** To flavor with sauce; ason. **2.** To give zest or piquancy to. **3.** _Informal_ To be ιucy to. [< OF < LL _salsa_, orig. fem. of L _salsus_ salted]

uce·pan (sôs′pan′) _n._ A metal or enamel pan with pro- cting handle, for cooking food.

u·cer (sô′sər) _n._ **1.** A small dish for holding a cup. **2.** ny small, round, shallow vessel of similar shape. [< OF < _uce_ sauce]

u·cy (sô′sē) _adj._ **·ci·er, ·ci·est 1.** Disrespectful to superi- ·s; impudent. **2.** Piquant; sprightly; amusing. — **sau′ci·** _adv._ — **sau′ci·ness** _n._

uer·bra·ten (sour′brätn, _Ger._ zou′ər·brätn′) _n._ Beef ιarinated in vinegar before being braised. [< G < _sauer_ ιur + _braten_ to roast]

uer·kraut (sour′krout′) _n._ Shredded and salted cabbage rmented in its own juice: also called _kraut._ [< G < _sauer_ ιur + _kraut_ cabbage]

uk (sôk) _n._ One of a tribe of North American Indians of lgonquian stock, formerly occupying Michigan, later Wis-

consin and the Mississippi valley, now on reservations in Oklahoma, Iowa, and Kansas. Also spelled _Sac._

Saul (sôl) **1.** The first king of Israel. _I Sam._ ix 2. **2.** The Hebrew name of the Apostle Paul (_Acts_ xiii 9): also **Saul of Tarsus.**

sau·na (sou′nə) _n._ A room or house for taking steam baths by the Finnish method, in steam produced by throwing water on hot stones; also, such a steam bath. [< Finnish]

saun·ter (sôn′tər) _v.i._ To walk in a leisurely or lounging way; stroll. — _n._ **1.** A slow, aimless manner of walking. **2.** An idle stroll. [ME _santren_ to muse, meditate]

sau·ri·an (sôr′ē·ən) _n._ One of a suborder of reptiles, includ- ing the lizards, geckos, and chameleons. — _adj._ Pertaining to saurians. [< NL < Gk. _sauros_ lizard]

sauro- _combining form_ Lizard. Also, before vowels, **saur-**. [< Gk. _sauros_ lizard]

-saurus _combining form_ _Zool._ Lizard: used to form genus names: _Brontosaurus._ [< Gk. _sauros_ lizard]

sau·sage (sô′sij) _n._ **1.** Finely chopped and highly seasoned meat, commonly stuffed into the cleaned entrails of some animal or into artificial casings. **2.** _Aeron._ A type of bar- rage or observation balloon, shaped like a sausage. [< AF < LL _salsicia_, orig. alt. < L _salsus_ salted]

sau·té (sō·tā′, sô-) _adj._ Fried quickly with little grease. — _v.t._ **·téed, ·té·ing** To fry quickly in a little fat. [< F, pp. of _sauter_ to leap < L _saltare_]

sau·terne (sō·tûrn′, sô-; _Fr._ sō·tern′) _n._ A sweet, white French wine. Also **sau·ternes′.** [after _Sauternes_, district in SW France]

sav·age (sav′ij) _adj._ **1.** Having a wild and untamed nature; not domesticated. **2.** Ferocious; fierce. **3.** Living in or be- longing to a primitive condition of human life and society; uncivilized: _savage_ tribes. **4.** Vicious; cruel; furious. **5.** Rude; uncultivated; rough. — _n._ **1.** A primitive or unciv- ilized human being. **2.** A brutal, fierce, and cruel person; a barbarian. — _v.t._ **·aged, ·ag·ing** To attack savagely, esp. with the teeth. [< OF < L _salvaticus, silvaticus_ < _silva_ a wood] — **sav′age·ly** _adv._ — **sav′age·ness** _n._

sav·age·ry (sav′ij·rē) _n._ _pl._ **·ries 1.** The state of being sav- age. **2.** Cruelty in disposition or action; a cruel or savage act. **3.** Savages collectively: also **sav′age·dom** (-dəm). Also **sav′ag·ism.**

sa·van·na (sə·van′ə) _n._ **1.** A tract of level country covered with low vegetation. **2.** Any large area of tropical or sub- tropical grassland, covered in part with trees and spiny shrubs. Also **sa·van′nah.** [Earlier _zavana_ < Sp. < Carib]

sa·vant (sə·vänt′, sav′ənt; _Fr._ sà·vän′) _n._ A man of excep- tional learning. [< F < L _sapere_ to be wise]

save[1] (sāv) _v._ **saved, sav·ing** _v.t._ **1.** To preserve or rescue from danger, harm, etc. **2.** To keep from being spent, ex- pended, or lost. **3.** To set aside for future use; accumulate: often with _up._ **4.** To treat carefully so as to avoid fatigue, harm, etc.: to _save_ one's eyes. **5.** To prevent by timely ac- tion: A stitch in time _saves_ nine. **6.** _Theol._ To deliver from spiritual death or the consequences of sin. — _v.i._ **7.** To avoid waste; be economical. **8.** To preserve something from danger, harm, etc. **9.** To admit of preservation, as food. [< OF < LL < L _salvus_ safe] — **sav′a·ble** or **save′a·ble** _adj._ — **sav′a·ble·ness** _n._ — **sav′er** _n._

save[2] (sāv) _prep._ Except; but. — _conj._ **1.** Except; but: usu. with _that._ **2.** _Archaic_ Unless. [< OF _sauf_ being ex- cepted, orig., safe < L _salvus_]

sav·ing (sā′ving) _adj._ **1.** That saves; preserving, as from destruction. **2.** Redeeming; delivering. **3.** Avoiding need- less waste or expense; economical; frugal. **4.** Incurring no loss, if not gainful: a _saving_ investment. **5.** Holding in re- serve; making an exception; qualifying: a _saving_ clause. — _n._ **1.** Preservation from loss or danger. **2.** Avoidance of waste; economy. **3.** The extent of something saved: a _saving_ of 16 percent. **4.** _pl._ Sums of money not expended. **5.** That which is saved. — _prep._ **1.** With the exception of; save. **2.** With due respect for: _saving_ your presence. — _conj._ Save; but. — **sav′ing·ly** _adv._ — **sav′ing·ness** _n._

savings account An account drawing interest at a bank.

savings bank 1. A bank whose chief functions are receiv- ing and investing savings and paying interest on deposits. **2.** A container with a slot for depositing coins.

sav·ior (sāv′yər) _n._ One who saves. Also _Brit._ **sav′iour.** [< OF < LL < L _salvare_ to save]

Sav·iour (sāv′yər) _n._ A title sometimes applied directly to God, but chiefly to Jesus Christ, as the Redeemer: usu. with _the._ Also **Sav′ior.**

sa·voir-faire (sà·vwàr·fâr′) _French_ Ability to say and do the right thing; tact; literally, to know how to act.

sa·vor (sā′vər) _n._ **1.** The quality of a thing that affects the sense of taste or smell, or both; flavor; odor. **2.** Specific or characteristic quality or approach to a quality; flavor. **3.** Relish; zest: The conversation had _savor._ — _v.i._ **1.** To have a specified savor; taste or smell: with *of*. **2.** To have a specified quality or character: with *of*. **—** *v.t.* **3.** To give flavor to; season. **4.** To taste or enjoy with pleasure; relish. **5.** To have the savor or character of. Also *Brit.* **sa'vour.** [< OF < L < *sapere* to taste, know] **— sa'vor.er** *n.* **— sa'. vor.ous** *adj.*

sa.vor.less (sā'vər.lis) *adj.* Tasteless; insipid.

sa.vor.y[1] (sā'vər.ē) *adj.* **1.** Of an agreeable taste and odor; appetizing. **2.** Piquant to the taste. **3.** In good repute; respectable. **—** *n. Brit.* A small, hot serving of food eaten at the end or beginning of a dinner. Also *Brit.* **sa'vour.y.** [< OF *savouré,* pp. of *savourer* to taste] **— sa'vor.i.ly** *adv.* **— sa'vor.i.ness** *n.*

sa.vor.y[2] (sā'vər.ē) *n.* A hardy, annual, aromatic herb of the mint family, used for seasoning. Also **summer savory.** [OE < L *satureia*]

sa.voy (sə.voi') *n.* A variety of cabbage with wrinkled leaves. [< F (*chou de*) *Savoie* (cabbage of) Savoy]

Sa.voy.ard (sə.voi'ərd, *Fr.* sȧ.vwä.yȧr') *n.* **1.** An actor or actress in the Gilbert and Sullivan operas. **2.** An admirer of these operas. [after the *Savoy* Theater in London]

sav.vy (sav'ē) *Slang v.i.* **.vied, .vy.ing** To understand; comprehend. **—** *n.* Understanding; good sense. [Alter. of Sp. *¿ Sabe* (usted)? Do (you) know? < L *sapere* to know]

saw[1] (sô) *n.* **1.** A cutting instrument with pointed teeth arranged continuously along the edge of the blade, used to cut or divide wood, bone, metal, etc. **2.** A machine for operating a saw or gang of saws. **3.** Any tool or instrument without teeth used like a saw. **—** *v.* **sawed, sawed** or **sawn, saw.ing** *v.t.* **1.** To cut or divide with a saw. **2.** To shape or fashion with a saw. **3.** To cut or slice (the air, etc.) as if using a saw. **4.** To cause to move with a to-and-fro motion like that of a saw. **—** *v.i.* **5.** To use a saw. **6.** To cut: said of a saw. **7.** To be cut with a saw: This wood *saws* easily. [OE *sagu*] **— saw'er** *n.*

saw[2] (sô) *n.* A proverbial or familiar saying; old maxim. **— Syn.** See PROVERB. [OE *sagu*]

saw[3] (sô) Past tense of SEE[1].

saw.bones (sô'bōnz') *n. Slang* A surgeon.

saw.buck (sô'buk') *n.* **1.** A sawhorse consisting of two X-shaped ends joined by a connecting bar or bars. **2.** *U.S. Slang* A ten-dollar bill: so called from the resemblance of X, Roman numeral ten, to the ends of a sawbuck. [Trans. of Du. *zaagbok*]

saw.dust (sô'dust') *n.* Small particles of wood produced by the action of sawing.

sawed-off (sôd'ôf', -of') *adj.* **1.** Having one end sawed off, as a shotgun. **2.** *U.S. Slang* Short; not of average height.

saw-fish (sô'fish') *n.* pl. **.fish** or **.fish.es** Any of various elongate, sharklike tropical fish with the snout prolonged into a flat blade with teeth on each edge.

saw.fly (sô'flī') *n.* pl. **.flies** Any of various winged insects having in the female a sawlike ovipositor for piercing plants, soft wood, etc.

saw.horse (sô'hôrs') *n.* A frame on which to rest wood, etc., for sawing, usu. consisting of a long wooden bar or plank supported by four straddled legs.

saw log A log of suitable size for sawing.

saw.mill (sô'mil') *n.* **1.** An establishment for sawing logs with power-driven machinery. **2.** A large sawing machine.

sawn (sôn) Alternative past participle of SAW[1].

saw-toothed (sô'tootht') *adj.* Serrate; having teeth or toothlike processes similar to those of a saw.

saw.yer (sô'yər) *n.* **1.** One whose occupation is the sawing of wood, as in lumbering or in a sawmill. **2.** Any of various longicorn beetles having larvae that bore into wood, as the pine sawyer. [Alter. of SAWER.]

sax (saks) *n. Informal* A saxophone.

sax.horn (saks'hôrn') *n.* Any of a family of valved brass instruments resembling the bugle, made in a wide series of ranges. [after the inventor, Antoine Joseph *Sax* (called Adolphe), 1814–94, Belgian instrument maker + HORN]

sax.i.frage (sak'sə.frij) *n.* Any of a large, widely distributed genus of herbaceous plants growing in rocky places, bearing small white, yellow, or purplish flowers. [< OF < L (*herba*) *saxifraga,* lit., stone-breaking (herb)]

Sax.on (sak'sən) *n.* **1.** A member of a Germanic tribal group formerly inhabiting what is now Schleswig-Holstein. **2.** A member of any of the offshoots of this group, as those who, with the Angles and Jutes, invaded England in the fifth and sixth centuries A.D. **3.** An Anglo-Saxon. **4.** An inhabitant of Saxony. **5.** The modern High German dialect of Saxony. **— Old Saxon** The dialect of Low German current in the valley of the lower Elbe in the early Middle Ages. **—** *adj.* **1.** Of or pertaining to the Saxons or to their language. **2.** Anglo-Saxon; English. **3.** Of or pertaining to Saxony, Germany. [< F < L *Saxo, Saxonis* < WGmc.]

sax.o.phone (sak'sə.fōn) *n.* Any of a family of metal wind instruments having a single reed and conical bore, made in a wide series of ranges. [after A. J. *Sax* (see SAXHORN) + -PHONE] **— sax'o.phon'ist** *n.*

say (sā) *v.* **said, say.ing** *v.t.* **1.** To pronounce or utter; speak. **2.** To declare or express in words; tell; state. **3.** state positively or as an opinion: *Say* which you prefer. **4.** To recite: to *say* one's prayers. **5.** To report; allege. **6.** assume; suppose. **—** *v.i.* **7.** To make a statement; spe **— that is to say** In other words. **—** *adv.* **1.** Approxima ly; at a guess: He is worth, *say,* a million. **2.** For examp Choose a number, *say,* ten. **—** *n.* **1.** What one has said has to say; word. **2.** Right or turn to speak or choose: have one's *say.* **3.** Authority: to have the *say.* **—** *int U.S. Informal* A hail or an exclamation to command att tion: also *Brit.* **I say.** [OE *secgan*] **— say'er** *n.*

say.ing (sā'ing) *n.* **1.** A maxim; adage. **2.** Something sa

says (sez) Third person singular, present indicative of s

say-so (sā'sō') *n. Informal* **1.** An unsupported assertion decision. **2.** Right or power to make decisions.

scab (skab) *n.* **1.** A crust formed on the surface of a wou or sore. **2.** *Vet.* Scabies. **3.** Any of certain plant disea characterized by a roughened or warty appearance. *Slang* A mean, contemptible fellow. **5.** *Informal* A wo man who will not join or act with a labor union; esp., a stri breaker. **—** *v.i.* **scabbed, scab.bing 1.** To form or beco covered with a scab. **2.** *Informal* To take the job of a stri [Fusion of ON *skabbr* (assumed) and OE *sceabb*]

scab.bard (skab'ərd) *n.* A sheath for a weapon, as fo bayonet or a sword. **—** *v.t.* To sheathe in or furnish wit scabbard. [< OF *escalberc,* prob. < OHG *scar* sword *bergan* to hide, protect]

scab.by (skab'ē) *adj.* **.bi.er, .bi.est 1.** Having, consist of, or resembling a scab or scabs. **2.** Having scabies. **3.** *formal* Contemptible. **— scab'bi.ly** *adv.* **— scab'bi.ness**

sca.bies (skā'bi.ēz, -bēz) *n.* **1.** A skin disease caused by itch mite; itch. **2.** *Vet.* A similar skin disease of sheep: called *scab.* [< L, roughness, an itch < *scabere* to scra scrape.] **— sca.bi.et.ic** (skā'bē.et'ik) *adj.*

sca.bi.ous[1] (skā'bē.əs) *adj.* **1.** Pertaining to or resembl scabies. **2.** Having scabs.

sca.bi.ous[2] (skā'bē.əs) *n.* Any of a genus of herbs allie the teasel, with heads of variously colored flowers. *sca'bi.o'sa* (-ō'sa). [< NL < Med.L (*herba*) *scabiosa,* f sing. of *scabiosus* scabious[1]]

sca.brous (skab'rəs, skā'brəs) *adj.* **1.** Roughened with nute points; scurfy. **2.** Off-color; risqué. **3.** Difficult to h dle tactfully; knotty. [< LL < *scabere* to scratch] **—** brous.ly *adv.* **— sca'brous.ness** *n.*

scads (skadz) *n.pl. Informal* A large amount or quant [? Var. of dial E *scald* a large amount, great number]

scaf.fold (skaf'əld, -ōld) *n.* **1.** A temporary elevated st ture for the support of workmen, materials, etc., as in bu ing. **2.** Any raised wooden framework. **3.** A platform the execution of criminals. **—** *v.t.* To furnish or supp with a scaffold. [< OF *eschaffaut*]

scaf.fold.ing (skaf'əl.ding) *n.* A scaffold, or system of s folds, or the materials for constructing them. Also **fold.age** (skaf'əl.dij).

sca.lar (skā'lər) *Math. adj.* Definable by a number c line or scale: said of a quantity having magnitude only, volume or mass: distinguished from *vector.* [< L < s ladder]

scal.a.wag (skal'ə.wag) *n.* **1.** *Informal* A worthless fell scamp. **2.** *U.S.* During the Reconstruction period, a na Southern white Republican: a contemptuous term. called *scallywag:* also spelled *scallawag.* [Origin uncert

scald (skôld) *v.t.* **1.** To burn with or as with hot liqui steam. **2.** To cleanse or treat with boiling water. **3.** heat (a liquid) to a point just short of boiling. **—** *v.i.* **4.** be or become scalded. **—** *n.* **1.** A burn or injury to the s by a hot fluid. **2.** A destructive parasitic disease of pla **3.** A discoloration of plant tissue due to improper condit of growth, storage, etc. [< AF < LL < L < *ex-* ver; *calidus* hot]

scale[1] (skāl) *n.* **1.** One of the thin, flat, horny, membrar or bony outgrowths of the skin of various animals, as r fishes, usu. overlapping and forming a nearly complete ering. **2.** Any similar thin, flat formation, piece, or part. A scab. **4.** A scale insect. **5.** *Bot.* A rudimentary or m morphosed leaf, as of a pine cone. **6.** *Metall.* The coatin oxide that forms on heated iron, etc. **7.** An incrusta formed on the inside of boilers, etc. **—** *v.* **scaled, scal** *v.t.* **1.** To strip or clear of scales. **2.** To form scales on. To take off in layers. **—** *v.i.* **4.** To come off in scales; **5.** To shed scales. **6.** To become incrusted with sc [< OF *escale* husk < Gmc.] **— scal'er** *n.*

scale[2] (skāl) *n.* **1.** Any instrument bearing accura spaced lines or gradations for use in measurement. **2.** series of marks so used. **3.** Any system of designating u of measurement: the Fahrenheit *scale.* **4.** A fixed pro tion used in determining measurements or dimension *scale* of one inch to the mile. **5.** Any progressive or gra classification: wage *scale.* **6.** Relative proportion, deg scope, etc.: with *on:* to live on a grand *scale.* **7.** *Mat* ystem of notation in which the successive places determine ιe value of the figures: the decimal *scale*. **8.** *Music* An arangement of tones in ascending or descending order through ιe interval of an octave: a diatonic *scale*. **— major scale** *lusic* A scale having semitones after the third and seventh εps, all the other intervals being whole tones. **— minor ale** A scale having semitones after the second and fifth εps (the natural form), or after the second, fifth, and sevιth steps (the harmonic form), or after the second and sevιth steps when ascending and the sixth and third when ιscending (the melodic form), all the other intervals being ιhole tones. **—** *v.* **scaled, scal·ing** *v.t.* **1.** To climb to the ρ of. **2.** To make according to a scale. **3.** To regulate or ljust according to a scale or ratio: with *up, down*, etc. **—** *ι.* **4.** To climb; ascend. **5.** To rise in steps or stages. [< al... < L *scandere* to climb] **— scal'a·ble** *adj.* **— scal'er** *n.*

ιle³ (skāl) *n.* **1.** Any weighing machine. **2.** A pan, oop, platform, etc., that holds the object or material to be ɛighed in a weighing instrument or balance. **3.** *Usu. pl.* A lance (defs. 1 & 2). **— to turn the scales** To determine; **—** *v.* **scaled, scal·ing** *v.t.* **1.** To weigh in scales. **2.** ɔ amount to in weight. **—** *v.i.* **3.** To be weighed. [< N *skāl* bowl, in pl., a weighing balance]

ιle insect One of numerous small insects that feed on ants and as adults have a scalelike, protective shield.

ι·lene (skā'lēn, skā·lēn') *adj. Geom.* Designating a triιgle having no two sides equal. [< LL < Gk. *skalēnos* unɛn]

ιles (skālz) *n.pl.* The constellation and sign of the zodiac bra.

ι·la·wag (skal'ə·wag) See SCALAWAG.

ιl·lion (skal'yən) *n.* **1.** A young, tender onion with a ιall white bulb. **2.** A shallot or leek. [< OF < L (*caepa*) *scalonia* (onion) of Ashkelon, a Palestinian seaport]

ιl·lop (skal'əp, skol'-) *n.* **1.** A bivalve molsk having a rounded, ridged shell whose valves e snapped together in swimming. **2.** The ible adductor muscle of certain species of this ollusk. **3.** The shell of a scallop; esp., one in ιich seafood is cooked or served. **4.** One of a ries of semicircular curves along an edge, as r ornament. **—** *v.t.* **1.** To shape the edge of th scallops. **2.** To bake (food) in a casserole ιth a sauce, often topped with bread crumbs. Also spelled *ιallop, scollop.* [< OF *escalope* < Gmc.] **— scal'lop·er** *n.*

SCALLOP SHELL

.l·ly·wag (skal'ē·wag) *n.* A scalawag.

ιlp (skalp) *n.* **1.** The skin of the top and back of the huan skull, usu. covered with hair. **2.** A portion of this, forɛrly cut or torn away as a war trophy among certain North nerican Indians. **—** *v.t.* **1.** To cut or tear the scalp from. *Informal* To buy and resell (tickets) at prices exceeding e established rate. **3.** *Informal* To buy and sell again ιickly in order to make a small profit. **4.** *Informal* To det utterly. **—** *v.i.* **5.** *Informal* To scalp bonds, tickets, ɔ. [ME, prob. < Scand.] **— scalp'er** *n.*

ιl·pel (skal'pəl) *n.* A small pointed knife with a very ιrp, thin blade, used in dissections and in surgery. [< L *ιlpere* to cut]

ι·ly (skā'lē) *adj.* **scal·i·er, scal·i·est** Having, resembling, incrusted with scales. **— scal'i·ness** *n.*

ιly anteater A pangolin.

ιmp¹ (skamp) *n.* A confirmed rogue; good-for-nothing low; rascal. [< obs. verb *scamp* to roam, contr. of SCAMP-) .] **— scamp'ish** *adj.*

ιmp² (skamp) *v.t.* To perform (work) carelessly or disnestly. [Orig. dial. E] **— scamp'er** *n.*

ι·per (skam'pər) *v.i.* To run quickly or hastily. **—** *n.* hurried run or departure. [< OF, ult. < L *ex* out from + *ιmpus* plain, battlefield] **— scam'per·er** *n.*

ιn (skan) *v.* **scanned, scan·ning** *v.t.* **1.** To examine in tail; scrutinize closely. **2.** To pass the eyes over quickly; ance at. **3.** To separate (verse) into metrical feet; ascerin or indicate the rhythm of. **4.** *Telecom.* To pass a beam light or electrons rapidly over every point of (a surface, ɔ.) for television, sound, or other reproduction. **—** *v.i.* **5.** ɔ conform to metrical rules: said of rse. [< LL < L *scandere* climb] **— scan'na·ble** *adj.* ** an'ner** *n.*

ιn·dal (skan'dəl) *n.* **1.** Heedless or malicious gossip. **2.** sgrace or reproach caused by outrageous or improper conιct. **3.** A discreditable circumstance, event, or action. **4.** ɛnsure or open disapproval. **5.** One whose conduct results disgrace or censure. [< AF < L < Gk. *skandalon* snare] **ιn·dal·ize** (skan'dəl·īz) *v.t.* **·ized, ·iz·ing** To shock the oral feelings of, as by improper, frivolous, or offensive conιct; outrage. **— scan'dal·i·za'tion** *n.* **— scan'dal·iz'er** *n.* **ιn·dal·mong·er** (skan'dəl·mung·gər, -mong'-) *n.* One ho spreads or repeats scandal.

scan·dal·ous (skan'dəl·əs) *adj.* **1.** Causing or tending to cause scandal; disgraceful. **2.** Consisting of or spreading scandal. **— scan'dal·ous·ly** *adv.* **— scan'dal·ous·ness** *n.*

Scan·di·na·vi·an (skan'də·nā'vē·ən) *adj.* Of or pertaining to Scandinavia, its people, or their languages. **—** *n.* **1.** A native or inhabitant of Scandinavia. **2.** The North Germanic group of languages: see under GERMANIC. Also *Norse*. **— Old Scandinavian** Old Norse. See under NORSE.

scan·di·um (skan'dē·əm) *n.* A metallic element (symbol Sc) of the lanthanide series. See ELEMENT. [< NL < L *Scandia* Scandinavia]

scan·sion (skan'shən) *n.* The division or analysis of lines of verse according to a metrical pattern. Compare METER² (def. 1). [< F < LL < L *scandere* scan]

scant (skant) *adj.* **1.** Scarcely enough; meager in measure or quantity. **2.** Being just short of the measure specified: a *scant* half-hour; a *scant* five yards. **3.** Insufficiently supplied with: with *of*: We were *scant* of breath. **—** *v.t.* **1.** To restrict or limit in supply; stint. **2.** To treat briefly or inadequately. **—** *adv. Dial.* Scarcely; barely. [< ON *skammr* short] **— scant'ly** *adv.* **— scant'ness** *n.*

scant·ling (skant'ling) *n.* **1.** A piece of lumber of small or moderate cross section, used for studding, etc. **2.** Such lumber collectively. [< OF *eschantillon* cornerpiece]

scant·y (skan'tē) *adj.* **scant·i·er, scant·i·est** **1.** Limited in extent. **2.** Restricted in quantity or amount; scarcely sufficient; meager. **— scant'i·ly** *adv.* **— scant'i·ness** *n.*

scape (skāp) *Archaic v.t. & v.i.* To escape. **—** *n.* An escape or means of escape. Also *'scape*.

scape·goat (skāp'gōt') *n.* **1.** In the Bible, the goat upon whose head the high priest symbolically laid the sins of the people on the day of atonement, after which it was led away into the wilderness. *Lev.* xvi. **2.** An animal, person, or group that bears the blame or suffers for the errors or sins of others.

scape·grace (skāp'grās') *n.* A mischievous or incorrigible person; rogue.

scapi- *combining form* A stalk, stem, or shaft. [< L *scapus* stalk]

scap·u·la (skap'yə·lə) *n.* *pl.* **·lae** (-lē) *Anat.* Either of a pair of large, flat, triangular bones in the back of the shoulder in man and having an analogous position in the skeleton of vertebrates: also called *shoulder blade*. [< LL < L *scapulae* shoulder blades]

scap·u·lar (skap'yə·lər) *n.* **1.** An outer garment consisting of two strips of cloth joined across the shoulders, worn by members of certain religious orders. **2.** A badge or sign of devotion worn about the neck by members of certain religious orders and groups. **3.** *pl. Ornithol.* The shoulder feathers of a bird. **—** *adj.* Of or pertaining to the scapula.

scap·u·lar·y (skap'yə·ler'ē) *n.* *pl.* **·ries** A scapular. **—** *adj.* Scapular.

scar (skär) *n.* **1.** The mark left on the skin after the healing of a wound or sore. **2.** Any mark, damage, or lasting effect resulting from past injury, stress, etc. **—** *v.t. & v.i.* **scarred, scar·ring** To mark or become marked with a scar. [< OF < LL *eschara* scab < Gk.]

scar·ab (skar'əb) *n.* **1.** A large, black beetle held sacred by the ancient Egyptians. **2.** A gem or ornament representing this beetle. [< MF < L *scarabaeus*]

scar·a·bae·us (skar'ə·bē'əs) *n.* *pl.* **·bae·us·es** or **·bae·i** (-bē'ī) A scarab. [< L]

scar·a·mouch (skar'ə·mouch, -mōōsh) *n.* A swaggering rascal. [< *Scaramouch*]

Scar·a·mouch (skar'ə·mouch, -mōōsh) In old Italian comedy, a stock character represented as a boastful, cowardly buffoon. [< F < Ital. *Scaramuccia*, lit., skirmish]

scarce (skârs) *adj.* **scarc·er, scarc·est** **1.** Rarely seen or found. **2.** Not plentiful; insufficient. **— to make oneself scarce** *Informal* To go away or stay away. [< OF, ult. < L < *ex-* out + *carpere* to pluck] **— scarce'ness** *n.*

scarce·ly (skârs'lē) *adv.* **1.** Only just; barely. **2.** Not quite; hardly.

scar·ci·ty (skâr'sə·tē) *n.* *pl.* **·ties** **1.** Inadequate supply; insufficiency; dearth. **2.** Infrequency of occurrence; rarity.

scare (skâr) *v.* **scared, scar·ing** *v.t.* **1.** To strike with sudden fear; frighten. **2.** To drive or force by frightening: with *off* or *away*. **—** *v.i.* **3.** To become scared. **— to scare up** *Informal* To get together or produce hurriedly. **—** *n.* Sudden fright, esp. from slight cause. **2.** Panic. [< ON < *skiarr* shy] **— scare'er** *n.* **— scar'ing·ly** *adv.*

scare·crow (skâr'krō') *n.* **1.** Any effigy set up to scare crows and other birds away from growing crops. **2.** Something frightening but not dangerous. **3.** A person of ragged or disreputable appearance.

scare·head (skâr'hed') *n.* *Informal* An exceptionally large newspaper headline giving news of sensational interest.

scarf¹ (skärf) *n.* *pl.* **scarfs** or **scarves** (skärvz) **1.** A band or square of cloth worn about the head, neck, etc., for warmth or protection, or as a decorative accessory. **2.** A necktie, cravat, kerchief, etc. **3.** A runner for a bureau or dresser. **4.** An official sash denoting rank. — *v.t.* To cover or decorate with or as with a scarf. [< OF *escharpe*]

scarf² (skärf) *n. pl.* **scarfs 1.** In carpentry, a lapped joint made by notching two timbers at the ends and joining them so as to form one continuous piece. Also **scarf joint. 2.** The notched end of a timber so cut. — *v.t.* **1.** To unite with a scarf joint. **2.** To cut a scarf in. [? < ON *skarfr* notch in a timber]

scar·i·fy (skar′ə-fī) *v.t.* **·fied, ·fy·ing 1.** To scratch or make slight incisions in, as the skin in surgery. **2.** To criticize severely. **3.** To stir or break up the surface of, as soil. [< MF < LL < L < Gk. < *skariphos* stylus] — **scar′i·fi′er** *n.* — **scar′i·fi·ca′tion** *n.*

SCARF JOINTS

scar·la·ti·na (skär′lə·tē′nə) *n. Pathol.* **1.** Scarlet fever. **2.** A mild form of scarlet fever. [< Ital. See SCARLET.]

scar·let (skär′lit) *n.* **1.** A brilliant red, inclining to orange. **2.** Cloth or clothing of this color. — *adj.* **1.** Being scarlet in color. **2.** Unchaste; whorish. [< OF < Med.L, prob. < Arabic < Persian *saqalāt* a rich, scarlet cloth]

scarlet fever *Pathol.* An acute infectious bacterial disease characterized by a diffused scarlet rash followed by scaling of the skin.

scarlet runner A tall climbing bean of tropical America, having vivid red flowers and long seed pods.

scarlet tanager An American tanager, the male of which has brilliant red plumage with black wings and tail.

scarp (skärp) *n.* **1.** A steep slope. **2.** An embankment or wall at the outer part of a fortification. — *v.t.* To cut or form to a steep slope. [< AF < Ital. *scarpa*]

scarves (skärvz) Alternative plural of SCARF¹.

scar·y (skâr′ē) *adj.* **scar·i·er, scar·i·est** *Informal* **1.** Easily scared; timid. **2.** Causing fear or alarm; frightening.

scat (skat) *v.i.* **scat·ted, scat·ting** *Informal* To go away; depart: usu. in the imperative. [? < SCATTER]

scathe (skāth) *v.t.* **scathed, scath·ing 1.** To criticize severely. **2.** To injure severely; harm. — *n.* Severe injury; harm. [< ON < *skathi* to harm] — **scathe′ful** *adj.*

scathe·less (skāth′lis) *adj.* Free from harm.

scath·ing (skā′thing) *adj.* Mercilessly severe; blasting; withering: a *scathing* rebuke. — **scath′ing·ly** *adv.*

scato- *combining form* Dung; excrement. Also, before vowels, **scat-.** [< Gk. *skōr* dung]

scat·o·log·i·cal (skat′ə·loj′i·kəl) *adj.* Of or pertaining to scatology; obscene. Also **scat′o·log′ic.**

sca·tol·o·gy (skə·tol′ə·jē) *n.* The study of, or a preoccupation with, excrement. — **sca·tol′o·gist** *n.*

scat·ter (skat′ər) *v.t.* **1.** To throw about in various places; sprinkle. **2.** To separate and drive away in different directions; disperse. — *v.i.* **3.** To separate and go in different directions. [ME *scateren* to squander] — **scat′ter·er** *n.*

scat·ter·brain (skat′ər·brān′) *n.* A flighty or forgetful person. — **scat′ter·brained′** *adj.*

scatter rug A small rug used to cover only part of a floor.

scaup (skôp) *n.* A sea duck of northern regions, related to the canvasback, having the head and neck black in the male. Also **scaup duck.** [Var. of SCALP]

scav·enge (skav′inj) *v.* **·enged, ·eng·ing** *v.t.* **1.** To remove filth, rubbish, and refuse from, as streets. — *v.i.* **2.** To act as a scavenger. **3.** To search or rummage, as for food. [Back formation < SCAVENGER]

scav·en·ger (skav′in·jər) *n.* **1.** An animal that feeds on carrion, as the buzzard. **2.** One who searches refuse, garbage, etc., for usable material. **3.** A street cleaner. [ME < AF < Flemish *scauwen* to see]

sce·nar·i·o (si·nâr′ē·ō, ·nä′rē·ō) *n. pl.* **·nar·i·os 1.** A summary or outline of the plot of a dramatic work. **2.** The written plot and arrangement of incidents of a motion picture. [< Ital. < LL < L < Gk. *skēnē* tent, stage]

sce·nar·ist (si·nâr′ist, ·nä′rist) *n.* One who writes scenarios.

scene (sēn) *n.* **1.** A locality as presented to view. **2.** The place in which the action of a drama is supposed to occur; setting. **3.** The surroundings of any event: the *scene* of the crime. **4.** A division of an act of a play; one comprehensive event in a play. **5.** Any incident or episode that may serve as the subject of a description. **6.** The painted canvas screens for the background for a play. **7.** Any striking display; esp., a display of excited feeling. — **behind the scenes 1.** Out of sight of a theater audience. **2.** Privately; in secret. [< OF < LL < Gk. *skēnē* tent, stage]

scen·er·y (sē′nər·ē) *n. pl.* **·er·ies 1.** The appearance or visible aspects of a landscape, locality, etc. **2.** The settings, backdrops, etc., of a theatrical production.

sce·nic (sē′nik, sen′ik) *adj.* **1.** Of or pertaining to natural scenery; picturesque. **2.** Relating to stage scenery. Also **sce′ni·cal.** — **sce′ni·cal·ly** *adv.*

scent (sent) *n.* **1.** A distinctive odor. **2.** A residual odor which an animal can be tracked. **3.** A trail, trace, or c aiding pursuit or investigation. **4.** A perfume. **5.** T sense of smell. — **Syn.** See SMELL. — *v.t.* **1.** To perce by the sense of smell. **2.** To form a suspicion of. **3.** cause to be fragrant; perfume. — *v.i.* **4.** To hunt by sense of smell: said of hounds. [< OF *sentir* to discern the senses, feel] — **scent′less** *adj.*

scep·ter (sep′tər) *n.* **1.** A staff carried as the badge of co mand or sovereignty. **2.** Kingly office or power. — *v.t.* confer the scepter on; invest with royal power. Also *e Brit.* **scep′tre** (-tər). [< OF < L < Gk. *skēptron* staff]

scep·tic (skep′tik), **scep·ti·cal,** etc. See SKEPTIC, etc.

sched·ule (skej′ool, -əl, -oo·əl; *Brit.* shed′yool) *n.* **1.** written or printed statement specifying the details of so matter. **2.** A list; catalogue. **3.** A timetable, as for a tra portation service. **4.** A detailed and timed plan; progr — *v.t.* **·uled, ·ul·ing 1.** To place in or on a schedule. **2.** make a schedule of. **3.** To appoint or plan for a specif time or date. [ME < OF < LL < L *scida, scheda* leaf paper]

sche·ma (skē′mə) *n. pl.* **·ma·ta** (-mə·tə) **1.** A scheme summary. **2.** A plan or diagram, of a process, organizati etc. [< Gk. See SCHEME.] — **sche·mat·ic** (skē·mat′ik) ·**i·cal** *adj.* — **sche·mat′i·cal·ly** *adv.*

sche·ma·tism (skē′mə·tiz′əm) *n.* **1.** A particular form disposition of anything. **2.** Orderly arrangement of pa

sche·ma·tize (skē′mə·tīz) *v.t.* **·tized, ·tiz·ing** To form i or arrange according to a scheme or schema.

scheme (skēm) *n.* **1.** A plan of something to be done plot or device for the accomplishment of an object. **2.** systematic arrangement, plan, or design. **3.** A secret or derhand plot or plan. **4.** An outline drawing or sketch; c gram. — *v.* **schemed, schem·ing** *v.t.* **1.** To make a sche for; plan. **2.** To plan or plot in an underhand manner. *v.i.* **3.** To make schemes; plan or plot. [< L < Gk. *sché -atos* a form, plan] — **schem′er** *n.*

scher·zan·do (sker·tsän′dō) *Music adv.* In a sportive playful manner. — *adj.* Sportive; playful. [See SCHERZ

scher·zo (sker′tsō) *n. pl.* **·zos** or **·zi** (-tsē) *Music* A pl ful or satirical movement, often following a slow moveme as in a symphony or sonata. [< Ital., a jest < G *sche*

Schick test (shik) A test to determine the susceptibility a person to diphtheria by the subcutaneous injection c diluted diphtheria toxin. [after Dr. Béla *Schick*, born 18 who devised it]

schil·ling (shil′ing) *n.* **1.** The standard monetary uni Austria: in 1960 worth about 4 U.S. cents; also, a coin of t value. **2.** Formerly, a minor coin of Germany. [< G]

schism (siz′əm) *n.* **1.** A division of a church or other org ized body into factions. **2.** The offense of causing such vision. **3.** Any group, esp., an ecclesiastical one, separa from a larger body. [< OF < LL < Gk. *schizein* to split

schis·mat·ic (siz·mat′ik) *adj.* Of, having the character implying, or promoting schism. Also **schis·mat′i·cal.** — One who makes or participates in a schism. — **schis·ma cal·ly** *adv.* — **schis·mat′i·cal·ness** *n.*

schist (shist) *n. Geol.* Any rock that readily splits or clea into parallel layers: also spelled *shist.* [< F < L < Gk. *schizein* to split] — **schist′ous, schist·ose** (shis′tōs) *adj.*

schizo- *combining form* Split; divided. Also, before vow **schiz-.** [< Gk. *schizein* to split]

schiz·o·carp (skiz′ə-kärp) *n. Bot.* A pericarp splitting maturity into two or more one-seeded indehiscent portic — **schiz′o·car′pous, schiz/o·car′pic** *adj.*

schiz·oid (skit′soid, skiz′oid) *Psychiatry n.* One who is normally shy and withdrawn. — *adj.* **1.** Of, pertaining or like a schizoid. **2.** Loosely, of or pertaining to sch phrenia. [< SCHIZ(OPHRENIA) + -OID]

schiz·o·phre·ni·a (skit′sō·frē′nē·ə, skiz′ō-) *n. Psychi* Any of a group of psychotic disorders characterized by lusions, withdrawal, conflicting emotions, and deteriorat of the personality. [< NL < Gk. *schizein* to split + *ph* mind] — **schiz′o·phren′ic** (-fren′ik) *adj. & n.*

schle·miel (shlə·mēl′) *n. Slang* An inept, easily duped t son; a bungler; dolt. Also **schle·mihl′.** [< Yiddish < brew *Shelumiēl*, a personal name]

schnapps (shnäps, shnaps) *n. pl.* **schnapps** Any stro liquor, esp. a type of gin. Also **schnaps.** [< G, < Du. sn gulp, mouthful]

schnau·zer (shnou′zər) *n.* A terrier originally develope Germany, having a wiry, black or pepper-and-salt coat. G *schnauzen* to growl, snarl]

schol·ar (skol′ər) *n.* **1.** A person eminent for learning, in the humanities. **2.** One who does authoritative resea and writing in some special field. **3.** The holder of a sch arship. **4.** A pupil. [See SCHOOL¹.]

schol·ar·ly (skol′ər·lē) *adj.* **1.** Of or befitting a schol *scholarly* methods. **2.** Having the qualities of a scholar. *adv.* After the manner of a scholar.

schol·ar·ship (skol′ər·ship) *n.* **1.** The mental attainme

qualities of a scholar; learning; erudition. **2.** Scholarly
uiry or research. **3.** Maintenance or a stipend awarded
, student; also, the position of such a student.

·las·tic (skŏ·las'tik, skə-) *adj.* **1.** Of, or characteristic
:holars, education, or schools. **2.** Of, or characteristic of
medieval schoolmen. **3.** Precise; pedantic. Also **scho·
ti·cal.** — *n.* **1.** *Often cap.* An advocate of scholasticism.
A pedant. [< L < Gk. < *scholazein* to be at leisure,
ote leisure to study] — **scho·las'ti·cal·ly** *adv.*

·las·ti·cism (skŏ·las'tə·siz'əm, skə-) *n.* **1.** *Often cap.*
systematized Christian logic, philosophy, and theology
iedieval scholars. **2.** Any system of teaching that insists
:raditional doctrines, etc.

ol¹ (skōol) *n.* **1.** Any institution devoted primarily to
arting knowledge or to developing certain skills or tal-
; esp., an educational institution for children. **2.** A
:e where formal instruction is given; a schoolhouse or
oolroom. **3.** A session or course of study at an education
istitution. **4.** The pupils in an educational institution.
A subdivision of a university: the *school* of medicine, law,
6. A body of disciples of a teacher or system; also, the
em, methods, or opinions characteristic of those thus as-
ated: a painting of the Flemish *school.* **7.** A general
e of life, manners, etc.: a gentleman of the old *school.* **8.**
, sphere or means of instruction: the *school* of hard
cks. — *v.t.* **1.** To instruct in or as in a school; train;
cate. **2.** To subject to rule or discipline. — **Syn.** See
CH. [OE < L < Gk. *scholē* leisure, school]

ol² (skōol) *n.* A large number of fish, whales, etc., swim-
together; shoal. — *v.i.* To swim together in a school.
Du., a crowd, school of fishes]

ol board A board of education.

ol·book (skōol'bŏok') *n.* A book for use in school.

ol·boy (skōol'boi') *n.* A boy attending school.

ol·girl (skōol'gûrl') *n.* A girl attending school.

ol·house (skōol'hous') *n.* A building in which a school
inducted.

ol·ing (skōol'ing) *n.* **1.** Instruction given at school.
!he process of teaching or being taught in a school.

ol·man (skōol'mən) *n.* *pl.* **·men** (-mən) One of the
·logians of the Middle Ages; a scholastic.

ol·marm (skōol'märm') *n.* *Informal* A woman school-
her. Also **school'ma'am'** (-mam').

ol·mas·ter (skōol'mas'tər, -mäs'-) *n.* **1.** A man who
hes in cr directs a school. **2.** Anything that instructs or
iplines: Necessity was his *schoolmaster.*

ol·mate (skōol'māt') *n.* A fellow pupil.

ol·mis·tress (skōol'mis'tris) *n.* A woman who teaches
ool.

ol·room (skōol'rōom', -rŏom') *n.* A room in which
ses are held or instruction is given.

ol·teach·er (skōol'tē'chər) *n.* One who gives instruc-
in a school below the college level.

ol year The part of the year during which a school or
schools of an educational system are in session.

on·er (skōo'nər) *n.* **1.** A fore-and-aft rigged vessel
ing two or more masts. **2.** A large
glass. [New England < dial.
n to skim on water]

t·tische (shot'ish) *n.* **1.** A round
:e similar to the polka, but slower.
!usic for this dance, in duple me-
[< G (*der*) *schottische* (*tanz*)
) Scottish (dance)]

va (shwä, shvä) *n.* *Phonet.* A
k, neutral vowel sound occurring
iost of the unstressed syllables in
lish speech, as the *a* in *alone*, the *e*
ippen, or the *u* in *circus*: written
[< G < Hebrew *shewa*]

t·ic (sī·at'ik) *adj.* Pertaining to
ffecting the hip or its nerves. —
i sciatic nerve or part. [< MF
Ved.L < Gk. < *ischion* hip, hip joint]

t·i·ca (sī·at'i·kə) *n.* *Pathol.* **1.** Neuralgia affecting the
:ic nerve. **2.** Any painful affection of the hip or adjoin-
areas. [See SCIATIC.]

nce (sī'əns) *n.* **1.** Any department of knowledge in
:h the results of investigation have been logically ar-
;ed and systematized. **2.** Knowledge of facts, phenom-
laws, and proximate causes, gained and verified by exact
rvation, organized experiment, and ordered thinking.
.n orderly presentation of facts, reasonings, doctrines,
beliefs concerning some subject or group of subjects. **4.**
ematic knowledge in general. **5.** Expertness or skill ow-
ig from knowledge. [< OF < L < *scire* to know]

ace fiction Fiction in which facts or theories of con-
porary science are imaginatively employed.

SCHOONER

a Jib topsail. *b*
Flying jib. *c* Jib.
d Foresail. *e* Fore
club topsail. *f*
Maintopmast stay-
sail. *g* Main club
topsail. *h* Mainsail.

sci·en·tif·ic (sī'ən·tif'ik) *adj.* **1.** Of, discovered by, derived
from, or used in science. **2.** Agreeing with the rules, principles, or methods of science; accurate; systematic; exact. **3.**
Versed in science or a science; eminently learned or skillful.
Also **sci'en·tif'i·cal.** [< LL < *scientia* knowledge + *facere*
to make] — **sci'en·tif'i·cal·ly** *adv.*

sci·en·tist (sī'ən·tist) *n.* One versed in science or devoted
to scientific study or investigation.

scil·i·cet (sil'ə·set) *adv.* Namely; to wit; that is to say. [<
L *scire licet* it is permitted to know]

scim·i·tar (sim'ə·tər) *n.* A curved Oriental sword or saber.
Also **scim'e·tar, scim'i·ter.** [< MF < Ital. *scimitarra*]

scin·til·la (sin·til'ə) *n.* A spark; trace; iota: a *scintilla* of
truth. [< L]

scin·til·late (sin'tə·lāt) *v.* **·lat·ed, ·lat·ing** *v.i.* **1.** To give
off sparks. **2.** To sparkle; glitter. **3.** To twinkle, as a star.
— *v.t.* **4.** To give off as a spark or sparks. [< L < *scintilla*
spark] — **scin'til·lant** *adj.* — **scin'til·lat'ing·ly** *adv.* —
scin'til·la'tion *n.*

sci·o·lism (sī'ə·liz'əm) *n.* Superficial knowledge; charlatan-
ism. [< L *scius* < *scire* to know] — **sci'o·lis'tic** *adj.*

sci·on (sī'ən) *n.* **1.** A twig or shoot cut from a plant or tree,
esp. for grafting. **2.** A child or descendant. [< OF < L *secare*
to cut]

scis·sile (sis'il) *adj.* Capable of being cut or split easily
and evenly. [< L *scindere* to cut]

scis·sion (sizh'ən, sish'-) *n.* **1.** The act of cutting or
splitting, or the state of being cut. **2.** Any division. [<
OF < LL < *scissus*, pp. of *scindere* to cut]

scis·sor (siz'ər) *v.t. & v.i.* To cut with scissors.

scis·sors (siz'ərz) *n.pl.* (*construed as sing. in defs. 2 & 3*) **1.**
A cutting implement with handles and a pair of blades pivoted face to face so that the opposed edges may be brought together on the object to be cut. Also **pair of scissors. 2.** In
wrestling, a hold secured by clasping the legs about the body
or head of the opponent. **3.** A gymnastic feat in which the
movement of the legs suggests that of scissors. [< OF <
LL *cisoria*, pl. of *cisorium* cutting instrument]

scissors kick In swimming, a kick performed usu. with the
side stroke, in which both legs are thrust apart, the upper
leg bent at the knee while the lower is kept straight, then
brought sharply together.

scis·sor·tail (siz'ər·tāl') *n.* A flycatcher of the SW U.S.
and Mexico, having a scissorlike tail.

scis·sure (sizh'ər, sish'-) *n.* **1.** A lengthwise cut; fissure.
2. Any division, rupture, or schism. [See SCISSION.]

scle·ra (sklir'ə) *n.* *Anat.* The hard, white, fibrous outer coat
of the eyeball, continuous with the cornea. For illus. see EYE.
[< NL < Gk. *sklēros* hard]

scle·ren·chy·ma (sklə·reng'kə·mə) *n.* *Bot.* A tough, thick-
walled tissue that protects and supports plants. [< NL <
Gk. *sklēros* hard + *enchyma* infusion]

sclero- *combining form* Hardness; hard. Also, before vowels, **scler-.** [< Gk. *sklēros* hard]

scle·rosed (sklə·rōst') *adj.* Affected with sclerosis; grown
abnormally hard.

scle·ro·sis (sklə·rō'sis) *n.* *pl.* **·ses** (-sēz) **1.** *Pathol.* The
thickening and hardening of a tissue or part. **2.** *Bot.* The
hardening of a plant cell wall by the formation of lignin in it.
[< Med.L < Gk. *sklēros* hard] — **scle·ro'sal** *adj.*

scle·rot·ic (sklə·rot'ik) *adj.* **1.** Dense; hard, as the sclera.
2. Of or pertaining to the sclera. **3.** *Pathol.* Pertaining to or
affected with sclerosis.

scle·rous (sklir'əs) *adj.* Hard or indurated; bony.

scoff (skôf, skof) *v.i.* **1.** To speak with contempt or derision; jeer: often with *at.* — *v.t.* **2.** To deride; mock. — *n.*
An expression or an object of contempt or derision. [ME
scof, prob. < Scand.] — **scoff'er** *n.* — **scoff'ing·ly** *adv.*

scoff·law (skôf'lô', skof'-) *n.* One who scoffs at or flouts
the law; esp., a habitual violator of traffic laws, etc.

scold (skōld) *v.t.* **1.** To find fault with harshly. — *v.i.*
2. To find fault harshly or continuously. — *n.* One who
scolds, esp. a shrewish woman. [Appar. < ON *skáld* poet,
satirist] — **scold'er** *n.* — **scold'ing·ly** *adv.*

scol·lop (skol'əp), etc. See SCALLOP, etc.

scom·broid (skom'broid) *adj.* Of or pertaining to a widely distributed family of fishes, including mackerels. — *n.*
A scombroid fish. [< NL < L < Gk. *skombros* mackerel]

sconce¹ (skons) *n.* **1.** A small earthwork or fort. **2.** A
protective shelter, covering, or screen. [< Du. *schanz*
fortress, wicker basket; infl. in form by SCONCE²]

sconce² (skons) *n.* An ornamental wall bracket for holding
a candle or other light. [< OF < Med.L *sconsa* < L *ab-
scondere* to hide]

scone (skōn, skon) *n.* A round tea cake or biscuit usu. eaten
with butter. [? < MDu. *schoonbrot* fine bread]

scoop (skōop) *n.* **1.** A shovellike instrument or large shovel
with high sides. **2.** A small shovellike implement or ladle

used by grocers, druggists, etc. **3.** An implement for bailing, as water from a boat. **4.** A spoon-shaped instrument for using in a cavity: a surgeons' *scoop*. **5.** An implement for dispensing uniform, spherical portions of ice cream, etc.; also, a portion thus dispensed. **6.** An act of scooping; a scooping movement. **7.** *Informal* A large gain, esp. in speculation. **8.** A bowl-shaped cavity. **9.** *Slang* In journalism, a news story obtained and published ahead of rival papers. **10.** *Slang* Any item of recent news. — *v.t.* **1.** To take or dip out with or as with a scoop. **2.** To hollow out, as with a scoop; excavate. **3.** To empty with a scoop. **4.** *Informal* To heap up or gather in or as in scoopfuls. **5.** *Slang* In journalism, to obtain and publish a news story before (a rival). [Fusion of MDu. *schope* vessel for bailing out water, and *schoppe* shovel] — **scoop'er** *n.*

scoot (skōōt) *v.i. Informal* To go quickly; dart off. — *n.* The act of scooting; a hurried darting off. [Prob. < Scand.]

scoot·er (skōō'tər) *n.* **1.** A child's vehicle consisting of a footboard mounted between two tandem wheels and steered by means of a long handle attached to the front axle. **2.** A motor scooter (which see). **3.** A sailboat with runners that may be used in water and on ice.

scope (skōp) *n.* **1.** Room for the exercise of faculties or function; capacity for achievement or effectiveness. **2.** Range of view or activity; outlook: a mind of limited *scope*. **3.** The area or sphere in which any activity takes place: the *scope* of a scientific work. **4.** *Naut.* The length or sweep of a cable at which a ship rides at anchor. **5.** *Informal* Any of various optical or detecting instruments, as a telescope. [< Ital. < L < Gk. < *skopeein* to look at]

-scope *combining form* An instrument for viewing, observing, or indicating: *telescope*. [< Gk. *skopeein* to watch]

sco·pol·a·mine (skō·pol'ə·mēn, -min, skō'pə·lam'ēn, -in) *n. Chem.* An alkaloid, $C_{17}H_{21}O_4N$, extracted from certain plants, the salts of which are used in medicine as a hypnotic and sedative. [< G < NL, after G. A. *Scopoli*, 1723–88, Italian naturalist]

-scopy *combining form* Observation; viewing: *microscopy*. [< Gk. < *skopeein* to watch]

scor·bu·tic (skôr·byōō'tik) *adj.* Relating to, characteristic of, or affected with scurvy: also **scor·bu'ti·cal.** [< NL < Med.L *scorbutus* scurvy] — **scor·bu'ti·cal·ly** *adv.*

scorch (skôrch) *v.t.* **1.** To change the color, taste, etc., of by slight burning; char the surface of. **2.** To wither or shrivel by heat. **3.** To criticize severely. — *v.i.* **4.** To become scorched. **5.** *Informal* To go at high speed. — *n.* **1.** A superficial burn. **2.** A mark caused by heat, as a slight burn. [Prob. akin to ME *skorken* < ON *skorpna* to dry up, shrivel] — **scorch'ing** *adj.* — **scorch'ing·ly** *adv.*

scorched-earth policy (skôrcht'ûrth') The military policy of destroying all crops, industrial equipment, dwellings, etc., so as to leave nothing for the use of the enemy.

scorch·er (skôr'chər) *n.* **1.** One who or that which scorches. **2.** *Informal* An extremely hot day. **3.** *Informal* Severe or caustic criticism. **4.** *Informal* One who or that which moves at great speed.

score (skôr, skōr) *n.* **1.** The record of the winning points in a competition or game; also, the total of such points made by a player or a team. **2.** *Psychol.* A quantitative value assigned to an individual or group response to a test or series of tests. **3.** Grade or rating in a test or examination. **4.** Any record, esp. of indebtedness. **5.** A notch or groove cut in something for keeping a tally. **6.** Something charged or laid up against one: to settle old *scores*. **7.** A set of twenty. **8.** *pl.* An indefinitely large number. **9.** *Music* The complete notation for a composition, showing the various instrumental or vocal parts. — **to know the score** *Informal* To be aware of the real facts of a situation. — *v.* **scored, scor·ing** *v.t.* **1.** To mark with notches, cuts, or lines. **2.** To mark with cuts or lines for the purpose of keeping a tally or record. **3.** To obliterate or cross out by means of a line drawn through: with *out*. **4.** To make or gain, as points, runs, etc. **5.** To count for a score of, as in games. **6.** To rate or grade, as an examination paper. **7.** *Music* a To orchestrate. b To arrange or adapt for an instrument. **8.** *Informal* To criticize severely. **9.** In cooking, to make superficial cuts in (meat, etc.). — *v.i.* **10.** To make points, runs, etc., as in a game. **11.** To keep score. **12.** To make notches, cuts, etc. **13.** To win an advantage or success. [OE < ON *skor* notch, tally] — **scor'er** *n.*

sco·ri·a (skôr'ē·ə, skō'rē·ə) *n. pl.* **·ri·ae** (-ri·ē) **1.** Refuse or slag remaining after metal has been smelted. **2.** Loose, clinkerlike pieces of lava. [< L < Gk. *skōria* refuse] — **sco'ri·a'ceous** (-ā'shəs) *adj.*

sco·ri·fy (skôr'ə·fī, skō'rə-) *v.t.* **·fied, ·fy·ing** *Metall.* **1.** To separate, as gold or silver, from an ore by smelting with lead, borax, etc. **2.** To reduce to scoria or dross. — **sco'ri·fi·ca'tion** *n.*

scorn (skôrn) *n.* **1.** A feeling of contempt or loathing, as for someone or something deemed inferior or unworthy of attention; disdain. **2.** Behavior characterized by such a

feeling; derision. **3.** An expression of contempt or disc**[text cut off]** **4.** An object of contempt. — *v.t.* **1.** To hold in or t**[cut off]** with contempt; despise. **2.** To reject with scorn; disc**[cut off]** spurn. [< OF < *escarnir* < Gmc.] — **scorn'er** *n.*
scorn'ful *adj.* — **scorn'ful·ly** *adv.* — **scorn'ful·ness** *n*

Scor·pi·o (skôr'pē·ō) *n.* A constellation, the Scor**[cut off]** containing the bright star Antares; also, the eighth sig**[cut off]** the zodiac. Also **Scor'pi·us** (-əs). See ZODIAC. [< L**[cut off]**

scor·pi·on (skôr'pē·ən) *n.* **1.** One of an order of arachnids found chiefly in warmer regions, having an elongated, lobsterlike body and a segmented tail that bears a venomous sting. **2.** An instrument of chastisement; a whip or scourge. I *Kings* xii 11. [< OF < L < Gk. *skorpios*]

SCORPION s Stinger. (To 8 inch long)

scot (skot) *n.* An assessment or tax. [Fusion of ON *skot* and OF *escot*]

Scot (skot) *n.* **1.** A native of Scotland: also called *Scotsman*. **2.** Formerly, a Gaelic Highlander. **3.** One of a Gaelic people who migrated i**[cut off]** fifth century to northwestern Britain from Ireland. *Scottas*, pl., the Irish < LL *Scotus, Scoti*]

scotch (skoch) *v.t.* **1.** To cut; scratch. **2.** To wound to maim or cripple. **3.** To put down; crush or suppress**[cut off]** *n.* **1.** A superficial cut; a scratch; notch. **2.** A line t**[cut off]** on the ground, as for hopscotch. [Origin uncertain]

Scotch (skoch) *n.* **1.** The people of Scotland collecti**[cut off]** with *the*. **2.** One or all of the dialects spoken by the p**[cut off]** of Scotland. **3.** Scotch whisky. — *adj.* Of or pertaini**[cut off]** Scotland, its inhabitants, or their language; Scottish; S**[cut off]**
Scotch·man (skoch'mən) *n. pl.* **·men** (-mən) A Scot; S**[cut off]** man. ♦ These forms are preferred to *Scotchman*.

Scotch tape A rolled strip of transparent cellulose having an adhesive on one side: a trade name.

Scotch terrier A Scottish terrier.

Scotch whisky Whisky made in Scotland from m**[cut off]** barley and having rather a smoky flavor.

sco·ter (skō'tər) *n.* Any of several dark sea ducks. dial. E *scote* scoot]

scot-free (skot'frē') *adj.* **1.** Without injury or loss**[cut off]** harmed; whole. **2.** Free from scot; untaxed.

Scot·land Yard (skot'lənd) The headquarters of the don Metropolitan Police and of the London Criminal In**[cut off]** gation Department, since 1890 located at the **New Sco**[cut off]** **Yard** on the Thames Embankment.

Scots (skots) *adj.* Scottish. — *n.* The Scottish dial**[cut off]** English. [Earlier *Scottis*, var. of SCOTTISH]

Scots·man (skots'mən) *n. pl.* **·men** (-mən) A Scot.

Scot·ti·cism (skot'ə·siz'əm) *n.* A form of expression idiom peculiar to the Scottish people.

Scot·tish (skot'ish) *adj.* Pertaining to or characteris**[cut off]** Scotland, its inhabitants, or their language: also *Scots*, *n.* **1.** The dialect of English spoken in Scotland, esp. i**[cut off]** Lowlands; Scots. **2.** The people of Scotland collecti**[cut off]** with *the*. [OE *Scottisc*]

Scottish Gaelic The Goidelic language of the Sc**[cut off]** Highlands: also called *Erse*.

Scottish terrier A small, short-legged terrier origin**[cut off]** in Scotland, having a large head and a wiry coat: also **[cut off]** *terrier*. Also *Informal* **Scot·tie** (skot'ē), **Scot'ty.**

scoun·drel (skoun'drəl) *n.* A mean, unprincipled r**[cut off]** a rogue. — *adj.* Of or characteristic of a scoundrel. AF, OF < L *ex-* off + *condere* to hide] — **scoun'drel·l**[cut off]**

scour[1] (skour) *v.t.* **1.** To clean or brighten by tho**[cut off]** washing and rubbing, as with sand or steel wool. **2.** remove dirt, etc., from; clean: to *scour* wool. **3.** To re**[cut off]** by or as by rubbing away. **4.** To clear by means of a s**[cut off]** current of water; flush. **5.** To purge the bowels of. clean (wheat) before milling. — *v.i.* **7.** To rub some vigorously so as to clean or brighten it. **8.** To become b**[cut off]** or clean by rubbing. — *n.* **1.** The act of scouring. place scoured, as by running water. **3.** A cleanser us**[cut off]** cleaning wool. **4.** *Usu. pl.* A watery diarrhea in c**[cut off]** [Prob. < MDu. < OF *escurer*, ult. < L *ex-* out + *cur*[cut off]** take care of] — **scour'er** *n.*

scour[2] (skour) *v.t.* **1.** To range over or through, as in ing a search. **2.** To move or run swiftly over or alon**[cut off]** *v.i.* **3.** To range about, as in making a search. **4.** To swiftly. [ME *scoure*] — **scour'er** *n.*

scourge (skûrj) *n.* **1.** A whip for inflicting sufferi**[cut off]** punishment. **2.** Any instrumentality or means for ca**[cut off]** suffering or death. **3.** Severe punishment. **4.** A ca**[cut off]** suffering or trouble. — *v.t.* **scourged, scourg·ing** **1.** whip severely; flog. **2.** To punish severely; afflict. [**[cut off]** < LL *excoriare* to flay] — **scourg'er** *n.*

scour·ings (skour'ingz) *n.pl.* **1.** The residue after ing grain. **2.** Dirt or other residue left after any scou**[cut off]**

scout[1] (skout) *n.* **1.** One who or that which is enga**[cut off]** scouting; esp., a person sent out to observe and get inf**[cut off]** tion, as of a war enemy, rival team in sports, etc. **2.** T**[cut off]** of scouting. **3.** *Slang* A fellow or friend. **4.** A Boy o**[cut off]**

ut. — *v.t.* **1.** To observe or spy upon for the purpose of ...ning information. — *v.i.* **2.** To go or act as a scout. — ...cout around To go in search. [< OF < L *auscultare* to ...en] — scout'er *n.*

...t² (skout) *v.t. & v.i.* To mock; jeer. [< Scand.]

...t car An armored motor car for reconnaissance work.

...t·ing (skout'ing) *n.* The activities of a scout, esp. of a ...y Scout or Girl Scout.

...t·mas·ter (skout'mas'tər, -mäs'-) *n.* The leader of a ...p of Boy Scouts.

...w (skou) *n.* A large boat with a flat bottom and square ...s, chiefly used for freight and usually towed. [< Du. ...*nw* boat propelled by a pole < MDu. *schoude*]

...wl (skoul) *n.* **1.** A lowering of the brows, as in anger, ...pproval, or sullenness. **2.** Gloomy aspect. — *v.i.* **1.** ...lower and contract the brows in anger, sullenness, or dis-...roval. **2.** To look threatening; lower. — *v.t.* **3.** To ...ct or express by scowling. [ME *skoul*, prob. < Scand.] ...cowl'er *n.* — scowl'ing·ly *adv.*

...b·ble (skrab'əl) *v.* ·bled, ·bling *v.i.* **1.** To scratch, ...pe, or paw, as with the hands. **2.** To make irregular or ...aningless marks; scribble. **3.** To struggle or strive. — **4.** To make meaningless marks on; scribble on. **5.** To ...her hurriedly; scrape together. — *n.* **1.** The act of ...bbling or scrambling. **2.** A scrawling character, mark, ...; scribble. **3.** A sparse growth, as of underbrush. [< ...*schrabbelen*, freq. of *schrabben* to scratch]

...g (skrag) *v.t.* scragged, scrag·ging *Informal* To use ...ghly; wring the neck of; esp., to kill by hanging. — *n.* ...omething thin or lean, as a person. **2.** *Slang* The human ...k. **3.** A lean or bony piece of meat. [? < Scand.]

...g·gly (skrag'lē) *adj.* ·gli·er, ·gli·est Unkempt; shaggy.

...g·gy (skrag'ē) *adj.* ·gi·er, ·gi·est **1.** Rough. **2.** Lean; ...wny; bony. — scrag'gi·ly *adv.* — scrag'gi·ness *n.*

...m (skram) *v.i.* scrammed, scram·ming *U.S. Slang* ...go away; leave quickly. [Prob. short for SCRAMBLE]

...m·ble (skram'bəl) *v.* ·bled, ·bling *v.i.* **1.** To move by ...mbering or crawling on hands and feet. **2.** To struggle ...h others in a disorderly manner; scuffle; also, to strive for ...mething in such a manner. **3.** *Aeron.* To put interceptor ...raft into the air hurriedly to meet enemy aircraft. — **4.** To mix together haphazardly. **5.** To gather or col-...hurriedly or confusedly. **6.** To fry (eggs) with the yolks ...whites stirred together. **7.** *Telecom.* To alter or garble ...ignal) so that a special receiving apparatus is needed to ...der it comprehensible. — *n.* **1.** The act of scrambling. ...A disorderly performance or struggle. **3.** A difficult ...b or trek, as over rocks or rough terrain. [Prob. nasal-...var. of SCRABBLE] — scram'bler *n.*

...p¹ (skrap) *n.* **1.** A small piece cut or broken from some-...g; fragment. **2.** A brief printed or written extract. **3.** ...Pieces of crisp fat tissue after the oil has been expressed ...cooking; also, any bits of food. **4.** Old or refuse metal. ...*t.* scrapped, scrap·ping **1.** To break up into scrap. **2.** ...discard. — *adj.* Having the form of scraps; discarded ...r use. [< ON *skrapa* to scrape]

...p² (skrap) *v.i.* scrapped, scrap·ping *Slang* To fight; ...rrel. — *n.* A quarrel, fight, or disagreement. [< ...APE (*n.* def. 2)] — scrap'per *n.*

...p·book (skrap'book') *n.* **1.** A blank book in which to ...te pictures, clippings, etc. **2.** A personal notebook.

...pe (skrāp) *v.* scraped, scrap·ing *v.t.* **1.** To rub, as with ...ething rough or sharp, so as to abrade or to remove an ...er layer or adherent matter. **2.** To remove thus: with ...*away*, etc. **3.** To rub (a rough or sharp object) across a ...ace. **4.** To rub roughly across or against (a surface). ...To dig or form by scratching or scraping. **6.** To gather ...ccumulate with effort or difficulty: usu. with *up* or *to*-...er. — *v.i.* **7.** To scrape something. **8.** To rub with a ...ting noise. **9.** To emit or produce a grating noise. **10.** ...draw the foot backward along the ground in bowing. **11.** ...manage or get along with difficulty. **12.** To be very or ...rly economical. — *n.* **1.** The act or effect of scraping; ..., the noise made by scraping. **2.** A difficult situation; ...dicament. **3.** A scraping or drawing back of the foot in ...ing. [Prob. fusion of OE *scrapian* and ON *skrapa* to ...pe, erase] — scrap'er *n.*

...p·ing (skrā'ping) *n.* **1.** The act of someone or some-...g that scrapes. **2.** The sound so produced. *Often pl.* ...t which is scraped off or together.

...p iron Old pieces of iron suitable for reworking.

...p·ple (skrap'əl) *n.* A mixture of meal or flour boiled ...h scraps of pork, seasoned, and allowed to set, usu. cooked ...frying. [Dim. of SCRAP¹]

...p·py¹ (skrap'ē) *adj.* ·pi·er, ·pi·est Composed of scraps; ...gmentary. — scrap'pi·ly *adv.* — scrap'pi·ness *n.*

...p·py² (skrap'ē) *adj.* ·pi·er, ·pi·est Pugnacious; given to ...king fights. — scrap'pi·ly *adv.* — scrap'pi·ness *n.*

scratch (skrach) *v.t.* **1.** To tear or mark the surface of with something sharp or rough. **2.** To scrape or dig with some-thing sharp or rough, as the claws or nails. **3.** To scrape lightly with the nails, etc., as to relieve itching. **4.** To rub with a grating sound; scrape. **5.** To write or draw awkward-ly or hurriedly. **6.** To erase or cancel by or as by scratches or marks. **7.** To erase or cancel the name of (a candidate) from a political ticket, while supporting the rest of the tick-et; also, to bolt (a ticket or party) in this way. **8.** To with-draw (an entry) from a race, game, etc. — *v.i.* **9.** To use the nails or claws, as in fighting or digging. **10.** To scrape the skin, etc., lightly, as to relieve itching. **11.** To make a harsh, grating noise. **12.** To manage or get along with dif-ficulty. **13.** To withdraw from a game, race, etc. **14.** In billiards and pool, to make a scratch. — *n.* **1.** A mark or incision made on a surface by scratching; also, a quick mark or scribble, as made by a pencil. **2.** A slight flesh wound or cut. **3.** A harsh, grating sound. **4.** The act of scratching. **5.** The line from which contestants start, as in racing. **6.** The contestant who competes against an allowance. **7.** In billiards, a chance shot; also, a fluke; in billiards and pool, a shot resulting in a penalty. — from scratch From the be-ginning; from nothing. — up to scratch *Informal* Meeting the standard or requirement in courage, stamina, or per-formance. — *adj.* **1.** Done by chance; haphazard. **2.** In sports, without handicap or allowance. **3.** Used for quick notes, a memorandum, etc.: a *scratch* pad. **4.** Chosen at random or by chance. [Prob. blend of ME *scratte* to scratch and *cracchen* to scratch] — scratch'er *n.*

scratch test *Med.* A test to determine the substances to which a person is allergic by rubbing allergens in small scratches made in his skin.

scratch·y (skrach'ē) *adj.* scratch·i·er, scratch·i·est **1.** Char-acterized by or covered with scratches. **2.** Making a scratch-ing noise. **3.** Straggling; shaggy; rough. **4.** That scratches or irritates. — scratch'i·ly *adv.* — scratch'i·ness *n.*

scrawl (skrôl) *v.t. & v.i.* To write hastily or illegibly. — *n.* Irregular or careless writing. [? < dial. E, var. of CRAWL]

scrawl·y (skrô'lē) *adj.* scrawl·i·er, scrawl·i·est Consisting of or characterized by ill-formed or irregular characters.

scraw·ny (skrô'nē) *adj.* ·ni·er, ·ni·est Skinny; thin. [< dial. E *scranny*, var. of SCRANNEL] — scraw'ni·ness *n.*

scream (skrēm) *v.i.* **1.** To utter a prolonged, piercing cry, as of pain, terror, or surprise. **2.** To make a prolonged, piercing sound. **3.** To laugh loudly or immoderately. **4.** To use heated, hysterical language. **5.** To have an odd or startling effect, as of screaming. — *v.t.* **6.** To utter with a scream. — *n.* **1.** A loud, shrill, prolonged cry or sound, generally denoting fear or pain. **2.** *U.S. Slang* A person or situation arousing great mirth. [ME *screamen*]

scream·er (skrē'mər) *n.* **1.** One who or that which screams. **2.** Any of various birds of South America related to the ducks.

screech (skrēch) *n.* **1.** A shrill, harsh cry; shriek. **2.** *Ca-nadian Slang* Cheap rum or wine. — *v.t.* **1.** To utter with or as with a screech. — *v.i.* **2.** To make a prolonged, harsh, piercing sound. [Var. of obs. *scritch*, prob. imit.] — screech'er *n.* — screech'y *adv.*

screech owl **1.** Any of various owls common from Canada to Brazil; esp. a small, gray species of the eastern U.S. **2.** The barn owl of England.

screed (skrēd) *n.* **1.** A prolonged tirade; harangue. **2.** A long piece of discursive prose. — *v.t.* To rend or tear into shreds. [Var. of SHRED]

screen (skrēn) *n.* **1.** That which separates or cuts off, shel-ters, or protects, as a light partition. **2.** A network, as of wire, forming a partition or panel in a window, door, etc., to exclude insects and admit air. **3.** A sieve or riddle for sift-ing. **4.** A smooth surface, on which motion pictures, etc., may be shown. **5.** A motion picture or motion pictures col-lectively. — *v.t.* **1.** To shield from observation or annoy-ance with or as with a screen. **2.** To cause to pass through a screen or sieve; sift. **3.** To show or exhibit on a screen, as a motion picture. **4.** To determine the competence or eligibil-ity of (an individual) for a specified task. — *v.i.* **5.** To be shown or be suitable for showing on a motion-picture screen. [Prob. < OF *escren, escrin*, prob. < OHG *skirm*] — screen'a·ble *adj.* — screen'er *n.*

screen·ing (skrē'ning) *n.* **1.** The act or instance of exhibit-ing a motion picture. **2.** The work of one who screens. **3.** Mesh, as of wire, fabric, or plastic, suitable for window screens and the like. **4.** *pl.* The residue of anything passed through a sieve; siftings.

screen play A motion picture.

screw (skrōō) *n.* **1.** A device resembling a nail but having a slotted head and a tapering grooved spiral for driving into wood with a screwdriver. **2.** A similar device of cylindrical form, for insertion into a corresponding grooved part: also

male or **external** screw. **3.** A cylindrical socket with a spiral groove: also **female** or **internal** screw. **4.** Anything having the form of a screw. **5.** A screw propeller. **6.** A turn of or as of a screw. **7.** Pressure; force. **8.** *Brit. Slang* Salary; pay. **9.** *Slang* A prison guard. **10.** A haggler over prices. — **to have a screw loose** *Slang* To be mentally deranged, eccentric, etc. — **to put the screws on** (or **to**) *Slang* To exert pressure or force upon. — *v.t.* **1.** To tighten, fasten, attach, etc., by or as by a screw or screws. **2.** To turn or twist. **3.** To force as if by the pressure of a screw; urge: to *screw* one's courage to the sticking point. **4.** To twist out of shape; contort, as one's features. **5.** To practice oppression or extortion on. **6.** To obtain by extortion. — *v.i.* **7.** To turn or admit of being turned as a screw. **8.** To be attached or become detached by means of screws: with *on, off,* etc. **9.** To practice oppression or extortion. [Appar. < OF *escroue* nut, female screw] — **screw′er** *n.*

screw·ball (skrōō′bôl′) *n.* *U.S. Slang* An unconventional or erratic person.

screw·driv·er (skrōō′drī′vər) *n.* **1.** A tool with a flattened metal end that fits into the slot of a screw in order to turn it. **2.** A cocktail consisting of vodka and orange juice.

screw·pile (skrōō′pīl′) *n.* A pile having a strong metal base with a screw thread to ensure firm penetration of hard ground or bedrock.

screw propeller A mechanism consisting of a revolving shaft with radiating blades set at an angle to produce a spiral action, used in propelling ships, etc.

screw thread **1.** The projecting spiral ridge of uniform pitch on the outer or inner surface of a screw or nut. **2.** A complete revolution of any point on this ridge.

screw·y (skrōō′ē) *adj.* **screw·i·er, screw·i·est** *Slang* Extremely irrational; crazy.

scrib·ble (skrib′əl) *v.* **·bled, ·bling** *v.t.* **1.** To write hastily and carelessly. **2.** To cover with careless or illegible writing or marks. — *v.i.* **3.** To write in a careless or hasty manner. **4.** To make illegible or meaningless marks. — *n.* **1.** Hasty, careless writing. **2.** Any scrawl. [< Med.L *scribillare*, freq. of L *scribere* to write] — **scrib′bler** *n.*

scribe (skrīb) *n.* **1.** One who writes or copies manuscripts. **2.** A clerk, public writer, or amanuensis. **3.** An ancient Jewish teacher, interpreter, or writer of the Mosaic law. — *v.* **scribed, scrib·ing** *v.t.* **1.** To mark or scratch with a pointed instrument. **2.** To write, inscribe, or engrave. — *v.i.* **3.** *Rare* To write; work as a scribe. [< L < *scribere* to write] — **scrib′al** *adj.*

scrim (skrim) *n.* **1.** A lightweight, open-mesh, cotton fabric, usu. white or ecru, used for draperies, etc. **2.** In the theater, a similar fabric, often painted, used as a transparency, to support artificial foliage, etc. [Origin unknown]

scrim·mage (skrim′ij) *n.* **1.** A rough-and-tumble contest; fracas. **2.** In American football, a mass play from the line of scrimmage after the ball has been placed on the ground and snapped back, the play ending when the ball is dead. **3.** In Rugby football, a scrummage. **4.** In football, a practice session or unofficial game played by opposing teams. — **line of scrimmage** In football, the hypothetic line on which the ball rests and along which the opposing linemen take position at the start of play. — *v.t. & v.i.* **·maged, ·mag·ing** To engage in a scrimmage. Also *scrummage.* [Alter. of *scrimish,* var. of SKIRMISH]

scrimp (skrimp) *v.i.* **1.** To be very or overly economical. — *v.t.* **2.** To be overly sparing with; skimp. **3.** To cut too small, narrow, etc. — *adj.* Scanty; scrimpy. [Prob. akin to OE *scrimman* to shrink, shrivel]

scrimp·y (skrim′pē) *adj.* **·i·er, ·i·est** **1.** Scanty; skimpy; short. **2.** Tending to scrimp; niggardly. — **scrimp′i·ness** *n.*

scrip[1] (skrip) *n.* **1.** A scrap of paper, esp. one containing writing. **2.** A writing; a certificate, schedule, or written list. **3.** A piece of paper money less than a dollar, formerly issued in the U.S. [< SCRIPT]

scrip[2] (skrip) *n.* A provisional document (or documents collectively) certifying that the holder is entitled to receive something else, as shares of stock or land. [Short for obs. *subscription receipt*]

script (skript) *n.* **1.** Writing of the ordinary cursive form. **2.** Type, or printed or engraved matter, in imitation of handwriting. **3.** *Law* A writing, esp. an original. **4.** A piece of writing; esp., a prepared copy of a play or dramatic role, for the use of actors. **5.** Alphabet; writing system: phonetic *script.* — *v.t. & v.i.* *U.S. Informal* To prepare a script for (a radio, television, or theatrical performance). [< OF < L *scribere* to write]

scrip·tur·al (skrip′chər·əl) *adj.* Relating to writing; written. — **scrip′tur·al·ly** *adv.* — **scrip′tur·al·ness** *n.*

Scrip·ture (skrip′chər) *n.* **1.** The books of the Old and New Testaments, including often the Apocrypha. **2.** A text or passage from the Bible. — **Scrip′tur·al** *adj.* — **Scrip′·tur·al·ly** *adv.* — **Scrip′tur·al·ness** *n.*

script·writ·er (skript′rī′tər) *n.* A writer who prepares copy for the use of an actor or announcer.

scrive (skrīv) *v.t.* **scrived, scriv·ing** To engrave. [? < L *scribere*]

scriv·en·er (skriv′ən·ər, skriv′nər) *n.* *Archaic* One ⟨ prepares deeds, contracts, and other writings; a clerk scribe. [< obs. *scrivein* < OF < Ital. < L *scribere* to wr⟩

scrod (skrod) *n.* A young codfish, esp. when split and ⟩ pared for broiling. [? < MDu. *schrode* piece cut off]

scrof·u·la (skrof′yə·lə) *n.* *Pathol.* A tuberculous condit⟨ of the lymphatic glands, characterized by enlargement, scesses, and cheeselike degeneration: also called *stru* [Orig. pl. < LL *scrofulae,* dim. pl. of *scrofa* breeding so⟩

scrof·u·lous (skrof′yə·ləs) *adj.* **1.** Pertaining to, affec⟨ with, or of the nature of scrofula. **2.** Morally corrupt; graded. — **scrof′u·lous·ly** *adv.* — **scrof′u·lous·ness** *n.*

scroll (skrōl) *n.* **1.** A roll of parchment, paper, or the ⟩ esp. one containing or intended for writing; also, the wri⟨ on such a roll. **2.** Anything resembling or suggestive ⟨ parchment roll; esp. a convoluted ornament or an o⟨ mental space or tablet on sculptured work. [Earlier *scro* alter. of obs. *scrow* < AF *escrowe*]

scroll saw A narrow-bladed hand or power saw for d⟨ curved or irregular work.

scroll·work (skrōl′wûrk′) *n.* Ornamental work of sc⟨ like pattern.

Scrooge (skrōōj), **Ebenezer** In Dickens's *A Christmas C⟨* a miser whose hard nature is transformed on Christmas ⟨

scro·tum (skrō′təm) *n.* *pl.* **·ta** (-tə), **·tums** *Anat.* ⟨ pouch of skin that contains the testicles in most mamm⟨ [< L] — **scro′tal** *adj.*

scrounge (skrounj) *v.t. & v.i.* **scrounged, scroung·ing** S⟨ **1.** To hunt about in order to take (something); pilfer. **2.** mooch; sponge; beg. — *n.* One who scrounges: also **scrou⟩ er.** [? < dial. E *scrunge* to steal]

scrub[1] (skrub) *v.* **scrubbed, scrub·bing** *v.t.* **1.** To rub orously in washing. **2.** To remove (dirt, etc.) by such tion. **3.** *U.S. Slang* To cancel; call off. — *v.i.* **4.** To something vigorously, as in washing. — *n.* The act of sc⟨ bing. [? < Scand. Cf. Dan. *skrubbe,* MDu. *shrubben.*] — **scrub′ber** *n.*

scrub[2] (skrub) *n.* **1.** A stunted tree; also, such trees co⟨ tively. **2.** A thicket or group of stunted trees or shrubs. A domestic animal of inferior breed. **4.** A poor, insignific⟨ person. **5.** In sports, a player not on the varsity or reg⟨ team. — *adj.* **6.** Undersized or stunted-looking; infe⟨ [Dial. var. of SHRUB[1]]

scrub·by (skrub′ē) *adj.* **·bi·er, ·bi·est** **1.** Of stunted gro⟨ **2.** Covered with or consisting of scrub or underbrush. — **scrub′bi·ness** *n.*

scrub·land (skrub′land′) *n.* Land covered with scrub⟨

scrub oak Any of various dwarf oaks of the United St⟨

scrub pine Any of several American pines having a t⟨ ency toward stunted or crowded growth.

scruff (skruf) *n.* The nape of the neck. [Earlier *scuff,* ON *skopt* hair]

scrum·mage (skrum′ij) *v.t. & v.i.* **·maged, ·mag·ing** scrimmage. — *n.* **1.** A scrimmage. **2.** In Rugby footba⟨ formation around the ball, out of which the ball is kicke⟨ begin play. [Var. of SCRIMMAGE] — **scrum′mag·er** *n⟩*

scrump·tious (skrump′shəs) *adj.* *Slang* Elegant or s⟨ ish; fine; delightful; splendid. [Prob. alter. of SUMPTUO⟨

scrunch (skrunch) *v.t. & v.i.* To crush; squeeze; cru⟨ — *n.* A crunch. [Imit. alter. of CRUNCH]

scru·ple (skrōō′pəl) *n.* **1.** Doubt or uncertainty regar⟨ a question of moral right or duty. **2.** An apothecar⟨ weight of twenty grains, or 1.296 grams (symbol: ℈). table front of book. **3.** A minute quantity. — *v.t. &* **·pled, ·pling** To have scruples (about). [< OF < L *scr⟨ lus* small sharp stone]

scru·pu·lous (skrōō′pyə·ləs) *adj.* **1.** Cautious in actio⟨ cause of a wish to do right; nicely conscientious. **2.** Re⟨ ing from the exercise of scruples; exact; careful. — ⟨ See METICULOUS. — **scru′pu·lous·ly** *adv.* — **scru′pu⟨ ty** (-ləs′ə·tē), **scru′pu·lous·ness** *n.*

scru·ti·nize (skrōō′tə·nīz) *v.t.* **·nized, ·niz·ing** To obs⟨ carefully; examine in detail. Also *Brit.* **scru′ti·nise.** **scru′ti·niz′er** *n.* — **scru′ti·niz′ing·ly** *adv.*

scru·ti·ny (skrōō′tə·nē) *n.* *pl.* **·nies** **1.** The act of sc⟨ nizing; close examination or investigation. **2.** A searc⟨ look or glance. [< OF < LL < L *scrutari* to examine⟨

scu·ba (skōō′bə, skyōō′-) *n.* *Sometimes cap.* An underw⟨ breathing apparatus needing no connection with the sur⟨ worn by divers. Also called *Aqua-Lung, aqualung.* *s(elf)-c(ontained)* *u(nderwater)* *b(reathing)* *a(pparatus)*⟨

scud (skud) *v.i.* **scud·ded, scud·ding** **1.** To move, run, ⟨ swiftly. **2.** *Naut.* To run rapidly before the wind. — ⟨ The act of scudding or moving swiftly. **2.** Light clouds ⟨ en rapidly before the wind. [Prob. < Scand.; ? infl. in m⟨ ing by *scut,* in earlier sense of "hare"]

scuff (skuf) *v.i.* **1.** To walk with a dragging movemen⟨ the feet; shuffle. — *v.t.* **2.** To scrape (the floor, ground,⟨ with the feet. **3.** To roughen or wear down the surface ⟨

bing or scraping. — *n.* **1.** The act of scuffing; also, the
se or mark so made. **2.** A flat slipper having no covering
the heel. [Prob. < ON *skúfa* to shove]

·fle (skuf′əl) *v.i.* **·fled, ·fling 1.** To struggle roughly or
tusedly. **2.** To drag one's feet; shuffle. — *n.* A disor-
y struggle. [Prob. freq. of SCUFF] — scuf′fler *n.*

l (skul) *n.* **1.** A long oar worked from side to side over
stern of a boat. **2.** A light, short-handled oar, used in
's by one person. **3.** A small boat for sculling. — *v.t. &*
To propel (a boat) by a scull or sculls. [ME *sculle, skulle;*
in unknown] — scull′er *n.*

·ler·y (skul′ər-ē) *n. pl.* **·ler·ies** A room where kitchen
nsils are kept and cleaned, vegetables washed, etc. [<
escuelerie care of dishes]

lion (skul′yən) *n. Archaic* **1.** A servant who washes
scours dishes, pots, and kettles. **2.** A base, contemptible
ion. [< OF *escouillon* mop < *escouve* broom]

·pin (skul′pin) *n. pl.* **·pins** or **·pin** One of several
ad-mouthed fishes with a large, spiny head. [Prob. alter.
escorpene < L *scorpaena* scorpionlike fish]

pt (skulpt) *v.t. & v.i. Informal* To sculpture.

p·tor (skulp′tər) *n.* One who creates sculpture by carv-
wood, modeling clay or plastics, working metal, or chis-
g stone, etc. — sculp′tress (-tris) *n.fem.*

p·ture (skulp′chər) *n.* **1.** The art of fashioning figures
ood, clay, plastics, metal, or stone. **2.** Figures or groups
ved, cut, hewn, cast, or modeled in such materials. **3.**
sed or incised lines or markings, as upon a shell. — *v.t.*
ed, ·tur·ing 1. To fashion, as statuary, by modeling,
ving, casting, or welding. **2.** To represent or portray in
pture. **3.** To embellish with sculpture. **4.** To change,
he face of a valley or canyon, by erosion and deposition.
L < *sculpere* to carve in stone] — sculp′tur·al *adj.*

p·tur·esque (skulp′chə·resk′) *adj.* Resembling sculp-
; coldly, calmly, or grandly beautiful; statuesque.

n (skum) *n.* **1.** Impure or extraneous matter that rises
he surface of boiling or fermenting liquids. **2.** Minute
 *etation on stagnant water. **3.** Worthless element; refuse.
vile or worthless person or group of persons: often in
phrase the scum of the earth. — *v.* **scummed, scum·ming
1.** To take scum from; skim. — *v.i.* **2.** To become
ered with or form scum. [< MDu. *schuum*] — scum′.
n.

n·my (skum′ē) *adj.* **·mi·er, ·mi·est 1.** Covered with,
taining, or resembling scum. **2.** Vile; contemptible.

p (skup) *n. pl.* **scup** or **scups** A food fish of the eastern
st of the U.S.: also called *porgy.* Also scup·paug (skup′ôg,
pŏg′). [< Algonquian (Narraganset) *mishcup* thick-
ed]

·per (skup′ər) *n. Naut.* A hole or gutter along the side
ship's deck, to let water run off. [? Short for *scupper*
< OF *escope* bailing scoop]

·per·nong (skup′ər·nông, -nong) *n.* **1.** A variety of
scadine grape cultivated in the southern United States.
A sweet, straw-colored wine made from this grape. [after
Scuppernong River in North Carolina]

f (skûrf) *n.* **1.** Loose outer skin thrown off in minute
es, as in dandruff. **2.** Any scaly matter. [OE] —
rf′y *adj.*

·ril·i·ty (skə·ril′ə·tē) *n. pl.* **·ties 1.** A scurrilous re-
k. **2.** The quality of being obscenely jocular.

·ri·lous (skûr′ə·ləs) *adj.* **1.** Grossly and offensively
sive. **2.** Expressed with or given to coarse jocularity.
> scur·rile (skûr′il), scur·ril [< L *scurrilis* buffoonlike]
scur′ri·lous·ly *adv.* — scur′ri·lous·ness *n.*

·ry (skûr′ē) *v.i.* **·ried, ·ry·ing** To move or go hurriedly;
mper. — *n. pl.* **·ries** The act or sound of scurrying.
ort for HURRY-SCURRY]

·vy (skûr′vē) *adj.* **·vi·er, ·vi·est 1.** Meanly low or con-
ptible; base. **2.** *Obs.* Scurfy; scabby. — *n. Pathol.* A
ase caused by lack of vitamin C in the diet, and charac-
zed by swollen and bleeding gums, and great weakness.
SCURF] — scur′vi·ly *adv.* — scur′vi·ness *n.*

t (skut) *n.* A short tail, as of a rabbit or deer. [ME,
hare, prob. < Scand. Cf. Icelandic *skott* fox's tail.]

tate (skyoō′tāt) *adj. Zool.* Covered with horny,
ldlike plates or large scales. **2.** *Bot.* Shaped like a shield.
L *scutatus* provided with a shield < *scutum* shield]

ch·eon (skuch′ən) *n.* An escutcheon.

tel·late (skyoō·tel′it, skyoō′tə·lāt) *adj. Zool.* **1.** Plat-
ike; shield-shaped. **2.** Covered with scales; scutate.
> scu·tel·lat·ed (-tə·lā′tid) [< NL *scutellatus* < L scu-
platter, dim. of *scutra* tray] — scu′tel·la′tion *n.*

tel·lum (skyoō·tel′əm) *n. pl.* **·la** (-lə) *Biol.* A small,
ldlike organ or part, as on the leg of a bird. [< NL, dim.
scutum shield] — scu·tel′lar *adj.*

·tle[1] (skut′l) *n.* **1.** A small opening or hatchway with
ovable lid or cover, esp. on the deck of a ship. **2.** The lid

closing such an opening. **3.** A sea cock in the bottom of a
ship. — *v.t.* **·tled, ·tling** To sink (a ship) by making holes in
the bottom or by opening the sea cocks. [< MF *escoutille*
hatchway]

scut·tle[2] (skut′l) *n.* A metal vessel or hod for coal. [OE
scutel dish, platter < L *scutella*]

scut·tle[3] (skut′l) *v.i.* **·tled, ·tling** To run in haste; scurry.
— *n.* A hurried run or departure. [? Var. of *scuddle*]

scut·tle·butt (skut′l·but) *n.* **1.** A drinking fountain aboard
ship. **2.** Formerly, a cask containing the day's drinking
water. **3.** *U.S. Slang* Rumor; gossip. [Orig. *scuttled butt* a
lidded cask for drinking water]

scu·tum (skyoō′təm) *n. pl.* **·ta** (-tə) **1.** *Zool.* A platelike
piece or part, as on a turtle. **2.** In ancient Rome, the large
oval or rectangular shield of the legionaries. [< L]

Scyl·la (sil′ə) In Greek mythology, a six-headed sea monster who dwelt in a cave on the Italian coast opposite the
whirlpool Charybdis. — between Scylla and Charybdis
Between two dangers, where one cannot be avoided without
incurring equally great peril from the other.

scythe (sīth, *sometimes* sī) *n.* An implement used for mowing, reaping, etc., consisting of a long, curved blade fixed at
an angle to a long bent handle. — *v.t.* **scythed, scyth·ing**
To cut or mow with or as with a scythe. [OE *sīthe*]

Scyth·i·a (sith′ē·ə) An ancient region of southern Europe,
generally considered as lying north of the Black Sea. —
Scyth′i·an *adj. & n.*

sea (sē) *n.* **1.** The great body of salt water covering the
larger portion of the earth's surface; the ocean. **2.** A large
body of oceanic water partly enclosed by land. **3.** A large
inland body of water, salt or fresh. **4.** The swell or surface
of the ocean: a calm *sea.* **5.** Anything that suggests the sea,
as something vast. **6.** The occupation of a seaman. — at
sea **1.** On the ocean. **2.** At a loss; bewildered. — to follow the sea To follow the occupation of a sailor. — to go
to sea **1.** To become a sailor. **2.** To take an ocean voyage.
— to put to sea To start on a voyage, as a ship. [OE *sǣ*]

sea anchor A large canvas bag or sail dragged from the
stern of a ship to reduce yawing, as in a gale.

sea anemone Any of various marine animals
that attach themselves to rocks, etc., suggesting flowers by their coloring and outspread
tentacles.

sea bass 1. Any of various large-mouthed food
fishes of Atlantic waters; esp., the black sea
bass. **2.** Any of various similar or related
fishes.

Sea·bee (sē′bē′) *n.* A member of the Construction Battalions of the U.S. Navy, organized to
build base facilities, airfields, etc. [< *C(on-
struction) B(attalion)*]

sea·board (sē′bôrd′, -bōrd′) *n.* The seashore
or seacoast; also, the land or region bordering
the sea. — *adj.* Bordering on the sea. [ME <
SEA + *board* border, OE *bord*]

sea breeze A cool breeze blowing inland from the ocean.

sea calf The harbor seal.

sea captain The captain of a seagoing vessel.

sea·coast (sē′kōst′) *n.* The seashore; seaboard.

sea cock A cock or valve controlling connection with the
water through a vessel's hull.

sea coconut The very large and heavy seed of a palm native to islands of the Indian Ocean.

sea cow 1. Any aquatic mammal, as the manatee or the
dugong. **2.** The walrus.

sea cucumber Any of a group of marine animals shaped
like a cucumber and having long branched tentacles.

sea dog 1. The harbor seal. **2.** The sea lion. **3.** An old or
experienced sailor.

sea·drome (sē′drōm′) *n. Aeron.* A floating airport for aircraft making overseas flights. [< SEA + -DROME]

sea duck Any of various diving ducks, esp. the eider.

sea·far·er (sē′fâr′ər) *n.* A seaman; a mariner.

sea·far·ing (sē′fâr′ing) *adj.* **1.** Following the sea as a calling.
2. Traveling by sea. — *n.* **1.** Travel by sea. **2.** The profession of a seaman.

sea·flow·er (sē′flou′ər) *n.* A sea anemone.

sea foam 1. Foam of the ocean. **2.** Meerschaum. **3.** A
fluffy candy made of spun sugar.

sea·food (sē′food′) *n. U.S.* Edible marine fish or shellfish.

sea·fowl (sē′foul′) *n.* A sea bird, or sea birds collectively.

sea front Land or buildings that border on the sea.

sea·girt (sē′gûrt′) *adj.* Surrounded by waters of the sea.

sea·go·ing (sē′gō′ing) *adj.* **1.** Adapted for use on the ocean.
2. Seafaring.

sea green A deep bluish green, like the color of sea water.

sea gull Any gull or large tern.

sea hog A porpoise.

SEA
ANEMONE
(3 to 5 in-
ches high)
a Tenta-
cles con-
tracted. *b*
Tentacles
extended.

sea horse 1. A marine fish, having a prehensile tail and a head resembling that of a horse. 2. A walrus. 3. A fabulous animal, half horse and half fish, driven by Neptune. 4. A large, white-crested wave.

Sea Islands A chain of small islands off the coast of South Carolina, Georgia, and northern Florida.

sea king A viking pirate king of the Middle Ages.

SEA HORSE (2 to 12 inches long)

seal[1] (sēl) n. 1. An instrument or device used for making an impression upon some plastic substance, as wax or a wafer; also, the impression made. 2. The wax, wafer, or similar token affixed to a document as a proof of authenticity; also, an impression, scroll, or mark on the paper. 3. A substance or device employed to secure a letter, door, etc., firmly or to prevent tampering. 4. Anything that confirms or ratifies; a pledge. 5. An ornamental stamp for packages, etc. — **under seal** Fastened or secured with an authoritative seal. — v.t. 1. To affix a seal to, as to prove authenticity or prevent tampering. 2. To stamp or impress a seal upon in order to attest to weight, quality, etc. 3. To fasten or close with or as with a seal. 4. To grant or assign under seal. 5. To establish or settle finally; determine. 6. In Mormon usage, to solemnize forever, as a marriage. 7. To secure, set, or fill up, as with plaster. 8. Mech. To supply with a device or trap for preventing a return flow of gas or air. [< OF < L sigillum small picture, seal] — **seal'a·ble** adj. — **seal'er** n.

seal[2] (sēl) n. 1. Any of a group of acquatic carnivorous mammals mostly of northern latitudes. 2. The fur of a fur seal; sealskin. 3. Leather made from the hide of a seal. 4. Any fur prepared so as to look like sealskin. — v.i. To hunt seals. [OE seolh]

sea legs Informal The ability to walk aboard ship, esp. in rough seas, without losing one's balance.

seal·er·y (sē'lər·ē) n. pl. ·er·ies 1. The occupation of hunting seals. 2. A place where seals are regularly hunted.

sea lettuce A green seaweed often used for food.

sea level 1. The assumed mean level of the ocean surface, esp. as used in determining elevation on maps, etc. 2. The actual mean level of the ocean surface.

sealing wax A mixture of shellac and resin with turpentine and pigment that is fluid when heated but becomes solid as it cools, used for sealing papers, packages, etc.

sea lion Any of various large, eared seals, esp., the **California sea lion**: also called sea dog.

seal ring A finger ring containing an engraved stone or signet: also called signet ring.

seal·skin (sēl'skin') n. 1. The under fur of the fur seal when prepared for use by removing the long hairs and dyeing dark brown or black. 2. A coat, etc., made of this fur. — adj. Made of this fur.

Sea·ly·ham terrier (sē'lē·ham, -əm) A breed of terrier first developed at Sealyham, Wales, having short legs and a wiry, usu. white coat.

seam (sēm) n. 1. A visible line of junction between parts, esp. the edges of two pieces of cloth sewn together. 2. A crack; fissure. 3. A ridge made in joining two pieces or left by a mold upon a casting. 4. A scar; also, a wrinkle. 5. A thin stratum of rock. — v.t. 1. To unite by means of a seam. 2. To mark with a cut, furrow, wrinkle, etc. 3. In knitting, to give the appearance of a seam to; purl. — v.i. 4. To crack open; become fissured. 5. In knitting, to form seams. [OE sēam] — **seam'er** n.

sea·man (sē'mən) n. pl. ·men (-mən) 1. A sailor. 2. Naval An enlisted man of any of the lowest grades. See tables at GRADE. — **sea'man·like'** (-līk') adj. — **sea'man·ly** adj. & adv.

sea·man·ship (sē'mən·ship) n. The skill and ability of a seaman in the operation and handling of a boat or ship.

seam·less (sēm'lis) adj. Having no seam.

seam·stress (sēm'stris, Brit. sem'-) n. A woman skilled in needlework, esp. one whose occupation is sewing. Also **sempstress**. [< OE sēamestre seamster + -ESS]

seam·y (sē'mē) adj. **seam·i·er**, **seam·i·est** 1. Full of seams, as the wrong side of a garment. 2. Showing the worst aspect; distasteful: the seamy side. — **seam'i·ness** n.

sé·ance (sā'äns, Fr. sā·äns') n. 1. A session or sitting. 2. A meeting of persons seeking spiritualistic manifestations. [< F < OF seoir to sit < L sedere]

sea onion Squill[1].

sea otter A large, nearly extinct marine animal of the North Pacific coast, having a valuable dark brown fur.

sea·plane (sē'plān') n. An airplane equipped to land on or take off from the water.

sea·port (sē'pôrt', -pōrt') n. 1. A harbor or port on a coast accessible to seagoing ships. 2. A town located on such a harbor.

sea purse Zool. The horny capsule enclosing the egg certain sharks, skates, and rays.

sea·quake (sē'kwāk') n. A seismic disturbance of ocean floor.

sear (sir) v.t. 1. To wither; dry up. 2. To burn the su of; scorch. 3. To burn or cauterize, as with a hot brand. 4. To make callous; harden. — v.i. 5. To c dryness. — adj. Poetic Dried or blasted; withered. A scar or brand. Also spelled sere. [OE sēarian to wit

search (sûrch) n. 1. The act of seeking or looking dilige 2. Investigation; inquiry. 3. A critical examination or s tiny. 4. Law Right of search. — v.t. 1. To look throu explore thoroughly in order to find something. 2. To ject (a person) to an examination, as for concealed wea etc. 3. To examine with close attention; probe. 4 penetrate or pierce. 5. To learn by investigation: with — v.i. 6. To make a search. [< OF < L circare t round, explore] — **search'a·ble** adj. — **search'er** n.

search·ing (sûr'ching) adj. 1. Investigating minutely Keenly penetrating; observant: a searching gaze. — sea **ing·ly** adv. — **search'ing·ness** n.

search·light (sûrch'līt') n. 1. An apparatus containi reflector and an intensely brilliant light that may be thi in various directions for search or signaling. 2. The bea light from this apparatus.

search warrant A warrant authorizing an officer to se a house or other specified place for things alleged to be lawfully concealed there.

sea·scape (sē'skāp') n. 1. An ocean view. 2. A pi presenting a marine view. [< SEA + (LAND)SCAPE]

sea·shell (sē'shel') n. The shell of any marine mollu

sea·shore (sē'shôr', -shōr') n. 1. Land adjacent to or dering on the ocean. 2. Law The ground between high-low-water marks.

sea·sick (sē'sik') adj. Suffering from seasickness.

sea·sick·ness (sē'sik'nis) n. Nausea, dizziness, and tration caused by the motion of a vessel at sea.

sea·side (sē'sīd') n. The seashore, esp. as a place of re — adj. Of or pertaining to the seashore.

sea·son (sē'zən) n. 1. A division of the year as detern by the earth's position with respect to the sun, and as ma by the temperature, moisture, vegetation, etc. 2. A p of time. 3. Any of the periods into which the Christian is divided. 4. A period of special activity: the hu season. 5. A fit or suitable time. 6. That which im relish; seasoning. — **in season** 1. In condition and ob able for use. 2. In good or sufficient time; opportunely Legally permitted to be killed or taken, as game. 4. R to mate or breed: said of animals. — v.t. 1. To increas flavor or zest of (food), as by adding spices, etc. 2. T zest or piquancy to. 3. To render more suitable for use To make accustomed or inured; harden. 5. To mitiga soften. — v.i. 6. To become seasoned. [< OF < L -onis sowing time < L, a sowing] — **sea'son·er** n.

sea·son·a·ble (sē'zən·ə·bəl) adj. 1. Being in keeping the season. 2. Done at the proper time. — **sea'son ness** n. — **sea'son·a·bly** adv.

sea·son·al (sē'zən·əl) adj. Characteristic of, affecte or occurring at a certain season. — **sea'son·al·ly** adv.

sea·son·ing (sē'zən·ing) n. 1. The act or process by something, as lumber, is rendered fit for use. 2. Some added to food to give relish; esp., a condiment. 3. S thing added to increase enjoyment, zest, etc.

season ticket A ticket or pass, usually at a reduced entitling the holder to daily trips on a train for a tain period or to admission to a series of sporting e etc.

seat (sēt) n. 1. That on which one sits, as a chair, ben stool. 2. The part of a thing upon which one rests in si or upon which an object or another part rests. 3. The tocks; also, the portion of a garment covering them. 4 place where anything is situated, settled, or established A place of abode. 6. The privilege or right of membe in a legislative body, stock exchange, etc. 7. The man sitting, as on horseback. 8. A surface or part upon the base of anything rests. — v.t. 1. To place on a se seats; cause to sit down. 2. To have seats for. 3. T or repair a seat on or in. 4. To locate, settle, or ce usually in the passive. 5. To fix or set firmly or in [< ON sæti. Akin to SIT.]

seat belt A safety belt.

seat·ing (sē'ting) n. 1. The act of providing with 2. Fabric for upholstering seats. 3. The arrangeme seats, as in a room, auditorium, etc.

sea urchin A marine animal having a soft rounded covered with a shell bearing numerous movable spines.

sea wall A wall or an embankment to prevent the encr ments of the sea, the erosion of the shore, etc.

sea·ward (sē'wərd) adj. 1. Going toward the sea. Blowing, as wind, from the sea. — adv. In the direct the sea: also **sea'wards** (-wərdz).

ay (sē′wā′) *n.* 1. A way or lane over the sea. 2. An
d waterway that receives ocean shipping. 3. The head-
made by a ship. 4. A rough sea: usu. in **in a seaway.**

eed (sē′wēd′) *n.* 1. Any of a widely distributed class
ants growing in the sea, including the kelps, rockweeds,
, etc. 2. Any marine plant.

or·thy (sē′wûr′t̶hē) *adj.* In fit condition for a voyage:
of a vessel. **— sea′wor′thi·ness** *n.*

ceous (si·bā′shəs) *adj. Physiol.* 1. Of, pertaining to,
e fat. 2. Designating any of the glands in the skin that
te sebum. [< NL *sebaceus* < L *sebum* tallow]

combining form Fat; fatty matter: also, before vowels,
Also **sebo-.** [< L *sebum* tallow]

m (sē′bəm) *n. Physiol.* A fatty matter secreted by
ebaceous glands. [< L, tallow]

ek) *adj. French* Dry: said of wines.

it (sē′kənt, -kant) *adj.* Cutting, esp. into two parts;
secting. **—** *n.* 1. *Geom.* **a** A straight line intersecting a
a curve. **b** A line drawn from the center of a circle
igh one extremity of an arc to the tangent drawn from
ther extremity of the same arc. 2. *Trig.* A function of
-ute angle, equal to the ratio of the hypotenuse to the
adjacent to the angle when the angle is included in a
triangle. [< L *secans, -antis*, ppr. of *secare* to cut]

de (si·sēd′) *v.i.* -ced·ed, ·ced·ing To withdraw formally
a union, fellowship, or association, esp. from a political
igious organization. [< L < *se-* apart + *cedere* to go]
·ced′er *n.*

;·sion (si·sesh′ən) *n.* 1. The act of seceding, esp. from
cal or religious association. 2. *Usually cap. U.S.* The
drawal of the Southern States from the Union in 1860–
— se·ces′sion·al *adj.* **— se·ces′sion·ist** *adj. & n.*

el (sek′əl, sik′əl) *n.* A variety of small, sweet pear.
r the Pennsylvania farmer who introduced it]

de (si·klo͞od′) *v.t.* ·clud·ed, ·clud·ing 1. To remove
keep apart from the company or society of others; iso-
2. To screen or shut off, as from view. [< L < *se-*
t + *claudere* to shut]

id·ed (si·klo͞o′did) *adj.* 1. Separated; withdrawn; liv-
part from others. 2. Protected or screened. **— se-**
ed·ly *adv.* **— se·clud′ed·ness** *n.*

i·sion (si·klo͞o′zhən) *n.* 1. The act of secluding, or the
or condition of being secluded; solitude; retirement.
secluded place. **— se·clu′sive** *adj.* **— se·clu′sive·ly**
— se·clu′sive·ness *n.*

nd¹ (sek′ənd) *n.* 1. A unit of time, ⅟₆₀ of a minute.
eom. A unit of angular measure, ⅟₆₀ of a minute of arc.
bol: *//*. [< OF *seconde*]

nd² (sek′ənd) *adj.* 1. Next in order, authority, respon-
ty, etc., after the first: the ordinal of *two.* 2. Ranking
to or below the first or best; secondary; subordinate.
lentical in character with another or preceding one; an-
r; other. 4. *Music* Designating one of two parts for like
uments or voices, usu. the one lower in pitch or in some
her subordinate. **—** *n.* 1. The one next after the first
osition, rank, importance, or quality. 2. An attendant
supports or aids another, as in a duel. 3. *pl.* Articles of
handise of imperfect manufacture or of inferior quality.
Music **a** The interval between any note and the next
e or below in the diatonic scale. **b** A note separated by
interval from any other. **c** Two notes at this interval
en or sounded together. **d** A second or subordinate part,
ument, or voice. In parliamentary law, an utterance
eby a motion is seconded: Do I hear a *second*? **—** *v.t.*
o act as a supporter or assistant of; promote; encourage.
1 deliberative bodies, to support formally, as a motion,
ution, etc. **—** *adv.* In the second order, place, or rank:
in formal discourse, **sec′ond·ly.** [< OF < L *secundus*
wing]

n·dar·y (sek′ən·der′ē) *adj.* 1. Of second rank, grade,
fluence; subordinate; auxiliary. 2. Depending on what
imary or original: *secondary* sources. 3. *Electr.* Of, per-
ing to, or noting an induced current or its circuit, esp.
n induction coil. **—** *n. pl.* ·dar·ies 1. One who acts
secondary or subordinate capacity; an assistant. 2.
thing of secondary size, position, or importance. 3.
ithol. One of the feathers that grow on the second joint
orearm of a bird's wing. **— sec′on·dar′i·ly** *adv.*

ndary accent See under ACCENT.

ndary cell *Electr.* A type of cell that can be recharged
he passage of direct current in reverse direction through
electrolyte: also called *storage cell.*

ndary education High school or preparatory school
cation between the elementary and college levels.

ndary school A high school or preparatory school
rmediate between the elementary and college school.

nd base In baseball, the base situated between first
third base.

second base·man (bās′mən) *n. pl.* ·men (-mən) A baseball player stationed at or near second base.

sec·ond-best (sek′ənd·best′) *adj.* Next to the best.

second childhood Senility; dotage.

sec·ond-class (sek′ənd·klas′, -kläs′) *adj.* 1. Ranking next
below the first or best; inferior; mediocre. 2. Of or pertaining to travel accommodations ranking between first class and
third class. 3. Of or pertaining to a class of mail including
all printed periodicals. **—** *adv.* By second-class ticket or by
using second-class conveniences.

Second Coming The expected second coming of Christ.

second estate The nobility.

second fiddle Any secondary or inferior status, esp. in the
phrase **to be (or play) second fiddle.**

sec·ond-guess (sek′ənd·ges′) *v.t. & v.i.* To judge or conjecture about (something) after it has occurred.

sec·ond-hand (sek′ənd·hand′) *adj.* 1. Having been previously owned, worn, or used by another; not new. 2. Received from another: *secondhand* information. 3. Handling
or dealing in merchandise that is not new.

second hand The hand that marks the seconds on a clock
or a watch.

second lieutenant *Mil.* The lowest grade of commissioned officer, ranking below first lieutenant.

second nature A disposition or character that is acquired
and not innate; deep-seated habits that have become fixed.

second papers A popular name for a certificate of naturalization.

sec·ond-rate (sek′ənd·rāt′) *adj.* Second in quality, size,
rank, importance, etc.; second-class. **— sec′ond-rat′er** *n.*

second sight The alleged power of seeing events occurring
at distant places, in the future, etc.; clairvoyance.

sec·ond-sto·ry man (sek′ənd-stôr′ē, -stō′rē) *U.S. Slang* A
burglar.

second-string (sek′ənd·string′) *adj. U.S. Informal* In
sports, ranking next to the regular or starting player or team.

Second World War See WORLD WAR II in table for WAR.

se·cre·cy (sē′krə·sē) *n. pl.* ·cies 1. The condition or
quality of being secret or hidden; concealment. 2. The
character of being secretive; secretiveness. 3. Privacy; retirement; solitude. Also **se·cret·ness** (sē′krit·nis).

se·cret (sē′krit) *adj.* 1. Kept separate or hidden from view
or knowledge; concealed; hidden. 2. Beyond normal comprehension; obscure; recondite. 3. Known or revealed only
to the initiated: *secret* rites. 4. Affording privacy; secluded.
5. Good at keeping secrets; close-mouthed. 6. *U.S. Mil.*
Denoting the second highest category of security classification. Compare TOP-SECRET. **—** *n.* 1. Something not to be
told. 2. A thing undiscovered or unknown. 3. An underlying reason; that which, when known, explains; key. 4. A
secret contrivance. 5. Secrecy. **— in secret** In privacy;
in a hidden place. [< OF < L < *se-* apart + *cernere* to
separate] **— se′cret·ly** *adv.*

sec·re·tar·i·at (sek′rə·târ′ē·it, -at) *n.* 1. A secretary's
position. 2. The place where a secretary transacts his business. 3. The executive department of an organization, esp.
of the United Nations. 4. The entire staff of secretaries in
an office. Also **sec′re·tar′i·ate.**

sec·re·tar·y (sek′rə·ter′ē) *n. pl.* ·tar·ies 1. A person employed to deal with correspondence, keep records, and handle clerical business for an individual, business, committee,
etc. 2. An executive officer presiding over and managing a
department of government. 3. A writing desk with a bookcase or cabinet. [< Med.L < L *secretum* secret] **— sec′re-**
tar′i·al (-târ′ē·əl) *adj.*

secretary bird A South African bird that has long legs and
a crest suggesting quill pens stuck behind the ear.

secretary general *pl.* **secretaries general** A chief secretary; an assistant to a governor general. **— sec′re·tar′y-**
gen′er·al·cy (-jen′ər·əl·sē) *n.*

se·crete (si·krēt′) *v.t.* ·cret·ed, ·cret·ing 1. To conceal; hide.
2. *Physiol.* To produce (a secretion). [See SECRET.] **—**
se·cre′tor *n.*

se·cre·tion (si·krē′shən) *n. Physiol.* 1. The process, generally glandular, by which materials are separated from the
blood and elaborated into new substances, as milk, etc. 2.
The substance secreted. [See SECRET.]

se·cre·tive (si·krē′tiv; *for def. 1, also* sē′krə·tiv) *adj.* 1. Inclined to secrecy; reticent. 2. *Physiol.* Producing or causing
secretion. **— se·cre′tive·ly** *adv.* **— se·cre′tive·ness** *n.*

se·cre·to·ry (si·krē′tər·ē) *adj.* Of, or functioning as, a secretion. **—** *n. pl.* ·ries A secreting organ or gland.

secret service 1. Investigation conducted secretly for a
government. 2. The secret or espionage work of various
government agencies in time of war.

Secret Service A section of the Department of the Treasury concerned with the suppression of counterfeiting, the
protection of the President of the United States, etc.

PRONUNCIATION KEY: add, āce, câre, pälm; end, ēven; it, īce; odd, ōpen, ôrder; to͝ok, po͞ol; up, bûrn; ə = a in *above*, e in *sicken*, i in *flex-*
in *melon*, u in *focus*; yo͞o = u in *fuse*; oil; pout; check; go; ring; thin; t̶his; zh, vision.

sect (sekt) *n.* **1.** A body of persons distinguished by peculiarities of faith and practice from other bodies adhering to the same general system, esp., the adherents of a particular religious creed. **2.** Any number of persons united in opinion, interest beliefs. [< OF < L < *sequi* to follow]

-sect *combining form* To cut; divide (in a specified manner): *vivisect, bisect*. [< L < *secare* to cut]

sec·tar·i·an (sek-târ′ē-ən) *adj.* **1.** Pertaining to or belonging to a particular sect. **2.** Adhering or confined to a specific group, party, etc.; partisan. — *n.* A member of a sect, esp. if bigoted. — **sec·tar′i·an·ism** *n.*

sec·ta·ry (sek′tər-ē) *n. pl.* **·ries 1.** A sectarian. **2.** A dissenter from an established church; a nonconformist. Also **sec′ta·rist.** [< MF or Med.L < L. See SECT.]

sec·tion (sek′shən) *n.* **1.** A separate part or division; as a portion of a book or a chapter. **2.** A distinct part of a country, community, etc. **3.** *U.S.* An area of land containing 640 acres, ⅟₃₆ of a township. **4.** Any of two or more trains, buses, airplanes, etc., represented by a single entry in a timetable or schedule. **5.** A portion of railroad track under the care of a particular set of men. **6.** In a sleeping car, a space containing two berths. **7.** A picture of a building, geological formation, etc., as if cut by an intersecting plane; also, the thing so viewed. **8.** The act of cutting; division by cutting. — *Syn.* see PORTION. — *v.t.* **1.** To cut or divide into sections. **2.** To shade (a drawing) so as to designate a section or sections. [< MF or L < *secare* to cut]

-section *combining form* The act or process of cutting or dividing: *vivisection.* [< L. See SECTION.]

sec·tion·al (sek′shən-əl) *adj.* **1.** Pertaining to a section, as of a country; local: a *sectional* dialect. **2.** Dividing or alienating one section from another. **3.** Made up of sections. — *n. U.S.* A long sofa having several separate units. — **sec′tion·al·ly** *adv.*

sec·tion·al·ism (sek′shən-əl-iz′əm) *n.* Undue concern for a particular section of the country; intense consciousness of sectional differences. — **sec′tion·al·ist** *n.*

sec·tor (sek′tər) *n.* **1.** *Geom.* A part of a circle or ellipse bounded by two radii and the arc subtended by them. **2.** A part or portion: a wooded *sector* of land; the conservative *sector* of the population. **3.** *Mil.* A defined area for which a unit is responsible. — *v.t.* To divide into sectors. [< LL < L < *secare* to cut] — **sec·to·ri·al** (sek·tôr′ē·al) *adj.*

SECTOR (*abc*) OF A CIRCLE

sec·u·lar (sek′yə·lər) *adj.* **1.** Of this world or the present life; temporal; worldly: distinguished from *spiritual*. **2.** Not under the control of the church; civil. **3.** Not concerned with religion; not sacred. **4.** Not bound by monastic vows. — *n.* **1.** One in holy orders who is not bound by monastic vows. **2.** A layman. [< OF < LL < L *saeculum* generation, an age]

sec·u·lar·ism (sek′yə·lə·riz′əm) *n.* **1.** The belief that morality should be determined without reference to religious systems. **2.** The view that religion should not be introduced into public education or civil affairs. — **sec′u·lar·ist** *n.*

sec·u·lar·ize (sek′yə·lə·rīz′) *v.t.* **·ized, ·iz·ing 1.** To convert from sacred to secular uses. **2.** To make worldly. — **sec′u·lar·i·za′tion** *n.*

se·cure (si·kyo͝or′) *adj.* **1.** Guarded against or not likely to be exposed to danger; safe. **2.** Free from fear, apprehension, etc. **3.** Fixed or holding firmly in place. **4.** So strong or well-made as to render loss, escape, or failure impossible. **5.** Assured; certain; guaranteed. — *v.* **·cured, ·cur·ing** *v.t.* **1.** To make secure; protect. **2.** To make firm or tight; fasten. **3.** To make certain; ensure. **4.** To obtain possession of; get. — *v.i.* **5.** To be or become secure; take precautions: with *against*, etc. [< L < *se-* without + *cura* care] — **se·cur′a·ble** *adj.* — **se·cure′ly** *adv.* — **se·cure′ment** *n.* — **se·cure′ness** *n.* — **se·cur′er** *n.*

se·cu·ri·ty (si·kyo͝or′ə·tē) *n. pl.* **·ties 1.** The state of being secure; freedom from danger, poverty, etc. **2.** One who·or that which secures or guarantees. **3.** Something deposited or pledged as a guarantee for payment. **4.** *pl.* Stocks, bonds, notes, etc. **5.** Protection of secrecy, as in wartime. — *Syn.* **2, 3.** Both *security* and *surety* may mean property given as a guarantee or the person who gives it, but *security* is chiefly used in the first sense, and *surety* in the second. A *bond* is a written promise to pay compensation for loss, damage, etc.

Security Council A permanent organ of the United Nations charged with the maintenance of international peace.

security risk *U.S.* A person regarded as unfit for employment in government or in a job connected with national defense, as because of dubious associations.

se·dan (si·dan′) *n.* **1.** A closed automobile having two or four doors and a front and back seat. **2.** A sedan chair. [? Ital. *sedere* to sit < L]

sedan chair A portable, enclosed chair, usu., for one passenger, carried by means of poles at the front and back.

se·date (si·dāt′) *adj.* **1.** Characterized by habitual composure; unhurried; calm. **2.** Sober and decorous. [< L *dere* to sit] — **se·date′ly** *adv.* — **se·date′ness** *n.*

se·da·tion (si·dā′shən) *n. Med.* The act or process ducing distress, irritation, excitement, etc., by adminis sedatives.

sed·a·tive (sed′ə·tiv) *adj.* **1.** Having a soothing effec *Med.* Allaying irritation; assuaging pain. — *n.* Any m as a medicine, of soothing distress or allaying pain.

sed·en·tar·y (sed′ən·ter′ē) *adj.* **1.** Characterized b quiring, or resulting from much sitting or a habitual s posture. **2.** Settled in one place, as certain tribes; slu inactive. **3.** Accustomed to sitting. **4.** *Zool.* Remain one place; attached or fixed to an object. [< L *sedere* t — **sed′en·tar′i·ly** *adv.* — **sed′en·tar′i·ness** *n.*

Se·der (sā′dər) *n. pl.* **Se·ders** or **Se·dar·im** (sə·där′i Judaism, the Passover feast commemorating the dep of the Israelites from Egypt. [< Hebrew *sedher* serv

sedge (sej) *n.* Any of various grasslike herbs widely uted in marshy places. [OE *secg*] — **sedg′y** *adj.*

sed·i·ment (sed′ə·mənt) *n.* **1.** Matter that settles bottom of a liquid; settlings; dregs; lees. **2.** *Geol.* Fra tary material deposited by water or air. — *Syn.* See M [< MF < L *sedere* to sit, settle] — **sed′i·men·ta·ry men′tal** *adj.*

se·di·tion (si·dish′ən) *n.* **1.** Language or conduct dir against public order and the safety of the state. **2** clandestine incitement of such disorder. **3.** Dissensio volt. [< OF < L < *sed-* aside + *itio, -onis* a going] **di′tion·ar·y, se·di′tion·ist** *adj. & n.*

se·di·tious (si·dish′əs) *adj.* **1.** Of, promoting, or havi character of sedition. **2.** Taking part in or guilty of tion. [See SEDITION.] — **se·di′tious·ly** *adv.*

se·duce (si·do͞os′, -dyo͞os′) *v.t.* **·duced, ·duc·ing 1.** T astray; entice into wrong, disloyalty, etc.; tempt. induce to engage in illicit sexual intercourse, esp. fo first time. [< L < *se-* apart + *ducere* to lead] — **se·d** *n.* — **se·duc′i·ble** or **se·duce′a·ble** *adj.*

se·duc·tion (si·duk′shən) *n.* **1.** The act of seducing Something that seduces; an enticement. Also **se·duce** (si·do͞os′mənt, -dyo͞os′-). [See SEDUCE.]

se·duc·tive (si·duk′tiv) *adj.* Tending to seduce; ent — **se·duc′tive·ly** *adv.* — **se·duc′tive·ness** *n.*

se·du·li·ty (si·do͞o′lə·tē, -dyo͞o′-) *n.* The state or cha of being sedulous.

sed·u·lous (sej′o͞o·ləs) *adj.* Constant in application tention; assiduous. [< L *sedulus* careful] — **sed′u·l** *adv.* — **sed′u·lous·ness** *n.* — *Syn.* diligent, persevering. Compare BUSY.

se·dum (sē′dəm) *n.* Any of a large genus of chiefly per plants, having very thick leaves and usu. white, yello pink flowers. [< L, houseleek]

see¹ (sē) *v.* **saw, seen, see·ing** *v.t.* **1.** To perceive wit eyes; gain knowledge or awareness of by means of one sion. **2.** To perceive with the mind; understand. **3.** T out or ascertain. **4.** To have experience or knowledg **5.** To encounter; chance to meet. **6.** To have a meeti interview with; visit or receive as a guest, patient, etc To attend as a spectator; view. **8.** To accompany; e **9.** To take care; be sure: *See* that you do it! **10.** In p to accept a bet by betting an equal sum. — *v.i.* **11.** have or exercise the power of sight. **12.** To find ou quire. **13.** To understand. **14.** To think; consider. **see about 1.** To inquire into the facts, causes, etc., o To take care of; attend to. — **to see (someone) off** T company to a point of departure, as for a journey. — (someone) through** To aid or protect, as throughout a od of difficulty or danger. — **to see through** To pene as a disguise or deception. — **to see to** To be respo for; give one's attention to. [OE *sēon*]

see² (sē) *n.* **1.** The local seat from which a bishop, bishop, or pope exercises jurisdiction. **2.** Episcopal or jurisdiction, authority, rank, or office. — **Holy See** Pope's jurisdiction or office. [< OF < L *sedes* seat]

seed (sēd) *n.* **1.** The ovule from which a plant may produced; the fertilized ovule containing an embryo. That from which anything springs; source. **3.** Offs children. **4.** The male fertilizing element; semen; mil Any small, usu. hard fruit; also, any part of a plant which it may be propagated, as bulbs, tubers, etc. **6.** collectively. **7.** Ancestry; stock. — **to go to seed 1.** velop and shed seed. **2.** To become shabby, useless, eto teriorate. — *v.t.* **1.** To sow with seed. **2.** To sow (s **3.** To remove the seeds from. **4.** In sports, to arrang sitions in a tournament, etc., so that the more skilled petitors meet only in the later events. **5.** To inters (clouds) with particles of silver iodide or other substan order to produce rainfall. — *v.i.* **6.** To sow seed. grow to maturity and produce or shed seed. [OE *sæd* **seed′er** *n.* — **seed′less** *adj.*

seed bud *Bot.* The germ within a seed; also, the ovul

seed cake A sweet cake containing aromatic seeds.

d·case (sēd′kās′) *n. Bot.* A pericarp.
d leaf *Bot.* A cotyledon.
d·ling (sēd′ling) *n.* **1.** *Bot.* A plant grown from seed, as stinguished from one propagated by grafting. **2.** A very mall or young tree or plant.
d oyster A young oyster, esp. one transplanted to another bed.
d pearl A small pearl, used in jewelry, embroidery, etc.
ds·man (sēdz′mən) *n. pl.* **·men** (-mən) **1.** A dealer in eds. **2.** A sower. Also **seed/man.**
d vessel *Bot.* A pericarp.
d·y (sē′dē) *adj.* **seed·i·er, seed·i·est 1.** Full of seeds. **2.** one to seed. **3.** Poor; shabby. **4.** *Informal* Feeling or oking wretched. **— seed′i·ly** *adv.* **— seed′i·ness** *n.*
·ing (sē′ing) *n.* The act of seeing; vision; sight. **—** *conj.* aking into consideration; since; in view of the fact.
k (sēk) *v.* **sought, seek·ing** *v.t.* **1.** To go in search of; look r. **2.** To strive for; try to get or obtain. **3.** To endeavor try: He *seeks* to mislead me. **4.** To ask or inquire for; re est. **5.** To go to; betake oneself to: to *seek* a warmer cli ate. **—** *v.i.* **6.** To make a search or inquiry. [OE *sēcan*] **seek′er** *n.*
m (sēm) *v.i.* **1.** To give the impression of being; appear. To appear to oneself: I *seem* to hear strange voices. **3.** To pear to exist. **4.** To be evident or apparent: It *seems* to be ining. [ME < ON *sǣma* to conform to] **— seem′er** *n.*
m·ing (sē′ming) *adj.* Having the appearance of reality; parent but not necessarily actual. **—** *n.* Appearance; mblance; esp., false show. **— seem′ing·ly** *adv.* **— seem′ g·ness** *n.*
m·ly (sēm′lē) *adj.* **·li·er, ·li·est** Befitting the proprieties; corous. **—** *adv.* Becomingly; decently; appropriately. ON < *sǣmr* fitting] **— seem′li·ness** *n.*
n (sēn) Past participle of SEE.
p (sēp) *v.i.* To soak through pores or small interstices; rcolate; ooze. **—** *n.* A small spring or a place out of which ater, oil, etc., oozes. [Alter. of OE *sypian* to soak]
p·age (sē′pij) *n.* **1.** The act or process of seeping or ooz g. **2.** The fluid or moisture that oozes.
r (sē′ər *for def. 1; also* sir *for defs. 2 and 3) n.* **1.** One who es. **2.** A prophet. **3.** One believed to have second sight. SEE¹ + -ER] **— seer′ess** *n. fem.*
r·suck·er (sir′suk′ər) *n.* A thin fabric of cotton, rayon, lon, etc., usu. striped in colors, with a crinkled surface. Hind. < Persian *shīr o shakkar,* lit., milk and sugar]
·saw (sē′sô′) *n.* **1.** A balanced plank or board made to ove alternately up and down by persons at opposite ends: o called *teeter.* **2.** The action or diversion of balancing on ch a board. **3.** Any up-and-down or to-and-fro move ent. **—** *v.t. & v.i.* **1.** To move or cause to move on or as if a seesaw. **2.** To alternate; fluctuate. **—** *adj.* Moving to d fro; vacillating. [Reduplication of SAW¹]
the (sēth) *v.* **seethed, seethed, seeth·ing** *v.i.* **1.** To boil. To foam or bubble as if boiling. **3.** To be agitated, as by ge. **—** *v.t.* **4.** To soak in liquid; steep. **—** *n.* The act or ndition of seething; turmoil. [OE *sēothan*]
·ment (seg′mənt) *n.* **1.** A part cut off or divided from e other parts of anything; a section. **2.** *Geom.* **a** A part of igure, esp., of a circle, cut off by a line or plane. **b** A finite rt of a line. **—** *v.t. & v.i.* To divide into segments. [< L *secare* to cut] **— seg·men·tar·y** (seg′mən·ter′ē) *adj.*
·men·tal (seg·men′təl) *adj.* **1.** Of a segment or seg ents. **2.** Divided into segments. **— seg·men′tal·ly** *adv.*
·men·ta·tion (seg′mən·tā′shən) *n.* **1.** The act of cut g or dividing into segments. **2.** The state of being so di ded. **3.** *Biol.* The cleavage of a cell.
go (sē′gō) *n. pl.* **·gos 1.** A perennial herb of the lily fam having white flowers: the State flower of Utah. **2.** Its ble bulb. [< Shoshonean (Ute) *sigo*]
·re·gate (seg′rə·gāt; *for adj. also* seg′rə·git) *v.* **·gat·ed, at·ing** *v.t.* **1.** To place apart from others or the rest; iso te. **2.** To subject to segregation. **—** *v.i.* **3.** To separate om a mass and gather about nuclei or along lines of frac re, as in crystallization. **4.** To undergo segregation. **—** *adj.* Set apart from others. [< L *se-* apart + *grex, gregis* ck] **— seg′re·ga′tive** *adj.* **— seg′re·ga′tor** *n.*
·re·ga·tion (seg′rə·gā′shən) *n.* **1.** The act or process of gregating. **2.** The practice of requiring separate facilities, in housing, schools, and transportation, for use by whites d nonwhites, esp. Negroes. **— seg′re·ga′tion·ist** *n.*
d·litz powder (sed′lits) An aperient consisting of two parate parts, tartaric acid, and sodium bicarbonate mixed th Rochelle salt, dissolved separately and then combined. fter *Seidlitz,* a Czech village, site of a medicinal spring]
gn·ior (sēn′yər) *n.* **1.** A lord; noble. **2.** A title of respect uivalent to *Sir.* Also **sei·gneur** (sēn·yûr′). [< AF, OF < *senior* older] **— sei·gnio·ri·al** (sēn·yôr′ē·əl, -yō′rē-) *adj.*
gn·ior·y (sēn′yər·ē) *n. pl.* **·ies 1.** The territory or juris

diction of a seignior; a manor. **2.** Right belonging to feudal superiority. Also **sei′gneur·y.**
seine (sān) *n.* A long fishnet hanging vertically in the water and having floats at the top edge and weights at the bottom. **—** *v.t. & v.i.* **seined, sein·ing** To fish or catch with a seine. [OE < L < Gk. *sagēnē* fishnet]
seis·mic (sīz′mik, sīs′-) *adj.* Of, characteristic of, or pro duced by earthquakes. Also **seis′mal, seis′mi·cal, seis·mat·i cal** (sīz·mat′ə·kəl, sīs-). [< Gk. < *seiein* to shake]
seismic sea wave A large and often destructive wave caused by a submarine earthquake; a tsunami.
seismo- *combining form* Earthquake. Also, before vowels, **seism-.** [< Gk. *seismos* earthquake]
seis·mo·gram (sīz′mə·gram, sīs′-) *n.* The record of an earthquake or earth tremor made by a seismograph.
seis·mo·graph (sīz′mə·graf, -gräf, sīs′-) *n.* An instrument for recording automatically the intensity, direction, and duration of an earthquake shock. **— seis′mo·graph′ic** *adj.* **— seis·mog·ra·pher** (sīz·mog′rə·fər, sīs-) *n.*
seis·mog·ra·phy (sīz·mog′rə·fē, sīs-) *n.* The study and recording of earthquake phenomena.
seis·mol·o·gy (sīz·mol′ə·jē, sīs-) *n.* The science of earth quake phenomena. **— seis·mo·log·ic** (sīz′mə·loj′ik, sīs′-) or **·i·cal** *adj.* **— seis′mo·log′i·cal·ly** *adv.* **— seis·mol′o·gist** *n.*
seize (sēz) *v.* **seized, seiz·ing** *v.t.* **1.** To take hold of sudden ly and forcibly. **2.** To grasp mentally; comprehend. **3.** To take possession of by authority or right. **4.** To take possession of by force. **5.** To take prisoner; capture; arrest. **6.** To act upon with sudden and powerful effect: Terror *seized* the ene my. **7.** To take advantage of immediately, as an opportunity. **8.** *Law* To put into legal possession. **9.** *Naut.* To fasten or bind by turns of cord, etc. **—** *v.i.* **10.** To take a sudden or forcible hold. [< OF < Med.L *ad propriam) sacire* to take (into one's own possession)] **— seiz′a·ble** *adj.* **— seiz′er** *n.*
sei·zure (sē′zhər) *n.* **1.** The act of seizing. **2.** A sudden or violent attack, as of epilepsy; fit; spell.
se·la·chi·an (si·lā′kē·ən) *adj.* Of or belonging to a group of fishes including the sharks, skates, and rays. **—** *n.* A sela chian fish. [< NL < Gk. *selachos* shark]
se·lah (sē′lə) A word of unknown meaning occurring often at the end of a verse in the Psalms, usu. considered as a direc tion to readers or musicians. [< Hebrew *selāh*]
sel·dom (sel′dəm) *adv.* At widely separated intervals, as of time or space; infrequently. [OE *seldum*]
se·lect (si·lekt′) *v.t.* **1.** To take in preference to another or others. **—** *v.i.* **2.** To make a choice. **—** *adj.* **1.** Chosen in preference to others; choice. **2.** Exclusive. **3.** Very partic ular in selecting. [< L < *se-* apart + *legere* to choose] **— se·lect′ness** *n.* **— se·lec′tor** *n.*
se·lec·tee (si·lek′tē′) *n.* One selected; esp., one drafted for military or naval service.
se·lec·tion (si·lek′shən) *n.* **1.** Choice. **2.** Anything se lected. **3.** A thing or collection of things chosen with care. **4.** *Biol.* The process by which certain organisms, or any of their characteristics, are favored in the struggle for survival.
se·lec·tive (si·lek′tiv) *adj.* **1.** Pertaining to selection; tend ing to select. **2.** Having or characterized by good selectivity.
selective service Compulsory military service according to specified conditions of age, fitness, etc.
se·lec·tiv·i·ty (si·lek′tiv′ə·tē) *n.* **1.** The state or quality of being selective. Also **se·lec′tive·ness. 2.** *Telecom.* That characteristic of a radio or television receiver, electrical cir cuit, etc., by which certain frequencies can be received to the exclusion of others.
se·lect·man (si·lekt′mən) *n. pl.* **·men** (-mən) In New Eng land, one of a board of town officers, elected annually to ex ercise executive authority in local affairs.
Se·le·ne (si·lē′nē) In Greek mythology, goddess of the moon: identified with the Roman *Luna.* Also **Se·le′na** (-nə). [< Gk. *Selēnē,* lit., the moon]
sel·e·nite (sel′ə·nīt) *n.* A pearly, usu. transparent variety of gypsum. [< L < Gk. *selēnitēs (lithos),* lit., moonstone < *selēnē* the moon]
se·le·ni·um (si·lē′nē·əm) *n.* A gray, crystalline, nonmetal lic element (symbol Se) of the sulfur group, varying greatly in electrical resistance under the influence of light. See ELE MENT. [< NL < Gk. *selēnē* the moon]
selenium cell A photoelectric cell in which plates of sele nium respond to the action of light upon them.
seleno- *combining form* Moon; pertaining to the moon; lu nar. Also, before vowels, **selen-.** [< Gk. *selēnē* the moon]
self (self) *n. pl.* **selves 1.** An individual known or consid ered as the subject of his own consciousness. **2.** Anything considered as having a distinct personality. **3.** Personal in terest or advantage. **4.** Any thing, class, or attribute that, abstractly considered, maintains a distinct and character istic individuality or identity. **—** *adj.* **1.** Being of the same color, substance, etc., throughout; uniform. **2.** Of a part,

accessory, etc., made of the same material as that with which it is used. [OE]

◆ *Self* may appear as a combining form with various meanings as shown in the list below:

1. Of the self (the object of the root word); as in:

self-abandonment	self-disclosure	self-murderer
self-abasing	self-discovery	self-mutilation
self-abhorrence	self-disgrace	self-neglect
self-accusation	self-disparagement	self-neglectful
self-adaptive	self-display	self-nourishment
self-admiration	self-disposal	self-observation
self-admission	self-disquieting	self-offense
self-adornment	self-dissolution	self-opinion
self-adulation	self-doubt	self-painter
self-advancement	self-easing	self-paying
self-advertisement	self-enriching	self-perceiving
self-advertising	self-estimate	self-perceptive
self-affliction	self-evacuation	self-perfecting
self-analysis	self-exalting	self-perfection
self-annihilation	self-exculpation	self-perpetuating
self-applause	self-excuse	self-perpetuation
self-appreciation	self-expansion	self-persuasion
self-approbation	self-expatriation	self-pleasing
self-approval	self-exploiting	self-praise
self-asserting	self-exposure	self-praising
self-awareness	self-fearing	self-preparation
self-bedizenment	self-flatterer	self-presentation
self-betrayal	self-flattering	self-preserving
self-blame	self-flattery	self-projection
self-castigation	self-folding	self-protecting
self-chastisement	self-forgetful	self-protection
self-cognizance	self-formation	self-punishment
self-commendation	self-glorification	self-raising
self-committal	self-gratification	self-recollection
self-comparison	self-guidance	self-reconstruction
self-condemnation	self-harming	self-reduction
self-condemning	self-helpful	self-regulation
self-conditioning	self-humbling	self-representation
self-confinement	self-humiliation	self-repressing
self-confounding	self-hypnosis	self-repression
self-conquest	self-hypnotism	self-reproach
self-conservative	self-hypnotized	self-reproachful
self-conserving	self-idolatry	self-restriction
self-consideration	self-idolizing	self-revealing
self-consoling	self-ignorance	self-revelation
self-consuming	self-ignorant	self-ruin
self-contempt	self-imitation	self-satirist
self-contradicting	self-immolation	self-scrutinizing
self-conviction	self-immurement	self-scrutiny
self-correction	self-impairment	self-searching
self-corruption	self-indignation	self-slaughter
self-creation	self-indulging	self-soothing
self-criticism	self-inspection	self-study
self-cure	self-instruction	self-subjection
self-damnation	self-insurer	self-subordination
self-debasement	self-integration	self-suppression
self-deceit	self-intensifying	self-surrender
self-deceiving	self-interrogation	self-suspicious
self-dedication	self-introduction	self-taxation
self-defeating	self-judgment	self-teacher
self-deflation	self-justification	self-terminating
self-degradation	self-justifying	self-tolerant
self-deifying	self-laudatory	self-torment
self-dejection	self-limitation	self-torture
self-delusion	self-limiting	self-treatment
self-deprecating	self-loss	self-trust
self-depreciation	self-maceration	self-trusting
self-depreciative	self-maintenance	self-undoing
self-destroying	self-martyrdom	self-upbraiding
self-destruction	self-mastery	self-valuing
self-destructive	self-mistrust	self-vaunting
self-direction	self-mortification	self-vindication
self-disapproval	self-murder	self-worship

2. By oneself or itself; by one's own effort (the agent of the root word); as in **self-employed.**

self-abandoned	self-doomed	self-named
self-administered	self-elaborated	self-offered
self-approved	self-elected	self-ordained
self-authorized	self-explained	self-paid
self-balanced	self-exposed	self-pampered
self-beguiled	self-furnished	self-performed
self-betrayed	self-generated	self-perpetuated
self-blinded	self-honored	self-perplexed
self-caused	self-idolized	self-planted
self-chosen	self-illumined	self-posed
self-condemned	self-imposed	self-powered
self-conducted	self-incurred	self-proclaimed
self-constituted	self-initiated	self-professed
self-convicted	self-instructed	self-punished
self-corrupted	self-invited	self-renounced
self-declared	self-judged	self-repressed
self-defended	self-justified	self-restrained
self-deluded	self-kindled	self-revealed
self-deprived	self-limited	self-schooled
self-destroyed	self-maimed	self-sown
self-determined	self-matured	self-subdued
self-devised	self-misused	self-sustained
self-divided	self-mortified	self-tempted

3. To, toward, in, for, on, or with oneself; as in:

self-absorbed	self-desire	self-permissic
self-aid	self-despair	self-pictured
self-aim	self-directed	self-pleased
self-amusement	self-direction	self-preferenc
self-application	self-disdain	self-prescribe
self-applied	self-disgust	self-pride
self-assumed	self-dislike	self-procured
self-assuming	self-dissatisfied	self-produced
self-benefit	self-elation	self-profit
self-care	self-enamored	self-purifying
self-comment	self-enclosed	self-reflection
self-communing	self-exultation	self-relation
self-compassion	self-focusing	self-relying
self-complacence	self-gain	self-repellent
self-complacency	self-helpfulness	self-repose
self-complacent	self-injurious	self-reproof
self-conflict	self-injury	self-repulsive
self-consistency	self-kindness	self-resentme
self-consistent	self-liking	self-resigned
self-content	self-loathing	self-respectfu
self-contented	self-oblivious	self-rigorous
self-delight	self-occupied	self-set
self-dependence	self-panegyrical	self-tenderne
self-dependent	self-penetration	self-vexation

4. From oneself or itself; from one's own nature or pow as in:

self-apparent	self-fruition	self-poise
self-arising	self-healing	self-poised
self-born	self-inclusive	self-refuting
self-coherence	self-initiative	self-renewing
self-complete	self-intelligible	self-resourcef
self-defining	self-issuing	self-resplende
self-derived	self-luminous	self-restoring
self-desirable	self-manifestation	self-reward
self-developing	self-moving	self-rewardin
self-effort	self-operative	self-sprung
self-evolving	self-opinionated	self-stability
self-explaining	self-originating	self-stimulate
self-forbidden	self-perfect	self-warranti

5. Independent; as in:

self-agency	self-dominance	self-existence
self-authority	self-dominion	self-ownershi
self-credit	self-entity	self-sovereigr

6. In technology, automatic or automatically; as in:

self-acting	self-cocking	self-moving
self-adapting	self-cooled	self-oiling
self-adjustable	self-defrosting	self-primer
self-adjusting	self-emptying	self-priming
self-aligning	self-feeder	self-recordin
self-burning	self-feeding	self-register
self-changing	self-filling	self-regulate
self-charging	self-inking	self-regulati
self-checking	self-lighting	self-righting
self-cleaning	self-locking	self-screwin
self-closing	self-lubricating	self-setting

self-a·base·ment (self′ə-bās′mənt) *n.* Abasement or d radation of oneself.

self-ab·ne·ga·tion (self′ab′ni-gā′shən) *n.* The compl putting aside of oneself and one's own claims for the sak some other person or object; self-sacrifice.

self-ab·sorp·tion (self′ab-sôrp′shən, -zôrp′-) *n.* Absorpt in or concentration on one's own affairs, work, interests,

self-a·buse (self′ə-byōōs′) *n.* **1.** The disparagement one's own person or powers. **2.** Masturbation.

self-ad·dressed (self′ə-drest′) *adj.* Addressed to onese

self-ap·point·ed (self′ə-poin′təd) *adj.* Appointed or de nated by oneself rather than by others: a *self-appointed* b

self-as·ser·tion (self′ə-sûr′shən) *n.* The asserting or p ting forward of oneself, one's opinions, claims, or rights. **self′-as·ser′tive** *adj.* — **self′-as·ser′tive·ly** *adv.*

self-as·sured (self′ə-shōórd′) *adj.* Confident in one's o abilities; self-reliant. — **self′-as·sur′ance** *n.*

self-cen·tered (self′sen′tərd) *adj.* Concerned chiefly w one's own affairs and interests, often with a lack of consi ation for others. Also *Brit.* **self·cen′tred.** — **self′-cen′ter** ness *n.* — **self′-cen′tered·ly** *adv.*

self-col·ored (self′kul′ərd) *adj.* **1.** Having the natural or. **2.** Of but one color or tint.

self-com·mand (self′kə-mand′, -mänd′) *n.* The state having all the faculties and powers fully at command.

self-con·ceit (self′kən-sēt′) *n.* An unduly high opinion oneself; vanity. — **self′-con·ceit′ed** *adj.*

self-con·fi·dence (self′kon′fə-dəns) *n.* Confidence in o self or in one's own unaided powers, judgment, etc. — **se con′fi·dent** *adj.* — **self′-con′fi·dent·ly** *adv.*

self-con·scious (self′kon′shəs) *adj.* **1.** Unduly consci that one is observed by others; ill at ease. **2.** Manifest embarrassment. — **self′-con′scious·ly** *adv.* — **self′-c scious·ness** *n.*

self-con·tained (self′kən-tānd′) *adj.* **1.** Keeping one thoughts and feelings to oneself. **2.** Exercising self-cont **3.** Complete and independent; self-sustaining. **4.** Hav all parts needed for working order, as a machine bearing own motor.

con·tra·dic·tion (self′kon′trə·dik′shən) *n.* **1.** The act ;ate of contradicting oneself or itself. **2.** That which radicts itself. — **self′-con′tra·dic′to·ry** *adj.*

con·trol (self′kən·trōl′) *n.* The act, power, or habit of ng one's faculties or energies under control of the will.

de·fense (self′di·fens′) *n.* Defense of oneself, one's erty, or one's reputation. — **self′-de·fen′sive** *adj.*

de·ni·al (self′di·nī′əl) *n.* The act or power of denying elf gratification. — **self′-de·ny′ing** *adj.* — **self′-de·ng·ly** *adv.*

de·ter·mi·na·tion (self′di·tûr′mə·nā′shən) *n.* **1.** The ciple of free will; decision by oneself. **2.** Decision by the ole of a country or section as to its future political status. elf′-de·ter′min·ing *adj. & n.*

de·vo·tion (self′di·vō′shən) *n.* Devotion of oneself, one's claims, wishes, or interests, to the service of a person or a cause. — **self′-de·vo′tion·al** *adj.*

dis·ci·pline (self′dis′ə·plin) *n.* The discipline or train- of oneself, often for improvement.

ed·u·cat·ed (self′ej′ŏŏ·kā′tid) *adj.* **1.** Educated ugh one's own efforts without the aid of instructors. **2.** icated at one's own expense. — **self′-ed′u·ca′tion** *n.*

ef·face·ment (self′i·fās′mənt) *n.* The keeping of one- in the background through modesty, timidity, etc.

es·teem (self′ə·stēm′) *n.* A good opinion of oneself; an ·estimate of oneself. — **Syn.** See PRIDE.

ev·i·dent (self′ev′ə·dənt) *adj.* Carrying its evidence or ·f in itself; requiring no proof of its truth. — **self′-ev′i·ce** *n.* — **self′-ev′i·dent·ly** *adv.*

·ex·am·i·na·tion (self′ig·zam′ə·nā′shən) *n.* Examina- of one's own motives, desires, habits, etc.

·ex·ist·ence (self′ig·zis′təns) *n.* Inherent, underived, ·pendent existence. — **self′-ex·ist′ent** *adj.*

·ex·plan·a·to·ry (self′ik·splan′ə·tôr′ē, -tō′rē) *adj.* Eas- comprehended without explanation; obvious.

·ex·pres·sion (self′ik·spresh′ən) *n.* Expression of one's temperament or emotions, as in art.

·fer·til·i·za·tion (self′fûr′təl·ə·zā′shən, -ī·zā′shən) *n.* ·l. Fertilization of an ovum by sperm from the same ani- or of a plant ovule by its own pollen.

·gov·ern·ment (self′guv′ərn·mənt, -ər·mənt) *n.* **1.** ·vernment of a country or region by its own people. **2.** state of being so governed. **3.** *Archaic* Self-control. — ·′-gov′erned, self′-gov′ern·ing *adj.*

heal (self′hēl′) *n.* Any of various weedy, perennial ·bs with violet flowers, formerly reputed to cure disease.

·help (self′help′) *n.* The act or condition of getting ·ng by one's own efforts without the aid of others.

·hood (self′hŏŏd) *n.* **1.** The state of being an individual; ·sonality. **2.** Selfishness; self-centeredness.

·im·por·tance (self′im·pôr′təns) *n.* Pompous self-con- — **self′-im·por′tant** *adj.*

·im·prove·ment (self′im·prōōv′mənt) *n.* Improvement ·ne's abilities or condition through one's own efforts.

·in·duced (self′in·dōōst′, -dyōōst′) *adj.* **1.** Induced by ·self or itself. **2.** *Electr.* Produced by self-induction.

·in·duc·tion (self′in·duk′shən) *n. Electr.* Induction ·hin the same circuit, causing it to resist any change in the ·ount of current flowing in it. — **self′-in·duc′tive** *adj.*

·in·dul·gence (self′in·dul′jəns) *n.* The indulgence or ·tification of one's own desires, weaknesses, etc. — **self′-·lul′gent** *adj.* — **self′-in·dul′gent·ly** *adv.*

·in·flict·ed (self′in·flik′tid) *adj.* Inflicted on oneself by ·self: a *self-inflicted* wound. — **self′-in·flic′tion** *n.*

·in·ter·est (self′in′tər·ist, -in′trist) *n.* Personal interest ·advantage, or the pursuit of it; selfishness. — **self′-in′·est·ed** *adj.*

·ish (sel′fish) *adj.* **1.** Caring chiefly for oneself or one's ·n interests or comfort, esp. to the point of disregarding · welfare or wishes of others. **2.** Proceeding from or char- ·erized by undue love of self. — **self′ish·ly** *adv.*

·ish·ness (sel′fish·nis) *n.* The quality of being selfish.

·knowl·edge (self′nol′ij) *n.* Knowledge of one's own ·aracter, motives, limitations, etc.

·less (self′lis) *adj.* Regardless of self; unselfish. — **self′·s·ly** *adv.* — **self′less·ness** *n.*

·load·ing (self′lō′ding) *adj.* Of firearms, utilizing a por- ·n of the force of the exploding gas or of recoil to extract ·d eject the empty case and chamber the next round.

·love (self′luv′) *n.* The desire or tendency that leads · e to seek his own well-being. — **self′-lov′ing** *adj.*

·made (self′mād′) *adj.* **1.** Having attained honor, ·alth, etc., by one's own efforts. **2.** Made by oneself.

·pit·y (self′pit′ē) *n.* The act or state of pitying oneself. **self′-pit′y·ing** *adj.* — **self′-pit′y·ing·ly** *adv.*

·pol·li·na·tion (self′pol′ə·nā′shən) *n. Bot.* The trans- · of pollen from stamens to pistils of the same flower. — **·lf′-pol′li·nat·ed** *adj.*

self-pos·ses·sion (self′pə·zesh′ən) *n.* **1.** The full possession or control of one's powers or faculties. **2.** Presence of mind; self-command. — **self′-pos·sessed′** *adj.*

self-pres·er·va·tion (self′prez′ər·vā′shən) *n.* **1.** The pro- tection of oneself from destruction. **2.** The urge to protect oneself, regarded as an instinct.

self-pro·nounc·ing (self′prə·noun′sing) *adj.* Having marks of pronunciation and stress applied to a word without pho- netic alteration of the spelling.

self-pro·pelled (self′prə·peld′) *adj.* **1.** Able to propel it- self. **2.** Having the means of propulsion contained within itself, as an automobile.

self-re·gard (self′ri·gärd′) *n.* **1.** Regard or consideration for oneself or one's own interests. **2.** Estimation of self.

self-re·li·ance (self′ri·lī′əns) *n.* Reliance on one's own abil- ities, resources, or judgment. — **self′-re·li′ant** *adj.*

self-re·spect (self′ri·spekt′) *n.* Proper respect for oneself and one's own character. — **self′-re·spect′ing** *adj.*

self-re·straint (self′ri·strānt′) *n.* Restraint, as of the pas- sions, by the force of one's own will; self-control.

self-right·eous (self′rī′chəs) *adj.* Righteous in one's own estimation; pharisaic. — **self′-right′eous·ly** *adv.* — **self′-right′eous·ness** *n.*

self-ris·ing (self′rī′zing) *adj.* **1.** That rises of itself. **2.** Having the leaven already added, as some flours.

self-sac·ri·fice (self′sak′rə·fīs) *n.* The sacrifice of one's self or one's personal welfare or wishes for the sake of duty or for the good of others. — **self′-sac′ri·fic′ing** *adj.*

self-same (self′sām′) *adj.* Exactly the same; identical. — **self′same′ness** *n.*

self-sat·is·fac·tion (self′sat′is·fak′shən) *n.* Satisfaction with one's own actions and characteristics; conceit; compla- cency. — **self′-sat′is·fied** *adj.* — **self′-sat′is·fy′ing** *adj.*

self-seek·ing (self′sē′king) *adj.* Exclusively seeking one's own interests or gain. — *n.* Actions, motives, etc., charac- teristic of a self-seeking person. — **self′-seek′er** *n.*

self-ser·vice (self′sûr′vis) *adj.* Designating a restaurant, store, etc., where patrons serve themselves.

self-ser·ving (self′sûr′ving) *adj.* Tending to advance one's own interests, often at the expense of others.

self-start·er (self′stär′tər) *n.* A starter (def. 3).

self-styled (self′stīld′) *adj.* Characterized (as such) by oneself: a *self-styled* gentleman.

self-suf·fi·cient (self′sə·fish′ənt) *adj.* **1.** Able to support or maintain oneself without aid or cooperation from others. **2.** Having overweening confidence in oneself. Also **self′-suf·fic′ing** (-sə·fī′sing). — **self′-suf·fi′cien·cy** *n.*

self-sup·port (self′sə·pôrt′, -pōrt′) *n.* The act or state of supporting oneself entirely by one's own efforts. — **self′-sup·port′ed, self′-sup·port′ing** *adj.*

self-sus·tain·ing (self′sə·stān′ing) *adj.* Sustaining oneself or itself without outside help; self-supporting.

self-taught (self′tôt′) *adj.* Taught by oneself or through one's own efforts, without the aid of formal instruction.

self-will (self′wil′) *n.* Strong or tenacious adherence to one's own will or wish, esp. with disregard of the wishes of others; obstinacy. — **self′-willed′** *adj.*

self-wind·ing (self′wīn′ding) *adj. Mech.* Having a device that automatically winds a clock or other mechanism.

sell (sel) *v.* **sold, sell·ing** *v.t.* **1.** To transfer (property) to another for money or for some other consideration. **2.** To deal in; offer for sale. **3.** To deliver, surrender, or betray for a price or reward: to *sell* one's honor. **4.** To promote the sale of: Good advertising *sells* many products. **5.** *Informal* To cause to accept or approve something: with *on:* They *sold* him on the scheme. **6.** *Informal* To cause the accept- ance or approval of: He always *sold* himself well. **7.** *Slang* To deceive; cheat. — *v.i.* **8.** To transfer ownership for money, etc.; engage in selling. **9.** To be on sale; be sold. **10.** *Informal* To attract buyers: This item *sells* well. **11.** *Informal* To gain acceptance or approval: Will his plan *sell*? — **to sell off** To get rid of by selling. — **to sell out** **1.** To sell all one's merchandise, possessions, etc. **2.** *Slang* To be- tray. — *n.* **1.** On the stock exchange, a stock that ought to be sold. **2.** *Slang* A trick; joke; swindle. [OE *sellan* to give]

sell·er (sel′ər) *n.* **1.** One who sells. **2.** Something with a measure of salability: This book is a good *seller.*

sell·out (sel′out′) *n.* **1.** An act of selling out. **2.** *Informal* A performance for which all seats have been sold. **3.** *Slang* A betrayal through a secret bargain or agreement.

Selt·zer (selt′sər) *n.* An effervescing mineral water. Also **Seltzer water.** [Alter. of G *Selterser,* from *Nieder Selters,* a village in SW Prussia, its place of origin]

sel·vage (sel′vij) *n.* The edge of a woven fabric so finished that it will not ravel. Also **sel′vedge.** [< SELF + EDGE, trans. of MDu. *selfegghe*]

selves (selvz) Plural of SELF.

se·man·tic (si·man′tik) *adj.* **1.** Of or pertaining to meaning. **2.** Of or relating to semantics. [< Gk. *sēmainein* to signify] **— se·man'ti·cal·ly** *adv.*

se·man·ti·cist (si·man'tə·sist) *n.* A specialist in semantics.

se·man·tics (si·man'tiks) *n.pl. (construed as sing.)* **1.** *Ling.* The study of the meanings of speech forms, esp. of the development and changes in meaning of words and word groups. **2.** *Logic* The relation between signs or symbols and what they signify or denote. **3.** Loosely, verbal trickery.

sem·a·phore (sem'ə·fôr, -fōr) *n.* An apparatus for making signals, as with movable arms, disks, flags, or lanterns. [< F < Gk. *sēma* a sign + -PHORE] **— sem'a·phor'ic** (-fôr'ik, -for'ik) or **·i·cal** *adj.*

sem·blance (sem'bləns) *n.* **1.** A mere show without reality; pretense. **2.** Outward appearance. **3.** A likeness or resemblance. [< OF < L *simulare, similare* to simulate]

se·men (sē'mən) *n.* The impregnating fluid of male animals that contains spermatozoa; seed. [< L < *serere* to sow]

se·mes·ter (si·mes'tər) *n.* **1.** A college half year. **2.** In U.S. colleges and universities, a period of instruction, usu. lasting 17 or 18 weeks. [< G < L (*cursus*) *semestris* (a period) of six months] **— se·mes'tral** *adj.*

sem·i (sem'ī) **1.** *U.S. Informal* A semitrailer. **2.** *Canadian Slang* An American.

semi- *prefix* **1.** Not fully; partially; partly: *semiautomatic, semicivilized.* **2.** Exactly half: *semicircle.* **3.** Occurring twice (in the periods specified): *semiweekly.* [< L]

◆ *Semi-* (def. 1) appears as a prefix in many words, as in the following words and in the list below. It is pronounced sem'ē, sem'ə, or sometimes sem'ī.

semiacquaintance	semidivine	semiovoid
semiadherent	semidomestic	semipagan
semiaffectionate	semidomesticated	semipanic
semiagricultural	semidry	semiparallel
semialcoholic	semi-Empire	semiparalysis
semiallegiance	semienclosed	semipastoral
semianarchist	semierect	semipeace
semiangular	semieremitical	semiperfect
semianimal	semiexposed	semiperishable
semianimated	semiextinction	semipermanent
semiarborescent	semifailure	semiperspicuous
semiarchitectural	semifatalistic	semipinnate
semiarid	semifeudalism	semiplastic
semiatheist	semifictional	semipolitical
semiattached	semifinished	semipolitician
semiautonomous	semifit	semiporous
semiautonomy	semifitting	semipublic
semibald	semifixed	semiradical
semibarbarian	semiflexed	semiraw
semibarbaric	semifluctuating	semireactionary
semibarbarism	semiforeign	semirebellion
semibarbarous	semifriable	semireligious
semibarren	semifrontier	semiresolute
semibleached	semifunctional	semirespectability
semiblind	semigala	semirespectable
semiblunt	semigenuflection	semiretirement
semiboiled	semi-Gothic	semiriddle
semibourgeois	semigranulate	semi-Romanesque
semichannel	semihard	semi-Romanized
semichaotic	semihigh	semiroyal
semichivalrous	semihistorical	semirustic
semi-Christian	semihobo	semisacred
semiclerical	semihostile	semisatiric
semiclosed	semihumanitarian	semisatirical
semiclosure	semihumorous	semiscientific
semicoagulated	semi-idle	semisecrecy
semicollapsible	semi-idleness	semisecret
semicolonial	semi-incandescent	semiserious
semicoma	semi-independence	semiseriousness
semicomplete	semi-independent	semisocial
semiconceal	semi-intoxicated	semisocialism
semiconfident	semi-intoxication	semisoft
semiconfinement	semi-invalid	semispontaneity
semiconformist	semileafless	semispontaneous
semiconnection	semilegendary	semistagnant
semiconservative	semiliberal	semistagnation
semiconversion	semilined	semistarvation
semicooperation	semiliterate	semistarved
semicooperative	semilucent	semisuccess
semicured	semimilitary	semisuccessful
semicylindrical	semimobile	semisuspension
semidangerous	semimodern	semisymmetric
semidarkness	semimonastic	semisymmetrical
semideaf	semimonopoly	semitailored
semidelirious	semimute	semitechnical
semidenatured	semimystical	semitrained
semidependent	seminecessary	semitruth
semidestructive	seminervous	semivirtue
semideveloped	semioblivious	semivital
semidiaphanous	semiobscurity	semivoluntary
semidigested	semiopened	semiwarfare
semidirect	semiorganized	semiwild

sem·i·an·nu·al (sem'ē·an'yōō·əl) *adj.* Issued or occurring twice a year; half-yearly. **— n.** A publication issued twice a year. **— sem'i·an·nu·al·ly** *adv.*

sem·i·au·to·mat·ic (sem'ē·ô'tə·mat'ik) *adj.* **1.** Partly au-

tomatic. **2.** Of firearms, self-loading but firing once at (pull on the trigger.

sem·i·breve (sem'ē·brēv', -brev') *n. Chiefly Brit. Mu:* whole note.

sem·i·cir·cle (sem'ē·sûr'kəl) *n.* **1.** A half-circle; an arc segment of 180°. **2.** Anything formed or arranged in a ' circle. **— sem'i·cir'cu·lar** (-kyə-lər) *adj.*

semicircular canal *Anat.* One of the three tubular st tures in the labyrinth of the ear, serving as the organ of (librium. For illus. see EAR.

sem·i·civ·i·lized (sem'ē·siv'ə·līzd) *adj.* Partly civilize

sem·i·co·lon (sem'ē·kō'lən, sem'ə-) *n.* A mark (;) of p tuation, indicating a greater degree of separation than comma.

sem·i·con·duc·tor (sem'ē·kən·duk'tər) *n. Physics* One class of substances whose electrical conductivity at ordi temperatures is between that of a metal and an insul used in the manufacture of transistors.

sem·i·con·scious (sem'ē·kon'shəs) *adj.* Partly consc

sem·i·de·tached (sem'ē·di·tacht') *adj.* Joined to anc on one side only; esp. designating a house having one w common with another house.

sem·i·fi·nal (sem'ē·fī'nəl) *n.* **1.** In sports, a compet that precedes the final event. **2.** One of two competitio a tournament, the winners of each meeting in the final. *adj.* Next before the final. **— sem'i·fi'nal·ist** *n.*

sem·i·flu·id (sem'ē·flōō'id) *adj.* Fluid, but thick and cous. Also **sem'i·flu·id'ic** (-flōō·id'ik). **— n.** A thick, cous fluid.

sem·i·month·ly (sem'ē·munth'lē) *adj.* Taking place t a month. **— n.** *pl.* **·lies** A publication issued twice a mo **— adv.** At half-monthly intervals.

sem·i·nal (sem'ə·nəl) *adj.* **1.** Of, pertaining to, or con ing seeds or semen. **2.** Having productive power; germ **3.** Not developed; rudimentary. Also *seminary.* [< OF < *semen, seminis* semen, seed] **— sem'i·nal·ly** *adv.*

sem·i·nar (sem'ə·när) *n.* **1.** A group of advanced stud at a college or university, meeting regularly and inform with a professor for discussion of research problems. **2.** course thus conducted or the room where it meets.

sem·i·nar·y (sem'ə·ner'ē) *n. pl.* **·nar·ies** **1.** A sp school, as of theology. **2.** A school of higher education The place where anything is nurtured. *— adj.* **1.** Sem **2.** Pertaining to a seminary. [< L *seminarium* seed p

sem·i·na·tion (sem'ə·nā'shən) *n.* **1.** The act of sowir spreading; dispersion of seeds. **2.** Propagation; repro tion. [< L *seminare* to sow < *semen* seed]

sem·i·nif·er·ous (sem'ə·nif'ər·əs) *adj.* **1.** Carrying or ducing semen. **2.** Bearing a seed or seeds.

Sem·i·nole (sem'ə·nōl) *n.* One of a Florida tribe of N American Indians of Muskhogean stock, an offshoot or Creeks, now chiefly in Oklahoma. [< Muskhogean (Cr *Simanóle*, lit., separatist, runaway]

sem·i·of·fi·cial (sem'ē·ə·fish'əl) *adj.* Having some off authority or sanction; official to a certain extent. **— s** of·fi'cial·ly *adv.*

sem·i·per·me·a·ble (sem'ē·pûr'mē·ə·bəl) *adj.* Part permeable, as membranes that separate a solvent from dissolved substance.

sem·i·pre·cious (sem'ē·presh'əs) *adj.* Of, pertaining t designating gemstones, as jade, garnet, opal, amethyst, that are somewhat less rare or valuable than precious sto

sem·i·pri·vate (sem'ē·prī'vit) *adj.* Partly but not wl private, as a hospital room for two or several patients.

sem·i·pro·fes·sion·al (sem'ē·prə·fesh'ən·əl) *adj.* Eng in a sport for profit, but not as a full-time occupation. **—** A semiprofessional athlete. Also *Informal* **sem'i·pro'** (-p **— sem'i·pro·fes'sion·al·ly** *adv.*

sem·i·qua·ver (sem'ē·kwā'vər) *n. Chiefly Brit. Mu:* sixteenth note.

sem·i·rig·id (sem'ē·rij'id) *adj. Aeron.* Partly rigid, a airship in which an exterior stiffener supports the load. *n.* A semirigid airship.

sem·i·skilled (sem'ē·skild') *adj.* Partly skilled.

sem·i·sol·id (sem'ē·sol'id) *adj.* Nearly solid; partly s

Sem·ite (sem'īt, sē'mīt) *n.* **1.** One of a people of Cauca stock, now represented by the Jews and Arabs, but origir including the ancient Babylonians, Assyrians, Arame Phoenicians, etc. **2.** A person believed to be a descendar Shem. Also *Shemite.* [< NL < Gk. < Hebrew *Shēm*]

Se·mit·ic (sə·mit'ik) *adj.* Of or pertaining to the Semite to any of their languages. **— n.** A subfamily of the Har Semitic family of languages.

Sem·i·tism (sem'ə·tiz'əm) *n.* **1.** A Semitic word or tri **2.** Semitic practices, opinions, or customs. **3.** Any pa favoring or thought to favor the Jews.

sem·i·tone (sem'ē·tōn') *n. Music* The smallest interv the chromatic scale; a minor second: also called *half step, tone.* **— sem'i·ton'ic** (-ton'ik) *adj.*

sem·i·trail·er (sem'ē·trā'lər) *n.* A trailer having wh only at the rear, the front end resting on the tractor.

i·vow·el (sem'ē-vou'əl) *n. Phonet.* A vowellike sound as a consonant, as (w), (y), and (r): also called *glide.*

i·week·ly (sem'ē-wēk'lē) *adj.* Issued or occurring a week. — *n. pl.* **·lies** A publication issued twice a . — *adv.* At half-weekly intervals.

i·year·ly (sem'ē-yir'lē) *adj.* Issued or occurring twice ar. — *n. pl.* **·lies** A semiyearly occurrence. — *adv.* alf-yearly intervals.

ɔ·li·na (sem'ə-lē'nə) *n.* The gritty or grainlike por-of wheat retained in the bolting machine after the fine has been passed through. [< L *simila* fine flour]

per fi·de·lis (sem'pər fi-dē'lis, fi-dā'lis) *Latin* Always ful: motto of the U.S. Marine Corps.

per pa·ra·tus (sem'pər pə-rā'təs) *Latin* Always pre-l: motto of the U.S. Coast Guard.

pi·ter·nal (sem'pə-tûr'nəl) *adj.* Eternal; everlasting. ɔF < L *sempiternus* everlasting] — **sem'pi·ter'ni·ty** *n.*

·stress (semp'stris, sem'-) *n.* A seamstress.

sen) *n. pl.* **sen** (sen) **1.** A former monetary unit and of Japan, equal to one hundredth of a yen. **2.** A mone-unit and coin of Indonesia.

te (sen'it) *n.* **1.** The governing body of some univer-s and institutions of learning. **2.** A council or legislative . [< OF < L *senatus*, lit., council of old men]

te (sen'it) *n.* **1.** The upper branch of national or state lative bodies of the U.S., Canada, France, and other rnments. The **United States Senate** is composed of two tors elected by popular vote from each State. **2.** In an-Rome, the state council.

·tor (sen'ə-tər) *n. Often cap.* A member of a senate. **·to·ri·al** (sen'ə-tôr'ē-əl, -tō'rē-) *adj.* Of, pertaining to, efitting a senator or senate. — **sen'a·to'ri·al·ly** *adv.*

(send) *v.* **sent, send·ing** *v.t.* **1.** To cause or direct (a ɔn or persons) to go; dispatch. **2.** To cause to be taken irected to another place; transmit; forward: sometimes *off.* **3.** To cause to issue; emit or discharge, as heat, , smoke, etc. **4.** To throw or drive by force; impel. **5.** ause to come, happen, etc.; grant. **6.** To bring into a ified state or condition. **7.** *U.S. Slang* To make raptur-with joy. — *v.i.* **8.** To dispatch an agent, messenger, or sage. — **to send (someone) about his (or her) business** dismiss with reproach or warning. — **to send down** To expel from a university. — **to send flying 1.** To ter or knock violently away. **2.** To cause to flee. — **to l for** To summon by a message or messenger. — **to send king** To dismiss quickly and forcefully. — **to send up** *rmal* To sentence to prison. [OE *sendan*] — **send'er** *n.*

-off (send'ôf', -of') *n.* **1.** The act of sending off; a start. farewell dinner or other celebration or demonstration at ing. **3.** Encouragement, as in starting a career.

e·ca (sen'ə-kə) *n.* One of a tribe of Indians of Iroquoian k formerly inhabiting western New York. [< Du. *Sen-ɪas* the Five Nations < Algonquian *A'sinnika*]

e·ga·lese (sen'gə-lēz', -lēs) *adj.* Of or pertaining to ɔgal, its inhabitants, customs, etc. — *n.* A native or in-itant of Senegal.

ɔs·cent (si-nes'ənt) *adj.* **1.** Growing old. **2.** Charac-stic of old age. [< L *senescere* to grow old] — **se·nes'.** :e *n.*

ɔschal (sen'ə-shəl) *n.* An official in the household medieval prince or noble, having charge of feasts, etc.; a ʋard or major-domo. **2.** *Brit.* A cathedral official. [< Gmc. Cf. OHG *siniskalk* old servant.]

le (sē'nīl, -nil, sen'īl) *adj.* **1.** Pertaining to, proceeding n, or characteristic of old age. **2.** Infirm; weak; doting. *ɪeog.* Almost worn away to base level. [< L *senilis* < *x* old] — **se'nile·ly** *adv.* — **se·nil·i·ty** (si-nil'ə-tē) *n.*

ɪor (sēn'yər) *adj.* **1.** Older in years or higher in rank. ɔenoting the older of two: opposed to *junior.* ♦ The ɪ used to distinguish a father from a son of the same ɪe is usu. written *Albert Jones, Sr.* or *Albert Jones, senior.* ɜelonging to maturity or later life. **4.** Pertaining to the year of a high-school or collegiate course of four years. . **1.** The older of two. **2.** One longer in service or higher tanding. **3.** A student in the senior year of a high-school, ɛge, or university. [< L, comparative of *senex* old]

ɪor high school A high school, in the U.S. typically ɪprising grades 10, 11, and 12.

ior·i·ty (sēn-yôr'ə-tē, -yor'-) *n. pl.* **·ties 1.** The state of ɪg senior; priority of age or rank. **2.** Precedence or pri-y due to length of service.

na (sen'ə) *n.* **1.** The dried leaflets of any of several le-ɪinous plants, used medicinally as purgatives. **2.** Any ɪt yielding senna. [< NL < Arabic *sanā*]

ɔr (sā-nyôr') *n. pl.* **·ño·res** (-nyō'rās) *Spanish* **1.** A tleman. **2.** Sir; Mr.: used as a title of address.

·o·ra (sā-nyō'rä) *n. Spanish* **1.** A lady. **2.** Mrs.; mad-

---

se·ño·ri·ta (sā'nyō-rē'tä) *n. Spanish* **1.** A young, unmar-ried lady. **2.** Miss.

sen·sate (sen'sāt) *adj.* Perceived by the senses. Also **sen'-sat·ed.** — *v.t.* **·sat·ed, ·sat·ing** To perceive by the senses. [< LL < L *sensus* sense]

sen·sa·tion (sen-sā'shən) *n.* **1.** The aspect of consciousness resulting from the stimulation of any of the sense organs, as hearing, taste, touch, smell, or sight. **2.** *Physiol.* The capac-ity to respond to such stimulation. **3.** That which produces great interest or excitement. **4.** An excited condition: to cause a *sensation.* [See SENSATE.]

sen·sa·tion·al (sen-sā'shən-əl) *adj.* **1.** Pertaining to emo-tional excitement. **2.** Of or pertaining to physical sensation. **3.** Causing excitement; startling; melodramatic. — **sen-sa'tion·al·ly** *adv.*

sen·sa·tion·al·ism (sen-sā'shən-əl-iz'əm) *n.* The use of sensational or melodramatic methods, words, etc. — **sen-sa'tion·al·ist** *n.* — **sen·sa'tion·al·is'tic** *adj.*

sense (sens) *n.* **1.** The faculty of sensation; sense percep-tion. **2.** Any of certain agencies by or through which an in-dividual receives impressions of the external world, as taste, touch, hearing, smell, or sight. **3.** *Physiol.* Any receptor, or group of receptors, specialized for the perception of external objects or internal bodily changes. **4.** Rational perception accompanied by feeling: a *sense* of wrong. **5.** *Often pl.* Nor-mal power of mind or understanding; sound or natural judg-ment: She is coming to her *senses.* **6.** Signification; import; meaning. **7.** Opinion, view, or judgment of the majority. **8.** Sound reason or judgment; wisdom. **9.** Capacity to per-ceive or appreciate: a *sense* of color. — *v.t.* **sensed, sens·ing 1.** To become aware of through the senses. **2.** *Informal* To comprehend; understand. [< F < L *sensus* perception]

sense·less (sens'lis) *adj.* **1.** Devoid of sense; making no sense; irrational. **2.** Unconscious. **3.** Incapable of feeling or perception. — **sense'less·ly** *adv.* — **sense'less·ness** *n.*

sense organ A structure specialized to receive sense im-pressions, as the eye, nose, ear, etc.

sen·si·bil·i·ty (sen'sə-bil'ə-tē) *n. pl.* **·ties 1.** The capability of sensation; power to perceive or feel. **2.** The capacity of sensation and rational emotion, as distinguished from intel-lect and will. **3.** *Often pl.* Susceptibility or sensitiveness to outside influences or mental impressions. **4.** Appreciation accompanying mental apprehension; discerning judgment.
— **Syn. 1, 3.** *Sensibility* may be used of mere physical sensa-tion, but more often denotes qualities of mind: *sensibility* to heat and cold, the *sensibility* of the artist to beauty. *Sensitivity* suggests great *sensibility*, and the readiness to be excited by small cause. *Susceptibility* is the capacity to receive, contain, or be influenced: *susceptibility* to colds. *Feeling* specifically refers to the tactile sense, but is also used in the sense of emotional response as a general, but less precise, substitute for the other words.

sen·si·ble (sen'sə-bəl) *adj.* **1.** Possessed of good practical judgment; exhibiting sound sense and understanding. **2.** Capable of physical sensation. **3.** Perceptible through the senses: *sensible* heat. **4.** Emotionally or mentally sensitive. **5.** Having a perception or cognition; fully aware; persuaded. **6.** Great enough to be perceived. [< OF < L < *sentire* to feel, perceive] — **sen'si·ble·ness** *n.* — **sen'si·bly** *adv.*

sen·si·tive (sen'sə-tiv) *adj.* **1.** Easily affected by outside operations or influences; excitable or impressionable; touchy. **2.** Reacting readily to external agents or forces: paper *sensi-tive* to light. **3.** Pertaining to or depending on the senses or sensation. **4.** Closing or moving when touched or irritated, as certain plants. **5.** Liable to fluctuation. **6.** Capable of indicating minute changes or differences; delicate. [See SENSIBLE.] — **sen'si·tive·ly** *adv.* — **sen'si·tive·ness** *n.*

sensitive plant 1. A shrubby tropical herb whose leaves close at a touch. **2.** Any of various similar or related plants.

sen·si·tiv·i·ty (sen'sə-tiv'ə-tē) *n. pl.* **·ties** The state or de-gree of being sensitive. — **Syn.** See SENSIBILITY.

sen·si·tize (sen'sə-tīz) *v.t.* **·tized, ·tiz·ing 1.** To render sen-sitive. **2.** *Photog.* To make sensitive to light, as a plate or film. — **sen'si·ti·za'tion** *n.* — **sen'si·tiz'er** *n.*

sen·sor (sen'sər) *n.* That which receives and responds to a stimulus or signal; esp., an instrument or device designed to detect and respond to some force, change, or radiation.

sen·so·ri·um (sen-sôr'ē-əm, -sō'rē-) *n. pl.* **·ri·a** (-rē-ə) **1.** *Anat.* The nervous system, including the cerebrum, as the collective organ of sensation. **2.** *Biol.* The entire sensory apparatus. [< LL < L *sensus* sense]

sen·so·ry (sen'sər-ē) *adj.* **1.** Of or pertaining to sensation. **2.** Conveying or producing sense impulses. **3.** Pertaining to the sensorium. Also **sen·so·ri·al** (sen-sôr'ē-al, -sō'rē-).

sen·su·al (sen'shoo-əl) *adj.* **1.** Unduly indulging the appe-tites or sexual pleasure; lewd. **2.** Pertaining to the body or to the physical senses; carnal. **3.** Pertaining to sensualism. ♦ See note under SENSUOUS. [< MF < LL < L *sensus* sense] — **sen'su·al·ly** *adv.*

---

sen·su·al·ism (sen'shōō·əl·iz'əm) n. **1.** Sensuality. **2.** A system of ethics predicating the pleasures of sense to be the highest good. — **sen'su·al·ist** n. — **sen'su·al·is'tic** adj.

sen·su·al·i·ty (sen'shōō·al'ə·tē) n. pl. **·ties 1.** The state of being sensual, or sensual acts collectively. **2.** Sensual indulgence. Also called sensualism: also **sen'su·al·ness.**

sen·su·al·ize (sen'shōō·əl·īz') v.t. **·ized, ·iz·ing** To make sensual. Also Brit. **sen'su·al·ise'.** — **sen·su·al·i·za'tion** n.

sen·su·ous (sen'shōō·əs) adj. **1.** Pertaining or appealing to or derived from the senses: used in a higher and purer signification than sensual. **2.** Keenly appreciative of and aroused by beauty, refinement, or luxury. **3.** Resembling imagery that appeals to the senses: a sensuous portrayal. — **sen'su·ous·ly** adv. — **sen'su·ous·ness** n.

◆ **sensuous, sensual** Sensuous refers not only to the physical senses but to any means of feeling, as intellectual or esthetic sensitivity, intuition, etc.: the sensuous pleasure of walking in the rain. Sensual is generally restricted to bodily sensations and to the satisfaction of physical appetites.

sent (sent) Past tense and past participle of SEND.

sen·tence (sen'təns) n. **1.** Gram. A group of words containing a subject and a predicate, as declarative, interrogative, imperative, and exclamatory sentences, or a single word in the case of the simple imperative. — **simple sentence** A sentence consisting of a subject and a predicate without any subordinate clauses. — **compound sentence** A sentence consisting of two or more independent clauses, usu. connected by a semicolon or a coordinating conjunction or both. — **complex sentence** A sentence consisting of an independent clause and one or more subordinate clauses. **2.** Law A penalty pronounced upon a person convicted. **3.** A formal determination or opinion. — v.t. **·tenced, ·tenc·ing** To pass sentence upon. [< OF < L < sentire to feel, be of opinion] — **sen'tenc·er** n. — **sen·ten'tial** (sen·ten'shəl) adj.

sen·ten·tious (sen·ten'shəs) adj. **1.** Abounding in or giving terse expression to thought; axiomatic. **2.** Habitually using terse, laconic, or aphoristic language. **3.** Pompously formal; moralizing. [< L sententia < sentire to feel, be of an opinion] — **sen·ten'tious·ly** adv. — **sen·ten·ti·os·i·ty** (sen·ten'shē·os'ə·tē), **sen·ten'tious·ness** n.

sen·ti·ent (sen'shē·ənt, -shənt) adj. Possessing powers of sense or sense perception; having sensation or feeling. — n. **1.** A sentient person or thing. **2.** The mind. [< L sentiens, -entis, ppr. of sentire to feel] — **sen'ti·ence, sen'ti·en·cy** n. — **sen'ti·ent·ly** adv.

sen·ti·ment (sen'tə·mənt) n. **1.** Noble, tender, or artistic feeling, or susceptibility to such feeling; sensibility. **2.** A verbal expression of such feeling. **3.** A mental attitude or response to a person, object, or idea, based on feeling instead of reason. **4.** An exaggerated emotional reaction. **5.** Often pl. An opinion or judgment. **6.** An expressive thought or idea in appropriate language [< OF < Med.L < L sentire to feel]

sen·ti·men·tal (sen'tə·men'təl) adj. **1.** Characterized by sentiment or emotion. **2.** Experiencing, displaying, or given to sentiment, often in an extravagant or mawkish manner: a sentimental novel. — **sen'ti·men'tal·ly** adv.

sen·ti·men·tal·i·ty (sen'tə·men·tal'ə·tē) n. pl. **·ties 1.** The state or quality of being mawkishly sentimental. **2.** Any expression of sentiment. Also **sen'ti·men'tal·ism** (-men'təl·iz'əm).

sen·ti·men·tal·ize (sen'tə·men'təl·īz) v. **·ized, ·iz·ing** v.t. **1.** To make sentimental. **2.** To cherish sentimentally. — v.i. **3.** To behave sentimentally. Also Brit. **sen'ti·men'tal·ise.**

sen·ti·nel (sen'tə·nəl) n. **1.** A sentry. **2.** Any watcher or guard. — v.t. **·neled** or **·nelled, ·nel·ing** or **·nel·ling 1.** To watch over as a sentinel. **2.** To furnish with sentinels. **3.** To station or appoint as a sentinel. [< OF < Ital. < LL sentinare to avoid danger]

sen·try (sen'trē) n. pl. **·tries 1.** A soldier placed on guard to see that only authorized persons pass his post and to warn of danger. **2.** The watch or guard kept by a sentry. [? Short for obs. centrenel, var. of SENTINEL]

se·pal (sē'pəl) n. Bot. One of the individual leaves of a calyx. [< F < NL < L sep(aratus) separate + (pet)alum petal]

sep·a·ra·ble (sep'ər·ə·bəl, sep'rə-) adj. Capable of being separated. — **sep'a·ra·bil'i·ty, sep'a·ra·ble·ness** n. — **sep'a·ra·bly** adv.

sep·a·rate (v. sep'ə·rāt; adj. sep'ər·it, sep'rit) v. **·rat·ed, ·rat·ing** v.t. **1.** To set asunder; disunite or disjoin; sever. **2.** To occupy a position between; serve to keep apart. **3.** To divide into components, parts, etc. **4.** To isolate or obtain from a compound, mixture, etc. **5.** To consider separately; distinguish between. **6.** Law To part by separation. — v.i. **7.** To become divided or disconnected; draw apart. **8.** To part company; withdraw from association or combination. — adj. **1.** Existing or considered apart from others; individual. **2.** Disunited from the body; disembodied. **3.** Separated; disjoined. [< L < se- apart + parare to prepare] — **sep'a·rate·ly** adv. — **sep'a·rate·ness** n. — **sep'a·ra'-**

tive, sep·a·ra·to·ry (sep'ər·ə·tôr'ē, -tō'rē, sep'rə-). — **s ra'tor** n.

sep·a·ra·tion (sep'ə·rā'shən) n. **1.** The act or proce separating; division. **2.** The state of being disconnect apart. **3.** Something that separates. **4.** Law Relinq ment of cohabitation between husband and wife by m consent: distinguished from divorce.

separation center A central army or navy point that dles the discharging and releasing of personnel.

sep·a·ra·tist (sep'ər·ə·tist, sep'rə-) n. One who advo or upholds separation, esp. one who secedes. Also **sep'** **tion·ist.** — **sep'a·ra·tism** n.

Se·phar·dim (si·fär'dim) n.pl. The Spanish and Portu Jews or their descendants. Also **Se·phar'a·dim** (-ə·dim) Hebrew sephārādhîm] — **Se·phar'dic** adj.

se·pi·a (sē'pē·ə) n. **1.** A reddish brown pigment prep from the inky secretion of the cuttlefish. **2.** The color c pigment. **3.** A picture done in this pigment. — adj. cuted in or colored like sepia; dark brown with a tinge o [< L < Gk. sēpia cuttlefish]

se·poy (sē'poi) n. A native Indian soldier who wa ployed in the former British Indian Army. [< Pg. si Urdu sipāhī soldier < Persian sipāh army]

sep·pu·ku (sep·pōō·kōō) n. Japanese Hara-kiri.

sep·sis (sep'sis) n. Pathol. Infection by pathogenic n organisms. [< NL < Gk. < sēpein to make putrid]

sep·ta (sep'tə) Plural of SEPTUM.

Sep·tem·ber (sep·tem'bər) The ninth month of the containing 30 days; the seventh month in the old R calendar. [< L septem seven]

sep·te·nar·y (sep'tə·ner'ē) adj. Consisting of, perta to, or being seven. — n. pl. **·nar·ies 1.** The number s **2.** Anything having a definite relation to the number s Also **sep'te·nar'i·us** (sep'tə·nâr'ē·əs). [< L < septem se

sep·ten·ni·al (sep·ten'ē·əl) adj. **1.** Recurring every years. **2.** Continuing or capable of lasting seven years. L < septem seven + annus year] — **sep·ten'ni·al·ly**

sep·tet (sep·tet') n. **1.** A group of seven persons, tl etc. **2.** Music A composition for seven singers or instru talists. Also **sep·tette.** [< G < L septem seven]

septi-¹ combining form Seven. Also, before vowels, [< L septem seven]

septi-² combining form A partition; fence. Also, before els, sept-. Also **septo-.** [< L septum enclosure, wall]

sep·tic (sep'tik) adj. **1.** Of, pertaining to, or caused by sis. **2.** Producing sepsis; infective. Also **sep'ti·cal.** Any agent producing sepsis. [< LL < Gk. sēpein to p fy] — **sep·tic·i·ty** (sep·tis'ə·tē) n.

sep·ti·ce·mi·a (sep'tə·sē'mē·ə) n. Pathol. An infecti the blood by pathogenic microorganisms; blood poiso Also **sep'ti·cae'mi·a.** [< NL < Gk. sēptikos putrefacti haima blood] — **sep'ti·ce'mic** (-sē'mik) adj.

septic tank A tank in which sewage is allowed to re until purified by the action of anaerobic bacteria.

sep·til·lion (sep·til'yən) n. **1.** U.S. A thousand sextil written as 1 followed by twenty-four zeros: a cardinal ber. **2.** Brit. A million sextillions (def. 2), written as lowed by forty-two zeros: a cardinal number. — adj. a septillion in number. [< MF < septi- seven + (mi million] — **sep·til'lionth** adj. & n.

sep·tu·a·ge·nar·i·an (sep'chōō·ə·jə·nâr'ē·ən, sep'tōō-) person 70 years old, or between 70 and 80. — adj. **1.** S ty years old, or between 70 and 80. **2.** Of or pertaining septuagenarian. [< L septuaginta seventy]

sep·tu·ag·e·nar·y (sep'chōō·aj'ə·ner'ē, sep'tōō-) adj. Septuagenarian.

Sep·tu·a·ges·i·ma (sep'chōō·ə·jes'ə·mə, sep'tōō-) n. third Sunday before Lent. Also **Septuagesima Sunday.** L, seventieth]

Sep·tu·a·gint (sep'chōō·ə·jint', sep'tōō-) n. An old G version of the Old Testament Scriptures. [< L septua seventy]

sep·tum (sep'təm) n. pl. **·ta** (-tə) Biol. **1.** A dividing between two cavities: the nasal septum. **2.** A partition, coral or in a spore. [< L < sepire to enclose] — **se sep'tate** adj.

sep·ul·cher (sep'əl·kər) n. **1.** A burial place; tomb; vaul A receptacle for relics, esp. in an altar slab. — v.t. **·ch** or **·chred, ·cher·ing** or **·chring 1.** To place in a sepulch Also Brit. **sep'ul·chre** (-kər). [< OF < L sepulcrum b place, tomb]

se·pul·chral (si·pul'krəl) adj. **1.** Pertaining to a sepulc **2.** Suggestive of the grave; dismal. **3.** Unnaturally low hollow in tone, as a voice. — **se·pul'chral·ly** adv.

sep·ul·ture (sep'əl·chər) n. **1.** The act of entombing; al. **2.** Archaic A sepulcher.

se·quel (sē'kwəl) n. **1.** Something that follows and se as a continuation; a development from what went before A narrative discourse that, though complete in itself, de ops from a preceding one. **3.** A consequence; upshot; re [< OF < L sequela < sequi to follow]

...uence (sē'kwəns) *n.* **1.** The process or fact of following ...pace, time, or thought; succession or order: also **se'quen-.** **2.** Order of succession; arrangement. **3.** A number of ...gs following one another, considered collectively; a se- **4.** An effect or consequence. **5.** In card games, a set of ...e or more cards next each other in value. **6.** A section of ...ion-picture film presenting a single episode, without time ...es or interruptions. **7.** *Math.* An ordered succession of ...ntities, as $2x$, $4x^2$, $8x^3$, $16x^4$. [< L < *sequi* to follow]
...ence of tenses See under TENSE².

...uent (sē'kwənt) *n.* That which follows; a consequence; ...lt. — *adj.* **1.** Following in the order of time; succeed- **2.** Consequent; resultant. [See SEQUENCE.]
...uen-tial (si-kwen'shəl) *adj.* **1.** Characterized by or ...ming a sequence, as of parts. **2.** Sequent. — **se-quen-ti-ty** (si-kwen'shē-al'ə-tē) *n.* — **se-quen'tial-ly** *adv.*
...ues-ter (si-kwes'tər) *v.t.* **1.** To place apart; separate. ...'o seclude; withdraw: often used reflexively. **3.** *Law* To ...e (property) into custody until a controversy, claim, etc., ...ttled or satisfied. **4.** In international law, to confiscate ...control (enemy property) by preemption. **5.** *Chem.* To ...der inactive, as by the process of chelation. [< OF < LL ...estrare to remove, lay aside < *sequester* trustee] — **se-s'tra-ble** *adj.* — **se-ques'tered** *adj.*
...ues-trate (si-kwes'trāt) *v.t.* **-trat-ed, -trat-ing** **1.** To ...e, esp. for the use of the government; confiscate. **2.** To ...e possession of for a time, with a view to the just settle-...t of the claims of creditors. **3.** To seclude; sequester. — **...e-ques-tra-tion** (sē'kwes-trā'shən, sek'wəs-) *n.* — **...s-tra-tor** (sē'kwes-trā'tər, si-kwes'trā-tər) *n.*
...uin (sē'kwin) *n.* A small coinlike ornament sewn on ...hing. [< F < Ital. < Arabic *sikka* coining-die]
...uoi-a (si-kwoi'ə) *n.* **1.** A gigantic evergreen tree of the ...tern U.S., with spreading, lanceolate leaves ...l small cones: also called *redwood.* **2.** A close-...elated tree of the Sierra Nevada mountains ...California, sometimes reaching a height of ...l feet. [< NL, after *Sequoyah*, 1770?–1843, ...alf-breed Cherokee Indian who invented the ...erokee alphabet]
...(sir) See SEER².
... Var. of SERO.
...a (sir'ə) Plural of SERUM.
...a-glio (si-ral'yō, -räl'-) *n.* **1.** The portion ...a Moslem house reserved for the wives and ...cubines; a harem. **2.** Any residence of a sul-...Also **se-rail** (se-rāl'). [< Ital. *serraglio* en-...sure, ult. < LL *serrare*, var. of L *serare* to ...k up]
...a-pe (sə-räp'ē) *n.* A blanketlike outer gar-...nt worn in Latin America, esp. in Mexico: ...o *sarape, zarape.* [< Am. Sp.]
...aph (ser'əf) *n.* *pl.* **ser-aphs** or **ser-a-phim** ...'ə-fim) A celestial being having three pairs ...wings. *Isa.* vi 2. [Back formation < *Sera-...m*, *pl.* < LL < Hebrew] — **se-raph-ic** (si-...'ik), **se-raph'i-cal** *adj.* — **se-raph'i-cal-ly** *adv.*
...a-phim (ser'ə-fim) *n.* **1.** Plural of SERAPH: ...o **ser'a-phin** (-fin). **2.** *pl.* **phims** A seraph: an ...oneous usage.
...bo-Cro-a-tian (sûr'bō-krō-ā'shən) *n.* **1.** ...e South Slavic language of Yugoslavia, including all the ...languages and dialects. **2.** One whose native tongue is ...bo-Croatian. Also **Ser'bo-Cro'at** (-krō'at, -ət). — *adj.* ...the Serbo-Croatian language or those who speak it.
...e¹ (sir) See SEAR¹.
...e² (sir) *n.* *Ecol.* The series of changes found in a given ...nt formation from the initial to the ultimate stage. [Back ...mation < SERIES] — **ser'al** *adj.*
...e-nade (ser'ə-nād') *n.* **1.** An evening song, usu. that of ...over beneath his sweetheart's window. **2.** Music per-...med in honor of some person in the open air at night. **3.** ...e music for such a song. **4.** *Music* A form of instrumental ...sic similar to the suite, and usu. including a march and a ...nuet: also called *serenata.* — *v.t. & v.i.* **-nad-ed, -nad-ing** ...entertain with a serenade. [< F < Ital. < L *serenus* ...ar, serene] — **ser'e-nad'er** *n.*
...e-na-ta (ser'ə-nä'tə) *n.* *pl.* **-tas, -te** (tā) *Music* **1.** A ...matic cantata on any imaginative or simple subject, ...en composed as a complimentary overture for a royal per-...age. **2.** A serenade. [< Ital. See SERENADE.]
...en-dip-i-ty (ser'ən-dip'ə-tē) *n.* The faculty of happen-...upon fortunate discoveries when not in search of them. ...oined by Horace Walpole (1754), in *The Three Princes of ...rendip* (Ceylon)] — **ser'en-dip'i-tous** *adj.*
...ene (si-rēn') *adj.* **1.** Clear; calm: a *serene* sky. **2.** ...arked by peaceful repose; tranquil; placid: a *serene* spirit. ...Of exalted rank: chiefly in the titles of certain European

princes: His *Serene* Highness. — **Syn.** See CALM. [< L *serenus*] — **se-rene'ly** *adv.* — **se-rene'ness** *n.*
se-ren-i-ty (si-ren'ə-tē) *n.* *pl.* **-ties** **1.** The state or quality of being serene; peacefulness; repose. **2.** Clearness; bright-ness. **3.** *Usu. Cap.* A title of honor given to certain mem-bers of royal families: preceded by *His, Your,* etc.
serf (sûrf) *n.* **1.** In feudal times, a person bound in servitude on an estate. **2.** Anyone in servile subjection. [< OF < L *servus* slave] — **serf'age, serf'dom, serf'hood** *n.*
serge (sûrj) *n.* **1.** A strong twilled fabric made of wool yarns and characterized by a diagonal rib on both sides of the cloth. **2.** A rayon lining fabric. [< OF < L *serica* (*lana*) (wool) of the Seres < *Seres* the Seres, an eastern Asian people]
ser-geant (sär'jənt) *n.* **1.** *Mil.* Any of several noncommis-sioned officer grades. See tables at GRADE. **2.** A police offi-cer ranking next below a captain (sometimes lieutenant) in the U.S., and next below an inspector in England. **3.** A ser-geant at arms. **4.** A constable or bailiff. Also, *esp. Brit.*, **ser-jeant.** [< OF < L *serviens, -entis,* ppr. of *servire* to serve] — **ser'gean-cy, ser'geant-cy, ser'geant-ship** *n.*
sergeant at arms **1.** An executive officer in a legislative body who enforces order. **2.** The title of certain court or city officials who have ceremonial duties.
sergeant major A noncommissioned officer in the highest enlisted grade of the U.S. Army and Marine Corps. See table at GRADE.
Sergeant Major of the Army The highest enlisted rank in the U.S. Army. See table at GRADE.
se-ri-al (sir'ē-əl) *adj.* **1.** Of the nature of a series. **2.** Pub-lished in a series at regular intervals. **3.** Arranged in rows or ranks; sucessive: also **se-ri-ate** (sir'ē-it, -āt). — *n.* **1.** A novel or other story regularly presented in successive instal-ments, as in a magazine, on radio or television, or in motion pictures. **2.** *Brit.* A periodical. [< NL < L *series* row, or-der] — **se'ri-al-ly** *adv.*
se-ri-al-ize (sir'ē-əl-īz') *v.t.* **-ized, -iz-ing** To arrange or pub-lish in serial form. — **se'ri-al-i-za'tion** *n.*
serial number A number assigned to a person, object, item of merchandise, etc., as a means of identification.
se-ri-a-tim (sir'ē-ā'tim, ser'ē-) *adv.* One after another; seri-ally. [< Med.L < L *series,* on analogy with *gradatim*]
ser-i-cul-ture (sir'ə-kul'chər) *n.* The raising and care of silkworms for the production of raw silk. [Contr. of F *séri-ciculture* < L *sericum* silk + *cultura* a raising, culture] — **ser'i-cul'tur-al** *adj.* — **ser'i-cul'tur-ist** *n.*
se-ries (sir'ēz) *n.* *pl.* **se-ries** **1.** An arrangement of one thing after another; a connected succession of persons, things, data, etc. on the basis of like relationships. **2.** *Math.* An ordered arrangement of terms the sum of which is indi-cated. **3.** *Electr.* **a** An arrangement of sources or utilizers of electricity in which the positive electrode of one is connected with the negative electrode of another. **b** The circuit so pro-duced. [< L < *serere* to join, weave together]
series winding *Electr.* The winding of a dynamo or an electric motor in such a way that the field circuit is connected in series with the armature circuit. — **se-ries-wound** (sir'-ēz-wound') *adj.*
ser-if (ser'if) *n.* *Printing* A light line or stroke crossing or projecting from the end of a main line or stroke in a letter: also spelled *ceriph.* [< Du. < L *scribere* to write]
se-ri-o-com-ic (sir'ē-ō-kom'ik) *adj.* Mingling the serious with the comic. Also **se'ri-o-com'i-cal.**
se-ri-ous (sir'ē-əs) *adj.* **1.** Grave and earnest in quality, feeling, or disposition; sober. **2.** Said, planned, or done with full practical intent; being or done in earnest. **3.** Of grave importance: a *serious* problem. **4.** Attended with considera-ble danger or loss: a *serious* accident. [< MF < LL < L *serius*] — **se'ri-ous-ly** *adv.* — **se'ri-ous-ness** *n.*
ser-jeant (sär'jənt) See SERGEANT.
ser-mon (sûr'mən) *n.* **1.** A discourse based on a passage or text of the Bible, delivered as part of a church service. **2.** Any discourse intended for the pulpit. **3.** Any speech of a serious or solemn kind, as a formal exhortation. [< AF, OF < L *sermo, -onis* talk] — **ser-mon'ic** (-mon'ik) or **-i-cal** *adj.*
ser-mon-ize (sûr'mən-īz) *v.t. & v.i.* **-ized, -iz-ing** **1.** To com-pose or deliver a sermon or sermons (to). **2.** To address at length in a moralizing manner. — **ser'mon-iz'er** *n.*
Sermon on the Mount The discourse of Jesus found re-corded in *Matt.* v, vi, vii: properly distinguished from the **Sermon on the Plain,** *Luke* vi 20–49.
sero- *combining form* Connected with or related to serum. Also, before vowels, **ser-.** [< L *serum* whey]
se-rol-o-gy (si-rol'ə-jē) *n.* The science of serums and their actions. — **se-ro-log-i-cal** (sir'ə-loj'i-kəl) *adj.*
se-ro-to-nin (ser'ə-tō'nin) *n.* *Biochem.* A crystalline protein found in many body tissues but chiefly in the brain and blood, a powerful vasoconstrictor. [< SERO- + TON- + -IN]
ser-pent (sûr'pənt) *n.* **1.** A scaly, limbless reptile; a snake.

SEQUOIA (To over 300 feet high)

2. Anything of serpentine form or appearance. **3.** An insinuating and treacherous person. **4.** Satan; the devil. [< OF < L < ppr. of *serpere* to creep]

ser·pen·tine (sûr′pən-tēn, -tīn) *adj.* **1.** Pertaining to or like a serpent; sinuous. **2.** Subtle; cunning. — *n.* A mottled green or yellow magnesium silicate, used as a source of asbestos, and as architecturally decorative stonework.

ser·rate (ser′āt, -it) *adj.* **1.** Toothed or notched like a saw. **2.** *Bot.* Having notched edges, as certain leaves. Also **ser′rat·ed.** [< L *serratus*, ult. < *serra* saw]

ser·ra·tion (se-rā′shən) *n.* **1.** The state of being serrated. **2.** One of the projections of a serrate formation, or a series of such projections. Also **ser·ra·ture** (ser′ə-chər).

ser·ried (ser′ēd) *adj.* Compacted in rows or ranks, as soldiers in company formation. [Pp. of obs. *serry* to press close together in ranks < MF *serré*, pp. of *serrer* to tighten]

se·rum (sir′əm) *n. pl.* **se·rums** or **se·ra** (sir′ə) **1.** The clear, slightly yellow portion of an animal liquid after separation from its solid constituents, esp. that formed by the clotting of blood. **2.** Loosely, an antiserum. **3.** Serum of milk; whey. **4.** Any similar secretion. [< L, whey, watery fluid]

ser·val (sûr′val) *n.* An African wildcat, yellow with black spots and having a ringed tail and long legs. [< F < Pg. *lobo cerval* lynx < *lobo* wolf + *cerval* stag]

ser·vant (sûr′vənt) *n.* **1.** A person hired to assist in domestic matters, sometimes living within the employer's house; hired help. **2.** A person employed to work for another; an employee. **3.** A slave or bondman. **4.** A public servant.

serve (sûrv) *v.* **served, serv·ing** *v.t.* **1.** To work for, esp. as a servant; be in the service of. **2.** To be of service to; wait on. **3.** To promote the interests of; aid. **4.** To obey and give homage to: to *serve* God. **5.** To satisfy the requirements of. **6.** To perform the duties connected with, as a public office. **7.** To go through (a period of enlistment, etc.). **8.** To furnish or provide, as with a regular supply. **9.** To offer or bring food or drink to (a guest, etc.). **10.** To bring and place on the table or distribute among guests, as food or drink. **11.** To operate or handle: to *serve* a cannon. **12.** To copulate with: said of male animals. **13.** In tennis, etc., to put (the ball) in play by hitting it to one's opponent. **14.** *Law* **a** To deliver (a summons or writ) to a person. **b** To deliver a summons or writ to. **15.** *Naut.* To wrap (a rope, stay, etc.), as with marlin or spun yarn, so as to strengthen or protect. — *v.i.* **16.** To work as or perform the functions of a servant. **17.** To wait at table; distribute food or drink. **18.** To perform the duties of any employment, office, etc. **19.** To go through a term of service, as in the army or navy. **20.** To be suitable or usable, as for a purpose. **21.** In tennis, etc., to put the ball in play. — *n.* **1.** In tennis, etc., the delivering of the ball by striking it toward an opponent. **2.** The turn of the server. [< OF < L *servus* slave]

serv·er (sûr′vər) *n.* **1.** One who serves. **2.** That which is used in serving, as a tray. **3.** The male of any domestic animal used for breeding. **4.** In games, the player who serves.

ser·vice (sûr′vis) *n.* **1.** Assistance or benefit afforded another. **2.** A useful result or product of labor that is not a tangible commodity. **3.** *pl.* Such products collectively, as distinguished from goods. **4.** The manner in which one is waited upon or served: The *service* in this restaurant is only fair. **5.** A system of labor and material aids for the public or a portion of it: telephone *service*. **6.** A division of public employment devoted to a particular function: the diplomatic *service*. **7.** Employment as a public servant in government. **8.** A public duty or function: jury *service*. **9.** Any branch of the armed forces. **10.** Military duty or assignment. **11.** Devotion to God, as demonstrated by obedience and good works. **12.** A formal and public exercise of worship. **13.** A ritual prescribed for a particular ministration or observance: a marriage *service*. **14.** The music for a liturgical office or rite. **15.** The state or position of a servant, esp. a domestic servant. **16.** A set of tableware for a specific purpose. **17.** Installation, maintenance, and repair of an article provided a buyer by a seller. **18.** *Law* The legal communication of a writ or process to a designated person. **19.** In tennis, etc., the act or manner of serving a ball. **20.** *Naut.* The protective cordage wrapped around a rope. **21.** In animal husbandry, the copulation or covering of a female. — *adj.* **1.** Pertaining to or for service. **2.** For the use of servants or tradespeople: a *service* entrance. **3.** Of, pertaining to, or belonging to a military service. — *v.t.* **viced, vic·ing** **1.** To maintain or repair. **2.** To supply service to. [< OF < L *servus* slave]

ser·vice·a·ble (sûr′vis-ə-bəl) *adj.* **1.** That can be made of service; beneficial; usable. **2.** Capable of rendering long service; durable. — **ser′vice·a·bil′i·ty, ser′vice·a·ble·ness** *n.* — **ser′vice·a·bly** *adv.*

ser·vice·ber·ry (sûr′vis-ber′ē) *n. pl.* **·ries 1.** A small tree bearing racemes of white flowers and purple edible berries; also called *service tree, shadbush.* **2.** A berry from this tree.

service cap A military uniform cap with a visor.

ser·vice·man (sûr′vis-man′) *n. pl.* **·men** (-men′) **1.** A

member of one of the armed forces. **2.** A man who perf[...] services of maintenance, supply, repair, etc. Also **se[...] man.** — **ser′vice·wom′an** (-woŏm′ən) *n.fem.*

service ribbon A distinctively colored ribbon worn o[...] U.S. service uniform to indicate the wearer's right to th[...] responding campaign medal or decoration.

service station A place for supplying automobiles, tr[...] etc., with gasoline, oil, water, etc.

service tree 1. Either of two deciduous trees of Eu[...] having alternate pinnate leaves and panicled cream-co[...] flowers. **2.** The serviceberry.

ser·vi·ette (sûr′vē-et′, -vyet′) *n. Brit. & Canadian* A [...] napkin. [< MF, prob. < *servir* to serve]

ser·vile (sûr′vīl, -vil) *adj.* **1.** Having the spirit of a s[...] abject: a *servile* flatterer. **2.** Pertaining to or appro[...] for slaves or servants. **3.** Being in a condition of serv[...] **4.** Obedient; subject: with *to.* [< L < *servus* slave[...] **ser′vile·ly** *adv.* — **ser′vile·ness, ser·vil·i·ty** (sûr-vil′ə-[...]

serv·ing (sûr′ving) *n.* A portion of food for one pe[...] — *adj.* Used for serving food at table: a *serving* platt[...]

ser·vi·tor (sûr′və-tər) *n.* One who waits upon and [...] another; an attendant; servant. — **ser′vi·tor·ship′** *n.*

ser·vi·tude (sûr′və-toōd, -tyoōd) *n.* **1.** The condition [...] slave; bondage. **2.** Enforced service as a punishmer[...] crime: penal *servitude.* **3.** A state of subjection to a p[...] or thing. **4.** The condition or duties of a servant; m[...] service. **5.** *Law* A right that one man may have to us[...] land of another for a special purpose.

ser·vo (sûr′vō) *n. pl.* **·vos** Any of various relay de[...] used in the automatic control of a complex machine, ir[...] ment, operation, or process. Also **ser′vo·mech′a·nism** (-[...] ə-niz′əm). [< L *servus* slave]

servo- *combining form* In technical use, auxiliary. [...] *servus* slave]

ser·vo·mo·tor (sûr′vō-mō′tər) *n.* An electric motor [...] nected with and supplying power for a servo.

ses·a·me (ses′ə-mē) *n.* **1.** An East Indian plant. **2.** [...] seeds of this plant, used as food and as a source of se[...] oil, an emollient. [< F < L < Gk. *sēsamon, sēsamē*]

sesqui- *prefix* One and a half; one and a half times: se[...] *centennial.* [< L < *semis* half + *que* and]

ses·qui·cen·ten·ni·al (ses′kwi-sen-ten′ē-əl) *adj.* Of or [...] taining to a century and a half. — *n.* A 150th annive[...] or its celebration.

ses·sile (ses′il) *adj.* **1.** *Bot.* Attached by its base, with [...] stalk, as a leaf. **2.** *Zool.* Firmly or permanently atta[...] fixed. [< L < *sessus*, pp. of *sedere* to sit] — **ses·sil′i[...]**

ses·sion (sesh′ən) *n.* **1.** The sitting together of a legis[...] assembly, court, etc., for the transaction of business. [...] single meeting or series of meetings of a group of pe[...] convened for a specific purpose or activity. **3.** A divisi[...] a school year; term. **4.** A part of a day during which c[...] meet in a school. [< F < L *sessio, -onis* < *sedere* to sit[...] **ses′sion·al** *adj.* — **ses′sion·al·ly** *adv.*

ses·tet (ses-tet′) *n.* **1.** The last six lines of a sonnet; [...] any six-line stanza. **2.** *Music* See SEXTET (def. 1). [< [...] *sesto* sixth (< L *sextus*) + *-etto,* dim. suffix]

set¹ (set) *v.* **set, set·ting** *v.t.* **1.** To put in a certain pla[...] position; place. **2.** To put into a fixed or immovable [...] tion or state: to *set* one's jaw. **3.** To bring to a spe[...] state: to *set* a boat adrift. **4.** To restore to proper pos[...] for healing, as a broken bone. **5.** To place in readines[...] operation or use: to *set* a trap. **6.** To adjust according [...] standard: to *set* a clock. **7.** To adjust (an instrument, [...] etc.) to a particular calibration or position. **8.** To p[...] knives, forks, etc., on (a table) in preparing for a meal. [...] To bend the teeth of (a saw) to either side alternately. [...] To appoint or establish: to *set* a time. **11.** To fix or e[...] lish a time for. **12.** To assign for performance, comple[...] etc.; allot: to *set* a task. **13.** To assign to some specific [...] or function; station: to *set* a guard. **14.** To cause t[...] **15.** To present or perform so as to be copied or emulate[...] *set* a bad example. **16.** To direct: He *set* his course fo[...] Azores. **17.** To put in place so as to catch the wind: t[...] the jib. **18.** To place in a mounting or frame, as a gem. [...] To stud or adorn with gems. **20.** To arrange (hair) in w[...] curls, etc., while moist. **21.** To place (a hen) on eg[...] hatch them. **22.** To place (eggs) under a fowl or in an [...] bator for hatching. **23.** To place (a price or value): wi[...] or *on.* **24.** To point (game): said of hunting dogs. [...] *Printing* **a** To arrange (type) for printing; compose. [...] put into type, as a sentence, manuscript, etc. **26.** *Mu[...]* To arrange (music) for words. **b** To write (words) to ac[...] pany music. **27.** To describe (a scene) as taking plac[...] *set* the scene in Monaco. **28.** In the theater, to arran[...] stage) so as to depict a scene. **29.** In some games, to c[...] to defeat. **30.** *Dial.* or *Illit.* To sit. — *v.i.* **31.** To g[...] pass below the horizon, as the sun. **32.** To wane; dec[...] **33.** To sit on eggs, as fowl. **34.** To become hard or [...] congeal. **35.** To begin a journey; start: with *forth, out[...]* etc. **36.** To have a specified direction; tend. **37.** To [...]

it, as clothes. **38.** To point game: said of hunting dogs. Bot. To begin development or growth, as a rudimentary it. **40.** Dial. or Illit. To sit. **— to set about** To start ng; begin. **— to set against 1.** To balance; compare. To make unfriendly to. **— to set aside 1.** To place .rt or to one side. **2.** To reject; dismiss. **3.** To declare l and void. **— to set back** To reverse; hinder. **— to set vn 1.** To place on a surface. **2.** To write or print; record. To judge or consider. **4.** To attribute; ascribe. **— to set th** To state or declare; express. **— to set in 1.** To begin occur: Rigor mortis set in. **2.** To blow or flow toward re, as wind or tide. **— to set off 1.** To put apart by it-. **2.** To serve as a contrast or foil for. **3.** To cause to .lode. **— to set on** To incite or instigate; urge. **— to set 1.** To present to view; exhibit. **2.** To establish the lim- or boundaries of, as a town. **3.** To plant. **4.** To start a rney, enterprise, etc. **— to set to 1.** To start; begin. **2.** start fighting. **— to set up 1.** To place in an upright .ition. **2.** To raise. **3.** To place in power, authority, etc. To construct or build; assemble. **5.** To establish. **6.** To vide with the means to start a new business. **7.** To cause be heard: to set up a cry. **8.** Informal **a** To pay for the nks, etc., of; treat. **b** To pay for (drinks, etc.). **— adj. 1.** .ablished by authority or agreement; appointed: a set .e; a set method. **2.** Customary; conventional: a set .ase. **3.** Deliberately and systematically conceived; for- l: a set speech. **4.** Fixed and motionless; rigid. **5.** Fixed)pinion or disposition. **6.** Formed; made: with a qualify- adverb: deep-set eyes. **7.** Ready; prepared: to get set. n. **1.** The act or condition of setting. **2.** Permanent .nge of form, as by chemical action, cooling, pressure, etc. The arrangement, tilt, or hang of a garment, sail, etc. **4.** rriage or bearing: the set of his shoulders. **5.** The sinking heavenly body below the horizon. **6.** The direction of a rent or wind. **7.** A young plant for setting out; a cutting. ., or seedlng. **8.** A group of games constituting a division tennis match. [OE settan to cause to sit]

(set) n. **1.** A number of persons regarded as associated ough status, common interests, etc. **2.** A social group ving some exclusive character; clique: the fast set. **3.** A mber of things belonging together and customarily used ether: a set of dishes. **4.** A number of specific things so uped as to form a whole: a set of lyrics. **5.** A group of umes issued together and related by common authorship subject. **6.** In motion pictures, television, etc., the com- te assembly of properties, structures, etc., required in a ne. **7.** Radio or television receiving equipment assem- d for use. **8.** Math. An array of objects, quantities, mag- udes, etc., arranged in some particular way: the set of egers. [< OF < L secta sect]

a (sē'tə) n. pl. **-tae** (-tē) Biol. **1.** A bristle, or slender, stlelike part or process of an organism. **2.** A slender ne or prickle. **3.** A coarse, rigid hair. [< L]

a·ceous (si·tā'shəs) adj. **1.** Bristly; more or less cov- d with bristles. **2.** Of the nature or form of setae. Also **tal** (sēt'l). [< NL < L seta bristle]

back (set'bak') n. **1.** An unexpected reverse or relapse. Archit. In tall buildings, the stepping of upper sections so t they progressively recede from the street line.

h (seth) The third son of Adam. Gen. v 3.

- combining form A bristle. Also, before vowels, **set-**. **L** seta bristle]

off (set'ôf', -of') n. **1.** That which offsets or counterbal- :es; a counterpoise. **2.** A counterclaim or the discharge a debt by a counterclaim.

screw (set'skrōō') n. A screw used as a clamp, esp. one d to screw through one part and slightly into another to d the parts tightly.

tee (se·tē') n. **1.** A long wooden seat with a high back. A sofa suitable for two or three people. [< SET¹ or SET- E). n. + -ee, dim. suffix]

ter (set'ər) n. **1.** One who or that which sets. **2.** One a breed of medium-sized, silky-coated, lithe hunting dogs ined to indicate the presence of game birds by standing id. See ENGLISH SETTER, GORDON SETTER, IRISH SETTER. **·ting** (set'ing) n. **1.** The act of anything that sets. **2.** insertion. **3.** That in which something is set; a frame; vironment. **4.** The act of indicating game like a setter. A number of eggs placed together for hatching. **6.** The lsic adapted to a song or poem. **7.** The scene or back-)und of a play or narrative. **8.** The apparent sinking of sun, etc., below the horizon. **9.** The tableware set out one person.

tle (set'l) v. **·tled**, **·tling** v.t. **1.** To put in order; set to hts. **2.** To put firmly in place: He settled himself on the uch. **3.** To free of agitation or disturbance; quiet: to set- one's nerves. **4.** To cause (sediment or dregs) to sink to bottom. **5.** To cause to subside or come to rest; make

firm or compact: to settle dust or ashes. **6.** To make clear or transparent, as by causing sediment or dregs to sink. **7.** Informal To make quiet or orderly: One blow settled him. **8.** To decide or determine finally, as an argument or difference. **9.** To pay, as a debt; satisfy, as a claim. **10.** To establish residents or residence in (a country, town, etc.). **11.** To es- tablish as residents. **12.** To establish in a permanent occu- pation, home, etc. **13.** To decide (a suit at law) by agree- ment between the litigants. **14.** Law To make over or as- sign (property) by legal act: with on or upon. **— v.i. 15.** To come to rest, as after moving about or flying. **16.** To sink gradually; subside. **17.** To sink or come to rest, as dust or sediment. **18.** To become more firm or compact. **19.** To become clear or transparent, as by the sinking of sediment. **20.** To take up residence. **21.** To come to a decision; re- solve: with on, upon, or with. **22.** To pay a bill, etc. **— to settle down 1.** To start living a regular, orderly life, esp. after a period of wandering or irresponsibility. **2.** To apply steady effort or attention. **— n. 1.** A long seat or bench, generally of wood, with a high back, often with arms and sometimes having a chest from seat to floor. **2.** A wide step; platform. [OE setl seat, setlan to seat]

set·tle·ment (set'l·mənt) n. **1.** The act of settling, or the state of being settled; esp., an adjustment of affairs by pub- lic authority. **2.** The settling of a new region; colonization. **3.** An area of country newly occupied by those who intend to live and labor there; a colony. **4.** A collection of frontier dwellings forming a community. **5.** Brit. A regular or set- tled place of living. **6.** An accounting; adjustment; liquida- tion in regard to amounts. **7.** The conveyance of property in such form as to provide for some future object, esp. the support of members of the settler's family; also, the property so settled. **8.** A welfare institution established in a congest- ed part of a city, that conducts educational and recreational activities for the community: also **settlement house.**

set·tler (set'lər) n. **1.** One who settles; esp., one who estab- lishes himself in a colony or new country; a colonist. **2.** One who or that which settles or decides something.

set-to (set'tōō') n. pl. **-tos** A bout at fighting, fencing, ar- guing, or any other mode of contest.

set-up (set'up') n. **1.** U.S. Informal The overall scheme or pattern of organization or construction; circumstances. **2.** U.S. Slang A contest or match arranged to result in an easy victory. **3.** U.S. Informal Ice, soda water, etc., provided for use in alcoholic drinks. **4.** Physique; physical build; make-up. **5.** Carriage of the body; bearing.

sev·en (sev'ən) n. **1.** The sum of six and one: a cardinal number. **2.** Any symbol of this number, as 7, vii, VII. **3.** Anything consisting of or representing seven units. **— adj.** Being one more than six. [OE seofon]

seven deadly sins Often cap. Pride, lust, envy, anger, cov- etousness, gluttony, and sloth: also called cardinal sins.

seven seas All the oceans of the world, now considered to be the North and South Atlantic, the North and South Pacific, the Indian, the Arctic, and the Antarctic oceans.

sev·en·teen (sev'ən·tēn') n. **1.** The sum of sixteen and one: a cardinal number. **2.** Any symbol of this number, as 17, xvii, XVII. **3.** Anything consisting of or representing seven- teen units. **— adj.** Being one more than sixteen. [OE seo- fontīene] **— sev·en·teenth'** adj. & n.

sev·en·teen-year locust (sev'ən·tēn'yir') A dark-bodied, wedge-shaped cicada native to the eastern U.S., having an underground nymphal stage of from 13 to 17 years.

sev·enth (sev'ənth) adj. **1.** Next after the sixth: the ordi- nal of seven. **2.** Being one of seven equal parts. **— n. 1.** One of seven equal parts. **2.** That which follows the sixth. **3.** Music **a** The interval between any tone and the seventh tone above it in the diatonic scale. **b** A tone separated by this interval from any other, considered with reference to that other. **— adv.** In the seventh order, place, or rank: also, in formal discourse, **sev'enth·ly.** [ME < seven + -TH, replacing OE seofotha]

sev·enth-day (sev'ənth·dā') adj. **1.** Pertaining to the sev- enth day of the week. **2.** Often cap. Advocating the observ- ance of this day as the Sabbath: a Seventh-Day Adventist. **seventh day** Saturday: a Quaker term.

Seventh-Day Adventist See under ADVENTIST.

seventh heaven 1. A condition of great happiness. **2.** The highest heaven according to various ancient systems of astronomy or in ancient theologies.

sev·en·ty (sev'ən·tē) n. pl. **·ties 1.** The sum of sixty and ten: a cardinal number. **2.** Any symbol of this number, as 70, lxx, LXX. **3.** Anything consisting of or representing seventy units. **— adj.** Being ten more than sixty. [OE (hund-) seofontig] **— sev'en·ti·eth** adj. & n.

Seven Wonders of the World The seven works of man considered the most remarkable in the ancient world: the Egyptian pyramids, the hanging gardens of Babylon, the temple of Diana at Ephesus, the statue of Zeus at Olympia, the mausoleum of King Mausolos at Halicarnassus, the Colossus of Rhodes, and the lighthouse of Alexandria.

Seven Years' War See table for WAR.

sev·er (sev'ər) *v.t.* **1.** To put or keep apart; separate. **2.** To cut or break into two or more parts. **3.** To break off; dissolve, as a relationship or tie. — *v.i.* **4.** To come or break apart or into pieces. **5.** To go away or apart; separate. [< AF, OF < L *separare* to separate] — **sev'er·a·ble** *adj.*

sev·er·al (sev'ər·əl, sev'rəl) *adj.* **1.** More than two, yet not many. **2.** Considered individually; single; separate. **3.** Individually different; various or diverse. — *n.* Several persons or things. [< AF < Med.L < L *separ* separate]

sev·er·al·ly (sev'ər·əl·ē, sev'rəl·ē) *adv.* **1.** Individually; separately. **2.** Respectively.

sev·er·ance (sev'ər·əns, sev'rəns) *n.* **1.** The act of severing, or the condition of being severed. **2.** Separation; partition. **3.** Extreme strictness; rigor; exactness. **4.** Seriousness; austerity. **5.** Strict conformity to truth or law.

se·vere (si·vir') *adj.* **·ver·er, ·ver·est** **1.** Rigorous in the treatment of others; unsparing. **2.** Conforming to rigid rules; accurate. **3.** Serious and austere in disposition or manner. **4.** Causing extreme pain: a *severe* pain. **5.** Causing extreme hardship; harsh: a *severe* snowstorm. [< MF < L *severus*] — **se·vere'ly** *adv.* — **se·vere'ness** *n.*

se·ver·i·ty (si·ver'ə·tē) *n.* *pl.* **·ties** **1.** The quality of being severe. **2.** Harshness or cruelty of disposition or treatment. **3.** Extreme strictness; rigor; exactness. **4.** Seriousness; austerity. **5.** Strict conformity to truth or law.

sew (sō) *v.* **sewed, sewed** or **sewn, sew·ing** *v.t.* **1.** To make, mend, or fasten with needle and thread. — *v.i.* **2.** To work with needle and thread. — **to sew up** *U.S. Informal* To conclude (a deal, etc.) successfully. [OE *siwian*] — **sew'-er** *n.*

sew·age (sōō'ij) *n.* The waste matter from domestic, commercial, and industrial establishments carried off in sewers.

sew·er (sōō'ər) *n.* **1.** A conduit, usu. laid underground, to carry off drainage and excrement. ◆ Collateral adjective: *cloacal.* **2.** Any large public drain. [< OF, ult. < L *ex-* off + *aqua* water]

sew·er·age (sōō'ər·ij) *n.* **1.** A system of sewers. **2.** Systematic draining by sewers. **3.** Sewage.

sew·ing (sō'ing) *n.* **1.** The act or occupation of one who sews. **2.** That which is sewed.

sewing circle A group of women, meeting periodically to sew, usu. for some charitable purpose.

sewing machine A machine for stitching or sewing.

sewn (sōn) Alternative past participle of SEW.

sex (seks) *n.* **1.** Either of two divisions, male and female, by which organisms are distinguished with reference to the reproductive functions. **2.** The character of being male or female. **3.** The activity or phenomena of life concerned with sexual desire or reproduction. **4.** *Informal* Sexual gratification. [< OF < L, prob. orig. < *secare* to divide]

sex- *combining form* Six: also *sexi-*. [< L *sex* six]

sex·a·ge·nar·i·an (sek'sə·jə·nâr'ē·ən) *n.* A person between sixty and seventy years of age. — *adj.* Sixty years old, or between sixty and seventy. [< SEXAGENARY]

sex·ag·e·nar·y (seks·aj'ə·ner'ē) *adj.* Sexagenarian. — *n. pl.* **·nar·ies** A sexagenarian. [< L < *sexaginta* sixty]

sex appeal A physical quality that attracts sexual interest.

sex chromosome *Genetics* A chromosome whose presence in the reproductive cells of certain plants and animals is associated with the determination of the sex of offspring.

sex gland A gonad; either of the testes or ovaries.

sexi- Var. of SEX-.

sex·less (seks'lis) *adj.* **1.** Having or appearing to have no sex; neuter. **2.** Provoking or showing little sexual desire. — **sex'less·ly** *adv.* — **sex'less·ness** *n.*

sex linkage *Biol.* That type of inheritance that is associated with the transmission of genes attached to the sex chromosomes. — **sex-linked** (seks'-lingkt') *adj.*

sex·ol·o·gy (seks·ol'ə·jē) *n.* The study of human sexual behavior. — **sex·o·log·ic** (sek'sə·loj'ik) or **·i·cal** *adj.* — **sex·ol'o·gist** *n.*

sext (sekst) *n.* *Often cap.* *Eccl.* Prescribed prayers constituting the fourth of the seven canonical hours. [< LL < L *sexta (hora)* the sixth (hour)]

sex·tant (seks'tənt) *n.* **1.** An instrument for measuring angular distance between two objects, as a heavenly body and the horizon, used esp. in determining latitude at sea. **2.** The sixth part of a circle; an arc of 60 degrees. [< L *sextus* sixth]

sex·tet (seks·tet') *n.* **1.** *Music* A group of six singers or players; also, a musical composition for six performers: also called *sestet.* **2.** Any collection of six persons or things. Also **sex·tette'.** [Alter. of SESTET; refashioned after L *sex* six]

sex·til·lion (seks·til'yən) *n.* **1.** *U.S.* A thousand quintillions, written as 1 followed by twenty-one zeros: a cardinal number. **2.** *Brit.* A million quintillions (def. 2), written as 1 followed by thirty-six zeros: a cardinal number. — *adj.* Being a sextillion in number. [< MF < *sexti-* six + (*mi*)*lion* million] — **sex·til'lionth** *adj. & n.*

sex·to·dec·i·mo (seks'tō·des'ə·mō) *n.* *pl.* **·mos** **1.** A page size made from a printer's sheet folded so as to have [16] leaves, usu. measuring 4½ x 6⅞ inches. **2.** A book or pa[mphlet] having pages this size. — *adj.* Having or consist[ing] of pages this size. Also *sixteenmo.* Also written **16mo.,** [< L < *sextus* sixth + *decimus* tenth]

sex·ton (seks'tən) *n.* A janitor of a church having cha[rge] also of ringing the bell, overseeing burials, etc. [< OF [<] Med.L *sacristanus*] — **sex'ton·ship** *n.*

sex·tu·ple (seks'tōō·pəl, -tyōō-, seks·tōō'-, -tyōō'-) *v.t.* **·p[led],** **·pling** To multiply by six. — *adj.* **1.** Consisting of six or six parts. **2.** Multiplied by six. **3.** *Music* Having six be[ats] to the measure. — *n.* A number or sum six times as gr[eat] as another. [< L *sex* six, formed on analogy with *quadru[ple], quintuple, etc.*] — **sex'tu·ply** *adv.*

sex·tu·plet (seks'tōō·plit, -tyōō-, seks·tōō'-, -tyōō'-) *n.* A set of six similar things. **2.** One of six offspring produ[ced] at a single birth. [< SEXTUPLE on analogy with *triplet*]

sex·u·al (sek'shōō·əl) *adj.* **1.** Of, pertaining to, or cha[rac]teristic of sex, the sexes, or the organs or functions of sex. Having sex. **3.** *Biol.* Designating a type of reproduction in[volving both sexes. [< LL < L *sexus* sex] — **sex'u·al**[·ly] (-al/ə·tē) *n.* — **sex'u·al·ly** *adv.*

sex·y (sek'sē) *adj.* **sex·i·er, sex·i·est** *Slang* **1.** Provoca[tive] of sexual desire. **2.** Concerned in large degree with sex[ual].

sfor·zan·do (sfôr·tsän'dō) *Music adj.* Accented more forci[bly] than the rhythm requires. — *adv.* In a sforza[ndo] manner. Also *sfor·za'to* (-tsä'tō). [< Ital. *sforzare* to fo[rce]]

shab·by (shab'ē) *adj.* **·bi·er, ·bi·est** **1.** Threadbare; rag[ged]. **2.** Wearing worn or seedy garments. **3.** Mean; paltry. [< *sceabb* scab + -Y[1]] — **shab'bi·ly** *adv.* — **shab'bi·ness** *n.*

Sha·bu·oth (shä·vōō'ōth, shä·vōō'əs) *n.pl.* The Jewish [fes]tival of Pentecost. [< Hebrew *shebuōth,* lit., weeks]

shack (shak) *n.* *U.S. & Canadian Informal* A rude ca[bin,] as of logs. [? < dial. Sp. (Mexican) *jacal* wooden hu[t,] Nahuatl *xacalli*]

shack·le (shak'əl) *n.* **1.** A ring, clasp, or bracketlike [fas]tening for encircling and fettering a limb. **2.** Impedim[ent] or restraint. **3.** One of various forms of fastenings. — [*v.t.*] **·led, ·ling** **1.** To restrain or confine with shackles. **2.** [To] keep or restrain from free action or speech. **3.** To con[fine] or fasten with a shackle. [OE *sceacul*] — **shack'ler** *n.*

shack·o (shak'ō) See SHAKO.

shad (shad) *n.* *pl.* **shad** Any of several food fishes rela[ted] to the herring. [OE *sceadd*]

shad·ber·ry (shad'ber'ē) *n.* *pl.* **·ries** The serviceberry.

shad·bush (shad'bŏŏsh') *n.* **1.** The serviceberry (def. [1)]. **2.** Any of various other related plants. Also **shad'bl** (-blō'). [< SHAD + BUSH[1]; so called because it flowers w[hen] the shad appear in U.S. rivers]

shade (shād) *v.* **shad·ed, shad·ing** *v.t.* **1.** To screen f[rom] light by intercepting its rays. **2.** To make dim; darken. To screen or protect with or as with a shade. **4.** To caus[e to] change by gradations. **5.** In graphic arts: **a** To repres[ent] (degrees of shade, colors, etc.) by gradations of light or d[ark] lines or shading. **b** To represent varying shades, colors, e[tc.] in (a picture, etc.) thus. **6.** To make slightly lower, a[s a] price. — *v.i.* **7.** To change or vary by degrees. — *n.* [**1.**] Relative obscurity due to interception of the rays of li[ght]; darkness. **2.** The state of being outshone. **3.** A sh[ady] place; secluded retreat. — *U.S.* A screen that shuts [out] light, heat, dust, etc. **5.** A gradation of color; also, sl[ight] degree; minute difference. **6.** The unilluminated part [of a] picture, etc. **7.** A disembodied spirit; ghost. — **the** [shades] The abode of departed spirits; Hades. [OE *sceadu*] — **shade'less** *adj.*

shad·ing (shā'ding) *n.* **1.** Protection against light or he[at]. **2.** The lines, dots, etc., by which degrees of darkness, co[lor,] or depth are represented in a picture. **3.** A slight variati[on].

shad·ow (shad'ō) *n.* **1.** A comparative darkness within [an] illuminated area, esp. that caused by the interception of li[ght] by a body. **2.** The dark image thus produced on a surf[ace] and representing the approximate shape of the intercept[ing] body. **3.** The shaded portion of a picture. **4.** A mirro[red] image. **5.** A delusive image or semblance. **6.** A phant[om;] ghost; shade. **7.** A faint representation or indication; a sy[m]bol. **8.** A remnant; vestige. **9.** An insignificant trace [or] portion. **10.** Gloom; a saddening influence. **11.** An ins[ep]arable companion. **12.** One who trails another, as a de[tec]tive. — *v.t.* **1.** To cast a shadow upon. **2.** To dark[en;] make gloomy. **3.** To represent or foreshow dimly: w[ith] *forth* or *out.* **4.** To follow closely or secretly. **5.** To sh[ade,] in painting, etc. [OE *sceadu* shade] — **shad'ow·er** *n.*

shad·ow·box (shad'ō·boks') *v.i.* To spar with an imagin[ary] opponent as a form of exercise. — **shad'ow·box'ing** *n.*

shad·ow·y (shad'ō·ē) *adj.* **·ow·i·er, ·ow·i·est** **1.** Full of affording shadow. **2.** Vague; dim. **3.** Unsubstantial or [il]lusory. — **shad'ow·i·ness** *n.*

shad·y (shā'dē) *adj.* **shad·i·er, shad·i·est** **1.** Full of sha[de;] casting a shade. **2.** Shaded, sheltered, or hidden. **3.** [In]*formal* Questionable as to honesty or legality; dubious.

he **shady side of** Older than; past the age of. — **shad′i·**
ly. — **shad′i·ness** n.

t¹ (shaft, shäft) n. 1. The long narrow rod of an arrow,
ar, etc. 2. An arrow. 3. Anything resembling a missile
ppearance or effect: *shafts* of ridicule. 4. A beam of
t. 5. A long handle, as of a hammer, etc. 6. *Mech.* A
bar, esp. if rotating and transmitting motive power. 7.
hit. a The portion of a column between capital and base.
slender column. 8. An obelisk or memorial column. 9.
stem of a feather. 10. One of two poles by which a
e is harnessed to a vehicle. [OE *sceat*]

t² (shaft, shäft) n. 1. A narrow, vertical or inclined,
vation connected with a mine. 2. The tunnel of a blast
ace. 3. An opening through the floors of a building, as
an elevator. [< LG *schacht* rod, shaft]

 (shag) n. 1. A rough coat or mass, as of hair. 2. A
growth, as of weeds. 3. A long nap on cloth. 4. Cloth
ing a rough or long nap. 5. A coarse, strong tobacco:
shag tobacco. — v. **shagged, shag·ging** v.t. To make
ggy; roughen. [OE *sceacga* rough hair, wool]

·**bark** (shag′bärk′) n. 1. A rough-barked hickory
ding high-grade, light-colored nuts. 2. Its tough, dura-
wood. Also called *shellbark.*

·**gy** (shag′ē) adj. **·gi·er, ·gi·est** 1. Having, consisting
r resembling rough hair or wool; rugged; rough. 2. Cov-
 with any rough, tangled growth; fuzzy; scrubby. 3.
kempt. — **shag′gi·ly** adv. — **shag′gi·ness** n.

green (shə-grēn′) n. 1. The rough skin of various sharks
rays. 2. A rough-grained leather, usu. dyed green. [<
 Turkish *săghrĭ* horse's hide]

 (shä) n. An eastern king or ruler, esp. of Iran. [<
sian *shäh*]

xe (shāk) v. **shook, shak·en, shak·ing** v.t. 1. To cause
ove to and fro or up and down with short, rapid move-
ts. 2. To affect in a specified manner by or as by vigor-
action: with *off, out, from,* etc. 3. To cause to tremble
uiver; vibrate. 4. To cause to stagger or totter. 5. To
ken or disturb: I could not *shake* his determination. 6.
agitate or rouse: often with *up.* 7. *Slang* To get rid of or
y from. 8. *Music* To trill. — v.i. 9. To move to and
or up and down in short, rapid movements. 10. To be
cted in a specified way by vigorous action: with *off, out,*
n, etc. 11. To tremble or quiver, as from cold or fear.
 To become unsteady; totter. 13. *Music* To trill on a
e, etc. — **to shake down 1.** To cause to fall by shaking;
g down. 2. To cause to settle. 3. *Slang* To extort
ney from. — **to shake hands** To clasp hands as a form
reeting, etc. — **to shake off** To rid oneself of by or as by
king. — **to shake up 1.** To shake, mix, or stir. 2. *U.S.*
ormal To shock or jar mentally or physically. — n. 1.
haking; concussion; agitation; vibration; shock; jolt. 2.
 state of being shaken. 3. *pl. Informal* The chill or ague
ntermittent fever. 4. A frost or wind crack in timber;
), a tight fissure in rock. 5. An earthquake. 6. *Slang*
instant. 7. *Music* A trill. — **no great shakes** *Infor-*
 Of no great importance; mediocre. [OE *scacan*] —
k′a·ble, shake′a·ble adj.

ke·down (shāk′doun′) n. *U.S. Slang* A swindle; extor-
. — adj. *U.S. Informal* For the purpose of adjusting
chanical parts or habituating people: a *shakedown* cruise.

k·er (shā′kər) n. 1. One who or that which shakes. 2. A
tainer for shaking or pouring something: cocktail *shaker.*

.k·er (shā′kər) n. One of a sect practicing celibacy and
mmunal living: so called from their characteristic bodily
vements during religious meetings. — **Shak′er·ism** n.

ke·spear·e·an (shāk·spir′ē·ən) adj. Of, pertaining to,
characteristic of Shakespeare, his work, or his style. — n.
 specialist on Shakespeare or his writings. Also **Shake·**
ar′i·an. — **Shake·spear′e·an·ism** n.

kespearean sonnet A sonnet having the rhyme
eme *ababcdcdefefgg:* also called *Elizabethan sonnet, Eng-*
 sonnet.

ke·up (shāk′up′) n. A radical change of personnel or or-
ization, as in a business office, etc.

k·o (shak′ō) n. pl. **·os** A kind of high, stiff military
address, originally of fur, having a peak and
upright plume: also spelled *shacko.* [< F <
ngarian *csákō*]

k·y (shā′kē) adj. **shak·i·er, shak·i·est 1.**
bitually shaking or tremulous; tottering;
ak; unsound. 2. Wavering; unreliable. —
ak′i·ly adv. — **shak′i·ness** n.

le (shāl) n. A fissile claylike rock resem-
 slate, with fragile, uneven laminae. —
al′y adj.

ll (shal) v. Present *3rd person sing.* **shall;**
st **should** A defective verb having a past tense
at is now used only as an auxiliary followed by

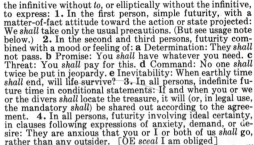

SHAKO

the infinitive without *to,* or elliptically without the infinitive,
to express: 1. In the first person, simple futurity, with a
matter-of-fact attitude toward the action or state projected:
We *shall* take only the usual precautions. (But see usage note
below.) 2. In the second and third persons, futurity combined with a mood or feeling of: a Determination: They *shall*
not pass. b Promise: You *shall* have whatever you need. c
Threat: You *shall* pay for this. d Command: No one *shall*
twice be put in jeopardy. e Inevitability: When earthly time
shall end, will life survive? 3. In all persons, indefinite future time in conditional statements: If and when you or we
or the divers *shall* locate the treasure, it will (or, in legal use,
the mandatory *shall*) be shared out according to the agreement. 4. In all persons, futurity involving ideal certainty,
in clauses following expressions of anxiety, demand, or desire: They are anxious that you or I or both of us *shall* go,
rather than any outsider. [OE *sceal* I am obliged]
 ♦ **shall, will** The formal view on the use of *shall* and *will*
is that to indicate simple futurity *shall* is used in the first person, *will* in the second and third; their roles are reversed to
express determination, command, inevitability, etc., while in
questions the choice depends on the form expected in the answer. These rules apply to American usage only at the most
formal level.

shal·lop (shal′əp) n. An open boat propelled by oars or sails.
 [< F < Du. *sloep.* See SLOOP.]

shal·lot (shə-lot′) n. 1. An onionlike vegetable allied to
garlic but having milder bulbs that are used in seasoning and
for pickles. 2. A small onion. [< OF *eschalotte*]

shal·low (shal′ō) adj. 1. Having the bottom not far below
the surface; lacking depth. 2. Lacking intellectual depth;
not wise; superficial. — n. A shallow place in a body of
water; shoal. — v.t. & v.i. To make or become shallow.
[ME *schalowe*] — **shal′low·ly** adv. — **shal′low·ness** n.

shalt (shalt) *Archaic* or *poetic* second person singular, present tense of SHALL: used with *thou.*

sham (sham) v. **shammed, sham·ming** v.t. 1. To assume or
present the appearance of; counterfeit; feign. 2. To represent oneself as; pretend to be. — v.i. 3. To make false pre-
tenses. — adj. False; counterfeit. — n. 1. A pretense; imposture; deception. 2. One who simulates a certain character; a pretender: also *sham′mer.* 3. A deceptive imitation.
[Prob. dial. var. of SHAME]

sha·man (shä′mən, shā′-, sham′ən) n. 1. A priest of Sha-
manism; a magician. 2. A North American Indian medicine
man. — adj. Of a shaman: also **sha·man·ic** (shə-man′ik).
[< Russian < Tungusic < Skt. *śamaṇa* ascetic]

Sha·man·ism (shä′mən·iz′əm, shā′-, sham′ən-) n. 1. A religion of NE Asia and Europe holding that gods and spirits
work only through the shamans. 2. Any similar religion, as
of certain Indians of the American Northwest. — **Sha′man·**
ist adj. & n. — **Sha′man·is′tic** adj.

sham·ble (sham′bəl) v.i. **·bled, ·bling** To walk with shuffling or unsteady gait. — n. A shambling walk; shuffling
gait. [Origin uncertain]

sham·bles (sham′bəlz) n.pl. (*usu. construed as sing.*) 1. A
place where butchers kill animals; slaughterhouse. 2. Any
place of carnage. 3. A place marked by great destruction or
disorder. [OE < L < *scamnum* bench, stool]

shame (shām) n. 1. A painful sense of guilt or of degradation
caused by consciousness of guilt or of anything degrading,
unworthy, or immodest. 2. Susceptibility to such feelings.
3. One who or that which brings reproach or disgrace. 4. A
state of regret, dishonor, or disgrace. — **to put to shame 1.**
To disgrace; make ashamed. 2. To surpass or eclipse. —
v.t. **shamed, sham·ing 1.** To make ashamed; cause to feel
shame. 2. To bring shame upon; disgrace. 3. To impel by
a sense of shame: with *into* or *out of.* [OE *scamu*]

shame·faced (shām′fāst′) adj. Easily abashed; showing
shame or bashfulness in one's face; modest; bashful. [<
ME < OE *scamfæst* abashed] — **shame·fac·ed·ly** (shām′·
fā′sid·lē, shām′fāst′lē) adv. — **shame′fac′ed·ness** n.

shame·ful (shām′fəl) adj. 1. Deserving or bringing shame
or disgrace; disgraceful; scandalous. 2. Exciting shame; indecent. — **shame′ful·ly** adv. — **shame′ful·ness** n.

shame·less (shām′lis) adj. 1. Impudent; brazen; immodest. 2. Done without shame; indicating a want of pride or
decency. — **shame′less·ly** adv. — **shame′less·ness** n.

sham·my (sham′ē), **sham·ois** (sham′ē) See CHAMOIS.

sham·poo (sham-pōō′) n. 1. Any of various liquid preparations of soap, chemical solvents, etc., used to cleanse the hair
and scalp. 2. The act or process of shampooing. — v.t. To
cleanse (the hair and scalp) with a shampoo. [< Hind.
chāmpnā to press] — **sham·poo′er** n.

sham·rock (sham′rok) n. Any of several trifoliate plants,
accepted as the national emblem of Ireland. [< Irish <
seamar trefoil]

shang·hai (shang′hī, shang·hī′) v.t. **·haied, ·hai·ing 1.** To

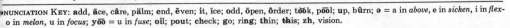

drug or render unconscious and kidnap for service aboard a ship. **2.** To cause to do something by force or deception. [after *Shanghai*, China]

Shan·gri·la (shang'grï·lä') *n.* Any imaginary hidden utopia or paradise. [after the locale of *Lost Horizon*, a novel by James Hilton, 1900–54, English author]

shank (shangk) *n.* **1.** The part of the leg between the knee and the ankle. **2.** A cut of meat from the leg of an animal; the shin. **3.** Something resembling a leg. **4.** The part of a tool connecting the handle with the working part. **5.** The projecting piece or loop by which some forms of buttons are attached. **6.** The straight part of a hook. **7.** *Printing* The body of a type. **13.** The narrow part of a shoe sole. [OE *scanca*]

sha'nt (shant, shänt) Shall not. Also **shan't.**

shan·tey (shan'tē) See CHANTEY.

shan·tung (shan'tung, shan·tung') *n.* A fabric with a rough, nubby surface, originally made of wild silk, now often made of rayon combined with cotton. [after the Chinese town *Shantung*]

shan·ty[1] (shan'tē) *n. pl.* **·ties** A hastily built shack or cabin; a ramshackle or rickety dwelling. [< F (Canadian) *chantier* lumberer's shack]

shan·ty[2] (shan'tē) See CHANTEY.

shape (shāp) *n.* **1.** Outward form or construction; configuration; contour. **2.** A developed expression or definite formulation; embodiment; cast: to put an idea into *shape*. **3.** A phantom. **4.** The character or form in which a thing appears; guise; aspect. **5.** A pattern or mold; in millinery, a stiff frame. **6.** The lines of a person's body; figure. **7.** Manner of execution. **8.** Condition: Everything is in good *shape*. — **to take shape** To have or assume a definite form. — *v.* **shaped, shaped** (*Rare* shap·en), **shap·ing** *v.t.* **1.** To give shape to; mold. **2.** To adjust or adapt; modify. **3.** To devise; prepare. **4.** To give direction or character to. **5.** To put into or express in words. — *v.i.* **6.** To take shape; develop; form: often with *up* or *into.* — **to shape up** *Informal* **1.** To proceed satisfactorily or favorably. **2.** To develop proper form. [OE < *scieppan* to create] — **shap'er** *n.*

shaped (shāpt) *adj.* **1.** Formed. **2.** Resembling in shape: used in compounds: leaf-*shaped.*

shape·less (shāp'lis) *adj.* Having no definite shape; lacking symmetry. — **shape'less·ly** *adv.* — **shape'less·ness** *n.*

shape·ly (shāp'lē) *adj.* **·li·er, ·li·est** Having a pleasing shape; well-formed; graceful. — **shape'li·ness** *n.*

shard (shärd) *n.* **1.** A broken piece of a brittle substance, as of an earthen vessel; a potsherd; a fragment: also called *sherd.* **2.** A hard, thin shell, or a wing cover, of a beetle. [OE *sceard.* Related to SHEAR.]

share[1] (shâr) *n.* **1.** A portion; allotted or equitable part. **2.** One of the equal parts into which the capital stock of a company or corporation is divided. **3.** An equitable part of something enjoyed or suffered in common. — **to go shares** To partake equally, as in an enterprise. — *v.* **shared, shar·ing** *v.t.* **1.** To divide and give out in shares or portions; apportion. **2.** To enjoy or endure in common; participate in. — *v.i.* **3.** To have a part; participate: with *in.* [OE < *scieran* to shear] — **shar'er** *n.*

share[2] (shâr) *n.* A plowshare.

share·crop·per (shâr'krop'ər) *n.* A tenant farmer who pays a share of his crop as rent for his land.

share·hold·er (shâr'hōl'dər) *n.* An owner of a share or shares of a company's stock; a stockholder.

shark[1] (shärk) *n.* One of a group of fishes, mostly marine, of medium to large size, having dun-colored bodies covered with plate-like scales. Some species are dangerous to man. — *v.i.* To fish for sharks. [Origin uncertain]

shark[2] (shärk) *n.* A bold and dishonest person; a rapacious swindler. Also **shark'er.** — *v.i.* To live by trickery. [Prob. < G *schürke* scoundrel; def. 2]

shark·skin (shärk'skin') *n.* **1.** The skin of a shark. **2.** A fabric with a smooth, almost shiny surface, made of acetate rayon and used for sports clothes.

sharp (shärp) *adj.* **1.** Having a keen edge or an acute point; capable of cutting or piercing. **2.** Coming to an acute angle; not obtuse; abrupt: a *sharp* peak. **3.** Keen of perception or discernment; also, shrewd in bargaining; artful; overreaching. **4.** Ardent; eager; keen; impetuous or fiery; attentive. **5.** Affecting the mind or senses, as if by cutting or piercing; poignant; acrimonious. **6.** Shrill. **7.** Pinching; cutting, as cold. **8.** Having an acrid or pungent taste. **9.** Distinct, as an outline. **10.** *Music* a Raised in pitch by a semitone. b Above the right, true pitch. c Having sharps in the key signature. **11.** Hard and rough; gritty. **12.** *Phonet.* Of consonants, voiceless: opposed to *flat.* — *adv.* **1.** In a sharp manner; sharply. **2.** Promptly; exactly: at 4 o'clock *sharp.* **3.** *Music* Above the proper pitch. — *n.* **1.** *Music* A sign (♯) placed before a note to indicate that the note is sharped; also, the note so altered. **2.** A cheat: a *cardsharp.* — *v.t.* *Music* To raise in pitch, as by a half step. [OE *scearp*] — **sharp'ly** *adv.* — **sharp'ness** *n.*

sharp·en (shär'pən) *v.t. & v.i.* To make or become sh — **sharp'en·er** *n.*

sharp·er (shär'pər) *n.* A swindler; cheat.

sharp-eyed (shärp'īd') *adj.* **1.** Having acute eyesight. Keenly observant; alert.

sharp·ie (shär'pē) *n.* A long, sharp, flat-bottomed sailb having a centerboard and one or two masts, each havin triangular sail, originally used for fishing. [< SHARP]

sharp·shoot·er (shärp'shoo'tər) *n.* A skilled marksm especially in the use of the rifle. — **sharp'shoot'ing** *n.*

sharp-tongued (shärp'tungd') *adj.* Bitter or causti speech.

sharp-wit·ted (shärp'wit'id) *adj.* Acute; intelligent. **sharp'-wit/ted·ness** *n.*

shat·ter (shat'ər) *v.t.* **1.** To break into pieces suddenly by a blow. **2.** To break the health or tone of, as the bod mind; disorder; damage. — *v.i.* **3.** To break into pie burst. [ME *schateren*]

shave (shāv) *v.* **shaved, shaved** or **shav·en, shav·ing** *v.i.* To cut hair or beard close to the skin with a razor. — *v.t.* To remove hair or beard from (the face, head, etc.) wit razor. **3.** To cut (hair or beard) close to the skin with a zor: often with *off.* **4.** To trim closely: to *shave* a lawn. To cut thin slices from, as in preparing the surface; p plane. **6.** To cut into thin slices. **7.** To touch or scrap passing; graze; come close to. — *n.* **1.** The act or opera of cutting off the beard with a razor. **2.** A knife or bl mounted between two handles, as for shaving wood: **draw shave, spoke shave. 3.** A shaving; thin slice. **4.** *formal* The act of barely grazing something; a narrow cape: a close *shave.* [OE *scafan* to shave]

shave·ling (shāv'ling) *n.* **1.** One who is shaven; oppr ously, a monk or priest. **2.** A youth.

shav·en (shā'vən) Alternative past participle of SHAVE. *adj.* **1.** Shaved; also, tonsured. **2.** Trimmed closely.

Sha·vi·an (shā'vē·ən) *n.* An admirer of George Bern Shaw, his books, or his theories. — *adj.* Of, pertaining or like George Bernard Shaw, or his style and methods.

shav·ing (shā'ving) *n.* **1.** The act of one who or that wl shaves. **2.** A thin paring shaved from anything, as a bo

shawl (shôl) *n.* A wrap, as a square cloth, or large sc worn over the upper part of the body. [< Persian *shā*

Shaw·nee (shô·nē') *n.* **1.** One of a tribe of North Ameri Indians of Algonquian stock, now living in Oklahoma. Algonquian (Shawnee) *Shawunogi* southerners]

she (shē) *pron., possessive* **her** or **hers,** *objective* **her;** *pl.* n *inative* **they,** *possessive* **their** or **theirs,** *objective* **them 1.** nominative singular pronoun of the third person, used of female person or being previously mentioned or underst or of things conventionally regarded as feminine, as sh machines, etc. **2.** That woman or female; any woman: who listens learns. — *n. pl.* **shes** A female person or be [ME < OE *sēo, sio,* fem. of *sē* the]

she- *combining form* Female; feminine: in hyphenated c pounds: *she-lion; she-devil.*

sheaf (shēf) *n. pl.* **sheaves** (shēvz) **1.** A quantity of stalks of cut grain or the like, bound together. **2.** Any lection of things, as papers, tied together. **3.** A quive of arrows. — *v.t.* To bind in a sheaf. [OE *scēaf*]

shear (shir) *n.* **1.** A two-bladed cutting instrument; o lete except in the plural. See SHEARS. **2.** *Physics* A de mation of a solid body, equivalent to a sliding over e other of adjacent laminar elements, with a progressive r tive displacement; also **shearing stress. 3.** The act or re of shearing. **4.** A plowshare. — *v.* **sheared, sheare shorn, shear·ing** *v.t.* **1.** To cut the hair, fleece, etc., fr **2.** To remove by cutting or clipping: to *shear* wool. **3.** deprive; strip, as of wealth. **4.** To cut or clip with o with shears. — *v.i.* **5.** To use shears. **6.** To slide or b from a shear (def. 2). **7.** To proceed by or as by cuttin way: with *through.* [OE < *scieran* to shear] — **shear'e**

shears (shirz) *n.pl.* **1.** Any large cutting or clipping inst ment worked by the crossing of cutting edges. Also **pai shears. 2.** The ways or guides, as of a lathe. [See SHE.

shear·wa·ter (shir'wô'tər, -wot'ər) *n.* Any of various ranging sea birds related to the fulmars and petrels: so ca because they skim close to the water.

sheath (shēth) *n. pl.* **sheaths** (shēthz, shēths) **1.** A velope or case, as for a sword; scabbard. **2.** A coverin plants or animals resembling a sheath. **3.** A close-fit dress having straight, unbroken lines. — *v.t.* To shea [OE *scæth*] — **sheath'less** *adj.*

sheathe (shēth) *v.t.* **sheathed, sheath·ing 1.** To put in sheath. **2.** To encase or protect with a covering. **3.** draw in, as claws. [< SHEATH]

sheath·ing (shē'thing) *n.* **1.** A protective covering, as ship's hull; that which sheathes; also, the material used. The act of one who sheathes. **3.** The covering or waterp material on outside walls or roofs.

sheave[1] (shēv) *v.t.* **sheaved, sheav·ing** To gather sheaves; collect. [< SHEAF]

ve² (shěv) *n.* A grooved pulley wheel; also, a pulley
el and its block. [ME *schive*]

ves (shēvz) Plural of SHEAF¹.

ba (shē′bə), **Queen of** A queen who visited Solomon to
his wisdom. I *Kings* x 1–3.

bang (shĭ·băng′) *n. U.S. Slang* 1. A building, vehicle,
2. Matter; affair: tired of the whole *shebang*.

bat (shĭ·băt′) *n.* The fifth month of the Hebrew year.
spelled *Sebat*. See (Hebrew) CALENDAR.

¹ (shed) *v.* **shed, shed·ding** *v.t.* 1. To pour forth in
s; emit, as tears. 2. To cause to pour forth. 3. To
forth; radiate. 4. To throw off without allowing to
etrate, as rain; repel. 5. To cast off by natural process,
air, etc. 6. To rid oneself of. — *v.i.* 7. To cast off or
skin, etc., by natural process. 8. To fall or drop, as
es. — **to shed blood** To kill. — *n.* 1. That which
ls, as a sloping surface or watershed. 2. That which has
n shed. [OE *scēadan* to separate, part]

² (shed) *n.* 1. A small low building, often with front or
s open; also, a lean-to: a wagon *shed*. 2. *Brit.* A barn.

d (shĕd) 1. Had. 2. She would.

·der (shĕd′ər) *n.* 1. One who sheds. 2. An animal
t sheds or has lately shed its skin, as a snake.

·n (shēn) *n.* 1. A glistening brightness, as if from reflec-
. 2. Shining attire. — *adj.* Shining; beautiful . — *v.i.*
shine; glisten. [OE *sciene* beautiful] — **sheen′y** *adj.*

p (shēp) *n. pl.* **sheep** 1. A medium-sized, domesticat-
even-toed ruminant, bred in many varieties for its flesh,
l, and skin. ◆ Collateral adjective: *ovine*. 2. Sheep-
. 3. A meek, bashful, or timid person. [OE *scēap*]

p·cote (shēp′kōt′) *n.* A small enclosure for the protec-
of sheep; a sheepfold. Also **sheep′cot′** (-kot′).

p dip Any of several liquid disinfectants containing
sote, nicotine, arsenic, etc., used for dipping sheep.

p dog A dog trained to guard and control sheep, often
llie, but also an **old English sheep dog**, a rough-coated,
vy, bobtailed dog much used by drovers in England: also
ed *shepherd dog, shepherd's dog*.

p·fold (shēp′fōld′) *n.* A pen for sheep.

p·herd·er (shēp′hûr′dər) *n.* A herder of sheep.
ep′herd′ing *n.*

p·ish (shē′pĭsh) *adj.* Foolish, as a sheep; awkwardly
dent; abashed. — **sheep′ish·ly** *adv.* — **sheep′ish·ness** *n.*

p ranch A ranch where sheep are bred and raised.
Brit. **sheep·walk** (shēp′wôk′), *Austral.* **sheep run**.

p's eyes (shēps) Bashful or amorous glances.

p·skin (shēp′skin′) *n.* 1. The skin of a sheep, tanned
untanned, or anything made from it. 2. A document
tten on parchment, as an academic diploma.

p sorrel An herb growing in dry places, and having
ves of an acrid taste.

r¹ (shir) *v.i.* To swerve from a course; turn aside. —
To cause to swerve. — *n.* 1. *Naut.* **a** The rise, or the
ount of rise from a level, of the lengthwise lines of a ves-
s hull. **b** A position of a vessel that enables it to swing
ar of a single anchor. 2. A swerving course. [< SHEAR]

r² (shir) *adj.* 1. Having no modifying conditions; un-
igated; absolute: *sheer* folly. 2. Exceedingly thin and
: said of fabrics. 3. Perpendicular; steep. 4. Pure; pel-
d. — *n.* Any very thin fabric used for clothes. — *adv.*
eply; perpendicularly. [ME *schere*] — **sheer′ness** *n.*
sheer′ly *adv.*

et (shēt) *n.* 1. A very thin and broad piece of any sub-
nce; as: **a** A large rectangular piece of bed linen. **b** A piece
paper. **c** A newspaper. **d** A piece of metal or other sub-
nce hammered, rolled, fused, or cut very thin. 2. A
ad, flat surface; superficial expanse: a *sheet* of water. 3.
ut. **a** A rope or chain from a lower corner of a sail to ex-
d it or move it. **b** *pl.* In an open boat, the space at the
w and stern not occupied by the thwarts. **c** A sail. 4. Any
erficial deposit, as of gravel left by a glacier, or of soil or
. 5. The large, unseparated block of stamps printed by
e impression of a plate. — **three sheets in the wind** *Slang*
sy; drunk. — *v.t.* 1. To cover with a sheet. 2. To
nish with sheets. [OE *scȳte* linen cloth]

et anchor 1. One of two anchors for use only in emer-
cy. 2. One who or that which can be depended upon in
ger or an emergency.

et bend *Naut.* A knot used to join two ropes' ends.

et·ing (shē′tĭng) *n.* 1. The act of sheeting, in any sense.
Cotton, muslin, etc., used for making sheets for beds.

et lightning Lightning appearing in sheetlike form as a
mentary and broadly diffused radiance in the sky, caused
the reflection of a distant lightning flash.

et metal Metal rolled and pressed into sheets.

et music Music printed on unbound sheets of paper.

ik (shēk, *Brit.* shāk) *n.* 1. A Moslem high priest or a
nerable man; also, the chief or head of an Arab tribe or

family. 2. *Archaic Slang* A man who fascinates women.
Also **sheikh**. [< Arabic *sheikh, shaykh,* lit., an elder, chief]

sheik·dom (shēk′dəm) *n.* The land ruled by a sheik. Also
sheikh′dom.

shek·el (shĕk′əl) *n.* 1. An Assyrian, Babylonian, and, later,
Hebrew unit of weight and money; also, a coin having this
weight. 2. *pl. Slang* Money. [< Hebrew *shāqal* to weigh]

shel·drake (shĕl′drāk′) *n.* 1. A large Old World duck of
southeastern Europe and North Africa. 2. A merganser.
[< dial. E *sheld* piebald, dappled + DRAKE]

shelf (shelf) *n. pl.* **shelves** (shelvz) 1. A board or slab set
horizontally against a wall, in a bookcase, etc., to support
articles, as books. 2. Contents of a shelf. 3. Any flat projecting ledge, as of rock. 4. A reef; shoal. 5. A stratum of
bedrock. — **on the shelf** No longer in use; discarded. [<
LG *schelf* set of shelves]

shell (shel) *n.* 1. Any of various hard structures encasing
an animal, as a mollusk or other shellfish. 2. The hard, relatively fragile outer coat of an egg. 3. The relatively hard
covering of a fruit, seed, or nut. 4. The material composing
a shell. 5. A hollow structure or vessel, generally thin and
weak; also, a case or mold for holding something: a pie *shell*.
6. A very light, long, and narrow racing rowboat. 7. A
hollow metallic projectile filled with an explosive or chemical. 8. A metallic or paper cartridge case for small arms.
9. A shape or outline that merely simulates a reality; hollow
form; external semblance. 10. A reserved or impersonal
attitude: to come out of one's *shell*. — *v.t.* 1. To divest of or
remove from a shell. 2. To separate from the cob, as corn.
3. To bombard with shells, as a fort. 4. To cover with
shells. — *v.i.* 5. To shed the shell or pod. 6. To fall off, as
a shell. — **to shell out** *Informal* To hand over, as money.
[OE *sciell* shell] — **shell′er** *n.* — **shell′y** *adj.*

she'll (shēl) She will.

shel·lac (shə·lak′) *n.* 1. A purified lac in the form of thin
plates, extensively used in varnish, sealing wax, insulators,
etc. 2. A varnishlike solution of flake shellac dissolved in
methylated spirit, used for coating floors, woodwork, etc.
— *v.t.* **lacked, ·lack·ing** 1. To cover or varnish with shellac.
2. *Slang* To belabor; beat. 3. *Slang* To defeat utterly. Also
shell′·lac′, shel·lack′. [< SHELL + LAC¹]

shel·lack·ing (shə·lak′ĭng) *n. U.S. Slang* 1. A beating;
assault. 2. A thorough defeat.

shell·back (shel′bak′) *n.* A veteran sailor; an old salt; esp.,
one who has crossed the equator. [Prob. with reference to
the shell of the sea turtle]

shell·bark (shel′bärk′) *n.* The shagbark or one of its nuts.

shell·fire (shel′fīr′) *n.* The firing of artillery shells.

shell·fish (shel′fish′) *n. pl.* **·fish** or **·fish·es** Any aquatic
animal having a shell, as a mollusk.

shell game 1. A swindling game in which the victim bets
on the location of a pea covered by one of three nutshells.
2. Any game in which the victim cannot win.

shell·proof (shel′prōof′) *adj.* Built to resist the destructive
effect of projectiles and bombs.

shell shock Formerly, combat fatigue. — **shell-shocked**
(shel′shokt′) *adj.*

shel·ter (shel′tər) *n.* 1. That which covers or shields from
exposure or danger; a place of safety. 2. The state of being
sheltered or protected. — *v.t.* 1. To provide protection or
shelter for; shield, as from danger or inclement weather. —
v.i. 2. To take shelter. [? Alter. of ME *scheltrun* < OE
sceld-truma a body of men armed with shields, phalanx, pro-
tection] — **shel′ter·er** *n.* — **shel′ter·less** *adj.*

shelter tent *Mil.* A tent for two men, divided into two
sections, each of which, called a **shelter half**, is carried as
part of a soldier's field equipment: also called *pup tent*.

shelve (shelv) *v.* **shelved, shelv·ing** *v.t.* 1. To place on a
shelf. 2. To postpone indefinitely; put aside. 3. To retire.
4. To provide or fit with shelves. — *v.i.* 5. To incline gradually; slope. [< SHELF] — **shelv′y** *adj.*

shelves (shelvz) Plural of SHELF.

shelv·ing (shel′ving) *n.* 1. Shelves collectively. 2. Material for shelves.

Shem (shem) The eldest son of Noah. *Gen.* v 32.

Shem·ite (shem′īt) See SEMITE.

she·nan·i·gan (shi·nan′ə·gən) *n. Often pl. Informal* Trickery; foolery; nonsense; also, treacherous action or a treacherous act. [? < Irish *sionnach* fox]

she·ol (shē′ōl) *n.* Hell. [< Hebrew *she'ōl* cave]

She·ol (shē′ōl) In the Old Testament, a place under the
earth where the departed spirits were believed to go.

shep·herd (shep′ərd) *n.* 1. A keeper or tender of sheep. 2.
A pastor, leader, or guide. — *v.t.* To watch and tend as a
shepherd. [OE *scēaphyrde*] — **shep′herd·ess** (-is) *n.fem.*

shepherd dog A sheep dog. Also **shepherd's dog**.

shep·herd's-purse (shep′ərdz-pûrs′) *n.* A weed bearing
small white flowers and notched triangular pods.

Sher·a·ton (sher'ə·tən) *adj.* Denoting the graceful, straight-lined, classically chaste style of English furniture developed by Thomas Sheraton, 1751–1806, English furniture designer.

sher·bet (shûr'bit) *n.* **1.** A flavored water ice. **2.** *Brit.* A drink made of sweetened fruit juice and sometimes cooled with snow. [< Turkish *sherbet*]

sherd (shûrd) *n.* A fragment of pottery: often in combination: *potsherd*: also called *shard*. [Var. of SHARD]

she·rif (she·rēf') *n.* **1.** A descendant of Mohammed through his daughter Fatima. **2.** An Arab chief. Also **she·reef'**. [< Arabic *sharîf* noble]

sher·iff (sher'if) *n.* The chief administrative officer of a county, who executes the mandates of courts, enforces order, etc. [OE *scīr-gerēfa* shire reeve] — **sher'iff·dom** *n.*

she·root (shə·rōōt') See CHEROOT.

Sher·pa (shûr'pə) *n.* One of a Tibetan tribe living on the southern slopes of the Himalayas in Nepal.

sher·ry (sher'ē) *n. pl.* **·ries** A fortified wine of Jerez, Spain; also, any similar wine. [after *Jerez*, Spain]

Sher·wood Forest (shûr'wōōd) A forest in Nottingham-shire, England, known as the home of Robin Hood.

she's (shēz) **1.** She is. **2.** She has.

Shet·land pony (shet'lənd) A small, hardy, shaggy breed of pony originally bred on the Shetland Islands.

shew (shō) *v.t. & v.i.* **shewed, shewn, shew·ing** *Archaic* To show. — **shew'er** *n.*

shew·bread (shō'bred') *n.* Unleavened bread formerly displayed in the Jewish temple: also spelled *showbread*.

Shi·ah (shē'ə) *n.* **1.** One of the two great sects of Islam. Compare SUNNI. **2.** A Shiite. [< Arabic *shi'i* follower, sect]

shib·bo·leth (shib'ə·leth) *n.* **1.** A test word or pet phrase of a party; a watchword: from the Hebrew word *shibboleth*, given by Jephthah (*Judges* xii 4–6) as a test to distinguish his own men from the Ephraimites, who used the pronunciation *sibboleth*. **2.** A custom or use of language regarded as distinctive of a particular social class, profession, etc. [< Hebrew *shibbōleth* ear of grain]

shied (shīd) Past tense and past participle of SHY.

shield (shēld) *n.* **1.** A broad piece of defensive armor, commonly carried on the left arm. **2.** Something that protects or defends. **3.** Any device for covering or protecting something. **4.** *Heraldry* An escutcheon. **5.** A conventional figure having an oval bottom and a cusp at the top, used in flags, emblems, etc. — *v.t.* **1.** To protect from danger as with a shield; defend; guard. — *v.i.* **2.** To act as a shield or safeguard. [OE *scīld*] — **shield'er** *n.*

shi·er (shī'ər) Comparative of SHY. — *n.* A horse in the habit of shying. Also spelled *shyer*.

shift (shift) *v.t.* **1.** To change or move from one position, place, etc., to another. **2.** To change for another or others of the same class. **3.** To change (gears) from one arrangement to another. **4.** *Ling.* To alter as part of a systematic change. — *v.i.* **5.** To change position, place, etc. **6.** To evade; equivocate. **7.** To shift gears. — **to shift for oneself** To do the best one can to provide for one's needs. — *n.* **1.** The act of shifting. **2.** A dodge; artifice; trick; evasion; expedient: We made *shift* to get along. **3.** *Archaic* or *Dial.* An undergarment; chemise. **4.** A straight, loosely hanging woman's garment, as a dress. **5.** A change of position, place, direction, or form: a *shift* in the wind. **6.** A relay of workers; also, the working time of each group. **7.** *Physics* Any of various displacements of spectral lines caused by velocity of the light source, gravitational effect, etc. See DOPPLER EFFECT. **8.** *Geol.* The relative displacement of areas on opposite sides of a rock fault. [OE *sciftan* to divide] — **shift'er** *n.*

shift·less (shift'lis) *adj.* **1.** Unable or unwilling to shift for oneself; inefficient or lazy. **2.** Showing lack of energy or resource. — **shift'less·ly** *adv.* — **shift'less·ness** *n.*

shift·y (shif'tē) *adj.* **shift·i·er, shift·i·est** **1.** Artful; tricky; fickle. **2.** Full of expedients; alert; capable. — **shift'i·ly** *adv.* — **shift'i·ness** *n.*

Shi·ite (shē'īt) *n.* A Moslem of the Shiah sect: distinguished from *Sunnite*: also *Shiah*. Also **Shie'ite, Shi'ite**.

shill (shil) *n. Slang* The assistant of a sidewalk peddler or gambler, who makes a purchase or bet to encourage onlookers to buy or bet; a capper. [Origin unknown]

shil·le·lagh (shi·lā'lə, -lē) *n.* In Ireland, a stout cudgel made of oak or blackthorn. Also **shil·e'lah**. [after *Shillelagh*, a town in Ireland famed for its oaks]

shil·ling (shil'ing) *n.* **1.** A British monetary unit, since the Norman Conquest equivalent to 12 pence or ⅟₂₀ pound; also, a coin of this value, first issued in 1504. **2.** A similar monetary unit of various other countries. **3.** A former coin of colonial America. [OE *scilling*]

shil·ly-shal·ly (shil'ē·shal'ē) *v.i.* **·lied, ·ly·ing** **1.** To act with indecision; be irresolute; vacillate. **2.** To trifle. — *adj.* Weak; hesitating. — *n.* Weak or foolish vacillation; irresolution. — *adv.* In an irresolute manner. [Dissimilated reduplication of *shall I?*] — **shil'ly-shal'li·er** *n.*

shi·ly (shī'lē) See SHYLY.

shim (shim) *n.* A piece of metal or other material use fill out space, for leveling, etc. — *v.t.* **shimmed, shim·m** To wedge up or fill out by inserting a shim. [Origin known]

shim·mer (shim'ər) *v.i.* To shine faintly; glimmer. — A tremulous shining or gleaming; glimmer; gleam. [OE *merian*] — **shim'mer·y** *adj.*

shim·my (shim'ē) *n. pl.* **·mies** *U.S.* **1.** *Informal* A mise. **2.** A former jazz dance accompanied by sha movements. **3.** Unusual vibration, as in automobile whe — *v.i.* **·mied, ·my·ing** **1.** To vibrate or wobble. **2.** To da the shimmy. [Alter. of CHEMISE]

shin (shin) *n.* **1.** The front part of the leg below the k also, the shinbone. **2.** The lower foreleg: a *shin* of beef. *v.t. & v.i.* **shinned, shin·ning** **1.** To climb (a pole) by ping with the hands or arms and the shins: often with *up*. **2.** To kick (someone) in the shins. [OE *scinu*]

shin·bone (shin'bōn') *n.* The tibia.

shin·dig (shin'dig) *n. U.S. Slang* A dance or noisy pa [< SHINDY, by folk etymology, suggesting a *dig on the s*]

shine (shīn) *v.i.* **shone** or (*esp. for def. 5*) **shined, shin·** **1.** To emit light; beam; glow. **2.** To gleam, as by refle light. **3.** To excel or be conspicuous in splendor, bea etc. — *v.t.* **4.** To cause to shine. **5.** To brighten by rub or polishing. — **to shine up to** *Slang* To try to please. — *n* **1.** The state or quality of being bright or shining; radia luster; sheen. **2.** Fair weather; sunshine. **3.** *U.S. Info* A liking or fancy. **4.** *U.S. Informal* A smart trick or pr **5.** A shoeshine. — **to take a shine to** *U.S. Informal* To come fond of. [OE *scīnan*]

shin·er (shī'nər) *n.* **1.** One who or that which shines. One of various silvery fresh-water fishes related to the nows. **3.** A silverfish, an insect. **4.** *Slang* A black eye.

shin·gle[1] (shing'gəl) *n.* **1.** A thin, tapering, oblong pie wood or other material, used in courses to cover roofs. small sign bearing the name of a doctor, lawyer, etc., placed outside his office. **3.** A short haircut. — *v.t.* · **·gling** **1.** To cover (a roof, building, etc.) with or as shingles. **2.** To cut (the hair) short. [ME < L *scan* shingle] — **shin'gler** *n.*

shin·gle[2] (shing'gəl) *n.* **1.** Rounded, waterworn gr found on the seashore. **2.** A place strewn with shingle, beach. [Cf. Norw. *singl* coarse gravel] — **shin'gly** *a*

shin·gles (shing'gəlz) *n.pl.* (*construed as sing. or pl.*) *Po* An acute inflammatory virus disease characterized by b ers along the course of the affected nerve ganglia and acc panied by pain: also called *herpes zoster*. [Alter. of M *cingulus* < L *cingulum* girdle < *cingere* to gird]

shin·ing (shī'ning) *adj.* **1.** Emitting or reflecting a cont ous light; gleaming; luminous. **2.** Of unusual brilliance excellence; conspicuous. — **shin'ing·ly** *adv.*

shin·ny[1] (shin'ē) *n.* **1.** A game resembling hockey; also of the sticks or clubs used by the players. **2.** *Canadian* hockey. [< SHINNY, a cry used in the ga

shin·ny[2] (shin'ē) *v.i.* **·nied, ·ny·ing** *U.S. Informal* To c using one's shins: usually with *up*.

shin·plas·ter (shin'plas'ter, -pläs'-) *n.* **1.** *U.S. Fract.* currency issued by other than the constituted author **2.** Any paper money issued by private enterprises. plaster for a sore shin.

Shin·to (shin'tō) *n.* A religion of Japan, consisting ch in ancestor worship, nature worship, and, formerly, a b in the divinity of the Emperor. Also **Shin'to·ism**. Japanese, way of the gods] — **Shin'to·ist** *n.*

shin·y (shī'nē) *adj.* **shin·i·er, shin·i·est** **1.** Glister glossy; polished. **2.** Bright; clear.

ship (ship) *n.* **1.** Any vessel suitable for deep-water na tion; also, its personnel. **2.** A large seagoing sailing with at least three masts, carrying square-rigged sail all three. **3.** An airship or airplane. — **when one's comes in** (or **home**) When one's fortune has been mad hopes realized. — *v.* **shipped, ship·ping** *v.t.* **1.** To tr port by ship or other mode of conveyance. **2.** To receive for service on board a vessel, as sailors. **3.** *Nau* receive over the side, as in rough weather: to *ship* a w **4.** *Informal* To get rid of. **5.** To set or fit in a prep place on a boat or vessel, as a mast, or a rudder. — *v.* To go on board ship; embark. **7.** To undergo shipm Raspberries do not *ship* well. **8.** To enlist as a sear usually with *out*. [OE *scip*]

-ship *suffix of nouns* **1.** The state, condition, or qualit *friendship*. **2.** Office, rank, or dignity of: *kingship*. **3.** art or skill of: *marksmanship*. [OE *-scipe*]

ship·board (ship'bôrd', -bōrd') *n.* **1.** The side or deck ship. **2.** A vessel: used only in the phrase **on shipboa**

ship·build·er (ship'bil'dər) *n.* One whose work is the b ing of vessels. — **ship'build'ing** *adj. & n.*

ship canal A waterway deep enough for seagoing ves

ship chandler One who deals in supplies for vessels.

ship·load (ship'lōd') *n.* The quantity that a ship carri can carry; a cargo.

ip·mas·ter (ship/mas/tər, -mäs/-) *n.* The captain or aster of a merchant ship.

ip·mate (ship/māt/) *n.* A fellow sailor.

ip·ment (ship/mənt) *n.* 1. The act of shipping. 2. That hich is shipped.

ip of the line Formerly, a man-of-war large enough to ke a position in a line of battle.

ip·owner (ship/ō/nər) *n.* One owning a ship or ships.

ip·pa·ble (ship/ə-bəl) *adj.* That can be shipped or trans-rted.

ip·per (ship/ər) *n.* One who ships goods.

ip·ping (ship/ing) *n.* 1. Ships collectively; also, tonnage. The act of shipping.

ip·shape (ship/shāp/) *adj.* Well arranged, orderly, and at, as on a ship, — *adv.* In an orderly manner; neatly.

ip's papers The documents required by international w to be carried by a ship.

ip·worm (ship/wûrm/) *n.* Any of various marine bi-lves, resembling worms, that burrow into the timbers of ips, piers, wharfs, etc.

ip·wreck (ship/rek/) *n.* 1. The partial or total destruc-on of a ship at sea. 2. Utter or practical destruction; ruin. Scattered remnants, as of a wrecked ship; wreckage. — 1. To wreck, as a vessel. 2. To bring to disaster; ruin.

ip·wright (ship/rīt/) *n.* One who builds or repairs ships.

ip·yard (ship/yärd/) *n.* A place where ships are built or paired.

re (shīr) *n.* A territorial division of Great Britain; a unty. [OE *scīr*]

rk (shûrk) *v.t.* 1. To avoid the doing of; evade doing omething that should be done). — *v.i.* 2. To avoid work evade obligation. — *n.* One who shirks: also **shirk'er.** < G *schürke* rascal]

rr (shûr) *v.t.* 1. To draw (material) into three or more rallel rows of gathers. 2. To bake with crumbs in a but-red dish, as eggs. — *n.* 1. A drawing of material into ree or more parallel rows of gathers. 2. A rubber thread oven into a fabric to make it elastic. [Origin unknown]

rt (shûrt) *n.* 1. A garment for the upper part of the dy, usu. having collar and cuffs and a front closing. 2. A osely fitting undergarment. 3. A shirtwaist. — **to keep e's shirt on** *Slang* To remain calm. — **to lose one's shirt** *ing* To lose everything. [OE *scyrte* shirt, short garment] **shirt'less** *adj.*

rt·ing (shûr/ting) *n.* Closely woven material of cotton, nen, silk, etc., used for making shirts, blouses, dresses, etc.

rt·waist (shûrt/wāst/) *n.* 1. A woman's tailored, sleeved ouse or shirt, usu. worn tucked in under a skirt or slacks. A woman's tailored dress having a bodice like a shirt-aist: also **shirtwaist dress.**

sh ke·bab (shish/kə·bob/) Meat roasted or broiled in all pieces on skewers and served with condiments. [< urkish *shish* skewer + *kebap* roast meat]

st (shist) See SCHIST.

·va (shē/və) Siva, a Hindu god.

·va·ree (shiv/ə·rē/) *n.* *U.S.* A charivari. [Alter. of HARIVARI]

·ver (shiv/ər) *v.i.* 1. To tremble; shake; quiver. — *v.t.* *Naut.* To cause to flutter in the wind, as a sail. — *n.* The t of shivering; a tremble. [ME *chivere*] — **shiv'er·y** *adj.*

·ver² (shiv/ər) *v.t. & v.i.* To break suddenly into frag-ents; shatter. — *n.* A splinter; sliver. [ME *schivere*] **iv'er·y** *adj.*

al¹ (shōl) *n.* 1. A shallow place in any body of water. A sandbank or bar, esp. one seen at low water. Compare EF¹. — *v.i.* 1. To become shallow. — *v.t.* 2. To make allow. 3. To sail into a lesser depth of (water): said of a ip. — *adj.* Shallow. [OE *sceald* shallow]

al² (shōl) *n.* 1. An assemblage or multitude; throng. 2. school of fish. — *v.i.* 1. To throng in multitudes. 2. To hool: said of fish. [OE *scolu* troop, multitude]

al·y (shō/lē) *adj.* Abounding in oals. — **shoal'i·ness** *n.*

ck¹ (shok) *n.* 1. A violent collision or concussion; im-ct; blow. 2. A sudden and violent sensation: a *shock* of ralysis. 3. A sudden and severe agitation of the mind or otions, as in horror or great sorrow. 4. *Pathol.* Prostra-n of bodily functions, as from sudden injury. 5. The ysical reactions produced by the passage of a strong elec-c current through the body, as involuntary muscular con-actions. — *v.t.* 1. To shake by sudden collision; jar. 2. disturb the emotions or mind of; horrify; disgust. 3. To ve an electric shock to. [< F < *choquer* < Gmc.] — **ock'er** *n.*

ck² (shok) *n.* A number of sheaves of grain, stalks of aize, or the like, stacked for drying upright in a field. — . & *v.i.* To gather (grain) into a shock or shocks. [ME *hokke* < Gmc. Cf. MLG *schok.*] — **shock'er** *n.*

shock³ (shok) *adj.* Shaggy; bushy. — *n.* A coarse, tangled mass, as of hair. [Back formation < *shock dog*]

shock absorber *Mech.* A device designed to absorb the force of shocks, as the springs of an automobile.

shock·ing (shok/ing) *adj.* 1. Causing a mental or emo-tional shock, as with horror or disgust. 2. *Informal* Terri-ble; awful. — **shock'ing·ly** *adv.* — **shock'ing·ness** *n.*

shock therapy *Psychiatry* The treatment of certain psy-chotic disorders by the injection of drugs, or by electrical shocks, both methods inducing coma, or with or without con-vulsions.

shock troops *Mil.* Seasoned men selected to lead an attack.

shock wave *Physics* A compression wave following a sud-den and violent disturbance of the transmitting medium, through which it is propagated with a velocity equal to or greater than that of sound.

shod (shod) Past tense and alternative past participle of SHOE.

shod·dy (shod/ē) *n.* *pl.* **·dies** 1. Wool obtained by shred-ding discarded woolens or worsteds; also, cloth made of such wool. 2. Any inferior goods made to resemble those of better quality. — *adj.* **shod·di·er, shod·di·est** 1. Made of or containing shoddy. 2. Sham; inferior. [Origin uncer-tain] — **shod'di·ly** *adv.* — **shod'di·ness** *n.*

shoe (shōō) *n.* *pl.* **shoes** 1. An outer covering, usu. of leather, for the human foot. 2. Something resembling a shoe in position or use. 3. A rim or plate of iron to protect the hoof of an animal. 4. A strip of iron, steel, etc., fitted under a sleigh runner to receive friction. 5. The part of the brake that presses upon a wheel or drum. 6. The tread or outer covering of a pneumatic tire, as for an automobile. 7. The sliding contact plate on an electric car or locomotive by which it obtains current from the third rail. — *v.t.* **shod, shod** or **shod·den, shoe·ing** 1. To furnish with shoes or the like. 2. To furnish with a guard of metal, wood, etc., for protection, as against wear. [OE *scōh*]

shoe·black (shōō/blak/) *n.* One who cleans or polishes shoes as an occupation.

shoe·horn (shōō/hôrn/) *n.* A smooth curved implement of horn, metal, etc., used to help put on a shoe.

shoe·lace (shōō/lās/) *n.* A lace or cord for fastening shoes.

shoe·mak·er (shōō/mā/kər) *n.* One who makes or repairs shoes, boots, etc. — **shoe'mak'ing** *n.*

sho·er (shōō/ər) *n.* One who shoes horses.

shoe·shine (shōō/shīn/) *n.* 1. The waxing and polishing of a pair of shoes. 2. The polished look of shined shoes.

shoe·string (shōō/string/) *n.* A shoelace. — **on a shoe-string** With a small sum of money with which to begin a business, etc.

shoe·tree (shōō/trē/) *n.* A form for inserting in a shoe to preserve its shape or to stretch it.

sho·far (shō/fär) *n.* A ram's horn used in Jewish ritual, sounded on solemn occasions and in war: also spelled *shop-har.* [< Hebrew *shōphār*]

sho·gun (shō/gun, -gōōn) *n.* Any of the hereditary military dictators who ruled Japan until the 19th century and under whom the emperor was a figurehead. [< Japanese < Chi-nese *chiang-chün* leader of an army]

sho·ji (shō/jē) *n.* A translucent paper screen forming a par-tition, door, etc., in a Japanese house. [< Japanese]

shone (shōn, shon) Past tense and past participle of SHINE.

shoo (shōō) *interj.* Begone! be off!: used in driving away fowls, etc. — *v.i.* 2. To cry "shoo." [Imit.] — *v.i.* 1. To drive away, as by crying "shoo."

shoo·fly (shōō/flī) *n.* *pl.* **·flies** *U.S.* 1. An enclosed child's rocker with sides representing horses, swans, etc. 2. A kind of pie with a syrupy filling made with molasses and brown sugar.

shoo-in (shōō/in/) *U.S. Informal* *n.* A contestant, candi-date, etc., who is certain to win.

shook (shook) Past tense of SHAKE.

shoot (shōōt) *v.* **shot, shoot·ing** *v.t.* 1. To hit, wound, or kill with a missile discharged from a weapon. 2. To dis-charge (a missile) from a bow, rifle, etc. 3. To discharge (a weapon): often with *off*: to *shoot* a cannon. 4. To take the altitude with a sextant, etc.: to *shoot* the sun. 5. To send forth as if from a weapon, as questions, glances, etc. 6. To pass over or through swiftly: to *shoot* rapids. 7. To go over (an area) in hunting game. 8. To emit, as rays of light. 9. To photograph; film. 10. To cause to stick out or protrude; extend. 11. To put forth in growth; send forth (buds, leaves, etc.). 12. To push into or out of the fastening, as the bolt of a door. 13. To propel, discharge, or dump, as down a chute or from a container. 14. To variegate, as with streaks of color: usually in the past participle: His paintings are *shot* with pink and brown. 15. In games: **a** To score (a goal, point, etc.) by kicking or otherwise forcing the ball, etc., to the objective. **b** To play (golf, craps, pool, etc.). **c**

To play (marbles). **d** To cast (the dice). —*v.i.* **16.** To discharge a missile from a bow, firearm, etc. **17.** To go off; discharge. **18.** To move swiftly; dart. **19.** To hunt game. **20.** To jut out; extend or project. **21.** To put forth buds, leaves, etc.; germinate; sprout. **22.** To take a photograph. **23.** To start the cameras, as in motion pictures. **24.** In games, to make a play by propelling the ball, puck, etc., in a certain manner. **— to shoot at** (or **for**) *Informal* To strive for; attempt to attain or obtain. **— to shoot down** To bring to earth by shooting. **— to shoot off one's mouth** *Slang* To talk too freely or too much. —*n.* **1.** A young branch or sucker of a plant; offshoot. **2.** A narrow passage in a stream; a rapid. **3.** An inclined passage down which anything may be shot; a chute. **4.** The act of shooting; a shot. **5.** A shooting match, hunting party, etc. **6.** *U.S. Informal* A rocket or missile launching. **7.** The thrust of an arch. **8.** Any new growth, as a new antler. **9.** Shooting distance; range. [OE *scēotan*] **— shoot'er** *n.*
shoot·ing (shoo'ting) *n.* The act of one who or that which shoots.
shooting gallery A place, usu. enclosed, where one can shoot at targets.
shooting star 1. A meteor. **2.** Any of certain small perennial herbs, having clusters of white, rose, or crimson flowers.
shop (shop) *n.* **1.** A place for the sale of goods at retail. Also **shoppe. 2.** A place for making or repairing any article, or the carrying on of any artisan craft: a blacksmith's *shop*. **3.** One's own craft or business as a subject of conversation: to talk *shop*. —*v.i.* **shopped, shop·ping** To visit shops or stores to purchase or look at goods. [OE *sceoppa* booth]
shop·girl (shop'gûrl') *n.* A girl who works in a shop.
sho·phar (shō'fär) See SHOFAR.
shop·keep·er (shop'kē'pər) *n.* One who runs a shop or store; a tradesman.
shop·lift·er (shop'lif'tər) *n.* One who steals goods exposed for sale in a shop. **— shop'lift'ing** *n.*
shop·per (shop'ər) *n.* **1.** One who shops. **2.** An employee of a store who compares the merchandise of competitors as to quality, price, etc. **— shop'ping** *n.*
shop steward A union worker chosen by fellow workers to represent them to management in seeking redress of grievances, etc. Also **shop chairman.**
shop·talk (shop'tôk') *n.* Conversation limited to one's job or profession.
shop·walk·er (shop'wô'kər) *n. Brit.* A floorwalker.
shop·worn (shop'wôrn', -wōrn') *adj.* **1.** Soiled or otherwise deteriorated from having been handled or on display in a shop. **2.** Worn out, as from overuse: stale.
shore¹ (shôr, shōr) *n.* **1.** The coast or land adjacent to an ocean, sea, lake, or large river. ◆ Collateral adjective: *littoral.* **2.** Land: to be on *shore.* **— in shore** Near or toward the shore. —*v.t.* **shored, shor·ing 1.** To set on shore. **2.** To surround as with a shore. [ME *schore*]
— Syn. (noun) **1.** *Shore, coast, beach,* and *bank* denote the land adjacent to a body of water. *Shore* is the general term; we speak of the *shore* of the sea, of a lake, or of a river. *Coast* is the ocean *shore*, especially along a great extent of land: the *coast* of Florida. A *beach* is a low, gently sloping expanse of sand or gravel; a *bank* is a more or less steep slope: the *banks* of the Red River.
shore² (shôr, shōr) *v.t.* **shored, shor·ing** To prop, as a wall, by a vertical or sloping timber: usu., with *up*. —*n.* A beam set endwise as a prop or temporary support against the side of a building, a ship in drydock, etc. [Cf. Du. *schoor* prop, ON *skortha* stay]
shore·less (shôr'lis, shōr'-) *adj.* **1.** Having no shore. **2.** Boundless.
shore·line (shôr'līn', shōr'-) *n.* The contour of a shore.
shore patrol A detail of the U.S. Navy, Coast Guard, or Marine Corps assigned to police duties ashore.
shore·ward (shôr'wərd, shōr'-) *adj. & adv.* Toward the shore. Also **shore'wards** (-wərdz).
shor·ing (shôr'ing, shō'ring) *n.* **1.** The operation of propping, as with shores. **2.** Shores, collectively.
shorn (shôrn, shōrn) Alternative past participle of SHEAR.
short (shôrt) *adj.* **1.** Having little linear extension; not long; of no great distance. **2.** Being below the average stature; not tall. **3.** Having little extension in time; of limited duration; brief. **4.** Abrupt in manner or spirit; cross. **5.** Not reaching or attaining a requirement, result, or mark; inadequate: often with *of*. **6.** Having a scant or insufficient amount: followed by *on*. **7.** Having little scope or breadth: a *short* view. **8.** In commerce: **a** Not having in possession when selling, but having to procure in time to deliver as contracted. **b** Of or pertaining to stocks or commodities not in possession of the seller: *short* sales. **9.** Not comprehensive or retentive; in error: a *short* memory. **10.** Breaking easily; crisp. **11.** *Phonet.* Denoting the vowel sounds of *Dan, den, din, don, duck,* as contrasted with those of *Dane, dean, dine, dome, dune.* **12.** In English prosody, unaccented. **13.** Less than: with *of*. **14.** Concise; compressed. —*n.* **1.** Anything that is short. **2.** A deficiency, as in a payment.

3. A short syllable or vowel. **4.** A short contract or sa one who has sold short; a bear. **5.** *pl.* Bran mixed w coarse meal or flour. **6.** *pl.* Trousers with legs extendi part way to the knees. **7.** *pl.* A man's undergarment cov ing the loins and often a portion of the legs. **8.** In baseb slang, shortstop. **9.** *Electr.* A short circuit. **10.** A sh subject. **— for short** For brevity: Edward was called *for short.* **— in short** In a word; briefly. —*adv.* **1.** Abru ly: to stop *short.* **2.** Curtly; crossly. **3.** So as not to rea or extend to a certain point, condition, etc.: to fall *short.* Without having in actual possession that which is sold: sell *short.* —*v.t. & v.i.* To short-circuit. [OE *sort*] **short'ness** *n.*
short·age (shôr'tij) *n.* The amount by which anything short; deficiency.
short·bread (shôrt'bred') *n.* A rich, dry cake or coo made with shortening.
short·cake (shôrt'kāk') *n.* **1.** A cake made short and cr with butter or other shortening. **2.** Cake or biscuit ser with fruit; strawberry *shortcake.*
short·change (shôrt'chānj') *v.t.* **·changed, ·chang·ing** *formal* To give less change than is due to; also, to cheat swindle. **— short'chang'er** *n.*
short-cir·cuit (shôrt'sûr'kit) *v.t. & v.i.* To make a sh circuit (in).
short circuit *Electr.* **1.** A path of low resistance est lished between any two points in an electric circuit, t shortening the distance traveled by the current. **2.** defect in an electric circuit or apparatus that may res in a dangerous leakage of current.
short·com·ing (shôrt'kum'ing) *n.* A failure or deficien in character, action, etc.
short-cut (shôrt'kut') *v.t. & v.i.* **-cut, -cut·ting** To tak short cut (in).
short cut 1. A byway or path between two places tha shorter than the regular way. **2.** Any means or meth that saves distance or time.
short·en (shôr'tən) *v.t.* **1.** To make short or shorter; c tail. **2.** To reduce; diminish; lessen. **3.** To furl or reef sail) so that less canvas is exposed to the wind. **4.** To ma brittle or crisp, as pastry, by adding shortening. —*v.i.* To become short or shorter. **— short'en·er** *n.*
short·en·ing (shôr'tən·ing) *n.* **1.** A fat, such as lard butter, used to make pastry crisp. **2.** An abbreviation. The act of one who shortens.
short·hand (shôrt'hand') *n.* Any system of rapid writi usu. employing symbols other than letters, words, etc. *adj.* **1.** Written in shorthand. **2.** Using shorthand.
short-hand·ed (shôrt'han'did) *adj.* Not having a su cient or the usual number of assistants, workmen, etc.
short·horn (shôrt'hôrn') *n.* One of a breed of cattle w short horns, originally from northern England.
short-lived (shôrt'līvd', -livd') *adj.* Living or lasting l a short time.
short·ly (shôrt'lē) *adv.* **1.** In a short time; quickly; so **2.** In few words; briefly. **3.** Curtly; abruptly.
short order Food requiring little time to prepare. —
short order Without any delay; quickly; abruptly. **short·or·der** (shôrt'ôr'dər) *adj.*
short shrift 1. A short time in which to confess be dying. **2.** Little or no mercy or delay, as in dealing wit person. **— to make short shrift of** To dispose of quick
short·sight·ed (shôrt'sī'tid) *adj.* **1.** Unable to see clea at a distance; myopic; near-sighted. **2.** Lacking foresig **3.** Resulting from or characterized by lack of foresig **— short'sight'ed·ly** *adv.* **— short'sight'ed·ness** *n.*
short-spo·ken (shôrt'spō'kən) *adj.* Characterized shortness or curtness of speech or manner; abrupt; gruff
short·stop (shôrt'stop') *n.* In baseball, an infielder s tioned between second and third bases; also, his positio
short story A narrative prose story shorter than a nove novelette, usu. under 10,000 words.
short subject A motion picture of relatively short durati often displayed between showings of the feature attract on a program: also called *short.*
short-tem·pered (shôrt'tem'pərd) *adj.* Easily angere
short-term (shôrt'tûrm') *adj.* In finance, due or paya within a short time, usu. one year: said of loans, etc.
short ton See under TON¹.
short waves Electromagnetic waves that are 60 meter less in length. **— short-wave** (shôrt'wāv') *adj.*
short-wind·ed (shôrt'win'did) *adj.* Affected with difficu of breathing; becoming easily out of breath.
Sho·sho·ne (shō-shō'nē) *n.* **1.** One of a large tribe of No American Indians of northern Shoshonean stock of the U Aztecan family, formerly occupying parts of Wyom Idaho, Nevada, and Utah. **2.** The Shoshonean languag this tribe. Also **Sho·sho'ni.**
Sho·sho·ne·an (shō-shō'nē-ən, shō'shə-nē'ən) *n.* largest branch of the Uto-Aztecan family of North Americ Indians, including the Comanche, Ute, and Shoshone p

u tribes, and the Hopi Indians. — *adj.* Of or pertaining this linguistic branch. Also **Sho·sho/ni·an.**

shot¹ (shot) *n.* *pl.* **shots;** *for def.* 1 **shot** 1. A solid missile, a ball of iron, or a bullet or pellet of lead, to be discharged from a firearm; also, such pellets collectively. 2. The act of shooting; any stroke, hit, or blow. 3. One who shoots; a marksman. 4. The distance traversed or that can be traversed by a projectile; range. 5. *U.S. Informal* The firing of a rocket, etc., that is directed toward a specific target: a moon shot. 6. A blast, as in mining. 7. A stroke, esp. in certain games, as in billiards. 8. A conjecture; guess. 9. An attempted performance or try. 10. A metal sphere that a competitor puts, pushes, or slings, in a distance contest. 11. *Informal* A hypodermic injection of a drug. 12. *Informal* A drink of liquor. 13. A single action or scene recorded on motion-picture or television film or tape. 14. A photograph or a snapshot. 15. *Naut.* A unit of chain length: in the U.S., 15 fathoms; in Great Britain, 12½ fathoms. — *v.t.* **shot·ted, shot·ting** 1. To load or weight with shot. 2. To clean, as bottles, by partially filling with shot and shaking. [OE *scot*]

shot² (shot) Past tense and past participle of SHOOT. — *adj.* Of changeable color, as when warp and weft are of different colors; also, streaked or mixed irregularly with other colors: a sky shot with pink. 2. *Informal* Completely done; ruined; also, worn out; completely broken.

shot³ (shot) *n. Brit. & Canadian* A reckoning or charge, or share of such a reckoning; scot. [Var. of SCOT]

shot effect *Electronics* The background noise resembling a patter of small shot, developed in an electron tube by a fluctuating emission of electrons from the heated filament. Also **shot noise.**

shot·gun (shot/gun/) *n.* A light, smoothbore gun, either single or double barreled, adapted for the discharge of shot at short range. — *adj.* 1. Having a clear passageway straight through: a shotgun house. 2. Coerced with, or as with, a shotgun: a shotgun wedding.

shot·put (shot/pŏŏt/) *n.* 1. An athletic contest in which a shot is thrown, or put, for distance. 2. A single put of the shot. — **shot/-put/ter** *n.*

shot·ten (shot/n) *adj.* Having spawned: said of a fish, esp. herring. [Obs. pp. of SHOOT]

should (shŏŏd) Past tense of SHALL, but rarely a true past, rather chiefly used as a modal auxiliary that, while conveying varying shades of present and future time, expresses a wide range of subtly discriminated feelings and attitudes: 1. Obligation or propriety in varying degrees, but milder than ought: You should write that letter; Should we tell him the truth about his condition? 2. Condition: a Simple contingency, but involving less probability than shall or the present with future sense: If I should go, he would go too. 3. Assumption: Should (Assuming that) the space platform prove practicable, as seems almost certain, a trip to the moon will be easy. 4. Surprise at an unexpected event in the past: When I reached the station, whom should I run into but the detective! 4. Expectation: I should be at home by noon. 5. *U.S. Informal* Irony, in positive statement with negative force: He'll be most happy, but with all his money he should (need not) worry! ◆ In American usage the first person may be followed by either should or would such expressions as I should/would be glad to see you. [OE *scolde*, pt. of *sculan* to owe]

shoul·der (shōl/dər) *n.* 1. The part of the trunk between the neck and the free portion of the arm or forelimb; also, the joint connecting the arm or forelimb with the body. 2. Anything that supports, bears up, or projects like a shoulder. 3. The forequarter of various animals. 4. An enlargement, projection, or offset, as for keeping something in place, or preventing movement past the projection. 5. Either edge of a road or highway. 6. The angle of a bastion included between a face and the adjacent flank; also **shoulder angle.** — **shoulder to shoulder** 1. Side by side and close together. 2. With united effort; in cooperation. — **straight from the shoulder** *Informal* Candidly; straightforwardly. — **to cry on (one's) shoulder** To seek sympathy and understanding from (one). — **to give the cold shoulder to** 1. To treat with scorn, contempt, or coldness. 2. To ignore, shun, or avoid. — **to put (one's) shoulder to the wheel** To work with great vigor and purpose. — *v.t.* 1. To assume as something to be borne; sustain; bear. 2. To push with or as with the shoulder or shoulders. 3. To fashion with a shoulder or abutment. — *v.i.* 4. To push with the shoulder or shoulders. — **shoulder arms** To rest a rifle against the shoulder, holding the butt with the hand. [OE *sculdor*]

shoulder blade *Anat.* The scapula.

shoulder patch A cloth insignia worn on the upper part of the sleeve of a uniform to indicate one's branch or unit.

shoulder strap 1. A strap worn on or over the shoulder

to support an article of dress. 2. A strap of cloth marked with insignia of rank, worn by army and navy officers.

should·n't (shŏŏd/nt) Should not.

shouldst (shŏŏdst) *Archaic* second person singular of SHALL: used with *thou.* Also **should·est** (shŏŏd/ist).

shout (shout) *n.* A sudden and loud outcry, often expressing joy, anger, etc., or used as a call or command. — *v.t.* 1. To utter with a shout; say or express loudly. — *v.i.* 2. To utter a shout. [Cf. ON *skūta* a taunt] — **shout/er** *n.*

shove (shuv) *v.t. & v.i.* **shoved, shov·ing** 1. To push, as along a surface. 2. To press forcibly (against); jostle. — **to shove off** 1. To push along or away, as a boat. 2. *Informal* To depart. — *n.* The act of pushing or shoving. [OE *scūfan*] — **shov/er** *n.*

shov·el (shuv/əl) *n.* A somewhat flattened scoop with a handle, as for digging, lifting earth, rock, snow, etc.; also, any large, usu. toothed device for extensive, heavy digging. — *v.* **shov·eled** or **·elled, shov·el·ing** or **·el·ling** *v.t.* 1. To take up and move with a shovel. 2. To toss hastily or in large quantities as if with a shovel. 3. To clear with a shovel, as a path. — *v.i.* 4. To work with a shovel. [OE *scofl*]

shov·el·board (shuv/əl-bôrd/, -bōrd/) *n.* Shuffleboard.

shov·el·er (shuv/əl-ər, shuv/lər) *n.* 1. One who or that which shovels. 2. A large river duck with a spatulate bill: also called *spoonbill:* also **shov·el·bill** (shuv/əl-bil/). Also **shov/el·ler.**

show (shō) *v.* **showed, shown** or, sometimes **showed, show·ing** *v.t.* 1. To cause or permit to be seen; exhibit, display. 2. To give in a marked or open manner; bestow: to show favor. 3. To cause or allow (something) to be understood or known; reveal; tell. 4. To cause (someone) to understand or see; teach. 5. *Law* To advance an allegation; plead: to show cause. 6. To make evident by logical process; demonstrate. 7. To guide; introduce, as into a room or building: with in or up; to show a caller in. 8. To indicate: The thermometer shows the temperature. 9. To enter in a show or exhibition. — *v.i.* 10. To become visible or known. 11. To seem. 12. To make one's or its appearance; be present. 13. *Informal* To give a theatrical performance; appear. 14. In racing, to finish third: distinguished from place, win. Also, *Archaic,* **shew.** — **to show off** 1. To exhibit proudly or ostentatiously. 2. To make an ostentatious display of oneself, or of one's accomplishments. — **to show up** 1. To expose or be exposed, as faults. 2. To be evident or prominent. 3. To make an appearance. 4. *Informal* To be better than; outdo. — *n.* 1. An entertainment or performance: a Broadway show. 2. Anything shown or manifested. 3. An elaborate display: a show of wealth. 4. A pretense or semblance: a show of piety. 5. Any public exhibition, contest, etc.: an art show. 6. An appearance: a bad show. 7. An indication; promise: a show of ore. 8. The third position among the first three winners of a race. 9. The act of showing. — **show of hands** A display of raised hands indicating the vote of a group. [OE *scēawian*] — **show/er** *n.*

show bill A poster announcing a play or show.

show·boat (shō/bōt/) *n.* A boat on which a traveling troupe gives a theatrical performance.

show·bread (shō/bred/) See SHEWBREAD.

show business The entertainment arts, esp. the theater, motion pictures, television, etc., collectively considered as an industry or profession.

show·case (shō/kās/) *n.* A glass case for exhibiting and protecting articles for sale.

show·down (shō/doun/) *n.* 1. In poker, the play in which the hands are laid on the table face up. 2. Any action or disclosure that brings an issue to a head.

show·er (shou/ər) *n.* 1. A fall of rain, hail, or sleet, esp. heavy rain of short duration within a local area. 2. A copious fall, as of tears, sparks, etc. 3. A shower bath. 4. An abundance or profusion of something. 5. A variety of fireworks for simulating a shower of stars. 6. A party for the bestowal of gifts, as to a bride; also, the gifts. — *v.t.* 1. To sprinkle or wet with or as with showers. 2. To discharge in a shower; pour out. 3. To bestow with liberality. — *v.i.* 4. To fall as in a shower. 5. To take a shower bath. [OE *scūr*] — **show/er·y** *adj.*

shower bath A bath in which water is sprayed on the body from an overhead, perforated nozzle; also, the area or room in which this is done.

show·ing (shō/ing) *n.* 1. A show or display, as of a quality. 2. A presentation or statement, as of a subject.

show·man (shō/mən) *n. pl.* **·men** (-mən) 1. One who exhibits or owns a show. 2. One who is skilled in presenting something. — **show/man·ship** *n.*

Show Me State Nickname of Missouri.

shown (shōn) Past participle of SHOW.

show·off (shō/ôf/, -of/) *n. Informal* 1. The act of showing off; ostentatious display. 2. One who shows off.

show·piece (shō′pēs′) *n.* **1.** A prized object considered worthy of special exhibit. **2.** An object on display.

show place   A place exhibited for its beauty, historic interest, etc.

show room   A room in which things, as merchandise, are displayed for sale or advertising.

show·y (shō′ē) *adj.* **show·i·er, show·i·est 1.** Making a great or brilliant display. **2.** Given to cheap display; gaudy; ostentatious. **— show′i·ly** *adv.* **— show′i·ness** *n.*

shrank (shrangk) Past tense of SHRINK.

shrap·nel (shrap′nəl) *n. pl.* **·nel** *Mil.* **1.** A field artillery projectile for use against personnel, containing a quantity of metal balls and a time fuse and base charge that expel the balls in mid-air. **2.** Shell fragments. [after Henry *Shrapnel*, 1761–1842, British artillery officer]

shred (shred) *n.* **1.** A small irregular strip torn or cut off. **2.** A bit; fragment; particle. **—** *v.t.* **shred·ded** or **shred, shred·ding** To tear or cut into shreds. [OE *scrēade*] **— shred′der** *n.*

shrew (shrōō) *n.* **1.** Any of numerous diminutive, chiefly insectivorous mammals having a long pointed snout and soft fur, as the **long-tailed shrew** of North America. Also **shrew/mouse/** (-mous′). **2.** A woman of vexatious, scolding, or nagging disposition. [OE *scrēawa*] **— Syn.** **2.** scold, vixen, termagant, virago.

shrewd (shrōōd) *adj.* **1.** Sharp or wise; sagacious. **2.** Artful; sly. [ME < *shrew* malicious person] **— shrewd′ly** *adv.* **— shrewd′ness** *n.*

shrew·ish (shrōō′ish) *adj.* Like a shrew; ill-tempered; nagging. **— shrew′ish·ly** *adv.* **— shrew′ish·ness** *n.*

shriek (shrēk) *n.* A sharp shrill outcry or scream. **—** *v.i.* **1.** To utter a shriek. **—** *v.t.* **2.** To utter with or in a shriek. [ME] **— shriek′er** *n.*

shrift (shrift) *n.* **1.** The act of shriving. **2.** Confession or absolution, as to or from a priest. [OE *scrift*]

shrike (shrīk) *n.* Any of numerous predatory birds with hooked bill, short wings, and long tail. [OE *scrīc* thrush]

shrill (shril) *adj.* **1.** Having a high-pitched and piercing tone quality. **2.** Emitting a sharp, piercing sound. **—** *v.t.* **1.** To cause to utter a shrill sound. **—** *v.i.* **2.** To make a shrill sound. **—** *adv.* Shrilly. [< Gmc.] **— shrill′ly** *adv.* **— shrill′ness** *n.*

shrimp (shrimp) *n. pl.* **shrimp** or **shrimps** for def. 1, **shrimps** for def. 2 **1.** Any of numerous small, long-tailed, principally marine animals, some species of which are used as food. **2.** *Slang* A small or unimportant person. [Akin to OE *scrimman* to shrink, G *schrimpfen*]

shrine (shrīn) *n.* **1.** A receptacle for sacred relics. **2.** A place, as a tomb or a chapel, sacred to some holy personage. **3.** A thing or spot made sacred by historic or other association. **—** *v.t.* **shrined, shrining** *Rare & Poetic* To enshrine. [OE < L *scrinium* case, chest]

SHRIMP
a Cephalothorax. *b* Abdomen. *c* Tail. *t* Telson.

shrink (shringk) *v.* **shrank** or **shrunk** or, sometimes, **shrunk·en, shrink·ing** *v.i.* **1.** To draw together; contract, as from heat, cold, etc. **2.** To diminish. **3.** To draw back, as from disgust, horror, or timidity; recoil: with *from.* **4.** To flinch; wince. **—** *v.t.* **5.** To cause to shrink, contract, or draw together. **—** *n.* **1.** The act of shrinking. **2.** *Slang* A psychiatrist. [OE *scrincan*] **— shrink′a·ble** *adj.*

shrink·age (shringk′ij) *n.* **1.** The act or fact of shrinking; contraction. **2.** The amount lost by such shrinking. **3.** Decrease in value; depreciation.

shrive (shrīv) *v.* **shrove** or **shrived, shriv·en** or **shrived, shriv·ing** *v.t.* **1.** To receive the confession of and give absolution to. **2.** To obtain absolution for (oneself) by confessing one's sins and doing penance. **—** *v.i.* **3.** To make confession. **4.** To hear confession. [OE *scrīfan,* ult. < L *scribere* to write, prescribe] **— shriv′er** *n.*

shriv·el (shriv′əl) *v.t. & v.i.* **shriv·eled** or **·elled, shriv·el·ing** or **·el·ling 1.** To contract into wrinkles; shrink and wrinkle: often with *up.* **2.** To make or become impotent; wither. [Origin uncertain]

shriv·en (shriv′ən) Alternative past participle of SHRIVE.

Shrop·shire (shrop′shir, -shər) *n.* A breed of black-faced, hornless sheep, noted for heavy fleece and superior mutton, originating in Shropshire.

shroud[1] (shroud) *n.* **1.** A dress or garment for the dead. **2.** Something that envelops or conceals like a garment: the *shroud* of night. **—** *v.t.* **1.** To dress for the grave; clothe in a shroud. **2.** To envelop, as with a garment. [OE *scrūd* garment] **— shroud′less** *adj.*

shroud[2] (shroud) *n.* **1.** *Naut.* One of a set of ropes, often of wire, stretched from a masthead to the sides of a ship, serving as means of ascent and as a support for the masts. **2.** *Usu. pl.* A guy, as a support for a smokestack. **3.** One of the supporting ropes attached to the edges of a parachute canopy. [< SHROUD[1]]

shrove (shrōv) Alternative past tense of SHRIVE.

Shrove·tide (shrōv′tīd′) *n.* The three days immediate preceding Ash Wednesday, **Shrove Sunday** (Quinquagesim Sunday), **Shrove Monday, Shrove Tuesday,** on which co fession is made in preparation for Lent. [ME *schroftide*

shrub (shrub) *n.* A woody perennial plant of low statu characterized by persistent stems and branches springi from the base. [OE *scrybb* brushwood]

shrub·ber·y (shrub′ər-ē) *n. pl.* **·ber·ies 1.** Shrubs c lectively. **2.** A collection of shrubs, as in a garden.

shrub·by (shrub′ē) *adj.* **·bi·er, ·bi·est 1.** Containing ma shrubs; covered with shrubs. **2.** Of, pertaining to, or like shrub. **— shrub′bi·ness** *n.*

shrug (shrug) *v.t. & v.i.* **shrugged, shrug·ging** To dr up (the shoulders), as in displeasure, doubt, surprise, et **—** *n.* **1.** The act of shrugging the shoulders. **2.** A ve short sweater or jacket, open in front. [ME *schrugge*]

shrunk (shrungk) Alternative past tense and past partici of SHRINK.

shrunk·en (shrungk′ən) Alternative past participle SHRINK. **—** *adj.* Contracted and atrophied.

shuck (shuk) *n.* **1.** A husk, shell, or pod. **2.** A shell of oyster or a clam. **—** *v.t.* **1.** To remove the husk or sh from (corn, oysters, etc.). **2.** *Informal* To take off or ca off, as clothes. [Origin unknown] **— shuck′er** *n.*

shucks (shuks) *interj.* *U.S. Informal* A mild ejaculati expressing annoyance, disgust, etc.

shud·der (shud′ər) *v.i.* To tremble or shake, as from frig or cold; shiver; quake. **—** *n.* The act of shuddering; a co vulsive shiver, as from horror or fear; tremor. [ME *shodde*

shuf·fle (shuf′əl) *n.* **1.** A mixing or changing of the ord of things, as of cards in a pack before each deal. **2.** hesitating, evasive, or tricky action; artifice. **3.** A scrapi of the feet, as in walking; a slow, dragging gait. **4.** A dan or the step used in it, where the dancer pushes his foot alo the floor at each step. **—** *v.* **·fled, ·fling** *v.t.* **1.** To shift t way and that; mix; confuse; disorder; esp. to change t order of by mixing, as cards in a pack. **2.** To move (t feet) along the ground or floor with a dragging gait. **3.** change from one place to another. **4.** To make up or move fraudulently or hastily; also, to put aside careless with *up, off,* or *out.* **—** *v.i.* **5.** To change position. **6.** resort to indirect methods. **7.** To dance the shuffle. **8.** scrape the feet along. **9.** To scrape or struggle along aw wardly. [Prob. < LG *schuffeln* to move with dragging fe mix cards, etc.] **— shuf′fler** *n.*

shuf·fle·board (shuf′əl-bôrd′, -bōrd′) *n.* **1.** A game which wooden or composition disks are slid by means of pronged cue along a smooth surface toward number spaces. **2.** The board or surface on which the game played. Also called *shovelboard.*

shun (shun) *v.t.* **shunned, shun·ning** To keep clear avoid; refrain from. [OE *scunian*] **— shun′ner** *n.*

shunt (shunt) *n.* **1.** The act of shunting. **2.** A railro switch. **3.** *Electr.* A conductor joining two points in a c cuit and serving to divert part of the current to an auxilia circuit: also called *by-pass.* **—** *v.t.* **1.** To turn aside. **2.** switch, as a train or car, from one track to another. **3.** *Electr.* To distribute by means of shunts. **4.** To evade turning away from; put off on someone else, as a task. **—** *v.i.* **5.** To move to one side. **6.** *Electr.* To be diverted b shunt: said of current. **7.** To shift or transfer one's view course. [ME *schunten*] **— shunt′er** *n.*

shunt-wound (shunt′wound′) *adj.* *Electr.* Designatin type of direct-current motor in which the armature circ and field circuit are connected in parallel.

shush (shush) *v.t.* To quiet, as by making the sound "sh

shut (shut) *v.* **shut, shut·ting** *v.t.* **1.** To bring into su position as to close an opening or aperture; close, as a do lid, or valve. **2.** To close (an opening, aperture, etc.) so to prevent ingress or egress. **3.** To close and fasten secure as with a latch or lock. **4.** To forbid entrance into or e from. **5.** To keep from entering or leaving: with *in, o from,* etc. **6.** To close, fold, or bring together, as extende expanded, or unfolded parts: to *shut* an umbrella. **7.** hide from view; obscure. **—** *v.i.* **8.** To be or become clos or in a closed position. **— to shut down 1.** To cease fr operating, as a factory or mine; close up; stop work. **2.** lower; come down close: the fog *shut down.* **3.** *Informal* suppress: with *on.* **— to shut one's eyes to** To ignore. **to shut out** In sports, to keep (an opponent) from scor during the course of a game. **— to shut up 1.** *Informal* stop talking or cause to stop talking. **2.** To close all t entrances to, as a house. **3.** To imprison; confine. **—** *adj.* **1.** Made fast or closed. **2.** Not sonorous; dull: said sound. **—** *n.* The act of shutting. **2.** The time or pla of shutting or closing. [OE *scyttan*]

shut·down (shut′doun′) *n.* The closing or ceasing work in a mine, mill, factory, or other industrial plant.

shut·eye (shut′ī) *n.* *Slang* Sleep.

shut-in (shut′in′) *n.* An invalid who is unable to go o **—** *adj.* Obliged to stay at home.

t·off (shut′ôf′, -of′) *n. Mech.* A device for shutting ...ething off.

t·out (shut′out′) *n.* **1.** A shutting out; esp., a lockout. In sports, a game in which one side is prevented from ...ring.

t·ter (shut′ər) *n.* **1.** One who or that which shuts. **2.** ...at which shuts out or excludes; esp., a cover or screen, ...a. hinged, for closing a window. **3.** *Photog.* Any of various ...chanisms for momentarily admitting light through a ...era lens to the film or plate. — *v.t.* To furnish, close, or ...ide off with shutters.

t·tle (shut′l) *n.* **1.** A device used in weaving to carry ...e weft to and fro between the warp threads. **2.** A similar ...ating or other device in a sewing machine or used in ...ting. **3.** A transport system operating between two ...rby points. — *v.t. & v.i.* ·tled, ·tling To move to and ...o, like a shuttle. [OE *scytel* missile]

t·tle·cock (shut′l·kok′) *n.* A rounded piece of cork, ...h a crown of feathers, used in badminton and battledore; ...o, the game of battledore. — *v.t.* To send or knock back ...d forth like a shuttlecock.

y (shī) *v.i.* shied, shy·ing **1.** To start suddenly aside, ...n fear: said of a horse. **2.** To draw back, as from doubt ...caution: with *off* or *away.* — *adj.* shi·er or shy·er, shi·est ...shy·est **1.** Easily frightened or startled; timorous. **2.** ...shful; coy. **3.** Circumspect, as from motives of caution; ...ry: with *of.* **4.** Not easy to perceive, seize, or secure; ...sive. **5.** Not prolific: said of plants, trees, or, rarely, ...ls. **6.** *Informal* Having less money than is called for or ...uired: to be *shy* a dollar. **7.** *Informal* Short; lacking: ...n with *on.* — *n.* A starting aside, as in fear. [OE *scēoh* ...id] — **shy′ness** *n.*

y (shī) *v.t. & v.i.* shied, shy·ing To throw with a swift ...long motion. — *n. pl.* shies A careless throw or fling. ...igin unknown]

·er (shī′ər) *n.* **1.** One who shies. **2.** See SHIER.

·lock (shī′lok) In Shakespeare's *Merchant of Venice*, a ...engeful usurer. — *n. Slang* Any relentless creditor.

·ly (shī′lē) *adv.* In a shy manner: also spelled *shily.*

·ster (shīs′tər) *n. Slang* Anyone, esp. a lawyer, who ...ducts his business in an unscrupulous or tricky manner. ...igin uncertain]

...sē) *n. Music* Formerly ti¹.

...sē) *adv.* Italian, Portuguese, Spanish, and sometimes ...nch, for "yes." [< L *sic* thus]

... *Chem.* Silicon.

...o- *combining form* Saliva; pertaining to saliva. Also, ...ore vowels, sial-. [< Gk. *sialon* saliva]

·mese (sī′ə·mēz′, -mēs′) *adj.* **1.** Pertaining to Thailand ...am), its people, or their language. **2.** Closely connected; ...te. — *n.* **1.** *pl.* ·mese A native of Siam, belonging to the ...ai stock. **2.** The Thai language of the people of Siam, ...w officially called *Thai.*

...nese cat A breed of short-haired cat, ...ically fawn-colored, with dark-tipped ...s, tail, feet, and face, and blue, gently ...ating eyes.

...nese twins Any twins joined togeth- ...at birth. [after the two Chinese males, ...g and Chang, 1811–74, born in Siam, ...ose bodies were joined by a fleshy band] ...sib) *Rare n.* **1.** A blood relation; kins- ...n. **2.** Kinsmen collectively; relatives. ...ed; similar. Also sibb. [OE *sibb*]

SIAMESE CAT
(About 11 inch-
es high at
shoulder)

·bo·leth (sib′ə·leth) See SHIBBOLETH.

·l·ant (sib′ə·lant) *adj.* **1.** Hissing. **2.** ...onet. Denoting those consonants pro- ...ced by the fricative passage of breath ...ough a very narrow orifice, in the front ...t of the mouth, as (s), (z), (sh), and (zh). — ...n. *Phonet.* A sibilant consonant. [< L *sibilans, -antis,* ...r. of *sibilare* to hiss] — **sib′i·lance, sib′i·lan·cy** *n.* ...i·lant·ly *adv.*

·ling (sib′ling) *n.* A brother or sister. [OE, a relative]

·yl (sib′əl) *n.* **1.** In ancient Greece and Rome, any of ...eral women who prophesied under the supposed inspira- ...n of some deity. **2.** A fortuneteller; sorceress. [< F ...ibylla < Gk.] — **sib′yl·line** (-īn, -ēn, in), **si·byl·ic** (si·bil′- ...; **si·byl′lic** *adj.*

... (sik) *adv.* So; thus: inserted in brackets after a quota- ...n to indicate that it is accurately reproduced even though ...may seem questionable or incorrect. [< L]

... (sik) *v.t.* sicked, sick·ing To sick. See SICK².

·il·i·an (si·sil′ē·ən, -sil′yən) *adj.* Of or pertaining to ...ily or its people: also **Si·ca′ni·an** (-ka′nē·ən). — *n.* An ...abitant or native of Sicily.

... (sik) *adj.* **1.** Affected with disease; ill. **2.** Of or used by ill persons: often used in combination: *sickroom.* **3.** Affected by nausea; desiring to vomit. **4.** Expressive of or experiencing disgust or unpleasant emotion. **5.** Impaired or unsound from any cause. **6.** Mentally unsound. **7.** Pallid; wan. **8.** Depressed and longing: *sick* for the sea. **9.** Disinclined by reason of satiety or disgust; surfeited: with *of.* **10.** Sadistic or macabre; morbid: *sick* jokes. — *n.* Sick people collectively: with *the.* [OE *sēoc*]
— **Syn. 2, 3.** In U.S. usage, *sick* is a general term that may refer to a slight ailment or the most severe illness; it may also mean nauseated, the sense it always bears in British usage. *Ill* is a close synonym but may refer to a greater variety of symptoms. *Unwell* is similar to *ill,* but is sometimes felt to be affected. *Ailing* and *indisposed* refer to slight illnesses. *Ailing* implies a minor, but chronic, condition; *indisposed* suggests a trivial or temporary illness that prevents normal activity.

sick² (sik) *v.t.* **1.** To attack: used in the imperative as an order to a dog. **2.** To urge to attack: I'll *sick* the dog on you. Also spelled *sic.* [Var. of SEEK]

sick·bay (sik′bā′) *n.* That part of a ship or of a naval base set aside for the care of the sick.

sick·bed (sik′bed′) *n.* The bed a sick person lies on.

sick call *Mil.* **1.** The daily period during which all non-hospitalized sick or injured personnel report to the medical officer. **2.** The call or signal that announces this.

sick·en (sik′ən) *v.t. & v.i.* To make or become sick or disgusted. — **sick′en·er** *n.*

sick·en·ing (sik′ən·ing) *adj.* Disgusting; revolting; nauseating. — **sick′en·ing·ly** *adv.*

sick headache Headache with nausea, esp., migraine.

sick·ish (sik′ish) *adj.* **1.** Somewhat sick. **2.** Slightly nauseating. — **sick′ish·ly** *adv.* — **sick′ish·ness** *n.*

sick·le (sik′əl) *n.* An implement with a curved or crescent-shaped blade mounted on a short handle, used for cutting tall grass, grains, etc. — *v.t.* ·led, ·ling To cut with a sickle, as grass. [OE < L *secare* to cut]

sickle cell A crescent-shaped red blood corpuscle containing a genetically transmitted type of hemoglobin in which the oxygen concentration is below normal, and causing an anemia (**sickle cell anemia**) occurring chiefly among Negroes.

sick·ly (sik′lē) *adj.* ·li·er, ·li·est **1.** Habitually indisposed; ailing; unhealthy. **2.** Marked by the prevalence of sickness: a *sickly* summer. **3.** Nauseating; disgusting. **4.** Pertaining to or characteristic of sickness: a *sickly* appearance. **5.** Weak; faint. — *adv.* In a sick manner; poorly: also **sick′li·ly.** — *v.t.* ·lied, ·ly·ing To make sickly, as in color or complexion. — **sick′li·ness** *n.*

sick·ness (sik′nis) *n.* **1.** The state of being sick. **2.** A particular form of disease. **3.** Nausea.

sick·room (sik′rōōm′, -rŏŏm′) *n.* A room in which a sick person lies or stays.

side (sīd) *n.* **1.** Any one of the bounding lines of a surface or of the bounding surfaces of a solid object; also, a particular line or surface other than top or bottom: the *side* of a mountain. **2.** A lateral part of a surface or object, usu. designated as *right* or *left.* **3.** Either of the two surfaces of a piece of paper, cloth, etc.; also, a specific surface of something: the rough *side* of sandpaper. **4.** One of two or more contrasted directions, parts, or places: the east *side* of town. **5.** A distinct party or body of competitors or partisans. **6.** An opinion, aspect, or point of view: my *side* of the question. **7.** Family connection, esp. by descent through one parent. **8.** The lateral half of a slaughtered animal. **9.** Either half of the human body. **10.** The space beside someone. **11.** In billiards, a lateral spin given to the cue ball. **12.** In sports, a team. — **side by side** Beside or next to each other. — **to take sides** To support a particular opinion, point of view, etc. — **Syn.** See PHASE. — *adj.* **1.** Situated at or on one side: a *side* window. **2.** Being or viewed as if from one side: a *side* glance. **3.** Directed towards one side: a *side* blow. **4.** Not primary; subordinate: a *side* issue. — *v.t.* **sid·ed, sid·ing** To provide with sides, as a building. — **to side with** To support or take the part of. [OE *sīde*]

side·arm (sīd′ärm′) *adj.* Executed with the hand level with the elbow, as a pitch. — *adv.* In a sidearm manner.

side arms Weapons worn at the side, as pistols, etc.

side·band (sīd′band′) *n. Telecom.* One of the two bands immediately adjacent to a carrier frequency, corresponding to the band-width of the modulating signal.

side·board (sīd′bôrd′, -bōrd′) *n.* A piece of dining-room furniture for holding tableware.

side·burns (sīd′bûrnz′) *n.pl. Chiefly U.S.* The hair growing on the sides of a man's face below the hairline, esp. when worn as whiskers. [Alter. of BURNSIDES]

side·car (sīd′kär′) *n.* A small, one-wheeled passenger car attached to the side of a motorcycle.

sid·ed (sī′did) *adj.* Having or characterized by (a specified kind or number of) sides: used in combination: *one-sided.*

side effect A secondary, usu. injurious effect, as of a drug.

side·kick (sīd′kik′) *n. U.S. Slang* A close friend; buddy.

side·light (sīd′līt′) *n.* **1.** A side window. **2.** A light coming from the side. **3.** Incidental facts or information.

side·line (sīd′līn′) *n.* **1.** An auxiliary line of goods sold by a store or a commercial traveler. **2.** Any additional or secondary work differing from one's main job. **3.** In sports: **a** One of the lines bounding the two sides of a football field, tennis court, etc. **b** *Often pl.* The area just outside these lines. Also **side line.** — *v.t.* **·lined, ·lin·ing** To prevent or remove (someone) from active participation.

side·long (sīd′lông′, -long′) *adj.* **1.** Inclining, tending or directed to one side. **2.** Indirect; sly. — *adv.* In a lateral or oblique direction.

side·piece (sīd′pēs′) *n.* A piece at or forming a side.

si·de·re·al (sī-dir′ē-əl) *adj.* **1.** Of or pertaining to stars. **2.** Measured by means of the stars: *sidereal* year. [< L < *sidus* star] — **si·de′re·al·ly** *adv.*

sidereal year The period of 365 days, 6 hours, 9 minutes, and 9 seconds in which the sun apparently returns to the same position among the stars.

sidero-[1] *combining form* Iron; of or pertaining to iron. Also, before vowels, **sider-.** [< Gk. *sidēros* iron]

sidero-[2] *combining form* Star; stellar. Also, before vowels, **sider-.** [< L *sidus* star]

sid·er·o·lite (sid′ər-ə-līt′) *n.* A meteorite consisting of iron containing embedded grains of certain minerals.

side·sad·dle (sīd′sad′l) *n.* A woman's saddle having one stirrup and designed so that both legs of the rider are on the same side of the horse. — *adv.* On or as on a sidesaddle.

side show **1.** A small show incidental to but connected with a larger or more important one: a circus *side show.* **2.** Any subordinate issue or attraction.

side·slip (sīd′slip′) *v.i.* **·slipped, ·slip·ping** To slip or skid sideways. — *n.* **1.** A lateral skid. **2.** *Aeron.* A downward, sideways slipping of an airplane along the lateral axis.

side·split·ting (sīd′split′ing) *adj.* **1.** Hearty and uproarious, as laughter. **2.** Causing great laughter or hilarity.

side·step (sīd′step′) *v.* **·stepped, ·step·ping** *v.i.* **1.** To step to one side. **2.** To avoid responsibility, conflict, etc. — *v.t.* **3.** To avoid, as an issue, or postpone, as a decision; evade.

side step **1.** A step to one side, as of a pugilist. **2.** *Usu. pl.* One of a series of steps at the side of a building, etc.

side·swipe (sīd′swīp′) *n.* A sweeping blow along the side. — *v.t. & v.i.* **·swiped, ·swip·ing** To strike or collide with such a blow.

side·track (sīd′trak′) *v.t. & v.i.* **1.** To move to a siding, as a railroad train. **2.** To divert or distract from the main issue or subject. — *n.* A railroad siding; also, a branch line.

side·walk (sīd′wôk′) *n. U.S.* A path or pavement at the side of the street, for the use of pedestrians.

side·ward (sīd′wərd) *adj.* Directed or moving toward or from the side; lateral. — *adv.* Toward or from the side; laterally: also **side′wards** (-wərdz).

side·ways (sīd′wāz′) *adv.* **1.** From the side. **2.** So as to incline toward the side, or with the side forward: Hold it *sideways.* **3.** Toward one side; obliquely. — *adj.* Moving to or from one side. Also **side′way′, side′wise′** (-wīz′).

side wheel A wheel at the side; esp., one of two paddle wheels on either side of a steamboat. — **side-wheel** (sīd′hwēl′) *adj.* — **side′-wheel′er** *n.*

sid·ing (sī′ding) *n.* **1.** A railway track by the side of a main track. **2.** The boarding that covers the side of a wooden house, etc.

si·dle (sīd′l) *v.i.* **·dled, ·dling** To move sideways, esp. in a cautious or stealthy manner. — *n.* A sideways movement. [Back formation < obs. *sidling* sidelong] — **si′dler** *n.*

siege (sēj) *n.* **1.** The act of surrounding any fortified area with the intention of capturing it. **2.** A steady attempt to win something. **3.** The time during which one undergoes a protracted illness or difficulty. — **to lay siege to** To attempt to capture or gain; besiege. — *v.t.* **sieged, sieg·ing** To lay siege to. [< OF < L < *sedere* to sit]

Sieg·fried (sēg′frēd, *Ger.* zēkh′frēt) The hero of the *Nibelungenlied* and several other Germanic legends.

si·en·na (sē-en′ə) *n.* **1.** A brownish yellow clay containing oxides of iron and manganese, used as a pigment. **2.** The brownish yellow color of this pigment. [< Ital. (*terra di*) *Siena* (earth of) Siena]

si·er·ra (sē-er′ə) *n.* A mountain range or chain, esp. one having a jagged outline. [< Sp. < L *serra* saw]

si·es·ta (sē-es′tə) *n.* A midday or afternoon nap. [< Sp. < L *sexta* (*hora*) sixth (hour), noon]

sieve (siv) *n.* A utensil for straining or sifting, consisting of a frame with a bottom of wire mesh, etc. — *v.t. & v.i.* **sieved, siev·ing** To pass through a sieve. [OE *sife* sieve]

sift (sift) *v.t.* **1.** To pass through a sieve in order to separate the fine parts from the coarse. **2.** To scatter as by a sieve. **3.** To examine carefully. **4.** To separate; distinguish: to *sift* fact from fiction. — *v.i.* **5.** To use a sieve. **6.** To fall through or as through a sieve. [OE *siftan*] — **sift′er** *n.*

sigh (sī) *v.i.* **1.** To draw in and exhale a deep, audible bre[...] as in expressing sorrow, weariness, etc. **2.** To make a so[...] suggestive of a sigh, as the wind. **3.** To yearn; long. — **4.** To express with a sigh. — *n.* The act or sound of sigh[...] [Back formation < ME *sighte* < OE *sīcan* to sigh]

sight (sīt) *n.* **1.** The act or fact of seeing. **2.** That whi[...] seen; a view. **3.** *pl.* Things worth seeing: the *sights* o[...] town. **4.** The faculty of seeing; vision. **5.** The rang[...] scope of vision. **6.** A device to assist aim, as on a gun, **7.** An aim or observation taken with a telescope or o[...] sighting instrument. **8.** *Informal* Something unusu[...] ugly to look at: He was a *sight.* **9.** *Dial.* A great quantit[...] number: a *sight* of people. — **at** (or **on**) **sight** As soo[...] seen. — **not by a long sight** **1.** Never; not at all. **2.** nearly. — **sight unseen** Without ever having seen th[...] ject in question. — *v.t.* **1.** To perceive with the eyes; serve. **2.** To take a sight of. **3.** To furnish with sight[...] adjust the sights of, as a gun. — *v.i.* **4.** To take aim. To make an observation or sight. [OE *gesiht*]

sight draft A draft or bill payable on presentation.

sight·less (sīt′lis) *adj.* **1.** Lacking sight; blind. **2.** In[...] ble. — **sight′less·ly** *adv.* — **sight′less·ness** *n.*

sight·ly (sīt′lē) *adj.* **·li·er, ·li·est** **1.** Pleasant to the v[...] comely. **2.** Affording a fine view. — **sight′li·ness** *n.*

sight·see·ing (sīt′sē′ing) *n.* The visiting of places of in[...] est. — **sight·seer** (sīt′sē′ər) *n.*

sig·ma (sig′mə) *n.* The 18th letter in the Greek alpha[...] written Σ (capital), σ (small initial or medial), or ς (s[...] final), and corresponding to English s in *so.* See ALPHA[...]

sig·moid (sig′moid) *adj.* Shaped like the Greek capital[...] ter sigma (Σ), or like the letter S. Also **sig·moi·dal** (-moid′l). [< Gk. *sigmoeidēs*]

sign (sīn) *n.* **1.** A motion or action indicating a thought, sire, command, etc. **2.** A board, placard, etc., gene[...] bearing an inscription conveying information of some k[...] a street *sign*; an advertising *sign.* **3.** Any arbitrary m[...] symbol, or token used to indicate a word, etc., or havin[...] own specific meaning: a *sign* of mourning. **4.** Any in[...] tion, trace, or evidence: *signs* of poverty. **5.** A vest[...] trace. **6.** Any omen or miraculous occurrence. **7.** On[...] the twelve equal divisions of the zodiac. — *v.t.* **1.** To w[...] one's signature or initials on. **2.** *Law* To acknowledg[...] instrument by affixing a mark or seal to. **3.** To mark or [...] secrate with a sign, esp. with a cross. **4.** To engage by [...] taining the signature of a contract; also, to hire (one[...] out for work: often with *on.* **5.** To dispose of or transfe[...] tle to by signature: with *off, over,* or *away.* **6.** To expres[...] indicate with a sign. — *v.i.* **7.** To make signs or sig[...] **8.** To write one's signature or initials. — **to sign off** T[...] *com.* To announce the close of a program from a broad[...] ing station and stop transmission. — **to sign up** To en[...] as in a military service. [< OF < L *signum*] — **sign′e[...]**

sig·nal (sig′nəl) *n.* **1.** A sign or means of communica[...] agreed upon or understood, and used to convey informa[...] a command, etc. **2.** *Telecom.* An electromagnetic imp[...] that transmits information, whether direct or in code. Anything that incites to action or movement. **4.** In s[...] card games, a lead or play that conveys certain informa[...] to one's partner. — *adj.* **1.** Notable; conspicuous. **2.** [...] to signal. — *v.* **sig·naled** or **·nalled, sig·nal·ing** or **·nal** *v.t.* **1.** To make signals to. **2.** To communicate by sig[...] — *v.i.* **3.** To make a signal or signals. [< F < L *sign[...] sign*] — **sig′nal·er** or **sig′nal·ler** *n.*

Signal Corps A branch of the U.S. Army responsible [...] communications equipment and systems, photography, [...] tronic reconnaissance devices, and related matters.

sig·nal·ize (sig′nəl-īz) *v.t.* **·ized, ·iz·ing** **1.** To render n[...] worthy. **2.** To point out with care.

sig·nal·ly (sig′nəl-ē) *adv.* In a signal manner; eminen[...]

sig·nal·man (sig′nəl-mən) *n. pl.* **·men** (-mən) One [...] makes or interprets signals, esp. railroad signals.

sig·na·to·ry (sig′nə-tôr′ē, -tō′rē) *adj.* Bound by the te[...] of a signed document; having signed: *signatory* powers. *n.* One who has signed or is bound by a document; es[...] nation so bound. [< L *signum* sign]

sig·na·ture (sig′nə-chər) *n.* **1.** The name of a person w[...] ten by himself; also, the act of signing one's name. **2.** A tinctive mark, characteristic, etc. **3.** *Printing* **a** A dis[...] guishing mark, letter, or number on the first page of e[...] form or sheet of a book, as a guide to the binder. **b** The f[...] or sheet on which this mark is placed. **c** A large printed s[...] that, when folded, forms four, or a multiple of four, page[...] a book. **4.** *Music* A symbol or group of symbols at the [...] ginning of a staff, indicating meter or key. **5.** *Telecom.* musical number or sound effect that introduces or clos[...] program. [< F < Med.L < L *signum* sign]

sign·board (sīn′bôrd′, -bōrd′) *n.* A board on which a s[...] direction, or advertisement is displayed.

sig·net (sig′nit) *n.* **1.** A seal, esp. one used to authenti[...] documents, etc. **2.** An impression made by or as by a s[...] [< F *signe* sign < L *signum*]

net ring A seal ring.

·nif·i·cance (sig·nif′ə·kəns) *n.* **1.** The character or state being significant. **2.** Meaning. **3.** Importance; consequence. Also **sig·nif′i·can·cy.**

·nif·i·cant (sig·nif′ə·kənt) *adj.* **1.** Having or expressing meaning; bearing or embodying a meaning. **2.** Conveying having some covert meaning: a *significant* look. **3.** Important; weighty; momentous. [< L < *signum* sign + *fa-re* to do, make] — **sig·nif′i·cant·ly** *adv.*

·ni·fi·ca·tion (sig′nə·fə·kā′shən) *n.* **1.** Meaning; sense; ·port. **2.** The act of signifying; communication. — **sig·**
·fi·ca·tive (sig·nif′ə·kā′tiv, -kə·tiv) *adj.*

·ni·fy (sig′nə·fī) *v.* **·fied, ·fy·ing** *v.t.* **1.** To make known ∙ signs or words; express. **2.** To betoken in any way; import. **3.** To amount to; mean. — *v.i.* **4.** To have some eaning or importance; matter. — **sig′ni·fi′er** *n.*

n language A system of communication by means of ∙ns, largely manual.

ːnor (sēn′yôr) *n.* An anglicized form of the Italian title ∙*nore.* Also **si′gnior.**

ːno·ra (sē·nyō′rä) *n. pl.* **·re** (-rā) *Italian* The Italian ∙le of courtesy for a married woman, equivalent to *Mrs.*

ːno·re (sē·nyō′rē) *n. pl.* **·ri** (-rē) The Italian title of ·urtesy for a man, equivalent to *Mr., sir.*

ːno·ri·na (sē′nyō·rē′nä) *n. pl.* **·ne** (-nā) The Italian title ∙ courtesy for an unmarried woman, equivalent to *Miss.*

·n·post (sīn′pōst′) *n.* **1.** A post bearing a sign. **2.** Any ∙n, clue, or indication.

·urd (sig′ōōrd) In German mythology, a hero who corresponds to Siegfried, the hero of the *Nibelungenlied.*

·h (sēk) *n.* One of a religious and military sect founded in ·dia early in the 16th century. — *adj.* Of or pertaining to ∙ Sikhs. [< Hind., lit., disciple] — **Sikh′ism** *n.*

·age (sī′lij) *n.* Ensilage. [< ENSILAGE]

·ence (sī′ləns) *n.* **1.** The state or quality of being silent. ∙ Absence of sound or noise; stillness. **3.** A failure to men-·n or take note of something. — *v.t.* **·lenced, ·lenc·ing** **1.** ∙ make silent. **2.** To stop the motion or activity of. **3.** ∙ force (guns, etc.) to cease firing, as by bombing, etc. — ·erj. Be silent. [< F < L *silere* to be silent]

·enc·er (sī′lən·sər) *n.* **1.** A tubular device attached to the ∙uzzle of a firearm to reduce the sound of the report. **2.** ·iefly *Brit.* A muffler (def. 1). **3.** One who or that which ·ences.

·ent (sī′lənt) *adj.* **1.** Not making any sound or noise; ·iseless; still; mute. **2.** Not given to speech; taciturn. **3.** ·aking no mention or allusion. **4.** Unspoken or unuttered: ·ent grief. **5.** Free from activity, motion, or disturbance: ∙lm; quiet: a *silent* retreat. [< L *silere* to be silent] — **si′·**
·t·ly *adv.* — **si′lent·ness** *n.*

·ent butler A small receptacle with a handle and hinged ∙, used for collecting refuse from ashtrays, etc.

·ent partner One who has invested money in a business ∙t does not participate in its management or its affairs.

·ex (sī′leks) *n.* **1.** Silica. **2.** Glass that is resistant to ∙at. [< L, flint]

·lex (sī′leks) *n.* A coffee maker: a trade name. Also **si′lex.**

·hou·ette (sil′ōō·et′) *n.* A profile drawing or portrait ·ving its outline filled in with uniform color, commonly ·ack, and often cut out of paper, etc. **2.** The figure cast by ∙ shadow; also, the outline of a solid figure. — *v.t.* **·et·ted,** **·ting** To cause to appear in silhouette; outline; make a ·houette profile of. [after Étienne de *Silhouette,* 1709–67, ·ench minister of finance]

·c- Var. of SILICO-.

·i·ca (sil′i·kə) *n.* A white or colorless, very hard, crystal-·e silicon dioxide, SiO₂, the principal constituent of quartz ∙d sand: also called *silex.* [< NL < L *silex, silicis* flint]

·cate (sil′i·kit) *n. Chem.* A salt or ester of silicic acid.

·ceous (si·lish′əs) *adj.* **1.** Pertaining to, resembling, or ·ntaining silica. **2.** Growing or living on soil rich in silica. ∙so **si·li′cious.** [< L *silex, silicis* flint]

·ic·ic (si·lis′ik) *adj.* Of, pertaining to, or derived from ·ica or silicon. [< SILIC- + -IC]

·cic acid *Chem.* Any of several gelatinous and easily de·mposed compounds of silica and water; esp., H₄SiO₄, asso-·ted in the formation of many metallic silicates.

·co- *combining form* Silicon; of, related to, or containing ·icon. Also, before vowels, **silic-.** [< L *silex, silicis* flint]

·i·con (sil′ə·kən, -kon) *n.* A widely distributed nonme-·llic element (symbol Si) prepared as a dull brown amor-·ous powder, or as shining metallic scales, or as a steel-gray ·ystalline mass. See ELEMENT. [< L *silex, silicis* flint]

·i·cone (sil′ə·kōn) *n. Chem.* Any of various compounds ·ntaining a silicon-carbon bond, used as lubricants, insula-∙g resins, waterproofing materials, etc. [< SILICON]

·i·co·sis (sil′ə·kō′sis) *n. Pathol.* A pulmonary disease ·used by the inhalation of finely powdered silica or quartz.

---

silk (silk) *n.* **1.** The creamy-white or yellowish, very fine natural fiber produced by the larvae of silkworms. **2.** A similar filamentous material spun by other insects. **3.** Cloth, thread, or garments made of silk. **4.** Anything resembling silk. — **to hit the silk** *Slang* To descend from an aircraft by parachute. — *adj.* **1.** Consisting of silk. **2.** Resembling silk. **3.** Of or pertaining to silk. — *v.t.* **1.** To clothe or cover with silk. — *v.i.* **2.** To produce the portion of the flower called silk: said of corn. [OE < L *sericus* silken]

silk cotton The silky seed covering of various tropical American trees; esp., kapok fiber.

silk·en (sil′kən) *adj.* **1.** Made of silk. **2.** Like silk; glossy; delicate; smooth. **3.** Dressed in silk. **4.** Luxurious.

silk hat A high cylindrical hat covered with fine silk plush, worn by men in dress clothes.

silk-screen process (silk′skrēn′) A stencil process that prints designs by forcing ink through the open meshes of a silk screen.

silk-stock·ing (silk′stok′ing) *adj.* **1.** Wearing silk stockings. **2.** Wealthy; luxurious. — *n.* One who wears silk stockings; a member of the wealthy class.

silk·worm (silk′wûrm′) *n.* The caterpillar of certain moths that spin a dense silken cocoon; esp., the **common silkworm,** yielding commercial silk.

silk·y (sil′kē) *adj.* **silk·i·er, silk·i·est** **1.** Made of or resembling silk; soft; lustrous. **2.** Long and fine, as hairs, or covered with such hairs, as leaves. **3.** Gentle or insinuating in manner. — **silk′i·ly** *adv.* — **silk′i·ness** *n.*

sill (sil) *n.* **1.** *Archit.* A horizontal, lower member of something, as the bottom of a door or window casing. **2.** A timber in the frame of the floor of a railroad car: end *sill.* [OE *syll*]

sil·ly (sil′ē) *adj.* **·li·er, ·li·est** **1.** Destitute of ordinary good sense; foolish. **2.** Stupid; absurd. **3.** *Informal* Stunned, as by a blow. — *n. pl.* **·lies** *Informal* A silly person. [OE *sǣsig* happy] — **sil′li·ly** *adv.* — **sil′li·ness** *n.*

si·lo (sī′lō) *n. pl.* **·los** A pit or tower in which fodder, grain, or other food is stored green to be fermented and used as feed for cattle, etc. — *v.t.* **·loed, ·lo·ing** To put or preserve in a silo; turn into ensilage. [< Sp. < L < Gk. *siros* pit for corn]

silt (silt) *n.* An earthy sediment consisting of fine particles of rock and soil suspended in and carried by water. — *v.i.* **1.** To become filled or choked with silt: usu. with *up.* **2.** To ooze; drift. — *v.i.* **3.** To fill or choke with silt or mud: usually with *up.* [ME *cylte*] — **silt′y** *adj.*

Si·lu·ri·an (si·lŏor′ē·ən, sī-) *adj. Geol.* Of the period or rock system of the Paleozoic era. See chart for GEOLOGY. — *n. Geol.* The Silurian period or system.

sil·ver (sil′vər) *n.* **1.** A white, ductile, and very malleable metallic element (symbol Ag) of high electric conductivity, found native as well as in combination, and used in medicine, industry, and the arts: also called *argentum.* See ELE-MENT. **2.** Silver regarded as a commodity or as a standard of currency. **3.** Silver coin; cash or change; money in general. **4.** Articles for domestic use made of silver or silver plate; silverware. **5.** A lustrous, pale gray color resembling that of silver. — *adj.* **1.** Made of or coated with silver. **2.** Of, containing, or producing silver. **3.** Having a silvery lustre. **4.** Having the soft, clear tones of a silver bell. **5.** Persuasive; eloquent. **6.** White or hoary, as the hair. **7.** Favoring the use of silver as a monetary standard. — *v.t.* **1.** To coat or plate with silver or with a silver-like substance. **2.** To make silvery. — *v.i.* **3.** To become silvery or white. [OE *seolfor*] — **sil′ver·er** *n.*

silver anniversary A 25th anniversary.

silver certificate *U.S.* Paper currency representing one dollar in silver bullion on deposit in the U.S. treasury, and valid as full legal tender.

sil·ver·fish (sil′vər·fish′) *n. pl.* **·fish** or **·fish·es** **1.** A silvery-white variety of the goldfish. **2.** Any of numerous flat-bodied, wingless insects that damage books, papers, etc.

silver fox A color phase of the red fox of North America, having fur that is interspersed with white-tipped hairs. **2.** The fur of this animal.

silver gray A light, slightly bluish gray, the color of silver.

silver nitrate *Chem.* A crystalline, poisonous compound, AgNO₃, obtained by treating silver with nitric acid, widely used in industry, photography, and medicine.

silver plate Articles, as table utensils, made of silver or metal plated with silver.

sil·ver·smith (sil′vər·smith′) *n.* A worker in silver; a maker of silverware.

silver standard A monetary standard or system based on silver.

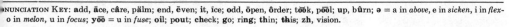

SILO
(Showing interior and pit)

Silver Star A U.S. military decoration, first issued in 1932, awarded for gallantry in action. See DECORATION.

Silver State Nickname of Nevada.

sil·ver-tongued (sil′vər-tungd′) *adj.* Eloquent.

sil·ver·ware (sil′vər-wâr′) *n.* Articles, esp., for table use, made of silver.

sil·ver·y (sil′vər-ē) *adj.* **1.** Containing or adorned with silver. **2.** Resembling silver, as in luster or hue. **3.** Soft and clear in sound. **— sil′ver·i·ness** *n.*

s'il vous plait (sēl vōō plė′) *French* If you please; please.

Sim·chath To·rah (sim′khäs tō′rə) A Jewish holiday; literally, the rejoicing over the Law. Also **Sim′hath To′rah.**

Sim·e·on (sim′ē·ən) In the Old Testament, a son of Jacob and Leah. *Gen.* xxix 33. **—** *n.* The tribe of Israel descended from him.

sim·i·an (sim′ē·ən) *adj.* Pertaining to, resembling, or characteristic of apes and monkeys. **—** *n.* An ape or monkey. [< L *simia* ape]

sim·i·lar (sim′ə·lər) *adj.* **1.** Bearing resemblance to one another or to something else; like, but not completely identical. **2.** Of like characteristics, nature, or degree; of the same scope, order, or purpose. **3.** *Geom.* Shaped alike, as figures that may become congruent by the alteration of linear dimensions, the angles remaining unchanged. [< F < L *similis* like] **— sim′i·lar·ly** adv.

sim·i·lar·i·ty (sim′ə·lar′ə·tē) *n. pl.* **·ties 1.** The quality or state of being similar. **2.** The point in which the objects compared are similar. **3.** *pl.* Things that coincide with or resemble each other. **— Syn.** See ANALOGY.

sim·i·le (sim′ə·lē) *n.* A figure of speech expressing comparison or likeness by the use of such terms as *like, as, so,* etc.: distinguished from *metaphor.* [< L, neut. of *similis* similar] **— Syn.** Simile is a literary device to conjure up a vivid picture; "an Alpine peak like a frosted cake" is a *simile.* A *metaphor* omits "like" or "as", the words of comparison; "the silver pepper of the stars" is a *metaphor.* A *comparison* brings together things of the same kind or class.

si·mil·i·tude (si·mil′ə·tōod, -tyōod) *n.* **1.** Similarity. **2.** A counterpart or likeness. [< OF < L *similis* like]

sim·mer (sim′ər) *v.i.* **1.** To boil gently or with a subdued sound; be or stay at or just below the boiling point. **2.** To be on the point of breaking forth, as with rage. **—** *v.t.* **3.** To keep at or just below the boiling point. **— to simmer down 1.** To reduce liquid content by boiling gently. **2.** *Informal* To subside from a state of anger or excitement. **—** *n.* The state or process of simmering. [< obs. *simper* to boil]

Si·mon Le·gree (si′mən li·grē′) **1.** A cruel overseer of slaves in Harriet Beecher Stowe's *Uncle Tom's Cabin.* **2.** Any brutal master.

Simon Peter See PETER.

si·mon-pure (si′mən·pyōor′) *adj.* Real; genuine; authentic. [after *Simon Pure,* a character in the comedy *A Bold Stroke for a Wife* (1718), who is impersonated by a rival]

si·mo·ny (si′mə·nē, sim′ə-) *n.* Traffic in sacred things; the purchase or sale of ecclesiastical preferment. [< Med.L < *Simon (Magus),* who offered Peter money for the gift of the Holy Spirit] **— si′mon·ist** *n.*

si·moom (si·mōom′, si-) *n. Meteorol.* A hot dry wind of the desert in northern Africa, Arabia, etc. Also **si·moon′** (-mōon′). [< Arabic < *samma* poison]

sim·per (sim′pər) *v.i.* **1.** To smile in a silly, self-conscious manner; smirk. **—** *v.t.* **2.** To say with a simper. **—** *n.* A silly, self-conscious smile. [< Scand. Cf. Sw. and Norw. *semper* coy.] **— sim′per·er** *n.* **— sim′per·ing·ly** *adv.*

sim·ple (sim′pəl) *adj.* **·pler, ·plest 1.** Consisting of one thing; single; uncombined. **2.** Not complex or complicated; easy. **3.** Without embellishment; plain; unadorned. **4.** Free from affectation; sincere; artless. **5.** Of humble rank; lowly. **6.** Silly; feeble-minded. **7.** Insignificant; trifling. **8.** Lacking luxury; frugal. **9.** Having nothing added; mere. **10.** *Chem.* Of one element; also, unmixed. **11.** *Bot.* Not divided; entire. **—** *n.* **1.** That which is simple; an uncomplex, or natural thing. **2.** A simpleton. [< OF < L *simplex*]

simple fraction *Math.* A fraction in which both numerator and denominator are integers.

simple interest Interest computed on the original principal alone.

simple machine Any of certain elementary mechanical contrivances, as the lever, the wedge, the inclined plane, the screw, the wheel and axle, and the pulley.

sim·ple-mind·ed (sim′pəl·mīn′did) *adj.* **1.** Artless or unsophisticated. **2.** Mentally defective. **3.** Stupid; foolish. **— sim′ple-mind′ed·ly** *adv.* **— sim′ple-mind′ed·ness** *n.*

simple sentence See under SENTENCE.

sim·ple·ton (sim′pəl·tən) *n.* A weak-minded or silly person.

simplici- *combining form* Simple. Also, before vowels, **simplic-.** [< L *simplex, simplicis* simple]

sim·plic·i·ty (sim·plis′ə·tē) *n. pl.* **·ties 1.** The state of being simple; freedom from admixture, ostentation, subtlety, difficulty, etc. **2.** Sincerity; unaffectedness. **3.** Lack of intelligence or good sense. [< OF < L *simplicitas*]

sim·pli·fy (sim′plə·fī) *v.t.* **·fied, ·fy·ing** To make more s[imple] ple or less complex. [< F < Med.L < L *simplex* simple *facere* to make] **— sim′pli·fi·ca′tion** *n.* **— sim′pli·fi′er** [

sim·plis·tic (sim·plis′tik) *adj.* Tending to ignore com[plications] cations or details. **— sim′plism** *n.* **— sim·plis′ti·cal·ly** [

sim·ply (sim′plē) *adv.* **1.** In a simple manner; intelligi[bly] **2.** Without ostentation or extravagance. **3.** Without s[ub]tlety or affectation; unassumingly. **4.** Merely. **5.** With [a] sense or discretion; foolishly. **6.** Really; absolutely: *sim[ply]* charming: sometimes used ironically.

sim·u·la·crum (sim′yə·lā′krəm) *n. pl.* **·cra** (-krə) **1.** [An] image. **2.** An imaginary, visionary, or shadowy semblan[ce] **3.** A sham. [See SIMULATE.]

sim·u·late (*v.* sim′yə·lāt; *for adj., also* -lit) *v.t.* **·lat·ed,** **·** **ing 1.** To have the appearance or form of, without the re[ali]ty; counterfeit; imitate. **2.** To make a pretense of. **—** Pretended. [< L < *similis* like] **— sim′u·la′tor** *n.*

sim·u·la·tion (sim′yə·lā′shən) *n.* **1.** The act of simulati[ng] counterfeit; sham. **2.** The taking on of a particular asp[ect] or form. **— sim′u·la′tive, sim′u·la·to′ry** (-lə·tôr′ē, -tō *adj.* **— sim′u·la·tive·ly** *adv.*

si·mul·cast (si′məl·kast′, -käst′) *v.t.* **·cast, ·cast·ing** broadcast by radio and television simultaneously. **—** *n.* [A] broadcast transmitted by radio and television simultaneo[usly] ly. [< SIMUL(TANEOUS) + (BROAD)CAST]

si·mul·ta·ne·ous (si′məl·tā′nē·əs, sim′əl-) *adj.* Occurri[ng] done, or existing at the same time. [< LL < L *simul* at same time] **— si′mul·ta′ne·ous·ly** *adv.* **— si′mul·ta′ne·o[us]ness, si′mul·ta·ne′i·ty** (-tə·nē′ə·tē) *n.*

sin (sin) *n.* **1.** A transgression, esp., when deliberate, [of a] law having divine authority. **2.** A particular instance [of] such transgression. **3.** Any offense against a standard [of] literary *sin.* **—** *v.* sinned, sin·ning *v.i.* **1.** To commit [a] transgress the divine law. **2.** To violate any requiremen[t of] right, duty, etc.; do wrong. **—** *v.t.* **3.** To commit or wrongfully. [OE *synn*]

Si·nai (si′nī, -nē·i′), **Mount** The mountain where Moses [re]ceived the law from God. *Ex.* xix.

since (sins) *adv.* **1.** From a past time, mentioned or refer[red] to, up to the present. **2.** At some time between a cert[ain] past time or event and the present. **3.** In time before [the] present; ago; before now. **—** *prep.* **1.** During or within [the] time after or later than: *since* you left. **2.** Continuou[sly] throughout the time after: *since* noon. **—** *conj.* **1.** Du[ring] or within the time after which. **2.** Continuously from [the] time when. **3.** Because of or following upon the fact th[at] inasmuch as. [ME < OE *siththan* afterwards]

sin·cere (sin·sir′) *adj.* **1.** Being in reality as it is in app[ear]ance; genuine. **2.** Free from hypocrisy; honest. [< L] *sin-* without + stem of *caries* decay] **— sin·cere′ly** *adv.*

sin·cer·i·ty (sin·ser′ə·tē) *n. pl.* **·ties** The state or qualit[y of] being sincere; honesty of purpose or character; freedom f[rom] hypocrisy, deceit, or simulation. Also **sin·cere′ness.**

sine[1] (sin) *n. Trig.* In a right triangle, a function of an ac[ute] angle, equal to the ratio of the side opposite the angle to [the] hypotenuse. [< L *sinus* a bend]

si·ne[2] (si′nē) *prep. Latin* Without.

si·ne·cure (si′nə·kyōor, sin′ə-) *n.* **1.** An office or posit[ion] for which recompense is received, but involving few or no [du]ties. **2.** *Eccl.* A benefice without cure of souls. [< L] without + *cura* care] **— si′ne·cur·ism** *n.* **— si′ne·cur·is**[t]

si·ne di·e (si′nē dī′ē) *Latin* Without setting a day for re[as]sembling; literally, without a day.

si·ne qua non (si′nē kwā non′) *Latin* That which is in[dis]pensable; an essential; literally, without which not.

sin·ew (sin′yōo) *n.* **1.** A tendon or similar fibrous cord. [2.] Strength, or that which supplies strength. **—** *v.t.* strengthen or knit together. [OE *seono*] **— sin′ew·less**

sin·ew·y (sin′yōo·ē) *adj.* **1.** Characteristic or consistin[g of] a sinew or sinews. **2.** Well supplied with sinews; str[ong] brawny. **3.** Forceful; vigorous: a *sinewy* style.

sin·ful (sin′fəl) *adj.* Characterized by, suggestive of, [or] tainted with sin; wicked; immoral. [OE *synfull*] **— sin**[′ful·] ly *adv.* **— sin′ful·ness** *n.*

sing (sing) *v.* sang *or* (*less commonly*) sung, sung, sing[ing] *v.i.* **1.** To produce word sounds that differ from speec[h in] that vowels are lengthened and pitches are clearly defin[ed] **2.** To use the voice in this manner for musical renditi[on or] performance. **3.** To produce melodious sounds, as a b[ird or] teakettle. **5.** To buzz or hum; ring. **6.** To be suitable [for] singing. **7.** To relate something in verse. **—** *v.t.* **8.** To [pro]duce (a tone or tones) with the voice. **9.** To render (a so[ng,] etc.) by singing. **10.** To chant, intone, or utter in a song[like] manner. **11.** To bring to a specified condition by sing[ing:] *Sing* me to sleep. **12.** To relate in or as in song; accla[im:] they *sing* his fame. **— to sing out** *Informal* To call loudly; shout. **—** *n.* **1.** A humming sound, as of a bulle[t in] flight. **2.** *Informal* A gathering for general participatio[n in] singing. [OE *singan*] **— sing′a·ble** *adj.*

singe (sinj) *v.t.* singed, singe·ing **1.** To burn slightly or [su]

-ficially; scorch. **2.** To remove bristles or feathers from passing through flame. **3.** To burn the ends of (hair, ...). — *n.* **1.** The act of singeing, esp. as performed by a -ber. **2.** A superficial burn; scorch. [OE *sengan* to -rch, hiss, causative of *singan* to sing]

-er (sing'ər) *n.* **1.** One who sings, esp. as a profession. That which produces a songlike utterance, as a songbird. **-er²** (sin'jər) *n.* One who or that which singes.

gha·lese (sing'gə·lēz', -lēs') *adj.* Of or pertaining to ylon, to a people constituting the majority of the inhabi- ts of Ceylon, or to their language. — *n.* **1.** One of the ghalese people. **2.** The Indic language of the Singhalese. o *Sinhalese*. [< Skt. *Siṅhala* Ceylon]

gle (sing'gəl) *adj.* **1.** Consisting of one only; individual. Having no companion or assistant; alone. **3.** Unmarried. Pertaining to the unmarried state. **5.** Consisting of only part. **6.** Unswerving in purpose, intention, etc.; sincere. Designed for use by only one person or individual: a *single* l. **8.** Engaged in by individuals in opposition to one ther: *single* combat. — *n.* **1.** One who or that which is gle; a unit. **2.** In baseball, a base hit that enables the ter to reach first base. **3.** A hotel room for one person. A golf match between two players only: opposed to *four-* ue. **5.** In cricket, a hit that scores one run. **6.** *pl.* In ten- , a game having one player on each side. — *v.* **·gled**, ng *v.t.* **1.** To choose or select (one) from others: usu. with — *v.i.* **2.** To single-foot. **3.** In baseball, to make a -base hit. [< OF < L *singulus*] — **sin'gle·ness** *n.*

gle bed A bed wide enough for one person.

gle-breast·ed (sing'gəl·bres'tid) *adj.* Having only one ckness of cloth over the breast and fastening in front with ngle set of buttons, loops, etc., as a coat or jacket.

gle file A line of people, animals, etc., disposed one ind the other, with no two abreast.

gle-hand·ed (sing'gəl·han'did) *adj.* **1.** Having no as- ance; unaided. **2.** Having or using but one hand. **3.** pable of being used with a single hand. **4.** Having only workman. — **sin'gle-hand'ed·ly** *adv.*

gle-heart·ed (sing'gəl·här'tid) *adj.* Sincere; straight- ward; loyal. — **sin'gle-heart'ed·ly** *adv.*

gle-mind·ed (sing'gəl·mīn'did) *adj.* **1.** Having but one pose or aim. **2.** Free from duplicity; sincere. — **sin'gle-mind'ed·ly** *adv.* — **sin'gle-mind'ed·ness** *n.*

gle-phase (sin'gəl·fāz') *adj. Electr.* Designating an alter- ing-current circuit having one phase at any given instant.

gle-stick (sing'gəl·stik') *n.* **1.** A cudgel. **2.** A stick h a basket-shaped hilt, used in fencing. **3.** The art or ctice of fencing with singlesticks.

gle tax A tax to be obtained from a single source, esp. m a levy on land and natural resources, as a substitute for other forms of taxation.

gle·ton (sing'gəl·tən) *n.* **1.** In a hand of cards dealt to player, a single card of a suit. **2.** Any single thing or in- idual, as distinguished from a pair or larger group.

gle·tree (sing'gəl·trē') *n.* A whiffletree.

gly (sing'glē) *adv.* **1.** Without companions or associates; ided, as an individual. **2.** One by one; one at a time.

·song (sing'sông', -song') *n.* **1.** Monotonous cadence peaking or reading. **2.** Inferior verse; doggerel. — *adj.* notonous; droning, as verse, speech, etc.

gu·lar (sing'gyə·lər) *adj.* **1.** Extraordinary; remarkable; ommon. **2.** Odd; peculiar; not customary or usual. **3.** resenting the only one of its type; unique. **4.** *Gram.* Of esignating a word form that denotes one person or thing, class considered as a unit: distinguished from *dual, plu-* — *n. Gram.* The singular number, or a singular word n. [< OF < L < *singulus* single] — **sin'gu·lar'i·ty** r'ə·tē) *n.* — **sin'gu·lar·ly** *adv.* — **sin'gu·lar·ness** *n.*

gu·lar·ize (sing'gyə·lə·rīz') *v.t.* **·ized**, **·iz·ing** To make lesignate as singular.

ha·lese (sin'hə·lēz', -lēs') *adj. & n.* Singhalese.

is·ter (sin'is·tər) *adj.* **1.** Underhandedly or suspiciously ng or wicked. **2.** Malevolent; evil. **3.** Boding, tending ard, or attended with disaster; unlucky: often with *to. Heraldry* Being on the wearer's left, and hence on the erver's right: opposed to *dexter.* [< F < L *sinister* left] **sin'is·ter·ly** *adv.* — **sin'is·ter·ness** *n.*

is·tral (sin'is·trəl) *adj.* **1.** Of, pertaining to, or turned ard the left. **2.** Left-handed. — **sin'is·tral·ly** *adv.*

is·trorse (sin'is·trôrs, sin'is·trôrs') *adj. Bot.* Twining rally toward the left, as certain climbing plants: opposed *dextrorse.* Also **sin'is·tror'sal.** [< L, ult. < *sinister* left *versum* turned] — **sin'is·tror'sal·ly** *adv.*

**** (singk) *v.* **sank** or (*less commonly*) **sunk**, **sunk** (*Obs.* **k·en**), **sink·ing** *v.i.* **1.** To go beneath the surface or to bottom, as of a liquid. **2.** To descend to a lower level; go vn, esp. slowly or by degrees. **3.** To descend toward or ow the horizon, as the sun. **4.** To incline downward;

slope, as land. **5.** To pass into a specified state: to *sink* into a coma. **6.** To fail, as from ill health or lack of strength; ap- proach death. **7.** To become less in force, volume, or de- gree: His voice *sank* to a whisper. **8.** To become less in value, price, etc. **9.** To decline in moral level, prestige, wealth, etc. **10.** To permeate: The oil *sank* into the wood. **11.** To become hollow; cave in, as the cheeks. **12.** To be impressed or fixed, as in the mind: with *in.* — *v.t.* **13.** To cause to go beneath the surface or to the bottom. **14.** To cause to fall or drop; lower. **15.** To force or drive into place: to *sink* a fence post. **16.** To make (a mine shaft, well, etc.) by digging or excavating. **17.** To reduce in force, vol- ume, or degree. **18.** To debase or degrade, as one's charac- ter or honor. **19.** To suppress, hide, or omit. **20.** To de- feat; ruin. **21.** To invest. **22.** To invest and subsequently lose. — *n.* **1.** A box-shaped or basinlike porcelain or metal receptacle with a drainpipe and usu. with a water supply. **2.** A cesspool, etc. **3.** A place where corruption and vice gather or are rampant. **4.** A natural pool, marsh, or basin in which a river terminates by evaporation or percolation. [OE *sincan*] — **sink'a·ble** *adj.*

sink·er (singk'ər) *n.* **1.** One who or that which sinks, or causes to sink. **2.** A weight for sinking a fishing line.

sink·hole (singk'hōl') *n.* A natural cavity, esp. a drainage cavity, as a hole worn by water through a rock along a joint.

sinking fund A fund established and invested so that its gradual accumulations will wipe out a debt.

sin·less (sin'lis) *adj.* Having no sin; guiltless; innocent. — **sin'less·ly** *adv.* — **sin'less·ness** *n.*

sin·ner (sin'ər) *n.* One who has sinned; esp., one who has transgressed against religious laws or moral principles.

Sinn Fein (shin fān) An Irish political society that originat- ed about 1905, having as its aims both independence and the cultural development of the Irish people. [< Irish, we our- selves] — **Sinn Fein'er** — **Sinn Fein'ism**

Sino- *combining form* Chinese; of or pertaining to the Chi- nese people, language, etc. Compare CHINO-. [< LL *Sinae* the Chinese]

Si·no-Ti·bet·an (sī'nō·ti·bet'n) *n.* A putative family of lan- guages spoken over a wide area in central and SE Asia, com- prising the two established subfamilies Sino-Thai (sī'nō·tī') and **Tibeto-Burman**: also called *Indochinese.* — *adj.* Of these languages or the people who speak them.

sin·ter (sin'tər) *n. Metall.* Metal particles made cohesive by sintering. — *v.t. & v.i. Metall.* To make or become co- hesive by the combined action of heat and pressure. [< G, dross of iron]

sin·u·ate (*adj.* sin'yōō·it, -āt; *v.* sin'yōō·āt) *adj.* **1.** Winding in and out; sinuous. **2.** *Bot.* Having a wavy or undulating margin, as a leaf. Also **sin'u·at'ed.** — *v.i.* **·at·ed**, **·at·ing** To curve in and out; wind. [< L *sinuatus*, pp. of *sinuare* to turn, wind] — **sin'u·ate·ly** *adv.* — **sin'u·a'tion** *n.*

sin·u·ous (sin'yōō·əs) *adj.* **1.** Characterized by bends, curves, or folds; winding; undulating. **2.** *Bot.* Sinuate. **3.** Devious; erring. [< L *sinus* bend] — **sin'u·os'i·ty** (-os'ə- tē) *n.* — **sin'u·ous·ly** *adv.* — **sin'u·ous·ness** *n.*

si·nus (sī'nəs) *n.* **1.** A recess formed by a bending or fold- ing; an opening or cavity. **2.** *Anat.* **a** Any of the air-filled cavities in the cranial bones, communicating with the nos- trils. **b** A channel or receptacle for venous blood. **c** A dilated part of a blood vessel. **3.** *Pathol.* Any narrow opening lead- ing to an abscess. **4.** *Bot.* A recess or rounded curve between two projecting lobes or teeth of a leaf. [< L]

si·nu·si·tis (sī'nə·sī'tis) *n. Pathol.* Inflammation of a sinus or sinuses, esp. in the cranial bones.

-sion Var. of -TION.

Si·on (sī'ən) See ZION.

Siou·an (sōō'ən) *n.* A large family of North American In- dian languages formerly spoken from the west banks of the Mississippi to the Rocky Mountains. — *adj.* Of or pertain- ing to this family of languages.

Sioux (sōō) *n., pl.* **Sioux** One of a group of North American Indian tribes formerly occupying the Dakotas and parts of Minnesota and Nebraska: also called *Dakota.*

sip (sip) *v.* **sipped**, **sip·ping** *v.t.* **1.** To drink by swallowing small quantities at a time. **2.** To drink from by sips. **3.** To imbibe. — *v.i.* **4.** To drink in sips. — *n.* **1.** A small amount of liquid swallowed at one time. **2.** The act of sip- ping. [ME < OE *sypian* to absorb] — **sip'per** *n.*

si·phon (sī'fən) *n.* **1.** A bent or flexible tube through which liquids may be passed from a higher to a lower level over an intervening elevation by making use of atmospheric pres- sure. **2.** A siphon bottle. **3.** *Zool.* A tubular structure in certain aquatic animals, as the squid, for drawing in or ex- pelling liquids: for illus. see SQUID. — *v.t.* **1.** To draw off or cause to pass through or as through a siphon. — *v.i.* **2.** To pass through a siphon. Also spelled *syphon.* [< F < L < Gk. *siphon*] — **si'phon·al** *adj.*

siphon bottle   A bottle containing aerated or carbonated water that can be expelled by pressure on a valve through a bent tube in the neck of the bottle.

sir (sûr)   *n.* The conventional term of respectful address to men, used absolutely, and not followed by a proper name. [< SIRE]

Sir (sûr)   *n.* A title of baronets and knights, used before the Christian name or the full name.

sire (sīr)   *n.* **1.** A father; begetter: sometimes used in combination: *grandsire.* **2.** The male parent of a mammal. **3.** A form of address to a superior, now used in addressing a king or sovereign. — *v.t.* **sired, sir·ing** To beget: now used chiefly of domestic animals. [< OF < L *senior* older]

si·ren (sī′rən)   *n.* **1.** In Greek legend, one of a group of nymphs living on an island, who lured sailors to destruction by their sweet singing. **2.** A fascinating, dangerous woman. **3.** An acoustical device having a perforated rotating disk or disks through which sharp puffs of steam or compressed air are permitted to escape so as to produce a continued musical note or a loud whistle, often used as a warning signal. **4.** *Zool.* Any of a family of eellike amphibians, as the mud eel. — *adj.* **1.** Of or pertaining to a siren. **2.** Alluring; dangerously fascinating. [< OF < L < Gk. *seirēn*]

Sir·i·us (sir′ē·əs)   The brightest star, −1.58 magnitude; Alpha in the constellation Canis Major: also called *Dog Star.* [< Gk. *seirios* hot, scorching]

sir·loin (sûr′loin)   *n.* A loin of beef, esp. the upper portion. [< OF < *sur-* over, above + *longe* loin]

si·roc·co (si·rok′ō)   *n. pl.* **·cos** *Meteorol.* **1.** A hot, dry, and dusty southerly wind blowing from the African coast to Italy, Sicily, and Spain. **2.** A warm, sultry wind blowing from a warm region toward a center of low barometric pressure. [< Ital. < Arabic *sharq* the east, the rising sun]

sir·rah (sir′ə)   *n. Archaic* Fellow; sir: a term of address expressing contempt or annoyance. [Var. of SIR]

sir·up (sir′əp)   See SYRUP.

sis (sis)   *n. Informal* Sister.

si·sal (sī′səl, sis′əl, sis′əl, sē′səl)   *n.* **1.** A strong fiber obtained from the leaves of an agave of the West Indies. **2.** The plant yielding this fiber. Also **sisal grass, sisal hemp.** [after *Sisal*, town in Yucatán, Mexico]

sis·si·fied (sis′i·fīd)   *adj. U.S. Informal* Effeminate.

sis·sy (sis′ē)   *n. pl.* **·sies** *U.S. Informal* **1.** An effeminate man or boy; a milksop. **2.** A coward or weakling. [< SIS] — **sis′sy·ish** *adj.*

sis·ter (sis′tər)   *n.* **1.** A female having the same parents as another or others of either sex. **2.** Something characterized as female, and closely associated with another of the same kind. **3.** A member of a sisterhood; a nun. **4.** *Brit.* A head nurse in the ward of a hospital; also, popularly, any nurse. — *adj.* Bearing the relationship of a sister or one suggestive of sisterhood. [OE *sweostor*]

sis·ter-ger·man (sis′tər·jûr′mən)   *n. pl.* **sis·ters-ger·man** A full sister.

sis·ter·hood (sis′tər·hŏŏd)   *n.* **1.** The relationship of or state of being sisters, esp. by blood. **2.** A body of women or girls united by some bond of fellowship or sympathy. **3.** A community of women bound by monastic vows or pledged to works of mercy and faith.

sis·ter-in-law (sis′tər·in·lô′)   *n. pl.* **sis·ters-in-law 1.** A sister of a husband or wife. **2.** A brother's wife. **3.** The wife of a wife's or husband's brother.

sis·ter·ly (sis′tər·lē)   *adj.* Pertaining to or characteristic of a sister. — *adv.* As a sister. — **sis′ter·li·ness** *n.*

Sis·y·phus (sis′ə·fəs)   In Greek mythology, a crafty, greedy king of Corinth, condemned in Hades forever to roll uphill a huge stone that always rolled down again.

sit (sit)   *v.* **sat** (*Archaic* **sate**), **sat, sit·ting** *v.i.* **1.** To rest with the buttocks on a supporting surface, with the body bent at the hips, and the spine nearly vertical. **2.** To occupy a chair, bench, etc., in such a position. **3.** To perch or roost, as a bird; also, to cover eggs so as to give warmth for hatching. **4.** To be or remain in a seated or settled position. **5.** To remain passive or inactive, or in a position of idleness or rest. **6.** To assume an attitude or take a position for a special purpose; pose, as for a portrait. **7.** To meet in assembly; hold a session. **8.** To occupy or be entitled to a seat in a deliberative body. **9.** To have or exercise judicial authority. **10.** To fit or be adjusted; suit: That hat *sits* well. **11.** To be suffered or borne, as a burden. **12.** To be situated or located: The wind *sits* in the east. **13.** To baby-sit; serve as company for someone ill, etc. — *v.t.* **14.** To have or keep a seat or a good seat upon: to *sit* a horse. **15.** To seat (oneself, etc.). — **to sit in** (on) *U.S.* To join or take part. — **sit out 1.** To sit or remain quietly till the end of: to *sit out* an entertainment. **2.** To sit aside during: They *sat out* a dance. **3.** To stay longer than. — **to sit tight** *Informal* To wait for the next move. [OE *sittan*]

si·tar (si·tär′)   *n.* An East Indian stringed instrument resembling a guitar. [< Hind. *sitār*]

sit-down strike (sit′doun′)   A strike during which strikers refuse to leave their place of employment until agreemen reached. Also **sit′-down′.**

site (sīt)   *n.* **1.** Place of location. **2.** A plot of ground apart for some specific use. [< F < L *situs* position]

sit-in (sit′in′)   *n.* A demonstration of protest, as by Neg in the southern U.S., in which participants enter and rem seated in a public place, commercial establishment, e from which they are customarily excluded.

sito-   *combining form* Food. [< Gk. *sitos* food]

sit·ter (sit′ər)   *n.* **1.** One who sits. **2.** A baby sitter. **3.** person posing as a model. **4.** A setting hen.

sit·ting (sit′ing)   *adj.* **1.** Being in a seated position. **2.** U for sitting: *sitting* room. — *n.* **1.** The act or position of who sits. **2.** A seat; also, the place of or the right to a s **3.** A single period of remaining seated for a specific purp **4.** A session or term. **5.** A period of hatching. **6.** The n ber of eggs on which a bird sits at one incubation.

sitting duck   *Informal* Any easy target.

sitting room   A parlor; living room.

sit·u·ate (sich′ŏŏ·āt)   *v.t.* **·at·ed, ·at·ing 1.** To fix a site locate. **2.** To place in a certain position or under cer conditions or circumstances. [< Med.L *situatus*, pp *situare* to place]

sit·u·at·ed (sich′ŏŏ·ā′tid)   *adj.* **1.** Having a fixed plac location; placed. **2.** Placed in (usu. specified) circ stances or conditions: He is *well* situated.

sit·u·a·tion (sich′ŏŏ·ā′shən)   *n.* **1.** Condition as modifie determined by surroundings or attendant circumstan status. **2.** A combination of circumstances, often leadin a complication, climax, or crisis. **3.** The place in wl something is situated; locality. **4.** A salaried post of ployment, usu. subordinate. — **sit′u·a′tion·al** *adj.*

Si·va (sē′və, shē′-)   The Hindu god of destruction and re duction, forming with Brahma and Vishnu the Hindu t ity: also *Shiva.* [< Hind. < Skt. *śivás* propitious] — **S** ism *n.* — **Si′va·ist** *n.* — **Si′va·is′tic** *adj.*

Si·van (sē·vän′)   *n.* The ninth month of the Hebrew y See (Hebrew) CALENDAR. Also **Si·wan′** (-vän′-)

six (siks)   *n.* **1.** The sum of five and one: a cardinal num **2.** Any symbol of this number, as 6, vi, VI. **3.** Anyt consisting of or representing six units. — **at sixes and ens 1.** In a state of confusion. **2.** At odds; estranged.

six of one, half-dozen of another   A situation offering no vious choice. — *adj.* Being one more than five. [OE

six·pence (siks′pəns)   *n.* A British silver coin of the valu six pennies, equivalent to half a shilling.

six·pen·ny (siks′pen′ē, -pən·ē)   *adj.* **1.** Worth or sold sixpence. **2.** Paltry; trashy. **3.** Denoting a size of nai

six-shoot·er (siks′shŏŏ′tər)   *n. Informal* A revolver may be fired six times without reloading.

six·teen (siks′tēn′)   *n.* **1.** The sum of fifteen and one: a car dinal number. **2.** Any symbol of this number, as 16, XVI. **3.** Anything consisting of or representing six units. — *adj.* Being one more than fifteen. [OE *sixt* — **six′teenth′** *adv. & n.*

six·teen·mo (siks·tēn′mō)   *adj. & n.* Sextodecimo.

sixteenth note   *Music* A note having one sixteenth time value of a whole note: also, *chiefly Brit.*, *semiquav*

sixth (siksth)   *adj.* **1.** Next after the fifth: the ordinal of **2.** Being one of six equal parts. — *n.* **1.** One of six e parts. **2.** That which follows the fifth. **3.** *Music* **a** Th terval between any tone and another tone five steps fro in a diatonic scale. **b** A tone separated by this interval f any other, considered with reference to that other; esp. sixth above the keynote. — *adv.* In the sixth order, p or rank: also, in formal discourse, **sixth′ly.**

sixth sense   Intuitive perception supposedly indepen of the five senses.

six·ty (siks′tē)   *n. pl.* **·ties 1.** The sum of fifty and te cardinal number. **2.** Any symbol of this number, as 6 LX. **3.** Anything consisting of or representing sixty u — *adj.* Being ten more than fifty. [OE *sixtig*] — **six′t** *adj. & n.*

six·ty-fourth note   (siks′tē·fôrth′, -fôrth′)   *Music* A having one sixty-fourth the time value of a whole note: *chiefly Brit.*, *hemidemisemiquaver.*

siz·a·ble (sī′zə·bəl)   *adj.* Of comparatively large size. **size′a·ble.** — **siz′a·ble·ness** *n.* — **siz′a·bly** *adv.*

size[1] (sīz)   *n.* **1.** Measurement or extent of a thing as pared with some standard. **2.** Comparative magnitu bulk. **3.** One of a series of graded measures, as of shoes, etc. **4.** A standard of measurement; specified q tity. **5.** Mental caliber; character. **6.** *Informal* State o fairs; true situation: That's the *size* of it. — *v.t.* **sized** ing 1. To estimate the size of. **2.** To distribute or cla according to size. **3.** To cut or otherwise shape (an ar to the required size. — **to size up** *Informal* **1.** To estimate, judgment, or opinion of. **2.** To meet spec tions. [< F *assise* to assize]

size[2] (sīz)   *n.* A solution of gelatinous material, usu. casein, wax, or clay, used to glaze paper, coat wall surf

. — *v.t.* sized, siz·ing 1. To treat with size. 2. To
ke plastic, as clay. [< OItal. *sisa* painter's glue]
·d (sīzd) *adj.* Being of a definite or specified size: often
·d in combination: *good-sized.*
·ing (sī'zing) *n.* 1. Size². 2. The process of adding or
plying size to a fabric, surface, etc.
·y (sī'zē) *adj.* siz·i·er, siz·i·est Glutinous. [< SIZE²]
·zle (siz'əl) *v.i.* ·zled, ·zling 1. To burn, fry, quench, etc.,
·h or as with a hissing sound; emit a hissing sound under
· action of heat. 2. To be extremely hot. — *n.* A hissing
·nd as from frying or effervescence. [Imit.]
·y (siz') *n. Informal* Something extremely hot, as a
·mmer day. [< SIZZLE]
·te¹ (skāt) *n.* 1. A device consisting of a metal runner at-
·hed to the sole of a boot or shoe, enabling the wearer to
·le over ice; also, such a runner. 2. A roller skate. — *v.i.*
·t·ed, skat·ing To glide or move over ice or some other
·ooth surface on or as on skates. [< earlier *skates* < Du.
OF escache stilt < Gmc.] — skat'er *n.*
·te² (skāt) *n.* Any of various ray fishes having large pec-
·al fins and a pointed snout. [< ON *skata*]
·dad·dle (ski-dad'l) *Informal v.i.* ·dled, ·dling To flee in
·te. — *n.* Hasty flight. [Origin unknown]
·et (skēt) *n.* A variety of trapshooting in which a succes-
·n of targets simulating the flight of birds are fired at from
·ious angles by the shooter. [Ult. < ON *skjota* to shoot]
·in (skān) *n.* 1. A quantity of yarn, thread, etc., wound
· loose, elongated coil. 2. Something resembling or sug-
·tive of this. 3. A flight of geese, etc. [< OF *escaigne*]
·l·e·ton (skel'ə·tən) *n.* 1. The supporting or protective
·mework of a human or animal body, consisting of the
·es and connective cartilage (endoskeleton) in man and
·vertebrates, or of a hard outer structure (exoskeleton), as
·rustaceans, insects, etc. 2. A sketch or outline, as of a
·tten work. 3. A very thin or emaciated person or ani-
·l. 4. A structure, group, etc., consisting of few parts, re-
·ed numbers, or bare essentials. — **skeleton in the closet**
·cret source of shame or discredit. — *adj.* 1. Consisting
·ely of a framework, outline, or few parts or members. 2.
·embling a skeleton in nature or appearance; meager;
·ciated. [< NL < Gk. *skeleton* (*sōma*) dried (body),
·mmy < *skeletos* dried up] — skel'e·tal *adj.*

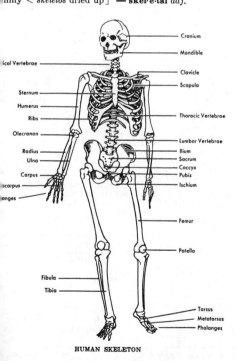

HUMAN SKELETON

Cranium
Mandible
·ical Vertebrae
Clavicle
Scapula
Sternum
Humerus
Ribs
Thoracic Vertebrae
Olecranon
Lumbar Vertebrae
Radius
Ilium
Ulna
Sacrum
Coccyx
Carpus
Pubis
·acarpus
Ischium
·anges
Femur
Patella
Fibula
Tibia
Tarsus
Metatarsus
Phalanges

·eton crew A work crew barely sufficient for the job.
·e·ton·ize (skel'ə·tən·īz') *v.t.* ·ized, ·iz·ing 1. To reduce
· skeleton, framework, or outline by removing soft tissues,

extraneous parts, etc. 2. To reduce greatly in size or numbers. 3. To draft in outline.
skeleton key A key filed to a slender shape, and used to
open a number of different locks.
skep·tic (skep'tik) *n.* 1. One who doubts, disbelieves, or
disagrees with generally accepted ideas. 2. One who by nature doubts or questions what he hears, reads, etc. 3. One
who questions the fundamental doctrines of a religion, esp.
the Christian religion. 4. *Sometimes cap.* An adherent of
any philosophical school of skepticism. Also spelled *sceptic.*
[< F < L < LGk. *skeptikos* reflective]
— **Syn.** *Skeptic* is a general term, and refers to a person who
does not feel that the state of human knowledge, or the evidence
available, is sufficient to establish the doctrine. A *freethinker* is
one who refuses to accept a doctrine, especially a religious doctrine, simply on authority, and demands empiric proof. An *agnostic*
rejects a doctrine because he believes that human knowledge is,
and always will be, incapable of determining its truth or falsity.
Skep·tic (skep'tik) *n.* In ancient Greek philosophy, a member of a school of skepticism. [< SKEPTIC]
skep·ti·cal (skep'ti·kəl) *adj.* 1. Doubting; questioning;
disbelieving. 2. Of, pertaining to, or characteristic of a
skeptic or skepticism. Also spelled *sceptical.* — skep'ti·cal·
ly *adv.* — skep'ti·cal·ness *n.*
skep·ti·cism (skep'tə·siz'əm) *n.* 1. A doubting or incredulous state of mind; disbelieving attitude. 2. *Philos.* The
doctrine that absolute knowledge is unattainable and that
judgments must be continually questioned and doubted.
Also spelled *scepticism.*
sketch (skech) *n.* 1. A rapid, incomplete, or hasty delinea-
tion or presentation, intended to give a general impression of
a work, study, etc., to be completed; an outline. 2. An artist's rough or rapid drawing or study. 3. A short, slight, or
unpretentious literary or dramatic composition. 4. A short
scene, play, or musical act in a revue, musical comedy, etc.
5. *Informal* An amusing person; joker. — *v.t.* 1. To make a
sketch or sketches of; outline. — *v.i.* 2. To make a sketch
or sketches. — **to sketch in** To present or explain (details)
in a rapid summary, way. — **to sketch out** To present or
explain in a rapid, summary way. [< Du. < Ital. < L <
Gk. *schedios* improvisation] — sketch'a·ble *adj.* —
sketch'er *n.*
sketch·book (skech'bŏŏk') *n.* 1. A book of paper used for
sketching. 2. A set or collection of literary sketches. Also
sketch book.
sketch·y (skech'ē) *adj.* sketch·i·er, sketch·i·est 1. Resembling or consisting of a sketch; roughly suggested without
detail. 2. Incomplete. — sketch'i·ly *adv.* — sketch'i·
ness *n.*
skew (skyōō) *v.i.* 1. To take an oblique direction; swerve.
2. To look obliquely or askance; squint. — *v.t.* 3. To give
an oblique position, direction, or form to; make lopsided.
4. To shift or twist the meaning or significance of; distort.
— *adj.* 1. Placed or turned obliquely; twisted to one side;
lopsided. 2. Distorted in effect or meaning. — *n.* A deviation from symmetry or straightness; oblique direction or position. [< AF *eskiuer*, OF *eschiuver* to shun < Gmc.]
skew·er (skyōō'ər) *n.* 1. A long pin of wood, or metal,
thrust into meat to hold it or keep it in shape while roasting
or broiling. 2. Any of various articles of similar shape or
use. — *v.t.* To run through or fasten with or as with a
skewer. [Var. of SKIVER]
ski (skē, *Norw.* shē) *n. pl.* **skis** or **ski** One of a pair of
wooden or metal runners with turned-up points, attached to
the feet and used in sliding over snow, esp. on slopes. — *v.i.*
skied (skēd), **ski·ing** 1. To glide or travel on skis. 2. To
engage in the sport of gliding over snow-covered inclines on
skis. [< Norw. < ON *skith* snowshoe]
skid (skid) *n.* 1. The act of skidding or slipping. 2. A small
frame or platform upon which merchandise is stacked to be
moved about or temporarily stored. 3. One of a pair of timbers used to support a heavy tilting or rolling object, or a log
used as a track in sliding heavy articles about, or forming an
inclined plane to ease their descent. 4. In lumbering, one of
several logs used to make a skid road or skidway. 5. A shoe
or drag on a wagon wheel. 6. *Aeron.* A runner in an airplane's landing gear. — **on the skids** *U.S. Slang* Rapidly
declining in prestige or power. — *v.* **skid·ded, skid·ding** *v.i.*
1. To slide instead of revolving, as a wheel that does not rotate. 2. Of a wheel, vehicle, etc., to slide or slip sideways
because of loss of traction. 3. *Aeron.* To move sideways, because of insufficient banking. — *v.t.* 4. To furnish with
skids; put, drag, or haul on skids. 5. To brake or hold back
with a skid. [? < ON *skith* piece of wood]
skid road A road or track along which logs are hauled.
skid row *U.S. Slang* An urban section inhabited by vagrants and derelicts. [< SKID ROAD]
ski·er (skē'ər) *n.* One who skis.

skiff (skif) *n.* A light rowboat or small, open sailing vessel light enough to be rowed with ease. [< F < Ital. < OHG *scif* ship, boat]

ski·ing (skē′ing) *n.* The act or sport of one who skis.

ski jump 1. A jump or leap made by a person wearing skis. **2.** A course prepared for making such jumps.

ski lift Any of various devices, usu. an endless cable running on towers, with attached bars or chairs, used to transport skiers to the top of a slope or trail.

skill (skil) *n.* **1.** Proficiency or technical ability in any art, science, handicraft, etc. **2.** A specific art, trade, or technique. — **Syn.** See DEXTERITY. [< ON *skil* knowledge]

skilled (skild) *adj.* **1.** Possessing or showing skill; proficient. **2.** Having specialized ability or training, as a worker. **3.** Requiring specialized ability or training, as a job.

skil·let (skil′it) *n.* A frying pan or similar cooking pot having a long handle. [ME *skelet*, ? < OF *esculette* dish]

skill·ful (skil′fəl) *adj.* **1.** Having skill; clever; dexterous; able. **2.** Characterized by or requiring skill. Also *Brit.* **skil′·ful.** — **skill′ful·ly** *adv.* — **skill′ful·ness** *n.*

skim (skim) *v.* **skimmed, skim·ming** *v.t.* **1.** To remove floating matter from the surface of, as with a ladle: to *skim* milk. **2.** To remove thus: to *skim* cream. **3.** To cover with a thin film, as of ice. **4.** To move lightly and quickly across or over. **5.** To cause to pass swiftly and lightly, as a flat stone across a pond. **6.** To read or glance over hastily or superficially. — *v.i.* **7.** To move quickly and lightly across or near a surface; glide. **8.** To make a hasty and superficial perusal; glance: with *over* or *through.* **9.** To become covered with a thin film. — *n.* **1.** The act of skimming. **2.** That which has been skimmed, as skim milk. **3.** A thin film or layer. — *adj.* Skimmed: *skim* milk. [Var. of SCUM]

skim·mer (skim′ər) *n.* **1.** A flat ladle or other utensil for skimming. **2.** One who or that which skims. **3.** A hat having a shallow crown and a wide, round brim.

skim milk Milk from which the cream has been removed.

skimp (skimp) *v.t. & v.i.* To scrimp or scamp. — *adj.* Scant; meager. [Prob. < ON *skemma* to shorten]

skimp·y (skim′pē) *adj.* **skimp·i·er, skimp·i·est 1.** Insufficient in size, amount, etc. **2.** Excessively saving or sparing. — **skimp′i·ly** *adv.* — **skimp′i·ness** *n.*

skin (skin) *n.* **1.** The membranous tissue covering the body of an animal; the integument. ◆ Collateral adjectives: *cutaneous, dermal.* **2.** The pelt of a small animal, removed from its body, whether raw or dressed. **3.** A vessel for holding liquids, made of skin. **4.** An outside layer, coat, or covering as the rind of a fruit, etc. **5.** One's life: to save one's *skin.* — **by the skin of one's teeth** Very closely or narrowly; barely. — **to get under one's skin 1.** To be provoking or irritating. **2.** To be an obsession. — **under the skin** In a close but not apparent figurative relationship: sisters *under the skin.* — *v.* **skinned, skin·ning** *v.t.* **1.** To remove the skin of; flay; peel. **2.** To cover with or as with skin. **3.** To remove or peel off hastily. **4.** *Slang* To cheat or swindle. — *v.i.* **5.** To shed the skin. [< ON *skinn*]

skin-deep (skin′dēp′) *adj.* Superficial. — *adv.* Superficially.

skin-dive (skin′dīv′) *v.i.* **-dived** (*U.S. Informal* **-dove**), **-dived, -div·ing** To engage in skin diving.

skin diving Underwater swimming or exploration in which the swimmer is equipped with goggles and foot fins, and sometimes with a scuba or snorkel. — **skin diver**

skin·flint (skin′flint) *n.* A miser or niggardly person.

skin game 1. A crooked or rigged gambling game in which the players have no chance. **2.** Any swindle.

skink (skingk) *n.* One of a group of lizards having smooth scales and short limbs. [< L < Gk. *skinkos* kind of lizard]

skin·ner (skin′ər) *n.* **1.** One who flays or sells the skins of animals. **2.** *U.S. Slang* A mule driver.

skin·ny (skin′ē) *adj.* **·ni·er, ·ni·est 1.** Very thin or emaciated; lean. **2.** Consisting of or resembling skin. — **skin′ni·ness** *n.*

skin·tight (skin′tīt′) *adj.* Fitting tightly to the skin.

skip (skip) *v.* **skipped, skip·ping** *v.i.* **1.** To move with light springing steps; caper. **2.** To bounce over, ricochet from, or skim a surface. **3.** To pass from one point to another omitting or not noticing what lies between. **4.** *Informal* To leave or depart hurriedly; flee. **5.** To be advanced in school beyond the next grade in order. — *v.t.* **6.** To leap lightly over. **7.** To cause to skim or ricochet. **8.** To pass over or by; omit. **9.** *Informal* To leave (a place) hurriedly. — *n.* **1.** A light bound or hop. **2.** A passing over without notice. [Prob. < Scand. Cf. Sw. *skuppa* to skip.]

ski pants Long trousers that fit snugly, esp. at the ankles, worn for skiing, etc.

skip·jack (skip′jak′) *n.* Any of various fishes that leap from or skip along the surface of the water, as the bonito.

skip·per¹ (skip′ər) *n.* **1.** One who or that which skips. **2.** Any of a family of small butterflies.

skip·per² (skip′ər) *n.* **1.** The captain of a ship. **2.** One in a position of leadership. [< Du. *schip* ship]

skirl (skûrl, skirl) *Scot. v.i.* To produce a shrill sound, a bagpipe. — *n.* A shrill cry or sound. [ME *scrille*]

skir·mish (skûr′mish) *v.i.* To fight in a preliminary or c ultory way. — *n.* **1.** A light engagement, as between sm parties or groups. **2.** Any encounter or action that eva the main contention or business. — **Syn.** See BATTLE. OF *eskermir* to fence, fight] — **skir′mish·er** *n.*

skirt (skûrt) *n.* **1.** The part of a dress, gown, or robe t hangs from the waist downward. **2.** A separate garm hanging from the waist and covering the lower portion of body. **3.** *pl.* The border, fringe, or edge of a particular a on the *skirts* of the town. **4.** One of the flaps or loose, ha ing parts of a saddle. **5.** *Slang* A woman or girl. — *v.t.* To lie along or form the edge of; to border. **2.** To surro or border: with *with.* **3.** To pass around or about. **4.** evade or avoid (a subject, issue, etc.). — *v.i.* **5.** To pass be near the edge or border of something. [ON *skyrt* sh

skit (skit) *n.* **1.** A short, usu. humorous dramatic scen presentation. **2.** A brief, humorous, often satirical piec writing. [< Scand. Cf. ON *skjota* to shoot]

ski tow A type of ski lift consisting of an endless rope.

skit·ter (skit′ər) *v.i.* **1.** To glide or skim along, touchin surface at intervals. — *v.t.* **2.** To cause to skitter. [F of SKITE]

skit·tish (skit′ish) *adj.* **1.** Easily frightened, as a horse. Capricious; uncertain; unreliable. **3.** Tricky; deceitful. dial. E *skit* to caper, as a horse] — **skit′tish·ly** *adv.* — **s tish·ness** *n.*

skit·tle (skit′l) *n.* **1.** *pl.* A game of ninepins, in which a tened ball or thick rounded disk is thrown to knock down pins. **2.** One of the pins used in this game. — **beer skittles** Carefree existence; drink and play. [Prob. < L *skyttel* a child's earthen ball]

skiv·vy (skiv′ē) *n.* *pl.* **·vies** *U.S. Slang* **1.** A man's sh sleeved undershirt. Also **skivvy shirt.** **2.** *pl.* Men's un wear. [Origin uncertain]

skoal (skōl) *interj.* To your good health: a toast in drink used esp. by Scandinavians. [< Scand.]

sku·a (skyoo′ə) *n.* A predatory gull-like bird of northerr gions. [< Faroese *skúgver* < ON *skúfr*]

skul·dug·ger·y (skul-dug′ər-ē) *n.* *U.S.* Trickery; un handedness. [Var. of dial. *sculduddery*; origin uncertai

skulk (skulk) *v.i.* **1.** To move about furtively; lie clos keep hidden. **2.** To shirk; evade work or responsibility. *n.* One who skulks. [< Scand.] — **skulk′er** *n.*

skull (skul) *n.* **1.** The bony framework of the head of a tebrate animal; the cranium. **2.** The head considered as seat of brain; the mind. [< Scand.]

skull and crossbones A representation of the human s over two crossed bones, used as a symbol of death, as a w ing label on poison, and as an emblem of piracy.

skull·cap (skul′kap′) *n.* A small, snug, brimless cap, o worn indoors.

skunk (skungk) *n.* **1.** A carnivorous mammal of N America, usu. black with a white stripe and a bushy tail, ejecting at will a malodorous liquid. **2.** *Informal* A ha or contemptible person. — *v.t. Slang* To defeat utterly game or contest. [< Algonquian *seganku*]

skunk cabbage A perennial plant of the arum family, e ting a strong odor, esp. when crushed or bruised. Also **sk weed** (skungk′wēd′).

sky (skī) *n.* *pl.* **skies 1.** The region of the upper air see a high vault or arch over the earth; the firmament. **2.** *pl.* Atmospheric condition or appearance of the upper cloudy *skies.* **3.** The celestial regions; heaven. — *v.t.* sk **sky·ing** *Informal* To bat or throw (a ball, etc.) high into air. [< ON *sky* cloup]

sky blue A blue like the color of the sky on a clear day. — **sky-blue** (skī′bloo′) *adj.*

sky·div·ing (skī′dī′ving) *n.* The sport of jumping fror airplane and performing various maneuvers and assur various positions before opening the parachute.

Skye terrier (skī) A small terrier having a long body, s legs, and long, straight hair.

sky-high (skī′hī′) *adj. & adv.* Extremely high.

sky·lark (skī′lärk) *n.* A lark of the Old World that sing it rises in flight. — *v.i.* To indulge in hilarious or boiste frolic. — **sky′lark′er** *n.*

sky·light (skī′līt′) *n.* A window in a roof or ceiling, ad ting daylight from above.

sky·line (skī′līn′) *n.* **1.** The visible horizon. **2.** The line of a group of buildings, etc., seen against the sky.

sky pilot *Slang* A clergyman or a chaplain.

sky·rock·et (skī′rok′it) *n.* A rocket, as in a fireworks play, projected so as to explode high in the air. — *v.i* rise rapidly or suddenly.

sky·sail (skī′səl, -sāl′) *n. Naut.* A light sail above the r in a square-rigged vessel.

sky·scrap·er (skī′skrā′pər) *n.* A very high building.

sky·ward (skī′wərd) *adv.* Toward the sky. Also **wards.** — *adj.* Moving or directed toward the sky.

·way (skī′wā′) n. 1. An air travel route. 2. An elevated highway.

·writ·ing (skī′rī′ting) n. 1. The forming of words in the by the release of vapor from an airplane. 2. The words letters thus formed. **— sky′writ′er** n.

· (slab) n. 1. A flat plate, piece, mass, or slice, as of metstone, etc. 2. The outside piece of a log sawed for lum-, often with the bark remaining on it. 3. U.S. Slang In eball, the pitcher's plate. **—** v.t. **slabbed, slab·bing** 1. make or form into slabs. 2. To cover with slabs. 3. To / slabs from, as a log. [ME. Origin uncertain.]

·k¹ (slak) adj. 1. Hanging or extended loosely. 2. ose or careless in performance; remiss; slovenly. 3. Flac-; loose: a slack mouth. 4. Lacking activity; not busy: a ·k season. 5. Listless; limp: a slack grip. 6. Flowing or ·ving sluggishly, as wind, water, etc. **—** v.t. 1. To slack-2. To slake, as lime. **—** v.i. 3. To be or become slack. **to slack off** To slow down; be less diligent. **—** n. 1. A ·t of a rope, sail, etc., that is slack or loose. 2. Slack con-ion; looseness. 3. A period of inactivity. 4. An extent of ter where there is no current. **—** adv. In a slack manner. E sleac] **— slack′ly** adv. **— slack′ness** n.

·k² (slak) n. Screenings or small pieces of coal. [Cf. mish slecke, LG slacke]

·k·en (slak′ən) v.i. 1. To become less active, produc-e, etc. 2. To become less tense or tight. 3. To become w or less intense. **—** v.t. 4. To become slow, negligent, or ·iss in: to slacken one's efforts. 5. To make slack.

·k·er (slak′ər) n. One who shirks his duties or avoids ·itary service in wartime; shirker.

·k-off (slak′ôf′) n. Informal A slowdown; abatement.

·ks (slaks) n.pl. Trousers worn by men or women for ·ual or sports wear.

· (slag) n. 1. Metall. The fused residue separated in the ·uction of metals from their ores. 2. Volcanic lava in all, cinderlike pieces. **—** v.t. & v.i. **slagged, slag·ging** To m into slag. [< MLG slagge] **— slag′gy** adj.

·n (slān) Past participle of SLAY.

·e (slāk) v. **slaked, slak·ing** v.t. 1. To quench or satisfy, ·hirst or an appetite. 2. To lessen the force or intensity 3. To moisten or refresh. 4. To mix with water or ·ist air, as in the preparation of slaked lime. **—** v.i. 5. become disintegrated and hydrated, as lime. [OE sla-·n to retard < sleac slack¹]

·ed lime See under LIME¹.

·lom (slä′ləm, slä′-) n. In skiing, a race or descent over a ·ding downhill course laid out between posts and marked h flags. **—** v.i. To ski in such a course. [< Norw.]

·n¹ (slam) v. **slammed, slam·ming** v.t. 1. To shut or push ·with violence and a loud noise. 2. To put, dash, throw, ·, with violence and a loud noise; bang. 3. Slang To hit ·trike violently. **—** v.i. 5. To close, swing, etc., with force and noise. 6. make a noisy entrance. **—** n. 1. The act or noise of ·nming. 2. Slang Harsh criticism; abuse. [< Scand. Cf. I. Norw. slamra slam.]

·n² (slam) n. In bridge, the winning of all (grand slam) or but one (little or small slam) of the tricks in a round of y; also, a bid to do so. [Origin uncertain]

·n-bang (slam′bang′) adv. Violently; noisily. **—** v.i. move with noise and violence.

·der (slan′dər) n. 1. Law a An oral statement of a ·e, malicious, or defamatory nature, tending to damage ·ther's reputation, means of livelihood, etc. **b** The utter-e of such a statement. 2. A maliciously false tale or re-t. **—** v.t. 1. To injure by maliciously uttering a false re-t. **—** v.i. 2. To utter slander. [< AF < L scandalum ·se of stumbling] **— slan′der·er** n.

·der·ous (slan′dər-əs) adj. 1. Uttering or containing nder. 2. Characterized by slander; calumnious. **— slan′·ous·ly** adv. **— slan′der·ous·ness** n.

·g (slang) n. 1. Language, words, or phrases of a vigor-·, colorful, facetious, or taboo nature, invented for specific ·asions or uses, or derived from the unconventional use of · standard vocabulary. 2. The special vocabulary of a ·tain class, group, or profession: college slang. 3. Former-the argot or jargon of thieves and vagrants. **—** v.t. & v.i. address with or use slang. [Origin uncertain]

·g·y (slang′ē) adj. **slang·i·er, slang·i·est** 1. Like or con-·ing of slang. 2. Using slang. **— slang′i·ly** adv. **—** ·ng′i·ness n.

·t (slant) v.t. 1. To give an oblique or sloping direction ·incline. 2. To write or edit (news or other literary mat-) so as to express a special attitude, bias, or opinion. **—** ·i. 3. To have or take an oblique direction; slope. 4. To ·ve a certain bias or attitude. **— Syn.** See TIP¹. **—** adj. ·ing at an angle; sloping. **—** n. 1. A slanting direction, ·irse, or plane; slope. 2. A bent, bias, or leaning. 3.

Point of view; attitude. [< earlier slent < Scand. Cf. Norw. slenta slope.] **— slant′ing·ly** adv.

slant·wise (slant′wīz′) adj. Slanting; oblique. **—** adv. At a slant or slope; obliquely. Also **slant′ways′** (-wāz′).

slap (slap) n. 1. A blow delivered with the open hand or with something flat. 2. A sharp rebuke; insult; slur. **—** v. **slapped, slap·ping** v.t. 1. To hit or strike with the open hand or with something flat. 2. To rebuff; insult. 3. To put or place violently or carelessly. **—** v.i. 4. To strike or beat as if with slaps. **—** adv. 1. Suddenly and forcibly; abruptly. 2. Informal Directly; straight. [< LG slapp] **— slap′·per** n.

slap·dash (slap′dash′) adj. Done or acting in a dashing or reckless way; impetuous; careless. **—** n. Offhand or care-less work, behavior, etc. **—** adv. In a careless manner.

slap·hap·py (slap′hap′ē) adj. **·pi·er, ·pi·est** Slang 1. Dazed or giddy from or as from repeated blows. 2. Silly; ir-responsible. **— slap′hap′pi·ness** n.

slap·jack slap′jak′) n. U.S. A griddlecake; flapjack.

slap·stick (slap′stick′) n. 1. Boisterous, loud comedy. 2. A flexible paddle formerly used in farces and pantomimes to make a loud report when an actor was struck with it. **—** adj. Using or suggestive of slapstick: slapstick humor.

slash (slash) v.t. 1. To strike or cut violently with or as with an edged instrument. 2. To whip; lash. 3. To make long gashes, cuts, or slits in. 4. To cut slits in, as a garment, so as to expose linings. 5. To criticize severely. 6. To re-duce sharply, as prices, wages, etc. **—** v.i. 7. To make sweeping, violent, or haphazard strokes with or as with something sharp. **—** n. 1. The act or result of slashing. 2. A slit or gash, esp. an ornamental slit in a garment. 3. An opening or gap left in a forest after logging, a destructive fire, or a high wind. 4. Printing A virgule. [? < OF escla-chier to break] **— slash′er** n.

slash·ing (slash′ing) adj. 1. Aggressively or destructively severe; violent. 2. Informal Very fine; splendid. **—** n. A slash. **— slash′ing·ly** adv.

slat (slat) n. A thin, narrow strip of wood or metal, as one of those in a crate, window blind, etc. **—** v.t. **slat·ted, slat·ting** To provide or make with slats. [< OF esclat splinter]

slate (slāt) n. 1. A compact, fine-grained rock that splits readily into thin and even layers. 2. A piece, slab, or plate of slate used for roofing, writing upon, etc. 3. A record of one's past performance or behavior: a clean slate. 4. A pre-arranged list, as of political candidates before their nomina-tion or election. 5. A dull bluish gray color resembling slate. **—** adj. 1. Made of slate. 2. Having the color of slate. **—** v.t. **slat·ed, slat·ing** 1. To roof with slate. 2. To put on a political slate or a list of any sort. 3. To designate or mark, as for a specific change in condition. [< OF esclate, fem. of esclat chip, splinter] **— slat′er** n. **— slat′y** adj.

slath·er (slath′ər) Informal or Dial. v.t. 1. To daub thickly. 2. To spend or use profusely. [Origin uncertain]

slat·tern (slat′ərn) n. An untidy or slovenly woman. **—** adj. Untidy; slovenly. [< dial. E slatter to slop, spill] **— slat′tern·li·ness** n. **— slat′tern·ly** adj. & adv.

slaugh·ter (slô′tər) n. 1. The act of killing; esp. the butch-ering of cattle and other animals for market. 2. Wanton or savage killing, esp. of human beings; massacre; carnage. **— Syn.** See MASSACRE. **—** v.t. 1. To kill for the market; butcher. 2. To kill wantonly or savagely. [< ON slätr butcher's meat] **— slaugh′ter·er** n. **— slaugh′ter·ous** adj. **— slaugh′ter·ous·ly** adv.

slaugh·ter·house (slô′tər·hous′) n. A place where animals are butchered; a scene of carnage.

Slav (släv, slav) n. A member of any of the Slavic-speaking peoples of northern or eastern Europe, comprising the Rus-sians, Poles, Czechs, Moravians, Wends, Slovaks, Bulgari-ans, Serbians, Croats, Slovenes, etc.

slave (slāv) n. 1. A person over whose life, liberty, and property someone has absolute control. 2. A person in men-tal or moral subjection to a habit, vice, or influence. 3. One who labors like a slave; a drudge. **—** v.i. **slaved, slav·ing** To work like a slave. [< F < Med.L slavus, sclavus]

slave driver 1. A person who oversees slaves at work. 2. Any severe or exacting employer.

slave·hold·er (slāv′hōl′dər) n. An owner of slaves. **— slave′hold′ing** adj. & n.

slav·er¹ (slav′ər) v.t. 1. To dribble saliva over. **—** v.i. 2. To dribble saliva; drool. **—** n. Saliva issuing or dribbling from the mouth. [Prob. < ON slafra] **— slav′er·er** n.

slav·er² (slā′vər) n. A person or a vessel engaged in the slave trade.

slav·er·y (slā′vər·ē, slāv′rē) n. 1. The holding of human beings as property or chattels; also, the condition of a slave. 2. Mental, moral, or spiritual bondage. 3. Slavish toil.

slave trade The business of dealing in slaves; esp. the bringing of Negro slaves to America. **— slave trader**

slav·ey (slā′vē, slav′ē) *n.* *pl.* **slav·eys** *Brit. Informal* A female servant, esp. a maid of all work.

Slav·ic (slä′vik, slav′ik) *adj.* Of or pertaining to the Slavs or their languages. — *n.* A branch of the Balto-Slavic sub-family of the Indo-European language family, consisting of the following groups: **East Slavic** (Russian, including Great Russian, Ukrainian, and Byelorussian); **West Slavic** (Czech, Slovak, Polish, Wendish); **South Slavic** (Serbo-Croatian, Bulgarian, Slovenian, Macedonian). — **Church Slavic** or **Church Slavonic** The liturgical language of the Eastern Orthodox Slavs and of certain Uniats: also called *Old Church Slavic, Old Church Slavonic, Old Slavic.*

slav·ish (slā′vish) *adj.* **1.** Pertaining to or befitting a slave; servile; base. **2.** Extremely hard or laborious. **3.** Dependent; imitative. — **slav′ish·ly** *adv.* — **slav′ish·ness** *n.*

Sla·von·ic (slə-von′ik) *adj. & n.* Slavic.

slaw (slô) *n.* Cole slaw.

slay (slā) *v.t.* **slew, slain, slay·ing** To kill, esp. by violence. [OE *slēan*] — **slay′er** *n.*

slea·zy (slē′zē, slā′-) *adj.* **·zi·er, ·zi·est** **1.** Lacking firmness of texture or substance; poorly made. **2.** Cheap; shoddy. [Origin uncertain] — **slea′zi·ly** *adv.* — **slea′zi·ness** *n.*

sled (sled) *n.* **1.** A vehicle on runners, designed for carrying people or loads over snow and ice; a sledge. **2.** A small, light frame mounted on runners, used by children for sliding on snow and ice. — *v.* **sled·ded, sled·ding** *v.t.* **1.** To convey on a sled. — *v.i.* **2.** To ride on a sled. [< MLG *sledde*] — **sled′der** *n.*

sled·ding (sled′ing) *n.* **1.** The condition of roads for sleds. **2.** The act of using a sled. **3.** State or circumstances of progress, work, etc.: hard *sledding.*

sledge¹ (slej) *n.* A vehicle or sled for moving loads over snow and ice. — *v.t. & v.i.* **sledged, sledg·ing** To travel or convey on a sledge. [< MDu. *sleedse*]

sledge² (slej) *n.* A heavy hammer wielded with one or both hands, for blacksmiths' use, or for breaking stone, coal, etc.: also **sledge hammer.** — *v.t.* **sledged, sledg·ing** To hammer, break, or strike with a sledge. [OE *slecg*]

sleek (slēk) *adj.* **1.** Smooth and glossy; polished. **2.** Smooth-spoken; flattering; unctuous. — *v.t.* **1.** To make smooth, even, or glossy. **2.** To soothe; mollify. [Var. of SLICK] — **sleek′ly** *adv.* — **sleek′ness** *n.* — **sleek′y** *adj.*

sleep (slēp) *n.* **1.** A state or period of reduced activity, accompanied by a complete or partial unconsciousness. **2.** A period of slumber. **3.** Any condition of inactivity, torpor, or rest. — *v.* **slept, sleep·ing** *v.i.* **1.** To be or fall asleep; slumber. **2.** To be dormant, inactive or quiet, or to rest in death. — *v.t.* **3.** To rest or repose in: to *sleep* the sleep of the dead. **4.** To provide with sleeping quarters; lodge. — **to sleep away** (or **off** or **out**) To pass or get rid of by or as by sleep: to *sleep off* a hangover. — **to sleep on** To postpone a decision upon. [OE *slǣp*]

sleep·er (slē′pər) *n.* **1.** One who or that which sleeps. **2.** A railroad sleeping car. **3.** *U.S. Informal* A play, motion picture, or book that achieves unexpected and striking success.

sleeping bag A large bag with a warm lining, used for sleeping, esp. out of doors.

sleeping car A passenger railroad car with accommodations for sleeping.

sleeping pill *Med.* A sedative; esp., one of the barbiturates taken to relieve acute or persistent insomnia.

sleeping sickness *Pathol.* The final stage of a disease prevalent in tropical Africa, marked by lethargy, fever and headaches and terminating in death.

sleep·less (slēp′lis) *adj.* Unable to sleep; wakeful; restless; unquiet. — **sleep′less·ly** *adv.* — **sleep′less·ness** *n.*

sleep·walk·ing (slēp′wô′king) *n.* The act or practice of one who walks while asleep. — **sleep′walk′er** *n.*

sleep·y (slē′pē) *adj.* **sleep·i·er, sleep·i·est** **1.** Inclined to sleep. **2.** Drowsy; sluggish; dull; heavy. **3.** Conducive to sleep. — **sleep′i·ly** *adv.* — **sleep′i·ness** *n.*

sleep·y·head (slē′pē-hed′) *n.* A sleepy person. — **sleep′y·head′ed** *adj.*

sleet (slēt) *n.* **1.** A mixture of snow or hail and rain. **2.** A drizzle or shower of partly frozen rain. **3.** A thin coating of ice. — *v.i.* To pour or shed sleet. [Akin to MLG *slōte* hail] — **sleet′y** *adj.*

sleeve (slēv) *n.* **1.** The part of a garment that serves as a covering for the arm. **2.** *Mech.* A tube surrounding something, as a shaft, for protection or connection. — **up one's sleeve** Hidden but at hand. — *v.t.* **sleeved, sleev·ing** To furnish or fit with a sleeve or sleeves. [OE *slīefe*] — **sleeve′less** *adj.*

sleigh (slā) *n.* A light vehicle, usu. drawn by a horse with runners for use on snow and ice. — *v.i.* To ride or travel in a sleigh. [< Du. *slee*, contr. of *slede* sledge] — **sleigh′er** *n.* — **sleigh′ing** *n.*

sleight (slīt) *n.* **1.** The quality of being skillful in manipulation. **2.** Craft; cunning. [< ON *slœgth* slyness]

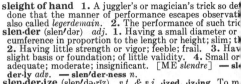

SLEIGH

sleight of hand **1.** A juggler's or magician's trick so deftly done that the manner of performance escapes observation: also called *legerdemain.* **2.** The performance of such tricks.

slen·der (slen′dər) *adj.* **1.** Having a small diameter or circumference in proportion to the length or height; slim; thin. **2.** Having little strength or vigor; feeble; frail. **3.** Having slight basis or foundation; of little validity. **4.** Small or inadequate; moderate; insignificant. [ME *slendre*] — **slen′der·ly** *adv.* — **slen′der·ness** *n.*

slen·der·ize (slen′də-rīz) *v.t. & v.i.* **·ized, ·iz·ing** To make or become slender.

slept (slept) Past tense and past participle of SLEEP.

sleuth (slooth) *n.* **1.** *U.S. Informal* A detective. **2.** A bloodhound. — *v.t.* **1.** To follow; track. — *v.i.* **2.** To play the detective. [< ON *slōth* track, trail]

slew¹ (sloo) Past tense of SLAY.

slew² (sloo) See SLOUGH (def. 2).

slew³ (sloo) *n.* *U.S. Informal* A large number, crowd, or amount; a lot: also spelled *slue.* [Cf. Irish *sluagh* crowd]

slew⁴ (sloo) See SLUE¹.

slice (slīs) *n.* **1.** A thin, broad piece cut off from a larger piece. **2.** Any of various tools or devices having a broad flat blade. **3.** In golf, a stroke that causes the ball to veer to the right. — *v.* **sliced, slic·ing** *v.t.* **1.** To cut or remove from a larger piece: often with *off.* **2.** To cut into broad, thin pieces; divide; apportion. **3.** In golf, to hit (the ball) with a slice. — *v.i.* **4.** In golf, to slice a ball. [< OF < OHG *zan* to slit] — **slic′er** *n.*

slick (slik) *adj.* **1.** Smooth; slippery; sleek. **2.** Flattering; obsequious. **3.** *Informal* Dexterously done; cleverly shrewd. **4.** Smart and clever, but often of little depth. **5.** Smooth; oily, as the surface of water. **6.** Glazed, as paper; printed on glazed paper: *slick* magazines. **7.** *Slang* Agreeable; excellent. — *n.* **1.** A smooth place on a surface, as water, as from oil. **2.** A broad chisel for paring or slicing: also **slick chisel.** **3.** *Usu. pl. U.S.* A magazine printed on glazed paper: distinguished from *pulp.* — *adv.* *Slang* In a slick or smooth manner; deftly. — *v.t.* **1.** To make smooth, trim, glossy, or oily. **2.** *Informal* To trim up; make presentable: often with *up.* [ME *slike*, ? < OE *nigslŷcod* glossy]

slick·er (slik′ər) *n.* **1.** *U.S.* A waterproof overcoat of skin, plastic, etc. **2.** *Informal* A clever, shifty person.

slide (slīd) *v.* **slid** (slid), **slid** or **slid·den** (slid′n), **slid·ing** **1.** To pass along over a surface with a smooth, slipping movement. **2.** To move easily or smoothly; pass gradually or imperceptibly. **3.** To proceed without being acted upon or directed: to let the matter *slide.* **4.** To lose one's equilibrium or foothold; slip. **5.** In baseball, to throw oneself along the ground toward a base. — *v.t.* **6.** To cause to slide over a surface. **7.** To move, put, enter, etc., with quietness or dexterity: with *in* or *into.* — *n.* **1.** An act of sliding. The slipping of a mass of earth, snow, etc., from a higher to a lower level; avalanche. **3.** An inclined plane or chute for sliding, as for children to slide upon. **4.** A small plate of glass on which a specimen is mounted and examined through a microscope. **5.** A small plate bearing a single image for projection on a screen. **6.** *Music* In a trumpet or trombone a U-shaped portion of the tubing that is pushed in and out to vary the pitch. **7.** *Mech.* A sliding part. [OE *slīdan*] — **slid′er** *n.*

slide fastener A zipper.

slide projector An optical device for projecting magnified images from transparent slides onto a wall or screen.

slide rule A device consisting of a rigid ruler with a central sliding piece, both ruler and slide being graduated in a similar logarithmic scale to permit rapid calculations.

sliding door A door that opens and closes by moving sidewise along grooves.

sliding scale A schedule affecting imports, prices, or wages varying under conditions of consumption, demand, or market price of some article.

slight (slīt) *adj.* **1.** Of small importance; trifling. **2.** Small in quantity, intensity, or degree; inconsiderable. **3.** Slender; frail; delicate; flimsy. — *v.t.* **1.** To manifest neglect or disregard for; ignore. **2.** To do imperfectly or thoughtlessly; shirk. **3.** To treat as trivial or insignificant. — *n.* An act or omission involving failure in courtesy or respect toward another. [ME] — **slight′ing** *adj.* — **slight′ing·ly** *adv.* — **slight′ly** *adv.* — **slight′ness** *n.*

sli·ly (slī′lē) See SLYLY.

slim (slim) *adj.* **slim·mer, slim·mest** **1.** Small in thickness in proportion to height or length, as a human figure or a tree. **2.** Insufficient; meager; slight: a *slim* attendance. — *v.t. & v.i.* **slimmed, slim·ming** To make or become thin or thinner. [Du. *slim* bad] — **slim′ly** *adv.* — **slim′ness** *n.*

slime (slīm) *n.* **1.** Any soft, sticky, or dirty substance. **2.** Soft, moist, adhesive mud or earth; muck. **3.** A mucous exudation from the bodies of certain animals, as fishes, snails, and certain plants. — *v.* **slimed, slim·ing** *v.t.* **1.** To smear or cover with or as with slime. **2.** To remove slime from. [OE *slīm*]

·y (slī′mē) *adj.* **slim·i·er, slim·i·est** **1.** Covered or be-bed with slime. **2.** Containing slime. **3.** Slimelike; foul. **lim′i·ly** *adv.* **— slim′i·ness** *n.*

z¹ (sling) *n.* **1.** A strap or pocket usu. with a string at-ed to each end, for hurling a stone or other missile by rling the whole and releasing one of the strings. **2.** Any various ropes, straps, etc., for suspending or hoisting ething, as for holding up an injured limb, carrying a rifle, **3.** The act of slinging; a sudden throw; cast; fling. **— slung, sling·ing** **1.** To fling from or as from a sling; hurl. Γo place or hang up in or as in a sling; move or hoist, as by pe or tackle. [OE *slingan*] **— sling′er** *n.*

z² (sling) *n.* *U.S.* A drink of brandy, whisky, or gin, sugar and nutmeg, lemon juice, and ice.

z·shot (sling′shot′) *n.* A weapon or toy consisting of a ed stick with an elastic strap attached to the prongs for pulting small missiles: also called *catapult.*

ζ (slingk) *v.i.* **slunk, slunk, slink·ing** To creep or steal g furtively or stealthily, as in fear. [OE *slincan* to creep] **link′ing·ly** *adv.*

ζ·y (slingk′ē) *adj.* **slink·i·er, slink·i·est** **1.** Sneaking; lthy. **2.** *Slang* Sinuous or feline in movement or form.

(slip) *v.* **slipped** or **slipt, slip·ping** *v.t.* **1.** To cause to ve smoothly and easily; cause to glide or slide. **2.** To put or off easily, as a loose garment. **3.** To convey slyly or etly. **4.** To free oneself or itself from, as a fetter or bri-**5.** To let loose; unleash, as hounds. **6.** To escape or s unobserved: It *slipped* my mind. **7.** To overlook; omit ligently. **— *v.i.*** **8.** To slide so as to cause harm or incon-ience; lose one's footing; become misplaced by failing to . **9.** To fall into an error or fault; err. **10.** To escape, ship. **11.** To move smoothly and easily. **12.** To get of restraint. **13.** To go or come stealthily or unnoticed: n with *off, away,* or *from.* **— to let slip** To say without nding to. **— to slip one over on** *Informal* To cheat; dwink. **— *n.*** **1.** An act of slipping; a sudden slide. **2.** apse or error in speech, writing, or conduct; a slight ake. **3.** *U.S.* A narrow space between two wharves. **4.** artificial pier sloping down to the water, serving as a ling place. **5.** An inclined plane leading down to the er, on which vessels are repaired or constructed. **6.** A aan's undergarment, usu. the length of a dress. **7.** A w case: also **pillow slip. 8.** A leash that permits quick ase of the dog. **9.** *Geol.* A joint or fissure where two strata have moved upon each other. **— to give (some-) the slip** To elude (someone). [< MLG *slippen*]

(slip) *n.* **1.** A cutting from a plant for planting or 'ting; a cion. **2.** A small, slender person, esp. a youthful **3.** A small piece of something, as of paper or cloth, er long relative to its width; a strip. **4.** A small piece of er for jotting down memoranda, a record, etc. **— *v.t.*** **ped, slip·ping** To cut off for planting; make a slip or slips [< MDu. *slippen* to cut]

cov·er (slip′kuv′ər) *n.* A fitted cloth cover for a chair, , etc., that can be readily removed.

knot (slip′not′) *n.* **1.** A knot having part of the mate-drawn through in a loop so that it is easily untied. For s. see KNOT. **2.** A running knot.

on (slip′on′, -ôn′) *adj.* Easily donned or taken off. **—** A slip-on garment, as a blouse.

o·ver (slip′ō′vər) *adj.* Easily donned by drawing over head: a *slipover* shirt. **— *n.*** A slipover garment.

per (slip′ər) *n.* A low, light shoe that is easily slipped on ff the foot. **— slip′pered** *adj.*

per·y (slip′ər·ē) *adj.* **·per·i·er, ·per·i·est** **1.** Having a so smooth that objects slip or slide easily on it. **2.** t evades one's grasp; tricky; elusive. **3.** Unreliable; un-endable. **— slip′per·i·ly** *adv.* **— slip′per·i·ness** *n.*

pery elm **1.** A tree of eastern North America. **2.** Its ilaginous inner bark, used in medicine.

shod (slip′shod′) *adj.* **1.** Carelessly done or wrought; ligent; slovenly. **2.** Down at the heel; ragged; seedy.

-stream (slip′strēm′) *n.* *Aeron.* The stream of air en backwards by the propeller of an aircraft.

-up (slip′up′) *n.* *Informal* A mistake; error.

(slit) *n.* A cut that is relatively straight and long; also, a , narrow opening. **— *v.t.*** **slit, slit·ting** **1.** To make a incision in; slash. **2.** To cut lengthwise into strips. *E slitten* to cut] **— slit′ter** *n.*

·er (slith′ər) *v.i.* **1.** To slide; slip, as on a surface where ing is insecure. **2.** To glide, as a snake. **— *v.t.*** **3.** To se to slither. [OE *slīdan* to slide] **— slith′er·y** *adj.*

er (sliv′ər) *n.* **1.** A slender piece cut or torn off length-; a splinter. **2.** Corded textile fibers drawn into a fleecy nd. **— *v.t. & v.i.* 3.** To cut or split into long thin pieces. dial. E *slive* to cleave < OE *tōflīfan*] **— sliv′er·er** *n.*

(slob) *n.* **1.** *Informal* A stupid, careless, or unclean per-**2.** *Irish* Mud; mire. [< Irish *slab*]

slob·ber (slob′ər) *v.t.* **1.** To wet and foul with, or as if with, liquids oozing from the mouth. **— *v.i.* 2.** To drivel; slaver. **3.** To talk or act gushingly. **— *n.* 1.** Liquid spilled as from the mouth; slaver. **2.** Gushing, sentimental talk. [Var. of SLABBER] **— slob′ber·er** *n.* **— slob′ber·y** *adj.*

sloe (slō) *n.* **1.** The blackthorn (defs. 1 & 2). **2.** Any of various related plants. [OE *slāh*]

sloe-eyed (slō′īd′) *adj.* Having dark, velvety eyes.

sloe gin A cordial with a gin base, flavored with sloes.

slog (slog) *v.t. & v.i.* **slogged, slog·ging** **1.** To strike hard; slug. **2.** To plod (one's way), as through deep mud. **— *n.*** A heavy blow. [Var. of SLUG] **— slog′ger** *n.*

slo·gan (slō′gən) *n.* **1.** A battle or rallying cry, originally of the Highland clans. **2.** A catchword or motto adopted by a group, as a political party. [< Scottish Gaelic *sluagh* army + *gairm* yell]

sloop (sloop) *n.* *Naut.* A single-masted, fore-and-aft rigged sailing vessel carrying at least one jib, now used principally as a racing vessel. [< Du. *sloep*]

SLOOP

slop (slop) *v.* **slopped, slop·ping** *v.i.* **1.** To splash or move through slush. **— *v.t.* 3.** To cause (a liquid) to spill or splash. **4.** To spill a liquid upon. **— to slop over** **1.** To overflow and splash. **2.** To do or say more than is necessary, be-cause of excess zeal, sentimentality, etc. **— *n.* 1.** Slush; watery mud. **2.** A puddle of liquid that has been slopped. **3.** An unappetizing liquid or watery food. **4.** Refuse liquid. **5.** *pl.* Waste food or swill, used to feed pigs, etc. [ME < OE *-sloppe*]

slope (slōp) *v.* **sloped, slop·ing** *v.i.* **1.** To be inclined from the level or the vertical; slant. **— *v.t.* 2.** To cause to slope. **— Syn.** See TIP. **— *n.* 1.** Any slanting surface or line. **2.** The degree of inclination of a line or surface from the plane of the horizon. [OE *āslūpan* to slip away] **— slop′er** *n.* **slop′ing·ly** *adv.* **— slop′ing·ness** *n.*

slop·py (slop′ē) *adj.* **·pi·er, ·pi·est** **1.** Slushy; splashy; wet. **2.** Watery or pulpy. **3.** Splashed with liquid or slops. **4.** *Informal* Messy; slovenly; untidy. **5.** *Informal* Slipshod; careless. **— slop′pi·ly** *adv.* **— slop′pi·ness** *n.*

slops (slops) *n.pl.* **1.** Articles of clothing, bedding, etc., supplied to sailors on shipboard. **2.** Cheap, ready-made clothes. [ME < OE *-slop*]

slosh (slosh) *v.t.* **1.** To throw about, as a liquid. **— *v.i.* 2.** To splash; flounder: to *slosh* through a pool. **— *n.*** Slush. [Var. of SLUSH] **— slosh′y** *adj.*

slot (slot) *n.* **1.** A long narrow groove or opening; notch or slit: the coin *slot* of a vending machine; the *slot* of a mailbox. **2.** A job opening or a place in a sequence. **— *v.t.* slot·ted, slot·ting** To cut a slot in; groove. [< OF *esclot* the hollow between the breasts]

sloth (slōth, slôth, sloth) *n.* **1.** Disinclination to exertion; habitual indolence; laziness. **2.** A slow-moving, tree-dwell-ing mammal of tropical America. [ME < OE *slǣwth*]

sloth·ful (slōth′fəl, slôth′-, sloth′-) *adj.* Sluggish; lazy; in-dolent. **— sloth′ful·ly** *adv.* **— sloth′ful·ness** *n.*

slot machine A vending machine or gambling machine having a slot in which a coin is dropped to cause operation.

slouch (slouch) *v.i.* **1.** To have a downcast or drooping gait, look, or posture. **2.** To hang or droop in a careless manner, as a hat. **— *v.t.* 3.** To cause to droop or hang down. **— *n.* 1.** A drooping of the head and shoulders caused by depres-tion, fatigue, etc. **2.** A drooping of the brim of a hat. **3.** An awkward, heavy, or incompetent person: usu. in the negative: He's no *slouch* at baseball. [Origin uncertain] **— slouch′y** *adj.* **— slouch′i·ness** *n.*

slough¹ (slou *for defs. 1 & 3;* slōo *for def. 2*) *n.* **1.** A place of deep mud or mire; bog. **2.** A stagnant swamp, backwater, bayou, inlet, or pond in which water backs up: also spelled *slew, slue.* **3.** A state or moral depravity or despair. [OE *slōh*] **— slough′y** *adj.*

slough² (sluf) *n.* **1.** Dead tissue separated and thrown off from the living parts, as in gangrene. **2.** The skin of a ser-pent that has been or is about to be shed. **— *v.t.* 1.** To cast off, as dead from living tissue: with *off.* **2.** To discard; shed, as a habit: with *off.* **— *v.i.* 3.** To be cast off. **4.** To cast off a slough or tissue. [ME *slouh*] **— slough′y** *adj.*

slough of despond (slōo) Deep despair or dejection; des-pondency. [after the *Slough of Despond* in John Bunyan's *Pilgrim's Progress*]

Slo·vak (slō′vak, slō-vak′) *n.* **1.** One of a Slavic people of eastern Czechoslovakia. **2.** The West Slavic language of the Slovaks. **— *adj.*** Of or pertaining to the Slovaks or to their language. Also **Slo·vak·i·an** (slō-vak′ē-ən, -vä′kē-ən). [< Czech *slovák* Slav]

slov·en (sluv′ən) *n.* One who is careless of dress or of clean-liness; one habitually untidy.

Slo·vene (slō′vēn, slō·vēn′) *n.* One of a group of southern Slavs now living in NW Yugoslavia. — *adj.* Of or pertaining to the Slovenes or to their language. [< G *Slovene*]

Slo·ve·ni·an (slō·vē′nē-ən) *adj.* Of or pertaining to Slovenia, its people, or their language. — *n.* The South Slavic language of the Slovenes.

slov·en·ly (sluv′ən-lē) *adj.* **·li·er, ·li·est** **1.** Having the habits of a sloven. **2.** Careless or slipshod in manner of work, etc. — *adv.* In a slovenly manner. — **slov′en·li·ness** *n.*

slow (slō) *adj.* **1.** Having relatively small velocity; not quick in motion, performance, or occurrence. **2.** Behind the standard time: said of a timepiece. **3.** Not precipitate or hasty: *slow* to anger. **4.** Dull or tardy in comprehending; mentally sluggish. **5.** Lacking promptness, spirit, or liveliness. **6.** *Informal* Dull or tedious in character: a *slow* party. **7.** Being in a condition that is not conducive to speed: a *slow* track. **8.** Inactive: Business is *slow* today. — *v.t.* **1.** To make slow or slower: often with *up* or *down*. — *v.i.* **2.** To go or become slow or slower: often with *up* or *down*. — *adv.* In a slow or cautious manner or speed. [OE *slǣw*] — **slow′ly** *adv.* — **slow′ness** *n.*

slow-mo·tion (slō′mō′shən) *adj.* Pertaining to or designating a motion picture filmed at greater than standard speed so that the action appears slow in normal projection.

slow·poke (slō′pōk′) *n.* *Informal* A person who works or moves at an exceedingly slow pace; a laggard.

sludge (sluj) *n.* **1.** Soft, water-soaked mud; mire. **2.** A slush of snow or broken ice. **3.** Muddy or pasty refuse, as that produced by sewage purification. **4.** The sediment in a water tank or boiler. [Earlier *slutch*] — **sludg′y** *adj.*

slue[1] (slōō) *v.* **slued, slu·ing** *v.t.* **1.** To cause to move sideways, as if some portion were pivoted. — *v.i.* **2.** To move sideways. — *n.* The act of sluing around sideways; also, the position of a body that has slued. Also spelled *slew*. [Origin unknown]

slue[2] (slōō) See SLEW[3].

slue[3] (slōō) See SLOUGH[1] (def. 2).

slug[1] (slug) *n.* **1.** A bullet or shot of irregular or oblong shape. **2.** *Printing* **a** A strip of type metal for spacing matter, etc. **b** A metal strip used as a compositor's mark. **3.** Any often counterfeit small chunk of metal; esp., one used as a coin in automatic machines. [Origin uncertain]

slug[2] (slug) *n.* **1.** Any of various mollusks related to the snail, having an elongated body and a rudimentary shell. **2.** The larva of a sawfly or other insect, resembling a slug. **3.** A sluggard. [ME *slugge* sluggard]

slug[3] (slug) *Informal* *n.* **1.** A heavy blow, as with the fist or a baseball bat. **2.** A drink of undiluted liquor. — *v.t.* **slugged, slug·ging** To strike heavily or brutally, as with the fist or a baseball bat. [Origin uncertain] — **slug′ger** *n.*

slug·gard (slug′ərd) *n.* A person habitually lazy or idle; a drone. — *adj.* Lazy; sluggish.

slug·gish (slug′ish) *adj.* **1.** Slow; inactive; torpid. **2.** Habitually idle and lazy. **3.** Not active; slow; stagnant: a *sluggish* season. — **slug′gish·ly** *adv.* — **slug′gish·ness** *n.*

sluice (slōōs) *n.* **1.** An artificial channel for conducting water, equipped with a valve or gate (**sluice gate**) to regulate the flow. **2.** The body of water so channeled. **3.** Any artificial channel, esp. one for excess water. **4.** A trough through which water is run to separate gold ore, to float logs, etc. **5.** That through which anything issues or flows. — *v.* **sluiced, sluic·ing** *v.t.* **1.** To wet, water, or irrigate by or as by means of a sluice. **2.** To wash in or by a sluice. **3.** To draw out or conduct by or through a sluice. **4.** To send (logs) down a sluice. — *v.i.* **5.** To flow out or issue from a sluice. [< OF < L *excludere* to shut out]

slum (slum) *n.* Often *pl.* A squalid, dirty, overcrowded section of a city, marked by poverty and poor living conditions. — *v.t.* **slummed, slum·ming** To visit slums for amusement or curiosity. [< cant, room] — **slum′mer** *n.*

slum·ber (slum′bər) *v.i.* **1.** To sleep, esp. lightly or quietly. **2.** To be inactive; stagnate. — *v.t.* **3.** To spend or pass in sleeping. — *n.* **1.** Sleep. **2.** A state of inactivity or quiescence. [OE *slūma* slumber] — **slum′ber·er** *n.* — **slum′ber·ing·ly** *adv.* — **slum′ber·less** *adj.*

slum·ber·ous (slum′bər-əs) *adj.* **1.** Inducing sleep. **2.** Sleepy; drowsy. **3.** Suggesting or resembling sleep. Also **slum′ber·y, slum·brous** (slum′brəs). — **slum′ber·ous·ly** *adv.* — **slum′ber·ous·ness** *n.*

slum·lord (slum′lôrd′) *n.* *U.S.* A landlord of slum property. [< SLUM + (LAND)LORD]

slump (slump) *v.i.* **1.** To break through a crust and sink. **2.** To slide with perceptible motion down a declivity: said of rock, etc. **3.** To fall or fail suddenly, as in value or quality. **4.** To stand or walk with a stooping posture. — *n.* The act of slumping; a collapsing fall; a failure; a decline.

slung (slung) Past tense and past participle of SLING.

slunk (slungk) Past tense and past participle of SLINK.

slur (slûr) *v.t.* **slurred, slur·ring** **1.** To slight; disparage; depreciate. **2.** To pass over lightly or hurriedly. **3.** To weaken and elide (speech sounds) by hurried articulation.

4. *Music* **a** To sing or play as indicated by the slur. **b** mark with a slur. — *n.* **1.** A disparaging remark or insi... tion. **2.** *Music* **a** A curved line (⌣ or ⌢) indicating that t... so tied are to be sung to the same syllable or performed w... out a break between them. **b** The legato effect indicate... produced by this mark. **3.** A blur. **4.** A slurred artic... tion. [< dial. E, orig., fluid mud]

slush (slush) *n.* **1.** Soft, sloppy material, as melting sno... soft mud. **2.** Grease. **3.** Overly sentimental talk or writ... drivel. [? Scand. origin] — **slush′y** *adj.*

slush fund *U.S.* Money collected or spent for corrupt ... poses, as bribery, etc.

slut (slut) *n.* **1.** A slatternly woman. **2.** A woman of l... character; hussy. **3.** A female dog. [ME *slutte*] — **s**... tish *adj.* — **slut′tish·ly** *adv.* — **slut′tish·ness** *n.*

sly (slī) *adj.* **sli·er** or **sly·er, sli·est** or **sly·est** **1.** Artf... dexterous in doing things secretly; cunning in evading de... tion. **2.** Playfully clever; mischievous. **3.** Meanl... stealthily clever. **4.** Done with or marked by artful secr... a *sly* trick. **5.** Skillful; wise. — **on the sly** In a stea... way; with concealment. [< ON *slǣgr*] — **sly′ness** *n.*

sly·ly (slī′lē) *adv.* In a sly manner: also spelled *slily.*

smack[1] (smak) *n.* **1.** A quick, sharp sound, as of the ... when separated rapidly. **2.** A sounding blow or slap. ... The sound of a blow, esp. with something flat. — *v.t.* &... To give or make a smack, as in tasting, kissing, etc.

smack[2] (smak) *v.i.* **1.** To have a taste or flavor, es... tested by smacking: usu. with *of.* **2.** To have or discl... slight suggestion: with *of.* — *n.* **1.** A suggestive taste ... flavor. **2.** A mere taste; smattering. [OE *smæc* the ta...

smack[3] (smak) *n.* A small, decked or half-decked vess... various rig used chiefly for fishing, esp. one having a we... fish in its hold. [< Du. *smak*]

smack·ing (smak′ing) *adj.* Brisk; lively: a *smacking* br...

small (smôl) *adj.* **1.** Comparatively less in size, quan... extent, etc.; diminutive. **2.** Being of slight moment, we... or importance. **3.** Narrow; ignoble; mean; paltry. **4.** L... ing in the qualities of greatness. **5.** Acting or transac... business in a limited way. **6.** Weak in characteristic pro... ties: said of liquors: *small* beer. **7.** Slender; fine; soft, ... voice. **8.** Of low degree; obscure. **9.** Lacking in pow... strength. — *adv.* **1.** In a low or faint tone. **2.** Into s... pieces. **3.** In a small way; trivially; also, timidly. — *n.* ... A small or slender part: the *small* of the back. **2.** A s... thing or quantity. [OE *smæl*] — **small′ness** *n.*

small arms Firearms of small caliber, as pistols, rifles, ... machine guns.

small capital A capital letter cut slightly larger than ... lower-case letters of a specified type size.

small change Coins of small denomination.

small craft Small boats or vessels collectively.

small fry **1.** Small, young fish. **2.** Young children. ... Small or insignificant people or things.

small hours The early hours of the morning.

small letter A lower-case letter, as *a* in *Ra.*

small-mind·ed (smôl′mīn′did) *adj.* **1.** Having a tri... petty mind. **2.** Narrow; intolerant; ungenerous. — **sm**... **mind′ed·ly** *adv.* — **small′-mind′ed·ness** *n.*

small potatoes *U.S. Informal* Insignificant person ... things.

small·pox (smôl′poks′) *n.* *Pathol.* An acute, highly co... gious virus disease, characterized by inflammatory fever ... the eruption of deep-seated pustules that usu. leave pe... nent scars: also called *variola.*

small talk Unimportant or trivial conversation.

small-time (smôl′tīm′) *adj.* *U.S. Slang* Petty; unim... tant: a *smalltime* hoodlum.

smart (smärt) *v.i.* **1.** To experience a stinging sensa... generally superficial, either bodily or mental. **2.** To ca... stinging sensation. **3.** To experience remorse. **4.** To ... one's feelings hurt. — *v.t.* **5.** To cause to smart. — ... **1.** Quick in thought or action; bright; clever. **2.** Imp... nently witty: often used contemptuously. **3.** Vigorous; ... phatic; severe; brisk. **4.** Causing a smarting sensa... stinging; pungent. **5.** Sharp, as at trade; shrewd. **6.** ... Large; considerable: a *smart* crop of wheat. **7.** Spru... dressed; showy. **8.** Belonging to the stylish classes; fas... able. — *n.* **1.** An acute stinging sensation, as fro... scratch or an irritant. **2.** Any distress; poignant me... suffering. [OE *smeortan*] — **smart′ly** *adv.* — **smart′ne**...

smart al·eck (al′ik) *Informal* A cocky, offensively ... ceited person. — **smart-al·eck·y** (smärt′al′ik-ē) *adj.*

smart·en (smär′tən) *v.t.* **1.** To improve in appeara... make smart: with *up.* **2.** To make more alert or cleve...

smart set Fashionable society.

smart-weed (smärt′wēd′) *n.* Any of several species of ... ly distributed marsh plants whose leaves cause itching...

smash (smash) *v.t.* **1.** To break in many pieces sudde... as by a blow, pressure, or collision. **2.** To flatten; cr... **3.** To dash or fling violently so as to crush or break. **4.** ... strike with a sudden, forceful blow. **5.** To make bankr...

'o destroy, as a theory. **7.** In tennis, etc., to strike (the
) with a hard, swift, overhand stroke. — *v.i.* **8.** To go
krupt; fail, as a business, etc. **9.** To come into violent
tact so as to crush or be crushed; collide. — **to go to
ash** *Informal* To be ruined; fail. — *n.* **1.** An act or
ance of smashing, or the state of being smashed. **2.** Any
ster or sudden breakup: a *smash* in business. **3.** In ten-
etc., a strong overhand shot. **4.** *Informal* Something
laimed by the public: a **smash hit.** [Prob. imit. Cf. Norw.
ska.] — **smash′er** *n.*

sh·ing (smash′ing) *adj.* *Informal* Extremely impres-
; overwhelmingly good: a *smashing* success.

sh·up (smash′up′) *n.* A smash; a disastrous collision.

t·ter (smat′ər) *v.t.* To talk of, dabble in, study, or use
erficially. — *n.* A smattering. [ME *smateren,* ? <
nd.] — **smat′ter·er** *n.*

t·ter·ing (smat′ər·ing) *n.* A superficial knowledge of
ething. — **smat′ter·ing·ly** *adv.*

ar (smir) *v.t.* **1.** To spread, rub, or cover with grease,
, dirt, etc.; bedaub. **2.** To spread or apply in a thick
r or coating: to *smear* grease on an axle. **3.** To defame;
der. **4.** *U.S. Slang* To defeat utterly. — *v.i.* **5.** To be
ecome smeared. — *n.* **1.** A soiled spot; stain. **2.** A
ll quantity of material, as blood, sputum, etc., placed on
icroscope slide for analysis. **3.** A substance to be
ared on something, as a glaze for pottery. **4.** A slander-
attack; defamation. [OE < *smeoru* grease]

ar·y (smir′ē) *adj.* **smear·i·er, smear·i·est** Greasy, vis-
, or staining; also, smeared. — **smear′i·ness** *n.*

ll (smel) *v.* **smelled** or **smelt, smell·ing** *v.t.* **1.** To per-
e by means of the nose and its olfactory nerves. **2.** To
eive the odor of; scent. **3.** To test by odor or smell. **4.**
discover or detect as if by smelling: often with *out.* —
5. To emit an odor or perfume: frequently with *of;* also,
ive indications of, as if by odor: to *smell* of treason. **6.**
oe malodorous. **7.** To use the sense of smell. **8.** To pry;
estigate: with *about.* — *n.* **1.** The special sense by means
which odors are perceived. **2.** The sensation excited
ugh the olfactory nerves. **3.** That which is directly per-
ed by this sense; an odor. **4.** A hint; trace. **5.** An act
melling. [ME *smellen*] — **smell′er** *n.*
- Syn. (noun) **3.** *Smell* often suggests a strong and slightly
easant sensation, and *odor,* a more delicate and pleasing one.
t is always delicate. *Aroma, fragrance,* and *perfume* are
sant. *Stench* and *stink* are sickening and unpleasant.

lling salts Pungent or aromatic salts, or mixtures of
h, often scented, used as stimulants by smelling.

l·ly (smel′ē) *adj.* **·li·er, ·li·est** *Informal* Having an un-
asant smell; malodorous.

lt¹ (smelt) *v.t. Metall.* **1.** To reduce (ores) by fusion in
rnace. **2.** To obtain (a metal) from the ore by a process
uding fusion. — *v.i.* **3.** To melt or fuse, as a metal. [<
u. *smelten* to melt]

lt² (smelt) *n.* *pl.* **smelts** or **smelt** Any of various small
ery food fishes of north Atlantic and Pacific waters. [OE]

lt³ (smelt) Alternative past tense and past participle of
LL.

lt·er (smel′tər) *n.* **1.** One engaged in smelting ore. **2.**
establishment for smelting: also **smelt′er·y.**

lg·en (smij′ən) *n.* *U.S. Informal* A tiny bit or part.

lax (smī′laks) *n.* **1.** Any of various shrubby or herba-
us plants of the lily family, having thorny stems, flowers
mbels, and globular fruit, esp. one yielding sarsaparilla.
A delicate twining greenhouse plant of the lily family,
h greenish flowers. [< L < Gk. *smilax* yew]

le (smil) *n.* **1.** A pleased or amused expression of the
, characterized by a raising up of the corners of the mouth.
A pleasant aspect: the *smile* of spring. **3.** Propitious dis-
ition; favor; blessing: the *smile* of fortune. — *v.* **smiled,**
·ing *v.i.* **1.** To give a smile; wear a cheerful aspect. **2.**
show approval or favor: often with *upon.* — *v.t.* **3.** To
ress by means of a smile. [ME *smilen,* prob. < LG] —
l′er *n.* — **smil′ing·ly** *adv.* — **smil′ing·ness** *n.*
- Syn. (noun) **1.** In a *smile,* the mouth is closed or slightly
ned; in a *grin* it is opened wide, displaying the teeth. A *smile*
gests pleasure, satisfaction, approval, or amity. A *grin* may
ote amusement, triumph, or irony.

rch (smûrch) *v.t.* **1.** To soil, as with grime; smear. **2.**
defame; degrade: to *smirch* a reputation. — *n.* The act
smirching, or the state of being smirched; a smear; a
al stain or defect. [ME < OF *esmorcher* to hurt]

rk (smûrk) *v.i.* **1.** To smile in a silly, self-complacent, or
cted manner. — *n.* An affected or artificial smile. [OE
arcian] — **smirk′er** *n.* — **smirk′ing·ly** *adv.*

te (smīt) *v.* **smote, smit·ten** or **smit** or **smote, smit·ing**
1. To strike (something). **2.** To strike a blow with
mething); cause to strike. **3.** To cut, sever, or break by
ow: usually with *off* or *out.* **4.** To strike with disaster;

afflict. **5.** To affect powerfully with sudden feeling. **6.** To
cause to feel regret or remorse. **7.** To affect as if by a blow:
The thought *smote* him. **8.** To kill by a sudden blow. — *v.i.*
9. To come with sudden force; also, to knock against something. [OE *smītan*] — **smit′er** *n.*

smith (smith) *n.* **1.** One who shapes metals by hammering:
goldsmith, tinsmith. **2.** A blacksmith. [OE]

smith·er·eens (smith′ə·rēnz′) *n.pl.* *Informal* Fragments
produced as by an explosion. Also **smith′ers** (-ərz). [Cf.
dial. E (Irish) *smidirin* fragment]

smith·y (smith′ē) *n.* *pl.* **smith·ies** A blacksmith's
shop; a forge. [< ON *smithja*]

smit·ten (smit′n) Alternative past participle of SMITE. —
adj. **1.** Struck with sudden force; gravely afflicted. **2.** Having the affections suddenly attracted.

smock (smok) *n.* A loose outer garment of light material
worn to protect one's clothes. — *v.t.* **1.** To clothe in a
smock. **2.** To decorate with smocking. [OE *smoc*]

smock·ing (smok′ing) *n.* Needlework in which the material is stitched into very small pleats or gathers, forming
a kind of honeycomb ornamentation.

smog (smog) *n.* A combination of smoke and fog, esp. as
seen in thickly populated industrial and manufacturing
areas. [Blend of SM(OKE) and (F)OG]

smoke (smōk) *n.* **1.** The volatilized products of the combustion of organic substances, as coal, wood, etc., forming a
suspension of carbon particles in a gas. **2.** Anything transient and unsubstantial; a useless or ephemeral result. **3.**
The act of smoking a pipe, cigar, etc. **4.** A period of time
during which one smokes tobacco. **5.** *Informal* A cigarette,
cigar, or pipeful of tobacco. — *v.* **smoked, smok·ing** *v.i.* **1.**
To emit or give out smoke. **2.** To inhale and exhale the
smoke from a pipe, cigarette, etc. — *v.t.* **3.** To inhale and
exhale the smoke of (tobacco, opium, etc.); also, to use (a
pipe, etc.) for this purpose. **4.** To cure (meat, fish, etc.) by
treating with smoke. **5.** To apply smoke to (animals) in
order to drive away: with *out.* **6.** To force out of hiding (a
criminal, etc.) or secrecy (information): with *out.* [OE *smoca*]

smoke·house (smōk′hous′) *n.* A building or closed room
in which meat, fish, hides, etc., are cured by smoke.

smoke·less (smōk′lis) *adj.* Having or emitting little or no
smoke: *smokeless* powder.

smok·er (smō′kər) *n.* **1.** One who or that which smokes. **2.**
A smoking car. **3.** A social gathering of men.

smoke screen A dense cloud of smoke used to prevent
enemy observation of a place, force, or operation. Also
smoke blanket, smoke curtain.

smoke·stack (smōk′stak′) *n.* **1.** An upright pipe, usu. of
sheet or plate iron, through which combustion gases from
a furnace and discharged into the air. **2.** The funnel of a
steamboat or locomotive, or the chimney of a factory, etc.

smoking jacket A short coat worn instead of a regular suit
coat as a lounging jacket.

smok·y (smō′kē) *adj.* **smok·i·er, smok·i·est 1.** Giving forth
smoke. **2.** Mixed with smoke: *smoky* air. **3.** Emitting
smoke improperly and unpleasantly, as from bad draft. **4.**
Discolored with smoke. **5.** Smoke-colored; dark gray. **6.**
Covered with mist. — **smok′i·ly** *adv.* — **smok′i·ness** *n.*

smol·der (smōl′dər) *v.i.* **1.** To burn and smoke with little
smoke and no flame. **2.** To exist in a latent state; to manifest suppressed feeling. — *n.* Smoke. [ME *smoldren*]

smolt (smōlt) *n.* A young salmon on its first descent from
the river to the sea. [? Akin to SMELT²]

smooth (smōōth) *adj.* **1.** Having a surface without irregularities; not rough; continuously even. **2.** Having no impediments or obstructions; easy; free from shocks or jolts.
3. Calm and unruffled; bland; mild. **4.** Flowing melodious-
ly: a *smooth* style. **5.** Suave, as in speech; flattering: often
implying deceit. **6.** Free from hair; beardless. **7.** Without
lumps; having the elements perfectly blended. **8.** Offering
no resistance to a body sliding along its surface; without
friction. — *adv.* Calmly; evenly. — *v.t.* **1.** To make
smooth or even on the surface. **2.** To make easy or less difficult: to *smooth* one's path. **3.** To free from or remove obstructions. **4.** To render less harsh or softer and more flowing. **5.** To soften the worst features of; palliate: usu. with
over. **6.** To make calm; mollify. — *v.i.* **7.** To become
smooth. — **to smooth (someone's) ruffled feathers** To
mollify. — *n.* **1.** The smooth portion or surface of anything. **2.** The act of smoothing. [OE *smōth*] — **smooth′er**
n. — **smooth′ly** *adv.* — **smooth′ness** *n.*

smooth·bore (smōōth′bōr′, -bôr′) *n.* A firearm with an un-
rifled bore. Also **smooth bore.** — **smooth′bored′** *adj.*

smooth breathing In classical Greek: **a** The absence of an
aspirated sound. **b** The symbol (′) indicating this.

smooth·en (smōō′thən) *v.t. & v.i.* To smooth.

smör·gås·bord (smôr′gəs·bôrd, *Sw.* smœr′gôs·bôrd) *n.* **1.**
Scandinavian hors d'oeuvres. **2.** A buffet supper consisting

of such hors d'oeuvres. **3.** A restaurant serving smörgåsbord. Also **smor′gas·bord.** [< Sw.]

smote (smōt) Past tense of SMITE.

smoth·er (smuth′ər) *v.t.* **1.** To prevent the respiration of; suffocate; stifle. **2.** To cover, or cause to smolder, as a fire. **3.** To hide or suppress: to *smother* one's feelings. **4.** To cook in a covered dish or under some other substance. — *v.i.* **5.** To suffocate, as from lack of air, etc. **6.** To be covered without air, as a fire. **7.** To be hidden or suppressed, as wrath. — *n.* **1.** That which smothers, as stifling vapor or dust. **2.** The state of being smothered; suppression. [Earlier *smorther*] — **smoth′er·y** *adj.*

smoul·der (smōl′dər) See SMOLDER.

smudge (smuj) *v.* **smudged, smudg·ing** *v.t.* **1.** To smear; soil. **2.** To protect (from frost, insects, etc.) by a heavy, smoky pall. — *v.i.* **3.** To cause a smudge. **4.** To be smudged. — *n.* **1.** A soiling, as of dry dirt or soot; smear; stain. **2.** A smoky fire or its smoke for driving away insects, preventing frost, etc. [Var. of SMUTCH]

smudg·y (smuj′ē) *adj.* **smudg·i·er, smudg·i·est** Full of or causing smudges. — **smudg′i·ly** *adv.* — **smudg′i·ness** *n.*

smug (smug) *adj.* **smug·ger, smug·gest** **1.** Characterized by a self-satisfied or complacent air. **2.** Trim; spruce. [Cf. LG *smuk* neat] — **smug′ly** *adv.* — **smug′ness** *n.*

smug·gle (smug′əl) *v.* **·gled, ·gling** *v.t.* **1.** To take (goods) into or out of a country without payment of lawful duties. **2.** To bring in illicitly. — *v.i.* **3.** To practice smuggling. [< LG *smuggeln*] — **smug′gler** *n.* — **smug′gling** *n.*

smut (smut) *n.* **1.** The blackening made by soot, smoke, etc. **2.** Obscenity; obscene language. **3.** Any of various fungus diseases of plants, in which the affected parts change into a dusty black powder. **4.** Any of the fungi causing such a disease. — *v.* **smut·ted, smut·ting** *v.t.* **1.** To blacken or stain, as with soot or smoke. **2.** To affect with smut, as growing grain. **3.** To pollute; defame. — *v.i.* **4.** To give off smut. **5.** To be or become stained. [< LG *schmutt* dirt]

smutch (smuch) *v.t.* To smudge; soil. — *n.* A smear; smudge. [Cf. MHG *smutzen* to smear] — **smutch′y** *adj.*

smut·ty (smut′ē) *adj.* **·ti·er, ·ti·est** **1.** Soiled with smut; black; stained. **2.** Affected with smut: *smutty* corn. **3.** Obscene; coarse; indecent. — **smut′ti·ly** *adv.* — **smut′ti·ness** *n.*

snack (snak) *n.* **1.** A slight, hurried meal. **2.** A share of something. [< MDu. *snacken* to bite]

snaf·fle (snaf′əl) *n.* A horse's bit without a curb, jointed in the middle. Also **snaf′fle·bit′** (-bit′). — *v.t.* **·fled, ·fling** To control with a snaffle. [Cf. Du. *snavel* muzzle]

sna·fu (sna-fōō′, sna′fōō) *Slang adj.* In a state of utter confusion. — *v.t.* **·fued, ·fu·ing** To put into confusion. [Acronym for "Situation normal, all fouled up"]

snag (snag) *n.* **1.** A jagged or stumpy knot or protuberance, esp. the stumpy base of a branch. **2.** A broken or projecting tooth. **3.** The trunk of a tree fixed in the bottom of a river, etc., by which boats are sometimes pierced. **4.** Any obstacle or difficulty. — *v.* **snagged, snag·ging** *v.t.* **1.** To injure, destroy, or impede by or as by a snag. **2.** To clear of snags. —*v.i.* **3.** To run upon a snag: said esp. of river craft. [Prob. < Scand.] — **snag′gy** *adj.*

snag·gle·tooth (snag′əl-tōōth′) *n.* *pl.* **·teeth** A tooth that is broken, projecting, or out of alignment with the others. — **snag′gle·toothed′** (-tōōtht′, -tōōthd′) *adj.*

snail (snāl) *n.* **1.** Any of a large class of slow-moving mollusks of aquatic and terrestrial habits and having a spiral shell. **2.** A slow or lazy person. [OE *snægl*]

snail pace A very slow gait or forward movement. Also **snail's pace.** — **snail-paced** (snāl′pāst′) *adj.*

SNAIL

snake (snāk) *n.* **1.** Any of a large order of scaly, legless reptiles with long, slim bodies and tapering tails; some kinds inject venom into the victim through tubular fangs. **2.** A treacherous person. **3.** A flexible, resilient wire used to clean clogged drains, etc. — *v.* **snaked, snak·ing** *v.t.* **1.** To drag by pulling forcibly from one end, as a log. **2.** To pull with jerks. —*v.i.* **3.** To move like a snake. [OE *snaca*]

snake·bite (snāk′bīt′) *n.* **1.** The bite of a snake. **2.** Poisoning caused by the venom of a snake.

snake charmer An entertainer who charms venomous snakes by rhythmic motions of his body and by music.

snake dance **1.** A ceremonial dance of the Hopi Indians of Arizona. **2.** A procession of persons moving in a winding or zigzag line to celebrate an athletic victory, etc.

snake·root (snāk′rōōt′, -rŏŏt′) *n.* **1.** Any of various plants having roots reputed to be effective against snakebite. **2.** The root of any of these plants.

snak·y (snā′kē) *adj.* **snak·i·er, snak·i·est** **1.** Of or like a snake; serpentine; winding. **2.** Insinuating; cunning; treacherous. **3.** Full of snakes. — **snak′i·ly** *adv.* — **snak′i·ness** *n.*

snap (snap) *v.* **snapped, snap·ping** *v.i.* **1.** To make a sharp, quick sound. **2.** To break suddenly with a cracking noise. **3.** To fly off or give way quickly, as when tension is suddenly

---

relaxed. **4.** To make the jaws come suddenly together in an effort to bite: often with *up* or *at.* **5.** To seize or sn suddenly: often with *up* or *at.* **6.** To speak sharply, har or irritably: often with *at.* **7.** To emit, or seem to em spark or flash of light: said of the eyes. **8.** To close, fa etc., with a click. **9.** To move or act with sudden, gestures: He *snapped* to attention. — *v.t.* **10.** To suddenly or eagerly, with or as with the teeth: often wit **11.** To sever with a snapping sound. **12.** To utter, ad or interrupt harshly, abruptly, or irritably. **13.** To cau make a sharp, quick sound: to *snap* one's fingers. **14** close, fasten, etc., with a snapping sound. **15.** To cau move suddenly, neatly, etc. **16.** To photograph w camera. **17.** In football, to put in play. — **to snap** **fingers at** To be unimpressed or unintimidated by. — **snap out of it** *Informal* **1.** To recover quickly, as fr state of depression. **2.** To change one's attitude. — *n.* The act of snapping, or a sharp, quick sound produced **2.** A sudden breaking of anything, or the sound so prod **3.** Any catch, fastener, or other similar device. **4.** A su seizing or effort to seize with or as with the teeth. quick blow of the thumb sprung from the finger or c finger from the thumb. **6.** The sudden release of the te of a spring or elastic cord. **7.** A small, thin, crisp ca cooky. **8.** Brisk energy; vigor; vim; zip. **9.** A brief a sudden turn: said chiefly of cold weather. **10.** *Inf* Any task or duty easy to perform. **11.** A bit: It is not a *snap.* **12.** A snapshot. — *adj.* **1.** Made or done sud and without consideration; offhand. **2.** Fastening w snap. **3.** *Informal* Easy; requiring little work. — With a snap; quickly. [< MDu. *snappen* to bite at]

snap·drag·on (snap′drag′ən) *n.* A plant of the fig family having solitary flowers likened to dragons' hea

snap·per (snap′ər) *n.* **1.** One who or that which s **2.** A large food fish of the Gulf Coast, as the **red sna 3.** A snapping turtle.

snapping turtle A large, voracious, fresh-water tur North America, much used as food.

snap·pish (snap′ish) *adj.* **1.** Apt to speak crossly or ta **2.** Disposed to snap, as a dog. — **snap′pish·ly** *adv.* **snap′pish·ness** *n.*

snap·py (snap′ē) *adj.* **·pi·er, ·pi·est** **1.** *Informal* energetic; vivacious. **2.** *Informal* Smart or stylish i pearance. **3.** Snappish. — **make it snappy** *Inf* Hurry up! — **snap′pi·ly** *adv.* — **snap′pi·ness** *n.*

snap·shot (snap′shot′) *n.* **1.** A photograph taken w small camera without timing. **2.** A shot made without

snare [1] (snâr) *n.* **1.** A device, as a noose, for catching or other animals; a trap. **2.** Anything by which c entangled or entrapped. **3.** *Surg.* A loop of wire used move tumors and other growths from the body. — **snared, snar·ing** **1.** To catch with a snare. **2.** To ca by trickery; entice. [OE < ON *snara*] — **snar′er** n

snare [2] (snâr) *n.* **1.** One of the cords or wires stre across one of the heads of a snare drum to increase the nance. **2.** A snare drum. [< MDu., a string]

snare drum A small drum having snares on one hea

snarl [1] (snärl) *n.* A sharp, harsh, angry growl; har quarrelsome utterance. — *v.i.* **1.** To growl harshly, dog. **2.** To speak angrily and resentfully. — *v.t.* utter or express with a snarl. [Freq. of obs. *snar* to g — **snarl′er** *n.* — **snarl′ing·ly** *adv.* — **snarl′y** *adj.*

snarl [2] (snärl) *n.* **1.** A tangle, as of hair or yarn. **2.** complication or entanglement. **3.** *Informal* A quarrel *v.i.* **1.** To get into a snarl or tangle. — *v.t.* **2.** To put a snarl or tangle. **3.** To confuse; entangle mentally. SNARE [1]] — **snarl′er** *n.* — **snarl′y** *adj.*

snatch (snach) *v.t.* **1.** To seize or lay hold of sudd hastily, or eagerly. **2.** To take or remove suddenly. — take or obtain as the opportunity arises. **4.** *Slang* To nap. — *v.i.* **5.** To attempt to seize swiftly and sudd with *at.* **6.** To be eager to accept: with *at.* — **Syn.** STEAL. — *n.* **1.** An act of snatching. **2.** A brief pe **3.** A small amount. **4.** *Slang* A kidnaping. **5.** In w lifting, a bringing of the weight from the floor to abov head in one motion. [ME *snacchen*] — **snatch′er** n

snatch block *Naut.* A single block having an opening one cheek to receive a rope. For illus. see BLOCK [1].

snatch·y (snach′ē) *adj.* **snatch·i·er, snatch·i·est** rupted; spasmodic.

sneak (snēk) *v.i.* **1.** To move or go in a stealthy ma **2.** To act with cowardice or servility. — *v.t.* **3.** To give, transfer, move, etc., secretly or stealthily. — *formal* To pilfer. — *n.* **1.** One who sneaks. **2.** An sneaking. — *adj.* Stealthy; covert. [OE *snican* to c

sneak·er (snē′kər) *n.* **1.** A sneak. **2.** *pl.* *U.S.* Rubber-soled canvas shoes esp. for sports.

sneak·ing (snē′king) *adj.* **1.** Acting in an underhand **2.** Secret: a *sneaking* suspicion. — **sneak′ing·ly** *adv.*

sneak preview *U.S.* The showing of a new motion p before its date of release.

k·y (snē′kē) *adj.* **sneak·i·er, sneak·i·est** Like a sneak;
aking. — **sneak′i·ly** *adv.* — **sneak′i·ness** *n.*
r (snir) *n.* **1.** A grimace of contempt or derision made
lightly raising the upper lip. **2.** A mean insinuation. —
1. To make or show a sneer. **2.** To express derision or
tempt in speech, writing, etc. — *v.t.* **3.** To utter with a
r or in a sneering manner. [ME *sneren*] — **sneer′er** *n.*
neer′ing·ly *adv.*

ze (snēz) **sneezed, sneez·ing** *v.i.* To drive air forcibly
audibly out of the mouth and nose by a spasmodic in-
intary action caused by irritation of the mucus mem-
nes. — **not to be sneezed at** *Informal* Worthy of consid-
ion. — *n.* An act of sneezing. [Alter. of ME *fnese,*
fnēosan to sneeze] — **sneez′er** *n.* — **sneez′y** *adj.*
1 (snel) *n.* A short line of gut, horsehair, etc., bearing a
hook, to be attached to a longer line. [Origin unknown]
k (snik) *n.* A small cut; nick; snip. — *v.t.* To cut a
in. [See SNICKERSNEE.]

k·er (snik′ər) *n.* A half-suppressed or smothered laugh,
n in derision. — *v.i.* **1.** To utter a snicker. — *v.t.* **2.**
utter or express with a snicker. [Imit.]
k·er·snee (snik′ər·snē′) *n.* A swordlike knife. [Alter.
arlier *snick* or *snee* to thrust or cut]
e (snīd) *adj.* Malicious or derogatory; nasty: *snide*
ments. [Origin unknown]
(snif) *v.i.* **1.** To breathe through the nose in short,
ek, audible inhalations. **2.** To express contempt, etc., by
s by sniffing: often with *at.* — *v.t.* **3.** To breathe in
ugh the nose; inhale. **4.** To smell with sniffs. **5.** To
eive as if by sniffs: to *sniff* peril. **6.** To express (con-
pt) by sniffs. — *n.* **1.** An act or the sound of sniffing.
erception by or as by sniffing. **3.** That which is inhaled
sniffing. [Appar. back formation < SNIVEL]
fle (snif′əl) *v.i.* **·fled, ·fling 1.** To breathe through the
e noisily. **2.** To snivel or whimper. — *n.* A snuffle.
— **sniffles** *Informal* A head cold or the sniffling that results.
eq. of SNIFF]
ter (snif′tər) *n.* **1.** A pear-shaped liquor glass. **2.**
. *Slang* A small drink of liquor. [< *snift*, var. of SNIFF]
·ger (snig′ər) *n.* A snicker. — *v.t. & v.i.* To snicker.
r. of SNICKER] — **snig′ger·er** *n.*
(snip) *v.* **snipped, snip·ping** *v.t.* **1.** To clip, remove, or
with a light stroke of shears: often with *off.* — *v.i.* **2.**
cut with small, quick strokes. — *n.* **1.** An act of snip-
. **2.** A small piece snipped off. **3.** *U.S. Informal* A
ll or insignificant person or thing. [< Du. *snippen*]
e (snīp) *n.* *pl.* **snipe** or **snipes** Any of various long-
ed shore or marsh birds, allied to the woodcock. — *v.i.*
ed, snip·ing 1. To hunt or shoot snipe. **2.** To shoot at
ick off individual enemies from hiding. [< ON *snipa*]
·er (snī′pər) *n.* One who shoots an enemy from hiding.
·pet (snip′it) *n.* **1.** A small piece snipped off. **2.** A
ll portion or share.
·py (snip′ē) *adj.* **·pi·er, ·pi·est** *Informal* **1.** Pert; im-
inent. **2.** Fragmentary; scrappy. Also **snip/pet·y** (-it-ē)
ch (snich) *Slang v.t.* **1.** To grab quickly; steal; swipe.
.i. **2.** To turn informer: with *on.* [Origin unknown]
·el (sniv′əl) *v.* **·eled** or **·elled, ·el·ing** or **·el·ling** *v.i.* **1.** To
cry in a snuffling manner. **2.** To whine. **3.** To run at
nose. — *v.t.* **4.** To utter with sniveling. — *n.* **1.** The
of sniveling. **2.** Nasal mucus. [OE *snyflung* mucus
n the nose] — **sniv′el·er** or **sniv′el·ler** *n.*
● (snob) *n.* **1.** One who makes birth, wealth, education,
ntelligence the sole criterion of worth. **2.** Any pretender
entility. [Origin uncertain] — **snob′ber·y** *n.*
·bish (snob′ish) *adj.* Characteristic of or befitting
ob or snobs. — **snob′bish·ly** *adv.* — **snob/bish·ness** *n.*
cat (snob′kat′) *n.* A trucklike vehicle used for traveling
rctic conditions: a trade name. Also **sno′cat.**
d (snood) *n.* A small, meshlike cap or bag, worn by
nen to keep the hair in place. — *v.t.* To bind (hair) with
ood. [OE *snōd*]
p (snoop) *Informal v.i.* To look or pry into things with
ch one has no business. — *n.* One who snoops: also
op′er. [< Du. *snoepen* to eat goodies on the sly]
·py (snoo′pē) *adj.* **snoop·i·er, snoop·i·est** *Informal*
en to snooping.
t (snoot) *Informal* **1.** The nose or face. **2.** A wry
; a grimace. [Var. of SNOUT]
t·y (snoo′tē) *adj.* **snoot·i·er, snoot·i·est** *U.S. Informal*
ceited or supercilious.
ze (snooz) *Informal v.i.* **snoozed, snooz·ing** To sleep
tly; doze. — *n.* A short nap. [Origin uncertain]
e (snôr, snōr) *v.i.* **snored, snor·ing** To breathe in sleep
a hoarse, rough noise, usu. with an open mouth. — *n.*
act or the noise of snoring. [ME *snoren*] — **snor′er** *n.*
·kel (snôr′kəl) *n.* A mouth tube permitting a skin
er to breathe while swimming on the surface with his face

under water. **2.** A tubelike apparatus for the ventilation of
a submerged submarine. [< G *schnörkel,* lit., spiral]
snort (snôrt) *v.i.* **1.** To force air violently and noisily
through the nostrils, as a horse. **2.** To express indignation,
ridicule, etc., by a snort. **3.** *Informal* To laugh with a boisterous outburst. — *v.t.* **4.** To utter or express by snorting.
— *n.* **1.** The act or sound of snorting. **2.** *Slang* A small
drink. [ME *snorten*] — **snort′er** *n.*
snot (snot) *n.* **1.** Mucus from or in the nose: a vulgar term.
2. *Slang* A low or mean fellow. [OE *gesnot*]
snot·ty (snot′ē) *adj.* **·ti·er, ·ti·est 1.** Dirtied with snot: a
vulgar term. **2.** *Slang* Contemptible; mean; paltry. **3.**
Slang Impudent; proudly conceited; saucy.
snout (snout) *n.* **1.** The forward projecting part of a
beast's head. **2.** Something resembling a hog's snout. **3.** A
person's nose: a contemptuous or humorous term. — *v.t.*
To provide with a snout. [ME *snūte*] — **snout′ed** *adj.*
snow (snō) *n.* **1.** Water vapor in the air precipitated in
the form of minute flakes when the temperature is below
32° F. ◆ Collateral adjective: *nival.* **2.** Anything resembling snow. **3.** A fall of snow; snowstorm. **4.** *Slang* Heroin
or cocaine. **5.** The pattern of snowlike flecks appearing on
a television screen. — *v.i.* **1.** To fall as snow. — *v.t.* **2.**
To scatter or cause to fall as or like snow. **3.** To cover, enclose, or obstruct with or as with snow. **4.** *U.S. Slang* To
subject to a snow job. [OE *snāw*]
snow·ball (snō′bôl′) *n.* A small round mass of snow compressed to be thrown, as in sport. — *v.i.* **1.** To throw
snowballs. **2.** To gain in size, importance, etc., as a snow-
ball that rolls over snow. — *v.t.* **3.** To throw snowballs at.
snow·bank (snō′bangk′) *n.* A large mound of snow.
snow·ber·ry (snō′ber′ē) *n.* *pl.* **·ries** A bushy American
shrub having white berries: also called *waxberry.*
snow·bird (snō′bûrd′) *n.* **1.** The junco. **2.** *Slang* A cocaine or heroin addict.
snow blindness A temporary dimming of the sight caused
by light reflected by snow. — **snow-blind** (snō′blīnd′) *adj.*
snow·bound (snō′bound′) *adj.* Hemmed in or forced to remain in a place because of heavy snow; snowed in.
snow bunting Any of various finches, the male of which in
the breeding season is snow-white with black markings.
snow·cap (snō′kap′) *n.* A crest of snow, as on a mountain
peak. — **snow′-capped′** *adj.*
snow-clad (snō′klad′) *adj.* Covered with snow.
snow·drift (snō′drift′) *n.* A snowbank made by the wind.
snow·drop (snō′drop′) *n.* A low, European, early-blooming
bulbous plant, bearing a single, white, drooping flower.
snow·fall (snō′fôl′) *n.* **1.** A fall of snow. **2.** The amount
of snow that falls in a given period.
snow fence *U.S. & Canadian* Portable fencing of thin,
closely placed slats, used to prevent the drifting of snow over
roads, fields, etc., by causing it to drift elsewhere.
snow·flake (snō′flāk′) *n.* **1.** One of the small, feathery
masses in which snow falls. **2.** Any of certain plants allied
to and resembling the snowdrop.
snow job *U.S. Slang* An elaborate, insincere speech contrived to impress or persuade.
snow line The limit of perpetual snow on the sides of
mountains. Also **snow limit.**
snow·mo·bile (snō′mō·bēl′) *n.* An enclosed vehicle used for
traveling over snow, ice, etc., often equipped with caterpillar treads. [< SNOW + (AUTO)MOBILE]
snow·plow (snō′plou′) *n.* Any plowlike device for turning
fallen snow aside from a road or railroad, or for the removal
of snow from surfaces. Also **snow/plough′.**
snow·shoe (snō′shoo′) *n.* A device, usu. a network of
thongs in a wooden frame, fastened on the foot and worn
in walking over snow. — *v.i.* **·shoed, ·shoe·ing** To walk
on snowshoes. — **snow′sho′er** (-shō′ər) *n.*
snow·storm (snō′stôrm′) *n.* A storm with a fall of snow.
snow·y (snō′ē) *adj.* **snow·i·er, snow·i·est 1.** Abounding in
or full of snow. **2.** Pure; unblemished; spotless: *snowy* linen.
— **snow′i·ly** *adv.* — **snow′i·ness** *n.*
snub (snub) *v.t.* **snubbed, snub·bing 1.** To treat with contempt or disdain, esp. by ignoring; slight. **2.** To rebuke
with a cutting remark. **3.** To stop or check, as a rope in
running out, by taking a turn about a post, etc.; also, to
make fast (a boat, etc.) thus. — *adj.* Short; pug: said of
the nose. — *n.* **1.** An act of snubbing; deliberate slight. **2.**
A sudden checking, as of a running rope or cable. [< ON
snubba to snub] — **snub′ber** *n.*
snub-nosed (snub′nōzd′) *adj.* Having a pug or snub nose.
snuff[1] (snuf) *v.t.* **1.** To draw in (air. etc.) through the nose.
2. To smell; sniff. — *v.i.* To snort; sniff. — *n.* An act
of snuffing. [< MDu. *snuffen*]
snuff[2] (snuf) *n.* The charred portion of a wick. — *v.t.* **1.**
To extinguish: with *out.* **2.** To crop the snuff from (a wick).
[Cf. G *schnuppe* snuff of a candle] — **snuf′fer** *n.*

snuff[3] (snuf)   *n.* Pulverized tobacco to be inhaled into the nostrils. **— up to snuff** *Informal* Meeting the usual standard, as in quality, health, etc. **—** *v.i.* To take snuff. [< Du. *snuf*] **— snuf′fer** *n.* **— snuff′y** *adj.* **— snuf′fi·ness** *n.*

snuff·box (snuf′boks′)   *n.* A small box for carrying snuff.

snuf·fle (snuf′əl)   *v.* **·fled, ·fling** *v.t.* **1.** To sniffle. **2.** To breathe noisily, as a dog following a scent. **3.** To talk through the nose; snivel. **—** *v.t.* **4.** To utter in a nasal tone. **—** *n.* **1.** An act of snuffing, or the sound made by it. **2.** An affected nasal or emotional voice or twang. [Freq. of SNUFF] **— snuf′fler** *n.* **— snuf′fly** *adj.*

snug (snug)   *adj.* **snug·ger, snug·gest 1.** Closely and comfortably sheltered, covered, or situated. **2.** Close or compact; comfortable; cozy. **3.** Having everything closely secured; trim: said of a ship. **4.** Fitting closely but comfortably. **—** *v.* **snugged, snug·ging** *v.t.* **1.** To make snug. **—** *v.i.* **2,** To snuggle; move close. **— to snug down** To make a vessel ready for a storm by reducing sail, etc. [Prob. < LG. Cf. Du. *snugger* clean, smooth.] **— snug′ly** *adv.* **— snug′ness** *n.*

snug·gle (snug′əl)   *v.t.* & *v.i.* **·gled, ·gling** To lie or draw close; cuddle: often with *up* or *together.*

so[1] (sō)   *adv.* **1.** To this or that or such a degree; to this or that extent. **2.** In this, that, or such a manner; in the same way: often following a clause beginning with *as,* or preceding one beginning with *that:* As the twig is bent, *so* is the tree inclined. **3.** Just as said, directed, suggested or implied: Do it *so;* I will do so. **4.** According to fact: That is not *so.* **5.** *Informal* To an extreme degree; very. **6.** About as many or as much stated: I shall stay a day or *so.* **7.** According to the truth of what is sworn or averred: *So* help me God. **8.** To such an extent: used elliptically for *so much:* I love him *so!* **9.** Too: used in emphatic contradiction of a negative statement: You can *so!* **10.** Consequently; thus; therefore. **11.** *Informal* It seems that; can it be that; apparently: *So* you don't like it here! **12.** Let it be that way; very well. **—** *conj.* **1.** With the purpose that; usu. with *that:* I came early *so* that they would avoid meeting him. **2.** As a consequence of which: He consented, *so* they left. **—** *interj.* **1.** Is that so! **2.** Hold still! [OE *swā*]
◆ Careful writers use *so that* rather than the informal *so* (conj. def. 1) to introduce clauses of result or purpose, as in "I want to leave now *so that* I won't be late."

so[2] (sō)   *n. Music* Sol.

soak (sōk)   *v.t.* **1.** To place in liquid until thoroughly saturated; steep. **2.** To wet thoroughly; drench. **3.** To suck up; absorb: with *in* or *up.* **4.** To take in eagerly or readily: with *up:* to *soak* up knowledge. **5.** *Informal* To drink, esp. to excess: with *up.* **6.** *U.S. Slang* To overcharge. **7.** *U.S. Slang* To strike hard. **—** *v.i.* **8.** To remain or be placed in liquid till saturated. **9.** To penetrate; pass: with *in* or *into.* **10.** *U.S. Slang* To drink to excess. **—** *n.* **1.** The act of soaking, or state of being soaked. **2.** Liquid in which something is soaked. **3.** *Slang* A hard drinker. [OE *socian*] **— soak′er** *n.*

so-and-so (sō′ən·sō′)   *n.* **1.** An unnamed person or thing. **2.** *Informal* A euphemism for many offensive epithets.

soap (sōp)   *n.* **1.** A cleansing agent made by decomposing the glyceryl esters of fats and oils with alkalis. **2.** A metallic salt of one of the fatty acids. **3.** *U.S. Slang* Money used for bribery. **— no soap** *U.S. Slang* **1.** No; not a chance. **2.** Futile. **—** *v.t.* To rub or treat with soap. [OE *sāpe*]

soap·ber·ry (sōp′ber′ē)   *n.* *pl.* **·ries 1.** The fruit of any of mostly tropical trees and shrubs, sometimes used as a substitute for soap. **2.** A tree or shrub bearing this fruit.

soap·box (sōp′boks′)   *n.* **1.** A box or crate for soap. **2.** Any box or crate used as a platform by street orators. Also **soap box.** **— soapbox oratory** Impromptu or crude oratory.

soapbox derby *U.S.* A race among unpowered racing cars, steered down a slope by the boys who have built them.

soap opera A daytime television or radio serial drama usu. dealing with highly emotional domestic themes.

soap·stone (sōp′stōn′)   *n.* Steatite.

soap·suds (sōp′sudz′)   *n.* *pl.* Suds of water and soap.

soap·y (sō′pē)   *adj.* **soap·i·er, soap·i·est 1.** Resembling or consisting of soap. **2.** Smeared with soap. **3.** *Slang* Flattering; unctuous. **— soap′i·ly** *adv.* **— soap′i·ness** *n.*

soar (sôr, sōr)   *v.i.* **1.** To rise high into the air. **2.** To sail through the air without perceptibly moving the wings, as a hawk or vulture. **3.** *Aeron.* To fly without power while gaining or holding altitude. **4.** To rise sharply above the usual level: Prices soared. **. 5.** To attain a lofty or exalted state. **—** *n.* The act of soaring; also, the height or range reached in soaring. [< F < L *ex* out + *aura* breeze, air] **— soar′er** *n.*

sob (sob)   *v.* **sobbed, sob·bing** *v.i.* **1.** To weep with audible, convulsive catches of the breath. **2.** To make a sound like a sob. **—** *v.t.* **3.** To utter with sobs. **4.** To bring to a specified condition by sobbing: to *sob* oneself to sleep. **—** *n.* The act of sobbing. [ME *sobben*] **— sob′bing·ly** *adv.*

so·be·it (sō·bē′it)   *conj. Archaic* If so; if only; provided.

so·ber (sō′bər)   *adj.* **1.** Possessing or characterized properly controlled faculties; well-balanced. **2.** G sedate. **3.** Not drunk. **4.** Moderate or abstinent. **5.** dued or modest in color, manner of dress, etc. **—** *v.t.* & To make or become sober. [< OF < L *sobrius*] **— so** ly *adv.* **— so′ber·ness** *n.*

so·bri·e·ty (sō·brī′ə·tē)   *n.* *pl.* **·ties 1.** The state or qu of being sober. **2.** Moderateness in temper or conduct

so·bri·quet (sō′bri·kā)   *n.* A fanciful or humorous app tion; a nickname: also *soubriquet.* [< F]

sob story *Slang* A sad personal narrative told to elicit

so-called (sō′kôld′)   *adj.* Called as stated; generally s thus: often implying a doubtful or incorrect designatio

soc·cer (sok′ər)   *n.* A form of football in which the b propelled toward the opponents' goal by kicking or by s ing with the body or head: officially called *association ball.* [Alter. of ASSOCIATION]

so·cia·ble (sō′shə·bəl)   *adj.* **1.** Inclined to seek comp social. **2.** Agreeable in company; genial. **3.** Characte by or affording occasion for agreeable conversation friendliness. **—** *n. U.S.* An informal social gathering: called *social.* [< F < L *socius* friend] **— so·cia·bil′i·t cia·ble·ness** *n.* **— so′cia·bly** *adv.*

so·cial (sō′shəl)   *adj.* **1.** Of or pertaining to society o organization. **2.** Disposed to hold friendly intercourse others; sociable; also, promoting friendly intercourse: *cial* club. **3.** Constituted to live in society: *social* be **4.** Of or pertaining to public welfare: *social* insurance. Of, pertaining to, or characteristic of persons consid aristocratic, fashionable, etc.: *social* register. **6.** Of ani or insects, living in communities. **7.** Venereal: *social* ease. **—** *n.* A sociable. [< L *socius* ally]

social disease A venereal disease.

so·cial·ism (sō′shəl·iz′əm)   *n.* **1.** Public collective ow ship or control of the basic means of production, distr tion, and exchange, with the avowed aim of operating use rather than for profit, and of assuring to each mer of society an equitable share of goods, services, etc. **2.** doctrines of those advocating this system.

so·cial·ist (sō′shəl·ist)   *n.* An advocate of socialism. Socialistic.

so·cial·is·tic (sō′shəl·is′tik)   *adj.* **1.** Of, pertaining to practicing socialism. **2.** Like or tending toward socia

Socialist Party The U.S. political party of socia formed in 1901 under the leadership of Eugene V. Deb

so·cial·ite (sō′shəl·īt)   *n. Informal* One who is promi in fashionable society.

so·ci·al·i·ty (sō′shē·al′ə·tē)   *n.* *pl.* **·ties** The state or c acter of being social; sociability.

so·cial·ize (sō′shəl·īz)   *v.* **·ized, ·iz·ing** *v.t.* **1.** To place u group or government control. **2.** To make friendly, operative, or sociable. **3.** To convert or adapt to the n of a social group. **—** *v.i.* **4.** *Informal* To take part in s activities. Also *Brit.* **so′cial·ise.** **— so′cial·i·za′tion** *n*

socialized medicine A system proposing to supply public with medical care at nominal cost, by regula services and fees, by government subsidies to physicians,

social register A directory of persons prominent in f ionable society.

social science 1. Sociology. **2.** Any field of knowl dealing with human society, as economics, history, sociol education, politics, ethics, etc.

social security *U.S.* A Federal program of old-age unemployment insurance, public assistance to the b disabled, and dependent, and maternal and child we services.

social service Organized activity intended to adv human welfare. **— so·cial-ser·vice** (sō′shəl·sûr′vis) ad

social studies *U.S.* In elementary and secondary sch a course or unit of study based upon the social sciences

social work Any clinical, social, or recreational servic improving community welfare, as through health cli recreational facilities, aid to the poor and the aged, etc

so·ci·e·ty (sə·sī′ə·tē)   *n.* *pl.* **·ties 1.** The system of c munity life in which individuals form a continuous and r latory association for their mutual benefit and protection The body of persons composing such a community; als people collectively. **3.** A number of persons regarde having certain common interests, similar status, etc. **4.** fashionable or aristocratic portion of a community. **5.** sociation based on friendship or intimacy; companions also, one's friends or associates. [< OF *societe* < L *soci ·tatis* < *socius* friend] **— so·ci·e·tal** (sō·sī′ə·tal) *adj.*

Society of Friends A Christian religious group fou in England by George Fox about 1650, and characterize the doctrine of "waiting upon the Spirit" for direct g ance and the repudiation of ritual, formal sacraments, o and violence: commonly known as *Quakers.*

Society of Jesus The religious organization of the Jes

socio- *combining form* **1.** Society; social. **2.** Sociol sociological. [< F < L *socius* companion]

.o·ec·o·nom·ic (sō′sē·ō·ek′ə·nom′ik, sō′shē-, -ē′kə-) *adj.* ial and economic: considered as a single factor: an upper *oeconomic* group. **— so′ci·o·ec′o·nom′i·cal·ly** *adv.*

.ol·o·gy (sō′sē·ol′ə·jē, sō′shē-) *n.* The science that ts of the origin and evolution of human society and al phenomena. **— so·ci·o·log·ic** (sō′sē·ə·loj′ik) or **·i·cal — so′ci·o·log′i·cal·ly** *adv.* **— so·ci·ol′o·gist** *n.*

.om·e·try (sō′sē·om′ə·trē, sō′shē-) *n.* The study of the rrelationships of individuals within a social group.

¹ (sok) *n. pl.* **socks**; *for def. 1 also* **sox** **1.** A short king reaching above the ankle or just below the knee. he light shoe worn by comic actors in the Greek and nan drama. [OE < L *soccus* slipper]

² (sok) *Slang v.t.* To strike or hit, esp. with the fist; to ch. **— n.** A hard blow. [Origin unknown]

·et (sok′it) *n.* **1.** *Mech.* A cavity or an opening adapted eceive and hold some corresponding piece or fixture. **2.** *t.* A cavity or hollowed depression for the reception of an n or part. **— v.t.** To furnish with, hold by, or put into cket. [< AF *soket*, dim. of OF *soc* plowshare]

·eye (sok′ī′) *n.* A salmon of the Pacific coast, highly ed as a food fish. [Alter. of Salishan *sukkegh*]

rat·ic (sō·krat′ik) *adj.* Pertaining to or characteristic ocrates: also **So·crat′i·cal.** **— So·crat′i·cal·ly** *adv.*

atic method The dialectic method of instruction by stions and answers, as adopted by Socrates.

(sod) *n.* **1.** A piece of grassy surface soil held together he matted roots of grass and weeds; a turf or divot. **2.** surface of the earth. **— v.t.** **sod·ded, sod·ding** To cover n sod. [< MDu. *sode* piece of turf]

a (sō′də) *n.* **1.** Any of several white, alkaline comnds widely used in medicine, industry, and the arts. **2.** ft drink containing soda water and flavoring: also **soda** **3.** A drink made from soda water, ice cream, and, etimes, flavoring. [< Med.L, ? < Ital. *soda* (*cenere*) d (ash) < L *solidus*]

ash Crude sodium carbonate, widely used in the mancture of glass, soaps, paper, etc.

cracker A thin, crisp cracker made with yeastened dough containing soda.

fountain 1. An apparatus from which soda water is wn, usu. containing receptacles for syrups, ice cream, **2.** A counter at which soft drinks, etc., are dispensed.

jerk *U.S. Slang* A clerk at a soda fountain.

al·i·ty (sō·dal′ə·tē) *n. pl.* **·ties 1.** Companionship. **2.** ociety; association. **3.** In the Roman Catholic Church, a ety organized for devotional and charitable purposes. L < *sodalis* companion]

water An effervescent drink consisting of water ged under pressure with purified carbon dioxide gas.

den (sod′n) *adj.* **1.** Soaked with moisture. **2.** Doughy; y, as bread, biscuits, etc. **3.** Flabby and pale, esp. from ipation. **4.** Dull; dreary. **— v.t. & v.i.** To make or bee sodden. [ME *soden*, orig. pp. of SEETHE] **— sod′ly** *adv.* **— sod′den·ness** *n.*

·um (sō′dē·əm) *n.* A silver-white, highly reactive, line, metallic element (symbol Na) that is soft and malle, and forms many compounds: also called *natrium*. See MENT. [< NL < SODA]

um bicarbonate *Chem.* A white crystalline comnd of alkaline taste, used in medicine and cookery: also d *baking soda, bicarbonate of soda.*

um carbonate *Chem.* A strongly alkaline compound : in crystalline hydrated form is known as washing soda, in the anhydrous form as soda ash.

um chloride Common salt.

um hydroxide *Chem.* A strongly basic compound,)H, used for bleaching, etc.: also called *caustic soda.*

um nitrate *Chem.* A white compound used as a ferer and in explosives.

um Pen·to·thal (pen′tə·thôl, -thal) *Proprietary* name a brand of thiopental sodium: also called *Pentothal son.* Also **sodium pent′o·thal.**

um thiosulfate *Chem.* A crystalline salt used inrially and medicinally and in photography as a fixing nt: also called *hypo.* Also **sodium hyposulfite.**

om (sod′əm) In the Bible, a city on the Dead Sea, royed with the city of Gomorrah because of the wicked of the people. *Gen.* xiii 10. **— Sod′om·ite** *n.*

om·y (sod′əm·ē) *n.* Unnatural sexual relations, esp. veen male persons or between a human being and an nal. [< OF < LL *Sodoma* Sodom, to whose people this ctice was imputed] **— sod′om·ite** *n.*

·er (sō·ev′ər) *adv.* To or in some conceivable degree: n added to *who, which, what, when, how,* etc.

a (sō′fə) *n.* A wide seat, upholstered and having a back raised ends. [< F < Arabic *soffah* a part of a floor ed to form a seat]

---

soft (sôft, soft) *adj.* **1.** Being or composed of a substance whose shape is changed easily by pressure, but without fracture; pliable, or malleable; easily worked: *soft* wood. **2.** Smooth and delicate to the touch. **3.** Gentle in its effect upon the ear; not loud or harsh. **4.** Mild in any mode of physical action; bland: a *soft* breeze. **5.** Of subdued coloring or delicate shading. **6.** Expressing mildness, sympathy, etc.; gentle: *soft* words. **7.** Giving or enjoying rest; placid: *soft* sleep. **8.** Easily or too easily touched in feeling; tender: a *soft* heart. **9.** Incapable of bearing hardship, strain, etc.; delicate: *soft* muscles. **10.** Of yielding character; weak; effeminate. **11.** *Informal* Involving little effort; easy: a *soft* job. **12.** Free from mineral salts that prevent the detergent action of soap: said of water. **13.** Bituminous, as opposed to anthracite: said of coal. **14.** *Phonet.* **a** Describing *c* and *g* when articulated fricatively as in *cent* and *gibe*: opposed to *hard.* **b** Voiced and weakly articulated. **15.** *Physics* Having relatively weak penetrating power: *soft* X-rays. **— n. 1.** That which is soft; a soft part or material. **2.** *Informal* One who is soft or foolish; a softy. **— adv. 1.** Softly. **2.** Quietly; gently. [OE *sôfte*] **— soft′ly** *adv. & interj.* **— soft′ness** *n.*

soft·ball (sôft′bôl′, soft′-) *n.* **1.** A variation of baseball, requiring a smaller diamond and a larger ball. **2.** The ball used in this game.

soft-boiled (sôft′boild′) *adj.* Boiled, as an egg, to an extent of incomplete coagulation of the albumen.

soft coal Bituminous coal.

soft drink A nonalcoholic drink, as ginger ale, etc.

soft·en (sôf′ən, sof′-) *v.t. & v.i.* To make or become soft or softer. **— soft′ten·er** *n.*

soft·heart·ed (sôft′här′tid, soft′-) *adj.* Tender-hearted; merciful. **— soft′heart′ed·ly** *adv.* **— soft′heart′ed·ness** *n.*

soft-ped·al (sôft′ped′l, soft′-) *v.t.* **·aled** or **·alled, ·al·ing** or **·al·ling 1.** To mute the tone of by depressing the soft pedal. **2.** *Informal* To render less emphatic; moderate.

soft pedal A pedal that mutes the tone, as in a piano.

soft-shell (sôft′shel′, soft′-) *adj.* Having a soft shell, as certain clams, or a crab or lobster after shedding its shell: also **soft′-shelled′** (-sheld′). **— n.** A soft-shelled crab.

soft-shelled crab A crab of North America after it has molted.

soft-shelled turtle Any member of a family of turtles having a long snout and a soft, leathery shell.

soft-soap (sôft′sōp′, soft′-) *v.t. Informal* To flatter; cajole. **— soft′-soap′er** *n.*

soft soap 1. Fluid or semifluid soap. **2.** *Informal* Flattery.

soft-spo·ken (sôft′spō′kən) *adj.* **1.** Speaking with a soft, low voice. **2.** Ingratiating; suave: said of speech.

soft·ware (sôft′wâr′, soft′-) *n.* Any of the programs used in operating a digital computer, as input and output programs: distinguished from *hardware* (def. 3).

soft·wood (sôft′wŏŏd′, soft′-) *n.* **1.** A coniferous tree or its wood. **2.** Any soft wood, or any tree with soft wood.

soft·y (sôf′tē, sof′-) *n. pl.* **soft·ies** *Informal* **1.** An extremely sentimental person. **2.** A sissy.

sog·gy (sog′ē) *adj.* **·gi·er, ·gi·est 1.** Saturated with water or moisture; wet and heavy; soaked. **2.** Heavy: said of pastry. **3.** Soft; boggy: said of land. Also **sog·ged** (sog′id). [< dial. E *sog* a swamp, bog < Scand.] **— sog′gi·ly** *adv.* **— sog′gi·ness** *n.*

soil¹ (soil) *n.* **1.** Finely divided rock mixed with vegetable or animal matter, constituting that portion of the surface of the earth in which plants grow. **2.** Land; country; native *soil.* **3.** A particular kind of earth. **4.** A medium for development or growth: Slums are fertile *soil* for disease. [< OF < L < *solum* the ground]

soil² (soil) *v.t.* **1.** To make dirty; smudge. **2.** To disgrace; defile. **— v.i. 3.** To become dirty. **— n. 1.** The act of soiling or the state of being soiled. **2.** A spot or stain. **3.** Filth; sewage. **4.** Manure used as fertilizer. [< OF, ult. < L *suculus*, dim. of *sus* pig]

soil·age (soi′lij) *n.* Green crops for feeding animals.

soi·ree (swä·rā′, Fr. swä·rā′) *n.* A party or reception given in the evening. Also **soi·rée′.** [< F < *soir* evening]

so·ja (sō′jə, sō′yä) *n.* The soybean. [< NL < Du. *soya*]

so·journ (*v.* sō′jûrn, sō·jûrn′; *n.* sō′jûrn) *v.i.* To stay or dwell temporarily; abide for a time. **— n.** A temporary residence or stay, as of one in a foreign land. [< OF, ult. < L *sub-* under + *diurnus* daily] **— so′journ·er** *n.*

sol¹ (sōl) *n. Music* The fifth of the syllables used in solmization; the fifth tone of a major scale; also, the tone G: also *so.* [See GAMUT.]

sol² (sōl, sol) *n.* A colloidal suspension of a solid in a liquid.

Sol (sol) **1.** The sun. **2.** In Roman mythology, the god of the sun. [< L]

sol·ace (sol′is) *n.* Comfort in grief, trouble, or calamity; also, that which supplies such comfort: also **sol′ace·ment.**

— *v.t.* **·aced, ·ac·ing 1.** To comfort or cheer in trouble, grief, or calamity. **2.** To alleviate, as grief; soothe. **— Syn.** See CONSOLE[1]. [< OF < L *solacium* comfort] **— sol'ac·er** *n.*

so·lar (sō'lər) *adj.* **1.** Pertaining to, proceeding from, or connected with the sun. **2.** Affected, determined, or measured by the sun. **3.** Operated by the action of the sun's rays: a *solar* engine. [< L *sol* sun]

solar battery An assembly of photovoltaic cells for the direct conversion of solar energy into electricity.

so·lar·i·um (sō·lâr'ē·əm) *n. pl.* **·i·a** (-ē·ə) or **·i·ums** A room or enclosed porch exposed to the sun's rays. [< L]

solar plexus 1. *Anat.* The large network of nerves found behind the stomach, and serving the abdominal viscera. **2.** *Informal* The pit of the stomach.

solar system The sun together with the heavenly bodies that revolve about it.

sold (sōld) Past tense and past participle of SELL.

sol·der (sod'ər) *n.* **1.** A fusible metal or alloy used for joining metallic surfaces or margins, applied in a melted state. **2.** Anything that unites or cements. **—** *v.t.* **1.** To unite or repair with solder. **2.** To join together. **—** *v.i.* **3.** To work with solder. **4.** To be united by or as by solder. [< OF < L *solidus* firm, hard] **— sol'der·er** *n.*

sol·dier (sōl'jər) *n.* **1.** A person serving in an army. **2.** An enlisted man, as distinguished from a commissioned officer. **3.** A brave, skillful, or experienced warrior. **4.** One who serves loyally in any cause. **5.** *Entomol.* An asexual form of a termite or of certain ants, in which the head and jaws are largely developed to defend the colony. **—** *v.i.* To be a soldier. [< OF *soude* wages < LL *solidus* a gold coin] **— sol'dier·ly** *adj.*

soldier of fortune An adventurous, restless person who is willing to serve wherever his services are well paid.

Soldier's Medal A U.S. military decoration awarded to any member of the army, or of a military organization connected with it, for heroism not involving actual conflict with the enemy. See DECORATION.

sol·dier·y (sōl'jər·ē) *n. pl.* **·dier·ies 1.** Soldiers collectively. **2.** Military service.

sole[1] (sōl) *n.* **1.** The bottom surface of the foot. ◆ Collateral adjective: *plantar.* **2.** The bottom surface of a shoe, boot, etc. **3.** The lower part of a thing, or the part on which it rests when standing; esp., the bottom part of a plowshare. **4.** The bottom part of the head of a golf club. **—** *v.t.* **soled, sol·ing** To furnish with a sole; resole, as a shoe. [< OF < Med.L *sola*, var. of L *solea* sandal]

sole[2] (sōl) *n.* **1.** Any of a family of flatfishes allied to the flounders, many of which are highly esteemed as food. **2.** One of various flounders of the Pacific coast of the U.S. [< OF < L *solea*]

sole[3] (sōl) *adj.* Being alone or the only one; only; individual. [< OF < L *solus* alone]

so·le·cism (sol'ə·siz'əm) *n.* **1.** A violation of grammatical rules or of the approved idiomatic usage of language. **2.** Any impropriety or incongruity. [< L < Gk. < *soloikos* speaking incorrectly < *Soloi*, a Cilician town whose people spoke a substandard Attic dialect] **— sol'e·cist** *n.* **— sol'e·cis'tic** or **·ti·cal** *adj.*

sole·ly (sōl'lē) *adv.* **1.** By oneself or itself alone; singly. **2.** Completely; entirely. **3.** Without exception; exclusively.

sol·emn (sol'əm) *adj.* **1.** Characterized by majesty, mystery, or power; impressive; awe-inspiring. **2.** Marked by gravity; serious. **3.** Characterized by ceremonial observances; sacred. **4.** *Law* Done in due form of law: a *solemn* protest. [< OF < L *solemnis*] **— sol'emn·ness, sol'-emn·ness** *n.* **— sol'emn·ly** *adv.*

so·lem·ni·ty (sə·lem'nə·tē) *n. pl.* **·ties 1.** The state or quality of being solemn; gravity; reverence. **2.** A rite expressive of religious reverence; also, any ceremonious observance. **3.** A thing of a solemn or serious nature.

sol·em·nize (sol'əm·nīz) *v.t.* **·nized, ·niz·ing 1.** To perform as a ceremony or solemn rite, or according to legal or ritual forms: to *solemnize* a marriage. **2.** To dignify, as with a ceremony; celebrate. **3.** To make solemn, grave, or serious. Also *Brit.* **sol'em·nise.** **— Syn.** See CELEBRATE. **— sol'em-ni·za'tion** *n.* **— sol'em·niz'er** *n.*

so·le·noid (sō'lə·noid) *n. Electr.* A conducting wire in the form of a helix, capable of setting up a magnetic field by the passage through it of an electric current. [< F < Gk. *sōlēn* a channel + -OID] **— so'le·noi'dal** *adj.*

so·lic·it (sə·lis'it) *v.t.* **1.** To ask for earnestly; seek to obtain by persuasion or entreaty. **2.** To beg or entreat (a person) persistently. **3.** To tempt; esp., to entice (one) to an unlawful or immoral act. **—** *v.i.* **4.** To make petition or solicitation. **— Syn.** See ASK. [< OF < L *sollicitare* to agitate] **— so·lic'i·ta'tion** *n.*

so·lic·i·tor (sə·lis'ə·tər) *n.* **1.** A person who solicits; esp., one who solicits gifts of money or subscriptions to magazines. **2.** The legal advisor to certain branches of the public service. **3.** In England, a lawyer who may advise clients or prepare cases for presentation in court, but who may appear

as an advocate in the lower courts only: distinguished *barrister.* Also **so·lic'i·ter.** **— so·lic'i·tor·ship'** *n.*

Solicitor General *pl.* **Solicitors General 1.** In the an officer who ranks after the Attorney General. **2.** principal law officer in some States, corresponding to Attorney General in others.

so·lic·i·tous (sə·lis'ə·təs) *adj.* **1.** Full of anxiety or con as for the attainment of something: *solicitous* of our will. **2.** Full of eager desire; willing. **— so·lic'i·tous·ly** **— so·lic'i·tous·ness** *n.*

so·lic·i·tude (sə·lis'ə·tōōd, -tyōōd) *n.* **1.** The state of b solicitous; anxiety or concern. **2.** *Usu. pl.* That w makes one solicitous.

sol·id (sol'id) *adj.* **1.** Having definite shape and vol not fluid. **2.** Substantial; firm and stable. **3.** Fillin whole of; not hollow. **4.** Having no aperture or cre compact. **5.** Manifesting strength and firmness; sound Characterized by reality; substantial or satisfactory. Exhibiting united and unbroken characteristics, opin etc.; unanimous: a *solid* vote. **8.** Financially sound or **9.** *U.S. Informal* Certain and safe in approval and sup They were *solid* with the boss. **10.** Having or relati the three dimensions of length, breadth, and thickness. Written without a hyphen: said of a compound word. Cubic in shape: a *solid* yard. **13.** Unadulterated; unallc *solid* gold. **14.** Carrying weight or conviction: a *solid* ment. **15.** Serious; reliable: a *solid* citizen. **16.** *Pri* Having no leads or slugs between the lines; not open. **1.** A state of matter characterized by definite shape volume. **2.** A magnitude that has length, breadth thickness, as a cone, cube, sphere, etc. [< F < L *solv* **— sol'id·ly** *adv.* **— sol'id·ness** *n.*

sol·i·dar·i·ty (sol'ə·dar'ə·tē) *n. pl.* **·ties** Coherence oneness in nature, relations, or interests, as of a class.

solid fuel *Aerospace* A rocket fuel in solid, rather liquid or gaseous, form. Also, **solid propellant.**

solid geometry The geometry that includes all dimensions of space in its reasoning.

so·lid·i·fy (sə·lid'ə·fī) *v.t. & v.i.* **·fied, ·fy·ing 1.** To r or become solid, hard, firm, or compact. **2.** To brir come together in unity. **— so·lid'i·fi·ca'tion** *n.*

so·lid·i·ty (sə·lid'ə·tē) *n. pl.* **·ties 1.** The quality or of being solid; extension in the three dimensions of sp **2.** Mental, moral, or financial soundness; stability.

solid state physics The branch of physics that deals the properties of solids, esp. at the atomic and mole levels.

sol·i·dus (sol'ə·dəs) *n. pl.* **·di** (-dī) The sign (/) to divide shillings from pence: 10/6 (10s. 6d.): sometimes used to express fractions: 3/4. [< LL]

so·lil·o·quize (sə·lil'ə·kwīz) *v.i.* **·quized, ·quiz·ing** To to oneself; utter a soliloquy. Also *Brit.* **so·lil'o·quise.**

so·lil·o·quy (sə·lil'ə·kwē) *n. pl.* **·quies** A talking or course to oneself, as in a drama; a monologue. [< LL *solus* alone + *loqui* to talk]

sol·ip·sism (sol'ip·siz'əm) *n. Philos.* The theory tha self is the only thing really existent. [< L *solus* alor *ipse* self] **— sol'ip·sist** *n.*

sol·i·taire (sol'ə·târ') *n.* **1.** A diamond or other ger alone. **2.** *Chiefly U.S.* One of many games, esp. of c played by one person: also, *Brit. patience.* **3.** *Brit.* board. [< F < L *solitarius* solitary]

sol·i·tar·y (sol'ə·ter'ē) *adj.* **1.** Living, being, or going a **2.** Made, done, or passed alone: a *solitary* life. **3.** U quented by human beings; secluded. **4.** Lonesome; lo **5.** Single; sole: Not a *solitary* soul was there. **—** *n.* **·tar·ies 1.** One who lives alone; a recluse. **2.** *Infc* Solitary confinement. [< L < *solus* alone] **— sol'i·ta** *adv.* **— sol'i·tar'i·ness** *n.*

solitary confinement The confining of a prisoner a from other prisoners, usu. as punishment.

sol·i·tude (sol'ə·tōōd, -tyōōd) *n.* **1.** The state of being tary; seclusion. **2.** A deserted or lonely place.

sol·mi·za·tion (sol'mə·zā'shən) *n. Music* The us syllables, most commonly *do, re, mi, fa, sol, la, ti* (si names for the tones of a major scale, with vowel chang indicate chromatic tones. [< SOL[1] + MI]

so·lo (sō'lō) *n. pl.* **·los** or **·li** (lē) **1.** A musical compos or passage for a single voice or instrument, with or wit accompaniment. **2.** Any of several card games, esp. o which one player may play alone against the other thre Any performance accomplished alone or without assist **—** *adj.* **1.** Composed or written for, or executed by, a s voice or instrument. **2.** Done by a single person alor *solo* flight. **—** *v.i.* **·loed, ·lo·ing** To fly an airplane alone, for the first time. [< Ital. < L *solus* alone] **— so'lo·i**

Sol·o·mon (sol'ə·mən) Tenth-century B.C. king of son of David and Bathsheba; noted for his wisdom.

Sol·o·mon's-seal (sol'ə·mənz·sēl') *n.* Any of sev rather large perennial herbs having tubular flowers and i stocks marked at intervals by circular scars.

ice (sol′stis) *n.* **1.** *Astron.* The time of year when the s at its greatest distance from the celestial equator; r the **summer solstice**, about June 22 in the northern sphere, or the **winter solstice**, about Dec. 22. **2.** Either e two points on the ecliptic marking these distances. **3.** minating or high point. [< F < L < *sol* sun + *sistere* use to stand] — **sol·sti·tial** (sol-stish′əl) *adj.*

bil·i·ty (sol′yə-bil′ə-tē) *n. pl.* **·ties** The state of being le; capability of being dissolved. Also **sol′u·ble·ness.**

ble (sol′yə-bəl) *adj.* **1.** Capable of being dissolved in a **.** **2.** Susceptible of being solved or explained. [< OF < *solvere* to solve, dissolve] — **sol′u·bly** *adv.*

e (sol′yо̄ot, sŏ′lо̄ot) *n.* The substance dissolved in a ion. — *adj.* Dissolved; in solution.

tion (sə-lо̄o′shən) *n.* **1.** A homogeneous mixture ed by dissolving one or more substances, whether solid, l, or gaseous, in another substance. **2.** The act or ss by which such a mixture is made. **3.** The act or ss of explaining, settling, or disposing, as of a difficulty, em, or doubt. **4.** The answer to a problem; also, the od of finding the answer. **5.** Separation; disruption. ▶F < L *solutus*, pp. of *solvere* to solve]

tre·an (sə-lо̄o′trē·ən) *adj. Anthropol.* Pertaining to aracteristic of a Paleolithic culture preceding the Mag-lian and typified by a skilled technique in the making of implements. Also **So·lu′tri·an.** [after *Solutré*, a village ntral France, where remains were found]

·ble (sol′və-bəl) *adj.* **1.** That may be solved. **2.** That be dissolved. — **solv′a·bil′i·ty, solv′a·ble·ness** *n.*

(solv) *v.t.* **solved, solv·ing** To arrive at or work out the ct explanation or solution of; find the answer to; re-. [< L *solvere* to solve, loosen] — **solv′er** *n.*

nt (sol′vənt) *adj.* **1.** Having means sufficient to pay bts. **2.** Having the power of dissolving. — *n.* **1.** That n solves. **2.** A substance, generally a liquid, capable of lving other substances. [< L *solvens, -entis*, ppr. of *e* to solve, loosen] — **sol′ven·cy** *n.*

a See -SOME².

a·li (sō-mä′lē) *n.* **1.** A member of one of certain Hamit-bes of Somalia, Kenya, Ethiopia, and French Somali-. **2.** Their Hamitic language. Also **So·mal** (sō-mal′).

at·ic (sō-mat′ik) *adj. Biol.* **1.** Of or relating to the ; physical; corporeal. **2.** Of or pertaining to the frame-or walls of a body. [< Gk. *sôma* body]

to- *combining form* Body; of, pertaining to, or denot-he body. Also, before vowels, **somat-.** [< Gk. *sôma*, *ίos* the body]

ber (som′bər) *adj.* **1.** Partially deprived of light or atness; dusky; murky; gloomy. **2.** Somewhat melan-r; depressing. Also *Brit.* **som′bre,** *Archaic* **som′brous.** ′ *sombre*]

bre·ro (som-brâr′ō) *n. pl.* **·ros** A broad-brimmed hat, of felt, much worn in Spain, Latin America, and the western U.S. [< Sp. < *sombra* shade]

(sum) *adj.* **1.** Of indeterminate or limited quantity, ber, or amount. **2.** Conceived or thought of, but not itely known: *some* person. **3.** Part (at least one) but ll of a class. **4.** *U.S. Informal* Worthy of notice: That *some* cake. — *pron.* **1.** A certain undetermined quan-or part. **2.** Certain particular ones not definitely known t specifically designated. — *adv.* **1.** In an approximate ee; about: *Some* eighty people were present. **2.** *In-il* or *Dial.* Somewhat. [OE *sum*]

e¹ *suffix of adjectives* Characterized by, or tending to be t is indicated by the main element): *blithesome, frolic-*. [OE *-sum* like, resembling]

e² *suffix of nouns* A body: *chromosome.* Also spelled **a.** [< Gk. *sôma* a body]

e³ *suffix of nouns* A group consisting of (a specified ber): *twosome, foursome.* [< SOME]

·bod·y (sum′bod′ē, -bəd-ē) *pron.* A person unknown named. — *n. pl.* **·bod·ies** A person of consequence.

·day (sum′dā′) *adv. U.S.* At some future time.

·how (sum′hou′) *adv.* In some manner not explained. A somebody.

·one (sum′wun′, -wən) *pron.* Some person; somebody.

·place (sum′plās′) *adv. Informal* Somewhere.

er·sault (sum′ər-sôlt) *n.* **1.** An acrobatic stunt in h a person either leaps or rolls from a sitting posture, ing heels over head. **2.** A complete reversal of opinion, ude, etc. — *v.i.* To perform a somersault. Also spelled *mersault.* Also **som′er·set** (-set). [< OF, ult. < L *supra* *e* + *saltus* leap]

·thing (sum′thing) *n.* **1.** A particular thing indefi-y conceived or stated. **2.** Some portion or quantity. **3.** rson or thing of importance. — *adv.* Somewhat: now in the phrase **something like.**

·time (sum′tīm′) *adv.* **1.** At some future time not

precisely stated; eventually. **2.** At some indeterminate time or occasion. — *adj.* Former; quondam: a *sometime* student.

some·times (sum′tīmz′) *adv.* At times; occasionally.

some·way (sum′wā′) *adv.* In some way or other; somehow. Also **some way, some′ways′** (-wāz′).

some·what (sum′hwot′, -hwət) *n.* **1.** An uncertain quan-tity or degree; something. **2.** An individual or thing of con-sequence. — *adv.* In some degree.

some·where (sum′hwâr′) *adv.* **1.** In, at, or to some place unspecified or unknown. **2.** In one place or another. **3.** In or to some existent place. **4.** Approximately: with *about*. — *n.* An unspecified or unknown place.

some·wheres (sum′hwârz′) *adv. Chiefly Dial.* Somewhere.

som·nam·bu·late (som-nam′byə-lāt) *v.i.* **·lat·ed, ·lat·ing** To walk or wander about while asleep. [< L *somnus* sleep + AMBULATE]

som·nam·bu·lism (som-nam′byə-liz′əm) *n.* The act or state of walking during sleep; sleepwalking. Also **som·nam′·bu·la′tion.** — **som·nam′bu·lant** (-lənt) *adj.* — **som·nam′·bu·list** *n.* — **som·nam′bu·lis′tic** *adj.*

somni- *combining form* Sleep; of or pertaining to sleep: *somniferous.* [< L *somnus* sleep]

som·nif·er·ous (som-nif′ər-əs) *adj.* Tending to produce sleep; soporiferous; narcotic. Also **som·nif′ic.**

som·no·lence (som′nə-ləns) *n.* Oppressive drowsiness or inclination to sleep. Also **som′no·len·cy.**

som·no·lent (som′nə-lənt) *adj.* **1.** Inclined to sleep; drow-sy. **2.** Tending to induce drowsiness. [< F < L < *somnus* sleep] — **som′no·lent·ly** *adv.*

son (sun) *n.* **1.** A male child considered with reference to either parent or to both parents. **2.** Any male descendant. **3.** One who occupies the place of a son, as by adoption, mar-riage, or regard. **4.** A person regarded as a native of a par-ticular country or place. **5.** A male person representing some quality or character. [OE *sunu*] — **son′ship** *n.*

-son A descendant of: English and Scandinavian patronymic suffix: *Anderson.*

Son (sun) Jesus Christ; the second person of the Trinity.

so·nant (sō′nənt) *adj.* **1.** Sounding; resonant. **2.** *Phonet.* Voiced. — *n. Phonet.* **1.** A voiced speech sound. **2.** A syl-labic sound. [< L *sonans, -antis*, ppr. of *sonare* to resound] — **so′nance** *n.*

so·nar (sō′när) *n.* A device using underwater sound waves for navigation, range finding, detection of submerged ob-jects, communication, etc. — *adj.* Of, or pertaining to this device. [< SO(UND) NA(VIGATION AND) R(ANGING)]

so·na·ta (sə-nä′tä) *n. Music* A composition for one, two, or in older music, three or more instruments. [< Ital. < *so-nare* to sound]

sonata form *Music* The outline upon which a movement, esp. the first, of a sonata, quartet, symphony, etc., is based.

so·na·ti·na (son′ə-tē′nə) *n. pl.* **·ti·nas** or **·ti·ne** (-tē′nä) *Music* A short or easy sonata. [< Ital., dim. of SONATA]

song (sông, song) *n.* **1.** A musical composition for one or more voices. **2.** The rendering of vocal music; more widely, any melodious utterance, as of a bird. **3.** A lyric or ballad. **4.** Poetry; verse. — **for a song** At a very low price. [OE]

song·bird (sông′bûrd′, song′-) *n.* A bird that utters a mu-sical call.

song·ful (sông′fəl, song′-) *adj.* Full of song or melody.

Song of Solomon A book of the Old Testament consisting of a Hebrew dramatic love poem attributed to Solomon: also, in the Douai Bible, *Canticle of Canticles*. Also **Song of Songs.**

song sparrow A common sparrow of the eastern U.S. noted for its song.

song·ster (sông′stər, song′-) *n.* **1.** A person or bird given to singing. **2.** A poet. — **song′stress** *n.fem.*

song thrush A bird of the thrush family, native in Europe and having brown wings and a spotted breast.

song·writ·er (sông′rī′tər) *n.* One who writes music or lyr-ics, or both, for songs, esp. popular songs. Also **song writer.**

son·ic (son′ik) *adj.* **1.** Of, pertaining to, determined or af-fected by sound. **2.** Having a speed approaching that of sound. [< L *sonus* sound]

sonic barrier *Aeron.* The transonic barrier.

son-in-law (sun′in-lô′) *n. pl.* **sons-in-law** The husband of one's daughter.

son·net (son′it) *n.* A poem usu. of fourteen decasyllabic lines, properly expressing two successive phases of a single thought or idea. — *v.t.* **1.** To celebrate in sonnets. — *v.i.* **2.** To compose sonnets. [< F < Ital. < Provençal *sonet*, dim. of *son* sound < L *sonus*]

son·net·eer (son′ə-tir′) *n.* A composer of sonnets. — *v.i.* To compose sonnets.

son·ny (sun′ē) *n. Informal* Youngster: a familiar form of address to boys.

so·nor·ant (sə-nôr′ənt, -nō′rənt) *n. Phonet.* A voiced con-sonant of relatively high sonority, as (l), (r), (m), (n).

so·nor·i·ty (sə-nôr′ə-tē, -nor′-) *n. pl.* **·ties** **1.** Sonorous quality or state; resonance; also **so·no′rous·ness**. **2.** A sound.

so·no·rous (sə-nôr′əs, -nō′rəs, son′ər-əs) *adj.* **1.** Productive or capable of sound vibrations. **2.** Loud and full-sounding; resonant. [< L *sonare* to resound] — **so·no′rous·ly** *adv.*

soon (sōōn) *adv.* **1.** At a future or subsequent time not long distant; shortly. **2.** Without delay; in a speedy manner. **3.** With ease; readily. **4.** With willingness or readiness: usu. preceded by *would as, had as,* etc. **5.** In good season; early. [OE *sōna* immediately]

Soon·er State (sōō′nər) Nickname for Oklahoma.

soot (sŏot, sōōt) *n.* A black substance, essentially carbon from the incomplete combustion of wood, coal, natural gas, etc., as deposited on the inside of chimneys and other surfaces. — *v.t.* To soil or cover with soot. [OE *sōt*]

sooth (sōōth) *Archaic adj.* True. — *n.* Truth. — **in sooth** In truth. [OE *sōth*] — **sooth′ly** *adv.*

soothe (sōōth) *v.* **soothed, sooth·ing** *v.t.* **1.** To restore to a quiet or normal state; calm. **2.** To mitigate, soften, or relieve, as pain or grief. — *v.i.* **3.** To have a calming or relieving effect. [OE *sōthian* to verify] — **sooth′er** *n.* — **sooth′-ing** *adj.* — **sooth′ing·ly** *adv.*

sooth·say·er (sōōth′sā′ər) *n.* One who claims to be able to foretell events. — **sooth′say′ing** *n.*

soot·y (sŏot′ē, sōō′tē) *adj.* **soot·i·er, soot·i·est** **1.** Blackened or stained by soot. **2.** Producing or consisting of soot. **3.** Black like soot. — **soot′i·ly** *adv.* — **soot′i·ness** *n.*

sop (sop) *v.* **sopped, sop·ping** *v.t.* **1.** To dip or soak in a liquid. **2.** To drench. **3.** To take up by absorption: often with *up*. — *v.i.* **4.** To be absorbed; soak in. **5.** To be or become drenched. — *n.* **1.** Anything softened in liquid, as bread. **2.** Anything given to pacify, as a bribe. [OE *sopp*]

soph·ism (sof′iz-əm) *n.* **1.** A false argument intentionally used to deceive. **2.** The doctrine or method of the sophists. [< F or L < Gk., ult. < *sophos* wise]

soph·ist (sof′ist) *n.* **1.** A philosopher; a learned man. **2.** One who argues cleverly but fallaciously or unnecessarily minutely. — *adj.* Pertaining to the art or method of sophists, or to sophistry. [< L < Gk., ult. < *sophos* wise]

Soph·ist (sof′ist) *n.* **1.** A member of a school of early Greek philosophy, preceding the Socratic school. **2.** One of the later Greek teachers of philosophy and rhetoric, who showed great skill in subtle disputation under logical forms.

so·phis·tic (sə-fis′tik) *adj.* Pertaining to a Sophist, sophists, or sophistry. — *n.* The art or method of the Sophists. Also **so·phis′ti·cal.** — **so·phis′ti·cal·ly** *adv.* — **so·phis′ti·cal·ness** *n.*

so·phis·ti·cate (*v.* sə-fis′tə-kāt; *n.* sə-fis′tə-kit, -kāt) *v.* **·cat·ed, ·cat·ing** *v.t.* **1.** To make less simple or ingenuous in mind or manner; render worldly-wise. **2.** *Rare* To mislead or corrupt (a person). **3.** To increase the complexity and capability of. — *v.i.* **4.** To indulge in sophistry; be sophistic. — *n.* A sophisticated person. [< Med.L < L *sophisticus* sophistic] — **so·phis′ti·ca′tor** *n.*

so·phis·ti·cat·ed (sə-fis′tə-kā′tid) *adj.* **1.** Having fine or subtle perceptions; cultured. **2.** Appealing to the intellect; not suited to popular tastes. **3.** Worldly-wise; deprived of natural simplicity. **4.** Very complicated in design, capabilities, etc.: said of mechanical and electronic devices.

so·phis·ti·ca·tion (sə-fis′tə-kā′shən) *n.* **1.** Sophisticated ideas, attitudes, etc., derived from education and culture. **2.** The act of sophisticating. **3.** Adulteration; falsification.

soph·is·try (sof′is-trē) *n. pl.* **·tries** **1.** Subtly fallacious reasoning or disputation. **2.** The art or methods of the Greek Sophists.

soph·o·more (sof′ə-môr, -mōr) *n.* In American high schools, colleges, and universities having a four-year course, a second-year student. [Earlier *sophumer* one who uses sophisms; later infl. in meaning by Gk. *sophos* wise + *mōros* fool]

soph·o·mor·ic (sof′ə-môr′ik, -mōr′-) *adj.* **1.** Of, pertaining to, or like a sophomore. **2.** Marked by a shallow assumption of learning or by empty grandiloquence; immature; callow. Also **soph′o·mor′i·cal.** — **soph′o·mor′i·cal·ly** *adv.*

Soph·o·ni·as (sof′ə-nī′əs) The Douai Bible name for ZEPHANIAH.

-sophy *combining form* Knowledge pertaining to a (specified) field: *theosophy.* [< Gk. *sophia* wisdom]

so·po·rif·ic (sō′pə-rif′ik, sop′ə-) *adj.* **1.** Causing or tending to cause sleep. **2.** Drowsy; sleepy. — *n.* A medicine that produces sleep. [< L *sopor* deep sleep]

sop·ping (sop′ing) *adj.* Wet through; drenched; soaking.

sop·py (sop′ē) *adj.* **·pi·er, ·pi·est** **1.** Very wet. **2.** Rainy. **3.** *Brit. Slang* Mawkish; sentimental.

so·pra·no (sə-pran′ō, -prä′nō) *n. pl.* **so·pran·os** or **so·pra·ni** (sə-prä′nē) **1.** A voice of the highest range. **2.** The music intended for such a voice. **3.** A person having a treble or high-range voice, or singing such a part. — *adj.* Of or pertaining to a soprano voice, part, etc. [< Ital. *sopra* above]

so·ra (sôr′ə, sō′rə) *n.* A small North American rail, esteemed as food. Also **sora rail.** [? < N.Am.Ind.]

Sorb (sôrb) *n.* A Wend.

Sor·bi·an (sôr′bē-ən) *adj.* Of or pertaining to the Sorbs, Wends or to their language. — *n.* **1.** A Sorb or Wend. **2.** The West Slavic language of the Sorbs; Wendish.

Sor·bonne (sôr-bôn′) The faculties of literature and science of the University of Paris.

sor·cer·er (sôr′sər-ər) *n.* A wizard; conjurer; magician. — **sor′cer·ess** *n.fem.*

sor·cer·y (sôr′sər-ē) *n. pl.* **·cer·ies** Alleged employment of supernatural agencies; witchcraft. [< OF < L *sors* — **sor′cer·ous** *adj.* — **sor′cer·ous·ly** *adv.*

sor·did (sôr′did) *adj.* **1.** Filthy; dirty. **2.** Mercenary. Of degraded character; vile; base. [< L *sordes* filth] **sor′did·ly** *adv.* — **sor′did·ness** *n.*

sore (sôr, sōr) *adj.* **sor·er, sor·est** **1.** Painful or tender to the touch as an inflamed or injured part of the body. **2.** Grieved; distressed: a *sore* heart. **3.** Arousing painful feelings; irritating: a *sore* point. **4.** Extreme or severe: in need. **5.** *Informal* Offended; aggrieved. — *n.* **1.** A sore on the body where the skin or flesh is bruised, broken, or inflamed. **2.** A painful memory; grief. — *adv. Archaic* ly. [OE *sār*] — **sore′ness** *n.*

sore·head (sôr′hed′, sōr′-) *U.S. Slang n.* A disgruntled offended person. — **sore′head·ed** *adj.*

sore·ly (sôr′lē, sōr′-) *adv.* **1.** Grievously; distressingly. **2.** Greatly; in high degree: His aid was *sorely* needed.

sor·ghum (sôr′gəm) *n.* **1.** Any of various stout, cane-like tropical grasses cultivated for their saccharine juices and as fodder. **2.** Syrup prepared from their sweet juices or plant. [< NL < Ital. *sorgo*]

so·ror·i·ty (sə-rôr′ə-tē, -ror′-) *n. pl.* **·ties** A sisterhood; a women's national or local association having chapters in secondary school, college, or university. [< Med.L *soror* sister]

sorp·tion (sôrp′shən) *n.* Any process by which one substance takes up and holds the molecules of another substance, as by absorption or adsorption. [< NL < L *sorptio*]

sor·rel[1] (sôr′əl, sor′-) *n.* Any of several herbs with leaves used in salads. [< F < OHG *sur* sour]

sor·rel[2] (sôr′əl, sor′-) *n.* **1.** A reddish or yellowish brown color. **2.** An animal of this color. [< OF *sor* hawk with plumage]

sor·row (sor′ō, sôr′ō) *n.* **1.** Pain or distress of mind because of loss, injury, or misfortune. **2.** An event that causes pain or distress of mind. **3.** The expression of grief. — *v.i.* To feel sorrow; grieve. [OE *sorg*] — **sor′row·er** *n.*

sor·row·ful (sor′ə-fəl, sôr′-) *adj.* Sad; unhappy; mournful. — **sor′row·ful·ly** *adv.* — **sor′row·ful·ness** *n.*

sor·ry (sor′ē, sôr′ē) *adj.* **·ri·er, ·ri·est** **1.** Grieved or pained, affected by sorrow from any cause. **2.** Causing sorrow; dismal. **3.** Pitiable or worthless; paltry. **4.** Painful; grievous. [OE *sār* sore] — **sor′ri·ly** *adv.* — **sor′ri·ness** *n.*

sort (sôrt) *n.* **1.** Any number or collection of persons or things characterized by the same or similar qualities; a class; species; class; set. **2.** Form of being or acting; character; quality; also, manner; style. **3.** *Usu. pl. Printing* A character or type considered as a portion of a font. — **sorts** Originally, of various or different kinds; now, of a poor or unsatisfactory sort: an actor *of sorts*. — **out of sorts** *Informal* In an ill humor; irritable. — **sort of** *Informal* Somewhat. — *v.t.* To arrange or separate into grades, kinds, sizes. [< OF < L *sors* lot, condition] — **sort′a·ble** *adj.* — **sort′a·bly** *adv.* — **sort′er** *n.*

sor·tie (sôr′tē) *n. Mil.* **1.** A sally of troops from a besieged place to attack the besiegers. **2.** A single trip of an aircraft on a military or naval mission. [< F *sortir* to go forth]

S O S (es′ō′es′) **1.** The code signal of distress adopted by the Radiotelegraphic Convention in 1912, and used by planes, ships, etc. **2.** Any call for assistance.

so-so (sō′sō′) *adj.* Passable; mediocre. — *adv.* Tolerably.

sot (sot) *n.* A habitual drunkard. [OE < OF < LL *sot* drunkard] — **sot′tish** *adj.* — **sot′tish·ly** *adv.* — **sot′tish·ness** *n.*

sot·to vo·ce (sot′ō vō′chē, *Ital.* sôt′tō vō′chā) Softly; in an undertone; privately. [< Ital., under the (normal) voice]

sou (sōō) *n.* A former French coin of varying value. [< LL *solidus* a gold coin]

sou·brette (sōō-bret′) *n.* **1.** In light opera or comedy, the role of a pert, intriguing lady's maid. **2.** An actress playing such a role. **3.** Any frivolous or coquettish young woman character. [< F < Provençal *soubret* shy, coy] — **bret′ish** *adj.*

sou·bri·quet (sōō′bri·kā) *n.* A sobriquet.

souf·flé (sōō-flā′) *adj.* Made light and frothy, and fixed in that condition by heat: also **souf·fléed′** (-flād′). — *n.* A light, baked dish made fluffy with beaten egg whites. [< L < *sub-* under + *flare* to blow]

sough (suf, sou) *v.i.* To make a sighing sound, as the wind. — *n.* A deep, murmuring sound. [OE *swōgan* to sound]

sought (sôt) Past tense and past participle of SEEK.

soul (sōl) *n.* **1.** The rational, emotional, and volitional

es in man, conceived of as forming an entity distinct
n the body. **2.** *Theol.* **a** The divine principle of life in
. **b** The moral or spiritual part of man as related to God.
The emotional faculty of man as distinguished from the
llect: He puts his *soul* into his acting. **4.** Fervor; emo-
al force; heartiness; vitality. **5.** An essential or vital
nent: Justice is the *soul* of law. **6.** The leading figure or
irer of a cause, movement, etc. **7.** A person considered
he embodiment of a quality or attribute: He is the *soul* of
rosity. **8.** A living person: Every *soul* trembled at the
st. **9.** The disembodied spirit of one who has died; a
st. [OE *sāwol*] — **souled** *adj.*

food Any of various Southern foods or dishes popular
American Negroes, as fried chicken, ham hocks, etc.

ful (sōl'fəl) *adj.* Full or expressive of deep feeling: a
ul gaze. — **soul'ful·ly** *adv.* — **soul'ful·ness** *n.*

less (sōl'lis) *adj.* **1.** Heartless; unemotional. **2.** Hav-
no soul. — **soul'less·ly** *adv.* — **soul'less·ness** *n.*

d[1] (sound) *n.* **1.** Any of a class of waves consisting of
hanical disturbances in an elastic system, esp. in air. **2.**
auditory stimulation produced by waves of this type
ing frequencies between about 20 and 20,000 cycles per
nd. **3.** An instance of this stimulation. **4.** A speech
nd. **5.** Significance; implication: The story has a sinister
nd. **6.** Sounding or hearing distance; earshot. **7.** Noise.
.i. **1.** To give forth a sound or sounds. **2.** To give a spe-
d impression; seem: The story *sounds* true. — *v.t.* **3.**
ause to give forth sound. **4.** To signal, order, announce
elebrate: to *sound* retreat, someone's praises, etc. **5.**
utter audibly; pronounce. **6.** To articulate a letter: to
nd the *r* in *park*. **7.** To test or examine by sound; auscul-
. [< OF < L *sonus*]
Syn. (noun) **3.** *Sound* is the general term embracing aural
ations of all qualities. A *tone* is a sound of definite pitch, caused
ibrations, predominantly of one frequency. *Noise* is a sound
ing pitch, caused by vibrations of dissonant frequencies.

d[2] (sound) *adj.* **1.** Having all the organs or faculties
plete and in normal action and relation; healthy. **2.**
e from injury, flaw, mutilation, or decay: *sound* timber.
'ounded in truth; valid; legal. **4.** Correct in views or
cesses of thought. **5.** Solvent. **6.** Profound, as rest;
p; unbroken. **7.** Complete and effectual; thorough. **8.**
d; stable; safe; also, trustworthy. **9.** Based on good
ment. [OE *gesund*] — **sound'ly** *adv.* — **sound'ness** *n.*
d[3] (sound) *n.* **1.** A long and narrow body of water, more
nsive than a strait, connecting larger bodies. **2.** The
bladder of a fish. [Fusion of OE and ON *sund*]

d[4] (sound) *v.t.* **1.** To test or measure the depth of (wa-
etc.), esp., by means of a lead weight at the end of a line.
'o explore or examine (the bottom of the sea, etc.) by
ns of a sounding lead adapted for bringing up adhering
ticles. **3.** To discover or try to discover the views, be-
, etc., of (a person) by means of conversation and round-
ut questions: usu. with *out.* — *v.i.* **4.** To sound depth.
'o dive down suddenly and deeply. **6.** To investigate;
uire. — *n. Surg.* An instrument for exploring a cavity.
OF < L *sub-* under + *unda* a wave] — **sound'a·ble** *adj.*
.ound'er *n.*

d barrier *Aeron.* The transonic barrier.

d effects In motion pictures, radio, etc., the incidental
often mechanically produced sounds, as of rain, hoof-
ts, explosions, etc., used to give the illusion of reality.

d·ing[1] (soun'ding) *adj.* **1.** Giving forth a full sound;
orous. **2.** Having much sound with little significance;
sy and empty. — **sound'ing·ly** *adv.*

d·ing[2] (soun'ding) *n.* **1.** The act of one who or that
ch sounds. **2.** Measurement of the depth of water. **3.**
The depth of water as sounded; also, water of such depth
t the bottom may be reached by sounding.

ding board A structure or dome over a pulpit or
aker's platform to amplify and clarify the speaker's voice.

d·less (sound'lis) *adj.* Having or making no sound;
nt. — **sound'less·ly** *adv.* — **sound'less·ness** *n.*

d·proof (sound'prōof') *adj.* Resistant to the penetra-
or spread of sound. — *v.t.* To make soundproof.

d track The portion along the edge of a motion-picture
that carries the sound record.

) (sōōp) *n.* **1.** Liquid food made by boiling meat, vege-
les, etc., in water. **2.** *Slang* A thick overcast or fog. —
he soup *U.S. Slang* In difficulties. — **to soup up** *U.S.
ng* To supercharge or otherwise modify (an automobile)
high speed. [< F *soupe* < Gmc.]

)·çon (sōōp·sôn') *n. French* A minute quantity; a taste;
rally, a suspicion.

r (sour) *adj.* **1.** Sharp to the taste; acid; tart, like vine-
. **2.** Having an acid or rancid taste as the result of fer-
ntation. **3.** Having a rancid smell or vapor; dank. **4.**
Misanthropic and crabbed; cross; morose: a *sour* person.

5. Cold and wet; unpleasant. **6.** Acid: said of soil. —
v.t. & v.i. To become or make sour. — *n.* **1.** Something
sour or distasteful. **2.** An acid solution used in bleaching,
etc. **3.** A sour or acid beverage: a whisky *sour.* [OE *sūr*]
— **sour'ly** *adv.* — **sour'ness** *n.*
— **Syn.** (adj.) *Sour* and *acid* refer to the taste of vinegar, but
acid stresses the natural composition and *sour* the result of fermentation or decay. *Bitter* suggests the taste of quinine or gall.

source (sôrs, sōrs) *n.* **1.** That from which any act, movement, or effect proceeds; a creator; origin. **2.** A place where
something is found or whence it is taken or derived. **3.** The
spring from which a stream of water proceeds; a fountain.
4. A person, writing, or agency from which information is
obtained. [< OF < L *surgere*]

sour·dough (sour'dō') *n.* **1.** *Dial.* Fermented dough for
use as leaven in making bread. **2.** *U.S. & Canadian Slang*
A pioneer or prospector.

sour grapes The attitude of affecting to despise something
one cannot do or have: an allusion to a fable of Aesop.

sour·puss (sour'pōōs') *n.* *Slang* A person with a sullen,
peevish expression or character.

souse (sous) *v.t. & v.i.* **soused, sous·ing** **1.** To dip or steep
in a liquid. **2.** To pickle. **3.** *Slang* To make or get drunk.
— *n.* **1.** The act of sousing. **2.** Something steeped in pickle,
esp., the feet and ears of a pig. **3.** A liquid used in pickling;
brine. **4.** *Slang* A drunkard. [< OF < OHG *sulza* brine]

sou·tane (sōō·tän') *n.* A Roman Catholic priest's cassock.
[< F < Ital. < *sotto* under < L *subtus*]

south (south) *n.* **1.** The direction along a meridian that
falls to the right of an observer on earth facing the sun at
sunrise. **2.** One of the four cardinal points of the compass,
directly opposite *north* and 90° clockwise from *east.* See
COMPASS CARD. **3.** Any direction near this point. **4.** *Sometimes cap.* Any region south of a specified point. — **the South**
In the U.S.: **a** The population or territory of the southern or
southeastern States. **b** The Confederacy. — *adj.* **1.** To,
toward, facing, or in the south; southern. **2.** Coming from
the south: the *south* wind. — *adv.* In or toward the south;
southward. [OE *sūth*]

south·east (south'ēst', *Naut.* sou'ēst') *n.* **1.** The direction
midway between south and east. **2.** A point on the mariner's compass, 12 points or 135° clockwise from due north.
See COMPASS CARD. **3.** Any region lying in or toward this
point. — *adj.* **1.** To, toward, facing, or in the southeast.
2. Coming from the southeast. — *adv.* In or toward the
southeast. — **south'east'ern** *adj.*

south·east·er (south'ēs'tər, *Naut.* sou'ēs'tər) *n.* A gale or
storm from the southeast.

south·east·er·ly (south'ēs'tər·lē, *Naut.* sou'ēs'tər·lē) *adj.*
1. In, of, or toward the southeast. **2.** From the southeast,
as a wind. — *adv.* Toward or from the southeast.

south·east·ward (south'ēst'wərd, *Naut.* sou'ēst'wərd) *adv.*
Toward the southeast. Also **south'east'wards.** — *adj.* To,
toward, facing, or in the southeast. — *n.* Southeast.

south·east·ward·ly (south'ēst'wərd·lē, *Naut.* sou'ēst'wərd·
lē) *adj. & adv.* Toward or from the southeast.

south·er (sou'thər) *n.* A gale or storm from the south.

south·er·ly (suth'ər·lē) *adj.* **1.** In, of, toward, or pertaining
to the south. **2.** From the south, as a wind. — *adv.* Toward
or from the south.

south·ern (suth'ərn) *adj.* **1.** To, toward, or in the south.
2. Native to or inhabiting the south. **3.** *Sometimes cap.* Of,
pertaining to, or characteristic of the south or South. **4.**
From the south, as a wind. [OE *sūtherne*] — **south'ern·**
most *adj.*

Southern Cross A southern constellation having four
bright stars in the form of a cross.

south·ern·er (suth'ərn·ər) *n.* **1.** One who is native to or
lives in the south. **2.** *Usu. cap.* One who lives in or comes
from the southern United States.

Southern Hemisphere See under HEMISPHERE.

southern lights The aurora australis.

south·land (south'land') *n. Sometimes cap.* A land or region in the south or South. — **south'land'er** *n.*

south·paw (south'pô') *Informal* *n.* **1.** In baseball, a left-
handed pitcher. **2.** Any left-handed person or player. —
adj. Left-handed.

South Pole The southern extremity of the earth's axis.

south·south·east (south'south'ēst', *Naut.* sou'sou'ēst') *n.*
1. The direction midway between south and southeast. **2.**
A point on the mariner's compass, 14 points or 157° 30' clockwise from due north. See COMPASS CARD. — *adj. & adv.* In,
toward, or from the south-southeast.

south·south·west (south'south'west', *Naut.* sou'sou'west')
n. **1.** The direction midway between south and southwest.
2. A point on the mariner's compass, 18 points or 202° 30'
clockwise from due north. See COMPASS CARD. — *adj. &
adv.* In, toward, or from the south-southwest.

south·ward (south′wərd, *Naut.* suth′ərd) *adv.* Toward the south. Also **south′wards.** — *adj.* To, toward, facing, or in the south. — *n.* A southward direction or point. — **south′ward·ly** *adj. & adv.*
south·west (south′west′, *Naut.* sou′west′) *n.* **1.** The direction midway between south and west. **2.** A point on the mariner's compass, 20 points or 225° clockwise from due north. See COMPASS CARD. **3.** Any region lying in or toward this point. — *adj.* **1.** To, toward, facing, or in the southwest. **2.** Coming from the southwest: a *southwest* wind. — *adv.* In or toward the southwest. — **south′west′ern** *adj.*
south·west·er (south′wes′tər, *Naut.* sou′wes′tər) *n.* **1.** A gale or storm from the southwest. **2.** A waterproof hat with a broad brim over the neck. Also **sou′′west′er.**
south·west·er·ly (south′wes′tər-lē, *Naut.* sou′wes′tər-lē) *adj.* **1.** In, of, or toward the southwest. **2.** From the southwest, as a wind. — *adv.* Toward or from the southwest.
south·west·ward (south′west′wərd, *Naut.* sou′west′wərd) *adv.* Toward the southwest. Also **south′west′wards.** — *adj.* To, toward, facing, or in the southwest. — *n.* Southwest. — **south′west′ward·ly** *adj. & adv.*
sou·ve·nir (soo′və-nir′, soo′və·nir′) *n.* A token of remembrance; memento. [< F < L *subvenire* to come to mind]
sov·er·eign (sov′rən, suv′-) *n.* **1.** A person, governing body, etc., in whom the supreme power or authority is vested; monarch; ruler. **2.** An English gold coin equivalent to one pound sterling or twenty shillings. — *adj.* **1.** Exercising or possessing supreme authority or jurisdiction. **2.** Independent, and free from external authority or influence: a *sovereign* state. **3.** Possessing supreme excellence or efficacy. [< OF, ult. < L *super* above] — **sov′er·eign·ly** *adv.*
sov·er·eign·ty (sov′rən-tē, suv′-) *n. pl.* **·ties 1.** The state of being sovereign; supreme authority. **2.** The supreme power in a state. **3.** A sovereign state, kingdom, etc. **4.** The status or dominion of a sovereign.
so·vi·et (sō′vē·et, -ət, sō′vē·et′) *n.* **1.** In the Soviet Union, any of the legislative bodies existing at various governmental levels. See SUPREME SOVIET. **2.** Any of various similar legislative bodies. [< Russian *soyvet* council]
So·vi·et (sō′vē·et, -ət, sō′vē·et′) *adj.* Of or pertaining to the Union of Soviet Socialist Republics.
so·vi·et·ism (sō′vē·ə·tiz′əm) *n.* The policies of or government by soviets, esp., as practiced in the Soviet Union. — **so′vi·et·ist** *n.* — **so′vi·et·is′tic** *adj.*
so·vi·et·ize (sō′vē·ə·tīz′) *v.t.* **·ized, ·iz·ing** To bring under a soviet form of government. — **so′vi·et·i·za′tion** *n.*
sow¹ (sō) *v.* **sowed, sown** or **sowed, sow·ing** *v.t.* **1.** To scatter (seed) over land for growth. **2.** To scatter seed over (land). **3.** To spread abroad; disseminate; implant: to *sow* the seeds of distrust. **4.** To cover or sprinkle. — *v.i.* **5.** To scatter seed. [OE *sāwan*] — **sow′er** *n.*
sow² (sou) *n.* A female hog. [OE *sū, sugu*]
sow·bel·ly (sou′bel′ē) *n. U.S. Dial.* Salt pork.
soy (soi) **1.** The soybean. **2.** An Asian sauce prepared from soybeans fermented and steeped in brine: also **soy sauce.** [< Japanese, short for *shōyu*]
soy·bean (soi′bēn′) *n.* **1.** An erect, leguminous herb native to China and India, and cultivated for forage. **2.** Its bean, a source of oil, flour, and other products. Also called *soy*: also **soy·a** (soi′ə). [< SOY + BEAN]
spa (spä) *n.* **1.** Any locality frequented for its mineral springs. **2.** A mineral spring. [from the Belgian town, *Spa*]
space (spās) *n.* **1.** That which is characterized by dimensions extending indefinitely in all directions from any given point, and within which all material bodies are located. **2.** An interval or area between or within points or objects. **3.** Area, room, or extent, as for some purpose: parking *space.* **4.** Outer space. **5.** An interval of time; period; while. **6.** An occasion or opportunity. **7.** *Printing* A piece of type metal used for spacing between words. **8.** A part of a musical staff included between two lines. **9.** Reserved accommodations, as on a train. **10.** Pages, linage, broadcasting time, etc., available for advertisements. — *v.t.* **spaced, spac·ing 1.** To separate by spaces. **2.** To divide into spaces. [< OF < L *spatium*] — **space′less** *adj.* — **spac′er** *n.*
space·craft (spās′kraft′, -kräft′) *n. Aerospace* Any vehicle, manned or unmanned, designed for research, exploration, or travel in outer space. Also **space·ship** (spās′ship′).
space·flight (spās′flīt′) *n.* Flight in outer space by a manmade object or vehicle.
space·man (spās′mən) *n. pl.* **·men** (-mən) *Aerospace* One who travels in outer space; an astronaut.
space medicine *Aerospace* medicine.
space·port (spās′pôrt′, -pōrt′) *n. Aerospace* A base for rockets and other spacecraft, with supporting equipment.
space probe *Aerospace* An artificial satellite or other spacecraft equipped to obtain data in outer space.
space-time (spās′tīm′) *n.* A four-dimensional continuum consisting of three spatial coordinates and one coordinate of time. Also **space-time continuum.**
spa·cial (spā′shəl) See SPATIAL.

spac·ing (spā′sing) *n.* **1.** The act, process, or result rangement by spaces. **2.** A space or spaces, as in prin
spa·cious (spā′shəs) *adj.* **1.** Of indefinite or vast exten Affording ample room; capacious. — **spa′cious·ly** *ad* **spa′cious·ness** *n.*
spade¹ (spād) *n.* **1.** An implement used for digging, cu turf, etc., heavier than a shovel and having a flatter **2.** Any of various tools or implements resembling a s — **to call a spade a spade** To speak the plain, uncom mising truth. — *v.t.* **spad·ed, spad·ing** To dig or cut w spade. [OE *spadu*] — **spad′er** *n.*
spade² (spād) *n.* **1.** A figure on playing cards, resemb heart with a stalk or handle at the juncture of the lobes A card so marked. **3.** *Usu. pl.* The suit of cards so ma [< Sp. < L < Gk. *spathē* sword]
spade·work (spād′wûrk′) *n.* **1.** Work done with a s **2.** Preliminary work necessary to get a project under
spa·dix (spā′diks) *n. pl.* **spa·di·ces** (spā·dī′sēz) B spike or head of flowers with a fleshy axis, usu. enclosed in a spathe. [< Gk. < *spaein* to break]
spa·ghet·ti (spə·get′ē) *n.* A food consisting of co strands of flour paste. [< Ital., pl. dim. of *spago* cord
spake (spāk) Archaic past tense of SPEAK.
span¹ (span) *v.t.* **spanned, span·ning 1.** To measure with the hand with thumb and little finger extended. encircle or grasp with the hand, as in measuring. **3.** stretch across: This road *spans* the continent. **4.** To pr with something that stretches across or extends over. — *n.* **1.** The extreme space over which the hand can be expan usu. considered as nine inches. **2.** Distance or exten tween any two extremities. **3.** Any small interval of tance, in space or in time. **4.** That which spans, as a bri [OE *spann*] — **span′less** *adj.*
span² (span) Archaic past tense of SPIN.
span·drel (span′drəl) *n. Archit.* **a** The triangular between the outer curve of an arch and the rectangular formed by the moldings or framework surrounding it. **b** space between the shoulders of two adjoining arches. **span′dril.** [Dim. of AF *spaundre*, prob. < OF *espano* expand]
spang (spang) *adv. U.S. Informal* Directly; exa straight: He ran *spang* into the wall. [Origin uncertai
span·gle (spang′gəl) *n.* **1.** A small bit of sparkling m plastic, etc., used for decoration in dress, as in thea costume. **2.** Any small sparkling object. — *v.* **·gled,** *v.t.* **1.** To adorn with or as with spangles; cause to g — *v.i.* **2.** To sparkle as spangles; glitter. [Dim. of N *spang* clasp, brooch] — **span′gly** *adj.*
Span·iard (span′yərd) *n.* A native or citizen of Spai
span·iel (span′yəl) *n.* **1.** Any of various breeds of sm medium-sized dogs having large pendulous ears and long silky hair. **2.** One who follows like a dog; an obseq follower. [< OF *espaignol* Spanish (dog)]
Span·ish (span′ish) *adj.* Of or pertaining to Spain, its ple, or their language. — *n.* **1.** The Romance langua Spain, Spanish America, and the Philippine Islands. **2.** inhabitants of Spain collectively: with *the.*
Span·ish-A·mer·i·can (span′ish·ə·mer′ə·kən) *adj.* **1.** pertaining to Spanish America. **2.** Designating or per ing to the war between the U.S. and Spain, 1898. — *n.* of Spanish origin living in America, esp. Central or S America; a citizen of a Spanish-American country.
Spanish-American War See table for WAR.
Spanish Main Loosely, the part of Caribbean thr which Spanish merchant vessels formerly sailed.
Spanish moss A long, pendent plant that grows on tre the southern U.S. near the seacoast.
spank (spangk) *v.t.* **1.** To slap or strike, esp. on the tocks with the open hand as a punishment. — *v.i.* **2.** move briskly. — *n.* A smack on the buttocks. [Imit.
spank·er (spangk′ər) *n.* **1.** One who or that which spa **2.** *Naut.* A fore-and-aft sail extended by a boom and a from the mizzenmast of a ship or boat. **3.** Any perso thing uncommonly large or fine.
spank·ing (spangk′ing) *adj.* **1.** Moving or blowing rap swift; dashing; lively; strong. **2.** *Brit. Informal* Un monly large or fine. — *n.* A series of slaps on the butt given as punishment. — *adv. Informal* Very: *spanking* c
span·ner (span′ər) *n.* **1.** One who or that which spans *Brit.* A hand tool used to turn nuts, bolts, etc. [< G]
spar¹ (spär) *n.* **1.** *Naut.* A round timber or pole for ext ing a sail, as a mast, yard, or boom. **2.** A similar pole for part of a derrick, crane, etc. **3.** *Aeron.* Any principal la member of an airplane wing. — *v.t.* **sparred, spar·ring** furnish with spars. [Cf. ON *sparri*, MDu. *sparre* bear
spar² (spär) *v.i.* **sparred, spar·ring 1.** To box, esp. care and adroitness. **2.** To bandy words; wrangle. — The act or practice of boxing. [? < OF < Ital. *sparar* kick < L *parare* to prepare]
spar³ (spär) *n.* A vitreous, crystalline, easily cleavable, trous mineral of varied composition. [< MDu.]

r (spär) *n.* A member of the women's reserve of the U.S.
st Guard. Also **SPAR**. [< L *s(emper) par(atus)* already, the motto of the U.S. Coast Guard]

deck *Naut.* The light upper deck of a vessel, extend-
from bow to stern.

'e (spär) *v.* **spared, spar·ing** *v.t.* 1. To refrain from in-
ng, molesting, or killing. 2. To free or relieve (someone)
n (pain, expense, etc.). 3. To refrain from using or ex-
sing; use frugally. 4. To part with; do without: Can you
re a dime? — *v.i.* 5. To be frugal. 6. To be lenient or
iving; show mercy. — *adj.* **spar·er, spar·est** 1. That
be spared or used at will; disposable; available. 2. Held
eserve; extra. 3. Having little flesh; lean. 4. Not lavish
abundant; scanty. 5. Economical; parsimonious. —
1. That which has been saved or stored away. 2. A
licate item kept as a substitute in case the original breaks
n, as an automobile tire. 3. In bowling, the knocking
n by a player of all the pins with the two bowls in any
ne; also, the score so made. [OE *sparian*] — **spare'ly**
— **spare'ness** *n.* — **spar'er** *n.*

'e·rib (spâr'rib') *n.* A cut of meat, esp. pork, consisting
losely trimmed ribs. [? Alter. of MLG *ribbespēr*]

·ing (spâr'ing) *adj.* 1. Scanty; slight. 2. Frugal. 3.
at spares. — **spar'ing·ly** *adv.* — **spar'ing·ness** *n.*

·k (spärk) *n.* 1. An incandescent particle thrown off
n a red-hot or burning substance or struck from a flint.
Any glistening or brilliant point or transient luminous
ticle. 3. Anything that kindles or animates. 4. *Electr.*
he luminous effect of a disruptive electric discharge, or
discharge itself. **b** A small transient arc or an incandes-
t particle thrown off from such an arc. 5. A small dia-
id or bit of diamond, as for cutting glass. 6. A small
e or indication. — *v.i.* 1. To give off sparks; scintillate.
at spares. 2. To activate or cause: to *spark* a revolution. [OE
arca] — **spark'er** *n.*

·kle (spär'kəl) *v.i.* **·kled, ·kling** 1. To give off flashes of
t; scintillate; glitter. 2. To emit sparks. 3. To bubble;
rvesce. 4. To be brilliant or vivacious. — *n.* A spark;
am. [Freq. of SPARK[1]]

·kler (spär'klər) *n.* 1. Something that sparkles. 2. A
rkling gem. 3. A thin, rodlike firework that emits sparks.

·kling (spär'kling) *adj.* 1. Giving out sparks or flash-
glittering. 2. Brilliant; vivacious. — **spar'kling·ly** *adv.*

·k plug An electrical device for igniting the explosive
es in an internal-combustion engine by means of a spark
sing between two terminals. Also *Brit.* **spark'ing plug.**

·ling (spär'ling) *n.* 1. A smelt, parr, or other young
. 2. A young herring. [< OF *esperlinge* < Gmc.]

·row (spar'ō) *n.* 1. A small hardy bird related to the
hes, grosbeaks, and buntings, introduced into the U.S.,
ere it is known as the **English sparrow.** 2. Any of sev-
l related North American birds. [OE *spearwa*]

row hawk 1. A small American falcon that preys on
er birds, mice, insects, etc. 2. A small European hawk
t preys on birds.

rse (spärs) *adj.* Scattered at considerable distances
art; not dense. [< L *sparsus*, pp. of *spargere* to scatter]
sparse'ly *adv.* — **sparse'ness, spar'si·ty** *n.*

r·ta (spär'tə) An ancient city in the Peloponnesus,
thern Greece; capital of ancient Laconia.

r·tan (spär'tən) *adj.* 1. Of or pertaining to Sparta or
Spartans. 2. Resembling the Spartans in character;
arageous, hardy, austere, stoical, and rigorous. — *n.* 1.
ative or citizen of Sparta. 2. A person of Spartan char-
er. — **Spar'tan·ism** *n.*

sm (spaz'əm) *n.* 1. Any sudden, transient burst of en-
y or activity. 2. *Pathol.* Any involuntary convulsive
scular contraction. When manifested by alternate con-
ctions and relaxations it is a **clonic spasm;** when persist-
and steady, it is a **tonic spasm.** [< L < Gk. < *span* to
aw, pull]

s·mod·ic (spaz·mod'ik) *adj.* 1. Of the nature of a spasm;
vulsive. 2. Violent; or impulsive and transitory. Also
as·mod'i·cal. — **spas·mod'i·cal·ly** *adv.*

s·tic (spas'tik) *adj.* Of, pertaining to, or characterized
spasms; spasmodic. — *n.* A person afflicted with cereal palsy. — **spas'ti·cal·ly** *adv.*

t[1] (spat) Past tense and past participle of SPIT[1].

t[2] (spat) *n.* 1. Spawn of shellfish; esp., spawn of the
ster. 2. A young oyster, or young oysters collectively. —
spat·ted, spat·ting To spawn, as oysters. [? Akin to
T[1]]

t[3] (spat) *n.* 1. A slight blow; slap. 2. A splash, as of
n; spatter. 3. A petty dispute. — *v.* **spat·ted, spat·ting**
1. To strike with a slight sound; slap. 2. To engage in a
tty quarrel. — *v.t.* 3. To slap. [Prob. imit.]

t[4] (spat) *n. Usu. pl.* A short gaiter worn over a shoe and
stened beneath with a strap. [Short for SPATTERDASH]

spate (spāt) *n. Chiefly Brit.* A sudden or vigorous outpouring, as of words, feeling, etc. Also **spait.** [Origin uncertain]

spathe (spāth) *n. Bot.* A large bract or pair of bracts
sheathing a flower cluster, spadix, etc. [< L < Gk. *spathē*
broadsword] — **spa·those** (spā'thōs, spath'ōs) *adj.*

spa·tial (spā'shəl) *adj.* Pertaining to, involving, or having
the nature of space. Also spelled *spacial.* [< L *spatium*
space] — **spa·ti·al·i·ty** (spā'shē·al'ə·tē) *n.* — **spa'tial·ly** *adv.*

spa·ti·o·tem·po·ral (spā'shē·ō·tem'pər·əl) *adj.* Of or pertaining to both space and time.

spat·ter (spat'ər) *v.t.* 1. To scatter in drops or splashes, as
mud or paint. 2. To splash with such drops. 3. To defame; slander. — *v.i.* 4. To throw off drops or splashes. 5.
To fall in a shower, as raindrops. — *n.* 1. The act of spat-
tering, or the matter spattered. 2. A pattering noise, as of
falling rain. [Cf. Frisian *spatterje*, Du. *spatten* to spatter]

spat·ter·dash (spat'ər·dash') *n.* A legging or puttee.

spat·u·la (spach'ŏŏ·lə) *n.* 1. A knifelike instrument with a
flat, flexible blade, used to spread plaster, cake icing, etc.
2. *Med.* An instrument used to press the tongue down or
aside, as in examinations. [< L, dim. of *spatha* spathe] —
spat'u·lar *adj.*

spawn (spôn) *n.* 1. *Zool.* The eggs of fishes, amphibians,
mollusks, etc., esp. in masses. 2. The offspring of any animal. 3. Outcome or results; yield. 4. The spat of the oyster. 5. Very small fish; fry. 6. *Bot.* The mycelium of mush-
rooms or other fungi. — *v.i.* 1. To produce spawn; deposit
eggs or roe. 2. To come forth as or like spawn. — *v.t.* 3.
To produce (spawn). 4. To give rise to. 5. To bring forth
abundantly or in great quantity. 6. To plant with spawn or
mycelium. [< AF, OF < L *expandere*]

spay (spā) *v.t.* To remove the ovaries from (a female animal). [< AF, OF < L *spatha* sword]

speak (spēk) *v.* **spoke** (Archaic **spake**), **spo·ken** (Archaic
spoke), **speak·ing** *v.i.* 1. To employ the vocal organs in ordinary speech; utter words. 2. To express or convey ideas,
opinions, etc., in or as in speech. 3. To make a speech. 4.
To talk together; converse. 5. To make a sound; also, to
bark, as a dog. — *v.t.* 6. To express or make known in or as
in speech. 7. To utter in speech. 8. To use or be capable of
using (a language) in conversation. 9. To speak to. — **to
speak for** 1. To speak in behalf of; represent officially. 2.
To lay claim to; engage. [OE *specan, sprecan*] — **speak'a·
ble** *adj.*

speak·eas·y (spēk'ē'zē) *n. pl.* **·eas·ies** *Slang* A place
where liquor is sold illegally.

speak·er (spē'kər) *n.* 1. One who speaks. 2. The presiding
officer in any one of various legislative bodies. 3. A loudspeaker. — **speak'er·ship** *n.*

speak·ing (spē'king) *adj.* 1. Having the power of effective
speech. 2. Expressive; telling. — *n.* 1. The act of utterance; vocal expression. 2. Oratory; public declamation. —
speak'ing·ly *adv.*

spear (spir) *n.* 1. A weapon consisting of a pointed head on
a long shaft. 2. A similar instrument, barbed and usu.
forked, as for use in spearing fish. 3. A leaf or slender stalk,
as of grass. — *v.t.* 1. To pierce or capture with a spear. —
v.i. 2. To pierce as a spear does. 3. To send forth spears or
spires, as a plant. [OE *spere* spear] — **spear'er** *n.*

spear·head (spir'hed') *n.* 1. The point of a spear. 2. One
who or that which leads, influences, or directs an action, etc.;
esp., a military force leading an attack on enemy positions.
— *v.t.* To be in the lead of (an attack, etc.).

spear·man (spir'mən) *n. pl.* **·men** (-mən) A man armed
with a spear. Also **spears'man** (spirz'-).

spear·mint (spir'mint') *n.* An aromatic herb similar to
peppermint.

spe·cial (spesh'əl) *adj.* 1. Having some peculiar or distinguishing characteristic or characteristics; particular. 2.
Designed for or assigned to a specific purpose; limited or specific in range, aim, or purpose. 3. Of, pertaining to, constituting, or designating a species; differential. 4. Unique; exceptional. 5. Extra or additional, as a dividend. 6. Intimate; beloved. — *n.* A person or thing made, detailed for,
or appropriated to a specific service or occasion, as a train, a
newspaper edition, etc. [< OF < L *species* kind, species]
— **spe'cial·ly** *adv.* — **spe'cial·ness** *n.*

special delivery *U.S.* Mail delivery by special courier, a
service obtained for an additional fee.

spe·cial·ist (spesh'əl·ist) *n.* 1. A person devoted to some
one line of study, occupation, or professional work; esp., a
physician who restricts his practice to one branch of medicine. 2. In the U.S. Army, an enlisted person in a technical
or administrative position, with pay equal to that of a noncommissioned officer in the same grade, but ranking below a
corporal and above a private first class. See table at GRADE.
— **spe'cial·ism** *n.* — **spe'cial·is'tic** *adj.*

spe·ci·al·i·ty (spesh'ē·al'ə·tē) *n. pl.* **·ties** 1. A specific or individual characteristic. **2.** Specialty (defs. 3, 4, 5). ◆ In British usage, this form is preferred to *specialty*.

spe·cial·i·za·tion (spesh'əl·ə·zā'shən, -ī·zā'-) *n.* **1.** The act or process of specializing; also, the state of being or becoming specialized. **2.** *Biol.* The development of a plant or animal organ or part in adaptation to environmental influences or for a special function.

spe·cial·ize (spesh'əl·īz) *v.* **·ized, ·iz·ing** *v.i.* **1.** To concentrate on one particular activity or subject; engage in a specialty. **2.** *Biol.* To take on a special form or forms by specialization. — *v.t.* **3.** To adapt for some special use or purpose. **4.** *Biol.* To modify or adapt by specialization. **5.** To endorse, as a check, to a particular payee. **6.** To mention specifically. Also *Brit.* **spe'cial·ise.**

spe·cial·ty (spesh'əl·tē) *n.* *pl.* **·ties 1.** A special occupation, craft, or study. **2.** The state of being special or of having peculiar characteristics. **3.** An individual characteristic or peculiarity; distinguishing mark. **4.** An article dealt in exclusively or chiefly, or having a special character.

spe·cie (spē'shē) *n.* Coined money; coin. — **in specie 1.** In coin. **2.** *Law* In kind. [< L (*in*) *specie* (in) kind]

spe·cies (spē'shēz, -shiz, -sēz) *n.* *pl.* **·cies 1.** *Biol.* A category of animals or plants subordinate to a genus but above a breed, race, strain, or variety. **2.** A group of individuals or objects agreeing in some common attribute or attributes and designated by a common name. **3.** *Eccl.* The visible form of bread or of wine retained by the eucharistic elements after consecration. **4.** A kind, sort, or variety. **5.** An image, form, or appearance. [< L, form, kind]

spec·i·fi·a·ble (spes'ə·fī'ə·bəl) *adj.* Such as can be specified.

spe·cif·ic (spi·sif'ik) *adj.* **1.** Distinctly and plainly set forth; definite or determinate. **2.** *Biol.* Of, pertaining to, or distinguishing a species. **3.** Peculiar or special, as characteristics, qualities, etc. **4.** Characteristic of or proper to a given substance or phenomenon, esp. in relation to some arbitrary but constant standard of comparison: *specific* gravity. **5.** *Med.* **a** Curing or alleviating a special disease or pathological condition: said of a remedy or medicine. **b** Caused by a particular condition, germ, etc.: said of a disease. — *n.* **1.** Anything specific or adapted to effect a specific result. **2.** A special medicine for a particular disease. **3.** *Usu. pl. U.S. Informal* A particular; item; instance. [< L < *species* kind, class + *facere* to make] — **spec·i·fic·i·ty** (spes'ə·fis'ə·tē) *n.*

spe·cif·i·cal·ly (spi·sif'ik·lē) *adv.* **1.** In a specific manner; explicitly; particularly; definitely. **2.** As to or in respect to species. **3.** In a particular sense or case.

spec·i·fi·ca·tion (spes'ə·fə·kā'shən) *n.* **1.** The act of specifying. **2.** Something specified, as in a contract, plans, etc.; also, one detail in such a statement. **3.** *Usu. pl.* A specific description of certain dimensions, types of material, etc., to be used in a manufacturing or engineering project.

specific gravity *Physics* The ratio of the mass of a body to that of an equal volume of some standard substance, water in the case of solids and liquids, and air or hydrogen in the case of gases; a measure of density.

spec·i·fy (spes'ə·fī) *v.t.* **·fied, ·fy·ing 1.** To mention specifically; state in full and explicit terms. **2.** To embody in a specification. [< OF < L < *species* species + *facere* to make]

spec·i·men (spes'ə·mən) *n.* **1.** One of a class of persons or things regarded as representative of the class; an example; sample. **2.** *Med.* A sample of body tissue or exudates taken for analysis and diagnosis. **3.** *Informal* A person of pronounced or curious type. [< L < *specere* to look at]

spe·ci·os·i·ty (spē'shē·os'ə·tē) *n.* *pl.* **·ties** One who or that which is plausible at first view but actually is not.

spe·cious (spē'shəs) *adj.* **1.** Apparently good or right, but actually not so; plausible: *specious* reasoning. **2.** Pleasing or attractive in appearance, but deceptive. **3.** Beguiling, but lacking in sincerity. [< L *speciosus* fair] — **spe'cious·ly** *adv.* — **spe'cious·ness** *n.*

speck (spek) *n.* **1.** A small spot, stain, or discoloration. **2.** Any very small thing; a particle. — *v.t.* To mark with spots or specks; speckle. [OE *specca*]

speck·le (spek'əl) *v.t.* **·led, ·ling** To mark with specks or speckles. — *n.* A small spot; speck. — **speck'led** *adj.*

specs (speks) *n.pl. Informal* **1.** Eyeglasses; spectacles. Also **specks.** **2.** Specifications (def. 3).

spec·ta·cle (spek'tə·kəl) *n.* **1.** That which is exhibited to public view, esp. something grand or showy. **2.** An unwelcome or deplorable exhibition. **3.** *pl.* A pair of eyeglasses. [< F < L < *spectare*, freq. of *specere* to see]

spec·ta·cled (spek'tə·kəld) *adj.* **1.** Wearing spectacles. **2.** Having markings resembling a pair of spectacles.

spec·tac·u·lar (spek·tak'yə·lər) *adj.* **1.** Characterized by or displaying unusual, exciting, or unexpected qualities, conditions, etc.: a *spectacular* rescue. **2.** Of, pertaining to, or like a spectacle. — *n.* **1.** In television, a lavish dramatic or musical production. **2.** An elaborate, illuminated sign. — **spec·tac'u·lar·ly** *adv.* — **spec·tac'u·lar'i·ty** (-lar'ə·tē) *n.*

spec·ta·tor (spek'tā·tər, spek·tā'-) *n.* **1.** One who beholds;

eyewitness; onlooker. **2.** One who is present at and vie[w]s show, game, spectacle, etc. [< L < *spectare* to look at]

spec·ter (spek'tər) *n.* **1.** A ghost or apparition. **2.** A[nything] thing of a fearful or horrible nature. Also *Brit.* **spec'tre.** F < L *spectrum* vision]

spec·tra (spek'trə) Plural of SPECTRUM.

spec·tral (spek'trəl) *adj.* **1.** Of, pertaining to, or li[ke a] specter; ghostly. **2.** Pertaining to a spectrum or spec[trum]. — **spec·tral·i·ty** (spek·tral'ə·tē) *n.* — **spec'tral·ly** *adv.*

spectro- *combining form* **1.** Radiant energy, as exhibite[d in] the spectrum. **2.** Spectroscope; spectroscopic. [< S[PEC-] TRUM]

spec·tro·gram (spek'trə·gram) *n.* A photograph made [by] spectrograph.

spec·tro·graph (spek'trə·graf, -gräf) *n.* **1.** An appar[atus] for photographing or forming a representation of the s[pec] trum. **2.** A spectrogram.

spec·tro·scope (spek'trə·skōp) *n.* An optical instru[ment] for forming and analyzing the spectrum emitted by bodies or substances. — **spec'· tro·scop'ic** (-skop'ik) or **·i·cal** *adj.* — **spec'· tro·scop'i·cal·ly** *adv.* **spec·tros·co·py** (spek· tros'kə·pē) *n.* The study and analysis of the phenomena observed with the spectroscope. — **spec· tros'co·pist** *n.*

SIMPLE SPECTROSCOPE

a Prism. *b* Telescope for viewing prism through eyepiece (*e*). *c* Collimator with slit (*d*).

spec·trum (spek'trəm) *n.* *pl.* **·tra** (-trə) **1.** *Physics* **a** band of color observed when a beam of white light is pa[ssed] through a prism that separates each component of the [light] according to wavelengths, ranging from long for red to s[hort] for violet. **b** An image formed by radiant energy dire[cted] through a spectroscope and brought to a focus, and in w[hich] each wavelength corresponds to a specific band or line [in a] progressive series characteristic of the emitting source. **2.** Any range of characteristics, values, activities, etc. **3.** [An] afterimage. [< L, vision]

spec·u·la (spek'yə·lə) Plural of SPECULUM.

spec·u·late (spek'yə·lāt) *v.i.* **·lat·ed, ·lat·ing 1.** To f[orm] conjectures regarding anything without experiment; t[heo-] rize; conjecture. **2.** To make an investment involvi[ng] risk, but with hope of gain. [< L *speculatus*, pp. of *specu[lari]* to look at] — **spec'u·la'tor** *n.*

spec·u·la·tion (spek'yə·lā'shən) *n.* **1.** The act of theoriz[ing] or conjecturing; speculating. **2.** A theory or conject[ure.] **3.** A conclusion reached by or based upon conjecture. [4.] An investment involving risk with hope of large profit. [5.] The act of engaging in risky business transactions that [offer] a possibility of large profit.

spec·u·la·tive (spek'yə·lā'tiv, -lə·tiv) *adj.* **1.** Of, pert[ain-] ing to, engaged in, or given to speculation, meditation, [etc.] **2.** Strictly theoretical or purely scientific. **3.** Engag[ing] or involving financial speculation. **4.** Involving risk. — **spec'u·la'tive·ly** *adv.* — **spec'u·la'tive·ness** *n.*

spec·u·lum (spek'yə·ləm) *n.* *pl.* **·la** (-lə) or **·lums** [A] mirror of polished metal or of glass coated with a metal [film] used for telescope reflectors, etc. **2.** *Med.* An instrument [that] dilates a passage of the body for examination. [< L, m[irror] < *specere* to see] — **spec'u·lar** *adj.*

sped (sped) Alternative past tense and past particip[le of] SPEED.

speech (spēch) *n.* **1.** The faculty of expressing thought [or] emotion by spoken words. **2.** The act of speaking. **3.** T[hat] which is spoken; a saying or remark. **4.** A public addre[ss or] talk. **5.** A characteristic manner of speaking. **6.** A par[ticu-] lar language, idiom, or dialect: American *speech.* **7.** [Any] audible or visible method of communication, including [also] gestures, and sign language. **8.** The study of oral comm[uni-] cation. [OE < *specan, sprecan* to speak]

speech clinic A place where speech disorders are trea[ted]

speech disorder Disorganization or impairment of sp[eech] caused either by physical defect or by mental disorder.

speech·i·fy (spē'chə·fī) *v.i.* **·fied, ·fy·ing** To make spee[ches;] a derisive or dialectal term. — **speech'i·fi'er** *n.*

speech·less (spēch'lis) *adj.* **1.** Unable to speak or tem[po-] rarily deprived of speech because of physical weakn[ess,] strong emotion, etc. **2.** Mute; dumb. **3.** Silent; reti[cent.] **4.** Unable to be expressed in words: *speechless* joy. — **speech'less·ly** *adv.* — **speech'less·ness** *n.*

speed (spēd) *n.* **1.** The act or state of moving or progr[ess-] ing swiftly; rapidity of motion; swiftness. **2.** Rate of [mo-] tion, esp., in physics, as considered without referenc[e to] direction. **3.** Rate of performance, as shown by the rat[e of] work done to time spent. **4.** *Mech.* A transmission gear [in a] motor vehicle. **5.** *Photog.* In a camera lens, the minim[um] time required for an effective exposure. — *v.* **sped** or **sp[eed-]** **ed, speed·ing** *v.t.* **1.** To move or go with speed. **2.** To [ex-] ceed a speed limit. — *v.t.* **3.** To promote the forward [move]

of; cause to move or go with speed. **4.** To promote the
ss of. **5.** To wish Godspeed to: *Speed* the parting guest.
speed up To accelerate in speed or action. — *adj.*
ing, pertaining to, characterized by, regulating, or indi-
ng speed. [OE *spēd* prosperity, power]
d·boat (spēd'bōt') *n.* A motorboat capable of high
d.
d·er (spē'dər) *n.* One who or that which speeds; esp., a
rist who exceeds a safe or legally specified limit.
d·om·e·ter (spi·dom'ə·tər) *n.* A device for indicating
speed of a vehicle, often combined with an odometer.
d·ster (spēd'stər) *n.* One who speeds.
d·up (spēd'up') *n.* An acceleration in work, output,
ement, etc.
d·way (spēd'wā') *n.* A specially reserved or prepared
for vehicles traveling at high speed.
d·well (spēd'wel) *n.* One of various low herbs of the
ort family, bearing blue or white flowers.
l·y (spē'dē) *adj.* **speed·i·er, speed·i·est 1.** Character-
by speed; rapid. **2.** Without delay; prompt. — **Syn.**
SWIFT. — **speed'i·ly** *adv.* — **speed'i·ness** *n.*
e·an (spi·lē'ən) *adj.* **1.** Of, or like a cave. **2.** Dwelling
cave or caves. [< L < Gk. *spēlaion* cave]
o- *combining form* Cave. [< L *spelaeum* cave < Gk.
ıion]
e·ol·o·gy (spē'lē·ol'ə·jē) *n.* **1.** The scientific study of
s in their physical, geological, and biological aspects. **2.**
exploration of caves as a sport or profession. — **spe'le-**
g'i·cal (-ə·loj'i·kəl) *adj.* — **spe'le·ol'o·gist** *n.*
l¹ (spel) *v.* **spelled** or **spelt, spell·ing** *v.t.* **1.** To name or
e the letters of (a word); esp., to do so correctly. **2.** To
t or be the letters of: C-a-t *spells* cat. **3.** To compose;
e up. **4.** To signify; mean. — *v.i.* **5.** To form words
of letters, esp. correctly. — **to spell out 1.** To read with
culty. **2.** To puzzle out and learn. **3.** To make clear
explicit. [< OF *espeler* < Gmc.]
l² (spel) *n.* **1.** A word formula used as a charm. **2.** An
istible fascination or attraction. — *v.t.* **spelled, spell·**
To cast a spell upon. [OE, statement.]
l³ (spel) *n.* **1.** A period of time, usu. of short length. **2.**
rmal A continuous period characterized by a certain type
eather. **3.** *Informal* A short distance. **4.** *Informal* A fit
ness, debility, etc. **5.** A turn of duty in relief of another.
period of work or employment. — *v.t.* **1.** To relieve
porarily from some work or duty. — *v.i.* **2.** To take a
[OE *gespelia* substitute]
l·bind (spel'bīnd') *v.t.* **·bound, ·bind·ing** To bind or en-
ll, as if by a spell. — **spell'bind'er** *n.*
l·bound (spel'bound') *adj.* Fascinated; enchanted.
l·er (spel'ər) *n.* **1.** One who spells. **2.** A spelling book.
l·ing (spel'ing) *n.* **1.** The act of one who spells. **2.** The
of correct spelling; orthography. **3.** The way in which a
d is spelled.
ling bee A gathering at which contestants engage in
ling words, those who spell wrongly usu. being retired
l only one remains.
t¹ (spelt) Alternative past tense and past participle of
LL.
t² (spelt) *n.* A species of wheat or any of its winter or
ng varieties. [OE]
lunk·er (spē·lung'kər) *n.* An enthusiast in the explora-
and study of caves; a speleologist. [< L *spelunca* cave]
pe·lunk'ing *n.*
d (spend) *v.* **spent, spend·ing** *v.t.* **1.** To pay out or dis-
se (money). **2.** To expend by degrees; use up. **3.** To ap-
or devote, as thought or effort, to some activity, purpose,
4. To pass: to *spend* one's life in jail. — *v.i.* **5.** To pay
or disburse money, etc. [OE < L *expendere* to expend]
spend'er *n.*
d·thrift (spend'thrift') *n.* One who spends money lav-
y or wastefully. — *adj.* Excessively lavish; prodigal.
t (spent) Past tense and part participle of SPEND. —
1. Worn out or exhausted. **2.** Deprived of force.
m¹ (spûrm) *n.* **1.** The male fertilizing fluid; semen. **2.**
ale reproductive cell; spermatozoon. [< OF < L <
sperma seed]
m² (spûrm) *n.* **1.** A sperm whale. **2.** Spermaceti. **3.**
rm oil. [Short for SPERMACETI]
rm *combining form Bot.* A seed (of a specified kind):
mosperm. [< Gk. *sperma, spermatos* seed]
r·ma·ce·ti (spûr'mə·sē'tē, -set'ē) *n.* A white, waxy sub-
nce separated from the oil contained in the head of the
rm whale, used for making candles, ointments, etc. [< L
rma ceti seed of a whale]
r·mat·ic (spûr·mat'ik) *adj.* Of, pertaining to, or like
rm; generative.
rmato- *combining form* **1.** Seed; pertaining to seeds.
Spermatozoa; of or related to spermatozoa. Also *spermo-*.

Also, before vowels, **spermat-**. [< Gk. *sperma, spermatos*
seed]
sper·ma·to·phyte (spûr'mə·tə·fīt', spər·mat'ə·fīt) *n. Bot.*
Any of a phylum or division of flowering and seed-bearing
plants. — **sper'ma·to·phyt'ic** (-fit'ik) *adj.*
sper·ma·to·zo·on (spûr'mə·tə·zō'on) *n. pl.* **·zo·a** (-zō'ə)
Biol. The male fertilizing element of an animal, usu. in the
form of a highly motile cell with a long flagellate process or
tail: also called *zoosperm.* [< SPERMATO- + Gk. *zōion* ani-
mal] — **sper'ma·to·zo'al, sper'ma·to·zo'ic** *adj.*
sper·mic (spûr'mik) *adj.* Spermatic.
spermo- See SPERMATO-.
-spermous *combining form* Having (a specified number or
kind of) seeds; seeded. Also **-spermal, -spermic.** [< -SPERM
+ -OUS]
sperm whale A large, toothed whale of warm seas, having a
huge truncate head containing a reservoir of sperm oil.
spew (spyōō) *v.t. & v.i.* To vomit; throw up. — *n.* That
which is spewed; vomit. Also spelled *spue.* [OE *spīwan*]
sphag·num (sfag'nəm) *n.* Any of a genus of whitish gray
mosses found in damp places; the bog or peat mosses, used as
packing and in surgical dressings. [< L < Gk. *sphāgnos,*
kind of moss] — **sphag'nous** *adj.*
sphal·er·ite (sfal'ər·īt) *n.* A resinous to adamantine native
zinc sulfide, ZnS, with traces of iron and cadmium; a principal ore of zinc: also called *zinc blende.* [< Gk. *sphaleros* deceptive + -ITE¹]
sphe·noid (sfē'noid) *n.* **1.** *Mineral.* A crystal form enclosed
by four faces, each of which cuts all three axes. **2.** *Anat.*
The sphenoid bone. — *adj.* Wedge-shaped. [< Gk. *sphēn*
wedge + -OID] — **sphe·noi·dal** (sfi·noid'l) *adj.*
sphenoid bone *Anat.* An irregular, compound bone situated at the base of the skull.
sphere (sfir) *n.* **1.** The surface described by a semicircle
making one complete rotation on its diameter. **2.** A solid or
hollow figure enclosed by a surface every point of which is
equidistant from the center. **3.** A globe; ball. **4.** Compass
or field of activity, endeavor, influence, etc.; range; scope;
province. **5.** A particular social rank or position. **6.** The
apparent outer dome of the heavens on which the heavenly
bodies appear to lie. — *v.t.* **sphered, spher·ing 1.** To place
in or as in a sphere. **2.** To set among the celestial spheres.
3. To make spherical. [< OF < L < Gk. *sphaira* ball]
-sphere *combining form* **1.** Denoting an enveloping spherical mass: *atmosphere.* **2.** Denoting a spherical form: *plani-
sphere.* [< Gk. *sphaira* ball, sphere]
spher·i·cal (sfir'i·kəl, sfer'-) *adj.* **1.** Shaped like a sphere;
globular. **2.** Pertaining to a sphere or spheres. **3.** Pertaining to the heavenly bodies; celestial. Also **spher'ic.** —
spher'i·cal·ly *adv.* — **spher'i·cal·ness** *n.*
sphe·ric·i·ty (sfi·ris'ə·tē) *n. pl.* **·ties** The state of being a
sphere; spherical form; roundness.
sphe·roid (sfir'oid) *n. Geom.* A body having nearly the
form of a sphere. — **sphe·roi'dal** (sfi·roid'l); **sphe·roi·dic**
or **·di·cal** *adj.* — **sphe·roi'dal·ly** *adv.*
sphe·roi·dic·i·ty (sfir'oi·dis'ə·tē) *n.* The state or character
of being a spheroid. Also **sphe·roi·di·ty** (sfi·roi'də·tē).
sphinc·ter (sfingk'tər) *n. Anat.* A band of muscle that surrounds an opening or tube in the body and serves to close it.
[< LL < Gk. < *sphingein* to bind fast] — **sphinc'ter·al**
adj.
sphinx (sfingks) *n. pl.* **sphinx·es** or **sphin·ges** (sfin'jēz) **1.**
In Egyptian mythology, a wingless monster with a lion's
body and the head of a man, a ram, or hawk. **2.** In Greek
mythology, a winged monster with a woman's head and
breasts and a lion's body, that destroyed those unable to
guess her riddle. **3.** A mysterious or enigmatical person. —
the Sphinx The colossal sphinx at Gizeh, having the body
of a lion. [< L < Gk. < *sphingein* to close, strangle]
sphyg·mo·ma·nom·e·ter (sfig'mō·mə·nom'ə·tər) *n.* An
instrument for measuring blood pressure in the arteries. [<
Gk. *sphygmos* pulse + MANOMETER]
Spi·ca (spī'kə) *n.* A star, one of the 20 brightest, 1.21 magnitude; Alpha in the constellation Virgo.
spi·cate (spī'kāt) *adj.* **1.** *Bot.* Arranged in spikes: said of
flowers. **2.** *Ornithol.* Having a spur, as the legs of some
birds. Also **spi'cat·ed.** [< L *spicatus* < *spica* spike]
spic·ca·to (spēk·kä'tō) *Music n. pl.* **·tos** A method of producing rapid, detached notes on a stringed instrument, by allowing the bow to rebound slightly. [< Ital.]
spice (spīs) *n.* **1.** An aromatic, pungent vegetable substance, as cinnamon, cloves, etc., used to flavor food and
beverages. **2.** Such substances collectively. **3.** That which
gives zest or adds interest. **4.** An aromatic odor. — *v.t.*
spiced, spic·ing 1. To season with spice. **2.** To add zest to.
[< OF *espice* < L *species*] — **spic'er** *n.*
spice·bush (spīs'bōosh') *n.* An aromatic American shrub of
the laurel family. Also **spice'wood** (-wōod').

spick (spik) *n. U.S. Slang* A Spanish-speaking person: an offensive term. Also **spic.**

spick-and-span (spik′ən-span′) *adj.* **1.** Neat and clean. **2.** Perfectly new, or looking as if new. [Prob. < *spick,* var. of SPIKE[1] +dial. E *span-new,* really or freshly new]

spic·ule (spik′yōōl) *n.* **1.** A small, slender, sharp-pointed body; a spikelet. **2.** *Zool.* One of the small, needlelike, growths supporting the soft tissues of certain invertebrates, as sponges. Also **spic·u·la** (spik′yə-lə). [< L *spicum* point, spike] — **spic′u·lar, spic′u·late** (-lāt, -lit) *adj.*

spic·u·lum (spik′yə-ləm) *n. pl.* **·la** (-lə) A spicule.

spic·y (spī′sē) *adj.* **spic·i·er, spic·i·est** **1.** Containing, flavored with, or fragrant with spices. **2.** Producing spices. **3.** Having zest or piquancy. **4.** Somewhat improper; risqué. — **spic′i·ly** *adv.* — **spic′i·ness** *n.*

spi·der (spī′dər) *n.* **1.** Any of a large number of eight-legged wingless arachnids having an unsegmented abdomen and capable of spinning webs for the capture of flies or other insects. **2.** A long-handled iron frying pan, often having legs. **3.** A trivet. [OE *spinnan* to spin] — **spi′der·y** *adj.*

spider crab Any of a genus of crustaceans with long legs, common on the Atlantic coast of North America.

spider monkey An arboreal South American monkey with very long limbs and a long prehensile tail.

spi·der·wort (spī′dər-wûrt′) *n.* Any of a genus of plants, esp., an American perennial with deep blue flowers.

spied (spīd) Past tense and past participle of SPY.

spiel (spēl, shpēl) *U.S. Slang v.i.* To talk; orate. — *n.* A speech; esp., a noisy, high-pressure sales talk. [< G, game, play < *spielen* to play] — **spiel′er** *n.*

spi·er (spī′ər) *n.* A spy; scout.

spiff·y (spif′ē) *adj.* **·fi·er, ·fi·est** *Slang* Smartly dressed; spruce. — **spiff′i·ness** *n.* [< dial. E *spiff* a dandy]

spig·ot (spig′ət) *n.* **1.** A faucet. **2.** A plug or valve for the bunghole of a cask. **3.** A turning plug fitting into a faucet. [ME *spigote*]

spike[1] (spīk) *n.* **1.** A long, thick metal nail. **2.** A projecting, pointed piece of metal, as in the soles of shoes to prevent slipping. **3.** A very narrow high heel, used on women's shoes. — *v.t.* **spiked, spik·ing** **1.** To fasten with spikes. **2.** To set or provide with spikes. **3.** To block; put a stop to. **4.** To pierce with or impale on a spike. **5.** *Informal* To add alcoholic liquor to. [ME < Scand.] — **spik′y** *adj.*

spike[2] (spīk) *n.* **1.** An ear of corn, barley, wheat, or other grain. **2.** *Bot.* A flower cluster having numerous flowers arranged closely on an elongated common axis. [< L *spica* ear of grain]

spike·let (spīk′lit) *n. Bot.* A small spike bearing few flowers.

spike·nard (spīk′nərd, -närd) *n.* **1.** A fragrant ointment of ancient times: also called *nard.* **2.** The East Indian herb that yields it. **3.** An American perennial herb having an aromatic root. [< L *spica* spike + *nardus* nard]

spile (spīl) *n.* **1.** A post or supporting timber; pile. **2.** A wooden pin or plug used as a vent in a cask; a spigot. **3.** A spout driven into a sugar maple to lead the sap to a bucket. — *v.t.* **spiled, spil·ing** **1.** To pierce for and provide with a spigot. **2.** To drive spiles into. [< MDu., skewer, splinter]

spill[1] (spil) *v.* **spilled** or **spilt, spill·ing** *v.t.* **1.** To allow or cause to fall or run out or over, as a liquid or a powder. **2.** To shed, as blood. **3.** *Naut.* To empty (a sail) of wind. **4.** To cause to fall, as from a horse. **5.** *Informal* To divulge; make known, as a secret. — *v.i.* **1.** To fall or run out or over: said of liquids, etc. — **to spill the beans** *Informal* To divulge a secret. — *n.* **1.** A fall to the ground, as from a horse; tumble. **2.** The act of spilling. [OE *spillan* to destroy] — **spill′er** *n.*

spill[2] (spil) *n.* **1.** A thin strip of wood or rolled paper, used for lighting fires, etc. **2.** A peg or plug. [< SPILE]

spill·way (spil′wā′) *n.* A passageway, as in a dam, to release the water in a reservoir.

spilt (spilt) Alternative past tense and past participle of SPILL[1].

spin (spin) *v.* **spun** (*Archaic* **span**), **spun, spin·ning** *v.t.* **1.** To draw out and twist into threads; also, to draw out and twist fiber into (threads, yarn, etc.). **2.** To make or produce as if by spinning. **3.** To form (a web, etc.): said of spiders, silkworms, etc. **4.** To tell, as a story or yarn. **5.** To protract; prolong, as a period of time: with *out.* **6.** To cause to whirl rapidly: to *spin* a top. — *v.i.* **7.** To make thread or yarn. **8.** To make a web or thread: said of spiders, etc. **9.** To whirl rapidly; rotate. **10.** To seem to be whirling, as from dizziness. **11.** To move rapidly. — *n.* **1.** An act or instance of spinning; a rapid whirling. **2.** Any rapid movement. **3.** *Informal* A ride or drive. **4.** *Aeron.* The descent of an airplane in a spiral curve about a vertical axis, with its nose steeply inclined. [OE *spinnan*]

spin·ach (spin′ich, -ij) *n.* **1.** A pot herb of the goosefoot family. **2.** Its fleshy leaves, used as a vegetable. [< OF *espinage* < LL *spinacia*]

spi·nal (spī′nəl) *adj.* **1.** Of or pertaining to the backbone;

vertebral. **2.** Resembling a spine, spines, or spinous ⸻ esses. — *n.* An injection for spinal anesthesia.

spinal anesthesia *Surg.* Anesthesia produced by th⸻ jection of an anesthetic into the spinal cord.

spinal column *Anat.* The series of articulated verte⸻ that enclose and protect the spinal cord and provide d⸻ support for the ribs; the backbone.

spinal cord *Anat.* That portion of the central ner⸻ system enclosed by the spinal column.

spin·dle (spin′dəl) *n.* **1.** A rod having a slit or catch i⸻ top and a whorl of wood or metal at its lower end, on w⸻ thread is wound from the distaff in hand spinning. **2.** ⸻ slender rod in a spinning wheel, containing a spool or bo⸻ on which the thread is twisted and wound; also, a simila⸻ vice on a spinning machine or shuttle. **3.** *Mech.* A rota⸻ rod, axis, or shaft, esp. when small and bearing somet⸻ that rotates: the *spindle* of a lathe. **4.** A needlelike ⸻ mounted on a weighted base, used for impaling bills, ch⸻ etc.: also **spindle file.** **5.** Any narrow, tapering objec⸻ sembling a spindle. **6.** A small shaft passing through ⸻ lock of a door and bearing the knobs or handles. — *v.* ⸻ **·dling** *v.i.* **1.** To grow into a long, slender stalk or body⸻ *v.t.* **2.** To form into a spindle. **3.** To provide with a spi⸻ **4.** To impale on a spindle. [OE *spinnan* to spin]

spin·dle-leg·ged (spin′dəl·leg′id, -legd′) *adj.* Having ⸻ slender legs. Also **spin′dle-shanked′** (-shangkt′).

spin·dle-legs (spin′dəl·legz′) *n. pl.* (construed as sin⸻ *def. 2*) **1.** Long, slender legs. **2.** *Informal* A person ha⸻ long, slender legs. Also **spin′dle-shanks′** (-shangks′).

spin·dling (spind′ling) *adj.* Long and thin; disproport⸻ ately slender. — *n.* A spindling person or plant shoot⸻

spin·dly (spind′lē) *adj.* **·dli·er, ·dli·est** Of a slender, t⸻ growth or form.

spin·drift (spin′drift) *n.* Blown sea spray: also called s⸻ *drift.* [Alter. of *spoondrift* < *spoon,* var. of SPUME + DR⸻

spine (spīn) *n.* **1.** The spinal column of a vertebrate; b⸻ bone. **2.** *Zool.* Any of various hard, pointed outgrowth⸻ the bodies of certain animals, as the fin ray of a fish. **3.** ⸻ A stiff, pointed woody process on the stems of certain pla⸻ thorn. **4.** The back of a bound book, usu. inscribed wit⸻ title and name of the author. **5.** A projecting eminenc⸻ ridge. [< OF < L *spina* spine]

spi·nel (spi-nel′, spin′əl) *n.* Any of a class of hard, vario⸻ colored minerals, some of which, as the **ruby spinel,** are ⸻ as gemstones. [< F < Ital. < L *spina* spine]

spine·less (spīn′lis) *adj.* **1.** Having no spine or backb⸻ invertebrate. **2.** Lacking spines. **3.** Lacking firmne⸻ will or steadfastness; cowardly. — **spine′less·ness** *n.*

spin·et (spin′it) *n.* **1.** A small musical keyboard instrum⸻ of the harpsichord class. **2.** A small upright piano. [< ⸻ G. *Spinetti,* 16th c. Venetian inventor]

spin·na·ker (spin′ə-kər) *n. Naut.* A large, bellying jib s⸻ times carried on the mainmast of a racing vessel opposite ⸻ mainsail, used when sailing before the wind. [? < a mis⸻ nunciation of *Sphinx,* the name of the first yacht to ⸻ this kind of sail, 1866]

spin·ner (spin′ər) *n.* **1.** One who or that which spins. ⸻ In angling, a whirling spoon bait.

spin·ner·et (spin′ə-ret′) *n.* **1.** An organ by which spide⸻ silkworms produce the filament for webs, cocoons, etc. **2⸻** pierced metal plate through which plastic material is fo⸻ so as to make rayon fibers.

spin·ning (spin′ing) *n.* The act of one who or that w⸻ spins. — *adj.* **1.** That spins. **2.** Of, belonging to, or ⸻ in the process of spinning.

spinning jenny A framed mechanism for spinning ⸻ than one strand of yarn at a time.

spinning wheel A device used for spinning yarn or thr⸻ a rotating spindle operated by a treadle and flywheel.

spin-off (spin′ôf′, -of′) *n.* An off-shoot or by-product.

spi·nose (spī′nōs) *adj.* Having many spines. — **spi′no⸻** *adv.* — **spi·nos′i·ty** (-nos′ə-tē) *n.*

spin·ster (spin′stər) *n.* **1.** A woman who has remained ⸻ married, esp. one no longer young; an old maid. **2.** A wo⸻ who spins; a spinner. [ME < SPIN + -STER] — **spin′s⸻** hood *n.* — **spin′ster·ish** *adj.*

spin·y (spī′nē) *adj.* **spin·i·er, spin·i·est** **1.** Having sp⸻ thorny. **2.** Difficult; perplexing. — **spin′i·ness** *n.*

spiny anteater The echidna.

spiny lobster Any of various marine crustaceans ha⸻ spiny shells but lacking large claws, valued as seafood: ⸻ called *crayfish, rock lobster.*

spir- Var. of SPIRO-.

spir·a·cle (spir′ə-kəl, spī′rə-) *n. Zool.* **1.** An aperture ⸻ the passage of air or water in the respiration of various ⸻ mals, as sharks, rays, tadpoles, and insects. **2.** A breat⸻ hole, as the nostril of a cetacean. [< OF < L *spiracu⸻* airhole]

spi·rae·a (spī-rē′ə) *n.* Any of a genus of shrubs of the ⸻ family, having clusters of small, white or pink flowers. ⸻ **spi·re′a.** [< L, meadowsweet]

ral (spī′rəl) *n.* **1.** *Geom.* Any plane curve formed by a 'nt that moves around a fixed center and continually in-·ases or decreases its distance from it. **2.** A curve winding e a screw thread. **3.** Something spirally wound or having piral shape, as a spring. **4.** A flight of an airplane in a ·ral path. — *adj.* **1.** Pertaining to or resembling a spiral. Winding and advancing; helical. **3.** Winding and rising a spire, as some springs. — *v.* ·raled or ·ralled, ·ral·ing ·ral·ling *v.t.* **1.** To cause to take a spiral form or course. *v.i.* **2.** To take a spiral form or course. **3.** To rise rply or disproportionately, as prices, costs, etc. [< d.L < L *spira* coil] — **spi′ral·ly** *adv.*

·e¹ (spir) *n.* **1.** The tapering or pyramidal roof or top of a ver. **2.** Any similar high, pointed formation; a pinnacle. A slender stalk or blade. — *v.* spired, spir·ing *v.t.* **1.** To nish with a spire or spires. — *v.i.* **2.** To shoot or point up or as in a spire. **3.** To put forth a spire or spires; sprout. E *spīr* stalk, stem]

·e² (spir) *n.* A spiral or a single turn of one; whorl; twist. F < L *spira* < Gk. *speira* coil]

·ril·lum (spī-ril′əm) *n. pl.* ·la (-lə) Any of a genus rigid, spirally twisted flagellate bacteria. [< NL, dim. of *pira* coil]

·it (spir′it) *n.* **1.** The vital essence or animating force in ng organisms, esp. man, often considered divine in origin. The part of a human being characterized by intelligence, sonality, self-consciousness, and will; the mind. **3.** The stance or universal aspect of reality, regarded as opposed matter. **4.** *Often cap.* In the Bible, the creative, animat-power of God. **5.** A supernatural or immaterial being, as angel, ghost, specter, etc. **6.** A person regarded with ref-nce to any particular activity, characteristic, or temper: a ding *spirit* in the community. **7.** *Usually pl.* A state of ıd; mood; temper. **8.** Vivacity or energy; ardor. **9.** Ar-t loyalty or devotion: school *spirit*. **10.** True intent or aning as opposed to outward, formal observance: the *spir*-f the law. **11.** The characteristic temper or disposition a period or movement: the *spirit* of the Reformation. **12.** Strong alcoholic liquor. **13.** *Usually pl. Chem.* The es-ce or distilled extract of a substance: *spirits* of turpentine. *Often pl.* In pharmacy, a solution of a volatile principle lcohol: *spirits* of ammonia. — *v.t.* **1.** To carry off secret-with *away*, *off*, etc. **2.** To infuse with spirit or anima-ı; inspirit; encourage: often with *up*. — *adj.* **1.** Of or per-ıing to ghosts; spiritualistic. **2.** Operated by the burning lcohol: a *spirit* lamp. [< OF < L *spiritus* breath, spirit]

·it (spir′it) *n.* In Christian theology, the Holy Spirit. ·it·ed (spir′it·id) *adj.* **1.** Full of spirit; animated. **2.** ving (a specified kind) of spirit or nature: high-*spirited*. **spir′it·ed·ly** *adv.* — **spir′it·ed·ness** *n.*

it gum A quick-drying solution of a gum in ether. ·it·less (spir′it·lis) *adj.* Lacking enthusiasm, energy, ; listless. — **spir′it·less·ly** *adv.* — **spir′it·less·ness** *n.*

it level An instrument used to determine any deviation n the horizontal or perpendicular by reference to the po-ın of a bubble of air in a tube of liquid.

·i·tu·al (spir′i·choo·əl) *adj.* **1.** Of, pertaining to, like, or sisting of spirit, as distinguished from matter; incorpo-l. **2.** Affecting the immaterial nature or soul of man. **3.** or pertaining to God; holy. **4.** Sacred or religious; not or temporal; ecclesiastical: *spiritual* authorities: distin-shed from *secular*. **5.** Marked or characterized by the ıest moral or intellectual qualities. — *n.* A religious ; song originating among the Negroes of the southern ; also, any similar song. — **spir′i·tu·al·ly** *adv.* — **spir-al·i·ty** (spir′i·choo·al′ə·tē), **spir′i·tu·al·ness** *n.*

·i·tu·al·ism (spir′i·choo·əl·iz′əm) *n.* **1.** The belief that spirits of the dead communicate with and manifest their sence to the living, usually through the agency of a medi-. **2.** *Philos.* A form of idealism that identifies the spirit as only ultimate reality. **3.** The state or character of being itual. — **spir′i·tu·al·ist** *n.* — **spir′i·tu·al·is′tic** *adj.*

·i·tu·al·ize (spir′i·choo·əl·īz′) *v.t.* ·ized, ·iz·ing **1.** To ce spiritual; free of grossness or materialism. **2.** To treat aving a spiritual meaning or sense. Also *Brit.* **spir′i·tu-se′**. — **spir′i·tu·al·i·za′tion** *n.* — **spir′i·tu·al·iz′er** *n.*

·i·tu·el (spir′i·choo·el′, *Fr.* spē·rē·tü·el′) *adj.* Charac-d by wit and by the higher and finer qualities of the d generally. [< F] — **spir′i·tu·elle′** *adj. fem.*

·i·tu·ous (spir′i·choo·əs) *adj.* Containing alcohol, as illed liquors; intoxicating. — **spir′i·tu·ous·ness** *n.*

o-¹ *combining form* Breath; respiration. Also, before vels, spir-. [< L *spirare* to breathe]

o-² *combining form* Spiral; coiled. Also, before vowels, ·. [< Gk. *speira* coil]

o·chete (spī′rə·kēt) *n.* **1.** Any of various motile bac-a having a corkscrewlike form and commonly found in er and sewage. **2.** Any similar bacteria including those

that cause syphilis, trench mouth, and yaws. Also **spi′ro·chaete**. [< Gk. *speira* coil + *chaitē* bristle]

spir·y (spīr′ē) *adj.* **1.** Pertaining to or having the form of a spire. **2.** Abounding in spires, as a city.

spit¹ (spit) *v.* spat or spit, spit·ting *v.t.* **1.** To eject (saliva, etc.) from the mouth. **2.** To eject or utter with violence. **3.** To light, as a fuse. — *v.i.* **4.** To eject saliva, etc., from the mouth. **5.** To make a hissing or sputtering noise. **6.** To fall in scattered drops or flakes, as snow. — *n.* **1.** Spit-tle; saliva. **2.** An act of spitting or expectorating. **3.** A light, scattered fall of snow or rain. **4.** *Informal* Exact like-ness; counterpart. [OE *spittan*] — **spit′ter** *n.*

spit² (spit) *n.* **1.** A pointed rod on which meat is turned and roasted before a fire. **2.** A point of low land extending from a shore into the water. — *v.t.* spit·ted, spit·ting To transfix or impale with or as with a spit. [OE *spitu*]

spit and image *Informal* An exact likeness; counterpart. Also **spitting image**. [See SPIT¹, n. (def. 4)]

spit·ball (spit′bôl) *n.* **1.** Paper chewed and shaped into a ball for use as a missile. **2.** In baseball, a pitched ball, now no longer legal, that is wet on one side with saliva, and devi-ates deceptively in its course.

spite (spīt) *n.* **1.** Malicious bitterness or hatred; grudge. **2.** That which is done in spite. — **in spite of** Notwith-standing. — **Syn.** See NOTWITHSTANDING. — *v.t.* spit·ed, spit·ing To show one's spite toward. [Short for DESPITE]

spite·ful (spīt′fəl) *adj.* **1.** Filled with spite. **2.** Prompted by spite. — **spite′ful·ly** *adv.* — **spite′ful·ness** *n.*

spit·fire (spit′fīr′) *n.* A quick-tempered person who is given to saying spiteful things.

spit·tle (spit′l) *n.* **1.** The fluid secreted by the mouth; sali-va; spit. **2.** The salivalike matter in which the larvae of spittle insects live. [OE *spātl*; infl. in form by SPIT¹]

spit·toon (spi·tōōn′) *n.* A receptacle for spit; a cuspidor.

spitz (spits) *n.* A small dog, a variety of Pomeranian, hav-ing long silky hair and a tapering muzzle. Also **spitz dog**. [< G, short for *spitzhund* < *spitz* pointed + *hund* dog]

splash (splash) *v.t.* **1.** To dash or spatter (a liquid, etc.) about. **2.** To spatter, wet, or soil with a liquid dashed about. **3.** To make (one's way) with splashes. **4.** To dec-orate or mark by or as by splashing. — *v.i.* **5.** To make a splash or splashes. **6.** To move, fall, or strike with a splash or splashes. — *n.* **1.** The act or noise of splashing. **2.** The result of splashing, as a spot. **3.** *Informal* A striking or os-tentatious impression, action, success, etc.: to make a *splash*. [Var. of PLASH¹] — **splash′er** *n.*

splash·down (splash′doun′) *n.* The setting down of a spacecraft or a part of it in the seas following its flight.

splash·y (splash′ē) splash·i·er, splash·i·est *adj.* **1.** Slushy; wet. **2.** Marked by or as by splashes; blotchy. **3.** *Informal* Sensational; showy: They made a *splashy* appearance.

splat (splat) *n.* A thin, broad piece of wood, as that forming the middle of a chair back. [Origin uncertain]

splat·ter (splat′ər) *v.t. & v.i.* To spatter or splash. — *n.* A spatter; splash. [Blend of SPLASH and SPATTER]

splay (splā) *adj.* **1.** Spread out; broad. **2.** Clumsily formed; awkward. — *n.* A slanted surface or beveled edge, as the sides of a doorway. — *v.t.* **1.** To make with a splay. **2.** To spread out; expand. — *v.i.* **3.** To spread out; open. **4.** To slant; slope. [Aphetic var. of DISPLAY]

splay·foot (splā′fŏŏt′) *n. pl.* ·feet (-fēt′) **1.** Abnormal flat-ness and turning outward of the feet. **2.** A foot so deformed. — **splay′foot′ed** *adj.*

spleen (splēn) *n. Anat.* **1.** A highly vascular, flattened, ductless organ located on the upper left side of the abdomi-nal cavity, and effecting certain modifications in the blood. **2.** Ill temper; spitefulness: to vent one's *spleen*. **3.** *Archaic* Low spirits; melancholy. [< OF < L < Gk. *splēn*] — **spleen′ful**, **spleen′ish**, **spleen′y** *adj.* — **spleen′ful·ly** *adv.*

splen·did (splen′did) *adj.* **1.** Magnificent; imposing. **2.** Inspiring to the imagination; glorious; illustrious. **3.** Giving out or reflecting brilliant light; shining. **4.** *Informal* Very good; excellent: a *splendid* offer. [< L *splendere* to shine] — **splen′did·ly** *adv.* — **splen′did·ness** *n.*

splen·dif·er·ous (splen·dif′ər·əs) *adj. Informal* Exhibiting great splendor; very magnificent: a facetious usage.

splen·dor (splen′dər) *n.* **1.** Exceeding brilliance from emit-ted or reflected light. **2.** Magnificence. **3.** Conspicuous greatness of achievement. Also *Brit.* **splen′dour**. [< L, brightness] — **splen′dor·ous**, **splen′drous** *adj.*

sple·net·ic (spli·net′ik) *adj.* **1.** Pertaining to the spleen. **2.** Fretfully spiteful; peevish. Also **sple·net′i·cal**. — *n.* A peevish person. — **sple·net′i·cal·ly** *adv.*

splen·ic (splen′ik, splē′nik) ° *adj.* Of, in, near, or pertaining to the spleen.

spleno- *combining form Anat. & Med.* The spleen; of or re-lated to the spleen. Also, before vowels, **splen-**. [< Gk. *splēn*, *splēnos* spleen]

splice (splīs) *v.t.* **spliced, splic·ing** **1.** To unite, as by twisting or intertwining the ends of rope, wires, etc. **2.** To connect, as timbers, by beveling, scarfing, or overlapping at the ends. **3.** *Slang* To join in marriage. — *n.* **1.** A union made by splicing. **2.** The place at which two parts are spliced. [< MDu. *splissen*] — **splic′er** *n.*

splint (splint) *n.* **1.** A thin, flat piece split off; a splinter. **2.** A thin, flexible strip of split wood used for basketmaking, chair bottoms, etc. **3.** *Surg.* An appliance, as of wood or metal, used for keeping a fractured limb or other injured part in a fixed or proper position. **4.** A splint bone. — *v.t.* To confine, support, or brace, as a fractured limb, with or as with splints. [< MDu. *splinte*]

splin·ter (splin′tər) *n.* A thin, sharp piece of wood, glass, metal, etc., split or torn off lengthwise; a sliver. — *v.t. & v.i.* To split into thin sharp pieces or fragments; shatter; shiver. [< MDu.] — **splint′er·y** *adj.*

split (split) *v.* **split, split·ting** *v.t.* **1.** To separate into parts by force, esp. into two approximately equal parts. **2.** To break or divide lengthwise or along the grain; separate into layers. **3.** To divide into groups or factions; disrupt, as a political party. **4.** To divide and distribute by portions or shares. — *v.i.* **5.** To break apart; divide lengthwise or along the grain. **6.** To become divided through disagreement, etc. **7.** To share something with others. — **to split hairs** To make fine distinctions; be unnecessarily precise. — **to split off** **1.** To break off by splitting. **2.** To separate by or as by splitting. — **to split the difference** To divide equally a sum in dispute. — **to split up** **1.** To separate into parts and distribute. **2.** To cease association; separate. — *n.* **1.** The act of splitting; also, the result of splitting, as a cleft or rent. **2.** Separation into factions; schism: a *split* in the church. **3.** A sliver; splinter. **4.** A share or portion, as of booty. **5.** *Informal* A bottle or a drink half the usual size. **6.** A confection made of a split banana, ice cream, syrup, chopped nuts, and whipped cream. **7.** In bowling, the position of two or more pins left standing on such spots so that a spare is nearly impossible. **10.** An acrobatic trick in which the legs are extended upon the floor in a straight line at right angles to the body: also **the splits.** — *adj.* **1.** Cleft, esp. longitudinally; fissured. **2.** Divided: a *split* ticket. [< MDu. *splitten*] — **split′ter** *n.*

split infinitive *Gram.* An infinitive in which the sign *to* is separated from the verb, generally by an adverb, as in "to really believe."

split level house A dwelling in which the floors of the several levels are less than a story above or below the adjoining one.

split ticket **1.** A ballot on which the voter has distributed his vote among candidates of different parties. **2.** A ballot containing names of candidates of more than one party or party faction. Compare STRAIGHT TICKET.

split·ting (split′ing) *adj.* **1.** Acute or extreme: a *splitting* shriek. **2.** That aches severely: a *splitting* head.

splotch (sploch) *n.* A discolored spot, as of ink, etc.; a daub; splash; spot. — *v.t.* To soil or mark with a splotch or splotches. [Cf. OE *splott* spot] — **splotch′y** *adj.*

splurge (splûrj) *Informal n.* **1.** An ostentatious display. **2.** An extravagant expenditure. — *v.i.* **splurged, splurg·ing** **1.** To show off; be ostentatious. **2.** To spend money lavishly or wastefully. [Origin uncertain] — **splurg′y** *adj.*

splut·ter (splut′ər) *v.i.* **1.** To make a series of slight, explosive sounds, or throw off small particles, as meat frying. **2.** To speak hastily, confusedly, or incoherently. — *v.t.* **3.** To utter excitedly or confusedly; sputter. **4.** To bespatter. — *n.* A noise as of spluttering; bustle; confused stir. [Blend of SPLASH and SPUTTER] — **splut′ter·er** *n.*

spoil (spoil) *v.* **spoiled** or **spoilt, spoil·ing** *v.t.* **1.** To impair or destroy the value, usefulness, or beauty of. **2.** To impair the character of, esp., by overindulgence: to *spoil* a child. **3.** *Obs.* To take property from by force; despoil. — *v.i.* **4.** To lose normal or useful qualities; esp., to become tainted or decayed, as food. — **Syn.** See DECAY. — **to be spoiling for** To long for; crave: He is *spoiling for* a fight. — *n.* **1.** *Often pl.* Plunder seized by violence; loot. **2.** *pl. Chiefly U.S.* The emoluments of public office. **3.** The act of pillaging; spoliation. [< OF < L < *spolium* booty] — **spoil′er** *n.*

spoil·age (spoi′lij) *n.* **1.** Spoiled material collectively. **2.** Something that is or has been spoiled. **3.** The process of spoiling. **4.** The state of being spoiled.

spoil·sport (spoil′spôrt′, -spōrt′) *n.* A person whose actions or attitudes spoil the pleasures of others.

spoils system *U.S.* In a political party after a victorious campaign, the system or practice of making public offices the rewards of partisan services.

spoke¹ (spōk) *n.* **1.** One of the rods or bars that serve to support the rim of a wheel by connecting it to the hub. **2.** A stick or bar for insertion in a wheel to prevent its turning. **3.** A rung of a ladder. — *v.t.* **spoked, spok·ing** **1.** To provide with spokes. **2.** To fasten (a wheel) with a stick or spoke to prevent its turning. [OE *spāca*]

spoke² (spōk) Past tense and archaic past participle of SPEAK.

spo·ken (spō′kən) Past participle of SPEAK. — *adj.* **1.** Uttered orally, as opposed to written. **2.** Speaking or having (a specified kind of) speech: *smooth-spoken.*

spoke·shave (spōk′shāv′) *n.* A planing tool having a blade set between two handles, used in rounding and smoothing wooden surfaces; originally used for shaping spokes.

spokes·man (spōks′mən) *n.* *pl.* **·men** (-mən) One speaks in the name and behalf of another or others. **spokes′wom·an** (-wŏm′ən) *n.fem.*

spo·li·a·tion (spō′lē·ā′shən) *n.* The act of despoiling; the authorized seizure of neutral ships by a belligerent. L < *spoliare* to despoil] — **spo′li·a′tor** *n.*

spo·li·a·tive (spō′lē·ā′tiv) *adj.* Tending to abstract from lessen.

spon·dee (spon′dē) *n.* A metrical foot consisting of long syllables or accented syllables. [< F < L < Gk. *spondē* libation; because used in the solemn chants accompanying a libation] — **spon·da·ic** (-dā′ik) *adj.*

sponge (spunj) *n.* **1.** Any of a varied group of aquatic, marine organisms, characterized by a highly porous body without specialized internal organs and incapable of movement. **2.** The skeleton or network of elastic fibers that remains after the removal of the living matter from certain sponges and that readily absorbs liquids, used as an absorbent for bathing, etc. **3.** Any spongelike substance used as an absorbent. **4.** Leavened dough, or dough in the process of leavening. **5.** *Surg.* An absorbent pad, as of sterile gauze. **6.** A sponge bath. **7.** *Informal* One who lives at the expense of another or others; a parasite. — **to throw (** or **in) the sponge** *Informal* To give up; abandon the struggle. — *v.* **sponged, spong·ing** *v.t.* **1.** To wipe, or clean with a sponge. **2.** To wipe out; expunge; erase. **3.** To absorb; suck in. **4.** *Informal* To get without cost at another's expense. — *v.i.* **5.** To be absorbent. **6.** *Informal* To live or get something at the expense of others. [OE < Gk. *spongos*] — **spong′er** *n.* — **spong′i·ness** *n.* **spong′y** *adj.*

sponge bath A bath taken by washing oneself with a cloth or sponge rather than in a bathtub or shower.

sponge cake A cake of sugar, eggs, and flour, containing shortening and beaten very light.

spon·son (spon′sən) *n.* **1.** A curved projection from the side of a vessel or seaplane, to give greater stability or increase the surface area. **2.** A similar protuberance on a ship's tank, for storage purposes or for the training of a gun. **3.** An air tank built into the side of a canoe, to improve stability and prevent sinking. [Appar. alter. of EXPANSION]

spon·sor (spon′sər) *n.* **1.** One who makes himself responsible for a statement by, or the debt or duty of, another; surety. **2.** A godfather or godmother. **3.** A business enterprise that finances a broadcast program that advertises its product or service. — *v.t.* To act as sponsor for; vouch for. [< L < *spondere* to be a security] — **spon·so·ri·al** (sôr′ē·əl, -sō′rē) *adj.* — **spon′sor·ship** *n.*

spon·ta·ne·i·ty (spon′tə·nē′ə·tē) *n. pl.* **·ties** **1.** The quality or fact of being spontaneous. **2.** A spontaneous act.

spon·ta·ne·ous (spon·tā′nē·əs) *adj.* **1.** Done or resulting from one's own impulse or desire; not premeditated; unconstrained. **2.** Arising from inherent qualities without external cause; self-generated. **3.** *Biol.* Growing without cultivation; wild; indigenous. [< LL < *spons*, *spontis* of free will] — **spon·ta′ne·ous·ly** *adv.* — **spon·ta′ne·ous·ness** *n.* — **Syn.** A *spontaneous* act seems to be prompted by inner feeling, rather than external stimulus: a *spontaneous* outburst of applause. An *impulsive* action comes from sudden inclination and lacks deliberation: an *impulsive* gesture of welcome.

spontaneous combustion The burning of a substance through the generation of sufficient internal heat to ignite, as masses of oiled rags, finely powdered ores, coal, etc.

spontaneous generation *Biol.* The doctrine of the generation of new organisms from putrid or decomposing organic matter assumed to be entirely devoid of life.

spoof (spoof) *Informal v.t. & v.i.* **1.** To deceive or hoax; parody. — *n.* Deception; parody; hoax. [after a game invented by Arthur Roberts, 1852–1933, English comedian]

spook (spook) *Informal n.* A ghost; an apparition; specter. — *v.t. Informal* To haunt (a person or place). [< Du.] **spook′i·ly** *adv.* — **spook′ish, spook′y** *adj.*

spool (spool) *n.* **1.** A small cylinder with a flange at each end and an axial bore, upon which thread or yarn is or may be wound. **2.** The quantity of thread held by a spool. **3.** Anything resembling a spool in shape or purpose. — *v.t.* To wind on a spool. [< MLG *spole*]

spoon (spoon) *n.* **1.** A utensil having a shallow, generally ovoid bowl and a handle, used in preparing, serving, or eating food. **2.** Something resembling a spoon or its bowl. **3.** A metallic lure attached to a fishing line: also **spoon, trolling spoon.** **4.** A wooden golf club with lofted face, comparatively short, stiff shaft. — *v.t.* **1.** To lift up or

:h a spoon. **2.** To hollow out like the bowl of a spoon. — **3.** *Informal* To make love, as by caressing or kissing.
Ξ spōn sliver, chip]
on·bill (spōō'bil) *n.* **1.** Any of various wading birds ated to the ibises, having the bill broad and flattened. **2.** e shoveler. — **spoon'-billed'** *adj.*
on·drift (spōōn'drift') *n.* Spindrift.
on·er·ism (spōō'nə·riz'əm) *n.* The unintentional transsition of sounds or of parts of words in speaking, as in alf-*warmed fish*" for "half-*formed wish*." [after William *Spooner,* 1884–1930, of New College, Oxford]
on-fed (spōōn'fed') *adj.* **1.** Fed with a spoon. **2.** Pamed; over-indulged. **3.** Not given the opportunity to act think for oneself.
on·ful (spōōn'fōōl') *n. pl.* **·fuls** As much as a spoon will d.
on·y (spōō'nē) *Informal adj.* spoon·i·er, spoon·i·est timental or silly, as in lovemaking; soft. — *n. pl.* on·ies A foolish, sentimental lover. Also **spoon'ey.**
or (spoor) *n.* Footprint or other trace of a wild animal. *v.t. & v.i.* To track by or follow a spoor. [< Du.]
·rad·ic (spô·rad'ik, spô-) *adj.* **1.** Occurring here and re; occasional. **2.** Separate; isolated. **3.** Neither epinic nor endemic: said of disease. Also **spo·rad'i·cal.** [< d.L < Gk. < *sporas* scattered] — **spo·rad'i·cal·ly** *adv.*
ran·gi·um (spô·ran'jē·əm, spō-) *n. pl.* **·gi·a** (-jē·ə) *Bot.* sac in which asexual spores are produced, as in certain al· and fungi: also called *spore case.* [< SPOR(O)- + Gk. *an*ɔn vessel] — **spo·ran'gi·al** *adj.*
·re (spôr, spōr) *n.* **1.** *Bot.* The reproductive body in cryp·ams, analogous to the seeds of flowering plants, but able develop asexually into an independent organism or indiual. **2.** *Bacteriol.* A strongly resistant body developed in ιe bacilli, able to become active under suitable conditions. *Biol.* Any cell or minute body capable of developing into a ·v organism; a germ, seed, etc. — *v.i.* spored, spor·ing To *velop spores: said of plants. [< NL < Gk. *seed, sowing*] **spo·ra·ceous** (spô·rā'shəs, spō-) *adj.*
·re case A sporangium.
·ro- *combining form* Seed; spore. Also, before vowels, ɔr-. [< Gk. *spora* seed]
·ro·phyte (spôr'ə·fīt, spō'rə-) *n. Bot.* The stage in which ɔres are produced in certain plants that reproduce by alnation of generations.
ɔrous *combining form* Having (a specified number or d of) spores. [< SPOR(O)- + -OUS]
·ro·zo·an (spôr'ə·zō'ən, spō'rə-) *adj. Zool.* Designating belonging to a class of parasitic protozoans reproducing by ɔres, as the malaria parasite. — *n.* A member of this ss. [< SPORO- + Gk. *zōion* animal]
r·ran (spor'ən) *n.* A purse, generally of fur, worn in nt of the kilt by Highlanders. For illus. see KILT. [< ɔttish Gaelic < LL *bursa* purse]
rt (spôrt, spōrt) *n.* **1.** That which amuses in general; di·sion; pastime. **2.** A particular game or play pursued for *version; esp.,* an outdoor or athletic game, as baseball, ten, swimming, etc. **3.** A spirit of jesting. **4.** That with ich one sports; a toy; plaything. **5.** Mockery; an object derision: to make *sport* of someone; also, a laughingstock; tt. **6.** *Biol.* An animal or plant that exhibits sudden and ntaneous variation from the normal type; a mutation. *Informal* One who lives a fast, gay, or flashy life. **8.** A ·son characterized by his observance of the rules of fair ·y, or by his ability to get along with others: a good *sport.* *v.i.* **1.** To amuse oneself; play; frolic. **2.** To participate games. **3.** To make sport or jest; trifle. **4.** *Biol.* To vary ldenly or spontaneously from the normal type; mutate. *v.t.* **5.** *Informal* To display or wear ostentatiously; show . — *adj.* Of, pertaining to, or fitted for sports; also, apɔpriate for informal wear: a *sport* coat: also **sports.** ɔhetic var. of DISPORT] — **sport'er** *n.* — **sport'ful** *adj.*
sport'ful·ly *adv.* — **sport'ful·ness** *n.*
·rt·ing (spôr'ting, spōr'-) *adj.* **1.** Of, engaged in, or con·ted with athletic games or field sports. **2.** Character·d by the spirit of sportsmanship; conforming to the codes standards of sportsmanship. **3.** Associated with sports gambling or betting: a *sporting* man. — **sport'ing·ly** *adv.*
rting chance *Informal* A chance involving the risk of s or failure.
r·tive (spôr'tiv, spōr'-) *adj.* **1.** Relating to or fond of ·rt or play; frolicsome. **2.** Interested in, active in, or re·ed to sports. — **sport'tive·ly** *adv.* — **sport'tive·ness** *n.*
rts car A low, rakish automobile, usu. seating two per·ıs, and built for high speed and maneuverability.
rts·man (spôrts'mən, spōrts'-) *n. pl.* **·men** (-mən) **1.** ne who pursues field sports, esp., hunting and fishing. **2.** ιe who abides by a code of fair play in games or in daily ιctice. — **sports'man·like** *adj.* — **sports'man·ship** *n.*

sports·wear (spôrts'wâr', spōrts'-) *n.* Clothes made for informal or outdoor activities.
sports·wom·an (spôrts'wōōm'ən, spōrts'-) *n. pl.* **·wom·en** (-wim'in) A woman who participates in sports.
sport·y (spôr'tē, spōr'-) *adj.* **sport·i·er, sport·i·est** *Informal* **1.** Relating to or characteristic of a sport. **2.** Gay, loud, or dissipated. — **sport'i·ly** *adv.* — **sport'i·ness** *n.*
spor·ule (spôr'yōōl, spor'-) *n.* A spore; esp., a little spore. [< F < NL < *spora* spore]
spot (spot) *n.* **1.** A particular place of small extent; a definite locality. **2.** Any small portion of a surface differing as in color from the rest; blot. **3.** A stain or blemish on character; a fault. **4.** *Slang* A currency note having a specified value: a ten *spot.* **5.** *U.S. Slang* A spotlight. — **in a spot** *Slang* In a difficult or embarrassing situation; in trouble. — **to hit the spot** *Slang* To gratify an appetite or need. — **to touch a** (or **one's**) **sore spot** To mention a topic that is painful to one. — **on the spot 1.** At once; immediately. **2.** At the very place. **3.** *Slang* In danger of death or of being held accountable for some action. — *v.* spot·ted, spot·ting *v.t.* **1.** To mark or soil with spots. **2.** To decorate with spots; dot. **3.** To place on a designated spot; locate; station. **4.** *Informal* To recognize or detect; see. — *v.i.* **5.** To become marked or soiled with spots. **6.** To make a stain or discoloration. — *adj.* **1.** Being on the place or spot. **2.** Paid or prepared for payment on delivery; spot cash. **3.** Made at random: a *spot* check. [ME < LG. Cf. MDu. *spotte.*] — **spot'less** *adj.* — **spot'ta·ble** *adj.*
spot check An inspection of one or a few typical things out of many, to insure quality and maintenance of standards.
spot·light (spot'līt') *n.* **1.** A circle of powerful light thrown on the stage to bring an actor or actors into clearer view. **2.** The apparatus that produces such a light. **3.** A pivoted automobile lamp. **4.** Notoriety; publicity.
spot·ted (spot'id) *adj.* **1.** Discolored in spots; stained; soiled. **2.** Characterized or marked by spots.
spotted fever *Pathol.* **1.** An epidemic form of cerebrospinal meningitis. **2.** Typhus.
spot·ter (spot'ər) *n.* **1.** *U.S. Informal* A detective; esp., one employed to discover dishonesty among employees. **2.** In civil defense, one who watches for enemy aircraft. **3.** In dry cleaning, one who removes spots.
spot·ty (spot'ē) *adj.* **·ti·er, ·ti·est 1.** Having many spots. **2.** Lacking uniformity. — **spot'ti·ly** *adv.* — **spot'ti·ness** *n.*
spous·al (spou'zal) *adj.* Pertaining to marriage. — *n. Often pl.* Marriage; espousal.
spouse (spouz, spous) *n.* A partner in marriage; one's husband or wife. [< OF < L *spondere* to promise, betroth]
spout (spout) *v.i.* **1.** To pour out copiously and forcibly, as a liquid under pressure. **2.** To discharge a fluid either continuously or in jets. **3.** *Informal* To speak or orate pompously; declaim. — *v.t.* **4.** To cause to pour or shoot forth. **5.** To utter grandiloquently or pompously. — *n.* **1.** A tube, trough, etc., for the discharge of a liquid. **2.** A continuous stream of fluid. [ME *spoute*] — **spout'er** *n.*
sprain (sprān) *n.* **1.** A violent straining or twisting of the ligaments surrounding a joint. **2.** The condition due to such strain. — *v.t.* To cause a sprain in; wrench the muscles of (a joint). [? < OF *espreindre* to squeeze]
sprang (sprang) Alternative past tense of SPRING.
sprat (sprat) *n.* **1.** A herringlike fish found in shoals on the Atlantic coast of Europe. [OE *sprott*]
sprawl (sprôl) *v.i.* **1.** To sit or lie with the limbs stretched out ungracefully. **2.** To be stretched out ungracefully, as the limbs. **3.** To move with awkward motions of the limbs. **4.** To spread out in a straggling manner, as handwriting, vines, etc. — *v.t.* **5.** To cause to spread or extend awkwardly or irregularly. — *n.* The act or position of sprawling. [OE *sprēawlian* to move convulsively] — **sprawl'er** *n.*
spray¹ (sprā) *n.* **1.** Liquid dispersed in fine particles. **2.** An instrument for discharging such particles. — *v.t.* **1.** To disperse (a liquid) in fine particles. **2.** To apply spray to. — *v.i.* **3.** To send forth spray. **4.** To go forth as spray. [Akin to MDu. *sprayen* to sprinkle] — **spray'er** *n.*
spray² (sprā) *n.* **1.** A small branch bearing dependent branchlets or flowers. **2.** Any ornament, pattern, etc., having a similar form. [ME]
spray gun A device that ejects liquids such as paint or insecticides in a fine spray by means of air pressure.
spread (spred) *v.* **spread, spread·ing** *v.t.* **1.** To open or unfold to full width or extent, as wings, sail, etc. **2.** To distribute over a surface, esp. in a thin layer; scatter or smear. **3.** To cover with a layer of something: to *spread* toast with marmalade. **4.** To force apart or farther apart. **5.** To extend over a period of time. **6.** To make more widely known, active, etc.: to *spread* a rumor; to *spread* contagion. **7.** To set (a table, etc.), as for a meal. **8.** To place on a table, etc., as a meal. — *v.i.* **9.** To be extended or expanded. **10.** To

be distributed. **11.** To become more widely known, active, etc. **12.** To be forced farther apart. — *n.* **1.** The act of spreading. **2.** An open extent or expanse. **3.** The limit of expansion of some designated object. **4.** A cloth or covering for a bed, table, etc. **5.** *Informal* An informal feast or banquet. **6.** Anything used to spread on bread or crackers. **7.** Two pages of a magazine or newspaper facing each other and covered by related material; also, print spread across two or more columns or on facing pages. — *adj.* Expanded; outstretched. [OE *sprædan*] — **spread′er** *n.*

spread·ea·gle (spred′ē′gəl) *adj.* **1.** Resembling the figure of an eagle with extended wings. **2.** *U.S. Informal* Bombastic: applied esp. to patriotic oratory. — *v.t.* **-ea·gled, -ea·gling** To lash to the mast or shrouds in spread-eagle position as a punishment.

spree (sprē) *n.* **1.** A drinking spell. **2.** A gay frolic. **3.** Excessive indulgence in an activity. [Origin uncertain]

sprig (sprig) *n.* **1.** A shoot or sprout of a tree or plant. **2.** An ornament in this form. **3.** A young man; a youth. — *v.t.* **sprigged, sprig·ging** To ornament with a design of sprigs. [ME *sprigge*] — **sprig′ger** *n.* — **sprig′gy** *adj.*

spright·ly (sprīt′lē) *adj.* **-li·er, -li·est** Full of animation; lively. — *adv.* Spiritedly; briskly; gaily. — **spright′li·ness** *n.*

spring (spring) *v.* **sprang** or **sprung, sprung, spring·ing** *v.i.* **1.** To move or rise suddenly and rapidly; leap; dart. **2.** To move suddenly as by elastic reaction. **3.** To move as if with a leap: An angry retort *sprang* to his lips. **4.** To work or snap out of place, as a mechanical part. **5.** To become warped or bent, as boards. **6.** To rise above surrounding objects. **7.** To come into being: New towns have *sprung* up. **8.** To originate; proceed, as from a source. **9.** To develop; grow. — *v.t.* **10.** To cause to spring or leap. **11.** To cause to act, close, open, etc., suddenly, as by elastic reaction: to *spring* a trap. **12.** To cause to happen, become known, or appear suddenly: to *spring* a surprise. **13.** To leap over; vault. **14.** To warp or bend; split. **15.** To cause to snap or work out of place. **16.** To undergo (a leak). **17.** *Slang* To obtain the release of (a person) from prison. — *n.* **1.** *Mech.* An elastic body or contrivance, as a coiled steel wire, that yields under stress, and returns to its normal form when the stress is removed. **2.** Elastic quality or energy. **3.** The act of flying back from a position of tension. **4.** A cause of action. **5.** The act of leaping up or forward suddenly; a jump. **6.** The season in which vegetation starts anew, occurring between winter and summer. ◆ Collateral adjective: *vernal.* **7.** A flow, as of water. **8.** Any source or origin. **9.** A crack or break, as of a plank, etc., or a thing sprung or warped. — *adj.* **1.** Pertaining to the season of spring. **2.** Acting like or having a spring. **3.** Hung on springs. [OE *springan*] — **spring′er** *n.*

SPRINGS
a Compression coil.
b Double spiral.
c Extension coil.

spring·board (spring′bôrd′, -bōrd′) *n.* **1.** A flexible, resilient board used by athletes and acrobats as an aid in leaping or tumbling. **2.** A diving board.

spring·bok (spring′bok′) *n.* A small South African gazelle noted for its ability to leap high in the air. Also **spring′buck′** (-buk′). [< Afrikaans]

spring chicken 1. A young chicken, 10 weeks to 10 months old, esp. tender for cooking. **2.** *Informal* A young, immature, or unsophisticated person.

spring fever The listlessness and restlessness that overtakes many people during the first warm days of spring.

spring lock A lock that fastens automatically by a spring.

spring tide 1. The tide occurring at or shortly after the new or full moon, when the rise and fall are greatest. **2.** Any great wave or flood, as of emotion.

spring·time (spring′tīm′) *n.* The season of spring. Also **spring′tide′** (-tīd′).

spring·y (spring′ē) *adj.* **spring·i·er, spring·i·est 1.** Elastic; resilient. **2.** Having many springs of water. — **spring′i·ly** *adv.* — **spring′i·ness** *n.*

sprin·kle (spring′kəl) *v.* **·kled, ·kling** *v.t.* **1.** To scatter in drops or small particles. **2.** To besprinkle. — *v.i.* **3.** To fall or rain in scattered drops. — *n.* **1.** A falling in drops or particles, or that which so falls; a sprinkling. **2.** A small quantity. [ME *sprenkelen*] — **sprin′kler** *n.*

sprin·kling (spring′kling) *n.* **1.** That which is sprinkled. **2.** A small number or quantity. **3.** A mottling. **4.** The act of scattering drops of liquid.

sprint (sprint) *n.* A short race run at top speed. — *v.i.* To run fast, as in a sprint. [< Scand.] — **sprint′er** *n.*

sprit (sprit) *n. Naut.* A spar reaching diagonally from a mast to the peak of a fore-and-aft sail. [OE *sprēot* pole]

sprite (sprīt) *n.* A fairy, elf, or goblin. [< OF < L *spiritus* breath, spirit]

sprit·sail (sprit′səl, sprit′sāl′) *n. Naut.* A sail extended by a sprit.

sprock·et (sprok′it) *n. Mech.* **1.** A projection, as on t rim of a wheel, for engaging with the links of a chain. **2.** wheel bearing such projections: also **sprocket wheel.** [O gin uncertain]

sprout (sprout) *v.i.* **1.** To put forth shoots; begin to gro germinate. **2.** To develop or grow rapidly. — *v.t.* **3.** cause to sprout. **4.** To remove shoots from. — *n.* **1.** A n shoot or bud on a plant. **2.** Something like or suggestive a sprout. **3.** *pl.* Brussels sprouts. [OE *sprūtan*]

spruce[1] (sprōōs) *n.* **1.** Any of a genus of evergreen trees the pine family, having a pyramidal crown, needle-shar leaves, and pendulous cones. **2.** The wood of these tre **3.** Any of certain coniferous trees, as the Douglas fir.

spruce[2] (sprōōs) *adj.* **1.** Having a smart, trim appearan **2.** Fastidious. — *v.* **spruced, spruc·ing** *v.t.* **1.** To m spruce: often with *up.* — *v.i.* **2.** To make oneself spru usu. with *up.* — **spruce′ly** *adv.* — **spruce′ness** *n.*

sprung (sprung) Past participle and alternative past te of SPRING.

spry (sprī) *adj.* **spri·er** or **spry·er, spri·est** or **spry·est** Qu and active; agile; brisk; energetic. [< dial. E *sprey* Scand.] — **spry′ly** *adv.* — **spry′ness** *n.*

spud (spud) *n.* **1.** A spadelike tool for removing the root weeds. **2.** *Informal* A potato. — *v.t.* **spud·ded, spud·d** To remove with a spud. [ME *spudde* < Scand.]

spue (spyōō) See SPEW.

spume (spyōōm) *n.* Froth, as on an agitated or effervesc liquid; foam; scum. — *v.i.* **spumed, spum·ing** To foa froth [< F < L *spuma* foam] — **spu′mous, spum′y** a

spu·mo·ne (spə-mō′nē, Ital. spoō-mō′nā) *n. pl.* **·ni** (-nē) dessert of ice cream or water ice containing fruit, nuts, Also **spu·mo′ni.** [< Ital. < L *spuma* foam]

spun (spun) Past tense and past participle of SPIN.

spunk (spungk) *n.* **1.** Punk or other tinder. **2.** A sn fire, spark, or flame; also, a match. **3.** *Informal* Met pluck; courage. [< Irish < L *spongia* sponge]

spunk·y (spungk′ē) *adj.* **spunk·i·er, spunk·i·est** *Infor* Spirited; courageous; also, touchy. — **spunk′i·ly** *adv.* **spunk′i·ness** *n.*

spur (spûr) *n.* **1.** A pricking or goading instrument worn a horseman's heel. **2.** Anything that incites or urges; inc tive. **3.** A part or attachment projecting like or suggest of a spur, as a crag or mountain peak. **4.** A stiff, sh spine, as on the legs of some insects and birds. **5.** *Bot.* A bular extension of some part of a flower, as in the larkspu **6.** A spur track. **7.** A pointed, curved cutting instrum fastened to each leg of a gamecock. — **on the spur of moment** Hastily; prompted by an impulse. — *v.* **spur·ring, spur·red** *v.t.* **1.** To prick or urge with or as with spurs. To furnish with spurs. — *v.i.* **3.** To spur one's horse. To hurry. [OE *spura*] — **spur′rer** *n.*

spurge (spûrj) *n.* A plant, euphorbia. [< OF < L < out + *purgare* to cleanse]

spur gear *Mech.* **1.** A spur wheel. **2.** Spur gearing.

spur gearing *Mech.* Gearing composed of spur wheels.

spu·ri·ous (spyoōr′ē·əs) *adj.* **1.** Not proceeding from source pretended; not genuine; false. **2.** Illegitimate. [*spurius*] — **spu′ri·ous·ly** *adv.* — **spu′ri·ous·ness** *n.*

spurn (spûrn) *v.t.* **1.** To reject with disdain; refuse c temptuously; scorn. **2.** To strike with the foot; kick. — **3.** To reject something with disdain. — *n.* The act of spi ing; also, a kick. [OE *spurnan*] — **spurn′er** *n.*

spurred (spûrd) *adj.* **1.** Wearing or having spurs. **2.** H ing sharp spikes, claws, or shoots.

spurt (spûrt) *n.* **1.** A sudden gush of liquid. **2.** Any s den outbreak, as of anger. **3.** An extraordinary effor brief duration. — *v.i.* **1.** To come out in a jet; gush fo **2.** To make a sudden and extreme effort. — *v.t.* **3.** To f out in a jet; squirt. [< OE *spryttan* to come forth]

spur track A short side track connecting with the m track of a railroad: also called *spur.*

spur wheel *Mech.* A wheel having radial teeth on the with their edges parallel to the axis; also called *spur gea*

sput·nik (spoot′nik, spoot′-; *Russ.* spoōt′nyik) *n.* A So artificial earth satellite, the first of which, **Sputnik I,** launched in 1957. [< Russian, satellite]

sput·ter (sput′ər) *v.i.* **1.** To throw off solid or fluid part in a series of slight explosions. **2.** To emit particles of sa from the mouth, as when speaking excitedly. **3.** To sp rapidly or confusedly. — *v.t.* **4.** To emit in small parti **5.** To utter in a confused or excited manner. — *n.* **1.** act or sound of sputtering; esp., excited talk. **2.** That w is ejected in sputtering. — **sput′ter·er** *n.*

spu·tum (spyōō′təm) *n. pl.* **·ta** (-tə) Saliva; spittle; ex torated matter. [< L *spuere* to spit]

spy (spī) *n. pl.* **spies 1.** One who enters an enemy's r tary lines covertly to get information. **2.** One who wat others secretly. — *v.* **spied, spy·ing** *v.i.* **1.** To keep wa closely or secretly; act as a spy. **2.** To make careful exa nation; pry: with *into.* — *v.t.* **3.** To observe stealthily with hostile intent: usu. with *out.* **4.** To catch sight of

To discover by careful or secret investigation: with *out.*
[OF *espier* to espy < Gmc.]

·glass (spī'glas', -gläs') *n.* A small telescope.

ab (skwob) *n.* **1.** A young pigeon, esp. when an unfledged
stling. **2.** A fat, short person. **3.** A soft, stuffed cushion.
A sofa; couch. — *adj.* **1.** Fat and short; squat. **2.** Un-
dged or recently hatched. [< dial. E < Scand.]

ab·ble (skwob'əl) *v.* **·bled, ·bling** *v.i.* **1.** To engage in a
tty wrangle or scuffle; quarrel. — *v.t.* **2.** *Printing* To dis-
range (composed type). — *n.* A petty wrangle. — **Syn.**
e QUARREL. — **squab'bler** *n.*

ad (skwod) *n.* **1.** A small group of persons organized for
e performance of a specific function. **2.** A small detach-
ent of troops or police; esp., the smallest tactical unit in
e infantry of the U.S. Army. **3.** A team: a football *squad.*
v.t. **squad·ded, squad·ding 1.** To form into a squad or
uads. **2.** To assign to a squad. [< F < OF < Ital. < L
attuor four]

ad car An automobile used by police for patrolling, and
uipped with radiotelephone: also called *patrol car.*

ad·ron (skwod'rən) *n.* **1.** In the U.S. Navy, two or more
visions of vessels or flights of naval aircraft. **2.** In the U.S.
r Force, a unit composed of two or more flights. **3.** A sub-
linate unit of a cavalry regiment. **4.** Any regularly ar-
ged or organized body. [< Ital. < L *quattuor* four]

adron leader In the Royal, Royal Canadian, and other
mmonwealth air forces, a commissioned officer ranking
xt below a wing commander. See table at GRADE.

al·id (skwol'id) *adj.* Having a foul appearance; dirty
d wretched. [< L *squalere* to be foul] — **squal'id·ly** *adv.*
squal'id·ness, squa·lid·i·ty (skwo·lid'ə·tē) *n.*

all¹ (skwôl) *n.* A loud, screaming outcry. — *v.i.* To cry
dly; scream; bawl. — **squall'er** *n.*

all² (skwôl) *n.* **1.** A sudden, violent burst of wind, often
companied by rain or snow. **2.** *Informal* A commotion.
v.i. To blow a squall. — **squall'y** *adj.*

al·or (skwol'ər) *n.* The state of being squalid; filth and
etched poverty. [< L *squalere* to be foul]

a·ma (skwā'mə) *n.* *pl.* **·mae** (-mē) *Biol.* A thin, scale-
e structure; a scale. [< L] — **squa'mate** (-māt), **squa'-
se** (-mōs), **squa'mous** *adj.*

an·der (skwon'dər) *v.t.* To spend (money, time, etc.)
stefully. — *n.* Prodigality; wasteful expenditure. [Ori-
unknown] — **squan'der·er** *n.* — **squan'der·ing·ly** *adv.*

are (skwâr) *n.* **1.** A parallelogram having four equal
es and four right angles. **2.** Any object, part, or surface
at has this form, or nearly so. **3.** An instrument having an
or T-shape by which to measure or lay out right angles.
An open area in a city or town formed by the intersection
several streets. **5.** An open area in a city or town formed
the intersection of four or more streets, often planted
th trees, flowers, etc. **6.** A section in a town bounded on
r sides by streets; also, the distance between one street
d the next. **7.** *Math.* The product of a number multiplied
itself. **8.** Formerly, a body of troops formed in a four-
ed array. **9.** *Slang* One not conversant with the latest
nds or fads. — **on the square 1.** At right angles. **2.** *In-
mal* In a fair and honest manner. — **out of square 1.** Not
right angles. **2.** Incorrectly; askew; out of order. — *adj.*
Having four equal sides and four right angles; also, re-
nbling a square in form. **2.** Formed with or characterized
a right angle; rectangular. **3.** Adapted to forming squares
computing in squares: a *square* measure. **4.** Direct; fair;
t; honest. **5.** Having debit and credit balanced. **6.** Ab-
ute; complete; unequivocal. **7.** Having a broad, stocky
me; strong; sturdy. **8.** *Informal* Solid; full; satisfying: a
are meal. — **square peg in a round hole** A misfit. — *v.*
ared, squar·ing *v.t.* **1.** To make or form like a square.
To shape or adjust so as to form a right angle. **3.** To
rk with or divide into squares. **4.** To test for the purpose
adjusting to a straight line, right angle, or plane surface.
To bring to a position suggestive of a right angle: *Square*
ur shoulders. **6.** To make satisfactory settlement or ad-
tment of: to *square* accounts. **7.** To make (the score of a
me, etc.) equal. **8.** To cause to conform; adapt; recon-
. **9.** *Math.* **a** To multiply (a number) by itself. **b** To de-
mine the area of. — *v.i.* **10.** To be at right angles. **11.**
conform; agree; harmonize. **12.** In golf, to make the
res equal. — **to square away 1.** *Naut.* To set (the
rds) at right angles to the keel. **2.** To square up. — **to
are off** To prepare to fight. — **to square the circle 1.**
construct a square equal in area to a given circle, an in-
uble problem. **2.** To attempt something impossible. —
. **1.** So as to be square, or at right angles. **2.** *Informal*
nestly; fairly. **3.** Directly; firmly. [< OF < L *quattuor*
r] — **square'ness** *n.* — **squar'er** *n.*

are-dance (skwâr'dans') *v.i.* **-danced, -danc·ing** *U.S.*
perform a square dance.

square dance *U.S.* Any dance, as a quadrille, in which the
couples form sets in squares.

square deal *Informal* **1.** In card games, an honest deal.
2. Fair or just treatment.

square knot A common knot, formed of two overhand
knots: also called *reef knot.* For illus. see KNOT.

square·ly (skwâr'lē) *adv.* **1.** In a direct or straight manner.
2. Honestly; fairly. **3.** *U.S.* Plainly; unequivocally. **4.** In
a square form. **5.** At right angles (to a line or plane).

square meal *Informal* A full and substantial meal.

square measure A unit or system of units for measuring
areas. See table front of book.

square-rigged (skwâr'rigd') *adj.* *Naut.* Fitted with square-
rigged sails as the principal sails.

square root *Math.* A number that, multiplied by itself,
produces the given number: 4 is the *square root* of 16.

square shooter *Informal* An upright person.

squash¹ (skwosh) *v.t.* **1.** To beat or press into a pulp or soft
mass; crush. **2.** To quell or suppress. — *v.i.* **3.** To be
smashed or squashed. **4.** To make a splashing or sucking
sound. — *n.* **1.** A soft or overripe object; also, a crushed
mass. **2.** The sudden fall of a heavy, soft body; also, the
sound made by such a fall. **3.** A sucking, oozy sound. **4.**
Either of two games played on an indoor court with rackets
and a ball. **5.** A beverage of which one ingredient is a fruit
juice. — *adv.* With a squelching, oozy sound. [< OF < L
ex- thoroughly + *quassare* to crush] — **squash'er** *n.*

squash² (skwosh) *n.* **1.** The edible fruit of various trailing
annuals of the gourd family. **2.** The plant that bears it. [<
Algonquian]

squash·y (skwosh'ē) *adj.* **squash·i·er, squash·i·est** Soft and
moist. — **squash'i·ly** *adv.* — **squash'i·ness** *n.*

squat (skwot) *v.* **squat·ted** *or* **squat, squat·ting** *v.i.* **1.** To
sit on the heels or hams, or with the legs near the body. **2.**
To crouch or cower down. **3.** To settle on a piece of land
without title or payment. **4.** To settle on government land
in accordance with certain government regulations that will
eventually give title. — *v.t.* **5.** To cause (oneself) to squat.
— *adj.* **1.** Short and thick; squatty. **2.** Being in a squatting
position. — *n.* **1.** A squatting attitude or position. **2.** The
act of squatting. [< OF < *es-* thoroughly + *quatir* to press
down] — **squat'ter** *n.*

squat·ty (skwot'ē) *adj.* Disproportionately short and thick.

squaw (skwô) *n.* **1.** An American Indian woman or wife.
2. *Informal* Any woman or girl. [< Algonquian, woman]

squawk (skwôk) *v.i.* **1.** To utter a shrill, harsh cry, as a
parrot. **2.** *Slang* To utter loud complaints or protests. —
n. **1.** The harsh cry of certain birds; also, the act of squawk-
ing. **2.** *Slang* A loud protest or complaint. [Prob. imit.]
— **squawk'er** *n.*

squeak (skwēk) *n.* A thin, sharp, penetrating sound. —
narrow (or **near**) **squeak** *Informal* A narrow escape. —
v.i. **1.** To make a squeak. **2.** *Slang* To let out information;
squeal. — *v.t.* **3.** To utter or effect with a squeak. **4.** To
cause to squeak. [ME *squeke*] — **squeak'er** *n.*

squeak·y (skwē'kē) *adj.* **squeak·i·er, squeak·i·est** Making
a squeaking noise. — **squeak'i·ly** *adv.* — **squeak'i·ness** *n.*

squeal (skwēl) *v.i.* **1.** To utter a sharp, shrill, somewhat
prolonged cry. **2.** *Slang* To turn informer; betray an accomplice or a plot. — *v.t.* **3.** To utter with a squeal. — *n.* A
shrill, prolonged cry, as of a pig. [Imit.] — **squeal'er** *n.*

squeam·ish (skwē'mish) *adj.* **1.** Easily disgusted or
shocked; modest; prudish. **2.** Overly fastidious. **3.** Easily
nauseated. [< earlier *squaymisch* < AF *escoymous*; ult. origin unknown] — **squeam'ish·ly** *adv.* — **squeam'ish·ness** *n.*

squee·gee (skwē'jē) *n.* **1.** An implement having a stout,
straight crosspiece edged with rubber or leather, used for removing water from decks or floors, window panes, etc. **2.**
Photog. A smaller similar implement. — *v.t.* **1.** To smooth
down, as a photographic film, with a squeegee. **2.** To
cleanse with a squeegee. [< SQUEEZE]

squeeze (skwēz) *v.* **squeezed, squeez·ing** *v.t.* **1.** To press
hard upon; compress. **2.** To extract something from by
pressure: to *squeeze* oranges. **3.** To draw forth by pressure;
express: to *squeeze* juice. **4.** To force or push; cram. **5.** To
oppress, as with burdensome taxes. **6.** To exert pressure
upon (someone) to act as one desires. **7.** To make a facsimile impression of. — *v.i.* **8.** To apply pressure. **9.** To force
one's way; push: with *in, through,* etc. **10.** To be pressed;
yield to pressure. — **to squeeze out** To force out of business, or ruin financially. — *n.* **1.** The act or process of
squeezing; pressure. **2.** A firm grasp of someone's hand;
also, an embrace; hug. **3.** Something, as juice, extracted or
expressed. **4.** A facsimile, as of a coin or inscription, produced by pressing some soft substance upon it. **5.** *Informal*
Pressure exerted for the extortion of money or favors; also,
financial pressure. [? < OF *es-* thoroughly + ME *queisen* to
crush] — **squeez'a·ble** *adj.* — **squeez'er** *n.*

squeeze play In baseball, a play in which the batter tries to bunt the ball so that a man on third base may score by starting while the pitcher is about to deliver the ball.

squelch (skwelch) *v.t.* 1. To crush; squash. 2. *Informal* To silence, as with a crushing reply. — *v.i.* 3. To make a splashing or sucking noise, as when walking in deep mud. 4. To walk with such a sound. — *n.* 1. A squelching sound. 2. A squelched or crushed mass of anything. 3. *Informal* A crushing reply. [Prob. imit.] — **squelch′er** *n.*

squib (skwib) *n.* 1. A firework to be thrown or rolled swiftly, finally exploding like a rocket. 2. A broken firecracker that burns with a spitting sound. 3. A short speech or writing in a satirical vein. — *v.* **squibbed**, **squib′bing** *v.i.* 1. To write or use squibs. 2. To fire a squib. 3. To explode or sound like a squib. 4. To move quickly or restlessly. — *v.t.* 5. To attack with squibs; lampoon. 6. To fire or use as a squib. [Origin unknown]

squid (skwid) *n.* Any of various ten-armed mollusks having a slender conical body, ink sac, and broad tail flukes, used as food and for bait. [Origin uncertain]

squig·gle (skwig′əl) *Informal n.* A meaningless scrawl. — *v.i.* To wriggle. [Blend of SQUIRM and WRIGGLE]

squig·gly (skwig′lē) *adj.* ·gli·er, ·gli·est Twisty; crooked.

squill (skwil) *n.* 1. The bulb of a plant of the lily family, found in the Mediterranean region, used chiefly as an expectorant: also called *sea onion.* 2. The plant itself. [< L < Gk. *skilla* sea onion]

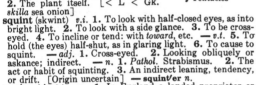

SQUID

a Arm. *b* Body. *c* Caudal fin. *d* Eye. *e* Mouth. *f* Siphon. *g* Tentacles

squint (skwint) *v.i.* 1. To look with half-closed eyes, as into bright light. 2. To look with a side glance. 3. To be cross-eyed. 4. To incline or tend: with *toward*, etc. — *v.t.* 5. To hold (the eyes) half-shut, as in glaring light. 6. To cause to squint. — *adj.* 1. Cross-eyed. 2. Looking obliquely or askance; indirect. — *n.* 1. *Pathol.* Strabismus. 2. The act or habit of squinting. 3. An indirect leaning, tendency, or drift. [Origin uncertain] — **squint′er** *n.*

squire (skwīr) *n.* 1. In England a landed proprietor or country gentleman. 2. *U.S.* A title often used in rural areas for justices of the peace, judges, lawyers, etc. 3. A young aspirant to knighthood serving as an attendant. 4. A man who escorts a woman in public; gallant. — *v.t. & v.i.* **squired**, **squir′ing** To attend or serve (someone) as a squire or escort. [Aphetic var. of ESQUIRE]

squirm (skwûrm) *v.i.* 1. To bend and twist the body; wriggle; writhe. 2. To show signs of pain or distress. — *n.* A squirming motion; a wriggle. [Origin uncertain] — **squirm′er** *n.* — **squirm′y** *adj.*

squir·rel (skwûr′əl, *Brit.* skwir′əl) *n.* 1. Any of various arboreal rodents having a long bushy tail and feeding chiefly on nuts, as the **red squirrel**, the **gray squirrel**, and the **fox squirrel** of North America. 2. Any of various related animals, as the chipmunk, flying squirrel, etc. 3. The fur of a squirrel. [< OF < LL < Gk. < *skia* shadow + *oura* tail]

squirt (skwûrt) *v.i.* 1. To come forth in a thin stream or jet; spurt out. 2. To eject water, etc., thus. — *v.t.* 3. To eject (water or other liquid) forcibly and in a jet. 4. To wet or bespatter with a squirt or squirts. — *n.* 1. The act of squirting; also, a jet of liquid squirted forth. 2. A syringe or squirt gun. 3. *Informal* A small, impudent, or presumptuous person. [Cf. LG *swirtjen*.] — **squirt′er** *n.*

squirt gun A child's toy gun used for squirting water.

squish (skwish) *v.t. & v.i. Informal* To squash. — *n.* A squashing sound. [Var. of SQUASH[1]] — **squish′y** *adj.*

stab (stab) *v.* **stabbed**, **stab′bing** *v.t.* 1. To pierce with or as with a pointed weapon; wound. 2. To thrust (a dagger, etc.), as into a body. 3. To penetrate; pierce. — *v.i.* 4. To thrust or lunge with a knife, sword, etc. 5. To inflict a wound thus. — **to stab in the back** To slander or injure in a treacherous, stealthy manner. — *n.* A thrust made with any pointed weapon. — **to have (or make) a stab at** To make an attempt at. [? < Scot. & dial. E *stob* to push, thrust, fix a stake < *stob* stake] — **stab′ber** *n.*

sta·bil·i·ty (stə-bil′ə-tē) *n.* *pl.* ·ties 1. The condition of being stable. 2. Steadfastness of purpose or resolution. 3. Continued existence; permanence. [See STABLE.[1]]

sta·bi·lize (stā′bə-līz) *v.t.* ·lized, ·liz·ing 1. To make firm or stable. 2. To keep steady; keep from changing or fluctuating: to *stabilize* prices. Also *esp. Brit.* **sta′bi·lise.** [< L *stabilis* steady + -IZE] — **sta·bi·li·za′tion** *n.*

sta·bi·liz·er (stā′bə-lī′zər) *n.* 1. One who or that which stabilizes. 2. *Aeron.* An airfoil serving to give an aircraft stability in flight. 3. A device in a ship or boat, as a gyroscope, to keep it from rolling. 4. *Chem.* A substance that increases the stability of another substance or compound.

sta·ble[1] (stā′bəl) *adj.* 1. Standing firmly in place; not easily moved, shaken, or overthrown; fixed. 2. Marked by fixity of purpose; steadfast. 3. Having durability or perma-

nence; abiding. 4. *Chem.* Not easily decomposed: said compounds. [< F < L *stabilis* < *stare* to stand] — **sta′**-(-blē) *adv.* — **sta′ble·ness** *n.*

sta·ble[2] (stā′bəl) *n.* 1. A building set apart for lodging a feeding horses or cattle; also, the animals. 2. Race hor belonging to a particular owner; also, the owner and pers nel collectively. 3. *U.S.* A group of writers, artists, ath letes, etc., under a single manager. — *v.t. & v.i.* **bled**, **bl** To put or lodge in a stable. [< OF < L *stare* to stand.

stac·ca·to (stə-kä′tō) *adj.* 1. *Music* Having or produc silence through most of the written time value of each n very short and detached. 2. Marked by abrupt, sharp phasis. — *adv.* In a staccato manner. — *n.* *pl.* **·tos** *Music* A staccato style or passage. 2. An abrupt, emph manner or sound. [< Ital., pp. of *staccare* to detach]

stack (stak) *n.* 1. A large, orderly pile of unthreshed gr hay, or straw, usu. conical. 2. Any systematic pile or he as a pile of poker chips. 3. A group of rifles (usu. three) upright and supporting one another. 4. A case compose several rows of bookshelves one above the other. 5. *pl.* T part of a library where most of the books are shelved. 6 chimney; smokestack. 7. *Informal* A great amount; ple — *v.t.* 1. To pile up in a stack. 2. To load (a vehicle, e with stacks of a material. — **to stack the cards** (or de 1. To arrange cards secretly in the pack in a manner fav able to the dealer. 2. To have an advantage secured bef hand. [< ON *stakkr*] — **stack′er** *n.*

sta·di·um (stā′dē-əm) *n.* *pl.* ·di·a (-dē-ə), *for def. 2* ·di 1. In ancient Greece, a course for foot races, with ban seats for spectators. 2. A similar modern structure in wl athletic games are played. [< L < Gk. *stadion*, meas of length]

staff (staf, stäf) *n.* *pl.* **staffs;** *for defs. 1, 2, & 3, also* sta (stävz) 1. A stick or piece of wood carried for some spe purpose. 2. A shaft or pole that forms a support or han 3. A stick used in measuring or testing. 4. *Mil.* A bod officers not having command but assigned in an executiv advisory capacity. 5. A body of persons associated in ca ing out some special enterprise. 6. *Music* The five horiz tal lines and four spaces used to represent the pitches tones: also called *stave.* — *v.t.* To provide (an office, e with a staff. [OE *stæf* stick]

staff officer 1. An officer on the staff of a military c mander. 2. In the U.S. Navy, an officer without comm or operational functions, as a doctor, dentist, chaplain,

stag (stag) *n.* 1. The male of the red deer. 2. The ma other large deer, as the caribou. 3. A swine castrated a maturity. 4. A man who attends a social function un companied by a woman. 5. A social gathering for r only. — *adj.* Of or for men only. — *v.i.* **stagged**, **stag**-To attend a social affair unaccompanied by a woman. *stagga*]

stage (stāj) *n.* 1. A raised platform, with its scenery mechanical appliances, on which the performance in a th ter or hall takes place. 2. The theater: to write for *stage.* 3. The drama; also, the dramatic profession. 4. field or plan of action of some event: to set the *stage* for 5. A definite portion of a journey. 6. A step in some de opment, progress, or process. 7. A water level: The r rose to flood *stage.* 8. A horizontal section or story building. 9. *Aerospace* One of the separate propulsion u of a rocket vehicle, each of which becomes operational a the preceding one reaches burnout and is jettisoned. Any raised platform or floor. 11. One of the regular st ping places on the route of a stagecoach or postrider. — **easy stages** Traveling or acting without hurry and v frequent stops. — *v.t.* **staged**, **stag·ing** 1. To put or exh on the stage. 2. To conduct; carry on. [< OF < L sta pp. of *stare* to stand]

stage·coach (stāj′kōch′) *n.* A large, horse-drawn, fo wheeled vehicle having a regular route from town to to

stage·craft (stāj′kraft′, -kräft′) *n.* Skill in writing or s ing plays.

stage door A door to a theater used by actors and sta hands that leads to the stage or behind the scenes.

stage fright A sudden panic that sometimes attacks th appearing before an audience.

stage·hand (stāj′hand′) *n.* A worker in a theater who h dles scenery and props, operates lights, etc.

stage manager One who superintends the stage during performance of a play.

stage-struck (stāj′struk′) *adj.* Struck with the idea of coming an actor or an actress; enamored of theatrical li

stage whisper 1. Any loud whisper intended to be o heard. 2. A direction by a prompter in the wings to an tor on the stage, intended not to be heard by the audie

stag·y (stā′jē) See STAGY.

stag·fla·tion (stag′flā′shən) *n.* An economic condition which inflation is combined with slow buying and h unemployment. [<STAG(NANT) + (IN)FLATION]

stag·ger (stag′ər) *v.i.* 1. To walk or run unsteadily; tot el. **2.** To become less confident or resolute; waver; hesi- te. — *v.t.* **3.** To cause to stagger. **4.** To affect strongly; erwhelm, as with grief. **5.** To place in alternating rows or ups. **6.** To arrange so as to prevent congestion or con- sion: to *stagger* lunch hours. — *n.* The act of staggering the condition of being staggered. [< ON *stakra*] — ag'ger·er *n.* — stag'ger·ing·ly *adv.*

g·gers (stag'ərz) *n.pl. (construed as sing.)* **1.** *Vet.* Any various diseases of domestic animals, as horses, character- d by staggering and sudden falling, due to disorder of the ain and spinal cord. **2.** A reeling sensation.

g·ing (stā'jing) *n.* **1.** A scaffolding or temporary plat- rm. **2.** The act of putting a play upon the stage. **3.** The siness of driving or running stagecoaches.

g line *U.S. Informal* A group of males at a dance who e without partners.

g·nant (stag'nənt) *adj.* **1.** Standing still; not flowing: d of water or air. **2.** Foul from long standing, as water. Lacking briskness or activity; dull; sluggish. — stag'- n·cy *n.* — stag'nant·ly *adv.*

g·nate (stag'nāt) *v.i.* ·nat·ed, ·nat·ing **1.** To be or be- me stagnant. **2.** To become dull or inert; vegetate. [< L *gnare* to stagnate] — stag·na·tion (stag·nā'shən) *n.*

g·y (stā'jē) *adj.* stag·i·er, stag·i·est Having a theatrical nner; of or suited to the stage: also spelled *stagey.* — g'i·ly *adv.* — stag'i·ness *n.*

id (stād) *adj.* **1.** Steady and sober. **2.** Fixed; established. rig. pt. and pp. of STAY¹] — staid'ly *adv.* — staid'ness *n.*

n (stān) *n.* **1.** A spot; smirch; blot. **2.** The act of dis- oring, or the state of being discolored. **3.** A dye or thin ment used in staining. **4.** A moral taint; tarnish. — *v.t.* To make a stain upon; discolor; soil. **2.** To color by the of a dye or stain. **3.** To bring a moral stain upon; blem- , — *v.i.* **4.** To take or impart a stain. [Aphetic var. of DAIN] — stain'a·ble *adj.* — stain'er *n.* — stain'less — stain'less·ly *adv.*

ned glass (stānd) Glass colored by the addition of pig- nts in the form of metallic oxides, used in church windows, , — stained-glass (stānd'glas', -gläs') *adj.*

nless steel A steel alloy made resistant to corrosion d atmospheric influences by the addition of chromium and er ingredients.

r (stâr) *n.* **1.** A step, or one of a series of steps, for unting or descending from one level to another. **2.** *Usu-* pl. A series of steps. [OE *stæger*]

r·case (stâr'kās') *n.* A flight or series of flights of stairs, ally from one floor to another.

r·way (stâr'wā') *n.* A flight of stairs; staircase.

ke (stāk) *n.* **1.** A stick or post sharpened at one end for ving into the ground, used as a boundary mark, support a fence, etc. **2.** A post to which a person is bound, to be cuted by being burned alive; also, execution in this man- e. **3.** Something wagered or risked, as money bet on a erprise. **6.** A grubstake. — at stake In hazard or jeop- y; in question: My whole future was *at stake.* — to pull stakes To wind up one's business in a place and move on. *v.t.* staked, stak·ing **1.** To fasten or support by means of take. **2.** To mark the boundaries of with stakes: often h *off* or *out.* **3.** *Informal* To put at hazard; wager; risk. *Informal* To grubstake; also, to supply with working capi- finance. [OE *staca*]

lac·tite (stə·lak'tīt, stal'ək·tīt') *n.* A long, tapering for- tion hanging from the roof of a cavern, produced by con- uous watery deposits containing certain minerals. [< < Gk. *stalassein* to trickle, drip] — stal·ac·tit·ic (stal'· tit'ik) or ·i·cal *adj.*

lag·mite (stə·lag'mīt', stal'əg- ') *n.* An incrustation, usu. cy- lrical or conical, on the floor of a ern, the counterpart of a stalac- . [< NL < Gk. < *stalassein* to] — stal·ag·mit·ic (stal'əg·mit'- or ·i·cal *adj.*

e (stāl) *adj.* stal·er, stal·est **1.** ving lost freshness; slightly nged or deteriorated, as air, beer, ad, etc. **2.** Lacking in interest n age or familiarity; worn out; e. **3.** Being in poor condition m prolonged activity or overstrain. nactive; dull, as after a period of ractivity. — *v.i.* staled, stal·ing become stale or trite. [Origin un- tain] — stale'ly *adv.* — stale'- s *n.*

e·mate (stāl'māt') *n.* **1.** In chess, a draw resulting en a player can make no move without placing his king in

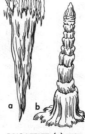

STALACTITE (*a*) AND
STALAGMITE (*b*)

check. **2.** Any tie or deadlock. — *v.t.* ·mat·ed, ·mat·ing **1.** To put into a condition of stalemate. **2.** To bring to a standstill. [< AF *estale* fixed position + MATE²]

stalk¹ (stôk) *n.* **1.** The stem or axis of a plant. **2.** A sup- porting or connecting part of a plant. **3.** *Zool.* Any support on which an organ is borne. **4.** Any stem or main axis, as of a goblet. [ME *stalke*] — stalked (stôkt) *adj.* — stalk'less *adj.* — stalk'y *adj.*

stalk² (stôk) *v.i.* **1.** To approach game, etc., stealthily. **2.** To walk in a stiff, dignified manner. — *v.t.* **3.** To approach (game, etc.) stealthily. **4.** To hover over. — *n.* **1.** The act of stalking game. **2.** A stately step or walk. [OE *bestealcian* to move stealthily] — stalk'er *n.*

stalk·ing-horse (stô'king·hôrs') *n.* **1.** Anything serving to conceal one's intention. **2.** In politics, a candidate put forth to divide the opposition or to hide another candidacy. **3.** A horse behind which a hunter conceals himself.

stall (stôl) *n.* **1.** A compartment in which a horse or bovine animal is confined and fed. **2.** A small sales booth or com- partment in a street, market, etc. **3.** A pew, as in a church. **4.** A space set aside for the parking of an automobile. **5.** *Aeron.* The condition of an airplane that, from loss of speed or excessive angle of attack, begins to drop. **6.** *Informal* An evasion. — *v.t.* **1.** To place or keep in a stall. **2.** To bring to a standstill; stop the progress or motion of, esp. uninten- tionally. — *v.i.* **3.** To come to a standstill; stop, esp. unin- tentionally. **4.** To stick fast in mud, snow, etc. **5.** *Infor- mal* To make delays; be evasive. **6.** To live or be kept in a stall. **7.** *Aeron.* To go into a stall. [OE *steall*]

stall-feed (stôl'fēd') *v.t.* -fed, -feed·ing To feed (cattle) in a stall or stable; fatten. — stall-fed (-fed') *adj.*

stal·lion (stal'yən) *n.* An uncastrated male horse. [< OF *estalon* < OHG *stal* stable]

stall shower A small enclosed place, with a glass door or curtain, for taking a shower bath.

stal·wart (stôl'wərt) *adj.* **1.** Strong and brawny; robust. **2.** Resolute; determined; unwavering. **3.** Brave; coura- geous. — *n.* **1.** A brave or stalwart person. **2.** An uncom- promising partisan, as in politics. [OE < *stæl* place + *wierthe* worth] — stal'wart·ly *adv.* — stal'wart·ness *n.*

sta·men (stā'mən) *n.* pl. sta·mens or Rare stam·i·na (stam'ə·nə) *Bot.* The pollen-bearing organ of a flower. For illus. see FLOWER. [< L, warp, thread]

stam·i·na (stam'ə·nə) *n.* Physical or moral capacity to en- dure or withstand hardship or difficulty; vitality; vigor. [< L, pl. of *stamen* warp, thread] — stam'i·nal *adj.*

stam·i·nate (stam'ə·nit, -nāt) *adj.* *Bot.* **1.** Having sta- mens. **2.** Having stamens but no pistils.

stam·mer (stam'ər) *v.t. & v.i.* To speak or utter haltingly, with involuntary repetitions or prolongations of a sound or syllable. — *n.* The act or condition of stammering. [OE *stamerian*] — stam'mer·er *n.*

stamp (stamp) *v.t.* **1.** To strike heavily with the sole of the foot. **2.** To bring down (the foot) heavily and noisily. **3.** To affect in a specified manner by or as by stamping with the foot: to *stamp* a fire out. **4.** To make marks or figures upon by means of a die, stamp, etc. **5.** To imprint or impress with a die, stamp, etc. **6.** To fix or imprint permanently: The deed was *stamped* on his memory. **7.** To assign a specified quality to; characterize; brand: to *stamp* a story false. **8.** To affix an official seal, stamp, etc., to. **9.** To crush, break, or pulverize, as ore. — *v.i.* **10.** To strike the foot heavily on the ground. **11.** To walk with heavy, resounding steps. — *n.* **1.** A die or block having a pattern or design for im- pressing upon a surface. **2.** The pattern, impression, de- sign, etc., so made. **3.** A weight or block for crushing ore. **4.** Any characteristic mark, as a label or imprint; a brand. **5.** Characteristic quality or form; kind; sort: men of his *stamp.* **6.** The act of stamping. **7.** A printed device pre- pared and sold by a government, for attachment to a letter, commodity, etc., as proof that the tax or fee has been paid. [ME *stampen*] — stamp'er *n.*

stam·pede (stam·pēd') *n.* **1.** A sudden starting and rush- ing off through panic, as a herd of cattle, horses, etc. **2.** Any sudden, tumultuous running movement of a crowd or mob. **3.** Any sudden mass movement. — *v.* ·ped·ed, ·ped·ing *v.t.* **1.** To cause a stampede or panic in. — *v.i.* **2.** To rush or flee in a stampede. [< Am. Sp. *estampida* crash] — stam- ped'er *n.*

stamp·ing ground (stam'ping) A favorite or habitual gath- ering place, for people or animals.

stance (stans) *n.* **1.** Mode of standing; posture. **2.** In golf, the relative positions of the player's feet and the ball, when making a stroke. [< OF < L *stare* to stand]

stanch (stanch, stänch) *v.t.* **1.** To stop or check the flow of (blood, etc.). **2.** To stop the flow of blood from (a wound). Also spelled *staunch.* — *adj.* See STAUNCH. [< OF *estan- chier* to halt] — stanch'er *n.*

stan·chion (stan′shən) *n.* **1.** An upright bar forming a principal support. **2.** A vertical bar or pair of bars used to confine cattle in a stall. — *v.t.* To provide or confine with stanchions. [< OF *estanchon* < *estance* situation, position]

stand (stand) *v.* **stood, stand·ing** *v.i* **1.** To assume or maintain an erect position on one's feet. **2.** To be in a vertical position; be erect. **3.** To measure a specified height when standing. **4.** To assume a specified position: to *stand* aside. **5.** To assume or have a definite opinion, position, or attitude: How do you *stand* on civil rights? **6.** To be situated; have position or location; lie. **7.** To remain unimpaired, unchanged, or valid: My decision still *stands*. **8.** To have or be in a specified state, condition, or relation: He *stood* in fear of his life. **9.** To be of a specified rank or class: He *stands* third. **10.** To assume an attitude for defense or offense: *Stand* and fight. **11.** To be or remain firm or resolute, as in determination. **12.** To be consistent; accord; agree. **13.** To collect and remain; also, to be stagnant, as water. **14.** To stop or pause; halt. **15.** To scruple; hesitate. **16.** *Naut.* To take a direction; steer: The brig *stood* into the wind. **17.** To point, as a hunting dog. **18.** *Brit.* To be a candidate, as for election. — *v.t.* **19.** To place upright; set in an erect position. **20.** To put up with; endure; tolerate. **21.** To be subjected to; undergo: He must *stand* trial. **22.** To withstand; resist. **23.** *Informal* To pay for; bear the expense of: to *stand* a treat. — **to stand a chance** (or **show**) To have a chance or likelihood, as of success. — **to stand by 1.** To stay near and be ready to help, operate, or begin. **2.** To help; support. **3.** To abide by; make good. **4.** To remain passive and watch, as when help is needed. — **to stand clear** To remain at a safe distance. — **to stand for 1.** To represent; symbolize. **2.** To put up with; tolerate. — **to stand in** *Informal* To cost. — **to stand in for** To act as a substitute for. — **to stand off** *Informal* **1.** To keep at a distance. **2.** To fail to agree or comply. — **to stand on 1.** To be based on or grounded in; rest. **2.** To insist on or demand observance of: to *stand on* ceremony. **3.** *Naut.* To keep on the same tack or course. — **to stand on one's own** (**two**) **feet** (or **legs**) To manage one's own affairs. — **to stand out 1.** To stick out; project or protrude. **2.** To be prominent; appear in relief or contrast. **3.** To refuse to consent or agree; remain in opposition. — **to stand over 1.** To remain near and watch, as a subordinate. **2.** To be postponed. — **to stand pat 1.** In poker, to play one's hand as dealt, without drawing new cards. **2.** To resist change. — **to stand to reason** To conform to reason. — **to stand up 1.** To stand erect. **2.** To withstand wear, criticism, analysis, etc. **3.** *Slang* To fail to keep an appointment with. — **to stand up for** To side with; take the part of. — **to stand up to** To confront courageously; face. — **to stand up with** To be best man or bridesmaid for. — *n.* **1.** The act of standing, esp. of standing firmly: to make a *stand* against the enemy. **2.** An opinion, attitude, or position, as in a controversy. **3.** A structure or platform upon which persons or things may sit or stand, or on which articles may be kept or displayed. **4.** A small table. **5.** A rack or other piece of furniture on which hats, canes, etc. may be hung or placed. **6.** A stall, counter, or the like, where merchandise is displayed. **7.** Any place where or in which something or someone stands. **8.** In the theater, a stop made while on tour to give a performance: a one-night *stand*. **9.** The growing trees in a forest. — **to take a stand** To have or reveal an opinion or attitude, as on a controversial issue. [OE *standan*] — **stand′er** *n.*

stan·dard (stan′dərd) *n.* **1.** A flag, ensign, or banner, used as a distinctive emblem of a government, body of men, military unit, etc. **2.** Any established measure of extent, quantity, quality, or value: a *standard* of weight. **3.** Any type, model, or example for comparison; a criterion of excellence: a *standard* of conduct. **4.** An upright timber, post, pole, or beam, esp. as a support. — *adj.* **1.** Serving as a gauge or model: a *standard* weight. **2.** Of recognized excellence or authority: a *standard* book or author. **3.** *Ling.* Designating or belonging to those usages or varieties of a language that have gained literary, cultural, and social acceptance and prestige: *standard* English. [< OF *estandard* banner]

stan·dard-bear·er (stan′dərd-bâr′ər) *n.* **1.** The member of a military unit who carries the flag or ensign. **2.** A leader or a candidate for a leading position, as for a presidency.

stan·dard·bred (*n.* stan′dərd·bred′; *adj.* stan′dərd·bred′) *n.* A breed of horse notable for its trotters and pacers. — *adj.* Bred so as to be of a required strain, quality, or pedigree, as poultry, horses, etc.

standard candle *Physics* A candle (def. 3).

standard English *Ling.* Those usages in English that have gained literary, cultural, and social acceptance and prestige, and are considered appropriate for educated speakers of the language. See LEVEL OF USAGE.

standard gauge A railroad having a track width of 56½ inches, considered as standard. — **stan·dard-gauge** (stan′·dərd·gāj′) *adj.*

stan·dard·ize (stan′dər·dīz) *v.t.* **ized, ·iz·ing** To make to

or regulate by a standard. — **stan′dard·iz′er** *n.*
stan′dard·i·za′tion *n.*

standard of living The average quantity and quality goods, services, luxuries, etc., that a person or group uses consumes in daily living.

standard time Time as reckoned from a meridian offici established as standard over a large area. In the conter nous U.S. the four standard time zones are the **East** (E.S.T.), **Central** (C.S.T.), **Mountain** (M.S.T.), and **Pac** (P.S.T.), using respectively the mean local time of the 7⁵ 90th, 105th, and 120th meridians west of Greenwich, a being 5, 6, 7, and 8 hours slower (or earlier) than Greenw time. Canada has a fifth zone, the **Atlantic** (or **Provinci** based on the local time of the 60th meridian, 4 hours slo than Greenwich time.

stand·by (stand′bī′) *n.* *pl.* **·bys** A person or thing on for emergency use.

stand·ee (stan·dē′) *n.* *Informal* A person who must st for lack of chairs or seats, as at a theater or on a train.

stand-in (stand′in′) *n.* **1.** A position of influence or fav a pull. **2.** A person who takes the place of a motion-pict player, as during waiting intervals or in hazardous actio

stand·ing (stan′ding) *adj.* **1.** Remaining erect; not p trated or cut down, as grain. **2.** For regular or perman use; not special or temporary: a *standing* army. **3.** Stagna not flowing. **4.** Begun while standing: a *standing* high ju **5.** Established; permanent. — *n.* **1.** High grade or ra good reputation: a man of *standing*. **2.** Time in which so thing goes on; duration: a feud of long *standing*. **3.** The of one who stands; erectness; stance.

standing army An army that is prepared at all times action, esp. during peacetime, and that consists of the re lar army plus reservists and conscripts.

standing room Place in which to stand, as in a build theater, etc., where the seats are all occupied.

stand·off (stand′ôf′, -of′) *n.* *Informal* **1.** A draw or tie in a game. **2.** A counterbalancing or neutralization. **3.** difference or coldness; aloofness. **4.** A postponement; de

stand·off·ish (stand′ôf′ish, -of′-) *adj.* Aloof; coolly reser — **stand′off′ish·ness** *n.*

stand·pat (stand′pat′) *adj.* Characterized by or pertain to the policy of opposition to change; conservative. — **stand′pat′ter** *n.*

stand·pipe (stand′pīp′) *n.* A vertical pipe into which water is pumped to give it a head; a water tower.

stand·point (stand′point′) *n.* A position from which th are viewed or judged; point of view.

stand·still (stand′stil′) *n.* A cessation; halt; rest. — In a state of rest or inactivity; standing still.

stand·up (stand′up′) *adj.* **1.** Having an erect positio *standup* collar. **2.** Done, consumed, etc., while standin

stank (stangk) Past tense of STINK.

stan·nic (stan′ik) *adj.* *Chem.* Of, pertaining to, or cont ing tin, esp. in its higher valence. [< L *stannum* tin + -

stan·nous (stan′əs) *adj.* *Chem.* Of, pertaining to, or taining tin, esp. in its lower valence. [< L *stannum* tir -OUS]

stan·num (stan′əm) *n.* Tin. [< L]

stan·za (stan′zə) *n.* A certain number of lines of v grouped in a definite scheme of meter and sequence; a me cal division of a poem. [< Ital., room, stanza < L *st stantis* standing] — **stan·za·ic** (stan·zā′ik) *adj.*

sta·pes (stā′pēz) *n.* *pl.* **sta·pes** or **sta·pe·des** (stə·pē′ *Anat.* The innermost ossicle of the middle ear of mamm also called *stirrup bone*. For illus. see EAR. [< LL *st stirrup*] — **sta·pe·di·al** (stə·pē′dē·əl) *adj.*

staph (staf) *n.* *Informal* Staphylococci; also, an infec caused by staphylococci.

staph·y·lo·coc·cus (staf′ə·lō·kok′əs) *n.* *pl.* **·coc·ci** (-ko Any of a genus of typically pathogenic bacteria occur singly, in pairs, or in irregular clusters; esp. an infec agent in boils and suppurating wounds. [< NL < *staphylos* bunch of grapes + *kokkos* berry] — **staph**′ **coc′cic** (-kok′sik) *adj.*

sta·ple[1] (stā′pəl) *n.* **1.** *Usu. pl.* A basic food or other c nary item of household use. **2.** A principal commodit production of a country or region. **3.** A main constitue something. **4.** The carded or combed fiber of cotton, or flax. **5.** Raw material. — *adj.* **1.** Regularly and stantly produced, used, or sold. **2.** Main; chief. **3.** Ha regular commercial channels; marketable. — *v.t.* ·pling To sort or classify according to length, as wool f [< OF *estaple* market, support < Gmc.] — **sta′pler** *n.*

sta·ple[2] (stā′pəl) *n.* **1.** A U-shaped piece of metal pointed ends, driven into a surface to secure a bolt, h hasp, etc. **2.** A thin piece of wire usu. shaped like a bra ([), driven into paper, fabrics, etc., to serve as a faster — *v.t.* **pled, ·pling** To fix or fasten by a staple or sta [OE *stapol* post, prop] — **sta′pler** *n.*

star (stär) *n.* **1.** Any of the heavenly bodies visible earth on clear nights as apparently fixed points of light, *stron.* One of a class of self-luminous celestial bodies, exclusive of comets, meteors, and nebulae; but including the ▪n. ◆ Collateral adjectives: *astral, sidereal, stellar.* **3.** A ▪nventional figure usu. having five or more radiating points, ▪ed as an emblem or device, as on the shoulder strap of a general. **4.** An actor or actress who plays the leading part. **5.** ▪nyone who shines prominently in a calling or profession: a ▪orts *star.* **6.** An asterisk (*). **7.** A heavenly body considered as influencing one's fate. **8.** *Often pl.* Fortune; destiny. — **to see stars** *Informal* To see bright spots before ▪e eyes, as from a sharp jolt to the head. — *v.* **starred,** **▪ar·ring** *v.t.* **1.** To set or adorn with spangles or stars. **2.** ▪ mark with an asterisk. **3.** To present as a star in a play ▪ motion picture. — *v.i.* **4.** To shine brightly as a star. **5.** ▪ play the leading part; be the star. — *adj.* **1.** Of or pertaining to a star or stars. **2.** Prominent; brilliant: a *star* ▪otball player. [OE *steorra*] — **star·less** *adj.* — **star·** ▪e′ *adj.*

▪r·board (stär′bərd) *Naut. n.* The right-hand side of a ▪ssel as one faces the front or bow. — *adj.* Being on or ▪ward the starboard. Opposed to *larboard, port.* [OE *steor-* ▪rd* steering side]

▪rch (stärch) *n.* **1.** *Biochem.* A white, odorless, tasteless, ▪anular carbohydrate ($C_6H_{10}O_5)_n$, found in most plants: ▪o called *amylum.* **2.** A preparation of this substance, used ▪ stiffening linen, and for many industrial purposes. **3.** ▪iffness or formality; a formal manner. **4.** *U.S. Slang* Energy; vigor. — *v.t.* To apply starch to; stiffen with or as ▪th starch. [OE *stercan* to stiffen < *stearc* stiff]

▪r Chamber **1.** Formerly, in England, a secret high ▪urt, abolished in 1641 because of abuses. **2.** Any court ▪gaged in arbitrary or illegal procedure.

▪rch·y (stär′chē) *adj.* **starch·i·er, starch·i·est** **1.** Stiffened with starch; stiff. Also **starched** (stärcht). **2.** Prim; ▪rmal; precise. **3.** Formed of or combined with starch; ▪rinaceous. — **starch′i·ly** *adv.* — **starch′i·ness** *n.*

▪re·dom (stär′dəm) *n.* The status of a star (defs. 4 & 5).

▪re (stâr) *v.* **stared, star·ing** *v.i.* **1.** To gaze fixedly, as ▪m admiration, fear, or insolence. **2.** To be conspicuously ▪unduly apparent; glare. **3.** To stand on end, as hair. — ▪. **4.** To stare at. **5.** To affect in a specified manner by ▪ring: to *stare* a person into silence. — *n.* The act of star-▪g; an intense gaze. [OE *starian*] — **star′er** *n.*

▪r·fish (stär′fish′) *n.* *pl.* ·fish or ·fish·es Any of various ▪dially symmetrical marine animals, commonly ▪th a star-shaped body having five or more ▪ms.

▪r·gaze (stär′gāz′) *v.i.* ·gazed, ·gaz·ing **1.** ▪ gaze at or study the stars. **2.** To engage in ▪verie; daydream. — **star′gaz·er** *n.* — **star′.** ▪z·ing *n.* & *adj.*

▪rk (stärk) *adj.* **1.** Without ornamentation; ▪nt; simple: the *stark* truth. **2.** Complete; ▪er: *stark* misery. **3.** Stiff or rigid, as in death. **4.** Severe; tempestuous, as weather. **5.** Strict ▪ grim, as a person. — *adv.* **1.** In a stark man-▪r. **2.** Completely; utterly: *stark* mad. [OE *stearc* stiff] **stark′ly** *adv.*

STARFISH (Ventral view showing tube feet)

▪r·let (stär′lit) *n.* **1.** A small star. **2.** *U.S. Informal* A ▪ung movie or television actress represented as a future star.

▪r·light (stär′līt′) *n.* The light given by a star or stars. ▪ *adj.* Lighted by or only by the stars: also **star′lit′** (-lit′).

▪r·ling (stär′ling) *n.* Any of various birds native to Europe and naturalized in North America, having a metallic ▪rple and green luster. [OE *stærling* < *stær* starling]

▪r-of-Beth·le·hem (stär′əv-beth′lē-əm, -lə-hem) *n.* A ▪ropean plant of the lily family having white stellate flow-▪r, naturalized in the eastern U.S.

▪r of Bethlehem The large star by which the three Magi ▪re guided to Jesus's manger in Bethlehem.

▪rred (stärd) *adj.* **1.** Spangled with stars. **2.** Presented ▪ advertised as the star of a play, motion picture, etc. **3.** ▪arked with an asterisk. **4.** Affected by astral influence: ▪efly in combination: *ill-starred.*

▪r·ry (stär′ē) *adj.* ·ri·er, ·ri·est **1.** Set with stars or star-▪e spots or points; abounding in stars. **2.** Lighted by the ▪rs. **3.** Shining as or like the stars. **4.** Shaped like a star. ▪ Of, pertaining to, proceeding from, or connected with ▪rs. **6.** Consisting of stars; stellar. — **star′ri·ness** *n.*

▪r·ry-eyed (stär′ē-īd′) *adj.* Given to fanciful wishes or ▪arnings.

▪rs and Bars, The The first flag of the Confederacy, ▪nsisting of a field of three bars and a circle of white stars.

▪rs and Stripes, The The flag of the U.S. of America, a ▪ld of thirteen horizontal stripes, alternately red and white, ▪d a blue union with 50 stars.

▪r-span·gled (stär′spang′gəld) *adj.* Spangled with stars ▪ starlike spots or points.

Star-Spangled Banner, The **1.** The flag of the U.S. **2.** The national anthem of the U.S. The poem was written by Francis Scott Key in 1814 during the bombardment by the British of Fort McHenry, Md.

start (stärt) *v.i.* **1.** To make a beginning or start; set out. **2.** To begin; commence. **3.** To make an involuntary, startled movement, as from fear or surprise. **4.** To move suddenly, as with a spring, leap, or bound; jump. **5.** To seem to bulge or protrude: His eyes *started* from his head. **6.** To be displaced or loosened. — *v.t.* **7.** To set in motion or circulation: to *start* an engine. **8.** To begin; commence: to *start* a lecture. **9.** To set up; establish. **10.** To introduce (a subject) or propound (a question). **11.** To displace or loosen, etc. **12.** To rouse from cover; cause to take flight; flush, as game. **13.** To draw the contents from; tap, as a cask. — **to start in** To begin; undertake. — **to start off** To begin a journey; set out. — **to start out** To make a beginning or start, as of a journey. — **to start up** **1.** To rise or appear suddenly. **2.** To begin or cause to begin operation, as an engine. — *n.* **1.** A setting out or going forth; beginning. **2.** A quick, startled movement, as at something unexpected. **3.** A temporary or spasmodic action or attempt; a brief, intermittent effort: by fits and *starts.* **4.** Advantage or distance in advance at the outset; lead. **5.** Impetus at the beginning of motion or course of action: to get a *start* in business. **6.** A loosened place or condition; crack. [ME *sterten* to start, leap]

start·er (stär′tər) *n.* **1.** One who or that which starts. **2.** One who sees to it that buses, etc., leave on schedule. **3.** A mechanism for starting an internal combustion engine without manual cranking: also called *self-starter.* **4.** A competitor at the start of a race. **5.** A person who gives the signal for the start of a race.

star·tle (stär′tal) *v.* ·tled, ·tling *v.t.* **1.** To arouse or excite suddenly; cause to start involuntarily; alarm. — *v.i.* **2.** To be aroused or excited suddenly; take alarm. — *n.* A sudden fright or shock; a scare. [OE *steartlian* to kick, struggle] — **star′tler** *n.*

star·tling (stär′tling) *adj.* Rousing sudden surprise, alarm, or the like. — **star′tling·ly** *adv.*

star·va·tion (stär-vā′shən) *n.* The act of starving, or the state of being starved.

starve (stärv) *v.* **starved, starv·ing** *v.i.* **1.** To perish from lack of food. **2.** To suffer from extreme hunger. **3.** To suffer from lack or need: to *starve* for friendship. — *v.t.* **4.** To cause to die of hunger; deprive of food. **5.** To bring to a specified condition by starving: to *starve* an enemy into surrender. [OE *steorfan* to die] — **starv′er** *n.*

starve·ling (stärv′ling) *n.* A person or animal that is starving, starved, or emaciated. — *adj.* **1.** Starving; emaciated; hungry. **2.** Failing to meet needs; inadequate.

stash (stash) *v.t.* *Slang* To hide or conceal (money, valuables, etc.), for storage and safekeeping: often with *away.* [? Blend of STORE + CACHE]

sta·sis (stā′sis, stas′is) *n.* *pl.* ·ses (-sēz) *Pathol.* **1.** Stoppage in the circulation of any of the body fluids. **2.** Retarded movement of the intestinal contents. [< NL < Gk., a standing < *histanai* to stand]

stat- Var. of STATO-.

-stat *combining form* A device that stops or makes constant: *thermostat; rheostat.* [< Gk. *-statēs* causing to stand]

state (stāt) *n.* **1.** Mode of existence as determined by circumstances, external or internal; nature; condition; situation. **2.** Frame of mind; mood. **3.** Mode or style of living; station. **4.** Grand and ceremonious style; pomp; formality. **5.** A sovereign political community organized under a distinct government recognized and conformed to by the people as supreme, and having jurisdiction over a given territory; a nation. **6.** *Usu. cap.* One of a number of political communities or bodies politic united to form one sovereign state; esp. one of the United States. **7.** *pl.* The legislative bodies of a nation; estates. **8.** The territorial, political, and governmental entity constituting a state or nation; authority of government. — **Syn.** See NATION. — **Department of State** An executive department of the U.S. government (established in 1789), headed by the Secretary of State, that supervises the conduct of foreign affairs, directs the activities of all diplomatic and consular representatives, protects national interests abroad, and assists in the formulation of policies in relation to international problems. Also **State Department.** — **to lie in state** To be placed on public view, with ceremony and honors, before burial. — *adj.* **1.** Of or pertaining to the state, nation, or government: *state* papers. **2.** Intended for use on occasions of ceremony. — *v.t.* **stat·ed, stat·ing** **1.** To set forth explicitly in speech or writing; assert; declare. **2.** To fix; determine; settle. [Aphetic var. of OF *estat* < L *status* condition, state] — **sta·tal** (stā′tal) *adj.*

state bank **1.** *U.S.* A bank that has a charter from a State government. **2.** Any bank that is owned or controlled by a state, esp. one that issues currency.

state·craft (stāt'kraft', -kräft') *n.* The art or practice of conducting affairs of state.

stat·ed (stā'tid) *adj.* **1.** Announced; specified. **2.** Established; regular; fixed. — **stat'ed·ly** *adv.*

State·hood (stāt'hŏŏd) *n.* The status of one of the United States, as distinguished from that of a Territory.

State House A building used for sessions of a State legislature and for other public purposes; State capitol.

state·less (stāt'lis) *adj.* **1.** Without nationality: a *stateless* person. **2.** Without a state or community of states.

state line In the U.S., any boundary between States.

state·ly (stāt'lē) *adj.* ·li·er, ·li·est Dignified; lofty. — *adv.* Loftily: also **state'li·ly** (-lə·lē). — **state'li·ness** *n.*

state·ment (stāt'mənt) *n.* **1.** The act of stating. **2.** That which is stated. **3.** A summary of the assets and liabilities of a bank or firm, showing the balance due. **4.** A report sent, usu. monthly, to a debtor of a business firm or to a depositor in a bank.

state park *U.S.* A tract of land provided and maintained by a State for conservation and recreation.

State policeman *U.S.* A member of the separate police force of a State; also called *State trooper, trooper.*

state·room (stāt'rōōm', -rŏŏm') *n.* **1.** A private room having sleeping accommodations on a passenger ship. **2.** A private sleeping compartment on a railroad car.

state's evidence **1.** Evidence produced by the State in criminal prosecutions. **2.** One who confesses himself guilty of a crime and testifies as a witness against his accomplices. — **to turn state's evidence** To become a witness for the state and inculpate one's accomplices.

state·side (stāt'sīd') *adj.* Of or in the continental U.S. — *adv.* In or to the continental U.S.

states·man (stāts'mən) *n.* *pl.* ·men (-mən) **1.** One who is skilled in government; a political leader of distinguished ability. **2.** One engaged in government, or influential in state affairs. — **states'man·like'**, **states'man·ly** *adj.* — **states'man·ship** *n.* — **states'wom'an** (-wŏŏm'ən) *n.fem.*

state socialism A political theory advocating government ownership of utilities and industries.

States' rights **1.** The rights and powers not delegated to the U.S. by the Constitution nor prohibited by it to the respective States. **2.** An interpretation of the Constitution that makes these rights and powers as large as possible. Also **State rights.**

State trooper *U.S.* A State policeman.

state-wide (stāt'wīd') *adj.* Throughout a state.

stat·ic (stat'ik) *adj.* **1.** At rest; dormant; not active, moving, or changing. **2.** Pertaining to bodies at rest or forces in equilibrium: opposed to *dynamic.* **3.** *Physics* Acting as weight, but not moving: *static* pressure. **4.** *Electr.* Pertaining to electricity at rest, or to stationary electric charges. Also **stat'i·cal.** — *n. Telecom.* A disturbance of a carrier wave caused by atmospheric or man-made sources; also, the noise caused by this. [< NL < Gk. *statikos* causing to stand] — **stat'i·cal·ly** *adv.*

stat·ics (stat'iks) *n.pl.* (*construed as sing.*) The branch of mechanics dealing with bodies at rest and with the interaction of forces in equilibrium.

sta·tion (stā'shən) *n.* **1.** The headquarters of some official person or body of men: a police *station.* **2.** An established building or place serving as a starting point, stage, stopping place, or post; terminal; depot. **3.** A place where a person or thing usu. stands or is; an assigned location. **4.** Social condition; rank. **5.** *Mil.* The place to which an individual, unit, or ship is assigned for duty; post. **6.** The offices, studios, and technical installations of a radio or television broadcasting unit. **7.** *Mining* A recess in a shaft or passage of a mine. **8.** *Austral.* A cattle or sheep ranch. — *v.t.* To assign to a station; place in a post or position. [< F < L < *stare* to stand]

sta·tion·ar·y (stā'shən·er'ē) *adj.* **1.** Remaining in one place; fixed. **2.** Not portable or not easily portable. **3.** Exhibiting no change of character or condition. — *n. pl.* ·ar·ies One who or that which is stationary.

sta·tion·er (stā'shən·ər) *n.* A dealer in stationery and related articles. [< Med.L *stationarius* stationary]

sta·tion·er·y (stā'shən·er'ē) *n.* **1.** Writing paper and envelopes. **2.** Writing materials, as pencils, notebooks, etc.

sta·tion·mas·ter (stā'shən·mas'tər, -mäs'-) *n.* The person having charge of a bus or railroad station.

Stations of the Cross The fourteen images or pictures representing successive scenes of the Passion of Christ, and before which devotions are performed.

station wagon A large automobile with one or more rows of removable or folding seats and a hinged tailgate.

stat·ism (stā'tiz·əm) *n.* **1.** A theory of government holding that the returns from group or individual enterprise are vested in the state. **2.** Loosely, adherence to state sovereignty, as in a republic. — **stat'ist** *n. & adj.*

sta·tis·tic (stə·tis'tik) *adj.* Statistical. — *n.* Any eleme entering into a statistical statement or array.

sta·tis·ti·cal (stə·tis'tə·kəl) *adj.* Of, pertaining to, consis ing of, or derived from statistics: also *statistic.* — **sta·tis** **cal·ly** *adv.*

stat·is·ti·cian (stat'is·tish'ən) *n.* One skilled in collecti and tabulating statistical data.

sta·tis·tics (stə·tis'tiks) *n.pl.* (*construed as sing. in def.* **1.** Quantitative data, pertaining to any subject or grou esp. when systematically gathered and collated. **2.** T science that deals with the collection, tabulation, and s tematic classification of quantitative data, esp. as a basis f inference and induction. [< G < Med.L, ult. < L *stat* state, condition]

stato- *combining form* Position. Also, before vowels, **sta** [< Gk. *statos* standing, fixed < *histanai* to stand]

sta·tor (stā'tər) *n. Mech.* The stationary portion of a namo, turbine, motor, etc.: distinguished from *rotor.* [NL < L, supporter < *stare* to stand]

stat·u·ar·y (stach'ōō·er'ē) *n. pl.* ·ar·ies **1.** Statues coll tively. **2.** The art of making statues. — *adj.* Of or suita for statues.

stat·ue (stach'ōō) *n.* A representation of a human or anir figure in marble, bronze, etc., esp. when nearly life-size larger, and preserving the proportions in all directions. [F < L < *status,* pp. of *stare* to stand]

Statue of Liberty A giant bronze statue on Liberty Islan depicting a crowned woman holding aloft a burning tor presented to the U.S. by France and unveiled in 1886.

stat·u·esque (stach'ōō·esk') *adj.* Resembling a statue, in grace, pose, or dignity. — **stat'u·esque'ly** *adv.* — **stat esque'ness** *n.*

stat·u·ette (stach'ōō·et') *n.* A small statue. [< F]

stat·ure (stach'ər) *n.* **1.** The natural height of an anim body, esp. of a human body. **2.** The height of anything, e of a tree. **3.** Development; growth: moral *stature.* [< < L < *status* state]

sta·tus (stā'təs, stat'əs) *n.* **1.** State, condition, or relati **2.** Relative position or rank. [< L < *stare* to stand]

sta·tus quo (stā'təs kwō, stat'əs) The condition or state which (a person or thing is or has been): often used with t to maintain the *status quo.* Also **status in quo.** [< L]

stat·ute (stach'ōōt) *n.* **1.** A legislative enactment d sanctioned and authenticated by constitutional rule; act Parliament, Congress, etc. **2.** Any authoritatively decla rule, ordinance, decree, or law. — *adj.* Consisting of or r ulated by statute. [< F < LL *statuere* to constitute]

statute law The law as set forth in statutes.

statute mile A mile (def. 1).

statute of limitations A statute that imposes time lim upon the right of certain actions, as by obliging a creditor demand payment of a debt within a specified time.

stat·u·to·ry (stach'ə·tôr'ē, -tō'rē) *adj.* **1.** Pertaining t statute. **2.** Created by or dependent upon legislation.

statutory rape The crime of having sexual relations w a girl who is under the age of consent.

staunch (stônch, stänch) *adj.* **1.** Firm and dependa constant; loyal: a *staunch* friend. **2.** Having firm const tion or construction: a *staunch* ship. **3.** Strong and vigoro Also spelled **stanch.** — *v.t.* See STANCH. [< OF *estanch* to make stand.] — **staunch'ly** *adv.* — **staunch'ness** *n.*

stauro- *combining form* Cross. [< Gk. *stauros* cross]

stave (stāv) *n.* **1.** A curved strip of wood, forming a par the sides of a barrel, tub, or the like. **2.** Any narrow stri material used for a like purpose. **3.** *Music* A staff. **4.** stanza; verse. **5.** A rod, cudgel, or staff. **6.** A rung o rack or ladder. — *v.* **staved** or **stove, stav·ing** *v.t.* **1.** break in the staves (of a cask or a boat). **2.** To crush shell or surface of; smash. **3.** To make (a hole) by crush or collision. **4.** To furnish with staves. **5.** To ward as with a staff: usu. with *off: to stave* off hunger. — *v.i* To be broken in, as a vessel's hull. [Back formation < *sta*

staves (stāvz) **1.** Alternative plural of STAFF. **2.** Plura STAVE.

stay¹ (stā) *v.i.* **1.** To cease motion; stop; halt. **2.** To c tinue in a specified place, condition, or state: to *stay* healt **3.** To remain temporarily as a guest, resident, etc. **4.** pause; wait; tarry. **5.** *Informal* To have endurance; l **6.** *Informal* To keep pace with a competitor, as in a race. In poker, to remain in a round by meeting an ante, bet raise. — *v.t.* **8.** To bring to a stop; halt; check. **9.** To der; delay. **10.** To postpone. **11.** To satisfy the dema of temporarily; to *stay* the pangs of hunger. **12.** To rem for the duration of: I will *stay* the night. **13.** To remain or beyond the end of: with *out*: to *stay* out one's welcome. **to stay put** *U.S. Informal* To remain or hold in spit everything. — *n.* **1.** The act or time of staying; sojou visit. **2.** That which checks or stops; esp., a suspensio judicial proceedings. **3.** Staying power; endurance. **4.** state of rest; standstill. [< AF *estaier,* OF *ester* < L *sta stand*] — **stay'er** *n.*

y² (stā) *v.t.* **1.** To be a support to; prop or hold up. **2.** support mentally; sustain. **3.** To cause to depend or y, as for support: with *on* or *upon.* — *n.* **1.** Anything t props or supports. **2.** A strip of plastic or metal, used stiffen corsets, girdles, etc. **3.** *pl.* Formerly, a corset. [< ' *estayer*]

y³ (stā) *Naut. n.* **1.** A strong rope, often of wire, used to port, steady, or fasten a mast or spar. **2.** Any rope sup- -ting a mast or funnel. — *v.t.* **1.** To support with a stay stays, as a mast. **2.** To put (a vessel) on the opposite k. — *v.i.* **3.** To tack: said of vessels. [OE *stæg*]

y·ing power (stā/ing) The ability to endure.

y·sail (stā/səl, -sāl/) *n. Naut.* A sail, usu. triangular, ex- ded on a stay.

ad (sted) *n.* **1.** Place of another person or thing: preced- by *in:* Serfdom came in the *stead* of slavery. Compare **TEAD. 2.** Place or attitude of support; service: chiefly in phrase **to stand one in (good) stead. 3.** A steading or m: used chiefly in compounds: *homestead.* [OE *stede*]

ad·fast (sted/fast/, -fäst/, -fəst) *adj.* **1.** Firmly fixed in h or devotion to duty; constant; unchanging. **2.** Di- ted fixedly at one point or to one end, as a gaze or pur- e; steady. Also spelled *stedfast.* [OE *stedefæst*] — **ad/fast·ly** *adv.* — **stead/fast·ness** *n.*

ad·y (sted/ē) *adj.* **stead·i·er, stead·i·est 1.** Stable in ition; firmly supported; fixed. **2.** Moving or acting with form regularity; unfaltering: a *steady* light. **3.** Not read- disturbed or upset: *steady* nerves. **4.** Free from intem- ance and dissipation: *steady* habits. **5.** Constant in mind conduct; steadfast. **6.** Regular; reliable: a *steady* cus- er. **7.** Uninterrupted; continuous. **8.** *Naut.* Having direction of the ship's head unchanged. — *v.t. & v.i.* **ad·ied, stead·y·ing** To make or become steady. — *in-* . Not so fast; keep calm: an order enjoining self-control composure. — *n. Slang* One's regular sweetheart. — **o steady** *Informal* To date only one person of the op- ite sex. [< STEAD + -Y³] — **stead/i·er** *n.* — **stead/i·ly** — **stead/i·ness** *n.*

k (stāk) *n.* **1.** A slice of meat or fish, usu. broiled or d. **2.** Meat chopped for cooking like a steak. [< ON *k*]

l (stēl) *v.* **stole, sto·len, steal·ing** *v.t.* **1.** To take from ther without right, authority, or permission, and usu. in ecret manner. **2.** To take or obtain in a surreptitious, ul, or subtle manner. **3.** To move, place, or convey lthily: with *away, from, in, into,* etc. **4.** In baseball, to ch (second base, third base, or home plate) without the of a hit, error, passed ball, or wild pitch: said of a base- ner. — *v.i.* **5.** To commit theft. **6.** To move secretly urtively. **7.** In baseball, to steal a base. — *n.* **1.** The of stealing. **2.** That which is stolen. **3.** *U.S. Slang* A gain. [OE *stelan*] — **steal/er** *n.*

lth (stelth) *n.* **1.** The quality or habit of acting secret- a concealed manner of acting. **2.** A secret or clandestine movement, or proceeding. [ME < OE *stelan* to steal]

lth·y (stel/thē) *adj.* **stealth·i·er, stealth·i·est** Moving cting secretly or slyly; done or characterized by stealth; ive. — **stealth/i·ly** *adv.* — **stealth/i·ness** *n.*

– Syn. Anything *stealthy* seeks to avoid notice; it may be ap- d to a worthy act or purpose. *Furtive* suggests the actions or ner of a thief; we speak of a *furtive* act, a *furtive* face. *Sur- litious* suggests quickness as well as concealment in action il- lly or improperly: a *surreptitious* glance into a neighbor's low. *Clandestine* describes that which is concealed because ally offensive or socially and politically dangerous: a *clandes- love* affair, a *clandestine* rally.

m (stēm) *n.* **1.** Water in the form of vapor. **2.** The or vapor into which water is changed by boiling, esp. n used under pressure as a source of energy. **3.** The ble mist into which aqueous vapor is condensed by cool- **4.** Any kind of vaporous exhalation. **5.** *Informal* Vig- force; speed. — **to let (or blow) off steam** *Informal* To e expression to pent-up emotions or opinions. — *v.i.* **1.** give off or emit steam or vapor. **2.** To rise or pass off as m. **3.** To become covered with condensed water vapor: n with *up.* **4.** To generate steam. **5.** To move or travel he agency of steam. — *v.t.* **6.** To treat with steam, as in ening, cooking, cleaning, etc. — *adj.* **1.** Of, driven, or rated by steam. **2.** Containing or conveying steam: a *m* boiler. **3.** Treated by steam. [OE *stēam*]

m·boat (stēm/bōt/) *n.* A steamship.

m engine An engine that derives its motive force from action of steam, usu. by pressure against a piston sliding hin a closed cylinder.

m·er (stē/mər) *n.* **1.** A ship propelled by steam. **2.** essel in which something is steamed, as for cooking.

mer trunk A trunk small enough to fit under a berth ship's cabin.

steam·fit·ter (stēm/fit/ər) *n.* A man who sets up or repairs steam pipes and their fittings. — **steam/fit/ting** *n.*

steam organ A calliope.

steam·roll·er (stēm/rō/lər) *n.* **1.** A road-rolling machine driven by steam. **2.** Any force that ruthlessly overcomes opposition. Also **steam roller.** — *v.t.* **1.** To work (a road, etc.) with a steamroller. **2.** To suppress; crush. **3.** To pro- vide a path for by crushing opposition. — *v.i.* **4.** To work with or as with a steamroller. — *adj.* Resembling the action of a steamroller; aggressive: *steamroller* tactics.

steam·ship (stēm/ship/) *n.* A large vessel used for ocean traffic and usu. propelled by steam; a steamer.

steam shovel A machine for digging and excavation, oper- ated by steam power.

steam table *U.S.* A long table, as in restaurants, with openings in which containers of food are placed to be kept warm by hot water or steam circulating beneath them.

steam turbine A turbine operated by steam power.

steam·y (stē/mē) *adj.* **steam·i·er, steam·i·est** Consisting of, like, or full of steam. — **steam/i·ly** *adv.* — **steam/i·ness** *n.*

ste·ar·ic (stē·ar/ik, stir/ik) *adj. Chem.* Of, pertaining to, or derived from stearin. [< F < Gk. *stear* suet]

stearic acid *Chem.* A white fatty acid, $C_{17}H_{35}COOH$, found in animal fats and in many vegetable oils.

ste·a·rin (stē/ə·rin) *n. Chem.* **1.** A white, crystalline compound $(C_{17}H_{35}COO)_3C_3H_5$, obtained from various ani- mal and vegetable fats. **2.** Stearic acid, esp. as prepared for making candles, etc. **3.** Fat in solid form. Also **ste/a·rine** (-rin, -rēn). [< F < Gk. *stear* suet]

ste·a·tite (stē/ə·tīt) *n.* Massive talc found in extensive beds and quarried for hearths, sink linings, coarse utensils, etc.: also called *soapstone.* [< L < Gk. *stear, steatos* suet, tallow] — **ste/a·tit/ic** (-tit/ik) *adj.*

sted·fast (sted/fast/, -fäst/, -fəst) See STEADFAST.

steed (stēd) *n.* A horse; esp., a spirited war horse: now chief- ly a literary term. [OE *stēda* studhorse]

steel (stēl) *n.* **1.** A tough alloy of iron containing carbon in variable amounts, malleable under proper conditions, and greatly hardened by sudden cooling. The addition of other components, as chromium and nickel, gives a large range of alloys having special properties. **2.** Something made of steel, as a sword. **3.** Hardness of character. **4.** A strip or band of steel, as for stiffening a corset. — *adj.* **1.** Made or composed of steel. **2.** Resembling steel, as in hardness. **3.** Adamant; unyielding. — *v.t.* **1.** To cover with steel; plate, edge, point, or face with steel. **2.** To make hard or strong like steel. **3.** To make unfeeling; harden. [OE *stÿle, stēle*]

steel blue A metallic blue, as of certain steels.

steel engraving **1.** The art and process of engraving on a steel plate. **2.** The impression made from such a plate.

steel gray Any of several dark shades of gray.

steel·head (stēl/hed/) *n. U.S. & Canadian* The rainbow trout, esp. in its migratory stage or when from the sea, highly esteemed as a game fish: also called *salmon trout.*

steel wool Steel fibers matted together for use as an abra- sive, as in cleaning, polishing, etc.

steel·work (stēl/wûrk/) *n.* **1.** Any article or construction of steel. **2.** *pl.* A shop or factory where steel is made or fabricated. — **steel/work/ing** *n.*

steel·work·er (stēl/wûr/kər) *n.* A worker in a steel mill.

steel·y (stē/lē) *adj.* **steel·i·er, steel·i·est 1.** Made of, con- taining, resembling, or suggesting steel. **2.** Having a steel- like hardness: a *steely* gaze. — **steel/i·ness** *n.*

steel·yard (stēl/yärd/, -yərd, stil/yərd) *n.* A weighing de- vice consisting of a scaled beam, counterpoise, and hooks. The article to be weighed is hung at the short end and the counterpoise weight on the long arm. Also **steel/yards.** [after *Steelyard,* formerly, the London headquarters for Hanseatic traders]

steen·bok (stān/bok, stēn/-) *n.* A small, fawn-colored African antelope: also called *steinbok.* [< Du. < *steen* stone + *bok* buck]

steep¹ (stēp) *adj.* **1.** Making a large angle with the plane of the horizon; precipitous. **2.** *Informal* Exorbitant; excessive; high, as a price. — *n.* A precipitous place, as a cliff or hill. [OE *stēap*] — **steep/ly** *adv.* — **steep/ness** *n.*

steep² (stēp) *v.t.* **1.** To soak in a liquid, as for softening, cleansing, etc. **2.** To imbue thoroughly; saturate: *steeped* in crime. — *v.i.* **3.** To undergo soaking in a liquid. — *n.* **1.** The process of steeping or the state of being steeped. **2.** A liquid or bath for steeping something; esp., a fertilizing liq- uid for seeds. [ME *stepen,* ? < Scand.] — **steep/er** *n.*

steep·en (stē/pən) *v.t. & v.i.* To make or become steep or steeper.

stee·ple (stē/pəl) *n.* A lofty, usu. tapering structure rising above the tower of a church; a spire. [OE *stÿpel*]

stee·ple·chase (stē/pəl·chās/) *n.* **1.** A race on horseback across country, in which obstacles are to be leaped. **2.** A race over a course artificially prepared, as with hedges, rails, etc. **3.** Any cross-country run. [So called because originally the goal of the racers was a distant church steeple] — **stee'ple·chas'er** n. — **stee'ple·chas'ing** n.

stee·ple·jack (stē'pəl·jak') n. A man whose occupation is to climb steeples and other tall structures to inspect or make repairs. [< STEEPLE + *jack* workman]

steer¹ (stir) v.t. **1.** To direct the course of (a vessel or vehicle) by means of a rudder, steering wheel, etc. **2.** To follow (a course). **3.** To direct; guide. — v.i. **4.** To direct the course of a vessel, vehicle, etc. **5.** To undergo guiding or steering. **6.** To follow a course: to *steer* for land. — **to steer clear of** To avoid. — n. U.S. Slang A piece of advice. [OE *stieran*] — **steer'a·ble** adj. — **steer'er** n.

steer² (stir) n. **1.** A male bovine animal, esp. when castrated and from two to four years old. **2.** An ox of any age raised for beef. [OE *stēor*]

steer·age (stir'ij) n. **1.** Formerly, the part of an ocean passenger vessel in the forward lower decks. **2.** Any markedly inferior, overcrowded, third-class accommodations. **3.** The act of steering. **4.** The effect of the helm on a vessel.

steer·age·way (stir'ij·wā') n. Naut. The lowest speed at which a vessel can be accurately steered.

steer·ing committee (stir'ing) A committee in a legislature or other assemblage that arranges or directs the course of the business to be considered.

steering gear The coordinated mechanism that steers a ship, automotive vehicle, aircraft, bicycle, etc.

steering wheel A wheel turned by the driver or pilot of a vehicle, ship, etc., to change its direction.

steers·man (stirz'mən) n. pl. ·men (-mən) One who steers a boat; a helmsman.

steg·o·my·ia (steg'ə·mī'ə) n. Aedes, a type of mosquito; a former name. [< NL < Gk. *stegos* roof + *myia* fly]

stein (stīn) n. A beer mug, esp. of earthenware. [< G]

stein·bok (stīn'bok) n. A steenbok.

stel·lar (stel'ər) adj. **1.** Of or pertaining to the stars; astral. **2.** Of or pertaining to a prominent actor or actress or to other persons in the arts. [< LL < L *stella* star]

stel·late (stel'it, -āt) adj. Star-shaped or starlike. Also **stel·lat·ed** (stel'ā·tid). [< L < *stella* star] — **stel'late·ly** adv.

stelli- combining form Star. [< L *stella* star]

St. El·mo's fire (sānt el'mōz) A luminous charge of atmospheric electricity sometimes appearing on the masts of ships, on church steeples, etc. Also **St. Elmo's light.**

stem¹ (stem) n. **1.** The main body or stalk of a tree, shrub, or other plant, rising above the ground. **2.** The relatively slender growth supporting the fruit, flower, or leaf of a plant. **3.** The long, slender, usu. cylindrical portion of an instrument, drinking vessels, etc. **4.** In a watch, the small, projecting, knobbed rod used for winding the mainspring. **5.** Printing The upright stroke of a type face or letter. **6.** Music The line attached to the head of a written musical note. **7.** Ling. A root plus a thematic vowel, as the Latin stem *luci-* ("light") in *lucifer* ("light-bearer"), composed of the root *luc-* plus the thematic vowel *-i-*. — v. stemmed, stem·ming v.t. **1.** To remove the stems of or from. **2.** To supply with stems. — v.i. **3.** To grow out of; develop or arise: usually with *from.* [OE *stemn, stefn* stem of a tree, prow of a ship] — **stem'mer** n. — **stem'less** adj.

stem² (stem) n. Naut. A nearly upright timber or metal piece uniting the two sides of a vessel at the bow. **2.** The bow or prow of a vessel. — **from stem to stern** From end to end; thoroughly. — v. stemmed, stem·ming v.t. **1.** To resist or make progress against, as a current: said of a vessel. **2.** To stand firm or make progress against (any opposing force): to *stem* the tide. [< STEM¹]

stem³ (stem) v.t. stemmed, stem·ming **1.** To stop, hold back, or dam up, as a current; stanch. **2.** To make tight, as a joint; to plug. [< ON *stemma* to stop]

stem·ware (stem'wâr') n. Drinking vessels with stems, as goblets, taken collectively.

stem-wind·er (stem'wīn'dər) n. A watch wound by turning the crown of the stem. — **stem'-wind'ing** adj.

stench (stench) n. A foul odor; stink. [OE *stenc*]

sten·cil (sten'səl) n. **1.** A sheet of paper, etc., in which a pattern is cut by means of spaces or dots, through which applied paint or ink penetrates to a surface beneath. **2.** A decoration or the like produced by stenciling. — v.t. sten·ciled or ·cilled, sten·cil·ing or ·cil·ling To mark with a stencil. [Prob. ME *stansel* to decorate with many colors < OF, ult. < L *scintilla* spark] — **sten'cil·er** or **sten'cil·ler** n.

steno- combining form Tight; narrow; contracted. Also, before vowels, **sten-.** [< Gk. *stenos* narrow]

ste·nog·ra·pher (stə·nog'rə·fər) n. One who writes stenography or is skilled in shorthand.

ste·nog·ra·phy (stə·nog'rə·fē) n. The art of writing by the use of contractions or arbitrary symbols; shorthand. — **sten·o·graph·ic** (sten'ə·graf'ik) or **·i·cal** adj. — **sten'o·graph'i·cal·ly** adv.

sten·o·type (sten'ə·tīp) n. **1.** A letter or combination of

letters representing a sound, word, or phrase, esp. in shorthand. **2.** A Stenotype.

Sten·o·type (sten'ə·tīp) n. A keyboard-operated machine used in stenotypy: a trade name. Also **stenotype.**

sten·o·typ·y (sten'ə·tī'pē) n. A system of shorthand employing ordinary letters alone or in various combinations to represent specific sounds, words, or phrases.

sten·tor (sten'tôr) n. One who possesses an uncommonly strong, loud voice. [< *Stentor*]

Sten·tor (sten'tôr) In the *Iliad*, a herald with a loud voice. **sten·to·ri·an** (sten·tôr'ē·ən, -tō'rē-) adj. Extremely loud.

step (step) n. **1.** An act of progressive motion that requires one of the supporting limbs of the body to be thrust in direction of the movement, and to reassume its function of support; a pace. **2.** The distance passed over in making such a motion. **3.** Any short distance; a space easily traversed. **4.** That which the foot rests upon in ascending or descending, as a stair or ladder rung. **5.** A single action or proceeding regarded as leading to something: a *step* toward emancipation. **6.** An advance or promotion that forms one of a series; grade. **7.** The manner of stepping; gait. **8.** The sound of a footfall. **9.** A footprint; track. **10.** pl. Progression by walking; walk. **11.** A patterned combination of foot movements in dancing: the tango *step.* **12.** Music An interval corresponding to one degree of a scale or staff; a major or minor second. **13.** Something resembling a step, a socket, supporting framework, etc.: the *step* of a mast. — **step 1.** Walking, dancing, marching, etc., in accord with proper rhythm or cadence, or in conformity with others. Informal In agreement or conformity. — **out of step** No step. — **to take steps** To adopt measures, as to attain end. — v. stepped, step·ping v.i. **1.** To move forward, backward by taking a step or steps. **2.** To walk a short distance: to *step* across the street. **3.** To move with measured, dignified, or graceful steps. **4.** To move or act quickly; briskly. **5.** To pass into a situation, circumstance, etc., if in a single step: He *stepped* into a fortune. — v.t. **6.** To take (a pace, stride, etc.). **7.** To perform the steps of: *step* a quadrille. **8.** To place or move (the foot) in taking a step. **9.** To measure by taking steps: often with *off.* **10.** To cut or arrange in steps. **11.** Naut. To place the lower end (a mast) in its step. — **to step down 1.** To decrease gradually, or by steps or degrees. **2.** To resign from an official position. — **to step in** To begin to take part; intervene. — **to step on** (or **upon**) **1.** To put the foot down on. **2.** To put the foot on so as to activate, as a brake or treadle. **3.** formal To reprove or subdue. — **to step on it** Informal To hurry; hasten. — **to step out 1.** To go outside, esp. for a short while. **2.** Informal To go out for fun or entertainment. **3.** To quit; resign. **4.** To walk vigorously and with long strides. — **to step up** To increase; accelerate. [OE *stæpe*]

step- combining form Related through the previous marriage of a parent or spouse, but not by blood. [OE < *stēp-* < *āstȳpan, āstēpan* to bereave, orphan]

step·broth·er (step'bruth'ər) n. The son of one's stepparent by a former marriage.

step·child (step'chīld') n. The child of one's husband or wife by a former marriage.

step·daugh·ter (step'dô'tər) n. A female stepchild.

step-down (step'doun') adj. **1.** Decreasing by stages. **2.** Electr. Converting a high voltage into a low voltage, as a transformer. **3.** Mech. Designating a gear that transfers motion at a reduced rate. Opposed to *step-up.*

step·fa·ther (step'fä'thər) n. The husband of one's mother other than one's own father.

step-in (step'in') n. **1.** A woman's brief underpants: also **step'-ins'.** **2.** A pumplike shoe.

step·lad·der (step'lad'ər) n. A set of portable steps with usu., a hinged frame at the back, that may be extended to support the steps in an upright position.

step·moth·er (step'muth'ər) n. The wife of one's father other than one's own mother.

step·par·ent (step'pâr'ənt) n. A stepfather or stepmother.

steppe (step) n. A vast plain devoid of forest; esp., one of the extensive plains in Russia and Siberia. [< Russian *step*]

step·per (step'ər) n. One who or that which steps: a horse is a high *stepper.* **2.** Slang A dancer.

step·ping-stone (step'ing-stōn') n. **1.** A stone affording footrest, as for crossing a stream. **2.** A preliminary step or stage in the fulfillment of a goal: *steppingstones* to success.

step·sis·ter (step'sis'tər) n. The daughter of one's stepparent by a former marriage.

step·son (step'sun') n. A male stepchild.

step-up (step'up') adj. **1.** Increasing by stages. **2.** Electr. Converting a low voltage into a high voltage, as a transformer. **3.** Designating a gear that transfers motion at an increased rate. Opposed to *step-down.*

-ster suffix of nouns **1.** One who makes or is occupied with: often pejorative: *songster, prankster.* **2.** One who belongs or is related to: *gangster.* **3.** One who is: *youngster.* [OE *-estre* fem. suffix expressing the agent]

e (stir) *n.* In the metric system, a measure of capacity
al to one cubic meter. See table front of book. [<
< Gk. *stereos* solid]

·e·o (ster′ē·ō, stir′-) *n.* A stereophonic system. — *adj.*
reophonic.

eo- *combining form* Solid; firm; hard; three-dimensional.
o, before vowels, stere-. [< Gk. *stereos* hard]

·e·o·chem·is·try (ster′ē·ō·kem′is·trē, stir′-) *n.* The
nch of chemistry that treats of the spatial arrangement of
ms and molecules.

·e·o·phon·ic (ster′ē·ə·fon′ik, stir′-) *adj.* 1. Pertaining
designed for, or characterized by the perception of sound
both ears; binaural. 2. *Electronics* Designing a system
sound reproduction in which two or more receivers or
dspeakers are so placed as to give the effect of hearing the
nd from more than one direction. Also *stereo.* — ster′e·
hon′i·cal·ly *adv.* — ster·e·o·phon·y (ster′ē·of′ə·nē, stir′-,
·′ē·ə·fō′nē, stir′-) *n.*

·e·op·ti·con (ster′ē·op′ti·kon, stir′-) *n.* A double magic
tern arranged to combine two images of the same object
scene, or used to bring one image after another on the
een. [< STEREO- + Gk. *optikos* of sight]

·e·o·scope (ster′ē·ə·skōp, stir′-) *n.* An instrument for
nding into one image two pictures of an object from
htly different points of view, so as to produce the impres-
s of relief and solidity. — ster′e·o·scop′ic (-skop′ik) or
al *adj.* — ster′e·o·scop′i·cal·ly *adv.*

·e·os·co·py (ster′ē·os′kə·pē, stir′-) *n.* 1. The art of
king or using stereoscopes and stereoscopic slides. 2. The
wing of objects as in three dimensions. — ster′e·os′co·
; *n.*

·e·o·type (ster′ē·ə·tīp′, stir′-) *n.* 1. A plate cast in type
al from a matrix and reproducing on its surface the com-
ed type or other material impressed upon the matrix. 2.
ything made or processed in this way. 3. Stereotypy. 4.
onventional or hackneyed expression, custom, mental
ge, etc. 5. A person possessing characteristics that typi-
particular group. — *v.t.* ·typed, ·typ·ing 1. To make a
eotype of. 2. To fix firmly or unalterably. — ster′e·o·
′er, ster′e·o·typ′ist *n.*

·e·o·typed (ster′ē·ə·tīpt′, stir′-) *adj.* 1. Formalized;
kneyed; trite. 2. Produced from a stereotype.

·e·o·typ·y (ster′ē·ə·tī′pē, stir′-) *n.* The art or act of
king stereotypes: also called *stereotype.*

·ile (ster′əl, *esp. Brit.* -īl) *adj.* 1. Having no reproduc-
power; barren. 2. *Bot.* Incapable of germinating. 3.
king productiveness: *sterile* soil. 4. Containing no bac-
a or other microorganisms. 5. Lacking in vigor or imagi-
ion: *sterile* verse. [< L *sterilis* barren] — ster′ile·ly
— ster′ile·ness, ste·ril·i·ty (stə·ril′ə·tē) *n.*

·il·ize (ster′əl·īz) *v.t.* ·ized, ·iz·ing 1. To free from in-
ive or pathogenic microorganisms. 2. To deprive of pro-
tive or reproductive power. 3. To make barren. Also
l. ster′il·ise. — ster′il·i·za′tion (-ə·zā′shən, -ī·zā′-) *n.* —
′il·iz′er *n.*

·ling (stûr′ling) *n.* 1. The official standard of fineness
British coins: for silver, 0.500; for gold, 0.91666. 2. Ster-
; silver, 0.925 fine, as used in manufacturing articles; also,
cles made of it. 3. A former silver penny of England·and
tland. — *adj.* 1. Made of or payable in sterling. 2.
de of sterling silver. 3. Genuine. 4. Valuable; es-
med: *sterling* qualities. [Prob. OE *steorra* star + -LING]
ause a star was stamped on some of the coins]

n[1] (stûrn) *adj.* 1. Marked by severity or harshness; unding. 2. Strict; severe. 3. Inspiring fear; awesome. 4.
solute; stout: a *stern* resolve. [OE *styrne*] — stern′ly
. — stern′ness *n.*

n[2] (stûrn) *n. Naut.* The aft part of a ship, boat, etc.
The hindmost part of any object. — *adj.* Situated at or
onging to the stern. [< ON *stȳra* to steer]

n·most (stûrn′mōst′, -məst) *adj.* Farthest to the rear
stern.

no- *combining form Anat.* The sternum. Also, before
vels, stern-. [< L *sternum* or Gk. *stérnon* breast]

n·post (stûrn′pōst′) *n. Naut.* The main vertical post
he stern frame of a vessel, to which the rudder is attached.

·num (stûr′nəm) *n. pl.* ·na (-nə) or ·nums *Anat.* The
astbone that covers the ventral support of the ribs in
tebrates. [< L < Gk. *stérnon* breast] — ster′nal *adj.*

n·ward (stûrn′wərd) *adj. & adv.* Toward the stern.

n·way (stûrn′wā′) *n. Naut.* Backward movement of
essel.

·n-wheel·er (stûrn′hwē′lər) *n.* A steamboat propelled
one large paddle wheel at the stern.

·oid (ster′oid) *n. Biochem.* Any of a large group of fat-
ble organic compounds, including the sterols, the bile
ds, and the sex hormones.

·ol (ster′ōl, -ol) *n. Biochem.* Any of a class of complex,

chiefly unsaturated solid alcohols, widely distributed in
plant and animal tissue, as cholesterol. [Contr. of CHOLES-
TEROL]

ster·to·rous (stûr′tər·əs) *adj.* Characterized by snoring or
accompanied by a snoring sound. [< NL < L *stertere* to
snore] — ster′tor·ous·ly *adv.* — ster′tor·ous·ness *n.*

stet (stet) Let it stand: a direction used in proofreading to
indicate that a word, letter, etc., marked for omission or
correction is to remain. — *v.t.* stet·ted, stet·ting To cancel
a former correction or omission by marking with the word
stet. Compare DELE. [< L < *stare* to stand, stay]

stetho- *combining form* The breast or chest; pectoral. Also,
before vowels, steth-. [< Gk. *stéthos* breast]

steth·o·scope (steth′ə·skōp) *n. Med.* An apparatus for
auscultation, adapted for conveying the sounds of the body
to the examiner's ear or ears. — steth′o·scop′ic (-skop′ik),
steth′o·scop′i·cal *adj.* — steth′o·scop′i·cal·ly *adv.* — ste·
thos·co·py (ste·thos′kə·pē) *n.*

ste·ve·dore (stē′və·dôr, -dōr) *n.* One whose business is
stowing or unloading the holds of vessels. — *v.t. & v.i.*
·dored, ·dor·ing To load or unload (a vessel). [< Sp. < L
stipare to compress, stuff]

stew (stōō, styōō) *v.t. & v.i.* 1. To boil slowly and gently;
seethe; keep or be at the simmering point. 2. *Informal* To
worry. — *n.* 1. Stewed food, esp. a preparation of meat or
fish and vegetables cooked together by stewing. 2. *Informal*
Mental agitation; worry. [< OF, prob. ult. < L *ex-* out +
Gk. *typhos* steam, vapor]

stew·ard (stōō′ərd, styōō′-) *n.* 1. One who is entrusted
with the management of property, finances, or other affairs
not his own. 2. One who has charge of buying provisions,
managing servants, etc., in a private residence or in a club,
hotel, etc. 3. One in charge of provisions and usu. of the
tables on a ship. 4. On an airplane, ship, or bus, one who
waits on the passengers. 5. One who manages any affair:
steward of the races. [OE < *stī* hall, sty + *weard* ward,
keeper] — stew′ard·ess *n.fem.* — stew′ard·ship *n.*

stewed (stōōd, styōōd) *adj.* 1. Cooked by stewing. 2.
Slang Drunk.

stew·pan (stōō′pan, styōō′-) *n.* A cooking vessel used for
stewing.

stib·i·um (stib′ē·əm) *n.* Antimony. [< L < Gk. *stibi*]
— stib′i·al *adj.*

-stichous *combining form* Having (a specified number of)
rows. [< Gk. *stichos* row, line]

stick (stik) *n.* 1. A slender piece of wood, as a branch cut
from a tree or bush, a baton or wand, etc. 2. *Brit.* A cane.
3. Anything resembling a stick in form: a *stick* of candy
or dynamite. 4. A piece of wood of any size, cut for fuel,
lumber, or timber. 5. *Aeron.* The control lever of an airplane, that operates the elevators and ailerons. 6. A poke,
stab, or thrust with a pointed instrument. 7. The state of
being stuck together; adhesion. 8. In sports, a baseball bat,
hockey stick, etc. 9. *Informal* A stiff, inert, or dull person.
10. A stalk, as of asparagus. — the sticks *Informal* An
obscure rural district; the backwoods or country. — *v.*
stuck or (*for def. 15*) sticked, stick·ing *v.t.* 1. To pierce, stab,
or penetrate with a pointed object. 2. To kill or wound by
piercing; stab. 3. To thrust or force, as a sword or pin, into
or through something else. 4. To force the end of (a nail,
etc.) into something so as to be fixed in place. 5. To fasten
in place with or as with pins, nails, etc.: to *stick* a ribbon on
a dress. 6. To cover with objects piercing the surface. 7.
To impale; transfix. 8. To put or thrust: He *stuck* his hand
into his pocket. 9. To fasten to a surface by or as by an
adhesive substance. 10. To bring to a standstill; obstruct;
halt: usu. in the passive: We were *stuck* in Rome. 11. *Informal* To smear or daub with something sticky. 12. *Informal* To
baffle; puzzle. 13. *Slang* To impose upon; cheat. 14.
Slang To force great expense, an unpleasant task, etc., upon.
15. To provide with sticks or brush on which to grow, as a
vine. — *v.i.* 16. To be or become fixed in place by being
thrust in: to *stick* in a cushion. 17. To become or remain
attached or close to something by or as by adhesion; adhere;
cling. 18. To come to a standstill; become blocked or obstructed. 19. To be baffled or disconcerted. 20. To hesitate; scruple: with *at* or *to*. 21. To persist; persevere: with
at or *to*. 22. To remain firm or resolute; be faithful. 23.
To be extended; protrude: with *from, out, through, up,* etc.
— to stick around *Slang* To remain near or near at hand. —
to stick by To remain faithful to; be loyal to. — to stick it
out To persevere to the end. — to stick up *Slang* To detain
and rob. — to stick up for *Informal* To take the part of;
defend. [OE *sticca*]

stick·er (stik′ər) *n.* 1. A gummed label, sign, etc. 2. One
who or that which fastens with or as with paste. 3. One
who holds tenaciously to anything. 4. *Informal* A puzzle.
5. A prickly stem, thorn, or bur.

stick·ing plaster (stik'ing) Adhesive tape.
stick·le (stik'əl) *v.i.* **-led, -ling** 1. To contend or argue about trifling matters. 2. To insist or hesitate for petty reasons. [ME *stighlen,* freq. of OE *stihtan* to arrange]
stick·le·back (stik'əl·bak') *n.* A small fresh- or salt-water fish, having sharp dorsal spines.
stick·ler (stik'lər) *n.* One who contends over or insists upon something: usu. with *for:* a *stickler* for details.
stick·pin (stik'pin') *n. U.S.* An ornamental pin for a necktie.
stick-to-it·ive (stik-tōō'it·iv) *adj. Informal* Persevering. — **stick-to'-it·ive·ly** *adv.* — **stick-to'-it·ive·ness** *n.*
stick·up (stik'up') *n. Slang* A robbery or holdup.
stick·y (stik'ē) *adj.* **stick·i·er, stick·i·est** 1. Adhering to a surface; adhesive. 2. Covered with something adhesive. 3. Warm and humid. — **stick'i·ly** *adv.* — **stick'i·ness** *n.*
stiff (stif) *adj.* 1. Resisting the action of a bending force; rigid. 2. Not easily moved: *stiff* brakes; also, moving or functioning painfully or without suppleness: a *stiff* neck. 3. Not natural, graceful, or easy; constrained and awkward; formal. 4. Not liquid or fluid; thick; viscous. 5. Taut; tightly drawn. 6. Having a strong, steady movement: a *stiff* breeze. 7. Firm in resistance; stubborn. 8. Harsh; severe: a *stiff* penalty. 9. High; dear: a *stiff* price. 10. Strong or potent, as in alcoholic content: a *stiff* drink. 11. Difficult; arduous: a *stiff* climb. — *n. Slang* 1. A corpse. 2. An awkward or unresponsive person; esp., a bore. 3. A man; fellow: working *stiff*; also, a roughneck. [OE *stif*] — **stiff'ly** *adv.* — **stiff'ness** *n.*
stiff·en (stif'ən) *v.t. & v.i.* To make or become stiff or stiffer. — **stiff'en·er** *n.*
stiff-necked (stif'nekt') *adj.* Not yielding; stubborn.
sti·fle (stī'fəl) *v.* **-fled, -fling** *v.t.* 1. To keep back; suppress or repress; check: to *stifle* sobs. 2. To suffocate; choke. — *v.i.* 3. To die of suffocation. 4. To experience difficulty in breathing, as in a stuffy room. [ME < OF *estouffer* to smother] — **sti'fler** *n.* — **sti'fling** *adj.* — **sti'fling·ly** *adv.*
stig·ma (stig'mə) *n. pl.* **stig·ma·ta** (stig'mə·tə, stig·mä'tə) or (*for defs. 1–3, usu.*) **stig·mas** 1. A mark of infamy, or token of disgrace. 2. A mark indicating a defect or something not normal. 3. *Bot.* The part of a pistil that receives the pollen. For illus. see FLOWER. 4. *Biol.* a A mark or spot. b An aperture or opening, as a pore. 5. *pl.* The wounds that Christ received during the Passion and Crucifixion. 6. Formerly, a brand made on slaves and criminals. [< L < Gk. *stizein* to prick, brand] — **stig·mat'ic** (-mat'ik), **stig·mat'i·cal** *adj.*
stig·ma·tize (stig'mə·tīz) *v.t.* **-tized, -tiz·ing** 1. To characterize or brand as ignominious. 2. To mark with a stigma. [< Med.L < Gk. *stigma* pointed end, mark] — **stig'ma·ti·za'tion** *n.* — **stig'ma·tiz'er** *n.*
stile (stīl) *n.* 1. A step, or series of steps, on each side of a fence or wall to aid in surmounting it. 2. A turnstile. [OE *stīgan* to climb]
sti·let·to (sti·let'ō) *n. pl.* **-tos** or **-toes** A small dagger with a slender blade. — *v.t.* **-toed, -to·ing** To pierce with a stiletto; stab. [< Ital. < L *stilus* writing instrument]
still[1] (stil) *adj.* 1. Making no sound; silent. 2. Peaceful; tranquil. 3. Without movement; motionless. 4. Low in sound; quiet; hushed. 5. Subdued; soft. 6. Dead; inanimate. 7. Having no effervescence: said of wines. 8. *Photog.* Of or designating a single photograph, as contrasted with a motion picture. — **Syn.** See CALM. — *n.* 1. *Poetic* Stillness; calm. 2. A still-life picture. 3. *Photog.* A still photograph. — *adv.* 1. Now as previously; up to this or that time: He is *still* here. 2. All the same: nevertheless. 3. Even; yet: *still* more. 4. *Poetic & Dial.* Always; constantly. — *conj.* Nevertheless; and yet. — *v.t.* 1. To cause to be still or calm. 2. To silence or hush. 3. To quiet or allay, as fears. — *v.i.* 4. To become still. [OE *stille*] — **still'ness** *n.*
still[2] (stil) *n.* 1. An apparatus in which a substance is vaporized by heat, and the vapor then liquefied in a condenser, used esp. for distilling alcoholic liquors. 2. A distillery. — *v.t. & v.i.* To distill. [< L < *stilla* drop]
still·born (stil'bôrn') *adj.* Dead at birth. — **still'birth'** *n.*
still life 1. In painting, the representation of objects, as tables, flowers, fruit, etc. 2. A picture of such a subject.
Still·son wrench (stil'sən) A wrench closely resembling a monkey wrench, but with serrated jaws, one of which is capable of slight angular movement, so that the grip is increased by pressure on the handle: a trade name.

STILLSON WRENCH

still·y (*adj.* stil'ē; *adv.* stil'lē) *adj.* Still; silent; calm. — *adv.* Calmly; quietly; without noise.
stilt (stilt) *n.* 1. One of a pair of long, slender poles made with a projection to support the foot some distance above the ground in walking. 2. A tall post or pillar used as a support, as for a dock. 3. Any of several long-legged, wading birds. — *v.t.* To raise on stilts. [ME *stilte,* ? < LG]

stilt·ed (stil'tid) *adj.* 1. Artificially formal or elevated manner; pompous. 2. Raised or built on or as on sti — **stilt'ed·ly** *adv.* — **stilt'ed·ness** *n.*
stim·u·lant (stim'yə·lənt) *n.* 1. Anything that quickens promotes the activity of some physiological process, a drug. 2. An alcoholic beverage. — *adj.* Acting as a stir lant; serving to stimulate. [See STIMULATE.]
stim·u·late (stim'yə·lāt) *v.* **-lat·ed, -lat·ing** *v.t.* 1. To ro to activity or to quickened action; spur. 2. *Physiol.* excite (an organ or tissue) by applying some form of stir lus. 3. To affect by alcoholic beverages. — *v.i.* 4. To as a stimulant. [< L < *stimulus* goad] — **stim'u·lat** **stim'u·la'tor** *n.* — **stim'u·la'tion** *n.* — **stim'u·la'tive** *& n.*
stim·u·lus (stim'yə·ləs) *n. pl.* **·li** (-lī) 1. Anything t rouses the mind or spirits; an incentive. 2. *Physiol.* agent or form of excitation that influences the activity o organism as a whole or in any of its parts. [< L]
sti·my (stī'mē) See STYMIE.
sting (sting) *v.* **stung, sting·ing** *v.t.* 1. To pierc prick painfully, as with a sharp, sometimes venomous org 2. To cause to suffer sharp, smarting pain from or as fro sting. 3. To cause to suffer mentally; pain: His heart *stung* with remorse. 4. To stimulate; goad; spur. 5. S To get the better of; also, to overcharge. — *v.i.* 6. To h or use a sting, as a bee. 7. To suffer or cause a sharp, sm ing pain. 8. To suffer or cause mental distress; pain. — 1. *Zool.* A sharp, pointed organ, as of a bee, able to infli wound. 2. The act of stinging; also, the wound or the p caused by a sting. 3. Any sharp, smarting sensation: *sting* of remorse. 4. A spur; goad. 5. *Bot.* One of the sh pointed hairs of a nettle, charged with an irritating fl also **stinging hair.** [OE *stingan*] — **sting'er** *n.* — **sti ing·ly** *adv.* — **sting'y** *adj.*
sting ray Any of a family of flat-bodied fishes having br pectoral fins and a whiplike tail capable of inflicting wou also called **sting·a·ree** (sting'ə·rē, sting'ə·rē') *n.*
stin·gy (stin'jē) *adj.* **-gi·er, -gi·est** 1. Unwilling to spen give; miserly. 2. Scanty; inadequate; meager. [< dia *stinge* sting + -Y[1]] — **stin'gi·ly** *adv.* — **stin'gi·ness** *n* — **Syn.** 1. niggardly, parsimonious, close, closefisted, tigh
stink (stingk) *n.* A strong, foul odor; stench. — **Syn.** SMELL. — *v.* **stank** or **stunk, stunk, stink·ing** *v.i.* 1. give forth a foul odor. 2. To be extremely offensive or h ful. 3. *Informal* To be of bad quality. — *v.t.* 4. To c to stink. — **to make** (or **raise**) **a stink** *Slang* To pr vehemently. — **to stink out** To drive out by a foul or focating odor. [OE *stincan* to smell] — **stink'ing·ly**
stink·bug (stingk'bug') *n.* Any of various large, flatt bugs that emit an unpleasant odor if disturbed.
stink·weed (stingk'wēd') *n.* Any of various plants ha a disagreeable odor, as the jimsonweed.
stint (stint) *v.t.* 1. To limit, as in amount or share; be st with. — *v.i.* 2. To be frugal or sparing. — *n.* 1. A l amount, as of work to be performed within a specified t 2. A bound; restriction; limit. 3. A small sandpiper. [*stynten* to cause to stop] — **stint'er** *n.*
stipe (stīp) *n.* 1. *Zool.* A stalk or support. 2. *Bot.* A st like support or stem, as that supporting a fern's frond. [< F < L *stipes* branch]
sti·pend (stī'pend) *n.* An allowance, salary, or pen esp., money paid under a scholarship. [< L < *stips* payment in coin + *pendere* to weigh, pay out]
sti·pen·di·ar·y (stī·pen'dē·er'ē) *ad.* 1. Receiving or forming services for a stipend. 2. Of or like a stipend. Paid for by a stipend, as services. — *n. pl.* **·ar·ies** who receives a stipend. See STIPEND.]
stip·ple (stip'əl) *v.t.* **-pled, -pling** To draw, paint, or eng with dots or short touches instead of lines. — *n.* method of painting, etc., by stippling. 2. A painting duced by stippling; also the effect of stippling. [< *stip dot*] — **stip'pler** *n.*
stip·u·late (stip'yə·lāt) *v.* **-lat·ed, -lat·ing** *v.t.* 1. To sp as the terms or as a condition for an agreement, contract 2. To promise; guarantee. — *v.i.* 3. To demand somet as a requirement: with *for.* 4. To make an agreement. L < *stipulari* to bargain] — **stip'u·la'tor** *n.*
stip·u·la·tion (stip'yə·lā'shən) *n.* 1. The act of stip ing, or the state of being stipulated. 2. That which is s lated; a condition. — **stip'u·la·to'ry** (-lə·tôr'ē, -tō'rē)
stip·ule (stip'yōol) *n. Bot.* One of a pair of leaflike app ages at the base of the petiole of certain leaves. [< L *st* stalk] — **stip·u·late** (stip'yə·lit, -lāt) *adj.*
stir[1] (stûr) *v.* **stirred, stir·ring** *v.t.* 1. To agitate so alter the relative position of the particles or componen as soup with a spoon. 2. To cause to move, esp., slight irregularly; disturb. 3. To move vigorously; bestir. 4 rouse, as from sleep, indifference, or inactivity; stimu 5. To incite; provoke: often with *up.* 6. To affect stror move with emotion. — *v.i.* 7. To move, esp., slightly To be active; move about. 9. To happen. 10. To und

ring: This molasses *stirs* easily. — *n.* **1.** The act of ring, or state of being stirred; activity. **2.** General inter- or commotion. **3.** Excitement or agitation. **4.** A poke; lge. [OE *styrian*] **— stir′rer** *n.*

² (stûr) *n. Slang* A jail; prison. [Origin uncertain]

·ring (stûr′ing) *adj.* **1.** Stimulating; inspiring. **2.** Full activity or stir; lively. **— stir′ring·ly** *adv.*

·rup (stûr′əp, stir′-) *n.* **1.** An inverted U-shaped sup- t hung from either side of a saddle to hold the rider's foot and after mounting. **2.** Any similarly shaped supports, for a beam. [OE *stigrāp* mounting rope]

·rup bone *Anat.* The stapes.

ch (stich) *n.* **1.** A single passage of a threaded needle ough fabric and back again, as in sewing or embroidery, in surgery, through skin or flesh. **2.** A single turn of ead or yarn around a needle, as in knitting or crocheting; o, the link or loop resulting from such a turn. **3.** Any ticular arrangement of a thread used in sewing, crochet- , etc.: a chain *stitch*. **4.** A sharp sudden pain, esp. in the k or side. **5.** *Informal* The slightest bit or fragment: not *itch* of work. — *v.t.* **1.** To join together or ornament h stitches. — *v.i.* **2.** To make stitches; sew. [OE *stice* a ck, stab] **— stitch′er** *n.*

·er (sti′vər) *n.* **1.** A small Dutch coin, ½₀ of a guilder. Anything of little value. [< Du. *stuiver*]

Johns·wort (sänt jonz′wûrt′) A hardy perennial with p yellow flowers. Also **St.-John's-wort.**

at (stōt) *n.* The ermine, esp. in its brown summer coat. E *stote*; origin uncertain]

k (stok) *n.* **1.** A quantity of something acquired or ·t for future use. **2.** The total merchandise or goods that ommercial establishment has on hand. **3.** Livestock. **4.** finance: **a** The capital or fund raised by a corporation ough the sale of shares. **b** The proportional part of this ·ital credited to an individual stockholder and repre- ·ted by the number of shares he owns. **c** A certificate wing ownership of shares. **5.** The trunk or main stem of ·ee or other plant. **6.** A line of familial descent. **7.** The inal progenitor of a family line. **8.** An ethnic group; ·e. **9.** A family of languages. **10.** A related group or ·ily of plants or animals; also, a type of animal or plant m which others are derived. **11.** *Bot.* **a** A rhizome. **b** In ·ticulture, a stem upon which a graft is made; also, a ·nt, tree, etc. that provides cuttings and slips. **12.** The ·th from boiled meat or fish used in preparing soups, etc. Raw material: paper *stock*. **14.** *pl.* A timber frame with ·es for confining the ankles, formerly used in punishing ·ty offenders. **15.** *pl.* The timber frame on which a vessel ·ts during construction. **16.** In firearms: **a** The rear ·oden portion of a rifle etc., to which the barrel and mech- ·sms are secured. **b** The arm on rapidfire guns connecting shoulder piece to the slide. **c** The handle of a pistol or ·ilar firearm. **17.** The handle of certain instruments, as of hip or fishing rod. **18.** A theatrical stock company; also, ·repertoire. **19.** A broad, stiffened band, formerly worn a cravat. **20.** An ornamental garden plant, as the gilly- ·ver. **— in stock** On hand and available for sale or use. **to take stock** 1. To take an inventory. 2. To estimate ·appraise. — *v.t.* **1.** To furnish with livestock or with ·rchandise. **2.** To keep for sale. **3.** To put aside for ·ure use. **4.** To provide with a handle or stock. **—** *v.i.* To lay in supplies or stock: often with *up.* — *adj.* **1.** ·t continually ready or constantly brought forth, like old ·ds: a *stock* joke. **2.** Kept on hand: a *stock* size. **3.** Banal; ·nmonplace: a *stock* phrase. **4.** Used for breeding pur- ·es. **5.** Employed in handling or caring for the stock. **—** . Motionlessly; like a stump: used in combination: *stock-* . [OE *stocc*]

·k·ade (sto·kād′) *n.* **1.** A line of stout posts, stakes, ·, set upright in the earth to form a fence or barrier; also, area thus enclosed, used as a prison, etc. **2.** Any similar ·a. — *v.t.* **·ad·ed, ·ad·ing** To surround or fortify with a ·kade. [< OF < Sp. < *estaque* stake < Gmc.]

·k·breed·er (stok′brē′dər) *n.* One who breeds and ·es livestock. **— stock′breed′ing** *n.*

·k·bro·ker (stok′brō′kər) *n.* One who buys and sells ·cks or securities for others. **— stock′bro′ker·age** (-ij), **ck′bro′king** *n.*

·k car An automobile, often a sedan, modified for racing.

·k company **1.** An incorporated company that issues ·ck. **2.** A more or less permanent dramatic company ·der one management, that presents a series of plays.

·k exchange **1.** A place where stocks and bonds are ·ight and sold. **2.** An association of stockbrokers who ·nsact business in stocks, bonds, etc.

·k farm A farm that specializes in breeding livestock.

·k·fish (stok′fish′) *n.* Cod, haddock, or the like, cured splitting and drying in the air, without salt.

stock·hold·er (stok′hōl′dər) *n.* One who holds certificates of ownership in a company or corporation. **— stock′hold· ing** *adj. & n.*

stock·i·net (stok′i·net′) *n.* An elastic knitted fabric, ma- chine-made and used for undergarments, stockings, etc. Also **stock′i·nette′.** [Alter. of *stockinget* < STOCKING + -ET]

stock·ing (stok′ing) *n.* **1.** A close-fitting woven or knitted covering for the foot and leg. **2.** Something resembling such a covering. **— in one's stocking feet** Wearing one's stock- ings or socks, but no shoes. [< STOCK, in obs. sense of "a stocking" + -ING³] **— stock′inged** (-ingd) *adj.*

stock·man (stok′mən) *n. pl.* **·men** (-mən) **1.** One who raises, owns, or has charge of livestock; a cattleman. **2.** One who works in a stockroom, warehouse, etc.

stock market **1.** A stock exchange. **2.** The business transacted in such a place: The *stock market* was active. **3.** The rise and fall of prices of stocks and bonds.

stock·pile (stok′pīl) *n.* A storage pile of materials or sup- plies. Also **stock pile.** — *v.t. & v.i.* **·piled, ·pil·ing** To ac- cumulate a supply or stockpile (of).

stock raising Breeding and raising of livestock.

stock·room (stok′rōōm′) *n.* A room where reserve stocks of goods are stored. Also **stock room.**

stock-still (stok′stil′) *adj.* Still as a post; motionless.

stock·y (stok′ē) *adj.* **stock·i·er, stock·i·est** Solidly built, thickset, and usu. short. **— stock′i·ly** *adv.* **— stock′i·ness** *n.*

stock·yard (stok′yärd′) *n.* A large yard where cattle, sheep, pigs, etc., are kept ready for shipping or slaughter.

stodg·y (stoj′ē) *adj.* **stodg·i·er, stodg·i·est 1.** Dull, stupid, and commonplace. **2.** Crammed full; distended; bulky. **3.** Indigestible and heavy: said of food. **4.** Thickset; stocky. **— stodg′i·ly** *adv.* **— stodg′i·ness** *n.*

sto·gy (stō′gē) *n. pl.* **·gies 1.** A long, slender, inexpensive cigar. **2.** A stout, heavy boot or shoe. Also **sto′gey, sto′gie.** [Earlier *stoga* < (CONE)STOGA (WAGON), because their driv- ers wore heavy boots and smoked coarse cigars]

sto·ic (stō′ik) *n.* A person apparently unaffected by pleasure or pain. — *adj.* Indifferent to pleasure or pain; impassive. Also **sto′i·cal.** **— sto′i·cal·ly** *adv.* **— sto′i·cal·ness** *n.*

Sto·ic (stō′ik) *n.* A member of a school of Greek philosophy founded by Zeno about 308 B.C., holding that wisdom lies in being superior to passion, joy, grief, etc. and in unper- turbed submission to the divine will. — *adj.* Of the Stoics or Stoicism. [< L < Gk. < *Stoa* (*Poikilē*) (Painted) Porch, the colonnade at Athens where Zeno taught]

sto·i·cism (stō′ə·siz′əm) *n.* Indifference to pleasure or pain; stoicalness.

Sto·i·cism (stō′ə·siz′əm) *n.* The doctrines of the Stoics.

stoke (stōk) *v.t. & v.i.* **stoked, stok·ing** To supply (a fur- nace) with fuel; stir up or tend (a fire or furnace). [Back formation < STOKER]

stoke·hold (stōk′hōld′) *n. Naut.* The furnace room of a steamship.

stoke·hole (stōk′hōl′) *n.* **1.** The space about the mouth of a furnace of the mouth itself. **2.** A stokehold.

stok·er (stō′kər) *n.* **1.** One who supplies fuel to a furnace; a fireman on a locomotive, etc. **2.** A device for feeding coal to a furnace. [< Du. < *stoken* to stir a fire]

stole¹ (stōl) *n.* **1.** *Eccl.* A long, narrow band of decorated cloth worn about the shoulders by officiating clergymen. **2.** A long scarf worn about the shoulders by women. [OE < L < Gk. *stolē* garment] **— stoled** (stōld) *adj.*

stole² (stōl) Past tense of STEAL.

sto·len (stō′lən) Past participle of STEAL.

stol·id (stol′id) *adj.* Having or showing little feeling or perception; impassive; dull. [< L *stolidus* dull] **— sto·lid· i·ty** (stə·lid′ə·tē), **stol′id·ness** *n.* **— stol′id·ly** *adv.*

sto·ma (stō′mə) *n. pl.* **sto·ma·ta** (stō′mə·tə, stom′ə·tə) **1.** *Bot.* A minute orifice or pore in the epidermis of plants, esp., of leaves and stems. **2.** *Biol.* **a** An aperture in the walls of blood vessels or in serous membranes. **b** A mouthlike opening in nematodes. [< NL < Gk. *stoma* mouth]

-stoma See -STOME.

stom·ach (stum′ək) *n.* **1.** The pouchlike, highly vascular enlargement of the alimentary canal, situated in man and vertebrates between the esophagus and the small intestine, and serving as one of the principal organs of digestion. ♦ Collateral adjective: *gastric.* **2.** Any digestive cavity. **3.** Loosely, the abdomen or belly. **4.** Desire for food; appe- tite. **5.** Any desire or inclination. — *v.t.* **1.** To put up with; endure. **2.** To take into and retain in the stomach; digest. [< OF < L < Gk. < *stoma* mouth]

stom·ach·er (stum′ək·ər) *n.* A former ornamental article of dress, worn over the breast and stomach.

sto·mach·ic (stō·mak′ik) *adj.* **1.** Pertaining to the stom- ach. **2.** Beneficial to or stimulating the activity of the stom- ach. Also **stom·ach·al** (stum′ək·əl), **sto·mach′i·cal.** **—** *n.* Any medicine strengthening or stimulating the stomach.

sto·ma·ta (stō′mə·tə, stom′ə·tə) Plural of STOMA.

stomato- *combining form* Of, like, or pertaining to the mouth. Also, before vowels, **stomat-**. [< Gk. *stoma, stomatos* mouth]

sto·ma·tous (stō′mə·təs, stom′ə-) *adj.* Having a stoma or stomata.

-stome *combining form* Mouth; mouthlike opening: *peristome.* Also spelled *-stoma.* [< Gk. *stoma* mouth]

-stomous *combining form* Having a (specified kind of) mouth: *microstomous.* Also **-stomatous.** [< Gk. *stoma, stomatos* mouth]

stomp (stomp) *v.t. & v.i.* **1.** To tread heavily or violently (upon); press down. **2.** *Dial.* To stamp. — *n.* A dance involving a heavy and lively step. [Var. of STAMP]

-stomy *combining form Surg.* An operation to form an artificial opening for or into (a specified organ or part): *colostomy.* [< Gk. *stoma* mouth]

stone (stōn) *n.* **1.** The hard, nonmetallic mineral or earthy matter of which rock is composed. **2.** A small piece of rock, as a pebble. **3.** Rock, or a piece of rock that has been hewn or shaped. **4.** A precious stone; gem. **5.** Anything resembling a stone in shape or hardness: a *hailstone.* **6.** A gravestone. **7.** A grindstone or millstone. **8.** *Pathol.* A stony concretion in the bladder, or a disease characterized by such concretions. **9.** *Bot.* The hard covering of the kernel in a fruit. **10.** (*pl.* **stone**) In England, 14 pounds avoirdupois. — *adj.* **1.** Made of stone: a *stone* ax. **2.** Made of coarse hard earthenware: a *stone* bottle. — *v.t.* **stoned, ston·ing 1.** To hurl stones at; pelt or kill with stones. **2.** To remove the stones or pits from. **3.** To furnish or line, as a well, with stone. [OE *stān*] — **ston′er** *n.*

Stone Age The earliest known period in human culture when stone implements and weapons were used.

stone-blind (stōn′blīnd′) *adj.* Totally blind.

stone-broke (stōn′brōk′) *adj. Informal* Without any money; having no funds. Also **ston′y-broke′** (stō′nē-).

stone-crop (stōn′krop′) *n.* Any of various plants having small fleshy leaves and yellow flowers, often grown in rock gardens.

stone-cut·ter (stōn′kut′ər) *n.* One who or that which cuts stone; especially, a machine for facing stone.

stone-deaf (stōn′def′) *adj.* Completely deaf.

Stone·henge (stōn′henj) A prehistoric structure on Salisbury Plain, England, consisting primarily of great circles of huge, dressed stones.

stone·ma·son (stōn′mā′sən) *n.* One who prepares and lays stones in building. — **stone′ma′son·ry** (-rē) *n.*

STONEHENGE

stone's throw A short distance.

stone·ware (stōn′wâr′) *n.* A variety of very hard pottery, made from siliceous clay or clay mixed with flint or sand.

stone·work (stōn′wûrk′) *n.* **1.** Work concerned with cutting or setting stone; also, something made of stone. **2.** *pl.* A place where stone is prepared for masonry. — **stone′·work′er** *n.*

ston·y (stō′nē) *adj.* **ston·i·er, ston·i·est 1.** Abounding in stone. **2.** Made or consisting of stone. **3.** Hard as stone. **4.** Unfeeling or inflexible. **5.** Converting into stone; petrifying. — **ston′i·ly** *adv.* — **ston′i·ness** *n.*

stood (stŏŏd) Past tense and past participle of STAND.

stooge (stōōj) *Informal n.* **1.** An actor placed in the audience to heckle a comedian on the stage. **2.** An actor who feeds lines to the principal comedian, acts as a foil for his jokes, etc. **3.** Anyone who acts as or is the tool or dupe of another. — *v.i.* **stooged, stoog·ing** To act as a stooge: usually with *for.* [Origin unknown]

stool (stōōl) *n.* **1.** A backless and armless seat, high or low, for one person. **2.** A low bench or support for the feet or for the knees in kneeling. **3.** A seat used in defecating; a privy. **4.** The matter evacuated from the bowels at each movement. **5.** *Bot.* **a** A stump or root from which suckers or sprouts shoot up. **b** The shoots from such a root or stump. **6.** A decoy. — *v.i.* **1.** To send up shoots or suckers. **2.** To decoy wild fowl with a stool. **3.** To void feces. **4.** *U.S. Slang* To be a stool pigeon. [OE *stōl*]

stool pigeon 1. A living or artificial pigeon attached to a perch to decoy others. **2.** *U.S. Slang* An informer or spy, esp. for the police.

stoop¹ (stōōp) *v.i.* **1.** To bend or lean the body forward and down; bow; crouch. **2.** To stand or walk with the upper part of the body habitually bent forward; slouch. **3.** To bend; lean; sink, as a tree. **4.** To lower or degrade oneself: to *stoop* to cheating. **5.** To swoop, as a hawk on prey. — *v.t.* **6.** To bend (one's head, shoulders, etc.) forward. — *n.* **1.** An act of stooping; a slouch. **2.** A habitual forward inclination of the head and shoulders. **3.** A decline from dignity or superiority. **4.** A swoop. [OE *stūpian*]

stoop² (stōōp) *n. U.S.* **1.** Originally, a platform at the door of a house approached by steps and having seats. **2.** A small porch at the entrance to a house. [< Du. *stoep*]

stoop³ (stōōp) See STOUP.

stop (stop) *v,* **stopped** or (*Chiefly Poetic*) **stopt, stop·ping 1.** To bring (something in motion) to a halt; arrest progress of. **2.** To prevent the doing or completion of. **3.** To prevent (a person) from doing something; restrain. **4.** To keep back, withhold, or cut off, as wages or supplies. **5.** To cease doing; desist from. **6.** To intercept in transit: a letter. **7.** To block up, obstruct, or clog (a passage, road, etc.): often with *up.* **8.** To cover over, or otherwise close, as a hole, cavity, etc. **9.** To close (a bottle, barrel, etc.) with a cork, plug, or other stopper. **10.** To stanch (a wound, etc.). **11.** To defeat; also, to kill. **12.** *Music* press down (a string) on the finger board, or to close (a hole) in order to vary the pitch produced by an instrument: finger. **13.** To punctuate. **14.** In boxing, etc., to parry. — *v.i.* **15.** To come to a halt; cease progress or motion. **16.** To cease doing something; pause or desist. **17.** come to an end. — **to stop off** *U.S. Informal* To cease traveling temporarily before reaching one's destination. **to stop over** *U.S. Informal* **1.** To stay at a place temporarily. **2.** To interrupt a journey; make a stopover. — *n.* **1.** act of stopping, or the state of being stopped; a halt; pause; end. **2.** That which stops or limits the range or time of movement: a camera *stop.* **3.** An obstruction or obstacle. **4.** *Music* **a** The stopping of a string or hole of an instrument. **b** In an organ or harpsichord, a knob controlling a register of pipes or strings; also the register so controlled. **5.** A punctuation mark, as a period. **6.** In telegrams and cablegrams, the word *stop* spelled out to indicate a punctuation mark. **7.** In joinery, a block, pin, or the like to check sliding motion, as of a drawer. **8.** *Phonet.* **a** Complete blockage of the breath stream (implosion), as with the lips or tongue, followed by a sudden release (plosion). **b** A consonant produced, as *p, b, t, d, k,* and *g.* [OE *-stoppian,* as in *stoppian* to stop up]

stop·cock (stop′kok′) *n.* A faucet or short pipe having a valve for stopping or regulating the passage of fluids.

stope (stōp) *Mining n.* An excavation from which the ore is removed in a series of steps. — *v.t. & v.i.* **stoped, stop·ing** To excavate in stopes. [Appar. akin to STEP]

stop·gap (stop′gap′) *n.* **1.** That which stops a gap. **2.** Something improvised to fill a need temporarily; an expedient. — *adj.* That serves as a stopgap.

stop·light (stop′līt′) *n.* **1.** The red light on a traffic light. **2.** A red light on the rear of a motor vehicle that shines upon application of the brakes.

stop order An order to an agent or broker to buy or sell stock at the market only when it reaches a specified price.

stop·o·ver (stop′ō′vər) *n.* **1.** The act of staying in a place for a brief period, esp. while traveling. **2.** The act of interrupting a journey without paying additional fare, as by taking a later train. Also **stop′-off′** (-ôf′, -of′).

stop·page (stop′ij) *n.* **1.** The act of stopping, or the state of being stopped. **2.** An obstruction of some kind; blockage.

stop payment An order to a bank to refuse payment of a certain check.

stop·per (stop′ər) *n.* **1.** Something that stops up or closes, as a plug or cork. **2.** One who or that which stops or checks a movement, action, etc. — *v.t.* To close with a stopper.

stop·ple (stop′əl) *n.* A stopper, plug, cork, or bung. — **·pled, ·pling** To close with or as with a stopple. [ME *stoppel,* prob. < *stoppen* to stop]

stopt (stopt) Alternative, chiefly poetic, past tense and participle of STOP.

stop·watch (stop′woch′) *n.* A watch that has a hand indicating fractions of a second and that may be instantaneously started or stopped, used for timing races, etc.

stor·age (stôr′ij, stō′rij) *n.* **1.** The depositing of articles in a warehouse for safekeeping. **2.** Space for storing goods. **3.** A charge for storing. **4.** The charging of a storage battery.

storage battery One or more secondary cells arranged as a single source of direct current and capable of being charged on reversal of the current.

storage cell *Electr.* A secondary cell.

store (stôr, stōr) *v.t.* **stored, stor·ing 1.** To put away for future use; accumulate. **2.** To furnish or supply; provide. **3.** To place in a warehouse or other place of deposit for safekeeping. — *n.* **1.** *U.S.* A place where merchandise of kind is kept for sale. **2.** That which is stored or laid up against future need. **3.** *pl.* Supplies, as of arms, or clothing. **4.** A place where commodities are stored; warehouse. — **in store** Set apart for the future; forthcoming; impending. — **to set store by** To value or esteem; regard. [< OF *instaurare* to restore, erect]

store·house (stôr′hous′, stōr′-) *n.* **1.** A building in which goods are stored; warehouse. **2.** A large or inexhaustible fund; reservoir: a *storehouse* of ideas.

store·keep·er (stôr′kē′pər, stōr′-) *n.* **1.** A person who keeps a retail store or shop; shopkeeper. **2.** One who has charge of stores or supplies.

·re·room (stôr′rōōm′, -rŏŏm′, stōr′-) *n.* A room in which ings are stored, as supplies.

·rey (stôr′ē, stō′rē) See STORY².

·ried¹ (stôr′ēd, stō′rēd) *adj.* Having or consisting of ·ries, as a building: usu. in compounds: a six-*storied* house. so **sto′reyed.**

·ried² (stôr′ēd, stō′rēd) *adj.* **1.** Having a notable his-·y. **2.** Related in a story. **3.** Ornamented with designs ›resenting scenes from history or story.

·rk (stôrk) *n.* Any of a family of large wading birds with ›g necks and long legs. [OE *storc*]

·rm (stôrm) *n.* **1.** A disturbance of the atmosphere, ›erally a great whirling motion of the air, accompanied ›rain, snow, etc. **2.** *Meteorol.* In the Beaufort scale, a ›d force of the 11th degree. **3.** A furious flight or shower ›objects, esp. of missiles. **4.** A violent outburst, as of ›ssion or excitement: a *storm* of applause. **5.** *Mil.* A ›lent and rapid assault on a fortified place. **6.** A violent ›nmotion, as in politics, society, or domestic life. — *v.i.* ›To blow with violence; rain, snow, hail, etc., heavily: ›d impersonally: It *stormed* all day. **2.** To be very angry; ›e. **3.** To move or rush with violence or rage. — *v.t. Mil.* To take or try to take by storm. [OE]

·rm·bound (stôrm′bound′) *adj.* Delayed, confined, or ›t off from communications because of a storm.

·rm center 1. *Meteorol.* The center or area of lowest ›ssure and comparative calm in a cyclonic storm. **2.** The ›tral point of a heated argument; the focus of any trouble.

·rm door A strong outer door for added protection ›ring storms and inclement weather.

·rm petrel Any of certain small petrels of the North At-›tic, thought to portend storm; Mother Carey's chicken: ›o called *stormy petrel.*

·rm trooper In Germany, a member of the Nazi party ›itia unit, the *Sturmabteilung:* also called *Brown Shirt.*

·rm warning A signal, as a flag or light, used to warn ›riners of coming storm. Also **storm signal.**

·rm window An extra window outside the ordinary one ›a protection against storms or for greater insulation.

·rm·y (stôr′mē) *adj.* **storm·i·er, storm·i·est 1.** Charac-ized by or subject to storms; tempestuous. **2.** Character-d by violent emotions or actions: a *stormy* life. — **storm′i-***adv.* — **storm′i·ness** *n.*

·rmy petrel 1. The storm petrel. **2.** One who portends ›uble or discord, as by rebelling against accepted ideas, ›actices, etc.

·ry¹ (stôr′ē, stō′rē) *n.* *pl.* **·ries** ›A narrative or recital of an event ›series of events, whether real or ›:titious. **2.** A narrative, usu. of ›:titious events, intended to entertain ›eader or hearer. **3.** A short story. ›A report. **5.** A news article in a ›wspaper or magazine; also, the ›terial for such an article. **6.** An ›ecdote. **7.** *Informal* A lie. **8.** The ›·ies of events in a novel, play, etc. **Syn.** See LIE². — *v.t.* **·ried, ·ry·ing** ›To relate as a story. **2.** To adorn ›th designs representing scenes from ›tory, legend, etc. [< OF < L *›toria* an account]

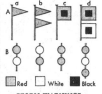

Red   White ■ Black

STORM WARNINGS
A Daylight. *B* Night. *a* Small-craft warn-ing. *b* Gale. *c* Whole gale. *d* Hurricane.

·ry² (stôr′ē, stō′rē) *n.* *pl.* **·ries 1.** A horizontal divi-›n in a building comprising the space between two suc-›ssive floors. **2.** Habitable rooms on the same level. Also, ›iefly Brit., storey. [Special use of STORY¹; ? from earlier ›se of "a tier of painted windows or sculptures that nar-›ted an event"]

·ry line The rough plot of a film, play, novel, etc.

·ry·tell·er (stôr′ē·tel′ər, stō′rē-) *n.* **1.** One who relates ›ories. **2.** *Informal* A liar. — **sto′ry·tell′ing** *n. & adj.*

·up (stōōp) *n.* **1.** *Eccl.* A basin for holy water at the en-›nce of a church. **2.** *Scot.* A pail, cup, etc.; also, its con-›its. Also spelled **stoop, stowp.** [< ON *staup* bucket]

·ut (stout) *adj.* **1.** Strong or firm of structure or material; ›und; tough. **2.** Determined; resolute. **3.** Fat. **4.** Sub-›ntial; solid: *stout* fare. **5.** Having muscular strength; ro-›st. **6.** Proud; stubborn. — *n.* **1.** A stout person. **2.** A ›ry dark porter or ale. [< OF *estout* bold, strong] — ›ut′ly *adv.* — **stout′ness** *n.*

·ut·heart·ed (stout′här′tid) *adj.* Brave; courageous. — ›ut′heart′ed·ly *adv.* — **stout′heart′ed·ness** *n.*

·ve¹ (stōv) *n.* **1.** An apparatus, usu. of metal, in which ›s, oil, electricity, etc., is consumed for heating or cook-›s. A portable kiln. [OE *stofa* heated room]

·ve² (stōv) Alternative past tense and past participle of ›AVE.

·ve·pipe (stōv′pīp′) *n.* **1.** A pipe, usu. of thin sheet iron,

---

for conducting the smoke and gases of combustion from a stove to a chimney flue. **2.** *U.S. Informal* A tall silk hat: also **stovepipe hat.**

stow (stō) *v.t.* **1.** To place or arrange compactly; pack. **2.** To fill by packing. **3.** To have room for; hold: said of a room, receptacle, etc. **4.** *Slang* To stop; cease. — **to stow away 1.** To put in a place of safekeeping, hiding, etc. **2.** To be a stowaway. [ME < OE *stōw* place]

stow·age (stō′ij) *n.* **1.** The act or manner of stowing, or the state of being stowed. **2.** Space for stowing goods; also, the goods stowed. **3.** Charge for stowing goods.

stow·a·way (stō′ə·wā′) *n.* One who conceals himself, as on a vessel, to obtain free passage or evade officials.

stowp (stōōp) See STOUP.

stra·bis·mus (strə·biz′məs) *n.* *Pathol.* A condition in which the eyes cannot be simultaneously focused on the same spot. When one or both eyes turn inward, the patient is *crosseyed,* when outward, *walleyed.* [< NL < Gk. *strabizein* to squint] — **stra·bis′mal, stra·bis′mic** or **·mi·cal** *adj.*

strad·dle (strad′l) *v.* **·dled, ·dling** *v.i.* **1.** To stand, walk, or sit with the legs spread apart. **2.** To stand wide apart: said of the legs. **3.** *Informal* To appear to favor both sides of an issue. — *v.t.* **4.** To stand, walk, or sit with the legs on either side of. **5.** To spread (the legs) wide apart. **6.** *Informal* To appear to favor both sides of (an issue). **7.** *Mil.* To fire shots both beyond and in front of (a target) so as to deter-mine the range — *n.* **1.** The act of straddling. **2.** The space between the feet or legs of one who straddles. **3.** A noncommittal or vacillating position on any issue. **4.** In the securities trade, a transaction in which the holder ob-tains the option of either delivering or buying a certain amount of stock or other commodity at a fixed price within a stipulated period. [OE *strīdan* to stride] — **strad′dler** *n.* — **strad′dling·ly** *adv.*

Strad·i·var·i·us (strad′i·vâr′ē·əs) *n.* One of the violins pro-duced by **Antonio Stra·di·va·ri** (strä′dē·vä·rē), 1644?–1737. Italian violinmaker noted for the fine quality of his instru-ments.

strafe (strāf, sträf) *v.t.* **strafed, straf·ing 1.** To attack (troops, emplacements, etc.) with machine-gun fire from low-flying airplanes. **2.** To bombard or shell heavily. **3.** *Slang* To punish. — *n.* A heavy bombardment. [< G *strafen* to punish] — **straf′er** *n.*

strag·gle (strag′əl) *v.i.* **·gled, ·gling 1.** To stray from or lag behind the main body. **2.** To wander aimlessly about. **3.** To occur at irregular intervals. [? Freq. of obs. *strake* to move, go about] — **strag′gler** *n.*

strag·gly (strag′lē) *adj.* **·gli·er, ·gli·est** Scattered or spread out irregularly.

straight (strāt) *adj.* **1.** Extending uniformly in one direc-tion without curve or bend. **2.** Free from kinks; not curly. **3.** Not stooped or inclined; erect, as in posture. **4.** Not de-viating from truth, fairness, or honesty. **5.** Clear; frank; direct. **6.** Free from obstruction; uninterrupted; unbroken. **7.** Correctly kept, ordered, or arranged: Are the facts *straight* in your mind? **8.** Sold without discount for number or quantity taken. **9.** *Informal* Strictly adhering to a par-ticular party or policy: a *straight* Democrat. **10.** In poker, consisting of five cards forming a sequence: a *straight* flush. **11.** Having nothing added; undiluted. — *n.* **1.** A straight part or piece. **2.** The part of a racecourse between the win-ning post and the last turn. **3.** In poker, a numerical se-quence of five cards not of the same suit, or a hand contain-ing this. **4.** A straight line. — *adv.* **1.** In a straight line or a direct course. **2.** Closely in line; correspondingly. **3.** At once; straightway. — **to go straight** To reform after a crim-inal career. [ME < OE *streccan* to stretch] — **straight′ly** *adv.* — **straight′ness** *n.*

straight angle *Geom.* An angle of 180°.

straight·a·way (strāt′ə·wā′) *adj.* Having no curve or turn. — *n.* A straight course or track. — *adv.* At once.

straight·edge (strāt′ej′) *n.* A bar of wood or metal having one edge true to a straight line, used for ruling, etc.

straight·en (strāt′n) *v.t.* **1.** To make straight. **2.** To lay out (a corpse). — *v.i.* **3.** To become straight. — **to straighten out** To restore order to; set right; rectify. — **to straighten up 1.** To make neat; tidy. **2.** To stand in erect posture. — **straight′en·er** *n.*

straight face A face that betrays no emotion, esp. amuse-ment. — **straight-faced** (strāt′fāst′) *adj.*

straight flush See under FLUSH³.

straight·for·ward (strāt′fôr′wərd) *adj.* **1.** Proceeding in a straight course. **2.** Honest; frank. — *adv.* In a straight course or direct manner: also **straight′for′wards.** — **straight′for′ward·ly** *adv.* — **straight′for′ward·ness** *n.*

straight man *U.S. Informal* An entertainer who acts as a foil for a comedian.

straight-out (strāt′out′) *adj. Informal* **1.** Showing the true sentiments or feelings; unreserved. **2.** Real; genuine. **3.** Uncompromising; all-out: a *straight-out* Republican.

straight ticket **1.** A political party ballot or ticket that presents the regular party candidates without addition or change. **2.** A ballot cast for all the candidates of one party.

straight·way (strāt′wā′) *adv.* Immediately; straightaway.

strain¹ (strān) *v.t.* **1.** To exert to the utmost. **2.** To injure by overexertion; sprain. **3.** To pull or draw tight; stretch. **4.** To stretch beyond the true intent, proper limit, etc.: to *strain* a point. **5.** To pass through a filtering agent or strainer. **6.** To remove by filtration. **7.** To alter or deform in structure or shape as a result of pressure or stress. **8.** To embrace tightly; hug. — *v.i.* **9.** To make violent efforts; strive. **10.** To be or become wrenched or twisted. **11.** To filter, trickle, or percolate. — **to strain at** **1.** To push or pull with violent efforts. **2.** To strive for. **3.** To scruple or balk at accepting. — *n.* **1.** An act of straining, or the state of being strained. **2.** The injury resulting from excessive tension or effort. **3.** Severe mental or emotional tension. [< OF < L *stringere* to bind tight]

strain² (strān) *n.* **1.** Line of descent, or the individuals, collectively, in that line; race; stock. **2.** Inborn or hereditary tendency; trace; element. **3.** *Biol.* A special line of animals or plants bred from a certain species or variety. **4.** *Often pl.* A passage of music or other sound when heard. **5.** Prevailing tone, style, or manner; mood. [? Var. of ME *strene*, OE *strēon* offspring]

strain·er (strā′nər) *n.* A utensil or device, containing meshes or porous parts, through which liquids are strained.

strait (strāt) *n.* **1.** *Often pl.* A narrow passage of water connecting two larger bodies of water. **2.** *Often pl.* A position of perplexity or distress. — *adj.* **1.** *Archaic* Narrow. **2.** *Archaic* Righteous; strict. **3.** Difficult. [< OF < L *stringere* to bind tight] — **strait′ly** *adv.* — **strait′ness** *n.*

strait·en (strāt′n) *v.t.* **1.** To make strait or narrow. **2.** To embarrass, as in finances; also, to distress.

strait·ened (strāt′nd) *adj.* **1.** Contracted; narrowed. **2.** Suffering privation or hardship, as from lack of money.

strait jacket A tight jacket of strong canvas, for confining the arms of violent patients.

strait-laced (strāt′lāst′) *adj.* Strict, esp. in morals.

strake (strāk) *n. Naut.* A breadth of planking or line of plating on a vessel's hull from stem to stern: also called *streak.* [Appar. akin to STRETCH; infl. in meaning by STREAK]

strand¹ (strand) *n.* A shore or beach, esp. that portion between high and low tides — *v.t. & v.i.* **1.** To drive or run aground. **2.** To leave or be left in straits or difficulties: usu. in the passive. [OE *strand*]

strand² (strand) *n.* **1.** One of the principal twists or members of a rope. **2.** A fiber, hair, or the like. **3.** Anything plaited or twisted. **4.** A string of beads or pearls — *v.t.* **1.** To break a strand of (a rope). **2.** To make by twisting strands. [? < OF *estran* < Gmc.]

strange (strānj) *adj.* **strang·er, strang·est** **1.** Previously unknown, unseen, or unheard of; unfamiliar. **2.** Not according to the ordinary way; unaccountable; remarkable. **3.** Of a different class, character, or kind. **4.** Foreign; alien. **5.** Distant in manner; reserved; shy. **6.** Inexperienced; unaccustomed. — *adv.* In a strange manner. [< OF < L *extraneus* foreign] — **strange′ly** *adv.* — **strange′ness** *n.*

stran·ger (strān′jər) *n.* **1.** One who is not an acquaintance. **2.** An unfamiliar visitor; guest. **3.** A foreigner. **4.** One unversed in or unfamiliar with something specified: with *to.*

stran·gle (strang′gəl) *v.* **·gled, ·gling** *v.t.* **1.** To choke to death; throttle; suffocate. **2.** To repress; suppress. **3.** To inhibit the action or development of — *v.i.* **4.** To suffer or die from strangulation. [< F < L < Gk. *strangalē* halter < *strangos* twisted] — **stran′gler** *n.*

strangle hold **1.** In wrestling, a usu. illegal hold that chokes one's opponent. **2.** Any influence or power that chokes freedom or progress.

stran·gu·late (strang′gyə·lāt) *v.t.* **·lat·ed, ·lat·ing** **1.** To strangle. **2.** *Pathol.* To compress, contract, or obstruct, esp. so as to cut off flow of a fluid. — *adj.* Strangulated. [See STRANGLE.] — **stran′gu·la′tion** *n.*

strap (strap) *n.* **1.** A long, narrow, and flexible strip of leather, etc., usu. having a buckle or other fastener, for binding about objects. **2.** A razor strop. **3.** Something resembling a strap and used as a fastening or support. **4.** A thin metal band. — *v.t.* **strapped, strap·ping** **1.** To fasten or bind with a strap. **2.** To beat with a strap. **3.** To embarrass financially. **4.** To sharpen or strop. [Var. of STROP] — **strap′less** *adj.* — **strap′per** *n.*

strap·hang·er (strap′hang·ər) *n.* A standee on a bus, etc., esp. one who holds on to an overhead strap.

strap·ping (strap′ing) *adj. Informal* Large and robust.

stra·ta (strā′tə, strat′ə) Alternative plural of STRATUM.

strat·a·gem (strat′ə·jəm) *n.* **1.** A maneuver designed to deceive or outwit an enemy in war. **2.** A device for obtaining advantage; trick. [< F < L < Gk. < *stratos* army + *agein* to lead]

stra·te·gic (strə·tē′jik) *adj.* **1.** Of or pertaining to strate **2.** Characterized by, used in, or having relation to strate Also **stra·te′gi·cal, strat·e·get·ic** (strat′ə·jet′ik) or **·i·cal. stra·te′gi·cal·ly, strat′e·get′i·cal·ly** *adv.*

stra·te·gics (strə·tē′jiks) *n.pl. (construed as sing.)* The or science of strategy; generalship.

strat·e·gist (strat′ə·jist) *n.* One versed in strategy.

strat·e·gy (strat′ə·jē) *n.* *pl.* **·ties** **1.** The science and ar conducting a military campaign on a broad scale: dis guished from *tactics.* **2.** The use of stratagem or artifice in business or politics. **3.** A plan or technique for achiev some end. [See STRATAGEM.]

strat·i·fy (strat′ə·fī) *v.* **·fied, ·fy·ing** *v.t.* **1.** To form or range in strata. **2.** To preserve (seeds) by spreading in ternating layers of earth and sand. — *v.i.* **3.** To form strata. **4.** *Geol.* To be formed in strata, as rocks. **5.** *So* To form social groups at different levels as determined class, caste, or status. [< F < Med.L < L *stratum* laye *facere* to make] — **strat′i·fi·ca′tion** *n.*

stra·to·cu·mu·lus (strā′tō·kyōō′myə·ləs) *n.* *pl.* **·li** *Meteorol.* Large globular masses of cloud (Symbol Sc), g to black in color, disposed in waves, groups, or bands, often covering the whole sky: also called *cumulostratus.* *strato-* (< STRATUS) + CUMULUS]

strat·o·pause (strat′ə·pôz) *n. Meteorol.* The zone of tra tion between the stratosphere and the mesosphere.

strat·o·sphere (strat′ə·sfir, strā′tə-) *n. Meteorol.* portion of the atmosphere beginning at a height of a seven miles and characterized by a more or less uniform t perature. — **strat′o·spher′ic** (-sfir′ik, -sfer′-) or **·i·cal**

stra·tum (strā′təm, strat′əm) *n.* *pl.* **·ta** (-tə) or **·tums** natural or artificial layer, bed, or thickness. **2.** *Geol.* A r or less homogeneous layer of rock, serving to identify a logical group, system or series. **3.** Something correspon to a layer, bed, or grade: a low *stratum* of society. [< L

stra·tus (strā′təs, strat′əs) *n.* *pl.* **·ti** (-tī) *Meteorol.* A c of foglike appearance, low-lying and arranged in a uni layer. [< L, orig. pp. of *sternere* to spread]

straw (strô) *n.* **1.** A slender tube of paper, glass, etc., to suck up a beverage. **2.** Stems or stalks of grain, co tively, after the grain has been thrashed out. **3.** A dry c pened stalk. **4.** A mere trifle. — **the last straw** The 1 test of patience or endurance: from the phrase **the st that broke the camel's back.** — **to clutch (grasp, ca** etc.) **at a straw** To try in desperation any solution or e dient. — *adj.* **1.** Like or of straw. **2.** Of no value; wo less; sham. **3.** Made of straw. **4.** Yellowish. [OE *strē*

straw·ber·ry (strô′ber′ē, -bər·ē) *n.* *pl.* **·ries** **1.** The e fruit of a stemless perennial herb of the rose family. **2.** plant bearing this fruit. [ME *strauberi*]

strawberry blond A person having reddish blond ha

straw color A pale yellow color, as of clean ripe straw. **straw-col·ored** (strô′kul′ərd) *adj.*

straw vote An unofficial vote to test the strength of op ing candidates, determine group opinion, etc.

straw·y (strô′ē) *adj.* **straw·i·er, straw·i·est** **1.** Of or straw. **2.** Covered or thatched with straw.

stray (strā) *v.i.* **1.** To wander from the proper course area, group, etc.; straggle; roam. **2.** To wander about; r **3.** To fail to concentrate; digress. **4.** To deviate from i or goodness; go astray. — *adj.* **1.** Having strayed; st ing. **2.** Irregular; occasional; casual; unrelated. — *n* A domestic animal that has strayed. **2.** A person wl lost or wanders aimlessly. **3.** The act of straying or wan ing. [< OF *estraier* to wander about, ult. < L *extra* no to wander outside] — **stray′er** *n.*

streak (strēk) *n.* **1.** A long, narrow, somewhat irregu shaped mark, line, or stripe: a *streak* of lightning. **2.** A or trace; dash: a *streak* of meanness; also, a transient m whim. **3.** A period of time; a spell. **4.** A strake. **5.** A or strip: meat with a *streak* of fat. — *v.t.* **1.** To mark a streak; form streaks in or on; stripe. — *v.i.* **2.** To for streak or streaks. **3.** To move at great speed. [OE *st* — **streaked** (strēkt) *adj.*

streak·y (strē′kē) *adj.* **streak·i·er, streak·i·est** **1.** Ma with or occurring in streaks. **2.** Of variable quality or c acter. — **streak′i·ly** *adv.* — **streak′i·ness** *n.*

stream (strēm) *n.* **1.** A current or flow of water or c fluid. **2.** Anything continuously flowing, moving, or p ing, as people. **3.** A trend; drift. **4.** Anything issuing or flowing from a source. — *v.i.* **1.** To pour forth or I a stream. **2.** To pour forth a stream: eyes *streaming* tears. **3.** To move in continuous succession. **4.** To with a waving movement, as a flag. **5.** To move with a of light, as a meteor. — *v.t.* **6.** To emit or exude. **7** cause (a flag, etc.) to stretch forth; display. [OE *stre* — **stream′y** *adj.*

stream·er (strē′mər) *n.* **1.** An object that streams fort hangs extended. **2.** A long, narrow flag or standard. shaft of light, such as shoots up from the horizon. newspaper headline that runs across the whole page.

eam·let (strēm′lit) *n.* A small stream; rivulet.

eam·line (strēm′līn′) *n.* **1.** *Physics* **a** The course of a id in which every particle maintains an identical speed d direction of flow; esp., a course free of turbulence or ed-·s. **b** The path traversed by one particle in such a course. Any shape or contour designed to offer minimum resis-ice to fluid flow. — *adj.* Designating an uninterrupted w or drift. —*v.t.* -**lined**, ·**lin·ing 1.** To design with a stream-ed shape. **2.** To make more simple, efficient, or up to date. **stream′lined′** *adj.*

eam of consciousness *Psychol.* The series of individu-conscious states moving continuously on in time as though a stream.

eet (strēt) *n.* A public way in a city or town, with build-·s on one or both sides; also. the roadway for vehicles, ·ween sidewalks. [OE *strǣt* < L *strata* (*via*) paved (road)] **eet·car** (strēt′kär′) *n.* A public passenger car of an elec-· railway that runs on tracks set into the streets: also ·led *trolley, trolley car, Brit., tramcar.*

eet·walk·er (strēt′wô′kər) *n.* A prostitute who solicits the streets. — **street′walk′ing** *n.* & *adj.*

·ngth (strengkth, strength) *n.* **1.** Muscular power; vig-· **2.** Durability; toughness. **3.** Power in general, or a irce of power. **4.** Binding force or validity, as of a law. Vigor or force of intellect, moral power, style, etc. **6.** ·ailable numerical force in a military unit or other organi-·ion. **7.** Degree of intensity; vehemence: *strength* of pas-n. **8.** The degree of intensity or concentration, as of a ·or, odor, etc. **9.** Potency, as of a drug, chemical, or ·uor. — **on the strength of** Based on or in reliance or de-·idence on. [OE *strengthu* < *strang* strong]

·ngth·en (strengk′thən, streng′-) *v.t.* **1.** To make strong. To encourage; hearten; animate. — *v.i.* **3.** To become grow strong or stronger. — **strength′en·er** *n.*

·n·u·ous (stren′yōō-əs) *adj.* **1.** Necessitating or charac-ized by strong effort or exertion. **2.** Vigorously active or ·lous. [< L *strenuus*] — **stren′u·ous·ly** *adv.* — **stren′u-i·ty** (-os′ə·tē), **stren′u·ous·ness** *n.*

·p·to·coc·cus (strep′tə·kok′əs) *n. pl.* ·**coc·ci** (-kok′sī) y of a genus of typically ovoid or spherical bacteria, ·uped in long chains, including species causing many dis-·es. [< NL < Gk. *streptos* twisted + COCCUS] — **strep′· ·oc′cal** (-kok′əl), **strep′to·coc′cic** (-kok′sik) *adj.*

·p·to·my·cin (strep′tō·mī′sin) *n.* A potent antibiotic ·ated from a moldlike organism. [< Gk. *streptos* twisted *mykēs* fungus]

·ss (stres) *n.* **1.** Special weight, importance, or signifi-·ce: to lay *stress* on the classics. **2.** In prosody, an em-·asis given to a specific word or syllable to indicate the ·trical pattern. **3.** *Mech.* **a** Force exerted between con-·uous portions of a body or bodies and generally expressed ·ounds per square inch. **b** A force or system of forces that ·ds to produce deformation in a body. **4.** Influence ex-·ed forcibly; pressure; compulsion. **5.** Emotional or in-·ectual strain or tension. **6.** *Phonet.* The relative force h which a sound, syllable, or word is uttered. — *v.t.* **1.** subject to mechanical stress. **2.** To put stress or empha-· accent, as a syllable. **3.** To put into straits or diffi-·ies; distress. [< OF < L *strictus*, pp. of *stringere* to draw ·nt] — **stress′ful** *adj.* — **stress′less** *adj.*

·ess *suffix of nouns* Feminine form of -STER: *songstress.* **·tch** (strech) *v.t.* **1.** To extend or draw out, as to full ·gth or width. **2.** To extend or draw out forcibly, esp. be-·d normal or proper limits. **3.** To cause to reach, as from · place to another or over an area; extend. **4.** To put ·h, hold out, or extend (the hand, an object, etc.): often h *out.* **5.** To tighten. **6.** To strain or exert to the ut-·st: to *stretch* every nerve. **7.** To make do with: to *stretch* ·'s salary with economies. — *v.i.* **8.** To reach or extend ·r an area or from one place to another. **9.** To become ex-·ded, esp. beyond normal or proper limits. **10.** To extend ·'s body or limbs, esp. to relieve stiffness. **11.** To lie down l extend one's limbs to full length: usu. with *out.* — *n.* The act of stretching, or the state of being stretched. **2.** ·ent or reach of that which stretches. **3.** A continuous ex-· of space or time. **4.** In racing, the part of the track ·t, being straight, permits the greatest speed. **5.** A par-·lar direction or course. **6.** *Slang* A term of imprison-·nt. — *adj.* Capable of stretching or of being stretched; ·stic: *stretch* pants. [OE *streccan*] — **stretch′a·ble** *adj.* **stretch′i·ness** *n.* — **stretch′y** *adj.*

·tch·er (strech′ər) *n.* **1.** One who or that which stretch-· **2.** Any device for stretching, as for loosening the fit of ·ves or shoes, for drying curtains, etc. **3.** A frame, as of ·tched canvas, for carrying the wounded, sick, or dead; a ·er. **4.** In masonry, a brick or stone lying lengthwise of a ·rse. **5.** A tie beam in the frame of a building.

·tch-out (strech′out′) *n.* **1.** A system of industrial op-

eration in which employees do more work without propor-tionate increase in pay. **2.** A slowdown practiced by em-ployees so as to make the work last longer.

strew (strōō) *v.t.* **strewed**, **strewed** or **strewn**, **strew·ing 1.** To spread about loosely or at random; scatter; sprinkle. **2.** To cover with something scattered or sprinkled. **3.** To be scattered over (a surface). [OE *strewian*]

stri·a (strī′ə) *n. pl.* **stri·ae** (strī′ē) **1.** A narrow streak, stripe, or band of distinctive color, structure, or texture, often parallel with others. **2.** *Geol.* A small groove, channel, or ridge on a rock surface, due to the action of glacier ice. [< L, groove]

stri·ate (strī′āt) *adj.* **1.** Having fine linear markings; striped or grooved. **2.** Constituting a stria or striae. Also **stri′at·ed.** — *v.t.* ·**at·ed**, ·**at·ing** To mark with striae. [< L < *stria* groove] — **stri·a′tion** *n.*

strick·en (strik′ən) Alternative past participle of STRIKE. ◆ *Stricken* is current in American English in certain senses: *stricken* with grief; a remark *stricken* from the record. — *adj.* **1.** Strongly affected or afflicted; overcome, as by calamity or disease. **2.** Wounded, esp. by a missile. [OE *stricen*, pp. of *strīcan* to strike]

strict (strikt) *adj.* **1.** Observing or enforcing rules exactly; severe. **2.** Containing exact or severe rules or provisions; exacting. **3.** Rigorously enjoined, maintained, and observed. **4.** Exactly defined, distinguished, or applied. **5.** Complete; absolute: *strict* attention. [< L *strictus*, pp. of *stringere* to draw tight] — **strict′ly** *adv.* — **strict′ness** *n.*

stric·ture (strik′chər) *n.* **1.** Severe criticism. **2.** *Pathol.* An abnormal contraction of some duct or channel.

stride (strīd) *n.* **1.** A long and sweeping or measured step. **2.** The space passed over by such a step. **3.** A progressive movement by an animal, completed when all the feet are re-turned to the same relative positions they occupied at the beginning of the movement. **4.** A stage of progress. — **to hit one's stride** To attain one's normal speed. — **to make rapid strides** To make quick progress. — **to take (some-thing) in one's stride** To do or react to (something) without undue effort or disturbance, as if part of one's normal activi-ty. — *v.* **strode**, **strid·den**, **strid·ing** *v.i.* **1.** To walk with long steps, as from haste or pride. — *v.t.* **2.** To walk through, along, etc., with long steps. **3.** To pass over with a single stride. **4.** To straddle. [OE *strīdan*] — **strid′er** *n.*

stri·dent (strīd′nt) *adj.* Having or making a high, harsh sound; shrill; grating. [< L *stridens, -entis*, ppr. of *stridere* to creak] — **stri′dence, stri′den·cy** *n.* — **stri′dent·ly** *adv.*

strid·u·late (strij′ōō-lāt) *v.i.* ·**lat·ed**, ·**lat·ing** To make a shrill, creaking noise, as a cicada or cricket. [< NL *stridere* to rattle, rasp] — **strid′u·la′tion** *n.* — **strid′u·la·to′ry** (-lə-tôr′ē, -tō′rē) *adj.* — **strid′u·lous** *adj.*

strife (strīf) *n.* **1.** Angry contention; fighting. **2.** Any con-test for advantage or superiority. [< OF *estriver* to strive]

strike (strīk) *v.* **struck**, **struck** or, sometimes, **strick·en**, **strik·ing** *v.t.* **1.** To come into violent contact with; hit. **2.** To hit with a blow; smite. **3.** To deal (a blow, etc.). **4.** To cause to hit forcibly: He *struck* his hand on the table. **5.** To attack; assault. **6.** To remove, separate, or take off by or as by a blow or stroke: with *off, from,* etc.: *Strike* it from the record. **7.** To ignite (a match, etc.); also, to produce (a light, etc.) thus. **8.** To form by stamping, printing, etc. **9.** To indicate (a specified time) by the sound of a stroke, bell, etc. **10.** To fall upon; reach: A sound *struck* his ear. **11.** To arrive at; come upon: to *strike* a trail. **12.** To find: to *strike* oil. **13.** To affect suddenly or in a specified manner: He was *struck* speechless. **14.** To come to the mind of; oc-cur to: An idea *strikes* me. **15.** To impress in a specified manner: He *strikes* me as an honest man. **16.** To attract the attention of; impress: The dress *struck* her fancy. **17.** To assume; take up: to *strike* an attitude. **18.** To cause to enter or penetrate deeply or suddenly: to *strike* dismay into one's heart. **19.** To lower or haul down, as a sail, or a flag in token of surrender. **20.** To cease working at in order to compel compliance to a demand, etc. **21.** In the theater, to dismantle (a set or scene). **22.** To make level (a measure of grain, etc.) **23.** To make and confirm, as a bargain. **24.** To harpoon (a whale). **25.** To hook (a fish that has taken the lure) by a sharp pull on the line. **26.** To arrive at by reck-oning: to *strike* a balance. — *v.i.* **27.** To come into violent contact; hit. **28.** To deal or aim a blow or blows. **29.** To make an assault or attack. **30.** To make a sound by or as by means of a blow or blows. **31.** To be indicated by the sound of blows or strokes: Noon has just *struck*. **32.** To ignite. **33.** To run aground, as on a reef or shoal. **34.** To lower a flag in token of surrender or in salute. **35.** To come sudden-ly or unexpectedly; chance: with *on* or *upon*. **36.** To start and proceed: to *strike* for home. **37.** To move quickly; dart. **38.** To cease work in order to enforce demands, etc. **39.** To snatch at or swallow the lure: said of fish. ◆ See note under STRICKEN. **— to strike camp** To take down the tents of a camp. **— to strike down 1.** To fell with a blow. **2.** To affect disastrously; incapacitate completely. **— to strike dumb** To astonish; amaze. **— to strike home 1.** To deal an effective blow. **2.** To have telling effect. **— to strike it rich** *Informal* **1.** To find a valuable vein or pocket of ore. **2.** To come into wealth or good fortune. **— to strike off 1.** To remove or take off by or as by a blow or stroke. **2.** To cross out or erase by or as by a stroke of the pen. **3.** To deduct. **— to strike out 1.** To strike off (def. 2). **2.** To aim a blow or blows. **3.** To make a start: *to strike out* on one's own. **4.** To originate; hit upon. **5.** In baseball: **a** To put out (the batter) by pitching three strikes. **b** To be put out because of having three strikes counted against one during a single turn at bat. **6.** In bowling, to complete a game by bowling three consecutive strikes. **— to strike up 1.** To begin to play, sing, or sound, as a band or musical instrument. **2.** To start up; begin, as a friendship. **— n. 1.** An act of striking or hitting; a blow. **2.** In baseball: **a** An unsuccessful attempt by the batter to hit the ball. **b** A pitched ball that passes over home plate not lower than the level of the batter's knees and not above that of his shoulders. **c** A foul bunt or any foul tip held by the catcher. **d** Any ball hit foul except when there have been two strikes. **3.** In bowling, the knocking down by a player of all the pins with the first bowl in any frame; also, the score so made: also called *ten-strike*: distinguished from *spare*. **4.** The quitting of work by a body of workers to enforce some demand. **5.** A new or unexpected discovery, as of oil or ore. **6.** Any unexpected or complete success. **7.** An air attack on a surface target. **8.** In fishing, a bite. [OE *strīcan* to stroke, move]

strike·bound (strīk′bound′) *adj.* Closed or immobilized by a strike: said of companies, equipment, workers, etc.

strike·break·er (strīk′brā′kər) *n.* One who takes the place of a workman on strike or who supplies workmen to take the place of strikers. **— strike′break′ing** *n.*

strike·out (strīk′out′) *n.* In baseball, an instance of striking out.

strik·er (strī′kər) *n.* **1.** One who or that which strikes. **2.** An employee who is on strike. **3.** The clapper of a bell, etc.

strik·ing (strī′king) *adj.* Notable; impressive. **— strik′ing·ly** *adv.* **— strik′ing·ness** *n.*

string (string) *n.* **1.** A slender line or strip, as of twine, cloth, leather, etc., thinner than a cord and thicker than a thread. **2.** The cord of a bow. **3.** Prepared wire or catgut for musical instruments. **4.** A stringlike organ or formation, as a vegetable fiber or fibers or an animal nerve or tendon. **5.** A thin cord upon which anything is strung; a row or series of things connected by a small cord: a *string* of pearls. **6.** A connected series or succession, as of things, acts, or events. sometimes implying unusual length: a *string* of lies. **7.** *U.S. Informal* A small collection of animals, esp. of racehorses. **8.** *pl.* Stringed instruments, esp. those of an orchestra; also, those who play on these. **9.** *Archit.* **a** A stringcourse. **b** A ramp or sidepiece supporting the steps of a stairway. **10.** In sports, a group of contestants ranked as to skill. **11.** *Usu. pl. Informal* A condition, limitation, or restriction attached to a proposition, gift, or donation. **— to pull strings** To manipulate or influence others to gain some advantage. **— v. strung, string·ing** *v.t.* **1.** To thread, as beads, on or as on a string. **2.** To fit with a string or strings, as a guitar. **3.** To cover, drape, or adorn with things attached to a string or strings. **4.** To tune the strings of (a musical instrument). **5.** To brace; strengthen. **6.** To make tense or nervous. **7.** To arrange or extend in a line or series. **8.** To remove the strings from (vegetables). **9.** *U.S. Informal* To hang: usu. with *up*. **10.** *Slang* To fool or deceive; hoax: often with *along*. **— v.i. 11.** To extend, stretch, or proceed in a line or series. **12.** To form into strings. **— to string along (with)** *Informal* To follow with trust or confidence. [OE *streng*]

string bean 1. Any of several varieties of beans cultivated for their edible pods. **2.** The pod itself.

string·board (string′bôrd′, -bōrd′) *n. Archit.* A board serving as a support for the ends of steps in a staircase.

string·course (string′kôrs′, -kōrs′) *n. Archit.* A horizontal molding or ornamental course, as of brick or stone, usu. projecting along the face of a building.

stringed instrument (stringd) A musical instrument that produces its tones by means of one or more vibrating strings, as a violin, cello, etc. Also **string instrument.**

strin·gent (strin′jənt) *adj.* **1.** Requiring or compelling adherence to strict requirements; severe, as regulations. **2.** Hampered by obstructions or scarcity of money. **3.** Convincing; forcible. [< L *stringens, -entis,* ppr. of *stringere* to draw tight] **— strin′gen·cy** *n.* **— strin′gent·ly** *adv.*

string·er (string′ər) *n.* **1.** One who or that which strings. **2.** *Archit.* A heavy timber, generally horizontal, supporting other members of a structure. **3.** A lengthwise timber on which rails are laid, as distinguished from a crosstie. **4.** *Informal* One having a specified numerical rank or degree of proficiency, as on a team: a second *stringer*.

string·piece (string′pēs′) *n. Archit.* A heavy support timber forming the margin or edge of a framework.

string tie A very narrow necktie, often tied in a bow with the ends hanging loosely.

string·y (string′ē) *adj.* **string·i·er, string·i·est 1.** Containing fibrous strings. **2.** Forming in strings; ropy. **3.** Having tough sinews. **— string′i·ly** *adv.* **— string′i·ness** *n.*

strip¹ (strip) *n.* **1.** A narrow piece, comparatively long, of cloth, wood, etc. **2.** A number of stamps attached in a row. **3.** A narrow piece of land. **4.** An airstrip or landing strip. **— v.t. stripped, strip·ping** To cut or tear into strips. [? < MLG *strippe* strap]

strip² (strip) *v.* **stripped** (*Rare* **stript**), **strip·ping** *v.t.* **1.** To pull the covering, clothing, etc., from; lay bare. **2.** To off (the covering or clothing). **3.** To rob or plunder. **4.** To make bare or empty. **5.** To remove; take away. **6.** To divest: He was *stripped* of his rank. **7.** *Mech.* To damage, break the teeth, thread, etc., of (a gear, bolt, or the like). **v.i. 8.** To remove one's clothing; undress. **9.** To undo stripping. [ME < OE *-strīepan,* as in *bestrīepan* to despoil, plunder] **— strip′per** *n.*

stripe¹ (strip) *n.* **1.** A line, band, or strip of different color, material, texture, etc., from the adjacent surface. **2.** Striped cloth. **3.** A piece of material or braid on the sleeve of a form to indicate rank, service, an award, etc.; a chevron. **4.** Distinctive quality or character; sort: a man of his *stripe*. **— v.t. striped, strip·ing** To mark with a stripe or stripes. [< MDu.] **— striped** *adj.*

stripe² (strip) *n.* A blow struck with a whip or rod, as in flogging. [Prob. < LG]

strip·ling (strip′ling) *n.* A mere youth.

strip mining The mining of coal by stripping off soil, to expose and dig out a vein.

strip·tease (strip′tēz′) *n.* In burlesque, etc., a gradual disrobing, interspersed with various movements of the torso. Also **strip tease. — strip′teas′er** *n.*

strip·y (strip′ē) *adj.* **strip·i·er, strip·i·est** Being in or suggesting stripes or streaks; having or marked with stripes.

strive (strīv) *v.i.* **strove** or (*less commonly*) **strived, striven** (striv′ən) or **strived, striv·ing 1.** To make earnest effort. **2.** To engage in strife; contend; fight. **3.** To vie; emulate. [OF *estriver,* prob. < Gmc.] **— striv′er** *n.*

strob·o·scope (strob′ə·skōp, strō′bə-) *n.* An instrument observing the motion of a body or object by rendering it visible only at intervals or at certain points of its path. [< *strobos* twisting + -SCOPE] **— strob′o·scop′ic** (-skop′ik) *adj.* **— strob·os′co·py** (-os′kə·pē) *n.*

strode (strōd) Past tense of STRIDE.

stroke (strōk) *n.* **1.** The act or movement of striking; impact. **2.** A single movement, as of the hand, arm, or an instrument, by which something is made or done. **3.** A blow or any ill effect caused as if by a blow. **4.** An attack of paralysis or apoplexy. **5.** A blow or the sound of a blow striking mechanism, as of a clock. **6.** A sudden or brilliant act; coup: a *stroke* of wit. **7.** A pulsation, as of the heart. **8.** A mark or dash of a pen or tool. **9.** A light, caressing movement; a stroking. **10.** A manner or technique of swimming. **11.** *Informal* A portion or stint, as of work: usu. with negative. **12.** *Mech.* **a** One of a series of alternating movements from one extreme position to another, as by a piston of an internal-combustion engine. **b** The distance covered by such a movement. **— v. stroked, strok·ing 1.** To pass the hand over gently or caressingly, or with pressure. **2.** To set the pace for (a rowboat or its crew) as stroke-oar. **— v.i. 3.** To perform strokes, as in swimming. [ME < OE *strācian* to strike]

stroll (strōl) *v.i.* **1.** To walk in a leisurely or idle manner; saunter. **2.** To go from place to place; wander. **— v.t.** To walk idly or wander over or through. **— n.** An idle, leisurely walk. [Origin uncertain]

stroll·er (strō′lər) *n.* **1.** One who strolls. **2.** A light, collapsible carriage in which a baby or child may sit upright. **3.** A wandering showman or player. **4.** A tramp.

strong (strông, strong) *adj.* **1.** Powerful in physique; muscular; vigorous. **2.** Healthy; robust: a *strong* constitution. **3.** Morally powerful; firm; resolute; courageous. **4.** Mentally powerful or vigorous. **5.** Especially competent or in a specified subject or field: *strong* in mathematics. **6.** Abundantly or richly supplied with something: often with *in*. **7.** Solidly made or constituted: *strong* walls. **8.** Powerful as a rival or combatant: a *strong* team. **9.** Easy to defend; difficult to capture: a *strong* military position. **10.** Having (a specified) numerical force: an army 20,000 *strong*. **11.** Capable of exerting influence, authority, etc.: a *strong* government. **12.** Financially sound: a *strong* bank. **13.** Powerful in effect: *strong* poison, medicine, etc. **14.** Concentrated; not diluted or weak: *strong* coffee. **15.** Containing much alcohol: *strong* drink. **16.** Powerful in flavor or odor; also, rank; unpleasant: a *strong* breath. **17.** Intense in degree or quality; not faint or mild: a *strong* pulse. **18.** Ardent and firm: a *strong* voice. **19.** Firm; tenacious: a *strong*

, Deeply earnest; fervid: a *strong* desire.   **21.** Cogent;
vincing: *strong* evidence.   **22.** Distinct; marked: a *strong*
emblance.   **23.** Extreme; forceful: *strong* measures.   **24.**
phatic; not moderate: *strong* language.   **25.** Moving
h great force: said of a wind, stream, or tide.   **26.** *Mete-
l.* Designating a breeze or gale on the Beaufort scale.   **27.**
aracterized by steady or rising prices: a *strong* market.
, *Gram.* In Germanic languages, denoting a strong verb.
adv. In a strong manner; so as to be strong.   [OE *strang,
ng*]   **—strong·ly** *adv.*

ng-arm (strông′ärm′, strong′-)   *Informal adj.* Violent;
ving and depending on physical power.   —*v.t.* To use
ysical force upon; assault.

ng-box (strông′boks′, strong′-)   *n.* A strongly built
st or safe for keeping valuables.

ng-hold (strông′hōld′, strong′-)   *n.* **1.** A strongly forti-
 place; fortress.   **2.** A place of security or refuge.

ng-man (strông′man′, strong′-) *n. pl.* ·**men** (-men′)   A
itical leader having considerable or preeminent power,
en derived from extralegal means, as a coup d'état.

ng-mind·ed (strông′mīn′did, strong′-)   *adj.* Having a
ermined, vigorous mind.   **—strong′-mind′ed·ly** *adv.* —
ong′-mind′ed·ness** *n.*

ng verb   A verb that forms its past tense and past par-
iple by internal vowel change, as *swim, swam, swum.*

ng-willed (strông′wild′, strong′-)   *adj.* Having a strong
l; decided; obstinate.

n·ti·um (stron′shē-əm, -shəm, -tē-əm)   *n.* A hard, yel-
ish, metallic element (symbol Sr) of the calcium group,
own chiefly through its salts, which burn with a red flame
d are used largely in pyrotechnics, but also in medicine
d ceramics. See ELEMENT.   [< NL, from *Strontian,* Argyll,
tland, where first discovered]   **—stron′tic** (-tik) *adj.*

ntium 90   *Physics* A radioactive isotope of strontium
emically resembling calcium and with a half life of about
years. Also called *radiostrontium.*

p (strop)   *n.* **1.** A strip of leather, canvas, etc., on which
sharpen a razor.   **2.** A strap.   —*v.t.* **stropped, strop·ping**
sharpen on a strop.   [OE < L < Gk. *strophos* band]

·phe (strō′fē)   *n.* **1.** In ancient Greek poetry, the verses
ng by the chorus in a play while moving from right to left.
In classical prosody, the lines of an ode constituting a
nza and alternating with the antistrophe.   **3.** The first of
o alternating metrical systems in a poem.   [< Gk. *stre-
in to turn*]   **—stroph·ic** (strof′ik, strō′fik) or ·**i·cal** *adj.*

ve (strōv)   Past tense of STRIVE.

w (strō)   *v.t.* **strowed, strowed** or **strown, strow·ing** *Ar-
ic* To strew.

ck (struk)   Past tense and past participle of STRIKE.
. Closed down or affected by a strike, as a factory.

ck measure   A measure having the contents level with
 edge of the container, rather than heaping.

c·tur·al (struk′chər-əl)   *adj.* Of, pertaining to, charac-
ized, or caused by structure.   **—struc′tur·al·ly** *adv.*

ctural steel   Rolled steel of considerable toughness and
ength, esp. adapted for use in construction.

c·ture (struk′chər)   *n.* **1.** That which is constructed; a
mbination of related parts, as a building or machine.   **2.**
e position and arrangement of parts, as of tissues in an
ganism, atoms within a molecule, etc.   **3.** The manner of
struction or organization: the social *structure* of a primi-
e society.   —*v.t.* **·tured, ·tur·ing 1.** To form into an or-
nized structure; build.   **2.** To conceive as a structural
ole; ideate.   [< L < *structus,* pp. of *struere* to build]

·del (strood′l, *Ger.* shtroo′dəl)   *n.* A kind of pastry made
a thin sheet of dough, spread with fruit or cheese, nuts,
., rolled, and baked.   [< G, lit., eddy]

ug·gle (strug′əl)   *n.* **1.** A violent effort or series of ef-
ts; a labored contest.   **2.** Conflict; strife; battle.   —*v.*
ed, ·gling *v.i.* **1.** To contend with an adversary in physical
mbat; fight.   **2.** To put forth violent efforts; strive: to
uggle against odds.   **3.** To make one's way by violent ef-
ts.   —*v.t.* **4.** To accomplish with a struggle.   [ME *stro-
en*]   **—strug′gler** *n.*   **—strug′gling·ly** *adv.*

m (strum)   *v.t. & v.i.* **strummed, strum·ming** To play a
inged instrument, a tune, etc.) idly, monotonously, or
hout technical skill.   —*n.* The act of strumming.   [Prob.
it.]   **—strum′mer** *n.*

um·pet (strum′pit)   *n.* A whore; harlot.   [? Ult. < OF
upe concubinage < L *stuprum* dishonor]

ung (strung)   Past tense and past participle of STRING.

ut (strut)   *n.* **1.** A proud or pompous step or walk.   **2.** A
ember in a framework, designed to relieve weight or pres-
re in the direction of its length. For illus. see ROOF.   —*v.*
ut·ted, strut·ting *v.i.* **1.** To walk pompously, conceitedly,
d affectedly.   —*v.t.* **2.** To brace or support, as a framing
structure, with or as with struts.   [OE *strūtian* to be rigid,
nd stiffly]   **—strut′ter** *n.*   **—strut′ting·ly** *adv.*

strych·nine (strik′nin, -nēn, -nīn)   *n.* A white, crystalline,
bitter, extremely poisonous alkaloid, $C_{21}H_{22}N_2O_2$, contained
in certain plants. Its salts are used in medicine, chiefly as a
neural stimulant. Also **strych′nin** (-nin).   [< F < L *strych-
nos* < Gk., nightshade]

Stu·art (stōō′ərt, styōō′-)   The royal family of Scotland,
1371–1603, and of England, 1603–1714.

stub (stub)   *n.* **1.** Any short projecting part or piece.   **2.**
The part of a tree trunk, bush, etc., that remains when the
main part is cut down.   **3.** A short or broken remnant, as of
a pencil, cigarette, or broken tooth.   **4.** *U.S.* In a checkbook,
one of the inner ends upon which a memorandum is entered,
and which remains when the check is detached; also, the detachable portion of a theater ticket, etc.   **5.** Anything blunt,
short, or stumpy, as a pen with a broad point.   —*v.t.*
stubbed, stub·bing 1. To strike, as the toe, against a low obstruction or projection.   **2.** To grub up, as roots.   **3.** To
clear or remove the stubs or roots from.   [OE *stubb*]

stub·ble (stub′əl)   *n.* **1.** The stubs of grain stalks, sugar
cane, etc., covering a field after the crop has been cut.   **2.**
The field itself.   **3.** Any surface or growth resembling stub-
ble, as short bristly hair or beard.   [< OF *stuble,* ult. < L
stipula stalk]   **—stub′bled** *adj.*   **—stub′bly** *adj.*

stub·born (stub′ərn)   *adj.* **1.** Inflexible in opinion or intention; unreasonably obstinate.   **2.** Difficult to handle, manage, or work with; resistant.   **3.** Characterized by perseverance or persistence: *stubborn* fighting.   [ME, ? < OE *stubb
stump*]   **—stub′born·ly** *adv.*   **—stub′born·ness** *n.*

stub·by (stub′ē)   *adj.* ·**bi·er,** ·**bi·est 1.** Short, stiff, and
bristling: a *stubby* beard.   **2.** Resembling or of the nature of
a stub: a *stubby* pencil.   **3.** Stocky; thickset.   **4.** Full of
stubs.   **—stub′bi·ly** *adv.*   **—stub′bi·ness** *n.*

stuc·co (stuk′ō)   *n. pl.* ·**coes** or ·**cos 1.** A fine plaster for
walls or their relief ornaments, usu. of Portland cement,
sand, and a small amount of lime.   **2.** Any plaster or cement
used for the external coating of buildings.   **3.** Ornamental
work made from stucco: also **stuc′co·work′** (-wûrk′).   —*v.t.*
·**coed,** ·**co·ing** To apply stucco to; decorate with stucco.   [<
Ital. < Gmc.]   **—stuc′co·er** *n.*

stuck (stuk)   Past tense and past participle of STICK.

stuck-up (stuk′up′)   *adj. Informal* Conceited; snobbish.

stud¹ (stud)   *n.* **1.** A short intermediate post, as in a
building frame; a post to which laths are nailed.   **2.** A
knob, round-headed nail, or small protuberant ornament.
3. A removable button used to fasten a shirt front, etc.   **4.**
A crosspiece in a link, as in a chain cable.   **5.** A small pin
such as is used in a watch.   —*v.t.* **stud·ded, stud·ding 1.** To
set thickly with small points, projections, or knobs.   **2.** To
be scattered or strewn over.   **3.** To support or stiffen by
means of studs or upright props.   [OE *studu* post]

stud² (stud)   *n.* **1.** A collection of horses and mares for
breeding.   **2.** The place where they are kept.   **3.** A collection
of horses for riding, hunting, or racing.   **4.** A studhorse or
other male animal used for breeding purposes.   **5.** Stud
poker.   **—at stud** Of a male animal, used or available for
breeding purposes.   —*adj.* **1.** Of or pertaining to a stud.
2. Kept for breeding: a *stud* mare.   [OE *stōd*]

stud·book (stud′book′)   *n.* A record of the pedigree of
thoroughbred stock.

stud·ding (stud′ing)   *n.* **1.** Studs or joists collectively.   **2.**
The material from which they are made.

stud·ding·sail (stun′səl, stud′ing·sāl′)   *n. Naut.* A light
auxiliary sail set out beyond one of the principal sails by extensible booms during a following wind.

stu·dent (stōōd′nt, styōōd′nt)   *n.* **1.** One engaged in a
course of study, esp. in a secondary school, college or university.   **2.** One devoted to study.   **3.** One who makes a thorough study of a particular subject.   [< OF < L *studens, -en-
tis,* ppr. of *studere* to be eager, study]   **—stu′dent·ship** *n.*
   — Syn. A *student* is one who studies, not necessarily under a
teacher: this is the common term for one enrolled in a secondary
school or college. A *pupil* is one under close supervision of a teacher; children in elementary schools are called *pupils,* but the term
is not synonymous with beginner. A concert violinist may be called
the *pupil* of some great master under whom he has studied.

student body   All the students attending a school.

stud·horse (stud′hôrs′)   *n.* A stallion kept for breeding.
Also **stud horse.**

stud·ied (stud′ēd)   *adj.* **1.** Deliberately designed or undertaken: a *studied* insult.   **2.** Lacking freshness, naturalness,
or spontaneity.   **—stud′ied·ly** *adv.*   **—stud′ied·ness** *n.*

stu·di·o (stōō′dē-ō, styōō′-)   *n. pl.* ·**os 1.** The workroom of
an artist, photographer, etc.   **2.** A place where motion pictures are filmed.   **3.** A room or rooms where radio or television programs are broadcast or recorded.   [< Ital., a study]

studio couch   A backless couch with a bed frame underneath that may be drawn out to form a double bed.

stu·di·ous (stōō′dē-əs, styōō′-)   *adj.* **1.** Given to study; devoting oneself to the acquisition of knowledge. **2.** Earnest in effort. **3.** Done with deliberation; studied: *studious* politeness. — **stu′di·ous·ly** *adv.* — **stu′di·ous·ness** *n.*

stud poker A game of poker in which the cards of the first round are dealt face down and the rest face up, betting opening on the second round. [< STUD²]

stud·y (stud′ē) *v.* **stud·ied, stud·y·ing** *v.t.* **1.** To apply the mind in acquiring a knowledge of. **2.** To examine: to *study* a problem. **3.** To look at attentively; scrutinize. **4.** To endeavor to memorize, as a part in a play. **5.** To give thought and attention to, as something to be done or devised. — *v.i.* **6.** To apply the mind in acquiring knowledge. **7.** To follow a regular course of instruction. **8.** To meditate. — *n.* *pl.* **stud·ies 1.** The act of studying; the process of acquiring information. **2.** A particular instance or form of mental work. **3.** Something to be studied; a branch of knowledge. **4.** A specific product of or work resulting from studious application. **5.** In art, a first sketch, exercise, etc. **6.** A carefully elaborated literary treatment of a subject. **7.** A room devoted to study, reading, etc. **8.** A state of deep thought or absent-mindedness. **9.** Earnest endeavor; thoughtful attention or care. **10.** Something worthy of close attention. **11.** *Music* An étude. [< OF < L < *studere* to apply oneself, be diligent]

stuff (stuf) *v.t.* **1.** To fill completely; pack; cram full. **2.** To fill (an opening, etc.) with something forced in; plug. **3.** To obstruct or stop up; choke. **4.** To fill or expand with padding, as a cushion. **5.** To fill (a fowl, roast, etc.) with stuffing. **6.** In taxidermy, to fill the skin of (a bird, animal, etc.) with a material preparatory to mounting. **7.** To fill too full; distend. **8.** To fill or cram with food. **9.** To fill with knowledge, ideas, or attitudes, esp. unsystematically. **10.** To force or cram, as into a small space. **11.** To put fraudulent votes into (a ballot box). — *v.i.* **12.** To eat to excess. — *n.* **1.** The material out of which something may be shaped or made; raw or unwrought material. **2.** The fundamental element or basic material of anything: the *stuff* of dreams. **3.** *Informal* Possessions generally, esp., household goods. **4.** A worthless collection of things; rubbish. **5.** Worthless ideas: often used as an interjection: *Stuff* and nonsense! **6.** Woven material, esp. of wool; also, any textile fabric. **7.** *Informal* Any unspecified or vaguely defined substance, activity, etc. [< OF *estoffe*, ? < L *stuppa* tow] — **stuff′er** *n.*

stuffed shirt (stuft) *Informal* A pompous person.

stuff·ing (stuf′ing) *n.* **1.** The material with which anything is stuffed. **2.** A mixture, as of bread or cracker crumbs with meat and seasoning, used in stuffing fowls, etc. **3.** The act or process of one who or that which stuffs.

stuff·y (stuf′ē) *adj.* **stuff·i·er, stuff·i·est 1.** Badly ventilated. **2.** Impeding respiration. **3.** *Informal* Pompous; smugly self-important. **4.** *Informal* Old-fashioned; stodgy; straight-laced. — **stuff′i·ly** *adv.* — **stuff′i·ness** *n.*

stul·ti·fy (stul′tə·fī) *v.t.* **·fied, ·fy·ing 1.** To cause to appear absurd; give an appearance of foolishness to. **2.** To make worthless or ineffectual. [< LL < L *stultus* foolish + *facere* to make] — **stul′ti·fi·ca′tion** *n.* — **stul′ti·fi′er** *n.*

stum·ble (stum′bəl) *v.* **·bled, ·bling** *v.i.* **1.** To miss one's step in walking or running; trip. **2.** To walk or proceed unsteadily. **3.** To speak, read, etc., falteringly. **4.** To happen upon something by chance: with *across, on, upon,* etc. **5.** To err. — *v.t.* **6.** To cause to stumble. — *n.* **1.** The act of stumbling. **2.** A blunder; false steps. [Cf. Norw. *stumla* to stumble in the dark] — **stum′bler** *n.* — **stum′bling·ly** *adv.*

stumbling block Any obstacle, hindrance, or impediment, as to the achievement of some end.

stump (stump) *n.* **1.** That portion of the trunk of a tree left standing when the tree is felled. **2.** The part of anything, as of a limb, tooth, pencil, etc., that remains when the main part has been removed; a stub. **3.** *pl. Informal* The legs: chiefly in the phrase **to stir one's stumps. 4.** A place or platform from which a political speech is made. **5.** In cricket, any one of the three posts forming the wicket. **6.** A pencil-like soft leather or rubber bar, with conical ends, used to shade drawings of crayon or charcoal or to apply powdered pigments. **7.** A short, thickset person or animal. **8.** A heavy step; a clump; also, the sound made by such a step. — **to take the stump** To electioneer in a political campaign. — *adj.* **1.** Being or resembling a stump; stumpy. **2.** Of or pertaining to political oratory or campaigning: a *stump* speaker. — *v.t.* **1.** To reduce to a stump. **2.** To remove stumps from (land). **3.** To canvass (a district) by making political speeches: The candidate *stumped* the State. **4.** *Informal* To bring to a halt by real or fancied obstacles; baffle. **5.** To strike against an obstacle; stub, as one's toe. — *v.i.* **6.** To go about on or as on stumps; also, to walk heavily, noisily, and stiffly. **7.** To go about making political speeches. [< MLG] — **stump′er** *n.*

stump·y (stum′pē) *adj.* **stump·i·er, stump·i·est 1.** Full of stumps. **2.** Like a stump; short and thick. — **stump′i·ness** *n.*

stun (stun) *v.t.* **stunned, stun·ning 1.** To render unconscious or incapable of action by a blow, fall, etc. **2.** To astonish; astound. **3.** To daze or overwhelm by loud or excessive noise. — *n.* A stupefying blow, shock, or concussion; also, the condition of being stunned. [< OF < L *ex-* roughly + *tonare* to thunder, crash]

stung (stung) Past tense and past participle of STING.

stunk (stungk) Past participle and alternative past tense of STINK.

stun·ner (stun′ər) *n.* **1.** One who or that which stuns. *Informal* A person of extraordinary beauty, etc.

stun·ning (stun′ing) *adj.* **1.** Rendering unconscious. *Informal* Impressively beautiful, etc. — **stun′ning·ly** *adv.*

stunt¹ (stunt) *v.t.* To check the natural development of; dwarf; cramp. — *n.* **1.** A check in growth, progress, or development. **2.** A stunted animal or thing. [OE *stunt* foolish] — **stunt′ed** *adj.* — **stunt′ed·ness** *n.*

stunt² (stunt) *U.S. Informal n.* **1.** A sensational feat, bodily skill. **2.** Any thrilling or unusual feat or undertaking. — *v.i.* **1.** To perform stunts. — *v.t.* **2.** To perform stunts with (an airplane, etc.). [? < G *stunde* lesson]

stunt man In motion pictures, a man employed to substitute for an actor in dangerous acts or situations.

stu·pe·fac·tion (stōō′pə·fak′shən, styōō′-) *n.* The act of stupefying or the state of being stupefied.

stu·pe·fy (stōō′pə·fī, styōō′-) *v.t.* **·fied, ·fy·ing 1.** To dull the senses or faculties of; stun. **2.** To amaze; astound. [< L < *stupere* to be stunned + *facere* to make] — **stu′pe·fi′er** *n.*

stu·pen·dous (stōō·pen′dəs, styōō-) *adj.* **1.** Of or characterized by any highly impressive or astonishing feature. Of prodigious size or bulk. [< L *stupere* to be stunned] — **stu·pen′dous·ly** *adv.* — **stu·pen′dous·ness** *n.*

stu·pid (stōō′pid, styōō′-) *adj.* **1.** Very slow of apprehension or understanding. **2.** Affected with stupor; stupefied. **3.** Marked by, or resulting from, lack of understanding, reason, or wit; senseless. **4.** Tedious; dull. — *n. Informal* A stupid person. [< L < *stupere* to be stunned] — **stu·pid′i·ty** *n.* — **stu′pid·ly** *adv.* — **stu′pid·ness** *n.*

stu·por (stōō′pər, styōō′-) *n.* **1.** A condition in which the senses and faculties are suspended or greatly dulled, as by drugs or liquor. **2.** Mental or moral dullness; gross stupidity. [< L < *stupere* to be stunned] — **stu′por·ous** *adj.* — **Syn. 1.** lethargy, torpor.

stur·dy (stûr′dē) *adj.* **·di·er, ·di·est 1.** Possessing rugged health and strength; hardy; vigorous. **2.** Firm and unyielding; resolute: a *sturdy* defense. [< OF *estourdir* to amaze] — **stur′di·ly** *adv.* — **stur′di·ness** *n.*

stur·geon (stûr′jən) *n.* A large, fresh-water and marine fish of northern regions, with coarse, edible flesh. It is valued as a source of isinglass and caviar. [< OF < Med.L < OHG *sturjo*]

Sturm·ab·teil·ung (shtŏŏrm′äp·tī′lŏŏngk) *n. pl.* **·teil·ung·en** A Nazi political militia: also called *Brown Shirts, Storm troopers*. [< G, storm detachment]

stut·ter (stut′ər) *v.t. & v.i.* To utter or speak with spasmodic repetition, blocking, and prolongation of sounds, esp. those in initial position in a word. — *n.* The act or habit of stuttering. [Freq. of ME *stutten* to stutter] — **stut′ter·er** *n.* — **stut′ter·ing** *adj. & n.* — **stut′ter·ing·ly** *adv.*

St. Vi·tus's dance (sānt vī′təs·iz) *Pathol.* Chorea. Also **Vi′tus' dance, St. Vi·tus dance** (vī′təs).

sty¹ (stī) *n. pl.* **sties 1.** A pen for swine. **2.** Any filthy place of bestiality or debauchery. — *v.t. & v.i.* **stied, sty·ing** To keep or live in a sty or hovel. [ME < OE *sti*]

sty² (stī) *n. pl.* **sties** *Pathol.* A small, inflamed swelling of a sebaceous gland on the edge of the eyelid. Also **stye.** [< *stīgan* to rise + *ye* eye]

styg·i·an (stij′ē·ən) *adj. Often cap.* **1.** Of or pertaining to the river Styx. **2.** Infernal; dark and gloomy.

style (stīl) *n.* **1.** Manner of expressing thought, in writing or speaking. **2.** A distinctive, characteristic, or suitable mode of expression: His writing lacks *style.* **3.** A particular or characteristic mode of composition, construction, or appearance, as in art, music, etc.: the Gothic *style.* **4.** The manner in which some action or work is performed: the horse ran in fine *style.* **5.** A good or exemplary manner of performing: a team with *style.* **6.** A mode of conduct; style of living: to live in makeshift *style.* **7.** A fashionable manner or appearance: to live in *style.* **8.** A particular fashion in clothing. **9.** A particular type or fashion suitable for a person. **10.** The conventions of typography, design, usage, punctuation, etc., observed by a given publishing house, printing office, or publication. **11.** The legal or official style or appellation of a person, organization, etc. **12.** A stylus. **13.** The gnomon of a sundial. **14.** *Surg.* A slender probe with a blunt point. **15.** *Bot.* The prolongation of a carpel or ovary, bearing the stigma. For illus. see FLOWER. **16.** A system of arranging the length of the calendar years so as to average that of the true solar year. See OLD STYLE, STYLE under CALENDAR. — *v.* **styled, styl·ing** *v.t.*

ne; give a title to. **2.** To make consistent in typography, lling, punctuation, etc. **3.** To give form, fashion, or le to. [< OF < L *stilus* writing instrument] —**styl′er** *n.*

le book A book containing rules of spelling, punctuation, ography, etc., used by printers, editors, etc.

·ish (stī′lish) *adj.* Having style or fashionableness in thes, etc. —**styl′ish·ly** *adv.* —**styl′ish·ness** *n.*

·ist (stī′list) *n.* **1.** One who is a master of literary or torical style. **2.** A designer or adviser of style in clothes, erior decoration, etc. —**sty·lis′tic** *adj.* —**sty·lis′ti·cal·** *adv.*

·ize (stī′līz) *v.t.* **·ized, ·iz·ing** To make conform to a dis- ctive mode or style; conventionalize. —**styl′i·za′tion** *n.* **styl′iz·er** *n.*

o— *combining form* **1.** A pillar. **2.** *Bot.* A style; of or ated to a style. Also, before vowels, **styl-**. [< Gk. *stylos* umn, pillar]

lus (stī′ləs) *n.* *pl.* **·lus·es** (-iz) or **·li** (-lī) **1.** An ancient ting instrument, having one end pointed for writing on k tablets. **2.** A pointed instrument for marking or en- ving. **3.** The needle of a record player or of a recording trument. Also called *style.* [< L] —**styl′lar** *adj.*

mie (stī′mē) *n.* A condition in golf when an opponent's l lies directly between the player's ball and the hole. — **·mied, ·my·ing 1.** To block or hinder by or as by a mie. **2.** To baffle or perplex. Also spelled *stimy.* Also **/my.** [Prob. use of earlier Scot. *styme,* to be unable to see]

·tic (stip′tik) *adj.* **1.** Causing contraction of tissues, as od vessels. **2.** Stopping hemorrhage or bleeding. Also **p′ti·cal.** — *n.* A styptic substance or agent. [< L < . *styphein* to contract] —**styp·tic·i·ty** (stip·tis′ə·tē) *n.*

x (stiks) *n.* In Greek mythology, the river of hate, one of five rivers surrounding Hades.

·sion (swā′zhən) *n.* Persuasion: archaic except in the rase **moral suasion.** [< L *suadere* to persuade] —**sua- e** (swā′siv), **sua·so·ry** (swā′sər·ē) *adj.*

ve (swäv, swäv) *adj.* Smoothly pleasant and ingratiating manner; blandly polite; urbane. [< F < L *suavis* sweet] **suave′ly** *adv.* —**suave′ness, suav·i·ty** (swä′və·tē) *n.*

(sub) *n.* *Informal* Short for any of various words begin- g with *sub-,* as: **a** A substitute. **b** A subordinate or subal- n. **c** A submarine.

— *prefix* Used to form words meaning: **a** Under; beneath: ow: *substratum.* **b** *Anat.* Situated under or beneath: *sub- ineous.* **c** Almost; nearly; slightly; imperfectly: chiefly in ntific terms: *subconical.* **d** Lower in rank or grade; sec- lary; subordinate: *subaltern, subcontract.* **e** Forming a sub- ision: *subsection.* **f** *Chem.* Present (in a compound) in less n normal amount: *subchloride, suboxide.* Also: *suc-* before s in *succumb; suf-* before *f,* as in *suffer; sug-* before *g,* as in *gest; sum-* before *m,* as in *summon; sup-* before *p,* as in *pport; sur-* before *r,* as in *surrogate; sus-* before *c, p, t,* as in *ceptible, suspect, sustain.* [< L *sub* under]

·ac·id (sub·as′id) *adj.* Slightly sour or acid. —**sub′a- /i·ty** (-ə·sid′ə·tē) *n.*

·al·tern (sub·ôl′tərn) *adj.* **1.** *Brit. Mil.* Ranking below aptain. **2.** Of inferior rank or position; subordinate. — **1.** A person of subordinate rank or position. **2.** *Brit. Mil.* officer ranking below a captain. [< LL < L *sub-* under < *alternus* alternate]

·ant·arc·tic (sub′ant·ärk′tik, -är′tik) *adj.* Of or per- ning to the region surrounding the Antarctic Circle.

·arc·tic (sub·ärk′tik, -är′tik) *adj.* Denoting or pertain- to the region surrounding the Arctic Circle.

·a·tom·ic (sub′ə·tom′ik) *adj.* Within the atom: *sub- mic* particle.

·base·ment (sub′bās′mənt) *n.* An underground story, any one of several below the first or true basement.

·clin·i·cal (sub·klin′i·kəl) *adj.* Having no symptoms ap- rent in clinical tests, as in the early stages of a disease.

·com·mit·tee (sub′kə·mit′ē) *n.* A subordinate commit- appointed from the members of the original committee special work.

·con·scious (sub·kon′shəs) *adj.* **1.** Not clearly or whol- conscious. **2.** *Psychol.* Denoting such phenomena of men- life as are not attended by full consciousness. —*n.* *Psy- l.* That portion of mental activity not directly in the focus consciousness but sometimes susceptible to recall by the per stimulus. —**sub·con′scious·ly** *adv.* —**sub·con′ ous·ness** *n.*

·con·ti·nent (sub·kon′tə·nənt) *n.* *Geog.* A great land ss forming part of a continent but having considerable ographical independence, as India.

·con·tract (*n.* sub·kon′trakt; *v.* sub′kən·trakt′) *n.* A ntract subordinate to another contract and assigning part all of the work to another party. —*v.t. & v.i.* To make a bcontract (for). —**sub′con·trac′tor** (-kən·trak′tər, -kon′- ak-) *n.*

sub·crit·i·cal (sub′krit′i·kəl) *adj.* *Physics* Of, pertaining to, or containing fissionable material in a quantity not suffi- cient to start or sustain a chain reaction: *subcritical* mass.

sub·cu·ta·ne·ous (sub′kyōō·tā′nē·əs) *adj.* **1.** Situated, found, or lying beneath the skin. **2.** Introduced or applied beneath the skin, as an injection. [< LL < L *sub-* under + *cutis* skin] —**sub′cu·ta·ne·ous·ly** *adv.*

sub·deb (sub′deb′) *n.* *Informal* **1.** A subdebutante. **2.** Any girl of this age. —*adj.* In a style suitable for girls of this age.

sub·deb·u·tante (sub′deb·ōō·tänt′, -deb′yōō·tant) *n.* A young girl the year before she becomes a debutante.

sub·di·vide (sub′di·vīd′) *v.t. & v.i.* **·vid·ed, ·vid·ing 1.** To divide (a part) resulting from a previous division; divide again. **2.** To divide (land) into lots for sale or improvement. [< LL < L *sub-* under + *dividere* to separate]

sub·di·vi·sion (sub′di·vizh′ən) *n.* **1.** Division following upon division. **2.** A part, as of land, resulting from subdi- viding. **3.** An area of land composed of subdivided lots.

sub·dom·i·nant (sub·dom′ə·nənt) *n.* *Music* The fourth tone or degree of a major or minor scale.

sub·due (sub·dōō′, -dyōō′) *v.t.* **·dued, ·du·ing 1.** To gain dominion over: subjugate; vanquish. **2.** To overcome by training, influence, or persuasion; tame. **3.** To repress (emo- tions, impulses, etc.). **4.** To reduce the intensity of; soften, as a color or sound. [< OF < L *subducere* to withdraw] — **sub·du′a·ble** *adj.* —**sub·du′al** *n.* —**sub·du′er** *n.* — **Syn. 1.** conquer. **2.** master, control, bridle. **3.** check, re- strain. **4.** moderate, temper.

sub·fam·i·ly (sub·fam′ə·lē, -fam′lē) *n.* *pl.* **·lies 1.** *Biol.* A division of plants or animals next below a family but above the genus. **2.** *Ling.* A division of languages below a family and above a branch.

sub·ge·nus (sub·jē′nəs) *n.* *pl.* **·gen·e·ra** (-jen′ər·ə) or, less commonly, **·ge·nus·es** *Biol.* A primary subdivision of a ge- nus including one or more species with common characters. —**sub′ge·ner′ic** (-ji·ner′ik) *adj.*

sub·head (sub′hed′) *n.* A heading or title of a subdivision. Also **sub′head′ing.**

sub·hu·man (sub·hyōō′mən) *adj.* **1.** Less than or imper- fectly human. **2.** Below the level of *Homo sapiens.*

sub·ja·cent (sub·jā′sənt) *adj.* **1.** Situated directly under- neath. **2.** Lower than but not directly below. [< L < *sub- under* + *jacere* to lie] —**sub·ja′cen·cy** *n.*

sub·ject (*adj.* sub′jikt; *v.* səb·jekt′) *adj.* **1.** Being under the power of another; owing or yielding obedience to sovereign authority. **2.** Liable to be affected by: with *to: subject* to dis- ease. **3.** Likely to bring about or incur: with *to: subject* to se- vere criticism. **4.** Dependent on; contingent on: with *to:* a treaty *subject* to ratification. —*n.* **1.** One who is under the governing power of another, as of a ruler or government, esp. of a monarch. **2.** One who or that which is employed or treated in a specified way, as a body for dissection, or a per- son used in psychological experiments. **3.** A topic or main theme, as of a discussion, written work, etc. **4.** Something represented by or serving as the basic idea for an artistic work. **5.** A branch of learning or course of study. **6.** An originating cause; motive. **7.** *Gram.* The word, phrase, or clause of a sentence about which something is stated or asked in the predicate. **8.** *Music* A melody on which a composi- tion or a part of it is based. **9.** *Philos.* The ego or self. **10.** *Logic* In a proposition, that term about which something is affirmed or denied. See PROPOSITION. —*v.t.* **1.** To bring under dominion or control. **2.** To cause to undergo some ex- perience or action. **3.** To offer for consideration or approval. **4.** To make liable; expose: His inheritance was *subjected* to heavy taxation. [< OF < L *sub-* under + *jacere* to throw] —**sub·jec′tion** *n.*

sub·jec·tive (səb·jek′tiv) *adj.* **1.** Relating to, proceeding from, or taking place within an individual's mind, emotions, etc.: opposed to *objective.* **2.** Originating from or influenced by one's personal interests, prejudices, etc. **3.** Introspec- tive. **4.** Of the mind or emotions only; illusory. **5.** In liter- ature and art, giving prominence to the subject or author as treating of his inner experience and emotion. **6.** *Gram.* Des- ignating the nominative case. —**sub·jec′tive·ly** *adv.* — **sub·jec′tive·ness, sub·jec·tiv·i·ty** (sub′jek·tiv′ə·tē) *n.*

sub·join (sub·join′) *v.t.* To add at the end; attach; affix. [< MF < L < *sub-* in addition + *jungere* to join]

sub·join·der (sub·join′dər) *n.* Something subjoined.

sub·ju·gate (sub′jōō·gāt) *v.t.* **·gat·ed, ·gat·ing 1.** To bring under dominion; conquer; subdue. **2.** To make subservient in any way. [< L < *sub-* under + *jugum* yoke] —**sub′ju· ga′tion** *n.* —**sub′ju·ga′tor** *n.*

sub·junc·tive (səb·jungk′tiv) *Gram. adj.* Of or pertaining to that mood of the finite verb that is used to express a future contingency, a supposition implying the contrary, a mere supposition with indefinite time, or a wish or desire. ◆ In

English the forms of the subjunctive mood are usu. introduced by conjunctions of condition, doubt, contingency, possibility, etc., as *if*, *though*, *lest*. *unless*, *that*, *till*, or *whether*, but verbs in conditional clauses are not always in the subjunctive mood, for the use of these conjunctions with the indicative is very common. — *n.* **1.** The subjunctive mood. **2.** A verb form or construction in this mood. [See SUBJOIN.]

sub·lease (*v.* sub·lēs′; *n.* sub′lēs′) *v.t.* **·leased**, **·leas·ing** To obtain or let (property) on a sublease. — *n.* A lease of property from a tenant or lessee. — **sub′les·see′** (-les-ē′), **sub·les·sor** (sub·les′ôr, sub′les·ôr′) *n.*

sub·let (sub·let′, sub′let′) *v.t* **·let**, **·let·ting** **1.** To let (property one holds on a lease) to another. **2.** To let (work that one has contracted to do) to a subordinate contractor.

sub·li·mate (sub′lə·māt) *v.* **·mat·ed**, **·mat·ing** *v.t.* **1.** *Chem.* To cause (a substance) to convert from the solid to the gaseous state by the application of heat or pressure, and then to solidify again. **2.** To refine; purify. **3.** *Psychol.* To convert the energy of (instinctual drives) into acceptable social manifestations. — *v.i.* **4.** To undergo sublimation. — *adj.* Sublimated; refined. — *n.* *Chem.* The product of sublimation, esp., when regarded as purified. [See SUBLIME.] — **sub′li·ma′tion** *n.*

sub·lime (sə·blīm′) *adj.* **1.** Characterized by elevation, nobility, etc.; grand; solemn. **2.** Inspiring awe, deep emotion, etc.; moving. **3.** Being of the highest degree; utmost. — *n.* That which is sublime; height, as of emotion, grandeur, etc.: often with *the.* — *v.* **·limed**, **·lim·ing** *v.t.* **1.** To make sublime; ennoble. **2.** *Chem.* To sublimate. — *v.i.* **3.** To become sublimated. [< L *sublimis* lofty, prob. < *sub-* up to, under + *limen* lintel] — **sub·lime′ly** *adv.* — **sub·lim′er** *n.* — **sub·lim·i·ty** (sə·blim′ə·tē), **sub·lime′ness** *n.*

sub·lim·i·nal (sub·lim′ə·nəl) *adj.* *Psychol.* Perceived below the threshold of consciousness, as images, etc., of too low an intensity to produce a clear awareness. [< SUB- + L *limen*, *liminis* threshold] — **sub·lim′i·nal·ly** *adv.*

sub·ma·chine gun (sub′mə·shēn′) A lightweight automatic weapon using pistol ammunition, designed to be fired from the shoulder or hip.

sub·mar·gi·nal (sub·mär′jən·əl) *adj.* **1.** Below the margin. **2.** Of low fertility; unproductive: *submarginal* land.

sub·ma·rine (*adj.* sub′mə·rēn′; *n.* sub′mə·rēn) *adj.* Existing, done, or operating beneath the surface of the sea: a *submarine* mine. — *n.* A ship designed to operate below the surface of the sea. — **sub·mar·i·ner** (sub·mar′ə·nər) *n.*

sub·max·il·lar·y (sub·mak′sə·ler′ē) *Anat.* *adj.* **1.** Of or situated beneath the lower jaw. **2.** Of one of the salivary glands on either side of the lower jaw. — *n.* *pl.* **·lar·ies** The lower jaw bone: also **sub·max·il·la** (sub′mak·sil′ə).

sub·merge (səb·mûrj′) *v.* **·merged**, **·merg·ing** *v.t.* **1.** To place under or plunge into water or other liquid. **2.** To cover; hide. — *v.i.* **3.** To sink or dive beneath the surface of water, etc. Also **sub·merse′** (-mûrs′). [< L < *sub-* under + *mergere* to plunge] — **sub·mer′gi·bil′i·ty** *n.* — **sub·mer′gi·ble** *adj.*

sub·mersed (səb·mûrst′) *adj.* **1.** *Bot.* Growing under water. **2.** Submerged. [See SUBMERGE.]

sub·mer·sion (səb·mûr′shən, -zhən) *n.* The act of submerging something in a liquid or the state of being submerged. Also **sub·mer′gence** (-jəns).

sub·mis·sion (səb·mish′ən) *n.* **1.** The act of submitting or yielding to the power or authority of another. **2.** The state or quality of being submissive. **3.** The act of presenting something for consideration, approval, decision, etc.

sub·mis·sive (səb·mis′iv) *adj.* Willing or inclined to submit; yielding; obedient; docile. — **sub·mis′sive·ly** *adv.* — **sub·mis′sive·ness** *n.*

sub·mit (səb·mit′) *v.* **·mit·ted**, **·mit·ting** *v.t.* **1.** To place under or yield to the authority, or power of another; surrender. **2.** To present for the consideration, decision, or approval of others; refer. **3.** To present as one's opinion; suggest. — *v.i.* **4.** To give up; surrender. **5.** To be obedient, submissive or acquiescent. [< L < *sub-* underneath + *mittere* to send] — **sub·mit′tal** *n.* — **sub·mit′ter** *n.*

sub·nor·mal (sub·nôr′məl) *adj.* **1.** Below the normal. **2.** *Psychol.* Less than normal in intelligence. — *n.* A subnormal individual. — **sub·nor·mal·i·ty** (sub′nôr·mal′ə·tē) *n.*

sub·or·di·nate (*adj.* & *n.* sə·bôr′də·nit; *v.* sə·bôr′də·nāt) *adj.* **1.** Belonging to an inferior or lower order in a classification; secondary; minor. **2.** Subject or subservient to another; inferior. **3.** *Gram.* **a** Of or designating a clause connected with and dependent upon another clause and functioning as a subject, object, or modifier. **b** Serving to introduce such a clause. — *n.* One who or that which is subordinate. — *v.t.* **·nat·ed**, **·nat·ing** **1.** To make subordinate; also, to hold as of less importance. **2.** To make subject or subservient. [< L < *sub-* under + *ordinare* to order] — **sub·or′di·nate·ly** *adv.* — **sub·or′di·nate·ness** *n.* — **sub·or′di·na′tion** *n.* — **sub·or′di·na·tive** *adj.*

subordinate clause *Gram.* A dependent clause. See under CLAUSE.

sub·orn (sə·bôrn′) *v.t.* **1.** To bribe or procure (someone) commit perjury. **2.** To incite to an evil act, esp. a crim act. [< L < *sub-* secretly + *ornare* to equip] — **sub·or tion** (sub′ôr·nā′shən) *n.* — **sub·orn′er** *n.*

sub·plot (sub′plot′) *n.* A plot subordinate to the princ one in a novel, play, etc.

sub·poe·na (sə·pē′nə, səb-) *n.* A judicial writ requiri person to appear in court to give testimony. — *v.t.* To r fy or summon by writ or subpoena. Also **sub·pe′na**. Med.L < L < *sub* under + *poena* penalty]

sub·ro·gate (sub′rō·gāt) *v.t.* **·gat·ed**, **·gat·ing** **1.** To sut tute (one thing) for another. **2.** To substitute (one pers for another when assigning rights or appointing to an of′ [< L < *sub-* in place of + *rogare* to ask]

sub·ro·ga·tion (sub′rō·gā′shən) *n.* The substitution of person, esp. a creditor, or thing for another.

sub ro·sa (sub rō′zə) *Latin* Confidentially; in secret: li ally, under the rose, the emblem of an Egyptian god, mis′ enly regarded by the Romans as the god of silence.

sub·scribe (səb·skrīb′) *v.* **·scribed**, **·scrib·ing** *v.t.* **1.** write, as one's name, at the end of a document; sign. **2.** sign one's name to as an expression of assent, etc.; attes by signing. **3.** To promise, esp., in writing, to pay (a su money). — *v.i.* **4.** To write one's name at the end of a d ment. **5.** To give sanction, support, or approval; agree. To promise to pay or contribute money. **7.** To agree to ceive and pay for issues of a newspaper, periodical, ∈ with *to*. [< L < *sub-* underneath + *scribere* to write] **sub·scrib′er** *n.*

sub·script (sub′skript) *adj.* Written below or lower an the right or left. — *n.* A subscript character. [See S SCRIBE.]

sub·scrip·tion (səb·skrip′shən) *n.* **1.** The act of subsc ing; signature. **2.** Consent, confirmation, or agreement. That which is subscribed; a signed paper or statement. **4** signature written at the end of a document. **5.** The i vidual or total sum or number subscribed for any purp **6.** A formal signed undertaking to pay for the receipt magazine, book, ticket, etc. — **to take up a subscription** collect money (for some special cause) from a large nur of people. — **sub·scrip′tive** *adj.* — **sub·scrip′tive·ly** *ad*

sub·se·quent (sub′sə·kwənt) *adj.* Following in time, pl or order, or as a result. [< L < *sub-* next below + *sequ* follow] — **sub′se·quence**, **sub′se·quen·cy** *n.* — **sub** **quent·ly** *adv.* — **sub′se·quent·ness** *n.*

sub·serve (səb·sûrv′) *v.t.* **·served**, **·serv·ing** **1.** To be of or help in furthering (a process, cause, etc.); serve; prom **2.** To serve as a subordinate to (a person). [< L < under + *servire* < *servus* slave]

sub·ser·vi·ent (səb·sûr′vē·ənt) *adj.* **1.** Adapted to prom some end or purpose; being of service; useful as a subo nate. **2.** Servile; obsequious. — *n.* One who or that wl subserves. — **sub·ser′vi·ent·ly** *adv.* — **sub·ser′vi·e** **sub·ser′vi·en·cy** *n.*

sub·side (səb·sīd′) *v.i.* **·sid·ed**, **·sid·ing** **1.** To become less olent or agitated; become calm or quiet; abate. **2.** To s to a lower level. **3.** To sink to the bottom; settle. [< l *sub-* under + *sidere* to settle < *sedere* to sit] — **sub·sid·e** (səb·sīd′ns, sub′sə·dəns).

sub·sid·i·ar·y (səb·sid′ē·er′ē) *adj.* **1.** Assisting or functi ing in a lesser capacity; supplementary; secondary. **2.** or in the nature of a subsidy; helping by a subsidy. — *n.* **·ar·ies** **1.** One who or that which furnishes aid or supp an auxiliary. **2.** A subsidiary company. [See SUBSIDE.]

subsidiary company A company controlled by anot company that owns the greater part of its shares.

sub·si·dize (sub′sə·dīz) *v.t.* **·dized**, **·diz·ing** **1.** To furr with a subsidy; grant a regular allowance or pecuniary to. **2.** To obtain the assistance of a subsidy: often imp ing bribery. — **sub′si·di·za′tion** *n.* — **sub′si·diz′er** *n.*

sub·si·dy (sub′sə·dē) *n.* *pl.* **·dies 1.** Pecuniary aid dire granted by government to a private commercial enterp deemed beneficial to the public. **2.** Any financial assista afforded by one individual or government to another. AF < L *subsidium* auxiliary forces, aid] — **Syn. 1.** A government *subsidy* supports a public service an airline. The word *subvention* is sometimes applied to a *sub* to an artistic enterprise. A *grant* is given by a government ∈ private institution to be spent for a specified purpose.

sub·sist (səb·sist′) *v.i.* **1.** To have existence or reality; c tinue to exist. **2.** To manage to live, often with *on* or *by subsist* on vegetables. **3.** To continue unchanged; ab **4.** To have existence in or by virtue of something; inh [< L < *sub-* under + *sistere* to cause to stand]

sub·sis·tence (səb·sis′təns) *n.* **1.** The act of subsisting. That on which one subsists; sustenance; livelihood. **3.** state of being subsistent; inherent quality. **4.** That wl subsists; real being. Also **sub·sis′ten·cy**. — **sub·sis′tent** *a*

sub·soil (sub′soil′) *n.* The stratum of earth next bene the surface soil: also called *undersoil*. — *v.t.* To plow s to turn up the subsoil. — **sub′soil′er** *n.*

son·ic (sub·son′ik) *adj.* 1. Designating those sound
ves beyond the lower limits of human audibility. 2.
on. Having a speed less than that of sound.

·stance (sub′stəns) *n.* 1. The material of which any-
ng consists; also, a material object as contrasted with
iething intangible. 2. Any type of matter of a specific
mical composition. 3. Density; body. 4. A substantial
lity; solidity. 5. The essential part of anything said or
tten; the gist. 6. Material wealth; property. [< OF <
< *sub-* under + *stare* to stand]

·stan·dard (sub′stan′dərd) *adj.* 1. Below the standard.
Lower than the established rate or authorized require-
nts. 3. *Ling.* Nonstandard.

stan·tial (səb·stan′shəl) *adj.* 1. Solid; strong; firm.
Of real worth and importance; of considerable value. 3.
nsiderable and real: *substantial* progress. 4. Possessed of
lth and influence. 5. Of or pertaining to substance; ma-
al. 6. Containing or conforming to the essence of a thing;
ing the correct idea; fundamental. 7. Ample and nour-
ng. — *n.* 1. That which has substance; a reality. 2.
e more important part. — **sub·stan′ti·al′i·ty** (-shē·al′ə-
sub·stan′tial·ness *n.* — **sub·stan′tial·ly** *adv.*

stan·ti·ate (səb·stan′shē·āt) *v.t.* ·at·ed, ·at·ing 1. To
ablish, as a position or a truth, by substantial evidence;
ify. 2. To give form to; embody. 3. To make substan-
, existent, or real; give substance to. [See SUBSTANCE.]
sub·stan′ti·a′tion *n.* — **sub·stan′ti·a′tive** *adj.*

stan·tive (sub′stən·tiv) *n.* 1. A noun or anything that
ctions as a noun, as a verbal form, phrase, or clause. 2.
e who or that which is independent. — *adj.* 1. Capable
eing used as a noun. 2. Expressive of or denoting exist-
e. The verb "to be" is called the *substantive* verb. 3.
ving substance or reality; lasting. 4. Essential. 5. In-
idual. 6. Independent; self-supporting. 7. Of consider-
e amount; substantial. [< OF < LL < L. See SUB-
ANCE.] — **sub·stan·ti′val** (-tī′vəl) *adj.* — **sub·stan·tive-**
v. — **sub′stan·tive·ness** *n.*

·sta·tion (sub′stā′shən) *n.* A subsidiary station, a
nch post office, etc.

·sti·tute (sub′stə·tōot, -tyōot) *v.* ·tut·ed, ·tut·ing *v.t.* 1.
put in the place of another person, constituent, or thing.
i. 2. To act as a substitute. — *n.* One who or that
ich takes the place of or serves in lieu of another. [< L <
- in place of + *statuere* to set up]

·sti·tu·tion (sub′stə·tōo′shən, -tyōo′-) *n.* 1. The act or
cess of substituting, or the state of being substituted. 2.
mething substituted. — **sub′sti·tu′tion·al** *adj.* — **sub′·**
tu′tional·ly *adv.*

·strate (sub′strāt) *n.* *Biochem.* The material or sub-
nce acted upon by an enzyme or ferment.

·stra·tum (sub·strā′təm, -strat′əm) *n.* *pl.* ·ta (-tə) or
ms 1. An underlying stratum or layer, as of earth or rock;
o, subsoil. 2. That which forms the foundation, ground-
rk, or basis. [< NL < L < *sub-* underneath + *sternere* to
ew] — **sub·stra′tive** *adj.*

·struc·ture (sub′struk′chər, sub·struk′-) *n.* A structure
ving as a foundation of a building, etc.

·ten·ant (sub′ten′ənt) *n.* A person who rents or leases
m a tenant: also called *undertenant*. — **sub·ten′an·cy** *n.*

·tend (sub·tend′) *v.t.* 1. *Geom.* To extend under or op-
site to, as the side of a triangle opposite to an angle. 2.
t. To enclose in its axil: A leaf *subtends* a bud. [< L <
- underneath + *tendere* to stretch]

·ter- *prefix* Under; less than. [< L *subter* below]

·ter·fuge (sub′tər·fyōoj) *n.* Any stratagem to avoid un-
easantness or difficulty. [< L < *subter-* below, in secret +
gere to flee]

·ter·ra·ne·an (sub′tə·rā′nē·ən) *adj.* 1. Situated or oc-
rring below the surface of the earth; underground. 2.
dden or secret. Also **sub·ter·ra′ne·al, sub′ter·ra′ne·ous.**

·tile (sut′l, sub′til) *adj.* 1. Delicate or tenuous in form,
aracter, etc.; ethereal. 2. Penetrating; pervasive. 3.
btle; wily. [< OF *subtil*, alter. of *soutil* subtle] — **sub′-**
·ly *adv.* — **sub·til·i·ty** (sub·til′ə·tē), **sub′tile·ness** *n.*

·til·ize (sut′l·īz, sub′tə·līz) *v.* ·ized, ·iz·ing *v.t.* 1. To
ake subtle or subtily; refine. 2. To make acute; sharpen,
the senses. 3. To argue subtly. — *v.i.* 4. To make sub-
distinctions; use subtlety. — **sub′til·i·za′tion** *n.*

·ti·tle (sub′tīt′l) *n.* 1. A subordinate or explanatory
le, as in a book, play, or document. 2. In motion pic-
res: **a** A running written translation of original dialogue
su. appearing at the bottom of the screen. **b** A written com-
ent or record of dialogue, as in a silent film.

·tle (sut′l) *adj.* 1. Characterized by cunning, or artifice;
afty. 2. Keen; discriminating. 3. Apt; skillful. 4. In-
nious; clever; refined. 5. Insidious; secretly active. 6.
struse. 7. Of delicate texture. [< OF < L *subtilis* orig.,
sely woven] — **sub′tle·ness** *n.* — **sub′tly** *adv.*

sub·tle·ty (sut′l·tē) *n.* *pl.* ·ties 1. The state or quality of
being subtle. 2. Something subtle, as a nice distinction.

sub·ton·ic (sub′ton′ik) *n.* *Music* The tone below the tonic;
the seventh tone of a major or minor scale.

sub·tract (səb·trakt′) *v.t. & v.i.* To take away or deduct, as
a portion from the whole, or one quantity from another. [<
L < *sub-* away + *trahere* to draw] — **sub·tract′er** *n.*

sub·trac·tion (səb·trak′shən) *n.* 1. The act or process of
subtracting; a deducting. 2. Something deducted. 3. *Math.*
The operation, indicated by the minus sign (−), of finding
the difference between two quantities.

sub·tra·hend (sub′trə·hend) *n.* *Math.* The number to be
subtracted from another. [See SUBTRACT.]

sub·treas·ur·y (sub′trezh′ər·ē) *n.* *pl.* ·ur·ies A branch of a
treasury.

sub·trop·i·cal (sub′trop′i·kəl) *adj.* 1. Of, pertaining to, or
designating regions adjacent to the Torrid Zone. 2. Having
characteristics intermediate between or common to both
Torrid and Temperate Zones. Also **sub′trop′ic.**

sub·trop·ics (sub′trop′iks) *n.pl.* Subtropical regions.

sub·urb (sub′ûrb) *n.* 1. A place adjacent to a city, esp., a
residential area. 2. *pl.* Outlying residential districts; outskirts. [< OF < L < *sub-* near to + *urbs, urbis* city]

sub·ur·ban (sə·bûr′bən) *adj.* 1. Of or pertaining to a suburb. 2. Dwelling or located in a suburb. — *n.* One who
lives in a suburb; suburbanite.

sub·ur·ban·ite (sə·bûr′bən·īt) *n.* A resident of a suburb.

sub·ur·bi·a (sə·bûr′bē·ə) *n.* Suburbs or suburbanites collectively and their social and cultural world.

sub·ven·tion (səb·ven′shən) *n.* 1. Giving of succor; aid.
2. A grant, as of money; subsidy. — **Syn.** See SUBSIDY. [<
OF < LL < L < *sub-* up from under + *venire* to come] —
sub·ven′tion·ar·y (-er′ē) *adj.*

sub·ver·sion (səb·vûr′shən, -zhən) *n.* 1. The act of sub-
verting, or the state of being subverted; a demolition; overthrow. 2. A cause of ruin. Also **sub·ver′sal** (-səl). [< OF
< LL < L. See SUBVERT.]

sub·ver·sive (səb·vûr′siv) *adj.* Tending to subvert or overthrow, as a government. — *n.* One who acts in accordance
with subversive principles. — **sub·ver′sive·ly** *adv.*

sub·vert (səb·vûrt′) *v.t.* 1. To overthrow; destroy utterly.
2. To undermine the morals, character, or faith of; corrupt.
[< OF < L < *sub-* up from under + *vertere* to turn] — **sub·**
vert′er *n.* — **sub·vert′i·ble** *adj.*
— **Syn.** 1. uproot, upset, overturn.

sub·way (sub′wā) *n.* 1. *U.S.* An underground railroad, usu.
electrically operated; also, a tunnel for such a railroad. 2.
An underground passage, as for cables, etc.

suc- Assimilated var. of SUB-.

suc·ceed (sək·sēd′) *v.i.* 1. To accomplish what is attempted
or intended; be successful. 2. To come next in order or sequence; follow; ensue. 3. To come after another into office,
etc.; be the successor: often with *to*. — *v.t.* 4. To come after;
follow. 5. To be the successor or heir of. [< OF < L *suc-
cedere* to follow after] — **suc·ceed′er** *n.*

suc·cess (sək·ses′) *n.* 1. A favorable or desired outcome of
something attempted. 2. A successful person, enterprise,
etc. 3. Attainment of wealth, etc. [< L. See SUCCEED.]

suc·cess·ful (sək·ses′fəl) *adj.* 1. Obtaining what one desires or intends. 2. Having reached a high degree of worldly
prosperity. 3. Terminating in success; resulting favorably.
— **suc·cess′ful·ly** *adv.* — **suc·cess′ful·ness** *n.*

suc·ces·sion (sək·sesh′ən) *n.* 1. The act of following in order, or the state of being successive; a following consecutively. 2. A series; sequence. 3. The act or right of legally or
officially coming into a predecessor's office, possessions, etc.;
also, that which is so acquired. 4. The order by which an
office, etc., changes hands. 5. Descendants collectively; issue. — **suc·ces′sion·al** *adj.* — **suc·ces′sion·al·ly** *adv.*

suc·ces·sive (sək·ses′iv) *adj.* Following in sequence; consecutive. — **suc·ces′sive·ly** *adv.* — **suc·ces′sive·ness** *n.*

suc·ces·sor (sək·ses′ər) *n.* One who or that which succeeds
or comes after; esp., a person who succeeds to a throne, property, or office.

suc·cinct (sək·singkt′) *adj.* Consisting of or characterized
by brief and meaningful language; terse; concise. — **Syn.**
See TERSE. [< L < *sub-* underneath + *cingere* to gird] —
suc·cinct′ly *adv.* — **suc·cinct′ness** *n.*

suc·cor (suk′ər) *n.* 1. Help or relief rendered in danger, difficulty, or distress. 2. One who or that which affords relief.
— *v.t.* To go to the aid of; help; rescue. Also *Brit.* **suc′cour**
[< OF < Med.L < L < *sub-* up from under + *currere* to
run] — **suc′cor·a·ble** *adj.* — **suc′cor·er** *n.*

suc·co·tash (suk′ə·tash) *n.* A dish of corn kernels and
beans, usu. lima beans, boiled together. [< Algonquian
(Narragansett) *misickquatash* ear of corn]

Suc·coth (sook′ōth, -ōs, -əs) See SUKKOTH.

suc·cu·bus (suk′yə·bəs) *n.* *pl.* ·bus·es or ·bi (bī) 1. In folklore, a female demon that has sexual intercourse with sleeping men. Compare INCUBUS. 2. Any evil spirit. [< Med.L < L < *sub-* underneath + *cubare* to lie]

suc·cu·lent (suk′yə-lənt) *adj.* 1. Full of juice; juicy. 2. *Bot.* Juicy; fleshy, as the tissues of certain plants. 3. Rich or vigorous; a *succulent* theme. [< L < *succus* juice] —**suc′·cu·lence, suc′cu·len·cy** *n.* —**suc′cu·lent·ly** *adv.*

suc·cumb (sə-kum′) *v.i.* 1. To give way; yield, as to force or persuasion. 2. To die. [< OF < L < *sub-* underneath + *cumbere* to lie]

such (such) *adj.* 1. Of that kind; of the same or like kind: often with *as* or *that* completing a comparison: *Such* wit as this is rare. 2. Being the same as what has been mentioned or indicated: *Such* was the king's command. 3. Being the same in quality: Let the truthful continue *such*. 4. Being the same as something understood by the speaker or the hearer, or purposely left indefinite: the chief of *such* a clan. 5. So extreme, unpleasant, or the like: We have come to *such* a pass. —**as such** 1. As being what is indicated or implied: An executive, *as such*, must take responsibility. 2. In or by itself: Clothes, *as such*, do not make the man. —**such as** 1. For example. 2. Of a particular kind or degree: The outcome of the trial was *such as* might be expected. —*pron.* 1. Such a person or thing, or such persons or things: The friend of *such* as are in trouble. 2. The same; the aforesaid: I bring good tidings, for *such* the general sent. —*adv. Informal* So: *such* awful manners. ♦ *Such* and *such a* are widely used in informal contexts to intensify the adjective or noun they precede: He was *such a* kind man; He had *such* wisdom. [OE *swelc, swilc, swylc*]

such and such Being a condition, person, thing, or time, not specifically named.

such·like (such′līk′) *adj.* Of a like or similar kind. —*pron.* Persons or things of that kind.

suck (suk) *v.t.* 1. To draw into the mouth by means of a partial vacuum created by action of the lips and tongue. 2. To draw in or take up in a manner resembling this; absorb. 3. To draw liquid or nourishment from with the mouth. 4. To take into and hold in the mouth. 5. To consume by licking, or by holding in the mouth: to *suck* candy. 6. To bring to a specified state or condition by sucking: He *sucked* the lemon dry. —*v.i.* 7. To draw in liquid, air, etc., by suction. 8. To suckle. 9. To draw in air instead of water, as a defective pump does. 10. To make the sound of sucking. —**to suck in** *Slang* To take advantage of. —*n.* 1. The act of sucking; suction. 2. That which is sucked or comes by sucking. 3. A slight draft or drink. [OE *sūcan*]

suck·er (suk′ər) *n.* 1. One who or that which sucks. 2. A North American fresh-water fish, having the mouth usu. protractile with thick and fleshy lips adapted for sucking in food. 3. *Zool.* An organ by which an animal adheres to other bodies by suction. 4. *U.S. Slang* One who is easily deceived; a foolish or gullible person. 5. A lollipop. 6. *Bot.* A shoot or sprout arising from the root near or remote from the trunk of certain trees. —*v.t.* 1. To strip of suckers or shoots. —*v.i.* 2. To form or send out suckers or shoots. [< SUCK]

suck·le (suk′əl) *v.* **·led, ·ling** *v.t.* 1. To allow or cause to take nourishment from the breast by sucking; nurse. 2. To bring up; nourish. —*v.i.* 3. To take nourishment at the breast: also *suck*. [ME *sucklen*, prob. back formation < SUCKLING] —**suck′ler** *n.*

suck·ling (suk′ling) *n.* 1. An unweaned mammal. 2. An infant. [ME < *soken* to suck + *-ling* -ling¹]

su·crose (sōō′krōs) *n. Biochem.* A crystalline disaccharide, C₁₂H₂₂O₁₁, forming the greater part of the sugar as obtained from the sugar cane, sugar beet, etc. Also called *saccharose*. [< F *sucre* sugar + *-ose* -ose²]

suc·tion (suk′shən) *n.* 1. The act or process of sucking. 2. The production of a partial vacuum in a space connected with a liquid or gas under pressure. 3. The tendency of a fluid to occupy all or part of a vacuum contiguous with it. [< OF < L *sugere* to suck]

suction pump A pump operating by suction, consisting of a piston working in a cylinder, both equipped with valves.

suc·to·ri·al (suk-tôr′ē-əl, -tō′rē-əl) *adj.* 1. Adapted for sucking or for adhesion. 2. *Zool.* Having organs for sucking.

Su·da·nese (sōō′də-nēz′, -nēs′) *adj.* Of or pertaining to the Sudan or its people. —*n. pl. ·nese* A native or inhabitant of the Sudan.

sud·den (sud′n) *adj.* 1. Happening quickly and without warning. 2. Hurriedly or quickly contrived, used, or done; hasty. 3. Come upon unexpectedly; causing surprise. 4. Quick-tempered; precipitate. —**all of a sudden** Without warning; suddenly. [< AF < OF < L < *sub-* secretly + *ire* to go] —**sud′den·ly** *adv.* —**sud′den·ness** *n.*

sudden infant death syndrome See CRIB DEATH.

su·dor·if·ic (sōō′də-rif′ik) *Med. adj.* Causing perspiration. —*n.* A medicine that produces or promotes sweating. [< NL < L *sudor, -oris* sweat + *facere* to make]

suds (sudz) *n.pl.* 1. Soapy water, or bubbles and froth on

its surface. 2. Foam; lather. 3. *Slang* Beer. [Pro
M Du. *sudde, sudae* marsh water] —**suds′y** *adj.*

sue (sōō) *v.* **sued, su·ing** *v.t.* 1. *Law* a To institute proc ings against for the recovery of some right or the redre some wrong. b To prosecute (an action). c To seek a g from (a court). 2. To endeavor to persuade by entreaty tition —*v.i.* 3. To institute legal proceedings. 4 make entreaty. [< AF *suer*, OF *sivre*, ult. < L *sequi* t low] —**su′a·ble** *adj.* —**su′er** *n.*

suede (swād) *n.* 1. A leather having a soft napped fi usu. on the flesh side. 2. A woven or knitted fabric fini to resemble this. Also **suède**. [< F *Suède* Sweden, in ph *gants de Suède* Swedish gloves]

su·et (sōō′it) *n.* The fatty tissues about the loins and kid of sheep, oxen, etc., used in cookery and to make ta [Dim. of AF *sue*, OF *seu* < L *sebum* fat] —**su′et·y** a

suf- Assimilated var. of SUB-.

suf·fer (suf′ər) *v.i.* 1. To feel pain or distress. 2. To b fected injuriously; experience loss or injury. 3. To und punishment; esp., to be put to death. —*v.t.* 4. To hav flicted on one; sustain, as an injury or loss. 5. To und pass through, as change. 6. To bear; endure: to *suffer* pain. 7. To allow; permit: Will he *suffer* us to leave? AF *suffrir*, OF *sofrir*, ult. < L < *sub-* up from under + to bear] —**suf′fer·er** *n.*

suf·fer·a·ble (suf′ər-ə-bəl, suf′rə-) *adj.* Such as can be fered or endured; tolerable. —**suf′fer·a·bly** *adv.*

suf·fer·ance (suf′ər-əns, suf′rəns) *n.* 1. Permission g or implied by failure to prohibit; passive consent. 2. act or state of suffering. 3. Power to endure pain or 4. Patience or endurance under suffering; submissiven

suf·fer·ing (suf′ər-ing, suf′ring) *n.* 1. The state of ang or pain of one who suffers. 2. The bearing of pain, injur loss. 3. Pain or distress borne or endured; injury. — Inured to pain and loss; submissive. —**suf′fer·ing·ly** — **Syn.** 1. *Suffering* is acute bodily or mental pain. *Dis* may be physical, but is more often mental, referring to any anxiety, or the external circumstances that may produc *Misery* is extreme *suffering* or abject hopelessness, as from so great loss, poverty, or the like.

suf·fice (sə-fīs′) *v.* **·ficed, ·fic·ing** *v.i.* 1. To be sufficie adequate; meet the requirements or answer the purpose. *v.t.* 2. To be satisfactory or adequate for; satisfy. [< L < *sub-* under + *facere* to make] —**suf·fic′er** *n.*

suf·fi·cien·cy (sə-fish′ən-sē) *n. pl. ·cies* 1. The state o ing sufficient. 2. That which is sufficient; esp., adequat cuniary means or income. 3. Full capability or quali tion; efficiency. 4. Conceit; self-sufficiency.

suf·fi·cient (sə-fish′ənt) *adj.* Being all that is needful; quate; enough. — **Syn.** See ADEQUATE. [See SUFFI — **suf·fi′cient·ly** *adv.*

suf·fix (suf′iks) *n.* 1. *Gram.* A bound form affixed to the of a base, stem, or root, functioning as a derivative or in tional element. Compare COMBINING FORM, PREFIX. 2. added title or the like. —*v.t.* To add as a suffix. [< N L < *sub-* underneath + *figere* to fix.] —**suf′fix·al** *adj* **suf·fix·ion** (sə-fik′shən) *n.*

suf·fo·cate (suf′ə-kāt) *v.* **·cat·ed, ·cat·ing** *v.t.* 1. To ki obstructing respiration in any manner. 2. To obstru oppress, as by an inadequate supply of air. 3. To s smother, as a fire. —*v.i.* 4. To become choked or st die from suffocation. [< L < *sub-* under + *fauces* thr — **suf′fo·cat′ing·ly** *adv.* —**suf′fo·ca′tion** *n.* —**suf′fo** tive *adj.*

Suf·folk (suf′ək) *n.* 1. A hardy English breed of wor horses, with a heavy body and rather short legs. Also **folk punch.** 2. A breed of hornless sheep producing mu of high quality. [after *Suffolk*, England]

suf·frage (suf′rij) *n.* 1. The right or privilege of vo franchise. 2. The act or process of voting. 3. A vote in port of some measure or candidate. 4. Approbation sent. [< OF < L *suffragium* voting tablet, vote]

suf·fra·gette (suf′rə-jet′) *n.* Formerly, a woman who a cated or agitated for female suffrage. —**suf′fra·get′ti**

suf·fra·gist (suf′rə-gist) *n.* An advocate of some parti form of suffrage, esp. of female suffrage.

suf·fuse (sə-fyōōz′) *v.t.* **·fused, ·fus·ing** To overspread with a vapor, fluid, or color. [< L < *sub-* underneat from under + *fundere* to pour] —**suf·fu·sive** (sə-fyōō *adj.*

suf·fu·sion (sə-fyōō′zhən) *n.* 1. The act of suffusing, or state of being suffused. 2. That which suffuses, as a b

sug- Assimilated var. of SUB-.

sug·ar (shŏŏg′ər) *n.* 1. *Biochem.* a A sweet, crystalline bohydrate, C₁₂H₂₂O₁₁, obtained from the juice of va plants, as from the sugar cane, the sugar beet, and the s maple. ♦ Collateral adjective: *saccharine.* b Any of a class of similar carbohydrates, widely distributed in p and animals. 2. Flattering or honeyed words. 3. *S* Sweet one: a pet name. —*v.t.* 1. To sweeten, cover, or with sugar. 2. To make agreeable or less distasteful, s

ery. — v.i. 3. Chiefly U.S. To make maple sugar. 4.
orm or produce sugar; granulate. [< OF < Med.L, ult.
rabic sukkar]

r beet A sugar-producing species of beet.

r·bush (shŏŏg′ər-bŏŏsh′) n. A grove of sugar maples.

r cane A tall, stout, perennial grass of tropical regions,
ng a solid jointed stalk constituting a major source of
mercial sugar.

r-coat (shŏŏg′ər-kōt′) v.t. 1. To cover with sugar. 2.
ause to appear attractive or less distasteful, as with eu-
nisms or flattery.

r-cured (shŏŏg′ər-kyŏŏrd′) adj. Cured by using sugar
ae curing process, as ham and pork.

red (shŏŏg′ərd) adj. 1. Sweetened with sugar; sugared. 2. Honeyed; pleasant; sweetened.

r loaf 1. A conical mass of hard refined sugar. 2. A
cal hat or hill. — **sug·ar·loaf** (shŏŏg′ər-lōf′) adj.

r maple A maple of eastern North America, yielding a
from which maple sugar is made.

ar·plum (shŏŏg′ər-plum′) n. A small ball or disk of
y; a bonbon.

r·y (shŏŏg′ər-ē) adj. 1. Composed of or as of sugar;
t. 2. Fond of sugar. 3. Insincerely or cloyingly sweet.
onsisting of grains; granular. — **sug′ar·i·ness** n.

zest (səg-jest′, sə-jest′) v.t. 1. To bring or put forward
onsideration, action, or approval; propose. 2. To bring
ind by association or connection; connote. 3. To give a
or indirect indication of; intimate: The simple house
ested a modest income. 4. To act as or provide a mo-
for; prompt: these events suggest a sequel. [< L < sub-
erneath + gerere to carry] — **sug·gest′er** n.

gest·i·bil·i·ty (səg-jes′tə-bil′ə-tē, sə-) n. 1. Psychol.
onsiveness to suggestion, esp. when heightened or ab-
nal, as in hypnosis and certain nervous conditions. 2.
diness to believe and agree without reflection.

gest·i·ble (səg-jes′tə-bəl, sə-) adj. 1. That can be sug-
ed. 2. Easily led; yielding: a suggestible patient.

ges·tion (səg-jes′chən, sə-jes′-) n. 1. The act of sug-
ing. 2. Something suggested. 3. A hint; insinuation.
The spontaneous calling up of an idea in the mind by a
nected idea.

ges·tive (səg-jes′tiv, sə-) adj. 1. Fitted or tending to
zest; stimulating to thought or reflection. 2. Hinting at
rousing indecent thoughts; suggesting the improper. —
·ges′tive·ly adv. — **sug·ges′tive·ness** n.

cide (sōō′ə-sīd) n. 1. The intentional taking of one's
life. 2. Self-inflicted political, social, or commercial
. 3. One who has taken his own life. — v.i. **·cid·ed**,
·ing Informal To commit suicide. [< NL < L < sui
self + caedere to kill] — **su′i·ci′dal** adj.

gen·e·ris (sōō′ī jen′ər-is) Latin Forming a kind by it-
; unique; literally, of its (his, or her) particular kind.

(sōōt) n. 1. A set of garments consisting of a coat and
users or skirt, made of the same fabric. 2. A group of
ags of like kind or pattern composing a series or set. 3.
cardplaying, one of the four sets of thirteen cards each
t make up a pack, as spades, hearts, diamonds, or clubs.
Law A proceeding in a court of law or chancery in which a
ntiff demands the recovery of a right or the redress of a
ng. 5. The courting or courtship of a woman. 6. Ar-
ic Entreaty; petition. — **to follow suit** 1. To play a card
ntical in suit to the card led. 2. To do as somebody or
ething else has done. — v.t. 1. To meet the require-
nts of, or be appropriate to. 2. To please; satisfy. 3. To
der appropriate or accordant; accommodate; adapt. —
4. To be befitting; agree. 5. To be or prove satisfactory.
AF < OF sieute, ult. < L sequi to follow]

·a·ble (sōō′tə-bəl) adj. Appropriate to a particular oc-
ion, condition, etc.; proper. — **suit′a·bil′i·ty, suit′a·ble-**
s n. — **suit′a·bly** adv.

·case (sōōt′kās′) n. A flat, rectangular valise.

e (swēt) n. 1. A succession of things forming a series
l usu. intended to go or be used together; a set. 2. A
nber of connected rooms. 3. A set of furniture designed
be used together in the same room. 4. A company of at-
dants or followers; retinue. 5. Music A form of instru-
ntal composition formerly consisting of a series of dances,
t now often varying freely in its construction. 6. Canadi-
In the West, an apartment. [< F < OF sieute]

·ing (sōō′ting) n. Cloth from which to make suits.

·or (sōō′tər) n. 1. A man who courts a woman; a wooer.
One who institutes a suit in court. 3. A petitioner. [<
< LL < L secutus, pp. of sequi to follow]

ki·ya·ki (sōō′kē·yä′kē, -yak′ē; skē-) n. A Japanese dish
de of meat in thin slices, vegetables, and condiments. [<
panese suki spade + yaki roast]

c·koth (sōōk′ōth, -ōs, -əs) n. The feast of Tabernacles, a
wish holiday beginning on the 15th of Tishri (late Septem-

ber–October), originally a harvest festival: also spelled Suc-
coth. Also **Suk′kos, Suk′kot.** [< Hebrew sukōth tabernacles]

sulfa- combining form Chem. Sulfur; related to or containing sulfur: also spelled sulpha-. Also, before vowels, **sulf-.**
See also SULFO-. [< SULFUR]

sul·fa drug (sul′fə) Chem. Any of a large group of organic
compounds consisting mainly of substituted sulfanilamide
derivatives, some of which are effective in the treatment of
certain bacterial infections.

sul·fa·nil·a·mide (sul′fə-nil′ə-mīd, -mid) n. Chem. A colorless, crystalline sulfonamide, $C_6H_8N_2O_2S$, used in the
treatment of various bacterial infections.

sul·fate (sul′fāt) n. Chem. A salt of sulfuric acid. — v.
·fat·ed, ·fat·ing v.t. 1. To form a sulfate of; treat with a sulfate or sulfuric acid. 2. Electr. To form a coating of lead sulfate on (the plate of a secondary battery). — v.i. 3. To
become sulfated. Also spelled sulphate.

sul·fide (sul′fīd) n. Chem. A compound of sulfur with an
element or radical: also sulphide, sulphid. Also **sul′fid** (-fid).

sul·fite (sul′fīt) n. Chem. A salt or ester of sulfurous acid:
also spelled sulphite. — **sul·fit′ic** (-fit′ik) adj.

sulfo- combining form Chem. Sulfur; containing sulfur.
Also spelled sulpho-. [< SULFUR]

sul·fon·a·mide (sul-fon′ə-mīd, sul′fən·am′īd, -id) n. Chem.
Any of a class of chemotherapeutic compounds containing
the univalent radical SO_2N, esp. those derived from sulfanilamide: also spelled sulphonamide.

sul·fur (sul′fər) n. A pale yellow, nonmetallic element
(symbol S), found both free and combined in the native state,
and existing in several forms, of which the best known is a
crystalline solid that burns with a blue flame and a suffocating odor. It is used for making matches, gunpowder, vulcanized rubber, and medicines. See ELEMENT. Also spelled
sulphur. [< AF sulfre, OF soufre < L sulfur, -uris]

sulfur dioxide Chem. A colorless, water-soluble, suffocating gas, SO_2, formed by the burning of sulfur and used in the
manufacture of sulfuric acid.

sul·fu·re·ous (sul-fyŏŏr′ē·əs) adj. Of or like sulfur: also
spelled sulphureous.

sul·fu·ret (sul′fyə·ret) v.t. **·fu·ret·ed** or **·ret·ted, ·fu·ret·ing**
or **·ret·ting** To sulfurize.

sul·fu·ric (sul-fyŏŏr′ik) adj. Chem. Pertaining to or derived
from sulfur, esp. in its higher valence: also sulphuric.

sulfuric acid Chem. A colorless, exceedingly corrosive, oily
liquid, H_2SO_4, extensively employed in the manufacture of
soda, batteries, guncotton, and in a great variety of industrial operations: formerly called oil of vitriol, vitriol.

sul·fur·ize (sul′fyə·rīz, -fə-) v.t. **ized, ·iz·ing** 1. To im-
pregnate, treat with, or subject to the action of sulfur. 2.
To bleach or fumigate with sulfur. Also spelled sulphurize.
Also **sul′fu·rate** (-rāt). — **sul′fur·i·za′tion** n.

sul·fur·ous (sul′fər·əs, sul-fyŏŏr′əs) adj. 1. Of, pertaining
to, derived from, or containing sulfur, esp. in its lower valence. 2. Fiery; hellish. Also spelled sulphurous.

sulfurous acid Chem. A compound corresponding to the
formula H_2SO_3, and known only in solution and by its salts.

sul·fur·y (sul′fər·ē) adj. Resembling or suggesting sulfur;
sulfureous: also spelled sulphury.

sulk (sulk) v.i. To be sulky or morose. — n. 1. Often pl. A
sulky mood or humor. 2. One who sulks. [Back formation
< SULKY]

sulk·y¹ (sul′kē) adj. **sulk·i·er, sulk·i·est** 1. Sullenly cross;
doggedly or resentfully ill-humored. 2. Dismal; gloomy:
said of weather. [? OE (ā)solcen, orig. pp. of (ā)seolcan to be
weak, slothful] — **sulk′i·ly** adv. — **sulk′i·ness** n.

sulk·y² (sul′kē) n. pl. **sulk·ies** A light, two-wheeled, one-
horse vehicle for one person. [< SULKY¹]

sul·len (sul′ən) adj. 1. Obstinately and gloomily ill-humored; morose; glum; melancholy. 2. Depressing; somber:
sullen clouds. 3. Slow; sluggish: a sullen tread. 4. Ill-
omened; threatening. [Earlier solein, appar. < AF < L solus alone] — **sul′len·ly** adv. — **sul′len·ness** n.

sul·ly (sul′ē) v. **·lied, ·ly·ing** v.t. 1. To mar the brightness or
purity of; soil; defile; tarnish. — v.i. 2. To become soiled
or tarnished. — n. pl. **·lies** Anything that tarnishes; a
stain; spot; blemish. [< MF souiller to soil]

sulpha- Var. of SULFA-.

sul·phur (sul′fər), **sul·phu·re·ous** (sul-fyŏŏr′ē·əs), etc. See
SULFUR, etc.

sulpho- Var. of SULFO-.

sul·tan (sul′tən) n. The ruler of a Moslem country. — **the
Sultan** Formerly, the title of the sovereign of Turkey. [< F
< Med.L sultanus < Arabic sultān]

sul·tan·a (sul-tan′ə, -tä′nə) n. 1. A sultan's wife, daughter,
sister, or mother. Also **sul·tan·ess** (sul′tən·is). 2. A variety
of raisin from around Smyrna, Asia Minor.

sul·tan·ate (sul′tən·āt, -it) n. The authority or territorial
jurisdiction of a sultan. Also **sul′tan·ship.**

sul·try (sul'trē) *adj.* **·tri·er, ·tri·est 1.** Hot, moist, and still; close: said of weather. **2.** Emitting an oppressive heat. **3.** Showing or suggesting passion; sensual. [< obs. *sulter*, var. of SWELTER] — **sul'tri·ly** *adv.* — **sul'tri·ness** *n.*

sum (sum) *n.* **1.** The result obtained by addition. **2.** The entire quantity, number, or substance. **3.** An indefinite amount, as of money. **4.** A problem in arithmetic propounded for solution. **5.** The topmost or highest point; also, the maximum. **6.** The pith or essence; summary. — *v.* **summed, sum·ming** *v.t.* **1.** To present in brief; recapitulate succinctly: usu. with *up*. **2.** To add into one total: often with *up*. **3.** To ascertain the sum of (the terms of a series). — *v.i.* **4.** To make a summation or recapitulation: usu. with *up*. [< AF, OF < L *summa* (*res*) highest (thing)]

sum- Var. of SUB-.

su·mac (soo'mak, shoo'-) *n.* **1.** Any of various woody, erect, or root-climbing plants, with panicles of small drupaceous fruits, and yielding a resinous or milky juice. **2.** The poison sumac. **3.** The dried and powdered leaves of certain species of sumac, used for tanning and dyeing. Also **su'mach.** [< OF < Med.L < Arabic *summāq*]

Su·mer (soo'mər) A region and ancient country of Mesopotamia, later the southern division of Babylonia.

Su·me·ri·an (soo·mir'ē·ən) *adj.* Of or pertaining to ancient Sumer, its people, or their language. — *n.* **1.** One of an ancient non-Semitic people formerly occupying a part of lower Babylonia. **2.** The unclassified language of these people, written in cuneiform characters and preserved on rocks and clay tablets that date from as early as 4000 B.C. Also **Su·mir'i·an.**

sum·mand (sum'and) *n.* That which is added; any of the numbers forming part of a sum.

sum·ma·rize (sum'ə·rīz) *v.t.* **·rized, ·riz·ing** To make a summary of; sum up. Also *Brit.* **sum'ma·rise.** — **sum'ma·rist** (-ə·rist), **sum'ma·riz'er** *n.* — **sum'ma·ri·za'tion** *n.*

sum·ma·ry (sum'ər·ē) *adj.* **1.** Giving the substance or sum; concise. **2.** Performed without ceremony or delay; offhand. — *n., pl.* **·ries** An abridgment or abstract. [< Med.L < L *summa* sum] — **sum·ma·ri·ly** (sum'ər·ə·lē, *emphatic* sə·mer'ə·lē) *adv.* — **sum'ma·ri·ness** *n.*

sum·ma·tion (sum·ā'shən) *n.* **1.** The act or operation of obtaining a sum; the computation of an aggregate sum; addition. **2.** A speech or a portion of a speech summing up the principal points.

sum·mer (sum'ər) *n.* **1.** The warmest season of the year, occurring between spring and autumn. ◆ Collateral adjective: *estival.* **2.** A year of life, esp. of early or happy life. **3.** A bright and prosperous period. — *v.t.* **1.** To keep or care for through the summer. — *v.i.* **2.** To pass the summer. — *adj.* Of, pertaining to, or occurring in summer. [OE *sumor*] — **sum'mer·ly** *adj. & adv.* — **sum'mer·y** *adj.*

sum·mer·house (sum'ər·hous') *n.* A rustic structure, as in a garden, for rest or shade.

sum·mer·sault (sum'ər·sôlt) See SOMERSAULT.

summer school A school, college, or university offering courses during the summer vacation period.

sum·mer·time (sum'ər·tīm') *n.* Summer; the summer season. Also **sum'mer·tide'.**

sum·mit (sum'it) *n.* **1.** The highest part; the top; vertex. **2.** The highest degree; maximum. **3.** The highest level or rank, as of government officials: a meeting at the *summit.* **4.** A meeting or discussion among the highest executives of government, esp. chiefs of state; also, the place where such a meeting is held. — *adj.* Of, pertaining to, or characterized by diplomacy at the highest level. [< OF < L *summum*, neut. of *summus* highest] — **sum'mit·al** *adj.*
— Syn. **1.** acme, climax, peak, pinnacle, apex, zenith.

sum·mit·ry (sum'ə·trē) *n.* The practice of conducting diplomacy by means of conferences between the highest executives of government, esp. chiefs of state.

sum·mon (sum'ən) *v.t.* **1.** To order to come; send for. **2.** To call together; cause to convene, as a legislative assembly. **3.** To order (a person) to appear in court by a summons. **4.** To call forth or into action; arouse: usu. with *up*: to *summon up* courage. **5.** To bid or call on for a specific act: The garrison was *summoned* to surrender. [< AF, OF < L *subsecretly + monere* to warn]

sum·mon·er (sum'ən·ər) *n.* **1.** One who summons. **2.** Archaic An officer who summons persons to appear in court.

sum·mons (sum'ənz) *n., pl.* **sum·mon·ses** (sum'ən·zəz) **1.** A call to attend or act at a particular place or time. **2.** *Law* A notice to a defendant summoning him to appear in court; any citation issued to a party to an action to appear before a court or judge at chambers. **3.** A notice to a person requiring him to appear in court as a witness or as a juror. **4.** A military demand to surrender. **5.** Any signal or sound that is a peremptory call.

sum·mum bo·num (sum'əm bō'nəm) *Latin* The chief, supreme, or highest good.

sump (sump) *n.* **1.** A small well, pit, or cavity to receive liquid wastes or serve as a reservoir for lubricating oil. **2.** A cesspool or other reservoir for drainage. [< MDu. *sump* marsh]

sump·ter (sump'tər) *n.* A pack animal; beast of bu[rden]. [< OF *sometier* driver of a pack horse]

sump·tu·ar·y (sump'chōo·er'ē) *adj.* Pertaining to exp[enses,] limiting or regulating expenditure, as some laws. [< *sumptus* expenditure]

sump·tu·ous (sump'chōo·əs) *adj.* **1.** Involving or sho[wing] lavish expenditure. **2.** Luxurious; magnificent. [See S[UMP-]TUARY.] — **sump'tu·ous·ly** *adv.* — **sump'tu·ous·ness**

sun (sun) *n.* **1.** The star that is the center of attractio[n,] the main source of radiant energy in the solar system, w[ith a] mean distance from the earth of about 93 million mil[es, a] diameter of 864,000 miles, and a mass 332,000 times th[at of] the earth. ◆ Collateral adjectives: *heliacal, solar.* **2.** [A] star, esp. one that is the center of a system revolving ar[ound] it. **3.** Sunshine. **4.** Anything brilliant and magnificen[t.] The time of the earth's revolution around the sun; a [year.] **6.** The daily appearance of the sun; a day; also, the tim[e of] its appearance or shining; sunrise. — **a place in the su[n]** A dominant position in international affairs. **2.** A po[sition] in the spotlight; publicity. — *v.* **sunned, sun·ning** *v.t.* **1.** To expose to the light or heat of the sun. **2.** To warm [or dry] (something) in the sun. — *v.i.* **3.** To bask in the sun. [OE *sunne*]

Sun may appear as a combining form or as the element in two-word phrases, with the following mean[ings:]
1. Of the sun: of sunshine:

sun blaze	sunland	sun worship[er]
sun-eclipsing	sun lover	sun worship[ing]
sun glare	sun-loving	sun-worship[]

2. By or with the sun:

sun-arrayed	sun-browned	sun-heated
sun-bake	sun-cracked	sun-kissed
sun-baked	sun-dappled	sunlit
sun-blanched	sun-dried	sun-scorche[d]
sun-blind	sun-dry	sun-scorchin[g]
sun-blinded	sun-filled	sun-streake[d]
sun-blistered	sun-flooded	sun-warmed
sun-brown	sun-gilt	sun-withere[d]

sun bath Exposure of the body to the direct rays of the [sun.]

sun-bathe (sun'bāth') *v.i.* **-bathed, -bath·ing** To ba[the in] the sun, esp., as a method of tanning the skin. — **bath'er** *n.* — **sun'bath'ing** *n.*

sun·beam (sun'bēm') *n.* A ray or beam of the sun; from the sun in a visible path.

Sun·belt (sun'belt') *n.* The southern part of the U.S.[, from] Virginia to southern California: also **sun'belt'.**

sun·bon·net (sun'bon'it) *n.* A bonnet of light mat[erial] with projecting brim and sometimes a cape over the nec[k.]

sun·burn (sun'bûrn') *n.* Discoloration or inflammati[on of] the skin from exposure to the sun. — *v.t. & v.i.* **·burn[ed or] ·burnt, ·burn·ing** To affect or be affected with sunbur[n.]

sun·burst (sun'bûrst') *n.* **1.** A strong burst of sunlig[ht] through rifted clouds. **2.** A jewelled brooch, etc., with [gems] shooting forth in all directions from a central disk.

sun·dae (sun'dē, -dā) *n.* A refreshment made of ice cr[eam,] crushed fruit, syrup, nuts, etc. [Prob. < SUNDAY]

Sun·day (sun'dē, -dā) *n.* The first day of the week[; the] Christian Sabbath. [OE < *sunnan* of the sun + *dæg* [day]]

Sunday school A school in which religious instructi[on is] given on Sunday, esp., to the young; also, the teachers [and] pupils collectively.

sun deck An exposed surface or platform suitable for [sun-]bathing, as on a ship or building; sun roof.

sun·der (sun'dər) *v.t.* **1.** To break apart; disunite; sever. — *v.i.* **2.** To be parted or severed. — *n.* Division into parts; separation. — **in sunder** Separate from other parts; apart. [OE *syndrian sundrian*] — **sun'der·ance** *n.*

sun·di·al (sun'dī'əl) *n.* A device that shows the time of day by the shadow of a gnomon thrown on a dial.

SUNDIAL
g Gnomo[n]

sun·down (sun'doun') *n.* *Chiefly U.S.* Sunset.

sun·down·er (sun'dou'nər) *n.* *Informal* A tramp.

sun·dries (sun'drēz) *n.pl.* Items or things too small or numerous to be separately specified. [< SUNDRY]

sun·dry (sun'drē) *adj.* Of an indefinite small number; ous; several; miscellaneous. [OE *syndrig* separate]

sun·fish (sun'fish') *n., pl.* **·fish** or **·fish·es 1.** Any of va[rious] large oceanic fishes having a deep, compressed body t[runcated] cated in the rear, and tough, leathery flesh. **2.** A[ny of a] family of North American fresh-water fishes.

sun·flow·er (sun'flou'ər) *n.* Any of various tall, stout h[erbs] with large leaves and circular heads of bright yellow flo[wers.]

Sunflower State Nickname of Kansas.

sung (sung) Past participle and occasional past ten[se of] SING.

Sung (soong) *n.* A dynasty in Chinese history, 960 to 1[279,] noted for its achievements in art and philosophy.

ı·glass (sun′glas′, -gläs′) *n.* **1.** *pl.* Spectacles that pro
-t the eyes from the glare of the sun by their colored lenses.
A burning glass.

ık (sungk) Past participle and alternative past tense of
ıK.

ık·en (sung′kən) Obsolete past participle of SINK. —
ı. **1.** Deeply depressed or fallen in; hollow: a *sunken*
eek. **2.** Located beneath the surface of the ground or the
ter. **3.** At a lower level: *sunken* gardens.

ı lamp A lamp radiating ultraviolet rays, used for therautic treatments or to acquire a sun tan.

ı·less (sun′lis) *adj.* **1.** Lacking sun or sunlight; overcast;
rk. **2.** Cheerless; gloomy. **— sun′less·ness** *n.*

ı·light (sun′līt) *n.* The light of the sun.

ı·ny (sun′ē) *adj.* **·ni·er, ·ni·est** **1.** Filled with the light
d warmth of the sun; also, exposed to the sun. **2.** Of or
embling the sun or sunlight. **3.** Bright; genial; cheery:
unny smile. **— sun′ni·ly** *adv.* **— sun′ni·ness** *n.*

ıny side **1.** The side, as of a hill, facing the sun. **2.** The
eerful view of any situation, question, etc.

ı parlor A room enclosed in glass and having a sunny exsure. Also **sun porch.**

ı·rise (sun′rīz′) *n.* **1.** The daily first appearance of the
ı above the horizon, with the atmospheric phenomena just
fore and after. **2.** The time at which the sun rises.

ı·set (sun′set′) *n.* **1.** The apparent daily descent of the
ı below the horizon. **2.** The time when the sun sets; the
·ly evening. **3.** The colors in the sky at sunset.

ı·shade (sun′shād′) *n.* Something used as a shade or
otection from the sun, as a parasol, an awning, etc.

ı·shine (sun′shīn′) *n.* **1.** The shining light of the sun;

the direct rays of the sun. **2.** The warmth of the sun's rays.
3. Brightness; cheerfulness. **— sun′shin′y** *adj.*

Sunshine State Nickname of Florida, New Mexico, and
South Dakota.

sun·spot (sun′spot′) *n. Astron.* One of many dark irregular
spots appearing periodically on the sun's surface.

sun·stroke (sun′strōk′) *n. Pathol.* A sudden onset of high
fever induced by exposure to the sun and often marked by
convulsions and coma. **— sun′struck′** (-struk′) *adj.*

sun tan A bronze-colored condition of the skin, produced
by exposure to the sun. **— sun′-tanned′** (-tand′) *adj.*

sun·up (sun′up′) *n. Chiefly U.S.* Sunrise.

sup¹ (sup) *v.t. & v.i.* **supped, sup·ping** To take (fluid food)
in successive mouthfuls, a little at a time; sip. **— n.** A
mouthful or taste of liquid or semiliquid food. [OE *sūpan*]

sup² (sup) *v.* **supped, sup·ping** *v.i.* To eat supper. [< OF
soper, super]

sup- Var. of SUB-.

su·per¹ (soō′pər) *n. Informal* A superintendent (def. 2).

su·per² (soō′pər) *n. Slang* A supernumerary (def. 2).

su·per³ (soō′pər) *n.* An article of superior size or quality;
also, such size or quality. **— adj.** *Slang* First-rate; superfine. [Short for SUPERIOR]

super- *prefix* **1.** Above in position; over: *superstructure.*
2. Above or beyond; more than: *supersonic.* **3.** Excessively:
supersaturate. **4.** Greater than or superior to others of its
class: *superhighway.* **5.** Extra; additional: *supertax.* [< L
super- < *super* above, beyond]

In the following list of words *super-* denotes excess or
superiority, as *supercritical* excessively critical, *superexcellence* superior excellence.

erabhor	superconformity	superextension	superlenient	superreliance
erabominable	superconfusion	superfecundity	superlie	superremuneration
erabsurd	supercongestion	superfeminine	superlogical	superrespectable
eraccession	superconservative	superfervent	superloyal	superresponsible
eraccommodating	supercontrol	superfoliation	superlucky	superrestriction
eraccomplished	supercordial	superfolly	superluxurious	superreward
eraccumulate	supercritic	superformal	supermagnificently	superrighteous
erachievement	supercritical	superformation	supermanhood	superromantic
eracquisition	supercultivated	superformidable	supermarvelous	supersacrifice
eracute	supercurious	superfriendly	supermasculine	supersafe
eradaptable	supercynical	superfructified	supermechanical	supersagacious
eradequate	superdainty	superfulfillment	supermediocre	supersanguine
eradmiration	superdanger	supergaiety	supermental	supersarcastic
eradorn	superdeclamatory	supergallant	supermentality	supersatisfaction
eraffluence	superdeficit	supergenerosity	supermetropolitan	superscholarly
eragency	superdejection	superglorious	supermishap	superscientific
eraggravation	superdelicate	supergoodness	supermodest	supersensitive
eragitation	superdemand	supergovernment	supermoisten	supersensitiveness
erambitious	superdemonic	supergratification	supermorose	supersensuousness
erangelic	superdesirous	supergravitation	supermundane	supersentimental
erappreciation	superdevelopment	superhandsome	supermystery	superserious
erarbitrary	superdevilish	superhearty	supernecessity	supersevere
erarduous	superdevotion	superhero	supernegligent	supersignificant
erarrogant	superdiabolical	superheroic	supernotable	supersimplify
eraspiration	superdifficult	superhistorical	supernumerous	supersmart
erastonish	superdiplomacy	superhypocrite	superobedience	supersolemn
erattachment	superdistribution	superideal	superobese	supersolemnly
erattraction	superdividend	superignorant	superobjectionable	supersolicitation
erattractive	superdonation	superillustrate	superobligation	superspecialize
erbelief	supereconomy	superimpending	superobstinate	superspiritual
erbeloved	supereffective	superimpersonal	superoffensive	superspirituality
erbenefit	supereffluence	superimportant	superofficious	superstimulation
erbenevolent	superelastic	superimprobable	superofficiousness	superstoical
erbenign	superelated	superimproved	superopposition	superstrain
erbias	superelegance	superincentive	superoratorical	superstrenuous
erblessed	supereligible	superinclination	superordinary	superstrict
erblunder	supereloquent	superinclusive	superorganize	superstrong
erbold	superemphasis	superinconsistent	superornamental	superstylish
erbrave	superendorsement	superindependent	superoutput	supersufficient
erbusy	superendow	superindifference	superpatient	supersurprise
ercandid	superenforcement	superindignant	superpatriotic	supersweet
ercapable	superenrollment	superindividualism	superpatriotism	supertension
ercatastrophe	superestablishment	superindividualist	superperfection	superthankful
ercatholic	superesthetic	superindulgence	superpious	superthorough
ercaution	superethical	superindustrious	superplease	supertoleration
erce remonious	superevident	superinference	superpolite	supertragic
erchivalrous	superexacting	superinfinite	superpositive	supertrivial
ercivil	superexalt	superinfirmity	superpraise	superugly
ercivilized	superexaltation	superinfluence	superprecise	superunity
erclassified	superexcellence	superingenious	superpreparation	superurgent
ercolossal	superexcellent	superinitiative	superpressure	supervexation
ercombination	superexcitation	superinjustice	superproduce	supervigilant
ercommendation	superexcited	superinquisitive	superprosperous	supervigorous
ercommercial	superexcitement	superinsistent	superpublicity	supervirulent
ercompetition	superexiguity	superintellectual	superpure	supervital
ercomplex	superexpansion	superintolerable	superpurgation	supervolume
ercomprehension	superexpectation	superjurisdiction	superradical	superwise
ercompression	superexpenditure	superjustification	superrational	superworldly
erconfident	superexpressive	superknowledge	super-refined	superwrought
erconformist	superexquisiteness	superlaborious	superreform	superzealous

su·per·a·ble (sōo′pər-ə-bəl) *adj.* That can be surmounted, overcome, or conquered. [< L < *superare* to overcome]

su·per·a·bun·dant (sōo′pər-ə-bun′dənt) *adj.* More than sufficient; excessive. — **su′per·a·bun′dance** *n.* — **su′per·a·bun′dant·ly** *adv.*

su·per·an·nu·ate (sōo′pər-an′yōo-āt) *v.t.* ·at·ed, ·at·ing 1. To permit to retire on a pension on account of age or infirmity. 2. To set aside or discard as obsolete or too old. [< Med.L < L *super* beyond + *annus* year]

su·per·an·nu·at·ed (sōo′pər-an′yōo-ā′tid) *adj.* 1. Retired on account of age, esp. with a pension. 2. Too old to be useful or efficient. 3. Obsolete; outdated.

su·perb (sōo-pûrb′, sə-) *adj.* 1. Having grand, impressive beauty; majestic; imposing. 2. Luxurious; rich and costly; elegant. 3. Very good; supremely fine. [< L *superbus* proud] — **su·perb′ly** *adv.* — **su·perb′ness** *n.*

su·per·car·go (sōo′pər-kär′gō) *n.* *pl.* ·goes or ·gos An agent on board ship in charge of the cargo and its sale and purchase. [< L *super-* over + CARGO]

su·per·charge (*v.* sōo′pər-chärj′; *n.* sōo′pər-chärj′) *v.t.* ·charged, ·charg·ing 1. To adapt (an engine) to develop more power by fitting with a supercharger. 2. To charge to excess; overload. — *n.* An excess charge.

su·per·charg·er (sōo′pər-chär′jər) *n.* *Mech.* A compressor for supplying air or combustible mixture to an internal-combustion engine at a pressure greater than that developed by the suction of the pistons alone.

su·per·cil·i·ous (sōo′pər-sil′ē-əs) *adj.* Exhibiting haughty contempt or indifference; arrogant. [< L *supercilium* eyebrow] — **su′per·cil′i·ous·ly** *adv.* — **su′per·cil′i·ous·ness** *n.*

su·per·con·duc·tiv·i·ty (sōo′pər-kon′duk-tiv′ə-tē) *n.* *Physics.* The property, exhibited by certain substances, of becoming almost perfect conductors of electricity at temperatures close to absolute zero. — **su′per·con·duc′tive** (-kən-duk′tiv) *adj.* — **su′per·con·duc′tor** *n.*

su·per·e·go (sōo′pər-ē′gō, -eg′ō) *n.* *Psychoanal.* The part of the psyche that acts to secure the conformity of the ego to parental, social, and moral standards.

su·per·em·i·nent (sōo′pər-em′ə-nənt) *adj.* Excelling or surpassing others; of a superior or remarkable quality. [< L *supereminere* to rise above] — **su′per·em′i·nence** *n.* — **su′per·em′i·nent·ly** *adv.*

su·per·er·o·gate (sōo′pər-er′ə-gāt) *v.i.* ·gat·ed, ·gat·ing To do more than is required or ordered. [< L *super-* over and above + *erogare* to pay out] — **su′per·er′o·ga′tion** *n.* — **su′per·e·rog′a·to′ry** (-ə-rog′ə-tôr′ē, -tō′rē) *adj.*

su·per·fi·cial (sōo′pər-fish′əl) *adj.* 1. Of, lying near, or forming the surface; affecting only the surface. 2. Of only the ordinary and the obvious; shallow: a *superficial* writer. 3. Marked by partial knowledge; cursory; hasty; slight: a *superficial* analysis. 4. Not real or genuine: a *superficial* likeness. 5. Square: said of measure. [< LL < L *super-* over + *ficies* face] — **su′per·fi′ci·al′i·ty** (-fish′ē-al′ə-tē), **su′per·fi′cial·ness** *n.* — **su′per·fi′cial·ly** *adv.*

su·per·fine (sōo′pər-fīn′) *adj.* 1. Of surpassing fineness and delicacy; of the best quality. 2. Overrefined; unduly elaborate; overnice. — **su′per·fine′ness** *n.*

su·per·flu·id (*n.* sōo′pər-flōo′id; *adj.* sōo′pər-flōo′id) *n.* *Physics.* Matter, as helium, cooled to within a degree of absolute zero, and characterized by an exceptional heat conductivity, a ready permeation of very dense substances, and the ability to flow upward against gravity. — *adj.* Of or pertaining to such a state.

su·per·flu·i·ty (sōo′pər-flōo′ə-tē) *n.* *pl.* ·ties 1. The state of being superfluous. 2. That which is superfluous. 3. Superabundance; plenty. [< OF < L *super-* over + *fluere* to flow]

su·per·flu·ous (sōo-pûr′flōo-əs) *adj.* 1. Exceeding what is needed; excessively abundant; surplus. 2. Unnecessary; uncalled for; irrelevant: a *superfluous* question. — **su·per′flu·ous·ly** *adv.* — **su·per′flu·ous·ness** *n.*

su·per·heat (*v.* sōo′pər-hēt′; *n.* sōo′pər-hēt′) *v.t.* 1. To heat to excess; overheat. 2. To raise the temperature of (a gas or vapor not in contact with water) above the saturation point for a given pressure. 3. To heat (a liquid) above the boiling point for a given pressure, but without conversion into vapor. — *n.* The degree to which steam has been superheated, or the heat so imparted. — **su′per·heat′er** *n.*

su·per·het·er·o·dyne (sōo′pər-het′ər-ə-dīn′) *adj.* *Electronics.* Pertaining to or designating a type of radio reception using heterodyne circuits between stages of amplification. Also **su′per·het′.** — *n.* A superheterodyne receiver. [< SUPER- (SONIC) + HETERODYNE]

su·per·high·way (sōo′pər-hī′wā′) *n.* A highway for high-speed traffic, generally with four or more traffic lanes divided by a safety strip.

su·per·hu·man (sōo′pər-hyōo′mən) *adj.* 1. Above the range of human power or skill; miraculous or divine. 2. Beyond normal human ability or power. — **su′per·hu·man′i·ty** (-hyōo·man′ə-tē) *n.* — **su′per·hu′man·ly** *adv.*

su·per·im·pose (sōo′pər-im-pōz′) *v.t.* ·posed, ·pos·ing To lay or impose upon something else. 2. To add to so thing else. — **su′per·im′po·si′tion** (-im′pə-zish′ən) *n.*

su·per·in·duce (sōo′pər-in-dōos′, -dyōos′) *v.t.* ·duced, ·ing To introduce additionally; bring in or cause as an a tion. — **su′per·in·duc′tion** (-duk′shən) *n.*

su·per·in·tend (sōo′pər-in-tend′) *v.t.* To have the ch and direction of; manage; supervise. [< LL < *super-* + *intendere* to aim at] — **su′per·in·ten′dence** *n.*

su·per·in·ten·dent (sōo′pər-in-ten′dənt) *n.* 1. One wh function is to superintend some particular work, office undertaking. 2. A person charged with supervising m tenance and repair in an office or apartment building. *adj.* Of or pertaining to superintendence or a superin dent; superintending. [< LL < *superintendere* to supe tend] — **su′per·in·ten′den·cy** *n.*

su·pe·ri·or (sə-pir′ē-ər, sōo-) *adj.* 1. Surpassing in quan quality, or degree; more excellent; preferable. 2. Of g worth or excellence; extraordinary. 3. Of higher gr rank, or dignity. 4. Too great or dignified to be influen serenely indifferent: with *to*: *superior* to envy. 5. Affec superiority; supercilious; disdainful. 6. Locally hig more elevated; upper. 7. *Printing* Set above the line C⁴Dⁿ, 4 and n are *superior.* — *n.* 1. One who surpa another in rank or excellence. 2. The ruler of an ecclesi cal order or house, as a convent, or monastery. [< OF < *super* above] — **su·pe′ri·or′i·ty** (sə-pir′ē-ôr′ə-tē, -sōo-) *n.* — **su·pe′ri·or·ly** *adv.*

su·per·la·tive (sə-pûr′lə-tiv, sōo-) *adj.* 1. Elevated to highest degree; of supreme excellence or eminence. 2. G Expressing the extreme degree of comparison of adjectiv adverbs. See COMPARISON (def. 3). 3. Excessive. — *n.* That which is superlative. 2. *Gram.* a The highest degre comparison of the adjective or adverb. b Any word or ph in this degree. [< OF < LL < L *super-* above + *l* pp. of *ferre* to carry] — **su·per′la·tive·ly** *adv.* — **su·pe tive·ness** *n.*

su·per·man (sōo′pər-man′) *n.* *pl.* ·men (-men′) 1. A pothetical superior being, regarded as the product of ev tionary survival of the fittest. 2. A man possessing su human powers. [Trans. of G *übermensch*]

su·per·mar·ket (sōo′pər-mär′kit) *n.* A large store sel food and household supplies and operating on a self-ser cash-and-carry basis. Also **super market.**

su·per·nal (sōo-pûr′nəl) *adj.* 1. Heavenly; celestial. Placed or located above; lofty; overhead; towering. [< < L *super-* over] — **su·per′nal·ly** *adv.*

su·per·nat·u·ral (sōo′pər-nach′ər-əl) *adj.* 1. Existin occurring through some agency beyond the known forc nature. 2. Believed to be miraculous or caused by the mediate exercise of divine power. 3. Of the miraculous. *n.* 1. That which is supernatural. 2. The action or ir vention of something supernatural: with *the.* [< Med. L *super-* above + *natura* (< *nasci* to be born)] — **su nat′u·ral·ly** *adv.* — **su′per·nat′u·ral·ness** *n.*

— **Syn.** (adj.) 1. A *supernatural* event is literally not boun explainable by known natural laws. *Preternatural* refers to which is superlative in degree, but not outside the known real nature: to display *preternatural* insight into a situation. Anyt *miraculous* is so marvellous or extraordinary that it is usu attributed to divine agency.

su·per·nat·u·ral·ism (sōo′pər-nach′ər-əl-iz′əm) *n.* 1. quality of being supernatural. 2. Belief in the doctrine a supernatural power guides the natural order. — **su nat′u·ral·ist** *adj. & n.* — **su′per·nat′u·ral·is′tic** *adj.*

su·per·nu·mer·ar·y (sōo′pər-nōo′mə-rer′ē, -nyōo′-) *adj* Being beyond a fixed or standard number. 2. Beyor customary or necessary number; superfluous. — *n.* *pl.* ies 1. A supernumerary person or thing. 2. A stage former, as in crowd scenes, without any speaking part. LL < L *super* over + *numerus* number]

su·per·pose (sōo′pər-pōz′) *v.t.* ·posed, ·pos·ing To lay or upon something else, as one layer upon another. [< *super-* over + *poser* to put] — **su′per·pos′a·ble** *adj* **su′per·po·si′tion** (-pə-zish′ən) *n.*

su·per·sat·u·rate (sōo′pər-sach′ōo-rāt) *v.t.* ·rat·ed, ·rat To saturate (a solution) beyond the point normal und given temperature. — **su′per·sat′u·ra′tion** *n.*

su·per·scribe (sōo′pər-skrīb′) *v.t.* ·scribed, ·scrib·in To write or engrave on the outside or upper part of. 2. inscribe with a name or address, as a letter. [< LL < L *per-* over + *scribere* to write] — **su′per·scrip′tion** (-sk shən) *n.*

su·per·script (sōo′pər-skript′) *adj.* Written above or o head. — *n.* 1. A superscript character. 2. *Math.* A c acter written above and to the right or left of a term to i cate a specific operation or characteristic of the term.

su·per·sede (sōo′pər-sēd′) *v.t.* ·sed·ed, ·sed·ing 1. To the place of, as by reason of superior worth, right, or ap priateness; replace; supplant. 2. To put something in place of; set aside; suspend; annul. [< OF < L < *sup*

ve, over + *sedere* to sit] — **su′per·sed′er** *n.* — **su′per·
ure** (-sē′jər), **su′per·ses′sion** (-sesh′ən) *n.*

er·son·ic (sōō′pər·son′ik) *adj.* 1. *Aeron.* Of, pertain-
to, or characterized by a speed greater than that of
nd. 2. Ultrasonic.

er·son·ics (sōō′pər·son′iks) *n.pl.* (construed as sing.)
· science that treats of supersonic speed.

er·sti·tion (sōō′pər·stish′ən) *n.* 1. A belief founded on
tional feelings, esp. of fear, and marked by a trust in
rms, omens, the supernatural, etc.; also, any rite or prac-
inspired by such belief. 2. Any unreasonable belief.
OF < L < *super-* over + *stare* to stand still]
er·sti·tious (sōō′pər·stish′əs) *adj.* 1. Disposed to be-
e in superstitions. 2. Of or manifesting superstition.
·er·sti′tious·ly *adv.* — **su′per·sti′tious·ness** *n.*

er·struc·ture (sōō′pər·struk′chər) *n.* 1. Any struc-
· or part of a structure considered in relation to its foun-
.on. 2. *Naut.* The parts of a ship's structure, as of a war-
·, above the main deck.

er·tax (sōō′pər·taks′) *n.* An extra tax in addition to
normal tax; a surtax.

er·vene (sōō′pər·vēn′) *v.i.* **·vened, ·ven·ing** 1. To fol-
closely upon something; come as something extraneous
·dditional. 2. To take place; happen. [< L < *super-*
· and above + *venire* to come] — **su′per·ven′ient**
n′yənt) *adj.* — **su′per·ven′tion** (-ven′shən) *n.*

er·vise (sōō′pər·vīz) *v.t.* **·vised, vis·ing** To have charge
lirecting (employees, an operation, etc.); superintend;
rsee. [< Med.L < L *super-* over + *videre* to see]

er·vi·sion (sōō′pər·vizh′ən) *n.* 1. The act of superg-
ng; superintendence. 2. The authority to supervise.

er·vi·sor (sōō′pər·vī′zər) *n.* 1. One who supervises or
rsees; superintendent; inspector; administrative officer.
A person supervising teachers of special subjects in a
.ool. — **su′per·vi′sor·ship** *n.* — **su′per·vi′so·ry** *adj.*

ine (sōō·pīn′) *adj.* 1. Lying on the back, or with the
· turned upward. 2. Inactive; indolent; listless. [< L
inus] — **su·pine′ly** *adv.* — **su·pine′ness** *n.*

per (sup′ər) *n.* The last meal of the day; the evening
l. [< OF *soper* to sup, dine] — **sup′per·less** *adj.*

plant (sə·plant′, -plänt′) *v.t.* 1. To take the place of;
lace. 2. To take the place of (someone) by scheming,
chery, etc. 3. To replace (one thing) with another; re-
ve; uproot. [< OF < L *supplantare* to trip up < *sub-*
from below + *planta* the sole of the foot] — **sup·plan·**
ion (sup′lan·tā′shən) *n.* — **sup·plant′er** *n.*

ple (sup′əl) *adj.* **sup·pler** (sup′lər), **sup·plest** (sup′ləst)
Easily bent; flexible; pliant. 2. Yielding to the humor or
hes of others; esp., servilely compliant. 3. Showing
ptability of mind. — *v.t. & v.i.* **·pled, ·pling** To make or
ome supple. [< OF < L < *sub-* under + stem of *plicare*
old] — **sup′ple·ly** *adv.* — **sup′ple·ness** *n.*

ple·ment (*v.* sup′lə·ment; *n.* sup′lə·mənt) *v.t.* To make
itions to; provide for what is lacking in. — *n.* 1. Some-
g that supplements; esp. an addition to a publication.
A supplementary angle. [See SUPPLY[1].]

ple·men·tal (sup′lə·men′təl) *adj.* Additional.

ple·men·ta·ry (sup′lə·men′tər·ē) *adj.* Functioning as
pplement; supplemental.

plementary angle *Geom.* Either of two angles whose
· is 180°: also called *supplement.*

pli·ant (sup′lē·ənt) *adj.* 1. Entreating earnestly and
ably; beseeching. 2. Manifesting entreaty or supplica-
· — *n.* One who supplicates. [< MF < L. See SUP-
CATE.] — **sup′pli·ant·ly** *adv.* — **sup′pli·ant·ness** *n.*

pli·cant (sup′lə·kənt) *n.* One who supplicates. — *adj.*
treating humbly; beseeching. [See SUPPLICATE.]

pli·cate (sup′lə·kāt) *v.* **·cat·ed, ·cat·ing** *v.t.* 1. To ask
humbly or by earnest prayer. 2. To beg something of;
reat. — *v.i.* 3. To beg or pray humbly. [< L < *sub-*
ler + *plicare* to bend, fold] — **sup′pli·ca′tion** *n.* —
·′pli·ca·to′ry (-kə·tôr′ē, -tō′rē) *adj.*

ply[1] (sə·plī′) *v.t.* **·plied, ·ply·ing** 1. To give or fur-
(something needful or desirable). 2. To furnish with
at is needed: to *supply* an army with ammunition. 3. To
vide for adequately; satisfy: to *supply* a demand. 4. To
ke good or compensate for, as a loss or deficiency. 5.
fill (the place of another); also, to fill (an office, etc.) or
upy (a pulpit) as a substitute. — *v.i.* 6. To take the
ce of another temporarily. — *n.* *pl.* **·plies** 1. That
ich is or can be supplied. 2. An amount sufficient for a
en use; store or quantity on hand. 3. *Usu. pl.* Accumu-
d stores reserved for distribution, as for an army. 4.
n. The amount of a commodity offered at a given price
available for meeting a demand. 5. A substitute or tem-
ary incumbent. 6. The act of supplying. [< OF < L
sub- up from under + *ple-*, root of *plenus* full]
·ply[2] (sup′lē) *adv.* In a supple manner; supplely.

sup·port (sə·pôrt′, -pōrt′) *v.t.* 1. To bear the weight of. 2.
To hold in position. 3. To bear or sustain (weight, etc.). 4.
To keep (a person, the mind, etc.) from failing or declining.
5. To serve to uphold or corroborate (a statement, etc.). 6.
To provide (a person, institution, etc.) with maintenance.
7. To give approval or assistance to; uphold. 8. To tolerate: I cannot *support* his insolence. 9. To carry on; keep
up: to *support* a war. 10. In the theater: **a** To act (a part).
b To act in a subordinate role to. — *n.* 1. The act of supporting, or the state of being supported. 2. One who or that
which supports. 3. Subsistence. [< OF < L < *sub-* up
from under + *portare* to carry]

sup·port·a·ble (sə·pôr′tə·bəl, -pōr′-) *adj.* Capable of being
supported or endured; bearable; endurable. — **sup·port′a·
ble·ness, sup·port′a·bil′i·ty** *n.* — **sup·port′a·bly** *adv.*

sup·port·er (sə·pôr′tər, -pōr′-] *n.* 1. One who or that which
supports. 2. An adherent. 3. An elastic or other support
for some part of the body. — **Syn.** See ADHERENT.

sup·pose (sə·pōz′) *v.* **·posed, ·pos·ing** *v.t.* 1. To think or
imagine to oneself as true. 2. To believe or believe probable; think. 3. To assume as true for the sake of argument
or illustration: *Suppose* he comes late. 4. To expect or require: used in the passive: He is *supposed* to be on time. 5.
To imply as cause or consequence; presuppose. — *v.i.* 6.
To conjecture. [< OF < *sup-* under (< L *sub-*) + *poser* to
put down] — **sup·pos′a·ble** *adj.* — **sup·pos′a·bly** *adv.* —
sup·pos′er *n.*

— **Syn.** 1. We *suppose* something to be true in expectation of
finding that it is true, or in order to ascertain what follows if it is
not true. We *conjecture* or *surmise* when the evidence is admittedly
insufficient for certainty: *surmise* suggests slighter grounds for a
conclusion than *conjecture.* Also, *conjecture* suggests that the
question is one of fact, while *surmise* may refer to questions of
interpretation or evaluation.

sup·posed (sə·pōzd′, -pō′zid) *adj.* Accepted as genuine or
true, often erroneously. — **sup·pos·ed·ly** (sə·pō′zid·lē) *adv.*

sup·po·si·tion (sup′ə·zish′ən) *n.* 1. The act of supposing.
2. That which is supposed. — **Syn.** See HYPOTHESIS. [<
Med.L < L < *sub-* under + *ponere* to place] — **sup′po·si′
tion·al** *adj.* — **sup′po·si′tion·al·ly** *adv.*

sup·pos·i·to·ry (sə·poz′ə·tôr′ē, -tō′rē) *n.* *pl.* **·ries** *Med.*
A solid, readily fusible, medicated preparation for introduction into the rectum, vagina, or urethra. [< LL < L < *sub-*
under + *ponere* to place]

sup·press (sə·pres′) *v.t.* 1. To put an end or stop to; quell;
crush, as a rebellion. 2. To stop or prohibit the activities of;
also, to abolish. 3. To withhold from knowledge or publication, as a book, news, etc. 4. To repress, as a groan or sigh.
5. To check or stop (a hemorrhage, etc.). [< L < *sub-*
under + *premere* to press] — **sup·press′er** or **sup·pres′sor**
n. — **sup·press′i·ble** *adj.* — **sup·pres′sive** *adj.*

sup·pres·sion (sə·presh′ən) *n.* 1. The act of suppressing,
or the state of being suppressed. 2. *Psychoanal.* The deliberate exclusion from consciousness and action of an idea,
emotion, or desire.

sup·pu·rate (sup′yə·rāt) *v.i.* **·rat·ed, ·rat·ing** To form or
generate pus; maturate. [< L < *sub-* under + *pus* pus]
— **sup′pu·ra′tion** *n.* — **sup′pu·ra′tive** *adj. & n.*

supra- *prefix* Above; beyond. [< L]

su·pra·re·nal (sōō′prə·rē′nəl) *Anat. adj.* 1. Situated above
the kidneys. 2. Of or pertaining to the suprarenal glands.
— *n.* A suprarenal gland. [< NL < L *supra-* above + *renes*
kidneys]

suprarenal gland *Anat.* An adrenal gland.

su·prem·a·cy (sə·prem′ə·sē, sōō-) *n.* *pl.* **·cies** 1. The state
of being supreme. 2. Supreme power or authority.

su·preme (sə·prēm′, sōō-) *adj.* 1. Highest in power or authority. 2. Highest in degree, importance, quality, etc.; utmost: *supreme* devotion. 3. Ultimate; last; final. [< L
super above] — **su·preme′ly** *adv.* — **su·preme′ness** *n.*

Supreme Being God.

Supreme Court In the U.S. and in various States, a court
of appellate jurisdiction and, in most cases, of last resort.

Supreme Soviet The highest legislative body of the Soviet
Union, consisting of two chambers, the **Soviet of the Union**
and the **Soviet of Nationalities.**

sur-[1] *prefix* Above; beyond; over: *surcharge; surcoat.* [<
OF < L *super* above]

sur-[2] Assimilated var. of SUB-.

su·rah (sŏŏr′ə) *n.* A soft, usu. twilled fabric of silk or silk
and rayon. Also **surah silk.** [after *Surat,* India]

sur·cease (sûr·sēs′, sûr′sēs) *Archaic n.* Absolute cessation;
end. — *v.t. & v.i.* **·ceased, ·ceas·ing** To cease; end. [< AF
< L < *super-* above + *sedere* to sit]

sur·charge (*n.* sûr′chärj; *v.* sûr·chärj′) *n.* 1. An excessive
burden, load, or charge. 2. An additional or excessive
amount charged; overcharge. 3. A new valuation or something additional printed on a postage stamp. — *v.t.*

·charged, ·charg·ing 1. To overcharge. **2.** To overload. **3.** To fill to excess. **4.** To imprint a surcharge on (postage stamps). [< F < *sur*- over + CHARGE] — **sur·charg′er** *n.*

sur·cin·gle (sûr′sing·gəl) *n.* A girth or strap encircling the body of a horse, etc., as for holding a saddle. [< OF < *sur*- over + L *cingulum* belt]

sur·coat (sûr′kōt′) *n.* **1.** An outer coat. **2.** A cloaklike garment worn over armor. [< OF < *sur*- over + *cot* coat]

surd (sûrd) *n.* **1.** *Math.* An irrational number, as √2. **2.** *Phonet.* A voiceless speech sound. — *adj.* **1.** *Math.* Incapable of being expressed in rational numbers; irrational. **2.** *Phonet.* Voiceless. [< L *surdus* deaf, silent]

sure (shŏŏr) *adj.* **sur·er, sur·est 1.** Free from doubt; certain; positive. **2.** Certain of obtaining, attaining, or retaining something: with *of*. **3.** Not liable to change; firm; stable. **4.** Bound to happen; inevitable. **5.** Not liable to fail or err; infallible. **6.** Reliable; trustworthy. **7.** *Rare* Secure; safe. — **to be sure** Indeed; certainly. — **to make sure** To make certain; secure. — *adv. Informal* Surely; certainly. [< OF < L *se*- without + *cura* care] — **sure′ness** *n.*

sure-e·nough (shŏŏr′i·nuf′) *U.S. Informal adj.* Real; genuine. — *adv.* Really; surely.

sure-foot·ed (shŏŏr′fŏŏt′id) *adj.* **1.** Not liable to fall or stumble. **2.** Not liable to fail or err.

sure·ly (shŏŏr′lē) *adv.* **1.** Certainly. **2.** Securely; safely.

sure·ty (shŏŏr′tē, shŏŏr′ə·tē) *n. pl.* **·ties 1.** One who agrees to be responsible for another; esp., one who engages to be responsible for the debt or default of another. **2.** A pledge or guarantee to secure against loss, damage, default, etc.; security. **3.** That which gives or serves as a basis for security or confidence; a guarantee. **4.** The state of being sure. [< OF < L *securus*. See SURE.] — **sure′ty·ship** *n.*

surf (sûrf) *n.* The swell of the sea that breaks upon a shore; also, the foam caused by such a swell. — *v.i.* To engage in surfing. — **surf′er** *n.* [Earlier *suff*, ? var. of SOUGH] — **surf′y** *adj.*

sur·face (sûr′fis) *n.* **1.** The exterior part or face of anything. **2.** A superficial aspect; outward appearance. **3.** That which has length and breadth, but not thickness. — *adj.* **1.** Of, pertaining to, or on a surface. **2.** Superficial; exterior; apparent. — *v.* **·faced, ·fac·ing** *v.t.* **1.** To put a surface on; esp., to make smooth. — *v.i.* **2.** To rise to the surface, as a submarine. [< F < *sur*- above + FACE]

sur·face-ac·tive (sûr′fis·ak′tiv) *adj. Chem.* Pertaining to any of a class of substances that have the property of reducing the surface tension of a liquid in which they are dissolved: said esp. of detergents.

surface tension *Physics* That property of a liquid by virtue of which the surface molecules exhibit a strong inward attraction, thus forming an apparent membrane that tends to contract to the minimum area.

sur·fac·tant (sûr·fak′tənt) *n. Chem.* A surface-active agent.

surf·board (sûrf′bôrd′, -bōrd′) *n.* A long, narrow board used in surfing.

surf·boat (sûrf′bōt′) *n.* A boat of extra strength and buoyancy, for launching and landing through surf.

sur·feit (sûr′fit) *v.t.* **1.** To feed or supply to fullness or satiety; satiate. — *v.i.* **2.** To partake of anything to excess; overindulge. — *n.* **1.** Excess in eating or drinking; also, the excessive quantity partaken of. **2.** The result of such excess; satiety. **3.** Oppressive fullness caused by excess in eating or drinking. [< OF *surfaire* to overdo < *sur*- above + *faire* to make] — **sur′feit·er** *n.*

surf·ing (sûrf′ing) *n.* A water sport in which a person standing on a surfboard is borne by the surf toward the shore. Also **surf·rid·ing** (sûrf′rī′ding).

surf·rid·er (sûrf′rī′dər) *n.* One who engages in surfing.

surge (sûrj) *v.i.* **surged, surg·ing 1.** To rise high and roll onward, as waves; swell or heave. **2.** To move or go in a manner suggestive of this. **3.** To increase or vary suddenly, as an electric current. — *n.* **1.** A large swelling wave; billow; also, such billows collectively. **2.** A heaving and rolling motion, as of great waves. **3.** *Electr.* A sudden fluctuation of voltage or current due to lightning, switching, etc. [< OF < L *surgere* to rise] — **surg′er** *n.* — **surg′y** *adj.*

sur·geon (sûr′jən) *n.* One who practices surgery, as distinguished from a physician. [See SURGERY.]

Surgeon General *pl.* **Surgeons General** or **Surgeon Generals** The chief officer of the Medical Department in the United States Army or Navy.

surgeon's knot A knot used in tying ligatures, stitching up wounds, etc. For illus. see KNOT.

sur·ger·y (sûr′jər·ē) *n. pl.* **·ger·ies 1.** The branch of medical science that relates to body injuries, deformities, and diseased conditions requiring treatment by operative procedures, with or without instruments. **2.** A place where surgical treatment is given, as an operating room. **3.** The work of a surgeon. [< OF, ult. < LL < Gk. < *cheir* hand + *ergon* work]

sur·gi·cal (sûr′ji·kəl) *adj.* Of, pertaining to, or used in surgery. — **sur′gi·cal·ly** *adv.*

sur·ly (sûr′lē) *adj.* **sur·li·er, sur·li·est** Characterized by rudeness, ill-humor, or gruffness. [Earlier *sirly* < *sir* + *-ly* like] — **sur′li·ly** (-lə·lē) *adv.* — **sur′li·ness** *n.*

sur·mise (sər·mīz′; *for n., also* sûr′mīz) *v.* **·mised, ·mi** *v.t.* **1.** To infer on slight evidence; guess. — *v.i.* **2.** To r a conjecture. — **Syn.** See SUPPOSE. — *n.* **1.** A conjec made on slight evidence. **2.** The act of surmising. [< *sur*- upon + *mettre* to put < L *mittere* to send]

sur·mount (sər·mount′) *v.t.* **1.** To overcome (a diffic etc.). **2.** To mount to the top or cross to the other si (an obstacle or mountain). **3.** To be or lie over or ab **4.** To place something on top of. [< OF < Med.L *super*- over + *mons* hill, mountain] — **sur·mount′a·ble** — **sur·mount′a·ble·ness** *n.* — **sur·mount′er** *n.*

sur·name (sûr′nām′; *for v., also* sûr·nām′) *n.* The nam a person's family; the last name of a person: also called *ily name.* — *v.t.* **·named, ·nam·ing** To give a surnam call by a surname. [Alter. of obs. *surnoun* < OF < above, beyond + *nom* name < L *nomen*] — **sur′nam** *n.*

sur·pass (sər·pas′, -päs′) *v.t.* **1.** To go beyond or pa degree or amount; excel. **2.** To go beyond the reach or ers of; transcend. — **Syn.** See EXCEED. [< MF < above + PASS] — **sur·pass′a·ble** *adj.*

sur·pass·ing (sər·pas′ing, -päs′-) *adj.* Preeminently e lent; exceeding. — *adv. Poetic* Exceedingly; excelle — **sur·pass′ing·ly** *adv.* — **sur·pass′ing·ness** *n.*

sur·plice (sûr′plis) *n. Eccl.* A loose white vestment full sleeves, worn over the cassock by the clergy and of some churches. [< AF or OF < Med.L < *super-* + *pellicia* fur garment]

sur·plus (sûr′plus) *adj.* Being in excess of what is use needed. — *n.* **1.** That which remains over and above has been used or is required; excess. **2.** Assets in exce liabilities. [< OF < Med.L < *super*- over and abov *plus* more]

sur·prise (sər·prīz′) *v.t.* **·prised, ·pris·ing 1.** To cau feel wonder or astonishment because unusual or unexpe **2.** To come upon suddenly or unexpectedly; take unaw **3.** To attack or capture suddenly and without warning To lead unawares, as into doing something not inten with *into*. **5.** To elicit in this manner: They *surprise* truth from him. — *n.* **1.** The act of surprising; a co upon unawares. **2.** The state of being surprised; asto ment. **3.** That which causes surprise, as a sudden and u pected event, fact, or gift. — **to take by surprise 1.** come upon without warning or unexpectedly. **2.** To astc or amaze; astonish. [< OF < Med.L < L *super*- ove *prehendere* to take] — **sur·pris′al** *n.* — **sur·pris′er** *n.*

sur·pris·ing (sər·prī′zing) *adj.* Causing surprise or won amazing. — **sur·pris′ing·ly** *adv.* — **sur·pris′ing·ness**

sur·re·al·ism (sə·rē′əl·iz′əm) *n.* A modern moveme literature and art that attempts to express the workin the subconscious mind, characterized by the incongruou rangement and presentation of subject matter. [< F < beyond, above + *réalisme* realism] — **sur·re′al·ist** *adj.* — **sur·re′al·is·tic** *adj.* — **sur·re′al·is·ti·cal·ly** *adv.*

sur·ren·der (sə·ren′dər) *v.t.* **1.** To yield possession power over to another; give up because of compulsion. To give up; abandon, as hope. **3.** To relinquish, es favor of another. **4.** To give (oneself) over to a passior fluence, etc. — *v.i.* **5.** To give oneself up, as to an enen warfare. — *n.* The act of surrendering. [< OF < *sur*- + RENDER]

sur·rep·ti·tious (sûr′əp·tish′əs) *adj.* **1.** Accomplishe secret or improper means; clandestine. **2.** Acting sec or by stealth. — **Syn.** See STEALTHY. [< L < *sub*- under + *rapere* to snatch] — **sur′rep·ti′tious·ly** *adv.* — **sur′rep·ti′tious·ness** *n.*

sur·rey (sûr′ē) *n.* A light vehicle, having two seats, wheels, and sometimes a top. [Prob. after *Surrey*, Engl

sur·ro·gate (sûr′ə·gāt; *for n., also* sûr′ə·git) *n.* **1.** A su tute; deputy. **2.** A probate judge. — *v.t.* **·gat·ed, ·gat 1.** To put in the place of another; substitute. **2.** To app (another) to succeed oneself. [< L < *sub*- in place of other + *rogare* to ask] — **sur′ro·gate·ship** *n.*

sur·round (sə·round′) *v.t.* **1.** To extend around; be o sides of; encircle; enclose. **2.** To shut in or enclose, a emy troops, so as to cut off retreat. [< OF < LL < su over + *undare* to rise in waves < *unda* a wave]

sur·round·ing (sə·roun′ding) *n.* **1.** *pl.* That which rounds; environment; conditions of life. **2.** The act of who surrounds. — *adj.* Encompassing; enveloping.

sur·tax (sûr′taks′) *n.* An extra tax; esp., a graduate come tax over and above the usual tax, levied on the am by which net income exceeds a certain sum. — *v.t.* T sess with a surtax. [< F < *sur*- above + TAX]

sur·veil·lance (sər·vā′ləns, -vāl′yəns) *n.* **1.** Close w kept over one, as a suspect. **2.** The act of watching, o state of being watched. [< F < *sur*- over + *veille* watch < L *vigilare*] — **sur·veil′lant** *adj. & n.*

sur·vey (sər·vā′; *for n., also* sûr′vā) *v.t.* **1.** To look at {

rety; view in a general way. **2.** To look at carefully and utely; scrutinize. **3.** To determine accurately the area, tour, or boundaries of (land) by measuring lines and les according to the principles of geometry and trigonom-. **—** *v.i.* **4.** To survey land. **—** *n.* **1.** The operation, process, or results of finding the contour, area, bound-s, etc., of a surface. **2.** A general or comprehensive v. **3.** A scrutinizing view; inspection. [< AF < OF < l.L < *super-* over + *videre* to look]

vey·ing (sər·vā'ing) *n.* **1.** The science and art of deter-ing the area and configuration of portions of the surface ne earth and representing them on maps. **2.** The act of who surveys.

vey·or (sər·vā'ər) *n.* **1.** One who surveys; esp., one who eys land. **2.** One who examines a thing for the purpose scertaining its condition, quality, or character; esp., a oms officer.

eyor's measure A system of measurement used in eying and based on the chain as a unit.

viv·al (sər·vī'vəl) *n.* **1.** The act of surviving, or the e of having survived. **2.** One who or that which sur-s; esp., a custom, belief, etc., persisting in society.

ival of the fittest The principle of natural selection pplied to living organisms, societies, etc.

vive (sər·vīv') *v.* **·vived**, **·viv·ing** *v.i.* **1.** To remain e or in existence. **—** *v.t.* **2.** To live or exist beyond the h, occurrence, or end of; outlive; outlast. [< AF < OF L < *super-* above, beyond + *vivere* to live] **— sur·viv'-** adj. **— sur·viv'er, sur·vi'vor** *n.*

Assimilated var. of SUB-.

ep·ti·bil·i·ty (sə·sep tə·bil'ə·tē) *n.* *pl.* **·ties 1.** The e or quality of being susceptible. **2.** The ability to re-e or be impressed by deep emotions or strong feelings; ibility. **3.** *pl.* Sensitive emotions; feelings. **4.** *Physics* ratio of the magnetization of a material to the magnetic e producing it. **— Syn.** See SENSIBILITY.

ep·ti·ble (sə·sep'tə·bəl) *adj.* **1.** Yielding readily; ca-of being influenced, acted on, or determined; open; le: usu. with *of* or *to*. **2.** Having delicate sensibility; im-sionable. [< Med.L < L < *sub-* under + *capere* to] **— sus·cep'ti·ble·ness** *n.* **— sus·cep'ti·bly** *adv.*

ect (*v.* sə·spekt'; *adj. & n.* sus'pekt) *v.t.* **1.** To think (a on) guilty as specified on little or no evidence. **2.** To e distrust or; doubt. **3.** To have an inkling or suspicion think possible. **—** *v.i.* **4.** To have suspicions. **—** *adj.* iting, open to, or viewed with suspicion; suspected. **—**)ne who is under suspicion, esp. for a crime. [< F < L ub- from under + *specere* to look]

end (sə·spend') *v.t.* **1.** To bar for a time from a privi-office, or function as a punishment. **2.** To cause to e for a time; withhold temporarily. **3.** To hold in a e of indecision; withhold or defer action on: to *suspend* a ence. **4.** To hang from a support so as to allow free ement. **5.** To sustain in a body of nearly the same spe-gravity; keep in suspension, as dust motes in the air. **—** **6.** To stop for a time. **7.** To fail to meet obligations; payment. [< OF < L *sub-* under + *pendere* to hang]

end·er (sə·spen'dər) *n.* **1.** *pl.* *U.S.* A pair of straps n over the shoulders for supporting the trousers. **2.** A garter.

ense (sə·spens') *n.* **1.** The state of being uncertain, ecided, or insecure, usu. accompanied by anxiety, appre-ention, etc. **2.** An uncertain or doubtful situation. [< < Med.L < L *suspendere*. See SUSPEND.]

en·sion (sə·spen'shən) *n.* **1.** The act of suspending, or state of being suspended. **2.** The state of deferment. **3.** *sics* A uniform dispersion of small particles in a medium, er by mechanical agitation or by molecular forces. **4.** sation of payments in business. **5.** Any device on or n which something is suspended. **6.** *Mech.* A system of ble members, as springs in a vehicle, intended to insulate chassis and body against road shocks. **7.** *Music* The ongation of a chord tone into the succeeding chord, re it forms a momentary dissonance; also, the tone so onged. **8.** The act of debarring from an office or its ileges.

ension bridge ridge in which the lway is hung from es anchored over ers and without rvening support a below.

en·sive (sə-/siv') *adj.* **1.** ding to suspend keep in suspense.)f or character-

SUSPENSION BRIDGE
(Brooklyn Bridge, New York)

ized by suspense. **3.** Having the power of suspending op-eration: a *suspensive* veto. **— sus·pen'sive·ly** *adv.* **— sus·pen'sive·ness** *n.*

sus·pen·so·ry (sə·spen'sər·ē) *adj.* Suspending; sustaining; delaying. **—** *n.* *pl.* **·ries** A truss, bandage, or supporter.

sus·pi·cion (sə·spish'ən) *n.* **1.** The act of suspecting, or the state of one who suspects; the imagining of something wrong without proof or clear evidence. **2.** *Informal* The least par-ticle, as of a flavor. **—** *v.t.* *Dial.* To suspect. [< OF < Med.L < L < *sub-* from under + *specere* to look] **— sus·pi'cion·al** *adj.*

— Syn. (noun) **1.** distrust, dubiety, skepticism. See DOUBT. **2.** soupçon, dash, touch, tinge, shade.

sus·pi·cious (sə·spish'əs) *adj.* **1.** Inclined to suspect; dis-trustful. **2.** Apt to arouse suspicion. **3.** Indicating suspi-cion. **— sus·pi'cious·ly** *adv.* **— sus·pi'cious·ness** *n.*

sus·tain (sə·stān') *v.t.* **1.** To keep from sinking or falling; uphold; support. **2.** To endure without yielding; withstand. **3.** To undergo or suffer, as loss or injury. **4.** To keep up the courage, resolution, or spirits of; comfort. **5.** To keep up or maintain; keep in effect or being. **6.** To maintain by provid-ing with food, drink, etc. **7.** To uphold or support as being true or just. **8.** To corroborate; confirm. [< OF < L *sub-* up from under + *tenere* to hold] **— sus·tain'a·ble** *adj.* **— sus·tain'er** *n.* **— sus·tain'ment** *n.*

sus·tain·ing program (sə·stā'ning) A radio or television program that has no commercial sponsor but is paid for by the network or station.

sus·te·nance (sus'tə·nəns) *n.* **1.** The act of sustaining, or the state of being sustained; esp., maintenance of life. **2.** That which sustains; esp., that which supports life; food. **3.** Means of support; livelihood. [See SUSTAIN.]

sut·ler (sut'lər) *n.* A peddler who sells goods and food to an army. [< Du. *soetelen* to perform mean duties]

sut·tee (su·tē', sut'ē) *n.* Formerly, the sacrifice of a Hindu widow on the funeral pyre of her husband; also, the widow so immolated. [< Hind. *satī* < Skt., a faithful wife] **— sut·tee'ism** *n.*

su·ture (sōō'chər) *n.* **1.** The junction of two contiguous surfaces or edges along a line by or as by sewing. **2.** *Anat.* The interlocking of two bones at their edges, as in the skull. **3.** *Surg.* **a** The operation of uniting the edges of a cut or wound by or as by stitching. **b** The thread, silver wire, or other material used in this operation. **—** *v.t.* **·tured**, **·tur·ing** To unite by means of sutures; sew together. [< MF < L *suere* to sew] **— su'tur·al** *adj.* **su'tur·al·ly** *adv.*

su·ze·rain (sōō'zə·rin, -rān) *n.* **1.** Formerly, a feudal lord. **2.** A nation having paramount control over a locally autono-mous region. [< F *sus* above < L *sursum* upwards; on anal-ogy with *souverain* sovereign] **— su'ze·rain·ty** *n.*

svelte (svelt) *adj.* Slender; slim; willowy. [< F < Ital. < L *ex-* out + *vellere* to pluck]

swab (swob) *n.* **1.** A small stick having a wad of cotton wound about one or both ends, used for cleansing the mouth of a sick person, applying medicines, etc.; also, a specimen of mucus, etc., taken with such a stick. **2.** A mop for cleaning decks, floors, etc. **3.** A cylindrical brush for cleaning fire-arms. **4.** *Slang* An awkward fellow; lout. **—** *v.t.* **swabbed**, **swab·bing** To clean, apply, medicate, etc., with or as with a swab. [? < MDu. *swabbe*] **— swab'ber** *n.*

swad·dle (swod'l) *v.t.* **·dled**, **·dling** To wrap with a band-age; esp., to wrap (an infant) with a long strip of linen or flannel; swathe. **—** *n.* A band used for swaddling. [OE *swathian* to swathe]

swaddling clothes Bands or strips of linen or other cloth wound around a newborn infant. Also **swaddling bands**, **swaddling clouts**.

swag (swag) *n.* **1.** *Slang* Property obtained by robbery or theft; plunder; booty. **2.** In Australia, a bundle or pack of personal belongings. [Prob. < Scand.]

swage (swāj) *n.* A tool or form, often one of a pair, for shaping metal by hammering or pressure. **—** *v.t.* **swaged**, **swag·ing** To shape (metal) with or as with a swage. [< OF *souage*]

swag·ger (swag'ər) *v.i.* **1.** To walk with a proud or insolent air; strut. **2.** To boast; bluster. **—** *n.* Expression of su-periority in words or deeds; braggadocio. [Appar. freq. of SWAG] **— swag'ger·er** *n.* **— swag'ger·ing·ly** *adv.*

swagger stick A short, canelike stick carried by army per-sonnel, esp. officers. Also **swagger cane**.

Swa·hi·li (swä hē'lē) *n.* *pl.* **·li 1.** A language of East Africa, basically Bantu with an admixture of Arabic elements, used widely as a lingua franca. **2.** A member of a Swahili-speak-ing group or community. [< Arabic < *sāhil* coast] **— Swa·hi'li·an** *adj.*

swain (swān) *n.* *Poetic* **1.** A youthful rustic. **2.** A young rustic gallant. **3.** A lover. [< ON *sveinn* boy]

swal·low¹ (swol'ō) *v.t.* **1.** To cause (food, etc.) to pass from the mouth into the stomach by means of muscular action of the gullet or esophagus. **2.** To take in or engulf; absorb; envelop: often with *up*. **3.** To put up with or endure. **4.** *Informal* To believe credulously. **5.** To refrain from expressing; suppress. **6.** To take back; recant: to *swallow* one's words. — *v.i.* **7.** To perform the act or the motions of swallowing. — *n.* **1.** The amount swallowed at once. **2.** The gullet; throat. **3.** The act of swallowing. [OE *swelgan* to swallow] — **swal·low·a·ble** *adj.* — **swal·low·er** *n.*

swal·low² (swol′ō) *n.* **1.** Any of various small birds with short bills, long, pointed wings, and forked tails, noted for their swiftness of flight and migratory habits. **2.** A similar bird, as the swift. [OE *swealwe*]

swal·low-tail (swol′ō-tāl′) *n.* **1.** The tail of a swallow, or a similar deeply forked tail. **2.** A butterfly having a taillike prolongation on each hind wing. **3.** *Informal* A swallow-tailed coat.

swal·low-tailed coat (swol′ō-tāld′) A man's formal dress coat with two long, tapering tails in the back.

swam (swam) Past tense of SWIM.

swa·mi (swä′mē) *n.* *pl.* **·mis** **1.** Master; lord: used by Hindus as a title of respect. **2.** A Hindu religious teacher. Also **swa′my.** [< Hind. < Skt. *swāmin* lord]

swamp (swomp, swômp) *n.* A tract or region of lowland saturated with water; a wet bog. Also **swamp/land/** (-land′). ◆ Collateral adjective: *paludal.* — *v.t.* **1.** To drench or submerge with water or other liquid. **2.** To overwhelm with difficulties; crush; ruin. **3.** *Naut.* To sink or fill (a vessel) with water. — *v.i.* **4.** To sink in or as in a swamp. — **swamp/ish** *adj.* — **swamp/y** *adj.*

swamp fever Malaria.

swan (swon, swôn) *n.* **1.** A large, long-necked, aquatic bird, noted for its brilliant white plumage and for its grace on the water. **2.** A poet or singer. [OE]

Swan (swon, swôn) *n.* The constellation Cygnus.

swan dive A dive performed with head tilted back and arms extended until near the water.

swang (swang) Dialectal past tense of SWING.

swank (swangk) *adj.* *Slang* Ostentatiously fashionable; pretentious. Also **swank/y.** — *n.* *Slang* **1.** Behavior, speech, etc., that is pretentious and overly stylish. **2.** Swagger; bluster. — *v.i.* To act in a pretentious or swaggering manner; show off. [< dial. E. Appar. akin to MLG *swank* flexible] — **swank/i·ly** *adv.* — **swank/i·ness** *n.*

swan's-down (swonz′doun′, swônz′-) *n.* **1.** The down of a swan, used for trimming, powder puffs, etc. **2.** A soft woolen cloth resembling down. Also **swans/down/.**

swan song A last or dying work, as of a poet or composer: from the fable that the swan sings only before dying.

swap (swop) *Informal* *v.t. & v.i.* **swapped, swap·ping** To trade (one thing for another). — *n.* An exchange or trade. Also spelled *swop*. [ME *swappen* to strike (a bargain)]

sward (swôrd) *n.* Land thickly covered with grass; turf: also called *swarth.* — *v.t. & v.i.* To cover or become covered with sward. [OE *sweard* skin]

swarm¹ (swôrm) *n.* **1.** A large number or body of insects or small living things of any kind. **2.** A hive of bees; also, a large number of bees leaving the parent stock at one time, to take up new lodgings, accompanied by a queen. **3.** A crowd or throng of persons, animals, or things. — **Syn.** See FLOCK. — *v.i.* **1.** To leave the hive in a swarm: said of bees. **2.** To come together, move, or occur in great numbers. **3.** To teem: with *with.* — *v.t.* **4.** To fill with a swarm or crowd; throng. [OE *swearm*] — **swarm/er** *n.*

swarm² (swôrm) *v.t. & v.i.* To climb (a tree, etc.) by clasping it with the arms and legs. [Prob. akin to SWARM¹.]

swart (swôrt) *adj.* *Dial.* or *Poetic* Swarthy. Also *swarth.* [OE *sweart*] — **swart/ness** *n.*

swarth¹ (swôrth) *n.* *Dial.* Sward. [OE *swearth*]

swarth² (swôrth) *adj.* Swart; swarthy. [? Var. of SWART]

swarth·y (swôr′thē) *adj.* **swarth·i·er, swarth·i·est** Having a dark hue; of dark or sunburned complexion; tawny: also *swart, swarth.* Also **swart/y.** [Var. of obs. *swarty* < SWART] — **swarth/i·ly** *adv.* — **swarth/i·ness, swarth/ness** *n.*

swash (swosh, swôsh) *v.i.* **1.** To move or wash noisily, as waves; splash. **2.** To swagger. — *v.t.* **3.** To splash (water, etc.). **4.** To splash or dash water, etc., upon or against. — *n.* **1.** The splash of a liquid. **2.** A narrow channel through which tides flow. **3.** A swaggerer or his behavior. [Imit.]

swash·buck·ler (swosh′buk/lər, swôsh′-) *n.* A swaggering or boasting soldier. [< SWASH + BUCKLER] — **swash/buck·ler·ing** *n.* — **swash/buck/ling** *adj. & n.*

swas·ti·ka (swos′ti·kə) *n.* **1.** A primitive religious ornament or symbol, consisting of a Greek cross with the ends of the arms bent at right angles. **2.** The emblem of the Nazis. [< Skt. *svastika* < *svasti* well-being, fortune]

swat (swot) *v.t.* **swat·ted, swat·ting** To hit with a sharp blow. — *n.* A smart blow. Also spelled *swot.* [Var. of SQUAT, in dial. sense of "squash"] — **swat/ter** *n.*

swatch (swoch) *n.* A strip, as of cloth, esp. one cut off for a sample. [< dial. E (Northern), a cloth tally]

swath (swoth, swôth) *n.* **1.** A row or line of cut grain, etc. **2.** The space or width of grass, grain, etc., cut by any of various mowing devices. **3.** A narrow belt or strip. Also called *swathe.* — **to cut a wide swath** To make a fine impression or display. [OE *swæth* a track]

swathe¹ (swāth) *v.t.* **swathed, swath·ing** **1.** To bind or wrap, as in bandages. **2.** To envelop; surround. — *n.* A bandage for swathing. [OE *swathian*] — **swath/er** *n.*

swathe² (swāth) *n.* A swath.

sway (swā) *v.i.* **1.** To swing from side to side or to and fro; oscillate. **2.** To bend or incline to one side; lean; veer. **3.** To tend in opinion, sympathy, etc. **4.** To have influence or control. — *v.t.* **5.** To cause to swing, bend, or incline. **6.** To influence (a person, opinion, etc.). **7.** To cause to swerve, as from a course of action. — *n.* **1.** Power exercised in governing; dominion; control. **2.** The act of swaying; a swaying, swinging, or turning from side to side. **3.** Overpowering force or influence. [Prob. fusion of ON *sveigja* to bend and LG *swajen* to be moved to and fro by the wind]

sway·back (swā′bak′) *n.* A hollow or unnaturally sagging condition of the back, as in a horse. — **sway/-backed/** *adj.*

swear (swâr) *v.* **swore** (*Obs.* **sware**), **sworn, swear·ing** **1.** To make a solemn affirmation with an appeal to some deity, etc., as in attestation of truth or proof of intentions. **2.** To utter a solemn promise. **3.** To use profanity; curse. **4.** *Law* To give testimony under oath. — *v.t.* **5.** To affirm or assert solemnly by invoking sacred beings or things. **6.** To vow. **7.** To declare or affirm upon oath. **8.** To take or utter (an oath). **9.** To administer a legal oath to. — **to swear by 1.** To appeal to by oath. **2.** To complete confidence in. — **to swear in** To administer a legal oath to. — **to swear off** *Informal* To promise to renounce or give up: to *swear off* drink. — **to swear out** To obtain (a warrant for arrest) by making a statement of charge under oath. [OE *swerian*] — **swear/er** *n.*

sweat (swet) *v.* **sweat** or **sweat·ed, sweat·ing** *v.i.* **1.** To exude or excrete sensible moisture from the pores of the skin; perspire. **2.** To exude moisture in drops; ooze. **3.** To gather and condense moisture in drops, as on the outer surface of a glass. **4.** To pass through pores or interstices in drops. **5.** To ferment, as tobacco leaves. **6.** *Informal* To work hard; toil; drudge. **7.** *Informal* To suffer: You will *sweat* for this. — *v.t.* **8.** To exude (moisture) from the pores. **9.** To gather or condense drops of (moisture). **10.** To soak or stain with perspiration. **11.** To cause to sweat. **12.** To cause to work hard. **13.** *Informal* To force (employees) to work for small wages and under unfavorable conditions. **14.** *Slang* To extort money from. **15.** To heat (solder, etc.) until it melts. **16.** To join, as metal objects, by applying heat. **17.** *Metall.* To heat so as to extract an element that is easily fusible. **18.** *Slang* To subject to torture or rigorous interrogation for the purpose of extracting information. — **to sweat (something) out** *U.S. Slang* To wait through anxiously and helplessly. — *n.* **1.** The act or state of sweating. **2.** That which is excreted from the sweat glands; perspiration. **3.** Any gathering in minute drops of moisture on a surface. **4.** An act of sweating. **5.** *Informal* Fuming impatience; worry; hurry. — **no sweat** *U.S. Slang* No difficulty whatever. [OE < *swāt* sweat] — **sweat/i·ly** *adv.* — **sweat/i·ness** *n.* — **sweat/y** *adj.*

sweat·band (swet′band′) *n.* A band, usu. of leather, inside the crown of a hat to protect it from sweat.

sweat·box (swet′boks′) *n.* **1.** A device for sweating products as hides and dried fruits. **2.** A narrow cell or box where an unruly prisoner is confined.

sweat·er (swet′ər) *n.* **1.** A knitted garment in the form of a jersey or jacket with or without sleeves. **2.** One who or that which sweats. **3.** An employer who underpays and overworks his employees. **4.** A sudorific.

sweat gland *Anat.* One of the convoluted tubules that secrete sweat, found in subcutaneous tissue.

sweat shirt A collarless pullover, sometimes lined with fleece, used by athletes.

sweat·shop (swet′shop′) *n.* A place where work is done for insufficient wages and for long hours.

Swede (swēd) *n.* A native or inhabitant of Sweden, or a person of Swedish descent.

Swe·den·bor·gi·an·ism (swē′dən·bôr′jē·ən·iz′əm) *n.* The system of philosophy or the theology developed by Emanuel **Swe·den·borg** (swēd′n·bôrg), 1688–1772, Swedish mystic, theologian and philosopher. — **Swe·den·bor·gi·an** (swē′dən·bôr′jē·ən) *adj. & n.*

Swed·ish (swē′dish) *adj.* Pertaining to Sweden, the Swedes, or their language. — *n.* **1.** The North Germanic language of Sweden. **2.** The inhabitants of Sweden collectively.

sweep (swēp) *v.* **swept, sweep·ing** *v.t.* **1.** To collect, move, or clear away with a broom, brush, etc. **2.** To clean with or as by a broom or brush: to *sweep* a room. **3.** To touch or brush: Her dress *swept* the ground. **4.** To pass over or through swiftly, as in searching: His eyes swept the sky. **5.** To cause to move with an even, continuous on: He *swept* the cape over her shoulders. **6.** To move, carry, bring, etc., with strong or continuous force: The flood *swept* the bridge away. **7.** To move over or through with strong or steady force: The gale *swept* the bay. **8.** To drag the bottom of (a body of water, etc.). — *v.i.* **9.** To clean or brush a floor or other surface with a broom, etc. **10.** To move or go strongly and evenly, esp. with speed: The train *swept* by. **11.** To walk with or as with trailing garments: She *swept* into the room. **12.** To trail, as a skirt. **13.** To extend with a long reach or curve: The road *sweeps* along the lake shore. — *n.* **1.** The act or result of sweeping. **2.** A swinging stroke or movement: a *sweep* of the hand. **3.** The act of clearing out or getting rid of, as a removal from office or place. **4.** A turning of the eye or of optical instruments over the field of vision. **5.** A great victory or success, as in an election. **6.** The range, area, or compass reached by sweeping, as extent of stroke, range of vision, etc. **7.** A curve or bend, as of a scythe blade, etc. **8.** *Brit.* A chimney sweep. **9.** A long, heavy oar. **10.** A well sweep. **11.** *pl.* Sweepings, as of a place where precious metals are worked. **12.** *Informal* Sweepstakes. [ME *swopen* to brush away] — **sweep′er** *n.* — **sweep′y** *adj.*

sweep·back (swēp′bak′) *n. Aeron.* The backward inclination of the leading edge of an airplane wing.

sweep·ing (swē′ping) *adj.* **1.** Carrying off or clearing away with a driving movement. **2.** Carrying all before it; covering a wide area; comprehensive. **3.** General and thorough-going. — *n.* **1.** The action of one who or that which sweeps. **2.** *pl.* Things swept up; refuse. — **sweep′ing·ly** *adv.* — **sweep′ing·ness** *n.*

sweep·stakes (swēp′stāks′) *n. pl.* **·stakes 1.** A gambling arrangement by which all the sums staked may be won by one or by a few of the betters, as in a horse race. **2.** A race or contest using this arrangement; also, the prize or prizes. Also **sweep′stake′.**

sweet (swēt) *adj.* **1.** Having an agreeable flavor of or like that of sugar. **2.** Containing or due to sugar in some form. **3.** Not fermented or decaying; fresh. **4.** Not salt or salty: *sweet* water. **5.** Gently pleasing to the senses. **6.** Arousing gentle, pleasant emotions. **7.** Having gentle, pleasing, and winning qualities. **8.** *Music Slang* a Designating jazz marked by blandness, moderate tempo, etc. **b** Playing or performing such jazz: a *sweet* trumpet. **9.** Sound; rich; productive: said of soil. **10.** Not dry: said of wines. — *n.* **1.** The quality of being sweet; sweetness. **2.** *Chiefly pl.* A confection, preserve, or piece of candy. **3.** A beloved person; darling. **4.** Something agreeable or pleasing; a pleasure. **5.** *Brit.* A dessert. [OE *swēte*] — **sweet′ly** *adv.* — **sweet′ness** *n.*

sweet alyssum A perennial Mediterranean herb having very fragrant white blossoms: also called *madwort*.

sweet bay A highly ornamental tree or shrub with large flowers.

sweet·bread (swēt′bred′) *n.* The pancreas (**stomach sweetbread**) or the thymus gland (**neck sweetbread** or **throat sweetbread**) of a calf or other animal, when used as food. [< SWEET + BREAD, in obs. sense of "a morsel"]

sweet·bri·er (swēt′brī′ər) *n.* A stout prickly rose native in Europe and Asia, with aromatic leaves: Also **sweet′bri′ar.**

sweet clover Any of several cloverlike herbs, used for fodder.

sweet corn Young ears of corn having sweet, milky kernels, boiled or roasted as food: also called *green corn*.

sweet·en (swēt′n) *v.t.* **1.** To make sweet or sweeter. **2.** To make more endurable; lighten. **3.** To make pleasant or gratifying. — *v.i.* **4.** To become sweet or sweeter. — **sweet′en·er** *n.*

sweet·en·ing (swēt′n·ing) *n.* **1.** The act of making sweet. **2.** That which sweetens.

sweet flag A marsh-dwelling plant, having long leaves and an aromatic rootstock: also called *calamus.*

sweet gum 1. A North American tree, the wood of which is sometimes used to imitate mahogany. **2.** The balsam or gum yielded by it.

sweet·heart (swēt′härt′) *n.* One who is particularly loved by or as a lover; a lover: often used as a term of endearment.

sweet·ie (swē′tē) *n. U.S. Informal* Darling; dear; honey.

sweet·ish (swē′tish) *adj.* Somewhat or rather sweet. — **sweet′ish·ly** *adv.* — **sweet′ish·ness** *n.*

sweet·meat (swēt′mēt′) *n.* **1.** A confection, preserve, candy, etc. **2.** *pl.* Very sweet candy, cakes, etc.

sweet pea An ornamental annual climber of the bean family cultivated for its varicolored flowers.

sweet pepper A mild variety of capsicum whose unripe green fruit is used as a vegetable.

sweet potato 1. A perennial tropical vine, with rose-violet or pink flowers and a fleshy tuberous root. **2.** The root itself, eaten as a vegetable. **3.** *U.S. Informal* An ocarina.

sweets (swēts) *n.pl.* **1.** Sweet things. **2.** *Brit.* Candy.

sweet tooth *Informal* A fondness for candy or sweets.

sweet william A perennial species of pink with closely clustered, showy flowers. Also **sweet William.**

swell (swel) *v.* **swelled, swelled** or **swol·len, swell·ing** *v.i.* **1.** To increase in bulk or dimension, as by inflation within; dilate; expand. **2.** To increase in size, amount, degree, etc. **3.** To grow in volume or intensity, as a sound. **4.** To rise in waves or swells, as the sea. **5.** To bulge, as a sail. **6.** To become puffed up with pride. **7.** To grow within one: My anger *swells* at the sight. — *v.t.* **8.** To cause to increase in size or bulk. **9.** To cause to increase in amount, extent, or degree. **10.** To cause to bulge; belly. **11.** To puff with pride. **12.** *Music* To crescendo and diminuendo in immediate succession. — *n.* **1.** The act, process, or effect of swelling; expansion. **2.** The long continuous body of a wave; a billow; also, a rise in the land. **3.** A bulge or protuberance. **4.** *Music* A crescendo and an immediate diminuendo; also, the signs (< >) indicating it. **5.** A device, as on an organ, by which the volume of a tone may be uninterruptedly varied. **6.** *Informal* A person of the ultrafashionable set. — *adj. Informal* **1.** Ultrafashionable; smart. **2.** First-rate; distinctive. [OE *swellan*]

swell·ing (swel′ing) *n.* **1.** The act of expanding, inflating, or augmenting. **2.** *Pathol.* Abnormal enlargement or protuberance of a part of the body. — *adj.* Increasing; bulging.

swel·ter (swel′tər) *v.i.* **1.** To suffer from oppressive heat; perspire from heat. — *v.t.* **2.** To cause to suffer or perspire from heat. — *n. Archaic* A hot, sweltering condition. [OE *sweltan* to die]

swel·ter·ing (swel′tər·ing) *adj.* **1.** Oppressive; overpoweringly hot. **2.** Overcome by or suffering with heat. Also **swel′try** (-trē). — **swel′ter·ing·ly** *adv.*

swept (swept) Past tense and past participle of SWEEP.

swept·back (swept′bak′) *adj. Aeron.* Having the leading edge inclined backward at an angle with the lateral axis of the airplane: said of a wing.

swerve (swûrv) *v.t. & v.i.* **swerved, swerv·ing** To turn or cause to turn aside from a course or purpose; deflect. — *n.* **1.** The act of swerving or turning aside. **2.** That which swerves. [OE *sweorfan* to file or grind away]

swift (swift) *adj.* **1.** Traversing space or performing movements in a brief time; rapid; quick. **2.** Capable of quick motion; fleet; speedy. **3.** Passing rapidly, as time or events; also, unexpected. **4.** Acting with readiness; prompt. — *n.* A bird of swallowlike form possessing extraordinary powers of flight; esp. the **chimney swift.** [OE] — **swift′ly** *adv.* — **swift′ness** *n.*

— **Syn.** (adj.) *Swift* and *fleet* are chiefly applied to moving persons or animals; *swift* suggests ease of motion, and *fleet*, nimbleness: a *swift* bird, a *fleet* horse. *Speedy* may be applied to that which moves or that which progresses: a *speedy* worker, *speedy* action. *Rapid* is applied to progress: *rapid* delivery of mail.

swig (swig) *Informal n.* A deep draft, as of liquor. — *v.t. & v.i.* **swigged, swig·ging** To drink deeply or greedily. [Origin unknown] — **swig′ger** *n.*

swill (swil) *v.t.* **1.** To drink greedily or to excess. **2.** *Brit.* To drench, as with water; rinse; wash. — *v.i.* **3.** To drink to excess; tope. — *n.* **1.** Liquid food for animals; esp., swine; slop. **2.** Any animal or vegetable refuse; garbage. **3.** A deep draft of liquor. [OE *swillan, swilian* to wash]

swim¹ (swim) *v.* **swam, swum, swim·ming** *v.i.* **1.** To propel oneself through water by organized bodily movement. **2.** To be supported on liquid; float. **3.** To move with a smooth or flowing motion, as if swimming. **4.** To be immersed in or covered with liquid; be flooded; overflow. — *v.t.* **5.** To traverse by swimming. **6.** To cause to swim. — *n.* **1.** The action, pastime, or period of swimming. **2.** A gliding, swaying movement. — **in the swim** *Informal* In the current of affairs. [OE *swimman*] — **swim′mer** *n.*

swim² (swim) *v.i.* **1.** To be dizzy; reel; have a giddy sensation. **2.** To seem to reel, whirl, or spin. — *n.* A sudden dizziness or swoon. [OE *swima* dizziness]

swim bladder The air bladder of a fish. Also **swimming bladder.**

swim·ming¹ (swim′ing) *n.* The act of one who or that which swims. — *adj.* **1.** Used for swimming. **2.** Having the capacity of swimming; natatorial. **3.** Watery; flooded with tears, as the eyes. [< SWIM¹]

swim·ming² (swim′ing) *n.* A state of dizziness or vertigo. — *adj.* Affected by dizziness. [< SWIM²]

swim·ming·ly (swim′ing·lē) *adv.* Easily, rapidly, and successfully.

swimming pool *U.S.* An indoor or outdoor tank designed for swimming, usu. equipped to cleanse the water.

swin·dle (swin′dl) *v.* **·dled, ·dling** *v.t.* **1.** To cheat of money or property by deliberate fraud; defraud. **2.** To obtain by such means. — *v.i.* **3.** To practice fraud or decep-

tion for gain. — *n.* **1.** The act of swindling. **2.** Anything that proves to be fraudulent or deceptive, esp., a deal or scheme. [Back formation < SWINDLER]
— **Syn.** (verb) **1.** fleece, cozen, bamboozle, hoodwink. — (noun) imposition, imposture.

swin·dler (swind′lər)   *n.*   One who swindles or deceives. [< G < *schwindeln* to act thoughtlessly, be giddy]

swine (swīn) *n. pl.* **swine 1.** A domesticated pig. **2.** Any of several related omnivorous mammals having a long mobile snout and cloven hoofs. **3.** A low, greedy, stupid, or vicious person. [OE *swīn*]

swine·herd (swīn′hûrd′)   *n.* A tender of swine.

swing (swing) *v.* **swung** (*Dial.* **swang**), **swung, swing·ing** *v.i.* **1.** To move to-and-fro or backward and forward rhythmically, as something suspended; oscillate. **2.** To ride in a swing. **3.** To move with an even, swaying motion. **4.** To turn; pivot. **5.** To be suspended; hang. **6.** *Informal* To be executed by hanging. — *v.t.* **7.** To cause to move to and fro or backward and forward. **8.** To cause to move with a sweeping motion, as a sword, ax, etc.; brandish; flourish. **9.** To cause to turn on or as on a pivot. **10.** To lift or hoist. **11.** *Informal* To bring to a successful conclusion; manage successfully. — *n.* **1.** The act, process, or manner of swinging; also, the distance covered. **2.** A free swaying motion. **3.** A seat hanging from ropes or chains on which a person may move to and fro as a pastime. **4.** Free course or scope; full liberty or license. **5.** Compass; sweep. **6.** The rhythm characterizing certain styles of poetry or music. **7.** A sweeping blow or stroke. **8.** The course of a career or period of activity; main current of business. **9.** In jazz: a development after about 1935, characterized by large bands, contrapuntal styles, etc. [OE *swingan* to scourge, beat up] — **swing′er** *n.*

swin·gle·tree (swing′gəl·trē′)   *n.* A whiffletree.

swing shift   *U.S. Informal* An evening work shift, usu. lasting from about 4 p.m. to midnight.

swin·ish (swī′nish) *adj.* Of, like, or fit for swine; degraded; sensual; beastly. — **swin′ish·ly** *adv.* — **swin′ish·ness** *n.*

swipe (swīp) *v.t.* **swiped, swip·ing 1.** *Informal* To give a strong blow; strike with a full swing of the arm. **2.** *Slang* To steal; snatch. — *n. Informal* A hard, sweeping stroke or blow. [Var. of SWEEP]

swirl (swûrl) *v.i.* **1.** To move with a whirling or twisting motion; whirl. **2.** To be dizzy; swim, as the head. — *v.t.* **3.** To cause to move in a whirling or twisting motion. — *n.* **1.** A whirling along, as in an eddy; whirl. **2.** A curl or twist; spiral. [< dial. E (Scottish) *swyrle*] — **swirl′ly** *adj.*

swish (swish) *v.i.* **1.** To move through the air with a hissing, whistling sound, as a slender, flexible rod. **2.** To rustle, as silk. — *v.t.* **3.** To cause to swish. **4.** To thrash; flog. — *n.* **1.** A hissing or rustling sound. **2.** A movement producing such a sound. [Imit.]

Swiss (swis) *adj.* Of or pertaining to Switzerland or its inhabitants. — *n. pl.* **Swiss** A native or naturalized inhabitant of Switzerland.

Swiss chard   Chard.

Swiss cheese   A pale yellow cheese with many large holes, made in, or similar to that made in, Switzerland.

Swiss steak   A thick cut of steak floured and braised, often with a sauce of tomatoes and onions.

switch (swich)   *n.* **1.** A small flexible rod, etc., used for whipping. **2.** A tress of false hair, used by women in building a coiffure. **3.** A mechanism for shifting a railway train from one track to another. **4.** The act or operation of shifting, or changing. **5.** The end of the tail in certain animals, as a cow. **6.** *Electr.* A device to make or break a circuit, or transfer a current from one conductor to another. — *v.t.* **1.** To whip with or as with a switch. **2.** To move, jerk, or whisk suddenly or sharply. **3.** To turn aside or divert; shift. **4.** To exchange: They *switched* plates. **5.** To shift (a railroad car) to another track by means of a switch. **6.** *Electr.* To connect or disconnect with a switch. — *v.i.* **7.** To turn aside; change; shift. **8.** To be shifted or turned. [Earlier *swits*] — **switch′er** *n.*

switch·back (swich′bak′)   *n.* **1.** A railway or road ascending a steep incline in a zigzag pattern. **2.** *Brit.* A roller coaster.

switch·board (swich′bôrd′, -bōrd′)   *n.* A panel or arrangement of panels bearing switches for connecting and disconnecting electric circuits, as a telephone exchange.

switch·man (swich′mən) *n. pl.* **·men** (-mən) One who handles railway switches.

switch·yard (swich′yärd′)   *n.* A railroad yard for the assembling and breaking up of trains.

swiv·el (swiv′əl) *n.* **1.** A coupling device, link, ring, or pivot that permits either half of a mechanism, as a chain, to rotate independently. **2.** A pivoted support on which a gun may be swung. **3.** A cannon that swings on a pivot: also **swivel gun.** — *v.* **swiv·eled** or **·elled, swiv·el·ing** or **·el·ling** *v.t.* **1.** To turn on or as on a swivel. **2.** To fit with or secure by a swivel. — *v.i.* **3.** To turn on or as on a swivel. [ME < OE < *swifan* to revolve]

swivel chair   A chair having a seat that turns horizontal on a swivel.

swob (swob), **swob·ber** (swob′ər)   See SWAB, etc.

swol·len (swō′lən)   Alternative past participle of SWELL.

swoon (swoon) *v.i.* To faint. — *n.* A fainting fit. [M < OE *geswōgen* unconscious] — **swoon′ing** *n.*

swoop (swoop) *v.i.* **1.** To drop or descend suddenly, as bird pouncing on its prey. — *v.t.* **2.** To take or seize suddenly: often with *up.* — *n.* The act of swooping. [< O *swāpan* to sweep]

swop (swop)   See SWAP.

sword (sôrd, sōrd) *n.* **1.** A weapon consisting of a long bla fixed in a hilt, as a rapier, etc. **2.** Power; esp., military po er. **3.** War; destruction; slaughter. — **at swords' poin** Hostile; ready for a fight. — **to put to the sword** To k with a sword; slaughter in battle. [OE *sweord*]

sword·fish (sôrd′fish′, sōrd′-)   *n. pl.* **·fish** or **·fish·es** A lar marine fish having the bones of the upper jaw consolidat to form an elongated swordlike process.

sword grass   **1.** Any of several varieties of grasses or sedg with sharp or serrated edges. **2.** The gladiolus.

sword·knot (sôrd′not′, sōrd′-)   *n.* Formerly, a loop of leat er used to fasten the hilt of a sword to the wrist; now, a tas of cord or ribbon tied to a sword hilt.

sword·play (sôrd′plā′, sōrd′-)   *n.* The act, art, or skill using the sword, esp. in fencing. — **sword′-play′er** *n.*

swords·man (sôrdz′mən, sōrdz′-) *n. pl.* **·men** (-mən) O skilled in the use of or armed with a sword. Also **swor man.** — **swords′man·ship** or **sword′man·ship** *n.*

swore (swôr, swōr)   Past tense of SWEAR.

sworn (swôrn, swōrn)   Past participle of SWEAR.

swot (swot)   See SWAT.

swounds (zwoundz, zoundz), **swouns** (zwounz, zoun See ZOUNDS.

swum (swum)   Past participle and dialectal past tense SWIM.

swung (swung)   Past tense and past participle of SWING

sy-   Var. of SYN-.

syb·a·rite (sib′ə·rīt)   *n.* One given to pleasure and luxu an epicure. [< L < Gk. < *Sybaris,* an ancient Greek c in southern Italy, famed for its luxury.] — **syb′a·rit′ic** (-r ik) or **·i·cal** *adj.* — **syb′a·rit′i·cal·ly** *adv.*

syc·a·more (sik′ə·môr, -mōr)   *n.* **1.** A medium-sized bus tree of Syria and Egypt allied to the common fig. **2.** Any various plane trees of the U.S., esp., the **American sy more:** also called *buttonwood.* **3.** An ornamental shade t of Europe and Asia. [< OF < LL < Gk. < *sykon* fig *moron* mulberry]

syc·o·phant (sik′ə·fənt)   *n.* A servile flatterer. [< L Gk. *sykophantēs* informer] — **syc′o·phan·cy** *n.* — **sy phan′tic** (-fan′tik) or **·i·cal** *adj.* — **syc′o·phan′ti·cal·ly** *ad*

syl·la·bar·y (sil′ə·ber′ē) *n. pl.* **·bar·ies** A list or table syllables; esp., a list of characters representing syllab [< NL < Med.L < L. See SYLLABLE.]

syl·lab·ic (si·lab′ik) *adj.* **1.** Of or consisting of a syllable syllables. **2.** *Phonet.* Designating a consonant capable forming a complete syllable, as *l* in *middle* (mid′l). **3.** H ing every syllable distinctly pronounced. Also **syl·lab′i·c** — *n. Phonet.* A sound of high sonority, usu., a vowel. **syl·lab′i·cal·ly** *adv.*

syl·lab·i·cate (si·lab′ə·kāt) *v.t.* **·cat·ed, ·cat·ing** To fo or divide into syllables. — **syl·lab′i·ca′tion, syl·lab′i·fi·c tion** *n.*

syl·lab·i·fy (si·lab′ə·fī) *v.t.* **·fied, ·fy·ing** To syllabicate. **syl·la·ble** (sil′ə·bəl) *n.* **1.** *Phonet.* A word or part of a wo uttered in a single vocal impulse, usu. consisting of a vo alone or with one or more consonants. **2.** A part of a writ or printed word corresponding, more or less, to the spok division. In this dictionary, syllable breaks are indica by centered dots. **3.** The least detail, mention, or tra Please don't repeat a *syllable* of what you've heard here. — *v.* **·bled, ·bling** *v.t.* **1.** To pronounce the syllables of. — **2.** To pronounce syllables. [< AF, OF < L < Gk. < *s together* + *lambanein* to take]

syl·la·bus (sil′ə·bəs) *n. pl.* **·bus·es** or **·bi** (-bī) A conc statement of the main points of a course of study, subje etc. [< NL < Med.L < L < *sittyba* label on a book < G

syl·lo·gism (sil′ə·jiz′əm)   *n.* **1.** *Logic* **a** A formula argument consisting of two propositions, called *premis* and a *conclusion,* logically drawn from them. Example: men are mortal (*major premise*); kings are men (*minor mise*); therefore, kings are mortal (*conclusion*). **b** Deduct reasoning. **2.** A subtle or crafty argument. [< OF < Gk. < *syn-* together + *logizesthai* to infer] — **syl′lo·gis** *adj. & n.* — **syl′lo·gis′ti·cal** *adj.* — **syl′lo·gis′ti·cal·ly** *a*

sylph (silf) *n.* **1.** An imaginary being, mortal but with a soul, living in the air. **2.** A slender, graceful young wom or girl. [< NL *sylphes,* pl.] — **sylph′like** *adj.*

syl·van (sil′vən) *adj. Chiefly Poetic* **1.** Of or located i forest or woods **2.** Composed of or abounding in trees woods. **3.** Characteristic of a forest or wood; rustic. [< NL

spirit, person or animal dwelling in the woods. [< MF L < *silva* wood]

n- Assimilated var. of SYN-.

n·bi·o·sis (sim/bī·ō/sis, -bē-)   *n. Biol.* The consorting gether, usu., in mutually advantageous partnership, of ssimilar organisms, as of the algae and fungi in lichens. ‹ NL < Gk. ult. < *syn-* together + *bios* life] — **sym/bi·ic** (-ot/ik) or **·i·cal** *adj.* — **sym/bi·ot/i·cal·ly** *adv.*

n·bol (sim/bəl) *n.* **1.** Something chosen to represent mething else; esp., an object used to typify a quality, stract idea, etc.: The oak is a *symbol* of strength. **2.** A aracter, mark, etc., indicating something, as a quantity mathematics. — *v.t.* To symbolize. — **Syn.** See EM-EM. [< L < Gk. < *syn-* together + *ballein* to throw]

n·bol·ic (sim·bol/ik) *adj.* **1.** Of, pertaining to, or ex-ssed by a symbol or symbols. **2.** Serving as a symbol: ‹th of. **3.** Characterized by or involving the use of sym-ls: *symbolic* poetry. Also **sym·bol/i·cal.** — **sym·bol/i·cal·**adv. — **sym·bol/i·cal·ness** *n.*

n·bol·ism (sim/bəl·iz/əm) *n.* **1.** Representation by sym-ls; treatment or interpretation of things as symbolic. **2.** ιe quality of being symbolic. **3.** A system of symbols. **4.** ɪe theories and practice of a group of symbolists.

n·bol·ist (sim/bəl·ist) *n.* One who uses symbols; esp., ɪe skilled in the interpretation or use of symbols, as in ‹rature and art.

n·bol·is·tic (sim/bəl·is/tik) *adj.* **1.** Expressed by sym-ls; characterized by the use of symbols **2.** Of or pertain-ʒ to symbolism; symbolic. Also **sym/bol·is/ti·cal.**

n·bol·ize (sim/bəl·īz) *v.* **·ized, ·iz·ing** *v.t.* **1.** To be a nbol of; represent symbolically; typify. **2.** To represent a symbol or symbols. **3.** To treat as symbolic or figura-e. — *v.i.* **4.** To use symbols. — **sym/bol·i·za/tion** *n.*

n·me·try (sim/ə·trē) *n. pl.* **·tries** **1.** An exact corre-ɔndence between the opposite halves of a figure, form, line, ·ttern, etc., on either side of an axis or center; the condition ιereby half of something is the mirror image of the other 1f. **2.** Beauty or harmony of form resulting from a sym-·trical or nearly symmetrical arrangement of parts; due or ht proportion. [< MF < LL < Gk. < *syn-* together + *tron* a measure] — **sym·met/ric** (-met/rik), **sym·met/ri·** ɪ (-met/ri·kəl) *adj.*

n·pa·thet·ic (sim/pə·thet/ik) *adj.* **1.** Of, expressing, or ɔceeding from sympathy. **2.** Having a fellow feeling for ιers; sympathizing; compassionate. **3.** Being in accord harmony; congenial. Also **sym/pa·thet/i·cal.** [< NL < ‹. See SYMPATHY.] — **sym/pa·thet/i·cal·ly** *adv.*

n·pa·thin (sim/pə·thin) *n. Biochem.* A substance lib-ιted by the stimulation of certain fibers of the sympathetic ·rvous system and acting as a chemical mediator in associ-ɪd nerve impulses. [< SYMPATH(ETIC) + -IN]

n·pa·thique (saṅ·på·tēk/) *adj. French* Pleasant; nice; ɪgenial: said of persons.

n·pa·thize (sim/pə·thīz) *v.i.* **·thized, ·thiz·ing** **1.** To ιre the sentiments, feelings, or ideas of another: with *with.* To feel or express compassion, as for another's sorrow or ʃliction: with *with.* **3.** To be in harmony or agreement. — **m/pa·thiz/er** *n.* — **sym/pa·thiz/ing·ly** *adv.*

n·pa·thy (sim/pə·thē) *n. pl.* **·thies** **1.** The quality of ʒng affected by the state of another with feelings corre-ɔndent in kind. **2.** A fellow feeling; esp., a feeling of com-ssion for another's sufferings; pity; commiseration. **3.** ι agreement of affections, inclinations, or temperaments ιt makes persons agreeable to one another; congeniality; cord. — **Syn.** See PITY. [< L < Gk. < *syn-* together + ιhos feeling]

npathy strike A strike in which the strikers support the ɪmands of another group of workers but demand nothing themselves.

n·pho·ny (sim/fə·nē) *n. pl.* **·nies** **1.** *Music* A composi-ι for orchestra, consisting usu., of four movements, that ɪ related by structure, key, etc. **2.** A symphony orches-ι. **3.** A harmonious or agreeable mingling of sounds, col-ε, etc.: *symphony* in gray. [< OF < L < Gk. < *syn-* ·gether + *phōnē* sound] — **sym·phon/ic** (fon/ik) *adj.* — **m/pho·nist** *n.*

nphony orchestra A large orchestra composed usu. of ε string, brass, woodwind, and percussion sections needed present symphonic works: also called *symphony.*

n·phy·sis (sim/fə·sis) *n. pl.* **·ses** (-sēz) *Anat.* A junc-ɪn of two parts of the skeleton, formed either by a growing ʒether of two bones or by the intervention of a layer of ɪtilage between them. [< NL < Gk. < *syn-* together + γein to grow] — **sym·phyt/ic** (sim·fit/ik) *adj.* — **sym·** yt/i·cal·ly *adv.*

n·po·si·um (sim·pō/zē·əm) *n. pl.* **·si·ums** or **·si·a** (-zē·ə) A meeting for discussion of a particular subject. **2.** A llection of comments or opinions brought together; esp., a

series of brief essays or articles on the same subject, as in a magazine. Also **sym·po/si·on** (-zē·on). [< L < Gk. < *syn-* together + *posis* a drinking < *po-*, stem of *pinein* to drink] — **sym·po/si·ac** (-ak) *adj.*

symp·tom (sim/təm) *n.* **1.** A sign, token, or indication. **2.** *Med.* Any observable alteration in bodily functions or men-tal behavior arising from and indicating the presence of dis-ease, esp. when regarded as an aid in diagnosis. [< L < Gk. < *syn-* together + *piptein* to fall]

symp·to·mat·ic (simp/tə·mat/ik) *adj.* **1.** Pertaining to, of the nature of, or constituting a symptom or symptoms. **2.** According to symptoms: a *symptomatic* classification of dis-eases. Also **symp/to·mat/i·cal.** — **symp/to·mat/i·cal·ly** *adv.*

syn- *prefix* With; together; associated with or accompany-ing: *syntax, syndrome.* Also: *sy-* before *sc, sp, st,* and *z,* as in *system; syl-* before *l,* as in *syllable; sym-* before *b, p,* and *m,* as in *sympathy; sys-* before *s.* [< L < Gk. < *syn* together]

syn·a·gogue (sin/ə·gòg, -gog) *n.* **1.** A place of meeting for Jewish worship and religious instruction. **2.** A Jewish con-gregation or assemblage for religious instruction and obser-vances. **3.** The Jewish religion or communion. Also **syn/a·gog.** [< OF < LL < Gk. *synagōgē* assembly < *syn-* togeth-er + *agein* to lead, bring] — **syn/a·gog/i·cal** (-goj/i·kəl), **syn/a·gog/al** (-gòg/əl, -gog/əl) *adj.*

syn·apse (si·naps/) *n. Physiol.* The junction point of two neurons, across which a nerve impulse passes. Also called **syn·ap·sis** (si·nap/sis). [< NL < Gk. < *syn-* together + *hapsis* a joining]

syn·carp (sin/kärp) *n. Bot.* **1.** A fruit composed of several carpels, as the blackberry. **2.** A multiple fruit, as the fig. Also **syn·car·pi·um** (sin·kär/pē·əm). [< NL < Gk. *syn-* to-gether + *karpos* fruit] — **syn·car/pous** *adj.*

syn·chro (sing/krō) *n.* Any of various electromagnetic de-vices for the remote control of complex operations.

syn·chro·mesh (sing/krə·mesh/) *n. Mech.* **1.** A gear sys-tem by which driving and driven members are brought to the same speed before engaging. **2.** Any gear in such a sys-tem. [< SYNCHRO(NIZED) + MESH]

syn·chro·nism (sing/krə·niz/əm) *n.* **1.** The state of being synchronous. **2.** Coincidence in time of different events or phenomena; simultaneousness. **3.** A tabular grouping of historic personages or events according to their dates. **4.** In art, representation in the same picture of events that oc-curred at different times. — **syn/chro·nis/tic** or **·ti·cal** *adj.* — **syn/chro·nis/ti·cal·ly** *adv.*

syn·chro·nize (sing/krə·nīz) *v.* **·nized, ·niz·ing** *v.i.* **1.** To occur at the same time; coincide. **2.** To move or operate in unison. — *v.t.* **3.** To cause (timepieces) to agree in keeping or indicating time. **4.** To cause to operate in unison. **5.** To assign the same time or period to. — **syn/chro·ni·za/tion** *n.* — **syn/chro·niz/er** *n.*

syn·chro·nous (sing/krə·nəs) *adj.* **1.** Occurring at the same time; coincident. **2.** Happening at the same rate. **3.** *Physics* Having the same period or rate of vibration, as waves or electric currents. Also **syn/chro·nal, syn/chro·nal.** [< LL < Gk. < *syn-* together + *chronos* time] — **syn/·chro·nous·ly** *adv.* — **syn/chro·nous·ness** *n.*

syn·cli·nal (sin·klī/nəl, sing-) *adj.* **1.** Sloping downward on each side toward a line or point. **2.** *Geol.* Inclining upward on each side from the axis of the fold, as rock strata. Also **syn·clin·i·cal** (sin·klin/i·kəl, sing-). — *n.* A syncline. [< Gk. < *syn-* together + *klinein* to incline]

syn·cline (sing/klīn) *n. Geol.* A trough or structural basin toward which rocks dip.

syn·co·pate (sing/kə·pāt) *v.t.* **·pat·ed, ·pat·ing** **1.** *Gram.* To contract (a word) by syncope. **2.** *Music* To treat or modify, as a tone, by syncopation. [< LL *syncopatus,* pp. of *synco-pare* to affect with syncope] — **syn/co·pat/or** *n.*

syn·co·pa·tion (sing/kə·pā/shən) *n.* **1.** The act of synco-pating or state of being syncopated. **2.** That which is syn-copated, as a dance or rhythm. **3.** *Music* **a** The rhythmic placement of a tone so that its accent does not coincide with the metric accent, as by beginning it on a weak beat or a fraction of a beat and continuing it through the next strong beat. **b** A tone so treated. **c** Any music featuring syncopa-tion, as ragtime, jazz, etc. **4.** *Gram.* Syncope.

syn·co·pe (sing/kə·pē) *n.* **1.** *Gram.* The elision of a sound or syllable in the middle part of a word, as *e'er* for *ever.* **2.** *Pathol.* A loss of consciousness caused by temporary cerebral anemia. [< OF, ult. < LL < Gk. < *syn-* together + *kop-*, stem of *koplein* to cut] — **syn/co·pal, syn·cop·ic** (sin·kop/-ik) *adj.*

syn·cre·tize (sing/krə·tīz) *v.t. & v.i.* **·tized, ·tiz·ing** To at-tempt to blend and reconcile, as various philosophies. [< NL < Gk. *synkrētizein* to combine] — **syn/cre·tism** *n.*

syn·det·ic (sin·det/ik) *adj.* Serving to unite or connect; con-nective, as a word. Also **syn·det/i·cal.** [< Gk. < *syn-* to-gether + *deein* to bind] — **syn·det/i·cal·ly** *adv.*

syn·dic (sin′dik) *n.* **1.** A civil magistrate or officer representing a government. **2.** One who is designated to transact business for others. [< Gk. *syndikos* defendant's advocate < *syn-* together + *dikē* judgment]

syn·di·cal·ism (sin′di·kəl·iz′əm) *n.* A social and political theory proposing the taking over of the means of production by syndicates of workers, preferably by means of the general strike, with consequent political control. — **syn′di·cal·ist** *adj. & n.* — **syn′di·cal·is′tic** *adj.*

syn·di·cate (*n.* sin′də·kit; *v.* sin′də·kāt) *n.* **1.** An association of individuals united to negotiate some business or to prosecute some enterprise requiring large capital. **2.** An agency that sells articles, etc., to a number of periodicals, as newspapers, for simultaneous publication. **3.** The office or jurisdiction of a syndic; also, syndics collectively. — *v.t.* **·cat·ed, ·cat·ing 1.** To combine into or manage by a syndicate. **2.** To sell (an article, etc.) for publication in many newspapers or magazines. [See SYNDIC.]

syn·drome (sin′drōm) *n. Med.* An aggregate or set of concurrent symptoms indicating the presence and nature of a disease. [< NL < Gk. < *syn-* together + *dramein* to run] — **syn·drom·ic** (sin·drom′ik) *adj.*

sy·nec·do·che (si·nek′də·kē) *n.* A figure of speech in which a part is put for a whole or a whole for a part, an individual for a class, or a material for the thing, as a *roof* for a *house.* [< LL < Gk. < *syn-* together + *ekdechesthai* to take from] — **syn·ec·doch·ic** (sin′ek·dok′ik) or **·i·cal** *adj.*

synfuel (sin′fyoo·əl) *n.* Synthetic fuel.

syn·i·ze·sis (sin′ə·zē′sis) *n.* **1.** *Biol.* The contractile massing of the chromatin in meiosis. **2.** *Med.* Contraction of the pupil of the eye. Also **syn′e·zi′sis** (-zi′sis). [< LL < Gk. < *syn-* together + *izanein* to settle down, sit]

syn·od (sin′əd) *n.* **1.** An ecclesiastical council. **2.** Any deliberative assembly. [OE < LL < Gk. *synodos*, lit., a coming together < *syn-* together + *hodos* way]

sy·nod·i·cal (si·nod′i·kəl) *adj.* **1.** Of, pertaining to, or of the nature of a synod; transacted in a synod. **2.** *Astron.* Pertaining to the conjunction of two heavenly bodies, one of which revolves round the other, or to the interval between two successive conjunctions. Also **syn·od·al** (sin′ə·dəl), **sy·nod′ic.** — **sy·nod′i·cal·ly** *adv.*

syn·o·nym (sin′ə·nim) *n.* **1.** A word having the same or almost the same meaning as some other: opposed to *antonym.* **2.** The equivalent of a word in another language. Also **syn′o·nyme.** [< LL < Gk. < *syn-* together + *onyma, onoma* name] — **syn/o·nym′ic** or **·i·cal** *adj.* — **syn/o·nym′i·ty** *n.*

sy·non·y·mize (si·non′ə·mīz) *v.t.* **·mized, ·miz·ing** To give the synonyms of; express by words of similar meaning.

sy·non·y·mous (si·non′ə·məs) *adj.* **1.** Being a synonym or synonyms; equivalent or similar in meaning. **2.** Closely related or alike in significance or effect. Also **syn·o·ny·mat·ic** (sin′ə·ni·mat′ik). — **sy·non′y·mous·ly** *adv.*

sy·non·y·my (si·non′ə·mē) *n. pl.* **·mies 1.** The quality of being synonymous. **2.** The science or systematic collection and study of synonyms; also, the use and discrimination of synonyms. **3.** A written analysis discriminating the meaning of synonyms. **4.** An index, list, or collection of synonyms, as in scientific nomenclature.

sy·nop·sis (si·nop′sis) *n. pl.* **·ses** (-sēz) A general view, as of a subject or its treatment; an abstract; syllabus; summary. [< LL < Gk. < *syn-* together + *opsis* view]

sy·nop·tic (si·nop′tik) *adj.* **1.** Giving or constituting a synopsis or general view. **2.** *Often cap.* Presenting the same or a similar point of view: said of the first three Gospels (**Synoptic Gospels**). Also **sy·nop′ti·cal.** — **sy·nop′ti·cal·ly** *adv.*

sy·no·vi·a (si·nō′vē·ə) *n. Physiol.* The viscid, transparent, albuminous fluid secreted by the **synovial membranes** at points where lubrication is necessary, as in joints. [< NL, appar. < Gk. *syn-* together + L *ovum* egg < Gk. *ōon*] — **sy·no′vi·al** *adj.*

syn·tax (sin′taks) *n.* **1.** The arrangement and interrelationship of words in phrases and sentences. **2.** The branch of linguistics dealing with such relationships. [< F < LL < Gk. < *syn-* together + *tassein* to arrange] — **syn·tac·tic** (sin·tak′tik) or **·ti·cal** *adj.* — **syn·tac′ti·cal·ly** *adv.*

syn·the·sis (sin′thə·sis) *n. pl.* **·ses** (-sēz) **1.** The assembling of separate or subordinate parts into a whole: opposed to *analysis.* **2.** A complex whole composed of originally separate parts. **3.** *Chem.* The building up of compounds from a series of reactions involving elements, radicals, or similar compounds. Compare ANALYSIS. [< L < Gk. < *syn-* together + *tithenai* to place] — **syn′the·sist** *n.*

syn·the·size (sin′thə·sīz) *v.t.* **·sized, ·siz·ing 1.** To unite or produce by synthesis. **2.** To apply synthesis to.

syn·thet·ic (sin·thet′ik) *adj.* **1.** Pertaining to, of the nature of, or characterized by synthesis. **2.** Tending to reduce particulars to inclusive wholes. **3.** *Chem.* Produced artificially by the synthesis of simpler materials or substances rather than occurring naturally. **4.** Artificial; spurious. — *n.* Anything produced by synthesis. — **syn·thet′i·cal·ly** *adv.*

synthetic fuel Fuel obtained by processing, such as cru oil obtained from shale or tar sands by extraction and fr coal by liquefaction, or natural gas obtained from coal gasification.

syph·i·lis (sif′ə·lis) *n. Pathol.* An infectious, chronic, nereal disease caused by a spirochete transmissible by dir contact or congenitally, and usu. progressing by three stag of increasing severity. [after a Latin poem published 1530, the hero of which, *Syphilus*, a shepherd, was the fi sufferer from the disease]

syph·i·lit·ic (sif′ə·lit′ik) *adj.* Relating to or affected w syphilis. — *n.* A person suffering from syphilis.

Syr·i·ac (sir′ē·ak) *n.* The language of the Syrians, belong to the eastern Aramaic subgroup of the Northwest Sem languages. [< L < Gk. *Syriakos*]

Syr·i·an (sir′ē·ən) *adj.* Of or pertaining to ancient or m ern Syria. — *n.* **1.** A native of Syria, esp. one of the Sem people of Arabic, Phoenician, and Aramean descent. **2.** (who is a member of a Christian church in Syria. [< OF < Gk. *Syria* Syria]

sy·rin·ga (si·ring′gə) *n.* **1.** Any of various ornamel shrubs of the saxifrage family, having fragrant cream-colo flowers. **2.** The lilac. [< NL < Gk. *syrinx, -ingos* a pi

sy·ringe (sir′inj, si·rinj′) *n.* **1.** *Med.* A small instrumen glass, metal, rubber, or plastic, consisting of a receptacle i which a liquid may be drawn for ejection in a fine jet stream, used for cleaning wounds, affected parts, etc. **2** hypodermic syringe. — *v.t.* **·inged, ·ing·ing** To spray or ject by a syringe; cleanse or treat with injected fluid. [< Med.L < Gk. *syrinx, -ingos* tube, pipe]

syr·inx (sir′ingks) *n. pl.* **sy·rin·ges** (sə·rin′jēz) or **sy′rinx 1.** *Ornithol.* A special modification of the windpipe servin the song organ in birds. **2.** *Anat.* The Eustachian tube. [< Gk., pipe] — **sy·rin·ge·al** (si·rin′jē·əl) *adj.*

syr·up (sir′əp) *n.* A thick, sweet liquid, as the boiled ju of fruits, sugar cane, etc.: also, *esp. U.S., sirup.* [< OF Arabic *sharāb*] — **syr′up·y** *adj.*

sys- Var. of SYN-.

sys·tal·tic (sis·tal′tik) *adj. Physiol.* Alternately contra ing and dilating, as the motion of the heart; pulsatory. [< LL < Gk. < *syn-* together + *stellein* to send]

sys·tem (sis′təm) *n.* **1.** Orderly combination or arrar ment of parts, elements, etc., into a whole; esp., such con nation according to some rational principle; any method arrangement of parts. **2.** Any group of facts, concepts, phenomena regarded as constituting a natural whole for p poses of philosophic or scientific investigation and consti tion: the Ptolemaic *system*; the solar *system.* **3.** The con tion or manner of connection of parts as related to a wh or the parts collectively so related: a railroad *system.* **4.** state or quality of being in order or orderly; method. *Physiol.* **a** An assemblage of organic structures compose similar elements and combined for the same general fu tions: the nervous *system.* **b** The entire body, taken a functional whole. **6.** *Physics* An aggregate or region of m ter considered as a unit with respect to specified factors s as mass, energy, gravitation, radioactivity, etc. **7.** *Chem* group of substances in one or more phases exhibiting tending to approach, equilibrium. **8.** *Mineral.* One of primary divisions into which all crystal forms may grouped, depending upon the relative lengths and mutua clinations of the assumed crystal axes. **9.** *Geol.* A catege of igneous and sedimentary rock strata corresponding wi period in the time scale. [< LL < Gk. < *syn-* togethei *histanai* to stand, set up]

sys·tem·at·ic (sis′tə·mat′ik) *adj.* **1.** Of, pertaining to the nature of, or characterized by system. **2.** Character by system or method; methodical: a *systematic* person. Forming a system; systematized. **4.** Carried out with ganized regularity. **5.** Taxonomic. Also **sys′tem·at·i** — **sys′tem·at′i·cal·ly** *adv.*

sys·tem·a·tism (sis′tə·mə·tiz′əm) *n.* **1.** Systematic rangement or classification. **2.** Adherence to or reducti principles, etc., to a system. — **sys′tem·a·tist** *n.*

sys·tem·a·tize (sis′tə·mə·tīz′) *v.t.* **·tized, ·tiz·ing** To red to a system. Also **sys′tem·ize,** *Brit.* **sys′tem·a·tise′.** — tem·a·ti·za′tion *n.* — **sys′tem·a·tiz′er** *n.*

sys·tem·ic (sis·tem′ik) *adj.* **1.** Of or pertaining to systei a system. **2.** *Physiol.* Pertaining to or affecting the bod a whole: a *systemic* poison. — **sys·tem′i·cal·ly** *adv.*

sys·to·le (sis′tə·lē) *n.* **1.** *Physiol.* The regular contrac of the heart, esp. of the ventricles, that impels the blood ward. Compare DIASTOLE. **2.** The shortening of a syll that is naturally or by position long. [See SYSTALTIC.] — **sys·tol·ic** (sis·tol′ik) *adj.*

syz·y·gy (siz′ə·jē) *n. pl.* **·gies** *Astron.* **a** One of two op site points in the orbit of a celestial body when it is in c junction with or in opposition to the sun. **b** The points on moon's orbit when the moon is most nearly in line with earth and the sun. [< LL < Gk. < *syn-* together + *zeu nai* to yoke] — **sy·zyg·i·al** (si·zij′ē·əl) *adj.*

T

T (tē) *n. pl.* **t's** or **ts, T's** or **Ts, tees** (tēz) **1.** The twentieth letter of the English alphabet. **2.** The sound represented by the letter *t*, the voiceless alveolar stop. **3.** Anything shaped like the letter T. — **to a T** Precisely; with exactness.

't Contraction for IT: used initially, as in *'tis* and finally, as in *on't.*

-t Inflectional ending used to indicate past participles and past tenses, and corresponding to *-ed*, as in *bereft, lost, spent.*

tab (tab) *n.* **1.** A flap, strip, tongue, or appendage of something, as a garment. **2.** A small, projecting part used as an aid in filing papers, etc. **3.** *Informal* Tally; total; bill: to pick up the *tab.* — **to keep tab** or **tabs (on) 1.** To watch or supervise closely. **2.** To maintain a factual record (of). [Origin uncertain]

tab·ard (tab′ərd) *n.* **1.** Formerly, a short, sleeveless or short-sleeved outer garment. **2.** A knight's cape or cloak, worn over his armor; also, a similar garment worn by a herald. [< OF *tabart*, ult. < L *tapete* tapestry]

Ta·bas·co (tə·bas′kō) *n.* A pungent sauce made from red pepper: a trade name. Also **Tabasco sauce.**

tab·by (tab′ē) *n. pl.* **·bies 1.** A brindled or striped cat. **2.** Any domestic cat, esp. a female. **3.** A gossiping old maid. **4.** Any of various plain-woven fabrics, as a watered taffeta. — *adj.* **1.** Having dark, wavy markings; brindled, as a cat. **2.** Watered or mottled, as a fabric. **3.** Made of tabby. — *v.t.* **·bied, ·by·ing** To give a wavy or watered appearance to (silk, etc.). [< F < Arabic *'Attābi*, name of a quarter of Baghdad where the cloth was manufactured]

tab·er·nac·le (tab′ər·nak′əl) *n.* **1.** A tent or similar temporary structure or shelter. **2.** A Jewish house of worship; a temple. **3.** Originally, the portable sanctuary used by the Jews in the wilderness. **4.** Any house of worship, esp. one of large size. **5.** The human body as the dwelling place of the soul. **6.** *Eccl.* The ornamental receptacle for the consecrated Eucharistic elements, or for the pyx. **7.** An ornamental recess or structure sheltering something. — *v.i. & v.t.* **·led, ·ling** To dwell or place in or as in a tabernacle. [< OF < L *tabernaculum*, dim. of *taberna* shed] — **tab·er·nac·u·lar** (tab′ər·nak′yə·lər) *adj.*

tab·la·ture (tab′lə·chər) *n.* *Music* A notation for instrumental music that indicates rhythm and fingering, but not the pitches produced. [< F < L *tabula* board]

ta·ble (tā′bəl) *n.* **1.** An article of furniture with a flat horizontal top upheld by one or more supports. **2.** Such a table around which persons sit for a meal. **3.** The food served or entertainment provided at a meal or dinner. **4.** The company of persons at a table. **5.** A collection of related numbers, values, signs, or items of any kind, arranged for reference or comparison, often in parallel columns: a *table* of logarithms. **6.** A synoptical statement; list: *table* of contents. **7.** A tableland; plateau. **8.** A tablet or slab bearing an inscription; esp., one of those that bore the Ten Commandments or certain Roman laws. — **to turn the tables** To thwart an opponent's action and turn the situation to his disadvantage. — *v.t.* **·bled, ·bling 1.** To place on a table, as a playing card. **2.** To postpone discussion of (a resolution, bill, etc.) until a future time, or for an indefinite period. **3.** *Rare* To tabulate. [Fusion of OF *table* and OE *tabule*, both < L *tabula* board]

tab·leau (tab′lō, ta·blō′) *n. pl.* **·leaux** (-loz, -lō) or **·leaus** (-lōz) **1.** Any picture or picturesque representation; esp., a scene presented dramatically. **2.** A tableau vivant. [< F, dim. of *table* table]

tableau vi·vant (tȧ·blō′ vē·vän′) *pl.* **ta·bleaux vi·vants** (tȧ·blō′ vē·vän′) *French* A picturelike scene represented by silent and motionless persons standing in appropriate attitudes: also called *tableau.*

ta·ble·cloth (tā′bəl·klôth′, -kloth′) *n.* A cloth covering a table, esp., at meals.

ta·ble d'hôte (tab′əl dōt′, tä′bəl; *Fr.* tȧ′blə dōt′) *pl.* **tab·les d'hôte** (tab′əlz dōt′, tä′bəlz; *Fr.* tȧ′blə dōt′) A complete meal served at a restaurant or hotel, the price of the entire meal being determined by the price of the entrée one

chooses. Compare À LA CARTE. [< F, lit., table of the host, as at an inn]

ta·ble·land (tā′bəl·land′) *n.* A broad, level, elevated region, usu. treeless; a plateau.

table linen Tablecloths, napkins, doilies, etc.

ta·ble·spoon (tā′bəl·spoon′, -spoon′) *n.* **1.** A fairly large spoon used for serving food and in measuring for recipes, etc. **2.** A tablespoonful, equivalent to three teaspoons.

ta·ble·spoon·ful (tā′bəl·spoon·fool′, -spoon-) *n. pl.* **·fuls** As much as a tablespoon will hold.

tab·let (tab′lit) *n.* **1.** A pad, as of writing paper or note paper. **2.** A small, flat surface, esp., one designed for containing an inscription or design. **3.** A definite portion of a drug, etc., pressed into a solid form. **4.** A small, flat, or nearly flat piece of some prepared substance, as chocolate or soap. **5.** A thin sheet or slab of solid material, as stone, wood, etc., used for writing, painting, or drawing. [< OF *tablete*, dim. of *table* table]

table tennis A table game resembling tennis, played usu. indoors with a small celluloid ball and wooden paddles: also called *ping-pong.*

ta·ble·ware (tā′bəl·wâr′) *n.* Dishes, knives, forks, spoons, etc., for table use, collectively.

tab·loid (tab′loid) *n.* A newspaper consisting of sheets one half the size of those in an ordinary newspaper, in which the news is presented by means of pictures and concise reporting. — *adj.* **1.** Compact; concise; condensed. **2.** Sensational: *tabloid* journalism. [< TABL(ET) + -OID]

Tab·loid (tab′loid) *n.* Proprietary name for any of various medical preparations and drugs in concentrated or condensed tablet form.

ta·boo (tə·boo′, ta-) *n.* **1.** Among primitive peoples, esp. the Polynesians, a religious and social interdict forbidding the mention of a certain person, thing, or place, the performance of a certain action, etc. **2.** The system or practice of such interdicts or prohibitions. **3.** Any restriction or ban founded on custom or social convention. **4.** The convention of avoiding certain words as profane, obscene, disagreeable, or otherwise socially unacceptable: compare EUPHEMISM. — *adj.* **1.** Consecrated or prohibited by taboo. **2.** Banned or forbidden by social authority or convention. — *v.t.* **1.** To place under taboo. **2.** To exclude; ostracize. Also **ta·bu′.** [< Tonga *tabu*]

ta·bor (tā′bər) *n.* A small drum or tambourine on which a fifer beats his own accompaniment. — *v.i.* To beat or play on a timbrel or small drum; beat lightly and repeatedly. Also **ta′bour.** [< OF *tabour*, prob. < Persian *tabīrah* drum] — **ta′bor·er** *n.*

tab·o·ret (tab′ər·it, tab′ə·ret′) *n.* **1.** A small tabor. **2.** A stool or small seat, usu. without arms or back. **3.** An embroidery frame. Also **tab·ou·ret** (tab′ər·it, tab′ə·ret′).

tab·u·lar (tab′yə·lər) *adj.* **1.** Pertaining to or consisting of a table or list. **2.** Computed from or with a mathematical table. **3.** Having a flat surface; tablelike. — **tab′u·lar·ly** *adv.*

tab·u·lar·ize (tab′yə·lə·rīz′) *v.t.* **·ized, ·iz·ing** To arrange in tabular form; tabulate. — **tab′u·lar·i·za′tion** *n.*

tab·u·late (tab′yə·lāt) *v.t.* **·lat·ed, ·lat·ing 1.** To arrange in a table or list: to *tabulate* results. **2.** To form with a tabular surface. — *adj.* Having a flat surface. — **tab′u·la′tion** *n.*

tab·u·la·tor (tab′yə·lā′tər) *n.* **1.** One who or that which tabulates. **2.** A device built into a typewriter, and used to present statistical matter in tabulated form. **3.** An automatic accounting machine for tabulating reports.

tac·a·ma·hac (tak′ə·mə·hak′) *n.* **1.** A yellowish, resinous substance with a strong odor, derived from various trees and used as incense. **2.** Any of the trees producing this substance. **3.** A tree of the U.S., having leaf buds exuding a gummy resin: also **tac·a·ma·hac′a** -hak′ə), **tac·a·ma·hack′, tac′ca·ma·hac′.** [< Sp. < Nahuatl *tecomahaca*, lit., fetid copal]

tace (tās) *n.* Tasset, a type of armor plate.

ta·chom·e·ter (te·kom′ə·tər) *n.* **1.** An instrument for measuring speed and velocity, as of a machine, the flow of a current, blood, etc. **2.** A device for indicating the speed of rotation of an engine, etc. [< Gk. *tachos* speed + -METER]

ta·chom·e·try (tə·kom′ə·trē) *n.* The art or science of using a tachometer. — **tach·o·met·ric** (tak′ə·met′rik) *adj.*

tachy- *combining form* Speed; swiftness. [< Gk. *tachys* swift]

tac·it (tas′it) *adj.* 1. Existing, inferred, or implied without being directly stated. 2. Making no sound; silent; noiseless. [< F < L *tacere* to be silent] — **tac′it·ly** *adv.* — **tac′·it·ness** *n.*

tac·i·turn (tas′ə·tûrn) *adj.* Habitually silent or reserved. — **tac·i·turn′i·ty** *n.* — **tac′i·turn·ly** *adv.*

tack¹ (tak) *n.* 1. A small sharp-pointed nail, commonly with tapering sides and a flat head. 2. *Naut.* **a** A rope that holds down the lower outer corner of certain sails. **b** The corner so held. **c** The direction in which a vessel sails when sailing close-hauled, considered in relation to the position of her sails. **d** The distance or the course run at one time in such direction. **e** The act of tacking. **f** Any veering of a vessel to one side, as to take advantage of a side wind. 3. A change of policy; a new course of action. 4. In sewing, a large, temporary stitch. — *v.t.* 1. To fasten or attach with tacks. 2. To secure temporarily, as with tacks or long stitches. 3. To attach as supplementary; append. 4. *Naut.* **a** To bring (a vessel) momentarily into the wind so as to go on the opposite tack. **b** To navigate (a vessel) to windward by making a series of tacks. — *v.i.* 5. *Naut.* **a** To tack a vessel. **b** To go on the opposite tack, or sail to windward by a series of tacks. 6. To change one's course of action; veer. [< AF *taque*, OF *tache* nail] — **tack′er** *n.*

tack² (tak) *n.* Food in general. [Origin uncertain]

tack·le (tak′əl) *n.* 1. A rope, pulley, or combination of ropes and pulleys used for hoisting or moving objects. 2. A windlass or winch, together with ropes and hooks. 3. The equipment used in any work or sport; gear; fishing *tackle*. 4. In football: **a** The act of tackling. **b** One of two linemen whose position is usu. between the guard and end. 5. A ship's rigging. — *v.t.* **·led**, **·ling** 1. To deal with; undertake to master, accomplish, or solve. 2. In football, to seize and stop (an opponent carrying the ball). — *v.i.* 3. In football, to tackle an opposing player. [< MLG *takel* < *taken* to seize] — **tack′ler** *n.*

tack·y¹ (tak′ē) *adj.* **tack·i·er**, **tack·i·est** Having adhesive properties; sticky, as a surface covered with partly dried varnish. Also **tack′ey**. [Prob. < TACK¹, v. (def. 2)]

tack·y² (tak′ē) *adj.* **tack·i·er**, **tack·i·est** *U.S. Informal* Shabby; neglected; shoddy. [Cf. dial. G *taklig* untidy]

tact (takt) *n.* A quick or intuitive appreciation of what is fit, proper, or right; esp., skill in avoiding what would offend or disturb. [< L *tactus* a touching]

tact·ful (takt′fəl) *adj.* Possessing or manifesting tact; considerate. — **tact′ful·ly** *adv.* — **tact′ful·ness** *n.*

tac·ti·cal (tak′ti·kəl) *adj.* 1. Pertaining to or like tactics. 2. Exhibiting adroit maneuvering. — **tac′ti·cal·ly** *adv.*

tac·ti·cian (tak·tish′ən) *n.* An expert in tactics.

tac·tics (tak′tiks) *n.pl.* (*construed as sing. in def. 1*) 1. The science and art of handling troops in the presence of the enemy or for immediate objectives: distinguished from *strategy*. 2. Any maneuvering to gain an objective. [< Gk. *taktikos* suitable for arranging or organizing]

tac·tile (tak′til, -təl, *esp. Brit.* -tīl) *adj.* 1. Pertaining to the organs or sense of touch; caused by or consisting of contact. 2. That may be touched; tangible. [< F < L *tactus* touch] — **tac·til′i·ty** *n.*

tact·less (takt′lis) *adj.* Lacking tact. — **tact′less·ly** *adv.* — **tact′less·ness** *n.*

tac·tu·al (tak′chōō·əl) *adj.* Tactile. — **tac′tu·al·ly** *adv.*

tad·pole (tad′pōl) *n.* The aquatic larva of an amphibian, as a frog or toad, breathing by external gills and having a tail: also called *polliwog*. [ME *taddepol* < *tadde* toad]

tael (tāl) *n.* 1. An Oriental weight varying from 1 to 2½ ounces, commonly about 1⅓ ounces. 2. A Chinese monetary unit of varying value. [< Pg. < Malay *tahil*]

ta'en (tān) *Scot.* Taken.

taf·fe·ta (taf′ə·tə) *n.* A fine, plain-woven, somewhat stiff fabric of silk, rayon, etc. — *adj.* Made of or resembling taffeta. [< OF < Med.L < Persian *tāftan* to twist]

taff·rail (taf′rāl′, -rəl) *n. Naut.* 1. The rail around a vessel's stern. 2. The upper part of a vessel's stern. [< MDu. *tafereel* panel, picture]

taf·fy (taf′ē) *n.* 1. A confection made of brown sugar or molasses, mixed with butter, boiled down, and pulled: also called *toffee*. 2. *Informal* Flattery. [Origin unknown]

tag¹ (tag) *n.* 1. Something tacked on or attached to something else; an appendage. 2. A label tied or attached loosely as to a piece of baggage. 3. A loose, ragged edge of anything; tatter. 4. The tail or tip of the tail of any animal. 5. The final lines of a speech in a play; catchword; cue. — *v.* **tagged**, **tag·ging** *v.t.* 1. To supply, adorn, fit, mark, or label with a tag. 2. To shear away matted locks of wool from (sheep). 3. To follow closely or persistently. — *v.i.* 4. To follow closely at one's heels. [Prob. < Scand.]

tag² (tag) *v.t.* **tagged**, **tag·ging** 1. In baseball, to touch (a player) with the ball or with the hand or glove in which the ball is held. 2. To overtake and touch, as in the game of tag. 3. *Informal* To make contact with; designate: *tagged* him for a loan. — *n.* 1. In baseball, the act or instance of tagging a player, esp., a base runner, in an attempt to retire him. 2. A children's running game in which a player who touched or caught (usu. called "it") tries to touch or catch the others. [< TAG¹]

Ta·ga·log (tä·gä′log, tag′ə·log, -lôg) *n.* 1. A member of Malay people native to the Philippines, esp., Luzon. 2. One of the principal native languages and, since 1940, the official language of the Philippines. Also **Ta·gal** (tä·gäl′).

tag day A day on which contributions are solicited for charitable and other institutions.

tag end 1. A loose end or tag of cloth, yarn, etc. 2. The endmost part of anything.

tagged atom A tracer.

tag·ger (tag′ər) *n.* One who or that which tags.

Ta·hi·ti·an (tä·hē′tē·ən, tə-, -shən) *adj.* Of or relating to Tahiti, its people, or their language. — *n.* 1. One of the native Polynesian people of Tahiti. 2. The Polynesian language of the Tahitians.

Tai (tī) See THAI.

tail¹ (tāl) *n.* 1. The hindmost part or rear end of an animal, esp., when prolonged beyond the rest of the body as a distinct, flexible member. ◆ Collateral adjective: *caudal*. 2. Any slender, flexible, terminal extension of the main part of an object: the *tail* of a shirt. 3. *Astron.* The luminous trail extending from the nucleus of a comet. 4. The bottom, back, or inferior portion of anything. 5. *pl. Informal* The reverse side of a coin. 6. Anything of taillike appearance, as a number of persons in single file. 7. A pigtail; braid. 8. *Aeron.* The rear end of an aircraft; also, the stabilizer and control surfaces at the rear of an aircraft. 9. The rear portion of a bomb, projectile, rocket, or guided missile. 10. *pl. Informal* A man's full-dress suit; also, a swallow-tailed coat. — *v.t.* 1. To furnish with a tail. 2. To cut off the tail of. 3. To be the tail or end of: to *tail* a procession. 4. To insert and fasten by one end, as a beam into a wall: with *in* or *on*. 5. *Informal* To follow secretly and stealthily; shadow. — *v.i.* 6. To extend or proceed in a line. 7. *Informal* To follow close behind. 8. To be inserted and fastened at one end, as a beam. — **to tail off** To diminish or recede gradually. — *adj.* 1. Rearmost; hindmost. 2. Coming from behind; following: a *tail* wind. [OE *tægl*] — **tail′less** *adj.*

tail² (tāl) *Law adj.* Restricted in succession to particular heirs: an estate *tail*. — *n.* A cutting off, abridgment, or limitation of ownership; an entail. [< OF *taillier* to cut]

tail·gate (tāl′gāt′) *n.* A hinged or vertically sliding board or gate closing the back end of a truck, wagon, etc. Also **tail board** (tāl′bôrd, -bōrd). — *v.t. & v.i.* **·gat·ed**, **·gat·ing** To drive too close behind for safety.

tail·ing (tāl′ing) *n.* 1. *pl.* Refuse or residue from grain after milling, or from ground ore after washing. 2. The inner covered portion of a projecting brick or stone in a wall.

tail·light (tāl′līt′) *n.* A light attached to the rear of a vehicle. Also **tail lamp**.

tai·lor (tā′lər) *n.* One who makes to order or repairs men's or women's outer garments. — *v.i.* 1. To do a tailor's work. — *v.t.* 2. To fit with garments: He is well *tailored*. 3. To work at or make by tailoring: to *tailor* a coat. ◆ Collateral adjective: *sartorial*. 4. To make, adjust, or adapt for a specific purpose. [< OF < LL *taliare* to split, cut]

tai·lor·bird (tā′lər·bûrd′) *n.* A passerine bird of Asia and Africa, that stitches leaves together to hold and hide its nest.

tai·lored (tā′lərd) *adj.* 1. Characterized by simple, severe style: said esp. of women's clothes. 1. Made by a tailor.

tai·lor-made (tā′lər·mād′) *adj.* 1. Made by a tailor. Made or as if made to order; perfectly fitted or suitable.

tail·piece (tāl′pēs′) *n.* 1. Any endpiece or appendage. 2. In a violin or similar instrument, a piece of wood, as ebony, at the soundboard end, having the strings fastened to it. For illus., see VIOLIN. 3. *Printing* An ornamental design at the lower blank portion of a page.

tail pipe An exhaust (n. def. 2).

tail·race (tāl′rās′) *n.* 1. That part of a millrace below the water wheel. 2. The channel for water to remove tailings.

tail·spin (tāl′spin′) *n.* 1. *Aeron.* The descent of a stalled airplane along a tight helical path at a steep angle. 2. *Informal* An emotional upheaval often resulting in loss of control.

tail wind A wind blowing in the same general direction as the course of an aircraft, ship, or other vehicle.

taint (tānt) *v.t.* 1. To imbue with an offensive, poisonous, or deteriorating quality or principle; infect with decay. 2. To render morally corrupt. — *v.i.* 3. To be or become tainted. — *n.* 1. A trace or germ of decay. 2. A moral stain or blemish; disgrace. [Fusion of ATTAINT and F *teint*, pp. of *teindre* to tinge, COLOR]

Taj Ma·hal (täzh′ mə·häl′, täj′) A mausoleum of white marble built (1631–45) at Agra, India.

take (tāk) *v.* **took**, **tak·en**, **tak·ing** *v.t.* 1. To lay hold sp. **2.** To get possession of; seize. **3.** To seize forcibly; ture. **4.** To catch in a trap or snare. **5.** To win in com- ition. **6.** To choose; select. **7.** To buy. **8.** To rent or e. **9.** To subscribe to, as a periodical. **10.** To assume upancy of: to *take* a chair. **11.** To assume the responsi- ties or duties of: to *take* office. **12.** To bring or accept) some relation to oneself: He *took* a wife. **13.** To assume s symbol or badge: to *take* the veil. **14.** To impose upon self: to *take* a vow. **15.** To remove or carry off: with *y.* **16.** To steal. **17.** To remove by death. **18.** To tract or deduct. **19.** To undergo: to *take* a beating. **20.** accept passively: to *take* an insult. **21.** To become af- ed with: He *took* cold. **22.** To affect: The fever *took* him lawn. **23.** To captivate; charm or delight. **24.** To react How did she *take* the news? **25.** To undertake to deal 1: to *take* an examination. **26.** To consider; deem. **27.** understand; comprehend. **28.** To strike in a specified ce; hit: The blow *took* him on the forehead. **29.** *Informal* aim or direct: He *took* a shot at the target. **30.** To carry 1 one: He *took* a briefcase along. **31.** To lead: This road s you to town. **32.** To escort; conduct: Who *took* her to dance? **33.** To receive into the body, as by eating, in- ng, etc. **34.** To accept, as something offered, due, or en: to *take* a degree. **35.** To let in; admit: The car will only six people. **36.** To indulge oneself in: to *take* a nap. To perform, as an action: to *take* a stride. **38.** To avail self of (an opportunity, etc.). **39.** To put into effect; ot: to *take* measures. **40.** To use up or consume: The 10 *takes* too much space. **41.** To make use of; apply: y *took* clubs to him. **42.** To travel by means of: to *take* ain. **43.** To go to; seek: to *take* cover. **44.** To ascertain obtain by measuring, computing, etc.: to *take* a census. To obtain or derive from some source; adopt or copy. To obtain by writing; write down or copy: to *take* notes. To obtain a likeness or representation of, by drawing photographing; also, to obtain (a likeness, picture, etc.) uch a manner. **48.** To experience; feel: to *take* pride. To conceive: to *take* a dislike. **50.** To absorb: The h will not *take* the pattern. **51.** In baseball, to allow (a h) to pass without swinging at it: said of a batter. **52.** ng To cheat; deceive. **53.** *Gram.* To require by construc- , or usage: The verb *takes* a direct object. — *v.i.* **54.** To possession. **55.** To engage; catch, as mechanical parts. To begin to grow; germinate. **57.** To have the intended ct: The vaccination *took.* **58.** To become popular; gain 1r or currency, as a play. **59.** To admit of being photo- ohed: His face *takes* well. **60.** To detract: with *from.* To become (ill or sick). **62.** To make one's way; go. In baseball, to allow a pitch to pass without swinging at aid of a batter. — **to take after 1.** To resemble. **2.** follow as an example. — **to take amiss** To be offended — **to take at one's word** To believe. — **to take back** To regain. **2.** To retract. — **to take breath** To pause, rom working. — **to take down 1.** To pull down, as a ding. **2.** To dismantle; disassemble. **3.** To humble. To write down; make a record of. — **to take heart** To courage or confidence. — **to take in 1.** To admit; re- e. **2.** To lessen in size or scope. **3.** To furl or haul in '). **4.** To include; embrace. **5** To understand; com- 1end. **6.** To receive into one's home for pay, as lodgers vork. **7.** *Informal* To cheat or deceive. **8.** *U.S. Infor-* To visit, as on a trip or tour: Did you *take in* the Louvre? o **take in vain** To use profanely or blasphemously, as the 1e of a deity. — **to take it 1.** To assume; understand. To endure hardship, abuse, etc. — **to take it out on** . *Informal* To vent one's anger, frustration, etc., on. — ake off **1.** To remove, as a coat. **2.** To carry away. **3.** kill. **4.** To deduct. **5.** *Informal* To mimic; burlesque. To rise from the ground or water in starting a flight, as an lane. **7.** *U.S. Informal* To leave; depart. — **to take on** o hire; employ. **2.** To undertake to deal with; handle. *nformal* To exhibit violent emotion. — **to take out 1.** extract; remove. **2.** To obtain from the proper authori- as a license or patent. **3.** To lead or escort. — **to take** r **1.** To assume control. **2.** To convey. — **to take** ce To happen. — **to take stock 1.** To make an inven- *.* **2.** To estimate probability, position, etc.; consider. — ake the field To begin a campaign or game. — **to take** 1. To have recourse to; go to: to *take* to one's bed. **2.** To elop the practice of, or an addiction to: He *took* to drink. To become fond of. — **to take to heart** To be deeply af- ed by. — **to take up 1.** To raise or lift. **2.** To make ller or less; shorten or tighten. **3.** To pay, as a mort- e. **4.** To accept as stipulated: to *take up* an option. **5.** begin or begin again. **6.** To reprove or criticize. **7.** To upy, engage, or consume, as space or time. **8.** To ac- e an interest in or devotion to: to *take up* a cause. — **to e up with** *Informal* To become friendly with. — *n.* **1.**

The act of taking, or that which is taken. **2.** An uninter- rupted run of a camera or recording apparatus in making a motion picture, television program, sound recording, etc. **3.** A quantity collected at one time: the *take* of fish. **4.** *U.S. Slang* Money collected, as the receipts of a sporting event. [OE *tacan* < ON *taka*]

take-down (tāk′doun′) *adj.* Fitted for being taken apart or easily down: a *takedown* rifle. — *n.* **1.** Any article so con- structed as to be taken apart easily. **2.** *U.S. Informal* The act of humiliating anyone.

take-home pay (tāk′hōm′) *U.S.* The remainder of one's wages or salary after tax and other payroll deductions.

take-in (tāk′in′) *n. Informal* An act of cheating or hoaxing. **take-off** (tāk′ôf′, -of′) *n.* **1.** The act of rising or leaping from the ground to begin flight; also, the spot where this happens. **2.** *Informal* A satirical imitation; caricature.

take-o-ver (tāk′ō-vər) *n.* An assuming or seizure of control, function, ownership, or rule.

tak-er (tā′kər) *n.* One who takes or collects.

tak-ing (tā′king) *adj.* **1.** Fascinating; captivating. **2.** *Informal* Contagious; infectious. — *n.* **1.** The act of one who takes. **2.** The thing or things taken. **3.** *pl.* Receipts. as of money. — **tak′ing-ly** *adv.* — **tak′ing-ness** *n.*

talc (talk) *n.* A soft, white or variously colored, hydrous magnesium silicate, $H_2Mg_3(SiO)_4$, used in making paper, soap, toilet powder, insulators, etc. Also **tal·cum** (tal′kəm). — *v.t.* **talcked** or **talced, talck·ing** or **talc·ing** To treat with talc. [< F < Med. L < Arabian *talq*]

talcum powder Finely powdered and purified talc, used as a dusting agent, filter, etc.

tale (tāl) *n.* **1.** That which is told or related; a story; reci- tal. **2.** A piece of gossip. **3.** A lie; falsehood. [OE *talu* speech, narrative]

tale-bear-er (tāl′bâr′ər) *n.* One who carries gossip; a tale- teller. — **tale′bear′ing** *adj. & n.*

tal·ent (tal′ənt) *n.* **1.** A particular and uncommon aptitude for some special work or activity. **2.** People of skill or abil- ity, collectively. **3.** An ancient weight and denomination of money. [OE < L < Gk. *talanton* weight]

tal·ent·ed (tal′ən-tid) *adj.* Having great ability; gifted.

talent scout One whose business is to discover talented people, esp. for the performing arts.

ta·ler (tä′lər) *n.* A former German silver coin, the proto- type of all dollars: also spelled *thaler.* [< G. See DOLLAR.]

ta·les (tā′lēz) *n. pl.* **·les** (-lēz) *Law* Persons to be sum- moned for jury duty to make up a deficiency when the regu- lar panel is exhausted by challenges. [< L *tales* pl. of *talis* such a one]

tales·man (tālz′mən) *n. pl.* **·men** (-mən) *Law* One of the tales.

tale·tel·ler (tāl′tel′ər) *n.* **1.** One who tells stories, etc.; a raconteur. **2.** A talebearer. — **tale′tell′ing** *adj. & n.*

tal·i·pes (tal′ə-pēz) *n. Pathol.* Clubfoot. [< NL < L *talus* ankle + *pes, pedis* foot] — **tal·i·ped** (tal′ə-ped) *adj.*

tal·i·pot (tal′ə-pot) *n.* A stately East Indian palm crowned by large leaves used as fans, umbrellas, writing material, and as coverings for houses. [< Bengali *tālipāt* palm leaf]

tal·is·man (tal′is-mən, -iz-) *n. pl.* **·mans 1.** Something supposed to produce extraordinary or magical effects; a charm or amulet. **2.** An astrological charm or symbol sup- posed to benefit or protect the possessor. [< F < Sp. < Arabic *tilsam, tilasm* magic figure] — **tal′is·man′ic** (-man′- ik) or **·i·cal** *adj.*

talk (tôk) *v.i.* **1.** To express or exchange thoughts in audi- ble words; communicate by speech. **2.** To make a speech. **3.** To communicate by means other than speech: to *talk* with one's fingers. **4.** To speak irreverently; prate; chatter. **5.** To confer; consult. **6.** To spread rumor; gossip. **7.** To make sounds suggestive of speech. **8.** *U.S. Informal* To give information, as to the police; inform. **9.** *Informal* To be effective or influential: money *talks.* — *v.t.* **10.** To ex- press in words; utter. **11.** To use in speaking; converse in: to *talk* Spanish. **12.** To converse about; discuss: to *talk* bus- iness. **13.** To bring to a specified condition or state by talk- ing: to *talk* one into doing something. **14.** To pass or spend, as time, in talking: usu. with *away.* — **to talk back To** answer impudently. — **to talk big** *Slang* To brag; boast. — **to talk down 1.** To silence by talking; outtalk. **2.** To direct (an aircraft) to a landing, in darkness, fog, etc., by giv- ing oral instructions to the pilot over the radio. — **to talk down to** To speak to in a condescending manner. — **to talk shop** To talk about one's work. — **to talk up 1.** To dis- cuss, esp. so as to promote; praise; extol. **2.** *Informal* To speak loudly or boldly. — *n.* **1.** The act of talking; conver- sation; speech. **2.** A speech or lecture, usu. informal. **3.** Report; rumor: We heard *talk* of war. **4.** That which is talked about; a topic; theme. **5.** A conference for discussion or deliberation; a council. **6.** Mere words; verbiage. **7.** A language, dialect, or lingo: baseball *talk*. [ME *talken*, prob. freq. of OE *talian* to reckon, speak] — **talk′er** *n.*

talk·a·tive (tô′kə·tiv) *adj.* Given to much talking. — **talk′a·tive·ly** *adv.* — **talk′a·tive·ness** *n.*

talking picture A motion picture with spoken words, music, sound effects, etc. Also *Informal* **talk·ie** (tô′kē).

talk·ing-to (tô′king·tōō′) *n. pl.* **-tos** *Informal* A scolding.

talk·y (tô′kē) *adj.* **talk·i·er, talk·i·est** Talkative.

tall (tôl) *adj.* **1.** Having more than average height; high or lofty. **2.** Having specified height: He is six feet *tall*. **3.** *Informal* Extravagant; boastful; also, unbelievable: a *tall* story. **4.** *Informal* Large; excellent; grand: a *tall* dinner. — *adv. Informal* Proudly: to stand *tall*. [OE *getæl* swift, prompt] — **tall′ness** *n.*

tall·ish (tô′lish) *adj.* Rather tall.

tal·lith (tal′ith, tä′lis) *n.* A fringed scarf or mantle worn around the shoulders by Orthodox and Conservative Jewish men when praying. [< Hebrew *tallīth* cover, robe]

tal·low (tal′ō) *n.* A mixture of the harder animal fats, as of beef or mutton, refined for use in candles, soaps, oleomargarine, etc. — *v.t.* To smear with tallow. [ME *talgh*] — **tal′low·y** *adj.*

tal·ly (tal′ē) *n. pl.* **·lies** **1.** A piece of wood on which notches or scores are cut as marks of number. **2.** A score or mark. **3.** A reckoning; account. **4.** A counterpart; duplicate. **5.** A mark indicative of a quantity or number, used to denote one in a series. **6.** A label; tag. — *v.* **·lied, ·ly·ing** *v.t.* **1.** To score on a tally; record. **2.** To reckon; count; estimate: often with *up*. **3.** To mark or cut corresponding notches in; cause to correspond. — *v.i.* **4.** To correspond; fit: The stories *tally*. **5.** To keep score. [< AF < L *talea* rod, cutting] — **tal′li·er** *n.*

tal·ly·ho (tal′ē·hō′) *interj.* A huntsman's cry to hounds when the quarry is sighted. — *n. pl.* **·hos** **1.** The cry of "tallyho." **2.** A four-in-hand coach. — *v.t.* **1.** To urge on, as hounds, with the cry of "tallyho." — *v.i.* **2.** To cry "tallyho." [Alter. of F *taïaut*, a hunting cry]

tal·ly·man (tal′ē·mən) *n. pl.* **·men** (-mən) **1.** One who keeps a count on a tally, esp., of votes. **2.** One who records number, volume, and measurement, as of timber.

Tal·mud (tal′mud, täl′mŏŏd) *n.* The body of Jewish civil and religious law (and related commentaries) not included in the Pentateuch. [< Hebrew *talmūdh* instruction] — **Tal·mud′ic** or **·i·cal** *adj.* — **Tal′mud·ist** *n.*

tal·on (tal′ən) *n.* **1.** The claw of a bird or other animal, esp. of a bird of prey. **2.** Anything resembling or suggesting a claw, as a grasping human hand. **3.** A projection on the bolt of a lock on which the key presses in shooting the bolt. [< OF < L *talus* heel] — **tal′oned** (-ənd) *adj.*

ta·lus (tā′ləs) *n. pl.* **·li** (-lī) **1.** *Anat.* The bone of the foot just above the heel bone: also called *anklebone, astragalus*. **2.** A slope, as of a tapering mass. **3.** *Geol.* The sloping mass of rock fragments below a cliff. [< L, ankle, heel]

tam (tam) *n.* A tam-o′-shanter.

ta·ma·le (tə·mä′lē) *n.* A Mexican dish made of crushed corn and meat, seasoned with red pepper, wrapped in corn husks, dipped in oil, and cooked by steam. Also **ta·mal** (tə·mäl′). [< Am. Sp. *tamales*, pl. of *tamal* < Nahuatl *tamalli*]

tam·a·rack (tam′ə·rak) *n.* **1.** The American larch, a tree common in northern North America. **2.** Its wood. Also called *hackmatack*. [< Algonquian]

tam·a·rind (tam′ə·rind) *n.* **1.** A tropical tree of the bean family, with hard yellow wood and showy yellow flowers striped with red. **2.** The fruit of this tree, a flat pod with soft acid pulp used in preserves and as a laxative. [< Sp. < Arabic *tamr hindī* Indian date]

tam·bour (tam′bŏŏr) *n.* **1.** A drum. **2.** A round wooden frame on which material for embroidering may be stretched; also, the fabric embroidered. — *v.t. & v.i.* To embroider on a tambour. [< F < Arabic *tambūr* a stringed instrument]

tam·bou·rin (tam′bə·rin) *n.* **1.** A long, narrow drum, originating in Provence. **2.** A gay, 18th-century Provençal dance, or the music for it. [< F < Provençal]

tam·bou·rine (tam′bə·rēn′) *n.* A musical instrument like the head of a drum, with jingles in the rim, played by striking it with the hand; a timbrel. [< F]

tame (tām) *adj.* **tam·er, tam·est** **1.** Having lost its native wildness or shyness; domesticated. **2.** In agriculture, brought under or produced by cultivation. **3.** Docile; tractable. **4.** Subdued or subjugated. **5.** Gentle; harmless. **6.** Lacking in effectiveness; uninteresting; dull. — *v.t.* **tamed, tam·ing** **1.** To domesticate. **2.** To bring into subjection or obedience; render spiritless. **3.** To tone down; soften, as glaring colors. [OE *tam*] — **tam′a·ble** or **tame′a·ble** *adj.* — **tame′ly** *adv.* — **tame′ness** *n.* — **tam′er** *n.*

tame·less (tām′lis) *adj.* Untamed or untamable. — **tame′-less·ness** *n.*

Tam·il (tam′əl, tum′əl) *n.* **1.** One of an ancient Dravidian people, and still the most numerous of the inhabitants of southern India and northern Ceylon. **2.** Their language.

Tam·ma·ny (tam′ə·nē) *n.* A fraternal society in New York

City (founded 1789) serving as the central organization of the city's Democratic party. Also called **Tammany Hall, Tammany Society.** [Alter. of *Tamanend*, name of a 17th Delaware Indian chief friendly toward white men]

Tam·muz (täm·mōōz′, täm′mōōz) The tenth month of the Hebrew year. See (Hebrew) CALENDAR. Also spelled *Thammuz:* also **Tam·uz.** [< Hebrew]

tam-o′-shan·ter (tam′ə·shan′tər) *n.* A Scottish cap with tight headband and a full, flat top, sometimes with a pompon or tassel. [after *Tam o′ Shanter,* a poem by Robert Burns]

tamp (tamp) *v.t.* **1.** To force down or pack closer by repeated blows. **2.** To ram down, as dirt, etc., on top of a charge in a blasthole. [Back formation < TAMPION]

tam·per (tam′pər) *v.i.* **1.** To meddle; interfere: usu. with *with*. **2.** To make changes, esp., so as to damage or corrupt: with *with*. **3.** To use corrupt measures, as bribery; scheme or plot. [Var. of TEMPER] — **tam′per·er** *n.*

tam·pi·on (tam′pē·ən) *n. Mil.* A stopper, as the plug into the mouth of a cannon to keep out moisture, etc. [< *tampion,* nasal var. of *tapon, tape* bung < Gmc]

tam·pon (tam′pon) *n. Med.* A plug of cotton or lint for insertion in a wound or body cavity. — *v.t.* To plug up, as a wound, with a tampon. [See TAMPION]

tan (tan) *v.* **tanned, tan·ning** *v.t.* **1.** To convert into leather, as hides or skins, by treating with tannin. **2.** To turn brown, as the skin, by exposure to sunlight. **3.** *Informal* To thrash; flog. — *v.i.* **4.** To become tanned, as hides or the skin. — *n.* **1.** A yellowish brown color tinged with red. **2.** A dark brown coloring of the skin, resulting from exposure to sun. **3.** Tanbark. — *adj.* **1.** Of the color tan; light brown. **2.** Used in or pertaining to tanning. [OE < Med.L *tanum* tanbark, prob. < Celtic]

tan·a·ger (tan′ə·jər) *n.* Any of a family of American songbirds noted for the brilliant plumage of the male. [< Pg. *tangara* < Tupi] — **tan′a·grine** (-grēn) *adj.*

tan·bark (tan′bärk′) *n.* **1.** The bark of certain trees, oak or hemlock, containing tannin, and used in tanning leather. **2.** Spent bark from the tan vats, used on circus arenas, racetracks, etc.

tan·dem (tan′dəm) *adv.* One in front of or before another. — *n.* **1.** Two or more horses harnessed in single file. **2.** A two-wheeled carriage drawn by a tandem of horses. **3.** A bicycle with seats for two persons, one behind the other: also **tandem bicycle. 4.** Any arrangement of two or more persons or things placed one before another. — *adj.* Arranged in tandem, or including parts so arranged. [< L, at length (of time); used in puns in sense of "lengthwise"]

tang (tang) *n.* **1.** A penetrating taste, flavor, or odor. **2.** A trace; hint. **3.** Any distinct taste, odor, quality, etc., other than one that is sweet. **4.** A slender shank or tongue projecting from some metal part, as the end of a sword blade or chisel, for inserting in or fixing upon a handle. — *v.t.* To provide with a tang. [< ON *tangi* point, dagger]

tan·gen·cy (tan′jən·sē) *n. pl.* **·cies** The state of being tangent. Also **tan′gence.**

tan·gent (tan′jənt) *adj.* Being in contact at a single point or along a line; touching. — *n.* **1.** *Geom.* **a** A straight line in contact with a curve at one point. **b** A straight line, curve, or surface touching another curve or surface at one or more consecutive points. **2.** *Trig.* A function of an acute angle equal to the ratio of the side opposite the angle to the side adjacent to the angle when the angle is included in a right triangle. — **to fly (or go) off on a tangent** *Informal* To make a sharp or sudden change in direction or course of action. [< L *tangens, -entis,* ppr. of *tangere* to touch]

tan·gen·tial (tan·jen′shəl) *adj.* **1.** Of, pertaining to, or moving in the direction of a tangent. **2.** Touching slightly. **3.** Only partially relevant to a subject. Also **tan·gen′tal** (-jen′təl). — **tan·gen′ti·al′i·ty** (-shē·al′ə·tē) *n.* — **tan·gen′tial·ly** *adv.*

tan·ger·ine (tan′jə·rēn′) *n.* **1.** A small, juicy orange with loose, easily removed skin: also called *mandarin.* **2.** A slightly burnt orange color. [after *Tangier*]

tan·gi·ble (tan′jə·bəl) *adj.* **1.** Perceptible by touch; within reach by touch. **2.** Capable of being apprehended by the mind; of definite shape; real: *tangible* evidence. **3.** Perceptible to the senses; corporeal; material: *tangible* property. — *n.* **1.** That which is tangible. **2.** *pl.* Material assets. [< F < L < *tangere* to touch] — **tan′gi·bil′i·ty, tan′gi·ble·ness** *n.* — **tan′gi·bly** *adv.*

tan·gle (tang′gəl) *v.* **·gled, ·gling** *v.t.* **1.** To twist or involve in a confused and not readily separable mass. **2.** To ensnare as in a tangle; enmesh. — *v.i.* **3.** To be or become entangled. — **to tangle with** *Informal* To come to blows with. — *n.* **1.** A confused intertwining, as of threads or hairs; a snarl. **2.** A state of confusion or complication; jumbled mess. **3.** A state of perplexity or bewilderment. [Nasalized var. of obs. *tagle* < Scand.] — **tan′gler** *n.*

tan·gly (tang′glē) *adj.* Consisting of or being in a tangle.

tan·go (tang′gō) *n. pl.* **·gos 1.** Any of several Latin-American dances in 2/4 time, characterized by deliberate glid-

ps and low dips. **2.** Any syncopated tune or melody to
ich the tango may be danced. — *v.i.* To dance the tango.
Am.Sp., fiesta, Negro drum dance]

g·y (tang′ē) *adj.* **tang·i·er, tang·i·est** Having a tang in
te or odor; pungent.

k (tangk) *n.* **1.** A large vessel, basin, or receptacle for
ding a fluid. **2.** Any natural or artificial pool or pond.
Mil. A heavily armored combat vehicle, moving on cater-
ar treads and mounting guns of various calibers. — *v.t.*
place or store in a tank. [< Pg. *tanque*, aphetic var. of
nque < L *stagnum* pool]

k·age (tangk′ij) *n.* **1.** The act, process, or operation of
ting in tanks. **2.** The price for storage in tanks. **3.** The
acity or contents of a tank. **4.** Slaughterhouse waste, as
es and entrails, used when dried as a fertilizer or feed.

k·ard (tangk′ərd) *n.* A large, one-handled drinking cup,
. made of pewter or silver, often with a cover. [< MDu.
Med.L *tancardus* large goblet]

k·er (tangk′ər) *n.* A cargo vessel specially constructed
the transport of liquids, esp. oil and gasoline.

k farm *U.S.* An area near a refinery, factory, port, etc.,
upied by large storage tanks.

k·ful (tangk′fool′) *n.* The quantity that fills a tank.

k town *U.S. Informal* A small town where trains for-
rly stopped to refill from a water tank.

nage (tan′ij) *n.* The act or operation of tanning.

ner (tan′ər) *n.* One who tans hides.

ner·y (tan′ər-ē) *n.* *pl.* **·ner·ies** A place where leather is
ned.

nic (tan′ik) *adj.* Pertaining to or derived from tannin
tanbark.

nic acid *n. Chem.* Any of a group of brownish astrin-
it compounds extracted from gallnuts, sumac, etc., used
:he preparation of ink and in the manufacture of leather.

nin (tan′in) *n.* Tannic acid.

ning (tan′ing) *n.* **1.** The art or process of converting
es into leather. **2.** A bronzing, as of the skin, by exposure
the sun, wind, etc. **3.** *Informal* A beating or thrashing.

sy (tan′zē) *n.* *pl.* **·sies** Any of various coarse perennial
bs with yellow flowers and an aromatic, bitter taste, used
medicine for its tonic properties. [< OF *tanesie*, aphetic
. of *athanasie* < LL < Gk., immortality]

ta·lize (tan′tə-līz) *v.t.* **·lized, ·liz·ing** To tease or tor-
it by repeated frustration of hopes or desires. Also *Brit.*
′ta·lise. [< TANTALUS] — **tan′ta·li·za′tion** *n.* — **tan′·**
iz′er *n.* — **tan′ta·liz′ing·ly** *adv.*

ta·lum (tan′tə-ləm) *n.* A silver-white, very heavy, duc-
. metallic element (symbol Ta), forming alloys with tung-
a, molybdenum, and iron. See ELEMENT. [< TANTALUS;
m its inability to absorb water]

·ta·lus (tan′tə-ləs) In Greek mythology, a rich king,
o was punished in Hades by being made to stand in water
it receded when he tried to drink, and under fruit-laden
nches he could not reach.

ta·mount (tan′tə-mount) *adj.* Having equivalent val-
effect, or import; equivalent: with *to.* [< AF < L *tantus*
much + OF *amonter* to amount]

trum (tan′trəm) *n.* A petulant fit of rage. [Origin un-
wn]

·ism (dou′iz-əm, tou′-) *n.* One of the principal religions
philosophies of China, founded by Lao-tse, who taught
it happiness could be acquired through obedience to the
uirements of man's nature in accordance with the **Tao**
u, tou), or Way, the basic principle of all nature. [<
nese *tao* way, road] — **Tao′ist** *adj. & n.* — **Tao·is′tic** *adj.*

(tap) *n.* **1.** An arrangement for drawing out liquid, as
r from a cask. **2.** A faucet or cock; spigot. **3.** A plug or
pper to close an opening in a cask or other vessel. **4.**
uor drawn from a tap; also, a particular liquor or quality
iquor contained in casks. **5.** *Brit.* A place where liquor is
ved; taproom. **6.** A tool for cutting internal screw
eads. **7.** A point of connection for an electrical circuit.
on tap 1. Contained in a cask; ready for tapping: beer *on*
. **2.** Provided with a tap. **3.** *Informal* Available; ready.
v.t. **tapped, tap·ping 1.** To provide with a tap or spigot.
To pierce or open so as to draw liquid from. **3.** To draw
uid) from a container. **4.** To make connection with: to
a gas main. **5.** To make connection with secretly: to *tap*
elephone wire. **6.** To make an internal screw thread in
h a tap. [OE *tæppa*]

(tap) *v.* **tapped, tap·ping** *v.t.* **1.** To touch or strike
tly. **2.** To make or produce by tapping. **3.** To apply
ther to (the sole or heel of a shoe) in repair. — *v.i.* **4.** To
ke a light blow or blows, as with the finger tip. — *n.* **1.**
gentle or playful blow; also, the sound made by such a
w. **2.** Leather, etc., affixed to a shoe sole or heel; also, a
tal plate on the toe or heel of a shoe. [< OF *taper*] —
′per *n.*

ta·pa (tä′pä) *n.* **1.** The inner bark of an Asian mulberry tree
used in making a kind of cloth. **2.** The cloth. [< native
Polynesian name]

tap-dance (tap′dans′, -däns′) *v.i.* **-danced, -danc·ing** To
dance or perform a tap dance.

tap dance A dance in which the dancer emphasizes his
steps by tapping the floor with the heels or toes of shoes designed to make the rhythm audible. — **tap dancer**

tape (tāp) *n.* **1.** A narrow strip of strong woven fabric. **2.**
Any long, narrow, flat strip of paper, metal, etc. **3.** A magnetic tape. **4.** A tapeline. **5.** A string stretched breast-
high across the finishing point of a racing track and broken
by the winner of the race. — *v.t.* **taped, tap·ing 1.** To wrap
or secure with tape. **2.** To apply a tape to; bandage: to *tape*
a boxer's hands. **3.** To measure with or as with a tapeline.
4. *Informal* To record on magnetic tape. [OE *tæppe* strip of
cloth] — **tape′less** *adj.*

tape·line (tāp′līn′) *n.* A tape for measuring distances. Also
tape measure.

ta·per[1] (tā′pər) *n.* One who or that which tapes.

ta·per[2] (tā′pər) *n.* **1.** A small candle. **2.** A burning wick or
other light substance giving but feeble illumination. **3.** A
gradual diminution of size in an elongated object: the *taper*
of a mast. **4.** Any tapering object, as a cone. — *v.t. & v.i.*
1. To make or become smaller or thinner toward one end.
2. To lessen gradually; diminish: with *off.* — *adj.* Growing
small by degrees in one direction; slender and conical or pyramidal. [OE, dissimilated var. of Med.L *papur* taper, wick
< L, papyrus] — **ta′per·ing·ly** *adv.*

tape recorder A device that converts sound into magnetic
patterns stored on a tape, reversing the process for playback.

tape recording 1. The process of transcribing music,
speech, etc., on a tape recorder. **2.** A transcription so made.

tap·es·try (tap′is-trē) *n.* *pl.* **·tries** A woven, ornamental
fabric, used for hangings, in which the woof is supplied by a
spindle, the design being formed by stitches across the warp.
— *v.t.* **·tried, ·try·ing 1.** To hang or adorn with tapestry. **2.**
To make or weave as tapestry. [< OF < L < Gk. *tapētion*,
dim. of *tapēs* rug]

tape·worm (tāp′wûrm′) *n.* Any of various worms with
segmented, ribbonlike bodies, parasitic on the intestines of
vertebrates and often infesting man.

tap·i·o·ca (tap′ē-ō′kə) *n.* A nutritious starchy substance
having irregular grains, obtained by drying cassava starch.
[< Sp. < Tupi < *ty* juice + *pŷa* heart + *oco* to be removed]

ta·pir (tā′pər) *n.* A large nocturnal mammal, having short
limbs and a flexible snout, native to South and Central
America and to the Malay Peninsula. [< Sp. < Tupi
tapy′ra]

tap·pet (tap′it) *n. Mech.* A lever or projecting arm of a
mechanism that moves or is moved intermittently by automatically touching another part. [< TAP[2]]

tap·ping (tap′ing) *n.* **1.** The act of one who or that which
taps. **2.** Something taken by tapping, or running from a tap.

tap·room (tap′rōōm′, -rōōm′) *n.* A bar or barroom.

tap·root (tap′rōōt′, -rōōt′) *n. Bot.* The principal descending root of a plant. — **tap′root′ed** *adj.*

taps (taps) *n.pl.* (*usu.* construed as *sing.*) A military signal
by bugle or beat of drum, regularly sounded after tattoo for
the extinguishing of all lights and sometimes played after a
military burial.

tap·ster (tap′stər) *n.* One who draws and serves liquor; a
bartender. [OE *tæppestre* barmaid]

tar[1] (tär) *n.* **1.** A dark, oily, viscid mixture of hydrocarbons,
obtained by the destructive distillation of resinous woods,
coal, etc. **2.** Coal tar. — *v.t.* **tarred, tar·ring** To cover
with or as with tar. — **to tar and feather** To smear (a person) with tar and then cover with feathers as a punishment.
— *adj.* Made of, derived from, or resembling tar. [OE *teoru*]

tar[2] (tär) *n. Informal* A sailor. [Short for TARPAULIN]

tar·an·tel·la (tar′ən-tel′ə) *n.* A lively Neapolitan dance in
6/8 time; also, the music written for it. [< Ital., dim. of
Taranto Taranto]

ta·ran·tu·la (tə-ran′chŏŏ-lə) *n.* *pl.* **·las** or **·lae** (-lē) **1.** A
large, hairy spider of southern Europe. **2.** Any of various
related spiders known for their painful but not dangerous
bite. [< Med.L < Ital. < *Taranto* Taranto]

tar·boosh (tär-bōōsh′) *n.* A brimless, usu. red, felt cap with
colored silk tassel, worn by Moslem men. Also **tar·bush′.**
[< Arabic *tarbūsh*]

tar·di·grade (tär′də-grād) *adj.* Slow in motion or action.
[< F < L < *tardus* slow + *gradi* to walk]

tar·dy (tär′dē) *adj.* **·di·er, ·di·est 1.** Not coming at the appointed time; late. **2.** Moving slowly. [< F < L *tardus*
slow] — **tar′di·ly** *adv.* — **tar′di·ness** *n.*

tare[1] (târ) *n.* **1.** An unidentified weed that grows among
wheat. **2.** A seed of wickedness. *Matt.* xiii 25. **3.** Any of
various species of vetch. [MDu. *tarwe* wheat]

tare[2] (târ) *n.* An allowance made to a buyer of goods by deducting from the gross weight of his purchase the weight of the container. — *v.t.* **tared, tar·ing** To weigh, as a package, in order to determine the amount of tare. [< F < Arabic < *taraha* to reject, throw away]

tar·get (tär′git) *n.* **1.** An object presenting a surface that may be used as a mark or butt, as in rifle or archery practice. **2.** Anything that is shot at. **3.** A person or thing made an object of attack or center of attention; a butt. — **on target 1.** Headed or aimed so as to hit a target. **2.** *Informal* Aptly directed or placed; to the point: The quip was right *on target*. [ME *targette, targuete,* dim. of *targa* shield]

Tar·heel (tär′hēl′) *n. Informal* A native of North Carolina. Also **Tar Heel.**

Tarheel State Nickname of North Carolina.

tar·iff (tar′if) *n.* **1.** A schedule of articles of merchandise with the rates of duty to be paid for their importation or exportation. **2.** A duty, or duties collectively. **3.** The law or principles governing the imposition of duties. **4.** Any schedule of charges. — *v.t.* **1.** To make a list or table of duties or customs on. **2.** To fix a price or tariff on. [< Ital. < Arabic *ta'rif* information]

tar·mac (tär′mak) *n. Brit. & Canadian* **1.** *Aeron.* **a** A hangar apron. **b** An asphalt runway. **2.** An asphalt road.

tarn (tärn) *n.* A small mountain lake. [ME < ON *tjörn*]

tar·na·tion (tär-nā′shən) *interj. & n. U.S. Dial.* Damnation: a euphemism.

tar·nish (tär′nish) *v.t.* **1.** To dim the luster of. **2.** To dim the purity of; stain; disgrace. — *v.i.* **3.** To lose luster, as by oxidation. — *n.* **1.** Loss of luster. **2.** A blemish or stain. **3.** The thin film of color on the exposed surface of a metal or mineral. [< OF < *terne* dull, wan] — **tar′nish·a·ble** *adj.*

ta·ro (tä′rō) *n. pl.* **·ros 1.** Any of several tropical plants of the arum family, grown for their edible, cornlike rootstocks. **2.** The rootstock of this plant. [< native Polynesian name]

tar·ot (tar′ō, -ət) *n.* One of a set of playing cards with grilled or checkered backs employed by fortunetellers and gypsies in foretelling future events. [< F < Ital. < *taroccaro* to wrangle, play at cards]

tar·pau·lin (tär-pô′lin, tär′pə-) *n.* **1.** A waterproof canvas impregnated with tar, used to cover merchandise, athletic fields, etc. **2.** A sailor's wide-brimmed storm hat. Also *Informal* **tarp.** [< TAR[1] + PALL[1] + -ING[1]]

tar·pon (tär′pon, -pən) *n. pl.* **·pon** or **·pons** A large marine game fish of the West Indies and the coast of Florida, having conspicuous silvery scales. [Origin unknown]

tar·ra·gon (tar′ə-gon) *n.* **1.** A European perennial plant allied to wormwood. **2.** The aromatic leaves of this plant, used as seasoning. [< Sp. < Arabic < Gk. *drakōn* dragon]

tar·ri·er (tar′ē-ər) *n.* One who or that which tarries.

tar·ry[1] (tar′ē) *v.* **·ried, ·ry·ing** *v.i.* **1.** To put off going or coming; linger. **2.** To remain in the same place, esp. longer than one expected. **3.** To wait; stay. — *n.* Sojourn; stay. [ME *tarien* to vex, hinder, delay, fusion of OE *tirgan* to vex + OF *targer* to delay < LL < L *tardare* to delay]

tar·ry[2] (tär′ē) *adj.* **·ri·er, ·ri·est** Covered with tar; like tar.

tar·sal (tär′səl) *adj.* Of, relating to, or situated near the tarsus or ankle.

tarso- *combining form* The tarsus; pertaining to the tarsus. Also, before vowels, **tars-.** [< Gk. *tarsos* flat of the foot, edge of the eyelid]

tar·sus (tär′səs) *n. pl.* **·si** (-sī) **1.** *Anat.* The ankle, or, in man, the group of seven bones of which it is composed. **2.** *Zool.* **a** The shank of a bird's leg. **b** The distal part of the leg in insects. [< NL < Gk. *tarsos* flat of the foot, any flat surface]

tart[1] (tärt) *adj.* **1.** Having a sharp, sour taste. **2.** Severe; cutting; caustic: a *tart* remark. [OE *teart*] — **tart′ly** *adv.* — **tart′ness** *n.*

tart[2] (tärt) *n.* **1.** A small pastry shell with fruit or custard filling and without a top crust. **2.** In England, an uncovered fruit pie. **3.** *Slang* A girl or woman of loose morals, as a prostitute. [< OF *tarte*]

tar·tan (tär′tən) *n.* **1.** A woolen fabric having varicolored lines or stripes at right angles, forming a distinctive pattern, the characteristic dress of the Scottish Highlanders, each clan having its particular pattern or patterns. **2.** Any similar pattern; a plaid. **3.** A garment made of tartan. For illus. see KILT. — *adj.* **1.** Made of tartan. **2.** Striped or checkered in a manner similar to the Scottish tartans. [? < OF *tiretaine* linsey-woolsey]

tar·tar[1] (tär′tər) *n.* **1.** An acid substance deposited from grape juice during fermentation as a pinkish sediment; crude bitartrate of potassium. **2.** *Dent.* A yellowish incrustation on the teeth, chiefly calcium phosphate. [< F < LL < Med.Gk. *tartaron,* ? < Arabic]

tar·tar[2] (tär′tər) *n. Often cap.* **1.** A person of intractable or savage temper. **2.** An unexpectedly formidable opponent. — **to catch a tartar** To take on or be matched with an unexpectedly strong opponent. [< TARTAR]

Tar·tar (tär′tər) *n.* A Tatar. — *adj.* Of or pertaining to the Tatars or Tartary: also **Tar·tar·i·an** (tär-târ′ē-ən). [F < LL < Persian *Tātar* Tatar]

Tar·tar·e·an (tär-târ′ē-ən) *adj.* Of or pertaining to Tartarus.

tartar emetic *Chem.* A white, crystalline, poisonous derivative of tartaric acid, used in medicine and in dyeing.

tar·tare sauce (tär′tər) A fish sauce made of mayonnaise, capers, chopped olives, and pickles. Also **tar′tar sauce.**

tar·tar·ic (tär-tar′ik, -tär′ik) *adj.* Pertaining to or derived from tartar or tartaric acid.

tartaric acid *Chem.* Any one of four organic compounds $C_4H_6O_6$, occurring in the free state or as a potassium or calcium salt, as in grape juice, various unripe fruits, etc.

tar·tar·ize (tär′tə-rīz) *v.t.* **·ized, ·iz·ing** To impregnate or treat with tartar, cream of tartar, or tartar emetic. — **tar·i·za′tion** *n.*

Tartar mink The kolinsky. Also **Tartar sable.**

tar·tar·ous (tär′tər-əs) *adj.* Of or derived from tartar.

Tar·ta·rus (tär′tər-əs) **1.** In Greek mythology, the abyss below Hades where Zeus confined the Titans. **2.** Hades.

Tar·ta·ry (tär′tər-ē) A region of Asia and eastern Europe ruled by the Tatars, under Mongol leadership, in the 13th and 14th centuries.

tart·let (tärt′lit) *n.* A small pastry tart.

tar·trate (tär′trāt) *n. Chem.* A salt or ester of tartaric acid.

task (task, täsk) *n.* **1.** A specific amount of labor or study imposed by authority or required by duty or necessity. **2.** Any work voluntarily undertaken. **3.** An exhausting or bothersome job or duty. **4.** A specific military mission. — **to take to task** To reprove; lecture. — *v.t.* **1.** To assign a task to. **2.** To overtax with labor; burden. **3.** To reprimand. [< AF < LL < L *taxare* to appraise]

task force *Mil.* A tactical unit consisting of elements drawn from different branches of the armed services and assigned to execute a specific mission.

task·mas·ter (task′mas′tər, täsk′mäs′tər) *n.* **1.** One who assigns tasks, esp. severe ones. **2.** One who or that which loads with heavy burdens.

Tass (täs, tas) *n.* A Soviet news agency. [< Russian *legrafnoe*) *A*(*gentstvo*) *S*(*ovetskovo*) *S*(*oyuza*)]

tas·sel (tas′əl) *n.* **1.** A dangling ornament for curtains, cushions, etc., consisting of a tuft of loose threads or cords. **2.** Any of various similar objects, as the inflorescence on the stalk of Indian corn. **3.** Formerly, a clasp for holding a cloak. — *v.* **tas·seled** or **·selled, tas·sel·ing** or **·sel·ling 1.** To provide or adorn with tassels. **2.** To form in a tassel or tassels. **3.** To remove the tassels from (Indian corn). — *v.i.* **4.** To put forth tassels, as Indian corn. [< OF, clasp < Med.L *tasselus,* var. of L *taxillus*]

taste (tāst) *v.* **tast·ed, tast·ing** *v.t.* **1.** To perceive the flavor of (something) by taking into the mouth or touching with the tongue. **2.** To take a little of (food or drink); eat or drink a little of. **3.** To test the quality of (a product) by tasting: His business is *tasting* tea. — *v.i.* **4.** To have a specific flavor: Sugar *tastes* sweet. **5.** To take a small quantity into the mouth; take a taste: usu. with *of.* **6.** To have experience or enjoyment; with *of:* to *taste* of great sorrow. — *n.* **1.** *Physiol.* Any of the four fundamental sensations, sweet, bitter, or sour, excited by the sole action of the gustatory nerves. **2.** A small quantity tasted, eaten, or sipped. **3.** A slight experience or sample of anything. **4.** Special fondness and aptitude for a pursuit; bent; inclination: *taste* for music. **5.** The faculty of discerning and appreciating what is beautiful, appropriate, or correct, as in nature, art, clothes, etc. **6.** Style or form with respect to the rules of propriety. **7.** Individual preference: That tie suits his *taste.* **8.** The act of tasting. [< OF *taster* to taste, try, feel] — **tast′a·ble** *adj.*

taste bud *Physiol.* One of the clusters of cells situated in the epithelial tissue, chiefly of the tongue, and containing sensitive receptors for the discriminatory perception of taste.

taste·ful (tāst′fəl) *adj.* **1.** Conforming to taste. **2.** Possessing good taste. — **taste′ful·ly** *adv.* — **taste′ful·ness** *n.*

taste·less (tāst′lis) *adj.* **1.** Having no flavor; insipid. **2.** Lacking, or showing a lack of, good taste. **3.** Devoid of esthetic taste. — **taste′less·ly** *adv.* — **taste′less·ness** *n.*

tast·er (tās′tər) *n.* One who tastes; esp., one who tests the quality of as an occupation: a *teataster.*

tast·y (tās′tē) *adj.* **tast·i·er, tast·i·est** *Informal* **1.** Having a fine flavor; savory. **2.** Tasteful. — **tast′i·ly** *adv.* — **tast′i·ness** *n.*

tat (tat) *v.* **tat·ted, tat·ting** *v.t.* **1.** To make, as an edging, by tatting. — *v.i.* **2.** To make tatting. [Back formation < TATTING] — **tat′ter** *n.*

Ta·tar (tä′tər) *n.* **1.** One belonging to any of the Tatar peoples of west central and southwest central U.S.S.R. **2.** Any of the Turkic languages of the Tatars, as Uzbek. — *adj.* Of or pertaining to the Tatars. Also *Tartar.* [< Persian] — **Ta·tar·i·an** (-tär′ē-ən) *adj.*

tat·ter (tat′ər) *n.* **1.** A torn and hanging shred; rag. **2.** Ragged clothing. — *v.t.* **1.** To make ragged; into

— *v.i.* **2.** To become ragged. [< Scand. Cf. ON *tö-rags*] — **tat′tered** *adj.*

er·de·mal·ion (tat′ər·di·māl′yən, -mal′-) *n.* A person ing ragged clothes; a raggamuffin. [Origin unknown]

ng (tat′ing) *n.* A lacelike threadwork, made by hand; the act or process of making it. [Origin unknown]

le (tat′l) *v.* **·tled, ·tling** *v.i.* **1.** To talk idly; prate; ter. **2.** To tell tales about others. — *v.t.* **3.** To reveal ossiping. — *n.* **1.** Idle talk or gossip. **2.** Prattling ch. [Prob. < MDu. *tatelen*] — **tat′tling·ly** *adv.*
Syn. (verb) **1.** prattle. **2.** blab, inform.

er (tat′ər) *n.* One who tattles; a talebearer.

le·tale (tat′l·tāl′) *n.* A talebearer; tattler.

00¹ (ta·too′) *v.t.* **1.** To prick and mark (the skin) with lible pigments. **2.** To mark the skin with (designs, etc.) is way. — *n. pl.* **·toos** A pattern or picture so made. Polynesian] — **tat·too′er** *n.* — **tat·too′ing** *n.*

00² (ta·too′) *n.* **1.** A continuous beating or drumming. military or naval usage, a signal by drum or bugle to ir to quarters, usu., occurring about 9 P.M. [< Du. < ap, faucet + *toe* to shut]

tou) *n.* The nineteenth letter in the Greek alphabet ·), corresponding to the English *t.* See ALPHABET.

ht (tôt) Past tense and past participle of TEACH.

t (tônt) *n.* A sarcastic, biting speech or remark; scorn-eproach. — *v.t.* **1.** To reproach with sarcastic or con-tuous words; mock; upbraid. **2.** To tease in any way; oke with taunts. [? < OF < L *temptare, tentare* to test, — **taunt′er** *n.* — **taunt′ing·ly** *adv.*

e (tōp) *n.* The color of moleskin; dark gray, often d with brown, purple, or yellow. [< F < L *talpa* mole] **)-** *combining form* Bull; ox; bovine. Also, before vow--aur-. [< Gk. *tauros* bull]

rus (tôr′əs) *n.* A constellation, the Bull, containing the ht star Aldebaran; also, the second sign of the zodiac. CONSTELLATION, ZODIAC. [< L]

t (tôt) *adj.* **1.** Stretched tight; not loose or slack. **2.** se; tight: *taut* muscles. **3.** In proper shape; tidy. [ME *toht*] — **taut′ly** *adv.* — **taut′ness** *n.*

en (tôt′n) *v.t. & v.i.* To make or become taut; tighten. **)-** *combining form* Same; identical. Also, before vow--taut-. [< Gk. *tauto* the same]

og (tô·tôg′, -tog′) *n.* A blackish, edible, fish of the th American Atlantic coast. Also **tau·taug′.** [< Algon-n pl. of *tautau*, a blackfish]

ol·o·gy (tô·tol′ə·jē) *n. pl.* **·gies** Unnecessary repe-n of the same idea in different words; pleonasm: *He is ng his own autobiography.* [< LL < Gk. < *tauto* the e + *logos* discourse] — **tau·to·log·ic** (tô′tə·loj′ik) or **l adj.** — **tau′to·log′i·cal·ly** *adv.*

rn (tav′ərn) *n.* **1.** A place licensed to retail liquors to drunk on the premises. **2.** A public house providing ing, food, and drink. [< OF < L *taberna* hut, booth]

tô) *n.* **1.** A game of marbles. **2.** The line from which ble-players shoot. **3.** A marble used for shooting. [< d. Cf. ON *taug* string.]

dry (tô′drē) *adj.* **·dri·er, ·dri·est** Showy and cheap; elessly ornamental. [< *St. Audrey's lace,* a type of neck-e sold at St. Audrey's Fair at Ely, England] — **taw′-y** *adv.* — **taw′dri·ness** *n.*

ny (tô′nē) *adj.* **·ni·er, ·ni·est** Tan-colored; brownish w. Also **taw′ney.** [< AF < OF < *tanner* to tan] — **′ni·ness** *n.*

taks) *n.* **1.** A compulsory contribution levied upon per-, property, or business for the support of government. iny proportionate assessment, as on the members of a ety. **3.** A heavy demand on one's powers or resources; nerous duty; a burden. — *v.t.* **1.** To impose a tax on. *aw* To settle or fix (costs) in any judicial matter. **3.** To ect to a severe demand; impose a burden upon: He *taxes* patience. **4.** To accuse; charge; blame: usu. with *with.* OF < L *taxare* to estimate, appraise] — **tax′a·bil′i·ty, ax′a·ble·ness** *n.* — **tax′a·ble** *adj.* — **tax′a·bly** *adv.*
ax′er *n.*
— **Syn.** (noun) **1.** assessment, custom, duty, excise, impost, , rate, tariff, tithe, tribute.
ax may appear as a combining form with the meaning of , as in the following list:

x assessor	tax evader	tax payment
x burden	tax-evading	tax proposal
x-burdened	tax-exempt	tax receipt
x claim	tax-free	tax repeal
x collecting	tax-laden	tax revenue
x collector	tax law	tax-ridden
x cut	tax levy	tax-supported
x dodger	taxman	tax system
x-dodging	taxpaid	taxwise

a·tion (tak·sā′shən) *n.* **1.** The act of taxing. **2.** The unt assessed as a tax.

tax-de·duct·i·ble (taks′di·duk′tə·bəl) *adj.* Legally deduct-ible from that portion of one's income or assets subject to taxes: Medical expenses are *tax-deductible.*

tax·i (tak′sē) *n. pl.* **tax·is** A taxicab. — *v.* **tax·ied, tax·i·ing** or **tax·y·ing** *v.i.* **1.** To ride in a taxicab. **2.** To move along the ground or on the surface of the water under its own power, as an airplane before taking off. — *v.t.* **3.** To cause (an airplane) to taxi. [< TAXI(CAB)]

tax·i·cab (tak′sē·kab′) *n.* An automobile available for hire, usually fitted with a taximeter. [Short for *taximeter cab*]

tax·i·der·my (tak′sə·dûr′mē) *n.* The art of stuffing and mounting the skins of dead animals for preservation or ex-hibition. [< Gk. *taxis* arrangement + *derma* skin] — **tax′-i·der′mal, tax′i·der′mic** *adj.* — **tax′i·der′mist** *n.*

tax·i·me·ter (tak′si·mē′tər) *n.* An instrument for measur-ing distances and recording fares, used in taxicabs. [< F < *taxe* tariff + *mètre* meter]

-taxis *combining form* Order; disposition; arrangement: *thermotaxis.* Also spelled **-taxy.** [< Gk. *taxis* arrangement]

tax·on·o·my (tak·son′ə·mē) *n.* **1.** The department of knowl-edge that embodies the laws and principles of classification. **2.** *Biol.* The systematic arrangement of plant and animal organisms according to established criteria in the following major groups, beginning with the most inclusive: kingdom, phylum or division, class, order, family, genus, and species. [< F < Gk. *taxis* arrangement + *nomos* law] — **tax·o·nom·ic** (tak′sə·nom′ik) or **·i·cal** *adj.* — **tax′o·nom′i·cal·ly** *adv.* — **tax·on′o·mer, tax·on′o·mist** *n.*

tax·pay·er (taks′pā′ər) *n.* One who pays a tax or is subject to taxation.

T-bone (tē′bōn) *n.* A beefsteak containing a T-shaped bone, taken from the loin. Also **T-bone steak.**

tea (tē) *n.* **1.** An evergreen Asian shrub having leathery, toothed leaves and white or pink flowers. **2.** The prepared leaves of this plant, or an infusion of them used as a bever-age. **3.** Any infusion, preparation, or extract used as a bev-erage or medicinally: beef *tea,* senna *tea.* **4.** *Brit.* A light evening or afternoon meal. **5.** A social gathering at which tea is served. [< dial. Chinese *t'e*]
Tea may appear as a combining form, as in **teacart, tea-taster, teaware.**

tea bag A small porous sack of cloth or paper containing tea leaves, immersed in water to make tea: also called *tea ball.*

tea ball **1.** A perforated metal ball that is filled with tea leaves and placed in hot water to make tea. **2.** A tea bag.

tea ceremony A ritual preparation and serving of tea, practiced by the Japanese.

teach (tēch) *v.* **taught, teach·ing** *v.t.* **1.** To impart knowl-edge by lessons; give instruction to: to *teach* a class. **2.** To give instruction in; communicate the knowledge of: to *teach* French. **3.** To train by practice or exercise. — *v.i.* **4.** To follow the profession of teaching. **5.** To impart knowledge or skill. [OE *tǣcan*] — **teach′a·bil′i·ty** *n.* — **teach′a·ble** *adj.* — **teach′a·bly** *adv.*
— **Syn. 1.** *Teach* embraces all methods of imparting knowledge, information, guidance, or counsel. To *instruct* is to give specific directions about a subject: to *instruct* recruits in the use of a rifle. *Educate* usu., means to instruct in a school or college. Both *school* and *discipline* refer to the teaching of certain patterns of behavior; they both connote authority: to *school* a child to obey promptly, to *discipline* oneself to eat sparingly. *Train* suggests the fitting of a person for a particular work; of all these words, *train* is preferred when reference is made to an animal.

teach·er (tē′chər) *n.* One who teaches; esp., one whose oc-cupation is to teach others; an instructor.

teach·ing (tē′ching) *n.* **1.** The act or occupation of a teach-er. **2.** That which is taught.

tea cozy A cozy.

tea·cup (tē′kup′) *n.* **1.** A small cup suitable for serving tea. **2.** As much as a teacup will hold, usu., four fluid ounces: also **tea′cup·ful′** (-fŏŏl′).

teak (tēk) *n.* **1.** A large East Indian tree, yielding a very hard, durable timber highly prized for shipbuilding. **2.** The wood of this tree: also **teak′wood** (-wŏŏd). [< Malayalam *tēkka*]

tea·ket·tle (tē′ket′l) *n.* A kettle with a spout, used for boil-ing water.

teal (tēl) *n.* **1.** Any of various small, short-necked river ducks of the Old World and North America. **2.** A dull blue color with a greenish cast: also **teal blue.** [ME *tele*]

team (tēm) *n.* **1.** Two or more beasts of burden harnessed together, often including harness and vehicle; also, a single horse and vehicle. **2.** A set of workers, or players competing in a game: a baseball *team.* — *v.t.* **1.** To convey with a team. **2.** To harness together in a team. — *v.i.* **3.** To drive a team as a business. **4.** To form a team; work as a team: to *team* up. — *adj.* Of or pertaining to a team: *team* spirit. [OE *tēam* offspring, succession, row]

---

team·mate (tēm′māt′) n. A fellow player on a team.

team·ster (tēm′stər) n. 1. One who drives or owns a team. 2. One who drives a truck or other commercial vehicle.

team·work (tēm′wûrk′) n. 1. Concerted action or effort by the members of a group to achieve some common end, as the coordinated play of an athletic team. 2. Work done or requiring to be done by or with a team.

tea party A social gathering at which tea and light sandwiches or cakes are the principal refreshments.

tea·pot (tē′pot′) n. A vessel with a spout and handle in which tea is made and from which it is served.

tear¹ (târ) v. tore, torn, tear·ing v.t. 1. To pull apart, as cloth; separate by pulling; rip; rend. 2. To make by rending or tearing: to tear a hole in a dress. 3. To injure or lacerate, as skin. 4. To divide; disrupt: a party torn by dissension. 5. To distress or torment: The sight tore his heart. — v.i. 6. To become torn or rent. 7. To move with haste and energy. — to tear into Informal To charge into or attack without restraint. — n. 1. A fissure made by tearing; a rent; an act of tearing. 2. Slang A spree; frolic. 3. A rushing motion: to start off with a tear. 4. Any violent outburst, as of anger, enthusiasm, etc. [OE teran]

tear² (tir) n. 1. A drop of the saline liquid secreted by the lachrymal gland, serving to moisten the eye, and stimulated to a flow by emotional distress. 2. Something resembling or suggesting a tear. 3. A drop of any liquid. 4. A droplike portion, as of glass, amber, etc. 5. pl. Sorrow; lamentation. — in tears Weeping; crying. — v.i. To shed or fill with tears. [OE tēar] — tear′less adj. — tear′y adj.

tear·drop (tir′drop′) n. A tear or tear-shaped object.

tear·ful (tir′fəl) adj. 1. Weeping abundantly. 2. Causing tears. — tear′ful·ly adv. — tear′ful·ness n.

tear gas (tir) Any of various chemicals that provoke a copious flow of tears, with irritation of the eyes.

tear·ing (târ′ing) adj. Informal 1. Violent; hasty; headlong. 2. Chiefly Brit. Tremendous; mighty.

tear-jerk·er (tir′jûr′kər) n. U.S. Slang A story, play, etc., full of sentimental sadness.

tea·room (tē′rōōm′, -rŏŏm′) n. A restaurant serving tea and other refreshments: also called teashop.

tease (tēz) v. teased, teas·ing v.t. 1. To annoy or harass with continual importunities, raillery, etc.; pester. 2. To scratch or dress in order to raise the nap, as cloth with teasels. 3. To comb or card, as wool or flax; also, to shred, as tobacco. 4. To comb (hair) so as to form fluffy layers and give an effect of fullness. — v.i. 5. To annoy a person in a facetious or petty manner. — n. 1. One who or that which teases. 2. The act of teasing, or the state of being teased. [OE tæsan to tease] — teas′er n. — teas′ing·ly adv.

tea·sel (tē′zəl) n. 1. A coarse, prickly Old World herb of which the flower head is covered with hooked bracts. 2. The rough bur of such a plant, or a mechanical substitute, used in dressing cloth. — v.t. tea·seled or ·selled, tea·sel·ing or ·sel·ling To raise the nap of with a teasel. Also tea′zel, tea′zle. [OE tæsel] — tea′sel·er or tea′sel·ler n.

tea·spoon (tē′spōōn′, -spŏŏn′) n. 1. A small spoon used for stirring tea, etc. 2. A teaspoonful.

tea·spoon·ful (tē′spōōn·fŏŏl′, -spŏŏn-) n. pl. ·fuls As much as a teaspoon will hold, ⅓ of a tablespoon.

teat (tēt, tit) n. The protuberance on the breast or udder of most female mammals, through which the milk is drawn; a nipple; pap; dug. [< OF tete < Gmc.]

tea wagon A table on wheels for use in serving tea, etc.

Te·bet (tā·vāth′, tā′ves) n. The fourth month of the Hebrew year. See (Hebrew) CALENDAR. Also Te·beth′.

tech·ne·ti·um (tek·nē′shē·əm) n. A chemical element (symbol Tc), artificially produced by the bombardment of molybdenum with neutrons or deuterons. It displaces the hypothetical element masurium. See ELEMENT. [< NL < Gk. technētos artificial]

tech·ni·cal (tek′ni·kəl) adj. 1. Pertaining to some particular art, science, or trade. 2. Peculiar to or used in a specialized field of knowledge. 3. Of or pertaining to the mechanical arts. 4. Considered in terms of an accepted body of rules: a technical defeat. [< Gk. < technē art] — tech′ni·cal·ly adv. — tech′ni·cal·ness n.

tech·ni·cal·i·ty (tek′ni·kal′ə·tē) n. pl. ·ties 1. The state of being technical. 2. The use of technical terms. 3. A technical point peculiar to some profession, art, trade, etc. 4. A petty distinction; quibble. Also tech·nism (tek′niz′əm).

technical knockout In boxing, a victory awarded when one fighter has been beaten so severely that the referee discontinues the fight.

tech·ni·cian (tek·nish′ən) n. One skilled in the handling of instruments or in the performance of tasks requiring specialized training.

Tech·ni·col·or (tek′ni·kul′ər) n. A motion-picture photographic process that reproduces the colors of the original scene: a trade name. Also tech′ni·col′or.

tech·nics (tek′niks) n.pl. (construed as sing.) 1. Practical method; technique. 2. The theory of an art or the arts; esp.,

the study of the techniques of an art. 3. Technical r[?] methods, etc. 4. Technology. — adj. Technical.

tech·nique (tek·nēk′) n. Working methods or manne[?] performance, as in art, science, etc. [< F < Gk. See TE NICAL.]

techno- combining form 1. Art; skill; craft. 2. Techni[?] technological. Also, before vowels, techn-. [< Gk. te[?] art, skill]

tech·noc·ra·cy (tek·nok′rə·sē) n. pl. ·cies A theory o[?] ciety and government that advocates control by an [?] ganized body of experts to achieve minimum waste and m[?] imum efficiency. — tech′no·crat (tek′nə·krat) n. — te[?] no·crat′ic adj.

tech·no·log·i·cal (tek′nə·loj′i·kəl) adj. Of, pertaining [?] associated with, produced or affected by technology. — tech′no·log′ic. — tech′no·log′i·cal·ly adv.

technological unemployment Unemployment bro[?] about by technical advances, as automation, etc.

tech·nol·o·gy (tek·nol′ə·jē) n. pl. ·gies 1. Theore[?] knowledge of industry and the industrial arts. 2. The [?] plication of science and of technical advances in indus[?] the arts, etc. 3. The technical language of an art, scie[?] etc. 4. The means by which material things are produ[?] as in a particular civilization. — tech·nol′o·gist n.

ted (ted) v.t. ted·ded, ted·ding To turn over and s[?] about, or spread loosely for drying, as newly mown g[?] [Prob. < Scand.] — ted′der n.

ted·dy bear (ted′ē) A toy bear, usu. covered with pl[?] Also **Teddy bear**. [after Teddy, a nickname of Theo[?] Roosevelt]

Te De·um (tē dē′əm) 1. An ancient Christian hymn be[?] ning with these words. 2. The music to which this hym[?] set. 3. Any thanksgiving service in which this hym[?] sung. [< L Te Deum (laudamus) (we praise) Thee, O [?]

te·di·ous (tē′dē·əs) adj. Causing weariness; boring. [?] TEDIUM.] — te′di·ous·ly adv. — te′di·ous·ness n. — Syn. tiresome, tiring, fatiguing, wearisome, irksome, du[?]

te·di·um (tē′dē·əm) n. The state of being tiresome or we[?] some; tediousness. [< L taedere to vex, weary]

tee¹ (tē) n. 1. A small peg with a concave top on whi[?] golf ball is placed in making the first play to a hole. [?] designated area within which the golf tee must be placed [?] v.t. & v.i. teed, tee·ing To place (the golf ball) on a tee. to tee off To strike (the golf ball) in starting play.

tee² (tē) n. In certain games, a mark toward which the b[?] quoits, etc., are directed, as in curling. — to a tee As cisely as possible; exactly.

teem¹ (tēm) v.i. To be full, as if at the point of produ[?] to be full to overflowing; abound. [OE tēam progeny] teem′er n. — teem′ing adj.

teem² (tēm) v.i. To come down heavily; pour: said of [< ON tœma empty]

-teen suffix Plus ten: used in cardinal numbers from 13 [?] inclusive: fifteen. [OE < tien ten]

teen age The age from 13 to 19 inclusive; adolescence teen-age (tēn′āj), teen′-aged′ (-ājd′) adj.

teen-ag·er (tēn′ā′jər) n. A person of teen age.

teens (tēnz) n.pl. 1. The numbers that end in -teen. 2. years of one's age from 13 to 19 inclusive.

tee·ny (tē′nē) adj. ·ni·er, ·ni·est Informal Tiny.

tee·pee (tē′pē) See TEPEE.

tee·ter (tē′tər) v.i. 1. To walk or move with a tottering [?] tion. 2. To seesaw; waver; vacillate. — v.t. 3. To c[?] to teeter. — n. 1. An oscillating motion. 2. A seesaw. dial. E titter, prob. < ON titra to tremble, shiver]

teeth (tēth) Plural of TOOTH.

teethe (tēth) v.i. teethed, teeth·ing To cut or develop t[?]

teeth·ing ring (tē′thing) A ring of hard rubber, bone, tic, etc., for a teething baby to bite on.

tee·to·tal (tē·tōt′l) adj. 1. Pertaining to total abstin[?] from intoxicants. 2. Total; entire. [< TOTAL, with [?] phatic repetition of initial letter] — tee·to′tal·ism n.

tee·to·tal·er (tē·tōt′l·ər) n. One who abstains totally [?] alcoholic drinks. Also tee·to′tal·ist, Brit. tee·to′tal·ler.

teg·u·ment (teg′yə·mənt) n. A covering or envelope; a tegument. [< L < tegere to cover] — teg·u·men·[?] (teg′yə·men′tər·ē), teg·u·men′tal adj.

tel- Var. of TELO-¹.

tele- combining form 1. Far off; at a distance: telegrap[?] Related to or transmitted by television: telecast. Also sp[?] telo-. Also, before vowels, tel-. [< Gk. tēle far]

tel·e·cast (tel′ə·kast, -käst) v.t. & v.i. ·cast or ·cas[?] ·cast·ing To broadcast by television. — n. A pro[?] broadcast by television.

tel·e·com·mu·ni·ca·tion (tel′ə·kə·myōō′nə·kā′shən) [?] The art and science of communicating at a distance, as [?] dio, radar, television, telegraphy, telephony, etc. Also [?] com·mu′ni·ca′tions. 2. Any message so transmitted.

tel·e·gram (tel′ə·gram) n. A message sent by telegra[?]

tel·e·graph (tel′ə·graf, -gräf) n. Any of various devic[?] systems, using a code; esp., one using coded impulses t[?]

itted by wire or radio. — *v.t.* **1.** To send (a message) by ⟨tele⟩graph. **2.** To communicate with by telegraph. — *v.i.* To transmit a message by telegraph. — **te·leg·ra·pher** ⟨ə·leg′rə·fər), **te·leg′ra·phist** *n.*

·e·graph·ic (tel′ə·graf′ik) *adj.* Of or pertaining to the ⟨tele⟩graph; transmitted by means of telegraphy. Also **tel′e·aph′i·cal.** — **tel′e·graph′i·cal·ly** *adv.*

·leg·ra·phy (tə·leg′rə·fē) *n.* **1.** The process of conveying ⟨me⟩ssages by telegraph. **2.** The art or science of the con⟨st⟩ruction and operation of telegraphs.

·lem·a·chus (tə·lem′ə·kəs)   In Greek legend, son of ⟨U⟩lysseus and Penelope.

·lem·e·ter (tə·lem′ə·tər) *n.* Any of various electronic de⟨vi⟩ces for indicating, measuring, recording, or integrating ⟨va⟩rious quantities and for transmitting the data to a distant ⟨po⟩int.

·lem·e·try (tə·lem′ə·trē) *n.* The theory and practice of ⟨us⟩ing telemeters, esp. in relation to rockets, space probes, ⟨gu⟩ided missiles, etc. Also **tel·e·me·ter·ing** (tel′ə·mē′tər·ing). — **tel′e·met′ric** (-met′rik) or **·ri·cal** *adj.* — **tel′e·met′ri·cal·** *adv.*

·eo- Var. of TELO-[1].

·e·ol·o·gy (tel′ē·ol′ə·jē, tē′lē-) *n. pl.* **·gies 1.** The branch ⟨of⟩ cosmology that treats of final causes. **2.** *Biol.* The doc⟨tri⟩ne that the phenomena of organic life and development ⟨ca⟩n be fully explained only by the action of design and pur⟨po⟩se and not by mechanical causes. Compare VITALISM. **3.** ⟨Th⟩e explanation of nature in terms of utility or purpose, esp. ⟨di⟩vine purpose. [< NL < Gk. *telos* end + *logos* discourse] **tel′e·o·log′i·cal** (-ə·loj′i·kəl) or **tel′e·o·log′ic** *adj.* — **tel′e·og′i·cal·ly** *adv.* — **tel′e·ol′o·gist** *n.*

·lep·a·thy (tə·lep′ə·thē) *n.* The supposed communication ⟨of⟩ one mind with another at a distance by other than normal ⟨sen⟩sory means. — **tel·e·path·ic** (tel′ə·path′ik) *adj.* — **tel′·** ⟨p⟩ath′i·cal·ly *adv.* — **te·lep′a·thist** *n.*

·e·phone (tel′ə·fōn) *n.* A device or system for transmit⟨tin⟩g sound over a wire or other communication channel. — **·phoned, ·phon·ing** *v.t.* **1.** To communicate with by tele⟨ph⟩one. **2.** To send by telephone, as a message. — *v.i.* **3.** ⟨To⟩ communicate by telephone. — **tel′e·phon′er** *n.* — **tel·** ⟨p⟩hon·ic (tel′ə·fon′ik) *adj.* — **tel′e·phon′i·cal·ly** *adv.*

·eph·o·ny (tə·lef′ə·nē) *n.* The science of designing, con⟨str⟩ucting, and operating telephones.

·e·pho·to (tel′ə·fō′tō) *adj.* **1.** Designating a lens system ⟨us⟩ed in connection with a camera to produce a large image of ⟨a⟩ distant object. **2.** Pertaining to telephotography.

·e·pho·to·graph (tel′ə·fō′tə·graf, -gräf) *n.* **1.** A picture ⟨tra⟩nsmitted by telephotography. **2.** A picture made with a ⟨tele⟩photo lens. — **tel′e·pho′to·graph′ic** *adj.*

·e·pho·tog·ra·phy (tel′ə·fə·tog′rə·fē) *n.* **1.** The art of ⟨pr⟩oducing photographic images of distant objects on a larger ⟨sc⟩ale than is possible with an ordinary camera. **2.** The fac⟨si⟩mile reproduction of photographs or other pictures by ra⟨di⟩o or telegraphic communication; phototelegraphy.

·le·prompt·er (tel′ə·promp′tər) *n.* A prompting device ⟨for⟩ television whereby a prepared script, unseen by the audi⟨en⟩ce, is shown to a speaker or performer, enlarged line by ⟨lin⟩e: a trade name. Also **tel′e·prompt′er.**

·e·ran (tel′ə·ran) *n. Telecom.* A system of air navigation ⟨th⟩at combines the principles of television and radar to trans⟨mit⟩ information gathered by ground stations to all air⟨cr⟩aft within range. [< TELE(VISION) + R(ADAR) + A(IR) ⟨N⟩AVIGATION)]

·e·scope (tel′ə·skōp) *n.* An optical instrument for en⟨lar⟩ging the image of a distant object, consisting of an object ⟨le⟩ns or concave mirror for collecting the light rays and a ⟨ma⟩gnifying eyepiece for viewing the image. — *v.* **·scoped, ·**⟨sc⟩op·ing *v.t.* **1.** To drive or slide together so that one part ⟨slide⟩s into another in the manner of the sections of a small tele⟨sco⟩pe. **2.** To crush by driving something into or upon. — ⟨*v.i.*⟩ **3.** To crash into one another, as railroad cars.

·e·scop·ic (tel′ə·skop′ik) *adj.* **1.** Pertaining to the tele⟨sco⟩pe. **2.** Visible only through a telescope. **3.** Farseeing. ⟨4.⟩ Having sections that slide within or over one another. ⟨Al⟩so **tel′e·scop′i·cal.** — **tel′e·scop′i·cal·ly** *adv.*

·es·co·py (tə·les′kə·pē) *n.* The art of using or making ⟨tel⟩escopes. — **te·les′co·pist** *n.*

·e·type (tel′ə·tīp) *v.t. & v.i.* **·typed, ·typ·ing** To commu⟨nic⟩ate (with) by teletypewriter or Teletype. — **tel′e·typ′·** *n.*

·e·type (tel′ə·tīp) *n.* A teletypewriter: a trade name. ⟨Al⟩so **tel′e·type.**

·e·type·writ·er (tel′ə·tīp′rī′tər) *n.* A telegraph system ⟨tra⟩nsmitting by means of a typewriter keyboard in which ⟨eac⟩h key produces a coded signal that activates a specific ⟨ch⟩aracter in a typewriterlike receiver.

·e·view (tel′ə·vyōō) *v.t. & v.i.* To observe by means of ⟨tele⟩vision. — **tel′e·view′er** *n.*

tel·e·vise (tel′ə·vīz) *v.t. & v.i.* **·vised, ·vis·ing** To transmit or receive by television.

tel·e·vi·sion (tel′ə·vizh′ən) *n.* **1.** The transmission of continuous visual images as a series of electrical impulses or a modulated carrier wave, restored to visual form on the cathode-ray screen of a receiver, often with accompanying sound. **2.** The television broadcasting industry. **3.** A television receiving set. Also called *TV*.

tel·fer (tel′fər) See TELPHER.

tell (tel) *v.* **told, tell·ing** *v.t.* **1.** To relate in detail; narrate, as a story. **2.** To communicate. **3.** To reveal: to *tell* secrets. **4.** To decide; ascertain: I cannot *tell* who is to blame. **5.** To express in words: to *tell* a lie. **6.** To give a command to; order: I *told* him to go home. **7.** To let know; inform. **8.** *Informal* To inform or assure emphatically: It's cold out, I *tell* you! **9.** To say (a rosary): to *tell* one's beads. — *v.i.* **10.** To give an account or description: usu. with *of.* **11.** To serve as indication or evidence: with *of.* **12.** To produce a marked effect: Every blow *told.* — **all told** In all. — **to tell off 1.** To count and set apart. **2.** *Informal* To reprimand severely. — **to tell on 1.** To tire; weary. **2.** *Informal* To inform against. [OE *tellan*] — **tell′a·ble** *adj.*

Tell (tel), **William** A legendary Swiss hero in the struggle for independence from Austria, forced to shoot an apple off his son's head with bow and arrow.

tell·er (tel′ər) *n.* **1.** One who relates or informs. **2.** A person who receives or pays out money, as in a bank. **3.** A person appointed to collect and count ballots in a legislative body or other assembly. — **tell′er·ship′** *n.*

tell·ing (tel′ing) *adj.* Producing a great effect; impressive; effective; striking. — **tell·ing·ly** *adv.*

tell·tale (tel′tāl′) *n.* **1.** One who improperly gives information concerning the private affairs of others; a tattler. **2.** That which conveys information, esp. in an involuntary way. **3.** An instrument or device for giving or recording information. — *adj.* That is or serves as a telltale.

tel·lu·ric (tə·lŏŏr′ik, tel·yŏŏr′-) *adj.* Of or pertaining to the earth; terrestrial; earthly.

tel·lu·ri·um (te·lŏŏr′ē·əm, tel·yŏŏr′-) *n.* A rare nonmetallic element (symbol Te) resembling sulfur and selenium in chemical properties, occasionally found native as white crystals, but usu. combined with metals. See ELEMENT. [< NL < L *tellus* the earth]

telo-[1] *combining form* Final; complete; perfect: also, before vowels, *tel-.* Also *teleo-.* [< Gk. *telos* end]

telo-[2] Var. of TELE-.

tel·pher (tel′fər) *n.* A light car suspended from cables and usu. propelled by electricity. — *v.t.* To transport by telpher. Also spelled *telfer.* [< TEL(E)- + Gk. *pherein* to bear] — **tel′pher·ic** *adj.* — **tel′pher·age** (-ij) *n.*

tel·son (tel′sən) *n. Zool.* The last abdominal segment of the body of an arthropod, as of a lobster, shrimp, or scorpion. For illus. see SHRIMP. [< Gk. *telson* boundary]

Tel·star (tel′stär′) The first artificial satellite for global communication, launched from Cape Canaveral, July 10, 1962.

Tel·u·gu (tel′ŏŏ·gŏŏ) *n. pl.* **·gu 1.** A Dravidian language used in NW Andhra Pradesh, India, and important in literary culture. **2.** One of a Dravidian people of Telugu speech. — *adj.* Of or pertaining to the Telugu or to Telugu.

te·mer·i·ty (tə·mer′ə·tē) *n.* Venturesome or foolish boldness; rashness. [< L *temere* rashly]
— **Syn.** *Temerity* is the quality of one who underestimates danger, or overrates his chances for success. *Audacity* refers (in its bad sense) to going beyond the decent restraints of social behavior. *Foolhardiness* characterizes the man who rushes into peril from lack of sense. — **Ant.** caution, wariness, timidity.

tem·per (tem′pər) *n.* **1.** Heat of mind or passion; disposition to become angry. **2.** Frame of mind; mood: to be in a bad *temper.* **3.** Composure of mind; self-command: to lose one's *temper.* **4.** *Metall.* The condition of a metal as regards hardness and elasticity, esp. when due to heating and sudden cooling. **5.** Something mixed with a substance to alter its properties or qualities. — *v.t.* **1.** To bring to a state of moderation or suitability, as by addition of another quality; moderate: to *temper* justice with mercy. **2.** To bring to the proper consistency, etc., by moistening and working: to *temper* clay. **3.** *Metall.* To bring (metal) to a required hardness and elasticity by heating and suddenly cooling. **4.** *Music* To adjust the tones of (an instrument) by temperament; tune. — *v.i.* **5.** To dry or become tempered. [OE and OF < L *temperare* to combine in due proportion] — **tem′per·a·bil′i·ty** *n.* — **tem′per·a·ble** *adj.* — **tem′per·er** *n.*
— **Syn.** (noun) **2.** temperament, mood, humor. — (verb) moderate, modify, qualify.

tem·per·a (tem′pər·ə, *Ital.* tem′pä·rä) *n.* **1.** A painting medium consisting of an emulsion prepared from a mixture of water and egg yolks, glue, gum, or casein solutions, etc.;

also, a method of painting with such a medium. **2.** Paint prepared by adding pigment to the medium of tempera. Also called *distemper*. [< Ital. *temperare* to temper < L]

tem·per·a·ment (tem′pər·ə·mənt, -prə-) *n.* **1.** The physical and mental peculiarities of an individual; nature. **2.** An intense, moody, and often rebellious nature. **3.** *Music* The tuning of an instrument or scale so that each semitone is a twelfth of an octave: also **equal temperament.** [< L *temperamentum* proper mixture]

tem·per·a·men·tal (tem′pər·ə·men′təl, -prə-) *adj.* **1.** Of or pertaining to temperament. **2.** Sensitive; easily excited. — **tem′per·a·men′tal·ly** *adv.*

tem·per·ance (tem′pər·əns) *n.* **1.** The state or quality of being temperate; habitual moderation. **2.** The principle or practice of total abstinence from intoxicants. [< OF < L < *temperare* to mix in due proportions]

tem·per·ate (tem′pər·it) *adj.* **1.** Observing moderation in the indulgence of an appetite, esp. in the use of intoxicating liquors. **2.** Moderate as regards temperature. **3.** Characterized by moderation; not excessive. **4.** Calm; restrained; self-controlled. **5.** *Music* Tempered: said of an interval or scale. [< L < *temperare* to mix in due proportions] — **tem′per·ate·ly** *adv.* — **tem′per·ate·ness** *n.*

tem·per·a·ture (tem′pər·ə·chər, -prə-) *n.* **1.** Condition as regards heat or cold. **2.** The degree of heat in a body or substance, as measured on the graduated scale of a thermometer. **3.** The degree of heat of an animal, esp. the human body; also, excess of this above the normal (which for the human body is 98.6° F, or about 37° C). [< L *temperatura* due measure]

tem·pered (tem′pərd) *adj.* **1.** Having temper or a specified disposition: used mainly in compounds: quick-*tempered.* **2.** *Music* Adjusted in pitch so as to produce or conform to temperament. **3.** Moderated by admixture. **4.** Having the right degree of hardness and elasticity.

tem·pest (tem′pist) *n.* **1.** A violent wind, usu. attended with rain, snow, or hail. **2.** A violent commotion or agitation; a fierce tumult. — **tempest in a teapot** A considerable uproar over a trivial matter. [< OF < L *tempestas* weather]

tem·pes·tu·ous (tem·pes′chŏŏ·əs) *adj.* Stormy; turbulent; violent. — **tem·pes′tu·ous·ly** *adv.* — **tem·pes′tu·ous·ness** *n.*

tem·plate (tem′plit′) *n.* **1.** A pattern or gauge, as of wood or metal, used as a guide in shaping something accurately. **2.** In building, a stout stone or timber for distributing weight or thrust. Also **tem·plet** (tem′plit). [< F < L *templum* small timber]

tem·ple[1] (tem′pəl) *n.* **1.** A stately edifice consecrated to the worship of one or more deities. **2.** In the U.S., a Reform synagogue. **3.** In France, a Protestant church. **4.** Any place considered as occupied by God. — **the Temple** Any of three sacred edifices built in Jerusalem for the worship of Jehovah. [OE < L *templum* temple]

tem·ple[2] (tem′pəl) *n.* The region on each side of the head above the cheek bone. [OF, ult. < L *tempus* temple]

tem·po (tem′pō) *n.* *pl.* **·pos** or **·pi** (-pē) **1.** *Music* Relative speed at which a composition is rendered. **2.** Characteristic manner or style. [< Ital. < L *tempus* time]

tem·po·ral[1] (tem′pər·əl) *adj.* **1.** Pertaining to affairs of the present life; earthly. **2.** Pertaining or related to time. **3.** Temporary; transitory. **4.** Civil; lay; secular. [< L < *temporis* time] — **tem′po·ral·ly** *adv.* — **tem′po·ral·ness** *n.*

tem·po·ral[2] (tem′pər·əl) *adj. Anat.* Of, pertaining to, or situated at the temple or temples.

temporal bone *Anat.* A compound bone situated at either side of the head, and containing the organ of hearing.

tem·po·ral·i·ty (tem′pə·ral′ə·tē) *n. pl.* **·ties 1.** *Usu. pl.* A temporal or material matter, interest, revenue, etc. **2.** The state of being temporal or temporary.

tem·po·ra·ry (tem′pə·rer′ē) *adj.* Lasting or intended to be used for a short time only; transitory. [< L < *tempus, temporis* time] — **tem·po·rar·i·ly** (tem′pə·rer′ə·lē, tem′pə·rer′-) *adv.* — **tem′po·rar′i·ness** *n.*

tem·po·rize (tem′pə·rīz) *v.i.* **·rized, ·riz·ing 1.** To act evasively so as to gain time or put off decision or commitment. **2.** To give real or apparent compliance to the circumstances; comply. **3.** To effect a compromise; negotiate: with *with* or *between.* Also *Brit.* **tem′po·rise.** [< F < L *tempus, temporis* time] — **tem′po·ri·za′tion** *n.* — **tem′po·riz′er** *n.* — **tem′·po·riz′ing·ly** *adv.*

tempt (tempt) *v.t.* **1.** To attempt to persuade (a person) to do something evil or unwise. **2.** To be attractive or invite: Your offers do not *tempt* me. **3.** To provoke or risk provoking: to *tempt* fate. [< OF < L *temptare, tentare* to test] — **tempt′a·ble** *adj.* — **tempt′er** *n.* — **tempt′ress** *n.fem.*

temp·ta·tion (temp·tā′shən) *n.* **1.** The act of tempting, or the state of being tempted. **2.** That which tempts.

tempt·ing (temp′ting) *adj.* Alluring; attractive; seductive. — **tempt′ing·ly** *adv.* — **tempt′ing·ness** *n.*

tem·pus fu·git (tem′pəs fyōō′jit) *Latin* Time flies.

ten (ten) *n.* **1.** The sum of nine and one: a cardinal number. **2.** Any symbol of this number, as 10, x, X. **3.** Anything

consisting of or representing ten units, as a playing card, b etc. — *adj.* Being one more than nine. [OE *tien*] — **tenth** (tenth) *adj. & n.*

ten- Var. of TENO-.

ten·a·ble (ten′ə·bəl) *adj.* Capable of being held, ma tained, or defended. [< F < L *tenere* to hold] — **ten′a·b i·ty, ten′a·ble·ness** *n.* — **ten′a·bly** *adv.*

te·na·cious (ti·nā′shəs) *adj.* **1.** Having great cohesiven of parts; tough. **2.** Adhesive; sticky. **3.** Holding or tendi to hold strongly, as opinions, rights, etc. **4.** Stubborn; c stinate. **5.** Apt to retain; strongly retentive, as memo [< L < *tenere* to hold, grasp, embrace] — **te·na′cious** *adv.* — **te·na′cious·ness** *n.*

te·nac·i·ty (ti·nas′ə·tē) *n.* The state or quality of being nacious.

ten·an·cy (ten′ən·sē) *n. pl.* **·cies 1.** The holding of lan houses, offices, etc.; occupancy. **2.** The period of holdi lands, houses, etc. **3.** The houses, lands, etc. so held.

ten·ant (ten′ənt) *n.* **1.** One who holds or possesses lands property by the payment of rent or other fee. **2.** A dwe in any place; an occupant. — *v.t.* **1.** To hold as tenant; cupy. — *v.i.* **2.** To be a tenant. [< F, orig. ppr. of *tenir* hold < L *tenere*] — **ten′ant·a·ble** *adj.* — **ten′ant·less** *a* — **ten′ant·ship** *n.*

tenant farmer One who farms land owned by another a pays rent, usu. in a share of the crops.

ten·ant·ry (ten′ən·trē) *n. pl.* **·ries 1.** Tenants collective **2.** The state of being a tenant; tenancy.

ten-cent store (ten′sent′) A five-and-ten-cent store.

Ten Commandments The set of injunctions given by G to Moses on Mount Sinai, constituting the moral code of Mosaic Law: also called *Decalogue. Ex.* xx 1–17.

tend[1] (tend) *v.i.* **1.** To have an aptitude, tendency, or c position; incline. **2.** To have influence toward a specified sult: Education *tends* to refinement. **3.** To go in a cert direction. [< OF < L *tendere* to extend, tend]

tend[2] (tend) *v.t.* **1.** To attend to the needs or requireme of; take care of; minister to: to *tend* a fire. **2.** To watch ov look after. — *v.i.* **3.** To be in attendance; serve or wa with *on* or *upon.* **4.** *Informal* To give attention or care: w to. [Aphetic var. of ATTEND]

ten·den·cy (ten′dən·sē) *n. pl.* **·cies 1.** An inclination ward some purpose, end, or result; bent; aptitude. **2.** T which tends to produce some specified effect. **3.** Bias; p pensity. [< Med.L < *tendere* to extend, tend]

ten·den·tious (ten·den′shəs) *adj.* Having a tendency to vor a particular point of view; biased. Also **ten·den′cio** [See TENDENCY.] — **ten·den′tious·ly** *adv.* — **ten·den′tio ness** *n.*

ten·der[1] (ten′dər) *adj.* **1.** Yielding easily to force that te to crush, bruise, break, or injure. **2.** Easily chewed or c said of food. **3.** Delicate or weak; not strong, rough, hardy. **4.** Youthful and delicate: a *tender* age. **5.** Kind; fectionate; gentle. **6.** Capable of arousing sensitive feelin touching: *tender* memories. **7.** Susceptible to spiritua moral feelings: a *tender* conscience. **8.** Painful if touchec *tender* sore. **9.** Of delicate effect or quality; soft: a *ten* light. **10.** Requiring deft or delicate treatment; tickli touchy: a *tender* subject. — *v.t.* To make tender; soft [< OF < L *tener, teneris* soft] — **ten′der·ly** *adv.* — **ten′der·ness** *n.*

ten·der[2] (ten′dər) *v.t.* **1.** To present for acceptance, a resignation; offer. **2.** *Law* To proffer, as money, in s charge of an obligation. — *n.* **1.** The act of tendering; offer. **2.** *Law* A formal offer of satisfaction. **3.** That wh is offered as payment: legal *tender.* [< F < L *tendere* to tend, tend] — **ten′der·er** *n.*

tend·er[3] (ten′dər) *n.* **1.** *Naut.* **a** A vessel used to bring s plies, passengers, etc. back and forth between a larger ve and shore. **b** A vessel that services another at sea. **2.** A hicle attached to the rear of a steam locomotive to carry and water. **3.** One who ministers to. [< TEND[2]]

ten·der·foot (ten′dər·fŏŏt′) *n. pl.* **·foots** or **·feet** (-fēt) L **1.** In the West, one not yet inured to the hardships of plains, the mining camp, etc.; a greenhorn. **2.** Any inexp enced person. **3.** A boy scout in the beginning class or gro

ten·der·heart·ed (ten′dər·här′tid) *adj.* Having deep quick sensibility, as to love, pity, etc.; compassionate. **ten′der·heart′ed·ly** *adv.* — **ten′der·heart′ed·ness** *n.*

ten·der·ize (ten′də·rīz) *v.t.* **·ized, ·iz·ing** To make ten as meat.

ten·der·iz·er (ten′də·rī′zər) A substance for softening tough fibers and connective tissues of meat.

ten·der·loin (ten′dər·loin′) *n.* The tender part of the loi beef, pork, etc., lying close to the ventral side of the lum vertebrae. — **the tenderloin district** Any urban dist noted for its night life, crime, etc.

ten·don (ten′dən) *n. Anat.* One of the bands of tough brous connective tissue forming the termination of a musc and serving to transmit its force to some other part; a sin [< Med.L < Gk. *tenōn* sinew < *tenein* to stretch]

a·dril (ten′dril) *n. Bot.* One of the slender, filamentous gans that serve a climbing plant as a means of attachment a wall, tree trunk, or other surface. [< F < *tendron* rout] **— ten′dril·lar, ten′dril·ous** *adj.*

e·brae (ten′a·brē) *n.pl. Eccl. Usu. cap.* The matins d lauds sung on the afternoons or evenings of Thursday, riday, and Saturday of Holy Week. [< L, darkness]

e·ment (ten′a·mant) *n.* **1.** An urban apartment build-g or rooming house that is poorly constructed or main-ined, typically overcrowded and often part of a slum: also **nement house. 2.** A room or set of rooms designed for one mily. **3.** *Law* Property held by one person of another, as nd, houses, offices, etc. **4.** Any dwelling place; abode. [< F < LL *tenementum* tenure] **— ten′e·men′tal** (-men′tal), n′e·men′ta·ry (-men′ta·rē) *adj.*

·et (ten′it, tē′nit) *n.* An opinion, principle, dogma, etc., at a person or organization believes or maintains as true. **Syn.** See DOCTRINE. [< L, he holds < *tenere* to hold]

·fold (ten′fōld′) *n.* An amount or number ten times as eat as a given unit. **— adv.** So as to be ten times as many as great. **— adj. 1.** Consisting of ten parts. **2.** Ten nes as many or as great.

·gal·lon hat (ten′gal′an) *U.S.* A wide-brimmed felt hat th a tall crown, traditionally worn by cowboys.

n·nes·se·an (ten′a·sē′an) *n.* A native or inhabitant of ennessee. **— adj.** Of or pertaining to Tennessee.

·nis (ten′is) *n.* A game played by striking a ball back d forth with rackets over a net stretched between two ual areas that together constitute a court. It has two rms, **court tennis**, played indoors, and **lawn tennis**, played t-of-doors on a court of grass, clay, concrete, etc. [< AF *netz* take, receive]

n·ny·so·ni·an (ten′a·sō′nē·an) *adj.* Relating to or char-teristic of Alfred Tennyson, or his verse or style.

o- *combining form Med.* Tendon; related to a tendon, or tendons: also *ten-.* Also **tenonto-.** [< Gk. *tenōn* tendon]

·on (ten′an) *n.* A projection on the end of a timber, etc., · inserting in a socket to form a joint. For illus. see MOR-SE. **— v.t. 1.** To form a tenon on. **2.** To join by a mor-e and tenon. [< F < *tenir* to hold]

·or (ten′ar) *n.* **1.** The adult male voice intermediate in nge between baritone and countertenor; also, a singer hav-g such a voice, or a part to be sung by it. **2.** *Music* Hav-rument playing the part intermediate between the bass and e alto. **3.** Course of thought; general purport. **4.** A set-d course or manner of progress. **5.** General character and ndency; nature. **— adj. 1.** Of or pertaining to a tenor. Having a relation to other instruments as the tenor bears other musical parts. [< OF < L *tenor* course]

·pen·ny (ten′pen′ē, -pa-nē) *adj.* **1.** Valued at tenpence. Designating the size of nails three inches long. See PENNY.

·pin (ten′pin′) *n.* One of the pins used in tenpins.

·pins (ten′pinz′) *n.pl.* (construed as sing.) A game ayed down ten pins set up at the far end of the alley. wl down ten pins set up at the far end of the alley.

·se¹ (tens) *adj.* **tens·er, tens·est 1.** Stretched tight; taut. Under mental or nervous strain; strained. **3.** *Phonet.* oduced with the tongue and its muscles taut, as (ē) and ō). **— v.t. & v.i.** tensed, tens·ing To make or become ained or drawn tight. [< L *tendere* to stretch] **— tense′·** *adv.* **— tense′ness** *n.*

·se² (tens) *n.* A form of a verb that relates it to time ewed either as finite past, a present, or future, or as non-ite. **— sequence of tenses** In inflected languages, the stomary choice of tense for a verb that follows another in a ntence, particularly in reported or indirect discourse. [< F < L *tempus* time, tense]

·si·ble (ten′sa·bal) *adj.* Tensile.

·sile (ten′sil, *Brit.* ten′sīl) *adj.* **1.** Of or pertaining to nsion. **2.** Capable of being drawn out or extended. **3.** oducing tones from stretched strings: said of instruments. ee TENSE¹.] **— ten·sil·i·ty** (ten·sil′a·tē) *n.*

·sile strength *Physics* The resistance of a material to rces of rupture and stress in the direction of length: usually pressed in pounds per square inch.

·sion (ten′shan) *n.* **1.** The act of stretching or the con-ion of being stretched tight. **2.** Mental strain; intense rvous anxiety. **3.** Any strained relation, as between gov-nments. **4.** *Physics* a Stress on a material caused by a rce pulling or stretching in one direction. **b** The stress on a body when acted on by such a force. **5.** A device for gulating the tension of something. **6.** *Electr.* Electromo-ve force; also, electric potential. **— Syn.** See STRESS. **—** n′sion·al *adj.*

·si·ty (ten′sa·tē) *n.* The state of being tense; tension.

·sive (ten′siv) *adj.* Of, like, or causing tension.

·sor (ten′sar, -sôr) *n. Anat.* A muscle that stretches part. [< NL < L *tensus.* See TENSE¹.]

---

ten-strike (ten′strīk′) *n.* **1.** In bowling, a strike (def. 3). **2.** *U.S. Informal* A totally successful stroke or act.

tent (tent) *n.* A shelter of canvas or the like, supported by poles and fastened by cords to pegs driven into the ground. **—** *v.t.* To cover with or as with a tent. **—** *v.i.* To pitch a tent; camp out. [< F < LL *tenta*, orig. neut. pl. of *tentus*, pp. of *tendere* to stretch]

TENTS
a Pup. *b* Pyramid. *c* Wall.

ten·ta·cle (ten′ta·kal) *n.* **1.** *Zool.* A pro-truding flexible proc-ess or appendage of invertebrate animals, functioning as an organ of touch or motion, as the arms of a cuttlefish. **2.** *Bot.* A sensitive glandular hair, as on the leaves of some plants. [< L < *tentare* to touch, try] **— ten·tac′u·lar** *adj.*

tent·age (ten′tij) *n.* **1.** The supply of tents available for any purpose. **2.** Tents collectively.

ten·ta·tive (ten′ta·tiv) *adj.* Provisional or conjectural; sub-ject to change; experimental. [< Med.L < L *tentare* to try, probe] **— ten′ta·tive·ly** *adv.* **— ten′ta·tive·ness** *n.*

tent caterpillar Any of the larvae of several North Ameri-can moths that spin silken webs to shelter the colony in which they live.

ten·ter (ten′tar) *n.* A frame or machine for stretching cloth to prevent shrinkage while drying. **—** *v.t.* **1.** To stretch on or as on a tenter. **—** *v.i.* **2.** To be or admit of being so stretched. [< L *tentus* extended]

ten·ter·hook (ten′tar·hŏŏk′) *n.* A sharp hook for holding cloth while being stretched on a tenter. **— to be on tenter-hooks** To be in a state of anxiety or suspense.

ten·u·ous (ten′yŏŏ-as) *adj.* **1.** Thin; slim; delicate; also, weak; flimsy; unsubstantial. **2.** Having slight density; rare. [< L *tenuis* thin] **— ten′u·ous·ly** *adv.* **— ten′u·ous·ness,** ten·u·i·ty (ten·yŏŏ′a·tē, ti·nŏŏ′-) *n.*

ten·ure (ten′yar) *n.* **1.** A holding, as of land. **2.** The act of holding in general, or the state of being held. **3.** The term during which a thing is held. **4.** The conditions or manner of holding. **5.** Permanent status granted to an employee, usu. after a trial period. [< L < L *tenere* to hold] **— ten·u·ri·al** (ten·yŏŏr′ē·al) *adj.* **— ten·u′ri·al·ly** *adv.*

te·nu·to (te·nōō′tō) *adj. Music* Sustained; held for the full time. [< Ital. < L *tenere* to hold]

te·pee (tē′pē) *n.* A conical tent of the North American Plains Indians, usu. covered with skins: also spelled *teepee.* [< Dakota < *ti* to dwell + *pi* used for]

tep·id (tep′id) *adj.* Moderately warm; lukewarm, as a liq-uid. [< L *tepere* to be lukewarm] **— te·pid·i·ty** (ta·pid′a·tē), **tep′id·ness** *n.* **— tep′id·ly** *adv.*

te·qui·la (ta·kē′la) *n.* **1.** A Mexican alcoholic liquor dis-tilled from the juices yielded by the roasted stems of an agave plant. **2.** The plant itself. [after *Tequila*, Jalisco, Mexico]

ter- *combining form* Three; third; threefold; three times: *tercentenary.* [< L *ter* thrice]

ter·a·tism (ter′a·tiz′am) *n.* A monstrosity; esp., a mal-formed human or animal fetus. [< Gk. *teras* monster]

terato- *combining form* A wonder; monster. Also, before vowels, **terat-.** [< Gk. *teras* wonder]

ter·bi·um (tûr′bē·am) *n.* A metallic element (symbol Tb) belonging to the lanthanide series, found in rare-earth min-erals. See ELEMENT. [< NL < *Ytterby*, town in Sweden] **—** ter′bic *adj.*

ter·cen·te·nar·y (tûr·sen′ta·ner′ē, tûr′sen·ten′ar·ē) *adj.* Of or pertaining to a period of 300 years or to a 300th anniver-sary. **—** *n. pl.* **·nar·ies** A 300th anniversary. Also *tricen-tennial.* Also **ter·cen·ten·ni·al** (tûr′sen·ten′ē·al).

ter·cet (tûr′sit, tûr·set′) *n.* **1.** A group of three lines rhym-ing together or connected with adjacent triplets by rhyme. **2.** *Music* A triplet. [< F < Ital. < L *tertius* third]

ter·gi·ver·sate (tûr′ji·var·sāt′) *v.i.* **·sat·ed, ·sat·ing 1.** To be evasive; equivocate. **2.** To change sides, attitudes, etc.; apostatize. [< L < *tergum* back + *versare* to turn] **— ter′-gi·ver·sa′tion** *n.* **— ter′gi·ver·sa′tor** *n.*

term (tûrm) *n.* **1.** A word or expression used to designate some definite thing: a scientific *term.* **2.** Any word or ex-pression conveying some conception or thought: to speak in general *terms.* **3.** *pl.* The conditions or stipulations accord-ing to which something is to be done or acceded to: the *terms* of sale. **4.** *pl.* Mutual relations: usu. preceded by *on* or *upon*: England was on friendly *terms* with France. **5.** *Math.* **a** The numerator or denominator of a fraction. **b** One of the quantities of an algebraic expression that are connected by the plus and minus signs. **c** One of the quantities that compose a series or progression. **6.** *Logic* Either the subject or predicate of a proposition. **7.** A fixed period or definite length of time: a *term* of office. **8.** One of the periods of the school year. **9.** *Law* **a** One of the prescribed periods during which a court may hold a session. **b** A specific extent of time for which an estate is granted. **c** An interval allowed a debtor to meet his obligation. **10.** *Med.* The time for childbirth. **— at term** At the end of a definite time. **— in terms of** With reference to; concerning. **— to bring to terms** To force to accede or agree. **— to come to terms** To reach an agreement. **—** *v.t.* To designate by means of a term; name or call. [< OF < L *terminus* limit] **— term'less** *adj.*

ter·ma·gant (tûr'mə·gənt) *n.* A scolding or abusive woman; shrew. **—** *adj.* Violently abusive and quarrelsome; vixenish. [after *Termagant*, an imaginary Moslem deity of overbearing character] **— ter'ma·gan'cy** *n.*

term·er (tûr'mər) *n. Informal* A prisoner serving a certain term: a first *termer.*

ter·mi·na·ble (tûr'mə·nə·bəl) *adj.* That may be terminated; limitable; not perpetual. **— ter'mi·na·bil'i·ty, ter'·mi·na·ble·ness** *n.* **— ter'mi·na·bly** *adv.*

ter·mi·nal (tûr'mə·nəl) *adj.* **1.** Of, pertaining to, or forming a boundary, limit, or end: a *terminal* railroad station. **2.** Pertaining to the delivery or storage of freight or baggage: *terminal* charges. **3.** Pertaining to a term or name. **4.** Situated at the end of a series or part. **5.** *Bot.* Borne at the end of a stem or branch. **6.** Of, pertaining to, or occurring in or at the end of a period of time. **7.** Ending in death: said of a disease. **—** *n.* **1.** That which terminates; a terminating point or part; end. **2.** *Electr.* A point at which a circuit element, as a battery, generator, resistor, capacitor, transistor, etc., may be connected to other elements. **3.** A railroad terminus. [< LL < L *terminus* boundary] **— ter'mi·nal·ly** *adv.*

ter·mi·nate (tûr'mə·nāt) *v.* **·nat·ed, ·nat·ing** *v.t.* **1.** To put an end or stop to. **2.** To form the conclusion of; finish. **3.** To bound or limit. **—** *v.i.* **4.** To have or come to an end. [< L *terminus* limit] **— ter'mi·na'tive** *adj.* **— ter'mi·na'·tor** *n.* **— ter'mi·na·to'ry** (-nə·tôr'ē, -tō'rē) *adj.*

ter·mi·na·tion (tûr'mə·nā'shən) *n.* **1.** The act of setting bounds or limits. **2.** The act of ending or concluding. **3.** That which bounds or limits; close; end. **4.** Outcome; result; conclusion. **5.** The final letters or syllable of a word; a suffix. **— ter'mi·na'tion·al** *adj.*

ter·mi·nol·o·gy (tûr'mə·nol'ə·jē) *n. pl.* **·gies** The technical terms used in a science, art, trade, etc.; nomenclature. [< L *terminus* + -LOGY] **— ter'mi·no·log'i·cal** (-nə·loj'i·kəl) *adj.* **— ter'mi·no·log'i·cal·ly** *adv.*

ter·mi·nus (tûr'mə·nəs) *n. pl.* **·nus·es** or **·ni** (-nī) **1.** The final point or goal; end. **2.** The farthermost station on a railway. **3.** A boundary or border. [< L]

ter·mite (tûr'mīt') *n.* Any of various small, whitish social insects native in warm regions, several species of which are very destructive of wooden structures, furniture, etc.: also, loosely, *white ant.* [< L *termes*]

tern (tûrn) *n.* Any of several birds allied to the gulls, but having a smaller bill and body, with wings more pointed, and the tail usu. deeply forked. [< Scand.]

ter·na·ry (tûr'nər·ē) *adj.* Formed or consisting of three; grouped in threes. **—** *n. pl.* **·ries** A group of three; a triad. [< L *terni* by threes]

ter·nate (tûr'nāt) *adj.* Arranged in threes. [< NL < L *terni* by threes] **— ter'nate·ly** *adv.*

ter·pene (tûr'pēn) *n. Chem.* Any of a class of isomeric hydrocarbons, $C_{10}H_{16}$, contained chiefly in the essential oils of coniferous plants. [< *terp(entin)*, earlier form of TURPENTINE + -ENE]

Terp·sich·o·re (tûrp·sik'ə·rē) The Muse of dancing. [< Gk. < *terpsis* enjoyment + *choros* dance] **— Terp·si·cho·re·an** (tûrp'si·kə·rē'ən) *adj.*

terp·si·cho·re·an (tûrp'si·kə·rē'ən) *adj.* Of or relating to dancing: also **terp'si·cho·re'al.** **—** *n. Informal* A dancer.

ter·race (ter'is) *n.* **1.** An artificial, raised, level space, as of lawn, having one or more vertical or sloping sides; also, such levels collectively. **2.** A raised level supporting a row of houses, or the houses occupying such a position. **3.** The flat roof of an Oriental or Spanish house. **4.** An unroofed, usu. paved area near a house. **5.** An open gallery. **—** *v.t.* **·raced, ·rac·ing** To form into or provide with a terrace or terraces. [< OF < Ital. < L *terra* earth]

ter·ra cot·ta (ter'ə kot'ə) **1.** A hard, durable clay, reddish brown in color and usu. unglazed, widely used as a structural material and in pottery, tiles, building façades, etc. **2.** Its brownish orange color. [< Ital., cooked earth]

ter·ra fir·ma (ter'ə fûr'mə) Solid ground. [< L]

ter·rain (te·rān', ter'ān) *n.* A piece or plot of ground; esp., a region or territory viewed with regard to its suitability for some particular purpose. [< F < L < *terra* earth]

Ter·ra·my·cin (ter'ə·mī'sin) *n.* Proprietary name for an antibiotic isolated from a soil mold and used in the treatment of a wide variety of bacterial infections. Also **ter'ra·my'cin.**

ter·ra·pin (ter'ə·pin) *n.* Any of several North Ameri- edible tortoises of fresh and brackish waters; esp., the c mond Back. [< Algonquian]

ter·rar·i·um (te·râr'ē·əm) *n. pl.* **·rar·i·ums** or **rar** (-râr'ē·ə) A place or enclosure for keeping land anim plants, etc. [< L *terra* earth + -ARIUM, on analogy w *aquarium*]

ter·res·tri·al (tə·res'trē·əl) *adj.* **1.** Of, pertaining to consisting of earth or land. **2.** Of, belonging to, or re senting the earth. **3.** *Biol.* Living on or growing in the ea or land. **4.** Belonging to or consisting of land, as disti from water, trees, etc. **5.** Worldly; mundane. **—** *n.* An habitant of the earth. [< L *terra* land] **— ter·res'tri·a** *adv.* **— ter·res'tri·al·ness** *n.*

ter·ret (ter'it) *n.* One of two metal rings projecting f the saddle of a harness, through which the reins are pas [ME < F *touret*, dim. of *tour* turn]

terri- *combining form* Earth; ground. [< L *terra* ear

ter·ri·ble (ter'ə·bəl) *adj.* **1.** Of a nature to excite terror; palling. **2.** *Informal* Characterized by excess; severe; treme. **3.** Inspiring awe. **4.** *Informal* Inferior. [< *terrere* to terrify] **— ter'ri·ble·ness** *n.* **— ter'ri·bly** *adv*

ter·ri·er (ter'ē·ər) *n.* Any of various small, active, wiry d of several breeds, formerly used to hunt burrowing anim [< OF < L *terra* earth]

ter·rif·ic (tə·rif'ik) *adj.* **1.** *Informal* **a** Extreme; inte tremendous. **b** Wonderful; great; splendid. **2.** Arousin calculated to arouse great terror or fear. **— ter·rif'i·cal·ly**

ter·ri·fy (ter'ə·fī) *v.t.* **·fied, ·fy·ing** To fill with extreme ror. [< L < *terrere* to frighten + *facere* to make]

ter·ri·to·ri·al (ter'ə·tôr'ē·əl, -tō'rē-) *adj.* **1.** Of or pert ing to a territory or territories. **2.** Limited to or within jurisdiction of a particular territory or region. **3.** Desig ing military forces intended for territorial defense. **4.** longing to a particular locality. **5.** *Often cap.* Organize intended primarily for national defense: the British T torial Army. **— ter'ri·to'ri·al·ism** *n.* **— ter'ri·to'ri·al·is — ter'ri·to'ri·al'i·ty** (-al'ə·tē) *n.* **— ter'ri·to'ri·al·ly** *adv.*

Ter·ri·to·ri·al (ter'ə·tôr'ē·əl, -tō'rē-) *adj.* Of any or al the Territories of the U.S., Great Britain, etc. **—** *n.* A m ber of the Territorial Army in Great Britain.

ter·ri·to·ry (ter'ə·tôr'ē, -tō'rē) *n. pl.* **·ries 1.** The dom over which a sovereign state exercises jurisdiction. **2.** considerable tract of land; a region; also, a sphere, provi **3.** An area assigned for a special purpose. [< L *terra* ea

Ter·ri·to·ry (ter'ə·tôr'ē, -tō'rē) *n. U.S.* A region havi certain degree of self-government but not having the stat of a State, as American Samoa.

ter·ror (ter'ər) *n.* **1.** An overwhelming impulse of fear; treme fright or dread. **2.** A person or thing that causes treme fear. **3.** *Informal* An intolerable nuisance. [< F *terrere* to frighten]

ter·ror·ism (ter'ə·riz'əm) *n.* **1.** The act of terrorizin the state of being terrorized. **2.** Unlawful acts of viol committed in an attempt to overthrow a government. : system of government that rules by intimidation. **— ror·ist** *n.* **— ter'ror·is'tic** *adj.*

ter·ror·ize (ter'ə·rīz) *v.t.* **·ized, ·iz·ing 1.** To reduce state of terror; terrify. **2.** To coerce through intimidat **— ter'ror·i·za'tion** *n.* **— ter'ror·iz'er** *n.*

ter·ry (ter'ē) *n. pl.* **·ries** A pile fabric in which the loops uncut: also **terry cloth.** [Prob. < F *tirer* to draw]

terse (tûrs) *adj.* **ters·er, ters·est** Short and to the p concise: a *terse* comment. [< L < *tergere* to rub off, down] **— terse'ly** *adv.* **— terse'ness** *n.*

— Syn. Terse, concise, pithy, and *succinct* characterize sp or writing that says much in relatively few words. *Terse* em sizes the finish and cogency of the result; *concise* suggest tha unnecessary words have been pruned away. *Pithy* describes so thing both brief and forceful, while *succinct* characterizes which is highly compact because all extraneous detail has removed. **— Ant.** diffuse, prolix, wordy.

ter·tial (tûr'shəl) *Ornithol. adj.* Tertiary. **—** *n.* A tert feather. [< L *tertius* third]

ter·tian (tûr'shən) *adj.* Recurring every other day, reckoned inclusively, every third day. **—** *n. Pathol.* A tian disease or fever. [< L *tertius* third]

ter·ti·ar·y (tûr'shē·er'ē, -shə·rē) *adj.* **1.** Third in poi time, number, degree, etc. **2.** *Ornithol.* Denoting one o flight feathers attached to a bird's wing: also called te **—** *n. pl.* **·ar·ies** *Ornithol.* A tertiary feather. [< L *tius* third]

Ter·ti·ar·y (tûr'shē·er'ē, -shə·rē) *Geol. adj.* Of the earli the two geological periods or systems comprising the C zoic era, following the Cretaceous and succeeded by the (ternary. **—** *n.* The Tertiary period or system, chara ized by the rise of mammals. See table for GEOLOGY.

tes·sel·late (tes'ə·lāt) *v.t.* **·lat·ed, ·lat·ing** To construe the style of checkered mosaic; lay or adorn with square tiles. [< L < dial. Gk. (Ionic) *tesseres* four] **— tes'sel ed** *adj.* **— tes'sel·la'tion** *n.*

test (test) *v.t.* **1.** To subject to a test or trial; try. **2.** *Chem.* To assay or refine (a precious metal). **b** To examine by means of some reagent. — *v.i.* **3.** *Chem.* **a** To undergo test- **b** To show specified qualities or properties under testing. *n.* **1.** Subjection to conditions that disclose the true character of a person or thing in relation to some particular quality. **2.** An examination made for the purpose of proving or disproving some matter in doubt: a sobriety *test.* **3.** A series of questions, problems, etc., intended to measure the extent of knowledge, aptitudes, intelligence, and other mental traits. **4.** A criterion or standard of judgment. **5.** *Chem.* A reaction by means of which the presence and identity of a compound or one of its constituents may be determined. **b** An agent or result of such a reaction. [< OF, vessel used in assaying metals < L *testum* earthen vessel] — **test′a·ble** — **test′er** *n.*

test (test) *n.* **1.** *Zool.* A rigid external case or covering of many invertebrates, as a sea urchin or mollusk; a shell: also **ed** *testa.* **2.** *Bot.* A testa. [< L *testa* shell]

tes·ta (tes′tə) *n. pl.* **·tae** (-tē) **1.** *Bot.* The outer, usu. hard brittle coat or integument of a seed: also called *test.* **2.** A test. [See TEST².]

tes·ta·ceous (tes·tā′shəs) *adj.* **1.** Of or derived from shells hellfish. **2.** Having a hard shell. [< L *testa* shell]

tes·ta·ment (tes′tə·mənt) *n.* **1.** *Law* The written declaration of one's last will: chiefly in the phrase **last will and testament. 2.** In Biblical use, a covenant. [< F < L < *testis* witness] — **tes′ta·men′tal** *adj.*

Tes·ta·ment (tes′tə·mənt) *n.* **1.** One of the two volumes of Bible, distinguished as the *Old* and the *New Testament.* **2.** A volume containing the New Testament.

tes·ta·men·ta·ry (tes′tə·men′tər·ē) *adj.* **1.** Derived from, bequeathed by, or set forth in a will. **2.** Appointed or provided by, or done in accordance with, a will. **3.** Pertaining to a will, or to the administration or settlement of a will.

tes·tate (tes′tāt) *adj.* Having made a will before decease. [< L *testis* witness]

tes·ta·tor (tes·tā′tər, tes′tā·ter) *n.* **1.** The maker of a will. **2.** One who has died leaving a will. [< L] — **tes·ta′trix** (-triks) *n.fem.*

tes·tes (tes′tēz) Plural of TESTIS.

tes·ti·cle (tes′ti·kəl) *n. Biol.* One of the two male sex glands enclosed in the scrotum and in which the spermatozoa and other secretions are formed: also called *testis.* [< L, dim. of *testis* testicle]

tes·ti·fy (tes′tə·fī) *v.* **·fied, ·fy·ing** *v.i.* **1.** To make solemn declaration of truth or fact. **2.** *Law* To give testimony; bear witness. **3.** To serve as evidence or indication: Her rags *testified* to her poverty. — *v.t.* **4.** To bear witness to; affirm positively. **5.** *Law* To state or declare on oath or affirmation. **6.** To be evidence or indication of. **7.** To make known publicly; declare. [< L < *testis* witness + *facere* to make] — **tes′ti·fi·ca′tion** (-fə·kā′shən) *n.* — **tes′ti·fi′er** *n.*

tes·ti·mo·ni·al (tes′tə·mō′nē·əl) *n.* **1.** A formal token or statement of regard. **2.** A written acknowledgment of services or worth; also, a letter of recommendation. — *adj.* Pertaining to or constituting testimony or a testimonial.

tes·ti·mo·ny (tes′tə·mō′nē) *n. pl.* **·nies 1.** A statement or affirmation of a fact, as offered in a court. **2.** Evidence; proof; specif., the aggregate of proof offered in a case. **3.** The act of testifying; attestation. **4.** Public declaration regarding some experience. [< L < *testis* witness]

— **Syn.** *Testimony* is the oral statements made by a witness under examination. A *deposition* or *affidavit* is *testimony* put into writing; *depositions* are made under formal questioning, and may be subject to cross-examination, while an *affidavit* is a sworn document that may be accepted when the testifier cannot appear in court in person.

tes·tis (tes′tis) *n. pl.* **·tes** (-tēz) A testicle. [< L]

tes·tos·ter·one (tes·tos′tə·rōn) *n. Biochem.* A male sex hormone, $C_{19}H_{28}O_2$, isolated as a white crystalline substance from the testes, and also made synthetically. [< TESTIS + $R(OL)$ + -ONE]

test pilot An aviator who tests aircraft of new design.

test tube A glass tube, open at one end and usu. with a rounded bottom, used in making chemical or biological tests.

tes·tu·do (tes·tōō′dō, -tyōō′-) *n. pl.* **·di·nes** (-də·nēz) **1.** A shed or screen used by the Romans for the protection of soldiers in siege operations. **2.** A protecting cover formed by soldiers in ranks by overlapping their shields above their heads. [< L < *testa* shell]

tes·ty (tes′tē) *adj.* **·ti·er, ·ti·est** Irritable in manner or disposition; touchy. [< AF *testif* heady < OF < L *testa* skull] — **tes′ti·ly** *adv.* — **tes′ti·ness** *n.*

te·tan·ic (ti·tan′ik) *adj.* Relating to or productive of tetanus. Also **te·tan′i·cal.** — *n.* A drug capable of causing convulsions, as strychnine or nux vomica.

tet·a·nus (tet′ə·nəs) *n.* **1.** *Pathol.* An acute infectious dis-

ease caused by a bacillus and characterized by rigid spasmodic contraction of various voluntary muscles, esp. those of the neck and jaw. Compare LOCKJAW. **2.** *Physiol.* A state of contraction in a muscle excited by a rapid series of shocks. [< L < Gk. *tetanos* spasm]

tetarto- *combining form* Four; fourth. Also, before vowels, **tetart-.** [< Gk. *tetartos* fourth < *tettares* four]

tetch·y (tech′ē) *adj.* **tetch·i·er, tetch·i·est** Peevishly sensitive; irritable; touchy. [< OF *teche* mark, quality] — **tetch′i·ly** *adv.* — **tetch′i·ness** *n.*

tête-à-tête (tāt′ə·tāt′, *Fr.* tet·à·tet′) *adj.* Confidential, as between two persons only. — *n.* **1.** A confidential interview between two persons; a private chat. **2.** An S-shaped sofa on which two persons may face each other. — *adv.* In or as in intimate conversation. [< F, lit. head to head]

teth·er (teth′ər) *n.* **1.** Something used to check or confine, as a rope for fastening an animal. **2.** The range, scope, or limit of one's powers or field of action. — **at the end of one's tether** At the extreme end or limit of one's resources, patience, etc. — *v.t.* To fasten or confine by a tether. [ME *tethir* < Scand.]

tetra- *combining form* Four; fourfold. Also, before vowels, **tetr-.** [< Gk.]

tet·ra·chord (tet′rə·kôrd) *n. Music* Four contiguous tones, of which the extreme tones are a perfect fourth apart. [< Gk. < *tetras* group of four + *chordē* string] — **tet′ra·chor′dal** *adj.*

tet·rad (tet′rad) *n.* A group or collection of four. [< Gk. *tetras, -ados* group of four]

tet·ra·eth·yl lead (tet′rə·eth′il led) *Chem.* A colorless, heavy, flammable, poisonous, liquid hydrocarbon $Pb(C_2H_5)_4$, used as an antiknock agent in internal-combustion engines.

tet·ra·he·dron (tet′rə·hē′drən) *n. pl.* **·drons** or **·dra** (-drə) *Geom.* A polyhedron bounded by four plane triangular faces. [< Gk. < *tetra-* four + *hedra* base] — **tet′ra·he′dral** *adj.*

TETRAHEDRON

te·tral·o·gy (te·tral′ə·jē) *n. pl.* **·gies 1.** A group of four dramas, including three tragedies and one satyr play, presented together at the festivals of Dionysus at Athens. **2.** Any series of four related dramatic, operatic, or literary works. [< Gk. < *tetra-* four + *logos* word]

te·tram·e·ter (te·tram′ə·tər) *n.* **1.** In prosody, a line of verse consisting of four metrical feet: Fúll fā│thóm fíve│thÿ fā│thḗr líes. **2.** Verse consisting of lines of four metrical feet. — *adj.* Consisting of four metrical feet or of lines containing four metrical feet. [< LL < Gk. < *tetra-* four + *metron* measure]

tet·rarch (tet′rärk, tē′trärk) *n.* **1.** The governor of one of four divisions of a country or province. **2.** A tributary prince under the Romans; a subordinate ruler. **3.** In ancient Greece, an army commander of a subdivision of a phalanx. [< LL < Gk. < *tetra-* four + *archos* ruler]

tet·rar·chy (tet′rär·kē, tē′trär-) *n. pl.* **·chies 1.** The rule, territory, or jurisdiction of a tetrarch. **2.** Government by a group of four; also, the four members of such a group. Also **tet′rar·chate** (-kāt, -kit).

tet·ra·stich (tet′rə·stik) *n.* A poem or stanza of four lines. [< TETRA- + Gk. *stichos* row, line] — **tet′ra·stich′ic** *adj.*

tet·ra·va·lent (tet′rə·vā′lənt) *adj. Chem.* Quadrivalent.

Teu·ton (tōōt′n, tyōōt′n) *n.* **1.** One of the Teutones. **2.** One belonging to any of the Teutonic peoples; esp., a German.

Teu·to·nes (tōōt′ə·nēz, tyōō′-) *n.pl.* An ancient German tribe that dwelt in Jutland north of the Elbe.

Teu·ton·ic (tōō·ton′ik, tyōō-) *adj.* **1.** Of, pertaining to, or designating the peoples of northern Europe, formerly the Angles, Saxons, Danes, Normans, Goths, etc., now embracing also the English, Germans, Dutch, etc. **2.** Of or pertaining to the Germanic languages. **3.** Of or pertaining to the Teutones. — *n.* The Germanic subfamily of languages.

Teu·ton·ism (tōōt′n·iz′əm, tyōōt′n-) *n.* **1.** A custom or mode of expression peculiar to Germans or Teutons; Germanism. Also **Teu·ton·i·cism** (tōō·ton′ə·siz′əm, tyōō-). **2.** A belief in the superiority of the Teutonic peoples. **3.** Teutonic character and civilization. — **Teu′ton·ist** *n.*

Teu·ton·ize (tōōt′n·īz, tyōōt′n-) *v.t. & v.i.* **·ized, ·iz·ing** To make or become Teutonic or German. — **Teu′ton·i·za′tion** *n.*

Texas fever A destructive cattle disease caused by a blood parasite transmitted by a tick.

Texas leaguer *U.S. Informal* In baseball, a fly ball that falls between an infielder and an outfielder for a base hit.

text (tekst) *n.* **1.** The body of matter on a written or printed page, as distinguished from notes, commentary, illustrations, etc. **2.** The actual or original words of an author. **3.** A written or printed version of the matter of an author's works: the folio *text* of Shakespeare. **4.** Any one of various recensions that are taken to represent the authentic words, or portion of the words, of the original Scriptures. **5.** A verse of Scripture, particularly when cited as the basis of a discourse or sermon. **6.** Any subject of discourse; a topic. **7.** A textbook. [< OF < L *textus* fabric < *texere* to weave]

text·book (tekst′bŏŏk′) *n.* A book used as a standard work or basis of instruction in any branch of knowledge.

tex·tile (teks′til, -tīl) *adj.* **1.** Pertaining to weaving or woven fabrics. **2.** Such as may be woven; manufactured by weaving. — *n.* **1.** A woven fabric. **2.** Material capable of being woven. [< L < *textus* fabric.]

tex·tu·al (teks′chŏŏ·əl) *adj.* **1.** Pertaining to, contained in, or based on the text of a book. **2.** Word for word; literal. **3.** Versed in texts. — **tex′tu·al·ly** *adv.*

tex·tu·al·ism (teks′chŏŏ·əl·iz′əm) *n.* Rigid adherence to a text. — **tex′tu·al·ist** *n.*

tex·ture (teks′chər) *n.* **1.** The arrangement or character of the threads, etc., of a woven fabric. **2.** The mode of union or disposition of elementary constituent parts, as in a photograph, surface of paper, etc. **3.** The structure of the surface of a painting, sculpture, etc.; also, the apparent surface structure of an object or part represented in a work of art, as skin, fur, etc. **4.** Any woven fabric; a web. — *v.t.* **.tured, .tur·ing** To give a particular texture to. [< L < *textus* fabric] — **tex′tur·al** *adj.* — **tex′tur·al·ly** *adv.*

tex·tured (teks′chərd) *adj.* **1.** Having a distinctive texture. **2.** Having (a specified kind of) texture: used in combination: *rough-textured.*

-th¹ *suffix of nouns* **1.** The act or result of the action expressed in the root word: *growth.* **2.** The state of being what is indicated in the root word: *health.* [OE *-thu, -th*]

-th² *suffix* Used in ordinal numbers: *tenth.* Also, after vowels, *-eth,* as in *fortieth.* [OE *-tha, -the*]

-th³ See -ETH¹.

Thai (tī) *n.* **1.** The people collectively of Thailand, Laos, and parts of Burma: preceded by *the.* **2.** A family of languages spoken by these people, considered by some to be a branch of the Sino-Tibetan family and by others to be affiliated with the Austronesian Polynesian family. **3.** The language of Thailand. — *adj.* Of or pertaining to the Thai, their culture, or their languages. Also spelled *Tai.*

tha·lam·ic (thə·lam′ik) *adj.* Of or pertaining to a thalamus, esp. to the thalamus of the brain.

thal·a·mus (thal′ə·məs) *n.* *pl.* **·mi** (-mī) **1.** *Anat.* A large, ovoid mass of gray matter at the base of the brain, the chief center for transmission of sensory impulses to the cerebral cortex: also called *optic thalamus.* **2.** *Bot.* The receptacle of a flower. [< L < Gk. *thalamos* chamber]

tha·las·sic (thə·las′ik) *adj.* **1.** Of or pertaining to the seas, as distinguished from the oceans. **2.** Pelagic; oceanic. [< F < Gk. *thalassa* sea]

thalasso- *combining form* The sea; of the sea. Also, before vowels, **thalass-, thalassi-.** [< Gk. *thalassa* sea]

tha·ler (tä′lər) See TALER.

thal·i·do·mide (thə·lid′ə·mīd) *n.* *Chem.* An organic compound, $C_{13}H_{10}N_2O_4$, originally a mild sedative and later withdrawn because its use by pregnant women was suspected of causing serious malformations in newborn children.

thal·li·um (thal′ē·əm) *n.* A soft, white, crystalline metallic element (symbol Tl), whose salts are used in rat poison, insecticides, and in making optical glass. See ELEMENT. [< NL < Gk. *thallos* green shoot; from the bright green line in its spectrum that led to its discovery]

thal·lo·phyte (thal′ə·fīt) *n.* Any of various plants belonging to a division including forms without true roots, stems, or leaves, comprising the bacteria, fungi, algae, and lichens. — **thal′lo·phyt′ic** (-fit′ik) *adj.*

thal·lus (thal′əs) *n.* *pl.* **·lus·es** or **·li** (-lī) *Bot.* A plant body without true root, stem, or leaf, as in thallophytes. [< L, shoot < Gk. < *thallein* to bloom]

Tham·muz (täm′mŏŏz, tam′uz) See TAMMUZ.

than (than, *unstressed* thən) *conj.* **1.** When, as, or if compared with: after an adjective or adverb to express comparison between what precedes and what follows: I am stronger *than* he (is). **2.** Except; but: used after *other, else,* etc.: no other *than* you. [OE *thonne* than]

◆ *Than* is usu. taken as a conjunction; as such, it may be followed by the nominative or the objective, depending on the nature of the ellipsis: You struck him harder *than* I (struck him) or You struck him harder *than* (you struck) me. A minority of grammarians and writers have accepted *than* as a preposition, in which case it is regularly followed by the objective: He is stronger *than me.*

thanato- *combining form* Death; of or pertaining to death. Also, before vowels, **thanat-.** [< Gk. *thanatos* death]

than·a·top·sis (than′ə·top′sis) *n.* A meditation upon death. [< THANAT(O)- + Gk. *opsis* appearance, sight]

thane (thān) *n.* **1.** A warrior companion of an English king before the Conquest. **2.** A man who ranked above an ordinary freeman or ceorl (churl) but below an earl or nobleman. **3.** *Scot.* The chief of a clan. Also **thegn.** [OE *thegn*]

thank (thangk) *v.t.* **1.** To express gratitude to. **2.** To hold

responsible; blame: often used ironically. — **thank** I thank you. [OE *thancian* < *thanc* thanks, thought]

thank·ful (thangk′fəl) *adj.* **1.** Appreciative of favor; ceived; grateful. **2.** Expressing thanks. — **thank′f** *adv.* — **thank′ful·ness** *n.*

thank·less (thangk′lis) *adj.* **1.** Not feeling or showing itude; ungrateful. **2.** Not gaining or likely to gain tha unappreciated. — **thank′less·ly** *adv.* — **thank′less·ne**

thanks (thangks) *n.pl.* Expressions of gratitude; gra adknowledgment. — *interj.* Thank you. — **thanks** Thanks be given to. **2.** Because of.

thanks·giv·ing (thangks′giv′ing) *n.* **1.** The act of g thanks, as to God; an expression of gratitude. **2.** A p celebration in recognition of divine favor.

Thanksgiving Day 1. *U.S.* The fourth Thursday in vember, set apart as an annual festival of thanksgiving *Canadian* The second Monday in October, a statutory day. Also **Thanksgiving.**

that (that, *unstressed* thət) *pl. for adj. and pron. def.* 1 (thōz) *adj.* **1.** Pertaining to some person or thing previ mentioned, understood, or specifically designated. **2** noting something more remote, or something contrasted another thing: distinguished from *this:* This house is b *that* one is red. — *pron.* **1.** As a demonstrative, the pe or thing implied, mentioned, or understood; the pers thing there or as distinguished from one already design *That* is the dress I like; Keep this and discard *that.* **2.** relative pronoun, who, whom, or which: the person I saw. — *adv.* **1.** To that extent: I can't see *that* far. **2** *formal* In such a manner or degree; so: He's *that* simpl can hardly read. — *conj.* **1.** As a fact: introducing a I tell you *that* it is so. **2.** As a result: introducing a r consequence, or effect: He bled so profusely *that* he died At which time; when: It was only yesterday *that* I saw **4.** So that: I tell you *that* you may know. **5.** For the r that; because. **6.** Introducing an exclamation: O th would come: — **so that 1.** To the end that. **2.** Wit result that. [OE *thæt,* neut. of *se* the, that]

thatch (thach) *n.* **1.** A covering of reeds, straw, etc ranged on a roof so as to shed water. **2.** Anything resem such a covering. **3.** Any of various palms whose leave used for thatching. — *v.t.* To cover with or as with th [OE *thæc* cover] — **thatch′er** *n.* — **thatch′y** *adj.*

thatch·ing (thach′ing) *n.* **1.** The act or process of cov a roof with thatch. **2.** Material used for thatch.

thaumato- *combining form* A wonder; a miracle. fore vowels, **thaumat-.** [< Gk. *thauma, -atos* wonder

thau·ma·tur·gy (thô′mə·tûr′jē) *n.* Magic; the worki wonders or miracles. — **thau′ma·tur′gic** or **·gi·cal** *ad*

thaw (thô) *v.i.* **1.** To melt or dissolve; become liqu semiliquid, as snow or ice. **2.** To rise in temperature to melt ice and snow: said of weather and used imperso **3.** To become less cold and unsociable. — *v.t.* **4.** To to thaw. — *n.* **1.** The act of thawing, or the state of thawed. **2.** Warmth of weather above the freezing following a colder period. **3.** A state of warmer feelin expression. [OE *thawian*] — **thaw′er** *n.*

the¹ (*stressed* thē; *unstressed before a consonant* thə; *uns* *before a vowel* thē or thi) *definite article or adj.* The posed to the indefinite article *a* or *an,* and is used, esp fore nouns, to render the modified word more particu individual. It is used specifically: **1.** When reference is to a particular person, thing, or group: He left *the* room To give an adjective substantive force, or render a notio stract: *the* doing of the deed; *the* quick and *the* dead. **3** fore a noun to make it generic: *The* dog is a friend of **4.** With the force of a possessive pronoun: He kicked *the* (my) leg. **5.** To give distributive force: equivalent *per,* each, etc.: a dollar *the* volume. **6.** To designate a p ular one as emphatically outstanding: usu. stressed in s and italicized in writing: He is *the* officer for the comm [OE, later form of *se*]

the² (thə) *adv.* By that much; by so much; to this ex used to modify words in the comparative degree: *the* v *the* merrier. [OE *thȳ,* instrumental case of *se* the¹]

the- Var. of THEO-.

the·a·ter (thē′ə·tər) *n.* **1.** A building especially adapt present dramas, operas, motion pictures, etc.; playhous The theatrical world and everything relating to it. room or hall arranged with seats that rise as they from a platform, esp. adapted to lectures, demonstra etc. **4.** Any place of semicircular form with seats rise easy gradations. **5.** Any place or region that is the sc events: a *theater* of operations in war. Also *esp. Brit.* tre. [< OF < L < Gk. < *theasthai* to behold]

the·a·ter·go·er (thē′ə·tər·gō′ər) *n.* One who goes oft regularly to the theater. Also *esp. Brit.* **the′a·tre·go′er**

the·a·ter-in-the-round (thē′ə·tər·in·thə·round′) *n.* theater.

the·at·ri·cal (thē·at′ri·kəl) *adj.* **1.** Pertaining to the th or to dramatic performances. **2.** Designed for show y, or effect; showy; artificial. **3.** Suited to dramatic presation. **4.** Resembling the manner of actors; histrionic. o **the·at'ric.** — *n.pl.* Dramatic performances, esp. by ateurs. — **the·at'ri·cal·ly** *adv.* — **the·at'ri·cal·ness** *n.*

at·ri·cal·ism (thē·at'ri·kəl·iz'əm) *n.* Theatrical or melamatic manner or style.

at·rics (thē·at'riks) *n.pl.* (*construed as sing.*) **1.** The ging of plays. **2.** The art of creating effects appropriate iramatic performances.

bes (thēbz) **1.** The ancient capital of Upper Egypt; xor and Karnak occupy part of its site on the Nile. **2.** e chief city of ancient Boeotia, Greece: also **The·bae** (thē'. , — **The·ban** (thē'bən) *adj. & n.*

ca (thē'kə) *n.* *pl.* **·cae** (-sē) **1.** *Biol.* A protective sheath :ase for an organ or part, as of the spinal cord, a follicle, insect pupa, etc. **2.** *Bot.* A spore case, sac, or capsule. L < Gk. *thēkē* case] — **the'ca** *adj.* — **the·cate** (thē'. -kāt)

e (thē' pron. **1.** *Archaic* The objective case of the pro-n *thou*. **2.** Thou: used by some Quakers with a verb in third person singular: *Thee knows my mind.* [OE *thē*, ;. dative, later accusative case of *thū* thou]

t (theft) *n.* **1.** The act or crime of thieving; larceny. **2.** That which is stolen. [OE *thēoft, thīefth*]

– Syn. 1. *Theft* is the general term for the crime of stealing. aw, larceny includes many forms of stealing, but not embezzle-it and swindling. *Burglary* is the crime of breaking into and ering another's home, place of business, or other property with nt to commit a felony. *Robbery* is stealing from the person, or he presence of, the victim.

·n (thān) See THANE.

ine (thē'ēn, -in) *n. Chem.* The alkaloid found in the tea nt, chemically identical with caffeine. Also **the'in** (-in). F < NL *thea* tea < dial. Chinese *t'e*]

·r (thâr) *pronominal adj.* The possessive case of the pro-n *they*, used attributively: *their homes.* [ME < ON *rra* of them]

rs (thârz) *pron.* **1.** The possessive case of the pronoun y, used predicatively: *That house is theirs.* **2.** The one or s belonging or relating to them: *our country and theirs.* **of theirs** Belonging or pertaining to them.

ism (thē'iz·əm) *n.* **1.** Belief in, or in the existence of, , a god, or gods. **2.** Belief in a personal God as creator supreme ruler of the universe, who transcends his crea-but works in and through it in revealing himself to men. Belief in one god; monotheism. [< Gk. *theos* god] — **'ist** *n.* — **the·is'tic** or **·ti·cal** *adj.* — **the·is'ti·cal·ly** *adv.*

m (them, *unstressed* thəm) *pron.* The objective case of pronoun *they.* [ME *theim* < ON, to them]

mat·ic (thē·mat'ik) *adj.* **1.** Of, constituting, or pertain-to a theme or themes. **2.** *Ling.* Constituting a stem. o **the·mat'i·cal.** — **the·mat'i·cal·ly** *adv.*

natic vowel *Ling.* A vowel added to a root to form a m.

me (thēm) *n.* **1.** A topic to be discussed or developed in ech or writing; a subject of discourse. **2.** Any topic. **3.** rief composition, esp. one written as an exercise as part of ourse of instruction. **4.** *Music* **a** A melody that is sub-ed to variation or elaboration; subject. **b** A musical fea-e, as a chordal sequence, rhythm, melody, etc. that forms basis of a composition. [< OF < L < Gk. *the-*, stem *'ithenai* to place]

me song 1. A melody used throughout a dramatic pres-ation to establish or maintain a mood. **2.** A strain of mu-that identifies a radio program, a dance band, etc.

m·selves (them'selvz', *unstressed* thəm-) *pron.* A form he third person plural pronoun, used: **1.** As a reflexive or object of a preposition in a reflexive sense: *They laughed themselves.* **2.** As an emphatic or intensive form of *they*: ey *themselves* are at fault. **3.** As a designation of a nor-l, proper, or usual state: *They were not themselves then.*

n (then) *adv.* **1.** At that time. **2.** Soon or immediately erward; next in space or time. **3.** At another time: often roducing a sequential statement following *now, at first,* . **4.** For that reason; as a consequence. **5.** In that case. *adj.* Being or acting in, or belonging to, that time: the n secretary of state. — *n.* A specific time already men-ed or understood; that time. [OE *thanne*]

nce (thens) *adv.* **1.** From that place. **2.** From the cir-nstance, fact, or cause; therefore. **3.** From that time; er that time. [ME < OE *thanon* from there + -*s³*]

nce·forth (thens'fôrth', -fôrth') **thens'fôrth', -fôrth')** . From that time on; thereafter.

nce·for·ward (thens'fôr'wərd) *adv.* **1.** Thenceforth. From that place or time forward. Also **thence'for'wards.**

o- *combining form* God; of or pertaining to God, a god, gods. Also, before vowels, *the-*. [< Gk. *theos* a god]

·oc·ra·cy (thē·ok'rə·sē) *n.* *pl.* **·cies 1.** A state, polity,

or group of people that claims a deity as its ruler. **2.** Gov-ernment of a state by a priesthood claiming divine authority, as in the Papacy. [< Gk. < *theos* god + *krateein* to rule] — **the·o·crat'ic** (-krat'ik) or **·i·cal** *adj.*

the·o·crat (thē'ə·krat) *n.* **1.** A theocratic or divine ruler. **2.** An advocate of theocracy.

the·od·o·lite (thē·od'ə·līt) *n.* In surveying, an instrument for measuring horizontal and vertical angles by means of a small telescope turning on a horizontal and a vertical axis. [An arbitrary formation] — **the·od'o·lit'ic** (-lit'ik) *adj.*

the·o·lo·gi·an (thē'ə·lō'jē·ən, -jən) *n.* One versed in theol-ogy, esp. that of the Christian church.

the·o·log·i·cal (thē'ə·loj'i·kəl) *adj.* Of or pertaining to the-ology or to divine revelation. Also **the'o·log'ic.** — **the'o·log'i·cal·ly** *adv.*

the·ol·o·gize (thē·ol'ə·jīz) *v.* **·gized, ·giz·ing** *v.t.* **1.** To de-vise or fit (something) into a system of theology. — *v.i.* **2.** To reason theologically. Also *Brit.* **the·ol'o·gise.**

the·ol·o·gy (thē·ol'ə·jē) *n.* *pl.* **·gies 1.** The study of re-ligion, culminating in a synthesis or philosophy of religion; also, a critical survey of religion, esp. of the Christian reli-gion. **2.** A body of doctrines as set forth by a particular church or religious group. [< OF < LL < Gk. < *theos* god + *logos* discourse]

the·oph·a·ny (thē·of'ə·nē) *n.* *pl.* **·nies** A manifestation or appearance of a deity or of the gods to man. [< L < Gk. < *theos* god + *phainein* to show]

the·o·rem (thē'ər·əm, thir'əm) *n.* **1.** A proposition demon-strably true or acknowledged as such. **2.** *Math.* **a** A prop-osition setting forth something to be proved. **b** A proposition that has been proved or assumed to be true. **c** A rule or state-ment of relations formulated in symbols. [LL < Gk. *the-ōrēma* sight, theory < *theōreein* to look at] — **the·o·re·mat·ic** (thē'ər·ə·mat'ik), **the'o·rem'ic** (-ə·rem'ik) *adj.*

the·o·ret·i·cal (thē'ə·ret'i·kəl) *adj.* **1.** Of, relating to, or consisting of theory. **2.** Relating to knowledge or science without reference to its application. **3.** Existing only in theory; hypothetical. **4.** Addicted to theorizing; impracti-cal; visionary. Also **the·o·ret'ic.** — **the·o·ret'i·cal·ly** *adv.*

the·o·re·ti·cian (thē'ər·ə·tish'ən) *n.* One who deals with the speculative, hypothetical, or ideal rather than with the prac-tical and executive aspects of a subject.

the·o·ret·ics (thē'ə·ret'iks) *n.pl.* (*construed as sing.*) The theoretical aspect of a science.

the·o·rist (thē'ər·ist) *n.* One who theorizes.

the·o·rize (thē'ə·rīz) *v.i.* **·rized, ·riz·ing** To form or express theories; speculate. Also *Brit.* **the'o·rise.** — **the'o·ri·za'·tion** *n.* — **the'o·riz'er** *n.*

the·o·ry (thē'ər·ē, thir'ē) *n.* *pl.* **·ries 1.** A plan or scheme existing in the mind only; a speculative or conjectural view of something. **2.** An integrated group of the fundamental principles underlying a science or its practical applications: the atomic *theory.* **3.** Abstract knowledge of any art as op-posed to the practice of it. **4.** A closely reasoned set of prop-ositions, derived from and supported by established evidence and intended to serve as an explanation for a group of phe-nomena: the quantum *theory.* — **Syn.** See DOCTRINE, HY-POTHESIS. [< LL < Gk. *theoria* view, speculation]

the·os·o·phy (thē·os'ə·fē) *n.* *pl.* **·phies 1.** Any of various religious systems that aim at establishing a direct relation between the individual soul and the divine principle through contemplation and speculation. **2.** *Often cap.* The doctrines of a modern religious sect (**Theosophical Society**), resem-bling those of Buddhism and Brahmanism. [< Med.L < Gk. < *theos* god + *sophos* wise] — **the·o·soph·ic** (thē'ə·sof'-ik) or **·i·cal** *adj.* — **the'o·soph'i·cal·ly** *adv.* — **the·os'o·phist** *n.*

ther·a·peu·tic (ther'ə·pyoo'tik) *adj.* **1.** Having healing qualities; curative. **2.** Pertaining to therapeutics. Also **ther'a·peu'ti·cal.** [< NL < Gk. < *therapeuein* take care of < *therapōn* an attendant] — **ther'a·peu'ti·cal·ly** *adv.*

ther·a·peu·tics (ther'ə·pyoo'tiks) *n.pl.* (*construed as sing.*) The branch of medical science dealing with the treatment of disease. — **ther'a·peu'tist** *n.*

ther·a·py (ther'ə·pē) *n.* *pl.* **·pies 1.** The treatment of disease: often used in combination: chemo*therapy.* **2.** Treat-ment, activity, etc., intended to remedy or alleviate a disor-der or undesirable condition. **3.** Healing or curative quality. — **ther'a·pist** *n.*

there (thâr) *adv.* **1.** In, at, or about that place: opposed to *here.* Also used to indicate or emphasize: *John there* is a good student. **2.** To, toward, or into that place; thither. **3.** At that stage or point of action or time. — *n.* That place: *Are you from there, too?* — *interj.* An exclamation of triumph, relief, etc.: *There!* It's finished. ◆ The adverb *there* cannot, in standard English, appear in the adjective position, as that. *there* girl. That girl *there* is the accepted order. *There* is very often used as an expletive introducing a clause or sentence, the subject usu. following the verb: *There* once were three bears. It is also used as an equivalent of the pronoun *that* in expressions of encouragement, approval, etc.: *There's* a good boy. [OE *thēr*]

there·a·bout (thâr′ə·bout′) *adv.* Near that number, quantity, degree, place, or time. Also **there′a·bouts′.**

there·af·ter (thâr·af′tər, -äf′-) *adv.* Afterward; from that time on.

there·at (thâr′at′) *adv.* At that event, place, or time; at that incentive; upon that.

there·by (thâr′bī′) *adv.* **1.** Through the agency of that. **2.** Connected with that. **3.** Conformably to that. **4.** *Archaic* Nearby; thereabout.

there·for (thâr′fôr′) *adv.* For this, that, or it.

there·fore (thâr′fôr′, -fōr′) *adv. & conj.* For that or this reason; on that ground or account; consequently: He did not run fast enough; *therefore* he lost the race.

there·from (thâr′frum′, -from′) *adv.* From this, that, or it; from this or that time, place, state, event, or thing.

there·in (thâr′in′) *adv.* **1.** In that place. **2.** In that time, matter, or respect.

there·in·af·ter (thâr′in·af′tər, -äf′-) *adv.* In a subsequent part of that (book, document, speech, etc.).

there·in·to (thâr′in·tōō′) *adv.* Into this, that, or it.

there·of (thâr′uv′, -ov′) *adv.* **1.** Of or relating to this, that, or it. **2.** From or because of this or that cause or particular.

there·on (thâr′on′, -ôn′) *adv.* **1.** On this, that, or it. **2.** Thereupon; thereat.

there's (thârz) There is.

there·to (thâr′tōō′) *adv.* **1.** To this, that, or it. **2.** In addition; furthermore. Also **there′un·to′** (-un·tōō′).

there·to·fore (thâr′tə·fôr′, -fōr′) *adv.* Before this or that; previously to that.

there·un·der (thâr′un′dər) *adv.* **1.** Under this or that. **2.** Less in number; fewer than that. **3.** In accordance with that; by that authority.

there·up·on (thâr′ə·pon′, -ə·pôn′) *adv.* **1.** Upon that; upon it. **2.** Following upon or in consequence of that. **3.** Immediately following; at once.

there·with (thâr′with′, -with′) *adv.* **1.** With this, that, or it. **2.** Thereupon; thereafter; immediately afterward.

there·with·al (thâr′with·ôl′) *adv.* With all this or that; besides.

therm- Var. of THERMO-.

therm. Thermometer.

ther·mal (thûr′məl) *adj.* **1.** Pertaining to, determined by, or measured by heat. **2.** Caused by, using, or producing heat. **3.** Hot or warm. Also **ther′mic.** — **ther′mal·ly** *adv.*

thermo- *combining form* Heat; of or caused by heat.] Also, before vowels, **therm-.** [< Gk. *thermos* heat, warmth]

ther·mo·coup·le (thûr′mə·kup′əl) *n.* A device for temperature measurement that depends upon the electric current or potential produced when joined conductors of two different metals have their ends at different temperatures. Also **thermoelectric couple.**

ther·mo·dy·nam·ics (thûr′mō·dī·nam′iks, -dī-) *n.pl.* (construed as sing.) The branch of physics dealing with the relations between heat and other forms of energy. — **ther′mo·dy·nam′ic** or **·i·cal** *adj.* — **ther′mo·dy·nam′i·cist** (-ə·sist) *n.*

ther·mo·e·lec·tric (thûr′mō·i·lek′trik) *adj.* **1.** Designating or associated with changes of electrical potential between two dissimilar metals in contact with each other as temperature varies. **2.** Designating or associated with the ability of an electric current to cause a flow of heat in a wire. Also **ther′·mo·e·lec′tri·cal.** — **ther′mo·e·lec′tri·cal·ly** *adv.*

ther·mo·e·lec·tric·i·ty (thûr′mō·i·lek′tris′ə·tē) *n.* Electricity generated by thermoelectric phenomena.

ther·mom·e·ter (thər·mom′ə·tər) *n.* An instrument for measuring temperature, usu. by means of a graduated glass capillary tube with a bulb containing a liquid, as mercury or alcohol, that expands or contracts as the temperature rises or falls. [< THERMO- + METER]

ther·mom·e·try (thər·mom′ə·trē) *n.* **1.** The measurement of temperature. **2.** The design and construction of thermometers. — **ther·mo·met·ric** (thûr′mō·met′rik) or **·ri·cal** *adj.* — **ther′mo·met′ri·cal·ly** *adv.*

ther·mo·nu·cle·ar (thûr′mō·nōō′klē·ər, -nyōō′-) *adj. Physics* Pertaining to or characterized by reactions involving the fusion of atomic nuclei at very high temperatures, esp. in stars and in the hydrogen bomb.

ther·mo·pile (thûr′mō·pīl) *n.* A group of thermocouples acting jointly to produce an electric current, esp. when used with a galvanometer to measure heat.

ther·mo·plas·tic (thûr′mō·plas′tik) *adj.* Plastic in the presence of or under the application of heat, as certain synthetic molding materials. — *n.* A thermoplastic substance.

Ther·mop·y·lae (thər·mop′ə·lē) A narrow mountain pass in Greece; scene of a battle, 480 B.C., in which the Spartans under the command of Leonidas held off the Persians under Xerxes and finally died to the last man rather than yield.

ther·mos bottle (thûr′məs) A bottle that keeps the contents hot or cold, consisting of two containers with a vacu between, the whole usu. enclosed in a metal cylinder. Gk. *thermos* hot]

ther·mo·set·ting (thûr′mō·set′ing) *adj.* Having the pr erty of assuming a fixed shape after being molded un heat, as certain plastics and urea resins.

ther·mo·stat (thûr′mə·stat) *n.* A device for the autom regulation of temperature, used for actuating fire ala starting or stopping heating plants, etc. [< THERMO-Gk. *statos* standing] — **ther′mo·stat′ic** *adj.* — **ther stat′i·cal·ly** *adv.*

ther·mot·ro·pism (thər·mot′rə·piz′əm) *n. Biol.* The pr erty whereby growing plants or other organisms turn tow or away from a source of heat. — **ther·mo·trop·ic** (thûr′ trop′ik) *adj.*

the·sau·rus (thə·sôr′əs) *n. pl.* **·sau·ri** (-sôr′ī) **1.** A b containing a store of words, esp., of synonyms and anton arranged in categories. **2.** A storehouse; treasury. [< Gk. *thesauros* treasure house]

these (thēz) *adj. & pron.* Plural of THIS.

The·seus (thē′sōōs, -sē·əs) In Greek mythology, the ki Athens, celebrated for killing the Minotaur and for unit Attica with Athens as its capital. See ARIADNE, PHAE

the·sis (thē′sis) *n. pl.* **·ses** (-sēz) **1.** A proposition. formal proposition, advanced and defended by argume tion. **3.** A formal treatise on a particular subject; es dissertation presented by a candidate for an academic gree. **4.** *Logic* An affirmative proposition; a premise or tulate. [< L < Gk. < *tithenai* to put, place]

Thes·pi·an (thes′pē·ən) *adj.* Of or relating to drama; matic; tragic. — *n.* An actor or actress. [after *The* Greek poet and actor, 6th century B.C.]

Thes·sa·lo·ni·an (thes′ə·lō′nē·ən) *n.* **1.** A native or in itant of ancient Thessalonica. **2.** *pl.* (construed as s Either of two books in the New Testament consistin epistles written by St. Paul to the Christians of Thessalo — *adj.* Of or pertaining to Thessalonica.

the·ta (thā′tə, thē′tə) *n.* **1.** The eighth letter in the G alphabet (Θ, ϑ, θ). See ALPHABET. **2.** *Math.* A symbo an angle of unknown value. [< Gk. *thēta*]

thew (thyōō) *n.* **1.** A sinew or muscle, esp., when stron well-developed. **2.** *pl.* Bodily strength. [ME < OE *t* habit, characteristic quality] — **thew′y** *adj.*

they (thā) *pron. pl., possessive* their or theirs, *objective* t **1.** The nominative plural of *he*, *she*, and *it*, used of the sons, beings, or things previously mentioned or underst **2.** People in general: *They* say this is his best book. *thei, thai* < ON *their*, pl. of *sā* this, that]

they'd (thād) **1.** They had. **2.** They would.

they'll (thāl) They will.

they're (thâr) They are.

they've (thāv) They have.

thi- Var. of THIO-.

thi·a·mine (thī′ə·mēn, -min) *n. Biochem.* A white cry line compound, $C_{12}H_{18}ON_4SCl_2$, vitamin B_1, found in ous natural sources and also made synthetically. Also **min** (-min). [< THI- + -AMINE]

Thi·bet·an (ti·bet′ən) See TIBETAN.

thick (thik) *adj.* **1.** Having relatively large depth or ex from one surface to its opposite; not thin. **2.** Having a ified dimension of this kind, whether great or small: an *thick.* **3.** Arranged compactly; close: a *thick* forest; also lowing at brief intervals; frequent, as blows, raindrops **4.** Set or furnished closely or abundantly with obj abounding. **5.** Having considerable density or consiste dense; heavy. **6.** Having the component particles cl packed together, as smoke, fog, etc. **7.** Dull; stupid. **8** distinct; muffled: a *thick* sound; also, guttural; husky *Informal* Very friendly; intimate. — **10.** *Brit. Informal* cessive; beyond what is tolerable. — *adv.* So as to be t thickly: bread sliced *thick.* — **to lay it on thick** *Info* **1.** To overstate; exaggerate. **2.** To flatter excessively. *n.* **1.** The dimension of thickness; the thickest part. **2** thickest or most intense time or place of anything: the of the fight. — **through thick and thin** Through good t and bad; loyally. [OE *thicce*] — **thick′ish** *adj.* — **thi** *adv.* — **thick′ness** *n.*

thick·en (thik′ən) *v.t. & v.i.* **1.** To make or become t or thicker. **2.** To make or become more intricate or int The plot *thickens.* — **thick′en·er** *n.*

thick·en·ing (thik′ən·ing) *n.* **1.** The act of making o coming thick. **2.** Something added to a liquid to inc its consistency. **3.** A thickened place or part.

thick·et (thik′it) *n.* A thick, dense growth, as of u brush; a coppice. [OE < *thicce* thick]

thick·head (thik′hed′) *n.* A stupid person; numskull. **thick′head′ed** *adj.* — **thick′head′ed·ness** *n.*

thick·set (thik′set′) *adj.* **1.** Having a short, thick b stout. **2.** Planted closely together. — *n.* A thicket.

thick·skinned (thik′skind′) *adj.* **1.** Having a thick pachydermatous. **2.** Insensitive; callous to hints or sim

-wit·ted (thik′wit′id) *adj.* Stupid; obtuse; dense. [**thēf**] *n.* *pl.* **thieves** (thēvz) One who takes some-
belonging to another; one who steals. [OE *thēof*]

e (thēv) *v.* **thieved, thiev·ing** *v.t.* **1.** To take by theft;
— *v.i.* **2.** To be a thief; commit theft. [OE *thēofian*]

iev′ish *adj.* — **thiev′ish·ly** *adv.* — **thiev′ish·ness** *n.*

·er·y (thē′vər·ē) *n.* *pl.* **·er·ies** The practice or act of
ving; theft.

h (thī) *n.* The leg between the hip and the knee of man
e corresponding portion in other animals. ◆ Collateral
ctive: *femoral.* [OE *thēoh*]

·bone (thī′bōn′) *n.* The femur.

(thil) *n.* Either of the shafts of a vehicle, between
h a horse is harnessed. [OE *thille* board]

·ble (thim′bəl) *n.* **1.** A caplike cover with a pitted
ice, worn in sewing to protect the end of the finger that
es the needle. **2.** *Mech.* A sleeve through which a bolt
es. **3.** *Naut.* **a** A metal antichafing ring forming a guard
a loop or eye in a sail. **b** The metal piece about which a
is bent and spliced. [OE < *thūma* thumb]

·ble·ful (thim′bəl·fŏŏl) *n.* **1.** As much as a thimble
hold. **2.** Any very small quantity.

·ble·rig (thim′bəl·rig′) *n.* A swindling trick in which a
is shifted from one to another of three inverted cups. —
·rigged, ·rig·ging To cheat by or as by thimblerig. —
′ble·rig′ger *n.*

(thin) *adj.* **thin·ner, thin·nest** **1.** Having opposite sur-
s relatively close to each other; being of little depth or
h; not thick. **2.** Lacking roundness or plumpness of
e; slender. **3.** Having the parts or particles scattered or
sed; sparse: *thin* ranks, *thin* gas. **4.** Small in number:
audience was *thin.* **5.** Having little substance: *thin*
ing. **6.** Having little or no consistency, as a liquid. **7.**
ing in essential ingredients: *thin* blood. **8.** Having
r volume or richness, as a voice. **9.** Not abundantly
·lied; scant: a *thin* table. **10.** Having little intensity:
: *thin* colors. **11.** *Photog.* Not having sufficient con-
t to print well: said of a negative. **12.** Feeble; superfi-
thin wit. — *adv.* So as to be thin; thinly: butter spread
— *v.t.* & *v.i.* **thinned, thin·ning** To make or become
or thinner. [OE *thynne*] — **thin′ly** *adv.* — **thin′ner** *n.*
hin·ness *n.*

e (thīn) *pron.* *Archaic* **1.** The possessive case of the
noun *thou*: used predicatively. **2.** The one or ones being or relating to thee: thou and *thine.* — *pronominal*
Thy: used before a vowel or *h*: *thine* eyes. [OE *thīn,*
tive of *thū* thou]

g (thing) *n.* **1.** That which exists as a separate entity;
inanimate object. **2.** That which is designated, as con-
ted with the word or symbol used to denote it. **3.** A
ter or circumstance; an affair; concern: *Things* have
ged. **4.** An act or deed; transaction. **5.** A statement;
rance: to say the right *thing.* **6.** An idea; opinion: Stop
ing *things* in her head. **7.** A quality; attribute; charac-
tic. **8.** An organic being: usu. with a qualifying word:
ry living *thing* dies. **9.** An object that is not or cannot
escribed or particularized: The *thing* disappeared in the
lows. **10.** A person, regarded in terms of pity, affection,
ontempt: that poor *thing.* **11.** *pl.* Possessions. **12.** The
·er or befitting act or result: with *the:* That was not the
g to do. **13.** The important point: with *the:* The *thing*
earned from the war was this. — **to see things** To have
ucinations. [OE, thing, cause, assembly]

g·a·ma·bob (thing′ə·mə·bob′) *n.* *Informal* A thing or
ific name of which is unknown or forgotten; a dingus.
◆ **thing′um·a·bob′, thing′um·bob, thing′a·ma·jig.**

k[1] (thingk) *v.* **thought** (thôt), **think·ing** *v.t.* **1.** To pro-
e or form in the mind; conceive mentally. **2.** To exam-
in the mind; determine by reasoning: to *think* a plan
ugh. **3.** To believe; consider: I *think* him guilty. **4.** To
ect; anticipate: They did not *think* to meet us. **5.** To
ember; recollect: I cannot *think* what he said. **6.** To
g about by thinking: to *think* oneself sick. **7.** To intend:
they *think* to rob me? — *v.i.* **8.** To use the mind in ex-
 sing judgment, forming ideas, etc.; reason. **9.** To have a
ticular opinion or feeling: I don't *think* so. — **to think**
ter of 1. To abandon or change a course of action. **2.**
form a better opinion of. — **to think fit (proper, right,**
) To regard as worth doing. — **to think nothing of** 1.
consider of no importance; ignore. **2.** To consider easy
lo. — **to think of** 1. To bring to mind; remember. **2.**
invent; imagine. **3.** To have a specified opinion or atti-
e toward; regard. **4.** To be considerate of; have regard
— **to think out** To devise, invent, or solve by thinking.
to **think over** To reflect upon. — **to think the world of**
To have a high opinion of. **2.** To love very much. — **to**
k **twice** To consider carefully. — **to think up** To de-
e, arrive at, or invent by thinking. — *n.* An act of think-

ing; a thought. [OE *thencean*] — **think′a·ble** *adj.* —
think′er *n.*

think[2] (thingk) *v.i.* **thought** (thôt), **think·ing** To seem; appear: now obsolete except in the combinations *methinks, me-
thought.* [OE *thyncan* to seem]

think·ing (thingk′ing) *adj.* **1.** Exercising the mental ca-
pacities. **2.** Capable of such exercise; rational. — *n.* **1.**
Mental action; thought. **2.** The product of such action, as
an idea. — **think′ing·ly** *adv.*

thin-skinned (thin′skind′) *adj.* **1.** Having a thin skin. **2.**
Easily hurt or offended; sensitive.

thio- *combining form* *Chem.* Containing sulfur; denoting a
compound of sulfur, esp., one in which sulfur has displaced
oxygen. Also, before vowels, sometimes *thi-.* [< Gk. *theion*
sulfur]

thi·o·pen·tal sodium (thī′ō·pen′tal) A yellowish white
powder, $C_{11}H_{17}N_2O_2SNa$, of the barbiturate group, used in-
travenously as a general anesthetic: also called *sodium pentothal.* Also *Chiefly Brit.* **thi′o·pen′tone sodium.**

thi·o·sul·fate (thī′ō·sul′fāt) *n.* *Chem.* A salt of thiosulfuric
acid.

thi·o·sul·fu·ric acid (thī′ō·sul·fyŏŏr′ik) *Chem.* An unstable acid, $H_2S_2O_3$, known chiefly by its salts, which have extensive applications in bleaching and photography.

third (thûrd) *adj.* **1.** Next after the second: the ordinal of
three. **2.** Being one of three equal parts. **3.** Pertaining to
the forward gears with the third highest ratio in an automobile transmission. — *n.* **1.** That which follows the second.
2. One of three equal parts. **3.** A unit of time or of an arc,
equal to one sixtieth of a second. **4.** *Music* **a** The interval
between a tone and another tone two steps from it in a diatonic scale. **b** A tone separated by this interval from any
other, considered in relation to that other; esp., the third
above the keynote. **5.** In baseball, the third base. **6.** *Mech.*
The forward gears with the third highest ratio in an automobile transmission. — *adv.* In the third order, rank, or place:
also, in formal language, **third′ly.** [OE *thridda* < *thrī* three]

third base In baseball, the third base reached by the runner, at the left-hand angle of the infield.

third base·man (bās′mən) *n.* *pl.* **·men** (-mən) A baseball
player stationed at or near third base.

third class **1.** In the U.S. postal system, a classification of
mail that includes all miscellaneous printed matter but not
newspapers and periodicals legally entered as second class.
2. A classification of accommodations on some ships and
trains, usu. the cheapest and least luxurious available. —
third-class (thûrd′klas, -klās) *adj.* & *adv.*

third degree **1.** *Informal* Severe or brutal examination of a
prisoner by the police for the purpose of securing information.
2. The third stage, order, step, etc., of something.

third estate The third political class of a kingdom, following the nobility and the clergy.

third rail A rail that supplies current to the trains of an
electric railway. — **third-rail** (thûrd′rāl′) *adj.*

third-rate (thûrd′rāt′) *adj.* **1.** Of the third rate or class.
2. Of poor quality; very inferior.

thirst (thûrst) *n.* **1.** An uncomfortable feeling of dryness
in the throat and mouth, accompanied by an increasingly
urgent desire for liquids. **2.** The physiological condition
that produces this feeling. **3.** Any longing or craving. —
v.i. **1.** To be thirsty. **2.** To have an eager desire or craving.
[OE *thurst, thyrstan*] — **thirst′er** *n.*

thirst·y (thûrs′tē) *adj.* **thirst·i·er, thirst·i·est** **1.** Affected
with thirst. **2.** Lacking moisture; arid; parched. **3.** Eagerly desirous. **4.** *Informal* Causing thirst. [OE *thurstig*] —
thirst′i·ly *adv.* — **thirst′i·ness** *n.*

thir·teen (thûr′tēn′) *n.* **1.** The sum of twelve and one: a
cardinal number. **2.** Any symbol of this number, as 13, xiii,
XIII. **3.** Anything consisting of or representing thirteen
units. — *adj.* Being one more than twelve. [OE *thrēotīne*]
— **thir′teenth′** *adj.* & *n.*

thir·ty (thûr′tē) *n.* *pl.* **·ties** **1.** The sum of twenty and ten:
a cardinal number. **2.** Any symbol of this number, as 30,
xxx, XXX. **3.** Anything consisting of or representing thirty
units. — *adj.* Being ten more than twenty. [OE *thrītig*]
— **thir′ti·eth** *adj.* & *n.*

thir·ty-sec·ond (thûr′tē·sek′ənd) *adj.* **1.** Being the second
after the thirtieth. **2.** Being one of thirty-two equal parts.
— *n.* A thirty-second note.

thirty-second note *Music* A note having a time value,
equal to one thirty-second of a whole note: also, *Chiefly Brit.,*
demisemiquaver.

thir·ty-two-mo (thûr′tē-tŏŏ′mō) *n.* *pl.* **·mos** **1.** The page
size (3⅛ x 4¾ inches) of a book made up of printer's sheets
folded into thirty-two leaves. **2.** A book consisting of pages
of this size. Also written **32mo.** — *adj.* Consisting of pages
of this size.

Thirty Years' War See table for WAR.

this (thĭs) *pl. for adj. and pron. def. 2* **these** (thēz) *adj.* **1.** That is near or present, either actually or in thought: *This* house is for sale; I shall be there *this* evening. **2.** That is understood or has just been mentioned: *This* offense justified my revenge. **3.** Denoting something nearer than or contrasted with something else: distinguished from *that*: *This* tree is still alive, but that one is dead. **4.** These: used of a number or collection considered as a whole: He has been dead *this* ten years. — *pron.* **1.** The person or thing near or present, being understood or just mentioned: *This* is where I live. **2.** The person or thing nearer than or contrasted with something else: opposed to *that*: *This* is a better painting than that. **3.** The idea, statement, etc., about to be made clear: I will say *this*: he is a hard worker. — *adv.* To this degree: I was not expecting you *this* soon. [OE]

this·tle (thĭs′əl) *n.* **1.** One of various prickly plants of the composite family, with cylindrical or globular heads of purple flowers; esp., the **bull thistle**, the national emblem of Scotland. **2.** Any of several other prickly plants. [OE *thistel*] — **this′tly** *adj.*

this·tle·down (thĭs′əl·doun′) *n.* The ripe silky fibers from the dry flower of a thistle.

thith·er (thĭth′ər, thĭth′-) *adv.* To or toward that place; in that direction. — *adj.* Situated or being on the other side; farther: the *thither* bank of the river. [OE *thider*]

thith·er·to (thĭth′ər·tōō′, thĭth′-) *adv.* Up to that time.

thith·er·ward (thĭth′ər·wərd, thĭth′-) *adv.* In that direction; toward that place. Also **thith′er·wards.**

tho (thō) See THOUGH.

thole (thōl) *n. Naut.* A peg or pair of pegs serving as a fulcrum for an oar in rowing. Also **thole pin.** [OE *thol* pin]

Thom·as (tŏm′əs) One of the twelve apostles, known for his doubting disposition: called **Saint Thomas.** Also *Didymus. John* xx 25.

Tho·mism (tō′mĭz·əm, thō′-) *n.* The system of dogmatic theology of St. Thomas Aquinas and his followers that formed the basis of 13th-century scholasticism. — **Tho′mist** *adj. & n.* — **Tho·mis′tic** *or* **·ti·cal** *adj.*

Thomp·son submachine gun (tomp′sən) A type of .45 caliber submachine gun: a trade name: also called *Tommy gun.*

thong (thông, thŏng) *n.* **1.** A narrow strip of leather, as for tying or fastening. **2.** A whiplash. [OE *thwang*]

Thor (thôr, tôr) In Norse mythology, the god of war, thunder, and strength. — *n.* An intermediate range, liquid-fueled ballistic missile of the U.S. Air Force.

tho·rac·ic (thō·răs′ĭk, thō-) *adj.* Of, relating to, or situated in or near the thorax. [< F < NL < Gk. *thōrax* chest]

thoraco- *combining form Med. & Surg.* The thorax or the chest; of or related to the thorax. Also, before vowels, **thorac-.** [< Gk. *thōrax* chest]

tho·rax (thôr′ăks, thō′răks) *n. pl.* **tho·rax·es** *or* **tho·ra·ces** (thôr′ə·sēz, thō′rə-) **1.** *Anat.* The part of the body between the neck and the abdomen, enclosed by the ribs and containing the lungs, heart, etc.; the chest. **2.** The corresponding part in other animals. **3.** *Entomol.* The middle region of the body of an insect. [< L < Gk. *thōrax*]

tho·ri·um (thôr′ē·əm, thō′rē-) *n.* A gray, radioactive, metallic element (symbol Th), found only in small quantities in certain rare minerals. See ELEMENT. [after *Thor*]

thorn (thôrn) *n.* **1.** A hard, leafless spine or sharp-pointed process from a branch. **2.** One of various other sharp processes, as the spine of a porcupine. **3.** Any of various thorn-bearing shrubs or trees; esp., a rosaceous plant, as the hawthorn. **4.** Anything or anyone that causes discomfort, pain, or annoyance. **5.** The name of the Old English rune þ; also, the corresponding Icelandic character. It was used originally to represent both voiceless and voiced *th*, as in *thin, then,* but finally only the voiceless sound. — *v.t.* To pierce or prick with a thorn. [OE] — **thorn′less** *adj.*

thorn apple 1. The jimsonweed. **2.** The fruit of the hawthorn; a haw.

thorn·y (thôr′nē) *adj.* **thorn·i·er, thorn·i·est 1.** Full of thorns; spiny. **2.** Sharp like a thorn. **3.** Presenting difficulties or trials; painful; vexatious. — **thorn′i·ness** *n.*

tho·ron (thôr′ŏn, thō′rŏn) *n.* A gaseous, radioactive isotope of radon, produced during the disintegration of thorium. [< NL < THOR(IUM) + -ON]

thor·ough (thûr′ō) *adj.* **1.** Carried to completion; thoroughgoing: a *thorough* search; also, persevering, accurate, and painstaking: a very *thorough* worker. **2.** Marked by careful attention throughout; complete. **3.** Completely (such and such); through and through: a *thorough* nincompoop. **4.** Painstakingly conforming to a standard. **5.** *Rare* Going or passing through. — *adv. & prep. Obs.* Through. Also *Rare* **thor′o.** [Emphatic var. of THROUGH] — **thor′ough·ly** *adv.* — **thor′ough·ness** *n.*

thor·ough·bred (thûr′ō·brĕd′, thûr′ə-) *n.* **1.** Pure and unmixed stock. **2.** *Informal* A person of culture and good breeding. — *adj.* **1.** Bred from pure stock. **2.** Possessing the traits of a thoroughbred; elegant; graceful.

thor·ough·fare (thûr′ō·fâr′, thûr′ə-) *n.* A road or street

through which the public has unobstructed passage; ▮ way. [ME < OE *thurh* through + *faru* going]

thor·ough·go·ing (thûr′ō·gō′ing, thûr′ə-) *adj.* **1.** Ch▮ terized by extreme thoroughness or efficiency. **2.** Un▮ gated: a *thoroughgoing* scoundrel.

those (thōz) *adj. & pron.* Plural of THAT. [OE *thās,* ▮ *this*]

thou (thou) *pron., possessive* **thy** *or* **thine,** *objective* **the**▮ *nominative* **you, ye,** *possessive* **your** *or* **yours,** *objective* **ye** *Archaic* The nominative singular pronoun of the se▮ person: formerly a familiar form, it has been replaced b▮ more formal singular *you,* and is no longer used exce▮ religious, elevated, or poetic language. [OE *thū*]

though (thō) *conj.* **1.** Notwithstanding the fact that: i▮ ducing a clause expressing an actual fact. **2.** Concedi▮ granting that; even if. **3.** And yet; still; however: i▮ ducing a modifying clause or statement: I am well, tho▮ do not feel very strong. **4.** Notwithstanding what has done or said; nevertheless. ◆ As used in this sense, th▮ is sometimes regarded as a conjunctive adverb. Also sp▮ *tho.* [Prob. fusion of OE *thēah* and ON *tho*]

thought[1] (thôt) *n.* **1.** The act or process of using the ▮ actively and deliberately; meditation; cogitation. **2.** product of thinking; an idea, concept, judgment, etc. **3** tellectual activity of a specific kind: Greek *thought.* **4.** sideration; attention. **5.** Intention or plan: All *thoug* returning was abandoned. **6.** Expectation: He ha▮ *thought* of finding her there. — **Syn.** See IDEA. [OE *t*▮

thought[2] (thôt) Past tense and past participle of TH▮

thought·ful (thôt′fəl) *adj.* **1.** Full of thought; medita▮ **2.** Showing, characterized by, or promotive of thinki▮ *thoughtful* book. **3.** Attentive; careful; esp., considera▮ others. — **thought′ful·ly** *adv.* — **thought′ful·ness** *n.*

thought·less (thôt′lĭs) *adj.* **1.** Manifesting lack of tho▮ or care; heedless. **2.** Lacking capacity for thought; st▮ — **thought′less·ly** *adv.* — **thought′less·ness** *n.*

thou·sand (thou′zənd) *n.* The product of ten and a dred; ten hundreds, written as 1,000 or M: a cardinal ▮ ber. — *adj.* Being a thousand in number. [OE *thūsend*] **thou·sandth** *adj. & n.*

thou·sand·fold (thou′zənd·fōld′) *n.* An amount or ▮ ber a thousand times as great as a given unit. — *adv.* ▮ to be a thousand times as many or as great. — *adj.* **1.** ▮ sisting of one thousand parts. **2.** One thousand tim▮ many or as great.

Thra·cian (thrā′shən) *adj.* Pertaining to Thrace or its ▮ ple. — *n.* **1.** One of the people of Thrace. **2.** The ▮ European language of the ancient Thracians.

thrall (thrôl) *n.* **1.** A person in bondage; a slave; serf The condition of bondage; thralldom. [OE *thrǣl* < O▮

thrall·dom (thrôl′dəm) *n.* **1.** The state of being a t▮ **2.** Any sort of bondage or servitude. Also **thral′dom.**

thrash (thrash) *v.t.* **1.** To beat as if with a flail; flog; ▮ **2.** To defeat utterly. — *v.i.* **3.** To move or swing a▮ with flailing, violent motions. — **to thrash out** To di▮ fully and to a conclusion. — *n.* The act of thrashing. [▮ var. of THRESH]

thrash·er[1] (thrash′ər) *n.* **1.** One who or that which th▮ es or threshes. **2.** A thresher (def. 2), a shark.

thrash·er[2] (thrash′ər) *n.* Any of several long-tailed A▮ can songbirds resembling the thrushes and related t▮ mockingbirds. [< dial. E *thresher* < THRUSH[1]]

thrash·ing (thrash′ing) *n.* A sound beating or whip▮

thread (thred) *n.* **1.** A very slender cord composed of or more filaments, as of flax, cotton, or silk, twisted toge▮ also, such twisted fibers used in sewing. **2.** A filame▮ any ductile substance, as of metal, glass, etc. **3.** A stream or beam: a *thread* of light. **4.** A fine line of ▮ **5.** Anything conceived of as serving to give sequence t▮ whole, as the course of existence represented by the an▮ Greeks as a thread spun and cut off by the three Fates▮ *Mech.* The spiral ridge of a screw. — *v.t.* **1.** To p▮ thread through the eye of (a needle). **2.** To arrang▮ string on a thread, as beads. **3.** To cut a thread on or ▮ a screw. **4.** To make one's way through or over: to thr▮ maze. **5.** To make (one's way) carefully. — *v.i.* **6▮** make one's way carefully. **7.** To drop from a spoon ▮ fine thread, as boiling syrup. [OE *thrǣd*] — **thread**▮

thread·bare (thred′bâr′) *adj.* **1.** Worn so that the th▮ show, as a rug or garment. **2.** Clad in worn garments▮ Commonplace; hackneyed. — **thread′bare′ness** *n.*

thread·y (thred′ē) *adj.* **thread·i·er, thread·i·est 1.** Re▮ bling a thread; stringy. **2.** Consisting of, containing, or ▮ ered with thread. **3.** *Med.* Weak and feeble: said of ▮ pulse. **4.** Weak and thin like a thread: a *thready* voic▮

threat (thret) *n.* **1.** A declaration of an intention to i▮ injury or pain. **2.** An indication of impending dang▮ harm. **3.** A person or thing regarded as endangering ▮ lives, peace of mind, etc., of others; menace. [OE *thr*▮

threat·en (thret′n) *v.t.* **1.** To utter threats against. **2** be menacing or dangerous to. **3.** To be ominous or appr▮

HUMAN THROAT
a Palate. *b*
Tongue. *c* Nasal
cavity. *d* Uvula. *e* Tonsils.
f Pharynx.
g Epiglottis.
h Esophagus.
i Larynx.
j Vocal cords.
k Trachea.

of. **4.** To utter threats of (injury, vengeance, etc.).
,i. **5.** To utter threats. **6.** To have a menacing aspect;
r: The rising waters seemed to *threaten*. [OE *thrēatnian*
rge, compel] — **threat/en·er** *n*. — **threat/en·ing·ly** *adv*.
e (thrē) *n*. **1.** The sum of two and one: a cardinal
ber. **2.** Any symbol of this number, as 3, iii, III. **3.**
thing consisting of or representing three units. — *adj*.
 g one more than two; ternary. [OE *thrie*]
e-base hit (thrē/bās/) In baseball, a base hit that
les the batter to reach third base; a triple.
e-D (thrē/dē/) *adj*. Three-dimensional. — *n*. A
e-dimensional representation; esp., a motion picture
gives the illusion of depth. Often written **3-D.**
e-deck·er (thrē/dek/ər) *n*. **1.** A vessel having three
s or gun decks. **2.** Any structure having three levels.
, sandwich made with three slices of bread.
e-fold (thrē/fōld/) *n*. An amount or number three
s as great as a given unit. — *adv*. So as to be three
s as many or as great. — *adj*. **1.** Consisting of three
s. **2.** Three times as many or as great.
e-mile limit (thrē/mīl/) A distance of three nautical
s from the shoreline seaward, allowed by international
for territorial jurisdiction.
e·pence (thrip/əns, threp/-, thrup/-) *n*. *Brit*. **1.** The
of three pennies. **2.** A small coin of Great Britain,
th three pennies: also **threepenny bit.**
e·pen·ny (thrip/ə·ni, threp/-, thrup/-, thrē/pen/ē) *adj*.
1. Worth or costing threepence. **2.** Of little value.
e-ply (thrē/plī/) *adj*. Consisting of three thicknesses,
nds, layers, etc.
e-point landing (thrē/point/) **1.** *Aeron*. A perfect
lane landing. **2.** Any successful outcome.
e-ring circus (thrē/ring/) **1.** A circus in which separate
are carried on simultaneously in three ringlike enclo-
s. **2.** Any situation characterized by simultaneous
vities, esp. of bewildering variety.
e·score (thrē/skôr/, -skōr/) *adj*. & *n*. Sixty.
e·some (thrē/səm) *adj*. **1.** Consisting of three. **2.**
ormed by three. — *n*. **1.** A group of three persons. **2.**
t which is played by three persons.
e-square (thrē/skwâr/) *adj*. Having a triangular cross
ion, as some files.
m·ma·tol·ogy (threm/ə·tol/ə·jē) *n*. The science of
ding domestic animals and plants. [< Gk. *thremma*,
os nursling + -LOGY]
n·o·dy (thren/ə·dē) *n*. *pl*. ·dies An ode or song of lam-
ation; a dirge. Also **thren/ode** (-ōd). [< Gk. < *thrēnos*
ent + *ōidē* song] — **thre·no·di·al** (thri·nō/dē·əl), **thre-**
ic (thri·nod/ik) *adj*. — **thren/o·dist** *n*.
sh (thresh) *v.t*. **1.** To beat stalks of (ripened grain) with
a flail or machine so as to separate the grain from the
w or husks. — *v.i*. **2.** To thresh grain. **3.** To move or
sh about. — *n*. The act of threshing. [OE *therscan*]
sh·er (thresh/ər) *n*. **1.** One who or that which threshes;
, a machine for threshing. **2.** A large shark of warm seas,
ing the dorsal lobe of the tail extremely long: also **thresh-**
hark.
sh·old (thresh/ōld, -hōld, -əld) *n*. **1.** The plank, timber,
tone lying under the door of a building. **2.** The entrance,
ring point, or beginning of anything. **3.** *Physiol*. &
chol. **a** The point at which a stimulus just produces a re-
nse. **b** The minimum degree of stimulation necessary for
scious perception: the *threshold* of consciousness. [OE
scold]
w (thrōō) Past tense of THROW.
ce (thrīs) *adv*. **1.** Three times. **2.** In a threefold man-
3. Extremely; very. [ME < OE *thriwa* + -s³]
ft (thrift) *n*. **1.** Care and wisdom in the management of
s resources; frugality. **2.** Vigorous growth, as of a
it. **3.** Any of a genus of tufted herbs, growing on moun-
s and the seashore and having white or pink flowers.
ON] — **thrift/less** *adj*.
ft·y (thrif/tē) *adj*. **thrift·i·er**, **thrift·i·est** **1.** Displaying
ft or good management; economical; frugal. **2.** Prosper-
; thriving. **3.** Growing vigorously. — **thrift/i·ly** *adv*.
hrift/i·ness *n*.
ll (thril) *v.t*. **1.** To cause to feel a sudden wave of emo-
; move to great or tingling excitement. **2.** To cause to
rate or tremble. — *v.i*. **3.** To feel a sudden wave of emo-
or excitement. **4.** To vibrate or tremble. — *n*. **1.** A
nor of feeling or excitement. **2.** A pulsation. [Var. of
. *thirl*] — **thrill/ing** *adj*. — **thrill/ing·ly** *adv*.
ll·er (thril/ər) *n*. **1.** One who or that which thrills. **2.**
ormal A sensational book, play, or motion picture.
ve (thrīv) *v.i*. **throve** (thrōv) or **thrived**, **thrived** or
iv·en (thriv/ən), **thriv·ing** **1.** To prosper; be successful.
To grow with vigor; flourish. [< ON *thrīfast*, orig. re-
ive of *thrīfa* to grasp] — **thriv/er** *n*. — **thriv/ing·ly** *adv*.

thro (thrōō) See THROUGH. Also **thro'.**
throat (thrōt) *n*. **1.** The passage leading
from the back of the mouth to the stomach
and lungs. **2.** The front of the neck, extending from below the chin to the collar-
bones. **3.** Any narrow passage resembling
the throat, as the entrance to a chimney.
— **to jump down one's throat** *Informal* To
criticize or berate one severely. — **to ram
(something) down one's throat** *Informal*
To force one to accept or hear something
against his will. — **to stick in one's throat**
To be difficult to utter, as from unwillingness or fear. [OE *throte*]
throat·y (thrō/tē) *adj*. **throat·i·er**,
throat·i·est Uttered in the throat; guttural. — **throat/i·ly** *adv*. — **throat/i-**
ness *n*.
throb (throb) *v.i*. **throbbed**, **throb·bing**
1. To beat rapidly or violently, as the
heart from exertion or excitement. **2.** To
pulsate. **3.** To feel or show great emotion.
— *n*. **1.** The act or state of throbbing. **2.** A pulsation or
beat, esp. one caused by excitement or emotion. [? Imit.]
— **throb/ber** *n*. — **throb/bing·ly** *adv*.
throe (thrō) *n*. **1.** A violent pang or pain. **2.** *pl*. The pains
of childbirth or death. **3.** *pl*. Any agonizing or violent activity. [ME *throwe*, prob. fusion of OE *thrōwian* to suffer
and *thrāwan* to twist, throw]
throm·bin (throm/bin) *n*. *Biochem*. The enzyme present in
blood serum that reacts with fibrinogen to form fibrin in the
process of clotting. [< THROMBUS]
throm·bo·cyte (throm/bə·sīt) *n*. A blood platelet. [< Gk.
thrombos clot + -CYTE]
throm·bo·sis (throm·bō/sis) *n*. *pl*. ·ses (sēz) *Pathol*. Local
coagulation of blood in the heart or blood vessels, forming
an obstruction to circulation. — **throm·bot/ic** (-bot/ik) *adj*.
throm·bus (throm/bəs) *n*. *pl*. ·bi (-bī) *Pathol*. The blood
clot formed in thrombosis. [< NL < Gk. *thrombos* clot]
throne (thrōn) *n*. **1.** The royal chair occupied by a sovereign on state occasions. **2.** The chair of state of a pope or of
some other dignitary, as a cardinal, bishop, etc. **3.** Royal
estate or dignity; sovereign power. **4.** One who occupies a
throne. — *v.t*. & *v.i*. **throned**, **thron·ing** To place or sit on
a throne; exalt. [< OF < L < Gk. *thronos* seat]
throng (thrông, throng) *n*. **1.** A multitude of people
crowded closely together. **2.** Any numerous collection. —
v.t. **1.** To crowd into; jam. **2.** To press or crowd upon. —
v.i. **3.** To collect or move in a throng. [OE *gethrang*]
— **Syn**. (noun) **1.** crowd, concourse, mob, host, horde, press.
thros·tle (thros/əl) *n*. The song thrush. [OE]
throt·tle (throt/l) *n*. *Mech*. **a** A valve controlling the
supply of steam to a steam engine, or of vaporized fuel to the
cylinders of an internal-combustion engine: also **throttle
valve. b** The lever that operates the throttle: also **throttle
lever.** — *v.t*. ·**tled**, ·**tling 1.** To press or constrict the throat
of; strangle; choke. **2.** To silence, stop, or suppress by or as
by choking. **3.** *Mech*. **a** To reduce or shut off the flow of
steam or fuel (in a steam or internal-combustion engine).
b To reduce the speed of by means of a throttle. — *v.i*. **4.**
To choke. [Dim. of ME *throte*] — **throt/tler** *n*.
through (thrōō) *prep*. **1.** Into one side, end, or point, and
out of the other. **2.** Covering, entering, or penetrating all
parts of; throughout. **3.** From the first to the last of; during
the time or period of. **4.** In the midst of; among. **5.** By
way of: He departed *through* the door. **6.** By means of; by
the instrumentality or aid of. **7.** Having reached the end of,
esp. with success: He got *through* his examinations easily.
8. On account of; because of or as a result of. — *adv*. **1.** From
one end, side, surface, etc., to or beyond another. **2.** From
beginning to end. **3.** To a termination or conclusion, esp.
a successful one: to pull *through*. **4.** Completely; entirely:
He is wet *through*. — **through and through** Thoroughly. —
adj. **1.** Going from beginning to end without stops or
with very few stops: a *through* train. **2.** Extending from one
side or surface to another. **3.** Unobstructed; open; clear: a
through road. **4.** Arrived at an end; finished. **5.** At the end
of all relations or dealings: He is *through* with school. Also
spelled *thro*, *thru*. [OE *thurh*]
through·out (thrōō·out/) *adv*. Through or in every part:
The house was searched *throughout*. — *prep*. All through;
everywhere in: *throughout* the nation.
through·way (thrōō/wā/) See THRUWAY.
throve (thrōv) Past tense of THRIVE.
throw (thrō) *v*. **threw** (thrōō), **thrown**, **throw·ing** *v.t*. **1.**
To launch through the air by means of a sudden straightening
or whirling of the arm. **2.** To propel or hurl. **3.** To put
hastily or carelessly: He *threw* a coat over his shoulders. **4.**

To direct or project (light, a glance, etc.). **5.** To bring to a specified condition or state by or as by throwing: to *throw* the enemy into a panic. **6.** To cause to fall; overthrow: The horse *threw* its rider. **7.** In wrestling, to force the shoulders of (an opponent) to the ground. **8.** To cast (dice). **9.** To make (a specified cast) with dice. **10.** To cast off or shed; lose. **11.** *Informal* To lose purposely, as a race, contest, etc., in accordance with a prearranged plan. **12.** To give birth to (young): said of domestic animals. **13.** To move, as a lever or switch, in connecting or disconnecting a circuit, mechanism, etc. **14.** *Slang* To give (a party, etc.). **15.** In card games, to play or discard. **16.** In ceramics, to shape on a potter's wheel. **17.** To spin (filaments, as of silk) into thread. — *v.i.* **18.** To cast or fling something. **— to throw away 1.** To discard. **2.** To waste; squander. **— to throw back 1.** To return by throwing. **2.** To revert to ancestral characteristics. **— to throw cold water on** To discourage. **— to throw in 1.** To cause (gears or a clutch) to mesh or engage. **2.** To contribute; add. **3.** To join with others. **— to throw in the towel** (or **sponge**) *Slang* To accept defeat; surrender. **— to throw off 1.** To cast aside; reject; spurn. **2.** To rid oneself of. **3.** To do or utter in an offhand manner. **4.** To disconnect, as a machine. **— to throw oneself at** To strive to gain the affections or love of. **— to throw oneself into** To engage or take part in vigorously. **— to throw oneself on** (or **upon**) To entrust oneself to; rely on. **— to throw open** To open suddenly or completely, as a door. **2.** To free from restrictions or obstacles. **— to throw the book at** *Slang* **1.** To sentence to the maximum penalty. **2.** To reprimand or castigate severely. **— to throw out 1.** To put forth; emit. **2.** To cast out or aside; discard; reject. **3.** To utter as if accidentally: to *throw out* hints. **4.** In baseball, to retire (a runner) by throwing the ball to the base toward which he is advancing. **— to throw over 1.** To overturn. **2.** To discard. **— to throw (something) up to (someone)** *Informal* To mention or repeat as a reproach. **— to throw together** To put together hastily or roughly. **— to throw up 1.** To construct hastily. **2.** To give up; relinquish. **3.** To vomit. — *n.* **1.** An act of throwing or hurling; a fling. **2.** The distance over which a missile may be thrown: a stone's *throw*. **3.** A cast of dice, or the resulting number. **4.** *Mech.* The radius of the circle described by a crank, cam, or the like. **5.** A scarf used for draping an easel or picture frame; also, a woman's scarf. **6.** *Geol.* **a** A faulting, or dislocation of rock strata. **b** The amount of vertical displacement produced by dislocation of strata. [OE *thrāwan* to turn, twist, curl] **— throw′er** *n.*

throw·a·way (thrō′ə·wā′) *n.* A free broadside or leaflet handed out for advertising or propaganda purposes.

throw·back (thrō′bak′) *n.* **1.** Reversion to an ancestral type or condition; also, an example of such reversion. **2.** A throwing back.

thru (thrōō) See THROUGH.

thrum¹ (thrum) *v.* **thrummed, thrum·ming** *v.t.* **1.** To play on or finger (a stringed instrument) idly and without expression. **2.** To drum or tap monotonously or listlessly. **3.** To recite or repeat in a droning, monotonous way. — *v.i.* **4.** To thrum a stringed instrument. **5.** To sound when played thus, as a guitar. — *n.* Any monotonous drumming. [Imit.]

thrum² (thrum) *n.* **1.** The fringe of warp threads remaining on a loom beam after the web has been cut off; also, one of such threads. **2.** Any loose thread or fringe, or a tuft of filaments or fibers; a tassel. — *v.t.* **thrummed, thrum·ming 1.** To cover or trim with thrums or similar appendages. **2.** *Naut.* To insert bits of rope yarn in (canvas) to produce a rough surface or mat to be used to prevent chafing. [OE -*thrum* ligament, as in *tungethrum* the ligament of the tongue]

thrush¹ (thrush) *n.* Any of numerous migratory birds having a long and slightly graduated tail, long wings, and spotted underparts, as the hermit thrush, wood thrush, and the song thrush of Europe. ◆ Collateral adjective: *turdine.* [OE *thrysce*]

thrush² (thrush) *n. Pathol.* A vesicular disease of the mouth, lips, and throat of infants caused by a fungus. [Cf. Dan, *tröske*, Sw. *trosk* mouth disease]

thrust (thrust) *v.* **thrust, thrust·ing** *v.t.* **1.** To push or shove with force or sudden impulse. **2.** To pierce or stab, as with a sword or dagger. **3.** To put (a person) forcibly into some condition or situation. **4.** To interpose; put in: to *thrust* in a remark. — *v.i.* **5.** To make a sudden push against something. **6.** To force oneself on or ahead: push one's way: with *through, into, on,* etc. — *n.* **1.** A sudden, forcible push, esp. with a pointed weapon. **2.** A vigorous attack. **3.** *Archit.* A stress or strain tending to push a member of a structure outward or sidewise: the *thrust* of an arch. **4.** *Mech.* The driving force exerted by a steam engine, motor, propeller, jet engine, etc. **5.** Salient force or meaning: the *thrust* of his remarks. [< ON *thrysta*] **— thrust′er** *n.*

thru·way (thrōō′wā′) *n. U.S.* A long-distance express highway: also spelled *throughway.*

thud (thud) *n.* **1.** A dull, heavy sound, as of a hard body

striking upon a comparatively soft surface. **2.** The causing such a sound; a thump. — *v.i.* **thud·ded, thud-** To make a thud. [OE *thyddan* to strike, thrust, press]

thug (thug) *n.* **1.** A cutthroat or ruffian. **2.** Formerly, of an organization of religious, professional assassin northern India. [< Hind. *thag* < Skt. *sthaga* swindler] **thug′ger·y** *n.* — **thug′gish** *adj.*

Thu·le (thōō′lē) In ancient geography, the northern limit of the habitable world.

thu·li·um (thōō′lē·əm) *n.* A metallic element (symbol of the erbium group in the lanthanide series. See ELEM [after *Thule*]

thumb (thum) *n.* **1.** The short, thick digit next to the finger of the human hand. **2.** The corresponding dig certain other animals, esp. primates. **3.** The division glove or mitten that covers the thumb. **— all thumbs** *formal* Clumsy with the hands. **— thumbs down** *Info* No; nix: from a sign used to indicate negation or disappr **— under one's thumb** Under one's influence or power. *v.t.* **1.** To press, rub, soil, or wear with the thumb in h ling, as the pages of a book. **2.** To perform clumsily or as with the thumbs. **3.** To run through the pages book, manuscript, etc.) rapidly and perfunctorily. **4** *formal* To solicit (a ride in an automobile) by signaling the thumb. — *v.i.* **5.** To hitchhike. **— to thumb one's** To show defiance or disgust by raising the thumb to the with the fingers extended. [OE *thūma*]

thumb-in·dex (thum′in′deks) *v.t.* To provide with a th index.

thumb index A series of scalloped indentations cut a the right-hand edge of a book and labeled to indicate its ous sections.

thumb·nail (thum′nāl′) *n.* **1.** The nail of the thumb. Anything as small and essentially complete as a thumb **— adj.** Small and essentially complete: a *thumbnail* sk

thumb·screw (thum′skrōō′) *n.* **1.** A screw to be turne thumb and fingers. **2.** An instrument of torture for pressing the thumb or thumbs: also **thumb′kin** (-kin).

thumb·tack (thum′tak′) *n. U.S.* A broad-headed that may be pushed in with the thumb.

thump (thump) *n.* **1.** A blow with a blunt or heavy ob **2.** The sound made by such a blow; a dull thud. — *v.* Informal To beat or defeat severely. — *v.i.* **3.** To s with a thump. **4.** To make a thump or thumps; pour throb. [Imit.] **— thump′er** *n.*

thump·ing (thum′ping) *adj.* **1.** That thumps. **2.** *I mal* Huge; whopping.

thun·der (thun′dər) *n.* **1.** The sound that accomp lightning, caused by the sudden heating and expansio the air along the path of the electrical discharge. **2.** loud, rumbling or booming noise, suggestive of thunder A denunciation or threat; a vehement utterance. **— to** one's thunder To take for one's own use anything po or effective originated by another: said esp. of an argun — *v.i.* **1.** To give forth a peal or peals of thunder: use personally: It *thunders.* **2.** To make a noise like thu **3.** To utter vehement denunciations or threats. — *v.t* To utter or express with a noise like or suggestive of thu [OE *thunor*] **— thun′der·er** *n.*

thun·der·bolt (thun′dər·bōlt′) *n.* **1.** An electric disch accompanied by a clap of thunder. **2.** An imaginary m ball or bolt hurled by the lightning flash. **3.** One wl that which acts with or as with the force and speed o structiveness of lightning.

thun·der·clap (thun′dər·klap′) *n.* **1.** A sharp, violen tonation of thunder. **2.** Anything having the violen suddenness of a clap of thunder.

thun·der·cloud (thun′dər·kloud′) *n.* A dark, heavy of cloud highly charged with electricity.

thun·der·head (thun′dər·hed′) *n. Meteorol.* A rou mass of cumulus cloud, either silvery white or dark silvery edges, often developing into a thundercloud.

thun·der·ing (thun′dər·ing) *adj.* **1.** Giving forth, o companied by, thunder. **2.** Resembling thunder in for effect; extremely violent. **3.** *Informal* Unusually gre extreme; superlative. — **thun′der·ing·ly** *adv.*

thun·der·ous (thun′dər·əs) *adj.* Producing a noise thunder. Also **thun′drous** (-drəs). **— thun′der·ous·ly**

thun·der·peal (thun′dər·pēl′) *n.* A clap of thunder.

thun·der·show·er (thun′dər·shou′ər) *n.* A shower of with thunder and lightning.

thun·der·storm (thun′dər·stôrm′) *n.* A local storm ac panied by lightning and thunder.

thun·der·struck (thun′dər·struk′) *adj.* **1.** Struc lightning. **2.** Amazed, astonished, or confounded, as fear, surprise, etc. Also **thun′der·strick′en** (-strik′ən)

thun·der·y (thun′dər·ē) *adj. Informal* **1.** Indicative accompanied by thunder. **2.** Ominous.

thu·ri·ble (thōōr′ə·bəl, thûr′-) *n.* A censer. [< L < *thuris* frankincense]

·rin·gi·an (thōō·rin'jē·ən) *adj. Geol.* Denoting the per division of the Permian in Europe. — *n.* One of a utonic tribe occupying central Germany until the sixth tury.

·rs·day (thûrz'dē, -dā) *n.* The fifth day of the week. usion of OE *Thunres dæg* of Thunor and ON *Thōrs-yr* day of Thor; trans. of LL *dies Jovis* day of Jove]

·s (thus) *adv.* **1.** In this, that, or the following way of anner. **2.** To such degree or extent; so: *thus* far. **3.** In ese circumstances or conditions; therefore. [OE]

·ack (thwak) *v.t.* To strike with something flat; whack. *n.* A blow with a flat or blunt instrument. [Prob. OE *ccian* to smack; infl. in form by *whack*] — **thwack'er** *n.*

·art (thwôrt) *v.t.* To prevent the accomplishment of, by interposing an obstacle; also, to prevent (one) from omplishing something; foil; frustrate; balk. — *n.* **1.** A sman's seat extending across a boat. **2.** A crosspiece or nsverse member in a boat. — *adj.* Lying, moving, or ending across something; transverse. — *adv. & prep.* hwart; across. [< ON *thvert*, neut. of *thverr* transverse] **·thwart'er** *n.*

(thī) *pronominal adj. Archaic* The possessive case of pronoun *thou*, used attributively: *Thy* kingdom come. pocopated var. of THINE]

·me (tīm) *n.* Any of various small shrubby plants of the nt family, having aromatic leaves and used in cookery. F < L < Gk. *thymon*] — **thym'y** *adj.*

·m·ic¹ (tī'mik) *adj.* Pertaining to or derived from thyme.
·mic² (thī'mik) *adj.* Of, pertaining to, or derived from thymus.

·mus (thī'məs) *n. Anat.* A glandular organ of man and ne other vertebrates, found behind the top of the breast-ne. [< NL < Gk. *thymos*]

·ro- *combining form Med. & Surg.* The thyroid; of or re-ed to the thyroid. Also, before vowels, **thyr-**. Also **·reo-**. [< Gk. *thyreoeidēs* thyroid]

·roid (thī'roid) *adj. Physiol.* Relating or pertaining to thyroid cartilage or the thyroid gland. — *n.* **1.** The yroid cartilage or gland. **2.** The dried and powdered yroid gland of certain domesticated food animals, used in treatment of hypothyroid disorders. [< Gk. < *thyreos* ge shield + *eidos* form]

·roid cartilage *Anat.* The largest cartilage of the larynx, nposed of two blades whose juncture in front forms the am's apple.

·roid gland *Anat.* An endocrine gland situated in front and on each side of the trachea, and secreting thyroxin, portant in the regulation of metabolism and body growth.

·rox·in (thī·rok'sin) *n. Biochem.* An odorless, crystal-e amino acid, $C_{15}H_{11}O_4NI_4$, obtained as the hormone of thyroid gland and used synthetically, used to treat yroid disorders. Also **thy·rox·ine** (-sēn, -sin). [< THYR(O)- OX(Y)- + -IN] — **thy·rox·in·ic** (thī'rok·sin'ik) *adj.*

·r·soid (thûr'soid) *adj.* Resembling or shaped like hyrsus. Also **thyr·soi·dal** (thûr·soid'l).

·r·sus (thûr'səs) *n., pl.* **·si** (-sī) A staff wreathed in ivy d crowned with a pine cone or a bunch of ivy leaves, as ried by Dionysus and the satyrs. [< L < Gk. *thyrsos*]

·self (thī·self') *pron. Archaic* A form of the second per-singular pronouns *thee* and *thou*, used: **1.** As a reflexive: ow *thyself*. **2.** As an emphatic or intensive form: I love e for *thyself*.

·ē) *n. Music* In solmization, a syllable representing the enth tone of the diatonic scale. [See GAMUT]

·r·a (tī·âr'ə, tē·är'ə, -ar'ə) *n.* **1.** The pope's triple crown; o, the papal dignity. Compare MITER. **2.** An ornamental, nicircular band of jewels, etc., worn by women for formal asions. [< L < Gk. *tiara* Persian headdress]

·et·an (ti·bet'n) *adj.* Of or pertaining to Tibet, the betans, or to their language, religion, or customs. — *n.* **1.** e of the native Mongoloid people of Tibet, now inter-xed with Chinese and various peoples of India. **2.** The o-Tibetan language of Tibet. Also **Thibetan**.

·i·a (tib'ē·ə) *n. pl.* **tib·i·ae** (tib'i·ē) or **tib·i·as 1.** *Anat.* e inner and larger of the two bones of the leg below the ee; the shin bone. **2.** The corresponding bone in the hind b of other animals. [< L] — **tib'i·al** *adj.*

(tik) *n.* An involuntary spasm or twitching of muscles, u. of the face and sometimes of neurotic origin. [< F]

·k¹ (tik) *n.* **1.** A light, recurring sound made by a watch, ck, or similar mechanism. **2.** A mark, as a dot or dash, ed in checking off something. — *v.i.* **1.** To make a re-rrent clicking sound, as a running watch or clock. — *v.t.* To mark or check with ticks. [Prob. imit.]

·k² (tik) *n.* **1.** One of numerous flat, bloodsucking arach-ls that attack the skin of man and other animals. **2.** Any certain two-winged or wingless insects, parasitic on sheep, rses, cattle, bats, and other animals. [OE *ticia*]

tick³ (tik) *n.* **1.** The stout outer covering of a mattress or pillow. **2.** *Informal* Ticking. [Earlier *teke, tyke*, ult. < L < Gk. *thēke* case]

tick⁴ (tik) *n. Brit. Informal* Credit; trust: to buy something on *tick*. [Short for TICKET]

tick·er (tik'ər) *n.* **1.** One who or that which ticks. **2.** A telegraphic instrument that records stock quotations on a paper ribbon. **3.** *Slang* A watch. **4.** *Slang* The heart.

ticker tape A paper ribbon that receives the printed information on a ticker. — **tick·er-tape** (tik'ər·tāp') *adj.*

tick·et (tik'it) *n.* **1.** A card showing that the holder is entitled to something, as transportation in a public vehicle, admission to a theater, etc. **2.** A label or tag for attachment or identification. **3.** A certificate or license, as of an airplane pilot or the captain of a ship. **4.** In politics: **a** A list of candidates of a single party on a ballot. **b** The group of candidates running for the offices of a party. **5.** *Informal* A legal summons, as for a traffic violation. — *v.t.* **1.** To fix a ticket to; label. **2.** To present or furnish with a ticket or tickets. [< MF < OF < *estiquer* to stick < OLG *stekan*]

ticket of leave Formerly, in Great Britain and Australia, a written permit granted to a penal convict to be at large before the expiration of his sentence.

tick·ing (tik'ing) *n.* A strong, closely woven cotton or linen fabric, used for ticks, awnings, etc. [< TICK³ + -ING¹]

tick·le (tik'əl) *v.* **·led, ·ling** *v.t.* **1.** To touch or scratch (someone) so as to produce a sensation resulting in spasmodic laughter or twitching; titillate. **2.** To arouse or excite agreeably; please: Compliments *tickle* our vanity. **3.** *Informal* To amuse or entertain; delight. **4.** To move, stir, or get by or as by tickling. — *v.i.* **1.** To have or experience a thrilling or tingling sensation. — *n.* **1.** The act of tickling or of being tickled; also the sensation produced. **2.** *Canadian* In Newfoundland, a narrow strait. [ME *tikelen*]

tick·ler (tik'lər) *n.* **1.** One who or that which tickles. **2.** A memorandum book or file, as of bills or notes due, etc.

tick·lish (tik'lish) *adj.* **1.** Sensitive to tickling. **2.** Liable to be upset or easily offended. **3.** Attended with risk; difficult; delicate. — **tick'lish·ly** *adv.* — **tick'lish·ness** *n.*

tick·tack·toe (tik'tak·tō') *n.* A game for two players who alternately put circles or crosses in the spaces of a figure formed by two parallel lines crossing at right angles two other parallel lines, each player trying to get a row of three circles or three crosses before his opponent does: also called *tit-tat-toe.* Also **tick'tack·too'** (-tōō'), **tic'tac·toe'** (-tō').

tick-tock (tik'tok') *n.* The sound of a clock or watch. — *v.i.* To make this sound. [Imit.]

tid·al (tīd'l) *adj.* **1.** Of, pertaining to, or influenced by the tides. **2.** Dependent on the rise of the tide as to time of starting or leaving: a *tidal* steamship.

tidal wave 1. Any great incoming rise of waters along a shore, caused by windstorms at sea or by excessively high tides. **2.** A great movement in popular feeling, opinion, action, etc. **3.** A tsunami.

tid·bit (tid'bit') *n.* A choice bit, as of food. Also, *Brit., titbit.* [< dial. E *tid* small object + BIT¹]

tid·dly·winks (tid'lē·wingks') *n.* A game in which the players attempt to snap little disks of bone, ivory, or the like, from a plane surface into a cup. Also **tid·dle·dy·winks** (tid'l·dē·wingks'). [Prob. < *tiddly* child's word for *little*]

tide (tīd) *n.* **1.** The periodic rise and fall of the surface waters of the oceans, caused by the attraction of moon and sun. In each lunar day of 24 hours and 51 minutes there are two high tides and two low tides, alternating at equal intervals of flood and ebb. **2.** Anything that rises and falls like the tide; also, the time at which something is most flourishing. **3.** A natural drift or tendency of events, opinions, etc. **4.** Season; time; esp., a season of the ecclesiastical year: used chiefly in combination: *Christmastide.* — *v.* **·tid·ed, tid·ing** *v.i.* **1.** To ebb and flow like the tide. **2.** To float with the tide. — *v.t.* **3.** To carry or help like a boat buoyed up by the tide: Charity *tided* us over the depression. **4.** To survive; endure, as a difficulty: with *over: to tide* over hard times. [OE *tīd* period, season] — **tide'less** *adj.*

tide·land (tīd'land') *n.* Land alternately covered and uncovered by the tide.

tide·rip (tīd'rip') *n.* Riptide. [< TIDE¹ + RIP²]

tide·wait·er (tīd'wā'tər) *n.* A customs officer who boards vessels entering port, to enforce customs regulations.

tide·wa·ter (tīd'wô'tər, -wot'ər) *n.* **1.** Water that inundates land at high tide. **2.** Water affected by the tide on the seacoast or in a river. **3.** Any area, as a seacoast, whose waters are affected by tides. — *adj.* Pertaining to the tidewater; also, situated on the tidewater: the *tidewater* country.

ti·dings (tī'dingz) *n.pl.* (*sometimes construed as sing.*) A report or information; news. [OE *tīdung*]

ti·dy (tī'dē) *adj.* **·di·er, ·di·est 1.** Marked by neatness and order; trim. **2.** Of an orderly disposition. **3.** *Informal*

Moderately large; considerable: a *tidy* sum.   **4.** *Informal* Tolerable; fairly good.   — *v.t.* & *v.i.* **·died, ·dy·ing** To make (things) tidy; put (things) in order.   — *n.*   *pl.* **·dies** A light, detachable covering, as of lace or embroidery, to protect the back or arms of a chair or sofa. [ME < OE *tīd* time] — **ti′di·ly** *adv.*   — **ti′di·ness** *n.*

tie (tī)   *v.* **tied, ty·ing** *v.t.*   **1.** To fasten with cord, rope, etc., the ends of which are then drawn into a knot.   **2.** To draw the parts of together or into place by a cord or band fastened with a knot: to *tie* one's shoes.   **3.** To form (a knot).   **4.** To form a knot in, as string.   **5.** To fasten, attach, or join in any way.   **6.** To restrain or confine; bind.   **7.** In sports, games, etc.: **a** To equal (a competitor) in score or achievement. **b** To equal (a competitor's score).   **8.** *Informal* To unite in marriage.   **9.** *Music* To unite by a tie.   — *v.i.*   **10.** To make a tie or connection.   **11.** To make the same score; be equal.   — **to tie down** To hinder; restrict.   — **to tie in** *Informal* To have a certain relationship or connection; often with *with.*   — **to tie (something) in** *Informal* To bring into a certain relationship or connection.   — **to tie up**   **1.** To fasten with rope, string, etc.   **2.** To moor (a vessel).   **3.** To block; hinder.   **4.** To have or be already committed, in use, etc., so as to be unavailable.   — *n.*   **1.** A string, cord, etc., with which something is tied.   **2.** Any bond or obligation, mental, moral, or legal: *ties* of affection.   **3.** An exact equality in number, as of a score, votes, etc.; esp., a contest which neither side wins; a draw.   **4.** A necktie.   **5.** A structural member fastening parts of a framework together and receiving tensile stress.   **6.** *Music* A curved line placed over or under two musical notes of the same pitch on the staff to make them represent one tone length.   **7.** *pl.* Low shoes fastened with lacings.   **8.** *U.S.* One of a set of timbers laid crosswise on the ground as supports for railroad tracks; a sleeper. [OE *tīegan* to bind]

tie·back (tī′bak′)   *n.* A piece of fabric, metal, etc., by which curtains are draped or tied back at the sides.

tie beam A timber that serves as a tie in a roof, etc. For illus. see ROOF.

tie-in (tī′in′)   *n.* A connection; association; relation.

tie-in sale A sale in which the buyer, in order to get the article he wants, is required to buy a second article.

tier (tir)   *n.* A rank or row of things, as seats, placed one above another.   — *v.t.* & *v.i.* To place or rise in tiers. [Earlier *tire* < OF, sequence < *tirer* to draw, elongate]

tierce (tirs)   *n.*   **1.** A former liquid measure equivalent in the U.S. to 42 wine gallons; a third of a pipe or butt.   **2.** A cask holding this amount.   **3.** *Often cap. Eccl.* Prescribed prayers constituting the third of the seven canonical hours: often called *undersong.*   [< OF *tierce, terce* a third < L *tertia*]

tie-up (tī′up′)   *n.*   **1.** A situation, resulting from a strike, mechanical breakdown, etc., in which progress or operation is impossible.   **2.** *Informal* A connection or relation.

tiff (tif)   *n.*   **1.** A peevish display of irritation; a pet; huff.   **2.** A light quarrel; a spat.   — *v.i.* To be in or have a tiff. [Origin unknown]

ti·ger (tī′gər)   *n.*   **1.** A large carnivorous feline of Asia, with vertical black wavy stripes on a tawny body and black bars or rings on the limbs and tail.   **2.** One of several other animals resembling the tiger.   **3.** A fierce, cruel person. [OE *tiger* or OF *tigre*, both < L < Gk. *tigris*]

ti·ger-eye (tī′gər·ī′)   *n.* A gemstone showing a changeable luster.   Also **ti′gers-eye′.**

ti·ger·ish (tī′gər·ish)   *adj.* Of or resembling the tiger or its habits; predacious; bloodthirsty: also **ti′grish** (-grish).

tiger lily A tall cultivated lily, with nodding orange flowers spotted with black.

tiger moth A stout-bodied moth with striped or spotted wings.

tight (tīt)   *adj.*   **1.** So closely held together or constructed as to be impervious to fluids, air, etc.: a *tight* vessel.   **2.** Firmly fixed or fastened in place; secure.   **3.** Fully stretched; taut: *tight* as a drum.   **4.** Closely drawn, packed, fastened, etc.: a *tight* weave.   **5.** Strict; stringent: to keep a *tight* rein over us.   **6.** Fitting closely; esp., fitting too closely.   **7.** *Informal* Difficult to cope with; troublesome: a *tight* spot.   **8.** *Informal* Parsimonious; tightfisted.   **9.** Characterized by a feeling of constriction: a *tight* cough.   **10.** *Slang* Drunk; intoxicated.   **11.** Evenly matched: said of a contest.   **12.** *Econ.* **a** Difficult to obtain. **b** Straitened from lack of money or commodities: a *tight* market.   **13.** Yielding very little or no profit: said of a bargain.   **14.** *Dial.* Well-built; compact.   **15.** *Dial.* Neat; tidy.   — *adv.*   **1.** Firmly; securely.   **2.** Closely; with much constriction.   — **to sit tight** To remain firm in one's position; refrain from taking action. [ME *thight*]   — **tight′ly** *adv.*   — **tight′ness** *n.*

-tight *combining form* Impervious to: *watertight.*

tight·en (tīt′n)   *v.t.* & *v.i.* To make or become tight or tighter.   — **tight′en·er** *n.*

tight·fist·ed (tīt′fis′tid)   *adj.* Stingy; parsimonious.

tight·lipped (tīt′lipt′)   *adj.*   **1.** Having the lips held tightly together.   **2.** Unwilling to talk; reticent or secretive.

tight·rope (tīt′rōp′)   *n.* A rope or cable stretched out t above the ground, on which acrobats do balancing acts,

tights (tīts)   *n.pl.* Skintight garments, commonly for legs and lower torso, worn by dancers, acrobats, etc.

tight·wad (tīt′wod′)   *n.* *U.S. Slang* A parsimonious son; miser.   [< TIGHT + WAD¹]

ti·gress (tī′gris)   *n.*   **1.** A female tiger.   **2.** A cruel, fi woman.

til·bur·y (til′ber-ē)   *n.*   *pl.* **·bur·ies** A form of gig for persons.   [after *Tilbury*, a 19th c. London coachmaker]

til·de (til′də, -dē)   *n.* A sign (~); used esp., in Spanish ov to represent the palatal nasal (roughly equivalent to n*y* in *cañón.*   [< Sp. < L *titulus* superscription, title]

tile (tīl)   *n.*   **1.** A thin piece of baked clay or other mate as asbestos, linoleum, etc., used for covering roofs, fl etc., and as an ornament.   **2.** A short earthenware used in forming sewers.   **3.** Tiles collectively; tiling. Any of the counters used in mahjong.   **5.** *Informal* A silk hat.   — *v.t.* **tiled, til·ing** To cover with tiles. [OE, < L < *tegere* to cover]   — **til′er** *n.*

til·ing (tī′ling)   *n.*   **1.** The act, operation, or system of tiles for roofing, drainage, etc.   **2.** Tiles collectively. Something made of or faced with tiles.

till¹ (til)   *v.t.* & *v.i.* To work (soil) for the productio crops, as by plowing, harrowing, hoeing, sowing, etc.; vate.   [OE *tilian* to strive, acquire]   — **till′a·ble** *adj.*

till² (til)   *prep.*   **1.** To the time of; until.   **2.** Before: with negative: I can't go *till* noon.   — *conj.*   **1.** Up to such as; until: *till* death do us part.   **2.** Before: with the nega They couldn't go *till* he came.   [OE *til* < ON, to]

till³ (til)   *n.* A drawer or tray in which money or valua are kept, as at a bank, store, etc.   [Origin uncertain]

till·age (til′ij)   *n.* The cultivation of land.   [< TILI -AGE]

till·er¹ (til′ər)   *n.* One who or that which tills.   [< T

till·er² (til′ər)   *n.* *Naut.* A lever to turn a rudder v steering.   [< OF < Med.L *telarium* weaver's beam]

tilt (tilt)   *v.t.*   **1.** To cause to rise at one end or side; in at an angle; slant; tip.   **2.** To aim or thrust, as a la **3.** To charge or overthrow in a tilt or joust.   — *v.i.*   **4** slope; lean.   **5.** To engage in a joust.   — Syn. See TIP¹. *n.*   **1.** A slant; slope.   **2.** The act of inclining, or the being inclined.   **3.** A medieval sport in which mou knights, charging with lances, endeavored to unseat other.   **4.** Any similar encounter, as a quarrel.   **5.** A th or blow, as with a lance.   **6.** A seesaw.   — **at full tilt** At speed.   [ME < OE *tealt* unsteady]   — **tilt′er** *n.*

tilth (tilth)   *n.*   **1.** The act of tilling; cultivation of soil; age.   **2.** Cultivated land.   [OE < *tilian* to till]

tim·bal (tim′bəl)   *n.* A kettledrum.   [< F < Sp. < A *at-tabl* a drum]

tim·bale (tim′bəl, *Fr.* tań·bàl′)   *n.*   **1.** A custardlik made of chicken, fish, cheese, or vegetables, cooked drum-shaped mold.   **2.** A small cup made of fried pastr which food may be served.   [< F. See TIMBAL.]

tim·ber (tim′bər)   *n.*   **1.** Wood suitable for building or st tural purposes.   **2.** Growing or standing trees; also, w land.   **3.** A single piece of prepared wood for use in a s ture.   **4.** *Naut.* Any principal beam of a vessel.   **5.** Pers character, talent, potentiality: presidential *timber.*   — To provide or shore with timber.   [OE]   — **tim′bered**

timber hitch *Naut.* A knot by which a rope is fast around a spar.

tim·ber·land (tim′bər·land′)   *n.* Land covered with tim

timber line The upper limit of tree growth on moun and in arctic regions.   — **tim′ber-line′** (-līn′) *adj.*

timber wolf The large gray or brindled wolf of the fo of the northern U.S. and Canada: also called *lobo.*

tim·bre (tim′bər, tam′-; *Fr.* tań′br′)   *n.* The attribute of a sound distinguishing one vowel sound from another, the tone of one musical instrument from another, etc.; quality; tone color.   [< F < OF < L *tympanum* kettledrum]

TIMBER WO (About 4 fe long)

tim·brel (tim′brəl)   *n.* An ancient instrument resembling a tambourine.   [< OF. See TIME

time (tīm)   *n.*   **1.** The general concept, relation, or fa continuous or successive existence, capable of division measurable portions, and comprising the past, present future.   **2.** Duration with reference to finite existenc distinguished from eternity.   **3.** A system of measuring ration: solar *time.*   **4.** A definite portion of duration; a specific hour, day, season, year, etc.: The *time* is : Autumn is my favorite *time.*   **5.** The moment or peri which something takes place, has taken place, or will place: at the *time* of his marriage.   **6.** That moment or tion of duration allotted to or sufficient for some speci tion, purpose, or event: *time* enough to catch the train The period of duration generally allotted to human life. Leisure: no *time* to read.   **9.** An instance or occasion o rence or repetition: next *time*; three *times* a day. **10.** A or proper moment or occasion: a *time* to plant. **11.** The iod of pregnancy or gestation; also, the moment of childth. **12.** The moment of death. **13.** A period considered h reference to one's personal experience: to have a good *e*. **14.** *Usu. pl.* An era marked by some cultural, hisical, or other special characteristics: ancient *times*; the *e* of Charlemagne. **15.** *Usu. pl.* The present period or or the period or era under consideration. **16.** *Usu. pl.* eriod of duration having some specific quality: *Times* are d. **17.** *Informal* A period of imprisonment. **18.** The iod during which work has been done or remains to be ne by a worker; also, the pay given for this. **19.** *Music* osely, meter, tempo, or the duration of a note. See METER. , Speed or rate of movement in marching, dancing, etc.: ble *time*. **21.** *Usu. pl.* In arithmetic, an instance of bemultiplied or added: How many *times* does three go into e? **— against time** With an imminent time limit; as ckly as possible. **— ahead of time** Before the time stated lue; early. **— at the same time 1.** At the same moment period. **2.** Despite that; however; nevertheless. **— at es** Now and then; occasionally. **— behind the times** d-fashioned. **— behind time** After the time stated or due; e. **— for the time being** Temporarily. **— from time to e** Now and then; occasionally. **— in good time 1.** ckly; fast. **2.** At the appropriate time; when properly e. **— in the nick of time** At just the right or critical mont. **— in time 1.** While time permits or lasts; before it oo late. **2.** In the progress of time; ultimately. **3.** In the per rhythm, tempo, etc. **— on time 1.** Promptly; acding to schedule. **2.** To be paid for, later or in installnts. **— time and again** Frequently; repeatedly: also e **after time**. **— to gain time 1.** To run fast: said of a epiece. **2.** To prolong an act or occasion so as to conr, decide, etc. **— to keep time 1.** To indicate time cortly, as a clock. **2.** To make rhythmic movements in uniwith others. **3.** To render or conduct a musical comition in the desired tempo or rhythm. **— to lose time** To run slow: said of a clock. **2.** To waste or miss opporuties; delay advancement. **— adj. 1.** Of or pertaining to e. **2.** Devised so as to operate at a specified time: a *time* mb. **3.** Of purchases, paid for in installments or at a ure date. **— v.t.** timed, tim·ing **1.** To regulate as to time. To cause to correspond in time: They *timed* their steps to music. **3.** To arrange the time or occasion for. **4.** To rk the rhythm or measure of. **5.** To ascertain or record speed or duration of: to *time* a race. [OE *tīma*] e·card (tīm′kärd′) *n.* A card for recording the time of val and departure of an employee. e clock A clock equipped for automatically recording es of arrival and departure. e exposure *Photog.* **1.** A film exposure made for a relaely long interval. **2.** A picture made by such an exposure. e·hon·ored (tīm′on′ərd) *adj.* Observed or honored be-se of long usage or existence. Also *Brit.* time′·hon′oured. e·keep·er (tīm′kē′pər) *n.* **1.** One who or that which ps time. **2.** One who declares the time in a race, game, ietic match, etc., or records the hours worked by employ-. **3.** A railroad train starter. **4.** A timepiece. e·less (tīm′lis) *adj.* **1.** Independent of or unaffected time; unending; eternal. **2.** Not limited to any special or era. **— time′less·ly** *adv.* **— time′less·ness** *n.* e·ly (tīm′lē) *adj.* ·li·er, ·li·est Being or occurring in good suitable time; opportune; seasonable; well-timed. **—** . Opportunely; seasonably; early. **— time′li·ness** *n.* e·out (tīm′out′) *n.* In sports, a short recess requested a team during play. Also **time out**. e·piece (tīm′pēs′) *n.* Something that records or meass time, as a clock or watch. ·er (tī′mər) *n.* **1.** A timekeeper. **2.** A stopwatch, as for ing a race. **3.** A device attached to an internal-combus- n engine so as to time the spark automatically. **4.** A ckwork or other device that signals the lapse of a time riod, controls an operation, etc. e·serv·er (tīm′sûr′vər) *n.* One who yields to the de- nds or opinions of the time, occasion, or authorities, with- t reference to principle. **— time′serv′ing** *adj. & n.* e signature *Music* A symbol placed on a musical staff indicate the meter. e·ta·ble (tīm′tā′bəl) *n.* A tabular schedule of the times which certain things are to take place, as arrivals and de- rtures of trains, times of high and low tides, etc. e·test·ed (tīm′tes′tid) *adj.* Having worth or efficiency oved by use over an extended period. e·work (tīm′wûrk′) *n.* Work paid for on the basis of a wage per hour, day, week, etc. **— time′work′er** *n.* e·worn (tīm′wôrn′, -wōrn′) *adj.* **1.** Showing the ravag- or effects of time. **2.** Trite; overused.

time zone One of the 24 sectors of 15° each, or a time interval of one hour, into which the earth is divided for reckoning standard time from the meridian of Greenwich. tim·id (tim′id) *adj.* **1.** Shrinking from danger or risk; fearful. **2.** Lacking self-confidence; shy. **3.** Characterized by fear or shyness: a *timid* voice. [< L < *timere* to fear] **— ti·mid·i·ty** (ti-mid′ə-tē), **tim′id·ness** *n.* **— tim′id·ly** *adv.* tim·ing (tī′ming) *n.* The act or art of regulating the speed of performance, utterance, a blow, stroke, etc., so as to insure maximum effectiveness; also, the effect so produced. tim·or·ous (tim′ər·əs) *adj.* **1.** Fearful of danger; timid. **2.** Indicating or produced by fear. [< OF < Med.L < L *timor, -oris* fear] **— tim′or·ous·ly** *adv.* **— tim′or·ous·ness** *n.* tim·o·thy (tim′ə-thē) *n.* A perennial fodder grass having long, cylindrical spikes. Also **timothy grass**. [after *Timothy* Hanson, who took seed to the Carolinas about 1720] Tim·o·thy (tim′ə-thē) A convert and companion of the apostle Paul. **— n.** Either of two books in the New Testament consisting of two epistles addressed to Timothy and attributed to Saint Paul. tim·pa·ni (tim′pə-nē) *n. pl.* of tim·pa·no (-nō) Kettledrums: also spelled *tympani*. [< Ital. < L *tympanum* drum] **— tim′pa·nist** *n.* tim·pa·num (tim′pə-nəm) See TYMPANUM. tin (tin) *n.* **1.** A white, malleable, metallic element (symbol Sn) of low tensile strength: also called *stannum*. See ELEMENT. **2.** Tin plate. **3.** A container or box made of tin. **4.** *Brit.* A can. **— v.t.** tinned, tin·ning **1.** To coat or cover with tin. **2.** To pack or put up in tins. **— adj.** Made of a tin. [OE] tin·a·mou (tin′ə-mōō) *n.* Any of certain South American birds resembling the partridge and hunted as game birds. [< F < Carib *tinamu*] tinc·ture (tingk′chər) *n.* **1.** A solution, usu., in alcohol, of some medicinal substance: *tincture* of iodine. **2.** A tinge of color; tint. **3.** A slight additional flavor, quality, etc. **—** *v.t.* ·tured, ·tur·ing **1.** To impart a slight hue or tinge to. **2.** To imbue with flavor, odor, etc. **3.** To imbue with a specified quality. [< L *tingere* to dye, color] tin·der (tin′dər) *n.* Any readily combustible substance, as charred linen or touchwood, that will ignite on contact with a spark. [OE *tynder*] **— tin′der·y** *adj.* tin·der·box (tin′dər·boks′) *n.* **1.** A portable metallic box containing tinder. **2.** Anything highly flammable, explosive, touchy, etc. tine (tīn) *n.* A spike or prong, as of a fork or an antler. [OE *tind*] **— tined** *adj.* tin·foil (tin′foil′) *n.* Tin or an alloy of tin made into thin sheets for use as wrapping material, etc. Also **tin foil**. ting (ting) *n.* A single high metallic sound, as of a small bell. [Imit.] **— v.t. & v.i.** To give forth or cause to give forth a ting. ting-a-ling (ting′ə-ling′) *n.* The sound of a little bell. tinge (tinj) *v.t.* tinged, tinge·ing or ting·ing **1.** To imbue with a faint trace of color; tint. **2.** To impart a slight characteristic quality of some other element to. **— n.** **1.** A faint trace of added color. **2.** A quality or peculiar characteristic imparted to something. [< L *tingere* to dye] tin·gle (ting′gəl) *v.* ·gled, ·gling *v.i.* **1.** To experience a prickly, stinging sensation, as from cold, or from a sharp blow. **2.** To cause such a sensation. **— v.t.** **3.** To cause to tingle. **— n.** A prickly, stinging sensation; a tingling. [Appar. var. of TINKLE] **— tin′gler** *n.* **— tin′gly** *adj.* tin·horn (tin′hôrn′) *U.S. Slang* *n.* One who is cheaply and noisily pretentious; also, a flashy, small-time gambler. tink·er (tingk′ər) *n.* **1.** An itinerant mender of domestic tin utensils, as pots and pans. **2.** Loosely, one who does repairing work of any kind; a jack-of-all-trades. **3.** A clumsy workman; a botcher. **4.** The act of roughly repairing; hasty workmanship. **— v.i.** **1.** To work as a tinker. **2.** To work in a clumsy makeshift fashion. **3.** To potter; fuss. **— v.t.** **4.** To mend as a tinker. **5.** To repair inexpertly. [Var. of earlier *tinekere* worker in tin] tinker's damn *Slang* The smallest, most contemptible bit: not worth a *tinker's damn*. Also **tinker's dam**. [< TINKER + DAMN; with ref. to the reputed profanity of tinkers] tin·kle (ting′kəl) *v.* ·kled, ·kling *v.i.* **1.** To produce slight, sharp, metallic sounds, as a small bell. **— v.t.** **2.** To cause to tinkle. **3.** To summon or signal by a tinkling. **— n.** A tinkling sound. [Imit.] **— tin′kly** *adj.* **— tink′ling** *n.* tin·ner (tin′ər) *n.* **1.** A miner employed in tin mines. **2.** A maker of or dealer in tinware; a tinsmith. tin·ny (tin′ē) *adj.* ·ni·er, ·ni·est **1.** Pertaining to, composed of, or abounding in tin. **2.** Resembling tin in lack of durability. **3.** Having a thin sound like that of tin being struck. **— tin′ni·ly** *adv.* **— tin′ni·ness** *n.* tin-pan alley (tin′pan′) **1.** A section of a city, esp., of New York, frequented by musicians and song writers and occupied by publishers of popular music. **2.** The composers and publishers of popular music, collectively.

tin-plate (tin′plāt′) *v.t.* **-plat·ed, -plat·ing** To plate with tin. **— tin′-plat′er** *n.*

tin plate Sheet iron or steel plated with tin.

tin·sel (tin′səl) *n.* **1.** Very thin, glittering bits of cheap metals used as decoration. **2.** A yarn containing gold or silver thread. **3.** Anything sparkling and showy, with little real worth. **4.** A fabric in which such spangles or bits of metal are woven. **—** *adj.* **1.** Made of, resembling, or covered with tinsel. **2.** Superficially brilliant; tawdry. **—** *v.t.* **·seled** or **·selled, sel·ing** or **sel·ling 1.** To decorate with or as with tinsel. **2.** To give a showy or gaudy appearance to. [< MF < OF < L *scintilla* spark]

tin·smith (tin′smith′) *n.* One who works with tin or tin plate: also called *whitesmith.*

tint (tint) *n.* **1.** A variety of color; tincture; esp., a slight admixture of a different color; tinge. **2.** A gradation of a color made by dilution with white. **3.** Any pale or delicate hue. **4.** In engraving, an effect of light, shade, texture, etc., produced by the spacing of lines or by hatching. **—** *v.t.* **1.** To give a tint to; tinge. **2.** In engraving, to form a tint upon. [< L *tingere* to dye, color] **— tint′er** *n.*

tin·tin·nab·u·la·tion (tin′ti·nab′yə·lā′shən) *n.* The pealing, tinkling, or ringing of bells. [< L *tintinnare* to ring]

tin·type (tin′tīp′) *n.* A photograph taken on a sensitized film supported on a thin sheet of enameled tin or iron.

tin·ware (tin′wâr′) *n.* Articles made of tin plate.

ti·ny (tī′nē) *adj.* **·ni·er, ·ni·est** Very small; minute; wee. [< obs. *tine* small amount, bit + -y³; ult. origin unknown]

-tion *suffix of nouns* **1.** Action or process of: *rejection.* **2.** Condition or state of being: *completion.* **3.** Result of: *connection.* Also **-ation, -cion, -ion, -sion, -xion.** [< F < OF < L *-tio, -tionis*]

tip¹ (tip) *n.* A slanting or inclined position; a tilt. **—** *v.* **tipped, tip·ping** *v.t.* **1.** To cause to lean by lowering or raising one end or side; tilt. **2.** To overturn or upset: often with *over.* **3.** To raise or touch (one's hat) in greeting. **—** *v.i.* **4.** To become tilted; slant. **5.** To overturn; topple: with *over.* [ME *tipen* to overturn; origin uncertain] **— tip′per** *n.* **— Syn. 1, 3.** Tilt, slant, slope.

tip² (tip) *n.* **1.** A small gift of money for services rendered, given to a servant, waiter, etc. **2.** A friendly, helpful hint; esp., information presumed to increase a better's or speculator's chance of winning. **—** *v.* **tipped, tip·ping** *v.t.* **1.** To give a small gratuity to. **2.** *Informal* To give secret information to, as in betting: often with *off.* **—** *v.i.* **3.** To give tips. [Orig. < thieves' cant, ? < TIP⁴] **— tip′per** *n.*

tip³ (tip) *n.* **1.** The point or extremity of anything tapering; end: the *tip* of the tongue. **2.** A piece or part made to form the end of anything, as a nozzle, ferrule, etc. **3.** The top or summit, as of a mountain. **—** *v.t.* **tipped, tip·ping 1.** To furnish with a tip. **2.** To form the tip of. **3.** To cover or adorn the tip of. [Prob. < MDu., point]

tip⁴ (tip) *v.t.* **tipped, tip·ping 1.** To strike lightly, or with something light; tap. **2.** In baseball, to strike (the ball) a light, glancing blow. **—** *n.* A tap; light blow. [Earlier *tippe*]

tip·off (tip′ôf′, -of′) *n. Informal* A hint or warning.

tip·pet (tip′it) *n.* **1.** An outdoor covering for the neck, or neck and shoulders, hanging well down in front. **2.** *Eccl.* A long scarf worn by Anglican clergymen. **3.** Formerly, a long, dangling part of a sleeve, hood, etc. [Prob. dim. of TIP³]

tip·ple (tip′əl) *v.t. & v.i.* **·pled, ·pling** To drink (alcoholic beverages) frequently and habitually. **—** *n.* Alcoholic liquor. **— tip′pler** *n.*

tip·ster (tip′stər) *n. Informal* One who sells tips, as for betting on a race. [< TIP³]

tip·sy (tip′sē) *adj.* **tip·si·er, tip·si·est 1.** Partially intoxicated; high. **2.** Apt to tip over; shaky; also, crooked; askew. [< TIP¹] **— tip′si·ly** *adv.* **— tip′si·ness** *n.*

tip·toe (tip′tō′) *v.i.* **·toed, ·toe·ing** To walk on tiptoe; go stealthily or quietly. **—** *n.* The tip of a toe. **— on tiptoe 1.** On one's tiptoes. **2.** Eagerly expectant. **3.** Stealthily; quietly. **—** *adj.* **1.** Standing or walking on tiptoe. **2.** Stealthy. **3.** Eager; excited. **—** *adv.* On tiptoe.

tip·top (tip′top′) *n.* **1.** The highest point; the very top. **2.** *Informal* The highest quality or degree. **—** *adj.* **1.** Located at the very top. **2.** *Informal* Best of its kind; first-rate. **—** *adv.* In a tiptop manner. [< TIP³ + TOP¹] **— tip′top′per** *n.*

ti·rade (tī′rād, tə·rād′) *n.* A prolonged declamatory outpouring, as of censure. [< F < Ital. *tirare* to fire, pull]

tire¹ (tīr) *v.* **tired, tir·ing** *v.t.* **1.** To reduce the strength of, as by toil; weary; fatigue. **2.** To reduce the interest or patience of, as with tediousness. **—** *v.i.* **3.** To become weary or exhausted. **4.** To lose patience, interest, etc. **— to tire of** To become weary of or impatient with. **— to tire out** To weary completely. [OE *tiorian*]

tire² (tīr) *n.* **1.** A pneumatic, doughnut-shaped structure, as of rubber, forming the outer part of the wheels of vehicles, serving to absorb shock and provide traction. **2.** A band or hoop of metal, etc. fixed tightly around the rim of a wheel.

— *v.t.* **tired, tir·ing** To furnish with a tire; put a tire on. [Aphetic var. of ATTIRE]

tired (tīrd) *adj.* Weary; exhausted; jaded; fatigued. **— tired′ly** *adv.* **— tired′ness** *n.*

tire·less (tīr′lis) *adj.* Proof against fatigue; untiring. **— tire′less·ly** *adv.* **— tire′less·ness** *n.*

tire·some (tīr′səm) *adj.* Tending to tire, or causing one tire; tedious. **— tire′some·ly** *adv.* **— tire′some·ness** *n.*

ti·ro (tī′rō) See TYRO.

'tis (tiz) *Archaic or Poetic* It is.

Tish'ah b'Ab (tish′ə·bäb′) *n.* In Judaism, a day of fast held on the 9th of Ab (July-August), to commemorate destruction of the Temple.

Tish·ri (tish·rē′, tish′rē) *n.* The first month of the Heb calendar. Also **Tis·ri.** See (Hebrew) CALENDAR. [< Heb < Aramaic *tishrī < sherā* to begin]

tis·sue (tish′ōō) *n.* **1.** *Biol.* One of the elementary aggreg of cells and their products, developed by plants and anim for the performance of a particular function: connective sue. **2.** A light, absorbent piece of paper, usu. consistin two or more layers, used as a disposable towel, handkerch etc. **3.** Tissue paper. **4.** A tissuelike typewriting paper onionskin, commonly used for making carbon copies. **5.** connected or interwoven series; chain: a *tissue* of lies. **6.** Any light or gauzy textile fabric. [< OF < *tistre* to wea

tissue paper Very thin, unsized, almost transparent pa for wrapping delicate articles, protecting engravings, et

tit¹ (tit) *n.* **1.** A titmouse. **2.** Any of various small birds a titlark. [Short for TITMOUSE, TITLARK, etc.]

tit² (tit) *n.* Teat; breast; nipple. [OE *titt*]

ti·tan (tīt′n) *n.* A person of gigantic size and strength. TITAN

Ti·tan (tīt′n) *n.* **1.** In Greek mythology, one of a rac giant gods who were vanquished and succeeded by the Ol pian gods. **2.** Helios: so called by some Latin poets. 3 liquid-fueled intercontinental guided missile of the U.S. Force. **—** *adj.* Titanic. **— Ti′tan·ess** *n.fem.*

Ti·ta·ni·a (ti·tā′nē·ə, tī-) Queen of fairyland and wif Oberon in Shakespeare's *A Midsummer Night's Dream.*

ti·tan·ic (tī·tan′ik) *adj.* Of great size; huge.

Ti·tan·ic (tī·tan′ik) *adj.* Of or resembling the Titans.

ti·ta·ni·um (tī·tā′nē·əm, ti-) *n.* A widely distributed c gray metallic element (symbol Ti), found in small quanti in many minerals and used to toughen steel alloys. See MENT. [< NL < L < Gk. *Titanes* the Titans]

tit·bit (tit′bit′) *n. Brit.* A tidbit.

tit for tat Retaliation in kind; blow for blow. [? Alte *tip for tap*]

tithe (tīth) *n.* **1.** A tax or assessment of one tenth; loos any ratable tax. **2.** In England, a tenth part of the ye proceeds arising from lands and from the personal indu of the inhabitants, for the support of the clergy and church. **3.** The tenth part of anything. **4.** A small part. *v.t.* **tithed, tith·ing 1.** To give or pay a tithe, or tenth par **2.** To tax with tithes. [ME *tithe*, OE *teogotha* tenth] **tith′a·ble** *adj.* **— tith′er** *n.*

ti·tian (tish′ən) *n.* A reddish yellow color much used by tian, esp. in painting women's hair. **—** *adj.* Having or taining to the color titian. [after *Titian*]

tit·il·late (tit′ə·lāt) *v.t.* **·lat·ed, ·lat·ing 1.** To cause a t ling sensation in. **2.** To excite pleasurably in any way. L *titillare* to tickle] **— tit′il·la′tion** *n.* **— tit′il·la′tive** a

tit·i·vate (tit′ə·vāt) *v.t. & v.i.* **·vat·ed, ·vat·ing** *Informa* put on decorative touches; dress up: also spelled *tittivate.* < TIDY, on analogy with *cultivate*] **— tit′i·va′tion** *n.*

tit·lark (tit′lärk′) *n.* A pipit. [ME *tit* little thing + *lark*]

ti·tle (tīt′l) *n.* **1.** The name of a book, play, poem, mo picture, etc. **2.** An appellation significant of office, ra etc.; esp., a designation of nobility. **3.** A characteristi descriptive name; epithet. **4.** A claim based on an ackn edged or alleged right. **5.** In some sports, a championsh **6.** The subtitle in a motion picture. **7.** *Law* The me whereby the owner of lands has the just possession of property; the union of possession, the right of possession, the right of property in lands and tenements; also, the l evidence of one's right of property, or the means by or so from which one's right to property has accrued: *title* by chase. **—** *v.t.* **·tled, ·tling** To give a name or title to; ent call. [< OF < L *titulus* label, inscription] **— ti′tled** a

title page A page containing the title of a work and names of its author and publisher.

title role The role of the character in a play, opera, or tion picture for whom it is named.

tit·mouse (tit′mous′) *n. pl.* **·mice** (-mīs′) Any of sev small birds related to the nuthatches; esp., the **tufted mouse** of the U.S., having a conspicuous crest. [Alter ME *titmuse < tit-* little + OE *mase* titmouse]

ti·trate (tī′trāt, tit′rāt) *v.i. & v.t.* **·trat·ed, ·trat·ing** *Ch* To determine the strength of (a solution) by means of sta ard solutions or by titration. [< F *titre* the fineness of g or silver alloy]

·a·tion (tī·trā′shən, ti-) *n. Chem.* The process of deter-
ning the strength or concentration of the ingredients of a
ution by adding measured amounts of a suitable reagent
:il the desired chemical reaction has been effected.
:at·toe (tit′tat·tō′) *n.* Ticktacktoe.
·er (tit′ər) *v.i.* To laugh in a suppressed way, as from
vousness or in ridicule; snicker; giggle. — *n.* The act of
ering. [Imit.] — **tit′ter·er** *n.* — **tit′ter·ing·ly** *adv.*
i·vate (tit′ə·vāt) See TITIVATE.
le (tit′l) *n.* **1.** The minutest quantity; iota. **2.** Origi-
ly, a very small mark in writing, as the dot over an *i*. **3.**
y diacritical mark. [< L *titulus* label, inscription]
le·tat·tle (tit′l·tat′l) *n.* **1.** Foolish or trivial talk; gos-
. **2.** An idle, trifling, or tattling talker. — *v.i.* **·tled, ·tling**
talk foolishly or idly; gossip. [Reduplication of TATTLE]
·lar (tich′oo·lər, tit′yə-) *adj.* **1.** Existing in name or
e only; nominal. **2.** Of, pertaining to, or like a title. **3.**
stowing or taking title. Also **tit′u·lar′y** (-ler′ē). [< L
lus title] — **tit′u·lar·ly** *adv.*
us (tī′təs) A disciple of the apostle Paul. — *n.* A book
the New Testament consisting of an epistle addressed to
us and attributed to Paul.
zy (tiz′ē) *n. pl.* **·zies** *Slang* A bewildered or excited
te of mind; a dither. [Origin unknown]
T (tē′en/tē′) *n.* **1.** Trinitrotoluene. **2.** *Informal* Any
losive and dangerous circumstance, force, or person.
:oo, *unstressed* tə) *prep.* **1.** In a direction toward or ter-
ating in: going *to* town. **2.** Opposite, in contact with, or
:r: face to face. **3.** Intending or aiming at; having as an
ect or purpose: Come *to* my rescue. **4.** Resulting in; hav-
as a condition or effect: frozen *to* death. **5.** Belonging or
d in connection with: the key *to* the door. **6.** Accompa-
d by; in rhythm with: March *to* the music. **7.** In honor
Drink *to* me only with thine eyes. **8.** In comparison, cor-
pondence, or agreement with: often denoting ratio: four
rts *to* the gallon. **9.** Approaching as a limit; until: five
utes *to* one. **10.** For the utmost duration of; as far as: a
er *to* the end of his days. **11.** In respect of; concerning:
d *to* her charms. **12.** In close application toward: Buck-
down *to* work. **13.** For; with regard for: The contest is
n *to* everyone. **14.** Noting an indirect or limiting object
:r verbs, adjectives, or nouns, and designating the recipi-
of the action: taking the place of the dative case in other
guages: Give the ring *to* me. **15.** By: known *to* the world.
. From the point of view of: It seems *to* me. **17.** About;
olved in: That's all there is *to* it. ◆ *To* also serves to in-
ate the infinitive, and is often used elliptically for it: You
y come if you care *to*. — *adv.* **1.** To or toward someng. **2.** In a direction, position, or state understood or im-
ed; esp., shut or closed: Pull the door *to*. **3.** Into a nor-
l condition; into consciousness: She soon came *to*. **4.**
ut. With head to the wind: said of a sailing vessel: to lie
5. Upon the matter at hand; into action or operation:
ey fell *to* with good will. **6.** Nearby; at hand. [OE *tō*]
l (tōd) *n.* **1.** A tailless, jumping, insectivorous amphib-
. resembling the frog but without teeth in the upper jaw,
d resorting to water only to breed. **2.** A lizard, the
rned toad. **3.** Any person regarded scornfully or con-
nptuously. [OE *tāde*]
d·fish (tōd′fish′) *n. pl.* **·fish** or **·fish·es** Any of various
hes of the Atlantic coast of the U.S., having scaleless skin,
d a mouth and head resembling those of a toad.
d·stool (tōd′stōol′) *n.* **1.** A mushroom. **2.** *Informal* A
isonous mushroom.
d·y (tō′dē) *n. pl.* **toad·ies** An obsequious flatterer; a
wning, servile person. — *v.t. & v.i.* **toad·ied, toad·y·ing**
· act the toady (to). [Short for *toadeater* an assistant to a
arlatan, who ate, or pretended to eat, toads to show the
icacy of a patent medicine] — **toad′y·ish** *adj.* — **toad′y-**
· *n.*
·and-fro (tōo′ən·frō′) *adj.* Moving back and forth.
and fro In opposite or different directions.
st¹ (tōst) *v.t.* **1.** To brown before or over a fire; esp., to
own (bread or cheese) before a fire or in a toaster. **2.** To
rm thoroughly before a fire. — *v.i.* **3.** To become warm
toasted. — *n.* Sliced bread browned in a toaster or at a
e. [< OF L *tostus*, pp. of *torrere* to parch, roast]
st² (tōst) *n.* **1.** The act of drinking to someone's health
to some sentiment. **2.** A person or sentiment named in so
inking. — *v.t.* **1.** To drink to the health of or in honor of.
v.i. **2.** To drink a toast. [< TOAST¹, in obs. sense of "a
.ced piece of toast put in a drink to flavor it"]
st·er¹ (tōs′tər) *n.* A device for making toast.
st·er² (tōs′tər) *n.* One who proposes a toast.
st·mas·ter (tōst′mas′tər, -mäs′tər) *n.* A person who, at
blic dinners, announces the toasts, calls upon the various
eakers, etc. — **toast′mis′tress** (-mis′tris) *n.fem.*
bac·co (tə·bak′ō) *n. pl.* **·cos** or **·coes** An annual plant

of the nightshade family. **2.** Its leaves prepared in various
ways, as for smoking, chewing, etc. **3.** The use of tobacco
for smoking. **4.** The various products prepared from tobacco leaves, as cigarettes, cigars, etc. [< Sp. *tabaco* < Carib, a
tube or pipe used in smoking tobacco]
to·bac·co·nist (tə·bak′ə·nist) *n.* One who sells tobacco.
To·bit (tō′bit) A pious Hebrew captive in Nineveh, hero of
the Apocryphal book of the Old Testament. — *n.* The Old
Testament book bearing his name. Also **To·bi·as** (tə·bī′əs).
to·bog·gan (tə·bog′ən) *n.* A light sledlike vehicle, consisting of a long thin board or boards curved upward at the forward end, used for transporting goods or coasting. — *v.i.*
1. To coast on a toboggan. **2.** To move downward swiftly:
Wheat prices *tobogganed*. [< dial. F (Canadian) *tabagan*
sleigh < Algonquian] — **to·bog′gan·er, to·bog′gan·ist** *n.*
to·by (tō′bē) *n. pl.* **·bies** A mug or jug for ale or beer, often
made in the form of an old man wearing a three-cornered
hat. [after *Toby*, dim. of *Tobias*, a personal name]
toc·ca·ta (tə·kä′tə, *Ital.* tōk·kä′tä) *n. Music* A free composition for a keyboard instrument, sometimes written to show
virtuosity. [< Ital., orig. pp. fem. of *toccare* to touch]
toco- *combining form* Child; pertaining to children or to
childbirth. Also, before vowels, **toc-**. [< Gk. *tokos* child]
to·coph·er·ol (tō·kof′ə·rōl, -rol) *n. Biochem.* Any of four
closely related alcohols, widely distributed in nature and
forming the active principle of vitamin E. [< TOCO- + Gk.
pherein to bear + -OL¹]
toc·sin (tok′sin) *n.* **1.** A signal sounded on a bell; alarm.
2. An alarm bell. [< MF < OF < Provençal < *tocar* to
strike, touch + *senh* bell < L *signum* sign]
to·day (tə·dā′) *adv.* **1.** On or during this present day. **2.**
At the present time; nowadays. — *n.* The present day,
time, or age. Also **to·day′**. [OE < *tō* to + *dæg* day]
tod·dle (tod′l) *v.i.* **·dled, ·dling** To walk unsteadily and with
short steps, as a little child. — *n.* The act of toddling; also,
a stroll. [Origin uncertain] — **tod′dler** *n.*
tod·dy (tod′ē) *n. pl.* **·dies 1.** A drink made with spirits, hot
water, sugar, and a slice of lemon. **2.** The sap or juice of
certain East Indian trees, the **toddy palms**. **3.** A spirituous
liquor distilled from these palms. [< Hind. *tārī* toddy (def.
2) < *tār* palm tree]
to-do (tə·dōō′) *n. Informal* Confusion or bustle; fuss. [OE
< *to-* asunder + *dōn* to do, put]
toe (tō) *n.* **1.** One of the digits of the foot. **2.** The forward
part of the foot, as distinguished from the heel. The portion
of a shoe, sock, stocking, skate, etc., that covers or corresponds in position with the toes. **3.** The lower end or projection of something, resembling or suggestive of a toe. — **on
one's toes** Alert; wide-awake. — **to tread on (someone's)
toes** To trespass on (someone's) feelings, opinions, prejudices, etc. — *v.* **toed, toe·ing** *v.t.* **1.** To touch with the toes:
to *toe* the line. **2.** To kick with the toe. **3.** To furnish with
a toe. **4.** To drive (a nail or spike) obliquely; also, to attach
(beams, etc.) end to end, by nails so driven. — *v.i.* **5.** To
stand or walk with the toes pointing in a specified direction:
to *toe* out. — **to toe the mark** (or **line**) To abide by the rules;
conform. [OE *tā*] — **toe′less** *adj.*
toed (tōd) *adj.* Having toes: chiefly in combination: *pigeon-
toed.*
toe-dance (tō′dans′, -däns′) *v.i.* **-danced, -danc·ing** To
dance on tiptoe; perform a toe dance. — **toe dancer**
toe dance A dance performed on tiptoe.
toe·hold (tō′hōld′) *n.* **1.** A small space that supports the
toes in climbing. **2.** Any means of entrance, support, etc.; a
footing: to gain a *toehold* on the island. **3.** A hold in which a
wrestler bends back the foot of his opponent.
toe·nail (tō′nāl′) *n.* **1.** A nail growing on the toe. **2.** A nail
driven obliquely to hold the foot of a stud or brace. — *v.t.*
To fasten with obliquely driven nails.
tof·fee (tôf′ē, tof′ē) *n.* Taffy. Also **tof′fy.**
tog (tog) *Informal n. pl.* Clothes; outfit. — *v.t.* **togged,
tog·ging** To dress; clothe: often with *up* or *out.* [Short for
vagabond's cant *togemans* < F < L *toga*]
to·ga (tō′gə) *n. pl.* **·gas** or **·gae** (-jē) **1.** The
distinctive outer garment worn in public by a
citizen of ancient Rome. **2.** Any gown or cloak
characteristic of a calling or profession: the lawyer's *toga*. [< L *tegere* to cover] — **to′gaed**
(-gəd) *adj.*
to·geth·er (tōō·geth′ər, tə-) *adv.* **1.** Into union
or contact with each other. **2.** In the same
place or at the same spot; with each other; in
company. **3.** At the same moment of time; simultaneously. **4.** Without cessation or intermission. **5.** With one another; mutually. [OE
< *tō* to + *gædre* together]
tog·ger·y (tog′ər·ē) *n. Informal* **1.** Togs collectively; clothes. **2.** A clothing shop.

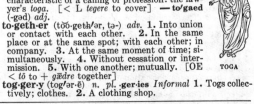

TOGA

tog·gle (tog′əl) *n.* A pin, or short rod, properly attached in the middle, as to a rope, and designed to be passed through a hole or eye and turned. — *v.t.* **·gled, ·gling** To fix, fasten, or furnish with a toggle. [Prob. var. of *tuggle*, appar. freq. of TUG]

toggle joint *Mech.* A joint having a central hinge like an elbow, and operable by applying the power at the junction, thus changing the direction of force and giving indefinite mechanical pressure.

toggle switch *Electr.* A switch in the form of a projecting lever whose movement through a small arc opens or closes an electric circuit.

toil[1] (toil) *n.* **1.** Fatiguing work; labor. **2.** Any oppressive task. **3.** Any notable work accomplished by labor. — *v.i.* **1.** To work arduously; labor painfully and tiringly. **2.** To progress or make one's way with slow and labored steps. [< AF < OF < L *tudiculare* to stir about] — **toil′er** *n.*
— **Syn.** (noun) **1.** Work, labor, drudgery.

toil[2] (toil) *n.* **1.** *Usu. pl.* Something that binds or ensnares, as a net. **2.** *Archaic* A net, snare, or other trap. [< MF < OF < L *tela* web]

toile (twäl) *n.* A sheer linen fabric; also, a fine cretonne with scenic designs printed in one color. [< F. See TOIL[2].]

toi·let (toi′lit) *n.* **1.** *U.S.* **a** A room with a washbowl, water closet, etc.: sometimes called *bathroom*. **b** A hopper flushed and discharged by means of water, into which one urinates or defecates: also called *water closet*. **2.** The act of dressing oneself; formerly, esp. of dressing the hair. **3.** Attire. — *adj.* Used in dressing or grooming: *toilet* articles. [< F *toilette* orig., cloth dressing gown, dim. of *toile* cloth]

toi·let·ry (toi′lit·rē) *n. pl.* **·ries** Any of the several articles used in making one's toilet, as soap, comb, brush, etc.

toi·lette (toi·let′, *Fr.* twà·let′) *n.* **1.** The act or process of grooming oneself, usu. including bathing, hairdressing, etc. **2.** A person's actual dress or style of dress; also, any specific costume or gown. [< F]

toilet water A scented liquid containing a small amount of alcohol, used in or after the bath, after shaving, etc.

toil·some (toil′səm) *adj.* Accomplished with fatigue; involving toil. — **toil′some·ly** *adv.* — **toil′some·ness** *n.*

toil·worn (toil′wôrn′, -wōrn′) *adj.* Exhausted by toil; showing the effects of toil.

To·kay (tō·kā′) *n.* **1.** A white or reddish blue grape. **2.** A wine made from it. [after *Tokay*, Hungary]

to·ken (tō′kən) *n.* **1.** Anything indicative of some other thing; a visible sign. **2.** A symbol: a *token* of my affection. **3.** Some tangible proof or evidence of a statement or of one's identity, etc. **4.** A memento; souvenir. **5.** A characteristic mark or feature. **6.** A piece of metal issued as currency and having a face value greater than its actual value. **7.** A piece of metal issued by a transportation company and good for one fare. — *v.t.* To evidence by a token; betoken. — *adj.* Done or given as a token, esp. in partial fulfillment of an obligation. [OE *tācen, tācn*]

told (tōld) Past tense and past participle of TELL.

To·le·do (tə·lē′dō) *n. pl.* **·dos** A sword or sword blade from Toledo, Spain. Also **to·le′do.**

tol·er·a·ble (tol′ər·ə·bəl) *adj.* **1.** Passably good; commonplace. **2.** Endurable. **3.** Allowable; permissible. **4.** *Informal* In passably good health. [< OF < L *tolerare* to endure] — **tol′er·a·ble·ness** *n.* — **tol′er·a·bly** *adv.*

tol·er·ance (tol′ər·əns) *n.* **1.** The character, state, or quality of being tolerant. **2.** Freedom from bigotry or from racial or religious prejudice. **3.** The act of enduring, or the capacity for endurance. **4.** A small permissible allowance for variations from the specified weight, dimensions, etc. **5.** *Med.* Ability to tolerate, as a drug.

tol·er·ant (tol′ər·ənt) *adj.* **1.** Disposed to tolerate beliefs, views, etc. **2.** Indulgent; liberal. **3.** *Med.* Capable of taking with impunity unusual or excessive doses of dangerous drugs. — **tol′er·ant·ly** *adv.*

tol·er·ate (tol′ə·rāt) *v.t.* **·at·ed, ·at·ing 1.** To allow to be or be done without active opposition. **2.** To concede, as the right to opinions or participation. **3.** To bear, sustain, or be capable of sustaining. **4.** *Med.* To endure, as a poisonous amount or dose, with impunity. [< L *toleratus*, pp. of *tolerare* to endure] — **tol′er·a′tive** *adj.* — **tol′er·a′tor** *n.*

tol·er·a·tion (tol′ə·rā′shən) *n.* **1.** The act or practice of tolerance. **2.** The recognition of the rights of the individual to his own opinions and customs, as in religious worship.

toll[1] (tōl) *n.* **1.** A fixed compensation for some privilege granted or service rendered, as passage on a bridge or turnpike. **2.** The right to levy such charge. **3.** Something taken or elicited like a toll; price: The train wreck took a heavy *toll* of lives. **4.** A due charged for shipping or landing goods. **5.** A charge for transportation of goods, esp. by rail or canal. **6.** A charge for a long-distance telephone call. [OE < LL < L < Gk. *telōnion* customhouse < *telos* tax]

toll[2] (tōl) *v.t.* **1.** To cause (a bell) to sound slowly and at regular intervals. **2.** To announce by tolling, as a death or funeral. **3.** To call or summon by tolling. **4.** To decoy

(game, esp. ducks). — *v.i.* **5.** To sound slowly and at re lar intervals. — *n.* The act or sound of tolling a bell. [*tollen, tullen*]

toll·bar (tōl′bär′) *n.* A tollgate, esp. one with a single

toll bridge A bridge at which a toll is charged for pass

toll call A long-distance telephone call, the charge for wl is higher than local rates.

toll collector A collector of tolls.

toll·er (tōl′ər) *n.* **1.** One who tolls a bell. **2.** A bell used tolling. **3.** A small dog trained to toll or decoy ducks.

toll·gate (tōl′gāt′) *n.* A gate at the entrance to a bridge on a road, at which toll is paid.

toll·house (tōl′hous′) *n.* A toll collector's lodge adjoini tollgate: also **toll′booth′** (-bō̄ōth′, -bō̄ōth̸′).

toll·keep·er (tōl′kē′pər) *n.* One who keeps a tollgate.

toll line A long-distance telephone line or channel for use of which a toll is charged.

toll road A road on which a toll is charged for each veh using it. Also **toll·way** (tōl′wā′).

Tol·tec (tol′tek, tōl′-) *n.* One of certain ancient Nahua tribes that dominated central and southern Mexico at A.D. 900–1100 and through contact with Mayan cul founded the highly civilized Nahua culture of the Aztecs. *adj.* Of or pertaining to the Toltecs. [< Nahuatl *Tolt* — **Tol′tec·an** *adj.*

tol·u·ene (tol′yŏō·ēn) *n. Chem.* A colorless, flammable uid hydrocarbon, $C_6H_5CH_3$, obtained from coal tar by tillation and used in making dyestuffs, explosives, etc.

tom (tom) *n.* The male of various animals, esp. the [after *Tom*, a personal name. See TOMCAT.]

tom·a·hawk (tom′ə·hôk) *n.* **1.** An axlike weapon used North American Indians, originally a carved club in whi piece of bone or metal was inserted. **2.** Any similar wea tool, etc. — *v.t.* To strike or kill with a tomahawk. [< gonquian < *tamahaken* he uses for cutting]

tom·al·ley (tom′al·ē) *n.* The liver of the lobster, con ered a delicacy. [Prob. < Carib]

Tom and Jer·ry (tom′ ən jer′ē) A drink made with bra rum, beaten egg, hot milk or water, sugar, and nutn [after two main characters in *Life in London*, 1821, Pierce Egan, 1772–1849]

to·ma·to (tə·mā′tō, -mä′-) *n. pl.* **·toes 1.** The large, pu edible berry, yellow or red when ripe, of a perennial plan the nightshade family, widely cultivated as a vegetable. The plant itself. **3.** *U.S. Slang* A girl or woman. [< < Nahuatl *tomatl*]

tomb (tōōm) *n.* **1.** A place for the burial of the dead, vault or grave. **2.** Any place or structure serving as a 1 repository for the dead. **3.** A monument, tombstone, commemorating the dead. **4.** Death: often preceded by [< AF *tumbe*, OF *tombe* < LL < Gk. *tymbos* mound]

tom·boy (tom′boi′) *n.* A girl who prefers boyish activi dress, etc. — **tom′boy·ish** *adj.* — **tom′boy·ish·ness** *n.*

tomb·stone (tōōm′stōn′) *n.* A stone, usu. inscribed, m ing a place of burial.

tom·cat (tom′kat′) *n.* A male cat. [after *Tom*, a male hero of *The Life and Adventures of a Cat*, 1760]

Tom Col·lins (tom kol′inz) A drink consisting of gin, le or lime juice, sugar, and carbonated water.

Tom, Dick, and Har·ry (dik; har′ē) Any persons take random from the general public: used disparagingly, often preceded by *every*.

tome (tōm) *n.* **1.** A volume; large book. **2.** One of a se of volumes. [< MF < L < Gk. *tomos* fragment]

-tome *combining form* A cutting instrument (of a speci kind). [< Gk. *tomos* a cutting < *temnein* to cut]

tom·fool (tom′fōōl′) *n.* An idiotic or silly person. — Very stupid or foolish. [after *Tom Fool*, a name form applied to mental defectives]

tom·fool·er·y (tom′fōō′lər·ē) *n. pl.* **·er·ies 1.** Nonsens or foolish behavior. **2.** Worthless or trivial stuff; fripp Also **tom′fool′ish·ness** (-fōō′lish·nis).

tom·my (tom′ē) *n. pl.* **·mies** *Brit. Informal* Often cap British soldier.

Tommy gun A Thompson submachine gun.

tom·my·rot (tom′ē·rot′) *n. Informal* Utter nonsense.

to·mor·row (tə·môr′ō, -mor′ō) *adv.* On or for the next after today. — *n.* **1.** The next day after today; the n row. **2.** Some time in the future. Also **to-mor′row.** [M OE < *tō* to + *morgen* morning, morrow]

tom·pi·on (tom′pē·ən) See TAMPION.

Tom Thumb 1. In English folklore, a hero who was no l ger than his father's thumb. **2.** A tiny person.

tom·tit (tom′tit′) *n.* Any of various small birds, as a chic dee or a wren. [< TOM + TIT[1]]

tom-tom (tom′tom′) *n.* A drum of India, Africa, etc., v ously shaped and usu. beaten with the hands. [< H *tamtam*, imit. of the instrument's sound]

-tomy *combining form* **1.** *Surg.* A cutting of a (specif part or tissue. **2.** A (specified) kind of cutting or divis *dichotomy*. [< Gk. *tomē* a cutting < *temnein* to cut]

ۀ (tun) *n.* **1.** Any of several large measures of weight; esp.: The **short ton** of 2000 pounds avoirdupois, commonly used in the U.S. and Canada. **b** The **long** or **gross ton** of 2240 pounds, used in Great Britain. See table front of book. **2.** A unit for reckoning the displacement or weight of vessels, 35 cubic feet of sea water weighing about one long ton: called in full a **displacement ton**. **3.** A unit for reckoning the freight-carrying capacity of a ship, usu. equivalent to 40 cubic feet of space but varying with the cargo: called in full a **freight ton** or **measurement ton**. **4.** A unit for reckoning the internal capacity of merchant vessels for purposes of registration, equivalent to 100 cubic feet or 2.8317 cubic meters: called in full a **register ton**. **5.** A metric ton. Var. of TUN]

ton- Var. of TONO-.

-ton *suffix* Town: used in place names: *Charleston*. [OE < *tūn*]

to·nal (tō′nəl) *adj.* Of or pertaining to tone or tonality. — **to′nal·ly** *adv.*

to·nal·i·ty (tō-nal′ə-tē) *n. pl.* **·ties** **1.** *Music* **a** The use of a system of tones so that one tone is the central or primary tone of the system. **b** Any particular arrangement of this type centering on a specific tone; key; mode. **2.** The general color or scheme or collective tones of a painting.

tone (tōn) *n.* **1.** Sound in relation to quality, volume, duration, and pitch. **2.** A sound having a definite pitch. **3.** *Music* **a** The timbre, or characteristic sound, of a voice, instrument, etc. **b** The interval between the first two degrees of a major scale: also called *whole tone*. **4.** A predominating disposition; mood. **5.** Characteristic style or tendency; tenor. **6.** Style or distinction; elegance. **7.** Vocal inflection as expressive of feeling: a *tone* of pity. **8.** *Phonet.* **a** The accentual pitch, or change in pitch, of a phrase or sentence. **b** The special stress or pitch accent given to a syllable or word. **9.** The prevailing impression of a picture, produced by effects of light and shadow, variations in color quality, etc. **10.** A shade, hue, tint, or degree of a particular color, or some slight modification of it: red with a purplish *tone*. **11.** *Physiol.* **a** The general condition of the body with reference to the vigorous and healthy discharge of its functions. **b** Firmness and resilience, as of a tissue. — **Syn.** See SOUND¹. — *v.* **toned, ton·ing** *v.t.* **1.** To give tone to. **2.** To modify in tone. **3.** To alter the color or increase the brilliancy of (a photographic print) by a chemical bath. **4.** *Rare* To intone. — *v.i.* **5.** To assume a certain tone or hue. **6.** To blend or harmonize, as in tone or shade. — **to tone down** **1.** To subdue the tone of (a painting). **2.** To moderate in quality or tone. — **to tone up** **1.** To raise in quality or strength. **2.** To gain in vitality. [< OF < L < Gk. *teinein* to stretch]

tone color The timbre of a voice, musical instrument, etc.

tone-deaf (tōn′def′) *adj.* Unable to perceive fine distinctions in pitch, as musical intervals. — **tone′deaf′ness** *n.*

tone·less (tōn′lis) *adj.* **1.** Having no tone; without tone. Lacking spirit or vivacity; listless. — **tone′less·ly** *adv.* — **tone′less·ness** *n.*

tong¹ (tông, tong) *v.t.* **1.** To gather, collect, or seize with tongs. — *v.i.* **2.** To use tongs, as for fishing. [< TONGS]

tong² (tông, tong) *n.* A Chinese secret society or fraternal association; esp., such a group formerly active in the U.S. [< Chinese *t'ang* hall, meeting place]

Ton·ga (tong′gə) *n.* A Polynesian language spoken in the Tonga Islands.

tongs (tôngz, tongz) *n.pl.* (*sometimes construed as sing.*) An implement for grasping, holding, or lifting objects, consisting usu. of a pair of pivoted levers: sometimes called a **pair of tongs**. [OE *tang, tange*]

tongue (tung) *n.* **1.** A protrusile, freely moving organ situated in the mouth of most vertebrates, highly developed in mammals, where it serves as an organ of taste, and in man also as an organ of speech. ◆ Collateral adjective: *lingual*. For illus. see THROAT. **2.** *Zool.* An analogous organ or part in the mouth of various insects, fishes, etc. **3.** An animal's tongue, as of beef, prepared as food. **4.** The power of speech or articulation: to lose one's *tongue*. **5.** Manner or style of speaking: a smooth *tongue*. **6.** Mere speech, as contrasted with fact or deed. **7.** Utterance. **8.** A language, vernacular, or dialect. **9.** *Archaic* A people or race, regarded as having its own language: a Biblical use. **10.** Anything resembling an animal tongue in shape or function. **11.** A slender projection of land, as a cape or small promontory. **12.** A long narrow bay or inlet of water. **13.** A jet of flame. **14.** A strip of leather for closing the gap in the front of a shoe. **15.** *Music* The free or vibrating end of a reed in a wind instrument. **16.** The clapper of a bell. **17.** The harnessing pole of a horse-drawn vehicle. **18.** Any flange or projecting part of a machine or mechanical device. **19.** A projecting edge or tenon on a board for insertion into a corresponding groove of another board, thus forming a **tongue-and-groove joint. — on the tip of one's tongue** On the verge of being recalled. — **to**

hold one's tongue To keep silent. — **(with) tongue in cheek** With ironical or facetious intent. — *v.* **tongued, tongu·ing** *v.t.* **1.** *Music* In wind-instrument playing: **a** To separate the tones played on (an instrument) by means of the tongue. **b** To begin (a tone) using the tongue. **c** To tongue the notes of (a phrase, etc.). **2.** To touch or lap with the tongue. **3.** In carpentry: **a** To cut a tongue on (a board). **b** To join or fit by a tongue-and-groove joint. **4.** *Poetic* To utter; articulate. — *v.i.* **5.** To use the tongue in playing a wind instrument. **6.** To talk or prattle. **7.** To extend as a tongue. [OE *tunge*]

tongued (tungd) *adj.* **1.** Having a tongue or tongues. **2.** Having or characterized by a (specified kind of) tongue or (a specified number of) tongues: *sharp-tongued*.

tongue-lash·ing (tung′lash′ing) *n. Informal* A severe or thoroughgoing reprimand; scolding.

tongue·less (tung′lis) *adj.* **1.** Having no tongue. **2.** Speechless; dumb.

tongue-tie (tung′tī′) *n.* Abnormal shortness of the frenum of the tongue, whereby its motion is impeded or confined. — *v.t.* **-tied, -ty·ing** To deprive of speech or the power of speech, or of distinct articulation.

tongue-tied (tung′tīd′) *adj.* **1.** Speechless or halting in speech, as from shyness, etc. **2.** Impeded by tongue-tie.

tongue twister A word or phrase difficult to articulate quickly, as "Miss Smith's fish-sauce shop."

ton·ic (ton′ik) *adj.* **1.** Having power to invigorate or build up; bracing. **2.** Pertaining to tone or tones. **3.** *Music* Pertaining to or in the key of the keynote. **4.** In art, denoting the general effect of color or of light and shade. **5.** *Physiol.* **a** Of or pertaining to tension, especially muscular tension. **b** Rigid; unrelaxing: *tonic* spasm. **6.** *Phonet.* Stressed, as a syllable. — *n.* **1.** A medicine that gradually restores the normal tone of organs from a condition of debility. **2.** Something imparting animation, vigor, or tone. **3.** *Music* The basic tone of a key or mode. **4.** Quinine water: gin and *tonic*. **5.** *U.S.* In the Boston area, soda (def. 2). [< Gk. < *tonos* sound, tone]

tonic accent An accent that is spoken or pronounced rather than written.

to·nic·i·ty (tō-nis′ə-tē) *n.* The resilience and elasticity of healthy muscles, arteries, and other bodily tissues.

tonic sol-fa A system of musical notation that uses the initial letters of the solmization syllables to indicate pitch, and dots and lines to indicate rhythm.

to·night (tə-nīt′) *adv.* In or during the present or coming night. — *n.* **1.** The night that follows this day. **2.** The present night. Also **to-night**′. [OE < *tō* + *niht* night]

ton·nage (tun′ij) *n.* **1.** The cubic capacity of a merchant vessel expressed in tons of 100 cubic feet each. **2.** The total carrying capacity of a collection of vessels, esp. of a country's merchant marine. **3.** A tax levied on vessels at a given rate per ton. **4.** Total weight in tons, as of materials produced, mined, or transported.

ton·neau (tu-nō′) *n. pl.* **·neaus** (-nōz′) or **·neaux** (-nōz′) The rear part of an early type of automobile or vehicle, with seats enclosed by low sides. [< F, lit., barrel]

tono- *combining form* **1.** Tension; pressure. **2.** *Music* Tone; pitch. Also, before vowels, **ton-**. [< Gk. *tonos* tension < *teinein* to stretch]

ton·sil (ton′səl) *n. Anat.* One of two oval lymphoid organs situated on either side of the passage from the mouth to the pharynx. For illus. see THROAT. [< L *tonsillae* tonsils] — **ton′sil·lar** or **ton′sil·ar** *adj.*

ton·sil·lec·to·my (ton′sə-lek′tə-mē) *n. pl.* **·mies** *Surg.* Removal of a tonsil or tonsils.

ton·sil·li·tis (ton′sə-lī′tis) *n. Pathol.* Inflammation of the tonsils. — **ton′sil·lit′ic** (-lit′ik) *adj.*

ton·so·ri·al (ton-sôr′ē-əl, sō′rē-) *adj.* Pertaining to a barber or barbering: chiefly in the humorous term **tonsorial artist**, a barber. [< L < *tonsus*, pp. of *tondere* to clip]

ton·sure (ton′shər) *n.* **1.** The shaving of the head, or of the crown of the head, as of a priest or monk. **2.** The state of being thus shaven. **3.** The part of a priest's or monk's head left bare by shaving. — *v.t.* **·sured, ·sur·ing** To shave the head of. [< OF < L. See TONSORIAL.]

ton·tine (ton′tēn, ton-tēn′) *n.* A form of collective life annuity, the individual profits of which increase as the number of survivors diminishes, the final survivor taking the whole. [< F, after Lorenzo *Tonti*, a Neapolitan banker who introduced it into France in about 1653]

ton·y (tō′nē) *adj.* **ton·i·er, ton·i·est** *Informal* High toned; fashionable; stylish. [< TONE (def. 6)]

too (tōō) *adv.* **1.** In addition; likewise; also. **2.** In excessive quantity or degree; more than sufficiently. **3.** *Informal* Very; extremely: That's not too likely. **4.** *Informal* Indeed: an intensive, often used to reiterate a contradicted statement: You are *too* going! [Stressed var. of OE *tō* to]

took (tŏŏk) Past tense of TAKE.

tool (tōōl) *n.* **1.** A simple mechanism or implement, as a hammer, saw, spade, or chisel, used chiefly in manual work. **2.** A power-driven apparatus, as a lathe, used for cutting and shaping the parts of a machine. **3.** The cutting or shaping part of such an apparatus. **4.** A bookbinder's hand stamp used in lettering or ornamenting book covers. **5.** A person used to carry out the designs of others or another; a dupe. **6.** Any instrument or means necessary to the efficient prosecution of one's profession or trade: Words are the writer's *tools.* — *v.t.* **1.** To shape, mark, or ornament with a tool. **2.** To provide with tools. **3.** To ornament or impress designs upon (leather, a book binding, etc.) with a roller bearing a pattern. — *v.i.* **4.** To work with a tool or tools. [OE *tōl*] — **tool′er** *n.*

tool·ing (tōō′ling) *n.* **1.** Ornamentation or work done with tools; esp., stamped or gilded ornamental designs on leather. **2.** The application of a tool or tools to any work.

tool·mak·er (tōōl′mā′kər) *n.* A maker of tools.

toot (tōōt) *v.i.* **1.** To blow a horn, whistle, etc., esp. with short blasts. **2.** To give forth a blast or toot, as a horn. **3.** To make a similar sound. — *v.t.* **4.** To sound (a horn, etc.) with short blasts. **5.** To sound (a blast, etc.). — *n.* **1.** A short note or blast on or as on a horn. **2.** *Slang* A spree; esp., a drinking spree. [? < MLG *tüten*; prob. orig. imit.] — **toot′er** *n.*

tooth (tōōth) *n. pl.* **teeth** (tēth) **1.** One of the hard structures in the mouth of most vertebrates, used for seizing and chewing food, as offensive and defensive weapons, etc. ◆ Collateral adjective: *dental.* **2.** One of various hard calcareous or chitinous bodies of the oral or gastric regions of invertebrates. **3.** Any small toothlike projection, as at the edge of a leaf. **4.** Something resembling a tooth in form or use; esp., a projecting point, tine, or cog, as on a saw, comb, fork, rake, or gearwheel. **5.** Appetite; liking: used chiefly in the expression *sweet tooth.* **6.** *pl.* Something that opposes in or as in a gnawing, biting, or piercing manner: the *teeth* of the wind. — **armed to the teeth** Completely or heavily armed. — **in the teeth of** Directly against, counter to, or in defiance of. — **to get one's teeth into** To achieve a solid grip or grasp of; engage completely with. — **to show one's teeth** To display a disposition to fight; threaten. — **to throw** (**cast, fling,** etc.) (**something**) **in one's teeth** To fling at one, as a challenge or taunt. — *v.t.* **1.** To supply with teeth, as a rake or saw. **2.** To give a serrated edge to; indent. — *v.i.* **3.** To become interlocked, as gear wheels. [OE *tōth*]

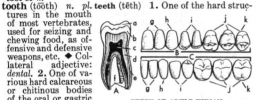

TEETH OF ADULT HUMAN

A Section of a molar: *a* Crown, *b* Enamel, *c* Pulp cavity, *d* Dentine, *e* Cementum, *f* Roots.

B and *C* Left upper and lower jaws: *g* Incisors, *h* Canines, *i* Bicuspids, *j* Molars, *k* Wisdom teeth.

tooth·ache (tōōth′āk′) *n.* Pain in a tooth or teeth.

tooth and nail With all possible strength and effort; fiercely: to fight *tooth and nail.*

tooth·brush (tōōth′brush′) *n.* A small brush used for cleaning the teeth.

toothed (tōōtht, tōōthd) *adj.* **1.** Having teeth. **2.** Having or characterized by a (specified kind or number of) teeth: used in combination: *sharp-toothed.* **3.** Notched or indented.

tooth·less (tōōth′lis) *adj.* **1.** Being without teeth. **2.** Lacking effective power or force; ineffectual. — **tooth′less·ly** *adv.*

tooth·paste (tōōth′pāst′) *n.* A paste used to clean teeth.

tooth·pick (tōōth′pik′) *n.* A small sliver of wood, plastic, etc., used for removing particles of food from between the teeth.

tooth·pow·der (tōōth′pou′dər) *n.* A powder used in cleaning the teeth.

tooth·some (tōōth′səm) *adj.* **1.** Having a pleasant taste. **2.** Appetizing; attractive. — **tooth′some·ly** *adv.* — **tooth′some·ness** *n.*

tooth·y (tōō′thē) *adj.* **tooth·i·er, tooth·i·est 1.** Having large or prominent teeth. **2.** Displaying the teeth: a *toothy* smile.

too·tle (tōōt′l) *v.t. & v.i.* **·tled, ·tling** To toot lightly or continuously, as on the flute. — *n.* The act or sound of tootling. [Freq. of TOOT]

top¹ (top) *n.* **1.** The uppermost or highest part, end, side, or surface of anything. **2.** The end or part regarded as the higher or upper extremity: the *top* of the street. **3.** A lid or cover: a bottle *top.* **4.** *U.S.* The roof of a vehicle, as an automobile. **5.** The crown of the head: from *top* to toe. **6.** *pl.* The aboveground part of a plant producing root vegetables. **7.** The highest degree or range: the *top* of one's ambition. **8.** The highest or most prominent place or rank. **9.** One who is highest in rank or position. **10.** The highest or loudest pitch: at the *top* of his voice. **11.** The choicest or best part: the *top* of the crop. **12.** In bridge, etc., the high card in a suit. **13.** In tennis, golf, etc.: **a** A stroke in wh the player hits the ball above the center or on the upper h **b** The forward spinning motion thus imparted to the b **14.** *Naut.* A platform at the head of the lower section ship's mast, used as a place to stand and for extending topmast rigging. — **to blow one's top** *Slang* **1.** To br out in a rage; flare up. **2.** To go insane. — **on top 1.** the highest point or position. **2.** In a situation of domina or power. **3.** Highly successful. — **on top of 1.** On highest point or upper surface of. **2.** In addition to; as a max to. — **over the top 1.** In trench warfare, over breastwork, as in an attack. **2.** Beyond a set goal, qu etc. — *adj.* **1.** Of or pertaining to the top. **2.** Formin comprising the top or upper part. **3.** Highest in rank quality; chief: *top* authors. **4.** Greatest in amount or gree: *top* prices. — *v.* **topped, top·ping** *v.t.* **1.** To rem the top or upper end of. **2.** To provide with a top, cap, **3.** To form the top of. **4.** To reach or pass over the top surmount. **5.** To surpass or exceed. **6.** In golf, tennis, e to hit the upper part of (the ball) in making a stroke. — **7.** To top someone or something. — **to top off 1.** something on the top of. **2.** To complete or finish with nal or crowning touch. [OE]

top² (top) *n.* A toy with a point on which it is made to s as by the unwinding of a string, spring, etc. [OE]

top- Var. of TOPO-.

to·paz (tō′paz) *n.* **1.** A native silicate of aluminum, occ ring in prismatic crystals of various colors, but chiefly low to brownish, that are valued as gemstones. **2.** A ye variety of sapphire. Also **Oriental topaz. 3.** A brownis grayish yellow. [< OF < L < Gk. *topazos*]

top boot A boot with a high top that is sometimes borde or decorated with material different from the rest of the b

top·coat (top′kōt′) *n.* A lightweight overcoat.

top dog *Informal* The leading or dominant individua group; the head; chief. — **top-dog** (top′dôg′, -dog′) *ad*

top-draw·er (top′drôr′) *adj. Informal* Of the highest sta ing, merit, excellence, etc.

top-dress (top′dres′) *v.t. Agric.* To apply top-dressing

top-dress·ing (top′dres′ing) *n.* A dressing of man spread over the surface of a field. Also **top′dress′ing, dressing.**

tope (tōp) *v.t.* **toped, top·ing** To drink (alcoholic bevera excessively and frequently. [? Akin to earlier *top* to ti

top·er (tō′pər) *n.* A habitual drunkard; sot. [< TOPE]

top·flight (top′flīt′) *adj.* Of the highest quality; super

top gal·lant (tə·gal′ənt, top′gal′ənt) *n. Naut.* **1.** mast, sail, yard, or rigging immediately above the topm and topsail. **2.** The parts of a deck that are higher than rest. — *adj.* Pertaining to the topgallants. [< TOP GALLANT; with ref. to "making a gallant show" compa with the lower tops]

top hat A man's hat, usu. made of silk, having a tall, cy drical crown and a narrow brim: also called *high hat.*

top-heav·y (top′hev′ē) *adj.* **-heav·i·er, -heav·i·est 1.** H ing the top or upper part too heavy for the lower part; proportioned or precariously balanced. **2.** In finance, o capitalized. — **top′-heav′i·ly** *adv.* — **top′-heav′i·ness**

to·pi (tō·pē′) *n.* A helmet made of pith, worn as protec against the sun: also called *pith helmet.* [< Hind., hat]

top·ic (top′ik) *n.* **1.** A subject of discourse or of a trea **2.** Any matter treated of in speech or writing; a theme discussion. **3.** A subdivision of an outline or a treatise. L < Gk. (*ta*) *topika,* title of a work by Aristotle, neut. p *topikos* of a place < *topos* place, commonplace]

top·i·cal (top′i·kəl) *adj.* **1.** Pertaining to a topic. **2.** Of nature of merely probable argument. **3.** Belonging t place or spot; local. **4.** Pertaining to matters of present terest: a *topical* song. **5.** *Med.* Local. — **top′i·cal·ly**

top kick *Slang* A top sergeant.

top·knot (top′not′) *n.* **1.** A crest, tuft, or knot on the of the head, as of feathers on the head of a bird. **2.** The of the human head when worn as a high knot.

top·less (top′lis) *adj.* **1.** Lacking a top. **2.** Having no the waist, or designed to include such nudity, as a bat suit. — **top′less·ness** *n.*

top·loft·y (top′lôf′tē, -lof′tē) *adj.* **·loft·i·er, ·loft·i·est** Towering very high. **2.** Very proud or haughty; infla pompous. — **top′loft′i·ly** *adv.* — **top′loft′i·ness** *n.*

top·mast (top′məst, top′mast′, mäst′) *n. Naut.* The n next above the lower mast.

top·most (top′mōst′) *adj.* Being at the very top.

top notch (top′noch′) *adj. Informal* Excellent; best.

topo- combining form A place or region; regional. Also, fore vowels, **top-.** [< Gk. *topos* place]

to·pog·ra·pher (tə·pog′rə·fər) *n.* An expert in topogra

to·pog·ra·phy (tə·pog′rə·fē) *n. pl.* **·phies 1.** The deta description of places. **2.** The art of representing on a the physical features of a place. **3.** The physical featu collectively, of a region. **4.** Surveying with reference to

hysical features of a region. **—top·o·graph·ic** (top′ə·graf′·
:) or **·i·cal** adj. **—top′o·graph′i·cal·ly** adv.
p·per (top′ər) n. **1.** One who or that which cuts off the
ɔp of something. **2.** Slang One who or that which is of su-
reme quality. **3.** Slang A top hat. **4.** A woman's short,
su. lightweight, coat.
p·ping (top′ing) adj. Brit. Informal Excellent; first rate.
— n. **1.** That which forms the top of anything. **2.** A sauce,
arnish, etc., put on a cake, portion of food, etc.
p·ple (top′əl) v. **·pled, ·pling** v.t. **1.** To push and cause to
ɔtter or fall by its own weight; overturn. **—** v.i. **2.** To tot-
r and fall, as by its own weight. **3.** To lean or jut out, as
about to fall. [Freq. of TOP¹, v.]
ps (tops) adj. Slang Excellent; first-rate.
p·sail (top′səl, top′sāl′) n. Naut. **1.** In a square-rigged
ɔssel, a square sail set next above the lowest sail of a mast.
. In a fore-and-aft-rigged vessel, a square or triangular sail
arried above the gaff of a lower sail.
p·se·cret (top′sē′krit) adj. U.S. Mil. Denoting the high-
t category of security classification. Compare SECRET.
p sergeant Informal The first sergeant of a company,
attery, or troop.
p·side (top′sīd′) n. Naut. The portion of a ship above the
ain deck. **—** adv. To or on the upper parts of a ship.
p·soil (top′soil′) n. The surface soil of land.
p·sy-tur·vy (top′sē·tûr′vē) adv. **1.** Upside-down; hind
de before. **2.** In utter confusion. **—** adj. **1.** Being in an
ɔset or disordered condition. **2.** Upside-down. **—** n. A
ate of confusion; disorder; chaos. [Prob. < TOP¹ + obs.
rve to turn, overturn] **—top′sy·tur′vi·ly** adv. **—top′sy-**
,r′vi·ness n. **—top′sy·tur′vy·dom** (-dəm) n.
[u]e (tōk) n. A close-fitting, brimless hat worn by women.
< F, cap < Sp. < Basque tauka, a kind of cap]
rah (tôr′ə, tō′rə) n. In Hebrew literature, a law; also,
ɔunsel or instruction proceeding from a specially sacred
ɔurce. Also **to′ra.** [< Hebrew tōrāh instruction, law]
·rah (tôr′ə, tō′rə) n. In Judaism, the Pentateuch: also
ɔlled the Law.
rch (tôrch) n. **1.** A source of light, as from flaming pine
1ots, or from some material dipped in tallow, etc., and
xed at the end of a handle. **2.** Anything that illuminates:
ɛ torch of science. **3.** A portable device giving off an in-
1nsely hot flame and used for burning off paint, melting
ɔlder, etc. **4.** Brit. A flashlight. **—to carry a** (or **the**)
rch **for** Slang To continue to love (someone), though the
ve is unrequited. [< OF torche, ult. < torquere to twist]
·ch·bear·er (tôrch′bâr′ər) n. **1.** One who carries a torch.
. One who imparts knowledge, truth, etc.
·chère (tôr·shâr′) n. A tall lamp giving light directed up-
ard by a bowllike shade. [< F, candelabrum]
·ch·light (tôrch′līt′) n. The light of a torch or torches.
— adj. Lighted by torches: a torchlight rally.
rch song A popular love song expressing sadness and
ɔpeless yearning. [< phrase to carry a torch for]
·e (tôr, tōr) Past tense of TEAR¹.
·e·a·dor (tôr′ē·ə·dôr′, Sp. tō′rä·ä·thôr′) n. A bullfighter.
< Sp. < torear to fight bulls < L taurus bull]
ri·i (tôr′ī·ē, tō′ri·ē) n. The gateway of a Shinto temple,
1nsisting of two uprights with one straight crosspiece, and
1other above with a concave lintel. [< Japanese]
·ment (n. tôr′ment; v. tôr·ment′) n. **1.** Intense bodily
ain or mental anguish; agony; torture. **2.** One who or that
hich torments. **—** v.t. **1.** To subject to excruciating physi-
l or mental suffering. **2.** To make miserable. **3.** To
ɔrass. [< OF < L tormentum rack < torquere to twist]
—tor·ment′er, tor·men′tor n. **—tor·ment′ing·ly** adv.
·n (tôrn, tōrn) Past participle of TEAR¹.
·na·do (tôr·nā′dō) n. pl. **·does** or **·dos** Meteorol. **1.** A
hirling wind of exceptional violence, accompanied by a pen-
ulous, funnel-shaped cloud marking the narrow path of
ɛatest destruction. **2.** Any whirlwind or hurricane. [Prob.
ter. of Sp. tronada thunderstorm < L tonare to thunder]
—tor·nad′ic (-nad′ik) adj.
·pe·do (tôr·pē′dō) n. pl. **·dos** or **·does** **1.** A device or
ɔparatus containing an explosive to be fired by concussion
' otherwise. **2.** An explosive, self-propelled, cigar-shaped
1derwater projectile, used to destroy enemy ships. **3.** A
1bmarine mine. **4.** The electric ray, a fish. **—** v.t. **·doed,**
o·ing To sink, damage, or wreck with or as with a torpedo.
< L, numbness < torpere to be numb]
·pedo boat A small, swift war vessel equipped with tubes
ɔr the discharge of torpedoes.
·pid (tôr′pid) adj. **1.** Inactive, as a hibernating animal.
. Dormant; numb. **3.** Sluggish; apathetic; dull. [< L
ɔrpere to be numb] **—tor·pid·i·ty** (tôr·pid′ə·tē), **tor′pid·**
ɛss n. **—tor′pid·ly** adv.
·por (tôr′pər) n. **1.** Complete or partial insensibility; stu-
ɔr. **2.** Apathy; torpidity. **—tor′po·rif′ic** adj.

torque (tôrk) n. Mech. Anything that causes or tends to
cause torsion in a body; the rotary force in a mechanism.
[< L torquere to twist]
tor·rent (tôr′ənt, tor′-) n. **1.** A stream, as of water, flowing
with great velocity or turbulence. **2.** Any abundant or tumultuous flow: a torrent of abuse. [< OF < L torrens, boiling, burning, ppr. of torrere to parch]
tor·ren·tial (tō·ren′shəl, to-) adj. **1.** Of, resembling, or resulting from the action of a torrent. **2.** Suggestive of a torrent; overpowering. **—tor·ren′tial·ly** adv.
tor·rid (tôr′id, tor′-) adj. **1.** Exposed to or receiving the
full force of the sun's heat. **2.** Very hot; scorching; burning.
3. Impassioned; ardent. [< L < torrere to parch] **—tor·**
rid·i·ty (tô·rid/ə·tē, to-), **tor′rid·ness** n. **—tor′rid·ly** adv.
tor·sion (tôr′shən) n. **1.** The act of twisting, or the state of
being twisted. **2.** Mech. Deformation of a body, as a thread
or rod, by twisting around its length as an axis. **3.** The
force with which a twisted cord or cable tends to return to
its former position. [< OF < L.L < torquere to twist]
—tor′sion·al adj. **—tor′sion·al·ly** adv.
tor·so (tôr′sō) n. pl. **·sos** or **·si** (-sē) **1.** The trunk of a human body. **2.** A sculptured representation of a human body
without the head or limbs. **3.** Any truncated or defective
thing. [< Ital. < L < Gk. thyrsos stalk]
tort (tôrt) n. Law Any private or civil wrong by act or
omission for which a civil suit can be brought, but not including breach of contract. [See TORSION.]
torte (tôrt, Ger. tôr′tə) n. A rich cake made with butter,
eggs, and often fruit and nuts. [< G < Ital. torta]
tor·til·la (tôr·tē′yä) n. In Mexico, a flat cake made of coarse
cornmeal baked on a hot sheet of iron or a slab of stone. [<
Sp., dim. of torta cake < LL < L torquere to twist]
tor·toise (tôr′təs) n. **1.** A turtle; esp., one of a terrestrial
species as distinguished from those that are aquatic. **2.** A
slow-moving person or thing. [< Med.L tortuca, ? < L tortus twisted; so called from its crooked feet]
tor·toise-shell (tôr′təs·shel′) adj. Made of or variegated
like tortoise shell. Also **tor′toise·shell′.**
tortoise shell The shell of a marine turtle, consisting of a
mottled, brownish, hornlike substance used for combs, etc.
tor·tu·ous (tôr′chŏŏ·əs) adj. **1.** Consisting of or abounding
in irregular bends or turns; twisting. **2.** Not straightforward; devious. **3.** Morally twisted or warped. [< AF <
L torquere to twist] **—tor′tu·os′i·ty** (-os′ə·tē) n. **—tor′tu·**
ous·ly adv. **—tor′tu·ous·ness** n.
tor·ture (tôr′chər) n. **1.** Infliction of or subjection to extreme physical pain. **2.** Great mental suffering; agony. **3.**
Something that causes severe pain. **—** v.t. **·tured, ·tur·ing**
1. To inflict extreme pain upon, as from cruelty. **2.** To
subject to judicial torture. **3.** To cause to suffer agony, extreme discomfort, etc. **4.** To twist or turn into an abnormal
form, meaning, etc. [< OF < L torquere to twist] **—tor′·**
tur·er n. **—tor′tur·ous** adj.
to·rus (tôr′əs, tō′rəs) n. pl. **to·ri** (tôr′ī, tō′rī) **1.** Archit. A
large convex molding used in bases as the lowest molding, or
in columns above the plinth. **2.** Bot. The swollen end of a
flower-stalk that bears the floral leaves. **3.** Geom. A solid
figure usu. resembling a doughnut. [< L, lit., a swelling]
To·ry (tôr′ē, tō′rē) n. pl. **·ries** **1.** A member of an English
political party, successor to the Cavaliers and opponent of
the Whigs, since about 1832 called the Conservative Party.
2. One who at the period of the American Revolution adhered to the cause of British sovereignty over the colonies.
3. One having very conservative beliefs, esp. in politics.
Also **to′ry.** [< Irish tóir to pursue] **—To′ry·ism** n.
toss (tôs, tos) v.t. **1.** To throw, pitch, or fling about. **2.** To
agitate; disturb. **3.** To throw with the hand, esp. with the
palm of the hand upward. **4.** To lift with a quick motion,
as the head. **5.** Informal To toss up with: I'll toss you to see
who pays. **—** v.i. **6.** To be flung to and fro, as a ship in a
storm. **7.** To throw oneself from side to side restlessly, as in
sleep. **8.** To go quickly or angrily, as with a fling of the
head. **9.** To toss up a coin. **—to toss off** **1.** To drink at
one draft. **2.** To utter, write, or do in an offhand manner.
—to toss up To throw a coin into the air to decide a wager
or choice, the outcome depending on the side on which the
coin falls. **—** n. **1.** The act of tossing; a pitch; also, the distance over which a thing is tossed. **2.** A quick upward or
backward movement, as of the head. **3.** A tossup or wager.
[Prob. < Scand.] **—toss′er** n.
toss·up (tôs′up′, tos′-) n. Informal **1.** The throwing up of a
coin to decide a bet, etc. **2.** An even chance.
tot¹ (tot) n. **1.** A little child; toddler. **2.** A small amount or
portion, as of liquor. [Origin unknown]
tot² (tot) v.t. **tot·ted, tot·ting** Informal To add; total: usu.
with up. [Short for TOTAL]
to·tal (tōt′l) n. The whole sum or amount. **—** adj. **1.** Constituting or comprising a whole. **2.** Complete; absolute: a

total loss. **—** *v.* **·taled** or **·talled, ·tal·ing** or **·tal·ling** *v.t.* **1.** To ascertain the total of. **2.** To come to or reach as a total. **—** *v.i.* **3.** To amount: often with *to*. [< OF < Med.L < L *totus* all] **— to′tal·ly** *adv.*

total eclipse *Astron.* An eclipse in which during some period the entire disk of a celestial body is hidden from view.

to·tal·i·tar·i·an (tō·tal′ə·târ′ē·ən) *adj.* Designating or characteristic of a government controlled exclusively by one party or faction, and maintained by political suppression. **—** *n.* An adherent of totalitarian government. **— to·tal′i·tar′i·an·ism** *n.*

to·tal·i·ty (tō·tal′ə·tē) *n. pl.* **·ties 1.** An aggregate of parts or individuals. **2.** The state of being total.

to·tal·i·za·tor (tōt′l·ə·zā′tər, -ī·zā′-) *n.* A pari-mutuel machine: also **to′tal·iz′er** (-ī′zər). Also *Brit.* **to′tal·i·sa′tor.**

tote (tōt) *U.S. Informal v.t.* **tot·ed, tot·ing 1.** To carry about or bear on the person. **2.** To haul, as supplies. **—** *n.* **1.** The act of toting. **2.** A load or haul. [? < West African] **— tot′er** *n.*

tote board *Informal* A board at a racetrack, etc., showing the betting odds and results of races.

to·tem (tō′təm) *n.* **1.** Among many primitive peoples, an animal, plant, or other natural object believed to be ancestrally related to a tribe, clan, etc. **2.** The representation of such an animal, plant, or object taken as an emblem. **3.** The name or symbol of a person, clan, or tribe. [< Algonquian] **— to·tem·ic** (tō·tem′ik) *adj.* **— to′tem·ism** *n.* **to′tem·ist** *n.* **— to′tem·is′tic** *adj.*

totem pole A tall post or pole carved or painted with totemic symbols, often erected outside a dwelling by North American Indians, esp. those of the NW coast.

toth·er (tuth′ər) *adj. & pron. Informal* The other; other. Also **t'oth′er.** [ME *the tother* < *thet other* the other]

toti- *combining form* Whole; wholly. [< L *totus* whole]

tot·ter (tot′ər) *v.i.* **1.** To walk feebly and unsteadily. **2.** To shake or sway, as if about to fall. **—** *n.* The act or condition of tottering. [Prob. < Scand.] **— tot′ter·er** *n.* **— tot′ter·y** *adj.*

— Syn. (verb) **2.** teeter, wobble, reel.

tou·can (tōō′kan, tōō·kän′) *n.* A large, fruit-eating bird of tropical America, with brilliant plumage and an immense, thin-walled beak. [< F < Pg. < Tupi *tucana*]

touch (tuch) *v.t.* **1.** To place the hand, finger, etc., in contact with. **2.** To be in or come into contact with. **3.** To bring into contact with something else. **4.** To hit or strike lightly. **5.** To lay the hand or hands on, esp. roughly. **6.** To border on; adjoin. **7.** To come to; reach. **8.** To attain to; equal. **9.** To mark or delineate lightly. **10.** To color slightly; tinge. **11.** To affect injuriously; taint: vegetables *touched* by frost. **12.** To affect by contact: The drill could not *touch* the steel. **13.** To affect the emotions of; move, esp. to pity, gratitude, etc. **14.** To relate to; concern. **15.** To treat or discuss in passing; deal with. **16.** To have to do with, use, or partake of I will not *touch* this food. **17.** To handle or appropriate improperly. **18.** *Slang* To be successful in borrowing from: used with *for*: He *touched* me for a loan. **19.** *Geom.* To be tangent to. **—** *v.i.* **20.** To touch someone or something. **21.** To come into or be in contact. **— to touch at** To stop briefly at (a port or place) in the course of a journey or voyage. **— to touch off 1.** To cause to explode. **2.** To cause to happen or occur. **— to touch on** (or **upon**) **1.** To relate to; concern. **2.** To treat briefly or in passing. **— to touch up** To improve or alter by slight additions or corrections. **—** *n.* **1.** The act or process of touching. **2.** The state of being touched. **3.** *Physiol.* That sense by which external objects are perceived through direct contact with any part of the body. ◆ Collateral adjective: *tactile*. **4.** The sensation conveyed by touching something: a smooth *touch*. **5.** A stroke; hit; blow. **6.** A perceptible effect or influence: He felt the *touch* of her wit. **7.** Any slight or delicate execution or effect, as of a brush, etc.; a light stroke or mark. **8.** Any slight detail or effort given to anything, as to a literary work. **9.** The manner or style in which an artist, etc. executes his work: a master's *touch*. **10.** A trace; tinge: a *touch* of irony. **11.** A slight attack or twinge: a *touch* of rheumatism. **12.** A small quantity or dash. **13.** Close communication or contact: to keep in *touch* with someone. **14.** A test; trial. **15.** *Music* **a** The resistance made to the fingers by the keys of a piano, etc. **b** The manner in which a player presses the keyboard. **16.** *Slang* A sum of money obtained by borrowing or mooching. **17.** *Slang* A request for such a sum of money. **18.** *Slang* A person who is an easy mark for a loan: an easy *touch*. [< OF *tochier*; prob. ult. imit.] **— touch′a·ble** *adj.* **— touch′a·ble·ness** *n.* **— touch′er** *n.*

touch-and-go (tuch′ən·gō′) *adj.* Risky; precarious.

touch and go An uncertain or precarious situation.

touch·back (tuch′bak′) *n.* In football, the act of touchi[ng] the ball to the ground behind the player's own goal line whe[n] it has been sent over the goal line by an opponent.

touch·down (tuch′doun′) *n.* In football, a scoring pla[y] worth six points, in which the ball is held on or over the o[p]ponent's goal line and is there declared dead.

tou·ché (tōō·shā′) *French adj.* In fencing, touched by t[he] point of an opponent's foil. **—** *interj.* You've scored point!: an exclamation to indicate an opponent's success.

touched (tucht) *adj.* **1.** Emotionally moved. **2.** Slight[ly] unbalanced in mind.

touch·hole (tuch′hōl′) *n.* The orifice in old-fashioned ca[n]non or firearms through which the powder was ignited.

touch·ing (tuch′ing) *adj.* Appealing to the sympathies emotions; affecting; pathetic. **—** *prep.* With regard to; co[n]cerning. **— touch′ing·ly** *adv.* **— touch′ing·ness** *n.*

touch-me-not (tuch′mē·not′) *n.* Any of various her[bs] whose ripe fruit bursts open on contact to discharge its see[ds]

touch·stone (tuch′stōn′) *n.* **1.** A fine-grained dark sto[ne] formerly used to test the fineness of gold and silver by t[he] color of the streak made on the stone. **2.** A criterion standard by which the qualities of something are tested.

touch·wood (tuch′wŏŏd′) *n.* **1.** Punk¹ (def. 1). **2.** A t[in]der prepared from fungus.

touch·y (tuch′ē) *adj.* **touch·i·er, touch·i·est 1.** Likely take offense easily; irritable. **2.** Risky; delicate: a *tou[chy]* subject. **— touch′i·ly** *adv.* **— touch′i·ness** *n.*

tough (tuf) *adj.* **1.** Capable of sustaining great tension strain without breaking. **2.** Firm and resilient in substa[nce] or texture. **3.** Not easily separated, softened, etc.: tou[gh] meat. **4.** Possessing great physical endurance: a *tough* co[n]stitution. **5.** Possessing moral or intellectual enduran[ce] steadfast; persistent. **6.** Unmanageably rough, unruly, vicious. **7.** Difficult to accomplish; laborious. **8.** Sever[e] rigorous. **9.** *Informal* Unfortunate; unpleasant: tough lu[ck] **—** *n.* A lawless person; a rowdy; ruffian. [OE *tōh*] **tough′ly** *adv.* **— tough′ness** *n.*

tough·en (tuf′ən) *v.t. & v.i.* To make or become tough tougher. **— tough′en·er** *n.*

tou·pee (tōō·pā′, -pē′) *n.* A wig worn to cover baldness o[r a] bald spot. [< F < OF *toup* tuft of hair]

tour (tōōr) *n.* **1.** A trip or rambling excursion. **2.** A [cir]cuit or passing through, as for inspection or sightseeing, for presenting a performance. **3.** A turn or shift, as of s[er]vice. **— on tour** Traveling from place to place giving per[formances, as a theatrical company, etc. **—** *v.t.* **1.** To ma[ke] a tour of. **2.** To present on a tour, as a play. **—** *v.i.* **3.** go on a tour. [< MF < OF < L *tornus* lathe < Gk. *torn[os]*]

tour de force (tōōr′ də fôrs′) *French* A feat of remarka[ble] strength or skill; esp., a work, performance, etc., that merely ingenious rather than intrinsically excellent.

tour·ing car (tōōr′ing) A large, open automobile for five more passengers and baggage. Also *Brit.* **tour′er.**

tour·ist (tōōr′ist) *n.* One who makes a tour or a pleas[ure] trip. **—** *adj.* Of or suitable for tourists.

tourist class A class of accommodations for steamship p[as]sengers, lower than cabin class.

tour·ma·line (tōōr′mə·lēn, -lin) *n.* A complex silicate aluminum occurring in various colors, the transparent va[ri]eties being esteemed as gemstones. Also **tour′ma·lin** (-l[in]) [< F, ult. < Singhalese *tōramalli* carnelian]

tour·na·ment (tûr′nə·mənt, tōōr′-) *n.* **1.** Any contest skill involving a number of competitors and a series games: a chess *tournament*. **2.** In medieval times, a page[ant] in which two opposing parties of men in armor contended horseback in mock combat. Also called **tourney.** [< OF *torneier, tornoi[er]* tourney]

tour·ney (tûr′nē, tōōr′-) *n.* A tournament. **—** *v.i.* To t[ake] part in a tournament; tilt. [See TOURNAMENT.]

tour·ni·quet (tōōr′nə·ket, -kā, tûr′-) *n. Surg.* A banda[ge] etc., for stopping the flow of blood through an artery by co[m]pression. [< F < *tourner* to turn]

tour of duty *Mil.* The hours or period of time during wh[ich] a serviceman is on official duty; also, an extended perio[d of] duty on a given assignment or in a particular group.

tou·sle (tou′zəl) *v.t.* **·sled, ·sling** To disarrange or disor[der] as the hair or dress. **—** *n.* A tousled mass or mop of h[air] Also **tou′zle.** [< ME *tusen, tousen*]

tout (tout) *Informal v.i.* **1.** To solicit patronage, custom[ers] votes, etc., esp., in an obtrusive or importunate manner. To spy on a racehorse so as to gain information for bett[ing] **—** *v.t.* **3.** To solicit; importune. **4.** In horse racing: **a** spy on (a horse) to gain information for betting. **b** To sell formation about (a horse). **—** *n.* One who touts. [M[E] < OE *tōtian*, to peep, look out] **— tout′er** *n.*

tout de suite (tōōt′swēt′) *French* Immediately; at onc[e]

tout en·sem·ble (tōō′tän sän′bl′) *French* **1.** All in everything considered. **2.** The general effect.

tow¹ (tō) *n.* Coarse, short hemp or flax fiber prepared spinning. [Prob. OE *tow-* for spinning] **— tow′y** *adj.*

tow² (tō) *v.t.* To pull or drag, as by a rope, chain, etc.—

The act of towing, or the state of being towed. **2.** That
hich is towed, as barges by a tugboat. **3.** That which tows.
The rope used; towline. **— to take in tow 1.** To take in
arge for or as for towing. **2.** To take under one's protec-
n; take charge of. [OE *togian*]

v·age (tō′ij)   *n.* **1.** The service of or charge for towing.
2. The act of towing. [< TOW²]

ward (tôrd, tōrd; *for prep., also* tə·wôrd′)   *prep.* **1.** In the
rection of; facing. **2.** With respect to; regarding: his atti-
de *toward* women. **3.** In anticipation of; for: He is saving
ward his education. **4.** Near in point of time; approaching;
out: arriving *toward* evening. **5.** Tending to result in; de-
ned to achieve: an effort *toward* mutual understanding.
so **to·wards′.** **—** *adj.* [OE < tō to + -*weard* -ward]
· to·ward′ness *n.*

v·a·way (tō′ə·wā)   *n.* The act of towing away a vehicle,
o. one illegally parked.

v·boat (tō′bōt′)   *n.* A tugboat.

v·el (toul, tou′əl)   *n.* A cloth or paper for drying any-
ing by wiping. **—** *v.t.* **tow·eled** or **·elled, tow·el·ing** or **·el·**
g To wipe or dry with a towel. [< OF *toaille*]
v·el·ing (tou′ling, tou′əl·ing)   *n.* Material used for tow-
s. Also **tow′el·ling.**

v·er (tou′ər)   *n.* **1.** A tall but relatively narrow structure,
metimes part of a larger building. **2.** Any similar tall
ucture or object, often erected for a specific use: a water
ver. **3.** A place or thing of security or defense; citadel. **—**
. To rise or stand like a tower: often with *over* or *above*.
E < OF < L *turris*] **— tow′er·y** *adj.*

v·ered (tou′ərd)   *adj.* Having a tower or towers.

v·er·ing (tou′ər·ing)   *adj.* **1.** Like a tower; lofty. **2.**
usually high or great; outstanding. **3.** Intense.

v·head (tō′hed′)   *n.* A head of very light-colored or flaxen
ir; also, a person having such hair. [< TOW¹ + HEAD] **—**
v′-head′ed *adj.*

·hee (tou′hē, tō′-)   *n.* Any of various American birds re-
d to the buntings and the sparrows; esp., the chewink.
so **towhee bunting.** [imit. of one of its notes]

·line (tō′līn′)   *n.* A towrope.

vn (toun)   *n.* **1.** Any considerable collection of dwellings
d other buildings larger than a village, but not incorporat-
as a city. **2.** The inhabitants of such a community;
wnspeople. **3.** A township (def. 1). **4.** Any closely set-
d urban district. **5.** The downtown or business section of
city. **— on the town** *Slang* On a round of pleasure. **—**
go to town *Slang* To act with speed and efficiency. [OE
n enclosure, group of houses]

vn clerk An official who keeps the records of a town.

vn crier Formerly, a person appointed to make procla-
ations through the streets of a town.

vn hall The building containing the public offices of a
wn and used for meetings of the town council.

vn house A residence in a town or city, as distinguished
m one in the country.

vn meeting 1. A general assemblage of the people of a
wn. **2.** An assembly of qualified voters for the purpose of
ansacting town business; also, the voters assembled.

vn·ship (toun′ship)   *n.* **1.** In the U.S.: **a** A territorial
bdivision of a county with certain corporate powers of mu-
cipal government. **b** In New England, a local political unit
verned by a town meeting. **2.** A unit of area in surveys of
S. public lands, normally six miles square. **3.** *Brit.* For-
rly, a parish. [OE < *tūn* village, group of houses]

vns·man (tounz′mən)   *n. pl.* **·men** (-mən) **1.** A resident
a town; also, a fellow citizen. **2.** In New England, a town
icer; a selectman.

vns·peo·ple (tounz′pē′pəl)   *n.pl.* People who live in
wns or in a particular town or city. Also **town′folk′** (-fōk′),
wns′folk′.

v·path (tō′path′, -päth′)   *n.* A path along a river or
nal used by draft animals, etc., for towing boats.

·rope (tō′rōp′)   *n.* A heavy rope or cable used in towing.

· truck (tō) A truck equipped to tow other vehicles.

·e·mi·a (tok·sē′mē·ə)   *n. Pathol.* Blood poisoning. Also
·ae′mi·a. [< NL < Gk. *toxicon* poison + *haima* blood]
tox·e′mic, tox·ae′mic *adj.*

·ic (tok′sik)   *adj.* Of or caused by poison; poisonous.
so **tox′i·cal.** [< Med.L < L < Gk. *toxicon* (*pharmakon*)
oison) for arrows] **— tox′i·cal·ly** *adv.* **— tox·ic′i·ty** *n.*

ico- *combining form* Poison; of or pertaining to poisons.
so, before vowels, **toxic-.** [< Gk. *toxicon* poison]

·i·col·o·gy (tok′sə·kol′ə·jē)   *n.* The science that treats of
e origin, nature, properties, etc., of poisons. [< F *toxico-*
ie] **— tox′i·co·log′i·cal** (-kō·loj′i·kəl) *adj.* **— tox′i·co-**
·′i·cal·ly *adv.* **— tox′i·col′o·gist** *n.*

·in (tok′sin)   *n.* **1.** Any of a class of more or less unstable
isonous compounds developed by animal, vegetable, or
cterial organisms and acting as causative agents in many

diseases. **2.** Any toxic matter generated in living or dead
organisms. Also **tox·ine** (tok′sēn). [< TOX(IC) + -IN]

tox·oid (tok′soid)   *n.* A toxin that has been specially treated
to remove toxicity, often used in immunization.

toy (toi)   *n.* **1.** A plaything for children. **2.** Any object of
little importance or value; a trifle. **3.** A small ornament or
trinket. **4.** Any diminutive object. **5.** A dog bred to extreme smallness: also **toy dog.** **—** *v.i.* To trifle; play. **—**
adj. Resembling a toy; of miniature size. [< ME *toye* sport
and Du. *tuig* tools] **— toy′er** *n.*

to·yon (tō′yən)   *n.* An evergreen shrub of the Pacific coast
of North America, having white flowers and bright red berries. [< Sp. *tollón* < N. Am. Ind. (Mexican)]

trace¹ (trās)   *n.* **1.** A vestige or mark left by some past event
or agent, esp., when regarded as a sign or clue. **2.** A barely
detectable quantity, quality, token, or characteristic; touch.
3. A proportion or ingredient too small to be weighed: a
trace of soda. **4.** An imprint or mark indicating the passage
of a person or thing, as a footprint, etc. **5.** A path or trail
through woods or forest beaten down by men or animals. **6.**
A lightly drawn line. **—** *v.* **traced, trac·ing** *v.t.* **1.** To follow the tracks, course, or development of. **2.** To follow
(tracks, etc.). **3.** To discover by examination or investigation; determine. **4.** To draw; sketch. **5.** To copy (a drawing, etc.) on a superimposed transparent sheet. **6.** To form
(letters, etc.) with careful strokes. **7.** To imprint (a pattern
or design). **8.** To mark or record by a curved or broken
line. **9.** To go or move over, along, or through. **—** *v.i.* **10.**
To make one's way; proceed. **11.** To have its origin; go
back in time. [< OF < L *trahere* to draw] **— trace′a·**
ble *adj.* **— trace′a·bil′i·ty, trace′a·ble·ness** *n.* **— trace′a·**
bly *adv.*

trace² (trās)   *n.* One of two side straps or chains for connecting the collar of a harness with the whiffletree. **— to kick
over the traces** To throw off control; become unmanageable. **—** *v.t.* **traced, trac·ing** To fasten with or as with traces.
[< OF < L. See TRACE¹.]

trace element *Biol.* Any of certain chemical elements
found in very small amounts in plant and animal tissues and
having a significant effect upon biochemical processes.

trac·er (trā′sər)   *n.* **1.** One who or that which traces. **2.**
One of various instruments used in tracing drawings, etc. **3.**
An inquiry forwarded from one point to another, to trace
missing mail matter, etc. **4.** *Mil.* A chemical incorporated
in certain types of ammunition used for ranging, signaling,
or incendiary purposes. **5.** A radioisotope introduced into
the body for the purpose of following the processes of metabolism, the course of a disease, etc. [< TRACE¹]

tracer bullet A bullet that leaves a line of smoke or fire in
its wake to indicate its course for correction of aim.

trac·er·y (trā′sər·ē)   *n. pl.* **·er·ies 1.** Ornamental stonework formed of ramifying lines. **2.** Any work, ornamentation, etc., resembling this.

tra·che·a (trā′kē·ə)   *n. pl.* **·che·ae** (-kī·ē) or **·che·as 1.**
Anat. The duct by which air passes from the larynx to the
bronchi and the lungs: also called *windpipe.* For illus. see
LUNG, MOUTH, THROAT. **2.** *Zool.* One of the passages by
which air is conveyed from the exterior in air-breathing arthropods, as insects and arachnids. [< Med.L < LL < Gk.
(*artēria*) *tracheia* a rough (artery)] **— tra′che·al** *adj.*

tracheo- *combining form* The trachea; of or pertaining to
the trachea. Also, before vowels, **trache-.** [< TRACHEA]

tra·che·ot·o·my (trā′kē·ot′ə·mē)   *n. pl.* **·mies** *Surg.* The
operation of cutting into the trachea.

tra·cho·ma (trə·kō′mə)   *n. Pathol.* A contagious virus disease characterized by the formation of hard granular excrescences on the conjunctiva of the eyelids, with inflammation of the lining. [< NL < Gk. < *trachys* rough] **— tra-**
chom·a·tous (trə·kom′ə·təs) *adj.*

trachy- *combining form* Rough; uneven. Also, before vowels, **trach-.** [< Gk. *trachys* rough]

trac·ing (trā′sing)   *n.* **1.** The act of one who traces. **2.** A
copy made by tracing on transparent paper. **3.** A record
made by a self-registering instrument.

track (trak)   *n.* **1.** A mark or trail left by the passage of
anything, as footprints. **2.** Any regular path; course. **3.**
Any kind of racecourse; also, sports performed on such a
course; track athletics. **4.** A set of rails or a rail on which
trains, etc., may travel. **5.** A trace or vestige. **6.** A sequence of events or ideas. **— to keep track of** To keep in
touch with. **— in one's tracks** Right where one is; on the
spot. **— to lose track of** To fail to keep in touch with; lose
sight of. **— to make tracks** To hurry; run away in haste.
— *v.t.* **1.** To follow, the tracks of; trail. **2.** To discover, pursue or follow by means of marks or indications. **3.** To make
tracks upon or with. **4.** To traverse, as on foot. **5.** To furnish with rails or tracks. [< OF *trac*] **— track′er** *n.* **—**
track′a·ble *adj.* **— track′less** *adj.*

track·age (trak′ij) *adj.* **1.** Railroad tracks collectively. **2.** The right of one company to use the track system of another company; also, the charge for this right.

track man An athlete who competes in a track or field event, as a runner, shot-putter, etc.

track meet An athletic contest made up of track and field events.

tract[1] (trakt) *n.* **1.** An extended area, as of land or water. **2.** *Anat.* An extensive region of the body, esp. one comprising a system of parts or organs: the alimentary *tract*. [< L < *trahere* to draw]

tract[2] (trakt) *n.* A short treatise; esp., a pamphlet on some question of religion or morals. [Short for L *tractatus* a handling, treatise]

tract·a·ble (trak′tə-bəl) *adj.* **1.** Easily led or controlled; manageable; docile. **2.** Readily worked or handled; malleable. [< L < *trahere* to draw] — **tract′a·ble·ness, tract′a·bil′i·ty** *n.* — **tract′a·bly** *adv.*

trac·tile (trak′til) *adj.* Capable of being drawn out; ductile. [< L < *trahere* to draw] — **trac·til′i·ty** *n.*

trac·tion (trak′shən) *n.* **1.** The act of drawing, as by motive power over a surface. **2.** The state of being drawn, or the power employed. **3.** Adhesive or rolling friction, as of wheels on a track. [< Med.L < L < *trahere* to draw] — **trac′tion·al** *adj.*

traction engine A locomotive for hauling on roads or ground, as distinguished from one used on a railway.

trac·tor (trak′tər) *n.* **1.** A powerful, motor-driven vehicle used, as on farms, to draw a plow, reaper, etc. **2.** An automotive vehicle with a driver's cab, used to haul trailers, etc. **3.** *Aeron.* An airplane with the propeller or propellers situated in front of the supporting surface: also **tractor airplane.** [< NL < L < *trahere* to draw]

trade (trād) *n.* **1.** A business; esp., a skilled handicraft; a craft. **2.** Mercantile traffic; commerce. **3.** An exchange, as in barter, buying and selling, etc.; also, a bargain or deal. **4.** The people following a particular calling. **5.** A firm's customers. **6.** Customary pursuit; occupation. **7.** *Usu. pl.* A trade wind. — **Syn.** See OCCUPATION. — *v.* **trad·ed, trad·ing** *v.t.* **1.** To exchange by barter, bargain and sale, etc. **2.** To exchange for something comparable. — *v.i.* **3.** To engage in commerce or in business. — **to trade in** To give in exchange as payment or part payment. — **to trade off** To get rid of by trading. — **to trade on** To make advantageous use of. [< MLG, track]

trade-in (trād′in′) *n.* Something given or accepted in payment or part payment for something else; an exchange.

trade journal A periodical publishing news and discussions of a particular trade or business.

trade-last (trād′last′, -läst′) *n. Informal* A favorable remark that one has heard and offers to repeat to the person complimented in return for a similar remark.

trade·mark (trād′märk′) *n.* **1.** A name, design, etc., often officially registered, used by a merchant or manufacturer to distinguish his goods from those made or sold by others. **2.** Any distinctive characteristic. — *v.t.* **1.** To label with a trademark. **2.** To register as a trademark.

trade name **1.** The name by which an article, process, service, or the like is designated in trade. **2.** A style or name of a business house.

trad·er (trā′dər) *n.* **1.** One who trades. **2.** Any vessel employed in a particular trade.

trade route A route, esp. a sea lane, used by traders.

trade school A school where a specific trade is taught.

trades·folk (trādz′fōk′) *n.pl.* People engaged in trade; esp., shopkeepers. Also **trades′peo′ple** (-pē′pəl).

trades·man (trādz′mən) *n. pl.* **·men** (-mən) A retail dealer; shopkeeper.

trade union A labor union. Also *Brit.* **trades union.**

trade wind *Meteorol.* Either of two steady winds blowing in the same course toward the equator from about 30° N and S latitude, one from the northeast on the north, the other from the southeast on the south side of the equator.

trading post A station for barter in unsettled territory set up by a trader or trading company.

trading stamp A stamp given by a tradesman to a purchaser, and exchangeable, in quantities, for merchandise.

tra·di·tion (trə-dish′ən) *n.* **1.** The knowledge, doctrines, customs, practices, etc., transmitted from generation to generation; also, the transmission of such knowledge, doctrines, etc. **2.** The body of unwritten Christian doctrine, handed down through successive generations. **3.** Among the Jews, an unwritten code said to have been handed down orally from Moses. **4.** The historic conceptions and usages of a school of art, literature, etc. **5.** A custom so long continued that it has almost the force of a law. [< OF < L < *trans-* across + *dare* to give]

tra·di·tion·al (trə-dish′ən-əl) *adj.* Relating or adhering to tradition. Also **tra·di′tion·ar′y** (-er′ē). — **tra·di′tion·al·ism** *n.* — **tra·di′tion·al·ist** *n.* — **tra·di·tion·al·ist′ic** *adj.* — **tra·di′tion·al·ly** *adv.* — **tra·di′tion·ist** *n.*

tra·duce (trə-dōōs′, -dyōōs′) *v.t.* **·duced, ·duc·ing** To d fame; slander. [< L *traducere* to transport, bring into d grace] — **tra·duc′er** *n.* — **tra·duc′i·ble** *adj.* — **tra·du ing·ly** *adv.* — **tra·duc·tion** (trə-duk′shən) *n.*

traf·fic (traf′ik) *n.* **1.** The movement or passage of ve cles, pedestrians, ships, etc., along a route; also, the vehicl pedestrians, etc. **2.** Buying and selling; trade. **3.** The b iness of transportation; also, the freight or passengers ca ried. **4.** The messages, signals, etc., handled by a comm nications system. **5.** Unlawful or improper trade. — *t* **·ficked, ·fick·ing 1.** To engage in buying and selling; do b iness, esp., illegally: with *in.* **2.** To have dealings: w *with.* [< MF < Ital. < *trafficare* < L *trans-* across + It *ficcare* to thrust in] — **traf′fick·er** *n.*

traffic light A signal light that, by changing color, dire the flow of traffic along a road or highway.

tra·ge·di·an (trə-jē′dē-ən) *n.* **1.** An actor in tragedy. **2** writer of tragedies.

tra·ge·di·enne (trə-jē′dē·en′) *n.* An actress of traged [< F]

trag·e·dy (traj′ə-dē) *n. pl.* **·dies 1.** An intensely sa calamitous, or fatal event or course of events; disaster. **2** A form of drama in which the protagonist comes to disas through a flaw in his nature or is crushed by social and ps chological forces. **3.** The branch of drama treating of su themes. **4.** The art or theory of acting or composing su drama. **5.** The sense of human life embodied in tra drama. [< OF < L < Gk. *tragōidia*, appar. < *tragos* go + *ōidē* song]

trag·ic (traj′ik) *adj.* **1.** Involving death, calamity, or s fering; fatal; terrible. **2.** Pertaining to or having the nat of tragedy. **3.** Appropriate to or like tragedy, esp., in dram Also **trag′i·cal.** [< L < Gk. *tragikos* pertaining to traged — **trag′i·cal·ly** *adv.* — **trag′i·cal·ness** *n.*

trag·i·com·e·dy (traj′i·kom′ə·dē) *n. pl.* **·dies 1.** A dra in which tragic and comic scenes are intermingled. **2.** situation or event suggestive of such a drama. [< MF LL < L < *tragicus* tragic + *comoedia* comedy] — **tra comic** or **·i·cal** *adj.* — **trag′i·com′i·cal·ly** *adv.*

trail (trāl) *v.t.* **1.** To draw along lightly over a surface; al to drag or draw after: to *trail* a robe. **2.** To follow the tr of; track. **3.** To follow or lag behind, esp., in a race. **4.** M To carry, as a rifle, with the muzzle to the front and the b nearly touching the ground. **5.** To tread or force down, grass into a pathway. — *v.i.* **6.** To hang or float loosely as to drag along a surface. **7.** To grow along the groun over rocks, bushes, etc., in a loose, creeping way. **8.** To low behind loosely; stream. **9.** To move along slowly, tir ly, or heavily. **10.** To lag behind; straggle. **11.** To fol or track game. — *n.* **1.** A path or track made by the pa sage of persons or animals. **2.** The spoor followed by hunter. **3.** Anything drawn behind or in the wake of sor thing. **4.** *Mil.* The inclined stock of a gun carriage, or tension of the stock that rests on the ground when the pi is not limbered up. — **to hit** (or **take**) **the trail** To set on a journey. [< AF < L < *trahere* to draw]

trail·blaz·er (trāl′blā·zər) *n.* **1.** One who blazes a trail. A pioneer in any field. — **trail′blaz·ing** *n.*

trail·er (trā′lər) *n.* **1.** One who or that which trails. **2** vehicle drawn by another having motive power. **3.** A ve cle drawn by a car or truck and used as a temporary or p manent dwelling. **4.** A short motion-picture film made of scenes from a coming feature picture, used for advertisi

trailer court A large area equipped with running wat electrical outlets, and other accommodations for the park of trailers. Also **trailer park.**

trail·ing arbutus (trā′ling) A perennial bearing fragr pink flowers: the State flower of Massachusetts.

train (trān) *n.* **1.** A continuous line of coupled railway ca **2.** A series, or set of connected things; a sequence; esp., procession of people or line of objects. **3.** A retinue or su **4.** Something pulled along with and in the track of anoth **5.** An extension of a dress skirt, trailing behind the wear **6.** Proper order; due course. **7.** *Mech.* A series of parts a ing upon each other, as for transmitting motion. **8.** M The men, animals, and vehicles, transporting military s plies, ammunition, etc. **9.** A succession or line of wag and pack animals en route. **10.** A line of gunpowder, e laid to conduct fire to a charge or mine. — *v.t.* **1.** To ren proficient or qualified by instruction, drill, etc.; educate. To make obedient or capable of performing tricks, as an mal. **3.** To bring into a required physical condition means of diet and exercise. **4.** To lead into taking a par ular course; develop into a fixed shape: to *train* a plant o trellis. **5.** To bring to bear; aim, as a cannon. — *v.i.* To undergo a course of training. **7.** To give a course training; drill. — **Syn.** See TEACH. [OF < L *trahere* draw] — **train′a·ble** *adj.* — **train′er** *n.*

train·ee (trā·nē′) *n.* One who undergoes training.

train·ing (trā′ning) *n.* **1.** The action of one who or t which trains. **2.** The state or condition of being trainee

in·man (trān'mən) *n. pl.* **·men** (-mən) A railway em-
oyee serving on a train; esp., a brakeman.
ipse (trāps) *v.i.* **traipsed, traips·ing** *Informal* To walk
out in an idle or aimless manner. [Earlier *trapass*]
it (trāt, *also Brit.* trā) *n.* A distinguishing feature or qual-
of character. — **Syn.** See CHARACTERISTIC. [< F <
F < L < *trahere* to draw]
i·tor (trā'tər) *n.* One who betrays a trust; esp., one who
mmits treason. [< OF < L < *trans-* across + *dare* to
ve] — **trai'tress** (-tris) *n.fem.*
i·tor·ous (trā'tər·əs) *adj.* **1.** Of or characteristic of a
aitor. **2.** Pertaining to or of the nature of treason. —
ai'tor·ous·ly *adv.* — **trai'tor·ous·ness** *n.*
·jec·to·ry (trə·jek'tər·ē) *n. pl.* **·ries** The path described
an object moving in space; esp., the path of a projectile.
Med.L < L < *trans-* over + *jacere* to throw]
m (tram) *n.* **1.** *Brit.* A streetcar or street railway: also
am'car (-kär'). **2.** A four-wheeled vehicle for conveying
als to or from a pit's mouth. [Short for *tramroad*, a road
th metal tracks]
m·mel (tram'əl) *n.* **1.** *Usu. pl.* That which limits free-
m or activity; an impediment; hindrance. **2.** A fetter,
ackle, or bond, esp., one used in teaching a horse to amble.
An instrument for describing ellipses. **4.** A hook used to
spend cooking pots from a fireplace crane. — *v.t.* **tram·
eled** or **·melled, tram·mel·ing** or **·mel·ling 1.** To hinder or
struct; restrict. **2.** To entangle in or as in a snare. Also
am'el or **tram'ell.** [< OF < LL < L *tri-* three + *macula*
esh] — **tram'mel·er** or **tram'mel·ler** *n.*
mp (tramp) *v.i.* **1.** To walk or wander, esp., as a vagrant
vagabond. **2.** To walk heavily or firmly. — *v.t.* **3.** To
lk or wander through. **4.** To walk on heavily; trample.
n. **1.** An indigent wanderer; a vagrant; vagabond. **2.** A
avy, continued tread. **3.** The sound of continuous and
avy marching or walking. **4.** A long walk; hike. **5.** A
eam vessel that picks up freight wherever it can be ob-
ned: also **tramp steamer.** **6.** *Informal* A sexually pro-
scuous girl or woman. [ME *trampen* < Gmc.]
m·ple (tram'pəl) *v.* **·pled, ·pling** *v.t.* **1.** To tread on
avily; injure, violate, or encroach upon by or as by tramp-
g. — *v.i.* **2.** To tread heavily or ruthlessly; tramp. — *n.*
e act or sound of treading under foot. [ME < *trampen*]
m·po·line (tram'pə·lin) *n.* A section of strong canvas
etched on a frame, on which an acrobat, athlete, etc., may
und or spring. [< Ital. *trampoli* stilts]
nce (trans, trăns) *n.* **1.** A condition intermediate be-
een sleep and wakefulness, characterized by dissociation
d automatisms of behavior, as in hypnosis and seances.
A dreamlike state marked by bewilderment and an in-
nsibility to ordinary surroundings. **3.** A state of deep ab-
·action. — *v.t.* **tranced, tranc·ing** To put into or as into
rance. [< OF < *transir* to pass, die]
n·quil (trang'kwil) *adj.* **·quil·er** or **·quil·ler, ·quil·est** or
uil·lest **1.** Free from mental agitation or disturbance;
lm. **2.** Quiet and motionless. — **Syn.** See CALM. [< L
nquillus quiet] — **tran'quil·ly** *adv.* — **tran'quil·ness** *n.*
n·quil·ize (trang'kwəl·īz) *v.t. & v.i.* **·ized, ·iz·ing** To
ake or become tranquil. Also **tran'quil·lize,** *Brit.* **tran'·
il·lise.** — **tran'quil·i·za'tion** *n.*
n·quil·iz·er (trang'kwəl·ī'zər) *n.* **1.** One who or that
ich tranquilizes. **2.** *Med.* Any of a class of drugs having
e property of reducing nervous tension and anxiety states.
so **tran'quil·liz'er.**
n·quil·li·ty (trang·kwil'ə·tē) *n.* The state of being tran-
il; calm; quiet. Also **tran·quil'i·ty.**
ns- *prefix* **1.** Across; beyond; through; on the other side
as in:

ransarctic	transcontinental	transfrontier
ransborder	transdesert	transisthmian
ranschannel	transequatorial	transpolar

adjectives and nouns of place, the prefix may signify "on
e other side of" (opposed to *cis-*) or "across; crossing."
rough long usage, certain of these are written as solid
rds, as *transalpine, transatlantic;* otherwise, words in this
ss are usually written with a hyphen, as in:

ns-African	trans-Baltic	trans-Iberian
ns-American	trans-Canadian	trans-Mediterranean
ns-Andean	trans-Germanic	trans-Scandinavian
ns-Arabian	trans-Himalayan	trans-Siberian

Through and through; changing completely; as in:

transcolor	transfashion

Surpassing; transcending; beyond; as in:

ansconscious	transmaterial	transnational
ansempirical	transmental	transphysical
anshuman	transmundane	transrational

Anat. Across; transversely; as in:

anscortical	transfrontal	transthoracic
ansduodenal	transocular	transuterine

L <*trans* across, beyond, over]

trans·act (trans·akt', tranz-) *v.t.* **1.** To carry through; accomplish; do. — *v.i.* **2.** *Rare* To do business. [< L <
trans- through + *agere* to drive, do] — **trans·ac'tor** *n.*
trans·ac·tion (trans·ak'shən, tranz-) *n.* **1.** The act of trans-
acting, or the state of being transacted. **2.** Something transacted; esp., a business deal. **3.** *pl.* Published reports, as of a
society. — **trans·ac'tion·al** *adj.*
trans·al·pine (trans·al'pīn, -pĭn, tranz-) *adj.* Of, pertaining
to, or situated on the northern side of the Alps. — *n.* A native or a resident of beyond the Alps. [< L < *trans-* across
+ *alpinus* alpine < *Alpes* the Alps]
trans·at·lan·tic (trans'ət·lan'tik, tranz'-) *adj.* **1.** On the
other side of the Atlantic. **2.** Across the Atlantic.
tran·scend (tran·send') *v.t.* **1.** To rise above in excellence
or degree. **2.** To overstep or exceed as a limit. **3.** *Philos. &
Theol.* To be independent of or beyond (the universe, experience, etc.) — *v.i.* **4.** To be transcendent; excel. [< L <
trans- beyond, over + *scandere* to climb]
tran·scen·dent (tran·sen'dənt) *adj.* **1.** Of very high and
remarkable degree; surpassing; excelling. **2.** *Theol.* Above
and beyond the universe: said of God. [See TRANSCEND.]
— **tran·scen'dence, tran·scen'den·cy, tran·scen'dent·ness**
n. — **tran·scen'dent·ly** *adv.*
tran·scen·den·tal (tran'sen·den'təl) *adj.* **1.** Of very high
degree; transcendent. **2.** Beyond or contrary to common
sense or experience. — **tran'scen·den'tal·ly** *adv.*
tran·scen·den·tal·ism (tran'sen·den'təl·iz'əm) *n.* **1.** *Philos.* Any of several doctrines holding that reality is essentially
mental or spiritual in nature, and that knowledge of it can be
attained by intuitive or a priori, rather than empirical, principles. **2.** The state or quality of being transcendental. —
tran'scen·den'tal·ist *n. & adj.*
tran·scribe (tran·skrīb') *v.t.* **·scribed, ·scrib·ing 1.** To copy
or recopy in handwriting or typewriting. **2.** *Telecom.* To
make an electrical recording of (a radio program). **3.** To
adapt (a musical composition) for a change of instrument or
voice. [< L < *trans-* over + *scribere* to write] — **tran·
scrib'a·ble** *adj.* — **tran·scrib'er** *n.*
tran·script (tran'skript) *n.* **1.** That which is transcribed;
esp., a written or typewritten copy. **2.** Any copy. **3.** A copy
of a student's academic record, listing courses and grades.
tran·scrip·tion (tran·skrip'shən) *n.* **1.** The act of transcribing. **2.** A copy; transcript. **3.** Phonetic notation of
speech sounds, also, a text containing such symbols. **4.**
Telecom. A recording of a performance made for a later
radio broadcast. **5.** *Music* The adaptation of a composition
for some instrument or voice other than that for which it was
written. — **tran·scrip'tion·al, tran·scrip'tive** *adj.*
trans·duc·er (trans·dōō'sər, -dyōō'-, tranz-) *n.* *Physics*
Any device whereby energy may be transmitted from one
system to another system, whether of the same or a different
type. [< L < *trans-* across + *ducere* to lead]
tran·sect (tran·sekt') *v.t.* To dissect transversely. [<
TRANS- + *sectus,* pp. of *secare* to cut] — **tran·sec'tion**
(-sek'shən) *n.*
tran·sept (tran'sept) *n. Archit.* One of the lateral projections between the nave and choir of a cruciform church.
[<Med.L < L <*transversus* lying across + *septum* enclosure]
— **tran·sep'tal** *adj.* — **tran·sep'tal·ly** *adv.*
trans·fer (trans'fər; *for v., also* trans-fûr') *v.* **·ferred, ·fer·
ring** *v.t.* **1.** To carry, or cause to pass, from one person,
place, etc., to another. **2.** To make over possession of to another. **3.** To convey (a drawing) from one surface to another. — *v.i.* **4.** To transfer oneself. **5.** To be transferred.
6. To change from one vehicle to another on a transfer (def.
4). **7.** To shift one's enrollment as a student from one
school to another. — **Syn.** See CONVEY. — *n.* **1.** The act of
transferring, or the state of being transferred. Also **trans·
fer'al** (-fûr'əl) or **trans·fer'ral.** **2.** That which is transferred
as a design. **3.** A place, method, or means of transfer. **4.** A
ticket entitling a passenger to change to another public
vehicle. **5.** *Law* A delivery of title or property from one person to another. **6.** An order transferring money or securities.
[< OF < L < *trans-* across + *ferre* to carry] — **trans·fer'a·
bil'i·ty** *n.* — **trans·fer'a·ble** *adj.* — **trans·fer'ence** (-fûr'
əns) *n.* — **trans·fer'rer** (-fûr'ər) *n.*
trans·fer·or (trans·fûr'ər) *n. Law* One who executes a
transfer of property, title, etc.
Trans·fig·u·ra·tion (trans'fig·yə·rā'shən) *n.* **1.** The supernatural transformation of Christ on the mount as recorded in
the Gospels. *Matt.* xvii 1–9. **2.** A church festival commemorating this, observed on August 6.
trans·fig·ure (trans·fig'yər) *v.t.* **·ured, ·ur·ing 1.** To change
the outward form or appearance of. **2.** To make glorious;
idealize. [< L < *trans-* across + *figura* shape] — **trans·fig·
ur·a'tion, trans·fig'ure·ment** *n.*
trans·fix (trans·fiks') *v.t.* **1.** To pierce through; impale. **2.**
To fix in place by impaling. **3.** To make motionless, as with

horror, awe, etc. [< L < *trans-* through + *figere* to fasten]
— **trans·fix′ion** (-fik′shən) *n*.
trans·form (trans-fôrm′) *v.t.* **1.** To give a different form or appearance to. **2.** To change the character, nature, condition, etc., of. **3.** *Math.* To change (one expression or operation) into another equivalent to it or similar. **4.** *Electr.* To change the potential or flow of (a current), as with a transformer. **5.** *Physics* To alter the energy form of, as electrical into mechanical. —*v.i.* **6.** To be or become changed. [< L < *trans-* over + *formare* to form] — **trans·form′a·ble** *adj.* — **trans′for·ma′tion** (-fər-mā′shən) *n.* — **trans·for′ma·tive** (-fôr′mə·tiv) *adj.*
trans·form·er (trans-fôr′mər) *n.* **1.** One who or that which transforms. **2.** *Electr.* A device for altering the ratio of current to voltage in alternating-current circuits, often consisting of two coils wound on the same iron core.
trans·form·ism (trans-fôr′miz-əm) *n. Biol.* The theory of the development of one species from another through successive gradual modifications.
trans·fuse (trans-fyōōz′) *v.t.* **·fused**, **·fus·ing 1.** To pour, as a fluid, from one vessel to another. **2.** To cause to be imparted or instilled. **3.** *Med.* To transfer (blood) from one person or animal to another. [< L < *trans-* across + *fundere* to pour] — **trans·fus′er** *n.* — **trans·fus′i·ble** *adj.* — **trans·fu′sive** (trans-fyōō′siv) *adj.*
trans·fu·sion (trans-fyōō′zhən) *n.* **1.** The act of transfusing. **2.** *Med.* The transfer of blood from one person or animal to the veins or arteries of another.
trans·gress (trans-gres′, tranz-) *v.t.* **1.** To break (a law, oath, etc.); violate. **2.** To pass beyond or over (limits); exceed; trespass. —*v.i.* **3.** To break a law; sin. [Appar. < OF < L < *trans-* across + *gradi* to step] — **trans·gres′si·ble** *adj.* — **trans·gress′ing·ly** *adv.* — **trans·gres′sive** *adj.* — **trans·gres′sor** *n.*
trans·gres·sion (trans-gresh′ən, tranz-) *n.* **1.** A violation of a law, command, etc.; esp., a violation of a divine law; sin. **2.** The act of transgressing.
tran·ship (tran-ship′), **tran·ship·ment** (tran-ship′mənt) See TRANSSHIP, etc.
tran·sient (tran′shənt) *adj.* **1.** Passing away quickly; of short duration; brief. **2.** Not permanent; temporary; transitory. —*n.* One who or that which is transient; esp., a lodger or boarder who remains for a short time. [< L < *trans-* across + *ire* to go] — **tran′sience, tran′sien·cy** *n.* — **tran′sient·ly** *adv.* — **tran′sient·ness** *n.*
— **Syn.** (adj.) **1, 2.** Something *transient* actually passes soon, while a *transitory* thing has the quality of impermanence: a *transient* visitor, a *transitory* stage of development. *Passing* is close to *transitory* but less formal: a *passing* fad.
tran·sis·tor (tran-zis′tər, -sis′-) *n. Electronics* A miniature device for the control and amplification of an electron current, made of semiconducting materials, and having three or more electrodes, the current between one pair controlling the amplified current between another pair, one electrode being common to each pair. [< TRANS(FER) (RES)ISTOR]
tran·sit (tran′sit, -zit) *n.* **1.** The act of passing over or through; passage. **2.** The act of carrying across or through; conveyance. **3.** A transition or change. **4.** *Astron.* **a** The passage of one heavenly body across the disk of another. **b** The moment of passage of a celestial body across the meridian. **5.** A surveying instrument for measuring horizontal and vertical angles: also **transit theodolite.** —*v.t.* To pass through or across. [< L < *trans-* across + *ire* to go]
tran·si·tion (tran-zish′ən) *n.* **1.** The act or state of passing from one place, condition, or action to another; change **2.** The time, period, or place of such passage. **3.** A sentence, paragraph, etc., that leads from one subject to another, as in an essay. **4.** *Music* A modulation or a passage connecting two themes or subjects. — **tran·si′tion·al, tran·si′tion·ar′y** (-er′ē) *adj.* — **tran·si′tion·al·ly** *adv.*
tran·si·tive (tran′sə·tiv) *adj.* **1.** *Gram.* Of transitive verbs. **2.** Capable of passing; effecting transition. —*n. Gram.* A transitive verb. [< LL < L. See TRANSIT.] — **tran′si·tive·ly** *adv.* — **tran′si·tive·ness, tran′si·tiv′i·ty** *n.*
transitive verb A verb that requires a complement to complete its meaning.
tran·si·to·ry (tran′sə·tôr′ē, -tō′rē) *adj.* Existing for a short time only. — **Syn.** See TRANSIENT. [< OF < L. See TRANSIT.] — **tran′si·to′ri·ly** *adv.* — **tran′si·to′ri·ness** *n.*
trans·late (trans-lāt′, tranz-, trans-lāt′, tranz-) *v.* **·lat·ed**, **·lat·ing** *v.t.* **1.** To express in another language; change into another language. **2.** To explain in other words; interpret. **3.** To change into another form; transform. —*v.i.* **4.** To act as translator. **5.** To admit of translation: This book *translates* easily. [? < OF *translater* < L < pp. of *transferre* < *trans-* across + *ferre* to carry] — **trans·lat′a·ble** *adj.* — **trans·lat′a·ble·ness** *n.* — **trans·la′tor** *n.*
trans·la·tion (trans-lā′shən, tranz-) *n.* **1.** The act of translating, or the state of being translated. **2.** That which is translated; esp., a work translated into another language; a version. — **trans·la′tion·al** *adj.*

trans·lit·er·ate (trans-lit′ə·rāt, tranz-) *v.t.* **·at·ed**, **·at·in** To represent (a letter or word) by the alphabetic characte of another language. [< TRANS- + L *litera* letter] — **tran lit′er·a′tion** *n.*
trans·lu·cent (trans-lōō′sənt, tranz-) *adj.* Allowing th passage of light, but not permitting a clear view of any ob ject; semitransparent. — **Syn.** See CLEAR. [< L < *tran* through, across + *lucere* to shine] — **trans·lu′cence, tran lu′cen·cy** *n.* — **trans·lu′cent·ly** *adv.*
trans·mi·grate (trans-mī′grāt, tranz-, trans′mə-, tranz′ *v.i.* **·grat·ed**, **·grat·ing 1.** To migrate from one place or co dition to another, esp., from one country to another. **2.** ′ pass into another body, as the soul at death. [< L < *tran* across + *migrare* to migrate] — **trans·mi′grant** *adj.* & — **trans′mi·gra′tion** *n.* — **trans·mi′gra·tor** *n.* — **trans·m gra·to·ry** (trans-mī′grə·tôr′ē, -tō′rē, tranz-) *adj.*
trans·mis·si·ble (trans-mis′ə·bəl, tranz-) *adj.* Capable being transmitted. Also **trans·mit′ti·ble** (-mit′ə·bəl). — **trans·mis′si·bil′i·ty** *n.*
trans·mis·sion (trans-mish′ən, tranz-) *n.* **1.** The act transmitting, or the state of being transmitted. **2.** Th which is transmitted. **3.** *Mech.* **a** A device that transm power from the engine of an automobile to the driving whee **b** The gears for changing speed. [See TRANSMIT.] — **tra mis′sive** *adj.*
trans·mit (trans-mit′, tranz-) *v.t.* **·mit·ted**, **·mit·ting 1.** send from one place or person to another; forward or conve dispatch. **2.** To pass on by heredity; transfer. **3.** To pa on or communicate (news, information, etc.). **4.** *Teleco* To send out (information, radio and television broadca etc.) by means of electromagnetic waves. **5.** *Physics* cause (light, sound, etc.) to pass through a medium. *Mech.* To convey (force, motion, etc.) from one part or mec anism to another. [< L < *trans-* across + *mittere* to se — **trans·mit′tal** *n.*
trans·mit·tance (trans-mit′ns, tranz-) *n.* The act or pr ess of transmitting.
trans·mit·ter (trans-mit′ər, tranz-) *n.* **1.** One who or th which transmits. **2.** A telegraphic sending instrument. The part of a telephone that converts sound waves into ele trical waves. **4.** *Telecom.* The part of a radio or televisi system that generates, modulates, and transmits elect magnetic waves to the antenna.
trans·mu·ta·tion (trans′myōō·tā′shən, tranz′-) *n.* **1.** T act of transmuting, or the state of being transmuted. *Physics* The change of one element into another through teration of its nuclear structure, as by bombardment w high-energy particles in an accelerator. **3.** *Biol.* Success change of form. **4.** In alchemy, the supposed change o base metal into gold, silver, etc. — **trans′mu·ta′tion** — **trans·mu·ta·tive** (trans-myōō′tə·tiv, tranz-) *adj.*
trans·mute (trans-myōōt′, tranz-) *v.t.* **·mut·ed**, **·mut·** To change in nature, form, quality, etc.; transform. A **trans·mu′tate.** [< L < *trans-* across + *mutare* to chang — **trans·mut′a·ble** *adj.* — **trans·mut′a·bil′i·ty, trans·m a·ble·ness** *n.* — **trans·mut′a·bly** *adv.* — **trans·mut′er** *n.*
trans·o·ce·an·ic (trans′ō·shē·an′ik, tranz′-) *adj.* **1.** Ly beyond or over the ocean. **2.** Crossing the ocean.
tran·som (tran′səm) *n.* **1.** A small window above a doo window, usu. hinged to a horizontal crosspiece; also, crosspiece. **2.** A horizontal construction dividing a wind into stages. **3.** *Naut.* A beam running across the st frame of a ship. **4.** The horizontal crossbar of a gallows cross. [< L *transtrum* crossbeam] — **tran′somed** *adj.*
tran·son·ic (tran·son′ik) *adj. Aeron.* Of or pertaining conditions encountered when passing to supersonic speed **transonic barrier** *Aeron.* A barrier to supersonic flight countered by aircraft designed for subsonic speed, caused turbulence of the airflow around different parts of the pla also called *sonic barrier, sound barrier.*
trans·pa·cif·ic (trans′pə·sif′ik) *adj.* **1.** Crossing the Pac Ocean. **2.** Situated across or beyond the Pacific.
trans·par·en·cy (trans-pâr′ən·sē, -par′-) *n.* pl. **·cies** The quality of being transparent. Also **trans·par′ence.** — Something transparent; esp., a picture on a substance, glass, intended to be viewed by shining a light through it
trans·par·ent (trans-pâr′ənt, -par′-) *adj.* **1.** Admitting passage of light, and permitting a clear view of objects yond. **2.** Easy to see through or understand; obvious. Without guile; frank; candid. **4.** Diaphanous; sheer. **Syn.** See CLEAR. [< Med.L < L *trans-* across + *parere* appear, be visible] — **trans·par′ent·ly** *adv.* — **trans·pa ent·ness** *n.*
trans·pierce (trans-pirs′) *v.t.* **·pierced**, **·pierc·ing** To pie through; penetrate completely. [< MF < *trans-* (across, through) + *percer* to pierce]
tran·spire (tran-spīr′) *v.* **·spired**, **·spir·ing** *v.t.* **1.** To g off (waste products) from the surface of the body, lea etc.; exhale. —*v.i.* **2.** To give off waste products, as surface of the body, leaves, etc. **3.** To become known. *Informal* To happen; occur. ◆ Although *transpire* is u

widely in this last sense, this usage is considered erroneous
y some. [< F < L *trans-* across, through + *spirare* to
reathe] —**tran′spi·ra′tion** n.

ans·plant (*v.* trans·plant′, -plänt′; *n.* trans′plant′, -plänt′)
t. **1.** To remove and plant in another place. **2.** To remove
nd settle or establish for residence in another place. **3.**
urg. To transfer (a portion of tissue) from its original site to
nother part of the same individual, or to another individual.
—*n.* **1.** That which is transplanted. **2.** The act of trans-
lanting. [< LL < L *trans-* across + *plantare* to plant] —
ans·plan·ta′tion n. —**trans·plant′er** n.

ans·port (*v.* trans·pôrt′, -pōrt′; *n.* trans′pôrt, -pōrt) *v.t.* **1.**
o carry or convey from one place to another. **2.** To carry
way with emotion. **3.** To carry into banishment; esp. be-
ond the sea. —**Syn.** See BANISH. —*n.* **1.** A vessel used
o transport troops, military supplies, etc. **2.** An aircraft
sed to transport passengers, mail, etc. **3.** The state of be-
ng transported with rapture; ecstasy. **4.** The act of trans-
orting. **5.** A deported convict. [< MF < L < *trans-* across
- *portare* to carry] —**trans·port′er** n.
ans·port·a·ble (trans·pôr′tə·bəl, -pōr′-) *adj.* Capable of
eing transported. —**trans·port′a·bil′i·ty** n.
ans·por·ta·tion (trans′pər·tā′shən) *n.* **1.** The act of
ransporting, or the state of being transported. **2.** A means
f transporting, as a vehicle. **3.** A charge for conveyance.
. A ticket, pass, etc., for travel.
ans·pose (trans·pōz′) *v.t.* ·**posed**, ·**pos·ing 1.** To reverse
he order or change the place of; interchange. **2.** To change
a place or order, as a word in a sentence. **3.** *Math.* To trans-
r (a term) with a changed sign from one side of an alge-
raic equation to the other, so as not to destroy the equality
f the members. **4.** *Music* To move (a chord, melody, com-
osition, etc.) upward or downward in pitch while retaining
s internal interval structure. —*v.i.* **5.** *Music* To play in a
ey other than the one notated: said of players or instru-
ents. [< OF < L *trans-* over + OF *poser* to place] —
ans·pos′a·ble *adj.* —**trans·pos′er** n. —**trans′po·si′tion,
ans·po′sal** n.

ans·sex·u·al (trans·sek′shoo·əl, -sek′shəl) *n.* **1.** A person
ho is genetically and physically of one sex but who
dentifies psychologically with the other. **2.** One whose sex
haracteristics have been altered by surgery and hormone
reatment.

ans·ship (trans·ship′) *v.t. & v.i.* ·**shipped**, ·**ship·ping** To
ransfer from one conveyance or line to another: also spelled
anship. —**trans·ship′ment** n.

an·sub·stan·ti·a·tion (tran′səb·stan′shē·ā′shən) *n.* **1.**
heol. The doctrine that the substance of the eucharistic ele-
ents is converted into that of the body and blood of Christ.
. A change of anything into something essentially different.
< Med.L < L *trans-* over + *substantia* substance] —
an·sub·stan′ti·a′tion·al·ist n.

ans·u·ra·ni·an (trans′yŏŏ·rā′nē·ən, tranz′-) *adj. Physics*
f or pertaining to any of those radioactive elements having
n atomic number greater than that of uranium. Also **trans′·
ran′ic** (-ran′ik).
ans·ver·sal (trans·vûr′səl, tranz·-) *adj.* Transverse. —
. Geom. A line intersecting a system of lines.
ans·verse (trans·vûrs′, tranz·-) *adj.* Lying or being across
r from side to side; athwart. —*n.* **1.** That which is trans-
erse. **2.** *Geom.* That axis of a hyperbola that passes
rough its foci. [< L < *trans-* across + *vertere* to turn] —
ans·verse′ly *adv.* —**trans·verse′ness** n.

ans·ves·tite (trans·ves′tīt, tranz·-) *n.* One who wears the
othes of the opposite sex. [< L *trans-* over + *vestire* to
othe + -ITE] —**trans·ves′tism, trans·ves′ti·tism** n.

ap¹ (trap) *n.* **1.** A device for catching game or other ani-
als, as a pitfall or snare. **2.** Any artifice or stratagem by
hich a person may be betrayed or taken unawares. **3.**
ech. A U- or S-bend in a pipe, etc., that fills with water or
her liquid for sealing the pipe against a return flow, as of
oxious gas. **4.** A contrivance for hurling clay pigeons or
ass balls into the air for sportsmen to shoot at. **5.** In some
ames, esp. golf, an obstacle or hazard: a sand *trap.* **6.** A
ght, two-wheeled carriage suspended by springs. **7.** *pl.*
ercussion instruments, as drums, cymbals, etc. **8.** A trap
oor. **9.** *U.S. Slang* The mouth: Shut your *trap.* —*v.*
apped, trap·ping *v.t.* **1.** To catch in a trap; ensnare. **2.**
o stop or hold (a gas, liquid, etc.) by some obstruction. **3.**
o provide with a trap. —*v.i.* **4.** To set traps for game.
. To be a trapper. [OE *treppe, træppe*]

ap² (trap) *n. Geol.* A dark, fine-grained igneous rock, of-
n of columnar structure, as basalt, dolerite, etc. Also **trap′·
ck′** (rok′). [< Sw. *trappa* stair; so·called from the step-
e arrangement of this rock in other rock]

ap door A door, hinged or sliding, to cover an opening, as
a floor or roof.

·peze (trə·pēz′, tra-) *n.* **1.** A short swinging bar, sus-

pended by two ropes, used by gymnasts, etc. **2.** *Geom.* A
trapezium. [< F < NL *trapezium* trapezium]
tra·pe·zi·um (trə·pē′zē·əm) *n. pl.* ·**zi·a** (-zē·ə) **1.** *Geom.* **a**
A four-sided plane figure of which no
two sides are parallel. **b** *Brit.* A trapezoid. **2.** *Anat.* The bone of the wrist
situated at the base of the thumb. [<
NL < Gk. *trapezion,* dim. of *trapeza*
table, lit., four-footed (bench) <
tetra- four, + *peza* foot]
trap·e·zoid (trap′ə·zoid) *n.* **1.** *Geom.*
a A quadrilateral of which two sides are parallel. **b** *Brit.* A
trapezium. **2.** *Anat.* An irregular bone near the base of the
forefinger. [< NL < Gk. < *trapeza* table + *eidos* form] —
trap′e·zoi′dal *adj.*

TRAPEZIUM (a) AND
TRAPEZOID (b)

trap·per (trap′ər) *n.* One whose occupation is the trapping
of fur-bearing animals.
trap·pings (trap′ingz) *n.pl.* **1.** An ornamental housing or
harness for a horse. **2.** Adornments of any kind; embellish-
ments; superficial dress. [< obs. *traps* < ME *trappe*]
Trap·pist (trap′ist) *n.* A member of an ascetic order of Cis-
tercian monks, noted for silence and abstinence. —*adj.* Of
or pertaining to the Trappists. [after *La Trappe* in Normandy, name of their first abbey, established 1664]
trap·shoot·ing (trap′shoo′ting) *n.* The sport of shooting
clay pigeons sent up from spring traps. —**trap′shoot′er** n.
trash (trash) *n.* **1.** Worthless or waste matter of any kind;
rubbish. **2.** A worthless or despicable individual or group of
individuals. **3.** Worthless or foolish writing, ideas, etc.; nonsense. **4.** That which is broken or lopped off; esp., the lop-
pings and trimmings of trees and plants. —*v.t.* **1.** To free
from trash. **2.** To strip of leaves; prune; lop. [Cf. dial.
Norw. *trask* lumber, trash, baggage]
trash·y (trash′ē) *adj.* **trash·i·er, trash·i·est** Resembling
trash or rubbish; worthless; cheap: *trashy* poetry. —**trash′·
i·ly** *adv.* —**trash′i·ness** n.
trau·ma (trô′mə, trou′-) *n. pl.* ·**mas** or ·**ma·ta** (-mə·tə) **1.**
Pathol. **a** Any injury to the body caused by shock, violence,
etc.; a wound. **b** The general condition of the system resulting from such an injury or wound. Also **trau′ma·tism** (-tiz′-
əm). **2.** *Psychiatry* A severe emotional shock having a deep,
often lasting effect upon the personality. [< NL < Gk.
trauma, -atos wound]
trau·mat·ic (trô·mat′ik) *adj.* Of, pertaining to, or caused
by a trauma. —**trau·mat′i·cal·ly** *adv.*
trav·ail (trav′āl, trə·vāl′) *v.i.* **1.** To toil; labor. **2.** To suffer
the pangs of childbirth. —*n.* **1.** Strenuous physical or mental labor. **2.** Anguish; pain. **3.** Labor in childbirth. [<
OF < *travaillier* to toil, ult. < LL *trepalium* instrument of
torture < *tres, tria* three + *palus* stake]
trav·el (trav′əl) *v.* **trav·eled** or ·**elled, trav·el·ing** or ·**el·ling**
v.i. **1.** To go from one place to another; make a journey or
tour. **2.** To proceed; advance. **3.** To go about from place
to place as a traveling salesman. **4.** *U.S. Informal* To move
with speed. **5.** To pass or be transmitted, as light, sound,
etc. **6.** *Mech.* To move in a fixed path, as part of a mechanism. —*v.t.* **7.** To move or journey across or through; traverse. —*n.* **1.** The act of traveling. **2.** *pl.* A trip or journey. **3.** A movement or progress of any kind. **4.** *Mech.* **a**
The full course of a moving part in one direction. **b** Length
of stroke, as of a piston. [Var. of TRAVAIL]
trav·eled (trav′əld) *adj.* **1.** Having made many journeys.
2. Experienced as the result of travel. **3.** Frequented or
used by travelers. Also **trav′elled.**
trav·el·er (trav′əl·ər, trav′lər) *n.* **1.** One who travels or
journeys. **2.** *Brit.* A traveling salesman. **3.** *Naut.* A metal
ring or thimble running freely on a rope, rod, or spar; also,
the rope, rod, or spar. Also **trav′el·ler.**
traveler's check A draft issued by a bank, express company, etc., having the bearer's signature, and payable when
the bearer signs it again in order to cash it.
traveling salesman A salesman who travels to various
places obtaining orders for his firm. Also **traveling man.**
trav·e·logue (trav′ə·lôg, -log) *n.* A lecture or film on travel.
Also **trav′e·log.**
tra·verse (trav′ərs; *for v. & adv., also* trə·vûrs′) *v.* ·**ersed**,
·**ers·ing** *v.t.* **1.** To pass over, across, or through. **2.** To move
back and forth over or along. **3.** To examine carefully; survey or scrutinize. **4.** To oppose; thwart. **5.** To turn (a gun,
lathe, etc.) to right or left; swivel. **6.** *Law* **a** In legal pleading, to deny (a matter of fact alleged by the opposite party).
b To impeach (the validity of an inquest of office). **7.** *Naut.*
To brace (a yard) fore and aft. —*v.i.* **8.** To move back and
forth. **9.** To move across; cross. **10.** To turn; swivel. —
n. **1.** A part, as of a machine or structure, placed across or
traversing another, as a crosspiece, crossbeam, transom, etc.
2. *Archit.* A gallery or loft communicating with opposite
sides of a building. **3.** Something serving as a screen or bar-

rier. **4.** _Geom._ A transversal. **5.** The act of traversing or crossing. **6.** A way or path across. **7.** _Mech._ Sidewise travel, as of the tool in a slide rest. **8.** _Law_ A formal denial. **9.** _Naut._ A zigzag track of a vessel while beating to windward. — _adj._ Transverse; lying or being across. [< OF < LL < L _trans-_ across + _vertere_ to turn] — **trav′ers·a·ble** _adj._ — **trav·er·sal** (trav′ər·səl, trə·vûr′səl) _n._ — **trav′ers·er** _n._

trav·er·tine (trav′ər·tin, -tēn, -tīn) _n._ A porous, light yellow, crystalline limestone deposited in solution from ground or surface waters, used for building purposes. Also **trav′er·tin** (-tin). [< Ital. < L _Tiburtinus_ Tiburtine < _Tiburs, -urtis_ of Tibur]

trav·es·ty (trav′is·tē) _n._ _pl._ **·ties 1.** A grotesque imitation; burlesque. **2.** In literature, a burlesque treatment of a lofty subject. — _v.t._ **·tied, ·ty·ing** To make a travesty on; parody. [< MF < Ital. < L _trans_ across + _vestire_ to dress]

trawl (trôl) _n._ **1.** A stout fishing line having many lines frequently spaced and bearing baited hooks: also called _trotline_. Also **trawl line. 2.** A great fishing net shaped like a flattened bag, for towing on the bottom of the ocean by a boat: also **trawl net.** — _v.t._ **1.** To catch (fish) with a trawl. — _v.i._ **2.** To fish with a trawl. [Cf. MDu. _traghel_ dragnet]

trawl·er (trô′lər) _n._ **1.** A vessel used for trawling. **2.** One who is engaged in trawling.

tray (trā) _n._ A flat receptacle with a low rim, made of wood, metal, etc., used to carry, hold, or display articles: a sandwich _tray_. [OE _trīg, trēg_ wooden board]

treach·er·ous (trech′ər·əs) _adj._ **1.** Traitorous; perfidious; disloyal. **2.** Having a deceptive appearance; unreliable; untrustworthy: a _treacherous_ path. — **treach′er·ous·ly** _adv._ — **treach′er·ous·ness** _n._

treach·er·y (trech′ər·ē) _n._ _pl._ **·er·ies** Violation of allegiance, confidence, or faith; perfidy; treason. [< OF < _tricher, trechier_ to cheat]

trea·cle (trē′kəl) _n._ **1.** _Brit._ Molasses. **2.** Formerly, a compound used as an antidote. [< OF < L < Gk. _thēriakē_ remedy for poisonous bites] — **trea′cly** _adj._

tread (tred) _v._ **trod** (_Archaic_ **trode**), **trod·den** or **trod, tread·ing** _v.t._ **1.** To step or walk on, over, along, etc. **2.** To press with the feet; trample. **3.** To accomplish in walking or in dancing: to _tread_ a measure. **4.** To copulate with: said of male birds. — _v.i._ **5.** To step or walk. **6.** To trample: usually with _on._ — **to tread water** In swimming, to keep the body erect and the head above water by moving the feet up and down as if walking. — _n._ **1.** The act, manner, or sound of treading or walking. **2.** The flat part of a step in a staircase. **3.** The part of a wheel that bears upon the ground or rails. **4.** The outer, often grooved surface of an automobile tire. **5.** That part of the sole of a shoe that treads upon the ground. **6.** The part of a rail on which the wheels bear. [OE _tredan_] — **tread′er** _n._

trea·dle (tred′l) _n._ A lever operated by the foot, usu. to cause rotary motion. For illus. see POTTER'S WHEEL. — _v.i._ **·led, ·ling** To work a treadle. [OE < _tredan_ to tread] — **tread′ler** _n._

tread·mill (tred′mil′) _n._ **1.** A mechanism rotated by the walking motion of one or more persons. **2.** A similar mechanism operated by a quadruped. **3.** Any wearisome or monotonous work, activity, routine, etc.

trea·son (trē′zən) _n._ **1.** Betrayal or breach of allegiance or of obedience toward one's sovereign or government. **2.** _Rare_ A breach of faith; treachery. [< AF _treyson_, OF _traison_ < L _traditio, -onis_ betrayal, delivery]

trea·son·a·ble (trē′zən·ə·bəl) _adj._ Of, involving, or characteristic of treason. Also **trea′son·ous.** — **trea′son·a·ble·ness** _n._ — **trea′son·a·bly** _adv._

treas·ure (trezh′ər) _n._ **1.** Riches accumulated or possessed, esp. in the form of money, jewels, or precious metals. **2.** One who or that which is regarded as valuable, precious, or rare. — _v.t._ **·ured, ·ur·ing 1.** To lay up in store; accumulate. **2.** To retain carefully, as in the mind. **3.** To set a high value upon; prize. [< OF < L < Gk. _thēsauros_]

treas·ur·er (trezh′ər·ər) _n._ An officer of a state, city, corporation, society, etc., who has charge of funds or revenues. **Treasure State** Nickname of Montana.

trea·sure-trove (trezh′ər·trōv′) _n._ **1.** _Law_ Any treasure found hidden in the earth, etc., the owner being unknown. **2.** Any discovery that proves valuable. [< AF < _tresor_ + _trové_, pp., of _trover_ to find]

treas·ur·y (trezh′ər·ē) _n._ _pl._ **·ur·ies 1.** The place where private or public funds or revenues are received, kept, and disbursed. **2.** Any public or private funds or revenues. **3.** Any group or collection of treasures or things regarded as treasures. **4.** A place or receptacle where treasures are kept. — **Department of the Treasury** An executive department of the U.S. government that superintends and manages the national finances. Also **Treasury Department.**

treasury note _U.S._ A note issued by the Treasury as legal tender for all debts, public and private.

treat (trēt) _v.t._ **1.** To conduct oneself toward in a specified manner. **2.** To look upon or regard in a specified manner:

They _treat_ the matter as a joke. **3.** To subject to chemic or physical action, as for altering or improving. **4.** To gi medical or surgical attention to. **5.** To deal with in writir or speaking. **6.** To deal with or develop (a subject in art literature) in a specified manner or style. **7.** To pay for t entertainment, food, or drink of. — _v.i._ **8.** To handle a su ject in writing or speaking: usu. with _of._ **9.** To negotiat **10.** To pay for another's entertainment or food. — _n._ Something that gives unusual pleasure. **2.** Entertainme furnished gratuitously to another. **3.** The act of treatin also, one's turn to treat. [< OF < L _tractare_ to handle] **treat′a·ble** _adj._ — **treat′er** _n._

trea·tise (trē′tis) _n._ A formal and systematic written a count of some subject. [< AF _tretiz_, OF _traitier_ to treat

treat·ment (trēt′mənt) _n._ **1.** The act, manner, or proce of treating. **2.** The care of an illness, by drugs, surgery, et **3.** The manner of handling an artistic or literary subject.

trea·ty (trē′tē) _n._ _pl._ **·ties** A formal agreement or compac duly concluded and ratified, between two or more state also, the document containing such an agreement or co pact. [< AF _treté_, OF _traitie_, pp. of _traitier_ to treat]

tre·ble (treb′əl) _v.t. & v.i._ **·led, ·ling** To multiply by thre triple. — _adj._ **1.** Threefold; triple. **2.** Soprano. — _n._ _Music_ **a** A soprano voice, part, or instrument; also, the sin er or player taking this part. **b** The highest register of an strument. **2.** High, piping sound. [< OF < L _triplus_] **treb′le·ness** _n._ — **treb′ly** _adv._

tree (trē) _n._ **1.** A perennial woody plant having usu. a sin self-supporting trunk of considerable height, with branch and foliage growing at some distance above the ground. Collateral adjective: _arboreal._ **2.** Any shrub or plant th assumes treelike shape or dimensions. **3.** Something rese bling a tree in form or outline, as a clothes tree, crosstre etc. **4.** A diagram or outline resembling a tree and showi family descent. **5.** A timber, post, pole, etc.: used in co bination: _axletree._ — **up a tree** _Informal_ In a position fr which there is no retreat; cornered: also, in an embarrassi position. — _v.t._ **treed, tree·ing 1.** To force to climb or ta refuge in a tree: to _tree_ an opossum. **2.** _Informal_ To g the advantage of; corner. **3.** To stretch, as a boot, on a bo tree. [OE _trēow, trīow, trēo_]

tree fern Any of various ferns with large fronds and woo trunks that often attain a treelike size.

tree frog An arboreal amphibian, having the toes dilat with viscous, adhesive disks: also called _tree toad._

tree of heaven The ailanthus.

tree of knowledge of good and evil In the Bible, a tr in Eden whose fruit Adam and Eve were forbidden to e _Gen._ iii 3, 6. Also **tree of knowledge.**

Tree-Plant·er State (trē′plan′tər, -plän′-) Nickname Nebraska.

tree sparrow A North American sparrow that nests Canada and migrates southward in winter.

tree surgery The treatment of disease conditions and c cay in trees by operative methods. — **tree surgeon**

tree toad A tree frog.

tree·top (trē′top′) _n._ The highest part of a tree.

tre·foil (trē′foil) _n._ **1.** Any of a genus of leguminous plan the clovers, with red, purple, pink, or yellow flowers and t foliate leaflets. **2.** A three-lobed architectural ornamer tion. [< AF, OF < L _trifolium_]

trek (trek) _v._ **trekked, trek·king** _v.i._ **1.** In South Africa, travel by ox wagon. **2.** To travel, esp. slowly or arduous — _v.t._ **3.** In South Africa, to draw (a vehicle or load): s of an ox. — _n._ **1.** In South Africa, a journey or any part it; esp., an organized migration, as for the founding o colony. **2.** A journey; esp., a slow or arduous journey. Du. < MDu. < OHG _trechan_ to draw] — **trek′ker** _n._

trel·lis (trel′is) _n._ **1.** A crossbarred structure or panel wood, metal, or other material, used as a screen or a supp for vines, etc. **2.** A summerhouse, archway, etc., made fr or consisting of such a structure. — _v.t._ **1.** To interlace so to form a trellis. **2.** To furnish with or fasten on a trel [< OF < L < _tri-_ three + _licium_ thread]

trel·lis·work (trel′is·wûrk′) _n._ Openwork made from, c sisting of, or resembling a trellis.

trem·a·tode (trem′ə·tōd) _n._ One of a class of parasitic fl worms, including the liver flukes. [< NL < Gk. < _trē -atos_ hole + _eidos_ form] — **trem′a·toid** (-toid) _adj._

trem·ble (trem′bəl) _v.i._ **·bled, ·bling 1.** To shake invol tarily, as with fear or weakness; be agitated. **2.** To ha slight, irregular vibratory motion, as from some jarr force; shake. **3.** To feel anxiety or fear. **4.** To quaver, the voice. — _n._ The act or state of trembling. [< OF LL _tremulus_ tremulous < _tremere_ to tremble] — **trem′b** _n._ — **trem′bling·ly** _adv._ — **trem′bly** _adj._

tre·men·dous (tri·men′dəs) _adj._ **1.** _Informal_ Extraor narily large; huge; vast. **2.** _Informal_ Unusual; amazi wonderful. **3.** Causing astonishment by its magnitu force, etc. [< L _tremendus_ to be trembled at < _tremere_ tremble] — **tre·men′dous·ly** _adv._ — **tre·men′dous·ness**

m·o·lo (trem/ə-lō) *n. pl.* ·los *Music* 1. In string instrument playing, a rapid reiteration of a tone caused by altering movements of the bow. 2. A tonal alternation of o tones, usu. a third or more apart. Compare TRILL. 3. device or stop for producing a vibrato effect on an organ ne. [< Ital. < L *tremulus*]

m·or (trem/ər, trē/mər) *n.* 1. A quick, vibratory movement; a shaking. 2. Any involuntary and continued quivng or trembling of the body or limbs; a shiver. 3. A quaring sound. 4. Any trembling, quivering effect. [< OF, ır, a trembling < L < *tremere* to tremble]

m·u·lous (trem/yə-ləs) *adj.* 1. Characterized or affected trembling: *tremulous* speech. 2. Showing timidity or ır. — **trem/u·lous·ly** *adv.* — **trem/u·lous·ness** *n.*

nch (trench) *n.* 1. A long narrow excavation in the ound; ditch. 2. A long irregular ditch, lined with a para- t of the excavated earth, to protect troops. — *v.t.* 1. To g a trench or trenches in. 2. To fortify with trenches. 3. cut deep furrows in; ditch. 4. To confine in a trench, as ster. — *v.i.* 5. To cut or dig trenches. 6. To cut; carve. To encroach. [< OF *trenchier* to cut, ult. < L *truncare* to) off < *truncus* tree trunk] — **trench/er** *n.*

nch·ant (tren/chənt) *adj.* 1. Cutting; incisive; keen: a *nchant* remark. 2. Forceful; vigorous; effective. 3. early defined; distinct. [< OF, ppr. of *trenchier* to cut] **trench/an·cy** *n.* — **trench/ant·ly** *adv.*

nch coat A loose-fitting overcoat of rainproof fabric.

nch·er (tren/chər) *n.* Formerly, a wooden plate or board which food was served or cut. [See TRENCH⁶]

nch·er·man (tren/chər-mən) *n. pl.* ·men (-mən) A eder; eater; esp., one who enjoys food.

nch fever *Pathol.* A remittent rickettsial fever trans- tted by body lice and common among soldiers assigned to olonged service in trenches during World War I.

nch foot *Pathol.* A disease of the feet caused by con- ued dampness and cold, and characterized by discolora- n, weakness, and sometimes gangrene.

nch mouth *Pathol.* A disease of the mouth, gums, and metimes the larynx and tonsils, caused by a soil bacillus. **nd** (trend) *n.* A general course, inclination, or deflection. *v.i.* To have or take a particular trend. [OE *trendan* to l]

·pan (tri-pan/) *n.* 1. An early form of the trephine. 2. large rock-boring tool. — *v.t.* ·panned, ·pan·ning 1. *Mech.* cut circular disks from (a rock or metal plate) by a rotary ol. 2. *Surg.* To trephine. [< OF, borer < Med.L < Gk. *trypaein* to bore] — **trep·a·na·tion** (trep/ə-nā/shən) *n.* — **tre·pan/ner** *n.*

·pang (tri-pang/) *n.* An East Indian sea cucumber, used China for making soup. [< Malay *tripang*]

·phine (tri-fīn/, -fēn/) *n. Surg.* A crown saw for remov- g a piece of bone from the skull so as to relieve pressure, c. — *v.t.* ·phined, ·phin·ing To operate on with a trephine. < earlier *trafine* < L *tres fines* three ends]

p·i·da·tion (trep/ə-dā/shən) *n.* 1. A state of agitation or ırm; perturbation. 2. An involuntary trembling. Also **e·pid·i·ty** (tri-pid/ə-tē). [< L < *trepidatus*, pp. of *trepidare* hurry, be alarmed < *trepidus* alarmed]

p·o·neme (trep/ə-nēm) *n.* Any of a group of bacteria in- uding the causative agent of syphilis. [< NL < Gk. *tre- in* to turn + *nēma* thread] — **trep/o·nem/a·tous** (-nem/ə- s) *adj.*

·s·pass (tres/pəs, -pas/) *v.i.* 1. *Law* To commit a tres- ıss; esp., to enter wrongfully upon another's land: with *on* upon. 2. To pass the bounds of propriety or rectitude, to e injury of another; intrude offensively; encroach: with *on* upon. 3. To transgress or sin. — *n.* 1. Any voluntary ınsgression of law or rule of duty; any offense done to other. 2. *Law* Any wrongful act accompanied with force, ther actual or implied, as wrongful entry on another's land. < OF < Med.L < L *trans-* across, beyond + to pass] — **es/pass·er** *n.*

·ss (tres) *n.* 1. A lock, or ringlet of human hair. 2. *pl.* he hair of a woman or girl, esp. when worn loose. [< OF *esce*] — **tress/y** *adj.*

·ess *suffix* Used to form many feminine nouns correspond- g to masculine nouns in *-ter, -tor: actress.* [Var. of -ESS]

·ssed (trest) *adj.* Wearing or arranged in tresses; braided.

·s·tle (tres/əl) *n.* 1. A beam or bar supported by four di- ergent legs, for bearing platforms, etc. 2. An open braced amework for supporting a railway bridge, etc. [< OF < , dim. of *transtrum* crossbeam]

·s·tle·work (tres/əl-wûrk/) *n.* 1. Trestles collectively. A bridge made of trestles. Also **tres/tling.**

·y (trā) *n.* A card, domino, or die having three spots or ps. [< OF *trei, treis* < L *tres* three]

· *prefix* 1. Three; threefold; thrice. 2. *Chem.* Contain- g three (specified) atoms, radicals, groups, etc.: *trioxide.*

3. Occurring every three (specified) intervals, or three times within an (assigned) interval: *tri-weekly.* [< L *tri-* threefold]

tri·a·ble (trī/ə-bəl) *adj.* 1. That may be tried or tested. 2. *Law* That may undergo a judicial examination or determi- nation. — **tri/a·ble·ness** *n.*

tri·ad (trī/ad) *n.* 1. A group of three persons or things. 2. *Music* A chord of three tones formed of superimposed thirds. [< L < Gk. *trias, -ados* < *treis* three] — **tri·ad/ic** *adj. & n.*

tri·al (trī/əl, trīl) *n.* 1. The examination before a court of the facts or law in a case in order to determine that case. 2. The act of testing or proving by experience or use. 3. The state of being tried or tested, as by suffering: hour of *trial.* 4. Experimental treatment or action performed to deter- mine a result: to learn by *trial* and error. 5. An attempt or effort to do something; a try: to make a *trial.* — **on trial** In the process of being tried or tested. — *adj.* 1. Of or per- taining to a trial or trials. 2. Made, used, or performed in the course of trying or testing. [< AF *trier* to try]

trial and error Experimentation, investigation, learning, etc., in which various methods, theories, or alternatives are tried and faulty or erroneous ones are rejected.

trial balance In double-entry bookkeeping, a draft or statement of the debit and credit footings or balances of each account in the ledger.

trial balloon 1. A balloon released in order to test atmos- pheric and meteorological conditions. 2. Any tentative plan or scheme advanced to test public reaction.

trial jury A petit jury.

tri·an·gle (trī/ang/gəl) *n.* 1. *Geom.* A figure, esp. a plane figure, bounded by three sides, and having three angles. 2. Something resembling such a figure in shape or arrange- ment. 3. A flat drawing implement for making parallel or diagonal lines, etc. 4. A group or set of three; a triad. 5. A situation involving three persons: the eternal *triangle.* 6. *Music* An instrument consisting of a metal bar bent into a tri- angle and sounded by being struck with a metal rod. [< OF < L < *tri-* three + *angulus* angle]

tri·an·gu·lar (trī-ang/gyə-lər) *adj.* 1. Pertaining to, like, or bounded by a triangle. 2. Concerned with or pertaining to three things, parties, or persons. — **tri·an/gu·lar/i·ty** (-lar/ə-tē) *n.* — **tri·an/gu·lar·ly** *adv.*

tri·an·gu·late (trī-ang/gyə-lāt) *v.t.* ·lated, ·lat·ing 1. To di- vide into triangles. 2. To survey by triangulation. 3. To make triangular. — *adj.* Of or marked with triangles.

tri·an·gu·la·tion (trī-ang/gyə-lā/shən) *n.* 1. The laying out and accurate measurement of a network of triangles. 2. A method of determining a position by taking bearings to two fixed points of known distance apart and computing it on the resultant triangle.

Tri·as·sic (trī-as/ik) *adj. Geol.* Of or pertaining to the earli- est of the three geological periods comprised in the Mesozoic era. — *n.* The Triassic period or rock system, following the Permian and succeeded by the Jurassic. Also **Tri·as** (trī/əs). See chart under GEOLOGY. [< LL *trias* triad]

tri·bal·ism (trī/bəl-iz/əm) *n.* Tribal organization, culture, or relations.

tribe (trīb) *n.* 1. A division, class, or group of people, esp. a primitive or nomadic people, usu. characterized by common ancestry, leadership, customs, etc. 2. In ancient states, an ethnic, hereditary, or political division of a united people; also, one of the twelve divisions of ancient Israel. 3. A num- ber of persons of any class or profession taken together: often an offensive term: the theatrical *tribe.* 4. *Biol.* A group of plants or animals of indefinite rank. [< L *tribus* tribe] — **tri/bal·ly** *adv.*

tribes·man (trībz/mən) *n. pl.* ·men (-mən) A member of a tribe.

trib·u·la·tion (trib/yə-lā/shən) *n.* A condition of affliction and distress; suffering; also, that which causes it. [< OF < LL < L < *tribulum* threshing floor < *terere* to rub, grind]

tri·bu·nal (tri-byōō/nəl, trī-) *n.* 1. A court of justice. 2. The seat set apart for judges, etc. [See TRIBUNE.]

trib·une¹ (trib/yōon) *n.* 1. In Roman history, a magistrate chosen by the plebeians to protect them against patrician op- pression. 2. Any champion of the people. [< L *tribunus* < *tribus* tribe] — **trib/u·nar/y** (-yə-ner/ē), **trib/u·ni/cial** (-yə- nish/əl, **trib/u·ni/cian** *adj.* — **trib/u·nate** (-yə-nit, -nāt), **trib/- une·ship** *n.*

trib·une² (trib/yōon) *n.* A rostrum or platform. [< MF < Ital. < L *tribunal* tribunal]

trib·u·tar·y (trib/yə-ter/ē) *adj.* 1. Bringing supply; con- tributory: a *tributary* stream. 2. Offered or due as tribute: a *tributary* payment. 3. Paying tribute, as a state. — *n. pl.* ·tar·ies 1. A person or state paying tribute. 2. A stream flowing into a larger stream or body of water. [See TRIB- UTE.] — **trib/u·tar/i·ly** *adv.* — **trib/u·tar/i·ness** *n.*

trib·ute (trib/yōot) *n.* 1. A speech, compliment, gift, etc., given in acknowledgment of admiration, gratitude, or respect. **2.** Money or other valuables paid by one state or ruler to another as an acknowledgment of submission or as the price of peace and protection; also, the taxes imposed to raise money to make such payment. **3.** Any enforced payment as by bribery. [< L *tribuere* to pay, allot]

trice (trīs) *v.t.* **triced, tric·ing** To raise with a rope; also, to tie or lash: usu. with *up.* — *n.* An instant: now only in the phrase **in a trice.** [< MDu. *trisen* to hoist]

tri·cen·ten·ni·al (trī′sen·ten′ē·əl) *adj. & n.* Tercentenary.

tri·ceps (trī′seps) *n. Anat.* A large muscle at the back of the upper arm, of which the function is to extend the forearm. [< L < *tri-* three + *caput* head]

tri·chi·na (tri·kī′nə) *n. pl.* **·nae** (-nē) A small nematode worm, parasitic in the intestines and muscles of man, swine, and other mammals. [< NL < Gk. *thrix* hair]

trich·i·no·sis (trik′ə·nō′sis) *n. Pathol.* The disease produced by trichinae in the intestines and muscles of the body, in man, usu. through eating improperly cooked meat, esp. pork. — **trich′i·nous** (-nəs) *adj.*

tricho- *combining form* Hair; of or resembling a hair or hairs. Also **trichi-:** also, before vowels, **trich-.** [< NL < Gk. *thrix* hair]

trick (trik) *n.* **1.** A device for getting an advantage by deception; a petty artifice; ruse. **2.** A malicious, injurious, or annoying act: a dirty *trick.* **3.** A practical joke; prank. **4.** A particular habit or manner; characteristic; trait. **5.** A peculiar skill or knack. **6.** An act of legerdemain or magic. **7.** In card games, the whole number of cards played in one round. — **to do** (or **turn**) **the trick** *Slang* To produce the desired result. — *v.t.* **1.** To deceive or cheat; delude. **2.** To dress or array: with *up* or *out.* — *v.i.* **3.** To practice trickery or deception. [< OF < *trichier* to cheat, prob. ult. < L < *tricae* trifles, tricks] — **trick′er** *n.* — **trick′less** *adj.*

trick·er·y (trik′ər·ē) *n. pl.* **·er·ies** The practice of tricks; artifice; stratagem; wiles.

trick·le (trik′əl) *v.* **·led, ·ling** *v.i.* **1.** To flow or run drop by drop or in a very thin stream. **2.** To move, come, go, etc., slowly or bit by bit. — *v.t.* **3.** To cause to trickle. — *n.* **1.** The act or state of trickling. **2.** Any slow and irregular movement. [ME *triklen*] — **trick′ly** *adj.*

trick·ster (trik′stər) *n.* One who plays tricks; a cheat.

trick·y (trik′ē) *adj.* **trick·i·er, trick·i·est** Disposed to or characterized by trickery; deceitful; wily. — **trick′i·ly** *adv.* — **trick′i·ness** *n.*

tri·col·or (trī′kul′ər) *adj.* Having or characterized by three colors: also **tri′col′ored.** — *n.* **1.** A flag of three colors. **2.** *Sometimes cap.* The French flag. Also *Brit.* **tri′col′our.** [< F < LL < L *tri-* three + *color* color]

tri·corn (trī′kôrn) *n.* A hat with the brim turned up on three sides. Also **tri′corne.** — *adj.* Having three hornlike processes. [< F < L < *tri-* three + *cornu* horn]

tri·cot (trē′kō, *Fr.* trē·kō′) *n.* **1.** A plain, knitted fabric, usu. machine made. **2.** A soft ribbed cloth. [< F < *tricoter* to knit]

tri·cus·pid (trī·kus′pid) *adj.* **1.** Having three cusps or points, as a molar tooth. **2.** *Anat.* Of the tricuspid valve. Also **tri·cus′pi·dal, tri·cus′pi·date.** — *n. Anat.* The tricuspid valve. [< L < *tri-* three + *cuspis* point]

tricuspid valve *Anat.* A three-segmented valve that controls the flow of blood from the right atrium to the right ventricle of the heart.

tri·cy·cle (trī′sik·əl) *n.* A three-wheeled vehicle; esp., such a vehicle with pedals. [< F < *tri-* three + Gk. *kyklos* circle]

tri·dent (trīd′nt) *n.* A three-pronged fork. — *adj.* Having three teeth or prongs: also **tri·den·tate** (trī·den′tāt), **tri·den′·tat·ed.** [< L < *tri-* three + *dens* tooth]

tried (trīd) Past tense and past participle of TRY. — *adj.* Tested; trustworthy.

tri·en·ni·al (trī·en′ē·əl) *adj.* **1.** Taking place every third year. **2.** Lasting three years. — *n.* **1.** A third anniversary. **2.** A ceremony, etc., celebrated every three years. **3.** A plant lasting three years. — **tri·en′ni·al·ly** *adv.*

tri·er (trī′ər) *n.* One who or that which tries.

tri·fa·cial (trī·fā′shəl) *adj. Anat.* Trigeminal.

tri·fid (trī′fid) *adj.* Divided into three parts or sections. [< L < *tri-* three + *findere* to split]

tri·fle (trī′fəl) *v.* **·fled, ·fling** *v.i.* **1.** To treat something as of no value or importance; dally: with *with.* **2.** To act or speak frivolously. **3.** To play; toy. **4.** To idle. — *v.t.* **5.** To pass (time) in an idle and purposeless way. — *n.* **1.** Anything of very little value or importance. **2.** A confection, usu. made of alternate layers of macaroons or ladyfingers with sugared fruit, covered with a custard and topped with meringue or whipped cream. — **a trifle** Slightly: *a trifle short.* [< OF *trufe* cheating, mockery] — **tri′fler** *n.*

tri·fling (trī′fling) *adj.* **1.** Frivolous. **2.** Insignificant. — **tri′fling·ly** *adv.*

tri·fo·cal (trī·fō′kəl) *adj.* **1.** Having three foci. **2.** *Optics* Pertaining to or describing eyeglasses or a lens ground in three segments, for near, intermediate, and far vision. — *n. pl.* Eyeglasses having trifocal lenses.

tri·fo·li·ate (trī·fō′lē·it, -āt) *adj. Bot.* Having three leav- or leaflike processes. Also **tri·fo′li·at·ed.**

tri·fo·ri·um (trī·fôr′ē·əm, -fō′rē-) *n. pl.* **·fo·ri·a** (-fôr′ē- -fō′rē-ə) *Archit.* A gallery above the arches of the nave i church. [< Med.L < L *tri-* three + *foris* a door]

trig (trig) *adj.* **1.** Trim; neat. **2.** Strong; sound. — **trigged, trig·ging** To make trig or neat: often with *out* or *u* [< ON *tryggr* true] — **trig′ly** *adv.* — **trig′ness** *n.*

tri·gem·i·nal (trī·jem′ə·nəl) *adj. Anat.* Of or pertaining the trigeminus: also *trifacial.* — *n.* The trigeminus. [< *tri-* + *geminus* a twin]

tri·gem·i·nus (trī·jem′ə·nəs) *n. pl.* **·ni** (-nī) *Anat.* T double-rooted fifth cranial nerve, whose three divisions, ma dibular, maxillary, and opthalmic, function as the great se sory nerve of the face. [See TRIGEMINAL.]

trig·ger (trig′ər) *n.* **1.** The lever or other device actuat manually to fire a firearm. **2.** Any lever, release, etc., th serves to initiate a process or operation. — **quick on t trigger 1.** Quick to shoot. **2.** Quick to act; alert. — *v* To initiate; precipitate. [< Du. *trekken* to pull]

trigonometric functions Certain functions of an angle arc, of which the most commonly used are the sine, cosi tangent, cotangent, secant, and cosecant.

trig·o·nom·e·try (trig′ə·nom′ə·trē) *n.* The branch of mat ematics that deals with the relations of the sides and ang of triangles. [< NL < Gk. *trigōnon* triangle + *metron* me ure] — **trig·o·no·met·ric** (trig′ə·nə·met′rik) or **·ri·cal** *a* — **trig′o·m·met′ri·cal·ly** *adv.*

tri·he·dron (trī·hē′drən) *n. pl.* **·dra** (-drə) *Geom.* A fig having three plane surfaces meeting at a point. [< NL Gk. *tri-* three + *hedra* a base] — **tri·he′dral** *adj.*

tri·lat·er·al (trī·lat′ər·əl) *adj.* Having three sides. [< L *tri-* three + *latus* a side] — **tri·lat′er·al·ly** *adv.*

trill (tril) *v.t.* **1.** To sing or play in a tremulous tone. *Phonet.* To articulate with a trill. — *v.i.* **3.** To give fort tremulous sound. **4.** *Music* To execute a trill. — *n.* **1.** tremulous utterance of successive tones, as of birds; a w ble. **2.** *Music* A rapid alternation of two tones either a to or a semitone apart. **3.** *Phonet.* A rapid vibration of t tongue in the articulation of *rr* in Spanish, or of the uvula the articulation of *r* in some varieties of German. **4.** A c sonant so uttered. [< Ital. *trillare*]

tril·lion (tril′yən) *n.* **1.** *U.S.* A thousand billions, writt as 1 followed by twelve zeros: a cardinal number: calle billion in Great Britain. **2.** *Brit.* A million billions (def. written as 1 followed by eighteen zeros: a cardinal numb — *adj.* Being a trillion in number. [< MF < *tri-* three (*mi)llion* million] — **tril′lionth** *adj. & n.*

tril·li·um (tril′ē·əm) *n.* Any of various herbs of the l family, having a stout stem bearing a whorl of three lea and a solitary flower. [< NL < L *tri-* three]

tri·lo·bate (trī·lō′bāt, trī′lə·bāt) *adj. Bot.* Having th lobes, as some leaves. Also **tri·lo′bal, tri·lo′bat·ed, tri′lob**

tri·lo·bite (trī′lə·bīt) *n. Paleontol.* Any of a group of tinct Paleozoic marine animals having a flattened body vided into a variable number of segments covered by a ha dorsal shield marked in three lobes. [< NL < Gk. three + *lobos* a lobe] — **tri·lo·bit′ic** (-bit′ik) *adj.*

tril·o·gy (tril′ə·jē) *n. pl.* **·gies** A group of three literary dramatic compositions, each complete in itself, but conti ing the same general subject. [< Gk. < *tri-* three + *logo* discourse]

trim (trim) *v.* **trimmed, trim·ming** *v.t.* **1.** To put in or store to order; make neat by clipping, etc. **2.** To remove cutting: usu. with *off* or *away.* **3.** To put ornaments decorate. **4.** In carpentry, to smooth; dress. **5.** *Infor* **a** To defeat. **b** To punish or thrash. **c** To rebuke. **d** To che **6.** *Naut.* **a** To adjust (sails or yards) for sailing. **b** To bala (a ship) by adjusting cargo, etc. — *v.i.* **7.** To act so as appear to favor both sides in a controversy. — *n.* **1.** Sta of adjustment or preparation; orderly disposition: All was good *trim.* **2.** Condition as to general appearance; dre **3.** *Naut.* **a** Fitness for sailing: said of a vessel in reference disposition of ballast, masts, cargo, etc. **b** Degree of imm sion. **4.** Particular character or nature. **5.** The moldi etc., as about the doors of a building. **6.** Ornament; tr ping; trimming; dress. — *adj.* **trim·mer, trim·mest 1.** justed to a nicety; being in perfect order; handsom equipped or of stylish and smart appearance; precise. Excellently fit; fine. — *adv.* In a trim manner: also **trim** [OE *trymman* to arrange, strengthen < *trum* strong] **trim′mer** *n.* — **trim′ness** *n.*

trim·e·ter (trim′ə·tər) *n.* In prosody, a line of verse c sisting of three metrical feet. — *adj.* In prosody, consist of three metrical feet or of lines containing three metri feet. [< L < Gk. < *tri-* three + *metron* measure] — **met·ric** (trī·met′rik), **tri·met′ri·cal** *adj.*

tri·meth·yl·pen·tane (trī′meth·il·pen′tān) *n. Chem.* of three isomeric hydrocarbon compounds, C_8H_{18}, which, often called isooctane, is used in rating motor fu **trim·ming** (trim′ing) *n.* **1.** Something added for orname *pl.* Articles or equipment; fittings, as the hardware of a use. **3.** *pl.* The usual or proper accompaniments or connents of an article or food. **4.** *pl.* That which is removed trimming. **5.** *Informal* A severe reproof; flogging; beat. **6.** *Informal* A defeat. **7.** The act of one who trims.

month·ly (trī·munth′lē) *adj. & adv.* Done or occurring ery third month.

nal (trī′nəl) *adj.* Having three parts; threefold. Also ne (trīn). [< LL < L *tres* three]

na·ry (trī′nər·ē) *adj.* Made up of three parts or proceed by threes; ternary. [See TRINAL.]

n·i·tar·i·an (trin′ə·târ′ē·ən) *adj.* **1.** Of or pertaining to Trinity. **2.** Holding or professing belief in the Trinity. mpare UNITARIAN. — *n.* A believer in the doctrine of Trinity. — **Trin′i·tar′i·an·ism** *n.*

ni·tro·tol·u·ene (trī·nī′trō·tol′yoō-ēn) *n. Chem.* A high losive, $C_7H_5N_3O_6$, made by treating toluene with nitric d, used in warfare, as a blasting agent, and as a base for asuring the explosive power of nuclear bombs: also called *T, trotyl.* Also **tri·ni′tro·tol′u·ol** (-yoō-ōl, -ol). [< TRI TRO- + TOLUENE]

·i·ty (trin′ə·tē) *n. pl.* **·ties** Any union of three parts or ments in one; a trio. [< OF < LL < L *trinus* triple]

n·i·ty (trin′ə·tē) *n. Theol.* A threefold personality exist in the one divine being or substance; the union in one God Father, Son, and Holy Spirit.

nity Sunday *Eccl.* The eighth Sunday after Easter, obved as a festival in honor of the Trinity.

·ket (tring′kit) *n.* **1.** Any small ornament, as of jewelry. A trifle; a trivial object; a toy. [< AF *trenquet,* OF *tren* a toy knife, ornament]

no·mi·al (trī·nō′mē·əl) *adj. Biol.* Of, having, or emying three terms or names in taxonomy, the generic, the cific, and the subspecific or varietal, as *Lynx rufus texen* the Texas bobcat. **2.** *Math.* Consisting of three terms nected by plus or minus signs or both. — *n.* **1.** *Math.* A omial expression, as $3x + y - 27z$. **2.** *Biol.* A trinomial ne. Also **tri·nom′i·nal** (-nom′ə-nəl), **tri·on′y·mal** (-on′əl). [< L *trinominus* having three names]

) (trē′ō; *for def.* 1, *also* trī′ō) *n. pl.* **tri·os** **1.** Any three ngs grouped or associated together. **2.** *Music* **a** A comsition for three performers. **b** The second part of a minuet, nerzo, etc. **c** A group of three musicians that plays trios. F < Ital. < L *tres* three]

ol *suffix Chem.* Denoting an organic compound contain three hydroxyl radicals.

ox·ide (trī·ok′sīd, -sid) *n. Chem.* An oxide containing ee atoms of oxygen in combination. Also **tri·ox′id** (-sid).

· (trip) *n.* **1.** A journey or voyage. **2.** A misstep or stumcaused by losing balance or striking the foot against an ect. **3.** An active, nimble step or movement. **4.** *Mech.* pawl or similar device that trips, or the action of such a vice. **5.** A sudden catch, esp. of the legs and feet, as of a estler. **6.** A blunder; mistake. **7.** *Slang* The taking of a rchedelic drug, or the resulting mental experience. — *v.* **pped, trip·ping** *v.i.* **1.** To stumble. **2.** To move quickly h light or small steps. **3.** To commit an error. **4.** *Mech.* be triggered, released, etc. — *v.t.* **5.** To cause to stum: often with *up.* **6.** To detect and expose in an error; de the purpose of. **7.** To perform (a dance) lightly. **8.** ech. To set free or in operation by releasing a stay, catch, gger, etc. **9.** *Naut.* To loosen (an anchor) from the botn. [< OF *treper, triper* to leap, trample]

par·tite (trī·pär′tīt) *adj.* Divided into three parts or isions; threefold: a *tripartite* leaf: also **tri·part·ed** (trī′pär. **2.** Pertaining to or executed between three parties. [< < *tri-* three + *partiri* to divide] — **tri·par′tite·ly** *adv.*

par·ti·tion (trī′pär·tish′ən) *n.* Division into three parts, o thirds, or among three.

e (trīp) *n.* **1.** A part of the stomach of a ruminant, used food. **2.** *Informal* Anything worthless; nonsense. [< < Arabic *tharb* entrails, a net]

hammer A heavy power hammer that is raised or tilt by a cam and then allowed to drop.

·le (trip′əl) *v.* **·led, ·ling** *v.t.* **1.** To make threefold in mber or quantity. — *v.i.* **2.** To be or become three times many or as large. **3.** In baseball, to hit a triple. — *adj.* Consisting of three things united or of three parts; three l. **2.** Multiplied by three; thrice said or done. — *n.* **1.** A or group of three. **2.** In baseball, a base hit that enables batter to reach third base. [< MF < L < Gk. *triplous* eefold] — **trip′ly** *adv.*

·le play In baseball, a play during which three men are out.

·let (trip′lit) *n.* **1.** A group of three of a kind. **2.** One three children born at one birth. **3.** A group of three med lines. **4.** *Music* A group of three equal notes per med in the time of two: also called *tercet.*

---

triple threat *U.S. Informal* **1.** A football player expert at kicking, running, and passing. **2.** One skillful in three areas of activity. — **trip·le-threat** (trip′əl-thret′) *adj.*

tri·plex (trī′pleks, trip′leks) *adj.* Having three parts. [< L < *tri-* three + *plicare* to fold]

trip·li·cate (*adj. & n.* trip′lə·kit; *v.* trip′lə·kāt) *adj.* Threefold; made in three copies. — *n.* One of or a set of three identical things. — *v.t.* **·cat·ed, ·cat·ing** To make three times as much or as many. [< L *triplicatus,* pp. of *triplicare* to triple] — **trip′li·cate·ly** *adv.* — **trip′li·ca′tion** *n.*

tri·plic·i·ty (tri·plis′ə·tē) *n. pl.* **·ties** **1.** Threefold character. **2.** A group or combination of three. **3.** In astrology, a combination of three of the twelve signs of the zodiac.

tri·pod (trī′pod) *n.* **1.** A utensil or article having three feet or legs. **2.** A three-legged stand for supporting a camera, transit, etc. [< L < Gk. < *tri-* three + *pous* foot]

trip·o·dal (trip′ə-dəl) *adj.* **1.** Of the nature or form of a tripod. **2.** Having three feet or legs. Also **tri·po·di·al** (tri·pō′dē-əl, trī-), **tri·pod′ic** (-pod′ik).

trip·o·dy (trip′ə·dē) *n. pl.* **·dies** A verse or meter having three feet.

trip·per (trip′ər) *n.* **1.** One who trips. **2.** *Brit. Informal* A traveler; tourist. **3.** *Mech.* A trip or tripping mechanism.

trip·ping (trip′ing) *n.* The act of one who or that which trips. — *adj.* Nimble. — **trip′ping·ly** *adv.*

trip·tych (trip′tik) *n.* **1.** A triple tablet; esp., a Greek or Roman hinged triple writing tablet. **2.** A triple picture or carving on three hinged panels, often depicting a religious subject. Also **trip′ty·ca** (-ti·kə), **trip′ty·chon** (-ti·kon). [< LL < Gk. < *tri-* thrice + *ptyssein* to fold]

tri·reme (trī′rēm) *n.* An ancient Greek or Roman warship with three banks of oars. [< L < *tri-* three + *remus* oar]

tri·sect (trī·sekt′) *v.t.* To divide into three parts, esp., as in geometry, into three equal parts. [< TRI- + L *sectus,* pp. of *secare* to cut] — **tri·sect′ed** *adj.* — **tri·sec′tion** (-sek′shən) *n.* — **tri·sec′tor** *n.*

tri·seme (trī′sēm) *n.* A syllable or foot consisting of or equivalent to three short syllables, as the trochee. — *adj.* Consisting of or equal to three short syllables: also **tri·se′mic.** [< Gk. < *tri-* three + *sēma* a sign]

tris·mus (triz′məs, tris′-) *n. Pathol.* Lockjaw. [< NL < Gk. *trismos* gnashing of teeth] — **tris′mic** *adj.*

Tris·tan (tris′tän, -tən) In medieval legend and Richard Wagner's *Tristan und Isolde,* a knight sent to Ireland to bring back the princess Iseult the Beautiful as a bride for his uncle, King Mark of Cornwall. Iseult and Tristan drink a magic love potion, and ultimately die together. Also **Tris·tram** (tris′trəm).

triste (trēst) *adj. French* Sorrowful; sad.

tris·tesse (trēs·tes′) *n. French* Sadness; melancholy.

tris·tich (tris′tik) *n.* A strophe or system of three lines; triplet. Compare COUPLET, DISTICH. [< TRI- + (DI)STICH]

tri·syl·la·ble (trī·sil′ə·bəl) *n.* A word of three syllables. — **tri·syl·lab·ic** (trī′si·lab′ik) or **·i·cal** *adj.* — **tri′syl·lab′i·cal·ly** *adv.*

trite (trīt) *adj.* Used so often as to be hackneyed; made commonplace by repetition. [< L *tritus,* pp. of *terere* to rub] — **trite′ly** *adv.* — **trite′ness** *n.*

— **Syn. 1.** *Trite* suggests merely a lack of freshness or originality. *Hackneyed* is stronger, suggesting something worn out from overuse; the extreme of *hackneyed* is *threadbare.* We speak of *hackneyed* expressions, and of *threadbare* subjects. *Stereotyped* describes that which uses clichés instead of seeking to evoke new images and ideas. — **Ant.** fresh, original, vivid, striking.

trit·i·cum (trit′ə·kəm) *n.* Any of a widely distributed genus of cereal grasses, the wheats, cultivated in many varieties. [< NL < L, wheat]

trit·i·um (trit′ē·əm, trish′ē-əm) *n. Physics* The isotope of hydrogen having the atomic weight 3. [< NL < Gk. *tritos* third]

tri·ton[1] (trīt′n) *n.* Any of a genus of marine gastropods having many gills and a trumpet-shaped shell. [< L < Gk. *Trītōn*]

tri·ton[2] (trī′ton) *n. Physics.* The nucleus of an atom of tritium. [< TRIT(IUM) + (ELECTR)ON]

Tri·ton (trīt′n) In Greek mythology, a son of Poseidon (Neptune) and Amphitrite, represented with a man's head and upper body and a dolphin's tail. — *n.* In Greek mythology, one of a race of attendants of the sea gods.

TRITON[1]

trit·u·rate (trich′ə·rāt) *v.t.* **·rat·ed, ·rating** To reduce to a fine powder or pulp by grinding or rubbing; pulverize. — *n.* That which has been triturated. [< LL < L *tritura* a rubbing, threshing < *terere* to rub] — **trit·u·ra·ble** (trich′ər·ə·bəl) *adj.* — **trit′u·ra′tion** *n.* — **trit′u·ra′tor** *n.*

tri·umph (trī′əmf) *v.i.* **1.** To win a victory; be victorious. **2.** To be successful. **3.** To rejoice over a victory; exult.

4. To celebrate a triumph, as a victorious Roman general. **— n. 1.** In Roman antiquity, the religious pageant of the entry of a victorious consul, dictator, or praetor into Rome. **2.** Exultation over victory. **3.** The condition of being victorious; victory. [< OF < L < Gk. *thriambos* a processional hymn to Dionysus] **— tri′umph·er** *n.*

tri·um·phal (trī-um′fəl) *adj.* **1.** Of, pertaining to, or of the nature of a triumph. **2.** Celebrating a victory.

triumphal arch A monumental arch erected to commemorate a great victory or achievement.

tri·um·phant (trī-um′fənt) *adj.* **1.** Exultant for or as for victory. **2.** Victorious. **— tri·um′phant·ly** *adv.*

tri·um·vir (trī-um′vər) *n. pl.* **·virs** or **·vi·ri** (-və·rī) One of three men united in public office or authority, as in ancient Rome. [< L < *tres, trium* three + *vir* a man] **— tri·um′vi·ral** *adj.*

tri·um·vi·rate (trī-um′vər·it, -və·rāt) *n.* **1.** A group or coalition of three men who unitedly exercise authority or control; government by triumvirs. **2.** The office of a triumvir. **3.** A group of three men; trio.

tri·une (trī′yo̅o̅n) *adj.* Three in one: said of God. **— n.** A group of three things united; triad; trinity in unity. [< TRI- + L *unus* one] **— tri·u′ni·ty** *n.*

tri·va·lent (trī-vā′lənt, triv′ə·lənt) *adj. Chem.* Having a valence or combining value of three. [< TRI- + L *valens*, ppr. of *valere* to be worth] **— tri·va′lence, tri·va′len·cy** *n.*

triv·et (triv′it) *n.* A stand, usu. three-legged, for holding cooking vessels in a fireplace, a heated iron, or a hot dish on a table. [OE < L < *tri-* three + *pes, pedis* a foot]

triv·i·a (triv′ē-ə) *n.pl.* Insignificant or unimportant matters; trifles. [See TRIVIAL.]

triv·i·al (triv′ē-əl) *adj.* **1.** Of little value or importance; trifling; insignificant. **2.** Such as is found everywhere or every day; commonplace. **3.** Occupied with trifles. [< L *trivialis* of the crossroads, commonplace < *tri-* three + *via* road] **— triv′i·al·ism** *n.* **— triv′i·al·ly** *adv.*

triv·i·al·i·ty (triv′ē-al′ə·tē) *n. pl.* **·ties 1.** The state or quality of being trivial: also **triv′i·al·ness. 2.** A trivial matter.

tri·week·ly (trī-wēk′lē) *adj.* **1.** Occurring three times a week. **2.** Done or occurring every third week. **— adv. 1.** Three times a week. **2.** Every third week. **— n.** A publication appearing triweekly.

-trix *suffix* A feminine termination of agent nouns the masculine form of which is *-tor: testatrix.* See -OR¹. [< L]

tro·cha·ic (trō-kā′ik) *adj.* Pertaining to, containing, or composed of trochees: a *trochaic* foot or verse. **— n.** A trochaic verse or line. [See TROCHEE.]

tro·chal (trō′kəl) *adj.* Shaped like a wheel; rotiform. [< Gk. *trochos* a wheel]

tro·che (trō′kē) *n.* A medicated lozenge, usu. circular: also called *pastille.* [Alter. of obs. *trochisk* < MF < L < Gk. < *trochos* wheel]

tro·chee (trō′kē) *n.* **1.** In prosody, a metrical foot consisting of one long or accented syllable followed by one short or unaccented syllable (—). **2.** A line or verse made up of or characterized by such feet: Nŏw thĕ| līght hăs| fāllĕn| frŏm thĕ| hēavĕns. [< L < Gk. < *trechein* to run]

trod (trod) Past tense and alternative past participle of TREAD.

trod·den (trod′n) Past participle of TREAD.

trog·lo·dyte (trog′lə·dīt) *n.* **1.** A cave man. **2.** A hermit; anyone of primitive habits. **3.** An anthropoid ape, as the chimpanzee. [< L < Gk. < *trōglē* hole + *dyein* to go into] **— trog′lo·dyt′ic** (-dit′ik) or **·i·cal** *adj.*

tro·gon (trō′gon) *n.* A tropical American bird noted for its resplendent plumage. [< NL < Gk. *trōgein* to gnaw]

troi·ka (troi′kə) *n.* A Russian vehicle drawn by a team of three horses driven abreast. [< Russian < *troie* three]

Tro·jan (trō′jən) *n.* **1.** A native of Troy. **2.** One who works earnestly or suffers courageously. **— adj.** Of or pertaining to ancient Troy. [< L < *Troja* Troy]

Trojan horse 1. In classical legend, a large, hollow wooden horse, filled with Greek soldiers and left at the Trojan gates. When it was brought within the walls the soldiers emerged at night and admitted the Greek army, who burned the city: also called *wooden horse.* **2.** A person, device, etc., intended to disrupt or undermine a plan.

Trojan War In Greek legend, the ten years' war waged by the confederated Greeks under their king, Agamemnon, against the Trojans to recover Helen, the wife of Menelaus, who had been abducted by Paris: celebrated esp. in the *Iliad* and the *Odyssey.*

troll¹ (trōl) *v.t.* **1.** To fish for with a moving lure, as from a slowly moving boat. **2.** To move (the line or lure) in fishing. **3.** To sing in succession, as in a round or catch. **4.** To sing in a full, hearty manner. **5.** To cause to roll; revolve. **— v.i. 6.** To fish with a moving lure. **7.** To sing a tune, etc., in a full, hearty manner. **8.** To be uttered in such a way. **9.** To roll; turn. **— n. 1.** A catch or round. **2.** A rolling movement or motion; also, repetition or routine.

3. In fishing, a spoon or other lure. [? < OF *troller* to qu... wander < Gmc.] **— troll′er** *n.*

troll² (trōl) *n.* In Scandinavian folklore, a giant; late... mischievous dwarf. Also **trold** (trōld). [< ON]

trol·ley (trol′ē) *n. pl.* **·leys 1.** *U.S.* A streetcar. **2**... grooved metal wheel for rolling in contact with a conduc... (the **trolley wire**), to convey the current to an electric... hicle. **3.** In a subway system, a device adapted to the sa... purpose attached to a current taker operating throug... third rail. **4.** A small truck or car for conveying mater... as in a factory, mine, etc. **5.** The mechanism of a travel... crane. **6.** A small car running on tracks and worked b... manually operated lever, used by workmen on a railway... *v.t. & v.i.* To travel by trolley. Also **trol′ly.** [< TROLL¹...

trolley bus A bus propelled electrically by current from... overhead wire by means of a trolley. Also **trolley coach...**

trolley car A car with a trolley for use on an electric... way; esp., *U.S.*, a streetcar.

troll·ing (trō′ling) *n.* The method or act of fishing... dragging a hook and line, as behind a boat and near... surface. [< TROLL¹]

trolling rod A strong fishing rod for trolling.

trol·lop (trol′əp) *n.* **1.** A slatternly woman. **2.** A pro... tute. [< dial. E (Scottish) < ME *trollen* to roll about... **trol′lop·ish, trol′lop·y, trol′lop·ing** *adj.*

trom·bone (trom-bōn′, trom′bōn′) A brass instrumen... the trumpet family, but larger and lower in pitch than... trumpet. A **slide trombone** changes pitch by means of a... shaped slide that can lengthen or shorten the air colum... **valve trombone** changes pitch by means of valves. [< I... aug. of *tromba* trumpet < Gmc.] **— trom·bon′ist** *n.*

trompe l'oeil (trônp lœ′y′) In art and decoration, the... curate representation of details, scenes, etc., to create... illusion of reality. [< F, lit., fool the eye]

-tron *suffix* **1.** Vacuum tube: *magnetron.* **2.** Device for... manipulation of subatomic particles: *cyclotron.* [< ... instrumental suffix]

troop (tro̅o̅p) *n.* **1.** An assembled company; gathering... herd or flock. **2.** *Usu. pl.* A body of soldiers; soldiers... lectively. **3.** The cavalry unit corresponding to a comp... of infantry. **4.** A body of Boy Scouts consisting of... patrols of eight scouts each. **— v.i. 1.** To move alon... gather as a troop or as a crowd. **— v.t. 2.** To form... troops. **3.** *Brit. Mil.* To carry ceremoniously before tro... to *troop* the colors. [< OF < LL *troppus* a flock < Gr...

troop carrier 1. A transport aircraft for carrying tro... and equipment. **2.** An armored vehicle for carrying tro...

troop·er (tro̅o̅p′ər) *n.* **1.** A cavalryman. **2.** A moun... policeman. **3.** A troop horse; charger. **4.** A troopship... A state policeman.

troop·ship (tro̅o̅p′ship′) *n.* A ship for carrying troop...

trope (trōp) *n.* **1.** The figurative use of a word. **2.** Loos... a figure of speech; figurative language in general. [< ... < Gk. *tropos* a turn < *trepein* to turn]

-trope *combining form* **1.** One who or that which turn... changes: *allotrope.* **2.** Turning; turned in a (specified) w... *hemitrope.* [< Gk. *tropos* a turning < *trepein* to turn]

troph·ic (trof′ik) *adj.* Pertaining to nutrition and its p... esses. Also **troph′i·cal.** [< Gk. < *trephein* to nourish]... **troph′i·cal·ly** *adv.*

tro·phied (trō′fēd) *adj.* Adorned with trophies.

tropho- *combining form* Nutrition; nourishment; of or... taining to food or nutrition. Also, before vowels, **tro**... [< Gk. *trophē* food, nourishment < *trephein* to feed, nour...

tro·phy (trō′fē) *n. pl.* **·phies 1.** Something symboli... victory or success; as: **a** A cup, statuette, etc., awarded... athletic or other achievement. **b** A mounted fish, anim... head, etc. **c** A weapon, etc., captured from an enemy... An ornamental symbolic group of objects hung together... wall. **3.** A memento or memorial. [< MF < L < Gk... *tropē* a defeat < *trepein* to turn, rout]

-trophy *combining form* A (specified) kind of nutritio... development: *hypertrophy.* Corresponding adjectives en... *-trophic.* [< Gk. *trophē.* See TROPHO-.]

trop·ic (trop′ik) *n.* **1.** *Geog.* Either of two parallels of latitude 23° 27′ north and south of the equator, on which the sun is seen in the zenith on the days of its greatest declination, called respectively **tropic of Cancer** and **tropic of Capricorn. 2.** *pl.* The regions of the earth's surface between the tropics of Cancer and Capricorn; the Torrid Zone. **— adj.** Of or pertaining to the tropics; tropical. [< L < Gk. *tropikos* (*kyklos*) the tropical (circle) < *tropē* a turning]

-tropic *combining form* Having a (specified) tropism; tu... ing or changing in a (particular) way, or in response... (given) stimulus: *phototropic.* Also *-tropal.*

trop·i·cal (trop′i·kəl) *adj.* **1.** Of, pertaining to, or cha... teristic of the tropics. **2.** Of the nature of a trope or m... phor. **— trop′i·cal·ly** *adv.*

pic bird A long-winged, oceanic bird, allied to the peli- ns, found mostly in the tropics, having the two middle tail thers elongated.

·pism (trō′piz·əm) *n. Biol.* **1.** The involuntary response an organism to an external stimulus. **2.** Any automatic ction to a stimulus. [< Gk. *tropē* a turning] — **tro·pis· (trō-pis′tik)** *adj.*

opism *combining form* A (specified) tropism: *phototro- m.* Also *-tropy.* [< TROPISM]

po·o·pause (trop′ə·pôz) *n. Meteorol.* A transition zone in e atmosphere between the troposphere and the strato- nere. [< TROPO(SPHERE) + Gk. *pausis* a ceasing]

po·o·sphere (trop′ə·sfir) *n. Meteorol.* The region of the nosphere beneath the stratosphere; it is characterized by rbulence and by decreasing temperature with increasing itude. [< F < Gk. *tropos* a turning + F *sphère* < L *haera* sphere] — **trop′o·spher′ic** (-sfir′ik, -sfer′-) *adj.*

t (trot) *n.* **1.** A gait of a quadruped, esp. a horse, in ich diagonal pairs of legs are lifted, thrust forward, and ced down almost simultaneously, also, the sound of this t. **2.** A race for trotters. **3.** A reasonably rapid run. **4.** *formal* A pony (def. 3). — *v.* **trot·ted, trot·ting** *v.i.* **1.** To at a trot. **2.** To hurry. — *v.t.* **3.** To cause to trot. **4.** ride at a trotting gait. — **to trot out** To bring forth for pection, approval, etc. [< OF < OHG *trottōn* to tread]

h (trôth, trŏth) *n.* **1.** Good faith; fidelity. **2.** The act pledging fidelity; esp., betrothal. **3.** Truth; verity. — *Archaic* To betroth; pledge. [ME *trowthe, trouthe,* var. OE *trēowth* truth; faith]

t·sky·ism (trot′skē·iz′əm) *n.* The doctrines of Trotsky d his followers; esp., his theory that Communism to suc- d must be international. — **Trot′sky·ist, Trot′sky·ite** & *adj.*

t·ter (trot′ər) *n.* One who or that which trots; esp., a rse trained to trot for speed.

tyl (trō′til) *n.* Trinitrotoluene. [< (TRINI)TROT(O- ENE) + -YL]

u·ba·dour (trōo′bə·dôr, -dōr, -dŏŏr) *n.* **1.** One of a class lyric poets, originating in Provence in the 11th century d flourishing in southern France, northern Italy, and east- Spain during the 12th and 13th centuries. **2.** A singer, e, of love songs. [< MF < Provençal < *trobar* to com- se, invent, find]

ub·le (trub′əl) *n.* **1.** The state of being distressed, an- yed, upset, afflicted, or confused. **2.** A difficulty, per- xity, annoyance, disturbance, etc. **3.** Toilsome exertion; ins: Take the *trouble* to do it correctly. **4.** A diseased con- ion: lung *trouble.* — **in trouble** **1.** Enmeshed in threaten- , difficulties. **2.** *Informal* Pregnant and unmarried. — *v.* **d, ·ling** *v.t.* **1.** To cause mental agitation to; distress; rry. **2.** To agitate or disturb; stir up or roil, as water. **3.** inconvenience or incommode. **4.** To bother. **5.** To se physical pain or discomfort to. — *v.i.* **6.** To take ins; bother. **7.** To worry. [< OF < L *turbula* mob, dim. *turba* crowd] — **troub′ler** *n.* — **troub′ling·ly** *adv.*

ub·led (trub′əld) *adj.* **1.** Beset with trouble. **2.** Dis- **3.** Agitated, disturbed, or roiled, as water. — **ub′led·ly** *adv.* — **troub′led·ness** *n.*

ub·le-shoot·er (trub′əl·shōō′tər) *n.* One who locates ficulties and seeks to remove them, esp., in the operation a machine, in an industrial process, etc. — **troub′le- oot′ing** *n.*

ub·le·some (trub′əl·səm) *adj.* **1.** Causing trouble; xatious; burdensome; trying. **2.** Marked by violence; multuous. **3.** Greatly agitated or disturbed; troublous. **troub′le·some·ly** *adv.* — **troub′le·some·ness** *n.*

ub·lous (trub′ləs) *adj.* **1.** Marked by commotion or mult; full of trouble: *troublous* times. **2.** Uneasy; restless.

ugh (trôf, trŏf) *n.* **1.** A long, narrow, open receptacle conveying a fluid or for holding food or water for animals. A long, narrow channel or depression, as between ridges land or waves at sea. **3.** A gutter (def. 3). **4.** *Meteorol.* ong, usu., narrow area having a low barometric pressure. *Econ.* A low or the lowest point reached in a business cle. [OE *trog*]

unce (trouns) *v.t.* **trounced, trounc·ing** **1.** To beat or rash severely; punish. **2.** *Informal* To defeat. [Ult. gin uncertain]

upe (trōop) *n.* A company of actors or other performers. *v.i.* **trouped, troup·ing** To travel as one of a theatrical mpany. [< MF < OF *trope* troop]

u·per (trōo′pər) *n.* **1.** A member of a theatrical com- ny. **2.** An actor of long experience.

u·sers (trou′zərz) *n.pl.* A garment, esp. for men and ys, covering the body from the waist to the ankles and ided so as to make a separate covering for each leg. Also **w′sers.** [Blend of obs. *trouse* breeches and DRAWERS]

us·seau (trōo′sō, trōo·sō′) *n. pl.* **·seaux** (-sōz, -sōz′) or

·seaus A bride's outfit, esp. of clothing, linens, etc. [< F *trousse* a packed collection of things]

trout (trout) *n.* **1.** A fish of the salmon family mostly found in fresh waters and highly esteemed as a game and food fish. The **brown** or **salmon trout** is common in Europe; the **cut-throat trout** and the **rainbow trout** or steelhead are species of western North America; the **speckled trout** or **brook trout** is common in eastern North America. **2.** A fish resembling, or supposed to resemble, the above, as the green- ling. [OE < LL < Gk. *trōktēs* nibbler < *trōgein* to gnaw]

trove (trōv) *n.* Something, esp. of value or pleasing quality, found or discovered. [< (TREASURE-)TROVE]

trow (trō) *v.t. & v.i. Archaic* To suppose; think; believe. [Fusion of OE *truwian* (< *truwa* faith) and *trēowan* to be- lieve < *trēowe* true]

trow·el (trou′əl, troul) *n.* **1.** A flat-bladed, sometimes pointed implement having an offset handle, used to smooth plaster, mortar, etc. **2.** A small concave scoop with a han- dle, used in digging about small plants, potting them, etc. — *v.t.* **trow·eled** or **·elled, trow·el·ing** or **·el·ling** To apply, dress, or form with a trowel. [< OF < LL < L *trulla,* dim. of *trua* stirring spoon, ladle] — **trow′el·er** or **trow′el·ler** *n.*

troy (troi) *n.* A system of weights in which 12 troy ounces make a pound, used by jewelers in England and the U.S. See table front of book. Also **troy weight.** [after *Troyes,* a city in France]

Troy (troi) An ancient city in NW Asia Minor of perhaps about 1200 B.C., the scene of the *Iliad:* also called *Ilium, Ilion.*

tru·an·cy (trōo′ən·sē) *n. pl.* **·cies** The state or habit of being truant; also, an act of being truant. Also **tru′ant·ry.**

tru·ant (trōo′ənt) *n.* One who absents himself, esp., from school, without leave. — *v.i.* To be truant. — *adj.* **1.** Be- ing truant; idle. **2.** Relating to or characterizing a truant. [< OF, vagabond, prob. < Celtic]

truant officer *U.S.* An official who investigates truancy from school.

truce (trōos) *n.* **1.** An agreement between belligerents for a temporary suspension of hostilities; an armistice. **2.** Tem- porary cessation or intermission. [Plural of ME *trew,* OE *trūwa* faith, a promise]

truck[1] (truk) *n.* **1.** *U.S. & Canadian* Any of various auto- motive vehicles designed to carry loads, freight, etc.: also, *Brit., lorry.* **2.** A two-wheeled barrowlike vehicle with a forward lip and no sides, used for moving barrels, boxes, etc., by hand. **3.** A vehicle used about railway stations, for mov- ing trunks, etc. **4.** *Brit.* An open or platform freight car. **5.** *Naut.* A disk at the top of a mast or flagpole through which the halyards of signals are run. **6.** One of the pivoting sets of wheels on a railroad car or engine. — *v.t.* **1.** To carry on a truck. — *v.i.* **2.** To carry goods on a truck. **3.** To drive a truck. [Appar. < L < Gk. *trochos* wheel]

truck[2] (truk) *v.t. & v.i.* **1.** To exchange or barter; also, to ped- dle. — *n.* **1.** Commodities for sale. **2.** *U.S.* Garden prod- uce for market. **3.** *Informal* Rubbish; worthless articles collectively. **4.** Barter. **5.** *Informal* Dealings: I will have no *truck* with him. [< OF *troquer* to barter]

truck·age[1] (truk′ij) *n.* **1.** Money paid for conveyance of goods on trucks. **2.** Such conveyance.

truck·age[2] (truk′ij) *n.* Exchange; barter.

truck·er[1] (truk′ər) *n.* One who drives or supplies trucks or moves commodities in trucks. Also **truck′man** (-mən).

truck·er[2] (truk′ər) *n.* **1.** *U.S.* A market gardener; truck farmer. **2.** One who barters or sells commodities; hawker.

truck farm *U.S.* A farm on which vegetables are produced for market. Also **truck garden.** — **truck farming**

truck·ing[1] (truk′ing) *n.* The act or business of transporta- tion by trucks.

truck·ing[2] (truk′ing) *n.* **1.** Exchanging or bartering; deal- ings. **2.** *U.S.* Cultivation of vegetables for market.

truck·le (truk′əl) *v.* **·led, ·ling** *v.i.* **1.** To yield meanly or weakly: with *to.* **2.** To roll on truckles or casters. — *v.t.* **3.** To cause to roll on truckles or casters. — *n.* A small wheel. [< AF < L *trochlea* a pulley] — **truck′ler** *n.* — **truck′ling·ly** *adv.*

truc·u·lence (truk′yə·ləns) *n.* Savageness of character, behavior, or aspect. Also **truc′u·len·cy.**

truc·u·lent (truk′yə·lənt) *adj.* **1.** Of savage character; awakening terror; cruel; ferocious. **2.** Scathing; harsh; violent: said of writing or speech. [< L < *trux, trucis* fierce] — **truc′u·lent·ly** *adv.*

trudge (truj) *v.i.* **trudged, trudg·ing** To walk wearily or laboriously; plod. — *n.* A tiresome walk or tramp. [Ear- lier *tredge, tridge*] — **trudg′er** *n.*

trudg·en (truj′ən) *n.* In swimming, a former racing stroke similar to the crawl but performed with a frog kick or a scissors kick. Also **trudgen stroke, trudg′eon.** [after John *Trudgen,* 19th c. British swimmer]

true (trōō) *adj.* **tru·er, tru·est** **1.** Faithful to fact or reality; not false. **2.** Being real or natural; genuine: *true* gold. **3.** Faithful; loyal; steadfast. **4.** Conformable to an existing standard type or pattern; exact: a *true* copy. **5.** Required by justice; legitimate: the *true* king. **6.** Truthful; honest. **7.** Indicating or predicting correctly: a *true* sign. **8.** *Biol.* **a** Of pure strain or pedigree. **b** Conformed to the structure of the type of a plant or animal: a *true* locust. **9.** In perfect tune: His voice is *true*. — *n.* Truth; pledge. — **in** (or **out of**) **true** In (or not in) line of adjustment: said of a mark or part. — *adv.* **1.** In truth; truly. **2.** In a true and accurate manner: The wheel runs *true*. — *v.t.* **trued, tru·ing** To bring to conformity with a standard; adjust: to *true* a frame. [OE *trēowe*] — **true′ness** *n.*

true bill *Law* **1.** The endorsement by a grand jury on a bill of indictment that the jurors find to be sustained by the evidence. **2.** A bill so endorsed.

true-blue (trōō′blōō′) *adj.* Staunch; faithful; genuine.

true-born (trōō′bôrn′) *adj.* Being such by birth or inheritance: a *trueborn* Scot.

true-lov·ers′ knot (trōō′luv′ərz) A complicated double knot, a symbol of fidelity in love.

truf·fle (truf′əl, trōō′fəl) *n.* Any of various edible fleshy underground fungi. [< OF *trufe, truffe*]

tru·ism (trōō′iz·əm) *n.* An obvious or self-evident truth.

trull (trul) *n. Archaic* A prostitute. [< G *trulle, trolle*]

tru·ly (trōō′lē) *adv.* **1.** In conformity with fact. **2.** With accuracy. **3.** With loyalty or fidelity. **4.** Legally.

trump[1] (trump) *n.* **1.** In various card games, a card of the suit selected to rank above all others temporarily. **2.** *Usu., pl.* The suit thus determined. **3.** A powerful or decisive stroke, resource, etc. **4.** *Informal* A good fellow. — *v.t.* **1.** To top (another card) with a trump. **2.** To surpass; excel; beat. — *v.i.* **3.** To play a trump. — **to trump up** To make up or invent for a fraudulent purpose. [Alter. of TRIUMPH]

trump[2] (trump) *n. Poetic* A trumpet. [< OF *trompe*]

trump·er·y (trum′pər·ē) *n. pl.* **·er·ies** **1.** Worthless finery. **2.** Rubbish; nonsense. **3.** Deceit; trickery. — *adj.* Showy but valueless. [< OF < *tromper* to deceive]

trum·pet (trum′pit) *n.* **1.** A soprano brass wind instrument with a flaring bell and a long, narrow-bored metal tube. **2.** Something resembling a trumpet in form; an ear trumpet. **3.** A loud penetrating sound like that of a trumpet; trumpeting. — *v.t.* **1.** To sound or proclaim by or as by a trumpet; publish abroad. — *v.i.* **2.** To blow a trumpet. **3.** To give forth a sound as if from a trumpet. [< OF *trompe*]

trumpet creeper A woody vine of the southern U.S., with scarlet, trumpet-shaped flowers. Also **trumpet vine.**

trum·pet·er (trum′pit·ər) *n.* **1.** One who plays a trumpet. **2.** One who publishes something loudly abroad. **3.** A large South American bird related to the cranes. **4.** A large North American wild swan, having a clarionlike cry: also **trumpeter swan.**

trun·cate (trung′kāt) *v.t.* **·cat·ed, ·cat·ing** To cut the top or end from. — *adj.* **1.** Truncated. **2.** *Biol.* Appearing as though cut or broken squarely off. [< L < *truncus* trunk] — **trun·ca·tion** (trung·kā′shən) *n.*

trun·ca·ted (trung′kā·tid) *adj.* **1.** Cut off; shortened. **2.** Describing a cone or pyramid whose vertex is cut off by a plane.

TRUNCATED PYRAMID

trun·cheon (trun′chən) *n.* **1.** A short, heavy stick; a club; staff. **2.** *Brit.* A policeman's club. — *v.t.* To beat as with a truncheon; cudgel. [< OF ult. < L *truncus* trunk]

trun·dle (trun′dəl) *n.* **1.** A small, broad wheel, as of a caster. **2.** The act, motion, or sound of trundling. **3.** A trundle bed. **4.** *Obs.* A small, low-wheeled truck. — *v.t. & v.i.* **·dled, ·dling** **1.** To roll along. **2.** To rotate. [ME < OE *trendel* circle] — **trun′dler** *n.*

trundle bed A bed with a very low frame resting upon casters, so that it may be rolled under another bed.

trunk (trungk) *n.* **1.** The main stem of a tree. **2.** A large box or case for carrying clothes, etc., as for a journey. **3.** *U.S. & Canadian* A large compartment of an automobile for storing luggage, etc., often at the rear. **4.** The human body, apart from the head, neck, and limbs; the torso. **5.** *Entomol.* The thorax. **6.** *Anat.* The main stem of a nerve, blood vessel, or lymphatic. **7.** The main line of a transportation system. **8.** The circuit connecting two telephone exchanges. **9.** The main body, line, or stem of anything. **10.** A proboscis, as of an elephant. **11.** *pl.* A close-fitting garment covering the loins, worn by male swimmers, etc. — *adj.* Being or belonging to a trunk or main body: a *trunk* railroad. [< OF < L *truncus* stem, trunk]

trunk·fish (trungk′fish′) *n. pl.* **·fish** or **·fish·es** A fish of warm seas, characterized by a covering of hard, bony plates.

trunk hose Full breeches extending to the middle of the thigh, worn by men in the 16th and early 17th centuries.

trunk line The main line of a transportation or communication system, as distinguished from a branch line.

trun·nion (trun′yən) *n.* One of two opposite cylind[rical] studs on a cannon, forming an axis on which it is elevate[d or] depressed. [< F *trognon* stump, trunk]

truss (trus) *n.* **1.** *Med.* A bandage or support for a rupt[ure]. **2.** A braced framework of ties, beams, or bars, as for the [sup]-port of a roof, bridge, etc. **3.** A package, bundle, esp[.] hay (usu. 56 or 60 pounds) or straw (usu. 36 pounds). *Naut.* A heavy iron piece by which a lower yard is [at]-tached to a mast. — *v.t.* **1.** To tie or bind; fasten: o[ften] with *up*. **2.** To support by a truss; brace, as a roof. **3** [To] fasten the wings of (a fowl) before cooking. **4.** To fas[ten,] tighten, or tie around one, as a garment. [< OF < *trou*[sse;] *trusser* to pack up, bundle] — **truss′er** *n.*

truss bridge A bridge supported chiefly by trusses.

trust (trust) *n.* **1.** A confident reliance on the integ[rity,] honesty, or justice of another; faith. **2.** Something c[om]-mitted to one's care; a charge; responsibility. **3.** The s[tate] or position of one who has received an important charge[.] **4.** A confidence in the reliability of persons or things with[out] careful investigation. **5.** Credit, in the commercial se[nse.] **6.** Custody; care; keeping. **7.** *Law* **a** The confidence [re]-posed in a person to whom the legal title to property is [con]-veyed for the benefit of another; also, the beneficial tit[le or] ownership of property of which the legal title is held [by] another. ◆ Collateral adjective: *fiducial*. **b** The proper[ty or] thing held in trust. **8.** A permanent combination, no[t] legal, for the purpose of controlling the production, p[rices,] etc., of some commodity or the management, profits, etc[., of] some business. **9.** A trust company. **10.** One who or [that] which is trusted. **11.** Confident expectation; belief; h[ope.] — *v.t.* **1.** To have trust in; rely upon. **2.** To commit t[o the] care of another; entrust. **3.** To commit something t[o the] care of: with *with*. **4.** To allow to do something wit[hout] fear of the consequences. **5.** To expect with confiden[ce or] with hope. **6.** To believe. **7.** To allow business credi[t to.] — *v.i.* **8.** To place trust or confidence; rely: with *in*. **9.** To hope: with *for*. **10.** To allow business credit. — **to t[rust] to** To depend upon; confide in. — *adj.* Held in trust: *trust* money. [< ON *traust*, lit., firmness] — **trust′er** *n.*

trust·bust·er (trust′bus′tər) *n. U.S. Informal* One [who] advocates or works for the dissolution of a trust (def. [8);] trusts, as by antitrust legislation. Also **trust buster.**

trust company An incorporated institution formed t[o ac]-cept and execute trusts, to manage money and prop[erty,] and to lend money.

trus·tee (trus·tē′) *n.* **1.** One who holds property in t[rust.] **2.** One of a body of men, often elective, who manage [the] affairs of a college, church, foundation, etc. — *v.t.* [·teed,] **·tee·ing** To place (property) in the care of a trustee.

trus·tee·ship (trus·tē′ship) *n.* **1.** The post or functio[n of a] trustee. **2.** Supervision and control of a Trust Territory[, a] country or countries commissioned by the United Nat[ions;] also, the Territory so controlled.

trust·ful (trust′fəl) *adj.* Disposed to trust. — **trust′[fully]** *adv.* — **trust′ful·ness** *n.*

trust fund Money, securities, etc., held in trust.

trust·ing (trus′ting) *adj.* Having trust; trustful. — **tr[ust]**-ing·ly *adv.* — **trust′ing·ness** *n.*

Trust Territory A dependent area administered by [a na]-tion under the authority of the United Nations.

trust·wor·thy (trust′wûr′thē) *adj.* Worthy of confide[nce;] reliable. — **trust′wor′thi·ly** (-wûr′thə·lē) *adv.* — **t[rust′]**-wor′thi·ness *n.*

trust·y (trus′tē) *adj.* **trust·i·er, trust·i·est** **1.** Faithf[ul to] duty or trust. **2.** Staunch; firm. — *n. pl.* **trust·ie[s]** A trustworthy person; esp., a convict who has been foun[d] liable and to whom special liberties are granted. — **tr[ust′i]-**ly *adv.* — **trust′i·ness** *n.*

truth (trōōth) *n. pl.* **truths** (trōōthz, trōōths) **1.** The [state] or character of being true in relation to being, knowled[ge, or] speech. **2.** Conformity to fact or reality. **3.** Conform[ity to a] rule, standard, pattern, or ideal. **4.** Steadfastness[; sin]-cerity. **5.** That which is true; a statement or belief [that] corresponds to the reality. **6.** Fact; reality. **7.** A dis[posi]-tion to tell only what is true; veracity. **8.** Fidelity; [con]-stancy. [OE < *trēowe* true] — **truth′less** *adj.*

truth·ful (trōōth′fəl) *adj.* **1.** Habitually telling the t[ruth.] **2.** Corresponding to the facts or to reality; true. — **t[ruth′]**-ful·ly *adv.* — **truth′ful·ness** *n.*

try (trī) *v.* **tried, try·ing** *v.t.* **1.** To make an attempt to [accomplish; undertake; endeavor. **2.** To make experi[men]-tal use or application of: often with *out*. **3.** *Law* **a** T[o de]-termine the guilt or innocence of by judicial trial. [b To] examine or determine judicially, as a case. **4.** To su[bject] to a test; put to proof. **5.** To put severe strain upon; t[ax:] to *try* the eyes. **6.** To subject to trouble or tribulation; a[fflict.] **7.** To extract by rendering or melting; refine: often [with] *out*: to *try* out oil. — *v.i.* **8.** To make an attempt [put] forth effort. **9.** To make an examination or test.

try on To put on (a garment) to test it for fit or appear[ance.] — **to try out** To attempt to qualify: He *tried out* [for] otball team. — *n. pl.* **tries** The act of trying; trial; ...periment. [< OF *trier* to sift, pick out]

·**ing** (tri'ing) *adj.* Testing severely; hard to endure.

·**out** (tri'out') *n. U.S. Informal* A test of ability, as of an ...tor or athlete, often in competition with others.

p·a·no·some (trip'ə-nə-sōm', tri·pan'ə-) *n.* Any of a ge-...us of protozoans parasitic in the blood of man and some ...wer animals and often causing serious and even fatal ...seases, as sleeping sickness. Also **tryp/a·no·so/ma** (-sō/mə). [< Gk. *trypanon* borer + -SOME (< Gk. *sōma* a body)]

p·sin (trip'sin) *n. Biochem.* A digestive enzyme con-...ined in the pancreatic juice. [< Gk. *tripsis* a rubbing ... *tribein* to rub) + (PEP)SIN] — **tryp/tic** (-tik) *adj.*

·**sail** (tri'səl, -sāl') *n. Naut.* A small sail bent to a gaff ...aft the foremast and mainmast of a ship: also called *spen-*...·. [< nautical phrase *(at) try* lying to in a storm + SAIL]

square A carpenter's square having usu. a wooden ...ck and a steel blade.

st (trist, trīst) *n.* **1.** An appointment, as between lovers, ... meet at a designated time and place; also, the meeting ...ce agreed upon; rendezvous. **2.** A prearranged meeting, ... of lovers. [< OF *triste, tristre* an appointed station in ...nting] — **tryst/er** *n.*

st·ing place (tris'ting) A meeting place, as of lovers.

·**se** (tset/sē) *n.* **1.** A small bloodsucking fly of southern ...rica, whose bite transmits disease in cattle, horses, etc. **2.** ... related species, that transmits the causative agent of ...eping sickness. Also spelled *tzetze.* Also **tsetse fly.** [< ...rikaans < Bantu]

·**hirt** (tē'shûrt') *n.* A cotton undershirt or sweater with ...rt sleeves. Also **T shirt.**

·**quare** (tē'skwâr') *n.* An instrument by which to meas-... or lay out right angles or parallel lines, consisting usu. ... a flat strip with a shorter head at right angles to it.

·**na·mi** (tsoo-nä'mē) *n.* An extensive and often very de-...uctive ocean wave caused by a submarine earthquake: ...o loosely called *tidal wave.* [< Japanese, a storm wave]

· (tub) *n.* **1.** A broad, open-topped vessel with handles ... the side. **2.** A bathtub. **3.** *Brit. Informal* A bath taken ...a tub. **4.** The amount that a tub contains. **5.** *Informal* ...ything resembling a tub, as a broad, clumsy boat. — ...*& v.i.* **tubbed, tub·bing** To wash, bathe, or place in a tub. ... MDu. *tubbe*] — **tub/ba·ble** *adj.* — **tub/ber** *n.*

·**ba** (too'bə, tyoo'-) *n. pl.* ·**bas** or ·**bae** (-bē) Any of vari-...s wide-bored, bass brass instruments whose pitch is varied ... means of valves. [< Ital. < L, a war trumpet]

·**by** (tub'ē) *adj.* ·**bi·er,** ·**bi·est** **1.** Resembling a tub in ...m. **2.** Short and fat; corpulent.

·**e** (toob, tyoob) *n.* **1.** A long, hollow, cylindrical body of ...tal, glass, rubber, etc., generally used for the conveyance ...something through it; a pipe. **2.** An electron tube. **3.** A ...lapsible metal cylinder for containing paints, toothpaste, ...e, etc. **4.** A thing or device having a tube or tubelike ...rt, as a telescope. **5.** *Zool.* Any elongated hollow part or ...gan: a bronchial *tube.* **6.** A subway or tunnel. — *v.t.* ...ed, **tub·ing** **1.** To fit or furnish with a tube. **2.** To en-...se in a tube or tubes. **3.** To make tubular. [< F < L ...us] — **tub/al** *adj.*

·**ber** (too'bər, tyoo'-) *n.* **1.** *Bot.* A short, thickened por-...n of an underground stem, as in the potato. **2.** *Anat.* A ...elling or prominence; tubercle. [< L, a swelling]

·**ber·cle** (too'bər-kəl, tyoo'-) *n.* **1.** A small rounded emi-...nce or nodule. **2.** *Bot.* A minute swelling on the roots of ...uminous plants. **3.** *Pathol.* **a** A small granular nodule or ...elling formed within an organ or plant. **b** The lesion of ...berculosis. **4.** *Anat.* A small knoblike excrescence, esp., ... the skin or on a bone. [< L < *tuber* a swelling] — **tu-**...**r·cu·loid** (too-bûr'kyə-loid, tyoo-) *adj.*

·**ercle bacillus** The rod-shaped bacterium that causes ...berculosis in man.

·**ber·cu·lar** (too-bûr'kyə-lər, tyoo-) *adj.* **1.** Covered with ...bercles; nodular. **2.** Tuberculous. — *n.* One affected ...th tuberculosis. — **tu·ber/cu·late** *adj.*

·**erculo-** *combining form* **1.** Tuberculosis; of tubercu-...is. **2.** Tuberculous. Also, before vowels, **tubercul-.** [< ...< *tuber* a swelling]

·**ber·cu·lo·sis** (too-bûr'kyə-lō'sis, tyoo-) *n. Pathol.* A ...mmunicable disease caused by infection with the tubercle ...cillus, characterized by the formation of tubercles within ...me organ or tissue. **2.** Tuberculosis affecting the lungs: ...o called *consumption, phthisis, pulmonary tuberculosis.* ... NL < L (See TUBERCLE) + -OSIS]

·**ber·cu·lous** (too-bûr'kyə-ləs, tyoo-) *adj.* Of, pertaining ... or affected with tuberculosis.

·**e·rose** (toob'rōz', tyoo'bə-rōs', tyoo'bə-rōs') *n.* A bul-...us plant of the amaryllis family, bearing fragrant white ...wers. [< NL < L *tuber* a swelling]

·**ber·ous** (too'bər-əs, tyoo'-) *adj.* **1.** Bearing projections

or prominences. **2.** Resembling tubers. **3.** *Bot.* Bearing tubers. Also **tu/ber·ose.** — **tu/ber·os/i·ty** (-bə·ros/ə·tē) *n.*

tub·ing (too'bing, tyoo'-) *n.* **1.** Tubes collectively. **2.** A piece of tube or material for tubes. **3.** Material for pillow-cases. **4.** The act of making tubes.

tu·bu·lar (too'byə-lər, tyoo'-) *adj.* **1.** Having the form of a tube. **2.** Made up of or provided with tubes. Also **tu/bu-lous, tu/bu·lose** (-lōs). [< L *tubulus* tube]

tu·bu·late (too'byə-lāt, tyoo'-) *v.t.* ·**lat·ed,** ·**lat·ing** **1.** To shape or fashion into a tube. **2.** To furnish with a tube. — *adj.* **1.** Shaped like or into a tube. **2.** Provided with a tube: also **tu/bu·lat/ed.** [< L *tubulus* tube] — **tu/bu·la/tion** *n.*

tuck (tuk) *v.t.* **1.** To fold under; press in the ends or edges of. **2.** To wrap or cover snugly. **3.** To thrust or press into a close place; cram; hide. **4.** To make tucks in, by folding and stitching. — *v.i.* **5.** To contract; draw together. **6.** To make tucks. — *n.* **1.** A fold stitched into a garment for a better fit or for decoration. **2.** Any tucked piece or part. [Fusion of OF *tūcian* to tuck up and MDu. *tucken* to pluck]

tuck·er[1] (tuk'ər) *n.* **1.** One who or that which tucks. **2.** A covering of linen, lawn, etc., formerly worn over the neck and shoulders by women.

tuck·er[2] (tuk'ər) *v.t. Informal* To weary completely; ex-haust: usu. with *out.* [Freq. of TUCK, v.]

-tude *suffix of nouns* Condition or state of being: *gratitude.* [< F < L *-tudo*]

Tu·dor (too'dər, tyoo'-) A royal family of England de-scended from **Sir Owen Tudor,** died 1461, a Welshman who married the widow of Henry V. — *adj.* Designating or per-taining to the architecture, poetry, etc., developed during the reigns of the Tudors.

Tues·day (tooz'dē, -dā, tyooz'-) *n.* The third day of the week. [OE *tiwesdæg* day of Tiw < *Tiw,* ancient Teutonic deity + *dæg* day]

tu·fa (too'fə, tyoo'-) *n.* **1.** A porous calcium carbonate, deposited from springs and streams. **2.** Tuff. [< Ital. < L *tofus*] — **tu·fa·ceous** (too-fā'shəs, tyoo-) *adj.*

tuff (tuf) *n.* A fragmentary volcanic rock composed of ma-terial varying in size from fine sand to coarse gravel. [< MF < Ital. *tufo.* See TUFA.] — **tuff·a/ceous** *adj.*

tuft (tuft) *n.* **1.** A collection or bunch of small, flexible parts, as hair, grass, or feathers, held together at the base. **2.** A clump or knot, as a cluster of threads drawn tightly through a quilt, mattress, or upholstery to secure the stuff-ing. — *v.t.* **1.** To separate or form into tufts. **2.** To cover or adorn with tufts. — *v.i.* **3.** To form tufts. [< OF *tuffe,* prob. < Gmc.] — **tuft/ed** *adj.* — **tuft/er** *n.* — **tuft/y** *adj.*

tug (tug) *v.* **tugged, tug·ging** *v.t.* **1.** To pull at with effort; strain at. **2.** To pull, draw, or drag with effort. **3.** To tow with a tugboat. — *v.i.* **4.** To pull strenuously: to *tug* at an oar. **5.** To strive; toil. — *n.* **1.** An act of tugging; a violent pull. **2.** A strenuous contest. **3.** A tugboat. **4.** A trace of a harness. [ME < OE < *lēon* to tow] — **tug/ger** *n.*

tug·boat (tug'bōt') *n.* A small, compact, ruggedly built vessel designed for towing: also *towboat, tug.*

tug of war **1.** A contest in which a number of persons at one end of a rope pull against a like number at the other end, each side endeavoring to drag the other across a line marked between. **2.** A hard struggle for supremacy.

tu·i·tion (too-ish'ən, tyoo-) *n.* **1.** The charge or payment for instruction, esp. formal instruction. **2.** Teaching; in-struction. [< AF & OF < L < *tueri* to look at, watch] — **tu·i/tion·al, tu·i/tion·ar/y** (-er/ē) *adj.*

tu·la·re·mi·a (too'lə-rē'mē-ə) *n.* A plaguelike disease of ro-dents, esp. rabbits, that may be transmitted to man; also called *rabbit fever.* Also **tu/la·rae/mi·a.** [< NL, after *Tulare* County, California + Gk. *haima* blood]

tu·lip (too'lip, tyoo'-) *n.* **1.** Any of numerous hardy, bul-bous herbs of the lily family, cultivated in many varieties for their large, variously colored, bell-shaped flowers. **2.** A bulb or flower of this plant. [< F < OF < Turkish < Per-sian *dulband* turban]

tulip tree **1.** A large tree of the magnolia family of the eastern U.S., with greenish cup-shaped flowers. **2.** Any of various other trees having tuliplike flowers.

tu·lip·wood (too'lip·wood', tyoo'-) *n.* **1.** The wood of the tulip tree. **2.** Any of several ornamental cabinet woods yielded by various trees. **3.** Any of the trees themselves.

tulle (tool, *Fr.* tül) *n.* A fine, silk, open-meshed material, used for veils, etc. [< F, after *Tulle,* city in France]

tum·ble (tum'bəl) *v.* ·**bled,** ·**bling** *v.i.* **1.** To roll or toss about. **2.** To perform acrobatic feats, as somersaults, etc. **3.** To fall violently or awkwardly. **4.** To move in a careless or headlong manner; stumble. **5.** *Informal* To understand: with *to.* — *v.t.* **6.** To toss carelessly; cause to fall. **7.** To throw into disorder or confusion; disturb; rumple. — *n.* **1.** The act of tumbling; a fall. **2.** A state of disorder or con-fusion. [ME < OE *tumbian* to fall, leap]

tum·ble·bug (tum′bəl·bug′) *n.* A beetle that rolls up a ball of dung to enclose its eggs.

tum·ble-down (tum′bəl·doun′) *adj.* Rickety, as if about to fall in pieces; dilapidated.

tum·bler (tum′blər) *n.* **1.** A drinking glass with a flat bottom. **2.** One who or that which tumbles; esp., an acrobat or gymnast. **3.** One of a breed of domestic pigeons noted for the habit of turning forward somersaults during flight. **4.** In a lock, a latch that prevents a bolt from being shot in either direction until it is raised by the key bit. For illus. see LOCK¹. **5.** In a firearm lock, a piece attached to the hammer and receiving the thrust of the mainspring.

tum·ble·weed (tum′bəl·wēd′) *n.* Any of various plants that, when withered, break from the root and are driven by the wind, scattering their seed.

tum·brel (tum′bril) *n.* **1.** A farmer's cart; esp., a boxlike cart for carrying and dumping dung. **2.** A rude cart in which prisoners were taken to the guillotine during the French Revolution. Also **tum′bril.** [< OF *tomber* to fall, ult. < Gmc.]

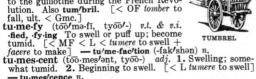

TUMBREL

tu·me·fy (tōō′mə·fī, tyōō′-) *v.t. & v.i.* **·fied, ·fy·ing** To swell or puff up; become tumid. [< MF < L *tumere* to swell + *facere* to make] — **tu′me·fac′tion** (-fak′shən) *n.*

tu·mes·cent (tōō·mes′ənt, tyōō-) *adj.* **1.** Swelling; somewhat tumid. **2.** Beginning to swell. [< L *tumere* to swell] — **tu·mes′cence** *n.*

tu·mid (tōō′mid, tyōō′-) *adj.* **1.** Swollen; enlarged, as a part of the body. **2.** Inflated or pompous in style. **3.** Bursting; teeming. [< L < *tumere* to swell] — **tu·mid′i·ty** *n.* — **tu′mid·ly** *adv.* — **tu′mid·ness** *n.*

tu·mor (tōō′mər, tyōō′-) *n. Pathol.* A local swelling on or in any part of the body, esp. from some abnormal growth of tissue that may or may not become malignant. Also *Brit.* **tu′mour.** [< L *tumere* to swell] — **tu′mor·ous** *adj.*

tu·mult (tōō′mult, tyōō′-) *n.* **1.** The commotion, disturbance, or agitation of a multitude; an uproar; turbulence; hubbub. **2.** Any violent commotion or agitation, as of the mind. [< OF < L *tumere* to swell]

tu·mul·tu·ous (tōō·mul′chōō·əs, tyōō-) *adj.* **1.** Characterized by tumult; disorderly. **2.** Causing or affected by tumult or agitation; agitated or disturbed. Also **tu·mul′tu·ar·y** (-er′ē). — **tu·mul′tu·ous·ly** *adv.* — **tu·mul′tu·ous·ness** *n.*

tun (tun) *n.* **1.** A large cask. **2.** A varying measure of capacity, usu. equal to 252 gallons. — *v.t.* **tunned, tun·ning** To put into a cask or tun. [OE *tunne*]

tu·na (tōō′nə) *n.* *pl.* **·na** or **·nas** **1.** Any of several large marine food fishes of the mackerel family. **2.** Any of various similar or related fishes. **3.** The flesh of any of these fishes processed and eaten as food: also **tuna fish.** Also called *tunny.* [< Am. Sp., ult. < L < Gk. *thynnos*]

tun·dra (tun′drə, tōōn′-) *n.* A treeless, often marshy plain of Siberia, arctic North America, etc. [< Russian < Lapp]

tune (tōōn, tyōōn) *n.* **1.** A melody or air, usu. simple and easy to remember. **2.** The state or quality of being at the proper pitch, or, loosely, in the proper key: out of *tune.* **3.** Concord or unison. **4.** Suitable temper or humor. — **to change one's tune** To assume a different manner, style, or attitude. — **to sing a different** (or **another**) **tune** To assume a different manner or attitude; change one's tune. — **to the tune of** To the price of. — *v.* **tuned, tun·ing** *v.t.* **1.** To adjust the pitch of to a standard. **2.** To adapt to a particular tone, expression, or mood. **3.** To bring into harmony. **4.** To express musically. — *v.i.* **5.** To be in harmony. — **to tune in** To adjust a radio receiver to the frequency of (a station, broadcast, etc.). — **to tune out** To adjust a radio receiver to exclude (interference, a station, etc.). — **to tune up 1.** To bring (musical instruments) to a standard or common pitch. **2.** To adjust (an engine, etc.) to proper working order. [Var. of TONE] — **tun′a·ble** or **tune′a·ble** *adj.*

tune·ful (tōōn′fəl, tyōōn′-) *adj.* **1.** Melodious; musical. **2.** Producing musical sounds. — **tune′ful·ly** *adv.* — **tune′·ful·ness** *n.*

tune·less (tōōn′lis, tyōōn′-) *adj.* **1.** Not employed in making music; silent. **2.** Lacking in rhythm, melody, etc. — **tune′less·ly** *adv.* — **tune′less·ness** *n.*

tun·er (tōō′nər, tyōō′-) *n.* **1.** One who or that which tunes. **2.** *Telecom.* A radio receiver without amplifiers.

tune-up (tōōn′up′, tyōōn′-) *n. Informal* An adjustment to bring a motor, etc., into proper operating condition.

tung oil (tung) A yellow to brown oil extracted from the seeds of a Chinese tree, used in paints, varnishes, etc. and also for waterproofing. [< Chinese *t′ung* tung tree]

tung·sten (tung′stən) *n.* A steel-gray, brittle, heavy metallic element of the chromium group (symbol W), having a high melting point and much used in the manufacture of filaments for electric lamps and high-speed cutting tools: also called *wolfram.* See ELEMENT. [< Sw. < *tung* weighty + *sten* stone] — **tung·sten·ic** (′tung·sten′ik) *adj.*

tu·nic (tōō′nik, tyōō′-) *n.* **1.** In ancient Greece and Rome, a garment with or without sleeves, reaching to the knees and usu. worn without a belt. **2.** A modern outer garment gathered at the waist, as a short overskirt or blouse. **3.** *Biol.* Any loose membranous skin or mantle of tissue enveloping an organ or part. [< L *tunica* < Semitic]

tu·ni·cate (tōō′nə·kit, -kāt, tyōō′-) *adj.* **1.** *Zool.* Of or pertaining to a group of small marine chordates, having in the adult stage a cylindrical saclike body covered with a parent membrane or tunic, as the ascidians. **2.** *Zool.* Having a tunic. — *n.* A tunicate animal. [< NL < L < *tu care* to clothe with a tunic < *tunica* tunic]

tuning fork (tōō′ning, tyōō′-) A fork-shaped piece of steel that produces a tone of definite pitch when struck.

Tu·ni·sian (tōō·nish′ən, -nē′zhən, tyōō-) *adj.* Of or relating to Tunisia, or Tunis, or their inhabitants. — *n.* **1.** An inhabitant or native of Tunisia or Tunis. **2.** The speech of Tunisia, a North Arabic dialect.

tun·nel (tun′əl) *n.* **1.** An artificial subterranean passageway or gallery, esp. one under a hill, etc., as for a railway. **2.** Any similar passageway under or through something, as in a mine. — *v.* **tun·neled** or **·nelled, tun·nel·ing** or **·nel·ling** *v.t.* **1.** To make a tunnel through. **2.** To shape or make in the form of a tunnel: to *tunnel* a passage. — *v.i.* **3.** To make a tunnel. [Fusion of OF *tonnelle* partridge net < dim. of *tonne* cask] — **tun′nel·er** or **tun′nel·ler** *n.*

tun·ny (tun′ē) *n.* *pl.* **·ny** or **·nies** The tuna, a fish. [< L < Gk. *thynnos*]

tup (tup) *n.* **1.** A ram, or male sheep. **2.** The striking face of a power hammer. — *v.t. & v.i.* **tupped, tup·ping** To copulate with (a female): said of the ram. [ME *tupe*]

Tu·pi (tōō·pē′) *n.* *pl.* **·pis** or **·pi 1.** A member of a group of South American Indian tribes, comprising the northern branch of the Tupian stock. **2.** The language spoken by the Tupis, used as a lingua franca along the Amazon. [< Tupi, comrade]

Tu·pi·an (tōō·pē′ən) *adj.* Of or pertaining to the Tupis or their language. — *n.* A large stock of South American Indians of some one hundred tribes of the Tupis and Guaranis: also **Tu·pi′-Gua′ra·ni′** (-gwä′rä·nē′).

tup·pence (tup′əns) *n. Brit. Informal* Twopence.

tuque (tōōk, tyōōk) *n. Canadian* A knitted cap, worn in tobogganing, etc. [< dial. F (Canadian) < F *toque* cap]

Tu·ra·ni·an (tōō·rā′nē·ən, tyōō-) *adj.* **1.** Of or pertaining to a hypothetical nomadic people who antedated the Aryans in Europe and Asia. **2.** Pertaining to the hypothetical Ural-Altaic family of languages. [< Persian *Tūrān*, country north of the Oxus River]

tur·ban (tûr′bən) *n.* **1.** An Oriental head covering consisting of a sash or shawl, twisted about the head or about a cap. **2.** Any similar headdress. **3.** A round-crowned brimless hat for women or children. [< F < Ital. < Turkish < Persian < *dul* turn + *band* band] — **tur′baned** (-bənd) *adj.*

tur·bid (tûr′bid) *adj.* **1.** Opaque or cloudy, as a liquid with a suspension of foreign particles. **2.** Thick and dense, as heavy smoke or fog. **3.** Being in a state of confusion. [< L *turbare* to trouble < *turba* crowd] — **tur′bid·ly** *adv.* — **tur·bid′ness, tur·bid′i·ty** (tûr·bid′ə·tē) *n.*

tur·bi·nate (tûr′bə·nit, -nāt) *adj.* Top-shaped; also, spinning like a top. [< L *turbo* whirlwind]

tur·bine (tûr′bin, -bīn) *n.* Any of various motors consisting of one or more rotary units, mounted on a shaft and provided with a series of curved vanes, actuated by the impulse of steam, water, gas, or other fluid under pressure. [< L *turbo* whirlwind, top]

turbo- *combining form* A turbine; related to or operated by a turbine or turbines. [< L *turbo* top]

tur·bo·gen·er·a·tor (tûr′bō·jen′ə·rā′tər) *n.* An electric power-generating machine adapted for direct coupling with a steam turbine.

tur·bo·jet engine (tûr′bō·jet′) *n. Aeron.* A type of jet engine using a gas turbine to drive an air compressor.

tur·bo·prop (tûr′bō·prop′) *n. Aeron.* A turbojet engine connecting directly with a propeller. Also called *propjet.*

tur·bot (tûr′bət) *n.* *pl.* **·bot** or **·bots 1.** A large European flatfish, esteemed as food. **2.** One of various related fishes. [< AF *turbut*, OF *tourbout*, or MDu. *turbot*]

tur·bu·lence (tûr′byə·ləns) *n.* **1.** The state or condition of being violently disturbed, restless, or confused. **2.** *Phys.* The irregular eddying flow of a gas or other fluid, especially caused by an obstacle or by friction, as of a ship or airplane in rapid motion. Also **tur′bu·len·cy.**

tur·bu·lent (tûr′byə·lənt) *adj.* **1.** Being in violent agitation or commotion. **2.** Inclined to rebel; insubordinate. **3.** Having a tendency to disturb or throw into confusion. [< MF < L *turbare.* See TURBID.] — **tur′bu·lent·ly** *adv.* — **Syn. 1.** agitated, boisterous, disorderly, disturbed, riotous, tumultuous, wild. **2.** insurgent, mutinous, refractory.

tur·dine (tûr′din, -dīn) *adj.* Belonging or pertaining to a large and widely distributed family of singing birds, including thrushes and bluebirds. [< NL < L *turdus* thrush]

een (tōō-rēn′, tyōō-) *n.* A deep, covered dish, as for holding soup to be served. [< F < LL < L *terra* earth]

·turf (tûrf) *n. pl.* **turfs** (*Archaic* **turves**) **1.** The grass or other fine plants with their matted roots filling the upper stratum of certain soils; sod. **2.** A piece of peat for burning as fuel. **— the turf 1.** A racetrack for horses. **2.** The practice of racing horses. [OE] **— turf′y** *adj.*

·man (tûrf′mən) *n. pl.* **·men** (-mən) A man who is devoted to or connected with horse racing.

·ges·cence (tûr·jes′əns) *n.* The process of swelling up. [Med.L < L *turgere* to swell] **— tur·ges′cent** *adj.*

gid (tûr′jid) *adj.* **1.** Unnaturally distended, as by contained air or liquid; swollen. **2.** Inflated; bombastic, as language, etc. [< L *turgere* to swell] **— tur·gid′i·ty, tur′gid·ness** (tûr′jid·nis) *n.* **— tur′gid·ly** *adv.*

·gor (tûr′gər) *n.* The state of being turgid; turgidity.

·k (tûrk) *n.* **1.** A native or inhabitant of Turkey; someone called Ottoman. **2.** One of any of the peoples speaking of the Turkic languages. **3.** A Moslem.

·key (tûr′kē) *n. pl.* **·keys 1.** A large American bird related to the pheasant, having the head naked and the tail extensible; esp., the American domesticated turkey, much esteemed as food. **2.** *U.S. Slang* A play that is a failure. **— to talk turkey** To discuss in a practical and direct manner. [Short for *turkey cock* the guinea fowl, after *Turkey*; formerly applied erroneously to the American bird]

·key buzzard A sooty black vulture of tropical America and the southern U.S., having a naked red head.

·ki (tōōr′kē) *adj.* **1.** Of or pertaining to Turkic. **2.** Of or pertaining to any of the peoples speaking a Turkic language, as the Osmanlis. **— n. pl. ·kis 1.** The Turkic languages. **2.** A member of any of the Turki peoples.

·k·ic (tûr′kik) *n.* A subfamily of the Altaic family of languages, including Osmanli or Turkish, Uzbek, etc. **— adj.** pertaining to this linguistic subfamily, or to any of the peoples speaking these languages.

·k·ish (tûr′kish) *adj.* **1.** Of or pertaining to Turkey or Turks. **2.** Of or relating to the Turkic subfamily of Altaic languages, esp. to Osmanli. **— n.** Osmanli.

·kish bath A bathing establishment where sweating is induced by exposure to high temperature, usu. in a room heated by steam, followed by washing, massage, etc.

·kish towel A heavy, rough towel with loose, uncut pile. Also **turkish towel.**

·mer·ic (tûr′mər·ik) *n.* **1.** The root of an East Indian plant, used as a condiment, aromatic stimulant, dyestuff, etc. **2.** The plant yielding this root. **— adj.** Of, pertaining to or saturated with turmeric. [? < F < Med.L *terra merita* deserving earth]

·moil (tûr′moil) *n.* Confused motion; disturbance; tumult. [? < OF < L *tremere* to tremble]

·turn (tûrn) *v.t.* **1.** To cause to rotate, as about an axis. **2.** To change the position of, as by rotating: to *turn* a trunk on its side. **3.** To move so that the upper side becomes the under and the under side becomes the upper: to *turn* a page; to *turn* the soil; to *turn* a shirt collar. **4.** To reverse the arrangement or order of. **5.** To cause to rotate in order to fasten, loosen, open, etc.: to *turn* a screw. **6.** To revolve mentally; ponder: often with *over*. **7.** To sprain or strain: to *turn* one's ankle. **8.** To nauseate (the stomach). **9.** To give rounded or curved form to, as by turning in a lathe. **10.** To make graceful or finished form to: to *turn* a phrase. **11.** To form by revolving: to *turn* cartwheels. **12.** To bend, curve, fold, twist, or blunt. **13.** To change or transform: to *turn* water into wine. **14.** To translate. **15.** To exchange for an equivalent: to *turn* stocks into cash. **16.** To adapt to the purpose; apply: to *turn* information to good account. **17.** To cause to become as specified: The sight *turned* him pale. **18.** To change the color of. **19.** To make sour or rancid. **20.** To change the direction or focus of. **21.** To direct; aim; point. **22.** To deflect or divert: to *turn* a blow. **23.** To repel: to *turn* a charge. **24.** To go around or to the other side of: to *turn* a corner. **25.** To pass or go beyond: to *turn* twenty-one. **26.** To cause to go; send; drive: to *turn* a beggar from one's door. **— v.i. 27.** To move around an axis; rotate; revolve. **28.** To move partially on or as if on an axis: He *turned* and ran. **29.** To change position; also, to turn from side to side. **30.** To reverse position; become inverted. **31.** To change or reverse direction or flow: We *turned* north. The tide has *turned*. **32.** To change the direction or focus of one's thought, attention, etc. **33.** To depend; hinge: with *on* or *upon*. **34.** To whirl, as the head. **35.** To become nauseated, as the stomach. **36.** To become hostile: to *turn* on one's neighbors. **37.** To change one's position in order to act in retaliation: The worm *turns*. **38.** To become transformed: The water *turned* into ice. **39.** To become as specified: His hair *turned* gray. **40.** To change color: said esp. of leaves. **41.** To become sour, rancid, or

fermented. **— to turn against** To become or cause to become opposed or hostile to. **— to turn down 1.** To diminish the flow, volume, etc., of. **2.** *Informal* To reject or refuse, as a request; also, to refuse the request, etc., of. **— to turn in 1.** To fold or double. **2.** To bend or incline inward. **3.** To deliver; hand over. **4.** *Informal* To go to bed. **— to turn loose** *Informal* To set free. **— to turn off 1.** To stop the operation, flow, etc., of. **2.** To leave the direct road. **— to turn on 1.** To set in operation, flow, etc. **2.** *Slang* To take or experience the effects of taking a psychedelic drug, as marijuana. **3.** *Slang* To evoke in (someone) a rapt response, as though under the influence of a psychedelic drug: Baroque music really *turned* him *on*. **— to turn out 1.** To turn inside out. **2.** To eject or expel. **3.** To dismiss. **4.** To stop the operation, flow, etc., of. **5.** To bend or incline outward. **6.** To produce; make. **7.** To come or go out, as for duty or service. **8.** To prove (to be). **9.** To become or result. **10.** To equip; dress. **11.** *Informal* To get out of bed. **— to turn over 1.** To change the position of; invert. **2.** To upset; overturn. **3.** To hand over; transfer or relinquish. **4.** To do business to the amount of. **5.** To invest and get back (capital). **6.** To buy and then sell: to *turn over* merchandise. **— to turn to 1.** To set to work. **2.** To seek aid from. **3.** To refer or apply to. **4.** To open a book, etc., to (a specified page). **— to turn up 1.** To bring or fold the under side upward. **2.** To bend or incline upward. **3.** To find or be found. **4.** To increase the flow, volume, etc., of. **5.** To put in an appearance; arrive. **— n. 1.** The act of turning, or the state of being turned. **2.** A change to another direction, motion, or position. **3.** A deflection or deviation from a course; change in trend. **4.** The point at which a change takes place: a *turn* for the better. **5.** A rotation or revolution. **6.** A bend, as in a road. **7.** A regular time or chance in some succession: It's my *turn* to play. **8.** A round; spell: a *turn* at painting. **9.** Characteristic form, shape, or style: the *turn* of a phrase. **10.** A knack or special ability: a *turn* for study. **11.** Tendency; direction: The talk took a serious *turn*. **12.** A deed performed: a good *turn*. **13.** An advantage: It served his *turn*. **14.** A walk, drive, or trip to and fro: a *turn* in the park. **15.** A round in a skein, coil, etc.; also, a twist. **16.** *Music* An ornament formed by a group of four rapid notes, the first a degree above and the third a degree below the principal tone, that occupies the second and fourth positions. In an *inverted turn* the tones are reversed in order. **17.** *Informal* A shock to the nerves, as from alarm. **18.** A short theatrical act. **— at every turn** On every occasion; constantly. **— by turns 1.** In alternation or sequence. **2.** At intervals. **— in turn** One after another; in proper order or sequence. **— out of turn** Not in proper order or sequence. **— to a turn** Just right: said esp. of cooked food. **— to take turns** To act, play, etc., one after another in proper order. [Fusion of OE *tyrnan* and *turnian* and OF *turner*, alt. < L *tornare* to turn in a lathe]

turn·a·bout (tûrn′ə·bout′) *n.* The act of turning completely about and taking the opposite direction, opinion, etc.

turn·a·round (tûrn′ə·round′) *n.* The act of unloading a ship, aircraft, etc., and loading it to begin its next trip.

turn·buck·le (tûrn′buk′əl) *n. Mech.* A form of coupling so threaded that when connected lengthwise between two metal rods or wires it may be turned so as to regulate the distance or tension between them.

TURNBUCKLES
a Insulated, for electric wires. *b* For metal tie rods. *c* For window shutters.

turn·coat (tûrn′kōt′) *n.* One who goes over to the opposite side or party; a renegade.

turn·down (tûrn′doun′) *adj.* Folded down, as a collar; also, capable of being turned down.

turn·er¹ (tûr′nər) *n.* One who turns; esp. one who fashions objects with a lathe.

turn·er² (tûr′nər) *n.* A gymnast; a member of a turnverein. [< G < *turnen* to engage in gymnastics < F *tourner*]

turn·ing (tûr′ning) *n.* **1.** The act of one who or that which turns. **2.** The art of shaping wood, metal, etc., in a lathe. **3.** Any deviation from a straight or customary course; a winding; bend. **4.** The point where a road forks. **5.** Fashioning or shaping, as of a literary work.

turning point 1. The point of a decisive change in direction of action; a crisis. **2.** The point at which the direction of a motion is reversed.

tur·nip (tûr′nip) *n.* **1.** The fleshy, globular, edible root of either of two biennial herbs, of the mustard family, the **white turnip,** and the rutabaga. **2.** Either of the plants yielding this root. [Earlier *turnepe*, ? < F *tour* turn (< L *turnus* lathe) + ME *nepe* < OE *nǣp* < L *napus* turnip]

turn·key (tûrn′kē) *n.* One who has charge of the keys of a prison; a jailer.

turn·off (tûrn′ôf′, -of′) *n. Informal* A road, path, or way branching off from a main thoroughfare.

turn·out (tûrn′out′) *n.* **1.** An act of turning out or coming forth. **2.** An assemblage of persons; attendance. **3.** A quantity produced; output. **4.** Array; equipment; outfit. **5.** A railroad siding. **6.** A carriage or wagon with its horses and equipage. **7.** *Brit.* A labor strike; also, a striker.

turn·o·ver (tûrn′ō′vər) *n.* **1.** The act or process of turning over; an upset or overthrow, as of a vehicle. **2.** The rate at which persons hired by a given establishment within a given period are replaced by others; also, the number of persons hired. **3.** A change or revolution. **4.** A small pie or tart made by covering half of a circular crust with fruit, jelly, or the like, and turning the other half over on top. **5.** The amount of business accomplished, or of work achieved. **6.** A completed commercial transaction or course of business; also, the money receipts of a business for a given period: also called *overturn.* — *adj.* **1.** Designed for turning over or reversing. **2.** Capable of being turned over or folded down. **3.** Made with a part folded down: a *turnover* collar.

turn·pike (tûrn′pīk′) *n.* **1.** A road, now esp. a superhighway, on which there are tollgates. **2.** Loosely, any highway: also **turnpike road.** **3.** A tollbar or tollgate. [ME *turnpyke* spiked road barrier < TURN + *pyke* pike[1]]

turn·stile (tûrn′stīl′) *n.* A gate, having revolving horizontal arms, that admits passengers to subways, buses, etc., on the deposit of fares, or registers the number of persons entering a building, or restricts passage to one direction only.

turn·stone (tûrn′stōn′) *n.* A ploverlike migratory bird of northern regions: so called from its habit of turning over stones to obtain its food.

turn·ta·ble (tûrn′tā′bəl) *n.* **1.** A rotating disk, as one that carries a phonograph record. **2.** A rotating platform arranged to turn a section of a bridge in order to open a passage for ships. **3.** Such a platform to turn a locomotive, car, etc. Also *Brit.* **turn′plate**′ (-plāt′).

turn·up (tûrn′up′) *n.* **1.** That which is turned up, as part of a garment. **2.** A particular card or die turned up in gambling. **3.** Pure chance; a tossup. — *adj.* Turned up.

turn·ver·ein (tōōrn′fə·rīn, tûrn′və·rīn) *n. Sometimes cap.* An athletic club. [< G < *turnen* to exercise + *verein* club]

tur·pen·tine (tûr′pən·tīn) *n.* An oleoresin obtained from any of several coniferous trees, esp. pines. — **oil of turpentine** The colorless essential oil formed when turpentine is distilled with steam; chiefly used to thin paint: also called *spirits of turpentine.* — *v.t.* **·tined, ·tin·ing** **1.** To put turpentine with or upon; saturate with turpentine. **2.** To obtain crude turpentine from (a tree). [< OF < L < Gk. *terebinthos,* a tree from which it was originally obtained]

tur·pi·tude (tûr′pə·tōōd, -tyōōd) *n.* Inherent baseness; vileness; depravity, or any action showing depravity. [< MF < L < *turpis* vile]

tur·quoise (tûr′koiz, -kwoiz) *n.* **1.** A blue or green aluminum phosphate, colored by copper, found massive, and in its highly polished blue varieties esteemed as a gemstone. **2.** A light greenish blue, the color of the turquoise: also **turquoise blue.** [< MF (*pierre*) *turquoise* Turkish (stone)]

tur·ret (tûr′it) *n.* **1.** *Mil.* **a** A rotating armored housing, large enough to contain a powerful gun or guns and gunners, forming part of a warship or of a fort. **b** A similar structure in a tank or a bombing or combat airplane. **2.** *Archit.* A small tower rising above a larger structure, as on a castle. **3.** *Mech.* In a lathe, a cylinder fitted with sockets or chucks for the reception of various tools, any one of which may be presented in the axial line of the work: also **turret head.** [< OF *torete,* dim. of *tor* tower] — **tur·ri·cal** (tûr′i·kəl) *adj.*

tur·ret·ed (tûr′it·id) *adj.* **1.** Provided with turrets. **2.** Having the form of a turret.

turret lathe A lathe having a turret.

tur·tle[1] (tûr′təl) *n.* **1.** Any of numerous reptiles having a horny, toothless beak, and a short, stout body enclosed within a carapace and plastron, into which all the members may be drawn for protection. **2.** A marine species as distinguished from a terrestrial or fresh-water species. **3.** The flesh of certain varieties of turtle, served as food. — **green turtle** An important food turtle of wide distribution in tropical and semitropical seas: so called from the greenish color of its flesh. — **to turn turtle** To capsize. — *v.i.* **·tled, ·tling** To hunt or catch turtles. [Appar. alter. of F *tortue* or Sp. *tortuga* < Med.L *tortuca* tortoise; infl. in form by TURTLE[2]]

tur·tle[2] (tûr′təl) *n. Archaic* A turtledove. [OE < L *turtur*]

tur·tle·back (tûr′təl·bak′) *n.* **1.** *Naut.* An arched covering, resembling the shell of a turtle, built over the bow or stern of a ship as protection against heavy seas. Also **turtle deck.** **2.** *Archeol.* A chipped stone implement rounded on one side.

tur·tle·dove (tûr′təl·duv′) *n.* A small Old World dove conspicuous for its white-edged black tail and soft, mournful coo. [< TURTLE[2] + DOVE]

turtle neck A high collar that fits snugly about the neck, usu. rolled or turned over double, used esp. on athletic sweaters. — **tur·tle·neck** (tûr′təl·nek′) *adj.*

Tus·can (tus′kən) *adj.* Pertaining to Tuscany. — *n.* native or inhabitant of Tuscany. **2.** Any Italian dia used in Tuscany; esp. the one spoken in Florence.

Tus·ca·ro·ra (tus′kə·rôr′ə, -rō′rə) *n. pl.* **·ra** or **·ras** Or a tribe of North American Indians of Iroquoian stock merly living in North Carolina, now surviving in New Y and Ontario.

tush (tush) *interj.* An exclamation expressing disappro impatience, etc. [ME *tussch*]

tusk (tusk) *n.* **1.** A long, pointed tooth, generally one pair, as in the boar, walrus, or elephant. **2.** A sharp, jecting, toothlike point. **3.** A shoulder on a tenon strengthen it at its base; also, a tenon having such a sh der. — *v.t.* **1.** To gore with the tusks. **2.** To root up the tusks. [Metathetic var. of OE *tūx*] — **tusked** (tu *adj.* — **tusk′less** *adj.*

tusk·er (tus′kər) *n.* A tusked elephant or boar.

tus·sah (tus′ə) *n.* **1.** An Asian silkworm that spins larg coons yielding a coarse, brownish or yellowish silk. **2.** silk, or the durable fabric woven from it. Also **tus·sar** (ər), **tus·sore** (tus′ôr, -ōr). [< Hind. < Skt. *tasara, tra* lit., shuttle]

tus·sis (tus′is) *n. Pathol.* A cough. [< NL < L] — **sal, tus′sive** *adj.*

tus·sle (tus′əl) *v.t. & v.i.* **·sled, ·sling** To fight or strugg a vigorous, determined way; scuffle; wrestle. — *n.* A d derly struggle, as in sport; scuffle. [Var. of TOUSLE]

tus·sock (tus′ək) *n.* **1.** A tuft or clump of grass or se **2.** A tuft, as of hair or feathers. Also **tus′suck.** [Prob. of obs. *tusk* tuft of hair, ? < TUSK] — **tus′sock·y** *adj.*

tut (tut) *interj.* An exclamation to check rashness or ex impatience. Also **tut tut.**

tu·te·lage (tōō′tə·lij, tyōō′-) *n.* **1.** The state of being u a tutor or guardian. **2.** The act or office of a guar guardianship. **3.** The act of tutoring; instruction. [< *tueri* to watch, guard]

tu·te·lar·y (tōō′tə·ler′ē, tyōō′-) *adj.* **1.** Invested with g dianship. **2.** Pertaining to a guardian. Also **tu′te·lar** (

tu·tor (tōō′tər, tyōō′-) *n.* **1.** One who instructs anoth one or more branches of knowledge; a private teacher. college teacher who gives individual instruction. **3.** *Br* college official entrusted with the tutelage and care of ur graduates assigned to him. **4.** *Law* A guardian of a min of a woman. — *v.t.* **1.** To act as tutor to; instruct; te train. **2.** To have the guardianship of. **3.** To treat sev or sternly, as a tutor might; discipline. — *v.i.* **4.** To d work of a tutor. **5.** To be tutored or instructed. [< OF < L < *tueri* to watch, guard] — **tu·to·ri·al** (tōō·tôr -tō′rē, tyōō′-) *adj.*

tu·tor·ship (tōō′tər·ship, tyōō′-) *n.* **1.** The office of a t or of a guardian. Also **tu′tor·age** (-ij). **2.** Tutelage.

tut·ti (tōō′tē) *Music adj.* All: a term used to indicate all performers are to take part. — *n. pl.* **·tis** A compos piece, movement, or passage for all the voices and in ments together. [< Ital., pl. of *tutto* all < L *totus*]

tut·ti-frut·ti (tōō′tē·frōō′tē) *n.* A confection, chewing ice cream, etc., made with a mixture of fruits. — *adj.* ing fruit flavors. [< Ital., all fruits]

tu·tu (tü·tü′) *n. French* A short, full, projecting skirt sisting of many layers of sheer fabric, worn by ballet dan

tu-whit tu-whoo (tōō·hwit′, tōō·hwōō′) The cry of an **tux·e·do** (tuk·sē′dō) *n. pl.* **·dos** **1.** *U.S.* A man's s formal dinner coat without tails: also called *dinner coat* ner jack′et. **2.** *U.S.* The suit of which the coat is a part. **Tux·e′do.** [after *Tuxedo* Park, N.Y.]

TV (tē′vē′) *n. pl.* **TVs** or **TV's** Television. — *adj.* pertaining to television.

twad·dle (twod′l) *v.t. & v.i.* **·dled, ·dling** To talk foo and pretentiously. — *n.* Pretentious, silly talk. [Pro ter. of TWATTLE] — **twad′dler** *n.*

twain (twān) *adj. Archaic & Poetic* Two. — *n.* **1.** A ple; two. **2.** In river navigation, two fathoms or twelve [OE *twēgen,* masculine of *twā* two]

twang (twang) *v.t. & v.i.* **twanged, twang·ing** **1.** To or cause to make a sharp, vibrant sound, as a bowstring To utter or speak nasally. — *n.* **1.** A sharp, vibr sound, as of a tense string plucked. **2.** Excessive nasali the voice. **3.** A sound resembling either of the foreg [Imit.] — **twang′y** *adj.*

twat·tle (twot′l) *v.t. & v.i.* **·tled, ·tling** *n.* Twaddle. for *twittle-twattle,* var. of TITTLE-TATTLE]

tweak (twēk) *v.t.* To pinch and twist sharply; twitch. A twisting pinch; twitch. [Var. of dial. *twick,* OE *twicci* twitch] — **tweak′y** *adj.*

tweed (twēd) *n.* **1.** A soft woolen fabric with a home surface, often woven in two or more colors to effect a c or plaid pattern. **2.** *pl.* Clothing of tweed. — **Harris t** A homespun woolen cloth, usu. of mixed colors, made at ris in the Hebrides. [Alter. of dial. E (Scottish) *tweel,* TWILL]

twee·dle (twēd′l) *v.* **·dling, ·dling** *v.t.* **1.** To play (a m trument) casually or carelessly. **2.** To wheedle; cajole. *v.i.* **3.** To produce a series of shrill tones. **4.** To play a sical instrument casually or carelessly. — *n.* A sound embling the tones of a violin. [Imit.]

e·dle·dum and twee·dle·dee (twēd'l·dum', twēd'l·) Two things between which there is only the slightest sible distinction. [Orig. imit. of low- and high-pitched sical instruments, respectively]

een (twēn) Contraction of BETWEEN.

et (twēt) *v.i.* To utter a thin, chirping note. — *n.* A ttering or chirping. Also **tweet'-tweet'.** [Imit.]

et·er (twē'tər) *n.* *Electronics* A small loudspeaker used reproduce high-pitched sounds in high-fidelity sound ipment. Compare WOOFER. [< TWEET]

eze (twēz) *v.t.* tweezed, tweez·ing *Informal* To handle, ck, etc., with tweezers. [Back formation < TWEEZERS]

ez·ers (twē'zərz) *n.pl.* Small pincers for grasping and ding small objects. Also called **pair of tweezers.** [Alter. *tweezes,* pl. of *tweeze,* earlier *etweese* case of small instru-nts < F *étuis,* pl. of *étui.*]

elfth-day (twelfth'dā') *n.* Epiphany.

elfth-night (twelfth'nīt') *n.* The evening (Jan. 5th) ore Epiphany; sometimes, the evening (Jan. 6th) of iphany. — *adj.* Of or pertaining to Twelfth-night.

lve (twelv) *n.* 1. The sum of eleven and one: a cardinal nber. **2.** Any symbol of this number, as 12, xii, XII. **3.** ything consisting of or representing twelve units. **— the elve** The twelve apostles. — *adj.* Being one more than ven. [OE *twelf*] **— twelfth** (twelfth) *adj. & n.*

lve Apostles The twelve disciples of Jesus: more com-nly *the Twelve.*

lve·mo (twelv'mō) *adj. & n.* Duodecimo.

lve-month (twelv'munth') *n.* A year.

lve-tone (twelv'tōn') *adj.* *Music* **1.** Of, using, or com-ed in the technique developed by Arnold Schönberg, in ich the tones of the chromatic scale are arranged in an ar-rary series, which is used as the basis of the composition. In 20th-century music, using or composed in a freely chro-tic style.

n·ty (twen'tē) *n.* *pl.* **·ties** **1.** The sum of nineteen and : a cardinal number. **2.** Any symbol of this number, as xx, XX. **3.** Anything consisting of or representing twenty ts. — *adj.* Being one more than nineteen. [OE *twēntig*] **twen'ti·eth** *adj. & n.*

n·ty-one (twen'tē-wun') *n.* A card game in which each yer bets against the dealer, the object being to draw cards ose value will equal or approach twenty-one without ex-ding that amount: also called *blackjack, vingt-et-un.*

- *prefix* Two; double; twice: *twibil.* Also spelled *twy-.* E, double < *twā* two]

·bil (twi'bil) *n.* **1.** A battle-ax with two cutting edges. A mattock having one blade like an ax and the other an z. Also **twi'bill.** [OE < *twi-* two + *bill* ax]

ce (twīs) *adv.* **1.** Two times. **2.** In double measure; ubly. [OE *twiges,* gen. of *twiga* twice]

ce-told (twīs'tōld') *adj.* Told more than once.

d·dle (twid'l) *v.* **·dled, ·dling** *v.t.* **1.** To twirl idly; toy or y with. — *v.i.* **2.** To revolve or twirl. **3.** To toy with nething idly. **4.** To be busy about trifles. **— to twiddle e's thumbs** **1.** To rotate one's thumbs idly around one ther. **2.** To pass time in doing nothing. — *n.* A gentle irling, as of the fingers. [Origin unknown] **— twid'dler** *n.*

g (twig) *n.* A small shoot or branchlet of a tree. [OE *gge*] **— twigged** *adj.* **— twig'less** *adj.*

·gy (twig'ē) *adj.* **·gi·er, ·gi·est** Like, or full of, twigs.

·light (twī'līt') *n.* **1.** The light diffused over the sky en the sun is below the horizon, esp. in the evening; also period during which this light is prevalent. **2.** Any faint ht. **3.** A condition following the waning of past glory, hievement, etc. — *adj.* Pertaining to, resembling, or aracteristic of twilight. [ME < OE *twi-* (< *twa* two) + GHT; used in the sense of "the light between the two," i.e., tween day and night]

light sleep *Med.* A light or partial anesthesia as by in-ction of morphine and scopolamine, sometimes used to re-ve childbirth pains. [Trans. of G *dämmerschlaf*]

ll (twil) *n.* **1.** A weave characterized by di-onal ribs or lines in fabrics. **2.** A fabric woven th a twill. — *v.t.* To weave (cloth) so as to oduce diagonal lines or ribs on the surface. ar. of ME *twile,* OE < *twa* two, partial trans. L *bilix* having a double thread]

lled (twild) *adj.* Woven so as to produce a agonal rib or line; ribbed or ridged.

in (twin) *n.* **1.** One of two young produced the same birth. **2.** The counterpart or exact ate of another. — *adj.* **1.** Being, or standing the relation of, a twin or twins. **2.** Consisting

TWILL
(Enlarged
to show
weave)

---

of, forming, or being one of a pair of similar and closely related objects; twofold. — *v.* **twinned, twin·ning** *v.i.* **1.** To bring forth twins. **2.** To be matched or equal; agree. — *v.t.* **3.** To bring forth as twins. **4.** To couple; match. [OE *twinn*]

twine (twīn) *v.* twined, twin·ing *v.t.* **1.** To twist together, as threads. **2.** To form by such twisting. **3.** To coil or wrap about something. **4.** To encircle by winding or wreathing. **5.** To enfold; embrace. — *v.i.* **6.** To interlace. **7.** To proceed in a winding course; meander. — *adj.* Of or like twine. — *n.* **1.** A string composed of two or more strands twisted together: loosely, any small cord. **2.** The act of twining or entwining. **3.** A form or conformation pro-duced by twining. **4.** An interweaving or interlacing. [OE *twin* twisted double thread < *twā* two] **— twin'er** *n.*

twinge (twinj) *n.* **1.** A sharp, darting, local pain. **2.** A mental or emotional pang. — *v.t. & v.i.* twinged, twing·ing To affect with or suffer a sudden pain or twinge. [OE *twen-gan* to pinch]

twin·kle (twing'kəl) *v.* ·kled, ·kling *v.i.* **1.** To shine with fitful, intermittent gleams, as a star. **2.** To be bright, as with amusement: Her eyes *twinkled.* **3.** To move rapidly to and fro; flicker: *twinkling* feet. — *v.t.* **4.** To emit or cause to flash out, as gleams of light. — *n.* **1.** A tremulous gleam of light; sparkle; glimmer. **2.** A wink or sparkle of the eye. **3.** An instant; a twinkling. [OE *twinclian*] **— twin'kler** *n.*

twin·kling (twing'kling) *n.* **1.** The act of scintillating. **2.** A wink or twinkle. **3.** The act of winking, or the time re-quired for it. **4.** A moment.

twin-screw (twin'skrōō') *adj.* *Naut.* Having two propeller shafts, one on each side of a vessel's keel, and two propellers, normally turning in opposite directions.

twin·ship (twin'ship') *n.* **1.** The character or condition of being a twin. **2.** The relation of a twin or twins.

twirl (twûrl) *v.t. & v.i.* **1.** To whirl or rotate. **2.** In base-ball, to pitch. — *n.* **1.** A whirling motion. **2.** A quick twisting action, as of the fingers. **3.** A curl; coil. [Alter. of ME *tirlen,* var. of *trillen* to roll] **— twirl'er** *n.*

twist (twist) *v.t.* **1.** To wind (strands, etc.) around each other. **2.** To form by such winding: to *twist* thread. **3.** To give spiral, circular, or semicircular form to, as by turning at either end. **4.** To force out of natural shape; distort or con-tort. **5.** To distort the meaning of. **6.** To confuse; perplex. **7.** To wreathe, twine, or wrap. **8.** To cause to revolve or rotate. **9.** To impart spin to (a ball) so that it moves in a curve. — *v.i.* **10.** To become twisted. **11.** To move in a winding course. **12.** To squirm; writhe. **13.** To dance the twist. — *n.* **1.** The act, manner, or result of twisting or turning on an axis. **2.** The state of being twisted. **3.** A curve; turn; bend. **4.** A contortion or twisting of a facial or bodily feature: a smile with a certain *twist.* **5.** A wrench; strain, as of a joint or limb. **6.** A peculiar or perverted in-clination or attitude: the *twist* of a criminal's mind. **7.** A deviation, variation, or distinctive difference: a *twist* of meaning. **8.** Thread or cord made of tightly twisted strands; also, one of the strands. **9.** A twisted roll or loaf of bread. **10.** Tobacco twisted in the form of a large cord. **11.** In baseball, tennis, etc.: **a** A spin or whirling motion given to a ball by a certain stroke or throw. **b** The stroke or throw pro-ducing such a spin. **12.** A dance characterized by a twisting or turning movement from side to side. [ME *twisten* to di-vide in two, combine two, etc. < OE *-twist* rope]

twist·er (twis'tər) *n.* **1.** One who or that which twists. **2.** A ball, as in cricket, bowled with a twist. **3.** In baseball, a curve; also, one who pitches a curve. **4.** *U.S.* A tornado.

twit (twit) *v.t.* twit·ted, twit·ting To taunt, reproach, or an-noy by reminding of a mistake, fault, etc. — *n.* A taunting allusion; reproach. [Aphetic var. of ME *atwite,* OE *ætwitan* to taunt < *æt-* at + *witan* to accuse]

twitch (twich) *v.t.* **1.** To pull sharply; pluck with a jerky movement. **2.** In lumbering, to drag or skid (logs) along the ground with a chain. — *v.i.* **3.** To move with a quick, spasmodic jerk. — *n.* **1.** A sudden involuntary contraction of a muscle. **2.** A sudden jerk or pull. [ME *twicchen*] — **twitch'ing·ly** *adv.*

twit·ter (twit'ər) *v.i.* **1.** To utter a series of light chirping or tremulous notes, as a bird. **2.** To titter. **3.** To be ex-cited; tremble. — *v.t.* **4.** To utter or express with a twitter. — *n.* **1.** The act of twittering. **2.** A succession of light, tremulous sounds. **3.** A state of nervous agitation. [Imit.] **— twit'ter·er** *n.* **— twit'ter·y** *adj.*

twixt (twikst) *prep. Poetic* Betwixt. Also **'twixt.**

two (tōō) *n.* **1.** The sum of one and one: a cardinal number. **2.** Any symbol of this number, as 2, ii, II. **3.** Anything con-sisting of or representing two units. **4.** A couple; pair. — **in two** So as to be in two parts or pieces; asunder. **— to put two and two together** To reach the obvious conclusion. — *adj.* Being one more than one. [OE *twā, tū*]

two-base hit (tōō′bās′) In baseball, a base hit that enables the batter to reach second base; a double.

two-bit (tōō′bit′) adj. U.S. Slang Cheap; small-time.

two bits U.S. Informal 1. Twenty-five cents. 2. A trifling or insignificant sum.

two-by-four (adj. tōō′bī-fôr′, -fōr; n. tōō′bī-fôr′, -fōr′) adj. 1. Measuring two inches by four inches. 2. U.S. Slang Of trifling size or significance. — n. A piece of lumber actually measuring 1⅝ inches by 3⅝ inches, much used in building.

two-edged (tōō′ejd′) adj. 1. Having an edge on each side, as a sword or knife blade. 2. Having two meanings, effects, etc., as an argument, supposed compliment, etc.

two-faced (tōō′fāst′) adj. 1. Having two faces. 2. Double-dealing. — **two′-fac′ed·ly** (-fā′sid-lē, -fāst′lē) adv.

two-fist·ed (tōō′fis′tid) adj. U.S. Informal Vigorous and aggressive.

two·fold (tōō′fōld′) n. An amount or number two times as great as a given unit. — adv. So as to be two times as many or as great. — adj. 1. Consisting of two parts. 2. Two times as many or as great.

two-hand·ed (tōō′han′did) adj. 1. Requiring both hands at once. 2. Constructed for use by two persons. 3. Ambidextrous. 4. Having two hands.

two-mas·ter (tōō′mas′tər, -mäs′-) n. A ship with two masts.

two·pence (tup′əns) n. Brit. 1. Money of account of the value of two pennies. 2. A silver coin of the same value, now issued only for alms money, distributed on Maundy Thursday. Also, Informal, tuppence.

two·pen·ny (tup′ən-ē) adj. Brit. 1. Of the price or value of twopence. 2. Cheap; worthless. Also, Informal, tuppenny.

two-ply (tōō′plī′) adj. 1. Made of two united webs; woven double: a two-ply carpet. 2. Made of two strands, layers, or thicknesses of material.

two·some (tōō′səm) n. 1. Two persons together; a couple. 2. A match with one player on each side.

two-spot (tōō′spot′) n. 1. A playing card having two pips; a deuce. 2. U.S. Slang A two-dollar bill.

two-step (tōō′step′) n. 1. A ballroom dance consisting of a sliding step in 2/4 meter; also, the music for it.

two-time (tōō′tīm′) v.t. -timed, -tim·ing Slang To be unfaithful in love; deceive. — **two′-tim′er** n.

two-way (tōō′wā′) adj. 1. Characterized by or permitting movement or communication in two directions. 2. Of cocks and valves, having an arrangement that will permit a fluid to be directed in either of two channels.

twy- See TWI-.

-ty[1] suffix of nouns The state or condition of being: sanity. [< F -té < L -tas]

-ty[2] suffix Ten; ten times: used in numerals, as thirty, forty, etc. [OE -tig ten]

ty·coon (tī-kōōn′) n. U.S. Informal A wealthy and powerful industrial or business leader. [< Japanese taikun mighty lord < Chinese ta great + kiun prince]

tyke (tīk) n. 1. Informal A small child. 2. A mongrel dog.

tym·bal (tim′bəl) See TIMBAL.

tym·pan (tim′pən) n. Printing A thickness of paper placed on the platen of a press to improve the quality of the presswork.

tym·pa·ni (tim′pə-nē) See TIMPANI.

tym·pan·ic (tim·pan′ik) adj. 1. Of or resembling a drum. 2. Of or pertaining to a tympanum or to the middle ear. Also **tym·pa·nal** (tim′pə-nəl).

tympanic membrane Anat. The membrane separating the middle ear from the external ear: also called eardrum. For illus. see EAR.

tym·pa·nist (tim′pə-nist) n. One who plays a kettledrum.

tym·pa·num (tim′pə-nəm) n. pl. **-na** (-nə) or **-nums** 1. Anat. **a** The middle ear. **b** The tympanic membrane. 2. Archit. An ornamental space, as over a doorway, enclosed by an arch or the coping of a pediment. 3. A drumlike membrane or part. Also spelled timpanum. [< NL < L, drum < Gk. < typtein to beat]

typ- Var. of TYPO-.

ty·pal (tī′pəl) adj. Of or pertaining to a type; typical.

type (tīp) n. 1. Class; category; kind; sort. 2. One who or that which has the characteristics of a group or class; embodiment. 3. Biol. **a** An organism whose structural and functional characteristics make it representative of a group, species, class, etc. **b** A taxonomic group considered as representative of the next higher category in a system of classification: the type genus. 4. Printing A piece or block of metal or of wood, bearing on its upper surface, usu. in relief, a letter or character for use in printing; also, such pieces collectively. 5. Printed or typewritten characters. 6. Informal A person. ◆ In business English and in informal speech, type is often used for type of, as in This type car is very popular. — v. typed, typ·ing v.t. 1. To typewrite (something). 2. To determine the type of; identify: to type a blood sample. 3. To assign to a particular type. 4. To represent; typify. 5. To prefigure. — v.i. 6. To typewrite. [< MF < L < Gk. < typtein to strike]

-type combining form 1. Representative form; type: pro type. 2. Printing; duplicating or photographic proce type: Linotype, collotype. [< Gk. typos stamp]

type·cast (tīp′kast′, -käst′) v.t. **·cast, ·cast·ing** To cast an actor, in a role suited to his appearance, personality, ●

type foundry An establishment in which metal typ● made. — **type founder** — **type founding**

type genus Biol. A genus that combines the essential ch acteristics of the family or higher group to which it belon●

type metal Printing The alloy of which type is made, u of lead, tin, and antimony, in various proportions.

type·script (tīp′skript′) n. Typewritten matter.

type·set·ter (tīp′set′ər) n. 1. One who sets type. 2● machine for composing type. — **type′set′ting** n.

type species Biol. The species regarded as most typica the genus to which its name is given.

type·write (tīp′rīt′) v.t. & v.i. **·wrote, ·writ·ten, ·writ** To write with a typewriter: also type.

type·writ·er (tīp′rī′tər) n. A machine equipped with a k board, that produces printed characters by impressing t upon paper through an inked ribbon.

type·writ·ing (tīp′rī′ting) n. 1. The act or operatio● one who uses a typewriter. 2. Typescript.

typhlo- combining form 1. Blindness. 2. Anat. & ● The cecum. Also, before vowels, **typhl-**. [< Gk. typ● blind]

typho- combining form Typhus; typhoid. Also, before v● els, **typh-**. [< Gk. typhos smoke, stupor]

ty·phoid (tī′foid) n. Typhoid fever. — adj. Of or like phoid fever: also **ty·phoi′dal**, **ty′phose** (-fōs). [< TYPH● + -OID]

typhoid bacillus A motile, flagellated bacterium, the p● ogen of typhoid fever.

typhoid fever Pathol. An acute, infectious fever caused the typhoid bacillus and characterized by severe intest● disturbances, an eruption of rose-red spots on the chest abdomen, and physical prostration.

ty·phoon (tī-fōōn′) n. Meteorol. A hurricane origina● over tropical waters in the western Pacific and the Chi● Sea. [< dial. Chinese tai feng, lit., big wind]

ty·phus (tī′fəs) n. Pathol. An acute, contagious ricket● disease, marked by high fever, with eruption of red sp● cerebral disorders, and extreme prostration. Also ca● spotted fever. Also **typhus fever**. [< NL < Gk. typhei● smoke] — **ty′phous** (-fəs) adj.

typ·i·cal (tip′i-kəl) adj. 1. Having the nature or chara● of a type; constituting a type or pattern. 2. Conformin● the essential features of a species, group, class, pattern o● tion or behavior, etc. Also typ′ic. [< Med.L < ● < typos type] — **typ′i·cal·ly** adv. — **typ′i·cal·ness** ●

typ·i·fy (tip′ə-fī) v.t. **·fied, ·fy·ing** 1. To represent by a t● signify, as by an image or token. 2. To constitute a typ● serve as a characteristic example of. — **typ′i·fi·ca′tio●** — **typ′i·fi′er** n.

typ·ist (tī′pist) n. 1. One whose occupation is operati● typewriter. 2. One who is able to operate a typewriter●

ty·po (tī′pō) n. Informal A typographical error.

typo- combining form Type; of or related to type. Also● fore vowels, **typ-**. [< Gk. typos stamp, type]

ty·pog·ra·pher (tī-pog′rə-fər) n. A printer.

ty·po·graph·i·cal (tī′pə-graf′i-kəl) adj. Of or relatin● typography or printing. Also **ty′po·graph′ic**. — ty● **graph′i·cal·ly** adv.

ty·pog·ra·phy (tī-pog′rə-fē) n. pl. **·phies** 1. The arra● ment of composed type. 2. The style and appearanc● printed matter. 3. The act or art of composing and prin● from type.

ty·pol·o·gy (tī-pol′ə-jē) n. pl. **·gies** 1. The study of ty● as in systems of classification. 2. A set or listing of ty●

Tyr (tûr, tir) In Norse mythology, the god of war and s● Odin: also **Tyrr**.

ty·ran·ni·cal (ti-ran′i-kəl, tī-) adj. Of or characteristic● tyrant; harsh; despotic. Also **ty·ran′nic**. — **ty·ran′ni·c●** adv. — **ty·ran′ni·cal·ness** n.

ty·ran·ni·cide (ti-ran′ə-sīd, tī-) n. 1. The killing of ● rant. 2. One who has killed a tyrant.

tyr·an·nize (tir′ə-nīz) v. **·nized, ·niz·ing** v.i. 1. To exe● power cruelly or unjustly: often with over. 2. To rule ● tyrant. — v.t. 3. To treat tyrannically. Also Brit. **ty●** nise. — **tyr′an·niz′er** n.

tyr·an·nous (tir′ə-nəs) adj. Despotic; tyrannical. — ● **an·nous·ly** adv. — **tyr′an·nous·ness** n.

tyr·an·ny (tir′ə-nē) n. pl. **·nies** 1. Absolute power ● trarily or unjustly administered; despotism. 2. An arbi● ily cruel exercise of power; a tyrannical act. 3. In G● history, the office or the administration of a tyrant. 4● verity; roughness. [< OF < L < tyrannus tyrant]

ty·rant (tī′rənt) n. 1. One who rules oppressively or c● ly; a despot. 2. One who exercises absolute power wit● legal warrant, whether ruling well or badly. [< OF ● Gk. tyrannos master, usurper]

(tīr) See TIRE[2].

·i·an purple (tir′ē-ən) **1.** A purple or crimson dyestuff ·ained by the ancient Greeks and Romans from certain ·cies of the murex. **2.** A violet purple color of high saut-·on and low brightness. Also **Tyrian dye**. [after *Tyre*, capital of ancient Phoenicia]

ty·ro (tī′rō) *n. pl.* **·ros** A beginner; novice: also spelled *tiro*. — **Syn.** See NOVICE. [< Med.L < L *tiro* recruit]

tzar (tsär) See CZAR.

tzet·ze (tset′sē) See TSETSE.

tzi·gane (tsē-gän′) *n. Sometimes cap.* A Gypsy, esp. a Hungarian Gypsy. [< F, < Hung. *czigány*]

U

U (yōō) *n. pl.* **u's, us, U's** or **Us** (yōōz) **1.** The twenty-· letter of the English alphabet. **2.** Any sound repre-·ted by the letter *u*. — *symbol.* **1.** Anything shaped like ·. **2.** *Chem.* Uranium (symbol U).

q·ui·tous (yōō-bik′wə-təs) *adj.* Existing, or seeming to ·st, everywhere at once; omnipresent. Also **u·biq′ui·tar′y** ·r′ē). — **u·biq′ui·tous·ly** *adv.* — **u·biq′ui·tous·ness** *n.*

q·ui·ty (yōō-bik′wə-tē) *n.* **1.** The state of being in an ·efinite number of places at once; omnipresence. **2.** The ·te of existing always without beginning or end. [< L < *que* everywhere]

oat (yōō′bōt′) *n.* A German submarine. [< G *U-boot*, ·tr. of *Unterseeboot* undersea boat]

·er (ud′ər) *n.* A large, pendulous gland, secreting milk · provided with nipples or teats for the suckling of off-·ing, as in cows. [OE *üder*]

· (ukh, u, ŏŏkh, ōō) *interj.* An exclamation of repugnance · disgust. [Imit.]

·i·fy (ug′lə-fī) *v.t.* **·fied, ·fy·ing** To make ugly. — **ug′li·fi·tion** (-fə-kā′shən) *n.*

·ly (ug′lē) *adj.* **·li·er, ·li·est 1.** Displeasing to the esthetic ·lings; distasteful in appearance; ill-looking; unsightly. **2.** ·pulsive to the moral sentiments; revolting. **3.** Bad in ·racter or consequences, as a rumor, wound, etc. **4.** *In-·mal* Ill-tempered; quarrelsome. **5.** Portending storms; ·reatening: said of the weather. [< ON *ugglígr* dreadful < ·r fear] — **ug′li·ly** *adv.* — **ug′li·ness** *n.*

·y duckling Any ill-favored or unpromising child who ·expectedly grows beautiful or remarkable, as did the little ·an in Hans Christian Andersen's story.

·ri·an (ōō′grē-ən, yōō′-) *n.* **1.** A member of any of the ·no-Ugric peoples of Hungary and western Siberia. **2.** ·ric. — *adj.* Of or pertaining to the Ugrians, their culture, ·their languages.

·ric (ōō′grik, yōō′-) *n.* A branch of the Finno-Ugric sub-·nily of Uralic languages, comprising Magyar, Ostyak, and ·gul. — *adj.* Of or pertaining to any of these languages.

·ro-Fin·nic (ōō′grō-fin′ik; yōō-) See FINNO-UGRIC.

·lan (ōō′län, ōō-län′, yōō′lən) *n.* **1.** A cavalryman and ·icer of a type originating in eastern Europe, formerly ·ominent in European armies, notably the German. **2.** ·e of a body of Tatar militia. Also **u′lan**. [< G < Polish · Turkish *öghlän* lad, servant]

·ase (yōō′kās, yōō-käz′) *n.* **1.** Any official decree. **2.** ·rmerly, an edict or decree of the imperial Russian govern-·ent. [< Russian *ukaz*]

·rain·i·an (yōō-krā′nē-ən, -krī′-) *adj.* Of or pertaining to ·e Ukraine, its people, or their language. — *n.* **1.** A na-·e or inhabitant of the Ukraine. **2.** The East Slavic lan-·age of the Ukrainians. Also *Little Russian, Ruthenian*.

·u·le·le (yōō′kə-lā′lē, *Hawaiian* ōō′kŏŏ-lā′lā) *n.* A small ·itarlike musical instrument having four strings. [< Ha-·iian, flea < *uku* insect + *lele* to jump]

·cer (ul′sər) *n.* **1.** *Pathol.* An open sore on an external or ·ternal surface of the body, usu. accompanied by disinte-·ation of tissue with the formation of pus. **2.** A corroding ·ult or vice; corruption; evil. [< L *ulcus, ulceris*]

·cer·ate (ul′sə-rāt) *v.t. & v.i.* **·at·ed, ·at·ing** To make or ·come ulcerous. [< L < *ulcus, ulceris* ulcer] — **ul′cer·a′·**·n *n.* — **ul′cer·a′tive** *adj.*

·cer·ous (ul′sər-əs) *adj.* **1.** Like an ulcer. **2.** Affected ·ith ulcers. — **ul′cer·ous·ly** *adv.* — **ul′cer·ous·ness** *n.*

·le *suffix of nouns* Small; little: used to form diminutives: ·anule. [< F < L *-ulus, -ula, -ulum*, diminutive suffix]

·lent *suffix of adjectives* Abounding in; full of: *opulent, truc-·ent.* Corresponding nouns are formed in **-ulence**, as in *opu-·nce, truculence*. [< L *-ulentus*]

·na (ul′nə) *n. pl.* **·nae** (-nē) or **·nas** *Anat.* **1.** That one of

the two long bones of the forearm that is on the same side as the little finger. **2.** The corresponding bone in the forelimb of other vertebrates. [< L, elbow] — **ul′nar** *adj.*

-ulose *suffix of adjectives* Marked by or abounding in: used in scientific and technical terms: *ramulose*. [< L *-ulosus*]

-ulous *suffix of adjectives* **1.** Tending to do or characterized by (what is indicated by the root): *meticulous, populous*. **2.** Full of: *meticulous, populous*. [< L *-ulus* and *-ulosus*]

ul·ster (ul′stər) *n.* A very long, loose overcoat, sometimes belted at the waist. [after *Ulster*, Ireland]

ul·te·ri·or (ul-tir′ē-ər) *adj.* **1.** More remote; not so perti-nent as something else: *ulterior* considerations. **2.** Inten-tionally unrevealed; hidden: *ulterior* motives. **3.** Later in time or secondary in importance; following; succeeding. **4.** Lying beyond or on the farther side of a certain bounding line. [< L < *ulter* beyond] — **ul·te′ri·or·ly** *adv.*

ul·ti·ma (ul′tə-mə) *n.* The last syllable of a word. [< L]

ul·ti·mate (ul′tə-mit) *adj.* **1.** Beyond which there is no other; last of a series; final. **2.** Not susceptible of further analysis; fundamental or essential. **3.** Most distant; farth-est; extreme. — *n.* **1.** The final result; last step; conclusion. **2.** A fundamental or final fact. [< LL < *ultimus* farthest, last] — **ul′ti·mate·ly** *adv.* — **ul′ti·mate·ness** *n.*

ul·ti·ma Thu·le (ul′tə-mə thōō′lē, tōō′lē) **1.** Farthest Thule; in ancient geography, the northernmost habitable re-gions of the earth. **2.** Any distant, unknown region. **3.** The farthest possible point, degree, or limit.

ul·ti·ma·tum (ul′tə-mā′təm, -mä′-) *n. pl.* **·tums** or **·ta** (-tə) A final statement, as concerning terms, conditions or conces-sions, esp., in diplomatic negotiations, the final terms offered. [< NL < LL. See ULTIMATE.]

ul·ti·mo (ul′tə-mō) *adv. Archaic* In the last month. [< L *ultimo* (*mense*) in the last (month)]

ul·tra (ul′trə) *adj.* Going beyond the bounds of moderation; extreme. — *n.* One who goes to extremes. [< L, beyond]

ultra- *prefix* **1.** On the other side of; beyond in space, as in: **ultra-Arctic, ultrastellar. 2.** Going beyond the limits of; surpassing, as in: **ultra-atomic, ultrahuman. 3.** Beyond what is usual or natural; excessively, as in: **ultra-ambitious, ultrafashionable.**

ul·tra·cen·tri·fuge (ul′trə-sen′trə-fyōōj) *n.* A centrifuge whose rotor will operate at extremely high velocities. — *v.t.* **·fuged, ·fug·ing** To subject to the action of an ultracen-trifuge. — **ul′tra·cen′tri·fu·ga′tion** (-fyōō-gā′shən) *n.*

ul·tra·con·ser·va·tive (ul′trə-kən-sûr′və-tiv) *adj.* Unusu-ally or excessively conservative. — *n.* An ultraconserva-tive person; a reactionary.

ul·tra·high frequency (ul′trə-hī′) *Telecom.* A band of wave frequencies between 300 and 3,000 megacycles per second.

ul·tra·ism (ul′trə-iz′əm) *n.* **1.** The policies or opinions of those who are in favor of extreme measures. **2.** An extreme view or action. — **ul′tra·ist** *n. & adj.* — **ul′tra·is′tic** *adj.*

ul·tra·ma·rine (ul′trə-mə-rēn′) *n.* **1.** A deep blue, perma-nent pigment made from powdered lapis lazuli. **2.** A similar pigment made artificially, as from kaolin, etc. **3.** A deep blue. — *adj.* Being beyond or across the sea. [< Med.L < L *ultra* beyond + *marinus* marine]

ul·tra·mi·crom·e·ter (ul′trə-mī-krom′ə-tər) *n.* A microm-eter designed for measurements requiring a high order of precision and accuracy.

ul·tra·mi·cro·scope (ul′trə-mī′krə-skōp) *n.* An optical in-strument for detecting objects too small to be seen with an ordinary microscope.

ul·tra·mi·cro·scop·ic (ul′trə-mī′krə-skop′ik) *adj.* **1.** Too minute to be seen by an ordinary microscope. **2.** Relating to the ultramicroscope. Also **ul′tra·mi′cro·scop′i·cal.** — **ul′tra·mi·cros′co·py** (-mī-kros′kə-pē) *n.*

ul·tra·mod·ern (ul′trə·mod′ərn) *adj.* Extremely modern. — **ul′tra·mod′ern·ism** *n.* — **ul′tra·mod′ern·ist** *n.* — **ul′·tra·mod′ern·is′tic** *adj.*

ul·tra·na·tion·al·ism (ul′trə·nash′ən·əl·iz′əm) *n.* Extreme devotion to or support of national interests or considerations. — **ul′tra·na′tion·al** *adj.* — **ul′tra·na′tion·al·ist** *n. & adj.* — **ul′tra·na′tion·al·is′tic** *adj.*

ul·tra·son·ic (ul′trə·son′ik) *adj. Physics* Pertaining to or designating sound waves having a frequency above the limits of human audibility, or in excess of about 20 kilocycles per second.

ul·tra·vi·o·let (ul′trə·vī′ə·lit) *adj. Physics* Lying beyond the violet end of the visible spectrum: said of high-frequency wavelengths ranging from about 3,900 to below 400 angstroms, the lower limit of X-rays. Compare INFRARED.

ul·u·late (yōōl′yə·lāt, ul′-) *v.i.* **·lat·ed, ·lat·ing** To howl, hoot, or wail. [< L < *ululare* to howl] — **ul′u·lant** *adj.*

U·lys·ses (yōō·lis′ēz) The Latin name for Odysseus.

um·bel (um′bəl) *n. Bot.* A flower cluster spreading outward from a small area at the top of a very short axis, giving an umbrellalike appearance. [< L *umbella* parasol] — **um′bel·lar, um′bel·late, um′bel·lat′ed.**

um·ber (um′bər) *n.* **1.** A brown ferric oxide, containing some manganese oxide and clay, and used as a pigment. **2.** The color of such a pigment. — *adj.* Of or pertaining to umber; of a dusky hue; brownish. — *v.t.* To color with umber. [< F (*terre d'*)*ombre* or Ital. *ombra*]

um·bil·i·cal (um·bil′i·kəl) *adj.* **1.** Pertaining to or situated near the umbilicus. **2.** Placed near the navel; central. [< LL < L *umbilicus* navel]

umbilical cord *Anat.* A ropelike tissue connecting the navel of the fetus with the placenta and serving to transmit nourishment to and remove wastes from the fetus.

um·bil·i·cus (um·bil′ə·kəs, um′bə·lī′kəs) *n. pl.* **·ci** (-sī) **1.** *Anat.* The navel. **2.** *Bot.* A hilum. [< L]

um·ble pie (um′bəl) See HUMBLE PIE.

um·bles (um′bəlz) *n.pl.* The entrails of a deer; humbles. [Var. of NUMBLES.]

um·bra (um′brə) *n. pl.* **·brae** (-brē) **1.** A shadow or dark area; esp., the portion of a shadow from which direct light is entirely cut off. **2.** *Astron.* In an eclipse, that part of the shadow of the earth or moon within which the moon or the sun is entirely hidden. [< L, shadow]

um·brage (um′brij) *n.* **1.** Resentment; a sense of injury; offense: now usu., in **to take umbrage.** **2.** That which gives

shade, as a leafy tree. **3.** *Poetic* Shade. [< F < L < *um* shade] — **um·bra′geous** (-brā′jəs) *adj.*

um·brel·la (um·brel′ə) *n.* A light, round, portable screen shade on a folding frame, carried as a protection against or rain. [< Ital. < L *umbella* parasol]

umbrella tree 1. A small magnolia of the southern U with fragrant white flowers and oval leaves crowded umbrellalike whorls. **2.** Any of several other trees.

u·mi·ak (ōō′mē·ak) *n. U.S. & Canadian* A large, open b made by drawing skins over a wooden frame, used by E mos. Also **u′mi·ack.** [< Eskimo]

um·laut (ōōm′lout) *n.* **1.** *Ling.* **a** The change in qualit a vowel sound caused by its partial assimilation to a vowe semivowel (often later lost) in the following syllable, esp the Germanic languages. **b** A vowel so altered. **2.** In G man, the two dots (¨) put over a vowel modified by umla Short for **umlaut-mark.** — *v.t.* To modify by umlaut. G, change of sound < *um* about + *laut* sound]

um·pire (um′pīr) *n.* **1.** In various games, as baseball, a son chosen to enforce the rules of the game and settle puted points. **2.** A person called upon to settle a disag ment in opinion. — Syn. See JUDGE. — *v.t. & v.i.* **·pi ·pir·ing** To decide as umpire; act as umpire (of or in). ME < OF < *non* not + *per* even, equal]

un-[1] *prefix* Not; opposed to. [OE] ◆ *Un-*[1] is used to press negation, lack, incompleteness or opposition. It is f ly attached to adjectives and adverbs, less often to no See UN-[2].

un-[2] *prefix* Back. [OE *un-, on-,* and-] ◆ *Un-*[2] is use express reversal of the action of verbs, or to form verbs fr nouns indicating removal from the state or quality pressed by the noun, or sometimes to intensify the forc negative verbs. At the bottom of this page and of follow pages is a partial list of words that are formed with *un-*[1] *un-*[2]. Other compounds of these prefixes, with strongly p tive, specific, or special meanings, will be found in voca lary place. In the verbs in the list, *un-* gives the sense of versal: *unchain* "to loose the chains of." In the nouns the adjectives it usually has negative or privative fo Thus, *unburdened* may be regarded as an adjective mean "not burdened," or as a participle of the verb *unbur* meaning "relieved of a burden."

◆ **un-, in-** *In-* as a prefix of adjectives expresses in us more of negation, *un-* more of mere lack or privation child's *unartistic* speech, a writer's *inartistic* diction.

unabashed	unanswerable	unbarbed	uncalendered	uncleared	unconciliated
unabated	unanswerably	unbeatable	uncanceled	uncleavable	unconcluded
unabetted	unanswered	unbeaten	uncandid	unclipped	uncondemned
unabolished	unapologetic	unbefitting	uncandidly	unclog	uncondensed
unabsolved	unappalled	unbeloved	uncanonic	unclogged	unconfined
unacademic	unapparent	unbeneficed	uncanonical	uncloud	unconfinedly
unaccented	unappeasable	unbenighted	uncarbureted	unclouded	unconfirmed
unacceptable	unappeased	unbenign	uncarpeted	uncloyed	unconfused
unaccepted	unappetizing	unbeseeming	uncastrated	uncoagulable	unconfusedly
unacclimated	unappreciated	unbesought	uncaught	uncoagulated	unconfuted
unacclimatized	unappreciative	unbespoken	unceasing	uncoated	uncongeal
unaccommodating	unapproached	unbetrayed	uncelebrated	uncocked	uncongealabl
unaccounted	unapproved	unbetrothed	uncensored	uncoerced	uncongealed
unaccredited	unarmored	unbewailed	uncensured	uncoffined	uncongenial
unacknowledged	unarrested	unblamable	uncertified	uncollectable	uncongenialit
unacquainted	unartful	unblamably	unchainable	uncollected	uncongenially
unacquitted	unartistic	unblamed	unchained	uncollectible	unconquerabl
unadaptable	unashamed	unbleached	unchallenged	uncolonized	unconquered
unadjustable	unasked	unblemished	unchambered	uncolored	unconscientio
unadjusted	unaspirated	unblissful	unchangeable	uncombed	unconsecrate
unadorned	unaspiring	unboastful	unchanged	uncombinable	unconsenting
unadulterated	unassailed	unbookish	unchanging	uncombined	unconsidered
unadvisable	unassignable	unborrowed	unchaperoned	uncomely	unconsoled
unadvisably	unassigned	unbottomed	uncharged	uncomforted	unconsonant
unaesthetic	unassumed	unbought	uncharted	uncomforting	unconstant
unaffiliated	unattainable	unbox	unchartered	uncommanded	unconstituted
unafraid	unattained	unboxed	unchary	uncommissioned	unconstrained
unaggressive	unattempted	unbraid	unchaste	uncompanionable	unconstricted
unagitated	unattended	unbranched	unchastened	uncomplaining	unconsumed
unaided	unattested	unbranded	unchastised	uncomplaisant	uncontaminat
unaimed	unattired	unbreakable	unchastity	uncomplaisantly	uncontemplat
unalike	unattracted	unbreathable	unchecked	uncompleted	uncontending
unalleviated	unattractive	unbreech	uncheerful	uncompliable	uncontested
unallied	unauspicious	unbreeched	uncheerfully	uncompliant	uncontradicta
unallowable	unauthentic	unbribable	uncheerfulness	uncomplicated	uncontradicte
unalloyed	unauthentical	unbridgeable	unchewed	uncomplimentary	uncontrite
unalterable	unauthenticated	unbridged	unchilled	uncomplying	uncontrolled
unaltered	unauthorized	unbridle	unchivalrous	uncompounded	uncontrolledly
unaltering	unavailability	unbrotherly	uncholeric	uncomprehended	uncontroverte
unambiguous	unavailable	unbruised	unchosen	uncomprehending	uncontrovertil
unambitious	unavailably	unbrushed	unchristened	uncomprehensible	uncontrovertil
unamiable	unavenged	unburied	unclaimed	uncomprehensibly	unconversant
unamplified	unavouched	unburned	unclarified	uncompressed	unconvinced
unamusing	unavowed	unburnt	unclassed	uncompromised	unconvincing
unanalytic	unavowedly	unbusinesslike	unclassic	uncomputed	unconvincingl
unanalyzable	unawaked	unbuttoned	unclassifiable	unconcealable	uncooked
unanimated	unawakened	uncage	unclassified	unconcealed	uncooperative
unannealed	unawed	uncalculate	uncleaned	unconcealed	uncoordinate
unannounced	unbaptized	uncalculating	uncleansed	unconcerted	uncordial

·ble (un·ā′bəl) *adj.* **1.** Lacking the necessary power or ·urces; not able: usu. used with an infinitive: *unable* to ·k. **2.** Lacking mental capacity; incompetent.

·bridged (un′ə·brijd′) *adj.* Not abridged or condensed; inal and complete: an *unabridged* dictionary.

·c·com·mo·dat·ed (un′ə·kom′ə·dā′tid) *adj.* **1.** Not ·le suitable; ill-adapted or -adjusted. **2.** Being without ·mmodations or conveniences.

·c·com·pa·nied (un′ə·kum′pə·nēd) *adj.* **1.** Proceeding, ·ng, or accomplished without an escort or companion. *Music* Performing or intended to be performed without ·mpaniment.

·c·com·plished (un′ə·kom′plisht) *adj.* **1.** Having fallen ·rt of accomplishment; not done or finished. **2.** Lacking ·mplishments.

·c·count·a·ble (un′ə·koun′tə·bəl) *adj.* **1.** Impossible ·e accounted for; inexplicable. **2.** Remarkable; extraor·ary. **3.** Not accountable; irresponsible. **—un′ac·count′·** ·le·ness *n.* **— un′ac·count′a·bly** *adv.*

·c·count·ed-for (un′ə·koun′tid·fôr′) *adj.* Unexplained.

·c·cus·tomed (un′ə·kus′təmd) *adj.* **1.** Not accustomed ·abituated: *unaccustomed* to hardship. **2.** Not familiar ·vell known; strange: an *unaccustomed* sight.

·d·vised (un′əd·vīzd′) *adj.* **1.** Not advised; not having ·ived advice. **2.** Rash or imprudent; ill-considered. **—** ·ad·vis′ed·ly (-vī′zid·lē) *adv.* **—un′ad·vis′ed·ness** *n.*

·f·fect·ed (un′ə·fek′tid) *adj.* **1.** Not showing affecta·; natural; sincere; real. **2.** Not influenced or changed. ·n′af·fect′ed·ly *adv.* **—un′af·fect′ed·ness** *n.*

·mer·i·can (un′ə·mer′ə·kən) *adj.* **1.** Not American in ·racter, style, etc. **2.** Not consistent with the ideals, ob·ives, spirit, etc., of the U.S.; lacking patriotism or nation·eeling; a derogatory term.

·nim·i·ty (yōō′nə·nim′ə·tē) *n.* The state of being unan·us; complete agreement in opinion, etc.

·n·i·mous (yōō·nan′ə·məs) *adj.* **1.** Sharing the same ·ws or sentiments; harmonious. **2.** Showing or resulting ·n the assent of all concerned. [< L < *unus* one + *ani·s* mind.] **— u·nan′i·mous·ly** *adv.* **— u·nan′i·mous·ness** *n.*

·p·proach·a·ble (un′ə·prō′chə·bəl) *adj.* **1.** Not easy to ·w or make personal contact with; aloof. **2.** Inaccessible. ·n′ap·proach′a·ble·ness *n.* **— un′ap·proach′a·bly** *adv.*

·rm (un·ärm′) *v.t.* To deprive of weapons; disarm. **—** ·armed′ *adj.*

·as·sail·a·ble (un′ə·sāl′ə·bəl) *adj.* **1.** Not capable of be·disproved, denied, or contested; incontrovertible. **2.** ·of against attack or destruction; impregnable. **— un′as·** ·l′a·ble·ness *n.* **— un′as·sail′a·bly** *adv.*

·as·sum·ing (un′ə·sōō′ming) *adj.* Unpretentious; mod·**— un′as·sum′ing·ly** *adv.*

·at·tached (un′ə·tacht′) *adj.* **1.** Not attached. **2.** Not ·aged or married.

·a·vail·ing (un′ə·vā′ling) *adj.* Futile; unsuccessful; inef·tive. **— un′a·vail′ing·ly** *adv.*

·a·void·a·ble (un′ə·voi′də·bəl) *adj.* That cannot be ·ided; inevitable. **— un′a·void′a·bil′i·ty, un′a·void′a·ble·** ·ss *n.* **— un′a·void′a·bly** *adv.*

·a·ware (un′ə·wâr′) *adj.* **1.** Not aware or cognizant, as ·something specified. **2.** Carelessly unmindful; inatten·e; heedless. **— adv.** *Archaic* Unawares.

·a·wares (un′ə·wârz′) *adv.* **1.** Unexpectedly; without ·rning. **2.** Without premeditation; unwittingly.

·bal·ance (un·bal′əns) *v.t.* **·anced, ·anc·ing 1.** To de·ve of balance. **2.** To disturb or derange, as the mind. **—** ·The state or condition of being unbalanced.

un·bal·anced (un·bal′ənst) *adj.* **1.** Not in a state of equi·librium. **2.** In bookkeeping, not adjusted so as to balance. **3.** Lacking mental balance; unsound; erratic.

un·bar (un·bär′) *v.* **·barred, ·bar·ring** *v.t.* **1.** To remove the bar from. **—** *v.i.* **2.** To become unlocked or unbarred; open.

un·bear·a·ble (un′bâr′ə·bəl) *adj.* That cannot be borne or tolerated; unendurable. **—un′bear′a·ble·ness** *n.* **— un′·bear′a·bly** *adv.*

un·be·com·ing (un′bi·kum′ing) *adj.* **1.** Not becoming; un·suited. **2.** Not befitting. **3.** Not decorous; improper. **— un′be·com′ing·ly** *adv.* **— un′be·com′ing·ness** *n.*

un·be·known (un′bi·nōn′) *adj.* Unknown: used with *to.* Also **un′be·knownst′** (-nōnst′).

un·be·lief (un′bi·lēf′) *n.* **1.** Absence of positive belief; in·credulity. **2.** A refusal to believe; disbelief, as in religion.

un·be·liev·er (un′bi·lē′vər) *n.* **1.** One who withholds be·lief. **2.** One who has no religious faith. **3.** One having a re·ligion different from that of the speaker or writer.

un·be·liev·ing (un′bi·lē′ving) *adj.* **1.** Doubting; skeptical; incredulous. **2.** Disbelieving, esp., in religious matters. **— un′be·liev′ing·ly** *adv.* **— un′be·liev′ing·ness** *n.*

un·bend (un·bend′) *v.* **·bent, ·bend·ing** *v.t.* **1.** To relax, as from exertion or formality. **2.** To straighten (something bent or curved). **3.** To relax, as a bow, from tension. **—** *v.i.* **4.** To become free of restraint or formality; relax. **5.** To become straight or nearly straight again.

un·bend·ing (un·ben′ding) *adj.* **1.** Not bending easily; stiff. **2.** Unyielding, as in character; resolute. **—** *n.* Relax·ation; ease. **— un·bend′ing·ly** *adv.* **— un·bend′ing·ness** *n.*

un·bi·ased (un·bī′əst) *adj.* Having no bias; esp., not preju·diced or warped; impartial; fair. Also **un·bi′assed.** **— un·bi′ased·ly** *adv.* **— un·bi′ased·ness** *n.*

un·bid·den (un·bid′n) *adj.* **1.** Not commanded; not in·vited. **2.** Not called forth: *unbidden* thoughts.

un·bind (un·bīnd′) *v.t.* **·bound, ·bind·ing 1.** To free from bindings; undo; also, to release. **2.** To remove, as some·thing that binds; unfasten. [OE *unbindan*]

un·blessed (un·blest′) *adj.* **1.** Deprived of a blessing. **2.** Unhallowed or unholy; evil. **3.** Deprived of good fortune; wretched. Also **un·blest′.**

un·blush·ing (un·blush′ing) *adj.* **1.** Not blushing. **2.** Im·modest; shameless. **— un·blush′ing·ly** *adv.*

un·bolt (un·bōlt′) *v.t.* To release, as a door, by withdrawing a bolt; unlock; open.

un·bolt·ed¹ (un·bōl′tid) *adj.* Not fastened by bolts.

un·bolt·ed² (un·bōl′tid) *adj.* Not sifted: *unbolted* flour.

un·born (un·bôrn′) *adj.* **1.** Not yet born; being of a future time or generation; future. **2.** Not in existence.

un·bos·om (un·bŏŏz′əm, -bōō′zəm) *v.t.* **1.** To reveal, as one's thoughts or secrets; disclose or give vent to: often used reflexively. **—** *v.i.* **2.** To say what is troubling one; tell one's thoughts, feelings, etc. **— un·bos′om·er** *n.*

un·bound·ed (un·boun′did) *adj.* **1.** Having no bounds; of unlimited extent; very great; boundless. **2.** Having no boundary, as a closed surface. **3.** Going beyond bounds; un·restrained. **— un·bound′ed·ly** *adv.* **— un·bound′ed·ness** *n.*

un·bowed (un·boud′) *adj.* **1.** Not bent or bowed. **2.** Not subdued; proud in defeat or adversity.

un·brace (un·brās′) *v.t.* **·braced, ·brac·ing 1.** To free from braces. **2.** To free from tension; loosen. **3.** To weaken.

un·bri·dled (un·brīd′ld) *adj.* **1.** Having no bridle on: an *unbridled* horse. **2.** Without restraint; unruly: an *unbridled* tongue. **— un·bri′dled·ly** *adv.* **— un·bri′dled·ness** *n.*

un·bro·ken (un·brō′kən) *adj.* **1.** Not broken; whole; en·tire. **2.** Unviolated. **3.** Uninterrupted; regular; smooth:

·orked	uncrystalline	undebatable	undelivered	undesignated	undignified
·rrected	uncrystallizable	undecayed	undemocratic	undesigned	undilated
·orroborated	uncrystallized	undecaying	undemonstrable	undesignedly	undiluted
·orrupt	uncultivable	undeceived	undemonstrably	undesired	undiminishable
·orrupted	uncultivated	undecipherable	undenied	undesirous	undiminished
·orruptly	uncultured	undeciphered	undenominational	undesisting	undimmed
·orruptness	uncumbered	undeclared	undenounced	undespairing	undiplomatic
·ountable	uncurable	undeclinable	undependable	undestroyed	undisbanded
·ourteous	uncurb	undeclined	undeplored	undetachable	undiscerned
·ourtliness	uncurbed	undecomposable	undeposed	undetached	undiscernedly
·ourtly	uncurdled	undecomposed	undepraved	undetectable	undiscernible
·overed	uncured	undecorated	undepreciated	undetected	undiscernibly
·rate	uncurious	undefaceable	undepressed	undetectible	undiscerning
·rated	uncurl	undefaced	undeputed	undeterminable	undischarged
·redited	uncurled	undefeated	underived	undetermined	undisciplined
·rippled	uncurrent	undefended	underogating	undeterred	undisclosed
·ritical	uncursed	undefensible	underogatory	undeveloped	undisconcerted
·riticizable	uncurtained	undefiled	undescribable	undeviating	undiscordant
·ropped	uncushioned	undefinable	undescribed	undevoured	undiscouraged
·ross	uncustomary	undefined	undescried	undevout	undiscoverable
·rossed	undamaged	undeformed	undeserved	undifferentiated	undiscoverably
·rowded	undated	undelayed	undeservedly	undiffused	undiscovered
·rown	undaughterly	undelineated	undeservedness	undigested	undiscredited
·rushable	undazzled	undeliverable	undeserving	undigestible	undiscriminating

unbroken sleep. **4.** Not weakened; firm. **5.** Not broken to harness or service, as a draft animal. **6.** Not disarranged. **— un·bro′ken·ly** *adv.* **— un·bro′ken·ness** *n.*
un·buck·le (un-buk′əl) *v.t. & v.i.* **·led, ·ling** To unfasten the buckle or buckles (of).
un·bur·den (un-bûr′dən) *v.t.* To free from a burden.
un·but·ton (un-but′n) *v.t. & v.i.* To unfasten the button or buttons (of).
un·caged (un-kājd′) *adj.* **1.** Not locked up in a cage; free. **2.** Released from a cage; freed.
un·called-for (un-kôld′fôr′) *adj.* Not justified by circumstances; improper; unnecessary; gratuitous.
un·can·ny (un-kan′ē) *adj.* **1.** Strange and inexplicable, esp. so as to excite wonder or dismay; weird; unnatural. **2.** So good as to seem almost supernatural in origin: *uncanny* accuracy. **— un·can′ni·ly** *adv.* **— un·can′ni·ness** *n.*
un·cap (un-kap′) *v.* **·capped, ·cap·ping** *v.t.* **1.** To take off the cap or covering of. **—** *v.i.* **2.** To remove the hat or cap, as in respect.
un·cer·e·mo·ni·ous (un′ser-ə-mō′nē-əs) *adj.* Informal; abrupt; discourteous. **— un′cer·e·mo′ni·ous·ly** *adv.*
un·cer·tain (un-sûr′tən) *adj.* **1.** That cannot be certainly predicted; doubtful. **2.** Not having certain knowledge or assured conviction. **3.** Not capable of being relied upon; variable. **4.** Not surely or exactly known: a lady of *uncertain* age. **5.** Having no exact or precise significance. **— un·cer′tain·ly** *adv.* **— un·cer′tain·ness** *n.*
un·cer·tain·ty (un-sûr′tən-tē) *n.* *pl.* **·ties** **1.** The state of being uncertain; doubt. **2.** A doubtful matter.
un·chain (un-chān′) *v.t.* To release from a chain; set free.
un·char·i·ta·ble (un-char′ə-tə-bəl) *adj.* Not charitable; harsh in judgment; censorious. **— un·char′i·ta·ble·ness** *n.* **— un·char′i·ta·bly** *adv.*
un·chris·tian (un-kris′chən) *adj.* **1.** Unbecoming to a Christian. **2.** Contrary to Christian precepts; uncharitable, ungracious, rude, etc. **3.** Non-Christian; pagan.
un·church (un-chûrch′) *v.t.* **1.** To deprive of membership in a church; expel from a church. **2.** To deny the validity of the sacraments and order of, as a sect.
un·cial (un′shəl, -shē·əl) *adj.* Pertaining to or consisting of a form of letters found in manuscripts from the fourth to the eighth century, and resembling rounded modern capitals. **—** *n.* **1.** An uncial letter. **2.** An uncial manuscript. [< L < *uncia* inch, ounce]
un·ci·nate (un′sə·nit, -nāt) *adj.* Hooked or bent at the end. Also **un′ci·nal, un′ci·nat′ed.** [< L < *uncus* hook]
un·cir·cum·cised (un-sûr′kəm·sīzd) *adj.* **1.** Not circumcised. **2.** Not Jewish; Gentile. **3.** Heathen; pagan. **—** *n.* Gentiles or heathens collectively: used with *the*.
un·civ·il (un-siv′əl) *adj.* Wanting in civility; discourteous; ill-bred. **— un·civ′il·ly** *adv.*
un·civ·i·lized (un-siv′ə·līzd) *adj.* Not civilized; barbarous.
un·clad (un-klad′) Alternate past tense and past participle of UNCLOTHE. **—** *adj.* Being without clothes; naked.
un·clasp (un-klasp′, -kläsp′) *v.t.* **1.** To release from a clasp. **2.** To release the clasp of. **—** *v.i.* **3.** To become released from a clasp.
un·cle (ung′kəl) *n.* The brother of one's father or mother; also, the husband of one's aunt. ◆ Collateral adjective: *avuncular.* [< F < L *avunculus* mother's brother]
un·clean (un-klēn′) *adj.* **1.** Not clean; foul. **2.** Characterized by impure thoughts; unchaste; depraved. **3.** Ceremonially impure. **— un·clean′ness** *n.*
un·clean·ly¹ (un-klen′lē) *adj.* **1.** Lacking cleanliness. **2.** Impure; indecent; not chaste. **— un·clean′li·ness** *n.*
un·clean·ly² (un-klēn′lē) *adv.* In an unclean manner.
un·clear (un′klir′) *adj.* **1.** Not clear. **2.** Not easily understandable; confused or muddled: *unclear* reasoning.

Uncle Sam (sam) The personification of the governmer the people of the U.S., represented as a tall, lean man chin whiskers, wearing a plug hat, a blue swallow-tailed c and red-and-white striped pants. [Nickname of *Sa* Wilson, 1766–1854, businessman]
Uncle Tom (tom) *U.S. Slang* A Negro who is servile white men: a contemptuous term. [After the chief chara in Harriet Beecher Stow's *Uncle Tom's Cabin*, a faith elderly Negro slave] **— Uncle Tom′ism**
un·cloak (un-klōk′) *v.t.* **1.** To remove the cloak or cove from. **2.** To unmask; expose. **—** *v.i.* **3.** To remove o cloak or outer garments.
un·close (un-klōz′) *v.t. & v.i.* **·closed, ·clos·ing** **1.** To o or set open. **2.** To reveal; disclose.
un·clothe (un-klōth) *v.t.* **·clothed** or **·clad** (klad), **·cloth** **1.** To remove clothes from; undress. **2.** To uncover.
un·coil (un-koil′) *v.t. & v.i.* To unwind or become unwov
un·com·fort·a·ble (un-kum′fər·tə·bəl, -kumpf′tə·bəl) **1.** Not at ease; feeling discomfort. **2.** Causing physica mental uneasiness; disquieting. **— un·com′fort·a·ble·**·· *n.* **— un·com′fort·a·bly** *adv.*
un·com·mit·ted (un′kə·mit′id) *adj.* Not committed; ε not pledged to a particular action, viewpoint, etc.
un·com·mon (un-kom′ən) *adj.* Not common or usual markable. **— un·com′mon·ly** *adv.* **— un·com′mon·ness**
un·com·mu·ni·ca·tive (un′kə·myōō′nə·kə·tiv, -nə·kā/ *adj.* Not communicative; silent; reserved. **— un′com·**·· **ni·ca·tive·ly** *adv.* **— un′com·mu′ni·ca·tive·ness** *n.*
un·com·pro·mis·ing (un-kom′prə·mī′zing) *adj.* Makin admitting of no compromise; inflexible; strict. **— un·c**· **pro·mis′ing·ly** *adv.* **— un·com′pro·mis/ing·ness** *n.*
un·con·cern (un′kən·sûrn′) *n.* Absence of or freedom f concern or anxiety; indifference.
un·con·cerned (un′kən·sûrnd′) *adj.* Undisturbed; anxious; indifferent. **— un′con·cern′ed·ly** (-sûr′nid·lē) **— un′con·cern′ed·ness** *n.*
un·con·di·tion·al (un′kən·dish′ən·əl) *adj.* Limited by conditions; absolute. **— un′con·di′tion·al·ly** *adv.*
un·con·di·tioned (un′kən·dish′ənd) *adj.* **1.** Not restric unconditional, absolute. **2.** *Psychol.* Not acquired; natu **3.** Admitted without reservation.
un·con·form·i·ty (un′kən·fôr′mə·tē) *n.* *pl.* **·ties** War conformity; nonconformity.
un·con·scion·a·ble (un-kon′shən·ə·bəl) *adj.* **1.** Going yond reasonable bounds; unjustifiable. **2.** Not governed prudence; unconscientious. **— un·con′scion·a·ble·ness** **— un·con′scion·a·bly** *adv.*
un·con·scious (un-kon′shəs) *adj.* **1.** Temporarily depri of consciousness. **2.** Unaware with *of*: *unconscious* of charm. **3.** Not known or felt to exist; not produced by c scious effort. **4.** Not endowed with consciousness o mind. **—** *n.* *Psychoanal.* That extensive area of the ps that is not in the immediate field of awareness. **— un·c**· **scious·ly** *adv.* **— un·con′scious·ness** *n.*
un·con·sti·tu·tion·al (un′kon·sti·tōō′shən·əl, -tyōō′-) Contrary to the constitution or basic law of a state. **—** **con·sti·tu′tion·al·i·ty** *n.* **— un′con·sti·tu′tion·al·ly** *adv.*
un·con·ven·tion·al (un′kən·ven′shən·əl) *adj.* **1.** Not hering to conventions. **2.** Not usual or ordinary. **—** **con·ven·tion·al′i·ty** *n.* **— un′con·ven′tion·al·ly** *adv.*
un·cork (un-kôrk′) *v.t.* To draw the cork from.
un·count·ed (un-koun′tid) *adj.* **1.** Not counted. **2.** yond counting; innumerable.
un·coup·le (un-kup′əl) *v.* **·led, ·ling** *v.t.* **1.** To disconnec unfasten. **2.** To set loose. **—** *v.i.* **3.** To break loose.
un·couth (un-kōōth′) *adj.* **1.** Rough; crude; unrefined. Awkward or odd; ungainly. [OE *uncūth* unknown] **— couth′ly** *adv.* **— un·couth′ness** *n.*

cov·er (un·kuv′ər) *v.t.* **1.** To remove the covering from. To make known; disclose. — *v.i.* **3.** To remove a cover-. **4.** To raise or remove the hat, as in respect.

·tion (ungk′shən) *n.* **1.** The state or quality of being **:tuous. 2.** *Eccl.* **a** A ceremonial anointing with oil. **b** The ramental rite of anointing those in danger of death: also led *extreme unction.* **3.** The act of anointing, as with oil. The unguent used in anointing; ointment. [< F < L < *ere* to anoint] — **unc′tion·less** *adj.*

·tu·ous (ungk′chōō·əs) *adj.* **1.** Characterized by affect-·emotion; oily-tongued; unduly suave. **2.** Characterized deep sympathetic feeling. **3.** Greasy; slippery to the **ich**, as an unguent [< Med.L < L < *ungere* to anoint] — **′tu·ous·ly** *adv.* — **unc′tu·os′i·ty** (-chōō·os′ə·tē), **unc′tu·-ness** *n.*

cut (un·kut′) *adj.* **1.** Not cut. **2.** In bookbinding, hav-·untrimmed margins. **3.** Unground, as a gem.

damped (un·dampt′) *adj. Physics* **1.** Pertaining to or ·ignating oscillations that continue without change in plitude. **2.** Not damped; unrepressed.

daunt·ed (un·dôn′tid, -dän′-) *adj.* Not daunted or in-·idated; fearless; intrepid. — **un·daunt′ed·ly** *adv.* — **un-·unt′ed·ness** *n.*

de·ceive (un′di·sēv′) *v.t.* **·ceived, ·ceiv·ing** To free from ·eption, error, or illusion.

de·cid·ed (un′di·sī′did) *adj.* **1.** Not having the mind ·de up. **2.** Not decided upon; not determined. — **un′de-·′ed·ly** *adv.* — **un′de·cid′ed·ness** *n.*

de·ni·a·ble (un′di·nī′ə·bəl) *adj.* **1.** That cannot be de-·d; indisputably true; obviously correct. **2.** Unquestion-·ly good; excellent. — **un′de·ni′a·bly** *adv.*

der (un′dər) *prep.* **1.** Beneath, so as to have something ·ectly above; covered by: layer *under* layer. **2.** In a place ·er than; at the foot or bottom of: *under* the hill. **3.** Be-·ath the shelter of. **4.** Beneath the guise or assumption of: *der* a false name. **5.** Less than in number, degree, etc.: ·der 10 tons. **6.** Inferior to in quality, character, or rank. Dominated by; owing allegiance to; subordinate to. **8.** ·oject to the guidance or tutorship of. **9.** Subject to the ·ral sanction of: *under* oath. **10.** With the liability of in-·rring: *under* penalty of the law. **11.** Subject to the pres-·e of; swayed by: *under* the circumstances. **12.** Driven or ·opelled by: *under* sail. **13.** In the group or class of: in-·ded *under* History. **14.** Being the subject of: *under* treat-·nt. **15.** During the period of; in the reign of. **16.** By ·tue of; attested or warranted by: *under* his own signa-·re. **17.** In conformity to or in accordance with. **18.** ·anted or sowed with. — *adv.* **1.** In or into a position be-·v something; underneath. **2.** In or into a lower degree or ·nk. **3.** So as to be covered or hidden. **4.** So as to be less ·an the required amount. — **to go under** To fail, as a busi-·ss. — *adj.* **1.** Situated or moving under something else; ·wer or lowermost. **2.** *Zool.* Ventral. **3.** Lower in rank; ·bordinate. **4.** Less than usual, standard, or prescribed; in-·fficient.

der- *combining form* **1.** Below in position; situated or ·rected beneath; on the underside, as in: **underlip, under-·le. 2.** Below a surface or covering; lower, as in: **under-·oring, underpainting. 3.** Inferior in rank or importance; ·bordinate; subsidiary, as in: **underofficer, undertreas-·er. 4.** Insufficient or insufficiently; less than is usual or ·oper, as in: **underpaid, underpopulated. 5.** Subdued; ·dden, as in: **underemphasis, underplot.

·der·age (un′dər·āj′) *adj.* Not of a requisite age; imma-·re. Also **un′der-age′.**

un·der·arm[1] (un′dər·ärm′) *adj.* Situated, placed, or used under the arm. — *n.* The armpit.

un·der·arm[2] (un′dər·ärm′) *adj.* In various sports, as ten-nis, baseball, etc., executed with the hand lower than the el-bow. — *adv.* In an underarm manner. Also *underhand.*

un·der·bid (un′dər·bid′) *v.t.* **·bid, ·bid·ding** To bid lower than, as in a competition. — **un′der·bid′der** *n.*

un·der·brush (un′dər·brush′) *n.* Small trees and shrubs growing beneath forest trees; undergrowth. Also **un′der·bush′** (-bŏŏsh′).

un·der·buy (un′dər·bī′) *v.t.* **·bought, ·buy·ing 1.** To buy at a price lower than that paid by (another). **2.** To pay less than the value for.

un·der·car·riage (un′dər·kar′ij) *n.* **1.** The framework sup-porting the body of a structure, as an automobile. **2.** The principal landing gear of an aircraft.

un·der·charge (*v.* un′dər·chärj′; *n.* un′dər·chärj′) *v.t.* **·charged, ·charg·ing 1.** To make an inadequate charge for. **2.** To load with an insufficient charge, as a gun. — *n.* An inadequate or insufficient charge.

un·der·class·man (un′dər·klas′mən, -kläs′-) *n. pl.* **·men** (-mən) A freshman or sophomore in a school or college.

un·der·clothes (un′dər·klōz′, -klōthz′) *n.pl.* Clothes de-signed for underwear, or to be worn next to the skin. Also **un′der·cloth′ing** (-klōth′ing).

un·der·coat (un′dər·kōt′) *n.* **1.** A coat worn under another coat. **2.** Underfur. **3.** A layer of paint, varnish, etc., be-neath another layer: also **un′der·coat′ing.** — *v.t.* To pro-vide with an undercoat (def. 3).

un·der·cov·er (un′dər·kuv′ər) *adj.* Secret; surreptitious; esp., engaged in spying or secret investigation.

un·der·cur·rent (un′dər·kûr′ənt) *n.* **1.** A current, as of water or air, below another or below the surface. **2.** A hid-den drift or tendency, as of popular sentiments.

un·der·cut (*n. & adj.* un′dər·kut′; *v.* un′dər·kut′) *n.* **1.** The act or result of cutting under. **2.** The tenderloin. **3.** Any part that is cut away below. **4.** In sports, a cut or backspin imparted to the ball. — *v.t.* **·cut ·cut·ting 1.** To cut under. **2.** To cut away a lower portion of. **3.** To work or sell for lower payment than (a rival). **4.** In sports, to give an under-cut to (the ball). — *adj.* Done by undercutting.

un·der·dog (un′dər·dôg′, -dog′) *n.* **1.** One who is at a dis-advantage in a struggle; a probable loser. **2.** One who is victimized or downtrodden by society.

un·der·done (un′dər·dun′) *adj.* **1.** Insufficiently done. **2.** Not cooked to the full; rare.

un·der·es·ti·mate (*v.* un′dər·es′tə·māt; *n.* un′dər·es′tə·mit) *v.t.* **·mat·ed, ·mat·ing** To put too low an estimate upon. — *n.* An estimate that is too low. — **un′der·es′ti·ma′tion** *n.*

un·der·ex·pose (un′dər·ik·spōz′) *v.t.* **·posed, ·pos·ing** *Pho-tog.* To expose (a film) less than is required for proper devel-opment. — **un′der·ex·po′sure** (-spō′zhər) *n.*

un·der·feed (un′dər·fēd′) *v.t.* **·fed, ·feed·ing 1.** To feed in-sufficiently. **2.** To fuel (an engine) from beneath.

un·der·foot (un′dər·fŏŏt′) *adv.* **1.** Beneath the feet; down on the ground; immediately below. **2.** In the way.

un·der·fur (un′dər·fûr′) *n.* The coat of dense, fine hair forming the main part of a pelt, as in seals.

un·der·gar·ment (un′dər·gär′mənt) *n.* A garment to be worn under the outer garments.

un·der·go (un′dər·gō′) *v.t.* **·went, ·gone, ·go·ing 1.** To be subjected to; have experience of; suffer. **2.** To endure.

un·der·grad·u·ate (un′dər·graj′ōō·it) *n.* A university or college student who has not received a bachelor's degree.

un·der·ground (*adj.* un′dər·ground′; *adv.* un′dər·ground′)

:expanded	**unfaded**	**unfetter**	**unforeseeable**	**unfreezable**	**ungirded**
:expectant	**unfading**	**unfettered**	**unforeseeing**	**unfreeze**	**ungladdened**
:expended	**unfallen**	**unfilial**	**unforeseen**	**un–French**	**unglazed**
:expendible	**unfaltering**	**unfilled**	**unforested**	**unfrequent**	**unglossed**
:expert	**unfashionable**	**unfilmed**	**unforetold**	**unfrequented**	**unglove**
:xpiated	**unfashioned**	**unfiltered**	**unforfeited**	**unfrequently**	**ungloved**
:xpired	**unfastened**	**unfired**	**unforged**	**unfrozen**	**unglue**
:xplainable	**unfatherly**	**unfittingly**	**unforgetful**	**unfruitful**	**ungoverned**
:xplained	**unfathomable**	**unfixed**	**unforgetting**	**unfulfilled**	**ungowned**
:xplicit	**unfathomed**	**unfixedness**	**unforgivable**	**unfunded**	**ungraced**
:xploded	**unfatigued**	**unflagging**	**unforgiven**	**unfurnished**	**ungraceful**
:xploited	**unfavored**	**unflaggingly**	**unforgiving**	**unfurrowed**	**ungracefully**
:xplored	**unfeared**	**unflattered**	**unforgot**	**ungallant**	**ungraded**
:xported	**unfearing**	**unflattering**	**unforgotten**	**ungalled**	**ungrafted**
:xposed	**unfeasible**	**unflavored**	**unformulated**	**ungarnished**	**ungrained**
:xpressed	**unfed**	**unflickering**	**unforsaken**	**ungartered**	**ungratified**
:xpunged	**unfederated**	**unfoiled**	**unfortified**	**ungathered**	**ungrounded**
:xpurgated	**unfeignedly**	**unforbearing**	**unfought**	**ungenerous**	**ungrudging**
:xtended	**unfelt**	**unforbidden**	**unfound**	**ungenial**	**ungrudgingly**
:xterminated	**unfeminine**	**unforced**	**unframed**	**ungenteel**	**unguided**
:xtinguishable	**unfenced**	**unforcedly**	**unfranchised**	**ungentle**	**unhackneyed**
:xtinguished	**unfermented**	**unfordable**	**unfraternal**	**ungentlemanly**	**unhailed**
:xtraditable	**unfertile**	**unforeboding**	**unfraught**	**ungently**	**unhalved**
:fadable	**unfertilized**	**unforeknown**	**unfree**	**ungifted**	**unhammered**

adj. **1.** Situated, done, or operating beneath the surface of the ground. **2.** Done in secret; clandestine. — *n.* **1.** That which is beneath the surface of the ground. **2.** A group secretly organized to oppose those in control of a government or country. **3.** *Brit.* A subway (def. 1). — *adv.* **1.** Beneath the surface of the ground. **2.** Secretly.

Underground Railroad A system of cooperation among antislavery people, before 1861, for assisting fugitive slaves to escape to Canada and the free States.

un·der·growth (un′dər-grōth′) *n.* **1.** A growth of smaller plants among larger ones; esp., a thicket or copse in or as in a forest. **2.** The condition of being undergrown.

un·der·hand (un′dər-hand′) *adj.* **1.** Done or acting in a treacherously secret manner; sly. **2.** In sports, underarm. — *adv.* **1.** Underhandedly; slyly. **2.** Underarm².

un·der·hand·ed (un′dər-han′did) *adj.* **1.** Underhand. **2.** Short-handed. — **un′der·hand′ed·ly** *adv.* — **un′der·hand′-ed·ness** *n.*

un·der·lay (*v.* un′dər-lā′; *n.* un′dər-lā′) *v.t.* **·laid, ·lay·ing 1.** To place (one thing) under another. **2.** To furnish with a base or lining. **3.** *Printing* To support or raise by underlays. — *n.* **1.** *Printing* A piece of paper, etc., placed under certain parts of a printing form.

un·der·lie (un′dər-lī′) *v.t.* **·lay, ·lain, ·ly·ing 1.** To lie below or under. **2.** To be the basis or support of: the principle that *underlies* a scheme. [OE *underlicgan*]

un·der·line (un′dər-līn′) *v.t.* **·lined, ·lin·ing 1.** To mark with a line underneath. **2.** To emphasize.

un·der·ling (un′dər-ling) *n.* A subordinate; an inferior.

un·der·ly·ing (un′dər-lī′ing) *adj.* **1.** Lying under. **2.** Fundamental. **3.** Prior in claim or lien.

un·der·mine (un′dər-mīn′, un′dər-mīn) *v.t.* **·mined, ·min·ing 1.** To excavate beneath; dig a mine or passage under: to *undermine* a fortress. **2.** To weaken by wearing away at the base. **3.** To weaken or impair secretly or by degrees: to *undermine* one's health. — **un′der·min′er** *n.*

un·der·most (un′dər-mōst′) *adj.* Having the lowest place or position.

un·der·neath (un′dər-nēth′, -nēth′) *adv.* **1.** In a place below. **2.** On the under or lower side. — *prep.* **1.** Beneath; under; below. **2.** Under the form or appearance of. **3.** Under the authority of; in the control of. — *adj.* Lower. — *n.* The lower or under part or side. [OE *underneothan*]

un·der·nour·ish (un′dər-nûr′ish) *v.t.* To provide with nourishment insufficient in amount or quality for proper health and growth. — **un′der·nour′ish·ment** *n.*

un·der·song (un′dərn-sông′, -song′) *n.* Tierce (def. 3). [OE *undern* midday, midday meal + SONG]

un·der·pants (un′dər-pants′) *n.pl. U.S.* An undergarment worn over the loins.

un·der·pass (un′dər-pas′, -päs′) *n. U.S.* A passage beneath; esp., the section of a way or road that passes under railway tracks or under another road.

un·der·pay (un′dər-pā′) *v.t.* **·paid, ·pay·ing** To pay insufficiently.

un·der·pin·ning (un′dər-pin′ing) *n.* **1.** Material or framework used to support a wall or building from below. **2.** *pl. Informal* The legs.

un·der·pitch vault (un′dər-pich′) *Archit.* A vault formed by the intersection of two vaults that spring from the same level but are of uneven widths. For illus. see VAULT¹.

un·der·priv·i·leged (un′dər-priv′ə-lijd) *adj.* Not privileged to enjoy certain rights to which everyone is theoretically entitled, as because of poverty, illiteracy, etc.

un·der·pro·duc·tion (un′dər-prə-duk′shən) *n.* Production below capacity or below requirements.

un·der·proof (un′dər-prōōf′) *adj.* Having less strength than proof spirit.

un·der·quote (un′dər-kwōt′) *v.t.* **·quot·ed, ·quot·ing** To undersell or offer to undersell, as goods or stocks.

un·der·rate (un′dər-rāt′) *v.t.* **·rat·ed, ·rat·ing** To rate low; underestimate. — *Syn.* See UNDERESTIMATE.

un·der·run (un′dər-run′) *v.t.* **·ran, ·run, ·run·ning 1.** run or pass beneath. **2.** *Naut.* To examine (a line, haw etc.) from below by drawing a boat along beneath it.

un·der·score (*v.* un′dər-skôr′, -skōr′; *n.* un′dər-skôr′, -sk *v.t.* **·scored, ·scor·ing** To underline. — *n.* A line drawn neath a word, etc., as for emphasis.

un·der·sea (un′dər-sē′) *adj.* Existing, carried on adapted for use beneath the surface of the sea. — *adv.* neath the surface of the sea: also **un′der·seas′** (-sēz′).

un·der·sec·re·tar·y (un′dər-sek′rə-ter′ē) *n. pl.* **·tar·ies** a government department, the official who ranks next be the secretary.

un·der·sell (un′dər-sel′) *v.t.* **·sold, ·sell·ing 1.** To sell lower price than. **2.** To sell for less than the real value. **un′der·sell′er** *n.*

un·der·set (un′dər-set′) *n.* An undercurrent in the oc

un·der·sher·iff (un′dər-sher′if) *n.* A deputy sheriff, one upon whom the sheriff's duties devolve in his absen

un·der·shirt (un′dər-shûrt′) *n.* A garment worn bene the shirt, generally of cotton.

un·der·shoot (un′dər-shōōt′) *v.* **·shot, ·shoot·ing** *v.t.* **1.** shoot short of or below (the mark, target, etc.). **2.** A To land an airplane or deliver a bomb short of (the ma — *v.i.* **3.** To shoot or land short of the mark.

un·der·shot (un′dər-shot′) *adj.* **1.** Propelled by water flows underneath: said of a water wheel. **2.** Projecting the lower jaw or teeth; also, having a projecting lower ja teeth.

un·der·side (un′dər-sīd′) *n.* The lower or under side or face.

un·der·sign (un′dər-sīn′) *v.t.* To sign at the foot, end bottom of: used chiefly in the past participle.

un·der·signed (un′dər-sīnd′) *adj.* **1.** Having one's si ture at the foot of a document. **2.** Signed at the foot document. — *n.* The subscriber or subscribers to a d ment: with *the*.

un·der·sized (un′dər-sīzd′) *adj.* Of less than the norma average size. Also **un′der·size′**.

un·der·slung (un′dər-slung′) *adj. Mech.* Having springs fixed to the axles from below, instead of resting u them: said of certain automobiles: also *underhung*.

un·der·soil (un′dər-soil′) *n.* Subsoil.

un·der·stand (un′dər-stand′) *v.* **·stood, ·stand·ing** *v.t.* To come to know the meaning or import of; apprehend. To comprehend the nature or character of. **3.** To have c prehension or mastery of: Do you *understand* German? To be aware of; realize: She *understands* her position. **5.** have been told: I *understand* that she went home. **6.** T fer the meaning of: How am I to *understand* that remark? To accept as a condition or stipulation: It is *understood* the tenant will provide his own heat. **8.** To suppl thought when unexpressed. **9.** To be in agreement with privately in sympathy with. — *v.i.* **10.** To have un standing; comprehend. **11.** To be informed; believe. **Syn.** See APPREHEND. [OE < *under-* under + *standa* stand] — **un′der·stand′a·ble** *adj.* — **un′der·stand′a** *adv.*

un·der·stand·ing (un′dər-stan′ding) *n.* **1.** The act of who understands, or the resulting state; comprehension. The power by which one understands. **3.** The sum of mental powers by which knowledge is acquired, retaine and extended. **4.** The facts or elements of a case as ap hended by any one individual. **5.** An informal or confi tial compact; also, the thing agreed on. **6.** An arrangem

unhampered	unheeding	unhuman	unimpeached	uninformed	unintention	
unhandicapped	unheedingly	unhumanize	unimpeded	uninfringed	uninterestin	
unhandled	unhelped	unhung	unimplored	uningenious	uninterestin	
unhang	unhelpful	unhurt	unimportant	uningenuous	unintermitte	
unhanged	unheralded	unhurtful	unimposing	uninhabitable	unintermitti	
unharassed	unheroic	unhygienic	unimpregnated	uninhabited	unintermitti	
unharbored	unheroically	unhygienically	unimpressed	uninhibited	uninterpola	
unhardened	unhesitant	unhyphenated	unimpressible	uninitiated	uninterpret	
unharmed	unhesitantly	unhyphened	unimpressionable	uninjured	uninterrupt	
unharmful	unhesitating	unideal	unimpressive	uninspired	unintimidat	
unharmfully	unhesitatingly	unidentified	uninaugurated	uninspiring	unintoxicate	
unharming	unhewn	unidiomatic	uninclosed	uninspiringly	uninvaded	
unharmonious	unhindered	unilluminated	unincorporated	uninstructed	uninvented	
unharnessed	unhired	unillumined	unincubated	uninstructive	uninventive	
unharrowed	unhistoric	unillustrated	unincumbered	uninsurable	uninventive	
unharvested	unhistorical	unimaginable	unindemnified	uninsured	uninverted	
unhastily	unhistorically	unimaginably	unindicated	unintellectual	uninvested	
unhasty	unhomogeneous	unimaginative	unindorsed	unintelligent	uninvited	
unhatched	unhonored	unimaginatively	uninfected	unintelligibility	uninviting	
unhealed	unhood	unimagined	uninfested	unintelligible	uninvitingly	
unhealthful	unhoped	unimbued	uninflammable	unintelligibleness	uninvoked	
unheated	unhostile	unimitated	uninflected	unintelligibly	uninvolved	
unheeded	unhouse	unimpaired	uninfluenced	unintended	unissued	
unheedful	unhoused	unimpassioned	uninfluential	unintentional	unjacketed	

settlement of differences, or of disputed points. — *adj.* Possessing comprehension and good sense. **2.** Tolerant; sympathetic. — **un·der·stand′ing·ly** *adv.* — **un′der·and′ing·ness** *n.*
— **Syn.** (noun) **2.** reason, intelligence, intuition, judgment.

der·state (un′dər·stāt′) *v.* **·stat·ed, ·stat·ing** *v.t.* **1.** To ite with less force than the truth warrants or allows. **2.** To ite, as a number or dimension, as less than the true one. *v.i.* **3.** To make an understatement.

der·state·ment (un′dər·stāt′mənt) *n.* A statement that deliberately unemphatic or restrained in tone.

der·stood (un′dər·stŏŏd′) Past tense and past participle UNDERSTAND. — *adj.* **1.** Assumed; agreed upon by all. **2.** sumed when unexpressed, as the subject of a sentence.

der·stra·tum (un′dər·strā′təm, -strat′əm) *n. pl.* **·stra-** (-strā′tə, -strat′ə) *or* **·stra·tums** A substratum.

der·stud·y (un′dər·stud′ē) *v.t. & v.i.* **·stud·ied, ·stud·y-** **g 1.** To study (a part) in order to be able, if necessary, to ke the place of the actor playing it. **2.** To act as an under- dy (to another actor). — *n. pl.* **·stud·ies 1.** An actor or tress who can take the place of another actor in a given e when necessary. **2.** A person prepared to perform the rk or fill the position of another.

der·take (un′dər·tāk′) *v.* **·took, ·tak·en, ·tak·ing** *v.t.* **1.** take upon oneself; agree or attempt to do; begin. **2.** To ntract to do; pledge oneself to. **3.** To guarantee or prom- **4.** To take charge or guidance. — *v.i.* **5.** To ke oneself responsible or liable: with *for*.

der·tak·er (un′dər·tā′kər *for def. 1*; un′dər·tā′kər *for def. n.* **1.** One who undertakes any work or enterprise. **2.** e whose business it is to arrange for the cremation or buri- of the dead and to oversee funerals.

der·tak·ing (un′dər·tā′king; *for def. 3* un′dər·tā′king) **1.** The act of one who undertakes any task or enterprise. The thing undertaken; a task. **3.** The business of an un- rtaker (def. 2). **4.** An engagement, promise, or guaranty.

der·ten·ant (un′dər·ten′ənt) *n.* A subtenant.

der·tone (un′dər·tōn′) *n.* **1.** A tone of lower pitch or udness than is usual; esp., the tone of a subdued voice or a nisper. **2.** A subdued shade of a color; also, a color upon nich other colors have been imposed and which is seen rough them. **3.** An implicit meaning or suggestion.

der·took (un′dər·tŏŏk′) Past tense of UNDERTAKE.

der·tow (un′dər·tō′) *n.* **1.** The flow of water beneath d in a direction opposite to the surface current. **2.** The award undercurrent below the surf.

der·val·ue (un′dər·val′yōō) *v.t.* **·ued, ·u·ing** To value o lightly; underrate; underestimate. — **Syn.** See UNDER- TIMATE. — **un′der·val·u·a′tion** *n.*

der·wa·ter (un′dər·wô′tər, -wot′ər) *adj. & adv.* Below e surface of a body of water; also, below the water line of a ip. — *n.* The region below the surface of water.

der·way (un′dər·wā′) *adv.* In progress or into operation: ne meeting was already *underway.* Also **under way.**

der·wear (un′dər·wâr′) *n.* Garments worn underneath e ordinary outer garments; underclothes.

der·weight (un′dər·wāt′) *adj.* Having less than the e normal weight. — *n.* Insufficiency of weight; also, weight low normal.

der·went (un′dər·went′) Past tense of UNDERGO.

der·wood (un′dər·wŏŏd′) *n.* Underbrush.

der·world (un′dər·wûrld′) *n.* **1.** In Greek and Roman ythology, the abode of the dead; Hades. **2.** The part of so- ety engaged in crime or vice; esp., organized criminals.

der·write¹ (un′dər·rīt′) *v.* **·wrote, ·writ·ten, writ·ing**

v.t. **1.** To write beneath; subscribe. **2.** In finance, to exe- cute and deliver (a policy of insurance on specified property); insure; assume (a risk) by way of insurance. **3.** To engage to buy, at a determined price and time, all or part of the stock in (a new enterprise or company) that is not sub- scribed for by the public. **4.** Loosely, to assume responsi- bility for, as an enterprise. **5.** To undertake to pay, as a written pledge of money. — **un′der·writ′er** *n.*

un·der·write² (un′dər·rīt′) *v.t. & v.i.* **·wrote, ·writ·ten, ·writ·ing** To write in a deliberately restrained style.

un·de·sir·a·ble (un′di·zīr′ə·bəl) *adj.* Not desirable; objec- tionable. — *n.* An objectionable person. — **un′de·sir′a· bil′i·ty, un′de·sir′a·ble·ness** *n.* — **un′de·sir′a·bly** *adv.*

un·did (un·did′) Past tense of UNDO.

un·dies (un′dēz) *n. pl. Informal* Women's or children's un- derwear.

un·do (un·dōō′) *v.t.* **·did, ·done, ·do·ing 1.** To cause to be as if never done; reverse; annul. **2.** To loosen or untie, as a knot, etc. **3.** To unfasten and open, as a parcel. **4.** To bring to ruin; destroy. [OE *undōn*] — **un·do′er** *n.*

un·do·ing (un·dōō′ing) *n.* **1.** Reversal, cancellation, etc., of what has been done. **2.** Destruction; ruin; also, the cause of ruin. **3.** The act or process of unfastening, etc.

un·done¹ (un·dun′) *adj.* **1.** Untied; unfastened. **2.** Ruined. [Orig. pp. of UNDO]

un·done² (un·dun′) *adj.* Not done. [< UN- + DONE]

un·doubt·ed (un·dou′tid) *adj.* Assured beyond question; being beyond a doubt; indubitable. — **un·doubt′ed·ly** *adv.*

un·draw (un·drô′) *v.t. & v.i.* **·drew, ·drawn, ·draw·ing** To draw open, away, or aside.

un·dreamed-of (un·drēmd′uv′, -ov′) *adj.* Not conceived of in the mind; unimaginable. Also **un·dreamt′-of** (-dremt′-).

un·dress (*v. & n.* un·dres′; *adj.* un′dres′) *v.t.* **1.** To divest of clothes; strip. **2.** To remove the dressing or bandages from, as a wound. — *v.i.* **3.** To remove one's clothing. — *n.* **1.** Ordinary attire, as distinguished from formal dress. **2.** Comfortable, informal clothing. — *adj. Informal.*

un·due (un·dōō′, -dyōō′) *adj.* **1.** Excessive; disproportion- ate. **2.** Not justified by law; illegal. **3.** Not due; not yet demandable. **4.** Not appropriate; improper.

un·du·lant (un′dyə·lənt, -də-) *adj.* Undulating; waving.

undulant fever *Pathol.* A disease transmitted to man in the milk of infected cows and goats, and characterized by re- current fever, swelling of the joints, neuralgic pains, etc.

un·du·late (*v.* un′dyə·lāt, -də-; *adj.* un′dyə·lit, -lāt, -də-) *v.* **·lat·ed, ·lat·ing** *v.t.* **1.** To cause to move like a wave or in waves. **2.** To give a wavy appearance to. — *v.i.* **3.** To move like waves. **4.** To have a wavy appearance. — *adj.* **1.** Having a wavy margin, as a leaf. **2.** Having wavelike markings, as of color: also **un′du·lat′ed** (-lā′tid). [< L *un- dulatus* having wavelike markings < *unda* wave]

un·du·la·tion (un′dyə·lā′shən, -də-) *n.* **1.** The act of un- dulating. **2.** A waving or sinuous motion. **3.** A wave. **4.** An appearance as of waves; a gentle rise and fall. — **un′du· la·to′ry** (-lə·tôr′ē, -tō′rē), **un′du·lous** (-ləs) *adj.*

un·du·ly (un·dōō′lē, -dyōō′-) *adv.* **1.** Excessively. **2.** In violation of a moral or of a legal standard; unjustly.

un·dy·ing (un·dī′ing) *adj.* Immortal; everlasting.

un·earth (un·ûrth′) *v.t.* **1.** To dig or root up from the earth. **2.** To reveal by or as by searching.

un·earth·ly (un·ûrth′lē) *adj.* **1.** Not earthly; sublime. **2.** Weird; terrifying; supernatural. **3.** *Informal* Ridiculously unconventional or inconvenient. — **un·earth′li·ness** *n.*

un·eas·y (un·ē′zē) *adj.* **·eas·i·er, ·eas·i·est 1.** Lacking ease, assurance, or security; disturbed. **2.** Not affording ease or

jaded	unlaundered	unlocated	unmannishly	unmenaced	unmoistened
joined	unleashed	unlocked	unmanufacturable	unmendable	unmold
jointed	unleased	unlovable	unmanufactured	unmended	unmolded
joyful	unled	unloved	unmarked	unmensurable	unmolested
joyfully	unlessened	unloveliness	unmarketable	unmentionability	unmollified
judged	unlessoned	unloverlike	unmarketed	unmentioned	unmolten
judicial	unlet	unloving	unmarred	unmercenary	unmortgaged
justifiable	unletted	unlovingly	unmarriageable	unmerchantable	unmotivated
justifiably	unlevel	unlubricated	unmarried	unmerited	unmounted
kept	unlevied	unmagnified	unmastered	unmeriting	unmourned
kindled	unlibidinous	unmaidenliness	unmatched	unmethodical	unmovable
kindliness	unlicensed	unmaidenly	unmated	unmilitary	unmoved
kingly	unlifelike	unmailable	unmaternal	unmilled	unmoving
kissed	unlighted	unmaileable	unmatted	unmingle	unmown
knelled	unlikable	unmanageable	unmatured	unmingled	unmurmuring
knightly	unlikeable	unmanful	unmeant	unmirthful	unmusical
knowing	unlined	unmanfully	unmeasurable	unmirthfully	unmuzzle
knowingly	unlink	unmanfulness	unmeasurably	unmistaken	unmuzzled
knowingness	unliquefiable	unmangled	unmeasured	unmitigable	unmystified
labeled	unliquefied	unmanifested	unmechanical	unmixed	unnail
labelled	unliquidated	unmanipulated	unmediated	unmixt	unnamable
ladylike	unlit	unmanned	unmedicated	unmodified	unnameable
lamented	unliveliness	unmannered	unmelodious	unmodish	unnamed
lash	unlively	unmannish	unmelted	unmodishly	unnaturalized

rest; causing discomfort. **3.** Showing embarrassment or constraint; strained. **— un·eas/i·ly** *adv.* **— un·eas/i·ness** *n.*

un·em·ploy·a·ble (un'əm-ploi'ə-bəl) *adj.* Not employable. **— n.** A person who, because of illness, age, mental or physical incapacity, etc., cannot be employed.

un·em·ployed (un'əm-ploid') *adj.* **1.** Having no remunerative employment; out of work. **2.** Not being put to use; idle. **— n.** A jobless person. **— the unemployed** Unemployed persons collectively. **— un'em·ploy'ment** *n.*

unemployment insurance *U.S.* A system of insurance authorized by the Federal Social Security Act of 1935, providing those who are involuntarily out of work with temporary compensation. Also **unemployment compensation.**

un·e·qual (un-ē'kwəl) *adj.* **1.** Not having equal extension, duration, proportions, amounts, etc. **2.** Not equal in strength, ability, status, etc. **3.** Inadequate for the purpose: with *to*. **4.** Inequitable; unfair. **5.** Varying; irregular. **6.** Not balanced; unsymmetrical. **— un·e/qual·ly** *adv.*

un·e·qualed (un-ē'kwəld) *adj.* Not equaled or matched; unrivaled; supreme. Also **un·e/qualled.**

un·e·quiv·o·cal (un'i-kwiv'ə-kəl) *adj.* Understandable in only one way; not equivocal. **— un'e·quiv·o·cal·ly** *adv.*

un·err·ing (un-ûr'ing, -er'-) *adj.* **1.** Making no mistakes; not erring. **2.** Certain; accurate. **— un·err'ing·ly** *adv.*

UNESCO (yōō-nes'kō) The United Nations Educational, Scientific and Cultural Organization. Also **U·nes/co.**

un·e·ven (un-ē'vən) *adj.* **1.** Not even, smooth, parallel, or level; rough. **2.** Not divisible by two without remainder; odd: said of numbers. **3.** Not uniform; variable; spasmodic. **— un·e/ven·ly** *adv.* **— un·e/ven·ness** *n.*

un·e·vent·ful (un'i-vent'fəl) *adj.* Devoid of noteworthy events; quiet. **— un/e·vent/ful·ly** *adv.*

un·ex·am·pled (un'ig-zam'pəld) *adj.* Having no precedent.

un·ex·cep·tion·a·ble (un'ik-sep'shən-ə-bəl) *adj.* That cannot be objected to; irreproachable. **— un'ex·cep'tion·a·ble·ness** *n.* **— un'ex·cep'tion·a·bly** *adv.*

un·ex·cep·tion·al (un'ik-sep'shən-əl) *adj.* **1.** Not exceptional; ordinary. **2.** Subject to no exception.

un·ex·pect·ed (un'ik-spek'tid) *adj.* Not expected; unforeseen. **— un'ex·pect/ed·ly** *adv.* **— un'ex·pect/ed·ness** *n.*

un·fail·ing (un-fā'ling) *adj.* **1.** Giving or constituting a supply that never fails; inexhaustible: an *unfailing* spring. **2.** Not falling short of need, hope, or expectation. **3.** Sure; infallible. **— un·fail/ing·ly** *adv.* **— un·fail/ing·ness** *n.*

un·fair (un-fâr') *adj.* **1.** Characterized by partiality or prejudice; not fair or just. **2.** Dishonest; fraudulent. **— un·fair/ly** *adv.* **— un·fair/ness** *n.*

un·faith·ful (un-fāth'fəl) *adj.* **1.** Not having kept faith; unworthy of trust; faithless. **2.** Not true to marriage vows; adulterous. **3.** Not accurate or exact. **— un·faith/ful·ly** *adv.* **— un·faith/ful·ness** *n.*

un·fa·mil·iar (un'fə-mil'yər) *adj.* **1.** Not having acquaintance: with *with*. **2.** Not known or recognizable. **— un/fa·mil/i·ar/i·ty** (-mil'ē-ar/ə-tē) *n.* **— un/fa·mil/iar·ly** *adv.*

un·fa·vor·a·ble (un-fā'vər-ə-bəl) *adj.* Not favorable; unpropitious; adverse. Also *Brit.* **un·fa/vour·a·ble. — un·fa/·vor·a·ble·ness** *n.* **— un·fa/vor·a·bly** *adv.*

un·feel·ing (un-fē'ling) *adj.* **1.** Not sympathetic; hard; cruel. **2.** Devoid of feeling or sensation. **— un·feel/ing·ly** *adv.* **— un·feel/ing·ness** *n.*

un·feigned (un-fānd') *adj.* Not feigned; not pretended; sincere; genuine. **— un·feign·ed·ly** (-fā'nid-lē) *adv.*

un·fin·ished (un-fin'isht) *adj.* **1.** Not finished; incomplete. **2.** Having no finish or special surface treatment, as wood. **3.** Of fabrics: **a** Not bleached. **b** Having a slight nap.

un·fit (un-fit') *adj.* **1.** Having no fitness; unsuitable. **2.** Not appropriate; improper. **3.** Not in sound physical condition. **— v.t. ·fit·ted** or **·fit, ·fit·ting** To make unfit; dis-

qualify. **— un·fit/ly** *adv.* **— un·fit/ness** *n.*

un·fix (un-fiks') *v.t.* **1.** To unfasten. **2.** To unsettle.

un·flap·pa·ble (un-flap'ə-bəl) *adj.* Characterized by unsh able composure; imperturbable. **— un·flap/pa·bil/i·ty** *n.*

un·fledged (un-flejd') *adj.* **1.** Not yet fledged, as a yo bird. **2.** Immature; inexperienced.

un·flesh·ly (un-flesh'lē) *adj.* Ethereal; spiritual.

un·flinch·ing (un-flin'ching) *adj.* Not shrinking from d ger, pain, etc.; brave. **— un·flinch/ing·ly** *adv.*

un·fold (un-fōld') *v.t.* **1.** To open or spread out (someth folded). **2.** To lay open to view. **3.** To make clear by tailed explanation; explain: to *unfold* a plan. **4.** To evo develop. **— v.i. 5.** To become opened; expand. **6.** To come manifest. [OE *unfealdan*] **— un·fold/er** *n.*

un·for·get·ta·ble (un'fər-get'ə-bəl) *adj.* Not forgettab memorable. **— un·for·get/ta·bly** *adv.*

un·formed (un-fôrmd') *adj.* **1.** Devoid of shape or fo **2.** Not fully developed in character. **3.** Unorganized.

un·for·tu·nate (un-fôr'chə-nit) *adj.* **1.** Not fortunate; happy, unsuccessful, etc. **2.** Causing or attended by ill tune; disastrous. **— n.** One who is unfortunate. **— for/tu·nate·ly** *adv.* **— un·for/tu·nate·ness** *n.*

un·found·ed (un-foun'did) *adj.* **1.** Having no foundati groundless; baseless. **2.** Not founded or established. **un·found/ed·ly** *adv.* **— un·found/ed·ness** *n.*

un·friend·ly (un-frend'lē) *adj.* **1.** Unkindly disposed; imical; hostile. **2.** Not favorable or propitious. **— adv.** an unfriendly manner. **— un·friend/li·ness** *n.*

un·frock (un-frok') *v.t.* **1.** To depose, as a monk or pri from ecclesiastical rank. **2.** To divest of a frock or gov

un·furl (un-fûrl') *v.t. & v.i.* **1.** To unroll, as a flag. **2.** spread out; expand; unfold.

un·gain·ly (un-gān'lē) *adj.* Lacking grace; awkward. **adv.** In an awkward manner. **— un·gain/li·ness** *n.*

un·gird (un-gûrd') *v.t.* **1.** To divest of or free from a b girdle, or confining band. **2.** To loosen or unfasten by o by removing a belt, etc.

un·god·ly (un-god'lē) *adj.* **1.** Having no reverence for G impious. **2.** Wicked; sinful. **3.** *Informal* Outrageous; seemly. **— un·god/li·ness** *n.*

un·gov·ern·a·ble (un-guv'ər-nə-bəl) *adj.* **1.** Not capabl being governed or controlled. **2.** Refractory; unruly. **un·gov/ern·a·ble·ness** *n.* **— un·gov/ern·a·bly** *adv.*

un·gra·cious (un-grā'shəs) *adj.* **1.** Lacking in graciousn of manner; unmannerly. **2.** Not pleasing; offensive; un ceptable. **— un·gra/cious·ly** *adv.* **— un·gra/cious·ness**

un·gram·mat·i·cal (un'grə-mat'i-kəl) *adj.* **1.** Not in cordance with the rules of grammar. **2.** Characterized b using grammar at variance with the rules. **— un/gr mat/i·cal·ly** *adv.*

un·grate·ful (un-grāt'fəl) *adj.* **1.** Not feeling or show gratitude; not thankful. **2.** Not pleasant; disagreeable. Unrewarding. **— un·grate/ful·ly** *adv.* **— un·grate/ful·nes**

un·guard·ed (un-gär'did) *adj.* **1.** Having no guard; be without protection. **2.** Characterized by lack of cautio discretion: *unguarded* speech. **— un·guard/ed·ly** *adv.* **un·guard/ed·ness** *n.*

un·guent (ung'gwənt) *n.* Any ointment or salve. [< I *unguere* to anoint]

un·gu·la (ung'gyə-lə) *n. pl.* **·lae** (-lē) **1.** *Zool.* A hoof, cla or nail. **2.** *Geom.* That which is left of a cone or cylin when the top is cut off by a plane oblique to the base. *Bot.* An unguis. [< L < *unguis* nail] **— un/gu·lar** *ad*

un·gu·late (ung'gyə-lit, -lāt) *adj.* **1.** Having hoofs. **2.** Designating, pertaining to, or belonging to a large grou hoofed mammals, including the elephant, rhinoceros, ho hog, and all the ruminants. **3.** Hoof-shaped. **— n.** hoofed mammal. [< LL < L *ungula* hoof]

unnavigable	unobtainable	unorthodoxy	unpatented	unphilological	unplowed
unnavigated	unobtained	unostentatious	unpatriotic	unphilosophic	unplucked
unneeded	unobtruding	unostentatiously	unpatriotically	unphilosophical	unplug
unneedful	unobtrusive	unostentatiousness	unpaved	unphonetic	unplugged
unnegotiable	unobtrusively	unowned	unpeaceable	unpicked	unpoetic
unneighborliness	unobtrusiveness	unoxidized	unpeaceful	unpicturesque	unpoetical
unneighborly	unoccasioned	unpacified	unpedigreed	unpierced	unpointed
unnoted	unoffended	unpaid	unpen	unpile	unpoised
unnoticeable	unoffending	unpainful	unpenetrated	unpitied	unpolarized
unnoticeably	unoffensive	unpainfully	unpensioned	unpitying	unpolished
unnoticed	unoffensively	unpainfulness	unperceivable	unpityingly	unpolitical
unnurtured	unoffered	unpaired	unperceived	unplaced	unpolluted
unobjectionable	unofficial	unpalatable	unperceiving	unplagued	unpondered
unobliged	unofficious	unpalatably	unperfected	unplait	unpopulated
unobliging	unofficiously	unparagraphed	unperformed	unplanned	unposted
unobligingly	unoiled	unpardonable	unperplexed	unplanted	unpractical
unobnoxious	unopen	unpardonably	unpersuadable	unplayed	unpracticality
unobscured	unopened	unpardoned	unpersuaded	unpleased	unpractically
unobservable	unopposed	unparental	unpersuasive	unpleasing	unpredictable
unobservant	unoppressed	unparted	unpersuasively	unpledged	unpredictably
unobservantly	unordained	unpartisan	unpersuasiveness	unpliable	unpreoccupied
unobserved	unoriginal	unpartizan	unperturbed	unpliant	unprepared
unobserving	unornamental	unpasteurized	unperused	unplighted	unprepossessin
unobstructed	unornate	unpatched	unphilanthropic	unploughed	unprepossessin

hal·lowed (un·hal'ōd) *adj.* **1.** Not consecrated or made
y. **2.** Unholy; wicked.

hand (un·hand') *v.t.* To remove one's hand from; rese from the hand or hands; let go.

hand·y (un·han'dē) *adj.* **·hand·i·er, ·hand·i·est 1.** Incon-
ient; hard to handle. **2.** Clumsy; lacking in manual skill.
— **un·hand'i·ly** *adv.* — **un·hand'i·ness** *n.*

hap·py (un·hap'ē) *adj.* **·pi·er, ·pi·est 1.** Sad; miserable;
pressed. **2.** Unlucky; unfortunate. **3.** Not tactful or ap-
priate. — **un·hap'pi·ly** *adv.* — **un·hap'pi·ness** *n.*

har·ness (un·här'nis) *v.t.* **1.** To remove the harness
m; unyoke; release. **2.** To remove the armor from.

health·y (un·hel'thē) *adj.* **·health·i·er, ·health·i·est 1.**
cking health or vigor; sickly; unsound: *unhealthy* animals
plants; also, indicating such a condition: *unhealthy* signs.
Injurious to health. **3.** Morally unsound; unwholesome.
— **un·health'i·ly** *adv.* — **un·health'i·ness** *n.*

heard (un·hûrd') *adj.* **1.** Not perceived by the ear. **2.**
t granted a hearing. **3.** Obscure; unknown.

heard-of (un·hûrd'uv', -ov') *adj.* Not known of before;
known or unprecedented.

hinge (un·hinj') *v.t.* **·hinged, ·hing·ing 1.** To take from
• hinges. **2.** To remove the hinges of. **3.** To detach; dis-
ge. **4.** To throw into confusion; disorder. **5.** To make
table; unsettle, as the mind.

hitch (un·hich') *v.t.* To unfasten.

ho·ly (un·hō'lē) *adj.* **·ho·li·er, ·ho·li·est 1.** Not sacred or
lowed. **2.** Lacking purity; wicked; sinful. **3.** *Informal*
rrible; dreadful: an *unholy* hour. [OE *unhālig*] — **un·**
li·ly *adv.* — **un·ho'li·ness** *n.*

hook (un·hŏŏk') *v.t.* **1.** To remove from a hook. **2.** To
`asten the hook or hooks of. — *v.i.* **3.** To become un-
oked.

hoped-for (un·hōpt'fôr') *adj.* Not expected or hoped
: an *unhoped-for* solution.

horse (un·hôrs') *v.*. **·horsed, ·hors·ing 1.** To throw
m a horse. **2.** To dislodge; overthrow. **3.** To remove a
rse or horses from: to *unhorse* a vehicle.

hur·ried (un·hûr'ēd) *adj.* Leisurely; not hurried.

· *combining form* Having or consisting of one only. [<
unus one]

i·at (yōō'nē·at) *n.* A member of the Uniat Church. —
•. Of or pertaining to the Uniats or the Uniat Church.
o U'ni·ate (-it, -āt). [< Russian < *uniya* union < L *unus*
e; from union with the Roman Catholic Church]

iat Church Any body of Eastern Christians forming a
irch that acknowledges the Pope as its supreme head and
it has its own distinctive liturgy: also called *Eastern
urch*. Also **Uniate Church.**

i·ax·i·al (yōō·nē·ak'sē·al) *adj.* Having one axis.

i·cam·er·al (yōō·na·kam'ar·al) *adj.* Consisting of but
e legislative chamber.

i·cel·lu·lar (yōō·na·sel'ya·lər) *adj. Biol.* Consisting of a
gle cell, as a protozoan; one-celled.

i·col·or (yōō'na·kul'ar) *adj.* Of one color.

i·corn (yōō'na·kôrn) *n.* A mythical horse-
e animal with one horn. [< OF < L < *unus*
• + *cornu* horn]

i·cy·cle (yōō'na·sī'kal) *n.* A vehicle consist-
• of a metal frame mounted on one wheel and
pelled by means of pedals.

i·di·rec·tion·al (yōō'na·di·rek'shan·al, -dī-) UNICORN
· **1.** Having or moving in only one direction.
Telecom. Designed or equipped to operate best in only
e direction, as a radio antenna.

u·ni·fi·a·ble (yōō'na·fī'a·bal) *adj.* That can be unified.

u·ni·fi·ca·tion (yōō'na·fa·kā'shən) *n.* The act of unifying,
or the state of being unified. — **u'ni·fi·ca'tion·ist** *n.*

unified command *Mil.* An armed force of two or more
U.S. military services under a single commander.

u·ni·form (yōō'na·fôrm) *adj.* **1.** Being always the same or
alike, as in form, appearance, quality, degree, etc.; not varying: *uniform* temperature. **2.** Agreeing or identical with
each other; alike: *uniform* tastes. — *n.* **1.** A distinctive
form of dress having a uniform style and appearance and
worn by members of the same organization or service, as soldiers, sailors, etc. **2.** A single suit of such clothes. — *v.t.*
1. To put into or clothe with a uniform. **2.** To make uniform. [< F < L < *unus* one + *forma* form] — **u'ni·form·**
ly *adv.* — **u'ni·form·ness** *n.*

u·ni·formed (yōō'na·fôrmd) *adj.* Dressed in uniform.

u·ni·form·i·ty (yōō'na·fôr'ma·tē) *n. pl.* **·ties 1.** The state
or quality of being uniform; also, an instance of it. **2.** Conformity, as in opinions or religion. **3.** Monotony; sameness.

u·ni·fy (yōō'na·fī) *v.t. & v.i.* **·fied, ·fy·ing** To combine into a
unit; become or cause to be one. [< F or LL < L *unus* one
+ *facere* to make] — **u'ni·fi'er** *n.*

u·ni·lat·er·al (yōō'na·lat'ar·al) *adj.* **1.** Of, pertaining to, or
existing on one side only. **2.** Made, undertaken, done, or
signed by only one of two or more people or parties. **3.** One-
sided. **4.** Relating to or concerned with only one side of a
question, dispute, etc. **5.** Turned to or showing only one
side. — **u'ni·lat'er·al·ly** *adv.* — **u'ni·lat'er·al·ism, u'ni·lat'·**
er·al'i·ty (-al'a·tē) *n.*

un·im·peach·a·ble (un'im·pē'cha·bal) *adj.* Not to be
called into question as regards truth, honesty, etc.; faultless;
blameless. — **un'im·peach'a·bly** *adv.*

un·im·proved (un'im·prōōvd') *adj.* **1.** Not improved, bet-
tered, or advanced. **2.** Having no improvements; not
cleared, cultivated, or built upon: *unimproved* land. **3.** Not
made anything of; unused: *unimproved* opportunities.

un·in·ter·est·ed (un·in'tar·is·tid, -tris-) *adj.* **1.** Having no
interest in, as in property. **2.** Taking no interest in; uncon-
cerned. — **un·in'ter·est·ed·ly** *adv.* — **un·in'ter·est·ed·ness** *n.*

un·ion (yōōn'yan) *n.* **1.** The act of uniting, or the state of
being united; also, that which is so formed. **2.**
A combining or joining of nations, states, parties, etc., for some mutual interest or purpose.
3. The harmony, agreement, or concord that results from such a combining or joining. **4.** The
joining of two persons in marriage; also, the
state of wedlock. **5.** A labor union. **6.** *Mech.*
A device for connecting parts of machinery;
esp., a coupling or connection for pipes or rods.
7. A device emblematic of union, used in a flag or emblem
and found in the corner near the staff or occupying the entire field. — *adj.* Of, pertaining to, or adhering to a union,
esp. a labor union. [< F < L < L *unus* one]

PIPE UNION

Un·ion (yōōn'yan) *n.* **1.** The U.S. regarded as a national
unit: with *the*. **2.** The former Union of South Africa. —
adj. Of, pertaining to, or loyal to the U.S.; esp., the Federal
government during the Civil War: a *Union* soldier.

union catalogue A library catalogue that contains the contents of more than one library.

un·ion·ism (yōōn'yan·iz'am) *n.* **1.** The principle of combining for unity of purpose and action. **2.** The principle or
the support of trade unions. **3.** *Usu. cap.* Adherence to the
federal union during the Civil War. — **un'ion·is'tic** *adj.*

un·ion·ist (yōōn'yan·ist) *n.* **1.** An advocate of union or
unionism. **2.** A member of a trade union.

---

rescribed	unprogressive	unpunishable	unreachable	unrecorded	unrelievable
resentable	unprohibited	unpunished	unreached	unrecounted	unrelieved
resentably	unpromising	unpurchasable	unreadable	unrecoverable	unrelished
reserved	unpromisingly	unpure	unrealizable	unrecruited	unremarkable
ressed	unprompted	unpurged	unrealized	unrectified	unremarked
resumptuous	unpronounced	unpurified	unreasoned	unredeemed	unremedied
retending	unpropitiated	unpurposed	unrebukable	unredressed	unremembered
retentious	unpropitiated	unpursuing	unrebuked	unreelable	unremittable
retentiously	unpropitious	unpuzzle	unreceipted	unrefined	unremitted
retentiousness	unpropitiously	unqauffed	unreceivable	unreflected	unremorseful
revailing	unproportionate	unquailing	unreceived	unreflecting	unremorsefully
reventable	unproportioned	unquaking	unreceptive	unreformed	unremorsefulness
revented	unproposed	unqualifying	unreceptively	unrefreshed	unremovable
rimed	unprosperous	unquelled	unreceptiveness	unrefreshing	unremoved
rincely	unprotected	unquenchable	unreciprocated	unregarded	unremunerated
rinted	unproved	unquenched	unreclaimable	unregistered	unremunerative
rivileged	unproven	unquestioning	unreclaimed	unregretted	unrendered
rized	unprovoked	unquotable	unrecognizable	unregulated	unrenewed
robed	unprovoking	unraised	unrecognizably	unrehearsed	unrenounced
rocessed	unpruned	unransomed	unrecognized	unrelated	unrenowned
rocurable	unpublishable	unrated	unrecommended	unrelatedness	unrent
rocured	unpublished	unratified	unrecompensed	unrelaxed	unrented
rofaned	unpucker	unravaged	unreconcilable	unrelaxing	unrepaid
rofited	unpunctual	unrazed	unreconciled	unreliable	unrepairable

---

Un·ion·ist (yōōn′yən·ist) *n.* During the U.S. Civil War, one who supported the Union cause and opposed secession.

un·ion·ize (yōōn′yən·īz) *v.* **·ized, ·iz·ing** *v.t.* **1.** To cause to join, or to organize into a union, especially a labor union. **2.** To make conform to the rules, etc., of a union. — *v.i.* **3.** To become a member of or organize a labor union. — **un′· ion·i·za′tion** *n.*

union jack A flag consisting of the union only.

Union Jack The British national flag, a combination of the flags of England, Scotland, and Ireland.

union shop An industrial establishment that hires only members of a labor union or those who promise to join a union within a specified time.

union suit A one-piece undergarment for men and boys consisting of shirt and drawers.

u·nip·a·rous (yōō·nip′ər·əs) *adj.* **1.** *Biol.* Bringing forth but one offspring at a time, or not having borne more than one. **2.** *Bot.* Having but one axis or stem at each branching.

u·ni·po·lar (yōō′nə·pō′lər) *adj. Physics* Showing only one kind of polarity.

u·nique (yōō·nēk′) *adj.* **1.** Being the only one of its kind; sole. **2.** Being without or having no equal or like. **3.** Loosely, unusual, rare, or notable: a *unique* opportunity. [< F < L < *unus* one] — **u·nique′ly** *adv.* — **u·nique′ness** *n.*

u·ni·sex·u·al (yōō′nə·sek′shōō·əl) *adj. Biol.* Of only one sex; also, having one kind of sexual organs only.

u·ni·son (yōō′nə·sən, -zən) *n.* **1.** A speaking or sounding the same words, tones, etc., simultaneously: with *in*: they answered in *unison*. **2.** Complete accord or agreement; harmony. **3.** *Music* **a** A state in which instruments or voices perform identical parts simultaneously, in the same or different octaves. **b** The interval formed by two tones at the same pitch. [< L < *uni-* one + *sonus* sound]

u·nit (yōō′nit) *n.* **1.** A single person or thing regarded as an individual but belonging to an entire group. **2.** A body or group, as of soldiers, considered as a subdivision of a similar but larger body or group. **3.** An apparatus or piece of equipment, usu. part of a larger object and having a specific function: the cooling *unit* of a freezer. **4.** A standard quantity with which others of the same kind are compared for purposes of measurement and in terms of which their magnitude is stated. **5.** *Math.* A quantity whose measure is represented by the number 1; a least whole number. **6.** *Med.* The quantity of a drug, vaccine, serum, or antigen required to produce a given effect. [Back formation < UNITY]

u·ni·tar·i·an (yōō′nə·târ′ē·ən) *n.* One who rejects the doctrine of the Trinity; a non-Trinitarian monotheist. — *adj.* Of or pertaining to a unit. [< NL *unitarius* unitary]

U·ni·tar·i·an (yōō′nə·târ′ē·ən) *n.* A member of a religious denomination that rejects the doctrine of the Trinity and emphasizes complete freedom of religious opinion, the importance of personal character, and the independence of each local congregation. — *adj.* Of or pertaining to the Unitarians, or to their teachings. — **U′ni·tar′i·an·ism** *n.*

u·ni·tar·y (yōō′nə·ter′ē) *adj.* **1.** Of or pertaining to a unit. **2.** Characterized by or based on unity, as a system of government. **3.** Having the nature of a unit; whole.

u·nite (yōō·nīt′) *v.* **u·nit·ed, u·nit·ing** *v.t.* **1.** To join together so as to form a whole; combine; compound. **2.** To bring into close connection, as by legal, physical, social, or other tie; join in action, interest, etc. **3.** To join in marriage. **4.** To attach permanently or solidly; cause to adhere; bond. **5.** To show or possess (characteristics, etc.) in combination: to *unite* wit and beauty. — *v.i.* **6.** To become or be merged into one; combine. **7.** To join together for action; concur. [< LL *unitus*, pp. of *unire* to make one < L *unus* one]

— **Syn. 1.** consolidate, amalgamate, merge, blend, fuse. **2.** connect, join, link, associate. — **Ant.** divide, separate, disconnect.

u·nit·ed (yōō·nī′tid) *adj.* Incorporated into one; allie combined. — **u·nit′ed·ly** *adv.* — **u·nit′ed·ness** *n.*

United Church of Canada A church made up of form denominational Methodists, Presbyterians, and others.

United Nations 1. A coalition to resist the aggression the axis powers in World War II, formed of 26 nations January, 1942. **2.** An organization of sovereign states, ha ing its permanent headquarters in an enclave of internatic al territory in New York City since 1951, created by t **United Nations Charter** drafted in September–October, 19 at Dumbarton Oaks, an estate in Washington, D.C., a adopted at San Francisco in May and June, 1945. T original membership was formed of 51 states. In 1964 th were 62 additional members. Formerly **United Natic Organization.** Abbr. *UN, U.N.*

United Nations Trust Territory See TRUST TERRITOR

United Press International An organization for colle ing and distributing news, formed in 1958 by a merger of t similar organizations, the International News Service a the United Press. Abbr. *UPI, U.P.I.*

unit modifier A conventional or improvised compou used adjectively before a substantive. Examples: *blue-gr* algae, *bitter-sweet* chocolate, *suit-coat* pattern.

◆ The use of the hyphen in the unit modifier is to av ambiguity in a word sequence where the relationship is immediately apparent from context: The house had fac red-brick walls (faded walls of red brick, *not* faded red wa of brick). The hyphen here is to be considered a nonce and not a spelling form or variant.

u·ni·ty (yōō′nə·tē) *n. pl.* **·ties 1.** The state or fact of be one. **2.** Something that is wholly united and complete wi in itself. **3.** A state or quality of general concord and m tual understanding; harmony. **4.** The harmonious agr ment of parts or elements into one united whole. **5.** T condition or fact of being free from variety or diversity. Singleness or constancy of purpose, action, etc. **7.** In and literature, the arrangement of parts into a homogene whole exhibiting oneness of purpose, thought, spirit, a style. **8.** *Math.* **a** The number one. **b** The element of number system that leaves any number unchanged und multiplication, that is, a number *e* such that $ex = xe = x$ all *x*. [< OF < L < *unus* one]

u·ni·va·lent (yōō′nə·vā′lənt) *adj. Chem.* Having a vale or combining value of one; monovalent. — **u/ni·va′len u/ni·va′len·cy** *n.*

u·ni·valve (yōō′nə·valv′) *adj.* Having only one valve, a mollusk. Also **u/ni·valved′, u/ni·val′vu·lar** (-val′vyə·lər). *n.* **1.** A mollusk having a univalve shell; a gastropod. **2.** shell of a single piece.

u·ni·ver·sal (yōō′nə·vûr′səl) *adj.* **1.** Of, pertaining to, typical of all or the whole: a *universal* reaction. **2.** Incl ing, involving, or intended for all: a *universal* law. **3.** plicable to everyone or to all cases: a *universal* cure. **4.** T can be used or understood by all: a *universal* language. Accomplished or interested in all or many subjects, acti ties, etc.: a *universal* genius. **6.** Of, pertaining to, or occ ring throughout the universe. **7.** Common to all in any s cific group or field: a *universal* practice of politicians. *Mech.* **a** Adapted or adaptable to a great variety of us shapes, etc., as certain machine parts. **b** Permitting f movement within fixed extremes, as a joint. **9.** *Logic* **a** cluding all the individuals of a class or genus; generic. **b** I proposition, predicable of all the individuals denoted by subject: opposed to *particular*: "All men are mortal" i *universal* proposition. — *n.* **1.** *Logic* A universal prop tion. **2.** Any general or universal notion, condition, pr ciple, etc. — **u/ni·ver′sal·ly** *adv.* — **u/ni·ver′sal·ness** *n.*

U·ni·ver·sal·ism (yōō′nə·vûr′səl·iz/əm) *n. Theol.* The d

ne that all souls will finally be saved and that good will tri-
ph universally. — U′ni·ver·sal·ist *adj. & n.*

i·ver·sal·i·ty (yōō′nə·vər·sal′ə·tē) *n. pl.* ·ties 1. The
te or quality of being universal. 2. Unrestricted fitness or
aptability. 3. An all-embracing range of knowledge, abil-
e, etc.

i·ver·sal·ize (yōō′nə·vûr′səl·īz) *v.t.* ·ized, ·iz·ing To
ke universal.

versal joint *Mech.* A joint that permits connected
rts of a machine to be turned in any direction within defi-
e limits. Also **universal coupling.**

i·ver·sal·ly (yōō′nə·vûr′sə·lē) *adv.* In a universal man-
r; on all occasions or in all places; without exception.

i·verse (yōō′nə·vûrs) *n.* 1. The aggregate of all existing
ings; the whole creation embracing all celestial bodies and
of space; the cosmos. 2. In restricted sense, the earth.
Human beings collectively; mankind. [< F < L < *unus*
e + *versus*, pp. of *vertere* to turn]

i·ver·si·ty (yōō′nə·vûr′sə·tē) *n. pl.* ·ties 1. An institu-
n for higher instruction that includes one or more schools
colleges for graduate or professional study, as well as an
dergraduate division, and grants master's and doctor's de-
ee. 2. The faculty and students of a university. 3. The
ildings and grounds of a university. [< OF < L *univer-*
as the whole, entire number]

iv·o·cal (yōō·niv′ə·kəl) *adj.* Having but one proper
se or meaning. — *n.* A word that has but one meaning.
LL < L *unus* one + *vox, vocis* voice]

just (un·just′) *adj.* 1. Not legitimate, fair, or just;
ongful. 2. Acting contrary to right and justice; unright-
us. — **un·just′ly** *adv.* — **un·just′ness** *n.*

kempt (un·kempt′) *adj.* 1. Not combed. 2. Not clean
neat; untidy. 3. Without polish or refinement; rough.
UN-¹ + *kempt* combed, pp. of dial. *kemb*, var. of COMB]

kind (un·kīnd′) *adj.* Showing lack of kindness; unsym-
thetic; cruel. — **un·kind′ly** *adv.* — **un·kind′ness** *n.*

knit (un·nit′) *v.* ·knit or ·knit·ted, ·knit·ting — *v.t.* 1.
untie or unravel (something tied or knit). 2. To smooth
t (something wrinkled). — *v.i.* 3. To become unknitted.

known (un·nōn′) *adj.* 1. Not known or apprehended;
t recognized, as a fact or person. 2. Not ascertained, dis-
vered, or established: an *unknown* element. — *n.* An un-
own person or quantity.

known Soldier One of the unidentified dead of World
ar I who is honored as a symbol of all his compatriots who
ed in action, extended to include unknown dead of World
ar II and the Korean conflict.

la·bored (un·lā′bərd) *adj.* 1. Produced without strain
effort; seemingly free and easy; natural. 2. Uncultivated
labor; unworked; untilled. Also *Brit.* **un·la′boured.**

lace (un·lās′) *v.t.* ·laced, ·lac·ing 1. To loosen or un-
ten the lacing of; untie. 2. To loosen or remove (armor
clothing) in this way.

lade (un·lād′) *v.t. & v.i.* ·lad·ed, ·lad·ing 1. To unload
e cargo of (a ship). 2. To unload or discharge (cargo, etc.).

laid (un·lād′) *adj.* 1. Not laid or placed; not fixed. 2.
t allayed or pacified. 3. Not twisted, as the strands of a
pe.

latch (un·lach′) *v.t.* 1. To open or unlock by releasing
e latch. — *v.i.* 2. To come open or unlocked.

law·ful (un·lô′fəl) *adj.* 1. Contrary to or in violation of
w; illegal. 2. Born out of wedlock; illegitimate. — **un·**
w′ful·ly *adv.* — **un·law′ful·ness** *n.*

lay (un·lā′) *v.t. & v.i.* ·laid, ·lay·ing To untwist: said of
e strands of a rope.

un·learn (un·lûrn′) *v.t. & v.i.* ·learned or ·learnt, ·learn·ing
To dismiss from the mind; forget.

un·learn·ed (un·lûr′nid; *for def. 3* un·lûrnd′) *adj.* 1. Not
possessed of or characterized by learning; illiterate; ignorant. 2. Unworthy of or unlike a learned man. 3. Not acquired by learning or study. — **un·learn′ed·ly** *adv.*

un·leash (un·lēsh′) *v.t.* To set free from or as from a leash.

un·leav·ened (un·lev′ənd) *adj.* Not leavened: said esp. of
the bread used at the feast of the Passover.

un·less (un·les′) *conj.* If it be not a fact that; supposing
that . . . not; except that: *Unless* we persevere, we shall lose.
— *prep.* Save; except; excepting: with an implied verb: *Un-*
less a miracle, he'll not be back in time. [Earlier *onlesse*
(*that*) (than) in a less case < ON + LESS]

un·let·tered (un·let′ərd) *adj.* Not educated; illiterate.

un·like (un·līk′) *adj.* Having little or no resemblance; different. — *prep.* Dissimilar to or different from; not like: It
was *unlike* him to say so. — **un·like′ness** *n.*

un·like·ly (un·līk′lē) *adj.* 1. Not likely; improbable. 2.
Not inviting or promising success. — *adv.* Improbably. —
un·like′li·ness, un·like′li·hood *n.*

un·lim·ber (un·lim′bər) *v.t. & v.i.* To disconnect (a gun or
caisson) from its limber; prepare for action.

un·lim·it·ed (un·lim′it·id) *adj.* 1. Having no limits in
space, number, or time; unbounded. 2. Not limited by restrictions. 3. Not limited by qualifications; undefined. —
— **un·lim′it·ed·ly** *adv.* — **un·lim′it·ed·ness** *n.*

un·load (un·lōd′) *v.t.* 1. To remove the load or cargo from.
2. To take off or discharge (cargo, etc.). 3. To relieve of
something burdensome or oppressive. 4. To withdraw the
charge of ammunition from. 5. *Informal* To dispose of. —
v.i. 6. To discharge freight, cargo, or other burden. — **un·**
load′er *n.*

un·lock (un·lok′) *v.t.* 1. To unfasten (something locked).
2. To open or undo; release. 3. To lay open; reveal or disclose. — *v.i.* 4. To become unlocked.

un·looked-for (un·lŏŏkt′·fôr′) *adj.* Not anticipated.

un·loose (un·lōōs′) *v.t.* ·loosed, ·loos·ing To release from
fastenings; set loose or free.

un·loos·en (un·lōō′sən) *v.t.* To loose; unloose.

un·luck·y (un·luk′ē) *adj.* ·luck·i·er, ·luck·i·est 1. Not favored by luck; unfortunate. 2. Resulting in or attended by
ill luck. 3. Ill-omened; inauspicious: an *unlucky* day. —
un·luck′i·ly *adv.* — **un·luck′i·ness** *n.*

un·make (un·māk′) *v.t.* ·made (-mād′), ·mak·ing 1. To reduce to the original condition or form. 2. To ruin; destroy.
3. To depose, as from a position of authority.

un·man (un·man′) *v.t.* ·manned, ·man·ning 1. To cause to
lose courage or fortitude; dishearten. 2. To render unmanly
or effeminate. 3. To deprive of virility; castrate.

un·man·ly (un·man′lē) *adj.* 1. Not masculine or virile; effeminate. 2. Not honorable. — **un·man′li·ness** *n.*

un·man·ner·ly (un·man′ər·lē) *adj.* Lacking manners; rude.
— *adv.* Impolitely; rudely. — **un·man′ner·li·ness** *n.*

un·mask (un·mask′, -mäsk′) *v.t.* 1. To remove a mask
from. 2. To reveal or disclose the truth about. — *v.i.* 3.
To remove one's mask or disguise.

un·mean·ing (un·mē′ning) *adj.* 1. Having no meaning.
2. Showing no expression of intelligence, interest, etc.; empty. — **un·mean′ing·ly** *adv.* — **un·mean′ing·ness** *n.*

un·meet (un·mēt′) *adj.* Not meet or suitable; not proper;
unbecoming. — **un·meet′ly** *adv.* — **un·meet′ness** *n.*

un·men·tion·a·ble (un·men′shən·ə·bəl) *adj.* Not proper to
be mentioned or discussed; embarrassing; shameful. — **un·**
men′tion·a·ble·ness *n.* — **un·men′tion·a·bly** *adv.*

hamed	unsisterly	unsolved	unsprinkled	unstripped	unsusceptible
hapely	unsized	unsoothed	unsprung	unstuffed	unsuspicious
hared	unskeptical	unsophistication	unsquandered	unstung	unsuspiciously
haved	unslacked	unsorted	unsquared	unsubdued	unsustainable
haven	unslaked	unsought	unstack	unsubmissive	unsustained
hed	unsleeping	unsounded	unstainable	unsubscribed	unswayed
helled	unslumbering	unsoured	unstained	unsubsidized	unsweetened
heltered	unsmiling	unsowed	unstalked	unsubstantiated	unswept
hielded	unsmilingly	unsown	unstamped	unsuccess	unswerving
hod	unsmirched	unspecified	unstandardized	unsuccessful	unsworn
horn	unsmoked	unspeculative	unstarched	unsuggestive	unsymmetrical
hrinkable	unsoaked	unspeculatively	unstarred	unsuited	unsymmetrically
hrinking	unsober	unspelled	unstated	unsullied	unsympathetic
hriven	unsocial	unspent	unstatesmanlike	unsunk	unsympathetically
hrouded	unsoftened	unspilled	unsteadfast	unsupportable	unsympathizing
hrunk	unsoiled	unspilt	unstemmed	unsupportably	unsympathizingly
hunned	unsold	unspiritual	unsterile	unsupported	unsystematic
hut	unsoldierly	unspirituality	unsterilized	unsupportedly	unsystematically
ifted	unsolicited	unspiritually	unstick	unsuppressed	unsystematized
igned	unsolicitous	unspiritualness	unstigmatized	unsure	untack
ilenced	unsolid	unspoiled	unstinted	unsurmountable	untactful
imilar	unsolidly	unspoilt	unstitched	unsurpassable	untactfully
ingable	unsoluble	unspoken	unstrained	unsurpassed	untactfulness
inkable	unsolvable	unsportsmanlike	unstressed	unsurprised	untainted

un·men·tion·a·bles (un-men′shən-ə-bəlz) *n.pl.* Things not ordinarily mentioned; usu., undergarments.

un·mer·ci·ful (un-mûr′sə-fəl) *adj.* Showing no mercy; pitiless. **—un·mer′ci·ful·ly** *adv.* **—un·mer′ci·ful·ness** *n.*

un·mind·ful (un-mīnd′fəl) *adj.* Neglectful; inattentive; careless. **—un·mind′ful·ly** *adv.* **—un·mind′ful·ness** *n.*

un·mis·tak·a·ble (un′mis-tā′kə-bəl) *adj.* That cannot be mistaken; evident; clear. **—un′mis·tak′a·bly** *adv.*

un·mit·i·gat·ed (un-mit′ə-gā′tid) *adj.* **1.** Not mitigated or lightened in effect: *unmitigated* sorrow. **2.** Absolute: an *unmitigated* rogue. **—un·mit′i·gat′ed·ly** *adv.*

un·mor·al (un-môr′əl, -mōr′-) *adj.* Having no moral sense; neither moral nor immoral. **—un·mo·ral·i·ty** (un′mə-ral′ə-tē) *n.* **—un·mor′al·ly** *adv.*

un·nat·u·ral (un-nach′ər-əl) *adj.* **1.** Contrary to the laws of nature. **2.** Monstrous; inhuman: *unnatural* crimes. **3.** Not having, or inconsistent with, those attitudes, feelings, etc., considered normal; abnormal. **4.** Artificial; affected; not essential. **—un·nat′u·ral·ly** *adv.* **—un·nat′u·ral·ness** *n.*

un·nec·es·sar·y (un-nes′ə-ser′ē) *adj.* Not required or necessary; not essential. **—un·nec′es·sar′i·ly** *adv.*

un·nerve (un-nûrv′) *v.t.* **·nerved**, **·nerv·ing** To deprive of strength; firmness, self-control, or courage; unman.

un·num·bered (un-num′bərd) *adj.* **1.** Not counted. **2.** Innumerable. **3.** Not marked with or assigned a number.

un·oc·cu·pied (un-ok′yə-pīd) *adj.* **1.** Empty; not dwelt in; uninhabited: an *unoccupied* house. **2.** Idle; unemployed.

un·or·gan·ized (un-ôr′gən-īzd) *adj.* **1.** Not organized in structure, system, government, etc. **2.** Not living; inorganic. **3.** Not unionized. Also *Brit.* **un·or′gan·ised**.

un·or·tho·dox (un-ôr′thə-doks) *adj.* Not orthodox in doctrine, manner, method, etc. **—un·or′tho·dox′ly** *adv.*

un·pack (un-pak′) *v.t.* **1.** To open and take out the contents of. **2.** To take out of the container, as something packed. **—v.i. 3.** To unpack a trunk, etc. **—un·pack′er** *n.*

un·paged (un-pājd′) *adj.* Having the pages unnumbered: said of a book, magazine, etc.

un·par·al·leled (un-par′ə-leld) *adj.* Without parallel; unmatched; unprecedented.

un·par·lia·men·ta·ry (un′pär-lə-men′tər-ē) *adj.* Contrary to the rules that govern parliamentary bodies. **—un′par·lia·men·ta·ri·ly** *adv.* **—un′par·lia·men′ta·ri·ness** *n.*

un·peg (un-peg′) *v.t.* **·pegged**, **·peg·ging** To open or unfasten by removing a peg or pegs.

un·peo·ple (un-pē′pəl) *v.t.* **·pled**, **·pling** To take or remove people from; depopulate. **—un·peo′pled** *adj.*

un·pin (un-pin′) *v.t.* **·pinned**, **·pin·ning** **1.** To remove the pins from. **2.** To unfasten by removing pins.

un·pleas·ant (un-plez′ənt) *adj.* Disagreeable; objectionable; not pleasing. **—un·pleas′ant·ly** *adv.* **—un·pleas′ant·ness** *n.*

un·plumbed (un-plumd′) *adj.* **1.** Not sounded or explored fully; unfathomed. **2.** Not furnished with plumbing.

un·polled (un-pōld′) *adj.* **1.** Not registered: an *unpolled* vote or voter. **2.** Not having voted at an election.

un·pop·u·lar (un-pop′yə-lər) *adj.* Having no popularity; generally disliked or condemned. **—un·pop′u·lar·ly** *adv.* **—un·pop·u·lar·i·ty** (-lar′ə-tē) *n.*

un·prac·ticed (un-prak′tist) *adj.* **1.** Being without practice, experience, or skill. **2.** Not carried out in practice; not used. **3.** Not yet tried.

un·prec·e·dent·ed (un-pres′ə-den′tid) *adj.* Being without precedent; unheard-of. **—un·prec′e·dent′ed·ly** *adv.*

un·prej·u·diced (un-prej′oo-dist) *adj.* **1.** Free from prejudice or bias; impartial. **2.** Not impaired, as a right.

un·priced (un-prīst′) *adj.* Having no fixed price.

un·prin·ci·pled (un-prin′sə-pəld) *adj.* Lacking in moral principles; unscrupulous. **—un·prin′ci·pled·ness** *n.*

un·print·a·ble (un-prin′tə-bəl) *adj.* Not fit to be printed.

un·pro·fes·sion·al (un′prə-fesh′ən-əl) *adj.* **1.** Having no profession or no professional status. **2.** Violating the rules or ethical code of a profession. **—un′pro·fes′sion·al·ly** *adv.*

un·qual·i·fied (un-kwol′ə-fīd) *adj.* **1.** Being without proper qualifications; unfit. **2.** Without limitation or restrictions; absolute; entire: *unqualified* approval. **—un·qual′i·fied′ly** *adv.* **—un·qual′i·fied′ness** *n.*

un·ques·tion·a·ble (un-kwes′chən-ə-bəl) *adj.* Too certain or sure to admit of question; being beyond a doubt; indisputable. **—un·ques′tion·a·bil′i·ty, un·ques′tion·a·ble·ness** *n.* **—un·ques′tion·a·bly** *adv.*

un·qui·et (un-kwī′ət) *adj.* **1.** Not at rest; disturbed; restless. **2.** Causing unrest or discomfort. **3.** Uneasy; disturbing. **—un·qui′et·ly** *adv.* **—un·qui′et·ness** *n.*

un·quote (un-kwōt′) *v.t. & v.i.* **·quot·ed**, **·quot·ing** To close (a quotation).

un·rav·el (un-rav′əl) *v.* **·eled** or **·elled**, **·el·ing** or **·el·ling** **1.** To separate the threads of, as a tangled skein or knitted article. **2.** To free from entanglement; unfold; explain, as a mystery or a plot. **—v.i. 3.** To become unraveled.

un·read (un-red′) *adj.* **1.** Not informed by reading; ignorant. **2.** Not yet perused.

un·read·y (un-red′ē) *adj.* **1.** Being without readiness or alertness. **2.** Not in a condition to act effectively; unprepared. **—un·read′i·ly** *adv.* **—un·read′i·ness** *n.*

un·real (un-rēl′, -rē′əl) *adj.* **1.** Having no reality or substance. **2.** Artificial; insincere; also, fanciful. **—un·re·al·i·ty** (un′rē-al′ə-tē) *n.* **—un·re′al·ly** *adv.*

un·rea·son·a·ble (un-rē′zən-ə-bəl) *adj.* **1.** Acting without or contrary to reason. **2.** Not according to reason; irrational. **3.** Immoderate; exorbitant. **—un·rea′son·a·bil′i·ty, rea′son·a·ble·ness** *n.* **—un·rea′son·a·bly** *adv.*

un·rea·son·ing (un-rē′zən·ing) *adj.* Not accompanied by reason or control. **—un·rea′son·ing·ly** *adv.*

un·reck·on·a·ble (un-rek′ən-ə-bəl) *adj.* That cannot be reckoned or computed; unlimited.

un·re·con·struct·ed (un′rē-kən-struk′tid) *adj.* **1.** Not constructed. **2.** Not reconciled to or accepting the conditions of the Reconstruction.

un·reel (un-rēl′) *v.t. & v.i.* To unwind, as from a reel.

un·re·gen·er·ate (un′ri-jen′ər-it) *adj.* **1.** Not having been changed spiritually; remaining unreconciled to God. **2.** Sinful; wicked. Also **un′re·gen′er·at′ed** (-ā′tid). **—un′re·gen′er·a·cy** (-ə·sē) *n.* **—un′re·gen′er·ate·ly** *adv.*

un·re·lent·ing (un′ri·len′ting) *adj.* **1.** Not relenting; pitiless; inexorable. **2.** Not diminishing, or not changing, as pace, effort, speed, etc. **—un·re·lent′ing·ly** *adv.*

un·re·li·gious (un′ri-lij′əs) *adj.* **1.** Irreligious; hostile to religion. **2.** Not connected in any way with religion.

un·re·mit·ting (un′ri-mit′ing) *adj.* Not relaxing or stopping; incessant. **—un′re·mit′ting·ly** *adv.* **—un′re·mit′ting·ness** *n.*

un·re·served (un′ri-zûrvd′) *adj.* **1.** Given or done without reserve; full; unlimited. **2.** Having no reserve of manner; informal; open; frank. **—un·re·serv·ed·ly** (un′ri-zûr′vid-) *adv.* **—un′re·serv′ed·ness** *n.*

un·rest (un-rest′) *n.* **1.** Restlessness, esp. of the mind.

untaken	unthriftily	untrimmed	unveiled	unwatched	unwomanish
untalented	unthriftiness	untroubled	unventilated	unwavering	unwomanishl
untamable	unthrifty	untrustful	unveracious	unwaveringly	unwomanly
untame	unthrone	untrustiness	unveraciously	unweakened	unwon
untameable	untillable	untrusty	unveraciousness	unweaned	unwooded
untamed	untilled	untuck	unverifiable	unwearable	unwooed
untangled	untilted	untufted	unverifiableness	unwearily	unworkabilit
untanned	untinged	untunable	unverifiably	unweary	unworkable
untarnished	untired	untuned	unverified	unwearying	unworkablen
untapped	untiring	untuneful	unversed	unwearyingly	unworked
untasted	untiringly	unturned	unvexed	unweathered	unworkmanl
untaxable	untouched	untwilled	unvext	unweave	unworn
untaxed	untraceable	untwisted	unvisited	unwed	unworshiped
unteachable	untraced	untypical	unvitiated	unwedded	unworshippe
untechnical	untracked	untypically	unvitrified	unweeded	unwound
untempered	untractable	untypicalness	unvocal	unwelcome	unwounded
untenanted	untrained	ununiform	unvocally	unwelded	unwoven
untended	untrammeled	ununiformly	unvolatilized	unwetted	unwreathe
unterrified	untrammelled	ununited	unvulcanized	unwhetted	unwrought
untested	untransferable	unurged	unwakened	unwhipped	unwrung
untether	untransferred	unusable	unwalled	unwifely	unyielding
untethered	untranslatable	unutilizable	unwanted	unwincing	unyieldingly
unthanked	untranslated	unuttered	unwarlike	unwinking	unyieldingne
unthatched	untransmitted	unvaccinated	unwarmed	unwinning	unyouthful
untheatrical	untrapped	unvacillating	unwarped	unwisdom	unyouthfully
unthinkable	untraversable	unvacillatingly	unwarranted	unwished	unyouthfulne
unthinkably	untraversed	unvalidated	unwashed	unwithered	unzealous
unthought	untreasured	unvanquished	unwasted	unwithering	unzealously
unthoughtful	untrim	unvaried	unwasting	unwitnessed	unzip

'rouble; turmoil, esp. with regard to public or political con-
itions and suggesting premonitions of revolt.

ɪ·rid·dle (un·rid′l) *v.t.* **·dled, ·dling** To solve, as a mys-
ery.

ɪ·ri·fled[1] (un·rī′fəld) *adj.* Smoothbored, as a gun.

ɪ·ri·fled[2] (un·rī′fəld) *adj.* Not rifled, seized, or plundered.

ɪ·right·eous (un·rī′chəs) *adj.* **1.** Not righteous; wicked;
nful. **2.** Contrary to justice; unfair. — **un·right′eous·ly**
dv. — **un·right′eous·ness** *n.*

ɪ·ripe (un·rīp′) *adj.* Not arrived at maturity; not ripe; im-
nature. [OE *unrīpe* untimely] — **un·ripe′ness** *n.*

ɪ·ri·valed (un·rī′vəld) *adj.* Having no rival or competitor;
nequaled; matchless. Also *Brit.* **un·ri′valled.**

ɪ·roll (un·rōl′) *v.t.* **1.** To spread or open (something rolled
p). **2.** To exhibit to view. — *v.i.* **3.** To become unrolled.

ɪ·ruf·fled (un·ruf′əld) *adj.* Not disturbed or agitated emo-
ionally; calm.

ɪ·ru·ly (un·rōō′lē) *adj.* **·li·er, ·li·est** Disposed to resist rule
r discipline; intractable; ungovernable. — **un·ru′li·ness** *n.*

ɪ·sad·dle (un·sad′l) *v.t.* **·dled, ·dling 1.** To remove a sad-
le from. **2.** To throw from the saddle; unhorse.

ɪ·sat·u·rat·ed (un·sach′ə·rā′tid) *adj.* **1.** Containing less
f a solute required for equilibrium, as a solution. **2.** *Chem.*
`apable of uniting with elements or radicals without loss of
he original constituents.

ɪ·sa·vor·y (un·sā′vər·ē) *adj.* **1.** Having a disagreeable
aste or odor. **2.** Suggesting something disagreeable, offen-
ve, or unclean; also, morally bad. Also *Brit.* **un·sa′vour·y.**
— **un·sa′vor·i·ly** *adv.* — **un·sa′vor·i·ness** *n.*

ɪ·say (un·sā′) *v.t.* **·said, ·say·ing** To retract (something
aid).

ɪ·scathed (un·skāthd′) *adj.* Uninjured.

ɪ·scram·ble (un·skram′bəl) *v.t.* **·bled, ·bling** *Informal*
o resolve the confused or disordered condition of.

ɪ·screw (un·skrōō′) *v.t.* **1.** To remove the screw or screws
om. **2.** To remove or detach by withdrawing screws, or by
urning. — *v.i.* **3.** To permit of being unscrewed.

ɪ·scru·pu·lous (un·skrōō′pyə·ləs) *adj.* Not scrupulous;
aving no scruples or morals; unprincipled. — **un·scru′pu-
us·ly** *adv.* — **un·scru′pu·lous·ness** *n.*

ɪ·seal (un·sēl′) *v.t.* **1.** To break the seal of. **2.** To open.

ɪ·search·a·ble (un·sûr′chə·bəl) *adj.* That cannot be
earched or explored; hidden; mysterious. — **un·search′a-
le·ness** *n.* — **un·search′a·bly** *adv.*

ɪ·sea·son·a·ble (un·sē′zən·ə·bəl) *adj.* **1.** Not being in or
haracteristic of the season. **2.** Inappropriate; ill-timed.
— **un·sea′son·a·ble·ness** *n.* — **un·sea′son·a·bly** *adv.*

ɪ·seat (un·sēt′) *v.t.* **1.** To remove from a seat or fixed posi-
on. **2.** To unhorse. **3.** To deprive of office or rank; depose.

ɪ·seem·ly (un·sēm′lē) *adj.* **·li·er, ·li·est** Not seemly or
roper; unbecoming; indecent. — *adv.* In an unseemly fash-
n. — **un·seem′li·ness** *n.*

ɪ·self·ish (un·sel′fish) *adj.* Not selfish; generous. — **un-
elf′ish·ly** *adv.* — **un·self′ish·ness** *n.*

ɪ·set·tle (un·set′l) *v.* **·tled, ·tling** *v.t.* **1.** To change or
ove from a fixed or settled condition. **2.** To confuse; dis-
urb. — *v.i.* **3.** To become unsteady or unfixed.

ɪ·sex (un·seks′) *v.t.* To deprive of the distinctive qualities
f a sex; esp., to render unfeminine or unwomanly.

ɪ·shack·le (un·shak′əl) *v.t.* **·led, ·ling** To unfetter; free
om or as from shackles.

ɪ·sheathe (un·shēth′) *v.t.* **·sheathed, ·sheath·ing** To take
om or as from a scabbard or sheath; bare.

ɪ·ship (un·ship′) *v.t.* **·shipped, ·ship·ping 1.** To unload
om a ship or other vessel. **2.** To remove from the place
here it is fixed or fitted, as a rudder or oar.

ɪ·sight·ly (un·sīt′lē) *adj.* **·li·er, ·li·est** Offensive to the
ght; ugly. — **un·sight′li·ness** *n.*

ɪ·skilled (un·skild′) *adj.* **1.** Destitute of skill or dexterity.
. Not requiring special skill or training: *unskilled* labor.

ɪ·skill·ful (un·skil′fəl) *adj.* Lacking or not evincing skill-
ulness; awkward. Also *Brit.* **un·skil′ful.** — **un·skill′ful·ly**
dv. — **un·skill′ful·ness** *n.*

ɪ·snap (un·snap′) *v.t.* **·snapped, ·snap·ping** To undo the
nap or snaps of; unfasten.

ɪ·snarl (un·snärl′) *v.t.* To disentangle.

ɪ·so·cia·ble (un·sō′shə·bəl) *adj.* **1.** Not sociable; not in-
lined to seek the society of others. **2.** Not congenial or in
ccord. **3.** Not encouraging social intercourse. — **un·so′-
ia·bil·i·ty, un·so′cia·ble·ness** *n.* — **un·so′cia·bly** *adv.*

ɪ·sol·der (un·sod′ər) *v.t.* **1.** To disunite or take apart
something soldered. **2.** To separate; sunder.

ɪ·so·phis·ti·cat·ed (un′sə·fis′tə·kā′tid) *adj.* **1.** Not so-
histicated; artless; simple. **2.** Free from adulteration; gen-
ine; pure. — **un′so·phis′ti·cat′ed·ly** *adv.* — **un′so·phis′ti-
at′ed·ness** *n.*

ɪ·sound (un·sound′) *adj.* **1.** Lacking in soundness; not
trong or solid; weak. **2.** Not sound in health; diseased. **3.**

Not logically valid; erroneous. **4.** Disturbed; not profound:
said of sleep. — **un·sound′ly** *adv.* — **un·sound′ness** *n.*

un·spar·ing (un·spâr′ing) *adj.* **1.** Not sparing or saving;
lavish; liberal. **2.** Showing no mercy. — **un·spar′ing·ly**
adv. — **un·spar′ing·ness** *n.*

un·speak·a·ble (un·spē′kə·bəl) *adj.* **1.** That cannot be expressed; unutterable. **2.** Extremely bad or objectionable.
— **un·speak′a·ble·ness** *n.* — **un·speak′a·bly** *adv.*

un·sta·ble (un·stā′bəl) *adj.* **1.** Lacking in stability or firmness; not stable. **2.** Having no fixed purposes; easily influenced; inconstant. **3.** *Chem.* Readily decomposable, as certain compounds. — **un·sta′ble·ness** *n.* — **un·sta′bly** *adv.*

un·stead·y (un·sted′ē) *adj.* **1.** Not steady or firm; shaky.
2. Not regular or constant; wavering: the motor's *unsteady*
movement. **3.** Inconstant and erratic in behavior, habits,
etc. — **un·stead′i·ly** *adv.* — **un·stead′i·ness** *n.*

un·stop (un·stop′) *v.t.* **·stopped, ·stop·ping 1.** To remove a
stopper from. **2.** To open by removing obstructions; clear.

un·strap (un·strap′) *v.t.* **·strapped, ·strap·ping** To unfasten
or loosen the strap or straps of.

un·string (un·string′) *v.t.* **·strung, ·string·ing 1.** To remove
from a string. **2.** To take the string or strings from. **3.** To
loosen the string or strings of. **4.** To weaken: usu., in the
passive: Her nerves were *unstrung.*

un·strung (un·strung′) *adj.* **1.** Having the strings removed
or relaxed. **2.** Unnerved; emotionally upset; weakened.

un·stud·ied (un·stud′ēd) *adj.* **1.** Not planned; unpremedi-
tated. **2.** Not stiff or artificial; natural. **3.** Not acquainted
through study; unversed: with *in.*

un·sub·stan·tial (un′səb·stan′shəl) *adj.* **1.** Lacking solidity, strength, or weight. **2.** Having no valid basis. **3.** Having no bodily existence; unreal; fanciful. — **un′sub·stan′-
tial·ly** *adv.* — **un·sub·stan·ti·al·i·ty** (-shē·al′ə·tē) *n.*

un·suit·a·ble (un·sōō′tə·bəl) *adj.* Not suitable; unfitting.
— **un·suit·a·bil·i·ty** (un′sōō·tə·bil′ə·tē), **un·suit′a·ble·ness** *n.*
— **un·suit′a·bly** *adv.*

un·sung (un·sung′) *adj.* **1.** Not celebrated in song or poetry; obscure. **2.** Not yet sung, as a song.

un·tan·gle (un·tang′gəl) *v.t.* **·gled, ·gling 1.** To free from
entanglement or snarls. **2.** To clear up; resolve.

un·taught (un·tôt′) *adj.* **1.** Not instructed; ignorant. **2.**
Acquired without training or instruction; natural.

un·ten·a·ble (un·ten′ə·bəl) *adj.* That cannot be maintained
or defended: *untenable* theories. — **un·ten′a·bil·i·ty, un·ten′-
a·ble·ness** *n.*

un·thank·ful (un·thangk′fəl) *adj.* **1.** Not grateful. **2.** Not
received with thanks; unwelcome. — **un·thank′ful·ly** *adv.*
— **un·thank′ful·ness** *n.*

un·think·ing (un·thingk′ing) *adj.* **1.** Not having the power
of thought. **2.** Thoughtless; careless; heedless; inconsider-
ate. — **un·think′ing·ly** *adv.* — **un·think′ing·ness** *n.*

un·thought-of (un·thôt′uv′) *adj.* **1.** Not remembered or
called to mind. **2.** Not conceived of; not discovered.

un·thread (un·thred′) *v.t.* **1.** To remove the thread from,
as a needle. **2.** To find one's way out of, as a maze.

un·ti·dy (un·tī′dē) *adj.* **·di·er, ·di·est** Showing lack of tidiness. [ME *untīdi*] — **un·ti′di·ly** *adv.* — **un·ti′di·ness** *n.*

un·tie (un·tī′) *v.* **tied, ·ty·ing** *v.t.* **1.** To loosen or undo, as a
knot. **2.** To free from restraint. **3.** To clear up or resolve.
— *v.i.* **4.** To become untied. [OE *untīgan*]

un·til (un·til′) *prep.* **1.** Up to the time of; till: We will wait
until midnight. **2.** Before: used with a negative: The music
doesn't begin *until* nine. — *conj.* **1.** To the time when:
until I die. **2.** To the place or degree that: Walk east *until*
you reach the river. **3.** Before: with a negative: He couldn't
leave *until* noon. [ME < *un-* up to, as far as + TILL]

un·time·ly (un·tīm′lē) *adj.* **1.** Before the proper or expected time; premature. **2.** At the wrong time; ill-timed. —
adv. Inopportunely. — **un·time′li·ness** *n.*

un·to (un′tōō) *prep.* **1.** *Poetic & Archaic* To. **2.** *Archaic*
Until. [ME *un-* up to, as far as + TO]

un·told (un·tōld′) *adj.* **1.** That cannot be revealed or described; inexpressible: *untold* misery. **2.** That cannot be
numbered or estimated: *untold* numbers. **3.** Not told.

un·touch·a·ble (un·tuch′ə·bəl) *adj.* **1.** Inaccessible to the
touch; out of reach. **2.** Intangible; unrivaled; unapproach-
able. **3.** Forbidden to the touch. **4.** Unpleasant, vile, or
dangerous to touch. — *n.* In India, a member of the lowest
caste, whose touch was formerly counted as pollution by
Hindus of higher station. — **un′touch·a·bil·i·ty** (-bil′ə·tē) *n.*

un·to·ward (un·tôrd′, -tōrd′) *adj.* **1.** Causing hindrance;
vexatious. **2.** Refractory; perverse. **3.** Unseemly; uncouth. — **un·to′ward·ly** *adv.* — **un·to′ward·ness** *n.*

un·trod·den (un·trod′n) *adj.* Not having been trodden
upon; also, unfrequented. Also **un·trod′.**

un·true (un·trōō′) *adj.* **1.** Lacking truth; not true; not corresponding with fact. **2.** Not conforming to rule or standard. **3.** Not faithful; disloyal. — **un·tru′ly** *adv.*

un·truss (un·trus**ʹ**) *v.t.* **1.** To unfasten. **2.** *Obs.* To undress.

un·truth (un·trōōth**ʹ**) *n.* *pl.* **·truths** (-trōōths**ʹ**, -trōōthz**ʹ**) **1.** The quality or character of being untrue; want of veracity. **2.** A lie. — **Syn.** See LIE². [OE *untrēowth*]

un·truth·ful (un·trōōth**ʹ**fəl) *adj.* **1.** Not truthful; untrue. **2.** Given to telling lies. — **un·truth**ʹ**ful·ly** *adv.* — **un·truth**ʹ**ful·ness** *n.*

un·tu·tored (un·tōō**ʹ**tərd, -tyōō**ʹ**-) *adj.* **1.** Having had no tutor or teacher. **2.** Naive; simple.

un·twine (un·twīn**ʹ**) *v.* **·twined, ·twin·ing** *v.t.* **1.** To undo (something twined); unwind by disentangling. — *v.i.* **2.** To become untwined.

un·twist (un·twist**ʹ**) *v.t.* & *v.i.* To unwind or untwine.

un·used (un·yōōzd**ʹ** *for def. 1*; un·yōōst**ʹ** *for def. 2*) *adj.* **1.** Not made use of; also, never having been used. **2.** Not accustomed or wont: with *to.*

un·u·su·al (un·yōō**ʹ**zhōō-əl) *adj.* Not usual, common, or ordinary; rare. — **un·u**ʹ**su·al·ly** *adv.* — **un·u**ʹ**su·al·ness** *n.*

un·ut·ter·a·ble (un·ut**ʹ**ər-ə-bəl) *adj.* **1.** Too great or deep for verbal expression; ineffable. **2.** Unpronounceable. — **un·ut**ʹ**ter·a·ble·ness** *n.* — **un·ut**ʹ**ter·a·bly** *adv.*

un·var·nished (un·vär**ʹ**nisht) *adj.* **1.** Having no covering of varnish. **2.** Having no embellishment; plain.

un·veil (un·vāl**ʹ**) *v.t.* **1.** To remove the veil from; reveal. — *v.i.* **2.** To remove one's veil; reveal oneself.

un·voiced (un·voist**ʹ**) *adj.* **1.** Not expressed. **2.** *Phonet.* **a** Voiceless. **b** Rendered voiceless: The final (v) in "have" is often heard *unvoiced* in "have to."

un·war·y (un·wâr**ʹ**ē) *adj.* Not careful or cautious; imprudent; rash; careless. — **un·war**ʹ**i·ly** *adv.* — **un·war**ʹ**i·ness** *n.*

un·well (un·wel**ʹ**) *adj.* Not well; ailing; sick. — **Syn.** See SICK¹. — **un·well**ʹ**ness** *n.*

un·wept (un·wept**ʹ**) *adj.* **1.** Not lamented or wept for, as a deceased person. **2.** Not shed, as tears.

un·whole·some (un·hōl**ʹ**səm) *adj.* **1.** Harmful to physical or mental health. **2.** Unsound in condition; diseased or decayed: *unwholesome* provisions. **3.** Suggestive of illness or disease: an *unwholesome* look. **4.** Morally bad; pernicious. — **un·whole**ʹ**some·ly** *adv.* — **un·whole**ʹ**some·ness** *n.*

un·wield·y (un·wēl**ʹ**dē) *adj.* Moved or managed with difficulty, as from great size or awkward shape; bulky; clumsy. — **un·wield**ʹ**i·ly** *adv.* — **un·wield**ʹ**i·ness** *n.*

un·will·ing (un·wil**ʹ**ing) *adj.* **1.** Not willing; reluctant; loath. **2.** Done, said, etc., with reluctance. — **un·will**ʹ**ing·ly** *adv.* — **un·will**ʹ**ing·ness** *n.*

un·wind (un·wīnd**ʹ**) *v.* **·wound, ·wind·ing** *v.t.* **1.** To reverse the winding of; untwist or wind off; uncoil. **2.** To disentangle. — *v.i.* **3.** To become unwound.

un·wise (un·wīz**ʹ**) *adj.* Showing a lack of wisdom; imprudent; foolish. [OE *unwīs*] — **un·wise**ʹ**ly** *adv.*

un·wit·ting (un·wit**ʹ**ing) *adj.* **1.** Having no knowledge or consciousness of the thing in question. **2.** Unintentional. [OE *unwitende*] — **un·wit**ʹ**ting·ly** *adv.*

un·wont·ed (un·wun**ʹ**tid, -wont**ʹ**-) *adj.* **1.** Not according to habit or custom; unusual. **2.** *Obs.* Not accustomed; unfamiliar. — **un·wont**ʹ**ed·ly** *adv.* — **un·wont**ʹ**ed·ness** *n.*

un·wor·thy (un·wûr**ʹ**thē) *adj.* **1.** Not deserving: usu., with *of.* **2.** Not befitting or becoming: often with *of*; improper. **3.** Lacking worth or merit. **4.** Shameful; contemptible. — **un·wor**ʹ**thi·ly** *adv.* — **un·wor**ʹ**thi·ness** *n.*

un·wound (un·wound**ʹ**) Past tense and past participle of UNWIND.

un·wrap (un·rap**ʹ**) *v.* **·wrapped, ·wrap·ping** *v.t.* **1.** To take the wrapping from. — *v.i.* **2.** To become unwrapped.

un·wrin·kle (un·ring**ʹ**kəl) *v.t.* **·kled, ·kling** To free from wrinkles; smooth.

un·writ·ten (un·rit**ʹ**n) *adj.* **1.** Not written or in writing. **2.** Not reduced to writing; traditional; customary. **3.** Having no writing upon it; blank.

unwritten law **1.** A rule or custom established by general usage. **2.** Common law (which see). **3.** A custom in some communities granting a measure of immunity to those who commit criminal acts of revenge in support of personal or family honor, esp., in cases of adultery, etc.

un·yoke (un·yōk**ʹ**) *v.* **·yoked, ·yok·ing** *v.t.* **1.** To release from a yoke. **2.** To separate; part. — *v.i.* **3.** To become unyoked. **4.** To stop work; cease. [OE *ungeocian*]

up (up) *adv.* **1.** From a lower to a higher place, level, position, etc.: Come *up.* **2.** In, on, or to a higher place, level, position, etc. **3.** Toward that which is figuratively or conventionally higher; as: **a** To or at a higher price. **b** To or at a higher place, rank, etc. **c** To or at a greater size or amount: to swell *up.* **d** To or at a place that is locally or arbitrarily regarded as higher: *up* north. **e** Above the surface or horizon. **f** From an earlier to a later period. **g** To a source, conclusion, etc.: Follow *up* this lead. **4.** To a vertical position; standing; also, out of bed. **5.** So as to be compact or secure: Tie *up* the boxes. **6.** So as to be even with in space, time, degree, etc.: *up* to date. **7.** In or into an excited state or some specific action: They were stirred *up* to mutiny. **8.** In or into view or existence: to draw *up* a will. **9.** In or into prominence; under consideration: *up* for debate. **10.** In or into a place of safekeeping; aside: Fruits are put *up* in jars. **11.** At an end: Your time is *up.* **12.** Completely; totally: The house was burned *up.* **13.** In baseball and cricket, at bat. **14.** In tennis and other sports: **a** In the lead; ahead. **b** Apiece; alike: said of a score. **15.** Running for as a candidate. **16.** *Naut.* Shifted to windward, as a tiller. ◆ In informal usage *up* is often added to a verb without affecting the meaning of the sentence: to light *up* a room. — **to be all up with** To be all over for. — **to be up against** *Informal* To meet with; confront. — **to be up against it** *Informal* To be in difficulty. — **to be up in** (or **on**) *Informal* To be well informed in or skilled at something. — **to be up to** *Informal* To be doing or plotting. **2.** To be equal to; capable of. **3.** To be incumbent upon; be dependent upon: It's *up* to him to save us. — *adj.* **1.** Moving, sloping, directed upward. **2.** At stake, as in gambling. **3.** *Informal* Going on; taking place: What's *up*? **4.** *Informal* Acquainted (with), equal (to): He is *up* in that subject. **5.** In golf, advance of an opponent by a specified number of holes. **6.** Rising, risen, overflowing, or at flood. **7.** In an active or excited state: His temper was *up.* — **up and around** *Informal* Sufficiently recovered to walk. — **up to no good** *Informal* Engaged in or contemplating some mischief. — *prep.* **1.** From a lower to a higher point or place of, on, or along. **2.** Toward a higher condition or rank on or in. **3.** To or at a point farther above or along: *up* the road. **4.** From the coast toward the interior of (a country). **5.** From the mouth toward the source of (a river). **6.** At, on, or near the height or top of. — *n.* **1.** A rise or ascent. **2.** A period of prosperity, etc., chiefly in the phrase **ups and downs**. — **to be on the up and up 1.** *Slang* To be honest. **2.** *Informal* Rising and improving. — *v.* **upped, up·ping** *Informal* *v.t.* **1.** To increase. **2.** To put or take up. — *v.i.* **3.** To rise. [OE *ūp*]

up- *combining form* As a combining element *up* has adverbial force with various meanings: **1.** To a higher place or level, as in: **upgaze, uprise. 2.** To a greater size or larger amount, as in: **upflooding, upswell. 3.** To a vertical position, as in: **upprop, upstand. 4.** In or into commotion or activity, in: **upboil, upstir. 5.** Completely; wholly, as in: **upbind, upgather.**

up-and-com·ing (up**ʹ**ən·kum**ʹ**ing) *adj.* Enterprising; energetic; promising.

up-and-down (up**ʹ**ən·doun**ʹ**) *adj.* **1.** Alternately rising and falling; fluctuating; varying: an *up-and-down* motion; an *up-and-down* career. **2.** Vertical; perpendicular.

u·pas (yōō**ʹ**pəs) *n.* **1.** A tall evergreen Javanese tree of the mulberry family, having an acrid, poisonous sap. **2.** The sap. [< Malay (*pohon*) *upas* poison (tree)]

up·beat (up**ʹ**bēt**ʹ**) *n.* *Music* The relatively unaccented beat that precedes the downbeat. — *adj.* *Slang* Characterized by a lively, swinging rhythm.

up·braid (up·brād**ʹ**) *v.t.* **1.** To reproach for some wrong doing; scold or reprove. — *v.i.* **2.** To utter reproaches. [< *up-* up + *bregdan* to weave, twist] — **up·braid**ʹ**er** *n.* — **up·braid**ʹ**ing** *n.* — **up·braid**ʹ**ing·ly** *adv.*

up·bring·ing (up**ʹ**bring**ʹ**ing) *n.* The rearing and training received by a person during childhood.

up·coun·try (*n.* & *adj.* up**ʹ**kun**ʹ**trē; *adv.* up**ʹ**kun**ʹ**trē) *Informal* *n.* Country remote from the coast or from lowlands; inland country. — *adj.* Living in, from, or characteristic of inland places. — *adv.* In or toward the interior.

up·date (up·dāt**ʹ**) *v.t.* **·dat·ed, ·dat·ing** To bring up to date, to revise, with corrections, additions, etc., as a textbook.

up·end (up·end**ʹ**) *v.t.* & *v.i.* To set or stand on end.

up·grade (*n.* up**ʹ**grād**ʹ**; *v.* up·grād**ʹ**) *adj.* up**ʹ**grād**ʹ**) *n.* An upward incline or slope. — *v.t.* **·grad·ed, ·grad·ing** To raise to a higher grade, rank, post, etc. — *adv.* Up a hill or slope. — **on the upgrade 1.** Improving. **2.** Rising.

up·heav·al (up·hē**ʹ**vəl) *n.* **1.** The act of upheaving, or the state of being upheaved. **2.** A violent disturbance or change.

up·heave (up·hēv**ʹ**) *v.* **·heaved** or **·hove, ·heav·ing** *v.t.* To heave or raise up. — *v.i.* **2.** To be raised or lifted.

up·held (up·held**ʹ**) Past tense and past participle of UPHOLD.

up·hill (*adv.* & *adj.* up**ʹ**hil**ʹ**; *n.* up**ʹ**hil**ʹ**) *adv.* Up or as up a hill or an ascent; against difficulties. — *adj.* **1.** Going up; ascent; sloping upward. **2.** Attended with difficulty or exertion. **3.** At a high place. — *n.* An upward slope.

up·hold (up·hōld**ʹ**) *v.t.* **·held, ·hold·ing 1.** To hold up; raise. **2.** To keep from falling. **3.** To support; agree with; encourage. **4.** To regard with approval. — **up·hold**ʹ**er** *n.*

up·hol·ster (up·hōl**ʹ**stər) *v.t.* To fit, as furniture, with coverings, cushioning, etc. [Back formation < UPHOLSTERER]

up·hol·ster·er (up·hōl**ʹ**stər-ər) *n.* One who upholsters. [alt. of < ME *upholder* tradesman]

up·hol·ster·y (up·hōl**ʹ**stər-ē, -strē) *n.* *pl.* **·ster·ies 1.** Fabric and fittings used in upholstering. **2.** The act, art, or business of upholstering.

up·keep (up**ʹ**kēp**ʹ**) *n.* The act or state of maintaining something; also, the cost of maintenance.

·land (up'lənd, -land') *n.* **1.** The higher portions of a region, district, farm, etc. **2.** The country in the interior. — *·j.* Pertaining to or situated in an upland.

·lift (*v.* up·lift'; *adj., n.* up'lift') *v.t.* **1.** To lift up; elevate. **,** To raise the tone of; put on a higher plane, mentally or orally. — *n.* **1.** The act of raising, or the fact of being ·ised. **2.** A movement upward. **3.** Mental or spiritual ·imulation or elevation. **4.** A movement aiming to improve ·e condition of the underprivileged. **5.** A brassiere de· ·gned to lift and support the breasts. — **up·lift'er** *n.*

·most (up'mōst') *adj.* Uppermost.

·on (ə·pon', ə·pôn') *prep.* On, in all its meanings. — *adv.* ·n: completing a verbal idea: The paper has been written *·on.* [ME]

upon, on *Upon* now differs little in use from *on*, the former ·ing sometimes used for reasons of euphony and also when ·otion into position is involved. When *upon* means *up* and **,** it is written as two words: Let's go *up on* the roof.

·ove (up'ər) *adj.* **1.** Higher than something else; being ·ove. **2.** Higher or further inland in location, place, etc. **,** Higher in station, rank, dignity, etc.; superior. — **to get ·e upper hand** To get the advantage. — *n.* **1.** That part **,** a boot or shoe above the sole; the vamp. **2.** *Informal* An ·pper berth. — **on one's uppers** *Informal* **1.** Having worn ·t the soles of one's shoes. **2.** At the end of one's resources; ·stitute. [ME, orig. compar. of UP]

·per (up'ər) *adj. Geol.* Designating a later period or a ·er formation of a specified period: the *Upper* Cambrian.

·per berth The top berth in a ship, railroad sleeping car, ·c., where two bunks or beds are built one above the other.

·per-brack·et (up'ər-brak'it) *adj.* Of or belonging to a ·gher bracket or level: an *upper-bracket* income.

·per case *Printing* **1.** Type for capital letters. See CASE[2]. The capital letters of the alphabet.

·per-case (up'ər-kās') *Printing adj.* Of, in, or indicating ·pital letters, as distinguished from small letters. — *v.t.* ·ased, **-cas·ing** To set as or change to capital letters.

·per class The socially or economically superior group in ·ciety. — **up'per-class'** (up'ər-klas', -kläs') *adj.*

·per-class·man (up'ər-klas'mən, -kläs'-) *n. pl.* **·men** ·mən) A junior or senior in a school or college.

·per·cut (up'ər·kut') *n.* In boxing, a swinging blow up· ·ard, delivered under or inside the opponent's guard. — *·t. & v.i.* **-cut, ·cut·ting** To strike with an uppercut.

·per hand Advantage: to get the *upper hand.*

·per House The branch, in a bicameral legislature, where ·embership is usu., smaller and more restricted, as the Brit· ·h House of Lords. Also **upper house.**

·per·most (up'ər·mōst') *adj.* **1.** Highest in place, rank, ·ithority, influence, etc. **2.** First to come into the mind: ·ie's *uppermost* thoughts. Also *upmost.* — *adv.* In the ·ghest place, rank, authority, etc.; also, first, as in time.

·pish (up'ish) *adj. Informal* Inclined to be self-assertive, ·etentious, or snobbish. Also **up·pi·ty** (up'ə·tē). — **up'· ·sh·ly** *adv.* — **up'pish·ness** *n.*

·raise (up·rāz') *v.t.* **·raised, ·rais·ing** To lift up; elevate.

·right (up'rīt') *adj.* **1.** Being in a vertical position; ·raight up; erect. **2.** Just and honest. — *n.* **1.** Something ·ving a vertical position, as an upright piano. **2.** The ·ate of being upright. **3.** In football, one of the goal posts. **·** *adv.* In an upright position; vertically. [OE < *ŭp-* up + *·it* right] — **up'right'ly** *adv.* — **up'right'ness** *n.*

·right piano A piano smaller than a grand piano, having ·rings arranged vertically in a rectangular case.

·ris·ing (up·rī'zing, up'rī'zing) *n.* **1.** The act of rising. **,** A revolt or insurrection. **3.** An ascent; a slope.

·roar (up'rôr', -rōr') *n.* A violent disturbance, noise, or ·mult. [< Du. < *op-* up + *roeren* to stir]

·roar·i·ous (up·rôr'ē·əs, -rō'rē-) *adj.* **1.** Accompanied by **·** making an uproar. **2.** Loud and noisy; tumultuous. **3.** ·ery funny: an *uproarious* play. — **up·roar'i·ous·ly** *adv.* **·** **up·roar'i·ous·ness** *n.*

·root (up·rōōt', -rŏŏt') *v.t.* **1.** To tear up by the roots. **2.** ·o destroy utterly; eradicate. — **up·root'er** *n.*

·set (*v.* up·set'; *adj.* up·set', up'set'; *n.* up'set') *v.* **·set, ·et·ting** *v.t.* **1.** To overturn. **2.** To throw into confusion **·** disorder. **3.** To disconcert, derange, or disquiet. **4.** To ·efeat, esp., unexpectedly. — *v.i.* To become over· ·urned. — *adj.* **1.** Tipped or turned over. **2.** Mentally or ·nysically disturbed or ill. **3.** Confused; disordered. — *n.* **.** The act of upsetting, or the state of being upset. **2.** *In· ·rmal* An unexpected defeat. **3.** A mental or physical dis· ·urbance or disorder. — **up·set'ter** *n.*

·shot (up'shot') *n.* The final outcome; result.

·side (up'sīd') *n.* The upper side or part.

·side-down (up'sīd'doun') *adj.* Having the upper side down ·own; in disorder. — *adv.* With the upper side down. Also **·pside down.** [< ME *up so down* up as if down]

up·si·lon (yōōp'sə·lon, up'sə·lon, *Brit.* yōōp·sī'lən) *n.* The twentieth letter and sixth vowel in the Greek alphabet (Υ, υ). See ALPHABET, Υ. [< Gk. < *u u* + *psilon* smooth]

up·stage (up'stāj') *adj.* **1.** Of the back half of a stage. **2.** *Informal* Haughty; supercilious. — *adv.* Toward or on the back of a stage. — *v.t.* **·staged, ·stag·ing 1.** To steal a scene from. **2.** *Informal* To treat in a haughty manner.

up·stairs (up'stârz') *adj.* Pertaining to an upper story. — *n.* An upper story; esp., the part of a building above the ground floor. — *adv.* In, to, or toward an upper story. — **to kick upstairs** To promote so as to get out of the way.

up·stand·ing (up·stan'ding) *adj.* **1.** Honest; upright; straightforward. **2.** Standing up; erect.

up·start (*v.* up·stärt'; *adj. & n.* up'stärt') *v.i.* To start or spring up suddenly. — *adj.* **1.** Suddenly raised to prominence, wealth, or power. **2.** Characteristic of an upstart; vulgar; pretentious. — *n.* **1.** One who or that which springs up suddenly. **2.** One who has suddenly risen from a humble position to one of wealth or importance and is usu. arrogant in tone or bearing.

up·state (up'stāt') *U.S. adj.* Of, from, or designating that part of a State lying outside, usu. north, of the principal city. — *n.* The outlying, usu. northern, sections of a State. — *adv.* In or toward such sections. — **up'stat'er** *n.*

up·stream (up'strēm') *adv.* Toward or at the source or upper part of a stream; against the current.

up·stretched (up'stretch') *adj.* Stretched or extended upward: *upstretched* arms.

up·stroke (up'strōk') *n.* An upward stroke, as of a pen.

up·surge (*v.* up·sûrj'; *n.* up'sûrj') *v.i.* **·surged, ·surg·ing** To surge up. — *n.* A surge or swell upward.

up·sweep (*n.* up'swēp'; *v.* up·swēp') *n.* A sweeping up or upward; esp., a hairdo that is swept upward smoothly in the back and piled high on the top of the head. — *v.t. & v.i.* **·swept, ·sweep·ing** To brush or sweep upward or up.

up·swing (*n.* up'swing'; *v.* up·swing') *n.* **1.** A swinging up· ward. **2.** An improvement. — *v.i.* **·swung, ·swing·ing 1.** To swing upward. **2.** To improve.

up·take (up'tāk') *n.* **1.** The act of lifting or taking up. **2.** A boiler flue that unites the combustion gases and carries them toward the smokestack. **3.** An upward ventilating shaft in a mine. — **to be on** (or **in**) **the uptake** *Informal* To demonstrate mental comprehension or perception.

up·throw (up'thrō') *n.* **1.** A throwing upward; an upheaval. **2.** *Geol.* An upward displacement of the rock on one side of a fault.

up·thrust (up'thrust') *n.* **1.** An upward thrust. **2.** *Geol.* An upheaval of rocks in the earth's crust.

up·tight (up'tīt') *adj. U.S. Slang* Uneasy, anxious, or tense; nervous. Also **up'-tight', up tight.**

up-to-date (up'tə·dāt') *adj.* **1.** Having the latest information, improvements, etc. **2.** Modern in manner.

up to date To the present time.

up·town (up'toun') *adv.* In or toward the upper part of a town. — *adj.* Of, pertaining to, or resident in the upper part of a town or city, or the part that is regarded as the upper part. — *n.* The upper part of a town or city.

up·turn (*v.* up·tûrn'; *n.* up'tûrn') *v.t.* **1.** To turn up or over, as sod with the plow. **2.** To overturn; upset. — *n.* A turning upward; an increase; an improvement.

up·ward (up'wərd) *adv.* **1.** In, to, or toward a higher place or position. **2.** To or toward the source, origin, etc.: to trace a stream upward. **3.** Toward a higher rank, amount, age, etc. **4.** Toward that which is better, nobler, etc. **5.** In excess; more. Also **up'wards.** — **upward** (or **upwards**) **of** Higher than; in excess of. — *adj.* In, on, turned, or directed toward a higher place. — **up'ward·ly** *adv.*

ur-[1] Var. of URO-[1].

ur-[2] Var. of URO-[2].

Ur (ûr) An ancient city of Sumer, southern Mesopotamia, the site of which is on the Euphrates in SE Iraq. Old Testament *Ur* of the Chal·dees (kal·dēz', kal'dēz).

u·rae·mi·a (yōō·rē'mē·ə), **u·rae·mic** (yōō·rē'mik) See URE· MIA, etc.

U·ral-Al·ta·ic (yōōr'əl·al·tā'ik) *n.* A hypothesized family of languages comprising the Uralic and Altaic subfamilies. — *adj.* **1.** Of or pertaining to the Ural and Altai mountain ranges. **2.** Of, pertaining to, or designating the Ural-Altaic languages or the peoples speaking these languages.

U·ral·ic (yōō·ral'ik) *n.* A family of languages comprising the Finno-Ugric and Samoyedic subfamilies: sometimes classified with Altaic in a Ural-Altaic family. — *adj.* Of or pertaining to this family. Also **U·ra·li·an** (yōō·rā'lē·ən).

u·ra·nal·y·sis (yōōr'ə·nal'ə·sis) See URINALYSIS.

U·ra·ni·a (yōō·rā'nē·ə) The Muse of astronomy. [< L < Gk. *ouranos* heaven]

U·ra·ni·an (yōō·rā'nē·ən) *adj.* **1.** Of or pertaining to the planet Uranus. **2.** Celestial.

u·ra·ni·um (yōō·rā′nē·əm) *n.* A heavy, white, radioactive, metallic element (symbol U), found only in combination. It is important in the generation of atomic energy. See ELEMENT. [< URANUS]

urano- *combining form Astron.* The heavens; of or pertaining to the heavens, or to celestial bodies. Also, before vowels, **uran-**. [< Gk. *ouranos* heaven]

U·ra·nus (yōō′rə·nəs) In Greek mythology, the son and husband of Gaea (Earth) and father of the Titans, Furies, and Cyclopes, overthrown by his son Cronus. — *n.* The third largest planet of the solar system and seventh in order from the sun. See PLANET. [< L < Gk. < *ouranos* heaven]

u·ra·re (yōō·rä′rē) *n.* Curare. Also **u·ra′ri.** [Var. of CURARE]

ur·ban (ûr′bən) *adj.* 1. Pertaining to, characteristic of, including, or constituting a city. 2. Situated or dwelling in a city. [< L *urbanus.* See URBANE.]

urban district An administrative subdivision of a county of England, Wales, or Northern Ireland, usu. comprising several thickly populated communities.

ur·bane (ûr·bān′) *adj.* Characterized by or having refinement or elegance, esp. in manner; suave. [< L *urbs, urbis* city] — **ur·bane′ly** *adv.* — **ur·bane′ness** *n.*

ur·ban·ism (ûr′bən·iz′əm) *n.* The character or condition of the life of people living in urban areas.

ur·ban·i·ty (ûr·ban′ə·tē) *n.* *pl.* **·ties** 1. The character or quality of being urbane; refined or elegant courtesy. 2. *pl.* Amenities or courtesies. [< F or L < *urbs, urbis* city]

ur·ban·ize (ûr′bən·īz) *v.t.* **·ized, ·iz·ing** To render urban, as in character or manner. — **ur·ban·i·za′tion** *n.*

urban renewal The planned upgrading of a deteriorating urban area, usu. using public funds and coordinated by a local government agency.

ur·chin (ûr′chin) *n.* 1. A roguish, mischievous boy. 2. A cylinder in a carding machine. 3. A sea urchin. [ME < OF < L *ericius* hedgehog < *er* hedgehog]

Ur·du (ōōr′dōō, ōōr·dōō′, ûr′dōō) *n.* A variety of Hindustani spoken by Moslems in India, containing many Persian and Arabic elements and written in a Persian-Arabic script: the official language of Pakistan. [< Hind. < Turkish *ordū* camp < Persian *urdū*]

-ure *suffix of nouns* 1. The act, process, or result of: *pressure.* 2. The function, rank, or office of: *prefecture.* 3. The means or instrument of: *ligature.* [< F < L *-ura*]

u·re·a (yōō·rē′ə) *n.* *Biochem.* A colorless crystalline compound, $CO(NH_2)_2$, formed in the body, and also made synthetically, used in medicine and in the making of plastics and fertilizers. [< NL < F < Gk. *ouron*] — **u·re′al** *adj.*

u·re·mi·a (yōō·rē′mē·ə) *n.* *Pathol.* A condition of the blood due to the presence of urinary constituents ordinarily excreted by the kidneys. Also **uraemia.** — **u·re′mic** *adj.*

-uret *suffix Chem.* Used to denote a compound: now replaced by *-ide.* [< F < *-ure.* See -URE.]

u·re·ter (yōō·rē′tər) *n.* *Anat.* The duct by which urine passes from the kidney to the bladder or the cloaca. For illus. see KIDNEY. [< NL < Gk. < *ourein* to urinate] — **u·re′ter·al, u·re·ter·ic** (yōō′rə·ter′ik) *adj.*

u·re·thra (yōō·rē′thrə) *n.* *Anat.* The duct by which urine is discharged from the bladder of most mammals, and which, in males, carries the seminal discharge. — **u·re′thral** *adj.*

urethro- *combining form Med.* The urethra; of or pertaining to the urethra. Also, before vowels, **urethr-**. [< Gk. *ourēthra* the urethra]

u·ret·ic (yōō·ret′ik) *adj.* *Med.* Of or pertaining to the urine; urinary. [< LL *ureticus* < Gk. *ourētikos* < *ouron* urine]

urge (ûrj) *v.* **urged, urg·ing** *v.t.* 1. To drive or force forward; impel; push. 2. To plead with or entreat earnestly, as with arguments or explanations. 3. To press or argue the doing, consideration, or acceptance of. 4. To move or force to some course or action. 5. To stimulate or excite. 6. To ply or use vigorously, as oars. — *v.i.* 7. To present or press arguments, claims, etc. 8. To exert an impelling or prompting force. — **Syn.** See ACTUATE. — *n.* 1. A strong impulse to perform a certain act. 2. The act of urging; the state of being urged. [< L *urgere* to drive, urge]

ur·gen·cy (ûr′jən·sē) *n.* *pl.* **·cies** 1. The quality of being urgent. 2. Pressure by entreaty; pressure of necessity. 3. The act of urging. 4. Something urgent.

ur·gent (ûr′jənt) *adj.* 1. Characterized by urging or importunity; requiring prompt attention; pressing. 2. Eagerly importunate or insistent. — **ur′gent·ly** *adv.*

-urgy *combining form* Development of or work with a (specified) material or product: *metallurgy, chemurgy.* [< Gk. *-ourgia* < *ergon* work]

-uria *combining form Pathol.* A (specified) condition of the urine: usu. used to indicate disease or abnormality. [< NL < Gk. *-ouria* < *ouron* urine]

U·ri·ah (yōō·rī′ə) A Hittite captain in the Israelite army, husband of Bathsheba, treacherously sent to his death by David, II *Sam.* xi 15–17.

u·ric (yōō′rik) *adj.* Of, pertaining to, or derived from urine.

uric acid *Biochem.* A colorless dibasic acid, $C_5H_4N_4O_3$, varying crystalline forms and slight solubility, found in th urine of man and animals and, in man, forming the nucle of most urinary and renal calculi.

u·ri·nal (yōō′rə·nəl) *n.* 1. An upright wall fixture with fa cilities for flushing, for men's use in urination; also the roo containing such a fixture. 2. A glass receptacle for urin

u·ri·nal·y·sis (yōō′rə·nal′ə·sis) *n.* *pl.* **·ses** (-sēz) Chemic analysis of the urine: also spelled *uranalysis.*

u·ri·nar·y (yōō′rə·ner′ē) *adj.* Of, pertaining to, or involve in the production and excretion of urine: the *urinary* organs — *n.* *pl.* **·nar·ies** 1. A reservoir for storing urine, etc., f use as manure. 2. A urinal.

u·ri·nate (yōō′rə·nāt) *v.i.* **·nat·ed, ·nat·ing** To void or pa urine. [< Med.L *urinatus*, pp. of *urinare* to pass urine *urina* urine] — **u′ri·na′tion** *n.*

u·rine (yōō′rin) *n.* A liquid containing body wastes, s creted by the kidneys, stored in the bladder, and void through the urethra. [< F < L *urina*]

urino- *combining form* Urine. Also, before vowels, **urin** as in *urinalysis.* [< L *urina* urine]

u·ri·no·gen·i·tal (yōō′rə·nō·jen′ə·təl) *adj.* Urogenital.

u·ri·nos·co·py (yōō′rə·nos′kə·pē) *n.* *pl.* **·pies** *Med.* Ur copy.

u·ri·nous (yōō′rə·nəs) *adj.* Of, pertaining to, containing, resembling urine. Also **u′ri·nose** (-nōs).

urn (ûrn) *n.* 1. A rounded or angular vase having a fo variously used in antiquity as a receptacle for the ashes the dead, a water vessel, etc. 2. A vessel for preserving t ashes of the dead. 3. In ancient Rome, a receptacle ha hold lots drawn in voting. 4. A vase-shaped receptacle ha ing a faucet, and designed for keeping tea, coffee, etc., h as by means of a spirit lamp. [< L *urna*]

uro-[1] *combining form* Urine; pertaining to urine or to t urinary tract: *urology.* Also, before vowels, **ur-**. [< G *ouron* urine]

uro-[2] *combining form* A tail; of or related to the tail; caud Also, before vowels, **ur-**. [< Gk. *oura* tail]

u·ro·gen·i·tal (yōō′rō·jen′ə·təl) *adj.* Of or pertaining to t urinary and genital organs and their functions.

u·rol·o·gy (yōō·rol′ə·jē) *n.* The branch of medicine th deals with the urine and the genitourinary tract. — **u·ro· log·ic** (yōō′rə·loj′ik) or **·i·cal** *adj.* — **u·rol′o·gist** *n.*

u·ros·co·py (yōō·ros′kə·pē) *n.* *pl.* **·pies** *Med.* Diagno by examination of the urine: also *urinoscopy.* — **u·ro·sc ic** (yōō′rə·skop′ik) *adj.* — **u·ros′co·pist** *n.*

ur·sa (ûr′sə) *n.* *Latin* A she-bear: used in the phrases *U Major* and *Ursa Minor.*

Ursa Major A constellation, the Great Bear, containing seven bright stars: also called *Big Dipper, Charles's Wain.* [< L]

Ursa Minor A constellation, the Lesser Bear, containing the polestar Polaris: also called *Cynosure, Little Bear, Little Dipper.* [< L]

URSA MAJOR (*a*) Ar
URSA MINOR (*b*)
c Polestar.
d,d Pointers.

ur·sine (ûr′sīn, -sin) *adj.* 1. Pertaining to or like a bear. 2. Clothed with dense bristles, as certain caterpillars. [< L *ursinus* < *ursus* bear]

Ur·su·line (ûr′syə·lin, -sə-, -līn) *adj.* Pertaining to Saint Ursula or to an order of nuns founded 1537, and engaged chiefly in the education of girls. — An Ursuline nun. [after Saint *Ursula,* 4th-c. Cornish pr cess and martyr]

ur·ti·car·i·a (ûr′tə·kâr′ē·ə) *n.* *Pathol.* A disease of the sk characterized by transient eruptions and attended with itc ing. Also called *hives, nettle rash.* [< NL < L *urtica* nett — **ur′ti·car′i·al** or **·i·ous** *adj.*

us (us) *pron.* The objective case of the pronoun *we.* [O

us·a·ble (yōō′zə·bəl) *adj.* 1. Capable of being used. That can be used conveniently. Also **use′a·ble.** — **us ble·ness** *n.* — **us′a·bly** *adv.*

us·age (yōō′sij, -zij) *n.* 1. The manner of using or treat a person or thing; treatment; also, the act of using. 2. C tomary or habitual practice, or something permitted by i done in accordance with it. 3. Uniform practice. 4. T customary way of using words, sounds, and grammat forms in a language. 5. A particular verbal or written pression or application of such an expression: a contemp ous *usage.*

us·ance (yōō′zəns) *n.* 1. A period of time, variable as tween various countries, that, by commercial usage, is lowed, exclusive of days of grace, for payment of bills of change, esp. foreign. 2. *Econ.* An income derived from possession of wealth, as by investment.

use (*v.* yōōz; *n.* yōōs) *v.* **used** (yōōzd; yōōst *for defs.* 5, 7) *v.t.* 1. To employ for the accomplishment of a purpo make use of. 2. To put into practice or employ habitua make a practice of: to *use* diligence in business. 3. To pend the whole of; consume: often with *up.* 4. To cond

•neself toward; treat: to *use* one badly. **5.** To make familiar by habit or practice; inure: now only in the past participle: He is *used* to exposure. **6.** To partake of; smoke or •hew: He does not *use* tobacco. — *v.i.* **7.** To do something ustomarily or habitually: now only in the past tense as an uxiliary to form a phrase equivalent to a frequentative past ense: I *used* to go there. — *n.* **1.** The act of using; the fact >r condition of being employed. **2.** Suitableness or adaptaility to an end: the *uses* of adversity. **3.** Way or manner of ising. **4.** Occasion or need to employ; purpose. **5.** Habital practice or employment; custom. **6.** Any special form, eremony, or ritual, or any individual service that arose in »r was perpetuated by a church, diocese, or branch of a hurch: Roman *use*. **7.** *Law* The permanent equitable right hat a beneficiary has to the enjoyment of the rents and profts of lands and tenements of which the legal title and posses->on are vested in another in trust for the beneficiary. **— to ave no use for 1.** To have no need of. **2.** *Informal* To ave a contempt or dislike for; want nothing to do with. < OF < L *usus*, pp. of *uti* to use]

•e·ful (yōōs′fəl) *adj.* Serviceable; serving a use or purpose, sp. a valuable one. **— use′ful·ly** *adv.* **— use′ful·ness** *n.*

•e·less (yōōs′lis) *adj.* **1.** Unserviceable; being of no use; ot capable of serving any beneficial purpose. **2.** Futile; in ain. **— use′less·ly** *adv.* **— use′less·ness** *n.*

•er (yōō′zər) *n.* **1.** One who or that which uses. **2.** *Law* he exercise or enjoyment of a right.

h·er (ush′ər) *n.* **1.** One who acts as doorkeeper, as of a ourt or other assembly room. **2.** An officer whose duty it s to introduce strangers or walk before a person of rank. **3.** ne who conducts persons to seats, etc., as in a church or heater. **4.** *Brit.* An assistant or subordinate teacher in a chool. — *v.t.* **1.** To act as an usher to; escort; conduct. **2.** o precede as a harbinger; be a forerunner of: usu. with *in*. < OF < L *ostiarius* doorkeeper < *ostium* door]

h·er·ette (ush′ə·ret′) *n.* A female usher, as in a theater.

•nic acid (us′nik) A yellow, crystalline substance, $_{18}H_{16}O_7$, derived from lichens, used as an antibiotic.

su·al (yōō′zhōō·əl) *adj.* Such as occurs in the ordinary ourse of events; frequent; common. [< OF < LL < L *usus* se] **— u′su·al·ly** *adv.* **— u′su·al·ness** *n.*

su·fruct (yōō′zyōō·frukt, yōō·syōō′-) *n.* *Law* The right of sing the property of another and of drawing the profits it roduces without wasting its substance. [< LL < L < *usus* + *fructus* use and fruit]

su·fruc·tu·ar·y (yōō′zyōō·fruk′chōō·er′ē, yōō′syōō-) *n.* *l. ·ar·ies* One who holds property for use by usufruct, as a enant. — *adj.* Of or pertaining to a usufruct.

su·rer (yōō′zhər·ər) *n.* One who practices usury; one who nds money, esp. at an exorbitant or illegal rate.

su·ri·ous (yōō·zhōōr′ē·əs) *adj.* Practicing usury; having he nature of usury. **— u·su′ri·ous·ly** *adv.* **— u·su′ri·ous· ess** *n.*

surp (yōō·zûrp′, -sûrp′) *v.t.* **1.** To seize and hold (the ffice, rights, or powers of another) without right or legal uthority; take possession of by force. **2.** To take arrogant-y, as if by right. — *v.i.* **3.** To practice usurpation; en-roach: with *on* or *upon*. [< OF < L, ? < *usus* use + *rapere* se] **— u·surp′er** *n.* **— u·surp′ing·ly** *adv.*

sur·pa·tion (yōō′zər·pā′shən, -sər-) *n.* The act of usurp-g; said esp. of unlawful or forcible seizure of kingly power.

su·ry (yōō′zhər·ē) *n.* *pl. ·ries* **1.** The act or practice of xacting a rate of interest beyond what is allowed by law. **.** A premium paid for the use of money beyond the rate of terest established by law. [< OF < L < *usus* used]

· (ōōt) *n.* *Music* The first syllable in the Guido solmization ystem: now commonly *do*. [See GAMUT.]

te (yōōt, yōō′tē) *n.* One of a group of tribes of North merican Indians of Shoshonean stock living in Colorado and tah.

ten·sil (yōō·ten′səl) *n.* A vessel, tool, implement, etc., erving a useful purpose, esp. for domestic or farming use. < OF < L *utensilis* fit for use < *utens*, ppr. of *uti* to use]

ter·ine (yōō′tər·in, -īn) *adj.* **1.** Pertaining to the uterus. **.** Born of the same mother, but having a different father. < LL *uterinus* born of the same mother]

ero– *combining form* The uterus; of or pertaining to the terus. Also, before vowels, **uter-**. [< L *uterus* uterus]

ter·us (yōō′tər·əs) *n.* *pl.* **u·ter·i** (yōō′tər·ī) *Anat.* The rgan of a female mammal in which the young are protected nd developed before birth; the womb. [< L]

tile (yōō′til) *adj.* *Rare* Useful. [< OF < L *uti* to use]

til·i·dor (yōō·til′i·dôr) *n.* *Canadian* A system of pipes,

cables, etc., raised and insulated to provide utilities to communities on the permafrost.

u·til·i·tar·i·an (yōō·til′ə·târ′ē·ən) *adj.* **1.** Relating to utility; esp., placing utility above beauty or the amenities of life. **2.** Pertaining to or advocating utilitarianism. — *n.* **1.** An advocate of utilitarianism. **2.** One devoted to mere material utility.

u·til·i·tar·i·an·ism (yōō·til′ə·târ′ē·ən·iz′əm) *n.* **1.** *Philos.* **a** The doctrine that actions derive their moral quality from their usefulness as means to some end, as happiness. **b** The ethical theory, held by Jeremy Bentham and John Stuart Mill, that the greatest human happiness determines the highest moral good. **2.** Devotion to mere material interests.

u·til·i·ty (yōō·til′ə·tē) *n.* *pl.* **·ties** **1.** Fitness for some desirable, practical purpose; also, that which is necessary. **2.** Fitness to supply the natural needs of man. **3.** A public service, as gas, water, etc. **4.** *pl.* Shares of utility company stocks. **5.** In utilitarianism, the greatest happiness for the greatest number of people. [< F < L *utilis* useful]

u·til·ize (yōō′təl·īz) *v.t.* **·ized, ·iz·ing** To make useful; turn to practical account; make use of. Also *Brit.* **u′til·ise**. — **u′til·iz′a·ble** *adj.* **— u′til·i·za′tion** *n.* **— u′til·iz′er** *n.*

ut·most (ut′mōst) *adj.* **1.** Of the highest degree or the largest amount or number; greatest. **2.** Being at the farthest limit or point. — *n.* The greatest possible extent; the most possible. Also *uttermost*. [OE *ūtmest, ȳtemest*]

U·to-Az·tec·an (yōō′tō·az′tek·ən) *n.* **1.** One of the chief stocks of North and Central American Indians, formerly occupying two large regions of the NW and SW U.S., comprising three branches (Shoshonean, Piman, and Nahuatlan) and embracing about fifty tribes, still surviving in the U.S. and Mexico. **2.** The family of languages spoken by these peoples. — *adj.* Of or pertaining to the Uto-Aztecans or their languages.

u·to·pi·a (yōō·tō′pē·ə) *n.* **1.** Any state, condition, or place of ideal perfection. **2.** A visionary, impractical scheme for social improvement. [after *Utopia*]

U·to·pi·a (yōō·tō′pē·ə) An imaginary island described as the seat of a perfect social and political life in a romance by Sir Thomas More, published in 1516. [< NL < Gk. *ou* not + *topos* place] **— U·to′pi·an** *n. & adj.*

u·to·pi·an (yōō·tō′pē·ən) *adj.* Excellent, but existing only in fancy or theory; ideal. — *n.* One who advocates impractical reforms; a visionary. **— u·to′pi·an·ism** *n.*

u·tri·cle (yōō′tri·kəl) *n.* *Anat.* The larger of two saclike cavities found in the bony vestibule of the inner ear. [< L *utriculus*, dim. of *uter* skin bag]

u·tric·u·lar (yōō·trik′yə·lər) *adj.* **1.** Resembling a utricle or small sac. **2.** Bladderlike; bearing or provided with utricles. Also **u·tric′u·late** (-lit, -lāt).

ut·ter[1] (ut′ər) *v.t.* **1.** To give out or send forth with audible sound; say. **2.** *Law* To put in circulation; now, esp. to deliver or offer (something forged or counterfeit) to another. [ME *outre*, freq. of obs. *out* to say, speak out < OE *ūt*] — **ut′ter·a·ble** *adj.* **— ut′ter·er** *n.*

ut·ter[2] (ut′ər) *adj.* **1.** Absolute; total: *utter* misery. **2.** Being or done without conditions or qualifications; final; absolute: *utter* denial. [OE *ūtera*, orig. compar. of *ūt* out]

ut·ter·ance (ut′ər·əns) *n.* **1.** The act of uttering; vocal expression; manner of speaking; also, the power of speech. **2.** A thing uttered or expressed. **3.** *Ling.* Any stretch of speech capable of being isolated from the flow of connected discourse, as a word, phrase, or sentence.

ut·ter·ly (ut′ər·lē) *adv.* Thoroughly; entirely.

ut·ter·most (ut′ər·mōst′) *adj. & n.* Utmost.

U-turn (yōō′tûrn′) *n.* *Informal* A continuous turn that reverses the direction of a vehicle on a road.

u·vu·la (yōō′vyə·lə) *n.* *pl.* **·las** or **·lae** (-lē) *Anat.* The pendent fleshy portion of the soft palate. For illus. see MOUTH, THROAT. [< LL, dim. of *uva* grape]

u·vu·lar (yōō′vyə·lər) *adj.* **1.** Pertaining to or of the uvula. **2.** *Phonet.* Produced by vibration of, or with the back of the tongue near or against, the uvula. — *n.* *Phonet.* A uvular sound.

ux·o·ri·al (uk·sôr′ē·əl, -sō′rē-, ug·zôr′ē·əl, -zō′rē-) *adj.* **1.** Of, pertaining to, characteristic of, or becoming to a wife. **2.** Uxorious. [< L *uxor* wife]

ux·o·ri·ous (uk·sôr′ē·əs, -sō′rē- ug·zôr′ē-, -zō′rē-) *adj.* Fatuously or foolishly devoted to one's wife. [< L *uxor* wife] **— ux·o′ri·ous·ly** *adv.* **— ux·o′ri·ous·ness** *n.*

Uz·bek (ōōz′bek, uz′-) *n.* **1.** A member of a Turkic people dominant in Turkestan; a native or inhabitant of the Uzbek S.S.R. **2.** The Turkic language of the Uzbeks. Also **Uz′beg**.

V

v, V (vē) *n. pl.* **v's** or **vs, V's** or **Vs, vees** (vēz) **1.** The twenty-second letter of the English alphabet. **2.** The sound represented by the letter *v*, the voiced, labiodental fricative. **3.** Anything shaped like a V. — *symbol* **1.** *Informal* A five-dollar bill. **2.** The Roman numeral five. **3.** *Chem.* Vanadium (symbol V).

va·can·cy (vā/kən·sē) *n. pl.* **·cies 1.** The state of being vacant; vacuity; emptiness. **2.** That which is vacant or unoccupied; empty space. **3.** An unoccupied post, place, or office; a place destitute of an incumbent.

va·cant (vā/kənt) *adj.* **1.** Containing or holding nothing; esp. devoid of occupants; empty. **2.** Occupied with nothing; unemployed; unencumbered; free. **3.** Being or appearing without intelligence; inane. **4.** Having no incumbent; unfilled: a *vacant* office. **5.** *Law* Unoccupied or unused, as land; also, abandoned; having neither claimant nor heir, as an estate. **6.** Free from cares. **7.** Devoid of thought. [< F < L *vacare* to be empty] — **va/cant·ly** *adv.* — **va/cant·ness** *n.*

va·cate (vā/kāt) *v.* **·cat·ed, ·cat·ing** *v.t.* **1.** To make vacant; surrender possession of by removal. **2.** To set aside; annul. **3.** To give up (a position or office); quit. — *v.i.* **4.** To leave an office, position, place, etc. **5.** *Informal* To go away; leave. — **Syn.** See ANNUL.

va·ca·tion (vā·kā/shən) *n.* **1.** An interlude, usu. of several days or weeks, from one's customary duties, as for recreation or rest. **2.** *Law* The period of time between stated terms of court. **3.** The intermission of the course of studies and exercises in an educational institution. **4.** The act of vacating. — *v.i.* To take a vacation. [< F < L *vacatio, -onis* freedom from duty] — **va·ca/tion·er** *n.*

va·ca·tion·ist (vā·kā/shən·ist) *n.* One who is taking a vacation or staying at a resort; a tourist.

vac·ci·nate (vak/sə·nāt) *v.* **·nat·ed, ·nat·ing** *Med. v.t.* **1.** To inoculate with a vaccine as a preventive measure; esp. to inoculate against smallpox. — *v.i.* **2.** To perform vaccination. — **vac/ci·na/tor** *n.*

vac·ci·na·tion (vak/sə·nā/shən) *n. Med.* The act or process of vaccinating, esp. against smallpox.

vac·cine (vak/sēn, -sin) *n.* **1.** The virus of cowpox, as prepared for or introduced by vaccination. **2.** Any preparation containing bacteria or viruses so treated as to give immunity from specific diseases when injected into the subject. [< L *vaccinus* pertaining to a cow] — **vac/ci·nal** (sə·nəl) *adj.*

vac·cin·i·a (vak·sin/ē·ə) *n. Vet.* Cowpox.

vac·il·late (vas/ə·lāt) *v.i.* **·lat·ed, ·lat·ing 1.** To sway one way and the other; totter; waver. **2.** To fluctuate. **3.** To waver in mind; be irresolute. [< L *vacillare* to waver] — **vac/il·lan·cy** (-lən·sē) *n.* — **vac/il·lant** (-lənt) *adj.* — **vac/·il·la/to·ry** (-lə·tôr/ē, -tō/rē) *adj.*
— **Syn. 3.** To *vacillate* is to incline to one alternative and then another, without coming to a decision. To *waver* is to be undecided whether to embark on a chosen course. *Falter* suggests failure to act through weakness, timidity, or fright.

vac·u·a (vak/yōō·ə) Alternative plural of VACUUM.

va·cu·i·ty (va·kyōō/ə·tē) *n. pl.* **·ties 1.** The state of being a vacuum; emptiness. **2.** Vacant space; a void. **3.** Freedom from mental exertion. **4.** Lack of intelligence. **5.** An inane or idle thing or statement. [< L *vacuus* empty]

vac·u·ole (vak/yōō·ōl) *n. Biol.* A minute cavity containing air, a watery fluid, or a chemical secretion of the protoplasm, found in an organ, tissue, or cell. For illus. see CELL. [< F < L *vacuus* empty] — **vac/u·o·lar** *adj.*

vac·u·ous (vak/yōō·əs) *adj.* **1.** Having no contents; empty. **2.** Lacking intelligence; blank. **3.** Idle; unoccupied. [< L *vacuus*] — **vac/u·ous·ly** *adv.* — **vac/u·ous·ness** *n.*

vac·u·um (vak/yōō·əm, -yōōm) *n. pl.* **·u·ums** or **·u·a** (-yōō·ə) **1.** A space absolutely devoid of matter. **2.** A space from which air or other gas has been exhausted to a very high degree. **3.** A void; an empty feeling. **4.** A condition of isolation from environmental influences. — *adj.* **1.** Of, or used in the production of, a vacuum. **2.** Exhausted or partly exhausted of gas, air, or vapor. **3.** Operated by suction to produce a vacuum. — *v.t. & v.i. Informal* To clean with a vacuum cleaner: to *vacuum* a rug. [< L, neut. of *vacuus* empty]

vacuum bottle A thermos bottle. Also **vacuum flask.**

vacuum cleaner A machine for cleaning carpets, furnishings, etc., by suction. — **vacuum cleaning**

vacuum pump A pulsometer.

vacuum tube *Electronics* **1.** A glass tube exhausted of [air] to a high degree and containing electrodes between whi[ch] electric discharges may be passed. **2.** An electron tube.

vacuum valve *Brit.* A vacuum tube.

va·de me·cum (vā/dē mē/kəm) *Latin* Anything carried [for] constant use, as a guidebook, manual, or bag; literally, [go] with me. Also **va/de·me/cum, va/de·me/cum.**

vag·a·bond (vag/ə·bond) *n.* **1.** One who wanders fr[om] place to place without visible means of support; a tramp. **2.** One without a settled home; a wanderer; nomad. **3.** [A] worthless fellow; rascal. — *adj.* **1.** Pertaining to a vaga[bond;] bond; nomadic. **2.** Having no definite residence; wand[er]ing; irresponsible. **3.** Driven to and fro; aimless. [< F < L *vagus* wandering] — **vag/a·bond·age** (-ij) *n.* — **vag/·bond/ish** *adj.* — **vag/a·bond·ism** *n.*

va·gar·y (və·gâr/ē, vā/gər·ē) *n. pl.* **·gar·ies** A wild fanc[y or] extravagant notion. [< L *vagari* to wander]

va·gi·na (və·jī/nə) *n. pl.* **·nas** or **·nae** (-nē) *Anat.* T[he] canal leading from the external genital orifice in fem[ale] mammals to the uterus. [< L, sheath] — **vag·i·nal** (vaj/nəl, və·jī/-) *adj.*

vag·i·nate (vaj/ə·nit, -nāt) *adj.* **1.** Having a sheath. **2.** Formed into a sheath; tubular. Also **vag/i·nat/ed** (-nā/ti[d]) [< NL < L *vagina* sheath]

vagino- *combining form Med.* The vagina; of or pertain[ing] to the vagina. Also, before vowels, **vagin-.** [< L *vagi[na]* sheath, vagina]

va·gran·cy (vā/grən·sē) *n. pl.* **·cies** The state of bein[g] vagrant. Also **va/grant·ness.**

va·grant (vā/grənt) *n.* **1.** A person without a settled hom[e;] an idle wanderer; vagabond; tramp. **2.** A roving perso[n.] — *adj.* **1.** Wandering about as a vagrant. **2.** Pertaining [to] one who or that which wanders; nomadic. **3.** Having [a] wandering course; capricious; wayward. [ME, alter. of *[a]wakerant* < OF *wacrer* to walk, wander < Gmc.; infl. in fo[rm] by L *vagari* to wander] — **va/grant·ly** *adv.*

vague (vāg) *adj.* **vagu·er, vagu·est 1.** Lacking definiten[ess] or precision. **2.** Of uncertain source or authority: a vag[ue] rumor. **3.** Not clearly recognized, understood, stated, [or] felt. **4.** Shadowy; hazy. [< F < L *vagus* wandering] — **vague/ly** *adv.* — **vague/ness** *n.*

va·gus (vā/gəs) *n. pl.* **·gi** (-jī) *Anat.* Either of the ten[th] pair of cranial nerves sending branches to the lungs, hea[rt,] stomach, and most of the abdominal viscera. Also **vag[us] nerve.** [< L, wandering]

vain (vān) *adj.* **1.** Filled with or showing undue admirat[ion] for oneself, one's appearance, etc.; conceited. **2.** Unprod[uc]tive; worthless; fruitless: a *vain* attempt. **3.** Having no [real] basis or worth; empty: *vain* hopes. **4.** Ostentatious; show[y.] — **in vain** To no purpose; without effect. [< F < L var[us] empty] — **vain/ly** *adv.* — **vain/ness** *n.*
— **Syn. 1.** proud, vainglorious. **2.** abortive. See FUTILE.

vain·glo·ry (vān·glôr/ē, -glō/rē) *n. pl.* **·ries** Excessive [and] groundless vanity; also, vain pomp; boastfulness. — **Sy[n.]** See PRIDE. [< OF < Med.L *vana gloria* empty pomp, sho[w]] — **vain·glo/ri·ous** (-glôr/ē·əs, -glō/rē-) *adj.* — **vain·glo[ri]ous·ly** *adv.* — **vain·glo/ri·ous·ness** *n.*

val·ance (val/əns) *n.* **1.** A hanging drapery, [us]from the framework of a bed to the floor, from a shelf, etc. A short drapery, board, or plate across the top of a wind[ow] — *v.t.* **·anced, ·anc·ing** To furnish with or as with a valan[ce.] [< OF *avaler* to descend, or after *Valence*, textile-manuf[ac]turing commune in France] — **val/anced** *adj.*

vale¹ (vāl) *n. Chiefly Poetic* A valley. [< OF < L *vallis*]

vale² (vā/lē) *interj. Latin* Farewell.

val·e·dic·tion (val/ə·dik/shən) *n.* A bidding farewell. [< L *valere* to be well + *dicere* to say]

val·e·dic·to·ri·an (val/ə·dik·tôr/ē·ən, -tō/rē-) *n.* A stud[ent] who delivers a valedictory at graduating exercises, usu. [the] graduating student ranking highest in scholarship.

val·e·dic·to·ry (val/ə·dik/tər·ē) *adj.* Pertaining to a lea[ve]taking. — *n. pl.* **·ries** A parting address, as by a mem[ber] of a graduating class.

va·lence (vā/ləns) *n. Chem.* **1.** The property possessed [by] an element or radical of combining with or replacing other [ele]ments or radicals in definite and constant proportion.

he number of atoms of hydrogen (or its equivalent) with hich an atom or radical can combine, or which it can re- lace. Also **va'len·cy.** [< LL < L *valere* to be strong]

l·en·tine (val'ən-tīn) *n.* 1. A greeting card or token of ffection sent on Saint Valentine's Day. 2. A sweetheart.

·le·ri·an (və-lir'ē-ən) *n.* Any of various perennial herbs; sp., one species with small pink or white flowers and a trong odor: also called *heliotrope.* [< OF < Med.L, ppar. ult. < *Valerius*, a personal name]

l·et (val'ā, val'it; *Fr.* và·le') *n.* 1. A gentleman's personal ervant. 2. A manservant in a hotel who performs personal ervices for patrons. — *v.t. & v.i.* To serve or act as a valet. [< F, a groom < OF *vaslet, varlet*, dim. of *vasal* vassal]

l·e·tu·di·nar·i·an (val'ə-tōō'də-nâr'ē-ən, -tyōō'/-) *n.* A hronic invalid; one unduly solicitous about his health. — *dj.* Seeking to recover health; infirm. Also **val'e·tu'di· ar'y.** [< L *valetudo* health, ill health < *valere* to be well] — **val'e·tu'di·nar'i·an·ism** *n.*

al·hal·la (val·hal'ə) *n.* In Norse mythology, the great hall ato which the souls of heroes fallen bravely in battle were orne by the valkyries and received and feasted by Odin. [< NL < ON < *valr* the slain + *höll* hall]

l·iant (val'yənt) *adj.* 1. Strong and intrepid; powerful nd courageous. 2. Performed with valor; bravely conduct- d; heroic. [< OF < L *valere* to be strong] — **val'iant·ly** *dv.* — **val'iance, val'ian·cy, val'iant·ness** *n.*

l·id (val'id) *adj.* 1. Based on evidence that can be sup- orted; acceptable; convincing. 2. Legally binding; effec- ve; warranted. 3. Properly derived from accepted prem- es by the rules of logic. [< F < L *validus* powerful < *alere* to be strong] — **val'id·ly** *adv.* — **val'id·ness** *n.*

l·i·date (val'ə-dāt) *v.t.* ·dat·ed, ·dat·ing 1. To make val- d; ratify and confirm. 2. To declare legally valid; legalize. — Syn. See RATIFY. — **val'i·da'tion** *n.*

·lid·i·ty (və-lid'ə-tē) *n.*, *pl.* ·ties 1. The state or quality f being valid; soundness, as in law or reasoning; efficacy. **·lise** (və-lēs') *n.* A portable case or bag for clothes, etc., sed when traveling; a suitcase. [< F < Ital. *valigia*]

l·kyr·ie (val-kir'ē, val'kir-ē) *n. Often cap.* In Norse ythology, one of the maidens who ride through the air and hoose heroes from among those slain in battle, and carry hem to Valhalla. Also **val'kyr.** [< ON < *valr* the slain + em of *kjósa* to choose, select] — **val·kyr'i·an** *adj.*

l·ley (val'ē) *n.*, *pl.* ·leys 1. A depression of the earth's urface, as one through which a stream flows; level or low nd between mountains, hills, or high lands. 2. Any de- ression or hollow like a valley. [< OF < L *vallis* valley] **l·or** (val'ər) *n.* Courage; personal bravery. Also *Brit.* **al'our.** [< OF < LL < L *valere* to be strong] — **val'or· us** *adj.* — **val'or·ous·ly** *adv.* — **val'or·ous·ness** *n.*

l·or·i·za·tion (val'ər·ə·zā'shən, -ī·zā'/-) *n.* The mainte- ance by governmental action of an artificial price for any roduct. [< Pg. *valorização* < *valor* value < LL. See VALOR.] **l·or·ize** (val'ə·rīz) *v.t.* ·ized, ·iz·ing To subject to valori- ation. Also *Brit.* **val'or·ise.**

l·u·a·ble (val'yōō·ə·bəl, val'yə·bəl) *adj.* 1. Having rela- vely great financial worth, price, or value; costly. 2. Of a ature or character capable of being valued or estimated. 3. aving moral worth, value, or importance; worthy. — *n.* su. pl.* An article of worth or value, as a piece of jewelry. — **val'u·a·ble·ness** *n.* — **val'u·a·bly** *adv.*

l·u·a·tion (val'yōō·ā'shən) *n.* 1. The act of valuing. 2. stimated worth or value. 3. Personal estimation; judgment f merit or character. — **val'u·a'tion·al** *adj.*

l·ue (val'yōō) *n.* 1. The desirability or worth of a thing; trinsic worth; utility. 2. *Often pl.* Something regarded as esirable, worthy, or right, as a belief, standard, or moral recept. 3. The rate at which a commodity is potentially xchangeable for others; a fair return in service, goods, tc.; worth in money; market price; also, the ratio of tility to price; a bargain. 4. Attributed or assumed val- ation; esteem or regard. 5. Exact meaning. 6. *Music* The elative length of a tone as signified by a note. 7. *Math.* The uantity, magnitude, or number an algebraic symbol or ex- ression is supposed to denote. 8. Rank in a system of classi- cation. 9. In the graphic arts, the relation of the elements of picture, as light and shade, to one another. 10. *Phonet.* he special quality of the sound represented by a written char- cter. — *v.t.* ·ued, ·u·ing 1. To estimate the value or worth f; appraise. 2. To regard highly; esteem; prize. 3. To lace a relative estimate of value or desirability upon. 4. o give a (specified) value to. [< OF *valoir* to be worth < L *alere*] — **val'ue·less** *adj.* — **val'u·er** *n.*

l·ued (val'yōōd) *adj.* 1. Regarded or estimated; much or ighly esteemed. 2. Having a (specified) value.

l·vate (val'vāt) *adj.* 1. Serving as or resembling a valve; aving a valve; valvular. 2. *Bot.* Meeting without overlap- ing, as petals. [< L *valvatus* with folding doors]

valve (valv) *n.* 1. *Mech.* Any contrivance or arrangement that regulates the amount and direction of flow of a liquid, gas, vapor, or loose material. 2. *Anat.* A structure formed by one or more loose folds of the lining membrane of a vessel or other organ, allowing flow of a fluid in one direction only, as blood to and from the heart. 3. *Zool.* One of the parts of a shell, as of a mollusk. 4. A device in certain brass instru- ments for lengthening the air column and lowering the pitch of the instrument's scale. — *v.t.* **valved, valv·ing** To fur- nish with valves; control the flow of by means of a valve. [< L *valva* leaf of a door] — **val'val** (-vəl), **val'var** (-vər) *adj.* — **valve'less** *adj.*

val·vu·lar (val'vyə·lər) *adj.* 1. Pertaining to or of the na- ture of a valve, as of the heart. 2. Having valves.

va·moose (va·mōōs') *v.t. & v.i.* ·moosed, ·moos·ing *U.S. Slang* To leave hastily or hurriedly; quit. Also **va·mose'** (-mōs'). [< Sp. *vamos* let us go < L *vadere* to go]

vamp[1] (vamp) *n.* 1. The piece of leather forming the upper front part of a boot or shoe. 2. Something added to give an old thing a new appearance. 3. *Music* A simple improvised accompaniment. — *v.t.* 1. To provide with a vamp. 2. To repair or patch. 3. *Music* To improvise an accompaniment to. — *v.i.* 4. *Music* To improvise accompaniments. [< OF < *avant* before + *pied* foot] — **vamp'er** *n.*

vamp[2] (vamp) *Informal v.t.* 1. To seduce (a man) by uti- lizing one's feminine charms. — *v.i.* 2. To play the vamp. — *n.* An unscrupulous flirt. [Short for VAMPIRE] — Syn. (noun) siren, temptress, gold-digger, femme fatale.

vam·pire (vam'pīr) *n.* 1. In folklore, a corpse that rises from its grave at night to feed upon the living, usu. by suck- ing the blood. 2. A man or woman who victimizes persons of the opposite sex; esp., a woman who brings her lover to a state of poverty or degradation. 3. A large bat of South or Central America, that drinks the blood of horses, cattle, and, sometimes, men. 4. An insectivorous or frugivorous bat formerly supposed to suck blood. [< F < G *vampir* < Slavic] — **vam·pir'ic** (vam-pir'ik), **vam'pir·ish** (-pir·ish) *adj.* — **vam'pir·ism** (-pī·riz'əm, -pə-) *n.*

van[1] (van) *n.* 1. A large covered vehicle for transporting furniture, livestock, etc. 2. *Brit.* A closed railway car for luggage, etc. [Short for CARAVAN]

van[2] (van) *n.* 1. The portion of an army, fleet, etc., that is nearest or in advance of the front: opposed to *rear.* 2. The leaders of a movement; those at the front of any line or unit. [Short for VANGUARD]

va·na·di·um (və·nā'dē·əm) *n.* A rare, silver-white metallic element (symbol V), used in steel alloys to increase tensile strength. See ELEMENT. [< NL < ON *Vanadīs*, a name of the Norse goddess Freya]

Van Al·len radiation (van al'ən) A high-intensity radia- tion consisting of charged atomic particles believed to circle the earth in an inner and outer belt conforming to the earth's magnetic field. Also **Van Allen belts.** [after James A. *Van Allen*, born 1914, U.S. physicist]

van·dal (van'dəl) *n.* One who willfully destroys or defaces property, esp. anything artistic. — *adj.* Wantonly destruc- tive. [< VANDAL] — **van·dal·ic** (van-dal'ik) *adj.*

Van·dal (van'dəl) *n.* One of a Germanic people who rav- aged Gaul and overran Spain and North Africa in the early part of the fifth century, and pillaged the city of Rome in 455. — **Van·dal·ic** (van-dal'ik) *adj.* — **Van'dal·ism** *n.*

van·dal·ism (van'dəl·iz'əm) *n.* Willful destruction or de- facement of artistic works, or of property in general.

Van·dyke beard (van·dīk') A short pointed beard resem- bling those depicted in the paintings of Anthony Van Dyck.

vane (vān) *n.* 1. A thin plate of metal or wood that pivots on a vertical rod to indi- cate the direction of the wind; weather vane. 2. An arm or blade extending from a rotating shaft, as of a windmill, propeller, turbine, etc. 3. *Ornithol.* The web of a feather. [OE *fana* flag] — **vaned** *adj.*

van·guard (van'gärd) *n.* 1. The advance guard of an army; the van. 2. Those in the forefront of a movement, as in art, etc. [< OF < *avant* before + *garde* guard]

WINDMILL VANES

va·nil·la (və·nil'ə) *n.* 1. A flavoring extract made from the podlike seed capsules of a climbing tropical orchid. 2. The seed capsule of this plant: also **vanilla bean.** 3. A food, as ice cream, flavored with vanilla. [< NL < Sp. dim. of *vaina* sheath, pod < L *vagina* sheath] — **va·nil'lic** (-ik) *adj.*

va·nil·lin (və·nil'in) *n. Chem.* A colorless, fragrant, crys- talline compound, $C_8H_8O_3$, contained in vanilla, and also made synthetically. Also **va·nil·line** (və·nil'in, -ēn)

van·ish (van'ish) *v.i.* 1. To disappear from sight; fade away; depart. 2. To pass out of existence; be annihilated. [< OF < L *evanescere* to fade away] — **van'ish·er** *n.*

van·ish·ing point (van'ish·ing) In perspective, the point at which parallel lines appear to converge.

van·i·ty (van'ə·tē) n. pl. **·ties** 1. The condition or character of being vain; excessive personal pride; conceit. 2. Ambitious display; ostentation; show. 3. The quality or state of being fruitless, useless, or destitute of reality, etc. 4. That which is vain or unsubstantial. 5. A bag or box containing cosmetics, comb, mirror, etc.: also **vanity case.** 6. A dressing table. [< OF < L < *vanus* empty, vain]

van·quish (vang'kwish, van'-) v.t. 1. To defeat in battle; overcome; conquer. 2. To suppress or overcome (a feeling). 3. To defeat, as in argument. [< OF < L *vincere* to conquer] — **van'quish·a·ble** adj. — **van'quish·er** n.

van·tage (van'tij) n. 1. Superiority over a competitor or opponent; advantage. 2. Advantage (def. 4). 3. An opportunity; chance. [OF < L *ab ante* from before]

vantage ground A position or condition that gives one an advantage.

vantage point A strategic position affording perspective; point of view.

van·ward (van'wərd) adj. Of or situated in the van or front. — adv. To or toward the van or front.

vap·id (vap'id) adj. 1. Having lost sparkling quality and flavor. 2. Flat; dull; insipid. [< L *vapidus* insipid] — **va·pid·i·ty** (ve·pid'ə·tē), **vap'id·ness** n. — **vap'id·ly** adv.

va·por (vā'pər) n. 1. Moisture in the air; esp., visible floating moisture, as light mist. 2. Any light, cloudy substance in the air, as smoke or fumes. 3. Any substance in the gaseous state, that is usu. a liquid or solid. 4. A gas below its critical temperature. 5. That which is fleeting and unsubstantial. — v.t. 1. To vaporize. — v.i. 2. To emit vapor. 3. To evaporate. 4. To brag. Also *Brit.* **va'pour.** [< AF < OF < L *vapor* steam] — **va'por·a·bil'i·ty** n. — **va'por·a·ble** adj. — **va'por·er** n. — **va'por·ish** adj.

vapori- combining form Vapor; of or related to vapor, steam, etc. Also, before vowels, **vapor-.** [< L *vapor* steam]

va·por·ize (vā'pə·rīz) v.t. & v.i. **·ized, ·iz·ing** To convert or be converted into vapor. — **va'por·iz'a·ble** adj. — **va'por·i·za·tion** (-ə·zā'shən, -ī·zā'-) **va'por·iz'er** n.

va·por·ous (vā'pər·əs) adj. 1. Of or like vapor; foggy; misty. 2. Full of or producing vapors. 3. Diaphanous; ethereal. 4. Vainly imaginative; whimsical. Also **va'por·y.** — **va·por·os·i·ty** (vā'pə·ros'ə·tē) n. — **va'por·ous·ly** adv. — **va'por·ous·ness** n.

vapor pressure *Physics* The pressure of a confined vapor in equilibrium with its liquid at any specific temperature. Also **vapor tension.**

vapor trail *Aeron.* A contrail.

va·que·ro (vä·kā'rō) n. pl. **·ros** (-rōz, *Sp.* -rōs) A herdsman; cowboy. [< Sp. < L *vacca* cow]

vari- combining form Various; different: *variform, varicolored.* Also **vario-.** [< L *varius* varied]

var·i·a·ble (vâr'ē·ə·bəl) adj. 1. Having the capacity of varying; alterable; mutable. 2. Having a tendency to change; not constant; fickle. 3. Having no definite value as regards quantity. 4. *Biol.* Prone to variation from a normal or established type. — n. 1. That which varies or is subject to change. 2. *Math.* A quantity susceptible of fluctuating in value or magnitude under different conditions. [< OF < L < *varius* various, diverse] — **var'i·a·bil'i·ty, var'i·a·ble·ness** n. — **var'i·a·bly** adv.

variable star *Astron.* Any of several groups of stars whose apparent magnitude varies at different times.

var·i·ance (vâr'ē·əns) n. 1. The act of varying, or the state of being variant; difference; discrepancy. 2. Dissension; discord. — **at variance** 1. Disagreeing or conflicting, as facts. 2. In a state of dissension or discord.

var·i·ant (vâr'ē·ənt) adj. 1. Having or showing variation; differing. 2. Tending to vary; changing. 3. Restless; fickle; inconstant. 4. Differing from a standard or type. — n. A thing that differs from another in form only; esp., a different spelling or pronunciation of a word. [See VARIABLE]

var·i·a·tion (vâr'ē·ā'shən) n. 1. The act, process, state, or result of varying; modification; diversity. 2. The extent to which a thing varies. 3. A repetition with its essential features intact and other features modified. 4. *Music* A modification of the rhythm, harmony, melodic pattern, etc., of a basic theme. 5. *Biol.* Deviation in structure or function from the type or parent form of an organism. [< F < L *variatio, -onis*] — **var'i·a'tion·al** adj.

varico- combining form *Med.* A varicose vein; varix. Also, before vowels, **varic-.** [< L *varix, -icis* varicose vein]

var·i·col·ored (vâr'i·kul'ərd) adj. Variegated in color; parti-colored; of various colors. Also *Brit.* **var'i·col'oured.**

var·i·cose (var'ə·kōs) adj. *Pathol.* Abnormally dilated, as veins. [< L < *varix, -icis* varicose vein] — **var'i·cos'i·ty** (-kos'ə·tē) n.

var·ied (vâr'ēd) adj. 1. Consisting of differing parts; diverse. 2. Partially or repeatedly altered, modified, etc. 3. Varicolored. — **var'ied·ly** adv.

var·i·e·gate (vâr'ē·ə·gāt') v.t. **·gat·ed, ·gat·ing** 1. To mark with different colors or tints; dapple; spot; streak. 2. make varied; diversify. [< LL < *varius* various + *agere* drive, do] — **var'i·e·ga'tion** n.

var·i·e·gat·ed (vâr'ē·ə·gā'tid) adj. 1. Having diverse colo— varied in color, as with streaks or blotches. 2. Having exhibiting different forms, styles, or varieties.

va·ri·e·tal (və·rī'ə·təl) adj. Of, pertaining to, or of the ture of a variety. — **va·ri'e·tal·ly** adv.

va·ri·e·ty (və·rī'ə·tē) n. pl. **·ties** 1. The state or charac of being various or varied; diversity. 2. A collection of verse things. 3. The possession of different characteristi by one individual. 4. A limited class of things that differ certain common peculiarities from a larger class to whi they belong. 5. *Biol.* An individual or a group that diff from the type species in certain characters; a subdivision a species. [< MF < L < *varius* various]

variety show A theatrical show, as in vaudeville, consi ing of a series of short, diversified acts or numbers.

vario- Var. of VARI-.

va·ri·o·la (və·rī'ə·lə) n. *Pathol.* Smallpox. [< Med.L, p tule < L *varius* speckled] — **va·ri'o·lar, va·ri'o·lous** ad

var·i·om·e·ter (vâr'ē·om'ə·tər) n. *Electr.* A variable ductance device composed of a fixed and a movable coil c nected in series, and capable of controlling the strength o current. [< VARIO- + -METER]

var·i·o·rum (vâr'ē·ôr'əm, -ō'rəm) adj. Having notes, comments by different critics or editors. — n. An editi containing various versions of a text, usu. with notes a commentary: also **variorum edition.** [< L (*cum no* *variorum* (with the notes) of various persons]

var·i·ous (vâr'ē·əs) adj. 1. Characteristically differe from one another; diverse. 2. More than one; several. Many-sided; varying. 4. Having a diversity of appearan variegated. 5. *Rare* Changeable; inconstant. [< L *vari* — **var'i·ous·ly** adv. — **var'i·ous·ness** n.

var·ix (vâr'iks) n. pl. **var·i·ces** (vâr'ə·sēz) *Pathol.* Permanent dilatation of a vein or other vessel of circulati **b** A vessel thus distorted, as a varicose vein. [< L, a va cose vein]

var·let (vär'lit) n. *Archaic* 1. A menial or subordina also, a page. 2. A knave or scoundrel. [< OF, groom

var·mint (vär'mənt) n. *Dial.* Any obnoxious or pestifer person or animal. [Alter. of VERMIN]

var·nish (vär'nish) n. 1. A solution of certain gums resins in alcohol, linseed oil, etc., used to produce a shini transparent coat on a surface. 2. Any natural or artifi product or surface resembling varnish. 3. Outward sh or any superficial polish, as of politeness. — v.t. 1. To c er with varnish. 2. To give a smooth or glossy appeara to. 3. To improve the appearance of; polish. 4. To hide a deceptive covering or appearance; gloss over. [< OF Med.L *vernicium* a resin] — **var'nish·er** n.

var·si·ty (vär'sə·tē) n. pl. **·ties** *Informal* The high ranking team that represents a university, college, or sch in sports, debating, etc. [< UNIVERSITY]

var·y (vâr'ē) v. **var·ied, var·y·ing** v.t. 1. To change form, nature, substance, etc., of; modify. 2. To cause to different from one another. 3. To impart variety to; div sify. 4. *Music* To modify (a melody) by changes of rhyth harmony, etc. — v.i. 5. To become changed in form, ture, substance, etc. 6. To be diverse; differ. 7. To de ate: with *from.* 8. *Math.* To be subject to continual char 9. *Biol.* To undergo variation. [< OF < L < *varius* verse] — **var'i·er** n.

vas (vas) n. pl. **va·sa** (vā'sə) *Biol.* A blood vessel or du [< L, vessel, dish]

vas- Var. of VASO-.

vas·cu·lar (vas'kyə·lər) adj. *Biol.* **a** Of, or consisting or containing ducts for the transport of body liquids, blood, lymph, etc. **b** Richly supplied with blood vess Also **vas'cu·lose** (-lōs), **vas'cu·lous** (-ləs). [< L < *vas* v sel] — **vas'cu·lar'i·ty** (-lar'ə·tē) n. — **vas'cu·lar·ly** a

vas def·er·ens (vas def'ər·enz) *Anat.* The duct by wh semen is conveyed from the testicles to the seminal vesic [< NL < L *vas* vessel + *deferens* leading down]

vase (vās, vāz, väz) n. A decorative container, usu., rou ed and of greater height than width, used as an ornam or for holding flowers. [< F < L *vas* vessel]

Vas·e·line (vas'ə·lēn, -lin) n. Proprietary name for a bra of petrolatum. Also **vas'e·line.**

vaso- combining form *Physiol.* 1. A vessel, esp., a blo vessel. 2. The vas deferens. Also, before vowels, *vas-.* L *vas* vessel]

vas·o·mo·tor (vas'ō·mō'tər) adj. *Physiol.* Producing c traction or dilatation in the walls of vessels.

vas·sal (vas'əl) n. 1. In the feudal system, one who h land of a superior lord by a feudal tenure; a liegeman or f dal tenant. 2. A dependent, retainer, or servant; a slave bondman. — adj. 1. Of or like a vassal. 2. Servile. OF < Med.L < LL *vassus* servant < Celtic]

vas·sal·age (vas'əl·ij) n. 1. The state of being a vass

so, the duties, and obligations of a vassal. **2.** The feudal system. **3.** Servitude in general. **4.** Land held by feudal tenure; a fief. **5.** Vassals collectively.

st (vast, väst) *adj.* **1.** Of great extent or size; immense; enormous; huge. **2.** Very great in number, quantity, or amount. **3.** Very great in degree, intensity, etc. [< L *stus* waste, empty, vast] — **vast′ly** *adv.* — **vast′ness** *n.*

t (vat) *n.* A large vessel, tub, etc., for holding liquids, as eing materials. — *v.t.* **vat·ted, vat·ting** To put into a at; treat in a vat. [OE *fæt*]

t·i·can (vat′ə·kən) *n.* **1.** The papal palace in Vatican ity, Rome. **2.** The papal government: distinguished from e *Quirinal.* [< L *Vaticanus* (*mons*) Vatican (hill) in ome]

ude·ville (vōd′vil, vô′də·vil) *n.* A miscellaneous theatrical entertainment, as a variety show; also, a theater presenting such shows. [< F < *Vau de Vire* the valley of the Vire ver (in Normandy)]

ult[1] (vōlt) *n.* **1.** n arched chamber; so, any subterranean compartment; cel**r. 2.** An arched structure, as a ceiling roof esp., of a cavi**3.** Any vaultlike vering, as the sky. An underground

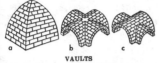

VAULTS
a Cove or cloister. *b* Groin.
c Underpitch or Welsh.

om or compartment for storing wine, etc. **5.** A strongly otected place for keeping valuables, as in a bank. **6.** A urial chamber. — *v.t.* **1.** To form with a vaulted roof; ver with or as with a vault. **2.** To construct in the form of vault. [< OF < L < *volvere* to roll]

ult[2] (vōlt) *v.t.* **1.** To leap over, esp. with the aid of a pole with the hands resting on something. **2.** To mount (a rse, etc.) with a leap. — *v.i.* **3.** To leap; spring. **4.** To a curvet. — *n.* **1.** A leap or bound, as one made with the d of a pole. **2.** The curvet of a horse. [< OF *volter* to ap, gambol, ? ult. < L *volutus*] — **vault′er** *n.*

ult·ing[1] (vōl′ting) *n.* **1.** Vaulted work, or vaults collecvely. **2.** The work or art of building a vault.

ult·ing[2] (vôl′ting) *adj.* **1.** That overleaps. **2.** Unduly nfident or presumptuous: *vaulting* ambition. **3.** That can used in vaulting, as in gymnastics.

unt (vônt, vänt) *v.i.* **1.** To speak boastfully. — *v.t.* **2.** boast of. — *n.* Boastful assertion or ostentatious disay. [< OF < LL *vanitare* to brag < L *vanus* empty, vain] **vaunt′er** *n.* — **vaunt′ing·ly** *adv.*

·a·dar (vē·ä·där′, vē′ä·där, vä′-) *n.* An intercalary onth of the Hebrew year. See (Hebrew) CALENDAR.

al (vēl) *n.* The flesh of a calf considered as food. — **bob al** The flesh of a calf too young to be eaten. [< OF < L *ellus,* dim. of *vitulus* calf]

·tor (vek′tər) *n.* **1.** *Math.* A physical quantity that has agnitude and direction in space, as velocity and accelera-
n. **2.** *Med.* A carrier of pathogenic microorganisms from e host to another. [L, carrier < *vehere* to carry] — **c·to·ri·al** (vek·tôr′ē·əl, -tō′rē-) *adj.*

·da (vā′də, vē′-) *n.* One of the collections of Indian cred writings, dating from the second millennium B.C., that rm the Hindu scriptures. **2.** The Vedas collectively. [< t., knowledge] — **Ve·da·ic** (vi·dā′ik) *adj.* — **Ve·da·ism** ā′də·iz′əm, vē′-) *n.*

·dan·ta (vi·dän′tə, -dan′-) *n.* Any of several schools of indu religious philosophy based on the Upanishads; esp., a onistic system that teaches the worship of Brahma as the eator and soul of the universe. [< Skt. < *Veda* Veda + *ta* end] — **Ve·dan′tic** *adj.* — **Ve·dan′tism** *n.* — **Ve·** an′tist *n.*

E Day (vē′ē′) May 8, the date of victory of the United ations in Europe in World War II, 1945.

dette (vi·det′) *n.* **1.** A mounted sentinel placed in ad-
nce of an outpost. **2.** A small vessel used to watch the ovements of the enemy: also **vedette boat.** Also spelled *lette.* [< F < Ital. *vedetta,* alter. (after *vedere* to see) of *letta,* dim. of Sp. *vela* vigil < L *vigilare* to watch]

·dic (vā′dik, vē′-) *adj.* Of or pertaining to the Vedas o' e language in which they were written.

er (vir) *v.i.* **1.** *Naut.* To turn to another course. **2.** To ange direction by a clockwise motion, as the wind. **3.** To ift from one position to another; be variable or fickle. — *t.* **4.** To change the direction of. — *n.* A change in direc-
n; a swerve. [< F *virer* to turn]

er·y (vir′ē) *n.* *pl.* **veer·ies** A melodious, tawny thrush eastern North America. [Prob. imit.]

·ga (vē′gə, vā′-) *n.* One of the 20 brightest stars, 0.14 agnitude; Alpha in the constellation Lyra. [< Med.L rabic (*al-Nasr*) *al-Waqi* the falling (vulture)]

veg·e·ta·ble (vej′ə·tə·bəl, vej′tə-) *n.* **1.** The edible part of any herbaceous plant, raw or cooked. **2.** Any member of the vegetable kingdom; a plant. — *adj.* **1.** Pertaining to plants, esp. garden or farm vegetables. **2.** Derived from, of the nature of, or resembling plants. **3.** Made from or consisting of vegetables. **4.** Resembling or like a vegetable in activity, etc.; dull; passive. [< OF < LL < L *vegetare* to animate < *vegere* to be lively] — **veg′e·ta·bly** *adv.*

vegetable kingdom The division of nature that includes all organisms classified as plants.

vegetable oil Any of various oils expressed from the seeds or fruits of plants and used in cooking, medicine, paints, and as lubricants, as corn oil, olive oil, linseed oil, etc.

veg·e·tal (vej′ə·təl) *adj.* **1.** Of or pertaining to plants or vegetables. **2.** Characterizing those vital processes that are common to plants and animals, esp., as distinguished from sensation and volition. [< L *vegetus* lively, vigorous]

veg·e·tant (vej′ə·tənt) *adj.* **1.** Invigorating; vivifying; stimulating growth. **2.** Of the nature of plant life.

veg·e·tar·i·an (vej′ə·târ′ē·ən) *adj.* **1.** Pertaining to or advocating vegetarianism. **2.** Exclusively vegetable, as a diet. — *n.* One who holds or practices vegetarianism.

veg·e·tar·i·an·ism (vej′ə·târ′ē·ən·iz′əm) *n.* The theory or practice of eating only vegetables and fruits.

veg·e·tate (vej′ə·tāt) *v.i.* **·tat·ed, ·tat·ing 1.** To grow, as a plant. **2.** To live in a monotonous, passive way. **3.** *Pathol.* To increase abnormally in size.

veg·e·ta·tion (vej′ə·tā′shən) *n.* **1.** The process of vegetating. **2.** Plant life in the aggregate. **3.** *Pathol.* An abnormal growth on the body. — **veg′e·ta′tion·al** *adj.*

veg·e·ta·tive (vej′ə·tā′tiv) *adj.* **1.** Of, pertaining to, or exhibiting the processes of plant life. **2.** Growing or capable of growing, as plants; productive. **3.** Having a mere physical or passive existence; showing little mental activity. **4.** Concerned with growth and nutrition. Also **veg·e·tive** (vej′ə·tiv). — **veg′e·ta′tive·ly** *adv.* — **veg′e·ta′tive·ness** *n.*

ve·he·ment (vē′ə·mənt) *adj.* **1.** Arising from or marked by impetuosity of feeling or passion; ardent. **2.** Acting with great force or energy; energetic; violent; furious. [< OF < L *vehemens, -entis* impetuous, rash; ult. origin uncertain] — **ve′he·mence, ve′he·men·cy** *n.* — **ve·he·ment·ly** *adv.*

ve·hi·cle (vē′ə·kəl) *n.* **1.** Any contrivance fitted with wheels or runners for carrying something; a conveyance, as, a car or sled. **2.** *Med.* An innocuous medium, as a liquid, with which is mixed some therapeutic substance that may be applied or administered more easily; an excipient. **3.** A liquid, as oil, with which pigments are mixed in painting. **4.** Anything by means of which something else, as power, thought, etc., is transmitted or communicated. **5.** In the performing arts, anything, as a play, musical composition, etc., that permits the performer to display his particular powers or talents. [< F < L < *vehere* to carry, ride] — **ve·hic·u·lar** (vi·hik′yə·lər) *adj.*

veil (vāl) *n.* **1.** A piece of thin and light fabric, worn over the face or head for concealment, protection, or ornament. **2.** Any piece of fabric used to conceal an object; a screen; curtain; mask. **3.** Anything that conceals from inspection; a disguise; pretext. **4.** The life of a nun; also, vows made by a nun. — **to take the veil** To become a nun. — *v.t.* **1.** To cover with a veil. **2.** To hide; disguise. [< OF < L *velum* piece of cloth, sail] — **veil′er** *n.*

veil·ing (vā′ling) *n.* **1.** Material for veils. **2.** A veil.

vein (vān) *n.* **1.** *Anat.* One of the muscular, tubular vessels that convey blood to the heart. **2.** Loosely, any blood vessel. **3.** *Entomol.* One of the radiating supports of an insect's wing. **4.** *Bot.* One of the slender vascular bundles that form the framework of a leaf. **5.** In mining, a lode. **6.** A long, irregular, colored streak, as in wood; marble, etc. **7.** A distinctive trait, tendency, or disposition. **8.** A temporary state of mind; humor; mood. — *v.t.* **1.** To furnish or fill with veins. **2.** To streak or ornament with veins. **3.** To extend over or throughout as veins. [< OF < L *vena* blood vessel] — **vein′y** *adj.*

veined (vānd) *adj.* **1.** Having, marked with, or abounding in veins. **2.** Marked with streaks of another color.

vein·ing (vā′ning) *n.* A network of veins.

vein·let (vān′lit) *n.* A small vein.

ve·lar (vē′lər) *adj.* **1.** Of or pertaining to a velum, esp. to the soft palate. **2.** *Phonet.* Formed with the back of the tongue touching or near the soft palate, as (k) in *cool,* (g) in *go:* sometimes *guttural.* — *n. Phonet.* **a** A velar consonant. **b** A back vowel. [< L *velum* a sail, curtain]

ve·lar·ize (vē′lə·rīz) *v.* **·ized, ·iz·ing** *Phonet. v.t.* To modify (a sound) by raising the back of the tongue toward the soft palate. — *v.i.* To be modified to a velar sound.

veldt (velt, felt) *n.* In South Africa, open country or grassland having few shrubs or trees. Also **veld.** [< Afrikaans *veld* < Du., field]

vel·lum (vel'əm) *n.* **1.** Fine parchment made from the skins of calves, used for expensive binding, printing, etc. **2.** A manuscript written on such parchment. **3.** Paper made to resemble parchment. [< OF < *veel, viel* calf]

ve·loc·i·pede (və-los'ə-pēd) *n.* **1.** An early form of bicycle or tricycle. **2.** A child's tricycle. **3.** A type of handcar. [< F < L *velox, velocis* swift + *pes, pedis* foot]

ve·loc·i·ty (və-los'ə-tē) *n. pl.* **·ties 1.** The state of moving or developing swiftly; rapidity; celerity; speed. **2.** The distance traveled by an object in a specified time. **3.** The time rate of motion in a stated direction; a vector quantity. [< L < *velox* swift]

ve·lours (və-lŏŏr') *n. pl.* **·lours** (-lŏŏrz) A soft, velvetlike, closely woven cotton or wool fabric having a short, thick pile. Also **ve·lour'.** [< F. See VELURE.]

ve·lum (vē'ləm) *n. pl.* **·la** (-lə) **1.** *Biol.* A thin membranous covering or partition. **2.** *Anat.* The soft palate: see under PALATE. [< L]

ve·lure (və-lŏŏr') *n.* **1.** Velvet, or a fabric resembling velvet. **2.** A velvet or silk pad for smoothing a silk hat. — *v.t.* **·lured, ·lur·ing** To smooth with a velure. [< F < L < *villus* shaggy hair]

vel·vet (vel'vit) *n.* **1.** A fabric of silk, rayon, cotton, etc., having on one side a thick, short, smooth pile, formed either of loops (**pile velvet**) or of single threads (**cut velvet**). **2.** Anything resembling such a fabric in softness, smoothness, etc. **3.** The furry skin covering a growing antler. — *adj.* **1.** Made of velvet. **2.** Smooth and soft to the touch; velvety. [< Med.L *velvetum*, ult. < L *villus* shaggy hair]

vel·vet·een (vel'və-tēn') *n.* **1.** A cotton fabric with a short, close pile like velvet. **2.** *pl.* Clothes, esp. trousers, made of this material. [< VELVET]

vel·vet·y (vel'vit-ē) *adj.* **1.** Smooth and soft like velvet. **2.** Mild and smooth to the taste: *velvety* liqueur.

ve·na ca·va (vē'nə kā'və) *pl.* **ve·nae ca·vae** (vē'nē kā'vē) *Anat.* Either of the two great venous trunks emptying into the right atrium of the heart. For illus. see HEART. [< L, hollow vein]

ve·nal (vē'nəl) *adj.* **1.** Ready to sell honor or principle, or to accept a bribe; mercenary; purchasable. **2.** Subject to sordid bargaining or to corrupt influences; salable. **3.** Characterized by corruption. [< L *venum* sale] — **ve·nal'i·ty** (-nal'ə-tē) *n.* — **ve'nal·ly** *adv.*

ve·na·tion (vē-nā'shən) *n. Biol.* The arrangement of veins, as in a leaf, an insect wing, etc.

vend (vend) *v.t.* **1.** To sell. **2.** To utter (an opinion); publish. — *v.i.* **3.** To be a vender. **4.** To be sold. [< F *vendre* < L < *venum* sale + *dare* to give] — **ven·di·tion** (ven-dish'ən) *n.*

ven·dee (ven-dē') *n. Law* The person or party to whom something is sold; a buyer.

vend·er (ven'dər) *n.* One who sells, as a hawker or peddler. Also **ven'dor** (-dər).

ven·det·ta (ven-det'ə) *n.* A blood feud in which the relatives of the killed or injured person take vengeance on the offender or his relatives. [< Ital. < L *vindicta* vengeance]

vend·i·ble (ven'də-bəl) *adj.* Capable of being vended or sold; marketable. — *n.* A vendible thing. — **vend'i·bil'i·ty, vend'i·ble·ness** *n.* — **vend'i·bly** *adv.*

vend·ing machine (ven'ding) A coin-operated device that dispenses some product or packaged article.

ve·neer (və-nir') *n.* **1.** A thin layer, as of choice wood, upon a commoner surface. **2.** Any of the thin layers glued together to strengthen plywood. **3.** Mere outside show or elegance. — *v.t.* **1.** To cover (a surface) with veneer; overlay for decoration or finer finish. **2.** To glue together to form plywood. **3.** To conceal, as something disagreeable or coarse, with an attractive or deceptive surface. [Earlier *fineer* < G < F *fournir* to furnish] — **ve·neer'er** *n.*

ve·neer·ing (və-nir'ing) *n.* **1.** The art of applying veneer. **2.** Material used for veneer. **3.** A surface of veneer.

ven·er·a·ble (ven'ər-ə-bəl) *adj.* **1.** Meriting or commanding veneration; worthy of reverence: now usu. implying age. **2.** Exciting reverential feelings because of sacred or historic associations. **3.** Revered: used as a title for an archdeacon in Anglican churches, and in the Roman Catholic Church, for one past the first stage of canonization, prior to beatification. [< OF < L *venerari* to revere] — **ven'er·a·ble·ness, ven'er·a·bil'i·ty** *n.* — **ven'er·a·bly** *adv.*

ven·er·ate (ven'ə-rāt) *v.t.* **·at·ed, ·at·ing** To look upon or regard with respect and deference; revere. [< L *veneratus,* pp. of *venerari* to revere]

— **Syn.** We *venerate* that which we judge objectively to be of great worth, as a great man, our ancestors, a holy person, or a sacred object. *Revere* and *reverence* imply respect, to which have been added personal affection and awe; *revere* is chiefly applied to persons or to a deity, and *reverence,* to places or objects: to *revere* God and the saints, to *reverence* a holy shrine. In strict usage, we *worship* or *adore* only that which we consider divine; *worship* refers to participation in religious ceremonies, and *adore,* to the sense of personal gratitude for divine favor which the worshiper feels.

ven·er·a·tion (ven'ə-rā'shən) *n.* **1.** The act of venerating or the state of being venerated. **2.** A feeling of profound respect and awe: reverence.

ve·ne·re·al (və-nir'ē-əl) *adj.* **1.** Pertaining to or proceeding from sexual intercourse. **2.** Communicated by sexual relations with an infected person: a *venereal* disease. **3.** Pertaining to or curative of diseases so communicated. **4.** Infected with venereal disease. [< L < *Venus*]

venereal disease *Pathol.* One of several diseases communicated by sexual intercourse, as syphilis, gonorrhea, and chancroid.

ven·er·y¹ (ven'ər-ē) *n. pl.* **·er·ies** *Archaic* Sexual indulgence, esp. when excessive. [< L *Venus*]

ven·er·y² (ven'ər-ē) *n. pl.* **·er·ies** *Archaic* The hunting of game. [< F < L *venari* to hunt]

Ven·e·ti (ven'ə-tī) *n.pl.* **1.** An ancient Celtic people of N Gaul, conquered by Caesar in 56 B.C. **2.** An ancient people of NE Italy, friendly to Rome.

Ve·ne·tian (və-nē'shən) *adj.* Pertaining to Venice, its inhabitants, art etc. — *n.* A native of Venice.

Venetian blind A flexible window screen that may be raised or lowered, having overlapping horizontal slats connected with a cord as to permit opening and closing.

Venetian carpet A worsted carpet for stairs and hallways, commonly of a simple striped pattern.

Venetian glass A delicate and fine glassware made at or near Venice.

ven·geance (ven'jəns) *n.* The act of revenging; retribution for a wrong or injury. — **Syn.** See REVENGE. — **with a vengeance** With great force or violence; to an unusual extent. [< AF < OF < L *vindicare* to defend, avenge]

venge·ful (venj'fəl) *adj.* **1.** Seeking to inflict vengeance; vindictive. **2.** Serving to inflict vengeance. — **venge'ful·ly** *adv.* — **venge'ful·ness** *n.*

veni- *combining form* Vein; also, vein in the earth. [< *vena* vein]

ve·ni·al (vē'nē-əl, vēn'yəl) *adj.* **1.** *Theol.* That may be easily pardoned or forgiven: distinguished from *mortal: venial* sin. **2.** Excusable; pardonable. [< OF < L *venia* forgiveness, mercy] — **ve'ni·al'i·ty** (-al'ə-tē), **ve'ni·al·ness** *n.* — **ve'ni·al·ly** *adv.*

ve·ni·re (vi-nī'rē) *n. Law* A writ issued to the sheriff summoning persons to serve as a jury. Also **ve·ni·re fa·ci·as** (fā'shi·as') [< L *venire facias,* that you cause to come]

ve·ni·re·man (vi-nī'rē-mən) *n. pl.* **·men** (-mən) One summoned to serve on a jury under a venire.

ven·i·son (ven'ə-zən, -sən; *Brit.* ven'zən) *n.* Deer flesh used for food. [< F < L *venatus,* pp. of *venari* to hunt]

ve·ni, vi·di, vi·ci (vē'nī, vī'dī, vī'sī; wā'nē, wē'dē, wē'kē) *Latin* I came, I saw, I conquered: words used by Julius Caesar to report a victory in Asia Minor.

ven·om (ven'əm) *n.* **1.** The poisonous liquid secreted by certain animals, as serpents and scorpions, and introduced into the victim by a bite or sting. **2.** Malice; malignity; spite. [< OF < L *venenum* poison]

ven·om·ous (ven'əm·əs) *adj.* **1.** Having glands secreting venom. **2.** Able to give a poisonous sting. **3.** Malignant; spiteful. — **ven'om·ous·ly** *adv.* — **ven'om·ous·ness** *n.*

ve·nous (vē'nəs) *adj.* **1.** Of, pertaining to, or marked with veins. **2.** *Physiol.* Designating the blood carried by veins, distinguished from arterial blood by its darker color and presence of carbon dioxide. [< L *venosus* < *vena* vein] — **ve'nous·ly** *adv.* — **ve'nous·ness** *n.*

vent (vent) *n.* **1.** An opening, commonly small, for the passage of liquids, gases, etc. **2.** Utterance; expression: chiefly in the phrase **to give vent to. 3.** *Zool.* The exterior opening of the alimentary canal, esp. of animals below mammals; the anus. — *v.t.* **1.** To give expression to: often with *on:* to *vent* one's rage on the cat. **2.** To relieve, as by giving vent to emotion. **3.** To permit to escape from an opening. [ME < OF *fente* cleft < L *findere* to split] — **ven'ter** *n.*

vent·age (ven'tij) *n.* **1.** A small opening. **2.** A finger hole in a musical instrument. [< VENT]

ven·tail (ven'tāl) *n.* The lower adjustable front of a medieval helmet. [< OF < *vent* wind]

ven·ti·late (ven'tə·lāt) *v.t.* **·lat·ed, ·lat·ing 1.** To produce free circulation of air in; admit fresh air into. **2.** To provide with a vent. **3.** To make widely known; expose to examination and discussion. **4.** To oxygenate, as blood. [< L *ventilatus,* pp. of *ventilare* to fan < *ventus* wind] — **ven'ti·la'tion** *n.* — **ven'ti·la'tive** *adj.*

ven·ti·la·tor (ven'tə·lā'tər) *n.* A device or arrangement for supplying fresh air. — **ven'ti·la·to·ry** (-lə·tôr'ē, -tō'rē) *adj.*

ven·tral (ven'trəl) *adj. Anat.* **a** Of, pertaining to, or situated on or near the abdomen. **b** On or toward the lower or anterior part of the body. [< L < *venter, ventris* belly] — **ven'tral·ly** *adv.*

ven·tri·cle (ven'trə·kəl) *n. Anat.* **1.** One of the two lower chambers of the heart, from which blood received from the atria is forced into the arteries. **2.** Any of various cavities e body, as of the brain, the spinal cord, etc. For illus. see ART. [< L *ventriculus*, dim. of *venter*, *ventris* belly]

·tric·u·lar (ven·trik′yə·lər) *adj.* **1.** Of, pertaining to, or the nature of a ventricle. **2.** Swollen and distended.

·tril·o·quism (ven·tril′ə·kwiz′əm) *n.* The art of speaking in such a manner that the sounds seem to come from me source other than the person speaking. Also **ven·tril′o·y** (-kwē). [< L < *venter* belly + *loqui* to speak] — **ven′l/o·quist** *n.* — **ven·tril′o·quis′tic** *adj.*

·tril·o·quize (ven·tril′ə·kwīz) *v.t.* & *v.i.* ·**quized**, ·**quiz·** g To speak as a ventriloquist. Also *Brit.* **ven·tril′o·quise.**

tro- *combining form Anat.* The abdomen; related to or ar the abdomen; ventral. [< L *venter*, *ventris* belly]

·ture (ven′chər) *v.* ·**tured**, ·**tur·ing** *v.t.* **1.** To expose to ance or risk; hazard; stake. **2.** To run the risk of; brave. To express at the risk of denial or refutation: to *venture* a gestion. — *v.i.* **4.** To take a risk; dare. — *n.* **1.** An dertaking attended with risk or danger; a risk; hazard; ., a business investment. **2.** That which is ventured; esp., perty risk. — **at a venture** At hazard; offhand. [Aphetic m of ADVENTURE] — **ven′tur·er** *n.*

·ture·some (ven′chər·səm) *adj.* **1.** Bold; daring. **2.** volving hazard; risky. — **ven′ture·some·ly** *adv.* — **ven′·e·some·ness** *n.*

·tur·ous (ven′chər·əs) *adj.* **1.** Adventurous; willing to ke risks and brave dangers; bold. **2.** Hazardous; risky; igerous. — **ven′tur·ous·ly** *adv.* — **ven′tur·ous·ness** *n.*

·ue (ven′yoō) *n. Law* The place where a crime is committed or a cause of action arises; also, the county or political division from which the jury must be summoned and in ich the trial must be held. — **change of venue** The ange of the place of trial. [< OF, orig. fem. pp. of *venir* to ne < L *venire*]

nus (vē′nəs) In Roman mythology, the goddess of love, ing, bloom, and beauty: identified with the Greek *Aphro-*. — *n.* **1.** The sixth largest planet of the solar system d second in order from the sun. See PLANET. **2.** A statue painting of Venus. **3.** A lovely woman. [< L]

ius of Mi·lo (mē′lō) A marble statue of Venus, with the ms missing, discovered in 1820 on the island of Milo and er placed in the Louvre. Also **Venus de Milo.**

nus's flytrap (vē′nəs·iz flī′trap′) *n.* A plant with clused leaves whose spiked blades instantly close upon insects ating upon them, found native chiefly in the sandy bogs of tern North and South Carolina.

·ra·cious (və·rā′shəs) *adj.* **1.** Habitually disposed to ak the truth; truthful. **2.** Conforming to or expressing th; true; accurate. [< L *verax*, *veracis* < *versus* true] **ve·ra′cious·ly** *adv.* — **ve·ra′cious·ness** *n.*

ac·i·ty (və·ras′ə·tē) *n. pl.* ·**ties 1.** The habitual regard truth; truthfulness; honesty. **2.** Agreement with truth; uracy. **3.** That which is true; truth.

an·da (və·ran′də) *n.* An open portico or balcony, usu. fed, along the outside of a building; a porch or stoop. Alve·ran′dah. [< Hind. < Pg. *varanda* railing, balustrade]

b (vûrb) *n. Gram.* **1.** The part of speech that expresses stence, action, or occurrence, as the English words *be, col-, think.* **2.** Any word or construction functioning simiy. [< F < L *verbum* word]

bal (vûr′bəl) *adj.* **1.** Of, pertaining to, or connected h words. **2.** Concerned with words rather than the ideas y convey: *verbal* distinctions. **3.** Expressed orally; not tten: a *verbal* contract. **4.** Having word corresponding h word; literal: a *verbal* translation. **5.** *Gram.* **a** Partak-of the nature of or derived from a verb: a *verbal* noun. **b** ed to form verbs: a *verbal* prefix. — *n. Gram.* A verb m that functions as a substantive (gerund and infinitive) as a modifier (present and past participles and infinitive), t retains some of the characteristics of a verb. [< F < L *verbum* word] — **ver′bal·ly** *adv.*

— **Syn.** (adj.) **2.** In strict usage, *verbal* refers to spoken or tten words, and *oral*, to spoken words only: a *verbal* dispute, *oral* examination. However, the distinction is often blurred, so t we speak of a *verbal* agreement, rather than of an *oral* agreemt. *Oral* and *verbal* always imply communication: *vocal* refers to use of the voice, whether for communicating thought or not: *cal* exercise, a *vocal* defect.

bal·ism (vûr′bəl·iz′əm) *n.* **1.** A verbal expression. **2.** meaningless form of words. **3.** Wordiness; verbiage.

bal·ist (vûr′bəl·ist) *n.* **1.** One who deals with words her than facts or ideas. **2.** One who is skilled in the use 1 meaning of words.

bal·ize (vûr′bəl·īz) *v.* ·**ized**, ·**iz·ing** *v.t.* **1.** To express in rds. **2.** *Gram.* To make a verb of; change into a verb. — **3.** To speak or write verbosely. **4.** To express oneself in rds. — **ver′bal·i·za′tion** *n.* — **ver′bal·iz′er** *n.*

·ba·tim (vər·bā′tim, -təm) *adj.* & *adv.* In the exact rds; word for word. [< LL < L *verbum* word]

ver·be·na (vər·bē′nə) *n.* Any of various American garden plants having dense terminal spikes of showy flowers. [< L, foliage, vervain]

ver·bi·age (vûr′bē·ij) *n.* **1.** Excess of words. **2.** Wordiness; verbosity. [< F *verbier* to gabble < L *verbum* word]

ver·bose (vər·bōs′) *adj.* Using or containing a wearisome and unnecessary number of words; wordy. [< L *verbosus* < *verbum* word] — **ver·bose′ly** *adv.* — **ver·bose′ness** *n.*
— **Syn.** Diffuse, prolix. Compare CIRCUMLOCUTION.

ver·bos·i·ty (vər·bos′ə·tē) *n. pl.* ·**ties** The state or quality of being verbose; wordiness.

ver·bo·ten (fer·bōt′n) *adj. German* Forbidden.

verb phrase *Gram.* A finite verb form, consisting of a principle verb and an auxiliary or auxiliaries.

ver·dant (vûr′dənt) *adj.* **1.** Green with vegetation; covered with grass or green leaves; fresh. **2.** Unsophisticated. [< F < L *viridis* green] — **ver′dan·cy** *n.* — **ver′dant·ly** *adv.*

ver·dict (vûr′dikt) *n.* **1.** The decision of a jury in an action. **2.** A conclusion expressed; judgment. [< AF *verdit*, OF *voirdit* < L < *verus* true + *dictum*, pp. of *dicere* to say]

ver·di·gris (vûr′də·grēs, -gris) *n.* The green or bluish patina formed on copper, bronze, or brass surfaces after long exposure to the air. [< OF *verd de Grice, vert de Grece*, lit., green of Greece]

ver·dure (vûr′jər) *n.* The fresh greenness of growing vegetation; also, such vegetation itself. [< F < L *viridis* green]

ver·dur·ous (vûr′jər·əs) *adj.* Covered with verdure; verdant. — **ver′dur·ous·ness** *n.*

Ver·ein (fer·īn′) *n. German* A society; association.

verge¹ (vûrj) *n.* **1.** The extreme edge of something having defined limits; brink; margin. **2.** The point at which some action, condition, or state is likely to occur: on the *verge* of bankruptcy. **3.** A bounding or enclosing line; a boundary; also, the space enclosed. **4.** A rod, wand, or staff as a symbol of authority or emblem of office. — *v.i.* **verged, verg·ing 1.** To come near; approach; border; usu. with *on*: His speech *verges* on the chaotic. **2.** To form the limit or verge. [< F, rod, stick < L *virga* twig]

verge² (vûrj) *v.i.* **verged, verg·ing** To slope; tend; incline. [< L *vergere* to bend, turn]

Ver·gil·i·an (vər·jil′ē·ən) *adj.* Pertaining to or in the style of Virgil: also spelled *Virgilian.*

ver·i·fi·a·ble (ver′ə·fī′ə·bəl) *adj.* Capable of being verified. — **ver′i·fi′a·ble·ness** *n.* — **ver′i·fi′a·bly** *adv.*

ver·i·fi·ca·tion (ver′ə·fə·kā′shən) *n.* **1.** The act of verifying, or the state of being verified. **2.** *Law* An oath appended to an account, petition, or plea, as to the truth of the facts stated in it.

ver·i·fy (ver′ə·fī) *v.t.* ·**fied**, ·**fy·ing 1.** To prove to be true or accurate; substantiate; confirm. **2.** To test or ascertain the accuracy or truth of. **3.** *Law* **a** To affirm under oath. **b** To add a confirmation to. [< OF < Med.L < *verus* true + *facere* to make] — **ver′i·fi′er** *n.*

ver·i·ly (ver′ə·lē) *adv. Archaic* In truth; really. [< VERY]

ver·i·sim·i·lar (ver′ə·sim′ə·lər) *adj.* Appearing or seeming to be true; likely; probable. [< L < *verus* true + *similis* like] — **ver′i·sim′i·lar·ly** *adv.*

ver·i·si·mil·i·tude (ver′ə·si·mil′ə·toōd, -tyoōd) *n.* **1.** Appearance of truth. **2.** That which resembles truth.

ver·i·ta·ble (ver′ə·tə·bəl) *adj.* Properly so called; unquestionable: a *veritable* villain. [< F *vérité* verity] — **ver′i·ta·ble·ness** *n.* — **ver′i·ta·bly** *adv.*

ver·i·ty (ver′ə·tē) *n. pl.* ·**ties 1.** The quality of being correct or true. **2.** A true or established statement, principle, etc.; a fact; truth. [< F < L *veritas* truth]

ver·juice (vûr′joōs) *n.* **1.** The sour juice of green fruit, as unripe grapes. **2.** Sharpness or sourness of disposition or manner; acidity. [< OF < *vert* green + *jus* juice]

ver·meil (vûr′mil) *n.* **1.** Silver or bronze gilt. **2.** *Poetic* Vermilion, or the color of vermilion. — *adj.* Of a bright-red color. [< OF < L *vermiculus*, dim. of *vermis* worm, the cochineal insect]

vermi- *combining form* A worm; of or related to a worm. [< L *vermis* worm]

ver·mi·cel·li (vûr′mə·sel′ē, *Ital.* ver′mē·chel′lē) *n.* A food paste made into slender cords thinner than spaghetti or macaroni. [< Ital., lit., little worms, pl. of *vermicello*]

ver·mi·cide (vûr′mə·sīd) *n.* Any substance that kills worms; esp., any drug destructive of intestinal worms. — **ver·mi·ci·dal** (vûr′mə·sīd′əl) *adj.*

ver·mic·u·lar (vər·mik′yə·lər) *adj.* **1.** Having the form or motion of a worm. **2.** Like the wavy tracks of a worm [< L < *vermis* worm] — **ver·mic′u·lar·ly** *adv.*

ver·mic·u·late (vər·mik′yə·lāt) *adj.* **1.** Covered with wormlike markings. **2.** Having the motions of a worm. **3.** Insinuating; tortuous. **4.** Worm-eaten.

ver·mi·form (vûr′mə·fôrm) *adj.* Like a worm in shape. [< Med.L < L *vermis* worm + *forma* form]

vermiform appendix *Anat.* A slender, wormlike vestigial structure, protruding from the end of the cecum in man and certain other mammals. For illus. see INTESTINE.

ver·mi·fuge (vûr′mə·fyōōj) *n.* Any remedy that destroys intestinal worms. — *adj.* Acting as a vermifuge. [< F < L *vermis* worm + *fugare* to expel]

ver·mil·ion (vər·mil′yən) *n.* **1.** A brilliant, durable red pigment, obtained naturally by grinding cinnabar to a fine powder, or made synthetically. **2.** The color of the pigment, an intense orange red. — *adj.* Of a bright-red color. — *v.t.* To color with vermilion; dye bright red. [See VERMEIL.]

ver·min (vûr′min) *n.* *pl.* **·min** **1.** Noxious small animals or parasitic insects, as lice, fleas, worms, rats, mice, etc. **2.** *Brit.* Certain animals injurious to game, as weasels, owls, etc. **3.** A repulsive or obnoxious human being; also, such persons collectively. [< OF < L *vermis* worm]

ver·min·ous (vûr′mən·əs) *adj.* **1.** Infested with vermin, esp. parasites. **2.** Relating to or caused by vermin. **3.** Of the nature of or resembling vermin. — **ver′min·ous·ly** *adv.* — **ver′min·ous·ness** *n.*

ver·mouth (vûr′mōōth, vər·mōōth′) *n.* A liqueur made from white wine flavored with aromatic herbs. Also **ver′·muth.** [< F < G *wermuth* wormwood]

ver·nac·u·lar (vər·nak′yə·lər) *n.* **1.** The native language of a locality. **2.** The common everyday speech of the people, as opposed to the literary language. **3.** The vocabulary or jargon of a particular profession or trade. **4.** An idiomatic word or phrase. **5.** The common name of a plant or animal as distinguished from its scientific designation. — *adj.* **1.** Originating in or belonging to one's native land; indigenous: said of a language, idiom, etc. **2.** Using everyday speech rather than the literary language. **3.** Written in the native language. **4.** Characteristic of a specific locality or country: *vernacular* arts. **5.** Designating the common name of a plant or animal. [< L *vernaculus* native < *verna* home-born slave, native] — **ver·nac′u·lar·ly** *adv.*

ver·nal (vûr′nəl) *adj.* **1.** Belonging to, appearing in, or appropriate to spring. **2.** Youthful; fresh. [< L *vernus* belonging to spring < *ver* spring] — **ver′nal·ly** *adv.*

ver·nal·ize (vûr′nəl·īz) *v.t.* **·ized, ·iz·ing** To accelerate the growth of (a plant) by subjecting the seeds to low temperatures. — **ver′nal·i·za′tion** *n.*

ver·na·tion (vər·nā′shən) *n.* *Bot.* The disposition of leaves within the leaf bud. [< NL < *vernare* to flourish]

ver·ni·er (vûr′nē·ər) *n.* **1.** The small, movable, auxiliary scale for obtaining fractional parts of the subdivisions of a fixed scale on a barometer, sextant, gauge, or other measure. Also **vernier scale.** **2.** *Mech.* An auxiliary device to insure fine adjustments in precision instruments. [after Pierre *Vernier*, 1580?–1637, French mathematician]

Ve·ro·nal (ver′ə·nəl) *n.* Proprietary name for a brand of barbital.

ver·sa·tile (vûr′sə·til) *adj.* **1.** Having an aptitude for various occupations; many-sided. **2.** Subject to change; variable. **3.** *Bot.* Attached so as to be freely swinging or turning. **4.** *Zool.* Capable of being turned forward or backward, as the toe of a bird. [< F < L *versatile* to turn] — **ver′sa·tile·ly** *adv.* — **ver′sa·til′i·ty, ver′sa·tile·ness** *n.*

verse (vûrs) *n.* **1.** A single metrical or rhythmical line. **2.** Metrical composition; poetry: distinguished from *prose.* **3.** A poem. **4.** A specified type of meter or metrical structure: iambic *verse.* **5.** One of the short divisions of a chapter of the Bible. **6.** A short division of any metrical composition, song, etc., esp., a stanza. — *v.t.* & *v.i.* **versed, vers·ing** *Rare* To versify. [OE and OF < L < *vertere* to turn]

versed (vûrst) *adj.* Thoroughly acquainted; adept; proficient: with *in.* [< L *versari* to occupy oneself]

versed sine *Trig.* A function of an angle, equal to one minus the cosine. Also **ver·sine** (vûr′sīn).

ver·si·cle (vûr′si·kəl) *n.* One of a series of lines said or sung alternately by minister and congregation. [< L. See VERSE.]

ver·si·fy (vûr′sə·fī) *v.* **·fied, ·fy·ing** *v.t.* **1.** To change from prose into verse. **2.** To narrate or treat in verse. — *v.i.* **3.** To write poetry. [< OF < L < *versus* verse + *facere* to make] — **ver′si·fi·ca′tion** (-fə·kā′shən) *n.* — **ver′si·fi′er** *n.*

ver·sion (vûr′zhən, -shən) *n.* **1.** A description or account as modified by a particular point of view. **2.** A translation. **3.** *Usu. cap.* A translation of the whole or part of the Bible: the Douai *version.* [< MF < Med.L < *vertere* to turn] — **ver′sion·al** *adj.*

vers li·bre (ver lē′br′) *French* Free verse.

ver·so (vûr′sō) *n.* *pl.* **·sos** **1.** A left-hand page of a book, or sheet of folded paper: opposed to *recto.* **2.** The reverse of a coin or medal. [< L *verso* (*folio*) a turned (leaf)]

verst (vûrst) *n.* A Russian measure of distance, about two thirds of a mile, or 1.067 kilometers. [< F and G < Russian *versta*, orig. a line]

ver·sus (vûr′səs) *prep.* **1.** In law and sports: against: Dempsey *versus* Tunney. **2.** Considered as the alternative of: free trade *versus* tariffs. [< L, toward, *vertere* to turn]

ver·te·bra (vûr′tə·brə) *n.* *pl.* **·brae** (-brē) or **·bras** *An*[.] Any of the segmented bones of the spinal column in man a[nd] the higher vertebrates. [< L, joint < *vertere* to turn] **ver′te·bral** *adj.*

ver·te·brate (vûr′tə·brāt, -brit) *adj.* **1.** Having a backbo[ne] or spinal column. **2.** Pertaining to or characteristic of ve[r]tebrates. — *n.* Any of a primary division of animals, ch[ar]acterized by a segmented spinal column, as fishes, birds, re[p]tiles, and mammals.

ver·tex (vûr′teks) *n.* *pl.* **·tex·es** or **·ti·ces** (-tə·sēz) **1.** T[he] highest point of anything; apex; top. **2.** *Astron.* The po[int] in the sky toward or from which a group of stars appears [to] be moving. **3.** *Geom.* **a** The point of intersection of the sid[es] of an angle. **b** The point of a triangle opposite to, and f[ar]thest from, the base. [< L, the top < *vertere* to turn]

ver·ti·cal (vûr′ti·kəl) *adj.* **1.** Perpendicular to the plane [of] the horizon, extending up and down; upright. **2.** Direc[tly] above or overhead. **3.** Of or at the vertex or highest poi[nt.] **4.** *Econ.* Of or pertaining to a group of business conce[rns] that handle all the stages of the manufacture and distri[bu]tion of a product. — *n.* **1.** A vertical line, plane, or circ[le.] **2.** An upright beam or rod in a truss. [< MF < L. S[ee] VERTEX.] — **ver′ti·cal′i·ty** (-kal′ə·tē), **ver′ti·cal·ness** *n.* **ver′ti·cal·ly** *adv.*

vertical union An industrial union.

ver·ti·ces (vûr′tə·sēz) Plural of VERTEX.

ver·ti·cil (vûr′tə·sil) *n.* *Biol.* **1.** A set of organs, as lea[ves] or tentacles, disposed in a circle around an axis; whorl. [2.] A volution of a spiral shell. [< L *verticillus* whorl]

ver·ti·cil·late (vər·tis′ə·lit, -lāt, vûr′tə·sil′it, -āt) *adj.* Arranged in a verticil. **2.** Having parts so arranged. A[lso] **ver·tic′il·lat·ed.** — **ver·tic′il·late·ly** *adv.* — **ver·tic′il**[·la]**tion** *n.*

ver·tig·i·nous (vər·tij′ə·nəs) *adj.* **1.** Affected by verti[go;] dizzy. **2.** Turning round; whirling; revolving. **3.** Liable [to] cause dizziness. [See VERTIGO.] — **ver·tig′i·nous·ly** *a*[dv.] — **ver·tig′i·nous·ness** *n.*

ver·ti·go (vûr′tə·gō) *n.* *pl.* **·goes** or **ver·tig·i·nes** (vər·tij′[ə]·nēz) *Pathol.* Any of a group of disorders in which a pers[on] feels as if he or his surroundings are whirling around; di[zzi]ness. [< L < *vertere* to turn]

ver·tu (vər·tōō′, vûr′tōō) See VIRTU.

ver·vain (vûr′vān) *n.* Any of a family of herbs, shrubs, a[nd] trees, including many cultivated ornamental verbenas. [< OF < L *verbena*]

verve (vûrv) *n.* **1.** Enthusiasm or energy, esp., as ma[ni]fested in artistic production. **2.** Spirit; vigor. [< F]

ver·y (ver′ē) *adv.* In a high degree; extremely: *very* gener[ous.] — *adj.* **ver·i·er, ver·i·est** **1.** Absolute; actual; simp[le:] the *very* truth. **2.** Identical: my *very* words. **3.** The (thi[ng]) itself: used as an intensive equivalent to *even*: The *very* sto[nes] cry out. **4.** Unqualified; utter; complete: a *very* rogue. [AF or OF < L *verus* true]

very high frequency *Telecom.* A band of radio wave [fre]quencies ranging from 30 to 300 megacycles.

very low frequency *Telecom.* A band of radio wave [fre]quencies ranging from 10 to 30 kilocycles.

ves·i·cant (ves′i·kənt) *adj.* Producing blisters. — *n.* Th[at] which produces blisters. [< NL < L *vesica* blister, bladd[er]] — **ves′i·ca′tion** *n.*

ves·i·cate (ves′i·kāt) *v.t.* & *v.i.* **·cat·ed, ·cat·ing** To blis[ter.] — **ves′i·ca′tion** *n.*

ves·i·ca·to·ry (ves′i·kə·tôr′ē, və·sik′ə·tôr′ē, -tō′rē) *adj.* [Ca]pable of producing blisters; vesicant. — *n.* *pl.* **·ries** A[ny] substance, as an ointment or plaster, that causes a bliste[r.] [< L *vesica* blister]

ves·i·cle (ves′i·kəl) *n.* **1.** Any small bladderlike cavity, c[yst] or cyst. **2.** *Anat.* A small sac, containing gas or fluid. [*Pathol.* A blister. [< L < *vesica* bladder] — **ve·sic·u·**[lar] (və·sik′yə·lər) *adj.*

vesico- *combining form* *Med.* The urinary bladder; of [or] pertaining to the urinary bladder. Also, before vow[els] **vesic-.** [< L *vesica* bladder]

ve·sic·u·late (*v.* və·sik′yə·lāt; *adj.* və·sik′yə·lit, -lāt) *v.t.* [&] *v.i.* **·lat·ed, ·lat·ing** To make or become vesicular. — [adj.] Having vesicles; vesicular. — **ve·sic·u·la′tion** *n.*

ves·per (ves′pər) *n.* **1.** A bell that calls to vespers. **2.** [An] evening service, prayer, or song. **3.** *Obs.* Evening. — [adj.] Of evening or vespers. [< L, the evening star]

Ves·per (ves′pər) *n.* The evening star; Hesperus; the pla[net] Venus when an evening star. [< OF < L]

ves·pers (ves′pərz) *n.pl. Often cap.* *Eccl.* **1.** The sixth of [the] seven canonical hours. **2.** A service of worship in the e[ve]ning. [< OF < Med.L < L *vespera* evening]

ves·sel (ves′əl) *n.* **1.** A hollow receptacle, esp. one capa[ble] of holding a liquid, as a bowl, pitcher, etc. **2.** A craft [de]signed to float on the water, usu. one larger than a rowbo[at:] a ship or boat. **3.** *Anat.* A duct or canal for transportin[g a] body fluid, as a vein. [< L < *vas* vessel]

vest (vest) *n.* *Chiefly U.S.* A man's short, sleeveless g[ar]ment, buttoning in front, commonly worn underneath a [suit] coat: also, *esp. Brit., waistcoat.* — *v.t.* **1.** To confer (ow[ner]ship, authority, etc.) upon some person or persons: u[pon] ith in. 2. To place ownership, or authority with (a person r persons). 3. To clothe, as with vestments. — v.i. 4. o clothe oneself, as in vestments. 5. To become vested; de- olve. [< F < Ital. < L vestis garment]

es·ta (ves′tə) n. In Roman mythology, the goddess of the earth and the hearth fire.

s·tal (ves′təl) n. 1. One of the virgin priestesses of Vesta. lso **vestal virgin.** 2. A woman of pure character; a virgin. A nun. — adj. 1. Pertaining to Vesta. 2. Chaste; pure.

st·ed (ves′tid) adj. 1. Law Held by fixed tenure. Estab- shed by law as a permanent right. 2. Dressed; robed, esp. church vestments.

sted interest 1. A strong commitment to a system or in- itution whose existence serves one's self-interest. 2. Usu. l. A financially powerful or influential group.

st·ee (ves·tē′) n. An imitation blouse-front worn in the ont of a suit or dress. [Dim. of VEST]

s·ti·bule (ves′tə·byōōl) n. 1. A small antechamber be- ind the outer door of a building; an entrance hall; lobby. The enclosed passage between railway passenger cars. Anat. Any of several chambers or channels adjoining or ommunicating with others: the vestibule of the ear. — v.t. uled, ·bul·ing To provide with a vestibule. [< L vestibu- m entrance hall] — ves·tib′u·lar (-tib′yə·lər) adj.

s·tige (ves′tij) n. 1. A visible trace, impression, or sign, f something absent or lost; trace. 2. Biol. A part or or- mall or degenerate, but well developed and functional in an- estral forms of organisms. [< F < L vestigium footprint] — ves·tig′i·al adj. — ves·tig′i·al·ly adv.

s·tig·i·um (ves·tij′ē·əm) n. pl. ·tig·i·a (-tij′ē·ə) Biol. A estigial part; vestige. [< L, footprint]

st·ment (vest′mənt) n. 1. An article of dress; esp., a be of office. 2. Eccl. One of the ritual garments of the ergy. [< OF < L vestire to clothe] — vest′ment·al adj.

st-pock·et (vest′pok′it) adj. Small enough to fit in a vest ocket; very small; diminutive: a vest-pocket edition.

s·try (ves′trē) n. pl. ·tries 1. A room, as in a church, here vestments and sacred vessels are kept: often called acristy. 2. A room in a church used for Sunday School, eetings, as a chapel, etc. 3. In the Anglican Church, a ody administering the affairs of a parish or congregation; lso, a meeting of such a body. [< OF vestiarie < Med.L stiarium wardrobe]

s·try·man (ves′trē·mən) n. pl. ·men (-mən) A member f a vestry.

s·ture (ves′chər) n. 1. Archaic Garments; clothing; a obe. 2. Archaic A covering or envelope. — v.t. ·tured, ur·ing Archaic To cover or clothe with vesture. [< OF < stir cloth < L vestire to clothe]

t¹ (vet) Informal n. A veterinarian. — v. vet·ted, vet· ng v.t. 1. To treat as a veterinarian does. — v.i. 2. To eat animals medically. [Short for VETERINARIAN]

t² (vet) n. Informal A veteran. [Short for VETERAN]

tch (vech) n. 1. Any of various climbing herbaceous nes of the bean family; esp., the common broad bean, own for fodder. 2. A leguminous European plant yielding lible seeds. [< AF veche, vecce < L vicia]

t·er·an (vet′ər·ən, vet′rən) n. 1. One who is much expe- enced in any service. 2. A former member of the armed rces. — adj. 1. Having had long experience or practice; d in service. 2. Of or pertaining to veterans. [< MF < L teranus < vetus, veteris old]

terans Administration An agency of the U.S. govern- ent that administers all federal laws relating to the relief of rmer members of the military and naval services.

terans Day A U.S. national holiday honoring veterans the armed forces, November 11, the anniversary of the ar- istice in World War I: formerly called Armistice Day.

terans of Foreign Wars A society of ex-servicemen ho have served in the U.S. armed forces in a war with and a foreign country; founded 1899.

t·er·i·nar·i·an (vet′ər·ə·nâr′ē·ən, vet′rə-) n. Chiefly U.S. practitioner of veterinary medicine or surgery.

t·er·i·nar·y (vet′ər·ə·ner′ē, vet′rə-) adj. Pertaining to the seases or injuries of animals, and to their treatment by edical or surgical means. — n. pl. ·nar·ies A veterinari- n. [< L veterinarius pertaining to beasts of burden]

terinary medicine The branch of medicine that deals ith the prevention, treatment, and cure of animal diseases.

·to (vē′tō) v.t. ·toed, ·to·ing 1. To refuse executive ap- roval of (a bill passed by a legislative body). 2. To forbid r prohibit authoritatively. — n. pl. ·toes 1. The preroga- ve of a chief executive to refuse to approve a legislative en- ctment by withholding his signature; also, the exercise of ich a prerogative: also veto power. 2. The official commu- ication containing a refusal to approve a bill and the rea- ons for refusing: also veto message. 3. Any authoritative rohibition. [< L, I forbid] — ve′to·er n.

vex (veks) v.t. 1. To provoke to anger or displeasure by small irritations; annoy. 2. To trouble or afflict. 3. To make a subject of dispute. [< OF < L vexare to shake] — **vexed** adj. — **vex′er** n.

vex·a·tion (vek·sā′shən) n. 1. A vexing or being vexed. 2. That which vexes.

vex·a·tious (vek·sā′shəs) adj. 1. Causing vexation. 2. Harassing; annoying. — **vex·a′tious·ly** adv. — **vex·a′· tious·ness** n.

vi·a (vī′ə, vē′ə) prep. By way of; by a route passing through: He went to Boston via New Haven. ◆ In informal usage, via can refer to the means of travel as well as the route: We went via train. [< L, ablative sing. of via way]

vi·a·ble (vī′ə·bəl) adj. 1. Capable of developing normally, as a newborn infant, a seed, etc. 2. Workable; practicable. [< F < vie life < L vita] — **vi·a·bil′i·ty** n.

vi·a·duct (vī′ə·dukt) n. A bridgelike structure, esp. a large one of arched mason- ry, to carry a road- way or the like over a valley or ravine. [< L via way + (AQUE)- DUCT]

vi·al (vī′əl) n. A small bottle for liq- uids: also phial. — **to pour out the vials of wrath upon** To in- flict retribution or vengeance on. See Rev. xvi. — v.t. vi· aled or ·alled, ·vi·al· ing or ·al·ling To put or keep in or as in a vial. [< OF < L < Gk. phialē shallow cup]

VIADUCT
(Pont du Gard, a Roman aqueduct at Nîmes, France)

vi·and (vī′ənd) n. 1. An article of food, esp. meat. 2. pl. Victuals; provisions; food. [< OF viande, ult. < L vivenda, neut. pl. gerundive of vivere to live]

vi·at·i·cum (vī·at′ə·kəm) n. pl. ·ca (-kə) or ·cums 1. Eccl. The Eucharist, as given on the verge of death. 2. Provisions for a journey. [< L, traveling money, neut. sing. of viaticus < via way]

vibes¹ (vībz) n.pl. Informal A vibraphone.

vibes² (vībz) n.pl. Slang Vibration (def. 3).

vi·bran·cy (vī′brən·sē) n. pl. ·cies The state or character of being vibrant; resonance.

vi·brant (vī′brənt) adj. 1. Vibrating. 2. Throbbing; pul- sing: vibrant with enthusiasm. 3. Rich and resonant, as a sound: vibrant tones. 4. Energetic; vigorous. 5. Phonet. Voiced. — n. Phonet. A voiced sound. [< L ppr. of vibrare to shake] — **vi′brant·ly** adv.

vi·bra·phone (vī′brə·fōn) n. A type of marimba in which a pulsating sound is produced by valves in the resonators. Also **vi′bra·harp′** (-härp′). [< VIBRA(TO) + -PHONE]

vi·brate (vī′brāt) v. ·brat·ed, ·brat·ing v.i. 1. To move back and forth rapidly; quiver. 2. To move or swing back and forth, as a pendulum. 3. To sound: The note vibrates on the ear. 4. To be emotionally moved; thrill. 5. To vacil- late; waver, as between choices. — v.t. 6. To cause to quiv- er or tremble. 7. To cause to move back and forth. 8. To send forth (sound, etc.) by vibration. [< L vibratus, pp. of vibrare to shake]

vi·bra·tile (vī′brə·til, -tīl) adj. 1. Adapted to, having, or used in vibratory motion. 2. Pertaining to or resembling vi- bration. — **vi·bra·til′i·ty** (vī′brə·til′ə·tē) n.

vi·bra·tion (vī·brā′shən) n. 1. The act of vibrating or the state of being vibrated. 2. Physics a Any physical process characterized by cyclic variations in amplitude, intensity, or the like, as wave motion or an electric field. b A single com- plete oscillation. 3. pl. The atmosphere of a place or the mood of a person as perceived by another person. — **vi·bra′tion·al** adj. — **vi′bra·to·ry** adj.

vi·bra·to (vē·brä′tō) n. pl. ·tos Music A trembling or pul- sating effect caused by rapid but minute variations in pitch during the production of a tone. [< Ital. < L, pp. of vi- brare to shake]

vi·bra·tor (vī′brā·tər) n. 1. That which vibrates. 2. An electrically operated massaging apparatus.

vib·ri·o (vib′rē·ō) n. pl. ·ri·os Any of various comma- shaped bacteria. [< L vibrare to shake] — **vib·ri·on′ic** adj.

vi·bur·num (vī·bûr′nəm) n. Any of a genus of shrubs or small trees related to the honeysuckle, bearing small flowers and berrylike fruit. [< L, the wayfaring tree]

vic·ar (vik′ər) n. 1. In the Anglican Church, the priest of a parish of which the main revenues are appropriated or im- propriated by a layman, the priest himself receiving but a stipend. 2. In the Roman Catholic Church, a substitute or representative of an ecclesiastical person. 3. In some parishes of the Protestant Episcopal Church, the clergyman who is the head of a chapel.   4. One authorized to perform functions in the stead of another; deputy.   [< AF, OF < L *vicarius* substitute < *vicis* change]

vic·ar·age (vik′ər·ij) *n.* 1. The benefice, office, or duties of a vicar.   2. A vicar's residence or household.

vicar general *pl.* **vicars general** 1. In the Roman Catholic Church, a functionary appointed by the bishop as assistant or representative in certain matters of jurisdiction.   2. In the Church of England, an official assisting the bishop or archbishop in ecclesiastical causes.

vi·car·i·al (vī·kâr′ē·əl) *adj.* 1. Vicarious; delegated.   2. Of, relating to, or acting as a vicar.

vi·car·i·ate (vī·kâr′ē·it, -āt, vi-) *n.* A delegated office or power; esp., the office or authority of a vicar. Also **vic·ar·ate** (vik′ər·it).

vi·car·i·ous (vī·kâr′ē·əs, vi-) *adj.* 1. Made or performed by substitution; suffered or done in place of another: a *vicarious* sacrifice.   2. Enjoyed, felt, etc., by a person as a result of his imagined participation in an experience not his own: *vicarious* gratification.   3. Filling the office of or acting for another.   [< L *vicarius* substitute] — **vi·car′i·ous·ly** *adv.* — **vi·car′i·ous·ness** *n.*

Vicar of Christ The Pope.

vic·ar·ship (vik′ər·ship) *n.* The office or position of a vicar.

vice[1] (vīs) *n.* 1. An immoral habit or trait.   2. A slight personal fault; foible.   3. Habitual indulgence in degrading or harmful practices.   4. Something that mars; a blemish or imperfection.   [< OF < L *vitium* fault]

vice[2] (vīs) See VISE.

vice[3] (*adj. & n.* vīs; *prep.* vī′sē) *adj.* Acting in the place of; substitute; deputy: *vice* president. — *n.* One who acts in the place of another; a substitute; deputy. — *prep.* Instead of; in the place of.   [< L, ablative of *vicis* change]

vice admiral *Naval* A commissioned officer ranking next below an admiral. Also *Brit. & Canadian* **vice-ad·mi·ral** (vīs′ad′mər·əl). See tables at GRADE.

vice-ad·mi·ral·ty (vīs′ad′mər·əl·tē) *n.* *pl.* **·ties** The office of a vice admiral.

vice consul One who exercises consular authority, either as the substitute or as the subordinate of a consul. — **vice-con·su·lar** (vīs′kon′sə·lər) *adj.* — **vice-con·su·late** (vīs′·kon′sə·lit) *n.* — **vice′-con′sul·ship** *n.*

vice·ge·ren·cy (vīs·jir′ən·sē) *n.* *pl.* **·cies** 1. The office or authority of a vicegerent.   2. A district ruled by a vicegerent.

vice·ger·ent (vīs·jir′ənt) *n.* One duly authorized to exercise the powers of another; a deputy; vicar. — *adj.* Acting in the place of another, usu. in the place of a superior.   [< Med.L < L *vice* in place + *gerens*, *-entis*, ppr. of *gerere* to carry, manage] — **vice·ge′ral** *adj.*

vic·e·nar·y (vis′ə·ner′ē) *adj.* 1. Consisting of or pertaining to twenty.   2. Relating to a system of notation based upon twenty.   [< L < *viceni* twenty each < *viginti* twenty]

vi·cen·ni·al (vī·sen′ē·əl) *adj.* 1. Occurring once in twenty years.   2. Lasting or existing twenty years.

vice president An officer ranking next below a president, and acting, on occasion, in his place. — **vice-pres·i·den·cy** (vīs′prez′ə·dən·sē) *n.* — **vice′-pres′i·den′tial** (-prez′ə·den′·shəl) *adj.*

vice-re·gal (vīs·rē′gəl) *adj.* Of or relating to a viceroy, his office, or his jurisdiction. Also **vice·roy′al** (-roi′əl). — **vice·re′gal·ly** *adv.*

vice regent A deputy regent. — **vice-re·gen·cy** (vīs′rē′jən·sē) *n.* — **vice′-re′gent** *adj.*

vice·roy (vīs′roi) *n.* 1. One who rules a country, colony, or province by the authority of his sovereign or king.   2. A North American nymphalid butterfly, orange red with black markings and a row of white marginal spots.   [< MF < *vice-*, *vis-* in place + *roy* king, ult. < L *rex*, *regis*]

vice·roy·al·ty (vīs·roi′əl·tē) *n.* *pl.* **·ties** 1. The office or authority of a viceroy.   2. The term of office of a viceroy.   3. A district governed by a viceroy. Also **vice′roy·ship**.

vice squad A police division charged with combating prostitution, gambling, etc.

vi·ce ver·sa (vī′sē vûr′sə, vīs′) The order being changed; conversely.   [< L]

vi·chy·ssoise (vē′shē·swäz′) *n.* A potato cream soup, usu. served cold.   [< F, of Vichy]

Vi·chy water (vish′ē, vē·shē′) The effervescent mineral water from the springs at Vichy, France; also, any mineral water resembling it. Also **Vi′chy, vi′chy.**

vic·i·nage (vis′ə·nij) *n.* 1. Neighboring places collectively; vicinity.   2. The state of being a neighbor or neighbors.   [< OF < L *vicinus* nearby]

vic·i·nal (vis′ə·nəl) *adj.* Neighboring; adjoining; near.

vi·cin·i·ty (vi·sin′ə·tē) *n.* *pl.* **·ties** 1. A region adjacent or near; neighborhood.   2. Nearness in space or relationship; proximity.   [< L < *vicinus* nearby]

vi·cious (vish′əs) *adj.* 1. Characterized by malice or spite; malicious.   2. Characterized by violence and fierceness: a *vicious* blow.   3. Addicted to vice; corrupt in conduct or

habits.   4. Morally injurious; vile.   5. Unruly or dangerou refractory, as an animal.   6. Defective or faulty: *vicious* a guments.   7. *Informal* Intense; severe; extreme: a *viciou* storm.   [< L *vitium* fault] — **vi′cious·ly** *adv.* — **vi′· cious·ness** *n.*

vicious circle 1. The process or predicament that aris when the solution of a problem creates a new problem an each successive solution adds another problem.   2. *Me* The accelerating effect of one disease upon another when th two are coexistent.

vi·cis·si·tude (vi·sis′ə·tood, -tyood) *n.* 1. *pl.* Irregula changes or variations, as of fortune: the *vicissitudes* of lif   2. A change; esp., a complete change; mutation or mutab ity.   3. Alternating change or succession, as of the season [< MF < L < *vicis* turn, change]

vi·cis·si·tu·di·nar·y (vi·sis′ə·too′də·ner′ē, -tyoo′-) *ac* Marked by or subject to change. Also **vi·cis′si·tu′di·nous.**

vic·tim (vik′tim) *n.* 1. One who is killed, injured, or su jected to suffering.   2. One who is swindled or tricked; dupe.   3. A living creature sacrificed to some deity or as a r ligious rite.   [< L *victima* beast for sacrifice]

vic·tim·ize (vik′tim·īz) *v.t.* **·ized, ·iz·ing** To make a victi of, esp. by defrauding or swindling; dupe; cheat. — **vic′ti i·za′tion** *n.* — **vic′tim·iz′er** *n.*

vic·tor (vik′tər) *n.* 1. One who vanquishes an enemy. One who wins any struggle or contest. — *adj.* Pertaini to a victor; victorious: the *victor* nation.   [< AF *victor*, *v* *tour*, OF *victeur* < L *victus*, pp. of *vincere* to conquer]

vic·to·ri·a (vik·tôr′ē·ə, -tō′rē·ə) *n.* A low, light, four-wheel carriage, with a calash top, a seat for two persons, and raised driver's seat.   [after Queen *Victoria*]

Vic·to·ri·a (vik·tôr′ē·ə, -tō′rē·ə) *n.* In Roman mytholog the winged goddess of victory: identified with the Gre Nike.

Victoria Cross A British military and naval decoration the form of a bronze Maltese cross, awarded for conspicuo bravery. Abbr. *V.C.*

Victoria Day In Canada, the Monday next before May 2 commemorating the birthday of Queen Victoria.

Vic·to·ri·an (vik·tôr′ē·ən, -tō′rē-) *adj.* 1. Of or relating Queen Victoria, or to her reign.   2. Pertaining to or chara teristic of the ideals and standards of morality and tas prevalent during the reign of Queen Victoria; prudish; co ventional; narrow. — *n.* Anyone, esp. an author, conte porary with Queen Victoria. — **Vic·to′ri·an·ism** *n.*

vic·to·ri·ous (vik·tôr′ē·əs, -tō′rē-) *adj.* 1. Having won v tory; triumphant.   2. Relating to or characterized by v tory. — **vic·to′ri·ous·ly** *adv.* — **vic·to′ri·ous·ness** *n.*

vic·to·ry (vik′tər·ē) *n.* *pl.* **·ries** The overcoming of an en my, opponent, or any difficulty; triumph.   [See VICTOR.

Victory Medal Either of two bronze medals awarded to who served in the U.S. armed forces in World War I World War II, worn with the **Victory Ribbon.**

vict·ual (vit′l) *n.* Food for human beings, as prepared eating: used in the plural. — *v.* **vict·ualed** or **·ualled, vi ual·ing** or **·ual·ling** *v.t.* 1. To furnish with victuals.   2. To lay in supplies of food.   [< OF < LL *victualia* pro sions < L < *victus* food]

vi·cu·ña (vi·kōōn′yə, -kyōō′nə) *n.* 1. A small ruminant the high Andes related to the llama and alpaca, having fi and valuable wool.   2. A textile made from this wool, some substitute. Also **vi·cu′gna.**   [< Sp. < Quechua]

vi·de (vī′dē) See: used to make a reference or direct atte tion to: *vide* p. 36.   [< L, imperative sing. of *videre* to se

vi·de an·te (vī′dē an′tē) *Latin* See before.

vi·de in·fra (vī′dē in′frə) *Latin* See below.

vi·de·li·cet (vi·del′ə·sit) *adv.* To wit; that is to say; name Abbr. *viz.*   [< L < *videre licet* it is permitted to see]

vid·e·o (vid′ē·ō) *adj.* Of or pertaining to television, esp. the picture portion of a program. — *n.* Television.   [< I see]

vi·de post (vī′dē pōst′) *Latin* See after; see what follo

vi·de su·pra (vī′dē sōō′prə) *Latin* See above.

vi·dette (vi·det′) See VEDETTE.

vi·de ut su·pra (vī′dē ut sōō′prə) *Latin* See what is writ above.

vie (vī) *v.* **vied, vy·ing** *v.i.* 1. To strive for superiority; co pete, as in a race: with *with* or *for.* — *v.t.* 2. *Rare* To forth in competition.   [< MF < L *invitare* to invite]

Vi·en·nese (vē′ə·nēz′, -nēs′) *adj.* Of or relating to Vien or its inhabitants. — *n.* *pl.* **·nese** A native or citizen Vienna.

Vi·et·nam·ese (vē·et′näm·ēz′, -ēs′) *n.* *pl.* **Vi·et·nam·** 1. A native or inhabitant of Vietnam.   2. The language Vietnam: formerly called *Annamese.* — *adj.* Of or perta ing to Vietnam, its inhabitants, or their language.

view (vyōō) *n.* 1. The act of seeing; survey; inspection. Mental examination or inspection.   3. Power or range vision.   4. That which is seen; outlook; prospect.   5. A resentation of a scene; esp., a landscape.   6. The object action; aim; intention; purpose.   7. Manner of looking

ngs; opinion; judgment. **8.** A general summary or ac-
nt. **— in view 1.** In range of vision. **2.** Under consid-
tion. **3.** As a goal or end. **— in view of** In consideration
— on view Open to the public; set up for public inspec-
1. **— with a view to 1.** With the aim or purpose of. **2.**
th a hope of. **—** *v.t.* **1.** To look at; see; behold. **2.** To
k at carefully; examine. **3.** To survey mentally; consider.
OF *veoir* to see < L *videre*] **— view′er** *n.*

v finder *Photog.* A finder (def. 3).

v·less (vyoo′lis) *adj.* **1.** Devoid of a view; that cannot
viewed. **2.** Having no views or opinions. **3.** Invisible;
een. **— view′less·ly** *adv.* **— view′less·ness** *n.*

v·point (vyoo′point′) *n.* Point of view.

es·i·mal (vī·jes′ə·məl) *adj.* **1.** Twentieth. **2.** Of or
taining to twenty; proceeding by twenties. [< L *viginti*
nty]

il (vij′əl) *n.* **1.** The act of staying awake in order to ob-
ve, protect, etc.; watch. **2.** *Eccl.* **a** The eve of a holy day.
l. Religious devotions on such an eve. [< OF < Med.L
L *vigil* wide-awake]

i·lance (vij′ə·ləns) *n.* The quality of being vigilant;
rtness; watchfulness in guarding against danger.

lance committee *U.S.* Formerly, a body of men self-
anized for the maintenance of order and the administra-
1 of summary justice.

i·lant (vij′ə·lənt) *adj.* Characterized by vigilance; being
the alert; watchful; heedful; wary. [< MF < L < *vigil*
ake] **— vig′i·lant·ly** *adv.* **— vig′i·lant·ness** *n.*
— Syn. *Vigilant* suggests action as well as attention: a riot was
rted by the *vigilant* police. *Watchful* suggests unremitting at-
tion: his *watchful* eye caught the covert signal. *Alert* stresses
speed of a response to necessity or opportunity: *alert* traders
de a killing on the stock market. **— Ant.** inattentive, heedless.

i·lan·te (vij′ə·lan′tē) *n. U.S.* **1.** One of a group who
e upon themselves the unauthorized responsibility of in-
preting and acting upon matters of law, public morality,
. **2.** A member of a vigilance committee: also **vigilance
n.** [< Sp., vigilant < L. See VIGILANT.]

nette (vin·yet′) *n.* **1.** A description, short literary work,
, that depicts something subtly and delicately. **2.** Any
rming, intimate scene, etc. **3.** A decorative design
ced on or before the title page of a book, at the end or be-
ning of a chapter, etc. **4.** An engraving, photograph, or
· like, having a background that shades off gradually. **—
·gnet·ted, ·gnet·ting 1.** To make with a gradually shaded
kground, as a photograph. **2.** To ornament with vi-
ttes. **3.** To depict in a vignette. [< F, dim. of *vigne
e*] **— vi·gnet′tist** *n.*

or (vig′ər) *n.* **1.** Active strength or force, physical or
ntal. **2.** Vital or natural power, as in a healthy animal or
nt. **3.** Forcible exertion of strength; energy; intensity.
Effective force; validity. Also *Brit.* **vig′our.** [< AF, OF <
igere to be lively, thrive]

or·ous (vig′ər·əs) *adj.* **1.** Full of physical or mental
or; robust. **2.** Performed or done with vigor. **3.** Show-
or exemplifying vigor. **4.** Forceful and effective: a *vigor-*
style. **— vig′or·ous·ly** *adv.* **— vig′or·ous·ness** *n.*

ing (vī′king) *n.* One of the Scandinavian warriors who
ried the coasts of Europe from the eighth to the tenth
turies. Also **Vi′king.** [< ON *vikingr* pirate]

· (vīl) *adj.* **vil·er, vil·est 1.** Morally base; shamefully
ked. **2.** Despicable; vicious. **3.** Loathsome; disgust-
. **4.** Degrading; ignominious: *vile* treatment. **5.** Fla-
ntly bad or inferior. **6.** Unpleasant; disagreeable. [<
, OF < L *vilis* cheap] **— vile′ly** *adv.* **— vile′ness** *n.*

·fy (vil′ə·fī) *v.t.* **·fied, ·fy·ing 1.** To abuse or characterize
th defamatory language; malign; slander. **2.** To make
se; degrade. [< LL < L *vilis* cheap + *facere* to make] **—
′i·fi·ca′tion** (-fə·kā′shən) *n.* **— vil′i·fi′er** *n.*

la (vil′ə) *n.* **1.** A comfortable or luxurious house in the
untry, at a resort, etc. **2.** *Chiefly Brit.* A modest suburban
idence. [< Ital. < L, a country house, farm]

lage (vil′ij) *n.* **1.** A collection of houses in a rural dis-
ct, usu. smaller than a town but larger than a hamlet. **2.**
S. In some States, a municipality smaller than a city,
metimes incorporated. **3.** Any comparatively small com-
nity. **4.** The inhabitants of a village, collectively. [<
′ < L < *villa* a country house]

lag·er (vil′ij·ər) *n.* One who lives in a village.

lain (vil′ən) *n.* **1.** An egregiously wicked, evil, or ma-
olent man. **2.** Such a man represented as a leading charter in a novel, play, etc., often in opposition to the hero.
A rogue; scoundrel: often used humorously. **4.** A villein.
AF, OF *vilein, vilain* farm servant < LL < L *villa* farm]
vil′lain·ess *n.fem.*

lain·ous (vil′ən·əs) *adj.* **1.** Having the nature of a vil-
n. **2.** Characteristic of a villain; evil. **3.** Very bad or un-
asant. **— vil′lain·ous·ly** *adv.* **— vil′lain·ous·ness** *n.*

vil·lain·y (vil′ən·ē) *n. pl.* **·lain·ies 1.** The quality of being
villainous. **2.** Conduct characteristic of a villain.

vil·lein (vil′ən) *n.* In the feudal system, a member of a class
of serfs who were regarded as freemen in respect to their legal
relations with all persons except their lord: also *villain.*
[See VILLAIN.] **— vil′lein·age, vil′lein·age, vil′len·age** *n.*

vil·lus (vil′əs) *n. pl.* **vil·li** (vil′ī) **1.** *Anat.* One of the short,
hai·like processes found on certain membranes, as of the
small intestine, where they aid in the digestive process. **2.**
Bot. One of the long, close, rather soft hairs on the surface of
certain plants. [< L, tuft of hair, shaggy hair, var. of *vellus*
fleece, wool] **— vil′lous** *adj.* **— vil′lous·ly** *adv.*

vim (vim) *n.* Force or vigor; energy; spirit. [< L, accusative of *vis* power]

vin (van) *n. French* Wine.

vin- Var. of VINI-.

vi·na (vē′nä) *n.* An East Indian musical instrument with
seven steel strings stretched on a long, fretted fingerboard
over two gourds. [< Hind. *vīnā* < Skt.]

vi·na·ceous (vī·nā′shəs) *adj.* **1.** Of or pertaining to wine or
grapes. **2.** Having the characteristic color of red wine. [<
L *vinaceous* < *vinum* wine]

vin·ai·grette (vin′ə·gret′) *n.* **1.** A small ornamental box or
bottle, used for holding smelling salts, or a similar pungent
restorative. **2.** Vinaigrette sauce. [< F, dim. of *vinaigre*
vinegar]

vinaigrette sauce A sauce made from vinegar, savory
herbs, etc., served with fish and cold meats.

vin·ci·ble (vin′sə·bəl) *adj. Rare* Capable of being conquered or overcome; conquerable. [< L *vincibilis* < *vincere*
to conquer] **— vin′ci·bil′i·ty, vin′ci·ble·ness** *n.*

vin·cu·lum (vingk′yə·ləm) *n. pl.* **·la** (-lə) *Math.* A straight
line drawn over several algebraic terms to show that all are
to be operated on together. [< L < *vincire* to bind]

vin·di·ca·ble (vin′də·kə·bəl) *adj.* Capable of being vindicated; justifiable.

vin·di·cate (vin′də·kāt) *v.t.* **·cat·ed, ·cat·ing 1.** To clear of
accusation, censure, suspicion, etc. **2.** To support or maintain, as a right or claim. **3.** To serve to justify. [< L *vindi-
catus,* pp. of *vindicare* to avenge, claim] **— vin′di·ca′tor** *n.*

vin·di·ca·tion (vin′də·kā′shən) *n.* **1.** A vindicating or being vindicated. **2.** Justification; defense.

vin·di·ca·to·ry (vin′də·kə·tôr′ē, -tō′rē) *adj.* **1.** Serving to
vindicate; justificatory. **2.** Punitive; avenging.

vin·dic·tive (vin·dik′tiv) *adj.* **1.** Having a revengeful spirit.
2. Revengeful or spiteful in quality, character, etc. [< L
vindicta revenge] **— vin·dic′tive·ly** *adv.* **— vin·dic′tive·
ness** *n.*

vine (vīn) *n.* **1.** Any of a large and widely distributed group
of plants having a slender flexible stem that may twine about
a support or clasp it by means of tendrils, petioles, etc.; also,
the slender flexible stem itself. **2.** A grapevine. [< OF
vigne, vine < L *vinea* vineyard < *vinum* wine]

vin·e·gar (vin′ə·gər) *n.* **1.** An acid liquid consisting chiefly
of dilute acetic acid, obtained by the fermentation of cider,
wine, etc., and used as a condiment and preservative. **2.**
Sourness of manner, speech, etc. [< OF < *vin* wine +
aigre,egre sour] **— vin′e·gar·y, vin′e·gar·ish** *adj.*

vin·er·y (vī′nər·ē) *n. pl.* **·er·ies 1.** A greenhouse for grapes;
grapery. **2.** Vines collectively.

vine·yard (vin′yərd) *n.* An area planted with grapevines.
[Earlier *wineyard,* OE *winegeard*]

vingt-et-un (van′tā·œn′) *n.* Twenty-one, a card game.
[< F, twenty-one]

vini- *combining form* **1.** Wine. **2.** Of or pertaining to wine
grapes. Also *vin-* (before vowels): also **vino-.** [< L *vinum*
wine]

vin·i·cul·ture (vin′ə·kul′chər) *n.* The cultivation of grapes
for wine. **— vin′i·cul′tur·al** *adj.* **— vin′i·cul′tur·ist** *n.*

vin or·di·naire (van ôr·dē·nâr′) *French* Cheap red wine;
literally, ordinary wine.

vi·nous (vī′nəs) *adj.* **1.** Pertaining to, characteristic of, or
having the qualities of wine. **2.** Caused by, affected by, or
addicted to wine. **3.** Tinged with dark red. [< L < *vinum*
wine] **— vi·nos·i·ty** (-nos′ə·tē) *n.*

vin·tage (vin′tij) *n.* **1.** The yield of a vineyard or wine-
growing district for one season; also, the wine produced from
this yield. **2.** The harvesting of a vineyard and the making
of wine. **3.** Wine of high quality or of an exceptionally good
year: also **vintage wine.** **4.** *Informal* The type popular at
a particular time of the past: a joke of ancient *vintage.* **—
** *adj.* Of exceptional quality or excellence; choice: a *vintage*
wine. [< AF, alter. of *vindage, vendage,* OF *vendage* < L <
vinum wine + *demere* to remove]

vint·ner (vint′nər) *n.* A wine merchant. [< OF *vinetier,
vinotier* < *vinot,* dim. of *vin* wine < L *vinum*]

vin·y (vī′nē) *adj.* **vin·i·er, vin·i·est 1.** Of, pertaining to, or
resembling a vine. **2.** Full of vines.

vi·nyl (vī′nəl, vin′əl) *n. Chem.* The univalent radical, CH_2:CH, derived from ethylene, and extensively used in organic synthesis. [< L *vinum* wine + -YL]

vi·ol (vī′əl) *n.* Any of a family of stringed musical instruments, predecessors of the violin family; also, any member of the violin family. [Earlier *vielle* < AF, OF < Med.L *vidula*, *vitula* < Gmc.]

vi·o·la (vē·ō′lə, vī-; *Ital.* vyō′lä) *n.* A musical instrument of the violin family, somewhat larger than the violin, and tuned a fifth lower, with a graver and less brilliant tone. [< Ital., orig., a viol < Med.L *vidula* < Gmc.]

vi·o·la·ble (vī′ə·lə·bəl) *adj.* Capable of being violated. [< L *violabilis* < *violare.* See VIOLATE.] **— vi′o·la·ble·ness, vi′o·la·bil′i·ty** *n.* **— vi′o·la·bly** *adv.* [< L *violaceus* < *viola* violet]

viola da gam·ba (dä gäm′bä) The bass of the viol family, held between the legs, and having a range similar to that of the cello, but with a thinner tone: also called *bass viol.* [< Ital., viol of the leg]

vi·o·late (vī′ə·lāt) *v.t.* **·lat·ed, ·lat·ing 1.** To break or infringe, as a law, oath, agreement, etc. **2.** To profane, as a holy place. **3.** To break in upon; disturb. **4.** To ravish; rape. **5.** To do violence to; offend grossly; outrage. [< L *violatus,* pp. of *violare* to use violence < *vis* force] **— vi′o·la′tive** *adj.* **— vi′o·la′tor** *n.*

vi·o·la·tion (vī′ə·lā′shən) *n.* **1.** The act of violating, or the state of being violated. **2.** Infringement or infraction, as of a law, regulation, etc. **3.** Profanation; desecration. **4.** Rape.

vi·o·lence (vī′ə·ləns) *n.* **1.** The quality or state of being violent; intensity; fury. **2.** An instance of violent action, treatment, etc. **3.** Violent or abusive exercise of power; injury; outrage. **4.** *Law* Physical force unlawfully exercised. **5.** Perversion or distortion of meaning, intent, etc. **— to do violence to 1.** To injure or damage by rough or abusive treatment. **2.** To distort the meaning of.

vi·o·lent (vī′ə·lənt) *adj.* **1.** Proceeding from or marked by great physical force or roughness; overwhelmingly forcible. **2.** Caused by or exhibiting intense emotional or mental excitement; passionate; impetuous; fierce. **3.** Characterized by intensity of any kind; extreme: *violent* heat. **4.** Marked by undue exercise of force; harsh; severe: to take *violent* measures. **5.** Resulting from unusual force or injury: a *violent* death. **6.** Tending to pervert the meaning or sense: a *violent* construction. [< OF < L *violentus* < *vis* force] **— vi′o·lent·ly** *adv.*

vi·o·let (vī′ə·lit) *n.* **1.** One of a widely distributed genus of herbaceous perennial herbs, bearing spurred flowers typically having a purplish blue color but sometimes yellow or white. The violet is the State flower of Illinois, New Jersey, Rhode Island, and Wisconsin. **2.** Any of several similar plants. **3.** A deep bluish purple color. **— adj.** Having a bluish purple color. [< OF < L *viola* violet]

violet rays 1. High-frequency radiation from the violet end of the visible spectrum. **2.** Loosely, ultraviolet rays.

vi·o·lin (vī′ə·lin′) *n.* A musical instrument having four strings and a sounding box of seasoned wood, held against the shoulder and played by means of a bow. It is the treble member of the violin family, which includes also the viola and cello: also called *fiddle.* [< Ital. *violino,* dim. of *viola*]

vi·o·lin·ist (vī′ə·lin′ist) *n.* One who plays the violin.

vi·o·list (vē·ō′list *for def. 1,* vī′əl·ist *for def. 2*) *n.* **1.** One who plays the viola. **2.** One who plays a viol.

vi·o·lon·cel·list (vē′ə·lən·chel′ist) *n.* A cellist.

vi·o·lon·cel·lo (vē′ə·lən·chel′ō) *n. pl.* **·los** A cello. [< Ital., dim. of *violone* double bass]

VIP or **V.I.P.** Very important person.

vi·per (vī′pər) *n.* **1.** Any of a family of venomous Old World snakes, esp. a small, variously colored snake native to Europe. **2.** Any of various similar or related snakes. **3.** Loosely, a pit viper. **4.** Any allegedly poisonous snake. **5.** A treacherous or spiteful person. [< OF < L *vipus* living + *parere* to bring forth] **— vi′per·ine** *adj.* **— vi′per·ish** *adj.*

vi·per·ous (vī′pər·əs) *adj.* **1.** Snakelike; viperine. **2.** Venomous; malicious. **— vi′per·ous·ly** *adv.*

vi·ra·go (vi·rä′gō, -rā′-, vī-) *n. pl.* **·goes** or **·gos** A noisy, sharp-tongued woman; a scold. [< L, mannish woman < *vir* man]

vi·ral (vī′rəl) *adj.* Of, pertaining to, caused by, or of the nature of a virus.

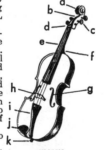

VIOLIN
a Scroll. *b* Peg box. *c* Peg. *d* Nut. *e* Fingerboard. *f* Neck plate. *g* Sound hole. *h* Bridge. *i* Tailpiece. *j* Chin rest. *k* Button.

vir·e·o (vir′ē·ō) *n. pl.* **·os** Any of various small, insectiv ous birds having predominantly dull green and grayish p mage. [< L, a small bird, ? the greenfinch]

vi·res·cence (vī·res′əns) *n.* The state or condition of coming green.

vi·res·cent (vī·res′ənt) *adj.* Greenish or becoming gre [< L *virescens, -entis,* ppr. of *virescere* to grow green]

vir·gin (vûr′jin) *n.* **1.** A person, esp. a young woman, w has never had sexual intercourse. **2.** A chaste young girl unmarried woman. **— adj. 1.** Being a virgin. **2.** Perta ing or suited to a virgin; chaste; maidenly. **3.** Uncorrupt pure; undefiled: *virgin* whiteness. **4.** Not hitherto us touched, tilled, or worked upon by man: *virgin* soil. **5.** N previously processed: *virgin* rubber; *virgin* wool. [< OF L *virgo, -inis* maiden]

Vir·gin (vûr′jin) *n.* **1.** Mary, the mother of Jesus: usu. p ceded by *the:* also *Virgin Mary.* **2.** The constellation a sign of the zodiac Virgo.

vir·gin·al (vûr′jin·əl) *adj.* Pertaining to or characteristic a virgin; chaste. [< OF < L *virginalis* < *virgo, -inis* virg

vir·gin·al (vûr′jin·əl) *n. Often pl.* A small, legless har chord of the 16th and 17th centuries: sometimes called a p **of virginals.** [< OF < VIRGINAL[1]; ? so called from its use young men and girls]

virgin birth *Theol.* The doctrine that Jesus Christ was vinely conceived without impairment of the virginity of mother Mary. Also **Virgin Birth.**

Virginia cowslip A smooth perennial herb having clus of tubular blue flowers. Also **Virginia bluebell.**

Virginia creeper A common American climbing vine the grape family, with compound toothed leaves and da blue berries: also called *five-fingers, woodbine.*

Vir·gin·ian (vər·jin′yən) *adj.* Of, pertaining to, or fr Virginia. **— n.** A native or inhabitant of Virginia.

Virginia reel A country-dance in which the perform stand in two parallel lines and perform various figures.

vir·gin·i·ty (vər·jin′ə·tē) *n. pl.* **·ties 1.** The state or con tion of being a virgin; maidenhood; virginal chastity. **2.** The state of being unsullied, unused, untouched, etc.

vir·gin·i·um (vər·jin′ē·əm) *n.* The former name of an e ment now identified as francium. [after the State of V ginia]

Virgin Mary Mary, the mother of Jesus: usu. with *the*

vir·gin's-bow·er (vûr′jinz·bou′ər) *n.* A species of clema bearing white flowers in leafy panicles.

Vir·go (vûr′gō) *n.* A constellation, the Virgin, contain the bright star Spica; also, the sixth sign of the zodi [< L, a virgin]

vir·gule (vûr′gyool) *n.* A slanting line (/) used to indic two alternatives, as in *and/or,* to set off phoneme symbe etc.: also called *slash.* [< L *virgula,* dim. of *virga* rod]

vir·i·des·cent (vir′ə·des′ənt) *adj.* Greenish, or becom slightly green. [< LL < *viridescere* to become green] **vir′i·des′cence** *n.*

vir·ile (vir′əl) *adj.* **1.** Having the characteristics of ad manhood; masculine. **2.** Having qualities considered ty cally masculine; vigorous; forceful. **3.** Capable of procr tion. [< OF < L *virilis* < *vir* man]

vi·ril·i·ty (və·ril′ə·tē) *n. pl.* **·ties** The state, character quality of being virile.

vi·rol·o·gy (və·rol′ə·jē, vī-) *n.* The study of viruses, esp their relation to disease. [< *viro-* (< VIRUS) + -LOGY] **vi·rol′o·gist** *n.*

vir·tu (vər·tōō′, vûr′tōō) *n.* **1.** Rare, curious, or beauti quality: usu. in the phrase **objects** or **articles of virtu. 2** taste for such objects. **3.** Such objects collectively. A spelled *vertu.* [< Ital. *virtù* merit < L *virtus* strength]

vir·tu·al (vûr′chōō·əl) *adj.* Having the effect but not actual form of what is specified: a *virtual* usurpation. [< VIRTUE.] **— vir′tu·al′i·ty** (-al′ə·tē) *n.*

vir·tu·al·ly (vûr′chōō·ə·lē) *adv.* In effect; for all practi purposes.

vir·tue (vûr′chōō) *n.* **1.** The quality of moral righteousn or excellence; rectitude. **2.** The practice of moral duties a the abstinence from immorality and vice. **3.** Chastity, e in women. **4.** A particular type of moral excellence, esp. of those considered to be of special importance in philosop cal or religious doctrine. Compare CARDINAL VIRTUES. Any admirable quality or trait. **6.** Inherent or essent quality, power, etc. **7.** Efficacy; potency. **— by** (or **in**) **v tue of** By or through the fact, quality, force, or authority **— to make a virtue of necessity** To seem to do freely from principle what is or must be done necessarily. [< *L virtus* manliness, bravery < *vir* man]

— Syn. We regard *virtue* as acquired through self-discipl and predicate it of human beings only. *Goodness* is an inn quality, and so may be ascribed to God as well as to man. *Mora* involves conformity to an accepted code of right conduct; it is elevated but more concrete than *virtue. Rectitude* also implies c formity to a moral code, but stresses intention or dispositi hence, a man's *morality* may arise from fear of punishment or sure, but his *rectitude* can come only from a love of the right y a conscious desire to follow it. **—Ant.** vice, sin, evil.

tu·os·i·ty (vûr/chōō·os/ə·tē) *n.* *pl.* **·ties** The skill, etc., a virtuoso; technical mastery of an art, as music.

tu·o·so (vûr/chōō·ō/sō) *n.* *pl.* **·si** (-sē) or **·sos** **1.** A ster of technique, as a skilled musician. **2.** One who dis- ys impressive or dazzling skill in any area of accomplish- nt. **3.** A connoisseur; a collector or lover of curios or ·ks of art. [< Ital., skilled, learned]

tu·ous (vûr/chōō·əs) *adj.* **1.** Characterized by, exhibit- , or having the nature of virtue. **2.** Chaste: now said esp. women. **—vir/tu·ous·ly** *adv.* **—vir/tu·ous·ness** *n.*

u·lent (vir/yə·lənt, vir/ə-) *adj.* **1.** Manifesting or char- erized by malignity; exceedingly noxious, harmful, etc. Bitterly rancorous; acrimonious. **3.** *Med.* Actively poi- ous or infective; malignant. **4.** *Bacteriol.* Having the ver to injure an organism by invasion of tissue and gener- n of internal toxins, as certain microorganisms. [< L s poison] **—vir/u·lence** *n.* **—vir/u·lent·ly** *adv.*

us (vī/rəs) *n.* **1.** Any of a class of filterable, submicro- pic pathogenic agents, chiefly protein in composition but n reducible to crystalline form, and typically inert except n in contact with certain living cells: also called *filterable s.* **2.** An illness caused by such an agent. **3.** Any viru- t substance developed within an animal body, and able of transmitting a specific disease. **4.** Venom, as snake. **—Syn.** See MICROBE. [< L, poison, slime]

(vis) *n.* *pl.* **vi·res** (vī/rēz) *Latin* Force; potency.

a (vē/zə) *n.* An official endorsement, as on a passport, tifying that it has been found correct and that the bearer y proceed. **—** *v.t.* **·saed, ·sa·ing** **1.** To put a visa on. To give a visa to. Also *visé.* [< F < L < *videre* to see]

age (viz/ij) *n.* The face or facial expression of a person; ntenance; distinctive aspect. [< OF < L *visus* look, ap- rance < *videre* to see] **—vis/aged** *adj.*

ard (viz/ərd) See VIZARD.

à-vis (vē/zə·vē/, *Fr.* vē·zà·vē/) *n.* *pl.* **vis-à-vis** **1.** One two persons or things that face each other from opposite es. **2.** One in a corresponding capacity, etc. **—** *adv.* Face ace. **—** *prep.* Regarding. [< F, face to face]

cer·a (vis/ər·ə) *n.* *pl. of* **vis·cus** (vis/kəs) *Anat.* The in- nal organs, esp. those of the great cavities of the body, as stomach, lungs, heart, intestines, etc. [< L, pl. of *viscus* ernal organ] **—vis/cer·al** *adj.*

cid (vis/id) *adj.* Sticky or adhesive; mucilaginous; vis- us. [< LL < L *viscum* birdlime] **—vis·cid·i·ty** (vi·sid/ə- , vis/cid·ness *n.* **—vis/cid·ly** *adv.*

cose (vis/kōs) *n.* *Chem.* A thick, honeylike substance duced by the action of caustic soda and carbon disulfide n cellulose, and constituting an important source of on. **—** *adj.* **1.** Viscous. **2.** Of, pertaining to, contain- , or made from viscose. [See VISCOUS.]

cos·i·ty (vis·kos/ə·tē) *n.* *pl.* **·ties** **1.** The state, quality, perty, or degree of being viscous. **2.** *Physics* That prop- y of fluids by virtue of which they offer resistance to flow to any change in the arrangement of their molecules.

count (vī/kount) *n.* In England, a title of nobility rank- between those of earl and baron. [< AF, OF < *vis*-in ce (< L *vice*) + *counte.* See COUNT².] **—vis/count·cy, /count·ship, vis/count·y** *n.*

count·ess (vī/koun·tis) *n.* **1.** The wife of a viscount. A peeress holding a corresponding title in her own right.

cous [vis/kəs] *adj.* **1.** Glutinous; semifluid; sticky. **2.** ysics Characterized by or having viscosity. [< LL < L *um* birdlime] **—vis/cous·ly** *adv.* **—vis/cous·ness** *n.*

cus (vis/kəs) Singular of VISCERA.

(vīs) *n.* A clamping device, usu. of two jaws made to be sed together with a screw, lever, etc., used for grasping holding objects being worked on, glued, etc. **—** *v.t.* ed, vis·ing To hold, force, or squeeze in or as in a vise. so, *Brit., vice.* [< OF < L *vitis* vine; with ref. to the spiral wth of vine tendrils]

é (vē/zā, vē·zā/) *v.t.* **·séed, ·sé·ing** To visa. **—** *n.* A visa.

·nu (vish/nōō) In Hindu theology, a major deity, the mber of the trinity also including Brahma and Siva, and ving many incarnations, of which the most famous is as ishna. **—Vish/nu·ism** *n.*

i·bil·i·ty (viz/ə·bil/ə·tē) *n.* *pl.* **·ties** **1.** Condition, capa- ity, or degree of being visible. **2.** The clarity of unaided ion as affected by distance, atmospheric conditions, etc.

i·ble (viz/ə·bəl) *adj.* **1.** Perceivable by the eye; capable being seen. **2.** Apparent; observable; evident. **3.** At nd; available; manifest. [< OF < L *visibilis* < *videre* to] **—vis/i·ble·ness** *n.* **—vis/i·bly** *adv.*

i·goth (viz/ə·goth) *n.* One of the western Goths, a Teu- ic people that invaded the Roman Empire in the third d fourth centuries and settled in France and Spain. [< *Visigothus*] **—Vis/i·goth/ic** *adj.*

vi·sion (vizh/ən) *n.* **1.** The faculty or sense of sight. **2.** The ability to anticipate and make provision for future events; foresight. **3.** Insight; imagination: a man of great *vision*. **4.** A mental representation of or as of external objects, scenes, etc., as in a religious revelation, dream, etc. **5.** A vividly imagined thing, state, occurrence, etc. **6.** Some- thing or someone very beautiful or pleasing. **—** *v.t.* *Rare* To see in or as in a vision. [< OF < L *visio* < *videre* to see] **—vi/sion·al** *adj.* **—vi/sion·al·ly** *adv.*

vi·sion·ar·y (vizh/ən·er/ē) *adj.* **1.** Not founded on fact; imaginary; impracticable. **2.** Affected by or tending toward fantasies; dreamy; impractical. **3.** Having idealistic goals or aims incapable of realization. **4.** Having or of the nature of apparitions, dreams, etc. **—** *n.* *pl.* **·ar·ies** **1.** One who has visions. **2.** A dreamer; an impractical schemer. **3.** One who is impracticably idealistic. **—vi/sion·ar/i·ness** *n.*

vis·it (viz/it) *v.t.* **1.** To go or come to see (a person) from friendship, on business, etc. **2.** To go or come to (a place, etc.), as for touring, etc. **3.** To be a guest of; stay with tem- porarily. **4.** To go or come to so as to make official inspec- tion or inquiry. **5.** To come upon or afflict. **6.** To inflict punishment upon or for. **7.** To inflict (punishment, wrath, etc.). **—** *v.i.* **8.** To make a visit; pay a call or calls. **9.** *In- formal* To chat or converse sociably. **—** *n.* **1.** The act of visiting a person or thing. **2.** A sojourn in a place or with a person. **3.** *Informal* A talk or friendly chat. **4.** An authori- tative personal call for inspection and examination, or dis- charge of an official or professional duty. [< OF < L *visi- tare* to go or come to see < *videre* to see] **—vis/it·a·ble** *adj.*

vis·i·tant (viz/ə·tənt) *n.* **1.** A visitor. **2.** A migratory ani- mal or bird stopping at a particular region.

vis·i·ta·tion (viz/ə·tā/shən) *n.* **1.** The act or fact of visiting; a visit; also, the state or circumstance of being visited. **2.** An official or authoritative inspection and examination. **3.** In Biblical and religious use, a visiting of blessing or afflic- tion. **—vis/i·ta/tion·al** *adj.* **—vis/i·ta/to/ri·al** (-tə·tôr/ē·əl, -tō/rē-) *adj.*

Vis·i·ta·tion (viz/ə·tā/shən) *n.* *Eccl.* **1.** The visit of the Virgin Mary to Elizabeth. *Luke* i 39–42. **2.** July 2, the church festival commemorating this visit.

vis·i·ting card (viz/i·ting) A calling card.

vis·i·tor (viz/ə·tər) *n.* One who visits.

vi·sor (vī/zər, viz/ər) *n.* **1.** A projecting piece at the front of a cap, etc., serving as a shade for the eyes. **2.** In armor, the movable front piece of a helmet, serving to protect the upper part of the face. **3.** A movable piece or part serving as a shield against glare, etc., as on the windshield of an au- tomobile. **—** *v.t.* To mask or cover with a visor. Also spelled *vizor*. [< AF & OF *vis* face]

vis·ta (vis/tə) *n.* **1.** A view or prospect, as along an avenue; an outlook. **2.** A mental view embracing a series of events. [< Ital. < L *videre* to see]

vis·u·al (vizh/ōō·əl) *adj.* **1.** Pertaining to, resulting from, or serving the sense of sight. **2.** Perceptible by sight; visible. **3.** Optical: the *visual* focus of a lens. **4.** Produced or in- duced by mental images: a *visual* conception. [< MF < LL < L *visus* sight < *videre* to see] **—vis/u·al·ly** *adv.*

visual aid *Often pl.* In education, a device or method de- signed to convey information by visible representation, as motion pictures, charts, etc.

vis·u·al·ize (vizh/ōō·əl·īz/) *v.t. & v.i.* **·ized, ·iz·ing** To form a mental image (of). **—vis/u·al·ist** (-ist) *n.* **—vis/u·al·i· za/tion** *n.* **—vis/u·al·iz/er** *n.*

vi·ta·ceous (vī·tā/shəs) *adj.* *Bot.* Of or belonging to the grape family of mostly woody and climbing vines. [< NL, family name < L *vitis* vine]

vi·tal (vīt/l) *adj.* **1.** Necessary to existence or continuance; essential. **2.** Of or pertaining to life: *vital* statistics. **3.** Es- sential to or supporting life. **4.** Affecting the course of life or existence, esp. so as to be dangerous or fatal: a *vital* error. **5.** Energetic; forceful; dynamic. **6.** Having immediate in- terest or importance: a *vital* question. [< OF < L *vita* life] **—vi/tal·ly** *adv.* **—vi/tal·ness** *n.*

vi·tal·ism (vīt/l·iz/əm) *n.* *Biol.* The doctrine that life and its phenomena arose from and are the product of a hypothet- ical **vital force** (or **vital principle**) regarded as acting inde- pendently of all physical and chemical forces. **—vi/tal·ist** *n.* **—vi/tal·is/tic** *adj.*

vi·tal·i·ty (vī·tal/ə·tē) *n.* **1.** The state or quality of being vi- tal. **2.** Vital or life-giving force, principle, etc. **3.** Vigor; energy; animation. **4.** Power of continuing in force or effect.

vi·tal·ize (vīt/l·īz) *v.t.* **·ized, ·iz·ing** To make vital; endow with life or energy. **—vi/tal·i·za/tion** *n.* **—vi/tal·iz/er** *n.*

vi·tals (vīt/lz) *n.pl.* **1.** The parts or organs necessary to life. **2.** The parts or qualities essential to the continued existence or well-being of anything.

vital statistics Quantitative data relating to certain as- pects and conditions of human life.

vi·ta·min (vī′tə·min) *n. Biochem.* Any of a group of complex organic substances found in minute quantities in most natural foodstuffs, and closely associated with the maintenance of normal physiological functions in man and animals. Also **vi′ta·mine** (-mēn, -min). [< NL *vit-* (< L *vita* life) + AMINE] — **vi′ta·min′ic** *adj.*

vitamin A A fat-soluble vitamin derived from carotene and occurring naturally in animal tissues, esp. egg yolk and fish-liver oils, essential to the prevention of atrophy of epithelial tissue and night blindness.

vitamin B complex A group of water-soluble vitamins widely distributed in plants and animals, most members of which have special names.

vitamin B₁ Thiamine.

vitamin B₂ Riboflavin.

vitamin B₃ Pantothenic acid.

vitamin B₆ Pyridoxine.

vitamin B₁₂ A dark red, crystalline vitamin, $C_{63}H_{90}N_{14}O_{14}PCo$, extracted from liver and certain mold fungi, and active against pernicious anemia.

vitamin B₆ Folic acid.

vitamin C Ascorbic acid.

vitamin D The antirachitic vitamin occurring chiefly in fish-liver oils.

vitamin D₁ An impure mixture of calciferol and irradiated ergosterol.

vitamin D₂ Calciferol.

vitamin D₃ A form of vitamin D₂ found principally in fish-liver oils.

vitamin E The antisterility vitamin, composed of three forms of tocopherol and found in whole grain cereals.

vitamin G Riboflavin.

vitamin H Biotin.

vitamin K₁ A vitamin, found in green leafy vegetables, that promotes the clotting of blood.

vitamin K₂ A form of vitamin K₁ prepared from fishmeal.

vitamin P complex A group of substances obtained from citrus fruits and promoting the normal permeability of capillary walls.

vi·ti·ate (vish′ē·āt) *v.t.* **·at·ed, ·at·ing** 1. To impair the use or value of; spoil. 2. To debase or corrupt. 3. To render legally ineffective. [< L < *vitium* fault] — **vi·ti·a·ble** (vish′-ē·ə·bel) *adj.* — **vi′ti·a′tion** *n.* — **vi′ti·a′tor** *n.*

vit·i·cul·ture (vit′ə·kul′chər, vī′tə-) *n.* The science and art of grape growing. [< L *vitis* vine + CULTURE] — **vit′i·cul′tur·al** *adj.* — **vit′i·cul′tur·er, vit′i·cul′tur·ist** *n.*

vit·re·ous (vit′rē·əs) *adj.* 1. Pertaining to glass; glassy. 2. Obtained from glass. 3. Resembling glass. 4. Pertaining to the vitreous humor. [< L < *vitrum* glass] — **vit′re·os′i·ty** (-os′ə·tē), **vit′re·ous·ness** *n.*

vitreous humor *Anat.* The transparent, jellylike tissue that fills the ball of the eye. Also **vitreous body.**

vitri- *combining form* Glass; of or pertaining to glass. Also, before vowels, **vitr-**. [< L *vitrum* glass]

vit·ri·fy (vit′rə·fī) *v.t. & v.i.* **·fied, ·fy·ing** To change into glass or a vitreous substance; make or become vitreous. [< MF < L *vitrum* glass + *facere* to make] — **vit′ri·fac′tion** (-fak′shən) *n.* — **vit′ri·fi′a·ble** *adj.* — **vit′ri·fi·ca′tion** (-fə·kā′shən) *n.*

vit·ri·ol (vit′rē·ōl, -əl) *n.* 1. *Chem.* **a** Sulfuric acid. **b** Any sulfate of a heavy metal, as *green vitriol* from iron, *blue vitriol* from copper, or *white vitriol* from zinc. 2. Anything sharp or caustic, esp. speech or writing. — *v.t.* **·oled** or **·olled, ·ol·ing** or **·ol·ling** 1. To injure (a person) with vitriol. 2. To subject (anything) to the agency of vitriol. [< OF < Med.L < L *vitrum* glass]

vit·ri·ol·ic (vit′rē·ol′ik) *adj.* 1. Derived from a vitriol. 2. Corrosive, burning, or caustic.

vit·ri·ol·ize (vit′rē·əl·īz′) *v.t.* **·ized, ·iz·ing** 1. To corrode, injure, or burn with sulfuric acid. 2. To convert into or impregnate with vitriol. — **vit′ri·ol·i·za′tion** *n.*

vit·tles (vit′əls) *n.pl. Informal* or *Dial.* Victuals.

vi·tu·per·ate (vī·tōō′pə·rāt, -tyōō′-, vi-) *v.t.* **·at·ed, ·at·ing** To find fault with abusively; rail at; berate; scold. [< L < *vitium* fault + *parare* to prepare, make] — **vi·tu′per·a′tion** *n.* — **vi·tu′per·a·tive** (-pər·ə·tiv) *adj.* — **vi·tu′per·a·tive·ly** *adv.* — **vi·tu′per·a′tor** *n.*

vi·va (vē′vä) *interj.* Live! Long live!: a shout of applause; an acclamation or salute. [< Ital. *vivere* to live < L]

vi·va·ce (vē·vä′chā) *adv. Music* Lively; quickly; briskly. Also **vi·va′ce·men′te** (-män′tā). [< Ital.]

vi·va·cious (vi·vā′shəs, vī-) *adj.* Lively; active. [< L < *vivere* to live] — **vi·va′cious·ly** *adv.* — **vi·va′cious·ness** *n.*

vi·vac·i·ty (vi·vas′ə·tē, vī-) *n., pl.* **·ties** 1. The state or quality of being vivacious. 2. Sprightliness, as of temper or behavior; liveliness. 3. A vivacious act, expression, etc.

vi·var·i·um (vī·vâr′ē·əm) *n., pl.* **·var·i·a** (-vâr′ē·ə) or **·var·i·ums** A place for keeping or raising live animals, fish, or plants, as a park, pond, aquarium, cage, etc. Also **viv·a·ry** (viv′ər·ē). [< L *vivere* to live]

vi·va vo·ce (vī′və vō′sē) *Latin* By spoken word; orally.

vive (vēv) *interj. French* Long live!: used in acclamations.

viv·id (viv′id) *adj.* 1. Very bright; intense: said of co[lor]. 2. Producing or evoking lifelike imagery, freshness, [or] *vivid* prose. 3. Clearly felt or strongly expressed, as e[motions]. 4. Full of life and vigor. 5. Clearly seen in the m[ind], as a memory. 6. Clearly perceived by the eye. [< L *vi*[vus] to live] — **viv′id·ly** *adv.* — **viv′id·ness** *n.* — **Syn.** 1. brilliant, clear. 2. lifelike. 4. animated, lively.

viv·i·fy (viv′ə·fī) *v.t.* **·fied, ·fy·ing** 1. To give life to; mate; vitalize. 2. To make more vivid or striking. [< LL < L *vivus* alive + *facere* to make] — **viv′i·fi·ca**[′tion] (-fə·kā′shən) *n.* — **viv′i·fi′er** *n.*

vi·vip·a·rous (vī·vip′ər·əs) *adj.* 1. *Zool.* Bringing forth [liv]ing young, as most mammals: distinguished from *ovipar*[ous.] 2. *Bot.* Producing bulbs or seeds that germinate while [at]tached to the parent plant. [< L < *vivus* alive + *pare*[re to] bring forth] — **vi·vip′a·rous·ly** *adv.* — **vi·vip′a·rism** (-[riz]əm), **viv·i·par·i·ty** (viv′ə·par′ə·tē), **vi·vip′a·rous·ness** *n.*

viv·i·sect (viv′ə·sekt) *v.t.* 1. To dissect or operate up[on a] living animal), with a view to exposing its physiological p[roc]esses. — *v.i.* 2. To practice vivisection. — **viv′i·sec′t**[or *n.*]

viv·i·sec·tion (viv′ə·sek′shən) *n.* 1. The act of cutting [in]or dissecting a living animal body. 2. Experimentatio[n on] living animals by means of operations designed to pro[mote] knowledge of physiological and pathological processes. [<] L *vivus* living, alive + SECTION.] — **viv′i·sec′tion·al** — **viv′i·sec′tion·ist** *n.*

vix·en (vik′sən) *n.* 1. A female fox. 2. A turbulent, q[uar]relsome woman; shrew. [Alter. of ME *fixen* she-fox < fem. of *fox*] — **vix′en·ish** *adj.* — **vix′en·ly** *adj. & ad*[v.]

viz·ard (viz′ərd) *n.* A mask; visor: also spelled *visard*. [Al]ter. of VISOR] — **viz′ard·ed** *adj.*

vi·zier (vi·zir′, viz′yər) *n.* A high official of a Moslem c[oun]try; esp., a minister of state. Also **vi·zir**. [< Turkis[h <] Arabic *wazīr* counselor, orig., porter < *wazara* to carry] — **vi·zier·ate** (vi·zir′it, -āt, viz′yər·it, -yə·rāt) *n.* The off[ice of] a vizier. Also **vi·zier′al, vi·zier′ship, vi·zir′ate, vi·zir′**[ship]

vi·zor (vī′zər, viz′ər) See VISOR.

V-J Day (vē′jā′) September 2, the official date of the [vic]tory over Japan in World War II, 1945.

V-mail (vē′māl′) *n.* Mail written on special forms, tr[ans]mitted overseas in World War II on microfilm, and enla[rged] for final delivery. [< V(ICTORY) + MAIL]

vo·ca·ble (vō′kə·bəl) *n.* 1. A spoken or written word [con]sidered only as a sequence of sounds or letters, witho[ut re]gard to its meaning. 2. A vocal sound. — *adj.* Capab[le of] being spoken. [< L < *vocabulum* name < *vocare* to ca[ll]

vo·cab·u·lar·y (vō·kab′yə·ler′ē) *n., pl.* **·lar·ies** 1. A li[st of] words, esp. one arranged in alphabetical order and define[d or] translated; a glossary. 2. All the words of a language. [3.] sum or aggregate of the words used by a particular pe[rson,] class, etc., or employed in some specialized field of kn[owl]edge. [< LL < L *vocabulum*. See VOCABLE.]

vocabulary entry 1. A word or term given in a vocabu[lary.] 2. A word, term, or phrase entered in a dictionary.

vo·cal (vō′kəl) *adj.* 1. Of or pertaining to the voice. [2.] Having voice; endowed with the power of utterance. [3.] Uttered or performed by the voice: *vocal music.* 4. [Con]cerned in the production of voice: the *vocal* organs. 5. [Made] of voices or sounds. 6. Freely expressing oneself in spe[ech:] the *vocal* segment. [< L *vocalis* speaking, sounding < [vox] voice] — **vo′cal·ly** *adv.* — **vo′cal·ness** *n.*

vocal cords Two membranous bands extending from [the] thyroid cartilage of the larynx and having edges that, w[hen] drawn tense, are caused to vibrate by the passage of air [from] the lungs, thereby producing voice. For illus. see THRO[AT.]

vo·cal·ic (vō·kal′ik) *adj.* Consisting of, like, or relati[ng to] vowel sounds.

vo·cal·ist (vō′kəl·ist) *n.* A singer.

vo·cal·ize (vō′kəl·īz) *v.* **·ized, ·iz·ing** *v.t.* 1. To make v[ocal;] utter, say, or sing. 2. To provide a voice for; render ar[ticu]late. 3. *Phonet.* **a** To change (a consonant) to a vowe[l or] some shift in the articulatory process. **b** To voice. — *v.[i.* 4.] To produce sounds with the voice, as in speaking or sin[ging.] — **vo′cal·i·za′tion** *n.* — **vo′cal·iz′er** *n.*

vo·ca·tion (vō·kā′shən) *n.* 1. A stated or regular occ[upa]tion; a calling. 2. A call to or fitness for a certain career. [3.] The work or profession for which one has a sense of sp[ecial] fitness. — **Syn.** See OCCUPATION. [< L < *vocare* to [call] — **vo·ca′tion·al** *adj.* — **vo·ca′tion·al·ly** *adv.*

vocational guidance A systematic program of tests [and] interviews to help a person find the occupation for whic[h he] is best suited.

vocational school A school, usu. on the secondary [level,] that trains students for special trades.

voc·a·tive (vok′ə·tiv) *adj.* 1. Pertaining to or used in [the] act of calling. 2. *Gram.* In some inflected languages, & [denot]ing the case of a noun, pronoun, or adjective used in d[irect] address. — *n. Gram.* 1. The vocative case. 2. A wo[rd in] this case. [< F, fem. of *vocatif* < L *vocare* to call]

vo·ces (vō′sēz) Plural of VOX.

if·er·ant (vō·sif′ər-ənt) *adj.* Viciferous; clamorous. —
A vociferous person. — **vo·cif′er·ance** *n.*

i·fer·ate (vō·sif′ə·rāt) *v.t. & v.i.* ·at·ed, ·at·ing To cry
; with a loud voice; shout. [< L < *vox, vocis* voice + *ferre*
carry] — **vo·cif′er·a′tion** *n.* — **vo·cif′er·a′tor** *n.*

if·er·ous (vō·sif′ər-əs) *adj.* Making or characterized by
)ud outcry; clamorous; noisy. — **vo·cif′er·ous·ly** *adv.* —
cif′er·ous·ness *n.*

·ka (vod′kə, *Russ.* vôd′kə) *n.* An alcoholic liquor, origi-
ly made in Russia from a fermented mash of wheat but
w also from other cereals and potatoes. [< Russian, dim.
voda water]

ue (vōg) *n.* **1.** The prevalent way or fashion; mode:
)n preceded by *in.* **2.** Popular favor; general acceptance.
F, fashion, orig., rowing < Ital. *vogare* to row]

gul (vō′gool) *n.* **1.** One of a Finno-Ugric people of the
al Mountains. **2.** The Ugric language of these people.

·e (vois) *n.* **1.** The sound produced by the vocal organs
a person or animal. **2.** The quality or character of such
und: a melodious *voice.* **3.** The power or faculty of vocal
erance; speech. **4.** A sound suggesting vocal utterance or
ech: the *voice* of the wind. **5.** Opinion or choice ex-
ssed; also, the right of expressing a preference or judg-
nt: to have a *voice* in the affair. **6.** Instruction; admoni-
n: the *voice* of nature. **7.** A person or agency by which the
)ught, wish, or purpose of another is expressed. **8.** Ex-
ssion of thought, opinion, feeling, etc.: to give *voice* to
's ideals. **9.** *Phonet.* The sound produced by vibration of
vocal cords in the production of most vowels and certain
)sonants. **10.** Musical tone produced by vibration of the
al cords and resonating in the cavities of the throat and
d; also, the ability to sing, or the state of the vocal organs
h regard to this ability: to be in poor *voice.* **11.** *Music* A
t (def. 11a), esp. as considered without regard to the par-
ılar instrument or human voice rendering it: also **voice
·rt. 12.** *Gram.* The relation of the action expressed by the
b to the subject, or the form of the verb indicating this re-
)onship. In most Indo-European languages, a distinction
ween an *active* and a *passive* voice is made, indicating, re-
ctively, that the subject of the sentence is either perform-
the action or is being acted upon. (Active: *He wrote the
er.* Passive: *The letter was written by him.*) — **in voice** In
)per condition for singing. — **with one voice** With one ac-
d; unitedly; unanimously. — *v.t.* **voiced, voic·ing 1.** To
: into speech; utter. **2.** *Music* To regulate the tones of;
e, as the pipes of an organ. **3.** *Phonet.* To utter with
ce or sonance. [< OF < L *vox, vocis*]
e box The larynx.

·ed (voist) *adj.* **1.** Having a voice; expressed by voice.
Phonet. Uttered with vibration of the vocal cords, as (b),
, (z); sonant: also *vocal.*

·e·less (vois′lis) *adj.* **1.** Having no voice, speech, or
e. **2.** *Phonet.* Produced without voice, as (p), (t), (s);
d. — **voice′less·ly** *adv.* — **voice′less·ness** *n.*

l (void) *adj.* **1.** No longer having force or validity, as a
ıtract, license, etc., that has lapsed; invalid; null. **2.**
)stitute; clear or free: with *of:* void of reason. **3.** Not occu-
d by matter; empty. **4.** Unoccupied, as a house or room.
Producing no effect; useless. — *n.* **1.** An empty space; a
:uum. **2.** A breach of surface or matter; a disconnecting
ce. **3.** Empty condition or feeling; a blank. — *v.t.* **1.** To
ke void or of no effect; invalidate. **2.** To empty or re-
ve (contents); evacuate, as urine. — **Syn.** See ANNUL.
OF, ult. < LL *vocuus* empty < L *vacuus*] — **void′er** *n.*

l·a·ble (voi′də·bəl) *adj.* **1.** Capable of being made void.
That may be evacuated. — **void′a·ble·ness** *n.*

l·ance (void′ns) *n.* **1.** The act of voiding, evacuating,
cting, or emptying. **2.** The state or condition of being
d; vacancy. [< AF < OF < *voider* to empty]

là (vwà·là′) *interj. French* There! behold!

le (voil, *Fr.* vwäl) *n.* A fine, sheer fabric like heavy veil-
, used for summer dresses and curtains. [< F, veil]

lant (vō′lənt) *adj.* **1.** Flying, or able to fly. **2.** Nimble.
OF, ppr. of *voler* to fly < L *volare*]

lan·te (vō·län′tā) *adj. Music* Swift and light. [< Ital.]

lar (vō′lər) *adj.* Pertaining to flight. [< L *volare* to fly]

·a·tile (vol′ə·til) *adj.* **1.** Evaporating rapidly at ordi-
ry temperatures on exposure to the air. **2.** Capable of be-
; vaporized. **3.** Easily influenced; changeable. **4.** Tran-
nt; ephemeral. [< OF < L *volare* to fly]

·a·til·i·ty (vol′ə·til′ə·tē) *n.* **1.** The state or quality of be-
; volatile. **2.** The property of being freely or rapidly dif-
ed in the atmosphere. — **vol′a·tile·ness.**

·a·til·ize (vol′ə·til·īz′) *v.t. & v.i.* ·ized, ·iz·ing **1.** To make
become volatile. **2.** To pass off or cause to pass off in va-
r; evaporate. — **vol′a·til·iz′a·ble** *adj.* — **vol′a·til·i·za′·
n** *n.* — **vol′a·til·iz′er** *n.*

·can·ic (vol·kan′ik) *adj.* **1.** Of, pertaining to, or charac-

---

teristic of a volcano or volcanoes. **2.** Produced by or emitted from a volcano. **3.** Eruptive. — **vol·can·ic·i·ty** (vol′kə·
nis′ə·tē) *n.* — **vol·can′i·cal·ly** *adv.*

vol·can·ism (vol′kən·iz′əm) *n.* The conditions and phenomena associated with volcanoes or volcanic action.

vol·can·ize (vol′kən·īz) *v.t.* ·ized, ·iz·ing To subject to the
action and effects of volcanic heat. — **vol′can·i·za′tion** *n.*

vol·ca·no (vol·kā′nō) *n. pl.* ·noes or ·nos *Geol.* **1.** An opening in the crust of the earth from which steam, hot gases,
ashes, etc., are expelled, forming a conical hill or mountain
with a central crater. **2.** The formation itself. [< Ital. <
L *Volcanus, Vulcanus* Vulcan]

vol·can·ol·o·gy (vol′kən·ol′ə·jē) *n.* The scientific study of
volcanoes. — **vol′can·o·log′i·cal** (-ə·loj′i·kəl) *adj.* — **vol′·
can·ol′o·gist** *n.*

vole (vōl) *n.* Any of various short-tailed, mouselike or ratlike rodents; esp., the **European vole** or the **North American
vole**: also called *field mouse, meadow mouse.* [Short for earlier *vole mouse* < *vole* field < Norw. *voll*]

vo·li·tion (və·lish′ən) *n.* **1.** The act or faculty of willing;
exercise of the will; esp., the termination of reasoning or uncertainty by a decision. **2.** Strength of will. **3.** That which
is willed or determined upon. [< F < Med.L < L *vol-*, stem
of *velle* will] — **vo·li′tion·al** *adj.* — **vo·li′tion·al·ly** *adv.*

vol·i·tive (vol′ə·tiv) *adj.* **1.** Of, pertaining to, or originating
in the will. **2.** Expressing a wish or permission.

vol·ley (vol′ē) *n. pl.* ·leys **1.** A simultaneous discharge of
many missiles; also, the missiles so discharged. **2.** Any discharge of many things at once: a *volley* of oaths. **3.** In tennis, a return of the ball before it touches the ground. **4.** In
soccer, a kick given the ball before its rebound. **5.** In cricket, a ball bowled so that it strikes the wicket before it touches
the ground. — *v.t. & v.i.* ·leyed, ·ley·ing **1.** To discharge or
be discharged in a volley. **2.** In tennis, to return (the ball)
without allowing it to touch the ground. **3.** In soccer, to
kick (the ball) before its rebound; in cricket, to bowl (a ball)
full pitch. [< MF < L *volare* to fly]

vol·ley·ball (vol′ē-bôl′) *n.* A game in which two teams on
either side of a high net strike a large ball with the hands in
an attempt to send the ball over the net without letting it
touch the ground; also, the ball used. Also **volley ball.**

vo·lost (vō′lost) *n.* In Russia, a district having one joint administrative assembly; a rural soviet. [< Russian *volost'*]

vol·plane (vol′plān) *Archaic v.i.* ·planed, ·plan·ing To
glide in an airplane. — *n.* An airplane glide. [< F *vol plané*
gliding flight < *vol* flight + *plané*, pp. of *planer* to glide]

Vol·sci (vol′sī) *n.pl.* A warlike people of ancient Italy, subdued by the Romans about 350 B.C. — **Vol·scian** (vol′shən)
adj. & n.

Vol·sun·ga Sa·ga (vol′sŏŏng-gə sä′gə) A prose version of
the Icelandic legends of the dwarf race, the Nibelungs, and
Sigurd, the grandson of Volsung. [< ON *Völsunga saga*, lit.,
saga of the Volsungs]

Vol·sungs (vol′sŏŏngz) *n.pl.* In Icelandic mythology, a
race of warriors descended from the hero **Vol′sung.**

volt[1] (vōlt) *n.* The unit of electromotive force, or that difference of potential that, when steadily applied against a resistance of one ohm, will produce a current of one ampere.
[after Alessandro *Volta,* 1745–1827, Italian physicist]

volt[2] (vōlt) *n.* **1.** In horse-training, a gait in which the horse
moves partially sidewise round a center. **2.** In fencing, a
sudden leap to avoid a thrust. [< F < Ital. *volta*, orig. pp.
fem. of *volvere* to turn]

volt·age (vōl′tij) *n.* Electromotive force expressed in volts.

vol·ta·ic (vol·tā′ik) *adj.* Pertaining to electricity developed
through chemical action or contact; galvanic.

voltaic battery *Electr.* A battery or primary cells.

voltaic cell *Electr.* A primary cell.

vol·ta·ism (vol′tə·iz′əm) *n.* Galvanism (def. 1).

volt·am·me·ter (vōlt′am′mē′tər) *n.* An instrument for
measuring either volts or amperes.

volt·am·pere (vōlt′am′pir) *n.* The rate of work in an electric circuit when the current is one ampere and the potential
one volt, equivalent to one watt.

volt·me·ter (vōlt′mē′tər) *n.* An instrument for determining
the voltage between any two points, generally consisting of a
calibrated galvanometer wound with a coil of high resistance.

vol·u·ble (vol′yə·bəl) *adj.* **1.** Having a flow of words or flu-
ency in speaking; garrulous. **2.** Turning readily or easily;
apt or formed to roll. **3.** Twining, as a plant. [< MF < L
< *volutus*, pp. of *volvere* to turn] — **vol′u·bil′i·ty, vol′u·ble·
ness** *n.* — **vol′u·bly** *adv.*

vol·ume (vol′yŏŏm, -yəm) *n.* **1.** A collection of sheets of
paper bound together; book. **2.** A separately bound part of
a work. **3.** Sufficient matter to fill a volume. **4.** Quantity of
sound or tone; loudness. **5.** A large quantity; a considerable
amount. **6.** Space occupied in three dimensions, as measured by cubic units. — **to speak volumes** To be full of

---

meaning; express a great deal. [< OF < L *volumen* roll, scroll < *volvere* to turn]

vo·lu·me·ter (və·lōō′mə·tər) *n.* Any of several instruments for measuring the volume of gases, liquids, or solids under specified conditions. [< VOLU(ME) + -METER]

vol·u·met·ric (vol′yə·met′rik) *adj. Chem.* Of or pertaining to measurement of substances by comparison of volumes. Also **vol′u·met′ri·cal.** — **vol′u·met′ri·cal·ly** *adv.* — **vol·u·me·try** (və·lōō′mə·trē) *n.*

vo·lu·mi·nous (və·lōō′mə·nəs) *adj.* 1. Having great quantity or volume. 2. Consisting of or capable of filling several volumes. 3. Writing or having written much; productive. 4. Having coils, folds, windings, etc. — **vo·lu′mi·nous·ly** *adv.* — **vo·lu′mi·nos′i·ty, vo·lu′mi·nous·ness** *n.*

vol·un·tar·y (vol′ən·ter′ē) *adj.* 1. Proceeding from the will or from one's own free choice; intentional; volitional. 2. Endowed with, possessing, or exercising will or free choice. 3. Effected by choice or volition. 4. *Law* a Unconstrained of will; done without compulsion. b Performed without legal obligation. — *n. pl.* **·tar·ies** 1. Any work or performance not compelled or imposed by another. 2. *Music* An organ solo, often improvised, played before, during, or after a service. [< OF < L *voluntas* will] — **vol′un·tar′i·ly** *adv.* — **vol′un·tar′i·ness** *n.*

vol·un·teer (vol′ən·tir′) *n.* One who enters into any service, esp. military service or a hazardous undertaking, of his own free will. — *adj.* 1. Pertaining to or composed of volunteers. 2. Springing up naturally or spontaneously, as from fallen or self-sown seed. — *v.t.* 1. To offer to give or do. — *v.i.* 2. To enter or offer to enter into some service or undertaking of one's free will; enlist. [< obs. F *voluntaire* < OF *voluntas* will]

Volunteer State Nickname of Tennessee.

vo·lup·tu·ar·y (və·lup′chōō·er′ē) *adj.* Pertaining to or promoting sensual indulgence and luxurious pleasures. — *n. pl.* **·ar·ies** One addicted to sensual pleasures; a sensualist.

vo·lup·tu·ous (və·lup′chōō·əs) *adj.* 1. Belonging to, producing, exciting, or yielding sensuous gratification. 2. Pertaining to or devoted to the enjoyment of pleasures or luxuries; luxurious; sensual. 3. Having a full and beautiful form, as a woman. [< OF < L *voluptas* pleasure] — **vo·lup′tu·ous·ly** *adv.* — **vo·lup′tu·ous·ness** *n.*

vo·lute (və·lōōt′) *n.* 1. *Archit.* A spiral, scroll-like ornament, esp. one characteristic of the Ionic capital. 2. *Zool.* One of the whorls or turns of a spiral shell. — *adj.* 1. Rolled up; forming spiral curves. 2. Having a spiral form, as a machine part. [< F < L *voluta* scroll, orig. fem. pp. of *volvere* to turn] — **vo·lut′ed** *adj.* — **vo·lu′tion** *n.*

VOLUTE

vom·it (vom′it) *v.i.* 1. To throw up or eject the contents of the stomach through the mouth. 2. To issue with violence from any hollow place; be ejected. — *v.t.* 3. To throw up or eject from the stomach, as food. 4. To discharge or send forth copiously or forcibly: The volcano *vomited* smoke. — *n.* Matter that is ejected, as from the stomach in vomiting. [< L *vomitare*, freq. of *vomere* to vomit] — **vom′it·er** *n.*

vom·i·tive (vom′ə·tiv) *adj.* Causing vomiting. — *n.* An emetic.

vom·i·to·ry (vom′ə·tôr′ē, -tō′rē) *adj.* Efficacious in producing vomiting. — *n. pl.* **·ries** 1. An emetic. 2. An opening through which matter is discharged. 3. In a Roman amphitheater, one of the entrances from the encircling arcades to the passages leading to the seats: so called because of the numbers of people who flowed forth from it: also **vom·i·tor·i·um** (vom′ə·tôr′ē·əm, -tō′rē-).

von (von, *Ger.* fôn, *unstressed* fən) *prep. German* Of; from: used in German and Austrian family names as an attribute of nobility, corresponding to the French *de.*

voo·doo (vōō′dōō) *n. pl.* **·doos** 1. A primitive religion of West African origin characterized by belief in sorcery and the use of charms, fetishes, witchcraft, etc. 2. One who practices voodoo. 3. A voodoo charm or fetish. — *adj.* Of or pertaining to the beliefs, ceremonies, or practices of voodoo. — *v.t.* **·dooed, ·doo·ing** To put a spell upon after the manner of a voodoo. [< Creole < Ewe (a W. African language) *vodu*]

voo·doo·ism (vōō′dōō·iz′əm) *n.* 1. The religion of voodoo. 2. Belief in or practice of this religion. — **voo′doo·ist** *n.* — **voo′doo·is′tic** *adj.*

-vora *combining form Zool.* Used to denote orders or genera when classified according to their food: *Carnivora.* An individual member of such an order or genus is denoted by **-vore:** *carnivore.* [< NL < L *-vorus.* See **-VOROUS.**]

vo·ra·cious (vô·rā′shəs, vō-, və-) *adj.* 1. Eating with greediness; ravenous. 2. Greedy; rapacious. 3. Ready to swallow up or engulf. 4. Insatiable; immoderate. [< L *vorare* to devour] — **vo·ra′cious·ly** *adv.* — **vo·rac·i·ty** (vô·ras′ə·tē, vō-, və-), **vo·ra′cious·ness** *n.*

-vorous *combining form* Consuming; eating or feeding upon: *omnivorous, carnivorous.* [< L *-vorus* < *vorare* to devour]

vor·tex (vôr′teks) *n. pl.* **·tex·es** or **·ti·ces** (-tə·sēz) mass of whirling gas or liquid, esp. when sucked spiral[ly] ward a central axis; a whirlwind or whirlpool. 2. Any [ac]tion or state of affairs that is similar to a vortex in viole[nce] force, etc. [< L, var. of *vertex* top, point] — **vor′t[ex]** (-ti·kəl) *adj.* — **vor′ti·cal·ly** *adv.*

vo·ta·ry (vō′tər·ē) *n. pl.* **·ries** 1. One bound by a vo[w or] promise, as a nun. 2. One devoted to some particular [wor]ship, pursuit, study, etc. Also **vo′ta·rist.** — **Syn.** See THUSIAST. — *adj.* Consecrated by a vow or promise [vo]tive. [< L *votus*, pp. of *vovere* to vow] — **vo·ta·ress** (vō′tə·ris) or **vo′tress** (vō′tris) *n. fem.*

vote (vōt) *n.* 1. A formal expression of will or opinion i[n re]gard to some question submitted for decision, as in elec[ting] officers, passing resolutions, etc. 2. That by which [the] choice is expressed, as a show of hands, or ballot. 3. Th[e re]sult of an election. 4. The number of votes cast; also, v[oters] collectively: a light *vote*; the farm *vote.* 5. The right to vo[te.] 6. A voter. — *v.* **vot·ed, vot·ing** *v.t.* 1. To enact or de[ter]mine by vote. 2. To cast one's vote for: to *vote* a stra[ight] ticket. 3. *Informal* To declare by general agreement: [We] *vote* a concert a success. — *v.i.* 4. To cast one's vote — [to] press opinion or preference by or as by a vote. — **to [vote] down** To defeat or suppress by voting against. — **to vo[te in]** To elect. [< L *votum* vow, wish, orig. pp. neut. of *vove[re* to] vow] — **vot′a·ble** or **vote′a·ble** *adj.* — **vot′er** *n.*

vote getter 1. A person who can win votes. 2. A [thing, event,] paign slogan, etc., that draws votes. — **vote getting**

voting machine A device which enables the voter to [indi]cate his choices by operating small levers and which regi[sters] and counts all votes.

vo·tive (vō′tiv) *adj.* Dedicated by a vow; performed in [ful]fillment of a vow. — **vo′tive·ly** *adv.* — **vo′tive·ness** *n.*

vouch (vouch) *v.i.* 1. To give one's own assurance or g[uar]antee; bear witness: with *for:* I will *vouch* for them. 2. [To] serve as assurance or proof: with *for.* — *v.t.* 3. To bear [wit]ness; to; attest or affirm. 4. To cite as support or justi[fica]tion. 5. To substantiate. — *n.* A declaration that att[ests] an assertion. [< OF < L *vocare* to call < *vox, vocis* v[oice]

vouch·er (vou′chər) *n.* 1. Any material thing, usu. a [writ]ing, that serves to vouch for the truth of something, or a[ffirm] an alleged act, esp. the payment or receipt of money. [2.] One who vouches for another; a witness.

vouch·safe (vouch′sāf′) *v. ·safed, ·saf·ing* *v.t.* 1. To g[rant] as with condescension; permit; deign. — *v.i.* 2. To co[nde]scend; deign. — **vouch′safe′ment** *n.*

vous·soir (vōō·swär′) *n. Archit.* A stone in an arch sh[aped] to fit its curve. [< OF *vausoir* < L *volvere* to turn]

vow (vou) *n.* 1. A solemn promise to God or to a dei[ty, as a] saint to perform some act or make some gift or sacrifice. [2.] A solemn engagement to adopt a certain course of life, [to pur]sue some end, etc.; also, a pledge of faithfulness. 3. A [sol]emn and emphatic affirmation. — **to take vows** To ent[er a] religious order. — *v.t.* 1. To promise solemnly, esp. to [God] or to some deity. 2. To declare with assurance or solem[nity.] 3. To make a solemn promise or threat to do, inflict, etc. [—] *v.i.* 4. To make a vow. [< AF *vu*, OF *vo, vou* < L *vot[um]* — **vow′er** *n.*

vow·el (vou′əl) *n.* 1. *Phonet.* A speech sound produce[d by] the relatively unimpeded passage of breath through [the] mouth, varying in quality according to the size, shape, [and] condition of the resonance cavities. Vowels may be cha[rac]terized by length (long or short), the height of the ton[gue] (high, mid, low), the place of articulation (front, cen[tral,] back), the tension of the tongue muscles (tense, lax), and [the] presence of lip rounding. Thus (ōō) is a long, high, b[ack,] tense, rounded vowel. 2. A letter representing such a so[und,] as *a, e, i, o, u,* and sometimes *y.* — *adj.* Of or pertaining [to a] vowel; vocal. [< OF < L *vox, vocis* voice, sound]

vox (voks) *n. pl.* **vo·ces** (vō′sēz) Voice; esp., in mus[ic a] voice; part. [< L]

vox po·pu·li (voks pop′yə·lī) *Latin* The voice of the peo[ple.]

voy·age (voi′ij) *n.* 1. A journey by water, esp. by sea: [com]monly used of a somewhat extended journey by water. [2.] Any journey. 3. A book describing a voyage or voyag[es.] 4. Any enterprise or project; also, course. — *v.* **·aged,** **·ag**[ing] *v.i.* 1. To make a voyage; journey by water. — *v.t.* [2.] To travel over. [< OF < L *viaticum*] — **voy′ag·er** *n.*

voy·age·a·ble (voi′ij·ə·bəl) *adj.* Navigable.

vo·ya·geur (vwä·yà·zhœr′) *n. pl.* **·geurs** (-zhœr′) *Cana*[dian] A boatman of Hudson's Bay Company or another fur c[om]pany, engaged in carrying men, supplies, etc., between [re]mote trading posts; also, a Canadian boatman or fur tra[der.] [< dial. F (Canadian)]

vo·yeur (vwä·yûr′) *n.* One who is sexually gratified by l[ook]ing at sexual objects or acts. [< F < L *videre* to see]

vo·yeur′ism *n.*

VTOL (vē′tôl) *n. Aeron.* An aircraft that takes off [and] lands vertically.

Vul·can (vul′kən) In Roman mythology, the god of fire [and] of metallurgy. — **Vul·ca′ni·an** (-kā′nē·ən) *adj.*

ca·ni·an (vul·kā′nē·ən) *adj.* Volcanic: also **vul·can·ic**
l·kan′ik). [< L < *Vulcanus* Vulcan]
can·ite (vul′kən·īt) *n.* A dark, hard variety of rubber
t has been vulcanized: also called *ebonite, hard rubber.* —
, Made of vulcanite. [after *Vulcan*]
can·ize (vul′kən·īz) *v.t.* **·ized, ·iz·ing** To treat (crude
ber) with sulfur or sulfur compounds in varying propor-
ns and at different temperatures, thereby increasing its
ength and elasticity. — **vul′can·iz′a·ble** *adj.* — **vul′·**
·i·za′tion *n.* — **vul′can·iz′er** *n.*
can·ol·o·gy (vul·kən·ol′ə·jē) *n.* Volcanology. — **vul′·**
·o·log′i·cal (-ə·loj′i·kəl) *adj.* — **vul′can·ol′o·gist** *n.*
gar (vul′gər) *adj.* **1.** Lacking in refinement, good taste,
sitivity, etc.; coarse; crude; boorish; also, obscene; inde-
t. **2.** Of, pertaining to, or characteristic of the people at
ge, as distinguished from the privileged or educated class-
popular; common. **3.** Written in or translated into the
mmon language or vulgate; vernacular. [< L < *vulgus*
common people] — **vul′gar·ly** *adv.*
gar·i·an (vul·gâr′ē·ən) *n.* A person of vulgar tastes or
nners.
gar·ism (vul′gə·riz′əm) *n.* **1.** Vulgarity. **2.** A word,
ase, or expression that is in nonstandard or unrefined
ge, though not necessarily coarse or gross.
gar·i·ty (vul·gar′ə·tē) *n.* *pl.* **·ties 1.** The quality or
racter of being vulgar. **2.** Something vulgar, as an ac-
n, word, etc. Also **vul·gar·ness** (vul′gər·nis).
gar·ize (vul′gə·rīz) *v.t.* **·ized, ·iz·ing 1.** To make vulgar.
To express and diffuse (something abstruse or complex)
a more widely comprehensible form; popularize. Also
t. **vul′gar·ise.** — **vul′gar·i·za′tion** *n.* — **vul′gar·iz′er** *n.*

Vulgar Latin See under LATIN.
vul·gate (vul′gāt) *adj.* Common; popular; generally accepted. — *n.* **1.** Everyday speech. **2.** Any commonly accepted
text. [< L < *vulgus* the common people]
Vul·gate (vul′gāt) *n.* A Latin version of the Bible, translated between A.D. 383 and 405, now revised and used as the
authorized version by the Roman Catholics. — *adj.* Belonging or relating to the Vulgate. [< Med.L *vulgata* (*editio*)
the popular (edition), fem. of L *vulgatus* common]
vul·ner·a·ble (vul′nər·ə·bəl) *adj.* **1.** Capable of being hurt
or damaged. **2.** Liable to attack; assailable. **3.** In contract bridge, having won one game of a rubber, and thus
receiving increased penalties and increased bonuses. [< LL
< L *vulnerare* to wound] — **vul′ner·a·bil′i·ty, vul′ner·a·**
ble·ness *n.* — **vul′ner·a·bly** *adv.*
vul·pine (vul′pin, -pīn) *adj.* **1.** Of or pertaining to a fox. **2.**
Like a fox; sly; crafty. [< L < *vulpes* fox]
vul·ture (vul′chər) *n.* **1.** Any of various
large birds related to the eagles, hawks,
and falcons, having the head and neck
naked or partly naked, and feeding mostly
on carrion. **2.** Someone or something dis-
gustingly predatory. [< AF, OF < L
vultur, vulturius] — **vul·tur·ine** (vul′chə·
rīn, -chər·in), **vul′tur·ous** *adj.*
vul·va (vul′və) *n.* *pl.* **·vae** (-vē) *Anat.*
The external genital parts of the female.
[< L, a covering, womb] — **vul′val,**
vul′var *adj.* — **vul′vi·form** (-və·fôrm) *adj.*
vy·ing (vī′ing) *adj.* Contending. — **vy′·**
ing·ly *adv.*

VULTURE
(To 55 inches
long; wing-
spread to
11 feet)

W

W (dub′əl·yōō, -yōō) *n.* *pl.* **w's** or **ws, W's** or **Ws, doub·**
ous 1. The twenty-third letter of the English alphabet;
able u: a ligature of vv or uu. **2.** The sound represented
the letter *w*, a voiced bilabial velar semivowel before
wels (*we, wage, worry*), and a *u*-glide in diphthongs (*how,*
w, dew, review). It often has no phonetic value before *r*
ist, write, wrong), and internally (*two, sword, answer*). ◆
e combination *wh*- (in Old English spelled *hw*-) is repre-
ted in this dictionary as (hw) because most Americans
d probably most Canadians use that pronunciation. In
me regions, however, *wh*- is consistently pronounced (w),
t the use cannot be considered nonstandard. — *symbol*
em. Tungsten (symbol W, for *wolfram*).
b·ble (wob′əl) *v.t.* & *v.i.* **·bled, ·bling** To wobble. — *n.*
wobble. — **wab′bler** *n.* — **wab′bly** *adj.*
C or **W.A.C.** (wak) *n.* A member of the Women's Army
rps. [< W(OMEN'S) A(RMY) C(ORPS)]
ck·y (wak′ē) *adj.* **wack·i·er, wack·i·est** *Slang* Extremely
ational or impractical; erratic; screwy. [Prob. < WHACK,
th ref. to damaging blows on the head]
d (wod) *n.* **1.** A small compact mass of any soft or flexi-
substance, esp. as used for stuffing, packing, or lining;
o, a lump; mass. **2.** A piece of paper, cloth, or leather
d to hold in a charge of powder in a muzzleloading gun;
o, a pasteboard or paper disk to hold powder and shot in
ce in a shotgun shell. **3.** Fibrous material for stopping
breaks, leakages, etc.; wadding. **4.** *Informal* A large
ount. **5.** *Informal* A roll of banknotes; also, money or
alth. **6.** A chew of tobacco. — *v.* **wad·ded, wad·ding**
. **1.** To press (fibrous substances, as cotton) into a mass
wad. **2.** To roll or fold into a tight wad, as paper. **3.** To
ck with wadding for protection, as valuables, or to stuff
line with wadding. **4.** To place a wad in, as a gun; hold
place with a wad. — *v.i.* **5.** To form into a wad. [Origin
certain] — **wad′dy** *adj.*
d·ding (wod′ing) *n.* **1.** Wads collectively. **2.** Any sub-
ance, as carded cotton, used as material for wads. **3.** The
t of applying a wad or wads.
d·dle (wod′l) *v.i.* **·dled, ·dling 1.** To walk with short
eps, swaying from side to side. **2.** To move clumsily; tot-
:. — *n.* A clumsy rocking walk, like that of a duck.
req. of WADE] — **wad′dler** *n.* — **wad′dly** *adj.*
d·dy (wod′ē) *n.* *pl.* **·dies** *Austral.* **1.** A thick war club

used by the aborigines. **2.** A walking stick; piece of wood.
— *v.t.* **·died, ·dy·ing** To strike with a waddy. [< native
Australian pronun. of *wood*]
wade (wād) *v.* **wad·ed, wad·ing** *v.i.* **1.** To walk through
water or any substance more resistant than air, as mud,
sand, etc. **2.** To proceed slowly or laboriously: to *wade*
through a book. — *v.t.* **3.** To pass or cross, as a river, by
walking on the bottom; ford. — **to wade in** (or **into**) *In-*
formal To attack or begin energetically or vigorously. — *n.*
1. The act of wading. **2.** A ford. [OE *wadan* to go]
wad·er (wā′dər) *n.* **1.** One who wades. **2.** A long-legged
wading bird, as a snipe, plover, or stork. **3.** *pl.* High waterproof boots, worn esp. by anglers.
wa·di (wä′dē) *n.* *pl.* **·dies 1.** In Arabia and northern Africa,
a ravine containing the bed of a watercourse, usu. dry except
in the rainy season; also, the watercourse. **2.** An oasis.
Also **wa′dy.** [< Arabic *wādī*]
WAF or **W.A.F.** (waf, wäf) *n.* A member of the Women in
the Air Force. [< W(OMEN IN THE) A(IR) F(ORCE)]
wa·fer (wā′fər) *n.* **1.** A very thin crisp biscuit, cooky, or
cracker; also, a small disk of candy. **2.** *Eccl.* A small flat
disk of unleavened bread stamped with a cross or the letters
IHS, and used in the Eucharist in some churches. **3.** A thin
disk of gelatin or other substance used for sealing letters,
attaching papers, or receiving a seal. — *v.t.* To attach,
seal, or fasten with a wafer. [< AF < MLG *wafel*]
waf·fle (wof′əl, wô′fəl) *n.* A batter cake, crisper than a pancake, baked between two hinged metal griddles marked with
regular indentations (**waffle iron**). [< Du. *wafel* wafer]
waft¹ (waft, wäft) *v.t.* **1.** To carry or bear gently or lightly
over air or water; float. **2.** To convey as if on air or water.
— *v.i.* **3.** To float, as on the wind. — *n.* **1.** The act of one
who or that which wafts. **2.** A current of air; also, something, as an odor, carried on a current of air. **3.** A wafting
or waving motion or movement. [Back formation < *wafter*,
in obs. sense, "an escort ship" < Du. *wachten* to guard]
waft² (waft, wäft) *n.* *Naut.* **1.** A signal flag or pennant,
sometimes used to indicate wind direction. **2.** A signal made
with a flag or pennant. Also called *weft.* [Alter. of dial. E
waff, var. of WAVE]
waft·er (waf′tər, wäf′-) *n.* **1.** One who or that which wafts.
2. A form of fan or revolving disk used in a blower.
wag¹ (wag) *v.* **wagged, wag·ging** *v.t.* **1.** To cause to move

lightly and quickly from side to side or up and down; swing: The dog *wags* its tail. **2.** To move (the tongue) in talking. — *v.i.* **3.** To move lightly and quickly from side to side or up and down. **4.** To move busily in animated talk: said of the tongue. — *n.* The act or motion of wagging. [ME *waggen*, prob. < Scand.]

wag² (wag) *n.* A humorous fellow; wit; joker. [? Short for obs. *waghalter* gallows bird < WAG¹ + HALTER¹]

wage (wāj) *v.t.* **waged, wag·ing** To engage in and maintain vigorously; carry on: to *wage* war. — *n.* **1.** Payment for service rendered; esp., the pay of artisans or laborers receiving a fixed sum by the hour, day, week, or month, or for a certain amount of work; hire. **2.** *pl. Econ.* The remuneration received by labor as distinguished from that received by capital. **3.** *pl.* Recompense or yield: formerly, often construed as sing.: The *wages* of sin is death. [< AF *wagier*, OF *guagier* to pledge]

wage earner One who works for wages.

wa·ger (wā'jər) *v.t. & v.i.* To bet. — *n.* **1.** A bet (defs. 1, 2, & 3). **2.** The act of giving a pledge. [< AF *wagier* to pledge] — **wa'ger·er** *n.*

wage scale A scale or series of amounts of wages paid.

wage·work·er (wāj'wûr'kər) *n.* An employee receiving wages.

wag·ger·y (wag'ər-ē) *n. pl.* **·ger·ies 1.** Mischievous jocularity; drollery. **2.** A jest; joke.

wag·gish (wag'ish) *adj.* **1.** Being or acting like a wag. **2.** Said or done in waggery. — **wag'gish·ly** *adv.* — **wag'gish·ness** *n.*

wag·gle (wag'əl) *v.* **·gled, ·gling** *v.t.* **1.** To cause to move with rapid to-and-fro motions; wag: The duck *waggles* its tail. — *v.i.* **2.** To totter; wobble. — *n.* The act of waggling. [Freq. of WAG¹] — **wag'gling·ly** *adv.* — **wag'gly** *adj.*

Wag·ne·ri·an (väg-nir'ē-ən) *adj.* Relating to Richard Wagner or to his style, theory, or works. — *n.* An admirer, performer, or advocate of Wagnerian works.

wag·on (wag'ən) *n.* **1.** Any of various four-wheeled horse-drawn vehicles used for carrying crops, goods, freight, etc. **2.** A child's four-wheeled toy cart. **3.** A stand on wheels or casters for serving food or drink. **4.** *Brit.* A railway freight car. **5.** *Informal* A patrol wagon. **6.** A station wagon. — **on the (water) wagon** *Informal* Abstaining from alcoholic beverages. — **to fix (someone's) wagon** *U.S. Slang* To ruin or punish. — *v.t.* To carry or transport in a wagon. Also *Brit.* **wag'gon.** [< Du. *wagen*]

wag·on·er (wag'ən-ər) *n.* One whose business is driving wagons. Also *Brit.* **wag'gon·er.**

wag·on-head·ed (wag'ən-hed'id) *adj. Archit.* Having a round-arched roof.

wa·gon-lit (vȧ-gôṅ-lē') *n. pl.* **-lits** (-lē') *French* A railway sleeping car.

wag·on·load (wag'ən-lōd') *n.* The amount that a wagon can carry.

wagon train A train or line of wagons.

wag·tail (wag'tāl') *n.* Any of several small singing birds having a long tail that is habitually wagged up and down.

Wa·ha·bi (wä-hä'bē) *n.* A member of an orthodox Moslem sect of Arabia. Also **Wa·ha'bee, Wah·ha'bi.**

wa·hoo (wä-hōo', wä'hōo) *n.* A deciduous North American shrub or small tree with purple flowers and scarlet fruit. [< Siouan (Dakota) *wānhu*, lit., arrowwood]

waif (wāf) *n.* **1.** A homeless, neglected wanderer; a stray. **2.** Anything found and unclaimed, the owner being unknown. — *v.t.* To throw away; cast off, as a waif. — *adj.* Stray; wandering; homeless. [< AF *waif*, OF *gaif*]

wail (wāl) *v.i.* **1.** To grieve with mournful cries; lament. **2.** To make a sad, melancholy sound, as if in grief. — *v.t.* **3.** To grieve on account of. **4.** To cry out in sorrow. — *n.* **1.** A prolonged, high-pitched sound of lamentation or grief. **2.** Any mournful sound, as of the wind. [< ON < *væ, vei* woe] — **wail'er** *n.* — **wail'ful** *adj.*

wain (wān) *n.* An open, four-wheeled wagon for hauling heavy loads. [OE *wægn, wæn*]

wain·scot (wān'skət, -skot, -skōt) *n.* **1.** A facing for inner walls, usu. of paneled wood. **2.** The lower part of an inner wall, when finished with material different from the rest of the wall. — *v.t.* **wain·scot·ed** or **·scot·ted, wain·scot·ing** or **·scot·ting** To face or panel with wainscot. [< MLG < *wagen* wagon + *schot* wooden partition]

wain·scot·ing (wān'skət·ing, -skot-, -skōt-) *n.* Material for a wainscot; a wainscot. Also **wain'scot·ting.**

wain·wright (wān'rīt) *n.* A maker of wagons.

waist (wāst) *n.* **1.** The part of the body between the chest and the hips. **2.** The middle part of any object, esp. if narrower than the ends. **3.** That part of a woman's dress covering the body from the waistline to the shoulders; a bodice. **4.** A waistband. [ME *wast*]

waist·band (wāst'band', -bənd) *n.* A band encircling the waist, esp., as part of a skirt or trousers.

waist·coat (wāst'kōt', wes'kit) *n. Chiefly Brit.* A vest (def. 1).

waist·line (wāst'līn') *n.* The line of the waist, between the ribs and the hips; in dressmaking, the line at which the s[k]irt of a dress meets the waist.

wait (wāt) *v.i.* **1.** To stay or remain in expectation, as o[f] anticipated action or event: with *for, until*, etc. **2.** To b[e] remain in readiness. **3.** To remain temporarily neglecte[d] undone. **4.** To perform duties of personal service or at[t] dance; esp., to act as a waiter or waitress. — *v.t.* **5.** To s[erve] or remain in expectation of; await. **6.** *Informal* To p[ost]pone; delay: Don't *wait* breakfast for me. — **to wait on** (**upon**) **1.** To act as a servant or attendant to. **2.** To g[o] see; call upon; visit. **3.** To attend as a consequence. — **wait up** To delay going to bed in anticipation of someon[e or] something. — *n.* **1.** The act of waiting, or the time spe[nt] waiting; delay. **2.** An ambush or trap: to lie in *wait* f[or a] victim. [< AF and OF < OHG < *wahta* guard]

wait·er (wā'tər) *n.* **1.** One who serves food and drink, a[s in] a restaurant. **2.** One who awaits something. **3.** A tray [for] dishes, etc.

wait·ing (wā'ting) *n.* The act of one who waits. — **waiting** In attendance, esp. at court. — *adj.* That w[aits;] expecting.

waiting room A room for the use of persons waiting, a[s for] a railroad train, a doctor, dentist, or the like.

wait·ress (wā'tris) *n.* A woman or girl employed to wai[t on] guests at table, as in a restaurant.

waive (wāv) *v.t.* **waived, waiv·ing 1.** To give up or re[lin]quish a claim to. **2.** To refrain from insisting upon or tak[e] advantage of; forego. **3.** To put off; postpone; delay. [< AF *weyver*, OF *gaiver* to abandon]

waiv·er (wā'vər) *n. Law* The voluntary relinquishmen[t of] a right or privilege; also, the instrument that evidences s[uch] relinquishment. [< AF < *weyver* to abandon]

wake¹ (wāk) *v.* **woke** (*Rare* **waked**), **waked** (*Dial.* and [al]ternative *Brit.* **woke, wok·en**), **wak·ing** *v.i.* **1.** To eme[rge] from sleep. **2.** To be or remain awake. **3.** To become [ac]tive or alert after being inactive or dormant. **4.** *Dial.* [To] keep watch at night; esp., to hold a wake (def. 1). — *v.t.* **5.** To rouse from sleep; awake. **6.** To stir up; excite[:] *wake* evil passions. **7.** *Dial.* To keep a vigil over; esp. [to] hold a wake over. — *n.* **1.** A watch over the body of a d[ead] person through the night, before burial. **2.** The act of [re]fraining from sleep, as on a solemn occasion. [Fusion of [OE] *wacan* to awake and *wacian* to be awake]

wake² (wāk) *n.* **1.** The track left by a vessel passing thro[ugh] the water. **2.** The area behind any moving thing. — **in the wake of 1.** Following close behind. **2.** In the aftermat[h of] as a result of. [< ON *vök* an opening in ice]

wake·ful (wāk'fəl) *adj.* **1.** Remaining awake, esp. at [the] ordinary time of sleep; not sleeping or sleepy. **2.** Watch[ful;] alert. **3.** Arousing from or as from sleep. — **wake'fu[l·ly]** *adv.* — **wake'ful·ness** *n.*

wak·en (wā'kən) *v.t.* **1.** To rouse from sleep; awake. [**2.**] To rouse to alertness or activity. — *v.i.* **3.** To cease sl[eep]ing; wake up. [OE *wæcnan, wæcnian*]

wake-rob·in (wāk'rob'in) *n.* Any species of trillium.

Wal·dorf salad (wôl'dôrf) A salad of chopped celery, [ap]ples, and walnuts, garnished with lettuce and mayonna[ise.] [after the first *Waldorf-*Astoria Hotel, New York City]

wale (wāl) *n.* **1.** A welt (def. 3). **2.** *Naut.* One of cer[tain] strakes of outer planking running fore and aft on a ves[sel.] **3.** A ridge on the surface of cloth. — *v.t.* **waled, wal·ing** [**1.**] To raise wales on by striking, as with a lash; beat. **2.** [To] manufacture, as cloth, with a ridge or rib. **3.** To weav[e, as] wickerwork with several rods together. [OE *walu*]

walk (wôk) *v.i.* **1.** To advance on foot in such a mann[er] that one part of a foot is always on the ground; of qua[dru]peds, to advance in such a manner that two or more feet [are] always on the ground. **2.** To move or go on foot for e[xer]cise or amusement. **3.** To proceed slowly. **4.** To ac[t or] live in some manner: to *walk* in peace. **5.** To return to ea[rth] and appear, as a ghost. **6.** In baseball, to achieve first b[ase] as a result of having been pitched four balls. — *v.t.* **7.** [To] pass through, over, or across at a walk: to *walk* the fl[oor.] **8.** To cause to go at a walk; lead, ride, or drive at a w[alk.] **9.** To accompany on a walk. **10.** To bring to a speci[fic] condition by walking: She *walked* me to death. **11.** In b[ase]ball, to allow to advance to first base by pitching four b[alls.] — **to walk off 1.** To depart, esp. abruptly or without wa[rn]ing. **2.** To get rid of (fat, etc.) by walking. — **to walk [off] with 1.** To win. **2.** To steal. — **to walk out** *Informal* [**1.**] To go out on strike. **2.** To keep company: with *with* or [to]*gether.* — **to walk out on** *Informal* To forsake; desert. **to walk over** To defeat easily; overwhelm. — *n.* **1.** [The] act of walking, as for enjoyment; a stroll. **2.** Manne[r of] walking; gait. **3.** Chosen profession or habitual spher[e of] action: the different *walks* of life. **4.** Distance as measu[red] by the time taken by one who walks: an hour's *walk.* **5.** [A] place set apart for walking; a path or sidewalk. **6.** A p[iece] of ground set apart for domestic animals; range; pasture. [**7.**] In baseball, an advancing to first base as a result of h[aving]

been pitched four balls. [OE *wealcan* to roll, toss] —
'er n.

.a·way (wôk'ə·wā') *n.* A contest won without serious
osition: also called *walkover.*

.ie-talk·ie (wô'kē-tô'kē) *n. Telecom.* A portable
ing and receiving radio set light enough to be carried by
man: also spelled *walky-talky.*

ing papers *Informal* Notice of dismissal from em-
ment, etc.

ing stick 1. A staff or cane. 2. Any of various in-
having legs, body, and wings resembling a twig.

-on (wôk'on', -ôn') *n.* A performer having a very
l part; also, the part.

-out (wôk'out') *n. Informal* A workmen's strike.

-o·ver (wôk'ō'vər) *n.* A walkaway.

-up (wôk'up') *Informal n.* An apartment house hav-
o elevator. — *adj.* Having no elevator.

.y-talk·y (wô'kē-tô'kē) See WALKIE-TALKIE.

(wôl) *n.* 1. A continuous structure designed to enclose
ea, to be the surrounding exterior of a building, to be a
ition between rooms, etc.; also, a fence separating fields,
◆ Collateral adjective: *mural.* 2. Something sugges-
of a wall: a *wall* of bayonets. 3. A rampart for defense;
e plural, fortifications. 4. A sea wall; levee. **— to
e, push,** or **thrust to the wall** To force (one) to an ex-
ity; crush. **— to go to the wall** To be driven to an
emity; be forced to yield. — *v.t.* 1. To provide, sur-
d, etc., with or as with a wall. 2. To fill or block with
all: often with *up.* — *adj.* Of, pertaining to, or on, a
[OE < L < *vallus* stake, palisade]

ia·by (wol'ə·bē) *n. pl.* **·bies** One of the smaller kan-
os. [< Australian *wolabá*]

·board (wôl'bôrd, -bōrd') *n.* A material composed of
ral layers of compressed wood chips and pulp, used as a
titute for wooden boards and plaster.

let (wol'it) *n.* 1. A pocketbook, usu. of leather, for
ing unfolded paper money, personal papers, etc.: also
d *billfold.* 2. A leather or canvas bag for tools, etc. 3.
apsack. [ME *walet*; ult. origin uncertain]

-eye (wôl'ī') *n.* 1. An eye in which the iris is light-
red or white. 2. Any of several walleyed fishes. [Back
ation < WALLEYED]

-eyed (wôl'īd') *adj.* 1. Having a whitish or grayish
. 2. Having large, staring eyes, as a fish. 3. *Slang*
nk. [< ON < *vagl* film on the eye + *eygr* < *auga* eye]

-eyed pike A fresh-water game fish of the Great Lakes,
ng large eyes. Also **walleyed perch.**

-flow·er (wôl'flou'ər) *n.* 1. Any of various European
s of the mustard family, having fragrant yellow, orange,
ed flowers. 2. *Informal* A person, esp. a woman, at a
y who stays by the wall for want of a dancing partner.

·loon (wo·loon') *n.* 1. One of a people inhabiting
hern and southeastern Belgium and the adjoining re-
s of France. 2. Their language, a dialect of French.
dj. Of or pertaining to the Walloons or their dialect.

lop (wol'əp) *v.t. Informal* 1. To beat soundly; thrash.
o hit with a hard blow. 3. To defeat soundly. — *v.i.*
. or *Informal* 4. To gallop. — *n. Informal* A severe
v. [< AF *waloper,* OF *galoper*]

lop·er (wol'əp·ər) *n. Informal* 1. One who or that
ch wallops. 2. A whopper.

lop·ing (wol'əp·ing) *Informal adj.* Very large; whop-
. — *n.* A beating; whipping.

low (wol'ō) *v.i.* 1. To roll about; be pleasurably and
vely immersed. 2. To thrash about; flounder. 3. To
ve with a heavy, rolling motion, as a ship in a storm. 4.
live self-indulgently: to *wallow* in sensuality. — *n.* 1.
act of wallowing. 2. A pool or hole in which animals
low; also, any depression or hollow made by or suggest-
such use. [OE *wealwian*] — **wal'low·er** *n.*

·pa·per (wôl'pā'pər) *n.* Paper specially prepared and
ted in colors and designs, for covering walls and ceilings
ooms. — *v.t.* To cover or provide with wallpaper.

l Street 1. A street in the financial district of New
k City. 2. The world of U.S. finance.

nut (wôl'nut', -nət) *n.* 1. Any of various trees of the
th temperate zone cultivated as ornamental shade trees
valued for their timber and their edible nuts. 2. The
od or nut of any of these trees, esp. the edible seed or
nel. 3. The shagbark hickory, or its nut. 4. The color
he wood of any of these trees, esp. of the black walnut, a
y dark brown. [OE < *wealh* foreign + *hnutu* nut]

·pur·gis Night (väl·poor'gis) The night before May 1,
ociated with a witches' Sabbath. [after St. *Walpurga* (or
lburga), whose feast day falls on this date]

·rus (wôl'rəs, wol'-) *n. pl.* **·rus·es** or **·rus** A large ma-
e mammal of arctic seas, having flippers, tusks in the
er jaw, and a thick neck. [< Du. *walrus* < Scand.]

waltz (wôlts) *n.* 1. A dance for couples to music in triple
time. 2. The music for such a dance, or any similar music
in triple time. — *v.i.* 1. To dance a waltz. 2. To move
quickly and boldly; flounce. 3. To move freely. — *v.t.* 4.
To cause to waltz. — *adj.* Of, or typical of, the waltz:
waltz time. [< G < *walzen* to waltz] — **waltz'er** *n.*

wam·pum (wom'pəm, wôm'-) *n.* 1. Beads made from
shells, often worked into ornaments, formerly used as currency by North American Indians. 2. *Informal* Money.
[< Algonquian *wampum(peage),* lit., a white string (of
beads)]

wan (won) *adj.* **wan·ner, wan·nest** 1. Pale, as from sickness or anxiety; pallid. 2. Indicating illness, unhappiness,
etc.: a *wan* smile. — *v.t. & v.i.* **wanned, wan·ning** *Poetic*
To make or become wan. [OE *wann* dark, gloomy] —
wan'ly *adv.* — **wan'ness** *n.*

wand (wond) *n.* 1. A slender rod waved by a magician;
also, any rod indicating an office or function of the bearer, as
a scepter. 2. A musician's baton. 3. A thin, flexible stick
or twig; also, a willow shoot; osier. [< ON *vöndr*]

wan·der (won'dər) *v.i.* 1. To move or travel about without
destination or purpose; roam; rove. 2. To go casually or
indirectly; idle; stroll. 3. To twist or meander. 4. To
stray. 5. To deviate in conduct or opinion; go astray. 6.
To think or speak deliriously or irrationally. — *v.t.* 7. To
wander through or across. — *n.* A ramble. [OE *wandrian*]
— **wan'der·er** *n.* — **wan'der·ing·ly** *adv.*
— Syn. (verb) 1. *Wander* implies no more than the absence of
purpose: to *wander* through the shops. *Ramble* tends to be dep-
recatory: the speaker *rambled* on for an hour. *Roam* and *rove* imply
travel through a large area, and suggest an irregular rather than a
purposeless course: the explorers *roamed* through the jungle,
pirates *roved* the sea.

wan·der·ing albatross (won'dər·ing) A large, whitish,
black-winged, web-footed sea bird.

wan·der·lust (won'dər·lust', *Ger.* vän'dər·lŏost) *n.* An
impulse to travel; restlessness combined with a sense of adventure. [< G < *wandern* to travel + *lust* joy]

wane (wān) *v.i.* **waned, wan·ing** 1. To diminish in size and
brilliance: opposed to *wax.* 2. To decline or decrease gradually; draw to an end. — *n.* 1. Decrease, as of power, prosperity, or reputation. 2. The decrease of the moon's visible
illuminated surface; also, the period of such decrease. —
on the wane Waning. [OE *wanian*]

wan·gle (wang'gəl) *v.* **·gled, ·gling** *Informal v.t.* 1. To
obtain or accomplish by indirect or irregular methods: to
wangle an introduction. 2. To manipulate or adjust, esp.,
dishonestly. — *v.i.* 3. To resort to indirect, irregular, or
dishonest methods. — *n.* An act of wangling. [? Alter. of
WAGGLE] — **wan'gler** *n.*

want (wont, wônt) *v.t.* 1. To feel a desire or wish for. 2.
To wish; desire: used with the infinitive: Your friends *want*
to help you. 3. To be deficient in; lack; be without. 4. To
be lacking to the extent of: He *wants* three inches of six feet.
5. *Brit.* To need; require. — *v.i.* 6. To have need: usu.
with *for.* 7. To be needy or destitute. 8. *Rare* To be lacking or absent. **— to want for** To be in need of; lack. **— to
want to** *Informal* Ought to: You *want to* eat well. — *n.* 1.
A lack; scarcity; shortage. 2. Privation; poverty; need. 3.
Something lacking; a need. 4. A conscious need of something; a craving. **— for want of** Because of the lack or absence of: The crop failed *for want of* rain. [Prob. < ON
vanta to be lacking] — **want'er** *n.*

wa'n't (wont, wônt) Was not: a dialectal contraction.

want ad *Informal* A classified advertisement for something wanted, as hired help, a job, a lodging, etc.

want column A column of want ads.

want·ing (won'ting, wôn'-) *adj.* 1. Not at hand; missing;
lacking. 2. Not coming up to need or expectation: His work
was found *wanting.* **— wanting in** Deficient in. — *prep.*
1. Without; lacking. 2. Minus; less.

wan·ton (won'tən) *adj.* 1. Licentious; lustful. 2. Unjust;
malicious; *wanton* savagery; also, unprovoked: a *wanton*
murder. 3. Of abundant growth; rank. 4. Extravagant;
excessive; unrestrained: *wanton* speech. 5. *Poetic* Not
bound or tied; loose: *wanton* curls; also, frolicsome. — *v.i.*
1. To act wantonly or playfully; revel or sport. 2. To grow
luxuriantly. — *v.t.* 3. To waste wantonly. — *n.* 1. A
licentious person, esp., a woman. 2. A playful or frolicsome
person or animal. 3. A trifler; dallier. [ME < OE *wan*
deficient + ME *towen* < OE < *tēon* to educate] — **wan'-
ton·ly** *adv.* — **wan'ton·ness** *n.*

wap·i·ti (wop'ə·tē) *n. pl.* **·tis** or **·ti** *U.S. & Canadian* A
large North American deer; an elk. [< Algonquian]

war (wôr) *n.* 1. An armed conflict between nations or
states, or between different parties in the same state. See
table MAJOR WARS OF HISTORY. 2. Any act or state of
hostility; enmity; also, a contest or conflict. 3. The science

MAJOR WARS OF HISTORY

NAME	CONTESTANTS (victor shown first)	NOTABLE BATTLES	TREATIES
Greco-Persian Wars 499–478 B.C.	Greek states — Persia	Marathon, 490; Thermopylae, Salamis, 480; Plataea, 479	
Peloponnesian War 431–404 B.C.	Sparta — Athens	Syracuse, 415; Cyzicus, 410; Aegospotami, 405	Peace of Nicias, 421
First Punic War 264–241 B.C.; Second Punic War 218–201 B.C.; Third Punic War 149–146 B.C.	Rome — Carthage	Drepanum, 249; Aegates, 241; Lake Trasimene, 217; Cannae, 216; Zama, 202	
Norman Conquest 1066	Normandy — England	Hastings, 1066	
Crusades 1096–1291	Christianity — Islam (indecisive)	Jerusalem, 1099; Acre, 1191	
Hundred Years' War 1338–1453	England — France	Crécy, 1346; Poitiers, 1356; Agincourt, 1415; Siege of Orléans, 1428–39	
Wars of the Roses 1455–85	Lancaster — York (indecisive)	St. Albans, 1455	
Thirty Years' War 1618–48	Catholics — Protestants	Leipzig, Breitenfeld, 1631; Lützen, 1632	Westphalia, 1648
Civil War (English) 1642–46	Roundheads — Cavaliers	Marston Moor, 1643; Naseby, 1645	
Second Great Northern War 1700–1721	Russia — Sweden and Baltic allies	Poltava, 1709	Nysted, 1721
War of the Spanish Succession 1701–14	England, Austria, Prussia, Netherlands — France, Spain	Blenheim, 1704	Utrecht, 1713
War of the Austrian Succession 1740–48	France, Prussia, Sardinia, Spain — Austria, England	Dettingen, 1743; Fontenoy, 1745	Aix-la-Chapelle, 1748
French & Indian War 1755–63	England — France	Plains of Abraham, 1759; Montreal, 1760	
Seven Years' War 1756–63	Prussia — Austria, France, Russia	Rossbach, Leuthen, 1757	Hubertusberg, 1763
Revolutionary War 1775–83	American Colonies — England	Lexington, Concord, Bunker Hill, 1775; Saratoga, 1777; Yorktown, 1781	Paris, 1783
Napoleonic Wars 1796–1815	England, Austria, Russia, Prussia, etc. — France	Nile, 1798; Trafalgar, 1805; Jena, Auerstädt, 1806; Leipzig, 1813; Waterloo, 1815	Campoformio, 1797; 1807; Schönbrunn, Paris, 1814–15; Vienna, Ghent, 1814
War of 1812 1812–15	United States — England	Lake Erie, 1813; New Orleans, 1815	
War of Independence (Greek) 1821–29	Greece, England, Sweden, Russia — Turkey	Navarino, 1827	London, 1827
Mexican War 1846–48	United States — Mexico	Resaca de la Palma, 1846; Chapultepec, 1847	Guadalupe Hidalgo, 184
Crimean War 1854–56	Turkey, England, France, Sardinia — Russia	Sevastopol, 1854	Paris, 1856
Civil War (United States) 1861–65	Union (North) — Confederate States (South)	Bull Run, 1861; Antietam, 1862; Chancellorsville, Gettysburg, Vicksburg, Chattanooga, 1863; Wilderness, 1864	
Franco-Prussian War 1870–71	Prussia — France	Sedan, 1870	Versailles, 1871
Spanish-American War 1898	United States — Spain	Manila Bay, Santiago, 1898	Paris, 1898
Boer War 1899–1902	England — Transvaal Republic & Orange Free State	Ladysmith, 1899	Vereeniging, 1902
Russo-Japanese War 1904–1905	Japan — Russia	Port Arthur, Mukden, Tsushima, 1905	Portsmouth, 1905
First Balkan War 1912–13; Second Balkan War 1913	Bulgaria, Serbia, Greece, Montenegro — Turkey	Scutari, 1912; Salonika, 1912; Adrianople, 1912	London, 1913
World War I 1914–18	Allies — Central Powers	Dardanelles, 1915; Verdun, Somme, Jutland, 1916; Caporetto, 1917; Vittorio Veneto, Amiens, Marne, Ypres, 1918	Versailles, Saint-Ger Neuilly, 1919; Triano Sèvres, 1920; Lausanne,
Civil War (Spanish) 1936–39	Insurgents — Loyalists	Teruel, 1937; Ebro River, 1938	
World War II 1939–45	United Nations — Axis 1939–45	Dunkirk, 1940; Crete, 1941; El Alamein, 1942; Tunis, 1943; Stalingrad, 1942–43; Kharkov, 1943; Cassino, 1943–44; Saint-Lô, 1944; Rhine, Ruhr, Berlin, 1945	Potsdam, 1945
	United Nations — Japan 1941–45	Pearl Harbor, 1941; Bataan, 1941–1942; Singapore, Coral Sea, Midway Island, Guadalcanal, 1942; Bismarck Sea, Tarawa, 1943; Leyte Gulf, 1944; Philippines, 1944–45; Okinawa, 1945	San Francisco, 1951
Korean War 1950–52	United Nations — North Korea	Inchon, Pyongyang, 1950; Seoul, 1951	Panmunjom, 1953
Viet Nam War 1958–1973	South Vietnam — North Vietnam (indecisive)	Pleiku, 1965; Dak To, 1966–68; Da Nang, 1968–69; Hue, 1968–69	Paris, 1973

of military operations; strategy. **— v.i. warred, war·ring**
1. To wage war; fight or take part in a war. **2.** To be in any state of active opposition. **— adj.** Of, used in, or resulting from war. [OE < AF < OHG *werra* strife]
war belt Among certain North American Indians, a belt of wampum sent to declare war, to invoke aid in war, etc.
War between the States The U.S. Civil War: used esp., in the former Confederate States.
war·ble (wôr′bəl) v. **·bled, ·bling** v.t. **1.** To sing with trills and runs, or with tremulous vibrations. **2.** To celebrate in song. **— v.i. 3.** To sing with trills, etc. **4.** To make a liquid, murmuring sound, as a stream. **5.** U.S. To yodel. **— n.** The act of warbling: a carol; song. [< AF and OF < *werble* warble]

war·bler (wôr′blər) n. **1.** One who or that which war
2. Any of various plain-colored, mostly Old World
noted for their song. **3.** Any of various small America
sectivorous birds, usu. brilliantly colored.
war bonnet The ceremonial head dress of the North A
ican Plains Indians.
war crime Any of various crimes considered in violatio
the rules of warfare, as atrocities against civilians, s
labor, genocide, and the mistreatment of prisoners.
war cry A rallying cry used by combatants in a war, o
participants in any contest.
ward (wôrd) n. **1.** A large room in a hospital, usu. fo
or more patients. **2.** An administrative or electoral divi
of a city. **3.** *Law* A person, often a minor, who is in

rge of a guardian. **4.** The act of guarding, or the state of
ng guarded; custody. **5.** A means of defense: a protec-
n. **6.** A defensive attitude, as in fencing; guard. **7.** Any
he separate divisions of a prison. — *v.t.* **1.** To repel or
n aside, as a blow: usu., with *off*. **2.** To keep in safety.
Archaic To guard. [OE < *weardian* to watch, guard]
rd *suffix* Toward; in the direction of: *upward*, *home-
-rd*. Also **-wards**. [OE *-weard*, *-weardes* at, toward]
·dance A dance of savage tribes before going to war or
celebration of a victory.
·den[1] (wôr′dən) *n.* **1.** *U.S.* The chief officer of a prison.
Brit. The head of certain colleges. **3.** In Connecticut, the
ef executive of a borough. **4.** A churchwarden. **5.** A
·der. [< AF *wardein*, OF *gardein*, *guarden* < Gmc]
war′den·ry, **war′den·ship** (-ship) *n.*
·den[2] (wôr′dən) *n.* A variety of pear used chiefly for
king. Also **War′den**. [ME *wardon*]
d·er (wôr′dər) *n.* **1.** A keeper; guard; sentinel; watch-
n. **2.** An official staff or baton; a truncheon. **3.** *Chiefly*
t. A prison official; warden. [< AF < *warder* to keep]
d heel·er *U.S. Slang* A hanger-on of a political boss,
o does minor tasks, canvasses votes, etc. [< WARD (def.
+ HEELER (def. 1)]
d·robe (wôrd′rōb′) *n.* **1.** All the garments belonging
any one person. **2.** An upright cabinet for clothes. **3.**
eatrical costumes; also, the room in which they are kept.
AF < OF < *warder* to keep + *robe* dress]
d·room (wôrd′rōōm′, -rōōm′) *n.* On a warship, the
nmon recreation area and dining room for the commis-
ned officers; also, these officers as a group.
·d·ship (wôrd′ship) *n.* **1.** The state of being a ward or
a guardian. **2.** Custody; guardianship.
·e (wâr) *n.* **1.** Articles of the same class; esp., manu-
tured articles: used collectively, often in combination:
leware, glassware. **2.** *pl.* Articles of commerce; goods;
rchandise. **3.** Pottery; earthenware. [OE *waru*]
·e·house (wâr′hous′) *n.* A storehouse for goods or
rchandise. — *v.t.* **·housed** (-houzd′), **·hous·ing** (-hou′-
g) To place or store in a warehouse.
·e·house·man (wâr′hous′mən) *n.* *pl.* **·men** (-mən)
e who works in, manages, or owns a warehouse.
·fare (wôr′fâr′) *n.* **1.** The waging or carrying on of
r; conflict with arms; war. **2.** Struggle; strife.
·game *pl.* Practice maneuvers imitating the conditions
actual warfare.
·head (wôr′hed′) *n.* *Mil.* The section at the nose of a
ded missile, bomb, etc., containing the explosive.
·horse **1.** *Informal* A veteran; esp., an aggressive or
teran politician. **2.** A horse used in combat; charger.
·like (wôr′līk) *adj.* **1.** Disposed to engage in war; bel-
erent. **2.** Relating to, used in, or suggesting war; mili-
y. **3.** Threatening war; pugnacious; hostile.
·lock (wôr′lok′) *n.* A wizard; sorcerer; also, a demon.
E < *wǣr* covenant + *lēogan* to lie, deny]
rm (wôrm) *adj.* **1.** Moderately hot; having heat some-
at greater than temperate. **2.** Imparting warmth or
at. **3.** Preserving warmth; preventing loss of bodily heat:
warm coat. **4.** Having a feeling of heat greater than
linary: *warm* from exertion. **5.** Affectionate; loving;
rmhearted. **6.** Possessing ardor, liveliness, etc.: a *warm*
gument. **7.** Excited; agitated; also, vehement; passion-
: a *warm* temper. **8.** United by affection. **9.** Having
dominating tones of red or yellow. **10.** Recently made;
sh: a *warm* trail. **11.** Near to discovering concealed fact
object. **12.** *Informal* Uncomfortable; dangerous. **13.**
aracterized by brisk activity: a *warm* skirmish. — *v.t.*
To heat slightly. **2.** To make ardent or enthusiastic; in-
est. **3.** To fill with kindly feeling. — *v.i.* **4.** To become
rm. **5.** To become ardent or enthusiastic: often with *to*.
To become kindly disposed or friendly: with *to* or *toward*.
to warm up 1. To warm. **2.** To exercise just before a
me, etc. **3.** To run an engine until it reaches operating
nperature. — *n.* *Informal* Warmth; a heating. [OE
arm] — **warm′er** *n.* — **warm′ly** *adv.* — **warm′ness** *n.*
rm-blood·ed (wôrm′blud′id) *adj.* **1.** *Zool.* Preserving
uniform body temperature, as man. **2.** Enthusiastic;
dent; passionate.
rm·heart·ed (wôrm′här′tid) *adj.* Kind; affectionate.
rm·ing pan (wôr′ming) A closed metal pan with a long
ndle, containing hot coals or water, for warming a bed.
·mon·ger (wôr′mung′gər, -mong′-) *n.* One who propa-
tes warlike ideas. — **war′mon′ger·ing** *adj. & n.*
rmth (wôrmth) *n.* **1.** The state, quality, or sensation of
ing warm. **2.** Ardor or fervidness of disposition or feel-
g; excitement of temper or mind. **3.** The effect produced
warm colors. [ME < OE *wearm* + *-thu*, *th* -th[1]]
rm-up (wôrm′up′) *n.* *Informal* The act of one who or
at which warms up.

warn (wôrn) *v.t.* **1.** To make aware of possible harm; caution. **2.** To advise; admonish. **3.** To give notice in advance. **4.** To notify (a person) to stay away etc.: with *off*,
away, etc. [OE *warnian*] — **warn′er** *n.*
warn·ing (wôr′ning) *n.* **1.** The act of one who warns; also,
notice of danger. **2.** That which warns or admonishes. —
adj. Serving as a warning. — **warn′ing·ly** *adv.*
War of 1812 See table for WAR.
War of American Independence *Brit.* The American
Revolution.
War of Independence The American Revolution.
War of Secession The Civil War in the U.S.
War of the Spanish Succession See table for WAR.
warp (wôrp) *v.t.* **1.** To turn or twist out of shape, as by
shrinkage or heat. **2.** To turn from a correct course; give a
twist or bias to; corrupt. **3.** To stretch (yarn) so as to form
a warp. **4.** *Naut.* To move (a vessel) by hauling on a rope
fastened to a pier or anchor. — *v.i.* **5.** To become turned
or twisted out of shape. **6.** To deviate from a proper
course; go astray. **7.** *Naut.* To move by means of ropes
fastened to a pier, etc. — *n.* **1.** The state of being warped;
a distortion, esp. in wood. **2.** A mental or moral deviation;
bias. **3.** The threads that run the long way of a fabric,
crossing the woof. **4.** *Naut.* A cable used for warping a
ship. [OE *weorpan* to throw] — **warp′er** *n.*
war paint **1.** Paint applied to faces and bodies by primitive peoples in token of going to war. **2.** *Informal* Cosmetics; finery; also, official garb or regalia.
war·path (wôr′path′, -päth′) *n.* The route taken by
American Indians going to war. — **on the warpath 1.** On
a warlike expedition. **2.** Ready for a fight; angry.
war·plane (wôr′plān′) *n.* An airplane equipped for fighting.
war·rant (wôr′ənt, wor′-) *n.* **1.** *Law* A judicial writ or
order authorizing arrest, search, seizure, etc. **2.** Something
that assures or attests; evidence; guarantee. **3.** That which
gives authority for some act; sanction; justification. **4.** A
certificate of appointment given to army and navy warrant
officers. **5.** A document giving a certain authority; esp., for
receipt or payment of money. — *v.t.* **1.** To guarantee the
quality, sufficiency, etc., of: to *warrant* a title to property.
2. To guarantee the character of; pledge oneself for. **3.** To
guarantee against injury, loss, etc. **4.** To be sufficient
grounds for; justify. **5.** To give legal authority; to em-
power; authorize. **6.** To say confidently; feel sure. [< AF
warant, OF *guarant*] — **war′rant·a·ble** *adj.* — **war′rant·
a·bly** *adv.* — **war′rant·er** *n.*
war·ran·tee (wôr′ən·tē′, wor′-) *n.* *Law* The person to
whom a warranty is given.
warrant officer *Mil.* An officer serving without a commission, but having authority by virtue of a certificate or warrant, with rank superior to that of a noncommissioned officer. See tables at GRADE.
war·rant·or (wôr′ən·tôr, wor′-) *n.* *Law* One who makes
or gives a warranty to another.
war·ran·ty (wôr′ən·tē, wor′-) *n.* *pl.* **·ties 1.** *Law* **a** An
assurance that facts regarding property, insurance risks,
etc., are as they are stated to be. **b** A covenant securing a
title of ownership. **2.** A guarantee (def. 1). **3.** Authorization; warrant. [< AF *warantie*, < OF *guarant* warrant]
war·ren (wôr′ən, wor′-) *n.* **1.** A place where rabbits live
and breed in communities. **2.** An enclosure for keeping
small game. **3.** An obscure, crowded place of habitation.
[< AF < *warir* to preserve]
war·ri·or (wôr′ē·ər, -yər, wor′-) *n.* A man engaged in or
experienced in warfare. [< AF < OHG *werra* strife]
war·ship (wôr′ship′) *n.* Any vessel used in naval combat.
Wars of the Roses See table for WAR.
wart (wôrt) *n.* **1.** A small, usu. hard and nonmalignant
bump formed on and rooted in the skin. **2.** A hard glandular protuberance on a plant. [OE *wearte*] — **wart′y** *adj.*
wart hog An African wild hog having warty excrescences
on the face and large tusks in both jaws.
war·time (wôr′tīm′) *n.* A time of war. — *adj.* Caused by
or related to a war, or occurring during a period of war.
war whoop A yell, as that made by American Indians, uttered as a signal for attack or to terrify opponents in battle.
war·y (wâr′ē) *adj.* **war·i·er**, **war·i·est 1.** Carefully watching and guarding. **2.** Shrewd; wily. [< OE *warian*] —
war′i·ly *adv.* — **war′i·ness** *n.*
was (wuz, woz, *unstressed* wəz) First and third person
singular, past indicative of BE. [OE *wæs*]
wash (wosh, wôsh) *v.t.* **1.** To cleanse by immersing in or
applying water or other liquid, often with rubbing. **2.** To
purify from defilement or guilt. **3.** To wet or cover with
liquid. **4.** To flow against or over: a beach *washed* by the
ocean. **5.** To remove by the action of water: with *away*,
off, *out*, etc. **6.** To form or wear by erosion: The storm
washed gulleys in the hillside. **7.** To purify, as gas, by passing

through a liquid. **8.** To coat with a thin layer of color or a thin coat of metal. **9.** *Mining* To subject (gravel, earth, etc.) to the action of water so as to separate the ore, etc. — *v.i.* **10.** To wash oneself. **11.** To wash clothes, etc. **12.** To withstand the effects of washing: That calico will *wash.* **13.** *Brit. Informal* To undergo testing successfully: That story won't *wash.* **14.** To flow with a lapping sound, as waves. **15.** To be removed by the action of water: with *away, off, out,* etc. **16.** To be eroded by the action of water. — **to wash down 1.** To drink liquid along with or right after (food) to facilitate swallowing. **2.** To scrub from top to bottom, as walls. — **to wash up 1.** To wash oneself. **2.** *Brit. Informal* To wash the dishes. — *n.* **1.** The act or process of washing; cleansing. **2.** A number of clothes, etc. set apart to be washed at one time; laundry. **3.** Liquid or semiliquid refuse; swill. **4.** A preparation used in washing or coating, as: **a** A mouthwash. **b** Water color spread on a picture. **5.** The breaking of a body of water upon the shore, or the sound made by waves breaking or surging against a surface; swash. **6.** Erosion of soil by the action of running water. **7.** Churned air, water, or other fluid resulting from the passage of an object through it. **8.** An area washed by a sea or river; a marsh; bog. — *adj.* Washable without injury: *wash* fabrics. [OE *wascan, wæscan*]
wash·a·ble (wosh′ə·bəl, wôsh′-) *adj.* That may be washed without fading or injury.
wash-and-wear (wosh′ən·wâr′, wôsh′-) *adj.* Designating or pertaining to a garment or fabric so treated as to require little or no ironing after washing.
wash·board (wosh′bôrd′, -bōrd′, wôsh′-) *n.* A board or frame having a corrugated surface on which to rub clothes while washing them.
wash·bowl (wosh′bōl′, wôsh′-) *n.* A basin or bowl used for washing the hands and face. Also **wash′ba′sin** (-bā′sən).
wash·cloth (wosh′klôth′, -kloth′, wôsh′-) *n.* A small cloth used for washing the body.
wash·day (wosh′dā′, wôsh′-) *n.* A day of the week set aside for doing household washing.
washed-out (wosht′out′, wôsht′-) *adj.* **1.** Faded; colorless; pale. **2.** *Informal* Exhausted; worn-out; tired.
washed-up (wosht′up′, wôsht′-) *adj.* **1.** *Slang* No longer successful, popular, etc.; finished. **2.** *Informal* Tired.
wash·er (wosh′ər, wô′shər) *n.* **1.** One who or that which washes. **2.** *Mech.* A small, flat, perforated disk of metal, leather, rubber, etc., used for placing beneath a nut or at an axle bearing or joint, to serve as a cushion, to prevent leakage, or to relieve friction. **3.** A washing machine.
wash·er·wom·an (wosh′ər·wŏŏm′ən, wô′shər-) *n. pl.* **·wom·en** (-wim′in) A laundress.
wash·ing (wosh′ing, wôsh′ing) *n.* **1.** The act of one who or that which washes. **2.** Things, as clothing, washed or to be washed on one occasion. **3.** That which is retained after being washed: a *washing* of ore. **4.** A thin coating of metal.
washing machine A machine for washing laundry.
washing soda Sodium carbonate in crystalline form, used for washing textiles and as a bleaching agent.
wash·out (wosh′out′, wôsh′-) *n.* **1.** A considerable erosion of earth by the action of water; also, the excavation thus made; a gully or gulch. **2.** *Slang* A failure. **3.** The act of one who or that which washes out.
wash·rag (wosh′rag′, wôsh′-) *n.* A washcloth.
wash·room (wosh′rōōm′, -rŏŏm′, wôsh′-) *n.* A lavatory.
wash·stand (wosh′stand′, wôsh′-) *n.* A stand for wash-bowl, pitcher, etc.
wash·tub (wosh′tub′, wôsh′-) *n.* A tub used for washing.
wash·wom·an (wosh′wŏŏm′ən, wôsh′-) *n. pl.* **·wom·en** (-wim′in) A washerwoman.
wash·y (wosh′ē, wô′shē) *adj.* **wash·i·er, wash·i·est 1.** Overly diluted; weak. **2.** Faded; wan. — **wash′i·ness** *n.*
was·n't (wuz′ənt, woz′-) Was not.
wasp (wosp, wôsp) *n.* Any of numerous stinging insects, including social wasps, that make nests of vegetable matter, and solitary wasps, living in mud or sand nests. [OE *wæsp*]
WASP (wosp, wôsp) *n. Slang* A white Protestant American: sometimes used contemptuously. Also **Wasp.** [Acronym formed from the initial letters of "white Anglo-Saxon Protestant"]
wasp·ish (wos′pish, wôs′-) *adj.* **1.** Having a nature like a wasp; irritable; irascible. **2.** Having a wasplike form or slender waist. — **wasp′ish·ly** *adv.* — **wasp′ish·ness** *n.*
wasp waist A waist so slender as to suggest that of a wasp. — **wasp-waist·ed** (wosp′wās′tid, wôsp′-) *adj.*
wasp·y (wos′pē, wôs′-) *adj.* **wasp·i·er, wasp·i·est** Like a wasp; waspish.
was·sail (wos′əl, was′-, wo·sāl′) *n.* **1.** An ancient salutation or toast to someone's health. **2.** The liquor, as spiced ale, prepared for a wassail. **3.** A festivity at which healths are drunk; a carousal. — *v.i.* **1.** To take part in a wassail; carouse. — *v.t.* **2.** To drink the health of; toast. [ME < ON *ves heill* be in good health] — **was′sail·er** *n.*
Was·ser·mann test (wos′ər·mən) A diagnostic test for syphi-

lis, based on the reaction of the blood serum of an infec individual. Also **Wassermann reaction.** [after August *Wassermann,* 1866–1925, German bacteriologist.]
wast (wost, *unstressed* wəst) Archaic second person gular, past indicative of BE: used with *thou.*
wast·age (wās′tij) *n.* That which is lost by wear, waste,
waste (wāst) *v.* **wast·ed, wast·ing** *v.t.* **1.** To use or exp thoughtlessly, uselessly, or without return; squander. To cause to lose strength, vigor, or bulk. **3.** To use up; sume. **4.** To fail to use or take advantage of, as an oppor nity. **5.** To lay waste; devastate. — *v.i.* **6.** To strength, vigor, or bulk: often with *away.* **7.** To dimin or dwindle gradually. **8.** To pass gradually: said of time. *n.* **1.** The act of wasting or the state of being wasted; less or unnecessary expenditure, consumption, etc. **2.** N use, neglect, or failure to take advantage of opportun etc. **3.** A place or region that is devastated or made desol desert. **4.** A continuous, gradual diminishing of streng vigor, or substance by use or wear. **5.** The act of lay waste or devastating. **6.** Something rejected as worth or unneeded; esp., tangled spun cotton thread. **7.** Garba rubbish; trash. — **to lay waste** To turn into ruins; dest utterly; devastate. — *adj.* **1.** Cast aside as worthless; w out; discarded. **2.** Excreted, as undigested material, **3.** Not under cultivation; unproductive; unoccupied. Made desolate; ruined. **5.** Containing or conveying wa products. **6.** Superfluous: *waste* energy. [< AF, ult. *vastare* to lay waste < *vastus* desert, desolate]
Waste, meaning containing or conveying refuse or wa may appear as a combining form or as the first element two-word phrases, as in:

| waste bin | waste heap | waste pipe |

waste·bas·ket (wāst′bas′kit, -bäs′-) *n.* An open contai for paper scraps and other waste. Also **wastepaper bas**
waste·ful (wāst′fəl) *adj.* **1.** Prone to waste; extravaga **2.** Causing waste. — **waste′ful·ly** *adv.* — **waste′ful·nes**
waste·land (wāst′land′) *n.* A barren or desolate land
waste·pa·per (wāst′pā′pər) *n.* Paper thrown away worthless. Also **waste paper.**
wast·er (wās′tər) *n.* One who wastes; a wastrel.
wast·ing (wās′ting) *adj.* **1.** Producing emaciation; feebling: a *wasting* fever. **2.** Laying waste; devastating
was·trel (wās′trəl) *n.* **1.** A waster; spendthrift. **2.** idler; loafer; vagabond. [Dim. of WASTER]
watch (woch) *v.i.* **1.** To look attentively. **2.** To wait pectantly: with *for.* **3.** To be constantly on the alert. To do duty as a guard or sentinel. **5.** To be an onloo **6.** To go without sleep; keep vigil. — *v.t.* **7.** To look steadily and attentively; observe. **8.** To keep inform concerning. **9.** To be alert for: to *watch* one's opportun **10.** To keep watch over; guard; tend. — **to watch out** be on one's guard. — *n.* **1.** The act of watching; close continuous attention; careful observation. **2.** A sm portable timepiece worn or carried on the person, and u actuated by a coiled spring. **3.** Position or service a guard. **4.** One or more persons set to watch. **5.** An ac period of wakefulness or attentive alertness, esp. during night; vigil. **6.** The period of time during which a gu is on duty. **7.** *Naut.* **a** One of the two divisions of a sh officers and crew, performing duty in alternation. **b** T period of time during which each division is on duty: u four hours. [OE *wæccan*] — **watch′er** *n.*
watch band A band to fasten a watch on the wrist.
watch·case (woch′kās′) *n.* The protecting case of a wat
watch·dog (woch′dôg′, -dog′) *n.* **1.** A dog kept to gu property. **2.** One who acts as a vigilant guardian.
watch·ful (woch′fəl) *adj.* Vigilant. — **watch′ful·ly** a — **watch′ful·ness** *n.*
watch·mak·er (woch′mā′kər) *n.* One who makes or pairs watches.
watch·man (woch′mən) *n. pl.* **·men** (-mən) Anyone v keeps watch or guard, as over a building at night.
watch night A religious service usu. held on New Ye Eve. Also **watch meeting.**
watch·tow·er (woch′tou′ər) *n.* A tower upon whic sentinel is stationed.
watch·word (woch′wûrd′) *n.* **1.** A password. **2.** A ra ing cry or maxim.
wa·ter (wô′tər, wot′ər) *n.* **1.** A limpid, tasteless, odor liquid compound of hydrogen and oxygen, H_2O, in proportion by weight of approximately 2 parts of hydro to 16 of oxygen. When pure, water has its maximum den at 4° C. or 39° F.; at normal atmospheric pressure it fre at 0° C. or 32° F., and boils at 100° C. or 212° F. **2.** A body of water, as a lake, river, or a sea. **3.** Any one of aqueous or liquid secretions of the body, as perspirati tears, urine, etc. **4.** Any preparation of water holdin gaseous or volatile substance in solution. **5.** The tra parency or luster of a precious stone or a pearl. **6.** Ex lence; quality: first *water.* **7.** An undulating sheen giver certain fabrics, as silk, etc. **8.** In commerce and finan

ck issued without increase of paid-in capital to represent
  — **above water** Out of danger; secure. — **like water**
ry freely or quickly: to spend money *like water*. — **of the**
st **water** Of the highest degree. — **to hold water** To
lid or effective: His argument doesn't *hold water*. — **to**
ake **water** To urinate. — *v.t.* **1.** To pour water upon;
isten; sprinkle. **2.** To provide with water for drinking.
To dilute with water: often with *down*. **4.** To give an
dulating sheen to the surface of (silk, etc.). **5.** To enlarge
e number of shares of (a stock company) without increas-
e the paid-in capital in proportion. **6.** To provide with
eams or sources of water; irrigate. — *v.i.* **7.** To secrete
discharge water, tears, etc. **8.** To fill with saliva, as the
uth, from desire for food. **9.** To drink water. **10.** To
ke in water, as a locomotive. [OE *wæter*] — **wa′ter·er** *n.*
Water may appear as a combining form, or as the first
ment in two-word phrases, as in:

water meter	water right
water motor	water supply
water-repellant	water system

ter Bearer   The constellation and sign of the zodiac
uarius.

·ter·borne (wô′tər-bôrn′, -bōrn′, wot′ər-) *adj.* **1.** Float-
e on water. **2.** Transported or carried by water.

·ter·buck (wô′tər·buk′, wot′ər-) *n.* Either of two large
rican antelopes frequenting the neigh-
rhood of rivers and swimming with ease.
Afrikaans *waterbok*]

ter buffalo   A large buffalo of Asia,
dia, and the Philippines, having a very
de spread of horns, and often domesti-
ed for use as a draft animal: also called
ter ox, carabao.

ter chestnut 1. The edible fruit of an
uatic plant contained in a hard, nutlike
sk. **2.** The plant itself.

ter clock   An instrument for measuring
ne by the regulated flow of water.

ter closet   A toilet.

ter color 1. A color prepared for painting with water as
e medium, as distinguished from one to be used with oil,
mpera, etc. **2.** A picture or painting done in water colors.
  wa·ter-col·or (wô′tər·kul′ər, wot′ər-) *adj.*

·ter-cool (wô′tər·kōōl′, wot′ər-) *v.t.* To cool by means of
ter, as by using a water jacket on an internal-combustion
gine. — **wa′ter-cooled′** *adj.* — **wa′ter-cool′ing** *adj.*

ter cooler   A vessel or apparatus for cooling and dispens-
g drinking water.

·ter-course (wô′tər-kôrs′, -kōrs′, wot′ər-) *n.* **1.** A
eam of water; river; brook. **2.** The course or channel of a
eam or canal.

·ter-craft (wô′tər-kraft′, -kräft′, wot′ər-) *n.* **1.** Skill in
ling boats or in aquatic sports. **2.** Any boat or ship; also,
ling vessels collectively.

·ter-cress (wô′tər-kres′, wot′ər-) *n.* A perennial herb of
e mustard family, growing in springs and clear, cool
eams and having edible, pungent leaves used as salad.

ter cure *Med.* Hydropathy.

·ter-fall (wô′tər-fôl′, wot′ər-) *n.* A steep fall of water,
of a stream over a dam or from a precipice; cascade.

·ter-fowl (wô′tər-foul′, wot′ər-) *n. pl.* **·fowl** or **·fowls**
A bird that lives on or about the water; esp., a swimming
me bird. **2.** Such birds collectively.

·ter-front (wô′tər-frunt′, wot′ər-) *n.* **1.** Real property
utting on or overlooking a natural body of water. **2.**
hat part of a town fronting on a body of water, esp. the
ea containing wharves, docks, etc.

ter gap   A deep ravine in a mountain ridge, giving pas-
ge to a stream.

ter gas   A poisonous mixture, chiefly of hydrogen and
rbon monoxide, produced by forcing steam over white-hot
rbon, as coal or coke, and used for cooking, heating, and as
illuminant. — **wa·ter-gas** (wô′tər·gas′, wot′ər-) *adj.*

ter gate   A floodgate (def. 1)

ter gauge   A gauge indicating the level of water, as in a
iler. Also **water gage.**

ter glass 1. A drinking glass. **2.** Any glass vessel for
lding water. **3.** Sodium silicate, a soluble silicate prepara-
n; esp., an aqueous solution used in preserving eggs, etc.
. A water gauge on a steam boiler, etc.

ter hole   A small pond, pool, or depression containing
ater; esp., one used by animals as a drinking place.

ter ice   A frozen dessert made with water, sugar, and
uit juice.

·ter·ing (wô′tər·ing, wot′ər-) *n.* **1.** The act of one who
that which waters. **2.** The process of producing a wavy,
namental effect on fabric, etc. — *adj.* **1.** That waters.
. Situated near the shore or near mineral springs.

WATER BUFFALO
(To 6 feet
high
at shoulder)

watering can   A container used for watering plants, etc.,
esp. one having a long spout. Also **watering pot.**

watering place 1. A place where water can be obtained,
as a spring. **2.** A health resort having mineral springs; also,
a pleasure resort near the water.

water jacket   A casing containing water and surrounding a
cylinder or mechanism, esp. the cylinder block of an internal-
combustion engine, for keeping it cool.

water jump   A water barrier, as a pool, stream, or ditch, to
be jumped over by the horses in a steeplechase.

water level 1. The level of still water in the sea or in any
other body of water. **2.** *Geol.* A water table. **3.** *Naut.* A
ship's water line.

water lily 1. Any of a genus of aquatic plants having
showy flowers with numerous white or pinkish petals: also
called *pond lily*. **2.** Any of various related plants.

water line 1. *Naut.* The part of the hull of a ship that corresponds with the water level at various loads: also called
water level. **2.** A line or demarcation corresponding to the
height to which water has risen or may rise.

wa·ter-logged (wô′tər-lôgd′, -logd′, wot′ər-) *adj.* **1.** Heavy
and unmanageable on account of the leakage of water into
the hold, as a ship. **2.** Water-soaked; saturated with water.

Wa·ter·loo (wô′tər-lōō) *n.* A final and decisive defeat: usu.
in the phrase **to meet one's Waterloo.** [after Napoleon's
defeat at *Waterloo*, Belgium]

water main   A large conduit for carrying water.

wa·ter·man (wô′tər-mən, wot′ər-) *n. pl.* **·men** (-mən) A
man who works with a boat or small vessel on the water; a
boatman. — **wa′ter·man·ship′** *n.*

wa·ter·mark (wô′tər-märk′, wot′ər-) *n.* **1.** A mark showing the extent to which water rises. **2.** In papermaking: **a**
A marking in paper, usu. produced by pressure of a projecting design on a processing roll or in the mold. **b** The metal
pattern that produces this marking. — *v.t.* **1.** To impress
(paper) with a watermark. **2.** To impress as a watermark.

wa·ter·mel·on (wô′tər-mel′ən, wot′ər-) *n.* **1.** The large,
edible fruit of a trailing plant of the gourd family, containing
a many-seeded red or pink pulp and a watery juice. **2.** The
plant on which this fruit grows.

water mill   A mill operated by waterpower.

water moccasin   A venomous pit viper of the southern
U.S.: also called *cottonmouth*.

water nymph   In classical mythology, any nymph or goddess living in or guarding a body of water.

water of crystallization *Chem.* Molecules of water forming part of certain crystallized salts. They may be eliminated
by heat, often with apparent loss of crystalline structure.

water ouzel   Any of various small birds adapted to feeding
under water. Also **water ousel.**

water ox   A water buffalo.

water pipe 1. A hookah. **2.** A conduit for water.

water polo   A game in which two teams of swimmers push
or throw a buoyant ball toward opposite goals.

wa·ter-pow·er (wô′tər-pou′ər, wot′ər-) *n.* **1.** The power of
water derived from its momentum, as applied to the driving
of machinery. **2.** A fall in a stream, yielding kinetic energy
from which motive power may be obtained.

wa·ter·proof (wô′tər-prōōf′, wot′ər-) *adj.* **1.** Permitting
no water to enter or pass through; impervious to water. **2.**
Coated with some substance, as rubber, that resists the passage of water. — *n.* **1.** Material or fabric rendered impervious to water. **2.** *Brit.* A raincoat or other garment made
of such fabric. — *v.t.* To render waterproof.

water rat 1. The muskrat. **2.** The European vole. **3.**
Any aquatic rodent. **4.** *Slang* A waterfront thief or tough.

wa·ter·shed (wô′tər-shed′, wot′ər-) *n.* **1.** The line of
separation between two contiguous drainage valleys. **2.**
The region from which a river receives its supply of water.

wa·ter·side (wô′tər-sīd′, wot′ər-) *n.* The shore of a body of
water; the water's edge. — *adj.* Of, pertaining to, or living,
growing, or working by the water's edge.

wa·ter-ski (wô′tər-skē′, wot′ər-) *v.i.* **-skied, -ski·ing** To
glide over water on water-skis, while being towed by a
motorboat. — *n. pl.* **-skis** or **-ski** A broad, skilike runner
with a fitting to hold the foot, worn when water-skiing: also
water ski. — **wa′ter-ski′er** *n.* — **wa′ter-ski′ing** *n.*

water snake   Any of various harmless snakes that live
chiefly in or near fresh water.

wa·ter·soak (wô′tər-sōk′, wot′ər-) *v.t.* To fill the pores or
crevices of with water; soak in water.

water softener   A substance added to hard water to
counteract the effect of its mineral content.

wa·ter-sol·u·ble (wô′tər-sol′yə-bəl, wot′ər-) *adj.* Soluble
in water: said esp. of certain organic compounds.

water spaniel   A large, reddish brown spaniel having a
curly, waterproof coat, used primarily for retrieving ducks.

wa·ter·spout (wô′tər-spout′, wot′ər-) *n.* **1.** A moving, whirling column of spray and mist, with masses of water in the lower parts, generated at sea or on other large bodies of water. **2.** A pipe for the free discharge of water.

water sprite A sprite living in the water; water nymph.

water table *Geol.* The surface marking the upper level of a water-saturated zone extending beneath the ground to depths determined by the thickness of the permeable strata.

wa·ter·tight (wô′tər-tīt′, wot′ər-) *adj.* **1.** So closely made that water cannot enter or leak through. **2.** Having no loopholes; foolproof: *watertight* tax laws.

water tower 1. A standpipe or tower, often of considerable height, used as a reservoir for a system of water distribution. **2.** A vehicular towerlike structure having an extensible vertical pipe from which water can be thrown on the upper floors of a burning building.

water vapor The vapor of water, esp. when below the boiling point, as in the atmosphere.

water wave An undulating effect of the hair, artificially produced when the hair is wet, and set by drying with heat.

wa·ter·way (wô′tər-wā′, wot′ər-) *n.* A river, channel, canal, etc., used as a means of travel.

water wheel A wheel so equipped with floats, buckets, etc., that it may be turned by flowing water, as a noria.

water wings A waterproof, inflatable device used as a support for the body while swimming or learning to swim.

wa·ter·works (wô′tər-wûrks′, wot′ər-) *n.pl.* A system of machines, buildings, and appliances for furnishing a water supply, esp. for a city.

wa·ter·worn (wô′tər-wôrn′, -wōrn′, wot′ər-) *adj.* Worn smooth by running or falling water.

wa·ter·y (wô′tər-ē, wot′ər-ē) *adj.* **1.** Containing or discharging water. **2.** Brimming; flowing. **3.** Resembling water; thin or liquid. **4.** Consisting of or pertaining to water. **5.** Diluted with water; weak. **— wa′ter·i·ness** *n.*

watt (wot) *n.* The practical unit of electric power, activity, or rate of work, equivalent to one joule per second, or one volt-ampere. [after James *Watt* 1736–1819, Scottish inventor]

wat·tage (wot′ij) *n.* **1.** Amount of electric power in terms of watts. **2.** The total number of watts needed to operate an appliance.

watt-hour (wot′our′) *n.* Electrical energy equivalent to one watt acting for one hour.

wat·tle (wot′l) *n.* **1.** A structure of rods or twigs woven together. **2.** A twig or withe. **3.** A naked, fleshy process, often wrinkled and brightly colored, hanging from the throat of a bird or snake. **4.** Any of various acacias of Australia, Tasmania, and South Africa. **— v.t. ·tled, ·tling 1.** To weave or twist, as twigs, into a network. **2.** To form, as baskets, by intertwining flexible twigs. **3.** To bind together with wattles. **— adj.** Made of or covered with wattles. [OE *watel, watul*] **— wat′tled** *adj.*

watt-me·ter (wot′mē′tər) *n.* An instrument for measuring electrical power in watts.

wave (wāv) *v.* **waved, wav·ing** *v.i.* **1.** To move freely back and forth or up and down, as a flag in the wind; fluctuate. **2.** To be moved back and forth or up and down as a signal; also, to make a signal by moving something thus. **3.** To have an undulating shape or form: Her hair *waves*. **— v.t. 4.** To cause to wave: to *wave* a banner. **5.** To form with an undulating surface or outline. **6.** To give a wavy appearance to; water, as silk. **7.** To form into waves: to *wave* one's hair. **8.** To signal by waving something: He *waved* me aside. **9.** To express by waving something: to *wave* farewell. **— n. 1.** A ridge or undulation moving on the surface of a liquid. **2.** One of the rising curves on an undulatory surface; one of a series of curves: *waves* of grain. **3.** Something that comes, like a wave, with great volume or power: a *wave* of enthusiasm. **4.** One of a series, as of events, occurring with wavelike fluctuations: He went ashore with the first *wave* of Marines. **5.** A progressive change in temperature or in barometrical condition: a heat *wave*. **6.** A wavelike tress or curl of hair. **7.** The act of waving; a sweeping or undulating motion, as with the hand. **8.** A wavelike stripe or undulation impressed on a surface. **9.** *Physics* One of the periodic vibratory impulses produced by a disturbance in and propagated through an elastic medium, as sound. **10.** *Usu. pl. Poetic* Any body of water, esp., the sea. [OE *wafian*] **— wav′er** *n.* **— wave′less** *adj.*

— Syn. (noun) **1.** *Wave* is the general term for an upheaval of the ocean's surface. A *ripple* is a very small *wave*, such as might be produced by a light breeze, or by an object dropping into still water. *Billow* is a poetic word for any *wave*, but esp., for a *wave* of great height. A *roller* is one of the long, irregular *waves* that move swiftly outward from a storm center.

Wave (wāv) *n.* A member of the WAVES.

wave band *Physics* A specified group of wave frequencies, esp. one assigned for radio or television broadcasting.

wave·length (wāv′length′) *n. Physics* The distance, measured along the line of propagation, between two points representing similar phases of two consecutive waves.

wave·let (wāv′lit) *n.* A little wave.

wave mechanics The branch of physics that investiga the wave characteristics ascribed to the atom and its as ciated particles, esp. with reference to the quantum theo

wa·ver (wā′vər) *v.i.* **1.** To move one way and the oth sway; flutter. **2.** To be uncertain or undecided; show resolution; vacillate. **3.** To show signs of falling back giving way; falter. **4.** To flicker; gleam. **5.** To quav tremble. **— n.** A wavering. [< ME *waveren*] **— wa′v er** *n.* **— wa′ver·ing·ly** *adv.*

WAVES or **W.A.V.E.S.** (wāvz) *n.* A corps of womer the U.S. Navy; officially, Women in the United States Na (1946). [< *W(omen) A(ccepted for) V(oluntary) E(merg cy) S(ervice)*, an earlier name]

wave set A preparation put on the hair before setting make waves and curls last.

wav·y (wā′vē) *adj.* **wav·i·er, wav·i·est 1.** Full of wav ruffled by or raised into waves. **2.** Undulatory; waving. Unstable; wavering. **— wav′i·ly** *adv.* **— wav′i·ness** *n.*

wax[1] (waks) *n.* *pl.* **wax·es 1.** Beeswax. **2.** *Chem.* An various natural substances consisting of the esters of fa acids and alcohols other than glycerol, including spermac and the secretions of certain plants and insects. **3.** A so mineral substance resembling wax, as paraffin. **4.** Seal wax. **5.** Earwax. **— v.t.** To coat or treat with wax. *adj.* Made of or pertaining to wax. [OE *weax*]

wax[2] (waks) *v.i.* **waxed, waxed** (*Poetic* **wax·en**)**, wax 1.** To become larger gradually; increase in size or numbe grow: said esp., of the moon as it approaches fullness. To become: to *wax* angry. [OE *weaxan* to grow]

wax bean A variety of string bean of a pale yellow co cultivated in the U.S.: also called *butter bean*.

wax·ber·ry (waks′ber′ē) *n.* *pl.* **·ries 1.** The wax myr **2.** Its wax-covered fruit. **3.** The snowberry.

wax·en (wak′sən) *adj.* **1.** Resembling wax. **2.** Consist wholly or in part of wax; covered with wax. **3.** Pale; pal a *waxen* complexion; also, pliable or impressible as wax.

wax myrtle Any of various North American shrubs small trees having fragrant leaves and small berries cove with wax, often used in making candles: also called *bayber candleberry, waxberry.*

wax palm 1. A South American palm with pinnate lea having a lofty straight trunk covered with a waxy, whit resinous substance. **2.** A Brazilian palm whose young lea yield a valuable wax.

wax paper Paper coated or treated with wax and used retain or protect against moisture. Also **waxed paper.**

wax·weed (waks′wēd′) *n.* An annual, clammy, hairy h of the loosestrife family with irregular purplish flowers.

wax·wing (waks′wing′) *n.* Any of various crested bi having soft, mainly brown plumage and wing feathers tip with appendages resembling red or yellow sealing wax.

wax·work (waks′wûrk′) *n.* **1.** Work produced in wax; ornaments or life-size figures of wax. **2.** *pl.* An exhibitio such figures. **— wax′work′er** *n.*

wax·y (wak′sē) *adj.* **wax·i·er, wax·i·est 1.** Like wax appearance, consistency, color, etc.; pliable; impressional pallid. **2.** Made of or abounding in wax; rubbed with w **— wax′i·ness** *n.*

way (wā) *n.* **1.** A manner or method of doing somethi procedure. **2.** Direction; turn; route; line of motion: Wh *way* is the city? **3.** A path, or track leading from one p to another or along which one goes. **4.** Space or room advance or work: Make *way* for the king. **5.** Length space passed over. **6.** Distance in general: a little *way* often popularly, **ways. 7.** Passage from one place to other. **8.** Headway; progress. **9.** A customary style manner peculiar to certain people: the British *way* of things. **10.** A point of relation; particular: He erred in ways. **11.** A course of life or experience: the *way* of sin. *Informal* State of health: to be in a bad *way*. **13.** A cou wished for or resolved upon: Have it your *way*. **14.** range of one's observation: An accident threw it in his u **15.** *Naut. pl.* A tilted framework of timbers upon whic ship slides when launched. **16.** *Law* A right of way. *Informal* Neighborhood, or route home: He lives out of *way*. **— by the way** In passing; incidentally. **— by w of 1.** With the purpose of; to serve as: by *way* of introd tion. **2.** Through; via. **— out of the way 1.** Remov as an obstruction. **2.** Remarkable; unusual. **3.** Impro wrong. **4.** Out of place; lost; remote. **— the way** *Infor* In the manner that; as: Do it *the way* I told you to. **under way** In motion; making progress. **— adv.** *Infor* Away; very much or very far. [OE *weg*]

way back *Informal* Long ago. [Short for AWAY BACK

way·bill (wā′bil′) *n.* A list describing or identifying go or naming passengers carried by a train, steamer, etc.

way·far·er (wā′fâr′ər) *n.* One who journeys.

way·far·ing (wā′fâr′ing) *adj. & n.* Journeying; being the road.

way·lay (wā′lā′, wā′lā′) *v.t.* **·laid, ·lay·ing 1.** To lie in a

sh for and attack, as in order to rob. **2.** To accost on the
...y. [< WAY + LAY[1]] **— way/lay/er** n.

...ys suffix of adverbs In a (specified) manner, direction,
position: nowadys, sideways: often equivalent to -wise.
so **-way.** [< WAY + -s[3]]

ys and means Means or methods of accomplishing an
...d or defraying expenses; esp., in legislation, methods of
...sing funds for the use of the government.

y·side (wā/sīd') adj. Standing or being near the side of
...oad. — n. The side or edge of the road or highway.

y station Any station between principal stations, esp.
a railroad; a local station.

y train A train stopping at way stations.

y·ward (wā/wərd) adj. **1.** Wanting its way; willful.
Without definite course; unsteady; capricious. **3.** Un-
...pected or unwished for. [ME < awei away + -WARD]
way/ward·ly adv. **— way/ward·ness** n.

y·worn (wā/wôrn', -wōrn') adj. Fatigued by travel.

(wē) pron. pl., possessive **our** or **ours**, objective **us** The
...minative plural pronoun of the first person, used by the
...rsons speaking or writing to denote themselves, by an in-
...vidual to refer to himself or herself and one or more others,
...an editor or other writer to give his words an impersonal
...aracter, or by a sovereign on formal occasions. [OE wē]

...ak (wēk) adj. **1.** Lacking in physical strength; wanting
energy or activity; feeble. **2.** Insufficiently resisting
...ess: a weak link or bridge. **3.** Lacking in strength of will
stability of character; pliable. **4.** Ineffectual, as from
...ficient supply: weak artillery support. **5.** Lacking in
...wer or sonorousness: a weak voice. **6.** Lacking a specified
...mponent or components in the proper amount; of less
...an customary potency: weak tea. **7.** Lacking the ability
...function properly: a weak heart. **8.** Lacking in mental
moral strength. **9.** Showing or resulting from poor judg-
...ent: a weak plan; unable to convince: a weak argument.
... Lacking in influence or authority. **11.** Deficient in
...ength, skill, experience, or the like. **12.** Gram. In Ger-
...anic languages, denoting a weak verb. **13.** Phonet. Un-
...essed; unaccented, as a syllable or sound. **14.** In prosody,
...dicating a verse ending in which the accent falls on a word
...syllable otherwise without stress. **15.** Wanting in im-
...essiveness or interest: a weak play. [< ON veikr] **—**
...ak/ly adv. **— weak/ness** n.

Weak may appear as a combining form, as in the following
...lf-explanatory compounds:

...eak-backed	weak-looking	weak-stemmed
...eak-bodied	weak-made	weak-tasting
...eakbrained	weak-muscled	weak-throated
...eak-brewed	weak-natured	weak-tinted
...eak-built	weak-nerved	weak-toned
...eak-colored	weak-seeming	weak-voiced
...eak-eyed	weak-sided	weak-walled
...eak-growing	weak-sighted	weak-willed
...eakhanded	weak-smelling	weak-winged
...eakhearted	weak-sounding	weak-witted
...eak-limbed	weak-spirited	weak-woven

...ak·en (wē/kən) v.i. v.t. & To make or become weak or
...eaker. **— weak/en·er** n.

...ak·fish (wēk/fish') n. pl. **·fish** or **·fish·es** Any of sev-
...al marine food fishes of the coastal waters of the eastern
...S.

...ak-kneed (wēk/nēd') adj. **1.** Weak in the knees. **2.**
...ithout resolution, strong purpose, or energy; spineless.

...ak·ling (wēk/ling) n. A feeble person or animal. **—**
...j. Having no natural strength or vigor.

...ak·ly (wēk/lē) adj. **·li·er, ·li·est** Sickly; feeble; weak.

...ak-mind·ed (wēk/mīn/did) adj. **1.** Indecisive; weak-
...lled. **2.** Feeble-minded. **— weak/mind/ed·ness** n.

...ak·ness (wēk/nis) n. **1.** The state, condition, or quality
being weak. **2.** A characteristic indicating feebleness.
A slight failing; a fault. **4.** A penchant or fondness: with
...r: a weakness for pastry.

...al[1] (wēl) n. Archaic A sound or healthy state; prosper-
...y; welfare. [OE wela]

...al[2] (wēl) n. A welt (def. 3). [Var. of WALE]

...ald (wēld) n, Chiefly Brit. An exposed forest area;
...aste woodland; also, an open region; down. [OE, a forest]

...alth (welth) n. **1.** A large aggregate of real and per-
...al property; riches; also, the state of being rich. **2.**
...con. All material objects having economic utility; also, in
...e private sense, all property possessing a monetary value.
... Great abundance of anything: usu. preceded by a: a
...ealth of learning. [ME < wele weal]
— Syn. 1. affluence, opulence. Compare PROPERTY.

...alth·y (wel/thē) adj. **wealth·i·er, wealth·i·est 1.** Pos-
...ssing wealth; affluent. **2.** More than sufficient; abound-
...g. **— wealth/i·ly** adv. **— wealth/i·ness** n.

...ean (wēn) v.t. **1.** To transfer (the young of any mammal)
...om dependence on its mother's milk to another form of

nourishment. **2.** To estrange from former habits or associations: usu. with from. [OE wenian to accustom]

wean·ling (wēn/ling) adj. Freshly weaned. — n. A child
or animal newly weaned.

weap·on (wep/ən) n. **1.** Any implement for fighting or
warfare. **2.** Any means that may be used against an adversary: verbal weapons. **3.** The sting, claw, spur, etc., of an
animal. — v.t. To furnish with a weapon or weapons. [OE
wǣpen] **— weap/on·less** adj.

weap·on·ry (wep/ən-rē) n. Weapons collectively.

wear[1] (wâr) v. **wore, worn, wear·ing** v.t. **1.** To carry or
have on the person as a garment, ornament, etc. **2.** To
bear on the person habitually: He wears a derby. **3.** To
have in one's appearance; exhibit: He wears a scowl. **4.** To
bear habitually in a specified manner; carry: She wears her
hair long. **5.** To display or fly: A ship wears its colors. **6.**
To impair, waste, or consume by use or constant action. **7.**
To cause by rubbing, etc.: to wear a hole in a coat. **8.** To
bring to a specified condition by wear: to wear a sleeve to
tatters. **9.** To exhaust; weary. — v.i. **10.** To be impaired
gradually by use, rubbing, etc. **11.** To withstand the effects
of use, wear, etc.: The skirt wears well. **12.** To become as
specified from use or attrition: His patience is wearing thin.
13. To pass gradually or tediously: with on or away. **— to
wear out 1.** To make or become worthless by use. **2.** To
waste gradually; use up: He wears out patience. **3.** To tire.
— n. **1.** The act of wearing, or the state of being worn. **2.**
The material or clothes to be worn: silk for summer wear:
also in compounds: footwear. **3.** The destructive effect of
use, work, or time. **4.** Capacity for resistance to use or impairment; durability. [OE werian] **— wear/a·bil/i·ty** n. **—
wear/a·ble** adj. **— wear/er** n.

wear[2] (wâr) v. **wore, worn, wear·ing** Naut. v.t. **1.** To turn
(a vessel) through an arc in which its head points momentarily directly to leeward. — v.i. **2.** To go about with the
wind astern. [Prob. alter. of VEER[1]]

wear and tear Loss by the service, exposure, decay, or
injury incident to ordinary use.

wear·ing (wâr/ing) adj. **1.** Fatiguing; exhausting; wasting:
a wearing job. **2.** Capable of being, or designed to be, worn.
— wear/ing·ly adv.

wearing apparel Clothing; garments.

wea·ri·some (wir/i·səm) adj. Causing fatigue; tiresome or
tedious. **— wea/ri·some·ly** adv. **— wea/ri·some·ness** n.

wea·ry (wir/ē) adj. **·ri·er, ·ri·est 1.** Tired; fatigued. **2.**
Discontented or vexed by continued endurance, as of something disagreeable, tedious, etc.: often with of: weary of life.
3. Indicating or characteristic of fatigue, boredom, etc. **4.**
Wearisome. — v.t. & v.i. **·ried, ·ry·ing** To make or become
weary; tire. [OE wērig] **— wea/ri·ness** adj. **— wea/ri·ly**
adv. **— wea/ri·ness** n.

wea·sel (wē/zəl) n. **1.** Any of certain small,
slender, predacious carnivores having brownish fur that in northern regions turns white in
winter. **2.** A sneaky, treacherous person. —
v.i. **·seled, ·sel·ing** U.S. Informal To speak or
act evasively, etc. [OE wesle]

WEASEL
(To 9 inch-
es long;
tail 2
inches)

weasel word A word that weakens a statement by rendering it ambiguous or equivocal.

weath·er (weth/ər) n. **1.** Atmospheric condition as regards temperature, moisture, winds,
or other meteorological phenomena. **2.** Bad
weather; storm. **— to keep one's weather eye
open** Informal To be alert. **— under the
weather** Informal **1.** Ailing; ill. **2.** Somewhat intoxicated.
— v.t. **1.** To expose to the action of the weather. **2.** To
discolor, crumble, or otherwise affect by action of the weather. **3.** To pass through and survive, as a crisis. **4.** Naut.
To pass to windward of: to weather Cape Horn. — v.i. **5.** To
undergo changes resulting from exposure to the weather.
6. To resist the action of the weather. — adj. Chiefly Naut.
Facing the wind. [OE weder] **— weath/ered** adj.

Weather may appear as a combining form or as the first
element in two-word phrases, as in **weather report, weather-
marked, weathertight.**

weath·er-beat·en (weth/ər-bēt/n) adj. **1.** Bearing or showing the effects of exposure to weather. **2.** Toughened or
tanned by or as by exposure to weather, as a face.

weath·er·board (weth/ər-bôrd', -bōrd') n. A clapboard.
— v.t. To fasten weatherboards on.

weath·er-bound (weth/ər-bound') adj. Detained by unfavorable weather, as a vessel in port.

Weather Bureau A bureau of the Department of Commerce in Washington, D.C., serving as headquarters for meteorological observation, the diffusion of information concerning the weather, etc.

weath·er·cock (weth/ər-kok') n. **1.** A weather vane in the
form of a cock. **2.** A fickle person or variable thing.

weath·er·glass (weth′ər·glas′, -gläs′)   *n.* An instrument for indicating the state of the weather; esp., a simple barometer showing falls in atmospheric pressure.

weath·er·man (weth′ər·man′) *n.* *pl.* **-men** (-men′) *n. Informal* A meteorologist, esp. one concerned with daily weather conditions and reports.

weather map A map or chart indicating weather conditions, as temperature, atmospheric pressure, wind velocity, precipitation, etc., for a given region and time.

weath·er·proof (weth′ər·proof′) *adj.* Capable of withstanding rough weather without appreciable deterioration. — *v.t.* To make weatherproof.

weather station A station or office where meteorological observations are taken and recorded.

weath·er·strip (weth′ər·strip′) *v.t.* **-stripped, -strip·ping** To equip or fit with weather strips.

weather strip A narrow strip of material placed over or in crevices, as at windows, to keep out drafts, rain, etc.

weather stripping 1. A weather strip. 2. Weather strips collectively.

weather vane A vane that indicates the direction from which the wind is blowing; weathercock.

weath·er·wise (weth′ər·wīz′) *adj.* 1. Experienced in observing or predicting the weather. 2. Skillful in predicting trends or shifts in public opinion, etc.

weave (wēv) *v.* **wove** or *for def. 10* **weaved, wo·ven** or (*less common*) **wove, weav·ing** *v.t.* 1. To form, produce, or manufacture as a textile, by interlacing threads or yarns; esp., in a loom. 2. To form by interlacing strands, strips, twigs, etc.: to *weave* a basket. 3. To produce by combining details or elements: to *weave* a story. 4. To bring together so as to form a whole. 5. To twist into, about, or through: to *weave* ribbons through one's hair. 6. To spin (a web). 7. To make or effect by moving from side to side or in a winding or zigzag course: to *weave* one's way through a crowd. — *v.i.* 8. To make cloth, baskets, etc., by weaving. 9. To become woven or interlaced. 10. To move from side to side or with a zigzagging motion. — *n.* A particular method or style of weaving. [OE *wefan*]

weav·er (wē′vər) *n.* 1. One who weaves; esp., one whose occupation is the weaving of textiles, etc. 2. A weaverbird.

weav·er·bird (wē′vər·bûrd′) *n.* Any of various finchlike birds, native to Asia, Africa, etc., and constructing intricately woven nests.

web (web) *n.* 1. Any fabric, structure, etc., woven of or as of interlaced or interwoven strands. 2. Textile fabric, esp. in the piece or being woven in a loom. 3. The network of delicate threads spun by a spider to entrap its prey, by certain caterpillars, other insect larvae, etc.; a cobweb. 4. Any complex network: a *web* of highways. 5. Anything artfully contrived or elaborated into a trap or snare: a *web* of espionage. 6. *Zool.* A membrane or fold of skin connecting the digits of an animal, as in aquatic birds, otters, bats, frogs, etc. 7. *Ornithol.* The series of barbs on either side of the shaft of a feather: also called **vane**. 8. A plate or sheet, as of metal, connecting the heavier sections, ribs, frames, etc., of any structural or mechanical element. 9. *Archit.* The part of a ribbed vault between the ribs. — *v.t.* **webbed, web·bing** 1. To provide with a web. 2. To cover or surround with a web; entangle. [OE]

webbed (webd) *adj.* 1. Having a web. 2. Having the digits united by a membrane, as the foot of a goose or duck.

web·bing (web′ing) *n.* 1. A woven strip of strong fiber, used for safety belts, in upholstery, etc. 2. Any structure or material forming a web.

web·by (web′ē) *adj.* **-bi·er, -bi·est** Resembling, having, or consisting of a web or membrane.

web·foot (web′foot′) *n.* *pl.* **-feet** 1. A foot with webbed toes. 2. A web-footed bird or animal.

web-foot·ed (web′foot′id) *adj.* Having the toes connected by a membrane, as many aquatic animals and birds.

Web·ste·ri·an (web·stir′ē·ən) *adj.* Of or pertaining to Daniel or Noah Webster.

wed (wed) *v.* **wed·ded, wed** or **wed·ded, wed·ding** *v.t.* 1. To take as one's husband or wife; marry. 2. To unite or give in matrimony; join in wedlock. 3. To join in a close relationship or attachment. — *v.i.* 4. To marry. [OE *weddian* to pledge]

we'd (wēd) 1. We had. 2. We would.

wed·ded (wed′id) *adj.* 1. Joined in wedlock; married. 2. Characteristic of marriage. 3. Having a close relationship or attachment: often with *to*: *wedded* to his work.

wed·ding (wed′ing) *n.* 1. The ceremony or celebration of a marriage. 2. The anniversary of a marriage: golden *wedding*. [OE *weddung* < *weddian* to pledge]

wedge (wej) *n.* 1. A piece of wood, metal, etc., that is V-shaped in longitudinal cross section, capable of being inserted into a narrow opening, and used as an aid in splitting substances, securing movable parts, raising weights, etc. 2. Anything in the form of a wedge, as a piece of pie, a formation of soldiers, etc. 3. An action, procedure, or idea constituting the earliest stage in a division of unity, change policy, intrusive action, etc. — *v.* **wedged, wedg·ing** 1. To force apart or split with or as with a wedge. 2. compress or fix in place with a wedge. 3. To crowd squeeze (something) into a narrow or confined space. *v.i.* 4. To jam or be forced in like a wedge. [OE *wecg*]

Wedg·wood (wej′wood) *n.* A type of fine, hard potte often of unglazed, tinted clay bearing small, white, finely tailed, classical figures in cameo relief. Also **Wedgwo ware.** [after Josiah *Wedgwood*, 1730–95, English potter]

wedg·y (wej′ē) *adj.* **wedg·i·er, wedg·i·est** Having the f or uses of a wedge.

wed·lock (wed′lok) *n.* The state or relationship of be married; matrimony. — **in wedlock** 1. With one's pare legally married to one another, as at the time of one's ception or birth. 2. In the married state. — **out of we lock** With one's parents not married to one another, as the time of one's conception or birth. [OE < *wed* pledge -*lāc*, suffix of nouns of action]

Wednes·day (wenz′dē, -dā) *n.* The fourth day of the we [OE *Wōdnesdæg* day of Woden]

wee (wē) *adj.* **we·er, wee·est** Very small; tiny. — *n. Chi Scot.* A short time or space; a bit: bide a *wee*. [ME *we* OE *wǣge* a quantity]

weed¹ (wēd) *n.* 1. Any common, unsightly, or troubleso plant that grows in abundance, esp. to injurious excess cultivated ground. 2. *Informal* Tobacco: usu. with *also*, a cigarette or cigar. 3. Any worthless animal or thi 4. The stem and leaves of any useful plant as distinguis from its flower and fruit: dill *weed*. 5. Thick, luxuri growth, as of underbrush or shrubs. — *v.t.* 1. To pull and remove weeds from. 2. To remove (a weed): often w *out.* 3. To remove (anything regarded as harmful or desirable): with *out.* 4. To rid of anything harmful or desirable. — *v.i.* 5. To remove weeds, etc. [OE *wē* — **weed′er** *n.* — **weed′less** *adj.*

weed² (wēd) *n.* 1. A token of mourning, as a band of cre worn as part of the dress. 2. *pl.* A widow's mourning ga [OE *wǣd* garment]

weed·y (wē′dē) *adj.* **weed·i·er, weed·i·est** 1. Havin growth of weeds; abounding in weeds. 2. Of or pertain to a weed or weeds. 3. Resembling a weed; weedlike, as rapid, ready growth. 4. *Informal* Gawky; awkward; gainly: *weedy* youths. — **weed′i·ly** *adv.* — **weed′i·ness**

wee folk Fairies, elves, etc.

wee hours The hours after midnight; early morning.

week (wēk) *n.* 1. A period of seven days; esp., suc period beginning with Sunday. ◆ Collateral adjecti *hebdomadal.* 2. The period of time within a week devo to work: a 35-hour *week*. 3. A period of seven days prec ing or following any given day or date: a *week* from Tuesd [OE *wucu, wicu, wice*]

week-day (wēk′dā′) *n.* Any day of the week except Sund

week-end (wēk′end′) *n.* The end of the week; esp., time from Friday evening or Saturday to the following M day morning. — *v.i. Informal* To pass the weekend: *weekended* in the country. — **week′end′er** *n.*

week-long (wēk′lông′, -long′) *adj.* Continuing for a we lasting all week.

week·ly (wēk′lē) *adv.* Once a week; esp., at regular sev day intervals. — *adj.* 1. Of or pertaining to a week or weekdays. 2. Done or occurring once a week. — *n.* **-lies** A publication issued once a week.

ween (wēn) *v.t. & v.i. Archaic* To suppose; guess; fan [OE *wēnan* to think]

ween·ie (wē′nē) *n. U.S. Informal* A wiener.

weep (wēp) *v.* **wept, weep·ing** *v.i.* 1. To manifest g or other strong emotion by shedding tears. 2. To mou lament: with *for*. 3. To ooze or shed liquid in drops. — 4. To weep for; mourn. 5. To shed (tears, or drops of ot liquid). 6. To bring to a specified condition by weeping *weep* oneself to sleep. — *n.* The act of weeping, or a fi tears. [OE *wēpan*] — **weep′er** *n.*

weep·ing (wē′ping) *adj.* 1. That weeps; crying; tear 2. Having slim, pendulous branches: *weeping* willow.

weeping willow A willow having long, slender, pendul branches.

weep·y (wē′pē) *adj.* **weep·i·er, weep·i·est** *Informal* clined to weep; tearful.

wee·vil (wē′vəl) *n.* 1. Any of numerous small beet many of them serious pests, having snoutlike heads a strong, pincerlike jaws, and feeding on plants and pl products. 2. Any of a family of small beetles that f principally on beans and seeds. [OE *wifel* beetle] — **w vil·y** or **wee′vil·ly** *adj.*

weft (weft) *n.* 1. The cross threads in a web of cloth; wo 2. A woven fabric; web. 3. *Naut.* A waft. [OE]

Wehr·macht (vâr′mäkht) *n. German* The armed forc collectively, of Germany; literally, defense force.

weigh¹ (wā) *v.t.* 1. To determine the weight of, as by m suring on a scale or balance. 2. To balance or hold in

and so as to estimate weight or heaviness.   3. To measure
a quantity or quantities of something) according to weight:
ith *out*.   4. To consider carefully; estimate the worth or
dvantages of: to *weigh* a proposal.   5. To press or force
own by weight or heaviness; burden or oppress: with *down*.
. To raise or hoist: now only in the phrase **to weigh anchor**.
- *v.i.*   7. To have weight; be heavy to a specified degree:
ne *weighs* ninety pounds.   8. To have influence or im-
ortance: The girl's testimony *weighed* heavily with the
ry.   9. To be burdensome or oppressive: with *on* or
pon: What *weighs* on your mind?   10. *Naut.* **a** To raise
nchor. **b** To begin to sail.   — **to weigh in** Of a prize fighter,
c., to be weighed before a contest.   — **to weigh one's
ords** To consider one's words carefully before speaking.
)E *wegan* to weigh, carry, lift]   — **weigh'er** *n.*

igh[2] (wā)   *n.* Way: used in the phrase **under weigh** by
istaken analogy with *aweigh*. [Var. of WAY]

ight (wāt)   *n.*   1. Any quantity of heaviness, expressed
definitely or in terms of standard units.   2. The measure
' the force with which bodies tend toward the center of the
arth or other celestial body, equal to the mass of the body
ultiplied by the acceleration due to gravitation; also, the
uality so measured.   3. Any object or mass that weighs a
efinite or specific amount.   4. A definite mass of metal,
c., equal to a specified unit or amount of heaviness, and
sed in scales as a standard; also, any unit of heaviness, as
pound, ounce, etc.   5. Any mass used as a counterpoise
' to exert pressure by force of gravity: a *paperweight*.   6.
urden; oppressiveness: the *weight* of care.   7. The relative
ndency of any mass toward a center of superior mass: the
eight of a planet.   8. A scale or graduated system of stand-
d units of weight: avoirdupois *weight*. [See tables front
' book.]   9. Influence; importance; consequence: a man
weight.   10. The comparative heaviness of clothes, as
propriate to the season: summer *weight*.   — **by weight**
easured by weighing.   — **to carry weight** To be of im-
ortance or significance.   — **to pull one's weight** To do one's
are; perform one's duty.   — **to throw one's weight
round** *Informal* To exercise one's authority more than is
ecessary or proper; make unwarranted use of position or
ower.   — *v.t.*   1. To add weight to; make heavy.   2. To
ppress or burden.   3. To adulterate or treat (fabrics, etc.)
ith extraneous substances. [OE *wiht, gewiht*]

ight·less (wāt'lis)   *adj.*   1. Having or seeming to have no
eight.   2. *Aerospace* Being at zero gravity.   — **weight'·
ss·ly** *adv.*   — **weight'less·ness** *n.*

ight·y (wā'tē)   *adj.* **weight·i·er, weight·i·est**   1. Having
eat weight; ponderous.   2. Having power to move the
ind; cogent.   3. Of great importance.   4. Influential, as in
ublic affairs.   5. Burdensome.   — **weight'i·ly** *adv.*
eight'i·ness *n.*

eimar Republic   A German Republic formed by a con-
itutional assembly at Weimar, 1919; dissolved 1933.

eir (wir)   *n.*   1. An obstruction or dam placed in a stream
' raise the water, divert it into a millrace or irrigation ditch-
, etc.   2. An aperture in such an obstruction, used to de-
rmine the quantity of water flowing through it.   3. A
ries of wattled enclosures in a stream to catch fish. [OE
er < *werian* to dam up]

ird (wird)   *adj.*   1. Concerned with the unnatural or with
itchcraft; unearthly; uncanny.   2. Strange; bizarre.   3.
ertaining to or having to do with Fate or the Fates. [OE
yrd fate]   — **weird'ly** *adv.*   — **weird'ness** *n.*

ird·ie (wir'dē)   *n.* **pl. weird·ies** *U.S. Slang* A bizarre or
eakish person, thing, or occurrence.   Also **weird'y.**

iss beer (vīs, wis)   A pale, effervescent beer, brewed usu.
om wheat.   [< G *weissbier*, lit., white beer]

lch (welch, welsh)   *v.i.* To welsh.   — **welch'er** *n.*

lch (welch, welsh)   See WELSH.

lch·man (welsh'mən, welch-)   See WELSHMAN.

l·come (wel'kəm)   *adj.*   1. Admitted gladly to a place or
stivity; received cordially: a *welcome* guest.   2. Producing
tisfaction or pleasure; pleasing: *welcome* tidings.   3. Made
ee to use or enjoy: She is *welcome* to my purse.   — **you are
or you're) welcome** You are under no obligation: a con-
entional response to "thank you."   — *n.* The act of bid-
ng or making welcome; a hearty greeting.   — **to wear out
ne's welcome** To come so often or to linger so long as no
nger to be welcome.   — *v.t.* **·comed, ·com·ing**   1. To give a
elcome to; greet hospitably.   2. To receive with pleasure.
)E < *will-* will, pleasure + *cuma* guest]   — **wel'come·ly**
lv.   — **wel'come·ness** *n.*   — **wel'com·er** *n.*

lcome mat   *Informal*   1. A doormat.   2. Any enthusi-
stic welcome or reception: chiefly in the phrase **to put (or
oll) out the welcome mat.**

ld (weld)   *v.t.*   1. To unite, as two pieces of metal, usu.
ith hammering or pressure, by the application of heat along
ie area of contact.   2. To bring into close association or

connection.   — *v.i.*   3. To be capable of being welded.   — *n.*
The consolidation of pieces of metal by welding; also, the
closed joint so formed.   [Alter. of WELL[1], v.]   — **weld'a·bil'
i·ty** *n.*   — **weld/a·ble** *adj.*   — **weld'er** *n.*

wel·fare (wel'fâr)   *n.*   1. The condition of faring well;
prosperity.   2. Welfare work.   3. Aid, as money, food, or
clothing, given to those in need.   — **on welfare** Receiving money, food, clothing, etc., from a government because of
need.   [ME < *wel* well + *fare* a going]

welfare state   A state or polity in which the government
assumes a large measure of responsibility for the social welfare of its members, as through unemployment and health
insurance, fair employment legislation, etc.

welfare work   Organized efforts carried on by government
or private organizations to improve the social and economic
condition of a group or class.   — **welfare worker**

wel·kin (wel'kin)   *n. Archaic* or *Poetic*   1. The vault of the
sky; the heavens.   2. The air.   [OE *wolcen, wolcn* cloud]

well[1] (wel)   *n.*   1. A hole or shaft sunk into the earth to obtain a fluid, as water, oil, brine, or natural gas.   2. A spring
of water; a fountain.   3. A source of continued supply, or
that which issues forth continuously; a wellspring: a *well* of
learning.   4. A depression, cavity, or vessel used to hold a
supply of liquid: an *inkwell*.   5. *Archit.* A vertical opening
descending through floors, or a deep enclosed space in a
building for light, ventilation, etc.: a *stairwell*; an elevator
well.   6. *Naut.* The enclosed space in a vessel's hold, housing
the pumps.   — *v.i.*   1. To pour forth or flow up, as water in a
spring.   — *v.t.*   2. To gush: Her eyes *welled* tears.   [OE <
weallan to boil, bubble up]

well[2] (wel)   *adv.* **bet·ter, best**   1. Satisfactorily; favorably;
according to one's wishes: Everything goes *well*.   2. In a
good or correct manner; expertly: to speak *well*.   3. Suitably; with reason or propriety: I cannot *well* remain here.
4. In a successful manner; also, agreeably or luxuriously:
He lives *well*.   5. Intimately: How *well* do you know him?
6. T a considerable extent or degree: *well* aware.   7. Completely; wholly.   8. Far; at some distance: He lagged *well*
behind us.   9. Kindly; generously; graciously.   — **as well**
1. Also; in addition.   2. With equal effect or consequence:
He might just as *well* have sold it.   — **as well as**   1. As
satisfactorily as.   2. To the same degree as.   3. In addition
to.   — *adj.*   1. Having good health.   2. Satisfactory; right:
All is *well*.   3. Prosperous; comfortable.   — *interj.* An
exclamation used to express surprise, expectation, resignation, doubt, indignation, acquiescence, etc., or merely to
preface a remark.   [OE *wel*]
    ◆ *Well* may be used in combination, as in *well-chosen,
well-informed*, etc. Such combinations are hyphenated before
the words they modify, as in *well-aimed* shots, but not when
used predicatively, as in: The shots were *well aimed*.

we'll (wēl)   1. We will.   2. We shall.

well-ap·point·ed (wel'ə·poin'tid)   *adj.* Properly equipped;
excellently furnished.

well·a·way (wel'ə·wā')   *interj. Archaic* Woe is me! alas!
Also **well'a·day'** (-dā').   [OE *wā lā wā* woe! lo! woe!]

well-bal·anced (wel'bal'ənst)   *adj.*   1. Evenly balanced or
proportioned.   2. Sensible; sane; sound.

well-be·ing (wel'bē'ing)   *n.* A condition of health, happiness,
or prosperity; welfare.

well-born (wel'bôrn')   *adj.* Of good birth or ancestry.

well-bred (wel'bred')   *adj.*   1. Characterized by or showing
good breeding; polite.   2. Of good stock, as an animal.

well-curb (wel'kûrb«)   *n.* The frame or stone ring around
the mouth of a well.

well-dis·posed (wel'dis·pōzd')   *adj.* Disposed or inclined to
be kind, favorable, etc.

well-do·er (wel'dōō'ər)   *n.* One who performs good deeds.
    — **well'-do'ing** *n.*

well-done (wel'dun')   *adj.*   1. Satisfactorily accomplished.
    2. Thoroughly cooked, as meat.

well enough   Tolerably good or satisfactory.   — **to let well
enough alone**   To leave things as they are lest the result of
interference be worse.

well-fa·vored (wel'fā'vərd)   *adj.* Of attractive appearance;
comely; handsome.   Also *Brit.* **well'-fa'voured.**

well-fed (wel'fed')   *adj.*   1. Plump; fat.   2. Properly nourished.

well-fixed (wel'fiskt')   *adj. Informal* Affluent; well-to-do.

well-found (wel'found')   *adj.* Well equipped or supplied.

well-found·ed (wel'foun'did)   *adj.* Based on fact, sound,
evidence, etc.: *well-founded* suspicions.

well-groomed (wel'grōōmd')   *adj.*   1. Carefully dressed,
combed, etc.; very neat.   2. Carefully curried, as a horse.

well-ground·ed (wel'groun'did)   *adj.*   1. Adequately
schooled in the elements of a subject.   2. Well-founded.

well-head (wel'hed')   *n.*   1. A natural source supplying
water to a spring or well.   2. Any source or fountainhead.

well-heeled (wel′hēld′) *adj. Slang* Plentifully supplied with money.

well-in·ten·tioned (wel′in·ten′shənd) *adj.* Having good intentions; well-meant: often with connotation of failure.

well-known (wel′nōn′) *adj.* 1. Widely known; famous. 2. Thoroughly or fully known.

well-man·nered (wel′man′ərd) *adj.* Characterized by good manners; courteous; polite.

well-mean·ing (wel′mē′ning) *adj.* 1. Having good intentions. 2. Done with or characterized by good intentions: also **well-meant′** (-ment′).

well-nigh (wel′nī′) *adv.* Very nearly; almost.

well-off (wel′ôf′, -of′) *adj.* In comfortable or favorable circumstances; fortunate.

well-read (wel′red′) *adj.* Having a wide knowledge of literature or books; having read much.

well-round·ed (wel′roun′did) *adj.* 1. Having or displaying diverse knowledge, interests, etc. 2. Wide in scope; comprehensive: a *well-rounded* program. 3. Fully formed or developed: a *well-rounded* figure.

well-spo·ken (wel′spō′kən) *adj.* 1. Fitly or excellently said. 2. Of gentle speech and manners.

well·spring (wel′spring′) *n.* 1. The source of a stream or spring; fountainhead. 2. A source of continual supply.

well sweep A device used for drawing water from a well, consisting of a pole swung on a pivot attached to a high post, and having a bucket suspended from one end.

well-thought-of (wel′thôt′uv′, -ov′) *adj.* In good repute; esteemed; respected.

well-to-do (wel′tə-dōō′) *adj.* Prosperous; affluent.

well-wish·er (wel′wish′ər) *n.* One who wishes well, as to another. — **well′-wish′ing** *adj. & n.*

welsh (welsh, welch) *v.i. Slang* 1. To cheat by failing to pay a bet or debt: often with *on.* 2. To avoid fulfilling an obligation: often with *on.* Also spelled **welch**. [? Back-formation < *welsher*, prob. < *Welsher* Welshman, with ref. to supposed national traits] — **welsh′er** *n.*

Welsh (welsh, welch) *adj.* Pertaining to Wales, its people, or their language. — *n.* 1. The Celtic people of Wales: with *the*: also called *Cymry.* 2. The Celtic language of Wales, belonging to the Brythonic or Cymric group: also called *Cymric.* Also spelled *Welch.* [OE *wealh* foreigner]

Welsh·man (welsh′mən, welch′-) *n. pl.* **·men** (-mən) A man of Welsh birth or ancestry. Also spelled *Welchman.*

Welsh rabbit A concoction of melted cheese cooked in cream or milk, often with ale or beer added, and served hot on toast or crackers. ◆ The form *rarebit* was a later development and is the result of mistaken etymology.

Welsh terrier A black-and-tan terrier having a flat skull and wiry coat, used for hunting.

welt (welt) *n.* 1. A strip of material, covered cord, etc., applied to a seam to cover or strengthen it. 2. A strip of leather set into the seam between the edges of the upper and the outer sole of a shoe. 3. A stripe raised on the skin by a blow: also called *wale, weal.* — *v.t.* 1. To sew a welt on or in; decorate with a welt. 2. *Informal* To flog severely, so as to raise welts. [ME *welte, walt*]

wel·ter (wel′tər) *v.i.* 1. To roll about; wallow. 2. To lie or be soaked in some fluid, as blood. 3. To surge or move tumultuously, as the sea. — *n.* 1. A rolling movement, as of waves. 2. A commotion; turmoil. [< MDu. *welteren*]

wel·ter·weight (wel′tər-wāt′) *n.* A boxer or wrestler whose fighting weight is between 136 and 147 pounds. [< *welter* heavyweight horseman + WEIGHT]

Welt·schmerz (velt′shmārts′) *n. German* Melancholy pessimism over the state of the world; literally, world pain.

wen (wen) *n. Pathol.* Any benign tumor of the skin containing sebaceous matter, occurring commonly on the scalp. [OE *wenn, wænn*] — **wen′nish, wen′ny** *adj.*

wench (wench) *n.* 1. A young woman; girl: a humorous term. 2. *Archaic* A young peasant woman; also, a female servant; maid. 3. *Archaic* A prostitute; strumpet. — *v.i. Archaic* To keep company with strumpets. [ME < OE *wencel* child, servant]

wend (wend) *Chiefly Poetic v.* **wen·ded** (*Archaic* went), **wend·ing** *v.t.* 1. To direct or proceed on (one's course or way). — *v.i.* 2. To travel; proceed; go. [OE *wendan*]

Wend (wend) *n.* One of a Slavic people now occupying the region between the Elbe and Oder rivers in eastern Germany: also called *Sorb, Sorbian.* [< G *Wende, Winde*]

Wend·ish (wen′dish) *adj.* Of or pertaining to the Wends or their language: also *Sorbian.* — *n.* The West Slavic language of the Wends; Sorbian. Also **Wend′ic.**

went (went) An archaic past tense and past participle of *wend*, now used as past tense of GO.

wept (wept) Past tense and past participle of WEEP.

were (wûr, *unstressed* wər) Plural and second person singular past indicative, and past subjunctive singular and plural of BE. [OE *wære, wæron*, pt. forms of *wesan* to be]

we're (wir) We are.

were·n't (wûr′ənt) Were not.

were·wolf (wir′wŏŏlf′, wûr′-) *n. pl.* **·wolves** (-wŏŏlvz′) European folklore, a human being transformed into a wolf one having power to assume the form of a wolf at will. Al **wer′wolf′.** [OE < *wer* man + *wulf* wolf]

wert (wûrt, *unstressed* wərt) Archaic second person sing lar, past tense of both indicative and subjunctive of BE: us with *thou.*

Wes·ley·an (wes′lē-ən, *Brit.* wez′lē-ən) *adj.* Of or perta ing to John Wesley or Methodism. — *n.* A disciple of Jo Wesley; a Methodist. — **Wes′ley·an·ism** *n.*

Wes·sex (wes′iks) The ancient kingdom of the West Saxo in southern England.

west (west) *n.* 1. The direction of the sun in relation to observer on earth at sunset. 2. One of the four cardi points of the compass, directly opposite *east* and 90° count clockwise from *north.* See COMPASS CARD. 3. Any directi near this point. 4. *Sometimes cap.* Any region west of specified point. — **the West** 1. The countries lying w of Asia and Turkey; the Occident. 2. The western hem sphere. — *adj.* 1. To, toward, facing, or in the west; we ern. 2. Coming from the west: the *west* wind. — *adv.* or toward the west; westward. [OE]

west·bound (west′bound′) *adj.* Going westward. A **west′-bound′.**

west·er·ing (wes′tər-ing) *adj.* Moving or turning we ward: the *westering* sun.

west·er·ly (wes′tər-lē) *adj.* 1. In, toward, or pertaining the west. 2. From the west, as a wind. — *n. pl.* **·lies** wind or storm from the west. — *adv.* Toward or from west. — **west′er·li·ness** *n.*

west·ern (wes′tərn) *adj.* 1. To, toward, or in the west. Native to or inhabiting the west: a *western* species. 3. *So times cap.* Of, pertaining to, or characteristic of the west the West. 4. From the west, as a wind. — *n.* 1. A we erner. 2. A type of fiction or motion picture using cowl and pioneer life in the western U.S. as its material.

Western Church 1. The medieval church of the West Roman Empire, now the Roman Catholic Church: dist guished from the church of the Eastern Empire, now Eastern Orthodox Church. 2. The Christian churches western Europe and America.

west·ern·er (wes′tər-nər) *n.* 1. One who is native to lives in the west. 2. *Usu. cap.* One who lives in or cor from the western U.S.

western frontier Formerly, the part of the U.S. border on the still unsettled regions of the west.

west·ern·ism (wes′tər-niz′əm) *n.* An expression or pr tice peculiar to the west, esp. the western U.S.

west·ern·ize (wes′tər-nīz) *v.t.* **·ized, ·iz·ing** To make we ern in characteristics, habits, etc. — **west′ern·i·za′tion**

west·ern·most (wes′tərn-mōst) *adj.* Farthest west.

Western Ocean In ancient geography, the ocean ly westward of the known world; the Atlantic Ocean.

Western (Roman) Empire The part of the Roman E pire west of the Adriatic that existed as a separate emp from A.D. 395 until the fall of Rome in A.D. 476.

West Highland white terrier A small, short-legged rier having a stiff, white coat.

west-north-west (west′north′west′) *n.* The direct midway between west and northwest, 26 points or 292° clockwise from due north. See COMPASS CARD. — *adj* *adv.* In, toward, or from the west-northwest.

West Saxon 1. One of a Saxon tribe that invaded Engl in the fifth and sixth centuries A.D. and settled in Wess 2. The dialect of Old English spoken in Wessex.

west-south-west (west′south′west′) *n.* The direct midway between west and southwest, 22 points or 247° clockwise from due north. See COMPASS CARD. — *adj* *adv.* In, toward, or from the west-southwest.

west·ward (west′wərd) *adv.* Toward the west: also **we wards.** — *adj.* To, toward, facing, or in the west. — *n* western part or region. — **west′ward·ly** *adv.*

wet (wet) *adj.* **wet·ter, wet·test** 1. Covered or satura with water or other liquid. 2. Not yet dry: *wet* varnish. Treated or separated by means of water or other liquids. Preserved in liquid; also, bottled in alcohol, as laborat specimens. 5. Marked by showers or by heavy rainf rainy. 6. *Informal* Favoring or permitting the manufact and sale of alcoholic beverages: a *wet* State. — **all —** *Slang* Quite wrong; crazy. — **wet behind the ears** Inexp enced or unsophisticated. — *n.* 1. Water; moisture; w ness. 2. Showery or rainy weather; rain. 3. *Informal* (opposed to prohibition. — *v.t. & v.i.* **wet** or **wet·ted, v ting** To make or become wet. — **to wet one's whi** *Informal* To take a drink. [OE *wæt*] — **wet′ly** *adv.* **wet′ness** *n.* — **wet′ta·ble** *adj.* — **wet′ter** *n.*

wet·back (wet′bak′) *n. U.S. Informal* A Mexican labo who enters the U.S. illegally. [So called because many cr the border by swimming or wading across the Rio Gran

wet blanket *Informal* One who or that which has a couraging effect on enthusiasm, activity, etc.

weth·er (weth′ər) *n.* A castrated ram. [OE]

wet-nurse (wet′nûrs′) *v.t.* **-nursed, -nurs·ing** **1.** To act as a wet nurse to. **2.** To attend to with painstaking care.

wet nurse A woman who is hired to suckle the child of another woman.

wet·ting (wet′ing) *n.* **1.** The act of one who wets, or the state of being wetted. **2.** A liquid, as water, used in moistening something, as flour in breadmaking.

wetting agent *Chem.* Any of a class of substances that, by reducing surface tension, enable a liquid to spread more readily over a solid surface.

we've (wēv) We have.

whack (hwak) *v.t. & v.i.* **1.** *Informal* To strike sharply; beat; hit. **2.** *Slang* To share: often with *up.* —*n.* **1.** *Informal* A sharp, resounding stroke or blow. **2.** *Slang* A share; portion. —**to have a whack at** *Slang* **1.** To give a blow to. **2.** To have a chance or turn at. —**out of whack** *Slang* Out of order. [? Var. of THWACK]

whack·ing (hwak′ing) *Chiefly Brit. Informal adj.* Strikingly large; whopping. —*adv.* Very; extremely.

whale¹ (hwāl) *n.* **1.** A marine mammal of fishlike form, esp. one of the larger pelagic species, having the fore limbs developed as paddles, a broad, flat tail, and a thick layer of fat or blubber immediately beneath the skin. The principal types are the toothless or whalebone whales and the toothed whales. **2.** *Informal* Something extremely good or large: a *whale* of a party. —*v.i.* **whaled, whal·ing** To engage in the hunting of whales. [OE *hwæl*]

whale² (hwāl) *v.t.* **whaled, whal·ing** *Informal* To strike as to produce wales or stripes; flog; wale. [? Var. of WALE¹, v.]

whale·back (hwāl′bak′) *n.* A steamship having a rounded main deck, used on the Great Lakes.

whale·boat (hwāl′bōt′) *n.* A long, deep rowboat, sharp at both ends, often steered with an oar, so called because first used in whaling, but now carried on steamers as lifeboats.

whale·bone (hwāl′bōn′) *n.* **1.** The horny substance developed in plates from the upper jaw on either side of the palate of certain whales; baleen. **2.** A strip of whalebone, used in stiffening dress bodies, corsets, etc.

whal·er (hwā′lər) *n.* **1.** A person or a vessel engaged in whaling. **2.** A whaleboat.

whal·ing (hwā′ling) *n.* The industry of capturing whales. —*adj. Slang* Huge; whopping.

wham·my (hwam′ē) *n. pl.* **·mies** *U.S. Slang* A jinx; hex: to put the *whammy* on someone. [< *wham*, informal interjection imit. of the sound of a hard blow]

whang (hwang) *Informal v.t. & v.i.* To beat or sound with resounding noise. —*n.* A heavy blow. [Imit.]

wharf (hwôrf) *n. pl.* **wharves** (hwôrvz) or **wharfs** A structure of masonry or timber erected on the shore of a harbor, river, etc., alongside which vessels may lie to load or unload cargo, passengers, etc.; also, any landing place for vessels, as a pier or quay. —*v.t.* **1.** To moor to a wharf. **2.** To provide or protect with a wharf or wharves. **3.** To deposit or store on a wharf. [OE *hwearf*]

—**Syn.** (noun) A *wharf* is usually a platform supported by wooden piles. A *pier* usually has a masonry foundation and projects into the water at right angles to the bank. A *dock* was originally the water between two *piers*, in which a vessel floated; by extension, any *pier* or *wharf* has come to be called a *dock*.

wharf·age (hwôr′fij) *n.* **1.** The use of wharves for unloading ships, storing goods, etc. **2.** Charge for the use of a wharf. **3.** Wharves collectively.

wharf·in·ger (hwôr′fin·jər) *n.* One who keeps a wharf or landing goods and collects wharfage fees. [Earlier *wharfager*]

wharf rat 1. A brown rat that inhabits wharves. **2.** *U.S. Slang* One who loiters about wharves, esp. with criminal intent.

wharf·side (hwôrf′sīd′) *n.* The space on or at the side of a wharf. —*adj.* On or at the side of a wharf.

wharve (hwôrv) In spinning, a round piece on a spindle, serving as a pulley. [OE *hweorfa*]

what (hwot, hwut) *pron.* **1.** Which specific thing or things, action, etc.: *What* does he do? I don't know *what* to do. **2.** That which: He knew *what* he wanted. —**and what not** *What* need not be mentioned in addition; and so forth. —**what for** *Slang* A punishment; scolding: I'll give him *what for*. —**what have you** What need not be mentioned in addition; and so forth. —**what if** What would happen if; suppose that. —**what's what** *Informal* The actual situation or state of affairs. —**what with** As a result of taking into consideration. —*adj.* **1.** In interrogative construction: **a** asking for information that will specify the person or thing qualified by it; which: Of *what* person do you speak? **b** How much; How much money has he? **2.** How surprising, ridiculous, great, etc.: *What* genius! **3.** Whatever: *What* money he had left was soon spent. —*adv.* **1.** In what respect; to what extent: *What* are you profited? **2.** For what reason; why: with *for*: *What* are you saying that for? —*conj. Informal* That: used only in negative expressions: I do not doubt but *what* he will come. [OE *hwæt*, neut. of *hwā* who]

what·ev·er (hwot′ev′ər, hwut′-) *pron.* **1.** As a compound relative, the whole that; anything that; no matter what: often added for emphasis to a negative assertion: *whatever* makes life dear; I do not want anything *whatever*. **2.** *Informal* What: usually interrogative: *Whatever* were you saying? Also *Poetic* **what′e′er′** (-âr′).

what·not (hwot′not′, hwut′-) *n.* An ornamental set of shelves for holding bric-à-brac, etc.

what·so·ev·er (hwot′sō·ev′ər, hwut′-) *adj. & pron.* Whatever: a more formal usage. Also *Poetic* **what′so·e′er′** (-âr′).

wheat (hwēt) *n.* **1.** The grain of a cereal grass, widely cultivated and providing a flour used for bread, pastries, etc. **2.** The plant producing this grain, bearing at its summit a dense spike called the ear or head, sometimes with awns (**bearded wheat**) and sometimes without awns (**beardless** or **bald wheat**). **3.** A field of wheat; crop of wheat. [OE *hwǣte*]

WHEAT
a Bearded.
b Beardless.
c,d Grain.

wheat·en (hwēt′n) *adj.* Belonging to or made of wheat.

whee·dle (hwēd′l) *v.* **·dled, ·dling** *v.t.* **1.** To persuade or try to persuade by flattery, cajolery, etc.; coax. **2.** To obtain by cajoling or coaxing. —*v.i.* **3.** To use flattery or cajolery. [? OE *wǣdlian* to beg, be poor] —**whee′dler** *n.* —**whee′dling·ly** *adv.*

wheel (hwēl) *n.* **1.** A circular rim and hub connected by spokes or a disk, capable of rotating on a central axis, as in vehicles and machines. **2.** An instrument or device having a wheel or wheels as its distinguishing characteristic, as a steering wheel, water wheel, spinning wheel, etc. **3.** Anything resembling or suggestive of a wheel; any circular object or formation. **4.** *Informal* A bicycle. **5.** An old instrument of torture or execution, consisting of a wheel to which the limbs of the victim were tied and then broken with an iron bar. **6.** A turning; rotation; revolution. **7.** *pl.* That which imparts or directs motion or controls activity; the moving force: the *wheels* of democracy. —**at the wheel 1.** Driving or steering a vehicle, boat, etc. **2.** In control. —*v.t.* **1.** To move or convey on wheels. **2.** To cause to turn on or as on an axis; pivot or revolve. **3.** To perform with a circular movement. **4.** To provide with a wheel or wheels. —*v.i.* **5.** To turn on or as on an axis; rotate or revolve. **6.** To take a new direction or course of action: often with *about*. **7.** To move in a circular or spiral course. **8.** To move on wheels. —**to wheel and deal** *U.S. Slang* To act freely and independently, without restrictions, as in business. [OE *hwēol*]

wheel·bar·row (hwēl′bar′ō) *n.* A boxlike vehicle ordinarily with one wheel and two handles, for moving small loads. —*v.t.* To convey in a wheelbarrow.

wheel·base (hwēl′bās′) *n.* The distance from the center of a back hub to the center of the front hub on the same side, as in an automobile.

wheel·chair (hwēl′châr′) *n.* A mobile chair mounted between large wheels, for the use of invalids. Also **wheel chair.**

wheel·er (hwē′lər) *n.* **1.** One who wheels. **2.** A wheel horse or other draft animal working next to the wheel. **3.** Something furnished with a wheel or wheels: a *side-wheeler*.

wheel·er-deal·er (hwē′lər-dē′lər) *n. U.S. Slang* One who wheels and deals; a shrewd, quick-witted person.

wheel horse 1. A horse harnessed to the pole or shafts when there is a leader or leaders in front. **2.** One who does the heaviest work or assumes the greatest responsibility.

wheel·house (hwēl′hous′) *n.* A pilothouse.

wheel of fortune The wheel represented as being turned in order to bring about changes in human destiny, and that symbolizes the uncertainty of fate.

wheel·wright (hwēl′rīt′) *n.* A man whose business is making or repairing wheels.

wheeze (hwēz) *v.t. & v.i.* **wheezed, wheez·ing** To breathe or utter with a husky, whistling sound. —*n.* **1.** A wheezing sound. **2.** A loud whisper. **3.** *Informal* A popular tale, saying, or trick, esp. a trite one. [Prob. < ON *hvǣsa* hiss] —**wheez′er** *n.* —**wheez′ing·ly** *adv.*

wheez·y (hwē′zē) *adj.* **wheez·i·er, wheez·i·est** Affected with or characterized by wheezing. —**wheez′i·ly** *adv.* —**wheez′i·ness** *n.*

whelk¹ (hwelk) *n.* Any of various large marine mollusks having whorled shells, that burrow in sand, esp. the common whelk, much eaten in Europe. [OE *weoloc*]

whelk[2] (hwelk) n. A swelling, protuberance, or pustule. [OE *hwylca* pustule] **—whelk'y** adj.

whelm (hwelm) v.t. 1. To cover with water or other fluid; submerge; engulf. 2. To overpower; overwhelm. —v.i. 3. To roll with engulfing force. [Prob. blend of OE *helmian* to cover and *gehwielfan* to bend over]

whelp (hwelp) n. 1. One of the young of a dog, wolf, lion, or other beast. 2. A dog. 3. A young fellow: a contemptuous term. —v.t. & v.i. To give birth (to): said of dogs, lions, etc. [OE *hwelp*]

when (hwen) adv. 1. At what or which time: *When* did you arrive? I know *when* he arrived. 2. At which: the time *when* we went on a picnic. —conj. 1. At what or which time: They watched until midnight, *when* they fell asleep. 2. As soon as: He laughed *when* he heard it. 3. Although: He walks *when* he might ride. 4. At the time that; while: *when* we were young. 5. If; considering that: How can I buy it *when* I have no money? 6. After which: We had just awakened *when* you called. —pron. What or which time: since *when*; until *when*. —n. The time; date: I don't know the *when* or the circumstances of it. [OE *hwanne, hwenne*]

whence (hwens) *Archaic* adv. From what place or source: *Whence* and what are you? —conj. 1. From what or which place, source, or cause; from which: the place *whence* these sounds arise. 2. To the place from which. 3. For which reason; wherefore. [ME < OE *hwanne* when]

whence·so·ev·er (hwens'sō·ev'ər) *Archaic* adv. & conj. From whatever place, cause, or source.

when·e'er (hwen'âr') adv. & conj. *Poetic* Whenever.

when·ev·er (hwen'ev'ər) adv. & conj. At whatever time.

when·so·ev·er (hwen'sō·ev'ər) adv. & conj. Whenever.

where (hwâr) adv. 1. At or in what place, relation, or situation: *Where* is my book? 2. To what place or end: *Where* are you going? 3. From what place: *Where* did you get that hat? 4. At or in which place: *where* men gather. 5. To a place or situation in or to which: Let us go *where* the mountains are. —conj. 1. At which place: Let us go home *where* we can relax. 2. With the condition that: xy = 4 *where* x = 2 and y = 2. —pron. 1. The place in which: The bear passed three yards from *where* we stood. 2. The point at which: That's *where* you are wrong. —n. Place; locality. ◆ *Where* has absorbed completely the sense of *whither* but not of *whence.* We must use a preposition to express the idea of motion from a place: *Where* did you come from? We do not use a preposition to show place at which: *Where* is the dog *at?* is not accepted in standard usage. [OE *hwǣr*]

where·a·bouts (hwâr'ə·bouts') adv. Near or at what place; about where. —n.pl. (construed as sing.) The place in or near which a person or thing is.

where·as (hwâr'az') conj. 1. Since the facts are such as they are; seeing that: used in the preamble of a resolution, etc. 2. The fact of the matter being that; when in truth: implying opposition to a previous statement. —n. pl. ·as·es A clause or item beginning with the word "whereas."

where·at (hwâr'at') *Archaic* or *Rare* adv. At what: *Whereat* are you angry? —conj. At which; for which reason.

where·by (hwâr'bī') adv. 1. By means of which; through which: the gate *whereby* he entered. 2. By what; how.

wher·e'er (hwâr'âr') adv. *Poetic* Wherever.

where·fore (hwâr'fôr', -fōr') *Archaic* adv. For what reason; why: *Wherefore* do you doubt me? —conj. For which reason: It began to rain, *wherefore* we called off the picnic.

where·from (hwâr'frum', -from') *Archaic* adv. Whence.

where·in (hwâr'in') adv. 1. In what: *Wherein* is the error? 2. In which: a marriage *wherein* there is discord.

where·of (hwâr'uv', -ov') *Archaic* adv. 1. Of or from what: *Whereof* did you partake? 2. Of which or whom.

where·on (hwâr'on', -ôn') *Archaic* adv. On what or on which.

where·so·ev·er (hwâr'sō·ev'ər) *Archaic* adv. & conj. In or to whatever place; wherever.

where·to (hwâr'tōō') *Archaic* adv. To what place or end: *Whereto* serves avarice? —conj. To which or to whom.

where·up·on (hwâr'ə·pon', -ə·pôn') adv. *Archaic* Upon what; whereon. —conj. Upon which or whom; in consequence of which; after which: *whereupon* they took in sail.

wher·ev·er (hwâr'ev'ər) adv. & conj. In, at, or to whatever place; wheresoever.

where·with (hwâr'with', -with') *Archaic* adv. Interrogatively, with what: *Wherewith* shall I do it? —conj. With which; by means of which: the food *wherewith* we abated hunger. —pron. That with or by which: with the infinitive: I have not *wherewith* to do it.

where·with·al (hwâr'with·ôl') n. The necessary means or resources; esp., the necessary money: with the definite article.

wher·ry (hwer'ē) n. pl. ·ries 1. A light, fast rowboat used on inland waters. 2. *Brit.* A fishing vessel with two sails. 3. A rowboat for racing or exercise, built for one person. 4. *Brit.* A very broad, light barge. —v.t. & v.i. ·ried, ·ry·ing To transport in or use a wherry. [Origin unknown]

whet (hwet) v.t. **whet·ted, whet·ting** 1. To sharpen, as a knife, by friction. 2. To make more keen or eager; excite, stimulate, as the appetite. —n. 1. The act of whetting. 2. Something that whets. [OE *hwettan*] **—whet'ter** n.

wheth·er (hweth'ər) conj. 1. If it be the case that: used to introduce an indirect question, often with the negative being implied: Tell me *whether* you are considering our plan. 2. In case; in either case: as the first alternative, followed by a correlative *or,* or *or whether: Whether* it rains or (*whether*) it snows, the roads become very slippery. 3. Either: *Wheth*- by luck or sheer determination, he will probably succee —whether or no In any case. [OE *hwæther*]

whet·stone (hwet'stōn') n. A fine-grained stone for whe ting knives, axes, etc.

whew (hwōō, hwyōō) *interj.* An exclamatory sound, e pressive of amazement, dismay, relief, admiration, etc.

whey (hwā) n. A clear, straw-colored liquid that separat from the curd when milk is curdled, as in making chee [OE *hwæg*] **—whey'ey, whey'ish** adj.

whey·face (hwā'fās') n. A pale, sallow face; also, a pers having such a face. **—whey'faced'** adj.

which (hwich) pron. & adj. 1. What particular person thing or collection of persons or things of a certain cla *Which* (or *which* apples) do you want? We don't know wh (or *which* story) to believe. 2. The thing designated; it relative pronoun whose antecedents refer now only to a mals or objects; that: the story *which* we preferred. *Which* sometimes has an entire clause or sentence as its an cedent: He raised his hand, *which* surprised me. See a usage note under WHO. [OE *hwilc*]

which·ev·er (hwich'ev'ər) pron. One or another (of t or of several). —adj. No matter which. Also **which'** ev'er.

whiff (hwif) n. 1. Any sudden or slight gust or puff of 2. A gust or puff of odor: a *whiff* of onions. 3. A single pulsion or inhalation of breath or smoke from the mou puff. —v.t. 1. To drive or blow with a whiff or puff. 2. exhale or inhale in whiffs. 3. To smell or sniff. 4. smoke, as a pipe. —v.i. 5. To blow or move in whiffs puffs. 6. To exhale or inhale whiffs. [Prob. ult. imit.] **whiff'er** n.

whif·fet (hwif'it) n. *Informal* 1. A trifling, useless pers 2. A small, snappish dog. [? Dim. of WHIFF]

whif·fle (hwif'əl) v. **·fled, ·fling** v.i. 1. To blow with pu or gusts; shift about, as the wind. 2. To vacillate; veer. v.t. 3. To blow or dissipate with or as with a puff. [Freq. WHIFF] **—whif'fler** n. **—whif'fler·y** n.

whif·fle·tree (hwif'əl·trē') n. A horizontal crossbar which the ends of the traces of a harness are attached: a called *singletree, swingletree, whippletree.* [Var. of WHIPPI TREE]

Whig (hwig) n. 1. An American colonist who support the Revolutionary War in the 18th century in opposition the Tories. 2. A member of an American political par (1834-1855) formed in opposition to the Democratic Par and in 1856 succeeded by the Republican Party. 3. England, a member of a more or less liberal political par in the 18th and 19th centuries, opposed to the Tories a later known as the Liberal Party. —adj. Consisting of supported by Whigs. [< ? *Whiggamore* < dial. E (Scotti < *Whig,* a cry to urge on a horse + *mere* horse] **— Wh ger·y** n. **— Whig'gish** adj. **— Whig'gish·ly** adv. **— Wh gish·ness** n. **— Whig'gism** n.

while (hwīl) n. 1. A short time; also, any period of tin Stay and rest a *while.* 2. Time or pains expended on a thi only in the phrase **worth while** or **worth one's while.** **between whiles** From time to time. **— the while** At the sa time. —conj. 1. During the time that; as long as. 2. the same time; although: *While* he found fault, he a praised. 3. Whereas: This man is short, *while* that one tall. ◆ This sense is widely used and is generally conside standard, although some authorities still disapprove of —v.t. **whiled, whil·ing** To cause (time) to pass lightly a pleasantly: usu. with *away.* [OE *hwil*]

whiles (hwīlz) *Archaic* or *Dial.* adv. 1. Occasionally. In the meantime. —conj. While; during the time that

whi·lom (hwī'ləm) *Archaic* adj. Former. —adv. For erly. [OE *hwīlum* at times, dative pl. of *hwīl* a while]

whilst (hwīlst) conj. *Chiefly Brit.* While.

whim (hwim) n. A sudden or unexpected notion or fanc idea; caprice. [Short for earlier *whim-wham* trifle]

whim·per (hwim'pər) v.i. 1. To cry or whine with pla tive broken sounds. —v.t. 2. To utter with a whimper. n. A low, broken, whining cry; whine. [Imit.] **— whi per·er** n. **— whim'per·ing** n. **— whim'per·ing·ly** adv.

whim·si·cal (hwim'zi·kəl) adj. 1. Having eccentric ide capricious. 2. Oddly constituted; fantastic; quaint. **whim'si·cal'i·ty** (-kal'ə·tē) n. **— whim'si·cal·ly** adv. **whim'si·cal·ness** n.

whim·sy (hwim'zē) n. pl. ·sies 1. A whim. 2. Quai fanciful humor, as in a literary work. Also **whim'sey.**

hin (hwin) *n.* Furze. [Prob. < Scand.]

hine (hwīn) *v.* **whined, whin·ing** *v.i.* **1.** To utter a low, laintive sound expressive of grief, peevishness, etc. **2.** To omplain in a tiresome or childish way. —*v.t.* **3.** To utter ith a whine. —*n.* The act or sound of whining. [OE *winan*] —**whin′er** *n.* —**whin′ing·ly** *adv.* —**whin′y** *adj.*

hin·ny (hwin′ē) *v.* **·nied, ·ny·ing** *v.i.* **1.** To neigh, esp. a low or gentle way. —*v.t.* **2.** To express with a whinny. —*n.* *pl.* **·nies** A neigh, esp. if low and gentle. [< WHINE]

ip (hwip) *v.* **whipped** or **whipt, whip·ping** *v.t.* **1.** To rike with a lash, rod, strap, etc. **2.** To punish by striking us; flog. **3.** To drive or urge with lashes or blows: with *on, o, off,* etc. **4.** To strike in the manner of a whip: The wind *hipped* the trees. **5.** To beat, as eggs or cream, to a froth. To seize, move, jerk, throw, etc., with a sudden motion: ith *away, in, off, out,* etc. **7.** In fishing, to make repeated asts upon the surface of (a stream, etc.). **8.** To wrap ope, cable, etc.) with light line so as to prevent chafing or ear. **9.** To wrap or bind about something. **10.** To sew, a flat seam, with a loose overcast or overhand stitch. **11.** *S. Informal* To defeat; overcome. —*v.i.* **12.** To go, me, move, or turn suddenly and quickly: with *away, in, , out,* etc. **13.** To thrash about in a manner suggestive of whip: pennants *whipping* in the wind. —**to whip up 1.** o excite; arouse. **2.** *Informal* To prepare quickly, as a eal. —*n.* **1.** An instrument consisting of a lash attached a handle, used for driving draft animals or for administer-g punishment. **2.** One who handles a whip expertly, as a iver. **3.** A stroke, blow, or lashing motion with, or as th, a whip. **4.** In politics, a member of a legislative body, Congress or Parliament, appointed unofficially to enforce e discipline and look after the interests of his party. **5.** dish or dessert containing cream or eggs and usu. fruit, ipped to a froth. [ME *wippen*] —**whip′per** *n.*

ip·cord (hwip′kôrd′) *n.* **1.** A strong, hard-twisted or aided hempen cord, used in making whiplashes. **2.** A orsted fabric with a pronounced diagonal rib.

ip hand 1. The hand that wields the whip in riding or iving. **2.** An instrument or means of mastery; advantage.

ip·lash (hwip′lash′) *n.* The lash of a whip.

iplash injury An injury to the neck caused by a sudden arking, as in an automobile collision.

ip·per·snap·per (hwip′ər·snap′ər) *n.* A pretentious but significant person, esp. a young one. [? Extension of *ipsnapper* a cracker of whips]

ip·pet (hwip′it) *n.* A small, swift breed of dog, probably cross between a greyhound and a terrier, used esp. in rac-g and coursing. [Dim. of WHIP]

ip·ping (hwip′ing) *n.* **1.** The act of one who or that ich whips; esp., a flogging. **2.** Cord or other material ed to whip or lash parts together.

ipping boy Anyone who receives punishment deserved another; scapegoat.

ipping post The post to which those sentenced to gging are secured.

ip·ple·tree (hwip′əl·trē′) *n.* A whiffletree. [Prob. < HIP]

ip·poor·will (hwip′ər·wil) *n.* A small nocturnal bird ied to the goatsuckers, common in the eastern U.S. [Imit. its reiterated cry]

ip·saw (hwip′sô′) *n.* A long, narrow, tapering saw, ounted in a wooden frame. —*v.t.* **·sawed, ·sawed** or **wn, ·saw·ing 1.** To saw with a whipsaw. **2.** To get the st of (an opponent) in spite of every effort he makes.

ip·stitch (hwip′stich′) *v.t.* To sew or gather with over-st stitches. —*n.* A stitch made in this way.

ip·stock (hwip′stok′) *n.* The handle of a whip.

ir (hwûr) *v.t. & v.i.* **whirred, whir·ring** To fly, move, or irl with a buzzing sound. —*n.* **1.** A whizzing, swishing und, as that caused by the sudden rising of birds. **2.** Con-sion; bustle. Also *Brit.* **whirr.** [Prob. < Scand.]

irl (hwûrl) *v.i.* **1.** To turn or revolve rapidly, as about a nter. **2.** To turn away or aside quickly. **3.** To move or swiftly. **4.** To have a sensation of spinning: My head irls. —*v.t.* **5.** To cause to turn or revolve rapidly. **6.** carry or bear along with a revolving motion: The wind irled the dust into the air. —*n.* **1.** A swift rotating or volving motion. **2.** Something whirling. **3.** A state of nfusion; turmoil. **4.** A rapid succession of events, social tivities, etc. **5.** *Informal* A brief drive or trip. **6.** *Infor-l* A try. [Prob. < ON *hvirfla* to revolve] —**whirl′er** *n.*

irl·i·gig (hwûr′lə·gig′) *n.* **1.** Any toy or small device at revolves rapidly on an axis. **2.** A merry-go-round. **3.** ything that moves in a cycle. **4.** A whirling motion. [< *irly* (< WHIRL) + obs. *gig,* a whirling toy]

irl·pool (hwûrl′pōōl′) *n.* **1.** A vortex where water oves with a whirling motion, as from the meeting of two rrents. **2.** Anything resembling the motion of a whirlpool.

whirl·wind (hwûrl′wind′) *n.* **1.** A funnel-shaped column of air, with a rapid, upward spiral motion and moving for-ward on the surface of the land or sea. **2.** Anything re-sembling a whirlwind, as rotary motion or violent activity. —*adj.* Extremely swift or impetuous: a *whirlwind* courtship.

whish (hwish) *v.i.* To move with a swishing, whistling sound. —*n.* A swishing sound. [Imit.]

whisk (hwisk) *v.t.* **1.** To bear along or sweep with light movements, as of a small broom: often with *away* or about. **2.** To cause to move with a quick sweeping motion. **3.** *Chiefly Brit.* To beat with a quick movement, as eggs, etc. —*v.i.* **4.** To move quickly and lightly. —*n.* **1.** A sudden, sweep-ing movement. **2.** A little broom or brush. **3.** *Chiefly Brit.* A small culinary instrument for rapidly whipping (cream, etc.) to a froth. [Prob. < Scand.]

whisk·broom (hwisk′brōōm′, -brŏŏm′) *n.* A small, short-handled broom for brushing clothing, etc.

whisk·er (hwis′kər) *n.* **1.** *pl.* The hair that grows on the sides of a man's face, as distinguished from that on his lips, chin, and throat; loosely, the beard or any part of the beard. **2.** A hair from the whiskers or beard. **3.** One of the long, bristly hairs on the sides of the mouth of some animals, as cats and rodents. —**whisk′ered, whisk′er·y** *adj.*

whis·key (hwis′kē) *n.* *pl.* **·keys 1.** An alcoholic liquor obtained by the distillation of certain fermented grains, as rye, barley, corn, etc., and containing about 40 to 50 per-cent of alcohol. **2.** A drink of whiskey. —*adj.* Pertaining to or made of whiskey. Also **whis′ky.** [Short for *usque-baugh* < Irish, water of life < *uisge* water + *beatha* life]

whis·per (hwis′pər) *n.* **1.** A low, soft, breathy voice. **2.** A low, rustling sound. **3.** *Phonet.* The sound produced by the passage of breath through the partially closed glottis. **4.** A whispered utterance; secret communication; hint; insinua-tion. —*v.i.* **1.** To speak in a whisper. **2.** To talk cau-tiously or furtively; plot or gossip. **3.** To make a low, rustling sound. —*v.t.* **4.** To utter in a whisper. **5.** To speak to in a whisper. [OE *hwisprian*] —**whis′per·er** *n.* —**whis′per·ing** *adj. & n.* —**whis′per·ing·ly** *adv.*

whispering campaign A deliberate spreading of rumors in order to discredit a person or group.

whist[1] (hwist) *n.* A game of cards, the forerunner of bridge, played by four persons. [Alter. of earlier *whisk*]

whist[2] (hwist) *interj.* Hush! be still! —*adj.* Silent or quiet.

whis·tle (hwis′əl) *v.* **·tled, ·tling** *v.i.* **1.** To make a musical tone, usu. shrill, by sending the breath through the teeth or through a small orifice formed by contracting the lips. **2.** To emit a sharp, shrill cry, as some birds and animals. **3.** To cause a sharp, shrill sound by swift passage through the air, as wind, etc. **4.** To blow or sound a whistle. —*v.t.* **5.** To produce (a tune) by whistling. **6.** To call, manage, or direct by whistling. **7.** To send or move with a whistling sound. —**to whistle for** To go without; fail to get. —*n.* **1.** A device for producing a shrill tone by forcing a current of air, etc., through a pipe or tube with a narrowed aperture, or against a thin edge. **2.** A whistling sound. **3.** The act of whistling. **4.** *Slang* The mouth and throat: to wet one's *whistle.* [OE *hwistle* shrill pipe]

whis·tler (hwis′lər) *n.* **1.** One who or that which whistles. **2.** Any of various birds so called from the noise of their wings in flight. **3.** A radio signal of very low frequency generated by atmospheric electricity.

whistle stop *U.S. Informal* A small town, where a train stops only on signal. —**whis·tle-stop** (hwis′əl·stop′) *adj.*

whit (hwit) *n.* The smallest particle; speck: not a *whit* abashed. [Var. of *wight* < OE *wiht* a certain amount]

white (hwīt) *adj.* **whit·er, whit·est 1.** Having the color produced by reflection of all of the visible solar spectrum, as from a bed of new-fallen snow. **2.** Light or comparatively light in color. **3.** Bloodless; ashen: *white* with rage. **4.** Very fair; blond. **5.** Silvery or gray. **6.** Snowy. **7.** Hab-ited in white clothing: *white* nuns. **8.** Not intentionally wicked; not harmful: a *white* lie. **9.** Free from spot or stain; innocent. **10.** Incandescent: *white* heat. **11.** Blank; un-marked by ink. **12.** Belonging to a racial group character-ized by light-colored skin; esp., Caucasian. **13.** Of, pertain-ing to, or controlled by white men: the *white* power structure. **14.** *Informal* Fair and honorable; honest. **15.** Designating any of various wines ranging in color from pale yellow to deep amber. —*n.* **1.** The color seen when light is reflected with-out sensible absorption of any of the visible rays of the spec-trum; the color of new-fallen snow. **2.** The state or condition of being white. **3.** *Biol.* The white or light-colored part of something, as the albumen of egg or the white part of the eyeball. **4.** A white or light-colored thing, as a white fabric, a white pigment, etc. **5.** *pl.* A white uniform or outfit: a sailor's summer *whites.* **6.** A member of the so-called white race. —*v.t.* **whit·ed, whit·ing** To make white; whiten. [OE *hwīt*] —**white′ly** *adv.* —**white′ness** *n.*

white ant Loosely, a termite.

white·bait (hwīt′bāt′) *n.* The young of various fishes, esp. of sprat and herring, netted in great quantities and much esteemed in Europe as a delicacy.

white bear The polar bear.

white birch 1. Birch. 2. The common European birch, having an ash-colored bark.

white·cap (hwīt′kap′) *n.* A wave with a crest of foam.

white cedar 1. An evergreen tree of the pine family, growing in moist places along the Atlantic coast: also called *cypress.* 2. Its soft, easily worked wood.

white clover A common variety of clover, with white flowers.

white coal Water considered as a source of power.

white-collar (hwīt′kol′ər) *adj.* Designating workers, jobs, attitudes, etc., associated with clerical, professional, and other nonmanual occupations.

whit·ed sepulcher (hwī′tid) A hypocrite. *Matt.* xxiii 27.

white elephant 1. A rare, pale gray variety of Asian elephant held sacred by the Burmese and Siamese. 2. Anything rare but expensive to keep. 3. Any burdensome possession.

white-faced (hwīt′fāst′) *adj.* 1. Pallid in countenance; pale. 2. Having a white mark or spot on the face or front of the head, as a horse. 3. Having a white facing or exposed surface.

white·fish (hwīt′fish′) *n. pl.* **·fish** or **·fish·es** 1. Any of various food fishes of North America, living mostly in lakes, some species of which are called chubs. 2. Any of various other fish having a silvery appearance, as the beluga. 3. A tropical marine food fish of California.

white flag 1. A flag of truce. 2. A white flag or cloth hoisted as a signal of surrender during a battle.

White Friar A Carmelite friar: so called from the color of his cloak.

white gold An alloy of gold with a white metal, usu. nickel and zinc, sometimes palladium and platinum.

white goods Household linens, such as sheets, towels, etc.

White·hall (hwīt′hôl′) 1. A street in Westminster, London, where a number of government offices are located. 2. The British government.

white heat 1. The temperature at which a body becomes incandescent. 2. Great excitement, intense emotion, etc.

white horse A wave crested with foam; whitecap.

white-hot (hwīt′hot′) *adj.* 1. Exhibiting the condition of white heat. 2. *Informal* Extremely angry.

White House, The 1. The official residence of the President of the U.S., at Washington, D.C., a white, colonial style building: officially called the *Executive Mansion.* 2. The executive branch of the U.S. government.

white lead A heavy, white, poisonous mixture of lead carbonate and lead oxide, used as a pigment and in some medicinal ointments for burns.

white lie See under LIE.

white-liv·ered (hwīt′liv′ərd) *adj.* 1. Having a pale and unhealthy look. 2. Base; cowardly.

white man 1. A person belonging to a racial group characterized by light-colored skin. 2. A male member of the so-called white race.

white man's burden The alleged duty of the white peoples to spread culture among the so-called backward peoples of the world: phrase originated by Rudyard Kipling.

white matter *Anat.* The portion of the brain and spinal cord composed mainly of medullated nerve fibers, giving it a white appearance.

white meat The light-colored meat or flesh of animals, as veal or the breast of turkey.

whit·en (hwīt′n) *v.t. & v.i.* To make or become white; blanch; bleach. — **whit′en·er** *n.*

— **Syn.** *Whiten, bleach,* and *blanch* mean to make nearly or completely white or colorless. *Whiten* implies overlay with a white paint or polish, while *bleach* and *blanch* refer to removal of color by sunlight, chemical agents, etc. Industrial products are *bleached,* while foodstuffs are *blanched.*

white oak 1. A North American oak of the eastern U.S. with long leaves having from five to nine entire, rounded lobes. 2. Any of several related species. 3. The wood of any species of white oak.

white pine 1. A pine widely distributed in eastern North America, with soft, bluish green leaves in clusters of five. The cone and tassel of this tree are the State emblem of Maine. 2. The light, soft wood of this tree. 3. Any of several similar species of pine.

white plague *Pathol.* Tuberculosis, esp. of the lungs.

white poplar A large, rapidly growing Old World tree, often planted in the U.S. for shade or for its ornamental green and silvery white leaves.

white potato The common potato.

white race The Caucasian ethnic division of mankind.

white rat One of a special breed of albino Norway rats much used in biological and medical experimentation.

White Russian Byelorussian.

white sale A sale of sheets, towels, etc., at reduced pri

white sauce A sauce made of butter, flour, milk, etc., u for vegetables, meats, and fish.

white slave A girl forced into or held in prostitution. **white-slave** (hwīt′slāv′) *adj.*

white slavery The business or practice of forced pro tution. — **white slaver**

white supremacy The doctrine arising from the be that the white race is superior to the Negro race and that latter must therefore be kept in an inferior economic a social position. — **white su·prem·a·cist** (sə-prem′ə-sist)

white-tailed deer (hwīt′tāld′) A common North Ameri deer, having a moderately long tail white on the undersi also called *Virginia deer.*

white-throat·ed sparrow (hwīt′thrō′tid) A comn North American sparrow, with a white patch on the thre

white tie 1. A white bow tie, worn with men's formal e ning attire. 2. A swallowtail coat and its correct accessor

white·wash (hwīt′wosh′, -wôsh′) *n.* 1. A mixture slaked lime and water, sometimes with salt, whiting, glue added, used for whitening walls, etc. 2. *Slang* A cov ing up or glossing over of reprehensible actions or ineffic cies, esp. of a political figure; also, a suppression of adv evidence, as in a legal matter. 3. *Informal* A failure score in a game. — *v.t.* 1. To coat with whitewash. *Slang* To gloss over; hide. 3. *Informal* In sports, to be without allowing the losing side to score. — **white′wash′e**

white water *U.S. & Canadian* Rapids in a river.

white whale The beluga.

whith·er (hwith′ər) *Archaic & Poetic adv.* 1. To wha which place? Where? 2. To what point, end, extent, e — *conj.* To which or what place, end, etc. [OE *hwider* **whith·er·so·ev·er** (hwith′ər-sō-ev′ər) *adv. Archaic* To wh ever place.

whit·ing (hwī′ting) *n.* A pure white chalk, powdered a washed, used in making putty and whitewash, as a pigme and for polishing.

whit·ish (hwī′tish) *adj.* Somewhat white or, esp., very li gray. — **whit′ish·ness** *n.*

whit·low (hwit′lō) *n. Pathol.* An inflammatory tun esp. on the terminal phalanx of a finger, seated between epidermis and true skin; a felon. [ME *whitflaw*]

Whit·mon·day (hwit′mun′dē, -dā) *n.* The Monday n following Whitsunday, observed in England as a holid Also **Whit-Monday, Whit′sun-Mon′day.**

Whit·sun (hwit′sən) *n.* Whitsunday: frequently used combination: *Whitsun-week.*

Whit·sun·day (hwit′sun′dē, -dā, hwit′sən-dā′) *n.* Per cost (def. 1). [OE *Hwíta Sunnandæg,* lit., white Sunday

Whit·sun·tide (hwit′sən-tīd′) *n.* The week that beg with Whitsunday, esp. the first three days. Also **Whit Tide.**

whit·tle (hwit′l) *v.* **·tled, ·tling** *v.t.* 1. To cut or shave from (wood, a stick, etc.). 2. To make or shape by carv or whittling. 3. To reduce or wear away by or as by pa a little at a time: with *down, off, away,* etc. — *v.i.* 4. whittle wood, usu. as an aimless diversion. [Alter. of N *thwitel* < OE *thwitan* to cut] — **whit′tler** *n.*

whit·tlings (hwit′lingz) *n.pl.* The fine chips and shavi made by a whittler.

whiz (hwiz) *v.* **whizzed, whiz·zing** *v.i.* 1. To make a hiss and humming sound while passing through the air. 2. move or pass with such a sound. — *v.t.* 3. To cause to wh — *n. pl.* **whiz·zes** 1. A whizzing sound. 2. *Slang* A person or thing of extraordinary excellence or ability. A **whizz.** [Imit.]

who (hoō) *pron. possessive case* **whose;** *objective case* **wh** 1. Which or what person or persons: *Who* said that? I kn *who* he is. 2. That; a relative pronoun: used when the an cedent refers to a human being. 3. He, she, or they th whoever: *Who* steals my purse steals my trash. — **as w should say** As if one should say. [OE *hwā*]

◆ In modern usage, *who* as a relative is applied only persons, *which* only to animals or to inanimate objects, to persons or things indiscriminately. The use of *whom* as interrogative pronoun in initial position, as in *Whom* did y see?, is supported by some grammarians, but the m natural *Who* did you see? *Who* did you give the book to? in wider use and are now considered acceptable. Howev when used after a verb or preposition, *whom* is still requir as in To *whom* did you give it? You saw *whom*?

whoa (hwō) *interj.* Stop! stand still! [Var. of HO]

who·dun·it (hoō-dun′it) *n. Informal* A type of myste fiction or dramatic production that challenges the rea or spectator to detect the perpetrator of a crime.

who·ev·er (hoō-ev′ər) *pron.* Any one without exception; a person who.

whole (hōl) *adj.* 1. Containing all the parts necessary make up a total; entire. 2. Having all the essential original parts unbroken and uninjured; intact. 3. In or ha ing regained sound health; hale. 4. Constituting the f

tent, amount, quantity, etc.; total; entire. **5.** Having the
me parents; full, as opposed to *half*: a *whole* brother. **6.**
ath. Integral. **— as a whole** Completely; altogether.
— on the whole Taking everything into consideration.
— out of whole cloth Fabricated; made up, without founda-
on in truth or fact. **—** *n.* **1.** All the parts or elements
tering into and making up a thing; totality. **2.** An organ-
of parts making a unity or system; an organism.
)E *hāl*] **— whole′ness** *n.*

ole blood Blood as taken directly from the body, esp.
at used in transfusions.

ole·heart·ed (hōl′här′tid) *adj.* Done or experienced
ith earnestness, sincerity, etc.; earnest. **— whole′heart′·**
·ly *adv.* **— whole′heart′ed·ness** *n.*

ole hog *Slang* The whole of anything; completeness. **—**
go the whole hog *Slang* To do something thoroughly;
come involved without reservation.

ole milk Milk containing all its constituents.

ole note *Music* A note having a time value equal to
e half of a breve: also, *Chiefly Brit., semibreve.*

ole number *Math.* An integer.

ole·sale (hōl′sāl′) *n.* The selling of goods in large bulk
quantity, esp. for resale: distinguished from *retail.* **—**
j. **1.** Pertaining to, involving, or engaged in the sale of
ods at wholesale. **2.** Made or done on a large scale or in-
scriminately: *wholesale* murder. **—** *adv.* **1.** In bulk or
antity. **2.** Indiscriminately. **—** *v.t. & v.i.* **·saled, ·sal·**
g To sell at wholesale. [ME < *by hole sale* in large quan-
ies] **— whole′sal′er** *n.*

ole·some (hōl′səm) *adj.* **1.** Tending to promote health;
ubrious; healthful: *wholesome* air or food. **2.** Favorable
virtue and well-being; beneficial: *wholesome* entertain-
ent. **3.** Indicative or characteristic of health: *wholesome*
d cheeks. **4.** Safe; free from danger or risk. [ME *holsum*]
whole′some·ly *adv.* **— whole′some·ness** *n.*

ole tone *Music* A tone (def. 3b).

ole-wheat (hōl′hwēt′) *adj.* Made from wheat grain
d bran.

o′ll (hōol) **1.** Who will. **2.** Who shall.

ol·ly (hō′lē, hōl′lē) *adv.* **1.** Completely; totally. **2.** Ex-
asively; only.

om (hōom) *pron.* The objective case of WHO.

om·ev·er (hōom′ev′ər), **whom·so** (hōom′sō′), **whom·**
·ev·er (hōom′sō·ev′ər) Objective cases of WHOEVER,
HOSO, etc.

oop (hōop, hwōop, hwoōp) *v.i.* **1.** To utter loud cries,
of excitement, rage, or exultation. **2.** To hoot, as an owl.
To make a loud, gasping inspiration, as after a paroxysm
coughing. **—** *v.t.* **4.** To utter with a whoop or whoops.
To call, urge, chase, etc., with whoops; hoot. **— to**
oop up *Slang* To arouse enthusiasm in or for. **— to**
oop it (or **things**) **up** *Slang* **1.** To make noisy revelry.
To arouse enthusiasm. **—** *n.* The cry, shout, or sound
one who or that which whoops. **— not worth a whoop**
formal Not worth anything. **—** *interj.* An exclamation of
y, enthusiasm, etc. [ME *whope*]

oop·ee (hwōo′pē, hwōop′ē) *interj. & n.* An exclamation
joy, excitement, etc. **— to make whoopee** To have a
isy, festive time. [< WHOOP?]

oop·er (hōo′pər, hwōo′pər, hwōo′p′r) *n.* **1.** One who or
at which whoops. **2.** A large Old World swan: so called
om its loud cry.

oop·ing cough (hōo′ping, hōop′ing) *Pathol.* A con-
gious respiratory disease of bacterial origin chiefly affect-
g children, marked in its final stage by violent coughing.

op (hwop) *Informal n.* A blow or fall, or the resulting
ise. **—** *v.* **whopped, whop·ping** *v.t.* **1.** To strike or beat.
To defeat convincingly. **—** *v.i.* **3.** To drop or fall sud-
nly; flop. [Prob. imit.]

op·per (hwop′ər) *n. Informal* Something large or
markable; esp., a big falsehood.

op·ping (hwop′ing) *adj.* Unusually large; great.

ore (hôr, hōr) *n.* A prostitute. **—** *v.i.* **whored, whor·ing**
To have illicit sexual intercourse, esp. with a prostitute.
To be a whore. [OE *hōre*, prob. < ON *hōra*]

ore·house (hôr′hous′, hōr′-) *n.* A house of prostitution.

ore·mas·ter (hôr′mas′tər, -mäs′-, hōr′-) *n. Archaic*
A procurer. **2.** A man who has intercourse with whores.

ore·mon·ger (hôr′mung′gər, -mong′-, hōr′-).

or·ish (hôr′ish, hōr′ish) *adj.* Characteristic of a whore;
vd. **— whor′ish·ly** *adv.* **— whor′ish·ness** *n.*

orl (hwûrl, hwôrl) *n.* **1.** The flywheel of a
spindle. **2.** *Bot.* A set of leaves, etc., on
e same plane with one another, distributed
a circle. **3.** *Zool.* A turn or volution, as
a spiral shell. **4.** Any of the convoluted
lges of a fingerprint. [ME *wharwyl, whor-*
il]

 WHORL (def. 2)

whorled (hwûrld, hwôrld) *adj.* Furnished with or arranged
in whorls.

whor·tle·ber·ry (hwûr′təl·ber′ē) *n. pl.* **·ries 1.** A European variety of blueberry. **2.** Its blue-black fruit. Also
called *bilberry.* [< OE *horta* + BERRY]

whose (hōoz) The possessive case of WHO and often of
WHICH. [ME < OE *hwæs*, altered by analogy with nominative form *hwo*]

whose·so·ev·er (hōoz′sō·ev′ər) Possessive case of WHO-
SOEVER.

who·so (hōo′sō) *pron.* Whoever; any person who. [Re-
duced form of OE *swā hwā swā*]

who·so·ev·er (hōo′sō·ev′ər) *pron.* Any person whatever;
who; whoever.

why (hwī) *adv.* **1.** For what cause, purpose, or reason?
wherefore? **2.** The reason or cause for which: I don't know
why he went. **3.** Because of which; for which: I know no
reason *why* he went. **—** *n. pl.* **whys 1.** An explanatory
cause; reason; cause. **2.** A puzzling problem; riddle; enigma. **—** *interj.* An introductory expletive, sometimes denoting surprise. ◆ The *why* in the expression *the reason why,*
though sometimes condemned as a redundancy, is commonly used in standard written English. [OE *hwȳ, hwī,*
instrumental case of *hwæt* what]

wich (wich) *n.* The wych-elm.

wich-elm (wich′elm′) See WYCH-ELM.

wick (wik) *n.* A wand of loosely twisted or woven fibers,
as in a candle or lamp, acting by capillary attraction to
convey oil or other illuminant to a flame. [OE *wēoce*]

wick·ed (wik′id) *adj.* **1.** Evil in principle and practice; vicious; sinful; depraved. **2.** Mischievous; roguish. **3.** Noxious; pernicious. **4.** Troublesome; painful. **5.** *Informal*
Done with great skill: a *wicked* game. [ME, alter. of *wikke,*
wicke] **— wick′ed·ly** *adv.* **— wick′ed·ness** *n.*

wick·er (wik′ər) *adj.* Made of twigs, osiers, etc. **—** *n.* **1.** A
pliant young shoot or rod; twig; osier. **2.** Wickerwork.
[Prob. < Scand.]

wick·er·work (wik′ər·wûrk′) *n.* A fabric or texture, as a
basket, made of woven twigs, osiers, etc.; basketwork.

wick·et (wik′it) *n.* **1.** A small door or gate subsidiary to or
made within a larger entrance. **2.** A small opening in a door.
3. A small sluice gate in a canal lock or at the end of a millrace. **4.** In cricket: **a** An arrangement of three stumps set
near together, with two bails laid over the top. **b** The place
at which the wicket is set up. **c** The right or turn of each
batsman at the wicket. **d** The playing pitch between the
wickets: a fast *wicket.* **e** An inning that is not finished or not
begun. **5.** In croquet, any one of the arches, usu. of wire,
through which the ball must be hit. [< AF *wiket*, OF *gui-*
chet, prob. < Gmc.]

wick·et-keep·er (wik′it·kē′pər) *n.* In cricket, the fielder
stationed behind the wicket that is being bowled at.

wide (wīd) *adj.* **wid·er, wid·est 1.** Having relatively great
extent between sides; broad. **2.** Extended far in every direction; ample; spacious: a *wide* expanse. **3.** Having a specified degree of width or breadth: an inch *wide.* **4.** Distant
from the desired or proper point by a great extent of space;
remote; wild: *wide* of the mark. **5.** Having intellectual
breadth; liberal: a man of *wide* views. **6.** Fully open; expanded or extended: *wide* eyes. **7.** Comprehensive; inclusive: *wide* learning. **8.** Loose; roomy: *wide* breeches. **—** *n.*
1. In cricket, a ball bowled too far over or on either side of
the wicket to be within the batsman's reach. **2.** Breadth of
extent; also, a broad, open space. **—** *adv.* **1.** To a great
distance; extensively. **2.** Far from the mark. **3.** To the
greatest extent; fully open. [OE *wīd*] **— wide′ly** *adv.* **—**
wide′ness *n.*

wide-an·gle lens (wīd′ang′gəl) *Photog.* A type of lens permitting an angle of view wider than that of the ordinary lens.

wide-a·wake (wīd′ə·wāk′) *adj.* **1.** Fully awake. **2.**
Marked by vigilance and alertness; keen.

wide-eyed (wīd′īd′) *adj.* With the eyes wide open, as in
wonder or surprise.

wid·en (wīd′ən) *v.t. & v.i.* To make or become wide or wider.
— wid′en·er *n.*

wide-o·pen (wīd′ō′pən) *adj.* **1.** Opened wide. **2.** *Informal*
Remiss in the enforcement of laws that regulate various
forms of vice, as gambling, etc.: a *wide-open* city.

wide-screen (wīd′skrēn′) *adj.* Designating a motion-picture process using an elongated screen designed to accommodate various systems of projection beyond 35 mm.

wide·spread (wīd′spred′) *adj.* **1.** Extending over a large
space or territory. **2.** Occurring, accepted, etc., among
many people; general: a *widespread* belief. Also **wide-spread′,**
wide′spread′ing.

widg·eon (wij′ən) *n.* Any of various river ducks with short
bill and wedge-shaped tail. [Cf. MF *vigeon* wild duck]

wid·ow (wid′ō) *n.* **1.** A woman who has lost her husband by death and has not remarried. **2.** In some card games, an additional hand dealt to the table; also, a kitty. **3.** *Printing* An incomplete line of type at the top of a page or column. — *v.t.* **1.** To make a widow of; deprive of a husband: usu. in the past participle. **2.** To deprive of something desirable; bereave. [OE *widewe, wuduwe*]

wid·ow·er (wid′ō·ər) *n.* A man whose wife is dead, and who has not married again. [ME < OE *widewe* widow]

wid·ow·hood (wid′ō·hŏŏd) *n.* The state or period of being a widow, or, rarely, of being a widower.

widow's mite A small but selfless contribution from one who can hardly afford it. *Mark* xii 42.

widow's peak A hairline growing in a V-shaped point from the forehead.

widow's walk A railed observation area built on the roof of a home near the sea giving the observer a clear view of incoming vessels: also called *captain's walk*.

width (width) *n.* **1.** Dimension or measurement of an object taken from side to side, and at right angles to the length. **2.** The state or fact of being wide; breadth. **3.** Something that has width; esp., one of the several pieces of material used in making a garment. [< WIDE]

width·wise (width′wīz′) *adv.* In the direction of the width; from side to side. Also **width′way′** (-wā′), **width′ways′**.

wield (wēld) *v.t.* **1.** To handle, as a weapon or instrument, esp. with full command and effect. **2.** To exercise (authority, power, etc.). [Fusion of OE *wealdan* to rule and OE *wieldan* to conquer] — **wield′a·ble** *adj.* — **wield′er** *n.*

wield·y (wēl′dē) *adj.* **wield·i·er, wield·i·est** Easily handled or managed; manageable.

wie·ner (wē′nər) *n. U.S.* A kind of sausage, often shorter than a frankfurter, made of beef and pork. Also **wie·nie** (wē′nē), **wie·ner·wurst** (wē′nər·wûrst′, *Ger.* vē′nər·vōōrst′). [Short for G *Wiener-wurst* Vienna sausage]

Wie·ner schnit·zel (vē′nər schnit′səl) A breaded veal cutlet, seasoned or garnished in any of several ways. [< G < *Wiener* Viennese + *schnitzel* cutlet, dim. of *schnitz* slice]

wife (wīf) *n. pl.* **wives** (wīvz) **1.** A woman joined to a man in lawful wedlock. ◆ Collateral adjective: *uxorial.* **2.** *Archaic* A grown woman; adult female: now usu. in combination or in certain phrases: *housewife*, old *wives'* tales. — **to take (a woman) to wife** To marry (a woman). [OE *wīf*] — **wife′dom, wife′hood** *n.* — **wife′ly** *adj.*

wig (wig) *n.* An artificial covering of hair for the head. — *v.t.* **wigged, wig·ging 1.** *Rare* To furnish with a wig or wigs. **2.** *Brit. Informal* To censure severely; berate or scold, esp. in public. [Short for PERIWIG]

wig·ging (wig′ing) *n. Brit. Informal* A rebuke; a scolding.

wig·gle (wig′əl) *v.t. & v.i.* **·gled, ·gling** To move or cause to move quickly and irregularly from side to side; squirm; wriggle. — *n.* A wiggling motion. — **to get a wiggle on** *Slang* To hurry up. [? < MLG *wiggelen*] — **wig′gly** *adj.*

wig·gler (wig′lər) *n.* **1.** One who or that which wiggles. **2.** The larva of a mosquito.

wig·wag (wig′wag′) *v.t. & v.i.* **·wagged, ·wag·ging** To send (a message) by moving hand flags, lights, etc., according to a code. — *n.* The act of wigwagging; also, a message so sent. [< dial. E *wig* to wiggle + WAG¹] — **wig′wag′ger** *n.*

wig·wam (wig′wom, -wôm) *n.* **1.** A dwelling or lodge of the North American Indians, commonly a conical framework of poles covered with bark, hides, etc. **2.** *U.S. Informal* A public building used for political gatherings, mass meetings, etc. [< Algonquian (Ojibwa) *wigwaum*, lit., their dwelling]

wild (wīld) *adj.* **1.** Inhabiting the forest or open field; not domesticated or tamed; living in a state of nature. **2.** Growing or produced without care or culture; not cultivated: *wild* flowers. **3.** Being without civilized inhabitants or cultivation; waste: *wild* prairies. **4.** Living in a primitive or savage way; uncivilized: the *wild* men of Borneo. **5.** Boisterous; unruly. **6.** Immoral; orgiastic: a *wild* affair. **7.** Affected with or originating violent disturbances; stormy; turbulent: a *wild* night, a *wild* crowd. **8.** Showing reckless want of judgment; extravagant: a *wild* speculation. **9.** Fantastically irregular or disordered; odd in arrangement or effect: a *wild* imagination, *wild* dress. **10.** Eager and excited, as by reason of joy, fear, desire, etc. **11.** Excited to frenzy or distraction; roused to fury or desperation; crazed or crazy: to drive one *wild.* **12.** Being or going far from the proper course or from the mark aimed at; erratic: a *wild* ball, a *wild* guess. **13.** In some card games, having its value arbitrarily determined by the dealer or holder. — **wild and wooly** *Informal* Untamed; reckless; boisterous. — *n. Often pl.* An uninhabited or uncultivated place; wilderness: the *wilds* of Africa. — **the wild** The wilderness; also, the free, natural, wild life: the call of the *wild.* — *adv.* In a wild manner; without control. [OE *wilde*] — **wild′ly** *adv.* — **wild′ness** *n.*

wild boar The native hog of continental Europe, southern Asia, North Africa, and formerly of Great Britain.

wild carrot An herb having filmy white flowers and from which the cultivated carrot is derived; also called *Queen Anne's lace.*

wild·cat (wīld′kat′) *n.* **1.** An undomesticated feline carnivore of Europe, resembling the domestic cat, but larger and stronger. **2.** The lynx. **3.** One of several other felines, as the ocelot and serval. **4.** An aggressive quick-tempered person, esp. a woman. **5.** An unattached locomotive and its tender, used on special work, as to haul trains, etc. **6.** A successful oil well drilled in an area previously unproductive. **7.** A tricky or unsound business venture; esp. a worthless mine: also **wildcat mine.** Also **wild cat.** — *adj.* **1.** Unsound; risky; esp. financially unsound or risky. **2.** Illegally made or carried on without official sanction or authorization. **3.** Not running on a schedule; also, running wild or without control, as a railroad train or engine. — *v.t. & v.i.* **cat·ted, ·cat·ting** To drill for oil in (an area not known to be productive). — **wild′cat′ting** *n. & adj.*

wildcat strike A strike unauthorized by regular union procedure.

wild·cat·ter (wīld′kat′ər) *n.* **1.** A promoter of mines of doubtful value. **2.** One who develops oil wells in unproven territory. **3.** One who manufactures illicit whisky.

wilde·beest (wīld′bēst, wil′də-; *Du.* vil′də·bāst) *n.* A gnu. [< Afrikaans < Du. *wild* wild + *beeste* beast]

wil·der·ness (wil′dər·nis) *n.* **1.** An uncultivated, uninhabited, or barren region. **2.** A waste, as of an ocean. **3.** A multitudinous and confusing collection: a *wilderness* of curiosities. [ME < OE *wilddēor* wild beast + -NESS]

wild·fire (wīld′fīr′) *n.* **1.** A raging, destructive fire: now generally in the phrase **to spread like wildfire. 2.** A composition of flammable materials, or the flame produced by any very hard to put out, as Greek fire. **3.** A phosphorescent luminousness; ignis fatuus.

wild·flow·er (wīld′flou′ər) *n.* Any uncultivated flowering plant; also, the flower of such a plant. Also **wild flower.**

wild·fowl (wīld′foul′) *n. pl.* **·fowl** (esp. for def. 2), or **fowls 1.** A wild game bird, esp. a wild duck or goose. **2.** *pl.* Wild game birds collectively. Also **wild fowl.**

wild-goose chase (wīld′gōōs′) **1.** Pursuit of the unknown or unattainable. **2.** Any strenuous and fruitless task.

wild·life (wīld′līf′) *n.* Wild animals, trees, and plants collectively.

wild oat 1. *Usually pl.* An uncultivated grass, esp. a common species of Europe. **2.** *pl.* Indiscretions of youth: usu. in the expression **to sow one's wild oats.**

wild pansy The pansy in its uncultivated state; esp. a European species from which the garden pansy is derived.

wild pitch In baseball, a misplay charged to the pitcher that allowing a runner to advance by throwing a pitch that the catcher does not and could not be expected to catch.

wild rice The grain of a tall aquatic grass of North America, esteemed as a table delicacy.

wild turkey A large North American turkey formerly ranging east of the Rocky Mountains from southern Canada to Florida and Mexico, and first domesticated in Mexico; now rare in the wild state.

Wild West The western U.S., esp. in its early period of Indian fighting, lawlessness, etc.

wild·wood (wīld′wŏŏd′) *n.* Natural forest land.

wile (wīl) *n.* **1.** An act or a means of cunning deception; also, any beguiling trick or artifice. **2.** Craftiness; cunning. — *v.t.* **wiled, wil·ing 1.** To lure, beguile, or mislead. **2.** To pass divertingly, as time: usu. with *away*: by confusion with *while.* [ME *wil*, prob. < Scand.]

wil·ful (wil′fəl), **wil·ful·ly, wil·ful·ness** See WILLFUL, etc.

will¹ (wil) *n.* **1.** The power of conscious, deliberate action; the faculty by which the mind makes choices and acts to carry them out. **2.** The act or experience of exercising this faculty. **3.** Strong determination; also, self-control. **4.** That which has been resolved or determined upon; a purpose. **5.** Power to dispose of a matter arbitrarily; discretion. **6.** *Law* The legal declaration of a person's intentions as to the disposal of his estate after his death. **7.** A conscious inclination toward any end or course; a wish. **8.** A request or command. — **at will** As one pleases. — *v.* **willed, will·ing** *v.t.* **1.** To decide upon; choose. **2.** To resolve upon as an action or course; determine to do. **3.** To give, devise, or bequeath by a will. **4.** To control, as a hypnotized person, by the exercise of will. **5.** *Archaic* To have a wish for. — *v.i.* **6.** To exercise will. [OE *willa*] — **will′a·ble** *adj.*

will² (wil) *v.* Present: *3rd person sing.:* **will;** *Archaic 2nd person sing.* **wilt;** past: **would;** *Archaic 2nd person sing.* **would·est** or **wouldst.** An auxiliary verb used with the infinitive without *to*, or elliptically without the infinitive, to express: **1.** Futurity: They *will* arrive by dark. **2.** Willingness or disposition: Why *will* you not tell the truth? **3.** Capability or capacity: The ship *will* survive any storm. **4.** Custom or habit: He *will* sit for hours and brood. **5.** *Informal* Probability or inference: I expect this *will* be the man in the street. ◆ See usage note under SHALL. — *v.t. & v.i.* To wish or have a wish; desire: As you *will.* [OE *willan*]

willed (wild) *adj.* Having a will, esp. one of a given character: usu. in combination: *self-willed.*

will·ful (wil'fəl) *adj.* **1.** Bent on having one's own way; headstrong. **2.** Resulting from the exercise of one's own will; voluntary; intentional. Also, *esp. Brit.*, *wilful*. [Cf. OE *wilfullice* willfully.] — **will'ful·ly** *adv.* — **will'ful·ness** *n.*

wil·lies (wil'ēz) *n.pl. Slang* Nervousness; jitters: with *the*. [? < WILLY-NILLY; with ref. to a state of indecision]

will·ing (wil'ing) *adj.* **1.** Having the mind favorably inclined or disposed. **2.** Answering to demand or requirement; compliant. **3.** Gladly proffered or done; hearty. **4.** Of or pertaining to the faculty or power of choice; volitional. — **will'ing·ly** *adv.* — **will'ing·ness** *n.*

will-o'-the-wisp (wil'ə-thə-wisp') *n.* **1.** Ignis fatuus. **2.** Any elusive or deceptive object. — *adj.* Deceptive; fleeting; misleading. [Earlier *Will with the wisp*]

wil·low (wil'ō) *n.* **1.** Any of various shrubs and trees, having generally smooth branches and often long, slender, pliant, and sometimes pendent branchlets. **2.** The soft white wood of the willow. **3.** *Informal* Something made of willow wood, especially a baseball or cricket bat. — *adj.* Of or pertaining to the willow; made of willow wood. [OE *welig*]
— **wil'low·ish** *adj.*

wil·low·y (wil'ō-ē) *adj.* **1.** Abounding in willows. **2.** Having supple grace of form or carriage.

will power Ability to control oneself; determination; strength or firmness of mind.

wil·ly-nil·ly (wil'ē-nil'ē) *adj.* Having no decisiveness; uncertain; irresolute. — *adv.* Willingly or unwillingly. [Earlier *will I, nill I* whether I will or not]

wilt¹ (wilt) *v.i.* **1.** To lose freshness; droop or become limp, as a flower that has been cut or that has not been watered. **2.** To lose energy and vitality; become faint or languid: We *wilted* under the hot sun. **3.** To lose courage or spirit; subside suddenly. — *v.t.* **4.** To cause to droop or wither. **5.** To cause to lose vitality and energy. — *n.* **1.** The act of wilting. **2.** Languor; faintness. **3.** *Bot.* Any of several plant diseases marked by a wilting of the leaves. [Prob. dial. var. of obs. *welk* to wither]

wilt² (wilt) Archaic second person singular, present tense of WILL²: used with *thou*.

Wil·ton (wil'tən) *n.* A kind of carpet having the loops of the pile cut, thus giving it a velvety texture. [after *Wilton*, England, where first made] Also **Wilton carpet, Wilton rug.**

Wilt·shire (wilt'shir) *n.* One of a breed of long-horned sheep. [after *Wiltshire*, England, where raised]

Wiltshire cheese A variety of Cheddar cheese.

wi·ly (wi'lē) *adj.* **-li·er, -li·est** Full of or characterized by wiles; sly; cunning. — **wi'li·ly** *adv.* — **wi'li·ness** *n.*

wim·ble (wim'bəl) *n.* Anything that bores a hole, esp. if turned by hand, as a brace and bit. — *v.t.* **·bled, ·bling** To bore or pierce, as with a wimble. [< AF, OF *quimbel* < MLG *wiemel*]

wim·ple (wim'pəl) *n.* **1.** A cloth, as of linen or silk, wrapped in folds around the neck close under the chin and over the head, exposing only the face, formerly worn as a protection by women outdoors, and still by nuns. **2.** *Scot.* A fold; plait; also, a curve; a winding turn, as in a river or road. — *v.* **·pled, ·pling** *v.t.* **1.** To cover or clothe with a wimple; veil. **2.** To make or fold into plaits, as a veil. **3.** To cause to move with slight undulations; ripple. — *v.i.* **4.** To lie in plaits or folds. **5.** To ripple. [OE *wimpel*]

win (win) *v.* **won, won, win·ning** *v.i.* **1.** To gain a victory; prevail, as in a contest. **2.** To succeed in an effort or endeavor. **3.** To succeed in reaching or attaining a specified end or condition; get: often with *across, over, through*, etc.: The fleet *won* through the storm. — *v.t.* **4.** To be successful in; gain victory in: to *win* an argument. **5.** To gain in competition or contest: to *win* the blue ribbon. **6.** To gain by effort, persistence, etc.: to *win* fame. **7.** To obtain the good will or favor of: often with *over*. **8.** To secure the love of; gain in marriage: He wooed and *won* her. **9.** To succeed in reaching; attain. **10.** To make (one's way), esp. with effort. **11.** To capture; take possession of. **12.** To earn or procure, as a living. — **to win out** *Informal* To succeed to the fullest extent. — *n.* **1.** A victory; success. **2.** Profit; winnings. **3.** The first position in a race. [OE *winnan* to contend]

wince (wins) *v.i.* **winced, winc·ing** To shrink back or start aside, as from a blow or pain; flinch. — *n.* The act of wincing. [< AF *wenchier*] — **winc'er** *n.*

winch (winch) *n.* **1.** A windlass used for hoisting, as on a crane, having usu., one or more hand cranks geared to a drum. **2.** A crank with a handle, used to impart motion to a grindstone or the like. [OE *vince*] — **winch'er** *n.*

Win·ches·ter (win'ches·tər) *n.* Originally, a repeating rifle, first produced in 1866: now a trade name applied to other firearms. [after Oliver F. *Winchester*, 1810–80, U.S. industrialist]

wind¹ (wind; *for n. also poetic* wīnd) *n.* **1.** Any movement of air, esp., a natural movement. **2.** Any powerful or destructive wind; a tornado; hurricane. **3.** Air in motion by artificial means. **4.** Air pervaded by a scent: The deer got *wind* of the hunter. **5.** A suggestion or intimation: to get *wind* of a plot. **6.** The power of breathing; breath. **7.** Idle chatter; also, vanity. **8.** *pl.* The wind instruments of an orchestra. **9.** The gaseous product of indigestion; flatulence. — **in the wind** Impending; astir; afoot. — **in the wind's eye** Directly opposed to the point from which the wind blows. — **to break wind** To expel gas through the anus. — **to get wind of** To receive a hint of. — **to have in the wind** To be on the track or scent of. — **to have the wind up** To be apprehensive or alarmed. — **to sail close to the wind** **1.** To sail in a direction as near as possible to that from which the wind blows. **2.** To come near to the limit, as of a danger line. **3.** To live economically. — *v.t.* **1.** To follow by scent; to catch a scent of on the wind. **2.** To exhaust the breath of, as by running. **3.** To allow to recover breath by resting. **4.** To expose to the wind, as in ventilating. [OE]

wind² (wīnd) *v.* **wound** (*Rare* **wind·ed**), **wind·ing** *v.t.* **1.** To coil (thread, rope, etc.) around some object or fixed core; twine; wreathe. **2.** To cover with something by coiling or wrapping: to *wind* a spool with thread. **3.** To renew the motion of, as a clock, by coiling a spring, etc. **4.** To cause to turn and twist. **5.** To make (one's way) by a twisting course. **6.** To introduce carefully or deviously; insinuate: He *wound* himself into my confidence. **7.** To raise or hoist, as by means of a capstan or windlass. — *v.i.* **8.** To move in a twisting course; meander. **9.** To coil or twine about some central object or core. **10.** To move in a circular or spiral course. **11.** To proceed carefully, subtly, or deviously. — **to wind up 1.** To coil or wind round and round. **2.** To excite; arouse. **3.** To bring to conclusion or settlement: He *wound up* his affairs. **4.** In baseball, to swing the arm preparatory to pitching. **5.** To hoist. — *n.* The act of winding, or the condition of being wound; a winding, turn, or twist. [OE *windan*] — **wind'a·ble** *adj.* — **wind'er** *n.*

wind³ (wīnd, wind) *v.t.* **wind·ed** *or* **wound, wind·ing** **1.** To blow, as a horn; sound. **2.** To give a (call or signal), as with a horn. [< WIND¹]

wind·age (win'dij) *n.* **1.** The rush of air caused by the rapid passage of an object, as a projectile or a railway train. **2.** Deflection of an object, as a bullet, from its natural course due to wind pressure. **3.** *Naut.* The surface offered to the wind by a vessel.

wind·bag (wind'bag') *n. Informal* A wordy talker.

wind·blown (wind'blōn') *adj.* **1.** Blown by the wind. **2.** Bobbed and brushed forward: said of a woman's hair.

wind·borne (wind'bôrn', -bōrn') *adj.* Carried or transported by the wind, as pollen.

wind·break (wind'brāk') *n.* Something, as a hedge or fence, that protects from or breaks the force of the wind.

Wind·break·er (wind'brā'kər) *n.* A sports jacket with fitted waistband: a trade name. Also **wind'break'er.**

wind·bro·ken (wind'brō'kən) *adj.* Asthmatic; broken-winded: said of a horse.

wind·ed (win'did) *adj.* Breathless, as from exercise.

wind·fall (wind'fôl') *n.* **1.** A piece of unexpected good fortune; esp., a sudden and substantial financial profit. **2.** Something, as ripening fruit, brought down by the wind.

wind·flaw (wind'flô) *n.* A sharp gust of wind.

wind·flow·er (wind'flou'ər) *n.* The anemone. [Trans. of Gk. *anemōnē* anemone < *anemos* the wind]

wind gauge A scale on a gunsight to allow for windage (def. 2). Also **wind gage.**

wind·hov·er (wind'huv'ər) *n. Brit.* The kestrel, a bird.

wind·ing (wīn'ding) *n.* **1.** The act or condition of one who or that which winds; a spiral turning or coiling. **2.** A bend or turn, or a series of them. — *adj.* **1.** Turning spirally about an axis or core. **2.** Having bends or lateral turns. — **wind'ing·ly** *adv.*

winding sheet (wīn'ding) The sheet that wraps a corpse.

wind instrument (wind) A musical instrument whose sounds are produced by vibrations of air injected by the lungs or by bellows. Compare ORGAN, WOODWINDS, etc.

wind·jam·mer (wind'jam'ər) *n.* **1.** *Naut.* A merchant sailing vessel. **2.** A member of its crew.

wind·lass (wind'ləs) *n.* Any of several devices for hauling or lifting, esp. one consisting of a drum or barrel on which the hoisting rope winds, and turned by means of cranking. — *v.t. & v.i.* To raise or haul with a windlass. [< ME < ON < *vinda* wind + *ass* beam]

wind·mill (wind'mil') *n.* **1.** A mill that operates by the action of the wind against adjustable slats, wings, or sails attached to a horizontal axis and that transmit motion to a pump, millstone, or the like. **2.** An imaginary wrong, evil, or foe: usu. in the phrase **to fight** (or **tilt at**) **windmills**, in allusion to Don Quixote's combat with windmills, which he mistook for giants. [< WIND¹ + MILL¹]

win·dow (win'dō) *n.* **1.** An opening in the wall of a building to admit light and air, commonly equipped with movable sashes that enclose one or more panes of glass. **2.** A sash. **3.** A windowpane. **4.** Anything resembling or suggesting a window. — *v.t.* To provide with a window or windows. [< ON < *vindr* wind + *auga* eye]

window box A box, generally long and narrow, along a window ledge or sill, for growing plants.

win·dow-dress·ing (win'dō-dres'ing) *n.* **1.** The act or art of arranging merchandise attractively in store windows; also, the goods so displayed. **2.** An appearance, statement, etc., that gives an unduly favorable impression of reality. — **win'dow-dress'er** *n.*

win·dow·pane (win'dō-pān') *n.* A single sheet of glass for a window. Also **window pane.**

window seat A seat in the recess of a window.

window shade A flexible shade or screen, usu., mounted on a spring roller, used to regulate light at a window.

win·dow-shop (win'dō-shop') *v.i.* **-shopped, -shop·ping** To look at goods shown in store windows without buying them. — **win'dow-shop'per** *n.*

wind·pipe (wind'pīp') *n.* The trachea.

wind·row (wind'rō') *n.* **1.** A long ridge or pile of hay or grain raked together preparatory to building into cocks. **2.** A row of Indian corn made by setting two rows together. **3.** A wind-swept line of dust, surf, leaves, etc. — *v.t.* To rake or shape into a windrow. — **wind'row'er** *n.*

wind·shield (wind'shēld') *n.* A transparent screen, usu. of glass, attached in front of the occupants of an automobile as protection against wind and weather.

wind·sock (wind'sok') *n. Meteorol.* A large conical bag open at both ends, mounted on a pivot and indicating the direction of wind by the current of air that blows through it. Also **wind sleeve.**

Wind·sor chair (win'zər) A wooden chair, common in the 18th century, typically with a spindle back, slanting legs, and a flat or slightly depressed seat.

Windsor tie A wide, soft necktie knotted loosely in a double bow, usu. of black silk cut on the bias.

wind·storm (wind'stôrm') *n.* A violent wind, usu. with little or no precipitation.

wind tunnel *Aeron.* A large cylindrical structure in which the aerodynamic properties of airplane models, airfoils, etc., can be observed under the effects of artificially produced winds of varying velocities.

wind·up (wīnd'up') *n.* **1.** The act of concluding or closing. **2.** A final act or part; conclusion. **3.** In baseball, the swing of the arm preparatory to pitching the ball.

wind·ward (wind'wərd) *adj.* **1.** Of the direction from which the wind is blowing. **2.** Being on the side exposed to the wind. — *n.* The direction from which the wind blows. — *adv.* In the direction from which the wind blows. Opposed to *leeward.*

wind·y (win'dē) *adj.* **wind·i·er, wind·i·est** **1.** Of, consisting of, or abounding in wind; stormy; tempestuous. **2.** Exposed to the wind; wind-swept. **3.** Suggestive of wind; boisterous; swift. **4.** Producing, due to, or troubled with gas in the stomach or intestines; flatulent. **5.** Bombastic; pompous. [OE *windig*] — **wind'i·ly** *adv.* — **wind'i·ness** *n.*

wine (wīn) *n.* **1.** The fermented juice of the grape, commonly used as a beverage and in cooking. **2.** The fermented juice of some other fruit as the elderberry, or of a plant. **3.** A dark purplish red, the color of certain wines. — *v.* **wined,** **win·ing** *v.t.* **1.** To entertain with wine. — *v.i.* **2.** To drink wine. [OE < L *vinum*]

wine·bib·bing (wīn'bib'ing) *adj.* Addicted to excessive drinking of wine. — *n.* The habitual, excessive drinking of wine. — **wine'bib'ber** *n.*

wine cellar **1.** A storage place for wines; also, the wines stored. **2.** Any stock of wines.

wine-col·ored (wīn'kul'ərd) *adj.* Having the color of certain red wines; dark purplish red.

wine·glass (wīn'glas', -gläs') *n.* A small goblet for drinking wine.

wine-grow·er (wīn'grō'ər) *n.* One who cultivates a vineyard and makes wine. — **wine'grow'ing** *adj. & n.*

wine·press (wīn'pres') *n.* An apparatus or a place where the juice of grapes is expressed. Also **wine'press'er.**

win·er·y (wī'nər·ē) *n. pl.* **·er·ies** **1.** An establishment for making wine. **2.** A room for fining and storing wines.

Wine·sap (wīn'sap) *n.* A U.S. variety of red winter apple.

wine·skin (wīn'skin') *n.* The skin of a domestic quadruped kept as entire as possible and made into a tight bag for containing wine, much used in the Orient.

wing (wing) *n.* **1.** An organ of flight; esp., one of the anterior movable pair of appendages of a bird or bat, homologous with the forelimbs of vertebrates but adapted for flight. **2.** An analogous organ in insects and some other animals. **3.** Anything resembling or suggestive of a wing, as in form or function. **4.** Flight or passage by or as by wings; also, the means or act of flying: to take *wing.* **5.** Something

regarded as conferring the power of swift motion or flight: on *wings* of song. **6.** Either of two extremist groups in a political or other organization: the left *wing.* **7.** *Archit.* A part attached to a side; esp., an extension of a building. **8.** *Aeron.* One of the main sustaining surfaces of an airplane. **9.** One of the sides of a stage; also, a piece of scenery for the side. **10.** *Mil.* Either division of a military force on either side of the center. **11.** An analogous formation in certain sports, as football. **12.** A side section of something that shuts or folds, as a screen, etc. **13.** A tactical unit of the U.S. Air Force, larger than a group. **14.** *Slang* An arm; esp., in baseball. **15.** One of the pectoral fins of a flying fish. **16.** *Anat.* An ala: a *wing* of the nose. **17.** *Bot.* Any thin membranous or foliaceous expansion of an organ, as of certain stems, seeds, etc. — **Syn.** See FACTION. — **on** (or **upon) the wing 1.** In flight. **2.** Departing; also, journeying. — **to take wing** To fly away. — **under one's wing** Under one's protection. — *v.t.* **1.** To pass over or through in flight. **2.** To accomplish by flying: the bird *winged* its way south. **3.** To enable to fly. **4.** To cause to go swiftly; speed. **5.** To transport by flight. **6.** To provide with wings for flight. **7.** To supply with a single body or part. **8.** To wound (a bird) in a wing. **9.** To disable by a minor wound. — *v.i.* **10.** To fly; soar. [< ON *vængr*] — **wing'less** *adj.*

wing chair A large armchair, upholstered throughout, with high back and side pieces designed as protection from drafts.

wing commander In the Royal, Royal Canadian, and other Commonwealth air forces, a commissioned officer ranking next below group captain. See table at GRADE.

winged (wingd; *for defs. 1, 2, & 3, also poetic* wing'id) *adj.* **1.** Having wings. **2.** Passing swiftly; soaring; lofty; rapt. **3.** Alive with creatures having wings. **4.** *Informal* Wounded or disabled in or as in the wing or arm.

wing·spread (wing'spred') *n.* The distance between the tips of the fully extended wings of a bird, insect, or airplane.

wink (wingk) *v.i.* **1.** To close and open the eye or eyelids quickly. **2.** To draw the eyelids of one eye together, as in conveying a hint or making a sign. **3.** To pretend not to see: usu. with *at.* **4.** To emit fitful gleams; twinkle. — *v.t.* **5.** To close and open (the eye or eyelids) quickly. **6.** To move force, etc., by winking: with *away, off,* etc. **7.** To signify or express by winking. — *n.* **1.** The act of winking. **2.** The time necessary for a wink. **3.** A twinkle; gleam. **4.** A hint conveyed by winking. — **forty winks** *Informal* A short nap. [OE *wincian* to close the eyes]

wink·er (wing'kər) *n.* **1.** One who winks. **2.** A blinder for a horse.

win·ner (win'ər) *n.* One who or that which wins.

win·ning (win'ing) *adj.* **1.** Successful in achievement, esp. in competition. **2.** Charming; attractive; winsome. — *n.* **1.** The act of one who wins. **2.** *Usu. pl.* That which is won; esp., money won in gambling. — **win'ning·ly** *adv.* — **win'ning·ness** *n.*

win·now (win'ō) *v.t.* **1.** To separate (grain, etc.) from the chaff by means of wind or a current of air. **2.** To blow away (the chaff) thus. **3.** To examine; analyse minutely; sift. **4.** To select or eliminate; distinguish; sort: often with *out.* **5.** To blow upon; cause to flutter. **6.** To beat or fan the air with the wings. **7.** To scatter by blowing; disperse. — *v.i.* **8.** To separate grain from chaff. **9.** To fly; flap. — *n.* **1.** Any device used in winnowing grain. **2.** The act of winnowing; also, a vibrating motion caused by a current of air. [OE < *wind* the wind] — **win'now·er** *n.*

win·some (win'səm) *adj.* Having a winning appearance or manner; pleasing; attractive. [OE < *wyn* joy] — **win'some·ly** *adv.* — **win'some·ness** *n.*

win·ter (win'tər) *n.* **1.** The coldest season of the year, occurring between autumn and spring. ◆ Collateral adjectives: *hibernal.* **2.** A period of time marked by lack of life, coldness, or cheerlessness. **3.** *Chiefly Poetic* A year of life: a man of ninety *winters.* — *v.i.* **1.** To pass the winter. — *v.t.* **2.** To care for, feed, or protect during the winter: to *winter* animals. — *adj.* **1.** Of or taking place in winter; hibernal. **2.** Suitable to or characteristic of winter. [OE] — **win'ter·er** *n.* — **win'ter·less** *adj.*

win·ter·green (win'tər·grēn') *n.* **1.** A small evergreen plant of North America, bearing a cluster of bell-shaped flowers and aromatic oval leaves that yield a colorless volatile oil (**oil of wintergreen**), used as a flavor. **2.** Any of various low evergreen herbs.

win·ter·ize (win'tə·rīz) *v.t.* **·ized, ·iz·ing** To prepare or equip (engines, etc.) for winter.

win·ter·kill (win'tər·kil') *v.t. & v.i.* To die or kill by exposure to extreme cold: said of plants and grains.

win·try (win'trē) *adj.* **·tri·er, ·tri·est** Belonging to winter; cold; frosty. Also **win'ter·y** (-tər·ē). [OE *wintrig*] — **win'tri·ly** (-trə·lē) *adv.* — **win'tri·ness** *n.*

win·y (wī'nē) *adj.* **win·i·er, win·i·est** Having the taste or qualities of wine.

wipe (wīp) *v.t.* **wiped, wip·ing** **1.** To subject to slight friction or rubbing, usu. with some soft, absorbent material. **2.**

To remove by rubbing lightly; brush: usu. with *away* or *off*. **3.** To move, apply, or draw for the purpose of wiping: He *wiped* his hand across his brow. **— to wipe out** To remove or destroy utterly. **— n. 1.** The act of wiping or rubbing. **2.** *Slang* A blow; a swipe. **3.** *Slang* A handkerchief. **4.** *Slang* A jeer. [OE *wīpian*] **— wip'er** *n.*

wire (wīr) *n.* **1.** A slender rod, strand, or thread of ductile metal. **2.** Something made of wire, as a fence, a snare, etc. **3.** A telegraph or telephone cable. **4.** The telegraph system as a means of communication. **5.** A telegram. **6.** *pl.* A secret means of exerting influence. **— under the wire** Just in time or barely within the limits. **— under wire** Fenced. **— v. wired, wir·ing** *v.t.* **1.** To fasten with wire. **2.** To furnish or equip with wiring. **3.** To transmit or send by electric telegraph: to *wire* an order. **4.** To send a telegram to. **5.** To place on wire, as beads. **6.** To catch, as a rabbit, with a snare of wire. **— v.i. 7.** To telegraph. [OE *wīr*]

wire-draw (wīr'drô') *v.t.* **-drew, -drawn, -draw·ing 1.** To draw, as a metal rod, through a series of holes of diminishing diameter to produce a wire. **2.** To treat (a subject) with excessive subtlety or overrefinement. **— wire'-draw'er** *n.*

wire gauge 1. A gauge for measuring the diameter of wire, usu. a round plate with calibrated numbered slots on its periphery, or a long graduated plate with a slot of diminishing width. **2.** A standard system of sizes for wire.

wire-haired terrier (wīr'hârd') A fox terrier having a wiry coat. Also **wire'hair'** (-hâr').

wire·less (wīr'lis) *adj.* **1.** Having no wire or wires. **2.** *Brit.* Radio. **— n. 1.** The wireless telegraph or telephone system, or a message transmitted by either. **2.** *Brit.* Radio. **— v.t. & v.i.** *Brit.* To communicate (with) by wireless telegraphy.

wireless telegraphy Telegraphy without wires, the message being transmitted through space by electromagnetic waves.

wireless telephony The transmission and reception of vocal messages by radio.

wire·pho·to (wīr'fō'tō) *n.* *pl.* **·tos** An apparatus and method for transmitting and receiving photographs by wire: a trade name. Also **wire/pho/to.**

wire·pull·er (wīr'pŏŏl'ər) *n.* **1.** One who pulls wires, as of a puppet. **2.** One who uses secret means to control others or gain his own ends; an intriguer. **— wire'pull'ing** *n.*

wire recorder *Electronics* A device for recording sounds by electromagnetic registration on a fine moving wire, the impulses being reconverted to sound as the magnetized wire is passed through a receiver.

wire service A news agency that collects and distributes news to subscribing newspapers, radio stations, etc.

wire-spun (wīr'spun') *adj.* **1.** Drawn out to form a wire. **2.** Spun or drawn out too fine; overrefined.

wire·tap (wīr'tap) *v.* **-tapped, -tap·ping** *v.t.* **1.** To intercept (information) by means of wiretapping. **— v.i. 2.** To engage in wiretapping. **— n.** Wiretapping. [Back formation < WIRETAPPING] **— wire'tap·per** *n.*

wire·tap·ping (wīr'tap'ing) *n.* The act, process, or practice of tapping telephone or telegraph wires for the purpose of secretly securing information: also called *wiretap*.

wire·work (wīr'wûrk) *n.* **1.** Small articles made of wire cloth. **2.** Wire fabrics in general.

wir·ing (wīr'ing) *n.* An entire system of wire installed for the distribution of electric power.

wir·y (wīr'ē) *adj.* **wir·i·er, wir·i·est 1.** Having great resisting power; thin, but tough and sinewy: said of persons. **2.** Like wire; stiff. **— wir'i·ly** *adv.* **— wir'i·ness** *n.*

wis·dom (wiz'dəm) *n.* **1.** The power of true and right discernment; also, conformity to the course of action dictated by such discernment. **2.** Good practical judgment; common sense. **3.** A high degree of knowledge; learning. **4.** A wise saying. [OE *wīsdōm* < *wīs* wise]

Wisdom of Solomon A book of the Old Testament Apocrypha, consisting of a hymn in praise of wisdom, ascribed by tradition to Solomon.

wisdom tooth The last molar tooth on either side of the upper and lower jaws in man, usu. appearing between the 17th and 22d year. For illus. see TOOTH. **— to cut one's wisdom teeth** To acquire mature judgment.

wise¹ (wīz) *adj.* **wis·er, wis·est 1.** Possessed of wisdom; having sound judgment. **2.** Sagacious; shrewd. **3.** Marked by wisdom; sensible. **4.** Having great learning; erudite. **5.** *Informal* Aware of; onto: *wise* to his motives. **6.** *U.S. Slang* Arrogant or sarcastic in manner; also, impudent. **— to get wise** *Slang* To know the true facts. **— v.t. wised, wis·ing** *Slang* To make cognizant of; inform. **— to wise up** *Slang* To make or become aware, informed, or sophisticated. [OE *wīs*] **— wise'ly** *adv.* **— wise'ness** *n.*

wise² (wīz) *n.* Way of doing; manner; method: chiefly in the phrases **in any wise, in no wise,** etc. [OE *wīse* manner]

-wise *suffix of adverbs* In a (specified) way or manner: no-

wise, likewise: often equivalent to *-ways.* [OE *wīse* manner]
◆ The suffix *-wise,* long considered archaic, has recently come back into fashion, and is now freely added to nouns, with the general meaning "with reference to": *Weather-wise,* it will probably snow. Such compounds often add no further information to a statement, and should be used with discretion.

wise·a·cre (wīz'ā'kər) *n.* **1.** One who affects great wisdom. **2.** A wise man; sage. [< MDu. *wijsseggher* soothsayer]

wise-crack (wīz'krak') *Slang n.* A smart or supercilious remark. **— v.i.** To utter a wisecrack. **— wise'crack'er** *n.*

wish (wish) *n.* **1.** A desire or longing, usu. for some definite thing. **2.** An expression of such a desire; petition. **3.** Something wished for. **— v.t. 1.** To have a desire or longing for; want: We *wish* to be sure. **2.** To desire a specified condition or state for (a person or thing): I *wish* this day were over. **3.** To invoke upon or for someone: I *wished* him good luck. **4.** To bid: to *wish* someone good morning. **5.** To request or entreat; also, to command: I *wish* you would be quiet. **— v.i. 6.** To have or feel a desire; yearn; long: usu. with *for.* **7.** To make or express a wish. **— to wish on** To impose (something or someone) on a person. [OE *wȳscan*]

wish·bone (wish'bōn') *n.* The forked bone formed by the united clavicles in many birds. [from the old belief that when pulled apart by two persons, each making a wish, the one who gets the longer part will have his wish fulfilled]

wish·ful (wish'fəl) *adj.* Having a wish or desire; full of longing. **— wish'ful·ly** *adv.* **— wish'ful·ness** *n.*

wishful thinking Thinking characterized by a conscious or unconscious attempt to impose upon reality conditions that, if true, would make it more pleasant or tolerable.

wish·y-wash·y (wish'ē-wosh'ē, -wôsh'ē) *adj.* *Informal* **1.** Thin; diluted, as liquor. **2.** Lacking character or resolution; indecisive; weak.

wisp (wisp) *n.* **1.** A small bunch, as of hay, straw, or hair. **2.** A small bit; a mere indication: a *wisp* of vapor. **3.** Will-o'-the-wisp. **— v.t. 1.** To dress, brush, or groom with a wisp or whisk. **2.** To fold and lightly twist into a wisp or wisplike form; crumple. [ME *wisp, wips*] **— wisp'y** *adj.*

wisp·ish (wis'pish) *adj.* Like or having the nature of a wisp.

wist (wist) Past tense and past participle of WIT².

wis·ter·i·a (wis-tir'ē-ə) *n.* Any of various woody twining shrubs of the bean family, with clusters of blue, purple, or white flowers. Also **wis·tar'i·a** (-târ'ē-ə). [after Caspar *Wistar,* 1761–1818, U.S. anatomist]

wist·ful (wist'fəl) *adj.* **1.** Wishful; longing. **2.** Musing; pensive. [Appar. < obs. *wistly* intently; infl. in form by WISHFUL] **— wist'ful·ly** *adv.* **— wist'ful·ness** *n.*

wit¹ (wit) *n.* **1.** The power of knowing or perceiving; intelligence; ingenuity. **2.** The power or faculty of rapid and accurate observation; the power of comprehending and judging. **3.** *pl.* The faculties of perception and understanding; to use one's *wits.* **4.** *pl.* The mental faculties with regard to their state of balance: out of her *wits.* **5.** The ready perception and happy expression of unexpected or amusing relations between apparently incongruous ideas. **6.** One who has a keen perception of the incongruous or ludicrous and makes skillful use of it in writing or speaking; also, a clever conversationalist. **7.** Significance; meaning. **— at one's wits' end** At the limit of one's devices and resources. [OE]

wit² (wit) *v.t. & v.i.* **wist, wit·ting** Present indicative: I wo' thou wost, he wot, we, you, they wite(n) *Archaic* To be or become aware (of); learn; know. **— to wit** That is to say; namely: used to introduce a detailed statement or explanation, especially in legal documents. [OE *witan* to know]

witch¹ (wich) *n.* **1.** A woman who practices sorcery; one having supernatural powers, esp. to work evil, and usu. by association with evil spirits or the devil. **2.** An ugly, malignant old woman; a hag. **3.** A bewitching or fascinating woman or girl. **— v.t. 1.** To work an evil spell upon. **2.** To effect by witchcraft. **3.** To fascinate or bewitch; enchant. [OE *wicce* witch, fem. of *wicca* wizard]

witch² (wich) *n.* The witch elm. [OE < *wīcan* to yield]

witch·craft (wich'kraft', -kräft') *n.* **1.** The practices or powers of witches or wizards, esp. when regarded as due to dealings with evil spirits or the devil: also called *black magic.* **2.** An instance of such practices. **3.** Extraordinary influence or fascination; witchery.

witch doctor 1. Among certain primitive peoples of Africa, a medicine man skilled in detecting witches and counteracting evil spells. **2.** Any medicine man or magician. **3.** One who professes to heal or cure by sorcery; a hex.

witch-elm (wich'elm') See WYCH-ELM.

witch·er·y (wich'ər-ē) *n.* *pl.* **·er·ies 1.** Witchcraft. **2.** Power to charm; fascination.

witches' Sabbath In medieval folklore, a midnight orgy of demons and witches, that in German folklore is believed to occur on Walpurgis Night.

---

witch hazel **1.** A shrub of the U.S. and Canada, with several branching crooked trunks and small yellow flowers. **2.** An ointment and extract derived from the bark and dried leaves of this shrub. Also **wychhazel.** [< WITCH¹ + HAZEL]

witch hunt *Informal* An investigation of persons ostensibly to uncover subversive activities, but intended for ulterior motives, such as harassing political opposition. — **witch-hunt-ing** (wich′hun′ting) *adj. & n.* — **witch-hunt-er** *n.*

witch-ing (wich′ing) *adj.* Having power to enchant; weird; fascinating. — *n.* Witchcraft; sorcery. — **witch′ing-ly** *adv.*

with (with, with) *prep.* **1.** In the company of; as a member or associate of. **2.** Next to; beside: Walk *with* me. **3.** Having; bearing: a hat *with* a feather. **4.** Characterized or marked by: the house *with* green shutters. **5.** In a manner characterized by; exhibiting: to dance *with* grace. **6.** Among; counted *with* the others. **7.** During; in the course of: We forget *with* time. **8.** From; so as to be separated from: to dispense *with* luxury. **9.** Against: to struggle *with* an adversary. **10.** In the opinion of: That is all right *with* me. **11.** Because of; as a consequence of: faint *with* hunger. **12.** In possession of: Leave the key *with* the janitor. **13.** Using; by means or aid of: to write *with* a pencil. **14.** By adding or having as a material or quality: trimmed *with* lace; endowed *with* beauty. **15.** Under the influence of: confused *with* drink. **16.** In spite of: *With* all his money, he could not buy health. **17.** At the same time as: to go to bed *with* the chickens. **18.** In the same direction as: to drift *with* the crowd. **19.** In regard to; in the case of: I am angry *with* them. **20.** Onto; to: Join this tube *with* that one. **21.** In proportion to: His fame grew *with* his deeds. **22.** In support of: He voted *with* the Left. **23.** Of the same opinion as: I'm *with* you there! **24.** Compared to; contrasted to: Consider this book *with* that one. **25.** Immediately after: *With* that, he slammed the door. **26.** Having received or been granted: *With* your consent I'll go. [OE]

with- *prefix* **1.** Against: *with*stand. **2.** Back; away: *with*hold. [OE *with-* < *with* against]

with-al (with-ôl′, with-) *Archaic adv.* With the rest; in addition. — *prep.* With: intensive form used after its object: a bow to shoot *withal.* [ME < *with* + *alle* all]

with-draw (with-drô′, with-) *v.* **-drew, -drawn, -draw-ing** *v.t.* **1.** To draw or take away; remove. **2.** To take back, as an assertion or a promise. **3.** To keep or abstract from use. — *v.i.* **4.** To draw back; retire.

with-draw-al (with-drô′əl, with-) *n.* The act or process of withdrawing. Also **with-draw′ment** (-mənt).

withdrawing room **1.** A room behind another room for retirement. **2.** A drawing room.

with-drawn (with-drôn′, with-) *adj. Psychol.* Lacking in responsiveness, esp. emotional responsiveness.

withe (with, with, with) *n.* **1.** A willowy, supple twig. **2.** A band made of twisted flexible shoots, straw, or the like. — *v.t.* **withed, with-ing** To bind with withes. [OE *withthe*]

with-er (with′ər) *v.i.* **1.** To become limp or dry, as a plant when cut down or deprived of moisture. **2.** To waste, as flesh. **3.** To droop or languish. — *v.i.* **4.** To cause to become limp or dry. **5.** To abash, as by a scornful glance. [Appar. var. of WEATHER, v.]

with-ers (with′ərz) *n.pl.* **1.** The highest part of the back of the horse between the shoulder blades. **2.** The similar part in some other animals, as the deer and ox. [OE *wither* against; so called because the horse opposes this part against the load he pulls]

with-hold (with-hōld′, with-) *v.* **-held, -hold-ing** *v.t.* **1.** To hold back; restrain. **2.** To keep back; decline to grant. — *v.i.* **3.** To refrain; forbear. — **with-hold′er** *n.*

withholding tax A part of an employee's wages or salary that is deducted as an installment on his income tax.

with-in (with-in′, with-) *adj.* **1.** In the inner part; interiorly. **2.** Inside the body, heart, or mind. **3.** Indoors. — *prep.* **1.** In the inner or interior part or parts of; inside. **2.** In the limits, range, or compass of (a specified time, space, or distance). **3.** Not exceeding (a specified quantity): Live *within* your means. **4.** In the reach, limit, or scope of: *within* my power. [OE < *with* with + *innan* in]

with-it (with′it) *adj. Slang* **1.** In touch with modern ways; hip. **2.** Lively and fashionably up-to-date. Also **with it.**

with-out (with-out′, with-) *prep.* **1.** Not having, as the result of loss, privation, negation, etc.; lacking: They are *without* a home. **2.** In the absence of: We must manage *without* help. **3.** Free from: *without* fear. **4.** At, on, or to the outside of. **5.** Outside of or beyond the limits of: living *without* the pale of civilization. **6.** With avoidance of: He listened *without* paying attention. — *adv.* **1.** In or on the outer part. **2.** Out of doors. [OE < *with* with + *utan* out]

with-stand (with-stand′, with-) *v.* **-stood, -stand-ing** *v.t.* **1.** To oppose with any force; resist successfully. — *v.i.* **2.** To endure. [OE < *with-* against + *standan* to stand]

with-y (with′ē, with′ē) *adj.* Made of withes; flexible and tough. — *n. pl.* **with-ies** **1.** A rope made of withes. **2.** A flexible twig; withe. [OE *withig*]

wit-less (wit′lis) *adj.* Lacking in wit; foolish. [OE *witleas*] — **wit′less-ly** *adv.* — **wit′less-ness** *n.*

wit-ling (wit′ling) *n.* One who considers himself a wit.

wit-ness (wit′nis) *n.* **1.** A person who has seen or know something, and is therefore competent to give evidence con cerning it; a spectator. **2.** That which serves as or furnishe evidence or proof. **3.** *Law* **a** One who has knowledge of fact relating to a given cause and is subpoenaed to testify. **b** A person who has signed his name to an instrument execute by another in order that he may testify to the genuinenes of the maker's signature. **4.** An attestation to a fact or a event; testimony: usu. in the phrase to bear witness. — *v.i.* **1.** To see or know by personal experience. **2.** To furnish o serve as evidence of. **3.** To give testimony to. **4.** To be th site or scene of: This spot has *witnessed* many heinous crime **5.** *Law* To see the execution of (an instrument) and subscrib to it for the purpose of establishing its authenticity. — *v.i.* **6.** To give evidence; testify. [OE *witnes* knowledge, test mony] — **wit′ness-er** *n.*

witness stand The place in a courtroom from which a wit ness gives evidence.

wit-ted (wit′id) *adj.* **1.** Having wit. **2.** Having (a specifie kind of) wit: used in combination: quick-*witted.*

wit-ti-cism (wit′ə-siz′əm) *n.* A witty saying. [< WITTY, b analogy with *criticism*; coined by Dryden]

wit-ting (wit′ing) *adj.* Done consciously, with knowledg and responsibility; deliberate. [< WIT²] — **wit′ting-ly** *ad*

wit-ty (wit′ē) *adj.* **-ti-er, -ti-est** **1.** Given to making origina or clever speeches; quick at repartee; humorous. **2.** Display ing or full of wit. — **Syn.** See HUMOROUS. [OE *wittig* wise] — **wit′ti-ly** *adv.* — **wit′ti-ness** *n.*

wives (wīvz) Plural of WIFE.

wiz (wiz) *n. Slang* A wizard (def. 2). [Short for WIZARD]

wiz-ard (wiz′ərd) *n.* **1.** A male witch; sorcerer. **2.** *Infor mal* A very skillful or clever person: He's a *wizard* with ma chinery. — *adj.* **1.** Having magical powers. **2.** Fascina ing; enchanting. [ME < OE *wis* wise]

wiz-ard-ry (wiz′ərd-rē) *n.* The practice or methods of wizard.

wiz-en (wiz′ən) *v.t. & v.i.* To become or cause to becom withered; shrivel. — *adj.* Wizened; shrunken; shrivele [OE *wisnian* to dry up, wither]

wiz-ened (wiz′ənd) *adj.* Shrunken; withered; dried up.

woad (wōd) *n.* **1.** An Old World herb of the mustard famil **2.** The blue dyestuff obtained from its leaves. [OE *wād*] — **woad′ed** *adj.*

wob-ble (wob′əl) *v.* **-bled, -bling** *v.i.* **1.** To move or swa unsteadily, as a top while rotating at a low speed. **2.** T show indecision or unsteadiness; waver; vacillate. — *v.t.* **3.** To cause to wobble. — *n.* An unsteady motion, as th of unevenly balanced rotating bodies. Also spelled *wabbl* [? < LG *wabbeln*] — **wob′bler** *n.* — **wob′bling-ly** *adv.*

wob-bly *adj.*

wob-bly (wob′lē) *n. pl.* **-blies** *U.S. Slang* A member of th Industrial Workers of the World (IWW).

Wo-den (wōd′n) The Old English name for Odin, the chi Norse god. Also **Wo′dan.**

woe (wō) *n.* **1.** Overwhelming sorrow; grief. **2.** Heavy a fliction or calamity; disaster. — *interj.* Alas! Also *Archa* **wo.** [OE *wā* misery]

woe-be-gone (wō′bi-gôn′, -gon′) *adj.* Overcome with wo mournful; sorrowful. Also **wo′be-gone′.**

woe-ful (wō′fəl) *adj.* **1.** Accompanied by or causing wo direful. **2.** Expressive of sorrow; doleful. **3.** Paltry; mise able; mean. — **woe′ful-ly** *adv.* — **woe′ful-ness** *n.*

wok (wok) *n.* A bowl-shaped pan used esp. in Chine cooking. [< Cantonese]

woke (wōk) Past tense of WAKE¹.

wok-en (wō′kən) Dialectal and alternative British pa participle of WAKE¹.

wold (wōld) *n.* An undulating tract of open upland; dow or moor. [OE *wald* forest]

wolf (woolf) *n. pl.* **wolves** (woolvz) **1.** Any of numerou carnivorous mammals related to the dog, especially the com mon European species or the timber wolf of North Americ ◆ Collateral adjective: *lupine.* **2.** Any ravenous, cruel, rapacious person or thing. **3.** *Slang* A man who habitual and aggressively flirts with women; a philanderer. — **to c wolf** To give a false alarm. — **to keep the wolf from th door** To avert want or starvation. — *v.t.* To devour rave ously; gulp down: He *wolfed* his food. [OE *wulf*]

wolf-ber-ry (woolf′ber′ē) *n. pl.* **-ries** A shrub of the hone suckle family, with pinkish flowers and white berries.

wolf-hound (woolf′hound′) *n.* Either of two breeds of lar dogs, the Russian wolfhound (or borzoi) and the Irish wo hound, originally trained to hunt and kill wolves.

wolf-ish (woolf′ish) *adj.* **1.** Having the qualities of a wo rapacious; savage. **2.** *Informal* Ravenously hungry. — **wolf′ish-ly** *adv.* — **wolf′ish-ness** *n.*

wolf-ram (woolf′rəm) *n.* **1.** Wolframite. **2.** Tungsten. [< G, prob. < *wolf* wolf + *rahm* cream, soot]

olf·ram·ite (wŏŏl′frəm·īt) *n.* A grayish black or brown mineral of iron and magnesium, an important source of tungsten. [< G < *wolfram* tungsten]

olf's-bane (wŏŏlfs′bān′) *n.* **1.** Aconite. **2.** A species of European arnica, a perennial herb, used as a lotion for bruises. [Trans. of NL *lycoctonum* < Gk. < *lykos* wolf + *teinein* to kill]

olv·er (wŏŏl′vər) *n.* One who hunts wolves.

ol·ver·ine (wŏŏl′və·rēn′) *n.* A rapacious carnivore of northern forests, with stout body and limbs and bushy tail. Also **wol′ver·ene′.** [Dim. f WOLF]

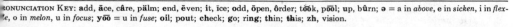

WOLVERINE
(To 3 feet long; tail to 1½ feet.)

olverine State   Nickname of Michigan.

olves (wŏŏlvz) Plural of WOLF.

om·an (wŏŏm′ən) *n. pl.* wom·en (wim′ən) **1.** An adult human female. **2.** The female part of the human race; women collectively. **3.** Womanly character; femininity: usu. with *the.* **4.** As applied to a man, one who is effeminate, timid, or weak. **5.** A female attendant or servant. **6.** A paramour or kept mistress. **7.** *Informal* A wife. — **the little woman** *U.S. Informal* One's wife. — *adj.* **1.** Feminine; characteristic of women. **2.** Female: a *woman* doctor. **3.** Affecting or pertaining to women. [OE < *wīf* wife + *mann* human being]

om·an·hood (wŏŏm′ən·hŏŏd) *n.* **1.** The state of a woman or of womankind. **2.** Women collectively.

om·an·ish (wŏŏm′ən·ish) *adj.* **1.** Characteristic of a woman; womanly. **2.** Effeminate; unmanly. — **wom′an·ish·ly** *adv.* — **wom′an·ish·ness** *n.*

om·an·ize (wŏŏm′ən·īz) *v.* **·ized, ·iz·ing** *v.t.* To make effeminate or womanish.

om·an·kind (wŏŏm′ən·kīnd′) *n.* Women collectively.

om·an·ly (wŏŏm′ən·lē) *adj.* Having the qualities natural, suited, or becoming to a woman; feminine. — *adv.* Like a woman. — **wom′an·li·ness** *n.*

omb (wŏŏm) *n.* **1.** The organ in which the young of higher mammals are developed; the uterus. **2.** The place where anything is engendered or brought into life. **3.** A cavity viewed as enclosing something. [OE *wamb* the belly]

om·bat (wom′bat) *n.* An Australian nocturnal marsupial resembling a small bear. [< Australian]

om·en (wim′in) Plural of WOMAN.

om·en·folk (wim′in·fōk′) *n.pl.* Women collectively. Also **om′en·folks′.**

on (wun) Past tense and past participle of WIN.

on·der (wun′dər) *n.* **1.** A feeling of mingled surprise and curiosity; astonishment. **2.** That which causes wonder; a strange thing; a miracle. — *v.t.* **1.** To have a feeling of doubt and strong curiosity in regard to. — *v.i.* **2.** To be affected or filled with wonder; marvel. **3.** To be doubtful; want to know. [OE *wundor*] — **won′der·er** *n.* — **won′der·ing** *adj.* — **won′der·ing·ly** *adv.*

on·der·ful (wun′dər·fəl) *adj.* Of a nature to excite wonder; marvelous. — **won′der·ful·ly** *adv.* — **won′der·ful·ness** *n.*

on·der·land (wun′dər·land′) *n.* A realm of fairy-tale romance or wonders.

on·der·ment (wun′dər·mənt) *n.* **1.** The emotion of wonder; surprise. **2.** Something wonderful; a marvel.

onder State   Nickname for Arkansas.

on·der·strick·en (wun′dər·strik′ən) *adj.* Suddenly smitten with wonder or admiration. Also **won′der·struck′** (-struk′).

on·der·work (wun′dər·wûrk′) *n.* A work inspiring wonder. — **won′der·work′er** *n.* — **won′der·work′ing** *adj.*

on·drous (wun′drəs) *adj.* Wonderful; marvelous. — *adv.* surprisingly. — **won′drous·ly** *adv.* — **won′drous·ness** *n.*

ont (wunt, wōnt) *adj.* Accustomed; used: He is *wont* to smoke after dinner. — *n.* Ordinary manner of doing or acting; habit. [OE pp. of *gewunian* to be accustomed]

on't (wōnt) Will not. [ME *woll not*]

ont·ed (wun′tid, wōn′-) *adj.* **1.** Commonly used or done; habitual. **2.** Habituated; accustomed. — **wont′ed·ness** *n.*

oo (wŏŏ) *v.t.* **1.** To seek the love or affection of, esp. in order to marry; court. **2.** To entreat earnestly; beg. **3.** To invite; seek. — *v.i.* **4.** To pay court. [OE *wōgian*]

ood¹ (wŏŏd) *n.* **1.** The hard, fibrous material beneath the bark of a tree or shrub. **2.** Lumber; timber; firewood. **3.** *Often pl.* A large and compact collection of trees; a forest; grove. **4.** Something made of wood. **5.** *pl.* A rural district; backwoods. — **out of the woods** Clear of difficulties; safe after peril. — *adj.* **1.** Made of wood. **2.** Made for using or holding wood. **3.** Living or growing in woods. — *v.t.* **1.** To furnish with wood for fuel. **2.** To plant with trees. — *v.i.* **3.** To take on a supply of wood. [OE *wudu*] — **wood′ed** *adj.* — **wood′less** *adj.*

wood alcohol   Methanol.

wood·bine (wŏŏd′bīn) *n.* **1.** The common honeysuckle of Europe. **2.** The Virginia creeper. Also called *bine:* also **wood′bind** (-bīnd). [OE < *wudu* wood + *bindan* to bind]

wood·block (wŏŏd′blok′) *n.* **1.** A block of wood prepared for engraving. **2.** A woodcut.

wood·chuck (wŏŏd′chuk′) *n.* A marmot of eastern North America, having a chunky body and a brown, bristly coat: also called *ground hog.* [By folk etymology < Ojibwa *wejack*]

wood·cock (wŏŏd′kok′) *n.* **1.** A small European game bird having the thighs entirely feathered. **2.** A related North American bird. [OE *wuducocc*]

wood·craft (wŏŏd′kraft′, -kräft′) *n.* **1.** Skill in things pertaining to woodland life, as hunting and trapping. **2.** Skill in woodwork or in constructing articles of wood. — **wood′crafts·man** (-krafts′mən, -kräfts′-) *n.*

wood·cut (wŏŏd′kut′) *n.* **1.** An engraved block of wood. **2.** A print from such a block. Also called *woodblock.*

wood·cut·ter (wŏŏd′kut′ər) *n.* One who cuts or chops wood. — **wood′cut′ting** *n.*

wood·en (wŏŏd′n) *adj.* **1.** Made of wood. **2.** Like a block of wood; stupid; mechanical; stiff; awkward. **3.** Dull; spiritless. — **wood′en·ly** *adv.* — **wood′en·ness** *n.*

wood engraving   **1.** The art of cutting designs on wood for printing. **2.** A woodcut. — **wood engraver**

wood·en·head (wŏŏd′n·hed′) *n.* *Informal* A stupid person; blockhead. — **wood′en·head′ed** *adj.*

wooden horse   Trojan horse.

wood·en·ware (wŏŏd′n·wâr′) *n.* Dishes, vessels, bowls, etc., made of wood.

wood·house (wŏŏd′hous′) *n.* A house or shed for storing firewood: also called *woodshed.*

wood·land (wŏŏd′lənd; *for n., also* wŏŏd′land′) *n.* Land occupied by or covered with woods or trees. — *adj.* Belonging to or dwelling in the woods. — **wood′land·er** *n.*

wood louse   Any of numerous small terrestrial flat-bodied crustaceans commonly found under old logs.

wood·man (wŏŏd′mən) *n. pl.* **·men** (-mən) A woodsman.

wood·note (wŏŏd′nōt′) *n.* A simple, artless, or natural song, as of a wild bird.

wood nymph   A nymph of the forest; a dryad.

wood·peck·er (wŏŏd′pek′ər) *n.* Any of various birds having stiff tail feathers for climbing, strong claws, and a sharp, chisellike bill for drilling holes in the wood of trees, etc., in search of insects.

wood·pile (wŏŏd′pīl′) *n.* A pile of wood, esp. of wood cut for burning.

wood pulp   Wood reduced to pulp, used for making paper.

woods·man (wŏŏdz′mən) *n. pl.* **·men** (-mən) **1.** A woodcutter; lumberman. **2.** A forester; also, a dweller in forests. **3.** A man skilled in woodcraft. **4.** A hunter of forest game. Also called *woodman.*

wood sorrel   A herb having purple, rose, or white flowers.

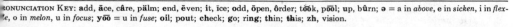

RED-HEADED WOODPECKER
(To 9½ inches long)

woods·y (wŏŏd′zē) *adj.* woods·i·er, woods·i·est *Informal* Of, like, or dwelling in the woods.

wood tar   A tar produced by the dry distillation of wood and containing turpentine, resins, and other hydrocarbons.

wood thrush   A large woodland thrush of North America, noted for the vigor and sweetness of its song.

wood·turn·ing (wŏŏd′tûr′ning) *n.* The process or art of shaping blocks of wood on a lathe. — **wood′turn′er** *n.*

wood·winds (wŏŏd′windz′) *n.pl. Music* Instruments in which a player's breath sets an air column into vibration by passing through a reed or striking a sharp edge, as oboes, bassoons, clarinets, flutes, etc. — **wood′wind′** *adj.*

wood·work (wŏŏd′wûrk′) *n.* **1.** The wooden parts of any structure, esp. interior wooden parts, as moldings or doors. **2.** Work made of wood. — **wood′work′er** *n.* — **wood′work′ing** *n.*

wood·y (wŏŏd′ē) *adj.* wood·i·er, wood·i·est **1.** Of the nature of or containing wood. **2.** Of or like wood. **3.** Wooded; abounding with woods. — **wood′i·ness** *n.*

woof (wŏŏf) *n.* **1.** The weft; the threads carried back and forth across the fixed threads of the warp in a loom. **2.** The texture of a fabric. [OE < *on* on + *wefan* to weave]

woof·er (wŏŏf′ər) *n. Electronics* A loudspeaker used to reproduce low frequencies in high-fidelity sound equipment. [< WOOF, imit. of a dog's growl]

wool (wŏŏl) *n.* **1.** The soft, curly or crisped hair obtained from the fleece of sheep and some allied animals. **2.** The underfur of a furbearing animal. **3.** Material or garments made of wool. **4.** A substance resembling wool. — **all wool and a yard wide** One hundred percent genuine. — **to pull**

the wool over one's eyes To deceive one. — *adj.* Of or made of wool or woolen material. [OE *wull*]

wool-clip (wŏol′klip′) *n.* The amount of wool clipped from the sheep in one year.

wool·en (wŏol′ən) *adj.* 1. Made of wool; like wool. 2. Of wool or its manufacture. — *n.pl.* Woolen cloth or clothing. Also **wool′len.** [OE *wullen, wyllen*]

wool·gath·er·ing (wŏol′gath′ər·ing) *n.* Any trivial or purposeless employment; esp., idle reverie. — *adj.* Idly indulging in fancies. — **wool′gath′er·er** *n.*

wool·grow·er (wŏol′grō′ər) *n.* A person who raises sheep for the production of wool. — **wool′grow′ing** *adj.*

wool·ly (wŏol′ē) *adj.* **·li·er, ·li·est** 1. Made of, covered with, or resembling wool; wool-bearing. 2. Soft and vaporous; lacking clearness; fuzzy; blurry. 3. Having a growth of woollike hairs. 4. Rough and exciting: usu. in the phrase **wild and woolly.** — *n. pl.* **·lies** A garment made of wool; esp., underwear. Also *esp. U.S.* **wool′y.** — **wool′li·ness** *n.*

wool·sack (wŏol′sak′) *n.* 1. A sack of wool. 2. The chair of the lord chancellor in the English House of Lords, a cushion stuffed with wool. 3. The office of lord high chancellor.

wooz·y (wŏo′zē) *adj.* **wooz·i·er, wooz·i·est** *Slang* Befuddled, esp. with drink; dazed. [Prob. < *wooze*, var. of OOZE] — **wooz′i·ly** *adv.* — **wooz′i·ness** *n.*

Worces·ter·shire sauce (wŏos′tər·shir) A piquant sauce made from vinegar and many other ingredients. Also **Worcestershire, Worcester sauce.** [after *Worcester*, England where originally made]

word (wûrd) *n.* 1. A linguistic form that can meaningfully be spoken in isolation. 2. The letters or characters that stand for such a linguistic form. 3. A mere sequence of sounds or letters; vocable: *words* rather than ideas. 4. *Usu. pl.* Conversation; talk: a man of few *words*. 5. A brief remark. 6. A short and pithy saying. 7. A communication or message; information: Send him *word*. 8. A command, signal, or direction: Give the *word* to start. 9. A promise; avowed intention: a man of his *word*. 10. A watchword. 11. *pl.* Language used in anger, rebuke, or otherwise emotionally: They had *words*. — **by word of mouth** Orally. — **in a word** In short; briefly. — **the Word** The Scriptures. — **to be as good as one's word** To keep one's promise. — **to break one's word** To violate one's promise. — **to eat one's words** To retract something that one has said. — **to have a word with** To have a brief conversation with. — **to mince words** To be evasive; avoid coming to the point. — **to take one at his word** To understand or deal with one literally in accordance with his own statement. — **to take the words out of one's mouth** To say what one was just about to say. — *v.t.* To express in a word or words, esp. in selected words; phrase. [OE]

word·age (wûr′dij) *n.* Words collectively.

word·book (wûrd′bŏok′) *n.* 1. A collection of words; vocabulary; lexicon; dictionary. 2. An opera libretto.

word for word In the exact words; literally; verbatim.

word·i·ness (wûr′dē·nis) *n.* The use of excessive words.

word·ing (wûr′ding) *n.* The act or style of expressing in words; phraseology; also, words used; expression.

word·less (wûrd′lis) *adj.* Having no words; inarticulate; silent. — **word′less·ly** *adv.* — **word′less·ness** *n.*

word order The sequence or order of words in a phrase, clause, or sentence.

word play 1. Fencing with words; repartee. 2. Subtle discussion on words and their meaning. 3. Play on words.

word square An arrangement of letters in rectangular form, so that they form the same words in either horizontal or vertical lines.

```
FRET
REAR
EASE
TREE
```
WORD SQUARE

word·y (wûr′dē) *adj.* **word·i·er, word·i·est** 1. Of the nature of words; verbal. 2. Expressed in many words. 3. Given to the use of words; verbose; prolix. [OE *wordig*] — **word′i·ly** *adv.*

wore (wôr, wōr) Past tense of WEAR¹ and WEAR².

work (wûrk) *n.* 1. Continued exertion or activity, whether physical or mental, directed to some purpose or end; labor. 2. The acts, obligations, etc., that one does or undertakes in return for something of value, as money; esp., the activities by which one earns one's livelihood; occupation. 3. A job or position; employment: to look for *work*. 4. A place of employment: Is he at home or at *work*? 5. That upon which labor is expended; task. 6. Exhausting or unrewarding effort; toil. 7. The matter at hand; the business that remains to be done: Get to *work*. 8. That which is produced by or as by labor, as an engineering structure, a design produced by a needle, etc.; also, a product of mental labor, as a book or opera. 9. A feat or deed. 10. *pl.* (*usu. construed as sing.*) A manufacturing or other industrial establishment, including buildings and equipment: a gas *works*. 11. *pl.* Running gear or machinery, as of a watch. 12. Manner of working, or style of treatment; workmanship. 13. *pl. Slang* The whole of anything: the whole *works*. 14. *pl. Theol.* Moral duties considered as external acts, especially as meritorious. 15. *Physics* A transference of energy from one body to another resulting in the motion or displacement of the body acted upon, expressed as the product of the force and the amount of displacement in the line of its action. — **in the works** *Informal* In progress or in preparation. — **to give (someone) the works** *Slang* 1. To maul or kill. 2. To be severe with. — **to shoot the works** *Slang* To make a supreme effort; risk one's all in a single attempt. — **worked** (*Archaic* **wrought**), **work·ing** *v.i.* 1. To perform work; labor; toil. 2. To be employed in some trade or business. 3. To perform a function; operate: The machine *works* well. 4. To prove effective; succeed: His stratagem *worked*. 5. To move or progress gradually or with difficulty: He *worked* up in his profession. 6. To become as specified, by gradual motion: The bolts *worked* loose. 7. To have some slight improper motion in functioning: The wheel *works* on the shaft. 8. To move from nervousness or agitation: His features *worked* with passion. 9. To undergo kneading, hammering, etc.; be shaped: Copper *works* easily. 10. To ferment. 11. *Naut.* To labor in a heavy sea so as to loosen seams and fastenings: said of a ship. — *v.t.* 12. To cause or bring about; accomplish: to *work* a miracle. 13. To direct the operation of: to *work* a machine. 14. To make or shape by toil or skill. 15. To prepare, as by manipulating, hammering, etc.: to *work* dough. 16. To decorate, with embroidery or inlaid work. 17. To cause to be productive, as by toil: to *work* a mine. 18. To cause to work: He *works* his employees too hard. 19. To cause to move as specified, usu. with effort: We *worked* the timber into position. 20. To make or achieve by effort: He *worked* his way through the narrow tunnel. 21. To carry on some activity in (an area, etc.); cover: to *work* a stream for trout. 22. To solve, as a problem in arithmetic. 23. To cause to move from nervousness or excitement: to *work* one's jaws. 24. To excite; provoke: He *worked* himself into a passion. 25. To influence or manage, as by insidious means; lead. 26. *Informal* To make use of for one's own purposes; use. — **to work in** To put in; insert or be inserted. — **to work off** To get rid of, as extra flesh by exercise. — **to work on** (or **upon**) 1. To try to influence or persuade. 2. To influence or affect. — **to work out** 1. To make its way out or through. 2. To effect by work or effort; accomplish. 3. To exhaust, as a mineral vein or a subject of inquiry. 4. To discharge, as a debt, by labor rather than by payment of money. 5. To develop; form, as a plan. 6. To solve. 7. To prove effective or successful. 8. To result as specified: It *worked* out badly. — **to work over** 1. To do again; repeat. 2. *U.S. Slang* To beat up; maul. — **to work up** 1. To excite; rouse. 2. To form or shape by working; develop. [OE *weorc*]

-work *combining form* 1. A product made from a (specified) material: *paperwork, brickwork*. 2. Work of a (given) kind: *piecework*. 3. Work performed in a (specified) place: *housework*. [< WORK]

work·a·ble (wûr′ka·bəl) *adj.* 1. Capable of being worked. 2. Capable of being put into effect, as a plan; practicable. — **work′a·bil′i·ty, work′a·ble·ness** *n.*

work·a·day (wûr′kə·dā′) *adj.* 1. Of, pertaining to, or suitable for working days; everyday. 2. Commonplace; prosaic. [Alter. of ME *werkeday* < OE *weorca* work + DAY]

work basket A basket for holding sewing materials.

work·bench (wûrk′bench′) *n.* A bench for work, as that of a carpenter or machinist.

work·book (wûrk′bŏok′) *n.* 1. A booklet based on a course of study and containing problems and exercises that a student works out directly on the pages. 2. A manual containing operating instructions. 3. A book for recording work performed or planned.

work·day (wûrk′dā′) *n.* 1. Any day not a Sunday or holiday; a working day. 2. The part of the day or number of hours of one day spent in work. — *adj.* Workaday.

work·er (wûr′kər) *n.* 1. One who or that which does work, esp., a laborer. 2. A female of an insect colony, as an ant, bee, or termite, with undeveloped sexual organs.

work force The total number of workers of a company, project, factory, region, etc.; staff. Also **working force.**

work·horse (wûrk′hôrs′) *n.* 1. A horse used for pulling loads, as a cart or plow. 2. A person who takes upon himself the hardest or most arduous part of an undertaking.

work·house (wûrk′hous′) *n.* 1. *Brit.* A house for paupers able to work. 2. An industrial prison for petty offenders.

work·ing (wûr′king) *adj.* 1. Engaged actively in some employment. 2. That works, or performs its function: This is a *working* model. 3. Sufficient for use or action: a *working* knowledge of French. 4. Relating to or occupied by work. 5. Throbbing with pain; also, twitching: said esp. of the facial muscles. 6. Fermenting, as wine. — *n.* 1. The act or operation of one who or that which works. 2. *Usu. pl.* The part of a mine or quarry where excavation is going on or has gone on.

working capital 1. That part of the finances of a business available for its operation. 2. The amount of quick assets that exceed current liabilities.

rking class The part of society consisting of working
ople paid in wages; esp., manual or industrial laborers. —
ork·ing-class (wûr′king·klas′, -kläs′) *adj.*

rking day 1. A day on which work is normally done, as
stinguished from a Sunday or holiday. 2. The number of
urs constituting a day's work: a four-hour *working day.*

rk·ing·man (wûr′king·man′) *n. pl.* **·men** (-men′) A
ale worker; laborer.

rking papers An age certificate and other official papers
rtifying that a minor may be legally employed.

rk·ing·wom·an (wûr′king·woom′ən) *n. pl.* **·wom·en**
wim′in) A female worker; laborer.

rk·less (wûrk′lis) *adj.* Jobless; unemployed.

rk·load (wûrk′lōd′) *n.* The amount of work apportioned
a person, machine, or department over a given period.

rk·man (wûrk′mən) *n. pl.* **·men** (-men′) One who earns
s living by manual labor; an artisan; mechanic; working-
an. — **work′man·ly** *adv.*

rk·man·like (wûrk′mən·līk) *adj.* Like or befitting a
illed workman; skillfully done. — **work′man·ly** *adv.*

rk·man·ship (wûrk′mən·ship) *n.* 1. The art or skill of a
orkman, or the quality of work. 2. The work or result pro-
ced by a worker.

rkmen's compensation 1. Damages recoverable from
employer by an employee in case of accident. 2. Govern-
ent insurance against illness, accident, or unemployment.

rk of art 1. A product of the fine arts, esp. of the graphic
ts and sculpture, but including literary and musical pro-
uctions. 2. Anything likened to an artistic work, as be-
use of great beauty, intricacy, etc.

rk·out (wûrk′out′) *n. Informal* A test, trial, practice
rformance, etc., to discover, maintain, or increase ability
some work or competition, as a practice boxing bout or
ce. 2. Any activity involving considerable effort or vigor.

rk·room (wûrk′room′, -room′) *n.* A room where work is
rformed.

rk·sheet (wûrk′shēt′) *n.* 1. A sheet of paper on which
actice work or rough drafts of problems are written. 2. A
eet of paper used to record work schedules and operations.

rk·shop (wûrk′shop′) *n.* A building or room where any
ork is carried on; workroom.

rk stoppage A stopping of work, as in industry, be-
use of a strike or layoff.

rk·ta·ble (wûrk′tā′bəl) *n.* A table with drawers for use
hile working, esp. while sewing.

rk·week (wûrk′wēk′) *n.* The number of hours worked in
week; also, the number of working hours in a week.

rld (wûrld) *n.* 1. The earth. 2. A part of the earth: the
d *World.* 3. The universe. 4. A division of existing or
eated things belonging to the earth: the animal *world.* 5.
he human inhabitants of the earth. 6. A definite class of
ople having certain interests or activities in common: the
ientific *world.* 7. A sphere or domain: the *world* of letters.
Man regarded socially. 9. Public or social life and inter-
urse: to go out into the *world.* 10. The practices, usages,
d ways of men: He knows the *world.* 11. A total of things
pertaining to or affecting an individual person: a child's
ivate *world* of fantasy. 12. A great quantity, number, or
ze: a *world* of trouble. 13. A scene of existence or of affairs
garded from a moral or religious point of view; worldly
ms, pleasures, or people collectively. 14. Earthly exist-
ace. — **for all the world** In every respect. — **on top of
e world** *Informal* Elated. — **out of this world** *Informal*
ery fine; extraordinarily good. — **to bring into the world**
o give birth to. [OE *weoruld, woruld*]

rld Court 1. The Permanent Court of International
ustice. 2. The International Court of Justice.

rld·ling (wûrld′ling) *n.* One who lives merely for this
orld; a worldly-minded person.

rld·ly (wûrld′lē) *adj.* **·li·er, ·li·est** 1. Pertaining to the
orld; mundane; earthly; not spiritual. 2. Devoted to tem-
oral things; secular. 3. Sophisticated; worldly-wise. —
dv. In a worldly manner. — **world′li·ness** *n.*

rld·ly-mind·ed (wûrld′lē·mīn′did) *adj.* Absorbed in the
ings of this world. — **world′ly-min′ded·ly** *adv.* — **world′·
·mind′ed·ness** *n.*

rld·ly-wise (wûrld′lē-wīz′) *adj.* Wise in the ways and
fairs of the world; sophisticated.

rld power A state or organization whose policy and ac-
on are of world-wide influence.

orld Series In baseball, the games played at the finish of
he regular schedule between the champion teams of the
merican and National Leagues, the first team to win four
ames being adjudged world champions. Also **world's
eries.**

rld's fair An international exhibit of the folk crafts and
rts, agricultural and industrial products, and scientific
rogress of various countries.

world-shak·ing (wûrld′shā′king) *adj.* Enormously significant or consequential; affecting the entire world.

World War See table for WAR.

world-wea·ry (wûrld′wir′ē) *adj.* **·ri·er, ·ri·est** Dissatisfied
and weary with life and its conditions.

world-wide (wûrld′wīd′) *adj.* Extended or spread throughout the world.

worm (wûrm) *n.* 1. A small, limbless invertebrate with an
elongated, soft, and usu. naked body, as a flatworm, round-
worm, or annelid. ◆ Collateral adjective: *vermicular.* 2.
Loosely, any small creeping animal having a slender body
and short or undeveloped limbs, as an insect larva, a grub,
etc. 3. That which suggests the action or habit of a worm as
eating away or as an agent of decay, as remorse, death, etc.
4. A despicable, groveling, or abject person. 5. Something
like a worm in appearance or movement. 6. *pl.* An intestinal disorder due to the presence of parasitic worms. — *v.t.*
1. To insinuate (oneself or itself) in a wormlike manner:
with *in* or *into.* 2. To draw forth by artful means, as a secret: with *out.* 3. To free from intestinal worms. 4. *Naut.*
To wind yarn, etc., along (a rope) so as to fill up the grooves
between the strands. 5. To remove the worms from, as a
dog. — *v.i.* 6. To move or progress slowly and stealthily.
7. To insinuate oneself by artful means: with *into.* [OE
wyrm] — **worm′er** *n.*

worm-eat·en (wûrm′ēt′n) *adj.* 1. Eaten or bored through
by worms. 2. Worn-out or decayed, as by time.

worm gear *Mech.* 1. A worm wheel. 2. The gear formed
by a worm wheel together with a worm screw.

worm·hole (wûrm′hōl′) *n.* The hole made by a worm or
termite, as in plants, timber, etc. — **worm′holed′** *adj.*

worm screw *Mech.* A short threaded portion of a shaft
constituting an endless screw formed to mesh with a worm
wheel.

worm wheel *Mech.* A toothed wheel gearing with a worm
screw.

worm·wood (wûrm′wood′) *n.* 1. Any of various European
herbs or small shrubs related to the sagebrush; esp., a common species that is aromatic and bitter and is used in making
absinthe. 2. That which embitters or makes bitter; bitterness. [Alter. of obs. *wermōd* < OE]

worm·y (wûr′mē) *adj.* **worm·i·er, worm·i·est** 1. Infested
with or injured by worms. 2. Of or pertaining to worms. 3.
Resembling a worm. 4. Mean; groveling. — **worm′i·ness** *n.*

worn (wôrn, wōrn) Past participle of WEAR. — *adj.* 1. Affected by use or any continuous action; as: **a** Threadbare: a
worn suit. **b** Exhausted, as from worry, anxiety, etc.: a *worn*
face. **c** Hackneyed: a *worn* phrase. 2. Used up; spent.

worn-out (wôrn′out′, wōrn′-) *adj.* 1. Used until without
value or effectiveness. 2. Thoroughly tired; exhausted.

wor·ri·some (wûr′i·səm) *adj.* 1. Causing worry or anxiety.
2. Given to worry. — **wor′ri·some·ly** *adv.*

wor·ry (wûr′ē) *v.* **·ried, ·ry·ing** *v.i.* 1. To be uneasy in the
mind; fret. 2. To pull or tear at something with the teeth:
with *at.* 3. *Informal* To advance or manage despite difficulties: with *along* or *through.* — *v.t.* 4. To cause to feel uneasy in the mind; trouble. 5. To bother; pester. 6. To
mangle or kill by biting, shaking, or tearing with the teeth.
— *n. pl.* **·ries** 1. A state of anxiety or vexation. 2. Something that causes anxiety. 3. The act of worrying. [OE
wrygan to strangle] — **wor′ri·er** *n.* — **wor′ri·ment** *n.*

worse (wûrs) Comparative of BAD and ILL. — *adj.* 1.
Bad or ill in a greater degree; more evil, etc. 2. Physically
ill in a greater degree. 3. Less favorably situated as to
means and circumstances. — *n.* Something worse. — *adv.*
In a manner more intense, severe, or evil. [OE *wiersa*]

wors·en (wûr′sən) *v.t. & v.i.* To make or become worse.

wor·ship (wûr′ship) *n.* 1. The adoration, homage, or
veneration given to a deity. 2. The rites, ceremonial forms,
prayers, etc., such adoration requires or assumes. 3. Excessive or ardent devotion or admiration. 4. The object of
such devotion or admiration. 5. *Chiefly Brit.* A title of
honor in addressing persons of rank or station: with *your,
his,* etc. — *v.* **wor·shiped** or **·shipped, wor·ship·ing** or
·ship·ping *v.t.* 1. To pay an act of worship to. 2. To have
an intense or exaggerated admiration or devotion for. — *v.i.*
3. To perform acts or have sentiments of worship. [OE *
weorth* value] — **wor′ship·er, wor′ship·per** *n.*

wor·ship·ful (wûr′ship·fəl) *adj.* 1. Giving or feeling reverence or adoration. 2. *Chiefly Brit.* Worthy of or entitled to
honor or respect: used as a title of respect for magistrates,
etc. — **wor′ship·ful·ly** *adv.* — **wor′ship·ful·ness** *n.*

worst (wûrst) Superlative of BAD and ILL. — *adj.* Bad,
ill, evil, harmful, etc., in the highest degree. — **in the worst
way** *Slang* Very much. — *n.* That which is worst. — **at
worst** By the most pessimistic estima·. — **if (the) worst
comes to (the) worst** If the worst imaginable thing comes
to pass. — **to get the worst of it** To be defeated or put at

a disadvantage. — *adv.* In the worst or most extreme manner or degree. — *v.t.* To defeat; vanquish. [OE *wierrest*]

wors·ted (woos′tid, wûr′stid) *n.* **1.** Woolen yarn spun from long staple, with fibers combed parallel and twisted hard. **2.** A fabric made from worsted yarns. — *adj.* Consisting of or made from this yarn. [after *Worsted*, former name of a parish in Norfolk, north of Norwich, England]

wort (wûrt) *n.* **1.** A plant or herb: usu. in combination: *liverwort.* **2.** The unfermented infusion of malt that becomes beer when fermented. [OE *wyrt* root, plant]

worth (wûrth) *n.* **1.** Value or excellence of any kind. **2.** The exchangeable or market value of anything. **3.** The quality or combination of qualities that makes one deserving of esteem. **4.** Wealth. **5.** The amount of something that can be had for a specific sum: three cents' *worth* of candy. — *adj.* **1.** Equal in value (to); exchangeable (for). **2.** Deserving of: to be *worth* seeing. **3.** Having possessions to the value of: He is *worth* a million. — **for all it is worth** To the utmost. — **for all one is worth** With every effort possible: to the utmost of one's capacity. [OE *weorth*] — **Syn.** (noun) **1.** *Worth* and *value* relate to the merit or excellence of a person or thing. In pecuniary matters, the words are usually equivalent: to get one's money's *worth*, to receive good *value* in a purchase. *Worth* often implies some intangible merit or efficacy, while *value* has reference to a measurable or precisely definable quality: ideas of little *worth*, the *value* of a house and its lot.

-worth *combining form* Of the value of: *pennyworth.* [OE *weorth* worth]

worth·less (wûrth′lis) *adj.* Having no worth, value, dignity, virtue, etc. — **worth′less·ly** *adv.* — **worth′less·ness** *n.*

worth·while (wûrth′hwīl′) *adj.* Sufficiently important to occupy the time; of enough value to repay the effort. — **worth′while′ness** *n.*

wor·thy (wûr′thē) *adj.* **·thi·er, ·thi·est 1.** Possessing worth or value; deserving of respect or honor. **2.** Having such qualities as to be deserving of or adapted to some specified thing; suitable: followed by *of* (rarely *for*) or sometimes by an infinitive: He is *worthy* of our prasie. — *n.* *pl.* **·thies 1.** A person of eminent worth. **2.** A person or character of local note: a humorous usage. [ME *wurthi, worthi*] — **wor′thi·ly** *adv.* — **wor′thi·ness** *n.*

-worthy *combining form* **1.** Meriting or deserving: *trustworthy.* **2.** Valuable as; having worth as: *newsworthy.* **3.** Fit for: *seaworthy.* [OE *wythe* worthy]

wot (wot) Present tense, first and third person singular, of WIT².

Wo·tan (vō′tän) In Wagner's *Ring of the Nibelung*, Woden.

would (wood) Past tense of WILL, but rarely a true past, rather chiefly used as a modal auxiliary expressing: **a** Desire or inclination: He *would* like to write. **b** Condition: He *could* give if he were able. **c** Futurity: He kept searching for something that *would* cure him. **d** Determination: He *would* not go. **e** Expectation or possibility: Letting him speak *would* have serious consequences. **f** Preference: We *would* have you succeed rather than fail. **g** Request: *Would* you give us a call? **h** Custom or habit: We *would* ride together each day. **i** Choice: He *would* never go if he could help it. **j** Uncertainty: It *would* seem to be wrong. ◆ See note under SHOULD. [OE *wolde*, pt. of *willan* to will]

would-be (wood′bē′) *adj.* **1.** Desiring or professing to be: a *would-be* poet. **2.** Intended to be.

would·n't (wood′nt) Would not.

wouldst (woodst) Archaic or poetic second person singular of WOULD: used with *thou.*

wound¹ (woond, *Poetic* wound) *n.* **1.** A hurt or injury to the body, usu. one in which the skin is cut or torn, as a stab, cut, etc. **2.** A similar injury to a tree or plant. **3.** Any injury or cause of pain or grief, as to the feelings, honor, etc. — *v.t. & v.i.* To inflict a wound or wounds (upon); cause injury or grief (to). [OE *wund*] — **wound′less** *adj.*

wound² (wound) Past tense and past participle of WIND².

wove (wōv) Past tense and alternative past participle of WEAVE.

wo·ven (wō′vən) Past participle of WEAVE.

wow (wou) *interj. Informal* An exclamation of wonder, surprise, pleasure, pain, etc. — *n. Slang* Something that is extraordinarily successful, amusing, etc. — *v.t. Slang* To be extraordinarily successful with.

wrack¹ (rak) *n.* **1.** Ruin; destruction: chiefly in the phrase **wrack and ruin.** **2.** A wrecked ship; wreckage. **3.** Marine vegetation and floating material cast ashore by the sea, as seaweed or eelgrass. — *v.t. & v.i.* To wreck or be wrecked. [Fusion of OE *wræc* revenge and MDu. *wrak* wreck]

wrack² (rak) *n.* See RACK³.

wraith (rāth) *n.* **1.** An apparition of a person thought to be alive, seen shortly before or shortly after his death. **2.** Any specter, ghost, or apparition. [Origin unknown]

wran·gle (rang′gəl) *v.* **·gled, ·gling** *v.i.* **1.** To argue or dispute noisily; brawl. — *v.t.* **2.** To argue; debate. **3.** *U.S.* To herd or round up (livestock). — *n.* An angry dispute. [Cf. LG *wrangeln* to quarrel] — **wran′gler** *n.*

wrap (rap) *v.* **wrapped** or **wrapt, wrap·ping** *v.t.* **1.** To su round and cover by something folded or wound about swathe; enwrap. **2.** To cover with paper, etc., folded abou and secured. **3.** To wind or fold (a covering) about som thing. **4.** To surround so as to obscure; blot out or concea envelop. **5.** To fold, wind, or draw together. — *v.i.* **6.** T be or become twined or coiled: with *about, around*, etc. — **to be wrapped up in 1.** To be clothed in or enveloped b (something). **2.** To be totally absorbed, involved, or inte ested in (something). — **to keep under wraps** To keep secre — *n.* **1.** An article of dress drawn or folded about a perso a wrapper. **2.** *pl.* Outer garments collectively, as cloak scarfs, etc. **3.** A blanket. [ME *wrappen*]

wrap·a·round (rap′ə·round′) *adj.* **1.** Designating a ga ment, as a skirt, dress, coat, etc., open down to the hem an made to fit by being wrapped around the body. **2.** E circling or overlapping: a *wraparound* windshield.

wrap·per (rap′ər) *n.* **1.** A paper enclosing a newspape magazine, or similar packet for mailing or otherwise. **2.** woman's dressing gown. **3.** One who or that which wrap

wrap·ping (rap′ing) *n. Often pl.* A covering; something which an object is wrapped.

wrath (rath, räth; *Brit.* rôth) *n.* **1.** Extreme or violent ra or fury; vehement indignation. **2.** An act done in viole rage, esp. in vengeance or punishment. [OE < *wrath* wrot

wrath·ful (rath′fəl, räth′-) *adj.* **1.** Full of wrath; extrem angry. **2.** Springing from or expressing wrath. — **wrat ful·ly** *adv.* — **wrath′ful·ness** *n.*

wrath·y (rath′ē, räth′ē) *adj.* **wrath·i·er, wrath·i·est** *Infc mal* Wrathful. — **wrath′i·ly** *adv.* — **wrath′i·ness** *n.*

wreak (rēk) *v.t.* **1.** To inflict or exact, as vengeance. **2.** give free expression to (anger, hatred, etc.); vent. [C *wrecan* to drive, avenge]

wreath (rēth) *n. pl.* **wreaths** (rēthz) **1.** A band or cir of flowers or greenery, often worn on the head as a crown placed on a grave or at a door, window, etc. **2.** Any cur band of circular or spiral shape, as of smoke. [OE < *writh* to bind, tie] — **wreath′y** *n.*

wreathe (rēth) *v.* **wreathed, wreath·ing** *v.t.* **1.** To fo into a wreath, as by twisting or twining. **2.** To adorn or e circle with or as with wreaths. **3.** To envelop; cover: I face was *wreathed* in smiles. — *v.i.* **4.** To take the form o wreath. **5.** To twist, turn, or coil, as masses of clou [< ME *writhen* to writhe]

wreck (rek) *v.t.* **1.** To cause the destruction or wreck of, a vessel. **2.** To bring ruin, damage, or destruction upc **3.** To tear down, as a building; dismantle. — *v.i.* **4.** suffer wreck; be ruined. — *n.* **1.** That which has be ruined or destroyed. **2.** Property cast upon land by the se either broken portions of a wrecked vessel or cargo from **3.** The accidental destruction or ruin of a ship; also, the sl so destroyed. **4.** One who is physically, mentally, or mor ly unsound or ruined. **5.** The act of wrecking, or the state being wrecked. [< AF < OF < ON *wrekan* to drive]

wreck·age (rek′ij) *n.* **1.** The act of wrecking, or the sta of being wrecked. **2.** Broken or disordered remnants fragments from a wreck.

wreck·er (rek′ər) *n.* **1.** One who or that which cau wreck, destruction, or frustration of any sort. **2.** One e ployed in tearing down and removing old buildings. **3.** person, train, car, or machine that clears away wrecks. One employed to recover disabled vessels or wrecked carg for the owners; also, a vessel employed in this service.

wreck·ing (rek′ing) *n.* The work or art of a wrecker. *adj.* Of, engaged in, or used in pulling down buildings or salvaging and clearing away wrecks.

wren (ren) *n.* **1.** Any of numerous small birds having sho rounded wings and a short tail, including the common ho wren. **2.** Any of numerous similar birds. [OE *wrenna*

wrench (rench) *n.* **1.** A violent twist. **2.** A sharp or olent twist or pull, as in the ankle, back, etc.; a sprain. Any sudden and violent emotion or grief. **4.** Any perv sion or distortion of an original meaning. **5.** Any of vari tools for twisting or turning bolts, nuts, pipe, etc. — *v.t.* To twist violently; turn suddenly by force; wrest. **2.** twist forcibly so as to cause strain or injury; sprain. **3.** twist from the proper meaning, intent, or use. **4.** To str or force the feelings, thoughts, etc., of: to *wrench* ones away from pleasure. — *v.i.* **5.** To give a twist or wren [OE *wrenc* trick]

wrest (rest) *v.t.* **1.** To pull or force away by violent twi ing or wringing; wrench. **2.** To turn from the true meanir character, intent, or application; distort. **3.** To seize for bly by violence, extortion, or usurpation. **4.** To extract toil and effort: to *wrest* a living from barren soil. — *n.* An act of wresting. **2.** A misapplication or perversion. A crooked act. **4.** A key for tuning a stringed instrument a harp. [OE *wræstan*] — **wrest′er** *n.*

wres·tle (res′əl) *v.* **·tled, ·tling** *v.i.* **1.** To engage in wr tling. **2.** To struggle, as for mastery; contend. — *v.t.* To engage in (a wrestling match), or wrestle with. **V.**

rrow (a calf) and hold it down for branding. —*n.* **1.** A
restling match. **2.** Any hard struggle. [OE *wræstlian*,
eq. of *wræstan* to wrest] — **wres′tler** *n.*

res·tling (res′ling) *n.* A sport or exercise in which each of
wo unarmed contestants endeavors to throw the other to
e ground or force him into a certain fallen position.

etch (rech) *n.* **1.** A base, vile, or contemptible person.
. A miserable or pitiable person. [OE *wrecca* outcast <
recan to drive]

etch·ed (rech′id) *adj.* **1.** Sunk in dejection; profoundly
nhappy. **2.** Causing misery or grief. **3.** Unsatisfactory or
orthless in ability or quality. **4.** Despicable; contemptible.
- **wretch′ed·ly** *adv.* — **wretch′ed·ness** *n.*

ig·gle (rig′əl) *v.* **·gled, ·gling** *v.i.* **1.** To twist in a sinuous
anner; squirm; writhe. **2.** To proceed as by twisting or
awling. **3.** To make one's way by evasive or indirect
eans. — *v.t.* **4.** To cause to wriggle. — *n.* The motion of
e who or that which wriggles; a squirm. [< MLG *wrig-
ln*, freq. of *wriggen* to twist] — **wrig′gly** *adj.*

ig·gler (rig′lər) *n.* **1.** One who or that which wriggles.
. A mosquito larva.

ight (rīt) *n.* One who constructs, contrives, or creates:
ed chiefly in compounds: *playwright.* [OE *wyrhta*]

ing (ring) *v.* **wrung** (*Rare* **winged**), **wring·ing** *v.t.* **1.** To
ueeze or compress by twisting. **2.** To squeeze or press
t, as water, by twisting. **3.** To extort; acquire by extor-
on. **4.** To distress; torment. **5.** To twist or wrest violent-
out of shape or place: to *wring* his neck. — *v.i.* **6.** To
rithe or squirm, as with anguish. — *n.* The act of wring-
g. [OE *wringan*]

ing·er (ring′ər) *n.* **1.** One who or that which wrings. **2.**
contrivance used to press water out of fabrics after wash-
g; also, the operator of such a machine.

in·kle[1] (ring′kəl) *n.* **1.** A small ridge, crease, or fold, as
a smooth surface. **2.** A small fold or crease in the skin,
u. produced by age or by excessive exposure to the ele-
ents. — *v.* **·kled, ·kling** *v.t.* **1.** To make a wrinkle or
rinkles in, as by creasing, folding, crumpling, etc. — *v.i.*
To be or become contracted into wrinkles or ridges. [OE
wrinclod, pp. of *gewrinclian* to wind] — **wrin′kly** *adj.*

in·kle[2] (ring′kəl) *n.* *Informal* A curious or ingenious
ethod, idea, device, etc. [Prob. dim. of OE *wrenc* trick]

ist (rist) *n.* **1.** The part or joint of the arm that lies be-
ween the hand and the forearm. ◆ Collateral adjective:
rpal. **2.** The part of a glove or garment that covers the
rist. **3.** A wrist pin. [OE, prob. < *writhan* to writhe]

ist·band (rist′band, -bənd, riz′-) *n.* The band of a sleeve
at covers the wrist or ends a shirt sleeve; a cuff.

ist·let (rist′lit) *n.* **1.** A flexible band worn on the wrist
· warmth. **2.** A bracelet. **3.** *Slang* A handcuff.

ist pin *Mech.* **1.** A pin holding together the piston and
nnecting rod of a steam engine. **2.** A similar pin in the
oss-head of an internal-combustion engine.

ist watch A watch set in a band or strap and worn at
e wrist.

it[1] (rit) *n.* **1.** *Law* A mandatory precept, under seal, is-
ed by a court, and commanding the person to whom it is
ddressed to do or not to do some act. **2.** That which is
ritten: now chiefly in the phrase *Holy Writ*, meaning the
ble. [OE, a writing < *writan* to write]

it[2] (rit) Archaic or dialectal past tense and past participle
WRITE.

ite (rīt) *v.* **wrote** (*Archaic* or *Dial.* **writ**), **writ·ten** (*Ar-
aic* or *Dial.* **writ**), **writ·ing** *v.t.* **1.** To trace or inscribe
tters, words, numbers, symbols, etc.) on a surface with
n or pencil, or by other means. **2.** To describe in writing.
To communicate by letter. **4.** *Informal* To communicate
th by letter: He *writes* her every day. **5.** To produce by
riting; be the author or composer of. **6.** To draw up;
aft: to *write* a check. **7.** To cover or fill with writing: to
rite two full pages. **8.** To leave marks or evidence of:
nxiety is *written* on his face. **9.** To spell or inscribe as
ecified: He *writes* his name with two *n's.* **10.** To entitle
designate in writing: He *writes* himself "General." **11.**
o underwrite: to *write* an insurance policy. — *v.i.* **12.**
) trace or inscribe letters, etc., on a surface, as of paper.
3. To communicate in writing. **14.** To be engaged in the
cupation of a writer or author. **15.** To produce a speci-
d quality of writing. — **to write down 1.** To put into
riting. **2.** To injure or depreciate in writing. — **to write
p 1.** To cancel or remove (claims, debts, etc.) from an
en account. **2.** To acknowledge the loss or failure of. —
write in 1. To insert in writing, as in a document. **2.** To
ame (a vote) for one not listed on a ballot by inserting his
ame in writing. — **to write out 1.** To put into writing.
. To write in full or complete form. — **to write up 1.** To
escribe fully in writing. **2.** To praise fully or too fully in
riting. [OE *writan*]

write-in (rīt′in′) *adj.* *Informal* Designating a method of
voting whereby a name not formally on the ballot is written
in by the voter. — *n.* In voting, a name thus written.

write-off (rīt′ôf′, -of′) *n.* **1.** A cancellation. **2.** An amount
canceled or noted as a loss.

writ·er (rī′tər) *n.* **1.** One who writes. **2.** One who engages
in literary composition.

writer's cramp *Pathol.* Spasmodic contraction of the
muscles of the fingers and hand, caused by excessive writing.
Also **writer's palsy** or **spasm**.

write-up (rīt′up′) *n.* *Informal* A written description,
record, or account, usu. laudatory, as of a town, manufacturing enterprise, or public institution.

writhe (rīth) *v.* **writhed, writhed, writh·ing** *v.t.* **1.** To
cause to twist or bend; distort. — *v.i.* **2.** To twist or distort the body, face, etc., as in pain. **3.** To suffer acutely, as
from embarrassment, anguish, etc. — *n.* An act of writh-
ing. [OE *writhan*] — **writh′er** *n.*

writ·ing (rī′ting) *n.* **1.** The act of one who writes. **2.** The
characters so made; handwriting. **3.** Anything written or
expressed in letters; esp., a literary production. **4.** The profession or occupation of a writer. **5.** The practice, art, form,
or style of literary composition.

writing paper Paper prepared to receive ink in writing.

writ·ten (rit′n) Past participle of WRITE.

wrong (rông, rong) *adj.* **1.** Not correct; mistaken; erroneous: a *wrong* estimate. **2.** Not suitable; inappropriate; improper: the *wrong* clothes; the *wrong* job. **3.** Not according
to the right, proper, or correct method, standard, intention,
etc.: the *wrong* way to do it. **4.** Not working or acting
properly or satisfactorily: Something is *wrong* with the lock.
5. Intended or made to be turned under, inward, or so as
not to be seen: the *wrong* side of the cloth. **6.** Not desired
or intended: the *wrong* road. **7.** Not favored by conventional social standards: the *wrong* side of town. **8.** Not
morally right, proper, or just. **9.** Unsatisfactory: the *wrong*
reply. — **to go wrong 1.** To lapse from the strict path of
rectitude. **2.** To turn out badly; go astray. — *adv.* In a
wrong direction, place, or manner; erroneously. — *n.* **1.**
That which is wrong, as an evil or unjust action. **2.** The
state or condition of being wrong: to be in the *wrong*. **3.**
Law An invasion or violation of one's legal rights. — *v.t.*
1. To violate the rights of; inflict injury or injustice upon.
2. To impute evil to unjustly; malign: If you think so, you
wrong him. **3.** To seduce or dishonor (a woman). [OE <
ON *rangr* awry, unjust] — **wrong′er** *n.* — **wrong′ly** *adv.*
— **wrong′ness** *n.*

wrong-do·er (rông′dōo′ər, rong′-) *n.* One who does wrong.
— **wrong′do′ing** *n.*

wrong·ful (rông′fəl, rong′-) *adj.* **1.** Characterized by
wrong or injustice; injurious; unjust. **2.** Unlawful; illegal.
— **wrong′ful·ly** *adv.* — **wrong′ful·ness** *n.*

wrong-head·ed (rông′hed′id, rong′-) *adj.* Stubbornly or
perversely erring in judgment, action, etc. — **wrong′-
head′ed·ly** *adv.* — **wrong′-head′ed·ness** *n.*

wrote (rōt) Past tense of WRITE.

wroth (rôth) *adj.* *Archaic* Filled with anger; furious; in-
censed. Also **wroth′ful** (-fəl). [OE *wrāth*]

wrought (rôt) *Archaic* past tense and past participle of
WORK. — *adj.* **1.** Beaten or hammered into shape by tools:
wrought gold. **2.** Worked; molded. **3.** Made with delicacy;
elaborated carefully. **4.** Made; fashioned; formed: often in
combination: *well-wrought*. — **wrought up** Excited; agitated. [ME < OE *geworht*, pp. of *wrycan* to work]

wrought iron Commercially pure iron, prepared from pig
iron and easily forged and welded into various shapes.

wrung (rung) Past tense and past participle of WRING.

wry (rī) *adj.* **wri·er** or **wry·er, wri·est** or **wry·est 1.** Bent
to one side or out of position; contorted; askew: a *wry* smile.
2. Deviating from that which is right or proper; warped.
3. Perverse, ironic, or bitter: *wry* humor. — *v.t.* **wried,
wry·ing** To twist; contort. [ME < OE *wrigian* to move,
tend] — **wry′ly** *adv.* — **wry′ness** *n.*

wry·neck (rī′nek′) *n.* **1.** A bird allied to the woodpeckers,
with the habit of twisting its head and neck. **2.** *Pathol.* A
spasmodic affliction that twists the neck muscles. — **wry-
necked** (rī′nekt′) *adj.*

Wy·an·dot (wī′ən·dot) *n.* *pl.* **·dot** or **·dots 1.** One of a
tribe of North American Indians of Iroquoian stock and
descendants of Hurons, presently settled in Oklahoma. **2.**
An Iroquoian language. Also spelled *Wyandotte*.

Wy·an·dotte (wī′ən·dot) *n.* **1.** One of an American breed
of domestic fowls. **2.** *pl.* **·dotte** or **·dottes** A Wyandot. **3.**
The Wyandot language. [after the *Wyandot* Indians]

wych-elm (wich′elm′) *n.* A widespreading elm, common
in the British Isles: also called *wich, witch*: also spelled *wich-
elm, witch-elm.* Also **wych.** [< *wych*, var. of WITCH[2] + ELM]

wych-ha·zel (wich′hā′zəl) *n.* Witch hazel.

X

x, X (eks) *n.* *pl.* **x's** or **xs, X's** or **Xs, ex·es** (ek'siz) **1.** The twenty-fourth letter of the English alphabet. **2.** The sounds represented by the letter *x*, in English variously sounded as (ks), as in *axle, box, next*; (gz), as in *executive, exert*; (ksh), as in *noxious*; (gzh), as in *luxurious*; and initially, always (z), as in *xenophobe, xylophone*. **3.** Anything shaped like an X. **4.** An unknown quantity, factor, result, etc. — *symbol* **1.** The Roman numeral ten. **2.** A mark shaped like an X, representing the signature of one who cannot write. **3.** A mark used in diagrams, maps, etc., to place some event or substance, or to point out something to be emphasized. **4.** A symbol used to indicate a kiss. **5.** Christ: an abbreviation used in combination: *Xmas*.

xan·the·in (zan'thē·in) *n.* *Biochem.* The water-soluble portion of the yellow coloring matter found in the cell sap of some plants. [< F < Gk. *xanthos* yellow]

xan·thic (zan'thik) *adj.* Having a yellow or yellowish color. [< F < Gk. *xanthos* yellow]

xan·thine (zan'thēn, -thin) *n.* *Biochem.* A crystalline nitrogenous compound, $C_5H_4N_4O_2$, contained in blood, urine, and other animal secretions, and in some plants.

xantho- *combining form* Yellow. Also, before vowels, **xanth-**. [< Gk. *xanthos* yellow]

xan·thous (zan'thəs) *adj.* **1.** Yellow. **2.** *Anthropol.* Of or pertaining to the yellow-skinned, or Mongoloid, ethnic division of mankind.

X-ax·is (eks'ak'sis) *n.* *pl.* **-ax·es** (-ak'sēz) The more nearly horizontal axis in a graph; the abscissa.

X-chro·mo·some (eks'krō'mə·sōm) *n.* *Genetics* One of the two types of chromosomes that determine the sex of an offspring.

xe·bec (zē'bek) *n.* A small, three-masted Mediterranean vessel, with both square and lateen sails, formerly used by Algerian pirates: also spelled *zebec*. [Earlier *chebec* < F < Sp. < Arabic *shabbāk*]

xeno- *combining form* Strange; foreign; different. Also, before vowels, **xen-**. [< Gk. *xenos* stranger]

xe·non (zē'non) *n.* A heavy, gaseous element (symbol Xe) occurring in extremely small quantities in the atmosphere and freezing at a very low temperature. See ELEMENT. [< Gk., neut. of *xenos* strange]

xen·o·phobe (zen'ə·fōb) *n.* One who hates or distrusts strangers or foreigners.

xen·o·pho·bi·a (zen'ə·fō'bē·ə) *n.* Hatred or distrust of foreigners or strangers. — **xen'o·pho'bic** (-fō'bik) *adj.*

xero- *combining form* Dry; dryness. Also, before vowels, **xer-**. [< Gk. *xēros* dry]

xe·rog·ra·phy (zi·rog'rə·fē) *n.* A method of printing in which a negatively charged ink powder is sprayed upon a positively charged metal plate, from which it is transferred to the printing surface by electrostatic attraction.

— **xe·ro·graph·ic** (zir'ō·graf'ik) *adj.* — **xe·rog'raph·er**

xe·roph·i·lous (zi·rof'ə·ləs) *adj.* *Biol.* Growing in or adap⟨ed to dry, hot climates.

xe·ro·phyte (zir'ə·fīt) *n.* *Bot.* A plant adapted to dry co⟨ ditions of air and soil. — **xe·ro·phyt'ic** (-fit'ik) *adj.*

xe·ro·print·ing (zir'ō·prin'ting) *n.* A simplified variati⟨ of xerography, using a suitably prepared plate on a rotati⟨ cylinder.

Xer·ox (zir'oks) *n.* A xerographic process for reproduci⟨ printed or pictorial matter: a trade name. — *v.t.* To ma⟨ or reproduce by Xerox: to *Xerox* 10 copies; to *Xerox* a do⟨ ment. Also **xer'ox**.

Xho·sa (kō'sä) *n.* The Bantu language of the Kaffirs, clos⟨ ly related to Zulu: also called *Kaffir*: also **Xosa**.

xi (zī, sī; *Gk.* ksē) *n.* The fourteenth letter in the Greek ⟨ phabet (Ξ, ξ), equivalent to the English *x*. See ALPHABE⟨

-xion Var. of -TION.

xiphi- *combining form* Sword. Also, before vowels, **xiph⟨** [< Gk. *xiphos* sword]

xiph·oid (zif'oid) *adj.* Shaped like a sword.

Xmas Christmas: popular abbreviation. ◆ *Xmas*, thou⟨ best avoided in formal contexts, has been used in writt⟨ English since the sixteenth century and cannot be co⟨ demned as a modern commercialism. [< *X*, abbr. for *Chr⟨* < Gk. *X*, chi, the first letter of *Christos* Christ + -MAS]

X-rat·ed (eks'rā'tid) *adj.* Of a motion picture, characteri⟨ by explicit sex.

X-ray (eks'rā') *v.t.* To examine, photograph, diagnose, treat with X-rays. — *n.* A picture made with X-ray⟨ roentgenogram: also **X-ray photograph**.

X-rays (eks'rāz') *n.pl.* Electromagnetic radiations of e⟨ tremely short wavelength, emitted from a substance when⟨ is bombarded by a stream of electrons moving in a vacuu⟨ at a sufficiently high velocity, as in an electron tube. T⟨ ability to penetrate solids, to ionize gases, and to act ⟨ photographic plates has many useful applications, especia⟨ in the detection, diagnosis, and treatment of certain orga⟨ disorders, chiefly internal. Also called *Roentgen rays*. [Tra⟨ of G *X-strahlen*, name coined by Roentgen, their discover⟨ because their nature was unknown]

xy·lem (zī'ləm) *n.* *Bot.* The portion of a vascular bundle⟨ higher plants that is made up of woody tissue, parenchym⟨ and associated cells, etc. [< G < Gk. *xylon* wood]

xylo- *combining form* Wood; woody. Also, before vowe⟨ **xyl-**. [< Gk. *xylon* wood]

xy·lo·phone (zī'lə·fōn) *n.* A musical instrument consisti⟨ of a row of wooden bars graduated in length to form a chromatic scale, and sounded by being struck with mallets. — **xy·lo·phon·ist** (zī'lə·fō'· nist, zī·lof'ə·nist) *n.*

XYLOPHONE

Y

y, Y (wī) *n.* *pl.* **y's** or **ys, Y's** or **Ys, wyes** (wīz) **1.** The twenty-fifth letter of the English alphabet. **2.** The sounds represented by the letter *y*. Initial *y* (introducing either a vowel or a syllable) represents a voiced palatal semivowel, as in *yet, you, yonder, beyond*. Final *y* represents either a vowel, pronounced (ē), as in *honey, pretty, steady*; a diphthong, pronounced (ī), as in *fly, my*; or the final glide of a diphthong, as in *gray, obey, annoy*. Internal *y* represents a vowel (i), as in *lyric, myth, syllable*; a diphthong (ī), as in *lyre, type, psychic*; an r-colored central vowel (ûr) or (ər), as in *myrtle, martyr*. **3.** Anything shaped like a Y, as: a pipe coupling, connection, etc. **b** A forked piece serving as a rest or support, as for some part of a sighting instrument. — *symbol Chem.* Yttrium (symbol Y).

y- *prefix* Used in Middle English as a sign of the past p⟨ ticiple, as an intensive, or without perceptible force: *ycl⟨ yclept*. It survives (as a-) in such words as *alike, aware, ⟨* Also spelled *i-*. [OE *ge-*]

-y¹ *suffix of adjectives* Being, possessing, or resembling wh⟨ is expressed in the root: *stony, rainy*. Also *-ey*, when ad⟨ to words ending in *y*, as in *clayey, skyey*. [OE *-ig*]

-y² *suffix* Th equality or state of being: *victory*: often used⟨ abstract nouns formed from adjectives in *-ous* and *-ic*. [<⟨ *-ie* < L *-ia*; also < Gk. *-ia, -eia*]

-y³ *suffix* Little; small: *kitty*: often used in nicknames or⟨ express endearment, as in *Tommy*. [Prob. < dial. E (Sc⟨ tish)]

yacht (yot) *n.* A vessel specially built or fitted for racing⟨

r private pleasure excursions. — *v.i.* To cruise, race, or
il in a yacht. [< Du. *jaghte*, short for *jaghtschip* pursuit
ıp < *jaght* hunting + *schip* ship]

·ht·ing (yot′ing) *n.* The act, practice, or pastime of
ıling a yacht.

·hts·man (yots′mən) *n.* *pl.* **·men** (-mən) One who
ıns or sails a yacht. Also **yacht′er, yacht′man.** — **yachts′·**
ɔm′an (-wŏŏm′ən) *n.fem.*

·hts·man·ship (yots′mən·ship) *n.* The art or skill of
ıchting. Also **yacht′man·ship.**

·¹ (yä, ya) *interj.* An exclamation of disgust or contempt.
·² (yä, yä) *interj.* *Informal* Yes. [Alter. of YES]

·hoo (yä′hŏŏ, yä′-, yä·hŏŏ′) *n.* 1. Any low, vicious person.
An awkward fellow; a bumpkin. [< YAHOO]

·hoo (yä′hŏŏ, yä′-, yä·hŏŏ′) *n.* In Swift's *Gulliver's*
avels, one of a race of brutish beings in human form.

·h·weh (yä′we) *n.* In the Old Testament, the national god
Israel; God. See JEHOVAH. Also **Yah·ve** (yä′ve), **Yah·veh.**
< Hebrew *YHWH*]

·¹ (yak) *n.* A large bovine ruminant of the higher re-
ɔns of central Asia, having long hair fringing the shoulders,
les, and tail, and often domesticated. [< Tibetan *gyag*]

·² (yak) *v.i.* **yakked, yak·king** *U.S. Slang* 1. To chatter
isily or constantly. 2. To laugh, esp. boisterously. [Imit.]

n (yam) *n.* 1. The fleshy, edible, tuberous root of any of
rious climbing tropical plants typical of a family of her-
ceous or somewhat woody vines. 2. Any of the plants
ɔwing this root. 3. A large variety of the sweet potato.
< Pg. < Senegal *nyami* to eat]

m·mer (yam′ər) *v.i. Informal* 1. To complain peevishly;
ıimper. 2. To howl; shout. — *v.t.* 3. To utter peevishly;
mplain. — *n.* The act of yammering. [OE *gēomrian* to
ment < *gēomor* sorrowful] — **yam′mer·er** *n.*

ıg (yang) *n.* In Chinese philosophy and art, the male
ment, source of life and heat. Compare YIN. Also **Yang.**
< Chinese]

ık (yangk) *v.t.* 1. To jerk or pull suddenly. — *v.i.* 2.
ɔ give a pull or jerk. 3. *Brit.* To be vigorously active. 4.
it. To jabber; scold. — *n. Informal* A sudden sharp pull.
< dial. E (Scottish) *yank* a sharp sudden blow]

ık (yangk) *n. & adj. Informal* Yankee.

·n·kee (yang′kē) *n.* 1. Originally, a native or inhabitant
New England. 2. A Northerner; esp., a Union soldier
ıring the Civil War; so called in the South. 3. Any citizen
the U.S.: a chiefly foreign usage. — *adj.* 1. Of, pertaining
, or characteristic of the Yankees. 2. American. [? Back
rmation < *Jan Kees* (taken as a plural), John Cheese,
ıg. a nickname for a Hollander; later applied by Dutch
ɔlonists in New York to English settlers in Connecticut]
› **Yan′kee·dom** *n.*

ınkee Doodle A song popular in pre-Revolutionary
mes and one of the national airs of the United States.

ɔ (yap) *n.* 1. *Slang* Talk; jabber. 2. A bark or yelp.
Slang The mouth. — *v.t.* **yapped, yap·ping** 1. *Slang*
ɔ talk idly or emptily; jabber. 2. *Informal* To bark or
ɪlp, as a cur. [Imit. of a dog's bark]

·qui (yä′kē) *n.* One of a tribe of North American Indians
ɪlonging to the Piman branch of the Uto-Aztecan stock,
ɔw living in southern Sonora, Mexico.

rd¹ (yärd) *n.* 1. A standard English and American meas-
·e of length; 3 feet, or 36 inches, or 0.914 meter. See table
ont of book. 2. A yardstick. 3. *Naut.* A long, slen-
·r, tapering spar set crosswise on a mast and used to sup-
ɔrt sails. [OE *gierd* rod, measure of length]

rd² (yärd) *n.* 1. A tract of ground, often enclosed, adja-
ınt to a residence, church, school, or other building. 2. An
ıclosure used for some specific work: often in combination:
ıckyard; shipyard. 3. An enclosure or piece of ground ad-
ıcent to a railroad station, used for making up trains and
·r storing the rolling stock. 4. The winter pasturing ground
· deer and moose. 5. An enclosure for animals, poultry, etc.
· *v.t.* 1. To put or collect into or as into a yard. — *v.i.* 2.
ɔ gather into an enclosure or yard. [OE *geard* enclosure]

rd·age (yär′dij) *n.* 1. The amount or length of some-
ıing expressed in yards. 2. Yard goods. [< YARD¹]

rd·arm (yärd′ärm′) *n. Naut.* Either end of a yard of a
ıuare sail.

rd goods Cloth that is sold by the yard.

rd·man¹ (yärd′mən) *n.* *pl.* **·men** (-mən) *Naut.* A sailor
ho works on the yards.

rd·man² (yärd′mən) *n.* *pl.* **·men** (-mən) A man em-
ɔyed in a yard, esp. on a railroad.

rd·mas·ter (yärd′mas′tər, -mäs′-) *n.* A railroad official
ıving charge of a yard.

rd·stick (yärd′stik′) *n.* 1. A graduated measuring stick
yard in length. 2. Any measure or standard of compari-
ɔn. Also *Archaic* **yard′wand′** (-wond′).

rn (yärn) *n.* 1. Any spun, threadlike material, natural or

synthetic, prepared for use in weaving, knitting, etc. 2.
Continuous strands of spun fiber, as wool, cotton, linen, silk,
etc. 3. A quantity of such material. 4. *Informal* A long,
exciting story of adventure, often of doubtful truth. — *v.i.*
Informal To tell a yarn or yarns. [OE *gearn*]

yarn-dyed (yärn′dīd′) *adj.* Made of yarn dyed before being woven into material.

yar·row (yar′ō) *n.* Any of various perennial herbs of
Europe and North America having finely dissected leaves,
small white flowers, and a pungent odor. [OE *gearwe*]

yat·a·ghan (yat′ə·gan, -gən; *Turkish* yä′tä·gän′) *n.* A
Turkish sword or scimitar with a double-curved blade and a
handle without a guard. Also **yat′a·gan.** [< Turkish]

yaw (yô) *v.i.* 1. *Naut.* To steer wildly, or out of its course,
as a ship when struck by a heavy sea. 2. To move unsteadily or irregularly. 3. *Aeron.* To deviate from the flight path
by angular displacement about the vertical axis; fishtail. —
v.t. 4. To cause to yaw. — *n.* 1. A movement of a ship by
which it temporarily alters its course. 2. *Aeron.* The angular movement of an aircraft, projectile, etc., about its vertical axis. 3. Any irregular, unsteady, or deviating motion.
[Cf. ON *jaga* to move to and fro]

yawl¹ (yôl) See YOWL.

yawl² (yôl) *n.* 1. A fore-and-aft rigged, two-masted vessel
having the mizzenmast or jiggermast abaft the rudder post.
2. A ship's small boat. 3. A small fishing boat. [Appar. <
Du. *jol*, orig. a boat used in Jutland]

yawn (yôn) *v.i.* 1. To open the mouth wide, usu. involuntarily and with a long, full inspiration of the breath, often
the result of drowsiness, fatigue, or boredom. 2. To be or
stand wide open, esp. as ready to engulf or receive something: A chasm *yawned* below. — *v.t.* 3. To express or
utter with a yawn. — *n.* 1. The act of yawning. 2. The
act of opening wide. [Prob. fusion of OE *geonian* to yawn
and *gānian* to gape] — **yawn′er** *n.*

yawp (yôp) *v.i.* 1. To bark or yelp. 2. *Informal* To gape;
yawn audibly. 3. *Brit. Informal* To bawl; talk loudly. — *n.* 1. A bark or yelp. 2. A shout; noise; noisy talking; also, a loud, uncouth outcry. Also **yaup.** [ME *golpen*,
pp. of *gelpen* to boast] — **yawp′er** *n.*

yaws (yôz) *n.pl. Pathol.* A contagious skin disease occurring in tropical and subtropical countries, caused by a
spirochete and resembling syphilis. [< Carib *yáya*]

Y-ax·is (wī′ak′sis) *n.* *pl.* **-ax·es** (-ak′sēz) The more nearly
vertical axis in a graph or coordinate system; the ordinate.

yay (yā) *U.S. Dial. adj.* 1. This many; this much. 2.
Ever so many: for *yay* years. — *adv.* 1. To this extent. 2.
Ever so: *yay* big. [Cf. G *je* ever]

Y-chro·mo·some (wī′krō′mə·sōm) *n. Genetics* One of the
two types of chromosome that determine the sex of an offspring.

y·clept (i·klept′) *adj. Archaic* Called; named. Also **y·**
cleped′. [OE *geclypod*, pp. of *clypian* to call]

ye¹ (thē) The: a mistaken form resulting from the substitution of the character *y* for the thorn (þ) of the Old and Middle English alphabet.

ye² (yē) *pron. Archaic* A pronoun of the second person, originally nominative plural: "Blessed are *ye* when men shall re-
vile you''; later, also nominative singular and objective singular and plural. [ME *ye, ȝe*, nominative pl. < OE *gē*]

yea (yā) *adv.* 1. *Archaic* A term of affirmation or assent,
now superseded by *yes*. 2. *Archaic* Not only so, but more
so: used to intensify or amplify: There were fifty, *yea*, a hundred archers. 3. In reality; indeed; verily: used to introduce a sentence, etc. — *n.* 1. An affirmative vote or voter:
opposed to *nay*. 2. An affirmation. [OE *gēa*]

yeah (yâ, ye′ə) *adv. Informal* Yes. [< YES]

yean (yēn) *v.t. & v.i.* To bear (young), as a goat or sheep.
[OE (assumed) *geēanian*]

yean·ling (yēn′ling) *n.* The young of a goat or sheep. —
adj. Young or newly born.

year (yir) *n.* 1. The period of time in which the earth com-
pletes one revolution around the sun, consisting of 365 or 366
days divided into 12 months and now reckoned as beginning
January 1 and ending December 31; also, a similar period in
other calendars. 2. Any period of 12 months, usu. reckoned
from a specific date or time: a *year* from now. 3. The period
of time during which a planet revolves once around the sun.
4. A specific period of time, usu. less than a year, given over
to some special work or activity: the school *year*. 5. *pl.* Age,
esp. old age: active for his *years*. 6. *pl.* Time: in *years* gone
by and *years* to come. — **year after year** Every year. —
year by year Each year; with each succeeding year. —
year in, year out From one year to the next; without cessation. [OE *gēar*]

year·book (yir′bŏŏk′) *n.* A book published annually, presenting information about the previous year.

year·ling (yir′ling) *n.* A young animal past its first year and not yet two years old; esp., a colt or filly a year old dating from January 1 of the year of foaling. — *adj.* Being a year old.

year·long (yir′lông′, -long′) *adj.* Continuing through a year.

year·ly (yir′lē) *adj.* **1.** Occurring, done, payable, seen, etc., once a year; annual. **2.** Continuing or lasting for a year: a *yearly* subscription. — *adv.* Once a year; annually.

yearn (yûrn) *v.i.* **1.** To desire something earnestly; long; hanker; pine: with *for.* **2.** To be deeply moved; feel sympathy. [OE *giernan, geornan*]

yearn·ing (yûr′ning) *n.* A strong emotion of longing or desire, esp. with tenderness. — **yearn′ing·ly** *adv.*

year-round (yir′round′) *adj.* Open, operating, or continuing for the entire year: a *year-round* health resort.

yeast (yēst) *n.* **1.** A substance consisting of minute cells of fungi that clump together in a yellow, frothy, viscous growth promoting fermentation in saccharine liquids, with the production of alcohol and carbon dioxide, as in the brewing of beer and the raising of bread. **2.** Such a substance mixed with flour or meal, and sold commercially. **3.** Froth or spume. **4.** Mental or moral ferment or agitation. — *v.i.* To foam; froth. [OE *gist*]

yeast cake A mixture of living yeast cells and starch in compressed form, suitable for use in baking or brewing.

yeast plant Any of a group of fungi that form yeast.

yeast·y (yēs′tē) *adj.* **yeast·i·er, yeast·i·est** **1.** Of, resembling, or containing yeast. **2.** Causing or characterized by fermentation. **3.** Restless; unsettled; frivolous. **4.** Covered with or consisting mainly of froth or foam. **5.** Light or unsubstantial. — **yeast′i·ness** *n.*

yegg (yeg) *n. Slang* A burglar or safe-cracker. Also **yegg′·man** (-mən) [Origin unknown]

yell (yel) *v.t. & v.i.* To shout; scream; roar; also, to cheer. — *n.* **1.** A sharp, loud, inarticulate cry, as of pain, terror, anger, etc. **2.** A rhythmic cheer composed of a series of words or nonsense syllables and shouted by a group in unison. [OE *giellan, gellan*] — **yell′er** *n.*

yel·low (yel′ō) *adj.* **1.** Having the color of ripe lemons, or sunflowers. **2.** Changed to a sallow color by age, sickness, or the like: a paper *yellow* with age. **3.** Having a yellowish complexion, as a member of the Mongoloid ethnic group. **4.** Melancholy or jealous. **5.** Sensational, esp. offensively so: said of newspapers: *yellow* journalism. **6.** *Informal* Cowardly; mean; dishonorable. — *n.* **1.** The color of the spectrum between green and orange. **2.** Any pigment or dyestuff having or producing such a color. **3.** The yolk of an egg. **4.** *pl. Bot.* Any of various unrelated plant diseases in which there is stunting of growth and yellowing of the foliage. **5.** *pl.* Jaundice, esp. a variety that affects domestic animals. — *v.t. & v.i.* To make or become yellow. [OE *geolu*] — **yel′low·ly** *adv.* — **yel′low·ness** *n.*

yel·low-bel·lied (yel′ō-bel′ēd) *adj.* **1.** *Slang* Cowardly; yellow. **2.** Having a yellow underside, as a bird.

yel·low·bird (yel′ō-bûrd′) *n.* Any of several yellow birds, as the American goldfinch or the yellow warbler.

yellow cake *Canadian Informal* Uranium ore; concentrated uranium oxide.

yel·low-dog contract (yel′ō-dôg′, -dog′) A contract with an employer, no longer legal, in which an employee agrees not to join a labor union during his term of employment.

yellow fever *Pathol.* An acute, infectious intestinal disease of tropical and semitropical regions, caused by a filterable virus transmitted by the bite of a mosquito and characterized by jaundice, vomiting, and fatty degeneration of the liver: also called *black vomit, vomito, yellow jack.*

yel·low·ham·mer (yel′ō-ham′ər) *n.* **1.** An Old World bunting having in the male bright yellow plumage and blackish head and tail feathers. **2.** The flicker, a bird. [prob. < OE *geolo* yellow + *amore*, a kind of bird]

yel·low·ish (yel′ō-ish) *adj.* Somewhat yellow. — **yel′low·ish·ness** *n.*

yellow jack **1.** A fish of the West Indies and Florida. **2.** The flag of the quarantine service. **3.** Yellow fever.

yellow jacket Any of various social wasps having bright yellow markings.

yellow metal **1.** A brass consisting of 60 parts copper and 40 parts zinc. **2.** Gold.

yellow peril The alleged power, both political and numerical, of the Oriental peoples of Asia, conceived of as threatening white or Western supremacy.

yellow pine **1.** Any of various American pines, as the loblolly pine. **2.** Their tough, yellowish wood.

yellow race The Mongoloid ethnic division of mankind.

yellow streak A tendency to be cowardly, mean, etc.

yellow warbler A warbler of the southern U.S., bright yellow with brown streaks underneath.

yel·low·wood (yel′ō-wŏŏd′) *n.* **1.** The yellow or yellowish wood of a medium-sized tree of the southern U.S., having a smooth bark, showy white flowers, and yielding a yellow dye. **2.** The tree. **3.** Any of several other trees with yellowish wood, as the Osage orange, buckthorn, smoketree, etc.

yel·low·y (yel′ō-ē) *adj.* Yellowish.

yelp (yelp) *v.i.* **1.** To utter a sharp, shrill cry or bark, a dog. — *v.t.* **2.** To express by a yelp or yelps. — *n.* A sha shrill cry or bark. [OE *gielpan* to boast] — **yelp′er** *n.*

yen[1] (yen) *Informal n.* An ardent longing or desire; inte want; infatuation. — *v.i.* **yenned, yen·ning** To yearn; lo [< Chinese, opium, smoke]

yen[2] (yen) *n. pl.* **yen** The standard monetary unit of pan, equal to 100 sen: in 1960 worth about 7⁄10 U.S. cent. Japanese < Chinese *yüan* round, dollar]

yeo·man (yō′mən) *n. pl.* **·men** (-mən) **1.** A petty officer the U.S. Navy or Coast Guard who performs clerical dut **2.** *Brit.* One who cultivates his own farm. **3.** *Brit.* A y man of the guard. **4.** Formerly, an attendant or serv in the service of a nobleman or of royalty. **5.** Formerly freeholder next below the gentry who owned a small lanc estate or farm. [ME *yeman, yoman*, prob. contr. of *yengm* young man < OE *geong* young + *mann* man]

yeo·man·ly (yō′mən·lē) *adj.* **1.** Of, pertaining to, or rese bling a yeoman. **2.** Brave; rugged; staunch. — *adv.* Lik yeoman; bravely; staunchly.

yeoman of the (royal) guard A member of the spec bodyguard of the English royal household, consisting of a hundred yeomen wearing medieval uniforms and first pointed by Henry VII: also called *beefeater.*

yeo·man·ry (yō′mən·rē) *n.* **1.** The collective body of y men; freemen; farmers. **2.** *Brit.* A home guard of volunt cavalry, created in 1761. In 1907 it became a part of Territorial Army.

yeoman's service Faithful and useful support or servi loyal assistance in need. Also **yeoman service.**

yep (yep) *adv. Informal* Yes. [Alter. of YES]

-yer Var. of -IER.

yes (yes) *adv.* As you say; truly; just so: a reply of affirr tion or consent: opposed to *no,* and sometimes used to force by repetition or addition something that precedes. *n. pl.* **yes·es** or **yes·ses** **1.** A reply in the affirmative. An affirmative vote or voter: often *aye.* — *v.t. & v i.* **yess yes·sing** To say "yes" (to). [OE *gēse*, prob. < *gēa* yea sī, third person sing. present subj. of *bēon* to be]

yes man *Informal* One who agrees without criticism; a s vile, acquiescent assistant or subordinate; toady.

yester- *prefix* Pertaining to the day before the present; extension of the preceding, used of longer periods than a d *yesteryear.* [< YESTER(DAY)]

yes·ter·day (yes′tər·dē, -dā′) *n.* **1.** The day preceding day. **2.** The near past. — *adv.* **1.** On the day before tod **2.** At a recent time. [OE < *giestran* yesterday + *dæg* day

yes·ter·year (yes′tər·yir′) *n.* Last year; yore. [Trans F *antan*; coined by D. G. Rossetti]

yet (yet) *adv.* **1.** In addition; besides; further: often wit comparative: They had twenty miles *yet* to go. **2.** Be or at some future time; eventually: He will *yet* succeed. In continuance of a previous state or condition; still: I hear him *yet.* **4.** At the present time; now: Don't go *yet.* After all the time that has or had elapsed: Are you not rea *yet*? **6.** Up to the present time; before: commonly wit negative: He has never *yet* lied to me. **7.** Than that wh has been previously affirmed: with a comparative: It v hot yesterday; today it is hotter *yet.* **8.** Nevertheless: was hot, *yet* not unpleasant. **9.** As much as; even: He not believe the reports, nor *yet* the evidence. — **as yet** to now. — *conj.* **1.** Nevertheless; notwithstanding: I sp to you peaceably, *yet* you will not listen. **2.** But: He is w ing, *yet* unable. **3.** Although: active, *yet* ill. — **Syn.** BUT[1]. [OE *giet, gieta*]

yew (yōō) *n.* **1.** Any of several evergreen trees or shru with flat, lanceolate leaves and a red berrylike fruit. **2.** hard, fine-grained, durable wood of the common yew. **3.** bow made from the wood of the yew tree. [OE *ēow, iw*]

Yid·dish (yid′ish) *n.* A Germanic language derived fr the Middle High German spoken in the Rhineland in thirteenth and fourteenth centuries, now spoken prima by Jews in eastern Europe, and by Jewish immigrants fr that region in other parts of the world. It contains eleme of Hebrew and the Slavic languages, and is written in brew characters. — *adj.* **1.** Of or pertaining to Yidd written or spoken in Yiddish. **2.** *Slang* Jewish. [< *jüdisch* Jewish < *Jude* Jew]

yield (yēld) *v.t.* **1.** To give forth by a natural process, o a result of labor or cultivation. **2.** To give in return, as investment; furnish: The bonds *yield* five percent inter **3.** To give up, as to superior power; relinquish: often v up: to *yield* a fortress. **4.** To concede or grant: to y precedence. — *v.i.* **5.** To provide a return; produce; be **6.** To give up; surrender. **7.** To give way, as to pressur force; bend, collapse, etc. **8.** To assent or comply, as un compulsion; consent: We *yielded* to their persuasion. **9.** give place, as through inferiority or weakness: with *to*: will *yield* to them in nothing. — *n.* **1.** The amount yield product, as of cultivation or mining. **2.** The profit deri

om invested capital. **3.** *Mil.* The explosive force of a
clear bomb as expressed in kilotons or megatons of TNT.
E *gieldan, geldan* to pay] — **yield′er** *n.*

ld·ing (yēl′ding) *adj.* Disposed to yield; flexible; obedi-
t. — **yield′ing·ly** *adv.* — **yield′ing·ness** *n.*

(yin) *n.* In Chinese philosophy and art, the female ele-
ent, that stands for darkness, cold, and death. Compare
NG. Also **Yin.** [< Chinese]

(yip) *n.* A yelp, as of a dog. — *v.i.* **yipped, yip·ping** To
lp. [Imit.]

e (yip) *interj. Often pl.* An exclamation of fear, surprise,
rror, etc.

suffix *Chem.* Used to denote a radical: *ethyl, butyl.* [<
s. *hylē* wood, matter]

del (yōd′l) *n.* A melody or refrain sung to meaningless
llables, with abrupt changes from chest to falsetto tones,
mmon among Swiss and Tyrolese mountaineers. — *v.i. &*
. **yo·deled** or **·delled, yo·del·ing** or **·del·ling** To sing with a
del, changing the voice quickly from its natural tone to a
lsetto and back. Also **yo′dle.** [< G *jodeln*, lit., to utter
e syllable *jo*] — **yo′del·er, yo′del·ler, yo′dler** *n.*

ga (yō′gə) *n.* **1.** A Hindu system of mystical and ascetic
ilosophy that involves certain physical and mental disci-
nes together with a withdrawal from the world and ab-
act meditation upon some spiritual principle or object.
A related system of exercises, the purpose of which is to
hieve both physical and spiritual well-being. [< Hind.
Skt., lit., union] — **yo·gic** (yō′gik) *adj.*

gh (yōkh) *n.* The Middle English letter, ȝ, ȝ, that repre-
nted a voiced or voiceless palatal fricative, or a voiced
lar fricative. It has been replaced in Modern English by *y*,
in *lay, w,* as in *law,* and *gh,* as in *daughter* and *enough.*

gi (yō′gē) *n. pl.* **·gis 1.** One who practices yoga. **2.**
ga. Also **yo′gee, yo′gin** (-gin). [< Hind. *yogi* < Skt.]

gurt (yō′goŏrt) *n.* A thick, curdled milk treated with
cteria, regarded as beneficial to the intestines. Also **yo′·
urt, yo′ghourt.** [< Turkish *yōghurt*]

cks (yoiks) *interj.* Hoicks. [Earlier *hoik,* var. of HIKE]

ke (yōk) *n. pl.* **yokes;** *for def. 3, often*
ke 1. A curved timber with attach-
ents used for coupling draft animals,
oxen, usu. having a bow at each end to
ceive the neck of the animal. **2.** Any of
rious similar contrivances, as a frame
ted for a person's shoulders and designed to carry a burden
either end, as a pail. **3.** A pair of draft animals coupled
th a yoke (def. 1). **4.** An oppressive force or influence:
der the *yoke* of tyranny. **5.** That which binds or con-
cts; a bond: the *yoke* of love. **6.** Servitude, or some visible
gn of it; bondage. **7.** A part of a garment designed to
pport a plaited or gathered part, as at the hips or shoul-
rs. **8.** *Naut.* A crosspiece on a rudderhead, carrying
bles for steering. — *v.* **yoked, yok·ing** *v.t.* **1.** To put a
ke upon. **2.** To join with or as with a yoke; couple or
k. **3.** To secure (a draft animal) to a plow, etc.; also, to
cure a draft animal to (a plow, etc.). — *v.i.* **4.** To be
ined or linked. [OE *geoc*]

YOKE (def. 1)

ke·fel·low (yōk′fel′ō) *n.* A mate or companion in labor.
lso **yoke′mate′** (-māt′).

kel (yō′kəl) *n.* A countryman; country bumpkin: a con-
mptuous term. [? < dial. E, green woodpecker, yellow-
mmer] — **yo′kel·ish** *adj.*

lk (yōk, yōlk) *n.* **1.** The yellow portion of an egg, as dis-
nguished from the white portion, used for the formation
d nourishment of the embryo. **2.** A yellow soapy
udation in sheep's wool. [OE *geol(o)ca,* lit., (the) yellow
art < *geolu* yellow]

lk·y (yō′kē, yōl′kē) *adj.* **yolk·i·er, yolk·i·est 1.** Of, like,
pertaining to yolk. **2.** Containing yolk: *yolky* wool.

m Kip·pur (yom kip′ər, *Hebrew* yōm ki-poŏr′) The Jew-
h Day of Atonement, the 10th of Tishri (September-
ctober), marked by continuous prayer and fasting for 24
ours from sundown on the evening previous. [< Hebrew
ōm kipūr day of atonement]

n (yon) *adj. & adv. Archaic, Dial. & Poetic* Yonder; that
r those over there: *yon* fine house. [OE *geon*]

n·der (yon′dər) *adj.* Being at a distance indicated. —
lv. In that place; there. [ME, prob. extension of *yone,* OE
eon yon]

re (yôr, yōr) *n.* Old time; time long past: in days of *yore.*
OE *gēara* formerly, prob. orig. genitive pl. of *gēar* year]

rk boat *Canadian* A type of heavy cargo canoe used by
ne Hudson's Bay Company. [after York Factory on Hud-
on Bay]

rk·shire pudding (yôrk′shir, -shər) A batter pudding
aked under roasting meat to catch the drippings.

rkshire terrier A toy breed of terrier having a long,
lky coat.

you (yoō) *pron., possessive* **your** or **yours 1.** The nominative
and objective singular and plural pronoun of the second person, used in addressing one or more persons, animals, or
things, and always taking a plural verb. **2.** An indefinite
pronoun equivalent to *one: You* learn by trying. [OE *ēow,*
dative and accusative pl. of *gē* ye]

you'd (yoōd, *unstressed* yoōd, yəd) **1.** You had. **2.** You
would.

you'll (yoōl, *unstressed* yoōl, yəl) You will.

young (yung) *adj.* **young·er** (yung′gər), **young·est** (yung′-
gist) **1.** Being in the early period of life or growth; not old.
2. Not having progressed far; newly formed: The day was
young. **3.** Pertaining to youth or early life. **4.** Full of vigor
or freshness. **5.** Being without experience; immature. **6.**
Denoting the younger of two persons having the same name
or title; junior. **7.** Radical or progressive in social or political aims: used with proper names: the *Young* Turks. —
Syn. See YOUTHFUL. — *n.* **1.** Young persons as a group;
youth. **2.** Offspring, esp. of animals. — **with young** With
child; pregnant. [OE *geong*] — **young′ish** *adj.*

young·ber·ry (yung′ber′ē) *n. pl.* **·ries** A large dark red
berry, hybridized from a trailing blackberry and a dewberry,
of the western U.S. [after B. M. *Young,* U.S. horticulturist]

young blood Youth; young people.

young-eyed (yung′īd′) *adj.* Having youthful eyes or fresh
vision; bright-eyed.

young·ling (yung′ling) *n.* **1.** A young person, animal, or
plant. **2.** An inexperienced person. — *adj.* Young.

young·ster (yung′stər) *n.* **1.** A young person; a child or
youth. **2.** A young animal, as a colt.

your (yôr, yoōr) *pronominal adj.* The possessive case of the
pronoun *you,* used attributively: *your* fate. [OE *ēower,* genitive of *gē* ye]

you're (yoōr, yôr, *unstressed* yər) You are.

yours (yôrz, yoōrz) *pron.* **1.** The possessive case of the
pronoun *you,* used predicatively: This room is *yours.* **2.** The
one or ones belonging or relating to you: a home as quiet as
yours; God bless you and *yours.* — **of yours** Belonging or
relating to you: a double possessive. [ME *youres*]

your·self (yôr-self′, yoōr-) *pron. pl.* **·selves** (-selvz′) A
form of the second person pronoun, used: **1.** As a reflexive or
as object of a preposition in a reflexive sense: Did you hurt
yourself? Look at *yourself* in the mirror. **2.** As an emphatic
or intensive form of *you:* You said so *yourself.* **3.** As a
designation of a normal, proper, or usual state: Why can't
you be *yourself* instead of putting on airs?

yours truly 1. A formal phrase used to close a letter, before the signature. **2.** *Informal* I; me.

youth (yoōth) *n. pl.* **youths** (yoōths, yoōthz) **1.** The
state or condition of being young. **2.** The period when one
is young; the part of life between childhood and manhood;
adolescence. **3.** The early period of being or development,
as of a movement. **4.** A young person, esp. a young man;
also, young persons collectively. [OE *geoguth*]

youth·ful (yoōth′fəl) *adj.* **1.** Having youth; being still
young. **2.** Characteristic of youth; fresh; vigorous. **3.** Of
or pertaining to youth. **4.** Not far advanced; early; new.
5. *Geol.* Young. — **youth′ful·ly** *adv.* — **youth′ful·ness** *n.*
— **Syn. 1.** *Youthful* describes character, manner, outlook, interests, appearance, and the like, while *young* refers merely to
chronological age. A mature or old person may properly be described as *youthful,* though he is no longer *young. Juvenile* emphasizes immaturity and is therefore often disparaging; *puerile* is
much the same, and is always uncomplimentary. *Adolescent* refers
to the age close to maturity, and may be disparaging or not:
adolescent pranks, *adolescent* energy and enthusiasm.

youth hostel A hostel.

you've (yoōv, *unstressed* yoōv, yəv) You have.

yowl (youl) *v.i.* To utter a yowl; howl; yell. — *n.* A loud,
prolonged, wailing cry; a howl. Also spelled *yawl:* also **yow.**
[Cf. ON *gaula* to howl, yell]

yo-yo (yō′yō′) *n. pl.* **-yos** A wheellike toy with a string
wound about it in a deep groove, commonly attached to the
operator's finger and spun up and down by manipulating
the string. [Origin unknown]

Y·quem (ē-kem′) *n.* A highly esteemed Sauterne wine.
[after Château *Yquem,* an estate in SW France]

yt·ter·bi·um (i-tûr′bē-əm) *n.* A rare metallic element (symbol Yb) of the lanthanide series, occurring in minute
amounts in gadolinite and certain other minerals. See ELE-
MENT. [< NL, from *Ytterby,* a town in Sweden where gadolinite was first found] — **yt·ter′bic** *adj.*

yt·tri·um (it′rē-əm) *n.* A rare element (symbol Y) of the
lanthanide series, found in gadolinite, samarskite, and other
minerals. See ELEMENT. Abbr. *Yt* [< NL < YTTRIA]

yuc·ca (yuk′ə) *n.* **1.** Any of various liliaceous plants of the
southern U.S., Mexico, and Central America, having a
woody stem that bears a large panicle of white, bell-shaped,

drooping flowers emerging from a crown of leaves. **2.** The flower of this plant, the State flower of New Mexico. [< NL < Sp. *yuca* < Taino]

Yu·go·slav (yōō'gō-släv, -slav) *adj.* Of or pertaining to Yugoslavia or its people. — *n.* A citizen or native of Yugoslavia. Also **Yu·go·sla'vi·an.**

yuk (yuk) *U.S. Slang n.* A loud, hearty laugh. — *v.i. & v.t.* **yukked, yuk·king** To laugh or cause to laugh loud and heartily.

Yule (yōōl) *n.* Christmas time, or the feast celebrating it. [OE *gēol* Christmas day, Christmastide]

yule log A large log or block of wood, brought in with much ceremony, and made the foundation of the Christmas Eve fire. Also **yule block, yule clog.**

Yule·tide (yōōl'tīd') *n.* Christmas time.

Yu·ma (yōō'mə) *n.* One of a tribe of North American I dians of Yuman stock, formerly living in northern Mexi and Arizona and in SE California.

Yu·man (yōō'mən) *n.* A North American Indian stock the SW U.S. and NW Mexico, including the Mohave a Yuma tribes.

yum·my (yum'ē) *Slang adj.* **·mi·er, ·mi·est** Gratifying the senses, esp. to the taste; delicious. — *n.* Somethi very gratifying; a delight. — *n.* **yum-yum,** an exclamati expressing delight at an agreeable taste]

yurt (yûrt) *n.* A portable tent made of felt laid on a fram work of branches, used by nomadic Mongols in central As [< Russian *yurta* < Turkic]

Z

z, Z (zē, *Brit.* zed) *n.* *pl.* **z's** or **zs, Z's** or **Zs, zees** (zēz) **1.** The twenty-sixth letter of the English alphabet. Also, *Brit.,* **zed.** **2.** The sound represented by the letter *z,* a voiced alveolar fricative corresponding to the voiceless *s.* — *symbol* **1.** *Physics* Atomic number. **2.** *Math.* An unknown quantity.

Zach·a·ri·ah (zak'ə-rī'ə) The last king of Israel of Jehu's race. II *Kings* xiv 29.

Zach·a·ri·as (zak'ə-rī'əs) **1.** The father of John the Baptist. *Luke* i 5. **2.** The Douai Bible name for ZECHARIAH.

zai·bat·su (zī-bät-sōō) *n. Japanese* The wealthy clique of Japan, representing four or five dominant families.

za·mar·ra (zə-mär'ə, -mar'ə) *n.* A sheepskin coat worn by Spanish shepherds. Also **za·mar'ro** (-mär'ō). [< Sp.]

za·ny (zā'nē) *adj.* **·ni·er, ·ni·est** Odd and comical; outlandish; ludicrous. — *n.* *pl.* **·nies 1.** A simpleton; buffoon; fool. **2.** In old comic plays, one who imitated the other performers, esp. the clown, with ludicrous failure. [< F < Ital. *zanni* servants who act as clowns in early Italian comedy]

zap·ti·ah (zup-tē'ä) *n.* A Turkish policeman. Also **zap·ti'e, zap·ti'eh.** [< Turkish *dabtiyeh* < Arabic *dabt* administration, regulation]

za·ra·pe (sä-rä'pā) See SERAPE.

za·re·ba (zə-rē'bə) *n.* **1.** In the Sudan, a stockade or other palisaded enclosure for protecting a village or camp. **2.** A village or camp so protected; also, any village. Also **za·ree'·ba.** [< Arabic *zarībah* pen for cattle < *zarb* sheepfold]

zarf (zärf) *n.* A metal cup-shaped holder, of open or ornamental filigree, for a hot coffee cup, used in the Levant. [< Arabic *zarf* vessel, sheath]

zar·zue·la (thär·thwä'lä) *n. Spanish* A form of lyrical theater in which song is intermingled with spoken dialogue.

za·yin (zä'yin) *n.* The seventh letter in the Hebrew alphabet. See ALPHABET.

zeal (zēl) *n.* Enthusiastic devotion; ardor, esp. for a cause. [< OF < L < Gk. *zēlos* < *zēein* to boil]

zeal·ot (zel'ət) *n.* **1.** An immoderate partisan; a fanatic. **2.** One who is zealous. [< LL < Gk. < *zēloein* to be zealous < *zēlos* zeal] — **zeal'ot·ry** *n.*

zeal·ous (zel'əs) *adj.* Filled with or incited by zeal; enthusiastic. — **zeal'ous·ly** *adv.* — **zeal'ous·ness** *n.*

ze·bec (zē'bek), **ze·beck** See XEBEC.

Zeb·e·dee (zeb'ə-dē) The father of James and John, disciples of Christ. *Matt.* iv 21.

ze·bra (zē'brə) *n.* Any of various African equine mammals resembling the ass, having a white or yellowish brown body fully marked with variously patterned, dark brown or blackish bands. [< Pg. < Bantu (Congo)] — **ze'brine** (-brēn, -brin), **ze'broid** (-broid) *adj.*

ze·bu (zē'byōō) *n.* The domesticated ox of India, China, and East Africa, having a hump on the withers, a large dewlap, and short horns. [< F *zébu* < Tibetan]

Zeb·u·lon (zeb'yə-lən) In the Old Testament, a son of Jacob and Leah. *Gen.* xxx 20. — *n.* The tribe of Israel descended from him. Also **Zeb'u·lun.**

Zech·a·ri·ah (zek'ə-rī'ə) Sixth-century B.C. Hebrew prophet who promoted the rebuilding of the Temple. — *n.* A book of the Old Testament bearing his name. Also, in the Douai Bible, *Zacharias.*

zed (zed) *n. Brit.* The letter Z. [< F < L < Gk. *zēta*]

zee (zē, *Du.* zā) *n. Dutch* Sea: used in geographic names: *Zuider Zee, Tappen Zee.*

Zeit·geist (tsīt'gīst) *n. German* The spirit of the time;

the intellectual and moral tendencies that characterize a age or epoch. [< G < *zeit* time + *geist* spirit]

zemst·vo (zem'stvō, *Russ.* zyem'stvô) *n.* Prior to 1917 Russian elective district. [< Russian *semlya* land]

ze·na·na (zə-nä'nə) *n.* In India, the women's apartmen the East Indian harem: also spelled *zanana.* [< Hir *zenāna* belonging to women < Persian *zanāna* < *zan* woma

Zen Buddhism (zen) A form of contemplative Buddhis whose adherents believe in and work toward abrupt e lightenment. It originated in China, and later spread Japan, where it greatly influenced Japanese culture. A **Zen.** [< Japanese *zen* meditation < Chinese < Skt. *dhyan*

Zend (zend) *n.* **1.** The ancient translation and comme tary, in a literary form of Middle Persian (Pahlavi), of t Avesta, the sacred writings of the Zoroastrian religion. Erroneously, the language of the Avesta; Avestan. [< < Persian, interpretation] — **Zend'ic** *adj.*

Zend-A·ves·ta (zend'ə·ves'tə) *n.* The Avesta, includi the later translation and commentary called the Zend. **Zend'-A·ves·ta'ic** (-ə·ves·tä'ik) *adj.*

ze·nith (zē'nith) *n.* **1.** The point of the celestial sphe that is exactly overhead, and opposite to the nadir. **2.** T highest or culminating point; peak: the *zenith* of one's care opposed to *nadir.* [< OF *cenit,* ult. < Arabic *samt* (ar-r the path (over the head)]

ze·o·lite (zē'ə·līt) *n.* Any of a large class of seconda minerals found in cavities and veins in eruptive rocks, us a hydrous silicate of aluminum and sodium. [< Sw. < G *zēein* to boil + *lithos* stone] — **ze'o·lit'ic** (-lit'ik) *adj.*

Zeph·a·ni·ah (zef'ə·nī'ə) Seventh-century B.C. Hebr prophet. — *n.* A book of the Old Testament bearing l name. Also, in the Douai Bible, *Sophonias.*

zeph·yr (zef'ər) *n.* **1.** The west wind. **2.** Any soft, gen wind. **3.** Worsted or woolen yarn of very light weight us for embroidery, shawls, etc.: also **zephyr worsted. 4.** An thing very light and airy. [< L < Gk. *zephyros*]

zephyr cloth Fine cassimere used for women's clothing

zep·pe·lin (zep'ə·lin, *Ger.* tsep'ə·lēn') *n. Often cap.* A lar dirigible having a rigid, cigar-shaped body. [after Cou Ferdinand von *Zeppelin,* 1838–1917, German general a aviator who designed it]

ze·ro (zir'ō, zē'rō) *n.* *pl.* **ze·ros** or **ze·roes 1.** The nume or symbol 0; a cipher. ◆ In nontechnical speech, th symbol is often pronounced (ō). **2.** *Math.* **a** A cardinal nu ber indicating the absence of quantity. **b** The point where continuous function changes its sign from plus to minus, vice versa. **3.** The point on a scale, as of a thermomet from which measures are counted; also, a temperature th registers zero on a thermometer. **4.** *Mil.* A setting for a gu sight that adjusts both for elevation and wind. **5.** The lowe point. **6.** Nothing. — *v.t.* **ze·roed, ze·ro·ing** To adjust (instruments) to an arbitrary zero point for synchroniz readings. — **to zero in 1.** To adjust the sight of (a gun) calibrated results of firings. **2.** To direct firepower exac on target. **3.** To approach or give one's attention to though directed to a target. — *adj.* Without value appreciable change. [< F < Ital. < Arabic *sifr*]

zero gravity *Aerospace* A condition in which the gra tational attraction of the earth or other celestial body nullified by inertial forces; weightlessness.

zero hour 1. H-hour. **2.** *Informal* The moment of unde taking something; any critical moment.

zest (zest) *n.* **1.** Invigorating excitement; keen enjoymer isto: often with *for*: a *zest* for reading. **2.** That which im- arts such excitement and relish. **3.** An agreeable and quant flavor in anything tasted, esp. if added to the usual avor. — *v.t.* To give zest or relish to; make piquant. [< *zeste* lemon peel (for flavoring)]

st·ful (zest′fəl) *adj.* Full of or marked by zest. Also ·st′y. — zest′ful·ly *adv.* — zest′ful·ness *n.*

ta (zā′tə, zē′-) *n.* The sixth letter (Z, ζ) in the Greek phabet, corresponding to English *z*. See ALPHABET. [< k. *zēta*]

ug·ma (zōog′mə) *n.* A rhetorical figure in which an ljective is made to modify, or a verb to govern, two nouns, hile applying properly only to one, as in *She was remem- red but they forgotten.* [< NL < Gk. < *zeugnymi* to yoke]

us (zōōs) In Greek mythology, the supreme deity, ruler the celestial realm, son of Kronos and Rhea and husband Hera: identified with the Roman *Jupiter.*

·et (zib′it) *n.* The Asian or Indian civet. Also zib′eth. < Med.L < Arabic *zabād* civet]

g·zag (zig′zag) *n.* **1.** A series of short, sharp turns or ngles from one side to the other in succession. **2.** Some- ing characterized by such angles, as a path or pattern. — *adj.* Having or proceeding in a zigzag. — *adv.* In a zig- g manner. — *v.t. & v.i.* ·zagged, ·zag·ging To form or ove in zigzags. [< F < G *zickzack*, prob. reduplication of *cke* sharp point] — zig′zag·ger *n.*

ic (zingk) *n.* A bluish white, metallic element (symbol n) occurring mostly in combination, widely used in indus- y, medicine, the arts, for roofing, and as the negative ectrode in electric batteries. See ELEMENT. — *v.t.* ncked or zinced, zinck·ing or zinc·ing To coat or cover ith zinc; galvanize. [< G *zink*; ult. origin unknown] — nc′ic *adj.* — zinck′y, zinc′y, zink′y *adj.*

ic blende Sphalerite.

ic ointment A medicated ointment for skin affections, ontaining zinc oxide mixed with petrolatum.

ic·ous (zingk′əs) *adj. Chem.* Pertaining to or derived om zinc.

ic oxide *Chem.* A white pulverulent compound ZnO, sed as a pigment, and in medicine as a mild antiseptic and stringent.

ic white Zinc oxide used as a pigment in paints.

n·fan·del (zin′fan·del) *n.* A dry, red or white claret-type ine made in California. [? after a European place name]

ng (zing) *Informal n.* **1.** A high-pitched buzzing or umming sound. **2.** Energy; vitality; vigor. — *v.i.* To ake a shrill, humming sound. [Imit.]

n·ga·ro (tseng′gä·rō) *n. pl.* ·ri (-rē) *Italian* A gypsy. lso zin′ga·no (-nō). — zin′ga·ra (-rä) *n.fem.*

n·ni·a (zin′ē·ə) *n.* Any of various American herbs, having nowy flowers; esp., the common zinnia, the State flower of ndiana. [< NL, after J. G. *Zinn*, 1727–59, German pro- essor of medicine]

on (zī′ən) **1.** A hill in Jerusalem, the site of the temple nd the royal residence of David and his successors, re- arded by the Jews as a symbol for the center of Jewish ational culture, government, and religion. **2.** The Jewish eople. **3.** Any place or community considered to be espe- ially under God's rule. **4.** The heavenly Jerusalem; eaven. Also Sion. [OE < LL < Gk. < Hebrew *tsiyôn* hill]

on·ism (zī′ən·iz′əm) *n.* A movement for a resettlement f the Jews in Palestine. Also Zion movement. — Zi′on·ist dj. & *n.* — Zi′on·is′tic *adj.*

p (zip) *n.* **1.** A sharp, hissing sound, as of a bullet passing hrough the air. **2.** *Informal* Energy; vitality; vim. — *v.* ipped, zip·ping *v.t.* **1.** To fasten with a zipper. — *v.i.* . *Informal* To be very energetic. **3.** To move or fly with zip. [Imit.]

P Code (zip) A numerical code devised by the U.S. Post ffice to aid in the distribution of domestic mail. Also Zip ode. [< Z(ONE) I(MPROVEMENT) P(LAN)]

p gun *U.S. Slang* A homemade pistol consisting of a mall pipe or other tube fastened to a block of wood and quipped with a firing pin actuated by a spring or rubber band.

p·per (zip′ər) *n.* A fastener having two rows of inter- ocking teeth that may be closed or separated by a sliding evice, used on clothing, boots, etc.: also called *slide fastener.*

p·py (zip′ē) *adj.* ·pi·er, ·pi·est *Informal* Brisk; energetic.

r·con (zûr′kon) *n.* A crystalline, variously colored, zir- onium silicate, ZrSiO₄; some translucent varieties of which re used as gems. [< G *zirken* or F *zircone* < Arabic *zarqūn* innabar < Persian < *zar* gold + *gūn* color]

r·co·ni·um (zûr·kō′nē·əm) *n.* A metallic element (symbol r) chemically resembling titanium, used in alloys, as an pacifier of lacquers, and as an abrasive. See ELEMENT. < NL < ZIRCON] — zir·con′ic (-kon′ik) *adj.*

th·er (zith′ər) *n.* A simple form of stringed instrument, aving a flat sounding board and from thirty to forty strings

---

that are played by plucking with a plectrum. Also zith′ern (-ərn). [< G < L < Gk. *kithara*]

zlo·ty (zlô′tē) *n. pl.* ·tys or ·ty The standard monetary unit of Poland, equal to 100 groszy: in 1960 worth about 25 U.S. cents. [< Polish, lit., golden]

zo- Var. of ZOO-.

zo·di·ac (zō′dē·ak) *n.* **1.** An imaginary belt encircling the heavens and extend- ing about 8° on each side of the ecliptic within which are the apparent orbits of the moon, sun, and larger planets. It is divided into twelve parts, called signs of the zodiac, that former- ly corresponded to twelve constellations bearing the same names. **2.** A figure or diagram repre- senting this belt and its signs, used in as- trology. **3.** A com- plete circuit. [< OF < L < Gk. (*kyklos*) *zōdiakos* (circle) of animals < *zōion* ani- mal] — zo·di·a·cal (zō-dī′ə-kəl) *adj.*

SIGNS OF THE ZODIAC

A Vernal equinox: Aries, Taurus, Gemini. *B* Summer solstice: Cancer, Leo, Virgo. *C* Autumnal equinox: Libra, Scorpio, Sagittarius. *D* Win- ter solstice: Capricorn, Aquarius, Pisces.

zom·bie (zom′bē) *n.* **1.** The supernatural power by which a dead body is believed to be reanimated. **2.** A corpse reactivated by sorcery, but still dead. **3.** Loosely, a ghost. **4.** A large, strong cocktail made from several kinds of rum, fruit juices, and liqueur. **5.** *Slang* An unattractive person. Also zom′bi. [< West African] — zom′bi·ism *n.*

zo·nal (zō′nəl) *adj.* Of, pertaining to, exhibiting, or marked by a zone or zones; like a zone. Also zo′na·ry (-nər·ē).

zone (zōn) *n.* **1.** An area, tract, or section distinguished from other or adjacent areas by some special quality, purpose, or condi- tion: a mountainous *zone*; a *zone* of disagreement. **2.** *Usu. cap.* Any of five divisions of the earth's surface, enclosed between two parallels of lati- tude and named for the prevailing climate: the Torrid Zone, extending on each side of the equator 23° 27′; the Temperate Zones, included between the parallels 23° 27′ and 66° 33′ on both sides of the equator, and the Frigid Zones, within the parallels 66° 33′ and the poles. **3.** An area of land designated as distinct from other areas because of its particular use or location: combat *zone*; school *zone*. **4.** *Ecol.* A belt or area delimited from others by the character of its plant or animal life, its climate, geological formations, etc. **5.** A concentric area or band; esp., any of a number of concentric areas used to de- termine the rate of charge for transporting something a specified distance, as in the U.S. parcel post system. **6.** A section of a city or town where only certain uses of the land or certain types of buildings are permitted by law: a resi- dential *zone*. **7.** A section of a city designated with a num- ber as an aid in the distribution of mail. **8.** A belt, band, stripe, etc., having a color or other characteristic that dis- tinguishes it from the object it encircles. **9.** *Geom.* A por- tion of the surface of a sphere enclosed between two parallel planes. **10.** *Archaic* or *Poetic* A belt or girdle. — *v.t.* zoned, zon·ing **1.** To divide into zones; esp., to divide (a city, etc.) into zones that are restricted as to types of con- struction and use, as residential or industrial. **2.** To desig- nate (an area, etc.) as a zone or part of a zone: to *zone* the waterfront district as commercial. **3.** To mark with or as with zones or stripes. **4.** To encircle with a zone or belt. [< L < Gk. *zōnē* girdle]

TERRESTRIAL ZONES

(labels on diagram: NORTH POLE, FRIGID ZONE, ARCTIC CIRCLE, NORTH TEMPERATE ZONE, TROPIC OF CANCER, EQUATOR, TORRID ZONE, EQUATOR, TROPIC OF CAPRICORN, SOUTH TEMPERATE ZONE, ANTARCTIC CIRCLE, FRIGID ZONE, SOUTH POLE)

zoo (zōō) *n.* A park or garden in which wild animals are kept for exhibition. Also zoological garden, zoological park.

zoo- *combining form* Animal; of or related to animals, or to animal forms. Also, before vowels, zo-. [< Gk. *zōion* ani- mal]

zo·o·ge·og·ra·phy (zō′ə·jē·og′rə·fē) *n.* The systematic study of the distribution of animals and of the relations be- tween animal groups and the land or aquatic areas in which

---

they predominate. **— zo′o·ge·og′ra·pher** *n.* **— zo′o·ge′o·graph′ic** (-jē′ə·graf′ik) or **·i·cal** *adj.* **— zo′o·ge′o·graph′i·cal·ly** *adv.*

zo·oid (zō′oid) *n.* **1.** *Biol.* Any animal or vegetable organism, usu. very small, capable of spontaneous movement and independent existence, as a spermatozoon, spermatozoid, etc. **2.** *Zool.* One of the distinct members of a compound or colonial organism. **—** *adj.* Having the nature of an animal: also **zo·oi·dal** (zō-oid′l).

zo·o·log·i·cal (zō′ə·loj′i·kəl) *adj.* **1.** Of or pertaining to zoology. **2.** Relating to or characteristic of animals. Also **zo′o·log′ic.** **— zo′o·log′i·cal·ly** *adv.*

zo·ol·o·gy (zō·ol′ə·jē) *n.* **1.** The science that treats of animals with reference to their structure, functions, development, evolution, and classification. **2.** The animal kingdom, or local examples of it, regarded biologically. [< NL < Gk. *zōion* animal + *logos* word, discourse] **— zo·ol′o·gist** *n.*

zoom (zoōm) *v.i.* **1.** To make a low-pitched but loud humming sound; also, to move with such a sound. **2.** To climb sharply in an airplane. **—** *v.t.* **3.** To cause to zoom. **—** *n.* The act of zooming. [Imit.]

zoom lens *Photog.* A lens, used chiefly on television and motion picture cameras, that permits the size of the image to be varied continuously without loss of focus.

zo·o·mor·phism (zō′ə·môr′fiz·əm) *n.* **1.** The conception, symbolization, or representation of a man or a god in the form of an animal; also, the attribution of divine or human qualities to animals. **2.** The representation of animals or animal forms in art or symbolism. **3.** Transformation into animals. Also **zo′o·mor′phy. — zo′o·mor′phic** *adj.*

zo·o·phyte (zō′ə·fīt) *n.* An invertebrate animal resembling a plant, as a coral or sea anemone. **— zo′o·phyt′ic** (-fit′ik) or **·i·cal** *adj.*

zo·o·spore (zō′ə·spôr, -spōr) *n.* **1.** *Bot.* A spore, produced among some algae and fungi, that is provided with cilia by means of which it can move about. **2.** *Zool.* A flagellate or ameboid motile body in certain protozoa. **— zo′o·spor′ic** (-spôr′ik, -spor′ik), **zo·os·po·rous** (zō-os′pər·əs) *adj.*

Zo·ro·as·tri·an (zō′rō·as′trē·ən) *n.* A follower of Zoroaster; an adherent of Zoroastrianism. **—** *adj.* Of or pertaining to Zoroaster or to the religion he founded.

Zo·ro·as·tri·an·ism (zō′rō·as′trē·ən·iz′əm) *n.* The religious system founded by Zoroaster and taught in the Zend-Avesta. It recognizes two creative powers, one good and the other evil, includes the belief in life after death, and teaches the final triumph of good over evil. Also **Zo′ro·as′trism.**

Zou·ave (zoō·äv′, swäv) *n.* **1.** A light-armed French infantryman wearing a brilliant Oriental uniform, originally an Algerian recruit. **2.** In the Civil War, a member of a volunteer regiment assuming the name and part of the dress of the French Zouaves. **3.** A woman's short, gaily embroid-ered jacket: also **Zouave jacket.** [< F < Arabic *Zouāoua*, Kabyle tribe]

zounds (zoundz, zoōndz) *interj.* *Archaic* A mild oath used to express surprise or anger. [Short for *God's wounds*]

zuc·chet·to (tsoōk·ket′tō) *n.* A skullcap worn by ecclesiastics in the Roman Catholic Church, black for a priest, purple for a bishop, red for a cardinal, and white for the pope. Also **zuc·chet′ta** (-tä). [Var. of Ital. *zucchetta*, < *cucutia* a kind of wood]

zuc·chi·ni (zoō·kē′nē, *Ital.* dzoōk·kē′nē) *n.* A type of green summer squash of cylindrical shape. [< Ital., pl. of *zucchino*, dim. of *zucca* gourd, squash]

Zu·lu (zoō′loō) *n.* *pl.* **Zu·lus** or **Zu·lu 1.** One of a Bantu nation of Natal, South Africa, sometimes included with the Kaffirs. **2.** The Bantu language of the Zulus. **—** *adj.* Of or pertaining to, or characteristic of the Zulus or their language.

Zu·ñi (zoō′nyē) *n.* **1.** One of a tribe of North American Indians of pueblo culture but comprising a distinct, ethnic stock, living in New Mexico. **2.** The language of this tribe. **— Zu′ñi·an** *adj. & n.*

zwie·back (zwī′bak, zwē′-, swī′, swē′-, -bäk; *Ger.* tsvē′bäk) *n.* A biscuit of wheaten bread or rusk baked yellow in the loaf and later sliced and toasted. [< G, twice baked < *zwei* twice (< *zwei* two) + *backen* to bake]

zygo- *combining form* Yoke; pair; resembling a yoke, in shape. Also, before vowels, **zyg-.** [< Gk. *zygon* yoke]

zy·gote (zī′gōt, zig′ōt) *n.* *Biol.* **1.** The product of the union of two gametes. **2.** A new organism developed from such a union. [< Gk. < *zygon* yoke] **— zy·got·ic** (zī-got′ik) *adj.*

zy·mase (zī′mās) *n.* *Biochem.* An enzyme, obtained principally from yeast, that induces fermentation by breaking down glucose and related carbohydrates into alcohol and carbon dioxide. [< F < Gk. *zymē* leaven]

zyme (zīm) *n.* A disease germ or virus supposed to be the specific cause of a zymotic disease. [< Gk. *zymē* leaven]

zymo- *combining form* Fermentation; of or related to fermentation. Also, before vowels, **zym-.** [< Gk. *zymē* leaven]

zy·mol·o·gy (zī·mol′ə·jē) *n.* The study of fermentation and the action of enzymes. **— zy·mo·log·ic** (zī′mə·loj′ik) or **·i·cal** *adj.* **— zy·mol′o·gist** *n.*

zy·mol·y·sis (zī·mol′ə·sis) *n.* Fermentation or the action of enzymes. **— zy·mo·lyt·ic** (zī′mə·lit′ik) *adj.*

zy·mo·sis (zī·mō′sis) *n.* *pl.* **·ses 1.** Any form of fermentation. **2.** *Med.* A process resembling fermentation formerly supposed to give rise to a diseased condition. [< NL < G < *zymoein* to leaven, ferment < *zymē* leaven] **— zy·mot·ic** (-mot′ik) *adj.*

zy·mur·gy (zī′mûr·jē) *n.* A branch of chemistry treating processes in which fermentation takes place, as brewing, winemaking, etc.

SUPPLEMENT

COMMON COMPUTER TERMS

This is a list of terms now common when speaking of or reading about home and office computers and word processors. Some of these terms have other meanings; only their computer-related meaning is given here. Pronunciations and syllabications of the following terms are given in the A–Z section of this Dictionary, as well as the other senses in which these words may be used. Terms not found there and all acronyms are pronounced here.

accumulator *n.* That part of a computer used for intermediate and short-term storage, where mathematical operations take place.

ACM Abbreviation for Association of Computing Machinery, an association whose objective is to facilitate the development of information processing.

acoustic coupler A device that connects a computer to a telephone, enabling signals to be transmitted over telephone lines to another computer; a modem.

acoustic modem A device that translates electrical signals to telephone tones and back to electrical signals.

address *n.* **1.** A specific location in computer memory where information is stored. **2.** A label, used as identification for a position in memory.

AI Abbreviation for *artificial intelligence.*

ALGOL (al′gôl) *n.* A computer programming language used primarily for mathematical and scientific applications. [*algo(rithmic) l(anguage)*]

algorithm *n.* A step by step problem-solving procedure, as with a computer.

alphanumeric *adj.* Consisting of the letters of the alphabet and numerals, as a computer code.

analog computer A computer that solves problems by substituting analogous quantities, as voltage, etc., for variables for the problems.

ANSI Abbreviation for American National Standards Institute, an organization that provides guidelines for standards for data processing and other computer-related industries in the United States.

array *n.* Two or more logically connected elements, arranged in a pattern.

artificial intelligence **1.** The use of computers for development of another machine, or for internal improvement and development. **2.** A machine that can perform functions resembling human intelligence, such as reasoning, learning, adapting, decision-making, etc. Abbr. *AI.*

ASCII (as′kē) *n.* A standard eight-bit code that is used in most computers to represent symbols, such as letters on a keyboard or binary digits. [*A(merican) S(tandard) C(ode) for I(nformation)*]

assembler *n.* A program whose function is to take symbolic code and translate it into machine code.

back-up *n.* A piece of hardware or software that is available in the event of a breakdown or loss of an original source. —*v.* To make a copy of a disk or program to prevent loss of information.

bar code A series of magnetic lines of varying thicknesses that can be scanned, read, and translated into a machine-readable form. The Universal Product Code (UPC), which appears on most supermarket items, is one example.

BASIC (bā′sik) *n.* A procedural programming language in which one command is executed before the next procedure is implemented. [*b(eginner's) a(ll-purpose) s(ymbolic) i(nstruction) c(ode)*]

batch *n.* A set of instructions or records that are considered part of the same group and that are processed by a computer at the same time. —*v.* To group for the purpose of processing together.

baud (bôd′) *n.* A unit that measures the speed of data transmission in bits per second.

bcd Abbreviation for binary-coded decimal, the code representing decimal numbers in a four-bit binary number.

benchmark *n.* A standard program that is run as a test to evaluate or compare software or hardware.

binary *adj.* **1.** Relating to a number system based entirely on two digits, 0 and 1. **2.** Relating to a system in which there are always only two possible choices: yes or no, on or off, true or false.

bisync (bī′singk) *n.* A system for synchronous exchange of information between two devices. [from *bi(nary) sync(hronous)*]

bit *n.* The smallest unit in binary notation, always a 0 or a 1. Different numbers of bits form other units: 4 bits is a nibble, 8 bits a byte. [from *b(inary) (dig)it*].

Boolean algebra (boo̅′lē·ən) A logical system that shows relationships between variables such as true, false or if, then. [after George Boole (1815–64), E. mathematician]

booting *n.* The use of a routine that can be initiated very simply, sometimes as simply as turning on a switch, which calls the rest of a routine or a program from a remote location into main memory. [from the phrase *to pull oneself up by the bootstraps*]

bps Abbreviation for bits per second, a term used to indicate how fast information can be transmitted.

branching *n.* An instruction in a computer program resulting in a choice between or among two or more options.

break *n.* The stopping of normal execution of a program caused by problems within the program or by human intervention.

bubble memory A highly accurate, often used, inexpensive method of memory storage composed of polarized bits (or bubbles) of magnetic material in a film of magnetic material.

buffer *n.* A place where data is temporarily stored between processes.

bug *n.* A miscalculation or error in a program or a defect in hardware that prevents a program from running properly.

bus *n.* A conduit or pathway created by a circuit, used for transfer of data from one device or location in memory to another.

byte *n.* A group of binary digits, usually eight, which a computer stores and treats as a unit.

C (sē) *n.* A high-level, general purpose programming language.

CAD Abbreviation for computer-aided design, the use of a computer to aid in the design of a product, such as a machine part, an airplane, etc.

CAD/CAM Abbreviation for computer-aided design/computer-aided manufacturing, a system that employs a computer to aid in the design and manufacture of complex products, such as the wiring of a chip.

CAI Abbreviation for computer-aided instruction, a system that utilizes a computer, frequently a microcomputer, as an instructional instrument.

card *n.* A form for storing information and instruction for processing on a computer. A card may be a **punch card,** in which the information is stored in the form of holes punched in a card which is inserted into a computer, or a **printed circuit board,** which is inserted into a computer to perform special functions.

central processing unit *See* CPU.

character *n.* A symbol that can be stored or processed by a computer.

chip *n.* A piece of silicon (a crystal) on which circuits are etched and integrated; an integrated circuit.

COBOL (kō′bôl) *n.* A computer programming language commonly used in business applications. [*c(ommon) b(usiness) o(riented) l(anguage)*]

code *n.* A symbolic representation of data, in a format usable by a machine. —*v.* To put a program into this form.

compiler *n.* A computer program that translates programming language into machine language so that it can be executed.

computer *n.* **1.** One who, or that which, computes. **2.** An electronic machine for the high-speed performance of mathematical and logical operations, or for the processing of large masses of coded information.

condition *n.* The state of a program at any given point in its execution.

configuration *n.* The way in which the physical units of the computer and its peripherals are designed to act as a system.

control unit That part of the computer that receives commands and directs the execution of the program.

CP/M Abbreviation for control program for microcomputers, an operating system or collection of programs for small computers allowing for the efficient handling of information by the computer.

CPU Abbreviation for central processing unit, which refers to the main storage and the place where the arithmetic and logical functions occur.

CRT Abbreviation for *cathode ray tube.*

cursor (kûr′sər) *n.* A small marker or pointer on a computer screen which indicates the user's position in what is displayed on the screen.

data *n., pl.* of **datum** The term used to designate that set of facts and symbols which describes a situation to a computer.

data base A collection of data, usually organized for more than one program.

data base management A system for storing and retrieving information in a data base.

data processing The operations involved in handling and storing information, using computers and other machines.

debugging *n.* The search for and correction of any errors in a computer program or a computer.

dedicated *adj.* Relating to a program, terminal, or machine that is set aside for a specific function.

diagnostics *n.* A program or set of programs whose function it is to find and isolate potential or actual problems in a program or in a computer.

digital *adj.* **1.** Relating to the representation of information in binary notation. **2.** Relating to the number of discrete signals used to transmit data.

digital computer A computing machine that receives problems and processes the answers in digital form.

direct access A method of storing information which allows the user to locate the desired information directly rather than sequentially.

disassembler *n.* A program used to translate from machine language to assembly language.

disk *n.* A magnetic storage medium, which allows direct access of information when used in a computer.

disk drive A device used to read disks and record information on them.

diskette (dis·ket′) *n.* A floppy disk.

documentation *n.* The written material that accompanies a program or a computer system and provides information about its use.

DOS (dos) *n.* An operating system consisting of a collection of programs managing disks and making possible the use of disks in a computer. [*d(isk) o(perating) s(ystem)*]

down load The transfer of material, sometimes whole systems, from one part of a computer network to another.

down time That time in which the computer cannot be used, usually because there is a malfunction.

dump *v.* **1.** To put all or part of storage on the screen or on paper for diagnostic purposes. **2.** To move all the contents of a program from one medium to another, such as from a disk to a tape, or from one location to another.

EBCDIC (eb′sə·dik) · *n.* An 8-bit code used for the representation of numbers, letters, and other symbols. [*e(xtended) b(inary) c(oded) d(ecimal) i(nterchange) c(ode)*]

echo check A method for checking a system in which data is sent to a point, returned, and then compared to the original for accuracy.

edit *v.* To change or correct (data or a program).

editor *n.* A program that allows a user to review, change, or correct data or another program.

erase *v.* To clear the computer memory and leave blank.

escape *v.* To leave one character set or part of a program to go to another.

execution *n.* The physical running of a program or routine in a computer.

field *n.* A part of a record, which allows the user to locate a defined unit. For example, in a record called "books," fields might be "author," "title," etc.

file *n.* A group of logically grouped records, dealt with as a unit.

firmware *n.* That set of instructions that is stored in a fixed form in a computer and used as part of the computer to control its functions.

floppy disk A round magnetized object usually made of plastic and resembling a small phonograph record, upon which data is stored.

flowchart *n.* A schematic diagram of the actions and interactions of a given program.

font *n.* A complete collection of characters of a given type, size, and style.

format *n.* A predetermined logical arrangement of a set of data. —*v.* To prepare a diskette for use with a particular operating system.

FORTRAN (fôr′tran) *n.* A computer programming language designed especially for scientific and mathematical notation, now used in many commercial applications. [*for(mula) tran(slator)*]

function key A key on a computer keyboard, used to indicate an entire command, such as "enter" or "run," allowing the user to perform a function in a program.

GIGO (gī′gō) *n.* A computer slang term used to explain errors. [*G(arbage) I(n) G(arbage) O(ut)*]

hang up The unexpected cessation of a program because of a faulty instruction code.

hard copy Data or other computer output printed on paper to be read or transported.

hard disk A magnetic disk made of rigid material, usually capable of storing more information than a floppy disk.

hardware *n.* The physical components of the computer, such as keyboard, memory storage drawers, circuitry, etc.

head *n.* The part of a disk or tape drive that reads, writes, and transfers information onto the magnetic field; an electromagnet.

heuristic *adj.* Describing an approach to problem solving which uses the trial-and-error method.

hexidecimal (hek″sə·des′ə·məl) *adj.* Describing a system which uses 16 digits in its notation: 0–9, A, B, C, D, E, F.

host *n.* A computer that has multiple users, either human or machine, and is usually the central or controlling computer in a system.

housekeeping *n.* Maintenance performed by a program, such as clearing memory, getting files, etc.

IC Abbreviation for *integrated circuit* or instruction counter.

increment *n.* A quantity which is added on to another quantity in a pattern sometimes used to determine patterns of information flow.

information *n.* Those data that have been processed by the computer and are now of use to the user.

input *n.* **1.** Information that is entered into the computer. **2.** The act of entering information into a computer —*v.* To enter data into a computer.

instruction *n.* A command given to the computer, telling it which action is to be performed on which data.

integrated circuit *n.* A circuit of electronic components formed in or on a tiny slice of material. Abbr. *IC*

interface *n.* The common boundary or interconnection of parts of a system. —*v.* To interact between two elements of a computer which cannot directly address one another.

interpreter *n.* That part of a computer which translates instruction into machine language and causes it to be executed.

interrupt *n.* A break in the normal flow of a program, usually to allow another program to run, after which the original program can resume running at the stopping point.

I/O Abbreviation for *input/output.*

item *n.* A piece or a set of information stored within a larger file or unit.

iteration *n.* The process of repeating an operation controlled by a set of instructions.

JCL Abbreviation for job control language, a command language that manages the use of time and resources of a machine, especially in timesharing.

joystick *n.* A stick-controlled device which may be hooked up to the machine to control the movement of a cursor in a video screen in games or in design.

K *n.* 1,000. In computer use, K refers to an actual value of 1,024. A computer with a 16K memory has 16,384 bytes of memory. [from *kilo*]

key *n.* **1.** The designation of a field in a database system to allow sorting and filing. **2.** A button on a keyboard. —**key in** To type data into a computer by using a keyboard.

keyboard *n.* A unit in a terminal designed to hold keys to be used for the inputting of data or other access.

keypad *n.* **1.** That part of a keyboard which contains numerical digits and functions. **2.** The mathematical and digit keys on a calculator or telephone.

language *n.* A set of commands, key words with a grammatical structure, used to communicate with the machine.

LISP (lisp) *n.* A symbolic computer programming language used for the manipulation of lists and strings. [*lis(t) p(rocessing)*]

load *n.* The transference of data or a program into a computer device, such as the copying of a program into the memory, the writing of data on a disk, etc. —*v.* To transfer data or a program.

loop *n.* A set of instructions to a computer which may be repeated either a given number of times or until a predetermined condition is fulfilled.

machine language The language, written in binary code, containing instructions that the computer can execute. Programming language is translated into machine language by compilers and interpreters.

macro *n.* A command or set of commands; a subroutine. [shortened form of *macroinstruction*]

mainframe *n.* Originally the main part of the central processing unit and its housing; commonly, a large computer as compared to a minicomputer or microcomputer.

matrix *n.* That part of the computer where data is stored.

matrix printer A printer that forms letters, numbers, and other symbols by patterns of dots.

memory *n.* The storage area of a computer.

menu *n.* A list of options available in a program, such list usually being displayed on the screen of a terminal when the program is being used.

merge *n.* The operation in which two or more files are combined to make one file. —*v.* To combine files.

MICR Abbreviation for magnetic ink character recognition, a system in which magnetic ink and machine-readable characters are imprinted on paper to be processed by machine, such as in checking accounts in banks.

microcircuit *n.* A miniaturized circuit.

microcomputer *n.* A small complete computor using a microprocessor. A personal computer is an example of a microcomputer.

microfiche *n.* A sheet of microfilm containing rows of reduced copy which can be read with a special device.

microfilm *n.* A photographic reproduction on film of a printed page, document, etc., highly reduced for ease in transmission and storage.

microprocessor *n.* A central processing unit, usually with a single integrated circuit-chip. Microprocessors are the basis of microcomputers.

mode *n.* That particular method used by a computer in its execution of processes.

model *n.* A visual or mathematical representation of a system.

modem (mō′dem) *n.* A device that converts output from one device into transportable form and translates the input at the other end. [*mo(dulator) dem(odulator)*]

modify *v.* To change the instructions in a program.

monitor *n.* The screen which the user sees when using a computer. —*v.* To watch and control a program to examine how it is performing.

mother board The main circuit board in a computer, into which all other boards connect.

mouse *n.* A small hand-held object, connected to a terminal by a wire, that when rolled across a surface, such as a desk top or special tablet, moves a cursor on the video screen.

multiprocessing *n.* A computer system with more than one central processing unit.

network *n.* A system of interconnected related units in a large computer system.

nibble *n. See* BIT.

number crunching The use of a computer to perform repetitive, routine calculations.

OCR Abbreviation for optical character recognition, a system for identifying characters imprinted on paper.

octal (ok′tal) *n.* **1.** A number system based on 8 digits or a system in which there are 8 possible states. **2.** A shorthand method for representing binary numbers.

off-line *adj.* Relating to that part of the system not connected to a computer.

on-line *adj.* Relating to a system directly connected to a computer.

operation *n.* An action performed in response to a command by a computer program.

output *n.* Computer-generated information, in the form of printing on paper, display on a screen, or a machine-readable tape or disk.

PASCAL *n.* A highly structured, logical computer programming language. [after Blaise Pascal, French mathematician (1623–62)]

password *n.* The group of letters or numbers, or a word or words, which allows a user to identify him- or herself to the computer system, used as a security measure.

peripheral *n.* A device used with but not directly part of the computer, such as a printer, modem, etc.

printer *n.* An output device used with a computer to provide readable copy of something in the machine, or of the results of a program.

program *n.* A set of instructions in a language that a computer uses, telling the computer how to perform a function. —*v.* To encode instructions into a computer.

program listing A program, printed out in the order in which it will be executed.

programming language A language used to develop instructions for a program to be used by a computer.

PROM (prom) *n.* A permanent memory chip for storage of programs designed to be modified to meet the customer's specifications. [*p(rogrammable) r(ead)-o(nly) m(emory)*]

protocol *n.* That set of rules which defines the uses and timing of a system when more than one device is in use.

pseudocode *n.* Procedures and steps in a program usually written in English statements rather than in programming language.

QUERTY (kwer′ tī) *adj.* Describing a standard keyboard for the English language in which the first letters in the top row are Q, W, E, R, T, and Y.

queue *n.* An ordered line of programs or processes waiting for processor time and attention.

RAM (ram) *n.* A memory device in which data or instructions are stored in a way that makes it possible to find any information in the memory, independent of how the memory is structured. [*r(andom) a(ccess) m(emory)*]

random access A system that provides direct access to a piece of information and is not dependent on surrounding information.

read *v.* To pick up data from a magnetic storage space and transfer them into a computer without destroying or changing the storage medium.

real-time *adj.* Referring to a computer system in which the response to user is immediate.

record *n.* A collection of related data.

recursion *n.* The deliberate repetition of a command or operation to determine the new result of the operation.

ROM (rom) *n.* Instructions placed in a computer memory at its manufacture. ROM cannot be changed by the user and no data can be stored in ROM. [*r(ead) o(nly) m(emory)*]

routine *n.* That part of a program which can be set apart as a set of instructions to perform one specific function.

screen *n.* The front of the display unit of a video terminal.

search *v.* To methodically check each piece of data for a specific piece of information.

seek *v.* To search on a diskette for a piece of information.

simulation *n.* The representation of a problem in mathematical terms in order that it might be more easily solved.

software *n.* Instructions to the computer; programs used on a computer.

sorting *n.* Rearrangement of information to a designated order, such as alphabetically or numerically.

source code The original programming-language version of a set of instructions for a system execution.

stand-alone *n.* That device which can function independently of the system.

statement *n.* The logical expression in a program.

storage *n.* A method or medium for retaining data in one place until they are needed again, by the user or by the machine.

subroutine *n.* A group of instructions in a program that performs a specific function that is usually repeated.

system *n.* Hardware and software used as a unit to perform specific tasks.

tape drive That device which pulls the tape past a magnetic head so that it may be read into the machine.

telecommunications *n. pl.* The transmission and reception of electronic signals over a distance.

terminal *n.* **1.** A device consisting of a keyboard and screen for writing with a computer. **2.** Any point at which I/O can occur in a system.

timesharing *n.* A system which allows more than one person to use the same computer at the same time.

truncate *v.* To drop one or more digits when a number is stored in a place too small to accommodate it.

unix (yōō′neks) *n.* An operating system that allows multi-users and sophisticated editing and compilation.

utility program A program which is provided to all users of a system to perform tasks that are commonly needed.

variable *n.* That part of a program or command which can change.

volatile memory A type of memory that does not retain its content without power.

word *n.* That set of characters or bits which fills up the capacity of a particular system; for example, a 16-bit system would have a 16-character word.

word processing A system that allows easy manipulation, storage, editing, and printing of text.

A PRONOUNCING GAZETTEER

This gazetteer lists states of the United States, its capital cities and cities with populations over 100,000, countries and other major political divisions of the world, world capitals, world cities, and Canadian provinces and their capitals. Included here also are the more important geographical features of the world. The population figures given for the United States are from the 1980 U.S. Census and those for the rest of the world are from 1982 estimates provided by the United Nations and other sources.

The following abbreviations are used in this section:

ab.	about	mi.	mile		
adm.	administrative	mtn(s).	mountain(s)		
betw.	between	N	north(ern)		
boro.	borough	penin.	peninsula		
cap.	capital	pop.	population		
cen.	central	prov.	province		
col.	colony	S	south(ern)		
dist.	district	terr.	territory		
E	east(ern)	U.S.	United States		
ft.	feet	U.S.S.R.	Union of Soviet		
isl(s).	island(s)		Socialist Republics		
met.	metropolitan	W	west(ern)		

Aar·hus (ôr′hōōs) city, E Denmark; pop. 244,839.
Ab·i·djan (ab·i·jän′) city, S Ivory Coast; cap.; pop. 1,500,000
A·bu Dha·bi (ä′bōō dä′bē) city, NE United Arab Emirates; cap.; pop. 300,000.
Ac·cra (ə·krä′, ak′rə) city, S Ghana; cap.; pop. 1,000,000.
A·con·ca·gua (ä′kôn·kä′gwä) extinct volcano, W cen. Argentina; highest point in South America; 22,834 ft.
Ad·dis Ab·a·ba (ä′dis ä′bə·bä, ad′is ab′ə·bə) city, cen. Ethiopia; cap.; pop. 1,200,000.
Ad·e·laide (ad′ə·lād) city, S Australia; pop. 952,700 (met.)
A·den (äd′n, ad′n) city, S Southern Yemen; cap.; pop. 343,000.
Ad·i·ron·dack Mountains (ad′ə·ron′dak) mtn. range, NE New York. Also **Adirondacks.**
A·dri·at·ic Sea (ā′drē·at′ik) inlet of the Mediterranean Sea, E of Italy.
Ae·ge·an Sea (i·jē′ən) inlet of the Mediterranean Sea betw. Greece and Asia Minor.
Af·ghan·i·stan (af·gan′ə·stan) country, S cen. Asia; pop. 16,750,000; cap. Kabul.
Af·ri·ca (af′ri·kə) second largest continent, S of Europe and W of Asia.
Ah·med·a·bad (ä′məd·ä·bäd′) city, W India; pop. 2,515,195.
Ak·ron (ak′rən) city, NE Ohio; pop. 237,177.
Al·a·bam·a (al′ə·bam′ə) state, SE U.S.; pop. 3,890,061; cap. Montgomery.
A·las·ka (ə·las′kə) state of U.S., NW North America; pop. 400,481; cap. Juneau.
Alaska Peninsula penin. of SW Alaska.
Al·ba·ni·a (al·bā′nē·ə, -bān′yə) country, S of Yugoslavia; pop. 2,875,000; cap. Tirana.
Al·ba·ny (ôl′bə·nē) city, E New York; cap.; pop. 101,727.
Al·ber·ta (al·bûr′tə) prov., W Canada; pop. 2,237,724; cap. Edmonton.
Al·bu·quer·que (al′bə·kûr′kē) city, NW New Mexico; pop. 331,767.
A·leu·tian Islands (ə·lōō′shən) isl. group, SW of Alaska.
Al·ex·an·dri·a (al′ig·zan′drē·ə) 1. city, NE Virginia; pop. 103,217. 2. city, N Egypt; pop. 2,320,000.
Al·ger·i·a (al·jir′ē·ə) country, NW Africa; pop. 20,000,000; cap. Algiers.
Al·giers (al·jirz′) city, N Algeria; cap.; pop. 2,200,000.
Al·le·ghe·ny Mountains (al′ə·gā′nē) mtn. range of Appalachian system; extends from Pennsylvania through Virginia.

Al·len·town (al′ən·toun′) city, E Pennsylvania; pop. 103,758
Alps (alps) mtn. system, S Europe; extends from S coast of France to W coast of Yugoslavia.
Al·tai Mountains (al′tī, äl′-) mtn. system, cen. Asia.
Am·a·ril·lo (am′ə·ril′ō) city, NW Texas; pop. 149,230.
Am·a·zon (am′ə·zon) river, N South America; 3,910 mi. long; carries the largest volume of water of all rivers.
A·mer·i·ca (ə·mer′ə·kə) 1. The United States of America. 2. North and South America; the Western Hemisphere.
American Samoa U.S. terr. consisting of 7 isls. in S Pacific; pop. 30,000; cap. Pago Pago.
Am·man (äm·män′) city, N cen. Jordan; cap.; pop. 650,000.
Am·ster·dam (am′stər·dam) city, W Netherlands; cap.; pop. 712,294.
A·mur (ä·mōōr′) river, E Asia; 2,700 mi. long.
An·a·heim (an′ə·hīm) city, SW California; pop. 221,847.
An·a·to·li·a (an′ə·tō′lē·ə) penin. at W end of Asia; comprises most of Turkey.
An·chor·age (äng′kər·ij) city, S Alaska; pop. 173,017.
An·des (an′dēz) mtn. range, W South America; connects with the Rockies.
An·dor·ra (an·dôr′ə, -dor′ə) country, SW Europe, betw. France and Spain; pop. 35,000; cap. Andorra la Vella.
Andorra la Vel·la (lä väl′yə) city, Andorra; cap.; pop. 13,500.
An·go·la (ang·gō′lə) country, SW Africa; pop. 7,450,000; cap. Luanda.
An·ka·ra (äng′kə·rə, ang′-) city, cen. Turkey; cap.; pop. 2,561,765.
An·nap·o·lis (ə·nap′ə·lis) city, cen. Maryland; cap.; pop. 31,740.
Ann Ar·bor (an′är′bər) city, SE Michigan; pop. 107,316.
An·ta·nan·a·ri·vo (an′tə·nan·ə·rē′vō) city, E cen. Madagascar; cap.; pop. 550,000. Also **Tananarive.**
Ant·arc·tic, the (ant·ärk′tik, -är′-) the regions around the South Pole.
Antarctic Circle parallel of latitude at 66°33′ S; the boundary of the South Frigid Zone.
Antarctic Ocean parts of Atlantic, Pacific, and Indian oceans bordering on Antarctica.
Ant·arc·ti·ca (ant·ärk′tə·kə, -är′-) continent surrounding the South Pole; also **Antarctic Continent.**
An·ti·gua and Bar·bu·da (an·tē′gwə, -gə, bär·bōō′də) country, isls. West Indies; pop. 80,000; cap. St. John's.
An·til·les (an·til′ēz) islands of the West Indies excluding the Bahamas; comprises *Greater Antilles:* Cuba, Hispaniola, Jamaica, and Puerto Rico, and *Lesser Antilles:* Trinidad, Tobago, Barbados, Virgin Islands, the Windward Islands, the Leeward Islands, and other small islands.
Ant·werp (ant′wûrp) city, N Belgium; pop. 197,000.
Ap·pa·la·chi·an Mountains (ap′ə·lā′chē·ən) mtn. system, E North America. Also **Appalachians.**
A·ra·bi·a (ə·rā′bē·ə) penin., SW Asia, betw. the Red Sea and Persian Gulf.
A·ra·bi·an Desert (ə·rā′bē·ən) desert, E Egypt, between Nile and Red Sea.
Arabian Sea part of the Indian Ocean betw. Arabia and India.
Ar·al Sea (ar′əl) salt inland sea, S cen. U.S.S.R.
Arc·tic, the (ärk′tik, är′-) the regions around the North Pole.
Arctic Circle parallel of latitude at 66°33′ N; the boundary of the North Frigid Zone.
Arctic Ocean sea, N of Arctic Circle, surrounding North Pole.
Ar·gen·ti·na (är′jən·tē′nə) country, S South America; pop. 27,900,000; cap. Buenos Aires.

PRONUNCIATION KEY: add, āce, câre, pälm; end, ēven; it; īce; odd, ōpen, ôrder; tŏŏk, pōōl; up, bûrn; ə = a in *above*, e in *sicken*, i in *flexible*, o in *melon*, u in *focus*; yōō = u in *fuse*; oil; pout; check; go; ring; thin; this; zh, vision. For à, œ, ü, kh, ṅ, see inside front cover.

807

Ar·i·zo·na (ar′ə-zō′nə) state, SW U.S.; pop. 2,718,425; cap. Phoenix.

Ar·kan·sas (är′kən-sô) **1.** river, cen. U.S.; 1,450 mi. long. **2.** state, S cen. U.S.; pop. 2,286,435; cap. Little Rock.

Ar·ling·ton (är′ling·tən) city, N Texas; pop. 160,123.

A·ru·ba (ä·rōō′bə) isl. in Netherlands Antilles.

A·sia (ā′zhə, ā′shə) largest of the continents; in the Eastern Hemisphere; part of a landmass with Europe and separated from Europe by Ural Mts.

Asia Minor penin. of extreme W Asia, comprising most of Turkey.

A·sun·ción (ä·sōōn·syôn′) city, SW Paraguay; cap.; pop. 530,000.

Ath·ens (ath′enz) city, SE Greece; cap.; pop. 3,000,000 (met.).

At·lan·ta (at·lan′tə) city, NW cen. Georgia; cap.; pop. 425,022.

At·lan·tic Ocean (at·lan′tik) ocean, extending from the Arctic to the Antarctic between the Americas and Europe and Africa.

At·las Mountains (at′ləs) mtn. range, NW Africa.

Auck·land (ôk′land) city, N New Zealand; pop. 818,000 (met.).

Au·gus·ta (ô·gus′tə, ə-) city, S Maine; cap.; pop. 21,819.

Au·ro·ra (ô·rôr′ə, ə-) city, N cen. Colorado; pop. 158,588.

Aus·tin (ôs′tən) city, cen. Texas; cap.; pop. 345,496.

Aus·tral·a·sia (ôs′trəl·ā·zhə, -shə) isls. of the South Pacific, including Australia, New Zealand, and New Guinea.

Aus·tral·ia (ôs·trāl′yə) **1.** isl. continent, South Pacific, SE of Asia. **2.** country comprising this continent and isl. of Tasmania; pop. 14,926,800; cap. Canberra.

Aus·tri·a (ôs′trē·ə) country, cen. Europe; pop. 7,515,000; cap. Vienna.

A·zores (ə·zôrz′, ā′zôrz) three isl. groups of Portugal, E Atlantic.

Bagh·dad (bag′dad, bäg·däd′) city, cen. Iraq; cap.; pop. 3,205,600 (met.).

Ba·ha·mas (bə·hä′məz, -hā′-) country, isl. SE of Florida; pop. 225,000; cap. Nassau.

Bah·rain (bä·rān′) country, isl. group in Persian Gulf off Saudi Arabia; pop. 360,000; cap. Manama.

Bai·kal (bī·käl′) freshwater lake, S U.S.S.R.

Ba·ja California (bä′hä) penin., NW Mexico; betw. the Gulf of California and the Pacific. Also **Lower California.**

Ba·kers·field (bā′kərz·fēld) city, S cen. California; pop. 105,611.

Ba·ku (bä·kōō′) city, U.S.S.R.; cap. of Azerbaidzhan Republic; pop. 1,550,000.

Bal·e·ar·ic Islands (bal′ē·ar′ik, bə·lir′ik) isl. group, W Mediterranean; prov. of Spain; comprising islands of Majorca, Minorca, Ibiza, and others.

Bal·ti·more (bôl′tə·môr) city, N Maryland; pop. 786,775.

Ba·ma·ko (bä·mä·kō′) city, S cen. Mali; cap.; pop. 450,000.

Ban·dung (bän′dōong) city, W Java, Indonesia; pop. 1,400,000.

Ban·ga·lore (bang′gə·lôr) city, S India; pop. 2,913,537.

Bang·kok (bang′kok) city, SW Thailand; cap.; pop. 5,000,000 (met.).

Ban·gla·desh (bäng′glä·desh′) country, S Asia; pop. 92,600,000; cap. Dacca. Formerly *East Pakistan.*

Ban·gui (bäng′gē) city, SW Central African Republic; cap.; pop. 375,000.

Ban·jul (bän·jōōl′) city, W Gambia; cap.; pop. 48,000. Formerly **Bath·urst** (bath′ərst).

Bar·ba·dos (bär·bā′dōs, -dōz) country, isl. in E Caribbean; pop. 275,000; cap. Bridgetown.

Bar·ce·lona (bär′sə·lō′nə) city, NE Spain; pop. 1,725,000.

Ba·sel (bä′zəl) city, N Switzerland; pop. 183,200.

Basse·terre (bas′tər, bäs′-) city, West Indies Associated States, on St. Kitts isl.; cap.; pop. 15,900.

Ba·su·to·land (bə·sōō′tō·land′) See Lesotho: *a former name.*

Bat·on Rouge (bat′n rōōzh′) city, SE cen. Louisiana; cap; pop. 219,486.

Beau·mont (bō′mont) city, SE Texas; pop. 118,102.

Bei·rut (bā′rōōt, bā·rōōt′) city, W Lebanon; cap.; pop. 702,000.

Bel·fast (bel′fast -fäst) city, E Northern Ireland; cap.; pop. 345,800.

Bel·gium (bel′jəm) country, NW Europe; pop. 9,830,000; cap. Brussels.

Bel·grade (bel′grād, bel-grād′) city, E Yugoslavia; cap.; pop. 1,000,000.

Be·lize (bə·lēz′) **1.** country, E cen. Central America; pop. 175,000; cap. Belmopan. Formerly *British Honduras.* **2.** city, E Belize; pop. 42,200.

Bel·mo·pan (bel·mō·pan′) city, cen. Belize; cap.; pop. 4,500.

Ben·ga·si (ben·gä′zē, beng-) city, N Libya; one of two caps; pop. 282,192.

Be·nin (be·nēn′) country, W Africa; pop. 3,725,000; cap. Porto-Novo. Formerly *Dahomey.*

Ber·gen (bûr′gən) city, SW Norway; pop. 208,910.

Ber·ing Sea (bâr′ing, bir′-) part of the North Pacific betw. Alaska and the U.S.S.R., joined to the Arctic by **Bering Strait.**

Berke·ley (bûrk′lē) city, W California; pop. 103,328.

Ber·lin (bər·lin′) city, E cen. Germany; cap. prior to 1945 when divided into the British, French, Soviet, and U.S. sectors. In 1949 the Soviet sector, *East Berlin,* was designated capital of East Germany; pop. 1,146,000. The remaining sectors formed *West Berlin,* associated with West Germany; pop. 1,900,000.

Bern (bûrn, bern) city, W cen. Switzerland; cap.; pop. 183,200. Also **Berne.**

Bhu·tan (bōō·tän′) country, S Asia; pop. 1,350,000; cap. Thimphu.

Bir·ming·ham (bûr′ming·ham) city, N cen. Alabama; pop. 284,413.

Bis·marck (biz′märk) city, S cen. North Dakota; cap.; pop. 44,485.

Bis·sau (bi·sō′) city, W Guinea-Bissau; cap.; pop. 109,500 (met.).

Bitterroot Range a range of Rocky Mtns. along the Idaho-Montana border.

Black Forest wooded mtn. reg., SW West Germany.

Black Sea inland sea betw. Europe and Asia, connects with the Aegean via the Bosporus, the Sea of Marmara, and the Dardanelles.

Blue Ridge Mountains. SW part of the Appalachians.

Bo·go·tá (bō′gə·tä′) city, E cen. Colombia; cap.; pop. 4,486,200.

Boi·se (boi′zē, -sē) city, SW Idaho; cap.; pop. 102,160.

Bo·liv·i·a (bə·liv′ē·ə) country, W cen. South America; pop. 5,900,000; cap. Sucre (constitutional), LaPaz (administrative).

Bo·lo·gna (bō·lō′nyä) city, N cen. Italy; pop. 455,853.

Bom·bay (bom·bā′) city, W India; pop. 8,200,000 (met.).

Bon·aire (bə·nâr′) isl. in Netherlands Antilles.

Bonn (bon) city, W West Germany; cap.; pop. 285,000.

Bor·deaux (bôr·dō′) city, SW France; pop. 226,300.

Bor·ne·o (bôr′nē·ō) isl. in Malay Archipelago, SW of the Philippines.

Bos·po·rus (bos′pə·rəs) strait, betw. the Black Sea and the Sea of Marmara.

Bos·ton (bôs′tən, bos′-) city, E Massachusetts; cap.; pop. 562,994.

Bot·swa·na (bot·swä′nä) country, S Africa; pop. 900,000; cap. Gaborone.

Bra·sí·li·a (brə·zē′lyə) city, cen. Brazil; cap.; pop. 1,202,683.

Bra·zil (brə·zil′) country, NE and N cen. South America; pop. 124,500,000; cap. Brasília.

Braz·za·ville (braz′ə·vil) city, SE Congo; cap.; pop. 200,000 (met.).

Brem·en (brem′en) city, NW West Germany; pop. 550,000.

Bridge·port (brij′pôrt) city, SW Connecticut; pop. 142,546.

Bridge·town (brij/toun) city, SW Barbados; cap.; pop. 8,000.

Bris·bane (briz/băn, -bən) city, E Australia; pop. 1,086,500.

Bris·tol (bris/təl) city, SW England; pop. 419,200.

Bristol Channel inlet of the Atlantic betw. Wales and SW England.

British Columbia prov., W Canada; pop. 2,744,467; cap. Victoria.

British Gui·an·a (gē·an/ə, -ä/nə) Guyana: *a former name.*

British Honduras Belize: *a former name.*

British Isles isl. group of W Europe comprising Great Britain, Ireland and adjacent islands.

British Virgin Islands British col., easternmost of the Virgin Islands.

British West Indies isl. group in the Caribbean including Jamaica, the Bahamas, Caymans, British Virgin Islands, British Leeward and Windward Islands and others.

Brno (bûr/nô) city, cen. Czechoslovakia; pop. 371,000.

Brus·sels (brus/əlz) city, cen. Belgium; cap.; pop. 1,008,715 (met.).

Bu·cha·rest (bōō/kə·rest, byōō/-) city, S Romania; cap.; pop. 1,861,007 (met.).

Bu·da·pest (bōō/də·pest) city, cen. Hungary; cap.; pop. 2,100,000.

Bue·nos Ai·res (bwā/nəs ī/riz, bō/nəs âr/ēz) city, E Argentina; cap.; pop. 3,000,000.

Buf·fa·lo (buf/ə·lō) city, W New York; pop. 357,870.

Bu·jum·bu·ra (bōō/jōom·bōōr/ə) city, W cen. Burundi; cap.; pop. 151,000.

Bul·gar·i·a (bul·gâr/i·ə, bōōl-) country, SE Europe; pop. 8,925,000; cap. Sofia.

Bur·ma (bûr/mə) country, SE Asia; pop. 37,500,000; cap. Rangoon.

Bu·run·di (bōō·rōōn/dē, -run/-) country, E cen. Africa; pop. 4,450,000; cap. Bujumbura.

Cai·ro (kī/rō) city, NE Egypt; cap.; pop. 5,423,000.

Cal·cut·ta (kal·kut/ə) city, NE India; pop. 9,165,650.

Cal·ga·ry (kal/gə·rē) city, S Alberta Canada; pop. 592,743 (met.).

Cal·i·for·nia (kal/ə·fôr/nyə) state, W U.S.; pop. 23,667,565; cap. Sacramento.

California, Gulf of inlet of the Pacific, W Mexico, betw. Lower California and the rest of Mexico.

Cam·bo·di·a (kam·bō/dē·ə) See KAMPUCHEA.

Cam·e·roon (kam/ə·rōōn/) country, W cen. Africa; pop. 8,800,000; cap. Yaoundé.

Can·a·da (kan/ə·də) country, N North America; pop. 24,343,181; cap. Ottawa.

Canary Islands isl. group of Spain near NW coast of Africa.

Ca·nav·er·al Cape (kə·nav/ər·əl), cape, E Florida; site of the John F. Kennedy Space Center, a space research and missiles installation.

Can·ber·ra (kan/bə·rə) city, SE Australia; cap.; pop. 246,100 (met.).

Can·ton (kan·ton/) city, S China; pop. 5,200,000. Pinyin spelling Guangzhou.

Cape Town city, S South Africa; legislative cap.; pop. 213,830. Also Cape·town (kāp/toun/).

Cape Verde (vûrd) country, isl. group off NW Africa; pop. 340,000; cap. Praia.

Ca·ra·cas (kə·rä/kəs, -rak/əs) city, N Venezuela; pop. 3,000,000 (met.).

Car·diff (kär/dif) city, SE Wales; cap.; pop. 273,860.

Car·ib·be·an Sea (kar/ə·bē/ən, kə·rib/ēən) part of the Atlantic betw. the West Indies and Central and South America.

Car·o·line Islands (kär/ə·līn) isl. group in the Pacific, E of the Philippines; part of the Trust Territory of the Pacific Islands.

Car·pa·thi·an Mountains (kär·pā/thē·ən) mtn. range, cen. and E Europe.

Carson City (kär/sən) city, W Nevada; cap.; pop. 32,022.

Cas·a·blan·ca (kas/ə·blang/kə, kä/sə·bläng/kə) city, NW Morocco; pop. 2,350,000 (met.).

Cascade Range mtn. range in Oregon, Washington, and British Columbia.

Cas·pi·an Sea (kas/pē·ən) saltwater lake in the S U.S.S.R. and N Iran.

Cas·tries (kas/trēz) city, St. Lucia; cap.; pop. 45,000.

Ca·ta·nia (kä·tä/nyä) city, E Sicily; pop. 378,521.

Cats·kill Mountains (kat/skil) range of the Appalachians in SE New York. Also Catskills.

Cau·ca·sus (kô/kə·səs) mtn. range between the Black and Caspian seas.

Cay·man Islands (kā/mən) Brit. dependency; three isls. in Caribbean, S of Cuba. Chief island *Grand Cayman;* pop. 15,000.

Cedar Rapids city, E Iowa; pop. 110,243.

Cel·e·bes (sel/ə·bēz, sə·lē/bēz) isl. of Indonesia, E of Borneo. Also Sulawesi.

Central African Republic country, cen. Africa; pop. 2,500,000; cap. Bangui. Formerly *Central African Empire.*

Central America S part of North America, betw. Mexico and Colombia.

Cey·lon (si·lon/) See SRI LANKA.

Chad (chad) country, cen. Africa; pop. 4,650,000; cap. N'Djamena.

Channel Islands British isl. group, English Channel; includes Jersey, Guernsey, Alderney, and Sark.

Charles·ton (chärl/stən, chärlz/tən) city, cen. West Virginia; cap.; pop. 63,968.

Char·lotte (shär/lət) city, S cen. North Carolina; pop. 314,447.

Char·lotte·town (shär/lət·toun) city, NE Canada; cap. of Prince Edward Island; pop. 17,063.

Chat·ta·noo·ga (chat/ə·nōō/gə) city, SE Tennessee; pop. 169,565.

Ches·a·peake (ches/ə·pēk) city, SE Virginia; pop. 114,226.

Chesapeake Bay inlet of the Atlantic in Virginia and Maryland.

Chey·enne (shī·an/, -en/) city, SE Wyoming; cap.; pop. 47,283.

Chi·ca·go (shə·kä/gō, -kô/-) city, NE Illinois; pop. 3,005,072

Chil·e (chil/ē) country, W South America; pop. 11,500,000; cap. Santiago.

China, People's Republic of (chī/nə) country, E and cen. Asia; pop. 1,020,000,000; cap. Peking (Pinyin spelling: Beijing).

Chi·na, Republic of country, on Taiwan and several smaller islands; pop. 18,350,000; cap. Taipei.

China Sea part of the Pacific bordering on China.

Chung·king (chŏong/king/) city, S cen. China; cap. during World War II; pop. 3,500,000. Pinyin spelling Chongqing.

Cin·cin·nat·i (sin/sə·nat/ē, -nat/ə) city, SW Ohio; pop. 385,457.

Ciu·dad Juá·rez (sē·yŏo·dä/ hwä·res/) city, N Mexico; pop. 500,000. Also Juárez.

Ciudad Tru·jil·lo (trōō·hē/yō) See SANTO DOMINGO.

Cleve·land (klēv/lənd) city, N Ohio; pop. 573,822.

Co·logne (kə·lōn/) city, W West Germany; pop. 975,000.

Co·lom·bi·a (kə·lum/bē·ə) country, NW South America; pop. 28,575,000; cap. Bogotá.

Co·lom·bo (kə·lum/bō) city, W Sri Lanka; cap.; pop. 640,000.

Co·lón (kō·lōn/) city, N Panama, on Caribbean at entrance to Panama Canal; pop. 117,000.

Col·o·ra·do (kol·ə·rad/ō, -rä/dō) state, W cen. U.S.; pop. 2,889,735; cap. Denver.

Colorado River river SW U.S. and NW Mexico, flowing from Colorado into Gulf of California; 1,400 mi. long.

PRONUNCIATION KEY: add, āce, câre, pälm; end, ēven; it; īce; odd, ōpen, ôrder; tŏŏk, pōōl; up, bûrn; ə = a in *above*, e in *sicken*, i in *flexible*, o in *melon*, u in *focus*; yōō = u in *fuse*; oil; pout; check; go; ring; thin; this; zh, vision. For à, œ, ü, kh, ṅ, see inside front cover.

Colorado Springs city, E cen. Colorado; pop. 215,150
Co·lum·bi·a (kə·lum′bē·ə) city, cen. South Carolina; cap.; pop. 99,296.
Columbia River river, SW Canada and NW U.S.; 1,200 mi. long.
Co·lum·bus (kə·lum′bəs) 1. city, W Georgia; pop. 169,441. 2. city, cen. Ohio; cap.; pop. 564,871.
Com·o·ros (käm′ə·rōs) country, isls. off SE Africa; pop. 375,000; cap. Moroni.
Con·a·kry (kän′ə·krē) city, W Guinea; cap.; pop. 575,000.
Con·cord (kong′kərd, kon′kôrd) 1. city, W California; pop. 103,251. 2. city, S cen. New Hampshire; cap.; pop. 30,400.
Con·go (kong′gō) country, W cen. Africa; pop. 1,625,000; cap. Brazzaville.
Congo River river, cen. Africa; 2,720 mi. long.
Con·nect·i·cut (kə·net′i·kət) state, NE U.S.; pop. 3,107,576; cap. Hartford.
Con·stan·ti·no·ple (kon′stan·tə·nō′pəl) Istanbul; *a former name*.
Continental Divide ridge of the Rockies separating W flowing and E flowing streams in North America.
Co·pen·ha·gen (kō′pən·hā′gən, -hä′-) city, E Denmark; cap.; pop. 654,437.
Cork (kôrk) city, SW Ireland; pop. 136,269.
Cor·pus Chris·ti (kôr′pəs kris′tē) city, S Texas; pop. 231,999.
Cor·si·ca (kôr′si·kə) isl., N Mediterranean; a dept. of France; pop. 229,400; cap. Ajaccio.
Cos·ta Ri·ca (kos′tə rē′kə) country, Central America; pop. 2,350,000; cap. San José.
Crac·ow See KRAKOW.
Crete (krēt) isl., E Mediterranean; adm. div. of Greece; cap. Canea.
Cu·ba (kyōō′bə) country, isl. in W Caribbean; pop. 9,850,000; cap. Havana.
Cum·ber·land Gap (kum′bər·lənd) passage through Cumberland Mts., betw. Tennessee and Virginia.
Cu·ra·çao (kyōor′ə·sō′, kōō′rä·sou′) largest isl. in Netherlands Antilles.
Cy·prus (sī′prəs) country, isl. E Mediterranean; pop. 650,000; cap. Nicosia.
Czech·o·slo·va·ki·a (chek′ə·slō·vä′ke·ə, -vak′ē·ə) country, E cen. Europe; pop. 15,400,000; cap. Prague.

Dac·ca (dä′kä) city, E cen. Bangladesh; cap.; pop. 2,500,000 (met.).
Da·ho·mey (də·hō′mē) Benin: *a former name*.
Da·kar (dä·kär′, də-) city, W Senegal; cap.; pop. 978,553.
Dal·las (dal′əs) city, N Texas; pop. 904,078.
Da·mas·cus (də·mas′kəs) city, SW Syria; cap.; pop. 1,200,000.
Da Nang (dä′näng′) city, cen. Vietnam; pop. 493,000. Also **Da′nang′**.
Dan·ube (dan′yōōb) river, cen. and E Europe; 1,770 mi. long.
Dan·zig (dan′sig, -tsig, -zig) Gdansk: *the German name*.
Dar·da·nelles (där′də·nelz′) strait, NW Turkey; connects Sea of Marmara with the Aegean.
Dar es Sa·laam (där′ es sə·läm′) city, E cen. Tanzania; cap.; pop. 700,000.
Dav·en·port (dav′ən·pôrt) city, E Iowa; pop. 103,264.
Day·ton (dā′tən, dāt′n) city, SW Ohio; pop. 203,588.
Dead Sea large salt lake on Israel-Jordan border; 1,292 ft. below sea level.
Death Valley desert basin, SE California; maximum depth 280 ft. below sea level; lowest point on North America.
Del·a·ware (del′ə·wâr) state, E U.S.; pop. 594,317; cap. Dover.
Del·hi (del′ē) city, NE cen. India; pop. 6,196,000.
Den·mark (den′märk) country, NW Europe; pop. 5,130,000; cap. Copenhagen.
Den·ver (den′vər) city, cen. Colorado; cap.; pop. 491,396.
Des Moines (də moin′) city, S cen. Iowa; cap.; pop. 191,003.

De·troit (di·troit′) city, SE Michigan; pop. 1,203,339.
Devil's Island rocky isl. off the coast of French Guiana; formerly a penal colony.
District of Columbia federal dist., E U.S.; has same boundaries as Washington, cap. of U.S.; pop. 637,651.
Dja·kar·ta (jä·kär′tä) See JAKARTA.
Dji·bou·ti (ji·bōō′tē) 1. country, NE Africa; pop. 335,000; cap. Djibouti. Formerly, *French Territory of the Afars and the Issas;* before 1967 known as *French Somaliland.* 2. city, E Djibouti; cap.; pop. 200,000 (met.).
Dnie·per (dnye′pər, nē′pər) river, SW U.S.S.R.; 1,420 mi. long. Also **Dne′pr.**
Dnies·ter (dnyes′tər, nē′stər) river, SW U.S.S.R.; 876 mi. long. Also **Dnes′tr.**
Do·ha (dō′hə) city, Qatar; cap.; pop. 190,000.
Do·min·i·can Republic (də·min′i·kən) country, West Indies, on E Hispaniola; pop. 5,575,000; cap. Santo Domingo.
Don (don) river, SW U.S.S.R.; 1,222 mi. long.
Do·ver (dō′vər) city, cen. Delaware; cap.; pop. 23,512.
Dres·den (drez′dən) city, S East Germany; pop. 516,000.
Dub·lin (dub′lin) city, E Ireland; cap.; pop. 525,360.
Dur·ban (dûr′bən) city, SE South Africa; pop. 505,963.
Dur·ham (dûr′əm, du′rəm) city, N cen. North Carolina; pop. 100,831.
Düs·sel·dorf (düs′səl·dôrf) city, W West Germany; pop. 590,000.
Dutch Gui·an·a (gē·an′ə, -ä′nə) Suriname: *a former name.*
Dutch West Indies See NETHERLANDS ANTILLES.

East Berlin See BERLIN.
East China Sea NE part of the China Sea.
Easter Island isl. of Chile, SE Pacific.
East Germany See GERMAN DEMOCRATIC REPUBLIC.
East Pakistan Bangladesh: *a former name.*
Ec·ua·dor (ek′wə·dôr) country, NW South America; pop. 8,350,000; cap. Quito.
Ed·mon·ton (ed′mən·tən) city, W Canada; cap. of Alberta; pop. 657,057 (met.).
E·gypt (ē′jipt) country, NE Africa; pop. 44,750,000; cap. Cairo. Formerly *United Arab Republic.*
El·be (el′bə) river, cen. Europe; 725 mi. long.
El·brus, Mount (el′brōōs) mtn. of the Caucasus range, U.S.S.R.; highest peak in Europe; 18,603 ft.
E·liz·a·beth (i·liz′ə·bəth) city, NE New Jersey; pop. 106,201.
El·lis Island (el′is) isl., upper New York Bay; former site of U.S. immigration station.
El Pas·o (el pas′ō) city, W Texas; pop. 425,259.
El Sal·va·dor (el sal′və·dôr) country, W Central America; pop. 5,150,000; cap. San Salvador.
Eng·land (ing′glənd) country, S Great Britain, W Europe, a division of the United Kingdom of Great Britain and Northern Ireland; pop. 46,221,000; cap. London.
English Channel strait, betw. England and France.
Equatorial Guinea country, W Africa; pop. 380,000; cap. Malabo. Formerly *Spanish Guinea.*
E·rie (ir′ē) city, NW Pennsylvania; pop. 119,123.
Erie, Lake southernmost of the Great Lakes.
Erie Canal waterway, betw. Albany and Buffalo, New York.
Es·sen (es′ən) city, W West Germany; pop. 650,000.
Es·to·ni·a (es·tō′nē·ə) constituent republic, W U.S.S.R., pop. 1,470,000; cap. Tallinn. Officially **Estonian SSR.**
E·thi·o·pi·a (ē·thē·ō′pē·ə) country, E. Africa; pop. 33,000,000; cap. Addis Ababa.
Eu·gene (yōō·jēn′) city, W Oregon; pop. 105,624.
Eu·phra·tes (yōō·frä′tēz) river, SW Asia; 1,740 mi. long.
Eu·rope (yōor′əp) continent, W part of landmass with Asia, bounded by Asia and Atlantic Ocean.
Ev·ans·ville (ev′ənz·vil) city, SW Indiana; pop. 130,496.
Ev·er·est, Mount (ev′ər·ist, ev′rist) mtn., E Nepal; highest point of the earth's surface; 29,028 ft.

Ev·er·glades (ev′ər·glādz) large swampy reg., S Florida.

Eyre, Lake (er) lake, NE South Australia.

Faer·oe Islands (fâr′ō) isl. group of Denmark, NE Atlantic.

Falk·land Islands (fôk′lənd) British col., SW Atlantic.

Fez (fez) city, NE Morocco; pop. 745,000. Also Fes.

Fi·ji (fē′jē) country, isl. group in South Pacific; pop. 650,000; cap. Suva.

Fin·land (fin′lənd) country, N Europe; pop. 4,825,000; cap. Helsinki.

Finland, Gulf of part of the Baltic Sea betw. Finland and U.S.S.R.

Flint (flint) city, E cen. Michigan; pop. 159,611.

Flor·ence (flôr′əns, flor′-) city, cen. Italy; pop. 453,300.

Flor·i·da (flor′ə·də, flôr′-) state, SE U.S.; pop. 9,745,000; cap. Tallahassee.

Florida Keys isl. group SW of Florida.

For·mo·sa (fôr·mō′sə) Taiwan: a former name.

Formosa Strait strait, betw. China and Taiwan.

Fort-La·my (fôr·lä·mē′) N'Djamena: the former name.

Fort Lau·der·dale (lô′dər·dāl) city, SE Florida; pop. 153,256.

Fort Wayne (wān) city, NE Indiana; pop. 172,196.

Fort Worth (wûrth) city, N Texas; pop. 385,141.

France (frans, fräns) country, W Europe; pop. 54,250,000; cap. Paris.

Frank·fort (frangk′fərt) city, N cen. Kentucky; cap.; pop. 25,973.

Frank·furt (frangk′fərt) city, cen. West Germany; pop. 630,000. Also Frankfurt-am-Main (-äm·mīn′).

Fred·er·ic·ton (fred′rik·tən, -ər·ik-) city, E Canada; cap. of New Brunswick; pop. 47,800.

Free·town (frē′toun′) city, W Sierra Leone; cap.; pop. 215,000.

Fre·mont (frē′mont) city, N California; pop. 131,945.

French Gui·an·a (gē·an′ə, -än′ə) French Overseas dept.; NE South America; pop. 70,000; cap. Cayenne.

French Indochina See INDOCHINA.

French Polynesia French Overseas terr., South Pacific; comprises the Society, Marquesas, Gambier, and other islands; pop. 160,000; cap. Papeete.

French So·ma·li·land (sō·mä′lē·land) Djibouti: a former name.

French Territory of the A·fars and the Is·sas (äf′ärz; ē′säz) See DJIBOUTI.

French West Indies isls. in the West Indies comprising Guadaloupe, Martinique and other islands.

Fres·no (frez′nō) city, cen. California; pop. 218,202.

Fris·ian Islands (frizh′ən, frizh′ē·ən) isl. group, North Sea near Germany, Denmark, and the Netherlands.

Front Range a range of Rocky Mtns. in N cen. Colorado.

Ful·ler·ton (fŏŏl′ər·tən) city, SW California; pop. 102,034.

Ga·bon (ga·bon′) country, W Africa; pop. 560,000; cap. Libreville. Formerly Ga·bo·nese Republic (gab′ə·nēz′).

Ga·bo·ro·ne (gä′bə·rō′nä) city, SE Botswana; cap.; pop. 60,000.

Galilee, Sea of freshwater lake; betw. NE Israel, SW Syria, and NW Jordan.

Gam·bi·a (gam′bē·ə) country, W Africa; pop. 640,000; cap. Banjul.

Gan·ges (gan′jēz) river, N India and E Pakistan; 1,560 mi. long.

Garden Grove city, SW California; pop. 123,351.

Gar·land (gär′lənd) city, N Texas; pop. 138,857.

Gar·y (gâr′ē) NW Indiana; pop. 151,953.

Gdansk (gdäny′sk) city, N Poland; pop. 443,200; Also Danzig.

Ge·ne·va (jə·nē′və) city, SW Switzerland; pop. 152,700.

Gen·o·a (jen′ō·ə) city, NW Italy; pop. 760,300.

George·town (jôrj′toun) city, N Guyana; cap.; pop. 200,000.

Geor·gia (jôr′jə) state, SE U.S.; pop. 5,463,105; cap. Atlanta.

German Democratic Republic country, cen. Europe; pop. 16,750,000; cap. East Berlin. Also East Germany.

Ger·ma·ny, Federal Republic of (jûr′mə·nē) country, cen. Europe; pop. 61,750,000; cap. Bonn; Also West Germany.

Gha·na (gä′nə) country, W Africa; pop. 500,000; cap. Accra.

Gi·bral·tar (ji·brôl′tər) Brit. col. on the Rock of Gibraltar; pop. 30,000.

Gibraltar, Rock of penin., S Spain; dominates the Strait of Gibraltar.

Gibraltar, Strait of strait, betw. Spain and Africa, W Mediterranean.

Gi·za (gē′zə) city, N Egypt; pop. 1,246,700.

Glen·dale (glen′dāl) city, SW California; pop. 139,060.

Go·bi Desert (gō′bē) desert, cen. Asia.

Golden Gate strait betw. San Francisco Bay and the Pacific.

Good Hope, Cape of penin. SW South Africa.

Gor·ki (gôr′kē) city, W cen. U.S.S.R.; pop. 1,344,000. Also Gor′kiy, Gor′ky.

Gö·te·borg (yœ′tə·bôr′ē) city, SW Sweden; pop. 443,000.

Gra·na·da (grə·nä′də) city, S Spain; pop. 246,640.

Grand Canyon gorge of the Colorado River, NW Arizona; ab. 250 mi. long.

Grand Cayman See CAYMAN ISLANDS.

Grand Rapids city, W Michigan; pop. 181,843.

Great Barrier Reef chain of coral reef off the coast of Queensland, Australia.

Great Bear Lake lake, Northwest Territories, Canada.

Great Brit·ain (brit′n) isl. W Europe; principal isl. of United Kingdom of Great Britain and Northern Ireland, comprising England, Scotland, and Wales.

Greater Antilles See ANTILLES.

Great Lakes chain of five lakes, cen. North America; on Canada–United States border; comprises Lakes Superior, Michigan, Huron, Ontario, and Erie.

Great Plains plateau, W North America; E of the Rockies.

Great Salt Lake salt lake, NW Utah.

Great Smoky Mountains mtn. range, North Carolina and Tennessee.

Greece (grēs) country, SE Europe; pop. 9,800,000; cap. Athens.

Green·land (grēn′lənd) isl. of Denmark in N Atlantic, near NE North America.

Green Mountains mtn. range, cen. Vermont.

Greens·boro (grēz′bûr′ō, -ə) city, N North Carolina; pop. 155,642.

Gre·na·da (gri·nä′də) country, isl. West Indies; pop. 110,000; cap. St. George's.

Gua·da·la·ja·ra (gwäd′ə·lə·här′ə) city, W cen. Mexico; pop. 2,100,000 (met.).

Gua·dal·ca·nal (gwä′dəl·kə·nal′) isl. in Solomon Islands in W Pacific.

Gua·de·loupe (gwä′də·lŏŏp′) French Overseas dept., Lesser Antilles.

Guam (gwäm) isl. in the Marianas in W Pacific; U.S. possession.

Gua·te·ma·la (gwä′tə·mä′lä) country, N Central America; pop. 7,700,000; cap. Guatemala City.

Guatemala City city, cen. Guatemala; cap.; pop. 1,250,000.

Guay·a·quil (gwī′ä·kēl′) city, W Ecuador; pop. 1,100,000.

Guin·ea (gin·ē) country, W Africa; pop. 5,300,000; cap. Conakry.

Guin·ea-Bis·sau (gin′ē·bi·sō′) country, W Africa; pop. 590,000; cap. Bissau. Formerly Portuguese Guinea.

Guy·a·na (gī·an′ə, -än′ə) country, N South America; pop. 925,000; cap. Georgetown. Formerly British Guiana.

PRONUNCIATION KEY: add, āce, câre, pälm; end, ēven; it; īce; odd, ōpen, ôrder; tŏŏk, pōōl; up, bûrn; ə = a in above, e in sicken, i in flexible, o in melon, u in focus; yōō = u in fuse; oil; pout; check; go; ring; thin; this; zh, vision. For à, œ, ü, kh, ṅ, see inside front cover.

Hague, The (hāg) city, W Netherlands; cap.; seat of the government; pop. 456,900.

Hai·fa (hī/fə) city, NW Israel; pop. 360,400 (met.).

Hai·ti (hā/tē) country, West Indies, W Hispaniola; pop. 5,200,000; cap. Port-au-Prince.

Hal·i·fax (hal/ə·fax) city, SE Canada; cap. of Nova Scotia; pop. 280,000 (met.).

Ham·burg (ham/bûrg) city, N West Germany; pop. 1,650,000.

Ham·il·ton (ham/əl·tən) **1.** city, cen. Bermuda; cap.; pop. 2,500. **2.** city, S Ontario, Canada; pop. 542,095 (met.).

Hamp·ton (hamp/tən) city, SE Virginia; pop. 122,617.

Ha·noi (hä·noi/) city, N Vietnam; cap.; pop. 2,600,000 (met.).

Han·o·ver (han/ō·vər) city, N cen. West Germany; pop. 535,000.

Ha·ra·re (hä·rä/rä) city, NE Zimbabwe; cap.; pop. 655,000 (met.). Formerly *Salisbury.*

Har·bin (här/bin) city, NE China; pop. 2,750,000. Pinyin spelling **Harbin.**

Har·ris·burg (har/is·bûrg) city, S cen. Pennsylvania; cap.; pop. 53,264.

Hart·ford (härt/fərd) city, cen. Connecticut; cap.; pop. 136,392.

Ha·va·na (hə·van/ə) city, W Cuba; cap.; pop. 2,000,000 (met.).

Ha·wai·i (hə·wä/ē, hə·wī/yē) state of U.S., North Pacific; pop. 964,691; cap. Honolulu.

Ha·wai·ian Islands (hə·wä/yən, -wī/-) chain of volcanic and coral isls. in N cen. Pacific Ocean. Formerly *Sandwich Islands.*

Heb·ri·des (heb/ri·dēz) isl. group off W coast of Scotland.

Hel·en·a (hel/ə·nə) city, W cen. Montana; cap.; pop. 23,938.

Hel·sin·ki (hel/sing·kē, hel·sing/-) city, S Finland; cap.; pop. 484,000.

Hi·a·le·ah (hī/ə·lē/ə) city, SE Florida; pop. 145,254.

Hi·ma·la·yas (him/ə·lā/əz, hi·mä/lə·yəz) mtn. chain between Tibet and India in Nepal, including *Mount Everest*, the world's highest point.

Hir·o·shi·ma (hir/ə·shē/mə, hi·rō/shə·mə) city, SW Honshu isl. Japan; pop. 899,000.

His·pa·nio·la (his/pə·nyō/lə) isl., West Indies; divided into Haiti and the Dominican Republic.

Ho·bart (hō/bärt) city, Tasmania; cap.; pop. 172,000.

Ho Chi Minh City (hō/chē/min/) city, S Vietnam; pop. 3,500,000. Formerly *Saigon.*

Hok·kai·do (hô·kī·dō) isl. of N Japan.

Hol·land (hol/ənd) See NETHERLANDS.

Hol·ly·wood (hol/ē·wŏŏd) city, SE Florida; pop. 117,188.

Hon·dur·as (hon·dŏŏr/əs, -dyŏŏr/-) country, NE Central America; pop. 3,900,000; cap. Tegucigalpa.

Hong Kong (hong/kong/, hông/kông) British crown colony, SE China; includes **Hong Kong Island** and some coastal terr.; pop. 5,250,000; cap. Victoria.

Hon·o·lu·lu (hon/ə·lōō/lōō) port city, SE Oahu; cap. of Hawaii; pop. 365,048.

Hon·shu (hon·shōō) isl. of cen. Japan.

Horn (hôrn) **, Cape** S extremity of South America.

Hous·ton (hyōōs/tən) city, SE Texas; pop. 1,594,086.

Hudson Bay inland sea; N cen. Canada; connected with the Atlantic by Hudson Strait.

Hun·ga·ry (hung/gə·rē) country, cen. Europe; pop. 10,800,000; cap. Budapest.

Huntington Beach (hunt/ing·tən) city, SW California; pop. 170,505.

Hunts·ville (hunts/vil, -vəl) city, N Alabama; pop. 142,513.

Huron, Lake one of the Great Lakes; betw. Michigan and Ontario.

Hwang Ho (hwäng/ hō/) river, N China; 2,900 mi. long. Also *Yellow River.*

Hy·der·a·bad (hī/dər·ə·bad/, -bäd/) **1.** city, S cen. India; pop. 1,500,000. **2.** city, SE Pakistan; pop. 795,000 (met.).

I·ber·i·a (ī·bir/ē·ə) penin. of SW Europe containing Spain and Portugal.

Ice·land (īs/lənd) country, isl., North Atlantic; pop. 235,000; cap. Reykjavik.

I·da·ho (ī/də·hō) state, NW U.S.; pop. 944,038; cap. Boise.

Il·lin·ois (il/ə·noi/, -noiz/) state, NE cen. U.S.; pop. 11,426,518; cap. Springfield.

In·chon (in/chon) city, NW South Korea; pop. 800,000.

In·de·pen·dence (in/di·pen/dəns) city, W Missouri; pop. 111,806.

In·di·a (in/dē·ə) country, S Asia; pop. 700,000,000; cap. New Delhi.

In·di·an·a (in/dē·an/ə) state, NE cen. U.S.; pop. 5,490,260; cap. Indianapolis.

In·di·a·nap·o·lis (in/dē·ə·nap/ə·lis) city, cen. Indiana; cap.; pop. 700,807.

Indian Ocean ocean betw. Africa, Asia, Australia, and Antarctica.

In·do·chi·na (in/dō·chī/nə) **1.** penin. of SE Asia, S of China, including Burma, Thailand, Cambodia, Laos, Vietnam and the Malay penin. **2.** part of this penin. consisting of Laos, Cambodia and Vietnam, formerly called *French Indochina.*

In·do·ne·sia (in/dō·nē/zhə, -shə) country, SE Asia in Malay Archipelago; consisting of Java, Sumatra, most of Borneo, and other islands; pop. 153,000,000; cap. Jakarta.

In·dus (in/dəs) river, S Asia, flowing from Tibet through Pakistan into Arabian Sea; 1,800 mi. long.

I·o·ni·an Sea (ī·ō/nē·ən) part of the Mediterranean betw. Greece and Sicily.

I·o·wa (ī/ə·wə, ī/ə·wä) state, N cen. U.S.; pop. 2,913,808; cap. Des Moines.

I·ran (i·ran/, ē·rän/) country, SW Asia; pop. 41,000,000; cap. Teheran. Formerly *Persia.*

I·raq (i·rak/, ī·räk/) country, SW Asia; pop. 14,000,000; cap. Baghdad.

Ire·land (īr/lənd) country, westernmost of the British Isles; pop. 3,480,000; cap. Dublin.

Irish Sea part of the Atlantic betw. Great Britain and Ireland.

Ir·ra·wad·dy (ir/ə·wä/dē) river, Tibet and Burma; 1,200 mi. long.

Ir·ving (ûr/ving) city, N Texas; pop. 109,943.

Is·lam·a·bad (iz·läm/ə·bäd) city, NE Pakistan; cap.; pop. 77,300.

Is·ra·el (iz/rē·əl) country, SW Asia; pop. 4,000,000; cap. Jerusalem.

Is·tan·bul (is/tan·bōōl/, -täm-) city, NW Turkey; pop. 2,990,680. Formerly *Constantinople.*

It·a·ly (it/ə·lē) country, S Europe; pop. 56,500,000; cap. Rome.

Ivory Coast country, W Africa; pop. 8,500,000; cap. Abidjan.

Iz·mir (ēz·mir/) city, W Turkey; pop. 1,049,000. Also **Smyrna.**

Jack·son (jak/sən) city, S cen. Mississippi; cap.; pop. 202,895.

Jack·son·ville (jak/sən·vil, -vəl) city, NE Florida; pop. 540,898.

Ja·kar·ta (jä·kär/tä) city, NW Java; cap. of Indonesia; pop. 5,500,000. Also **Djakarta.**

Ja·mai·ca (jə·mā/kə) country, isl. West Indies; pop. 2,250,000; cap. Kingston.

Ja·pan (jə·pan/) country, E Asia; isl. chain; pop. 118,500,000; cap. Tokyo.

Japan, Sea of part of the Pacific betw. Japan and the Asian mainland.

Ja·va (jä/və, jav/ə) isl. of Indonesia; SE of Sumatra.

Jef·fer·son City (jef/ər·sən) city, cen. Missouri; cap.; pop. 33,619.

Jer·sey City (jûr/zē) city, NE New Jersey; pop. 223,532.

Je·ru·sa·lem (ji·rōō/sə·ləm, -lem) city, Israel; cap.; pop. 412,000.

Jid·da (jid′ə) city, W Saudi Arabia; pop. 750,000. Also **Jed′dah.**

Jo·han·nes·burg (jō·han′is·burg, jə-, yō·hän′is-) city, NE South Africa; cap.; pop. 1,536,457 (met.).

Jor·dan (jôr′dən) country, SW Asia; pop. 3,500,000; cap. Amman.

Jordan River river, SW Asia, flowing from mts. in Syria through Jordan into Dead Sea; over 200 mi. long.

Ju·neau (jōō′nō) city, SE Alaska; cap.; pop. 19,528.

Jut·land (jut′lənd) penin., N Europe; comprises continental Denmark and part of Germany.

Ka·bul (kä′bəl) city, E cen. Afghanistan; cap.; 891,750 (met.).

Kam·pa·la (käm·pä′lä) city, S Uganda; cap.; pop. 330,700.

Kam·pu·che·a (kam·pōō·chē′ə, -sē′ə) country, SW Indochina penin.; pop. 7,000,000; cap. Phnom Penh. Also **Cambodia.**

Kan·sas (kan′zəs) state, cen. U.S.; pop. 2,364,236; cap. Topeka.

Kansas City 1. city, NE Kansas; pop. 161,087. 2. city, W Missouri; pop. 448,159.

Ka·ra·chi (kə·rä′chē) city, S Pakistan; pop. 5,100,000 (met.).

Kat·man·du (kät′män·dōō′) city, cen. Nepal; cap.; pop. 171,400.

Kat·te·gat (kat′ə·gat) strait of the North Sea betw. Sweden and Jutland.

Kau·ai (kou′ī) one of the Hawaiian Islands.

Ken·ne·dy, Cape (ken′ə·dē) Cape Canaveral: *the former name.*

Ken·tuck·y (kən·tuk′ē) state, E cen. U.S.; pop. 3,660,257; cap. Frankfort.

Ken·ya (kēn′yə, ken′-) country, E Africa; pop. 17,600,000; cap. Nairobi.

Key West southwesternmost of the Florida Keys.

Khar·kov (kär′kôf) city, NE Ukraine, U.S.S.R., pop. 1,444,000.

Khar·toum (kär·tōōm′) city, cen. Sudan; cap.; pop. 333,921.

Khartoum North city, cen. Sudan; pop. 150,991.

Ki·ev (kē·ev′, kē′ev) city, U.S.S.R.; cap. of Ukraine; pop. 2,144,000.

Ki·ga·li (ki·gä′lē) city, cen. Rwanda; cap.; pop. 155,000 (met.).

Kil·i·man·ja·ro, Mount (kil′ē·män·jär′ō) mtn., NE Tanzania; highest point in Africa; 19,565 ft.

Kings·ton (kingz′tən, king′stən) city, SE Jamaica; cap.; pop. 671,000 (met.).

Kings·town (kingz′toun) city, St. Vincent; cap.; pop. 23,650.

Kin·sha·sa (kēn·shä′sä) city, W Zaire; cap.; pop. 2,500,000. Formerly *Léopoldville.*

Knox·ville (noks′vil, -vəl) city, E Tennessee pop. 183,139.

Ko·be (kō·bē) city, S Japan; pop. 1,375,000.

Ko·re·a, Democratic People's Republic of (kô·rē′ə, kō-) country, E Asia; pop. 18,750,000; cap. Pyongyang. Also **North Korea.**

Korea, Republic of country, E Asia; pop. 39,350,000; cap. Seoul. Also **South Korea.**

Korea Strait strait, betw. the Sea of Japan and the East China Sea.

Kos·ci·us·ko, Mount (kos′ē·us′kō) mtn. SE Australia; highest peak in Australia; 7,316 ft.

Kra·kow (krak′ou, krä′kō) city, S Poland; pop. 706,100 (met.). Also **Cracow.**

Kua·la Lum·pur (kwä′lə lōōm′pŏor) city, cen. Malaya, cap. of Malaysia; pop. 452,000.

Ku·wait (kōō-wät′) 1. country, NE Arabia; pop. 1,550,000; cap. Kuwait. 2. city, E Kuwait; cap.; pop. 60,000.

Kyo·to (kyō·tō) city, SW Japan; pop. 1,475,000.

Kyu·shu (kyōō·shōō) isl., S Japan.

La·do·ga (lä′də·gə), **Lake** lake, NW U.S.S.R.

La·gos (lä′gōs, lä′-) city, SW Nigeria; cap.; pop. 4,000,000 (met.).

La·hore (lə·hôr′) city, Bangladesh; pop. 2,900,000 (met.).

Lake·wood (lāk′wŏod) city, cen. Colorado; pop. 112,848.

La·nai (lə·nī′) isl. of the Hawaiian Islands.

Lan·sing (lan′sing) city, S cen. Michigan; cap.; pop. 130,414.

La·os (lä′ōs) country, NW Indochina; pop. 3,900,000; cap. Vientiane.

La Paz (lä päz′) city, W Bolivia; administrative cap.; pop. 700,000.

La Pla·ta (lä plä′tä) city, E Argentina; pop. 391,200.

Las Ve·gas (läs vā′gəs) city, SE Nevada; pop. 164,674.

Lat·vi·a (lat′vē·ə) constituent republic, NE U.S.S.R.; pop. 2,506,000; cap. Riga. Officially **Latvian SSR.**

Lau·sanne (lō·zàn′) city, W Switzerland; pop. 131,000.

Leb·a·non (leb′ə·nən) country, SW Asia; pop. 2,700,000; cap. Beirut.

Lee·ward Islands (lē′ward) isl. group, of N Lesser Antilles.

Leip·zig (līp′sik, -sig) city, S cen. East Germany; pop. 563,000.

Len·in·grad (len′in·grad) city, NW U.S.S.R.; pop. 4,600,000 (met.). Formerly *St. Petersburg* (1703–1914) and *Petrograd* (1914–1924).

Lé·o·pold·ville (lē′ə·pōld/vil) Kinshasa: *a former name.*

Le·so·tho (lə·sō′tō, -thō) country, S Africa; pop. 1,400,000; cap. Maseru. Formerly *Basutoland.*

Lesser Antilles See ANTILLES.

Lex·ing·ton (lek′sing·tən) city, N cen. Kentucky; pop. 204,165.

Lha·sa (lä′sə) city, SE Tibet; cap.; pop. 70,000.

Li·ber·i·a (lī·bir′ē·ə) country, W Africa; pop. 2,150,000; cap. Monrovia.

Li·bre·ville (lē·brə·vēl′) city, W Gabon; cap.; pop. 225,200.

Lib·y·a (lib′ē·ə) country, N Africa; pop. 3,250,000; cap. Tripoli and Bengasi.

Lib·y·an (lib′ē·ən) **Desert** desert, N Africa.

Liech·ten·stein (lik′tən·stīn) country, cen. Europe; pop. 30,000; cap. Vaduz.

Li·ège (lē·ezh′, lyezh) city, E Belgium; pop. 220,000.

Lille (lēl) city, N France; pop. 189,555.

Li·long·we (li·lông′wä) cap. of Malawi; pop. 102,900.

Li·ma (lē′mə) city, W Peru; cap.; pop. 4,900,000 (met.).

Lim·er·ick (lim′rik, -ə·rik) city, W Ireland; pop. 62,140.

Lin·coln (ling′kən) city, SE Nebraska; cap.; pop. 171,932.

Lis·bon (liz′bən) city, W Portugal; cap.; pop. 861,500.

Lith·u·a·ni·a (lith′ōō·ā′nē·ə) constituent republic, NW U.S.S.R.; pop. 3,400,000; cap. Vilna. Officially **Lithuanian SSR.**

Little Rock city, cen. Arkansas; cap.; pop. 158,461.

Li·vo·ni·a (li·vō′nē·ə) city, SE Michigan; pop. 104,814.

Lodz (lŏoj) city, cen. Poland; pop. 830,000.

Loire (lwàr) river, SE France; 620 mi. long.

Lo·mé (lō·mā′) city, S Togo; cap.; pop. 285,000.

Lon·don (lun′dən) 1. city, Ontario, Canada; pop. 283,668. 2. city, SE England; pop. 6,696,000.

Long Beach city, SW California; pop. 361,334.

Long Island isl., SE New York.

Long Island Sound inlet of the Atlantic betw. Long Island and Connecticut.

Los An·ge·les (lôs an′jə·lēz, ang′gə·ləs) city, SW California; pop. 2,966,763.

Lou·i·si·an·a (lə·wē′zē·an′ə, lōō′zē-) state, S U.S.; pop. 4,206,312; cap. Baton Rouge.

Lou·is·ville (lōō′ē·vil, lyōō′-, -vəl) city, N Kentucky; pop. 298,451.

Lower California See BAJA CALIFORNIA.

Lu·an·da (lōō·än′də) city, NW Angola; cap.; pop. 500,000.

Luang Pra·bang (lwäng prä·bang´) city, N cen. Laos; site of royal residence; pop. 25,000.

Lub·bock (lub´ək) city, NW Texas; pop. 173,979.

Luck·now (luk´nou) city, N cen. India; pop. 883,400.

Lu·sa·ka (lōō·sä´kə) city, cen. Zambia; cap.; pop. 684,000 (met.).

Lü·ta (lōō·tä´) city, NE China; pop. 4,000,000. Pinyin spelling **Lüda.**

Lux·em·bourg (luk´səm·bûrg) 1. country, W Europe; pop. 365,000; cap. Luxembourg. 2. city, S cen. Luxembourg; cap.; pop. 80,000.

Lu·zon (lōō·zon´) isl., N Philippines; largest of the Philippine Islands.

Ly·ons (lē·ōn´, li´ənz) city, E cen. France; pop. 463,000.

Ma·cao (mə·kou´, -kä´ō) 1. isl., Canton river delta, China. 2. Portuguese overseas prov. comprising a penin. of Macao isl. and two small isls.; pop. 300,000; 3. city; cap. of Macao.

Mac·ken·zie (mə·ken´zē) river, NW Canada; 2,640 mi. long.

Mc·Kin·ley, Mount (mə·kin´lē) mtn. S cen. Alaska; 20,320 ft.; highest peak in North America.

Ma·con (mā´kən) city, cen. Georgia; pop. 116,860.

Mad·a·gas·car (mad´ə·gas´kər) country, isl., Indian Ocean off SE Africa; pop. 9,190,000; cap. Antananarivo. Formerly *Mal·a·gas·y Republic* (mal´ə·gas´ē).

Ma·dei·ra (mə·dir´ə) Portuguese isl. group in N Atlantic, W of Morocco.

Mad·i·son (mad´ə·sən) city, S cen. Wisconsin; cap.; pop. 170,616.

Ma·dras (mə·dras´, -dräs´, mad´rəs) city, S India; pop. 4,276,635 (met.).

Ma·drid (mə·drid´) city, cen. Spain; cap.; pop. 3,275,000.

Ma·du·ra (mä·dōō´rä) isl. of Indonesia E of Java.

Ma·gel·lan, Strait of (mə·jel´ən) channel betw. the Atlantic and Pacific, separating the South American mainland from Tierra del Fuego.

Maine (mān) state, NE U.S.; pop. 1,125,027; cap. Augusta.

Ma·jor·ca (mə·jôr´kə, -yôr´-) largest of the Balearic Islands.

Malacca, Strait of (mə·lak´ə) strait betw. Sumatra and the Malay Peninsula.

Mál·a·ga (mal´ə·gə) city, S Spain; pop. 502,200.

Ma·la·wi (mä´lä·wē, mə·lä´-) country, SE Africa; pop. 6,275,000; cap. Lilongwe.

Ma·lay Archipelago (mä´lā, mə·lā´) isl. group off SE Asia; includes isls. of Indonesia, Malaysia, and the Philippines.

Malay Peninsula S penin. of Asia; includes Malaysia and part of Thailand.

Ma·lay·sia (mə·lā´zhə, -shə) country, SE Asia; pop. 14,750,000; cap. Kuala Lumpur.

Mal·dives (mal´dīvz) country, atolls in Indian Ocean; pop. 160,000; cap. Malé. Formerly *Maldive Islands.*

Ma·lé (mäl´ē) chief isl. and cap. of Maldives; pop. 29,600.

Ma·li (mä´lē) country, W Africa; pop. 7,350,000; cap. Bamako.

Mal·ta (môl´tə) country, isl. in Mediterranean, SE of Sicily; pop. 375,000; cap. Valletta.

Man, Isle of (man) one of the British Isles, cen. Irish Sea; pop. 70,000; cap. Douglas.

Ma·na·gua (mä·nä´gwä) city, SW Nicaragua; cap.; pop. 517,500.

Ma·na·ma (mə·nam´ə) city, Bahrain; cap.; pop. 150,000.

Man·da·lay (man´də·lā, man´də·lā´) city, cen. Burma; pop. 458,000.

Man·hat·tan (mən·hat´ən, man-) isl., SE New York; boro. New York City.

Ma·nil·a (mə·nil´ə) city, SW Luzon, Philippines; pop. 1,600,000.

Man·i·to·ba (man´ə·tō´bə, -tō·bä´) prov., cen. Canada; pop. 1,026,241; cap. Winnipeg.

Ma·pu·to (mə·pōōt´ō) city, S Mozambique; cap.; pop. 750,000.

Ma·ra·cai·bo (mä´rä·kī´bō) city, NW Venezuela; pop. 820,000.

Maracaibo, Lake lake, NW Venezuela.

Ma·ri·a·nas Islands (mär´ē·ä´näs) isl. group, W Pacific; including Guam, Saipan, Tinian, and Rota; part of the U.S. Trust Terr. of the Pacific Islands (excluding Guam).

Mar·ma·ra, Sea of (mär´mə·rə) sea betw. Europe and Asia, connecting the Bosporus and the Dardanelles. Also **Marmo·ra** (mär´mə·rə, mär·môr´ə, -mō·rə).

Marne (märn) river, NE France; 325 mi. long.

Mar·que·sas Islands (mär·kā´säs, -kē´-) isl. group S Pacific in French Polynesia.

Mar·ra·kesh (mä·rä´kesh, mar·ə·kesh´) city, SW Morocco; pop. 1,225,000 (met.).

Mar·seille (mår·sā´y) city, SE France; pop. 914,350. Also **Marseilles** (mär·sā´, -sälz).

Mar·shall Islands (mär´shəl) isl. group in Pacific; part of the Trust Territory of the Pacific Islands.

Mar·ti·nique (mär´ti·nēk´) isl., French Overseas dept.; Lesser Antilles.

Mar·y·land (mâr´i·lənd, mer´i-) state, E U.S.; pop. 4,216,975; cap. Annapolis.

Ma·se·ru (maz´ə·rōō´) city, NW Lesotho; cap.; pop. 75,000.

Mas·sa·chu·setts (mas´ə·chōō´sits) state, NE U.S.; pop. 5,737,037; cap. Boston.

Mat·ter·horn (mat´ər·hôrn) mtn. in the Alps on the Swiss-Italian border; 14,701 ft.

Mau·i (mou´ē) isl. of the Hawaiian Islands.

Mau·ri·ta·ni·a (môr´ə·tā´nē·ə) country, W Africa; pop. 1,725,000; cap. Nouakchott.

Mau·ri·ti·us (mô·rish´ē·əs, mô·rish´əs) country, isl. in Indian Ocean, E of Madagascar; pop. 950,000; cap. Port Louis.

M·ba·bane (em·bə·bän´) cap. of Swaziland; pop. 23,000.

Mec·ca (mek´ə) city, W Saudi Arabia; pop. 500,000.

Me·di·na (mə·dē´nə) city, W Saudi Arabia; pop. 198,200.

Med·i·ter·ra·ne·an Sea (med´ə·tə·rān´ē·ən) sea betw. Europe, Asia, and Africa.

Me·kong (mā·kong´) river, SE Asia; 2,500 mi. long.

Mel·a·ne·sia (mel´ə·nē´zhə, -shə) isls. of the W Pacific S of the Equator; including Bismarck Archipelago, the Solomon Islands, New Hebrides, New Caledonia and the Fijis.

Mel·bourne (mel´bərn) city, S Australia; pop. 2,803,600 (met.).

Mem·phis (mem´fis) city, SW Tennessee; pop. 646,356.

Me·sa (mā´sə) city, S cen. Arizona; pop. 152,453.

Meuse (myōōz) river, W Europe; 580 mi. long.

Mex·i·co (mek´sə·kō) country, S North America; pop. 72,900,000; cap. Mexico City.

Mexico, Gulf of inlet of the Atlantic, betw. the United States, Mexico, and Cuba.

Mexico City city, S cen. Mexico; cap.; pop. 9,200,000.

Mi·am·i (mi·am´ē, -am´ə) city, SE Florida; pop. 346,931.

Mich·i·gan (mish´ə·gən) state, N U.S.; pop. 9,262,078; cap. Lansing.

Michigan, Lake one of the Great Lakes; betw. Michigan and Wisconsin.

Mi·cro·ne·sia (mī´krə·nē´zhə, -shə) See PACIFIC ISLANDS, TRUST TERRITORY OF THE.

Mid·way Islands (mid´wā´) isls. in N Pacific, NW of Honolulu; in Hawaiian group, but not part of state of Hawaii; U.S. terr.

Mi·lan (mi·lan´, -län´) city, N Italy; pop. 1,635,000.

Mil·wau·kee (mil·wô´kē) city, SE Wisconsin; pop. 636,212.

Min·ne·ap·o·lis (min´ē·ap´ə·lis) city, E Minnesota; pop. 370,951.

Min·ne·so·ta (min´ə·sō´tə) state, N U.S.; pop. 4,075,970; cap. St. Paul.

Minsk (minsk) city, U.S.S.R.; cap. Belorussia; pop. 1,276,000.

Mis·sis·sip·pi (mis´ə·sip´ē) state, S U.S.; pop. 2,520,638; cap. Jackson.

Mississippi River river, cen. U.S.; 2,350 mi. long.

Mis·sou·ri (mi·zoor´ē, -zoor´ə) state, W cen. U.S.; pop. 4,916,759; cap. Jefferson City.

Missouri River river, NW cen. U.S.; 2,470 mi. long.

Mo·bile (mō·bēl′, mō′bēl) city, SW Alabama; pop. 200,452.

Mo·des·to (mə·des′tō) city, cen California; pop. 106,105.

Mog·a·di·shu (mog′ə·dish′ōō) city, E Somalia; cap.; pop. 500,000. Also **Mog′a·di′sco** (-dē′shō).

Mo·ja·ve Desert (mō·hä′vē) desert, S California.

Mo·lo·kai (mō′lə·kī′) isl. cen. Hawaiian Islands.

Mo·luc·ca Islands (mə·luk′ə) isl. group of Indonesia, betw. Celebes and New Guinea. Formerly *Spice Islands.*

Mon·a·co (mon′ə·kō, me·nä′kō) country, S Europe; pop. 30,000.

Mon·go·li·a (mong·gō′lē·ə, mon-) country, E Asia; pop. 1,725,000; cap. Ulan Bator. Formerly *Outer Mongolia.*

Mon·ro·vi·a (mən·rō′vē·ə) city, E Liberia; cap.; pop. 229,300.

Mon·tan·a (mon·tan′ə) state, NW U.S.; pop. 786,690; cap. Helena.

Mont Blanc (mont blangk′) highest mountain of the Alps, on the French-Italian border; 15,781 ft.

Mon·te Car·lo (mon′tē kär′lō) city, Monaco; pop. 9,950.

Mon·ter·rey (mont′tə·rā′) city, NE Mexico; pop. 1,300,000.

Mon·te·vid·e·o (mon′tə·vi·dā′ō -vid′ē·ō) city, S Uruguay; cap.; pop. 1,250,000.

Mont·gom·er·y (mont·gum′ər·ē, mənt-) city, E cen. Alabama; cap.; pop. 178,157.

Mon·ti·cel·lo (mon′tə·sel′ō, -chel′ō) estate and residence of Thomas Jefferson, near Charlottesville, Virginia.

Mont·pel·ier (mont·pēl′yər) city, N cen. Vermont; cap.; pop. 8,241.

Mon·tre·al (mon′trē·ôl′) city, S Quebec, Canada; pop. 2,802,547 (met.).

Mont·ser·rat (mont′sə·rat′) isl. of Leeward group, West Indies; cap. Plymouth.

Mo·roc·co (mə·rok′ō) country, NW Africa; pop. 21,275,000; cap. Rabat.

Mos·cow (mos′kou, -kō) city, W U.S.S.R.; cap.; pop. 8,011,000 (met.).

Mount Ver·non (vûr′nən) home and burial place of George Washington, near Washington, D.C.

Mo·zam·bique (mō′zam·bēk′) country, SE Africa; pop. 11,100,000; cap. Maputo.

Mu·nich (myōō′nik) city, SE West Germany; pop. 1,314,500.

Murray River river, SE Australia; 1,600 mi. long.

Mus·cat (mus·kät′) cap. of Oman; pop. 15,000. Also **Mas·qat′.**

Muscat and Oman Oman: *a former name.*

Na·go·ya (nä·gō·yä) city, S cen. Honshu isl., Japan; pop. 2,100,000.

Nag·pur (näg′pŏŏr) city, cen. India; pop. 1,300,000.

Nai·ro·bi (ni·rō′bē) city, SW Kenya; cap.; pop. 835,000.

Na·mib·i·a (nə·mib′ē·ə) country, SW Africa; pop. 1,000,000; cap. Windhoek.

Nan·king (nan′king′, nän′-) city, E China; cap. 1928–37; pop. 2,000,000. Pinyin spelling **Nanjing.**

Nantes (nants) city, W France; pop. 255,700.

Na·ples (nā′pəlz) city, SW Italy; pop. 1,210,500.

Nash·ville (nash′vil) city, N cen. Tennessee; cap.; pop. 455,651 (met. Nashville-Davidson).

Nas·sau (nas′ô) city, cap. of Bahamas; on New Providence isl.; pop. 135,500 (met.).

Na·u·ru (nä·ōō′rōō) country, isl. in W Pacific; pop. 8,000; cap. Yaren.

N'Dja·me·na (en·jä′mə·nə) city, SW Chad; cap.; pop. 300,000. Formerly *Fort-Lamy.*

Ne·bras·ka (nə·bras′kə) state, cen. U.S.; pop. 1,569,825; cap. Lincoln.

Neg·ev (neg′ev, ne·gev′) desert reg., S Israel. Also **Neg·eb** (neg′eb, nə·geb′).

Ne·pal (ne·päl′) country, S Asia; pop. 15,325,000; cap. Katmandu.

Neth·er·lands (neth′ər·landz) country, NW Europe; pop. 14,350,000; cap. Amsterdam; seat of government, The Hague. Also **Holland.**

Netherlands Antilles 6 isls. belonging to the Netherlands, in the West Indies, N of Venezuela, including Aruba, Bonaire, Curaçao, Saba, St. Eustatius, and part of St. Martin. Also **Dutch West Indies.**

Ne·vad·a (nə·vad′ə, -vä′də) state, W U.S.; pop. 800,493; cap. Carson City.

New·ark (nōō′ərk, nyōō′-) city, NE New Jersey; pop. 329,248.

New Brunswick (brunz′wik) prov., SE Canada; pop. 696,403; cap. Fredericton.

New Cal·e·don·i·a (kal′ə·dō′nē·ə, -nyə) isl. E of Australia; comprising with adjacent isls. a French Overseas terr.; cap. Nouméa.

New·cas·tle (nōō′kas·el, nyōō′-) city, NE England; pop. 192,460.

New Del·hi (del′ē) city, N cen. India; cap. pop. 619,417.

New England NE section of the United States, including Maine, New Hampshire, Vermont, Massachusetts, Rhode Island, and Connecticut.

New·found·land (nōō′fənd·land′, nyōō′-) prov., E Canada; comprising the island of Newfoundland and Labrador on the mainland; pop. 567,681; cap. St. John's.

New Guinea isl., N of Australia; world's second largest island.

New Hamp·shire (hamp′shir) state, NE U.S.; pop. 126,109; cap. Concord.

New Ha·ven (hā′vən) city, S Connecticut; pop. 126,109.

New Heb·ri·des (heb′ri·dēz) Vanuatu: *a former name.*

New Jer·sey (jûr′zē) state, E U.S.; pop. 7,364,823; cap. Trenton.

New Mex·i·co (mek′sə·kō) state, SW U.S.; pop. 1,302,981; cap. Santa Fe.

New Or·le·ans (ôr′lē·ənz, ôr·lēnz′, ôr′lənz) city, SE Louisiana; pop. 557,482.

New·port News (nōō′pôrt, nyōō′-) city, SE Virginia; pop. 144,903.

New York (yôrk) 1. state, NE U.S.; pop. 17,558,072; cap. Albany. 2. city, SE New York; pop. 7,071,030.

New Zea·land (zē′lənd) country, isl. group SE of Australia; pop. 3,175,000; cap. Wellington.

Nia·mey (nyä·mā′) city, W Niger; cap.; pop. 225,000.

Nic·a·ra·gua (nik′ə·rä′gwə) country, Central America; pop. 2,900,000; cap. Managua.

Nice (nēs) city, SE France; pop. 347,000.

Nic·o·si·a (nik′ə·sē′ə) city, N cen. Cyprus; cap.; pop. 161,000 (met.).

Ni·ger (nī′jər) 1. country, W cen. Africa; pop. 5,650,000; cap. Niamey. 2. river, W Africa; ab. 2,600 mi. long.

Ni·ge·ri·a (nī·jir′ē·ə) country, W Africa; pop. 88,600,000; cap. Lagos.

Nile (nīl) river, E Africa; 4,130 mi. long; longest river in the world.

Nor·folk (nôr′fək) city, SE Virginia; pop. 266,979.

North America N continent of the Western Hemisphere.

North Car·o·li·na (kar′ə·li′nə) state, SE U.S.; pop. 5,881,813; cap. Raleigh.

North Da·ko·ta (də·kō′tə) state, N U.S.; pop. 652,717; cap. Bismarck.

Northern Ire·land (īr′lənd) part of the United Kingdom in N reg. of Ireland; pop. 1,540,000; cap. Belfast.

North Korea See KOREA, DEMOCRATIC PEOPLE'S REPUBLIC OF.

North Pole N extremity of the earth's axis.

North Sea part of the Atlantic betw. Great Britain and Europe.

Northwest Territories adm. div., N Canada; pop. 45,741; cap. Yellowknife.

Northwest Territory reg. awarded to the United States by Britain in 1783, extending from the Great Lakes S to the Ohio River and from Pennsylvania W to the Mississippi.

Nor·way (nôr′wā) country, N Europe; pop. 4,125,000; cap. Oslo.

Nouak·chott (nwäk·shôt′) city, W Mauritania; cap.; pop. 250,000.

No·va Sco·tia (nō′və skō′shə) prov., E Canada; pop. 847,442; cap. Halifax.

Nu·ku'a·lo·fa (noō′kə·wə·lō′fə) cap. of Tonga; pop. 18,300.

Ny·asa, Lake (nī·as′ə) lake, SE Africa.

O·a·hu (ō·ä′hoō) isl., N cen. Hawaiian Islands.

Oak·land (ōk′lənd) city, W California; pop. 339,288.

O·ce·an·i·a (ō′shē·an′ē·ə) isls. of Melanesia, Micronesia, and Polynesia, and sometimes the Malay Archipelago and Australasia.

O·der (ō′dər) river, cen. Europe; 563 mi. long.

O·des·sa (ō·des′ə) city, S Ukraine, U.S.S.R., pop. 1,046,000.

O·hi·o (ō·hī′ō) state, NE cen. U.S.; pop. 10,797,624; cap. Columbus.

Ohio River river, E cen. U.S.; 981 mi. long.

O·kee·cho·bee (ō·kə·chō′bē) lake, S cen. Florida.

O·ki·na·wa (ō′ki·nä′wä) The largest of the Ryukyu Islands.

O·kla·ho·ma (ō′klə·hō′mə) state, S cen. U.S.; pop. 3,025,290; cap. Oklahoma City.

Oklahoma City city, cen. Oklahoma; cap.; pop. 403,213.

O·lym·pi·a (ō·lim′pē·ə) city, W Washington; cap.; pop. 27,447.

O·lym·pus (ō·lim′pəs), **Mount** mtn., N Greece; regarded in Greek mythology as the home of the gods.

O·ma·ha (ō′mə·hä, -hô) city, E Nebraska; pop. 311,681.

O·man (ō′man, ō·man′, ō·män′) country, SE Arabian penin., in SW Asia; pop. 950,000; cap. Muscat. Formerly *Muscat and Oman.*

On·tar·i·o (on·târ′ē·o) prov., SE Canada; pop. 8,625,107; cap. Toronto.

Ontario, Lake easternmost of the Great Lakes.

O·por·to (ō·pôr′tō) city, W Portugal; pop. 335,700.

Orange River river, S Africa; 1,300 mi. long.

Or·e·gon (ôr′ə·gən, -gon, or′-) state, NW U.S.; pop. 2,633,149; cap. Salem.

O·ri·no·co (ôr′ə·nō′kō, or′-) river, Venezuela; ab. 1,700 mi. long.

Ork·ney Islands (ôrk′nē) isl. group, N of Scotland comprising Orkney; a county of Scotland.

Or·lan·do (ôr·lan′dō) city, E cen. Florida; pop. 128,394.

O·sa·ka (ō·sä·kä) city, S Honshu, Japan; pop. 2,600,000.

Os·lo (os′lō, oz′-) city, SE Norway; cap.; pop. 454,872.

O·tran·to, Strait of (ō·trän′tō) strait betw. the Adriatic and Ionian seas.

Ot·ta·wa (ot′ə·wə) city, SE Ontario, Canada; cap.; pop. 717,978 (met.).

Ot·to·man Empire (ot′ə·mən) former empire (1300–1919) of the Turks in Asia Minor, NE Africa, and SE Europe.

Oua·ga·dou·gou (wä′gə·doō′goō) city, cen. Upper Volta; cap.; pop. 235,000.

Outer Mongolia See MONGOLIA.

Ox·nard (oks′närd) city, S California; pop. 108,195.

O·zark Mountains (ō′zärk) highland region in SW Missouri, NW Arkansas, and NE Oklahoma. Also **Ozarks.**

Pa·cif·ic Islands, Trust Territory of the (pə·sif′ik) isl. groups in W Pacific; U.S. Trust Terr.; including the Caroline Islands, the Marshall Islands, and the Marianas, except Guam. Also called **Micronesia.**

Pacific Ocean ocean betw. the American continents and Asia and Australia; extending betw. the Arctic and Antarctic regions.

Pa·go Pa·go (päng′ō päng′ō) town, SE Tutuila isl. of American Samoa; pop. 2,450.

Painted Desert desert plateau in N cen. Arizona.

Pa·ki·stan (pä′ki·stän′, pak′i·stan′) country, S Asia; pop. 85,500,000; cap. Islamabad.

Pa·lau Islands (pä·lou′) isl. group, W Caroline Islands.

Pa·ler·mo (pä·ler′mō) city, NW Sicily; pop. 699,691.

Pal·es·tine (pal′is·tīn) terr., E Mediterranean; divided (1947) by the United Nations into Israel and a terr. that became part of Jordan.

Pan·a·ma (pan′ə·mä, -mô) country, Central America; pop. 2,000,000; cap. Panama City.

Panama, Isthmus of isthmus connecting North and South America.

Panama Canal ship canal connecting Atlantic and Pacific, extending across Isthmus of Panama.

Panama City city, near the Pacific end of the Panama Canal; pop. 655,000.

Pap·u·a New Guinea (pä′poō·ə, pap′oō·ə, -yoō·ə) country, isl., N of Australia; pop. 3,250,000; cap. Port Moresby.

Par·a·guay (par′ə·gwä, -gwī) country, S cen. South America; pop. 3,375,000; cap. Asunción.

Paraguay River river, S cen. South America ab. 1,300 mi. long.

Par·a·mar·i·bo (par′ə·mar′i·bō) city, N Suriname; cap.; pop. 150,000.

Pa·ra·ná (pä′rä·nä′) river, S cen. South America; ab. 2,800 mi. long.

Par·is (par′is) city, N France; cap.; pop. 2,300,000.

Par·nas·sus Mount (pär·nas′əs), mtn., cen. Greece; anciently regarded as sacred to Apollo and the Muses.

Pas·a·de·na (pas′ə·dē′nə) **1.** city, SW California; pop. 119,374. **2.** city, SE Texas; pop. 112,560.

Pat·er·son (pat′ər·sən) city, NE New Jersey; pop. 137,970.

Pearl Harbor inlet, S Oahu, Hawaii.

Pe·king (pē·king′) city, N China; cap.; pop. 9,000,000. Pin-yin spelling **Beijing.**

Pel·o·pon·ne·sus (pel′ə·pə·nē′səs) penin. betw. Aegean and Ionian seas; one of the main divisions of S Greece.

Penn·syl·va·ni·a (pen·səl·vā′nē·ə, -vān′yə) state, E U.S.; pop. 11,863,895; cap. Harrisburg.

Pe·o·ri·a (pē·ôr′ē·ə) city, N cen. Illinois; pop. 124,160.

Per·sia (pûr′zhə, -shə) Iran: *a former name.*

Persian Gulf inlet of the Arabian Sea betw. Iran and Arabia.

Perth (pûrth) city, SW Australia; pop. 918,000 (met.).

Pe·ru (pə·roō′) country, W South America; pop. 18,850,000; cap. Lima.

Phil·a·del·phi·a (fil′ə·del′fē·ə) city, SE Pennsylvania; pop. 1,688,210.

Phil·ip·pines (fil′ə·pēnz) country, a Pacific archipelago SE of China; pop. 50,500,000; cap. Quezon City; seat of administration, Manila.

Phnom Penh (pə·nôm′pen′) city, S cen. Kampuchea (Cambodia); cap.; pop. 500,000. Also **Pnom Penh.**

Phoe·nix (fē′niks) city, S cen. Arizona; cap.; pop. 789,704.

Pierre (pir) city, cen. South Dakota; cap.; pop. 11,973.

Pillars of Hercules 2 promontories on opposite sides of the E end of the Strait of Gibraltar.

Pi·rae·us (pi·rē′əs) city, S Greece; pop. 439,100 (met.).

Pit·cairn Island (pit′kârn) isl., S Pacific; Brit. col.

Pitts·burgh (pits′bûrg) city, SW Pennsylvania; pop. 423,959.

Plymouth Colony colony on the shore of Massachusetts Bay founded by the Pilgrim Fathers in 1620.

Po·land (pō′lənd) country, N cen. Europe; pop. 36,300,000; cap. Warsaw.

Pol·y·ne·sia (pol′i·nē′zhə, -shə) isls. of Oceania, cen. and SE Pacific; E of Melanesia and Micronesia.

Poo·na (poō′nə) city, W India; pop. 1,700,000.

Port-au-Prince (pôrt′ō·prins′) city, S Haiti; cap.; pop. 790,000 (met.).

Port·land (pôrt′lənd) city, NW Oregon; pop. 366,383.

Port Lou·is (loō′is, loō′ē) city, SW Mauritius; cap.; pop. 155,000.

Port Mores·by (môrz′bē) city, SE New Guinea; cap. of Papua New Guinea; pop. 120,000 (met.).

Port-of-Spain (pôrt′əv·spän′) city, NW Trinidad; cap. of Trinidad and Tobago; pop. 62,700 (met.).

Por·to-No·vo (pôr′tō-nō′vō) port city, SE Benin; cap.; pop. 125,000.
Port Sa·id (sä-ēd′) city, NE Egypt; pop. 263,000.
Ports·mouth (pôrts′məth) city, SE Virginia; pop. 104,577.
Por·tu·gal (pôr′chə·gəl) country, SW Europe; pop. 10,000,000; cap. Lisbon.
Portuguese Guinea Guinea-Bissau: *a former name.*
Prague (präg) city, W Czechoslovakia; cap.; pop. 1,182,000.
Pre·to·ri·a (pri·tôr′ē-ə, -tō′rē-ə) city, NE cen. South Africa: adm. cap.; pop. 600,000.
Prince Ed·ward Island (ed′wərd) prov., NE Canada; pop. 122,506; cap. Charlottetown.
Prince Ru·pert (rōō′pərt) city, W British Columbia, Canada; pop. 14,754.
Prov·i·dence (prov′ə-dəns) city, NE Rhode Island; cap.; pop. 156,804.
Pueb·lo (pweb′lō) city, S cen. Colorado; pop. 101,686.
Puer·to Ri·co (pwer′tō rē′kō, pôr′-, pōr′-) isl., Greater Antilles; a Commonwealth of the United States; cap. San Juan.
Pu·get Sound (pyōō′jit) inlet of the Pacific, NW Washington.
Pu·san (pōō′sän) city, SE South Korea; pop. 3,000,000.
Pyong·yang (pyông·yäng′) city, W North Korea; cap.; pop. 1,500,000.
Pyr·e·nees (pir′ə·nēz) mtn. chain betw. France and Spain.

Qa·tar (kä′tär) country, W coast of the Persian Gulf; pop. 260,000; cap. Doha.
Que·bec (kwi·bek′) 1. prov., E Canada; pop. 6,438,403; cap. Quebec. Also *Fr.* **Qué·bec** (kā·bek′). 2. city; E Canada; cap of Quebec prov.; pop. 542,158 (met.). Also *Fr.* **Qué·bec′.**
Que·moy Islands (ki·moi′) 2 isls. of the Republic of China in Formosa Strait.
Que·zon City (kā′sôn) city, N cen. Philippines; cap.; pop. 1,100,000.
Qui·to (kē′tō) city, N cen. Ecuador; cap.; pop. 800,000.
Qum (kōōm) city, NW Iran; pop. 110,000. Also spelled **Qom.**

Ra·bat (rä·bät′) city, N Morocco; cap.; pop. 865,000 (met.).
Rai·nier (ra·nir′) Mount, mtn., W cen. Washington; highest point in Cascade Range.
Ra·leigh (rô′lē, rä′lē) city, cen. North Carolina; cap.; pop. 149,771.
Ran·goon (rang·gōōn′) city, S Burma; cap.; pop. 2,200,000.
Re·ci·fe (rä·sē′fə) city, NE Brazil; pop. 1,240,897.
Red River 1. river in Texas, Arkansas, and Louisiana; 1,018 mi. long. 2. river in U.S. and Canada; 540 mi. long. Also called **Red River of the North.**
Red Sea sea betw. Egypt and Arabia.
Re·gi·na (ri·jī′nə) city, W cen. Canada; cap. of Saskatchewan; pop. 164,313 (met.).
Re·no (rē′nō) city, W Nevada; pop. 100,756.
Ré·un·ion (rē-yōōn′yən) French Overseas dept.; isl., E Indian Ocean, E of Madagascar.
Rey·kja·vik (rā′kyə·vik) city, SW Iceland; cap.; pop. 83,500.
Rhine (rīn) river, W cen. Europe; 810 mi. long.
Rhode Island (rōd) state, NE U.S.; pop. 947,154; cap. Providence.
Rhodes (rōdz) Greek island of the Dodecanese group; SE Aegean; cap. Rhodes.
Rho·de·sia (rō-dē′zhə, -zhē-ə) See ZIMBABWE.
Rhône (rōn) river, Switzerland and SE France; 504 mi. long. Also **Rhone.**
Rich·mond (rich′mənd) city, E cen. Virginia; cap.; pop. 219,214.
Ri·o de Ja·nei·ro (rē′ō də jə·nâr′ō, zhə·nâr′ō) city, SE Brazil; former cap.; pop. 5,184,292.

Ri·o de la Pla·ta (rē′ō thä lä plä′tä) estuary of the Paraná and Uruguay rivers betw. Argentina and Uruguay; 170 mi. long.
Ri·o Grande (rē′ō grand′) river betw. Texas and Mexico; 1,890 mi. long.
Riv·er·side (riv′ər·sīd′) city, SW California; pop. 170,876.
Ri·yadh (rē·yäd′) city, E `Saudi Arabia; cap.; pop. 1,250,000.
Ro·a·noke (rō′ə·nōk) city, W Virginia; pop. 100,427.
Roch·es·ter (roch′es/tər, -is·tər). city, W New York; pop. 241,741.
Rock·ford (rok′fərd) city, N Illinois; pop. 139,712.
Rocky Mountains mtn. system, W North America, extends from the Arctic to Mexico. Also **Rockies.**
Ro·ma·nia (rō·mā′nyə) country, SE Europe; pop. 22,700,000; cap. Bucharest. Also **Rumania.**
Rome (rōm) city, W Italy; cap.; pop. 2,830,569.
Ro·sa·rio (rō·sä′ryō) city, E cen. Argentina; pop. 750,000.
Ro·seau (rō·zō′) city, Dominica; cap.; pop. 20,000.
Rot·ter·dam (rot′ər·dam) city, W Netherlands; pop. 579,200.
Rou·en (rōō·än′) city, N France; pop. 113,740.
Ru·ma·ni·a (rōō·mā′nē·ə, -mān′yə) See ROMANIA.
Rus·sia (rush′ə) see UNION OF SOVIET SOCIALIST REPUBLICS.
Rwan·da (rwän′dä, rōō·än′dä) country, cen. Africa; pop. 5,200,000; cap. Kigali.
Ryu·kyu Islands (ryōō′kyōō) Japanese isl. group in W Pacific; chief isl. Okinawa.

Sac·ra·men·to (sak′rə·men′tō) city, N cen. California; cap.; pop. 275,741.
Sa·har·a (sə·har′ə, -hä′rə) desert area, N Africa from Atlantic Ocean to Red Sea.
Sai·gon (sī·gon′) See HO CHI MINH CITY.
St. Croix (kroi′) the largest of the Virgin Islands of the United States.
St. George's (jôr′jiz) city, Grenada; cap.; pop. 30,000.
St. He·le·na (hə·lē′nə) isl., South Atlantic; Brit. col.; pop. 7,300; cap. Jamestown.
St. John (jon) one of the Virgin Islands of the United States.
St. John's (jonz) 1. city, SE Canada; cap. of Newfoundland; pop. 83,770. 2. city, on Antigua isl.; cap. of Antigua and Barbados; pop. 25,000.
St. Kitts (**St. Chris·to·pher**)**-Ne·vis-An·guil·la** (kits, kris′tə·fər, nē′vis, ang·gwil′ə) isl. group, Leeward Islands, West Indies; pop. 71,000; cap. Basseterre. Also **West Indies Associated States.**
St. Law·rence River (lor′əns, lôr′-) river, SE Canada; the outlet of the Great Lakes system, flowing NE from Lake Ontario to the **Gulf of St. Lawrence,** an inlet of the N Atlantic.
St. Lawrence Seaway A system of ship canals extending along the St. Lawrence River above Montreal to Lake Ontario.
St. Lou·is (lōō′is, lōō′ē) city, E Missouri; pop. 453,085.
St. Lu·cia (lōō′shə) country, isl. West Indies; pop. 125,000; cap. Castries.
St. Mar·tin (mart′ən) isl. of the Leeward group, West Indies; N part belongs to France, S part to the Netherlands and is part of the Netherlands Antilles. **Du. St. Maar·ten** (sint mär′tən).
St. Paul (pôl) city, SE Minnesota; cap.; pop. 270,230.
St. Pe·ters·burg (pē′tərz·bûrg) 1. city, W Florida; pop. 236,893. 2. Leningrad: *a former name.*
St. Thom·as (tom′əs) one of the Virgin Islands of the United States.
St. Vin·cent (vin′sənt) country, isl. West Indies; pop. 150,000; cap. Kingstown.
Sa·lem (sā′lem) city, NW Oregon; cap.; pop. 89,233.

Salis·bury (sôlz**′**ber·ē, -brē) Harare: *a former name.*
Sa·lo·ni·ka (sə·lon**′**i·kə, sal**′**ə·nē**′**kə) city, NE Greece; pop. 800,000 (met.).
Salt Lake City city, N cen. Utah; cap.; pop. 163,033.
Salz·burg (sälz**′**boorg) city, W Austria; pop. 139,000.
Sa·mo·a (sə·mō**′**ə) isl. group, SW Pacific. See AMERICAN SAMOA and WESTERN SAMOA.
Sa·na (sä·nä**′**) city, cen. Yemen (Yemen Arab Republic); cap.; pop. 210,000. Also **Sa·naa′**.
San An·to·ni·o (san**′**an·tō**′**nē·ō) city, S cen. Texas; pop. 785,410.
San Ber·nar·di·no (san**′** bûr**′**nə·dē**′**nō) city, SW California; pop. 118,057.
San Di·e·go (san**′** dē·ā**′**gō) city, SW California; pop. 875,504.
Sand·wich Islands (sand**′**wich) Hawaiian Islands: *the former name.*
San Fran·cis·co (san**′** frən·sis**′**kō) city, W California; pop. 678,974.
San Francisco Bay inlet of the Pacific, W California.
San Jose (san**′** hō·zā**′**) city, W California; pop. 636,550.
San Jo·sé (san**′** hō·zā**′**) city, cen. Costa Rica; cap.; pop. 800,000 (met.).
San Juan (sän hwän) city, NE Puerto Rico; cap.; pop. 435,000.
San Ma·ri·no (mä·rē**′**nō) **1.** country, an enclave in NE Italy; pop. 20,500; cap. San Marino. **2.** city, San Marino; cap.; pop. 8,500.
San Sal·va·dor (san**′** sal**′**və·dôr) **1.** city, S El Salvador; cap.; pop. 430,000. **2.** isl., cen. Bahamas.
San·ta An·a (san**′**tə an**′**ə) city, SW California; pop. 203,713.
San·ta Cruz (san**′**tə krōōz**′**) city, E Bolivia; pop. 237,128.
San·ta Fe (san**′**tə fā**′**) city, N New Mexico; cap.; pop. 48,953.
San·ti·a·go (sän**′**tē·ä**′**gō) city, cen. Chile; cap.; pop. 3,850,000.
San·to Do·min·go (sän**′**tō dō·ming**′**gō) city, S Dominican Republic; cap.; pop. 1,250,000. Formerly *Ciudad Trujillo.*
São Pau·lo (souṅ pou**′**lŏŏ) city, SE Brazil; pop. 8,585,000.
São To·mé (souṅ tə·mā**′**) city, São Tomé and Principe; cap.; pop. 20,000.
São Tomé and Prin·ci·pe (prin**′**sə·pə) country, isls. on the equator, W of Africa; pop. 90,000; cap. São Tomé.
Sap·po·ro (säp·pō·rō**′**) city, SW Hokkaido isl., Japan; pop. 1,400,000.
Sa·ra·je·vo (sä**′**rä·ye·vô) city, cen. Yugoslavia; pop. 400,000.
Sar·din·i·a (sär·din**′**ē·ə) isl., E cen. Mediterranean; with adjacent isls. a region of Italy.
Sas·katch·e·wan (sas·kach**′**ə·won) prov., W cen. Canada; pop. 968,313; cap. Regina.
Sas·ka·toon (sas**′**kə·tōōn**′**) city, S cen. Saskatchewan, Canada; pop. 154,210.
Sau·di Arabia (sou**′**dē, sä·ōō**′**dē) country, Arabian penin., SW Asia; pop. 10,400,000; cap. Riyadh.
Sa·van·nah (sə·van**′**ə) city, E Georgia; pop. 141,634.
Scan·di·na·vi·a (skan**′**də·nā**′**vē·ə) reg., NW Europe; includes Sweden, Norway, and Denmark and sometimes Finland, Iceland, and the Faeroe Islands.
Scot·land (skot**′**lənd) country, N Great Britain, W Europe, a division of the United Kingdom of Great Britain and Northern Ireland; pop. 5,117,000; cap. Edinburgh.
Se·at·tle (sē·at**′**l) city, W cen. Washington; pop. 493,846.
Seine (sān) river, NE France; 482 mi. long.
Sen·e·gal (sen**′**ə·gal, -gôl) country, NW Africa; pop. 5,950,000; cap. Dakar.
Seoul (sōl) city, NW South Korea; cap.; pop. 8,000,000.
Se·ville (sə·vil**′**) city, SW Spain; pop. 630,000.
Sey·chelles (sā**′**shelz) country, isl. group in Indian Ocean, NE of Madagascar; pop. 70,000; cap. Victoria.
Shang·hai (shang**′**hī) city, E China; pop. 12,000,000 (met.). Pinyin spelling **Shanghai.**
Shan·non (shan**′**ən) river, cen. Ireland; 224 mi. long.

Shen·yang (shun**′**yäng) city, NE China; pop. 4,800,000. Pinyin spelling **Shenyang.**
Shet·land Islands (shet**′**lənd) isl. group NE of the Orkney Islands, comprising **Shetland,** a county of Scotland.
Shreve·port (shrēv**′**pôrt) city, NW Louisiana; pop. 205,815.
Si·am (sī·am**′**) Thailand: *a former name.*
Siam, Gulf of part of the South China Sea betw. the Malay Peninsula and Indochina.
Sic·i·ly (sis**′**ə·lē) isl. of Italy, cen. Mediterranean.
Si·er·ra Le·o·ne (sē·er**′**ə lē·ō**′**nē, lē·ōn**′**) country, W Africa; pop. 3,675,000; cap. Freetown.
Si·er·ra Ne·vad·a (sē·er**′**ə nə·vad**′**ə, -vä**′**də) mtn. range, E California.
Si·nai (sī**′**nī) penin., E Egypt, betw. the Mediterranean and the Red Sea.
Sin·ga·pore (sing**′**ə·pôr, sing**′**gə-) **1.** country, isl. in South China Sea off Malay penin.; pop. 2,500,000; cap. Singapore. **2.** city, S Singapore; cap.; pop. 2,450,000 (met.).
Smyr·na (smûr**′**nə) See IZMIR.
So·ci·e·ty Islands (sə·sī**′**ə·tē) isl. group, S Pacific, part of French Polynesia.
So·fi·a (sō**′**fēə, sō·fē**′**ə) city, W Bulgaria; cap.; pop. 965,355.
Sol·o·mon Islands (sol**′**ə·mən) country, isl. group, SW Pacific; pop. 250,000; cap. Honiara.
So·ma·li·a (sō·mä**′**lyə, -lē·ə) country, E Africa; pop. 5,150,-000; cap. Mogadishu.
South Africa country, S Africa; pop. 29,000,000; seat of government Pretoria; seat of legislature Cape Town.
South America S continent of the Western Hemisphere.
South Bend city, N Indiana; pop. 109,727.
South Car·o·li·na (kar**′**ə·lī**′**nə) state, SE U.S.; pop. 3,121,833; cap. Columbia.
South China Sea part of the Pacific betw. SE Asia and the Malay Archipelago.
South Da·ko·ta (də·kō**′**tə) state, N cen. U.S.; pop. 690,768; cap. Pierre.
Southern Yemen See YEMEN, PEOPLE'S DEMOCRATIC REPUBLIC OF.
South Island one of the two main isls. of New Zealand.
South Korea See KOREA, REPUBLIC OF.
South Pole S extremity of the earth's axis.
South Sea Islands isls. of the South Pacific.
South Seas waters of the Southern Hemisphere, esp. the South Pacific Ocean.
South-West Africa Namibia: *a former name.*
So·vi·et Union (sō**′**vē·et, -ət) See UNION OF SOVIET SOCIALIST REPUBLICS.
Spain (spān) country, SW Europe; pop. 37,900,000; cap. Madrid.
Spanish Guinea Equatorial Guinea: *a former name.*
Spice Islands Molucca Islands: *the former name.*
Spo·kane (spō·kan**′**) city, E Washington; pop. 171,300.
Spring·field (spring**′**fēld) **1.** city, cen. Illinois; cap.; pop. 99,637. **2.** city, SW Massachusetts; pop. 152,319. **3.** city, SW Missouri; pop. 133,116.
Sri Lan·ka (srē lang**′**kə) country, isl. S of India; pop. 15,250,000; cap. Colombo. Formerly *Ceylon.*
Stam·ford (stam**′**fərd) city, SW Connecticut; pop. 102,453.
Stat·en Island (stat**′**n) isl. SE New York, at the entrance to New York Harbor.
Ster·ling Heights (stur**′**ling hīts) city, SE Michigan; pop. 108,999.
Stock·holm (stok**′**hōm) city, SE Sweden; cap.; pop. 1,400,000 (met.).
Stock·ton (stok**′**tən) city, cen. California; pop. 149,779.
Stras·bourg (stras**′**bûrg, sträz**′**-) city, NE France; pop. 257,300.
Strat·ford-upon-A·von (strat**′**fərd·əpon·ā**′**von) town, S cen. England; pop. 20,860.
Stutt·gart (stut**′**gärt) city, SW West Germany; pop. 590,100.
Su·cre (sōō**′**krā) city, S cen. Bolivia; constitutional cap.; pop. 90,000.

Su·dan (sō͞o·dan′) country, NE Africa; pop. 19,150,000; cap. Khartoum.

Su·ez (sō͞o·ez′, sō͞o′ez) city, NE Egypt; pop. 381,000.

Suez, Gulf of inlet of the Red Sea; NE Egypt.

Suez, Isthmus of a strip of land joining Asia and Africa, between the Gulf of Suez and the Mediterranean; traversed by the Suez Canal.

Suez Canal ship canal across the Isthmus of Suez; 107 mi.

Su·la·we·si (sō͞o·lä·wä′sē) See CELEBES.

Su·ma·tra (sō͞o·mä′trə) isl. of Indonesia S of the Malay Peninsula.

Sun·ny·vale (sun′ē·vāl) city, W California; pop. 106,618.

Superior, Lake largest of the Great Lakes.

Su·ra·ba·ya (sō͞o′rä·bä′yä) city, NE Java, Indonesia; pop. 2,000,000.

Su·ri·name (sŏŏr′ə·näm′) country, NE South America; pop. 420,000; cap. Paramaribo. Formerly Dutch Guiana.

Su·va (sō͞o′vä) cap. of Fiji, on Viti Levu Island; pop. 65,000.

Swa·zi·land (swä′zē·land) country, SE Africa; pop. 600,000; cap. Mbabane.

Swe·den (swēd′n) country, NW Europe; pop. 8,330,000; cap. Stockholm.

Swit·zer·land (swit′sər·lənd) country, cen. Europe; pop. 6,475,000; cap. Bern.

Syd·ney (sid′nē) city, SE Australia; pop. 3,280,900 (met.).

Syr·a·cuse (sir′ə·kyō͞os) city, cen. New York; pop. 170,105.

Syr·i·a (sir′ē·ə) country, SW Asia; pop. 9,650,000; cap. Damascus.

Ta·briz (tä·brēz′) city, NW Iran; pop. 598,600.

Ta·co·ma (tə·kō′mə) city, W Washington; pop. 158,501.

Ta·hi·ti (tä·hē′tē, tə-, tī′tē) isl., Society group.

Tai·pei (tī′pā′) city, N Taiwan; cap. of Republic of China; pop. 2,250,000.

Tai·wan (tī′wän) isl. of SE coast of China, seat of govt. of Republic of China. Formerly Formosa.

Tal·la·has·see (tal′ə·has′ē) city, N Florida; cap.; pop. 81,548.

Tam·pa (tam′pə) city, W Florida; pop. 271,523.

Ta·na·na·rive (tä·nä′nä·rēv′) See ANTANANARIVO.

Tan·gan·yi·ka, Lake (tang′gan·yē′kə) lake, E cen. Africa.

Tan·gier (tan·jir′) city, N Morocco; pop. 291,400.

Tan·za·ni·a (tan′zə·nē′ə, tän′-) country, E Africa; pop. 19,000,000; cap. Dar es Salaam.

Tash·kent (təsh·kyent′) city, U.S.S.R.; cap. of Uzbekistan Republic; pop. 1,779,000.

Tas·ma·ni·a (taz·mā′nē·ə) 1. isl. S of Australia. 2. A State of Australia comprising this isl. and other small isls.; pop. 422,000; cap. Hobart.

Tbi·li·si (tbi′li·sē) city, U.S.S.R.; cap. of Georgia; pop. 1,042,000.

Te·gu·ci·gal·pa (tä·gō͞o′sē·gäl′pä) city, S cen. Honduras; cap.; pop. 375,000.

Te·he·ran (te′ə·rän′, -ran′) city, N cen. Iran; cap.; pop. 6,000,000. Also Teh′ran.

Tel A·viv (tel′ä·vēv′) city, W Israel; includes Jaffa; pop. 343,300.

Tem·pe (tem·pē′) city, S cen. Arizona; pop. 106,743.

Ten·nes·see (ten′ə·sē′) state, SE cen. U.S.; pop. 4,591,120; cap. Nashville.

Tennessee River river, E U.S.; 652 mi. long.

Te·ton Range (tē′ton) range of the Rocky Mtns. in NW Wyoming.

Tex·as (tek′səs) state, S U.S.; pop. 14,229,288; cap. Austin.

Thai·land (tī′land) country, SE Asia; pop. 49,000,000; cap. Bangkok. Formerly Siam.

Thames (temz) river, S England; 209 mi. long.

Thim·phu (thim′bŏŏ) cap. of Bhutan; pop. 10,000.

Thousand Islands group of ab. 1,500 isls. in the St. Lawrence River.

Ti·ber (tī′bər) river, cen. Italy; 125 mi. long.

Ti·bet (ti·bet′) autonomous reg. of SW China; pop. 1,270,000; cap. Lhasa; formerly independent.

Tien·tsin (tin′tsin′) city, NE China; pop. 7,200,000. Pinyin spelling Tianjin.

Tier·ra del Fue·go (tyer′ä del fwā′gō) 1. Archipelago at S tip of South America, belonging to Chile and Argentina; separated from mainland by Strait of Magellan. 2. Largest isl. in this group.

Ti·gris (tī′gris) river, SW Asia, ab. 1,150 mi. long.

Ti·jua·na (tē·wä′nə, tē·ə·wä′nə) city, NW Mexico; pop. 750,000.

Ti·ra·na (tē·rä′nä) city, cen. Albania; cap.; pop. 200,000.

To·go (tō′gō) country, W Africa; pop. 2,800,000; cap. Lomé.

To·ky·o (tō′kē·ō) city, E Japan; cap.; pop. 8,350,000.

To·le·do (tə·lē′dō) 1. city, NW Ohio; pop. 354,635. 2. city, cen. Spain; pop. 54,350.

Ton·ga (tong′gə) country, isl. group in South Pacific, SE of Fiji; pop. 100,000; cap. Nuku'alofa.

To·pe·ka (tə·pē′kə) city, NE Kansas; cap.; pop. 115,266.

To·ron·to (tə·ron′tō) city, SE Canada; cap. of Ontario; pop. 2,998,947 (met.).

Tor·rance (tor′əns, tôr′-) city, SW California; pop. 131,497.

Tou·louse (tō͞o·lō͞oz′) city, S France; pop. 383,176.

Tren·ton (trent′n, tren′tən) city, W New Jersey; cap.; pop. 92,124.

Trin·i·dad and To·ba·go (trin′ə·dad, tō·bä′gō) country, isls. off N Venezuela; pop. 1,200,000; cap. Port-of-Spain.

Trip·o·li (trip′ə·lē) 1. city, NW Lebanon; pop. 127,600. 2. city, NW Libya, cap.; pop. 1,000,000.

Trust Territory of the Pacific Islands See PACIFIC ISLANDS, TRUST TERRITORY OF THE

Tsing·tao (ching′dou′) city, E China; pop. 1,121,000; Pinyin spelling Qingdao.

Tuc·son (tō͞o·son′, tō͞o′son) city, SE Arizona; pop. 330,537.

Tul·sa (tul′sə) city, NE Oklahoma; pop. 360,919.

Tu·nis (tō͞o′nis, tyō͞o′-) city, NE Tunisia cap.; pop. 960,000 (met.).

Tu·ni·sia (tō͞o·nē′zhə, -nish′ə, -nish′ē·ə) country, N Africa; pop. 6,650,000; cap. Tunis.

Tu·rin (tŏŏr′in, tyŏŏr′-, tŏŏ·rin′, tyŏŏ-) city NW Italy; pop. 1,103,520.

Tur·key (tûr′kē) country, SE cen. Eurasia; pop. 47,500,000; cap. Ankara.

U·gan·da (yō͞o·gan′də, -gän′dä) country, E cen. Africa; pop. 14,000,000; cap. Kampala.

U·lan Ba·tor (ō͞o′län bä′tôr) city, N cen. Mongolian People's Republic; cap.; pop. 435,000.

Union of Soviet Socialist Republics country E Europe and N Asia; a union of 15 constituent republics; pop. 269,850,000; cap. Moscow. Also Soviet Union.

United Arab E·mir·ates (i·mir′its, -āts) country, E Arabian penin.; pop. 800,000; cap. Abu Dhabi.

United Arab Republic Egypt: a former name.

United Kingdom of Great Britain and Northern Ireland country, W Europe, consisting of England, Scotland, Wales, and Northern Ireland; pop. 56,252,000; cap. London.

United States of America country, North America; 226,545,805; cap. Washington.

Upper Vol·ta (vol′tə, vōl′-) country, W Africa; pop. 7,170,000; cap. Ougadougou.

U·ral Mountains (yŏŏr′əl) mtn. system, U.S.S.R., regarded as boundary betw. Europe and Asia.

U·ral River (yŏŏr′əl) river, U.S.S.R.; flowing from Ural Mts. to Caspian Sea; 1,574 mi. long.

U·ru·guay (yŏŏr′ə·gwā) country, SE South America; pop. 2,950,000; cap. Montevideo.

Uruguay River river, SE South America; 1,000 mi. long.

U·tah (yōō′tô, -tä) state, W cen. U.S.; pop. 1,461,037; cap. Salt Lake City.
U·trecht (yōō′trekt) city, cen. Netherlands; pop. 476,400.

Va·duz (vä′dōōts) cap. of Liechtenstein; pop. 4,700.
Va·len·ci·a (və·len′shē·ə, -shə) city, E Spain; pop. 770,000.
Val·pa·rai·so (val′pə·rä′zō, -sō, -rī′-) city, cen. Chile; pop. 248,200.
Van·cou·ver (van·kōō′vər) city, SW British Columbia, Canada; pop. 1,268,183 (met.).
Va·nu·a·tu (vä·nōō′a·tōō) country, isls. S Pacific; pop. 125,000; cap. Vila. Formerly *New Hebrides.*
Vat·i·can City (vat′ə·kən) papal state, within Rome, Italy; pop. 1,000.
Ven·e·zue·la (ven′ə·zwā′lə, -zwē′lə) country, N South America; pop. 14,700,000; cap. Caracas.
Ven·ice (ven′is) city, NE Italy; pop. 341,400.
Verde (vûrd), **Cape** westernmost point of Africa; a peninsula.
Ver·mont (vər·mont′) state, NE U.S.; pop. 511,456; cap. Montpelier.
Ver·sailles (vər·sī′, -sālz′) city, N France; pop. 93,370.
Ve·su·vi·us (və·sōō′vē·əs) active volcano, W Italy.
Vic·to·ri·a (vik·tôr′ē·ə) **1.** city, W Canada, on Vancouver isl.; cap. of British Columbia; pop. 233,481 (met.). **2.** city, Hong Kong isl., cap. of Hong Kong; pop. 633,150. **3.** town on Mahé isl.; cap. of Seychelles; pop. 23,000.
Vi·en·na (vē·en′ə) city, NE Austria; cap.; pop. 1,504,200.
Vien·tiane (vyan·tyän′) city, NW cen. Laos; adm. cap.; pop. 200,000.
Vi·et·nam (vē·et·näm′) country, SW Indochina; pop. 56,250,000; cap. Hanoi. Also **Viet-Nam** or **Viet Nam.**
Vi·la (vē′lä) city, Vanuatu; cap.; pop. 15,000.
Vir·gin·ia (vər·jin′yə) state, E U.S.; pop. 5,346,818; cap. Richmond.
Virginia Beach city, SE Virginia; pop. 262,199.
Virgin Islands isl. group, West Indies, E of Puerto Rico.
Virgin Islands of the United States the W isls. of the Virgin Islands, comprising St. Croix, St. Thomas and St. John; a U.S. terr.
Vol·ga (vol′gə, vôl′gə) river, W U.S.S.R.; 2,290 mi. long.

Wa·co (wā′kō) city, cen. Texas; pop. 101,261.
Wake Island (wāk) isl., N Pacific; U.S. terr.
Wales (wālz) penin., SW Britain; comprising a division of the United Kingdom; pop. 2,790,000; cap. Cardiff.
War·ren (wor′ən, -in) city, SE Michigan; pop. 161,134.
War·saw (wôr′sô) city, E cen. Poland; cap.; pop. 1,576,600.
Wash·ing·ton (wosh′ing·tən, wô′shing-) **1.** state, NW U.S.; pop. 4,132,180; cap. Olympia. **2.** city, E U.S.; cap. of U.S.; has same boundaries as District of Columbia; pop. 637,651.
Wa·ter·bur·y (wô′tər·ber′ē, wot′ər-) city, W Connecticut; pop. 103,266.
Wa·ter·ford (wô′tər·fərd, wot′-) city, S Ireland; pop. 33,340.
Wa·ter·loo (wô′tər·lōō, wô′tər·lōō′) vill., cen. Belgium; pop. 21,725.
Wel·ling·ton (wel′ing·tən) city, cen. New Zealand; cap.; pop. 342,000 (met.).
Western Samoa country, isls. in S Pacific; pop. 160,000; cap. Apia.
West Germany See GERMANY, FEDERAL REPUBLIC OF.
West Indies series of isl. groups separating the North Atlantic from the Caribbean.

West Indies Associated States See ST. KITTS-NEVIS-ANGUILLA.
West Point U.S. military reservation, SE New York; seat of the U.S. Military Academy.
West Vir·gin·ia (vər·jin′yə) state, E U.S.; pop. 1,950,279; cap. Charleston.
White·horse (hwīt′hôrs) cap. of Yukon Territory, NW Canada; pop. 14,814.
White Mountains range of the Appalachians, N cen. New Hampshire.
Wich·i·ta (wich′ə·tô) city, S cen. Kansas; pop. 279,272.
Wight, Isle of (wīt) isl. off the S coast of England.
Wind·hoek (vint′hŏŏk) city, cen. Namibia; cap.; pop. 85,000.
Wind·sor (win′zər) city, SE Ontario, Canada; pop. 246,110.
Wind·ward Islands (wind′wərd) isl. group, S Lesser Antilles.
Win·ni·peg (win′ə·peg) city, cen. Canada; cap. of Manitoba; pop. 584,842 (met.).
Win·ston-Sa·lem (win′stən·sā′ləm) city, NW cen. North Carolina; pop. 131,885.
Wis·con·sin (wis·kon′sən) state, N U.S.; pop. 4,705,521; cap. Madison.
Worces·ter (wŏŏs′tər) city, cen. Massachusetts; pop. 161,799.
Wro·claw (vrô′tswäf, -tsläf) city, SW Poland; pop. 609,100.
Wu·han (wōō′hän′) city, E cen. China; pop. 4,400,000. Pinyin spelling **Wuhan.**
Wy·o·ming (wī·ō′ming) state, NW U.S.; pop. 469,557; cap. Cheyenne.

Yang·tze (yang′tsē′) river flowing from Tibet to the East China Sea; 3,600 mi. long.
Ya·oun·dé (yà·ōōn·dā′) city, S cen. Cameroon; cap.; pop. 350,000.
Yel·low·knife (yel′ō·nīf) cap. of Northwest Territories, Canada; pop. 9,483.
Yellow River Hwang Ho; *an alternate name.*
Yellow Sea inlet of the Pacific betw. Korea and China.
Yem·en, People's Democratic Republic of (yem′ən) country, S Arabian Penin.; pop. 2,100,000; cap. Aden. Also **Southern Yemen.**
Yemen Arab Republic country, SW Arabian penin.; pop. 8,575,000; cap. Sana. Also **Yemen.**
Yo·ko·ha·ma (yō′kə·hä′mə) city, cen. Honshu, Japan; pop. 2,775,000.
Yon·kers (yong′kərz) city, SE New York; pop. 195,351.
Youngs·town (yungz′toun′) city, NE Ohio; pop. 115,436.
Yu·ca·tán (yōō′kə·tan′) penin., SE Mexico and NE Central America.
Yu·go·sla·vi·a (yōō′gō·slä′vē·ə) country, SE Europe; pop. 22,412,000; cap. Belgrade.
Yu·kon River (yōō′kon) river, NW Canada and cen. Alaska; 2,300 mi. long.
Yukon Territory terr., NW Canada; pop. 23,153; cap. Whitehorse.

Za·greb (zä′greb) city, N Yugoslavia; pop. 700,000
Za·ire (zä·ir′) country, cen. Africa; pop. 28,150,000; cap. Kinshasa.
Zam·be·zi (zam·bē′zē) river, S Africa; 1,700 mi. long.
Zam·bi·a (zam′bē·ə) country, S cen. Africa; pop. 6,100,000; cap. Lusaka.
Zim·ba·bwe (zim·bä′bwē) country, S Africa; pop. 7,850,000; cap. Harare. Formerly *Rhodesia.*
Zu·rich (zŏŏr′ik) city, NE Switzerland; cap.; pop. 377,300.

BIOGRAPHIES

Ad·ams (ad'əmz) A prominent Massachusetts family, including **John**, 1735–1826, second president of the U.S. 1797–1801, signer of the Declaration of Independence; his son **John Quincy**, 1767–1848, sixth president of the U.S. 1825–1829; **Henry**, 1838–1918, historian and author; **Samuel**, 1722–1803, patriot, signer of the Declaration of Independence.

Ad·en·au·er (ad'n·ou'ər, *Ger.* ä'dən·ou'ər), **Konrad**, 1876–1967, Chancellor of the Federal Republic of Germany, 1949–1963.

Ad·ler (ad'lər), **Alfred**, 1870–1937, Austrian psychiatrist.

Aes·chy·lus (es'kə·ləs), 525–456 B.C., Gk. tragic dramatist.

Ae·sop (ē'səp, ē'sop), 6th-c. B.C. Gk. compiler of fables.

Ag·as·siz (ag'ə·sē, *Fr.* à·gà·sē'), **(Jean) Louis (Rodolphe)**, 1807–73, U.S. naturalist born in Switzerland.

Al·a·ric (al'ə·rik), 370?–410, Visigoth king; sacked Rome.

Al·cott (ôl'kət, -kot), **Louisa May**, 1832–88, U.S. novelist.

Al·den (ôl'dən), **John**, 1599–1687, Pilgrim settler in Plymouth Colony (1620); a character in Longfellow's poem *The Courtship of Miles Standish.*

Al·ex·an·der VI (al'ig·zan'dər, -zän'-) See (Rodrigo) **BORGIA.**

Alexander Nev·ski (nev'skē, nef'-), 1220?–63, Russ. hero.

Alexander the Great, 356–323 B.C., king of Macedon 336–323; conqueror of the Persian Empire.

Al·fred (al'frid), 849–899, king of Wessex and overlord of England 871–899: called **the Great.**

Al·len (al'ən), **Ethan**, 1737–89, Amer. soldier.

Am·brose (am'brōz), **Saint**, 340?–397, bishop of Milan; one of the Latin church fathers.

Amerigo Vespucci See **VESPUCCI.**

A·mund·sen (ä'mŏŏn·sən), **Roald**, 1872–1928, Norw. explorer; discovered South Pole, 1911.

An·der·sen (an'dər·sən), **Hans Christian**, 1805–75, Dan. writer of fairy tales.

An·dro·pov (än·drô'pôf), **Yuri Vladimirovich**, born 1914, Soviet statesman, general secretary of the Communist party 1982–, chairman of the Presidium of the Supreme Soviet 1982–1984.

An·gel·i·co (än·jel'i·kō), **Fra**, 1387–1455, Giovanni da Fiesole, Florentine painter and monk: original name **Guido di Pi·e·tro** (dē pē·ā'trō).

Anne (an), 1665–1714, queen of Great Britain and Ireland 1702–14.

An·tho·ny (an'thə·nē, -tə-), **Saint**, 250?–356?, Egyptian hermit and monk; founder of monastic life.

An·tho·ny (an'thə·nē), **Susan Brownell**, 1820–1906, U.S. suffragist.

An·to·ni·nus (an'tə·nī'nəs) See **AURELIUS.**

An·to·ny (an'tə·nē), **Mark**, Anglicized name of **Marcus An·to·ni·us** (an·tō'nē·əs), 83–30 B.C., Roman general; triumvir.

A·qui·nas (ə·kwī'nəs), **St. Thomas**, 1225?–74, Ital. Dominican monk and theologian: called **the Angelic Doctor.**

Ar·chi·me·des (är'kə·mē'dēz), 287?–212 B.C., Gk. mathematician born in Sicily.

Ar·is·toph·a·nes (ar'is·tof'ə·nēz), 450?–380? B.C. Gk. comic dramatist.

Ar·is·tot·le (ar'is·tot'l), 384–322 B.C., Gk. philosopher; pupil of Plato and teacher of Alexander the Great.

Arm·strong (ärm'strông'), **Neil Alden**, born 1930, U.S. astronaut; first man to walk on the moon, July 20, 1969.

Ar·nold (är'nəld), **Matthew**, 1822–88, Eng. poet and critic.

A·rou·et (à·rwe'), **François Marie** See **VOLTAIRE.**

Ar·thur (är'thər), **Chester Alan**, 1830–86, 21st president of the U.S. 1881–85.

A·ta·türk (ä·tä·türk') See **KEMAL ATATÜRK.**

At·ti·la (at'ə·lə, ə·til'ə), 406?–453, king of the Huns.

Attlee, Clement Richard, Earl, 1883–1967, Eng. statesman; prime minister 1945–51.

Au·den (ô'dən), **W(ystan) H(ugh)**, 1907–1973, U.S. poet born in England.

Au·du·bon (ô'də·bon), **John James**, 1785–1851, U.S. ornithologist born in Haiti.

Au·gus·tine (ô'gəs·tēn, ô·gus'tin), **Saint**, 354–430, bishop of Hippo; one of the Latin church fathers.

Au·gus·tus Cae·sar (ô·gus'təs sē'zər), 63 B.C.–A.D. 14, Gaius Julius Caesar Octavianus, the first Roman emperor 27 B.C.–A.D. 14: before 27 B.C. called *Octavian.*

Au·re·li·us (ô·rē'lē·əs, ô·rēl'yəs), **Marcus**, 121–180, Roman emperor, 161–180, and Stoic philosopher: full name **Marcus Aurelius An·to·ni·nus** (an'tə·nī'nəs).

Aus·ten (ôs'tən), **Jane**, 1775–1817, Eng. novelist.

A·vo·ga·dro (ä'vō·gä'drō), **Amedeo**, 1776–1856, Conte de Quaregna, Ital. physicist.

Bach (bäkh) A family of Ger. musicians and composers, of whom the best known are **Johann Sebastian**, 1685–1750, and his sons, **Karl Philipp Emanuel**, 1714–88, and **Johann Christian**, 1735–82.

Ba·con (bā'kən), **Francis**, 1561–1626, first Baron Verulam, Viscount St. Albans, Eng. philosopher, essayist, and statesman. — **Roger**, 1214?–94, Eng. scientist and philosopher.

Bal·bo·a (bal·bō'ə, *Sp.* bäl·vō'ä), **Vasco Núñez de**, 1475–1517, Sp. explorer; discovered the Pacific Ocean, 1513.

Bal·zac (bal'zak, bôl'-; *Fr.* bȧl·zȧk'), **Honoré de**, 1799–1850, Fr. novelist.

Bar·ba·ros·sa (bär'bə·ros'ə) Nickname of **FREDERICK I.**

Bar·ber (bär'bər), **Samuel**, born 1910–1981, U.S. composer.

Bar·num (bär'nəm), **P(hineas) T(aylor)**, 1810–91, U.S. showman.

Barth (bärt), **Karl**, 1886–1968, Swiss theologian.

Bar·tók (bär'tôk), **Béla**, 1881–1945, Hung. composer.

Bar·ton (bär'tən), **Clara**, 1821–1912, U.S. founder of the Amer. Red Cross.

Baude·laire (bōd·lâr'), **Charles Pierre**, 1821–67, Fr. poet.

Beard (bird), **Charles Austin**, 1874–1948, U.S. historian.

Beau·har·nais (bō·ȧr·ne'), **Josephine de** See **JOSEPHINE.**

Beck·et (bek'it), **Saint Thomas à** See **THOMAS À BECKET.**

Beck·ett (bek'it), **Samuel**, born 1906, Irish poet, novelist, and playwright.

Becque·rel (bek·rel'), **Antoine Henri**, 1852–1908, Fr. physicist.

Bede (bēd), **Saint**, 673?–735, Eng. theologian and historian: called **the Venerable Bede.** Also **Be·da** (bē'də).

Bee·be (bē'bē), **(Charles) William**, 1877–1962, U.S. naturalist and explorer.

Bee·tho·ven (bā'tō·vən), **Ludwig van**, 1770–1827, Ger. composer.

Bell (bel), **Alexander Graham**, 1847–1922, U.S. scientist born in Scotland; inventor of the telephone.

Ben·e·dict of Nur·si·a (ben'ə·dikt əv nûr'se·ə, nur'shē·ə, -shə), **Saint**, 480?–543, Ital. monk; founder of the Benedictine Order.

Ben·Gur·i·on (ben gŏŏr'ē·ən), **David**, 1886–1973, Israeli statesman born in Poland; prime minister 1948–53, 1955–57, 1958–1963.

Ben·tham (ben'thəm), **Jeremy**, 1748–1832, Eng. jurist and philosopher.

Berg (berkh), **Alban**, 1885–1935, Austrian composer.

Berg·son (berg'sən, *Fr.* berg·sôn'), **Henri Louis**, 1859–1941, Fr. philosopher.

Berke·ley (bûrk'le, *Brit.* bärk'-), **George**, 1685–1753, Irish Anglican prelate and philosopher.

Ber·li·oz (ber'lē·ōz), **Hector**, 1803–69, Fr. composer.

Bern·hardt (bûrn'härt, *Fr.* ber·nȧr'), **Sarah**, 1884–1923, Fr. actress: orig. name **Rosine Ber·nard** (ber·nȧr').

Ber·ni·ni (ber·nē'nē), **Giovanni Lorenzo**, 1598–1680, Ital. sculptor and architect.

Ber·noul·li (bûr·nōō'le, *Fr.* ber·nōō·ye'), **Daniel**, 1700–82, Swiss mathematician.

Ber·ze·li·us (bər·zē'lē·əs, *Sw.* ber·sā'lē·ŏŏs), **Baron Jöns Jacob**, 1779–1848, Sw. chemist.

Bes·se·mer (bes'ə·mər), **Sir Henry**, 1813–98, Eng. engineer.

Beyle (bāl), **Marie Henri** See **STENDHAL.**

Bis·marck (biz'märk) **Prince Otto Eduard Leopold von**, 1815–98, Ger. statesman; founder of the Ger. Empire: called **the Iron Chancellor.**

Bi·zet (bē·zā'), **Georges**, 1838–75, Fr. composer: orig. name **Alexandre César Léopold Bizet.**

Black·stone (blak'stōn', -stən), **Sir William**, 1723–80, Eng. jurist.

Blake (blāk), **William**, 1757–1827, Eng. poet and artist.

Blas·co-I·bá·ñez (bläs'kō·ē·vä'nyäth), **Vicente**, 1867–1928, Sp. novelist.

Blé·riot (blā·ryō'), **Louis**, 1872–1936, Fr. aviator and inventor.

Boc·cac·ci·o (bō·kä'chē·ō, *Ital.* bōk·kät'chō), **Giovanni**, 1313–75, Ital. writer and poet; author of the *Decameron.*

Bohr (bōr), **Niels**, 1885–1962, Dan. physicist.

Bol·eyn (bŏŏl'in, bŏ·lin'), **Anne**, 1507–36, second wife of Henry VIII of England; beheaded.

Bol·ing·broke (bol'ing·brŏŏk, bŏl'-) See **HENRY IV** (of England).

Bol·í·var (bol'ə·vər, -vär; *Sp.* bō·lē'vär), **Simón**, 1783–1830, Venezuelan general and statesman; liberated South America.

Bo·na·parte (bō'nə·pärt) A prominent Corsican Fr. family including: **Napoleon**, 1769–1821, Fr. military leader and conqueror; emperor of France 1804–15 as **Napoleon I**; **Joseph**, 1768–1844, king of Naples 1806–08, of Spain 1808–1813; and **Louis Napoleon**, 1808–73, emperor of France 1852–70 as **Napoleon III.** Also **Buonaparte.**

Boone (bōōn), **Daniel**, 1735?–1820, Amer. frontiersman in Kentucky and Missouri.

Booth (bōōth), **William**, 1829–1912, Eng. religious leader, founder of the Salvation Army: called **General Booth.** — **Edwin Thomas**, 1833–93, U.S. actor; his brother **John Wilkes**, 1838–65, U.S. actor; assassinated Abraham Lincoln.

Bor·gia (bôr'jä) An Italian aristocratic family of Spanish origin, including **Rodrigo**, 1431?–1503, pope 1492–1503 as *Alexander VI:* his children, **Cesare**, 1475?–1507, soldier and statesman, and **Lucrezia**, 1480–1519, duchess of Ferrara.

Bor·o·din (bôr′ə·dēn), **Aleksandr Porfirevich**, 1834–87, Russ. composer.
Bosch (bos), **Hieronymus**, 1450?–1516, Du. painter.
Bos·well (boz′wel, -wəl), **James**, 1746–95, Scot. lawyer and writer; biographer of Samuel Johnson.
Bot·ti·cel·li (bot′ə·chel′ē), **Sandro**, 1447?–1515, Florentine painter: orig. name **Alessandro di Mariano dei Fi·li·pe·pi** (fē·lē·pā′pē).
Boyle (boil), **Robert**, 1627–91, Eng. chemist and physicist, born in Ireland.
Boz (boz) See DICKENS.
Brahms (brämz, *Ger.* bräms), **Johannes**, 1833–97, Ger. composer.
Bra·man·te (brä·män′tä), **Donato d'Agnolo**, 1444–1514, Ital. architect and painter.
Braque (bräk), **Georges**, 1882–1963, Fr. painter.
Brecht (brekht), **Bertolt**, 1898–1956, Ger. playwright and poet.
Breu·ghel (brœ′gəl) See BRUEGHEL.
Brezh·nev (bryezh·nyôf′), **Leonid Ilyich**, born 1906, Soviet statesman; first secretary of the Communist party 1964–1982; president 1977–1982.
Bron·të (bron′tē), **Anne**, 1820–49, and her sisters, **Charlotte**, 1816–55, and **Emily Jane**, 1818–48, Eng. novelists. Pseudonyms, respectively, **Acton**, **Currer**, and **Ellis Bell**.
Brown (broun), **John**, 1800–59, U.S. abolitionist; led raid on arsenal at Harper's Ferry; hanged for treason.
Brown·ing (brou′ning), **Elizabeth Barrett**, 1806–61, Eng. poet; wife of Robert. — **Robert**, 1812–89, Eng. poet.
Broz (brôz), **Josip** See TITO.
Brue·ghel (brœ′gəl) A family of Flemish painters, esp., **Pieter**, 1520?–69, known as the **Elder**, and his sons, **Pieter**, 1564?–1638?, known as the **Younger**, and **Jan**, 1568–1625. Also spelled *Breughel:* also **Brue′gel**.
Bru·nel·les·chi (broō·nāl·les′kē), **Filippo**, 1377–1446, Florentine architect and sculptor. Also **Bru·nel·les′co** (-les′kō).
Bru·tus (broō′təs), **Marcus Junius**, 85?–42 B.C., Roman politician and general; one of Caesar's assassins.
Bry·an (brī′ən), **William Jennings**, 1860–1925, U.S. statesman and orator.
Bu·ber (boō′bər), **Martin**, 1878–1965, Austrian Jewish religious philosopher.
Buchanan (byoō·kan′ən), **James**, 1791–1868, 15th president of the U.S. 1857–61.
Bud·dha (bŏŏd′ə, boō′də) **Gautama** or **Gotama Siddhartha**, 563?–483? B.C., the founder of Buddhism.
Buf·fa·lo Bill See CODY.
Bun·yan (bun′yən), **John**, 1628–88, Eng. preacher and author of *Pilgrim's Progress.*
Buo·na·par·te (bwô′nä·pär′tā) See BONAPARTE.
Buo·nar·ro·ti (bwô′när·rō′tē) See MICHELANGELO.
Bur·bank (bûr′bangk), **Luther**, 1849–1926, U.S. horticulturist.
Burg·er (bûr′gər), **Warren Earl**, born 1907, U.S. jurist; chief justice of the Supreme Court 1969–.
Bur·goyne (bər·goin′), **John**, 1722–92, Brit. general in the Amer. Revolution.
Burke (bûrk), **Edmund**, 1729–97, Brit. statesman, writer, and orator born in Ireland.
Burns (bûrnz), **Robert**, 1759–96, Scot. poet.
Burr (bûr), **Aaron**, 1756–1836, Amer. lawyer and statesman, vice president of the U.S. 1801–05.
But·ler (but′lər), **Samuel**, 1835–1902, Eng. novelist.
Byrd (bûrd), **Richard Evelyn**, 1888–1957, U.S. rear admiral, aviator, polar explorer, and writer.
By·ron (bī′rən), **Lord**, 1788–1824, George Gordon Noel, 6th Baron Byron, Eng. poet.

Cab·ot (kab′ət), **John**, Anglicized name of **Giovanni Ca·bo·to** (kä·bô′tō), 1451?–98, Venetian seafarer and explorer.
Cæd·mon (kad′mən), 7th-c. Eng. poet.
Cae·sar (sē′zər), **Gaius Julius**, 100–44 B.C., Roman general, statesman, and historian.
Cal·vin (kal′vin), **John**, 1509–64, Fr. Protestant reformer.
Ca·mus (kä·mü′), **Albert**, 1913–60, Fr. writer.
Ca·pet (kā′pit, kap′it; *Fr.* kà·pe′) See HUGH CAPET
Ca·ra·vag·gio (kä′rä·väd′jō), **Michelangelo Amerighi da**, 1569–1609, Ital. painter.
Car·lyle (kär·līl′), **Thomas**, 1795–1881, Scot. essayist.
Car·ne·gie (kär·nā′gē, -neg′ē, kär′nə·gē), **Andrew**, 1835–1919, U.S. industrialist and philanthropist born in Scotland.
Car·roll (kar′əl), **Lewis** Pseud. of *Charles Lutwidge Dodgson,* 1832–98, Eng. mathematician; author of *Alice in Wonderland.*
Car·ter (kär′tər), **Jimmy** (James Earl, Jr.), born 1924, 39th president of the U.S., 1977–1981.
Ca·ru·so (kə·roō′sō, *Ital.* kä·roō′zō), **Enrico**, 1873–1921, Ital. operatic tenor.

Car·ver (kär′vər), **George Washington**, 1864–1943, U.S. botanist and chemist.
Ca·sals (kä·säls′), **Pablo**, 1876–1973, Sp. violoncellist, conductor, and composer.
Cas·a·no·va (kas′ə·nō′və, kaz′-; *Ital.* kä′sä·nō′vä), **Giovanni Giacomo**, 1725–98, Ital. adventurer; known for his *Memoirs;* full surname **Casanova de Sein·galt** (dä sīn′gält).
Cas·tro (käs′trō, kas′-), **Fidel**, born 1926, Cuban revolutionary leader; premier 1959–: full name **Fidel Castro Ruz** (roōth).
Cath·e·rine II (kath′rin, -ər·in), 1729–96, empress of Russia: called **Catherine the Great.**
Ca·to (kā′tō), **Marcus Porcius**, 234–149 B.C., Roman statesman: called **the Elder** or **the Censor.** — **Marcus Porcius**, 95–46 B.C., Roman patriot and Stoic philosopher: called **U·ti·cen·sis** (yoō′ti·ken′səs) or **the Younger.**
Cav·en·dish (kav′ən·dish), **Henry**, 1731?–1810, Eng. chemist.
Cel·li·ni (chə·lē′nē, *Ital.* chel·lē′nē), **Benvenuto**, 1500–71, Ital. sculptor and goldsmith; known for his autobiography.
Cer·van·tes (sər·van′tēz, *Sp.* ther·vän′tās), **Miguel de**, 1547–1616, Sp. novelist and dramatist; author of *Don Quixote:* full surname **Cervantes Sa·a·ve·dra** (sä′ä·vā′thrä).
Cé·zanne (sā·zàn′), **Paul**, 1839–1906, Fr. painter.
Chap·lin (chap′lən), **Charles Spencer**, 1889–1977, Eng. motion-picture actor and producer formerly active in the U.S.: called **Charlie Chaplin.**
Char·le·magne (shär′lə·mān), 742?–814, king of the Franks 768–814; emperor of the West as **Charles I** 800–814: called **Charles the Great.**
Charles I (chärlz), 1600–49, Charles Stuart, king of England 1625–49; beheaded.
Charles II, 1630–85, king of England 1660–85.
Chat·ham (chat′əm), **Earl of** See PITT.
Chau·cer (chô′sər), **Geoffrey**, 1340?–1400, Eng. poet.
Che·khov (chek′ôf), **Anton Pavlovich**, 1860–1904, Russ. dramatist and story writer: also *Tchekhov.* Also **Che′kov.**
Che·ops (kē′ops) Egyptian king of the 4th dynasty (about 2900 B.C.), builder of the Great Pyramid at Giza: also **Khu·fu** (koō′foō).
Chiang Kai-shek (chyäng′ kī′shek′, chang′; *Chinese* jyäng′) 1886–1975, Chinese generalissimo; head of the Republic of China: orig. name Chiang Chung-cheng.
Cho·pin (shō′pan, *Fr.* shô·pan′), **Frédéric François**, 1810–1849, Polish composer and pianist active in France.
Chou En-lai (jō′en′lī′), 1898–1976, Chinese statesman; foreign minister 1949–58; premier of the People's Republic of China 1949–1976.
Christ (krīst) See JESUS.
Chris·to·pher (kris′tə·fər), **Saint**, 3rd-c. Christian martyr.
Church·ill (chûrch′il, -əl), **Sir Winston** (Leonard Spencer), 1874–1965, Brit. statesman and author; prime minister 1940–45, 1951–55.
Cic·e·ro (sis′ə·rō), **Marcus Tullius**, 106–43 B.C., Roman statesman, orator, and author; also called *Tully.*
Cid (sid, *Sp.* thēth), **the**, 1040?–99, Rodrigo Díaz de Bivar, Sp. epic hero; champion in wars against the Moors. Also called **El Cid Cam·pe·a·dor** (kam′pä·ä·thôr′).
Ci·ma·bu·e (chē′mä·boō′ā), **Giovanni**, 1240?–1302?, Florentine painter.
Clark (klärk), **Charles Joseph**, born 1939, Canadian statesman; prime minister 1979.
Clau·se·witz (klou′zə·vits), **Karl von**, 1780–1831, Prussian general and military scientist.
Clay (klā), **Henry**, 1777–1852, U.S. statesman and orator.
Cle·men·ceau (klem′ən·sō′, *Fr.* kle·män·sō′), **Georges Eugène**, 1841–1929, Fr. statesman; premier 1906–09, 1917–20: called **the Tiger.**
Clem·ens (klem′ənz), **Samuel Langhorne** See MARK TWAIN.
Cle·o·pa·tra (klē·ə·pat′rə, -pā′trə, -pä′trə), 69–30 B.C.; queen of Egypt 51–49 B.C., 48–30 B.C.; committed suicide.
Cleve·land (klēv′lənd), **(Stephen) Grover**, 1837–1908, 22nd and 24th president of the U.S. 1885–89, 1893–97.
Co·dy (kō′dē), **William Frederick**, 1846–1917, U.S. plainsman, army scout, and showman: called *Buffalo Bill.*
Cœur de Li·on (kûr′ də lē′ən) See RICHARD I.
Cole·ridge (kōl′rij), **Samuel Taylor**, 1772–1834, Eng. poet and critic.
Co·lum·bus (kə·lum′bəs), **Christopher**, 1446?–1506, Genoese seafarer and explorer; discovered America for Spain Oct. 12, 1492. Sp. **Cristóbal Co·lón** (kō·lōn′), Ital. **Cristoforo Co·lom·bo** (kō·lōm′bō).
Comte (kônt, *Fr.* kônt), **Auguste**, 1798–1857, Fr. philosopher.
Con·fu·cius (kən·fyoō′shəs), 551?–478? B.C., Chinese philosopher and teacher. Chinese **K'ung Fu-tse** (koōng′ foō′tse′).
Con·rad (kon′rad), **Joseph**, 1857–1924, Eng. author born in

Poland: orig. name **Teodor Józef Konrad Kor·ze·niow·ski** (kôr/ze·nyôf/skē).

Con·stan·tine I (kon/stən·tēn, -tīn), 288?–337, first Christian emperor of Rome; founder of the Byzantine Empire: called **the Great**.

Cook (kŏŏk), **Captain James**, 1728–79, Eng. seafarer and explorer.

Coo·lidge (kōō/lij), (**John**) **Calvin**, 1872–1933, 30th president of the U.S. 1923–29.

Coop·er (kōō/pər, kŏŏp/ər), **James Fenimore**, 1789–1851, U.S. novelist.

Co·per·ni·cus (kō·pûr/nə·kəs), **Nicholas**, Lat. name of **Mikołaj Ko·per·nik** (kô·pûr/nĕk), 1473–1543, Polish astronomer.

Cop·land (kōp/lənd), **Aaron**, born 1900, U.S. composer.

Cor·neille (kôr·nā/, Fr. kôr·nā/y/), **Pierre**, 1606–84, Fr. dramatist.

Corn·wal·lis (kôrn·wôl/is, -wol/-), **Charles**, 1738–1805, first Marquis Cornwallis, Eng. general and statesman.

Co·ro·na·do (kôr/ə·nä/dō, Sp. kô/rō·nä/thō), **Francisco Vásquez de**, 1510–54, Sp. explorer.

Cor·tés (kôr·tez/, Sp. kôr·tās/), **Hernando**, 1485–1547, Sp. conquistador; conqueror of Mexico. Also **Cor·tez/**.

Cra·nach (krä/näkh), **Lucas**, 1472–1533, Ger. painter.

Crane (krān), (**Harold**) **Hart**, 1899–1932, U.S. poet. — **Stephen**, 1871–1900, U.S. writer.

Crock·ett (krok/it), **David**, 1786–1836, Amer. frontiersman and politician; killed at the Alamo: called **Davy Crockett**.

Crom·well (krom/wel), **Oliver**, 1599–1658, Eng. general and statesman; lord protector of England 1653–58.

Crookes (krŏŏks), **Sir William**, 1832–1919, Eng. physicist and chemist.

Cu·rie (kyŏŏr/ē, kyŏŏr·ē/; Fr. kü·rē/), 1867–1934, **Marie**, née Sklodowska, born in Poland, and her husband **Pierre**, 1859–1906, Fr. physicists, discoverers of radium.

Cu·vi·er (kōō/vē·ā, Fr. kü·vyā/), **Baron Georges**, 1769–1832, Fr. naturalist.

Cyr·il (sir/əl), **Saint**, 827–869, Christian scholar and missionary: called **Apostle of the Slavs**.

Dal·ton (dôl/tən), **John**, 1766–1844, Eng. chemist and physicist.

Dan·te A·li·ghie·ri (dän/tä ä/lē·gyä/rē, dan/tē), 1265–1321, Ital. poet; author of the *Divine Comedy*: orig. name **Durante Alighieri**.

Dar·win (där/win), **Charles Robert**, 1809–82, Eng. naturalist.

Dau·mier (dō·myā/), **Honoré**, 1808–79, Fr. painter and caricaturist.

da Vin·ci (də vin/chē, Ital. dä vēn/chē), **Leonardo**, 1452–1519, Florentine painter, sculptor, architect, and inventor.

Da·vis (dā/vis), **Jefferson**, 1808–89, U.S. statesman; president of the Confederacy 1862–65.

Da·vy (dā/vē), **Sir Humphry**, 1778–1829, Eng. scientist.

De·bus·sy (də·byōō/sē, Fr. də·bü·sē/), **Claude** (**Achille**), 1862–1918, Fr. composer.

De·foe (di·fō/), **Daniel**, 1660–1731, Eng. novelist and political journalist. Also **De Foe**.

De For·est (di fôr/est, for/-), **Lee**, 1873–1961, U.S. inventor; pioneer in radio transmission.

De·gas (də·gä/), (**Hilaire Germaine**) **Edgar**, 1834–1917, Fr. impressionist painter.

de Gaulle (də gōl/, Fr. də gôl/), **Charles André Joseph Marie**, 1890–1970, Fr. general and statesman; president 1944–45, 1959–1969.

De·la·croix (də·là·krwä/), (**Ferdinand Victor**) **Eugène**, 1799–1863, Fr. painter.

del Sar·to (dĕl sär/tō), **Andrea** See SARTO.

De Quin·cey (di kwin/sē), **Thomas**, 1785–1859, Eng. essayist.

Des·cartes (dā·kärt/), **René**, 1596–1650, Fr. mathematician and philosopher.

De So·to (də sō/tō), **Hernando**, 1500?–42, Sp. explorer; discovered the Mississippi River, 1541.

De Va·le·ra (dev/ə·lâr/ə, dā/və·lir/ə), **Eamon**, 1882–1975, Irish statesman born in the U.S.; prime minister 1937–48, 1951–54, 1957–59, president 1959–73.

Dew·ey (dōō/ē, dyōō/ē), **George**, 1837–1917, U.S. admiral in the Spanish-Amer. War. — **John**, 1859–1952, U.S. philosopher, psychologist, and educator.

Dí·az de Bi·var (dē/ath thä bē·vär/) See CID.

Dick·ens (dik/ənz), **Charles** (**John Huffam**), 1812–70, Eng. novelist: pseud. **Boz** (boz).

Dick·in·son (dik/ən·sən), **Emily** (**Elizabeth**), 1830–86, U.S. poet.

Di·de·rot (dē·drō/), **Denis**, 1713–84, Fr. philosopher and encyclopedist.

Di·og·e·nes (dī·oj/ə·nēz), 412?–323 B.C., Gk. Cynic philosopher, reputed to have lived in a tub.

Dis·rae·li (diz·rā/lē), **Benjamin**, 1804–81, first Earl of Beaconsfield, Eng. statesman and novelist; prime minister 1868, 1874–80.

Dob·zhan·sky (dŏb·zhän/skē), **Theodosius**, born 1900, U.S. geneticist born in Russia.

Dodg·son (doj/sən), **Charles Lutwidge** See (Lewis) CARROLL.

Dom·i·nic (dom/ə·nik), **Saint**, 1170–1221, Sp. friar; founded the Dominican Order: orig. name **Domingo de Gus·mán** (gōōth·män/).

Don·a·tel·lo (don/ə·tel/ō, Ital. do/nä·tel/lō), 1386?–1466, Florentine sculptor: orig. name **Donato di Niccolò di Bet·to Bar·di** (dē bät/tō bär/dē).

Donne (dun), **John**, 1573–1631, Eng. poet and clergyman.

Dop·pler (dôp/lər), **Christian Johann**, 1803–53, Ger. physicist and mathematician active in Austria.

Dos·to·ev·ski (dôs/tô·yef/skē), **Feodor Mikhailovich**, 1821–1881, Russ. novelist. Also **Dos/to·yev/sky**.

Doug·las (dug/ləs), **Stephen Arnold**, 1813–61, U.S. senator; opposed Lincoln in a series of debates, 1858. — **William Orville**, 1898–1980, U.S. jurist, associate justice of the Supreme Court 1939–1975.

Doyle (doil), **Sir Arthur Conan**, 1859–1930, Eng. physician and novelist; creator of detective Sherlock Holmes.

Drake (drāk), **Sir Francis**, 1540?–96, Eng. admiral; first Englishman to sail round the world.

Drei·ser (drī/sər, -zər), **Theodore** (**Herman Albert**), 1871–1945, U.S. novelist.

Drey·fus (drā/fəs, drī-; Fr. dre·füs/), **Alfred**, 1859–1935, Fr. army officer; wrongfully convicted of treason in 1894; vindicated in 1906.

Dry·den (drīd/n), **John**, 1631–1700, Eng. poet, critic, and dramatist; poet laureate 1670–88.

Dul·les (dul/əs), **John Foster**, 1888–1959, U.S. lawyer and diplomat; secretary of state 1953–59.

Du·mas (dōō·mä/, dōō/mä; Fr. dü·mà/), **Alexandre**, 1802–1870, **Dumas père**, and his son **Alexandre**, 1824–95, **Dumas fils**, Fr. novelists and dramatists.

Duns Sco·tus (dunz skō/təs), **John**, 1265?–1308, Scot. scholastic theologian: called **the Subtile Doctor**.

Dü·rer (dü/rər), **Albrecht**, 1471–1528, Ger. painter and engraver.

Dzhu·ga·shvi·li (jōō/gä·shvē/lē), **Iosif Vissarionovich**. See STALIN.

Ear·hart (âr/härt), **Amelia**, 1898–1937, Mrs. George Palmer Putnam, U.S. aviatrix.

Ed·dy (ed/ē), **Mary Baker**, 1821–1910, née Mary Morse Baker, U.S. religious leader; founder of Christian Science.

Ed·i·son (ed/ə·sən), **Thomas Alva**, 1847–1931, U.S. inventor.

Ed·ward VII (ed/wərd), 1841–1910, king of England 1901–10; called the Peacemaker.

Edward VIII See (Duke of) WINDSOR.

Ein·stein (īn/stīn), **Albert**, 1879–1955, U.S. physicist born in Germany; developed the theory of relativity.

Ei·sen·how·er (ī/zən·hou/ər), **Dwight David**, 1890–1969, U.S. general; 34th president of the U.S. 1953–61.

El Gre·co (el grek/ō, grā/ko), 1548?–1614, Sp. painter born in Crete: orig. name **Domenicos The·o·to·co·pou·los** (thä/ō·tô·kô/pōō·lôs).

E·li·a (ē·lyē/ä) See (Charles) LAMB.

El·i·ot (el/ē·ət), **George** Pseud. of *Mary Ann Evans*, 1819–1880, Eng. novelist. — **T**(**homas**) **S**(**tearns**), 1888–1965, Brit. poet, dramatist, and critic born in the U.S.

E·liz·a·beth I (i·liz/ə·bəth), 1533–1603, queen of England 1558–1603.

Elizabeth II, born 1926, queen of England 1952–.

Em·er·son (em/ər·sən), **Ralph Waldo**, 1803–82, U.S. essayist, philosopher, and poet.

En·gels (eng/əls), **Friedrich**, 1820–95, Ger. socialist and theoretician; collaborated with Karl Marx.

Ep·i·cu·rus (ep/ə·kyŏŏr/əs), 342?–270? B.C., Gk. philosopher.

E·ras·mus (i·raz/məs), **Desiderius**, 1466?–1536, Du. theologian, classical scholar, and humanist: orig. name **Geert Geerts** (gerts) or **Gerhard Ger·hards** (ger/harts).

Er·ic·son (er/ik·sən), **Lief**, 11th-c. Norse adventurer; son of Eric the Red; probably discovered North America about 1000. Also **Er/ics·son**.

Er·ic the Red (er/ik), 950?–?1003, Scandinavian adventurer; colonizer of Greenland.

Eu·clid (yōō/klid), Gk. mathematician of about the 3rd-c. B.C.; developed the basic principles of geometry.

Eu·ler (oi/lər), **Leonhard**, 1707–83, Swiss mathematician.

Eu·rip·i·des (yŏŏ·rip/ə·dēz), 480?–406? B.C., Gk. dramatist.

Ev·ans (ev/əns), **Mary Ann** See (George) ELIOT.

Far·a·day (far/ə·dā), **Michael**, 1791–1867, Eng. chemist and physicist; discovered properties of electromagnetism.

Far·ra·gut (far/ə·gət), **David Glasgow**, 1801–70, Union admiral in the Amer. Civil War.

Faulk·ner (fôk/nər), **William**, 1897–1962, U.S. novelist. Also **Falk/ner**.

Fer·di·nand V (fûr/di·nand), 1452–1516, king of Spain; husband of Isabella I: called **the Catholic**.

Fer·mi (fer'mē), **Enrico**, 1901–54, Ital. nuclear physicist active in the U.S.

Fich·te (fikh'tə), **Johann Gottlieb**, 1762–1814, Ger. patriot and philosopher.

Fill·more (fil'môr), **Millard**, 1800–74, 13th president of the U.S. 1850–53.

Fitz·Ger·ald (fits'jer'əld), **Edward**, 1809–83, Eng. poet.

Fitzgerald, F(rancis) Scott (Key), 1896–1940, U.S. writer.

Flau·bert (flō-bâr'), **Gustave**, 1821–80, Fr. novelist.

Flem·ing (flem'ing), **Sir Alexander**, 1881–1955, Brit. physician and bacteriologist; discoverer with Florey of penicillin.

Flo·rey (flôr'ē, flō'rē), **Sir Howard Walter**, 1898–1968, Brit. pathologist born in Australia; collaborated with Fleming in the discovery of penicillin.

Foch (fôsh), **Ferdinand**, 1851–1929, Fr. general; commander in chief of the Allied armies, 1918.

Fok·ker (fok'ər), **Anthony Herman Gerard**, 1890–1939, Du. airplane designer.

Ford (fôrd, fōrd), **Gerald Rudolph**, born 1913, U.S. representative; 38th president of the United States 1974–77.
— **Henry**, 1863–1947, U.S. automobile manufacturer.

Fos·ter (fôs'tər, fos'-), **Stephen (Collins)**, 1826–64, U.S. songwriter.

Fou·cault (fōō-kō'), **Jean Bernard Léon**, 1819–68, Fr. physicist.

Fou·rier (fōō-ryā'), **Jean Baptiste Joseph**, 1768–1830, Fr. mathematician and physicist.

Fox (foks), **George**, 1624–91, Eng. preacher; founded the Society of Friends.

Fra (frä) **Angelico** See ANGELICO.

France (frans, fräns), **Anatole** Pseud. of **Jacques Anatole Thi·bault** (tē-bō'), 1844–1924, Fr. novelist and critic.

Fran·ces·ca (frän-ches'kä), **Piero della** See PIERO DELLA FRANCESCA.

Fran·cis of As·si·si (fran'sis, frän'-; ə-sē'zē), **St.**, 1182?–1226, Ital. friar and preacher: orig. name **Giovanni Francesco Ber·nar·do·ne** (bâr'när-dō'nā).

Francis Xavier, Saint See XAVIER.

Franck (fräṅk), **César Auguste**, 1822–90, Fr. composer born in Belgium.

Fran·co (fraṅg'kō, Sp. fräṅg'kō), **Francisco**, 1892–1975, Sp. political and military leader; chief of state 1939–1975; called **el Cau·dil·lo** (el kou·thē'lyō, -thē'yō): full surname **Fran·co-Ba·ha·mon·de** (-bä'ä·môn'dä).

Frank·lin (fraṅk'lin), **Benjamin**, 1706–90, Amer. patriot, writer, scientist, and diplomat: pseud. **Richard Saun·ders** (sôn'dərz, sän'-).

Fred·er·ick I (fred'ər·ik, fred'rik), 1123?–90, emperor of the Holy Roman Empire 1152–90: called *Barbarossa* (Redbeard).

Frederick II, 1712–86, king of Prussia 1740–86: called **Frederick the Great.**

Fres·nel (frā-nel'), **Augustin Jean**, 1788–1827, Fr. physicist.

Freud (froid), **Sigmund**, 1856–1939, Austrian neurologist; founded modern theory of psychoanalysis.

Frost (frôst, frost), **Robert (Lee)**, 1875–1963, U.S. poet.

Ful·ton (fōōl'tən), **Robert**, 1765–1815, U.S. engineer and inventor.

Funk (fuṅk), **Isaac Kauffman**, 1839–1912, U.S. publisher and lexicographer.

Ga·len (gā'lən), 130?–200?, Gk. physician and medical writer.

Gal·i·le·o (gal'ə·lē'ō, Ital. gä'lē·lā'ō), 1564–1642, Florentine astronomer and physicist: full name **Galileo Gal·i·le·i** (gal'·ə·lā'ē).

Gal·va·ni (gäl·vä'nē), **Luigi**, 1737–98, Ital. physiologist.

Ga·ma (gam'ə, Pg. Gä'mə), **Vasco da**, 1469?–1524, Pg. seafarer and explorer.

Gan·dhi (gän'dē, gan'-), **Mohandas Karamchand**, 1869–1948, Indian politician and Hindu spiritual leader: called **Mahatma Gandhi**; — **In·di·ra** (in·dir'ə), born 1917, Indian stateswoman; prime minister 1966–77, 1980–.

Gar·cí·a Lor·ca (gär·thē'ä lôr'kä), **Federico**, 1899–1936, Sp. poet, dramatist, and essayist.

Gar·field (gär'fēld), **James Abram**, 1831–81, 20th president of the U.S. 1881; assassinated.

Gar·i·bal·di (gar'ə·bôl'dē, Ital. gä'rē·bäl'dē), **Giuseppe**, 1807–82, Ital. patriot and general; worked to unite Italy.

Gar·rick (gar'ik), **David**, 1717–79, Eng. actor, manager, and author.

Gau·guin (gō·gaṅ'), **Paul**, 1848–1903, Fr. painter: full name **Eugène Henri Paul Gauguin.**

Gauss (gous), **Karl Friedrich**, 1777–1855, Ger. mathematician and astronomer.

Gau·ta·ma (gō'tə·mə, gou'-) See BUDDHA.

Gay-Lussac (gā·lü·sak'), **Joseph Louis**, 1778–1850, Fr. chemist and physicist.

Gen·ghis Khan (jen'giz kän', jeng'gis, geng'gis), 1167?–1227, Mongol conqueror: orig. name **Te·much·in** (tə·mōō'·chin). Also **Jen'ghiz Khan.**

George (jôrj), **St.**, died 303?, Christian martyr; patron of England.

George III, 1738–1820, king of England 1760–1820.

George VI, 1895–1952, king of England 1936–52.

Ge·ron·i·mo (jə·ron'ə·mo), 1829–1909, Apache Indian chief.

Gide (zhēd), **André**, 1869–1951, Fr. writer.

Gil·bert (gil'bərt), **Sir William Schwenck**, 1836–1911, Eng. librettist; collaborator with Sir Arthur Sullivan.

Gior·gio·ne (jôr·jō'nā), 1477?–1511, Venetian painter: orig. name **Giorgio Bar·ba·rel·li** (bär'bä·rel'lē).

Giot·to (jôt'tō), 1266?–1337, Florentine painter, architect, and sculptor: full name **Giotto di Bon·do·ne** (dē bōn·dō'nä).

Glad·stone (glad'stōn, -stən), **William Ewart**, 1809–98, Eng. statesman and political leader; prime minister 1868–1874, 1880–85, 1886, 1892–94.

Goe·thals (gō'thəlz), **George Washington**, 1858–1928, U.S. army engineer; builder of the Panama Canal.

Goethe (gœ'tə), **Johann Wolfgang von**, 1749–1832, Ger. poet, dramatist, and novelist.

Gogh (gō, gôk; Du. khôkh), **Vincent van** See VAN GOGH.

Go·gol (gō'gəl, Russ. gô'gōl), **Nikolai Vasilievich**, 1809–52, Russ. writer and dramatist.

Gom·pers (gom'pərz), **Samuel**, 1850–1924, U.S. labor leader.

Gor·ki (gôr'kē), **Maxim** Pseud. of **Alexei Maximovich Pyesh·kov** (pyesh'kôf), 1868–1936, Russ. author. Also **Gor'ky.**

Gou·nod (gōō·nō'), **Charles François**, 1818–93, Fr. composer.

Go·ya (gō'yə), **Francisco José de**, 1746–1828, Sp. painter and etcher: full surname **Goya y Lu·cien·tes** (ē lōō·thyen'täs).

Gra·ham (grā'əm), **William Franklin**, born 1918, U.S. evangelist: called **Billy Graham.**

Grant (grant), **Ulysses S(impson)**, 1822–85, U.S. general in the Civil War; 18th president of the U.S. 1869–77: orig. name **Hiram Ulysses Grant.**

Gray (grā), **Thomas**, 1716–71, Eng. poet.

Gre·co (grek'ō, grā'kō), **El**, See EL GRECO.

Gregory I (greg'ə·rē), **St.**, 540?–604, pope 590–604; reformed the church service: called **Gregory the Great.**

Gregory XIII, 1502–85, pope 1572–85; reformed the calendar: orig. name **Ugo Buon·cam·pag·ni** (bwôn'cäm·pän'yē).

Grieg (grēg), **Edvard (Hagerup)**, 1843–1907, Norw. composer.

Grimm (grim), **Jakob (Ludwig Karl)**, 1785–1863, and his brother **Wilhelm (Karl)**, 1786–1859, Ger. collectors of fairy tales.

Gro·pi·us (grō'pē·əs), **Walter**, 1883–1969, Ger. architect active in the U.S.

Grü·ne·wald (grü'nə·vält), **Mathias**, 1480?–1530?, Ger. painter.

Gu·ten·berg (gōōt'n·bûrg), **Johann**, 1400?–68?, Ger. printer; inventor of movable type: orig. name **Johannes Gens·fleisch** (gens'flīsh).

Ha·ber (hä'bər), **Fritz**, 1868–1934, Ger. chemist.

Haeck·el (hek'əl), **Ernst Heinrich**, 1834–1919, Ger. naturalist and philosopher.

Hai·le Se·las·sie (hī'lē sə·las'ē, -läs'ē), 1891–1975, emperor of Ethiopia 1930–74; in exile 1936–41: orig. name **Taffari Ma·kon·nen** (mä·kôn'nen).

Hal·dane (hôl'dān), **J(ohn) B(urdon) S(anderson)**, 1892–1964, Eng. geneticist.

Hale (hāl), **Nathan**, 1755–76, Amer. Revolutionary patriot; hanged as a spy by the British.

Hals (häls), **Frans**, 1580?–1666, Du. painter.

Hal·sey (hôl'zē), **William Frederick**, 1882–1959, U.S. admiral in World War II.

Ham·il·ton (ham'əl·tən), **Alexander**, 1757–1804, Amer. statesman born in the British West Indies.

Ham·mar·skjöld (häm'är·shuld), **Dag**, 1905–61, Sw. statesman; UN Secretary General 1953–61.

Ham·mu·ra·bi (hä'mōō·rä'bē, ham'ə-), king of Babylonia in the first dynasty, about 2000 B.C.; promulgator of a system of laws called the **Code of Hammurabi.**

Han·cock (han'kok), **John**, 1737–93, U.S. patriot; signer of the Declaration of Independence.

Han·del (han'dəl), **George Frideric**, 1685–1759, Ger. composer active in England and Italy: orig. name **Georg Friedrich Hän·del** (hen'dəl): called **George Frederick Handel.**

Han·ni·bal (han'ə·bəl), 247?–183? B.C., Carthaginian general; invaded Italy by crossing the Alps.

Har·ding (här'ding), **Warren Gamaliel**, 1865–1923, 29th president of the U.S. 1921–23.

Har·ri·son (har′ə·sən), **Benjamin**, 1833–1901, 23rd president of the U.S. 1889–93; his grandfather, **William Henry**, 1773–1841, military commander; ninth president of the U.S. for a month in 1841.

Harte (härt), **Bret**, 1836–1902, U.S. novelist and short-story writer: orig. name **Francis Brett Harte**.

Har·vey (här′vē), **William**, 1578–1657, Eng. physician; discovered the circulation of the blood.

Haw·thorne (hô′thôrn), **Nathaniel**, 1804–64, U.S. novelist and short-story writer.

Hay·dn (hīd′n), **Franz Joseph**, 1732–1809, Austrian composer.

Hayes (hāz), **Rutherford Birchard**, 1822–93, 19th president of the U.S. 1877–81.

Hearst (hûrst), **William Randolph**, 1863–1951, U.S. newspaper publisher.

He·gel (hā′gəl), **Georg Wilhelm Friedrich**, 1770–1831, Ger. philosopher.

Hei·ne (hī′nə), **Heinrich**, 1797–1856, Ger. lyric poet.

Helm·holtz (helm′hōlts), **Hermann Ludwig Ferdinand von**, 1821–94, Ger. physiologist and physicist.

Hé·lo·ïse (ā·lō·ēz′), died 1164?, Fr. abbess, mistress and then wife of Abelard.

Hem·ing·way (hem′ing·wā), **Ernest**, 1899–1961, U.S. writer.

Hen·ry (hen′rē), **O.** See O. HENRY. — **Patrick**, 1736–99, Amer. revolutionary statesman and orator.

Henry II, 1133–89, king of England 1154–89; first Plantagenet king: called **Henry Plantagenet**.

Henry IV, 1367–1413, king of England 1399–1413.

Henry V, 1387–1422, king of England 1413–22.

Henry VIII, 1491–1547, king of England 1509–47, asserted royal supremacy over the Catholic Church in England.

Her·od An·ti·pas (her′əd an′ti·pas), died A.D. 39?, tetrarch of Galilee 4 B.C.–A.D. 39; the Herod of the Gospels.

He·rod·o·tus (hi·rod′ə·təs), 5th-c. B.C. Gk. historian: called **the Father of History**.

Her·rick (her′ik), **Robert**, 1591–1674, Eng. lyric poet.

Her·zl (her′tsəl), **Theodor**, 1860–1904, Austro-Hung. journalist; founded the Zionist movement.

Hin·de·mith (hin′də·mit), **Paul**, 1895–1963, Ger. composer.

Hin·den·burg (hin′den·bûrg, Ger. hin′dən·bŏŏrkh), **Paul von**, 1847–1934, Ger. general and statesman; president of the Weimar Republic 1925–34.

Hip·poc·ra·tes (hi·pok′rə·tēz), 460?–377? B.C., Gk. physician: called **the Father of Medicine**.

Hi·ro·hi·to (hir·ō·hē·tō), born 1901, emperor of Japan 1926–.

Hit·ler (hit′lər), **Adolf**, 1889–1945, Ger. Nazi dictator born in Austria; chancellor 1933–45: called **der Fuhrer** (the Leader).

Hobbes (hobz), **Thomas**, 1588–1679, Eng. philosopher.

Ho·garth (hō′gärth), **William**, 1697–1765, Eng. painter and engraver.

Hol·bein (hōl′bīn, Ger. hôl′bīn), **Hans**, 1465?–1524, **the Elder**, and his son **Hans**, 1497?–1543, **the Younger**, Ger. painters.

Holmes (hōmz), **Oliver Wendell**, 1809–94, U.S. physician, poet, and essayist. — **Oliver Wendell**, 1841–1935, U.S. jurist; associate justice of the Supreme Court 1902–32; son of the preceding.

Ho·mer (hō′mər), 9th-c. B.C. Gk. epic poet; trad. author of the *Iliad* and the *Odyssey*.

Hooke (hŏŏk), **Robert**, 1635–1703, Eng. physicist.

Hoo·ver (hŏŏ′vər), **Herbert Clark**, 1874–1964, U.S. mining engineer and statesman; 31st president of the U.S. 1929–33. — **J(ohn) Edgar**, 1895–1972, U.S. lawyer; director of the Federal Bureau of Investigation 1924–72.

Hor·ace (hôr′is, hor′-) · Anglicized name of **Quintus Horatius Flac·cus** (flak′əs), 65–8 B.C., Roman poet.

Hou·di·ni (hŏŏ·dē′nē), **Harry**, 1874–1926, U.S. magician: orig. name **Erich Weiss** (wīs).

Hous·man (hous′mən), **A(lfred) E(dward)**, 1859–1936, Eng. poet.

Hous·ton (hyŏŏs′tən), **Sam**, 1793–1863, U.S. general and politician; first president of the Republic of Texas 1836–38, 1841–44.

Hud·son (hud′sən), **Henry**, died 1611?, Eng. navigator and explorer; discovered the Hudson River for the Dutch, 1609, and Hudson Bay for the English, 1610.

Hugh Ca·pet (hyŏŏ kā′pit, kap′it; Fr. kà·pe′), 938?–996, king of France 987–996; founder of the Capetian dynasty.

Hu·go (hyŏŏ′gō, Fr. ü·gō′), **Victor (Marie)**, 1802–85, Fr. poet, novelist, and dramatist.

Hume (hyŏŏm), **David**, 1711–76, Scot. historian and philosopher.

Hux·ley (huks′lē) An Eng. family prominent in science and literature, notably **T(homas) H(enry)**, 1825–95, biologist and Darwinian; and his grandsons **Julian (Sorell)**, born 1887, biologist, and **Aldous (Leonard)**, 1894–1963, novelist and critic.

Huy·gens (hī′gənz), **Christian**, 1629–95, Du. mathematician, physicist, and astronomer. Also **Huy′ghens**.

I·bá·ñez (ē·vä′nyeth), **Vicente Blasco** See BLASCO·IBÁÑEZ.

Ib·sen (ib′sən), **Henrik**, 1828–1906, Norw. dramatist.

Ig·na·ti·us Loyola (ig·nā′shē·əs, -shəs), **Saint** See LOYOLA.

Ir·ving (ûr′ving), **Washington**, 1783–1859, U.S. writer, historian, and humorist.

Is·a·bel·la I (iz′ə·bel′ə), 1451–1504, queen of Castile; aided Christopher Columbus: called **Isabella the Catholic**.

I·van IV (ī′vən, Russ. i·vän′), 1530–84, first czar of Russia 1547–84: called **the Terrible**.

Jack·son (jak′sən), **Andrew**, 1767–1845, U.S. general; seventh president of the U.S. 1829–37: called **Old Hickory**. — **Thomas Jonathan**, 1824–63, Confederate general in the Civil War: called **Stonewall Jackson**.

James (jāmz), **Henry**, 1843–1916, U.S. writer and critic active in England. — **Jesse (Woodson)**, 1847–82, U.S. outlaw. — **William**, 1842–1910, U.S. philosopher and psychologist; brother of Henry.

James I, 1566–1625, 1st Stuart king of England 1603–25; as **James VI** king of Scotland 1567–1625.

James II, 1633–1701, king of England 1685–88; deposed.

Jeanne d'Arc (zhän dark) See JOAN OF ARC.

Jeans (jēnz), **Sir James (Hopwood)**, 1877–1946, Eng. astronomer, physicist, and philosopher.

Jef·fer·son (jef′ər·sən), **Thomas**, 1743–1826, Amer. statesman, diplomat, and writer; third president of the U.S. 1801–1809.

Jen·ner (jen′ər), **Edward**, 1749–1823, Eng. physician; discovered vaccination.

Je·sus (jē′zəs) Founder of Christianity, 6? B.C.–29? A.D., son of Mary; regarded in the Christian faith as Christ, the Messiah. Also **Jesus Christ, Jesus of Nazareth**.

Joan of Arc (jōn), 1412?–31, Fr. heroine and martyr; burned as a heretic; canonized 1920; also called the **Maid of Orléans**.

John (jon), 1167?–1216, king of England 1199–1216, signed the Magna Carta 1215: called **John Lack·land** (lak′land).

John XXIII, 1881–1963, pope 1958–63: orig. name **Angelo Giuseppe Ron·cal·li** (rōn·käl′lē).

John Paul I (jon pôl), 1912–78, pope Aug.–Sept. 1978: orig. name **Albino Lu·cia·ni** (lŏŏ·chä′nē).

John Paul II, born 1920, pope 1978–: orig. name **Karol Woj·ty·la** (voi′tē·vä, -tē·ä).

John·son (jon′sən), **Andrew**, 1808–75, 17th president of the U.S. 1865–69; impeached. — **Lyndon Baines**, 1908–1973, 36th president of the U.S. 1963–69. — **Samuel**, 1709–84, Eng. lexicographer, poet, man of letters: called **Dr. Johnson**.

Jones (jōnz), **John Paul**, 1747–92, Amer. Revolutionary naval officer born in Scotland: orig. name **John Paul**.

Jon·son (jon′sən), **Ben**, 1573?–1637, Eng. poet and dramatist.

Jo·seph·ine (jō′zə·fēn, Fr. zhô·zä·fēn′), **Empress**, 1763–1814, widow of Vicomte Alexandre de Beauharnais, married Napoleon Bonaparte 1796, divorced 1809.

Joule (joul, jŏŏl), **James Prescott**, 1818–89, Eng. physicist.

Joyce (jois), **James (Augustine Aloysius)**, 1882–1941, Irish writer and poet active in Zurich and Paris.

Jul·ius (jŏŏl′yəs) **Caesar** See (Gaius Julius) CAESAR.

Jung (yŏŏng), **Carl Gustav**, 1875–1961, Swiss psychologist.

Jus·tin·i·an I (jus·tin′ē·ən), Anglicized name of **Flavius Anicius Jus·tin·i·a·nus** (jus·tin′ē·ā′nus), 483–565, Byzantine emperor 527–565; codified Roman laws.

Kaf·ka (käf′kä), **Franz**, 1883–1924, Austrian writer born in Prague.

Kant (känt), **Immanuel**, 1724–1804, Ger. philosopher.

Keats (kēts), **John**, 1795–1821, Eng. poet.

Ke·mal A·ta·türk (ke·mäl′ ä·tä·türk′), 1881–1938, Turkish general and statesman; founder of modern Turkey. Also **Mus·ta·fa Ke·mal** (mŏŏs′tä·fä ki·mäl′).

Ken·ne·dy (ken′ə·dē), **John Fitzgerald**, 1917–63, 35th president of the U.S. 1961–63; assassinated. — **Robert Francis**, 1925–68, U.S. senator and political leader; brother of the preceding; assassinated.

Kep·ler (kep′lər), **Johann**, 1571–1630, Ger. astronomer; formulated laws of planetary motion.

Key (kē), **Francis Scott**, 1779–1863, Amer. lawyer and poet; wrote *The Star-Spangled Banner*.

Keynes (kānz), **John Maynard**, 1883–1946, first Baron of Tilton, Eng. economist.

Khay·yám (kī·äm′), **Omar**. See OMAR KHAYYÁM.

Khrush·chev (krŏŏsh·chôf′, Russ. khrŏŏ·shchôf′), **Nikita Sergeyevich**, 1894–1971, Soviet statesman; first secretary of the Communist Party 1953–1964; premier 1958–1964.

Kidd (kid), **William**, 1645?–1701, Brit. sea captain and pirate; hanged: called **Captain Kidd**.

Kier·ke·gaard (kir′kə·gôr), **Søren Aabye**, 1813–55, Dan. philosopher and theologian.

King (king), **Martin Luther, Jr.**, 1929–68, U.S. leader of nonviolent civil rights movement for Negroes; assassinated.

Kip·ling (kip′ling), **(Joseph) Rudyard**, 1865–1936, Eng. author and poet.

Klee (klä, klē), **Paul,** 1879–1940, Swiss painter and etcher.

Knox (noks), **John,** 1505?–72, Scot. Calvinist reformer, theologian, and historian.

Koest·ler (kest′lər), **Arthur,** 1905–1983, Hung. writer active in England.

Kos·ci·us·ko (kos′ē·us′kō), **Thaddeus,** 1746–1817, Polish patriot and general born in Lithuania; fought in the Amer. Revolution. *Polish* **Koś·ciusz·ko** (kōsh·chōōsh′kō).

Ko·sy·gin (ko·sig′in), **Alexei Nikolayevich,** 1904–1980, Soviet statesman; premier 1964–1980.

Kra·nach (krä′näkh), **Lucas** See CRANACH.

Ku·blai Khan (kōō′blī kän′), 1216?–94, Mongol emperor, founder of the Mongol dynasty of China. Also **Kub·la Khan** (kōō′blə).

La·fay·ette (lä′fē·et′, laf′ē·et′; *Fr.* là·fâ·yet′), **Marquis de,** 1757–1834, Fr. general, revolutionist, and statesman; fought in the Amer. Revolution. Also **La·Fay·ette′.**

La Fon·taine (lä fon·tān′, *Fr.* là fôn·ten′), **Jean de,** 1621–1695, Fr. writer, noted for his fables.

La·marck (là·märk′), **Chevalier de,** 1744–1829, Fr. naturalist; orig. name **Jean Baptiste Pierre Antoine de Mo·net** (də mō·ne′).

Lamb (lam), **Charles,** 1775–1834, Eng. essayist: pseud. *Elia.*

Lao·tse (lou′ə:u′), 604?–531? B.C., Chinese philosopher and mystic; founder of Taoism. Also **Lao-tze, Lao-tzu.**

Lard·ner (lärd′nər), **Ring,** 1885–1933, U.S. journalist and short-story writer: full name **Ringgold Wilmer Lardner.**

La Roche·fou·cauld (lä rōsh·fōō·kō′), **Duc François de,** 1613–80, Prince de Marcillac, Fr. moralist and writer.

La Salle (là säl′), **Sieur Robert Cavelier de,** 1643–87, Fr. explorer in America.

Lau·trec (lō·trek′) See TOULOUSE-LAUTREC.

Law·rence (lôr′əns, lor′-), **D**(avid) **H**(erbert), 1885–1930, Eng. novelist and poet. — **T**(homas) **E**(dward), 1885–1935, Eng. archaeologist, soldier, and writer; led Arab revolt against Turkey in World War I; after 1927 changed his name to Shaw (shô): called **Lawrence of Arabia.**

Lee (lē), **Robert E**(dward), 1807–70, Confederate commander in chief in the Civil War.

Leeu·wen·hoek (lā′vən·hōōk), **Anton van,** 1632–1723, Du. naturalist; pioneer in microscopy.

Leib·nitz (līb′nits), **Baron Gottfried Wilhelm von,** 1646–1716, Ger. philosopher and mathematician. Also **Leib′niz.**

Leif Er·ic·son (lēf er′ik·sən) See ERICSON.

Le·nin (len′in), **Vladimir Ilyich,** 1870–1924, Russ. statesman; chief leader and theorist of the Bolshevik Revolution; head of the U.S.S.R. 1917–24: original name **Vladimir Ilyich Ul·ya·nof** (ōōl·ya′nəf). Also, erroneously, **Nikolai Lenin.**

Leo X, 1475–1521, pope 1513–21: orig. name *Giovanni de' Medici.*

Le·o·nar·do da Vin·ci (lē′ə·när′dō də vin′chē, *Ital.* lā′ō·när′dō dä vēn′chē) See DA VINCI.

Les·seps (les′əps, *Fr.* le·seps′), **Vicomte Ferdinand Marie de,** 1805–94, Fr. engineer and diplomat; supervised building of the Suez Canal.

Lew·is (lōō′is), **Sinclair,** 1885–1951, U.S. novelist.

Lie (lē), **Trygve Halvdan,** 1896–1968, Norw. statesman; first secretary general of the U.N., 1946–53.

Lil·i·en·thal (lē′lē·ən·täl′), **Otto,** 1848–98, Ger. inventor.

Lin·coln (ling′kən), **Abraham,** 1809–65, U.S. statesman; 16th president of the U.S. 1861–65; assassinated.

Lind·bergh (lind′bûrg), **Charles Augustus,** 1902–74, U.S. aviator.

Lin·nae·us (li·nē′əs), **Carolus,** Latinized name of **Karl von Lin·né** (lē·nā′), 1707–78, Sw. botanist and taxonomist.

Lis·ter (lis′tər), **Joseph,** 1827–1912, first Baron Lister of Lyme Regis, Eng. surgeon; founder of antiseptic surgery.

Liszt (list), **Franz,** 1811–86, Hung. composer and pianist.

Lloyd George (loid jôrj), **David,** 1863–1945, first Earl of Dwyfor, Brit. statesman; prime minister 1916–22.

Locke (lok), **John,** 1632–1704, Eng. philosopher.

Lon·don (lun′dən), **Jack,** 1876–1916, U.S. author: orig. name **John Griffith London.**

Long (lông, long), **Huey Pierce,** 1893–1935, U.S. politician; assassinated.

Long·fel·low (lông′fel·ō, long′-), **Henry Wadsworth,** 1807–1882, U.S. poet.

Lo·pe de Ve·ga (lō′pā thä vā′gä) See (Lope de) VEGA.

Lor·ca (lôr′kä), **Federico García** See GARCIA LORCA.

Lo·rentz (lō′rents), **Hendrik Antoon,** 1853–1928, Du. physicist.

Lou·is XIV (lōō′ē, lōō′is; *Fr.* lwē), 1638–1715, king of France 1643–1715; called *le Roi Soleil* (the Sun King).

Louis XV, 1710–74, king of France 1715–74.

Louis XVI, 1754–93, king of France 1774–92, dethroned by the French Revolution; guillotined.

Louis Napoleon See (Louis Napoleon) BONAPARTE.

Louis Phi·lippe (fē·lēp′), 1773–1850, king of France 1830–1848; abdicated: called **le Roi Ci·toy·en** (lə rwä sē·twä·yan′) (the Citizen King).

Lo·yo·la (loi·ō′lə), **St. Ignatius,** 1491–1566, Sp. soldier, priest, and mystic; founder of the Society of Jesus: original name **Inigo de Oñez y Loyola.**

Lu·cre·tius (lōō·krē′shəs, -shē·əs), 96–55 B.C., Roman poet: full name **Titus Lucretius Car·us** (kâr′əs).

Lu·ther (lōō′thər), **Martin,** 1483–1546, Ger. monk, theologian, and reformer; leader of the Reformation; excommunicated 1520.

Mac·Ar·thur (mək·är′thər), **Douglas,** 1880–1964, U.S. general.

Mach·i·a·vel·li (mäk′ē·ə·vel′ē, *Ital.* mä′kyä·vel′lē), **Niccoló,** 1469–1527, Florentine statesman and writer on politics.

Mac·mil·lan (mak·mil′ən), **Harold,** born 1894, Brit. statesman; prime minister 1957–63.

Mad·i·son (mad′ə·sən), **James,** 1751–1836, 4th president of the U.S. 1809–17: called **the Father of the Constitution.**

Ma·gel·lan (mə·jel′ən), **Ferdinand,** 1480?–1521, Pg. navigator in the service of Spain.

Mah·ler (mä′lər), **Gustav,** 1860–1911, Austro-Hung. composer and conductor active in Austria and Germany.

Ma·hom·et (mə·hom′it) See MOHAMMED.

Mai·mon·i·des (mī·mon′ə·dēz), 1135–1204, Sp. rabbi, physician, and philosopher: orig. name **Moses ben Mai·mon** (mī′mōn). Called **RaM·BaM** (ram·bam′).

Mal·colm X (mal′kəm eks) Name adopted by *Malcolm Little,* 1925–65, U.S. political and religious leader, active in the Black Muslim movement; assassinated.

Mal·o·ry (mal′ər·ē), **Sir Thomas,** died 1470, Eng. author and translator.

Mal·pi·ghi (mäl·pē′gē), **Marcello,** 1628–94, Ital. anatomist.

Mal·raux (mäl·rō′), **André,** 1901–1967, Fr. novelist, art critic, and politician: full name **Georges André Malraux.**

Mal·thus (mal′thəs, môl′-), **Thomas Robert,** 1766–1834, Eng. political economist.

Mann (män), **Thomas,** 1875–1955, Ger. novelist active in the U.S.

Mao Tse-tung (mou′dzu′dōōng′), 1893–1976, Chinese Communist leader; chairman of the People's Republic of China 1949–59.

Marc Antony (märk) See (Mark) ANTONY.

Mar·co·ni (mär·kō′nē), **Marchese Guglielmo,** 1874–1937, Ital. inventor; developed a system of wireless telegraphy.

Mar·co Po·lo (mär′kō pō′lō) See POLO.

Ma·rie An·toi·nette (mä·rē′ än·twä·net′), 1755–93, queen of France; wife of Louis XVI; guillotined.

Ma·ri·tain (mä·rē·tan′), **Jacques,** 1882–1973, Fr. philosopher.

Mark Twain (märk twān) Pseud. of Samuel Langhorne Clemens, 1835–1910, U.S. humorist and novelist.

Mar·lowe (mär′lō), **Christopher,** 1564–93, Eng. poet.

Mar·ti (mär·tē′), **José Julian,** 1853–95, Cuban patriot.

Mar·vell (mär′vəl), **Andrew,** 1621–78, Eng. poet.

Marx (marks), **Karl** (**Heinrich**), 1818–83, Ger. philosopher and theorist of modern socialism.

Ma·ry (mâr′ē) **I,** 1516–58, queen of England 1553–58: called **Mary Tudor, Bloody Mary.**

Mary, Queen of Scots, 1542–87, queen of Scotland 1542–1567; beheaded. Also **Mary Stuart.**

Ma·sac·cio (mä·sät′chō), 1401–29?, Florentine painter: orig. name **Tommaso Gui·di** (gwē′dē).

Ma·tisse (mä·tēs′) **Henri,** 1869–1954, Fr. painter.

Mau·pas·sant (mō·pà·säñ′), (**Henri René Albert**) **Guy de,** 1850–93, Fr. writer.

Max·well (maks′wel), **James Clerk,** 1831–79, Scot. physicist.

Maz·zi·ni (mät·tsē′nē), **Giuseppe,** 1805?–72, Ital. patriot and revolutionary.

Mc·Cor·mick (mə·kôr′mik), **Cyrus** (**Hall**), 1809–84, U.S. inventor; developed the reaping machine.

Mc·Kin·ley (mə·kin′le), **William,** 1843–1901, 25th president of the U.S. 1897–1901; assassinated.

Mead (mēd), **Margaret,** 1901–78, U.S. anthropologist.

Med·i·ci (med′ə·chē, *Ital.* mä′dē·chē) A family of Florentine bankers and statesmen, notably **Giovanni de' Medici,** died 1429, and his sons **Cosimo,** 1389–1464, and **Lorenzo,** 1395–1440; **Lorenzo,** 1449?–92, grandson of Cosimo, patron of the arts, called **the Magnificent;** his son **Giovanni,** 1475–1521 (see LEO X); **Cosimo,** 1519–74, grand duke of Tuscany: called **the Great.**

Me·ir (mä·ir′), **Golda,** 1898–1978, Israeli politician and stateswoman; prime minister 1969–74; born **Golda Mabovitz** in Kiev, Russia.

Mel·ville (mel′vil), **Herman,** 1819–91, U.S. novelist.

Mem·ling (mem′ling), **Hans,** 1430?–95?, Flemish painter.

Menck·en (meng′kən), **H(enry) L(ouis)**, 1880–1956, U.S. author and editor.

Men·del (men′dəl), **Gregor Johann**, 1822–84, Austrian monk and botanist; formulated laws of genetics.

Men·de·ley·ev (men′də·lā′əf), **Dmitri Ivanovich**, 1834–1907, Russ. chemist; developed the periodic law. Also **Men′de·le′ev**.

Men·dels·sohn (men′dəl·sən, *Ger.* men′dəl·zōn), **Felix**, 1809–47, Ger. composer: full name **Jakob Ludwig Felix Men′dels·sohn-Bar·thol·dy** (-bär·tōl′dē).

Mer·ca·tor (mər·kā′tər, *Flemish* mer·kä′tôr), **Gerardus**, 1512–94, Flemish geographer and cartographer: orig. name **Gerhard Kre·mer** (krā′mər).

Mes·sa·li·na (mes′ə·lī′na), **Valeria**, died 48 A.D., Roman empress; notorious for profligacy; executed. Also **Mes′sal·li′na**.

Metch·ni·koff (mech′ni·kôf), **Élie**, 1845–1916, Russ. physiologist and bacteriologist active in France: orig. name **Ilya Ilich Mechnikov**.

Met·ter·nich (met′ər·nikh), **Prince von**, 1773–1859, Klemens Wenzel Nepomuk Lothar von Metternich-Winneburg, Austrian statesman and diplomat.

Mi·chel·an·ge·lo (mī′kəl·an′jə·lō, *Ital.* mē′kel·än′je·lō), 1475–1564, Ital. sculptor, painter, architect, and poet: full name **Michelangelo Buo·nar·ro·ti** (bwô′när·rô′tē).

Mi·chel·son (mī′kəl·sən), **Albert Abraham**, 1852–1931, U.S. physicist born in Germany.

Mill (mil), **John Stuart**, 1806–73, Eng. philosopher and political economist.

Mil·lay (mi·lā′), **Edna St. Vincent**, 1892–1950, U.S. poet.

Mil·ler (mil′ər), **Arthur**, born 1915, U.S. novelist and playwright. **— Henry**, 1891–1980, U.S. author.

Mil·li·kan (mil′ə·kən), **Robert Andrews**, 1868–1955, U.S. physicist.

Mil·ton (mil′tən), **John**, 1608–74, Eng. poet and essayist.

Mo·ham·med (mō·ham′id), 570?–632, Arabian founder and prophet of Islam whose revelations are collected in the Koran: also **Mahomet, Muhammad**.

Mo·lière (mō·lyâr′) Pseud. of **Jean Baptiste Po·que·lin** (pô·klän′), 1622–73, Fr. dramatist and actor.

Mon·dri·an (môn′drē·än), **Piet**, 1872–1944, Du. painter. Also **Mon′dri·aan**.

Mo·net (mō·ne′), **Claude**, 1840–1926, Fr. painter.

Mon·roe (mən·rō′), **James**, 1758–1831, 5th president of the U.S. 1817–25.

Mon·taigne (mon·tān′, *Fr.* môn·ten′y′), **Michel Eyquem de**, 1533–92, Fr. essayist.

Mon·tes·quieu (mon′təs·kyōō′, *Fr.* môn·tes·kyœ′), **Baron de la Brede et de**, 1689–1755, Charles de Secondat, Fr. jurist, political philosopher and man of letters.

Mon·te·ver·di (mon′tə·vûr′dē, *Ital.* môn′tā·ver′dē), **Claudio (Giovanni Antonio)**, 1567–1643, Ital. composer.

Mon·te·zu·ma II (mon′tə·zōō′ma), 1479?–1520, last Aztec Emperor of Mexico, dethroned by Cortés. Also **Moctezuma**.

Moore (mōōr, môr, mōr), **Henry**, born 1898, Eng. sculptor. **— Marianne (Craig)**, 1887–1972, U.S. poet.

More (môr, mōr), **Sir Thomas**, 1478?–1535, Eng. statesman and author: beheaded by Henry VIII; canonized 1935.

Mor·gan (môr·gən), **John Pierpont**, 1837–1913, U.S. banker, art collector and philanthropist.

Mor·ris (môr′is, mor′-), **William**, 1834–96, Eng. poet, painter, and socialist writer.

Morse (môrs), **Samuel Finley Breese**, 1791–1872, U.S. artist and inventor; constructed the first practical telegraph.

Mose·ley (mōz′lē), **Henry Gwyn-Jeffreys**, 1887–1915, Eng. physicist.

Mous·sorg·sky (mōō·sôrg′skē), **Modest Petrovich**, 1835–1881, Russ. composer. Also **Mus·sorg′sky**.

Mo·zart (mō′tsärt, -zärt), **Wolfgang Amadeus**, 1756–91, Austrian composer.

Mus·so·li·ni (mōōs′ə·lē·nē), **Benito**, 1883–1945, Ital. Fascist leader; premier 1922–43; executed: called **Il Du·ce** (ēl dōō′chā).

Mu·ham·mad (mōō·ham′əd) See MOHAMMED.

Na·pi·er (nā′pē·ər, nə·pir′), **John**, 1550–1617, Scot. mathematician.

Na·po·le·on I (nə·pō′lē·ən; *Fr.* nȧ·pô·lā·ôn′) See under BONAPARTE.

Napoleon III See under BONAPARTE.

Nas·ser (näs′ər, nas′-), **Gamal Abdel**, 1918–1970, Egyptian army officer and political leader; chief of state 1954–1970; president of the United Arab Republic 1958–1970.

Neb·u·chad·nez·zar (neb′yŏō·kəd·nez′ər), died 562 B.C., king of Babylonia 605–562 B.C.; conquered Judea and destroyed Jerusalem. Also **Neb′u·chad·rez′zar** (-rez′ər).

Neh·ru (nā′rōō), **Ja·wa·har·lal** (jə·wä′hər·läl), 1889–1964, Indian nationalist leader and statesman; 1st prime minister 1947–64.

Nel·son (nel′sən), **Viscount Horatio**, 1758–1805, Eng. admiral; killed at the battle of Trafalgar.

Ne·ro (nir′ō), 37–68, Nero Claudius Caesar Drusus Germanicus, Roman emperor 54–68; committed suicide: orig.

name **Lucius Domitius A·he·no·bar·bus** (ə·hē·nō·bär′bus).

New·man (nyōō′mən, nōō′-), **John Henry**, 1801–90, Eng. cardinal and theologian.

New·ton (nōō′tən, nyōō′-), **Sir Isaac**, 1642–1727, Eng. philosopher and mathematician.

Nei·buhr (nē′bōōr), **Reinhold**, 1892–1971, U.S. Protestant theologian.

Nie·tzsche (nē′chə), **Friedrich Wilhelm**, 1844–1900, Ger. philosopher.

Night·in·gale (nī′tən·gāl, nī′ting-), **Florence**, 1820–1910, Eng. pioneer of modern nursing, born in Italy.

Nix·on (nik′sən), **Richard Milhous**, born 1913; 37th president of the U.S. 1969–74; resigned.

No·bel (nō·bel′), **Alfred Bernhard**, 1833–96, Sw. industrialist; inventor of dynamite; founded the Nobel Prizes.

Nos·tra·da·mus (nos′trə·dā′məs), 1503–66, Fr. astrologer: orig. name **Michel de No·tre·dame** (də nō′trə·däm′).

O'Ca·sey (ō·kā′sē), **Sean** (shôn), 1880–1964, Irish playwright.

Ock·ham (ok′əm), **William of**, 1300?–49?, Eng. Franciscan and scholastic philosopher; opponent of Duns Scotus: called **the Invincible Doctor**. Also spelled **Oc′cam**.

Oc·ta·vi·an (ok·tā′vē·ən) See AUGUSTUS CAESAR.

O. Henry (ō hen′rē) Pseud. of *William Sydney Porter*, 1862–1910, U.S. short-story writer.

Ohm (ōm), **Georg Simon**, 1787–1854, Ger. physicist.

O·li·vi·er (ō·liv′ē·ā), **Sir Laurence** (Kerr), born 1907, Eng. actor.

O·mar Khay·yám (ō′mär kī·äm′, ō′mər), died 1123?, Persian poet and astronomer: author of the *Rubáiyát*.

O'Neill (ō·nēl′), **Eugene** (Gladstone), 1888–1953, U.S. playwright.

Or·te·ga y Gas·set (ôr·tā′gä ē gä·set′), **José**, 1883–1955, Sp. philosopher, writer, and statesman.

Or·well (ôr′wel), **George**, pseud. of Eric Blair (blâr), 1903–1950, Brit. novelist and essayist.

Ov·id (ov′id), 43 B.C.–A.D. 18, Roman poet: full name **Publius O·vid·i·us Na·so** (ō·vid′i·əs nā′sō).

Ow·en (ō′in), **Robert**, 1771–1858, Brit. manufacturer and social reformer.

Paine (pān), **Thomas**, 1737–1809, Amer. patriot, author, and political philosopher born in England.

Pa·les·tri·na (pä′les·trē′nä), **Giovanni Pierluigi da**, 1524?–1594, Ital. composer: called **Prin·ceps Mu·si·cae** (prin′seps myōō′zi·sē) (Prince of Music).

Pas·cal (pas·kal′, pas·kəl; *Fr.* pȧs·kȧl′), **Blaise**, 1623–62, Fr. mathematician, philosopher, and author.

Pas·teur (pas·tœr′), **Louis**, 1822–95, Fr. chemist; founder of modern bacteriology.

Pat·rick (pat·rik), **St.**, 389?–461?, Christian missionary; patron of Ireland: called **the Apostle of Ireland**.

Paul VI (pôl), 1897–1978, pope 1963–78: orig. name Giovanni Battista Mon·ti·ni (môn·tē′nē).

Pav·lov (päv′lôf), **Ivan Petrovich**, 1849–1936, Russ. physiologist.

Pearson, **Lester Bowles**, 1897–1972, Can. statesman; prime minister of Canada 1963–68.

Pea·ry (pir′ē), **Robert Edwin**, 1856–1920, U.S. Arctic explorer; first to reach the North Pole, April 6, 1909.

Penn (pen), **William**, 1644–1718, Eng. Quaker; founder of Pennsylvania.

Pepys (pēps, pep′is), **Samuel**, 1633–1702, Eng. diarist.

Pérez de Cuellar (pā′rez dā kwä′yär), **Javier**, born 1920, Peruvian statesman, UN Secretary General 1982–.

Per·i·cles (per′ə·klēz), died 429 B.C., Athenian statesman, orator, and general.

Pe·rón (pā·rōn′), **Juan Domingo**, 1895–1974, Argentine politician; president 1946–55, 1973–74.

Per·ry (per′ē), **Oliver Hazard**, 1785–1819, U.S. naval commander during Amer. Revolution.

Per·shing (pûr′shing), **John Joseph**, 1860–1948, U.S. General of the Armies: called **Black Jack**.

Peter I (pē′tər), 1672–1725, czar of Russia 1682–1725: called **Peter the Great**.

Pe·trarch (pē′trärk), **Francesco**, 1304–74, Ital. poet and scholar. Also **Pe·trar·ca** (pā·trär′kä).

Phid·i·as (fid′ē·əs), 5th-c. B.C. Gk. sculptor and architect.

Pi·cas·so (pē·kä′sō), **Pablo**, 1881–1973, Sp. painter and sculptor active in France: full surname **Ru·iz y Picasso** (rōō·ēth′ē).

Pierce (pirs), **Franklin**, 1804–69, 14th president of the U.S. 1853–57.

Pie·ro del·la Fran·ces·ca (pyä′rō del′lä fran·ches′kä) 1420?–92, Ital. painter.

Pis·sar·ro (pē·sä·rō′), **Camille**, 1830–1903, Fr. painter born in West Indies.

Pitt (pit), **William**, 1708–78, first Earl of Chatham, Eng. statesman, prime minister 1766–68: called **the Elder, the Great Commoner**. **— William**, 1759–1806, Eng. statesman, prime minister 1783–1801, 1804–1806, son of the preceding: called **the Younger**.

Pi·us V, Saint, 1504–72, pope 1566–72: orig. name **Michele Ghi·lie·ri** (gēz·lyã'rē).

Pius IX, 1792–1878, pope 1846–78; orig. name **Giovanni Maria Ma·stai-Fer·ret·ti** (mäs·tā'ē·fer·ret'te).

Pius XII, 1876–1958, pope 1939–58: orig. name **Eugenio Pa·cel·li** (pä·chel'lē).

Pi·zar·ro (pi·zär'ō, *Sp.* pē·thär'rō), **Francisco,** 1471?–1541, Sp. conquistador, conqueror of Peru.

Planck (plängk), **Max (Karl Ernst Ludwig),** 1858–1947, Ger. physicist; formulated the quantum theory.

Pla·to (plā'tō), 427?–347? B.C., Gk. philosopher.

Plu·tarch (plōō·tärk), A.D., 46?–120?, Gk. biographer.

Po·ca·hon·tas (pō·ka·hon'tas), 1595?–1617, Amer. Indian princess in Virginia; reputedly saved the life of Captain John Smith.

Poe (pō), **Edgar Allan,** 1809–49, U.S. writer and critic.

Polk (pōk), **James Knox,** 1795–1849, 11th president of the U.S. 1845–49.

Pol·lock (pol'ak), **Jackson,** 1912–56, U.S. painter.

Po·lo (pō'lō), **Marco,** 1254?–1323?, Venetian traveler.

Pom·pey (pom'pē) Anglicized name of **Gnaeus Pompeius Mag·nus** (mag·nəs), 106–48 B.C., Roman general and statesman; defeated by Julius Caesar: called **the Great.**

Ponce de Le·ón (pons' də lē'ən, *Sp.* pōn'thã thã lã·ōn'), **Juan,** 1460?–1521, Sp. explorer; discovered Florida, 1513.

Pon·tius Pilate (pon'shəs, -tē·əs), Roman procurator of Judea 26–36 A.D., condemned Jesus to be crucified. Also called **Pilate** (pī'lat).

Pope (pōp), **Alexander,** 1688–1744, Eng. poet and satirist.

Por·ter (pôr'tər, pōr'-), **William Sydney** See O. HENRY.

Pound (pound), **Ezra (Loomis),** 1885–1972, U.S. poet.

Priest·ley (prēst'lē), **Joseph,** 1733–1804, Eng. clergyman, philosopher, and chemist; discovered oxygen.

Pro·kof·iev (prō·kôf'yəf), **Sergei Sergeyevich,** 1891–1953, Soviet composer. Also **Pro·kof·ieff.**

Ptol·e·my (tol'ə·mē) 2nd-c. Gk. astronomer, mathematician, and geographer in Alexandria: full name **Claudius Ptol·e·mae·us** (tol'ə·mē'əs).

Puc·ci·ni (pōōt·chē'nē), **Giacomo,** 1858–1924, Ital. operatic composer.

Pu·las·ki (pōō·las'kē, pə-; *Polish* pōō·läs'kē), **Casimir,** 1748–1779, Polish general in the Amer. Revolution.

Pur·cell (pûr'səl), **Henry,** 1658?–95, Eng. composer.

Push·kin (pōōsh'kin), **Aleksander Sergeyevich,** 1799–1837, Russ. poet.

Py·thag·o·ras (pi·thag'ər·əs) 6th-c. B.C. Gk. philosopher and mathematician.

Rab·e·lais (rab'ə·lā, *Fr.* rà·ble'), **François,** 1494?–1553?, Fr. humorist and satirist: pseud. **Al·co·fri·bas Na·sier** (ál·kō·frē·bas' nä·zyã').

Rach·ma·ni·noff (räkʰ·mä'ni·nôf), **Sergei Vassilievich,** 1873–1943, Russ. pianist and composer.

Ra·cine (rà·sēn'), **Jean Baptiste,** 1639–99, Fr. dramatist.

Ra·leigh (rô'lē), **Sir Walter,** 1552–1618, Eng. courtier, colonizer, admiral, and poet; beheaded. Also *Brit.* **Ra'legh.**

Ram·e·ses II (ram'ə·sēz), 1292–1225 B.C., Egyptian king; allegedly the pharaoh who oppressed the Israelites. Also **Ram·ses II** (ram'sēz).

Ran·dolph (ran'dolf), **A(sa) Philip,** 1889–1979, U.S. labor leader.

Raph·a·el (raf'ē·əl, rä'fē-), 1483–1520, Ital. painter: full name **Raphael (or Raffaello) San·zio** (sän'tsyō).

Ra·vel (rà·vel'), **Maurice Joseph,** 1875–1937, Fr. composer.

Rea·gan (rā'gən), **Ronald Wilson,** born 1911, 40th president of the United States, 1981–.

Reed (rēd), **Walter,** 1851–1902, U.S. army surgeon.

Rem·brandt (rem'brant), 1606–69, Du. painter: full name **Rembrandt Harmenszoon van Rijn** (vän rīn) or **van Ryn.**

Re·noir (rə·nwàr'), **Pierre Auguste,** 1840–1919, Fr. Impressionist painter.

Re·vere (ri·vir'), **Paul,** 1735–1818, Amer. Revolutionary patriot and silversmith; famous for his ride the night of April 18, 1775, to warn of the approach of British troops.

Rhee (rē), **Syngman,** 1875–1965, Korean statesman; president of the Republic of Korea 1948–60.

Rhodes (rōdz), **Cecil John,** 1853–1902, Brit. colonial statesman, financier, and philanthropist, active in S. Africa.

Rich·ard I (rich'ərd), 1157–99, king of England 1189–99: called **the Lion-Heart.** Also called *Coeur de Lion.*

Richard III, 1452–85, duke of Gloucester, king of England 1483–85; killed at Bosworth Field: called **Crouch·back** (krouch'bak/).

Ri·che·lieu (rē·shə·lyœ'), **Duc de,** 1585–1642, Armand Jean du Plessis, Fr. cardinal and statesman: called **E·mi·nence Rouge** (ã·mē·näns' rōōzh').

Ril·ke (ril'kə), **Rainer Maria,** 1875–1926, Austrian poet born in Prague.

Rim·baud (ran·bō'), **Arthur,** 1854–91, Fr. poet: full name **Jean Nicholas Arthur Rimbaud.**

Rim·sky-kor·sa·kov (rim'skē·kôr'sə·kôf), **Nicholas An·dreievich,** 1844–1908, Russ. composer.

Ri·ve·ra (rē·vä'rä), **Diego,** 1886–1957, Mexican painter.

Robes·pierre (rōbz'pē·âr), 1758–94, Fr. Revolutionary leader; guillotined: full name **Maximilien François Marie Isidore de Robespierre:** called the **Incorruptible.**

Rock·e·fel·ler (rok'ə·fel'ər), **John D(avison),** 1839–1937, U.S. industrialist and philanthropist.

Ro·din (rō·dan'), **Auguste,** 1840–1917, Fr. sculptor.

Roent·gen (rent'gən, runt'-; *Ger.* rœnt'gən), **Wilhelm Kon·rad,** 1845–1923, Ger. physicist. Also **Rönt'gen.**

Rog·ers (roj'ərz), **Will,** 1879–1935, U.S. actor and humorist: full name **William Penn Adair Rogers.**

Roi So·leil (rwä sô·lã'), le see LOUIS XIV.

Rom·u·lo (rōm'yōō·lō), **Carlos Pena,** born 1899, Philippine statesman, general and writer.

Ron·sard (rôn·sàr'), **Pierre de,** 1524–85, Fr. poet.

Roo·se·velt (rō'zə·velt, rōz'velt, -vəlt), **(Anna) Eleanor,** 1884–1962, *née* Roosevelt, U.S. lecturer, writer, and diplomat; wife of Franklin Delano. — **Franklin Delano,** 1882–1945, U.S. statesman, 32nd president of the U.S. 1933–45. — **Theodore,** 1858–1919, U.S. army officer and statesman; 26th president of the U.S. 1901–09.

Ross (rôs), **Betsy,** 1752–1836, *née* Griscom, Amer. patriot; reputed to have made the first American flag.

Ros·si·ni (rôs·sē'nē), **Gioacchino Antonio,** 1792–1868, Ital. composer.

Roth·schild (rôth'chīld, *Ger.* rōt'shilt), **Mayer Anselm,** 1743–1812, founder of the worldwide banking enterprise **(House of Rothschild)** at Frankfort on the Main, Germany.

Rou·get de Lisle (roo·zhē' də lēl'), **Claude Joseph,** 1760–1836, Fr. army officer and composer; wrote the *Marseillaise,* 1792.

Rous·seau (rōō·sō'), **Henri,** 1844–1910, Fr. painter: called **le Dou·an·ier** (lə dwä·nyã') (the customs officer). — **Jean Jacques,** 1712–78, Fr. philosopher and author, born in Switzerland.

Ru·bens (rōō'bənz. *Flemish* rü'bəns), **Peter Paul,** 1577–1640, Flemish painter.

Rus·kin (rus'kin), **John,** 1819–1900, Eng. art critic and author.

Rus·sell (rus'əl), **Bertrand (Arthur William),** 1872–1970, 3rd Earl Russell, Eng. mathematician and philosopher.

Ruth (rōōth), **George Herman,** 1895–1948, U.S. baseball player: called **Babe Ruth.**

Ruth·er·ford (ruth'ər·fərd), **Sir Ernest,** 1871–1937, first Baron Rutherford, Brit. physicist born in New Zealand.

Sade (såd), **Comte Donatien Alphonse François de,** 1740–1814, Fr. novelist and libertine: called **Marquis de Sade.**

Sal·a·din (sal'ə·din), 1137?–93, sultan of Egypt and Syria, 1174?–93: full name **Sa·lah-al-Din Yusuf ibn-Ayyud** (sə·lä'ä·dēn').

Salk (sôk, sôlk), **Jonas,** born 1914, U.S. bacteriologist; developed injected vaccine for poliomyelitis.

Sand·burg (sand'bûrg, san'-), **Carl,** 1878–1967, U.S. poet and biographer.

Sang·er (sang'ər), **Margaret,** 1883–1966, *née* Higgins, U.S. leader in birth-control education.

San·ta·ya·na (sän'tä·yä'nä), **George,** 1863–1952, U.S. philosopher and author born in Spain.

Sap·pho (saf·ō) 6th-c. B.C. Gk. lyric poetess.

Sar·to (sär'tō), **Andrea del,** 1486–1531, Florentine painter: orig. name **Andrea d'Angelo di Fran·ces·co** (frän·ches'kō).

Sar·tre (sàr'tr'). **Jean Paul,** 1905–1980, Fr. philosopher, novelist, and dramatist.

Scar·lat·ti (skär·lät'tē), **Alessandro,** 1659–1725, and his son, **Domenico,** 1685–1757, Ital. composers.

Schil·ler (shil'ər), **Johann Christoph Friedrich von,** 1759–1805, Ger. poet and dramatist.

Schlie·mann (shlē'män), **Heinrich,** 1822–90, Ger. merchant and archaeologist.

Schön·berg (shoen'berkʰ), **Arnold,** 1874–1951, Austrian composer and conductor active in the U.S.

Scho·pen·hau·er (shō'pən·hou'ər), **Arthur,** 1788–1860, Ger. philosopher.

Schrö·ding·er (shroe'ding·ər), **Erwin,** 1887–1961, Austrian physicist.

Schu·bert (shōō'bərt), **Franz Peter,** 1797–1828, Austrian composer.

Schu·mann (shōō'män), **Robert,** 1810–56, Ger. composer.

Schwann (shvän), **Theodor,** 1810–82, Ger. physiologist.

Schweit·zer (shvī'tsər), **Albert,** 1875–1965, Fr. (Alsatian) clergyman, physician, missionary, philosopher, and musicologist; founder and director of the hospital at Lambaréné, Gabon.

Scott (skot), **Sir Walter,** 1771–1832, Scot. novelist and poet.

Se·go·via (sā·gō′vyä), Andrés, born 1893, Sp. classical guitarist.

Sen·e·ca (sen′ə·kə), **Lucius Annaeus,** 4? B.C.–A.D. 65, Roman Stoic philosopher, statesman and dramatist: called **Seneca the Younger.**

Shake·speare (shāk′spir), **William,** 1564–1616, Eng. poet and dramatist. Also **Shake′spere, Shak′speare, Shak′spere.**

Shaw (shô), **George Bernard,** 1856–1950, Brit. dramatist, critic, and novelist born in Ireland.

Shel·ley (shel′ē), **Mary Wollstonecraft,** 1797–1851, *née* Godwin, Eng. novelist; wife of Percy Bysshe. — **Percy Bysshe,** 1792–1822, Eng. poet.

Sher·man (shûr′mən), **William Tecumseh,** 1829–91, Union general in the Civil War.

Shos·ta·ko·vich (shos′tə·kō′vich), Dimitri, 1906–75, Soviet composer.

Si·be·li·us (si·bā′lē·əs, –bāl′yəs), **Jean,** 1865–1957, Finnish composer.

Sitting Bull, 1834?–90, Sioux Indian chief; won battle of Little Big Horn in 1876.

Sit·well (sit′wel, –wol), **Edith,** 1887–1964, Eng. poet.

Smith (smith), **Adam,** 1723–90, Scot. moralist and political economist. — **Alfred E(manuel),** 1873–1944, U.S. political leader. — **Captain John,** 1580–1631, Eng. adventurer; president of the Virginia colony 1608–1609. — **Joseph,** 1805–1844, founder and first prophet of the Mormon Church; assassinated.

Smuts (smuts), **Jan Christiaan,** 1870–1950, S. African general and statesman; prime minister 1919–24, 1939–48.

Soc·ra·tes (sok′rə·tēz), 469?–399 B.C., Gk. philosopher; forced to commit suicide by drinking hemlock.

Soph·o·cles (sof′ə·klēz), 496?–406 B.C., Athenian tragic poet.

Spal·lan·za·ni (späl′län·dzä′nē), **Lazzaro,** 1729–99, Ital. biologist.

Spen·cer (spen′sər), **Herbert,** 1820–1903, Eng. philosopher.

Speng·ler (speng′glər), **Oswald,** 1880–1936, Ger. philosopher and historian.

Spen·ser (spen′sər), **Edmund,** 1552?–99, Eng. poet.

Spi·no·za (spi·nō′zə), **Baruch,** 1632–77, Du. philosopher. Also **Benedict Spinoza.**

Sta·lin (stä′lin), **Joseph,** 1879–1953, Soviet statesman; chief of state 1924–53: orig. name *Iosif Vissarionovich Dzhugashvili.*

Stein (stīn), **Gertrude,** 1874–1946, U.S. writer active in France.

Sten·dhal (stań·dål′) Pseud. of *Marie Henri Beyle,* 1783–1842, Fr. novelist and critic.

Sterne (stûrn), **Laurence** 1713–68, Brit. novelist, born in Ireland.

Steu·ben (stōō′bən, *Ger.* shtoi′bən), **Baron Friedrich Wilhelm Ludolph Gerhard Augustin von,** 1730–94, Prussian general, served under Washington in the Amer. Revolutionary War.

Ste·ven·son (stē′vən·sən), **Adlai Ewing,** 1900–65, U.S. lawyer and political leader. — **Robert Louis (Balfour),** 1850–94, Scot. novelist and essayist active in the U.S. and Samoa.

Stowe (stō), **Harriet Beecher,** 1811–96, U.S. novelist and humanitarian: orig. name **Harriet Elizabeth Bee·cher** (bē′chər).

Stra·di·va·ri (strä′dē·vä′rē), **Antonio,** 1644?–1737, Ital. violinmaker. Also **Strad·i·var·i·us** (strad′i·vâr′ē·əs).

Strauss (strous), **Johann,** 1804–49, Austrian composer. — **Johann,** 1825–99, Austrian composer; son of Johann: called **the Waltz King.** — **Richard,** 1864–1949, Ger. composer.

Stra·vin·sky (strə·vin′skē), **Igor Fëdorovich,** 1882–1971, U.S. composer born in Russia.

Strind·berg (strind′bûrg), **August,** 1849–1912, Sw. dramatist and novelist.

Sul·li·van (sul′ə·vən), **Sir Arthur (Seymour),** 1842–1900, Eng. composer.

Sun Yat·sen (sŏon′ yät′sen′), 1866–1925, Chinese political leader; founder of the Kuomintang 1912.

Swift (swift), **Jonathan,** 1667–1745, Eng. clergyman, satirist, and man of letters born in Ireland: called **Dean Swift.**

Swin·burne (swin′bûrn), **Algernon Charles,** 1837–1909 Eng. poet and critic.

Tac·i·tus (tas′ə·təs), **Cornelius,** 55?–117?, Roman historian.

Taft (taft), **Robert Alphonso,** 1899–1953, U.S. legislator; son of William Howard. — **William Howard,** 1857–1930, U.S. statesman and jurist, 27th president of the U.S. 1909–13.

Tal·ley·rand-Pe·ri·gord (tä·le·räñ′pā·rē·gôr′), **Charles Maurice de,** 1754–1838, Prince de Bénévent, Fr. statesman and diplomat: often called **Tal·ley·rand** (tal′ē·rand).

Tam·er·lane (tam′ər·lān), 1336?–1405, Mogul conqueror: also called **Tam·bur·laine** (tam′bər·lān).

Tar·king·ton (tär′king·tən), **Booth,** 1869–1946, U.S. novelist: full name **Newton Booth Tarkington.**

Tay·lor (tā′lər), **Zachary,** 1784–1850, U.S. general, 12th president of the U.S. 1849–50: called **Old Rough and Ready.**

Tchai·kov·sky (chī·kof′skē), **Pëtr Ilich,** 1840–93, Russ. composer.

Tche·khov (chek′ôf), **Anton** See CHEKHOV.

Ten·ny·son (ten′ə·sən), **Alfred,** 1809–92, 1st Baron Tennyson, Eng. poet; poet laureate 1850–92: called **Alfred, Lord Tennyson.**

Ter·ence (ter′əns), 185?–159? B.C., Roman comic playwright born in Africa: full name **Publius Terentius A·fer** (ā′fər).

Thack·er·ay (thak′ə·rē), **William Makepeace,** 1811–63, Eng. author.

Thant (thont), U, 1909–74, Burmese statesman; secretary general of the United Nations 1961–71.

Thatch·er (thach′er), **Margaret Hilda,** born 1925, Brit. stateswoman; prime minister 1979–.

Tho·mas (tom′əs), **Dylan (Marlais),** 1914–53, Brit. poet and author born in Wales. — **Norman (Mattoon),** 1884–1968, U.S. socialist leader and writer.

Thomas à Becket, St., 1118–70, Eng. prelate; archbishop of Canterbury 1162–70; murdered for opposing Henry II; called **Saint Thomas Becket, Saint Thomas of London.**

Tho·reau (thôr′ō, thô′rō, thə·rō′), **Henry David,** 1817–62, U.S. author: orig. name **David Henry Thoreau.**

Thu·cyd·i·des (thōō·sid′ə·dēz, thyōō–), 471?–401? B.C., Gk. historian.

Til·lich (til′ik, –ikh), **Paul,** 1886–1965, Ger. Protestant theologian and philosopher active in the U.S.

Tin·to·ret·to (tin′tə·ret′ō, *Ital.* tēn′tō·ret′tō), 1518–94, Venetian painter: orig. name **Jacopo Ro·bus·ti** (rō·bōōs′tē).

Ti·tian (tish′ən), 1477?–1576, Venetian painter: orig. name **Ti·zia·no Ve·cel·lio** (tē·tsä′nō vā·chel′lyō).

Ti·to (tē′tō), **Marshal,** 1892–1980, Yugoslav Communist statesman and leader; prime minister 1945–53; president 1953–80: orig. name **Josip Broz.**

Tocque·ville (tōk·vēl′), **Alexis Charles Henri Maurice Clérel de,** 1805–59, Fr. statesman and political writer.

Tol·stoy (tōl′stoi, tol′–), **Count Leo Nikolaevich,** 1828–1910, Russ. novelist and social reformer. Also **Tol′stoi.**

Tor·que·ma·da (tôr′kwə·mä′də, *Sp.* tôr′kä·mä′thä), **Tomás de,** 1420?–98, Dominican monk; head of the Inquisition in Spain.

Tos·ca·ni·ni (tôs′kə·nē′nē; *Ital.* tôs′kä·nē′nē), **Arturo,** 1867–1957, Ital. orchestra conductor active in the U.S.

Tou·louse-Lau·trec (tōō·lōōz′lō·trek′), **Henri Marie Raymond de,** 1864–1901, Fr. painter and lithographer.

Tra·jan (trā′jən), 53?–117, Roman emperor 98–117: full name **Marcus Ulpius Tra·ja·nus** (trā·jā′nəs).

Trot·sky (trot′skē), **Leon,** 1879–1940, Russ. Revolutionist and Bolshevist leader; banished 1929; murdered: orig. name **Lev Davidovitch Bron·stein** (brun′shtīn).

Tru·deau (trōō·dō′), **Pierre Elliott,** born 1919, Canadian statesman; prime minister 1968–79, 1980–: full name **Joseph Phillippe Pierre Ives Elliotte Trudeau.**

Tru·man (trōō′mən), **Harry S,** 1884–1972, 33rd president of the U.S. 1945–53.

Tul·ly (tul′ē) See CICERO.

Tur·ge·nev (tŏŏr·gā′nyef), **Ivan Sergeyevich,** 1818–83, Russ. novelist. Also **Tur·ge′niev.**

Tut·ankh·a·men (tŏŏt′ängk·ä′min), 14th-c. B.C. Egyptian pharaoh. Also **Tut′ankh·a′mon.**

Twain (twān), **Mark** See MARK TWAIN.

Ty·ler (tī′lər), **John,** 1790–1862, 10th president of the U.S. 1841–45.

U·na·mu·no (ōō′nä·mōō′nō), **Miguel de,** 1864–1936, Sp. philosopher, novelist and poet.

U·rey (yŏŏr′ē), **Harold Clayton,** 1893–1981, U.S. chemist.

U·tril·lo (ōō·trē′lyō, ōō·tril·ō; *Fr.* ü·trē·lō′), **Maurice,** 1883–1955, Fr. painter.

Val·en·tine (val′ən·tīn), **St.** 3rd-c. Christian martyr.

Va·le·ra (və·ler′ə), **Eamon De** See DE VALERA.

Van Bu·ren (van byŏŏr′ən), **Martin** 1782–1862, 8th president of the U.S. 1837–{ 1.

Van Dyck (van dīk′), **Sir Anthony,** 1599–1641, Flemish painter active in England. Also **Van·dyke′.**

van Eyck (van īk′), **Jan,** 1385?–1440, Flemish painter.

van Gogh (van gō′, gōkh), **Vincent,** 1853–90, Du. painter.

Va·sa·ri (vä·zä′rē), **Giorgio,** 1511–74, Ital. painter, architect, and biographer of artists.

Veb·len (veb′lən), **Thorstein Bunde,** 1857–1929, U.S. economist and sociologist.

Ve·ga (vā′gə, *Sp.* bā′gä), **Lope de,** 1562–1635, Sp. dramatist and poet. Full name **Lope Félix de Vega Car·pio** (kär′pyō).

Ve·lás·quez (və·las′kwiz, *Sp.* bā·läth′käth), 1599–1660, Sp. painter: full name **Diego Rodriguez de Silva y Velásquez.** Also **Ve·láz·quez** (bä·läth′käth).

Ver·di (ver′dē), **Giuseppe,** 1813–1901, Ital. composer.

Ver·gil (vûr′jil) Anglicized name of **Publius Vergilius Ma·ro** (mâ′rō), 70–19 B.C., Roman epic poet. Also *Virgil.*

Ver·laine (ver·len′), **Paul,** 1844–96, Fr. poet.

Ver·meer (vər·mãr′), **Jan,** 1632–75, Du. painter. Also **Jan van der Meer van Delft** (vän dər mãr vän delft′).

Verne (vûrn, *Fr.* vern), **Jules,** 1828–1905, Fr. novelist.

Ve·ro·ne·se (vā′rō·nā′zā), **Paolo,** 1528–88, Venetian painter: orig. name **Paolo Ca·glia·ri** (kä′lyä·rē).

Ve·sa·li·us (vi·sā′lē·əs), **Andreas,** 1514–64, Belgian physician; founder of modern anatomy.

Ves·puc·ci (ves·pōōt′chē), **Amerigo,** 1451–1512, Ital. explorer for whom America was named.

Vic·to·ri·a (vik·tôr′ē·ə, -tō′rē·ə), 1819–1901, queen of England 1837–1901: full name **Alexandrina Victoria.**

Vin·ci (vēn′chē), **Leonardo da** See DA VINCI.

Vir·gil (vûr′jəl) See VERGIL.

Vi·val·di (vē·väl′dē), **Antonio,** 1675?–1743, Ital. violinist and composer: called **the Red Priest.**

Vol·taire (vol·tãr′; *Fr.* vôl·tãr′) Pseud. of *François Marie Arouet,* 1694–1778, Fr. author and philosopher.

Wag·ner (väg′nər), **Richard,** 1813–83, Ger. composer, poet, and critic: full name **Wilhelm Richard Wagner.**

Waks·man (waks′mən), **Selman Abraham,** 1888–1973, U.S. biochemist and microbiologist born in Russia.

Wald·heim (vält′hīm), **Kurt,** born 1918, Austrian statesman; secretary general of the United Nations 1972–1981.

War·ren (wôr′ən, wor′-), **Earl,** 1891–1974, U.S. administrator and jurist; chief justice of the Supreme Court 1953–1969.

Wash·ing·ton (wosh′ing·tən, wô′shing-), **Booker T**(**alia·ferro**), 1856–1915, U.S. educator. — **George,** 1732–99, Amer. Revolutionary patriot, general, and statesman; 1st president of the U.S. 1789–97.

Watt (wot), **James,** 1736–1819, Scot. inventor and engineer.

Web·ster (web′stər), **Daniel,** 1782–1852, U.S. statesman and orator. — **Noah,** 1758–1843, U.S. lexicographer.

Wel·ling·ton (wel′ing·tən), **Duke of,** 1769–1852, Arthur Wellesley, Brit. general and statesman born in Ireland; prime minister 1828–30: called **the Iron Duke.**

Wells (welz), **H**(**erbert**) **G**(**eorge**), 1866–1946, Eng. author.

Wes·ley (wes′lē, *Brit.* wez′lē), **John,** 1703–91, Eng. clergyman; founder of Methodism.

Whis·tler (hwis′lər), **James Abbott McNeill,** 1834–1903, U.S. painter and etcher, active in England.

White·head (hwīt′hed), **Alfred North,** 1861–1947, Eng. mathematician and philosopher active in the U.S.

Whit·man (hwit′mən), **Walt,** 1819–92, U.S. poet: full name **Walter Whitman.**

Whit·ney (hwit′nē), **Eli,** 1765–1825, U.S. inventor and manufacturer; devised the cotton gin.

Wie·ner (wē′nər), **Norbert,** 1894–1964, U.S. mathematician.

Wilde (wīld), **Oscar,** 1856–1900, Irish poet, dramatist, and novelist: full name **Oscar Fingal O'Flahertie Wills Wilde.**

Wil·kins (wil′kinz), **Roy,** 1901–1981, U.S. civil rights leader for Negroes.

Wil·liam I (wil′yəm), 1027?–87, Duke of Normandy; invaded England 1066; king of England 1066–87: called **William the Conqueror, William the Norman.**

Wil·liams (wil′yəms), **Roger,** 1603?–83, Eng. clergyman in New England; founded Rhode Island. — **Tennessee,** born 1916, U.S. playwright: orig. name **Thomas Lanier Williams.**

Wil·son (wil′sən), (**Thomas**) **Woodrow,** 1856–1924, U.S. educator and statesman; 28th president of the U.S. 1913–21.

Wind·sor (win′zər), **Duke of,** 1894–1972; King of England as *Edward VIII* 1936; abdicated.

Witt·gen·stein (wit′gən·stīn, *Ger.* vit′gen·shtīn), **Ludwig Joseph Johann,** 1889–1951, Brit. philosopher, born in Austria.

Words·worth (wûrdz′wûrth), **William,** 1770–1850, Eng. poet; laureate 1843–50.

Wren (ren), **Sir Christopher,** 1632–1723, Eng. architect.

Wright (rīt), **Frank Lloyd,** 1869–1959, U.S. architect. — **Orville,** 1871–1948, U.S. pioneer in aviation. — **Wilbur,** 1867–1912, U.S. pioneer in aviation; brother of Orville.

Wyc·liffe (wik′lif), **John,** 1324?–84, Eng. religious reformer; first translator of entire Bible into English. Also **Wyc′lif.**

Xa·vi·er (zā′vē·ər, zav′ē-), **Saint Francis,** 1506–52, Sp. Jesuit missionary in the orient; one of the founders of the society of Jesus: called **the Apostle of the Indies.**

Yeats (yāts), **William Butler,** 1865–1939, Irish poet, dramatist, and essayist.

Young (yung), **Brigham,** 1801–77, U.S. Mormon leader.

Za·ra·thus·tra (zä′rä·thōōs′trä, zar′ə·thōōs′trə) See ZORO-ASTER.

Zeng·er (zeng′ər), **John Peter,** 1697–1746, Amer. printer and newspaper publisher born in Germany; noted as the central figure in a lawsuit that helped establish the freedom of the press.

Ze·no of Elea (zē′nō) 5th c. B.C. Gk. philosopher.

Zeno the Stoic, died 264? B.C., Gk. philosopher; founder of the Stoic school.

Zo·la (zō′lə, zō·lä; *Fr.* zō·lä′), **Émile,** 1840–1902, Fr. novelist and journalist.

Zo·ro·as·ter (zō′rō·as′tər) 6th- or 7th-c. B.C. Iranian religious reformer; founder of Zoroastrianism. Also *Zarathustra.*

ABBREVIATIONS AND ACRONYMS

A or Å angstrom unit
A or A. ace; America(n)
a. or A. or A acre; alto; ampere; answer; are (metric measurement); area
AA or A.A. Alcoholics Anonymous; antiaircraft
A.A. Associate in Arts
AAA antiaircraft artillery
AAA or A.A.A. American Automobile Association
AAAS or A.A.A.S. American Association for the Advancement of Science
AAM air-to-air missile
A and M Agricultural and Mechanical (College)
A and R or A & R artists and repertory
AAU or A.A.U. Amateur Athletic Union
AAUP or A.A.U.P. American Association of University Professors
AAUW or A.A.U.W. American Association of University Women
ab. about
ab. or a.b. (times) at bat
AB Alberta (Canada)
A.B. Bachelor of Arts (L *Artium Baccalaureus*)
AB or A.B. able-bodied seaman
ABA or A.B.A. American Bar Association; American Basketball Association; American Booksellers Association; American Bankers Association
abbr. or abbrev. abbreviated; abbreviation
ABC American Broadcasting Company
abl. ablative
ABM antiballistic missile
Abp. or abp. archbishop
abr. abridged; abridgment
abs. absolute(ly)
abstr. abstract
abt. about
Ac actinium
AC or A.C. before Christ (L *ante Christum*)
AC or A.C. or a.c. alternating current
a/c or A/C account; account current
a.c. before meals (L *ante cibum*)
acad. academic; academy
acc. acceleration; account; accountant
acc. or accus. accusative
acct. account; accountant
ack. acknowledge; acknowledgment
ACLU or A.C.L.U. American Civil Liberties Union
ACM Association of Computing Machinery
ACP or A.C.P. American College of Physicians
ACS or A.C.S. American Chemical Society; American College of Surgeons
ACT or A.C.T. Australian Capital Territory
act. active
actg. acting
AD or A.D. active duty; assembly district; of the Christian era (L *anno Domini* in the year of our Lord)
ADA or A.D.A. Americans for Democratic Action
add. addenda; addition
addn. or addnl. additional
ad int. in the meantime (L *ad interim*)
adj. adjacent; adjective; adjutant
ad loc. at the place (L *ad locum*)
adm. or admin. administration; administrative
Adm. or ADM Admiral
ADP automatic data processing
adv. adverb; advertisement
ad val. according to value (L *ad valorem*)
advt. advertisement
AEC Atomic Energy Commission
AEF or A.E.F. American Expeditionary Force(s)
aeq. equal (L *aequales*)
aero. or aeron. aeronautical; aeronautics
aet. or aetat. at the age of; of age; aged (L *aetatis*)
AF Air Force

AF or A.F. or a.f. audio frequency
AF or AFr. Anglo-French
AFB Air Force Base
AFC automatic frequency control
AFC or A.F.C. American Football Conference
afft. affidavit
Alc. Airman, first class
AFL or A.F.L. American Football League
AFL-CIO American Federation of Labor and Congress of Industrial Organizations
Afr. Africa(n)
AFSCME or A.F.S.C.M.E. American Federation of State, County, and Municipal Employees
AFT or A.F.T. American Federation of Teachers
aft. afternoon
AFTRA or A.F.T.R.A. American Federation of Television and Radio Artists
Ag silver (L *argentum*)
Ag. or Ag August
A.G. Adjutant General; Attorney General
agcy. agency
agr. or agric. agricultural; agriculture
agt. agent
A.H. in the year of the Hegira (L *anno hegira*)
AI artificial intelligence
AID Agency for International Development
AK Alaska
a.k.a. also known as
AKC or A.K.C. American Kennel Club
Al aluminum
AL Alabama
AL or A.L. American League; American Legion
ALA or A.L.A. American Library Association
Ala. Alabama
Alas. Alaska
alc. alcohol
ald. alderman
alg. algebra
ALGOL algorithmic language
alk. alkali(ne)
alt. alternate; altitude; alto
alt. or alter. alteration(s)
Alta. Alberta (Canada)
alum. aluminum
Am americium
AM or A.M. or a.m. amplitude modulation; before noon (L *ante meridiem*)
Am. America(n)
A.M. Master of Arts (L *Artium Magister*)
AMA or A.M.A. American Medical Association
amb. ambassador
AMDG or A.M.D.G. to the greater glory of God (L *ad majorem Dei gloriam*)
amdt. amendment
AME or A.M.E. African Methodist Episcopal
Amer. America(n)
amp. amperage; ampere
amt. amount
AMVETS American Veterans of World War II and Korea
anal. analogous; analogy; analysis; analytic
anat. anatomical; anatomist; anatomy
anc. ancient
ann. annals; annual; annuity
anon. anonymous(ly)
ans. answer
ANSI American National Standards Institute
ant. antenna; antonym
Ant. Antarctica
ANTA American National Theatre and Academy
anthrop. anthropological; anthropology
antiq. antiquarian; antiquity

ANZAC or **A.N.Z.A.C.** Australian and New Zealand Army Corps
A/O or **a/o** account of
AP antipersonnel
AP or **A.P.** Associated Press
A/P account paid; accounts payable
ap. or **Ap.** apothecaries' (weight or measure)
Ap. Apostle
Ap. or **Ap** April
a.p. additional premium
APA or **A.P.A.** American Philological Association; American Philosophical Association; American Psychiatric Association; American Psychological Association
APB all points bulletin
API or **A.P.I.** American Petroleum Institute
APO Army Post Office
Apoc. Apocalypse; Apocrypha; Apocryphal
app. apparatus; appendix; apprentice
appl. applied
approx. approximate(ly)
appt. appoint; appointment
Apr. April
apt. apartment
Ar argon
AR Arkansas
A/R account receivable
ar. arrival; arrive(s)
Ar. Arabic
ARC or **A.R.C.** American Red Cross
arch. archaic; architect; architectural; architecture
archaeol. archaeology
archit. architecture
arith. arithmetic; arithmetical
Ariz. Arizona
Ark. Arkansas
arr. arranged; arrival; arrive(d)
art. article; artificial; artillery; artist
As arsenic
AS Anglo-Saxon; antisubmarine
ASCAP or **A.S.C.A.P.** American Society of Composers, Authors and Publishers
ASCII American Standard Code for Information Interchange
ASPCA or **A.S.P.C.A.** American Society for the Prevention of Cruelty to Animals
assn. association
assoc. associate; association
ASSR or **A.S.S.R.** Autonomous Soviet Socialist Republic
asst. assistant
ASTM American Society for Testing Materials
astrol. astrologer; astrological; astrology
astron. astronomer; astronomical; astronomy
A.S.V. American Standard Version (of the Bible)
At astatine
at. atomic
Atl. Atlantic
atm. atmosphere; atmospheric
at. no. atomic number
att. attached
att. or **attn.** attention
att. or **atty.** attorney
Att. Gen. or **Atty. Gen.** Attorney General
attrib. attributive(ly)
ATV all-terrain vehicle
at. wt. atomic weight
Au gold (L *aurum*)
aud. audit; auditor
Aug. August
AUS Army of the United States
Aust. Austria(n)
auth. authentic; author; authority; authorized
auto. automatic; automobile; automotive
aux. or **auxil.** auxiliary
A/V according to value (L *ad valorem*)
A/V or **A-V** or **AV** or **A.V.** audiovisual

av. avenue; average; avoirdupois
A.V. Authorized Version (of the Bible)
avdp. avoirdupois
ave. avenue
avg. average
A/W actual weight
awol or **AWOL** absent without leave
ax. axiom
AZ Arizona
az. azimuth

B bishop; boron
b. or **B.** bachelor; base; baseman; bass; basso; book; born
B. bacillus; Bible; British
Ba barium
B.A. Bachelor of Arts; British Academy; Buenos Aires
bal. balance
b and w black and white
Bap. or **Bapt.** Baptist
bar. barometer; barometric
Bar. Baruch
Bart. Baronet
BASIC beginner's all-purpose symbolic instruction code
bb ball bearing; base on balls
B.B.A. Bachelor of Business Administration
BBB or **B.B.B.** Better Business Bureau
BBC British Broadcasting Corporation
bbl. barrel
BC or **B.C.** before Christ; British Columbia (Canada)
B.C. Bachelor of Commerce
bcd binary-coded decimal
BCE or **B.C.E.** before the Common Era
B.C.S. Bachelor of Commercial Science
B/D or **B.D.** bank draft; bills discounted; brought down
bd. board; bond; bound
B.D. Bachelor of Divinity
bd. ft. board foot
bdl. or **bdle.** bundle
bdrm. bedroom
Be beryllium
B/E or **B.E.** bill of exchange
B.E. Bachelor of Engineering; Board of Education
bef. before
BEF or **B.E.F.** British Expeditionary Force(s)
Belg. Belgian; Belgium
bet. between
BeV or **Bev** or **bev** billion electron volts
bf or **bf.** or **b.f.** boldface
B/F brought forward
B.F.A. Bachelor of Fine Arts
BG Brigadier General
bg. bag
bhd. bulkhead
bhp or **b.hp** brake horsepower
Bi bismuth
Bib. Bible
Bib. or **Bibl.** Biblical
bibl. or **bibliog.** bibliographer; bibliographical; bibliography
b.i.d. twice a day (L *bis in die*)
biog. biographer; biographical; biography
biol. biologic(al); biologist; biology
Bk berkelium
bk. bank; book
bkg. banking
bkgd. background
bkpg. bookkeeping
bks. barracks
bkt. basket; bracket
bl. bale; barrel; black; block; blue
B/L bill of lading
bldg. building
bldr. builder
blk. black; block; bulk

B.L.S. Bachelor of Library Science
BLT bacon, lettuce, and tomato (sandwich)
blvd. boulevard
BM basal metabolism; bowel movement
BMR basal metabolism rate
bn. or **Bn.** battalion
BO or **B.O.** body odor; box office
b.o. or **B.O.** or **BO** branch office; broker's order; buyer's option
Bol. Bolivia
BOQ bachelor officers' quarters
bor. borough
bot. botanical; botanist; botany; bottle
BP or **B.P.** blood pressure; British Pharmacopoeia
B/P or **BP** or **B.P.** or **b.p.** bills payable
bp. bishop
bp. or **bpl.** birthplace
b.p. boiling point
bpi bits per inch; bytes per inch
BPOE or **B.P.O.E.** Benevolent and Protective Order of Elks
bps bits per second; bytes per second
Br bromine
B/R or **b.r.** bills receivable
br. branch; brass; brown
Br. Britain; British; Brother
brig. brigade; brigadier
Brig. Gen. Brigadier General
Brit. Britain; British
bro. brother
bros. brothers
b.s. or **B.S.** balance sheet; bill of sale
B.S. or **B.Sc.** Bachelor of Science
BSA or **B.S.A.** Boy Scouts of America
bsh. bushel
bskt. basket
Bt. Baronet
btry. battery
Btu or **BTU** British thermal unit
bu. bushel
Bulg. Bulgaria(n)
bull. bulletin
bur. or **bu.** bureau
bus. business
BV or **B.V.** Blessed Virgin
Bvt. Brevet
BW black and white
B.W.I. British West Indies
BX base exchange
bx. box

C carbon
C or **C.** Celsius; centigrade; coulomb
c. or **C.** carat; cent; century; chapter; circa; copy; copyright; cup
C. Cape; Catholic; Church; City; Corps; Court
ca or **ca.** centiare
Ca calcium
CA California
ca. circa
C.A. chartered accountant; chief accountant; chronological age
CAB Civil Aeronautics Board
CAD Computer-Aided Design
CAD/CAM Computer-Aided Design/Computer-Aided Manufacturing
CAF or **C.A.F.** cost and freight
CAI computer-aided instruction
cal. calendar; caliber; calorie
Cal. or **Calif.** California
calc. calculate(d)
can. canon; canto
can. or **canc.** cancel(ed); cancellation
Can. or **Canad.** Canada; Canadian
C and W country and western

Cant. Canticle of Canticles; Cantonese
CAP Civil Air Patrol
cap. capacity; capital city; capitalize(d); capital letter
caps capital letters; capsule
Capt. or **CAPT** Captain
car. carat
Card. Cardinal
CARE Cooperative for American Relief Everywhere, Inc.
CAT clear air turbulence
cat. catalog
cath. cathedral; cathode
Cath. Catholic
CATV community antenna television
cav. cavalry
Cb columbium
CB citizens band
CBC Canadian Broadcasting Corporation
C.B.D. or **c.b.d.** cash before delivery
CBS Columbia Broadcasting System
C.B.W. chemical and biological warfare
cc or **cc.** cubic centimeter
cc or **c.c.** or **CC** or **C.C.** carbon copy
cc. chapters
CCC Civilian Conservation Corps; Commodity Credit Corporation
CCTV closed-circuit television
ccw or **cckw** counterclockwise
Cd cadmium
CD or **C.D.** Civil Defense
C/D or **CD** or **C.D.** certificate of deposit
cd. cord
c.d. cash discount
CDR Commander
Ce cerium
C.E. Chemical Engineer; Civil Engineer; Common Era; Corps of Engineers
CEA Council of Economic Advisors
CEC Commodity Exchange Commission
cen. or **cent.** central; century
cent. centigrade
CEO chief executive officer
cert. or **certif.** certificate; certification; certified; certify
CETA Comprehensive Employment and Training Act
Cf californium
C/F or **c/f** or **C.F.** or **c.f.** carried forward
cf. compare (L *confer*)
C.F. or **c.f.** cost and freight
C.F.I. or **c.f.i.** cost, freight, and insurance
CFL or **C.F.L.** Canadian Football League
cg or **cg.** centigram
c.g. center of gravity
C.G. Coast Guard; Commanding General; Consul General
cgs or **CGS** centimeter-gram-second
ch. or **Ch.** chain (measurement); champion; (television) channel; chaplain; chapter; child(ren); church
C.H. clearing-house; courthouse; customhouse
Chanc. Chancellor; Chancery
chap. chapter
chem. chemical; chemist; chemistry
chg. change; charge
Chin. China; Chinese
chm. chairman
chron. or **chronol.** chronicle; chronological; chronology
Chron. Chronicles
C.I. certificate of insurance; cost and insurance
Cia Company (Sp. *Compañía*)
CIA Central Intelligence Agency
CID or **C.I.D.** Criminal Investigation Department (of Scotland Yard)
Cie Company (F *Compagnie*)
C.I.F. cost, insurance, and freight
C. in C. Commander in Chief
cir. or **circ.** circa; circular; circulation

circum. or **cir.** or **circ.** circumference
cit. citation; cited; citizen
civ. civil; civilian
CJ or **C.J.** Chief Justice
ck. cask; check
cl or **cl.** centiliter
Cl chlorine
cl. class; classification; clause; clearance; clerk
c.l. carload; civil law; common law
cld. called; cleared
clk. clerk
clo. clothing
clr. clear
CLU or **C.L.U.** Chartered Life Underwriter; Civil Liberties Union
cm or **cm.** centimeter
cm² or **cm.²** square centimeter
cm³ or **cm.³** cubic centimeter
Cm curium
cmdg. commanding
Cmdr. Commander
cml. commercial
C/N or **CN** circular note; credit note
CNO Chief of Naval Operations
CNS or **C.N.S.** central nervous system
Co cobalt
CO Colorado
CO or **C.O.** Commanding Officer; conscientious objector
c/o care of
C/O or **c/o** or **C.O.** or **c.o.** cash order; carried over
Co. or **co.** company; county
COBOL common business oriented language
COD or **C.O.D.** or **c.o.d.** cash on delivery; collect on delivery
C. of C. Chamber of Commerce
C. of S. Chief of Staff
cog. cognate
COL Colonel
COL or **C.O.L.** cost of living
col. colonial; colony; color(ed); column
col. or **coll.** collect(ed); college; collegiate
Col. Colonel; Colorado; Colossians
collat. or **coll.** collateral
colloq. or **coll.** colloquial
Colo. Colorado
com. or **comm.** command; commander; commerce; commercial; commission; committee; common
Com. Commander; Commission; Commissioner; Committee; Commonwealth
comb. combination; combining
comdg. commanding
Comdr. Commander
coml. commercial
comp. compilation; compiled; compiler; complete; composition; compositor; compound
comp. or **compar.** comparative
Comdt. Commandant
Con. Consul
conc. concentrated
conf. conference
Confed. Confederate; Confederation
Cong. Congregational; Congress; Congressional
conj. conjugation; conjunction
Conn. Connecticut
cons. consonant
Cons. Constable; Consul
consol. consolidated
const. constant
const. or **constr.** construction
Const. Constable; Constitution(al)
cont. containing; contents; continent; continental; continue(d); contract; contraction; control
contd. continued
contemp. contemporary

contg. containing
contr. contract; contraction; contralto
contrib. contribution; contributor
CONUS continental United States
coop. cooperative
cop. or **copr.** copyright
cor. corner; corpus
cor. or **corr.** correct(ed); correction; correspond; correspondence; correspondent; corresponding
Cor. Corinthians; Coroner
CORE Congress of Racial Equality
corp. or **corpn.** corporation
C.O.S. cash on shipment; Chief of Staff
cp. compare; coupon
c.p. candlepower; chemically pure
C.P. Command Post; Common Prayer; Communist Party
CPA or **C.P.A.** Certified Public Accountant
cpd. compound
CPFF cost plus fixed fee
cpi characters per inch
CPI Consumer Price Index
Cpl. or **CPL** Corporal
CP/M control program for microcomputers
CPO Chief Petty Officer
CPR cardiopulmonary resuscitation
cps or **c.p.s.** cycles per second; characters per second
CPT Captain
CPU central processing unit
CQ charge of quarters
Cr chromium
cr. credit; creditor; crown
CRC Civil Rights Commission
cres. or **cresc.** crescendo
crit. critic; critical; criticism
CRT cathode ray tube
cryst. crystalline
Cs cesium
C/S cycles per second
cs. case
c.s. capital stock
C.S. Chief of Staff; Christian Science; Christian Scientist; Civil Service; county seat
C.S.A. Confederate States of America
CSC Civil Service Commission
CST or **C.S.T.** or **c.s.t.** Central Standard Time
CT or **C.T.** or **c.t.** Central Time
ct. carat; cent
Ct. or **CT** Connecticut
Ct. or **ct.** count; county; court
ctf. certificate
ctg. or **ctge.** cartage
ctn. carton
ctr. center
Cu copper (L *cuprum*)
cu. cubic
cum. cumulative
cur. currency; current
cw clockwise
CWO Chief Warrant Officer
C.W.O. or **c.w.o.** cash without order
cwt. hundredweight
cyc. or **cycl.** cyclopedia
cyl. cylinder
CYO or **C.Y.O.** Catholic Youth Organization
C.Z. or **CZ** Canal Zone

d *Brit.* penny (L *denarius*)
D or **D.** December
d. or **D.** date; daughter; day; deceased; degree; diameter; died; dose; drachma
D. Democrat(ic); Doctor (in academic degrees); Dutch
D/A or **D.A.** days after acceptance; deposit account
D.A. Department of Agriculture; District Attorney; Doctor of Arts; doesn't (or don't) answer

dag or **dag.** dekagram
dal or **dal.** dekaliter
dam or **dam.** dekameter
dam² or **dam.²** square dekameter
dam³ or **dam.³** cubic dekameter
Dan. Daniel; Danish
DAR or **D.A.R.** Daughters of the American Revolution
DAT Differential Aptitude Test
dat. dative
dau. daughter
db or **dB** decibel
D.B. Bachelor of Divinity
d.b.a. doing business as
dbl. double
DC or **D.C.** District of Columbia
DC or **D.C.** or **d.c.** direct current
D.C. Doctor of Chiropractic; from the beginning (Ital. *da capo*)
D/D or **DD** or **D.D.** days after date; demand draft
DD or **D.D.** dishonorable discharge; Doctor of Divinity
D.D.S. Doctor of Dental Science; Doctor of Dental Surgery
DDT dichlorodiphenyltrichloroethane
DDVP dichlorvos (dimethyldichlorovinyl phosphate)
DE Delaware
deb. debenture
dec. deceased; decorated; decrescendo
Dec. December
decl. declension
def. defendant; defense; definite; definition
deg. degree
del. delegate; delegation
del. or **dely.** delivery
Del. Delaware
Dem. Democrat; Democratic
Den. Denmark
dent. dental; dentist; dentistry
dep. or **Dep.** depart; departure; deposit; depot; deputy
depr. depreciation
dept. or **Dept.** department
der. or **deriv.** derivation; derivative; derive(d)
det. detached
Deut. Deuteronomy
dev. deviation
DEW Distant Early Warning (Line)
DF or **D.F.** damage free; direction finder
DFC Distinguished Flying Cross
DFM Distinguished Flying Medal
dg or **dg.** decigram
D.G. by the grace of God (L *Dei gratia*); Director General
DH designated hitter
dia. diameter
diag. diagonal; diagram
dial. dialect; dialectal; dialectic(al)
diam. diameter
dict. dictation; dictionary
diff. or **dif.** difference; different
dig. digest
dil. dilute
dim. dimension; diminished; diminuendo; diminutive
dipl. diplomat(ic)
dir. or **Dir.** director
disc. discount
dist. distance; district
distn. distillation
distr. distribute; distribution; distributor
div. divided; dividend; division; divisor; divorced
DJ or **D.J.** disk jockey; District Judge; Doctor of Laws (L *Doctor Juris*)
dk. dark; deck; dock
dkg or **dkg.** dekagram
dkl or **dkl.** dekaliter
dkm or **dkm.** dekameter
dkm² or **dkm.²** square dekameter

dkm³ or **dkm.³** cubic dekameter
dl or **dl.** deciliter
D.Lit. or **D.Litt.** Doctor of Letters; Doctor of Literature (L *Doctor Litterarum*)
DLO Dead Letter Office
dlr. dealer
dlvy. delivery
dm or **dm.** decimeter
dm² or **dm.²** square decimeter
dm³ or **dm.³** cubic decimeter
DM Deutsche mark
D.M.D. Doctor of Dental Medicine
DMZ demilitarized zone
dn. down
DNA deoxyribonucleic acid
do. ditto
D.O. Doctor of Osteopathy
DOA or **D.O.A.** dead on arrival
DOB or **D.O.B.** or **d.o.b.** date of birth
doc. document
DOD Department of Defense
DOE Department of Energy
dol. dollar
dom. domestic; dominant; dominion
DOS disk operating system
DOT Department of Transportation
doz. dozen
DP or **D.P.** data processing; dew point; displaced person
D.P.H. Doctor of Public Health
dpt. department
DR or **D.R.** dead reckoning; dining room
dr. debit; debtor; drachma; dram; drum
Dr. Doctor; Drive
D.S. or **d.s.** days after sight; document signed; repeat from the sign (Ital. *dal segno*)
DSC Distinguished Service Cross
D.S.C. Doctor of Surgical Chiropody
DSM Distinguished Service Medal
DSO Distinguished Service Order
d.s.p. died without issue (L *decessit sine prole*)
DST or **D.S.T.** or **d.s.t.** Daylight Saving Time
D.S.T. Doctor of Sacred Theology
Du. Duke; Dutch
dup. duplex; duplicate
D.V. God willing (L *Deo volente*); Douay Version (of the Bible)
D.V.M. Doctor of Veterinary Medicine
dwt. pennyweight (*d* < L *denarius*)
DX distance
Dy dysprosium
dz. dozen

e electron
E energy; excellent
E or **E.** Earth; east(ern); English
e. or **E.** eldest; engineer(ing); error
ea. each
E. & O.E. errors and omissions excepted
EBCDIC extended binary coded decimal interchange code
E by N east by north
E by S east by south
eccl. or **eccles.** ecclesiastic(al)
Eccles. Ecclesiastes
Ecclus. Ecclesiasticus
ECG electrocardiogram
ECM or **E.C.M.** European Common Market
ecol. ecological; ecology
econ. economics; economist; economy
Ecua. Ecuador
ED or **E.D.** Election District
ed. edited; edition; editor; education
EDA Economic Development Administration
EDP electronic data processing
EDT or **E.D.T.** or **e.d.t.** Eastern Daylight Time

educ. education; educational
EE Early English
E.E. Electrical Engineer
EEC or **E.E.C.** European Economic Community
EEG electroencephalogram
EENT eye, ear, nose, and throat
EEO equal employment opportunity
EEOC Equal Employment Opportunity Commission
eff. efficiency
EFT or **E.F.T.** electronic funds transfer
Eg. Egypt(ian)
e.g. for example (L *exempli gratia*)
Egypt. Egyptian
EHF extremely high frequency
EHS Environmental Health Service
EKG electrocardiogram
el. elevation
elec. or **elect.** electric; electrical; electrician; electricity
elem. element; elementary
elev. elevation
ELF extremely low frequency
EM enlisted man
emer. emeritus
emf or **EMF** electromotive force
Emp. Emperor; Empire; Empress
emu or **EMU** electromagnetic unit
enc. or **encl.** enclosed; enclosure
ency. or **encyc.** or **encycl.** encyclopedia
ENE east-northeast
eng. engine; engineer; engineering
Eng. England; English
engr. engineer; engraved; engraver; engraving
enl. enlarge(d); enlisted
Ens. or **ENS** Ensign
entom. or **entomol.** entomological; entomology
env. envelope
EOM or **E.O.M.** or **e.o.m.** end of the month
EPA Environmental Protection Agency
Eph. Ephesians
Episc. Episcopal(ian)
EPROM erasable programmable read only memory
eq. equal; equation
eq. or **equiv.** equivalent
equip. equipment
Er erbium
ERA Equal Rights Amendment
ERIC Educational Resources Information Center
erron. erroneous(ly)
E.R.V. English Revised Version (of the Bible)
Es einsteinium
Esd. Esdras
ESE east-southeast
Esk. Eskimo
ESL English as a second language
ESP extrasensory perception
esp. especially
Esq. or **Esqr.** Esquire
EST or **E.S.T.** or **e.s.t.** Eastern Standard Time
est. estate; estimate; estimated
est. or **estab.** established
Esth. Esther
ET or **E.T.** or **e.t.** Eastern Time
ETA estimated time of arrival
et al. and others (L *et alii*)
etc. et cetera (L, and the rest, and so on)
ETD estimated time of departure
et seq. and the following (L *et sequens*)
ETV educational television
ety. or **etym.** etymological; etymology
Eu europlum
Eur. Europe(an)
eV or **ev** or **ev.** electron volt
EVA extravehicular activity
evap. evaporate
evg. evening

EW enlisted woman
ex. example; except(ed); exception; exchange; executive; express; extra
Ex. Exodus
exam. examination; examiner
exc. excellent; except; exception; excursion
exch. exchange; exchanged; exchequer
excl. exclamation; excluding; exclusive
exec. executive
exec. or **exor.** executor
Exod. Exodus
exp. expenses; expired; export; exporter; express
expt. experiment
exptl. experimental
expwy. expressway
ext. extension; exterior; external(ly); extinct; extra; extract
Ezech. Ezechiel
Ezek. Ezekiel

f focal length; forte; function
f or **F** farad
F fluorine
F or **F.** Fahrenheit; false; February; French; Friday
f. folio; following (page, etc.)
f. or **F.** or **F** family; female; feminine; franc; frequency
f/ f number
FAA Federal Aviation Agency
fac. facsimile; factor; factory; faculty
FADM Fleet Admiral
FAO Food and Agriculture Organization (of the United Nations)
FAS Foreign Agricultural Service
F.A.S. or **f.a.s.** free alongside ship
fasc. fascicle
fath. fathom
f.b. or **fb.** freight bill
FBI Federal Bureau of Investigation
FCA Farm Credit Administration
FCC Federal Communications Commission
fcp. foolscap
fcy. fancy
FD or **F.D.** Fire Department
FDA Food and Drug Administration
FDIC Federal Deposit Insurance Corporation
FDPC Federal Data Processing Centers
Fe iron (L *ferrum*)
FEA Federal Energy Administration
Feb. February
fec. he (or she) made it (L *fecit*)
fed. or **Fed.** federal; federated; federation
fedn. or **Fedn.** federation
fem. female; feminine
FEPC Fair Employment Practices Committee
FET or **F.E.T.** Federal Excise Tax
ff fortissimo
ff. folios; following (pages, etc.)
FHA Federal Housing Administration
FIC Federal Information Centers
FICA Federal Insurance Contribution Act
FIFO first in, first out
fig. figurative(ly); figure
fin. finance; financial; finish
Fin. Finland
Fin. or **Finn.** Finnish
F.I.O. free in and out
1st Lt. First Lieutenant
FL Florida
fl. floor; florin; flourished (L *floruit*); fluid
Fla. Florida
fl. dr. fluid dram
Flem. Flemish
fl. oz. fluid ounce
Fm fermium
FM or **F.M.** or **f.m.** frequency modulation

fm. fathom
fn. footnote
fo. folio
F.O. field office; field order; Flight Officer; Foreign Office; forward observer
F.O.B. or **f.o.b.** free on board
fol. folio
fol. or **foll.** following
for. foreign; forester; forestry
F.O.R. free on rails
FORTRAN Formula translator
F.O.S. free on steamer
F.O.T. free on truck
FP or **F.P.** or **f.p.** or **fp** foot-pound; freezing point
FPC Federal Power Commission
FPC or **F.P.C.** or **f.p.c.** fish protein concentrate
fpm or **f.p.m.** feet per minute
FPO field post office; Fleet Post Office
fps or **FPS** foot-pound-second
fps or **f.p.s.** feet per second
Fr francium
fr. fragment; franc; from
Fr. Father; France; French; Friar; Friday
freq. frequency; frequent(ly)
Fri. Friday
front. frontispiece
FRS Federal Reserve System
frt. freight
frwy. freeway
FSLIC Federal Savings and Loan Insurance Corporation
ft. foot; feet
ft.² square foot
ft.³ cubic foot
Ft. Fort
FTC Federal Trade Commission
ft.-lb. or **ft-lb** foot-pound
fur. furlong
fut. future
fwd. forward
FWD four-wheel drive
FY or **F.Y.** fiscal year
FYI or **F.Y.I.** for your information

g or **g.** acceleration due to gravity; gauge; gram
G good
G or **G.** German
Ga gallium
GA or **G.A.** General Agent; General Assembly; general average; General of the Army
ga. gauge
Ga. or **GA** Georgia
Gael. Gaelic
gal. gallon
Gal. Galatians
galv. galvanized
GAO General Accounting Office
GAR or **G.A.R.** Grand Army of the Republic
gar. garage
GATT General Agreement on Tariffs and Trade
GAW or **G.A.W.** guaranteed annual wage
gaz. gazette; gazetteer
G.B. Great Britain
GCA ground-controlled approach
g.c.d. greatest common divisor
GCT or **G.C.T.** or **G.c.t.** Greenwich civil time
Gd gadolinium
gd. good; guard
gds. goods
Ge germanium
gen. gender; genus
gen. or **genit.** genitive
gen. or **genl.** general
Gen. General; Genesis
Gen AF General of the Air Force

geog. geographer; geographic(al); geography
geol. geologic(al); geologist; geology
geom. geometric(al); geometry
ger. gerund
Ger. German; Germany
GHQ general headquarters
GHz gigahertz
GI or **G.I.** galvanized iron; gastrointestinal; general issue; government issue
gi. gill
GIGO garbage in, garbage out
Gk. Greek
gm or **gm.** gram
GM guided missile
G.M. General Manager; Grand Master
Gmc. Germanic
GMT or **G.M.T.** or **G.m.t.** Greenwich mean time
GNP gross national product
GO general order
GOP or **G.O.P.** Grand Old Party (Republican Party)
Goth. Gothic
gov. or **govt.** government
Gov. Governor
gp. group
G.P. general practitioner
GPO general post office; Government Printing Office
GQ general quarters
gr. or **gr** grade; grain; gram; gravity; gross; group
Gr. Greece; Greek
grad. graduate; graduated
gram. grammar; grammatical
Gr. Brit. Great Britain
GRE Graduate Record Exam
gro. gross
gr. wt. gross weight
GSA General Services Administration
GSA or **G.S.A.** Girl Scouts of America
GT or **G.T.** gross ton
gt. a drop (L *gutta*); great
Gt. Brit. Great Britain
gtd. guaranteed
gtt. drops (L *guttae*)
GU Guam
guar. guaranteed
gyn. gynecology
Gy. Sgt. Gunnery Sergeant

H henry; hydrogen
h. or **H.** or **H** harbor; hard; hardness; height; high; hit; hot; hour; humidity; husband
ha or **ha.** hectare
Hab. Habakkuk
Hag. Haggai
Hb hemoglobin
H.B.M. Her (or His) Britannic Majesty
h.c. with due respect (L *honoris causa* for the sake of honor)
H.C. Holy Communion; House of Commons
h.c.f. highest common factor
HCL or **H.C.L.** or **h.c.l.** high cost of living
HD or **H.D.** or **h.d.** heavy duty
hd. hand; head
hdbk. handbook
hdkf. handkerchief
hdwe. hardware
He helium
HE high explosive
H.E. His Eminence; His (or Her) Excellency
Heb. or **Hebr.** Hebrew; Hebrews
HEW Department of Health, Education, and Welfare
hex. hexagon; hexagonal
Hf hafnium
HF high frequency
hf. half
hg or **hg.** hectogram

Hg mercury (L *hydrargyrum* water silver)
HG High German
hgt. height
hgwy. highway
H.H. Her (or His) Highness; His Holiness
hhd. hogshead
HHFA Housing and Home Finance Agency
HI Hawaii
Hind. Hindi; Hindustani
hist. historian; historical; history
HJ or **H.J.** here lies (L *hic jacet*)
hl or **hl.** hectoliter
H.L. House of Lords
hm or **hm.** hectometer
H.M. Her (or His) Majesty
H.M.S. Her (or His) Majesty's Ship
H.N. head nurse
Ho holmium
hon. or **Hon.** honorable; honorary
HOPE Health Opportunity for People Everywhere
hor. horizon; horizontal
horol. horology
hort. horticultural; horticulture
Hos. Hosea
hosp. hospital
HP or **H.P.** or **hp** or **h.p.** high pressure; horsepower
HQ headquarters
hr. hour
H.R. House of Representatives
H.R.H. Her (or His) Royal Highness
hrzn. horizon
HS or **H.S.** High School
HST hypersonic transport
HST or **H.S.T.** or **H.s.t.** Hawaiian Standard Time
ht. height
H.T. high-tension; high tide
Hts. Heights
HUD Department of Housing and Urban Development
Hung. Hungarian; Hungary
H.V. or **h.v.** high velocity; high voltage
hvy. heavy
hwy. highway
hyp. hypotenuse
hyp. or **hypoth.** hypothesis; hypothetical
Hz hertz

I iodine
I. Island; Isle
Ia. or **IA** Iowa
ibid. or **ib.** in the same place (L *ibidem*)
IC or **I.C.** integrated circuit
ICBM intercontinental ballistic missile
ICC Interstate Commerce Commission
Ice. or **Icel.** Iceland(ic)
ICJ International Court of Justice
ICU intensive-care unit
ID Idaho
ID or **I.D.** identification
id. the same (L *idem*)
i.d. inside diameter
Ida. Idaho
IE Indo-European
i.e. that is (L *id est*)
I.E. Industrial Engineer
IF intermediate frequency
I.G. association; trust (G *interessengemeinschaft*)
IGY International Geophysical Year
IHP indicated horsepower
IHS symbol and monogram for Jesus, derived from the Greek IH ((ΣΟΥ) Σ, Jesus
IL Illinois
ILGWU or **I.L.G.W.U.** International Ladies' Garment Workers' Union
ill. or **illus.** or **illust.** illustrated; illustration; illustrator
Ill. Illinois

ILS instrument landing system
IMF or **I.M.F.** International Monetary Fund
imit. imitative
imp. imperial; import(ed); important
imp. or **imper.** imperative
imp. or **imperf.** imperfect
In indium
IN Indiana
in. inch
in.² square inch
in.³ cubic inch
inc. increase
Inc. or **inc.** incorporated
incl. including; inclusive
incog. incognito
incr. increase(d); increasing
ind. independence; independent; index; industrial; industry
Ind. Indian; Indiana
indic. indicative
inf. below (L *infra*); infantry; inferior; information
inf. or **infin.** infinitive
infl. influence(d)
init. initial
INP International News Photo
I.N.R.I. Jesus of Nazareth, King of the Jews (L *Iesus Nazarenus, Rex Iudaeorum*)
ins. inches; insurance
insol. insoluble
insp. inspected; inspector
Insp. Gen. Inspector General
inst. instant
Inst. or **inst.** institute; institution
instr. instructor; instrument; instrumental
int. interest; interior; internal; international; intransitive
inter. intermediate; interrogation; interrogative
interj. interjection
internat. international
INTERPOL International Criminal Police Organization
interrog. interrogative
intl. or **intnl.** international
intr. or **intrans.** intransitive
intro. or **introd.** introduction; introductory
inv. invoice
I/O input/output
IOOF or **I.O.O.F.** Independent Order of Odd Fellows
IOU or **I.O.U.** I owe you
IP innings pitched
IPA International Phonetic Alphabet
ips or **i.p.s.** inches per second
IQ or **I.Q.** intelligence quotient
i.q. the same as (L *idem quod*)
Ir iridium
IR or **I.R.** information retrieval
Ir. Irish
IRA or **I.R.A.** individual retirement account; Irish Republican Army
IRBM intermediate range ballistic missile
Ire. Ireland
IRO International Refugee Organization
irreg. irregular(ly)
IRS Internal Revenue Service
IS or **I.S.** Intermediate School
Is. or **is.** or **Isl.** or **isl.** island; isle
Isa. Isaiah
ISBN International Standard Book Number
Isr. Israel(i)
ital. italic(s); italicized
Ital. or **It.** Italian; Italy
ITV instructional television
IUD intrauterine device
IV or **I.V.** or **i.v.** intravenous
IWW or **I.W.W.** Industrial Workers of the World

J or **j** joule
J or **J.** jack; Journal; Judge; Justice
JA or **J.A.** joint account; Judge Advocate
Ja. or **Ja** January
JAG Judge Advocate General
Jam. Jamaica
Jan. January
Jap. Japan(ese)
Jas. James
J.C.C. Junior Chamber of Commerce
JCL job control language
JCS or **J.C.S.** Joint Chiefs of Staff
jct. or **jctn.** junction
JD or **J.D.** Justice Department; juvenile delinquent
J.D. Doctor of Jurisprudence (L *Juris Doctor*); Doctor of Laws (L *Jurum Doctor*)
JDL or **J.D.L.** Jewish Defense League
Je. or **Je** June
Jer. Jeremiah; Jeremias
jg or **jg.** or **j.g.** junior grade
JHS or **J.H.S.** Junior High School
Jl. or **Jl** July
jnt. joint
Jon. Jonah
Josh. Joshua
jour. journal
JP jet propulsion
J.P. Justice of the Peace
jr. or **Jr.** junior
Jr. Journal
JRC or **J.R.C.** Junior Red Cross
Jth. Judith
Judg. Judges
Judge Adv. Gen. Judge Advocate General
Jul. July
jun. or **Jun.** junior
Jun. June
Junc. or **junc.** junction
juv. juvenile
JV or **J.V.** junior varsity

K Kelvin; king; knit; potassium (L *kalium*); thousand *(kilo-)*
K or **K.** kindergarten
k. karat; kilo; kilogram; kitchen
Kans. Kansas
KB king's bishop
KBP king's bishop's pawn
kc kilocycle
KC or **K.C.** Kansas City; King's Counsel; Knights of Columbus
kc/s kilocycles per second
KD or **K.D.** kiln-dried; knocked down
kg or **kg.** kilogram
KGB (Soviet) Committee of State Security (Russ. *Komitet Gosudarstvennoy Bezopasnosti*)
kHz kilohertz
KIA killed in action
K.J.V. King James Version (of the Bible)
KKK or **K.K.K.** Ku Klux Klan
KKt king's knight
KKtP king's knight's pawn
kl or **kl.** kiloliter
km or **km.** kilometer
km² or **km.²** square kilometer
km³ or **km.³** cubic kilometer
kn or **kn.** knot
KN king's knight
KNP king's knight's pawn
Knt. Knight
K. of C. Knights of Columbus
KP king's pawn
KP or **K.P.** kitchen police
kPa kilopascal
KPH or **K.P.H.** or **kph** or **k.p.h.** kilometers per hour

Kr krypton
KR king's rook
KRP king's rook's pawn
KS Kansas
Kt knight
kt. karat
kV or **kv** kilovolt
kW or **kw** kilowatt
kWh or **kwhr** or **K.W.H.** kilowatt-hour
Ky. or **KY** Kentucky

l or **l.** or **L** liter
L large; *Brit.* pound (sterling)
L or **L.** Latin; left
l. or **L.** or **L** lake; latitude; left; length; line
La lanthanum
La. or **LA** Louisiana
LA or **L.A.** Los Angeles
Lab. Labrador
lam. laminated
Lam. Lamentations
lang. language
lat. latitude
Lat. Latin
LB Labrador
lb. or **lb** pound (L *libra*)
lc or **l.c.** lower case
L/C or **l/c** letter of credit
L.C. Library of Congress
LCD liquid-crystal diode
l.c.d. least common denominator; lowest common denominator
LCDR Lieutenant Commander
L.C.L. or **l.c.l.** less than carload lot
l.c.m. least common multiple
LD lethal dose
ld. load
Ld. Lord
ldg. landing; loading
lect. lecture; lecturer
LED light-emitting diode
leg. legal; legato; legend
leg. or **legis.** legislation; legislative; legislature
LEM lunar excursion module
Lev. Leviticus
lex. lexicon
lf or **l.f.** lightface
LF low frequency
LG Low German
lg. long
lg. or **lge.** large
LGk Late Greek
LH or **L.H.** or **l.h.** left hand; lower half
L.H.D. Doctor of Humane Letters (L *Litterarum Humaniorum Doctor*)
Li lithium
L.I. Long Island
Lieut. Lieutenant
LIFO last in, first out
lim. limited
lin. lineal; linear
ling. linguistics
liq. liquid; liquor
LISP list processing
lit. literally
lith. or **litho.** or **lithog.** lithograph; lithographic; lithography
Litt.D. or **Lit.D.** Doctor of Letters; Doctor of Literature (L *Lit(t)erarum Doctor*)
Lk. Luke
LL Late Latin
ll. lines
LL.B. Bachelor of Laws (L *Legum Baccalaureus*)
LL.D. Doctor of Laws (L *Legum Doctor*)
LM lunar module

LNG liquefied natural gas
loc. cit. in the place cited (L *loco citato*)
Lond. London
long. or **lon.** longitude
loq. he (or she) speaks (L *loquitur*)
LP long-playing record
LP or **L.P.** or **l.p.** low pressure
LPG liquefied petroleum gas
LPGA or **L.P.G.A.** Ladies Professional Golfers' Association
LPN or **L.P.N.** Licensed Practical Nurse
Lr lawrencium
LR or **L.R.** living room
L.S. left side; letter signed; place of the seal (L *locus sigilli*)
LSAT Law School Admissions Test
LSD lysergic acid diethylamide
LSS life-support system
LST landing ship, tank
LST or **L.S.T.** or **l.s.t.** local standard time
LT or **L.T.** or **l.t.** local time
lt. light
Lt. or **LT** Lieutenant
L.T. long ton; low-tension
Lt. Col. or **LTC** Lieutenant Colonel
Lt. Comdr. or **Lt. Com.** or **LTC** Lieutenant Commander
Ltd. or **ltd.** limited
Lt. Gen. or **LTG** Lieutenant General
Lt. Gov. Lieutenant Governor
Lt. (jg.) or **LTJG** Lieutenant junior grade
L.T.L. or **l.t.l.** less than truckload
ltr. letter
Lu lutetium
lv. leave
LZ landing zone

m or **m.** meter
m² or **m.²** square meter
m³ or **m.³** cubic meter
M Mach; mass; thousand (L *mille*)
M or **M.** Medieval; Monday; Monsieur
M or **M.** or **m.** male; married; masculine; mile; minim; minute; month; moon; noon (L *meridies*)
MA Massachusetts
M.A. Master of Arts (L *Magister Artium*)
Macc. Maccabees
mach. machine; machinery; machining; machinist
Mach. Machabees
mag. magazine; magnetism; magneto; magnitude
Maj. or **MAJ** Major
Maj. Gen. Major General
Mal. Malachi
man. manual
Man. Manitoba (Canada)
manuf. manufacture(r); manufacturing
mar. maritime; married
Mar. March
masc. masculine
MASH mobile army surgical hospital
Mass. Massachusetts
math. mathematical; mathematician; mathematics
Matt. Matthew
max. maximum
MB Manitoba (Canada)
M.B.A. Master of Business Administration
mc megacycle
MC Marine Corps; Medical Corps
MC or **M.C.** master of ceremonies; Member of Congress
MCAT Medical College Admissions Test
MCPO Master Chief Petty Officer
Md mendelevium
Md. or **MD** Maryland
M/D or **MD** or **m/d** months after date
M.D. Doctor of Medicine (L *Medicinae Doctor*)
mdnt. midnight

mdse. merchandise
ME Middle English
Me. or **ME** Maine
M.E. Mechanical Engineer; Medical Examiner; Mining Engineer
meas. measure
mech. mechanical; mechanics
med. median; medical; medicine; medieval; medium
M.Ed. Master of Education
meg. megohm
mem. member; memoir; memorial
mep or **m.e.p.** mean effective pressure
meq. milliequivalent
mer. meridian
Messrs. pl. of *Mr.*
met. metropolitan
metall. metallurgical; metallurgy
meteorol. meteorological; meteorology
MeV or **Mev** or **mev** or **MEV** million electron volts
Mex. Mexican; Mexico
MF medium frequency; Middle French
M.F.A. Master of Fine Arts
mfd. manufactured
mfg. manufacturing
mfr. manufacture(r)
mg or **mg.** milligram
Mg magnesium
MG machine gun; Major General; military government
Mgr. Manager; Monseigneur; Monsignor
mgt. management
MHz megahertz
MI Michigan; Military Intelligence
mi. mile; mill
mi.² square mile
MIA missing in action
Mic. Micah
Mich. Micheas; Michigan
MICR magnetic ink character
mid. middle
mil. military
min. minim; minimum; mining; minister; minor; minute
Minn. Minnesota
MIRV multiple independently targeted reentry vehicle
misc. miscellaneous; miscellany
Miss. Mississippi
mixt. mixture
mk. mark
Mk. Mark
mks or **MKS** meter-kilogram-second
mkt. market
mktg. marketing
ml or **ml.** or **mL** milliliter
ML Medieval (or Middle) Latin
MLD minimum lethal dose
Mlle. or **Mlle** Mademoiselle
mm or **mm.** millimeter
mm² or **mm.²** square millimeter
mm³ or **mm.³** cubic millimeter
MM. or **MM** Messieurs (pl. of *Monsieur*)
Mme. or **Mme** Madame
Mn manganese
MN Minnesota
Mo molybdenum
MO or **M.O.** or **m.o.** mail order; modus operandi; money order
mo. month
Mo. Monday
Mo. or **MO** Missouri
M.O. Medical Officer
mod. moderate; modern
mod. or **modif.** modification; modified
modem modulator demodulator
mol. molecular; molecule
MOM or **M.O.M.** or **m.o.m.** middle of month
Mon. Monday; Monsignor

Mont. Montana
MP or **M.P.** Member of Parliament; Metropolitan Police; Military Police(man); Mounted Police
m.p. or **mp.** melting point
MPG or **mpg** or **m.p.g.** miles per gallon
MPH or **mph** or **m.p.h.** miles per hour
Mr. title prefixed to a man's surname (contraction of *Mister*)
Mr. or **Mr** March
Mrs. title prefixed to a married woman's surname (contraction of *Mistress*)
MS Mississippi
MS or **M.S.** motor ship; multiple sclerosis
Ms. or **Ms** title prefixed to a woman's name regardless of her marital status
MS. or **MS** or **Ms.** or **Ms** or **ms.** or **ms** manuscript
M.S. Master of Science
msec. or **msec** millisecond
MSG monosodium glutamate
msg. message
Msgr. Monseigneur; Monsignor
M. Sgt. or **MSgt** or **M/Sgt** Master Sergeant
m.s.l. or **M.S.L.** mean sea level
MST or **M.S.T.** or **m.s.t.** Mountain Standard Time
MT Montana
MT or **M.T.** or **m.t.** Mountain Time
Mt. or **mt.** mount; mountain
M.T. metric ton
mtg. meeting
mtg. or **mtge.** mortgage
Mt. Rev. Most Reverend
mun. or **munic.** municipal
mus. museum; music; musical; musician
MV motor vehicle
MVP most valuable player
MX missile experimental
My. or **My** May
myth. mythological; mythology

N knight; nitrogen
N or **N.** Navy; New; normal (solution); Norse; north(ern); November
n. born (L *natus*)
n. or **N.** or **N** name; net; neuter; nominative; noon; note; noun; number
Na sodium (L *natrium*)
n/a no account
N.A. National Association; North America; not applicable; not available
NAACP or **N.A.A.C.P.** National Association for the Advancement of Colored People
Nah. Nahum
NAM or **N.A.M.** National Association of Manufacturers
NAS National Academy of Sciences; Naval Air Station
NASA National Aeronautics and Space Administration
NASL or **N.A.S.L.** North American Soccer League
nat. native; natural
nat. or **natl.** national
NATO North Atlantic Treaty Organization
naut. nautical
nav. naval; navigable; navigation
Nb niobium
N.B. or **NB** New Brunswick (Canada)
NB or **N.B.** or **n.b.** note well (L *nota bene*)
NBA or **N.B.A.** National Basketball Association; National Boxing Association
NBC National Broadcasting Company
NBS National Bureau of Standards
N by E north by east
N by W north by west
N/C or **NC** no charge; no credit
N.C. or **NC** North Carolina
NCAA or **N.C.A.A.** National Collegiate Athletic Association
NCO noncommissioned officer

NCTE or **N.C.T.E.** National Council of Teachers of English
NCV no commercial value
Nd neodymium
n.d. no date
N.D. or **ND** or **N.Dak.** North Dakota
NDEA National Defense Education Act
Ne neon
NE Nebraska; northeast(ern)
N.E. New England
NEA or **N.E.A.** National Education Association
N.E.B. New English Bible
Nebr. Nebraska
NE by N northeast by north
NE by E northeast by east
neg. negative
Neh. Nehemiah
NEI or **n.e.i.** not elsewhere included
NES or **n.e.s.** not elsewhere specified
NET National Educational Television
Neth. Netherlands
neurol. neurology
neut. neuter
Nev. Nevada
NF Newfoundland (Canada); Norman French
N.F. National Formulary
N.F. or **n.f.** no funds
NFC or **N.F.C.** National Football Conference
NFL or **N.F.L.** National Football League
Nfld. Newfoundland (Canada)
NG or **N.G.** or **n.g.** no good
N.G. National Guard
NGC New General Catalog (of Astronomy)
NGk. New Greek
N.H. or **NH** New Hampshire
NHI National Health Insurance
NHL or **N.H.L.** National Hockey League
NHS National Health Service
Ni nickel
NIH National Institutes of Health
N.J. or **NJ** New Jersey
NL New Latin
NL or **N.L.** National League
n.l. it is not permitted (L *non licet*)
NLRB National Labor Relations Board
N/M no mark; not marked
n.m. nautical mile
N.M. or **NM** or **N.Mex.** New Mexico
NMI no middle initial
NNE north-northeast
NNW north-northwest
No nobelium
No. or **no.** north(ern); number (L *numero*)
nom. nominative
non seq. it does not follow (L *non sequitur*)
Nor. or **Norw.** Norway; Norwegian
NORAD North American Air Defense Command
NOS or **n.o.s.** not otherwise specified
nos. or **Nos.** numbers
Nov. November
NOW or **N.O.W.** National Organization of Women; negotiable order of withdrawal
Np neptunium
n.p. no pagination; no place (of publication)
N.P. notary public
NPN nonprotein nitrogen
NRA or **N.R.A.** National Recovery Administration; National Rifle Association
NRC Nuclear Regulatory Commission
ns nanosecond
N.S. or **NS** Nova Scotia (Canada); nuclear ship
N.S. or **n.s.** new series; not specified
NSC National Security Council
nsec. or **nsec** nanosecond

NSF National Science Foundation; not sufficient funds
NT Northwest Territories (Canada)
NT or **N.T.** New Testament
N.T.P. normal temperature and pressure
nt.wt. or **n.wt.** net weight
NU or **n.u.** name unknown
num. numeral
Num. Numbers
numis. numismatic
NV Nevada
NW northwest(ern)
NW by N northwest by north
NW by W northwest by west
N.W.T. Northwest Territories (Canada)
N.Y. or **NY** New York
N.Y.C. or **NYC** New York City
N.Z. or **NZ** New Zealand

O oxygen
O or **Ō.** Ocean; October; Ohio; Old; order
o/a on or about
OAS Organization of American States
OB or **O.B.** obstetrician; obstetrics
ob. died (L *obiit*); incidentally (L *obiter*)
Ob. or **Obad.** Obadiah
obj. object(ive)
obl. oblique; oblong
obs. obsolete
OCAS Organization of Central American States
occ. occupation
occas. occasional(ly)
OCD Office of Civil Defense
OCR optical character recognition
OCS Officer Candidate School
Oct. October
OD or **O.D.** Officer of the Day; olive drab; overdraft; overdrawn; right eye (L *oculus dexter*)
o.d. or **O.D.** outside diameter
O.D. Doctor of Optometry
OE Old English
OED or **O.E.D.** Oxford English Dictionary
OEO Office of Economic Opportunity
OEP Office of Emergency Preparedness
O.E.S. Order of the Eastern Star
off. office; officer; official
OFr. or **OF** Old French
O.F.S. Orange Free State
o.g. or **O.G.** original gum
OH Ohio
OJT on-the-job training
Okla. or **OK** Oklahoma
OL or **O.L.** left eye (L *oculus laevus*)
OMB Office of Management and Budget
ON Old Norse
Ont. or **ON** Ontario (Canada)
Op. or **op.** opus
O.P. observation post; Order of Preachers
O.P. or **o.p.** out of print
op. cit. in the work cited (L *opere citato*)
OPEC Organization of Petroleum Exporting Countries
opp. opposite
opt. optical; optician; optics; optional
OR operating room; Oregon
OR or **O.R.** or **o.r.** owner's risk
orch. orchestra
ord. order; ordnance
Ord. Sgt. Ordnance Sergeant
Ore. or **Oreg.** Oregon
org. organic; organization; organized
orig. origin; original(ly)
ornith. ornithology
orth. orthopedic; orthopedics
ORV off-the-road vehicle
Os osmium
OS Old Saxon

OS or **O.S.** left eye (L *oculus sinister*); ordinary seaman
o/s or **OS** out of stock
O.S.F. Order of St. Francis
OSHA Occupational Safety and Health Administration
OT or **O.T.** Old Testament; overtime
OTB off-track betting
OTC over-the-counter
OTS Officers' Training School
oz. or **oz** ounce
oz. ap. ounce apothecaries'
oz. av. ounce avoirdupois

p pence; proton
p. page; participle; past; pence; penny; per; peseta; peso; pint; pitcher; population; pressure
P pawn; phosphorus; purl
P. President
Pa protactinium
PA public address (system)
PA or **P.A.** Parents Association; power of attorney; press agent; private account; purchasing agent
Pa. or **PA** Pennsylvania
p.a. per annum
PAC or **P.A.C.** political action committee
Pac. Pacific
paleon. paleontology
pam. pamphlet
Pan. Panama
P and L or **P. and L.** or **P & L** or **P. & L.** profit and loss
par. paragraph; parallel; parish
Par. Paralipomenon
paren. parenthesis
Parl. Parliament(ary)
part. participial; participle; particular
pass. passenger; passive; throughout (L *passim*)
pat. patent(ed)
path. or **pathol.** pathological; pathology
pat. pend. patent pending
payt. payment
Pb lead (L *plumbum*)
PBA or **P.B.A.** Patrolmen's Benevolent Association; Permanent Budget Account; Professional Bowling Association
PBS Public Broadcasting Service
PBX private branch (telephone) exchange
PC Peace Corps
p.c. after meals (L *post cibum*); percent(age); petty cash; postal card
PCB polychlorinated biphenyl
PCP phencyclidine
pct. percent
Pd palladium
PD or **P.D.** Police Department
pd. paid
p.d. per diem; potential difference
PDT or **P.D.T.** or **p.d.t.** Pacific Daylight Time
PE Prince Edward Island (Canada)
PE or **pe** printer's error
P.E. physical education; Professional Engineer; Protestant Episcopal
P.E.I. Prince Edward Island (Canada)
PEN or **P.E.N.** International Association of Poets, Playwrights, Editors, Essayists, and Novelists
Pen. or **pen.** peninsula
Penn. or **Penna.** Pennsylvania
per. period; person
Per. Persia(n)
perf. perfect; perforated
perh. perhaps
perm. permanent
perp. perpendicular
pers. person; personal
Pers. Persia(n)
pert. pertaining
pet. petroleum

Pet. Peter
pf. pfennig
pf. or **pfd.** preferred
Pfc. or **PFC** Private, first class
pg. page
P.G. postgraduate
PGA or **P.G.A.** Professional Golfers' Association
pharm. pharmaceutical; pharmacist; pharmacy
Ph.D. Doctor of Philosophy (L *Philosophiae Doctor*)
phil. or **philol.** philological; philology
phil. or **philos.** philosophical; philosopher; philosophy
Phil. Philippians
Philem. Philemon
phon. or **phonet.** phonetics
photog. photographer; photographic; photography
phr. phrase
PHS Public Health Service
phys. physical; physician; physicist; physics
physiol. physiological; physiologist; physiology
pinx. he (or she) painted it (L *pinxit*)
pk. pack; park; peak; peck; pike
pkg. package
pkt. packet; pocket
pkwy. parkway
pl. plate; plural
Pl. or **pl.** place
PLO Palestine Liberation Organization
Pm promethium
PM or **P.M.** Paymaster; Police Magistrate; Postmaster; post-mortem; Prime Minister; Provost Marshal
PM or **P.M.** or **p.m.** afternoon (L *post meridiem*)
pm. premium
pmk. postmark
pmt. payment
P/N or **p.n.** promissory note
pnxt. he (or she) painted it (L *pinxit*)
Po polonium
PO or **P.O.** petty officer; postal order; post office
POB or **P.O.B.** post office box
POC or **P.O.C.** port of call
POD or **P.O.D.** pay on delivery; port of debarkation
POE or **P.O.E.** port of embarkation; port of entry
pol. or **polit.** political; politician; politics
Pol. Poland; Polish
POP or **P.O.P.** point of purchase
pop. population
P.O.R. or **p.o.r.** pay on return
Port. Portugal; Portuguese
POS or **P.O.S.** point of sale
pos. position; positive
poss. possession; possessive; possible; possibly
pot. potential
POW prisoner of war
pp pianissimo
pp. pages; past participle
P.P. parcel post
ppd. or **P.P.** postpaid; prepaid
ppm part per million
ppr. or **p.pr.** present participle
PPS or **P.P.S.** or **p.p.s.** additional postscript (L *post postscriptum*)
ppt. precipitate
pptn. precipitation
PQ Province of Quebec (Canada)
Pr praseodymium
PR or **P.R.** payroll; proportional representation; public relations; Puerto Rico
pr. pair; present; price; printed; pronoun
prec. preceded; preceding
pred. predicate
pref. preface; preference; preferred; prefix
prelim. preliminary
prem. premium
prep. preparatory; preposition
pres. present

Pres. President
prev. previous(ly)
prim. primary; primitive
prin. principal; principle
print. printing
p.r.n. when needed (L *pro re nata*)
prob. probable; probably; problem
proc. procedure; proceedings
prod. produce; produced; producer; product; production
Prof. Professor
PROM programmable read-only memory
pron. pronoun; pronounced; pronunciation
prop. property; proposition; proprietary; proprietor
pros. prosody
Prot. Protestant
prov. province; provincial; provisional; provost
Prov. Proverbs
prox. in the next month (L *proximo mensa*)
ps picosecond
PS or **P.S.** or **p.s.** postscript
Ps. or **Psa.** Psalm; Psalms
P.S. Public School
PSAT Preliminary Scholastic Aptitude Test
pseud. pseudonym
psf or **p.s.f.** pounds per square foot
psi or **p.s.i.** pounds per square inch
PST or **P.S.T.** or **p.s.t.** Pacific Standard Time
psych. or **psychol.** psychologist; psychology
Pt platinum
PT or **P.T.** or **p.t.** Pacific Time
pt. part; payment; pint; point; port
PTA or **P.T.A.** Parent-Teachers Association
Pte. *Brit.* Private
ptg. printing
P.T.O. please turn over (a page)
PTV public television
pty. proprietary
Pu plutonium
pub. public; publication; published; publisher; publishing
PVC polyvinyl chloride
Pvt. or **PVT** Private
PW prisoner of war
pwt. pennyweight
PX post exchange

Q or **Q.** queen
Q or **Q.** or **q.** quarto; question
q quart; quire
QB queen's bishop
Q.B. Queen's Bench
QBP queen's bishop's pawn
Q.C. Queen's Counsel
Q.E.D. which was to be demonstrated (L *quod erat demonstrandum*)
q.i.d. four times a day (L *quater in die*)
QKt queen's knight
QKtP queen's knight's pawn
QM Quartermaster
QMC Quartermaster Corps
QMG or **Q.M. Gen.** Quartermaster General
QMS or **Q.M. Sgt.** Quartermaster Sergeant
QN queen's knight
QNP queen's knight's pawn
QP queen's pawn
qq.v. which (things) see (L *quae vide*)
QR queen's rook
qr. quarter; quire
QRP queen's rook's pawn
qt. quart
qt. or **qty.** quantity
qto. quarto
qu. question
quad. quadrangle; quadrant

Que.   Quebec (Canada)
ques.   question
quot.   quotation
q.v.   which see (L *quod vide*)
qy.   query

r or **R**   resistance; roentgen
R   rook
R or **R.** or **r.**   radius; rare; right; run
r.   ruble; rupee
R.   Railroad; Railway; Republican; River
Ra   radium
RA   Regular Army
R.A.   Royal Academy
RAAF   Royal Australian Air Force
rad.   radical; radio; radius
RADM   Rear Admiral
RAF   Royal Air Force
RAM   random access memory
R and B or **R&B**   rhythm and blues
R and D or **R&D**   research and development
R and R or **R&R**   rest and recreation; rest and recuperation
Rb   rubidium
RBC or **R.B.C.**   red blood cell; red blood count
RBI or **R.B.I.** or **r.b.i.** or **rbi**   run(s) batted in
RC or **R.C.**   Red Cross; Roman Catholic
RCAF   Royal Canadian Air Force
R.C.Ch.   Roman Catholic Church
rcd.   received; record
RCMP   Royal Canadian Mounted Police
RCN   Royal Canadian Navy
rct.   recruit
RD or **R.D.**   rural delivery
rd.   rod; round
Rd. or **rd.**   road
Rdm.   Radarman
Re   rhenium
REA   Railway Express Agency; Rural Electrification Administration
Rear Adm.   Rear Admiral
rec.   receipt; record; recorder; recording; recreation
recd. or rec'd.   received
recip.   reciprocal; reciprocity
Rec. Sec.   Recording Secretary
rect.   receipt; rectangle; rectangular; rectified; rector; rectory
ref.   referee; reference; referred; refining; reformation; reformed; refund; refunding
refl.   reflective; reflex; reflexive
refr.   refraction
refrig.   refrigeration; refrigerator
reg.   region; register; registry; regular(ly); regulation
reg. or regd.   registered
Reg.   Regent; Registrar
Reg. or **Regt.**   Regiment
REIT   real-estate investment trust
rel.   relating; relative; released
rel. or relig.   religion
rep.   repair; repeat; report(ed); reporter; representative; republic
Rep.   Representative; Republic; Republican
repl.   replace(ment)
rept.   report
req.   request; require(d); requisition
res.   research; reserve(d); residence; resigned; resolution
resp.   respective(ly)
retd.   retained; retired; returned
rev.   revenue; reverse; review; reviewed; revise(d); revision; revolution
Rev.   Revelation; Reverend
RF   radio frequency
RFD or **R.F.D.**   rural free delivery
Rh   rhodium
RH or **R.H.** or **r.h.**   right hand

rhet.   rhetoric; rhetorical
R.I. or **RI**   Rhode Island
RIP or **R.I.P.**   may he (or she) rest in peace (L *requiescat in pace*)
Riv. or **riv.**   river
rm.   ream; room
Rn   radon
RN or **R.N.**   registered nurse
RNA   ribonucleic acid
rnd.   round
ROG or **R.O.G.**   receipt of goods
ROI   return on investment
rom.   roman (type)
Rom.   Roman; Romance; Romania(n); Romans
ROM   read only memory
ROTC   Reserve Officers' Training Corps
rpm or r.p.m.   revolutions per minute
rps or r.p.s.   revolutions per second
rpt.   repeat; report
RR or **R.R.**   railroad; rural route
R.S.   Recording Secretary; Revised Statutes; right side; Royal Society
R.S.V.   Revised Standard Version (of the Bible)
RSVP or **R.S.V.P.** or **r.s.v.p.**   please reply (F *répondez s'il vous plait*)
RSWC   right side up with care
RT   radiotelephone
rt.   right
rte.   route
Rt. Rev.   Right Reverend
Ru   ruthenium
Rum.   Rumania(n)
Russ.   Russia(n)
RV   recreational vehicle
R.V.   Revised Version (of the Bible)
R.W.   Right Worshipful; Right Worthy
Rwy. or **Ry.**   Railway

S   sulfur
S or **S.**   Saint; Saturday; School; Sea; Senate; September; South(ern); Sunday
s.   scruple; section; series; shilling; signed; singular; small; son; stere; substantive
Sa. or **Sa**   Saturday
s.a.   subject to approval; without year (or date) (L *sine anno*)
S.A.   Salvation Army; seaman apprentice; sex appeal; Société Anonyme; Sociedad Anonima; South Africa
SAC   Strategic Air Command
SALT   Strategic Arms Limitation Talks
SAM   surface-to-air missile
Sam. or **Saml.**   Samuel
S and L or **S&L**   Savings and Loan (Association)
S and M or **S&M**   sadism and masochism; sadist and masochist
sanit.   sanitary; sanitation
Sask.   Saskatchewan (Canada)
SAT   Scholastic Aptitude Test
sat.   saturate(d); saturation
Sat.   Saturday
Sb   antimony (L *stibium*)
sb.   substantive
S.B.   Bachelor of Science (L *Scientiae Baccalaureus*)
SBA   Small Business Administration
S by E   south by east
S by W   south by west
sc or s.c.   small capitals
Sc   scandium
sc.   namely (L *scilicet*); scale; scene; science
Sc.   Scots
S.C. or **SC**   South Carolina
Scand.   Scandinavia(n)
sch.   school
sci.   science; scientific
scil.   namely (L *scilicet*)

Scot. Scotland; Scottish
SCPO Senior Chief Petty Officer
Script. Scriptural; Scripture
SD or **S.D.** special delivery; standard deviation
s.d. without setting a day (L *sine die* without a day)
S.D. or **SD** or **S.Dak.** South Dakota
SDA or **S.D.A.** Students for Democratic Action
SDS or **S.D.S.** Students for a Democratic Society
Se selenium
SE southeast(ern)
SEATO Southeast Asia Treaty Organization
SE by E southeast by east
SE by S southeast by south
SEC Securities and Exchange Commission
sec. according to (L *secundum*); second; secondary; sector
sec. or **sect.** section
Sec. or **sec.** or **Secy.** or **secy.** secretary
sel. select(ed); selection
sem. seminary
Sen. or **sen.** senate; senator; senior
sep. separate(d)
sepn. separation
Sept. or **Sep.** September
seq. the following (one) (L *sequens*)
seqq. the following (ones) (L *sequentia*)
ser. serial; series; sermon
Serg. or **Sergt.** Sergeant
serv. service
SF or **sf** science fiction
Sfc. or **SFC** Sergeant first class
SG Secretary General; senior grade; Solicitor General; Surgeon General
sgd. signed
Sgt. or **SGT** Sergeant
Sgt. Maj. Sergeant Major
sh. share; sheet
SHAPE Supreme Headquarters Allied Powers (Europe)
SHF superhigh frequency
shpt. shipment
shr. share
sht. sheet
shtg. shortage
Si silicon
SI International System of Units (F *Système International d'Unités*)
S.I. or **SI** Staten Island
sig. signal; signature
sing. singular
S.J. Society of Jesus
S.J.D. Doctor of Juridical Science (L *Scientiae Juridicae Doctor*)
SK Saskatchewan (Canada)
Skt. Sanskrit
S.L. salvage loss
Slav. Slavic
sld. sailed; sealed
Sm samarium
sm. small
S.M. Master of Science (L *Scientiae Magister*); Society of Mary
SMaj or **SM** Sergeant Major
SMSgt Senior Master Sergeant
Sn tin (L *stannum*)
So. or **so.** south(ern)
S.O. or **s.o.** seller's option; strikeout
soc. social; socialist; society
sociol. sociological; sociology
sol. soluble
sol. or **soln.** solution
Sol. Solicitor; Solomon
SOP standard operating procedure; standing operating procedure
soph. sophomore
SP Shore Patrol; Specialist

sp. special; species; specimen; spelling; spirit
Sp. Spain
Sp. or **Span.** Spanish
s.p. without offspring (L *sine prole*)
SPCA or **S.P.C.A.** Society for the Prevention of Cruelty to Animals
SPCC or **S.P.C.C.** Society for the Prevention of Cruelty to Children
spec. special; specifically; specification
specif. specific(ally)
sp. gr. specific gravity
spp. species
Sq. or **sq.** squadron; square
Sr strontium
SR Seaman Recruit
SR or **S.R.** shipping receipt
Sr. Senior; Sister
SRO or **S.R.O.** standing room only
SS. Saints
S.S. or **SS** steamship; Sunday School; sworn statement
SSA Social Security Administration
SSE south-southeast
SSG or **SSgt** or **S. Sgt.** Staff Sergeant
ssp. subspecies
SSR or **S.S.R.** Soviet Socialist Republic
SSS Selective Service System
SST supersonic transport
SSW south-southwest
st. stanza; statute; stitch; stone
St. Saint; State; Strait; Street
s.t. short ton
sta. station; stationary
stat. immediately (L *statim*); statute
stbd. starboard
std. standard
S.T.D. Doctor of Sacred Theology (L *Sacrae Theologiae Doctor*)
Ste. Saint (F *sainte*)
ster. or **stg.** sterling
STOL short takeoff and landing
STP or **S.T.P.** standard temperature and pressure
stud. student
Su. or **Su** Sunday
sub. subscription; subtract; suburb(an); subway
subj. subject; subjunctive
suf. or **suff.** suffix
suff. sufficient
Sun. Sunday
sup. supra (L, above)
sup. or **super.** superior
sup. or **superl.** superlative
supp. or **suppl.** supplement(ary)
Supt. or **supt.** superintendent
supvr. supervisor
surg. surgeon; surgery; surgical
Surg. Gen. Surgeon General
surv. survey; surveying; surveyor
s.v. under the word (L *sub verbo* or *sub voce*)
svc. or **svce.** service
svgs. savings
SW shipper's weight; shortwave; southwest(ern)
Sw. or **Swed.** Sweden; Swedish
SW by S southwest by south
SW by W southwest by west
Switz. Switzerland
syl. or **syll.** syllable; syllabus
sym. symbol; symmetrical
syn. synonym; synonymous; synonymy
synd. syndicate(d)
syst. system

T or **T.** tablespoon; Territory; Testament; time; Township; transit; true; Tuesday
t. teaspoon; temperature; tense; ton; transitive; troy
Ta tantalum

TA transactional analysis
TAC Tactical Air Command
TAG The Adjutant General
tan tangent
Tb terbium
TB or **T.B.** tuberculosis
T.B. or **t.b.** trial balance
TBA to be announced
tbs. or **tbsp.** or **tb.** tablespoon
Tc technetium
TC Teachers College
TD touchdown; Treasury Department
TDY temporary duty
Te tellurium
tech. technical(ly); technician; technological; technology
tel. telegram; telegraph; telephone
teleg. telegraphy
temp. in the time of (L *tempore*); temperature; temporary
ten. tenor
Tenn. Tennessee
ter. or **terr.** territorial; territory
Ter. or **ter.** terrace
TESL teaching English as a second language
test. testator; testimony
Test. Testament
Teut. Teuton(ic)
Tex. Texas
Th thorium
Th. or **Th** Thursday
THC tetrahydrocannabinol
Th.D. Doctor of Theology (L *Theologiae Doctor*)
theat. theatrical
theol. theologian; theological; theology
therm. thermometer
Thess. Thessalonians
Thurs. or **Thur.** or **Thu.** Thursday
Ti titanium
t.i.d. three times a day (L *ter in die*)
Tim. Timothy
Tit. Titus
tk. tank; truck
TKO technical knockout
Tl thallium
T.L. or **t.l.** total loss; truck load
TLC tender loving care
Tm thulium
TM trademark; transcendental meditation
TMO or **T.M.O.** telegraph money order
TN Tennessee
tn. ton; town; train
tng. training
tnpk. turnpike
TNT trinitrotoluene
T.O. telegraph office
T.O. or **t.o.** turn over
Tob. Tobias; Tobit
topog. topographical; topography
tot. total
Tp. or **tp.** township
t.p. title page
tpk. or **tpke.** turnpike
tr. transitive; translated; translation; translator; transpose; transposition; treasurer; troop; trustee
trans. transaction; transitive; translated; translation; translator; transportation; transverse
transl. translated; translation
transp. transportation
Treas. or **treas.** treasurer; treasury
trib. tributary
trop. tropic(al)
TSgt or **T.Sgt.** Technical Sergeant
tsp teaspoon
Tues. or **Tue.** or **Tu.** or **Tu** Tuesday

Turk. Turkey; Turkish
TV television
TVA Tennessee Valley Authority
Twp. or **twp.** township
TWX teletypewriter exchange
TX Texas
typ. or **typo.** or **typog.** typographer; typographical; typography

U uranium
U or **U.** union; unit; university; unsatisfactory; upper
UAR or **U.A.R.** United Arab Republic
UAW or **U.A.W.** United Automobile Workers
uc or **u.c.** upper case
UFO unidentified flying object
UH or **U.H.** or **u.h.** upper half
UHF ultrahigh frequency
UK or **U.K.** United Kingdom
UL Underwriters' Laboratories
ult. ultimate(ly)
ult. or **ulto.** last month (L *ultimo mense*)
UMT universal military training
UMTS Universal Military Training Service
UMW or **U.M.W.** United Mine Workers
UN United Nations
UNESCO United Nations Educational, Scientific, and Cultural Organization
UNICEF United Nations Children's Fund (< its original name, United Nations International Children's Emergency Fund)
univ. universal
Univ. or **univ.** university
UNRWA United Nations Relief and Works Agency
UPC universal product code
UPI or **U.P.I.** United Press International
UPS United Parcel Service
US or **U.S.** United States
u.s. as above (L *ut supra*); where mentioned above (L *ubi supra*)
USA or **U.S.A.** United States Army; United States of America
USAF United States Air Force
USAREUR United States Army, Europe
USCG United States Coast Guard
USDA United States Department of Agriculture
USES United States Employment Service
USIA United States Information Agency
USLTA or **U.S.L.T.A.** United States Lawn Tennis Association
USM United States Mail
USMC United States Marine Corps
USN United States Navy
USO United Service Organizations
USP or **U.S.P.** United States Pharmacopeia
USS or **U.S.S.** United States Ship
USSR or **U.S.S.R.** Union of Soviet Socialist Republics
USTA or **U.S.T.A.** United States Tennis Association
usu. usual(ly)
UT Utah
ut sup. as above (L *ut supra*)
UV ultraviolet
UW or **U/W** underwriter
ux. wife (L *uxor*)

V vanadium; vector; victory; volt
v. velocity; verb; verse; version; versus; vide (L, see); voice; voltage; volume; vowel
VA Veterans Administration; Vice Admiral
Va. or **VA** Virginia
VADM Vice Admiral
val. valuation; value; valued
var. variable; variant; variation; variety
VAT or **V.A.T.** value added tax
vb. verb
VC or **V.C.** Vice-Chancellor; Vice-Consul; Vietcong

VD venereal disease
vel. vellum; velocity
Ven. Venerable
ver. verse; version
vert. vertical
VF video frequency; visual field; voice frequency
VFD or **V.F.D.** volunteer fire department
VFW or **V.F.W.** Veterans of Foreign Wars
VG or **V.G.** very good; Vicar General
VHF very high frequency
v.i. see below (L *vide infra*); verb intransitive
V.I. or **VI** Virgin Islands; volume indicator
vic. vicinity
Vic. Vicar; Victoria
Vice Adm. Vice Admiral
vil. village
VIP very important person
vis. visibility; visual
VISTA Volunteers in Service to America
viz. namely (L *videlicet*)
VL Vulgar Latin
VLF very low frequency
VOA Voice of America
voc. or **vocat.** vocative
vocab. vocabulary
vol. volume; volunteer
vou. voucher
VP or **V.P.** verb phrase; Vice-President
vs. verse; versus
v.s. see above (L *vide supra*)
vss. verses; versions
V/STOL vertical short takeoff and landing
Vt. or **VT** Vermont
v.t. verb transitive
VTOL vertical takeoff and landing
VTR video tape recorder; video tape recording
Vulg. or **Vul.** Vulgate
vv. verses
v.v. vice versa

W tungsten (G *wolfram*)
W or **W.** Wednesday; Welsh; west(ern)
w. or **W.** or **W** water; watt; week; weight; wide; width; wife; with
w/ with
WA Washington
WAC Women's Army Corps
WAF Women in the Air Force
war. warrant
Wash. Washington
WATS Wide Area Telecommunications Service
WAVE Women in the United States Navy (< Women Accepted for Volunteer Emergency Service)
W/B or **W.B.** waybill
WBA or **W.B.A.** World Boxing Association
WBC or **W.B.C.** white blood cell; World Boxing Council
W by N west by north
W by S west by south
WC or **W.C.** or **w.c.** water closet; without charge
WCTU or **W.C.T.U.** Women's Christian Temperance Union
Wed. Wednesday
wh. which
WHA or **W.H.A.** World Hockey Association
whf. wharf
WHO World Health Organization

whse. or **whs.** warehouse
whsle. wholesale
WI Wisconsin
W.I. West Indies
wid. widow; widower
Wis. or **Wisc.** Wisconsin
Wisd. Wisdom
wk. week; work
wkly. weekly
WL water line; wavelength
wmk. watermark
WMO World Meteorological Organization
WNW west-northwest
WO Warrant Officer
w/o without
WP word processing
WPM or **wpm** words per minute
wpn. weapon
wrnt. warrant
WSW west-southwest
wt. weight
W.Va. or **WV** West Virginia
WW or **W.W.** World War
Wyo. or **WY** Wyoming

x or **X** experimental; extra; times
X Christ; Christian
X-C cross-country
xd or **x.d.** or **XD** or **X.D.** or **x.div.** without dividend
Xe xenon
x.i. or **XI** or **X.I.** or **x.in.** or **x.int.** without interest
XL extra large
Xmas Christmas
Xn. or **Xtian.** Christian
Xnty. or **Xty.** Christianity
x-ref. cross-reference

Y yttrium
y. yard; year; yen
Yb ytterbium
Y.B. yearbook
yd. yard
yd.^{2} square yard
yd.^{3} cubic yard
YMCA or **Y.M.C.A.** Young Men's Christian Association
YMHA or **Y.M.H.A.** Young Men's Hebrew Association
y.o.b. year of birth
yr. year; your
yrbk. yearbook
yrs. years; yours
Y.T. or **YT** Yukon Territory (Canada)
YTD or **Y.T.D.** year to date
YWCA or **Y.W.C.A.** Young Women's Christian Association
YWHA or **Y.W.H.A.** Young Women's Hebrew Association

Z atomic number; zenith distance
z. or **Z.** zero; zone
Zach. Zacharias
Zech. Zechariah
Zeph. Zephaniah
Zn zinc
zool. zoological; zoology
ZPG zero population growth
Zr zirconium

SECRETARIAL HANDBOOK

SECRETARIAL HANDBOOK

by Alice Ottun

Secretaries, even though well-educated and experienced, encounter problems in their everyday dictation, transcription, and office work. It is the purpose of this Secretarial Handbook to help solve these problems by presenting clear, concise statements, along with recommendations on preferred usage, about traditionally troublesome areas of language.

The author of this Handbook, Alice Ottun, is a leading authority on secretarial and office procedures. For twenty years the Administrative Dean of Pace College, she is at present the Director of Business Education of the Middle Country School District in Centereach, Long Island. Miss Ottun has served as President of the Commercial Education Association of New York City, of the Business Institutes of the State of New York, and of the Private Schools Association of New York City. She is listed in *Who's Who in American Education* and in *Who's Who of American Women*. She has for many years taught business subjects and English and has an intimate knowledge of the type of information that secretaries and other office workers need and want.

Throughout the years Funk & Wagnalls' Dictionary Department has been called upon to answer a great many inquiries, many of them from secretaries, about various problems relating to language. Records have been kept of these inquiries, and a report based upon them has been made available to the author of this Handbook, thus providing her with original, practical data to aid her in selecting the categories that secretaries and others will find most useful.

WORD USAGE AND WORD RELATIONSHIPS

Agreement of Subject and Verb

It may seem needless to say that a singular subject takes a singular verb, while a plural subject takes a plural verb; however, many errors occur in this respect.

The small table *was* in the hall.
The small tables *were* in the hall.

In some instances, when phrases or other elements come between the subject and the verb, the agreement may not be so clear.

The small table around which the children play *was* in the hall.
The small tables owned by the church *were* in the hall.
The men, as well as the policeman, *were* aghast at the sight.

The following words are generally considered singular and take the singular form of the verb: *each, either, neither, one, someone, anyone, everybody, nobody, somebody, much, anybody, everyone.*

The following words are plural and take the plural form of the verb: *both, few, many, several.*

The following pronouns may be singular or plural depending on the meaning intended: *all, most, some, every, none, any, half, more.*

When one is referring to two or more persons who are of different sexes, or to a group of people whose gender one has no way of determining, the pronouns *they, them,* and *their* are often used to refer to *anyone, each, everybody,* etc., in order to avoid the awkward *he or she, him or her, his or her.* Strictly speaking, one should use the masculine singular pronouns (*he, him, his*) in such cases, but in practice they are used consistently only in formal usage. Which procedure you follow will depend on how formal a style you wish to employ.

Either—Or; Neither—Nor

Neither always takes *nor*; *either* takes *or*.

When a subject is compounded with *neither . . . nor* or *either . . . or*, the verb is normally singular if the nouns joined are singular, and plural if they are plural. If, however, one noun is singular and one plural, the verb agrees with the second or nearer subject.

Either Bill or Ralph *is* lying.
Neither she nor her sisters *skate* well.

A collective noun, such as *class, company, club, crew, jury, committee,* takes a singular verb when the whole is considered as a unit, and a plural verb when part of the whole is considered separately.

The jury *has* deliberated for six hours.
The crew *were* near exhaustion after their many hours of exposure.

Some collective nouns, as *police* and *cattle,* are used only in the plural form; others, as *mankind* and *wildlife,* are generally used in the singular form.

The cattle *were* almost destroyed by the severe storm.
The New England wildlife *has* been protected.

Agreement of Pronoun with Its Antecedent

If the antecedent is singular, the pronoun is singular; if the antecedent is plural, the pronoun is likewise plural.

The *boy* did *his* best in the contest.
The *boys* in the school did *their* best.
The *boy* and the *girl* did *their* best.
Neither one of the boys did *his* best.

PUNCTUATION

For practical purposes, it is best to keep in mind that too much punctuation is as confusing as too little. The current trend is toward a minimum of punctuation, just enough to make the writer's meaning clear. This can best be accomplished by cultivating a simple, straightforward style that flows as naturally as ordinary speech.

Where a sentence is so complicated that no amount of punctuation seems adequate, a writer would be wise to reorganize his thoughts. Punctuation can help to guide a reader to the meaning of a sentence; it cannot, however, make order out of confused thinking and expression.

End Punctuation

Because the sentence is a grammatically complete and separate unit of utterance, it is necessary to show where one sentence ends and another begins. In speech, this is accomplished by falling pitch, intonation, and a full pause. In written discourse, the reader is guided by a period, a question mark, or an exclamation point, depending on the nature of the sentence.

The Period [.] The period is used at the end of a declarative sentence, an imperative sentence, an indirect question, and after a polite request that resembles a question. It is also used after initials and most abbreviations.

Mrs. Morris placed the book on the table.
The members of the committee asked when the meeting would take place.
Will you open the door for me, please.

If a sentence ends in an abbreviation, only one period is needed.

The bus will arrive at 8:30 A.M.

Do not use a period and two zeros after even amounts of money, except in tabulation.

$25, not $25. or $25.00

The period should not be used in centered headings, such as manuscript and chapter headings; in the various elements in an outline; or in the items in a tabulation.

Do not use periods between the call numbers of broadcasting stations: WABC, WQXR; or between the letters indicating government agencies: FBI, CIA, FAA, IRS.

Three dots (. . .), called an *ellipsis,* are used to indicate an omission in quoted matter. When the omission comes at the end of the line, use the three dots together with the sentence period, making a total of four dots. If one or more paragraphs are omitted in the quoted matter, show the omission by using seven dots across the page.

The Question Mark [?] The question mark signifies that the sentence preceding it does not make a statement, but asks a question. This punctuation serves the same purpose in writing that rising or sustained pitch intonation of the voice does in speaking.

When may we expect to receive your check?

If a sentence consists of several questions, the question mark should appear at the close of each question within the sentence and also at the close. The separate questions within the sentence do not begin with a capital since they are part of the larger and complete question.

Who will attend the conference—the president? the vice president? or the secretary?

The Exclamation Point [!] This is used at the end of a statement denoting a strong emotional experience or a sense of urgency or excitement. If spoken, it would be gasped, shouted, groaned, or cried. Written, the exclamation point, and the reader's imagination, must suffice.

Watch out!
Oh, my head!

An interjection at the beginning of a sentence is usually followed by a comma, and the sentence is ended with an exclamation point. The interjection may, however, be immediately followed by an exclamation mark, and the following sentence punctuated without reference to it.

Oh, what a day this is!
Oh! How could you do that?

Exclamation points should be used with discretion and for particular emphasis. Excessive use tends to lessen the impact of this device.

Internal Punctuation

When sentences become more complex and deal with two or more closely related ideas, internal punctuation is necessary to show the relation between the various parts. Authorities differ in some respects on the rules applying to the use of the comma and the semicolon. Since this Handbook is a secretarial guide, however, some specific rules should be laid down, but with the understanding that research may indicate differences of opinion.

The Comma [,] The comma is used to separate the various elements in a series—either words, phrases, or clauses—when there are at least three units.

The torn, tattered, soaking flag was lowered.
The dog jumped up, barked ferociously, bared his teeth, and took off after the rabbit.

Formal punctuation requires that a comma be inserted between the last two elements of a series even when a conjunction is used; this rule is generally followed in letter writing. An informal style of writing, such as newspaper and editorial work, does not require the comma before the conjunction.

The flag is red, white and blue.

Sometimes the conjunction is used with each element in the series. When this occurs, no comma is used to separate the elements.

The banner will be red or blue or white or a combination of these colors.

When *etc.* is the concluding element in a series, it should be preceded by a comma. A comma should also follow *etc.* when it is not the last word in a sentence.

She stopped off at the supermarket to get some fruit, vegetables, etc., on the way home.

Use the comma to set off an introductory sentence element (word, phrase, clause) which is out of its natural order. Of all the comma rules, this is probably the most difficult to master. Some words, like *however*, are not always used as introductory words and would not then be followed by the comma.

Obviously, we cannot meet your request.
In order to meet the deadline, we shall have to work overtime.
When you go to see him in the hospital, bring along a few magazines.
However well you meant, it was the wrong thing to do.

When the main clause in the sentence comes first, do not use the comma between the main clause and the dependent clause.

Bring along a few magazines when you go to visit him in the hospital.

As a general rule, an introductory phrase which contains a verb should be followed with a comma.

After *making* the survey, the committee will publish the report.
To *complete* the survey, the officers worked overtime.

If the introductory phrase does not contain a verb, it should not be followed by a comma unless the phrase is parenthetical or explanatory.

After much debate the meeting was adjourned.
As an act of mercy the sick animal was killed.
Under separate cover we are sending you a catalogue.
On the contrary, I believe the President was absolutely right.

For example, consider the boy's attitude toward his parents.
In the second place, watch his behavior with his peers.

Use the comma to set off introductory *yes* or *no* or light exclamations in a sentence.

No, we shall not be ready on time.
Oh, what a wonderful day this has been!

A parenthetical expression (word, phrase, or clause) that can be omitted without changing the meaning of the sentence should be set off by commas.

The king, who was very ill, was not present at the ceremony.
Something may, of course, turn up to change what seems now to be the obvious outcome.

Note: When the information has little connection with the thought expressed in the main clause, it is usually enclosed in parentheses rather than in commas.

The strike (which began on the President's birthday) completely paralyzed the nation.

Dashes may also be used to set off any sort of nonrestrictive or parenthetical matter. Some writers feel that dashes lend a more personal dramatic effect to their writing.

The earth—all parched and dry—yearns for moisture.

Use the comma before short, direct quotations.

She asked, "Is the train on time?"

Use the comma to set off words in direct address.

We are certain, Mr. Long, that you will be satisfied with our product.

The comma or commas should be used to set off an identifying or explanatory word or phrase (called an *appositive*) which helps to make the meaning of the sentence clearer. This rule applies to a person's title or degree and to the abbreviation "Inc." when used in a company name.

Our salesman, Mr. Brown, will call on you tomorrow.
We shall write a letter to Ray Smith & Company, Inc., in New York City.
Harold Brown, Ph.D., has been appointed to the faculty.

Separate contrasting expressions—word, phrase, or clause—by using the comma.

We shall leave today, not tomorrow.

Use the comma to separate two or more parallel adjectives.

Their sleeping bags kept them warm during the long, cold nights.

Note: If the word *and* can be inserted between the two adjectives or if the two adjectives can be reversed, they are parallel and the comma should be used.

The comma is *not* used when the order of the adjectives helps to determine the meaning of the sentence.

They built the building with wide open stairways.

The comma should be used before a conjunction (*but, and, or,* etc.) that connects two independent clauses.

We have had the pleasure of counting you as one of our members for many years, but we notice that you have not yet renewed your membership.

If the clauses are short and uncomplicated, the comma may be omitted.

We were drenched but arrived safely.

The Semicolon [;] The semicolon is used to separate two independent clauses when the conjunction is omitted.

We are enclosing an envelope for your convenience; it requires no postage.

Use the semicolon to separate the members of a compound sentence when one or both members contain other punctuation marks.

If he is nominated, he will run; but his chances seem dim.

Use the semicolon to separate the members of a compound sentence when the clauses are connected by such words as *however, nevertheless, consequently,* etc.

He paid little attention to details; consequently, he failed to be promoted.

Phrases or clauses in a series are separated by the semicolon when any one or more of the phrases or clauses contain a comma.

Our profits for the three successive years were: 1960, $2,345,000; 1961, $2,070,400; 1962, $2,545,000.

The Colon [:] The colon is used most often to indicate that a list, example, strong assertion, or the like will follow to complete or fulfill some introductory statement.

The bride takes three vows: to love, honor, and obey.
We have only one goal: to win.

The colon is also used outside the sentence in certain purely conventional ways: after the salutation of a formal letter; between elements of a Biblical or bibliographical citation; after the name or other identification of the speaker in a dialogue or in a transcript of speech.

Use the colon to separate hours and minutes when time is expressed in figures. When no minutes are expressed, it is not necessary to use two zeros with the number designating the hour. When the word *o'clock* is used, do not indicate the time in figures but express the time in words.

We shall be there at 3:30 P.M.
We shall be there at 3 P.M.
We shall be there at three o'clock.

The Apostrophe [']

To Indicate Possession Apostrophes are employed most commonly to form the possessive of nouns and pronouns. In words not ending with an *s* or *z* sound, *'s* is added; in those ending with an *s* or *z* sound, the common practice is to add only an apostrophe at the end. Most singular nouns take the *'s*, and most plural forms add only *'*.

Words not ending in s or z:
the children's playroom
somebody's hat

Words ending in s or z:
the babies' bottles
for goodness' sake

Exceptions may be found in the possessive form of proper names ending in *s* or *z*. There is a growing tendency to add *'s* to a name having one syllable even though it ends with an *s* sound, thus making James *James's*, Marx *Marx's*, and Schultz *Schultz's*. With names of more than one syllable, either form may be used unless the additional *s* makes the word difficult to pronounce. Then only the apostrophe is used.

Thomas's *or* Thomas'
Adams's *or* Adams'
Titus's *or* Titus'

but only Genesis'
Exodus'
Moses'

Personal pronouns do not take the apostrophe in the possessive form.

my, mine
your, yours
her, hers

our, ours
their, theirs
his, its, whose

To Indicate Omission An apostrophe is also used to show that one or more letters have been omitted from a word, or that numerals have been omitted from a number.

it's—it is; can't—cannot; you're—you are;
we'll—we will; where'er—wherever; '29—1929

Plurals of Letters or Numbers The plural of a letter or a number is formed by adding *'s*, although it should be noted that there is a growing trend to drop the apostrophe where years are concerned. Abbreviations form the plural by adding *'s*.

Dot your i's and cross your t's.
There are four s's, four i's, and two p's in Mississippi.
Watch your ABC's.
6's and 7's
a company of GI's
a carload of VIP's

Quotation Marks [" "] [' ']

There are two classes of quotations: *direct* and *indirect*. Quotation marks are required at the beginning and end of a word or words spoken in direct discourse.

Roy said, "I am reading a good book."

Indirect quotations require no quotation marks, and are commonly introduced by the word *that*.

Roy said that he was reading a good book.

If a direct quotation is interrupted by one or more words, the quotation marks are placed around the quoted matter only and not around the interrupting words.

"Hurry along," said the coach, "or we shall not make the game in time."

When quoting material, be careful to include every detail of punctuation even though you may not wholly agree with the details involved.

"Stir not up agitation! Give us peace!"

The use of slang, humor, and colloquial expressions is unsuited to formal speech or writing. If used, such words should be enclosed in quotation marks.

It was a "whale" of a story.

Translations of foreign words and phrases should be enclosed in quotations marks.

Au revoir means "till we meet again" or "good-bye."
Laissez faire means "noninterference."

In manuscripts and business correspondence, the title of a book, a booklet, a magazine, or a newspaper should be typed in capital and small letters (or all in capitals) and underlined. Enclose in quotation marks and type in capital and small letters the titles of essays, magazine articles, lectures, term papers, and the titles of chapters. The first letter of the first word and the first letter of every important word following is capitalized.

I have just finished reading Why England Slept.
The "Foreword to the Memorial Edition," written by Robert F. Kennedy, shows great depth of feeling and love for his brother, John F. Kennedy.
Did you read the article "One Man's Opinion" in this morning's New York Times?

When a lengthy quotation of two or more paragraphs is used, beginning or opening quotation marks are used at the start of each paragraph, and closing quotation marks appear only at the very end of the quoted passage.

No quotation marks are necessary in interviews, dramatic dialogues, or legal testimony where the name of the speaker or other identification precedes the speech, or where question and answer are clearly marked.

Judge: How do you plead, guilty or not guilty?
Defendant: Not guilty, Your Honor.
Q.: Where were you on the night of June 26?
A.: I don't remember.

Quotation marks are used to set off words or phrases that the writer wishes not to claim as his own. These may be the words of other persons, or they may be jargon, slang, barbarisms, figures of speech, and the like, which he "decontaminates" by using quotation marks.

Let my opponent produce his "incontrovertible evidence."
The young men apparently did it "for kicks."

A quotation within a quotation is enclosed by single quotation marks.

Jack remarked, "I believe Patrick Henry said, 'Give me liberty or give me death.' "

Note: The period within the quotation marks serves as end punctuation both for the sentence spoken by Jack and that spoken by Patrick Henry. The period is never doubled at the end of a quotation within a quotation.

The rule for punctuating quoted matter is quite simple. The period and comma are always *inside* the closing quotation marks; the colon and semicolon are always *outside* the closing quotation marks; the question mark and exclamation point will be inside or outside the closing quotation marks depending on whether they are or are not part of the quoted matter.

He said, "Call the police."
He said, "Who called the police?"
Who said, "Call the police"?
He said, "Call the police"; but the sirens were already wailing.

The Hyphen [-]

The hyphen is used primarily for end-of-line word divisions and for hyphenation of compound words.
Words may be divided *only* between syllables.
Words pronounced as one syllable may never be divided.
Words may not be divided in groups of fewer than three letters.
Abbreviations should never be carried over from one line to the next, and every attempt should be made to include the initials or first name of a person's name on the same line with his surname.

For book editing, and when preparing a manuscript, hyphens should not be used at the end of more than two successive lines. (This rule should also be followed for letter writing.) Breaking the last word of a paragraph is also considered bad form.

Do not hyphenate a word at the end of a page.

Dividing a compound word or a word already hyphenated should be avoided.

If numbers must be divided, the break should be made after a comma: There are 35,675,-
545 chickens in Nebraska.

The general rule in the hyphenation of compound words is this: When two or more words precede a noun and together form a single idea modifying the noun, they should be hyphenated; they are usually not hyphenated if they follow the noun. In many instances only the context of the sentence will determine whether a hyphenated compound is required, or whether the words should remain separate.

He said it in a very matter-of-fact way.
He knew that to be true as a matter of fact.
As a matter of fact, he knew that to be true.
Her dress was green and white.
Her green-and-white dress was pretty.

Note: Do not confuse the adverb and the adjective when they precede a noun—these are not hyphenated.

The beautifully illustrated book was enjoyed by the membership.

Hyphens are used to separate prefixes from words where the writer's meaning would otherwise be distorted.

The upholsterer re-covered the chair.
The police recovered the typewriter.

The hyphen is also used to separate a prefix from a proper noun, or to simplify a confusing combination.

anti-American, pre-Renaissance, mid-ocean

Hyphens are also used in all numbers ranging from twenty-one to ninety-nine, and in fractions: one-half, three-quarters. Hyphens are also used in designating years: nineteen-sixties, nineteen sixty-two (*not* nineteen-sixty-two).

The hyphen is used in titles when combined with *elect* or *ex*.

President-elect
ex-President

The hyphen is generally used when words are compounded with the prefix *self*.

self-satisfied, self-confident, self-possessed, self-starter

The Dash [—]

A word of caution against confusing the hyphen (-) and the dash (—). The hyphen connects, while the dash separates. The dash is formed on the typewriter with two hyphens, no space before, between, or after.

If properly used, the dash is effective to secure emphasis but has only a few legitimate uses in business letters. It may be used in place of the comma and parentheses in handling appositive and parenthetical expressions. It is also used to mark intentional repetition.

Exercise every day—*every* day—and find out for yourself how beneficial it is to your health and well being.

The dash may be used to show an abrupt change in thought.

We do not know when we shall go—here is the bus.

Parentheses [( )]

Parentheses are used to enclose words which give additional information but have little, if any, direct connection with the main thought expressed. Commas and dashes have already been discussed in this relationship. Material enclosed in commas or separated from the rest of the sentence by dashes adds something to the main thought expressed, although not something essential; material enclosed in parentheses adds nothing to the main thought and has no direct relationship to the rest of the sentence.

If we win the contest (and I feel certain we will), we shall compete in the national contest in Chicago.

Parentheses are widely used to enclose references to statements, authors, etc.

"How to Express Thoughts Properly" is outlined in full in our text (see page 124).
We are using *Effective Business English* (Jones and Smith) for reference.

The Underscore

Underscoring a word or a group of words may be done for emphasis, but this device should be used with caution. There are a few fundamental rules, however, which should be followed.

Underline the title of a book, a booklet, essay, play, magazine, or newspaper. (Full capitals are also acceptable.)

Note: This rule is discussed more fully under the subject of Quotation Marks.

When preparing copy for the printer, underline material which is to be printed in italics.

Do not use underscoring for emphasis in the body of the letter.

Do not break the underscoring when underscoring headings.

Do not break the underscoring of parts of the text unless each part or each word is intended to be emphasized separately.

Do not include the punctuation at the end of the sentence in the underscoring.

CAPITALIZATION

Conventions governing the use of capital letters are quite clear.

Capitalize the first word of every sentence.

The first person singular pronoun *I* and the vocative *O* are generally capitalized.

Unless style requires a different form, *a.m.* and *p.m.* are set in small letters without a space between them. Capital letters are used for B.C. and A.D. but, again, there is no space between them.

9:30 a.m.   10:30 p.m.
A.D. 1760 *or* 1760 A.D.
76 B.C.

Note: Although A.D. should technically precede the number of the year, popular usage permits it to follow the date. In printed matter B.C., A.D., a.m., and p.m. usually appear in small capitals (B.C., A.D., A.M., P.M.).

The first letter of a line of conventional poetry is capitalized. Much modern poetry, however, ignores this convention.

Hickory, dickory, dock
The mouse ran up the clock.

The first word after a colon should be capitalized only when it begins a complete sentence.

The candidate made only one promise: If elected, he would fight for better conditions.
The list contained these items: five pounds of flour, two dozen eggs, and a pound of butter.

Every direct quotation should begin with a capital, except where the quoted passage is grammatically woven into the text preceding it.

The announcer shouted, "There it goes, over the back wall for a home run!"
The announcer saw the ball going "over the back wall for a home run."

Capitalize the first letters of all important words in the titles of books, newspapers, magazines, chapters, poems, articles. Short conjunctions and prepositions are generally not capitalized.

How to Win Friends and Influence People

Geographical divisions and regions require capitals.

Arctic Circle   the Atlantic Seaboard
the Orient   the Great Plains

Compass points are capitalized when they are part of a generally accepted name, but not when they denote direction, or are used with common nouns.

Middle East   eastern New York
Old South   Head west for twenty-five miles.

Capitalize names of streets, parks, buildings, but not the general categories into which they fall.

General Post Office *but* We went to the *post office*.
Metropolitan Museum of Art *but* Some *museums* are open until five.
Empire State Building *but* Which is the tallest *building* in New York City?

Religions, religious leaders, the various appellations for God and the Christian Trinity require capitalization, as do all names for the Bible and its parts.

the Father, the Son, and the Holy Ghost
Virgin Mary, the Immaculate Virgin
Yahweh, Jehovah, Saviour, Messiah

Buddhism, Shintoism, Taoism
New Testament
Exodus
Sermon on the Mount
Ten Commandments

Capitalize the names of political parties, classes, clubs, organizations, movements, and their adherents. Use small letters for the terms that refer generally to ideology (bolshevism, fascism, socialism).

Democratic Party
the Right Wing
Farm Bloc
Boy Scouts of America

Political divisions are capitalized.

Holy Roman Empire	the Colonies
French Republic	Suffolk County
the Dominion	Eighth Congressional District

Government bodies, departments, bureaus, and courts are capitalized.

the Supreme Court	the Cabinet
House of Representatives	Census Bureau
Department of Labor	British Parliament

Capitalize the titles of all high-ranking government officials, and all appellations of the President of the United States. Many publishers, it should be pointed out, prefer small letters for titles that are not accompanied by the name of the official.

President	Commander-in-Chief
Secretary of State	Chief Justice
Undersecretary	Prime Minister
Ambassador to India	Minister of War

Capitalize the names of treaties, documents, and important events.

Second World War	Declaration of Independence
Treaty of Versailles	Boston Tea Party

Family designations, when used without a possessive pronoun, take a capital letter.

I sent Mother home by taxi.
I sent my mother home by taxi.

Capitalize seasons only when they are personified. All personifications require capitals.

The frosty breath of Winter settled on the land.
The voice of Envy whispered in her ear.
The mother of Invention is Necessity.
When Headquarters commands, we jump.
He saw Mother Nature's grim visage.

Names and epithets of peoples, races, and tribes are capitalized.

Caucasian	Sioux
Negro	Cliff Dwellers

Articles and prepositions are generally capitalized in the names of Englishmen and Americans, and are not capitalized in French, Italian, Spanish, German, and Dutch names, unless otherwise specified by family usage.

Thomas De Quincey	Ludwig van Beethoven
Martin Van Buren	Leonardo da Vinci
Fiorello La Guardia	San Juan de la Cruz

Capitalize the names of holidays and festivals.

Christmas Eve	Shrove Tuesday
Yom Kippur	New Year's Day

Capitalize such parts of a book as the Glossary, Contents, Index, and Preface.
Capitalize the first and last words in the salutation in business letters, and all titles.

My dear Sir	Dear Doctor Brown
My dear Reverend Lothrop	Dear Reverend Father

Capitalize only the first word of the complimentary close of a letter.

Very truly yours	Sincerely yours

SPELLING

General Suggestions

When in doubt as to the correct spelling of a word, consult the dictionary; do not take anything for granted.

Keep a list of your spelling errors and study them.
Learn the available lists of the most commonly misspelled words—there are many such lists.
Learn to spell by syllables, carefully pronouncing each syllable. Faulty spelling is often due to faulty pronunciation.
Use newly acquired words and make them part of your oral and written vocabulary.
Do not use the simplified or modern forms of spelling in business correspondence, as *thru* for *through*.
Learn some basic spelling rules such as the following.

cede, ceed, and sede endings According to the Government Style Manual, there is only one word which ends in *sede—supersede*, and three that end in *ceed—proceed* (but *procedure*), *exceed*, *succeed*. All other words using this combination end in *cede—precede*, *secede*, *recede*.

ie and ei a. After *c*, when the sound is long *e* (ē), the *e* usually precedes the *i*: *receive*, *deceive*, *ceiling*, *receipt*.
b. After most other letters, the *i* precedes the *e* (*ie*): *thief*, *grief*, *believe*, *achieve*, *lien*.
The exceptions must be learned, since they follow no rule: *neither*, *leisure*, *weird*, *seize*.
c. When the sound is *not* long *e* (ē), and especially if the sound is long *a* (ā), the *e* precedes the *i* (*ei*): *sleigh*, *veil*.

Beginnings and Endings of Words (Prefixes and Suffixes)

a. As a general rule, drop the final *e* in the base word when a suffix beginning with a vowel is added: decide—deciding; write—writing; type—typing. (When in doubt, use the dictionary.)
b. As a rule, retain the final *e* in the base word when a suffix beginning with a consonant is added: remote—remotely; care—carefully; adverse—adversely.
c. In applying the rule for adding *ed* or *ing*, the accent (or lack of it) may serve as a guide. Words of one syllable (and most words of more than one syllable) that end in a single consonant (except *f*, *h*, or *x*), preceded by a single vowel, double the final consonant *if the accent falls on the last syllable.*

plan—planned, planning; whet—whetted, whetting; bet—betting; can—canning
transfer—transferred, transferring; excel—excelled, excelling
omit—omitted, omitting; begin—beginning

d. When the word is *not* accented on the last syllable, the consonant is usually not doubled.

travel—traveled, traveling; benefit—benefited, benefiting; profit—profited, profiting; gossip—gossiped, gossiping

e. When the endings *ness* and *ly* are added to a word not ending in *y*, the base word rarely changes. In most words ending in *y*, the *y* changes to *i* when *ly* is added.

natural—naturally; similar—similarly; genuine—genuineness; blessed—blessedness; hazy—hazily; body—bodily

If the base word ends in *n* and the suffix *ness* is added, the *n* is doubled: sudden—suddenness; mean—meanness; vain—vainness.
f. In regard to the word endings *ise*, *ize*, *yze*, the most common form is *ize*, but here again the dictionary should be consulted if there is doubt.

legalize, fraternize, criticize, jeopardize
advertise, merchandise, surmise, enterprise
paralyze, analyze

◆ In British English *ise* is sometimes used for *ize*, as *realise* for *realize*. See the note under -IZE in the dictionary.
g. When the word beginnings (prefixes) *in*, *en*, *im*, *em*, *un*, *dis*, *mis*, *be*, *de*, *re*, *il*, and *over* are added to a word, the spelling of the base word is not changed.

inactive, enjoy, impending, embrace, uneasy
dismiss, mistrust, beguile, degrade, retreat, illegal, overhaul

h. When adding the suffix *ful*, the *l* is single except when *ly* is also added (*fully*): care—careful—carefully; hope—hopeful—hopefully.

Forming the Plurals of Nouns

a. Most nouns form the plural by simply adding *s*: table—tables; house—houses.
b. Some nouns, especially those ending in *s*, form the plural by adding *es*: class—classes; glass—glasses.
c. Words ending in *y* preceded by a consonant form the plural by changing the *y* to *i* and adding *es*: candy—candies; study—studies; secretary—secretaries.

d. Words ending in *y* preceded by a vowel form the plural without any change in the word: key—keys; boy—boys; money—moneys (monies when referring to "sums of money").

e. Nouns ending in *o* preceded by a vowel form the plural by adding *s*: rodeo—rodeos; radio—radios.

When the *o* is preceded by a consonant, the plural is formed by adding *es*: hero—heroes; torpedo—torpedoes.

f. Nouns referring to music which end in *o* preceded by a consonant form the plural by simply adding *s*: piano—pianos; oratorio—oratorios; contralto—contraltos; soprano—sopranos.

g. Some few nouns follow none of the above rules but form the plural in an unusual way: child—children; tooth—teeth; mouse—mice; ox—oxen.

h. Compound nouns (more than one noun) form the plural from the main word: notary public—notaries public; trade-union—trade-unions; father-in-law—fathers-in-law; court-martial—courts-martial.

i. When a solid compound ends in *ful*, the plural is formed at the end of the solid compound and not within the word: basketfuls, spoonfuls, pocketfuls.

j. Words taken from another language sometimes form the plural as they would in the original language: stratum—strata; addendum—addenda; datum—data.

k. When the words in compounds are of almost equal importance, both parts of the compound are pluralized: heads of departments; women operators.

◆ For further information, see the note under PLURAL in the body of this dictionary.

CONFUSING WORDS

[Including words that have different meanings but are pronounced the same (*homophones*) or similarly]

accept See EXCEPT.

addition, edition *addition* means the process of joining together or finding the sum of. *edition* refers to the form in which a book, magazine, or other literary work is published: first *edition*.

advice, advise *advice* is the noun: to give *advice*. *advise* is the verb: to *advise* a person.

affect See EFFECT.

all ready See ALREADY.

all right, alright *all right* is the only spelling to be used: It is *all right* to do so. The spelling *alright* is not yet considered acceptable and should not be used.

allude, elude *allude* means to make indirect or casual reference: He *alluded* to one of Shakespeare's sonnets. *elude* means to avoid or escape: The meaning *eludes* me.

already, all ready *already* means before or by this time or the time mentioned: The group has *already* gone. *all ready* (two words) means that everyone is ready to do a given thing: We are *all ready* to go.

among, between *among* is used when referring to more than two persons or things. *between* is usually preferable when referring to only two persons or things.

appraise, apprise *appraise* means to make an official valuation of. *apprise* means to notify or inform.

ascent, assent *ascent* means rising, soaring, or climbing: the *ascent* of the mountain. *assent* means to express agreement, consent, sanction: to *assent* to a course of action.

between See AMONG.

can See MAY.

capital, capitol *capital* means (*n.*) property, chief city: Albany is the *capital* of New York; and (*adj.*) of chief importance. *capitol*, always a noun, means a building in which a State legislature meets: The *capitol* is on Chamber Street.

censor, censure *censor* means (*n.*) an official examiner of manuscripts, plays, etc.; (*v.*) to act as a censor; delete; suppress. *censure* means (*v.*) to express disapproval of; condemn; (*n.*) the expression of disapproval or blame.

census See SENSES.

cite, sight, site *cite* means to quote or to summon: to *cite* an incident. *sight* means a view, a vision: a beautiful *sight*. *site* means a place or location: the *site* of the church.

compliment, complement *compliment* means praise or congratulation. *complement* means one of two parts that mutually complete each other.

consul See COUNCIL.

correspondents, correspondence *correspondents* refers to people who communicate by means of letters. *correspondence* refers to the letters written.

council, counsel, consul *council* means an assembly convened for consultation. *counsel* means guidance, advice; also, a lawyer. *consul* means an officer residing in a foreign country to protect his own country's interests.

creditable, credible *creditable* means deserving credit or esteem; praiseworthy: a *creditable* project for reducing poverty. *credible* means capable of being believed; reliable: a *credible* alibi.

decent, descent, dissent *decent* means proper; respectable. *descent* means the act of descending or going downward. *dissent* means (*v.*) to disagree; (*n.*) a disagreement.

device, devise *device* is the noun: a handy *device* for opening bottles. *devise* is the verb: He *devised* a new way to open bottles.

dissent See DECENT.

edition See ADDITION.

effect, affect *effect*, both a noun and a verb, means (*v.*) to bring about; to cause or achieve: The treatments will *effect* an early cure; and (*n.*) result, outcome. *affect*, a verb only, means to influence or act upon: Fear *affects* the mind.

effective, effectual *effective* means producing a desired result: *Effective* action averted the strike. *effectual* means having the power to produce a desired result: *effectual* legal steps.

elicit, illicit *elicit* means to bring to light: to *elicit* the truth. *illicit* means unlawful or unauthorized.

elude See ALLUDE.

eminent, imminent *eminent* means high in station; distinguished; prominent: an *eminent* statesman. *imminent* means about to happen (said especially of danger): an *imminent* calamity.

except, accept *except* means with the exclusion or omission of. *accept* means to receive or agree to; acknowledge: to *accept* an invitation.

farther, further *farther* refers to distance. *further* means to a greater degree; more; in addition.

formerly, formally *formerly* means some time ago; once: He was *formerly* a judge. *formally* means with formality or with regard to form: *formally* dressed.

further See FARTHER.

illicit See ELICIT.

imminent See EMINENT.

lay, lie See below, under CONSISTENCY OF TENSE AND PERSON OF VERBS.

learn See TEACH.

lesson, lessen *lesson* refers to instructive or corrective example. *lessen* means to make less; decrease.

loose, lose *loose* means not fastened or attached. *lose* means to part with; to be deprived of.

may, can *may* expresses permission: The child *may* play in the yard. *can* expresses ability to do: The child *can* do better than he is doing at present.

past, passed *past* means (*adj.*) ended or finished: His hopes are *past*; and (*n.*) time gone by: He dreams of the *past*. *passed*, the past tense and past participle of *pass*, means went (or gone) beyond or farther than: The car, which was going at high speed, *passed* him easily.

persecute, prosecute *persecute* means to maltreat or oppress; to harass. *prosecute* is generally used in a legal sense—to bring suit against.

personal, personnel *personal* pertains to a person: *personal* matters, *personal* opinions. *personnel* pertains to a body or group of persons: *personnel* problems, *personnel* department.

practical, practicable *practical* pertains to actual use and experience. *practicable* means feasible or usable. A *practicable* plan is a workable plan, but a *practical* plan is one based on experience rather than theory, or one that can easily be put into effect.

principal, principle *principal* means (*n.*) head or leader: The *principal* of the school will give the order; and (*adj.*) highest in rank; chief: The *principal* member of an orchestra is the concertmaster. *principle*, always a noun, means a fundamental truth or law: We cannot sacrifice the *principle* for which we stand.

prosecute See PERSECUTE.

rise, raise See below, under CONSISTENCY OF TENSE AND PERSON OF VERBS.

senses, census *senses*, the plural of *sense*, refers to the faculty of sensation, as through taste, touch, hearing, smell, or sight. *census* refers to an official count of the people of a country or district, etc.

sight See CITE.

sit, set See below, under CONSISTENCY OF TENSE AND PERSON OF VERBS.

site See CITE.

stationery, stationary *stationery* refers to writing supplies. *stationary* means remaining in one place.

sweet, suite *sweet* means agreeable to the sense of taste. *suite* refers to a set or series of things intended to be used together: *suite* of rooms, *suite* of furniture.

teach, learn The teacher *teaches*; the student *learns*.

CONSISTENCY OF TENSE AND PERSON OF VERBS

Care should be given not to change the *tense* or *form* of the verb or the *person* of a pronoun in the middle of a sentence. Such violation is generally due to carelessness.

The *tense* of a verb indicates the time when something took place; and the three main tenses are *present*, *past*, and *future*.

I *eat* my dinner.
I *ate* my dinner.
I *shall eat* my dinner.

The form of the verb indicates *active voice* when the subject of the verb is acting, and the *passive voice* when the subject of the verb is acted upon.

I *am helping.*
I *am being helped.*

The *person* of a pronoun denotes the speaker (*first person* I, we); the person spoken to (*second person* you); and the person spoken of (*third person* he, she, it, they). The writer of the letter should never refer to himself in the third person (as "the writer" or "the undersigned") but should use the first person.

Some verbs cause confusion in both writing and speaking because of the similarity in spelling and in principal parts.

The most common verbs in this group are: **lie—lay; rise—raise; and sit—set.**

The principal parts of these verbs are as follows:

lie—meaning to rest or recline
lay—meaning to place or put
Present: lie—I *lie* down to rest at ten o'clock each morning.
lay—I *lay* the wood for the fire each day.
Past: lay—I *lay* in bed too long.
laid—I *laid* the book on the table.
Past Participle: lain—She has *lain* there for an hour.
laid—She has *laid* the book on the table.
◆ For further information, see the note under LAY¹ in the body of this dictionary.

rise—meaning to move upward
raise—meaning to cause to rise up, to arouse or awaken
Present: rise—I *rise* at six o'clock in the morning.
raise—I *raise* the flag each morning.
Past: rose—I *rose* at six o'clock today.
raised—I *raised* the flag this morning.
Past Participle: risen—I shall have *risen* by six o'clock.
raised—I shall have *raised* the prices on these articles by then.

sit—meaning to seat oneself
set—meaning to fix firmly or make fast or place
Present: sit—I like to *sit* in the sun.
set—I plan to *set* the table for six persons.
Past: sat—I *sat* in the sun.
set—He *set* the alarm for four o'clock.
Past Participle: sat—I have *sat* in the sun one hour.
set—The sun has *set* in a bright glow.

shall—will ◆ See the note under SHALL in the body of this dictionary.

BUSINESS CORRESPONDENCE

Let it be stated at the outset that there are no unimportant letters. Good letters help to increase business, make friends, and influence people favorably; sloppy letters have the opposite effect.

Good letters are not written in haste. Often, they are written, revised, and rewritten until they express clearly the meaning the writer wishes to convey to his reader. As one authority puts it: "You must write not so that you can be understood but so that you cannot possibly be misunderstood."

The formalities of letter writing are definite and rigid. Brevity and clarity are the prime virtues. Carbon copies are made to give the sender an up-to-date file of his correspondence. The number of copies made will depend on the number of persons concerned with the information, but one office copy must be made of every letter or document sent out, either interoffice or through the mail.

Letter Styles The most common letter styles are the Block, Modified Block with Paragraph Indentions, Modified Block without Paragraph Indentions, and the Indented; but there are also the Inverted Paragraph style and the NOMA Simplified. (NOMA stands for National Office Management Association.)

Forms of Punctuation—Open, Closed, and Mixed
When the (Strictly) Open punctuation is used, no punctuation is used after the date line, after the inside address (unless there is an abbreviation), after the salutation, or after the complimentary close.

When Closed punctuation is used, place a period after the date line, and a comma (unless there is an abbreviation) after each line in the inside address except the last, where there is a period. Place a colon after the salutation and a comma after the complimentary close. Closed punctuation is generally

used with the Indented letter style and rarely ever used with the Block style.

When Mixed punctuation is used, only two marks are involved unless abbreviations in the inside address dictate otherwise—a colon goes after the salutation and a comma after the complimentary close.

Letter Placement on the Standard-Size Letterhead
Letters are classified as short, average, and long. Short letters generally have wider side margins and are placed lower on the page than the long letters. The side (horizontal) margins should not vary by more than two or four spaces. The top and bottom (vertical) spacing should not vary by more than six lines to look well on the page.

In determining the placement of the letter on the page, the size of the typewriter type (pica or elite) must be considered. Pica type has ten spaces to the inch, whereas elite type has twelve spaces to the inch.

The following letter is in the Modified Block style. The date line is to the right and the complimentary close begins at or about the center of the letter. (The close may begin at the center of the horizontal line, five spaces to the left of center, or five spaces to the right of center, depending on the signature and title of the sender. Try to begin at the center, if possible.)

SAMPLE LETTER

(The address of the sender or merely the date line should begin eighteen or fewer spaces from the top of the page, depending on the depth of the letterhead and the length of the letter.)

811 Cedar Street (*Heading*)
San Francisco, California 94125
July 21, 1963 (*Date line*)

(leave 3 or more lines blank)

Mr. Jack Armstrong, President (*Inside Address*)
American Steel Foundation
355 Lexington Avenue
New York, New York 10017 (leave 2 spaces between State
(leave 1 line blank) and ZIP Code)
Attention: Transportation Manager
(leave 1 line blank)
Dear Mr. Armstrong: (*Salutation*)
(leave 1 line blank)
Two spaces below the Salutation begins the body of the letter, which is single-spaced, with a double space between paragraphs. Each paragraph including the first begins flush with the left-hand margin. The spacing between the Heading and the Inside Address, and also between the top of the page and the Date Line, may be expanded if the letter is short so as to improve the appearance of the page. The Attention line is used to alert a particular member of the company, as the personnel manager, the purchasing agent, etc. Where it is customary to cite the subject of the correspondence separately from the text, it may appear on the same line with the Salutation, flush against the margin on the right; or it may be centered between the Salutation and the Body of the letter; or it may be placed flush with the left-hand margin between the Salutation and the Body of the letter, depending on the style of letter used.

(leave 1 line blank between paragraphs)
Two spaces below the body of the letter, centered, or five spaces to the right or left of center (depending on the signature and title of the sender), is placed the Complimentary Close. In formal correspondence this is *Yours truly, Very truly yours*; for a person of sufficient rank, *Respectfully yours* is appropriate.

(leave 1 line blank)

Yours truly, (*Complimentary Close*)
(leave 1 line blank)
(full caps) J & B BOILER CORPORATION

(leave 3 lines blank)

(capitals and small letters) John J. Little (*Signature*)
(capitals and small letters) Chairman (*Title*) (no space
between name and title)
(leave 1 line blank)
JJL: bp (*Identifying Initials*)
(leave 1 line blank)
Enclosure (*Enclosures*)
(leave 1 line blank)
cc: Mr. George Phipps (*Notation of Copies Sent*)

Elements of a Business Letter

Heading This consists of the address of the sender (often part of the letterhead) and the date of the letter. The date line ends flush with the right-hand margin except in the strictly Block and the NOMA styles.

Inside Address This identifies the recipient of the letter, and enables the sender to identify the file copy. It includes the name of the recipient, his title, if any, and the address.

Salutation For letters addressed to a company, *Gentlemen* is a suitable greeting. Where an individual is addressed, any one of the following may be appropriate: *Dear Sir, Dear Madam, Dear Mr.* (or *Mrs.* or *Miss*) (name of the person specifically addressed). When the marital status of a woman is unknown, she is addressed as *Miss* or simply by the letter *M*. The Salutation in business letters is always followed by a colon except in the Strictly Open form. The NOMA form uses no Salutation.

Complimentary Close The flowery close that was considered good form at one time, and is still used in many European countries, is a thing of the past in this country. The most-used closings are: Yours very truly, Very truly yours, Yours truly, Sincerely yours, Very sincerely yours. Except in extremely formal contexts, it is *not* considered good form to run the Body of the letter into the Complimentary Close, such as: Awaiting your decision, I remain, Very truly yours, etc. (The NOMA style letter uses no Close.)

Signature The name of the sender is usually typed in capitals and small letters, but sometimes in full capitals, four spaces below the Complimentary Close. On the line following is typed, always in capitals and small letters, the position he occupies in the firm, unless, of course, this information is included in the letterhead. When the company name is typed at the bottom of the letter, as well as the name and title of the writer, the company name is typed in full capitals two spaces below the Complimentary Close. Four spaces below this is the name of the writer in capitals and small letters; the writer's title appears on the line below the writer's name, always typed in capitals and small letters.

Identifying Initials In the lower left-hand corner of the letter, two spaces below the writer's title or name, it is customary to put the initials or name of the sender and the initials of the secretary. Full capitals or capital and small letters may be used, and the identification of the writer and secretary separated by the colon or diagonal (: /).

Enclosures Enclosures, if any, are indicated two spaces below the identification letters. If there is only one enclosure, the word "Enclosure" or merely "Enc." may be used. If more than one enclosure is being sent, the number must be indicated (Enclosures 4). Identifying the enclosure or enclosures may also be done (as Enclosure: Invoice, Number 642).

Postcript Generally, postcripts are not used in routine business correspondence. They are, however, used in sales letters for emphasis or to call attention to matters which, if placed in the body of the letter, might be overlooked. When a postcript is used, it should be prefaced by the letters P.S. (two spaces follow) and be placed two spaces below the Identification, or the Enclosure, if there is one. If the Block style is used, the letters P.S. are flush with the left-hand margin. If the Indented form of letter is used, the letters P.S. are indented five spaces from the left margin. The second and following lines are flush with the left margin, even with the lines in the body of the letter. The Postscript is not generally signed but should be initialed by the writer.

Notation of Copies Sent When a copy of a letter is sent to one or more persons, notation of this fact is usually made on the original letter and on all carbons. In this way, all parties concerned with the original letter know what other person or persons received copies. The notation is made two spaces below the Identification initials or two spaces below the last item in the letter, such as Enclosure or Postscript. The words "Copy to" or "Copies to" or the abbreviation "cc" may be used. If for some reason the writer does not wish to make known to whom copies were sent, the notation may be made only on the office file copy and is usually placed in a position other than the lower left—it may be placed in the upper left corner, which is not used for any other part of the letter. This position of the carbon notation signifies that the distribution of the carbon(s) is confidential but the notation keeps the information in the office files for future reference.

Business Envelopes The address on the envelope will coincide in all particulars with the Inside Address. Double spacing is preferred in order to expedite the mailman's task, even in the four-line address. The size of the envelope to be used (regular or legal—No. 6¾ or No. 10 being the most common with the standard 8½ by 11 inch paper) will be determined by the material to be sent. Letters of two pages or longer, or a one-page letter with an enclosure, should be sent in the larger envelope. The first line of the address should be written one or two lines below the horizontal center and five spaces to the left of the vertical center on the No. 6¾ envelope and at the center of the No. 10 envelope. If one or more of the lines in the address are particularly long or short, some adjustment should be made in placing the address properly on the envelope. The style of punctuation must agree with the inside address in the letter. The ZIP Code number is typed two spaces below the state (two spaces after the state in the inside address of the letter with no punctuation between the state and the ZIP Code number), whereas the Zone number is written between the city and state with a comma after the number (San Diego 3, California). Names of states must always be written in full on the envelope as well as in the inside address. The words *Street, Court, Boulevard, Avenue*, etc., must always be written in full. Do not use *th, st, rd* with street numbers; write the address as follows: 125 East 45 Street.

Paragraphing in Business Letters There is no one rule for paragraphing in business letters. Most letters are of the short or medium length; therefore, plan on a short opening paragraph which states the purpose of the letter, or reason for writing, in clear, concise English. Avoid trite expressions. One or two paragraphs will probably be needed to carry the message, and a short closing should suggest action. Avoid overparagraphing; on the other hand, the busy executive has to absorb the substance of the letter as quickly as possible, and the long, involved paragraph tends to lose the reader. It is better to break up one main thought into two or three paragraphs than to make it difficult for the reader to grasp your message. Enumerations and quotations should be indented at the right of the letter as well as at the left-hand margin; enumerations may be numbered as well, and each enumeration should be treated as a paragraph. If numbers are used with the enumerations, two spaces are left after the period following the number, except in the NOMA letter, where no period follows the number.

Spacing in Business Letters The single-spaced letter is almost invariably used, with two spaces between paragraphs. In the first place, single spacing gives a better appearance; in the second place, it saves expensive stationery, tissues, and carbon, as well as filing space, since many of the single-spaced letters would go to two or more pages if they were double-spaced. If other than the Block paragraph is used, the indention may be five or ten spaces, but most writers prefer five spaces. When the Inverted Paragraph style is used, the overhang is also five spaces.

When a letter requires two or more pages, the second and subsequent pages must be identified with the first. There are various methods of doing this, but the two neatest and quickest styles are as follows:

Acme Products -2- Date
or
Acme Products—Page 2—Date

Spacing for Rough Drafts When preparing technical or otherwise difficult and important matter for printing or mailing, the copy should be double- or triple-spaced to leave room for corrections. Single-spaced copy is very difficult to correct.

Stationery Sizes The different sizes of letterheads can be identified by name. The common terms and dimensions are as follows:

Standard	8½ x 11 inches
Half-sheet	8½ x 5½ "
Monarch	7¼ x 10½ "
Baronial	5½ x 8½ "

The Standard and Half-sheet size stationery take the No. 10 and No. 6¾ envelopes respectively.

The Monarch and Baronial, which are used for personal letters and frequently by top executives in the firm, take their own special size envelopes—7½ x 3⅞ inches and 6 x 4⅝ inches, respectively.

Having various sizes of stationery is costly and time-consuming in handling, and the pages that are smaller than the standard file-folder size are troublesome in the files.

Carbon Paper and Carbon Packs To produce good clear carbon copies, care must be given to the selection of the weight and grade of the original copy, the tissue sheets, and the carbon paper. Most typewriters have a "copy set" which makes provision for space and pressure with respect to the cylinder, and the adjustment should be made to produce the best copies.

When only one copy is required for the files and the letter will be only one page in length, many offices use the back of the incoming letter for the file copy of the reply in order to save filing space as well as time.

In offices where it is standard procedure to make many carbons, ready-made carbon packs are used. The carbon paper and tissue sheets are fastened together at the bottom and save a great deal of time because the typist does not have to collate the papers. The carbons are thrown away after one using, since an inexpensive grade of carbon paper is used. The packs may be purchased in any number of sheets.

Making Corrections by Spreading and Squeezing Letters Stenographers should learn the device for making corrections by spreading or squeezing letters instead of retyping the page containing the error. This is a difficult matter and takes a little skill. By erasing all or part of the word containing the error, and by manipulating the spacer, the word can be contracted or spread, thus concealing the insertion or deletion of a letter.

Erasing If there is a movable carriage on the machine, move the carriage to the right or to the left to prevent the erasure particles from falling into the interior of the machine. If the carriage is stationary, move the writing unit away from the place in the copy containing the error in order to avoid having the erasure particles fall into the writing unit. Use the eraser shield, which has various slots to protect the typed words not to be erased. Be careful not to smudge the paper, particularly when correcting errors on carbon copies. A softer eraser should be used on the carbon tissues than the eraser used on the original.

FORMS OF ADDRESS

President of the United States
Address: Business: The President
The White House
Washington, D.C.
Social: The President
and Mrs. Washington
The White House
Washington, D.C.
Salutation: Formal: Sir:
Informal: My dear Mr. President:
Closing: Formal: I have the honor to remain,
Most respectfully yours,
Informal: Very respectfully yours,
In Conversation: Mr. President or Sir
Title of Introduction: *Only the name of the person being introduced is spoken*

Vice President of the United States
Address: Business: The Vice President
United States Senate
Washington, D.C.
Social: The Vice President
and Mrs. Hope
Home Address
Salutation: Formal: Sir
Informal: My dear Mr. Vice President:
Closing: Formal: Very truly yours,
Informal: Sincerely yours, or Faithfully yours,
In Conversation: Mr. Vice President or Sir
Title of Introduction: The Vice President

Chief Justice of the United States
Address: Business: The Chief Justice
The Supreme Court
Washington, D.C.
Social: The Chief Justice
and Mrs. Page
Home Address
Salutation: Formal: Sir
Informal: My dear Chief Justice
Closing: Formal: Very truly yours,
Informal: Sincerely yours, or Faithfully yours,
In Conversation: Chief Justice or Sir
Title of Introduction: The Chief Justice

Associate Justice of the Supreme Court
Address: Business: Justice Katsaros
The Supreme Court
Washington, D.C.
Social: Justice Katsaros   or Justice Daly and
and Mrs. Katsaros   Mr. Jay Daly
Home Address   Home Address
Salutation: Formal: Sir or Madam
Informal: My dear Justice Katsaros
Closing: Formal: Very truly yours,
Informal: Sincerely yours,
In Conversation: Justice or Justice Daly or Sir or Madam
Title of Introduction: Justice Katsaros

Informal: Sincerely yours,
In Conversation: Mr. Justice or Mr. Justice Katsaros or Sir
Title of Introduction: Mr. Justice Katsaros

Cabinet Officer
Address: Business: The Honorable Gary George Gussin
The Secretary of the Treasury
or The Attorney General
or The Postmaster General
Washington, D.C.
Social: The Secretary of the Treasury
and Mrs. Gussin
Home Address
or (for a woman cabinet member)
Mr. and Mrs. Henry Leo Woods
Salutation: Formal: Sir: or Dear Sir: or Madam:
Informal: My dear Mr. Secretary:
or My dear Mr. Attorney General:
or My Dear Mr. Postmaster General:
or Madam Secretary:
Closing: Formal: Very truly yours,
Informal: Sincerely yours,
In Conversation: Mr. Secretary or Madam Secretary or
Mr. Attorney General or
Mr. Postmaster General or Sir
Title of Introduction: The Secretary of the Treasury or
The Attorney General

Former President
Address: Business: The Honorable
Alfred Edward Work
Office Address
Social: The Honorable
Alfred Edward Work
and Mrs. Work
Home Address
Salutation: Formal: Sir:
Informal: My dear Mr. Work:
Closing: Formal: Very truly yours,
Informal: Sincerely yours,
In Conversation: Mr. Work or Sir
Title of Introduction: The Honorable Alfred Edward Work

United States Senator
Address: Business: The Honorable
John Wandzilak
United States Senate
Washington, D.C.
Social: The Honorable
John Wandzilak
and Mrs. Wandzilak
Home Address
or (for a woman senator)
Mr. and Mrs. John Row Doe
Salutation: Formal: Sir: or Madam:
Informal: My dear Senator Wandzilak:
Closing: Formal: Very truly yours,
Informal: Sincerely yours,
In Conversation: Senator or Senator Wandzilak or Sir
Title of Introduction: Senator Wandzilak of Alaska

Speaker of the House of Representatives
Address: Business: The Honorable
Walter Grevesmuhl
The Speaker of the House of
Representatives
Washington, D.C.
Social: The Speaker
and Mrs. Grevesmuhl
Home Address
Salutation: Formal: Sir:
Informal: My dear Mr. Speaker:
Closing: Formal: Very truly yours,
Informal: Sincerely yours,
In Conversation: Mr. Speaker or Sir
Title of Introduction: The Speaker of the House of
Representatives

Member of the House of Representatives
Address: Business: The Honorable
Henry Cobb Wellcome
United States House of Representatives
Washington, D.C.

Social: The Honorable
Henry Cobb Wellcome
and Mrs. Wellcome
Home Address
or (for a woman member)
Mr. and Mrs. John Knox Jones
Salutation: Formal: Sir: *or* Madam:
Informal: My dear Mr. Wellcome:
Closing: Formal: Very truly yours,
Informal: Sincerely yours,
In Conversation: Mr. Wellcome *or* Mrs. Jones *or* Sir
or Madam
Title of Introduction: Representative Wellcome from
Nebraska

Ambassador of the United States
Address: Business: The Honorable
John Wilson Smith
The Ambassador of the United States
American Embassy
London, England
Social: The Honorable
John Wilson Smith
and Mrs. Smith
Home Address
or (for a woman ambassador)
Mr. and Mrs. Joseph Leeds Walker
Home Address
Salutation: Formal: Sir: *or* Madam:
Informal: My dear Mr. Ambassador: *or* My dear
Madam Ambassador:
Closing: Formal: Very truly yours,
Informal: Sincerely yours,
In Conversation: Mr. Ambassador *or* Madam Ambassa-
dor *or* Sir *or* Madam
Title of Introduction: The American Ambassador *or (if neces-
sary)* Our Ambassador to England

Minister Plenipotentiary of the United States
Address: Business: The Honorable
James Lee Row
The Minister of the United States
American Legation
Oslo, Norway
Social: The Honorable
James Lee Row
and Mrs. Row
Home Address
or (for a woman minister)
Mr. and Mrs. Arthur Johnson
Home Address
Salutation: Formal: Sir: *or* Madam:
Informal: My dear Mr. Minister *or* My dear
Madam Minister:
Closing: Formal: Very truly yours,
Informal: Sincerely yours,
In Conversation: Mr. Row *or* Mrs. Johnson
Title of Introduction: Mr. Row, the American Minister *or
(if necessary)* Mrs. Johnson, the
American Minister to Denmark

Consul of the United States
Address: Business: Mr. John Smith
American Consul
Rue de Quelque Chose
Paris, France
Social: Mr. and Mrs. John Smith
Home Address
Salutation: Formal: Sir: *or* My dear Sir:
Informal: Dear Mr. Smith:
Closing: Formal: Sincerely yours,
Informal: Sincerely yours,
In Conversation: Mr. Smith
Title of Introduction: Mr. Smith

Ambassador of a Foreign Country
Address: Business: His Excellency
Juan Luis Ortega
The Ambassador of Mexico
Washington, D.C.
Social: His Excellency
The Ambassador of Mexico
and Señora Ortega
Home Address

Salutation: Formal: Excellency:
Informal: My dear Mr. Ambassador:
Closing: Formal: Very truly yours,
Informal: Sincerely yours, *or* Faithfully yours,
In Conversation: Mr. Ambassador *or* Excellency *or* Sir
Title of Introduction: The Ambassador of Mexico

Minister of a Foreign Country
Address: Business: The Honorable
Carluh Matti
The Minister of Kezeah
Washington, D.C.
Social: The Honorable
Carluh Matti
and Mrs. Matti
Home Address
Salutation: Formal: Sir:
Informal: My dear Mr. Minister:
Closing: Formal: Very truly yours,
Informal: Sincerely yours,
In Conversation: Mr. Minister *or* Sir
Title of Introduction: The Minister of Kezeah

Governor of a State
Address: Business: The Honorable
Joseph L. Marvin
Governor of Idaho
Boise, Idaho
Social: The Honorable
Joseph L. Marvin
and Mrs. Marvin
Home Address
Salutation: Formal: Sir:
Informal: Dear Governor Marvin:
Closing: Formal: Very truly yours,
Informal: Sincerely yours,
In Conversation: Governor Marvin *or* Sir
Title of Introduction: The Governor *or (if necessary)* The
Governor of Idaho

State Senators and Representatives are addressed like U.S.
Senators and Representatives, with appropriate addresses.

Mayor
Address: Business: His [or Her] Honor the Mayor
City Hall
Easton, Maryland
Social: His Honor the Mayor
and Mrs. Lake
Home Address
or (for a woman mayor)
Mr. and Mrs. L. T. Wayne
Home Address
Salutation: Formal: Sir: *or* Madam:
Informal: Dear Mayor Lake:
Closing: Formal: Very truly yours,
Informal: Sincerely yours,
In Conversation: Mr. Mayor *or* Madam Mayor
Title of Introduction: Mayor Lake

Judge
Address: Business: The Honorable
Carson Little
Justice, Appellate Division
Supreme Court of the State of New York
Albany, New York
Social: The Honorable
Carson Little
and Mrs. Little
Home Address
Salutation: Formal: Sir:
Informal: Dear Judge Little:
Closing: Formal: Very truly yours,
Informal: Sincerely yours,
In Conversation: Mr. Justice
Title of Introduction: The Honorable Carson Little, Judge of
the Appellate Division of the Su-
preme Court

Protestant Bishop
Address: Business: The Right Reverend John S. Bowman
Bishop of Rhode Island
Providence, Rhode Island
Social: The Right Reverend John S. Bowman
and Mrs. Bowman

Salutation: Formal: Right Reverend Sir:
    Informal: My dear Bishop Bowman:
  Closing: Formal: Respectfully yours,
    Informal: Faithfully yours, or Sincerely yours,
In Conversation: Bishop Bowman
Title of Introduction: Bishop Bowman

Protestant Clergyman
Address: Business: The Reverend David Dekker
    Address of his church
    or (if he holds the degree)
    The Reverend David Dekker, D.D.
    Address of his church
  Social: The Reverend David Dekker and Mrs.
    Dekker
    Home Address
Salutation: Formal: Sir: or My dear Sir:
    Informal: Dear Mr. [or Dr.] Dekker:
  Closing: Formal: Sincerely yours, or Faithfully yours,
    Informal: Sincerely yours, or Faithfully yours,
In Conversation: Mr. [or Dr.] Dekker
Title of Introduction: Mr. [or Dr.] Dekker

Rabbi
Address: Business: Rabbi Paul Aaron Fine
    Address of his synagogue
    or (if he holds the degree)
    Dr. Paul Aaron Fine, D.D.
    Address of his synagogue
  Social: Rabbi [or Dr.] and Mrs. Paul Aaron Fine
    Home Address
Salutation: Formal: Dear Sir:
    Informal: Dear Rabbi [or Dr.] Fine:
  Closing: Formal: Sincerely yours,
    Informal: Sincerely yours,
In Conversation: Rabbi [or Doctor] Fine
Title of Introduction: Rabbi [or Doctor] Fine

The Pope
Address: His Holiness Pope Paul VI
  or His Holiness the Pope
    Vatican City
Salutation: Your Holiness:
Closing: Your Holiness' most humble servant,
In Conversation: Your Holiness

Cardinal
Address: His Eminence Alberto Cardinal Vezzetti
    Archbishop of Baltimore
    Baltimore, Maryland
Salutation: Your Eminence:
  Closing: I have the honor to remain,
    Your Eminence's humble servant,
In Conversation: Your Eminence
Title of Introduction: One is presented to: His Eminence,
    Cardinal Vezzetti

Roman Catholic Archbishop
Address: The Most Reverend Preston Lowen
Salutation: Formal: Your Excellency: or Most Reverend Sir:
    Informal: Most Reverend and dear Sir:
Closing: I have the honor to remain,
    Your Excellency's humble servant,
In Conversation: Your Excellency
Title of Introduction: One is presented to: The Most Reverend
    The Archbishop of San Francisco

Roman Catholic Bishop
Address: The Most Reverend Matthew S. Borden
    Address of his church
Salutation: Formal: Most Reverend Sir:
    Informal: My dear Bishop Borden:
  Closing: Formal: I have the honor to remain,
    Your obedient servant,
    Informal: Faithfully yours,
  In Conversation: Your Excellency
Title of Introduction: Bishop Borden

Monsignor
Address: The Right Reverend Monsignor Ryan
    Address of his church
Salutation: Formal: Right Reverend and dear Monsignor
    Ryan:
    Informal: Reverend and dear Monsignor Ryan:

Closing: Respectfully yours,
In Conversation: Monsignor Ryan
Title of Introduction: Monsignor Ryan

Priest
Address: The Reverend John Matthews [and the initials of
    his order]
    Address of his church
Salutation: Formal: Reverend Father:
    Informal: Dear Father Matthews:
  Closing: Formal: I remain, Reverend Father, yours faith-
    fully,
    Informal: Faithfully yours,
In Conversation: Father or Father Matthews or Your
    Reverence
Title of Introduction: The Reverend Father Matthews

Member of Religious Order
Address: Sister Angelica [and initials of order] or
    Brother James [and initials]
    Address
Salutation: Formal: My dear Sister: or My dear Brother
    Informal: Dear Sister Angelica: or Dear Brother
    James
  Closing: Formal: Respectfully yours,
    Informal: Faithfully yours,
In Conversation: Sister Angelica or Brother James
Title of Introduction: Sister Angelica [or Brother James],
    may I present Mrs. Jones

University Professor
Address: Business: Professor Robert Knowles
    Office Address
    or (if he holds the degree)
    Dr. Robert Knowles or
    Mr. Robert Knowles
    Office Address
  Social: Professor [or Dr. or Mr.] and Mrs.
    Robert Knowles
    Home Address
Salutation: Formal: Dear Sir:
    Informal: Dear Professor [or Dr. or Mr.] Knowles:
  Closing: Formal: Very truly yours,
    Informal: Sincerely yours,
In Conversation: Professor [or Doctor] Knowles (within
    the college); Mr. Knowles (elsewhere)
Title of Introduction: Professor [or Doctor] Knowles

Physician
Address: Business: William L. Barnes, M.D.
    Office Address
  Social: Doctor and Mrs. William L. Barnes
    Home Address
Salutation: Formal: Dear Sir:
    Informal: Dear Doctor Barnes:
  Closing: Formal: Very truly yours,
    Informal: Sincerely yours,
In Conversation: Doctor Barnes
Title of Introduction: Doctor Barnes

CANADA

Prime Minister
Address: Business: The Right Hon. John Smith, P.C., M.P.,
    Prime Minister of Canada
    Parliament Building
    Ottawa, Ontario
  Social: The Hon. John Smith and Mrs. Smith
    Home Address
Salutation: Formal: Sir: or Dear Sir:
    Informal: Dear Mr. Prime Minister: or
    Dear Mr. Smith:
  Closing: Formal: I am, Sir,
    Yours very truly,
    Informal: With kind regards,
    Yours very sincerely,
In Conversation: Sir or Mr. Smith or Mr. Prime Minister

Governor General—The Commonwealth
Address: Business: His Excellency
    John Smith (or his personal title)
    Government House
    Ottawa, Ontario

Social: Their Excellencies
  The Governor General and Mrs. John
  Smith
  Home Address
Salutation: Formal: Sir:
  Informal: My dear Mr. Smith:
Closing: Formal: I have the Honour to be, Sir,
  Your Excellency's obedient servant
  Informal: With kind regards,
  Yours very sincerely,
In Conversation: Your Excellency

Cabinet Officer
Address: Business: The Hon. John Smith, P.C., M.P.,
  Minister of Forestry
  Ottawa, Ontario
  Social: The Hon. John Smith and Mrs. Smith
  Home Address
  or (for a woman cabinet member)
  Mr. and Mrs. John Smith
Salutation: Formal: Sir: *or* Dear Sir: *or* Madam *or* Dear
  Madam:
  Informal: Dear Mr. Smith: *or* Dear Mrs. Smith
Closing: Formal: I am, Sir *or* Madam,
  Informal: Yours very sincerely,
In Conversation: Sir *or* Madam, formal; Mr. *or* Mrs. Smith
  or Mr. Minister; informal.

Former Prime Minister
Address: The Honourable (or Right Honourable)
  John Smith
  Home Address (or Office Address)

Judges
Judges of the following federal and provincial courts have the
title The Honourable, and are addressed as Mr. Justice:
  Supreme Court of Canada, Exchequer Court of Canada,
Courts of appeal of the provinces of British Columbia,

Manitoba, and Saskatchewan, Court of Chancery of the
province of Prince Edward Island, Courts of Queen's Bench
of the provinces of Manitoba, Quebec, and Saskatchewan
Superior Court of the province of Quebec, Supreme courts of
the provinces of Alberta, British Columbia, New Brunswick
Nova Scotia, Ontario, Prince Edward Island, and Newfound
land; and the territorial courts.
Address: Business: The Hon. Mr. Justice John Smith
  Social: The Hon. Mr. Justice John Smith and
  Mrs. Smith
Salutation: Formal: Sir:
  Informal: Dear Mr. Justice Smith:
Closing: Formal: I am, Sir,
  Yours sincerely,
  Informal: Believe me,
  Dear Mr. Justice Smith,
  Yours very sincerely,
In Conversation: Sir (formal); Mr. Justice Smith (informal).

Mayor
Address: His Worship
  The Mayor of St. Lazare
Salutation: Formal: Dear Sir:
  Informal: Dear Mr. Mayor:
Closing: Formal: Yours sincerely,
  Informal: Believe me, Dear Mr. Mayor,
  Yours very sincerely,
In Conversation: Sir (formal); Mr. Mayor (informal).

Member of Parliament
Address: John Smith, Esq. M.P.
  House of Commons
  Ottawa, Ontario
Salutation: Formal: Dear Sir:
  Informal: Dear Mr. Smith
Closing: Formal: Yours sincerely,
  Informal: Believe me,
  Yours very sincerely,

MANUSCRIPT PREPARATION

A writer must bear in mind that strangers will be evaluating his manuscript. It is unreasonable to assume that editors will take time out from a busy schedule to unscramble a poorly constructed manuscript when the author himself did not care sufficiently to make it presentable. A carbon copy smudged from handling and chewed around the edges is not likely to encourage an editor to read very far into it. By exerting a little effort to learn the fundamental conventions of style required by publishers and printers, a writer may save himself much time and effort later.

Before a final copy is typed, the typewriter keys should be thoroughly cleaned. A black, almost new ribbon is preferable, because the ink is too dense on a brand new ribbon. Good quality carbon paper will help to get the clearest possible impression. It is also common sense to submit the original copy to the publisher, and a carbon copy if possible. One carbon should always be retained by the author to protect against loss in transit. Radical innovations in style should be avoided, except where absolutely necessary to achieve a particular effect. More often than not, these innovations confuse the reader and distract him from the meaning of the text.

Paper Paper should be of a standard size, preferably 8½ x 11 inches, and of a good opacity, sixteen- or twenty-pound weight. Onionskin is too flimsy to serve as a printer's copy, and publishers are often put to the additional expense of retyping a manuscript for the printer.

Margins Liberal margins on both sides of the sheet are essential. The copy editor needs this space to make corrections to query the author, and to give instructions to the printer A six-inch line (seventy-two elite spaces, or sixty pica spaces centered on the page will insure sufficient margins. The line should be made as even as possible, without sacrificing the rules governing word division. This will help the editor to estimate the length of the manuscript in its printed form.

Spacing Text, bibliography, and table of contents should be double-spaced. Long footnotes also require double-spacing Shorter footnotes may be single-spaced with a double space separating them. Single-spacing is also permitted for long excerpts, thereby setting them apart from the rest of the text The number of lines on a page should be uniform, generally twenty-five for a standard eleven-inch sheet. Some brands of carbon paper include a guide sheet which, when set in the platen behind the paper, helps to achieve the desired uniformity

Indentation All paragraphs start seven spaces from the left-hand margin. This is true for quoted matter and foot notes. For long quotations, single-spaced, the opening line is indented the same seven spaces, but then a new margin is set four spaces from the left-hand side, and is maintained until the excerpt is concluded.